LOVE SIGNS & YOU

THE ULTIMATE ASTROLOGICAL GUIDE TO LOVE, SEX, AND RELATIONSHIPS

Skye Alexander, Frank Andrews, Frank Don,
Rochelle Gordon, Wendy C. Hawks,
Jean Mars, Sophia Mason

EDITOR-IN-CHIEF – ROCHELLE GORDON
EDITORIAL DIRECTOR – NADIA STIEGLITZ

ATRIA BOOKS

NEW YORK • LONDON • TORONTO • SYDNEY • SINGAPORE

ATRIA BOOKS

1230 Avenue of the Americas
New York, NY 10020

ISBN 0-7434-7649-2

Library of Congress/Cataloguing-in-Publication Data is available on file

First Atria Books hardcover printing October 2003

10 9 8 7 6 5 4 3 2 1

ATRIA BOOKS is a trademark of Simon & Schuster, Inc.

For further information regarding special discounts for bulk purchases,
please contact Simon & Schuster Special Sales at 1-800-456-6798
or business@simonandschuster.com

Manufactured in the United States of America

This book was created and produced for ATRIA BOOKS by
Pasteur Publishing Group, Inc., PO Box 3227, East Hampton, NY 11937
www.lovesigns and you.com

The authors wish to acknowledge the dedicated hard work of the following
people, without whom this book could never have come into being:

CONTRIBUTORS
Maggie Anderson, Martin Branch-Shaw, Blythe Camenson, Andrea Dawn, Jill Dearman, Stephanie L. Dempsey,
Ronnie Gale Dreyer, Heather Fenby, Nancy Frederick, Andi Frolich, Molly Hall, Elaine Harrison, Barbara Herel,
Madalyn Hillis-Dineen, Summer Hung, Bethea Jenner, Jo-ann Langseth, Suzanne Munshower, Ramita Navai,
Michael O'Reilly, Jill M. Phillips, Kim Rogers-Gallagher, Stefanie Iris Weiss, Jennie Misson Williams, Sherie Winslow

ASSISTANT EDITORS
Gigi Branch-Shaw, Blythe Camenson, Kathleen Crepeau, Susan Forney,
Roya Ireland, Jo-ann Langseth, Paul Watson, Sherie Winslow

DESIGN Bill Mason
COVER DESIGN Jon Glick
ILLUSTRATIONS Anelia Davidson

DEVELOPMENT
Gigi Branch-Shaw, Kathleen Crepeau, Andrea Dawn, Stephanie L. Dempsey,
Rochelle Gordon, Sandra Horth, Bill Mason, Nadia Stieglitz

SPECIAL THANKS TO
Michel Benarrosh, David Crane, Carol Mansfield, Daniel Melamud, Time Cycles Inc.

PHOTOGRAPHY CREDITS
All pictures supplied by Topham Picturepoint.
On page 96 (Margot Fonteyn picture courtesy of ArenaPAL/TopFoto)
On page 670 (*The Matrix* WB/Village Roadshow/TopFoto)
Authors' photographs by Julia Maloof and Michael Trevillion

*Every effort has been made to verify the historical and astrological information contained
in this book and the publisher accepts no responsibility for inaccuracies or errors.*

CONTENTS

THE ULTIMATE ASTROLOGICAL GUIDE TO LOVE, SEX, AND RELATIONSHIPS

THE ASTROLOGY OF ROMANCE

Loving and being loved are what everyone desires. This craving is hardwired into our genes. It is within every cell of our bodies. When love is found, it is precious and delicate and should be treated with special care. Unfortunately, that is not always what happens. Why? Life intervenes. Those same forces that brought us love can also take it away.

We can understand our lives' circumstances better by studying our astrological genes. Your astrological inheritance, as seen in your natal chart—your horoscope—reflects the inner and outer circumstances poised to influence your life. In **LOVE SIGNS & YOU** we reveal your chances and choices for love under all circumstances.

When an astrologer "reads" your chart, it is not just your Zodiac Sign that is being studied. All of the planets are considered for their roles in how you express and experience love, sex, romance, and relationships. Venus informs you about your love and relationship needs, while Mars provides insight into your sexual desires along with how you go after what you want. Your relationship karma with a partner can be read from your Saturn, a strong indicator of circumstance—circumstance often stemming from a past life relationship.

Whether you accept the Eastern mystical-based belief of reincarnation and having been reborn into another life with a partner from a past life or not, Saturn often reveals roadblocks to love. All of these vital planetary findings can be found on pages 696 through 863. Here we provide readings for your Venus and Mars Signs, along with readings for Saturn. To determine your Venus, Mars, and Saturn Signs, look to the pink side panel next to your Zodiac Sign reading.

Your Zodiac Sign, which tells of basic identity and deep needs, is where you should begin your exploration into your love desires or another's secrets. Armed with Venus, Mars, and Saturn Signs, you can find planetary readings for yourself and a partner—or anyone you are curious about. You can also match your planets up with those of a lover. Find out just how compatible you really are!

Understanding your astrological makeup, which describes your relationship potentials and more, can take you a long way toward altering your circumstances—karmic or otherwise! This is why we created insightful astrological readings for each Zodiac Sign from 1920 through 2002. Now you can discover pertinent astrological information about your family's love history. You can go back in time to see what mores and social settings were influencing your parents to discern their approaches to love and sex. Check it out.

And also check out the cultural influences surrounding your choices in love by reading about the Hot Couples and Sex Idols of your impressionable adolescent years. Read our Hot Topics and information on those Celebrities who put their personal style and stamp on relationship trends in each decade. We've added astrological insights about the Celebrities whose lives we cover. You'll see how the signs and planets influenced their relationships and why they were attracted to each other—adding further depth to the understanding of your own love life. These fascinating features are found on the last page of each year.

There are many factors that go into making our personal love stories. With **LOVE SIGNS & YOU**, the ultimate astrological guide to love, sex, and relationships, we hope you will enjoy your love story that much more—or perhaps even rewrite some of the chapters!

**SKYE ALEXANDER • FRANK ANDREWS • FRANK DON • ROCHELLE GORDON •
WENDY C. HAWKS • JEAN MARS • SOPHIA MASON**

LOVE SIGNS & YOU
IN 5 EASY STEPS

LOVE SIGNS & YOU contains all the insights you'll ever need to find out about anyone's true romantic nature… including your own! Written by seven Master Astrologers, you will discover how the astrological forces of your Zodiac Sign and your Love Planets—Venus, Mars, and Saturn—affect what you want, need, and expect from relationships. You'll also delve into fascinating astrological facts and stories that our Master Astrologers uncovered about the most famous couples and sex idols of the last 80 years.

HERE ARE THE 5 SIMPLE STEPS TO UNCOVER
EVERY SECRET ABOUT YOUR LOVE LIFE

1
DISCOVER THE HIGHLIGHTS OF YOUR DECADE

From the Roaring '20s to the Millennium Madness of the 2000s, read the captivating highlights of the cultural, economic, and sexual mores of the decade you were born in!

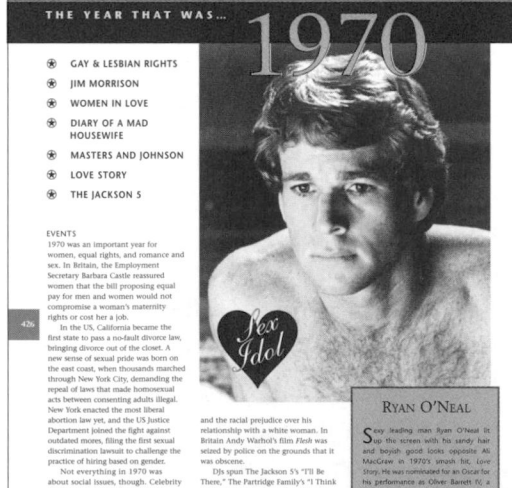

2
FIND OUT ABOUT THE EVENTS OF YOUR BIRTH YEAR

What news and pop culture impacted the world during the year you were born? Which Sex Idols, Hot Couples, or Hot Movies stirred the times? Find out all about it on your Birth Year Events page.

1964 CAPRICORN

From December 22, 1963 14:02 through January 21, 1964 0:40 (December 1964 Capricorns, see 1965 Capricorn)

The Committed Partner

You're a determined Capricorn born in 1964, and to you a relationship must be totally committed and focused. You believe in strong, long-lasting connections and you have no patience at all with frivolous romantic dalliance. In your opinion, life's too short. You're a team player, and a relationship is the ultimate team in which both people help each other to achieve mutually supported goals.

Good communication is essential to you. Being able to connect intellectually is crucial or else why would you bother staying with this person? Honest communication leads to a comforting sense of camaraderie and friendship, probably the most essential components of your relationship. Being able to depend upon your partner is another significant aspect of a strong relationship. You want to be there for the one you love, and expect to have that favor returned.

You have a distinct sense of your preferred "type" in every walk of life, and it's not so much what a mate might do, as what he or she is. To sustain your interest, your mate must be a true partner, on your side in every situation, ready to do battle for you, if need be. "You and me against the world," just might be your motto. You enjoy sharing social activities and like being active in your community. Pitching in together to host a charity event or even to make a good impression on the boss—that's what it's all about.

Male goats born in 1964 need a woman who is sparkling and communicative. From the moment you meet, she has what it takes to be your best friend. Your lady is a people-person, and her social skills come in handy when you need to favorably impress someone. Highly intelligent, your gal is keenly aware of what's going on. She is committed to you, and you know you can always count on her no matter what.

Female Capricorns born in 1964 expect a man to be assertive and intelligent. Your guy knows his own mind and he expresses his ideas aggressively, and with verve. He's strong and determined and an excellent leader, inspiring confidence in all whom he meets. He's achieved success in his field, and you feel instantaneously that he's your perfect partner.

CAPRICORN ZODIAC SIGN

YOUR LOVE PLANETS

YOUR ROMANTIC SIDE p. 696
- ▶ VENUS IN CAPRICORN *Born Dec. 22, 1963 14:02 - Dec. 23, 1963 18:52*
- ▶ VENUS IN AQUARIUS *Born Dec. 23, 1963 18:53 - Jan. 17, 1964 2:53*
- ▶ VENUS IN PISCES *Born Jan. 17, 2:54 - Jan. 21, 0:40*

YOUR SEX DRIVE p. 722
- ▶ MARS IN CAPRICORN *Born Dec. 22, 1963 14:02 - Jan. 13, 1964 6:12*
- ▶ MARS IN AQUARIUS *Born Jan. 13, 6:13 - Jan. 21, 0:40*

YOUR CELEBRITY TWINS p. 760
Find out the astrological similarities you have with famous people.

YOUR COMPATIBILITY p. 780
Compare planets to find out how compatible you are in a relationship.

YOUR RELATIONSHIP KARMA p. 824
- ▶ SATURN IN AQUARIUS *Born Dec. 22, 1963 14:02 - Jan. 21, 1964 0:40*

TIPPI HEDREN
American Actress
Sun in Capricorn

377

1964 AQUARIUS

From January 21, 0:41 through February 19, 14:56

Seeker of Perfection

As a responsible Aquarius born in 1964, you require a relationship that is passionate, supportive, and romantic. You believe in true love, and that each of us has a perfect partner—which is just the sort of relationship you want to have. You hate the idea of compromise, and want to be with your soulmate because you feel it's your destiny. Although responsibility is also important to you and you believe in loving and caring for someone, you feel that it has to be just right, or you'd rather keep looking.

Sensitivity is another important component of your relationship. You want to know and be known, and the only way to accomplish this goal is to be willing to open up and share everything, without feeling it's a risk. A little intuition is essential, and you feel that being able to know each other by means that can best be described as psychic is just another reasonable expectation of true love.

To sustain your interest, a mate must be intense, passionate, and sensitive. You want to feel that electrical buzz, the chemistry that holds everything in place, the connection that you know was somehow always meant to be. Tender moments of passion mean a lot, but so does sharing the serious responsibilities of life. That a mate will offer praise and give your spirits a boost is a big plus, because you like emotional support and compliments. You also like sharing romance—you'll willingly go dancing, sneak into a closet at a party for a quick kiss, or plan a trip around the world together.

Male Aquarians born in 1964 like a woman who is sensitive and passionate, yet also bold and outgoing. Your lady has a lot of pizzazz, and you appreciate those special qualities that make her so intense and interesting. Her love for you is boundless, and you feel happy simply because she's in the same room.

Female Aquarians born in 1964 like a man to be sensitive yet stable. Your guy has strong intuition and he's quite musical, so if you're crabby or feeling blue he just might sing you a tune to calm your nerves. He's dependable, and you know that if you ask him to do a favor, he will never forget to carry through.

AQUARIUS ZODIAC SIGN

YOUR LOVE PLANETS

YOUR ROMANTIC SIDE p. 696
- ▶ VENUS IN PISCES *Born Jan. 21, 0:41 - Feb. 10, 21:08*
- ▶ VENUS IN ARIES *Born Feb. 10, 21:09 - Feb. 19, 14:56*

YOUR SEX DRIVE p. 722
- ▶ MARS IN AQUARIUS *Born Jan. 21, 0:41 - Feb. 19, 14:56*

YOUR CELEBRITY TWINS p. 760
Find out the astrological similarities you have with famous people.

YOUR COMPATIBILITY p. 780
Compare planets to find out how compatible you are in a relationship.

YOUR RELATIONSHIP KARMA p. 824
- ▶ SATURN IN AQUARIUS *Born Jan. 21, 0:41 - Feb. 19, 14:56*

1 Read Your Sign 2 Look Up Your Love Planets 3 Go to Pages Shown

3

READ ABOUT YOUR ZODIAC SIGN

Find out all the secrets of love and sex your Zodiac Sign holds. Interpreted by one of seven Master Astrologers, your Reading will tell you how the astrological forces on your date of birth played a unique role in shaping your love life.

AQUARIUS ZODIAC SIGN

YOUR LOVE PLANETS

YOUR ROMANTIC SIDE p. 696
- ▶ **VENUS IN PISCES**
  Born Jan. 21, 0:41 - Feb. 10, 21:08
- ▶ **VENUS IN ARIES**
  Born Feb. 10, 21:09 - Feb. 19, 14:56

YOUR SEX DRIVE p. 722
- ▶ **MARS IN AQUARIUS**
  Born Jan. 21, 0:41 - Feb. 19, 14:56

YOUR CELEBRITY TWINS p. 760
Find out the astrological similarities you have with famous people.

YOUR COMPATIBILITY p. 780
Compare planets to find out how compatible you are in a relationship.

YOUR RELATIONSHIP KARMA p. 824
- ▶ **SATURN IN AQUARIUS**
  Born Jan. 21, 0:41 - Feb. 19, 14:56

4

UNCOVER THE SECRETS OF YOUR LOVE PLANETS

Unveil your Love Planets located to the side of your Zodiac Sign Reading. Turn to the pages indicated to discover what Venus, Mars, and Saturn mean and how they can affect Your Romantic Side, Sex Drive, Romantic and Sexual Compatibility, and Relationship Karma. Also find out which signs you share with famous people in Your Celebrity Twins.

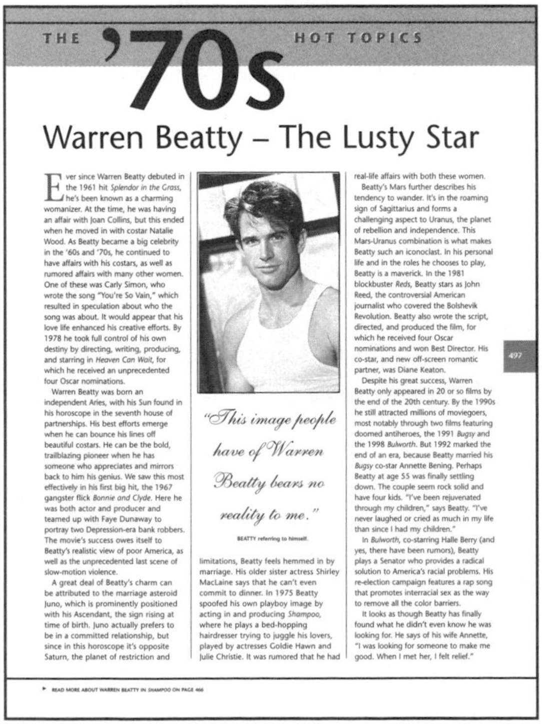

THE '70s HOT TOPICS

Warren Beatty – The Lusty Star

Ever since Warren Beatty debuted in the 1961 hit *Splendor in the Grass*, he's been known as a charming womanizer. At the time, he was having an affair with Joan Collins, but this ended when he moved in with costar Natalie Wood. As Beatty became a big celebrity in the '60s and '70s, he continued to have affairs with his costars, as well as rumored affairs with many other women. One of these was Carly Simon, who wrote the song "You're So Vain," which resulted in speculation about who the song was about. It would appear that his love life enhanced his creative efforts. By 1978 he took full control of his own destiny by directing, writing, producing, and starring in *Heaven Can Wait*, for which he received an unprecedented four Oscar nominations.

Warren Beatty was born an independent Aries, with his Sun found in his horoscope in the seventh house of partnerships. His best efforts emerge when he can bounce his lines off beautiful costars. He can be the bold, trailblazing pioneer when he has someone who appreciates and mirrors back to him his genius. We saw this most effectively in his first big hit, the 1967 gangster flick *Bonnie and Clyde*. Here he was both actor and producer and teamed up with Faye Dunaway to portray two Depression-era bank robbers. The movie's success owes itself to Beatty's realistic view of poor America, as well as the unprecedented last scene of slow-motion violence.

A great deal of Beatty's charm can be attributed to the marriage asteroid Juno, which is prominently positioned with his Ascendant, the sign rising at time of birth. Juno actually prefers to be in a committed relationship, but since in this horoscope it's opposite Saturn, the planet of restriction and limitations, Beatty feels hemmed in by marriage. His older sister actress Shirley MacLaine says that he can't even commit to dinner. In 1975 Beatty spoofed his own playboy image by acting in and producing *Shampoo*, where he plays a bed-hopping hairdresser trying to juggle his lovers, played by actresses Goldie Hawn and Julie Christie. It was rumored that he had real-life affairs with both these women.

"This image people have of Warren Beatty bears no reality to me."

BEATTY referring to himself.

Beatty's Mars further describes his tendency to wander. It's in the roaming sign of Sagittarius and forms a challenging aspect to Uranus, the planet of rebellion and independence. This Mars-Uranus combination is what makes Beatty such an iconoclast. In his personal life and in the roles he chooses to play, Beatty is a maverick. In the 1981 blockbuster *Reds*, Beatty stars as John Reed, the controversial American journalist who covered the Bolshevik Revolution. Beatty also wrote the script, directed, and produced the film, for which he received four Oscar nominations and won Best Director. His co-star, and new off-screen romantic partner, was Diane Keaton.

Despite his great success, Warren Beatty only appeared in 20 or so films by the end of the 20th century. By the 1990s he still attracted millions of moviegoers, most notably through two films featuring doomed antiheroes, the 1991 *Bugsy* and the 1998 *Bulworth*. But 1992 marked the end of an era, because Beatty married his *Bugsy* co-star Annette Bening. Perhaps Beatty at age 55 was finally settling down. The couple seem rock solid and have four kids. "I've been rejuvenated through my children," says Beatty. "I've never laughed or cried as much in my life than since I had my children."

In *Bulworth*, co-starring Halle Berry (and yes, there have been rumors), Beatty plays a Senator who provides a radical solution to America's racial problems. His re-election campaign features a rap song that promotes interracial sex as the way to remove all the color barriers.

It looks as though Beatty has finally found what he didn't even know he was looking for. He says of his wife Annette, "I was looking for someone to make me good. When I met her, I felt relief."

497

▶ READ MORE ABOUT WARREN BEATTY IN SHAMPOO ON PAGE 466

5

EXPLORE THE HOTTEST TOPICS OF THE TWENTIETH CENTURY

Revealed at the end of each scintillating year are the provocative astrological insights into the romantic nature and sexual prowess of the hottest celebs throughout that decade! Read about the most spectacular, as well as the most heartfelt, love stories of all time. Also catch a glimpse into the hottest cultural and sexual trends that inspired the generations!

Now that you know how easy to use and how informative **LOVE SIGNS & YOU** really is, keep all of your personal astrological information handy for easy reference.

As you use **LOVE SIGNS & YOU** over and over again, you'll discover for yourself all the entertaining ways that you, your friends and family can enjoy it.

You can even throw your very own **LOVE SIGNS & YOU** party! Everyone will have so much fun reading about themselves and about the people—lovers, friends, bosses—in their lives!

YOUR TIME OF BIRTH AND FINDING YOUR PLANETARY AND ZODIAC SIGNS

A major factor used by astrologers when reading a horoscope is the Zodiac Sign that each planet was "traveling through" at the time of birth. We are all familiar with our Zodiac Sign (or Sun Sign), but not so with the signs of the other planets when we were born. In *Love Signs & You*, we use your Zodiac, Venus, Mars, and Saturn Signs to gain insights into your love life.

Because planets move around the sun, they can be in any of the twelve signs of the zodiac at any given time. Which sign that is must be determined. We provide the means for you to do so. We supply the planetary signs, and you supply your birth data. We list the planets as observed from Greenwich, England in universal Greenwich Mean Time (GMT). All that is left for you to do to find out your Venus, Mars, and Saturn Signs—including your Zodiac Sign if you were born on the cusp—is to make a little mathematical adjustment to equate your local time to GMT.

When we say someone was born "on the cusp," we mean they were born on the day when the sun was leaving one Zodiac Sign and entering the next. The cusp is like the dividing line. We have provided the exact time the divider is crossed—not only for your Zodiac Sign, but for Venus, Mars, and Saturn as well. You will need to

know this to get your love readings.

If you are born on the cusp, this book will provide the means to determine your true sign. Let's say you were born on February 19, 1964. Does that make you an Aquarius or a Pisces? It all depends on where and when you were born. For example, if you were born at 7:15 am in Miami, it would be Eastern Standard Time (EST). You need to convert your local time to Greenwich Mean Time (GMT). Looking at the Time Zone Chart below for Eastern Standard Time, you'll see that you need to add 5 hours to your original time of birth, making it 12:15 pm. Using this 12:15 pm time, turn to page 376, where you will find that you are an Aquarius Zodiac Sign. If you look at Figure 1, you will see that the sun was in Aquarius from January 21, at 00:41 through February 19, 14:56 (military time) GMT. It did not go into Pisces until 14:57 GMT.

Next you will want to find your Venus, Mars, and Saturn signs. They are located in the pink panel to the side of the Zodiac Sign reading (see

Figure 2). Under *Your Romantic Side*, you see that Venus was in Pisces through February 10, but that it was in Aries from February 10, 21:09 through the 19th at 14:56. Therefore, you know that your Venus sign would be Aries. Looking under *Your Sex Drive*, you see that your Mars is in Aquarius, and continuing down you note under *Your Relationship Karma* that your Saturn is in Aquarius. It is that simple.

If you don't know your time of birth or the time of the person you are wishing to read about, simply use 6 am as the birth time and proceed as above to determine the signs. If you do not know the place of birth, as in the case of a new friend, use 6 am GMT.

Figure 2

AQUARIUS ZODIAC SIGN
YOUR LOVE PLANETS

YOUR ROMANTIC SIDE   p. 696
> ▶ **VENUS IN PISCES**
> *Born Jan. 21, 0:41 - Feb. 10, 21:08*
> ▶ **VENUS IN ARIES**
> *Born Feb. 10, 21:09 - Feb. 19, 14:56*

YOUR SEX DRIVE   p. 722
> ▶ **MARS IN AQUARIUS**
> *Born Jan. 21, 0:41 - Feb. 19, 14:56*

YOUR CELEBRITY TWINS   p. 760
> *Find out the astrological similarities you have with famous people.*

YOUR COMPATIBILITY   p. 780
> *Compare planets to find out how compatible you are in a relationship.*

YOUR RELATIONSHIP KARMA   p. 824
> ▶ **SATURN IN AQUARIUS**
> *Born Jan. 21, 0:41 - Feb. 19, 14:56*

Figure 1

AQUARIUS   *From January 21, 0:41 through February 19, 14:56*
Seeker of Perfection

TIME ZONE CHART

WESTWARDS				EASTWARDS			
Meridian	**GMT + or -**	**Zone**	**Zone Name**	**Meridian**	**GMT + or -**	**Zone**	**Zone Name**
0	0	WET	Western Europe Time	0	0	WET	Western Europe Time
15	+ 1	WAT	West Africa Time	15	- 1	CET	Central Europe Time
30	+ 2	AT	Azores Time	30	- 2	EET	Eastern Europe Time, USSR Zone 1
45	+ 3	BST	Brazil Standard Time	45	- 3	BT	Baghdad Time, USSR Zone 2
52.30	+ 3.5	NFT	Newfoundland Time	52.30	- 3.5	IR	Iran Time
60	+ 4	AST	Atlantic Standard Time	60	- 4		USSR Zone 3
75	+ 5	EST	Eastern Standard Time	75	- 5		USSR Zone 4
90	+ 6	CST	Central Standard Time	90	- 6	NST	North Sumatra Time
105	+ 7	MST	Mountain Standard Time	105	- 7	SST	So. Sumatra Time, USSR Zone 6
120	+ 8	PST	Pacific Standard Time	112.30	- 7.5	JT	Java Time
135	+ 9	YST	Yukon Standard Time	120	- 8	CCT	China Coast Time, USSR Zone 7
150	+10	CAT	Central Alaska Time	127.30	- 8.5	MT	Moluccas Time
157.30	+10.5	HST	Hawaiian Standard Time	135	- 9	JST	Japan Standard Time, USSR Zone 8
165	+11	IN/BT	Nome time / Bering Time	142.30	- 9.5	SAST	South Australia time
180	+12	IDLW	International Dateline West	150	-10	GST	Guam Standard Time, USSR Zone 9
				165	-11.5		USSR Zone 10
				172.30	-11.5	NZT	New Zealand Time
				180	-12	IDLE	International Dateline East

Simply by looking at the chart, you'll see that you can determine whether to add or subtract in order to get the equivalent of your local time to Greenwich Mean Time. You will also need to know the local time zone of birth for this. If this is unclear, we have listed the meridian to provide further help in determining the local time zone.

ABOUT THE AUTHORS
AND EDITORS

ROCHELLE GORDON

Rochelle, Editor-in-Chief of *Love Signs & You*, has been a leading expert in astrology, tarot, acrophonology (alphabet/zodiac correspondences), and clairvoyance for over thirty years. Author of several books, including *Body Talk* and *Personal Power Is in Your Name*, and a former editor of *Body Mind Spirit* magazine, she is an influential voice both in popular astrology as well as the study of the mind/body connection. She was also editor of *Astro Signs Digest*, *Horoscope Guide* and *Astro Signs* magazines and has contributed articles to *Cosmopolitan*, *Dell Horoscope*, *National Astrology*, and *American Astrology*.

SKYE ALEXANDER

A highly respected astrologer, author, and advisor for over twenty years, Skye has published several books, including the classic *Planets in Signs* and the award-winning astrological mystery *Hidden Agenda*. She is a frequent contributor to the Llewellyn annual *Sun Signs and Moon Signs* books and has written articles for *Better Homes and Gardens*, *Dell Horoscope*, and *Magical Blend* magazines. Skye is also a well-known authority on Wicca and frequently speaks on magick and witchcraft at New Age conferences, workshops, and events. She recently appeared in a television program on magick for the *Discovery Channel*, filmed at Stonehenge.

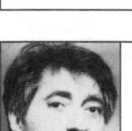

FRANK ANDREWS

World-renowned astrologer, tarot expert, lecturer, consultant, and columnist, Frank Andrews has advised so many famous people for so long that he is a celebrity in his own right. He has appeared on national TV shows including *Good Morning America*, *The Phil Donahue Show*, and *Fox News* and has been featured on PBS. He wrote the Sunday "Tarot to Go" column for *The New York Post* as well as a column for *Elegant Bride* magazine. He has been profiled by dozens of magazines including *Marie Claire*, *Cosmopolitan*, *Redbook*, and *Harper's Bazaar*. *New York* magazine named him "Best Psychic in New York."

FRANK DON

As a professional astrologer for thirty years, Frank Don has a worldwide clientele including Academy Award, Tony Award, and Emmy Award winners, sports figures, corporate executives, and government officials. Frank is also an international lecturer, consultant, and author of *Earth Changes Ahead*, *Color Magic*, and *Color Your World*. He has accurately forecasted weather and changing earth patterns and economic conditions for the *Los Angeles Weekly* and *The New York Times Magazine*. Frank is also very civic-minded and ran for the US Congress as an independent candidate.

WENDY C. HAWKS

Wendy has been a nationally published astrologer and consultant for over twenty-three years. She is the author of numerous popular horoscope booklets and three Mini-Mags, including *An Astro Guide to Healing Herbs* and *Get Rich for the New Millennium*. Her book, *The Nuts and Bolts of Running an Astrology Practice*, is one of the American Federation of Astrologers' most in-demand titles. Wendy is perhaps best known for correctly predicting O. J. Simpson's acquittal in a *National Examiner* column in 1994, nearly a year before the trial ended.

JEAN MARS

A lifelong student of the prophecies of Nostradamus, Swiss astrologer and numerologist Jean Mars was for many years the resident astrologer for the French magazine *Ici Paris* and for Europe's *Radio Monte Carlo*. He has been a member of the American Mentalists Association for forty-five years and the American Federation of Astrologers for over twenty-five years. Jean is also a well-known figure on the international conference circuit, where he has given readings and telepathy demonstrations for many years. His *One Man Mental Show* is especially renowned as a "must-see" event!

SOPHIA MASON

A Master Astrologer, Sophia's passion for astrology spans over thirty years. She is a two-time winner of the American Federation of Astrologers' Best Astrologer, Lecturer, and Teacher awards and specializes in "astrological detective" work and card divination. She lectures at astrology conferences throughout the US and is the author of several books, including *Playing Your Cards Right: Finding Your Destiny in Playing Cards*, and *Sexuality, an In-depth Astrological Study of Sexual Compatibility*.

NADIA STIEGLITZ

Editorial Director for the Pasteur Publishing Group, French born, Nadia Stieglitz has been the creative force behind many publishing successes such as *Your Birthday Signs Through Time*, *Supermarket Remedies*, *OmniForce*, *Feng Shui Solutions*, and *Your Spirit Animal Helpers*. Prior to joining the Pasteur Publishing Group, Nadia utilized her creative talents in advertising and marketing in Paris. An experienced Feng Shui practitioner, she lives with her husband and three children in London.

1900-1909

INVENTIONS, GADGETS ... AND PURITY

New inventions

brought music, film,

and communication

to the marketplace.

Appearance was everything at the beginning of the century, from physical appearance to the image of propriety. And the image to be fostered was one of female purity. Unmarried women didn't venture out unless chaperoned, lest their reputations suffer. After all, a stolen kiss was the same as a marriage proposal. Many women married simply for the freedom, after years of sitting safely at home trying to maintain an image.

The 1900s was a decade of invention, and new gadgets exploded onto the marketplace. Electricity was coming to homes, slowly replacing oil lamps and wood stoves, and the homes of the rich had running water. Inventors felt free to take the wildest idea and run with it, creating the telegraph, record player, transcontinental communication, and the horse-drawn vacuum cleaner. The Kodak Brownie camera sold for a dollar, and by the end of the decade, Ford's Model A had provided a popular means of transportation.

The Victrola phonograph brought music to the parlors. From "The Maple Leaf Rag" and "You Can't Keep a Good Man Down" to patriotic songs like "You're a Grand Ole Flag," people were singing and asking for more. Irving Berlin published the first of his eventual 800 tunes.

Magazines of the day printed how-to articles covering everything from cooking to furniture placement, determined to keep women busy—and informed. But they took it too far. In 1906 *The Ladies Home Journal* printed articles on venereal disease and lost 75,000 subscribers. Other more famous guides were also established, as in Britain where the *Oxford English Dictionary* published letters 'A' to 'H' and in Paris the *Michelin Guide* was born.

Protecting a woman's purity was a problem in the workplace. With 18.3 percent of women employed, US moralists were concerned that women would be "sullied" by contact with men on the job. If a woman was forced by "unfortunate circumstances" to seek employment, the only suitable jobs were as school teacher, nurse, or artist. One woman, Olga Nethersole, threw caution (and her reputation) to the wind and starred as Fanny in the Broadway play *Sapho* in 1900. In one offending scene, Fanny is carried up a flight of stairs—by a man who is not her husband. She was arrested during one show and jailed for violating public decency, but the jury only took 15 minutes to find her innocent.

Clothing helped maintain not only the illusion but the reality of purity. Dresses went from the collar to the ground. If the neck-to-floor outfits weren't enough to stop inappropriate sexual contact, the underwear surely was, with whalebone corsets and layers of petticoats. Men's fashions were almost as restricting, with high, stiff collars and suits with waistcoats. And not every inventor was a man. In 1903 Mary Anderson was granted a patent for an automobile windshield wiper, having gotten the idea during a stormy ride on a streetcar. By 1916, every car had wipers.

Although stifled, women still wanted a say in government. In the US, Carrie Chapman Catt developed

◄◄ Isadora Duncan, corsetless, in
revolutionary classical pose

▲ Mme du Gaste, France's first
woman racing driver

◄ Modesty was the key to
bathing fashion in the 1900s

a plan to use a constitutional amendment as a way to win women's voting rights, and in 1920 the 19th Amendment guaranteed women the right to vote.

During the early 1900s, motion pictures became entertainment for the masses. For the price of a nickel, people could watch silent films to the accompaniment of a piano. The first movie, a 12-minute western called *The Great Train Robbery*, opened in 1903.

The decade also saw literary works on the rise. Produced during that time were enduring classics, such as Jack London's *Call of the Wild*, Upton Sinclair's *The Jungle*, Booker T. Washington's *Up From Slavery* and Rudyard Kipling's *Kim*. The first Nobel Prize in literature was won by French poet Sully Prudhomme and, also in France, Andre Gide wrote *The Immoralist*.

In Europe there was an artistic boom—Rodin completed one of the world's most famous sculptures, *The Thinker*, Henri Matisse began the Fauvist movement in painting, Pablo Picasso entered his blue period, and in Berlin, Isadora Duncan opened the first school of modern dance.

1910 -1919

THE COMING OF AGE

From industrial superiority

to war, this was the decade

of extremes, ending

dramatically with a stock

market crash in 1919.

The inventions of the previous decade continued to be perfected and expanded, women's fashions became a bit more comfortable as styles loosened and waistlines dropped. Cars turned up in more and more driveways, producers churned out an endless stream of movies for the public, airmail delivery began, a phone company vowed to bring service to rural areas ... and then we went to war.

The decade began so brightly. Sarah Bernhardt starred in the first full-length motion picture, *Queen Elizabeth*. Life expectancy had increased to 48 for men and 51 for women. But that same year the *Titanic*, promoted as unsinkable, struck an iceberg and sank, killing more than 1,500 people. A year later, Americans started paying income tax for the first time. But Americans were still riding high on the prosperity and good feelings of the previous decade.

The one millionth Ford Model T rolled off the assembly line. The rate of manufacture was attributed to Ford's innovative mass-production methods and the fact that workers were being paid an eye-popping $5 for an 8-hour day. The first grocery store opened, selling among other things the newly developed LifeSavers candy. It became possible to place calls from coast to coast with long-distance lines connecting New York and California.

Many books of the decade became classics. Zane Grey's *Riders of the Purple Sage*, Lawrence's *Sons and Lovers*, and Burroughs' *Tarzan of the Apes* shared fiction lists with Maugham's *Of Human Bondage*, Joyce's *A Portrait of the Artist as a Young Man* and Thomas Mann wrote *Death in Venice*. The bestseller at the end of the decade was *The Four Horsemen of the Apocalypse*, which sold for $1.90 per copy. J.M. Barrie wrote *Peter Pan*, magnanimously leaving the copyright to Great Ormond Street Hospital for Children—Britain's first children's hospital.

Cinemas, which replaced the informal storefront nickelodeons, continued to be packed, with 30 million tickets sold weekly. Serials such as *The Perils of Pauline* kept audiences coming back to see what would happen next. *Quo Vadis* ran for a whopping two hours, and in 1917 one enterprising theater discovered a way to keep its seats filled—they installed air conditioning.

Sexy Theda Bara, hilarious Fanny Brice, and the dazzling Ziegfeld Follies girls kept people titillated, both at movie theaters and stage performances. George Bernard Shaw's *Pygmalion* was produced—it would eventually become *My Fair Lady*.

Art covered the spectrum, from futurism, realism, and cubism to symbolism, dadaism, and Fauvism. At the same time, Norman Rockwell began his career painting homey covers for *The Saturday Evening Post*.

Billboard magazine began tracking the most popular songs and *Publishers Weekly* kept a list of bestsellers, stopped for four years as readership declined, then began again in 1917 when fiction and nonfiction became popular again.

This was also the decade for thinkers—Carl Jung's *Psychology of the Unconscious* helped found analytical psychology, Einstein added the General Theory of

Relativity and Lenin's *State and Revolution* put Marx's theories into practice.

In Germany, the 35mm Leica camera was invented and the hand-crank Victrola of the previous decade grew to the size of a piece of furniture, and the record industry finally settled on the 78 rpm format, with 100 million records and two million record players being sold each year. By the end of the decade, people were spending more on records than on books. Sheet music was a

◄◄ An erotic Christmas card sent during World War I

▲ *The All-Story*, showing the world's first picture of Tarzan

◄ Sarah Bernhardt, French stage actress

popular item, too, with printed hits such as, "He's Got Those Big Blue Eyes Like You Daddy Mine" and "Sweet Cider Time When You Were Mine."

But the decade ended on a down note. World War I broke out, with America entering in 1917. President Wilson signed the Selective Service Act, and General Pershing estimated that the war effort would require an eventual 3 million US soldiers. By 1918 the US Food Administration was handing out pamphlets urging "voluntary" rationing. "Meatless" and "wheatless" meals were promoted according to a weekly schedule. Factories east of the Mississippi shut down to save power. And to make matters even tougher, Prohibition began in 1919 with the banning of alcohol production, transport, and sale.

The decade that had dawned so brightly, hit rock bottom in November 1919 with the fifth worst stock market crash on record.

1920 -1929

THE ROARING TWENTIES

Hemlines fell as fast as

the stock market with the

Crash of 1929—

a new age of decadence

was dawning.

The decade of prosperity and peace between two world wars was marked by rapid advances in technology, new musical and art forms, and widespread moral, sexual, and political challenges to the social code.

During the twenties, innovations in recording and broadcast technology, airplane and automobile travel, and sound synchronization with image ("talking pictures") allowed a more mobile and faster-paced life. What had been novelties became essential and commonplace. Radio broadcasts, phonograph records, and films let people at great geographic distances enjoy the same entertainment simultaneously, and this instantaneous sharing led to hits, crazes, stars, and fads. Recognizable brand-name products were created: Band-Aid, Scotch tape, Trojan, Kleenex, and Maidenform. The fashions were provocative, the dancing was uninhibited, and in the US alcohol was forbidden, which gave rise to speakeasies, gangster culture, and a widespread sense of reckless, lawless anti-authoritarianism, culminating in the American decade ending with a crash—of the stock market in 1929.

The twenties was the decade of feminism and of suffrage, finally allowing women the vote. Vocal, articulate women advocated birth control and workplace equality. Dr. Marie Stopes bravely opened Britain's first birth control clinic in London and a few years later she daringly wrote a series of sex manuals for women—emancipation had truly begun. Women's behavior and dress broke so many taboos that church and society traditionalists resorted to censorship, edicts, and frequent lamentations at the breakdown in decorum and social order.

Even literature was pushing back the boundaries—D.H. Lawrence shook respectable English society with his audacious novels of erotic love such as *Women in Love*. But this was nothing compared to the reception the explicit *Lady Chatterley's Lover* received. Needless to say, it was promptly banned.

But forces other than literature, fashion and loose morals were challenging old assumptions. The powerful new ideas of Freud and Darwin rocked the very foundations of human identity. Artists, from filmmakers to writers, were breaking the confines of traditional form. Isadora Duncan danced barefoot and corsetless in flowing Grecian dress. European surrealists drew on dream imagery and the unconscious. And jazz, the first indigenous American art form, arose out of African-American blues and spiritual traditions. Music was the harbinger of a larger social change. African-American musicians and singers became the first of their race to receive respect and societal acclaim. Although bands and venues were strictly segregated, black entertainers often performed for all-white audiences. Louis Armstrong, Duke Ellington, Count Basie, and Bessie Smith all came of age in the twenties.

The great orator and defense attorney Clarence Darrow was involved in two sensational trials—the Scopes Monkey Trial, a test case for the teaching of the theory of evolution, and the Leopold and Loeb murder trial, over the "thrill kill" of a schoolboy by two very rich young Jewish men. Charles

Lindbergh and Amelia Earhart flew the Atlantic and became heroes. Al Capone and his gang ran Chicago's prostitution, gambling, and bootleg liquor underworld.

Songwriting was in its heyday, from New York's Tin Pan Alley and Broadway to blues, ragtime, folk, and jazz innovators. Some of the most enduring songs of modern time came from the twenties, from "Ain't She Sweet," to "Downhearted Blues" and song titles like "I Need Some Petting" and "Makin' Whoopie" reflected the decade's mood of naughty abandon.

THE SILVER SCREEN
Garbo, Chaplin, Keaton, Valentino, Louise Brooks, and Clara Bow—the stars of the silent screen—vamped, clowned, and smoldered. Exotic locales, World War I, and the ceaseless tortures and delights of love were perennial subjects. From *Nosferatu* to *The Jazz Singer*, great directing, acting, and increasingly sophisticated camera techniques and effects created lasting works of art and cultural time capsules.

BETWEEN THE PAGES
Hemingway, Woolf, Mencken, Wharton, Faulkner, and Fitzgerald dazzled with titillating accounts of nightlife debauchery and tell-alls about the fast crowd. Bisexual French literary genius Colette penned her most scandalous novel, *Cheri*, based on her incestuous affair with her stepson.

PEOPLE
Margaret Sanger tirelessly lobbied for the availability of birth control in the US, while celebrities such as Charlie Chaplin and Fatty Arbuckle scandalized with their very public falls from grace. Dancer, entertainer and all-round *provocateur* Josephine Baker took Paris by storm, dancing bare-breasted with only a string of bananas around her waist.

15

▲▲ The Charleston

◄◄ Marie Stopes arriving at the Law Courts for the hearing of her appeal

▲ Sigmund Freud, founder of psychoanalysis

1920

- ★ **F. SCOTT AND ZELDA FITZGERALD**
- ★ **MODIGLIANI DIES**
- ★ **LILLIAN GISH ON ICE**
- ★ **APPLE BLOSSOM TIME**
- ★ **WOMEN IN LOVE**
- ★ **THIS SIDE OF PARADISE**
- ★ **BLISS**

EVENTS

Newlyweds F. Scott and Zelda Fitzgerald defined the spirit of the "Jazz Age." Their uninhibited escapades included riding atop taxis down 5th Avenue and diving into the Plaza Hotel fountain. An International Feminist Conference took place in Geneva, and the League of Nations was formed, also to be based in Geneva. Trojan condoms made their debut, and abortion was legalized in the Soviet Union but outlawed in France. Italian painter of nudes Modigliani died at the age of thirty-five. The following day, his pregnant mistress committed suicide. Pope Benedict XV banned the film *Holy Bible* for its naked portrayal of Adam and Eve.

In Britain, the novelist Agatha Christie created one of the most famous detectives in literary history, when she wrote the first of the Hercule Poirot novels. Dr. Marie Stopes wrote *Radiant Motherhood*, a progressive self-help manual for women.

POP CULTURE

Melodramatic silent films paired compelling imagery with gloriously expressive acting. In D.W. Griffith's *Way Down East*, a seduced and abandoned Lillian Gish flees across ice floes. In *Suds*, London laundry girl Mary Pickford misses out on true love by overreaching her class. In Cecil B. DeMille's *Why Change Your Wife?*, Gloria Swanson recaptures the love of her ex-husband. *Neighbors* starred the great Buster Keaton in a tenement neighborhood version of Romeo and Juliet.

Songs of the era included the lush strains of "I'll Never Love Again," "I'll Be With You in Apple Blossom Time," and "The Love Nest." Large dance orchestras played "The Lamp of Love" and "My Baby's Arms." A federation of American women's clubs campaigned to replace popular tunes with more wholesome fare like "Keep the Home Fires Burning."

Bestsellers included *Women in Love* by D. H. Lawrence, a critique of England's class system via the love and sexual relationships between two couples, and *This Side of Paradise* by F. Scott Fitzgerald, which captured the post-war ennui and narcissism of the "younger generation." *The Bachelor Girl* described the hedonistic life of a young woman in Paris, while in Katherine Mansfield's *Bliss*, a young married woman's sexual awakening leads to disappointment and disillusionment.

Hot Couple

DOUGLAS FAIRBANKS & MARY PICKFORD

Swashbuckling movie star Douglas Fairbanks and America's first sweetheart Mary Pickford were the apple of Hollywood's eye in the late teens and early twenties. Both still married to others, they lived in scandalous secret sin until they divorced their respective spouses and married each other on March 28th, 1920.

Their lavish Beverly Hills mansion, dubbed "Pickfair," was the meeting place for the elite of the time. They were thought of as the unofficial King and Queen of Hollywood. Pickford said of their life at that time: "We were pioneers in a brand new medium. Everything's fun when you're young." They divorced in 1936.

SEE ALSO

▶ KATHARINE HEPBURN & SPENCER TRACY *Page 196*
▶ HUMPHREY BOGART & LAUREN BACALL *Page 235*

1920 CAPRICORN

From December 22, 1919 21:27 through January 21, 1920 8:03
(December 1920 Capricorns, see 1921 Capricorns)

♑ *The Challenging Companion*

You're likely to take any road leading to a relationship, Capricorn of 1920, as long as that road promises to bring you endless thrills and adventure. You view every close relationship in your life as a challenge, a contest in which each person wants something just a little bit different from what the other one wants. For you there's nothing so refreshing and invigorating as a friendly clash with a romantic edge to it, which tunes, tones, and even titillates the minds, wills, and senses of the two people involved.

You definitely are not the shy, flirtatious type who is afraid of becoming involved, but at the same time your standards are high. Though others may at times think you're standoffish, you're probably sizing everyone up, ready to plunge in headlong when just the right one comes along. And once you commit to someone, you're in it for the long haul.

Those who get your attention are those who, at first, seem to be least interested in having it, and whom you know will test every one of your social and romantic skills. You want someone to remind you that your attention needs to stray from work at the end of the day and be redirected straight into someone's loving arms. Once that person sees they have you where they want to, you are like putty in their hands, for you know they will always keep you on your toes.

For the 1920 Capricorn male, the right woman can be either plain or beautiful, but she definitely has to have that extra something— that unique combination of aloofness, mystery, and sex appeal that tells you this lady has to be won with finesse, style, and flair. She's not the kind people would describe as accessible, but you know that once you've won her by using all your considerable charm, you'll have a partner you appreciate every moment you're with her.

The perfect man for the 1920 Capricorn woman is one of few words, who exudes confidence and sex appeal. Someone who is perfectly content with his own company is the type who will be a good, steady, companion for life. You may just have to work overtime convincing him that you're the right one to be by his side.

CAPRICORN ZODIAC SIGN
YOUR LOVE PLANETS

YOUR ROMANTIC SIDE   p. 696
▶ **VENUS IN SCORPIO**
Born Dec. 22, 1919 21:27 - Jan. 04, 1920 9:19
▶ **VENUS IN SAGITTARIUS**
Born Jan. 04, 9:20 - Jan. 21, 8:03

YOUR SEX DRIVE   p. 722
▶ **MARS IN LIBRA**
Born Dec. 22, 1919 21:27 - Jan. 21, 1920 8:03

YOUR CELEBRITY TWINS   p. 760
Find out the astrological similarities you have with famous people.

YOUR COMPATIBILITY   p. 780
Compare planets to find out how compatible you are in a relationship.

YOUR RELATIONSHIP KARMA   p. 824
▶ **SATURN IN VIRGO**
Born Dec. 22, 1919 21:27 - Jan. 21, 1920 8:03

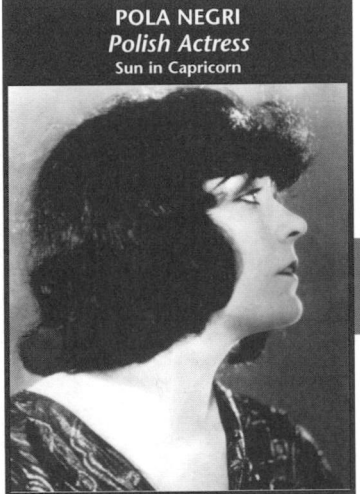

POLA NEGRI
Polish Actress
Sun in Capricorn

17

1920 AQUARIUS

From January 21, 8:04 through February 19, 22:28

♒ *The Sociable Samaritan*

Relationships don't come easy for you, Aquarius of 1920. With all your community activities, social engagements, and the hours spent helping friends in need, you never seem to have enough time to devote to those you love. That's why your ideal relationship is with someone who has an equally busy life. When each of you finally have time to pause in your busy schedules, you savor your moments together, filling your time with the things that matter most to the two of you.

For you, a relationship is something that helps two people to grow and to learn from one another. More than a lover, your partner is your friend, and your relationship must always reflect the loyalty and honesty that exists between two people who offer respect to the same degree that they offer love. Talkative and probing, you need to speak your mind freely, without worrying how tactful you might or might not be.

A creative mind and a romantic soul are the two primary requirements for anyone who wants to catch your eye and hold your interest. Reading your favorite love poems in a quiet and romantic setting makes you quiver every time, and to hear them read aloud by someone you care about longingly, arouses your deepest passions. Touch, too, is important, and anyone who offers a nice neck rub along with romantic words is a friend for life.

The perfect woman for you, Aquarian male of 1920, is one who is interested in everything you are doing, and all you have to say. You love women who are artistic and perhaps a bit reserved, though not too shy. In any case, your closest lady must be independent, and someone who won't worry if you're off on one of your projects, having lost track of time.

A 1920 Aquarian female wants a man who has an ability to ease her sometimes worrisome nature, making her feel cool, calm, and collected. Though talkative and often high-strung, your secret desire is to be with a man to whom you don't have to say a word, someone whose eyes are hypnotic and whose arms are soothing and strong. That kind of security allows you to give the best of yourself to him and to the world around you.

AQUARIUS ZODIAC SIGN
YOUR LOVE PLANETS

YOUR ROMANTIC SIDE   p. 696
▶ **VENUS IN SAGITTARIUS**
Born Jan. 21, 8:04 - Jan. 29, 11:54
▶ **VENUS IN CAPRICORN**
Born Jan. 29, 11:55 - Feb. 19, 22:28

YOUR SEX DRIVE   p. 722
▶ **MARS IN LIBRA**
Born Jan. 21, 8:04 - Jan. 31, 23:17
▶ **MARS IN SCORPIO**
Born Jan. 31, 23:18 - Feb. 19, 22:28

YOUR CELEBRITY TWINS   p. 760
Find out the astrological similarities you have with famous people.

YOUR COMPATIBILITY   p. 780
Compare planets to find out how compatible you are in a relationship.

YOUR RELATIONSHIP KARMA   p. 824
▶ **SATURN IN VIRGO**
Born Jan. 21, 8:04 - Feb. 19, 22:28

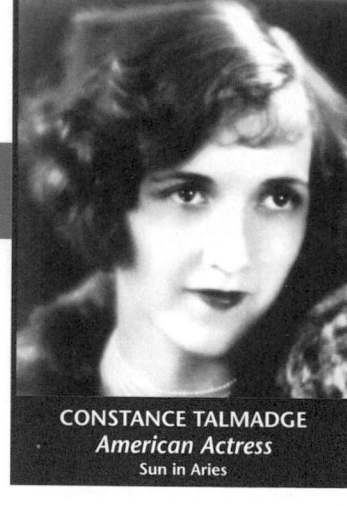

CONSTANCE TALMADGE
American Actress
Sun in Aries

1920 PISCES
From February 19, 22:29 through March 20, 21:58

The Sensitive Gardener

You're a deep and sensitive person, Pisces of 1920, but your view of a close relationship is probably more practical than most people would think. You understand that being with someone requires a good deal of adjustment, and that it's a situation in which little weeds in the garden of love can grow into tree-sized ones if you don't nip them in the bud right at the beginning.

You're an attentive, caring person who listens intently to those you care about most, and you expect the same in return from the one you have chosen to share your life with. You like to know that you're appreciated and that the two of you are working together in order to make sure that the road ahead is as smooth as it has been in the past. When that happens, your sensual side emerges and love takes on deeper meaning.

You are attracted not to looks or superficial behavior, but rather to sincerity and caring. A pretty or handsome face is nice, but when you're close up and begin to talk, the real attraction begins. For you, what's simple is most important. If the one who catches your eye takes a genuine interest in your cares, your problems, and your joys by listening and asking questions, you're hooked for life.

For the Pisces man of 1920, the ideal woman is immediately attentive the first time you meet. She is intuitive and sympathetic enough to know you aren't as cool and carefree as your subdued personality might make it seem. Any woman sensitive enough to see through your veneer is yours, since she will be the one who lets you open up and be your real self. When you feel like this, you can be an attentive, ardent lover, a man that every woman wants to be with.

If you're a 1920 Pisces woman, the man of your dreams sees right into your heart and cares deeply about what he finds there. Someone who can meet you on that level can be trusted to always be there for you. The perfect man will consider you a partner and a friend, not someone to fetch coffee and put your own feelings aside to tend to his. You don't unlock your heart easily, but the right kind of man can open both your mind and your senses.

1920 ARIES
From March 20, 21:59 through April 20, 9:38

The Secret Rebel

Love is a truly liberating force for you, Aries of 1920, and a relationship is the highest form and best expression of love you know. Even though you are an independent soul, you understand that no person is an island, and having someone else in your life will surely complete you emotionally, intellectually, and physically. A partner gives your life form and purpose and makes you a better person.

What you value most in someone close to you is how it opens your mind and lets you see beyond the simple needs of everyday life. You love the idea of sharing and caring, as well as those wonderful, sensual moments being close to someone brings. Like a teenager, you still revel at the fact that you can coo and cuddle all you like at any time of day and night. A relationship that brings both touching and closeness adds dimension and depth not only to your life, but to your character as well.

The person who most draws your eye is someone who is spontaneous and creative, not bound by conventional ways of thinking. The moment that special someone approaches you and takes your hand, you will know if he or she is the one by the warm touch and whether or not your heart skips a beat. Anyone with artistic or literary talent is a sure bet, but someone with a wild and crazy sense of humor can also fill the bill.

As an Aries male of 1920, the lady you most like to be with is warm, witty, compassionate, and not at all bound by a conventional viewpoint. A woman like this lets you express a side of yourself that others rarely see. Her disarming manner and·willingness to let you be yourself can sometimes shock and delight you when the touching and kissing begin.

Your ideal match and perfect man, Aries lady of 1920, is the fellow who manages to take that pompous boor at a party down a notch or two, or the one who stands up at a meeting and says out loud what's on everyone else's mind. He's not bound by convention, but he takes that attitude just far enough to amuse or to defuse a tense situation. He has a good heart, a twinkle in his eye—and you just can't wait to get your arms around him.

1920 TAURUS
From April 20, 9:39 through May 21, 9:21

The Self-Made Dreamer

A relationship for you, 1920 Taurus, is the bedrock on which you can build the foundation of the rest of your life. Though you can be as romantic and sexy as the next person when it comes to love, what makes a relationship especially attractive to you is togetherness, and that includes making the most of your present, as well as planning for the future. Your mate thinks like you do, and knows that when jobs, money, and even retirement accounts are in place, love can blossom in an atmosphere free from want and care.

Once the basics are in place and you are free to express your inner emotions to your soul mate, you are thoughtful and attentive to the one you love. You have a deep sensuality that shows itself in the bedroom, but is also evident in the way you treat your soul mate at every moment. You like to touch, to hug, to exchange little kisses when the mood strikes you.

You are certainly attracted by good looks, and by someone who knows how to dress well. However, anyone who wants to draw your eye and hold your attention needs to first and foremost appear confident and organized. Just a little bit of sloppiness or too much of a casual air is a quick turn-off for you, as it often indicates a person who will let the important things of life slide.

The woman who attracts you most, Taurus man of 1920, is probably a bit on the conservative side in dress and appearance, for you understand that beneath her businesslike appearance is someone who just loves to let her hair down and have fun. Trueness to her values comes first with this lady, as she knows what she's about and where she's headed, qualities that you find irresistible.

The ideal for the 1920 Taurus female, like yourself, is the self-made man. This doesn't mean you need a captain of industry or a billionaire to stir the fires of your romantic soul. But if you meet someone who started from poverty and wound up as a success story, with financial security, this man is just your type. But you don't need to see his resume. You'll know he's the one, the minute he walks in the room, and you're ready to get to know him.

RICHARD BARTHELMESS
American Actor
Venus in Gemini

1920 GEMINI
From May 21, 9:22 through June 21, 17:39

The Heart Talker

The key to your heart, Gemini of 1920, is communication, the right kind at the right time. You see a relationship as a meeting of minds and hearts, so anyone you get close to will hear openly and honestly what's on your mind at any moment. In turn, you expect the same, but you're not just looking for conversation, as the times when you and your love open up to each other are intimate and heartfelt moments in which you share your deepest hopes, fears, and secrets.

When it comes to loving and relating, communication extends well beyond words for you, as you understand that those little everyday gestures say much more than words ever could. You're always ready with a smile, a little gift, an unexpected kiss on the cheek, or just a little touch here and there that lets the person you love most know how much you really care.

The cool, silent type might attract you for a moment or two, but the person who turns your head and wins your heart has a warm, winning smile, and can knock you right off your feet with just a kind "Hello, how are you?" This person doesn't have to be a brilliant conversationalist, holding forth on great literary works, or the events of the day. But the eyes, the smile, the words have to say, "I'm interested in you, and you alone."

If you're a 1920 Gemini man, others probably see your gal as modest, and perhaps even a bit shy, but what others see as shyness is just her way of saving what's inside her for just the right man. She's pleasant, charming, and often people like to be around her without quite knowing why. But you know why, as you can see right to her heart, and you know that she can see to yours.

Your perfect man, 1920 Gemini lady, may not be movie-star handsome, or a man of great accomplishments, though it's okay if he has such qualities. He may appear to others as a man of few words, though he is someone who can command attention just by his presence. He is self-confident and comfortable in his own skin, as the saying goes. And when he talks to you, perhaps the very first time, you can feel it all the way down to the very center of heart.

19

---

1 Read Your Sign   **2** Look Up Your Love Planets   **3** Go to Pages Shown

COCO CHANEL
French Designer
Sun and Venus in Leo

1920 CANCER
From June 21, 17:40 through July 23, 4:34

♋ The Creative Nurturer

For you, Cancer of 1920, a relationship provides an emotional cushion, which makes you comfortable being yourself at any time and anywhere. You need to be with someone whose values are as strong as yours, and who will, like yourself, stop at nothing to hold the family together, whatever it takes. In return, you are ready to work hard and long to build a good home and make it a solid foundation for your love and for your lives together.

As a caring and nurturing soul, you want a relationship where jealousy is absent and loyalty is never questioned. Any time both of you spend exploring your own interests only makes the heart grow fonder and the intimacy more exciting once you are back together. You need to know that your partner will support all your activities, even those that might seem a bit strange or out of the mainstream. Your quirky, creative nature is what makes you so unique, and in understanding this about you, your partner will love you even more intently.

To catch your eye, someone who wants to be with you must have a well-kept appearance, exuding both beauty and simplicity at the same time. You are not impressed with expensive accessories nor fashionable clothing that masks the essence of the real person within. The special someone whose appearance and bearing say firmly, "This is the real me," will win your heart every time.

If you are a Cancerian male born in 1920, you want a woman who is imaginative and kind, whose mind is whimsically creative rather than deeply intellectual. Sensuality and mystery, combined with loyalty and affection, are qualities that surely win you over. You like to be pampered and flattered, so the woman who knows how to cater to your needs without being subservient to them is the one for you.

The man who catches your eye, if you are a Cancerian female from 1920, is gentle and soft-spoken with an easygoing stay-at-home nature. Those hunky he-man types are good for the movies, but sharing your life requires someone with much more sensitivity than that, and who especially values the meaning of family, which you are too happy to provide.

1920 LEO
From July 23, 4:35 through August 23, 11:20

♌ The Adventurous Romantic

A relationship for you, 1920 Leo, is something that makes you feel good all over. A true romantic, you like nothing better than that tingling "love makes me feel brand new" sensation from the top of your head to the bottom of your toes. But relating is more than romance for you, so more than just a sweetheart, you need someone who can match your drive and enthusiasm, as well as share your adventurous love of life.

You need commitment, but not if it ties you together at the ankles, so that neither of you can move too far from the other. You want someone both devoted and infatuated, no matter how old, and who is not afraid to hold hands, to kiss you when the mood strikes, or to dance cheek to cheek in public. You are proud of being in love and want to share that special feeling with the entire world.

Anyone can catch your eye and draw your interest if they focus a lot of attention on you in a sincere way. Once that person gets through the front door and keeps you interested for more than one evening, he or she needs to be forthright and unafraid to say what is on his or her mind. Honesty truly makes someone sexy and intriguing in your eyes, though generosity runs a close second. Someone who likes to surprise you with little gifts or to whisk you away for a day outside your normal routine is sure to win your heart.

As a 1920 Leo male, you love women who can hold their own in life and in love. The more confident a woman is, the more you are attracted to her. If a woman can challenge you on an intellectual level, you are likely to find her truly desirable. At the same time, though, she has to know when to challenge and when to compromise, as you're looking for love, not a contest.

If you are a Leo female born in 1920, you like a man with ambition and desires for the finer things in life. A perfectionist by nature, you will never be happy with someone who muddles his way through life satisfied with the status quo. The man who strives for something bigger and better not only inspires your love and affection, but also inspires you to be the best you can be, in every way.

1920 VIRGO
From August 23, 11:21 through September 23, 8:27

The Serious Lover

As a Virgo of 1920, your idea of a lasting relationship is simple. Two people make a commitment to one another, and take it as seriously as one possibly could. To you, a partnership means that both people support each other equally, and work hard to reach mutual goals. While that may sound boring to some, you actually find it exciting, gratifying, and satisfying to see your long-held dreams turn into realities.

When you're in a good, loving relationship, you look forward to coming home at night to a warm embrace, so you can forget about all the things that stressed you out during the day. Sharing quiet moments cuddling on the sofa, nuzzling with your significant other like an adolescent, or giving each other long, sensual foot massages helps make your life (and your love life) well worthwhile.

Though you often take life far too seriously, you always have a soft spot for someone who is lighthearted, playful, and can make you smile with a quick one-liner or silly gesture. Nothing makes you feel more alive and engaged than walking arm-in-arm with that special person, the two of you laughing out loud together like giddy school children.

As a Virgo male born in 1920, you like a woman who is sweet and good-natured, yet intelligent enough to engage you in stimulating conversation. You are secure enough not to be threatened by a woman who has both brains and beauty, and in fact become bored if she doesn't have some mental and emotional depth. You like good looks, but you're most attracted to someone who knows how to complement her looks by dressing in a fashionable and tasteful way.

You want a man who is sexy and seductive, yet gentle and subtle at the same time, if you're a 1920 female Virgo. You'll walk right out the door if someone comes on too strong, but a man who eases his way slowly into your good graces with sincere compliments made over intimate dinners can melt your heart. A great conversationalist is not your main preference, as you like to be with someone who is more of a listener than a talker, but who still knows how to say the right thing at the right time.

H. L. MENCKEN
American Writer
Sun in Virgo

1920 LIBRA
From September 23, 8:28 through October 23, 17:12

The Seductive Romantic

With your seductive smile and charming manner, Libra of 1920, you know how to make others fall madly in love with you, and can have anyone you want at the snap of a finger. But you want your closest and longest-lasting relationship to bring out more in you than just your seductive ability. Once you get under someone's skin, they will never be able to leave you alone, and you want that special someone to make you feel the very same way.

For you, it's important that your closest relationship helps you escape from the world. When you close the door to the day's stress and responsibility, you want to know that the world is outside, and you and your partner are the only ones inside. In your own private world for two, you think nothing of chilling a bottle of champagne before dinner, and using a good hearty meal to work up an appetite of love and desire.

Anyone who wants to win you over, must shower you with romance, romance, and even more romance. In fact, to keep your relationship fresh and spontaneous, you need to fall in love anew each and every day. You

need to know that holidays and birthdays will be remembered with special surprises, and that each day of love will feel like Christmas, bringing out the wide-eyed child in you no matter what your age.

As a Libra male of 1920, your perfect companion is a woman completely traditional and feminine, whose soft-spoken manner, inviting eyes, and loving smile make you feel as if you are the only man on earth. You want someone to give you a back rub when you feel tense, and give you reassuring words when things look bleak. Most of all, a woman who supports you through thick and thin is one who will capture your heart and soul.

The most desirable man for a 1920 Libra female is unpredictable in his actions, yet unswerving in his loyalty and love for you. You are best suited to a man who is physically strong and pushes his body to the absolute limits. At the same time, he will be health conscious and aware that the more he takes care of himself, the longer he will be around to service your needs and fulfill your desires.

PABLO CASALS
Spanish Musician
Venus in Sagittarius

1920 SCORPIO
From October 23, 17:13 through November 22, 14:14

♏ The Sensual Sleuth

As a Scorpio of 1920, you view every relationship as a fascinating enigma waiting for you to unravel it, slowly but surely. What makes any partnership appealing for you is taking it one spoonful at a time, and never swallowing everything all at once. The more you don't know about the emotional depth of your partner, and the more you can discover through your own detective work, the greater your interest and the less likely you'll be bored.

An ideal relationship inspires you, always pushing you to the limits of your creativity and ingenuity. What makes a long-lasting union most satisfying are those moments you spend with your love, locked away from the world, and you may have a secret hideaway that only the two of you know about. You probably have your own affectionate terms that you call one another, and special gestures and facial expressions that are yours alone.

If someone wants to keep you interested, they should never reveal everything about themselves, at least not at first. The prospect of discovering something new about someone is exciting to you, especially when the two of you take time to work slowly from the emotional to the physical. Allowing your fingertips to touch, relaxing with a sensual massage to ease your tension—these are the things that keep you coming back for more, again and again.

A Scorpio man of 1920 likes a woman of mystery, but is also attracted to someone who likes adventure. The superficialities of perfect clothing and a well-groomed appearance are nice, but not if that's all there is to the lady. For you, it's what's inside that counts most, even if (and in fact especially if) you're not sure what that inside might be!

If you are a feminine Scorpio born in 1920, you like your men rugged, and you're drawn to the type who is not afraid to take risks both at his work and in his private life. He must give you strength when you feel most vulnerable, but be compassionate and not afraid to be openly sensitive when you need it. Yet at the same time, there must always be some side of his personality that stays at a distance, intriguing you always.

1920 SAGITTARIUS
From November 22, 14:15 through December 22, 3:16

♐ The Adventurous Enthusiast

Exuberant and enthusiastic, you will try almost anything at least once, Sagittarius of 1920, so you want a partner who will take you to places you'd never dream of going, and do things with you that you'd never dare dream of doing on your own. The thought of opening up new vistas and exploring far-off exotic places with someone you love comes close to your ideal lifestyle. Prospective mates who are more comfortable sitting at home and exploring only the television need not apply.

A partnership for you is a meeting of the minds, a space in which you are free to express all your opinions, even when the two of you don't quite agree. You love learning from the views and ideas of someone close to you, so it doesn't matter if you differ on the details. And besides, even if you do disagree a little too vehemently at times, it is nice to kiss and make up afterwards, isn't it?

If someone wants to tug at your heartstrings, he or she needs to be fit and trim. Flabby bodies are definitely a turn-off for you, and bad heating habits or sloppy appearance will never get anyone to first base with you. It is not that you are vain or superficial, as you're just using your common sense. Unless someone is physically fit, he or she could never keep pace with you, nor be able to accompany you on life's shared journey.

As a 1920 Sagittarian male, you love all types of women. What attracts you most, though, is someone boldly individual, who isn't afraid to surprise you day after day, even after you think you have learned all there is to know about her. What makes a woman sexy in your eyes is her soft yet firm touch, shown in the way she rubs her fingers through your hair, or kisses you long and lovingly.

The man perfectly suited for a Sagittarian female born in 1920 should be gregarious, friendly, and comfortable in a variety of social settings, especially since you have a range of friends and family, and varied interests. Being with someone who is unafraid to show his affection, and who seems to have something in common with everyone makes you confident, and ready to meet the world head on.

Colette – The Bold Provocateur

A feminist icon, bisexual heroine, literary genius, and all-round provocateur, Sidonie Gabrielle Colette, or simply Colette, as she was known, was the New Woman of the swinging Belle Epoque in France, wreaking scandal and outrage wherever she went.

Born in a rural town in Burgundy, France, she left for Paris at the age of twenty to marry the writer Henri Gauthier-Villars. It was at his insistence that her writing career began. *Claudine* was her first book, written under Henri's pen name Willy, about the sexual adventures of a teenage girl. It was an instant hit and spawned a whole series of *Claudine* spin-offs—everything from a theatre show to *Claudine* soap.

The marriage disintegrated after twelve years and Colette took to the stage, giving risqué and hypnotic music hall performances, baring her breasts, and appearing nude. At the famous Moulin Rouge cabaret, she famously peeled bandages off her female lover and ended by kissing her on the mouth—while she was cross-dressed as a male archaeologist. The show was banned by the police for indecency.

Colette embarked on a series of public affairs with both men and woman—no one could escape her palpable sexual energy. Her sexuality was magnetic, her presence mesmerising. Also a brilliant journalist, Colette worked as a theatre critic for the French daily newspaper *Le Matin* where she embarked on a fervent affair with the editor, Henry de Jouvenel. Her next moment of disrepute happened when she had his child out of wedlock—they did eventually marry but Colette's scandalizing was far from

over. She was about to break the biggest taboo of them all.

Tired of Henry's constant womanizing and infidelities, Colette threw herself passionately into a new relationship—with her sixteen-year-old stepson, who lost his virginity to her on a family holiday. She was forty-seven. The incestuous affair lasted four years and inspired one of her greatest and most erotic literary works, *Chéri*, in which a sexually inexperienced young man has an affair with an older woman. Colette's second marriage ended when her husband discovered she had been bedding his son.

Railing against society's dictates, she enticed another younger man—this time all the way down the aisle. She married pearl dealer Maurice Goudeket at the age of 62.

From the late nineteen twenties onward, Colette finally gained recognition for her writing, which had developed into rich and sensuous prose, captivating readers in a blurring of boundaries between fact and fiction—most of her work was closely based on her life and her real-life exploits.

Responsible for bringing pornographic literature into the mainstream, Colette's arousing fictional fantasies were often narrations of her private world. This was how she came to epitomize the liberated woman, unafraid to reveal her carnal desires and expose her lustful life. Awarded countless honors, on her death in 1954, she was the first woman to be honored with a French state funeral. But the Church hadn't forgotten her promiscuous past, refusing her final rites.

A sexual pioneer of her time, she never feared public outrage, openly flouting her conquests and revelling in her sexuality. Her life challenged social boundaries, fusing erotica with art with a shameless, guilt-free conscience. The ultimate sybarite, Colette was unrelenting in her pursuit of pleasure and paved the way for generations of women to come.

"I love my past. I love my present. I'm not ashamed of what I've had, and I'm not sad because I have it no longer."

COLETTE, *THE LAST OF CHERI*, 1926

23

▶ READ ABOUT THE RISE OF FEMINISM ON PAGE 449

⭐ **SKIRTS**

⭐ **MISS AMERICA**

⭐ **BIRTH CONTROL PIONEERS**

⭐ **VALENTINO, "THE GREAT LOVER"**

⭐ **FANNY BRICE IN THE FOLLIES**

⭐ **MAIN STREET**

⭐ **AGE OF INNOCENCE**

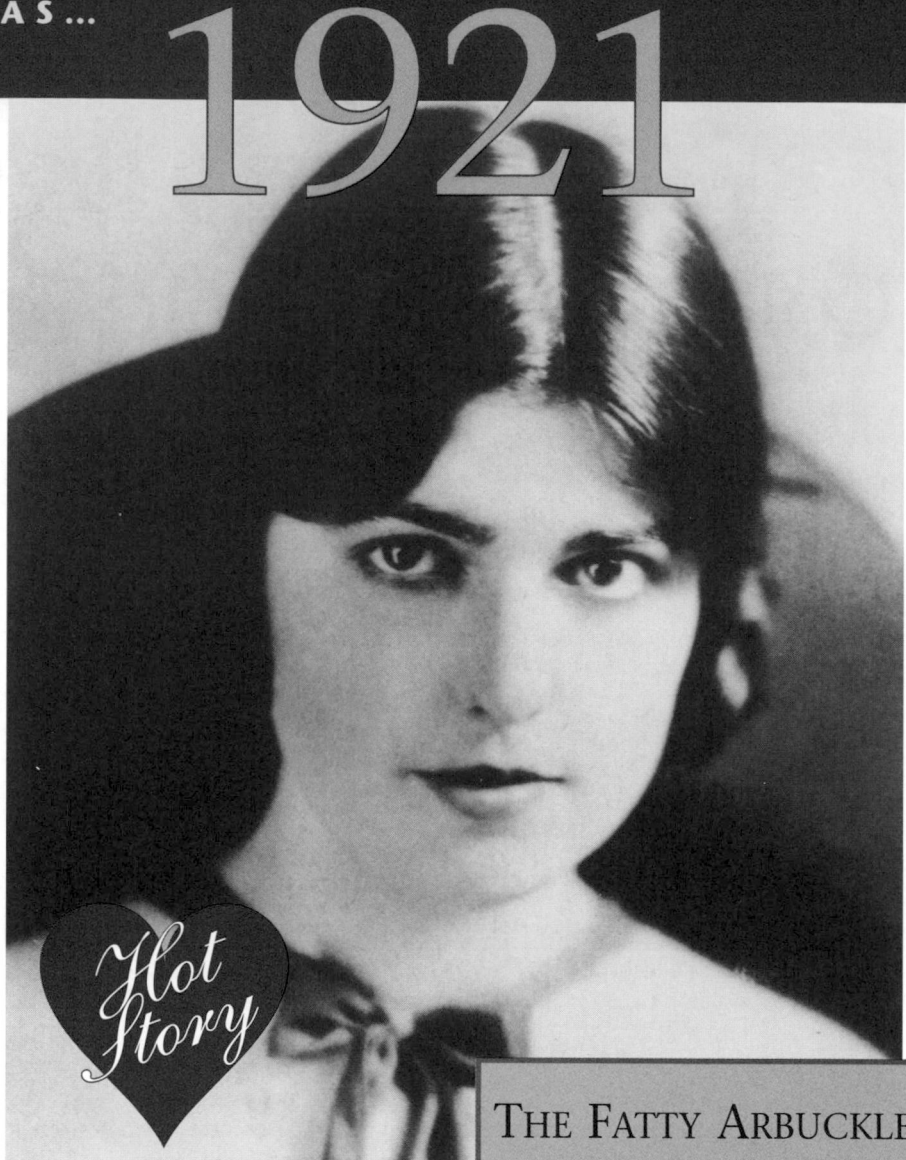

Hot Story

EVENTS

Skirts were big news. As fashions dictated their rise from the ankle to the calf, a bill in Utah proposed to imprison any woman wearing a skirt three inches above the ankle. Men adopted a new slang word for women, referring to them as "skirts." Following the Great War, however, there were less of them to do so—two million less men than women in Britain. Margaret Sanger held the first American Birth Control Conference in New York, and in Britain Dr. Marie Stopes faced fierce opposition in opening the first birth control clinic in London.

In Michigan the Supreme Court ruled that the husband was the master in his own home, and Atlantic City staged the first Miss America Bathing Beauty contest.

POP CULTURE

Rudolph Valentino burst on the scene as leading man in both *The Four Horsemen of the Apocalypse*, a sprawling, international epic with plenty of tango action, and *The Sheik*, in which he spirits a feisty British socialite off to his luxurious desert tent-palace. In Sven Gade's gender-bending *Hamlet*, Danish star Asta Nielsen is a princess forced by her scheming mother to masquerade as Hamlet and secretly vies with Ophelia for Horatio's love.

In Cecil B. Demille's *The Affairs of Anatol,* a socialite husband embarks on a series of affairs to seek a better version of his wife.

Audiences enjoyed upbeat sing-along tunes like "Ma! (He's/She's Makin' Eyes at Me)" and "Ain't We Got Fun?" "I'm Just Wild About Harry" and "Daddy, Won't You Please Come Home?" were penned by Eubie Blake, a black ragtime pianist and composer. W.C. Handy's version of an old folk tune, "Careless Love," became a jazz standard. Fanny Brice popularized the French torch song "My Man" in the Ziegfeld Follies.

Great books of the year included Sinclair Lewis's *Main Street*, a satire of small-town American life, and *The Age of Innocence* by Edith Wharton, a New York high-society vignette set in the 1870s. *The Sheik*, by Edith M. Hull, the book on which the Valentino movie was based, sold well. In *Rubé* by Guiseppe Antonio Borgese, a wounded soldier struggles with post-war life, and abandons his wife in favor of a Parisian courtesan.

THE FATTY ARBUCKLE SCANDAL

Roscoe "Fatty" Arbuckle was in the throes of a thriving movie career when infamy swept in and destroyed his life. He was one of the silent screen's first big stars. But on Labor Day, 1921, he was arrested on manslaughter charges for the murder of starlet Virginia Rappe.

The jovial Arbuckle had thrown a party a few days before. Rappe crashed it, and ended up dead. It was Hollywood's first major scandal—the papers seized on it and his career was effectively ended, despite the fact that he was eventually acquitted. It would take three trials for Arbuckle to win back his good name.

SEE ALSO

▶ **LANA TURNER** *Page 333*

▶ **THE LONELY HEARTS KILLERS** *Page 259*

1921 CAPRICORN

From December 22, 1920 3:17 through January 20, 1921 13:54
(December 1921 Capricorns, see 1922 Capricorn)

♑ *The Compassionate Realist*

As a 1921 Capricorn, you have every reason to take pride in being a bit old fashioned. You've experienced a lot in the world. And looking around, you may wonder how relationships got so complex and confusing. Once you make a commitment, you honor it, because you are highly responsible. This doesn't preclude having fun, however! You have made sacrifices, but you are no stranger to romance!

It would be understandable if you find yourself toying with the belief that each person should shoulder equal responsibility in a relationship, since that is what you demand of yourself and you're willing to do your part. Yet, your softer side says, "There but for the grace of God, go I." Therefore you give others the benefit of the doubt, especially when a loved one is in need.

You are most responsive to a partner who shares your sense of tradition and has similar values related to family and responsibility. Yet, you also love to be swept away by glamor and romance. It is important for suitors to see that you are more sensitive below the surface than

you may initially appear. Because you have high ideals, love prospects must respect you and be true to themselves to earn your respect in return. You know that fairy tales are meant to come true, and the lucky person who earns your love may just live happily ever after!

As a 1921 male Capricorn you want a woman you can be proud of, with a healthy sense of dignity and self-esteem. You want her to be comfortable knowing that she has a special place in your heart and is loved for her strengths and compassion. You prefer a woman who can read your body language, since words aren't always easy for you. To hold your interest a woman must have a touch of mystique and keep you guessing a little.

If you are a 1921 female Capricorn, you need a man you can rely on and who has a lot of practical skills, as well as being simply a good person. You have a way of bringing out the best in the men you attract, so you want to invest your time in a man who has the greatest potential, not only to make you happy, but to do good things in the world.

CAPRICORN ZODIAC SIGN

YOUR LOVE PLANETS

YOUR ROMANTIC SIDE   p. 696
- ▶ VENUS IN AQUARIUS
  Born Dec. 22, 1920 3:17 - Jan. 06, 1921 20:32
- ▶ VENUS IN PISCES
  Born Jan. 06, 20:33 - Jan. 20, 13:54

YOUR SEX DRIVE   p. 722
- ▶ MARS IN AQUARIUS
  Born Dec. 22, 1920 3:17 - Jan. 05, 1921 7:38
- ▶ MARS IN PISCES
  Born Jan. 05, 7:39 - Jan. 20, 13:54

YOUR CELEBRITY TWINS   p. 760
Find out the astrological similarities you have with famous people.

YOUR COMPATIBILITY   p. 780
Compare planets to find out how compatible you are in a relationship.

YOUR RELATIONSHIP KARMA   p. 824
- ▶ SATURN IN VIRGO
  Born Dec. 22, 1920 3:17 - Jan. 20, 1921 13:54

MAURICE RAVEL
French Composer
Venus in Aquarius

1921 AQUARIUS

From January 20, 13:55 through February 19, 4:19

♒ *The Surprising Romantic*

No matter what the rules or traditions were when you were growing up, as a 1921 Aquarian, you've always done thing in your own unique fashion. Everything that you've experienced, including love, has been on your own terms. You've never liked being tied down—you still don't—and relationships need to reflect that need for freedom. For you, variety is the spice of life, and you aren't willing to settle for things boring and commonplace.

Relationships that are the most comfortable for you are the ones that almost aren't there. The longer the leash a partner gives you, the happier you are. Yet sharing things of common interest with someone you love makes you the most content. The best pairings are the ones that combine explorations of the intellect, shared visits to odd and obscure places, and a sense of acceptance for who and what you are.

For a potential mate to capture your attention and your affections, you need to feel as though you could have an intelligent conversation, but also that the elements of

whimsy and fun are always near at hand. You want a partner who can see the possibilities that exist and not get mired down by a few limitations. You know that obstacles are always a challenge, and you want a partner who would like to rise to the challenges together with you.

As a 1921 Aquarius male, the female who captures your heart must first capture your mind. You want a woman who is a fun companion and friend to you, and who will never take you for granted. She'll have interests separate from yours, and won't give you the third degree about where you are every single second of the day. Her sense of self is solid—and so is her love for you.

For females born in 1921, the kind of man who can steal your heart is one who is able to balance his actions with emotions. A man who likes to cuddle and snuggle with you is most appealing—even better if he reads aloud from your favorite books. If he willingly goes along with you on jaunts to antique stores, so much the better.

AQUARIUS ZODIAC SIGN

YOUR LOVE PLANETS

YOUR ROMANTIC SIDE   p. 696
- ▶ VENUS IN PISCES
  Born Jan. 20, 13:55 - Feb. 02, 18:34
- ▶ VENUS IN ARIES
  Born Feb. 02, 18:35 - Feb. 19, 4:19

YOUR SEX DRIVE   p. 722
- ▶ MARS IN PISCES
  Born Jan. 20, 13:55 - Feb. 13, 5:20
- ▶ MARS IN ARIES
  Born Feb. 13, 5:21 - Feb. 19, 4:19

YOUR CELEBRITY TWINS   p. 760
Find out the astrological similarities you have with famous people.

YOUR COMPATIBILITY   p. 780
Compare planets to find out how compatible you are in a relationship.

YOUR RELATIONSHIP KARMA   p. 824
- ▶ SATURN IN VIRGO
  Born Jan. 20, 13:55 - Feb. 19, 4:19

CONRAD NAGEL
American Actor
Sun in Pisces

26

1921 PISCES
From February 19, 4:20 through March 21, 3:50

◊◊ A Considerate Lover

As a 1921 Pisces, you've had a wide romantic streak your whole life, with a vivid imagination that has allowed you to immediately sense when the perfect mate is near. Because you are so psychically sensitive, you often feel what your partner is feeling, even without realizing that you are absorbing the other person's emotions. Because of that, and because you give more than 100% in a relationship, it is important that you give your heart to someone who is worthy of it, and who will not take your love and concern for granted.

In many respects you are a loner, because you are comfortable doing your own thing. You prefer a relationship that allows both of you enough emotional breathing room to be separate individuals. Yet on a much deeper level, you and your partner are joined together. Depending on your mood, you can be either a leader or a follower. The best relationship for you is one in which there is lots of give and take—but always that psychic connection.

For you, love is sparked largely by the sense of inner compassion and beauty. If your partner shares your love of music, theater, and the arts, you may have a match made in heaven. To keep your attention, a mate should remain just a bit mysterious.

As a 1921 Pisces male, the perfect partner is one who is ready when you are to engage in sensual delights. She may have a fondness for gardening, flower arranging, and cooking. You want a woman who is secure and comfortable within herself. An appreciation for fine music will make her a sure winner in your heart.

For 1921 Pisces females, the perfect man for you is one who is fearlessly self-reliant and action oriented. He will enjoy keeping things simple with a "what you see is what you get" quality. Your perfect mate loves to tinker with repairs and problem solving, and prefers being useful than lazy. He will put duty before pleasure and be your rock to rely on when life's storms pull you in different directions, and he knows the value of a well-timed hug.

1921 ARIES
From March 21, 3:51 through April 20, 15:31

♈ The Restless Leader

While you may be glad to spend time alone because you are very good company for yourself, you are happiest when you are in a committed relationship. You're extremely giving by nature, and having someone to give to is important for your emotional well-being. Freedom is important to you, yes, but more important is the feeling of security from being in a long-term relationship.

You are passionate about the things you care about. No half measures here. The perfect relationship for you is one where your goals and desires are respected, as is your tendency to stand up for the underdog. With a partner who is right there with you every step of the way, happily helping and supporting you, there's no end to the good you can accomplish.

The person who will get a second glance and a more than passing chance with you is one who respects your independent nature, and who has hobbies or interests that are different than yours. This will keep the sparks from dimming. A love of nature may be a key as the glue that holds a relationship together for you,

because you have a wonderful appreciation for all things earthy and solid. Not the least in importance, too, is being able to communicate about money—where it's coming from and where (and how fast) it's going.

For 1921 Aries males, your interest in the fairer sex has a touch of nostalgia connected to it. She'll have a solid sense of self and a quiet demeanor, and while she's usually willing to let you lead in public, you are tantalized by the spicy things that sometimes come out of her prim and proper mouth in private. She may appear to be a lady to the rest of the world, but she can make you laugh with the occasional risqué joke.

For Aries women born in 1921, the man in your life will compete to win your affections, though not necessarily against another male. He may have to compete with your own interests and pastimes, since you have so many of them. If he is able to follow your lead without complaint, he has a chance of winning you over. But he'll stop you in your tracks the first time he brings you a single red rose.

1921 TAURUS
From April 20, 15:32 through May 21, 15:16

♉ Steady and Secure

As a 1921 Taurus, you have the advantage of many years of good common sense on your side. You are an excellent judge of character, so you aren't about to be snowed over today, tomorrow, or any day by someone who puts on airs or is flighty. In your ideal relationship, you achieve a sense of balance by being with someone who complements your passions and desires, and who loves to share with you the good things in life that you both work hard to acquire.

Security (getting it and keeping it) is an important theme in any relationship, and not just financial security. Emotional security is high on your list, too. You prefer knowing that there won't be any surprises sprung on you, so you may be slow to commit. You want a relationship that is a good balance between being alone and time spent with your partner. Your home (and all its comforts) is the center of your world, and you'll happily work alongside a partner when it comes to cooking and shopping—but only as long as the duties are equally shared.

For someone to capture your heart, you must feel that it is safe to express your true feelings, no matter what they are. You have strong beliefs and want a partner who has equally strong opinions. This doesn't mean, however, that you are overly serious. Not at all! You have a terrific sense of wit and charm and sociability, and you want to be with someone who can bring out the playful side of you as well.

As a male Taurus born in 1921, the perfect woman is someone who appreciates the value of a dollar, and who values a sense of order in the physical world. She loves to have a good time and is open to being spontaneous in the right circumstances. She'll shock you just often enough to keep you on your toes!

As a 1921 female Taurus, your attractions to a man are tied to his ability to follow through with promises, as well as being a good problem solver. Your best guy is a patient man, willing to let you move at your own pace in life. At the same time his varied interests bring a new dimension of excitement to your days, and you find yourself saying "yes" more often than "no."

TAURUS ZODIAC SIGN
Your Love Planets

YOUR ROMANTIC SIDE   p. 696
▶ **VENUS IN TAURUS**
Born Apr. 20, 15:32 - Apr. 25, 23:45
▶ **VENUS IN ARIES**
Born Apr. 25, 23:46 - May 21, 15:16

YOUR SEX DRIVE   p. 722
▶ **MARS IN TAURUS**
Born Apr. 20, 15:32 - May 06, 1:44
▶ **MARS IN GEMINI**
Born May 06, 1:45 - May 21, 15:16

YOUR CELEBRITY TWINS   p. 760
Find out the astrological similarities you have with famous people.

YOUR COMPATIBILITY   p. 780
Compare planets to find out how compatible you are in a relationship.

YOUR RELATIONSHIP KARMA   p. 824
▶ **SATURN IN VIRGO**
Born Apr. 20, 15:32 - May 21, 15:16

NORMA TALMADGE
American Actress
Sun and Venus in Taurus

27

1921 GEMINI
From May 21, 15:17 through June 21, 23:35

♊ A Versatile Lover

As a Gemini born in 1921, you exude a quality of sociability, curiosity, and wit, all attributes that are capable of making your attractive to a broad range of love prospects. Being able to have solid communication with a partner is key to your happiness, since you take great pleasure in being able to share your observations, feelings, interests, and desires.

Central in importance to a successful and long-lasting love relationship is valuing self-awareness and self-improvement, along with staying well connected within the broader family circle. Like the sign of the "twins" you are, Gemini, you thrive on the dynamics of many social interactions, so your ideal relationship is one that includes many kinds of people from different walks of life.

Because you have a touch of a dramatic flair, you want to know that your partner still has the fires of desire for you, no matter how long you've been together. To keep you interested, your partner needs most of all to be a good conversationalist with an interest in current events and literature, in addition to the more

sensual delights and playfulness of time in the bedroom. And because variety for you is indeed the spice of life, you crave the thrill of erotic opportunities in unusual places or settings, such as on vacation or while traveling.

As a 1921 male Gemini, one of your greatest challenges may have been less finding and keeping a woman's interest but how to narrow the field to just one who can satisfy enough of your interests and appetites. While a woman's physical beauty is important to you, it pales in comparison to the importance you place on the qualities of her mind and speech, which is what really turns you on.

You women born in 1921 have the advantage of wit and keen observational skills to help you know when a man is telling you the truth or not, and your partner will quickly learn that honesty is always the best policy with you! Your perfect guy willingly goes along on long rides to visit family and view changes of scenery, knowing how that sparks your mind. He'll even surprise you with a trip now and then.

GEMINI ZODIAC SIGN
Your Love Planets

YOUR ROMANTIC SIDE   p. 696
▶ **VENUS IN ARIES**
Born May 21, 15:17 - June 02, 4:20
▶ **VENUS IN TAURUS**
Born June 02, 4:21 - June 21, 23:35

YOUR SEX DRIVE   p. 722
▶ **MARS IN GEMINI**
Born May 21, 15:17 - June 18, 20:33
▶ **MARS IN CANCER**
Born June 18, 20:34 - June 21, 23:35

YOUR CELEBRITY TWINS   p. 760
Find out the astrological similarities you have with famous people.

YOUR COMPATIBILITY   p. 780
Compare planets to find out how compatible you are in a relationship.

YOUR RELATIONSHIP KARMA   p. 824
▶ **SATURN IN VIRGO**
Born May 21, 15:17 - June 21, 23:35

BARBARA LAMARR
American Actress
Sun and Venus in Leo

1921 CANCER
From June 21, 23:36 through July 23, 10:29

A Sensitive Sweetheart

As a Cancerian born in 1921, you have a soft touch and a romantic soul. You naturally want to create a nest for family and a home as a sanctuary in a world that is too often inhospitable or harsh. Your idea of the perfect relationship is one in which you are joined in this endeavor and take comfort in the many ways you can build a sense of security and a warm, private life.

You also have a powerful desire for emotional intimacy within a relationship. It is important to you that your relationship provide emotional support in gentle ways so that, as a couple, your kindness will endear others to you both. Because you have a relatively shy and sometimes retiring nature, you prefer a relationship that helps you balance these tendencies, and bring you more into the world than you would on your own.

For a mate to capture and keep your interest, listening to you is foremost in importance, not only to what you say but to how you say it, reading your body language. Because good food is central to your well-being, you will delight in a relationship where you enjoy meals together in a relaxed atmosphere. Finding the right balance between creativity and maintaining a sense of order is also key. It is important for you to negotiate how you share your living space, so that you each know where you can keep your personal belongings. Stability is more exciting to you than excitement.

For you male Cancers born in 1921, your heart is stirred by a woman who has good old-fashioned values. The one you commit to is gentle, supportive, and nurturing and makes you feel secure enough to open your heart. A sense of humor is a must, too, and your best gal keeps you laughing. You'll never have to wonder where you stand with her, because she'll tell you—frequently.

Female Cancers born in 1921 have a lot to offer a man when it comes to nurturing, and the one who catches your eye is the one who wants to take care of you for a change! He's spirited, loving, and a bit headstrong, but you'll sense his love in everything he does for you. If you feel a blush on your cheek after his kiss, he's a keeper.

1921 LEO
From July 23, 10:30 through August 23, 17:14

A Powerful Player

You know in your heart, as a 1921 Leo, that love makes the world go 'round and that you in particular have lots of love to give. Love comes as naturally to you as breathing in and out. You wouldn't dream of living just a solitary life and depriving someone of all you have to offer! That would be a terrible waste!

But in all seriousness, Leo, because you love to share your heartfelt emotions with others, it is important for you to be in a relationship that will not stifle your creativity, but which, on the contrary, allows it to flourish. Like the Sun associated with the sign Leo, you need to shine, so it is also desirable for you to be in a relationship that, in a sense, showcases your many talents and your personality. As Shakespeare said, all the world's a stage, and you certainly thrive on life's dramatic ups and downs when it comes to love and romance.

Because you are a winner, you're attracted to a partner who similarly has a winning attitude. You're smitten by someone who's in your cheering section, and lets you know it. It's not that you need constant reassurance of your greatness. It's just that it can help to know that the object of your affection is aware that good fortune was smiling when it brought you together. Anyone who wants to keep your attention needs a strong sense of self and interests that don't include you. Even adoration can get boring when it's a steady diet.

As a male Leo born in 1921, your ideal female understands your sense of pride and does her best not to step on the lion's tail. She knows that as long as you feel that you have most of the control in the relationship, you're happy. At the same time, she's got a mind of her own and isn't afraid to stand up to you.

As a female 1921 Leo, you may have a hard time convincing a man that he "wears the pants" in the relationship, because it's so natural for you to take charge. The ideal man for you is happier following your lead, rather than being in control himself, and knows how to make you feel like a queen. However, a bit of dissension now and then lets the making up be all that sweeter.

1921 VIRGO

From August 23, 17:15 through September 23, 14:19

A Meticulous Mate

While the typical adjectives often describe Virgo as practical, useful, analytical, perfectionist, and detailed-oriented, you are much more than that when it comes to romance. Whatever you do, and whomever you do it with, you want to share a sense of style, sophistication, and panache. Your ideal relationship is one that allows you to set an example of good grooming and good taste for the rest of the world, or whatever part of it you influence.

In affairs of the heart, little things make all the difference. You are committed to investing all your strength and energy into a relationship and you expect the same in return. You will give 100% as long as you feel confident that the effort will be well rewarded. With the right partner, this will be automatic.

In order for you to be swept off your feet, and to keep the sparks flying, a suitor would do well to take you to the theater or to a new showing at the museum. You have a fondness for nature, too, so simple walks in the park or a trip to the flower show or nearby zoo could put you in a romantic mood. No doubt some of your fondest romantic memories include scenery that is full of nature. Comparison-shopping is another favorite pastime for you to be able to share the process of discovery with a mate. Most of all, your suitor had better know right from wrong, as you have a highly developed conscience and expect your partner to have one, too.

As a Virgo man born in 1921, your preferred Goddess of Love comes in a neat package, well groomed and organized, but with a playful spirit that loves to tease and laugh at your jokes. She takes pride in her appearance, and you're always proud to be seen with her because she's a true lady in public. Behind closed doors she's a bit earthy!

As a female Virgo born in 1921, you are most attracted to a true "he-man" in a classical sense. Your heart flutters when a man is courteous enough to open the door for you and offer you his arm when crossing the street. His jokes will be tasteful and refined, too. If he treats you like a queen, you will bestow many loving favors upon him!

VIRGO ZODIAC SIGN
YOUR LOVE PLANETS

YOUR ROMANTIC SIDE   p. 696
▶ **VENUS IN CANCER**
Born Aug. 23, 17:15 - Aug. 31, 22:23
▶ **VENUS IN LEO**
Born Aug. 31, 22:24 - Sept. 23, 14:19

YOUR SEX DRIVE   p. 722
▶ **MARS IN LEO**
Born Aug. 23, 17:15 - Sept. 19, 11:39
▶ **MARS IN VIRGO**
Born Sept. 19, 11:40 - Sept. 23, 14:19

YOUR CELEBRITY TWINS   p. 760
Find out the astrological similarities you have with famous people.

YOUR COMPATIBILITY   p. 780
Compare planets to find out how compatible you are in a relationship.

YOUR RELATIONSHIP KARMA   p. 824
▶ **SATURN IN VIRGO**
Born Aug. 23, 17:15 - Sept. 23, 14:19

ELINOR GLYN
English Writer
Sun in Libra

29

1921 LIBRA

From September 23, 14:20 through October 23, 23:01

The Refined Lover

No sign more than you understands the value of a relationship, and for 1921 Libras, that is especially true, because you not only want to have a relationship, but you understand the importance of working to make it last. You know that compromise is an essential element in getting along, but you also know how to balance work with pleasure. Life with you is a refreshing fountain of intellectual, spiritual, and social stimulation.

You love bringing people together, whether it's for fun or work, making sure things run smoothly. While commitment isn't always easy for you, especially in romance, once you've made a decision, you stick with it. You're loyal, devoted, and most of all, fair, especially in matters of the heart. Your partner doesn't have to wonder about your love, because you show it in your actions.

To keep your attention, a mate needs to share your love of social projects and work alongside you to aid the less fortunate. You enjoy hosting gracious parties, and your partner is as skilled as you are in making guests feel welcome. You have a penetrating mind, one that knows intuitively if someone is keeping a secret. This can be a double-edged sword, because while you love to be surprised by grand gestures, it is hard for someone to fool you.

As a male born with the Sun in Libra in 1921, you have a distinctly artistic flair, which can be expressed in love, as you find colorful ways to please your partner. The woman who can most inspire you is one who is beautiful inside as well as outside, skilled in the social arts, and able to make quick decisions.

Female Libras born in 1921 truly are beautiful inside and out. A man who can appreciate your many charms is lucky indeed, because you will always keep life interesting for him. For him to keep life interesting for you takes some practical know-how. Something about a man who knows how to fix things and put them together after he's taken them apart is apt to light a fire of desire under you. Remembering your birthday and/or anniversary in special ways is a must, but that should be easy, given how memorable you are.

LIBRA ZODIAC SIGN
YOUR LOVE PLANETS

YOUR ROMANTIC SIDE   p. 696
▶ **VENUS IN LEO**
Born Sept. 23, 14:20 - Sept. 26, 4:07
▶ **VENUS IN VIRGO**
Born Sept. 26, 4:08 - Oct. 20, 17:34
▶ **VENUS IN LIBRA**
Born Oct. 20, 17:35 - Oct. 23, 23:01

YOUR SEX DRIVE   p. 722
▶ **MARS IN VIRGO**
Born Sept. 23, 14:20 - Oct. 23, 23:01

YOUR CELEBRITY TWINS   p. 760
Find out the astrological similarities you have with famous people.

YOUR COMPATIBILITY   p. 780
Compare planets to find out how compatible you are in a relationship.

YOUR RELATIONSHIP KARMA   p. 824
▶ **SATURN IN VIRGO**
Born Sept. 23, 14:20 - Oct. 7, 17:21
▶ **SATURN IN LIBRA**
Born Oct. 7, 17:22 - Oct. 23, 23:01

EZRA POUND
American Poet
Venus in Sagittarius

30

1921 SCORPIO
From October 23, 23:02 through November 22, 20:04

♏ *The Intense Charismatic*

As a Scorpio born in 1921 you have the capacity to charm and allure because you have a keen awareness of what you and others desire. This helps you establish a relationship, because your sixth psychic sense knows if your love prospect is on track with your intentions. You are prone to emotional extremes, so a relationship that offers a safe haven of relatively neutral ground may be appealing. It helps if in a relationship you can share some of the same interests in metaphysics, art and culture, and of course, most importantly, sex.

Your ideal relationship is one in which sexuality plays a primary role and where you can share the intimacies of sexual exploration at any age. Even when you may not be in the mood for it, you can thrive on the sexual stimulation that comes from watching a romantic or semi-erotic movie together. You are interested in a wide range of people and in understanding what makes them tick, and your ideal relationship is one in which you can share the fun of people

watching and discussing the dynamics of complex social interactions.

To pique your interest, a prospective partner would have to understand the game of seduction in all its nuances, or at least be willing to learn them from you. You want a partner whose will is as strong as yours so that when you argue, it will be fiery, and when you make up it will be equally intense and passionate.

As a Scorpio man born in 1921, you have known your share of interesting experiences in love and sexuality. Because of your fascination with money, your ideal woman is cagey with a buck and knows how to invest it. It turns you on to know that she's wise enough to teach you a few things about money, and woman enough to welcome your sexual advances.

As a woman Scorpio born in 1921, you expect a lot from your man, and Mr. Right is equal to the task. He's smart, attentive, intuitive, and treats you as an equal, frequently soliciting your opinion. He's also charming and knows just the right words to make you smile.

1921 SAGITTARIUS

♐ *A Principled Explorer*

For all Sagittarians born in 1921, you are naturally optimistic in love as you are in all other areas of your life, and chances are you have probably enjoyed one or many affairs of the heart—and still do. You know how to have a good time and you love to share your joy with someone who is equally enthusiastic about all that life has to offer. Life is one interesting experience after the other for you! And romance is a necessary part of it.

Your ideal relationship is one in which you can travel together and expand your repertoire of experiences and memories with many journeys near and far. You're not the stay at home type, but you do want to know that there is a home (or two) to come back to. That is an important element in cementing a relationship that the two of you share a sense of knowing where you belong together.

To keep your attention a partner needs to be intelligent and well informed about the world in general. You love to engage in lively conversations and bantering, especially about philosophy, religion, and even sports. Your

ideal partner is one who can keep up with you, and sometimes offer a new challenge that stretches your mind and heart a bit. Because you also have a keen awareness of fair play and justice, your relationship must be a companionship between mental equals.

As a man born during the Sagittarius month in 1921, your interest in love may be a bit like your interests in sports and philosophy. You are most attracted to a woman who is not too easy to get, because you love the chase and the anticipation of getting together at least as much as the time you actually spend together. Your ideal woman is mature in a spiritual sense, and lives by a good set of principles, and perhaps a faith, that resonate with yours.

As a woman Sagittarius born in 1921, you are happy to be swept off your feet, in a literal sense, with a man who loves to take you on trips, and can trip the light fantastic with you on the dance floor where you can express yourself in movement and rhythm. Your best guy is always full of surprises and plans for little adventures.

Rudolph Valentino – The Latin Lover

When the legendary Latin Lover Valentino died on August 23, 1926, he was the most famous silent screen actor of the day. His sudden, unexpected death created a Valentino cult, as tens of thousands of weeping women paid tribute at his open coffin at Campbell's Funeral Home in Manhattan. Around the world several crazed women committed suicide in the mass hysteria that followed. A mysterious "Lady in Black" laid flowers on his grave every week for many years to come. Some say he never really died, that he had gone into hiding under an assumed name. Many reported seeing his ghost in his Beverly Hills mansion and along the beach in Oxnard, California, where he filmed his most famous movie, *The Sheik*.

Rudolph Valentino was born a sensuous Taurus, with his Mars in emotional Cancer. Mars here makes a man unusually sensitive to a woman's moods and, consequently, a great lover. In the Roaring Twenties women had just received the vote and were allowed for the first time to go to the movies unaccompanied by a male escort. And women went in droves and found Valentino to be the most captivating male figure Hollywood had ever produced. He alone among the silent film stars could dance the tango, and it gave him a grace and finesse in his movements that other actors couldn't match.

Valentino made a dozen films before he landed a starring role in the 1921 classic *The Four Horsemen of the Apocalypse*. His exotic appearance and unconventional mannerisms brought a new kind of sex appeal to the screen,

"Women are not in love with me but the picture of me on the screen."

RUDOLPH VALENTINO

which became firmly established in his next movie, the desert romance tale of *The Sheik*. In this adventure story a cultured English woman meets the young Arab sheik at a desert gambling casino. Once the dark-skinned Sheik

sees the beautiful white woman, he wants her and plots to abduct her. Over the course of the movie, her fear turns to trust and attraction, and his compulsive lust turns to tenderness and affection.

Valentino did not consider himself a great conqueror of women. And while he may have made women swoon on screen and in the movie theaters, his relationships off-screen reveal a different persona. In 1919 he met Jean Acker at a Hollywood party, and the two spent the entire night together. They married shortly after, but abruptly separated just a month later. Valentino's second wife, the set designer Natacha Rambova, micromanaged her husband's film career, and effeminized him with the movies she convinced him to make. Valentino eventually left Rambova, wanting to change his image.

While women absolutely loved Valentino's subtle, sensitive screen roles, male filmgoers did not. The actor didn't project the he-man image, and many columnists of the day questioned his virility. One reporter called him a "pink powder puff." According to rumors in Hollywood, his two wives were lesbians, and he never consummated his marriage with either of them. At one point in his career, he wore heavy perfumes, mink coats, and gold jewelry.

In 1926 Valentino made his last movie, *The Son of The Sheik*. His style is smoother and cooler in this film, but his seduction techniques reveal the same intense stare and flaring nostrils. He looks fabulously handsome and slightly dangerous, and this is the way his fans remember him.

31

▶ READ ABOUT SEX ICON JOHN BARRYMORE ON PAGE 48

1922

- ★ PARAMOUNT BIGWIG SLAIN

- ★ SOCIETY FOR THE SUPPRESSION OF VICE

- ★ NOSFERATU

- ★ TOOT, TOOT, TOOTSIE

- ★ IN DEFENSE OF WOMEN

- ★ LESBIANISM

Hot Couple

EVENTS

1922 was marked by vice and scandal. Police arrived at William Desmond Taylor's bungalow to find the Paramount studio director shot dead and Paramount executives burning papers in the fireplace. Police found pornography, and lingerie monogrammed MMM, the initials of actress Mary Miles Minter.

A historical fantasy sex novel deemed obscene by the Society for the Suppression of Vice was exonerated by a New York judge. The author clarified the difference between pornography and literature saying, "Everybody enjoys the first, while few care one way or another about the second."

Pope Pius XI condemned immodest fashions for women and launched a crusade against them.

In Britain Edith Thompson and her lover Frederick Bywaters were sentenced to death for the murder of Edith's husband. Letters shown to the jury proved the plot to kill Percy Thompson so that the new couple could marry.

POP CULTURE

Films, while silent and black-and-white, didn't lack plot complexity or visual allure. Rudolph Valentino smoldered as a famous Spanish toreador torn between his wife and an upper-class woman in *Blood and Sand*. Erich von Stroheim's *Foolish Wives* featured faux nobility, gambling in Monte Carlo, and a hapless American "mark." F. W. Murnau's *Nosferatu*, a stylish, scary adaptation of Bram Stoker's *Dracula*, became a silent film classic.

Music continued to blend ragtime, blues, jazz, and dance hall influences, with light, up-tempo love songs dominating the brand-new medium of radio. "The Sheik (of Araby)" appealed to the craze for faux-exotica, "Fascination" and "Toot, Toot, Tootsie" were dance orchestra favorites, and "L'Amour-Toujours L'Amour" was a sentimental chanson.

The novel *If Winter Comes* by A. S. M. Hutchinson described a love triangle during World War I. The preeminent essayist and satirist of the day, H. L. Mencken, took on the changing role of women in society in a series of essays called *In Defense of Women*. *The Psychology of Misconduct, Vice, and Crime* was scandal-as-scholarship as Bernard Hollander "uncovered" rampant lesbianism and seduction of pupils by teachers in Britain's girls' schools. In that same vein, Victor Margueritte's novel *La Garçonne (Bachelor Girl)* described love and lesbianism in Paris.

ISADORA DUNCAN & SERGEI ESENIN

Acclaimed bohemian dancer Isadora Duncan married famous Russian poet Sergei Esenin on May 2, 1922. He was 17 years her junior. Although anti-marriage, she married him so he could legally accompany her on dance tours. It was the height of the Red Menace, and when they traveled to the US in 1924 they were scorned by the press as Bolsheviks.

When they returned to Europe, Duncan said, "Good-bye America. I shall never see you again!" A year later Esenin deserted her to return to his native country. He committed suicide at age thirty in 1925. Duncan died in a tragic car accident in 1927.

SEE ALSO

▶ FRED ASTAIRE & GINGER ROGERS *Page 130*

▶ DAVID SELZNICK & JENNIFER JONES *Page 252*

32

1922 CAPRICORN

From December 22, 1921 9:07 through January 20, 1922 19:47 (December 1922 Capricorns, see 1923 Capricorn)

♑ *The Serious Pussycat*

You see relationships as serious business, 1922 Capricorn, and you probably are the first to admit that your standards for a long-lasting one may be rather high. Yet despite that serious edge to your nature, your life is far from being all work and no play. In fact, the person with whom you've made a lifetime commitment knows that play often is what you need most—especially in those quiet times you share together at night.

Your closest partnership is your safety net, a quiet place where you are free to be what you like, not having to worry what others think. And the person you are closest to always makes you crack a smile, even when the going gets tough in the world outside. You may seem independent and assertive to the outside world, but in the bedroom you're a pussycat, needing to be gently stroked and treated with tender, loving care.

The person who wants to get close to you understands that keeping you happy and satisfied is not that difficult. Laughing and having fun are what you look for most when you're with that special someone. You do have your gloomy moments, so the person who keeps the love fires burning longest is someone who can snap you out of such a mood before it takes hold.

The woman in your life, Capricorn male of 1922, knows how to follow a game plan from start to finish, and you can rely on her through thick and thin. She will be there for you, matching your pace and helping you out while providing much-needed emotional support, love and constancy. You never have to think twice about her loyalty, but she will tell you in no uncertain terms when to leave your work behind, and she never lets you forget who is most important.

As a female Capricorn born in 1922, you really want someone to sweep you off your feet, and to encourage your interest in those activities you'd never do on your own. The man who best complements your own serious nature has a passion for life, and a penchant for spontaneity, especially when it comes to being in love. The one you need most makes you feel light and alive, and he opens your heart in a way that nobody else can.

CAPRICORN ZODIAC SIGN
YOUR LOVE PLANETS

YOUR ROMANTIC SIDE   p. 696
► **VENUS IN CAPRICORN**
Born Dec. 22, 1921 9:07 - Jan. 20, 1922 19:47

YOUR SEX DRIVE   p. 722
► **MARS IN SCORPIO**
Born Dec. 22, 1921 9:07 - Jan. 20, 1922 19:47

YOUR CELEBRITY TWINS   p. 760
Find out the astrological similarities you have with famous people.

YOUR COMPATIBILITY   p. 780
Compare planets to find out how compatible you are in a relationship.

YOUR RELATIONSHIP KARMA   p. 824
► **SATURN IN LIBRA**
Born Dec. 22, 1921 9:07 - Jan. 20, 1922 19:47

1922 AQUARIUS

From January 20, 19:48 through February 19, 10:15

♒ *The Warm Rationalist*

Emotional, intellectual, yet very rational, you, Aquarius of 1922, pride yourself on running a tight ship, with every aspect of your life neatly in place. In contrast, your idea of a perfect relationship is one that brings a spontaneous, exhilarating feeling into one corner of your life. Having this is a way of making your life well rounded and complete.

You may be assertive in some life situations, but someone you love never has to guess or to play games in order to find out how you feel—they'll know right from the start. You see emotional and romantic communication as sharing simple everyday experiences, as well as deep, passionate conversations. That kind of communication really makes your blood flow and arouses your passion, almost more than anything else you can name.

To keep your interest at an all-time high, a life partner must be completely attentive to you. You are attracted to independent thinkers who judge each situation on its own merit. Someone who thinks for him or herself, and is not afraid to challenge the status quo, will catch your eye and hold your attention. Whoever can pierce, ever so gently, the wall that you often build around your heart is the one for you.

The woman who plays a central role in your life, Aquarius male of 1922, should be intelligent, strong-minded, and never afraid to say what she really thinks. If she is the one for you, she knows that expressing herself with complete candor is a complete turn-on. What someone looks like counts less with you than what is inside her mind and her heart. She is a sucker for sad tales, and people in need, and, as a result, will be a shoulder to lean on.

Without uttering a word, the man of your dreams lets you know that he is committed to you for life, Aquarius female of 1922. You are attracted to the strong, silent type who listens to you speak your mind and compliments you for doing so, even if his own opinions differ from yours. This charming guy makes you feel beautiful, loved, and wanted every minute of the day. Most important, he can ease your mind and calm you down with just a warm hug.

JAMES JOYCE
Irish Writer
Sun and Venus in Aquarius

AQUARIUS ZODIAC SIGN
YOUR LOVE PLANETS

YOUR ROMANTIC SIDE   p. 696
► **VENUS IN CAPRICORN**
Born Jan. 20, 19:48 - Jan. 24, 13:12
► **VENUS IN AQUARIUS**
Born Jan. 24, 13:13 - Feb. 17, 11:05
► **VENUS IN PISCES**
Born Feb. 17, 11:06 - Feb. 19, 10:15

YOUR SEX DRIVE   p. 722
► **MARS IN SCORPIO**
Born Jan. 20, 19:48 - Feb. 18, 16:14
► **MARS IN SAGITTARIUS**
Born Feb. 18, 16:15 - Feb. 19, 10:15

YOUR CELEBRITY TWINS   p. 760
Find out the astrological similarities you have with famous people.

YOUR COMPATIBILITY   p. 780
Compare planets to find out how compatible you are in a relationship.

YOUR RELATIONSHIP KARMA   p. 824
► **SATURN IN LIBRA**
Born Jan. 20, 19:48 - Feb. 19, 10:15

EDNA ST. VINCENT MILLAY
American Poet
Sun in Pisces

1922 PISCES
From February 19, 10:16 through March 21, 9:48

 The Affectionate Dreamer

As a Pisces of 1922, you tend to dive right into relationships head first, without much reflection, and certainly very little worry about how they will turn out. Your tendency to love first, and ask questions later, reflects your truest ideas about love—that it is something unique you should follow wherever you find it.

For you, a partnership isn't on the right track if you have to spend time analyzing it. But though you may be impulsive when it comes to falling in love, once you've opened your heart to someone, it is not likely you will close it back up anytime soon. When you face disagreements, your answer is to put on some mood music, or watch a romantic movie, knowing that making up makes everything all right.

Anyone who wants to hold on to you should simply envelop you with love and affection. The person vying for your attention need not say a word, or even be a great conversationalist, as this is someone who can communicate with body language, which says all that needs to be said. When you hold this person's hand, the thrill of getting to know one another is a high like nothing else.

Pisces man of 1922, you are not ashamed to say that you are traditional and old-fashioned, or that you desire a woman who is soft-spoken, loving, and kind. You want someone who looks up to you, and though she is capable of making up her own mind and thinking for herself, she never makes any major decision without asking for your input. However, while she always ask for your opinion, and values it, her most admirable trait is the way in which she sticks to her guns when she is certain that she is right.

According to you, Pisces female of 1922, the most wonderful man in the world penetrates your heart and soul in a way that nobody else can. He encourages you to stay physically fit, and gets you out and about when your first urge is to wake up late, and lounge around the house. Your ideal man finds your propensity for dreaming and your fertile imagination most endearing, but also recognizes that providing an anchor for your sea of dreams is what will ultimately solidify your union.

1922 ARIES
From March 21, 9:49 through April 20, 21:28

♈ *The Headstrong Activist*

As a 1922 Aries, you can be quite headstrong, direct, and passionate, and once you meet someone with whom you want to spend the rest of your life there is just no stopping you. You do not hesitate to go after what you want. And since you live much of your life that way, always going for broke, you definitely need and want someone who can keep pace with you.

Although you do seem to come on quite strong, especially to those who do not know you well, you really are quite vulnerable. Because of this, you find that an ideal relationship is one that bolsters your confidence and strengthens your emotions. What you like most are those lighthearted games that lovers play, where you can tease each other endlessly, and then kiss and make up all night to show it was all in fun.

The person who wants to hold your attention must have an active mind, capable of challenging and stimulating you mentally. Anyone who is equally comfortable at the ballet or an action movie certainly is capable of sharing your own eclectic interests. Add a night on the town to the mix—cocktails, dinner at a trendy restaurant, and a nightcap after a good show—and you will be all revved up and raring to go.

Your ideal woman, Aries male of 1922, loves to get involved in outdoorsy activities like walking, swimming, bicycling, or anything else that lets her keep up with you, and share your active lifestyle. She might even teach you a thing or two about easing the tension that sometimes overtakes you, though you might have to wait to get home for that! Whatever method she uses, this woman is always able to tame your wild side, turning the roaring tiger into a little cub.

The man you most want in your life, Aries lady of 1922, definitely must have a spiritual side, but he also can equal you in both physical stamina and mental curiosity. You are a strong presence, and need someone who is no shrinking violet and can hold his own when he escorts you to social events, from public functions to family dinners. The perfect man will bring you flowers, take you dancing, and tell you how special you are all in the same day!

1922 TAURUS

From April 21, 21:29 through May 21, 21:09

The Sweet Sensualist

As silly as it may seem, Taurus of 1922, you approach relationships as if entering a large candy store. Everywhere you turn there is something sweet and forbidden to sample, especially if you have been especially good and deserve a reward. Like that candy store, your relationship should be a place where you never have to feel guilty partaking of those "sinful" little pleasures.

If this sounds like wishful thinking, you may be right, yet on the other hand you may be fortunate enough to find someone who shares your proclivity for touching, warmth, and generally leaving unpleasantries and arguments at the door. Taureans have never liked confrontation, and the person most suited for you will make sure that your life stays sweet.

While you love surprise gifts and spontaneous romantic evenings, what attracts you most to someone is knowing that he or she will always be there. You like to know that someone will call when they say they will, and be on time for dates. If someone is unreliable or forgets to phone that he or she will be late, then you'd better find someone else to cozy up to. Of course, those wonderful words "I love you" can never be repeated too often to suit you!

For you, Taurus man of 1922, the ideal woman is someone who has variety in her tastes, and knows how to get you on your feet and out of the house. You love being lazy and following a predictable path, so the woman of your dreams has an exciting mixture of intensity and originality that really shakes your tree. She should have a great sense of humor, and have enough interests to keep her busy. Most of all, she needs to be confident and secure in your love for her.

A man who always speaks the truth and tells you what he really thinks, and not just what you want to hear, is most appealing to you, Taurus lady of 1922. While you want to be flattered, you do not want to be treated as a fragile lady, but one whose intelligence and depth are equal to his. When he treats you with respect, and makes you feel you are the most beautiful, sensual woman in the world, this will sweep you off your feet every time.

TAURUS ZODIAC SIGN
YOUR LOVE PLANETS

YOUR ROMANTIC SIDE   p. 696
- ▶ VENUS IN TAURUS
  Born Apr. 20, 21:29 - May 01, 1:21
- ▶ VENUS IN GEMINI
  Born May 01, 1:22 - May 21, 21:09

YOUR SEX DRIVE   p. 722
- ▶ MARS IN SAGITTARIUS
  Born Apr. 20, 21:29 - May 21, 21:09

YOUR CELEBRITY TWINS   p. 760
Find out the astrological similarities you have with famous people.

YOUR COMPATIBILITY   p. 780
Compare planets to find out how compatible you are in a relationship.

YOUR RELATIONSHIP KARMA   p. 824
- ▶ SATURN IN LIBRA
  Born Apr. 20, 21:29 - May 21, 21:09

BILLIE DOVE
American Actress
Sun in Taurus

1922 GEMINI

From May 21, 21:10 through June 22, 5:26

The Spicy Dish

Variety is your spice of life, Gemini of 1922, and you embrace relationships that promise you a life free from boredom and endless routine. You have a good and successful life on your own, but unraveling life's mysteries with a partner who is always full of love and surprises is something that really appeals to you, and your ideal model for a relationship.

Restless though you may be, you are still somewhat of a homebody. For you, the most romantic place in the world is your own living space, and nothing is more comforting and sexy than a sprawling sofa that you and your partner can sink yourselves into, while you watch a romantic movie or perhaps listen to some of your favorite mood music. That kind of scene is heaven to you—and you don't have to travel far to find it!

Someone who wants to grab your attention and hold it must make you feel at ease, accommodating your initial shyness, and later, when the ice is broken, listening to you for hours—completely fascinated. Whispering sweet nothings in your ear in a silky voice, and running his or her fingers through your hair, is certain to melt you every time. You may be initially attracted to smooth talkers with just the right lines, but there must be substance beneath the charm to qualify someone for a permanent place in your heart.

The woman you are most attracted to, 1922 male Gemini, exudes sex appeal, yet retains an air of mystery, keeping you guessing even when you think you know her inside and out. The fact that you can never fully know her contributes to her charm, and to her ability to excite and stimulate you. Along with that quality, a woman who loves entertaining you at home, with creative "recipes" both before and after dinner, is the obvious one for you.

The man for you, female Gemini of 1922, has just the right dose of imagination and reality, creates an atmosphere all his own, and sends shivers up and down your spine. He makes you feel as if you are the star in a romantic movie, no matter where you are or what you are doing, and his special brand of optimism can lift you right out of your occasional doldrums.

GEMINI ZODIAC SIGN
YOUR LOVE PLANETS

YOUR ROMANTIC SIDE   p. 696
- ▶ VENUS IN GEMINI
  Born May 21, 21:10 - May 25, 17:03
- ▶ VENUS IN CANCER
  Born May 25, 17:04 - June 19, 16:31
- ▶ VENUS IN LEO
  Born June 19, 16:32 - June 22, 5:26

YOUR SEX DRIVE   p. 722
- ▶ MARS IN SAGITTARIUS
  Born May 21, 21:10 - June 22, 5:26

YOUR CELEBRITY TWINS   p. 760
Find out the astrological similarities you have with famous people.

YOUR COMPATIBILITY   p. 780
Compare planets to find out how compatible you are in a relationship.

YOUR RELATIONSHIP KARMA   p. 824
- ▶ SATURN IN LIBRA
  Born May 21, 21:10 - June 22, 5:26

EDNA FERBER
American Writer
Mars in Cancer

1922 CANCER
From June 22, 5:27 through July 23, 16:19

 The Intimate Wonder

Intensity by day, and intimacy by night, are key phrases that describe your ideal relationship, Cancer of 1922. It doesn't matter what else occurs in your lives—if the two of you do not have that quiet time at the end of the day, or even in the middle of it, so you can make the world go away, look into each other's eyes, and just commune with one another, then sharing your life is not as much fun as it should be.

Your days together must be filled with wondrous moments, from walks by the ocean to drives in the country to getaway weekends where the two of you can discover a little country inn or a charming restaurant that you can call your own. At night, you love nothing more than sharing some fine wine, listening to soft music, and falling asleep in one another's arms. Creating a secret language that the two of you share is most important to keeping the fires burning.

Sensitive, and deeply emotional, you tend to be a person of very few words. The person to whom you give your heart instinctively knows what you think and feel, and has the uncanny ability to finish your sentences. The person who knows you that well, and never asks you to explain yourself, is very likely the one who wins your heart in the end.

The woman who sweeps you off your feet, Cancerean male of 1922, is proud, regal, and beaming with self-confidence. You want someone who is just as comfortable taking the lead in making decisions, as she is with letting you take the lead, and without any argument in either case. She loves taking care of you, whether in the kitchen or the bedroom. She's somewhat vulnerable, without being overly sensitive, and she makes you feel like a knight in shining armor.

For you, 1922 Cancerean female, the perfect man is truly a leader in his chosen field, one who is a commanding presence and is admired and loved by both colleagues and friends. With the world at his fingertips, he is a powerhouse at work and on the playing field. Yet, when he walks through the front door, the lion turns into a lamb, and he surrenders to you, making you feel as if your every wish is his command.

1922 LEO
From July 23, 16:20 through August 23, 23:03

The Loving Heart

Loving, generous, yet serious, you, Leo of 1922, want a relationship to fill your heart with happiness, and to put you in a good mood 24 hours a day. When you are in love, you want to share it with the world. You want to be able to leave home in a good mood each morning, and return to loving arms at the end of the day.

Since you like sharing, you want someone who will remind you that life is best lived through the eyes of others. You have a tendency to do things on your own, and to be quite subjective without asking others for their opinions. That can sometimes make you appear insensitive when you are really not. But a loving partner opens your eyes and keeps you focused on things other than yourself.

As a hopeless romantic, you want to hear those bells ringing all the time. You are not someone who falls in love easily, and anyone who wants to stay in your life has to find ways to make you fall in love with him or her over and over again. Bringing you flowers when you least expect it, surprising you with tickets to that concert you've wanted to attend, or simply whispering sweet nothings in your ear, are ways to make your heart skip many beats.

The woman who wins your love, Leo man of 1922, has a detailed and organized way of seeing the world, and yet knows how to be charming, sexy, and intelligent at the very same time. It could even be she has spent the better part of her life rehearsing for your meeting. Someone who is succinct yet expressive, and dresses impeccably, might be the woman of your dreams. You want someone who will challenge your mind, but will be putty in your hands in the bedroom.

The perfect man for you, Leo lady of 1922, is a combination of brawn and brains. He should melt you with his charm, since you just love submitting to the tingly feelings it brings. At the same time, you should both be able to laugh, when you both know he is laying it on too thick. The perfect man is doesn't take himself too seriously, and yet he is responsible, dependable, and not the least bit afraid to express his feelings for you, nor commit to you for a lifetime.

1922 VIRGO
From August 23, 23:04 through September 23, 20:09

The Flawless Romantic

As a Virgo of 1922, you want everything in life, especially your closest relationship, to be flawless. From the moment you take a vow of undying love, you want to hear bells ringing and romantic guitars strumming. Life has much more meaning for you when it plays out like the script of a romantic movie in which guy meets girl, guy gets girl, and both live happily ever after.

Your life with your partner is one that you can willingly share with an extended family of relatives and friends. Though you love sharing your every thought and feeling with that special someone, that's just the beginning of your life together. Your home is likely to be a center of activity, and the more people who pass through it, the more satisfying it is for you and your mate.

If someone wants to win you over, that person definitely must have a great sense of humor. You love to laugh, so anyone who wants to be a permanent fixture in your life knows how to make you smile at a moment's notice. Since you are bored rather easily, this person must be ready to go the extra mile in pleasing you, never taking you for granted.

With so many social and familial engagements, Virgo male of 1922, you want the perfect escort, a woman who is intelligent, cultured, and can strike up a conversation with almost anyone at all. She need not be classically beautiful, but must take pride in her appearance, and dress stylishly with impeccable taste. As an added touch, she puts on a social face at a moment's notice, knowing full well that however much you ask of her—and you may ask quite a bit—you give 150 percent in return.

The man who's willing to move mountains for you, has social graces, is utterly charming, and—though everyone he meets falls madly in love with him—only has eyes for you, is the man for you, Virgo female of 1922. This man need not be erudite or intellectual, but has his finger on the pulse of current events, and shares the same social values as you. Most important, he is comfortable in his own skin, does not always need to be right, and respects what you have to say whether you agree with him or not.

VIRGO ZODIAC SIGN
Your Love Planets

YOUR ROMANTIC SIDE   p. 696
▶ **VENUS IN LIBRA**
Born Aug. 23, 23:04 - Sept. 07, 7:14
▶ **VENUS IN SCORPIO**
Born Sept. 07, 7:15 - Sept. 23, 20:09

YOUR SEX DRIVE   p. 722
▶ **MARS IN SAGITTARIUS**
Born Aug. 23, 23:04 - Sept. 13, 13:01
▶ **MARS IN CAPRICORN**
Born Sept. 13, 13:02 - Sept. 23, 20:09

YOUR CELEBRITY TWINS   p. 760
Find out the astrological similarities you have with famous people.

YOUR COMPATIBILITY   p. 780
Compare planets to find out how compatible you are in a relationship.

YOUR RELATIONSHIP KARMA   p. 824
▶ **SATURN IN LIBRA**
Born Aug. 23, 23:04 - Sept. 23, 20:09

BUSTER KEATON
American Comedian
Sun and Mars in Libra

1922 LIBRA
From September 23, 20:10 through October 24, 4:52

The Love Bug

Love and romance comprises the center of your world, Libra of 1922, even though most people you know might not suspect just how important a place it occupies. One reason it may appear to be downplayed is because you spend a good deal of time very quietly adjusting your relationships in order to make them work as smoothly and magically as they possibly can.

With you, even a small glare or a flare of anger will stay with you all day, unless you turn it over in your mind, try to understand the reason for it, and come up with a way of keeping it from happening again. Taking care of the little things before they turn into big ones means that, by the end of the day, misunderstandings are gone and your affection has accelerated. You appreciate the same kind of attentiveness to detail and harmony from your partner, as well. You know that the better you get along on the little things, the more fun it will be when you get to your quiet, sensual times alone together.

You certainly have a keen eye for good looks, and you really love it when someone attractive and well groomed casts an inviting glance your way. But someone who really wants to attract you, and hold on to you, needs above all to be honest, fair-minded, and even-tempered, without a hint of any aggressive behavior that might lie underneath the surface.

If you're a 1922 Libra male, the kind of lady you want to be with has a genuine charm that is much more than skin deep. If you put that together with a nice (and kind) face, topped by a little twinkle in her eye, you've got the woman who can melt your heart on the spot. When you meet someone like this, your first impulse is to be gallant, and to sweep her off her feet.

For the 1922 lady Libra, the smile, the eyes, and the sense of humor are good indicators that a man is the one for you. What has to shine through in all of those is a compassionate nature, and you most want someone who is at ease with himself, and thus with you. Mostly, you are drawn to the man who can talk to you for hours about any subject under the sun—all the while listening well to what you have to say.

LIBRA ZODIAC SIGN
Your Love Planets

YOUR ROMANTIC SIDE   p. 696
▶ **VENUS IN SCORPIO**
Born Sept. 23, 20:10 - Oct. 10, 22:32
▶ **VENUS IN SAGITTARIUS**
Born Oct. 10, 22:33 - Oct. 24, 4:52

YOUR SEX DRIVE   p. 722
▶ **MARS IN CAPRICORN**
Born Sept. 23, 20:10 - Oct. 24, 4:52

YOUR CELEBRITY TWINS   p. 760
Find out the astrological similarities you have with famous people.

YOUR COMPATIBILITY   p. 780
Compare planets to find out how compatible you are in a relationship.

YOUR RELATIONSHIP KARMA   p. 824
▶ **SATURN IN LIBRA**
Born Sept. 23, 20:10 - Oct. 24, 4:52

EUGENE O'NEILL
American Playwright
Mars in Sagittarius

38

1922 SCORPIO
From October 24, 4:53 through November 23, 1:54

♏ The Artful Entertainer

As a 1922 Scorpio, you can't help but compare relationships to a trip to a grandiose casino or splashy floorshow. You don't take any sight or sound for granted, and you want excitement and liveliness every minute. And though your passionate nature is often reflected in the outer events—the places and the things you see together—it really runs deep within you and can be felt through the long stares into one another's eyes.

For you, being with and interacting with someone you love is an event that opens up new vistas in your life. Learning the ways of another person helps you grow and develop, a process that you see as continuing at every stage of life. Each day that your partner surprises you with some new thought, your own reaction changes you just a little bit.

Someone who wants to attract you must above all be exciting, constantly active, and even a little mysterious. The dull homebody type is not for you, unless he or she happens to have another, more hidden, side, especially one that's artistic or creative. Since as a matter of course you always look underneath the surface, qualities of value not immediately obvious in someone—like helping the underdog or others in need—will pique your interest every time.

For the 1922 Scorpio man, you particularly like the woman who has made her own way in life, even maintaining her own separate career or artistic interest while tending to home and family. Though you like physical attractiveness as much as the next man, this probably rates a little lower on the scale than it does with other men, so while it's a nice part of the total package, it's not the first thing you look for.

A guy with a good deal of dash, a bit of panache, and handsome to boot is just your style, Scorpio lady of 1922. If you can't get all of that in one great, big lovely package, then you definitely put the dash and the panache at the top of the list because more than anything else you need someone who will keep you interested, excited and feeling really alive every minute you are with him. The fellow who not only excites your senses but also your mind is just your type.

1922 SAGITTARIUS
From November 23, 1:55 through December 22, 14:56

♐ The Soulful Communicator

The art of communication is foremost in your mind when you think of a relationship, Sagittarius of 1922, and in most areas of your life you are accommodating and especially diplomatic. When you are deeply in love, and in the company of that special someone, you hold nothing back. Not only do you say what's on your mind, but you expect the same of your partner, and the most exciting part of your life together is not knowing what you might hear next.

Despite this, you believe strongly in communing on an emotional level without ever having to say a word. Your innermost feelings are especially clear when you are in any kind of sensual contact, and you let your dear love know how you feel with every touch. This doesn't all have to happen in the bedroom, either, as just a touch of your hand and a little look can set your partner on fire.

The person most likely to attract you and to hold your interest responds most directly to this side of your soul, and greets it with true understanding. Your mate may say what they feel to match your own honesty, or their witty remarks will alert you to the fact that there is something special. The one who returns your deep glance, who responds in a direct way to a touch of the hand, will be the one you are taken with.

For the 1922 Sagittarius man, the woman you like best is one who is confident, perhaps even a bit proud, and very independent, while at the same time able to share with ease and grace. Someone like this is also able to plumb your emotional depths and welcome what she finds there. You want someone who can know you deeply, share all of your secrets, and who is not afraid to dive into the deepness of your soul.

You like a man with a little bit of mystery, Sagittarius lady of 1922, but one who also considers you an attractive mystery yourself. In fact, the more each of you thinks of the other in this way, the more likely you are to get lost in each other's arms in a wonderful, deliciously sensual exploration of the depths of the other. If he is all that, and a bit of a looker, it's likely you'll be hooked the first time you see him!

F. Scott and Zelda Fitzgerald

Born a Libra in 1896, F(rancis) Scott (Key) Fitzgerald chronicled the glittering Roaring Twenties "Jazz Age" from the inside and achieved literary success in the process. Named after the composer of the US's national anthem (a distant relative), he married a beautiful and vivacious Leo woman, Zelda Sayre, the same year his first and astoundingly popular novel *This Side of Paradise* was published. In 1921, their only child, daughter Scottie, was born. Their world seemed good; the sky was the limit.

From the beginning, the Fitzgeralds embarked upon a life together that epitomized those in his novels. The glamorous couple divided their time between the Riviera, Paris, New York, and Washington, DC, frequenting posh European resorts and fashionable American speakeasies where they hobnobbed with the rich and famous. On any given night, the pair could be found dancing the Charleston, drinking bathtub gin, partying, and socializing with other society folk who mirrored the characters in Fitzgerald's novels, such as the highly acclaimed *The Great Gatsby*.

"Their life together was one great, gaudy spree," writes astrological biographer Lois M. Rodden. Their marriage inspired several of Scott's novels including *The Beautiful and the Damned*—not surprising, as Libra is the sign of relationships. It's interesting, too, that Scott's birth chart featured Jupiter, the planet of good luck, in the 7th house, the sector of marriage—and indeed, Zelda was a fortunate influence who enriched his writing.

But while their glitzy life seemed like a fairytale come true to outsiders, underneath it was riddled with suffering and tragedy. Zelda, whose Moon and

"It is in the thirties that we want friends. In the forties we know they won't save us anymore than love did."

F. SCOTT FITZGERALD,
shortly before he died at age forty-four

Venus (the two heavenly bodies associated with women) were in the maternal sign Cancer, wanted more children, but her husband did not. Consequently, she underwent several illegal abortions. By the late '20s, Scott's drinking had evolved into alcoholism. In 1930, Zelda was diagnosed with schizophrenia, a condition that would grow steadily worse in the coming years.

Zelda's mental illness strained not only their marriage, but also Scott's writing. She entered a sanitarium in Switzerland in 1930, the first of several institutions she would go in and out of during the rest of her short and troubled life. In his novel *Tender Is the Night* (published in 1934), Scott grappled with the turmoil caused by Zelda's condition. For most of the decade, the Fitzgeralds lived apart as Zelda's schizophrenia required her to be hospitalized. By 1935, Scott's life had hit rock bottom. The strain of his wife's illness brought Scott to a crisis of the soul. "In the real dark night of the soul," he wrote, "it is always three o'clock in the morning, day after day." He described his despair and personal struggle in *The Crack-Up* (published in 1936).

Nevertheless, Scott managed to pull himself together to write his last, and some say his best, novel *The Last Tycoon*, published after his death from a heart attack in 1940. Zelda died tragically in 1948 in a fire at a mental hospital in Asheville, NC. Their brilliant run had come to an end. Yet to this day, F. Scott Fitzgerald is considered to be one of America's most gifted writers and their relationship—as well as the literature it inspired—continues to provide a vivid picture of one of America's most colorful periods.

► READ ABOUT ERNEST HEMINGWAY AND MARTHA GELLHORN ON PAGE 180

39

- ⍟ DIAPHRAGM
- ⍟ STOCKINGS
- ⍟ CHORUS GIRLS
- ⍟ FLAMING YOUTH
- ⍟ DOWNHEARTED BLUES
- ⍟ BREAKING POINT
- ⍟ THE CONFESSIONS OF ZENO

Hot Couple

EVENTS

Authorities were stymied and vexed by rapid social change. A Broadway show featuring bare-breasted chorus girls set off a censorship drive and the Supreme Court of Arkansas upheld a school board ban on "...any style of dress tending toward immodesty ... or the use of face paint or cosmetics."

Synthetic, seamless, sheer stockings, the Maidenform bra, and the rubber diaphragm debuted, the latter thanks to Margaret Sanger, founder of the American Birth Control League.

Family planning advocates in Britain were also making progress, with The National Birthrate Commission encouraging sex education in the schools and homes. Dr. Marie Stopes won a libel battle against Dr. Halliday Sutherland, who argued that her birth control clinics encouraged immorality, and that her book *Married Love* was obscene. A breakthrough was made for women with the passing of The Matrimonial Causes Bill, which permitted women to divorce their husbands for adultery.

POP CULTURE

Buster Keaton's *The Three Ages* found the comedian perplexed by love in three historical periods. *A Woman of Paris*, directed by Charles Chaplin, was a tragic tale of transcontinental heartache. John Francis Dillon's *Flaming Youth* chronicled the coming of age of the daughter of well-to-do parents,

amid wild parties with jazz bands, Prohibition booze, nude swimming, and debauchery.

Black music, both blues and jazz, influenced white bands and was popular in its own right. Bessie Smith became a star when "Downhearted Blues" sold 780,000 copies. "St. Louis Blues" and "Aggravatin' Papa (Don't You Try to Two-Time Me)" were covered by both black and white artists. The vaudeville tradition continued with "Who's Sorry Now?" and "You've Got to See Mama Every Night (Or You Can't See Mama at All)."

1923 books included *This Freedom* by A. S. M. Hutchinson, a morality tale in which a career woman is "punished" by the death of her daughter due to an illicit abortion. In the classic *La Coscienza Di Zeno (The Confessions of Zeno)* by Italo Svevo, a fictional businessman, Zeno Cosini, records his life, including marriage and infidelity.

ELIZABETH BOWES-LYON & THE DUKE OF YORK

When Elizabeth Bowes-Lyon married Prince Albert Windsor in April of 1923 in the first royal marriage to take place at Westminster Abbey in over 400 years, little did she know that she would become the "Queen Mum," beloved by all.

When King George died in 1936, his oldest son, Edward, became King. A short time later he abdicated the throne to marry American divorcee Wallis Simpson. Albert became King George the VI, and Elizabeth became the Queen Consort. Their first child, Elizabeth, was crowned Queen at age 26 when her father died. The Queen Mum died in 2002 at age 101.

SEE ALSO

▶ EDWARD VIII & WALLIS SIMPSON *Page 154*
▶ GRACE KELLY & PRINCE RAINIER *Page 310*

1923 CAPRICORN

From December 22, 1922 14:57 through January 21, 1923 1:34 (December 1923 Capricorns, see 1924 Capricorn)

♑ *The Quiet Fireball*

Initial impressions of you may be misleading, Capricorn of 1923. When it comes to outward appearances though, you can be the embodiment of a cool and shrewd operator. However, your emotional life is a very different affair. You have never been one to avoid a chance to make new and interesting personal connections. You may have taken your time before settling on your life partner—there have been so many attractive possibilities out there. Even when you have been disappointed by love, your romantic optimism has allowed you to pick yourself up and explore the next delicious opportunity. However, once you make the ultimate emotional commitment, you do your utmost to keep the relationship secure.

Paradoxically, it may have been your willingness to constantly renew and refresh your relationship that has allowed it to continue to change and grow. You know romantic surprises continue to keep love alive. Perhaps the secret to your success has been the clear-eyed way you have always kept business and pleasure separate. You have never forgotten that you can always operate better from the basis of a supportive and stable relationship.

Attracting your attention may have been quite simple, but keeping it may have been a different matter. Someone who shares your love of nature and enjoys discussing the ways of the world deep into the night would have a head start over a pretty face or a gorgeous physique. A jealous nature would be an equal turn-off—you are loyal and hate any game-playing.

Independent, athletic women have always been hard for you to resist, Capricorn men of 1923. You relish the company of a woman who is unafraid to speak her mind, and it helps if she dresses in a classic and unfussy style. You adore knowing that beneath her calm exterior, only you understand her true sensuality.

As a Capricorn woman of 1923, it is vital that your mate has emotional integrity. Generosity is also a quality you admire and value. It is important he has the self-confidence to let you in on his deepest feelings and concerns. And you still love to be swept away by passion from time to time!

CAPRICORN ZODIAC SIGN
YOUR LOVE PLANETS

YOUR ROMANTIC SIDE   p. 696
> ► VENUS IN SCORPIO
> *Born Dec. 22, 1922 14:57 - Jan. 02, 1923 7:26*
> ► VENUS IN SAGITTARIUS
> *Born Jan. 02, 7:27 - Jan. 21, 1:34*

YOUR SEX DRIVE   p. 722
> ► MARS IN PISCES
> *Born Dec. 22, 1922 14:57 - Jan. 21, 1923 1:34*

YOUR CELEBRITY TWINS   p. 760
> *See what your Venus-Mars combination does for your sexual allure and satisfaction!*

YOUR COMPATIBILITY   p. 780
> *Compare planets to find out how compatible you are in a relationship.*

YOUR RELATIONSHIP KARMA   p. 824
> ► SATURN IN LIBRA
> *Born Dec. 22, 1922 14:57 - Jan. 21, 1923 1:34*

1923 AQUARIUS

From January 21, 1:35 through February 19, 15:59

♒ *The Ambitious Companion*

Love makes the world go round, but friendship is just as important to you, Aquarius 1923. You have a wide and diverse cross section of friends who continue to enhance the quality of your life. There may have been many times when you were tempted to pursue someone impulsively, but you have always needed to know that they were really worth the effort as a long-term prospective. Not that you are in any sense calculating. But you do have an innate awareness of the true meaning of emotional commitment. A flash in the pan is not your idea of true love. Once you set your heart on your partner, nothing puts you off. And a partnership is what your closest relationship has always had to be. As far as you are concerned, the most important ingredient of a happy relationship is that you both continue to see the world in a similar way.

Mutual support is the glue that binds you to your partner. Just knowing that he or she will never let you down in public and will always take your side in the face of opposition is crucial. Of course, in private you are aware that the occasional disagreement can add spice to the relationship. In any event, you always respect your partner's individuality.

To get you to take notice, any potential partner must tread a fine line between being available and playing hard to get. If you know someone is right, you are happy to do most of the running. You are attracted to material stability because you know the damage that can be done to any relationship when money is short.

You will shower your affection and your money on your woman, Aquarius man of 1923. Your ideal partner would be happy to entertain your colleagues, if that was how you could sustain your standing in society. Nevertheless, you are appreciative of her own aspirations and will actively support them.

As an Aquarius woman of 1923, your man must be a real man. You need to know above all that his caring arms, intelligence, and ambition will give you the security that you crave above everything. You've never been afraid to fight to keep him and show your appreciation in every way you can.

SERGE DIAGHILEV
Russian Ballet Impresario
Venus in Aquarius

AQUARIUS ZODIAC SIGN
YOUR LOVE PLANETS

YOUR ROMANTIC SIDE   p. 696
> ► VENUS IN SAGITTARIUS
> *Born Jan. 21, 1:35 - Feb. 06, 14:33*
> ► VENUS IN CAPRICORN
> *Born Feb. 06, 14:34 - Feb. 19, 15:59*

YOUR SEX DRIVE   p. 722
> ► MARS IN PISCES
> *Born Jan. 21, 1:35 - Jan. 21, 10:06*
> Mars in Aries
> *Born Jan. 21, 10:07 - Feb. 19, 15:59*

YOUR CELEBRITY TWINS   p. 760
> *See what your Venus-Mars combination does for your sexual allure and satisfaction!*

YOUR COMPATIBILITY   p. 780
> *Compare planets to find out how compatible you are in a relationship.*

YOUR RELATIONSHIP KARMA   p. 824
> ► SATURN IN LIBRA
> *Born Jan. 21, 1:35 - Feb. 19, 15:59*

ALDOUS HUXLEY
English writer
Mars in Aries

42

1923 PISCES
From February 19, 16:00 through March 21, 15:28

♓ The Good Listener

You do your best to appreciate everyone's most attractive qualities. Your inquiring mind leads you to mix with many different types and you number among your friends those from all walks of life. You can sometimes get a bit lost in your own dream world, Pisces 1923, and anyone who has shared his or her life with you has learned to accept the endearingly vague way you can operate. It helps if your partner is happy to take care of the more mundane aspects, especially the purse strings. Your other talents contribute to your relationship. You know that the direct approach is not always the fastest one, and you often surprise and delight your partner with your unique solutions to problems you've encountered over the years.

Romance is one area where you may be far more direct. You have always sensed right away when you've met someone, if you wanted to get to know him or her on a deeper level. While the person may not always be aware of it, once a potential companion is in your sights, you rarely miss your target. If you are interested in more than friendship, you have an arsenal of romantic weaponry to capture your objective.

You may go out of your way to help others and you can be attracted to people who have a slightly lost look about them. You may find it hard to tell others the truth, if it could hurt their feelings. You may sometimes be misunderstood, but your ideal partner knows that, while you can lavish attention on someone who needs your help, your commitment to your closest relationship is unwavering.

As a male Piscean of 1923, you can be dazzled by beauty. But what you find beautiful may not be to everyone's taste. Your ideal partner is in tune with your need to stop and smell the roses, even in the midst of a crisis. She responds to your belief that everything will turn out for the best.

Pisces woman of 1923, you know that love can conquer all, but you also know that a little money in the bank helps as well, even if you're the one to ensure it stays there! Your man can keep you content, if he is sympathetic to your feelings and open and honest with his own.

1923 ARIES
From March 21, 15:29 through April 21, 3:05

♈ The Fierce Provider

Aries of 1923, you may have found that your love for your closest partner has grown stronger and more profound as the years have gone by. While you can be very sure of yourself in your dealings with the outside world, you may have been a great deal more cautious when choosing your mate. For you love must last a lifetime—you would never give your heart away too soon. A relationship has to be all encompassing—from the heady elevation of a spiritual connection to the deep sharing of physical love. But, you can also be a devoted friend and you are generous to a fault.

Betrayal is one thing you may never forgive. When you love someone, whether it is your partner, child, or a close friend, there is a line that you'd rather no one would cross. You may have had to cope with disappointment at times because others can't always reach the high standards you set yourself. Your faith in the enduring bonds of marriage and family may have been tested over the years, but never broken.

You may be attracted by physical beauty because your taste is exquisite. You want to be proud of your partner and thrill to the admiring glances directed his or her way by others. However, the compliments should stay at a distance—people who attempt to come between you and your loved one will be put in their place very firmly. 1923 Aries, you'll fight to keep your relationship secure. You want your partnership to be close—you and I against the world could be your credo.

If you are an Aries man born in 1923, you want your woman to respond to you on every level possible. You are very tactile and often touch and cuddle your partner, as if to reassure yourself that she is really there. You enjoy being the provider and protector, and you are proud that you have never dodged your responsibility.

As an Arien woman of 1923, you want nothing more than to be your husband's most prized possession. This in no way implies that he has always gotten his own way. Far from it—behind closed doors you can stand up for yourself quite well! But isn't it funny how so many arguments have turned into lovemaking?

1923 TAURUS

From April 21, 3:06 through May 22, 2:44

The Idealistic Explorer

You have always needed a quest and finding the love of your life has been no exception. While emotional security may have been the ultimate goal, your impulsive nature and low boredom threshold may have meant that you were not easily satisfied. You are a romantic at heart and possibly a little too idealistic for your own good. You can also be direct when you find someone interesting or attractive. You maintain a child-like excitement at the prospect of making new friends and acquaintances. If you can help them in some way, it is all the more satisfying.

In your closest relationship you continue to contribute fresh and unorthodox ideas. You love to do your own thing, but you hate to be ignored. Ideally, you go out into the world and bring back new friends and concepts that you can show to your partner. Your home may be constantly filled with the laughter of different generations mixing and mingling. Couch potatoes need not apply! Your children and grandchildren may be surprised at how up-to-date you always are.

You may at times appreciate good looks, but that has never been your main consideration. To get your attention, Taurus 1923, someone must be witty and independent. People unsure of themselves or who need constant attention never got a second date! Your ideal partner keeps pace with your need to expand your world. He or she shares your love of novelty and can talk the talk as well as you can.

A male born under Taurus in 1923, you want a woman who can match you stride for stride. While shrinking violets may have your sympathy, you probably wouldn't want to live with one. You are proud that your partner has strong principles and applaud her when she stands by them. You adore the direct way she shows her continuing affection for you.

Romance and sensuality are only part of the formula for you, Taurus woman of 1923. A man who can open your eyes to something new every day is far more attractive than obvious strength and traditional good looks. You want a man who can talk you into bed rather than carry you there. After all, sexual attraction begins in the mind.

TAURUS ZODIAC SIGN
YOUR LOVE PLANETS

YOUR ROMANTIC SIDE — p. 696
▶ VENUS IN PISCES
Born Apr. 21, 3:06 - Apr. 26, 13:35
▶ VENUS IN ARIES
Born Apr. 26, 13:36 - May 21, 14:49
▶ VENUS IN TAURUS
Born May 21, 14:50 - May 22, 2:44

YOUR SEX DRIVE — p. 722
▶ MARS IN GEMINI
Born Apr. 21, 3:06 - May 22, 2:44

YOUR CELEBRITY TWINS — p. 760
Find out the astrological similarities you have with famous people.

YOUR COMPATIBILITY — p. 780
Compare planets to find out how compatible you are in a relationship.

YOUR RELATIONSHIP KARMA — p. 824
▶ SATURN IN LIBRA
Born Apr. 21, 3:06 - May 22, 2:44

HAROLD LLOYD
American Comedian
Mars in Gemini

43

1923 GEMINI

From May 22, 2:45 through June 22, 11:02

The Sociable Homebody

You may possess all the smooth social skills associated with your sign, but under the surface there lurks profound depths. You approach relationships with caution, at least until you are certain that your affection or love will be returned. It may have taken quite a while before you made the ultimate commitment. Once you did, however, you remained faithful to the end. Along with your brilliant conversation, you bring kindness, warmth, and generosity to your relationship. You know the value of an arm around the shoulder and a simple gesture of sympathy.

Once you know you belong, you feel confident enough to reveal your true sensuality. Lovemaking completes the union that you crave. Far from being something separate from the day to day business of living together or a pleasant diversion, showing your love physically is an intrinsic part of your relationship. You feel lost if kissing and cuddling don't happen every day. And you probably still hold hands!

You have expensive tastes, Gemini of 1923, and people who take time and trouble over their appearance always catch your eye. Your lively mind is a given because exchanging opinions continues to stimulate and intrigue you. However, you are passionate and people who live in their head and lack your need for physical reassurance can sometimes make you feel insecure. You hate to be kept guessing— you need to know you are loved.

The ability to organize a comfortable and attractive home is a great asset in your partner, Gemini man of 1923. You may be modern in your outlook, but you also appreciate the traditional feminine qualities such as great cooking and an affinity to children. You notice a new hairdo or dress, and you can usually pick the perfect gift.

As a Gemini woman of 1923, your ideal partner is unafraid to let you know how much you are valued. You are happiest when you feel both materially and emotionally secure. This allows you the freedom to explore your passionate side. You still thrill to your partner's touch and hate ending the day on an angry word. In return you make sure you always look your best.

GEMINI ZODIAC SIGN
YOUR LOVE PLANETS

YOUR ROMANTIC SIDE — p. 696
▶ VENUS IN TAURUS
Born May 22, 2:45 - June 15, 11:45
▶ VENUS IN GEMINI
Born June 15, 11:46 - June 22, 11:02

YOUR SEX DRIVE — p. 722
▶ MARS IN GEMINI
Born May 22, 2:45 - May 30, 21:18
▶ MARS IN CANCER
Born May 30, 21:19 - June 22, 11:02

YOUR CELEBRITY TWINS — p. 760
Find out the astrological similarities you have with famous people.

YOUR COMPATIBILITY — p. 780
Compare planets to find out how compatible you are in a relationship.

YOUR RELATIONSHIP KARMA — p. 824
▶ SATURN IN LIBRA
Born May 22, 2:45 - June 22, 11:02

COLLEEN MOORE
American Actress
Venus and Mars in Cancer

1923 CANCER
From June 22, 11:03 through July 23, 22:00

The Constant Charmer

As a Cancer born in 1923, you have an inexhaustible capacity to make friends and keep them. You like nothing more than to draw others out—you know that everyone has something unique to contribute. You intuitively sense how to please others and you love to hear the sound of laughter and conversation at home. You may have lost count of the number of happy gatherings you have shared with family and friends in your home. You are intrigued at the new world that your grandchildren and other youngsters can show you. And you need a partner who shares your love and interest in the world around you.

Your light touch may give the impression that your passions are fleeting. That is misleading—you operate best from a secure base. Your loyalty is never in question, and you get the greatest pleasure from sharing your thoughts and ideas with your partner. Your sensuality runs like a river through your veins, and you understand the joy that comes from a deep and complete relationship. Physical contact every day is as natural to you as breathing.

There are many facets to your character, and you require a partner who can equal that quality. If your partner is a touch unpredictable, that adds fuel to the fire. You want to be constantly surprised and can't bear to spend too much time around people who live their life by the numbers. Boredom and pointless routine are guaranteed to send you straight out the door. However, you may meet any threat to your emotional security with a steely determination to keep the relationship intact.

As a man born under Cancer in 1923, your woman must sparkle brightly. She should combine femininity with brains. You take a fierce pride in her intelligence and social skills. You love to talk to her about anything and everything, and she must be your best friend as well as wife.

The strong, silent type has never really appealed to you, Cancer woman of 1923. You demand a response, and you appreciate physical affection. You treasure your love letters. Words are precious and you never get tired of being told by your partner just how much he adores you.

1923 LEO
From July 23, 22:01 through August 24, 4:51

The Passionate Partner

You may have been with your partner for as long as 60 years, but for you, Leo of 1923, your relationship may still be your grand passion. You throw yourself headlong into all of your undertakings—and romance is no exception. You are affectionate and playful, and your warm heart attracts others to you. Your loyalty to your partner and your friends is second to none. You are incapable of small-minded pettiness and you can easily be hurt by thoughtless criticism. Your sense of drama spills onto every area of your life, and you can sometimes over-react when you are upset. Nevertheless, you demand respect and your pride can suffer if you feel you have been made to look foolish.

You expect a great deal from your loved one, but you are fully prepared to give in equal measure. You are an attentive partner and show through both word and deed that your most treasured possession remains your partner's love. You can be a considerate lover and your love of luxury means that the marital bedroom may be the most beautifully decorated and welcoming room in your home. You adore setting the scene for a romantic evening.

Mutual respect is vital for any relationship to flourish. Integrity, loyalty, and kindness are the cornerstones of a relationship in your eyes. You'd always rather leave the chores to spend quality time with your partner. Your dignity is one of your most attractive traits and you applaud courtesy and grace in your partner.

As a male Leo born in 1923, you know how much you want to be appreciated. Your partner will be skilled at expressing her love with more than words and gestures. Aware that you want to be proud of her, she maintains her sense of style and a whiff of glamour that can still make you catch your breath.

You are attracted by self-confidence, Leo woman of 1923, and any man who shies away from a real relationship with its dizzy mixture of highs and lows is not for you. You love to be the center of his universe, and you never tire of hearing him tell you so. As long as his interest in you remains constant, you are happy to stick with him no matter what.

44

1923 VIRGO
From August 24, 4:52 through September 24, 2:03

The Steadfast Supporter

You take relationships very seriously, Virgo of 1923. This in no way implies, however, that you don't know how to have fun. After all, as an earth sign, you are bound to enjoy the physical side of love as much as anyone else. But you may have put practical considerations fairly high up on your list of desired qualities in a mate. You can be hard-working and you are willing to take the bad along with the good in your relationship. You are unafraid to work through the inevitable difficulties that occur in a long relationship, especially when raising a family. Your readiness to talk through your children's problems may have made you an exceptional parent and a much-loved grandparent.

You are quite self-contained and could endure a single life comfortably. You may have been cautious when choosing your life's companion. Once you embarked on a commitment, it was for the long term, and you preferred to be safe rather than sorry. Your ideal relationship involves lots of meaningful conversation and a realistic approach to shared goals—eyes focussed on the same objective rather than only on each other.

It's a cliché that Virgos require perfection, and as a Virgo of 1923, you are far more likely to find your partner's quirks and imperfections endearing. You need a lot of space in your relationship and you are prepared to let your partner pursue his or her own hobbies and interests. However, you might find it difficult to respect a partner who wastes too much time, energy, and money chasing unrealistic dreams.

As a Virgo man born in 1923, you are attracted by a woman who initially appears demure and youthful. You are fascinated that in private she can be spontaneous and warm. You love the way she fusses over you and takes care of the little things that cement and enhance your relationship.

A healthy attitude and a healthy appearance may have drawn you to your partner initially, Virgo woman of 1923. Your man may sometimes have his head in the clouds, but his feet never really leave the ground. And he never forgets that marriage is, first and foremost, a working partnership.

VIRGO ZODIAC SIGN
YOUR LOVE PLANETS

YOUR ROMANTIC SIDE   p. 696
- ▶ **VENUS IN LEO**
  Born Aug. 24, 4:52 - Aug. 27, 23:58
- ▶ **VENUS IN VIRGO**
  Born Aug. 27, 23:59 - Sept. 21, 3:28
- ▶ **VENUS IN LIBRA**
  Born Sept. 21, 3:29 - Sept. 24, 2:03

YOUR SEX DRIVE   p. 722
- ▶ **MARS IN LEO**
  Born Aug. 24, 4:52 - Sept. 01, 0:56
- ▶ **MARS IN VIRGO**
  Born Sept. 01, 0:57 - Sept. 24, 2:03

YOUR CELEBRITY TWINS   p. 760
Find out the astrological similarities you have with famous people.

YOUR COMPATIBILITY   p. 780
Compare planets to find out how compatible you are in a relationship.

YOUR RELATIONSHIP KARMA   p. 824
- ▶ **SATURN IN LIBRA**
  Born Aug. 24, 4:52 - Sept. 24, 2:03

DR. MARIE STOPES
English Birth Control Pioneer
Sun and Mars in Libra

1923 LIBRA
From September 24, 2:04 through October 24, 10:50

The Peace Maker

It is probably fair to say that life is much less enjoyable without a partner with whom to share it. You weren't meant to live alone, Libra of 1923, and while you were unlikely to rush into the first relationship that came your way, you may always have had an ideal scenario in the back of your mind. Your quiet charm is very attractive and you are never short of friends. But it is within your closest relationship that you become more alive and more completely yourself. You possess a layer of reserve only a select few can ever hope to penetrate. Although you know exactly what to say to put others at ease, only that special someone may be able to do the same for you.

Your taste is second to none and you may believe that beautiful surroundings can contribute to a more loving atmosphere. With impeccable manners you can get genuine pleasure from making others feel comfortable, especially your partner. You are happiest when you know that you have given your partner something to smile about.

You may be attracted to that special someone who comes across as refined. Outrageous behavior may be amusing to some, but for you it can be the height of embarrassment. You are gently considerate as a lover, but the merest hint of sordidness can dissolve your desire in a flash. Companionship is possibly more important to you than physical love would be. A similar outlook is high on your list of needs—and a squeeze of the hand can convey a lifetime of love.

As a Libra man born in 1923, you always perk up when a serene woman in well-tailored clothes comes into view. Your partner probably takes a keen interest in her appearance and won't leave the house without her lipstick. Ideally, she has her own ideas and convictions, but doesn't force them on to you.

A man who is polite, well groomed, and well mannered will always grab your attention, if you are a Libra woman of 1923. Your soul mate is respectful of your sensitivity and uses gentle persuasion rather than overbearing force to get you to see his point of view. You are not demanding, but you can be hurt if your efforts go unnoticed.

LIBRA ZODIAC SIGN
YOUR LOVE PLANETS

YOUR ROMANTIC SIDE   p. 696
- ▶ **VENUS IN LIBRA**
  Born Sept. 24, 2:04 - Oct. 15, 4:48
- ▶ **VENUS IN SCORPIO**
  Born Oct. 15, 4:49 - Oct. 24, 10:50

YOUR SEX DRIVE   p. 722
- ▶ **MARS IN VIRGO**
  Born Sept. 24, 2:04 - Oct. 18, 4:17
- ▶ **MARS IN LIBRA**
  Born Oct. 18, 4:18 - Oct. 24, 10:50

YOUR CELEBRITY TWINS   p. 760
Find out the astrological similarities you have with famous people.

YOUR COMPATIBILITY   p. 780
Compare planets to find out how compatible you are in a relationship.

YOUR RELATIONSHIP KARMA   p. 824
- ▶ **SATURN IN LIBRA**
  Born Sept. 24, 2:04 - Oct. 24, 10:50

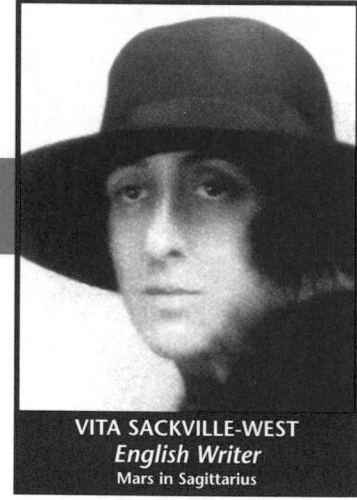

VITA SACKVILLE-WEST
English Writer
Mars in Sagittarius

1923 SCORPIO
From October 24, 10:51 through November 23, 7:53

♏ *The Fearless Defender*

Born under the sign of Scorpio in 1923, you have never been one to squander your feelings. You may not have loved very often, but you have always loved—and continue to love—very deeply. Above all, you desire intensity in your closest relationship and any indication of betrayal could cut you like a knife. You have always chosen the mind-blowing highs and dark lows of a grand passion over some meaningless flirtation. You may still find it difficult to put into words exactly how much you value your partner, but you are able to demonstrate this by your actions and deeds.

You may be accused occasionally of being possessive, but you almost always put your partner's needs ahead of your own. You know intuitively when to allow space and when to provide a comforting embrace. You are considerate and have a clever knack for being able to create a romantic atmosphere in the most unpromising circumstances. You can be quite sweet in your desire to please your loved one—and sweet is not a word usually associated with Scorpio!

You shy away from anything superficial and to catch your eye, potential partners would have to impress you with their own capacity for deep feelings. They don't have to have film star good looks or a brilliant mind. It is beyond that. What fascinates you is the assurance that they are genuinely prepared to enter into and sustain true intimacy. Any relationship that relies on partners doing their own thing doesn't seem to be a real relationship in your eyes.

A woman who appreciates being protected and provided for is the kind of woman who suits you, Scorpio man of 1923. She still responds to your intimate needs and understands that the most important aspect of your relationship is the complete merging of mind, body, and spirit.

If you are a Scorpio woman born in 1923, you want to know that your man will always be there for you. The memories of the difficulties you have faced together through the years are just as valuable to you as the good times when problems were at a minimum. These are just two sides of the same wonderful coin.

1923 SAGITTARIUS
From November 23, 7:54 through December 22, 20:52

♐ *The Serious Joker*

Initial impressions may lead others to wrongly believe that you are as free and easy in your relationships as you appear in public. Nothing could be further from the truth, Sagittarian of 1923. You delight in mixing with people who can open your eyes to new ideas. You may be a witty companion yourself, and humor is vital in your closest relationships. The talent to make you laugh is one of the qualities you love best in your partner. But you also appreciate his or her willingness to go beneath the surface whenever necessary. An optimistic attitude to setbacks has kept you and your loved one close through the most difficult times.

A relationship for you is not even worth contemplating, unless it is set for the long term. Your partner must be prepared to commit to you unreservedly. In return, you are willing to provide stability and security and a lifetime of unwavering loyalty. Because you would never be happy with a relationship that lacked physical intimacy, you may have chosen to wait a long time before you found the one special person who could match your integrity and desire.

You were always attracted to people with immediate warmth and friendliness. However, for friendships to develop, they had to gradually let you see that they had hidden depths. The person you would choose as your partner had to have the ability to continually surprise you. And it is crucial that you are trusted completely by your partner and are able to trust in return.

As a Sagittarius man of 1923, your woman is more attractive if she has some of the practical skills you may occasionally lack. She may gently bring some viability to your more fantastic schemes and plans. You still adore that she is unshockable and has taken in stride every setback life has dealt.

If you are a woman born under Sagittarius in 1923, your man must be powerful and charismatic. It may be important that he was also able to take care of your material needs and that he was straightforward in all his undertakings. You are more than willing to provide him with strong emotional support and intense and loving intimacy.

Georgia O'Keeffe and Alfred Stieglitz

Best known for her radiant, vulva-like depiction of flowers, Georgia O'Keeffe holds a unique place in the history of American art. But it was her partnership with Alfred Stieglitz, the preeminent photographic artist of his time, that helped to shape many of her attitudes and professional accomplishments. Born and reared in Wisconsin, O'Keeffe was teaching art in South Carolina when her work was brought to Stieglitz's attention by a friend. The famous photographer and art exhibitor was 23 years her senior and married. He became her mentor, exhibiting her paintings and introducing her to some of the most influential members of the New York intellectual, artistic, and literary world, which comprised his social circle.

The two quickly became lovers, but their relationship transcended just a sexual affair. She became his inspiration, his muse. Obsessed by her unconventional beauty, he took hundreds of photographs of her, many of them focused on her body parts and many of them highly erotic.

They had already been living together for six years when Stieglitz's wife divorced him. He wanted marriage with O'Keeffe but O'Keeffe was wary of a fulltime commitment and for a time she resisted. Finally, in December 1924, they married. For the next twelve years they spent the majority of their time in New York City, enjoying their summers at Stieglitz's family home at Lake George in the Adirondack mountains. He loved New York City and didn't feel the need to leave it for artistic inspiration, except for the yearly trek to Lake George. But O'Keeffe needed a reprieve from the insular world they lived in, and in 1929, she sought new vistas on her first trip to New Mexico. She visited novelist D.H.

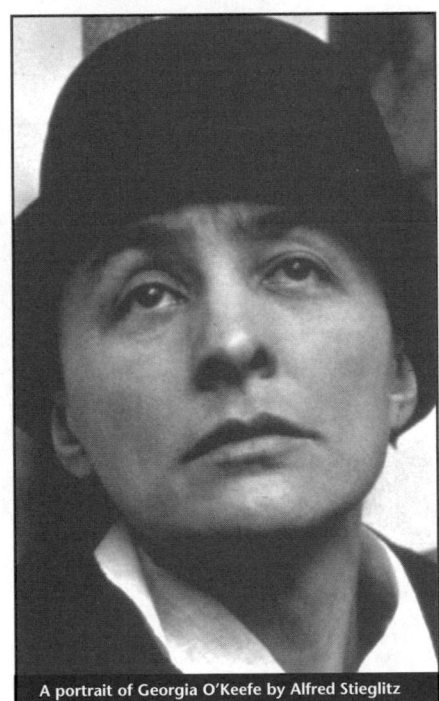

A portrait of Georgia O'Keefe by Alfred Stieglitz

"He was much more wonderful in his work than as a human being ... I believe it was the work that kept me with him."

GEORGIA O'KEEFFE
about husband Alfred Stieglitz

Lawrence's home in Taos, and Ghost Ranch, near Santa Fe. She began summering there each year, instead of going with Stieglitz to the Adirondacks.

Despite the inspiration they gave to one another, O'Keeffe's marriage to Stieglitz was anything but congenial. It was often tempestuous and complicated by those yearly separations. Biographers speak of the couple's unconventional relationship—they both reportedly experimented with extramarital liaisons and Georgia was said to have lesbian attachments.

O'Keeffe's independent, loner nature is characteristic of a Scorpio, her zodiacal sign. As a Capricorn, Stieglitz was equally uncompromising and demanding. His Venus in Scorpio explains the powerful artistic and sexual attraction to her, since Scorpio is the sign of obsession.

Stieglitz died of a cerebral hemorrhage in July 1946. As his widow and the executor of his will, O'Keeffe spent the next three winters cataloguing his works and writings. After his death she relocated permanently to her beloved New Mexico. She summed up their marriage by saying, "Though I loved him as a human being ... I put up with what seemed to me a good deal of contradictory nonsense because of what seemed clear and bright and wonderful."

O'Keeffe's life post-Steiglitz produced some of her most noteworthy works, inspired by the New Mexico landscape she loved so much. Her last relationship, a platonic one begun in 1972, was with Juan Hamilton, who served as her confidante and business manager until the end of her life. Her eyesight began to fade in the 1970s, but with Juan's help she took up pottery and wrote her autobiography. She died in 1986 at the age of 98.

47

▶ READ ABOUT D. H. LAWRENCE ON PAGE 87

1924

- ⭐ **GOLD DIGGERS**
- ⭐ **HIGH SOCIETY WHODUNIT**
- ⭐ **THE COAST OF FOLLY**
- ⭐ **BEAU BRUMMEL**
- ⭐ **IT HAD TO BE YOU**
- ⭐ **TEA FOR TWO**

EVENTS

Although "blackface" comedy was popular, black actor Paul Robeson drew the wrath of the Ku Klux Klan while playing a black man married to a white woman in Eugene O'Neill's *All God's Chillun Got Wings*. The *New York Evening Graphic* warned against opportunistic "gold diggers," reminding readers that "of all the gifts that can be offered to a woman, love is the most precious." Producer/director Thomas H. Ince died after a party aboard William Randolph Hearst's yacht. Rumor was that Hearst had shot Ince after mistaking him for Chaplin, whom he suspected of having an affair with his mistress. Charlie Chaplin himself, 35, married 16-year-old Lita Gray, his second marriage to a girl that age.

The fashion for nightclubbing grew in Britain and took hold among the country's youth.

In Italy Mussolini introduced a bill allowing women to vote, while Irishman P. S. O'Hegarty argued vehemently against giving women the vote in his home country.

POP CULTURE

John Barrymore embodied gentlemanly derring-do in the title role of *Beau Brummel*. In *He Who Gets Slapped*, the "man of a thousand faces," Lon Chaney, was a heartbroken inventor who becomes a clown. Douglas Fairbanks headlined the elaborate—and moneymaking—swashbuckler *The Thief of Bagdad*. In Buster Keaton's classic *The Navigator*, the comedian played a brokenhearted young millionaire on a solitary sea voyage.

Sex Idol

Hits included "It Had to Be You," "Tea for Two," "How Come You Do Me Like You Do?" featuring Louis Armstrong and the Fletcher Henderson Orchestra, and the Gershwin show tunes "The Man I Love" and "Oh, Lady Be Good." "Hard Hearted Hannah (The Vamp of Savannah)" and Bix Beiderbecke's "I Need Some Petting" captured the mood of the times.

Morality tales amid modern excess dominated the year's novels. In *The Coast of Folly* by Coningsby Dawson, a woman abandons her daughter to live a carefree life in France. One of the decade's bestsellers, *The Green Hat* by Michael Arlen, told a story of sexual liberation and disappointment. Dorothy Canfield Fisher's *The Home-Maker* featured a married couple's role reversal.

JOHN BARRYMORE

The dashing, dapper John Barrymore was one of the first of his famous thespian family to make it on the big screen. His siblings, Lionel and Ethel, were also well-known on stage and screen. John was so handsome that his nickname was "The Great Profile." He was as famous for his conquests of beautiful actresses as he was for his films.

Despite his talent, Barrymore chose a destructive path. As a serious alcoholic, he squandered much of his film fortune on drinking and cavorting. The height of his career stood in stark contrast to his dark later years. He died in 1942.

SEE ALSO
▶ RUDOLPH VALENTINO *Page 31*
▶ GARY COOPER *Page 146*

48

1924 CAPRICORN

*From December 22, 1923 20:53 through January 21, 1924 7:27
(December 1924 Capricorns, see 1925 Capricorn)*

♑ *The Lifelong Comrade*

As a 1924 Capricorn, it's likely that loyalty is your hallmark, and you may still be involved with colleagues and acquaintances whose beliefs chime with your own. Your address book could be filled with contacts whose ages span the generations, but it's likely that they all share a similar outlook or point of view. And your criteria are probably no different when it comes to choosing a mate. Above all, you want a friend, and it's important that you respect them. Equality is vital in all your relationships, and that may very well filter through to your closest relationship. You could be the man whose masculinity is not threatened if he does the dishes or the woman that finds fulfillment through a career.

It takes a special person to penetrate your cool and self-contained exterior. You don't wear your heart on your sleeve, and you may prefer to let others win your affections, rather than trying to please them. Once someone has won your heart, however, you will be a steadfast and loyal partner. It is also sometimes easier for you to show your feelings through actions rather than words. You love deeply, but can sometimes be tongue-tied when you try express it.

You admire independence and those with the courage of their convictions. For relationships to develop you must know that someone won't back down when principles are at stake. Your partner must accept that you have many interests outside the home and possessiveness can sour any relationship.

As a Capricorn man of 1924, you may set less store by good looks than good character, so someone who is constantly fussing over her appearance might be a major turn off. You know the real value of a lifelong partnership is that your outlook and vision is in harmony and that you treat each other with respect.

As a woman born under Capricorn in 1924, your man must make you proud. But this is not necessarily in terms of material success. No, so long as you are not too broke, it's his attitude to his principles and the causes he supports that are important, and you're likely to applaud him when he goes out on a limb for his beliefs.

CAPRICORN ZODIAC SIGN
YOUR LOVE PLANETS

YOUR ROMANTIC SIDE   p. 696
▶ VENUS IN AQUARIUS
Born Dec. 22, 1923 20:53 - Jan. 19, 1924 13:44
▶ VENUS IN PISCES
Born Jan. 19, 13:45 - Jan. 21, 7:27

YOUR SEX DRIVE   p. 722
▶ MARS IN SCORPIO
Born Dec. 22, 1923 20:53 - Jan. 19, 1924 19:05
▶ MARS IN SAGITTARIUS
Born Jan. 19, 19:06 - Jan. 21, 7:27

YOUR CELEBRITY TWINS   p. 760
Find out the astrological similarities you have with famous people.

YOUR COMPATIBILITY   p. 780
Compare planets to find out how compatible you are in a relationship.

YOUR RELATIONSHIP KARMA   p. 824
▶ SATURN IN SCORPIO
Born Dec. 22, 1923 20:53 - Jan. 21, 1924 7:27

BEBE DANIELS
American Actress
Sun in Capricorn

1924 AQUARIUS

From January 21, 7:28 through February 19, 21:50

♒ *The Casual Idealist*

Born an Aquarius of 1924, you remain upbeat and cheerful, whatever blows life may have dealt you. Your optimistic attitude helps you always to look forward to the next experience and the next potential pal. Deep in your heart you may secretly treasure one far distant romantic moment, but living in the past is not really your style. You love meeting the many friends and colleagues that first your children and now your grandchildren may bring home. Your warmth can make the generation gap seem non-existent, and you may be fascinated by their attitude to relationships and envy—a little—the freedom they enjoy.

Your spontaneity and enthusiasm draw people to you, and you know just how to make them feel good about themselves. In your closest relationship you are non-judgmental, and you continue to be thankful that you chose such a wonderful companion as your partner. You always keep up with what's going on in the world and, while you may only be an armchair traveler, you love exploring different cultures.

With a social life as busy as yours, you can always find someone to connect with. No matter what their background you can usually find common ground to keep the conversation flowing. However, you may drift away from shy and silent types that expect you to entertain them and do all of the talking. For you, being tied down is a major no-no. Your partner understands your need for interaction and knows that if you are allowed unlimited freedom to roam you will always come home in the end.

As an Aquarius man of 1924, you love sporty-looking women. Ideally your partner is comfortable and confident with her body and enjoys every aspect of your relationship as much as you do. Sometimes you have to yank your foot out of your mouth, so your ideal woman will need a robust sense of humor.

Aquarius woman of 1924, you have a spiritual attitude to lovemaking. Your man must be able to open your eyes to the beauty of a truly committed relationship. You love a man who is confident and enjoys going out as much as you. Someone that demands his dinner on time may have to rely on take-outs!

AQUARIUS ZODIAC SIGN
YOUR LOVE PLANETS

YOUR ROMANTIC SIDE   p. 696
▶ VENUS IN PISCES
Born Jan. 21, 7:28 - Feb. 13, 4:09
▶ VENUS IN ARIES
Born Feb. 13, 4:10 - Feb. 19, 21:50

YOUR SEX DRIVE   p. 722
▶ MARS IN SAGITTARIUS
Born Jan. 21, 7:28 - Feb. 19, 21:50

YOUR CELEBRITY TWINS   p. 760
See what your Venus-Mars combination does for your sexual allure and satisfaction!

YOUR COMPATIBILITY   p. 780
Compare planets to find out how compatible you are in a relationship.

YOUR RELATIONSHIP KARMA   p. 824
▶ SATURN IN SCORPIO
Born Jan. 21, 7:28 - Feb. 19, 21:50

BESSIE SMITH
American Blues Singer
Sun in Aries

1924 PISCES
February 19, 21:51 through March 20, 21:19

 ## The Demanding Romantic

Under absolutely no circumstances could you be described as a cold fish, Pisces of 1924. You may sometimes require periods of solitude, but the dance of love is your very favorite step. You can be impulsive and direct when you are attracted to someone, and your lifelong partner can still light up your soul. You are demonstrative and straightforward in your affections and all who know you appreciate your child-like quality of openness. Of course, if you should turn against someone, they also know it pretty quickly! But that rarely seems to happen. You fall all over yourself to seek out the very best qualities in your many friends and acquaintances.

Younger people are a great source of pleasure for you, and the joy of having a family is to watch them grow and learn—and then discover it all over again with your grandchildren. But most of all you cherish your partner. You have a very free spirit and love to investigate anything new that catches your eye. It's most satisfying when you can share your discoveries with your partner, who is as fascinated as you are.

Independence and joie de vivre have always attracted you, Pisces of 1924. Unsociable types with nothing to say can't hold your attention. Your interests are so varied, from art to sports to the latest movie, that you can usually find some common ground. You like to know how people feel, what turns them on, and what their aspirations are, and a person who refuses to open up can be a depressing dinner companion.

If you are a man born a Pisces in 1924, you find creative women irresistible. If they are headstrong and independent, so much the better! You have no problem with making the first move and, if you get turned down occasionally, you probably see it as an exciting challenge. Your partner knows that "No" can be as exciting as "Yes"!

As a Pisces woman of 1924, you want a man that can open your eyes to emotional magic. He's 100 percent masculine and gives you plenty of freedom to be yourself. He shares your love of exploring life to the full. The pipe and slippers are never a match for the plane ticket to distant lands.

1924 ARIES
From March 20, 21:20 through April 20, 8:58

 ## The Quiet Dynamo

As an Aries of 1924, you are as serious and clear thinking about relationships as you are about most other aspects of your life. You may be cautious when approaching a prospective partner as you loathe rejection of any kind. Your friends may be those that you made in your twenties and thirties, as you choose carefully and for keeps. Your determination to make something of your life may be reflected in the people you mix with and also your partner. "For better or for worse" is a phrase that echoes your attitude to your closest relationship. Naturally, you prefer the good times, but you remain constant during the bad.

You may have expensive tastes and appreciate material luxury. This is sure to be reflected in your home, which will be comfortable and welcoming. However, when times were hard you probably still had the ability to turn the humblest dwelling into an attractive and desirable residence. Physical comfort is something you give with ease, and you also enjoy receiving it. You need to know your loved one is close and you touch and

caress your partner unselfconsciously. The physical connection between you is always an intrinsic part of your relationship.

Your attention can be caught by ambitious and determined types. You appreciate their desire to get ahead and you enjoy lending a helping hand. Anyone that is lazy and expects you to do all the work doesn't seem very attractive somehow. You need to be appreciated and you hate to be just one of a crowd. You have never been able to tolerate mind games either.

As an Aries man of 1924, you like your woman to be supportive. She must understand that all you do is for the good of the family and that you may expect her to play a traditional role. You know that without the stability she provides at home your effectiveness in the world will suffer.

Born under Aries in 1924, you are a woman that loves your man to show his appreciation with gifts and tokens. He doesn't have to keep telling you he loves you–that is clear from the way he treats you. You love his quiet authority and you take pleasure in his reassuring touch.

1924 TAURUS
From April 20, 8:59 through May 21, 8:39

The Comfortable Companion

You enjoy company, Taurus of 1924, mixing and matching your friends in your own unique way. You can usually find common ground when you meet new people but you may not give away very much about yourself. Your method is to draw others out and get them to talk about themselves. Without realizing it, you can be very flirtatious. In your eyes most people are kept at a distance and only the chosen few really get close to you. Once you take someone to your heart, however, they remain there forever. You need to trust your friends and loved ones, and any hint of betrayal can damage a relationship.

Despite your upbeat and cheerful manner, you need to be appreciated. You don't place too high a value on money and possessions, despite your Taurean reputation. What is important to you is that your partner shares your outlook and even your political viewpoint. Not that you are intent on changing minds—it's just that people aren't attractive in the first place if their beliefs are too far away from your own. Sharing a cause keeps your relationship fresh and strong.

It may be true for you that attraction is more mental than physical. You may have noticed how good looking your partner is only after you have been turned on by what they had to say. You love to get a response from your partner and need to be sure of their loyalty. But you prefer it if they allow you some space and freedom to do your own thing. You may begin to panic if you know they are sitting, waiting for your return, unable to enjoy their own company.

Your woman must endlessly surprise you, Taurus man of 1924. Predictability and an emphasis on routine can be major turn offs. You may not be too worried if the physical side of love has slowed down a little but you need to know that your lifelong conversation will continue to excite you.

As a Taurus woman of 1924, you desire feedback and conversation. You want your man to tell you that he loves you, but also to tell you what he has seen and done during the day. You love to share every aspect of his life— although too many questions about yours can be claustrophobic!

THOMAS MANN
German Writer
Venus in Taurus

51

1924 GEMINI
From May 21, 8:40 through June 21, 16:58

The Idealistic Flirt

Gemini of 1924, you have probably always been at your happiest when you were involved in a loving and committed relationship. Despite your astrological reputation as a flirtatious butterfly, your loyalty has never been in question. In fact, you may have chosen as a life mate someone who, like you, can enjoy many and varied friendships, not only with your contemporaries but also with people older and much younger than yourself. You haven't stopped learning about what makes others tick—and you never intend to either. If they can teach you something new, so much the better!

You have a robust romantic side, but rather than hearts and flowers it is likely to be the romance of a shared vision or a devotion to a cause, either political or social. Equality has always been vital in your relationships, and you won't hesitate to show the door to anyone that comes across as bigoted or selfish. You've always had the big picture in your sights, and nitpicking or nagging is the biggest turn off for you.

A suitor that wears their ideals as well as their heart on their sleeve is guaranteed a second look from you. It is always helpful if your admirer has the ability to make you laugh out loud as well. You'll always notice if a potential partner is good with children, as family life remains a big attraction for you.

As a male Gemini of 1924 your ideal partner would have to be a woman that combines sensuality, self-confidence, and a youthful outlook. She would share your vision but also sew on your buttons, feed you three meals a day, and occasionally bring you down to earth. For you, sex has always been as much about the meeting of mind and spirit as well as the body.

As a Gemini woman of 1924 you need to be proud of your man. He doesn't have to be the strongest or handsomest guy on the block, but it is important that he has confidence, both intellectually and spiritually. You're comfortable taking care of the practical side, just so long as he stays true to his principles. You've always enjoyed lovemaking, but a loving word or a shared intimacy can warm your heart just as much.

1924 CANCER
From June 21, 16:59 through July 23, 3:57

♋ *The Eternal Lover*

As a Cancer born in 1924, the desire to love and be loved is at the core of your being. You may have married early or alternatively held out in the belief that you would meet your ideal partner. Either way, the quest for the kind of relationship that keeps you totally absorbed and enthralled has been at the heart of your psyche. Once you find your soul mate, nothing and no one can persuade you to change your mind. Commitment for you is a lifelong affair, and you have always been well able to withstand the ups and downs that most relationships encounter. And, despite your gentle demeanor, you are quite capable of fighting to keep your loved one.

For you, a family has always been the natural extension of a relationship. Far from damaging the bond between you and your partner, as far as you were concerned it could only strengthen it. Now your children may have grown, and you may be reliving the joy you felt as a parent through your grandchildren. In some ways you have never needed an extensive social life, preferring to delight in and grow with those closest to you. Entertaining the local high-flyers never has been your idea of a special evening!

It may be difficult to put into words exactly what attracted you to your partner but an ability to convey the same sense of wonder at the meeting of two hearts could give an indication. You know just how to keep your partner happy and in return you require loyalty above all. You still prefer a moonlight stroll or an intimate dinner to dancing the night away.

As a man born under Cancer in 1924, your woman has to be just that–all woman! If she can bake an apple pie and keep you entertained in the bedroom, she's more than halfway there! While you may still appreciate a pretty face or a shapely leg, your heart remains true.

Cancer woman of 1924, you love to be needed. Under that demure exterior there beats the heart of a siren. Sex for you is symbolic of the deepest sharing and it has always been the glue that held you together. It must always be beautiful and romantic. Any coarseness or off-color behavior can kill the moment for you.

WILLIAM BUTLER YEATS
Irish Writer
Mars in Leo

1924 LEO
From July 23, 3:58 through August 23, 10:47

♌ *The Proud Dreamer*

Of course you have many friends, Leo of 1924, but your family is the axis on which your life revolves. You are happy to see yourself as the proud matriarch surrounded by successive generations of her family. Or as the cherished father and grandfather to whom all can turn for advice. Love for you is expressed through nurture and you can empathize with the most wayward of your grandchildren. You know that the family bonds remain strong regardless of any minor rifts along the way.

You are always aware of and attentive to your partner's needs. Your sensitivity coupled with your Leonine pride leads you to treat others with respect. You expect that to be reciprocal, and it can take you a while to recover your dignity if someone offends you. But your generous spirit means that you rarely stay mad for long. You know that the most important people in your life need to be aware of how much they matter, and you do your utmost to show your concern for them. Your closest relationship still retains its early magical fairy-tale quality and lovemaking symbolizes the unity of your souls.

Your sympathetic and kindly nature has sometimes drawn you to those that need a helping hand. You instinctively know how to boost their self-esteem and rekindle their optimism. And you remain convinced that even through difficult times, keeping your eyes fixed firmly on the silver lining can minimize those more threatening clouds. However, your relationship must be mutually supportive—you can't do all the work!

As a Leo man of 1924, you adore a woman who combines a charming sensuality with a poetic soul. Tender caresses and a romantic atmosphere are far more appealing than obvious glamor. You want your woman to center her world around you. For you, your chosen mate remains a goddess on a pedestal.

Born a Leo woman in 1924, you want your man to sweep you off your feet, Rhett Butler style. You are happy to drown in a sea of kisses and, regardless of circumstances, your man must live up to your romantic ideals. For you to shine, he must give you his undivided attention and unconditional love.

52

1924 VIRGO

From August 23, 10:48 through September 23, 7:57

The Discreet Dramatic

Beneath that cool, calm, and unruffled exterior, you are passionate and idealistic. You choose your friends with the utmost care, Virgo of 1924, and you need to respect your life partner above all. Loyalty and an inquiring mind are two of the many qualities you insist on for a relationship to work. In return you are a devoted, considerate, and selfless companion. Your attention to detail results in perfectly chosen gifts and exquisite meals shared with great company. You love to spoil people and, while you are realistic about the many failings and foibles of those you love, your support is unstinting.

You are not afraid to put in the effort required to make your marriage work, but you resent being taken for granted. If your efforts are overlooked once too often, you can be quite capable of staging an uncharacteristic and highly dramatic tantrum! But you rarely bear a grudge, so long as those close to you reassure you that you have not been forgotten. You may not be the most physical of partners, but you show you care with well-chosen words of encouragement

or a discreet squeeze of the hand.

A knack of making you laugh will always attract your attention, Virgo of 1924. But you must know that those you connect with have a code of ethics in tune with your own. Once you're at ease, you are an open and inspiring companion and you continue to expand your circle of acquaintances. You may feel uncomfortable with lavish displays of public affection, even from your partner.

As a Virgo man of 1924, you are proud of your woman. In your eyes she is still the best looking girl in the room and you love it when she makes a special effort to shine. Her loyalty to you is one of the joys of your partnership and you know that she will always be in your corner cheering you on.

To win your respect, Virgo woman of 1924, your man must stick to his principles. It's okay if he flirts a little, but any real disloyalty is hard for you to forgive. For you, marriage should last a lifetime, and you need him to demonstrate that he is worthy of the love and support you are so willing to give him.

VIRGO ZODIAC SIGN
YOUR LOVE PLANETS

YOUR ROMANTIC SIDE   p. 696
- ▶ **VENUS IN CANCER**
  Born Aug. 23, 10:48 - Sept. 08, 21:42
- ▶ **VENUS IN LEO**
  Born Sept. 08, 21:43 - Sept. 23, 7:57

YOUR SEX DRIVE   p. 722
- ▶ **MARS IN PISCES**
  Born Aug. 23, 10:48 - Aug. 24, 15:37
- ▶ **MARS IN AQUARIUS**
  Born Aug. 24, 15:38 - Sept. 23, 7:57

YOUR CELEBRITY TWINS   p. 760
Find out the astrological similarities you have with famous people.

YOUR COMPATIBILITY   p. 780
Compare planets to find out how compatible you are in relationship.

YOUR RELATIONSHIP KARMA   p. 824
- ▶ **SATURN IN LIBRA**
  Born Aug. 23, 10:48 - Sept. 13, 21:58
- ▶ **SATURN IN SCORPIO**
  Born Sept. 13, 21:59 - Sept. 23, 7:57

BETTY BRONSON
American Actress
Mars in Libra

1924 LIBRA

From September 23, 7:58 through October 23, 16:43

The Disarming Opponent

As a Libran, you have all the charm and social skills that are linked to your sign, but you are likely to be far more discriminating in your relationships if you were born in 1924. You count as friends only those that reach your own high standards of behavior. Loud-mouthed show offs are not your chosen companions, although you are far too polite to tell them so. You may take great pains to sound out potential companions before giving away any of your inner feelings. You are adept at steering the conversation away from yourself and onto subjects of mutual interest instead. And you have no qualms about taking a discussion as far as an argument!

Duty is not a chore for you when it comes to your partner and your family. You are happy to do more than your share of the work needed to keep your relationship running smoothly. You know when to compromise and you know when to stand your ground. While it is sometimes tricky to tell someone a few home truths, you ultimately have the courage to do so if necessary. Of course, you let people

know that they have overstepped the mark in the most charming way!

You are always attracted to smartly dressed people. You may believe that a tidy appearance symbolizes a tidy mind. But it takes much more than beauty to keep you interested. You have a strong sense of justice and you love nothing more than a cause you can get your teeth into. You won't waste your time on people who only think about their own needs. But you don't hesitate to help when a loved one needs your support.

If you were born a Libra man of 1924, you can't help but notice if a woman is intelligent. You appreciate a lovely face, but what goes on behind the smile is far more intriguing. Your closest relationship remains fresh as you both continue to look outward as well as at each other.

Libra woman of 1924, you love a fighter. Your man may lose as many battles as he wins, but the fact that he keeps on fighting them is what makes you love him. His eccentric streak is as endearing to you now as it was when you first set eyes on him. His honesty is his finest quality.

LIBRA ZODIAC SIGN
YOUR LOVE PLANETS

YOUR ROMANTIC SIDE   p. 696
- ▶ **VENUS IN LEO**
  Born Sept. 23, 7:58 - Oct. 07, 14:15
- ▶ **VENUS IN VIRGO**
  Born Oct. 07, 14:16 - Oct. 23, 16:43

YOUR SEX DRIVE   p. 722
- ▶ **MARS IN AQUARIUS**
  Born Sept. 23, 7:58 - Oct. 19, 18:41
- ▶ **MARS IN PISCES**
  Born Oct. 19, 18:42 - Oct. 23, 16:43

YOUR CELEBRITY TWINS   p. 760
Find out the astrological similarities you have with famous people.

YOUR COMPATIBILITY   p. 780
Compare planets to find out how compatible you are in a relationship.

YOUR RELATIONSHIP KARMA   p. 824
- ▶ **SATURN IN SCORPIO**
  Born Sept. 23, 7:58 - Oct. 23, 16:43

53

SCORPIO ZODIAC SIGN

YOUR LOVE PLANETS

YOUR ROMANTIC SIDE   p. 696
- ▶ **VENUS IN VIRGO**
  Born Oct. 23, 16:44 - Nov. 02, 14:43
- ▶ **VENUS IN LIBRA**
  Born Nov. 02, 14:44 - Nov. 22, 13:45

YOUR SEX DRIVE   p. 722
- ▶ **MARS IN PISCES**
  Born Oct. 23, 16:44 - Nov. 22, 13:45

YOUR CELEBRITY TWINS   p. 760
Find out the astrological similarities you have with famous people.

YOUR COMPATIBILITY   p. 780
Compare planets to find out how compatible you are in a relationship.

YOUR RELATIONSHIP KARMA   p. 824
- ▶ **SATURN IN SCORPIO**
  Born Oct. 23, 16:44 - Nov. 22, 13:45

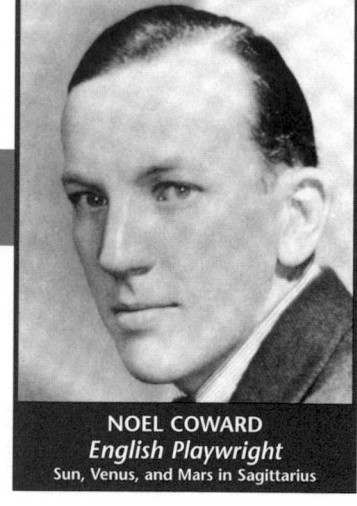

NOEL COWARD
English Playwright
Sun, Venus, and Mars in Sagittarius

SAGITTARIUS ZODIAC SIGN

YOUR LOVE PLANETS

YOUR ROMANTIC SIDE   p. 696
- ▶ **VENUS IN LIBRA**
  Born Nov. 22, 13:46 - Nov. 27, 11:47
- ▶ **VENUS IN SCORPIO**
  Born Nov. 27, 11:48 - Dec. 21, 19:55
- ▶ **VENUS IN SAGITTARIUS**
  Born Dec. 21, 19:56 - Dec. 22, 2:44

YOUR SEX DRIVE   p. 722
- ▶ **MARS IN PISCES**
  Born Nov. 22, 13:46 - Dec. 19, 11:08
- ▶ **MARS IN ARIES**
  Born Dec. 19, 11:09 - Dec. 22, 2:44

YOUR CELEBRITY TWINS   p. 760
Find out the astrological similarities you have with famous people.

YOUR COMPATIBILITY   p. 780
Compare planets to find out how compatible you are in a relationship.

YOUR RELATIONSHIP KARMA   p. 824
- ▶ **SATURN IN SCORPIO**
  Born Nov. 22, 13:46 - Dec. 22, 2:44

1924 SCORPIO
From October 23, 16:44 through November 22, 13:45

♏ *The Devoted Supporter*

Once you found your mate, you didn't really have to maintain a huge circle of friends, Scorpio of 1924. Your home and family and a few trusted pals give you all the emotional support you need. You are capable of emotional and material comfort to your loved ones that occasionally borders on the superhuman. Your loyalty is such that it would take years of mistreatment before you would cast someone aside. Those who know you well appreciate your capacity for boundless love and also your ability to say and do exactly what is necessary for them.

Your closest relationship is one of touching devotion. Your partner really is everything to you and you never knowingly cause them hurt—although you can sometimes wield a sharp tongue if you're caught off guard! Yours is a sensual sign, but you may have enjoyed the physical side of love only when you felt completely secure in your relationship—and knowing that you can completely open up to another human being may still be an enormous source of comfort to you. You may even feel during those special moments that

you are touching the divine.

You may notice intense good looks but you don't really go for "cute." You want to know, when you look into your partner's eyes, that you really are seeing a window to their soul. You have chosen to contribute total commitment to your relationship, and nothing less will suffice in return. A flirtatious partner can cause you far too much grief—security and depth are what you seek in relationships.

Scorpio man of 1924, your partner is a woman who knows her own mind but listens to your opinions. Of course, she may frequently disagree with them, but you don't mind the discussions that follow, however heated! To be able to trust her completely with your heart is your constant source of joy and wonderment.

Born under Scorpio in 1924, you are a woman who just can't resist charisma. A man that has a sense of mystery can't help but be intriguing. Your partner may have opened your eyes to many aspects of relationships that you never even dreamed of, and his touch remains your greatest source of fulfillment.

1924 SAGITTARIUS
From November 22, 13:46 through December 22, 2:44

♐ *The Grounded Philosopher*

You may sometimes be a quiet one, Sagittarius of 1924. You can be optimistic but you play your cards close to your chest and never commit yourself until you are certain it is for the long term. Casual acquaintances may see your sunny side, but those who know you well understand your hidden depths. You are serious about many things, and relationships come close to the top of your list. You approach new people with caution and you may need to mull over in private how far you want to take a relationship. Your partner may be used to those times when you want solitude rather than company.

To you, feelings are personal, and it can take a while before you let an admirer know how you feel. While you don't always show it, you are extremely sensitive. A thoughtless remark can cut you to the quick, and sometimes you don't care to take the risk. But to your loved ones you can be generous to a fault—for example, it's likely that you'd sacrifice almost anything to put your kids through college. You never close off the learning process and you are

eager for your children and grandchildren to share their knowledge with you.

Gentleness may be what first attracted you to your partner. You can be protective of your loved ones, and knowing you can provide for them heightens your self-esteem. You try to be truthful in all you do and say, and people that leave you guessing are not your ideal companions. For you, a friendship must be above board—you are dismayed by lies.

As a Sagittarius man born in 1924, you love women who are sure of themselves. Your soul mate will have her feet on the ground but she never tires of looking at the stars. For you, making love is the merging of two souls. It delights you that your woman has a discreet sensuality that is known to you alone.

If you are a Sagittarius woman of 1924, you want your partner to continually delight in love's mysteries. A healthy bank balance is attractive but does not compare to a partner who can read you poetry in bed. Your man must be an artist— even if he's a lawyer. There must be some magic in his spirit to keep you happy.

Gertrude Stein and Alice B. Toklas

Expatriate lesbian lovers Gertrude Stein and Alice Babette Toklas met in 1907 in Paris when they were 33 and 30, respectively. Both women were Jewish and from the San Francisco area, and both had fled the more conventional paths their well-to-do families had urged on them for lives of bohemian freedom. Gertrude Stein was already an established writer, acclaimed author of *Three Lives* and *Tender Buttons*, known for experimenting with form, selecting words for their rhythm and sound rather than for their meanings. Even her narrative works sang with poetry. She often used repetition with slight variation to create texture, or used repetition to call meaning into question as in her famous epigram "A rose is a rose is a rose."

At first, Toklas worked as Stein's secretary, but the two soon fell in love and, after a honeymoon vacation, Toklas moved in with Stein at 27 Rue de Fleuris. They lived in remarkable domestic harmony for 38 years, Stein as the "genius" and Toklas in the helpmate's role, managing the household, the accounts, and doing the cooking. She also typed and proofread Stein's manuscripts. They had an astonishing array of pet names for one another—Stein called Toklas "wifie" and "pussy" while Toklas called Stein "hubbie" and "lovey." They wrote love notes to one another almost daily, some of which survived when Toklas mistakenly included them among manuscripts she donated to Yale after Stein's death.

The couple received medals from the French government for their help during World War I, when they transported medical supplies and wounded soldiers in their car, "Auntie." During the 1920s, they hosted a thriving salon to which flocked writers,

Paris in the 20's, where Toklas and Stein first met

artists, and flamboyant characters such as F. Scott Fitzgerald, Ernest Hemingway, and Paul Bowles—post–World War I expatriates whom Stein famously called the "lost generation." Stein, along with her brother Leo, was one of the first to support emerging modern artists, buying works by Picasso, Matisse, Renoir, and Gaugin, and Picasso painted a brooding portrait of bulky, severe-faced, crop-haired Gertrude.

In 1933, Stein wrote *The Autobiography of Alice B. Toklas*, a clever faux-memoir of Alice's life that was actually all about Gertrude. Its interweaving of fact and fiction, and Stein's attribution of her own thoughts and observations to Toklas, still keep literary scholars busy reading between the lines. At the time of publication, it was the only one of Stein's books that had achieved public acclaim.

Despite the rise of Nazism, the couple, now in their sixties, stayed in Paris, moving to the countryside during the German occupation of France, and miraculously managing to avoid harm despite the period's anti-Semitic and anti-homosexual purges. They extended their famous hospitality to American soldiers during and after the war.

Gertrude Stein died of cancer on July 27, 1946, Alice B. Toklas by her side. Her famous last words to Alice were: "What is the answer?" and, receiving no answer, "In that case, what is the question?"

After Stein's death, Toklas was the loyal and faithful companion, serving as literary executor and sharing her memories of her more famous partner in her book *What Is Remembered*. She died in 1967 at the age of 90, and joined Stein in eternal rest in Paris's Pere Lachaise Cemetery, where they share a tombstone, an epitaph for each on either side.

55

> *"She was a golden brown presence, burned by the Tuscan sun and with a golden glint in her warm brown hair."*
>
> **ALICE BABETTE TOKLAS' MEMOIRS**

▶ READ ABOUT F. SCOTT AND FITZGERALD ON PAGE 39 ▶ READ ABOUT JEAN COCTEAU ON PAGE 161 ▶ READ ABOUT ERNEST HEMINGWAY ON PAGE 180

1925

- ⊛ PETTING PARTIES
- ⊛ PORT OF LOVE
- ⊛ JOSEPHINE BAKER
- ⊛ BURLESQUE
- ⊛ THE BIG PARADE
- ⊛ SWEET GEORGIA BROWN
- ⊛ MRS. DALLOWAY

EVENTS

Trends this year in the US included nightclubbing, tanning, and slimming. Outraged by "petting parties," a US judge condemned the automobile as a "house of prostitution on wheels."

Nellie Ross of Wyoming was sworn in as first woman governor in the US and the Protestant Episcopal Church dropped the word "obey" from wedding vows, but bishops in northern Italy excluded women with bare legs or immodest dress from Catholic churches.

In Britain, the Dean of Durham added his voice to the debate over women's modesty by condemning the fashion in which English women shamelessly confessed their infidelity in the divorce courts, and the backlash against women continued with the condemnation of contraceptives by The National Council of Public Morals.

Meanwhile, American burlesque star Carrie Finnel twirled tassels from her breasts and buttocks while Josephine Baker, the "Black Venus," became a Paris sensation for her bare-breasted "jungle" dances.

POP CULTURE

Costume melodrama films were all the rage. Valentino starred in *The Eagle* as a Russian lieutenant who spurns the Czarina and becomes an outlaw. *The Phantom of the Opera*, based on Gaston Leroux's novel, features Lon Chaney as a disfigured phantom pining for love. King Vidor's *The Big Parade* was a WWI weeper about an American soldier and a

Sex Idol

beautiful French peasant woman.

Songs ranged from swing tunes like "Sweet Georgia Brown" and "Dinah" to the jaunty "Yes Sir, That's My Baby," "Five Foot Two, Eyes of Blue," and "If You Knew Susie." Hit songs, often with risqué lyrics, poured from New York's "Tin Pan Alley," from Broadway, dance orchestras, and folk traditions, and were promptly recorded by an array of singers and musicians, and sold as sheet music.

Novels included Margaret Kennedy's *The Constant Nymph*, about a young girl's love for her father's friend, and Giovanni Comisso's *Port of Love*, which contrasts emotion and sensual experience with bourgeois values. Virginia Woolf's groundbreaking *Mrs. Dalloway* used stream-of-consciousness to follow a day in the stifled life of an upper-class British matron.

JOHN GILBERT

Sexy silent film star John Gilbert was a devastatingly handsome leading man. Despite his talent, his career was short-lived. It was rumored that his high voice kept him from succeeding in the "talkies," but another rumor was that studio head Louis B. Mayer ruined him because of a dispute over starlet Greta Garbo.

The on-screen romance he'd shared with Garbo had blossomed into a torrid off-screen affair. But when their relationship ended, so did his career. Mayer's powerful influence in Hollywood made sure of it. Gilbert barely worked again and died in 1936 from a heart attack at the age of 37.

SEE ALSO

▶ JOHN BARRYMORE *Page 48*
▶ GRETA GARBO *Page 153*

1925 CAPRICORN

From December 22, 1924 2:45 through January 20, 1925 13:19
(December 1925 Capricorns, see 1926 Capricorn)

♑ *The Creative Romancer*

For you, Capricorn of 1925, the central theme in a successful relationship is keeping you on the edge of your seat, so you both feel there is something fresh and new to learn from each other every day. You want someone with whom you can share wonderfully inventive ideas about love and life, and be engaged at every moment, taking nothing for granted.

You look for a friend, a lover, and an intellectual equal who can keep a good flow of conversation and mutual activities going. You basically want the kind of relationship that keeps both of you on your toes. Whatever differences you have will add an element of excitement that will show itself when you touch or kiss, or when you simply look into each other's eyes. This is what you need more than anything else being with someone.

A person who wants to attract your eye and your interest needs to be accessible, but not accommodating. Someone you can talk to, but who is self-possessed and secure in his or her own skin, will keep you interested for more than just a casual conversation. You're most transfixed when you feel there is something deeper to this person than meets the eye, and if he or she showers you with surprises each time you are together, you will surely keep coming back.

The woman who really turns you on the most, and in every way, Capricorn man of 1925, is the one who combines good looks, good taste, and an independent soul that you feel is always just a little beyond your reach. No matter what you do, you are never quite in the center of this lady's radar screen, and that's both maddening and exciting to you—and very likely she knows it. You need to get close to her, ultimately that is what makes her want to be close to you.

For the Capricorn woman of 1925, a man with a big heart who shows it in a quiet way is just the one to pluck at your heartstrings. He has an air of kindness about him that everyone senses, yet at the same time he is just a little aloof from the scene around him—something that intrigues you more than you can put into words. This is someone you want to be with in mind, body, and spirit.

CAPRICORN ZODIAC SIGN

YOUR LOVE PLANETS

YOUR ROMANTIC SIDE   p. 696
  ▶ **VENUS IN SAGITTARIUS**
  Born Dec. 22, 1924 2:45 - Jan. 14, 1925 22:27
  ▶ **VENUS IN CAPRICORN**
  Born Jan. 14, 22:28 - Jan. 20, 13:19

YOUR SEX DRIVE   p. 722
  ▶ **MARS IN ARIES**
  Born Dec. 22, 1924 2:45 - Jan. 20, 1925 13:19

YOUR CELEBRITY TWINS   p. 760
  Find out the astrological similarities you have with famous people.

YOUR COMPATIBILITY   p. 780
  Compare planets to find out how compatible you are in a relationship.

YOUR RELATIONSHIP KARMA   p. 824
  ▶ **SATURN IN SCORPIO**
  Born Dec. 22, 1924 2:45 - Jan. 20, 1925 13:19

VILMA BANKY
Hungarian Actress
Sun, Venus, and Mars in Capricorn

57

1925 AQUARIUS

From January 20, 13:20 through February 19, 3:42

♒ *The Passionate Dreamer*

As an Aquarius of 1925, you are quite a heady mixture of hot passions and dreamy romanticism that makes you very exciting, mysterious, and even a bit vexing to anyone you're involved with. You are the ultimate romantic, someone who sees even a small flirtation as a major event, because it inspires a kind of emotional poetry inside you. When you were younger, this feeling might have been distracting, no matter how pleasant it was, and though it's more manageable as you've matured, it still can knock you for a loop.

You find romance in everything you do, even when you are just hanging around in the same space, sharing coffee in the morning, and having a laugh now and again. The icing on top is that the two of you can relate, way down deep, where your minds mingle and your senses are challenged. Physical passion is the best part of it all, but it never overshadows the sharing, and the mental closeness of being together.

If someone wants to attract you, he or she needs to penetrate your heart and your mind. This is not the kind of thing most people can do just by walking in a room, saying hello, or shaking your hand. Someone who really wants to get close to you has to understand that with you it takes a bit of time. However, the quickest way for someone to get on your good, romantic side is to exude a bit of passion beneath a cool exterior.

For you, Aquarian man of 1925, you are attracted to the woman who has a subtle quality in the way she carries herself, and in the way she looks at you. She has a passion for life, and a passion for sharing her life with someone like you. Even if she's not "picture perfect" attractive, you're not likely to see this, as you're looking well below the surface, more than skin deep.

As an Aquarian woman of 1925, your ideal man may seem a little unusual to others, someone with interests off the beaten track. It's not that you're attracted to odd types—you're more interested in his heart and his mind, not his resume or his public image. You need a man who can share your heart and who will share his with you, so whatever else he may be, that's just gravy.

AQUARIUS ZODIAC SIGN

YOUR LOVE PLANETS

YOUR ROMANTIC SIDE   p. 696
  ▶ **VENUS IN CAPRICORN**
  Born Jan. 20, 13:20 - Feb. 07, 23:15
  ▶ **VENUS IN AQUARIUS**
  Born Feb. 07, 23:16 - Feb. 19, 3:42

YOUR SEX DRIVE   p. 722
  ▶ **MARS IN ARIES**
  Born Jan. 20, 13:20 - Feb. 05, 10:16
  ▶ **MARS IN TAURUS**
  Born Feb. 05, 10:17 - Feb. 19, 3:42

YOUR CELEBRITY TWINS   p. 760
  See what your Venus-Mars combination does for your sexual allure and satisfaction!

YOUR COMPATIBILITY   p. 780
  Compare planets to find out how compatible you are in a relationship.

YOUR RELATIONSHIP KARMA   p. 824
  ▶ **SATURN IN SCORPIO**
  Born Jan. 20, 13:20 - Feb. 19, 3:42

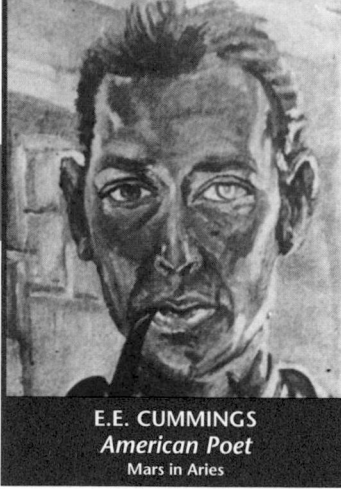

E.E. CUMMINGS
American Poet
Mars in Aries

1925 PISCES
From February 19, 3:43 through March 21, 3:11

The Quintessential Romantic

As a Pisces of 1925, you are a curious combination of someone who is cuddly and sensual, yet unconventional and always unpredictable. For that reason you demand a lot from a relationship. You want to be showered with unconditional love by someone who won't question the independent part of your life. At the same time, you want the fires burning on the home front, with someone to love you through thick and thin, regardless of how much or how little time you spend together.

You are the quintessential romantic, and when you fall for someone, you fall long and hard. You want to know that no matter how many years you are together, both your hearts will skip a beat whenever the other walks in the room. Nonetheless, you can be insecure and shy, needing assurances that you'll never be alone, and that the two of you can always work through any disagreements that come your way.

For you love has to come on strong or not at all, with nothing in between. To make a relationship work with you, your partner must be as intense as he or she is loving, and willing to confront any emotional challenge the two of you might face. Someone with boundless energy, who can make you laugh and sweep you off your feet, interests you right from the start.

As a 1925 Pisces man, you look for a woman who is compassionate, soft-spoken, and sensitive, but not so sensitive that you have to be careful about everything you say. An intuitive woman suits you best, one whose judgment you can rely upon, so you are not always the one who makes the decisions. If she is strong-willed and strong-minded, yet able to yield on occasion, she's the one for you.

The man who thrills you, 1925 Pisces, and makes you feel as if you're the only woman on earth, is steadfast and reliable and has the patience of a saint. He accepts your moods, and when you change your mind three or four times a day, he finds it endearing. This man thinks your creativity and emotional fluttering are wonderful, since it enlivens his life. He is incredibly sensual, and the thought of his fingertips on your face sends your heart into a tailspin.

1925 ARIES
From March 21, 3:12 through April 20, 14:50

The Attentive Listener

It's pretty easy for you to become completely lost in love, Aries of 1925, because that's the real reason for two people coming together. Being involved in a long-term relationship is a wonderful means of making the world go away and forgetting all the responsibilities of your everyday life. It is also the best way to practice the art of compromise, and to cultivate respect for your partner's opinions—even when you don't agree.

Because of this, you will likely devote a great deal of attention to making sure things work the way they should between you and your partner, especially when it comes to taking turns talking and listening to one another. What you are most attentive to, though, are the sounds your loved one makes when the two of you are softly caressing and cuddling, and the warm, sensual response that you give in return.

Anyone who wants to attract you needs to look good, but also needs to defer to you from time to time, letting you be the one who sets the pace that the other must match. At the same time, you like someone who is ready and able to speak up and say what's on his or her mind. And the more purposeful and directed someone is, the more that person will hold your interest.

If you're a 1925 Aries man, the woman who interests you most is well spoken and educated, perhaps even someone who has been at the top of a social or business ladder. While she may have drive and direction, she's not a competitor as such, and will let you know that she wants to hook up with you as a partner. Above all, she has to have some depth because the superficial type who's all giggles and flashy makeup turns you right off.

The perfect man for a 1925 Aries woman is someone who is confident, well groomed, and perhaps a success in his own right and in his own field. Although he is someone used to getting his own way, the man you dream about has to switch gears on the home front. He must listen to you and respond to your needs and feelings. He may be one of the guys, but when he is around you, he has no problem letting you lead, at least occasionally, in the dance of romance.

58

1925 TAURUS *From April 20, 14:51 through May 21, 14:32*

The Social Lover

The best relationship in the world for you, Taurus of 1925, is one that does as much for you outside as inside. Not only do you like to have a personal connection with someone who fulfills you and satisfies you in an emotional way, but you like knowing that the two of you together look like the perfect duo to everyone you meet. Knowing the world approves makes you feel absolutely certain that you are with the right person.

This is not to say that you're all show when it comes to sharing a close bond with someone. What matters to you most when it comes to love is what lies beneath the surface, and what you both share in your own private home. You love a home-cooked meal to stimulate your taste buds, topped with an especially sweet dessert of kisses and hugs.

Anyone who wants to attract you first and hold on to you later needs to look especially good in manner, in dress, and in general appearance. However, looking good also has to come from inside, because you never looked just for a model or a clotheshorse type to dress

up your appearance. You need someone who can share both the moonlight and the limelight, someone at ease in settings both private and public.

If you're a 1925 Taurus man, the lady who sweeps into the room with charm, grace, and just a dash of pizzazz can catch your eye and win your heart at a moment's notice. But winning and keeping are two different things. She needs to have a good mind, be a good conversationalist, and be willing to defer to you at key times, though without really giving in. If she's comfortable being a public person, that's fine with you—the two of you need to be able to stand before the world as a winning couple.

For the 1925 Taurus woman, a man with a good, firm voice, strong, chiseled looks, and a really good wardrobe is right up your alley, but only if he has a warm heart to go along with the package. Even if he doesn't look like a movie star now, or never did, if he's the kind who turns heads when he walks in the room, you know he's the one for you. He's just the type of fellow who makes you feel good to be beside him.

VIRGINIA WOOLF
English Writer
Mars in Gemini

59

1925 GEMINI  *From May 21, 14:33 through June 21, 22:49*

The Passionate Player

The way you relate to someone you love is interesting and, to some people, a bit contradictory, 1925 Gemini. On the one hand, you see a romantic relationship as a way of freeing your mind and spirit, a kind of playground for the heart and soul. On the other hand, you tend to be very serious and deeply passionate about your closest bond with another person.

In reality, these things are not contradictory at all, because both come from the deep need you have to get all you can out of knowing and being with someone who is very special to you. If you do that just right, then you will run the gamut of thoughts and emotions from the silly to the serious, enjoying every moment along the way. Anyone lucky enough to be your partner will understand sooner rather than later that a relationship to you is not just a social occasion.

The person who wants to attract you has to meet you on one of your two romantic levels, or at least at some distance in between. When you spot a person who can be romantic, yet playful, and who also has a spark of intensity—

that flair of passion that perhaps defies definition—this is someone who will certainly interest you. In fact, someone with those qualities will likely spot you in no time, and know just how to project these qualities out there so you can see and appreciate them.

Your dream girl, 1925 Gemini, is the one who can sing a song, tell a story, and, if you are lucky, be an incredibly good dancer. At the same time, she is someone who knows how to take advantage of those private and sensual moments the two of you share together. To this unique woman, passion is as important as play, and she knows how to bring out your romantic soul.

For you, 1925 Gemini lady, the man you want most is a charmer and a talker and the kind of man who can make not just you, but everyone in the room, feel completely at ease. The first time he touches your hand you know he has a sensual and emotional side that he is unafraid to express. This is someone who is interesting on a variety of levels, and you're ready to meet him and match him on each and every one.

CANCER ZODIAC SIGN
YOUR LOVE PLANETS

YOUR ROMANTIC SIDE   p. 696
▶ **VENUS IN CANCER**
Born June 21, 22:50 - July 03, 14:30
▶ **VENUS IN LEO**
Born July 03, 14:31 - July 23, 9:44

YOUR SEX DRIVE   p. 722
▶ **MARS IN CANCER**
Born June 21, 22:50 - June 26, 9:07
▶ **MARS IN LEO**
Born June 26, 9:08 - July 23, 9:44

YOUR CELEBRITY TWINS   p. 760
Find out the astrological similarities you have with famous people.

YOUR COMPATIBILITY   p. 780
Compare planets to find out how compatible you are in a relationship.

YOUR RELATIONSHIP KARMA   p. 824
▶ **SATURN IN SCORPIO**
Born June 21, 22:50 - July 23, 9:44

LOUIS ARMSTRONG
American Musician
Sun in Leo

LEO ZODIAC SIGN
YOUR LOVE PLANETS

YOUR ROMANTIC SIDE   p. 696
▶ **VENUS IN LEO**
Born July 23, 9:45 - July 28, 5:24
▶ **VENUS IN VIRGO**
Born July 28, 5:25 - Aug. 22, 0:27
▶ **VENUS IN LIBRA**
Born Aug. 22, 0:28 - Aug. 23, 16:32

YOUR SEX DRIVE   p. 722
▶ **MARS IN LEO**
Born July 23, 9:45 - Aug. 12, 21:11
▶ **MARS IN VIRGO**
Born Aug. 12, 21:12 - Aug. 23, 16:32

YOUR CELEBRITY TWINS   p. 760
Find out the astrological similarities you have with famous people.

YOUR COMPATIBILITY   p. 780
Compare planets to find out how compatible you are in a relationship.

YOUR RELATIONSHIP KARMA   p. 824
▶ **SATURN IN SCORPIO**
Born July 23, 9:45 - Aug. 23, 16:32

1925 CANCER
From June 21, 22:50 through July 23, 9:44

♋ The Caring Sharer

As a Cancer of 1925, you are charismatic and caring, and have an enormous impact on everyone you meet. Because you view love relationships as a place where both of you can have an almost hypnotic effect upon each other, it is likely that those you've had throughout life have been anything but dull.

You see a close romance as a partnership that allows you to let loose and pour out all your feelings, whether it's through honest, heart-to-heart dialogue, or through silence—fingers running through your hair, lips touching each other's lips, and vibrations throughout your body. When you can share your heart and soul verbally, sensually, and in every other way possible, you have created a bond for life, one that will never be broken.

Someone who wants to attract you should be a good listener, and should be able to talk to you in a way that allows you to bring to the surface all the frustrations and problems you may have bottled up inside you. Once these things are out in the open, you can deal with them, and the person who wants you needs to know and understand that. A twinkle in the eye, a smile, and good looks all help, but are not as important as being able to talk to you and soothe you.

For the 1925 Cancer man, the woman you most want to be with is someone whose voice may be just as appealing as her face, her figure, or the way she dresses. There's a certain quality you can't put your finger on, but it comes from deep inside. There's something about her that tells you she cares about listening to your every want and need. Whatever you do together, the key to everything is sharing your feelings, and the one meant for you instinctively knows that.

A 1925 Cancer female loves to be with a guy who is all heart and unafraid to show it. He has a way of being interested, and sincerely so, in everyone he meets, though he is even more interested in you. He can listen to your tales of happiness, or your stories of disappointments, and respond to them in a way that lets you know everything is all right. And while he is good at getting you to share his feelings, he is not afraid to share his.

1925 LEO
From July 23, 9:45 through August 23, 16:32

♌ The Generous Showoff

For you, 1925 Leo, there is no greater good than being involved in a close relationship with someone whose heart is in the right place, mostly because it brings out the best in your feelings for yourself and for your fellow human beings. Love and romance for you make up just one big cycle of giving and receiving, the best in the human spirit.

You are a very generous and attentive partner to someone you care deeply about, prone to giving gifts on the spur of the moment, or doing little things to make the other person's life easier. As a lover you're among the most responsive around. You may even feel that if everyone had someone to love, the world would be a more peaceful and less trouble-prone place overall.

Someone who wants your heart needs to show his or her good side as quickly as possible. You like the nice surface things, such as good looks, but those just arouse more admiration than interest in you. Anyone who can demonstrate a deep and warm sympathy for other people will win your heart and your devotion in short order. As magnanimous as being in love makes you feel, it also reminds you that you can be enormously sensual. Part of what you give lies in your warm touch.

Aside from a warm and human heart, the perfect lady for the 1925 Leo man is someone with a lively personality, who likes to have fun, and who can enjoy herself no matter what she is doing. There should be somewhere in the depths of her eyes a little come-hither look that only you can see, and one that is reserved only for you. You want someone whose idea of fun includes lots of touching and kissing, and who will perk up both your days and your nights.

For the 1925 Leo woman, the man who fits her needs and desires is someone whose heart may have more depth than his resume. You certainly admire a man who has outward achievements. But that kind of man is not for you unless he exhibits a great humanity and a caring he gives first to you, while reserving a large portion for others around him as well. If someone asked you to describe the kind of man you wanted, you'd have to say, "He's gotta have heart."

1925 VIRGO

From August 23, 16:33 through September 23, 13:42

♍ *The Energetic Lover*

Intensity characterizes much of your approach to life, Virgo of 1925, and it also marks a central theme in your approach to love. You see a love connection as something that deserves your attention, and you will never shortchange anyone with whom you form a romantic bond. Your lover gets the most you can give every day the two of you are together.

Of course, you do expect the same in return. For you relationships are definitely two-way streets. You are not the kind of person who considers "giving" and "sacrifice" to be synonymous, so it is important to you that whoever you're with do his or her best to give you the full measure of love you need and deserve. Love is a way of learning and growing for you, and you do this best when the two of you are on the same wavelength.

The person who would like to come into your life needs to show that he or she really is interested in more than just a good time. Someone who wants to win your heart must first of all give a good deal of attention to you and to you alone. Taking you to a restaurant

that serves your favorite cuisine or driving to your favorite spot where you can cuddle and even make out like two randy teenagers are ways that person reads your mind, and shows openness to you and your needs.

For the 1925 Virgo male, the woman best suited to you lights up the room the moment she walks through the door. She has a great capacity to give, receive, and enjoy love with everything that goes with it. Any woman for you must be independent, not the clingy type. At the same time she knows that two people together are more and better than either of them alone might be.

Your man, 1925 Virgo lady, has to be someone who is a success in the outer world, but who knows he can do better if someone is standing with him as he moves quickly and firmly down the road of life. It raises your energy level and makes you feel alive just to be with him, especially during those moments the two of you have to yourselves. He is someone who can share both his life and his feelings without worrying that he might be losing something in the process.

VIRGO ZODIAC SIGN
YOUR LOVE PLANETS

YOUR ROMANTIC SIDE   p. 696
► VENUS IN LIBRA
Born Aug. 23, 16:33 - Sept. 16, 2:04
► VENUS IN SCORPIO
Born Sept. 16, 2:05 - Sept. 23, 13:42

YOUR SEX DRIVE   p. 722
► MARS IN VIRGO
Born Aug. 23, 16:33 - Sept. 23, 13:42

YOUR CELEBRITY TWINS   p. 760
Find out the astrological similarities you have with famous people.

YOUR COMPATIBILITY   p. 780
Compare planets to find out how compatible you are in a relationship.

YOUR RELATIONSHIP KARMA   p. 824
► SATURN IN SCORPIO
Born Aug. 23, 16:33 - Sept. 23, 13:42

T.S. ELIOT
Anglo-American poet
Sun and Venus in Libra

1925 LIBRA

From September 23, 13:43 through October 23, 22:30

♎ *The Smiling Face*

Some people become lost in love, Libra of 1925, but for you, love is the way in which you come one step closer to finding yourself. Without someone in your life, you tend to feel a little bit lost and somewhat unconnected with the rest of the world. This is not to say that you can't function without a partner, but you do understand and appreciate how much richer and better your life is when you have one.

Your real goal in a relationship is a shared experience, a way of seeing and facing the world that lets you and your closest loved one learn and grow each day you are together. That learning and growing is on a variety of levels, of course, and particularly the emotional level. You understand that you learn at least as much by exploring the world of touch, sense, and physical love, as you do from the other parts of your lives together.

If someone wants to attract you, that person needs to be able to tap into that lonely part you hide so well from most people, and touch it in a way that lets you know you have met someone who can be both friend, lover, and

soul mate. You don't need sparks flying or the earth moving—at least not right away—but you do need a certain look or smile that lets you know everything will be all right—and in fact more than all right.

For the 1925 Libra man, the kind of woman you seek is someone who can fill in all the little gaps in your life that you feel are missing. She has her own inner strength, and doesn't feel challenged about having to share some of it with you. More often than not, she will put your own interests ahead of hers, but she'll also remind you when it's time for you to support her and help her on an emotional level.

A 1925 Libra lady likes a man others might describe as a tower of strength. He's self-assured, but not in an arrogant way, and he's firmly supportive of you, considering your feelings and needs at least as important as his own, if not more so. Though he's probably been a great success in the world, he has never been too busy being Mr. Big that he didn't have time to listen to what's on your mind—and what's in your heart.

LIBRA ZODIAC SIGN
YOUR LOVE PLANETS

YOUR ROMANTIC SIDE   p. 696
► VENUS IN SCORPIO
Born Sept. 23, 13:43 - Oct. 11, 14:09
► VENUS IN SAGITTARIUS
Born Oct. 11, 14:10 - Oct. 23, 22:30

YOUR SEX DRIVE   p. 722
► MARS IN VIRGO
Born Sept. 23, 13:43 - Sept. 28, 19:00
► MARS IN LIBRA
Born Sept. 28, 19:01 - Oct. 23, 22:30

YOUR CELEBRITY TWINS   p. 760
Find out the astrological similarities you have with famous people.

YOUR COMPATIBILITY   p. 780
Compare planets to find out how compatible you are in a relationship.

YOUR RELATIONSHIP KARMA   p. 824
► SATURN IN SCORPIO
Born Sept. 23, 13:43 - Oct. 23, 22:30

RENEE ADOREE
French Actress
Venus in Scorpio

62

1925 SCORPIO
From October 23, 22:31 through November 22, 19:34

♏ *The Deep Seeker*

As a Scorpio of 1925, you view relationships the way you do the ocean—deep, vast and filled with mysteries that could take a lifetime for you to understand. You love getting to know your partner, even if it takes forever. If you knew everything there is to know about the person you're with, you would have to look elsewhere for the challenges that keep you going on a daily basis.

Serious and optimistic, you pay attention to life's details. Plotting out what you will do on your next vacation or asking for input on a remodeling decision are the little things you enjoy doing with the one you're connected to. You also love being involved in invigorating activities in which you inhale fresh, cold air, listen to your hearts beating fast, and then later retreat to a warm inn with a large fireplace. Nothing is more romantic than that.

The person who keeps you coming back for more knows how to love unconditionally, and is your number one fan, whatever you choose to do. The perfect mate teases you lightly with soft caresses and light kisses, getting to know you a little at a time both emotionally and physically. The less said in the getting to know you phase, the more your interest is piqued and the likelihood you will hang around waiting for more.

The woman you've been waiting for, Scorpio male of 1925, is one who takes life by the hand, and yearns to find out all there is about the world. She is someone who is cultured, educated, and what she does not know she will find out, either by traveling—with you of course—or reading. Once she is interested in something, and that something definitely will include you, all that attention and ability to focus appeals to you.

Your perfect man, Scorpio female of 1925, is kind and considerate, but has higher standards than most people. He places great value on honesty and integrity, and most important, will give that in return. With his charming nature, he knows just how to be complimentary, so much so that some people do not even realize how direct he actually is. Most important, he is never afraid to say, "I love you" over and over again.

1925 SAGITTARIUS
From November 22, 19:35 through December 22, 8:36

♐ *The Best Friend*

The world of relationships is no different for you, Sagittarius of 1925, than life's many adventures, and the only way you can live in a heart to heart bond with someone else is if you both have the same love affair with life. You view a partnership simply and idealistically, seeing it as a way of sharing with your very best friend the joy and wonderment of every new day and of each new thing you both learn.

In addition to being friends and intellectual equals, you cannot live without the touching and light kisses on the cheek that spark your mornings, and the ones on the lips that heighten your nights. More than anything, you want to share as much of your time as possible, and that means accompanying each other even when you don't share the same interests.

The person who wants to catch your eye needs to be a lover of the arts, and must enjoy the latest cultural and artistic trends. To solidify the relationship this person can simply recite some poetry from a book of great love poems, or perhaps play some romantic music to put you in just the right mood—a mood that will last for a long time to come. And you will be at the beck and call of anyone who knows how to massage your tired feet after a long day.

The perfect woman for you, male Sagittarius of 1925, might tend to arouse some jealousy, as she is graceful, beams with self-confidence, and absolutely glows with an inner beauty all her own. You are secure enough to want a woman you can boast about to your friends, and you want her to be extremely social so that the people you know can see for themselves how good your taste is, and how good her taste in a man is as well.

The man of your dreams, Sagittarius lady of 1925, has always made himself known to you by that endearing smile, cute laugh, and his hypnotic stare. That may have gotten him through the door to your heart, but what keeps you with him day in and day out is his honesty, his good nature, and that he knows how to say just the right thing on nearly every occasion. He has a sympathetic ear, and a kind heart you can turn to for support and encouragement.

1 Read Your Sign   **2** Look Up Your Love Planets   **3** Go to Pages Shown

'20s

Charlie Chaplin – The Little Tramp

Charlie Chaplin became one of the most famous and wealthy men in the world, as well as the most innovative pioneer in the fledgling moviemaking industry. This is an impressive achievement for someone who was virtually orphaned as a young child after his father died and lived as a street urchin for a while. As a young man, he became involved with a musical troupe, and in 1913, at age 24 he found his way to Hollywood, where he earned an impressive $150 a week as an actor. Ambitious and talented, within two years Chaplin would become a major screen comedian, making an astronomical $10,000 per week. In 1919, he helped to start the United Artists Corporation (UA), and by the early 1920s, he was so popular that no one could afford him, and he only appeared in films that he produced.

While Chaplin was undoubtedly successful in his career, much of his love

> *"Oona may have screamed, in her last days, 'What the f did I do with my life!'"*
>
> from the *Kirkus* review of Scovell's book,
> *Oona: Living in the Shadows*

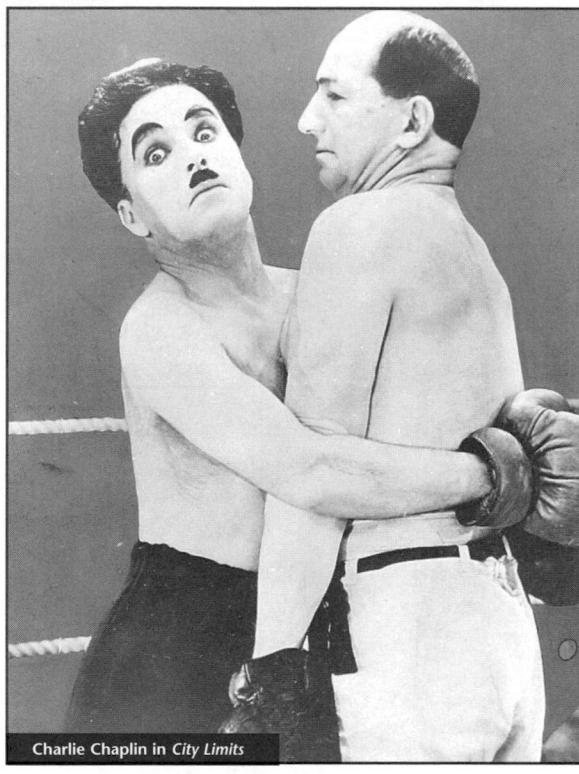

Charlie Chaplin in *City Limits*

life was unsettled and troubled. His first three marriages all ended in messy divorces, and he was once sued for statutory rape. His many scandalous affairs led to some harsh criticism about his private life, and he was accused of having loose morals, of being a "lecherous hound," and "Hollywood's busiest satyr." Yet through these difficult affairs, Chaplin remained Hollywood's first celebrity comic.

Chaplin's Moon and horoscope Rising Sign are both in Scorpio. Either one of these placements would indicate a healthy sexual appetite, but together they create a powerful hunger for sex. Chaplin's first marriage was in 1918 to the 16-year-old actress Mildred Harris. He married her because he thought she was pregnant and wanted to avoid a scandal. The pregnancy turned out to be a false alarm, and they divorced two years later,

with Mildred eventually receiving a $100,000 settlement.

A few years later, Chaplin chose the 16-year-old Lita Grey as his lead in *The Gold Rush* but managed to get her pregnant. Faced with statutory rape charges, Chaplin secretly married her in Mexico in November 1924. That marriage lasted only two years before she filed for divorce. She claimed that Chaplin was having affairs with other women. Her lengthy 52-page complaint was filled with accusations of his behavior, details of which were copied and reprinted everywhere. The highly publicized ordeal was eventually resolved for $600,000, which at the time was the largest divorce settlement ever. A third marriage to the young actress Paulette Goddard became complicated by a paternity suit filed by actress Joan Barry. Blood tests proved Chaplin could not be the father of Barry's baby, but the court ordered him to pay child support anyway.

In 1943 at age 53, after having established a track record of being attracted to very young actresses, Chaplin married a fourth time to 18-year-old aspiring actress Oona O'Neill, the daughter of playwright Eugene O'Neill. When Charlie and Oona eloped, O'Neill was so enraged that he disinherited his daughter. Unlike his preceding marriages, Chapin's marriage to Oona lasted. Their intense love affair produced eight children and rescued him from his reputation as a womanizer and his disturbing habit of getting underage women pregnant. "I was constantly surprised by her sense of humor and tolerance," he wrote in his 1964 autobiography. "She could always see the other person's point of view."

63

▶ READ ABOUT PAULETTE GODDARD ON PAGE 326

1926

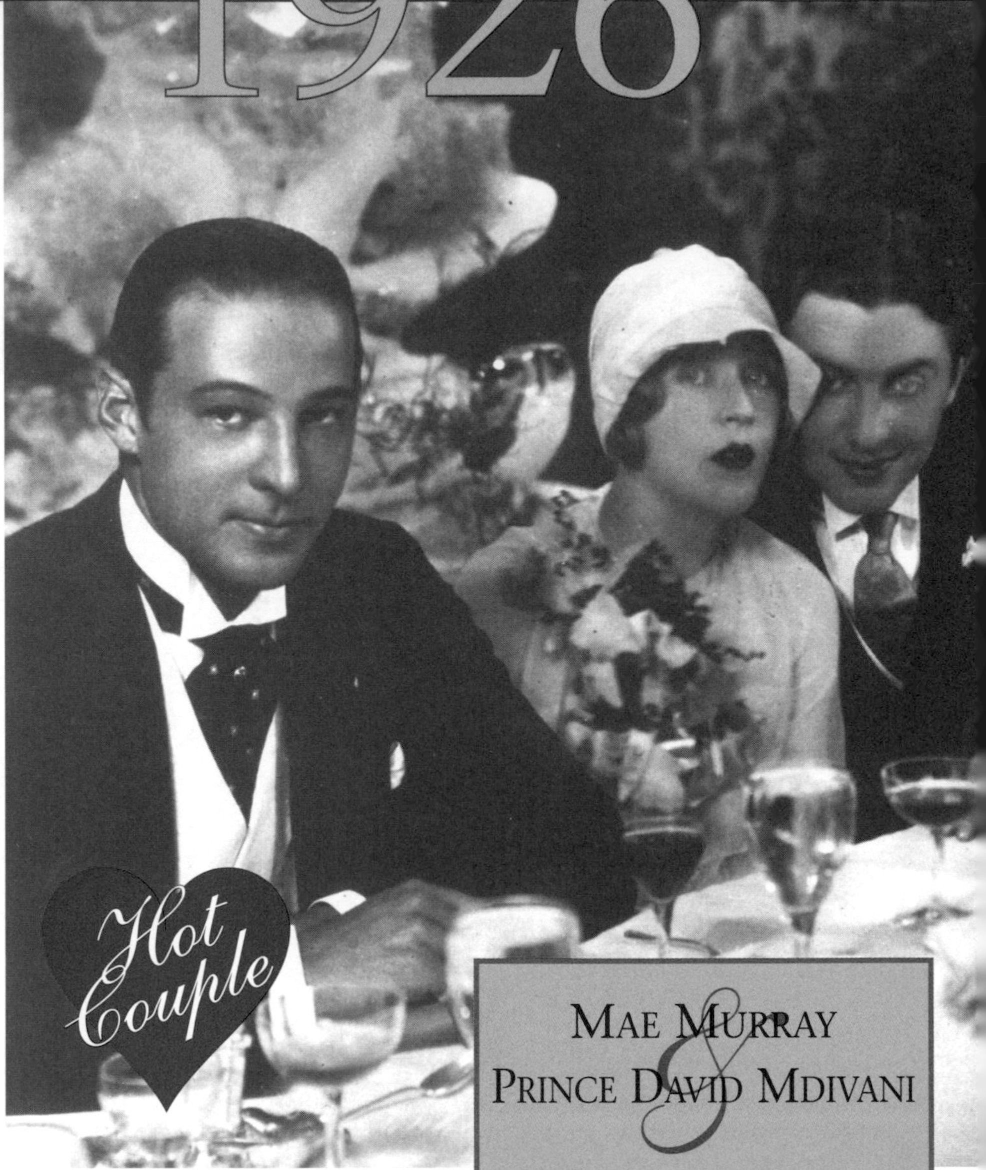

- ⊛ IT GIRL
- ⊛ SEX
- ⊛ GENTLEMEN PREFER BLONDES
- ⊛ FLESH AND THE DEVIL
- ⊛ SOMEONE TO WATCH OVER ME
- ⊛ THE SUN ALSO RISES

EVENTS

Both the great escape artist, Houdini, and the great lover, Valentino, died. 40,000 people turned out for Valentino's spectacular funeral in New York, almost causing a riot with dozens injured in the crush. Police reported at least a dozen suicides by distraught female fans. Only recently, Valentino had declared: "Women are not in love with me but with the picture of me on the screen. I am merely the canvas on which women paint their dreams."

Skirt lengths rose to just below the knee, the shortest length yet. Author Elinor Glyn coined the term "It Girl" to describe Clara Bow, "it" being "the same as before but more of it showing…a little more available."

A leading British doctor warned against the fashion for dieting to excess, saying that it would merely increase the risk of suffering from consumption.

Writing for *Good Housekeeping* magazine, Dr. Cecil Webb-Johnson warned married women who might be planning to broaden their horizons that "The constant craving for change, for amusement, for excitement at any cost" resulted in "the lined and weary face, the constant headaches and…uncertainty and irritability of temper."

POP CULTURE

Greta Garbo smoldered as the center of a love triangle in *Flesh and the Devil*. Clara Bow competed with her mother for the same man in *Dancing Mothers*. Lillian Gish starred as adulteress Hester Prynne in *The Scarlet Letter*. Jean Renoir directed a lush adaptation of Émile Zola's *Nana*, the tale of a would-be actress who becomes a kept woman.

The year's hits included Irving Berlin's "Blue Skies," "Bye Bye Blackbird," the blues vamp "I Ain't Got Nobody," and the Gershwin show tune "Someone to Watch Over Me."

In 1926 notable books included *Gentlemen Prefer Blondes* by Anita Loos, featuring Lorelei Lee, the archetypal "dumb blonde," and *The Sun Also Rises* by Ernest Hemingway, about cynical, hard-drinking expatriates in Paris and Spain. A. A. Milne wrote the enduring children's classic *Winnie-the-Pooh*, inspired by his son's stuffed animals.

64

Hot Couple

MAE MURRAY & PRINCE DAVID MDIVANI

She was known as "the girl with the bee-stung lips." A stunning beauty, Mae Murray was a dancer in the Ziegfield Follies. She made many silent movies in the 1920s and as her star rose, so did her status. But she would eventually become too big for her beautiful britches.

When she wed Prince David Mdivani in 1926, her friend Rudolph Valentino was the best man. But this would be the last of the glitter and glamour for Murray. She turned down an important film and was blackballed in Hollywood. Soon after, the prince divorced her and took custody of their son.

SEE ALSO

▶ RUDOLPH VALENTINO *Page 31*
▶ JOSEPHINE BAKER *Page 79*

1926 CAPRICORN
From December 22, 1925 8:37 through January 20, 1926 19:11
(December 1926 Capricorns, see 1927 Capricorn)

♑ A Wise Owl

As a Capricorn born in 1926, you rise to challenges, including the realm of relationships. You realize that everyone comes with some "baggage" of personal history, which must be understood and accepted, including your own. You must feel comfortable with the personal background of your loved one, in order to build a relationship on a solid foundation. You want to be with someone who has a good family history and impressive credentials. You are happiest when you are with someone who shares your work ethic and respect for tradition.

Because you want a relationship to take you to a higher level intellectually and socially, it must offer you opportunities to grow in these areas. This could include involvement with different groups and mutually fostered friendships. The more light social connections you make together, the happier you are. This doesn't mean that you want no quality time alone. On the contrary—as a 1921 Capricorn, you must balance your sense of social obligations with your urges for independence, both within and beyond your primary relationship.

To keep your interest, someone would have to show you in deeds more than words how much you matter and that promises made are faithfully kept, in all regards. In order to satisfy your appetite for worldly experiences, your ideal partner loves to travel as much as you do, and keep abreast of current events so that you can have thoughtful conversations about the state of the world in all its aspects, political and otherwise.

If you are a 1926 Capricorn male, your ideal woman appreciates the value of all of your experience, but is secure in herself as well. You want a woman who knows what she wants out of life and is open to letting you help her get there by acting as her mentor along the way.

As a Capricorn woman born in 1926, you are happiest with a man who is respectful, mature, and wise. To stoke the fires of your passion, he needs to care as much about your feelings and concerns as he does about his own. He makes you proud of his accomplishments because you know he has earned them with hard work and ingenuity.

CAPRICORN ZODIAC SIGN
YOUR LOVE PLANETS

YOUR ROMANTIC SIDE   p. 696
► **VENUS IN AQUARIUS**
Born Dec. 22, 1925 8:37 - Jan. 20, 1926 19:11

YOUR SEX DRIVE   p. 722
► **MARS IN SCORPIO**
Born Dec. 22, 1925 8:37 - Dec. 28, 1925 00:35
► **MARS IN SAGITTARIUS**
Born Dec. 28, 1925 00:36 - Jan. 20, 1926 19:11

YOUR CELEBRITY TWINS   p. 760
Find out the astrological similarities you have with famous people.

YOUR COMPATIBILITY   p. 780
Compare planets to find out how compatible you are in a relationship.

YOUR RELATIONSHIP KARMA   p. 824
► **SATURN IN SCORPIO**
Born Dec. 22, 1925 8:37 - Jan. 20, 1926 19:11

65

1926 AQUARIUS
From January 20, 19:12 through February 19, 9:34

♒ An Independent Spirit

As an Aquarius born in 1926, you are the ultimate individualist and free thinker, which means that your views of relationships are guided by your desire to remain true to yourself at all costs. Even if it means periods of time when you are dating more than one person, and committed to no one in particular, you need to feel that you are choosing your circumstance and not the other way around.

First and foremost, you value friendship within a relationship. It is essential for a relationship to provide good company, along with respect for privacy. You want to be with a person who shares your ideals and helps you aspire to loftier heights. This person must feel as passionate as you do about social issues. You may be happiest in a relationship where you can both participate in work (paid or volunteer) that has socially redeeming qualities.

The best way for a partner to keep your interest is to mix up the routine. You never want to feel as though you are settling into a repetition of the same thing day in and day out. You love to surprise others, and be surprised in return, and you are most likely to enjoy a partner who has an element of eccentricity. Perhaps you even share an interest in astrology, computers, fashion trends, and air travel.

As a man Aquarius born in 1926, your perfect female partner is one who breaks the mold and shows you that you can never second guess her. She has an exotic quality about her that makes heads turn when she comes into the room, as they wonder what it is about her that seems so different. She can match wits with you any day, although you'd prefer that she knows you are right, of course.

For a 1926 Aquarius woman, your ideal man is one who can recognize you as an equal and is not surprised by how capable and strongly individualistic you are. He is secure in himself and has many interests of his own that keep him occupied when you are busy. He will have to accept you for who you are and not expect to change you to fit any external expectations or social stereotypes. He also understands and accepts that at times you may prefer to be alone.

GILBERT ROLAND
Mexican Actor
Mars in Aquarius

AQUARIUS ZODIAC SIGN
YOUR LOVE PLANETS

YOUR ROMANTIC SIDE   p. 696
► **VENUS IN AQUARIUS**
Born Jan. 20, 19:12 - Feb. 19, 9:34

YOUR SEX DRIVE   p. 722
► **MARS IN SAGITTARIUS**
Born Jan. 20, 19:12 - Feb. 09, 3:34
► **MARS IN CAPRICORN**
Born Feb. 09, 3:35 - Feb. 19, 9:34

YOUR CELEBRITY TWINS   p. 760
Find out the astrological similarities you have with famous people.

YOUR COMPATIBILITY   p. 780
Compare planets to find out how compatible you are in a relationship.

YOUR RELATIONSHIP KARMA   p. 824
► **SATURN IN SCORPIO**
Born Jan. 20, 19:12 - Feb. 19, 9:34

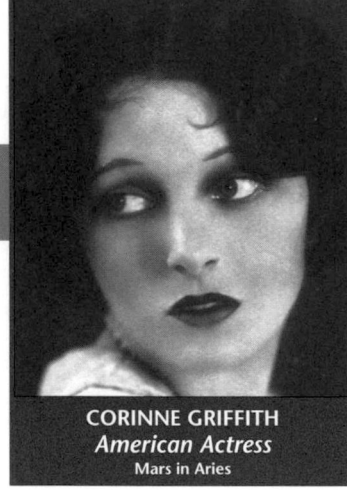

CORINNE GRIFFITH
American Actress
Mars in Aries

1926 PISCES
From February 19, 9:35 through March 21, 9:00

A Novel Romancer

The adjectives sweet, endearing, and quirky come to mind for Pisces born in 1926. You have a sixth sense about knowing when to be by yourself and when to engage with others. This comes strongly into play with love relations. You want a love connection that can nurture your spiritual and your physical self. At times that can be a very tall order. As such, it is easy for you to become disappointed or disillusioned in love because you see that a relationship is capable of being so much more than it usually is, in terms of intimacy, mutual sharing, and growth.

You won't give up, however, which is a good thing, because the world would be a bit bleak without souls like you willing to keep taking a chance on love. You have a profound sense of destiny, and you want a relationship that activates that feeling. Your ideal partnership is one in which your psychic sensitivity is appreciated, and where you make the most of your time together, for however long that is meant to be.

As a Pisces born in 1926, you are not typical of your sign, as you have a good deal of focus and decisiveness. Because you have a clear sense of what is and isn't acceptable within a relationship, you want to be with someone who does not expect you to be the only one making sacrifices for the relationship. The person who will keep your attention and loyalty appreciates and respects all that you do. To satisfy your more pragmatic side, this person will want to show you in many small ways that your trust is well deserved.

The perfect love match for a 1926 Pisces man is a woman who is bright, witty, and knows how to keep up her end of the conversation in any social environment. She is open to trying new things, traveling to new places, and meeting new people. If she is exotic and seductive, all the better.

As a woman Pisces born in 1926, your ideal partner understands that you have worked hard for what you have achieved, and he accepts your decisions on matters that are important to you. He treats you like the princess that you are, and has enough charm and dignity to seem like a real prince to you.

1926 ARIES
From March 21, 9:01 through April 20, 20:35

A Fiery Lover

Like the season that you are associated with—early springtime—your sparkling and effervescent qualities shine in the realm of relationships along with everything else that you do. Because you are so action-oriented, you have little patience for people who are slow on the uptake, so to speak. Since you want to experience as much of life as possible, it is important to you that your love relationships foster the qualities of fun, adventure, and spontaneity.

Your physical needs are probably as (or nearly as) vital today as in your youth. Because of this, you must feel that a love relationship is capable of sustaining the physical and sexual side of it along with the rest. You have no doubt also known your share of hurts in love, and you want a relationship that allows you to apply all of the lessons you have learned from the past. The relationship that brings you happiness includes forgiveness, understanding, and compassion.

The key to a love prospect being able to spark and keep your interest is perhaps most of all a sense of honesty and integrity. Because your gut-level instincts tell you quickly if someone is not being on the up-and-up with you, that person may quickly go off of your radar screen. An abiding sense of passion helps, too, because you need lots of heat in your life to keep stoking the fires that burn in your heart.

Being a 1926 Aries man, you may yearn for the great outdoors, because you are in touch with your natural, animal instinct to a great degree. Your ideal woman is somewhat of a pioneer woman in the respect that she is well able to manage with simple tools and is inventive and self-reliant when she needs to be. She knows how to manage money as well, in order to help you keep track of the expenses and budget.

As a woman Aries born in 1926, you are the fire that lights the match, and your ideal man is one who can fan the flames with his own brand of passion and desire. He is not afraid to show his romantic side, as he is sincere and loving. Giving you fresh flowers now and then and making sure to stay in touch if he is away can make your day.

66

1926 TAURUS
From April 20, 20:36 through May 21, 20:14

A Pleasurable Partner

Romance blooms eternal for you as a Taurus born in 1926, as your natural sensuality leads you easily into love and helps you stay there for enduring relationships. As long as you can feel comfortable in a relationship, you remain steady and faithful to it, and expect to grow gracefully old together until the end.

You know that a good relationship is a matter of give and take, and seeing it through when the going gets rough, as it has for you now and then. However, even in the best of times and when you feel the closest within a relationship, a part of you remains reserved and aware that you are fundamentally alone on a spiritual plane. Nurturing the love you want to share in a relationship is a top priority, so finding ways to do things together, both work and play, is important for building lasting memories.

The kinds of things that win your attention and your heart are the simple things that show you that the other person really cares. A small gesture, a gift, and a home cooked meal all say that you are accepted and appreciated just for who you are. Walks along the ocean, near a body of water or the chance to swim at the beach or in a pool can stir romance for you. A good glass of wine or special dessert now and then is also a plus. And the magic of Hollywood in a good movie does the trick as well, as you love to share both sentimental and humorous moments with your mate.

For men born with the Sun in Taurus in 1926, your ideal woman knows how to please you in many practical ways, just like a gardener nurturing a beautiful bouquet. She will be a quick study and on the ball, especially with regard to how to coordinate social engagements to make them a great success. She gets along well with most people but is happiest putting her attentions on you.

As a Taurus woman born in 1926, you want a man who displays sensitivity to your feelings as well as to the feelings of others. He is most likely glad to let you take the lead when you are ready. While he knows how to follow, he is also sensitive to seeing when it is time for him to take control and steer the course.

TAURUS ZODIAC SIGN
YOUR LOVE PLANETS

YOUR ROMANTIC SIDE   p. 696
► **VENUS IN PISCES**
Born Apr. 20, 20:36 - May 06, 15:12
► **VENUS IN ARIES**
Born May 06, 15:13 - May 21, 20:14

YOUR SEX DRIVE   p. 722
► **MARS IN AQUARIUS**
Born Apr. 20, 20:36 - May 03, 17:02
► **MARS IN PISCES**
Born May 03, 17:03 - May 21, 20:14

YOUR CELEBRITY TWINS   p. 760
Find out the astrological similarities you have with famous people.

YOUR COMPATIBILITY   p. 780
Compare planets to find out how compatible you are in a relationship.

YOUR RELATIONSHIP KARMA   p. 824
► **SATURN IN SCORPIO**
Born Apr. 20, 20:36 - May 21, 20:14

MARION DAVIES
American Actress
Mars in Gemini

1926 GEMINI
From May 21, 20:15 through June 22, 4:29

An Avid Conversationalist

As a Gemini born in 1926, your needs and wishes in love relationships are as varied as your interests. The idea that only one right person exists for you is hard to accept, and you may have remained ambivalent about your feelings toward commitment. You are a creature of the intellect, so it is important for you to feel that you can always have someone to turn to for a good conversation, someone who knows the details of your history and can understand the context of your thought patterns.

Mobility is also vital to your sense of well being. Your ideal relationship is one in which you can share hobbies that get you out and about. You enjoy interacting with people and exercising body and mind, be it with walks, dancing, hiking, bicycling, or other fresh air activity. An occasional picnic in the park or dining al fresco can light your romantic fires.

When it comes to romance, the person who can attract and keep your attention is a great conversationalist and is never boring. The person thrives on the stimulation of a healthy discussion on a range of topics. Given your natural sense of humor, your ideal partner has a good funny bone, too, and knows how to lighten things up when they start to drag. He or she is able to discuss the latest news from around the world and the newest novel or literary work that offers new thoughts or theories.

As a Gemini man born in 1926, your ideal woman is uninhibited in love and sexuality. She also has a good sense of timing and tradition. One of her attributes may represent in some way the idea of a forbidden fruit, as you would define it. She helps you to distinguish between what is and is not worth desiring. She understands that there is an emotional cost as well as a financial cost to many decisions.

1926 Gemini woman, your ideal man does not need for you to diminish your own intelligence just to reinforce his ego. He is secure in himself and is proud of your talents and gifts. He has an impressive intellect that can match wits with you. He shares many of your interests and has interests of his own that keep him happily involved.

GEMINI ZODIAC SIGN
YOUR LOVE PLANETS

YOUR ROMANTIC SIDE   p. 696
► **VENUS IN ARIES**
Born May 21, 20:15 - June 02, 19:58
► **VENUS IN TAURUS**
Born June 02, 19:59 - June 22, 4:29

YOUR SEX DRIVE   p. 722
► **MARS IN PISCES**
Born May 21, 20:15 - June 15, 0:49
► **MARS IN ARIES**
Born June 15, 0:50 - June 22, 4:29

YOUR CELEBRITY TWINS   p. 760
Find out the astrological similarities you have with famous people.

YOUR COMPATIBILITY   p. 780
Compare planets to find out how compatible you are in a relationship.

YOUR RELATIONSHIP KARMA   p. 824
► **SATURN IN SCORPIO**
Born May 21, 20:15 - June 22, 4:29

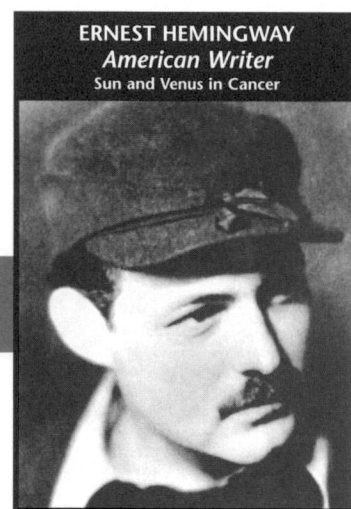

ERNEST HEMINGWAY
American Writer
Sun and Venus in Cancer

1926 CANCER
From June 22, 4:30 through July 23, 15:24

An Intense Player

Sensitive, kind, and caring all describe your soulful nature as a 1926 Cancer. These qualities permeate everything you do, and within the realm of love relationships in particular. In addition, you have a playful and whimsical side to your personality that thrives in a relationship where you can both take pleasure in lavishing attention on each other and the extended family that you create together.

Unlike the typical image of Cancer, you are not only devoted to family. Your humanitarian impulses incline you to want to reach out beyond your immediate circle to shine a distant light for others who may be in need. This humanitarian impulse comes into play within love relationships for you, too, because you want to share your passion for truth and justice with someone who is similarly inclined.

The person who is likely to attract and keep your attention is complex and deep. His or her personality has twists and turns that keep you puzzling and wondering what will come next, surprising you. He or she is open to negotiating, to come to a mutual understanding about what you each expect from the other. A little jealousy can actually be a turn-on for you, when your partner reminds you that you are the only one desired. Your ideal partner will help you move on after a difficult time, clearing the way for long lasting intimacy and fidelity.

As a man born with the Sun in Cancer in 1926, your ideal Goddess of Love may be just a bit on the flirty side, because you want a woman who knows she has something special to offer, but that only you are privy to it. Ideally, she will enjoy sex as much as you do and is open to exploring new ways of being physical together, to keep your interest alive, such as role-playing.

As a Cancer woman born in 1926, your ideal man is okay with you being the head of the household and letting you take charge of matters large and small. He is comfortable trusting your instincts and offering you his advice when you could use it. He is also aware of the importance of taking good care of his health so he can maintain a high quality of life with you.

1926 LEO
From July 23, 15:25 through August 23, 22:13

A Willing Lover

Romance and love come almost too easily to you as a 1926 Leo, but this does not mean that it is without challenges. In fact, your impulse to be "blinded" by love can sometimes interfere with your ability to be objective when it comes to seeing things in a clear light. For that reason, you know that it is wise to take your time before committing to a relationship. You want a person who is open and honest without a lot of skeletons in the closet.

You think more with your heart than your head, and your heart is often right. You know that the best relationship takes time to mature, like a fine wine, and you want to be with someone who understands this, too. You want a love relationship to intoxicate you with the fragrance of all of life's joys and delights. Having a good time is a top priority for you, and you always make time for leisure, recreation, and entertainment in your weekly schedule. The more you take the initiative to do the things together that make you happy being with your partner, the more your relationship is bound to thrive.

You have an endearing child-like quality that translates into a fondness for children and all things related to enjoying the process of raising them together in your relationship. Whether the children are your biological ones or come to you from the grace of good fortune is less important to you than the love that you share in the context of a complete family life. Because you are also very strong willed, you are happiest with a partner who has enough flexibility to allow you the room you need to feel that you are more or less in control.

1926 male Leo, your ideal woman freely showers you with affection and warmth. She inspires confidence in her abilities and character, and knows how to balance your intensity with a bit of lightheartedness. She brings a smile to your face!

As a 1926 Leo woman, you expect your man to be the Rock of Gibraltar for you. He is steady, reliable, and very down to earth, and he lights your romantic fires by his goodness and solid, practical qualities. He is open and lets you know how things stand with him.

1926 VIRGO
From August 23, 22:14 through September 23, 19:26

A High Standard-bearer

Neat and well organized describes how a 1926 Virgo likes to conduct relationships as well as other aspects of life. You want things to run like a well-oiled machine with as few problems as possible, and ones that crop up being handled immediately. You want to be with someone who is a realist and who is purposeful, efficient and well organized about life's many small details. Your ideal love relationship allows you to enjoy the good feeling that comes with seeing how often the proverbial two heads are better than one.

You want to be with someone who shares your practical approach to love and your common sense. This person understands that life's many requirements are best fulfilled with a partner, and has a healthy heart that pounds with passion for the simple pleasures of love and romance. Your ideal relationship fills your imagination with fairy tale happily-ever-after pictures. Your partnership allows for the inevitable adjustment now and then, when human flaws soil the ideal of perfection. You want to be with someone who accepts your weaknesses and helps you work with them to strengthen the bonds.

Building lasting security within a partnership is important to you, and your ideal mate shares this priority. Your ideal partner knows that commitment means seeing it through when the going gets rough. Your perfect mate balances optimism and hope with a sense of natural conservatism.

As a Virgo man born in 1926, your ideal woman can swing back and forth between being passionate, sexy, and sure of herself, and then also showing her shy side at times. She can be demure and almost self-depreciatingly humble. She can recognize the difference between constructive and non-helpful criticism and is generous with the former, sparing with the latter.

As a 1926 Virgo woman, you prefer a man who is good looking, well mannered, loyal, and with a strong sense of duty and integrity. He must be strong of body and will, with an appreciation for the value of discipline and hard work. He recognizes that there is always more to do, and he balances the work load with enough leisure time, too.

VIRGO ZODIAC SIGN
YOUR LOVE PLANETS

YOUR ROMANTIC SIDE   p. 696
- ▶ **VENUS IN LEO**
  Born Aug. 23, 22:14 - Sept. 11, 16:36
- ▶ **VENUS IN VIRGO**
  Born Sept. 11, 16:37 - Sept. 23, 19:26

YOUR SEX DRIVE   p. 722
- ▶ **MARS IN TAURUS**
  Born Aug. 23, 22:14 - Sept. 23, 19:26

YOUR CELEBRITY TWINS   p. 760
Find out the astrological similarities you have with famous people.

YOUR COMPATIBILITY   p. 780
Compare planets to find out how compatible you are in a relationship.

YOUR RELATIONSHIP KARMA   p. 824
- ▶ **SATURN IN SCORPIO**
  Born Aug. 23, 22:14 - Sept. 23, 19:26

1926 LIBRA
From September 23, 19:27 through October 24, 4:17

A Tireless Lover

Beauty, charm, and culture come so naturally to 1926 Libras that it may have been hard for you to narrow down the best candidate on whom to bestow your favors. No doubt, many were equally eager to tie a knot with you. It is important for you to be with someone who is also experienced in love and is no stranger to the efforts that go into developing and keeping a relationship strong.

Your image of the perfect relationship is one in which you share not only good times and the day-to-day chores of living, but more importantly, a spiritual kinship where you know without speaking that your destiny feels guided by higher powers. True love for you includes feeling that fate has put you together for a higher purpose, which can only be fully revealed over time by living out your daily lives.

In order for someone to keep your interest, he or she shows that they appreciate your efforts and talents, and do not take you for granted. This person is warm hearted and generous in paying you sincere compliments and thanking you often. He or she also prizes intellectual knowledge and stimulation, and loves to develop interests and hobbies together with you, to combine mental and social activities. He or she loves to join groups, perhaps a couples' bridge club, dance club, or other pleasant social organization.

As a Libra man born in 1926, you are ready and able, as long as your partner is willing. She knows how to spark the right mood for love, and is regularly available and open to sharing intimacies. Her beauty inspires you to want to create, as she brings out your artistic impulses. She makes life easier to accept during hard times, as her softer qualities remind you that she loves you for who you are and not for what you have.

1926 Libra woman, you have a keen sense of justice, fair play, and compromise, and your ideal man is equally sensitive to these important values. His earthy kind of lust appeals to you, because it tells you that you're still appealing. But his manners are impeccable out in public, where you pride yourself on always projecting the image of being a lady.

FANNIE HURST
American Writer
Sun in Libra

LIBRA ZODIAC SIGN
YOUR LOVE PLANETS

YOUR ROMANTIC SIDE   p. 696
- ▶ **VENUS IN VIRGO**
  Born Sept. 23, 19:27 - Oct. 05, 21:06
- ▶ **VENUS IN LIBRA**
  Born Oct. 05, 21:07 - Oct. 24, 4:17

YOUR SEX DRIVE   p. 722
- ▶ **MARS IN TAURUS**
  Born Sept. 23, 19:27 - Oct. 24, 4:17

YOUR CELEBRITY TWINS   p. 760
Find out the astrological similarities you have with famous people.

YOUR COMPATIBILITY   p. 780
Compare planets to find out how compatible you are in a relationship.

YOUR RELATIONSHIP KARMA   p. 824
- ▶ **SATURN IN SCORPIO**
  Born Sept. 23, 19:27 - Oct. 24, 4:17

69

GEORGE GERSHWIN
American Composer
Venus in Scorpio

1926 SCORPIO
From October 24, 4:18 through November 23, 1:27

♏ A Powerful Playmate

As a 1926 Scorpio, you seem to live between states of very dynamic and powerful tensions followed by brief releases and relaxation, only to build up more tension again. This pattern may also describe how relationships tend to go for you, where the bonds of love take many unusual twists and turns that keep things interesting, and often intriguing.

Because you have strong opinions about things, you want a relationship where you can set the tone philosophically and ethically, and perhaps religiously, too. You want to be with someone who respects the rules by which you feel life must be lived, yet is also flexible enough to change the rules if they interfere with pursuing happiness and fulfilling desires. Because this sense of personal authority to make and break rules can challenge the stability of a relationship, it is vital that you reserve time together to clear the air often. You want to be able to get any irritations off of your chest and work them out rationally instead of emotionally. You know that love is only one of a whole spectrum of emotions that a good

relationship experiences, and you welcome the chance to experience the rest of them, too.

For someone to capture your mind and heart, he or she would have to fully convince you of their honesty and devotion to you by the things that they say and do. More importantly, he or she must follow through on promises made to earn your trust over time with consistent and sincere demonstrations of good character.

1926 red-blooded Scorpio man, your ideal woman matches your sexual impulses within the relationship. She considers sex to be a natural part of life, and enjoys spicing things up with a bit of seduction and role-play. She can send you a "certain look" across a crowded room, and you instantly know what she's thinking.

As a woman born with the Sun in Scorpio in 1926, your ideal man will give his all to whatever and whomever you are involved in together. He appreciates your level of intensity and passion. He's a bit of a closed book, but you are skillful enough to discover most any secret that he tries to keep!

1926 SAGITTARIUS
From November 23, 1:28 through December 22, 14:32

♐ A Bold Adventurer

Although as a Sagittarian you are poised to think about and plan for tomorrow, with lofty visions of hope and optimism, you are also quite a realist in love. You expect to invest your energies and resources in a relationship with consistent, practical effort. In love, you aspire to find the right balance between your hopes and the steadfast effort it takes to realize them.

Because you recognize that romance takes work, you want a relationship that allows you to grow together. Your ideal partnership includes many kinds of travel experiences that are well planned and carefully executed. Because you may have a special fondness for a particular foreign land or culture, you may even want to have two homes great distances apart so that you can have the freedom to live together in different settings. You avoid boredom at all costs!

With your penetrating mind, your relationship must allow you room to cultivate and consider many points of view and explore together philosophical and physical realms. Your prospective partner should feel and act as

if a lot is much better than a little, be generous, and have a high sense of self-esteem. Your ideal partner wants you to have the best, and expects all the right doors to open at the right time for him or her to take advantage of many good opportunities.

As a 1926 Sagittarius man, your ideal woman rises to the challenge of a good chase, and is not too easily caught. She keeps you slightly guessing about her intentions and her next moves. She wants to climb new mountains with you and challenge you to grow psychologically and materially. She is so convincing and persuasive, that she can make you feel as if it was your idea all along.

For a Sagittarius woman born in 1926, the ideal man knows the value of money and building on a solid foundation. He loves to see new sights—even if it's via the armchair with a stack of travel videos. He'll keep you intellectually challenged, especially when it comes to spirited discussions of current events. You won't have to wonder what he's thinking because he'll tell you, even if it's not with words.

The Disappearance of Agatha Christie

Born under the Zodiac sign Virgo in 1890, Dame Agatha Christie, the First Lady of Crime, knew what she was talking about when she made that statement. Her second husband, Sir Max Mallowan, was a respected British archaeologist who specialized in excavations in Mesopotamia and the Middle East. He was also 14 years younger than Christie.

Christie accompanied her Taurus mate on some of his "digs," serving as his assistant. While he searched for ancient artifacts, she dug up plots for her extremely popular mystery novels, including *Death on the Nile*, which was made into a movie in 1978. Mallowan's knowledge provided authenticity to Christie's tales of mayhem in the Middle East and their journeys together enriched her novels, giving them a sense of place as well as fascinating storylines.

But it was while she was married to her first husband, a dashing World War I fighter pilot named Archie Christie whom she'd wed at the age of 24, that Agatha became the protagonist in her own personal mystery. On December 3, 1926, the best-selling author disappeared near her Berkshire, England home. She'd gone out for a drive late in the evening, but didn't return. The next morning her car was discovered abandoned, her clothes and other personal items scattered about near a lake where a character in one of Christie's novels had drowned. Police launched a search of the surrounding countryside, enlisting the help of 15,000 fans, and drained the lake, but found nothing.

The press had a field day with the story. Before the lady vanished, she'd written several letters to her husband, who was involved in a 'none-too-discreet

love affair with Nancy Neele. On the night his wife disappeared, Archie was entertaining his lover. His affair compounded the depression sensitive Agatha was experiencing over her mother's recent demise. Had the grand dame of death done herself in? Had her philandering husband murdered the queen of murder? Or was the whole escapade an elaborate publicity scheme?

Upon learning of Archie Christie's infidelity, police tapped his phone line and tailed him—as if he were a suspect in one of Agatha's popular crime novels. For eleven days, the novelist's family and fans held their breath and feared the worst.

Finally, the missing author surfaced at a Yorkshire health spa where she'd registered under the name of Teresa Neele. She claimed amnesia, a condition that was verified by doctors who suggested she was grief stricken over her

mother's death. But few people believed the excuse, and secretive Agatha, whose Venus (planet of love and creativity) was in the privacy-loving sign Scorpio, refused to discuss the incident further—nor did she mention it in her autobiography (published in 1977). Although the mystery remains unsolved, most likely Christie needed an escape from a painful situation and, at the same time, saw a way to embarrass her husband—women with Venus in Scorpio, as astrologers know, can be vindictive. Talk about vengeance with style and intrigue!

Two years later, the Christies were divorced, although Agatha retained her married name for professional reasons. She went on to become the most popular mystery writer of all time. Her books have sold more than 1 billion copies, surpassed only by the *Bible* and the works of William Shakespeare. In 1971, she was awarded the honor of Dame of the British Empire.

> *"An archaeologist is the best husband a woman can have. The older she gets, the more interested he is in her."*
>
> AGATHA CHRISTIE, in the news 1954

71

▶ READ ABOUT ANOTHER WRITER'S LOVE TRIANGLE ON PAGE 145

1927

- ⭐ LINDY HOP
- ⭐ DUKE ELLINGTON AT THE COTTON CLUB
- ⭐ THE JAZZ SINGER
- ⭐ AIN'T SHE SWEET
- ⭐ LOST ECSTASY
- ⭐ TWILIGHT SLEEP

Sex Idol

EVENTS

1927 saw Charles Lindbergh complete the first solo transatlantic flight (apocryphally sparking the "Lindy Hop" dance craze), the development of Movietone, which allowed for synchronized sound in "talking pictures," and the first long distance television broadcast. The Duke Ellington Orchestra played at the Cotton Club, a happening Harlem nightspot where the clientele was white and the entertainers black, and CBS radio broadcast the show nationwide. Charlie Chaplin was divorced by his second child bride—this time it cost him $600,000, sealed his reputation as a womanizing philanderer, and turned his hair white. Film censors prohibited "any licentious or suggestive nudity," "miscegenation," and "inference of sexual perversion." The Church of England's changes to the *Book of Common Prayer* included sex equality in the marriage service. German physiologists identified a sex hormone that made early pregnancy testing possible. In her privately printed and covertly distributed book *The President's Daughter*, Nan Britton revealed she'd had President Warren Harding's love child. She crusaded for every child born to be recorded as legitimate, whether born in or out of wedlock.

POP CULTURE

Clara Bow starred in both *It*, as a salesgirl with plenty of "it" (sex appeal), and *Wings*, a war aviation drama. After passionate scenes between Garbo and Gilbert in *Flesh and the Devil* sparked a real-life romance, their next film was re-titled *Love* so that the billboards could read "Greta Garbo and John Gilbert in Love." Alexandre Volkoff directed *Casanova*, the action-packed epic tale of the famous Italian lover. Josef von Sternberg took on gangsters and their molls in *Underworld*. Al Jolsen starred in *The Jazz Singer*, the first full-length sound film.

In 1927, popular songs included "'S Wonderful," "Can't Help Lovin' Dat Man" from the musical *Show Boat*, "My Blue Heaven," first popularized in the *Ziegfeld Follies of 1927*, the swinging "Ain't She Sweet?" and the ballad "Are You Lonesome Tonight?"

Notable novels included Sinclair Lewis's *Elmer Gantry* about a philandering minister, Mary Roberts Rinehart's *Lost Ecstasy*, about love between the classes in ranch country, and Edith Wharton's *Twilight Sleep*, about a disfunctional family who numbs life's pains with addictions.

CLARA BOW

She was literally the "It Girl" of the 1920s. Clara Bow personified the height of flapper fashion. When she starred in the screen version of Elinor Glyn's book *It*, she skyrocketed to superstardom. "It" was the quality that attracted the opposite sex, and Bow had loads and loads of it.

Her fame came almost overnight, and she partook of much hedonistic overindulgence. She gambled and had love affairs and sped around Hollywood in a red convertible. Her excesses were legendary. Success left her just as suddenly as it found her, though. When the Roaring Twenties ended, so did her career.

SEE ALSO
► GARY COOPER *Page 146*
► JEAN HARLOW *Page 113*

72

1927 CAPRICORN

♑ *The Committed Sensualist*

From December 22, 1926 14:33 through January 21, 1927 1:11
(December 1927 Capricorns, see 1928 Capricorn)

You're an indomitable Capricorn born in 1927, and to you a relationship is all about passion and intensity. Right from the start you must feel that electric spark of chemistry or you simply aren't interested. A relationship must tease your imagination and tantalize your senses. You've always felt that chemistry is essential because it's important to you to be able to feel you belong with your partner and in your relationship.

Commitment is another essential to you. Knowing that you're loved and that your relationship is stable and reliable is important. You can understand how someone could get swept along on a tide of passion, which is why you believe in chemistry, but ultimately you insist on being able to pledge ongoing devotion. Emotional and physical compatibility are also essential to you. Your feeling is get it right from the beginning, then it will continue to make sense forever.

A partner who is stable, reliable and sexy can sustain your interest. You always enjoy a lively conversation but you admit that the real exchange goes on below the surface, and you've always felt that being attuned to that mutual chemistry is how any love story should begin. You do like socializing and good opening gambits have usually included an invitation to a romantic meal or a business acquaintance that sparked and grew.

Male Goats born in 1927 prefer a woman who is traditional, stable and down to earth. Your lady dresses in proper clothes and her style is always classic and tasteful. She looks elegant and worthy of respect, and you're always glad to introduce her to friends and associates. Even though she looks sedate, deep inside this woman is quite passionate, often very intense and sometimes downright possessive.

Female Capricorns born in 1927 prefer a man who is solid, reliable, and an excellent provider. You always know where you stand with this fellow because he makes his likes and dislikes clearly known. He has a vision of the life you'll share and that is very comforting because you know he'll always take care of you. Although he's stable, he's also sensual and sexy.

WILLIAM HAINES
American Actor
Sun in Capricorn

73

1927 AQUARIUS

♒ *The Magnanimous Mate*

From January 21, 1:12 through February 19, 15:33

As an altruistic Aquarius born in 1927, to you a relationship must provide tenderness and security. You believe that to give and receive is the most important dynamic in a good relationship. Being able to know that you will always love and be loved is what makes a good relationship great.

Self-sacrifice is another worthy dimension of your relationship. You believe it's quite worthwhile to focus much energy on your partner's wishes and needs, and in knowing that your mate returns the favor, you feel secure and beloved. Being loved and nurtured is the best feeling in the world and it gives you the strength and confidence to go out into the world and make a success of your life. You'd hate to be trapped in a shallow relationship in which neither partner was the other's best friend and most ardent support. In your opinion, that's not love!

You rely on intuition when assessing a potential partner's possibilities. You've always felt that you could just tell if someone were right for you. Being invited to a dance or elegant social event has always appealed to you and you enjoy when someone cares enough to fuss over a scrumptious meal. Even so, you admit that it's never been about what a partner does to impress you but rather about how you feel when you're in each other's company.

Male Aquarians born in 1927 prefer a woman to be tender and gentle, the sort of soft creature you automatically want to nurture and protect. Your lady is intelligent, though, and she often inspires you with the things she says. It's just her way of looking at the world that appeals to you and, from the moment you met, you felt she could be your forever best friend.

Female Aquarians born in 1927 like a man to be strong and solid, very romantic and a bit complicated. Your guy is sensitive but he can also be stubborn and, although he often goes out of his way to please you, sometimes he's more demanding than he should be. You don't mind his quirks because he's always so interesting and you enjoy his company. He loves to surprise you and sometimes twirls you around the living room in an impromptu waltz.

BETTY COMPSON
American Actress
Sun in Pisces

1927 PISCES
From February 19, 15:34 through March 21, 14:58

The True Original

You're an intense Pisces born in 1927 and to you a relationship must have passion as well as stability. You've always had to fight your impetuous heart and you can understand how someone might elope on a first date, although you would never allow that sort of thing to happen in your own life. You do admire people who can pull off that much spontaneity!

A feeling of belonging and acceptance is very important to you in a relationship. There has to be a secure bond and the sense that your partnership can survive whatever storms life might inflict. It is in knowing and being known that you most appreciate a relationship because it provides you with the stage on which you can express your most private self. Feeling that you're getting what you want and that your needs are being met is also so important. Without that feeling, you'd never make a commitment.

Challenging conversation has always been the best opening gambit for a partner who wants to win your heart. When you think of the great loves in your life, you always recall the clever bon mots you two exchanged and the heady feelings they inspired. You enjoy trying new things and being tempted to go a bit farther, and doing something new and different continues to appeal to you. Fast cars, stolen kisses, and travel adventures are fun for you to share with a special someone.

Male Pisces born in 1927 like a woman who is a bit brash and impulsive. Your lady is tempestuous, outgoing, exciting, and sometimes a little self-centered. She never minds expressing her feelings or her desires and sometimes she's rather demanding and even quite possessive. Yes, you admit she's a whirlwind and you love the thrilling way she keeps life exciting and new each and every day.

Female Fish born in 1927 prefer a man who is a bit complicated. He's impetuous and hasty by nature, but he restrains himself and that way you know he's exciting but that he'll never completely lose control. Your guy knows what's appropriate yet he likes to challenge people and sometimes seems like quite the rebel. He follows his own code rather than arbitrary rules.

1927 ARIES
From March 21, 14:59 through April 21, 2:31

The Fun-Lover

As a pleasure-loving Aries born in 1927, your relationship must provide lots of good fun. You're very skilled at pleasure and all aspects of enjoying life, and a relationship that didn't include those things wouldn't appeal to you at all. A fun lifestyle is just as important to you as a solid life. In fact, you may have waited rather late to settle down, simply because you were having too much fun.

Shared interests are also very important to you because you love going to fun places and doing exciting things. Being on the same level is essential to you in a relationship because otherwise one person is out having fun while the other is home napping. What good is that! A penetrating intellectual connection is important to you in a relationship as well. That way there's always something amusing to say— and to hear.

A partner who has spunk and sensuality appeals to you. Even when it was a risqué gesture, you admired a potential partner nervy enough on a first date to reach out and hold your hand or to steal a kiss. Having a sense of adventure and boldness appeals to you because it lets you anticipate exciting possibilities. You love being playful, so being asked on a picnic, to go bike or horseback riding, or simply taking a stroll arm in arm have always been good ways to pique your interest.

Male Rams born in 1927 prefer a woman to be soft and sensual. Your lady is completely female and she radiates a sweet tenderness that touches your heart. She may be a bit plump because she loves to eat and together you share lots of delightful pleasures. She is a bit slow and deliberate and sometimes she teases you for being an irresponsible boy but her kisses are so sweet you don't mind at all.

Female Aries born in 1927 need a man to keep up with you. Spry and athletic, your guy is a little impatient, quite playful, and an all around fun companion. He is always willing to try something new and, when a challenge is offered, he steps right up. He changes his mind often and that keeps life interesting for you, even if you dress for one event and suddenly find yourself attending another.

1927 TAURUS *From April 21, 2:32 through May 22, 2:07*

The Fierce Enthusiast

You're a bold Taurus born in 1927, and your relationship must be liberating and intense. In every aspect of life you need to feel profusely and your relationship must provide you with the strongest connection you could ever possibly experience. You believe in destiny and want to feel that you have connected with the one and only person with whom you were meant to be. The idea of belonging together is, in your opinion, what it's all about.

Security is another important dimension to your relationship. Although you believe in passion and chemistry, without security and devotion it's just like playing with fire. There must be control and sanity within your relationship for you to feel happy and relaxed. Because you believe in commitment, you share a relationship in which both partners have freedom to take risks, to share needs unapologetically, and to make love with abandon.

A passionate, dramatic gesture has always appealed to you as part of the ritual of courting. A mate bold enough to walk over to you and say something enticingly absurd—such as "last night I dreamt of you and today here we are meeting"—well, that partner certainly gets your attention. Deep conversation about serious subjects appeals to you more than chitchat. You have always known right from the start that you were seeking a tango, not a waltz.

Male Bulls born in 1927 like a woman who is charming, literate, and humorous. Your lady is lively and outgoing and talking with her is always a pleasure. Her ideas are interesting and well thought out. Although this woman has a light and engaging quality, under the surface there is also depth and a sense of responsibility. You know she will remain devoted.

Female Taureans born in 1927 prefer a man to be sensitive yet intense. Your guy is a volcano of passion and desire, and he expresses his needs and wishes without apology. He is fiercely protective and you know that he will go to the ends of the earth to serve and protect those he loves. You adore the way his mind works but most compelling is his unwavering instinct, the compass that guides him all his life.

1927 GEMINI *From May 22, 2:08 through June 22, 10:21*

The Steadfast Heart

As a passionate Gemini born in 1927, your relationship must have a sense of total togetherness, chemistry, and stability. A strong fated quality is one of the most significant aspects of your relationship. Right from the moment you met, you felt you belonged with this person. In your relationship there is a tight bond and together you become a strong and steadfast team, always looking out for each other's needs and wants.

Love is, of course, the most important thing of all. You have always known that there is no substitute for that feeling of caring that binds you close with your significant other. You feel sorry for people who marry for security because you realize that the only true security arises when you hold tightly in your heart someone who does the same for you. Passion and chemistry are other important aspects of your relationship. It must always be deep, true, and intense.

You have always responded most reliably to the partner who causes you to feel those delightful butterflies in your stomach. It's chemistry that makes you feel all abuzz. Being invited to a nice dinner, being pampered and fussed over appeal to you as well, and you enjoy family events as much as fancy dress balls. But the one true test of whether someone can gain your interest and subsequently your heart has always been whether or not you remain mesmerized after the evening ends.

Male Geminis born in 1927 seek a woman who is passionate and intense. Your lady is deep and serious yet she has a tender, generous side. She's the sort of person who can always be counted upon and you know that the depth of her love is immeasurable. She has a tender heart where children and pets are concerned and she loves nurturing others, especially you.

Female Geminis born in 1927 like a man who is strong and secure. Your guy is macho and confident and he has a nice aura of confidence. From the moment you met, you suspected he was your destiny and you could imagine him in every part of your life. He is strong enough to be a solid success and tender enough to hold you gently in his arms whenever life gets messy.

TAURUS ZODIAC SIGN
YOUR LOVE PLANETS

YOUR ROMANTIC SIDE   p. 696
- ▶ **VENUS IN GEMINI**
  Born Apr. 21, 2:32 - May 12, 8:32
- ▶ **VENUS IN CANCER**
  Born May 12, 8:33 - May 22, 2:07

YOUR SEX DRIVE   p. 722
- ▶ **MARS IN CANCER**
  Born Apr. 21, 2:32 - May 22, 2:07

YOUR CELEBRITY TWINS   p. 760
Find out the astrological similarities you have with famous people.

YOUR COMPATIBILITY   p. 780
Compare planets to find out how compatible you are in a relationship.

YOUR RELATIONSHIP KARMA   p. 824
- ▶ **SATURN IN SAGITTARIUS**
  Born Apr. 21, 2:32 - May 22, 2:07

IGOR STRAVINSKY
Russian Composer
Sun in Gemini

GEMINI ZODIAC SIGN
YOUR LOVE PLANETS

YOUR ROMANTIC SIDE   p. 696
- ▶ **VENUS IN CANCER**
  Born May 22, 2:08 - June 08, 2:50
- ▶ **VENUS IN LEO**
  Born June 08, 2:51 - June 22, 10:21

YOUR SEX DRIVE   p. 722
- ▶ **MARS IN CANCER**
  Born May 22, 2:08 - June 06, 11:35
- ▶ **MARS IN LEO**
  Born June 06, 11:36 - June 22, 10:21

YOUR CELEBRITY TWINS   p. 760
Find out the astrological similarities you have with famous people.

YOUR COMPATIBILITY   p. 780
Compare planets to find out how compatible you are in a relationship.

YOUR RELATIONSHIP KARMA   p. 824
- ▶ **SATURN IN SAGITTARIUS**
  Born May 22, 2:08 - June 22, 10:21

75

 Read Your Sign   Look Up Your Love Planets   3 Go to Pages Shown

HERMAN HESSE
German Writer
Sun and Venus in Cancer

1927 CANCER
From June 22, 10:22 through July 23, 21:16

♋ *The Cherished Mate*

You're an unselfish Cancer born in 1927 and your relationship must be tender and nurturing. To give selflessly to a true love is what you feel a relationship is all about and there is no greater comfort than knowing you will always care for and be cared for by someone you love. Building a family and a home together are other significant aspects of your good relationship. Selfish preoccupations have no place in your relationship.

You also believe that sharing common interests helps keep you close. Always having something to discuss and to do together is important in any relationship, but you also believe that it's meaningful to be supportive of each other's separate interests as long as they don't become more important than what you share as a team. Building a sense of mutual history is important to you because you enjoy looking back over the warm and happy years you've shared.

A partner who performs an act of kindness gets your attention rather quickly. Something as simple as giving you a seat on a bus or pitching in to help you with a project

impressed you forty years ago and it still touches your heart today. You also enjoy the company of someone who lets you offer a helping hand. A charity event is one perfect way to connect with a like-minded partner, and a casual discussion in which you share your views of life is a great opener.

Male Crabs born in 1927 like a woman who is kind and generous. A helpful spirit is just as important to you as a pretty face, and the woman who radiates good cheer and kindness is better than any glamour girl. Your lady is graceful, sometimes musical, often organized and practical, and quite romantic. She is shy at the core and deep in her heart are the tender, romantic feelings you prize so deeply.

Female Cancers born in 1927 believe a man should be debonair but also a sensitive champion of the underdog. Your guy can waltz you across the floor and listen to your most serious problems with interest and compassion. He's confident also and you get the sense that he has what it takes to get the job done—as long as it's the right thing to do.

1927 LEO
From July 23, 21:17 through August 24, 4:04

♌ *The Devoted Paramour*

As a nurturing Leo born in 1927, devotion is the most meaningful aspect of your relationship. You believe in loving with your whole heart and soul, and that means putting your partner first. In your relationship, each person looks out for the needs and desires of the other and that creates a wonderful sense of symbiosis—and true love. Being in a relationship where each person was selfish would just not appeal to you at all.

Fidelity and commitment are other aspects of your good relationship. You believe in holding your partner deeply in your heart. Working devotedly together you can build a much better life, a stronger family, and more secure future. Communication is the key, but you believe communication isn't just about the spoken word but about paying attention to the other person and hearing also what hasn't been said but is strongly felt.

A partner who is courteous and considerate always has impressed you. Good manners are very important, and a sweet and thoughtful gesture is the perfect way to connect. Someone

who brings you a drink at a party simply to be kind or who knows you need something and offers to provide it—that's the sort of person you want to know better. You enjoy simple things and good conversation but what's most important is who the person actually is.

Male Leos born in 1927 prefer a woman who is helpful, kind, and sweet. Your lady knows how to reach out when someone is in need and she effortlessly glides into complicated situations and sets them to rights. Her style is elegant yet understated and she's always tasteful and well bred. She is subtle yet sexy and from the moment you met she inspired you to create a few fantasies with her in the starring role.

Lady Lions born in 1927 need a man who is practical and down to earth. Your guy has a deep and penetrating intellect and he always has something interesting to say. He loves solving problems and is organized and efficient. He always seems to know the swiftest route to any solution but he's never speedy or careless. This fellow knows how to please you and is tireless in seeking your happiness.

1927 VIRGO
From August 24, 4:05 through September 24, 1:16

♍ The Inspired Idealist

You're an idealistic Virgo born in 1927, and you feel a relationship must be all about true love and sharing something perfect. There must be meaning and resonance in everything you do—and your relationship is no exception. You want to feel you're making a difference in your mate's life and that the same is true in yours. Casual or insignificant connections don't appeal to you at all.

True love is a very meaningful concept to you and you're sorry for people who just don't understand the depth, intensity, and sheer perfection involved when love is that genuine. You believe in two people sharing everything and creating a union of mutual generosity and self-sacrifice. Giving your all to love is very meaningful to you. Of course, that doesn't mean that the obvious things are any less important. Communication, mutual interests, and having a good time together are also significant in your relationship.

A deep and compelling conversation has always been a good opening gambit where you're concerned. A partner who has something meaningful to say interests you. Cultural events like concerts and movies are pleasant ways to get to know someone new and in an ongoing relationship they give you and a mate some enjoyable interaction. You like sharing creative projects and interesting points of view.

Male Virgos born in 1927 like a woman of many mysteries. Your lady seems deceptively normal, rather staid on the outside—but there is a mystique to her and right from the start you suspected she was one of those still waters run deep kind of gals. She is classically dressed, but under it all is a romantic heart and sexy soul. There's always something interesting to learn about her because she's so deep you can keep discovering new things.

Female Virgins born in 1927 prefer a man to be earthy and practical, precise and organized, but never too fussy or picky. Your guy has multiple dimensions. He can be practical, but also lively and outgoing. He's courtly but also athletic and fun loving. He's intellectual but also humorous. Most of all he's courteous, considerate, and loving.

VIRGO ZODIAC SIGN
Your Love Planets

YOUR ROMANTIC SIDE   p. 696
▶ **VENUS IN VIRGO**
Born Aug. 24, 4:05 - Sept. 24, 1:16

YOUR SEX DRIVE   p. 722
▶ **MARS IN VIRGO**
Born Aug. 24, 4:05 - Sept. 10, 14:18
▶ **MARS IN LIBRA**
Born Sept. 10, 14:19 - Sept. 24, 1:16

YOUR CELEBRITY TWINS   p. 760
Find out the astrological similarities you have with famous people.

YOUR COMPATIBILITY   p. 780
Compare planets to find out how compatible you are in a relationship.

YOUR RELATIONSHIP KARMA   p. 824
▶ **SATURN IN SAGITTARIUS**
Born Aug. 24, 4:05 - Sept. 24, 1:16

DOROTHY PARKER
American Writer
Sun and Mars in Virgo

77

1927 LIBRA
From September 24, 1:17 through October 24, 10:06

♎ The Sizzling Romantic

As an intense Libra born in 1927, your relationship must be passionate and meant to be. A casual connection is not for you. You must feel that there is a whisper of destiny in your relationship and that you searched for ages until, like magic, you connected with that one perfect soulmate. In fact, you may have been one of the first people to use the term soulmate, and even before there was a word to describe it, in your heart you knew such a partner was your destiny.

Passion and romance are very important to you in a good relationship, and even if there are quarrels, that only serves to heighten the intensity you share with your partner. Being electrified and swept off your feet is the level of emotion that feels normal to you and a relationship of any lesser magnitude just seems dull. You love flirting and manage to have a great deal of that sort of communication in your relationship, something that keeps the magic alive.

A clever come-on has always been an excellent opening gambit by a partner who wanted to gain your attention. You love romance and every aspect of the mating game is quite titillating to you, so even if you're not all that attracted to someone who is taken with you, usually you'll enjoy the flirting for quite a while before moving on. Of course, what you really seek is chemistry, and no gesture or invitation can create that.

Male Libras born in 1927 prefer a woman who is elegant and genteel but under the surface you know she is passionate and intense. It's much more thrilling for you to be with someone who seems quite demure to other people but to you is clearly a tigress. Your lady is also courteous and kind, and she can make people feel better just by spending time with them.

Lady Libras born in 1927 want your man to be intense and passionate. He is a strong leader but he's never coarse or tacky. He has a natural gentility, but under it all you know that, no matter what, he will achieve his goals and win any battle he enters. This guy has stamina and endurance and, although he's a bit bossy, he's very sexy and exciting so that keeps life fun.

LIBRA ZODIAC SIGN
Your Love Planets

YOUR ROMANTIC SIDE   p. 696
▶ **VENUS IN VIRGO**
Born Sept. 24, 1:17 - Oct. 24, 10:06

YOUR SEX DRIVE   p. 722
▶ **MARS IN LIBRA**
Born Sept. 24, 1:17 - Oct. 24, 10:06

YOUR CELEBRITY TWINS   p. 760
Find out the astrological similarities you have with famous people.

YOUR COMPATIBILITY   p. 780
Compare planets to find out how compatible you are in a relationship.

YOUR RELATIONSHIP KARMA   p. 824
▶ **SATURN IN SAGITTARIUS**
Born Sept. 24, 1:17 - Oct. 24, 10:06

JANET GAYNOR
American Actress
Venus in Scorpio

1927 SCORPIO
From October 24, 10:07 through November 23, 7:13

♏ ## The Passionate Communicator

You're an assertive Scorpio born in 1927, and for you a relationship must be positive and deep. You believe in love and feel that as long as there is deep caring, what follows naturally will be nurturing, support, and romance. The emotional connection in your relationship is of course the most important thing, because that is the foundation for all you will share. Without that strong bond, you feel a relationship is just uselessly casual.

Communication and intellectual understanding are other significant dimensions of your relationship. You feel that it's so rewarding to be with someone who knows what you mean when you speak and whose viewpoints are compatible with your own. That way your conversations lead to intimacy and deep understanding. Devotion and unselfish concern for each other are very important and you feel a sense of ongoing joy because of the one you love.

A partner who can engage you in fascinating conversation has always been your first choice. Clever repartee is not as appealing to you as a genuine exchange. You enjoy knowing someone is interested in you and like showing your interest in return. Discussing literature or art is fun too, and it keeps your mind lively. You also enjoy sharing pleasant social activities, perhaps something romantic like a high tea or a simple outing such as a stroll through the neighborhood.

Male Scorpions born in 1927 prefer a woman who is gracious and demure but also friendly and social. Your lady knows how to behave in every situation and you're always proud to introduce her to the people you know. She has a subtle way about her, but she always manages to cheer you up on a gray day and you feel confident that your needs will always matter deeply to her.

Female Scorpios born in 1927 like a man who is sensitive yet manly. Your guy is deeply emotional and he seems to go on instinct. He trusts his gut feelings and you trust them as well. This fellow is passionate and intense and he makes you feel safe because he's so confident, devoted, and steady. He's a one-woman man—and he has a few secrets and is fun to unravel.

1927 SAGITTARIUS
From November 23, 7:14 through December 22, 20:18

♐ ## The Dedicated Detective

As a restrained Sagittarius born in 1927, you believe a relationship is in part a vehicle for personal growth. Loving someone means you must learn to be responsible to and for that person, and you feel you've learned so much because of the people you've loved. Intense passion and deep devotion are another significant aspect of your relationship. You have always felt that it's almost as if there's no choice where love is concerned—you meet your partner, fall in love, and everything goes from there.

Commitment is very important to you. There is so much comfort in stability, even if it doesn't come naturally at first. You love knowing that you're in a relationship with someone who is reliable and who will keep the pledge to be there for you forever. You would not feel comfortable at all in a relationship with someone who seemed flighty or unreliable, and chances are you learned this the hard way through experience!

You have always found it appealing to connect with someone sexy and attractive who has interesting things to say. A total stranger at a party who whispers something fascinating, perhaps even a secret—well, that person is someone you're willing to know a little better. Thrillers appeal to you and you like discussing a good mystery novel. You may even have attended one of those murder weekends with a mate and laughed together as you sleuthed.

Male Archers born in 1927 like a woman who is intense and passionate. Your lady is deep and magnetic and you felt the chemistry between you the moment you met. She is clever and socially adept and just seems to draw people out. Everyone you know tells her their secrets and you do too! She's somewhat possessive and may be a bit bossy but she's so sexy you don't mind.

Female Sagittarians born in 1927 prefer a man to be outgoing and freewheeling. Your guy has a mind of his own and he knows just how he wants things done. Sometimes he's too picky, sometimes he's domineering, but you always know that his heart is in the right place. He is comfortingly stable and, no matter his quirks, you feel you can always count on him.

Josephine Baker – The Black Pearl

Hemingway called her "the most beautiful woman there is, there ever was, or ever will be." Even if these words were an exaggeration, it is certainly true that the sensational and uninhibited Josephine Baker had a style all her own, both on stage and off. From a St. Louis slum, this talented and beautiful American woman of color—limited by racial discrimination in her own country—rose to become a show-stopping performer who achieved real stardom in France.

The daughter of a drummer, Josephine began performing at age thirteen with a group of street performers. She got her first real break in 1921 when she filled in for an ailing chorus member of the Dixie Steppers. By the mid-1920s she joined *La Revue Negre*, which was booked for a Paris engagement.

And it was in Paris, the City of Light, that Baker really began to shine as a solo performer. She joined *Les Follies Bergères* where she originated her "Danse Sauvage"—a savage dance wherein her willowy, undulating figure was covered with feathers and very little else. An even more risqué act, her famous "banana dance," featured Baker wearing only a belt of the phallic-shaped yellow fruit. Parisians were fascinated by the woman the press nicknamed "the Black Pearl." In her heyday the sexy, contortionist poses she struck on stage were the talk of Paris. The French lavished on her the kind of celebrity status she could never have found in America, and as a result she became an expatriate.

But true to her Gemini Zodiac sign, Baker had the ability to reinvent herself on a regular basis, and by 1930, with the help of her lover and manager, Pepito Abatino, she had transformed herself into a more glamorous and sophisticated stage performer—a combination of French chanteuse and American torch singer. She became legendary for her exotic lifestyle, which included walking her pet leopard on a diamond-studded leash along the fashionable Champs Elysées.

Returning to the US in 1936 to star in the Ziegfield Follies, her presence was met with disdain and outright cruelty by the New York critics, who called her a "Negro wench." This blatant hostility convinced her to become a French citizen, which she did the following year by marrying French industrialist Jean Lion. During the Nazi Occupation she was instrumental in working with the Resistance and she was awarded the Legion of Honor. She later worked to advance the cause of civil rights in the United States.

Baker had four husbands, including French bandleader Jo Bouillon, who helped her raise the dozen orphans of ethnic backgrounds she adopted and called her "rainbow tribe." Her generosity had nearly bankrupted her by the late '50s and she was forced to begin performing again. Near the end of her life she was provided a villa and a pension by Monaco's Princess Grace, a fellow American expatriate.

Her last relationship was basically a platonic one with American artist Robert Brady, whom she met in 1973. The two exchanged vows in an empty church but were never legally wed. Baker died in Paris in 1975 shortly after a party given in her honor. Twenty-thousand people attended her funeral. She is remembered for her talent, her commitment to causes, and as the first black female sex symbol of the twentieth century.

79

> *"Since I personified the savage on stage, I tried to be as civilized as possible in daily life."*
>
> **JOSEPHINE BAKER**

► READ ABOUT PRINCESS GRACE OF MONACO ON PAGE 310

1928

- ★ AMELIA EARHART
- ★ PICKLE OR PEACH?
- ★ WEST END BLUES
- ★ STAR DUST
- ★ MAKIN' WHOOPIE
- ★ BAD GIRLS OF ALL KINDS

EVENTS

Amelia Earhart became the first woman to fly solo across the Atlantic, and the first women's events were held at Amsterdam's summer Olympic Games. Britain had its lowest birthrate on record. While one German bureaucracy required skirts to be at least eight inches below the knee, playwright George Bernard Shaw praised women's fashions as suitable for "real human beings" instead of "upholstery for Victorian angels." The Equal Franchise Bill gave British women the same voting rights as men, but female suffrage was abolished in Italy. Student slang for undesirable girls included: pill, pickle, priss, drag, oilcan, and nutcracker. Popular girls were called: peach, whiz, sweet patootie, pippin, choice bit of calico, and snappy piece of work. New York had less street prostitution, but plenty of hostesses, cigarette and checkroom girls, or outright hustlers provided "companionship" at speakeasies.

POP CULTURE

Films of the day included Josef von Sternberg's romantic working-class melodrama *The Docks of New York*, King Vidor's *The Crowd*, about a young man's disillusionment with career and family, and Charlie Chaplin's *The Circus*, where the "Tramp" falls for the circus owner's acrobat daughter. Carl Dreyer's *The Passion of Joan of Arc* is still considered a film masterpiece.

Louis Armstrong recorded his groundbreaking jazz masterpiece "West End Blues." The year's bumper crop of enduring tunes included "Star Dust," "Get Out and Get Under the Moon," "I Can't Give You Anything But Love,"

Hot Couple

"Let's Do It," "Love Me or Leave Me," and "Makin' Whoopee."

People were reading *Bad Girl* by Vina Delmar, chronicling a young couple's emotional and financial struggles, Booth Tarkington's *Claire Ambler*, in which a young woman toys with lovers before marrying conventionally, and Anne Parrish's *All Kneeling*, about a beautiful, selfish woman and her circle of sycophants. Eugene O'Neill's play *Strange Interlude*, about a woman's heartbreak in love and family, broke new ground by having characters speak their thoughts. *Extraordinary Women*, by Compton Mackenzie, a study of intimate relationships between women, sold out, while Radclyffe Hall's *The Well of Loneliness*, the story of lesbian love between a young girl and older woman, was put on trial for obscenity.

SINCLAIR LEWIS & DOROTHY THOMPSON

When brilliant satirist Sinclair Lewis married distinguished suffragist and journalist Dorothy Thompson on May 14, 1928, they were one of the smartest, coolest couples of the decade. She was known as the "blue-eyed tornado," and her feisty attitude was well matched with Lewis' fiery, progressive spirit.

Lewis asked Thompson to marry him the same day she obtained a divorce from her previous husband, poet Joseph Bard. She tried domestic life with Lewis for a brief time, but quickly tired of it and went abroad, where she got an interview with Adolph Hitler. Thompson and Lewis divorced in 1942, in part because of Lewis' struggle with alcoholism.

SEE ALSO
▶ ALFRED STIEGLITZ & GEORGIA O'KEEFFE *Page 47*

1928 CAPRICORN

From December 22, 1927 20:19 through January 21, 1928 6:56
(December 1928 Capricorns, see 1929 Capricorn)

♑ *The Brilliant Builder*

Capricorns of 1928, you have always had big dreams and you don't let anything stand in the way of your achieving them. With your legendary determination and your ability to see the big picture, you are a powerful inspiration to those around you. You take relationships as seriously as you do the other aspects of your life, and you are likely to proceed with caution before giving your heart. But, once you are committed, you are a devoted partner, who is consistently eager to please your mate.

Though you are generally reserved when it comes to your emotions, in the bedroom, you are quite demonstrative. You are a powerhouse of sexual energy, using your incredible stamina to build slowly, reaching the peak of pleasure each and every time. Typically, you like to be in control in sexual situations but, now and again, you enjoy it when your partner takes charge and leads the way. In fact, you welcome it.

In order to catch your eye, a would-be partner might suggest going to the opera, where you can fill your senses with the powerful music and the opulent costumes. Or, a visit to the museum, feasting on the works of the great masters would be just as delightful. But, to really capture your heart, he or she should share your respect for traditional values and your passion for history.

The perfect woman for the 1928 Capricorn male has a positive and optimistic outlook on life. She needs to be able to counterbalance your instinctually serious nature and your cautious attitude with a touch of her own lightheartedness and spontaneity. Together, you will strike a wonderful balance, and the belief that your ladylove has in you will give you the encouragement and confidence you need to reach your highest goals.

The 1928 Capricorn female wants a man who is a bit of an adventurer, someone who can take her to new and exciting realms. He needs to be a bit of a risk-taker and his ambition should match your own. But, the bottom line for you is security. Ultimately, your man must be a success in whatever path he chooses and he should have a strong regard for family and roots as well.

CAPRICORN ZODIAC SIGN
YOUR LOVE PLANETS

YOUR ROMANTIC SIDE   p. 696
▶ **VENUS IN SCORPIO**
Born Dec. 22, 1927 20:19 - Jan. 04, 1928 0:05
▶ **VENUS IN SAGITTARIUS**
Born Jan. 04, 0:06 - Jan. 21, 6:56

YOUR SEX DRIVE   p. 722
▶ **MARS IN SAGITTARIUS**
Born Dec. 22, 1927 20:19 - Jan. 19, 1928 2:01
▶ **MARS IN CAPRICORN**
Born Jan. 19, 2:02 - Jan. 21, 6:56

YOUR CELEBRITY TWINS   p. 760
Find out the astrological similarities you have with famous people.

YOUR COMPATIBILITY   p. 780
Compare planets to find out how compatible you are in a relationship.

YOUR RELATIONSHIP KARMA   p. 824
▶ **SATURN IN SAGITTARIUS**
Born Dec. 22, 1927 20:19 - Jan. 21, 1928 6:56

NILS ASTHER
Swedish Actor
Sun in Capricorn

81

1928 AQUARIUS

From January 21, 6:57 through February 19, 21:18

♒ *The Experimental Genius*

Innovative and downright brilliant, 1928 Aquarius, you are a visionary. Your view of the world is often offbeat and forward thinking, keeping you wonderfully youthful no matter what age you reach. Fun-loving and sociable, people are undoubtedly drawn to your easygoing nature. You want a relationship that is energetic and vibrant—one that keeps your curiosity and interest alive through the years.

You love to try new things and your need for experimentation certainly applies to your sex life. Your fondness for the unusual coupled with your penchant to sample the unknown make you a tantalizing and exciting lover. You can be somewhat detached and cool and, therefore, mistakenly send out the message that you are not as sexual as some other sun signs. But, once you are alone with your beloved, you are a determined and inventive partner.

Communication is essential for you in a relationship and a prospective mate must be able to stimulate your mind before there can be the slight hope of stimulating anything else. Once you have determined that the two of you are on the same page, you are ready for whatever your new love may suggest—especially if it involves learning something new. But, what really turns you on is someone who can give freely to others, without expecting something in return.

As a 1928 Aquarian male, you want a woman that can be a true friend as well as a loyal mate. It is important that she at least shares a few of your wide range of interests and not be intimidated by your unconventional behavior. You hate to feel hemmed in, and it is very important that she is able to give you the freedom to do your own thing without sulking or heavy emotional displays.

The ideal man for the 1928 Aquarian female is a combination of resourceful intelligence and driving ambition. You want someone who is grounded and practical, giving you the freedom to indulge your enormous creativity and more fanciful notions. Most of all, he needs to be patient, understanding, and supportive of your need to help the underdog, because service to others is one of your highest ideals.

AQUARIUS ZODIAC SIGN
YOUR LOVE PLANETS

YOUR ROMANTIC SIDE   p. 696
▶ **VENUS IN SAGITTARIUS**
Born Jan. 21, 6:57 - Jan. 29, 1:12
▶ **VENUS IN CAPRICORN**
Born Jan. 29, 1:13 - Feb. 19, 21:18

YOUR SEX DRIVE   p. 722
▶ **MARS IN CAPRICORN**
Born Jan. 21, 6:57 - Feb. 19, 21:18

YOUR CELEBRITY TWINS   p. 760
See what your Venus-Mars combination does for your sexual allure and satisfaction!

YOUR COMPATIBILITY   p. 780
Compare planets to find out how compatible you are in a relationship.

YOUR RELATIONSHIP KARMA   p. 824
▶ **SATURN IN SAGITTARIUS**
Born Jan. 21, 6:57 - Feb. 19, 21:18

KURT WEILL
German Composer
Sun and Mars in Pisces

1928 PISCES
From February 19, 21:19 through March 20, 20:43

♓ The Creative Feeler

Blessed with a vivid imagination and a truly unique way of looking at life, 1928 Pisces, you are someone who feels your emotions to the very depths of your soul. Though you may not always be able to express it in words, you are very aware of each and every magical moment in a relationship. Your intuition is highly developed, and you know right off the bat whether you will hit it off with someone.

You enjoy all the accoutrements of romance and really yearn for a dramatic declaration of undying love from your partner. Consciously or unconsciously, you have the ability to absorb the very essence of your beloved into your being. And, your partner cannot help but respond to your magnetic dreaminess. When you are intimate with someone, you are able to share your innermost secrets and fantasies without any hesitation.

In social situations, you are dazzlingly charming and polished. In order to get your attention, a potential partner needs to approach you in a sensitive and sophisticated way. Once you are smitten by his or her enticements, you're likely to respond favorably to an invitation to see a film or play. Glamour and glitziness intrigue you, and you would be captivated by a night out on the town, complete with dancing in the moonlight to a romantic tune from the past.

The ideal woman for the 1928 Pisces male has an indomitable spirit and a mind of her own. She's a marvelous blend of idealism and practicality, sensitivity and curiosity. Flexibility is an important trait too, for she needs to be able to keep up with your seemingly divergent inclinations. And, you need someone who is understanding and compassionate, undaunted by an all-encompassing love and the depth of the wellspring of your emotions.

The 1928 Pisces female wants a man who is courageous and willing to march to the beat of a much different drummer. You are motivated by love and are not terribly impressed with the material things in life. Instead, you want someone who can give you the spiritual fulfillment that you so strongly desire—a commodity more precious and valuable than anything money can buy.

1928 ARIES
From March 20, 20:44 through April 20, 8:16

♈ The Fiery Innovator

You are a leader, 1928 Aries, daring to tread where no one has ever gone before. A take-charge individual, you usually know exactly what you want. And, you have a surprisingly idealistic streak, helping you to see the best in others. In relationships, you don't hesitate to take the plunge, especially if you are challenged by the lure of an interesting pursuit. In fact, you may enjoy the chase more than you do the catch.

You like to make the first move, setting the tempo for whatever may happen next. You are an invigorating and insatiable lover, anxious to explore all the delights that another has to offer. With your tendency to move too quickly at times, you may burn yourself out before your partner even gets heated up. But, when you've found someone who likes things just as fast-paced and exciting as you do, it's full speed ahead and no turning back.

There is a dreamy, romantic side to you that is decidedly attractive to others, so it is not likely that you are ever lacking attention from potential partners. But first they need to get your attention, and this can be most easily accomplished by being straightforward and honest with you. If there's one thing that's sure to turn you off, it's deception. You love to be where the action is and, to a large extent, you make things even more exhilarating just by your sheer presence.

As a 1928 Aries male, you need a woman who enjoys your impetuous, spontaneous side and doesn't mind going with the flow. Since you like to be in control, it helps if she is willing to follow your lead, especially when it comes to steering the course of the relationship. Most of all, your perfect mate has a sensitive, compassionate nature and can understand your need to be number one.

The ideal man for the 1928 Aries female loves being outdoors and is an adventurer who doesn't mind pushing the envelope just a bit. You love surprises and he needs to be able to keep you guessing about what may come next. And, you place a high value on personal freedom, so he definitely needs to be able to accept and appreciate your need to be your own person.

1928 TAURUS
From April 20, 8:17 through May 21, 7:51

♉ *The Devoted Charmer*

Born with more than your share of charisma, 1928 Taurus, you have an irresistible and magnetic personality. People are drawn to your quiet reserve and your placidly calm exterior. Nothing shakes your resolve and you are a loyal, trustworthy friend and a devoted mate. Rarely impulsive, your down-to-earth, somewhat cautious approach to relationships ensures that your commitment is long lasting and genuine.

Affectionate and giving, you like the simple pleasure of hugging or holding hands with your beloved. But, you are also an ardent lover who truly takes pleasure in gratifying another. Sensuality is your middle name, and you employ all of your senses in your loving encounters with others. You can't help but be aware of the smell and feel of everything around you. Therefore, the setting must be just right and appeal to your love of comfort and luxury.

Because you take relationships very seriously and fear rejection, you are naturally reticent about jumping into a situation too quickly. A would-be mate would be wise to let you know

that they are interested in you. Since you dislike bold or brash behavior of any kind, a potential partner needs to be subtle in their approach. You have a taste for fine food, and an invitation to dine on sumptuous cuisine in beautiful surroundings is one you'd find hard to refuse.

The 1928 Taurus male wants a woman who enjoys the creature comforts of life. Harmony is very important to you and she must be able to make your home both beautiful and serene. She should also understand your occasional need for solitude and allow you the space you need to feel your emotions. Above all, you expect your woman to be faithful to you and, in return, you will pledge yourself to her.

As a 1928 Taurus female, you need a man who can feed your romantic nature with tenderness and sensitivity. While there is no doubt that you want a man who is confident and self-assured, you need someone who is also compassionate towards others. Most of all, your man must be able to provide you with both emotional and financial security in order for you to feel safe.

YOUR LOVE PLANETS

1928 GEMINI
From May 21, 7:52 through June 21, 16:05

♊ *The Bold Thinker*

You are quick and versatile, 1928 Gemini, and you have a vibrant imagination that enlivens your every conversation. Irrepressibly charming and flirtatious, you are a welcome addition in any social situation. Because you are acutely aware that relationships require responsibility, you may have been reluctant to settle down until you had the opportunity to sow a few wild oats. And, once you do make a commitment, you still need to feel free to relate to others without constraints.

Restless and curious, you are apt to try almost anything once, especially in the bedroom. While you may have been more reticent in your youth, as you grew older and more confident, it is likely that it became easier for you to express your needs and desires to your partner. Mental stimulation is foreplay for you and you can get a considerable amount of enjoyment just thinking about your next meeting with your beloved.

A prospective suitor will undoubtedly catch your eye by stimulating your mind. Clever conversation or even a good old-fashioned

debate is one way to get you to notice someone. You really admire a fine intellect and are impressed with someone who is well read and knowledgeable. A would-be partner would be smart to brush up on a few of your interests or, better yet, genuinely enjoy similar pastimes.

As a 1928 Gemini male, there is nothing you dislike more than boredom. You need a woman that can give you the illusion that she is constantly new and different. She should also share your love for games and other hobbies and not mind that you may spend a good deal of time and money on your toys. Like you, she should love traveling and be able to pack a week's worth of fun into a day.

The ideal man for the 1928 Gemini female is someone who knows what they want and is motivated enough to go get it. It is likely that your man likes to be in control and you find his masterful approach to life exciting and invigorating. But, he also needs to respect your independence and your need to explore new territory. You dislike jealousy so he should be tolerant of your playfully coy nature.

ELEANOR BOARDMAN
American Actress
Mars in Gemini

p.G. WODEHOUSE
English Writer
Mars in Cancer

1928 CANCER
From June 21, 16:06 through July 23, 3:01

The Powerful Giver

Cancer of 1928, you are blessed with a tremendous capacity for taking care of those around you. Intensely nurturing, above all else, you want to be needed by another. And, in return, you will generously bestow all the love and tenderness you have within you upon the object of your affection. Sentimental and conventional, you become easily attached to others. But, you can just as easily withdraw into your own shell if you feel threatened.

If you give yourself to someone, you expect your gift to be treasured by the other. Casual encounters are not your style, and you need to feel safe from rejection and secure in the good intentions of the other before you can really relax in a sexual situation. But, once you do, you make up in passionate eagerness what you may lack in sheer experience. You are a tender, giving lover who delights in the spiritual, physical, and emotional bonds that come with lovemaking.

Because Cancer is a water sign, you'd be delighted to go to the beach or sailing for the afternoon. You'd also enjoy an outing to the aquarium where you can watch the "other" water creatures in their natural habitat. If someone really wants to capture your interest, they might try asking your advice on a personal matter. You love to be helpful and asking for your assistance makes you feel important to your prospective partner.

The perfect woman for the 1928 Cancer male is someone who can understand your sensitive temperament and isn't put off by your periodic mood swings. She should share your enjoyment of good food, your love of children, and a stable home life. You are conservative, especially about money, and she needs to respect your need to save for a rainy day.

As a 1928 Cancer female, you want a man who is solid, stable, and willing to give you the security you so desire. You are a traditionalist who has a strong work ethic and you absolutely need someone who is ambitious and hard working. Faithfulness is also important to you and he must be capable of making you his one and only. Likewise, he shouldn't mind being the recipient of your powerful capacity for love.

1928 LEO
From July 23, 3:02 through August 23, 9:52

The Cheerful Performer

Your warm hearted nature and your wry sense of humor guide your way through the inevitable ups and downs of life, 1928 Leo. With your considerable magnetism and inner strength, your metal has been tested on more than one occasion. As bright as the sun itself, you are able to use your stellar quality to assure those around you that all is well with the world. In relationships, you give your heart completely and can be counted on to stick like glue to your beloved.

You tend to dominate in most situations and the bedroom is not an exception. When it comes to lovemaking, your appetites are large and the portions you mete out to others are generous. You graciously take the lead and keep it, directing your lover to heavenly blissful heights. And, because you are the first to admit that you have a deep desire to be adored, you do all that you can to make sure that your yearnings are met.

Because you are usually the center of attention, it is easy for others to become smitten with you. The easiest way for someone to get your attention is by praising you, and you make it easy for others with your significant accomplishments. You also have a strong need to be right and you love it when others notice your mental prowess. Happiest when the spotlight is on you, intimate cocktail parties are the perfect venue for you to show off your sunny personality.

1928 Leo male, your perfect woman is blessed with graceful good looks and a regal stature. But, you also need someone who has a good deal of inner beauty and possesses a magnanimous and giving spirit. You are very aware that this priceless inner quality can really bolster you through thick and thin. She should also be demonstrative with her affections and be willing to happily follow you into the sunset.

You, 1928 Leo female, want a man whose aura is larger than life. Because you can easily overpower others with the sheer force of your personality, he needs to be powerful and passionate enough to match your own intensity. You also want someone who is versatile, interesting and full of surprises to intrigue and delight you.

1928 VIRGO

From August 23, 9:53 through September 23, 7:05

The Artistic Thinker

You are a marvelous combination of discriminating thinking and artistic sensibility, 1928 Virgo. You are able to analyze any situation and are a stickler for details. But, you also have a creative flare that helps you shift perspective to readily see what others might miss. When it comes to relationships, you can blend your enormous communication skills with a calm and pleasant demeanor, to be an interesting and appealing partner.

You are a methodical yet inventive lover, making sure that you have explored every inch of your partner. Because you place such a high value on service, you are quite willing to go above and beyond to please another. Settling for nothing less than perfection, you are a practiced lover who prides yourself on your ability to be versatile and flexible.

In order to catch your eye, a prospective mate should impress you with their love of work and possess a high degree of ambition. Shy and reserved, you are not likely to initiate a conversation with someone you don't know. But, you can be quite taken with a person's intellectual gifts and like nothing better than a gripping discussion with just one other person. You'd also love to spend a cozy morning at home sipping gourmet coffee, reading the newspaper and discussing current events.

As a 1928 Virgo male, you want a woman that is refined and tasteful in her mannerisms and appearance. You also need someone who appreciates harmony and serenity as much as you do and you don't respond very well to pushing and prodding. Though you are not likely to make a scene, you will secretly feel undermined and harbor feelings of resentment. Only a true gentlewoman understands how fragile you are and how much you need to feel loved.

The 1928 Virgo female wants a man who is as multi-faceted and polished as the finest jewel. You are not likely to settle for an imitation and can spot a phony a mile away. Because you place such store in character and integrity, your ideal man must be above reproach. But, most of all, he needs to be exciting and lively—someone who can keep your quick mind stimulated and enthralled.

1928 LIBRA

From September 23, 7:06 through October 23, 15:54

The Mysterious Mediator

You like to think of yourself as a bit of an enigma, 1928 Libra. On the one hand, you seem to be open and forthright, yet one can't help but feel that you are keeping some part of yourself secret. You both love a mystery and love being a mystery to others, making you totally irresistible. Though you dislike confrontation, you will not shy away from fighting for what you believe to be right, especially when you believe that the issue is vitally important.

You thrive on romance and you love to fall in love. There is a teasing, flirtatious quality to your encounters, especially when you are trying to woo someone into the bedroom. But, once there, you are an intense and passionate lover who doesn't fail to deliver what you promised. And, since you are attracted to what's considered taboo, you may be a bit of a sexual explorer, all to the delight of your partner.

In order for a would-be partner to get your attention, they should appeal to your highly developed artistic sense. You love beauty in all its forms, and so it is important that they share your appreciation of art, music, and architecture. But, since you are also excited about the unknown and untried, it is important that they keep you guessing about themselves and not show all their cards at once.

The perfect woman for the 1928 Libra male is passionate about love and life. She should be willing to surprise you with a romantic evening filled with all the sensual delights—aromatic candlelight, enchanting music, and a delectable potpourri of edible goodies. But, you are not merely satisfied with external beauty and superficial interests. Therefore, she also needs to be able to touch you on a deeper, soul level with her spiritual outlook and her selfless dedication to others.

As a 1928 Libra female, you need a man who has a high degree of integrity and is interested in searching for the truth. It is important that you be able to communicate with each other on a mental, emotional, and spiritual level. But, most of all, you want your man to be responsible for his actions and to take an interest in home and family.

IRENE RICH
American Actress
Sun and Venus in Libra

DOLORES COSTELLO
American Actress
Mars in Scorpio

1928 SCORPIO
From October 23, 15:55 through November 22, 12:59

♏ The Profound Spellbinder

Mesmerizing and hypnotic, 1928 Scorpio, you have an alluring persona that others simply cannot resist. You are a determined and powerful individual who needs to have a higher purpose and focus for your life. In relationships, you can be remarkably devoted and loyal, making your beloved the center of your personal universe. Truth is a holy grail for you and if you find out that you've been deceived by someone, it is not likely that you will ever be able to trust that individual again.

When you stare deeply into another's eyes, it is as if you can read their soul. Most people will simply melt at your look and any request you make will certainly be granted. Sexy and dramatic, your lovemaking ability is, without question, legendary. But, you are more than just a seeker of physical pleasure. Your ultimate desire is spiritual union.

There's one sure way to capture your attention, 1928 Scorpio, and that is to be seductive. You like someone who is overtly sexual, and a prospective partner would do well to make a provocative suggestion or two in your ear. And, you need to know that you are being taken seriously. Anyone truly interested in captivating you needs to let you know that they understand that you are a person who has a message of depth and weight.

1928 Scorpio male, your ideal woman is someone who wants to journey with you, both literally and metaphorically. She should share your love of knowledge and your desire to go beneath the surface to find the real meaning in any situation. Your shared communication will be equally important to both of you and she needs to be able to help you sort out the myriad of possibilities that you perceive. A lover of serene and magnificent surroundings, the woman for you is capable of truly making your home your castle.

As a 1928 Scorpio female, the perfect man for you is one who can match your passionate and forceful nature. He needs to be able to shower you with physical affection and lavish attention to your every desire. You are lover of luxury and your mate should be generous to a fault, willing to indulge your every whim.

1928 SAGITTARIUS
From November 22, 13:00 through December 22, 2:03

♐ The Dedicated Explorer

You were born to go through life searching for the answer to the mystery of existence, 1928 Sagittarius. And, you take your quest very seriously, looking for significance in everyday acts. Ultimately, you may find your truth in a meaningful relationship with another human being. Herein lies the gate to your authentic self, the door to understanding that the meaning of life lies in union with another soul.

Being with you is apt to make any partner feel more alive and they will certainly appreciate your inclination to please. And, because you are an adventurer at heart, you are wonderfully willing to try anything new or unusual. Variety is an essential ingredient in your lovemaking style, and you make sure that it never becomes routine. You are an expert at foreplay, tantalizingly leading your partner to a smorgasbord of sensual delights.

One sure way to attract your attention is to first become your friend. You will go to any lengths for a friend and, of course, companionship is an excellent foundation for intimacy. You love being outdoors and an afternoon communing with nature is an excellent way to get you to open up and share your deepest thoughts. You are an avid traveler and will enjoy both short weekend getaways as well as trips to exotic destinations.

The ideal woman for a 1928 Sagittarius male is surprisingly conservative and traditional. You really want someone that you can depend upon and who is able to bring you down to earth when you drift too far from reality. Since you are often impractical, it helps if your woman is a realistic counterbalance to your unbridled enthusiasm. And, since you tend to overlook details, you need someone who can point out the trees while you are preoccupied with seeing the forest.

The 1928 Sagittarius female wants a man who is even-tempered and able to understand that freedom is essential for you to feel content. It is important that he be willing to let you spread your wings without feeling threatened or jealous. You want your mate to be a trusted and loyal companion, someone with whom you can share your innermost feelings.

D.H. Lawrence – The Erotic Trailblazer

From *Penthouse* magazine, to X-rated films, to the *Diary of Anais Nin*, to Nancy Friday's collections of women's sexual fantasies—all have followed a path first cleared by D.H. Lawrence, whose novels, essays, and poetry broke societal barriers against obscenity and defined the contours of a new realm of erotic expression. By today's standards, Lawrence's works remain surprisingly titillating and erotic. Depicting explicit sexual subject matter with originality, lyricism, and brilliance, the literature of D.H. Lawrence never loses its arousing ability, especially in contrast to the often base and predictable formula of modern pornography. At the dawn of the 21st century, Lawrence is still hot, hot, HOT!

Born on September 11, 1885, at Eastwood in Nottinghamshire, Lawrence was the sickly child of a poor coal miner and a teacher. Extremely close to his mother, Lydia, who encouraged his intellectual aspirations, Lawrence helped her escape the pain of terminal cancer in 1910 with a fatal dose of sleeping pills. He immortalized this event in his 1913 novel *Sons and Lovers*. Plagued by tuberculosis throughout his life, Lawrence wrote prolifically, as if there were no tomorrow.

Although Lawrence's poetry earned him early recognition in London literary circles, his impoverished background left him feeling like an outsider. In 1912, he ran off to continental Europe with Frieda Weekly, the wife of his professor at University College, Nottingham. They married in 1914 in England. Due to Lawrence's opposition to the war and Frieda's identity as a German national, the couple was denied passage from England until 1919. In search of hospitable environments for Lawrence's failing health after the war, they traveled

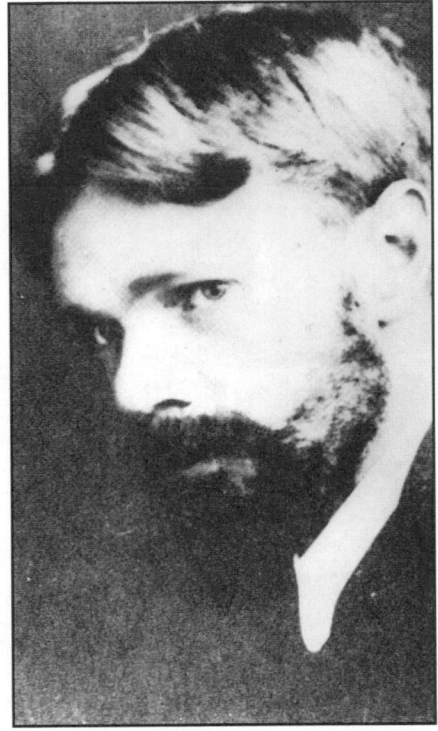

"John Thomas says good-night to Lady Jane, a little droopingly, but with a hopeful heart."

D.H. LAWRENCE in *Lady Chatterley's Lover*

extensively, spending time in continental Europe, Australia, and Taos, New Mexico.

1928 marked the publication of Lawrence's last (and many believe his best) novel, *Lady Chatterley's Lover*. The title character, Lady Constance Chatterley, is the restless wife of an English aristocrat. Lady Chatterley's husband, wounded in World War I, is paralyzed from the waist down and incapable of sexual performance. Hungry for the exhilaration of sex, Constance has affairs, first with a gentleman intellectual, and then with the gamekeeper on her estate. Commentators have suggested that Lawrence conceived the novel while living in Taormina, Sicily, a town frequented by British artists and adventurers.

British publishers recoiled not only from the depiction of raw sexuality in *Lady Chatterley's Lover*, but from the fact that the heroine goes unpunished for her scandalous rebellion against her husband and society. It was not the first time Lawrence slammed into a wall of rejection from prudish publishers. Upon the initial rejection of *Sons and Lovers* in 1913, Lawrence wrote: "Curse the blasted, jelly-boned swines, the slimy, the belly-wriggling invertebrates, the miserable sodding rutters, the flaming sods, the sniveling, dribbling, dithering, palsied, pulse-less lot that make up England today. They've got the white of egg in their veins and their spunk is that watery it's a marvel they can breed."

Forced to publish *Lady Chatterley's Lover* privately, through a Florentine printing house, Lawrence was unable to secure copyright protection for the novel. Bootleg copies of various versions of the novel flooded European and American markets. On March 2, 1930, Lawrence died at a sanitarium in Vence, France. In 1959 in America and in 1960 in London, free speech lawsuits finally cleared the way for the book's first legitimate publication.

87

▶ READ ABOUT ANAIS NIN ON PAGE 145

1929

- ★ VALENTINE'S MASSACRE
- ★ ACADEMY AWARDS
- ★ BROADWAY MELODY
- ★ AIN'T MISBEHAVIN'
- ★ MEAN TO ME
- ★ A ROOM OF ONE'S OWN
- ★ IS SEX NECESSARY?

EVENTS

The decade darkened at its close. Chicago gangster Al Capone's turf war left seven dead in the "St. Valentine's Day Massacre." On October 29, "Black Tuesday," the New York stock market crashed to the tune of $30 billion. Police raided New York's Birth Control Research Center, arresting medical personnel and confiscating records.

Women in Romania were granted equal suffrage and a congress on women's work opened in Berlin.

The celebrated actress and beauty Lillie Langtry died. She was infamous for having attracted keen attention from the Prince of Wales and other notables during her lifetime.

Police seized twelve paintings from an exhibition in Mayfair on the grounds that they were obscene. All were the work of celebrated novelist D.H. Lawrence, and all depicted nudes.

POP CULTURE

In the first Academy of Motion Picture Arts and Sciences awards (Academy Awards), the World War I film *Wings* won best picture. *The Broadway Melody*, an extravaganza about love and hard luck in vaudeville, and the first talkie musical, earned $3 million for MGM and later won the second Oscar for best picture. Louise Brooks stormed the big screen in *Pandora's Box* as an innocent, sensual beauty for whom men destroy themselves. Luis Bunuel and Salvador Dali created the surrealistic film classic *Un Chien Andalou (An Andalusian Dog)*.

Jazz pianist/composer Fats Waller's "Ain't Misbehavin'" was a big hit.

Other stellar songwriters produced "Am I Blue?" "Honeysuckle Rose," "Mean to Me," "You Do Something to Me," "Daddy, Won't You Please Come Home?" and "What Is This Thing Called Love?"

It was a year of great literature, including Ernest Hemingway's *A Farewell to Arms*, following a tragic wartime love affair, Erich Maria Remarque's anti-war *All Quiet on the Western Front*, and Virginia Woolf's *A Room Of One's Own*, a meditation on women's education and writing. Julia Peterkin's *Scarlet Sister Mary*, about a free-spirited black woman in the post-Emancipation South, was both banned in Boston and winner of the year's Pulitzer Prize. In *Womanliness as a Masquerade*, Joan Riviere deconstructed the "career woman." Essayists E.B. White and James Thurber asked, tongue-in-cheek, *Is Sex Necessary?*

Hot Couple

CHARLES LINDBERGH & ANNE MORROW

Anne Morrow was the highly educated and refined daughter of a poet and a banker. When she met Charles Lindbergh in 1927, he'd just completed the first nonstop transatlantic flight. They were instantly smitten and wed two years later on May 27, 1929.

She became his constant in-flight companion, and was the first American woman to obtain her own glider pilot's license in 1930. But tragedy struck in 1932 when their first child, Charles, was abducted and murdered. It was the crime of the century. Devastated by the murder and threats against their other son, they moved to England, where Anne became a best-selling author.

SEE ALSO
► SINCLAIR LEWIS & DOROTHY THOMPSON *Page 80*

88

1929 CAPRICORN

♑

*From December 22, 1928 2:04 through January 20, 1929 12:41
(December 1929 Capricorns, see 1930 Capricorn)*

The Reliable Romantic

You're an energetic Capricorn born in 1929, and you believe a relationship must be dynamic and exciting, as well as stable and reliable. There's no question that chemistry has always been important to you in all your involvements, from friendships and family to romance. You feel there's either a certain spark between two people or there isn't, and if nothing special is pulling you together, then why waste the time.

Stability is another important quality to you in relationships. Knowing you can count on each other—and feeling that ongoing commitment to stay together and be there for each other—is what makes a relationship special and worthwhile. Looking back over shared history has always meant a great deal to you because it's the living example of how love has bound you together.

A partner who is outgoing and exciting has always been your favorite type. You enjoy traveling, strolling along together and sharing stimulating conversation, because you feel that as long as there's something interesting to say to each other, there's a good reason to remain together. Sharing common interests is also very important because working together side by side to build a warm and happy life is very rewarding. It's always been the balance of romance and obligation that has kept you involved.

Male goats born in 1929 like a woman who is sparkly and sexy. Your lady has a certain flair that makes other people seek her out as a companion. She is interested in life and has amusing comments to share; her creativity keeps her involved in any number of interesting projects. Her joie de vivre is infectious, and no matter how long you've known her, you still expect some surprises.

Female Cappies born in 1929 like a man who is clever but also responsible. Your guy has charm and flair and sometimes he's downright boyish, so he always knows how to keep you laughing. His playfulness is adorable, yet he is reliable as well, so you know you can always count on him to remember and to fulfill his obligations. His conversation is lively, and he always wants to share an interesting point of view.

CAPRICORN ZODIAC SIGN
YOUR LOVE PLANETS

YOUR ROMANTIC SIDE   p. 696
▶ **VENUS IN AQUARIUS**
Born Dec. 22, 1928 2:04 - Jan. 06, 1929 12:00
▶ **VENUS IN PISCES**
Born Jan. 06, 12:01 - Jan. 20, 12:41

YOUR SEX DRIVE   p. 722
▶ **MARS IN GEMINI**
Born Dec. 22, 1928 2:04 - Jan. 20, 1929 12:41

YOUR CELEBRITY TWINS   p. 760
Find out the astrological similarities you have with famous people.

YOUR COMPATIBILITY   p. 780
Compare planets to find out how compatible you are in a relationship.

YOUR RELATIONSHIP KARMA   p. 824
▶ **SATURN IN SAGITTARIUS**
Born Dec. 22, 1928 2:04 - Jan. 20, 1929 12:41

BERTOLT BRECHT
German Writer
Sun and Venus in Aquarius

89

1929 AQUARIUS

♒

From January 20, 12:42 through February 19, 3:06

The Orderly Communicator

As a disciplined Aquarius born in 1929, your relationship must make sense. A connection that allows you to express your own interests yet also to build something warm and happy with a partner is your recipe for romantic perfection. Although you believe in personal self-expression, you also feel that responsibility and obligation are important. You wouldn't enjoy being attached to a flake at all.

Good communication is essential in any relationship, and you feel that being able to share interesting ideas nourishes a strong bond. Acceptance is also important because it's warm and comforting to be in a relationship in which you're appreciated for all the special qualities that make you unique. Although you don't have to like all the same things as your partner, it's always been good to feel that together you're building a mutually rewarding life.

You best appreciate a partner who maintains a sparkling intellect and you love being engaged in stimulating conversations. You have many interests and you're always eager to hear about something new and fascinating. You enjoy art and culture as well, and perhaps even science, so sharing an interesting movie or television documentary, and even working together on a picture puzzle is lots of fun for you.

Male Aquarians born in 1929 prefer a stimulating woman who's dynamic and has a mind of her own. Although it can sometimes be relaxing to hear, "Yes, dear," you'd almost always rather hear an interesting comment that gives you something to ponder. Your lady is witty and passionate and she has the sort of flair that makes other people notice and admire her. In fact, you feel like a bit of a sex symbol just because she's yours.

Female Aquarians born in 1929 feel that their man should be agile, intelligent, and dependable. A man who is strong, perhaps formerly in the military, is your sort of fellow. The dashing hero in uniform always seems sexy and appealing to you. Your guy is organized, and whatever he does he does well, and with much care and attention to detail. He makes you feel safe and secure, and you have a great deal of confidence in him.

AQUARIUS ZODIAC SIGN
YOUR LOVE PLANETS

YOUR ROMANTIC SIDE   p. 696
▶ **VENUS IN PISCES**
Born Jan. 20, 12:42 - Feb. 02, 14:33
▶ **VENUS IN ARIES**
Born Feb. 02, 14:34 - Feb. 19, 3:06

YOUR SEX DRIVE   p. 722
▶ **MARS IN GEMINI**
Born Jan. 20, 12:42 - Feb. 19, 3:06

YOUR CELEBRITY TWINS   p. 760
Find out the astrological similarities you have with famous people.

YOUR COMPATIBILITY   p. 780
Compare planets to find out how compatible you are in a relationship.

YOUR RELATIONSHIP KARMA   p. 824
▶ **SATURN IN SAGITTARIUS**
Born Jan. 20, 12:42 - Feb. 19, 3:06

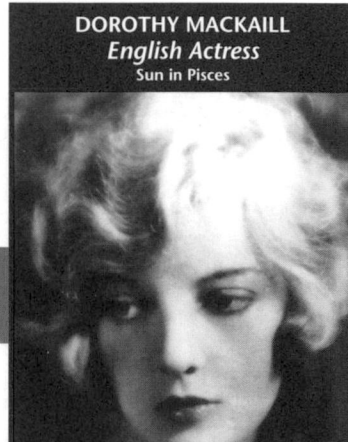

DOROTHY MACKAILL
English Actress
Sun in Pisces

1929 PISCES
From February 19, 3:07 through March 21, 2:34

Practical Passionate Fish

You're an affectionate Pisces born in 1929, and for you a relationship must combine the best of pleasure and commitment. Chemistry and passionate feelings of attraction are essential in getting any relationship off the ground, but you've always realized that without work and commitment, even the hottest romance can sizzle, then fizzle. Feeling that you're on the same team and working side by side is essential to you.

Personal freedom and acceptance are other important qualities for you in any good relationship. Each person much feel that it's all right to express all those little eccentricities, and that there will still be affection and support. You believe in responsibility, but you would hate to feel that you always had to toe the line and could never just be zany now and then.

You appreciate a partner whose affection for you is unbounded. A little unrestrained extravagance isn't so hard to take, and you enjoy receiving generous gifts, warm bear hugs and well-placed words of flattery. Someone who knows what you like and makes a special effort gets an A-plus. Traveling together, exploring new places in the neighborhood, and sharing a good meal are also simple pleasures.

Male Pisces born in 1929 like a woman who isn't too shy. Your lady is assertive, outgoing, and very affectionate. You're never embarrassed when she smothers you with kisses and you enjoy knowing that you're always in her heart. This woman is always a bit independent and charmingly confident—she knows her own mind and isn't shy about expressing thoughts and feelings. Yet, under it all, she's passionate and sentimental, capable of intense love and always aiming to please you.

Female fishies born in 1929 need a man who is charmingly unpredictable, occasionally eccentric and a little temperamental; yet, deep down, he must also be solid as a rock and utterly dependable. Your guy is multidimensional and has some amusing personality quirks that keep life interesting. He loves practical jokes and goofy stories, yet he is always on your side and you know in your heart that he will never, ever let you down.

1929 ARIES
From March 21, 2:35 through April 20, 14:09

The Intense Sensualist

As a passionate Aries born in 1929, you expect a relationship to be so compelling you'd never want to leave. Although you believe strongly in commitment and obligation, you also realize that you must have excitement and an intense connection in your relationship. Passion and sensuality have always been important to you because you absolutely refuse to buy into the idea of love growing from obligation.

Personal freedom and self-expression are other important dimensions to you in a good relationship. You like to feel that you are more yourself because of your relationship, rather than that you must restrain yourself to fit in. As you change and grow, so must the relationship. You also appreciate longevity, and the fact that you've shared so much over a long period of time makes the relationship even more dear.

A partner who is sexy and outgoing sustains your interest most easily. You like to be connected to someone who has lots of pizzazz so that you're always eager to see what's coming next. You also appreciate tender bits of attention, like a foot rub when you're tired, or being treated to your favorite dinner with just the right loving touches. And if you have separate interests from your partner's, you appreciate so much being given the green light to go off on your own and enjoy them.

Male rams born in 1929 like a woman who is sensual and devoted. Your lady has a softness about her and you love the way she feels in your arms. She may be a bit plump—giving you that much more to love—and she's a great cook, She is practical, reliable and steady, and you know that once she declares her affection for you, she will always hold you close in her heart.

Female Aries born in 1929 need a man who is sensitive yet dynamic, a bit eccentric, a strong individualist, but also solid as a rock. Your guy is very family-oriented but he also needs his space. Sometimes he's bossy and certain he knows it all, but before you decide to strangle him, he cracks a joke and all is forgiven. There's a certain mystique about him and it was this power and veiled sexiness that first attracted you.

1929 TAURUS
From April 20, 14:10 through May 21, 13:47

The Devoted Romantic

As an ardent Taurus born in 1929, you believe a relationship must be passionate, romantic, and lots of fun. Loving someone intensely is what it's always been about for you, and you believe wholeheartedly in devotion and true love. "All for one and one for all" is your credo, and you enjoy a relationship in which each person's needs are met and there is mutual support and affection.

Family values are important to you, but you'd never say the main reason for marriage is to raise a family. You realize only too well that you start out as a couple before the children come, and if you can't enjoy being a couple after the kids are grown then something has been missing right from the start. You believe romance is the spark that brings you together, and, when things are right, it's the guiding light that keeps the love alive.

A partner who loves you heart and soul is someone who sustains your interest. You know the value of love and devotion and that's worth more to you than all the gifts and fancy dates in the world. You enjoy sharing a brisk walk or a concert, and might even fondly remember when an impetuous lover sang beneath your window or dedicated a poem to you. You don't mind admitting that you're sentimental and enjoy being with a partner equally tender of heart.

Male bulls born in 1929 like a woman who is passionate and romantic. Your lady has real depth of feeling and when you met her it felt like you were tumbling into a volcano. When it comes to her, the phrase "falling in love" applies totally. This woman trusts in her feelings, believes in destiny, and told you early and often that the two of you were meant to be together. She's a little headstrong and sometimes possessive, but she's always worth loving.

Female Taureans born in 1929 think a man should be sensitive and emotional, yet outgoing, courageous and true blue. Your guy is family-oriented and he cares about making loved ones happy. He loves to cook with you in the kitchen and is a genuine nurturer. He seeks closeness and companionship and will go out of his way to provide whatever he believes will make you happy.

TAURUS ZODIAC SIGN
YOUR LOVE PLANETS

YOUR ROMANTIC SIDE   p. 696
► VENUS IN ARIES
Born Apr. 20, 14:10 - May 21, 13:47

YOUR SEX DRIVE   p. 722
► MARS IN CANCER
Born Apr. 20, 14:10 - May 13, 2:32
► MARS IN LEO
Born May 13, 2:33 - May 21, 13:47

YOUR CELEBRITY TWINS   p. 760
Find out the astrological similarities you have with famous people.

YOUR COMPATIBILITY   p. 780
Compare planets to find out how compatible you are in a relationship.

YOUR RELATIONSHIP KARMA   p. 824
► SATURN IN CAPRICORN
Born Apr. 20, 14:10 - May 5, 3:56
► SATURN IN SAGITTARIUS
Born May 5, 3:57 - May 21, 13:47

DOROTHY SEBASTIAN
American Actress
Sun in Taurus

91

1929 GEMINI
From May 21, 13:48 through June 21, 22:00

The Impulsive Lover

You're a deep-thinking Gemini born in 1929, and you believe that a relationship should express the personalities of each of the partners involved. Despite the fact that you require relevant conversation, where love is concerned you're more in favor of action than talk. You've always acted on impulse and you believe that's what a relationship is all about—two people who feel a connection reaching out to each other without explanation or apology.

Commitment and devotion are important to you, but you also insist on an ongoing sense of choice. Humdrum routine does not appeal to you, and you prefer to believe that a relationship can change and grow just as the people involved do. True love is another significant component of your romance. You've always chosen to share a lifelong connection with someone just right for you, a mate who completes your destiny.

A partner who is exciting appeals to you most, and will sustain your interest more because of what changes than what stays the same. You adore a sense of ongoing excitement and electricity between yourself and your mate, and a partner who does sweet things to surprise you gets high marks. You enjoy culture, and an impromptu trip to the theater or a gift-wrapped copy of the first song you ever danced to are excellent ways to hold your heart.

Male Geminis born in 1929 need a woman who is a bit mystical, rather musical and totally devoted to you. Your lady has a few quirks and she sometimes flaunts them but you find that stimulating rather than annoying. She believes in true love, which means that from the moment you met, she insisted you were destined to be together forever—something you may have resisted at first, but ultimately you realized she was right.

Female Geminis born in 1929 need a man who is self-assured. He's also a bit self-centered, but he has a kind and generous heart and will walk a mile to help out a stranger. He's stubborn on some days but then he surprises you by changing his mind and going in a completely different direction. You love the way he makes your heart pound with excitement in and out of the bedroom.

GEMINI ZODIAC SIGN
YOUR LOVE PLANETS

YOUR ROMANTIC SIDE   p. 696
► VENUS IN ARIES
Born May 21, 13:48 - June 03, 9:47
► VENUS IN TAURUS
Born June 03, 9:48 - June 21, 22:00

YOUR SEX DRIVE   p. 722
► MARS IN LEO
Born May 21, 13:48 - June 21, 22:00

YOUR CELEBRITY TWINS   p. 760
Find out the astrological similarities you have with famous people.

YOUR COMPATIBILITY   p. 780
Compare planets to find out how compatible you are in a relationship.

YOUR RELATIONSHIP KARMA   p. 824
► SATURN IN SAGITTARIUS
Born May 21, 13:48 - June 21, 22:00

ROBERT GRAVES
English Writer
Sun and Mars in Leo

1929 CANCER
From June 21, 22:01 through July 23, 8:52

The Tender Romantic

As a devoted Cancer born in 1929, you believe a relationship must be filled with tenderness, nurturing, and emotional support. More than anything, you've always believed in true love and building a life with the partner who is your destiny. There is no substitute for that deep, emotional connection and the instantaneous feeling of having known each other all your lives—right from the start.

Sentiment and self-sacrifice seem quite normal to you because that's what true love is all about. To you, love is a shelter where you both can live, knowing that each one will nurture and take care of the other. Focusing on each other's perfect happiness has always led to your own fulfillment and you feel sorry for people who turn a relationship into a quagmire of selfishness. Mutual interests are also important to you, as is a sense of common goals and expectations. All together it means harmony, happiness, and true contentment.

More than anything a partner could do to sustain your interest, you respond to the emotions that pass between you like an electrical current. A casual glance, a secret smile, a pat on the cheek, a squeeze of the hand such is the unspoken language of love in your relationship. Of course, you enjoy tender gestures too, and being taken out for a nice meal, receiving a gift of sweet sentiment, and being told how wonderful you are—well, these are the icing on the cake.

Male Crabs born in 1929 prefer a woman who is sensitive and emotional, sensual and passionate, outgoing and friendly. Your lady is soft and sweet and, because she is filled with devotion and the fullness of life and love, you enjoy spending time with her. She is never shy about showing how she feels and she adores giving of herself. She is musical and often hums a sweet tune.

Female Cancers born in 1929 feel a man can be both strong and sensitive. Your guy has great intuition and knows how you feel and what you need. It's important to him that you're happy, and he goes out of his way to nurture and please you. He's talented and outgoing, often a good dancer, and he just naturally finds the key to your heart.

1929 LEO
From July 23, 8:53 through August 23, 15:40
The Reliable Mate

You're a responsible Leo born in 1929, and you believe in a relationship that is a strong and solid partnership. Two people working together to create a good and stable life really appeals to you, and you feel that without effort and commitment a relationship won't work. It's important to take life seriously, and a partner who understands who you are and is willing always to stand by your side is a source of comfort and joy.

Affection is very important to you too, and you feel it's always worthwhile to go out of your way to make your partner happy. That's what keeps a relationship sailing smoothly along, in your opinion. Having independent interests is also important, and you feel that each partner must always give the other the freedom to enjoy those things that make him or her special. What comes first, however, is the good of the team.

A partner who is clever and sensitive sustains your interest. You like to feel you're connecting with someone of value, someone you can always admire. Being given sentimental mementos is a sweet touch that you appreciate and you also enjoy sharing mutually interesting activities. Just a simple television show that you can watch and enjoy together brings you closer, and reminds you of what brought you together in the first place.

Male lions born in 1929 like a woman who is intelligent and sentimental. Your lady has a sweet side and she's always willing to give her all to loved ones. She is kind and caring and she enjoys being there for you when you need a helping hand. She needs security and appreciates your effort to fill her life with happiness and safety. You know she is completely committed to you and the relationship, and that you can always count on her.

Lady Leos born in 1929 feel a man should be practical and hard-working. Your guy is skilled and thorough, yet never full of himself because he prizes modesty. He is kind and caring, always willing to pitch in when help is needed. He has a special way of understanding you and your needs, often stepping in with an unexpected thoughtful gesture that makes you love him even more.

1929 VIRGO
From August 23, 15:41 through September 23, 12:51

The Fun-Lover

As a sociable Virgo born in 1929, you believe a relationship must provide pleasure, companionship and fun. Although you work hard, you feel that a relationship should be bliss rather than labor. Who wants to punch a time clock at home! Connecting positively with a mate is what romance is all about, and you feel that, right from the start, you've always known who would be a good romantic partner. To you it makes sense to follow your instincts where love is concerned, and that means focusing on happiness.

Being able to socialize as a team is very important to you. By going out together as a couple you have more fun, and later on you laugh and share lots of nonsensical details of the evening. Raising a family together is another joy, and being able to talk about the children and grandchildren keeps you close. But even if you didn't have children you'd still be happy as a couple, because you've always made it a priority to focus on a joyous relationship.

To sustain your interest a partner must be sociable and outgoing. Being charming and attractive appeals to you, and you enjoy going out and sharing lots of social activities. Going to the theater, dining out, dancing, entertaining, and being entertained keep you happy as a couple. Having fun keeps you youthful and sustains the joy you felt when first you got together.

Male Virgos born in 1929 like a woman who is beautiful and sparkly. Your lady is a glamour girl at any age, and you appreciate the effort she expends to remain attractive and appealing. She's an excellent hostess and she loves entertaining. That makes her a perfect partner because you know she will favorably impress friends, family, and business associates.

Female Virgos born in 1929 feel a man should be elegant, sophisticated, and an excellent dancer. This fellow is assertive but he never seems rude or aggressive. He's an inspirational leader because he simply has a way of making the perfect suggestion. Your guy has superlative manners, finely developed social graces, and he knows how to be polite to all your friends—whether he likes them or not!

VIRGO ZODIAC SIGN
Your Love Planets

YOUR ROMANTIC SIDE   p. 696
▶ VENUS IN CANCER
Born Aug. 23, 15:41 - Aug. 31, 11:23
▶ VENUS IN LEO
Born Aug. 31, 11:24 - Sept. 23, 12:51

YOUR SEX DRIVE   p. 722
▶ MARS IN LIBRA
Born Aug. 23, 15:41 - Sept. 23, 12:51

YOUR CELEBRITY TWINS   p. 760
Find out the astrological similarities you have with famous people.

YOUR COMPATIBILITY   p. 780
Compare planets to find out how compatible you are in a relationship.

YOUR RELATIONSHIP KARMA   p. 824
▶ SATURN IN SAGITTARIUS
Born Aug. 23, 15:41 - Sept. 23, 12:51

ANTONIO MORENO
Spanish Actor
Venus in Virgo

1929 LIBRA
From September 23, 12:52 through October 23, 21:40

The Generous Lover

You're an amorous Libra born in 1929, and to you a relationship must provide a worthwhile and passionate connection. Falling in love has always been as important to you as being loved in return, and you enjoy every moment of luxuriating in those intense emotions. Giving and sharing are other significant dimensions of your relationship. Loving is about making someone else happy, and you enjoy being part of that ultimate sharing.

Communication is essential to you because it keeps the interaction lively and exciting. Being able to share ideas and insights is important in a relationship because that way you can understand each other, and see how much you're each growing and changing. Commitment is another important aspect of your relationship. You've never wanted to worry what tomorrow would bring, and so knowing you'll always be there for each other is a source of comfort.

A partner who is loving and considerate sustains your affection and devotion. You appreciate so much when someone who loves you makes an effort to please you. Small gestures designed to make you happy get high marks. A gift-wrapped book, sharing a class, or playing bridge together keep the energy and the happiness flowing between you. You also appreciate it when your own gestures of affection are accepted with pleasure.

Male Libras born in 1929 like a woman to be modest and conservative, yet also pretty and affectionate. Your lady has many special rainbows inside her heart and so she never has to be flashy or demanding. Her energy is gentle and kind, and she loves to help someone in need. You're always impressed by the depth of her love and the way she always makes you feel noticed, appreciated, and adored.

Female Libras born in 1929 feel a man should be sensitive and spiritual. Your guy trusts his instincts and he just knows what's appropriate behavior. Sometimes he can be bossy or demanding, but you find that macho and sexy, as long as he doesn't go too far overboard. He is on your side and completely devoted to making you happy, so you always know that his heart is in the right place—and that it belongs to you alone.

LIBRA ZODIAC SIGN
Your Love Planets

YOUR ROMANTIC SIDE   p. 696
▶ VENUS IN LEO
Born Sept. 23, 12:52 - Sept. 25, 16:12
▶ VENUS IN VIRGO
Born Sept. 25, 16:13 - Oct. 20, 5:11
▶ VENUS IN LIBRA
Born Oct. 20, 5:12 - Oct. 23, 21:40

YOUR SEX DRIVE   p. 722
▶ MARS IN LIBRA
Born Sept. 23, 12:52 - Oct. 06, 12:26
▶ MARS IN SCORPIO
Born Oct. 06, 12:27 - Oct. 23, 21:40

YOUR CELEBRITY TWINS   p. 760
Find out the astrological similarities you have with famous people.

YOUR COMPATIBILITY   p. 780
Compare planets to find out how compatible you are in a relationship.

YOUR RELATIONSHIP KARMA   p. 824
▶ SATURN IN SAGITTARIUS
Born Sept. 23, 12:52 - Oct. 23, 21:40

1 Read Your Sign   **2** Look Up Your Love planets   **3** Go to Pages Shown

LEATRICE JOY
American Actress
Sun in Scorpio

1929 SCORPIO
From October 23, 21:41 through November 22, 18:47

♏ *The True Romantic*

As a romantic Scorpio born in 1929, you believe a relationship should be about true love. Even though in your day few people called them soul mates, you always knew there was such a connection and that it was your destiny to find it. Romance is the heart and soul of a relationship to you, and being with someone you adore is what life is about. How can people marry for security rather than passion? You can't imagine.

Commitment is another serious matter, and you believe in giving your heart totally and forever. Social interaction and good conversation are important in your relationship because they bring you closer together and provide the fun that is the consolation for whatever bad times life makes you endure. Sharing common interests is another positive aspect of a good relationship, but you also feel that some time apart renews you for when you reconnect.

A partner who is romantic and passionate holds your interest. You believe strongly in love at any age, and no matter how long you've been together, it's the hearts and flowers that mean the most to you. Being given a sweet, sentimental present like a silk scarf, going out on the town for a memorable evening, or even dancing together in the living room appeal to you because these are the things that keep the magic alive.

Male Scorpios born in 1929 like a woman to be graceful, lovely and delicate. Your lady is well-dressed, beautiful and elegant, and her popularity is legendary. Everyone you know adores her, and you feel incredibly lucky that she chose you. She is affectionate, a wonderful hostess who knows how to impress the most finicky guest, and she makes the world a kinder and more romantic place just by being in it.

Female Scorpions born in 1929 expect a man to be masculine, passionate and intense. When you first met him he may have reminded you of your favorite movie idol, and his ability to make you swoon just by touching your hand was quite mesmerizing. He is strong and secure, and just has a way of making things work out. When you're with him you feel safe, and you know he will always be there to take care of you.

1929 SAGITTARIUS
From November 22, 18:48 through December 22, 7:52

♐ *The Playful Partner*

You're a fun-loving Sagittarius born in 1929, and to you a relationship must be a jolly good time. Being able to express yourself without restraint is the mark of a good relationship, in your opinion. Playing and laughing together make life warm and happy, and being able to do so helps your relationship endure. Common interests are also important to you in a relationship, but you feel that there's also room for separate pursuits, so that there's always something to talk about with each other.

You believe in true love and feel that it's only right to share your life with the partner who genuinely touches your soul. Settling down just to have a mate never appealed to you because it seemed like selling yourself short. Passion and commitment have always been very important to you in a relationship. You feel that when the emotions are right, everything else just falls into place.

A partner who remains youthful and exciting sustains your interest. Knowing you're loved for yourself is a big plus as well, and you appreciate being told just how your mate feels about you.

Sharing fun adventures also appeals to you and you feel that no matter how old you get, there is always something exciting to interest you and your mate. Traveling, sharing secrets, discussing detective novels, and raising pets together can also enrich your life and your love.

Male archers born in 1929 like a woman to be intense and passionate. Your lady has a special aura and she's deep and loving. Sometimes she's a bit too possessive, but you know that just means she loves you to distraction. You can always calm her down with a joke or goofy gesture and then she laughs as intensely as she loves. Winning her heart was very important to you, and each day you're together you appreciate her.

Female Sagittarians born in 1929 like a man who is lively, athletic, and optimistic. Your guy is playful and boyish and he always has something interesting to say and do. He's hasty and impatient and he keeps life exciting when he says one thing and does another. It's fun not to know what to expect at every moment of the day.

Louise Brooks – The Free-Spirited Flapper

One of the enduring images of the 20th century is the free-spirited flapper, the independent, sexually liberated woman who made the 1920s roar. Louise Brooks, a dancer for Ziegfeld's Follies and a silent picture star, was at the center of that decade, but she is remembered not so much for her luminous presence on film, but for her trademark hair. Her sleek black hair framed a beautiful face, at once inviting and enigmatic. Her signature bob known as the Black Helmet was the most copied hairstyle of the day. Brooks' wild love life, her dancing career, and her defiant flapper attitude was the inspiration behind the long-running comic strip "Dixie Dugan." Most recently Catherine Zeta-Jones reprised the role in *Chicago*.

Brooks was born with her Sun in passionate Scorpio, and her Venus in uninhibited, trendy Sagittarius. Restless and full of enthusiasm, Louise Brooks took the train out of Wichita, Kansas in the summer of 1922 and at the age of 15 headed for Manhattan. She learned modern dance and met Martha Graham, who decades later recalled her first impression of Brooks. "Louise stood out in two ways, because she was so extraordinarily beautiful and because of a deep inner power that stood her all of her life."

By 1925 Brooks had achieved some notoriety for the male company she kept. She dated some of New York's most prominent people in show business, including a two-month fling with Charlie Chaplin. She met a laundry tycoon named George Preston Marshall and had

affairs with *New York Times* critic Herman Mankiewicz and the young radio pioneer William Paley. While filming *It's the Old Army Game* with W.C. Fields in 1926, she became involved with that film's director, Eddie Sutherland. She eventually married Sutherland, but while they were engaged she scandalously fell in love with Buster Collier, her leading man in another

movie directed by her fiancé.

Brooks' Mars forms a challenging square to Uranus, the planet of rebellious independence. This combination makes it difficult for her to play a traditional role in life or in the movies. In 1928 she divorced Sutherland after only two years of marriage and headed for Berlin. It was there that she would make the most important movie of her film career, *Pandora's Box*, and where she would become an international film star in Europe. Under the intelligent guidance of director G.W. Pabst, Brooks played the temptress Lulu, with her sexual escapades designed to outrage Victorian morality. In an interview, Brooks said, "I revered Pabst for the truthful picture of the world of pleasure which let me play Lulu naturally."

Unfortunately for Brooks, talking pictures had just become all the rage, and not many people saw this film, which also suffered from deep censorship. Furthermore, critics of the time said her acting was too natural and complained that she couldn't act at all. When Brooks returned to Hollywood, her outspokenness brought her into conflict with studio heads, and she gave up her acting career in 1937. After a series of various jobs and careers, she ended up in Rochester, NY where she became a successful and respected film critic. *Pandora's Box* is now recognized as being one of the great classics of the silent movie era, and film scholars and journalists consider Brooks' subtle, erotic style of acting ahead of its time.

▶ READ ABOUT CHARLIE CHAPLIN ON PAGE 63   ▶ READ ABOUT CATHERINE ZETA-JONES ON PAGE 688   ▶ READ ABOUT JOSEPHINE BAKER ON PAGE 79

Oxford  Mail

No. 2,497.   TELEPHONE 4141.   THURSDAY, 10 DECEMBER, 1936.   PRICE ONE PENNY.

KING EDWARD ABDICATES
Dramatic Message Read To Parliament

"FINAL AND IRREVOCABLE DECISION"

CAN NO LONGER DISCHARGE THIS HEAVY TASK

DUKE OF YORK NEW MONARCH

IN ...NSELY PACKED HOUSE OF COMMONS THIS AFTER-
...OON ...E SPEAKER ANNOUNCED KING EDWARD'S DECISION
...BDICA ... AND THE DUKE OF YORK'S SUCCESSION TO THE
...ONE.

THE P... MINISTER HANDED THE FOLLOWING MESSAGE TO
SPEAKE ... D THE SPEAKER THEN READ IT TO THE HOUSE:—

...FOR   ...fter long and anxious consideration, I have determined
... the Throne, to which I succeeded on the death of
...y fath ... I am now communicating this, my final and
... irrevoca... ...sion.

Mrs. Simpson

MRS. SIMPSON WILL

1930 -1939

THE TUMULTUOUS THIRTIES

World-wide economic

depression, political ferment,

artistic flowering, and

lighthearted entertainment

made for a fascinating decade.

The 1930s saw a great Depression and the gathering clouds of war. Yet it was a decade of cultural and political intensity, of radical ideas and behaviors, and of joyful, frivolous entertainments that delighted and distracted.

Nazism and Fascism took root in economically shattered and demoralized parts of Europe, and in England, King Edward VIII astounded the nation when he abdicated the throne to marry American divorcee Wallis Warfield Simpson.

In the US, intellectuals were embracing Marx and Freud, but more Americans were finding pure escapism appealing, with Broadway and film musical extravaganzas, society scandals, and sports fitting the bill.

The thirties sparkled with character and characters, from baseball greats Babe Ruth and Lou Gehrig, African-American boxing champion Joe Louis and track star Jesse Owens (whose prowess humiliated the Aryan supremacist Germans at the 1936 Berlin Olympics), to tunesmiths Cole Porter, Irving Berlin, the Gershwins, Rodgers, Hart, and Hammerstein and bandleaders Count Basie, Benny Goodman, Tommy Dorsey, Duke Ellington, and Glenn Miller.

President Franklin Delano Roosevelt's New Deal pioneered American social programs, including the WPA, which put artists, craftspeople, writers, and photographers to work making public art and documenting folk music and everyday life. The fine arts also flourished, with the work of artists such as Picasso, Diego Rivera, Matisse, and Georgia O'Keefe, architect Frank Lloyd Wright, and modern choreographer Martha Graham. Hard-boiled detective fiction was born, Disney began producing early animated classics such as *Pinocchio*, the art-deco Chrysler Building and the Golden Gate Bridge were constructed, and Albert Einstein revolutionized physics. Women began to hold elected office, and divorce, birth control, and respect were all a little easier to come by.

The guilt of German immigrant Bruno Hauptmann, executed for the kidnap and murder of the Lindbergh baby, is still disputed today. Radio reporter Herb Morrison, emotional eyewitness to the explosion of the dirigible *Hindenburg*, uttered the famous line "Oh, the humanity."

This was the golden age of songwriting, as vaudeville, black spiritual, ragtime, and jazz influences combined with Eastern European folk traditions in the tunes of Tin Pan Alley and Broadway. Enduring standards of the decade include "My Funny Valentine," "These Foolish Things," "My Baby Just Cares for Me," and "Moonlight Serenade." Music offered a path for African Americans to flourish, and Billie Holiday, Ethel Waters, Louis Armstrong, and Paul Robeson became mainstream entertainers. African-American life also became a legitimate theme for stage and page. *Showboat* and *Porgy and Bess* set recent American history to music.

THE SILVER SCREEN
Despite, or perhaps because of, reinvigorated censorship regulations, films of the thirties included some of Hollywood's most innuendo-laden dialogue and inventively suggestive scenes. The "screwball comedy" was born in the work of directors like Frank Capra and Howard Hawks. Directors like Bunuel, Renoir, Eisenstein, Lubitsch,

and Hitchcock crafted some of the finest films ever made. And talkies created a new crop of stars, including Fred Astaire, Bette Davis, Orson Welles, Marlene Dietrich, Jean Gabin, Cary Grant, Norma Shearer, John Barrymore, James Cagney, Clark Gable, and Edward G. Robinson. Shirley Temple and the Three Stooges provided lighter antics for audiences.

BETWEEN THE PAGES
Dashiell Hammett and James Cain carved out new literary terrain with their detective noir tales. Thomas Wolfe explored the disorientation created by the mobility of modern society, and John Steinbeck cast an unsentimental eye on the disenfranchised. Great works came from Hemingway, Lewis, West, Powell, and writers of the Harlem Renaissance such as Langston Hughes. And Daphne du Maurier wrote *Rebecca*.

PEOPLE
First Lady Eleanor Roosevelt became a role model for her independence, compassion, and dedication to human rights. "Poor Little Rich Girl" Gloria Vanderbilt was removed from the care of her famously sexually adventurous mother. Mae West offered a robust, taboo-breaking antidote to the traditional feminine image, and the young ballerina Margot Fonteyn embarked on her remarkably long career.

▲ Louis Armstrong, legendary jazz pioneer

◄◄ The *Oxford Mail* of December 10, 1936, announcing Edward VIII's abdication

◄ Margot Fonteyn in *Swan Lake*

97

1930

- ⊛ LEGION OF DECENCY
- ⊛ RHYTHM METHOD
- ⊛ THE BLUE ANGEL
- ⊛ HELL'S ANGELS
- ⊛ MOOD INDIGO
- ⊛ SAM SPADE
- ⊛ VILE BODIES

EVENTS

Hollywood found itself in hot water when the Catholic Legion of Decency threatened to boycott the movie industry if moral standards in films were not imposed. The UK board of censors seemed to agree, revealing that over 350 films were cut during the year and that "sordid themes" had been a particular problem. However, there was a happy couple in Hollywood—the writers Dashiell Hammett and Lillian Hellman met for the first time, sparking a long-term relationship. Scientists viewed a human egg cell through a microscope for the first time and Pope Pius XI declared only the "rhythm" method of birth control was acceptable to the Church. After fierce debate, the Church of England approved the use of contraceptives if the circumstances were deemed to be "moral."

POP CULTURE

It was a good year for bad girls in film. Norma Shearer gave an Academy Award–winning performance in *The Divorcee*. Its divorce theme paled in comparison to *The Blue Angel*, in which a good professor goes bad for the love of cabaret singer, played by the gender bending Marlene Dietrich. Platinum blonde Jean Harlow raised eyebrows and increased pulse rates in *Hell's Angels*. In Luis Bunuel's *L'Age d'Or*, a couple's passion is absurdly thwarted by their families, the Church, and bourgeois society.

Ruth Etting sang Rodgers and Hart's lament of the taxi dancer, "Ten Cents a Dance." Maurice Chevalier worked his French accent in "You Brought a New Kind of Love to Me." Composer Duke Ellington recorded "Mood Indigo," and Red Nichols' band included future big-band stars Benny Goodman, Gene Krupa, Tommy Dorsey, Glenn Miller, and Jack Teagarden.

Dashiell Hammet's hard-boiled detective Sam Spade fends off a vamp in *The Maltese Falcon*. Evelyn Waugh's *Vile Bodies*, about heavy-drinking, promiscuous partying "Bright Young Things," foretold another world war. Margaret Ayer Barnes took the Pulitzer Prize for *Years of Grace*, about a woman who really knew how to carry a torch, and Edna Ferber's bestseller *Cimarron* chronicled a family of Oklahoma homesteaders.

Sex Idol

NORMA SHEARER

In 1927 actress Norma Shearer married Irving Thalberg, the "boy wonder" of MGM. His loving attention to every detail of his wife's career made her a bona fide star. In 1930, she received an Oscar for *The Divorcee*, portraying a young wife who repays her husband's infidelities in kind.

His premature death at age 36 devastated Shearer, who was in the midst of filming *Marie Antoinette*, Thalberg's final project. Her career floundered after she turned down the lead in *Gone with the Wind*. Shearer quit films in the early '40s and married again, to a man much younger than herself.

SEE ALSO
▶ THE GAY DIVORCEE *Page 130*

98

1930 CAPRICORN

From December 22, 1929 7:53 through January 20, 1930 18:32
(December 1930 Capricorns, see 1931 Capricorn)

♑ *The Eclectic Conservative*

As a 1930 Capricorn, you want relationships that serve a purpose. Freedom loving and unpredictable, you yearn for the perfect blend of personal independence and the traditional commitments that you grew up believing in. Your relationships must challenge your thinking and encourage you to grow and expand as a person as well as a lover. You want a relationship that respects core values as much as it respects your right to be an individual.

Your sexuality can express itself as hot or cold like a water faucet and, as a result, lend itself to an exciting game of never-ending anticipation for the right partner. For you, the perfect lover is a dichotomy between sheer savage passion privately and ultra-sophisticated manners publicly. The cooler you behave, the hotter your passions are when you misbehave. The challenge of keeping up appearances keeps you creatively amused.

You love intriguing people who are unique because they are exceptional and know how to express their bold individuality with a playful wink at society. For someone to keep your attention though, they must also be open minded and young at heart. You love to spend time in the company of people who are brilliant at whatever it is that they do best and who aren't afraid of new ideas. Seeing things in new and innovative ways is your lifeblood and creative thinkers always make your heart beat faster.

The ideal match for a male 1930 Capricorn is a woman who loves him for his madcap, inventive mind and knows how to keep him mentally stimulated as well as sane. He is bound by his sense of duty and is happiest with an independent woman who encourages his need for personal space and self-expression while maintaining the integrity of the relationship.

For a 1930 female Capricorn, the ideal man is ambitious, driven, and committed to maintaining a stable home environment. You thrive when you have the freedom to do your own things at home, unfettered by his, or anyone else's presence. The epitome of social grace and classic, feminine style, you also require a partner who can respect your feisty spirit.

CAPRICORN ZODIAC SIGN
YOUR LOVE PLANETS

YOUR ROMANTIC SIDE   p. 696
▶ **VENUS IN SAGITTARIUS**
Born Dec. 22, 1929 7:53 - Dec. 31, 1929 3:43
▶ **VENUS IN CAPRICORN**
Born Dec. 31, 1929 3:44 - Jan. 20, 1930 18:32

YOUR SEX DRIVE   p. 722
▶ **MARS IN CAPRICORN**
Born Dec. 22, 1929 7:53 - Jan. 20, 1930 18:32

YOUR CELEBRITY TWINS   p. 760
Find out the astrological similarities you have with famous people.

YOUR COMPATIBILITY   p. 780
Compare planets to find out how compatible you are in a relationship.

YOUR RELATIONSHIP KARMA   p. 824
▶ **SATURN IN CAPRICORN**
Born Dec. 22, 1929 7:53 - Jan. 20, 1930 18:32

KAY FRANCIS
American Actress
Sun in Capricorn

99

1930 AQUARIUS

From January 20, 18:33 through February 19, 8:59

♒ *The Original Thinker*

As a 1930 Aquarius, you want a relationship that offers genuine friendship and companionship. You are not overly concerned with traditional social roles or expectations, and prefer a relationship that allows you the freedom to explore and discuss a variety of romantic expressions. Romantic and intellectual needs merge for you, and the key to keeping a loving gleam in your eye is the ability of your partner to engage you mentally. The ideal lover for you is bright, witty, and stimulating.

You can be sexually detached, and while this can confuse more sensual types, it doesn't make the experience less than amazing for you. While you are more moved by mental acumen than physical appeal, your expression in matters of a more carnal nature still retains the wide-eyed freshness of perspective and curiosity that is almost virginal. For you, sex is considered a delightful distraction from your other favorite activity—thinking.

The easiest way to get your attention is to show as much of an interest in your current pet project as in romancing you. You delight in the opportunity to share an experience with a buddy, friend, or a whole group of people. Keeping your attention is more complicated only because it involves learning to love (or at least tolerate) your eclectic and wide assortment of friends. An amazingly social creature, the partner who holds your genuine affection is the one that is not uncomfortable with your need to bond with humanity, one person at a time.

The male 1930 Aquarian is best paired with a female who has more than enough of her own interesting friends and hobbies. More than anything else, you want a woman who piques your interest in her life as much as your own projects. Reasonableness is the key trait that you look for in a love match.

As a female 1930 Aquarian, your best match is a man who can respect you as the bright, creative, and highly independent individual that you are. A confident, tolerant man who is secure himself and can celebrate your uniqueness is the only type that can truly capture your affections and your heart.

AQUARIUS ZODIAC SIGN
YOUR LOVE PLANETS

YOUR ROMANTIC SIDE   p. 696
▶ **VENUS IN CAPRICORN**
Born Jan. 20, 18:33 - Jan. 24, 0:21
▶ **VENUS IN AQUARIUS**
Born Jan. 24, 0:22 - Feb. 16, 22:10
▶ **VENUS IN PISCES**
Born Feb. 16, 22:11 - Feb. 19, 8:59

YOUR SEX DRIVE   p. 722
▶ **MARS IN CAPRICORN**
Born Jan. 20, 18:33 - Feb. 06, 18:20
▶ **MARS IN AQUARIUS**
Born Feb. 06, 18:21 - Feb. 19, 8:59

YOUR CELEBRITY TWINS   p. 760
Find out the astrological similarities you have with famous people.

YOUR COMPATIBILITY   p. 780
Compare planets to find out how compatible you are in a relationship.

YOUR RELATIONSHIP KARMA   p. 824
▶ **SATURN IN CAPRICORN**
Born Jan. 20, 18:33 - Feb. 19, 8:59

DASHIELL HAMMETT
American Writer
Venus in Aries

1930 PISCES
From February 19, 9:00 through March 21, 8:29

 ## The Driven Humanitarian

As a 1930 Pisces, you crave a relationship that is a total spiritual and emotional bonding experience that borders on telepathy. You are not interested in relationships that require you to curb your natural humanitarian and charitable instincts, and yearn for someone who can be gentle with your kind nature. You are looking for someone who is a strong and stable buoy for you when you are overcome by the harshness of the world. You need a special person who will understand your need to do good things in the world and support your efforts.

For you, sex is meant to be a psychic communion between kindred souls. At once detached and, conversely, united, you transcend worlds and boundaries through the act of intimacy. For you, flesh is a mere distraction from the real magic occurring between two people. Playful exploration of mind and body are the keys to gaining entry to the magical, fantasy world in your heart, mind, and soul.

If someone wants to get your attention, they must first capture your imagination.

Offering you entry into a mysterious and unusual world that is not your own always draws you like a moth to a flame. You are attracted to dramatic, colorful, or problematic personalities, but it is the gentle and kind heart that inspires you to stay. Taking the time to dream a better world with you is the secret to inspiring your devotion.

As a male 1930 Pisces, you are attracted to versatile women who are colorful, independent, and gentle by nature. You prefer women who wield their power with the feminine grace and restraint of a tigress. Your ideal woman inspires poetry in you as well as unrepentant adoration and knows the value of a genuinely absolute romantic in a cold, unforgiving world.

A female 1930 Pisces is happiest when she can relinquish the functions of daily survival to a stronger, more dynamic partner. You want a man who navigates the outer world as comfortably as you navigate your inner one. Ideally, you are seeking someone who cherishes your sensitivity enough to offer you the shelter you need from the buffeting of daily life.

1930 ARIES
From March 21, 8:30 through April 20, 20:05

The Sensitive Warrior

As a 1930 Aries, you want a challenging relationship that keeps you on your toes and challenges you to be your very best. Your ideal relationship will do this while still maintaining the solid comfort of the traditional roles and values that you hold dear to your heart. You are not one to settle for a boring life and because of that, your ideal relationship is as much of a friendship and spirited companionship as it is a love match.

For you, sex in a relationship is secondary to mental intimacy. You yearn for someone who understands you and offers you more than physical gratification. For you, sex is as much a spiritually and emotionally bonding experience as it is an expression of your more imaginative desires. Relationships for you, on all levels, are about sharing and discovering new things every day.

To catch and keep your attention, a potential mate should polish off their best conversational skills. You thrill at the opportunity of having a lively chat with someone who knows how to keep the conversation interesting and doesn't

want to monopolize your time. Good talkers and good kissers are the ones that put a sparkle in your eye. Someone who knows how to make you feel special with forget-me-not gifts and sweet treats is a star player in your book of love.

If you are a male 1930 Aries, you prefer your women feminine and old-fashioned with just enough fire to keep you feeling young as the years roll on. You want a woman who understands that in a relationship with you, following your lead should be natural. A healthy appreciation for your imagination and spontaneity is the only reminder that you need that she is the right woman.

As a 1930 female Aries, you are looking for the hero of your dreams. Your measure of the ideal mate is the right blend of masculine courage and romantic sensuality. You are not one to settle for anything less than embodiment of your romantic dreams and absolutely crave someone who knows how to tame your free spirit. Only if they also offer a passionate life filled with commitment and tenderness is your heart truly conquered.

1930 TAURUS

From April 21, 20:06 through May 21, 19:41

The Mischievous Flirt

As a 1930 Taurus, relationships are where you make your mischief as well as your magic. Building a home and a family comes naturally to you. Establishing a secure home base is your first priority but your flirtatious nature doesn't end where your domestic duties begin. Your infectious laugh and warm smile will always leave more than a few admirers wishing that they were the one you were coming home to.

Sexually, you are a dynamo and love the thrill of the seductive chase. If things get a little too sedate in your relationship, you are just as likely to flirt with someone else to encourage a little jealous passion in your partner as you are likely to have an inspired moment that demands his or her total amorous desire. You know how to make private moments sizzle.

If someone wants to get your attention, the eyes have it. While a little flash and pizzazz will always turn your head, it is the eyes themselves that get a second look from you. No matter what kind of eyes they have, they must have the quality of lights dancing in them

as if they were magical orbs intended to keep you entranced. Keeping your attention is as simple as not giving in to your charismatic sway too easily. You want someone who can hold their ground and prove to you that they are your better half.

As a 1930 male Taurus, the perfect woman for you sparkles inside and out. Your rambunctious nature is best suited to a woman who enjoys your physical expressions of love and affection. A schoolgirl giggle and a love of flirty, feminine things are what truly brings forth the better man in you. A healthy sense of humor and a love of your manly style are all you need to remember where your heart is.

A 1930 female Taurus is looking for a man who isn't afraid to be all man, all the time. You want someone that you can lean on and count on to take care of life's little problems. A charming and gracious helpmate, you prefer the role of social director and secretary to the "man in charge." Someone who keeps you smiling and feeling safe are your top ingredients for a lifetime of happiness.

TAURUS ZODIAC SIGN

YOUR LOVE PLANETS

YOUR ROMANTIC SIDE   p. 696
- ▶ VENUS IN TAURUS
  Born Apr. 20, 20:06 - Apr. 30, 12:36
- ▶ VENUS IN GEMINI
  Born Apr. 30, 12:37 - May 21, 19:41

YOUR SEX DRIVE   p. 722
- ▶ MARS IN PISCES
  Born Apr. 20, 20:06 - Apr. 24, 17:26
- ▶ MARS IN ARIES
  Born Apr. 24, 17:27 - May 21, 19:41

YOUR CELEBRITY TWINS   p. 760
Find out the astrological similarities you have with famous people.

YOUR COMPATIBILITY   p. 780
Compare planets to find out how compatible you are in a relationship.

YOUR RELATIONSHIP KARMA   p. 824
- ▶ SATURN IN CAPRICORN
  Born Apr. 20, 20:06 - May 21, 19:41

JEANETTE MACDONALD
American Singer
Sun in Gemini

101

1930 GEMINI
From May 21, 19:42 through June 22, 3:52

The Secret Dreamer

As a 1930 Gemini, you want a relationship that can keep you coming back for more. A restless, sensitive soul, you seek out people who will understand your need for emotional security and your simultaneous desire for variety and change. Your ideal relationship is on the spicy, saucy side with just enough stability to keep you well grounded and happily nurtured. You are a powerhouse of raw creativity and sheer determination that sees life and relationships as a constant process of building and growth.

Romantically and sexually, you are slow to warm up but long lasting in your affections. Sweet nothings whispered in your ear during a slow, loving dance are the sort of thing that enchants your finicky heart. For you, sex is a private, playful thing that is best with someone you cherish and adore. Cuddling is your favorite activity next to spooning.

People often think they have your attention because you are such a good listener, but for someone who really wants to stand up and be noticed by you, the secret is in the silence.

Because you are intensely private and emotional, you are a boiling pot of feelings and dreams that are rarely discussed with anyone. A person who knows how to listen sensitively to your carefully guarded displays of feeling and sentiment is the one who gets your special attention.

The ideal woman, for a 1930 Gemini male, embodies the perfect blend of dynamic, feminine power and a healthy preservation of nurturing wisdom. She knows how to keep your home life balanced and sacrosanct from the outside world while she maneuvers through it like a warrior. Your dream woman can handle your intense emotional nature and still offer you the tender loving care that you thrive with.

If you are a female 1930 Gemini, you are a dynamic champion of the home and a true domestic goddess. You prefer a man that shares and upholds your family values and are drawn to creative and challenging personalities whose top priorities are their current worldly passion and you. A man who maintains an upbeat youthful personality with mature values is your best match.

GEMINI ZODIAC SIGN

YOUR LOVE PLANETS

YOUR ROMANTIC SIDE   p. 696
- ▶ VENUS IN GEMINI
  Born May 21, 19:42 - May 25, 4:35
- ▶ VENUS IN CANCER
  Born May 25, 4:36 - June 19, 4:38
- ▶ VENUS IN LEO
  Born June 19, 4:39 - June 22, 3:52

YOUR SEX DRIVE   p. 722
- ▶ MARS IN ARIES
  Born May 21, 19:42 - June 03, 3:14
- ▶ MARS IN TAURUS
  Born June 03, 3:15 - June 22, 3:52

YOUR CELEBRITY TWINS   p. 760
Find out the astrological similarities you have with famous people.

YOUR COMPATIBILITY   p. 780
Compare planets to find out how compatible you are in a relationship.

YOUR RELATIONSHIP KARMA   p. 824
- ▶ SATURN IN CAPRICORN
  Born May 21, 19:42 - June 22, 3:52

MAURICE CHEVALIER
French Entertainer
Sun and Venus in Leo

1930 CANCER
From June 22, 3:53 through July 23, 14:41

♋ ## The Dramatic Nurturer

As a 1930 Cancer, you see relationships as a romantic journey of self-expression and drama. You are drawn to people who need your ability to speak the language of the heart fluently and also respect your ability to keep both feet on the ground. You are an irrepressible champion of motivation and self-initiative who is committed to only the best quality in all aspects of life and love. Your ideal relationship is a combination of bold, passionate drama interwoven with delicate, intricate moments of genuine caring.

Sexually, you appear complex because you require the extended time of courtship to determine whether you want to enter into a love relationship with someone. Once you do get involved, you are a constant and faithful lover who takes great care in making everything a total, sensual experience. Not one to be rushed, you prefer tender moments that gradually develop and allow time for complete self-expression along the way.

In your mind, keeping your attention is the same thing as getting it. For you, the whole picture is as important as the parts, so a well-groomed and visually pleasing palette of colors and textures in appearance are requirements for you. Gentle behaviors and/or good social manners are also important in the efforts to keep you happily engaged in a relationship. Good kissers get special consideration from you, always.

If you are a 1930 male Cancer, your ideal woman is the personification of grace, beauty, and self-control. You see women as living works of art and in the same vein, understand women who enjoy being on display and admired as the beautiful creatures they are. Still, in the end, you are happiest with the same kind of woman who also knows that her home and heart are with you.

A female 1930 Cancer thrives in a relationship that encourages celebration and adornment of warmth and loyalty. You are happiest with a man who knows how to give genuine compliments and encouragement as well as loving support. Your best match is a man who appreciates and supports your efforts toward constant self-renewal and personal rejuvenation.

1930 LEO
From July 23, 14:42 through August 23, 21:25

♌ ## The Spirited Player

As a 1930 Leo, you see relationships as both serious business and a playful game of romance. You want the kind of relationship that helps you transform life into a wonder filled, amazing test of both skill and insight. A social dynamo, you need a relationship that allows you the freedom to interact with a variety of people in many different situations. Your flirtatious charm endears you to everyone and you seek relationships that understand and support your need to keep life entertaining and light.

Sexually, you are a delightful mixture of entertainment and naughtiness that is constantly seeking new twists on old games. You are not one to let life get stale, and with the winsome wink of an eye, you can change personalities and desires faster than the flip of a coin. Your intimate life is your antidote for life's insanities and you are happiest with someone who can keep up with your ever changing fascinations.

It is no simple matter to get and keep your attention when there is so much for you to see and do. You crave someone who can keep your pace and introduce you to new things, often. Spontaneous personalities always keep you happily intrigued and wondering what will happen next. Upbeat and optimistic friends are your cure for a dull life and your answer to staying delightfully committed.

A male born in the sign of Leo in 1930 wants a woman who is upbeat, sassy and, most of all, someone he can learn from. You prefer women who radiate from the inside out with total health and beauty and aren't afraid to show off their brains. If she can keep you laughing while helping you manage your endless list of projects, then you become happily hooked for life.

If you are a 1930 female Leo, you are looking for a man who knows how to wear his attitude well. The ability to ask your opinion and advice on even the smallest matters (and listen) is the thing that you look for and expect from your ideal man. Good-natured and well-intentioned, he should also be a little dramatic with a playful spirit that understands your need for constant communication.

1930 VIRGO
From August 23, 21:26 through September 23, 18:35

The Idealistic Pragmatist

As a 1930 Virgo, you are committed to healthy and fruitful relationships that nurture the mind and body as well as the spirit. What you seek is an extraordinary kind of intimacy that transcends mere words and borders on emotional telepathy. Nurturing and growth oriented, you stay committed to the path of self-improvement and better living and see your relationship as a springboard from which you move past your personal challenges.

Sex is a deep, intimate, and extraordinarily emotional activity for you that unleashes a sensitive side that is rarely seen in public. Your attention to nuances and subtleties create hypersensitivity with a lover who knows immediately when something is amiss. Your fidelity is legendary and you require someone who appreciates and upholds the sanctity of your type of bonding.

For you, competence and efficiency are things to be celebrated, and if someone wants to get your attention, giving you an opportunity to display your amazing problem solving skills is the fastest way to get noticed. If they are sure to appreciate and cherish you for these very same gifts, then they are guaranteed to stay in the best places of your heart. You are a secret sentimentalist and are genuinely thrilled with love notes and simple, well considered tokens of appreciation that show how much someone cares about you.

A Virgo male born in 1930 relishes his role as family provider and looks for a woman who can offer graciousness, support, and an innovative perspective to a strong sense of home and family. The first qualities you look for in a female are sensitivity and fidelity. Ideally, you are best matched with a woman who can create an environment where your creative side can flourish and thrive.

As a 1930 female Virgo, you are best matched with a traditional type of man who is earthy, sensual, and pays attention to important romantic details. You will not settle for anything less than someone who is capable of making life run smoother for you. You are happiest with someone who has a strong character and is genuinely devoted to home and family.

EMIL JANNINGS
German Actor
Mars in Virgo

1930 LIBRA
From September 23, 18:36 through October 24, 3:25

The Complicated Sensualist

As a 1930 Libra, you seek a deeper kind of relationship with more emotional substance than most people. You are an intense idealist and will work ceaselessly at expanding your relationship into a meaningful, balanced expression of both love and fairness. You are generous with your time and affections when you have decided that you are, definitely, involved with someone and not casually spending time with each other. You need someone who understands the intense intimacy that you demand as well as the equal measure of personal space that you need to stay emotionally balanced.

You are a sensualist and the act of intimacy is something that you would create into an art form, each and every time, if you could. Sensitive to all of the subtleties and intricacies in a good seduction, you need to be able to set the right mood or you feel as if something was irrevocably lost in the moment. You see yourself as an artist when it comes to love and will not allow your creative inspirations to be rushed or treated casually.

You are sensitive to first impressions and a well-presented package gets your attention immediately. For you, elegantly coordinated sight, sound, and smell create an unmistakable symphony in your mind that leave a lasting impression. You are searching for an oasis of beautiful feelings and will only surrender completely and commit to someone with whom you can create this delicate emotional garden.

A 1930 male born in the sign of Libra flourishes under the attention of a secure woman who understands his emotional complexity. Your best match is with a woman who will enjoy analyzing with you all the nuances of your relationship and appreciates your refined sensibilities tailored into a masculine exterior.

A 1930 female Libra dreams of a man who is a combination of definable, gentle masculinity and poetic, emotional expression. You are seeking a man who believes in chivalry and courtly love, someone who can thrive in his role of protector and still seize those unexpected moments of romantic opportunities that ignite your passionate fire.

Your Love Planets

YOUR ROMANTIC SIDE   p. 696
▶ **VENUS IN SAGITTARIUS**
Born Oct. 24, 3:26 - Nov. 22, 7:43
▶ **VENUS IN SCORPIO**
Born Nov. 22, 7:44 - Nov. 23, 0:33

YOUR SEX DRIVE   p. 722
▶ **MARS IN LEO**
Born Oct. 24, 3:26 - Nov. 23, 0:33

YOUR CELEBRITY TWINS   p. 760
Find out the astrological similarities you have with famous people.

YOUR COMPATIBILITY   p. 780
Compare planets to find out how compatible you are in a relationship.

YOUR RELATIONSHIP KARMA   p. 824
▶ **SATURN IN CAPRICORN**
Born Oct. 24, 3:26 - Nov. 23, 0:33

FRANCES DEE
American Actress
Sun and Venus in Sagittarius

104

SAGITTARIUS ZODIAC SIGN

Your Love Planets

YOUR ROMANTIC SIDE   p. 696
▶ **VENUS IN SCORPIO**
Born Nov. 23, 0:34 - Dec. 22, 13:39

YOUR SEX DRIVE   p. 722
▶ **MARS IN LEO**
Born Nov. 23, 0:34 - Dec. 22, 13:39

YOUR CELEBRITY TWINS   p. 760
Find out the astrological similarities you have with famous people.

YOUR COMPATIBILITY   p. 780
Compare planets to find out how compatible you are in a relationship.

YOUR RELATIONSHIP KARMA   p. 824
▶ **SATURN IN CAPRICORN**
Born Nov. 23, 0:34 - Dec. 22, 13:39

1930 SCORPIO
From October 24, 3:26 through November 23, 0:33

The Willful Romantic

As a 1930 Scorpio, your relationships must be as fiery, dramatic, and intense as every great romance story you have ever heard—or you are simply not getting involved. You seek out a relationship that challenges you to the point of being impossible for weaker mortals, and you never flinch at the thought of possibly getting in over your head. For you, real love is a monumental experience filled with intense emotional and life defining moments—or it is not love at all.

A sexual dynamo, you have a lusty and extravagant appetite that is only matched by your determination to conquer your lover's heart, mind, and fantasies and be the "one and only." Once committed, your dramatic and impulsive side shows. Your moments of unpredictable and voracious appetite ensure your lover's complete and rapt consideration.

If someone really wanted to get and keep your attention, all they need to do is have the kind of inner strength that can look you in the eye and mean every word they are saying. Pride and bravery are big words in your vocabulary, and being able to respect someone for exactly those things get a nod of approval and a second look from you. You want someone who will not be conquered by you, and someone who is polished on the outside and tougher than nails on the inside.

A male 1930 Scorpio is looking for a strong personality paired with classic beauty and an undying loyalty. Like Bogey and Bacall, you want the kind of woman who can love as passionately as she fights and is always in your corner when the chips are down. Your ideal match is a woman who understands your passionate personality and inspires you to be the larger than life hero that you believe in.

If you are a female 1930 Scorpio, you inspire men to fall in love with you, yet search for a man that you can fall head over heels for, deeply and totally. Freedom loving and completely indomitable, you may commit but you will never allow yourself to be conquered. You are looking for a man who can accept your strength and power without ever letting you forget that you are all woman, all the time.

1930 SAGITTARIUS
From November 23, 0:34 through December 22, 13:39

The Passionate Explorer

As a 1930 Sagittarius, you are looking for the kind of relationship that offers complete freedom of movement and a secure, uncompromising bond that knows no boundaries or limitations in time or space. You love as passionately as you play and because of this, you seek out a relationship that offers you a complete range of new challenges and experiences. More than a lover, you are seeking a sexy and secure traveling partner in your endless adventurous quest for a fully lived life.

You are a physically passionate person with a sexually competitive nature. Easily bored with an appetite for novelty, you crave someone who not only can keep pace with you but can also serve you a few surprises. You like your intimate relationships to have an edge that keeps you completely focused on the moment. Your appetites are strong and undeniable and you prefer partners who can handle both the volume and the intensity of your desires.

A good challenge is always the best way to get your attention and being a good sport is the only way to keep it. You love the novel and the exciting and will often be drawn to people who know how to push your buttons in all the right ways. You want someone who pushes you to be bigger, better, and more of who you are in every way and knows how to keep the sense of fun and adventure in your romance.

A male 1930 Sagittarius is a hunter, an explorer, and an action hero. Your ideal woman is a magnetic combination of intensely confident sexiness and passionate life-loving drama. She is the beautiful, no-nonsense, take-charge heroine of your dreams who could keep up with your wildest ways if she wanted to, always keeps you covered in a crisis, and never lets you forget that she is all woman, always.

As a female 1930 Sagittarius, you are looking for the kind of man that sets your imagination on fire. You like your men rough and tumble with just a little bit of bad boy humor thrown in for good measure. No shrinking violet yourself, your perfect match is someone who can appreciate an all-weather kind of girl who knows how to make anything exciting.

Marlene Dietrich – Queen of Illusion

Marlene Dietrich made her entrance into the world on December 27, 1901, in Berlin, under a Capricorn Sun and a Leo Moon. Legendary star of stage and screen, famous for her steely looks, smoky voice, and marvelous legs, she lived her life as an orchestrated illusion and image, aided by her innate self-discipline and personal courage.

Trained as a violinist, a wrist injury caused her to change direction and she set her sights on acting. Berlin was a wild, decadent town in the early 1920s, and Dietrich, though married to casting director Rudy Sieber and the mother of a newborn, absorbed the eroticism around her, working in the cabarets and visiting the clubs. Her persona appealed equally to men and women, and she embarked on many affairs with lovers of both sexes.

Director Josef von Sternberg arrived in Germany on the hunt for a new actress, but not just any actress. Dietrich's cultivated air of indifference and cool contempt was the quality he was looking for, and he took control of every aspect of her life to turn her into a screen goddess. In *The Blue Angel*, Dietrich played Lola Lola, a cabaret dancer. The film opened to rave reviews, and with a contract from Paramount in hand, Dietrich left for the US.

Her first American film, *Morocco*, had her playing yet another cabaret dancer, this time one who appeared wearing white tie and tails and kissing a female member of the audience on the lips. Her androgynous appearance and behavior struck a chord with males and females

alike. The tux and tails became a major component of her image.

It was from von Sternberg that she learned about film lighting to achieve a certain look. She became so knowledgeable that she carried her own lighting fixtures with her and was even made an honorary member of the technicians' union.

After her initial success in the US, her penchant for being difficult during filming was bad enough that Paramount bought out her contract. She was bombarded by offers from Joseph Goebbels, Hitler's minister of propaganda, to come home to Germany to make films. Dietrich detested the Nazis and when the US entered WWII, she abandoned her

failing movie career to join the USO and perform for the Allies in Europe. She was declared a traitor by Germany and she risked her life to perform for the US troops in often primitive and dangerous conditions. In 1947 the US War Department gave her the Medal of Freedom for her efforts, and France made her a Chevalier of the Legion d'Honneur.

At loose ends after the war, she missed the close contact and rapport she had developed with the soldiers, her "boys." Film work held no more attraction for her and at the suggestion of her friend Noel Coward, she developed her own one-woman show, eventually becoming the world's highest paid nightclub entertainer. But alcohol and stage falls took their toll and she performed her last show in 1975.

In 1984 she agreed to a documentary, but only if she wasn't filmed. She refused to let her deteriorating image be shown. She spent the rest of her life virtually alone, struggling to maintain the illusion of "Dietrich"—her creation—and died in Paris in 1992.

> *"If she had nothing more than her voice she could break your heart with it."*
>
> ERNEST HEMINGWAY

105

▶ READ ABOUT ERNEST HEMINGWAY ON PAGE 180 ▶ READ ABOUT LOUISE BROOKS, ANOTHER DARING ACTRESS, ON PAGE 95

1931

- ⭐ GAMBLING ON DIVORCE
- ⭐ SEX CHANGE
- ⭐ PRIVATE LIVES
- ⭐ GRAND HOTEL
- ⭐ THE THRILL IS GONE
- ⭐ BACK STREET

EVENTS

It was quite a year for the institution of marriage. Irish author James Joyce made an honest woman of Nora Barnacle, his companion of 26 years. Aviator Amelia Earhart also married— but not before asking her fiance, publisher George Putnam, for an amicable split if it didn't work out. And Mrs. Josef von Sternberg initiated proceedings against Marlene Dietrich, the star of the film *The Blue Angel*, for the "alienation of her husband's affection." The Republican government of Spain legalized divorce, though all divorces and remarriages were nullified years later under the fascist Franco regime. The National Education Association reported that 75 percent of all cities banned the employment of married women. Scientific progress was made when the male sex hormone androgen was isolated, while Einar Weigner, a Danish painter, had his sex altered in the first surgical procedure of its kind.

POP CULTURE

In Charlie Chaplin's silent *City Lights*, his Little Tramp falls in love with a blind girl who mistakes him for a rich man. Noel Coward's play *Private Lives*, about a divorced couple who honeymoon with their new spouses at the same resort, hit the big screen, to critical acclaim. Cult horror characters were brought to life when both *Dracula* and *Frankenstein* premiered. Perhaps the year's most memorable screen scene was James Cagney smashing a grapefruit into Mae Clarke's face in *The Public Enemy*.

Hot Couple

With the Depression in full swing, a hit song assured that "Life Is Just a Bowl of Cherries." Cab Calloway crooned about "Minnie the Moocher," Kate Smith had a hit with "When the Moon Comes Over the Mountain," and an accordion standard was born with "Lady of Spain." The year's hits also included "You Rascal You," "Dream A Little Dream of Me," and "The Thrill Is Gone."

Pearl Buck's *The Good Earth* told the story of a Chinese farmer and his selfless wife. Vicki Baum's *Grand Hotel* explored tales of love lost and found by the transient occupants of a lavish Berlin hotel. Daphne du Maurier's *The Loving Spirit* was a family melodrama spanning three generations. Graham Greene's *Rumor at Nightfall* focused on a dangerous love triangle, while in Fannie Hurst's *Back Street*, a woman makes sacrifices for her long-term affair with an unavailable man.

AMELIA EARHART & GEORGE PUTNAM

On the morning of February 7, 1931, their wedding day, Amelia Earhart gave husband-to-be publisher George Putnam a short note explaining her fears about marriage. "Let us not interfere with the other's work or play, nor let the world see our private joys or disagreements." She asked to be let go in a year if they were not happy. But after a year they were still together.

In 1937 she disappeared somewhere over the South Pacific on a flight around the world—her fate became one of the great mysteries of the 20th century. *Soaring Wings*, published two years later, was Putnam's biographical tribute to her.

SEE ALSO
▶ CHARLES LINDBERGH & ANNE MORROW *Page 88*

1931 CAPRICORN

From December 22, 1930 13:40 through January 21, 1931 0:17
(December 1931 Capricorns, see 1932 Capricorn)

♑ *The Quiet Adventurer*

Capricorn of 1931, you are as steady and reliable as the proverbial Swiss watch and when it comes to relationships, you are just as steadfast. Though you may have had a wandering eye in your younger years, once you have made a commitment, you can be relied upon to fulfill your promises. Though you may be a bit reticent to express your feelings, all you need is the time and space to thoroughly examine your innermost thoughts. Then, you are quite willing to demonstrate your ardor to your loved one.

Passionate and confident, you need a partner who can match your strong desires. And, even though you are traditional, you do have an adventurous spirit that occasionally seeks to express itself. As long as you are with a partner whom you trust, you are not afraid to let this zany side show. Through the years, you have learned many ways to delight yourself and your partner in order to keep your desire for each other fresh and alive.

To really get your attention, a prospective mate should be acquainted with all the finer things that life has to offer. Nothing pleases you more than to share a bottle of fine wine, a sumptuous dinner, and good conversation with a kindred soul. Whether it is a trip to Zanzibar or trying out the latest chic ethnic cuisine, your companion should be ready to travel with you, both physically and philosophically.

The ideal female for the 1931 male Capricorn is one who constantly seeks to grow as a person. You place a high value on intellectual pursuits and you really enjoy a woman who is interesting and well read. It also helps if she shares your point of view, has similar values and priorities, and doesn't mind letting you take the lead when it comes to making major decisions for the two of you.

Female Capricorns born in 1931 desire a man who is strong, proud, and determined. After all, they need to be able to stand up to your own strong personality. Your mate should possess a high degree of integrity and be willing to take responsibility seriously. Likewise, they can count on you to do the right thing and to be ever faithful to those you love.

CAPRICORN ZODIAC SIGN
YOUR LOVE PLANETS

YOUR ROMANTIC SIDE   p. 696
▶ **VENUS IN SCORPIO**
Born Dec. 22, 1930 13:40 - Jan. 03, 1931 20:02
▶ **VENUS IN SAGITTARIUS**
Born Jan. 03, 20:03 - Jan. 21, 0:17

YOUR SEX DRIVE   p. 722
▶ **MARS IN LEO**
Born Dec. 22, 1930 13:40 - Jan. 21, 1931 0:17

YOUR CELEBRITY TWINS   p. 760
Find out the astrological similarities you have with famous people.

YOUR COMPATIBILITY   p. 780
Compare planets to find out how compatible you are in a relationship.

YOUR RELATIONSHIP KARMA   p. 824
▶ **SATURN IN CAPRICORN**
Born Dec. 22, 1930 13:40 - Jan. 21, 1931 0:17

PEARL BUCK
American Writer
Mars in Aquarius

107

1931 AQUARIUS

From January 21, 0:18 through February 19, 14:39

♒ *The True Companion*

You place a high value on friendship, 1931 Aquarius and, therefore, your partner must be your best friend as well as your lover. Never content with things as they are, you also want a relationship that challenges you and stimulates you to achieve new heights. The freedom to express yourself is paramount and you need to be in a relationship that gives you the space to explore your wide range of interests.

Communication and intellectual compatibility are of primary importance to you, making you quite unlikely to be interested in the more superficial qualities that attract most people. What really turns you on is the mental union you can forge with another. Once you've achieved that connection, the physical allure attraction grows quickly. Your sexuality is as unconventional as you are and you are willing to try anything once, especially if it will please your partner.

In order to tickle your fancy, a potential partner should engage you in conversation. Talking about anything unusual—avant-garde theater or art, astrology, science fiction—is sure to capture your attention. Over the long haul, however, you are more likely to become involved with someone who feels as deeply as you do about humanitarian causes and world affairs.

As a 1931 Aquarian male, your ideal partner is an independent woman who can give you both the companionship and freedom you need. Finding this delicate balance is likely to take a lifetime with you, Aquarius, as teacher, friend, and lover. You also need a woman who has a sense of adventure and enjoys the outdoors. Though you love to be different, you are most comfortable, however, with someone who is a bit more traditional.

The perfect male for the 1931 Aquarian female is one who is sociable, generous, and warm-hearted. You like it when your partner is the center of attention as long as you are the one that he adores. Though you don't like to be told what to do, you respect a man who knows his own mind and will fight for his beliefs. The man for you is unquestionably honest and loyal, a hard worker who enjoys the simple things in life.

AQUARIUS ZODIAC SIGN
YOUR LOVE PLANETS

YOUR ROMANTIC SIDE   p. 696
▶ **VENUS IN SAGITTARIUS**
Born Jan. 21, 0:18 - Feb. 06, 12:24
▶ **VENUS IN CAPRICORN**
Born Feb. 06, 12:25 - Feb. 19, 14:39

YOUR SEX DRIVE   p. 722
▶ **MARS IN LEO**
Born Jan. 21, 0:18 - Feb. 16, 14:26
▶ **MARS IN CANCER**
Born Feb. 16, 14:27 - Feb. 19, 14:39

YOUR CELEBRITY TWINS   p. 760
Find out the astrological similarities you have with famous people.

YOUR COMPATIBILITY   p. 780
Compare planets to find out how compatible you are in a relationship.

YOUR RELATIONSHIP KARMA   p. 824
▶ **SATURN IN CAPRICORN**
Born Jan. 21, 0:18 - Feb. 19, 14:39

GEORGE BRENT
Irish Actor
Sun in Pisces

1931 PISCES
From February 19, 14:40 through March 21, 14:05

♓ The Determined Dreamer

You, 1931 Pisces, are a marvelous combination of intuitive thought and strong-mindedness. Once you decide what you want, you are able to bring it into your life. This gift extends to relationships and you know just how to use your uncanny instincts for understanding what makes another tick to make them yours. Though you possess considerable charm and can be very flirtatious in social situations, you are, at heart, as faithful and true as they come.

Intimacy comes quite naturally to you and when you connect with a person, you are willing to share all of yourself—physically, mentally, emotionally, and spiritually. In fact, you may find it hard to separate where you end and your loved one begins. But, your ability to invest yourself emotionally in another makes you an attentive and supportive lover and mate. In fact, your private moments are likely to be utterly blissful and intense.

Though you are quite romantic, you have a practical side as well. A potential lover would do well to appeal to both sides of your contradictory nature. They might suggest working together on a household project by day. After all, two can work twice as quickly as one. Then, there will be plenty of time and energy left over for a quiet candlelight dinner and the two of you may even dance the night away.

As a 1931 Pisces male, you are attracted to a woman who is ambitious, strong, and practical but can still be feminine and soft. You want to be able to stare deeply into her eyes and see the compassion and gentleness you so desperately need. But, you also want to know that you can count on her enormous strength to bolster you when the going gets tough.

The ideal male for you, 1931 Pisces female, has a gentle certainty that can see you through the inevitable ups and downs of life. You respect hard work and ambition and need the security of knowing that you are ready for whatever may come your way. Your man should be able to move mountains, if necessary, in order to overcome any difficulties. But, you also want someone who is affectionate and knows how to relax and enjoy life with you.

1931 ARIES
From March 21, 14:06 through April 21, 1:39

♈ The Inspired Go-getter

Aries of 1931, you are usually the first in your group to try something new. A true leader, you are a stimulating blend of daredevil action and brilliant perception. You crave excitement and, especially in your youth, the thrill of the chase may have been more enjoyable than the nitty-gritty reality of an ongoing relationship. But, you have a deep sensitivity that yearns to love and be loved.

Your appetites are large and you approach relationships with the enthusiasm of a child on their first outing to the amusement park. Anxious to experience all that there is and willing to try anything once, you are an exhilarating partner. For you, there is nothing worse than boredom and routine and you will try your best to keep that spark of interest glowing and growing.

A prospective partner can first interest you with a bit of old-fashioned flirting and some clever verbal repartee. Then, they might propose a day at a casino, a racetrack, or a sporting event. As long as the action is fast and there's a crowd, you are game. But, to hold your attention for the whole nine yards, they will need to be able to make every day seem like a new challenge and every night seem like the first.

As a 1931 Aries male, you want a woman who is imaginative, kindhearted, and giving. You look for a dreamy, delicate quality in your mate, one who can counterbalance your take-charge attitude. And, it is important that she can handle your spontaneity and that she is able to surprise you on occasion as well. Above all, she must be willing to let you take the lead and have the freedom to be your own man, while she remains a constant source of support and love.

The perfect man for a 1931 Aries woman is one who can allow you to be as independent as you like. You equate dependency with weakness and you need a man that not only understands this, that but also knows that your strength does not make him weak. While you love competition, you do not appreciate it when it comes to love. You must know that your man is devoted to you and that no other woman could ever compare in his eyes.

1931 TAURUS

From April 21, 1:40 through May 22, 1:14

The Thoughtful Pragmatist

Taurus of 1931, you are thoughtful and resourceful, and you place a great value on your home and family life. In fact, it is likely that you have devoted yourself to your loved ones and that you derive a great deal of pleasure from what has taken you a lifetime to build. You understand the importance of having a firm foundation in a relationship and you possess the patience necessary to build upon that foundation to create your very own Taj Mahal.

Earthy and passionate by nature, you enjoy the closeness that romantic love has to offer. You are loving and sensual, and pleasing your partner is paramount in your mind. Your style is slow and deliberate and, as you steadily stoke the fire of desire, you take pleasure in knowing that you are quietly building a raging inferno. Of course, you will happily go to any lengths to make sure that your lover is satisfied.

You are quiet and reserved, and a wise potential lover makes sure that you are not put off by grand gestures or brashness. You are much more receptive to someone who has a simple and down-to-earth approach. Since you love beautiful things, a visit to a museum or art gallery may be the ticket to stir your soul and your emotions. But, most of all, anyone interested in capturing your heart needs to be patient while you take the time to be absolutely sure of your feelings.

The perfect woman for the 1931 Taurus male is one who is romantic, loyal, and able to express her feelings. While you want someone who is exciting and fun, you also need to feel secure and know that you are loved and can safely express your innermost thoughts. Most of all, she should enjoy making a comfortable home for you and your family and be content with the simple pleasures that life has to offer.

As a 1931 female, you need a mate who is fiery and strong, someone who is confident and can take charge in any situation. Your ideal man is friendly, generous, and willing to indulge your exquisite tastes. But, you also value financial security and it is important that he know how to balance his spending impulses with careful planning for the future.

TAURUS ZODIAC SIGN
YOUR LOVE PLANETS

YOUR ROMANTIC SIDE   p. 696
- ▶ **VENUS IN PISCES**
  Born Apr. 21, 1:40 - Apr. 26, 2:09
- ▶ **VENUS IN ARIES**
  Born Apr. 26, 2:10 - May 21, 2:37
- ▶ **VENUS IN TAURUS**
  Born May 21, 2:38 - May 22, 1:14

YOUR SEX DRIVE   p. 722
- ▶ **MARS IN LEO**
  Born Apr. 21, 1:40 - May 22, 1:14

YOUR CELEBRITY TWINS   p. 760
Find out the astrological similarities you have with famous people.

YOUR COMPATIBILITY   p. 780
Compare planets to find out how compatible you are in a relationship.

YOUR RELATIONSHIP KARMA   p. 824
- ▶ **SATURN IN CAPRICORN**
  Born Apr. 21, 1:40 - May 22, 1:14

MARTHA GRAHAM
American Dancer
Sun in Taurus

1931 GEMINI

From May 22, 1:15 through June 22, 9:27

The Versatile Communicator

Gemini of 1931, you are blessed with the ability to communicate with almost anyone, delighting listeners with your quick wit and clever use of language. Interesting and vivacious, you have a gift of making others feel as if they are the most fascinating person alive. This is quite an asset when it comes to relationships and it is likely that you have never lacked for admirers. But, you also treasure the intimacy that can only come from a long-term relationship with one special person.

Agile and versatile, you seek variety in all things and lovemaking is no exception. You are naturally youthful and have an irrepressible way of making the most mundane activities seem fresh and new. Though you are quite sensual and enjoy the physical pleasures that love has to offer, you also have a strong mental component to your sexuality and are quite likely to be excited by the whisper of "sweet nothings" in your ear.

In order to be of interest to you, a would-be partner should engage you in a conversation about current events, the latest hit film, or hottest celebrity gossip. It is also important that they share some of your many interests and have a zest for trying new things. They would do well to suggest an afternoon perusing the stacks at the used bookstore. Or, you certainly would enjoy walking through the city, browsing in the shops and sharing a drink at a sidewalk café.

As a 1931 Gemini male, you want a woman that can be both playful and spontaneous as well as solid and reliable. She should be a good conversationalist but also be secure enough in herself to be comfortable with the quieter moments that inevitably follow your bursts of activity. But, most of all, the woman for you is one who doesn't mind giving you the freedom you need to be yourself.

The perfect man for the 1931 Gemini female is one that has an adventurous spirit, is fond of travel, and likes to be on the move. Though you love your home and family, you also need a lot of stimulation to keep life interesting. It helps if your man understands this and has a similar thirst for exploring the wonders of the world.

GEMINI ZODIAC SIGN
YOUR LOVE PLANETS

YOUR ROMANTIC SIDE   p. 696
- ▶ **VENUS IN TAURUS**
  Born May 22, 1:15 - June 14, 23:03
- ▶ **VENUS IN GEMINI**
  Born June 14, 23:04 - June 22, 9:27

YOUR SEX DRIVE   p. 722
- ▶ **MARS IN LEO**
  Born May 22, 1:15 - June 10, 14:57
- ▶ **MARS IN VIRGO**
  Born June 10, 14:58 - June 22, 9:27

YOUR CELEBRITY TWINS   p. 760
Find out the astrological similarities you have with famous people.

YOUR COMPATIBILITY   p. 780
Compare planets to find out how compatible you are in a relationship.

YOUR RELATIONSHIP KARMA   p. 824
- ▶ **SATURN IN CAPRICORN**
  Born May 22, 1:15 - June 22, 9:27

JAMES CAGNEY
American Actor
Sun and Venus in Cancer

110

1931 CANCER
From June 22, 9:28 through July 23, 20:20

The Tender Nurturer

You have a kind and gentle temperament, 1931 Cancer, and you are very protective of those you love. Born to take care of others, you are a loving and sensitive partner in a relationship. You have a compassionate nature giving you the ability to really understand the feelings of others. Emotional security is important to you and when you feel threatened, you may, like a crab, either withdraw into your shell or use your sharp pinchers to defend yourself.

When you are first getting to know someone, you are likely to be quite cautious about giving yourself to him or her fully. But, once you feel safe, there is nothing that you like more than to lavish affection and attention on your loved one. Thanks to a highly developed intuitive sense, you can easily read your lover. And, because you are so ready to please another, you are willing to adapt yourself to their needs.

A prospective mate can get your notice by showing an interest in your family and sharing stories of their childhood with you. Roots are important to you and knowing about your mate's background helps you to really understand them. Afterwards, they might offer to prepare a home cooked meal for you, making sure to include all the yummy comfort foods that you love so much.

As a 1931 Cancer man, you need a woman who understands how truly sensitive you are and who is not intimidated by your powerful feelings. She should also make you feel comfortable enough to share your emotions with her. Your ideal woman is an excellent listener but is also able to draw you out of your shell when you are in a sullen mood. Most of all, you need someone who doesn't mind being taken care of and won't rebel at your protective behavior.

The perfect man for a 1931 Cancer woman is hard working and resourceful and someone who doesn't mind spending a lot of time at home working on household projects or gardening. It's important that he be practical about money since security is such an important issue with you. Because you hate stinginess of any type, it is important that he be generous in spirit as well as with his time and money.

1931 LEO
From July 23, 20:21 through August 24, 3:09

The Noble Superstar

You are larger than life, 1931 Leo, and you really know how to make the most of every day. Warm and generous, others can't help but want to bask in the glow of your sunny personality, making you the center of attention in most social situations. An optimist at heart, you tend to give others the benefit of the doubt. In relationships, you are caring, open, and loyal, and expect the same in return.

Straightforward and unafraid, you are willing to plunge into intimacy with complete abandon. Once you feel confident about your partner's feelings towards you, nothing can hold back your ardor. You take a great deal of pride in being able to please your partner and your approach to lovemaking is as powerful as you are. Experience is a wonderful teacher and, like a fine wine, your style improves with age.

To capture your attention, a potential partner should always make sure to look his or her best. It is important to flatter you, building your confidence and allowing you to beam with self-assurance. To appeal to your dramatic nature, tickets to a play or a concert would be right up your alley. Or, since you love sports, you would certainly enjoy a good tennis match or a round or two of golf. Of course, the end to the perfect day would be dinner with friends at the most popular eatery in town.

As a 1931 Leo male, you need a woman that you can be proud of and that will create a warm and cozy atmosphere for you, your family, and friends. It is important that your lady is friendly, well spoken, and confident enough to be at your side on center stage. But, above all, you need a woman who can devote herself to you and give you the loving attention you require.

The ideal man for the 1931 Leo female is imaginative enough to help inspire your creativity and practical enough to be able to make all your dreams come true. You have a great deal of inner strength and you need a man who is able to match your intensity. He should enjoy entertaining and socializing with friends as much as you do. Most importantly, you need someone who has the capacity to be faithful to you for a lifetime.

1931 VIRGO

From August 24, 3:10 through September 24, 0:22

The True Perfectionist

With your ability to pay attention to every detail, 1931 Virgo, you notice things that most people miss. Careful, considerate, and thoughtful, you try to treat others with the respect and dignity that you want for yourself. You are quite self-sufficient and may find it hard to let your guard down enough to really allow yourself to need another person. But, once you do, you are able to give yourself in a relationship without reservation.

Being aware of every nuance is a decided advantage when it comes to lovemaking. You can sense how well your partner responds to each and every touch and you are sure to store this knowledge in your memory bank for future use. You are never careless and you always strive for perfection—two traits that are likely to be quite appreciated by your partner. In return, however, you expect the same attentive care that you are so willing to give.

A prospective mate might capture your interest by appealing to your strong work ethic and your desire to achieve results. Therefore, they would do well to tell you the details of their latest endeavors and be sure to ask for your advice on how to better streamline their task. Since your critical eye is sure to notice every one of their strong points as well as each imperfection, they would be wise to go over their appearance very carefully to make sure that they are as fastidiously groomed as you.

The ideal female for the 1931 Virgo male is someone who shares your same high standards of perfection. You want a woman who is orderly and thorough, not afraid of hard work, and someone who enjoys doing things the right way. She also needs to be tough enough to withstand your occasional criticism, which you offer in the spirit of helping her to do her best.

1931 Virgo female, your ideal man is fair and balanced and someone who doesn't go to extremes. You need a man who is soft-spoken and gentle, one that is careful not to offend your delicate sensibilities. Confrontation is not your style and you need someone who is capable of discussing problems rather than bullying you into doing things their way.

VIRGO ZODIAC SIGN
YOUR LOVE PLANETS

YOUR ROMANTIC SIDE   p. 696
▶ VENUS IN LEO
Born Aug. 24, 3:10 - Aug. 27, 10:41
▶ VENUS IN VIRGO
Born Aug. 27, 10:42 - Sept. 20, 14:14
▶ VENUS IN LIBRA
Born Sept. 20, 14:15 - Sept. 24, 0:22

YOUR SEX DRIVE   p. 722
▶ MARS IN LIBRA
Born Aug. 24, 3:10 - Sept. 17, 8:42
▶ MARS IN SCORPIO
Born Sept. 17, 8:43 - Sept. 24, 0:22

YOUR CELEBRITY TWINS   p. 760
Find out the astrological similarities you have with famous people.

YOUR COMPATIBILITY   p. 780
Compare planets to find out how compatible you are in a relationship.

YOUR RELATIONSHIP KARMA   p. 824
▶ SATURN IN CAPRICORN
Born Aug. 24, 3:10 - Sept. 24, 0:22

MAE CLARK
American Actress
Mars in Virgo

1931 LIBRA

From September 24, 0:23 through October 24, 9:15

The Passionate Artisan

You, 1931 Libra, are blessed with an uncanny ability for diplomacy, grace, and determination. One of your greatest gifts is to be able to find the balance between two extremes. Like Buddha, you know that walking the middle ground is one of life's great challenges. You are exceptionally fair and understand the give-and-take that is necessary to keep a relationship strong and vital. And, because you love the idea of love, you know that a relationship is necessary for you to fulfill your potential as an individual.

An ardent lover, you are quite passionate and intense about your sensuality. Capable of reaching great heights of ecstasy, you thoroughly enjoy all the accoutrements of romance—sweet smelling flowers, silky sheets, and sultry candlelight. Once the stage is set, you are ready to indulge all your senses in the satisfying pleasure that your partner has to offer.

Communication is very important to you and a potential partner first needs to reach you mentally. Once the mental connection is made, you are open to exploring what other possibilities for relationship may exist. An engaging conversation about current events, pop culture, or the "good old days" is likely to tantalize and delight you and you are apt to be quite willing to come back for more. But, to really capture your heart, there needs to be a deeper, more spiritual link, a soul connection that cannot be planned or contrived.

The perfect woman for the 1931 Libra male shares your high regard for harmony in your environment. Never brash or boisterous, your ideal has an ethereal quality to her movements and approaches life with grace. Not only can she charm you but others are sure to notice just how lucky you are to have such a captivating partner.

As a 1931 Libra female, you want a man who is deeply ambitious. It is also important for you to be with someone who is decisive and confident and who can lead you through the more mundane details of existence. That way, you are free to concentrate on what you do best—making your environment a serene and peaceful oasis from the realities of everyday life.

LIBRA ZODIAC SIGN
YOUR LOVE PLANETS

YOUR ROMANTIC SIDE   p. 696
▶ VENUS IN LIBRA
Born Sept. 24, 0:23 - Oct. 14, 15:44
▶ VENUS IN SCORPIO
Born Oct. 14, 15:45 - Oct. 24, 9:15

YOUR SEX DRIVE   p. 722
▶ MARS IN SCORPIO
Born Sept. 24, 0:23 - Oct. 24, 9:15

YOUR CELEBRITY TWINS   p. 760
Find out the astrological similarities you have with famous people.

YOUR COMPATIBILITY   p. 780
Compare planets to find out how compatible you are in a relationship.

YOUR RELATIONSHIP KARMA   p. 824
▶ SATURN IN CAPRICORN
Born Sept. 24, 0:23 - Oct. 24, 9:15

ANDRE GIDE
French Writer
Sun and Mars in Sagittarius

1931 SCORPIO
From October 24, 9:16 through November 23, 6:24

The Earnest Enigma

Scorpio of 1931, you are a powerful blend of mystery and sincerity who is able to enchant a room with the force of your magnetic personality. You take relationships very sincerely and you are not the type to have casual flings. In fact, you feel your emotions so deeply that you may find that you are too intense for others to understand. But, for those who are unafraid to explore the deep recesses of the soul, you are a marvelous and willing trail guide, for you have been there many times.

With your enormous stockpile of charisma, you attract others like the proverbial moth to a flame. As you might expect, you are as passionate about lovemaking as you are about everything else. Not content with any superficial efforts, you use your special verve to unabashedly make each encounter an exciting adventure. And, when you find someone with whom to share these escapades into ecstasy, you expect them to be totally committed to you in return.

In order for someone to get your attention, they should make sure to surround themselves in an air of secrecy. You really love to peel each layer of the onion and enjoy discovering something new about your partner at each level. Once you are a bit enthralled with a potential mate, they might suggest spending a mystery weekend at a secluded country inn where you can use your talent for digging deep to ferret out the truth in any situation.

As a 1931 Scorpio male, your ideal woman is intuitive and emotional but also has her feet planted firmly on the ground. You need a woman who has the patience and fortitude to draw you out since you don't easily share what you are feeling. And, she needs to be able to help you see the lighter side of things, to help you think of the glass as half full rather than half empty.

The perfect man for the 1931 Scorpio female is generous, trustworthy, and outgoing. He should be able to give you confidence in the fact that he will be there for you during those inevitable dark moments that we all must face. In return, he can be secure in the fact that you will be a devoted helpmate to him for the rest of your life.

1931 SAGITTARIUS
From November 23, 6:25 through December 22, 19:29

The Practical Optimist

You are a fascinating blend of hopefulness and common sense, 1931 Sagittarius, making you able to easily meet whatever challenges life throws in your path. You use this same matter-of-fact approach in relationships and, while some may think that you are a bit too like Pollyanna, you have found that giving someone the benefit of the doubt often pays off nicely. You dislike manipulation and, since you are essentially without guile, you are open and honest with others.

When you find someone exciting, you don't keep it a secret. You are always prepared to seize an opportunity to have a good time and you really enjoy the company of an interesting partner. Your lovemaking style is as generous and open as you are. And, because you have a surprising amount of focus and strength, you can happily climb to the top of the mountain with your beloved.

In order to catch your eye, a potential mate should be friendly and outgoing, and demonstrate that they have a positive outlook on life. You really enjoy the great outdoors and actually are rejuvenated and uplifted by the wonders of nature. An invitation for a sunset walk on the beach or a stroll along a bubbling mountain stream are a perfect way to get to know you better. Since you also enjoy intellectual pursuits, a would-be suitor might suggest going to a poetry reading or a lecture by a famous author.

For a 1931 Sagittarius male, the ideal woman is someone who is even-tempered and up-front. Heavy emotions or dramatic scenes turn you off and you much prefer a philosophical and rational approach to any problems that might come up. You are a big picture person, a sort of visionary, and you need a woman who is grounded enough to help you through the sometimes-boring details.

The 1931 Sagittarius female needs a man who is adventurous and fun and has the spontaneity you need to keep life from getting too monotonous or routine. But, you also want someone who is reliable and dependable. Though you may seem a bit devil-may-care, you require the stability of a fellow traveler in order to feel free enough to explore the journey of life.

Jean Harlow – The Blonde Bombshell

In an all too brief ten-year span making Hollywood films, Jean Harlow became a great star, known as much for her clever dialogue and revealing costumes as for her skill in comedy and drama. Her 1931 hit *Platinum Blonde* captivated audiences, and peroxide sales around the country soared. Yet as she succeeded professionally, her private life was filled with tragedy and disappointment. At sixteen she married a wealthy businessman to escape her controlling mother, but that relationship soured after a few years. Her second marriage ended when her husband committed suicide two months later. A third marriage lasted less than a year, and she was plagued with health problems and financial parasites, including her stepfather and mother.

Harlow was born with her Sun in the intuitive sign of Pisces and Venus in boldly flirtatious Aries. Women with Venus in Aries know how to strut their stuff, and Harlow's Aries Moon only added spice and confidence to her sexual advances. She came to Hollywood with her first husband and found some small parts in silent pictures, but in 1930 was noticed by billionaire entrepreneur and producer Howard Hughes.

Hughes was making a big production movie about World War I aerial dogfights called *Hell's Angels* and signed Harlow as the love interest of two brothers, one good and one evil. The most famous line of the movie is delivered by Harlow who plays the sexy, voluptuous fiancée of one brother, but during a dance asks the other brother to take her home. In this scene, the two-timing Harlow is wearing a tremendously controversial evening dress with a plunging neckline that barely covers her breasts. After she invites him up to her room and serves him a drink, she coyly asks, "Would you be shocked if I put on something more comfortable?"

The film was a big hit and secured Harlow's reputation as a sex symbol. Over the next few years she made nothing but box-office successes, but it wasn't until Hughes sold her contract to MGM in 1932 that she was recognized for her talent as a wisecracking comedienne. She made *Red-Headed Woman* in 1932, in which her character happily sleeps her way to the top, as well as *Red Dust*, the second of six films with Clark Gable. Harlow's saucy characters were instrumental in the Catholic Church's efforts to screen and rate films, which led to the 1934 establishment of the Hays Production Code and the beginning of film censorship.

It was while she was filming *Red Dust* that her second husband, MGM executive Paul Bern, committed suicide. The reason for this is controversial, with many gossipers asserting that he felt humiliated for being impotent. Others claim he did it to protect Harlow from a secret affair he had been having. Harlow did eventually find the love of her life, the popular actor William Powell, but their story is a sad one. She reportedly aborted a child that he fathered, and while she was filming *Saratoga* in 1937, she came down with kidney poisoning and died before they could marry.

Harlow died young, and her successful film career was relatively short. Nevertheless, she made her mark on the silver screen. She is the blonde bombshell that all other blonde bombshells have measured themselves up to, including Marilyn Monroe.

113

▶ READ ABOUT CLARK GABLE ON PAGE 170 ▶ READ ABOUT MARILYN MONROE ON PAGES 293, 294, AND 334

1932

- ★ LINDBERGH BABY
- ★ TESTOSTERONE
- ★ BARBARA CARTLAND
- ★ BLONDE VENUS
- ★ ALL OF ME
- ★ APRIL IN PARIS
- ★ TOBACCO ROAD

EVENTS

The Lindbergh baby's kidnapping and murder riveted the world. Salacious suicide stories included 21-year-old actress Jean Harlow's producer husband, Broadway singer Libby Holman's tobacco heir husband, and Stalin's wife, Nadezhda Alliluyeva. Efforts to combat venereal disease made it acceptable for the first time for newspapers to print the word syphilis. With the recent discovery of the male hormone testosterone, animal gonad transplants provoked a great deal of interest. In the UK, novelist Barbara Cartland won a lengthy court battle and was granted a divorce from her adulterous husband, Alexander McCorquodale. The fashion for backless gowns for women, once considered shocking, found acceptance and permanence in society.

POP CULTURE

Sex symbol Cary Grant hit the silver screen in a total of seven films, including *Madame Butterfly* (as Lt. Pinkerton) and *Blonde Venus*, in which he romances married nightclub singer Marlene Dietrich. Helen Hayes and Gary Cooper starred in the film adaptation of Hemingway's *A Farewell to Arms*, a tragic tale of love during WWI. Mae West gave the censors a run for their money with her salty innuendoes in her screen debut *Night After Night*. In Ernst Lubitsch's *Trouble in Paradise*, a high-class thief falls for a pickpocket masquerading as a countess.

Rudy Vallee had hits with "If You Were the Only Girl," and "Let's Put Out the Lights (and Go to Sleep)."

Hot Couple

Duke Ellington let everyone know that "It Don't Mean a Thing If It Ain't Got That Swing," Louis Armstrong sang "All of Me," and Guy Lombardo asked "How Deep Is the Ocean?" "Night And Day" and "April in Paris" were among the year's memorable songs.

Aldous Huxley painted an eerie picture of the future in *Brave New World*, which foresaw state control of human reproduction. James T. Farrell's *Young Lonigan*, the first in a trilogy, detailed a young man's coming of age in Chicago. In *The Sheltered Life*, by Ellen Glasgow, several young women in early 1900s Virginia explore relationships with men. *Mary's Neck*, by Booth Tarkington, detailed the rivalries that arise in a summer resort, and Erskine Caldwell's *Tobacco Road* depicted the depravities of a family of Georgia sharecroppers.

JEAN HARLOW & PAUL BERN

By the early '30s gorgeous Jean Harlow was MGM's biggest draw, known as the "Blonde Bombshell." She could have had just about any man, but she chose Paul Bern, a studio executive 22 years her senior.

They married in July 1932 and two months later he was found dead at their home from a self-inflicted gunshot wound. Gossip circulated that he had been unable to satisfy the sex goddess in bed and killed himself out of humiliation. In recent years stories of murder and conspiracy have shrouded the tale in deeper mystery. Harlow died five years later from kidney disease.

SEE ALSO
▶ JEAN HARLOW *Page 113*

1932 CAPRICORN
From December 22, 1931 19:30 through January 21, 1932 6:06
(December 1932 Capricorns, see 1933 Capricorn)

The Traditional Partner

As a 1932 Capricorn, you place great value on a lasting relationship. You are happiest when playing a traditional role within a caringly-crafted loving lifestyle. However, you want your special person to understand that yours is a partnership between equals. Somewhat parental, you love to pamper and please your beloved and are happy to receive similar attention in return. You want to be able to count on your one special person for both emotional support and friendship. You're not comfortable with a partner that is too eccentric or self-centered or one that shows signs of being fickle.

It's important to you to keep the lines of communication open with the one you love. You can discuss challenging issues with an open mind so your sweetheart won't hesitate to share his or her thoughts. You willingly make significant life changes in order to please or accommodate your mate, but you also expect any sacrifices to be reciprocated. The passion you feel for your lover never wanes. Yours is a lasting partnership with true romance.

You're most attracted to a loving mate that is earthy, sensuous, and physically self-assured. This person can entice you with a bold glance, a gentle touch, and words of devotion. You relax and respond, not only to the special one next to you, but also to romantic surroundings. Beautiful music and satin sheets help you get into the right mood for lovemaking.

As a male Capricorn born in 1932, you're most attracted to women that are physically fit and intelligent. You love a lady with a mind of her own who is well informed about current events and is willing to share her opinions. A sexy voice is especially pleasing to you. If your darling can sing a love song just for you, she'll always have your heart and soul.

Because you're a 1932 Capricorn woman, you're drawn to men with high ideals and positive goals. He is ambitious, but not necessarily for worldly goods. Rather, your man has a sense of life purpose and a good reputation within your community. You may even share a special calling or vocation and build bonds by working well together.

1932 AQUARIUS
From January 21, 6:07 through February 19, 20:27

A Mindful Lover

As a 1932 Aquarian, you thrive in an intimate relationship built on mutual trust and respect. You need someone close that will provide balance for your serious approach to life. Throughout good times and those that are challenging, you'll be supportive of the one you love. You realize the value of teamwork and know that you can go far with the encouragement of your special partner. You and your true love may live an unconventional lifestyle but you will be old-fashioned in your devotion to the object of your affections.

While you thoroughly enjoy a little intellectual sparring with your partner, you would prefer that this person have a mind-set similar to your own. You enjoy stimulating conversation, not willful battles over opposing ideas. Although you may occasionally pick a small fight in order to kiss and make up later, you do this just to keep things interesting. In general, you need a harmonious relationship and will avoid being near to anyone who is negative or critical.

Youthful, curious, and bright individuals are very appealing to you. Your favorite person may be older or younger than you by many years—it's the ability to remain young at heart that you continue to find most desirable. Your ideal partner is a good conversationalist and usually has something meaningful to relate. Sharing life stories and special memories brings you even closer together.

Aquarian males born in 1932 are attracted to shy, gentle, and artistic women. Your best gal is sensuous but never flamboyant, saving her most precious charms for you only. You appreciate her emotional support and the behind-the-scenes influence she has on your life. Your lover is a true helpmate and a dear companion.

If you're a 1932 Aquarian female, you more than likely became friends with the love of your life first before entering into a more intimate arrangement. Looks are not as important to you in a man as character—you might become completely fascinated by a man with great moral integrity. You put your partner on a pedestal and want to share your life with someone that will take the high road.

CAPRICORN ZODIAC SIGN
YOUR LOVE PLANETS

YOUR ROMANTIC SIDE   p. 696
- ► **VENUS IN CAPRICORN**
  Born Dec. 22, 1931 19:30 - Dec. 25, 1931 19:43
- ► **VENUS IN AQUARIUS**
  Born Dec. 25, 1931 19:44 - Jan. 19, 1932 1:51
- ► **VENUS IN PISCES**
  Born Jan. 19, 1:52 - Jan. 21, 6:06

YOUR SEX DRIVE   p. 722
- ► **MARS IN CAPRICORN**
  Born Dec. 22, 1931 19:30 - Jan. 18, 1932 0:34
- ► **MARS IN AQUARIUS**
  Born Jan. 18, 0:35 - Jan. 21, 6:06

YOUR CELEBRITY TWINS   p. 760
Find out the astrological similarities you have with famous people.

YOUR COMPATIBILITY   p. 780
Compare planets to find out how compatible you are in a relationship.

YOUR RELATIONSHIP KARMA   p. 824
- ► **SATURN IN CAPRICORN**
  Born Dec. 2, 1931 19:30 - Jan. 21, 1932 6:06

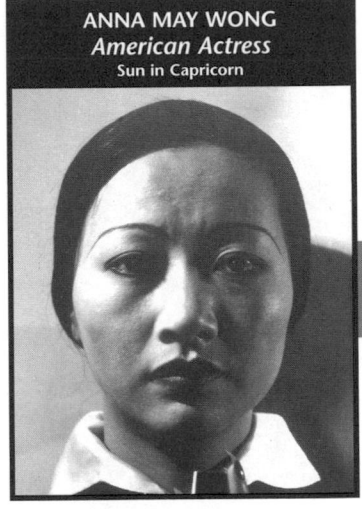

ANNA MAY WONG
American Actress
Sun in Capricorn

AQUARIUS ZODIAC SIGN
YOUR LOVE PLANETS

YOUR ROMANTIC SIDE   p. 696
- ► **VENUS IN PISCES**
  Born Jan. 21, 6:07 - Feb. 12, 16:57
- ► **VENUS IN ARIES**
  Born Feb. 12, 16:58 - Feb. 19, 20:27

YOUR SEX DRIVE   p. 722
- ► **MARS IN AQUARIUS**
  Born Jan. 21, 6:07 - Feb. 19, 20:27

YOUR CELEBRITY TWINS   p. 760
Find out the astrological similarities you have with famous people.

YOUR COMPATIBILITY   p. 780
Compare planets to find out how compatible you are in a relationship.

YOUR RELATIONSHIP KARMA   p. 824
- ► **SATURN IN CAPRICORN**
  Born Jan. 21, 6:07 - Feb. 19, 20:27

MAUREEN O'SULLIVAN
Irish Actress
Mars in Pisces

116

1932 PISCES
From February 19, 20:28 through March 20, 19:53

The Tender Idealist

As a Piscean born in 1932, you have firm ideas about what a perfect relationship should be and how to achieve it. Your desire for a true and enduring love could be the subject of poetry and song. You want a partner that is a soul mate and who also shares your worldly values. At the same time, you are independent and self-assured and expect your beloved to be also. Above all, you want your partnership to be very easy and loving. It should never feel as if you have to work hard to make it successful.

As in other areas of life, you follow your intuition when choosing a partner. You know instantly when the right one comes across your path. The physical, mental, and emotional attraction is there. It might be hard to recall afterward which of you made the first move. Rather, it is a simple coming together of two people who are made for one another. You find insensitivity a real turn-off and appreciate a tender and thoughtful lover.

What will your dearest person do to please you? You won't keep this a secret that requires guessing. You're fond of traditional courtship rituals and also like surprises. Your lover should give you lots of attention and never forget a birthday, anniversary, or other special occasion. The one you cherish will celebrate life along with you. You will be the center of his or her life and you'll adore your partner in return.

Good humored, happy-go-lucky, women appeal to Pisces males born in 1932. Your ideal gal is an adventuress, willing to join in your explorations of the unknown. She is sexy and fearless but never ill tempered or negative about life. Your special lady compliments your gentle personality with her feisty disposition. The two of you make a great team.

Pisces women born in 1932 prefer men that take the lead in love. He is somewhat protective of you but supports your varied interests outside the relationship. The ideal mate for you leads a very public life and wants you to share it with him. He's handsome but hardly ever silent. You always know what he's thinking because you're his best friend and he keeps nothing from you.

1932 ARIES
From March 20, 19:54 through April 20, 7:27

An Independent Romantic

Life as a 1932 Aries is never simple, especially when it comes to love and romance. You want a stable, committed relationship but with someone that allows you infinite freedoms. You'll remain forever faithful and loyal. However, your independent spirit may prompt you to live a lifestyle that involves being away from home for long periods of lime. Luckily, absence really does make your heart, and that of your special person, grow fonder. It may even seem as if you're on a continual honeymoon.

Yours is a life with a mission and it's important that the one you love share it with you. The two of you may embrace a meaningful humanitarian, political, or business cause and work together for the benefit of others. You need a like-minded person who shares your enthusiasm for fresh ideas that can change the world. Boredom will not be tolerated. Your relationship must never lapse into discussions of such mundane issues as who needs to take out the garbage.

To keep the flames burning, your lover must be playful, imaginative, and adventurous. You respond readily to lavish displays of affection. Your partner should never hold back when demonstrating how much you're cared for. Bold pronouncements of love are the best. You'd like to see your names in a heart written in the sky or on a big billboard. It's important that the two of you are known in public as a happy couple.

Well-grounded women that can act as a touchstone are attractive to 1932 Aries males. You're drawn to one who is sensual and a lover of luxury. Your sexy woman dresses well and appreciates the finer things of life, including good music and fine art. She is down-to-earth and practical, a perfect counter-balance for your free-spirited ways.

A rare type of man appeals to Aries women born in 1932. He is a brave risk-taker and a physically active, dynamic guy who embraces all the joys life has to offer. He's also a kind and gentle lover, one that is fiercely devoted to you. When this relationship is at it's best, you'll feel as if you and your irresistible hero are living the story line in a captivating romance novel.

1932 TAURUS
From April 20, 7:28 through May 21, 7:06

The Steady Heart

When considering romance as a 1932 Taurus, recall the fervent desire you experience in love. You think about your dear one always and hold that person always close to your heart. Through this intense longing, you literally draw your lover to you. You want a totally committed relationship with one person that lasts forever. At the same time, you realize that personal growth is a good thing. Each of you will change through the years and you try to do this together and in harmony.

You will exhibit strength of character under all conditions and expect your partner to do the same. He or she should stand by your side and fight the good fight when necessary. Anyone who withers and gives up when life becomes challenging will not keep your affection. Although the dynamics between you and your true love will alter and mature, your attachment grows stronger each year as you build a history together.

In order to keep the passion alive, the one you care for must be daring and bold. You will be charmed by declarations of love and intimate pillow talk. Your lover should share your passion for the simple things in life as well as the unique experiences. For you, home cooked meals and breezy rides through the countryside are as romantic as an elaborate trip around the world—so long as you're with your real true love.

Women that are talkative, friendly, and easy to get to know will appeal to shy 1932 Taurus males. It's likely that your best gal is someone you attended school with or who lived in your neighborhood. You'll especially appreciate one that gets along well with your family and friends. She's a real tease who is always physically active, hoping you'll keep up with her. And you'll want to.

As a female Taurus of 1932, perhaps Marlon Brando was your favorite star of the silver screen. Any man who comes close to him in looks or attitude may still catch your eye. While you find the super macho man attractive, your chosen partner is one that is more domesticated and traditional. You don't mind when your special guy wanders away from home, just so long as he takes you with him!

TAURUS ZODIAC SIGN
YOUR LOVE PLANETS

YOUR ROMANTIC SIDE — p. 696
► VENUS IN GEMINI
Born Apr. 20, 7:28 - May 06, 9:03
► VENUS IN CANCER
Born May 06, 9:04 - May 21, 7:06

YOUR SEX DRIVE — p. 722
► MARS IN ARIES
Born Apr. 20, 7:28 - May 12, 10:52
► MARS IN TAURUS
Born May 12, 10:53 - May 21, 7:06

YOUR CELEBRITY TWINS — p. 760
Find out the astrological similarities you have with famous people.

YOUR COMPATIBILITY — p. 780
Compare planets to find out how compatible you are in a relationship.

YOUR RELATIONSHIP KARMA — p. 824
► SATURN IN AQUARIUS
Born Apr. 20, 7:28 - May 21, 7:06

JOAN MIRO
Spanish Artist
Mars in Gemini

117

1932 GEMINI
From May 21, 7:07 through June 21, 15:22

A Kindred Spirit

As a 1932 Gemini, you continue to have great expectations and enthusiasm for your relationship. Fortunately, you are lucky in love. One reason for this is that you knew everything important about your partner before making a commitment. You are forthright and honest and never hesitate to speak your mind, so your partner always knows where you stand on any issue. Your generosity and kindness to the one you love makes that person want to treat you well, too. You seem to have discovered the formula for a successful union.

However, your relationship will not be so perfect that it becomes stale. You and your partner will have some disagreements, but they'll be more like sibling rivalry than lover's quarrels, with just enough friction to clear the air. It's important to you that your dear one help you create a pleasant daily environment where you both feel supported. You are totally turned off by negative thinking, complaints, and whining.

To keep the infatuation alive, your lover should say those three little words often and with passion. When traveling, you'll fall in love all over again once you're in the heart-shaped bed in the Honeymoon Suite. At home your romantic hideaway should be a completely private place for you and your sweetheart, one where the world cannot interrupt you. A relaxed setting and beautiful music will put both of you in the right mood for making love.

The Earth Mother type of woman is attractive to male Geminis born in 1932. She is shy, gentle, and emotionally nurturing to all those that cross her path. You always feel pampered when you're with her. Your favorite lady wants to make you comfortable and she's proud of her extraordinary domestic skills. It's a real plus that she's a superior cook.

Female Geminis of 1932 are fond of outdoorsmen that live in harmony with nature. He will be down-to-earth and exceptionally intelligent but slow and deliberate in his speech. Your perfect guy may have an unwavering daily routine of physical exercise. He is mentally agile, curious about the world around him, and a good intellectual match for you.

GEMINI ZODIAC SIGN
YOUR LOVE PLANETS

YOUR ROMANTIC SIDE — p. 696
► VENUS IN CANCER
Born May 21, 7:07 - June 21, 15:22

YOUR SEX DRIVE — p. 722
► MARS IN TAURUS
Born May 21, 7:07 - June 21, 15:22

YOUR CELEBRITY TWINS — p. 760
Find out the astrological similarities you have with famous people.

YOUR COMPATIBILITY — p. 780
Compare planets to find out how compatible you are in a relationship.

YOUR RELATIONSHIP KARMA — p. 824
► SATURN IN AQUARIUS
Born May 21, 7:07 - June 21, 15:22

HELEN HAYES
American Actress
Mars in Leo

1932 CANCER
From June 21, 15:23 through July 23, 2:17

Faithful in Love

Cancers born in 1932 thrive in a secure, loving relationship. You appreciate traditional male/female roles and enjoy domestic life most with your special partner. Your nesting instinct is very strong and there's nothing you love more than getting cozy at home with your sweetheart. Your devotion to your partner's happiness is sincere. As one of the most nurturing signs of the zodiac, you really know how to care for the one you love.

As a kind and sensitive person, you need a mate that is considerate of your emotional life. You put your faith in a lover only after receiving a total commitment. Once you form this bond, your darling will have your loyalty forever. It's best if this person supports your worldly and professional goals too. You'll do the same in return. Because you are cautious in love, you may marry late in life when you're wise enough to make a choice that's perfect for you.

Your heart will never turn away from one that cherishes you above all others. He or she must not hesitate to tell you often how much you are loved and cared for. Then, actions should follow those words of love. Physical affection is important to you and the intimate moments you share ought never become routine or predictable. You like surprises and want your lover to do the unexpected when the two of you are alone.

As a Cancer male born this year, you have a real appreciation of the opposite sex. It makes no difference to you if a woman is a beauty queen or not. You respond positively to female energy. You may have met your special gal while you were working or in a recreational setting. Your sweetheart is brilliant but shy. She understands your needs and appreciates the love and affection you show her.

The ideal guy for a 1932 Cancer woman is a good communicator, young at heart, and full of nervous energy. His personality may remind you of one of your family members, perhaps your father or brother. Your guy can be playful and fun to have near. It's the little acts of kindness he shows on a regular basis that will keep you falling in love with him over and over and over again.

1932 LEO
From July 23, 2:18 through August 23, 9:05

The Royal Charmer

Ardent 1932 Leos are curiously unaware of their exceptional power to enchant members of the opposite sex. You have a natural animal magnetism and a charming personality that is irresistible to your partner. You do your best to create a happy relationship, one in which every day together is exciting. As a result, the one you love is happy when you're near and willing to please you, too. You are most alive when you're in love and some of your favorite memories are of your exciting romantic times with your partner.

You are generous to a fault with your sweetheart. You'll deny this person nothing and will always give more of your time and attention than is asked for. An unappreciative or withholding partner can easily wound your pride, even though your dignity won't allow you to show it. There's a sense of playfulness in your relationship with the one you love. You can be a tease and it's important to you that your partner has fun. Life with you will be joyful and never mundane.

To ensure that you stay interested, the one you care for should always laugh at your jokes and enjoy it when you're the life of the party. When the two of you are alone, you're very pleased when the one you adore makes the first move. The more passion your lover shows for you, the better you respond. You are romantically energized when your partner reaffirms that you're desirable.

If you're a male Leo born in 1932 you're drawn to graceful women that are physically active and mentally alert. You want your lady to have classic good looks whether wearing her little black dress or casual blue jeans. She is sexy but in an understated way. Above all, you need your special gal to keep you on a pedestal long after the honeymoon is over.

Female Lionesses born this year prefer men that have gregarious and joyful personalities. You respond to one with a melodious voice and an interesting way of communicating. Your man's body language appeals to you. He stands tall and confident in all social situations. When you're alone, it's obvious that his mind, body, and spirit are focused on no one but you.

1932 VIRGO

From August 23, 9:06 through September 23, 6:15

The Discriminating Lover

Virgos born in 1932 remain forever optimistic about love. You strive for perfection in your relationship, not for your own peace of mind but for your sweetheart's happiness. At the same time, you're very self-sufficient and don't actually need someone in your life for you to be content. However, you are truly happy once you're in a mutually devoted partnership—you thrive in married life. Your lover adores you for your rare combination of independence and romantic passion.

Well-grounded and extremely sensuous, you take very seriously your commitment to the one you love. In return, you expect your partner to be a faithful companion and willing helpmate. Your social and family ties are important so you want your mate to share these interests. You have exquisite taste and are quite turned off by anyone that is loud or ill mannered, or someone who might embarrass you in public.

Your sensuality finds full expression only within a secure relationship. You don't especially care for public demonstrations of affection. Once behind closed doors,

however, there should be no doubt that your partner finds you the most desirable person on earth. To hold your interest, your lover must never forget the intimacies you prefer. You respond to obvious flirtations, hugs, and snuggles, and those special pet names your darling has given you.

Virgo men born this year are drawn to complicated and sensitive women. Your perfect mate is modest and a bit reserved, but curious about life and love. Since you find pleasure in watching bathing beauties at play, your gal should enjoy swimming and other water sports. She makes the time you spend together in a hot tub so memorable that you'll never stray.

If you're one of the 1932 Virgo gals, you're attracted to men that are down-to-earth and practical, very helpful, and healthy conscious. He is kind, nurturing, and fastidious about his looks and dress. You're lucky because your guy may be one of the few of his generation comfortable in the kitchen and a really great cook! Having this man serve you breakfast in bed could be your favorite treat!

VIRGO ZODIAC SIGN
Your Love Planets

YOUR ROMANTIC SIDE — p. 696
- ▶ **VENUS IN CANCER**
  Born Aug. 23, 9:06 - Sept. 08, 19:44
- ▶ **VENUS IN LEO**
  Born Sept. 08, 19:45 - Sept. 23, 6:15

YOUR SEX DRIVE — p. 722
- ▶ **MARS IN CANCER**
  Born Aug. 23, 9:06 - Sept. 20, 19:42
- ▶ **MARS IN LEO**
  Born Sept. 20, 19:43 - Sept. 23, 6:15

YOUR CELEBRITY TWINS — p. 760
Find out the astrological similarities you have with famous people.

YOUR COMPATIBILITY — p. 780
Compare planets to find out how compatible you are in a relationship.

YOUR RELATIONSHIP KARMA — p. 824
- ▶ **SATURN IN CAPRICORN**
  Born Aug. 23, 9:06 - Sept. 23, 6:15

FREDRIC MARCH
American Actor
Sun in Virgo

1932 LIBRA

From September 23, 6:16 through October 23, 15:03

The Lasting Lover

Librans born in 1932 have a special talent. You know how to create lasting, loving relationships. Completely open and self-confident, you inspire your sweetheart to be genuine, open, and at ease. This makes for an honest partnership, one where each person can be truly authentic and totally loved—human imperfections included. You're keenly aware of your partner's needs and will do your best to meet them. You're happiest in an equitable partnership. You expect the one you care for to be attentive and loving, too.

It's important for you to achieve harmony in your everyday life. You will not be happy with an individual that has a sullen disposition or is generally down. You will avoid anyone that is unforgiving or who dwells on negative events. More than most people, you are able to find the good in others and in the world around you. The one who loves you will support you by doing the same. The two of you share common values.

If you have your way, the time you spend alone will always be exciting no matter how

long you and your partner are together. You're well suited to a life of passion and are pleased to be in the presence of a bold and dynamic lover. You respond best to one who is physically appealing, charming, and flirtatious. Romance is best for you if your surroundings are pleasing and serene. Candlelight and soft music playing in the background help make intimacy and your nights together wondrous.

Love is a great adventure for the 1932 male Libra. You're drawn to beautiful and artistic women with an uncommon sense of style. Your special lady has sparkling eyes and a flirtatious smile. It's possible that you met her through close friends. You expect your darling to be your intimate companion for a lifetime.

Happy-go-lucky, outgoing men appeal to Libra women born in 1932. You love a happy guy that is entertaining, one whose joy for life is so boundless that it infects everyone around him. Your relationship is not a meeting of opposites but of like-minded soul mates. You and your true love have a great deal in common and similar emotional expressions.

LIBRA ZODIAC SIGN
Your Love Planets

YOUR ROMANTIC SIDE — p. 696
- ▶ **VENUS IN LEO**
  Born Sept. 23, 6:16 - Oct. 07, 5:45
- ▶ **VENUS IN VIRGO**
  Born Oct. 07, 5:46 - Oct. 23, 15:03

YOUR SEX DRIVE — p. 722
- ▶ **MARS IN LEO**
  Born Sept. 23, 6:16 - Oct. 23, 15:03

YOUR CELEBRITY TWINS — p. 760
Find out the astrological similarities you have with famous people.

YOUR COMPATIBILITY — p. 780
Compare planets to find out how compatible you are in a relationship.

YOUR RELATIONSHIP KARMA — p. 824
- ▶ **SATURN IN CAPRICORN**
  Born Sept. 23, 6:16 - Oct. 23, 15:03

EVELYN WAUGH
English Writer
Sun in Scorpio

120

1932 SCORPIO
From October 23, 15:04 through November 22, 12:09

♏ *A Lifetime Lover*

The emotional intensity of Scorpios born in 1932 is focused on love and romance. You will never enter into a relationship quickly. Rather, you must know everything about your lover before revealing the depth of your feelings. Once trust between you is established, it can endure forever. You require lasting emotional stability in your life and a partner you can count on at all times. This requires the unwavering loyalty of your sweetheart and repeated affirmations of his or her love. Your goal is total union with your special person.

Your partnership may not be lighthearted but it certainly has depth. Your significant other must respect your rare sensitivity and never wound your pride—not even in jest. You avoid linking up with anyone that is critical or not pleased with you exactly the way you are. You're happiest with a supportive lover that is also an asset to you out in public. Together you will enjoy an active life in your community and may even establish a successful business.

Naturally, the one you love should be physically passionate. You'll also respond to daily, small shows of affection—hugs, kisses, and loving terms of endearment. Your special darling should recognize that you're a complicated individual and be attuned to your various moods. You expect your mate to read your body language well enough to know when you're inclined to intimacy—without having to spell it out.

Women with discriminating taste appeal to male Scorpios born in 1932. Your perfect lady does not have to be a heart-stopping beauty. However, she should have classical features, a good character, rare wit, and wisdom. She'll tell you how smart and lucky she was to have captured your heart and, of course, you know she's right!

Scorpio females born in 1932 have an ideal mate in mind, one that has a rare combination of personality traits. He is at times very outgoing and playful, and makes you laugh a lot. He can also be mysteriously reserved about certain areas of his life. Above all, you know he loves you and is someone you can count on to be there for you when you need him.

1932 SAGITTARIUS
From November 22, 12:10 through December 22, 1:13

♐ *The Spirited Playmate*

As a discriminating 1932 Sagittarius, you keep your romantic options open until the perfect partner comes along. Before making a commitment, you are quite happy to play in the big wide world on your own, without any emotional involvements. When you do finally give your heart to someone special, you continue to require lots of private time to follow your intellectual and spiritual pursuits. For you, love is to be held lightly, without possessiveness, jealously, or mistrust.

It's best if your true love shares your large range of interests and hobbies. You especially enjoy lively discussions around the dinner table. The great outdoors holds fascination for you, too, and you're never happier than when walking in the woods with your sweetheart. You will not respond well to homebodies or anyone that tries to domesticate you. Rather, you need a partner who appreciates your playful approach to life.

You will usually take the initiative in love but also appreciate a lover that is direct, even bold. You never want your love life to decrease as you age. To keep you coming back for more, your mate should be full of sexy surprises. This might include romancing you in a variety of settings outside of the bedroom. You consider sex to be a form of recreation and want it to always be fun.

Beautiful, athletic women cause male Sagittarians born in 1932 to turn their heads. You like gals that can take part in healthy outdoor activities with you. In your youth, you wanted a perky cheerleader on your arm. Later in life, you're happy to be with a sexy, good-natured woman that is a loving companion. She is an inspiration to you, one that helps you achieve your highest goals.

As a 1932 model Sagittarius female, you are drawn to sporting men with fiery, happy dispositions. An outdoor, field-and-stream kind of guy suits you best. Your perfect man will be actively involved in your community and will also enjoy traveling. He is a bit of a perfectionist and extraordinarily intelligent. When you meet him, you know immediately that this rare individual is capable of having an expansive influence on your life.

Eleanor and Franklin D. Roosevelt

While a student at Harvard, Franklin D. Roosevelt became attracted to Eleanor, Theodore Roosevelt's niece and Franklin's fifth cousin. At first glance, the match between the handsome, charming, wealthy bon vivant and the shy, plain Eleanor may have seemed odd to some—especially to Franklin's mother, Sara, who was far from enthusiastic about their union. But FDR, born under the zodiac sign Aquarius in 1882, probably prized intelligence more highly than beauty in a woman. The pair were married in 1905 and had six children together between 1906 and 1916 (one died in infancy).

During those years, Eleanor Roosevelt led the life of supportive wife and mother, while Franklin climbed the career ladder, rising from New York State Senator to Assistant US Secretary of the Navy. But in September of 1918, Eleanor made a startling discovery that shook the foundations of her marriage. While unpacking her husband's suitcase after a business trip to Europe, she came upon a packet of love letters between FDR and Eleanor's own social secretary, Lucy Mercer. The correspondence revealed that their love affair had been going on for years.

Eleanor was crushed. She offered her husband a divorce, but he refused. In their upper-class social circle, divorce was frowned upon. A divorce would also have damaged the ambitious young man's political prospects. Additionally, both Eleanor and FDR had their Zodiac moons in Cancer, which shows a strong emotional bond between them as well as a shared desire for security and a stable family structure. Franklin promised never to see Mercer again.

FDR's betrayal profoundly changed not only their relationship, but also Eleanor's vision of herself and her role in

life. She returned to New York where she grew friendly with Esther Lape and Elizabeth Read, and became active in the women's suffrage movement. Her interest and involvement in politics would increase in the coming years, leading her to champion peace and later civil rights.

In 1921, the Roosevelt's marriage suffered another blow when FDR was stricken with polio. Eleanor cared for him devotedly—ironically, the illness that crippled FDR strengthened their relationship. Years later, *Time* magazine wrote: "They made an exceptional team.... Together they mobilized the American people to effect enduring changes in the political and social landscape of the nation."

Eleanor continued her political activism and her associations with other powerful, intelligent women. In 1932, journalist Lorena Hickok attracted Eleanor's attention while covering FDR's presidential campaign. The two became intimate friends and wrote long, passionate letters to one another that, when publicized in 1978, suggested a lesbian relationship between the First Lady and the AP reporter.

Although the sexual nature of their companionship was never proved, the love and respect the two women shared was evident. According to biographer Blanche Wiesen Cook, the friendship "empowered and emboldened" Eleanor, encouraging her to even greater achievements during a time when the nation was in crisis. Theirs was "an ardent, loving relationship between two adult women."

For Eleanor, born in 1884 under Libra, the zodiac sign that rules relationships, relationships truly were the hub around which her rich and influential life turned.

Few couples have made such an impact on world events and American politics as Franklin and Eleanor Roosevelt. Likewise, few have experienced such complexity in their personal relationships.

121

▶ READ ABOUT JOHN AND JACQUELINE KENNEDY AND THE TRIALS OF THEIR MARRIAGE ON PAGE 351

- ⊛ **RISE OF NAZISM**
- ⊛ **ESQUIRE**
- ⊛ **GOLD DIGGERS**
- ⊛ **SHE DONE HIM WRONG**
- ⊛ **BILLIE HOLIDAY**
- ⊛ **SMOKE GETS IN YOUR EYES**
- ⊛ **MISS LONELYHEARTS**

Hot Movie

EVENTS

The Nazi Party, under newly elected Chancellor Adolf Hitler, proposed an end to women's suffrage in Germany, while state marriage loans were awarded to newly married couples, provided that the woman left her job. With unemployment in the US at 15 million, the marriage rate was down 40% from 1920s levels. Sally Rand was the biggest hit at the Chicago World's Fair. With only her face, bare arms and legs visible from behind a giant balloon as she crossed the stage, she proved the power of suggestion. *Esquire*, the first magazine for men, began publication and featured scantily clad women. And in Paris, Marlene Dietrich turned heads when she arrived wearing men's clothing. Parisian law penalized women who sought attention by wearing male attire in public.

POP CULTURE

Busby Berkeley's musical *Gold Diggers of 1933* ushered in an era of lavishly choreographed and costumed production numbers. Fay Wray was helpless in King Kong's grip, but Mae West was in complete control of Cary Grant as she uttered the oft-misquoted "Why don't you come up sometime and see me?" in *She Done Him Wrong*. The Marx Brothers romped it up in *Duck Soup*, Katharine Hepburn starred in *Little Women*, and Fred Astaire and Ginger Rogers first danced together in *Flying Down to Rio*. In Camden, New Jersey, the first drive-in theater opened.

Billie Holiday, making her first recordings (with Benny Goodman), sang to the man of her dreams, "Can't you see, you've got to be my mother's son-in-law!" Jimmy Durante had a hit with "Inka Dinka Doo." Chart toppers of the year also included "Stormy Weather," "Smoke Gets in Your Eyes," and "It's Only a Paper Moon." American musicians organized a campaign to cable protests to Hitler after black jazz and Jewish music and musicians were banned in Germany.

James Hilton introduced the world to Shangri-La in *Lost Horizon*. Far from such utopia, Nathanael West's *Miss Lonelyhearts* told the tawdry tale of the life and death of an advice-to-the-lovelorn columnist. Sinclair Lewis tackled marriage, divorce, sexual rights, and abortion in *Ann Vickers*. Caroline Miller won the Pulitzer for *Lamb in His Bosom*, while literary experimentalist Gertrude Stein penned *The Autobiography of Alice B. Toklas*.

KING KONG

The ultimate Beauty and the Beast theme, this RKO Radio Pictures film contains one of the most iconographical moments in cinema history: King Kong atop the Empire State Building with a terrified Fay Wray clutched in his fist.

Talk about sweeping a woman off her feet! In its time there was something ultimately lurid and sexual about a ferocious primate holding a beautiful woman as his hostage.

One censored scene, too risqué and disturbing for 1933, showed Kong taking off unconscious Fay Wray's clothing. The scene was restored in a version released in 1971, but had lost its shock value.

SEE ALSO
▶ **SEX AND THE CITY** *Page 679*

1933 CAPRICORN

From December 22, 1932 1:14 through January 20, 1933 11:52
(December 1933 Capricorns, see 1934 Capricorn)

The Power Broker

As a 1933 Capricorn, you want a relationship that won't distract you from your ambitious climb toward excellence. Your ideal relationship is one that is built on a mutual commitment to common goals. More than anything else, you want someone that you can share your life work with. Given to long periods of deep reflection, an almost telepathic understanding with someone who truly shares your vision is your assurance that you have the right partner for life.

Underneath that ultra-controlled exterior, you are intensely sexual and see intimacy as a profound and deeply emotionally purging experience. You are discriminating because of your sensitivity to other people's motivations and will happily opt for celibacy rather than compromise or lower your standards for the ideal partner. If someone meets your high standards for intimacy, you will go to great lengths to keep your partner happy and satisfied with the relationship.

You are attracted to a person who hints of unbridled, simmering sexual passion. Underneath your own "take it or leave it" sexual exterior beats the heart of someone who lives for a spicier, more decadent expression of sensuality—spontaneous and unconventional moments of passion and daring. Such private explorations keep your attention fixed on tempting adventures with your partner instead of on tempting strangers.

A male 1933 Capricorn knows what he likes in his women even though he may give the appearance of utter, romantic befuddlement. You prefer your women to have the clean, elegant lines that speak of natural sophistication. Whether she is a glamour girl or a wholesome beauty, she must be someone who isn't afraid to surrender herself to the power of your love.

If you are a female born in 1933 under the sign of Capricorn, you decided when you were a little girl what your ideal partner would be like. You are a firm believer in shaping your own destiny and know that a partner with real potential is sometimes better than the illusion of perfection. For the right person, your ability to help anyone realize their dreams is a magic potion for happiness.

LORETTA YOUNG
American Actress
Sun in Capricorn

123

1933 AQUARIUS

From January 20, 11:53 through February 19, 2:15

The Gentle Perfectionist

If you are a 1933 Aquarius, you want a relationship that is a true meeting of the minds. Armed with a hearty appetite for life and all that it has to offer, you need someone who understands your drive to be the best at anything you do. Your perfectionist tendencies and commitment to self-sufficiency require someone who is sensitive enough to recognize your genuine desire to do the right thing and your deep disappointment when others do not value your efforts or your time.

Sexually shy, you are often seen as a late bloomer or slightly repressed. In reality, you are sexually sensitive and see intimacy as a glorious act of creativity that is not to be taken for granted or sullied with vulgarity. You have a natural approach to sexuality and, once comfortable with someone, you are perfectly accepting of the less than perfect human condition. For you, sexuality is a revered form of playful quality time that is always welcome with the right person.

The best way to get your attention is to offer an interesting piece of useful information about anything. Not one for meaningless banter, anyone that expands your body of useful knowledge is always someone to admire, even briefly. To hold your long-term interest in a relationship, someone would have to make him or herself indispensable to you. Making your life function more smoothly and efficiently, so that you can relax occasionally, always holds your attention and your heart.

As a male 1933 Aquarius, you are happiest with a woman who is an equal, mentally, and a helpmeet, spiritually. Your ideal woman is, foremost, logical, bright, and organized in her thinking. A woman with a gentle nature and a quiet, competent approach to managing your mutual needs is your formula for a happy life.

If you are a 1933 Aquarius woman, your ideal man is someone who excites you on a mental level and complements your existing skills on a physical level. A pragmatist from an early age, you cherish the ideal companionship more than you do an idyllic romance. A sensual man that inspires both passion and respect on your part is your heart's desire.

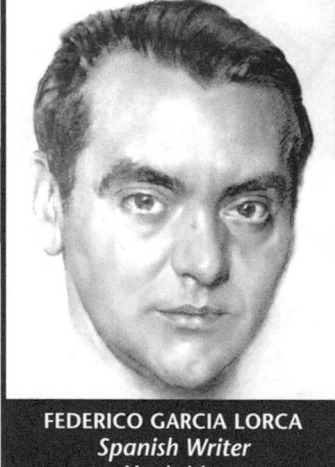

FEDERICO GARCIA LORCA
Spanish Writer
Mars in Aries

124

1933 PISCES
From February 19, 2:16 through March 21, 1:42

 The Seductive Psychic

A 1933 Pisces wants a relationship that is akin to the respect and passion between an artist and patron. A passive soul, you naturally gravitate toward assertive, sure-footed folks who can appreciate your creative musings and musical nature. You have no problem leaving the business of living in someone else's hands. You are a charming romantic who can slip between dry realism and fantastic imaginings at the drop of a hat and are happiest with someone who can take the reins of the relationship and lead with integrity and commitment.

For you, intimacy is a psychic reunion that strengthens your love bonds over time and reinforces your already strong telepathic understanding of your lover's needs. Sexually intuitive and passive, you read the unspoken feelings and desires of others as if they had been openly and clearly expressed. Innuendo and suggestion are your favored methods of seduction and a hint of mystery always ignites the flames of your desire.

If someone wants to capture your attention, they must first tune into and turn on your imagination. Deeply emotional and psychic, you are often conflicted by the differences between what you feel from other people and what they show you. A person who is unafraid to express their thoughts and feelings creates a feeling of immediate trust and respect. You long for someone whom you can count on to be honest, in action and words.

A 1933 Pisces man needs a muse that inspires his creative genius, every day. The best match for this sensitive and poetic personality is a kind and supportive woman who is capable of being an assertive problem solver and champion of the domestic fortress. More than anything else, you yearn for a woman that you can wrap your dreams around.

As a female 1933 Pisces, you have an endearing helplessness that attracts men like bees to honey. You are often on the arm of a stronger, more dramatic personality but cruel or aggressive behavior will destroy any romantic feelings you had for the person. In the end, you are happiest with a strong, silent type whose need for you is only matched by his reticence to say it.

1933 ARIES
From March 21, 1:43 through April 20, 13:17

♈ *The Confident Troubleshooter*

If you are a 1933 Aries, it is the relentless pursuit of the ideal in a relationship that drives you. The perfect partnership for you is a fiery one that is peppered with intense exchanges and allows you to emotionally purge and renew yourself, time and again. You need a partner who can handle your bold confidence and not be overwhelmed by your impatient desires. Happiness comes when you find someone who has enough of a sharp or exciting edge on his or her personality that becoming complacent is never an option for you.

Sexually, you can express yourself as a wide-eyed innocent or a sybaritic glutton and both would be true. You have a healthy sexual appetite coupled with a very physical approach to intimacy, and you are not afraid to pursue the path that meets your needs. Secretly, you long for a passion that will transform you and your lover into pure and primal need and, once found, you are addicted to the heady experience of your newly discovered passion.

To get your attention, one must first radiate a cheeky kind of arrogance. You love the challenge a strong and healthy ego offers. Playful competitiveness keeps you hanging around for the next exciting episode in the relationship but being magnanimous during those exceptional moments when you are wrong and unperturbed when you are right engages you for a lifetime.

If you are a 1933 Aries man, you adore the "girl next door" type. A big smile and a sunny disposition with a child-like enthusiasm always puts a spring in your step and makes your heart skip a beat. You are a man of simple pleasures and honest appreciation. Your happiness is found with a wholesome girl who reminds you of the country and wide-open spaces in both heart and body.

A female 1933 Aries swoons for the kind of old-fashioned man that sets her imagination on fire. A heart of gold and a hard worker, your ideal man never shrugs off his cosmic duty to help someone in need and relishes his role of protector and servant of the weak. The perfect man for you is an ardent champion outside the home and a strong father figure and playful husband inside it.

1933 TAURUS
From April 20, 13:18 through May 21, 12:56

The Sybaritic Traditionalist

As a 1933 Taurus, you want a relationship that supports your need for security and routine. You are an organized and thorough person and want someone who can respect these personal qualities and add to your life without disrupting it. Your ideal relationship is built on a mutual love of longevity and quality and you are looking for someone who has your necessary hallmarks of lasting endurance and timelessness. A traditionalist, you are happiest with a mutual understanding about your roles in the relationship.

Sex for you is a natural and healthy expression of affection that is best when it is familiar. You are most excited by the delicious familiarity that comes with time invested into one person. You believe that there is no need to improve upon a good thing and once you have mastered the rituals of intimacy with your partner, you delight in testing the hedonistic boundaries of time, endurance, and, of course, mutual gratification.

If someone wants to get your attention, they must first smell exquisite. You are an earthy, sensual person and have a heightened sense of touch and smell. You live for the smell and feel of natural goodness as much as expensive quality and are easily intoxicated by someone who knows how to become a sensual panorama of delights. Paying attention to your list of favorite things along with this has you swimming in a heady sea of bliss for life.

A man born as a 1933 Taurus is happiest with a woman who is a sensual garden of delights and feels as good as she looks. From the smell of clean soap and water to the comforting feeling of flesh, you want a woman that you can lose yourself in. If she is also a domestic goddess who knows how to bewitch a man with her cooking, then you are totally devoted.

A 1933 Taurus woman is a tempting vixen and has an ample share of suitors who would love to curl up at her hearthside. You need only one man to be happy though, and your best match is with someone who understands your delight in creature comforts and also appreciates what you offer in return. Your desire is for someone who will amply provide sustenance for your love.

BING CROSBY
American Singer
Sun in Taurus

125

1933 GEMINI
From May 21, 12:57 through June 21, 21:11

The Sprightly Reporter

A 1933 Gemini needs an active relationship that offers stimulation and variety on a daily basis. You have a genuine need to communicate on many different levels and are best matched with someone who understands the sheer volume of conversation that you thrive on. Your ideal relationship is with someone who will not handicap your ability to satisfy your "need to know" curiosity. You want someone who can appreciate your enthusiastic approach to life as a constant source of discovery and amusement.

You are sexual quicksilver and change with mood, whim, and inspiration. Your immense exhilarating curiosity keeps your intimate life spontaneous and invigorating. Your love of variation always manages to put a fresh twist on a familiar subject. You crave someone who is as open-minded and imaginative as you are, but are happiest with someone who knows that sex is a game that is best played by the rules, between two loving and committed hearts.

If someone wants to get your attention, they should whisper or perhaps whistle but only nonchalantly. Arousing your curiosity is the fastest way to catch your kaleidoscopic attention and, once engaged, keeping a few surprises handy is the only way to keep it. You believe in savoring your experiences and like to enjoy your new love in small, delicate morsels, saving the best parts of their heart and mind for later. You want someone who knows how to dish out sweet enticements over a lifetime.

A 1933 Gemini man is happiest with a perpetual playmate. Your ideal woman has just enough capriciousness to keep life entertaining without being fickle or unreliable. She should share your love of novelty and your interest in the community at large. Your ideal woman is a lively conversationalist wrapped in a colorful, girlish package.

A woman born as a 1933 Gemini yearns for someone that is willing to share with her and enjoys his inner child. He knows that the secret to your happiness is not in the trappings of a successful life but in the stories you build along the way. Your ideal man is a unique and scintillating blend of man, boy, friend, and lover.

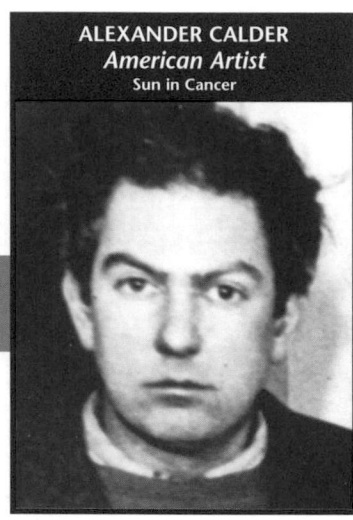

ALEXANDER CALDER
American Artist
Sun in Cancer

126

1933 CANCER
From June 21, 21:12 through July 23, 8:04

 The Affectionate Sentimentalist

If you are a 1933 Cancer, your best relationship takes you to the heights of amorous feelings. You are a dreamy romantic that sees every small detail of your new relationship as momentous and filled with meaning. You need a singular type of person who can understand the dramatic depths that your emotional intensity can reach and the breathless heights to which your adoration can soar. To you, the dance of love is a romantic musical set against the scenery of daily life.

You are a sexually conservative lover who is open to creative variations of love if they are a natural part of genuine commitment with your lover. You thrill for the trappings of a good seduction with soft lights, slow music, and gentle words because intimacy for you is a sensually amorous expression of loving. You yearn for the experience of sex being transformed into a magical, romantic union between hearts.

If someone wants to get your attention, they should master the art of paying a sincere compliment. You adore people who are able to lavish just the right amount of attention in any situation and know how to make others feel good about themselves. Remembering sentimental anniversaries and other emotionally endearing reasons for celebration assure you that you have found the one you can be happy with for life.

As a 1933 Cancer man, you are an old-fashioned gentleman who believes in wooing his beloved with all the splendor and grand magnificence of a great romantic story. Your ideal partner is a soft and kind woman whose affection is only rivaled by her desire to protect her loved ones. A homebody and nurturer at heart, she is the only kind of woman you can imagine falling in love with.

A woman born as a 1933 Cancer is an exquisite flower of femininity and domestic grace. Your ideal man is someone who only needs the restorative power of your love and nurturing to excel and fulfill his real potential in life. You believe in the power of believing in dreams and having faith renewed by the smallest of miracles. A man who shows a genuine desire to be all that you need in life is your idea of a love partner.

1933 LEO
From July 23, 8:05 through August 23, 14:51

 The Romantic Connoisseur

As a 1933 Leo, your ideal relationship satisfies your need for idyllic romance. You are an artist and a lover at heart and live for the beauty of perfect moments. You are a visual person and are attracted to natural beauty and elegant grace in all things. Your ideal relationship is a careful courtship that lasts a lifetime. Your commitment to self-improvement and higher ideals is reflected not only in your work but also in the delicate crafting of a genuinely loving partnership.

You see sex as an intimate dance that is thoughtfully orchestrated with tempo, rhythm, sound, and light to create a harmonic exchange between hearts and souls. Your careful total attention to the details surrounding the experience of intimacy creates an atmosphere that transports your lover into a poetic panorama of the senses. Refined and gentle, you prefer sweet nothings to private obscenity and you are completely chilled by vulgarity and less than tender behavior in bed.

Getting your attention requires a finesse and sense of decorum that is almost Victorian. Your discerning approach to socializing is always impressed by someone who truly comprehends and employs a more genteel approach to being in the world. If someone wants to keep your attention for a lifetime, they must share your connoisseur's ability to lose themselves in the sensual pleasures of exquisiteness when it is found.

If you are a man born as a 1933 Leo, you are the consummate gentleman and are looking for a woman who is the personification of feminine poise and natural beauty. Your best match is with a woman who complements your unparalleled taste, sense of design, and stylized masculinity with her own superb sense of elegance, refinement, and sophistication.

As a 1933 Leo woman, you present yourself as an exquisite and rare flower that needs careful grooming and special care. Your ideal man is handsome, perfectly groomed, and has that necessary touch of nobility in his carriage. You can be extremely selective, but once you have found the embodiment of masculine courtliness, you are ready to bloom under his exquisite lifelong care.

1933 VIRGO

From August 23, 14:52 through September 23, 12:00

The Secret Debauchee

Underneath the prim and decorous behavior of a 1933 Virgo beats the heart of a romantic hunter who enjoys power games of seduce, capture, and conquer. You want a relationship that satisfies your very private desires of intrigue and hedonistic pleasure. Complicated dramas keep you amused but you need a special partner to discover lasting relationship bliss. You are happiest with someone who is both an equal and a partner in your life's escapades. Your best match is with someone who plays love games as enthusiastically as you do, only better.

Your sexuality radiates from every pore and veritably shimmers in your aura. In private, there is nothing you won't try and no taboo you won't break in your pursuit of gratification. The more daring something is, the more excited you are. For you, there is no such thing as "inappropriate" so long as it is something that enhances the sexual experience.

If someone wants to get your attention, sending you discrete messages that are carefully laced with hidden sexual promise will always have you ready to solve the secret riddle. Keeping your attention, however, requires a certain amount of immunity from your best manipulations and the ability to retain their integrity no matter what the temptation. People who have immovable boundaries and an open mind always keep you standing ready.

A male Virgo born in 1933 has an innate sexual charisma and will happily explore the boundaries of social and sexual convention while he looks for the virgin that will not be seduced and the wife that will not betray. Your ideal partner is a chameleon who can play the chaste, blushing bride as flawlessly as she can the wanton, jaded sinner without ever raising an eyebrow.

A 1933 Virgo woman is a siren calling out to sea for the one man who can claim her without capitulating to her charms. Your ideal mate is a formidable, masculine fortress of self-control and intense sexual desire. His ability to handle any crisis situation with a cool, competent hand inflames your ardor for him and his loyalty to the relationship creates an inferno of reverence in your heart.

VIRGO ZODIAC SIGN
YOUR LOVE PLANETS

YOUR ROMANTIC SIDE — p. 696
► VENUS IN LIBRA
Born Aug. 23, 14:52 - Sept. 15, 14:53
► VENUS IN SCORPIO
Born Sept. 15, 14:54 - Sept. 23, 12:00

YOUR SEX DRIVE — p. 722
► MARS IN LIBRA
Born Aug. 23, 14:52 - Aug. 26, 6:33
► MARS IN SCORPIO
Born Aug. 26, 6:34 - Sept. 23, 12:00

YOUR CELEBRITY TWINS — p. 760
Find out the astrological similarities you have with famous people.

YOUR COMPATIBILITY — p. 780
Compare planets to find out how compatible you are in a relationship.

YOUR RELATIONSHIP KARMA — p. 824
► SATURN IN AQUARIUS
Born Aug. 23, 14:52 - Sept. 23, 12:00

JOAN BLONDELL
American Actress
Sun in Virgo

127

1933 LIBRA

From September 23, 12:01 through October 23, 20:47

The Sexy Gambler

If you are a 1933 Libra, your ideal partner has the ability to transport you to the next level of sensational, corporeal ecstasy. You love to push the boundaries of an experience and see how far limitation will take you and often venture where more conservative folks would not dare to go. You need an inexhaustible partner who will readily accept the challenge of keeping up with you. Your ideal relationship is an intense and fiery roller coaster ride that always keeps you anticipating the next enthralling chapter of love.

Sexually, you are a fireball of passionate ardor. Love is a thrilling quest for you. Your competitive and jealous nature shows when you decide that the experience of intimacy with you must, and will, obliterate the memories of anyone before you. For you, sex is the ultimate expression of love's power, and you want a lover who can join you in your complete submission to the corybantic delights it promises.

If someone wants to get your attention, intensity is the key to catching your eye. If someone wants to keep your attention, integrity is the rule. You are not immune to the physical laws of attraction, but ultimately you will be more attracted to and remain with someone who has a strong personality and a stronger code of ethics. When you do find someone that you can admire as well as find incredibly sexually attractive, then you are completely besotted.

As a 1933 male Libra, you are a sexy devil who knows what women want. Your ideal woman is a powerful and enthusiastic player in the game of life. Like the heroines of the big screen, she is a "tough tomato" who isn't afraid of gambling on her big dreams or you. A femme fatale with a heart of gold is your dream girl.

If you are a 1933 Libra woman, you are a risk taker when it comes to love and life. Your ideal man is brave, strong, and a classic tough guy when it comes to any challenges that come his way. Your best match is with a man who can set your imagination on fire with his animal magnetism—and who ignites the fires of your wild, untamed heart with his powerful character and masculinity.

LIBRA ZODIAC SIGN
YOUR LOVE PLANETS

YOUR ROMANTIC SIDE — p. 696
► VENUS IN SCORPIO
Born Sept. 23, 12:01 - Oct. 11, 4:31
► VENUS IN SAGITTARIUS
Born Oct. 11, 4:32 - Oct. 23, 20:47

YOUR SEX DRIVE — p. 722
► MARS IN SCORPIO
Born Sept. 23, 12:01 - Oct. 09, 11:34
► MARS IN SAGITTARIUS
Born Oct. 09, 11:35 - Oct. 23, 20:47

YOUR CELEBRITY TWINS — p. 760
Find out the astrological similarities you have with famous people.

YOUR COMPATIBILITY — p. 780
Compare planets to find out how compatible you are in a relationship.

YOUR RELATIONSHIP KARMA — p. 824
► SATURN IN AQUARIUS
Born Sept. 23, 12:01 - Oct. 23, 20:47

HELEN TWELVETREES
American Actress
Mars in Scorpio

128

1933 SCORPIO
From October 23, 20:48 through November 22, 17:52

 ## The Fearless Gallivanter

The ideal relationship for a 1933 Scorpio is one that presents a never-ending horizon of entertaining challenges. You are a ball of boisterous and optimistic confidence and are happiest when you have ample freedom within a relationship to pursue your ambitious or playful adventures. Your ideal partner is someone who places the same high value on personal integrity that you do and recognizes that, sometimes, the only way to keep you home is to take home with you.

You are a sexual barnstormer who thrills and delights with your wide-eyed and open-minded attitude. You see sex as a wonderful sport to be enjoyed and entertained by. You have a refreshingly wholesome and exuberant quality about your sexuality that relaxes the uptight and can enchant the most cynical of lovers. The ability to laugh during affectionate moments is the hallmark of your casual and guileless approach to love.

If someone wants to get your attention, they should show that they are able to laugh at themselves first. Your keen sense of comedy often can't resist a good joke, especially at the expense of someone else's ego. If a person can handle your good-humored approach to life, keeping your attention is simple because your ideal partner is a true friend. Cherishing your companionship as much as they cherish you is your sign that you have the right mate for life.

If you are a 1933 Scorpio man, your ideal woman can roll with the punches and travel life's bumpy roads without reservation. You love women whose personalities sparkle like diamonds and who come endowed with a great sense of humor and a better sense of direction. Couple this with the unique ability to maintain hope for you in the worst of times and you know have your true love.

A 1933 Scorpio woman understands men, perhaps a little too well. Your tomboy style may have given way to a more femme fatale glamour but you have never forgotten what you have learned along the way. Your ideal man is the embodiment of every good thing you still believe about manhood. Honorable, true, and brave, you are looking for a champion among men who you can trust.

1933 SAGITTARIUS
From November 22, 17:53 through December 22, 6:57

The Ambitious Achiever

A 1933 Sagittarius has an ambitious nature that often creates caution regarding relationships. You need someone who understands the importance you place on a true partnership and who will not shirk their duties during difficult times. Your ideal partner is conservative and has enough life experience to act as a trusted advisor when you need it. You are a long-term planner who is looking for a true friend and life partner to share your successes with.

You are a sensual, tactile lover with a sexuality that is slow to unleash. When you do allow yourself the privilege of uninhibited intimate expression, you are a tender, considerate, and caring lover whose goal is the pleasure of your partner. You believe that sexual gratification is love's reward for fidelity and trust and prefer not to waste your time with meaningless trysts or unwanted emotional entanglements. Once you feel secure in a relationship, you are an imaginative virtuoso of sensuality.

If someone wants to get your attention, they should ask you about your plans. Whether you are building a future or creating a legacy, you reserve your quality time for people who are willing to go the extra mile and contribute to the richness and successes of your life. If someone can understand your need for goals in every stage of life and stand by you during the lean times, then you can be convinced that they are worth establishing as an integral part of your life.

A 1933 Sagittarius man wants a woman whose support of him is motivated by her love for him, not his achievements. Your ideal mate believes in your ability to achieve your lofty goals and will never fail you when you need her most. Duty bound and traditional in her sense of loyalty, she is an icon of marital fidelity and trustworthiness in marriage for you.

As a 1933 Sagittarius woman, you have social savvy and want a man who knows that the best things in life start with commitment. Your ideal man is industrious and has mature values. He believes in his role of father, provider, and husband and invests as much quality time into your relationship as he does elsewhere.

Mae West – The Wisecracking Sexpot

Mae West was the queen of the wisecracking sexpots in the '20s and '30s. Even toward the end of her career when she was playing Las Vegas nightclubs, Mae West had 'em rolling in the aisle with great one-liners, such as her signature ending, "When I was good, I was very good. But when I was bad, I was better." She believed, long before the social revolution of the '60s, that a woman could be intelligent, strong, and sexually independent all at the same time. Virtually alone among the great women stars of the '20s and '30s, she never allowed herself to become dependent on a man, either financially or sexually.

Mae West married only once, to her burlesque song-and-dance partner Frank Wallace. She was only 17 at the time and left him a few months later. Her mother had advised her to enjoy boys, but not to get too involved with them, a policy she kept for most of her life. West did have a long relationship with New York lawyer Jim Timony, but it evolved from being lovers into a platonic friendship based on mutual trust and respect. West was very liberated when it came to sex. One friend recalled about her earlier years that "Mae West slept with any man she chose to, and no man she chose not to."

Mae West was determined to have a life that counted, one that ultimately meant something, and she found meaning by pioneering sex onstage and in the movies. Her 1927 Broadway play *Sex*, which she wrote, produced, and starred in, was a huge hit, but landed her

"Why don't you come up sometime 'n see me?"

MAE WEST as Lou in *She Done Him Wrong*

in jail for performing an obscene dance onstage. That's when she realized she had become a star. Her next play, *Diamond Lil*, in 1928 , was even more successful. She portrayed what one biographer described

as an "insouciant, insinuating, sashaying, tough-talking, sultry-voiced, golden-wigged, diamond encrusted, bone-corseted, wasp-waisted, flare-hipped, and balloon-bosomed 1890s Bowery saloon hostess and singer."

Building on her Broadway reputation, Mae West went to Hollywood in 1932 to make a movie with former lover George Raft. Although that film was a dud (she had only fourth billing), she had insisted on writing her own lines and was recognized for creating a sensational bit role. The studio then offered her a movie of her own with total script control. She remade *Diamond Lil*, calling it *She Done Him Wrong*, and it became an instant box office hit. She picked the unknown actor Cary Grant for her co-star, having spotted him in the studio lot. "If he can talk, I'll take him," she said.

Her next film, made in 1933 and again co-starring Cary Grant, was *I'm No Angel* and was also a smash hit. The picture was produced for $225,000 and earned over $3 million. However, her famous double entendres and blatant sexuality contributed to a conservative backlash. By 1937 censorship and changing public attitudes had tarnished her star power, and she faded from the limelight.

Mae West achieved cult status in World War II when the inflatable life preservers used by the RAF were named after her. She was a true sex pioneer, perhaps more so than the famed sexologists Freud, Jung, and Kinsey. As she said, "They may have been the generals, but I was on the front lines."

► READ ABOUT CARY GRANT ON PAGES 244 AND 384 ► READ ABOUT MARLENE DIETRICH, ANOTHER POPULAR ACTRESS IN WWII, ON PAGE 105

1934

- ★ DIONNE QUINTS
- ★ HAYS OFFICE
- ★ SCREWBALL COMEDIES
- ★ BING CROSBY
- ★ BLUE MOON
- ★ HONEYSUCKLE ROSE
- ★ I, CLAUDIUS

EVENTS

The birth of the Canadian Dionne quintuplets caused a worldwide stir, turning the girls' childhoods into a carnival freak show. In the US, under pressure from the Catholic Legion of Decency, the Hays Office imposed restrictions on film, prohibiting long kisses, double beds, naked babies, and any suggestion of seduction or cohabitation. Real life was a different matter—*Photoplay* ran an article outing "Unmarried [Hollywood] Husbands and Wives," and contraceptives were sold in the Sears, Roebuck catalog. In Italy, marriage was encouraged by increasing the tax imposed on bachelors, while in Germany, Hitler announced that unemployed fathers would have priority over bachelors in the job market. In the UK, disputes broke out over the decency of dress required by sunbathers on the Thames, but women players at the Wimbledon tennis tournament were allowed to wear shorts for the first time, despite opposition from officials. The Prince of Wales had openly supported the change in rules.

POP CULTURE

Frank Capra's *It Happened One Night*, a screwball comedy about the unlikely romance between a spoiled heiress and a hardboiled reporter, swept the Academy Awards and sent men's undershirt sales south after Clark Gable went without in the film. Poets Elizabeth Barrett and Robert Browning fell in love in *The Barretts of Wimpole Street*, Bette Davis tormented Leslie Howard in *Of Human Bondage*, and high-society detectives Nick and Nora Charles (and their dog

Asta) debuted in *The Thin Man*.

Bing Crosby hosted radio's Kraft Music Hall and people tuned in to hear such pop songs as "Blue Moon" and "I Only Have Eyes for You." The Dorsey Brothers topped the charts with "Honeysuckle Rose." America's Sweetheart Shirley Temple minced through "On the Good Ship Lollipop."

In James Cain's noir novel *The Postman Always Rings Twice*, a drifter and the sultry wife of a roadside restaurant owner plot to murder her husband. James Hilton's book *Goodbye, Mr. Chips* explored the life of a well loved private school teacher, while Robert Graves plumbed the depths of Roman depravity and double dealing in *I, Claudius*. John O'Hara savaged the suburban country club set in *Appointment in Samarra*. Walter B. Pitkin's *Life Begins at Forty* was a bestseller, and moody Welsh poet Dylan Thomas published his *Eighteen Poems*.

FRED ASTAIRE & GINGER ROGERS

Depression-era audiences wanted to forget their problems by being swept up in movie magic and no couple did that better than Fred Astaire and Ginger Rogers. *The Gay Divorcee* in 1934 was their first starring film, where they did their famous "Continental" dance routine. They were never an item, yet their onscreen chemistry was magical.

Rogers went on to win a Best Actress Oscar and Astaire's career lasted almost until his death in 1987, but their names remained linked by the legendary partnership. Explaining why they "clicked," Katharine Hepburn said, "Astaire gave her class and Rogers gave him sex appeal."

SEE ALSO
▶ KATHARINE HEPBURN & SPENCER TRACY *Page 251*

1934 CAPRICORN

From December 22, 1933 6:58 through January 20, 1934 17:36
(December 1934 Capricorns, see 1935 Capricorn)

♑ *The Devoted Intellectual*

As a zesty 1934 Capricorn, your relationship must keep you riveted and be full of snap, crackle and pop. Although security is important to you, a ho-hum partnership that merely endures has no appeal at all. You value change and excitement and require ongoing personal growth to keep things lively. Mutual support and involvement make sharing a life particularly meaningful and give validation to you as an individual.

Friendship to you is an important component of any relationship, so you need to feel that your lover is also your best pal. By sharing common interests and lively conversation, you maintain the sparkle that initially brought you together. Give-and-take is important in any relationship and you enjoy the friction that comes before a compromise is struck. Mutual respect is another significant component of any relationship and even when you disagree, you allow each other the freedom to share your ideas.

You appreciate challenging intellectual interaction, and want your partner to maintain an interesting outlook and have stimulating verbal skills. Passion is less likely to fade when you can share a political debate, giggle over a goofy joke, conduct a chess tournament or debate the merits of a point of view. Working together toward a mutual cause is another way you bond, and of course being part of a group makes you feel closer as a couple because that way you're working together on the same team.

Male goats born in 1934 like a woman who is their intellectual equal. She may be younger, but her verbal pizzazz and challenging point of view keep you endlessly fascinated. You're quite tolerant when your partner is capricious or even a spendthrift because that's all part of the feminine aspects of her nature that you find so appealing, year after year.

As a female Cappie born in 1934, you appreciate masculine men who are stable, hard-working and practically skilled. Your partner's macho qualities endear him to you, even when he's being too bossy, because that increases his sex appeal. Soft and sentimental men annoy you; a guy should be a guy and your guy is always a man's man.

CAPRICORN ZODIAC SIGN
YOUR LOVE PLANETS

YOUR ROMANTIC SIDE — p. 696
▶ **VENUS IN AQUARIUS**
Born Dec. 22, 1933 6:58 - Jan. 20, 1934 17:36

YOUR SEX DRIVE — p. 722
▶ **MARS IN CAPRICORN**
Born Dec. 22, 1933 6:58 - Dec. 28, 1933 3:42
▶ **MARS IN AQUARIUS**
Born Dec. 28, 1933 3:43 - Jan. 20, 1934 17:36

YOUR CELEBRITY TWINS — p. 760
Find out the astrological similarities you have with famous people.

YOUR COMPATIBILITY — p. 780
Compare planets to find out how compatible you are in a relationship.

YOUR RELATIONSHIP KARMA — p. 824
▶ **SATURN IN AQUARIUS**
Born Dec. 22, 1933 6:58 - Jan. 20, 1934 17:36

JESSIE MATTHEWS
English Dancer
Venus in Aquarius

131

1934 AQUARIUS

From January 20, 17:37 through February 19, 8:01

♒ *The Impassioned Romantic*

The 1934 Aquarian understands the power of sentiment. You are a giver and your relationship is about your need to share love and give devotion. Connecting deeply with other people is your special talent and you enjoy being able to bond on every level with your partner. Commitment and security are essential to you and you believe in a relationship that lasts a lifetime rather than any sort of short fling.

Your nature is spiritual and your view of love equally tender. You believe in true love and in destiny and always want to know that your relationship was meant to be. By giving affection and love, you make the world a better place, and you like being in a relationship that provides you an oasis of happiness. Sharing mutual pleasures is always worthwhile, but a connection below the surface that can be intuited is the real glue that holds your romance in place.

Good times and shared laughter are so important to you, and you enjoy a sense of mutual happiness and lively anticipation. Similar interests give you something to talk about and you love sharing details about computers, charities, or local points of interest. Enjoying your partner's company is what love is all about, and you find that as long as there's happy chemistry, you remain love-struck. You have a well-defined view of life and the world, and by sharing that with your true love, you feel that together you're more than just a couple, but a force for good in the world.

As a male Aquarian born in 1934, you appreciate a woman with a well-defined sense of self who is clever, affectionate and committed to a better world. A perky personality, good sense of humor and the ability to entrance you with sparkle and down-to-earth seriousness inspire your ongoing devotion.

Female Aquarians born in 1934, you enjoy a sensitive man who appreciates your sparkle and wants to lavish you with devotion. You feel that excessively macho men don't have the depth that you require of a true love. A partner who is a good dancer, shares impassioned ideas, and encourages you to be your best self, ever keeps you happy, year after year.

AQUARIUS ZODIAC SIGN
YOUR LOVE PLANETS

YOUR ROMANTIC SIDE — p. 696
▶ **VENUS IN AQUARIUS**
Born Jan. 20, 17:37 - Feb. 19, 8:01

YOUR SEX DRIVE — p. 722
▶ **MARS IN AQUARIUS**
Born Jan. 20, 17:37 - Feb. 04, 4:12
▶ **MARS IN PISCES**
Born Feb. 04, 4:13 - Feb. 19, 8:01

YOUR CELEBRITY TWINS — p. 760
Find out the astrological similarities you have with famous people.

YOUR COMPATIBILITY — p. 780
Compare planets to find out how compatible you are in a relationship.

YOUR RELATIONSHIP KARMA — p. 824
▶ **SATURN IN AQUARIUS**
Born Jan. 20, 17:37 - Feb. 19, 8:01

BETTE DAVIS
American Actress
Sun in Aries

1934 PISCES
From February 19, 8:02 through March 21, 7:27

The Generous Lover

As a Pisces born in 1934, you demand a relationship that reflects your social consciousness. To you, a partnership must embody the motto of the Three Musketeers—"All for one and one for all"—although you'd prefer to nurture a relationship of only two rather than three participants! A strong sense of friendship and camaraderie makes a relationship happy and long-lasting, and you are content to frequently put your own needs aside when it makes sense to focus on what's best for the team.

Consideration and harmony are very important to you, and a happy partnership means being selfless some of the time. The ideals of truth, beauty and, most of all, true love are so meaningful to you. Causal flings can occasionally be tempting, but you realize deep in your heart that they don't give you the depth of commitment that is so much more heartwarming.

A partner who keeps you on your toes makes life challenging and much more fun. You don't expect life or love to be easy but you do enjoy working to make a relationship happy. A mate with an interesting point of view is your preference and you don't mind a lively debate now and then. Music and dance really speak to your soul, so attending a concert and holding hands keeps the melody of love alive in your heart.

Male fish born in 1934 like a woman who is sparkly, smart, and who has a tender heart. Your lady wants to make the world a better place and you enjoy being involved with her in those good works. You like to know that there's more to her than a pretty face or sparkling wit, because you want a union to last a lifetime. Therefore she must also be your very best pal. Together you form an unbeatable team and you gather strength from each other.

Female Pisceans of 1934, you seek a sensitive, sentimental, musical fellow who can twirl you around the dance floor and massage your aching feet. You need someone who is as devoted a nurturer as you are, a man who will love you tenderly and long. A guy who is sometimes willing to put his own needs aside will generate a great deal of devotion and strongly inspire you to make him number one in your heart.

1934 ARIES
From March 21, 7:28 through April 20, 18:59

The Romantic Individualist

Being a firecracker Aries born in 1934, you insist on a relationship that lets you be yourself. A little friction isn't always a bad thing in a relationship, because it allows each person to develop greater self-expression, something you deeply prize. Although you find boredom an unbearable affliction, you still believe in commitment and devotion. That's why a lasting relationship must grow and change along with the participants. You want to know that you're appreciated and that your mate will remain devoted, even if you make an occasional mistake.

Life becomes dull for you when it's too predictable, and you're equally willing to have a few surprises in your love life. A relationship is most fun when you're kept on your toes, and the more surprises in the partnership, the greater your willingness to stick around for the long haul. Occasional "words" aren't threatening—you're one of those people who revels in the quarrels as a prelude to the making up.

A partner who expresses admiration for you gains your trust and tenderness, and you feel confident to take risks when you know that someone who loves you is there in your life, providing ongoing devotion. Imagination is one of your strong suits, and a mate who listens with glee to your lively tales provides you with the audience you need. You enjoy concerts and dancing, but devotion, trust and encouragement are what you really require.

Male rams born in 1934 enjoy the company of a woman who is intelligent, clever and committed. You don't mind at all if she sometimes treats you as a recalcitrant little boy during the daytime, as long as she's soft as a lamb at night. You're macho and sexy, and your woman appreciates your sizzling lovemaking as much as your clever mind.

Female Ariens born in 1934 are assertive and it takes a strong man to keep up with you. Soft and sentimental guys bore you because you're more macho than they are. You want an equal who can challenge your mind and toss you into bed for a lively romp in the hay. A guy who is brave, willful and uproarious is man enough to maintain your interest and hold your heart.

1934 TAURUS
From April 20, 19:00 through May 21, 18:34

The Destiny-Seeker

A single-minded Taurus born in 1934, you believe that relationships should just fall into place. What's meant to be will naturally work out, and you would never immerse yourself in a commitment unless you were sure it was the best choice for you. Love and happiness are out there, available to us all, and your strong belief in the goodness of life brings you the commitment and devotion you seek.

A relationship is a partnership in which both people work together to make a life that is just what each one needs. You believe in giving your all to your partnership and you find that following your instincts guarantees you will make good choices, time and time again. Love and devotion are very important to you and casual flings are a total waste of time. You want to love and know your perfect partner, for an entire lifetime.

Good conversation, delicious food, laughter and passionate sensuality appeal to you, and a partner who wants to share those things with you can gain your heart forever. Making life rich and well-lived is also meaningful to you, and a partner who shares this philosophy enriches your life even more. You enjoy wooing and being wooed and it's a great deal of fun to plan a romantic evening or to be on the receiving end of one. Each detail is special to you, and seeing a partner go all-out for you makes your heart go pitapat.

A male bull born in 1934 likes a woman who is passionate. Her verve for life and love excites you and whether or not a tango is playing on the stereo, you feel like dancing. Your lady's depth of feeling is legendary and you enjoy the way she draws you out, encouraging you to try new lovemaking techniques that elevate your passions.

A female Taurus born in 1934 wants her man to be solid, stable and reliable. You know where you stand with this guy and what he thinks about pretty much everything. He helps you build a family, a home, and keeps track of the nest egg. When you're tired he cradles your head and when you're in the mood, he knows how to rev your engine. In short, he's the perfect husband and father and the man you will always love.

TAURUS ZODIAC SIGN
YOUR LOVE PLANETS

YOUR ROMANTIC SIDE   p. 696
► VENUS IN PISCES
Born Apr. 20, 19:00 - May 06, 8:53
► VENUS IN ARIES
Born May 06, 8:54 - May 21, 18:34

YOUR SEX DRIVE   p. 722
► MARS IN ARIES
Born Apr. 20, 19:00 - Apr. 22, 15:39
► MARS IN TAURUS
Born Apr. 22, 15:40 - May 21, 18:34

YOUR CELEBRITY TWINS   p. 760
Find out the astrological similarities you have with famous people.

YOUR COMPATIBILITY   p. 780
Compare planets to find out how compatible you are in a relationship.

YOUR RELATIONSHIP KARMA   p. 824
► SATURN IN AQUARIUS
Born Apr. 20, 19:00 - May 21, 18:34

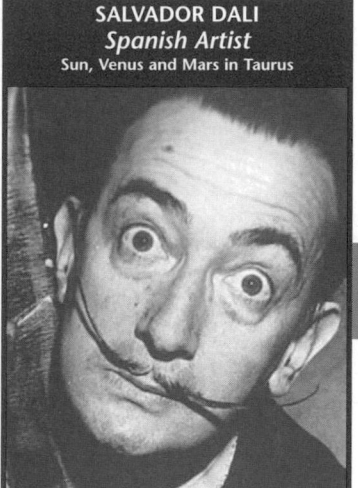

SALVADOR DALI
Spanish Artist
Sun, Venus and Mars in Taurus

133

1934 GEMINI
From May 21, 18:35 through June 22, 2:47

The Free Spirit

A s an excitement-loving Gemini born in 1934, you require a relationship that maintains your interest. Commitment just for the sake of continuity bores you. You need to feel that something exciting can happen in each and every day, and having someone in your life makes it more fun. You're not always sure that you believe in marriage, and even if you've been a couple for what seems like your entire life, you may enjoy baiting your mate and decrying marriage as an institution.

Lively give-and-take is what partnership should be all about. Learning and changing are important parts of life and of any good relationship. Compromise and flexibility are very important to you and you need to know that you have the freedom to change your mind.

A partner must change and grow to maintain your interest, and staying active intellectually is the first step. Lively conversation, good jokes, and clever repartee keep you actively involved with that special someone. If you never know what you're going to hear, you're happy to keep listening. Being part of a group of friends is also important because you're such a social person that you demand lots of social and intellectual stimulation. That way, you can go home with your mate and share lots of delicious gossip.

Male Geminis born in 1934 enjoy a woman who is so smart and lively she seems to change on a daily basis. You don't care at all that she be solid or stable and if she's a little ditzy, so much the better because then you'll keep laughing together. You enjoy sharing music and dancing, the arts and the theatre, but you also require the occasional company of other people. You need a woman who understands this and doesn't object to sharing your attentions now and then.

Female Geminis born in 1934, you like a man to be clever and creative, a good dancer, socially adept and not too demanding. You need your space and your freedom and you like flirting now and then with other guys. Your man knows this and finds it charming. He's never possessive or demanding but instead always lets you be the breath of fresh air who first won his heart.

GEMINI ZODIAC SIGN
YOUR LOVE PLANETS

YOUR ROMANTIC SIDE   p. 696
► VENUS IN ARIES
Born May 21, 18:35 - June 02, 10:10
► VENUS IN TAURUS
Born June 02, 10:11 - June 22, 2:47

YOUR SEX DRIVE   p. 722
► MARS IN TAURUS
Born May 21, 18:35 - June 02, 16:20
► MARS IN GEMINI
Born June 02, 16:21 - June 22, 2:47

YOUR CELEBRITY TWINS   p. 760
Find out the astrological similarities you have with famous people.

YOUR COMPATIBILITY   p. 780
Compare planets to find out how compatible you are in a relationship.

YOUR RELATIONSHIP KARMA   p. 824
► SATURN IN AQUARIUS
Born May 21, 18:35 - June 22, 2:47

LUIGI PIRANDELLO
Italian Writer
Sun in Cancer

134

1934 CANCER
From June 22, 2:48 through July 23, 13:41

 The Sentimental Prankster

As a loquacious Cancer born in 1934, you need a relationship that provides devotion and intellectual stimulation in equal measure. Connecting with other people is the most important thing in your life, and your relationship must be well-balanced and interesting. Nothing is as satisfying as sharing life's little moments with that special someone, and you know that when you can love and play together, you can stay together forever.

You believe in true love and always want to feel that your relationship was meant to be. Commitment is very important to you, but not as important as the sense that destiny is on your side. Belonging together and to each other is what a relationship is really all about and you feel sorry for people who don't share that sense of everlasting devotion and camaraderie.

You're tender and sentimental, it's true, but you also have a wicked sense of humor and respond with raucous good cheer to a mate who brings out the good times in life. Culture and artistic pursuits appeal to you and you enjoy sharing those interests with a mate who is as involved with them as you are. What a bore it must be to wrestle over the remote control! In your household, it's more fun to watch something you both enjoy. You love children, and playing fun games with or without youngsters keeps you youthful—and in love.

Male crabs born in 1934 like a woman who is a smart and clever wordsmith, whose youthful enthusiasm for life makes her enduringly special. Although she must be cultured and appreciative of the arts, your lady is also quite spiritual and sexy in her own special way. It's not so much what she does that makes you love her, but you give your heart because of the tender way she makes you feel.

Female Cancers born in 1934 like a man who is playful, intelligent, well-informed and a good dancer. He's witty and urbane, and you know that his heart is in the right place. Even if you seldom leave your own hometown, this man makes you feel as if you've traveled the world and made love in every exotic port. He's as much fun as a circus, and tender as a flaky piece of pastry.

1934 LEO
From July 23, 13:42 through August 23, 20:31

 The Tender Paramour

A generous Leo born in 1934, your relationship must be filled with tenderness, devotion and joy. You love sharing happiness and enjoy being in a partnership in which you both revel in the good life. Building a home and family together is what life is all about and you love seeing children, grandchildren, and even great-grandchildren come into your happy world.

Other people may live for appearances, but you exist for joy, and you love loving and being loved. The goodness of life is reflected in your relationship, and nothing makes you happier than giving joy to someone who lives to return the favor. It's not enough that you believe in true love (of course you do), but in living every day and giving your heart and soul each time as you did when you first met, you reaffirm the principles of all that is good and holy about life and love.

To maintain your devotion, a partner must be genuine, sincere and loving. Although you appreciate a pleasant appearance, you're much more interested in a pure heart. A mate whose heart is always in the right place will gain and hold your love forever. You enjoy cooking, playing games, and shopping as much as you like romance, and you feel that maintaining that childlike spirit of pleasure will keep you forever youthful and in love.

Male lions born in 1934 appreciate a woman who is tender-hearted, motherly and generous of spirit. Your lady is a woman, not a girl, though she never loses her ability to play. She can wipe away a child's tear, feed you a sinful morsel while naked in bed, and converse on a variety of significant topics. She is the girl of your dreams and the woman who will forever hold your heart gently in her hand.

Female Leos born in 1934 like a man who is gentle and kind yet outgoing and sexy. Your man is secure and generous, as boisterous as Santa Claus, and he knows how to touch all the tender places you're so shy about revealing. His heart is sweetly sentimental and he is eternally dedicated only to you. You know he's the perfect man for you because he's a thrilling lover, a devoted dad, and the best provider on earth.

1934 VIRGO

From August 23, 20:32 through September 23, 17:44

The Spiritual Giver

A creative Virgo born in 1934, you need a relationship that stimulates your imagination. You believe in commitment that's born of devotion rather than obligation. A relationship to you is one of the ways in which you grow and thrive as an individual. Giving and sharing are essential dimensions of any relationship, and you enjoy being able to make your partner's life happier.

You believe in destiny and you want to feel that you belong with your partner. A relationship fulfills a spiritual need in your life to be part of something meaningful and greater than just yourself. It's not enough to share your life as a way to avoid being lonely; you must feel that you're on the right track, that there's comfort and contentment as well as joy and playfulness, and a relationship that gives you all that will inspire eternal devotion.

A partner whose intuition matches your own is the perfect choice. You want to feel that some things can remain unspoken, that you're both dancing to the same drummer without ever having to negotiate terms. You have an artistic and playful side and like being with a mate who can share your love of culture and music. You enjoy attending concerts and dancing, and may make it your life's mission to capture your mate on film. You also enjoy being wooed and lavished with clever gifts, but you'd never give your heart for a mere bauble.

Male Virgos born in 1934 appreciate a woman who is as fun-loving as she is beautiful. Your artistic sensibilities respond to beauty and you can't help admiring a pretty face. Your lady must also be a bit unpredictable, have a mind of her own, and give you a good surprise now and then. She's playful in bed, likes being a sex object, and knows how to turn the tables on you.

Female Virgos born in 1934, you prefer a man who is macho enough to allow you to enjoy being feminine. He's clever and creative and sexy enough to make you quiver in delight, even when you're just remembering what happened once upon a time. He's smart enough to keep you guessing and a bit of a bad boy, but you know that under it all, he's a good guy.

VIRGO ZODIAC SIGN
YOUR LOVE PLANETS

YOUR ROMANTIC SIDE   p. 696
- ▶ VENUS IN LEO
  Born Aug. 23, 20:32 - Sept. 11, 3:31
- ▶ VENUS IN VIRGO
  Born Sept. 11, 3:32 - Sept. 23, 17:44

YOUR SEX DRIVE   p. 722
- ▶ MARS IN CANCER
  Born Aug. 23, 20:32 - Aug. 30, 13:42
- ▶ MARS IN LEO
  Born Aug. 30, 13:43 - Sept. 23, 17:44

YOUR CELEBRITY TWINS   p. 760
Find out the astrological similarities you have with famous people.

YOUR COMPATIBILITY   p. 780
Compare planets to find out how compatible you are in a relationship.

YOUR RELATIONSHIP KARMA   p. 824
- ▶ SATURN IN AQUARIUS
  Born Aug. 23, 20:32 - Sept. 23, 17:44

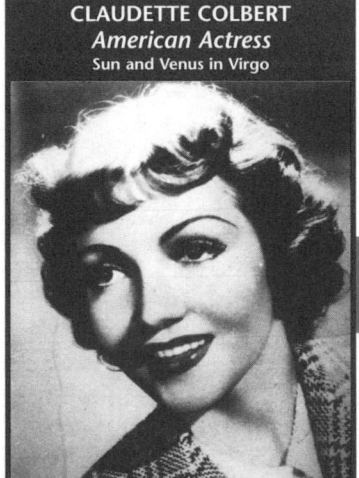

CLAUDETTE COLBERT
American Actress
Sun and Venus in Virgo

135

1934 LIBRA

From September 23, 17:45 through October 24, 2:35

The Genteel Romantic

A s a conservative Libra born in 1934, your relationship must embody good taste and decorum. You care deeply about balance and harmony and feel most comfortable in a relationship that is genteel and amicable. You could never endure a public shouting match and feel badly for people whose lives have gotten so messy. You believe in compromise and are willing to give up your own preference in favor of your mate's, when necessary.

You believe that compatibility is essential in any relationship; that way, fewer compromises are necessary and everyone's needs are met. Stability, commitment and building a solid life together are essential to you, and you will work very hard to ensure the success of your relationship. You may be a bit old-fashioned and if so, you gladly champion the family values of bygone days. We all have our roles to play and our responsibilities, and you're committed to upholding your own.

A partner must be up to your standards to gain and maintain your devotion. You would never align your destiny with someone who was crude or tacky. Of course, you're a Libra, and that means you love romance, being taken out to cultural events, being wined and dined and given sweet mementos of affection. But it's not just the hearts and flowers to which you respond. Instead, when you see worthwhile behavior and words backed up by deeds, you feel respect, and then enduring affection. Pitching in together, making a difference in your neighborhood, these are the things worth sharing.

A male Libran born in 1934 appreciates a woman who is sweet, kind and pretty. Your lady is charming, adorable and a social asset. She knows how to entertain your contacts, whether they be family or business. She appreciates how hard you work and how much effort you put into the family.

Female Librans born in 1934 want a man who is stable, reliable and a success. He may be older, he's secure in himself and his life, and he looks to you for beauty and comfort. This man is a great provider and he gives you the security you crave and the freedom to explore your artistic and cultural interests.

LIBRA ZODIAC SIGN
YOUR LOVE PLANETS

YOUR ROMANTIC SIDE   p. 696
- ▶ VENUS IN VIRGO
  Born Sept. 23, 17:45 - Oct. 05, 7:55
- ▶ VENUS IN LIBRA
  Born Oct. 05, 7:56 - Oct. 24, 2:35

YOUR SEX DRIVE   p. 722
- ▶ MARS IN LEO
  Born Sept. 23, 17:45 - Oct. 18, 4:58
- ▶ MARS IN VIRGO
  Born Oct. 18, 4:59 - Oct. 24, 2:35

YOUR CELEBRITY TWINS   p. 760
Find out the astrological similarities you have with famous people.

YOUR COMPATIBILITY   p. 780
Compare planets to find out how compatible you are in a relationship.

YOUR RELATIONSHIP KARMA   p. 824
- ▶ SATURN IN AQUARIUS
  Born Sept. 23, 17:45 - Oct. 24, 2:35

SCORPIO ZODIAC SIGN
YOUR LOVE PLANETS

YOUR ROMANTIC SIDE   p. 696
▶ **VENUS IN LIBRA**
Born Oct. 24, 2:36 - Oct. 29, 7:36
▶ **VENUS IN SCORPIO**
Born Oct. 29, 7:37 - Nov. 22, 4:58
▶ **VENUS IN SAGITTARIUS**
Born Nov. 22, 4:59 - Nov. 22, 23:43

YOUR SEX DRIVE   p. 722
▶ **MARS IN VIRGO**
Born Oct. 24, 2:36 - Nov. 22, 23:43

YOUR CELEBRITY TWINS   p. 760
*Find out the astrological similarities you have
with famous people.*

YOUR COMPATIBILITY   p. 780
*Compare planets to find out how compatible
you are in a relationship.*

YOUR RELATIONSHIP KARMA   p. 824
▶ **SATURN IN AQUARIUS**
Born Oct. 24, 2:36 - Nov. 22, 23:43

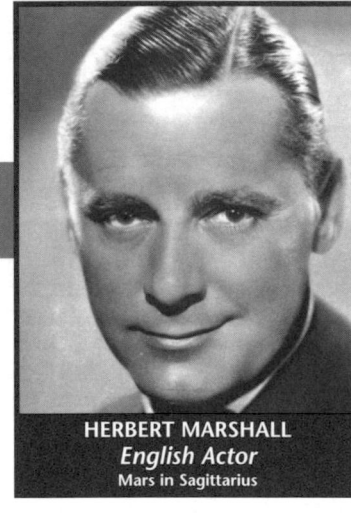

HERBERT MARSHALL
English Actor
Mars in Sagittarius

SAGITTARIUS ZODIAC SIGN
YOUR LOVE PLANETS

YOUR ROMANTIC SIDE   p. 696
▶ **VENUS IN SAGITTARIUS**
Born Nov. 22, 23:44 - Dec. 16, 1:38
▶ **VENUS IN CAPRICORN**
Born Dec. 16, 1:39 - Dec. 22, 12:48

YOUR SEX DRIVE   p. 722
▶ **MARS IN VIRGO**
Born Nov. 22, 23:44 - Dec. 11, 9:31
▶ **MARS IN LIBRA**
Born Dec. 11, 9:32 - Dec. 22, 12:48

YOUR CELEBRITY TWINS   p. 760
*Find out the astrological similarities you have
with famous people.*

YOUR COMPATIBILITY   p. 780
*Compare planets to find out how compatible
you are in a relationship.*

YOUR RELATIONSHIP KARMA   p. 824
▶ **SATURN IN AQUARIUS**
Born Nov. 22, 23:44 - Dec. 22, 12:48

136

1934 SCORPIO
From October 24, 2:36 through November 22, 23:43

The Joyous Soulmate

An exuberant Scorpio born in 1934, you require a relationship to stimulate you on every level. To you a relationship should be as much fun as attending summer camp as a child, as sweetly optimistic as a first date, and as passionate as sex with the perfect soulmate. You are direct, open and honest, and you want a relationship to be happy, joyous and perfection itself.

You believe in commitment, but not because you fear solitude. Instead you know that when you're with the soulmate who completes your destiny, it just feels right to stay together forever. Love is the perfect form of self-expression and it provides a bountiful river of joy in which you and your mate choose to swim together. You feel sorry for those sad folks who stay together merely for the kids or for the sake of appearances. You'd never do that. Your heart is your own until you give it to the soulmate who will hold you forever entranced.

There are lots of ways a partner can hold your interest. Being charming, sexy, a good conversationalist, sharing funny tidbits, planning a romantic evening and taking you dancing all tickle your fancy. But when it comes right down to it, it's not about what your lover does, but who he or she is. You believe that we all make our own fun, and our own happiness, and by being with the right person, everything in your world comes into focus.

Male Scorpions born in 1934 love women. You can't help it—you're entranced by their beauty, the yin perfection of their natures, the softness of their skin. You could rhapsodize forever about the perfection that is woman. Your chosen partner must be all that and more. It's the light in her eyes that gets you and holds you. All the rest is just fluff!

Female Scorpios born in 1934 like a man who's sparkly, fun and intuitive. Nothing appeals to you more than when he whispers a fantasy into your ear and you recognize it as your own, without ever having to inform him of the slightest detail. He is a giver and he knows how to make you smile. Being in the same room gives you comfort and joy, and you know he is what makes your world feel right.

1934 SAGITTARIUS
From November 22, 23:44 through December 22, 12:48

The Loving Conversationalist

An unassuming Sagittarius born in 1934, you need a relationship that lets you go with the flow. You want your world and your love life to be relaxed and comfortable. That's much more important to you than stability or commitment. As long as things feel happy, you're content to remain in a relationship, but you'd never want to endure years of acrimony just to preserve a few unimportant mutual assets.

There's a spiritual side to your nature and you must feel that there's some element of destiny in your relationship. You've come together for a purpose that serves each of you and that also makes the world a little bit better. Love is a powerful force for growth and healing, and that's what you appreciate most about being connected to someone special. You gain emotional sustenance and a sense of comfort from being romantically entwined.

To maintain your interest, a partner must continue to have something worthwhile to say. You are deep, and you appreciate a mindset that observes and comments on the profundities of life. You're a good conversationalist and banalities bore you. Sharing interests also appeals to you and it's lots of fun to walk along a beach at sunset, to explore interesting places, or travel to faraway spots. Sex is another way a partner sustains your interest. Being creative in bed keeps you wanting more.

Male Sagittarians born in 1934 enjoy a woman who is spiritual, creative and sensitive. A sweet nature and clever wit endear her to you, but you respond even more strongly to the kindnesses she does for you and other people. Knowing in your heart that she is someone special and that the world is a better place because she's here makes you love her all the more.

Female archers born in 1934 need a man who owns his own power. He is confident and capable and has a way of sparking your imagination—in bed and out. You enjoy sharing activities with your guy and as long as he's willing to give your newest interest a try, you're willing to cut him a lot of slack. He can be bossy and eccentric and that's okay too, because to you that keeps him interesting.

Bonnie and Clyde – Outlaw Lovers

Two lovers with a death-defying love, wild, defiant, willing to go down together in a hail of glory—such is the stuff of Hollywood romance. But for outlaws Bonnie Parker and Clyde Barrow, real life on the run was nowhere near as glamorous as it appeared in the 1967 film *Bonnie and Clyde*. Lacking the height of the willowy Faye Dunaway, Parker, born on October 1, 1910 in Rowena, Texas, was a tiny thing—only four-foot-ten-inches tall and 85 pounds in weight. The love of her life, Clyde Chestnut Barrow, born on March 24, 1909 in Telico, Texas, was no Warren Beatty. At five-foot-seven-inches, he weighed 125 pounds.

Feeding speculation about the outlaws' sexuality, the movie suggested that Bonnie was a frustrated nymphomaniac and that Barrow was impotent, if not homosexual. "I ain't much of a lover boy," says Beatty. Dunaway's Bonnie rages at Clyde's inability to perform, and the movie implies something of a sexual ménage à trois between Bonnie, Clyde, and their accomplice, C.W. Moss, a composite character based on two members of the actual Barrow gang, W.D. Jones and Henry Methvin.

Clyde Barrow was, in fact, a normal heterosexual male. At Christmas time in 1929, he met Bonnie at a mutual friend's home. It was love at first sight for both of them, even though Parker was married and remained so until her death. Her husband was Roy Thornton, a convict serving time for theft. Bonnie and Clyde saw each other daily until early February 1930 when Clyde was arrested for petty thievery. Bonnie helped him escape from the Waco County lockup, but he was

"Mama, when they kill us, don't ever say anything ugly about Clyde."

BONNIE PARKER shortly before her death

caught and sentenced to 14 years at Eastham Prison Farm, a notoriously brutal Texas facility, where he was likely the victim of jailhouse rape. A desperate move appears to confirm Clyde's revulsion at his treatment. In early 1932 he gained early medical release by having a fellow prisoner chop off two of his toes with an axe. Shortly thereafter, the lovers made off on a two-year spree of robbery and murder that would end in an orgy of violence on May 23, 1934.

The charts of Bonnie and Clyde indicate that Bonnie got an emotional charge from Clyde's violent impulses and that he found her to be a sympathetic and nurturing mate. Clyde's Mars, planet of aggression, stands directly next to his Uranus, which rules sudden outbursts. Bonnie's Moon, which rules feelings and motherly care, makes an exact angle to Clyde's Mars and Uranus. Uranus rules rebels, and the Barrow Gang enjoyed a Robin Hood-like reputation for defying the government and stealing from banks that profited from Depression-era foreclosures.

The harsh conditions and close quarters of fugitive life limited opportunities for normal intimacy, let alone any three-way hanky panky with fellow gang members. For all the brutality of their way of life, the Barrow Gang was remarkably family-oriented. In March 1933, Clyde's brother, Buck, and his wife, Blanche, joined them. Along their criminal path through Texas and other states they would frequently arrange family gatherings with the parents and siblings of various gang members. One visit to the Louisiana home of Iverson Methvin, father of gang member Henry Methvin, enabled famed bounty hunter Frank Hamer to arrange the ambush that brought the story of Bonnie and Clyde to a fatal climax in a hail of bullets.

137

▶ READ ABOUT FAYE DUNAWAY ON PAGE 458 AND WARREN BEATTY ON PAGE 497 ▶ READ ABOUT THE LONELY HEARTS KILLERS, ANOTHER CRIME COUPLE, ON PAGE 259

⭐ **LADY GODIVA**

⭐ **PORGY AND BESS**

⭐ **TIME AND LIFE**

⭐ **BRIDE OF FRANKENSTEIN**

⭐ **CHEEK TO CHEEK**

⭐ **BEGIN THE BEGUINE**

⭐ **TORTILLA FLAT**

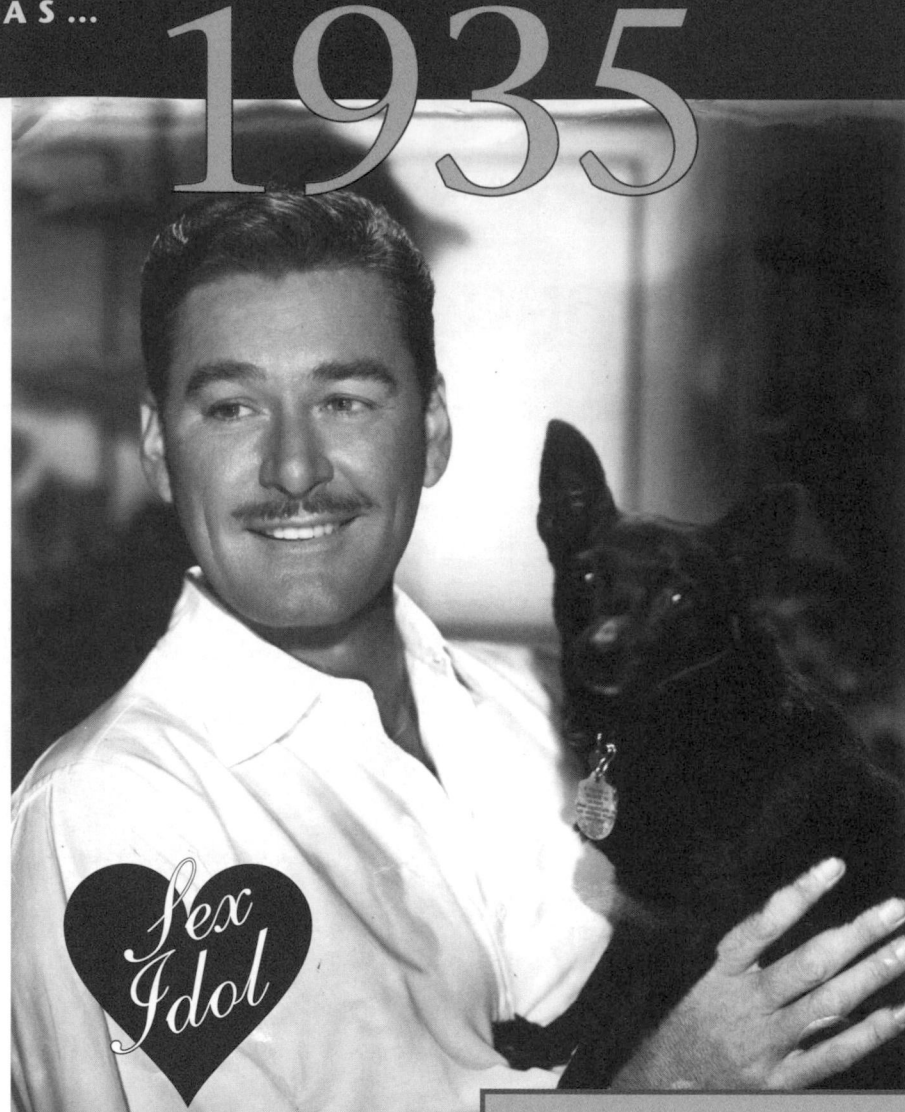

Sex Idol

EVENTS

A jubilee pageant in Brighton, England found its volunteer Lady Godiva got cold feet at the last moment. Desperate appeals were made for a replacement— even if it had to be a man dressed in flesh-colored tights. Unity Mitford, daughter of Lord Redesdale, showed no hesitation when she met Adolf Hitler for the first time and fell head over heels in love with him. She became a keen assistant of the Nazi Party. The Gershwins, whose work was banned in Germany, jolted the opera world with the premiere of *Porgy and Bess*. Playwright and *Vanity Fair* Managing Editor Claire Boothe married Henry Luce, founder of *Time* magazine. Together they launched *Life* magazine, and Clare went on to become a war correspondent and later the first American female ambassador (to Mexico). In Germany Hitler banned all marriages between Aryan Germans and Jews. If Jewish boys so much as walked together with German girls, they risked being sent to a concentration camp.

POP CULTURE

Hollywood went for the classics with adaptations of *A Midsummer Night's Dream*, *Anna Karenina*, and *Les Misérables*. Boris Karloff got a custom-built dream girl in *Bride of Frankenstein*, and Charles Laughton and Clark Gable had it out in *Mutiny on the Bounty*. Alfred Hitchcock hit his stride with spy thriller *The 39 Steps*. The operetta *Naughty Marietta* brought Jeanette MacDonald and Nelson Eddy together on film, while the Marx Brothers offered a decidedly twisted take on the

world of divas in *A Night at the Opera*.

Hollywood stars hit the pop charts with songs like Fred Astaire's *Top Hat* number "Cheek to Cheek." Opera made the crossover, too, as "Summertime" became a hit. People also were listening to "Begin the Beguine," "Stairway to the Stars," "These Foolish Things," and "Zing! Went the Strings of My Heart."

The year's books explored pressing social issues. Fascism came under attack in Sinclair Lewis's *It Can't Happen Here*. John Steinbeck set his *Tortilla Flat* in a mixed-race community in California. Horace McCoy's noir *They Shoot Horses, Don't They?* took place in a world of dance marathon desperation. Thomas Wolfe's *Of Time and the River* followed a young southerner in New York City, and Edna Ferber chronicled a Wisconsin family's fortunes in the first decades of the century in *Come and Get It*.

ERROL FLYNN

I n *Captain Blood*, Errol Flynn achieved overnight success in the 1935 film and brought his own unique swashbuckling style and sex appeal to the adventurous characters he portrayed. One of Hollywood's lovable "bad boys," Flynn was married three times. His first marriage was to French movie star Lili Damita.

Notorious for drinking, carousing, and living life on his own terms, Flynn found himself accused of statutory rape in 1942. In 1958, shortly before his death, he portrayed friend and idol John Barrymore in *Too Much, Too Soon*. The popular phrase "in like Flynn" derives from his reputation for sexual conquests.

SEE ALSO

▶ **TYRONE POWER** *Page 188*

▶ **JOHN GILBERT** *Page 56*

1935 CAPRICORN

From December 22, 1934 12:49 through January 20, 1935 23:27
(December 1935 Capricorns, see 1936 Capricorn)

♑ The Elegant Sophisticate

You're a romantic Capricorn born in 1935 and your relationship must have just the right balance of sentimentality and stability. You believe in congeniality and happiness without strife or aggravation. Love, in your opinion, is just supposed to work out and that's that. Although you recognize the deep importance of reliability and commitment, you don't feel a relationship should endure out of obligation but rather because it just hums along naturally.

Good communication is important to you in a relationship because you feel that being creative intellectually is a good way to connect and life is much more fun when you share fascinating ideas with an interesting partner. Magic within a relationship is another very important facet. You feel that there should just be a sense of distinctiveness between you, a feeling that is there from the moment you meet and lasts as long as you're together.

A clever mind and a good grasp of the social graces in a mate has always appealed to you. Someone who tickles your fancy with an amusing conversational tidbit is sure to hold your interest. A warm and friendly feeling brings you together and keeps you involved. You enjoy being wooed and entertained and you don't mind at all if someone dresses elegantly to impress you and takes you to a pricey restaurant.

Male goats born in 1935 like a solid, practical, down to earth sort of woman who is more than just what she seems. Your lady has skills and intelligence but she's also romantic and even a little quirky now and then. That's because she expresses herself with unembarrassed flair—you know from the moment you meet that she could be an enduring part of your life and you suspect she was meant to be your best pal.

Female Cappies born in 1935 feel a man should be elegant and socially adept. You love the heroes from old movies because they were so sophisticated and could twirl a woman around on a dance floor. That to you is the epitome of taste and refinement. Your guy is a good leader but he's never overly aggressive. He just knows the way to get things done—and the way to your heart.

1935 AQUARIUS

From January 20, 23:28 through February 19, 13:51

♒ The Easygoing Intellectual

As a steadfast Aquarius born in 1935, your relationship must be friendly and reliable. You want to feel that you've connected with someone who is not only your best friend but the person without whom your life wouldn't be the same. It's not so much that you're obsessed with true love—to you it's not really about hearts and flowers but rather about just being peaceful with someone truly congenial. Being just right for each other is your frame of reference.

Good communication is important to you because you enjoy clever repartee, intellectual exchanges and political discussions, and you'd never be happy with an attractive but dull-witted partner. You need someone on your own level who can continue to stimulate you. Sharing mutual interests is also important and there's no substitute at all for the feeling that together you're building a worthwhile and happy life.

You've always appreciated people with substance and that's what you find most important in a partner. Knowing that you've connected with a quality individual whom you can respect and trust is what love is all about, in your opinion. A partner who invites you to pitch in on a charity drive, be part of a neighborhood group, or attend an interesting lecture knows what makes you tick. You like best the quiet moments in which your friendship deepens.

Male Aquarians born in 1935 like a woman who is intelligent and refined. Your lady is practical and informed and she may have had a career in the sciences and the arts, even in the days when such was unheard of. A woman who can build something on her own is someone you want in your corner. This lady is interesting and you always have something to talk about.

Female Aquarians born in 1935 like a man to be refined and elegant but also stable and reliable. Your guy can whirl you around on the dance floor but he's no dandy. He's a solid guy you can always count on. His values are sound and he inspires confidence in all who know him. You enjoy his company in social situations, he's easy to love, and he brings abundant charm and good cheer to any situation you share.

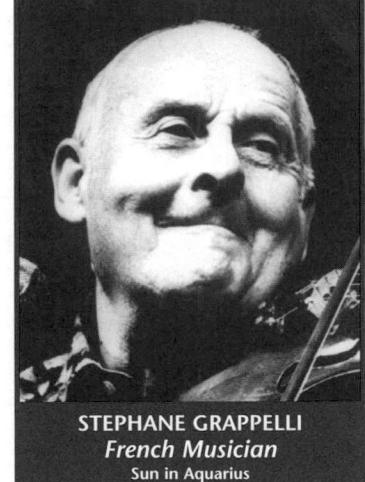

STEPHANE GRAPPELLI
French Musician
Sun in Aquarius

MADELEINE CARROLL
English Actress
Sun and Venus in Pisces

1935 PISCES
From February 19, 13:52 through March 21, 13:17

The Sexy Rebel

You're an independent Pisces born in 1935, and to you a relationship must be very stimulating and exciting. You find that you learn so much about life through relating seriously to a mate and you enjoy a relationship that is somewhat challenging. Dull and routine are not your preference at all!

Sharing interesting ideas with a mate is the foundation of your relationship. You enjoy being able to talk and to enjoy each other's points of view. Compromise is another important feature of your relationship, and you realize that sometimes you have to fight for what you want. That doesn't mean the relationship has gone sour though, but rather that it's always lively and interesting. Each time you work through a compromise you feel that the relationship is a source of learning and inspiration.

Although the sweet, sentimental aspects of love do appeal to you, the mate who is challenging and makes you think is really more likely to sustain your interest. You like surprises and enjoy pointing out to today's unruly youngsters that you were a rebel ahead of your time. Thus a mate with the nerve to steal a kiss in a public place, or even to do something a bit more risqué—that's a partner you could love forever. An impromptu invitation has always appealed to you, and you enjoy fast cars, scavenger hunts, masquerade balls, and anything out of the ordinary.

If you're a male Pisces born in 1935, you like a woman with pizzazz. Your lady is outgoing and assertive, and she can give any man a run for his money. Shy wallflowers don't appeal to you at all. You prefer a woman who can stand up for herself—and stand up to you as well. She knows her own mind and she's as willing to drag you back to her cave as she is to be dragged back to yours.

As a female Pisces born in 1935, you demand that a partner be on your own level. Your guy can be original, quirky, and a bit eccentric and you feel all the richer for knowing him. Dull or ordinary is not your ideal fellow at all. Your man has excellent social graces, but often he laughs at convention. He's an independent thinker and wickedly sexy in bed.

1935 ARIES
From March 21, 13:18 through April 21, 0:49

The Chic Sensualist

As a social Aries born in 1935, you value romance, sensuality, and pleasure in a relationship. Being able to socialize with your mate is important to you, and you like being a glamorous couple others admire. You also like to feel the intense chemistry that draws you together and believe that good chemistry can heal many of the problems that occur in a long-term partnership.

Having similar tastes and a good level of compatibility is another plus in your love relationship. You feel that some compromise is in order, but you'd never want to wrangle with a partner whose taste or lifestyle were at odds with your own. Wanting the same things out of life and being able to build something together has always appealed to you. You feel that stability and commitment are essential in a relationship, and a like-minded partner is the best way to accomplish that goal. That way life and love are easy and it all feels right, year after year.

The social graces are important to you, and a mate whose style and flair complement your own has always appealed most to you. That doesn't mean you'd choose to fall for someone who blandly follows the rules, because you enjoy a partner who is sexy and who isn't shy about it. A partner who sensually strokes your hand or offers an impromptu backrub has always been able to get your attention rather quickly.

You male Aries born in 1935 prefer a woman to be beautiful and sensual. Your lady is elegant and stylish, and she isn't shy about giving into her passions. She loves to eat, to touch, and be touched and even if she's a bit overweight, you feel that makes her more sensual and sexy. Your beloved is soft and sweet, she has a beautiful voice, and she knows how to make you feel safe, secure and desired.

Female Rams born in 1935 feel that a man should have excellent social graces but a wicked side as well. You guy is well-mannered and elegant and he loves to dress well. You can shop together endlessly and you each love dressing the other up—and undressing each other as well. Sometimes he's bossy and demanding, but you enjoy that macho side of his nature.

1935 TAURUS *From April 21, 0:50 through May 22, 0:24*

The Memory Maker

You're a communicative Taurus born in 1935 and your relationship must keep you interested. Sharing is very important to you and, whether you're discussing interesting ideas, doing fun things together, or building a new home, it's all about the harmonious interaction resulting from doing it together as a team. A relationship lacking a positive team spirit mentality would not be your choice at all.

Being with a mate you love who loves you equally is what makes your relationship special. Knowing that you're compatible, and that you like each other as much as you love each other, gives you a sense of security. Good conversation is the light in your relationship, and each day you look forward to sharing your thoughts and feelings with that perfect partner. Social activities that you share are also important to you because they provide the foundation of memories that fill your life.

A clever partner who has something interesting to say has always appealed to you. You enjoy being engaged in conversation and a date comprising little more than a stroll through the park can be made special by the nice chit chat you share. You enjoy being invited to a lecture, going to a party, or doing something where children are. Going to a dance recital of your grandchildren can be just as special as a date from your youth because of the energy you exchange with your true love.

If you're a male Bull born in 1935, you like a woman who remains girlish all her life. Your sweetheart is fun, and her ideas are youthful, and filled with sparkle. Her peppiness is endearing to you because you know that no matter how many years you share, she'll always have something interesting to say and she'll keep you involved and amused.

As a female Taurus born in 1935, your guy must be willing to compromise. You like to feel there's a real partnership in your relationship and that you're both equally involved in making the decisions. Your man is tasteful and pleasant and he never offends anyone. He's kind to your friends, willingly attends the social events you enjoy, and he likes wearing nice clothes.

TAURUS ZODIAC SIGN
YOUR LOVE PLANETS

YOUR ROMANTIC SIDE — p. 696
▶ VENUS IN GEMINI
Born Apr. 21, 0:50 - May 11, 22:00
▶ VENUS IN CANCER
Born May 11, 22:01 - May 22, 0:24

YOUR SEX DRIVE — p. 722
▶ MARS IN LIBRA
Born Apr. 21, 0:50 - May 22, 0:24

YOUR CELEBRITY TWINS — p. 760
Find out the astrological similarities you have with famous people.

YOUR COMPATIBILITY — p. 780
Compare planets to find out how compatible you are in a relationship.

YOUR RELATIONSHIP KARMA — p. 824
▶ SATURN IN PISCES
Born Apr. 21, 0:50 - May 22, 0:24

141

1935 GEMINI  *From May 22, 0:25 through June 22, 8:37*

The Adoring Lover

As a responsible Gemini born in 1935, you believe a relationship must be passionate and fiery enough to inspire a lifetime commitment. Love to you has always been about that struck-by-a-thunderbolt feeling that makes a connection unavoidable, as though you're both being carried along on an emotional tidal wave. If you have to ask yourself what you're feeling, it's not for you! Your relationship features such an intense connection that it binds you together forever.

You're quite serious and you believe in building a relationship on a solid foundation. Giving and receiving a sacred promise to love and trust forever is very meaningful to you. You feel that being connected to a mate means that sometimes you have to compromise and give up what you want as an individual. There is never any sense of sacrifice in that for you because of the intensity of the love you share.

Your first rule in choosing a partner has always been to ask is he or she a person of substance. Someone deep and solid is your preference and that's something you discover over time. Feeling the chemistry has always been the first step and so the particular event you share is less important than the electricity between you. It is fun to get dressed up and go to a fancy dress ball or other elegant event. You also like being given nice gifts and sharing deep and relevant conversation.

You male Geminis of 1935 like a woman who is passionate and intense. Your sweetie has a deep and loving heart and you adore the way she makes you feel as though her love is never-ending sunshine that warms your world. This lady is kindly, generous, and nurturing, and she adores your children as intensely as she loves you. Creating a happy family is very important to her.

Female Geminis feel a man should be well-mannered and orderly. Your fellow is a good leader and he has strong, solid values. He believes in doing the right thing and you know you can always trust his sense of ethics. This man is a responsible partner and always upholds his end of the bargain, whether socially, personally, at home, or in the business world.

BENNY GOODMAN
American Musician
Sun and Venus in Gemini

GEMINI ZODIAC SIGN
YOUR LOVE PLANETS

YOUR ROMANTIC SIDE — p. 696
▶ VENUS IN CANCER
Born May 22, 0:25 - June 07, 19:10
▶ VENUS IN LEO
Born June 07, 19:11 - June 22, 8:37

YOUR SEX DRIVE — p. 722
▶ MARS IN LIBRA
Born May 22, 0:25 - June 22, 8:37

YOUR CELEBRITY TWINS — p. 760
Find out the astrological similarities you have with famous people.

YOUR COMPATIBILITY — p. 780
Compare planets to find out how compatible you are in a relationship.

YOUR RELATIONSHIP KARMA — p. 824
▶ SATURN IN PISCES
Born May 22, 0:25 - June 22, 8:37

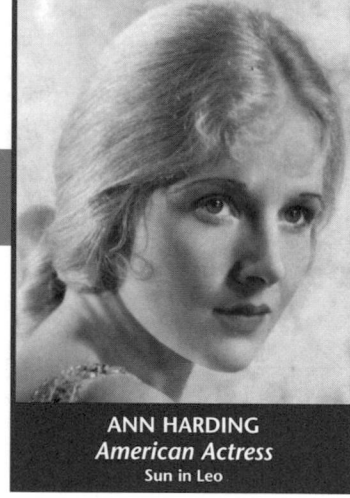

ANN HARDING
American Actress
Sun in Leo

1935 CANCER
From June 22, 8:38 through July 23, 19:32

The Loyal Lover

You're a devoted Cancer born in 1935, and you feel most comfortable in a relationship that features equal give-and-take. To you, a partnership is about taking care of and supporting each other and you enjoy the feeling that you and your mate are tightly bonded. Nurturing and being nurtured is the best feeling in the world and by providing that for each other, you gain the necessary emotional strength to succeed in the world. You wouldn't enjoy a relationship that failed to provide that sort of security.

Mutual responsibility is another important feature of your relationship. You feel that each partner must always take into account the other's needs and wishes. Compromise is part of the give-and-take you regard as essential and you believe in working through any difficulties in the relationship through honest sharing of ideas and feelings.

You've always preferred a partner with depth of feeling as well as an interesting history. Blank people don't appeal to you and a rousing conversation in which you share amusing life events has always been an excellent opening gambit. Cleverness stimulates you, and the partner who can make you laugh is a good choice. You enjoy a little drama in your romance, so having to fight for your lover's attention is exciting to you.

If you're a male Cancer born in 1935, you prefer a woman capable of deep devotion and loyalty. Your mate is pretty and sparkling, but what really endears her to you is the tender way she holds you in her heart. You know that no matter what, day in and day out, she will be there loving you and looking out for your best interests. She is sweet and generous and has a way of making things work out just right.

As a female Crab born in 1935, you like a man who can balance graciousness with machismo. Your fellow is a good leader but he tries not to seem bombastic about it. He is confident and people just find him charismatic, which you find sexy. This sweetheart has well-developed social graces, he realizes the importance of good manners. and when he sweeps you off your feet, it feels like you're dancing a waltz.

1935 LEO
From July 23, 19:33 through August 24, 2:23

The Devoted Mate

As a loving Leo born in 1935, you believe a relationship should be filled with generosity and tenderness. You believe in true love and feel that once you give your heart to a soul mate, you've also pledged loyalty, devotion, and emotional support. All good things come through love and you believe in giving everything you have to make your partner's life happy and wonderful. And because you have such a beautiful outlook where love is concerned, you receive in equal measure. A shallow, self-centered attachment would never be right for you.

Sharing a similar viewpoint and a compatible sense of taste are also important to you. Being with a soul mate means sharing your life with someone who fits perfectly, like a comfy sweater. Although good verbal interaction is meaningful to you, you also feel that the real communication happens below the surface on a psychic and emotional level.

You've always been attracted to someone sweet and sensitive and, by offering you a kindness or a helping hand, a partner holds your attention and admiration. You enjoy sharing pleasant conversation, but you also like being invited to casual social activities. You and a mate develop and maintain romantic closeness while attending a concert or movie, or going on a picnic or walk together.

You male Leos born in 1935 prefer a woman who is deep and sensitive. Your lady is romantic, and her heart and soul are filled with poetry. She's also practical and down to earth and the two sides of her nature keep you bemused. When you need a helping hand, she pitches right in, and she's always there hoping for the best in everything you attempt. Her faith in you is touching and she enriches your world.

Lady Lions born in 1935 feel that a man should be playful yet also serious and stable. Your fellow is deep and emotional and most of the time he goes on instinct. He makes decisions based on gut reactions, but even if he's occasionally too hasty, he has the wisdom and determination to follow through and make sure everything comes out right. Your guy loves to play and he's always optimistic and cheerful.

1935 VIRGO
From August 24, 2:24 through September 23, 23:37

The Comfortable Idealist

You're an optimistic Virgo born in 1935, and to you a relationship is a source of love and joy. You believe in developing a foundation of closeness and sharing within your relationship, and by focusing on your partner's needs, you know that the favor will be returned to you. That way you both feel nurtured and beloved. A deep connection is always what you seek—anything less is of no interest to you at all. You want to feel that you're seen and understood, and you do the same for your partner.

Your relationship must also feature an easygoing sense of compatibility. You are reassured by the knowledge that you both like similar things and can share mutually enjoyable activities. That keeps the love alive and gives your relationship a sense of ongoing excitement and personal involvement. Being comfortable together is very important to you because then you share a sense of peace, relaxation, and security.

You most appreciate the mate continues to engage you in play, as long as there is a deeper emotional current under the surface right from the start. Talking and laughing together, being invited to a movie or concert, strolling along a romantic byway—these things warm your heart and keep you together. You like the unspoken feeling of walking through life, side by side, emotionally bonded, all the while doing casual things.

As a male Virgo born in 1935, you prefer a woman who is securely in touch with reality but who never loses the stars in her eyes. Your lady is helpful and kind yet always practical, and she is willing to aid someone in need, even if she knows they might be better off struggling alone. Her heart is tender and romantic and because she loves music and poetry, she makes you her hero.

If you're a female Virgin born in 1935, you like a man who is intense yet playful. Your fellow is passionate and emotional and he understands that aspect of your personality. Acting on instinct is quite normal and you enjoy his playful, impatient nature. Even when takes action too hastily, your guy is also solid and responsible. He's a good playmate, life mate and bedmate.

VIRGO ZODIAC SIGN

YOUR LOVE PLANETS

YOUR ROMANTIC SIDE p. 696
► **VENUS IN VIRGO**
Born Aug. 24, 2:24 - Sept. 23, 23:37

YOUR SEX DRIVE p. 722
► **MARS IN SCORPIO**
Born Aug. 24, 2:24 - Sept. 16, 12:58
► **MARS IN SAGITTARIUS**
Born Sept. 16, 12:59 - Sept. 23, 23:37

YOUR CELEBRITY TWINS p. 760
Find out the astrological similarities you have with famous people.

YOUR COMPATIBILITY p. 780
Compare planets to find out how compatible you are in a relationship.

YOUR RELATIONSHIP KARMA p. 824
► **SATURN IN PISCES**
Born Aug. 24, 2:24 - Sept. 23, 23:37

GRAHAM GREENE
English Writer
Sun in Libra

1935 LIBRA
From September 23, 23:38 through October 24, 8:28

The Thrill Seeker

As an idealistic Libra born in 1935, you prefer a relationship to be thrilling and romantic. A dull, quiet love story never appealed to you because you're much more interested in the drama that plays out before happily-ever-after begins. Your relationship must feature a few ups and downs to maintain your interest!

You also believe in the importance of chemistry, and that means more than just a little friction feels quite comfortable to you. The passion, the quarrels, the intense make-up sessions—these are the things you love to experience and remember. You've probably often said that your diary could become a best seller! Give and take are also important to you and you recognize the value of compromise, although you sometimes wish it weren't necessary.

A mate must spark your imagination to hold your heart. You love being invited to enjoy super romantic outings and would gladly spend your life dancing the night away under twinkling stars. You adore sharing walks by the seaside and attending concerts, and you may have laughed your way through a hay ride or taffy pull. As long as the chemistry is right, the activity is secondary.

If you're a male Libra born in 1935, you love the idea of sweeping your perfect lady off her feet. Her romantic outlook meshes strongly with your own and from the moment she meets you, her eyes sparkle and she glows. This woman is soft and tender, she has a gentle, nurturing side, and everyone admires her kindness and generosity. To other people your sweetheart seems demure and conservative, but under your influence she turns into a passionate, sexy tigress.

As a female Libra born in 1935, you like a man to be youthful, playful, and outgoing. Your guy maintains a puppy dog quality all his life, and no matter how difficult life gets, his optimism sees you through. He is athletic and jaunty and he loves to take you on adventures. You sense that he's your guy from the moment you meet, although you wonder along the way if you made the correct choice. He's musical and sexy and he has a way of seeing life agreeably through rose colored glasses.

LIBRA ZODIAC SIGN

YOUR LOVE PLANETS

YOUR ROMANTIC SIDE p. 696
► **VENUS IN VIRGO**
Born Sept. 23, 23:38 - Oct. 24, 8:28

YOUR SEX DRIVE p. 722
► **MARS IN SAGITTARIUS**
Born Sept. 23, 23:38 - Oct. 24, 8:28

YOUR CELEBRITY TWINS p. 760
Find out the astrological similarities you have with famous people.

YOUR COMPATIBILITY p. 780
Compare planets to find out how compatible you are in a relationship.

YOUR RELATIONSHIP KARMA p. 824
► **SATURN IN PISCES**
Born Sept. 23, 23:38 - Oct. 24, 8:28

143

IRENE DUNNE
American Actress
Sun and Venus in Sagittarius

1935 SCORPIO
From October 24, 8:29 through November 23, 5:34

♏ *The Congenial Cohabitant*

You're a gracious Scorpio born in 1935, and to you chemistry is a very important aspect of your relationship. You have always liked to feel that electric zing between yourself and a lover and without that, it wouldn't even progress to a first date, let alone beyond it. You need to feel there is a strong bond in your relationship and you want to connect on many levels, including intellectual and emotional, but chemistry comes first.

Good taste and good manners are important to you, and although you admit that some friction feels normal in a relationship, you also believe that there is a time and place for a lovers' quarrel and that shouldn't be in public. You care strongly about building a solid foundation together as partners, and that means having a sense of compatibility and agreement about mutually significant choices.

A mate who is graceful, intelligent, cultured, and tasteful gains your attention quite easily, but to sustain that interest, sex appeal is most important. You want to feel electricity crackling between you each time

you connect. You enjoy doing things together and have always liked working on practical projects as a team, hosting social events together, and being the couple everyone envies in the business world.

As a male Scorpion born in 1935, you prefer a woman who is magical enough to spark your imagination. Your lady could inspire a poet's verse or a musician's song and you feel that her special qualities are unique enough to maintain your interest forever. She is genteel and artistic, a caring hostess and loving mate. Your sweetheart takes pleasure in giving to others and she loves to see you smiling and happy.

If you're a female Scorpio born in 1935, you relate well to a man who is grounded and down to earth yet also sensitive. You believe a man must be a success, and a hard worker has always impressed you. Even though your guy was always committed to his career, spending time with you and the family never ceased to be a priority. This fellow is earthy and passionate about life, love, and sex, and he has a second sense about how to please you.

1935 SAGITTARIUS
From November 23, 5:35 through December 22, 18:36

⚹ *The Passionate Romancer*

As an intense Sagittarius born in 1935, you feel a relationship must be challenging and interesting. You have always sought a strong and passionate bond in all your relationships and even your friendships are dynamic. The dull and commonplace never appeal to you at all. You need passion, energy, and excitement to keep you coming back for more. A strong emotional connection is number one in your book.

Although you recognize the need for compromise when two people are bound together in a relationship, you also feel there is space for each one to focus on individual needs and concerns. Therefore you insist on plenty of space and autonomy as part of your happy relationship. Chemistry is another essential dimension of your relationship. Even if there's a quarrel, those intense feelings of attraction keep you together year after year.

You enjoy the company of an attractive mate who is fascinating and quirky. Someone who isn't shy about expressing an interest in you has always gained your attention quickly. You love being dragged onto the dance floor or kissed in

an impromptu fashion by someone you barely know. Sharing clever conversation or a game of wits also appeal to you.

Male Archers born in 1935 choose a woman who is sexy and passionate. Your lady is magnetic and intense, and you love the way she has always made you feel, like a knight in shining armor, jousting to win her hand. Your sweetheart is beautiful and electric and everyone wants to share her company. Her heart is deep, and you recognize right from the first meeting that she will love you longer and more intensely than any woman you've ever met.

If you're a female Sagittarian born in 1935, your guy is quite a dynamo. He's bossy, intense, quirky, and temperamental, but he's also the best time you've ever had. He makes a decision, insists on having it all his way, and then just as you're accepting his choice, he changes his mind. Because of these ups and downs, your life is never dull. Your sweetie is ultra-masculine, a take charge fellow who delights in running your world, and in bed he makes you swoon.

144

Anaïs Nin and Henry Miller

Henry Miller and Anaïs Nin made great erotica together. Their personal affair and literary collaboration in the 1930s was one of the great romances of the 20th century. The written record left by these two passionately autobiographical writers and sexual adventurers was so revolutionary and artistically important, it ultimately overshadowed the outrageous promiscuity from which they gained their inspiration.

Born on February 21, 1903, in Neuilly, France, Anaïs Nin traveled Europe with her musician parents. Her career as a diarist began in 1914 in New York, where her mother settled after her father abandoned the family. In 1923 Nin married Hugh Guiler, a wealthy banker, and moved with him from New York to Paris. In a marriage that lasted fifty years, Guiler was a stable, supportive husband, who allowed his wife unlimited freedom to pursue her artistic and erotic passions.

Henry Miller was a native of New York City, born in 1891. He grew up in Brooklyn and lived a conventional life, marrying in 1917, siring a daughter, and working for Western Union. At a dance hall in 1923, Miller met the woman who would be his love, his hate, the bane of his existence, and his muse—June Smith. He divorced his wife to marry Smith in 1924. To support Miller's literary ambitions, she worked odd scams to send him to Paris in 1930, where his writing talent would come to fruition.

In late 1931, Miller and Nin met in Paris and struck up an instant attraction. June soon arrived for a month-long visit, and the three plunged into an emotional and physical ménage à trois, painstakingly documented in the unexpurgated version of Nin's diary, published after her death. Nin portrays

Henry Miller

"*Woman does not forget she needs the fecundator, she does not forget that everything that is born of her is planted in her.*"

THE DIARY OF ANAÏS NIN,
Vol. 2 (1967), August 1937 entry.

two conflicting versions of June—one the romanticized object of Nin's lustful, lesbian fantasies, the other the real woman, who, having discovered her husband in the throes of adulterous infatuation, tries to get in on the game. The mutual seduction between Nin and June never progressed beyond flirtatious kissing and petting. After a second visit in October 1932, June returned to New York, divorced Miller in absentia, and never spoke to him until 1977.

Nin and Miller's frenzied literary collaboration drew from the sexual awakening they shared together and with other lovers. Nin provided the financial backing for the Parisian publication of *Tropic of Cancer* (1934), Miller's breakthrough masterpiece, a fictionalized account of his life in the degenerate cultural atmosphere of Europe prior to World War II. Miller's sexually explicit style kept *Tropic of Cancer* from publication in the United States until 1961. Miller's nine years in Paris produced *Black Spring* (1936), dedicated to Nin, and *Tropic of Capricorn* (1939). Beat Generation writers later adopted the warts-and-all truthfulness and the poetic, stream-of-consciousness technique that Miller pioneered.

Nin published her celebrated diaries (1914-1974) in edited form. She wished to protect June and conceal her own infidelities, including affairs with two psychoanalysts and, most notably, with her father in 1933. *Delta of Venus: Erotica* is a famous collection of sexually explicit stories that Nin wrote for a private client. Interestingly, Nin took the project from Miller, who found such "literary prostitution" to be a "castrating operation" and proved inept as a pornography writer. Nin and Miller's relationship faded during the war. She died in 1977, and Miller died in 1980.

145

▶ READ ABOUT D.H. LAWRENCE ON PAGE 87   ▶ READ ABOUT THE BOOK *THE SECRET SEX LIFE OF CATHERINE M.* ON PAGE 695

1936

- ⭐ THE LINDY HOP
- ⭐ MARY ASTOR'S PURPLE PROSE
- ⭐ SWING TIME
- ⭐ CAMILLE
- ⭐ INDIAN LOVE SONG
- ⭐ GONE WITH THE WIND
- ⭐ LIVE ALONE AND LIKE IT

EVENTS

In the UK, Stella Browne, Dora Russell, Frida Laski, and Joan Malleson founded the Abortion Law Reform Association, arguing that the legalization of abortion would cut the number of deaths caused by illegal and unprofessional attempts. A *Fortune* poll in the US indicated that 67 percent favored birth control. The Lindy Hop was a popular dance craze, along with the conga, and seven million women paid more than $2 billion for hair permanents. Tampons were invented. The 1934 world shot-putting champion, Edith Louise Weston, became Mark Weston following two operations at a London hospital. Actress Mary Astor was the center of an adultery scandal in which "purple passages" from her diary, describing her sexual liaison with playwright, critic, and director George S. Kaufman, became public. "Remarkable staying power. I don't see how he does it!" she rhapsodized.

POP CULTURE

In Frank Capra's *Mr. Deeds Goes to Town*, a man who inherits a fortune is nearly found insane because he wants to give it away to poor people. In the Fred Astaire-Ginger Rogers musical *Swing Time*, a dancer is torn between his fiancée and his new dancing partner. William Powell, as a mysterious butler, wins Carole Lombard's heart in *My Man Godfrey*. The year's hits also included *Camille* (with an unforgettable Garbo) and Charlie Chaplin's silent classic *Modern Times*.

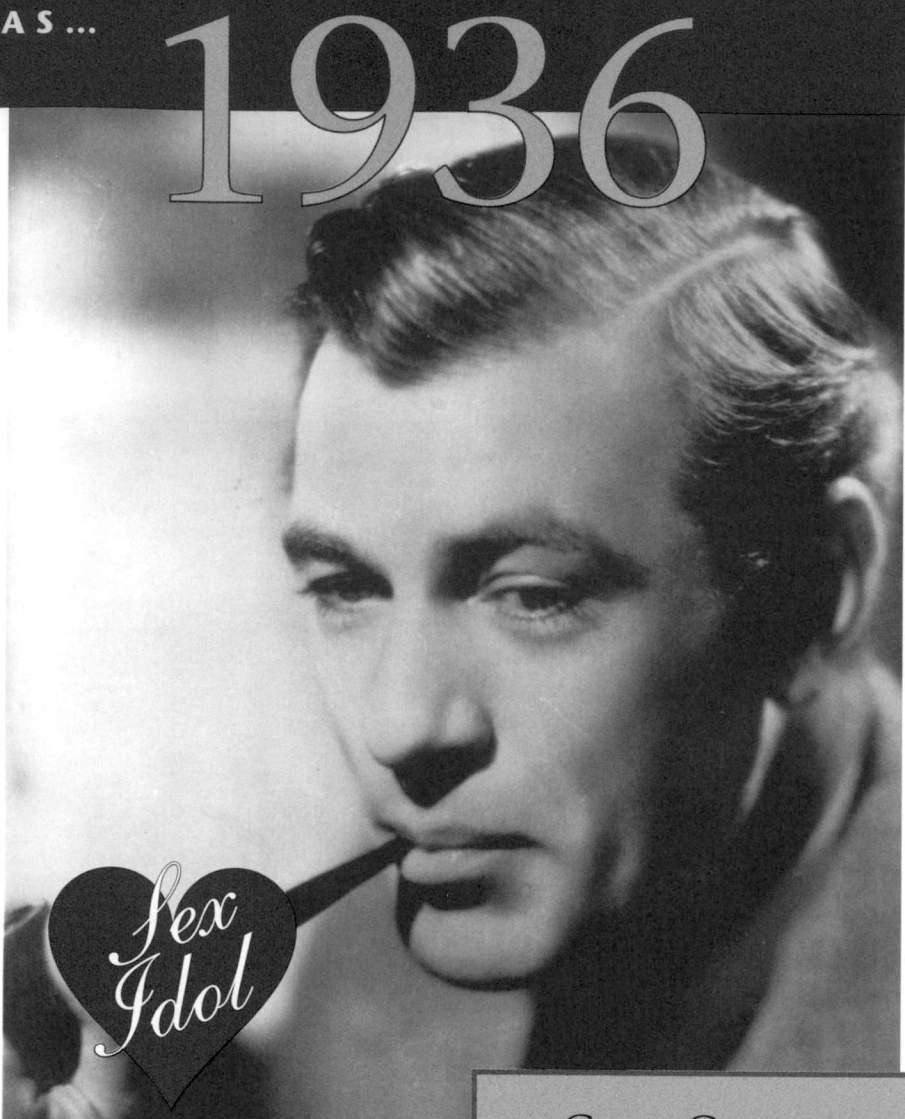

Sex Idol

Songs included "The Wiffenpoof Song" and the Jeanette MacDonald-Nelson Eddy duet "Indian Love Song." Bing Crosby sang "Pennies from Heaven," and Fred Astaire's string of hits included "Let's Face the Music and Dance" and "The Way You Look Tonight." Big band and jazz classics like "Stompin' at the Savoy" were hits.

Margaret Mitchell's *Gone with the Wind*, the saga of Scarlett O'Hara and her family during the Civil War, sold a record million copies in six months. In James Cain's *Double Indemnity*, a woman schemes to have her husband killed. Marjorie Hills's *Live Alone and Like It* was a bestseller as were Rebecca West's *The Thinking Reed* and Booth Tarkington's *The Lorenzo Bunch*. Kate O'Brien's novel *Mary Lavelle* was banned in Ireland due to a sympathetic lesbian character and an adulterous romance.

GARY COOPER

Gary Cooper had a very good year in 1936. Starring for the second time with the beautiful Marlene Dietrich in *Desire*, then with the gorgeous Madeleine Carroll in *The General Died at Dawn*, he topped it off with *Mr. Deeds Goes to Town*, earning his first Oscar nomination. Married to Sandra Shaw for almost thirty years, "Coop" was nonetheless rumored to be a Hollywood heartbreaker, having affairs with several of his female co-stars, including Clara Bow, Lupe Velez, Grace Kelly, and Patricia Neal. Ingrid Bergman said of Cooper, "Every woman who knew Gary fell in love with him."

SEE ALSO
- ▶ CLARA BOW *Page 72*
- ▶ MARLENE DIETRICH *Page 105*
- ▶ GRACE KELLY *Page 310*
- ▶ INGRID BERGMAN *Page 203*

1936 CAPRICORN

From December 22, 1935 18:37 through January 21, 1936 5:11
(December 1936 Capricorns, see 1937 Capricorn)

The Caring Sweetheart

Compassionate and intuitive, you 1936 Capricorns are a comforting lot. You enjoy nothing more than serving humankind. And although your selfless attitude is admirable, you have to admit that you get burned out from time to time. That's why it's so important for you to have an intimate relationship. A partner who recognizes your personal needs is an ideal match for you. You thrive in a relationship based on kindness, consideration, and mutual respect. A tempestuous union would drain you of valuable energy, so you probably tried to avoid such a partnership.

You can be quite impulsive when it comes to romance, and have a hard time keeping your feelings hidden. A mate who enjoys your passionate outbursts helps you feel less self-conscious. You're also extremely insightful, and enjoy discussing philosophical matters with your partner. Sex is a sacred expression of love for you, so you do best with a mate who feels strongly about fidelity.

A good way to catch your eye is to get involved with charitable works. You really appreciate someone who is dedicated to making the world a better place. Exhibiting a passionate interest in people also impresses you, because you're always eager to talk about the little idiosyncrasies of the folks around you. Your admirer should take a slow and considerate approach when it comes time to take your relationship to the physical level. You hate to be rushed into sex, and prefer to be slowly seduced with tender words and passionate kisses.

If you're a 1936 male Goat, you admire friendly women with upbeat attitudes. Sometimes you have a tendency to brood, so you do best with a mate who reminds you to look on the bright side. You also like serious females who have profound inner depths. Superficial women hold no charm for you.

As a woman Capricorn who was born in 1936, you want a man who is social but independent. You really admire a free-spirited guy who can maintain his own identity in a crowd. Men who are easygoing and sensitive also appeal to you. If there's anything you can't stand, it's a man who complains when things don't go his way.

CAPRICORN ZODIAC SIGN
Your Love Planets

YOUR ROMANTIC SIDE — p. 696
▶ **VENUS IN SCORPIO**
Born Dec. 22, 1935 18:37 - Jan. 03, 1936 14:15
▶ **VENUS IN SAGITTARIUS**
Born Jan. 03, 14:16 - Jan. 21, 5:11

YOUR SEX DRIVE — p. 722
▶ **MARS IN AQUARIUS**
Born Dec. 22, 1935 18:37 - Jan. 14, 1936 13:58
▶ **MARS IN PISCES**
Born Jan. 14, 13:59 - Jan. 21, 5:11

YOUR CELEBRITY TWINS — p. 760
Find out the astrological similarities you have with famous people.

YOUR COMPATIBILITY — p. 780
Compare planets to find out how compatible you are in a relationship.

YOUR RELATIONSHIP KARMA — p. 824
▶ **SATURN IN PISCES**
Born Dec. 22, 1935 18:37 - Jan. 21, 1936 5:11

WILLIAM POWELL
American Actor
Mars in Aquarius

147

1936 AQUARIUS

From January 21, 5:12 through February 19, 19:32

The Resourceful Lover

As a 1936 Aquarius, you are one of the most trustworthy and reliable folks around, especially with regard to love. Your partner can be assured that when you say something, you mean it. You're not the type to play games with someone's heart, and you expect your partner to return the same courtesy. Although you have a serious attitude towards romance, that doesn't mean you're incapable of having fun. In fact, you're one of the most playful lovers around, provided you're in a stable relationship.

To some extent, you see marriage as an economic arrangement. A fiscally responsible spouse brings out the best in you. You wouldn't do well with a loose partner who squanders your hard-earned money. Retiring in leisure with the one you love may be your primary objective in life. You have many interests and hobbies, and enjoy pursuing them with your beloved. You're not the type to become idle in your golden years. Consequently, you benefit from a mate who intends to keep up with you, both physically and intellectually. There's a good chance that you will take up a sport with your spouse after you retire.

Anybody seeking to attract your interest should be hardworking, honest, and true. You admire people who share your work ethic, and welcome the chance to join forces with a partner who wants to be of service to others. When it comes time to make the first move toward you, your admirer would be well advised to move boldly. You can't abide hesitant lovers. A person who treats you like a powerful sex magnet is bound to get an enthusiastic response.

If you're a male Water Bearer who was born in 1936, you appreciate a woman who is sexy but dignified. You enjoy the challenge of melting an elegant woman's reserve. Idealistic, principled females also appeal to you. Ultimately, you want a mate who has a good sense of herself.

You 1936 female Aquarians enjoy a man who is thoughtful, reflective, and gracious. Males who feel like they have to flaunt their masculinity completely turn you off. You prefer the company of a man who is not ashamed to cry at the movies or quote poetry at parties.

AQUARIUS ZODIAC SIGN
Your Love Planets

YOUR ROMANTIC SIDE — p. 696
▶ **VENUS IN SAGITTARIUS**
Born Jan. 21, 5:12 - Jan. 28, 13:59
▶ **VENUS IN CAPRICORN**
Born Jan. 28, 14:00 - Feb. 19, 19:32

YOUR SEX DRIVE — p. 722
▶ **MARS IN PISCES**
Born Jan. 21, 5:12 - Feb. 19, 19:32

YOUR CELEBRITY TWINS — p. 760
Find out the astrological similarities you have with famous people.

YOUR COMPATIBILITY — p. 780
Compare planets to find out how compatible you are in a relationship.

YOUR RELATIONSHIP KARMA — p. 824
▶ **SATURN IN PISCES**
Born Jan. 21, 5:12 - Feb. 19, 19:32

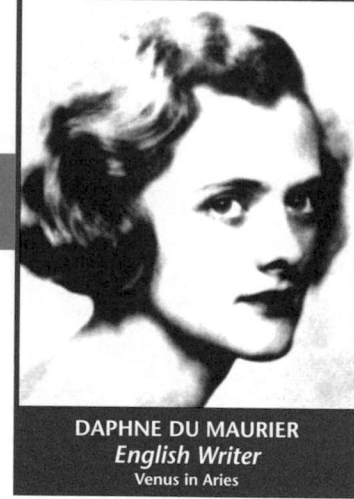

DAPHNE DU MAURIER
English Writer
Venus in Aries

148

1936 PISCES
From February 19, 19:33 through March 20, 18:57

The Controlled Sentimentalist

As a 1936 Piscean, you have admirable reserve, especially when it comes to love. Although you possess powerful feelings, you're able to express them in a way that makes your partner feel appreciated and valued. You're not the type to lash out at your lover when things go wrong. A relationship that features lots of honest dialogue is best for you.

You have idealistic views about marriage, and believe in staying together for life. The idea of divorce disturbs you, and you're likely to accept difficult aspects of your relationship in order to maintain it. A spouse who encourages you to change and grow with the times is ideal. You have a tendency to cling to old habits and patterns, which can undermine the health of your marriage. By opening yourself to your partner's suggestions, you can enjoy the long and fruitful partnership you desire. The more sexually vigorous your relationship, the longer it will thrive. You're quite a dynamo in the bedroom!

When somebody wants to capture your heart, he or she should express an interest in practical reform. Although you enjoy the prospect of making the world a better place, you want to do so in a way that helps people in material ways, like providing permanent homes and teaching valuable skills. You're also a very spiritual person, and are drawn to suitors who base their lives around moral principles. You like to make the first move in a relationship, but appreciate an admirer who makes their romantic desires obvious. You probably love having your ears nibbled as a prelude to lovemaking!

If you're a male Fish who was born in 1936, you admire a wide range of women. Although you appreciate females who are independent and original, you also admire women who are traditional. Females who are mischievous and whimsical also appeal to you. Ultimately, you want a partner who seeks to build a happy, prosperous life with you.

As a 1936 female Pisces, you want a man who is either romantic and yielding or forceful and ardent. In the end, you seek a relationship in which one partner is the clear leader. You love a man who is spontaneous.

1936 ARIES
From March 20, 18:58 through April 20, 6:30

The Loving Optimist

Open-minded, lighthearted, and bursting with enthusiasm, you 1936 Rams are an irresistible herd. You're determined to make the most of life while it lasts, and that includes leading a rewarding love life. A partner who shares your insatiable curiosity for different cultures, peoples, and lands is best suited to you. You want a relationship that involves plenty of travel. Interestingly, you probably have powerful ties to home, and may return to a particular place time after time. A mate who combines domestic skills with a spirit of adventure is ideal for you.

You don't have any set ideas about marriage, and prefer to let your relationship evolve naturally. Although you may seem like a carefree character on the outside, you do harbor some nagging fears in private. Therefore, it's a wise idea to pair up with someone who has good instincts. Such a spouse can detect when you're in a blue mood, and help talk you through your anxieties. When it comes to making love, you'll try anything once, and often do! Consequently, it is best that your marriage partner is enthusiastic about experimenting in the bedroom.

Intelligent, spiritual people attract your attention. Someone doesn't have to be book smart in order to impress you. Actually, you have great respect for self-taught people. Your admirer would be wise to ask you lots of questions about your past. You love to tell entertaining stories about your exploits! An aggressive character like you is apt to make the first sexual move, although you don't mind if your admirer makes subtle overtures toward you. You're extremely turned on when your partner strokes your hair.

You 1936 male Rams appreciate a woman who is sensitive, sensuous, and creative. You also admire females who are headstrong and outgoing. A partner who shares your sense of wonder about the world is best suited to you.

As a female Aries who was born in 1936, you want a man who likes to take the initiative. Although you enjoy exerting your power, you are secretly turned on by a guy who takes charge. Men who are cuddly like teddy bears also win your affection.

1936 TAURUS

From April 20, 6:31 through May 21, 6:06

The Independent Romantic

As a 1936 Taurus, you are a free-spirited soul who shies away from serious attachments. Although you are intensely romantic, you fear that making a commitment to a partner will take all the spontaneity out of the relationship. You want a partnership that is fluid and ever-changing. You wouldn't have any qualms if your mate changed careers after many years in a particular field. For you, personal happiness is more important than stability. You also appreciate the finer things in life, and benefit from a partner who enjoys good food and fine wine as much as you do.

Your attitude toward making love could be best described as "more is better." A mate with a strong sex drive can satisfy your physical needs. Marriage may not be very important to you, but you may decide to exchange vows as a means to please your partner. You detest barriers in a relationship, and will do everything in your power to promote a spirit of intimacy within it. No matter how important your spouse is, you still manage to make friends a priority in your life.

The best way to win your heart is to make a friendly overture toward you. It's hard for you to develop romantic feelings for someone until you've known that person for quite a while. Therefore, inviting you to a movie, photo exhibit, or dance performance may be a good way to make inroads with you, as you're probably interested in the arts. Because you find it difficult to cross the barrier between friendship and romance, your admirer should be prepared to make the first move. You enjoy massage as a prelude to lovemaking.

If you're a 1936 male Bull, you want a woman who is a self-starter. You admire any female who takes the initiative, whether in work, love, or both. You also feel a kinship with females who have a strong appreciation for beauty. Ultimately, you desire a partner who is intent on leading a life of luxury with you.

Men who are affectionate and cuddly bring out the best in you female 1936 Taureans. You're also turned on by males who are lighthearted and versatile. A mate who makes you laugh at life's absurdities is your ideal match.

JESSE OWENS
American Olympic Champion
Mars in Gemini

1936 GEMINI

From May 21, 6:07 through June 21, 14:21

The Effusive Lover

You 1936 Geminis have no problem expressing your feelings, especially to your loved ones. You're always pouring out your heart to your beloved, and rarely fail to say "I love you" at least once a day. Although you're very ambitious, you make time for your romantic partner. As far as you're concerned, no amount of success is worth sacrificing your personal relationships. Dividing time between your private and professional lives can be quite stressful at times, because you're in great demand. However, you usually manage to satisfy the needs of both your sweetheart and the public.

You've probably held a somewhat idealized view of domestic life since childhood. Being greeted at home by hugs and the aroma of freshly baked cookies may be your idea of heaven. A partner who helps promote a warm and harmonious living space is ideal for you. Sexually, you're extremely giving, and tend to put your spouse's needs before your own. You would do well to marry a person who is just as mindful of your physical needs. You want

relationship that is based on plenty of affection, both verbal and physical.

An admirer who is enthusiastic and outgoing is sure to catch your attention. Laid-back types make you nervous. Inviting you to an athletic game is a good bet, as you probably enjoy sports quite a bit. You're also a fan of the outdoors, and love taking strolls through the park. Making the first move isn't easy for you, so it's best that your suitor takes the initiative. You like lots of sex play before having actual intercourse, and respond beautifully to teasing, persistent kisses.

Women who are grounded, committed, and tender appeal to you 1936 male Twins. You're also drawn to females who are witty and talkative. In the final analysis, you do best with a mate who lets you know where you stand at all times.

If you're a female Gemini who was born in 1936, you prefer men who are communicative, intelligent, and flirtatious. You love it when a man looks you up and down appreciatively when you walk into the room. A partner who stimulates both your brain and body is ideal for you.

149

MYRNA LOY
American Actress
Sun in Leo

1936 CANCER
From June 21, 14:22 through July 23, 1:17

The Strong-willed Softy

As a 1936 Crab, you're determined to lead a life that is meaningful, rewarding, and spiritually fulfilling. Love plays large and important role in this equation. Therefore, you treat your beloved with a great deal of sincere tenderness and respect. You want a relationship in which both partners can freely express their feelings without fear of reprisal. Clinging stubbornly to destructive habits out of sheer egotism is not your style. You intend to keep changing and growing along with your mate as the years go by.

You have very set ideas about how life should be conducted, and do well with a mate who can show you viable alternatives. A relationship that helps you let go of your assumptions draws fresh energy in your life, and encourages you to take risks that you might otherwise avoid. When it comes to making love, you're a bit reserved, and benefit from a mate who helps you to drop your inhibitions in the bedroom.

Winning your heart takes strategy. You're deeply impressed by people who are intent on improving themselves. Therefore, an admirer would be wise to ask you for advice on anything from losing weight to expanding one's vocabulary. Being treated like an authority figure makes your ego soar. Making the first move is never easy for you, so it's best that your admirer makes their sexual intentions known by caressing your hand in a darkened movie theater. Such a subtle invitation can break down barriers and take the relationship to a whole new phase.

If you're a male Crab who was born in 1936, you're intrigued by a wide spectrum of women. Upbeat, social types thrill you, as do moody, romantic females. You also have a weakness for passionate, flamboyant women who enjoy making dramatic entrances. A partner who makes you feel like the center of the Universe is best suited to you.

As a 1936 female Cancer, you want a guy who is young at heart. Such a man can help you look at the world through new eyes. You also are drawn to men who are sentimental, reserved, and introspective. A mate who makes you feel intensely feminine and desirable makes you glow with happiness.

1936 LEO
From July 23, 1:18 through August 23, 8:10

The Sexual Powerhouse

You 1936 Lions have strong physical needs, and make no bones about advertising this fact. For you, one of the most important aspects of a relationship is sexual attraction. You're capable of being aroused by the same partner for many years, provided your lover reminds you of your desirability. It disturbs you to see married couples who no longer seem to have any passion for each another. You'll do anything and everything to keep your mate interested in you sexually, including working out at the gym and keeping yourself well-groomed and attractive at all times. For you, sex is not only a means to forge an intimacy with your partner, but a way to stay vital.

You're quite playful and do well with a partner who shares your love of spontaneity and mischief. A partnership that is filled with love, laughter, and fun is your greatest desire. One of your biggest delights is making your mate smile. You'll even resort to making a spectacle of yourself if it will make your partner break out with a chuckle. At times you have difficulty dealing with serious issues. A mate who can bring you gently down to earth in order to deal with these problems is a decided asset.

Clowning around never fails to catch your eye. You appreciate an admirer who has a keen sense of the absurd. Throwing a party, proposing a game of tennis, or buying two tickets for the theater are also good ways to capture your heart, as you adore recreation in all forms. You don't care who makes the first move, and are often eager to get things heated up in the early stages of a relationship. You enjoy marathon lovemaking sessions.

Women who are impetuous and unpredictable have a strong appeal for you 1936 male Lions. You're also drawn to females who hide their smoldering sensuality beneath a smooth, dignified exterior. A mate who is both passionate and funny brings out the best in you.

If you're a 1936 female Leo, you want a man who is tough on the outside but tender on the inside. Guys who are energetic and loving also turn you on. A partner who makes you feel like a queen wins your undying devotion.

1936 VIRGO
From August 23, 8:11 through September 23, 5:25

♍ *The Passionate Volcano*

You 1936 Virgos are a deceptively quiet bunch. Although you seem so calm and assured on the outside, you're really a smoldering volcano on the inside, particularly with regard to love. Sometimes you're so suffused with passion for your partner that you can't speak or move. A relationship is what gives life meaning for you. Although you believe in being of service to others, it's hard for you to put your heart into your work unless you have someone special waiting for you at home.

You're an entirely different person in private than you are in public, and let your reserved demeanor drop as soon as you and your lover are behind closed doors. You're extremely passionate in the bedroom, and often won't stop making love until you're completely drained of energy. Marriage is a serious business for you, so it's not likely that you'd stray from your partner. Still, you want a mate who enjoys sex as much as you do. A spouse who has a strong sense of self is a good match for you.

A suitor with a strong love of home and family is sure to attract your attention. You love the cozy companionship of a close-knit household, and appreciate being included in clannish traditions and celebrations. Anyone possessing strong artistic or musical talent is also sure to find favor with you. When it comes to taking your relationship to the next level, your admirer should be advised to go slowly. You're not the type to rush into a romance. You do like having your knees and lower back stroked as a form of foreplay.

If you're a 1936 male Virgin, you admire women who are pragmatic, polished, and purposeful. Nothing turns you on like a lady who knows what she wants and knows how to get it. You're also attracted to females who are courteous, persuasive, and tactful. A mate who can make harmonious compromises brings out the best in you.

As a 1936 female Virgo, you want a man who is ambitious, visionary, and authoritative. You like a guy who can take charge through the sheer force of his personality. Bullies hold no charms for you. A partner who makes you feel loved and protected suits you best.

VIRGO ZODIAC SIGN
YOUR LOVE PLANETS

YOUR ROMANTIC SIDE   p. 696
▶ VENUS IN VIRGO
Born Aug. 23, 8:11 - Sept. 04, 10:01
▶ VENUS IN LIBRA
Born Sept. 04, 10:02 - Sept. 23, 5:25

YOUR SEX DRIVE   p. 722
▶ MARS IN LEO
Born Aug. 23, 8:11 - Sept. 23, 5:25

YOUR CELEBRITY TWINS   p. 760
Find out the astrological similarities you have with famous people.

YOUR COMPATIBILITY   p. 780
Compare planets to find out how compatible you are in a relationship.

YOUR RELATIONSHIP KARMA   p. 824
▶ SATURN IN PISCES
Born Aug. 23, 8:11 - Sept. 23, 5:25

WILLIAM FAULKNER
American Writer
Sun in Libra

151

1936 LIBRA
From September 23, 5:26 through October 23, 14:17

♎ *The Sociable Flirt*

You 1936 Librans have a talent for witty banter. This comes in extremely handy when dealing with your partner. It's virtually impossible for your mate to stay mad at you for long, thanks to your ability to make even the most serious situations seem funny and light. Relationships that are based on hard work and sacrifice hold no charms for you. You want a partnership that celebrates triumphs and downplays tragedies. A mate who shares your optimistic view of life is your ideal match.

It's very possible that you don't have strong feelings about marriage one way or the other. As far as you're concerned, a piece of paper doesn't make a relationship valid. Rather, it's the feelings that two people have for one another that cause a union to flourish or flounder. Your sex drive can be a bit erratic. Sometimes you go through long periods of passionate frenzy, and others you are more interested in intellectual pursuits. You benefit greatly from a partner who can keep your physical desires on an even keel.

A suitor who expresses frank interest in you has a good chance of winning your heart. You love being admired, and especially enjoy being told how beautifully you dress and how charming you are. Someone who is well read and widely traveled will also win favor with you. You can't abide people who refuse to look beyond their own back yard for lack of interest. When it comes time to make the first move, the element of surprise usually works best with you. Nothing thrills you more than being swept up in a passionate embrace when you least expect it.

Women who are feminine, elegant, and intelligent appeal most to you 1936 male Librans. You want a partner who is so dainty that she makes you feel like a real man. Females who are sultry and sensual also turn you on. You do best with an alluring partner who brings your sexual side.

Men who are idealistic, honest, and friendly attract you as a 1936 female Libran. You can't abide cynics. A guy who is self-motivated and amusing also attracts you. In the final analysis, you want a humorous mate who shares your optimistic view of the world.

LIBRA ZODIAC SIGN
YOUR LOVE PLANETS

YOUR ROMANTIC SIDE   p. 696
▶ VENUS IN LIBRA
Born Sept. 23, 5:26 - Sept. 28, 18:35
▶ VENUS IN SCORPIO
Born Sept. 28, 18:36 - Oct. 23, 4:59
▶ VENUS IN SAGITTARIUS
Born Oct. 23, 5:00 - Oct. 23, 14:17

YOUR SEX DRIVE   p. 722
▶ MARS IN LEO
Born Sept. 23, 5:26 - Sept. 26, 14:50
▶ MARS IN VIRGO
Born Sept. 26, 14:51 - Oct. 23, 14:17

YOUR CELEBRITY TWINS   p. 760
Find out the astrological similarities you have with famous people.

YOUR COMPATIBILITY   p. 780
Compare planets to find out how compatible you are in a relationship.

YOUR RELATIONSHIP KARMA   p. 824
▶ SATURN IN PISCES
Born Sept. 23, 5:26 - Oct. 23, 14:17

RUTH CHATTERTON
American Actress
Mars in Scorpio

152

1936 SCORPIO
From October 23, 14:18 through November 22, 11:24

♏ *The Unpredictable Lover*

You can never tell what you 1936 Scorpions are going to do next. You delight in confounding the public, and it's especially rewarding when you astonish your beloved. For you, the fastest way to kill a relationship is by being predictable. Maybe that's why you're always springing surprises on your partner, whether it's switching jobs or buying tickets for a luxury cruise. Although the effect of your actions is jolting, you always put a lot of thought into romantic gestures. You are the last person who would take your mate for granted once you've made a commitment to one another.

It takes a long time for you to warm up sexually, so you benefit most from a partner who enjoys the challenge of seducing you. Nobody could ever accuse you of being a cold fish. It's just that you have such an active mind that it can be difficult for you to turn off your brain and focus on your body instead. Conventional marriages don't interest you in the slightest. You'd rather have a committed relationship that affords both parties plenty of freedom.

Suitors who are brilliant or unusual in some way generally attract your attention. You have little interest in preserving the status quo, and appreciate someone who is able to defy it in a good-natured way. Stating unusual opinions or proposing an unconventional outing is sure to win favor with you. When it comes time to take the relationship to the physical level, you respond beautifully to a paramour whose desire is obvious. Your suitor may want to prolong a friendly embrace as a means to get the message across.

As a male Scorpio who was born in 1936, you want a woman who is emotional, fervent, and restless. Such a female can awaken the passions that are buried deep within you. Women who are witty but polite also turn you on. You do best with a partner who can seduce you with words.

Men who are progressive but principled really appeal to you 1936 female Scorpions. You're not impressed by thoughtless radicals, but you do admire a reflective guy who wants to change the world by setting an impressive example. You want a mate you admire.

1936 SAGITTARIUS
From November 22, 11:25 through December 22, 0:26

♐ *The Amiable Romantic*

You 1936 Sagittarians are among the friendliest folks around. It's no surprise that many of your pals may have become lovers, and vice-versa. You take great delight in all levels of companionship, and treat relationships as your most precious possessions. An intimate partnership with your best friend is your ideal. Above all, you need a mate who shares your love of people. As someone who delights in other cultures, you may have a strong desire to travel. A mate who shares this interest brings out the best in you.

Sexually, you are extremely free-spirited, and enjoy making love whenever the mood seizes you. You do best with a partner who is extremely receptive to your overtures, even when they're made at inconvenient times. For you, the best marriage is one that thrives on spontaneity. You couldn't abide a partnership wherein routine meals, talk, and sex follow a predictable pattern. A spouse who prefers to go with the flow wins your respect and sincere admiration. As an avid outdoors person, you also enjoy a mate who enjoys camping

trips and nature walks as a means to unwind.

A suitor who is sociable and sincere has a good chance of winning your heart. You can't abide snobbery. Taking you to a place where you can people-watch, like a neighborhood fair or an outdoor market, would be a good way to get to know you. You're not fussy about who makes the first move in a relationship, but your admirer should understand that you like sex that is intense, heated, and long-lasting. You especially enjoy deep kissing and can linger on foreplay for hours.

If you're a male Archer who was born in 1936, you want a woman who is a good judge of character. You admire a lady who can spot a fake in a crowd of sincere people. You are also drawn to women who are philosophical but irreverent. A partner who is friendly but discerning gives you a thrill.

Men who are romantic and visionary have a strong appeal for you 1936 female Sagittarians. You want a gregarious partner with humanitarian instincts who enjoys making friends. A mate who treats you as his sexy equal brings out the best in you.

Greta Garbo – The Swedish Sphinx

Whether by design or pathology, Greta Garbo's wish for absolute privacy during the last 50 years of her life sealed her fate as one of Hollywood's most glamorous goddesses of the 20th century. From the mid-1920s to 1941 Garbo starred in 24 movies for MGM, all of them love stories. Her ethereal screen presence in the silent movies carried her into the 1930s "talkies," with her ability to be simultaneously inscrutable and expressive helping her through a technological transition other actors found impassable. And when she spoke her first line in 1930, "Give me a viskey!" her husky, androgynous voice only added to her appeal to both genders.

Garbo was capable of the minutest nuances in facial expression. Of the great silent stars, she alone sensed that the greatest cinematic scene was to share a private moment with the audience, which she did during her famous close-ups. The camera absolutely loved her face, and audiences were captivated by the Garbo mystique. Her onscreen image projected a rare luminosity reflecting a kaleidoscope of contradictory emotions. She could portray desire and aloofness, severity and fickleness, femininity and bisexuality. She eventually became a Hollywood goddess, an unattainable star known for her allure as much as for her cunning (or pathological) reclusive nature.

She most often co-starred with matinee idol John Gilbert, and their offscreen romance heightened public interest in their torrid, onscreen love scenes. Garbo moved in with Gilbert and had agreed to marry him, but she never showed up on her wedding day. Later she insisted that they were just friends. Another friend who was also a lover was the bisexual set designer Cecil Beaton. He thought she was "as beautiful as the aurora borealis," but after a disastrous vacation with her was not so kind. "She is incapable of love and she does not know the meaning of friendship," he said. "She would make a secret out of whether she had an egg for breakfast." In the 1930s Garbo became the master at creating the illusion of romantic love, but in her private life she seemed fearful of true intimacy, whether with a man or a woman.

Her best-loved performances can be found in the 1935 classic *Anna Karenina*, as well as the 1939 *Ninotchka*. Perhaps her most famous role was when she played a dying courtesan opposite her love interest Robert Taylor in the 1936 three-hankie romance *Camille*. One critic described the knotty combination of paradoxes she managed to portray as "a sublime, ironic performance."

During her heyday Garbo had many devoted companions. They may have been friends or lovers, but nothing that might be called a committed relationship. She most likely had a cozy romance with the lesbian writer Mercedes de Acosta, who is probably best known for her affairs with Marlene Dietrich and Isadora Duncan. Among her closest associates were the renowned composer Leopold Stokowski, the writer Erich Maria Remarque, co-star Nils Asther, and the homosexual nutritionist Gayelord Hauser. Though she was surrounded by friends and lovers, she never really liked the adulation. In 1941 she made her final movie at the age of 36 and retired behind a thick veil of secrecy for her last 50 years. She remains legendary today, thanks in part to the combination of glamour and mystery she exuded.

"You must realize I am a sad person. I am a misfit in life."

GRETA GARBO, to set designer Cecil Beaton

▶ READ ABOUT MARLENE DIETRICH ON PAGE 105 ▶ READ ABOUT FRIDA KAHLO ON PAGE 177

1937

- ★ THE DUKE OF WINDSOR
- ★ HITLER AS WEDDING WITNESS
- ★ THE AWFUL TRUTH
- ★ GLENN MILLER
- ★ THE LADY IS A TRAMP
- ★ L'AMOUR FOU

EVENTS

Sex made headlines as the American Medical Association endorsed doctors' dispensing birth control advice, and results of a *Fortune* poll showed that 50 percent of college men and 25 percent of college women had had premarital sex (and two-thirds of the women would for "true love"). No longer Edward VIII, the Duke of Windsor married American divorcee Wallis Simpson and the pair began a tour of Europe that included meetings with Hitler. Other British visitors included Sir Oswald Mosely, the founder of the British Union of Fascists, who married Diana Mitford in Berlin, with Hitler as as a witness. In the UK, the Marriage Bill was passed, allowing a divorce to occur three years after a marriage, rather than five. The Italian government declared that interracial marriages in its African colonies were henceforth illegal. Eighteen-year-old British ballerina Margot Fonteyn starred in *Giselle* and the French fashion magazine *Marie-Claire* made its first appearance.

POP CULTURE

Cary Grant haunted a couple in *Topper* and engaged in pre-divorce wrangling with Irene Dunne in *The Awful Truth*. Spencer Tracy, Lionel Barrymore, and Freddy Bartholomew took to the sea in *Captains Courageous*. Jean Renoir directed his gorgeous, profound anti-war classic *La Grande Illusion*. Enduring favorites *A Star Is Born*, *Stage Door*, and *The Life of Emile Zola* were also 1937 box-office hits.

Glenn Miller formed a new band, Charlie Parker joined the Jay McShann band, and Ella Fitzgerald was among the top performers named by *Downbeat*. Benny Goodman's band made "Sing, Sing, Sing" its own. Chart toppers of the year also included "Nice Work If You Can Get It," "They Can't Take That Away from Me," "The Lady Is a Tramp," "In the Still of the Night," and "Where or When."

The year's great books included Zora Neale Hurston's Harlem Renaissance classic *Their Eyes Were Watching God* and Christopher Isherwood's tale of cabaret life in Nazi Germany, *Sally Bowles*. André Breton produced his *L'Amour Fou*, poems about love's delights and madness. Bestsellers of the year also included *Of Mice and Men*, *Northwest Passage*, *Drums Along the Mohawk*, and Dale Carnegie's *How to Win Friends and Influence People*.

Hot Couple

EDWARD VIII & WALLIS SIMPSON

Edward VIII of England, not yet crowned, shocked the world in December 1936 when he abdicated the throne of England for "the woman I love," a twice-divorced American, Wallis Simpson. They married the following June 3, 1937 at a French chateau. As the Duke and Duchess of Windsor, they became, essentially, the royal family in exile.

They pursued an envied lifestyle in Paris and New York, entertaining "the best people" at sumptuous parties. Wallis was a style-setter well into old age. Edward died in Paris in 1972. She died fourteen years later. They are buried together on the grounds of Windsor Castle.

SEE ALSO

▶ QUEEN ELIZABETH & PRINCE PHILIP *Page 236*

▶ LADY DI & PRINCE CHARLES *Page 516*

154

1937 CAPRICORN
From December 22, 1936 0:27 through January 20, 1937 11:00
(December 1937 Capricorns, see 1938 Capricorn)

♑ *The Kind Conservative*

You command respect wherever you go, 1937 Capricorn, because you are a trusted and responsible individual as well as one who is kind and considerate. With this unbeatable combination, you can often open the hearts of those who have long ceased to trust anyone with their feelings. A loyal friend and a faithful lover, your relationships can be a solid foundation upon which you may build the rest of your life.

Though you are generally characterized by your pensive and reserved nature, when it comes to lovemaking, you can easily let your partner know just how much they mean to you. You have a need to be in control but you also have a kinder, gentler side that really wants to know what your mate is thinking and feeling. A talented and passionate lover, you are capable of putting your great powers of concentration to constructive use by focusing on providing exquisite pleasure for both you and your partner.

You admire those who can see the truth and are not afraid to tell it. A potential partner would be wise to always be upfront and honest with you. If you notice that someone lacks integrity in their dealings with you or with others, you are not likely to stick around for very long. But, once a prospective partner shows that they can be trusted, you are remarkably easy to please. All you want is to love and be loved in return.

The ideal woman for you, 1937 Capricorn male, is one who is not only romantic and dreamy but also has courage and faith. She is able to inspire you to believe in yourself as well as in the basic goodness of others. With her by your side, there is no obstacle too great for you to overcome. Her deep and abiding love is the foundation of your life and you want nothing more than to make her the center of your world.

1937 Capricorn female, your perfect man is someone who is full of surprises and enjoys living life to the fullest. You want someone who is magnetic and powerful and isn't afraid to take a risk, especially when it comes to love. Most of all, he should possess a strong character and be able to meet life's challenges with grace and equanimity.

CAPRICORN ZODIAC SIGN
YOUR LOVE PLANETS

YOUR ROMANTIC SIDE — p. 696
▶ VENUS IN AQUARIUS
Born Dec. 22, 1936 0:27 - Jan. 06, 1937 3:17
▶ VENUS IN PISCES
Born Jan. 06, 3:18 - Jan. 20, 11:00

YOUR SEX DRIVE — p. 722
▶ MARS IN LIBRA
Born Dec. 22, 1936 0:27 - Jan. 05, 1937 20:38
▶ MARS IN SCORPIO
Born Jan. 05, 20:39 - Jan. 20, 11:00

YOUR CELEBRITY TWINS — p. 760
Find out the astrological similarities you have with famous people.

YOUR COMPATIBILITY — p. 780
Compare planets to find out how compatible you are in a relationship.

YOUR RELATIONSHIP KARMA — p. 824
▶ SATURN IN PISCES
Born Dec. 22, 1936 0:27 - Jan. 20, 1937 11:00

LUISE RAINER
German Actress
Sun in Capricorn

155

1937 AQUARIUS
From January 20, 11:01 through February 19, 1:20

♒ *The Headstrong Intellect*

It is likely that in your lifetime you have developed from being an angry and rebellious recalcitrant to someone with a single-minded desire to improve humanity, 1937 Aquarius. Because of your understanding of the benefits of personal transformation, you may find that you are a tremendous catalyst for change in others as well. With you as a power of example, others may feel compelled to pursue what you seem to have—a sense of purpose and inner peace in your life.

You are eager to take the jump in romantic matters and simply adore the thrill of the chase. Your penchant for always trying to improve yourself is a definite asset in lovemaking. Anything but detached when it comes to the pleasures of sexual gratification, you are a skillful lover who is quite willing to learn a new technique to please a mate. Striving for the ultimate union, you are someone who wants to connect on every level with your partner—physically, mentally, emotionally, and spiritually.

You are a lifelong learner and, if someone wants to get your attention, they might suggest enrolling in a course together. Knowledge is power in your book and, with knowledge, you feel better equipped to achieve your fullest potential. On the lighter side, you are a fan of new technology and would enjoy an afternoon at a computer show or a visit to the mall to drool over the latest in TV and sound systems.

For the 1937 Aquarius male, the ideal woman is someone who is independent and fun loving and possesses a sense of adventure. Unconventional to the core, your lady is probably not willing to be defined by society's standards and has worked hard on her own personal development. Like you, she marches to the beat of her own drummer and has a visionary, forward-thinking attitude about life and love.

The perfect man for the 1937 Aquarius female is someone who has a strong sense of his own identity and is not concerned with what others may think of him. He is likely to know his own mind and may be quite fixed in his opinions. Practical and resourceful, he is capable of living life in an intense and purposeful manner.

AQUARIUS ZODIAC SIGN
YOUR LOVE PLANETS

YOUR ROMANTIC SIDE — p. 696
▶ VENUS IN PISCES
Born Jan. 20, 11:01 - Feb. 02, 10:38
▶ VENUS IN ARIES
Born Feb. 02, 10:39 - Feb. 19, 1:20

YOUR SEX DRIVE — p. 722
▶ MARS IN SCORPIO
Born Jan. 20, 11:01 - Feb. 19, 1:20

YOUR CELEBRITY TWINS — p. 760
Find out the astrological similarities you have with famous people.

YOUR COMPATIBILITY — p. 780
Compare planets to find out how compatible you are in a relationship.

YOUR RELATIONSHIP KARMA — p. 824
▶ SATURN IN PISCES
Born Jan. 20, 11:01 - Feb. 19, 1:20

RONALD COLMAN
English Actor
Mars in Aries

156

1937 PISCES
From February 19, 1:21 through March 21, 0:44

The Imaginative Romantic

Dreamy and idealistic, 1937 Pisces, you have a strong desire to see the best in others. Though you certainly have had your share of disappointments, you are still the eternal optimist, always looking for the bright side in any situation. In relationships, your forgiving, live-and-let-live attitude makes you seem easygoing and accepting. Yet, beneath the surface, you really do have a strong idea of what you need and want from others.

Magnetic and mysterious, others can't help but succumb to the power of your charms. Sexually, you are a powerhouse of stored emotional energy that can finally be expressed through the act of physical love. You need physical union in the way that birds need to fly. It is through sensuality that you can find your true self. When you find the partner that can satisfy your profound need for love and affection, you can be a faithful and devoted lover.

In order to catch your eye, a potential lover should try to engage your childlike curiosity about the miracle of life. A visit to the aquarium to see the latest exotic addition or a trip to an inspiringly beautiful natural wonder is sure to get your juices flowing. Above all, they need to show that they can take responsibility for their own actions because, when it comes right down to it, you are a conscientious person who respects that same quality in others.

The ideal woman for you, 1937 Pisces male, is someone who is spirited and exhilarating. You have a secret desire to try new things but may lack the confidence you need to take the plunge. Your lady should be someone who can give you the encouragement you need to go for it. Most of all, you want a woman who is exciting enough to keep your fires burning only for her.

1937 Pisces female, your perfect man is someone who is unafraid of your penetrating emotional nature and is secure enough to express his feelings without reservation. You want a man who is able to stand up for what he believes, without losing his sensitivity. Finally, he needs to be a genuinely giving and caring person, capable of putting the needs of others first.

1937 ARIES
From March 21, 0:45 through April 20, 12:18

The Daring Connoisseur

You were born ready for the world 1937 Aries, gifted with an uncanny sense of timing and a genial and courageous personality. You always seem to know exactly what to do in any given situation, and you move through life with confidence and ease. Always ready to speak up for what you believe is right, you are a wanderer at heart and value your freedom above all else. Therefore, in relationships, it is important that you are able to maintain your independent spirit.

Others admire you for your steely nerves and your willingness to take the lead in precarious situations. You are also very eager to be the initiator when it comes to lovemaking and you will dare to go where others may fear to tread. As a surprising and innovative lover, you instinctively know what will work and what will not. Excitement is one of your favorite aphrodisiacs, and you can usually be counted on to keep things moving fast.

As someone who thoroughly enjoys the thrill of the chase, you like it when a potential partner plays a little hard to get. A suitor who is sincerely interested in you will need to be aware that beneath your brave and bold exterior beats the heart of someone who truly believes that love conquers all. Presenting you with a few seemingly insurmountable challenges may be just what is needed for a prospective mate to capture and hold your interest.

For you, 1937 Aries male, the ideal woman is someone who can help you to keep your feet firmly planted on the ground. While you certainly want a woman who is sensual and fun, you want someone who is grounded enough to pay attention to the essentials of everyday life—and who will remind you to eat properly, take your vitamins, and get some rest.

The perfect man for you, 1937 Aries female, is a dashing adventurer who will sweep you off your feet and take you to exotic and romantic places. He needs to be an explorer, ready to seek out the uncharted territory of your heart and mind. And, it is important that your man can be as spontaneous and impulsive as you are, equipped for all the twists and turns on the roller-coaster of life.

1937 TAURUS
From April 20, 12:19 through May 21, 11:56

The Fiery Realist

Practical and down-to-earth, 1937 Taurus, you are a tender and hardworking individual who is grateful for all that you've achieved in your life. It has not always been easy, but somehow you have managed to maintain a joyful outlook despite all of the frustrations. In relationships, you have the capacity to be a committed and loyal partner once you learn how to love and accept yourself for who you are.

Sensual and romantic, others are irresistibly drawn to the twinkle in your eye and your somewhat devilish personality. When it comes to sex, your appetite is enormous and may even border on the insatiable. Always ready for more, you are likely to exhaust even the most energetic of partners. Not only do you have an immeasurable hunger but, in lovemaking, you also demand quality in addition to quantity from both yourself and your partner.

Unwilling to compromise your vision, you can be a bit difficult to approach. Therefore, anyone who wants to get your attention needs to be, first and foremost, patient and persevering. You enjoy being where the action is and love sporting events, concerts, and crowded nightclubs. A potential lover might suggest an afternoon at the races but the suitor that really wants to win your heart might invite you on a trip to Las Vegas or the Super Bowl.

Your ideal woman, 1937 Taurus male, is an ambitious dynamo of energy and drive. You need someone whose cravings for the good life can match your own and who is able to satisfy your wildest fantasies. Intrigued by power and money, you want a woman who will support your quest to reach your goals. But most of all, she needs to be able to understand your tenacity and be able to ease your disappointment should you fall short of your objectives.

1937 Taurus female, your perfect man is a combination of sensitive philosopher and determined go-getter. Because financial security is so important to you, you want someone who also aspires to attaining material prosperity. But because you also need the companionship that your lover has to offer, he should to be able to balance family, social, and private time.

TAURUS ZODIAC SIGN
YOUR LOVE PLANETS

YOUR ROMANTIC SIDE   p. 696
- ▶ **VENUS IN ARIES**
Born Apr. 20, 12:19 - May 21, 11:56

YOUR SEX DRIVE   p. 722
- ▶ **MARS IN SAGITTARIUS**
Born Apr. 20, 12:19 - May 14, 22:51
- ▶ **MARS IN SCORPIO**
Born May 14, 22:52 - May 21, 11:56

YOUR CELEBRITY TWINS   p. 760
Find out the astrological similarities you have with famous people.

YOUR COMPATIBILITY   p. 780
Compare planets to find out how compatible you are in a relationship.

YOUR RELATIONSHIP KARMA   p. 824
- ▶ **SATURN IN PISCES**
Born Apr. 20, 12:19 - Apr. 25, 6:26
- ▶ **SATURN IN ARIES**
Born Apr. 25, 6:27 - May 21, 11:56

SERGEI PROKOFIEV
Russian Composer
Sun in Taurus

157

1937 GEMINI
From May 21, 11:57 through June 21, 20:11

The Relentless Competitor

You are an interesting blend of dogged determination and versatility, 1937 Gemini, giving you the ability to take on a variety of tasks and bring them to completion. With your piercing intelligence and logical brilliance, you are a master debater who can ultimately bring anyone around to your side of an issue. You bring this same fervor to your relationships and are not likely to shrink from confrontation when you feel that you are right.

When it comes to lovemaking, you can alternate between being impishly playful and utterly serious. And, to the delight of your partner, they usually can't tell which you'll be at any given encounter. But, it doesn't really matter because you can always be counted on to deliver a fine performance. You regard sex as a sporting event and though you will definitely jockey for control, you know when to surrender and are willing to accept defeat very graciously.

You can be very reserved, especially when you are in an unfamiliar situation. A potential partner should recognize that they might need to make the first approach. However, once you are comfortable with someone, you are likely to have a lot to say. Mental stimulation is the key to your heart and you would naturally enjoy a spirited and smart discussion about politics, religion, or the state of the world. And, of course, any activity that affords you the opportunity to expand your mind is sure to get your interest.

The perfect woman for you, 1937 Gemini male, is someone who can easily adapt to suit your mood, whether it be a quiet evening spent at home or a rollicking night on the town. She probably has her own dualistic nature and is likely to be practical and efficient by day. Then, by night, she's sultry and loving, endearing herself to you all over again.

Your ideal man is someone who simply drips with captivating charm and mystery, Gemini female of 1937. You love a man who is complex, just about unfathomable, someone with whom you can use your own highly developed analytical abilities. Like a great chess player, he should be able to lure you into his own very tender trap.

GEMINI ZODIAC SIGN
YOUR LOVE PLANETS

YOUR ROMANTIC SIDE   p. 696
- ▶ **VENUS IN ARIES**
Born May 21, 11:57 - June 04, 6:40
- ▶ **VENUS IN TAURUS**
Born June 04, 6:41 - June 21, 20:11

YOUR SEX DRIVE   p. 722
- ▶ **MARS IN SCORPIO**
Born May 21, 11:57 - June 21, 20:11

YOUR CELEBRITY TWINS   p. 760
Find out the astrological similarities you have with famous people.

YOUR COMPATIBILITY   p. 780
Compare planets to find out how compatible you are in a relationship.

YOUR RELATIONSHIP KARMA   p. 824
- ▶ **SATURN IN ARIES**
Born May 21, 11:57 - June 21, 20:11

SYLVIA SIDNEY
American Actress
Venus in Cancer

1937 CANCER
From June 21, 20:12 through July 23, 7:06

♋ The Affectionate Protector

You are the epitome of warm and fuzzy, 1937 Cancer, and others can't help but respond to your kindliness and sincerity. Home and family are your first priority and you will go to any lengths to protect them from harm, real or imagined. In fact, you may worry a bit too much about those you love and you definitely need to learn to let go. But, your love is so all encompassing and generous that those around you are likely to overlook any of your shortcomings.

Tender and gentle, you needs are simple and uncomplicated. You just want to be loved. When it comes to lovemaking, passion is your middle name. Though, at first, you may be reluctant to fully express the breadth of your desires, once you feel loved and accepted, anything goes. There is no limit to your willingness to please a partner and sex becomes a mutually pleasurable vehicle through which you can express your boundless love.

You don't like wasting time, or any resource for that matter, so anyone who is interested in you needs to let you know as soon as possible.

Once you're certain that someone is definitely attracted to you, you are very open to letting things evolve in a natural way. A prospective lover should remember to bring you little, sentimental gifts for you to cherish. And, they need to demonstrate an interest in getting to know your family and friends.

1937 Cancer male, your ideal woman is a faithful and loving partner who values emotional security as much as you do. Affectionate and attractive, she will draw you to her like a magnet and you will be comforted by her subtle and calm manner. She is likely to have a strong artistic sense that is reflected both in her personal style of dress and in her surroundings.

For you, 1937 Cancer female, strength and determination are important qualities that you look for in a man. You want your partner to be someone who can help you to feel safe and warm when the harsh realities of the world encroach upon your sheltered environment. Above all, he needs to be unafraid of your powerful emotions and be able to give you the all-embracing love that you desire.

1937 LEO
From July 23, 7:07 through August 23, 13:57

♌ The Leading Light

You seem to have been born with a guardian angel to watch over you always 1937 Leo. Whenever you may be in trouble, you somehow always manage to miraculously come through with flying colors. You are a very bright and luminous power of example for those around you and you are more than willing to light the way for others to follow. A giving and caring individual, you use your myriad of talents to help others live up to their own potential.

In relationships, you like to keep things enthralling and exciting. But, for you to feel completely satisfied, there needs to be an emotional component to your lovemaking in addition to physical attraction. You are a polished, smooth as silk lover who knows how to keep romance alive in a relationship. When it comes to sex, you appreciate experimentation and variety. However, once committed, you are not likely to stray.

You are both elegant and imaginative, and you like to see those same qualities in a potential partner. Taste and class are a turn-on for you, and you appreciate when things are done in a

big way. You love to be wined and dined in opulence—no discount coupons or TV dinners for you! And, on a mental level, a would-be suitor who is interested in you needs to demonstrate an ability to think on their feet and apply creative solutions to life's little dilemmas.

For the 1937 Leo male, the perfect woman is one who is compassionate and kindhearted, as well as communicative and interesting. You want a woman who is able to discuss world events with clarity and intelligence but who can also be tender and soft when you need her comfort and attention. Above all else, you want a woman who understands and supports your need to give of yourself to others.

The ideal man for the 1937 Leo female is one who approaches life with an all or nothing attitude. He believes that if a goal is truly worthwhile, it only makes sense to stop at nothing to achieve it. His powerful emotions and desires can't help but touch you, and you are likely to respond in kind. Most of all, you want someone who can act from the higher motivations of idealism and altruism.

1937 VIRGO
From August 23, 13:58 through September 23, 11:12

♍ The Reticent Perfectionist

Blessed with a critical eye, exacting standards and exquisite taste, 1937 Virgo, you bring panache to all you do. Though you are a skilled communicator, you may often be reluctant to say what is on your mind. Your reserve is probably due to both your dislike of confrontation and your need to be precise. You have the ability to really focus on details, but you may sometimes get bogged down in trivialities.

When it comes to relationships, you apply the same rigorous standards that you do in the other areas of your life. You expect your partner to be sophisticated, mannerly, flawlessly groomed, and well educated. In lovemaking, you pride yourself on your dexterity and ability to please your partner. A passionate and determined lover, you are a blend of earthy sensuality and heated fervor.

You are impressed with eloquence, and a would-be paramour who wants to get your attention should practice the nuances of conversational technique. One thing is certain—nothing turns you off more than vulgarity in any form. Since you have a strong interest in health matters, it is important that any prospective suitor share your desire to observe good eating habits and regular exercise. You would enjoy browsing through the alternative health section at a bookstore or taking a yoga class with your potential beloved.

1937 Virgo male, the perfect woman for you needs to be just that—perfect. Your ideal woman is interesting and lively, and knows how to make your home environment comfortable and serene. It's important that she has a gift for entertaining and that she is sexy and alluring as well. You want a woman that you can cherish and adore, one who doesn't mind being the focus of your wholehearted attention.

Your perfect man, 1937 Virgo female, is one who has an aesthetic flair and does not offend your delicate sensibilities. You want someone who is what used to be known as "a man of the world," since nothing short of dashing sophistication would appeal to your discriminating taste. Most of all, you want someone you can talk to and who will help you develop confidence in your abilities.

CONSTANCE BENNETT
American Actress
Sun and Venus in Libra

159

1937 LIBRA
From September 23, 11:13 through October 23, 20:06

♎ The Cultured Friend

You have always seemed wiser than your years, 1937 Libra, and others admire your judicious and well-balanced approach to life. Hardworking and industrious, you have a decidedly playful streak and an infectious smile. You make friends easily and they naturally seek out your advice, especially when it comes to romance. More than most, you have a deep-seated need for partnership, yet you may sometimes be disappointed because most people will fail to live up to your high expectations.

With your sparkling personality and your refined intelligence, you have no trouble adapting to any social situation. Expert at "working a crowd," you can easily move from an offbeat gathering at a coffeehouse to a traditionally chic cocktail party. You bring this same versatility to your lovemaking, which is sure to delight and intrigue your partner. Capable of complete abandon, you approach lovemaking with the same finesse and elegance you would bring to any situation.

If a prospective partner wants to catch your notice, they should approach you in a lighthearted and joyful manner. It's not that you can't be serious and, in fact, the opposite is true. You enjoy clever and witty banter and you pride yourself on your great sense of humor. A night at a comedy club is perfect for getting you in the mood for love. But, to really capture your heart, a would-be lover really needs to be the one who is able to make you laugh.

"Work hard, play hard" is your creed, 1937 Libra male, and your woman needs to be respectful of that balance. She should be able to understand your need for success and, in addition, be ready to party when the time is right. Most importantly, you want a woman who always knows precisely the appropriate thing to do or wear or say to fit any situation.

1937 Libra female, your ideal man has a strong desire for recognition and needs to know that you are proud of his accomplishments. A master of self-control, he is likely to be quite disciplined and somewhat aloof. What he may lack in tenderness, he will certainly make up for with his powerful devotion to you and your family.

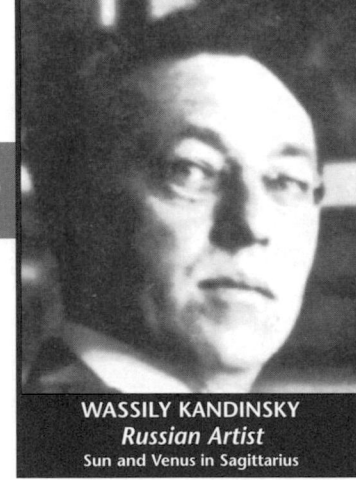

WASSILY KANDINSKY
Russian Artist
Sun and Venus in Sagittarius

1937 SCORPIO
From October 23, 20:07 through November 22, 17:16

♏ *The Unsolvable Riddle*

Baffling and incomprehensible, 1937 Scorpio, you are as difficult to understand as the Great Sphinx. There are times when you can be astonishingly open and accessible and then, without warning, you can simply erect an impenetrable wall designed to keep others at arm's length. As you might expect, any sort of inconsistent behavior can be somewhat disconcerting for those around you. Yet, there are those brave souls who will find your unpredictability diabolically intriguing.

When you meet someone that you want in your life, you will stop at nothing to make the relationship a reality. You will even be ruthless, if necessary, for you believe that "all's fair in love and war." A five-star general in the battle of the sexes, you are a sexual dynamo who is able to make each encounter seem unforgettable and amazing. And, once you find the person that you really love, you are ready to commit yourself to a lifetime of love and passion.

There's no reason to be subtle when someone wants to get your attention. You like it when a would-be partner puts it all on the line, and you will respect and probably respond favorably to a frank, all-or-nothing approach. The air of mystery with which you surround yourself certainly makes you enticing to others. But, it's the person who can find the secret to what makes you tick that you will find downright irresistible.

The perfect woman for the 1937 Scorpio male is both a seductress and a confidante. You want a woman that you can tell your secrets to—someone who won't blink when she hears your deepest and darkest inner thoughts. For you, trust is the most essential ingredient in a relationship and your woman needs to be brave enough to tell you the truth about what she thinks.

Your ideal man, 1937 Scorpio female, is a no-nonsense, practical achiever. He is someone with significant energy and ambition, which he probably directs towards his career. It's quite likely that your man is as proficient as you are at seeing the deeper motivations in the actions of others. But, most of all, you want a man who not only respects your strength but welcomes it.

1937 SAGITTARIUS
From November 22, 17:17 through December 22, 6:21

♐ *The Truth Seeker*

Integrity and honesty are the foundation of your character, 1937 Sagittarius, making you a highly idealistic and ethical individual. Sometimes, however, you may be more interested in adhering to an abstract idea or philosophy than you are in the personal side of life. It's important that you remember to stay connected with others or you may find yourself alone with your ideas. In relationships, you may certainly be trusted to live up to your promises and you expect the same from others.

On the exterior, you have a breezy and laid-back demeanor that is quite appealing and alluring. But, just beneath the surface lies a much more demanding and passionate part of your personality. You may even be somewhat possessive, which comes as a surprise to everyone except those who know you exceptionally well. Once you are intimate with someone, there is a part of you that wants to keep them all to yourself.

You are a lover of animals and would probably enjoy an afternoon of horseback riding or just walking around the zoo. Game playing is also fun and you would be delighted with a good round of chess or Trivial Pursuit. Intellectual jousting is foreplay for you, so a would-be lover needs to be up to the challenge. And, since you are not known for your tolerance when it comes to differing points of view, a potential partner should definitely share your beliefs.

The perfect woman for you, 1937 Sagittarius male, is someone who can connect with you on both a mental and spiritual plane. It's likely that she'll share your love of travel and want to explore the far corners of the earth with you. She should be able to handle your detachment and your occasional blunt remarks. But, most of all, you want a woman who shares your strong ideals and your passion for reform.

1937 Sagittarius female, your perfect man has an inventive genius combined with a practical business sense. He is interested in anything new and unusual, and he may even be an expert in technology. In his youth, he may have been a bit of a revolutionary but, with age, it is likely that his focus is on humanitarian ideals.

Jean Cocteau and Jean Marais

Writer, artist, filmmaker, poet, choreographer Jean Cocteau explored every artistic medium the world had to offer, placing him firmly at the head of the avant-garde movement.

His eccentric and original approach was fitting of a man with an unconventional childhood. Born into a middle-class Parisian family, his father committed suicide when Cocteau was nine. It was then that Jean started writing. School bored him, and it was maybe for this reason that he was an unexceptional student expelled at fifteen. He ran away to Marseilles in search of more entertaining forms of education—and this he received in full force, living with prostitutes and partying hard with sailors. Police discovered him, and the young Cocteau was sent packing back to Paris. But his life was about to change irrevocably. He had formed several relationships with older men, and one of the first of these, Edouard de Max, a star of the Parisian stage, encouraged his young protégé to write. At the age of nineteen Cocteau's career as an artiste began when his first volume of poems was published.

From that moment on, Cocteau began to explore all his artistic capabilities—no medium was out of bounds, including the ballet, for which he was challenged to write by the impresario of Russian ballet, Sergei Diaghilev.

Permeating the essence of his work was sexuality—in Cocteau's case, homosexuality. Cocteau was a proud and outspoken homosexual, and striking homoerotic imagery pervaded his work.

By the '30s, he had cultivated a rich coterie of friends, all talented pioneers of the avant-garde scene. Pablo Picasso, Erik Satie and Marcel Proust were some of the greats he collaborated with, confirming his artistic prowess. Living an indulgent, hedonistic lifestyle, Cocteau had also developed a serious addiction, which

161

"Tact in audacity consists in knowing how far we may go too far."

JEAN COCTEAU

inspired him to the write the cult classic of drug literature, *Opium.*

Among his collaborators was a string of younger men he would take on as lovers and whom he called his "enfants," and by far the most famous of these was the actor Jean Marais. Cocteau first set eyes on him in 1937 when Marais was auditioning for a role in his play. Although there was a twenty-four-year age difference between them, it was love at first sight. The handsome, athletic twenty-four-year-old blonde was to be Cocteau's inspiration and muse for the rest of his life. Cocteau immediately set to work writing a screenplay aimed at catapulting his young lover into the spotlight. The movie, *The Eternal Return,* was an instant success, and sealed their professional and personal partnership.

Marais encouraged Cocteau to develop filmmaking skills. Movies like *Beauty and the Beast* and *Orpheus* exposed the pair to an international audience, cementing Cocteau's reputation as a visionary and spectacular cinematic innovator, and Marais as a superstar pinup with credible acting ability. Their intense love affair lasted over ten years, but even after their separation the two men remained close friends until the day Cocteau died—only hours after the death of his great friend Edith Piaf—in 1963. Marais died in 1998.

A fearless experimenter knowing no boundaries, Cocteau was an artistic revolutionary, fusing surrealism, cubism, and poetic and magical realism, refusing to be restricted or pigeonholed by a single movement. He remains, to this day, one of France's most loved cultural icons.

▶ READ ABOUT EDITH PIAF ON PAGE 269 ▶ READ ABOUT PABLO PICASSO ON PAGE 352

1938

- ⭐ **SEXUAL MISCONDUCT**
- ⭐ **CENSORSHIP**
- ⭐ **BRINGING UP BABY**
- ⭐ **PYGMALION**
- ⭐ **HOTEL DU NORD**
- ⭐ **BEI MIR BIST DU SCHÖN**
- ⭐ **REBECCA**

Sex Idol

EVENTS

Amid plans for invasion and annexation, Hitler found time to sack two of his closest allies after they were accused of sexual misconduct. General Werner von Fritsch was said to be a homosexual, while Field Marshal Verner von Blomberg was married to a one-time prostitute. In the US, film censorship continued with the re-release of *King Kong*. A scene was cut in which Kong rips at Fay Wray's dress and then sniffs his finger. After Mae West and Don Ameche exchanged risque banter during an Adam and Eve radio sketch, 130 radio stations banned the very mention of West's name. But censorship did not extend to the Broadway stage, where Mary Martin, sitting on a trunk and wearing a very short coat and little else, stopped the show singing "My Heart Belongs to Daddy."

POP CULTURE

Two screwball classics hit the silver screen—paleontologist Cary Grant, socialite Katharine Hepburn, and a leopard made for madcap mayhem in *Bringing Up Baby*, and James Stewart contended with Jean Arthur's wacky family in *You Can't Take It with You*. George Bernard Shaw was outraged that the film adaptation of his play *Pygmalion* ended with Eliza Doolittle returning to Henry Higgins. Bette Davis was Southern not-so-belle *Jezebel*. Marcel Carné's *Hotel du Nord* intertwined the stories of a despairing young couple in love and a pimp and prostitute, while in *The Divorce of Lady X*, Laurence

Olivier and Merle Oberon were paired for the first time in a frothy comedy of love and disguises.

Ella Fitzgerald's "A-Tisket, A-Tasket" was a big hit, as was the Andrew Sisters' "Bei Mir Bist du Schön." "Jeepers Creepers," "My Heart Belongs to Daddy," and "You Must Have Been a Beautiful Baby" were popular, and radio star Bob Hope sang "Thanks for the Memory."

Phyllis Bottome's *The Mortal Storm* told the tale of a Nazi storm trooper, a freedom fighter, and the woman they both love. Dawn Powell depicted New York City's cafe society in *The Happy Island*, Rachel Field's *All This, and Heaven Too* was about a French governess who becomes a small-town American minister's wife, and in Daphne du Maurier's gothic romance, *Rebecca*, a charismatic first wife's malevolent influence reaches from beyond the grave.

CHARLES BOYER

Although he never actually said the famous line "Come with me to the Casbah" in his 1938 film *Algiers*, for a whole generation of moviegoers, Charles Boyer was the quintessential Frenchman. Distinguished by his good looks, velvet voice, and suave European manners, Boyer became an American citizen in 1942.

He could play a womanizing cad in movies, but in his private life he was a loving and faithful husband, married for forty-four years to English actress Patricia Paterson. When she died from cancer in 1978, Boyer was so desolate he killed himself with sleeping pills just two days later.

SEE ALSO

▶ **MARCELLO MASTROIANNI** *Page 367*

▶ **GARY COOPER** *Page 146*

1938 CAPRICORN

From December 22, 1937 6:22 through January 20, 1938 16:58
(December 1938 Capricorns, see 1939 Capricorn)

♑ *The Generous Lover*

You are among the most generous folks on the planet 1938 Capricorn. You're always thinking of new ways to bestow kindnesses on your lover. As far as you're concerned, relationships are about giving, not receiving. You benefit from a partner who not only enjoys being pampered, but thrives on it. A mate who is remarkable in some way gives you special joy. There's nothing you love more than providing a genius with a sense of normalcy. In exchange, you get the benefit of your lover's extraordinary insights. A partnership that offers an interesting blend of different personalities works best for you.

As someone with a strong sex drive, you enjoy a partner whose physical needs are equal to your own. Sex has a transforming effect on you. One of the best ways for your mate to get you out of a bad mood is to lure you into the bedroom. As far as the household is concerned, you're not particularly connected to it. You could live in a variety of places and still be happy, provided your mate is by your side. You hate being separated from your spouse for long periods of time.

Anyone who is inventive, expressive, and utterly unique has a good chance of winning your heart. Voicing dissent in a crowd is an excellent way to get your attention. So is proposing an outing to an unusual, out-of-the-way place. You love seeing how the other half lives! Your admirer should let you make the first move, as you prefer to be the aggressor. The best way to invite a pass is to look soulfully into your eyes while talking about some perfectly innocent topic, like the weather.

If you're a male Goat who was born in 1938, you want a woman who is willful, magnetic, and ambitious. Females who are goal-oriented and enthusiastic never fail to win your admiration. You do best with a mate who welcomes your generosity and uses it to her benefit.

Female 1938 Capricorns seek a man who is fanciful, eccentric, and humorous. Offbeat types really turn you on, because they can show you different ways of thinking and feeling. A partner who provides you with loving companionship is just your cup of tea.

CAPRICORN ZODIAC SIGN
YOUR LOVE PLANETS

YOUR ROMANTIC SIDE — p. 696
► VENUS IN SAGITTARIUS
Born Dec. 22, 1937 6:22 - Dec. 30, 1937 14:41
► VENUS IN CAPRICORN
Born Dec. 30, 1937 14:42 - Jan. 20, 1938 16:58

YOUR SEX DRIVE — p. 722
► MARS IN PISCES
Born Dec. 22, 1937 6:22 - Jan. 20, 1938 16:58

YOUR CELEBRITY TWINS — p. 760
Find out the astrological similarities you have with famous people.

YOUR COMPATIBILITY — p. 780
Compare planets to find out how compatible you are in a relationship.

YOUR RELATIONSHIP KARMA — p. 824
► SATURN IN PISCES
Born Dec. 22, 1937 6:22 - Jan. 14, 1938, 10:32
► SATURN IN ARIES
Born Jan. 14, 10:33 - Jan. 20, 16:58

JOHN STEINBECK
American Writer
Venus in Aquarius

163

1938 AQUARIUS

From January 20, 16:59 through February 19, 7:19

♒ *The Inventive Romantic*

As a 1938 Aquarius, you have unusual ideas about love that are quite refreshing. Conventional relationships don't really interest you. You do far better with a partner who treats your union as something that is special and unique. Keeping up with the neighbors doesn't interest you in the slightest. You'd rather carve out a lifestyle that supports and inspires both you and your mate, whether that means living in a remote area or keeping unusual hours. An insightful, dynamic lover suits you very well.

Sexually, you are quite idealistic, and want to share yourself with one partner. You don't even like to utter the word "betrayal," much less contemplate it. Sex transports you to a place where cruelty doesn't exist. A mate who shares your dreamy attitude toward making love brings you much joy. Your partnership may be the primary focus of your life. There is little chance that career or family concerns will ever take priority over your lover. Hopefully, your spouse shares this same sense of loyalty and devotion to you.

A suitor with no pretensions stands a good chance of winning your affection. You respect a person who sees equal merit in a rock concert and an opera. An admirer who is upbeat and social is also attractive to you. You can't stand pessimists! You're shy when it comes to initiating romance. When it's time to make the first move, your suitor would be wise to place a gentle kiss on the inside of your palm, and then let their lips travel upward. You're extremely turned on by soft caresses.

1938 male Aquarians like all sorts of women. You enjoy reflective, dreamy females, as well as off-the-wall, rebellious types. Women who are sensual and sensitive also find favor with you. Ultimately, you want a mate who seeks to create a private world of pleasure with you.

If you're a female Water-bearer who was born in 1938, you desire a man who is either caring and capable or clever and witty. Whichever kind of guy you choose, your lover should be the sort of man who celebrates your uniqueness. You have no desire to be shaped into some kind of feminine ideal.

AQUARIUS ZODIAC SIGN
YOUR LOVE PLANETS

YOUR ROMANTIC SIDE — p. 696
► VENUS IN CAPRICORN
Born Jan. 20, 16:59 - Jan. 23, 11:15
► VENUS IN AQUARIUS
Born Jan. 23, 11:16 - Feb. 16, 8:59
► VENUS IN PISCES
Born Feb. 16, 9:00 - Feb. 19, 7:19

YOUR SEX DRIVE — p. 722
► MARS IN PISCES
Born Jan. 20, 16:59 - Jan. 30, 12:43
► MARS IN ARIES
Born Jan. 30, 12:44 - Feb. 19, 7:19

YOUR CELEBRITY TWINS — p. 760
Find out the astrological similarities you have with famous people.

YOUR COMPATIBILITY — p. 780
Compare planets to find out how compatible you are in a relationship.

YOUR RELATIONSHIP KARMA — p. 824
► SATURN IN ARIES
Born Jan. 20, 16:59 - Feb. 19, 7:19

JOAN BENNETT
American Actress
Sun and Venus in Pisces

1938 PISCES
From February 19, 7:20 through March 21, 6:42

 The Retiring Romantic

You prefer to operate from behind the scenes rather than center stage as a 1938 Pisces. For you, relationships are private matters that should not be subjected to public scrutiny. A low-key but communicative partner works best for you. Although you are quite reflective, you have a hard time expressing your ideas. Having a partner who can draw out your emotions helps you to lead a richer, more fulfilling life. Because you are such an observant person, you enjoy drawing your mate's attention to details that would be otherwise overlooked. A relationship in which each partner can draw on the other's strengths is your idea of paradise.

When it comes to making love, you are both earthy and idealistic. At times you want sex to satisfy your physical desires, and at others you want to meld souls with your partner. Either way, the experience is a profoundly satisfying one for you. Although you're a private person, you do enjoy sudden spurts of social activity. A mate who is content to break up prolonged periods of privacy with festive parties brings out the best in you. Since you have a cautious attitude toward finances, you do well with a mate who shows you how to spend money on things that give you pleasure.

Dreamy philosophers are guaranteed to attract your attention. You admire a suitor who is eager to explore the big questions of life. Someone with strong spiritual values also has a good chance of winning your heart. You're the type of lover who enjoys being seduced with a candlelit meal, fine wine, and soft music. Like all Pisceans, you enjoy a languorous foot massage as a prelude to making love.

Women who are romantic, independent, and sensitive really appeal to you 1938 male Fish. You're also drawn to females who are gentle yet tough. A woman who knows when to draw you out and when to leave you alone is your ideal mate.

If you're a woman Piscean who was born in 1938, you want a man who is confident but down-to-earth. Cowboy types really turn you on. Alternately, you enjoy a guy who is charming, witty, and persuasive. You want a mate who treats you like a lady.

1938 ARIES
From March 21, 6:43 through April 20, 18:14

♈ *The Reserved Suitor*

Rams of 1938 dislike grand displays of emotion, especially in love. You prefer to show your devotion through impressive actions, not words. A relationship in which both partners work to relieve each other of duties and hardships is ideal for you. As a person who believes in the value of hard work, you really appreciate a partner who makes you feel as though your contributions are noble and worthy. You're capable of earning and spending lots of money, and do best with a mate who knows how to balance the budget in both good times and bad.

Most people would be surprised to learn what a passionate lover you are. You take sex very seriously, and prefer to devote your attentions to a single partner. A mate who makes you feel irresistibly sexy brings out the best in you. When you're ill, you love to be babied and pampered by your partner. Teaming up with someone who loves to be of service gives you the love and attention you crave. You're also quite gregarious, and enjoy having lots of friends visit your home. You benefit from a spouse who smiles on your ever-expanding social circle.

A bold and determined suitor is bound to attract your attention. Although you're very reserved, you admire daring people who know what they want. You're deeply interested in humanitarian causes, and are sure to feel a kinship with someone who believes as you do. A good first move is stroking your cheek. As far as you're concerned, there is nothing as fascinating as the human face, and you love it when a suitor pays attention to yours.

Male Rams who were born in 1938 like women who are innovative, extroverted, and blunt. It's important for you to know where you stand with a lady. You also appreciate females who are practical and supportive. A mate who has both her feet planted firmly on the ground suits you best.

Men who are sensual, sexy, steady, and loyal find favor with you 1938 female Ariens. You can't stand a man with roving eyes. You need a partner who focuses on you like a laser. A spouse who values your hard work but can convince you to take occasional breaks is your ideal match.

1938 TAURUS
From April 21, 18:15 through May 21, 17:49

The Popular Lover

As a 1938 Bull, you're usually the center of attention. And although your magnetic personality draws plenty of admirers, you benefit most from being with one devoted partner. Flirting is a means for you to stay young and vibrant, but when you go home, you want only to be wrapped in the arms of your beloved. For you, a relationship is a safe haven from the uncertainties of the outside world. Having a warm, loving home life is very important to you. You do best with a partner who enjoys making your domestic environment comfortable, cozy, and welcoming.

You have a strong desire for romance that spills over in practically everything you do. You're always quick with a compliment or a tender tribute. A lover who makes a big deal out of anniversaries, birthdays, and special occasions makes your heart sing. At home, you like to occupy the dominant position, and delight in spoiling your lover with lavish treats. Sexually, you can be a bit coy. You'd rather have your mate seduce you than the other way around. Still, you respond beautifully when you're kissed, cuddled, and caressed. When it comes to making love, quality is more important than quantity for you.

Outrageous flirting is always an effective way of attracting your interest. So is talking about the distant past or the distant future. You're very interested in speculating about other people's lives, either what they were like or how they will evolve. An admirer would also be wise to confess hidden fears to you, as this is another topic that you love to explore. When it comes time to make the first move, you enjoy having your neck kissed and caressed as a prelude to lovemaking.

Women who are artistic, enduring, and enthusiastic appeal to you 1938 male Taureans. You're also drawn to witty ladies who are flirtatious but faithful. A mate who makes you feel young, sexy, and important is best suited to you.

If you're a female Bull who was born in 1938, you want a man who is ambitious, steadfast, and forceful. Take-charge types really turn you on. Sensual men who are loaded with practical knowledge also appeal to you.

ELLA FITZGERALD
American Singer
Sun and Venus in Taurus

165

1938 GEMINI
From May 21, 17:50 through June 22, 2:03

The Sentimental Dreamer

You are among the most visionary people in the zodiac, 1938 Gemini. You always have your head in the clouds, and that's especially true with regard to romance. Although you are extremely sentimental towards your partner, it's easy for you to get distracted by the fascinating concepts that are always flitting through your brain. A partner who understands your need to retreat to a world of fantasy for long periods of time is ideal for you. You want a relationship that affords plenty of intellectual freedom and personal space.

As far as you're concerned, the brain is the sexiest organ in the human body. There's a good chance you enjoy acting out fantasies with your partner, and thinking up new ways to titillate each other. It may take a while for you to get heated up in the bedroom, but when you do, the results are spectacular. Because you have such strong opinions, it helps for you to be with a mate who can argue without taking such debates personally. A relationship that thrives on plenty of lively discussion suits you very well.

Demonstrating mental resourcefulness is a wonderful way to get your attention. You greatly admire problem-solvers, and usually try to integrate these folks into your social circle. Because you prefer being friends before becoming lovers, it's a good idea to take a casual approach with you in the early stages. When it comes time to make the first move, your suitor would be wise to take you to an erotic movie, and let things develop naturally from there. You're very impressionable!

As a 1938 male Gemini, you are attracted to lots of different women. The first type is a good storyteller. The second is emotional but realistic. Ladies who are restless and sociable also appeal to you. Ultimately, you want a partner who encourages your visionary mind.

Men who are expressive and vivacious are extremely attractive to you 1938 female Geminis. You adore a man who keeps you on the edge of your seat with hair-raising tales. Guys who are nurturing and protective also warm your heart. A mate who celebrates your intelligence is your best match.

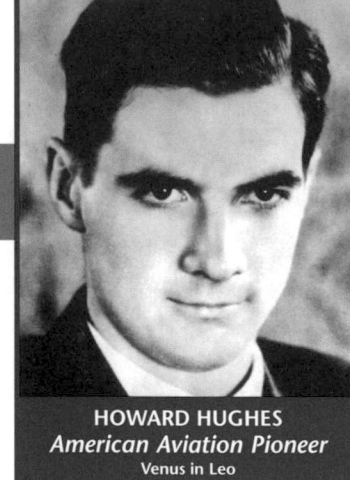

HOWARD HUGHES
American Aviation Pioneer
Venus in Leo

1938 CANCER
From June 22, 2:04 through July 23, 12:56

 ## The Enterprising Suitor

Enjoying a rewarding romance has always been the guiding principle in your life as a 1938 Cancer. A lover who shares your deep love of philosophy, religion, and culture suits you best. You want a partnership that allows you to explore the bigger questions in life through study, travel, or both. There's a good chance you'll devote much of your time exploring curious corners of the world with your mate. A lover who is willing to drop everything in order to pursue a fresh adventure is a perfect match for you. You view these sudden trips as a means to keep your partnership exciting.

Although you enjoy taking risks, you probably have conventional views with regard to marriage. It's likely that you view your wedding day as the most important in your life. As someone who is bound to achieve success in your career, you benefit from a spouse who can handle living in the spotlight. Having a solid relationship earns you the respect and admiration of the public, while providing the support you need to withstand the pressures of your position. Sexually, you can be quite shy, and need a mate who is able to melt your considerable reserve.

Discussing subjects like religion, mysticism, and the occult is a good way to catch your eye. You're extremely interested in these subjects, and feel a strong bond with anyone who demonstrates a fair amount of knowledge in any one of them. Civic-minded people also appeal to you, as they share your humanitarian streak. Turning your friendship into a romance is as simple as turning a platonic hug into a passionate embrace. Your admirer should be advised that you want an exclusive relationship.

If you're a male Crab who was born in 1938, you enjoy women who are generous, magnetic, and stubborn. You also appreciate ladies with refined tastes. A partner who enjoys exploring new vistas with you is your ideal.

As a female Cancer who was born in 1938, you want a man who is powerful and confident. A guy who can make an impressive entrance never fails to take your breath away. You do best with a mate whose masculinity emphasizes your femininity.

1938 LEO
From July 23, 12:57 through August 23, 19:45

The Energetic Paramour

Bursting with vitality, you 1938 Lions are a thrilling lot. You manage to stir up excitement wherever you go, and this is especially true with regard to your love life. No matter how long you've been with your partner, the relationship manages to stay fresh. That's because you have a zest for romance that is impossible to resist. Once you capture someone's heart, you're intent on keeping it. Showering your lover with flowers, candy, jewelry, and poetry is a regular habit of yours, but it's one that never grows stale.

It also helps if your mate is as active as you are, especially in the bedroom! You have a strong sex drive that demands expression. There's little chance of your slowing down as you get older. You will probably get even more potent with age! When you're not having fun with your in the boudoir, you can be found at some public event. As someone who loves to be the center of attention, you need a spouse who doesn't mind yielding the spotlight to you. You need a partnership that allows you to showcase your many talents.

The best way to win your heart is to express admiration for your gifts. You pride yourself on being an innovative person, and like to be recognized as such. A suitor who is well-educated also attracts your interest, as you admire anyone who has the tenacity to get a degree. Playing hard-to-get is always a good idea, since you love the thrill of the chase. Your admirer would be wise to let you make the first move, although giving you a little encouragement wouldn't hurt. You're especially turned on when the object of your affection wets their lips in anticipation of a kiss.

Male Lions who were born in 1938 like women who are dependable, kind-hearted, and restrained. You also admire clever females who have a love of words and ideas. In the end, you do best with a devoted mate who delights in your crazy antics.

Men who are passionate, adventurous, and idealistic appeal to you 1938 female Leos. You need a partner who encourages your ideas, and is eager to follow through with them. If there's anything you can't stand, it's a wet blanket!

1938 VIRGO
From August 23, 19:46 through September 23, 16:59

The Romantic Go-getter

You don't let the grass grow under your feet when it comes to romance 1938 Virgo. Forthright, determined, and directed, you'll do anything in your power to serve the object of your affection, even if it means putting your own dreams on hold. A relationship in which both partners are constantly working to make each other happy is your ideal. You're not interested in resting on your laurels once you've won your beloved's heart. Rather, you will continue to reinforce your love and devotion through kind gestures and helpful acts.

Although you are delighted to share your life with your partner, you may find it a bit difficult to open up sexually. It can be difficult to reconcile your respect for your mate with your passionate impulses. A spouse who encourages you to express your sexual desires brings you a great deal of happiness and comfort. Because you are very sensitive to your mate's needs, you can often anticipate them. This makes you a very pleasing and sympathetic partner, and helps to keep your bond strong through good times and bad.

A suitor seeking to attract your attention would be wise to bring up subjects like telepathy, extrasensory perception, or even extraterrestrial life. You've always been fascinated with esoteric concepts like these. Inquiring after your creative pursuits is also a smart idea, as there is a good chance you are artistic. Before making the first move, your admirer should take pains to make the atmosphere as romantic as possible, complete with soft music and candlelight. These touches will go a long way toward putting you in the mood for love. Gentle kisses to your inner wrist drive you wild.

If you're a 1938 male Virgo, you enjoy diplomatic women who have a love of art and music. You're also drawn to ladies who are quick-witted and intense. A partner who makes you feel wanted and needed is your ideal match.

As a 1938 female Virgo, you are attracted to warm, compassionate men. Self-motivated, intellectual types also turn you on. You do best with a mate who helps boost your self-esteem with encouraging words and honest compliments.

VIRGO ZODIAC SIGN
YOUR LOVE PLANETS

YOUR ROMANTIC SIDE   p. 696
▶ **VENUS IN LIBRA**
Born Aug. 23, 19:46 - Sept. 07, 1:35
▶ **VENUS IN SCORPIO**
Born Sept. 07, 1:36 - Sept. 23, 16:59

YOUR SEX DRIVE   p. 722
▶ **MARS IN LEO**
Born Aug. 23, 19:46 - Sept. 07, 20:21
▶ **MARS IN VIRGO**
Born Sept. 07, 20:22 - Sept. 23, 16:59

YOUR CELEBRITY TWINS   p. 760
Find out the astrological similarities you have with famous people.

YOUR COMPATIBILITY   p. 780
Compare planets to find out how compatible you are in a relationship.

YOUR RELATIONSHIP KARMA   p. 824
▶ **SATURN IN ARIES**
Born Aug. 23, 19:46 - Sept. 23, 16:59

HELEN WILLS MOODY
American Tennis Champion
Venus in Virgo

167

1938 LIBRA
From September 23, 17:00 through October 24, 1:53

The Suave Heartbreaker

No matter where you go or what you do, 1938 Librans will always have a sizable crowd of admirers. That's the price you have to pay for being so charming and appealing. And although you enjoy all the attention, your heart probably belongs to one person. You take partnerships very seriously, and believe in the concept of soul mates. For you, a romantic relationship should have an exclusive quality. Swapping one partner for another is not your style. When you commit yourself to somebody, you mean it with every fiber of your being.

Few lovers are as exciting as you are. True, you can go through periods when you're not the least bit interested in making love. Then, your partner will do something to fuel your passion, and you become insatiable. You may be very inventive when it comes to making love. When you're not expressing your physical desire for your partner, you're probably doing something recreational together. Taking up a sport together is a good means to keep your intimacy alive as you get older. Travel is another means to promote togetherness later in life.

Expressing originality is an excellent means to catch your eye. You've always been attracted to people who have unconventional interests or unusual talents. A suitor with a childlike spirit also has a good chance with you. You can't abide stodgy, stuffy types who never want to try anything new. As a means to express desire, your admirer might want to rub their foot against yours while you dine at a fancy restaurant. You love naughty behavior like this, and will respond enthusiastically when you're finally able to freely express your passion in private.

If you're a man who was born under the sign of the Scales in 1938, you want a quiet woman who has profound inner depths. You're also drawn to ladies who are curious and intelligent. A mate who makes you think is your ideal match.

Men who are insightful, kind-hearted, and modest attract you 1938 female Librans. You do best with a man who pushes you to be the best that you can be. A partner that appreciates your inner beauty makes your spirits soar.

LIBRA ZODIAC SIGN
YOUR LOVE PLANETS

YOUR ROMANTIC SIDE   p. 696
▶ **VENUS IN SCORPIO**
Born Sept. 23, 17:00 - Oct. 13, 18:48
▶ **VENUS IN SAGITTARIUS**
Born Oct. 13, 18:49 - Oct. 24, 1:53

YOUR SEX DRIVE   p. 722
▶ **MARS IN VIRGO**
Born Sept. 23, 17:00 - Oct. 24, 1:53

YOUR CELEBRITY TWINS   p. 760
Find out the astrological similarities you have with famous people.

YOUR COMPATIBILITY   p. 780
Compare planets to find out how compatible you are in a relationship.

YOUR RELATIONSHIP KARMA   p. 824
▶ **SATURN IN ARIES**
Born Sept. 23, 17:00 - Oct. 24, 1:53

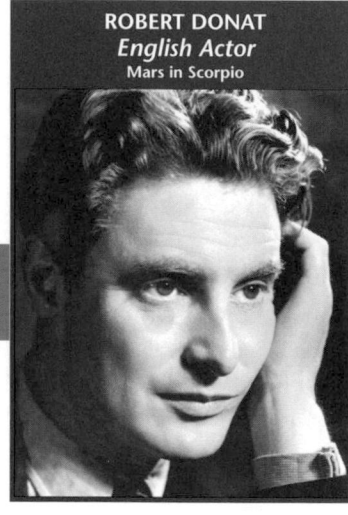

ROBERT DONAT
English Actor
Mars in Scorpio

168

1938 SCORPIO
From October 24, 1:54 through November 22, 23:05

♏ *The Strong-willed Swain*

Few folks are as determined as you 1938 Scorpions are, particularly with regard to love. Your greatest desire is to live happily ever after with your partner. As someone with a strong drive to succeed, it can be difficult for you to balance your public and private lives, but that doesn't stop you from trying. A mate who is intimately involved in your work is a good match for you. By engaging your mate in your professional affairs, it is easier to achieve the trust and intimacy you need. You want a relationship that touches every area of your life, not just the domestic sphere.

Entertaining in your home is one of your favorite ways to unwind. Consequently, you greatly benefit from a spouse who knows how to throw a fun party. Teaming up with a detail-oriented partner works well for you, because you prefer thinking about the big picture. When it comes to making love, you enjoy being in control. A lover who enjoys following your lead really fuels your passion. Prolonged, intense sessions in the bedroom satisfy your considerable sexual appetite.

Attracting your attention takes skill and cunning. You don't like admirers who wear their hearts on their sleeves. You far prefer subtle forms of seduction, like a handshake that lingers a second too long, or a deep gaze that seems to be making a mute appeal for love. Your suitor need not worry that you won't pick up these signals. As someone whose intuition borders on psychic, it is impossible for you to miss such messages. Once your admirer sends out the signal, you'll make the first move towards the bedroom. Sexy underclothes may only make your sexual fire burn brighter.

Women with a large appetite for life appeal most to you 1938 Scorpions. You also appreciate ladies who are self-confident and romantic. A partner who supports your professional aspirations brings out the best in you.

As a 1938 female Scorpion, you want a man who is a purist in both love and work. You detest guys who play games. You're also drawn to dreamy idealists. A mate who always makes you feel loved, cherished, and respected is your ideal.

1938 SAGITTARIUS
From November 22, 23:06 through December 22, 12:12

♐ *The Intuitive Partner*

As a 1938 Sagittarian, you've got uncanny instincts with regard to romance. You know just what to say to bring out the best in your partner from moment to moment. That's because you make it your business to know your beloved, both inside and out. Studying your partner's movements, body language, and voice inflections helps you understand when compassion, guidance, or sympathy are needed. A relationship that is based on mutual care and respect is your ideal. You have no desire for a tempestuous union that makes you feel unsettled and nervous. You'd rather explore your partner's needs from a position of safety and security.

At times, you put your partner on a pedestal. This can create barriers between you in the bedroom if you're not careful. You greatly benefit from a mate who invites you to take a more down-to-earth approach to sex. A spouse who has a strong spiritual foundation supports your desire to lead a meaningful life. Acquiring lots of material goods has little interest for you. Consequently, you do best in a marriage that is

founded on mutual beliefs, rather than a desire to build wealth.

An accomplished, serious-minded suitor has a good chance of attracting your attention. Flirtatious games have no appeal for you, though. You appreciate and respect an admirer who expresses a desire for romance from the outset. You're also impressed by folks who express interest in education, philosophy, and self-improvement. A suitor would be well advised to take the initiative with you when it comes to sex. Asking permission for a kiss is a good idea, as you dislike presumptuous lovers.

As a 1938 male Archer, you want a woman who is hard-working and dedicated. A lady who is deeply motivated to make the world a better place speaks to your heart. You want a partner that can provide you with a close, enduring relationship.

1938 female Sagittarians are drawn to men who are rational, outgoing, and communicative. Brooding, moody types leave you cold. You're also attracted to men who are disciplined and compassionate. A mate who values your interests is your ideal.

'30s

Big Band Music Is for Swingers

Throughout the 20th century, new trends in dance and music allowed young people to vent their energy in ways that often caused societal anxiety. By the mid 1990s, fans of alternative rock music were throwing themselves, half-naked, into mosh pits and bouncing off each other with chaotic abandon. The same time period saw a parallel trend that was reassuring to members of older generations. The revival of Big Band music and swing dance in Europe and America provided an alternative to the alternative—the sensual satisfaction of high-energy partner dancing to lushly orchestrated music with a melody and contagious beat. The stylish evening dress seen in Big Band venues contrasted drastically with the torn jeans and grungy tee shirts of the alternative scene.

When Big Band music and Swing Dance first emerged in the 1930s and '40s, it did not enjoy the same kind of cross-generational acceptance that it does today. Parents and community leaders fretted over the opportunity swing dancing provided for casual physical contact between strangers. The rhythmic intensity and acrobatic moves seemed sexually charged and dangerously wild for their time. Rooted in jazz, Big Band music reflected African-American influence, inspiration, and participation—a factor that provoked alarm about the integration of the races and the potential for miscegenation. Many Big Band orchestras, such as Benny Goodman's, and some clubs, such as the Savoy in Harlem, were integrated.

For young adults in the Depression Era, Big Band music and swing dancing provided an escape into a realm of eye-catching opulence and dizzying excitement. With Big Band members in tuxedos, men in sharp suits and ties, and

The Duke Ellington Orchestra

ladies in light, flowing dresses, everyone could strut with refinement. The social ease of swing dancing, known in the '30s and '40s as the "Lindy Hop," reinforced its popularity through World War II, as soldiers, nurses, and civilians boogied their blues away.

The Big Band craze of the 1930s was a Jazz Age descendent, incubated in New Orleans, Chicago, Kansas City, New York, and Paris—cities that welcomed African-American musical innovators. The "hot jazz" ensembles of the 1920s expanded into larger, more elaborate companies of musicians eager to push the music in new and exciting directions. The expansive Swing "sound" was characterized by the bright sound of brass, sassy clarinets and sax, and anchored in the rich rhythms of piano, string bass, and drums. Led by a charismatic bandleader, the orchestras of the Big Band era featured thrilling solos by individual "sidemen," who became

famous in their own right for their instrumental virtuosity.

The growth of radio, the recorded music industry, and jukeboxes contributed dramatically to the popularity of Swing music. In 1938, Big Band music was in its heyday. That year, the Benny Goodman Orchestra played Carnegie Hall in New York. Glenn Miller, known for choreographing dance moves for his band members, formed a new orchestra and secured a contract with NBC Radio, which provided national broadcasts of Miller's concerts at the Paradise Restaurant, also in New York. Of course, no account of the Big Band Era can be complete without mention of the monumental contribution of Duke Ellington and Count Basie, whose orchestras generated interracial "crossover" appeal. For the ultimate Big Band experience, downtown New Yorkers would "Take the A Train" on a pilgrimage to the "Mecca of Swing" in Harlem.

► READ ABOUT BILLIE HOLIDAY ON PAGE 187 ► READ ABOUT JOSEPHINE BAKER, THE BLACK PEARL ON PAGE 79 ► READ ABOUT SWINGING LONDON ON PAGE 383

1939

- ⍟ **ARTIFICIAL INSEMINATION**
- ⍟ **SEX HORMONES**
- ⍟ **WUTHERING HEIGHTS**
- ⍟ **RULES OF THE GAME**
- ⍟ **IN THE MOOD**
- ⍟ **OVER THE RAINBOW**
- ⍟ **GRAPES OF WRATH**

EVENTS

The first animal conceived by artifical insemination—appropriately, a rabbit—was born, while Adolf Butenandt was awarded the Nobel Prize in chemistry for his work on sexual hormones, but declined to accept it.

In Germany, the birth rate reached a peak, despite the forcible sterilization of "undesirables." The 13-year-old Princess Elizabeth caught the first glimpse of her future husband Prince Philip while on a family holiday. And the Bastardy Bill was passed in the House of Lords, which made blood tests an essential factor in paternity suits.

A flurry of marriages among the famous included: Erskine Caldwell and Margaret Bourke-White; Tyrone Power and French actress Annabella; Merle Oberon and producer Alexander Korda; and Janet Gaynor and film costume designer Adrian.

POP CULTURE

Gone with the Wind dominated the Academy Awards. The producers needed permission for Clark Gable to say "Frankly, my dear, I don't give a damn." Norma Shearer, Joan Crawford, Joan Fontaine, and Rosalind Russell fought for their men in *The Women*. Greta Garbo had an international affair in *Ninotchka*, and Laurence Olivier and Merle Oberon loved and lost in *Wuthering Heights*. Jean Renoir's *La Règle du Jeu (Rules of the Game)* cast a cynical eye on the upper-class participants in a weekend shooting party.

Jazz and big band sounds were red hot, including Count Basie's "Miss Thing," Glenn Miller's "In the Mood," and Billie Holiday's "Strange Fruit." The Ink Spots had a chart-topper with "If I Didn't Care." Judy Garland sang "Over the Rainbow." Bandleader Ruth Lowe wrote the song "I'll Never Smile Again" in memory of her late husband.

John Steinbeck's *The Grapes of Wrath* told the story of the Joad family, driven by dust storms to migrant life in California. In Stefan Zweig's *Beware of Pity*, a crippled girl is in love with an Austrian officer. Christopher Morley offered the complication of romance between Philadelphia's social classes in *Kitty Foyle*, and felines of another sort came to life in T.S. Eliot's *Old Possum's Book of Practical Cats*.

Hot Couple

CLARK GABLE & CAROLE LOMBARD

Already christened by *Photoplay* magazine one of Hollywood's "Unmarried Husbands and Wives," Gable and Lombard tied the knot for real in March 1939. This marriage was a true love match. They called each other "Ma" and "Pa" and played extravagant practical jokes on one another. They bought a ranch in the Valley, and Lombard insisted she was going to retire from movies, stay home, knit, and raise kids.

But the good times ended in January 1942 when her plane crashed into a mountain outside Las Vegas. Gable died in 1960, a few days after filming wrapped on *The Misfits*.

SEE ALSO
▶ **MARILYN MONROE** *Page 293*

1939 CAPRICORN

From December 22, 1938 12:13 through January 20, 1939 22:50
(December 1939 Capricorns, see 1940 Capricorn)

The Vintage Valentine

Like a fine wine, 1939 Capricorn, you get better and better over the years. When you first set out on the road to romantic fulfillment, you may have been a bit shy and inhibited, willing to let parents and social mores dictate the big decisions of when to commit and with whom. Because you tend to learn best by doing, a relationship may have provided a kind of "on-the-job" training for you in intimacy, responsibility, sex, and asserting yourself. What you are "supposed to do" in relationships and parenting may matter a lot less to you now than what you do because you want to and because it's a joy.

For you, success boosts your self-assurance, and as you enjoy greater personal satisfaction in love and romance, you tend to become a more daring and adventurous partner, able to trust your judgment and make quick decisions. You are likely to have a strong sense of humor, a trait that allows you and your mate to take challenges in stride and have a great time, wherever you go. You may love to socialize and entertain together. As a guest or co-host, you can be indulgent and extravagant, lavishing loved ones with gifts, delicious treats, and affection. Lovemaking can be a highly charged experience for you, as you may be especially sensitive to sensual stimulation.

You may have a bit of a sweet tooth, and sharing delectable treats with your mate can be almost as good as sex itself. Exotic settings can stir your passions, and a vacation to a distant land or a day at the museum may inspire you and your mate to expand your erotic repertoire.

The 1939 Capricorn man enjoys a woman who is outgoing and openly affectionate. You appreciate someone who is eager to learn new things and to discover a range of interesting activities that the two of you can enjoy together. Her enthusiasm can keep you energized and excited.

Female Capricorns born in 1939 like the man who is passionate and industrious. You may find it so inspiring to be around someone who has the courage to pursue the causes and activities that stir his emotions. His support can spur you to follow your heart in everything you do.

CAPRICORN ZODIAC SIGN
YOUR LOVE PLANETS

YOUR ROMANTIC SIDE   p. 696
- ▶ VENUS IN SCORPIO
  Born Dec. 22, 1938 12:13 - Jan. 04, 1939 21:47
- ▶ VENUS IN SAGITTARIUS
  Born Jan. 04, 21:48 - Jan. 20, 22:50

YOUR SEX DRIVE   p. 722
- ▶ MARS IN SCORPIO
  Born Dec. 22, 1938 12:13 - Jan. 20, 1939 22:50

YOUR CELEBRITY TWINS   p. 760
Find out the astrological similarities you have with famous people.

YOUR COMPATIBILITY   p. 780
Compare planets to find out how compatible you are in a relationship.

YOUR RELATIONSHIP KARMA   p. 824
- ▶ SATURN IN ARIES
  Born Dec. 22, 1938 12:13 - Jan. 20, 1939 22:50

GLENN MILLER
American Musician
Venus in Aquarius

171

1939 AQUARIUS

From January 20, 22:51 through February 19, 13:08

The Reborn Romantic

You may joke, 1939 Aquarius, that you are a late bloomer and shy when it comes to relationships, and you are likely to keep on blooming in wondrous ways. Love and romance may have made an enormous difference in your life, indeed, making a new person of you. While you may have had the potential for willfulness, youthful arrogance, and a bit of a temper early on, a relationship may have mellowed any such traits. The love of your mate brings out a side of you that is sympathetic, imaginative, and affectionate. For you, partnership tends to bring gains that make compromise or self-sacrifice well worthwhile.

To be needed can inspire you to faithfully devote yourself to the well-being of your mate and family. You may strongly believe that steady effort over time ultimately leads to greater and more enduring rewards—and to the stability and longevity of your partnership. Your emotional attachment gives you a reason to see what is unique and precious about your loved ones. Tending to be a rebel and trendsetter yourself, you may encourage your mate and any children you may have to be true to themselves. Such support can inspire your mate and blow the minds of young whippersnappers, who might expect you to disapprove of offbeat pursuits. Lovemaking lets you express your creative imagination by exploring ways to please your partner.

Getting a rise out of your partner can rouse your passions. Vocal approval of a certain move or technique can make your adrenaline surge. Music can strongly influence your mood, and an evening concert can be a wonderfully romantic outing for the two of you.

The Aquarian man of 1939 appreciates a woman who is fun-loving and a true friend. You tend to be a bit eccentric, and you can prosper with someone who recognizes you as a true original. With this lady you can enjoy healthy helpings of laughter and excitement.

An enthusiastic, idealistic man is a superb counterpart for the 1939 Aquarian woman. You tend to admire someone with an expansive intellect and an ability to appreciate your point of view. Together, you can enjoy thought-provoking conversations.

AQUARIUS ZODIAC SIGN
YOUR LOVE PLANETS

YOUR ROMANTIC SIDE   p. 696
- ▶ VENUS IN SAGITTARIUS
  Born Jan. 20, 22:51 - Feb. 06, 9:19
- ▶ VENUS IN CAPRICORN
  Born Feb. 06, 9:20 - Feb. 19, 13:08

YOUR SEX DRIVE   p. 722
- ▶ MARS IN SCORPIO
  Born Jan. 20, 22:51 - Jan. 29, 9:48
- ▶ MARS IN SAGITTARIUS
  Born Jan. 29, 9:49 - Feb. 19, 13:08

YOUR CELEBRITY TWINS   p. 760
Find out the astrological similarities you have with famous people.

YOUR COMPATIBILITY   p. 780
Compare planets to find out how compatible you are in a relationship.

YOUR RELATIONSHIP KARMA   p. 824
- ▶ SATURN IN ARIES
  Born Jan. 20, 22:51 - Feb. 19, 13:08

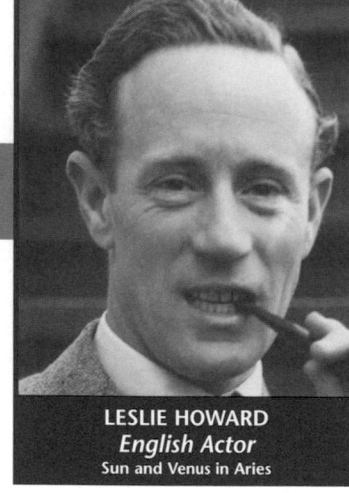

LESLIE HOWARD
English Actor
Sun and Venus in Aries

172

1939 PISCES
From February 19, 13:09 through March 21, 12:27

The Lusty Lover

For you, 1939 Pisces, the ups and downs of relationships can be as thrilling as a roller coaster ride—and as suitable for youngsters. You tend to thrive on intensity, and early on, you may have reckoned that the ecstasy of a passionate romance was a fair trade-off for an occasional case of the blues. You may have crossed paths with the old silver-tongued devil and impulsively spent a lot of time, energy, and resources before experience made you wise. A sense of urgency can energize you, and you tend to rise to the occasion in times of crisis—a gift you may now prefer to share with a reliable partner who satisfies your need for tender-loving care.

A serious relationship brings out your affinity for organization, discipline, and follow-through. Home, family, and respect for others may be very important to you, and you—probably work hard to provide your mate and children with good, orderly direction and a stable household. Idealism about romance can lead you to expect a lot from your relationship. Still, your sensitivity to your mate's feelings and willingness to make sacrifices enable you to work out compromises that strengthen your bond over time. You may have a strong sex drive, and the privacy of the bedroom allows you to embrace your mate with passion, gusto, and lusty intensity.

Lovemaking can give you the chance to make a spiritual connection with your mate. Spontaneity can be exhilarating for you, and you may respond well to romantic surprises. A weakness for beauty can leave you susceptible to seduction, especially when your mate is dressed to impress.

An unconventional woman can exude a magnetic attraction for the 1939 Piscean man. You may love the thrill of being around someone with an unorthodox outlook, especially if she is artistically creative. This ravishing rebel tends to stir your imagination.

The 1939 Piscean woman tends to revel in the attention of a man who is passionate and generous with attention. You appreciate self-assurance and integrity in a man. His hands-on approach to love can make you feel safe and adored. His lust for life can energize you.

1939 ARIES
From March 21, 12:28 through April 20, 23:54

The Ingenious Improviser

For Aries of 1939, the thrill of the chase is not enough. You're likely to be a faithful and devoted partner, more willing to invest your time and energy in enhancing a sure thing than wasting it on a lost cause. With maturity you can enjoy greater romantic satisfaction, as it allows you to leave any youthful impulses or exaggerated yearnings in the dust and to outgrow any tendency to want what you can't have. The hunter spirit in you is alive and well, but you are more likely to use it in finding creative ways to woo and seduce a steady love interest and to keep a relationship hot, upbeat and spicy. You tend to find your greatest satisfaction in a romantic partnership based on the empathy and reliability of friendship.

You may love a vigorous debate and can thrive with a partner who can think at your speed and keep you on your competitive toes. A little bit of appreciation goes a long way with you, and the mate who notices your hard work and loving favors can look forward to more of the same. Likely to be witty and innovative, you can find all kinds of creative ways to reinvent your relationship through the years. With every milestone you reach, you and your mate may fall in love over and over again. In the bedroom, you can improvise brilliant variations on your lovemaking themes. With you, it often feels like the first time.

Physical exercise can be both arousing and relaxing for you, and you may enjoy sex that allows you to work up a sweat. Tactile pleasures can turn you on, and you may be highly responsive to stroking and caressing, or a long massage with scented oils.

The 1939 Aries man can hardly resist a woman who is empathetic and idealistic. You may have an unusual outlook and appreciate someone who can understand where you're coming from. Without compromising her own standards, this sweet lady can be a compelling ally.

The Aries woman of 1939 adores a man who is persistent and protective. You tend to be attracted to a self-made man who has a take-charge charisma. With his initiative and staying power, he can win you over and prove himself worthy of your affection.

1939 TAURUS

From April 20, 23:55 through May 21, 23:26

The Delightful Darling

In your ideal relationship, 1939 Taurus, you meet your dreamboat and sail off on a date that never ends. To have such an enduring commitment (for you, almost always a marriage) can be the fulfillment of your most heartfelt wishes. You're likely to be a tender and dependable partner, devoted to your home, mate, and family. With your lovely flair for romancing a mate through every milestone of your life together, you can keep the passion fresh and stay together for years. You are likely to have good instincts for business matters and investments, and providing for your loved ones' security tends to be a high priority that lends greater stability to your household.

Charming and generous, you may enjoy attending social events or entertaining at home with your mate. Your penchant for extravagance can make you a popular guest or host, but you must take care not to let others take advantage of your kindness. As can be common with Taureans, you may show greater caution and concern when it comes to managing your partner's resources than you do

with your own. You may find it hard to spare yourself the pleasure of lavishing loved ones with gifts and fine foods, and providing the most comfortable furnishings in your home. In the bedroom, you tend to be equally bighearted. Making love provides an opportunity to show how much you adore your mate.

You need a lover who is openly affectionate, and you may be just as satisfied with cuddling, stroking, and kissing as with the ultimate act. Lush natural settings, such as gardens or forest trails, can stir your romantic passions.

The Taurean man of 1939 appreciates a woman who is ardent and artistic. Her drive can energize you, and you may rely on her to give you the impetus to get out there and apply your talents. Her creative touches can add beauty and a personal charm to your home.

A man with a good mind for the value of things can win the heart of the 1939 Taurean woman. You may have great respect for someone who shares your appreciation for the finer things in life. His thrifty sensibility can gently counterbalance your predisposition to spend.

FATS WALLER
American Musician
Sun and Venus in Taurus

173

1939 GEMINI

From May 21, 23:27 through June 22, 7:38

The Loving Lyricist

When your heart is set on romance, 1939 Gemini, you are likely to make an offer that no one can refuse to accept. Your powers of seduction have a subtle, lyrical, and compelling appeal. Your astrological sign rules communication, and with your artful flair for painting lovely pictures with words, you can sweet-talk a mate into blissful submission. You can be highly perceptive, usually knowing when not to push your luck, but sometimes you can come on too strong and ride roughshod over others' feelings or sensitivities. Tending to be fiercely protective of your mate and family, your anger and forcefulness is most likely to arise when you detect any threat to loved ones.

A serious romance can surely bring you to happiness and profound contentment. You can be an optimistic and open-minded partner. Sometimes you can become a bit too settled and complacent in your comfort, therefore you may appreciate a mate who speaks frankly and encourages you to get out there and make the best use of your talents. Energizing and emboldening you, such honesty can reinforce the trust between

you and your mate and infuse your relationship with dynamism. For you, lovemaking allows you to share feelings of romantic and spiritual attachment with your beloved.

You can be a daring and adventurous lover, keeping things interesting with a variety of techniques. Likely to have a strong sex drive, you may hunger for your mate's body and feed off the passion you enjoy together. Fine dining can be an intensely erotic experience, and food may play a role in enhancing foreplay.

A sensual, refined woman may be highly enticing to the 1939 Gemini man. Her charitable instincts can be inspiring, as you appreciate someone who has the grace to be kind, even to people she may not like. Poetic and musical, she can softly soothe your sometimes sensitive nerves.

The man with an idealistic outlook and high principles presents the 1939 Gemini woman with a delightfully stimulating challenge. You may gravitate towards someone who can expand your perspectives, and with his sophisticated intellect, this man gives you plenty of food for thought.

JEAN ARTHUR
American Actress
Mars in Leo

174

1939 CANCER
From June 22, 7:39 through July 23, 18:36

The Thoughtful Heartthrob

For the 1939 Cancerian in love, it's the little things that matter and the thought that counts. Sensitivity to your mate and a long memory allow you to notice and keep track of the things that please your partner. Without calling attention to your generosity, you may lavish your mate with thoughtful favors and meaningful gifts—perhaps leaving an item where your sweetheart is most likely to find it during the day. Such understatement and subtlety tend to be the key elements in your seductive chemistry. You may fiercely guard your privacy as it allows you to feel safe enough to let your hair down and revel in the joys of intimacy with your mate.

While you can be indulgent of your partner, your sense of value keeps you from being wasteful. Your desire to provide security for your partner and family may compel you to maintain some resources in reserve, in case of emergency. To be helpful to your loved ones, you might accumulate useful, practical knowledge on health, nutrition, family leisure, and home care. When you don't feel appreciated, you can become insecure, temperamental, and uncommunicative. Your mate can break any standoff by simply raising the subject, talking things through, and following up with liberal doses of tenderness, empathy, and physical affection.

The seclusion of the boudoir can free you and your mate to explore the mysteries of sexuality. A night in a luxury hotel can rejuvenate your desire. Exotic practices may stir your passions, and you might enjoy probing the secrets of Tantrism or the Kama Sutra.

For the Cancerian man of 1939, a curious, imaginative woman can be incredibly refreshing. Because you can be a visionary and a daydreamer, you may find her mental flights of fancy to be utterly charming. The fantasies you share together can fill your relationship with romance.

The Cancerian woman born in 1939 can find a perfect match in the man with strong humanitarian sympathies. He can appreciate your ability to provide a stable home front, and you may rely on him to inspire you to extend your caring hands to the world, where you can be of service.

1939 LEO
From July 23, 18:37 through August 24, 1:30

The Extravagant Enchanter

You may bring a gargantuan passion to life, Leo of 1939, and any partner you have will enjoy some large living. Without a clearly defined sense of direction, you may have been prone to scatter your energies and make your way through a series of intense but short-lived love affairs. It may have taken a serious relationship to get you to narrow your focus and team up with a partner who fit your unique personality and helped you to channel your desires. You and your mate may cut a striking figure together at social affairs and public events, and your capabilities as a leader may cause you to spend much of your life together in the spotlight.

You may have so much energy that you need your mate to share you with various outside associates—ideally, to join you in your pursuits. Spirituality may play a central role in your life together, guiding you in your outreach to your community and in your emotional commitment to each other. You can be an extravagant partner, conveying the depth of your affection with a broad gesture, creative flair, and dramatic impact. Communication between you and your mate can be quite animated at times, but any outbursts of passion tend to release tension and restore calm. You can be a highly physical lover, likely to make love with ardor and great staying power.

Sex tends to put you at ease, and you may prefer soothing pleasures. A long bath or massage with scented oils can thrill and relax you. Atmospheric touches—candlelight, soft music, satin sheets, incense—inspire you and your mate to focus in on each other.

A hearty and theatrical woman can capture the attention of the 1939 Leo man. You appreciate an exciting partner who can keep up with your expansive energy level. Thrilled by you and proud of you, she can offer the recognition and applause that tend to make you thrive.

The Leo woman of 1939 adores the man who has excellent managerial skills. His competence and attention to detail can make you feel well cared for. His talent for defining priorities and devising strategies for meeting them can help you to realize your greatest goals.

1939 VIRGO
From August 24, 1:31 through September 23, 22:48

♍ ## *The Intimate Idealist*

Likely to be sensitive and attentive, 1939 Virgo, you are a good listener, with great enthusiasm for a mate's sweetest dreams. Pleasing your partner tends to be very important to you, and you can be very good at it. A relationship can make you feel more yourself, but it can also throw you off balance. Earlier in life, you may have been tempted to remake yourself to suit your partner's needs and preferences. By merging so powerfully with your mate, you may have lost a firm sense of your own identity and needs. With maturity, you tend to focus your energies on your own talents, and your accomplishments and greater independence can shift the balance of power in your relationship.

You thrive with a mate who affords you the same trust, support, and encouragement that you so generously give. Gentle honesty can go a long way with you. Likely to be idealistic, you can benefit from a mate who offers you objective feedback without dampening your dreams. Ideally, a romance allows you to fully express your creativity. Your powers of attraction and seduction peak when you are inspired. You can be an ideas person, with a taste for the finer things in life. Indulging in luxurious pleasures can enhance the intimacy you share with your mate.

An evening of art, music, theater, or poetry can make for a perfect date with you. Anything that captures your imagination can ease you into the mood for love. Virtuosity tends to turn you on, and you appreciate a lover who remembers exactly what you like and does it the way you like it.

For you, Virgo man of 1939, a healthy, well-groomed woman can stir your animal passions. Someone who takes good care of herself tends to inspire your confidence in her ability to take good care of you. With her instinctive organization and good habits, she offers a desirable lifestyle.

The man with a fine sense of timing appeals to the Virgo woman born in 1939. You may admire someone with a well-honed feel for what is appropriate in any given situation. With his flair for making the right gesture at the right moment, he can be supportive without being intrusive.

VIRGO ZODIAC SIGN
Your Love Planets

YOUR ROMANTIC SIDE   p. 696
> ▶ **VENUS IN LEO**
Born Aug. 24, 1:31 - Aug. 26, 21:23
> ▶ **VENUS IN VIRGO**
Born Aug. 26, 21:24 - Sept. 20, 1:01
> ▶ **VENUS IN LIBRA**
Born Sept. 20, 1:02 - Sept. 23, 22:48

YOUR SEX DRIVE   p. 722
> ▶ **MARS IN CAPRICORN**
Born Aug. 24, 1:31 - Sept. 23, 22:48

YOUR CELEBRITY TWINS   p. 760
Find out the astrological similarities you have with famous people.

YOUR COMPATIBILITY   p. 780
Compare planets to find out how compatible you are in a relationship.

YOUR RELATIONSHIP KARMA   p. 824
> ▶ **SATURN IN TAURUS**
Born Aug. 24, 1:31 - Sept. 22, 5:17
> ▶ **SATURN IN ARIES**
Born Sept. 22, 5:18 - Sept. 23, 22:48

MIRIAM HOPKINS
American Actress
Sun and Venus in Libra

1939 LIBRA
From September 23, 22:49 through October 24, 7:45

♎ ## *The Compelling Mate*

You may have an intimate appreciation for the power of love, 1939 Libra. A relationship may not be worth your time unless the passion you share with a mate can be deep and enduring. Ideally, your love should inspire you and your lover to grow to your fullest potential. Experience may have been your best teacher on the subject of love. Early on, you may have had a weakness for charismatic lovers who promised the moon with dazzling persuasiveness. One or two disappointments were likely all you needed to hone your personal judgment and swear off contact with any hawkers of seductive snake oil. You may have a long memory and a sharp nose for dishonesty. For you, trust is the very lifeblood of a relationship.

You thrive in a partnership rich with passion, harmony, and mutual respect. Because you tend to have keen sensitivity to your mate's concerns and a talent for speaking gently but persuasively, your relationship can enjoy the advantage of a balanced flow of communication. In a rough patch, you may be willing to swallow your pride and go out on an emotional limb for the sake of your mate, and such courage can deepen your bond and hold you together for the long haul. You can be a mesmerizing lover, able to cast a romantic spell that entices you and your mate to escape into pleasure.

You may approach sex with a certain delicacy, and tend to feel most comfortable opening up in a cozy, private setting. Exotic fantasies can stir your passions, and you may enjoy a partner with a fertile imagination for role-playing and wish fulfillment.

The Libra man born in 1939 enjoys a woman who makes a gracious, elegant impression. You tend to admire someone who has good manners and shows respect for all people, regardless of their station. With this lovely lady, you can rest assured that you are in the finest of company.

An ingenious, friendly man can be the perfect partner for the 1939 Libra woman. You can benefit from having a mate who shares your social inclinations and who stimulates your intellectual abilities. The originality of his ideas can spark your most creative impulses.

LIBRA ZODIAC SIGN
Your Love Planets

YOUR ROMANTIC SIDE   p. 696
> ▶ **VENUS IN LIBRA**
Born Sept. 23, 22:49 - Oct. 14, 2:40
> ▶ **VENUS IN SCORPIO**
Born Oct. 14, 2:41 - Oct. 24, 7:45

YOUR SEX DRIVE   p. 722
> ▶ **MARS IN CAPRICORN**
Born Sept. 23, 22:49 - Sept. 24, 1:12
> ▶ **MARS IN AQUARIUS**
Born Sept. 24, 1:13 - Oct. 24, 7:45

YOUR CELEBRITY TWINS   p. 760
Find out the astrological similarities you have with famous people.

YOUR COMPATIBILITY   p. 780
Compare planets to find out how compatible you are in a relationship.

YOUR RELATIONSHIP KARMA   p. 824
> ▶ **SATURN IN ARIES**
Born Sept. 23, 22:49 - Oct. 24, 7:45

LILLIAN HELLMAN
American Writer
Mars in Scorpio

1939 SCORPIO
From October 24, 7:46 through November 23, 4:58

The Sympathetic Soulmate

In love and romance, Scorpio of 1939, a little less self-control can be a very good thing for you. It's likely you've already happened upon this seemingly counterintuitive nugget of wisdom. Early on, when you fell in love, you may have fallen hard. To avoid overwhelming a mate with demands, you may have struggled to hold back your feelings. You may have powerful self-control, but holding back for too long can make you snap and unleash a flood of unsatisfied needs. With the intensity of your passions, you benefit from a regular dose of pampering, attention, and desire-indulgence. You may be a tireless worker, willing to do just about anything to keep a mate happy. You thrive in a partnership that allows you to rely on the same in return.

Your own ups and downs in love may have made you a sympathetic mate and true-blue friend. Just about nothing can shock you because, honey, you've been there yourself. With you, putting on airs is for the birds. Your tender empathy can make you completely accessible to others, and your mate may be the first to agree that you are about as real as they come. Your romantic aura can infuse the most ordinary experiences with a greater sense of meaning and intensity. In the bedroom, you tend to bring a hypnotic enchantment to lovemaking.

For you, sex is an activity that may consume all of you—heart, body, and soul. For you, spirituality and mysticism can turn fooling around into divine ecstatic union with your mate. Sharing secrets can put both partners at ease and drench you in passion.

A woman who is deep and nonjudgmental can be the ideal mate for the 1939 Scorpio man. You flourish with someone who knows everything about you and whose attachment to you is unquestionable. With her willingness to take account of your needs, you can enjoy a harmonious relationship.

An idealistic, sincere man can bring comfort and excitement to the Scorpio woman of 1939. It's impossible to quantify the benefits you gain from having a mate who is absolutely trustworthy. With this open and caring man, you need never have to worry about where you stand.

1939 SAGITTARIUS
From November 23, 4:59 through December 22, 18:05

The Heartfelt Healer

In an intimate relationship, 1939 Sagittarius, your true powers as a healer can emerge. With your faith and unusual insights, you tend to have an exceptional talent for comforting a friend or lover. You may carry your own memory of a painful ending, one that may have changed your outlook. By sensitizing you to the preciousness and fragility of life and relationships, such an experience can galvanize you into action and bring out your greatest potentials. When a loss or setback arises in the course of your relationship, you can show heartfelt empathy and exude a quiet assurance that inspires trust and the courage to begin again. Innate vitality and deep spiritual motivation tend to fuel your determination to live and love fully and completely.

Likely to be reliable, responsible, and a good judge of character, you can be a sustaining force in your relationship. Always optimistic and understanding, you tend to adjust naturally to your mate's needs and the demands of your partnership. Good instincts for taking full advantage of opportunities as they arise allow you to provide a stable household for your mate and family. Your partner may appreciate your knack for doing the right thing at the right time, especially in the bedroom, where you can be a doting lover, eager to please.

A habit of holding hands, hugging, and kissing can keep your relationship warm and intimate. Expressing your deep affection for your partner, both verbally and physically, may be the best thing about sex for you. An enthusiastic response from your mate can really thrill you.

The Sagittarius man of 1939 thrives with a woman who takes a cheerful and positive approach to life. You appreciate someone who has a good sense of humor and can see the possibilities in any situation. Her encouraging outlook can boost your spirits and keep you motivated.

The Sagittarius woman born in 1939 adores a man who is romantic and perceptive. You thrive with someone who can sense your feelings and respond with loving-kindness. His flair for dreams and fantasy can inspire you to get out there and fulfill your most ambitious ideas.

Frida Kahlo – The Tortured Artist

If it's true that the greatest artists suffer during their lives, and only after their death is their art recognized as being great, then Frida Kahlo is the perfect great artist. A grisly trolley accident at age 18 created tremendous physical and psychological trauma, leaving her an invalid for life, but inspiring her to paint. Nowadays the Mexican painter Kahlo is a phenomenon, a veritable cult, with her fans reveling in her tragic, personal tale and fascinating friends and lovers, as much as her actual paintings. Her marriage to famed Mexican muralist Diego Rivera was tumultuous and contributed to her reputation as a tragic victim. Yet he also supported her and encouraged her to explore her creative imagination.

Frida Kahlo first met the love of her life while she was only 15 and a student in middle school. Diego Rivera was commissioned to paint a mural depicting the Mexican Revolution on the school walls, and Frida knew right away that she wanted to have a baby with him. Three years later this dream crumbled when her accident prevented Frida from bearing children. Over the next 30 years she would have several miscarriages, and more than 30 operations on her spine, leg, and foot. During the first few years of her recuperation she was forced to wear restrictive body casts, but her mother helped rig up an easel over her bed so she could paint.

In 1928 Frida persuaded Rivera to critique her art and give her an honest assessment on whether she had talent. He assured her that she did indeed have what it takes and encouraged her to

"He never has been, nor will he ever be, anybody's husband."

FRIDA KAHLO speaking of her husband, Diego Rivera

pursue painting. They married in 1929 when she was 22 and he was 43. Although they respected and supported each other artistically, the emotional bond between them was turbulent. Rivera had numerous affairs, and Frida suffered from his infidelity. In 1939 they divorced, but remarried the next year. In spite of her illnesses, Frida had some

rather famous friends. Among her better known were the Soviet photographer and spy Tina Modotti, painter Georgia O'Keeffe, and Russian revolutionary Leon Trotsky.

When together, Frida and Rivera entertained some of the most glamorous politicians and artists of their time, including surrealist Andre Breton, Soviet filmmaker Sergei Eisenstein, and billionaire industrialist Nelson Rockefeller. Their mutual interest in the progressive political ferment of their time kept them together as much as their passion for art. Mexico was in an intellectual and cultural renaissance, and both Diego Rivera and Frida Kahlo were at the vanguard of this movement.

One big difference between them was that Rivera was internationally recognized during his lifetime as a creative genius, while Frida, whose work was groundbreaking from several perspectives, obtained her status posthumously. Many of her paintings focused on her own life, but carried metaphorical dimensions later praised by sociologists, psychologists, political analysts, and feminists. Her depiction of her own miscarriage, the border scene between the US and Mexico, and her own native jewelry make up her more famous works.

Rivera and Frida's life was an odd mixture of political fire and mutually inflicted pain. Not until Frida's death from an overdose of painkillers in 1954 could Rivera admit how much she meant to him. He wrote in his autobiography, "Too late I realized the most wonderful part of my life had been my love for Frida."

177

▶ READ ABOUT GEORGIA O'KEEFFE AND ALFRED STIEGLTIZ ON PAGE 47

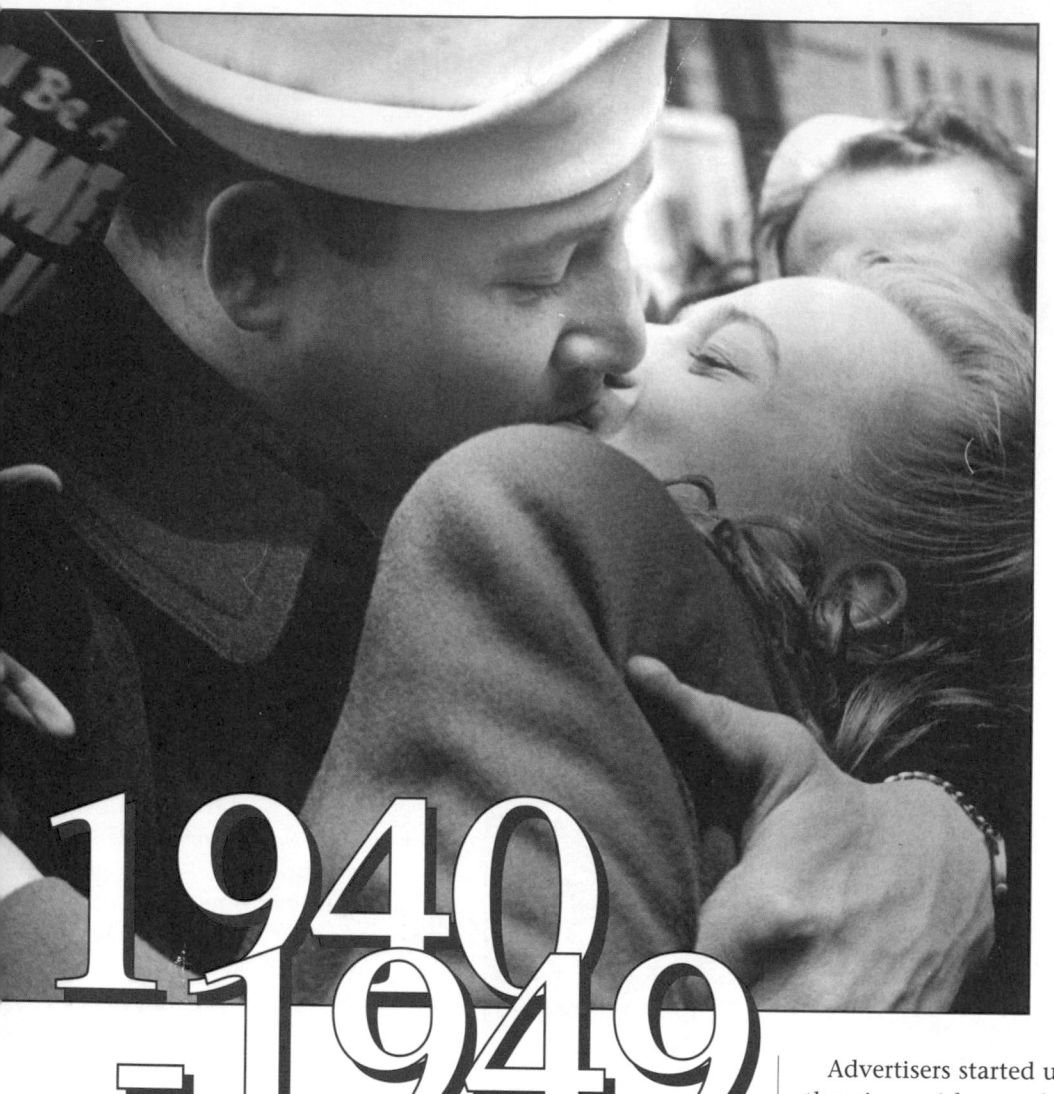

1940 -1949

THE WAR YEARS

Movies, music, and shorter hemlines eased the stresses of war, and women began to demand equality in all areas of life.

The war years tore people and countries apart, then later brought them together again in an even stronger bond.

People learned to make sacrifices during the war. Families said good-bye to loved ones who went off to fight. Women made do without cosmetics, stockings, and fabric for new clothes, creating makeup from the juice of red beets and new fashions using potato sacks. The British government urged women not to wear high heels in order to save wood.

Fashion designers rose to the task and raised hemlines and designed the bikini bathing suit to conserve on fabric. A generation of more confident women started demanding equality across the board. Countries in Europe finally gave women the right to vote and most western countries welcomed women into the work force. Unmarried women between the ages of twenty and thirty were called up for war work in Britain.

Advertisers started using sex to sell their products and the pinup girls were launched. Rita Hayworth and Betty Grable became household names.

Attitudes toward homosexuality started to relax— it was decriminalized in Sweden, and the US War Department recommended discharge and treatment instead of court martial.

War themes understandably dominated movies throughout the '40s, reflecting the world's fears and hopes. Onscreen couples such as Humphrey Bogart and Ingrid Bergman, Cary Grant and Ginger Rogers, and Judy Garland and Robert Walker portrayed both the serious and lighter sides of life during the war.

Big band music topped the charts and people danced to bandleaders Glenn Miller, Benny Goodman, Guy Lombardo, and Artie Shaw. The Ink Spots, Vaughn Monroe, and Perry Como crooned their way into the hearts of listeners on both sides of the Atlantic. Frank Sinatra became a teen idol, and later in the decade Nat King Cole soothed wounded hearts. The Andrews Sisters, Doris Day, Peggy Lee, and Ella Fitzgerald represented the females in '40s music.

The end of the war was a joyous time and the start of the baby boom in the United States. Couples long separated reunited with abandon—with the predictable result of the largest rise in the birthrate ever recorded.

THE SILVER SCREEN

In the theaters, in addition to war love stories such as *Casablanca*, suspense and lighthearted films also drew in moviegoers. Director Alfred Hitchcock gave us *Rebecca* and *Spellbound*. *Meet Me in St. Louis* let viewers fall in love with Judy Garland all over again, and the Christmas classic, *It's a Wonderful Life*, still touches our hearts every year. In Europe, Jean Cocteau's poetic masterpiece *La Belle et la Bête* appeared. And this was the decade that the epic *Les Enfants du Paradis* was finally released, after an extraordinary production—not only was it the most expensive film to date, but it was made during the Occupation in France with hundreds of resistance fighters working undercover as extras.

BETWEEN THE PAGES

The 1940s was a decade for books that would become staples in high school and college literature courses, with classics such as *The Heart Is a Lonely Hunter* (Carson McCullers), *For Whom the Bell Tolls* (Ernest Hemingway) and *You Can't Go Home Again* (Thomas Wolfe). Evelyn Waugh found fame with *Brideshead Revisited*, a depiction of love and student life at Oxford University in the late twenties. Early sex manuals such as *Living with a Husband and Liking It*, *The Function of the Orgasm*, and *The Hygiene of Marriage* began to make an appearance.

PEOPLE

The decade brought us some notable pairings. Ronald Reagan married film star Jane Wyman. Marilyn Monroe married for the first time in this decade, as did Elizabeth

◄◄ A couple celebrating the end of World War II

▲ Count Basie and his Band

► Pinup Betty Grable

Taylor. Laurence Olivier was divorced by his first wife on the grounds of adultery with his onscreen lover Vivien Leigh. Princess Elizabeth married Lieutenant Philip Mountbatten and was granted an extra hundred clothing coupons for her dress. And while one famous German was becoming an official citizen of the United States—actress and sex symbol Marlene Dietrich—another was having his relationship scrutinized by the world. Adolf Hitler's marriage to Eva Braun only lasted a couple of days, was probably never consummated, and ended in the suicide of both newlyweds. The war was finally over.

1940

- ⭐ RONALD REAGAN AND JANE WYMAN
- ⭐ REBECCA
- ⭐ MY FAVORITE WIFE
- ⭐ ERNEST HEMINGWAY
- ⭐ YOU CAN'T GO HOME AGAIN
- ⭐ FOOLS RUSH IN

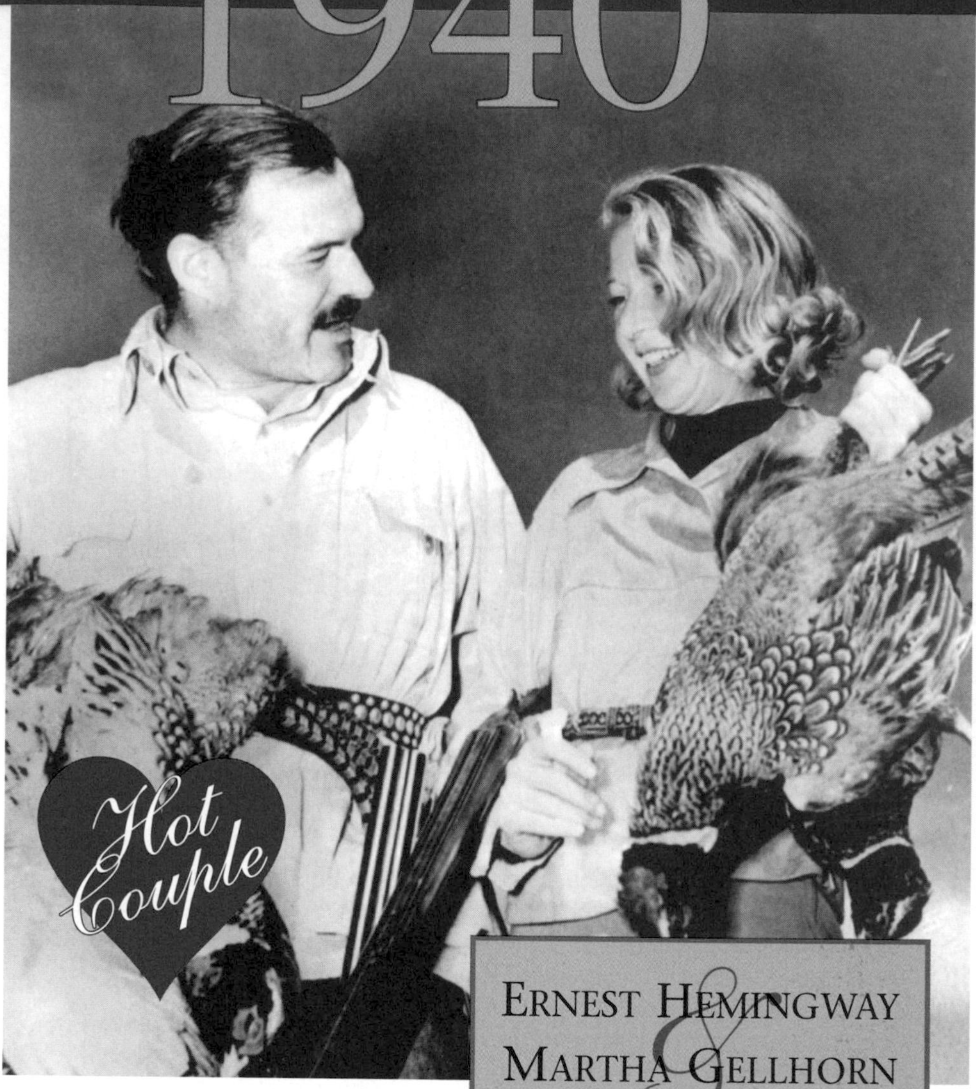

EVENTS

Two US presidents-to-be got married: Ronald Reagan to Jane Wyman, and Richard Nixon to Pat Ryan. After the 1937 scandal caused by King Edward VIII of England marrying an American and abdicating the throne, Winston Churchill made him governor of the Bahamas for five years, where he sat out the war.

While women in Britain demanded equal pay for war work, the French Vichy regime banned women from working in public services.

Englishwoman Unity Mitford, whose love for Hitler led her to attempt suicide when war broke out, arrived home after being granted permission by Hitler to leave.

POP CULTURE

Movies played with the marriage theme in 1940. In *Rebecca*, directed by Alfred Hitchcock and based on the Daphne du Maurier novel, a British gentleman's innocent bride grapples with intrusive reminders of his deceased wife. *My Favorite Wife* gave us a man whose wife had been on an island with another man for seven years, then finally returns to her husband, who has remarried. In *He Married His Wife,* the leading man tries to get out of paying alimony by marrying off his ex-wife, who still loves him.

1940 was a debut year for some soon-to-be classic books. *The Heart Is a Lonely Hunter* by Carson McCullers told of a town helping a deaf-mute and finding love and fulfillment. Ernest Hemingway's *For Whom the Bell Tolls* was about a US teacher who joins the Spanish Civil War and falls in love with the daughter of a mayor. In *You Can't Go Home Again* Thomas Wolfe wrote about a young writer from the south who has an affair with a married woman in New York in the 1920s. The *Encyclopedia of Sexual Knowledge* was an early *Everything You Wanted to Know About Sex...* anthology.

Glenn Miller had the spotlight on the hit parade in 1940 with four popular songs: "Blueberry Hill," "Careless," "Fools Rush In," and "In the Mood." Tommy Dorsey had two: "I'll Never Smile Again" and "All the Things You Are." Benny Goodman's "Darn That Dream" was a hit, as were "Maybe" by the Ink Spots and "Only Forever" by Bing Crosby.

Hot Couple

ERNEST HEMINGWAY & MARTHA GELLHORN

On November 5, 1940, author Ernest Hemingway married his third of four wives, Martha Gellhorn. A journalist, Gellhorn had met Hemingway in 1936 in Key West where he lived with his wife, Pauline Pfeiffer. Gellhorn became a fixture in the Hemingway home.

The two traveled to Spain, where their affair continued against the backdrop of the Spanish Civil War. Their wedding took place one day after Hemingway's divorce from Pfeiffer was final. During the marriage, Hemingway wrote *For Whom the Bell Tolls*, a novel he dedicated to Gellhorn. The marriage proved too small for two careers. They divorced in 1945.

SEE ALSO

▶ F. SCOTT AND ZELDA FITZGERALD *Page 39*

▶ ANAIS NIN AND HENRY MILLER *Page 145*

1940 CAPRICORN
From December 22, 1939 18:06 through January 21, 1940 4:43
(December 1940 Capricorns, see 1941 Capricorn)

The Responsible Romantic

Bright lights and big cities aren't enough to lure 1940 Goats away from home. You adore domestic comforts, and do best in a relationship that uses a cozy abode as its foundation. A partner who has a deep respect for tradition is your ideal. However, you also benefit when your mate encourages you to try a few unfamiliar things, as you can be cautious about making changes. A lover with a creative streak helps you to loosen up a bit. The one area in which you enjoy experimenting is romance. You love thinking up new ways to delight and enrapture your beloved.

Sex is a profound experience for you. You don't like sharing your body with anybody other than your mate. You've got lots of stamina in the bedroom, and can go all night if you so desire. You do best with a lover whose staying power matches yours. The idea of growing old with your spouse is an extremely attractive one to you. You have a very responsible attitude towards your relationship, and will weather any storms with your mate in the interest of having many years together. A partner with good communication skills is a definite asset.

Fix-it-yourself types have a good chance of winning your heart. You've always admired folks who learn how to do complicated jobs on their own. Kooky artists also turn you on, because they serve as an effective counterbalance to your practical personality. When it comes time to make the first move, your suitor would be wise to create a comfortable setting for your first sexual encounter. It's hard for you to loosen up in unfamiliar surroundings. Abandoning yourself to pleasure on a soft, yielding bed with plenty of pillows is easy.

Women who are friendly, trustworthy, and innovative appeal most to you 1940 male Capricorns. You're also attracted to ladies who are talkative, fanciful, and intuitive. A versatile homebody is the ideal partner for you.

If you're a female Goat who was born in 1940, you want a man who is strong, unwavering, and gentle. Protective men with rich imaginations also turn you on. A mate who encourages you to take risks brings out the best in you.

CAPRICORN ZODIAC SIGN
YOUR LOVE PLANETS

YOUR ROMANTIC SIDE   p. 696
- ▶ **VENUS IN CAPRICORN**
  Born Dec. 22, 1939 18:06 - Dec. 25, 1939 7:24
- ▶ **VENUS IN AQUARIUS**
  Born Dec. 25, 1939 7:25 - Jan. 18, 1940 13:59
- ▶ **VENUS IN PISCES**
  Born Jan. 18, 14:00 - Jan. 21, 4:43

YOUR SEX DRIVE   p. 722
- ▶ **MARS IN PISCES**
  Born Dec. 22, 1939 18:06 - Jan. 04, 1940 0:04
- ▶ **MARS IN ARIES**
  Born Jan. 04, 0:05 - Jan. 21, 4:43

YOUR CELEBRITY TWINS   p. 760
Find out the astrological similarities you have with famous people.

YOUR COMPATIBILITY   p. 780
Compare planets to find out how compatible you are in a relationship.

YOUR RELATIONSHIP KARMA   p. 824
- ▶ **SATURN IN ARIES**
  Born Dec. 22, 1939 18:06 - Jan. 21, 1940 4:43

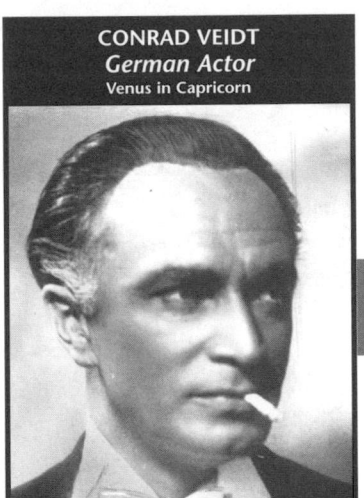

CONRAD VEIDT
German Actor
Venus in Capricorn

181

1940 AQUARIUS
From January 21, 4:44 through February 19, 19:03

The Chatty Suitor

As a 1940 Aquarian, you are a smart cookie. Relationships are one of your favorite topics to ponder. You're always questioning why certain couples do well versus others who don't. Fortunately, you have at your disposal great communication skills, which is half the battle in a successful partnership. You do best with a mate who is deep, reflective, and decisive. Such a partner helps direct your own train of thought, which threatens to go off in several different directions without the proper guidance. You want a partnership that gives you a sense of direction and purpose.

Sexually, you are a real chameleon. At times you prefer to the aggressor, at others, the object of desire. One thing is for sure: You love to make love! You do best with a partner who enjoys indulging your fantasies. Being anchored to a single home doesn't particularly appeal to you. If you do happen to stay in one place, it's likely that your home will be filled with lots of different visitors. A spouse who enjoys entertaining is a good match for you. You love a good party!

Powerful, magnetic figures have the best chance of attracting your attention. You admire people who conduct themselves with a confident air of authority. A suitor who tells you that you're going on a date, rather than asking for one, could easily win your heart. You also enjoy quick thinkers who can think of snappy comebacks at the drop of a hat. When it comes time to take your relationship to the physical level, your admirer would be wise to knock your socks off with an overpowering kiss. You love it when an uncontrollable wave of passion washes over you.

As a male Water-bearer who was born in 1940, you enjoy a woman who is charming, seductive, and capable. You're also drawn to ladies who are direct, humorous, and deft. Nothing turns you on like a woman who takes charge of a situation.

If you're a 1940 female Aquarius, you want a guy who is talkative, friendly, and aggressive. Men who are nurturing and grounded also appeal to you. Ultimately, you want a partner who provides you with a secure foundation from which you can dream.

AQUARIUS ZODIAC SIGN
YOUR LOVE PLANETS

YOUR ROMANTIC SIDE   p. 696
- ▶ **VENUS IN PISCES**
  Born Jan. 21, 4:44 - Feb. 12, 5:50
- ▶ **VENUS IN ARIES**
  Born Feb. 12, 5:51 - Feb. 19, 19:03

YOUR SEX DRIVE   p. 722
- ▶ **MARS IN ARIES**
  Born Jan. 21, 4:44 - Feb. 17, 1:53
- ▶ **MARS IN TAURUS**
  Born Feb. 17, 1:54 - Feb. 19, 19:03

YOUR CELEBRITY TWINS   p. 760
Find out the astrological similarities you have with famous people.

YOUR COMPATIBILITY   p. 780
Compare planets to find out how compatible you are in a relationship.

YOUR RELATIONSHIP KARMA   p. 824
- ▶ **SATURN IN ARIES**
  Born Jan. 21, 4:44 - Feb. 19, 19:03

CARSON McCULLERS
American Writer
Sun and Mars in Pisces

182

1940 PISCES
From February 19, 19:04 through March 20, 18:23

The Esteemed Lover

You demand respect, especially from your romantic partner, 1940 Pisces. Getting the love you deserve may have been your primary focus in life. As far as you're concerned, a good relationship can heal all wounds. A partner who is nurturing, attentive, and compassionate brings out the best in you. You want to lead a comfortable lifestyle, and benefit from a mate who knows how to apply your resources in a way that meets both of your needs. A romantic union that provides you with both security and acceptance fills your heart with joy. Fickle partners don't thrill you in the slightest.

You're a sensitive, sensuous, and creative lover. In order for you to get in the mood, however, you need to feel as though you're appreciated and admired. A partner who constantly reassures you of your sexiness and desirability fuels the flames of your passion. Because you are extremely service oriented, you and your spouse may get involved with humanitarian causes that reflect your values. A mate who wants to be a force for positive change in the world is your ideal.

Someone who is visionary, dreamy, and idealistic has a good chance of catching your eye. You can't abide folks who resign themselves to life's ugly realities. You far prefer being with a suitor who is looking for new possibilities and fresh vistas. A suitor who is also heavily involved in community affairs also appeals to you, because you like folks who value strong social networks. When you meet someone attractive, you waste no time making the first move. Your admirer would be wise to reciprocate your advances with some passionate kisses to your neck and shoulders.

As a male Piscean who was born in 1940, you admire a woman who is witty, irreverent, and service-oriented. Ladies who are both sensual and intellectual also light your fire. You do best with a mate whose big heart matches her brain.

Men who are charming, persuasive, and practical draw you 1940 female Fish like magnets. Dull, predictable types leave you cold. You benefit from a partner who expresses his love for you a thousand different ways each day.

1940 ARIES
From March 20, 18:24 through April 20, 5:50

The Giving Heartthrob

You are always first to volunteer your services when someone is in need, 1940 Aries. Maybe that's why you have so many admirers, romantic and otherwise. Despite the throngs of suitors that are always hovering near your door, you prefer to devote attentions to one single partner. There is no limit to your affection. A mate who returns your love in full measure is your ideal. You dislike stingy, distrustful types who are incapable of giving you the benefit of the doubt. For you, the best relationship is founded on trust.

Following your own unique value system is important with regard to romance. You're not interested in mirroring everybody else's relationships. A spouse who isn't bothered by leading an unconventional lifestyle suits you best. You're quite intuitive about your mate's needs, and enjoy adjusting your behavior to suit their requirements. Sexually, you're quite a powerhouse, and probably enjoy making love for hours on end. You're an extremely attentive lover, provided you get the love and attention you crave on a daily basis.

Getting your attention is a matter of principles. You've always been attracted to folks who have strong moral codes and follow them. An admirer won't get very far with you by engaging in duplicitous business practices or smothering you with false compliments. You're also drawn to people who are involved with spiritual work in some way. And although you enjoy taking the lead when it comes to sex, your suitor would be wise to give you encouragement in this area. Making a bet wherein the prize is a kiss could be a good way to motivate you.

If you're a male Ram who was born in 1940, you enjoy women who are practical, sensual, and reassuring. Females who are expressive, vivacious, and childlike also appeal to you. You do best with a partner who is as generous with her heart as you are.

Men who have a raw enjoyment of physical pleasures greatly appeal to you 1940 female Ariens. You're also attracted to guys who are suave, charming, and sophisticated. An affectionate mate who celebrates your allure brings out the best in you.

1940 TAURUS

From April 20, 5:51 through May 21, 5:22

The Stable Sensualist

As a 1940 Taurus, you enjoy nothing more than standing still and smelling the flowers. You're not the type to engage in tumultuous love affairs. A comfortable, loving partnership with few surprises is your ideal. You do best with a mate who takes comfort in your calm approach to life. It's easy to rely on you, and you often enjoy it when your partner rests problems on your capable shoulders. As a person with an inventive and independent mind, you benefit from a romance that allows you to do things in your own unique style. You don't want to conform your relationship to a set ideal.

A love of pleasure and luxury draws you to a partner who can help you enjoy a lavish lifestyle. You're an idealist when it comes to romance, and enjoy it when your mate takes great pains to look wonderful at all times. At home, you can be rather demanding, and want everything just so. You appreciate a partner who is content to let you rule the roost. You're a connoisseur when it comes to lovemaking. Quality is always more important than quantity when it comes to sex. You'd rather have one breathtaking encounter a week than a quick session every day.

A good opening move is to compliment you on your good taste. It's easy for you to open up to somebody who shares your refined sensibilities. Going to you for comfort is also a good idea, because you love soothing troubled minds. If your admirer asks you on a date, it should be to a gourmet restaurant or an elegant art gallery. You can't relax in dingy surroundings. Your suitor would be wise to make the first move. You enjoy long, sliding kisses down your neck as a prelude to making love.

You 1940 male Bulls want a woman who is loyal, dependable, and intellectual. You're also attracted to ladies who are expressive, vivacious, and clever. A partner who is both intelligent and nurturing is your ideal.

As a female Taurus who was born in 1940, you want a man who is affectionate, friendly, and popular. Versatile men with a childlike sense of fun also appeal to you. You want a playmate who will kiss your tears away when you fall down.

TAURUS ZODIAC SIGN
YOUR LOVE PLANETS

YOUR ROMANTIC SIDE   p. 696
▶ **VENUS IN GEMINI**
Born Apr. 20, 5:51 - May 06, 18:46
▶ **VENUS IN CANCER**
Born May 06, 18:47 - May 21, 5:22

YOUR SEX DRIVE   p. 722
▶ **MARS IN GEMINI**
Born Apr. 20, 5:51 - May 17, 14:44
▶ **MARS IN CANCER**
Born May 17, 14:45 - May 21, 5:22

YOUR CELEBRITY TWINS   p. 760
Find out the astrological similarities you have with famous people.

YOUR COMPATIBILITY   p. 780
Compare planets to find out how compatible you are in a relationship.

YOUR RELATIONSHIP KARMA   p. 824
▶ **SATURN IN TAURUS**
Born Apr. 20, 5:51 - May 21, 5:22

MARGARET SULLAVAN
American Actress
Sun in Taurus

1940 GEMINI

From May 21, 5:23 through June 21, 13:35

The Persistent Partner

Wistful, sentimental, and loyal, you are very tenderhearted, 1940 Gemini. You cherish the people in your life, especially your romantic partner. As far as you're concerned, love is what makes the world go around. When you don't have your mate by your side, you feel incomplete. A partnership that provides you with a sense of grounding and permanence is best for you. Having someone who understands your dreams and fears gives you a great deal of comfort. You appreciate a compassionate partner who enjoys talking with you, regardless of the subject.

Sexually, you're a very private person. You'd never discuss your love life with anybody but your partner. It's possible that you're a bit shy in the bedroom. You benefit tremendously from a lusty partner who is capable of melting your reserve, and have a somewhat idealized notion of what home life should be. A spouse who reassures you that the occasional domestic squabble is perfectly healthy helps balance your view. You're also an extremely curious person, and enjoy exploring unfamiliar areas and meeting new folks with your beloved. A sociable partner who is good at breaking the ice with strangers is a perfect match for you.

A suitor who wants to catch your eye should draw you out of your shell. You tend to be a bit shy at social gatherings, and appreciate a person who can put you at ease. Movies, books, and current events are all topics that will make you open up. It's preferable if your admirer makes the first move toward a physical relationship. You love being touched and enjoy it when your lover explores every inch of your body with their hands.

If you're a 1940 male Gemini, you enjoy a woman who is sincere, gentle, and sensitive. A lady who lets you know where you stand brings out the best in you. You want an expressive partner who constantly reassures you of her love and devotion.

Men who are sweet, thoughtful, and charming appeal most to you 1940 female Geminis. Bad boys don't interest you in the slightest. You far prefer a considerate guy who comes to your door with flowers and helps you on with your coat.

GEMINI ZODIAC SIGN
YOUR LOVE PLANETS

YOUR ROMANTIC SIDE   p. 696
▶ **VENUS IN CANCER**
Born May 21, 5:23 - June 21, 13:35

YOUR SEX DRIVE   p. 722
▶ **MARS IN CANCER**
Born May 21, 5:23 - June 21, 13:35

YOUR CELEBRITY TWINS   p. 760
Find out the astrological similarities you have with famous people.

YOUR COMPATIBILITY   p. 780
Compare planets to find out how compatible you are in a relationship.

YOUR RELATIONSHIP KARMA   p. 824
▶ **SATURN IN TAURUS**
Born May 21, 5:23 - June 21, 13:35

JAMES STEWART
American Actor
Venus in Cancer

184

1940 CANCER
From June 21, 13:36 through July 23, 0:33

The Sentimental Suitor

Friendships play a very important part in the life of a 1940 Crab. You take great pleasure in surrounding yourself with sensitive, tasteful people who share your romantic nature. There's a very good chance that you and your partner started out as friends. That's because you're not the type of person to jump straight into a love affair. You prefer to get to know a person's views before joining hearts. A relationship that is based on mutual tastes is your ideal. A mate who is sociable, refined, and affectionate brings out the best in you. Stuffy, repressed types leave you cold.

You probably have a strong interest in the arts and enjoy the company of a partner who enjoys going to museums, movies, and plays. As you may rely a great deal on your mate, you may benefit from a spouse who encourages you to become more self-sufficient. When it comes to sex, you can feel quite vulnerable. A lover who offers continual praise, admiration, and encouragement in the bedroom brings out the best in you. You prefer tender, sweet encounters to hot, torrid ones. For you, making love is a means to intimacy, rather than physical release.

Expressing an interest in charities or social clubs is a sure way to win your approval. You enjoy an admirer with community spirit. Anyone who is interested in you would be wise to appeal to your nurturing side. Expressing desire for a home cooked meal or an old-fashioned remedy will cause you to jump to your suitor's aid. You prefer taking the lead when it comes to romance. Pretending to stumble and fall can give you a convenient opening to sweep your sweetheart into a passionate embrace.

If you're a male Crab who was born in 1940, you want a woman who is sociable, shrewd, and sensitive. Ladies who are sentimental, versatile, and talkative also appeal to you. You do best with a partner who enjoys your solicitous attentions.

As a 1940 female Cancer, you admire men who are generous, regal, and loyal. Rugged guys who are assertive and friendly also turn you on. You want a mate who makes you feel like you're his favorite person in the entire world.

1940 LEO
From July 23, 0:34 through August 23, 7:28

The Love Magnet

It's hard to conceive of a more lovable group than the 1940 Lions. You simply ooze charm from every pore, and have a bunch of admirers to prove it! Although you're probably very popular, you do best with one committed partner. You don't want to share your lover with anybody else. A mate who is shy, retiring, and a little aloof brings out the best in you. That's because you love a challenge. A partner who tries to resist your alluring persuasions never fails to arouse your passion. You want a partnership that feels like it is always in the courtship phase.

You're rather idealistic about money, and benefit from a partner who can provide a more realistic view of how your funds should be spent. As someone with an incredibly strong will, you need to be mindful of giving way to your spouse every once in a while. This should not be difficult, as you are famous for your generous, loving heart. You're an incredibly ardent lover who enjoys having sex at every available opportunity. A partner who enjoys making love all day and night is best suited to your sexual style.

Putting up an initial resistance to your charms is a surefire way to win your heart. Offering just a slight smile at one of your jokes is enough to make you redouble your attentions. You're also interested in the latest forms of entertainment, so discussing upcoming movie stars and musical acts can lure you into a romance. You prefer to have your admirer make the first move toward the bedroom. It really turns you on when your suitor gazes deeply into your eyes just before a kiss.

As a male Lion who was born in 1940, you want a woman who is young at heart. Ladies who are always yearning for "the good old days" have little appeal for you. You're also drawn to women who are shy but romantic. A mate who wants to be cherished and protected is your perfect match.

Men who are authoritative in a quietly confident manner excite you 1940 female Leos. Overtly macho behavior really turns you off. Men who are cerebral and sophisticated also attract you. You want a partner who loves your considerable star power.

1940 VIRGO
From August 23, 7:29 through September 23, 4:45

The Earthy Sensualist

As a 1940 Virgo, you've got a down-to-earth attitude that is most attractive. You cherish both your partner's strengths and weaknesses, reasoning that a perfect human being would be a pretty boring lover. A relationship that allows you to take plenty of time to smell the flowers is your ideal. Although you're extremely hard working and service-oriented, your first priority is to enjoy everything that life has to offer, including love. Teaming with a reflective mate helps you to appreciate everyday blessings even more.

Because you're highly attuned to your partner's needs, you make an excellent lover. You enjoy taking your mate to new heights in the bedroom. Playing out sexual fantasies may be one of your favorite forms of recreation. Deep down inside, you have tremendous emotional reserves that can support and sustain your relationship in times of trouble. You're not the type of partner to abandon a union just because it is experiencing difficulty. You do best with a trusting mate who isn't afraid to lean on you when times are tough.

Asking you to work out the details of a large project is a good way of winning your affection. You take pride in your ability to execute plans in a careful, systematic manner. Coming to a disorganized person's aid really boosts your ego. There's a very good chance you enjoy sports, too, and would never turn down tickets to watch your favorite team. Because you enjoy being the aggressor in love, your suitor should let you make the first move. Inviting you over just after having taken a shower is a good idea, since you're extremely turned on by cleanliness.

If you're a 1940 male Virgo, you want a woman who is both nurturing and intellectual. Ladies who are warm but have a strong sense of privacy also attract you. A partner who enjoys basking in the sensual pleasures of life is ideal for you.

A man who is self-motivated, skillful, and pragmatic fills you 1940 female Virgos with admiration. You love a guy who has strong leadership qualities, but doesn't use brute force to exert them. You do best with a mate who respects your opinion.

VIRGO ZODIAC SIGN
Your Love Planets

YOUR ROMANTIC SIDE   p. 696
- ▶ VENUS IN CANCER
  Born Aug. 23, 7:29 - Sept. 08, 16:58
- ▶ VENUS IN LEO
  Born Sept. 08, 16:59 - Sept. 23, 4:45

YOUR SEX DRIVE   p. 722
- ▶ MARS IN VIRGO
  Born Aug. 23, 7:29 - Sept. 23, 4:45

YOUR CELEBRITY TWINS   p. 760
Find out the astrological similarities you have with famous people.

YOUR COMPATIBILITY   p. 780
Compare planets to find out how compatible you are in a relationship.

YOUR RELATIONSHIP KARMA   p. 824
- ▶ SATURN IN TAURUS
  Born Aug. 23, 7:29 - Sept. 23, 4:45

COUNT BASIE
American Musician
Venus in Virgo

1940 LIBRA
From September 23, 4:46 through October 23, 13:38

The Sexy Dish

When it comes to having sex appeal, you have been blessed with a double dose of desirability, 1940 Libra. You have an animal magnetism that is virtually impossible to ignore. And although you probably enjoy an active social life, you really prefer a relationship that affords a great deal of privacy. Unless you're alone with your partner, it can be difficult for you to express the depths of your devotion. In private, however, you're extremely affectionate.

As a person with a tremendous sexual appetite, you need a lover with plenty of stamina. Pairing up with an open-minded, nonjudgmental spouse is ideal, because you sometimes are shy about articulating your physical desires. A partner who encourages you to act out your fantasies wins your everlasting devotion. Since you're probably very artistic, you need a mate who is willing to give you plenty of space to just dream and create. A partner who has their own interests and hobbies gives you the inspiration and understanding you need to thrive.

Winning your heart is a matter of serious flirting. You love it when an admirer expresses obvious interest in you through lavish compliments and appreciative glances. Some sexy verbal sparring never fails to turn you on. You're also attracted to powerful types who can advance your interests in some way. Offering to promote your work or put you in touch with the right people is a good way to embark on a relationship with you. When it comes time to make the first move, your suitor should act with confidence and purpose. You can't abide wishy-washy lovers.

If you're a male Libran who was born in 1940, you desire a woman who is truthful, friendly, and broad-minded. You're also drawn to ladies who are insightful, modest, and compassionate. You do best with a partner who loves both your private and public personas.

As a 1940 female Libra, you want a man who is giving, practical, and creative. Guys who are diplomatic and independent also attract you. Ultimately, you want a partner who not only enjoys taking you out on the town, but loves spending quiet evenings with you, too.

LIBRA ZODIAC SIGN
Your Love Planets

YOUR ROMANTIC SIDE   p. 696
- ▶ VENUS IN LEO
  Born Sept. 23, 4:46 - Oct. 06, 21:09
- ▶ VENUS IN VIRGO
  Born Oct. 06, 21:10 - Oct. 23, 13:38

YOUR SEX DRIVE   p. 722
- ▶ MARS IN VIRGO
  Born Sept. 23, 4:46 - Oct. 05, 14:20
- ▶ MARS IN LIBRA
  Born Oct. 05, 14:21 - Oct. 23, 13:38

YOUR CELEBRITY TWINS   p. 760
Find out the astrological similarities you have with famous people.

YOUR COMPATIBILITY   p. 780
Compare planets to find out how compatible you are in a relationship.

YOUR RELATIONSHIP KARMA   p. 824
- ▶ SATURN IN TAURUS
  Born Sept. 23, 4:46 - Oct. 23, 13:38

CARMEN MIRANDA
Brazilian Entertainer
Mars in Sagittarius

186

1940 SCORPIO
From October 23, 13:39 through November 22, 10:48

♏ ## The Proud Partner

Partnerships are your lifeblood, 1940 Scorpio. You want a union that completes you as a person. A mate that is practical, grounded, and stable is best suited to you. Because you probably possess a tremendous amount of authority, it can be hard for you to tell your real friends from folks who just want favors. An intuitive partner can help guide you to people who truly appreciate your wit, compassion, and wisdom. As far as you're concerned, your mate is as essential to you as breathing.

You're the type of lover who prefers to devote yourself to a single partner. The thought of sharing your mate with anybody else is very distasteful. Your approach to lovemaking is passionate and ardent. A spouse who is willing to abandon work for pleasure brings out the best in you. Spirituality plays a very important role in your life, and you benefit from a partner who shares your beliefs. Having a relationship that is solely focused on earthy pleasures would not suit you at all. You also do well with a mate who, like you, is very civic-minded.

An admirer who expresses an interest in serious romance has a good chance of capturing your heart. Frivolous flirtations hold little interest for you. You want to build a life with somebody, not just have a few laughs together. A suitor who has a profound appreciation for beauty is also bound to attract your attention. Your admirer should make sure to get plenty of sleep the night before making a move on you. Your sexual stamina is extremely high. Kissing your neck is a good way to get an enthusiastic response from you.

Women who are idealistic, progressive, and passionate appeal most to you 1940 male Scorpions. You're also attracted to sensitive, creative ladies. A partner who is willing to join her life to yours on every possible level is your ideal match.

As a 1940 female Scorpion, you desire a man who is charming and idealistic. Intense, emotional guys also turn you on. You want a man who makes you feel sexy, desirable, and smart. You're not interested in a mate who takes you for granted after your courtship is over.

1940 SAGITTARIUS
From November 22, 10:49 through December 21, 23:54

♐ ## The Loving Helper

You 1940 Sagittarians are always looking for ways to help your loved ones. For you, the surest sign of devotion is making sacrifices for your beloved. Perhaps that is why you do best with a partner who is slightly scatter-brained. Helping to organize your mate's life makes you feel needed and productive. Because you're such a practical person, you enjoy the company of a spiritual partner who shows you that there is more to life than just work and service.

Although you enjoy earthly pleasures, sex isn't your highest priority in life. You're sometimes so focused on assisting others that you forget to attend to your own physical needs. A mate who reminds you of your sexual needs brings you much joy. As someone who enjoys legal, educational, and moral issues, you do best with a partner who is also engaged by these concepts. You want a relationship that encourages you to aspire to a higher level of humanity. Joining forces with a self-satisfied partner would not afford you much pleasure.

Drawing on your desire to help others is a good way to catch your eye. An admirer who seems disorganized brings out your protective side. You're also attracted to people who are somewhat private about their desires. Such folks never fail to pique your curiosity, and you'll stop at nothing to discover their secret hopes and wishes. A suitor would be wise to make the first move, as you can be somewhat unsure when a person is sexually interested in you. You are extremely turned on by light, lingering kisses that slowly grow deeper. Physical intimacy is a gradual process for you.

As a 1940 male Archer, you want a woman who loves people. Self-centered ladies hold little attraction for you. You're also drawn to females with powerful personalities that are just a little bit secretive. A mate who engages your mind and spirit is your ideal.

Enigmatic men really excite you 1940 female Sagittarians. You love probing the depths of your mate's soul. Shallow guys leave you completely cold. A spiritual partner who draws your attention to life's little miracles brings out the best in you.

Billie Holiday – Lady Day Sings the Blues

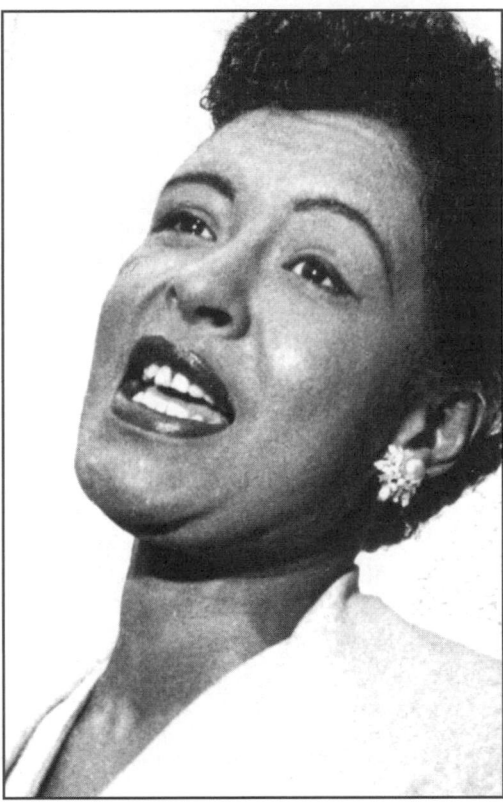

Raped when she was only eleven and a street-wise prostitute by fourteen, Billie Holiday was invariably drawn to abusive men. Yet calling on some inner strength and determination to rise from her desperate roots, she eventually became one of the most famous jazz singers of the 20th century. Her love life was one disastrous affair after another, and her music career was often blocked by racism and her own addiction to alcohol and heroin. These personal vices and social injustices fueled her passion for singing the blues and always left audiences feeling the deep ecstasy and pain that she knew so intimately.

With her Sun in bold, original Aries, Billie Holiday fearlessly began singing in New York clubs as a teenager. Even though her range was only about an octave, she had natural talent and created a personal style based on Bessie Smith's big voice and Louis Armstrong's depth of feeling. By the time she was eighteen she had established herself as a stirring singer with an earthy, searching honesty in her voice. She made some recordings with Bennie Goodman and record producer John Hammond, and by twenty she was known as "Lady Day" and the hottest young singer in Harlem.

Holiday has a boat-load of planets in sentimental, impressionable Pisces that tune her to the subtle vibrations beyond physical appearances. Musicians, artists, and all kinds of creative people benefit by planets in Pisces, but they have a downside. Pisces feels the pain of the world, and often the only relief is found in drugs and alcohol. An additional, major factor in Holiday's case is that her Mars in Pisces squares Saturn. Women with Mars square Saturn often have trouble with brutal men and experience

the cruelty of life in a variety of ways.

By the late 1930s Holiday had toured with the best musicians of her day, singing with the bands of Artie Shaw, Count Basie, and Duke Ellington. Then in 1939 Holiday opened as a solo act in the Café Society, a progressive, racially mixed club in Greenwich Village. Here she introduced what eventually became her signature song, "Strange Fruit," penned by Abel Meeropol in 1939. The words tell a stark tale of a lynching: "Southern trees bear a strange fruit, Blood on the leaves and blood at the root, Black body swinging in the Southern breeze. Strange fruit hanging in the poplar trees."

This revolutionary protest song received a wide range of reactions. Of course it was banned on the radio and the label that had her under contract would not record it. Audiences were often deeply moved by Holiday's wrenching performance. One club owner noted at the song's conclusion that "a moment of oppressively heavy silence followed, and then a kind of rustling sound I had never heard before. It was the sound of almost two thousand people sighing." Others perceived "Strange Fruit" as a sexy song, or felt that way about it because that's the way Holiday sang it.

Probably Holiday's best years, both professionally and personally, were between 1938 and 1943 when she teamed up with saxophonist Lester Young. In 1941 she married Jimmy Monroe, the younger brother of a club owner she knew. The couple parted company soon after, but he introduced her to heroin. Although she was voted Best Jazz vocalist in 1943, her downward spiral had already begun.

> *"When Billie sang, you could see the emotion in her face. She didn't choreograph a song or act it."*
>
> **MILT GABLER**
> **Commodore label record producer**

187

▶ READ ABOUT THE SWINGING MUSIC OF THE TIMES ON PAGE 169

1941

Sex Idol

- ⭐ SEXUAL IMMORALITY
- ⭐ SUMNER WELLES
- ⭐ PINUPS
- ⭐ RANDOM HARVEST
- ⭐ KISSES FOR BREAKFAST
- ⭐ JIMMY DORSEY
- ⭐ STAR DUST

EVENTS

US Under-Secretary of State Sumner Welles was a lifetime chum of Franklin D. Roosevelt, and when FBI Director J. Edgar Hoover told Roosevelt that Welles was a homosexual, Roosevelt was unfazed—until the resulting scandal forced him to fire his "criminal" friend.

Across the ocean thousands of British women were interviewed at military bases to discover whether accusations of sexual immorality amongst women were justified. It was concluded they were not.Unmarried women between the ages of twenty and thirty were called up for war work. Married women with young children were assisted in volunteering by the establishment of widespread nursery provision.

Actress Gene Tierney married designer Oleg Cassini—it was a stormy marriage with a divorce, a remarriage, and another divorce. Pinup star Betty Grable divorced former child star Jackie Coogan, then married band leader Harry James.

POP CULTURE

Bookstores featured Carson McCullers' *Reflections in a Golden Eye*. In the 1940s South an Army major with a passionate wife realizes he's a homosexual. In *This Above All* we read about a deserter during World War II who resents the upper class, then falls for a WAAF private who turns out to be a British aristocrat. In *Random Harvest* by James Hilton, an amnesiac British veteran of

World War I marries a showgirl—then loses any memory of her.

In the movie *Kisses for Breakfast* we met another man with amnesia. This one also forgets he's newly married, but ends up marrying his bride's sister. Set in Chicago during the '20s *Tall, Dark, and Handsome* gave us a gangster with a heart of gold who falls for his children's governess. *The Farmer's Wife* was about a British farmer who proposes to three women, then realizes it's really his housekeeper he loves.

At the top of the Hit Parade we had all the big band leaders. Jimmy Dorsey gave us four hits: "Blue Champagne," "I Heard a Rhapsody," "Yours," and "High on a Windy Hill," and from Tommy Dorsey we heard "This Love of Mine." Other hits were "Star Dust" by Artie Shaw and Glenn Miller's "You and I."

TYRONE POWER

In *Witness for the Prosecution*, Tyrone Power had the role of a sexy, scheming husband, but in real life, this Hollywood heartthrob had secrets even more shocking and sordid. Known as the swashbuckling hero of *The Mark of Zorro*, Power was married three times and had numerous affairs with legendary actresses such as Lana Turner, Judy Garland, and Rita Hayworth.

But Power's libido swung both ways. He was rumored to have had affairs with Errol Flynn, Howard Hughes, and Cesar Romero. Biographers have speculated that fear of exposure as a bisexual led Power to grant an outrageously generous divorce settlement to his second wife.

SEE ALSO

▶ LANA TURNER *Page 333*

▶ JUDY GARLAND *Page 219*

1941 CAPRICORN

From December 21, 1940 23:55 through January 20, 1941 10:33
(December 1941 Capricorns, see 1942 Capricorn)

♑ *The Sensitive Steady*

You can afford to be permissive with your mate, 1941 Capricorn. With you, mutual trust and respect tend to be staples of your relationship. Sensitive and perceptive, you may have a nose for sincerity and the excellent judgment to give it high priority in a romantic partnership. You're likely to be a reliable partner, showing your love through concrete acts rather than words. Compromise may come to you naturally, and you thrive in a romantic relationship rich with compassion and kind tolerance. Even when a partner's quirks or failings get on your nerves, you may find it easy to shift your focus to the qualities you adore. With your vision and imagination, you can bring out the best in your mate.

Having a steady routine allows you to provide your mate and family with a stable lifestyle, but you may overreact to any slight disruption to the status quo. Being in control of your circumstances may make you feel safe. Your mate's empathy and reassurance can help to calm any fears you may have about change. Facing challenges together can reinforce your optimism and faith in your abilities to make the most of every situation. You may have strong physical and emotional needs, but you tend to be discreet about satisfying them. The privacy of the bedroom frees you to let your hair down.

For you, lovemaking can provide you and your mate with a blissful, dreamy escape. Sharing only the best in sensual pleasures—fine wine, candlelit dinners, perfumed sheets, beautiful music—can stir your passions. Next to sex, dancing can be your favorite form of intimate exercise.

The 1941 Capricorn man enjoys a woman who is flexible and broadminded. She may be content to follow your lead most of the time, but her big picture perspective can come in handy when you need to improvise. With her ideas and your practical skills, you can be a perfect team.

The Capricorn woman born in 1941 admires a truthful man with a strong sense of humor. Together, you are likely to find something to laugh about even in the toughest situations. With his honest feedback and bright outlook, you can face challenges with confidence and grace.

CAPRICORN ZODIAC SIGN
YOUR LOVE PLANETS

YOUR ROMANTIC SIDE .... p. 696
► **VENUS IN SAGITTARIUS**
Born Dec. 21, 1940 23:55 - Jan. 13, 1941 21:28
► **VENUS IN CAPRICORN**
Born Jan. 13, 21:29 - Jan. 20, 10:33

YOUR SEX DRIVE .... p. 722
► **MARS IN SCORPIO**
Born Dec. 21, 1940 23:55 - Jan. 04, 1941 19:41
► **MARS IN SAGITTARIUS**
Born Jan. 04, 19:42 - Jan. 20, 10:33

YOUR CELEBRITY TWINS .... p. 760
Find out the astrological similarities you have with famous people.

YOUR COMPATIBILITY .... p. 780
Compare planets to find out how compatible you are in a relationship.

YOUR RELATIONSHIP KARMA .... p. 824
► **SATURN IN TAURUS**
Born Dec. 21, 1940 23:55 - Jan. 20, 1941 10:33

IDA LUPINO
English Actress
Sun and Venus in Aquarius

189

1941 AQUARIUS

From January 20, 10:34 through February 19, 0:55

♒ *The Aspiring Amour*

You may have always aspired for one great love, 1941 Aquarius, and pledged your heart only to the partner who proved worthy of you. As you're likely to be fiercely protective of your independence, you thrive with a stout-hearted mate who respects your need for freedom. You tend to resist any attempt to control you or cramp your style, but you can mistake a partner's genuine concern as an attempt to interfere in your business. With the confidence that a particular admirer is your soul mate, you can let down your guard and rest easy that this person is on your side. You thrive with a partner who is patient, determined, and up to the challenge of a little friendly sparring.

In a serious relationship, you can be a deeply devoted mate, and you are capable of having enormous success in romance. Your willingness to make a partnership work is what turns a commitment into your one great love. Open communication and trust may be your highest priorities, and your creative imagination can dream up a variety of ways to please your mate. Your partner's love can bring out your soft, receptive side, and you may show great sensitivity to your mate's desires. You tend to be a passionate lover, with a strong need for physical affection and a healthy taste for sensual pleasures.

Lovemaking can be intoxicating for you, and you may respond well to romantic atmospheric touches. Music can strongly influence your mood, especially any songs that are sentimental favorites for you and your mate. Soft light can be relaxing for you, and a long massage can ease you into languid bliss.

The Aquarian man of 1941 appreciates a woman who is true to herself and loyal to him. You can be idealistic, and you tend to have great respect for someone who conducts herself with integrity. With this trustworthy lady, you can open up and share your feelings.

An optimistic, open-minded man is a superb counterpart for the 1941 Aquarian woman. You admire someone who understands your original points of view and offers constructive feedback. Wonderfully encouraging, this fellow can inspire you to take action on your ideas.

AQUARIUS ZODIAC SIGN
YOUR LOVE PLANETS

YOUR ROMANTIC SIDE .... p. 696
► **VENUS IN CAPRICORN**
Born Jan. 20, 10:34 - Feb. 06, 21:48
► **VENUS IN AQUARIUS**
Born Feb. 06, 21:49 - Feb. 19, 0:55

YOUR SEX DRIVE .... p. 722
► **MARS IN SAGITTARIUS**
Born Jan. 20, 10:34 - Feb. 17, 23:31
► **MARS IN CAPRICORN**
Born Feb. 17, 23:32 - Feb. 19, 0:55

YOUR CELEBRITY TWINS .... p. 760
Find out the astrological similarities you have with famous people.

YOUR COMPATIBILITY .... p. 780
Compare planets to find out how compatible you are in a relationship.

YOUR RELATIONSHIP KARMA .... p. 824
► **SATURN IN TAURUS**
Born Jan. 20, 10:34 - Feb. 19, 0:55

ORSON WELLES
American Director
Venus and Mars in Aries

1941 PISCES
From February 19, 0:56 through March 21, 0:19
The Lucky Lover

You have a great talent for making your own luck in love, 1941 Pisces. As a partner, you are diligent, reliable, sincere, and fair, and these qualities enable you to keep a fortunate opportunity—or a good mate—from slipping through your fingers. Because an overflow of passion can color your perception, too much intensity can be distracting and even disturbing for you. An overly-demanding partner can trigger fears of entrapment, leading you to emotionally distance yourself and run. You can be at your easygoing best with an understanding sweetheart who knows better than try to force issues when tempers are high. Once you've had a chance to think a bit and let your feelings settle, you can be a good problem solver.

You can be kind, sympathetic, and generous with praise, but you rarely impose yourself or express feelings unless they are mutual. A stable relationship can bring out your ability to make sacrifices, provided they'll bring greater benefits for you, your partner, and family over the long term. Such an approach allows you to provide a secure emotional and material environment in which love and loved ones can flourish. For you, lovemaking allows you to express feelings of mental, physical, and spiritual attachment to your mate.

An intimate dinner allows you and your mate to enjoy fine food and drink and the pleasure of each other's company. Thoughtful gifts can warm your heart, especially if they have sentimental meaning. Sex is best for you when there is a slow, gentle build-up, with affectionate kissing, caressing, and whispers in the dark.

A quiet, compassionate woman can offer comfort and enchantment to the 1941 Piscean man. You may love the ease of being around someone who has an intuitive understanding of how you feel about things. Her sensitivity allows you to enjoy a harmonious bond.

The 1941 Piscean woman tends to enjoy a good-humored man who can keep things orderly and under control. You may prefer life to proceed with a certain delicacy and refinement. With his exquisite sense of timing, this fellow enables the two of you to share the good life.

1941 ARIES
From March 21, 0:20 through April 20, 11:49
The Vivacious Valentine

A love affair with you, Aries of 1941, sparkles with the same innate vitality that makes you shine. As far as you're concerned, a relationship should expand each partner's opportunities for enjoyment and personal growth. Still, in your zeal to protect your freedom and keep your options open, you could miss out on some opportunities to deepen the intimacy you share. Sometimes you may mistake your sweetheart's interest in your daily life as an attempt to control you or cramp your style. Open-hearted communication can nip your worries in the bud, allowing you to define the boundaries of your relationship and to enjoy greater support from your partner. Your native Aries bravery may embolden you to let down your guard with your mate. Taking the initiative to share your needs and feelings can strengthen your bond.

You are perfectly capable of carrying on a serious relationship, but it must reflect your individuality and leave plenty of room for spontaneity. The better you and your mate get in working out compromises, the more you can harmonize outside engagements with your personal commitment. You thrive with a partner who finds it energizing to come up with original and creative responses to whatever challenges you two may face. A sexy improvisational approach can enhance your enjoyment in the boudoir.

You and your mate might like to "mix it up" every now and then with new techniques or different locales—in your home or on a vacation escape. With your boundless and adventurous imagination, you might occasionally enjoy the thrill of taking naughty liberties.

The 1941 Aries man can hardly resist a woman who is daring and determined. Her willfulness can offer a provocative challenge that brings out your warrior spirit. With her restless and impulsive spirit, you can enjoy the thrill of the chase and the joys of the catch.

The Aries woman of 1941 adores a man who is innovative and self-motivated. You have a talent for getting things started, and this man has the genius, vision, and persistence to see things through to the end. Together, you can successfully realize your goals.

1941 TAURUS
From April 20, 11:50 through May 21, 11:22

The Enriching Comrade

On many levels, 1941 Taurus, a love affair with you can be an enriching experience. You are likely to be benevolent, kind, and sympathetic. In a new relationship, you may work overtime to win the affections of your beloved, perhaps even molding your personality to impress the object of your affections. A serious commitment can provide the safety and stability you tend to crave, but you can't enjoy true contentment if you sell your needs short just to hold things together. At a key point in your romantic career, you may have resolved never to settle for an unequal relationship with someone who was not worthy of you. A dependable, compassionate partner allows you to relax, open up, and just be yourself.

You may pride yourself on being self-sufficient, but your mate can inspire you to embrace the benefits of mutual support and interdependence. Your gift for enthusiastic listening ensures a smooth flow of communication. The warmth and empathy you show for each other tends to make a lasting impression, and you and your partner may have

a network of supportive friends who can ease your burdens in any rough patches and multiply your happiness in times of joy. For you, lovemaking can be a sensuous celebration.

Lavishing you with luxurious pleasures is a surefire way to stir your passions. The wealth of the good earth can turn you on. An evening of intimacy may begin with a bouquet of fragrant flowers, a walk in the park, or a garden picnic. Gourmet foods add spice to your love life, and a walk through the produce aisle can make your mouth water.

The Taurean man of 1941 appreciates a woman who is warm and approachable. You're not quite yourself without your minimum daily requirement of hugs and open affection. With this earthy mama, you may never miss a chance to smell the roses or to enjoy the sweetness of life.

A social charmer is the man for the 1941 Taurean woman. With you, affection tends to be a forever thing, and you thrive with a partner who is gracious and generous with your friends. With this affable fellow by your side, you can surround yourselves with love.

TAURUS ZODIAC SIGN
YOUR LOVE PLANETS

YOUR ROMANTIC SIDE   p. 696
- ▶ **VENUS IN TAURUS**
  Born Apr. 20, 11:50 - May 14, 13:35
- ▶ **VENUS IN GEMINI**
  Born May 14, 13:36 - May 21, 11:22

YOUR SEX DRIVE   p. 722
- ▶ **MARS IN AQUARIUS**
  Born Apr. 20, 11:50 - May 16, 5:04
- ▶ **MARS IN PISCES**
  Born May 16, 5:05 - May 21, 11:22

YOUR CELEBRITY TWINS   p. 760
Find out the astrological similarities you have with famous people.

YOUR COMPATIBILITY   p. 780
Compare planets to find out how compatible you are in a relationship.

YOUR RELATIONSHIP KARMA   p. 824
- ▶ **SATURN IN TAURUS**
  Born Apr. 20, 11:50 - May 21, 11:22

HENRY FONDA
American Actor
Sun in Taurus

1941 GEMINI
From May 21, 11:23 through June 21, 19:32

The Idealistic Romantic

The most exciting relationship for you, Gemini of 1941, is one where you feel you can learn a lot from your partner. Intellectual stimulation is a big turn-on for most Geminis, but for you it can be just as important to connect with your mate on a spiritual and emotional level. Likely to be idealistic about love, you may have once assumed that partners should know everything about each other and have no secrets. Maturity tends to temper Geminian curiosity, and you may now believe that there is such a thing as "too much information," even in an intimate relationship. The give-and-take of a loving commitment allows you to consider the effect of what you say or don't say on your sweetheart's feelings.

You thrive in a relationship that is based on honesty, realistic expectations, and respect for each partner's individuality. You may appreciate a mate who encourages you to trust your best instincts and gives you gentle feedback about your capabilities and limitations. With your partner's support, you can focus your energy and creativity with brilliant success. You may

have a mesmerizing way with words that enables you to inspire a partner's confidence in the face of a challenge or to arouse your mate's passion when you're in the mood for love.

In bed with your beloved, you can lose all sense of time. For you, sex can offer a pleasure-filled escape, a chance to let your imagination run wild. Sharing and fulfilling fantasies allows you to engage your body, mind, and spirit in an endless variety of erotic possibilities.

An open, perceptive woman can be highly enticing to the 1941 Gemini man. Sharing ideas can be exhilarating for you, and you may enjoy someone who can offer insightful observations and clever conversation. With so much food for thought, you can fill your life together with meaning.

An intuitive and empathetic man can be a wonderful complement for the 1941 Gemini woman. With his ability to pick up on your thoughts and emotions, you can enjoy the feeling of being truly in tune with your partner. With her poetic skills, she can seduce you with dreamy verses.

GEMINI ZODIAC SIGN
YOUR LOVE PLANETS

YOUR ROMANTIC SIDE   p. 696
- ▶ **VENUS IN GEMINI**
  Born May 21, 11:23 - June 07, 23:52
- ▶ **VENUS IN CANCER**
  Born June 07, 23:53 - June 21, 19:32

YOUR SEX DRIVE   p. 722
- ▶ **MARS IN PISCES**
  Born May 21, 11:23 - June 21, 19:32

YOUR CELEBRITY TWINS   p. 760
Find out the astrological similarities you have with famous people.

YOUR COMPATIBILITY   p. 780
Compare planets to find out how compatible you are in a relationship.

YOUR RELATIONSHIP KARMA   p. 824
- ▶ **SATURN IN TAURUS**
  Born May 21, 11:23 - June 21, 19:32

DUKE ELLINGTON
American Musician
Mars in Leo

192

1941 CANCER
From June 21, 19:33 through July 23, 6:25

♋ The Magnetic Mate

Only the ultimate in romantic indulgence will do for you, 1941 Cancerian. You may often develop ardent attachments to partners, causes, activities, even pets. With your magnetic charisma, you can arouse strong reactions in others. Your mate is likely to number among those who find you irresistibly enticing and compellingly persuasive. Taking care of loved ones comes instinctively to most Cancerians, but in your zeal to rescue a partner in need, you can sometimes end up undermining the very person you are trying to help. Over time, you may have learned that the best way to keep those good intentions from backfiring is to talk to your mate first and find out whether emotional support or material aid is in order.

Able to see your mate's greatest potentials and to visualize solutions to problems, you can inspire your mate to rise to any occasion, a skill that can bring success and make you a stronger couple. You can be a deeply sympathetic and understanding partner, and your flair for self-expression can be endearing. With your unusually creative mind, you can enchant your mate with romantic musings, pet names, and tender gestures. Your bedroom may be well-appointed for the occasional in-home pleasure cruise.

For you, creature comforts can lend an indulgent sweetness to lovemaking. You may set the tone for passion with soft cushions, satin sheets, scented candles, beautiful music. On a hot night, you might spoon-feed each other ice cream. If you're feeling randy, you can always find more erotic uses for any tasty confection.

For the Cancerian man of 1941, a tender, receptive woman can be a soothing presence. Coming home to a peaceful atmosphere may be a necessity for you, and this lovely lady shares your flair for gracious living. With her, you can share the good life with friends and family.

The Cancerian woman born in 1941 can find a perfect match in the man with strong passions. You appreciate someone whose physical appetite can match your own, and this fellow can provide you with plenty of action. With his romantic firepower, he can stir your soul and energize you.

1941 LEO
From July 23, 6:26 through August 23, 13:16

♌ The Courageous Charmer

The history of your love life, 1941 Leo, is likely to have all the elements of a blockbuster movie, with you, of course, in the starring role. Early on, you may have been a bit rowdy, a youth with extreme passions, intense likes and dislikes, and not a whole lot of common sense. Any reckless tendencies likely smoothed out with maturity, and you may have come away with valuable lessons and some amazing stories to tell. You may still have strong desires and a hypnotic animal magnetism that your mate is bound to find outrageously charming. These days your hunter instincts may get more use in finding creative ways to seduce your partner and to fill your partnership with romance and adventure.

In a loving relationship, you tend to be an honorable partner, with great courage, endurance, and optimism. Likely to be fiercely protective of your mate and family, you may roar with fury at any threat to a loved one's well-being. With your marvelous sense of humor and breezy disposition, you can help your mate to face any challenge with poise and aplomb. Because you may become impatient with routine, you thrive with a partner who likes to socialize, travel, and go out on the town. Your fertile imagination can keep passions high in the boudoir and elsewhere.

You tend to be a playful lover, with strong physical desires and an insatiable curiosity about erotic possibilities. Exploring various techniques with your mate keeps lovemaking fresh. Fulfilling fantasies can be an enormous turn-on, allowing you and your partner to enjoy your dramatic skills.

A modest woman with refined tastes can be alluring to the 1941 Leo man. You enjoy sharing the good life, and her nose for quality can keep you well-indulged. With her understated appeal and hard-to-get aura, the thrill of the chase will always stay fresh for you.

The Leo woman of 1941 adores the man who can be active and competitive. You may get a charge out of being around someone with intense desires, and this fellow can bring out your best. With this exciting go-getter, you can enjoy a romance packed with interest and excitement.

1941 VIRGO
From August 23, 13:17 through September 23, 10:32

The Substantive Sweetheart

A pretty mate is like a melody, 1941 Virgo, but the substance behind the sweet smile is what keeps your interest. You tend to be knowledgeable and to speak only when you know what you're talking about. A mate who can appreciate the fine points of any subject is a rare find. A good debate keeps a relationship interesting for you. Sometimes your flair for playing devil's advocate can go too far, and you may find yourself making amends to frazzled mate, especially if you mistakenly treated a plea for emotional support as a topic for intellectual discussion. Your mate's feelings tend to matter to you a lot more than being right about something, and you can be flexible in making adjustments to soothe your sweetheart and restore peace.

You are a loyal mate, willing to work long and hard to meet common goals and support your partner. Good timing and thriftiness enable you to manage shared resources and provide a comfortable home life for your mate and family. Steady habits can make you feel secure, but sometimes you can fall into a rut. You flourish with a mate who can pick up on any brewing frustrations and suggest a refreshing change of pace. Lovemaking provides a very pleasant way to blow off some steam and renew your passions.

About once every quarter, you and your mate can benefit from a total escape. Anything from a day trip to an extended vacation allows you to relax, reconnect, and enjoy intimate moments alone. Music and dancing cheek-to-cheek can be a wonderfully romantic warm-up to an erotic interlude.

For the Virgo man of 1941, a bright, artistic woman can be a perfectly delightful mate. You may find it stimulating to be in the company of someone with a refined appreciation of the arts and a taste for beauty. With her elegance and creativity, she can offer you a gracious lifestyle.

The man who channels his passions into productive ventures can win the admiration of the Virgo woman born in 1941. You tend to have a strong work ethic and good manners, and you appreciate a man with discipline. His originality in expressing himself can motivate and inspire you.

VIRGO ZODIAC SIGN
YOUR LOVE PLANETS

YOUR ROMANTIC SIDE   p. 696
▶ **VENUS IN LIBRA**
Born Aug. 23, 13:17 - Sept. 15, 4:00
▶ **VENUS IN SCORPIO**
Born Sept. 15, 4:01 - Sept. 23, 10:32

YOUR SEX DRIVE   p. 722
▶ **MARS IN ARIES**
Born Aug. 23, 13:17 - Sept. 23, 10:32

YOUR CELEBRITY TWINS   p. 760
Find out the astrological similarities you have with famous people.

YOUR COMPATIBILITY   p. 780
Compare planets to find out how compatible you are in a relationship.

YOUR RELATIONSHIP KARMA   p. 824
▶ **SATURN IN TAURUS**
Born Aug. 23, 13:17 - Sept. 23, 10:32

VERONICA LAKE
American Actress
Venus in Libra

1941 LIBRA
From September 23, 10:33 through October 23, 19:26

The Romantic Rebel

Love tends to change everything for you, 1941 Libra, and you may mark various stages in your life by who you were with or where you were in a relationship. Meeting a soul mate can be liberating for you, encouraging you to shed inhibitions and restrictions. In a serious romance, your emotional attachment to your mate may have a deep intensity, a feeling that you were fated to meet and learn something from each other. Likely to have the heart of a rebel, you may have benefited from social changes that expanded your options in relationships and freed you to enjoy greater sexual satisfaction.

You thrive with a partner who is open-minded, adventurous, and willing to come along with you on an exciting journey of growth and self-discovery. In your zeal to pursue your passions, you and your mate may have been unable to avoid a clash of wills. Your talent for compromise and harmonious communication allows you and your partner to support each other as you adapt to new situations and challenges. In a trusting relationship, you can be loyal and devoted.

Surviving a few power struggles can actually deepen your commitment. In the privacy of your bedroom, you and your mate may explore the outer limits of erotic pleasure.

The sexual energy between you and your partner can inspire your creativity, and you can be an electrifying lover when you set your creativity loose on your sexual relations. For you, sex manuals may be old-but-enjoyable news, and you may have a great time exploring new positions, techniques, accessories, and other enhancements.

The Libran man born in 1941 enjoys a woman who has an hypnotic, seductive allure. Her mystical aura of sensuality can intrigue you, and her intense passions can energize and empower you. With this charismatic lady you can feel intimately connected to the cycles of life.

An innovative man with a healthy curiosity can be a stimulating partner for the 1941 Libran woman. You can find it exciting and inspiring to be with a mate who pushes you to try new things. Exploring the world with him can provoke you to realize your greatest abilities.

LIBRA ZODIAC SIGN
YOUR LOVE PLANETS

YOUR ROMANTIC SIDE   p. 696
▶ **VENUS IN SCORPIO**
Born Sept. 23, 10:33 - Oct. 10, 19:20
▶ **VENUS IN SAGITTARIUS**
Born Oct. 10, 19:21 - Oct. 23, 19:26

YOUR SEX DRIVE   p. 722
▶ **MARS IN ARIES**
Born Sept. 23, 10:33 - Oct. 23, 19:26

YOUR CELEBRITY TWINS   p. 760
Find out the astrological similarities you have with famous people.

YOUR COMPATIBILITY   p. 780
Compare planets to find out how compatible you are in a relationship.

YOUR RELATIONSHIP KARMA   p. 824
▶ **SATURN IN TAURUS**
Born Sept. 23, 10:33 - Oct. 23, 19:26

DOROTHY LAMOUR
American Actress
Sun and Mars in Sagittarius

1941 SCORPIO
From October 23, 19:27 through November 22, 16:37

♏ The Generous Giver

For you, Scorpio of 1941, love can be an all-or-nothing proposition. Over time, you may have strived to bring greater balance, more compromise, and moderation into your relationships. You may have strong passions and can fall deeply for a partner. Early on, you may have been vulnerable to a personality more powerful than yours. If all the support and affection goes to your partner's side and nothing to yours, a rush of anger can help you to muster the courage you need to confront an unworkable situation. Speaking truthfully and with sensitivity to each other can empower you and a mate to face any problems together and create (or recreate) a relationship based on mutual support, trust, and respect.

In a long term partnership, you can be warm, affectionate, and congenial. A generous soul, you are usually willing to give your mate the benefit of the doubt in hard times. You have the ability to take on some tremendous responsibilities in relationships. Your instincts can help you understand your mate's reactions and responses, and your resourcefulness enables you to make a tangible difference. You can thrive with sympathetic mate who makes you feel valued and secure. Lovemaking allows you to renew deep feelings of emotional connection with your partner.

You tend to be a giving lover, and a positive response from your mate can make you feel wonderful. Pillow talk enhances the intimacy of an encounter for you. "Firsts" can be so exciting for you. A caring partner would be wise to find out what you've always wanted but never had—and then give it to you.

A woman who is dedicated and sincere can be a comforting mate for the 1941 Scorpio man. You flourish with someone who can be gently frank with you. Her openness can win your trust, but the kind things she does for you gives you concrete proof of her affection.

A passionate, direct man allows the Scorpio woman of 1941 to know exactly where she stands. His willingness to take the initiative in your partnership assures you of the security of your relationship. His enthusiasm for life and for you can encourage you to express yourself.

1941 SAGITTARIUS
From November 22, 16:38 through December 22, 5:43

♐ The Meaning Magnifier

Sharing can make everything seem better to you, 1941 Sagittarius. With a loving partner by your side, experiences tend to feel more meaningful and sensual pleasures seem more intense. In your relationship, the expansive rewards of love can go well beyond good feelings. Because you can be such an encouraging partner, your mate can take on greater challenges, realize more impressive results, and turn around and push you to higher heights. For you, effort tends to matter more than results. Even in a setback, you can find a positive learning experience that benefits you and your mate.

In a lasting commitment, you may go through periods of high energy and enthusiasm, but you can lose interest once you and your mate fall into a comfortable groove. In the down times, your mate may wonder what happened to the buoyant, ardently devoted person you can be. Sharing an active spiritual life with your mate can provide you with an ongoing source of energizing food for your soul. You are likely to have an impressive imagination that allows you to come up with creative ways to enchant and seduce your partner. You tend to enlist both your mind and body in communicating with your partner, and for you, lovemaking allows you make a deep emotional connection.

You can be an adventurous lover, and you and your mate may enjoy exploring a variety of erotic possibilities, and you can be especially receptive to sensual pleasures. You may have a fascination for exotic influences, and the food, drink, and music of a distant culture can make for a sexy vacation.

The Sagittarian man of 1941 thrives with a woman who has a charming personality and an enthusiastic approach to romance. You appreciate someone who has a cheerful attitude and loves to learn. With her optimistic outlook, you can fill your days with fun and excitement.

The Sagittarian woman born in 1941 adores a man who is passionate and energetic. You thrive with someone who can inspire your competitive spirit and your pride in fully expressing your talents. With his empowering faith in you, this man can inspire you to give your all.

Film Noir – Hollywood's Dark Side

Treacherous, sexually unbound, and all-too-attainable, the Femme Fatale was the most seductively memorable character of Film Noir, a cinematic genre that emerged in the early 1940s. Unique for its dark visual perspective, story lines, and characterizations, Film Noir movies eschewed the sunny escapism of mainstream Hollywood films, especially in the treatment of romantic relationships. The classic Hollywood story line was, "Boy meets girl. Boy loses girl. Boy wins girl back. Boy and girl ride off together into the sunset." Love and marriage is the ultimate happy ending.

Film Noir rejects these Hollywood values and portrays a dark, gritty world of danger and alienation. Relations between men and women are tense, distrustful, fraught with obsession and betrayal—and ultimately doomed. Artistically indebted to German expressionism, Film Noir reflects the historical backdrop of World War II—a time when real life horror and uncertainty seemed to hover in the air. Themes and character types reflected the impact of the war on families, with many husbands leaving home to serve in distant lands.

In 1941 two breakthrough films paved the way for the ripening of Film Noir into a cinematic phenomenon that would enjoy an eighteen-year-long golden age. Orson Welles' *Citizen Kane* pioneered shooting techniques and black-and-white visual style, and John Huston's *The Maltese Falcon* furnished the standard elements of plotline, atmosphere, and characterization.

Women fell into two categories: the traditional woman and the dangerous seductress. In early noir films, the

Humphrey Bogart and Mary Astor in *The Maltese Falcon*

"I don't care who loves who. I won't play the sap for you!"

HUMPHREY BOGART as Sam Spade in
The Maltese Falcon

traditional woman was an idealized object of longing and nostalgia—the goodness and purity of the family back home. In contrast, the femme fatale character embodied both the dangers and temptations the men would face while separated from their families.

In *The Maltese Falcon*, Humphrey Bogart's hardboiled detective, Sam Spade,

set the standard for the Film Noir hero, whose seduction by the femme fatale subjected him to dangerous situations. This treacherous female strikes again in Billy Wilder's *Double Indemnity*, when Barbara Stanwick's character persuades insurance agent/lover Fred McMurry to kill her husband. By the end of the classic genre story, the femme fatale would be jailed or killed, and the male hero would learn a hard lesson about the hazards of falling for such a woman. While the fascinating bad-girl qualities and sexual independence of the femme fatale afforded the thrill of vicarious infidelity, her disastrous fate reinforced the family values and moral sensibilities of the movie audience.

In the post-war period, as soldiers returned home to their families, the moral center of gravity between the good girl and the femme fatale character in Film Noir began to shift. With the ascendancy of the traditional nuclear family through the 1950s, the girl-next-door type became dangerous and treacherous, while the femme fatale became the whore with a heart of gold, giving respite and comfort to the hero. As in *The Postman Always Rings Twice* (1946), the husband of the evil wife was often aging, paralyzed, or confined to a wheel chair. He deprived his wife of affection or treated her as a possession.

By depicting traditional family life as sterile, suffocating, and confining and by transforming husbands and wives into villains, Film Noir began to reflect a simmering real world disillusionment with traditional marriage and the nuclear family, a sentiment that would anticipate the seismic changes to come in family life in the 1960s.

195

▶ READ ABOUT BARBARA STANWYCK AND FRED MACMURRAY ON PAGE 238 ▶ READ ABOUT HUMPHREY BOGART ON PAGE 235

★ BARE LEGS

★ AVA GARDNER

★ CARY GRANT

★ THE FUNCTION OF THE ORGASM

★ DON'T SIT UNDER THE APPLE TREE

★ JUDY GARLAND

EVENTS

Because of wartime rationing, both inhibitions and hemlines started to lift, but no one complained. Women were encouraged to be patriotic and accept bare legs instead of stockings. But the Pope announced that women without stockings were not permitted in St. Peter's. Yet the Church of England abandoned its regulation that women must wear hats in church. The shortage of cosmetics led British women to use soot for eye shadow and beet juice for lipstick, and the British government banned embroidery on women's undergarments.

A petition demanded that men and women receive equal compensation for injuries sustained during air raids. Concern was voiced that British women were becoming the victims of the lust of American soldiers, with high numbers of "half-caste" babies being born to white Britons and black Americans.

In Hollywood love marched on. Mickey Rooney and Ava Gardner married and at the age of 16 Marilyn Monroe married 21-year old James Dougherty—she called him "Daddy" and the marriage lasted four years. Leading man Cary Grant married heiress Barbara Hutton, while author Sinclair Lewis divorced his second wife.

POP CULTURE

War-related films dominated. In *For Me and My Gal,* World War I separates vaudeville song-and-dance partners, who later are reunited in love on Broadway. *To the Shores of Tripoli* gave

Hot Couple

us a playboy who joins the Marines, then learns to shape up after he tries to woo a nurse and clashes with his sergeant. In *Once Upon a Honeymoon* a US reporter working in Europe informs a stripper from Brooklyn she has just married a Nazi.

Publishers looked to sex to help readers forget about the war. *Living with a Husband and Liking It* was an early self-help marital guide for women. In *The Function of the Orgasm*, by Wilhelm Reich, the author, a student of Freud, held that libido energy is the most important factor in human development.

At the top of the charts were lighthearted fare such as "Don't Sit Under the Apple Tree" by Glenn Miller, "For Me and My Gal" by Judy Garland and Gene Kelly, and "I Left My Heart at the Stage Door Canteen" by Sammy Kaye.

KATHARINE HEPBURN & SPENCER TRACY

He was a scruffy kid from a working-class Irish Catholic family who got expelled from a dozen schools. She was the plucky daughter of Connecticut white-shoe aristocrats. But when their lips locked on the silver screen, the electricity between Spencer Tracy and Katharine Hepburn was for real.

The best unkept-secret in Hollywood, the twenty-five-year love affair between Tracy and Hepburn lent a highly charged authenticity to their portrayals as romantic partners in films such as *Woman of the Year*, *Adam's Rib*, and *Guess Who's Coming to Dinner*. With their feisty chemistry, they put the "sex" in "the battle of the sexes."

SEE ALSO
► HEPBURN AND TRACY *Page 251*

1942 CAPRICORN

From December 22, 1941 5:44 through January 20, 1942 16:23
(December 1942 Capricorns, see 1943 Capricorn)

♑ The Extravagant Sweetheart

Generous, refined, and social, you 1942 Goats are extremely popular, especially on the romantic front. And while it's easy for you to attract admirers, you are selective about your mate. You do best with a partner you can admire and respect. A relationship in which your aspirations are encouraged and supported is your ideal. Your romantic partner understands that just because you enjoy the good life doesn't mean you dislike work. A mate who enjoys going off in another direction from time to time complements you perfectly.

Although you love to shower your spouse with gifts, you want a relationship that isn't solely based on materialism. You're quite spiritual and benefit from a mate who shares your sacred beliefs. When it comes to sex, you want pleasure more than excitement. A long afternoon of making love is preferable to a hurried morning session. A lover who enjoys lingering over sex is a perfect match for you. On another front, it would be nice if your mate is health-conscious and encourages you to get plenty of exercise each day, because you may

have a tendency to overindulge.

Expressing interest in "taboo" subjects such as religion, politics, and sex is a good way to get your attention. You enjoy exploring such topics with an admirer who shares your love of the forbidden. A suitor who is cooperative and helpful to others also attracts you. You can't abide egotistical types. Your admirer would be well-advised to make the first move, because you like take-charge types in the bedroom. A partner who takes time getting you in the mood wins your undying loyalty.

Women who are unusual, independent, and friendly appeal most to you 1942 male Goats. You love a lady who values relationships more than material goods. Your ideal partner enjoys the creature comforts you provide, but appreciates your mind, too.

If you're a 1942 female Capricorn, you want a man who is a bit of a warrior. You're also turned on by sensual, traditional types. Ultimately, you want a mate who makes you feel loved and protected, but also gives you credit for being just as strong as he is.

CAPRICORN ZODIAC SIGN
YOUR LOVE PLANETS

YOUR ROMANTIC SIDE   p. 696
▶ VENUS IN AQUARIUS
Born Dec. 22, 1941 5:44 - Jan. 20, 1942 16:23

YOUR SEX DRIVE   p. 722
▶ MARS IN ARIES
Born Dec. 22, 1941 5:44 - Jan. 11, 1942 22:20
▶ MARS IN TAURUS
Born Jan. 11, 22:21 - Jan. 20, 16:23

YOUR CELEBRITY TWINS   p. 760
Find out the astrological similarities you have with famous people.

YOUR COMPATIBILITY   p. 780
Compare planets to find out how compatible you are in a relationship.

YOUR RELATIONSHIP KARMA   p. 824
▶ SATURN IN TAURUS
Born Dec. 22, 1941 5:44 - Jan. 20, 1942 16:23

PAUL HENREID
Austrian Actor
Sun in Capricorn

197

1942 AQUARIUS

From January 20, 16:24 through February 19, 6:46

♒ The Glamorous Lover

Dynamic, glamorous, and aloof, you 1942 Aquarians are an intriguing group. You're the type who can take romance or leave it, as long as you are surrounded by plenty of creature comforts. You want a lover who provides companionship above all else. When you want flowers and candy, you'll buy them yourself, but you can't purchase a soul mate. To you the ideal relationship consists of exchanging unusual ideas and exploring new vistas. Although you're a very independent person, you do benefit from a mate who affirms your belief that the world is an unpredictable place inhabited by extraordinary people.

Exploring all avenues of sexual enjoyment is important for you. A lover who is open-minded and uninhibited really turns you on. Sometimes you can go without sex for weeks, so you benefit from a partner who can seduce you out of your complacency with promises of bedroom bliss. Although you don't want a conventional home life, you do have a strong devotion to domestic bliss. A partner who helps you create a household routine that is both spontaneous and

comforting brings out the best in you.

A suitor with an original mind has an excellent change of winning your affection. You aren't impressed by folks who can't think for themselves, or feel the need to parrot the majority opinion. Expressing an interest in a specialized subject such as archaeology, astronomy, or physics is sure to excite you. When it comes time to make the first move toward a physical relationship, your suitor should be the aggressor. You may enjoy having your ankles and calves stroked as a prelude to lovemaking.

If you're a male Water-bearer who was born in 1942, you want a woman who is inventive, inquisitive, and friendly. Ladies with an air of intrigue have no appeal for you. You do best with a partner who means what she says and says what she means.

Nurturing and determined men are extremely attractive to you 1942 female Aquarians. Macho, aggressive types rub you the wrong way. A mate who is hard-working but tender-hearted brings out the best in you. You want a strong guy who isn't afraid to cry.

AQUARIUS ZODIAC SIGN
YOUR LOVE PLANETS

YOUR ROMANTIC SIDE   p. 696
▶ VENUS IN AQUARIUS
Born Jan. 20, 16:24 - Feb. 19, 6:46

YOUR SEX DRIVE   p. 722
▶ MARS IN TAURUS
Born Jan. 20, 16:24 - Feb. 19, 6:46

YOUR CELEBRITY TWINS   p. 760
Find out the astrological similarities you have with famous people.

YOUR COMPATIBILITY   p. 780
Compare planets to find out how compatible you are in a relationship.

YOUR RELATIONSHIP KARMA   p. 824
▶ SATURN IN TAURUS
Born Jan. 20, 16:24 - Feb. 19, 6:46

ANN SHERIDAN
American Actress
Sun in Pisces

198

1942 PISCES
From February 19, 6:47 through March 21, 6:10

The Loving Homebody

As a 1942 Pisces, you are sociable, clever affectionate, and utterly domestic. While you enjoy taking frequent short trips with your partner, your favorite spot on earth is home. Therefore, you do best with a mate who enjoys maintaining a domestic environment that is warm and welcoming. Because you have tons of friends, you're bound to have houseguests often, so it helps to have a partner who enjoys playing host. You're also extremely curious and need a relationship that can provide you with plenty of mental stimulation. A lover who likes comfort and adventure in equal amounts brings out the best in you.

Sex and love are interchangeable terms for you. Making love in a romantic, candlelit atmosphere is one of your greatest delights. You do best with a partner whose attitude toward sex is as reverent as yours. As a civic-minded person, you benefit from a spouse who values having strong roots in your community. As far as you are concerned, your partnership can only be enhanced by forming strong, nurturing friendships with your neighbors.

Performing charitable works with your partner also nourishes and strengthens your union.

A good way to get your attention is to discuss your dreams. You love analyzing a person's subconscious in this manner. Inviting you to a beach or lake is also a good idea, because you enjoy the water immensely. Having a strong love of home and family is definitely a plus when it comes to courting you. You're not an especially aggressive lover, so it is wise for your suitor to make the first move toward a physical relationship. Being kissed in a darkened movie theater is one way to make your heart skip a beat.

If you're a 1942 male Fish, you desire a woman who is idealistic, principled, and sociable. You don't want a lady who always needs to cling to your arm. A partner who is independent but affectionate suits you best.

As a 1942 female Pisces, you like two types of men. The first is gentle, cuddly, and laid-back. The second is energetic, witty, and intelligent. Whichever type you choose as a mate, he should encourage your vibrant social life.

1942 ARIES
From March 21, 6:11 through April 20, 17:38

The Frank Admirer

Honest and forthright, you 1942 Rams are always very clear about where you stand, especially with regard to romance. You're the last person to string an admirer along for sheer amusement. You want a relationship that doesn't involve role playing or mind games. A partner who is communicative and fair-minded always brings out the best in you. Your greatest desire is to create a life with your mate that is financially secure. This will enable you both to live according to your own values, instead of following the herd.

Sex is a healthy form of recreation for you. You view making love as the best remedy for stress or exhaustion. A lover who shares your playful attitude toward sex can give you much joy. You may have a very delicate nervous system, and need a partner who can help you take the edge off. Taking up a sport with your spouse is an ideal way to strengthen your system while promoting togetherness. Going on short trips together can also ease your restless spirits. As far as you're concerned, one of the best things about a relationship is always

having company for your favorite activities.

A guaranteed way to catch your eye is to blurt out the truth when everybody else is trying to be diplomatic. You admire a courageous person who is willing to take the heat for voicing unpleasant realities. You also enjoy the company of an admirer who always tries to stay mentally engaged through studies of some kind. Although you enjoy being the one to make the first move in a relationship, you don't mind a little encouragement. Your suitor would be wise to ask you for a neck or shoulder rub as a means to becoming physically intimate.

If you're a 1942 male Ram, you want a woman who is observant, gregarious, and a little eccentric. You're also attracted to easy-going, emotionally receptive ladies. A mate who celebrates your individuality makes you thrive.

Men who are expressive, vivacious, and thoughtful greatly appeal to you 1942 female Rams. You can't stand stolid, plodding types. You want a partner who welcomes adventure, as long as he takes you along for the ride.

1942 TAURUS

From April 20, 17:39 through May 21, 17:08

The Expansive Suitor

All Taureans love luxury, but none as much as you 1942 Bulls do. Not only do you pamper yourself, but you lavish your partner with creature comforts, too. With regard to relationships, you feel more comfortable giving than receiving. You do best in a partnership in which you can make your mate feel adored, comfortable, valued, and safe. A lover who appreciates your creative talents more than the gifts you give is your ideal match. You have keen artistic sensibilities that are quite often channeled into touching expressions of true romance. You can pen a truly beautiful love letter or poem when the mood strikes you.

Your sex life is bound to be colorful because you enjoy injecting an element of fantasy into lovemaking. A versatile partner who has fun role playing and acting out various scenarios with you gives you much pleasure. Romantic atmospheres never fail to fuel your passion. At home you could tend be set in your ways. You prefer a mate who is willing to let you call all the shots regarding domestic affairs. Creating a home that is elegant, sumptuous, and

comfortable is a means of honoring your spouse. You want nothing but the best for your beloved.

Expressing admiration for your considerable knowledge is a good way to win your affection. Although most folks are distracted by your lavish lifestyle, few people recognize what a sharp and clever mind you have. Because you have a profound respect for nature, an admirer would do well to express an interest in ecology or the environment. Your suitor should take pains to create an elegant atmosphere for your first kiss. A candlelit room filled with flowers is sure to put you in the proper mood for romance.

A male Bull born in 1942 would want a woman who is intuitive and philosophical. Timid but imaginative ladies also attract you. A partner who returns your generosity with love and affection is a good match for you.

As a 1942 female Taurus, you enjoy a man who is intelligent, versatile, and adaptable. A nurturing, ambitious guy also turns you on. You benefit most from a talkative mate who enjoys exchanging ideas with you.

TAURUS ZODIAC SIGN
YOUR LOVE PLANETS

YOUR ROMANTIC SIDE   p. 696
▶ **VENUS IN PISCES**
Born Apr. 20, 17:39 - May 06, 2:25
▶ **VENUS IN ARIES**
Born May 06, 2:26 - May 21, 17:08

YOUR SEX DRIVE   p. 722
▶ **MARS IN GEMINI**
Born Apr. 20, 17:39 - Apr. 26, 6:17
▶ **MARS IN CANCER**
Born Apr. 26, 6:18 - May 21, 17:08

YOUR CELEBRITY TWINS   p. 760
Find out the astrological similarities you have with famous people.

YOUR COMPATIBILITY   p. 780
Compare planets to find out how compatible you are in a relationship.

YOUR RELATIONSHIP KARMA   p. 824
▶ **SATURN IN TAURUS**
Born Apr. 20, 17:39 - May 8, 19:39
▶ **SATURN IN GEMINI**
Born May 8, 19:40 - May 21, 17:08

SIMONE SIMON
French Actress
Mars in Gemini

1942 GEMINI

From May 21, 17:09 through June 22, 1:15

The Visionary Lover

As a 1942 Gemini, you're always thinking about new ways to improve old traditions. A conventional relationship has little interest for you. You do best in a partnership that gives both people plenty of space to dream, create, and reflect. A mate who appreciates your inventive mind would be your perfect match. You're passionately interested in people, and would benefit from a mate who likes mixing with folks from all different walks of life. It would be very difficult for you to thrive in a claustrophobic relationship.

When it comes to making love, you can be a little absent-minded. You're so immersed in the intellectual realm of life that you often forget its physical aspects. A sensual spouse who can draw out this side can help you lead a more balanced and pleasurable existence. Unless you team up with an organized partner, your home life could be a little chaotic. You're often so engrossed in creative pursuits that you might forget practical matters such as keeping the refrigerator stocked. A nurturing mate who enjoys

attending to domestic affairs is a wonderful counterbalance to your dreamy ways.

Any suitor who wants to attract your attention should express a great deal of creative power. You're enormously attracted to people who enjoy visual arts such as painting, fashion, and photography. Stable, grounded people also have a good chance with you, because you enjoy the secure feeling such folks provide. Your admirer should make the first move because you tend to be a bit hesitant when it comes to romance. Surprising you with a kiss at a mundane place such as the supermarket is sure to pique your interest.

Women who are athletic, friendly, and outgoing appeal to 1942 male Geminis. You're also attracted to ladies who are voluptuous and sensual. Ultimately, you want a partner who balances your intellect with common sense.

If you're a female Gemini born in 1942, you enjoy a man who is warm, affectionate, and sensitive. Passionate males who are dynamic and larger-than-life also intrigue you. You do best with a mate who reminds you of your feminine charms.

GEMINI ZODIAC SIGN
YOUR LOVE PLANETS

YOUR ROMANTIC SIDE   p. 696
▶ **VENUS IN ARIES**
Born May 21, 17:09 - June 02, 0:25
▶ **VENUS IN TAURUS**
Born June 02, 0:26 - June 22, 1:15

YOUR SEX DRIVE   p. 722
▶ **MARS IN CANCER**
Born May 21, 17:09 - June 14, 3:55
▶ **MARS IN LEO**
Born June 14, 3:56 - June 22, 1:15

YOUR CELEBRITY TWINS   p. 760
Find out the astrological similarities you have with famous people.

YOUR COMPATIBILITY   p. 780
Compare planets to find out how compatible you are in a relationship.

YOUR RELATIONSHIP KARMA   p. 824
▶ **SATURN IN GEMINI**
Born May 21, 17:09 - June 22, 1:15

200

WALTER PIDGEON
Canadian Actor
Venus in Leo

1942 CANCER
From June 22, 1:16 through July 23, 12:06

 The Private Partner

You 1942 Crabs are very selective about the people you spend time with. Although there are plenty who enjoy your warm, bubbly expansive outlook, you prefer to be with a small group of loved ones. The most important member of your social circle is your romantic partner. You want a mate who is not only your lover, but your best friend as well. Because you've been blessed with a very strong intuition, you may be very good at choosing a partner who can provide you with that privacy you need. Even though you love spending time with your mate, you need plenty of time alone to develop creative ideas.

Affectionate and physically demonstrative, you are an extremely enthusiastic lover. You can't go for a long time without making love. A mate who shares your playful, ardent attitude toward sex keeps your passion alive. You don't especially enjoy traveling, preferring to stay close to home with your beloved. A spouse who enjoys maintaining a cozy private sanctuary from the outside world is your ideal. Visiting nearby friends allows you to get a change of scenery together.

Expressing compassion for others is an excellent way to win your heart. You feel a kinship with fellow humanitarians, and may go out of your way to become friends with such a person. Your admirer should know that you don't jump into romance very quickly. Rather, you prefer letting a relationship develop slowly over time. When it comes time to take your relationship to a physical level, you will make the first move. Your suitor can make it easier for you by entwining arms in a rainstorm. Such close physical proximity could prompt you to place a kiss on your beloved's lips.

As a 1942 male Cancer, you want a woman who is sweet-tempered, seductive, and yielding. You also admire ladies who are intelligent, open, and friendly. A mate who makes you feel confident, and vibrant is your ideal match.

You 1942 female Crabs enjoy men who have a flair for a dramatic. It's hard for you to resist a man who draws admiring stares wherever he goes. You do best with a partner who celebrates your tender, nurturing instincts.

1942 LEO
From July 23, 12:07 through August 23, 18:57

The Friendly Flirt

Vibrant, unusual, and outgoing, you 1942 Lions are an exciting bunch. Although romance isn't first on your list of priorities, you do value your partner greatly. As far as you're concerned, relationships are a means to soften the harsher aspects of life. Because you are drawn to humanitarian causes, you are often confronted with unpleasant realities. A mate who reminds you of the joyous aspects of life helps balance your perspective. You do best in a union that supports your social ideals. Cynics and complainers hold no charm for you. You have much more in common with a partner who is intent on changing things for the better.

You have a strong sex drive, but sometimes have difficulty expressing your desires. An intuitive lover who encourages you to abandon yourself to pleasure is an ideal match for you. Likely you've become more easygoing with regard to sex as you've gotten older. Because you can be a strong-willed individual with intense desires, you benefit from a partner who is able to stand up to you from time to time. Secretly, you enjoy it when your mate defies your wishes or

contradicts your opinion. You love a debate.

Cool, confident, and controlled suitors usually attract your attention. You can't help admire somebody who seems self-assured. Expressing an interest in the dramatic arts is also a good way to win your heart, because you probably love movies and plays. Although you prefer to make the first move in a romance, you can get swept away by an admirer who draws you into a passionate embrace when you least expect it. You love it when your partner makes you feel absolutely irresistible.

If you're a male Lion who was born in 1942, you want a lady who is old-fashioned and nurturing. You're also drawn to women who are extraordinarily glamorous. Ultimately, you want a mate who makes you feel like her knight in shining armor.

Men who are warm, loving, and dynamic thrill you 1942 female Leos. You're also drawn to guys who are modest, unassuming, and shy. Whichever type of man you choose for your partner, he should share your compassion for humankind.

1942 VIRGO
From August 23, 18:58 through September 23, 16:15

The Stimulating Suitor

Intelligent and determined, you 1942 Virgins are an impressive group. You require a special partner who is not intimidated by your unique originality or your ambition. Because you're focused on being the best at what you do, you benefit from a mate who admires and supports your goals. You're a real visionary, and are happiest with a lover who enjoys building castles in the air with you. A cynical partner would dampen your enthusiasm for making the world a kinder, gentler place. Because you can be progressive in your thinking and actions it helps if your mate isn't too concerned about upholding conventional appearances.

Friends play an important part in your life, and your partner should celebrate this. Being part of a large group gives you comfort and security, and you enjoy a spouse who is willing to be a team player. Intimacy could be a challenge for you, though. You benefit most from a lover who helps let your defenses down. Your earthy sexuality may only be apparent to your partner because you prefer to keep this side of yourself private. Secretly, you long to be

a dynamic and exciting lover, and are drawing closer to this as you get older.

A charming and witty conversationalist will get your attention quickly. You appreciate someone who is able to put others at ease in a social setting. Inviting you to a concert is a good idea, because you most likely have a great passion for music. Any admirer of yours should have beautifully polished manners. You can't abide rude, gauche types. When it comes time to take your relationship to the physical level, your suitor should ask permission before bestowing a kiss. You don't enjoy being taken by surprise.

If you're a 1942 male Virgo, you want a woman who is unassuming, conscientious, and practical. Warm, friendly ladies also appeal to you. A loving partner with great integrity is your ideal match.

Men who are gentle, considerate, and hard-working attract you 1942 female Virgos. You also like gentlemen with perfect manners and good taste. A mate who admires your intelligence will always have a chance at winning your heart.

GREER GARSON
English Actress
Sun and Venus in Libra

201

1942 LIBRA
From September 23, 16:16 through October 24, 1:14

The Cosmopolitan Romantic

As a 1942 Libra, you've got an active mind that needs stimulation. A partner who enlightens and entertains brings out the best in you. You want a relationship that allows you to explore new ideas and examine different vistas. Building a solid foundation for your partnership is important and that could include embarking on adventures together. You would not to well in a union that thrives on routine. You're always looking for inspiration in different places, and your partner should have as much wanderlust as you.

You're an affectionate person who enjoys making love, but needs to be in the right mindset to feel passionate. If you're not looking or feeling your best, you're apt to forestall sex until you're in top form again. You thrive with a lover who makes you less self-conscious. Your social life means a great deal to you, and you enjoy entertaining friends quite often in your home. A spouse who enjoys throwing both big, lavish parties and small, elegant dinners is a good match for you. Because you are quite active, you may want to

take up a sport such as tennis or golf with your partner to promote togetherness.

A suitor who makes you feel as though you're the center of attention at all times has a good chance of winning your heart. You love being admired and appreciated. Entertaining you with stories about the world of arts is also a good way to catch your eye. Juicy tales about celebrities and public figures probably make your eyes sparkle with delight. Making the first move with you is a matter of timing. Waiting for a moonlit night or a romantic interlude to bestow the first kiss can be frustrating, but the rewards will be worth it.

If you're a male Libran who was born in 1942, you enjoy a woman who is ladylike and shy. You're also drawn to females who are refined and elegant. A partner who makes heads turn fills you with pride.

Men who are intelligent, sociable, and tasteful excite you 1942 female Librans. You want a mate who looks great in a tuxedo. Boorish, slovenly types really turn you off. You need a man who has an air of romance about him.

CLAUDE RAINS
English Actor
Sun in Scorpio

1942 SCORPIO
From October 24, 1:15 through November 22, 22:29

♏ *The Secret Lover*

Few people are as secretive about their emotions as you 1942 Scorpions. Because your desires are so powerful, you like to keep a tight lid on them, even around your partner. You want a relationship that is passionate, but not turbulent. Sudden surprises can upset you, so you benefit most from a mate who is serene, stable, and secure.

Because you have a strong desire to succeed, you appreciate a lover who supports you from behind the scenes. You are never stingy about your achievements, and take great pains to let everybody know just how much your partner has contributed to them.

Intimacy is both exciting and intimidating for you. You view sex as a means to merge souls with your partner. This can be a scary prospect, so you are wise to team up with a lover who is completely trustworthy. You can be quite experimental in the bedroom, and enjoy a mate who is as open-minded as you are. Expanding your horizons is important to you, and you prefer a partner who would join you on visits to exotic locales. Studying philosophy, religion, and foreign languages together are all good ways to keep your love alive. You want a permanent partnership.

A suitor who is adept in the art of teasing has a good chance of winning your affection. You love the thrill of the chase, and are never more excited than when an admirer plays hard-to-get. Cultivating a mysterious air is also alluring because you probably pride yourself on being a born detective. An admirer won't have to wait long for you to make the first move. When you see somebody you want, you move with the speed and determination of a jungle cat. Ardent kisses and passionate embraces make you wild with desire.

Women who are intense, intriguing, and sexually enticing give you 1942 male Scorpions a thrill. You're also drawn to females who are elegant and proper. You want a partner who strives to know you, inside and out.

If you're a female Scorpion who was born in 1942, you enjoy a man who projects an image of power. You're also attracted to guys with impeccable manners. A mate who is excited by your passion is ideal for you.

1942 SAGITTARIUS
From November 22, 22:30 through December 22, 11:39

♐ *The Elusive Mate*

Relationships can be a tricky business for you 1942 Sagittarians. On the one hand, you love the comfort and stability of a committed partnership. On the other, you enjoy being free to come and go as you please. A mate who is loyal, adventurous, and open-minded is your perfect match. Feeling joined at your spouse's hip does not suit you at all. You far prefer joining forces with your partner for an adventure, then separating for a while as a means to gather your thoughts. Because you are very sensitive to the needs of humankind, you would benefit from a mate who shares your desire to make the world a kinder place.

Your sex drive is extremely high, and you appreciate a partner who likes to make love as much as you do. Passion can overtake you quite suddenly, and you're apt to make overtures toward your mate at the unlikeliest times and places. A relationship that thrives on spontaneity works for you. Group activities also bring you lots of pleasure, and it's possible that you and your mate will spend lots of time playing sports, taking trips, and having meals with friends. A social-minded spouse suits you very well.

Telling a good joke is a great way to win your affection. You value a sense of humor in an admirer above all else. A suitor who demonstrates leadership skills also impresses you. You love a person who can take charge of a situation without bruising anybody else's feelings. You can be quite aggressive when it comes to romance, although you wouldn't object if your admirer made the first move. You are most receptive to a suitor who kisses your ears and neck as a prelude to lovemaking.

As a 1942 male Archer, you want a woman who projects powerful sensuality and magnetism. You are also attracted to women who are active, fun-loving, and vivacious. A partner who fills your life with a sense of adventure is perfect for you.

Men who are authority figures have a strong attraction for you 1942 female Sagittarians. Guys who are humorous and upbeat win your admiration, too. You do best with a mate who is stable in his affections, but surprising in his actions.

Ingrid Bergman – Saint and Sinner

When it comes to natural allure, there are few actresses past or present who can hold a candle to Ingrid Bergman. Her scrubbed-clean Scandinavian beauty projected an onscreen sensuality that was the ideal of that time. Tall and big-boned, she possessed a warm and unassuming charm that was at odds with the artificial sex appeal displayed by most of Hollywood's female stars of her era. Married to fellow Swede Dr. Peter Lindstrom, Bergman was already the mother of a daughter, Pia, when she became a movie star in American films like *Intermezzo*, *Casablanca*, and *Gaslight*, for which she won her first Oscar in 1944.

This legendary actress was a Virgo, sign of the virgin—a good symbolic fit for the woman who played heroine Joan of Arc in two different movies. But Virgo is an earth sign, full of healthy and uncomplicated sensual appetites. So, after more than a decade of playing nuns, saints, virgins, and emotionally repressed or nobly self-sacrificing heroines, the still-married Bergman changed her on- and offscreen image and shocked Hollywood by having an illicit affair with Roberto Rossellini, her director on the film *Stromboli*. This "betrayal" was a slap in the face to America's smug post-war morality, causing her to be denounced on the floor of the US Senate by Senator Edwin C. Johnson as an "apostle of degradation." Almost overnight her popularity turned to outright infamy when it was revealed she was pregnant with her lover's child. In the moral climate of the time, Bergman's attitudes toward love and sex were perceived as too sophisticated and permissive for American tastes, and it would be six

"When I was very young in Sweden, I used to pray, 'God, please don't let me have a dull life.' And He obviously heard me."

INGRID BERGMAN,
told to *The New York Times* before her death

years before she would work in the film capital again.

In the vernacular of the day her son was born "out of wedlock." Soon afterwards she divorced Lindstrom and married her lover in 1950. She and Rossellini continued to make films together in Europe, though none of these were commercial or artistic successes. In June 1952 she gave birth to twin girls, Isabella and Isotta, but her marriage was already in trouble. She and Rossellini split in 1957. Speaking of the relationship years later she declared, "I have no regrets. I wouldn't have lived my life the way I did if I was going to worry about what people were going to say." Although she was never able to regain her pre-*Stromboli* reputation, in 1956 Bergman returned to the same Hollywood that had denounced her nearly a decade earlier to star in *Anastasia*. The role won her a second Oscar and the grudging forgiveness of the American public. By that time, social mores were beginning to change, catching up with the actress' honesty and lifestyle.

Bergman had Venus in Virgo, epitomizing a naturalistic style of sensuality. She had a sunny, earth mother quality that was irresistible on the screen, and the gift of combining wholesome sex appeal with ladylike charm was her special talent as an actress and personality. Despite her statuesque appearance, on screen she could often seem femininely fragile. Some of her luminous beauty can be seen in the face of her daughter, actress Isabella Rossellini—but there was only one Ingrid.

In 1995 *Empire* magazine rated Bergman thirtieth on their list of the "Sexiest Stars in Film History." The actress died on her birthday in 1982 after a small party with friends.

203

▶ READ ABOUT INGRID BERGMAN AND HITCHCOCK ON PAGE 341 ▶ READ ABOUT INGRID BERGMAN AND ROBERTO ROSSELLINI ON PAGE 262

1943

- ★ RITA HAYWORTH
- ★ BETTY GRABLE'S LEGS
- ★ CASABLANCA
- ★ A TREE GROWS IN BROOKLYN
- ★ AS TIME GOES BY
- ★ PAPER DOLL
- ★ BING CROSBY

EVENTS

It was announced in Germany that women who had an abortion could be executed for threatening the well-being of the German race. Alarmed by a report of the increase in venereal disease in the UK, the Archbishops of Canterbury and York appealed for moral self-control in the nation's interests. The Court of Appeal ruled that any money saved by a wife from the housekeeping budget is the property of the husband.

In the US pinup girl Rita Hayworth's lip prints and autograph appeared in the February issue of *Photoplay*. A few months later she married Orson Welles. Betty Grable's legs were insured with Lloyd's of London for one million dollars. The same year Kirk Douglas married his first wife, Diana, and Dinah Shore married actor George Montgomery.

Film star Charlie Chaplin was well-known for his predilection for young girls, but when Joan Barry accused him of fathering her child, the subsequent trial and scandal ended his career.

POP CULTURE

Moviegoers viewed *Casablanca* with Humphrey Bogart playing an American nightclub owner in French Morocco. In this classic film he sacrifices the love of his life to continue his fight against the Nazis. In *When We Are Married*, set in late 19th century Yorkshire, three couples discover the invalidity of their marriages on their silver wedding anniversary. In the original *Heaven Can Wait*, set in the 1890s, Satan reviews the life of a playboy to see if he deserves to go to Hell or not.

In the bookstores readers were buying *A Tree Grows in Brooklyn* by Betty Smith. In this classic coming-of-age novel, Katie marries a charming dreamer and accepts her fate, but vows that things will be better for her children. A Belgian aristocrat falls in love with a concert pianist who is also a German colonel and living in her family's chateau in *So Little Time* by John P. Marquand.

DJs were spinning "As Time Goes By" by Rudy Vallee, "Don't Get Around Much Anymore" by the Ink Spots, "Paper Doll" by the Mills Brothers, and two hits by Bing Crosby: "Moonlight Becomes You" and "Sunday, Monday, or Always."

Hot Couple

BETTY GRABLE & HARRY JAMES

Band leader Henry James lived the fantasy harbored by millions of World War II GIs. As the husband of pinup girl Betty Grable, James had exclusive access to her magnificent "gams," those long, shapely legs that 20th Century Fox insured for a million dollars.

The couple married in 1943, the year of publication of Grable's celebrated poster—a rear view, with the blond, bathing-suited bombshell peering seductively over her shoulder. The marriage lasted twenty-two years, but Grable wasn't James' only successful discovery. He signed Frank Sinatra to his band after spying "Old Blue Eyes" working in a New Jersey eatery.

SEE ALSO
▶ FRANK SINATRA *Page 211*

204

1943 CAPRICORN

From December 22, 1942 11:40 through January 20, 1943 22:18
(December 1943 Capricorns, see 1944 Capricorn)

♑ *The Serious Sensualist*

You may have heard that Capricorns are cold and stodgy, but that description probably doesn't sound much like you, Capricorn of 1943-at least not where relationships are concerned. Instead, you tend to be quite friendly and enjoy sharing the good things in life with an appreciative partner. In fact, you are likely to be more fun-loving and outgoing now than you were in your youth. Many might say you are more attractive, too, for you tend to get better with age, like fine wine.

Although discriminating in many ways, you try to keep an open mind—and an open heart—when it comes to romance. Usually you give others the benefit of the doubt and bring out the best in your partners. Your curiosity might be piqued by people who are different from you or those who can teach you things. Whether you choose to spend your time with one significant other or many different companions, you like to explore new territory in order to broaden your horizons.

Variety, you realize, keeps you young at heart and keeps love—and life—from getting dull. As a result, you've probably had your share of romantic adventures and could have many more. You enjoy a partner who is both inventive and entertaining in the bedroom, someone who takes an uninhibited approach to sex and likes to experiment. Like all earth signs, you have a strong sensual nature and an appreciation for the physical side of love.

Intelligent, independent women generally appeal to you Capricorn men born in 1943. A person who projects her own style, has her own ideas, and doesn't always follow the rules is likely to attract your interest. A few little idiosyncrasies might make her all the more intriguing. Cookie-cutter cuties can leave you cold—you want someone who is uniquely herself.

A sense of humor is high on the list of priorities for most female Capricorns of 1943. A lively, upbeat partner can offset your somewhat serious nature and help you to laugh at life's little annoyances. A worldly individual with a questing spirit, who likes to range far and wide—both physically and mentally—could also score points with you.

CAPRICORN ZODIAC SIGN
YOUR LOVE PLANETS

YOUR ROMANTIC SIDE   p. 696
- ▶ **VENUS IN CAPRICORN**
  Born Dec. 22, 1942 11:40 - Jan. 08, 1943 10:02
- ▶ **VENUS IN AQUARIUS**
  Born Jan. 08, 10:03 - Jan. 20, 22:18

YOUR SEX DRIVE   p. 722
- ▶ **MARS IN SAGITTARIUS**
  Born Dec. 22, 1942 11:40 - Jan. 20, 1943 22:18

YOUR CELEBRITY TWINS   p. 760
Find out the astrological similarities you have with famous people.

YOUR COMPATIBILITY   p. 780
Compare planets to find out how compatible you are in a relationship.

YOUR RELATIONSHIP KARMA   p. 824
- ▶ **SATURN IN GEMINI**
  Born Dec. 22, 1942 11:40 - Jan. 20, 1943 22:18

MICHELE MORGAN
French Actress
Venus in Aquarius

205

1943 AQUARIUS

From January 20, 22:19 through February 19, 12:39

♒ *The Creative Idealist*

Those who know you casually might only see your independent side and think you are perfectly content to go your own way alone. But that's not a fair analysis of you, Aquarius of 1943. Underneath your self-possessed exterior lies a romantic, serious side that you reveal to the people near and dear to you. In truth, relationships are quite important to you—so important that if you are unattached, it's probably because you haven't found the perfect partner, not because you don't want one.

Like all Water Bearers, you prize your freedom and don't want anyone to tell you how to live your life. Even though you value stability and closeness, you need to be able to express your individuality, and might have rebelled against lovers who tried to corral you. You see relationships as partnerships, in which both of you are on an equal footing. Ideally, you want someone who is also on the same spiritual, creative, and emotional wavelength. But sometimes you may set the bar too high, so that partners fear they might not be able to live up to your expectations.

Your somewhat aloof, detached persona tends to fall away once you leave the public arena and enter the private realm. Lovers may be pleasantly surprised at how deftly you blend sensuality with imagination, affection, and boldness. A partner who recognizes your taste for romance and feeds you good-sized helpings of it has a good chance of winning you over.

As an Aquarian male of 1943, you appreciate a compassionate woman with whom you can let down your guard, knowing she'll listen, sympathize, and provide comfort. You may also be drawn to delicate, sensitive partners whose femininity brings out your protective side. Artistic women who can bring beauty into your life and inspire your own creative spirit get high marks, too.

1943's women Water Bearers usually find that stable, mature, responsible men provide a nice counterpoint to their free-spirited personality. You need to be able to depend on your partner, and value someone who is practical as well as intelligent. It doesn't hurt if he's financially secure and well-respected to boot.

AQUARIUS ZODIAC SIGN
YOUR LOVE PLANETS

YOUR ROMANTIC SIDE   p. 696
- ▶ **VENUS IN AQUARIUS**
  Born Jan. 20, 22:19 - Feb. 01, 9:01
- ▶ **VENUS IN PISCES**
  Born Feb. 01, 9:02 - Feb. 19, 12:39

YOUR SEX DRIVE   p. 722
- ▶ **MARS IN SAGITTARIUS**
  Born Jan. 20, 22:19 - Jan. 26, 19:09
- ▶ **MARS IN CAPRICORN**
  Born Jan. 26, 19:10 - Feb. 19, 12:39

YOUR CELEBRITY TWINS   p. 760
Find out the astrological similarities you have with famous people.

YOUR COMPATIBILITY   p. 780
Compare planets to find out how compatible you are in a relationship.

YOUR RELATIONSHIP KARMA   p. 824
- ▶ **SATURN IN GEMINI**
  Born Jan. 20, 22:19 - Feb. 19, 12:39

PAUL ROBESON
American Actor
Sun in Aries

206

1943 PISCES
From February 19, 12:40 through March 21, 12:02

♓ *The Imaginative Giver*

Like most high-minded Piceans of 1943, you have much to offer, and you give generously of yourself. Your heart is as big as the ocean, and those you love rarely doubt your affection. You believe in the power of love to bring out the best in people, and might see human love as a reflection of divine love. But sometimes you can be too benevolent, letting others take advantage of you. As a result, you may have experienced some frustrations or disappointments in love.

Despite occasional setbacks, you tend to retain a positive attitude toward love and can see the silver lining inside any cloud. Your feelings run deep, but you also have an optimistic and playful side that keeps you in the game of love even if you do get hurt now and again. A romantic at heart, you may hold an idealized vision of the perfect love and continue searching for it, rather than settling for something less than your dream. Some might call you a "Pollyanna" and at times your expectations may be a bit too high. But with your wonderful imagination, you can keep romance alive in a relationship.

There might be some disparity between your chronological age and your "amorous age," for you are inclined to stay young at heart regardless of your years. You know that routine can ruin a partnership, so you try to keep things fresh and exciting by thinking outside the box. A partner who can be spontaneous and sees sex as an adventure is likely to brighten your days—and your nights.

Men born in 1943 under the sign of the fishes generally like outgoing, independent women who have a sense of daring. She doesn't have to be a perfect 10, but if she isn't physically fit you might not give her a second look. Athletic, outdoorsy types who have a bit of the tomboy in them might appeal to you more than beauty queens.

Female Piceans of 1943 are usually drawn to men who blend strength with sensitivity. You want your partner to know his own mind and stand on his own two feet, but he shouldn't be too emotionally cool or controlled. If he can combine intelligence and common sense, idealism with pragmatism, so much the better.

1943 ARIES
From March 21, 12:03 through April 20, 23:31

♈ *The Excitement-Craver*

A life in the fast lane probably appeals to you, Aries of 1943, for few people require as much excitement as you do. Always on the lookout for adventure, you eagerly embrace new challenges in life and in love. At times, you can be a bit excessive, but the thrill of the chase is what gets your blood flowing. Easily bored, you might be happiest in a somewhat volatile relationship or one that involves an element of risk. If things get too comfortable, you may stir up a little controversy just for fun. Your daring approach to romance can enable you to soar to great heights, or crash and burn.

Regardless of your age, you retain a childlike playfulness that other people find endearing. Your upbeat, irrepressible nature has a way of making partners forget their troubles, at least for a while. Although your quixotic nature has probably led you to change partners frequently over the years, you are capable of staying in a long-term relationship that offers plenty of action and variety. But you don't want anyone to put his or her brand on your flank—there's a bit of wild mustang in your soul.

It doesn't take much to kindle your flame, but your enthusiasm tends to flare up suddenly and may burn itself out just as quickly. A partner who wants to hold your interest has to keep updating the old game with new, enticing features. Your ardor may cool some in your middle years, but you still appreciate someone who can show you a new trick or two.

Although male rams born in 1943 may insist on having their freedom, you might not want your partner to enjoy the same flexibility. You like to feel secure about her affection and might appreciate someone who can hold down the fort while you go off in search of adventure. Sensual, affectionate women usually appeal to you—especially if they can cook.

Women born under the sign of the ram in 1943 are often fascinated by men who can't be tamed—James Dean-types who like to live on the wild side offer the challenge you thrive on. Intelligence is a turn-on for you, too, especially if it's coupled with a humanitarian spirit or an avant-garde perspective.

1943 TAURUS

From April 20, 23:32 through May 21, 23:02

The Earthy Homebody

You know a good thing when you see it, Taurus of 1943, and when you meet the right person you do whatever is necessary to make the relationship work. Few people are more caring and affectionate than you, or more generous with their love. You go to great lengths to please your partner—cooking favorite meals, writing love songs, and giving beautiful gifts are some of the ways you may choose to demonstrate your love. Therefore, it's no surprise that a relationship with you is likely to have an enduring quality that can withstand many tests.

Although you may have engaged in your share of flirtations in your youth, you value commitment and usually prefer a close, stable partnership to playing around. So long as a relationship offers romance, sensual pleasure, and creature comforts, you probably won't look elsewhere—why complicate matters? A bit of a homebody, you are generally content to spend time with your loved ones and don't require a steady diet of excitement. A peaceful, secure domestic life suits you well. But you can use your creativity to keep a relationship from growing dull.

Physical contact nourishes you, for no sign is more sensual than Taurus. Anything that gives pleasure is okay in your book. But as important as sex is to you, it's only part of the equation. You enjoy all forms of affection, including holding hands, snuggling, and back rubs. Although the physical side of love may top your list of priorities, your ideal partner is one who also connects with you mentally and emotionally.

Friendship scores high with male Tauruses of 1943. You enjoy the company of a woman you can talk to and with whom you can share good times. You may also be intrigued by an intelligent woman with a youthful spirit, who can teach you things, bring new people into your life, and keep you from getting in a rut.

Romantic men who express their love in all sorts of creative ways can melt the hearts of female Tauruses born in 1943. You may not be able to resist poets, artists, and musicians who share their love of beauty with you and inspire you to express your own artistic side.

TAURUS ZODIAC SIGN

YOUR LOVE PLANETS

YOUR ROMANTIC SIDE   p. 696
▶ **VENUS IN GEMINI**
Born Apr. 20, 23:32 - May 11, 11:55
▶ **VENUS IN CANCER**
Born May 11, 11:56 - May 21, 23:02

YOUR SEX DRIVE   p. 722
▶ **MARS IN PISCES**
Born Apr. 20, 23:32 - May 21, 23:02

YOUR CELEBRITY TWINS   p. 760
Find out the astrological similarities you have with famous people.

YOUR COMPATIBILITY   p. 780
Compare planets to find out how compatible you are in a relationship.

YOUR RELATIONSHIP KARMA   p. 824
▶ **SATURN IN GEMINI**
Born Apr. 20, 23:32 - May 21, 23:02

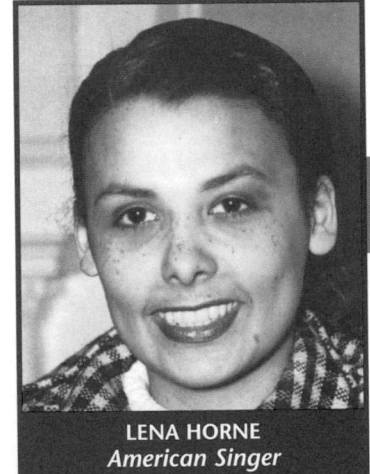

LENA HORNE
American Singer
Mars in Gemini

207

1943 GEMINI
From May 21, 23:03 through June 22, 7:11

The Versatile Companion

Mercurial is perhaps the best word to use when describing your approach to relationships, Gemini of 1943. That's not surprising, as your sign is ruled by the quixotic planet, Mercury. Sometimes you can be quite outgoing, friendly, and spontaneous, but other times you seem rather cautious, sensitive, even shy. One part of you might want to be free to enjoy all the flowers in the field, while another part longs for the security of a steady relationship. As a result, your partners may have some difficulty figuring you out—even you might feel there are two "yous," as your zodiac symbol, the twins, suggests.

One thing most people agree on, though, is that you are an interesting companion, and life with you is rarely dull. Your boundless curiosity has probably brought many different people and experiences into your life, but you can never have too many friends or too much knowledge. Being able to share ideas with a partner is key to the success of a relationship with you. When troubles arise, your well-honed communication skills enable you to discuss problems openly

with a lover and find solutions to most of them.

Your changeable, inquisitive nature could have led you to be something of a flirt in your youth, for you don't like to miss out on anything that might be fun or educational. Most likely, you've had your share of admirers who marveled at your sexual cleverness and versatility (for you learn something from everyone you meet). A partner who can show you a thing or two and whose curiosity matches your own would probably suit you well.

1943's Gemini men admire women who combine intellect with emotional depth. It helps if she likes kids and is a competent homemaker. A caring, compassionate partner who nurtures you and makes your life comfortable in every way could be the answer to your prayers.

Gemini women of 1943 appreciate males who exhibit a playful, fun-loving side. Athletes, adventurers, and men who don't run away from challenges usually appeal to you, too. An assertive, decisive partner can provide direction for you and keep you from vacillating endlessly.

GEMINI ZODIAC SIGN

YOUR LOVE PLANETS

YOUR ROMANTIC SIDE   p. 696
▶ **VENUS IN CANCER**
Born May 21, 23:03 - June 07, 12:08
▶ **VENUS IN LEO**
Born June 07, 12:09 - June 22, 7:11

YOUR SEX DRIVE   p. 722
▶ **MARS IN PISCES**
Born May 21, 23:03 - May 27, 9:24
▶ **MARS IN ARIES**
Born May 27, 9:25 - June 22, 7:11

YOUR CELEBRITY TWINS   p. 760
Find out the astrological similarities you have with famous people.

YOUR COMPATIBILITY   p. 780
Compare planets to find out how compatible you are in a relationship.

YOUR RELATIONSHIP KARMA   p. 824
▶ **SATURN IN GEMINI**
Born May 21, 23:03 - June 22, 7:11

MAUREEN O'HARA
Irish Actress
Sun in Leo

208

1943 CANCER
From June 22, 7:12 through July 23, 18:04
♋ The Loyal Supporter

Home and family are the hub around which your life revolves, Cancer of 1943. You and a partner may differ in other areas, but your common ground is likely to be the value you place on the security and connectedness you derive from your family, friends, and community. The "American Dream" is probably your dream, too, and you want a mate who helps you make that dream come true. Those closest to you know they can depend on your love and support, for when you make a commitment to someone you do your best to honor it.

Of course you realize that change is inevitable, but you try to establish constancy and stability in your personal life as much as possible, preferring one significant other to playing the field. This doesn't mean you don't have other opportunities or that you might not be tempted from time to time, but loyalty is one of your strong suits. You may be deeply devoted to your mate and do everything you can to make sure the relationship lasts. Intensely emotional, once you invest yourself in a relationship it's hard for you to live alone—being separated from your partner might seem as if you'd lost a part of yourself.

You tend to be quite demonstrative, showing affection for your partner in lots of little ways. No matter how long you've been together, you still try to keep romance alive between you. Physical contact is a form of communication for you, and touching, hugging, or curling up together in bed might be just as important to you as sex. For you, sex is best when it's combined with love and affection.

A woman who makes him feel important, without diminishing herself in the process, could claim the heart of a male Cancer born in 1943. Your ideal woman can run a household or a business efficiently, entertain with panache, and comfort you when you feel the world is against you.

Strong, vigorous men who exude sex appeal might make a female Cancer of 1943's blood race. You don't want someone who's too complicated. Give you a good-natured guy who likes kids and has a childlike joie de vivre himself—computer geeks and pretty boys had better look elsewhere.

1943 LEO
From July 23, 18:05 through August 24, 0:54
♌ The Roaring Romantic

Love is a colorful production for you, Leo of 1943, and you really get into the theatrics of romance. In love, as in other areas of life, you do things in a big way. Your relationships might sometimes resemble a Verdi opera or a Shakespearean drama, more show than substance, but at least they aren't dull. Of course, you like to star in the lead role and really shine when your lover's attention is focused on you. Love can produce the spark that fires up your creativity, and you infuse your partnerships with imagination.

You enjoy showering your partner with beautiful gifts and amorous affection. Few people are as generous as you toward those they love. It could even be said that you treat your partner like a king or queen—so long as that person shows you the respect and gratitude you crave. Like the lion, which is your zodiac symbol, you can be loyal to a partner and value the security a steady relationship offers. Family life, too, can bring you comfort and joy. But occasionally, your head might be turned by a pretty face or fine physique, for you are a true connoisseur of beauty.

Adulation is perhaps the biggest turn-on for you. A partner who worships you and makes you feel special can bring out the best in you. Your sensual nature needs to be fed, too, and you revel in all kinds of physical demonstrations of affection. A lover who uses an artistic touch to set the scene for romance can inspire an Academy Award-winning performance from you.

Leo males of 1943 appreciate women who make them feel like your symbol, the king of beasts. Your heart goes out to a partner who can take care of the details of daily life while also paying attention to your every need. Though you may admire glamorous women, you tend to prefer a modest, reserved mate who doesn't try to hog the spotlight.

Lionesses born in 1943 may adore affectionate men of substance who dote on them. Easy-going family men also score high on your list. Your best bets are often practical, down-to-earth types you can depend on for financial and emotional support, leaving you free to pursue your creative endeavors.

1943 VIRGO

From August 24, 0:55 through September 23, 22:11

The Indispensable Partner

The smallest details matter to you, Virgo of 1943, and you probably know more about your partners than they know about themselves. You notice what makes a lover happy and try your best to please. Kind-hearted and compassionate, you enjoy taking care of those you love and tend to their every need. With your efficiency, competence, and beneficence, you often make yourself indispensable to a mate. But you can also be quite critical in your attempt to perfect your partner, and although you mean well, others sometimes feel you expect too much.

Communication is one of your fortés, and you may frequently tell your partner how much he or she means to you. Sharing ideas, interests, and activities provides the glue that holds your relationship together—a partner who works in the same field as you or who enjoys your favorite hobby might suit you best. Because you are so good at examining the inner dynamics of a relationship, you can usually work through any problems that arise and find satisfactory solutions. However, you can be a bit too analytical at times, letting your head rule your heart.

It's said that the mind is the most sensitive erogenous zone, and that's probably true of you. Discussing your sexual interests and experiences might be your favorite form of foreplay. Of course, physical pleasure matters to you, too—you're an earth sign, after all. But you need a companion you can talk to, who is a friend as well as a lover.

Shy, sensitive women who possess a quiet dignity often appeal to male Virgos of 1943. You usually give your seal of approval to practical, orderly individuals who can keep a business or household running smoothly—you want a partner you can rely on to take care of every aspect of life, without a lot of fanfare.

Intelligence is the mark of a man in a 1943 female Virgo's book. Like Marilyn Monroe, you might find Einstein sexy. You want a friendly, multifaceted companion who can teach you things and share your many interests with you. A man who opens up to you and tells you what he's thinking and feeling is likely to get the "thumbs up" sign.

VIRGO ZODIAC SIGN
YOUR LOVE PLANETS

YOUR ROMANTIC SIDE — p. 696
▶ VENUS IN VIRGO
Born Aug. 24, 0:55 - Sept. 23, 22:11

YOUR SEX DRIVE — p. 722
▶ MARS IN GEMINI
Born Aug. 24, 0:55 - Sept. 23, 22:11

YOUR CELEBRITY TWINS — p. 760
Find out the astrological similarities you have with famous people.

YOUR COMPATIBILITY — p. 780
Compare planets to find out how compatible you are in a relationship.

YOUR RELATIONSHIP KARMA — p. 824
▶ SATURN IN GEMINI
Born Aug. 24, 0:55 - Sept. 23, 22:11

209

MICKEY ROONEY
American Actor
Sun and Venus in Libra

1943 LIBRA

From September 23, 22:12 through October 24, 7:07

The Discriminating Lover

It's hard to imagine you being alone for long, Libra of 1943, for love is almost as important to you as breathing. A real "people person," you like to surround yourself with amiable companions and usually have a significant other in your life. It might even be said that you seek the admiration and affection of others to reinforce your sense of self. You can be quite romantic and know how to make a partner feel special. Your charming personality, generous spirit, and easy-going nature attract many devotees, so you've probably had your share of romantic liaisons.

Despite your need to be in a relationship, you can be emotionally detached and tend to intellectualize love. Before someone gets the "go" sign from you, he or she might have to jump through a few hoops, for your standards are quite high. You might enjoy flirting (to reassure yourself that you still have "it"), but you only allow a few people to get really close to you.

Your affection can lack intensity, and in time a relationship with you may settle into a comfortable routine. In your youth, you may have seen love and sex as a game, and you played it with great skill. But later in life, you might tire of the chase, preferring a friendly alliance to grand passion. Someone with whom you can socialize and share good times, but who doesn't make too many demands on you emotionally or physically, might be an excellent partner for you.

Libra men born in 1943 tend to seek perfection and can be quite choosy about their partners. Your feminine ideal combines beauty with brains, competence with modesty, and practicality with sensitivity. You want her to be devoted to you, but clinginess can send you into a panic. Orderliness counts in your book, and you quickly hand out black marks to messy or "flaky" women.

You Libra women of 1943 prize brains over brawn or beauty. Lively, quick-witted males who keep you guessing—and laughing—rank among your favorite companions. A sense of adventure is important, too. Versatile yourself, you appreciate a partner who has many sides to his personality and is as inquisitive as you are.

LIBRA ZODIAC SIGN
YOUR LOVE PLANETS

YOUR ROMANTIC SIDE — p. 696
▶ VENUS IN VIRGO
Born Sept. 23, 22:12 - Oct. 24, 7:07

YOUR SEX DRIVE — p. 722
▶ MARS IN GEMINI
Born Sept. 23, 22:12 - Oct. 24, 7:07

YOUR CELEBRITY TWINS — p. 760
Find out the astrological similarities you have with famous people.

YOUR COMPATIBILITY — p. 780
Compare planets to find out how compatible you are in a relationship.

YOUR RELATIONSHIP KARMA — p. 824
▶ SATURN IN GEMINI
Born Sept. 23, 22:12 - Oct. 24, 7:07

JOSEPH COTTEN
American Actor
Mars in Scorpio

210

1943 SCORPIO
From October 24, 7:08 through November 23, 4:21

♏ The Ultimate Embracer

Underneath your cool, controlled exterior beats a passionate heart that feels love's joys and sorrows with great intensity. You may try to remain detached, but once Cupid's arrow strikes you, you are anything but aloof, Scorpio of 1943. Because you know how deeply you can care—and how much love can sometimes hurt—you tend to be a bit skeptical and choose your companions carefully. Only a select few are ever allowed into your inner circle. However, those who do make the cut know they can rely on your love and loyalty.

You may expect a lot from your partner, but you are usually willing to give a lot, too. Fiercely protective of your loved ones, you try your best to care and provide for them. Sometimes your caring might be viewed as possessiveness, however. You tend to be rather controlling, perhaps because you value security—and emotions, as you well know, aren't orderly or predictable. Therefore, you generally develop your partnerships slowly and cautiously. A lover who earns your trust, however, has a chance to enjoy a passionate romance with you forever.

Scorpios are known for their sex appeal, and you certainly have yours. Intimacy, however, is usually what you seek, and sex is a way of expressing your desire for closeness with the person you love. Romance and affection are just as important to you. Physical pleasure without an emotional component might not be very fulfilling to you.

Male Scorpions of 1943 usually enjoy the company of women who are analytical, sensitive, and introspective, like you. You might also appreciate someone with a caring, compassionate nature, who binds up your emotional, physical, and psychological wounds. A practical, orderly woman could help to balance your extremist tendencies.

An outgoing, sociable man with a good head on his shoulders could bring you private, sensitive Scorpio females of 1943 out of your shells. You might appreciate someone who is easy to talk to and who eagerly shares his ideas with you. Because you tend to be rather stubborn, a flexible partner who adapts to changes gracefully could be a good match for you.

1943 SAGITTARIUS
From November 23, 4:22 through December 22, 17:28

♐ The Restless Initiator

Love is a fascinating journey for you, Sagittarius of 1943. Like the rolling stone that gathers no moss, you like to stay on the move and might feel that marriage and family life limit your freedom. Your boundless curiosity and thirst for excitement could have led you to travel far and wide, and you've probably met many interesting partners along the way. Even in midlife, your restless spirit keeps you gazing at the far horizon and fantasizing about adventure. Therefore, you might be happiest with a partner who understands your independent nature and doesn't make too many demands on you.

Although you may be hard to pin down for long, you are an entertaining and fun-loving companion, so you usually find plenty of admirers with whom to share a few laughs. You're likely to be the one who initiates romance, for you tend to be impatient and seek immediate gratification. Once your interest is whetted, you can shift into high gear and go after the object of your fancy. You probably believe that variety is the spice of life, and even

if you're in a monogamous relationship you can be a bit of a flirt. You might wear a wedding ring, but that doesn't mean you stop looking.

For the most part, you take a playful approach to sex and like to have fun with your lover. A partner who wants to hold your attention might have to keep introducing new and different enticements, for you quickly grow bored. Your enthusiasm could wane if routine sets in or if a lover takes matters too seriously.

Changeable Sagittarian males of 1943 may like to experiment with all kinds of women. Often you enjoy the company of sociable, easy-going partners, but sometimes you might not be able to resist the mystery and challenge of an intensely passionate female who seems to offer a bit of danger.

Men who are as changeable and free-spirited as you are, Sagittarian women of '43, tend to appeal to you. You want a companion who can keep up with you, who's always ready to go places and do things. An intelligent man who can expand your mental horizons as well as your physical ones could be your Prince Charming.

Frank Sinatra – The Loving Crooner

Frank Sinatra, often referred to as the "Chairman of the Board" or "The Voice," was born under the freedom-loving sign of Sagittarius in humble Hoboken, New Jersey. His romantic escapades are almost as legendary as his unlikely rise to fame and fortune, and his "string of broads" reads like a who's who in Hollywood, ranging from Lauren Bacall, Ava Gardner, Angie Dickinson, Juliet Prowse, and Mia Farrow, alongside numerous cocktail waitresses, showgirls, and just about any woman who caught his eye. After all, who could resist his irresistible combination of good looks, talent, and charm. And adding to his mystique was his connection to power at both dizzying heights and depths—from Presidents Kennedy and Reagan to Mafia dons.

During the tumultuous years of World War II, the skinny crooner became the heartthrob of "bobbysoxers" all over the country who not only screamed but also swooned when "Old Blue Eyes" sang his songs of love in an easy, conversational style. And when he flashed that boyish, sexy grin, they surely thought that he was singing just to them. That feeling of being singled out as if you are the only woman in the room is typical of his Moon, which rules women as well as the emotions, in the sensitive and empathetic sign of Pisces.

As a Sagittarian, Sinatra possessed a carefree, relaxed attitude as well as a sense of wanderlust. For his first wife, Nancy Barbato, it was impossible to keep her husband in check. Though she answered the marriage proposals that were included in his voluminous fan mail with a polite rejection coupled with thanks, she was not able to stop her husband's dalliances with the beautiful women that Hollywood would offer him—Lana Turner, Marlene Dietrich and,

Frank Sinatra and his first wife Nancy at the Stork Club

211

of course, the love of his life, Ava Gardner.

After divorcing Nancy, his marriage to Gardner was tempestuous to say the least. Sexually, they were a match made in heaven but, according to Sinatra, "the quarreling started on the way to breakfast." After his divorce from Gardner, Sinatra was involved with a number of women including Lauren Bacall and Marilyn Monroe. It was Sinatra who introduced Monroe to both John and Robert Kennedy and he may have even thought of marrying her in order to keep anyone, presumably the Kennedy brothers, from bothering her again. Though that was never to pass, Sinatra did take a very unlikely bride in Mia Farrow, who was 30 years his junior and not at all the voluptuous sex goddess that Sinatra usually courted. In fact, his ex-wife Ava Gardner is said to have quipped, "I always knew Frank would end up in bed with a little boy."

But, with his Venus the planet of love in traditional Capricorn, Sinatra also married two very conventional women—Nancy Barbato, his childhood sweetheart

and mother of his three children, and Barbara Marx, his fourth wife to whom he was married from 1976 until his death in 1998. The success of his last marriage was probably due to the fact that Barbara was both a dutiful wife who made a comfortable home yet was able to give Sinatra the freedom he needed to pursue other women. So, it seems that Bacall really did understand the man even if she couldn't tame him.

"Behind that swinging facade lies a lonely, restless man . . ."

LAUREN BACALL
in her 1979 autobiography, *By Myself*

► READ ABOUT MIA FARROW AND WOODY ALLEN ON PAGE 587 ► READ ABOUT FRANK SINATRA AND AVA GARDNER ON PAGE 270

1944

- ✪ HOMOSEXUALITY
- ✪ MEET ME IN ST. LOUIS
- ✪ GASLIGHT
- ✪ GIGI
- ✪ ELLA FITZGERALD
- ✪ IS YOU IS OR IS YOU AIN'T?

Hot Movie

EVENTS

During the war, Germany tried to control its youth, saying "they get together dressed in notorious baggy or loose clothing, and under the spell of English music and dance, they attend parties full of sexual mischief." To the delight of all, clothing restrictions were lifted in Britain, leaving women free to sport pleats and men double-breasted jackets and lined pockets.

Attitudes toward homosexuality were relaxing a little. In Sweden the 1864 law that criminalized homosexuality was abolished. US War Department Circular No. 3 recommended discharge and/or hospitalization rather than court martial for the "true or confirmed homosexual."

In the UK the Queen offered thanks to all the women who had undertaken war work, and Italian women took up arms alongside their men to drive the occupiers out of their territory. Meanwhile, Martin Bormann, the German Chancellor, established a ménage à trois with his wife and mistress, justifying his actions by claiming the procreation of more children was in the national interest. His wife supported the claim.

POP CULTURE

Meet Me in St. Louis, directed by Vincente Minnelli, showcased his soon-to-be-wife Judy Garland. The classic *Gaslight* debuted, about a sociopathic husband who tries to drive his wife crazy. In *Here Come the Waves*, the hero signs up for the Navy with his buddy—they share everything including a set of twin sisters. *Bride by Mistake* gave us a pilot courting a woman posing as an heiress—he mistakenly elopes with the heiress.

Before the movie came the book. In *Gigi* by Colette, Gigi's aunt has trained her niece to be a courtesan, but the rebellious girl chooses marriage with a womanizer she reforms. In *Forever Amber* by Kathleen Winsor a poor but beautiful English girl loses her lover on her way to becoming Charles II's mistress. Elizabeth Goudge's *Green Dolphin Street* was the story of two sisters and the odd twists of fate that send them down different roads.

Duets reigned in 1944. Ella Fitzgerald teamed up with the Ink Spots for "I'm Making Believe," and Bing Crosby and the Andrews Sisters paired for "Is You Is or Is You Ain't?"

DOUBLE INDEMNITY

The careers of Barbara Stanwyck and Fred MacMurray reached a simultaneous climax in 1944, the year in which they co-starred in *Double Indemnity*. One of the finest examples of Film Noir, *Double Indemnity* featured Stanwyck as the ultimate femme fatale who seduces insurance salesman MacMurray into murdering her uncaring husband and collecting on a double indemnity insurance policy.

The plot, the love affair, and the lovers were doomed from the start, but how they met their doom made for riveting entertainment and earned the film seven Academy Award nominations, including ones for Best Picture and Best Actress for Stanwyck.

SEE ALSO

▶ **FILM NOIR** *Page 195*

▶ **HUMPHREY BOGART** *Page 235*

1944 CAPRICORN

From December 22, 1943 17:29 through January 21, 1944 4:06
(December 1944 Capricorns, see 1945 Capricorn)

♑ *The Busy Beloved*

As a 1944 Capricorn, you are always looking for ways to be of service to others. This is especially true with regard to your romantic partner. You want a relationship that makes you feel useful, valued, and productive. A mate who enjoys leaning on you for support is the perfect match for you. Because you enjoy keeping busy, you do best in a partnership that is grounded in work. Volunteering together at a charitable organization is a good way to maintain a vibrant, fulfilling union. You also enjoy intellectual challenges and may take classes with your mate as a means of entertainment.

Serving humanity is one of the guiding principles of your life, as well as your marriage. A spouse who respects your values helps you to fulfill your considerable potential as a compassionate human being. You enjoy drawing on your partner's strengths as a means of becoming a more complete person. Sexually, you can be a bit reserved and abandoning yourself to pleasure can be difficult for you. But a lover who teaches you to embrace your physical needs can allow you to thrive.

Expressing admiration for your organized mind is a good way to win your affection. You love coming to a scatterbrain's rescue. An admirer would be wise to nurture you at every opportunity. You secretly love being pampered with hot meals, comfortable surroundings, and soothing reassurances. Telling stories that are short, sweet, and to the point also wins your approval, because you are frequently pressed for time. Your admirer should make the first move toward a physical relationship. Stealing a kiss while you're focused on some small task may prove very effective.

If you're a male Goat born in 1944, you want a woman who is intelligent, loyal, and principled. You also admire spiritual ladies with deep convictions. A partner who makes you feel strong and reliable brings out the best in you.

As a 1944 female Capricorn, you enjoy a man who is restless, pensive, and smart. You love a guy who doesn't think twice about helping his fellow human beings. A mate who shares your ideals is perfectly suited to you.

CAPRICORN ZODIAC SIGN
YOUR LOVE PLANETS

YOUR ROMANTIC SIDE   p. 696
▶ **VENUS IN SCORPIO**
Born Dec. 22, 1943 17:29 - Jan. 03, 1944 4:42
▶ **VENUS IN SAGITTARIUS**
Born Jan. 03, 4:43 - Jan. 21, 4:06

YOUR SEX DRIVE   p. 722
▶ **MARS IN GEMINI**
Born Dec. 22, 1943 17:29 - Jan. 21, 1944 4:06

YOUR CELEBRITY TWINS   p. 760
Find out the astrological similarities you have with famous people.

YOUR COMPATIBILITY   p. 780
Compare planets to find out how compatible you are in a relationship.

YOUR RELATIONSHIP KARMA   p. 824
▶ **SATURN IN GEMINI**
Born Dec. 22, 1943 17:29 - Jan. 21, 1944 4:06

DANA ANDREWS
American Actor
Sun in Capricorn

213

1944 AQUARIUS

From January 21, 4:07 through February 19, 18:26

♒ *The Witty Romantic*

You 1944 Aquarians are more fun than a barrel of monkeys! Quick with jokes and compliments, it is easy to see why you have so many admirers. You prefer a romantic partner who is as clever and versatile as you are, but a little more grounded. A relationship that gives your life structure is enormously beneficial. You thrive with a mate who establishes firm ground rules. As an utterly charming person, you can be extremely flirtatious. Secretly, you love it when your beloved chastises such irreverent behavior, because you see this as a sign of love.

Most people would be surprised to know what an ardent, passionate lover you are, because you tend to hold yourself apart from crowds. Behind closed doors, however, it's easy for you to be intimate with your partner. You are extremely open-minded when it comes to sex and enjoy a mate who shares your sense of bedroom adventure. Sports and entertainment probably play a big role in your life, and can be a source of mutual pleasure for you and your partner. Taking up tennis and attending the theater together can help you keep the sparks flying.

An admirer who is heavily involved with group activities has a good chance of catching your eye. You can't help but appreciate somebody who enjoys good relationships with friends, relatives, and neighbors. Making you feel like a member of the team is a wonderful idea, because you sometimes have difficulty integrating with large crowds. You're usually eager to make the first move in a relationship. Your suitor would be wise to let the foreplay stretch out as long as possible—this can be your favorite stage of lovemaking.

Women who are friendly, visionary, and independent really excite you 1944 male Aquarians. You're also drawn to females who are tough on the outside but tender at heart. A partner who indulges your playful antics is best for you.

As a 1944 female Water-bearer, you want a man who is a colorful conversationalist. You can't abide bores. A guy whose warm affection melts your friendly reserve brings exciting new elements to your life. You do best with a loving mate.

AQUARIUS ZODIAC SIGN
YOUR LOVE PLANETS

YOUR ROMANTIC SIDE   p. 696
▶ **VENUS IN SAGITTARIUS**
Born Jan. 21, 4:07 - Jan. 28, 3:10
▶ **VENUS IN CAPRICORN**
Born Jan. 28, 3:11 - Feb. 19, 18:26

YOUR SEX DRIVE   p. 722
▶ **MARS IN GEMINI**
Born Jan. 21, 4:07 - Feb. 19, 18:26

YOUR CELEBRITY TWINS   p. 760
Find out the astrological similarities you have with famous people.

YOUR COMPATIBILITY   p. 780
Compare planets to find out how compatible you are in a relationship.

YOUR RELATIONSHIP KARMA   p. 824
▶ **SATURN IN GEMINI**
Born Jan. 21, 4:07 - Feb. 19, 18:26

MERLE OBERON
Anglo-Indian Actress
Venus in Pisces

1944 PISCES
From February 19, 18:27 through March 20, 17:48

The Restless Lover

It's not easy for you 1944 Pisceans to stand in one place. You're always on the go—which can be quite a challenge for your romantic partner. You prefer a relationship that affords plenty of freedom and movement. A mate who is content to keep the home fires burning while you explore your interests is ideal for you. Although you don't like being cooped up inside, you do want a stable, secure domestic environment. Because you probably thrive on stress in your public life, you appreciate a nurturing partner who helps you to relax after hours. You want a soothing union.

You have tremendous powers of seduction that serve you well in the bedroom. Making love is a transcendent experience for you. A warm, responsive lover brings out the best in you. You use sex as a means to connect with your partner on a spiritual level, rather than as a mere physical release. As somebody with a profound appreciation for the arts, you enjoy a partner who shares your interest in film, dance, photography, and the like. Working on creative projects with your spouse is a good way to keep your relationship healthy.

A potential mate who enjoys reading books, magazines, or newspapers has a good chance of winning your heart. You collect facts and figures with zeal, and appreciate a suitor who shares this mania. Visionaries also turn you on. You aren't impressed by stuffy folks who follow convention blindly. Your admirer would be wise to let you make the first move because you have fantastic romantic instincts. If your suitor wants to fuel the flames of your passion, a sensuous hand massage will do the trick.

If you're a 1944 male Fish, you are attracted to a wide variety of women. Private, self-contained ladies excite you, as do inventive, compassionate types. You also have a weakness for females with vivid imaginations. Your ideal partner cherishes you.

As a female Pisces who was born in 1944, you want a man who is intelligent and highly intuitive. A guy who can communicate with his eyes absolutely thrills you. You do best with a mate who can anticipate your needs and engage your thoughts.

1944 ARIES
From March 20, 17:49 through April 20, 5:17

The Affectionate Communicator

As a 1944 Ram, you love exchanging ideas with people, and particularly your romantic partner. You want a relationship that features plenty of open, honest communication. You can be quite idealistic when it comes to love partnerships, so it helps if your beloved is more grounded in reality. A spouse who reminds you of the practical concerns of a union such as paying bills and doing housework gives you a more balanced perspective on love. For this you provide your mate with generous doses of romance—which keeps your relationship exciting.

You're a very vigorous and enthusiastic sexual partner. You thrive with a spouse who enjoys your spontaneous and often humorous approach to lovemaking. For you sex is a primarily physical release that has the added benefit of drawing you closer to your mate. At heart, you're just a great big kid, and probably enjoy going on fun romps with your beloved. A lover who shares your childlike sense of joy wins your everlasting affection. You want a partnership that is firmly founded on optimism.

Attracting your attention is as simple as proposing fun outings. Visiting a carnival, zoo, or circus is a great way to forge a romance with you. You also enjoy the performing arts, and would welcome an invitation to a play or a concert. There's a good chance you're a big sports fan, so attending a football or tennis match is a fine idea, too. You don't care who makes the first move in a relationship, as long as it's done fairly quickly. Because you like to know where you stand, it's a good idea for your admirer to respond to your initial kisses with energy and enthusiasm. Playing hard-to-get doesn't interest you at all.

Women who are easy-going and generous really appeal to you 1944 male Rams. You can't abide high maintenance types. You also enjoy feisty, aggressive ladies. A partner who makes you laugh is your ideal match.

Men who are talkative, playful, and lively attract you 1944 female Ariens. You're also drawn to tender, nurturing types. Ultimately, you want a mate who is both a lover and a playmate. Pessimistic guys leave you cold.

1944 TAURUS
From April 20, 5:18 through May 21, 4:50

The Enterprising Sweetheart

Quick-thinking and resourceful, you 1944 Bulls always know what your priorities are. At the top of your list is romance. You value a partner who is loyal, steady, and magnetic. Flighty types make you nervous. You want a relationship you can rely on for love, support, and comfort. You probably spend lots of time working so that you and your partner can lead a life of luxury. Consequently, you do best with a mate who encourages your efforts and appreciates all the luxuries it affords. Your home is a source of pride for you, and you benefit from a spouse who enjoys turning your abode into a showplace for guests.

It takes you a while to get in the mood for love. A partner who is proficient in the fine art of seduction brings out the best in you. You enjoy having sex for hours, and hate being hurried in bed. Although you are undeniably sensual, that doesn't mean you are selfish. You give as much as you receive. You are also an extremely compassionate person, and may perform charitable works with your partner as a means to strengthen your relationship. You

have no desire for a partnership that is based only on materialism.

Someone with a profound sense of inner peace can win your heart. There's a good chance you have a delicate nervous system, so you appreciate an admirer whose very presence puts you at ease. As you may be somewhat of a chatterbox, you also enjoy a suitor who is a good listener. You'd rather have your partner make the first move toward a physical relationship. Lingering over foreplay is advised, since this is probably your favorite phase of lovemaking.

If you're a male Bull who was born in 1944, you want a woman who is romantic, imaginative, and affectionate. You're also drawn to sensual ladies with strong desires. A mate who constantly reassures you of her love and devotion is your perfect match.

Men who are vivacious, clever, and sensitive excite you female Taureans who were born in 1944. You love a good storyteller. Moody, silent types drive you to distraction. A partner who entertains and engages you is sure to win your lifelong devotion.

TAURUS ZODIAC SIGN
YOUR LOVE PLANETS

YOUR ROMANTIC SIDE   p. 696
► VENUS IN ARIES
Born Apr. 20, 5:18 - May 04, 22:03
► VENUS IN TAURUS
Born May 04, 22:04 - May 21, 4:50

YOUR SEX DRIVE   p. 722
► MARS IN CANCER
Born Apr. 20, 5:18 - May 21, 4:50

YOUR CELEBRITY TWINS   p. 760
Find out the astrological similarities you have with famous people.

YOUR COMPATIBILITY   p. 780
Compare planets to find out how compatible you are in a relationship.

YOUR RELATIONSHIP KARMA   p. 824
► SATURN IN GEMINI
Born Apr. 20, 5:18 - May 21, 4:50

LAURENCE OLIVIER
English Actor
Sun in Taurus

215

1944 GEMINI
From May 21, 4:51 through June 21, 13:01

The Loving Inquisitor

As a 1944 Gemini, you have an insatiable need to know everything about everybody, especially your romantic partner. You love trying to figure out what makes your mate tick, and enjoy peppering your beloved with a slew of questions. A relationship that provides you with constant mental stimulation is your idea of heaven. You do well with a mate who has a wide variety of interests. As someone who enjoys creature comforts, you do your best to create a luxurious lifestyle for you and your mate. You secretly think of your life as a spectacular movie and want both a household and relationship that supports this fantasy. Glamorous surroundings bring out the romantic in you.

Because practicality may not be your strong suit, you do benefit from a spouse who attends to mundane matters such as paying bills, making appointments, and completing chores. In return, you pamper your beloved with sentimental gestures. When it comes to sex, you need a little motivation. Books and movies may be your chief sexual inspiration. A lover who keeps you in a sensual mindset brings out

the best in you. You enjoy most a partnership that emphasizes both your sexual and intellectual appeal.

Discussing current events is a surefire way to win your approval. You admire a person who is engaged with the world. Asking you for a good book recommendation is also advised because you're probably an extremely avid reader. Celebrity gossip may be one of your favorite topics, so your suitor would be wise to peruse the tabloids before meeting with you. When you're attracted to somebody, you don't waste any time making the first move. Nothing turns you on like a talkative lover. You can't abide silent sex.

As a 1944 male Gemini, you appreciate a woman who is responsive yet reserved. You're also drawn to enthusiastic, decisive ladies. A smart partner who can hold your interest is ideal for you.

Men who are down-to-earth but imaginative captivate you 1944 female Geminis. Guys who are warm and spontaneous also attract you. You want a mate who is both a good conversationalist and an affectionate lover.

GEMINI ZODIAC SIGN
YOUR LOVE PLANETS

YOUR ROMANTIC SIDE   p. 696
► VENUS IN TAURUS
Born May 21, 4:51 - May 29, 8:38
► VENUS IN GEMINI
Born May 29, 8:39 - June 21, 13:01

YOUR SEX DRIVE   p. 722
► MARS IN CANCER
Born May 21, 4:51 - May 22, 14:15
► MARS IN LEO
Born May 22, 14:16 - June 21, 13:01

YOUR CELEBRITY TWINS   p. 760
Find out the astrological similarities you have with famous people.

YOUR COMPATIBILITY   p. 780
Compare planets to find out how compatible you are in a relationship.

YOUR RELATIONSHIP KARMA   p. 824
► SATURN IN GEMINI
Born May 21, 4:51 - June 20, 7:49
► SATURN IN CANCER
Born June 20, 7:50 - June 21, 13:01

AARON COPLAND
American Composer
Mars in Leo

1944 CANCER
 From June 21, 13:02 through July 22, 23:55

The Conservative Suitor

You 1944 Crabs aren't terribly forthcoming about your feelings, at least not in words. You prefer to demonstrate your affection through your actions. A partner who craves both emotional and financial stability is best suited to you. You want a relationship based on a mutual desire to build time-honored traditions and solid foundations. You probably have a strong subconscious need to create a happy family with your partner, whether that means having lots of children or building a loving community of faithful friends. You appreciate a spouse who provides you with a warm and comfortable domestic environment.

Although you may be somewhat shy, you are definitely highly sexual. An intuitive, seductive lover never fails to bring out your sensual side. Sexual fidelity is very important to you, and it's highly unlikely you'd ever stray from your marriage. You may possess hidden creative talents that only your partner recognizes. A supportive mate who encourages you to exercise your imagination wins a special place in your heart.

An admirer who is intent on understanding your thoughts and feelings is sure to make a good impression on you. You have no interest in conducting a relationship based on sheer physical attraction. Expressing an interest in home and family is also a plus—you're quite domestic at heart. Your suitor would be wise to make the first move with you because you can be uncertain in the initial stages of a romance. Creating a romantic setting for your first kiss is sure to get an enthusiastic response from you.

As a 1944 male Cancer, you are attracted to a wide variety of women. Sentimental, versatile ladies turn you on, as do sociable and insightful females. You're also drawn to generous, loving women. You do best with a partner who believes in the enduring power of love.

You 1944 female Crabs enjoy men who are magnetic, traditional, and sensual. Refined, intellectual guys also can turn you on. A mate who is eager to accept all the love you have to give brings out the best in you. You have no interest in a partner who is independent and aloof.

1944 LEO   *From July 22, 23:56 through August 23, 6:45*

The Quiet Admirer

Although you 1944 Lions aren't very effusive about your affections, you do have a profound capacity for love. Your partner is probably the most important person in the world to you. A relationship that has a karmic quality about it appeals to you the most. There's a good chance you believe in pre-ordained romances. And although you enjoy spending plenty of private time with your beloved, an active social life is still important to you. A gregarious mate who shares your appreciation for unusual, visionary people brings out the best in you. Because you're quite a forceful personality, it helps if your partner lets you take the lead in most situations.

You positively exude sex appeal and may enjoy seducing your partner whenever and wherever possible. A lover who wants to be sexually overpowered thrills you to no end. For you making love is both a divine physical release and a means to maintain intimacy with your mate. You're an extremely visual person and appreciate a well-dressed, perfectly groomed partner. Since you have a tendency to daydream,

it is wise that you pair up with a practical spouse who can bring you back down to earth.

Admirers with a flair for the dramatic may appeal to you. You're turned on by folks who aren't afraid to express their passion for life. A suitor who makes you feel needed and appreciated also has a good chance of winning your heart. You enjoy nothing more than coming to the rescue of a love interest. Your admirer should make the first move toward a physical relationship, as you prefer being pursued. A lover who plants hot kisses on your ears and neck is sure to make sexual headway with you.

If you're a male Lion born in 1944, you want a woman who is exceptionally glamorous and beautiful. You're also attracted to prim, ladylike females. A partner who makes you feel you're all man is your perfect match.

Men who are shy, reliable, and considerate excite you 1944 female Leos. You can't abide a rude man who always wants to dominate the conversation. You do best with an attentive mate who is willing to yield center stage to you.

216

1944 VIRGO

From August 23, 6:46 through September 23, 4:01

The Sociable Seducer

As a 1944 Virgo, you're apt to make friends wherever you go. There's a good chance that your romantic partner started out as one of your many pals. Even if your mate wasn't a member of your social circle originally, you probably consider your beloved to be your best friend. You want a relationship that is based on mutual respect and affection. A tempestuous partnership wouldn't suit you at all. Because you're likely to be a visionary, you need a mate who supports your ground-breaking ideas. Such a spouse prevents you from feeling alienated in a world that can be slow to change.

You're a dedicated, serious lover who demands total fidelity from your partner. Although you appear to prize independence, an open relationship is not for you. You've got an earthy sensuality that becomes richer with age. It's likely that you have a driving ambition to attain material wealth, and benefit from a partner who draws you closer to this goal. Although you're extremely resourceful, you need a mate who encourages you to take occasional risks as a means to get bigger and better earning opportunities.

A fun-loving admirer with loads of creative talent is bound to attract your attention. You sometimes have difficulty letting go of your reserve, and admire unselfconscious folks. Imaginative types also turn you on, probably because there is an artist that is buried deep within you. Such a suitor can help liberate your creativity. You don't feel comfortable making the first move in a relationship. An admirer would be wise to initiate a physical relationship with a gentle kiss, and then let your natural giving instincts take over.

Women who are resourceful, creative, and analytical really excite you 1944 male Virgos. You're also attracted to graceful, intelligent ladies. A loving mate who is both a good conversationalist and a loyal friend is your ideal.

If you're a female Virgo who was born in 1944, you want a man who is tastefully discriminating. Men who are gracious and proper also turn you on. You do best with a partner whose wit and elegance softens the harsher aspects of life.

JOAN FONTAINE
American Actress
Sun in Libra

1944 LIBRA

From September 23, 4:02 through October 23, 12:55

The Sexy Superstar

You 1944 Librans have a tendency to draw admiring stares wherever you go. Your animal magnetism could have attracted many romantic opportunities throughout your lifetime. A partner who understands your need to be praised and appreciated by the public is the perfect match for you. You have no desire for a possessive relationship. One of the best ways to promote togetherness with your mate is through travel. You dislike staying in one place for too long and appreciate a fun-loving spouse who is as adventurous as you are when it comes to seeing the world.

Although you are likely attractive, you may be a little self-conscious when it comes to sex. A spouse who helps you see what a sexy, desirable creature you are brings out the best in you. When given the proper encouragement, you can be a tender and enthusiastic lover. There's a good chance you've been blessed with a strong intuition—which helps you sense whenever your partner is troubled or sad. In exchange for your compassion, your mate should encourage you to use your talents to

help others. A relationship that treats your sensitivity as an asset allows you to thrive.

Inviting you for a home-cooked gourmet meal is a surefire way to win your affection. An admirer who fixes something special makes you feel honored and privileged. Asking you for wardrobe or decorating advice is also a way to catch your interest because you pride yourself on your impeccable taste. Your suitor should make an extra effort to ensure that the surroundings of your first physical encounter are beautiful and romantic. Kissing beneath the light of a full moon is sure to fuel your passion.

If you're a male Libra born in 1944, you want a woman who is sensitive, artistic, and smart. Ladies who are passionate and intense also can turn you on. A partner who helps you to further appreciate the beauty of life is your ideal.

As a 1944 female Libra, you want a guy who is diplomatic, social, and solicitous. You're also drawn to perceptive, moody men who can go to romantic extremes. You need a mate who makes you feel you're the sexiest woman alive.

HEDY LAMARR
Austrian Actress
Sun in Scorpio

218

1944 SCORPIO
From October 23, 12:56 through November 22, 10:07

♏ ## The Patient Paramour

The motto for you 1944 Scorpions may be "Good things come to those who wait." You set high standards, especially when it comes to romance. A relationship with an exceptional partner is your ideal. Pairing up with someone just for the sake of companionship is not your style at all. You won't settle. You may be a passionate lover, and you'd benefit from a mate who likes being pursued. The thrill of the chase makes your eyes sparkle. You also enjoy asserting your authority and thrive with a partner who is turned on by your powerful personality.

You're one of the most inventive lovers around and are always eager to try different techniques to excite your mate. A partner who is willing to make love at any time in any place is best suited to you because you can become aroused very quickly. You might think nothing of waking your mate in the middle of the night to have sex. You are also quite a spiritual person and appreciate a spouse who encourages you to explore your beliefs. Although you don't care whether your partner shares your faith, you do want your beloved to respect it.

Eluding your probing questions is a sure way to spark your interest. The more elusive your admirer, the more attracted you can become. Expressing an interest in philosophy or religion is also a good way to win your heart—you enjoy discussing the meaning of life with others. Superficial conversation leaves you cold. Your suitor would be wise to let you make the first move because you prefer to call the shots in a relationship. Following your sexual lead is sure to bring about pleasing results. For a passionate encounter your admirer should drop all inhibitions.

If you're a male Scorpion who was born in 1944, you want a feisty woman who knows her own mind. You're also attracted to strong-willed females who are extremely ambitious. A mate who poses a challenge is perfect for you.

Men who are secretive and mysterious give you 1944 female Scorpions a thrill. As far as you're concerned, a guy who wears his heart on his sleeve is a supreme bore. You want a partner who always keeps you guessing.

1944 SAGITTARIUS
From November 22, 10:08 through December 21, 23:14

♐ ## The Nurturing Partner

Sweet, giving, and tender, you 1944 bold Sagittarians are true treasures in the romance department. Your first priority is to make your partner feel happy, valued, and comfortable. You want a relationship that thrives on give-and-take. One-sided partnerships hold no charm for you. Although you do need a union that affords you plenty of personal freedom, you have no intention of leaving your mate out in the cold. Rather, you pursue solitary hobbies as a means to keep your relationship from going stale. As far as you're concerned, there is nothing more stifling than being joined to your partner at the hip.

Sex may be one of the most important aspects of a relationship for you. As far as you're concerned, making love isn't merely a physical release, but a means to maintain intimacy with your beloved. You appreciate a lover who is enthusiastic and responsive in bed. It helps if your spouse is quite social, since you probably have loads of friends. A partner who enjoys entertaining your pals into the wee hours of the night wins both your admiration and loyalty.

A good way to catch your eye is to reach out to underprivileged people. You feel a strong kinship with humanitarians. Nurturing you is also a wise idea because you tend to get burned out from caring for everybody else. Because you are probably quite active, expressing an interest in sports and outdoor activities may win your heart, too. You're apt to make the first move toward a physical relationship quite soon—you tend to act on your impulses. A suitor would be wise to pay special attention to your calves and thighs during foreplay—those are most likely very sensitive parts of your body.

Women who are romantic, traditional, and practical are extremely attractive to you 1944 male Archer. You're also drawn to intelligent, visionary ladies. A mate who celebrates your tender, protective ways is your ideal.

If you're a female Archer born in 1944, you want a man who is social and spiritually substantial. Guys who are sexy and intense also appeal to you. Ultimately, you want a partner with profound emotional depths.

Judy Garland – The Rainbow Goddess

From her stage debut at two years old to her death from a drug overdose at 47, Judy Garland lived her life onstage. She was constantly in the public eye, and the pressures to perform made her personal relationships difficult and short-lived. A psychologist could easily make the connection between her troubled childhood and her string of five unsuccessful marriages, and perhaps her self-destructive habits of binge-and-purge eating, drinking, and pill-popping. Yet in spite of her personal problems, Garland had millions of fans and made some of the most memorable films in Hollywood history.

As a fast-paced Gemini, Garland took making more than one movie at a time in stride. From 1938 to 1948 she made 25 films, often moving from one set to the next in the course of a day. Her big break in showbiz came along when she teamed up with Mickey Rooney in the fourth installment of the Andy Hardy movies. The two made several more Andy Hardy flicks and musicals over the next few years, but her 1939 role as Dorothy in *The Wizard of Oz* became an instant classic and confirmed her status as a star. One critic wrote, "In Judy's Dorothy there is a plea for love and protection which communicated itself with alarming depth." For this role she received her only Oscar—for Best Juvenile Performance.

Astrologically, one of the most significant factors in Garland's horoscope is Pluto, which was right on her Cancer Rising sign when she was born. Pluto Rising is all about power. As a youngster, Garland was totally under someone else's

"I can live without money, but I cannot live without love."

JUDY GARLAND

219

power. Her mother pushed her onstage, and when she was at MGM her entire existence was controlled by L.B. and Ethel Mayer, the studio owners. The Mayers forced her to give up dating Tyrone Power because they thought it was bad for her image. She was given diet pills to help her lose weight, and when she couldn't sleep at night, she was given sedatives.

Garland found it difficult to seize control of her own life. The only time she felt her own power was when she was singing. Her voice mysteriously, magically tapped into the fathomless depths of the soul, so that she sang with an intensity and passion that touched others deeply,

often moving them to tears of joy. In 1944 she starred in *Meet Me in St. Louis*, a charming, heart-warming musical that became MGM's best-selling box office hit after *Gone With the Wind*. This movie highlights the Judy Garland we like to remember best, the singing and dancing actress who brought freshness and sincerity to her roles.

The next year she married Vincente Minnelli, the director of *Meet Me in St. Louis*, and the following year gave birth to Liza. This new responsibility left her in a state of confusion and depression. In 1949 Garland's film career hit rock bottom when her pill habit prevented her from making *Annie Get Your Gun,* and she was fired. However, Pluto Rising is like the legendary phoenix, and after flaming out in Hollywood, she rose again in the 1950s by performing concerts onstage. Her signature song "Over the Rainbow" created an emotional rapport with audiences that was peerless, and she is generally regarded as one of the greatest stage performers of the 20th century.

► READ ABOUT TYRONE POWER ON PAGE 188 ► READ ABOUT EDITH PIAF ON PAGE 269

1945

- ⍟ FRENCH CENSORSHIP
- ⍟ ALFRED EISENSTAEDT
- ⍟ BLITHE SPIRIT
- ⍟ ALFRED HITCHCOCK
- ⍟ IMMORTAL WIFE
- ⍟ PORTRAIT OF A MARRIAGE
- ⍟ IT'S ONLY A PAPER MOON

EVENTS

At the end of the war the French government censored all movies shown in France and previewed scripts before filming began, but finally gave women the right to vote.

Adolf Hitler described his relationship with Eva Braun as nothing more than her having given him "many years of loyal friendship." He then married her, but according to many authorities, they never consummated their marriage and two days later they both committed suicide.

Professional photographer Alfred Eisenstaedt snapped one of the most famous photographs in history—a sailor kissing a nurse—and it appeared on the cover of *Life* magazine.

POP CULTURE

Based on the popular Noel Coward play, the movie *Blithe Spirit* debuted, about a novelist and his second wife who are visited by the ghost of his first wife. *Spellbound*, directed by Alfred Hitchcock, was about a female psychiatrist with an amnesiac patient who is a murder suspect. *Mildred Pierce* featured a businesswoman's daughter and second husband who embark on a romantic affair with predictably unhappy results. In *The Enchanted Cottage* a disfigured war veteran and his less than perfect bride find each other beautiful in their special beach cottage.

Irving Stone's bestselling book, *Immortal Wife*, is a biographical novel and love story about Jessie Benton Fremont, one of the strongest women

in American history. In *Cass Timberlane* by Sinclair Lewis a respectable Minnesota judge marries a sexy younger woman who has trouble mixing with his snobby, middle-aged friends. Evelyn Waugh's *Brideshead Revisited* gave us Charles Ryder, who forms a romantic friendship with Lord Sebastian Flyte, the charming son of an old Catholic family verging on dissolution, then falls in love with Sebastian's sister. *Portrait of a Marriage* by Pearl S. Buck was set in the early 1900s and follows the ups and downs of a marriage between a poor hard-working girl and a wealthy man.

On the radio we heard Bing Crosby croon "It's Been a Long, Long Time" and Perry Como sang "If I Loved You" and "'Til the End of Time." Ella Fitzgerald released "It's Only a Paper Moon," and "There, I've Said It Again" by Vaughn Monroe became a hit.

Hot Couple

ADOLF HITLER & EVA BRAUN

The wedding of Adolph Hitler and Eva Braun, on April 29, 1945, brought a strange and morbid conclusion to Germany's involvement in World War II and to history's most puzzling romance.

Capping a relationship that lasted sixteen years, the marriage was followed by a suicide pact carried out on April 30. With Allied forces bearing down on Berlin, Eva Braun took poison and Hitler shot himself in the head. British comedian Eddie Izzard captured the absurd futility of the Hitler family nuptials by noting that the two spent their "honeymoon in a bunker, covered with petrol, and on fire."

SEE ALSO

▶ *LES ENFANTS DU PARADIS* Page 227

▶ MARLENE DIETRICH *Page 105*

1945 CAPRICORN

From December 21, 1944 23:15 through January 20, 1945 9:53
(December 1945 Capricorns, see 1946 Capricorn)

♑ *The Loving Traditionalist*

You, 1945 Capricorn, are a complex blend of tenderness and reserve, making it difficult for others to know where they stand with you. Though you have a tough exterior and don't often let your feelings show, you are quite compassionate and gentle at heart. You don't let compliments fall easily from your lips, so when you do flatter others, they can be sure that you are sincere in your praise and that you really appreciate them.

You are as reserved when it comes to lovemaking as you are in other situations. But, your beloved would be seriously in error if your formality is mistaken for detachment. Once you are emotionally involved with someone, you are as ardent and passionate as anyone. A determined and faithful lover, you can be depended upon to use both your sensitivity and incredible staying power to know how to please and delight your partner.

To get your attention, a prospective mate should demonstrate that they have a healthy respect for work and a dedication for service to others. They might suggest spending an afternoon volunteering at the local Habitat for Humanity construction site. Or, because you also love history and tradition, you would enjoy an afternoon shopping for antiques or even rummaging through the memorabilia in the attic.

The ideal woman for the 1945 Capricorn male is someone who has a dreamy and romantic nature yet understands and supports your driving ambition. You want a woman who is as flexible as you are uncompromising and who can be a compassionate counterpart to your stern and disciplined nature. Since you are a perfectionist, she needs to be a gentle soul who can encourage you through your darker moments when you may be feeling less than ideal.

1945 Capricorn female, your perfect man is goal-oriented and someone who is willing to go the extra mile to achieve his dreams. He should be capable of hard work, patience, and perseverance, all qualities that you possess in great abundance. You also want someone who matches your passion and is secure enough in his own right to honor your need to be independent and in control of your own life.

CAPRICORN ZODIAC SIGN
Your Love Planets

YOUR ROMANTIC SIDE   p. 696
- ▶ **VENUS IN AQUARIUS**
  Born Dec. 21, 1944 23:15 - Jan. 05, 1945 19:17
- ▶ **VENUS IN PISCES**
  Born Jan. 05, 19:18 - Jan. 20, 9:53

YOUR SEX DRIVE   p. 722
- ▶ **MARS IN SAGITTARIUS**
  Born Dec. 21, 1944 23:15 - Jan. 05, 1945 19:30
- ▶ **MARS IN CAPRICORN**
  Born Jan. 05, 19:31 - Jan. 20, 9:53

YOUR CELEBRITY TWINS   p. 760
Find out the astrological similarities you have with famous people.

YOUR COMPATIBILITY   p. 780
Compare planets to find out how compatible you are in a relationship.

YOUR RELATIONSHIP KARMA   p. 824
- ▶ **SATURN IN CANCER**
  Born Dec. 21, 1944 23:15 - Jan. 20, 1945 9:53

JAMES MASON
English Actor
Mars in Aquarius

1945 AQUARIUS

From January 20, 9:54 through February 19, 0:14

♒ *The Original Thinker*

You are definitely one of a kind, 1945 Aquarius, and you can always be counted on to surprise others with your unique point of view. Since you love to be a wee bit contrary, just when someone thinks they know how you'll react, you love to shift gears and take off in a different direction. Methodical and discriminating, you are at your best when you use your fine mind to discover a new perspective or solution for routine problems.

Your lovemaking style is as interesting, original, and unpredictable as you are. Always ready for fun and trying something new, you are not afraid of experimentation. In fact, you depend on it to keep things from getting too monotonous. Though you are inventive and kinky, you are also surprisingly comfortable in a traditionally romantic setting complete with flowers, candlelight, and soft music.

A rebel at heart, the best way to get your attention is to engage you in conversation about your favorite cause. Whether it is vegetarianism, the environment, or social justice, you throw yourself passionately into your beliefs and are all too happy to tell others about them as well. You admire creativity so a prospective partner needs to demonstrate that they can use their imagination. They'd do well to share their latest inspiration with you— poetry, arts and crafts, or even nouvelle cuisine would strike your fancy.

1945 Aquarius male, your perfect woman is someone who enjoys exploring the unusual and the unknown. She should be an intelligent, lively conversationalist who loves to socialize as much as you do. And, she needs to be down to earth so that she can relate to people from all walks of life with ease. But, most of all, she needs to genuinely be herself for if there is anything you can't abide it is a phony.

The ideal man for you, 1945 Aquarius female, is someone who is energetic, dynamic, and fiercely determined. In order to gain your respect and devotion, he also needs to possess a great deal of integrity. Discipline is also very important to you and you need to be around a man who knows how to channel his energy in a constructive manner.

AQUARIUS ZODIAC SIGN
Your Love Planets

YOUR ROMANTIC SIDE   p. 696
- ▶ **VENUS IN PISCES**
  Born Jan. 20, 9:54 - Feb. 02, 8:06
- ▶ **VENUS IN ARIES**
  Born Feb. 02, 8:07 - Feb. 19, 0:14

YOUR SEX DRIVE   p. 722
- ▶ **MARS IN CAPRICORN**
  Born Jan. 20, 9:54 - Feb. 14, 9:57
- ▶ **MARS IN AQUARIUS**
  Born Feb. 14, 9:58 - Feb. 19, 0:14

YOUR CELEBRITY TWINS   p. 760
Find out the astrological similarities you have with famous people.

YOUR COMPATIBILITY   p. 780
Compare planets to find out how compatible you are in a relationship.

YOUR RELATIONSHIP KARMA   p. 824
- ▶ **SATURN IN CANCER**
  Born Jan. 20, 9:54 - Feb. 19, 0:14

JOAN CRAWFORD
American Actress
Sun in Aries

222

1945 PISCES
From February 19, 0:15 through March 20, 23:36

The Intuitive Revolutionary

Restless and rebellious, 1945 Pisces, you are on a lifelong quest to change the status quo. Never content with things as they are, you have an insatiable need to make the world a better place. When it comes to relationships, you may find that you are constantly searching for something more. And, the deeper intimacy that you are looking for may elude you until you begin to understand yourself more fully.

Blessed with a great deal of intuition, you are one of those people who can sense what others want. Gifted at unspoken communication, you can read your partner's desires quite easily as well as to transmit your own needs. Your lovemaking style is passionate and all encompassing, making you an electrifying lover. And, the act of merging with another both empowers you and leaves you yearning for your next encounter.

In order to catch your eye, a prospective mate needs to be graceful and understated. Though you are very comfortable in social situations, you also really enjoy one-on-one communication most. Sharing their innermost secrets and fantasies is a great way for a loved one to draw you to them for you can't resist these gestures of closeness. But, to really capture your heart, a partner needs to be spiritually in tune with you.

The perfect woman for a 1945 Pisces male is one who is high-spirited and a bit impulsive. You want someone who can be wild and carefree and who has a way of making everyday things seem like a grand adventure. But, you also want a woman who can be levelheaded when necessary—someone with common sense, who knows how to solve problems. Above all, you need a woman who can be a source of strength during difficult times and multifaceted enough to hold your interest.

1945 Pisces female, your ideal man is someone who enjoys intellectual pursuits as much as you do. It is also important for him to be broadminded enough to accept some of your more far-reaching, zany ideas. He should share your compassion for those who are less fortunate and be a stable and supportive shoulder for you to lean on when the harsh realities of the world get you down.

1945 ARIES
From March 20, 23:37 through April 20, 11:06

The Reluctant Leader

You alternate between feeling comfortably in control and not knowing what you want at all, Aries of 1945. Others depend on you to set the pace but often you may feel as if it is a case of "the blind leading the blind." Feelings are hard for you to express and, therefore, you may seem aloof or dispassionate. But, nothing could be further from the truth. You want nothing more than to be fully engaged in an intimate relationship with another.

Your lovemaking style is as complex and enigmatic as you are. It's not that you intentionally try to baffle your mate but they can never be sure of your shifting moods. Sometimes you enjoy taking the lead in the bedroom but you often like to surrender control to your partner. Either way, you easily immerse yourself in whichever role you are playing and thoroughly enjoy the pleasure of being one with your beloved.

You are uncharacteristically reserved for an Aries and you may wait for a prospective partner to let you know that they are interested before you make a move. Since you place a high regard on honesty and straightforwardness, it is always wise to approach you in an open and friendly way. But, you do enjoy the challenge of the chase and so it is best for a potential lover to keep you guessing just a little bit about their feelings. In other words, you need both encouragement and mystery from a mate.

1945 Aries male, your ideal woman is patient, reliable, and able to recognize that you are a man of complex emotions and varied interests. It is important that she give you the encouragement that you need to pursue your favorite leisure activities, especially the physical ones. She's strong in her own way and is an equal partner, seeming to know instinctively how to make you laugh.

The perfect man for the 1945 Aries female is one who is easygoing, flexible, and able to adapt to your varying wants and needs. He needs to be secure enough to let you have your own way and understands your strong need for independence. Yet, he should also be savvy enough to be aware of the times when what you really want is for him to take control.

1945 TAURUS

From April 20, 11:07 through May 21, 10:39

The Beauty Seeker

You are quite creative, 1945 Taurus, and have a wonderful way of seeing the splendor and majesty in everyday things. Blessed with an exquisite, elegant sense of style and a childlike curiosity about life, you possess a quiet self-confidence that is quite attractive to others. You may sometimes be a bit too self-indulgent but you easily make up for it with your charm and grace. Eager to participate in all that life has to offer, money is very important to you, both for what it can buy and the security it provides.

When it comes to lovemaking, you have a voracious appetite and you are always ready to feast on the sumptuously sensual banquet that your lover has to offer. Physical intimacy invigorates you and you need to express yourself in lovemaking in order to be productive in the other areas of your life. It is in those intimate moments that you share with another that you feel most alive and fulfilled.

The best way for a prospective partner to get your attention is to be well dressed and self-assured. It is not that you are shallow—you just have an aesthetic awareness that must be satisfied before you can venture any deeper into a relationship. You love the outdoors, so a potential lover would be wise to suggest a picnic in an extraordinarily beautiful setting, complete with delectable food and drink to delight all your senses.

1945 Taurus male, you place a high value on harmony and tranquility, and your ideal woman needs to appreciate your need for a calm and serene environment. It is also very important that she shares your fondness for beautiful things and enjoys entertaining. Above all, you are quite traditional and you want a woman that understands your need to be close to your family.

Your perfect man, 1945 Taurus female, knows what he wants and knows how to get it. You want your man to be powerful and overflowing with confidence and savoir-faire, one who is a brilliant thinker and has the perseverance to finish what he starts. Ambition and decisiveness is important to you and you would easily lose respect for a man who lacked strength of character.

223

JEAN-PAUL SARTRE
French Writer
Sun in Gemini

1945 GEMINI

From May 21, 10:40 through June 21, 18:51

The Versatile Raconteur

Born with the proverbial gift of gab, you pride yourself on your ability to converse intelligently on just about any topic, 1945 Gemini. You are full of surprises and may even have been a bit of a radical in your early years. Inventive and original, you certainly have your share of fascinating stories to tell. Communication is an essential ingredient in relationships and, more than anything, you want someone with whom you can talk as well as being able to share the comfortable silences.

Magnetic and sexy, others are drawn to your irrepressible charm and wit. But, you don't take yourself too seriously and find it difficult to understand what all the fuss is about. You carefully guard your personal freedom and heavy emotional scenes and clinging partners are a sure turn-off. The same is true for your lovemaking style—you like to keep things light and breezy and, most of all, fun.

You have a seemingly inexhaustible storehouse of energy and a potential partner needs to be able to keep up with you. In order to get your attention, they might suggest boating, golfing, tennis, or bicycling—anything that keeps you in motion. And, an evening out with friends, dancing to some good old rock and roll or taking in the latest hot concert group, is sure to win your heart.

The ideal woman for the 1945 Gemini male is someone who is quick-witted and able to juggle a busy schedule. You want someone with a daring spirit, who likes to experiment and with whom you can share your many interests. But, you also need someone who can keep her feet on the ground, especially during those times when you have taken on too much. She needs to understand that, for you, variety is the spice of life and not force you into a rigid routine.

1945 Gemini female, your perfect man is a pioneer and someone who definitely walks to the beat of a different drummer. You enjoy someone who is not likely to accept the status quo and is willing to question why things are the way they are. He should be as high-spirited and freedom loving as you and be ready to share a lifetime of hilarious escapades.

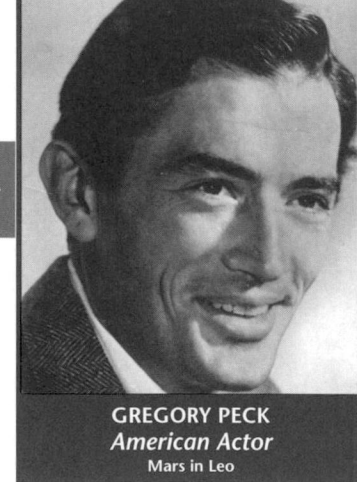

GREGORY PECK
American Actor
Mars in Leo

1945 CANCER  *From June 21, 18:52 through July 23, 5:44*

 ## The Sentimental Collector

Sensitive and protective, 1945 Cancer, you are blessed with the power to soothe and comfort others. You love to be needed and are at your best when you are taking care of those you love. In relationships, you are dependable and faithful, and you are capable of great sacrifice. Known for your incredible memory, you love to reminisce by looking through the photo album or rearranging cherished mementoes given to you by dear friends or souvenirs you picked up on vacations.

You are extremely sensuous, appreciative of varying smells, tastes, and textures, and especially enjoy anything soft and lush. You attach a great deal of sentimentality to your belongings, especially if a loved one gave them to you. Though you may seem reserved, you are a passionate and tender lover who is always ready to give anything in order to please your partner. You take lovemaking seriously and are not the type to engage in sex without love or commitment.

To get your attention, a potential partner might suggest an afternoon trip shopping for antiques or a visit to a museum for a special showing of vintage clothing and toys. Any prospective lover should share your appreciation for the past. Or you might enjoy seeing a classic black and white film, or visiting a cooking school to see how the pros do it.

1945 Cancer male, your ideal woman is as solid as the rock of Gibraltar. You want someone who is patient, kind, and giving and who makes home and family a priority. She should share your love of the finer things in life and understand your need to maintain your connections with your family. Once you have found your ladylove, you are not likely to stray and you need someone who is as loyal as you.

The perfect man for the 1945 Cancer female is one who is compassionate and understanding of your emotional nature. Your man should be able to safeguard your feelings and allow you the latitude you need to express them fully. He should also be hardworking, determined, and steadfast—in short, someone you can count on. Most of all, he should share your need to create a stable and traditional family life.

1945 LEO *From July 23, 5:45 through August 23, 12:34*

 ## The Generous Analyst

A commanding presence, when you enter the room, 1945 Leo, most eyes turn in your direction. You are graced with a detailed mind and a warm and cheerful personality, making you an interesting and lively companion. In relationships, you are giving and considerate, making a real effort to please your partner. And, you absolutely sparkle and shine when you have a partner who unabashedly adores and worships you.

You are a dramatic and demonstrative lover, wanting only to soar to the heights of ecstasy with your partner. Blessed with versatility and grace, you can easily move through different rhythms and adapt to whatever pace your partner requires. And, you have a way with words that is sure to arouse even the most reticent partner. Glamour definitely turns you on and the stage should be appropriately set so that you can give your best performance.

Your piercing intelligence is one of your finest assets and a prospective partner would do well to notice just how bright you are. You like recognition and when you feel appreciated by someone, you are apt to be as sweet as a kitten in return. With your analytical ability, would-be lovers would be wise to consult you about their current dilemmas. A master critic, you would thoroughly enjoy seeing the latest "art" film and dissecting its meaning over a fine glass of brandy.

The perfect woman for you, 1945 Leo male, is someone who is willing to let you have the limelight. She needs to be secure enough to not be distressed by your numerous admirers. You want a soft, feminine woman who will let you take the lead in the relationship. But, above all, you want someone who is compassionate, giving, and fond of a strong family life.

1945 Leo female, your ideal man is a witty conversationalist who has a fondness for discussing current events and pop culture. It's important that his intellect is as highly developed and refined as your own. He is likely to be quite versatile and possess a variety of talents and hobbies. Most of all, you also want someone who likes to be on the move and makes life fast-paced and exciting.

1945 VIRGO
From August 23, 12:35 through September 23, 9:49

The Proper Expert

Practical and ambitious, 1945 Virgo, you are a discerning and discriminating critic. You can't help but notice the fine details and can be counted on to have an opinion on just about everything. Typically, you are quite resourceful and may find that it hard to ask for help from others. Your mere presence is a comfort since you always make others feel that you can handle just about any eventuality. But, your amazing ability to stand on your own may be disconcerting to a partner who also wants to feel needed.

You approach lovemaking the way you would approach any other project—with meticulous organization and thorough precision. Once you find the way to please your partner, you will practice each technique until you reach perfection. Though you may not be known for having a varied repertoire, you will certainly be proficient at whatever skills you've made your own.

Boastful or ribald stories are not likely to impress you half as much as tasteful and clever repartee. A prospective partner should never be ostentatious nor try to impress you by spending money lavishly. Though you have an appreciation of quality, you abhor waste. You enjoy any activity that allows you to expand your knowledge. A lecture about saving money on taxes or how to create your own backyard lily pond would be ideal.

As a 1945 Virgo male, you want a woman who is expressive, generous, and regal in stature. It is important that she pride herself on always doing the right thing just as you do. And, she must surely appreciate your mental prowess and be able to keep up with your razor sharp mind. Once you have found the love of your life, she can be sure that you will treat her like a queen.

The ideal man for you, 1945 Virgo female, is responsible and diligent, much like yourself. He should possess a high degree of propriety and a respect for social mores and customs. But, he also needs to have a compassionate and gentle nature and be able to encourage you when you might be too self-critical. He needs to assure you that while you may not be perfect, you are as close to it as humanly possible.

VIRGO ZODIAC SIGN
YOUR LOVE PLANETS

YOUR ROMANTIC SIDE   p. 696
- ▶ VENUS IN CANCER
Born Aug. 23, 12:35 - Aug. 30, 13:04
- ▶ VENUS IN LEO
Born Aug. 30, 13:05 - Sept. 23, 9:49

YOUR SEX DRIVE   p. 722
- ▶ MARS IN GEMINI
Born Aug. 23, 12:35 - Sept. 07, 20:55
- ▶ MARS IN CANCER
Born Sept. 07, 20:56 - Sept. 23, 9:49

YOUR CELEBRITY TWINS   p. 760
Find out the astrological similarities you have with famous people.

YOUR COMPATIBILITY   p. 780
Compare planets to find out how compatible you are in a relationship.

YOUR RELATIONSHIP KARMA   p. 824
- ▶ SATURN IN CANCER
Born Aug. 23, 12:35 - Sept. 23, 9:49

MARGARET LOCKWOOD
English Actress
Sun in Virgo

225

1945 LIBRA
From September 23, 9:50 through October 23, 18:43

The Amiable Gambler

You are not afraid to take a calculated risk in order to achieve what you want, Libra of 1945. And, you are able to use your excellent judgment to know when to go after something and when to retreat. Justice is very important to you and you firmly believe that life should be as fair as possible. You are brimming with confidence, illusiveness, and charm, an appealing combination that is apt to attract others to you like the moth to proverbial flame.

You take a balanced approach to relationships, making sure that the two of you have the right combination of friendship, passion, and communication in order to create a lasting commitment. When it comes to lovemaking, you are a refined and polished lover, sensitive to the desires of your partner. Passionate and romantic, you need a partner that can match your ardor. Once you find that individual, you can be intensely loyal and devoted.

In order to catch your eye, a prospective partner should dazzle you with their intellectual brilliance or creative abilities. You are fond of all art forms and enjoy the theatre, ballet, opera, and exploring art galleries. But, to really capture your heart, a would-be lover needs to demonstrate that they have a compassionate and understanding nature and want to be in a relationship that is harmonious and relaxed.

1945 Libra male, your ideal woman is refined and graceful, and has a strong desire to serve. You need a woman who strives for excellence and is able to understand that you may be critical at times because you are constantly seeking perfection yourself. Above all, you want a woman who has a great sense of purpose and can dedicate herself to the higher principles of fairness and self-sacrifice.

As a 1945 Libra female, you want a tender and thoughtful man, someone who is more interested in others than he is in getting ahead. It's not that you don't admire ambition—it's just that you don't believe it is more important than human dignity. You also want someone who is a willing participant in a full relationship—a man who is eager to express his feelings and be there to listen to yours.

LIBRA ZODIAC SIGN
YOUR LOVE PLANETS

YOUR ROMANTIC SIDE   p. 696
- ▶ VENUS IN LEO
Born Sept. 23, 9:50 - Sept. 24, 16:05
- ▶ VENUS IN VIRGO
Born Sept. 24, 16:06 - Oct. 19, 4:08
- ▶ VENUS IN LIBRA
Born Oct. 19, 4:09 - Oct. 23, 18:43

YOUR SEX DRIVE   p. 722
MARS IN CANCER
Born Sept. 23, 9:50 - Oct. 23, 18:43

YOUR CELEBRITY TWINS   p. 760
Find out the astrological similarities you have with famous people.

YOUR COMPATIBILITY   p. 780
Compare planets to find out how compatible you are in a relationship.

YOUR RELATIONSHIP KARMA   p. 824
- ▶ SATURN IN CANCER
Born Sept. 23, 9:50 - Oct. 23, 18:43

ELEANOR ROOSEVELT
American Humanitarian
Mars in Scorpio

1945 SCORPIO
From October 23, 18:44 through November 22, 15:54

♏ The Spiritual Artist

Passionate, emotional, and unpredictable, 1945 Scorpio, you are a wonderful example of power and courage for your friends and family. You have an enormous urge to create—whether it be a work of art or a loving family, the process of bringing something to life is what matters to you. Your remarkable gift of clarity allows you to see the essence of what is important in your relationships and allows you to transform a negative situation into a positive agent for change.

You are a strong and attentive lover and you eagerly participate in all of the delights that sexuality has to offer. Affectionate and demonstrative, you need to be reassured of your partner's love and may grow sullen if your physical needs are not met. Lovemaking is a transcendental, mystical experience for you, especially when you are with someone whose abilities and appetites are as great as your own.

If someone wants to get your attention, they need to be provocative and seductive. You will always respond to a challenge and a potential lover might spark your interest by daring you to ensnare them in your very sultry web. A romantic soul at heart, you prefer spending a cozy evening at home, listening to music and making love. It is also important for a prospective partner to be truthful with you—once you have reason to distrust another person, it is not likely that you will give them a second chance to hurt you.

The perfect woman for the 1945 Scorpio male is artistic, spiritual, and full of grace and charm. She is also likely to be much lighter and cheerful than you, a perfect counterbalance to your serious demeanor. Most of all, you need someone who is as interested in the physical aspects of love as you and who is capable of giving you a tremendous amount of affection.

1945 Scorpio female, your ideal man is one who is courageous yet gentle, powerful yet compassionate. You want to be proud of your man and need someone who has a generous and abundant spirit. It is important that he benefits from a tremendous amount of belief in himself and that he has faith in the fact that love can conquer all.

1945 SAGITTARIUS
From November 22, 15:55 through December 22, 5:03

♐ The Passionate Explorer

You are on a lifelong quest for knowledge and truth, 1945 Sagittarius, giving you the ability to always see that there is light at the end of the tunnel. Your philosophical outlook is likely to have seen you through the most difficult of circumstances and you are someone who has an uncanny ability to land on your feet. You are blessed with strong integrity and a sense of honor, making you a sincere and committed partner in a relationship.

Day-to-day life is never boring since you bring your incredible sense of humor and your enthusiastic inquisitiveness into everything you do. The same is true of your lovemaking style—it is as receptive, giving, and imaginative as you are. Broadminded by nature, you are willing to try anything once, especially if it will please your partner. You approach sex the way you do life—you want to experience it to the fullest.

In order to get your attention, a would-be lover needs to first engage you in an interesting conversation. A lover of nature, you are sure to enjoy hiking through the woods. While you'd love to go on safari, you might also settle for a trip to the zoo. But, most of all, you value your freedom, and a potential mate should remember that it is important not to make you feel trapped or restricted.

The ideal woman for you, 1945 Sagittarius male, is one who is as open and adventurous as you are. You want a companion as you travel through life and it helps if she is willing to explore the road less taken with you. Your ideal woman has a positive outlook and believes that all things work together for the good. But, above all, you need a woman who has an unshakeable faith and deals with life as wholeheartedly as you do.

Your perfect man, 1945 Sagittarius female, is someone who stands out in a crowd. Gregarious and charming, he is likely to be quite confident and self-assured. He may be interested in working out, sports, or martial arts, yet is surprisingly gentle when it comes to you. But, above all, your ideal man is one who really wants to be your friend and enjoys spending his days and nights by your side.

Les Enfants du Paradis

A sweeping, romantic epic of love, betrayal, tragedy and farce, *Les Enfants du Paradis* is a multi-layered French masterpiece whose making was as intriguing as the plot itself.

Set in the 1820s theatre world of Paris, with showgirls, artists, and actors indulging in a life of flamboyance and hedonism, *Les Enfants* is the story of a beautiful actress, Garance, who is loved by four men. Each man represents the different facets of love. There is the debonair actor Frédérick, the fiendish criminal Lacenaire, and the jealous Count de Montray, who Garance eventually marries. But destiny will never let her be with the man she loves—Baptiste, a mime, who is the embodiment of purity and goodness.

With a rich script by Jacques Prévert, reminiscent of 19th century literature, director Marcel Carné created a vision of poetic-realism—a movement in French film in the late '30s and '40s that dealt with "realistic" subjects in a poetic and lyrical way.

Almost all the main characters were inspired by real people, and Jean-Louis Barrault, who played Baptiste, was himself a famous Parisian mime artist. The enigmatic French movie star Arletty played the part of Garance, creating a captivating and ravishing beauty who, even in marriage, could not be owned. This theme of ownership and freedom is the subversive undercurrent that drives the movie—which is immediately significant considering that the filming of *Les Enfants* began in 1943, during the Nazi occupation of France.

Carné made sure that the Nazis, who carefully monitored his work, did not impinge on the movie's creative force nor his own political beliefs. His

"Beauty, blood, glory, adjoining hotel rooms, the backstage wings, that's life which has neither start nor finish: love and death, yesterday as today."

JACQUES PRÉVERT

production designer and composer were Jewish and bravely worked undercover even as they were being hunted by the Gestapo. He employed nearly 2,000 extras, most of whom were members of the Resistance, using filming as a subterfuge for their underground work. The pro-Nazi collaborators he was forced to hire had no idea they were working alongside Resistance fighters. He even cut the movie into two parts so as not to contravene German laws—the Nazis banned all films over ninety minutes—certain that he would show them together after the war. And no expense was spared—*Les Enfants* was to become the most expensive French film of its time, with extravagant sets and exquisite costumes creating a visual opulence never seen before.

As soon as France was liberated, Carné's wish came true, when he was able to premiere *Les Enfants* to a free France. The film ran for 54 weeks and is still said to be shown at least once everyday somewhere in Paris.

But that was not the end of the story. In a poignant twist, Arletty had fallen in love with a Nazi officer during the making of the movie. After the Liberation she was shunned by her once adoring French public, who named her the "horizontal collaborator." She was arrested and sent to a concentration camp and then to a prison, where she spent 120 days. She was then put under house arrest for another two years and forbidden from working for three years. She was not invited to the premiere of *Les Enfants du Paradis*.

A triumph of art over repression, of political resistance, and of decadent filmmaking, *Les Enfants du Paradis* is considered by many to be the best French film ever made.

227

▶ READ ABOUT ADOLF HITLER AND EVA BRAUN ON PAGE 220 ▶ READ ABOUT LOUISE BROOKS ON PAGE 95

1946

- ⭐ BABY BOOM
- ⭐ THE BIKINI INTRODUCED
- ⭐ MAHATMA GANDHI
- ⭐ IT'S A WONDERFUL LIFE
- ⭐ TAYLOR CALDWELL
- ⭐ NAT KING COLE
- ⭐ DOIN' WHAT COMES NATURALLY

Sex Idol

EVENTS

1946 was the first year of the Baby Boom. So many couples reunited after long separations because of the war that the result was the biggest birthrate rise in history. One couple got together only by phone, though. A telephone wedding took place between a British bride and her American fiancé from opposite sides of the Atlantic. At the same time in Britain thirty-five legal teams were appointed to deal with the fifty thousand divorce cases waiting to be heard.

The bikini was introduced, making a trip to the beach more than just a trip to the beach. Women in Italy received the vote, and the first Miss Italia contest was held.

Indian leader Mahatma Gandhi confessed he'd been taking naked girls to bed with him for years to test his ability to remain celibate. In the US, Massachusetts attempted to ban the sale of *Forever Amber* by Kathleen Winsor, charging that the book was obscene. The attorney general, George Rowell, supported the ban, and at great personal discomfort, itemized each sexual scene or reference—93 in all.

POP CULTURE

The annual Christmas classic, *It's a Wonderful Life*, showcased James Stewart as a family man contemplating suicide on Christmas Eve. He gets another chance with the help of his guardian angel. In *Duel in the Sun*, two sons, one good, the other bad, of a Texas cattle baron battle each other and the railroad over a dark beauty. In *The Gentleman Misbehaves* a producer marries a woman he thinks is rich—turns out he was wrong.

Carson McCullers filled bookstores with *The Member of the Wedding*, following the life of a 12-year-old as she grows up in small-town Georgia. In Frank Yerby's *The Foxes of Harrow* an Irish gambler marries an aristocrat in 1820s New Orleans to raise his social status. *This Side of Innocence* by Taylor Caldwell was about a post-Civil War family, its conflicts and loves and romances.

Frank Sinatra dominated jukeboxes with three hits: "Five Minutes More," "Oh! What It Seemed to Be," and "They Say It's Wonderful." Dinah Shore sang "Doin' What Comes Naturally," and Nat King Cole had a hit with "For Sentimental Reasons."

RITA HAYWORTH

In 1946, Rita Hayworth, made her name as a cinema sex goddess in her role as the title character in *Gilda*, a film noir classic set in Argentina. As the ultimate femme fatale, Hayworth played the sexually experienced wife of a shady casino owner. A tense ménàge à trois develops when her husband, a.k.a. Gilda's meal ticket, hires her ex-lover as his right-hand man.

Hayworth not only stops the show with a mock striptease, she steals the movie outright by radiating the energy of a caged tigress in heat. In that famous closeup on her bare shoulders, Hayworth flipped her red locks into cinema history.

SEE ALSO

▶ BETTY GRABLE *Page 204*

▶ MARILYN MONROE *Pages 293 & 294*

▶ SHARON STONE *Page 606*

1946 CAPRICORN

From December 22, 1945 5:04 through January 20, 1946 15:44
(December 1946 Capricorns, see 1947 Capricorn)

♑ The Ambitious Partner

Tough like steel on the outside and soft like custard on the inside—that's you, 1946 Capricorn! You are determined to get ahead in the world, but not without the help of a loving partner. For you, relationships are all about teamwork. You do best with a mate who is willing to boost you up the ladder of success, and nurse your wounds when you occasionally slide down. A lover who is attentive, nurturing, and supportive brings out the best in you. You never turn down a kiss or a cuddle.

You have a powerful sex drive that is breathtaking. Therefore, finding a spouse whose sexual appetite matches your own is very satisfying. You care too much about your reputation to conduct extramarital affairs. As far as you're concerned, marriage is a sacred institution. You're not about to cheapen it by betraying your mate. One of the ways in which you like to keep your relationship alive and vibrant is always to set mutual goals together. It's very important that you and your mate are on the same page with regard to your wants and needs.

Active, vibrant suitors always win favor with you. Nothing turns you off more than a couch potato. You're enormously taken by people who keep themselves in shape through sports activities and workout routines. When it comes to making love, you like to be the aggressor. An admirer can encourage you to make the first move by asking you to smooth their hair or remove a speck of dust from their eye. The head is the most attractive part of the body for you!

Women who are energetic, ambitious, and playful appeal most to you 1946 male Capricorns. You want a partner who is able to keep up with you, whether it's scaling mountains or landscaping the yard. A capable partner who welcomes your tender loving care is best suited to you.

As a 1946 female Goat, you desire a man who is charming, enterprising, and persuasive. You love suave guys with old-world manners. If there's anything you can't stand, it's someone who makes crass jokes and off-color remarks. A spouse who makes you feel like your contributions are valued and needed does well with you.

CAPRICORN ZODIAC SIGN
YOUR LOVE PLANETS

YOUR ROMANTIC SIDE   p. 696
▶ VENUS IN CAPRICORN
Born Dec. 22, 1945 5:04 - Jan. 20, 1946 15:44

YOUR SEX DRIVE   p. 722
▶ MARS IN CANCER
Born Dec. 22, 1945 5:04 - Jan. 20, 1946 15:44

YOUR CELEBRITY TWINS   p. 760
Find out the astrological similarities you have with famous people.

YOUR COMPATIBILITY   p. 780
Compare planets to find out how compatible you are in a relationship.

YOUR RELATIONSHIP KARMA   p. 824
▶ SATURN IN CANCER
Born Dec. 22, 1945 5:04 - Jan. 20, 1946 15:44

JOHN GARFIELD
American Actor
Mars in Aquarius

1946 AQUARIUS

From January 20, 15:45 through February 19, 6:08

♒ The Mystical Mate

Dreamy, idealistic, and spiritual, you 1946 Water Bearers look like you're walking on air. There's a sort of wistful nobility about you that draws admirers like bees to a flower. And although you appreciate all the attention, you really want to focus on one special person in your life. For you, relationships imply exclusivity and devotion. You do best with a mate with whom you feel a karmic kinship. You're not the type to marry out of a desire for companionship. You want to say your marriage vows out of love, not loneliness. You do best with a partner who stimulates your intellect.

You're an inspired lover who likes to surprise your partner with amorous advances in unusual places. You're not the type to wait until bedtime to make your first move. Nothing gives you more pleasure than making love at unconventional times in unusual places. Your spontaneous nature is best suited to a partner who enjoys living in the moment. And although you're quite whimsical, you do believe in the value of work. You do very well with someone who also likes to work hard and play hard.

Having unusual viewpoints is a surefire way to catch your attention. You always admire an independent thinker. You're also drawn to people who put great emphasis on spirituality. An admirer would be wise to take note of your favorite kinds of music. You're very sexually responsive when certain albums are playing. You've also got very sensitive nerve endings, and like to be gently stroked all over as a prelude to lovemaking.

As a 1946 Water Bearer, you're attracted to a wide variety of women. You admire self-assured females, as well as brilliant, zany types. Soft, poetic creatures also warm your heart. You do best with a partner who sees beauty in seemingly mundane things. Cynics turn you off.

Men who are unpretentious, pleasant, and tender appeal to you 1946 female Aquarians. You can't abide show-offs. Conversely, a guy who underplays his accomplishments really impresses you. You want a mate who takes great pleasure in living a simple life. You are not in the market for a restless malcontent!

AQUARIUS ZODIAC SIGN
YOUR LOVE PLANETS

YOUR ROMANTIC SIDE   p. 696
▶ VENUS IN CAPRICORN
Born Jan. 20, 15:45 - Jan. 22, 22:27
▶ VENUS IN AQUARIUS
Born Jan. 22, 22:28 - Feb. 15, 20:10
▶ VENUS IN PISCES
Born Feb. 15, 20:11 - Feb. 19, 6:08

YOUR SEX DRIVE   p. 722
▶ MARS IN CANCER
Born Jan. 20, 15:45 - Feb. 19, 6:08

YOUR CELEBRITY TWINS   p.760
Find out the astrological similarities you have with famous people.

YOUR COMPATIBILITY   p. 780
Compare planets to find out how compatible you are in a relationship.

YOUR RELATIONSHIP KARMA   p. 824
▶ SATURN IN CANCER
Born Jan. 20, 15:45 - Feb. 19, 6:08

NAT KING COLE
American Singer
Sun in Pisces

230

1946 PISCES
From February 19, 6:09 through March 21, 5:32

The Romantic Go-Getter

There's very little you wouldn't do for love as a 1946 Pisces. Romance is what inspires your sentimental soulful soul. You do best in a relationship that makes you feel sinfully sexy, cherished, and admired. When life gets grim or serious, you want your partner to liven things up with a joke and a smile. Partnerships that are based on work and self-sacrifice don't appeal to you in the slightest. You far prefer a romance that uplifts and inspires you. Perhaps that's why your relationships have always had a playful element to them. Deep down inside, you're just a fun-loving kid.

A marriage that takes place on the spur of the moment isn't out of the question for you. You've always trusted your intuition, and have very good instincts regarding love. A partner who is stable but indulgent of your whimsical behavior suits you best. You don't want your creativity to be stifled, but welcome soothing reassurances from your spouse. Sexually, you're quite a dynamo, and need a mate who enjoys making love several times a day. When you love a person, you want to merge with them as often as possible, both emotionally and physically.

Playing hard-to-get is a good strategy for getting your attention. You love the thrill of the chase, and are especially attentive to people who are spiritual without being stodgy. Although you like to make the first move, you can be inspired by being pulled onto a darkened dance floor. Swaying to the music with a partner never fails to arouse you. Watching a steamy but tasteful movie can also put you in the mood for love.

If you're a male Fish who was born in 1946, you want a woman who is outgoing but ladylike. You love it when a soft, shy female goes after something she really wants. You also enjoy daredevils. Ultimately, you want a partner who enjoys adventure without compromising her femininity.

You female Pisceans who were born in 1946 want a man who is playful, funny, and tender. Class-clown types usually appeal to you, although you can't stand overbearing buffoons. The ideal match for you knows when you want to kid around and when you want to be held.

1946 ARIES
From March 21, 5:33 through April 20, 17:01

The Devoted Partner

Love is a religion for you 1946 Rams. Nothing is more important to you than having a stable romantic relationship. You have a tendency to put your partner on a pedestal, and look the other way at their shortcomings. If someone dares criticize your mate, your normally warm tone turns chilly. You simply can't bear to hear anything negative about your beloved. Relationships are about loyalty for you. Therefore, you take every opportunity to praise and promote your partner, even for small gestures that most people would take for granted.

You have ardent passions that you prefer to direct toward one person. Sex is a very special bond for you. You need to trust your partner implicitly before letting go of your inhibitions. Once you do commit your life to another person, your beautiful sexual nature bursts into flower. Although marriage for you is a serious business, you enjoy injecting plenty of levity into your relationship. Springing surprise vacations, gifts, and treats on your partner is a regular habit for you. No gesture is too extravagant for your beloved!

A suitor who seeks your protection has a good chance of winning your heart. Asking to share your umbrella on a rainy day is a good way to break the ice with you. So is requesting assistance with a tricky gadget. Your suitor should take great pains with creating a romantic atmosphere for your first sexual encounter. Dim lights, soft music, and clean sheets help put you in the mood. You love it when your partner goes out of the way to make you feel special. Deep kissing turns you on tremendously.

As a 1946 male Ram, you want a woman who is bright, enthusiastic, and athletic. You're also drawn to iron-willed ladies with a strong sense of beauty. A partner who is proud to be on your arm suits you best. When you love a woman, you want the world to know it!

You 1946 female Ariens seek a man who is devoted, loving, and tender. Macho guys who are always trying to establish their superiority really make you angry. You far prefer a man who is willing to show his vulnerable side. Fatherly types also thrill you.

1946 TAURUS *From April 21, 17:02 through May 21, 16:33*

The Harmony Lover

You 1946 Taureans have no intention of rocking the boat, especially when it comes to romance. When you find someone who makes your heart pound with excitement, you'll do everything possible to keep their heart. Flirting as a means to evoke jealousy is not your style at all. Neither is taking your partner for granted. As far as you're concerned, relationships are a means of stability. Having a rocky one would greatly upset your desire for balance and harmony. You do best with a partner who likes to build bridges, rather than tear them down.

It might take you a long time to get in the mood for love. You're usually so preoccupied with daily chores that you put sex on the back burner. A mate who can distract you from your lists of chores is ideal for you. When you are aroused, you are extremely sensual and responsive. Having a secure and comfortable home is very important for you. You glow with pleasure when your partner compliments you on your domestic skills. The more you feel like your marriage is an equal partnership, the happier you are. You want a spouse who you value, and vice-versa.

If someone wants to seduce you, they should put themselves at your service. Too often, you busy yourself attending to others. Having a suitor pamper you for a change would be most refreshing. Sexually, your most sensitive spot is your throat. Your admirer would be well advised to slide their mouth from your lips to your neck during your first embrace. You're also very receptive to sensual massages and foot rubs, preferably enhanced with scented oils.

As a 1946 male Bull, you like women who are robust, sexy, and good-humored. Females who have a deep appreciation for nature also appeal to you. A partner who can remind you that all work and no play makes a dull relationship brings out the best in you.

If you're a female Taurus who was born in 1946, you like a man who is intelligent and sensitive. A guy who is filled with goofy schemes never fails to get a smile out of you. You also like men who are sincere and loyal. Suave, sophisticated types have very little appeal for you.

TAURUS ZODIAC SIGN
YOUR LOVE PLANETS

YOUR ROMANTIC SIDE   p. 696
▶ VENUS IN TAURUS
Born Apr. 20, 17:02 - Apr. 29, 10:58
▶ VENUS IN GEMINI
Born Apr. 29, 10:59 - May 21, 16:33
YOUR SEX DRIVE   p. 722
▶ MARS IN CANCER
Born Apr. 20, 17:02 - Apr. 22, 19:30
▶ MARS IN LEO
Born Apr. 22, 19:31 - May 21, 16:33
YOUR CELEBRITY TWINS   p. 760
Find out the astrological similarities you have with famous people.
YOUR COMPATIBILITY   p. 780
Compare planets to find out how compatible you are in a relationship.
YOUR RELATIONSHIP KARMA   p. 824
▶ SATURN IN CANCER
Born Apr. 20, 17:02 - May 21, 16:33

231

ROSALIND RUSSELL
American Actress
Sun in Gemini

1946 GEMINI *From May 21, 16:34 through June 22, 0:43*

The Flirty Sweetheart

That sexy twinkle in your eyes is positively devastating, and you 1946 Geminis know it. You can make someone in a slovenly bathrobe feel like a glamorous movie star with just one wink. And though you like to spread love wherever you go, it may have taken you a while to settle down into a committed relationship. You do best with a mate who doesn't mind your flirtatious ways. Fortunately, you never forget to pay tribute to your beloved, and probably delight in penning beautiful love letters.

As far as sex is concerned, you believe that more is better. Consequently, you thrive with a partner whose sexual appetite matches your own. You desire a marriage filled with romance. You have no intention of treating your mate like an old shoe after your vows have been taken. In fact, your relationship may be the source of envy for settled couples who have forgotten the joys of courtship. One way you keep your love alive is through frequent travel. Another is through games. Playing bridge, charades, and Scrabble with your partner teaches you both valuable teamwork skills.

If someone wants to catch your eye, they should wear bright colors and flashy clothes. You've always had a flair for fashion, and enjoy suitors who know how to dress. You also admire storytellers, and are likely to fall head over heels in love with a good raconteur who makes you laugh. You don't mind who makes the first move in a relationship, so long as it's spontaneous. It thrills you when an admirer gets overcome by passion and plants a kiss on your lips at an unexpected moment.

You male Twins who were born in 1946 like a variety of women. Whether she's chatty and mirthful or sweet and sensitive makes no difference to you. Your greatest desire is for a partner who makes life fun. You're also attracted to women with a dramatic flair.

As a 1946 female Gemini, you desire a man who is light-hearted and playful. You also adore guys who are reserved and bashful. Ultimately, you want a mate who revels in your high spirits. It gives you great pleasure to add generous splashes of color to your partner's life.

GEMINI ZODIAC SIGN
YOUR LOVE PLANETS

YOUR ROMANTIC SIDE   p. 696
▶ VENUS IN GEMINI
Born May 21, 16:34 - May 24, 3:38
▶ VENUS IN CANCER
Born May 24, 3:39 - June 18, 4:59
▶ VENUS IN LEO
Born June 18, 5:00 - June 22, 0:43
YOUR SEX DRIVE   p. 722
▶ MARS IN LEO
Born May 21, 16:34 - June 20, 8:30
▶ MARS IN VIRGO
Born June 20, 8:31 - June 22, 0:43
YOUR CELEBRITY TWINS   p. 760
Find out the astrological similarities you have with famous people.
YOUR COMPATIBILITY   p. 780
Compare planets to find out how compatible you are in a relationship.
YOUR RELATIONSHIP KARMA   p. 824
▶ SATURN IN CANCER
Born May 21, 16:34 - June 22, 0:43

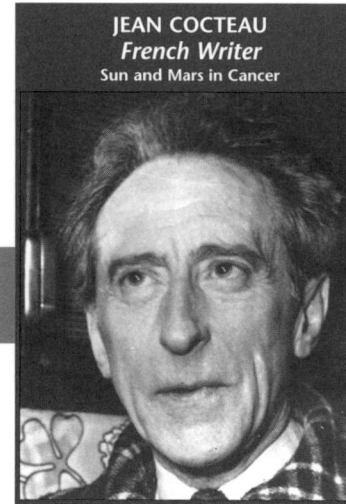

JEAN COCTEAU
French Writer
Sun and Mars in Cancer

1946 CANCER
From June 22, 0:44 through July 23, 11:36

 The Dignified Sentimentalist

You 1946 Crabs take it upon yourselves to nurture the world. You're so tender and caring that you often neglect yourself for the sake of others. A protective, loving partner brings out the best in you. You benefit from a relationship in which kindness and compassion are the founding principles. Rough, indifferent lovers aren't your cup of tea. You far prefer a mate who eases your anxieties and champions your needs. The more secure and happy your household, the happier you are.

You take a great deal of pride in your family and make it the focus of your marriage. If you have children, you probably idealize them. A spouse who understands and supports your need for a harmonious domestic life has your lifelong affection and devotion. You're very ardent in love, and enjoy pouring out your emotions during sex. For you, physical intimacy is a means to reveal your emotions to your partner. You love letting down your guard in bed.

If someone wants to catch your eye, they should express admiration for your caring, responsible ways. You pride yourself on being a good friend and neighbor, although you'd never brag about your nurturing qualities. Therefore, it's gratifying to be singled out for your loving heart. Before making the first move, your admirer should take care to create an environment in which you feel comfortable. Inviting you over for a home cooked meal is a good prelude to sex for you. Nothing puts you in the mood for love like good food served in cozy surroundings. Slow, languorous foreplay also excites you.

If you're a male Crab who was born in 1946, you want a woman who loves living the good life. Such a female can help you relax and appreciate luxuries of which you would normally deprive yourself. A charming, expressive female also warms your heart. You want a partner who makes you feel confident, loved, and valued.

Men who are stable but stimulating appeal to you 1946 female Cancereans. You love a guy with a curious mind who is content to pursue his interests from home. A mate who willingly lifts burdens from your shoulders is the ideal match for you.

1946 LEO
From July 23, 11:37 through August 23, 18:25

The Persistent Pursuer

When you 1946 Leos see something you want, you go for it. You're always determined to win, especially when it comes to love. Seduction is an art form to you. When you have the object of your affection in your sights, the rest of the world disappears. You do best with a partner who understands that their destiny is linked with yours. Casual attachments have no interest for you. You intend to know your mate inside and out, and you often succeed. Because you love a challenge, it is very possible that you bond with a partner who has an element of mystery.

Marriage may be a mere formality for you. It's possible that you don't place much value on a piece of paper that ties you to your lover. What's important for you is that there is an emotional intensity between you and your soul mate that transcends all laws and social conventions. If you do make things legal, it may be for the purpose of satisfying family members or protecting each other from an economic point of view. Sexually, you have a voracious appetite. When you're in the mood for love, you can pursue your mate with the intensity of a jungle cat!

If someone wants to capture your heart, your admirer would be wise to hang on your every word. You love it when an admirer looks up to you, seeking your advice and citing your opinions. Embarking on a physical relationship can be tricky with you. You like to be the aggressor, but enjoy stringing your intended along before making the first move. A smart suitor will remain cool in the face of your indifference. If there's anything that turns you on, it's a lover who seems calm on the outside but smolders within.

As a male Lion who was born in 1946, you enjoy a woman who is sedate, lovely, and a little imposing. You also appreciate females who are witty and talkative. In the end, you want a partner who makes you feel like the sexiest man on Earth.

If you're a 1946 female Leo, you desire a man who is sensual, organized, and practical. Guys who are heartbreakingly charming also turn you on. A partner who enjoys falling under your spell is the ideal match for you.

1946 VIRGO

From August 23, 18:26 through September 23, 15:40

The Extravagant Sweetheart

There's no doubt about it, 1946 Virgo—you love living the good life. Your refined tastes extend to your romantic life as well. You want a relationship that is rooted in beauty, elegance, and luxury. Starving in a garret with your lover is not really a possibility for you. You'll go above and beyond the call of duty to provide your mate with a superior lifestyle. If that means working overtime or embarking on a career that is lucrative but boring, so be it. A partner who shares your appreciation for the finer things and appreciates your efforts to obtain them is best for you.

You value partnerships. As far as you're concerned, two heads are better than one. Maybe that's why you are such a satisfying marriage partner. You really value your spouse's opinion, and often seek it when faced with a moral dilemma. You may not be the world's most passionate lover, but you are extremely attentive to your mate's physical needs. Mastering your mate's favorite lovemaking techniques is no problem for you. Any sexual activity that gives your partner pleasure satisfies you.

Getting your attention takes work. You appreciate someone who demonstrates good taste and impeccable manners over time. You're not the type to fall head-over-heels in love at the first sight of an admirer. Rather, your suitor's charms will gradually grow on you over a prolonged courtship. When it comes to making the first move, you prefer a courtly technique. Soft kisses and passionate sighs summon your passion more readily than an ardent, aggressive approach.

As a male Virgo who was born in 1946, you prefer women who are romantic and ultra feminine. Women who are thoughtful but fun also appeal to you. Ultimately, you desire a partner who enhances your enjoyment of life. An exuberant mate suits you best.

Men who are sentimental, intelligent, and tasteful never fail to attract you 1946 female Virgos. You love a guy who appreciates the arts, but doesn't take himself too seriously. You do best with a mate who is able to enjoy a refined lifestyle in an easygoing way. You can't abide repressed, stuffy snobs.

VIRGO ZODIAC SIGN
YOUR LOVE PLANETS

YOUR ROMANTIC SIDE — p. 696
▶ **VENUS IN LIBRA**
Born Aug. 23, 18:26 - Sept. 07, 0:15
▶ **VENUS IN SCORPIO**
Born Sept. 07, 0:16 - Sept. 23, 15:40

YOUR SEX DRIVE — p. 722
▶ **MARS IN LIBRA**
Born Aug. 23, 18:26 - Sept. 23, 15:40

YOUR CELEBRITY TWINS — p. 760
Find out the astrological similarities you have with famous people.

YOUR COMPATIBILITY — p. 780
Compare planets to find out how compatible you are in a relationship.

YOUR RELATIONSHIP KARMA — p. 824
▶ **SATURN IN LEO**
Born Aug. 23, 18:26 - Sept. 23, 15:40

OLIVIA DE HAVILLAND
American Actress
Mars in Virgo

1946 LIBRA

From September 23, 15:41 through October 24, 0:34

The Romantic Philosopher

For you 1946 Librans, nothing is as inspirational as the idea of true love. It may take years for you to find it, but that just sweetens your search. You believe anything precious is worth waiting for. A partner who shares your exalted view of romance is bound to bring you happiness. You do best in a relationship that is courtly and dignified. You're not the type of lover who delights in seeing your partner let down his or her guard. Rather, you prefer maintaining an idealized vision of your mate. You may benefit from having separate bathrooms and dressing areas as a means to maintain the illusion of always being impeccably groomed.

For you, partnerships are a means to explore exciting ideas. You enjoy having a sounding board in your spouse, and may decide to travel or study together. You wouldn't benefit from a relationship that feels as though it's remained the same since the day you met. Sexually, you're quite adventurous and may enjoy experimenting with various lovemaking techniques. You're a whimsical lover.

Anybody wanting to seduce you should

know that you consider the brain to be the most erogenous part of the body. Therefore, it's a wise idea to bring up subjects like philosophy, religion, and the law while in your company. You appreciate a suitor with an open mind. Making the first move on you can be difficult, because you don't wear your heart on your sleeve. The best approach may be to make a whispered request for a kiss while you're out walking in the moonlight. A romantic atmosphere makes all the difference with you.

If you're a 1946 male Libran, you admire a woman who is intuitive, sexy, and smart. You're not intimidated by a female with a powerful personality. You also enjoy women with a wild streak. A partner who works to keep the freshness alive in your relationship is best suited to you.

As a 1946 female Libra, you are drawn to guys who are charming but ambitious. You're not impressed by men who get by on their good looks. Men who are earthy and passionate also appeal to you. You thrive with a mate who makes you feel like a natural woman.

LIBRA ZODIAC SIGN
YOUR LOVE PLANETS

YOUR ROMANTIC SIDE — p. 696
▶ **VENUS IN SCORPIO**
Born Sept. 23, 15:41 - Oct. 16, 10:44
▶ **VENUS IN SAGITTARIUS**
Born Oct. 16, 10:45 - Oct. 24, 0:34

YOUR SEX DRIVE — p. 722
▶ **MARS IN LIBRA**
Born Sept. 23, 15:41 - Sept. 24, 16:34
▶ **MARS IN SCORPIO**
Born Sept. 24, 16:35 - Oct. 24, 0:34

YOUR CELEBRITY TWINS — p. 760
Find out the astrological similarities you have with famous people.

YOUR COMPATIBILITY — p. 780
Compare planets to find out how compatible you are in a relationship.

YOUR RELATIONSHIP KARMA — p. 824
▶ **SATURN IN LEO**
Born Sept. 23, 15:41 - Oct. 24, 0:34

CELIA JOHNSON
English Actress
Venus and Mars in Scorpio

234

1946 SCORPIO
From October 24, 0:35 through November 22, 21:45

♏ *The Powerful Lover*

As a 1946 Scorpion, you are a force with which to contend. You can be especially awe-inspiring when you're in love. It's almost impossible to resist your ardor. A partner who adores being enveloped by your passionate aura does best with you. You possess powerful passions, and need to release them in your relationship. That's probably why you are drawn to a mate who is receptive and intuitive. You want your mate to treat your love as a precious gift that is as essential to life as food, water, and sunlight.

Your sex drive has an electric intensity that is quite exciting. All you may have to do to get your partner in the mood is to fix them with a penetrating stare. The sparks between you and your spouse may continue to fly long after you've said your marriage vows. That's because you make a concerted effort to keep the physical side of your relationship exciting. It's very possible that you will hold a career that puts in you the spotlight. Therefore, you do best with a mate who is comfortable living part of your life together in the public eye.

Demonstrating a love of challenge is a surefire way to get your attention. You always admire and respect somebody who is willing to put their talents to the test. An admirer who isn't afraid to vent their emotions also appeals to you. Strong displays of passion or anger really turn you on. When it comes time to take your relationship to the physical level, your suitor should pace themselves accordingly. A first kiss could easily lead to an all night marathon of lovemaking. You're especially responsive to a lover who seeks to explore every inch of your body.

If you're a male Scorpion who was born in 1946, you want an outgoing woman who is athletic and daring. You're also drawn to females who are impulsive and passionate. Ultimately, you need a partner who longs to be swept away by a tide of passion.

As a 1946 female Scorpio, you desire a man who is ambitious and intense. Friendly guys with leadership potential also appeal to you. You want an appreciative mate who sees you as an essential ingredient to his success.

1946 SAGITTARIUS
From November 22, 21:46 through December 22, 10:52

♐ *The Closet Romantic*

Although you 1946 Archers like to keep things casual on the surface, you're really quite romantic by nature. Friends would be shocked to see how tender and sentimental you are with your partner. It's not that you're ashamed of your emotions. Rather, you prefer reserving your soft side for the sole enjoyment of your mate. A partner who is unusual or unconventional in some way does best with you. You want to seek adventure with your beloved!

Marriage might not be high on your list of priorities. You love your freedom, and prefer a partnership that isn't bogged down by legal commitments. If you do decide to wed, it may be on the spur of the moment. You love spontaneous gestures of love, so getting married at midnight in a Las Vegas chapel may be the preferred way for you to tie the knot. Your sex drive is dependant on your mindset. When you're optimistic, you can make love all night. When you're moody, it can be hard getting a kiss from you. Consequently, you would be wise to pair with a mate who keeps you in good spirits and knows how to make you laugh.

If someone wants to seduce you, they should express interest in you as a person first. An admirer who has "I want a relationship!" stamped on their forehead won't get very far with you. You find it arousing when someone expresses interest in your spiritual side. Introducing sex into your relationship shouldn't be difficult. You prefer the direct approach, and don't mind if your partner makes the first move. You especially enjoy having your thighs stroked.

You 1946 male Archers want a woman who is sexy, mysterious, and elusive. Although you don't like intrigues in a relationship, you are drawn to females who have an indefinable air about them. You want a partner who keeps your sentimental side a secret.

As a 1946 female Sagittarian, you enjoy two types of men. The first is energetic, outgoing, and optimistic. The second is earthy, sensual, and strong. Whichever kind of guy you pick, he should give you a measure of freedom. A giving partner who encourages your many interests and hobbies suits you very well.

Bogart and Bacall – Legendary Lovers

"...he leaned over, put his hand under my chin and kissed me."

From her autobiography,
LAUREN BACALL: By Myself

235

Who would have thought that the willowy 19-year-old model Lauren Bacall and the grizzled, seasoned actor Humphrey Bogart would make such a fabulous couple? When studio executives spotted Bacall on the cover of *Harper's Bazaar*, she had no acting experience. Director Howard Hawks told her he wanted to cast her with either Cary Grant or Humphrey Bogart. She was excited about Grant, but her first reaction to Bogart was "Yuck!" Bogart was more enthusiastic after he saw her audition tape. "I just saw your test," he said when they bumped into each other on the studio lot. "We'll have a lot of fun together."

In this first film they made, *To Have and to Have Not*, the physical attraction leaps off the screen, making it obvious that these two had something going. Within three weeks on the set together they were falling in love, but they had to meet secretly over the next year because Bogey was married. In reality Bacall was sexually inexperienced, and she trembled during the more intimate scenes. She developed the habit of lowering her head and looking up at Bogart to control the shaking, a tactic which was soon heralded as a great seduction technique and became known as "the Look." This film has one of the greatest come-ons in Hollywood movies when she plays a slinky exit scene, saying, "You know how to whistle, don't you Steve? You just put your lips together and blow."

Although she's a modest Virgo, her Moon in fiery, headstrong Aries gives her the courage and boldness to go after what she wants. (Aries is associated with the sex planet Mars.) His Capricorn Zodiac sign is connected with Mars, the sexy planet of war. Bogey's Sun-Mars connection is great for playing the independent hero, but in his personal life, this combination led to plenty of disagreements and fights with his previous three wives. Bogart and Bacall utilized their Martian energy in some exquisite snappy dialogue and fast-paced, action-oriented plot development.

Their cinematic chemistry can be seen in three more films, *The Big Sleep*, *Dark Passage*, and *Key Largo*.

The sign rising at the time of Bacall's birth was Cancer, the sign of home and family. His Mars in Capricorn perfectly harmonized with her seventh house of marriage. They married on May 21, 1945, only 11 days after Bogart received the divorce decree from his third wife. When they weren't making movies or cruising on their yacht, the two were perfectly content to stay at home. Bogart received hormone injections to increase his sperm count, and they then had two children. He boasted to his friends about his wonderful relationship, "She's my wife, so she stays home and takes care of me. Maybe that's the way you tell the ladies from the broads in this town."

Still, considering their mutually feisty nature, they did clash from time to time. Bogart took Bacall along when he went to the Congo to film with Katharine Hepburn. Hepburn noticed their frequent spats, but also how quickly they blew over. "They seemed to have the most enormous opinion of each other's charms," she said. "And when they fought it was with the utter confidence of two cats locked deliciously in a cage." Bogart and Bacall remained best sparring partners, friends, and lovers until he died in 1957 of cancer.

► READ ABOUT FILM NOIR CLASSICS ON PAGE 195 ► READ ABOUT CARY GRANT ON PAGES 244 & 384 ► READ ABOUT KATHARINE HEPBURN ON PAGES 196 & 251

1947

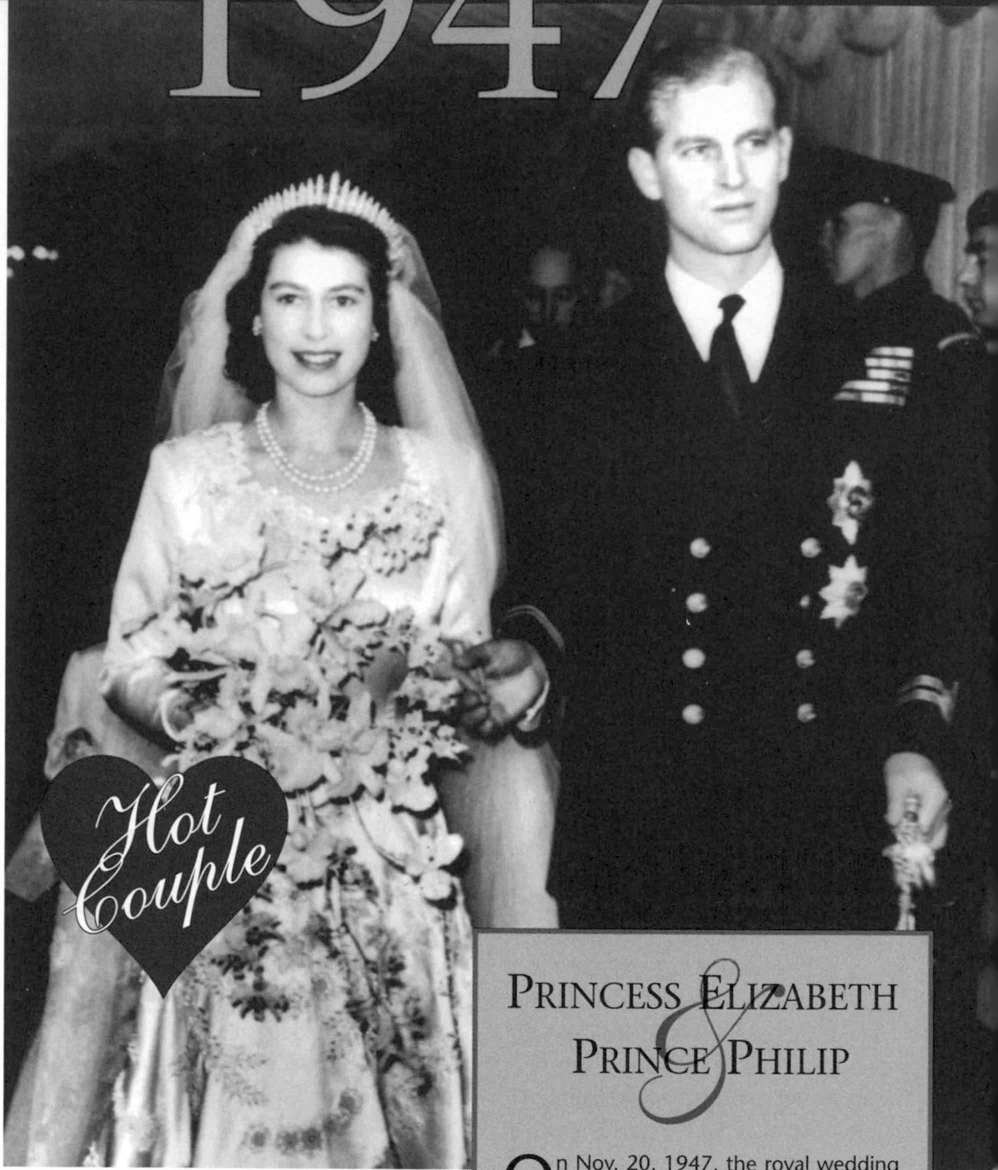

- ✪ CHRISTIAN DIOR
- ✪ ARTIFICIAL INSEMINATION
- ✪ TALES OF THE SOUTH PACIFIC
- ✪ TRY A LITTLE TENDERNESS
- ✪ I'M IN THE MOOD FOR LOVE

EVENTS

The war was over and the availability of fabric inspired Dior to create ankle-length dresses—many men protested the change. UK Prime Minister Harold Wilson described the "New Look" as wasteful and frivolous.

In the US, Springmaid sheets shocked the business community with its daring ad—a cartoon of an Indian couple on a sheet hammock with the caption: "A buck well spent on a Springmaid sheet."

True Romance started publication and remained popular through to the mid-70s. Elizabeth Short, the "Black Dahlia," was found nude and murdered in Los Angeles—and the case is still unsolved.

Film producer Michael Todd took actress Joan Blondell as his second wife. The marriage lasted three years. He later married Elizabeth Taylor and stayed with her until his death. The Bishop of London condemned the high divorce rate in Britain and lay the blame on the influence of Hollywood. Artificial insemination was considered adulterous by the Public Morality Council in Britain.

POP CULTURE

In the movie *The Bachelor and the Bobby-Soxer* a playboy is court-ordered to date the judge's younger sister. In *Cynthia*, a teenager sheltered by her over-protective parents is finally allowed to go out on a date. In *Desire Me* a Frenchwoman's husband, long thought to be dead, returns from war and finds his wife in love with one of his friends. *The Ghost and Mrs. Muir*, later made into a TV series, was about a widow who falls in love with the sea captain's ghost haunting her cottage.

In the bestseller *Lydia Bailey* a lawyer is jailed, then escapes to Haiti to find his client's daughter—a woman he has fallen in love with, although they've never met. *Tales of the South Pacific* by James Michener tells a tale of soldiers, nurses, and islanders dealing with the war and waiting for love and romance in a tropical paradise. *Love Without Fear* is an early how-to manual about achieving a happy marital sex life.

Filling the airwaves were the Harmonicats singing "Peg O' My Heart," Paul Carpenter and his "Try A Little Tenderness," and Ivy Benson's "I'm in the Mood for Love."

Hot Couple

PRINCESS ELIZABETH & PRINCE PHILIP

On Nov. 20, 1947, the royal wedding of Princess Elizabeth to Philip, Duke of Edinburgh, at Westminster Abbey uplifted a war-weary Britain with pageantry and dreams of a hopeful future.

Embroidered with 10,000 seed pearls, the ivory silk bridal gown recalled the goddess Flora of Botticelli's Primavera. The groom cut a dashing figure in full dress garb of the Royal Navy, of which he was a lieutenant and World War II hero. His royal blood, athletic carriage, and continental education—not to mention his titles as prince of Greece and Denmark—made Philip a glamorous match for Britain's future queen.

SEE ALSO

▶ QUEEN ELIZABETH'S PARENTS *Page 40*
▶ LADY DI & PRINCE CHARLES *Page 516*

236

1947 CAPRICORN

From December 22, 1946 10:53 through January 20, 1947 21:31
(December 1947 Capricorns, see 1948 Capricorn)

♑ The Inspired Intimate

Your dreams about romance allow you to share an inspired intimacy with your sweetheart, 1947 Capricorn, but they are unlikely to cloud your ability to handle the nuts-and-bolts of keeping a relationship healthy and happy. What you want from love may seem to just come to you, but it's really the good karmic payoff for all the work you tend to put into a relationship. Sometimes you may act on an assumption about what a mate wants. If you don't get the reaction you expected, you can wind up feeling frustrated and disappointed. A few rounds of wasted effort may be all you need to make a point of consulting with your mate on any issues that may arise.

Expressing your needs with grace and poise, you may exude an easy confidence—an approach that makes it a pleasure for your mate to try to satisfy your requests. Treating your relationship as a team effort strengthens your bond. Your emotional intensity and eagerness to share new experiences allow you and your mate to keep the passion alive through the years. For you lovemaking can be a way to provide comfort in hard times, to celebrate your happiness in good times or simply to enjoy a thrilling physical release.

Assurance of your mate's devotion warms you up and eases you into the mood for love. Loving gestures—hand holding, sweet kisses on the cheek, a peck on the lips—can rouse your passion, but more blatant displays of affection may offend your need for privacy. Behind closed doors you can be an earthy lover, open to almost anything, and highly responsive to sensual pleasures.

The 1947 Capricorn man admires an optimistic woman with a philosophical outlook on the ups and downs of love. Her sense of humor enables her to put a positive spin on any situation. With a flair for spontaneity she can keep your relationship moving at a healthy pace.

The Capricorn woman born in 1947 enjoys a man who is self-assured and confident. You appreciate someone with a practical outlook, and this fellow fits the bill. His faith in your abilities can buttress your determination to reach for higher goals and greater levels of achievement.

CAPRICORN ZODIAC SIGN
Your Love Planets

YOUR ROMANTIC SIDE   p. 696
▶ VENUS IN SCORPIO
Born Dec. 22, 1946 10:53 - Jan. 05, 1947 16:44
▶ VENUS IN SAGITTARIUS
Born Jan. 05, 16:45 - Jan. 20, 21:31

YOUR SEX DRIVE   p. 722
▶ MARS IN CAPRICORN
Born Dec. 22, 1946 10:53 - Jan. 20, 1947 21:31

YOUR CELEBRITY TWINS   p. 760
Find out the astrological similarities you have with famous people.

YOUR COMPATIBILITY   p. 780
Compare planets to find out how compatible you are in a relationship.

YOUR RELATIONSHIP KARMA   p. 824
▶ SATURN IN LEO
Born Dec. 22, 1946 10:53 - Jan. 20, 1947 21:31

LIZABETH SCOTT
American Actress
Mars in Capricorn

237

1947 AQUARIUS

From January 20, 21:32 through February 19, 11:51

♒ The Erotic Eccentric

An eccentric or unorthodox relationship may feel perfectly natural to you, 1947 Aquarian. You may have chosen an unusual mate, perhaps someone from a different culture or religion. What other people think about your romantic choices tends not to matter much to you. Your determination to be true to yourself, in all your original glory, appeals to your mate and keeps things interesting. Intense affection tends to seal your bond with your mate, but the trade-off for such deep passion can be the occasional power struggle. Because you have the will to get at the root of any issue, you and your mate can weather the storm and become closer for having made the effort.

Friendship can be exciting and erotic for you, and while your mate is probably your best pal, the two of you are likely to enjoy a sparkling social life. The longevity of your relationship rests on your ability to strike a healthy balance between breathing space for each partner and time together to nurture and renew your commitment. Day-to-day life with your mate is rarely boring for you because you can be so creative finding ways to jazz up your routine. Animal attraction tends to be a running undercurrent that draws you and your mate together like magnets.

Indulging your sensual side can put you in the mood for love. You most likely adore romantic getaways that allow you and your mate to luxuriate—feasting your eyes on scenic views, your stomach on luscious cuisine, and your body on special spa treatments. A nice hot soak for your feet and ankles is welcome anytime.

The Aquarian man of 1947 is drawn to a woman who pursues her ideals with passion and conviction. You admire someone who backs up her beliefs with concrete actions and results. Her illuminating insights and devotion can inspire you to pursue a path that is meaningful to you.

An empathic, intuitive man is a superb counterpart for the 1947 Aquarian woman. His ability to combine gut instincts with a sense of spiritual mission is a perfect complement for your sharp intellectual mind. Together, you can devote your relationship to a higher cause.

AQUARIUS ZODIAC SIGN
Your Love Planets

YOUR ROMANTIC SIDE   p. 696
▶ VENUS IN SAGITTARIUS
Born Jan. 20, 21:32 - Feb. 06, 5:40
▶ VENUS IN CAPRICORN
Born Feb. 06, 5:41 - Feb. 19, 11:51

YOUR SEX DRIVE   p. 722
▶ MARS IN CAPRICORN
Born Jan. 20, 21:32 - Jan. 25, 11:43
▶ MARS IN AQUARIUS
Born Jan. 25, 11:44 - Feb. 19, 11:51

YOUR CELEBRITY TWINS   p. 760
Find out the astrological similarities you have with famous people.

YOUR COMPATIBILITY   p. 780
Compare planets to find out how compatible you are in a relationship.

YOUR RELATIONSHIP KARMA   p. 824
▶ SATURN IN LEO
Born Jan. 20, 21:32 - Feb. 19, 11:51

ALIDA VALLI
Italian Actress
Venus in Aries

238

1947 PISCES
February 19, 11:52 through March 21, 11:12

The Fantasy Fulfiller

A stable relationship can be as essential to you, 1947 Pisces, as the air you breathe. To be truly at one with your mate—in heart, mind, body, and soul—can be the fulfillment of a life-long dream. While you may have a flair for fantasy, once assured of your partner's devotion, you tend to shed romantic illusions and create a practical reality as tender, harmonious, and comforting as anything you might imagine. Forsaking all others can be a relief for you, allowing you to focus your energies on taking care of your mate and family, an occupation you most likely find deeply satisfying.

You may have chosen a mate who was older than you or who exuded an air of authority and self-assurance. Such a take-charge personality can make you feel safe and sheltered from a sometimes cruel world. While you may thrive within the security of a loving commitment, you can become too isolated and drift away from dear friends and pursuits. Entertaining with your mate allows you to invite the world into your home and stay close to the people you love. You may find it highly enriching to team up with your partner and other family members in outside activities.

Your physical attraction to your mate tends to be strong. Indulging your sweetheart's body may be your favorite hobby, and sex may be your favorite form of exercise. Because you are likely to have great erotic stamina, a lover with staying power can give you big thrills. Sensitive to atmospheric touches, you can absorb the mood set by lovely music, soft lighting, and sweet aromas.

A fiercely devoted woman creates an alluring aura of romance for the 1947 Piscean man. You enjoy someone who pursues her passions with determination and tenacity, especially when you are the object of her desire. Her hypnotic powers of seduction can be utterly electrifying.

The 1947 Piscean woman can relate best to a protective man who is sensitive to the feelings of others. You appreciate a good listener, one who is willing to make an effort to find out what you care about. The pleasure he gets from satisfying your desires assures you of a win-win relationship.

1947 ARIES
March 21, 11:13 through April 20, 22:38

The Instant Inamorata

For you, Aries of 1947, love at first sight can be a happy way of life. You can fall in love instantly with a new friend, a movie, an activity, a car, a pet—almost anything! First impressions tend to capture your interest, and you may sometimes base your expectations on hopes more than reality. Only the test of time can prove whether a new preoccupation will become an enduring part of your life. When you first laid eyes on your partner, you may have sensed that destiny had something in mind for the two of you. Your dreams of perfect romance fill a relationship with enchantment, and a mate's persistence may play an important role in getting your partnership over the hump from hot-and-heavy to serious, substantive, and lasting.

As your emotional attachment deepens, your mate's little flaws, foibles, and quirks become more endearing to you. Your sensitivity to the feelings of others ensures you will consult with your mate before making any moves that could affect both of you. Because you tend to take on new challenges with great enthusiasm and you have an iron will for follow-through, you leave your mate no room to doubt your ability to realize shared goals. The passion you bring to life in general gains its most intense expression for you in lovemaking.

Non-verbal communication allows you to feel completely in tune with your mate. Little signals and gestures known only to the two of you can add a flirtatious sense of fun to your bond. Pleasing your mate boosts your excitement, and you may love it when your partner moans in ecstasy.

The 1947 Aries man can hardly resist a woman who is starry-eyed and idealistic. The originality of her ideas can complement your own talents as a pioneer and trendsetter. With her wild imagination, this lovely lady can inspire you to blaze new and exciting romantic trails together.

The Aries woman of 1947 adores a man who is protective and empathetic. You appreciate someone who is attentive to your needs and watches out for you, even when you're not looking. With this fellow's ardent devotion to you, he assures you of support in all your pursuits.

1947 TAURUS
From April 20, 22:39 through May 21, 22:08

The Comforting Creature

Sheer animal attraction could set a romance in motion for you, 1947 Taurus, and it can mature into a stable, affectionate love affair. You tend to be confident and self-assured, and you set about pursuing your passions with a calm determination. With your subtle, sexy seductive appeal you can often get what you want to come to you—a gift that can bring great satisfaction, as long as you don't expect your mate to read your mind. You needn't shy away from directly asking your partner for anything you want. Your demands are rarely unreasonable, and, after all, why deny your mate an opportunity to make you happy?

You can flourish with a mate who is energetic and intense—someone who can stir your deeper impulses, inspire you to take action, and turn you on to new challenges. Your practical outlook allows you to support your partner as you progress through different stages in life. Over time, your mate is likely to gain an intimate familiarity with more than a few of your favorite things. Indulging you may become a regular part of your mate's romantic routine because you can be so tender, amorous, and just plain sexy when contented. Because you tend to be very comfortable in your own skin, lovemaking may be the perfect creature comfort for you.

For you, sex allows you to satisfy basic cravings for physical contact, warmth, and affection. You may like it when your mate introduces new techniques or turns you on to a bodily response you didn't know you had, but what matters most to you is to know and hear how much your partner loves you.

The Taurean man of 1947 appreciates a woman who is spirited and passionate. Someone who takes the initiative in your relationship allows you the luxury of sitting back and enjoying yourself. With her lust for life she can introduce you on to pleasures beyond your wildest dreams.

An active, spontaneous man tends to complement the more laid-back style of the 1947 Taurean woman. Someone with a fervent interest in you assures you of the security of your bond. With his strength and vigor he can keep you moving and fill you with an invigorating spirit.

GLENN FORD
American Actor
Sun in Taurus

239

1947 GEMINI
From May 21, 22:09 through June 22, 6:18

The Spontaneous Sweetheart

You bring a refreshing spontaneity to any relationship, 1947 Gemini. Unlikely to worry about things that only might happen, you offer a mate the promise of a carefree existence. And because you tend not to dwell on the past, you don't burden your relationship with blame or recriminations. Your ability to focus on what's in front of you frees you and your mate to enjoy all of the pleasures and opportunities of the moment. Still, too much resistance to planning for the future can create tension in your relationship and raise a mate's concerns about your ability to honor commitments. Your empathy for a mate's concerns allows you to work out compromises and defuse any conflicts that might wear on your sensitive Geminian nerves.

Flexible and forgiving, you can openly discuss issues with your mate and improvise creative solutions to any problems. You are likely to be a highly principled person, and your shared spiritual values may be the glue that holds your partnership together over time. The passion you and your mate share tends to be deep and steady. Facing challenges together brings you even closer and strengthens your bond. Lovemaking allows you to express your affection through meaningful and poignant touching.

Taking time to talk and reconnect with your honey can be the foreplay to your foreplay. You respond well to mood music, soft lighting, and lavish treats that cater to each of your senses. A natural setting with flowers, gentle breezes, and singing birds is a perfect location for a romantic date.

A sensuous, nurturing woman can be highly enticing to the 1947 Gemini man. You appreciate a lover with a serene disposition, someone who is willing to assume the best about any given situation. Providing a comforting, harmonious home life comes naturally to her and brings you peace.

The man who takes time to smell the roses can offer a meaningful life to the 1947 Gemini woman. You admire someone who has a clear sense of what really matters in life and who makes the most of the joyous times you share. His easygoing style brings welcome relief on stressful days.

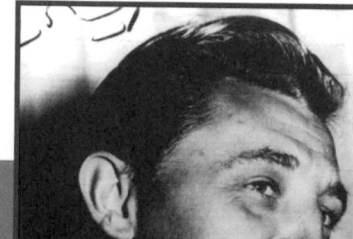

ROBERT MITCHUM
American Actor
Sun in Leo

240

1947 CANCER
From June 22, 6:19 through July 23, 17:13

♋ The Empathetic Enthusiast

Your rich imagination can fill your relationship with sweetness and enchantment, 1947 Cancer, and yet you know how to keep fantasy safely in its place. While great passion may heave in your heart, it does not rule you. Rather, you may have very firm ideals about how lovers should treat one another, and living up to your own standards comes naturally to you. Sometimes your expectations may exceed your mate's abilities and lead to disappointment. Charitable impulses prevent you from being overly judgmental, though, and enable you to shift your focus to what you love best about your partner.

Your ability to truly empathize with your mate's feelings, even when you disagree with each other, is one of your most admirable qualities—and the key to the longevity of your relationship. Your positive outlook brings wonderful karmic rewards because it brings out the very best from your sweetheart. A marvelous enthusiasm for learning may liven up your romance, and you and your mate may enjoy reading, taking courses, or vacationing together in locales that offer intellectual inspiration. In the sanctity of the bedroom you can be an uninhibited and adventurous lover.

Going with your mate to socialize and enjoy outside activities can make you eager to get home and enjoy some one-on-one intimacy. Your sexual curiosity may keep you young-at-heart. In the privacy of your bedroom you can explore a range of erotic possibilities. You may get a charge out of inventive techniques, interesting accessories, and creative variations in your routine.

The Cancerian man of 1947 appreciates a woman who is bright and playful. Ideally, she stays on the alert for the kinds of things that can bring you pleasure and enjoyment. Her thoughtful way of keeping you in mind as she goes through her day assures you of her devotion.

The Cancerian woman born in 1947 enjoys a man who appreciates the fine points of love and romance. Able to remember the little things, he can surprise and impress you with his thoughtfulness. His astute perception assures you that he can deal with any situation and keep you safe.

1947 LEO
From July 23, 17:14 through August 24, 0:08

♌ The Resilient Romantic

Your desires run deep, Leo of 1947, and you may pursue what you want with ardent determination and enchanting subtlety. At its peak your passion can be all-encompassing, burning in your heart, mind, soul—even in your bones. Early on, a mad, dramatic romance may have held you in thrall, but with maturity you may tend to avoid pushing your resilience to its limits. You exude a compelling elegance that spares you the need to be pushy or obvious, and you may have long since left any youthful impulsiveness behind you. With your unusual ability to convey your needs you can be a master in the art of seduction, capturing your mate's attention with a look, smile, or gesture.

Conversations between you are likely to be animated, and an interesting debate can provide you with an entertaining way to blow off steam. Because you tend to consult each other extensively about decisions affecting your relationship or family, you most likely excel in working out solutions to any problems together. Intimate familiarity with each other's perspectives may be a point of pride, but the feeling of being truly understood keeps your love strong. A secure commitment allows you and your partner to create a natural rhythm for the ebb and flow of erotic energies.

You may love it when your partner dares you to turn your pillow talk into action. Open to suggestion, you may be willing to try anything once, especially if it's fun. Experimenting with new techniques can be highly exciting for you, and the two of you might occasionally make room in bed for an open sex manual.

A striking woman who carries herself with dignity can be alluring to the 1947 Leo man. Behind closed doors, her kittenish, playful ways offer you a delightful surprise, but you may most appreciate her fierce loyalty to you. Her affection can make you feel like a king.

The Leo woman of 1947 adores the man who can be clever and mischievous. You may get a charge out of being around someone with a sharp mind and a great sense of humor. With his insight he can find a valuable lesson in any situation and help you to rebound from any setback.

1947 VIRGO

From August 24, 0:09 through September 23, 21:28

The Affable Amour

In your modesty, Virgo of 1947, you might wave off any likeness between you and columnist Will Rogers, but you do have the grace and kindness to be able to see at least something to like in any person. Your demure discretion and aversion to conflict may prompt you to follow the maxim, "If you don't have something nice to say, say nothing at all." Your affable style lends harmonious flow to your relationship because you are more likely to let your mate know what you do need and like, as opposed to what you don't. Should you catch yourself voicing a criticism, you and you mate should take it as a sign that you are under stress. Rather than arguing over whether your disapproval is justified, you may need to look deeper, talk it over, and find out what is really bothering you.

The romance you share with your sweetheart may have begun as a friendship that grew into a deeply passionate bond. Socializing with others allows you and your mate to enjoy a lifestyle filled with warmth and excitement. Time alone together allows the most special and unique aspects of your personalities to emerge in all their glory. Lovemaking allows you and your partner to lavish each other with penetrating attention and tender empathy.

Taking care of your mate's needs—in your daily routine or in bed—can be satisfying for you, but open appreciation of your efforts can make your spirits and passions soar. You may have a weakness for outfits that tastefully show off a mate's build. Fine food can add to the pleasure of entertaining in, going out, or fooling around.

For the Virgo man of 1947, a refined woman with a strong sense of personal character can be a highly attractive mate. You admire someone who has a lot of class in the way she carries herself and treats others. Her integrity provides a rock solid foundation for lasting love.

A considerate and accommodating man is the ideal match for the Virgo woman born in 1947. The nicest thing he can do is to show generosity and affection to the people dearest to you. With his open-hearted spirit he supports and enhances your ability to care for your loved ones.

VIRGO ZODIAC SIGN
YOUR LOVE PLANETS

YOUR ROMANTIC SIDE   p. 696
- ▶ **VENUS IN LEO**
  Born Aug. 24, 0:09 - Aug. 26, 8:16
- ▶ **VENUS IN VIRGO**
  Born Aug. 26, 8:17 - Sept. 19, 12:00
- ▶ **VENUS IN LIBRA**
  Born Sept. 19, 12:01 - Sept. 23, 21:28

YOUR SEX DRIVE   p. 722
- ▶ **MARS IN CANCER**
  Born Aug. 24, 0:09 - Sept. 23, 21:28

YOUR CELEBRITY TWINS   p. 760
Find out the astrological similarities you have with famous people.

YOUR COMPATIBILITY   p. 780
Compare planets to find out how compatible you are in a relationship.

YOUR RELATIONSHIP KARMA   p. 824
- ▶ **SATURN IN LEO**
  Born Aug. 24, 0:09 - Sept. 23, 21:28

LINDA DARNELL
American Actress
Sun in Libra

241

1947 LIBRA

From September 23, 21:29 through October 24, 6:25

The Playful Partner

Although you can be a starry-eyed romantic, 1947 Libra, time and experience may have given you a first-hand appreciation of those immortal lyrics by the Rolling Stones: "You can't always get what you want..." But blessed with a strong spirit, you are not one to give up on love. Able to combine your dreams of the ideal with an appreciation for what you actually have, you might often find, "...you get what you need." An attitude of gratitude enables you to be an inspiring partner, bringing out the best in your mate, setting a standard for mutual generosity in your relationship, and creating a solid foundation for love that lasts.

It may not take a village to raise your romance, but you and your mate may rely on a community of friends and loved ones who watch out for you, lend moral support, and celebrate your milestones. Your commitment thrives on the encouragement you and your sweetheart give each other in pursuing new challenges and realizing your best potentials as individuals. As the two of you continue to grow and change over the years, your enchanting flair for romance can still fill your relationship with new sources of interest and excitement. For you lovemaking is best when it engages your body and imagination equally.

The bedroom is one place where you and your mate can be forever young. You may love to share and fulfill fantasies, role-playing elaborate scenarios. You might keep a private toy box well stocked with accessories and enhancements that can provide you and your partner with hours of fun.

The Libran man born in 1947 enjoys a woman who has a compelling inner beauty. You admire someone who can take a variety of competing perspectives or opinions and blend them into an harmonious whole. She can bring peace to family relations and lovely atmospheric touches to your home.

An affectionate man with a flamboyant air can be an utterly charming partner for the 1947 Libran woman. You may have a weakness for someone willing to go to rather elaborate lengths to woo you. With his creative sensibility and your artistic talents, he can be your biggest fan.

LIBRA ZODIAC SIGN
YOUR LOVE PLANETS

YOUR ROMANTIC SIDE   p. 696
- ▶ **VENUS IN LIBRA**
  Born Sept. 23, 21:29 - Oct. 13, 13:48
- ▶ **VENUS IN SCORPIO**
  Born Oct. 13, 13:49 - Oct. 24, 6:25

YOUR SEX DRIVE   p. 722
- ▶ **MARS IN CANCER**
  Born Sept. 23, 21:29 - Oct. 01, 2:30
- ▶ **MARS IN LEO**
  Born Oct. 01, 2:31 - Oct. 24, 6:25

YOUR CELEBRITY TWINS   p. 760
Find out the astrological similarities you have with famous people.

YOUR COMPATIBILITY   p. 780
Compare planets to find out how compatible you are in a relationship.

YOUR RELATIONSHIP KARMA   p. 824
- ▶ **SATURN IN LEO**
  Born Sept. 23, 21:29 - Oct. 24, 6:25

VAN HEFLIN
American Actor
Sun and Venus in Sagittarius

242

1947 SCORPIO
From October 24, 6:26 through November 23, 3:37

♏ The Desiring Darling

Healthy balance is the key to romantic success for you, Scorpio of 1947. Your passions run deep and your desires may run even deeper—so much so, that the intensity of your personality may have been hard for you to manage when you were younger. Likely to have been unusually sensitive to others' reactions, you might have allowed the slightest rejection to shut you down completely. By now you may be perfectly comfortable leaving the safe, predictable relationships to the wilting lilies of this world. The best mate for you is a hearty soul, someone not easily cowed, and who can't get enough of you.

With your expansive appetite for adventure and meaningful experiences, you thrive with a partner eager to go for the gusto in life. For you the feeling of being truly understood may be the most precious thing about your relationship. In return, you tend to be a profoundly loyal and reliable partner, tender and caring toward your mate and family. An equal partnership can even out any extremes in your moods, feelings, or sex drive. When your energy level is dragging, you can rely on your mate to pick up the slack, take care of business, and uncurb your enthusiasm. If your engine is revving too high, your honey can help you unwind and relax.

Lovemaking may be your favorite tool for stirring up your passions or venting excess energy. To fully unleash your inhibitions you must be able to trust your mate with your deepest emotions and secrets. Experimenting with different techniques can be exciting, and the practices of exotic cultures may inspire you.

A woman with a virtually insatiable capacity for pleasure can be a stimulating match for the 1947 Scorpio man. Her powerful drives can keep you on your toes. A lady like this practically dares you to go for the maximum joy in life, a challenge you may embrace with glee.

A generous, courageous man allows the Scorpio woman of 1947 to enjoy an inspired romance. You treasure someone who is fiercely protective of you and the private life you share. With his sunny disposition and animal magnetism he can brighten even your darkest day.

1947 SAGITTARIUS
From November 23, 3:38 through December 22, 16:42

♐ The Freedom Lover

Freedom is the air that fans the flames of romance for you, 1947 Sagittarius. The more space your mate allows you, the closer you become. The irony of that little insight on love may amuse you, and your partner's ability to accept it can sustain your relationship over time. Insecure, possessive, or controlling suitors need not apply. With you, affection tends to come in big bursts and with grand gestures. You can be a generous mate, lavishing your beloved with gifts and attention. Once the high degree of passion levels off, you may include other interests in your relationship and share these with your partner.

Once you pledge your love, your mate need never doubt your ability to be faithful. Your word is your bond. To cheat on your beloved can be painful for you because it forces you to go against your nature. A committed relationship works best when your partner has plenty of activities to pursue in addition to what you are involved in together. A little absence may make you impatient to see your mate so you can update each other on the latest developments. Sharing ideas with your mate can be as fun as opening a stack of birthday presents. A healthy sense of humor can help your partner adapt to the unusual rhythm of your relationship.

As much as you enjoy spontaneity, your mate should make sure you're well-equipped to make the most of the moment. You can never have too many lotions, potions, candles, music, sex manuals, accessories, or erotic enhancements. Finding creative ways to use them keeps lovemaking fresh and exciting for you.

The Sagittarian man of 1947 thrives with a woman who has a dry wit and a practical, no-nonsense outlook on life. You appreciate someone who can take your ambitious ideas and produce concrete results. This patient lady can help you see your visions through to completion.

The Sagittarian woman born in 1947 can have a well-rounded relationship with a man who pays attention to detail. You enjoy a partner who takes care of the finer points of daily life. With his refined tastes this man makes it his business to give you the very best.

THE '40s

Juan and Eva Peron – A Powerful Love

On January 15, 1944 a major earthquake shook Argentina, killing some 7,000 people and injuring another 12,000. Colonel Juan Peron, the Secretary of Labor and Social Welfare, organized a benefit concert at which the popular actress and radio personality Eva Duarte performed. After the show, Eva elbowed her way through the crowd to sit next to him and get an introduction. They instantly fell in love and began the most dramatic relationship in Argentine history.

Although their backgrounds were very different, both Juan and Eva had Sun and Mars together in each of their horoscopes, giving them extraordinary drive and ambition to get ahead. Eva's parents were never married, so for her entire life she carried the stigma of being an illegitimate child. With her Sun and Mars in Taurus, Eva naturally became a singer and was also gifted at dancing. She moved to Buenos Aires to make her mark in show business, and by the time she met Juan Peron at age 24 she had found success in a radio soap opera and performing in a series called *The Biographies of Illustrious Women* where she played characters like Elizabeth I, Sarah Bernhardt, and Catherine the Great.

Juan Peron was born with his Sun and Mars in Libra, the love sign of partnership. This combination works best through marriage, although Eva was his mistress for two years before they married. He excelled at military school, becoming a champion fencer, and was also a skilled boxer and skier. In 1943 he participated in a coup that overthrew the ineffective civilian government and soon gained popular recognition for his support of the underprivileged class of laborers. In October 1945 a 'counter-coup forced

Peron to resign, and he was exiled to the island of Martin Garcia.

The events that followed were dramatically portrayed in the operatic movie *Evita*, starring Madonna in her most successful cinematic effort. Evita, as she was called, worked with the leaders of the labor unions to get Juan released on October 17, 1945. That evening Peron addressed a crowd of 300,000 supporters from the balcony of the presidential palace. His speech was broadcast on live radio as well. He promised to win the upcoming Presidential election, and a few days later he married Eva to thank her and legitimize their relationship.

The extraordinary teamwork of Eva and Juan Peron can be seen in their horoscopes. His Mars trines her Venus, a perfectly harmonious interchange between these love planets. Then,

adding a synergistic boost to their chemistry, her Mars trines his Venus, making a double dose of love and physical compatibility. The next time Juan Peron faced a Presidential election in 1951, he asked his wife to run as his Vice President. On August 22 one million of her ardent supporters gathered outside the presidential palace, chanting for her to accept the offer.

However, on August 31 she announced on national radio that she would not run for the office. Insiders claim that army officers forced her out of the race, but she was also becoming gravely ill. She finally agreed to see a doctor and was told that she had uterine cancer, too far advanced to treat. Juan Peron was re-elected. She made her last public appearance at his inauguration in June 1952 and died the next month.

243

▶ READ ABOUT MADONNA ON PAGES 548 & 555

1948

- ⊛ ORAL SEX
- ⊛ DICK VAN DYKE
- ⊛ JOHNNY BELINDA
- ⊛ SEXUAL BEHAVIOR IN THE HUMAN MALE
- ⊛ WALDEN TWO
- ⊛ PEGGY LEE

EVENTS

The US Congress was busy in 1948. The Assimilative Crimes Act from 1909, which allowed the federal government to prosecute sodomy, was amended by Congress to increase the jurisdictions in the US where oral sex would be considered illegal. The Miller Act was ostensibly introduced to increase penalties for sex crimes against minors, but was in fact aimed at homosexuals.

The rising film star Carole Landis committed suicide at age 29, reportedly over an affair gone wrong with actor Rex Harrison.

In Britain the Women's Service Bill was passed, making the wartime ATS and WAAF permanent bodies. Lillian Penson became the first woman to hold the post of vice-chancellor of London University. The future queen, Princess Elizabeth, gave birth to her first child, Prince Charles.

POP CULTURE

In *Johnny Belinda* a Nova Scotia doctor helps a deaf-mute rape victim with a baby to love again. *Anna Karenina*, starring Vivian Leigh, was Tolstoy's story of a woman who abandons her husband and child for the man she loves. *The Pirate*, directed by Vincente Minnelli, gave us an actor who courts a Caribbean islander by posing as the pirate of her dreams. In *Easter Parade* a dancer in New York who is dumped by his partner trains a chorus girl to take her place. In *Every Girl Should Be Married* a heroine uses strategy and her rich boss to lure an eligible doctor into marriage.

Sex Idol

The bestseller *Dinner at Antoine's*, by Frances Parkinson Keyes, was a story of love, deception, and murder. *Sexual Behavior in the Human Male* by Alfred C. Kinsey both shocked and intrigued Americans enough to make it a bestseller and revealed that Americans who claim to be prudish about sex are anything but. *Walden Two* by B.F. Skinner was the author's idea of Utopia, with early marriage and childbearing strongly encouraged.

Dinah Shore was on the Hit Parade again with "Buttons and Bows." Doris Day with Buddy Clark sang "Love Somebody," Peggy Lee belted out "Manana," and Al Trace sang "You Call Everybody Darlin'." Nat King Cole's "Nature Boy" and Kay Kyser's "Woody Woodpecker" were also hits.

CARY GRANT

A third marriage, in 1948, did not turn out to be the charm for silver screen legend Cary Grant. The bride, Betsy Drake, was Grant's co-star in the ironically titled film that year, *Every Girl Should Be Married*. Having accumulated five wives before his death in 1986, perhaps the urbane, witty actor thought every girl should be married to Cary Grant.

He would have had plenty of takers. Projecting a suave, gentlemanly air, Grant was the model for the James Bond character created by author Ian Fleming, although he turned down the opportunity to play Agent 007 in the movies.

SEE ALSO
▶ THE BOND GIRLS *Pages 687*
▶ HITCHCOCK & HIS BLONDES *Pages 341*

1948 CAPRICORN

From December 22, 1947 16:43 through January 21, 1948 3:17
December 1948 Capricorns, see 1949 Capricorn

The Happy Individual

Over the course of your love life, 1948 Capricorn, your relationships may have fallen into two categories—the easy-going affair that provided comfort and stability, versus the high-intensity romance that brought growth and change. At this point in your life, you may be more focused on a having relationship that allows you to combine and harmonize both extremes. Likely to prize individuality over social as you are conventions, you can flourish with a mate who prizes your unique loveableness. You tend to be a diligent, reliable, and methodical partner. You may enjoy a steady flow of sexual energy that you can channel into wooing your mate or providing security for your relationship and family life.

Still, you can get set in your ways, and too much routine can leave you in a rut. The passion of a soul mate attraction can add spice and momentum to your partnership. There may be some turbulence and growing pains, but the exhilaration of the highs can justify the lows. Entrusting your partner with your deepest feelings—allowing yourself to be raw and vulnerable—can jolt your relationship into a new period of growth and evolution. Your desire to make a true, intimate connection with your mate can move you to overcome any emotional or sexual inhibitions.

You may be a real softie for the traditional trappings of romance. Candlelight, sentimental music selections, and thoughtful gifts can ease you into the mood for love. Physical affection outside the bedroom makes you feel loved and keeps the passion flowing between you and your mate.

The Capricorn man of 1948 admires a woman who can be a good friend and a bit of a rebel. Her naughty impulses can give you a welcome rise from time to time. With her loyalty and trustworthiness you can enjoy the comfort level necessary to allow her to take some liberties.

The Capricorn woman born in 1948 enjoys a man who can be meticulous but also flexible. You can relax with someone who is sensitive to your need for privacy and discretion. With attention to detail that assures you of his competence, his take-charge confidence can be downright sexy.

CAPRICORN ZODIAC SIGN
YOUR LOVE PLANETS

YOUR ROMANTIC SIDE   p. 696
- ▶ VENUS IN CAPRICORN
  Born Dec. 22, 1947 16:43 - Dec. 24, 1947 19:12
- ▶ VENUS IN AQUARIUS
  Born Dec. 24, 1947 19:13 - Jan. 18, 1948 2:13
- ▶ VENUS IN PISCES
  Born Jan. 18, 2:14 - Jan. 21, 3:17

YOUR SEX DRIVE   p. 722
- ▶ MARS IN VIRGO
  Born Dec. 22, 1947 16:43 - Jan. 21, 1948 3:17

YOUR CELEBRITY TWINS   p. 760
  Find out the astrological similarities you have
  with famous people.

YOUR COMPATIBILITY   p. 780
  Compare planets to find out how compatible
  you are in a relationship.

YOUR RELATIONSHIP KARMA   p. 824
- ▶ SATURN IN LEO
  Born Dec. 22, 1947 16:43 - Jan. 21, 1948 3:17

MOIRA SHEARER
Scottish Dancer
Sun in Capricorn

245

1948 AQUARIUS

From January 21, 3:18 through February 19, 17:36

The Romantic Radical

Love and romance may have opened up a brave new world of personal enrichment for you, Aquarius of 1948. During your lifetime, shifting societal standards on sexuality and sex roles granted you unprecedented freedom and invited you to express your individuality. Likely to reject tradition and social conventions unless there's a rational reason for them, you may be flexible about the part each mate should play and the necessity of a permanent commitment. Your approach to relationships may have seemed radical to your elders. Tending to expect sexual satisfaction, you and your mate may openly discuss matters that would make your granny faint.

Spontaneity keeps love interesting for you. Your mate may inspire you to experiment with different lifestyles and to make conscious decisions about the kind of commitment that works for both of you. Because your passion can come in bursts, and because you thrive with a lot of breathing space, you may cope well with the on-again-off-again dynamic of a long-distance relationship. Open communication and shared ideals can keep your romance going. The feeling that your mate is unique—that nobody does it better—tends to create a deep sense of attachment between the two of you.

Because your mind plays as important a role in lovemaking as any other part of your body, intellectual pursuits can rouse your passions. You can fall in love with a good idea or be open to the seductive suggestion of a poem or a song. The rebel in you may get a charge out of naughty acts with a risk of discovery.

The Aquarian man of 1948 is drawn to a woman who has high ideals and the determination to pursue them. You admire someone who can bring a spiritual perspective into your relationship mix. With her empathy and compassion for others this lady can be a most inspiring partner.

A caring, nurturing man can be a superb counterpart for the 1948 Aquarian woman. You may enjoy the unique and original appeal of a man who has a well-developed feminine side. Because it takes guts to be a nonconformist, he exudes a strength that is as unusual as it is admirable.

AQUARIUS ZODIAC SIGN
YOUR LOVE PLANETS

YOUR ROMANTIC SIDE   p. 696
- ▶ VENUS IN PISCES
  Born Jan. 21, 3:18 - Feb. 11, 18:50
- ▶ VENUS IN ARIES
  Born Feb. 11, 18:51 - Feb. 19, 17:36

YOUR SEX DRIVE   p. 722
- ▶ MARS IN VIRGO
  Born Jan. 21, 3:18 - Feb. 12, 10:27
- ▶ MARS IN LEO
  Born Feb. 12, 10:28 - Feb. 19, 17:36

YOUR CELEBRITY TWINS   p. 760
  Find out the astrological similarities you have
  with famous people.

YOUR COMPATIBILITY   p. 780
  Compare planets to find out how compatible
  you are in a relationship.

YOUR RELATIONSHIP KARMA   p. 824
- ▶ SATURN IN LEO
  Born Jan. 21, 3:18 - Feb. 19, 17:36

GEORGE BALANCHINE
Russian Ballet Choreographer
Mars in Pisces

246

1948 PISCES
From February 19, 17:37 through March 20, 16:56

The Liberated Lover

As quiet and subtle as you may be, 1948 Pisces, you have the makings to be a true warrior of the Sexual Revolution. The rules about relationships that you learned in childhood may have proved unworkable for you in adulthood, especially if they forced you to repress any healthy need for sex and intimate satisfaction. You may have struggled a bit with the uncertainty that comes with making up your own laws on love. In the end, though, your values were likely to lead you to a mate who would share your outlook and support you in being true to yourself. Erotic freedom can be energizing for you because it provides a physical outlet for your strong spiritual and emotional impulses.

An active sex life with a loving mate can inspire you to fully express your creativity in every aspect of your life. The security of a committed relationship gives you a stable home base from which you and your sweetheart can explore opportunities for personal growth and pursue shared goals in the world. You tend to be a flexible partner, sensitive to your mate's feelings and needs, and willing to compromise on important issues. Having defined your expectations about love together, the two of you can create a partnership that allows you to thrive.

For you lovemaking can be an adventure in erotic discovery, and you may experiment with different positions and techniques. Mystical influences can spice up an encounter, especially those reflecting the traditions of exotic cultures. Tantrism and the Kama Sutra can take your sex life into a new dimension.

An ardent, passionate woman can be an exciting partner for the 1948 Piscean man. You enjoy someone who approaches intimacy with a fiery sensuality. Her forward, daring style can embolden you to open up and take a few risks. With this wild child you can let it all hang out.

The 1948 Piscean woman relates best to a man who exudes an animal magnetism and makes love like a big teddy bear. You appreciate someone who is big-hearted and fiercely devoted to you. His warmth and sunny smile can cut through the gloom on a rainy day and utterly enchant you.

1948 ARIES
From March 20, 16:57 through April 20, 4:24

The Homey Hunter

The thrill of the chase can hold a spellbinding allure for you, 1948 Aries, but the love of your life is likely to turn you on to the thrill of staying put. The drama of being a star-crossed lover may have been captivating in your youth. But to lust after the impossible may have proved so frustrating, you were likely to ultimately abandon pursuits that promised no reward at their end. You are not one to run around in romantic circles. In a loving relationship you have an amazing ability to inspire a partner to break out of a rut and head in a new direction. Conversely, your soul mate can awaken you to the joy of standing still—enabling you to discover and express the part of you that is patient, serene, happy to just let things happen, and enjoy the moment.

As a partner you tend to be warm, open, and friendly. Perhaps to your surprise, a serious commitment can bring you a feeling of completion. Chasing after dreams and fantasies can be more worthwhile for you when it is a team effort. Your animal magnetism can excite a lover's interest. In the privacy of the bedroom you may exude a languid sensuality, like a lion sunning itself on the savanna, but once aroused, you can spring into action like a tiger.

Indulging your senses can stir your desires. Strong feelings—including the anger of an argument—tend to intensify the passion and pleasure of sex for you, but lovemaking can soothe tempers and deepen your emotional attachment to your mate. An unfailing kiss goodnight or goodbye assures you of your mate's devotion.

An earthy, luscious woman can be irresistibly seductive to the 1948 Arien man. Her easy, laid-back attitude can help you to power down after a long day running from one task to another. With her capacity for sensory pleasure, she can entice you into the bliss of utter contentment.

The Arien woman of 1948 can thrive with a man who is playful and proud. You appreciate someone with a flair for the broad theatrical gesture. His ability to attract attention may delight you, and his big-hearted generosity ensures that you'll always know how special you are.

1948 TAURUS

From April 20, 4:25 through May 21, 3:57

The Erotic Explorer

Taurus of 1948, you are not one to let something unique and original slip between your fingers. Your one and only is that special person who fits you like a warm, cashmere glove. Romance is ideal for you when your lover is a best friend with tastes and desires compatible with your own. You sometimes resist change and feel uncomfortable in unfamiliar situations, but with a trusted partner by your side, you can try things that you might avoid on your own. A serious relationship opens up all kinds of avenues for personal growth for you. Secure in your mate's encouragement, you can take risks and pursue opportunities that allow you to push the envelope of your talents.

Over time your relationship goes through its stages at a natural and steady pace. Boredom is rarely a problem for you and your mate because there is always something new and unusual to discover and learn together. Because the two of you tend to agree on what is beautiful and delightful, turning each other on to different ideas for fun and pleasure can keep your partnership exciting. Physical affection may be a part of your daily health regimen with a good-morning snuggle, goodbye hugs and kisses, and lots of friendly stroking and handholding in between.

You tend to be an uninhibited lover, eager to explore and probe every part of your mate's body. An open attitude and enthusiastic response from your partner can be like cheerleading for you. You may love going out together to sample fine foods, cultural events, and artistic forms of entertainment.

The Taurean man of 1948 can get along famously with a woman who is brilliant and charming. Her adaptability can be a welcome complement to your sometimes settled ways. With her keen perception she can sense when you're getting into a rut and draw you out for some needed stimulation.

An adventurous, fun-loving man can indulge the exotic tastes of the 1948 Taurean woman. You enjoy someone who can furnish you with a wide variety of ways to thrill your senses. With his easy sense of humor he can help you laugh off any reluctance to venture into unknown territory.

TAURUS ZODIAC SIGN
YOUR LOVE PLANETS

YOUR ROMANTIC SIDE — p. 696
▶ **VENUS IN GEMINI**
Born Apr. 20, 4:25 - May 07, 8:26
▶ **VENUS IN CANCER**
Born May 07, 8:27 - May 21, 3:57

YOUR SEX DRIVE — p. 722
▶ **MARS IN LEO**
Born Apr. 20, 4:25 - May 18, 20:53
▶ **MARS IN VIRGO**
Born May 18, 20:54 - May 21, 3:57

YOUR CELEBRITY TWINS — p. 760
Find out the astrological similarities you have with famous people.

YOUR COMPATIBILITY — p. 780
Compare planets to find out how compatible you are in a relationship.

YOUR RELATIONSHIP KARMA — p. 824
▶ **SATURN IN LEO**
Born Apr. 20, 4:25 - May 21, 3:57

TENNESSEE WILLIAMS
American Playwright
Venus in Taurus

247

1948 GEMINI

From May 21, 3:58 through June 21, 12:10

The Talkative Companion

Some love affairs begin with a conversation that lasts until dawn, but in your case, 1948 Gemini, the ideal romance starts with a meeting of the minds and continues with dialogue that lasts until death do you part. You simply must have a partner who can be a good listener and an enthusiastic audience for your ideas and the charming way you deliver them. Your mate's approving responses can leave you beaming with confidence and ready to take on the world. Sometimes you can get fixated on tiny details or fine distinctions. A mate with a broad outlook can keep you from sweating the small stuff.

Together you can be a highly effective team, able to scan your environment for opportunities, and swoop down with eagle-like precision to meet shared goals and seize your rewards. For you talking things out can be a cure-all for everything from a case of the blues, to a lover's quarrel, to a family crisis requiring mutual support and cooperation to make it through. Your own gifts of empathy and keen perception make you a sensitive partner, willing and able to satisfy a mate's need for romance and tender loving care. In the bedroom body language allows you to relate to your sweetheart on an intuitive, emotional level.

Your partner's attention to the little things can stir your passions. A thoughtful gift or gesture can assure you that your mate is paying close attention to your needs and preferences. Sex should have a certain refinement for you, like a beautiful art form with poetic suggestion and gentle physical interplay.

A nurturing, imaginative woman can be a soothing influence on the 1948 Gemini man. You appreciate someone who can provide you with a home life that is peaceful, harmonious, and secure. When your nerves are on edge, this lovely lady can furnish you with the serenity and comfort you need.

A man with sophisticated sensibilities can be a stimulating match for the 1948 Gemini woman. You admire someone who has a taste for only the best things in life. When it comes to romancing and enchanting you, this man knows exactly how to create the perfect atmosphere for love.

GEMINI ZODIAC SIGN
YOUR LOVE PLANETS

YOUR ROMANTIC SIDE — p. 696
▶ **VENUS IN CANCER**
Born May 21, 3:58 - June 21, 12:10

YOUR SEX DRIVE — p. 722
▶ **MARS IN VIRGO**
Born May 21, 3:58 - June 21, 12:10

YOUR CELEBRITY TWINS — p. 760
Find out the astrological similarities you have with famous people.

YOUR COMPATIBILITY — p. 780
Compare planets to find out how compatible you are in a relationship.

YOUR RELATIONSHIP KARMA — p. 824
▶ **SATURN IN LEO**
Born May 21, 3:58 - June 21, 12:10

JANE WYMAN
American Actress
Mars in Cancer

1948 CANCER
From June 21, 12:11 through July 22, 23:07

The Soothing Sweetheart

When life gets you down, 1948 Cancer, you can find "a paradise that's trouble-proof," and like the famous song by the Drifters, "there's room enough for two." A romance with you is like a soothing retreat into a world of imagination and enchantment, where you can give and receive comfort and make everything right again. With a gift for making someone feel truly and deeply understood, you can offer unusually tender insights and help a mate to recover from any setback. Because you have an amazing ability to heal breaches in relationships, loved ones may depend on you for advice and assistance in hard times.

The aid and loyalty you give to others can bring its own karmic rewards—a circle of friends who support your relationship and provide a range of resources for you and your mate. Your natural openness and vulnerability may inspire your partner to watch out for you, without needing to be asked. In this way a serious commitment can make you feel secure and protected. Around your mate you may have little need to withdraw into your own shell, but if you do, it's a red flag that you need some attention. Talking things through makes it easy for you to reconnect with your sweetheart, and you respond well to tender, physical affection. For you, lovemaking can be healthy for your body and soul, and a good wellness regimen can enhance the quality of your sex life. A nice, brisk walk will loosen you up and get your blood flowing. Natural settings can create a romantic mood. You may love to hold hands and look at the stars.

The Cancerian man of 1948 can completely relax with a woman who is caring and flexible. You may especially appreciate someone who never holds a grudge and is eager to resolve any issues as they arise. Sensitive to your moods and feelings, she can ease your mind and please your body.

The Cancerian woman born in 1948 enjoys a man who is somewhat predictable in his habits. With his reliable routine you can always know where he is and how you can find him. His diligence in handling responsibilities assures you that your relationship is on equal footing.

1948 LEO
From July 22, 23:08 through August 23, 6:02

The Instinctive Intimate

You were born to love, Leo of 1948, and a relationship allows you to grow and experience life in all its glory. An instinctive wisdom seems to guide you in caring for a mate and creating a solid partnership. You and your mate are likely to share an easy, friendly compatibility that allows you to relax and be yourselves when you're together. Differing points of view are a plus, as a little bit of healthy competitiveness can liven up your relationship and inspire each of you to do your best. It's all in good fun, but sometimes you may let a contest go too far. Your empathy for each other's feelings enables you to make peace, strike a fair compromise, and ensure that neither partner's needs will be neglected.

You may find change to be energizing and exciting, a necessary part of keeping a romance moving ahead through the years. At the same time, you can also appreciate the benefits of slowing things down and focusing in on one-on-one intimacy. You tend to have an excellent sense of timing that allows you and your mate to create a healthy rhythm for working, playing, reaching out to new friends and opportunities, or scaling back ambitions and expenditures.

For you, lovemaking can be good theatre—sometimes a melodrama, sometimes a comedy—but always sure to take you to a new and awesome place. Sharing and fulfilling fantasies can rouse your passions. You may love to be romanced in grand style. The ideal date caters to your artistic sensibilities—a night at the opera, a play, a concert—anything involving creativity.

A perceptive, imaginative woman can be the perfect object of desire for the 1948 Leo man. You tend to appreciate someone who exudes a sense of wonder and joy, especially in response to your attempts to woo her. Responsive to your needs, she assures you of mutual satisfaction.

The Leo woman of 1948 can shine in the presence of a man who is eager to please. You can flourish with someone who sees your inner beauty and tells you sincerely and often how lovely you are. With his kind words he can tell you what you need to know without ever hurting your feelings.

1948 VIRGO

From August 23, 6:03 through September 23, 3:21

♍ The Poetic Partner

Your ideal romance, Virgo of 1948, is like a beautiful piece of poetry come to life. With every act of kindness and grace you and your mate can add another verse. You thrive in a relationship that allows you to share your fantasies and make your dreams come true. The best partner for you should be nonjudgmental, easy to talk to, but alert to the practical details of any situation. Because your expectations tend to be high, a sweetheart's down-to-earth perspective can provide you with a gentle reality check and protect you from disappointment and disillusionment. Whenever things turn out to be less than perfect, your mate can help you shift your focus to what is good and valuable, right now, in the present.

An active spiritual life may be the bond that holds your relationship together over the long term. While the beliefs you share can increase your chances of success in realizing your objectives, devotion to higher principles makes the effort meaningful, even when an outcome falls short of your goals. Friendship and trust in a partnership tend to be more important to you than fiery sexual passion, but you may be open to a lover's attempts to turn you on to something new—as long as it's not vulgar or liable to attract outside attention.

For the mate determined to seduce you, sweet words can soften your heart and open your body to suggestion. Warm, affectionate gestures—hugs, kisses, a long cuddling session—can be just as satisfying for you as all-out lovemaking. Intimacy is best for you when it's about true love.

The Virgo man of 1948 prizes a romantic woman who is discreet and trustworthy. You feel most comfortable with someone who is fiercely protective of the privacy you share. With her dreamy imagination and sensitivity to your needs, this tender lady can bring you an inspired love.

An elegant and courteous man can satisfy the exacting standards of the Virgo woman born in 1948. You tend to admire someone who's got his act together and shows consideration for others' feelings. With his good manners this fellow can treat you to some good old-fashioned romance.

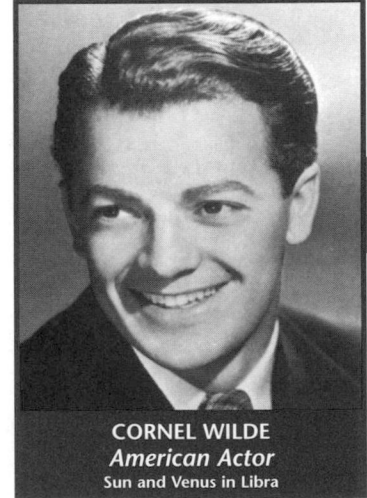

CORNEL WILDE
American Actor
Sun and Venus in Libra

249

1948 LIBRA

From September 23, 3:22 through October 23, 12:17

♎ The Fiery Friend

For you, 1948 Libra, a relationship may begin with fireworks and passion, but over time you and your mate tend to settle into a more stable and comfortable routine. This does not mean your partnership becomes boring—no way! As you get to know each other better, your love and sense of connection gain in depth and durability. What started as a bunch of sparks becomes an eternal flame in your hearts and souls. You and your partner are likely to share a friendship that is different from all others because of its intimacy and intensity. Every new phase in your lives together tends to bring opportunities to reinvent your relationship and rediscover each other, as if for the first time. Such an approach keeps your bond fresh and exciting.

A certain principled neutrality may temper the way you treat each other. That is, no matter how close you become, you are likely to show each other the same kind of genteel politeness you would give to a casual friend or new acquaintance. By relating to each other with courteousness and tact, you can make it easy to discuss sensitive issues and solve problems that might spell the end for other couples. Lovemaking allows you and your mate to rekindle your sparks together on a regular basis.

In the privacy of the bedroom you can abandon yourself to the joy of merging with your soul mate, an experience that may take on mystical dimensions for you. You can be highly sensitive to atmospheric influences and respond well to soft lighting, mood music, and the aromas of flowers, incense, or your lover's body.

The Libran man born in 1948 enjoys a woman who exudes a striking beauty in the way she carries herself and in her openhearted tenderness toward her loved ones. You admire someone who can be creative, caring, and compassionate, and this lovely lady can bring it all home to you.

A passionate man with a smoldering sensuality can seduce the 1948 Libran woman into sweet submission. You tend to appreciate someone who takes the romantic lead with total confidence, allowing you to enjoy the ride. With this man intimacy can be inviting and energizing.

NORMAN MAILER
American Writer
Venus in Sagittarius

250

1948 SCORPIO
From October 23, 12:18 through November 22, 9:2

♏ *The Daring Darling*

You may be the strong, silent type in a relationship, 1948 Scorpio, but you find plenty of ways to express yourself without wasting a lot of energy on idle chatter. Chances are, your mate is just fine with that because you tend to be extremely creative in finding ways to generate passion and excitement. Non-verbal communication may be a highly stimulating specialty of yours. Early on in life you may have been a starry-eyed romantic, a role that could have led to disappointment and heartbreak. For you, though, the combination of a broken heart, time, and maturity can make you stronger than you were before. Besides, you may be just too plumb stubborn to give up on love.

Today you may be as much of a starry-eyed romantic as you ever were, but you're wiser and more discriminating. One thing's for sure—that compassion of yours is as deep as the ocean and one-hundred-percent authentic. You have seen it all. As a result, you tend to be gentle and nonjudgmental with your beloved. Your mate may cherish the ability to share secrets and desires with you without shame or fear of

disclosure. You are the Fort Knox of confidential information. Lovemaking allows you and your mate to push the outer envelope of erotic possibility.

With your adventurous spirit you may enjoy experimenting with all kinds of techniques, positions, and toys—the more exotic, the better. Vacations to distant locales can provide fresh material to inspire your imagination. Going out and having fun together can be the perfect lead-in to a night of intimacy.

A woman who gives top priority to the growth and development of your relationship can be a perfect match for the 1948 Scorpio man. Her devotion and concern for your needs allow you to enjoy a harmonious bond. With total trust in you this lovely lady can bring out your best.

An optimistic, confident man inspires the Scorpio woman of 1948 to take the kind of emotional risks that allow love to grow and thrive. You can flourish with someone who dares you to plunge into life with both arms. With this brave beau you can make every day better than the last.

1948 SAGITTARIUS
From November 22, 9:29 through December 21, 22:32

♐ *The Secret Sweetheart*

Love can rock your world or make it go round, 1948 Sagittarius. Either way, you're liable to get something good out of the exchange. You tend to be a stable soul, and you may enjoy a partner who can come in and shake things up for you from time to time. Left to your own devices, you can get locked into a routine, especially if work or outside projects begin to consume your attention. While your mate may admire your diligence and productivity, there's no substitute for intimacy and sweet love. Sometimes you may need a little help in making sure to channel your passions in the right place. Fortunately, you've got plenty of passion to go around.

You can thrive in a relationship that gives you lots of breathing space, but you remain a faithful and devoted mate. The security of a serious commitment gives you the support you need to give your all in the world. To outsiders the freedom you enjoy may mask the depth and intensity of the love you share with your partner. But the two of you are privy to a precious secret—the emotional attachment between you tends to be an enormous source of

strength and inspiration in your life. Lovemaking allows you to reconnect with the romantic current that flows from your mate, to you, and back again.

Behind closed doors you can be a stunningly uninhibited lover with a healthy appetite for fun, pleasure, and sensory indulgences. Plentiful food, wine, and merry music can provide a luscious build-up to sex. Even so, nothing may turn you on as much as the sound of your partner's laughter.

The Sagittarian man of 1948 enjoys a woman with a smoldering sensuality that can burst into a volcano of erotic expression. You appreciate a mate who is fervently and fearlessly devoted to you. With her private nature you can trust her to respect your sense of propriety.

The Sagittarian woman born in 1948 adores a man with a take-charge confidence and the competence to get things done. You admire someone with an ironic sense of humor because it assures you he can rise to any occasion. With this capable companion your needs are in the best of hands.

Hepburn and Tracy – A Private Affair

At first glance, Katharine Hepburn and Spencer Tracy may have seemed an unlikely match. They came from different backgrounds—her father was a surgeon, his a truck salesman—and displayed distinctly different acting styles—Hepburn often portrayed educated, classy characters, Tracy played a "tough guy." But their strong wills and eccentricity bound them to one another. During their 25-year romance, they formed a dynamic team, on- and offstage.

The two met in 1942, while filming *Woman of the Year*, the first of nine movies they starred in together. Both Hepburn and Tracy were already major box-office draws and highly acclaimed stars, even though neither fit the typical Hollywood image of a leading lady or leading man. And although their talents and willfulness earned them the respect of studio executives, both actors were considered difficult. Hepburn, a Taurus born in 1907, wasn't a voluptuous beauty like many popular actresses of the day, but she combined a sense of dignity with sharp spirited independence, an image that made her attractive to both male and female fans. Stocky and gruff, Tracy's success lay in his ability to project strength and sincerity in an understated, masterful and unaffected way—traits characteristic of his Capricorn Ascendant (which is the sign rising at his time of birth). Laurence Olivier said "I've learned more about acting from watching Tracy than in any other way."

Typical of her secretive Scorpio Ascendant, Hepburn cherished her privacy, avoiding the Hollywood crowd and socializing with a select group of intellectuals. One of her biggest "open

"I have had twenty years of perfect companionship with a man among men."

KATHARINE HEPBURN said of Spencer Tracy

secrets" was her relationship with the married Tracy, born an Aries in 1900. Although Hepburn and Tracy were almost always seen together, few people—not even the Hollywood gossip columnists—knew much about the couple's private life.

Their birth charts, however, reveal the inside story. Tracy's Zodiac sign and Hepburn's Venus (planet of love) join up in Aries. Likewise, Hepburn's Zodiac sign and Tracy's Venus are linked in Taurus. These factors explain their strong attraction to one another—each fulfilled the other's romantic ideal—and suggest that not only a deep and abiding affection existed between them, but also genuine passion.

Despite their profound personal love and professional chemistry, the pair never married. Tracy, a devout Catholic who had studied for the priesthood as a young man, would not divorce his wife, former stage actress Louise Treadwell, although they no longer lived together.

When Tracy became ill in the 1960s with lung problems and complications due to alcoholism, Hepburn put her own career on hold to care for him. In 1965, during one of his lowest points, Hepburn and his wife Louise took turns keeping vigil at his bedside.

Hepburn and Tracy returned to the silver screen for one last picture together, *Guess Who's Coming to Dinner*, for which Hepburn won an Academy Award. Gravely ill, Tracy could only work a few hours a day and his scenes had to be shot between 9 A.M. and noon. He died just three weeks after the filming was completed. Out of respect for his wife and family, his long-time companion, Katharine Hepburn, did not attend the funeral. In 1971, writer-director Garson Kanin, who helped bring the pair together for their first movie, wrote a tribute to their love, *Tracy and Hepburn: An Intimate Memoir*, which became an immediate bestseller.

251

▶ READ MORE ABOUT KATHARINE HEPBURN AND SPENCER TRACY ON PAGE 196

1949

- ✪ LACE-TRIMMED PANTIES
- ✪ NUDE CALENDAR
- ✪ ADAM'S RIB
- ✪ A RAGE TO LIVE
- ✪ THE SECOND SEX
- ✪ SOME ENCHANTED EVENING
- ✪ FRANKIE LAINE

EVENTS

Gussie Morgan raised eyebrows and opposition—and apparently her skirt—when she appeared on court at Wimbledon with lace-trimmed panties under her skirt.

Married film star Ingrid Bergman began an affair with Italian film director Roberto Rossellini. A year later she gave birth to their first child. Zsa Zsa Gabor and George Sanders married. Italian film star turned US sex symbol Gina Lollobrigida married fellow European Milko Skofic. Rita Hayworth married playboy Prince Aly Aga Khan, son of the Aga Khan, after failed marriages to director Orson Welles and promoter Edward Judson, as well as romances with Howard Hughes and Victor Mature.

California photographer Tom Kelly snapped the famous nude photograph of Marilyn Monroe that was later featured on the most publicized calendar in history.

POP CULTURE

Moviegoers enjoyed Katharine Hepburn and Spencer Tracy in *Adam's Rib*, a romance with married lawyers clashing both in and out of court over a case involving a woman shooting her husband and his girlfriend. In *And Baby Makes Three* a recently divorced couple have second thoughts when they learn there's a baby on the way. *The Good Old Summertime* gave us co-workers at odds in a Chicago music store, but unwittingly falling in love as secret pen pals.

Readers were raving over *A Rage to Live*, by John O'Hara. Grace Caldwell Tate's lust for life carries her through marriage, violent extramarital affairs, scandal, disaster, and a special kind of triumph. Frank Yerby's *Pride's Castle* was the story of the relationship between a black jazz musician and a white southern woman in Paris. In *The Man with the Golden Arm*, addiction, adultery, alcoholism, murder, and gambling play a part in the lives of Frankie Machine, his complaining wheelchair-bound wife Sophie and his sweet girlfriend Molly. Simone de Beauvoir's *The Second Sex* was an early spark to the battle of the sexes, discussing how women had been subjected to male oppression.

Perry Como had two hits on the charts this year: "A, You're Adorable" and "Some Enchanted Evening." Frankie Laine did too with "Mule Train" and "That Lucky Old Sun."

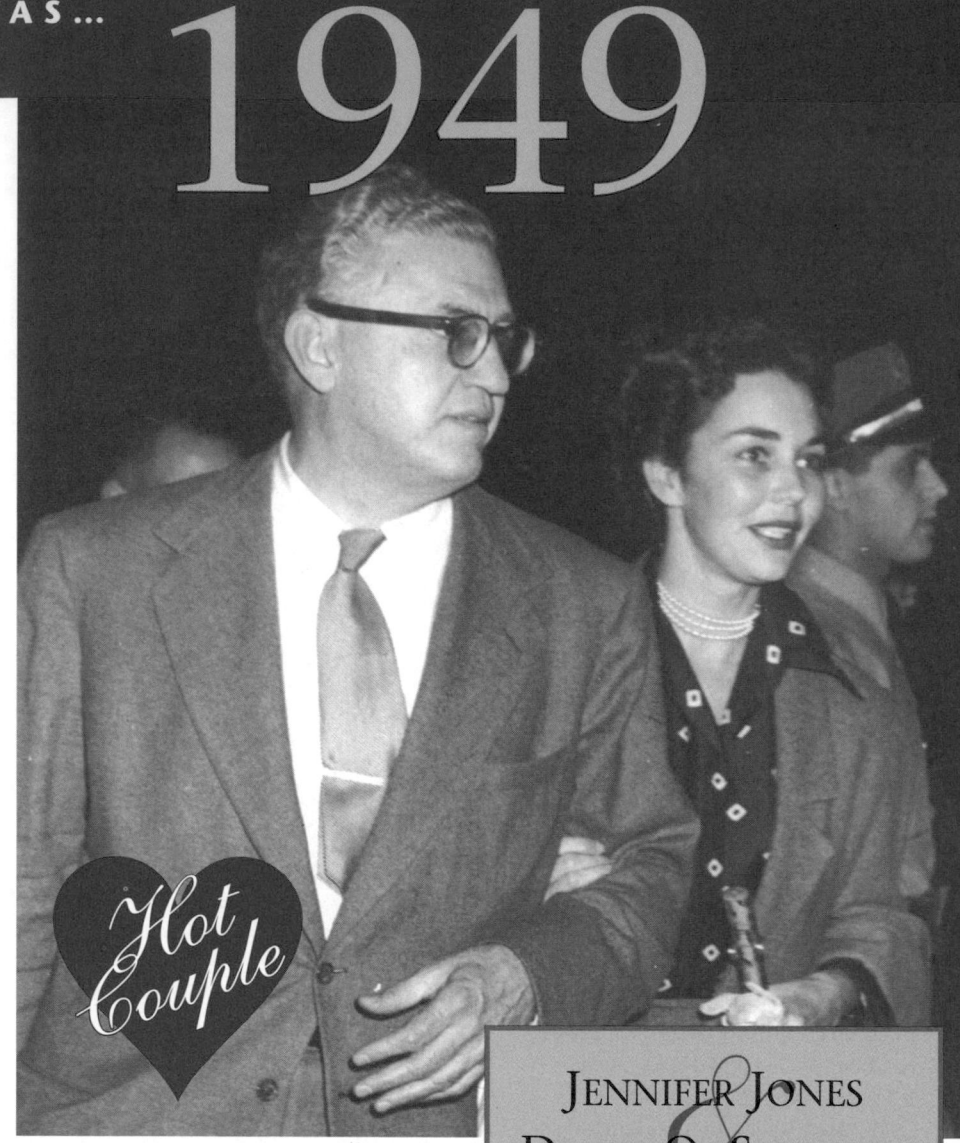

Hot Couple

JENNIFER JONES & DAVID O. SELZNICK

The wedding of legendary producer David O. Selznick and actress Jennifer Jones, on July 13, 1949, consummated a decade-long romantic obsession. Having noticed Jones fresh from drama school, Selznick took a personal interest in her career. Gossip columnists claimed he "stole" Jones from her first husband.

He cast Jones as the lead in *Song of Bernadette* for which she won an Oscar. Selznick produced costly cinematic vehicles for Jones, including *Duel in the Sun*, derisively nicknamed "Lust in the Dust." A jealous Selznick allowed only happily married actors to play opposite Jones. They remained married until Selznick's death in 1965.

SEE ALSO
► LLOYD WEBBER & BRIGHTMAN *Page 540*

252

1949 CAPRICORN

From December 21, 1948 22:33 through January 20, 1949 9:08
(December 1949 Capricorns, see 1950 Capricorn)

♑ *The Wry Romantic*

Always quick with a dry remark or witty reply, you 1949 Goats are spunky amusing characters. You use your wry humor as a means to mask your romantic nature. Few people realize how tender and sentimental you really are, preferring to think of you as a sophisticated cynic. Actually, you're quite idealistic when it comes to love, and want a relationship that allows you to express your sweet side. A partner who is able to uphold your reputation as a comic in public and then cuddle with you in private is your perfect match.

You're not the type to be physically intimate with somebody unless you are in love. For you sex is a means of making yourself vulnerable to another person. Therefore, you do best with a partner who makes you feel safe and secure in the bedroom. As a 1949 Goat, you're also somewhat philosophical, and enjoy the company of a lover who likes to ponder the meaning of life with you. Although you don't take marriage lightly, you do believe that your happiest moments should be spent with your spouse. Taking lots of vacations together may be one of your greatest priorities.

The best way to attract your attention may be to bring up subjects such as art, poetry, and music. Normally, folks think you prefer to keep the conversation light with witty observations about politics. Talking about art gives you a welcome opportunity to show off your sensitive side. Sexually, you're very passionate but slow to trust. Asking permission to kiss you is a good first move, because this gives you an element of control over the physical aspect of a relationship.

As a male Capricorn who was born in 1949, you adore a woman who is upbeat, independent, and fun-loving. You also gravitate toward females who hide deep emotions behind a wall of reserve. Whichever kind of woman you choose as a partner, she should possess a terrific sense of humor.

You female 1949 Goats enjoy a man who is visionary, idealistic, and somewhat aloof. Guys who are strong and authoritative also win favor with you. In the final analysis, you do best with a man who recognizes and enjoys your many thrilling facets.

CAPRICORN ZODIAC SIGN
YOUR LOVE PLANETS

YOUR ROMANTIC SIDE — p. 696
▶ **VENUS IN SAGITTARIUS**
Born Dec. 21, 1948 22:33 - Jan. 13, 1949 9:00
▶ **VENUS IN CAPRICORN**
Born Jan. 13, 9:01 - Jan. 20, 9:08

YOUR SEX DRIVE — p. 722
▶ **MARS IN CAPRICORN**
Born Dec. 21, 1948 22:33 - Jan. 04, 1949 17:49
▶ **MARS IN AQUARIUS**
Born Jan. 04, 17:50 - Jan. 20, 9:08

YOUR CELEBRITY TWINS — p. 760
Find out the astrological similarities you have with famous people.

YOUR COMPATIBILITY — p. 780
Compare planets to find out how compatible you are in a relationship.

YOUR RELATIONSHIP KARMA — p. 824
▶ **SATURN IN VIRGO**
Born Dec. 21, 1948 22:33 - Jan. 20, 1949 9:08

KATHRYN GRAYSON
American Singer
Sun and Venus in Aquarius

253

1949 AQUARIUS

From January 20, 9:09 through February 18, 23:26

♒ *The Visionary Lover*

As a 1949 Aquarius, you're a wild-eyed dreamer who enjoys thinking about possibilities, not problems. Your upbeat optimism is enormously attractive, and probably draws a nice variety of admirers to your side. Although you're quite a free spirit, a monogamous relationship is the only kind that makes you happy. You would hate sharing your lover with anybody else. For you a committed partnership reflects an exclusivity that is both precious and profound.

A mate who is bold, magnetic, and powerful is best suited to you. Although you're incredibly smart and accomplished, you enjoy looking up to your partner. You want a relationship in which your creativity is not only encouraged, but channeled in positive directions. Therefore, your marriage partner could be someone who is always thinking in terms of the latest technologies or the newest opportunities. You thrive with a partner who looks toward the future with eager anticipation. Pairing up with a mate who yearns for the "good old days" would give you very little satisfaction.

When potential partners wants to catch your eye, they should try to dominate the room with colorful conversation and profound insights. You're enormously attracted to big personalities. In terms of lovemaking, you're somewhat reserved, so it's best that your admirer takes things slowly with you. Murmuring encouraging words between kisses gives you the encouragement you need to let go of your inhibitions. You also like talking in soft whispers after making love, and may enjoy sneaking out to the kitchen with your lover for a post-coital feast.

You male Water Bearers who were born in 1949 admire women who are well-versed in the ways of the world. Innocent, naïve types leave you cold. You also appreciate females who are outspoken and intelligent. A take-charge partner is best suited to you.

Men who are unconventional and open-minded appeal greatly to you 1949 female Aquarians. You are also drawn to guys who are spiritual and intuitive, but you benefit most from a mate who is strong and self-assured. Secretly, you like a man who takes charge.

AQUARIUS ZODIAC SIGN
YOUR LOVE PLANETS

YOUR ROMANTIC SIDE — p. 696
▶ **VENUS IN CAPRICORN**
Born Jan. 20, 9:09 - Feb. 06, 9:04
▶ **VENUS IN AQUARIUS**
Born Feb. 06, 9:05 - Feb. 18, 23:26

YOUR SEX DRIVE — p. 722
▶ **MARS IN AQUARIUS**
Born Jan. 20, 9:09 - Feb. 11, 18:04
▶ **MARS IN PISCES**
Born Feb. 11, 18:05 - Feb. 18, 23:26

YOUR CELEBRITY TWINS — p. 760
Find out the astrological similarities you have with famous people.

YOUR COMPATIBILITY — p. 780
Compare planets to find out how compatible you are in a relationship.

YOUR RELATIONSHIP KARMA — p. 824
▶ **SATURN IN VIRGO**
Born Jan. 20, 9:09 - Feb. 18, 23:26

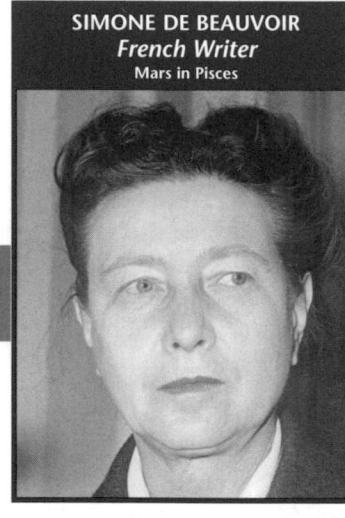

SIMONE DE BEAUVOIR
French Writer
Mars in Pisces

254

1949 PISCES
From February 18, 23:27 through March 20, 22:47

The Sensitive Sensualist

You 1949 Pisceans are awash with emotion, and your admirers wouldn't have it any other way. You're a romantic, sentimental soul who enjoys cooing over both your partner's strengths and shortcomings. Unconditional love is a living reality for you, and you're proud to say that you wouldn't change a thing about your lover. Ideally, your mate feels the same way about you, allowing you to enjoy a relationship in which both partners feel valued, appreciated, and accepted. Couples who exchange sarcastic remarks and barbed insults are a mystery to you. You wouldn't dream of being disrespectful to your partner under any circumstance.

All forms of sensuous expression are thrilling for you, including sex. You enjoy the intimacy that comes from sharing your body with another. A lover who likes to linger over your sensitive spots will get a very enthusiastic response from you. Having a sexually active marriage is very important for you, and you are likely to enjoy frequent relations with your spouse well into old age. You definitely get sexier as you get older! Being physically close to

your partner helps you tune into their emotions, and makes for a very sympathetic relationship.

Merging physicality with creativity is a great way to seduce you. An admirer would be wise to invite you out dancing or ice skating as a first date. During breaks, your suitor should explore your ideas about esoteric subjects such as ESP, astrology, and metaphysics. When it comes time to make the first move, it's a good idea to take a masterful approach. You adore feeling overwhelmed by an amorous partner.

If you're a male Fish who was born in 1949, you do best with a woman who is spiritual, compassionate, and intelligent. Females who are sensitive and poetic also appeal to you. A partner who enjoys your dreamy ways is ideal for you.

Men who are intuitive and romantic suit you 1949 female Pisceans best. You're not impressed by macho displays of aggression. Rather, you're moved by a guy who can express his emotions through words, images, or music. A mate who invites you into his fantasy world thrills you.

1949 ARIES
From March 20, 22:48 through April 20, 10:16

The Idealistic Partner

As a 1949 Aries, you have an exalted view of romantic partnerships. As far as you're concerned, your mate should be a best friend, lover, and spiritual counselor rolled into one. You are best suited to a relationship that features unselfish love and understanding. Making sacrifices for your mate is no problem. You've always believed that putting your own needs aside is a small price to pay for love. The sacrifices you make for your lover are effortless.

Sex plays a powerful part in your life. When you give yourself to somebody physically, it's with the expectation that your relationship will undergo a beautiful transformation. Nobody could accuse you of being fickle. You would greatly benefit from a partner who shares your reverent attitude toward making love. A marriage that is solely based on sex would have little value for you, however. You would rather have a spouse who is an excellent conversationalist than a breathtaking lover. Of course, you welcome a mate who combines both qualities!

Seducing you is a matter of living up to your ideals. Expressing a desire to lead a harmonious,

balanced life together is an excellent beginning. You also appreciate admirers who are adept at the art of lively conversation. Letting you make the first move is a wise idea. You like to call the shots sexually, and feel intimidated and confused when an admirer makes aggressive moves toward you. When things have progressed to the bedroom, your suitor would be wise to admire your physique, as you probably spend a great deal of time and effort staying in shape.

Women who are headstrong and opinionated excite you 1949 male Rams. You're not interested in a female who feels the need to parrot your ideas. You also admire women with colorful imaginations. A partner who is willing to pair her strengths with yours to make an unbeatable team is an ideal match for you.

If you're a female Ram who was born in 1949, you admire men who are directed, determined, and dashing. Occasionally, you'll be drawn to a dreamy, poetic type. The most important quality your mate must have is loyalty.

1949 TAURUS
From April 20, 10:17 through May 21, 9:50

The Ambitious Homebody

As excellent providers, you 1949 Bulls are wonderful partners. If only you could spend more time with your family, life would be perfect! Although you greatly desire domestic bliss, career demands can keep you far from home. You do best with a partner who can withstand long separations. When you are very comfortably ensconced at home with your beloved, you are as happy as a clam. In fact, nobody is as tender or devoted as you during such times. Your relationship may be a welcome escape from the many career pressures you continually experience.

A warm, lavish home is very important to you. Consequently, you admire a mate who is skilled in the domestic arts. Although you have a tendency to spoil your children, you put your spouse's needs higher than theirs. As far as you're concerned, a household can't fully thrive without a successful marriage. Therefore, you go out of your way to cater to your partner's needs. Expensive gifts and luxurious vacations may be some of the ways you pay tribute to your lover's contributions. One thing is for sure: you spare no expense when it comes to making your partner happy!

If potential mates wants to catch your eye, they should defer to your authority. You take great pride in your leadership skills, and are very flattered when an admirer takes your advice. Sexually, you may go through cycles. One minute, you're burning with passion, and the next, you're cool as a cucumber. A suitor who can discern your physical desires by just looking into your eyes has a good chance of winning your heart. In bed your ardor is increased by tactile sensations that material such as satin and silk provide.

If you're a male Bull who was born in 1949, you want a woman who is attentive, loving, and understanding. Females with a wide variety of interests also turn you on. Ultimately, you desire a partner who won't hold your career demands against you.

Men who are impulsive and confident greatly appeal to you 1949 female Taureans. You also like guys who are tasteful and considerate. A mate who respects and encourages your ambition is a perfect match for you.

TAURUS ZODIAC SIGN
YOUR LOVE PLANETS

YOUR ROMANTIC SIDE   p. 696
▶ **VENUS IN TAURUS**
Born Apr. 20, 10:17 - May 14, 0:24
▶ **VENUS IN GEMINI**
Born May 14, 0:25 - May 21, 9:50

YOUR SEX DRIVE   p. 722
▶ **MARS IN ARIES**
Born Apr. 20, 10:17 - Apr. 30, 2:32
▶ **MARS IN TAURUS**
Born Apr. 30, 2:33 - May 21, 9:50

YOUR CELEBRITY TWINS   p. 760
Find out the astrological similarities you have with famous people.

YOUR COMPATIBILITY   p. 780
Compare planets to find out how compatible you are in a relationship.

YOUR RELATIONSHIP KARMA   p. 824
▶ **SATURN IN LEO**
Born Apr. 20, 10:17 - May 21, 9:50

SARAH VAUGHAN
American Singer
Venus in Taurus

255

1949 GEMINI
From May 21, 9:51 through June 21, 18:02

The Spiritual Suitor

Philosophical, gentle, and kind, you 1949 Geminis are the salt of the earth. You extend your tender behavior to your mate, believing that compassion is the cornerstone of any fulfilling relationship. You do best with a mate who doesn't ridicule your philanthropic instincts. In fact, you and your partner may decide at some point to perform volunteer work together as a means of keeping your bond strong and purposeful. Talented egotists hold no charms for you. You far prefer the company of a humble humanitarian.

Making love may not be high on your list of priorities, but that doesn't mean you're not passionate. Rather, you need the right setting in which to get in touch with your physical side. Nothing gives you more pleasure than falling into an amorous embrace with your lover beneath the light of a full moon. Sex can also be a means for you to release subconscious fears. A partner who knows when and how to approach you will be pleasantly surprised by just how amorous you can be. You may be especially responsive when your mate blows softly in your ear.

Demonstrating a commitment to social causes is a wonderful way to catch your eye. You feel a kinship with people who dedicate their lives to worthy causes. Sometimes you're uncertain about when to take a friendship to the next level, so it's a good idea for your suitor to initiate the physical aspect of your relationship. Turning a casual hug goodbye into a passionate clinch may be the best way to break past the platonic barrier.

As a male 1949 Gemini, you do best with women who are versatile, witty, and charming. You appreciate a female who is up on current events. You also admire nurturing women who are adept in the domestic arts. A mate who wants to make the world a kinder, gentler place is your ideal.

You female Geminis who were born in 1949 want a man who is steady, reliable, and strong. Faithless flirts really turn you off. You're also drawn to guys who are constantly trying to improve themselves through study, athletics, and prayer. Ultimately, you want a partner who makes you feel intelligent and worthy.

GEMINI ZODIAC SIGN
YOUR LOVE PLANETS

YOUR ROMANTIC SIDE   p. 696
▶ **VENUS IN GEMINI**
Born May 21, 9:51 - June 07, 10:46
▶ **VENUS IN CANCER**
Born June 07, 10:47 - June 21, 18:02

YOUR SEX DRIVE   p. 722
▶ **MARS IN TAURUS**
Born May 21, 9:51 - June 10, 0:56
▶ **MARS IN GEMINI**
Born June 10, 0:57 - June 21, 18:02

YOUR CELEBRITY TWINS   p. 760
Find out the astrological similarities you have with famous people.

YOUR COMPATIBILITY   p. 780
Compare planets to find out how compatible you are in a relationship.

YOUR RELATIONSHIP KARMA   p. 824
▶ **SATURN IN LEO**
Born May 21, 9:51 - May 29, 12:59
▶ **SATURN IN VIRGO**
Born May 29, 13:00 - June 21, 18:02

TREVOR HOWARD
English Actor
Mars in Cancer

256

1949 CANCER
From June 21, 18:03 through July 23, 4:56

♋ *The Energetic Romantic*

Brimming with ingenuity, you 1949 Cancerians are a creative lot. Even your love life has a unique quality to it. You'd hate your partner to think you're boring. Therefore, you like to come up with a variety of ways to keep your relationship alive with excitement. Trying new activities, traveling to foreign lands, and altering your domestic routine together are just some of the ways you like to introduce fresh energy into your partnership. You want emotional security and intellectual stimulation from your partner.

You have an optimistic attitude about relationships that makes it easy for you to make a long-term commitment. As far as you are concerned, love can only enhance your life. You're not the type to team up with a mate who is always creating drama in your life. Rather, you do best with a lover who is interested in blending your personalities to create joy and harmony. Sexually, you can be probably quite vigorous, and prefer a spouse who likes to spend plenty of time between the sheets.

Exhibiting inventive behavior is a good way to catch your eye. You're attracted to people who are able to think outside the box. When it comes to lovemaking, you like to be caught by surprise. An admirer who plants a swift kiss on your lips when you're not expecting it is sure to excite you. Your passion can ignite with rapid intensity, given the proper encouragement. You're not averse to trying new things in the bedroom, or anyplace else for that matter. Making love in unusual places gives you a special thrill.

If you're a 1949 male Crab, you are happiest with a woman who is sensitive and nurturing, with a goofy sense of humor. You also admire passionate, straightforward females with a flair for drama. Your mate should look on your relationship as constantly evolving. You can't stand being taken for granted.

Men who are wired and restless really appeal to you 1949 female Cancerians. You detest stolid, boring types. You want a guy who is excited about the future and ready to take risks, both intellectual and emotional. Your partner should be lighthearted and independent.

1949 LEO
From July 23, 4:57 through August 23, 11:47

♌ *The Impatient Lover*

You 1949 Lions have tons of personal magnetism that others find absolutely riveting. You have never lacked for admirers, and may have led quite an active love life in your youth. And while a free-wheeling lifestyle has always been within your reach, your very romantic nature is such that you prefer to devote your energies to one person. A love relationship that provides you with a sense of security and permanence makes you thrive. You do best with a partner who is loyal, vibrant, and loving.

It's important for you to take the lead position in romance. Although you would never abuse your power, you definitely feel more comfortable when you are in the driver's seat. A mate who welcomes living beneath your very protective influence is best suited to you. Your sex drive is pretty strong, and you may enjoy making love several times a day. Your spouse needs plenty of stamina to keep up with you!

If potential partners want to win your heart, they should express a strong interest in mystical or occult subjects. You may be very interested in these topics, and feel a bond with people with similar passions. With regard to sex, you feel comfortable making the first move, but always will welcome a little encouragement. Suitors who make direct eye contact or wet their lips in anticipation of your first kiss could attract you like a magnet. You enjoy making love in rich, sumptuous environments such as luxury hotel rooms.

You 1949 male Lions prefer a woman who is dynamic, strong-willed, and passionate. You're also turned on by females who are pretty, witty, and vivacious. Ultimately, you seek a mate who wants to devote her life completely to you and only you. Being treated like the king you are brings out your kind and generous spirit.

As a 1949 female Leo, you want a man who is insightful, tender, and somewhat secretive. You enjoy a guy who has a mysterious cast to his personality. Above all, you want a partner who will pamper and coddle you like a child. Deep inside you there's a little girl who doesn't want to grow up. Your mate should recognize and celebrate your youthful spirit within.

1949 VIRGO

♍ *The Tasteful Suitor*

You 1949 Virgos have impeccable taste, and it's especially evident with regard to your love life. You hold out for a partner who is as elegant and refined as you are. It is your intention to have a relationship that is based on love, loyalty, and mutual respect. And although you have a somewhat serious attitude toward love, your romantic impulses are very strong. Showing and telling your lover how much they mean to you has never been a problem. For all your dignity and reserve, you're extremely affectionate. Your partner will never be starved for love.

A relationship that has a spiritual foundation suits you best. You like to ponder the mysteries of life with your partner. Sexually, you are a bit shy and reserved. Therefore, you may attract a spouse who enjoys stripping away your mannerly outer layers to reveal the ardent lover within. One of the ways you like to keep your relationship strong is by also participating in lasting, supportive friendships. You wouldn't want a marriage that feels like a free-floating life raft on a sea of uncertainty. Having good

pals in whom you can confide gives you a profound sense of reassurance.

Demonstrating good taste in art, music, and movies is an excellent way to win favor with you. You have admiration for anyone whose sensibilities are both refined and individual. Making the first move can be a daunting prospect for you. A suitor who makes their sexual interest known in a respectful but ardent way is sure to capture your heart. Kissing for hours as a prelude to lovemaking really heats you up.

Women who are gracious, pretty, and gentle attract you 1949 male Virgoes. You're very turned on by soft, feminine types. Sexy, intellectual types also intrigue you. A mate who adds a touch of elegance to life is the perfect match for you.

If you're a female Virgo who was born in 1949, you want a man who is intuitive, imaginative, and friendly. You can't abide aloof, brooding guys. A man who is generous and compassionate can also steal your heart. Ultimately, you need a partner who provides you with a gracious, comfortable lifestyle.

VIRGO ZODIAC SIGN
YOUR LOVE PLANETS

YOUR ROMANTIC SIDE   p. 696
  ▶ **VENUS IN LIBRA**
  Born Aug. 23, 11:48 - Sept. 14, 17:11
  ▶ **VENUS IN SCORPIO**
  Born Sept. 14, 17:12 - Sept. 23, 9:05

YOUR SEX DRIVE   p. 722
  ▶ **MARS IN CANCER**
  Born Aug. 23, 11:48 - Sept. 07, 4:50
  ▶ **MARS IN LEO**
  Born Sept. 07, 4:51 - Sept. 23, 9:05

YOUR CELEBRITY TWINS   p. 760
  Find out the astrological similarities you have with famous people.

YOUR COMPATIBILITY   p. 780
  Compare planets to find out how compatible you are in a relationship.

YOUR RELATIONSHIP KARMA   p. 824
  ▶ **SATURN IN VIRGO**
  Born Aug. 23, 11:48 - Sept. 23, 9:05

PETER LAWFORD
English Actor
Sun, Venus and Mars in Virgo

257

1949 LIBRA

♎ *The Captivating Swain*

Independent but romantic, you 1949 Librans are in much demand. People can't help be attracted to your carefree charm. You may have enjoyed basking in the admiration of others for many years before you finally settled down. You thrive on a great variety of friendships, but when you find that one special person, that relationship takes precedence over all others. You have an idealistic view of love, believing that it can solve all of your problems.

No matter how close you are to your partner, you need an element of freedom within your relationship. Taking separate vacations is a good way to recharge your individual batteries and keep your romance alive. It's also important for you to have interests apart from your spouse. Having something of your own to cherish makes it possible for you to share other elements of your personality with your beloved. When it comes to sex, you may be very discerning. You do best with a mate who enjoys looking their best at all times as a means to arouse your passion.

People with strong leadership skills tend to attract your attention. You really appreciate a

suitor who can command authority without being mean-spirited or autocratic. Taking charge of you at a swanky function is a good way to win your heart. You love it when an admirer takes the trouble to introduce you around and ensure that you're having fun. A suitor who murmurs words of admiration when offering you a nuzzle has a good chance of becoming your permanent lover.

If you're a male Libran who was born in 1949, you admire women who are street smart. Gullible females make you impatient and annoyed. You also appreciate restless, unpredictable women who add an element of whimsy to life. In the final analysis, you do best with a partner who is a good friend and a sensitive lover, in that order.

Men who are idealistic, inventive, and romantic attract you 1949 female Librans. You want a guy who is always looking for new, better ways of living. Men who sit around all day watching television are definite turn-offs. You want a mate who will engage both your mind and heart.

LIBRA ZODIAC SIGN
YOUR LOVE PLANETS

YOUR ROMANTIC SIDE   p. 696
  ▶ **VENUS IN SCORPIO**
  Born Sept. 23, 9:06 - Oct. 10, 10:17
  ▶ **VENUS IN SAGITTARIUS**
  Born Oct. 10, 10:18 - Oct. 23, 18:02

YOUR SEX DRIVE   p. 722
  ▶ **MARS IN LEO**
  Born Sept. 23, 9:06 - Oct. 23, 18:02

YOUR CELEBRITY TWINS   p. 760
  Find out the astrological similarities you have with famous people.

YOUR COMPATIBILITY   p. 780
  Compare planets to find out how compatible you are in a relationship.

YOUR RELATIONSHIP KARMA   p. 824
  ▶ **SATURN IN VIRGO**
  Born Sept. 23, 9:06 - Oct. 23, 18:02

DIZZY GILLESPIE
American Musician
Venus in Sagittarius

1949 SCORPIO
From October 23, 18:03 through November 22, 15:15

♏ ## The Disciplined Lover

As a 1949 Scorpio, you are extremely determined to succeed, both in work and love. Sometimes career can get in the way of your relationship, and vice-versa, but you enjoy the challenge of leading a balanced life. You're not the type to be in a relationship just because you're lonely. In fact, you're remarkably self-sufficient, and enjoy a little solitude. However, you do have a deep interest in finding a soul mate who intuits your needs and understands your moods. A partner who is compassionate and caring best suits you.

You're not interested in having sex unless it is with someone whose soul touches yours in some meaningful way. A lover who shares your interest in psychology, the occult, or spiritual transcendence arouses your urge to merge. You are extremely possessive toward your mate, and will not tolerate infidelity. For you love is about respect and devotion, not fun and games. You thrive in a relationship that makes you feel special, wanted, and needed. Nothing makes you happier than providing your spouse with love and comfort, especially when life becomes difficult.

If someone wants to seduce you, he or she should express interest in unusual subjects. Reincarnation, ESP, and alien life forms are all ideas that intrigue you. You may also be interested in crime stories, and enjoy discussing famous trials. Taking things slow and steady on the sexual front is a wise idea. You do best with a lover who takes time to win your trust. Jumping into bed on the first date isn't your style. You do like it when your admirer lingers over one spot on your body, lavishing it with kisses and caresses.

As a male Scorpion who was born in 1949, you want a woman who is spiritual, adventurous, and philosophical. You also like females who possess strong survival skills. Ultimately, you need a partner who is willing to stick by you in both good times and bad.

You 1949 female Scorpions prefer men who are charming, capable, and ambitious. You are also drawn to guys who are innovative and a little eccentric. A mate who has a distinctive air about him does best with you.

1949 SAGITTARIUS
From November 22, 15:16 through December 22, 4:22

♐ ## The Sexy Humanitarian

As a 1949 Sagittarian, you have a passionate investment in humankind. You believe it is your mission to serve the world in some material way, and that includes spreading love to all who need it. Although you might have postponed getting into a serious relationship for the sake of your career, that doesn't mean you're not romantic. It is just an indication of your investment in the public's welfare. A partner who shares your commitment to social justice is an ideal match for you. You couldn't bear being with somebody who is totally self-involved.

You do best in a relationship that features an ongoing exchange of ideas. You're always eager to hear your partner's opinion, and rely heavily on your mate for moral guidance. Sexually, you're extremely open-minded, and enjoy experimenting with your lover in the bedroom. A spouse who is as highly free-spirited and adventurous as you are will keep your passion alive. For you making love is both an enjoyable means to achieve intimacy and release stress. Travel may play an important part in your relationship, as you enjoy exchanging notes on exotic lands with your beloved.

Someone who expresses interest in world religions, different belief systems, and unusual cultural practices has a good chance of capturing your attention. You respect an admirer who is curious about people's similarities and differences. It doesn't matter who makes the first move in a relationship, because you possess few sexual hang-ups. You're equally delighted to be the pursuer or the pursued. An admirer whose sexual style is playful and lighthearted is sure to feel a kinship with you.

Women who are sensible, straightforward, and honest attract you 1949 male Archers. You also admire females who are funny and adventurous. Ultimately, you are looking for a partner who shares your belief that humans were put here to make the world a better place.

As a 1949 female Sagittarian, you want a man who is a born leader. You really admire a guy who can rally the troops for a good cause. A partner who sets a good moral example for others to follow is the ideal mate for you.

The Lonely Hearts Killers

Bigamist and serial con artist Raymond Fernandez wooed women through lonely hearts advertisements. Enticing his victims with promises of marriage, he would earn their trust, raid their bank accounts, and skip town. But once he met Martha Beck, Fernandez' depredations turned murderous. The fatal chemistry of their relationship earned the duo infamy as the "Lonely Hearts Killers."

Born in Hawaii in 1914, Raymond Fernandez served as a spy for the British government during World War II. Returning to America aboard a freighter after the war, he was struck in the head by a heavy steel hatch cover. The impact fractured his skull and damaged his frontal lobes—the section of the brain associated with impulse control.

When Fernandez arrived in the United States, he was caught at customs with a load of items stolen from his ship's storeroom. He served a one-year sentence for the theft in a federal penitentiary, where his cellmate initiated him into various occult practices, including voodoo. Upon his release, Fernandez settled in Brooklyn, New York and began corresponding with women in lonely hearts clubs. Fancying himself as a voodoo priest, he wielded supernatural power by having the women send him locks of hair and personal effects that he would use in mystical rituals. Fernandez succeeded in seducing and defrauding dozens of women before he met Martha Beck.

In 1942, Florida native Martha Seabrook was working as a nurse in a California army hospital and trolling the local bars for sexual encounters with soldiers on leave. When she became pregnant by one soldier, he rejected marriage and attempted to kill himself.

Raymond Fernandez (3rd from left) and Martha Beck (right) are charged with murder

Returning to Florida to have her child, Martha told her family that she had married a soldier who had been killed in Pacific combat. In late 1944, Martha became pregnant by Alfred Beck, a Pensacola bus driver who agreed to marry her. By 1945, Martha was a 250-pound divorcee, isolated, with two children and no job.

Escaping into romance novels and true confession magazines, Martha Beck posted a personal advertisement in "Mother Dinene's Family Club for Lonely Hearts." The only suitor to reply, Raymond Fernandez, met Beck in Jacksonville, Florida in late 1947. After two weeks of romance and sexual intimacy, Fernandez—probably realizing that Beck had no money—left for home. Ultimately, Beck chased Fernandez down in New York. In order to stay with him, Beck abandoned her two children at the Salvation Army.

Fernandez openly continued with his lonely hearts depredations. Posing as his sister, Beck assisted him with his scams, even as he married various women. But Beck could not contain her jealousy about the intimacy and sex Fernandez lavished on their victims. While his con jobs had once concluded with abandonment and humiliation, Beck's involvement changed everything. Victims started dying—usually after an angry confrontation between the victim and Beck.

Myrtle Young died after Fernandez drugged her. Beck killed Janet Fay with strangulation and a ball peen hammer. The most heinous crime occurred when Fernandez shot Delphine Downing in the head. Two days later, Beck drowned Downing's two-year child, Rainelle. Alerted by Rainelle's crying, suspicious neighbors called police. Beck and Fernandez were arrested. Following a sensational trial, they were convicted of capital murder on August 18, 1949. They died in the electric chair, at Sing Sing prison, on March 8, 1951.

▶ READ ABOUT BONNIE AND CLYDE AND THEIR GANG ON PAGE 137

1950 -1959

A TIME OF INNOCENCE

Peacetime brought new prosperity, ideas, music, morals—and censorship. Repression also came in the form of "blacklisting" of Communists and homosexuals.

After almost a whole decade of war, the 1950s allowed the world to recover and experience a time of innocence.

In the US, the new baby boomer generation was young and growing up with fun around them—American Bandstand and rock 'n' roll music, hula hoops, Barbie dolls, poodle skirts, and saddle shoes with bobby sox.

Disney released *Cinderella*, the original animated film about the unloved stepsister who finds her Prince Charming. The *I Love Lucy* show debuted, starring comedienne Lucille Ball and her husband Desi Arnaz.

With a misguided attempt at keeping the US innocent as long as possible, censorship became rampant. Radio stations played most of the hip new rock 'n' roll, but banned Dottie O'Brien's "Four or Five Times" and Dean Martin's "Wham Bam, Thank You Ma'am" because they were considered too suggestive, as was "Wake Up, Little Susie" by the Everly Brothers, a song about two teens who fall asleep at a movie and miss curfew. Crooners at the beginning of the decade gave way to teen idols. Music lovers propelled Elvis Presley to the top of the charts with major hits such as "Don't Be Cruel" and "Jailhouse Rock." Other singing sensations included the Everly Brothers, Bobby Darin, and the Platters. "The Chipmunks" (Alvin!) capped off the decade with a continued spirit of fun. When Elvis Presley appeared on *The Ed Sullivan Show*, Sullivan was so disturbed by his raunchy hip thrusting that he instructed the crew not to shoot Elvis below the waist.

Racy literature was treated with the same contempt—authorities banned the bestselling *Catcher in the Rye* by J.D. Salinger for sexual content and vulgarity, and 31 years after it was written, D.H. Lawrence's *Lady Chatterley's Lover* (about a married woman and her gamekeeper lover) was banned from the US mails.

More repression came in the form of "witch hunts" for alleged communists and homosexuals. The purge focused mainly on Hollywood, while the US government held congressional hearings that resulted in unjustified firings and "blacklistings."

In Europe, boundaries were also being pushed. Britain was to be the first to transmit a live birth on television—until it had to be stopped when a Caesarean was carried out, to the relief of outraged viewers. In France, Christian Dior presented the short skirt, which fell just above the knees, creating a fashion revolution. Faced with criticism, Dior answered insouciantly, "Women don't wear what they like, they like what they wear."

Although still following the TV "Donna Reed" housewife model for much of the decade, women also made some grand strides. Margaret Sanger started the International Planned Parenthood Federation to help women with birth control and abortions. French feminist Simone de Beauvoir won the Prix Goncourt—France's most prestigious literary award—for *The Mandarins*, about a woman torn between love and politics. Women demanded equal pay for equal work—and equality in the bedroom, too. Kinsey's *Sexual Behavior in the Human Female* shook up middle-America with its survey results, indicating that one-half of

Gene Kelly and Leslie Caron share the romance as well as the dancing in Metro Goldwyn Mayer's love story set to an all-Gershwin score, *An American in Paris*

French couturier Christian Dior with two of his models

▼ Elvis Presley, the King of Rock'n'Roll

American women were not virgins when they married and one-fourth of married women had committed adultery by the age of 40.

THE SILVER SCREEN
Some classic films came out of the '50s: *The African Queen*, *An American in Paris*, *A Place in the Sun*, *A Streetcar Named Desire*, and *Some Like It Hot*, which helped to lower some taboos thanks to its references to homosexuality and seduction. In France, Louis Malle's *Les Amants* caused controversy over its long love scene.

BETWEEN THE PAGES
Bestseller lists gave us many classic books, too, including *From Here to Eternity* by James Jones, *East of Eden* by John Steinbeck, *My Cousin Rachel* by Daphne du Maurier, *Giant* by Edna Ferber, and the Nobel Prize winning saga *Doctor Zhivago* by Boris Pasternak.

PEOPLE
John F. Kennedy married Jacqueline Bouvier, Marilyn Monroe married baseball great Joe Di Maggio, with the marriage only lasting nine months, and Janet Leigh married heartthrob Tony Curtis, later giving birth to film star Jamie Lee Curtis.

American actress Ingrid Bergman gave birth to Italian director Rossellini's child while she was still married to someone else, prompting a US Senator to attack her loose morals. There were also a few royal couplings: the Shah of Iran married Princess Soraya Esfandiari and actress Grace Kelly married Prince Rainier of Monaco.

1950

- ⭐ **INGRID BERGMAN**
- ⭐ **SEX PERVERTS**
- ⭐ **CINDERELLA**
- ⭐ **ALL ABOUT EVE**
- ⭐ **JOY STREET**
- ⭐ **GOODNIGHT, IRENE**
- ⭐ **MONA LISA**

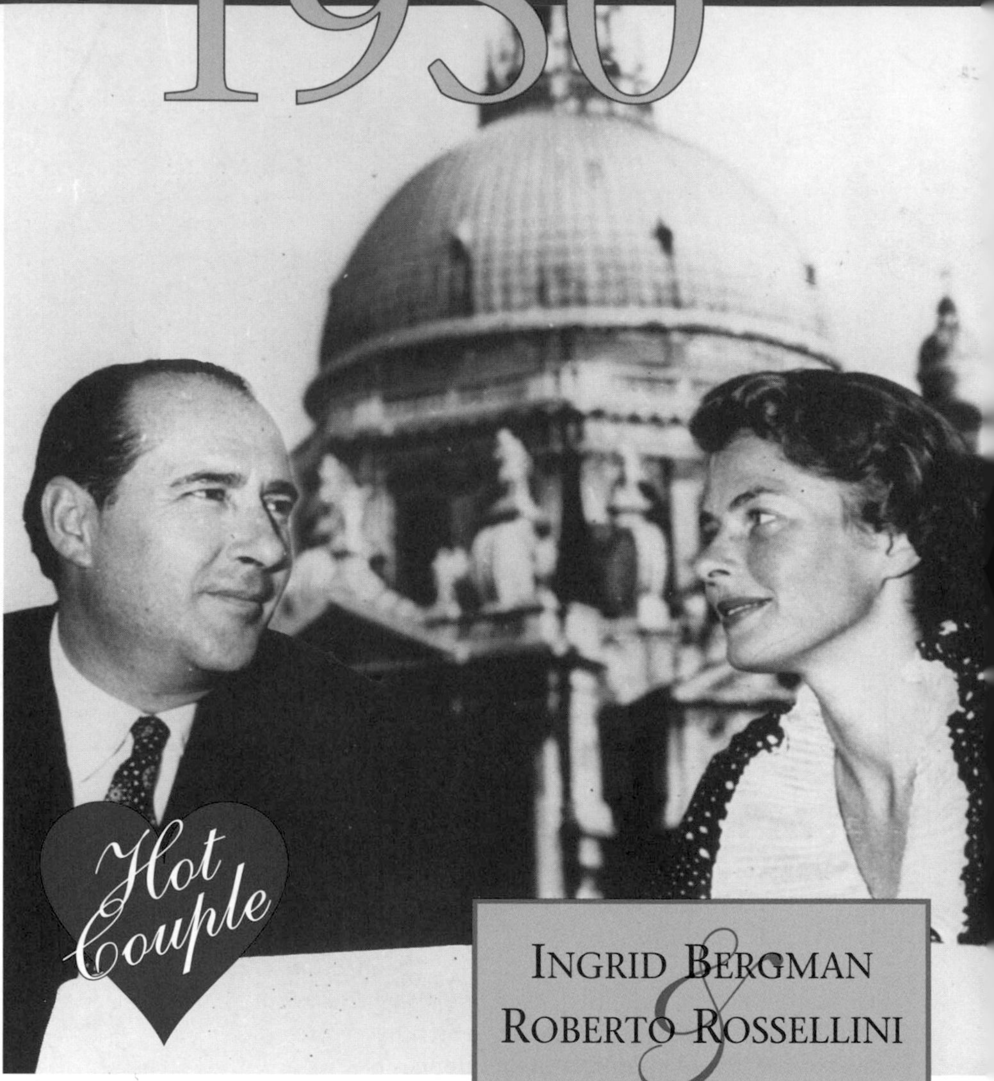

EVENTS

Yale anthropologist George Murdoch said that in three generations society would accept pre-marital sex as the way to select a mate. But society wasn't ready for that kind of attitude in 1950. Actress Ingrid Bergman gave birth to a child fathered by Italian director Rossellini—while still married to someone else. US Senator Edwin Johnson attacked her morality.

Other government officials were also showing little tolerance. The Congressional Record (March 29 to April 24), referring to homosexuals, reported that "...91 sex perverts had been located and fired from the Department of State ...But have they gone far enough?" Senate testimony indicated there were 400 more in the State Department and 4,000 in Government. "Where are they? Who hired them? Do we have a cell of these perverts hiding...?"

Meanwhile in Britain a study of 2,000 convictions for sex offences revealed that the youngest offender was just nine years of age, the oldest, 90. Most offenders, however, were between the ages of 21 and 50.

POP CULTURE

Charming audiences at the movies in 1950 was *Cinderella*, the original animated Disney story of the stepdaughter who meets Prince Charming. *Madeleine* chronicled the true story of a young woman in Glasgow on trial for the murder of her lover in 1857. In *Cyrano de Bergerac* the ugly Cyrano uses a handsome man to tell his feelings to the beautiful Roxanne, who doesn't realize that the words are someone else's. *All About Eve* was the story of an aspiring actress who schemes to enter the magic circle of directors and stars in the theatre world.

In the bookstores readers were grabbing *The Roman Spring of Mrs. Stone* by Tennessee Williams off the shelves. In this story an American actress with a failing career begins a moral decline while in Rome. In *Joy Street*, set in Boston, a young wife finds herself in love with her husband's best friend.

Topping the charts in 1950 were Patti Page's two hits, "The Tennessee Waltz" and "All My Love." Also popular were "Goodnight, Irene," by the Weavers, "Mona Lisa," by Nat King Cole, and "If I Knew You Were Comin' I'd've Baked a Cake."

Hot Couple

INGRID BERGMAN & ROBERTO ROSSELLINI

She was the most beloved movie star of her day, a glamorous Swedish beauty on screen, a devoted wife and mother in private life. He was a temperamental Italian director, known for his gritty, realistic films. Ingrid Bergman and Roberto Rossellini fell in love on the island of Stromboli while working together on a movie of the same name.

She was a Virgo, he a Taurus—the perfect blend of sensual earth sign energy. Their affair rocked Hollywood when she bore his love child in 1950. They married and had two more children, including the actress Isabella Rossellini, before divorcing in 1957.

SEE ALSO

▶ INGRID BERGMAN *Page 203*
▶ ALFRED HITCHCOCK *Page 341*

1950 CAPRICORN

From December 22, 1949 4:23 through January 20, 1950 14:59
(December 1950 Capricorns, see 1951 Capricorn)

♑ *The Sexy Idealist*

You're a dynamic Capricorn born in 1950 and you expect a happy relationship to give you the freedom to express all the intensity and passion that are so deeply a part of your nature. The give and take of relating is very important because you feel it's vital to connect on all levels. You really believe in true love and can be very romantic.

Sexual compatibility is an essential dimension of any relationship. You want to look in your lover's eyes and quiver all over. Good feelings and a happy level of optimism is another important factor. But even more so, you value the friendship aspect of romance. You'd never make a commitment just because of passion. You have to feel you'd be friends with this person, even if sex never entered into it at all.

A partner has to have many different layers to sustain your interest. Remaining static doesn't appeal to you at all, and you encourage your mate to change and grow and to be well-rounded. You love good conversation and sharing common pursuits. Socializing together is always fun because then you can come home and talk about the great time you had. You love music and find a romantic evening of dancing or holding hands at a concert very special. Doing something athletic together is also high on your list.

Male Goats born in 1950 prefer a woman who has sparkle and passion. Your lady is a dreamy idealist, but can also be a wanton woman. She radiates sex appeal and you love trying to keep up with her in bed. Occasionally she's possessive, but you love that about her because it makes you feel adored. You may fight sometimes, but when you make up, your love life really sizzles.

Female Capricorns born in 1950 like a man to be socially adroit, yet a little unpredictable. He should be outgoing, athletic, and a bit of a jokester. It's fun that he likes to show off and allows you to be his adoring audience. He inspires your imagination and you enjoy a rich fantasy life with him at the center. Sometimes he can be a bit temperamental or touchy. You don't mind, though, because you believe it's true love or you wouldn't bother at all.

CAPRICORN ZODIAC SIGN
YOUR LOVE PLANETS

YOUR ROMANTIC SIDE — p. 696
► VENUS IN AQUARIUS
Born Dec. 22, 1949 4:23 - Jan. 20, 1950 14:59

YOUR SEX DRIVE — p. 722
► MARS IN VIRGO
Dec. 22, 1949 4:23 - Dec. 26, 1949 5:22
► MARS IN LIBRA
Dec. 26, 1949 5:23 - Jan. 20, 1950 14:59

YOUR CELEBRITY TWINS — p. 760
Find out the astrological similarities you have with famous people.

YOUR COMPATIBILITY — p. 780
Compare planets to find out how compatible you are in a relationship.

YOUR RELATIONSHIP KARMA — p. 824
► SATURN IN VIRGO
Born Dec. 22, 1949 4:23 - Jan. 20, 1950 14:59

JOSE FERRER
Puerto Rican Actor
Sun in Capricorn

263

1950 AQUARIUS

From January 20, 15:00 through February 19, 5:17

♒ *The Idealistic Romantic*

As an optimistic Aquarius born in 1950, you believe a relationship is one way to bring harmony to the earth. Being with someone you cherish, and who loves you just as much, creates a positive vibration that makes other people happy, too. You're an incredible idealist and you bring all your positive notions into a partnership.

You believe in tenderness and true love and would never fall for anything less. Friendship is another positive dimension of your relationship and you feel that your mate is your best pal as well as your soul mate. Doing what's best for the team is high on your list of priorities and you are willing at times to put your personal needs aside in favor of your mate's needs. Making the one you love happy gives you the utmost pleasure.

To sustain your interest a mate must have a positive vibration. If asked, you could come up with a long list of qualities that appeal to you, such as intelligence, kindness, generosity, sparkle, sex appeal, and pizzazz, but what matters most to you is the energy you exchange. As long as that's working, you easily forgive any minor flaws. You enjoy sharing hobbies and doing good works together, such as organizing and attending charitable events. You're also very romantic, so candlelit dinners enhanced by a singer and a dance floor keep the magic alive.

If you're a male Aquarius born in 1950, you prefer a partner to be intelligent and forward-thinking. Old-fashioned or staid won't snag your attention. Your lady can remain front and center in your heart by staying youthful, sharing clever ideas, and lavishing you with devotion. She's sexy, but never crass, because she knows how to entice you subtly.

As a female Aquarius born in 1950 you want your man to be socially adept, courtly and sincere, but also magnetic, outgoing, and charismatic. Your guy can twirl you around the dance floor, help you shop for something sexy to wear, and decorate a bedroom, all without sacrificing a bit of machismo. He's cheerful, intelligent, and optimistic. He is your soul mate, and when you're together, the world shines a little brighter.

AQUARIUS ZODIAC SIGN
YOUR LOVE PLANETS

YOUR ROMANTIC SIDE — p. 696
► VENUS IN AQUARIUS
Born Jan. 20, 15:00 - Feb. 19, 5:17

YOUR SEX DRIVE — p. 722
► MARS IN LIBRA
Born Jan. 20, 15:00 - Feb. 19, 5:17

YOUR CELEBRITY TWINS — p. 760
Find out the astrological similarities you have with famous people.

YOUR COMPATIBILITY — p. 780
Compare planets to find out how compatible you are in a relationship.

YOUR RELATIONSHIP KARMA — p. 824
► SATURN IN VIRGO
Born Jan. 20, 15:00 - Feb. 19, 5:17

TOSHIRO MIFUNE
Japanese Actor
Sun in Aries

264

1950 PISCES
From February 19, 5:18 through March 21, 4:34

The Passionate Idealist

As a hard-working Pisces born in 1950, your relationship must be idealistic, passionate, and romantic. You believe in commitment and true love, but you also need time for your career and personal freedoms. That means you require a relationship that allows you to express all sides of your nature. Being shipwrecked on a desert island is a romantic idea, but you prefer to build a solid relationship in the real world.

Generosity and friendship are also very important to you and you believe that true love means you each look out for the other's needs. Taking care of that special someone is quite heartwarming, and doing so for each other creates a positive atmosphere of mutual support and caring. Romance is also very important and you work hard to keep the hearts and flowers alive in your love story.

A mate must also spark your imagination to sustain your interest. You like to believe that there are mysteries below the surface, and being able to keep on discovering new facets is quite a thrill. You enjoy being wooed with passion and determination, and it's a lot of fun to realize a mate has planned a special evening with you at the center. Sharing New Age activities can be enjoyable, too, and you're willing to try astral projection or even hypnosis together. Holding hands in the movies may be more traditional, but can be equally pleasant.

Male Fish born in 1950 need a woman who is romantic, idealistic, and passionate. She can sometimes be serene and devoted and at other times knocks you off your heels with an amusing bout of possessiveness and temper tantrums. Your lady has her moments! She's never dull and that's what makes her endlessly appealing.

If you're a female Pisces born in 1950, you expect a man to have a mind of his own. Of course, he must understand the social graces, because, after all, why would you fall for someone who doesn't? But he is also sexy, unpredictable, and he surprises you more often than not. Sometimes he needs his space for his own interests, but that gives you time for your activities, too. When you reconnect, there's always a lot to share.

1950 ARIES
From March 21, 4:35 through April 20, 15:58

The Practical Dreamer

You're a creative Aries born in 1950 and to you a relationship is a comfortable connection in which you can grow as a person and share good feelings. Feeling understood is an important dimension of your relationship, and you believe that being best pals as well as lovers keeps you together. A positive vibration you share is also important. This helps to give you a sense of simpatico.

Romance is a component of easy mutual idealism, and by sharing your vision of life with someone compatible, you feel that all's right with the world. Working together side by side, being on the same team, and giving and receiving support and devotion is what love is all about for you. You like excitement, but in a relationship you prefer a quiet sense of security that gives way to comfort, happiness, and contentment.

To sustain your interest a mate has to be on the same wavelength as you are. You support innovative ideas, but you like to feel your partner is connected and intelligent, and that there's a strong basis for continued intellectual compatibility. Goofing off, sharing those long talks in front of the fire, or recounting stories from your past can be fun and bring you both closer. You also like projects you can complete side by side, such as charitable events. And you enjoy social activities so you can go out together and share good times with friends.

If you're a male Aries born in 1950, you like a woman who sparkles with life. Her ideas are clever, and she communicates them adroitly and with humor. A happy personality is number one in your book. You'd rather she be interesting than a mere babe, because after all, you can't make love every minute of the day. She's good with kids and kind to strangers, and she makes you feel happy and centered.

As a female Aries born in 1950, you prefer your guy to be imaginative, yet also realistic. He has lots of creative ideas and you enjoy hearing him speak. He is fluid in thought and one other plus—his voice is so sexy. He isn't just a beautiful dreamer, though. He's practical and hardworking, and knows how to solve a variety of problems.

1950 TAURUS

From April 20, 15:59 through May 21, 15:26

The Intense Sexpot

You're a dynamic Taurus born in 1950, and you expect your relationship to meet your needs. You have a strong belief in hard work and achievement, and you like to share your life with someone who not only agrees, but is committed to helping you meet your goals. A positive intellectual connection combined with good chemistry makes you happy. Having your world in order is important to you and your relationship must be reliable and steady. You'd hate to be uncertain about love or your partner.

Sexual compatibility is also essential to you. You realize that the best sex happens when both partners find the same turn-ons mutually stimulating. Of course, that doesn't mean you believe it's possible to build an enduring relationship without an occasional difference of opinion. Strong wills can lead to disagreements at times, but the making up part afterwards is always worthwhile. You expect a relationship to be a bit larger than life, just as you, yourself, are.

A partner must be sexy and engaging to sustain your interest. You want to feel that your partner continues to be a good catch. You love a good debate and it's fun for you to sway your mate to your point of view. That means he or she must have the moxie to stand up to you and challenge your ideas now and then. Marathon lovemaking sessions are very appealing and you might be content to forego romantic outings in favor of hot sex.

As a male Bull born in 1950, you need a woman to be sexy and stimulating. She is sweet, but also seductive. Your lady understands the mating dance and loves enticing you. She follows your orders—sometimes—but often speaks her mind and causes you to refine your position. This woman cooperates willingly and enjoys working by your side.

If you're a female Taureans born in 1950, you need a strong, macho guy who is down to earth. You believe in the give and take of any relationship and you don't mind jockeying for position now and then. That means your guy must be strong enough to stand up to you. He's skilled and can solve problems. You know he'll always be there for you when you need him.

TAURUS ZODIAC SIGN
YOUR LOVE PLANETS

YOUR ROMANTIC SIDE   p. 696
▶ VENUS IN PISCES
Born Apr. 20, 15:59 - May 05, 19:18
▶ VENUS IN ARIES
Born May 05, 19:19 - May 21, 15:26

YOUR SEX DRIVE   p. 722
▶ MARS IN LIBRA
Born Apr. 20, 15:59 - May 21, 15:26

YOUR CELEBRITY TWINS   p. 760
Find out the astrological similarities you have with famous people.

YOUR COMPATIBILITY   p. 780
Compare planets to find out how compatible you are in a relationship.

YOUR RELATIONSHIP KARMA   p. 824
▶ SATURN IN VIRGO
Born Apr. 20, 15:59 - May 21, 15:26

ANNE BAXTER
American Actress
Sun in Taurus

265

1950 GEMINI

From May 21, 15:27 through June 21, 23:35

The Sensual Cut-up

You are a stable Gemini born in 1950 and you expect a relationship to provide happiness and pleasure. While you believe in commitment, you also expect to have your own way, so that means you must have the right partner or you feel like calling it quits. Acceptance and understanding are essential to you because that means you're free to try new things and still come home to the same mate.

Good communication is important, but a relationship can't always be about the serious things in life. Having fun together and sharing lighthearted chit chat make you happy because it brings sparkle back into your life after a long, hard workday. You also believe in sharing good sex within a relationship because that way you each provide the other with an oasis of relaxation and affection.

To sustain your interest a partner must have sweet and interesting things to say. A clever turn of phrase appeals to you, but something as simple as a greeting card expressing ongoing devotion in a meaningful way really touches your heart and keeps you coming back for more. You enjoy art and good writing and are excited by a mate who can engage you in an interesting debate about a good book or television show. Sex is important too, and you love being surprised by a mate whose needs are expressed in new and stimulating ways.

Male Geminis born in 1950 like a woman who is clever, sensual, and down to earth. She can be ribald or practical, but she loves to please you. Her sweet, sexy ways bring a kind of rhythm to your world. Your lady adores music and art and may be a professional in a creative field. Her voice is soft and melodious and her touch entrances you, as though you're being caressed with silk and velvet.

Female Geminis born in 1950 expect a man to be a hard working, practical sort of fellow who has his own ideas and isn't shy about expressing them. He's often busy, may be somewhat of an absent-minded professor, but he knows what he's doing, and is never a fool. Your guy gives you the space you need, doesn't infringe on your private time, and offers enough surprises to keep life from getting dull.

GEMINI ZODIAC SIGN
YOUR LOVE PLANETS

YOUR ROMANTIC SIDE   p. 696
▶ VENUS IN ARIES
Born May 21, 15:27 - June 01, 14:18
▶ VENUS IN TAURUS
June 01, 14:19 - June 21, 23:35

YOUR SEX DRIVE   p. 722
▶ MARS IN LIBRA
Born May 21, 15:27 - June 11, 20:26
▶ MARS IN LIBRA
Born June 11, 20:27 - June 21, 23:35

YOUR CELEBRITY TWINS   p. 760
Find out the astrological similarities you have with famous people.

YOUR COMPATIBILITY   p. 780
Compare planets to find out how compatible you are in a relationship.

YOUR RELATIONSHIP KARMA   p. 824
▶ SATURN IN VIRGO
Born May 21, 15:27 - June 21, 23:35

JUDY HOLLIDAY
American Actress
Mars in Cancer

1950 CANCER
From June 21, 23:36 through July 23, 10:29

The Tender Sweetheart

As a creative Cancer born in 1950, your relationship must be both spiritual and stimulating. You want to feel that you are truly connected and that there is a purpose to your union. Your belief in destiny and true love is profound and you seek a relationship that makes you feel safe and secure. Good communication is the cornerstone of any good relationship and sharing your ideas with a receptive partner makes you feel like a real couple.

Keeping the spirit of romance alive is important to you, and you believe that there's more to a relationship than just stability. There has to be a sense of joy and the feeling that you are the only two people out on the dance floor, perpetually in rhythm. You need a gentle kind of love and never want to feel you're being coerced or overpowered.

To sustain your interest a partner must have sincerity and more than a little flair and magic. Sharing music and dance is fun. You love being engaged in interesting conversation and it's fun to attend a play, a movie, or even watch television together because afterward there's always so much to say. Knowing that you are loved is very important to you, so a mate who offers tender gestures and verbal assurances makes you feel committed and secure.

Male Cancers born in 1950 need a woman who is youthful, communicative, yet also reliable and stable. You want to know where her heart is and you don't want to have to beg for her affection because you need security. Your lady is sparkling and fun, cherishes fond memories of her childhood, and shares interesting stories. She's romantic and sexy, and when you think of her you hum a happy tune.

Female Crabs born in 1950 need a man who is intellectual and spiritual. He's so intuitive he seems to know what's in your heart from the moment you meet—and that makes you feel cozy and content. He is good on the dance floor and even when you're just hugging, he sways in a way that's hypnotic. He knows how to please you in bed without making too big a deal of his own prowess. His desire to see you happy is quite endearing and it makes you love him all the more.

1950 LEO
From July 23, 10:30 through August 23, 17:22

The Determined Idealist

As a protective Leo born in 1950, you want a relationship to be spiritual, idealistic, and an oasis of tenderness. Nothing is more meaningful to you than the idea of true love, and you're determined to live your life with that one special soul mate. You believe in intelligence and fidelity, and feel that people who take love lightly end up miserable. You would never do that—trust and commitment are too important to you.

Love can also be an illusion, as you know only too well. While on the path to true love you may have stumbled a few times, believing you'd found your perfect partner, but ended up being fooled instead. In your opinion it takes time to create perfection, so a few missteps are not uncommon along the way. Building a solid home and family are important to you in a romance, but you also believe it comes down to what you feel for your mate that defines whether or not the relationship will work.

To maintain your interest a partner must be sensitive and caring, tender and gentle, and determined to make you happy. Kind gestures mean a lot to you and being given a sweet treat helps you open your heart. A compatible level of emotionality is essential, and you want to be with a mate for whom the same things are meaningful and important. You enjoy music and art and it's fun to dress up and go out and do all those classically romantic things, but you're just as content to stay home and snuggle.

Male Leos born in 1950 like a woman who is soft and lovable. Your lady is a natural mother, she's kind and nurturing, and it's impossible not to want to hug her. Children flock to her side, pets sit contentedly at her feet, and all who know her love her. You sense that when you meet she has the depth of emotion you need, and in looking into her eyes you feel contentment and devotion.

Lady Lions born in 1950 need a man who is intense and magnetic, yet he must also have a spiritual leaning. Your guy is sensitive and his energy is fluid. He's intuitive and has a way of knowing what will please you. He's courtly and gentle, yet you feel he'll always come through for you.

1 Read Your Sign   **2** Look Up Your Love Planets   **3** Go to Pages Shown

1950 VIRGO
From August 23, 17:23 through September 23, 14:43

The Liberated Lover

You're an intense Virgo born in 1950, and for you a relationship must be sexy, passionate, and your true destiny. You believe in loving with your whole heart. Connecting with that one right soul mate is what a relationship is all about. Why settle for anything less? You'd never commit just to stave off loneliness or because the time is right. You are an all or nothing kind of lover, and that's the way you like it.

Sexual compatibility is very important to you because you feel that it's a significant path to true intimacy. You're liberal and will try most anything. You believe a good relationship provides each partner the chance to open up and share ideas, needs, and desires without judgment or fear. Compromise and caring are also important, but when strong-willed people mate, there's bound to be some friction. However, you feel friction can be a good thing—especially in the incendiary make up sessions that follow any argument.

A partner must be magnetic, sexy, and unapologetic to sustain your interest. A strong-willed person is always more interesting to you than someone quiet or demure, because you like being with someone who is your equal. You're willing to go a few rounds with a partner who continues to captivate you. You love being pampered, worshiped, and lavished with gifts, and are willing to return the favor.

Male Virgos born in 1950 like a woman who is gorgeous and sizzling. No matter how long you've been together, she continues to spark your imagination. Your gal is a sexy beauty and when she walks into the room, heads turn. She's also generous and loving, and she pulls out all the stops to show you how she feels. She's playful, fun-loving, and the envy of all your friends.

Female Virgos born in 1950 like a man who is strong and macho. Your guy knows what he wants and he never hesitates to make his desires known. He has a simmering kind of sexuality and every woman you know has asked you what he's like in bed. You feel safe around him and you know that he's in it for the long haul. This is a guy who improves with age and makes you feel ageless.

VIRGO ZODIAC SIGN
YOUR LOVE PLANETS

YOUR ROMANTIC SIDE — p. 696
▶ VENUS IN LEO
Born Aug. 23, 17:23 - Sept. 10, 1:36
▶ VENUS IN LIBRA
Born Sept. 10, 1:37 - Sept. 23, 14:43

YOUR SEX DRIVE — p. 722
▶ MARS IN SCORPIO
Born Aug. 23, 17:23 - Sept. 23, 14:43

YOUR CELEBRITY TWINS — p. 760
Find out the astrological similarities you have with famous people.

YOUR COMPATIBILITY — p. 780
Compare planets to find out how compatible you are in a relationship.

YOUR RELATIONSHIP KARMA — p. 824
▶ SATURN IN VIRGO
Born Aug. 23, 17:23 - Sept. 23, 14:43

GLORIA GRAHAME
American Actress
Mars in Libra

267

1950 LIBRA
From September 23, 14:44 through October 23, 23:44

The Destiny Seeker

You're a sensitive Libra born in 1950, and for you a relationship must provide a sense of destiny and belonging. You care so much about security and believe that only love can provide you with the sanctuary you need. You also realize that love is complicated and admit that on the path to that perfect connection, you may have had to kiss a few frogs. From that you learned that it takes time to ascertain who a person is, and now you are deeper and wiser as a result.

Tolerance and acceptance are other essential dimensions to your relationship. You want to know that you can express all the aspects of your nature and that you will not only be allowed to do so, but will be encouraged. The freedom to act independently is meaningful in a relationship, but you also care about sharing common interests. Love requires balance and that's always your goal. Living in harmony is important and you'd hate to have a relationship that was always in chaos or filled with strife.

To keep your interest a mate must be trustworthy. You connect on a psychic level and just seem to know what matters. You appreciate kindness and personal sparkle, though, and you enjoy being drawn out by a mate who wants to know what you think and how you feel. Outdoor activities are fun to share and you love pitching in together on worthwhile projects.

Male Librans born in 1950 need a woman who is reliable and sparkling. You want to feel that she will always be there for you, but you're also willing to compromise if she has an agenda of her own. Being loved and appreciated is important to you and you seek a woman with whom you can forge a lasting bond. She may be a little older than you are or else perhaps a bit of a rebel.

Lady Librans want a man who is playful and boyish, yet also macho and manly. Your guy is sensitive and he knows who you are and what you need. But he's also a bit of a handful and sometimes he keeps you guessing. He's trustworthy, though, and you feel he'd never do anything deliberately to disappoint you. Instead, he just wants you to be happy and to express the many aspects of his nature.

LIBRA ZODIAC SIGN
YOUR LOVE PLANETS

YOUR ROMANTIC SIDE — p. 696
▶ VENUS IN LIBRA
Born Sept. 23, 14:44 - Oct. 04, 5:50
▶ VENUS IN LIBRA
Born Oct. 04, 5:51 - Oct. 23, 23:44

YOUR SEX DRIVE — p. 722
▶ MARS IN SCORPIO
Born Sept. 23, 14:44 - Sept. 25, 19:47
▶ MARS IN SAGITTARIUS
Born Sept. 25, 19:48 - Oct. 23, 23:44

YOUR CELEBRITY TWINS — p. 760
Find out the astrological similarities you have with famous people.

YOUR COMPATIBILITY — p. 780
Compare planets to find out how compatible you are in a relationship.

YOUR RELATIONSHIP KARMA — p. 824
▶ SATURN IN VIRGO
Born Sept. 23, 14:44 - Oct. 23, 23:44

RICARDO MONTALBAN
Mexican Actor
Sun in Sagittarius

1950 SCORPIO
From October 23, 23:45 through November 22, 21:02

♏ ## The Amorous Conversationalist

As a devoted Scorpio born in 1950, your relationship must be loving and stable. Commitment is essential to you. Good communication is important and you feel that it makes a relationship happy and positive. You also believe humor is the cornerstone of any romance, so that means the couple who laughs together stays together.

Self-expression is another significant issue. You believe that each partner must have the right to open up and share ideas, and also be encouraged to follow his or her own personal star. That doesn't mean you're in favor of chaos within a relationship, because you certainly are not. You realize the importance of cooperation and know that sometimes one mate must give in because the other's needs or desires should take precedence.

A mate who is a pleasant and amusing conversationalist can hold your interest. Warm moments of intellectual interaction, amusing little stories, and even a limerick now and then keep you happy and involved. You love it when your partner is brave enough to whisper a fantasy into your ear, because then you feel you're making a genuine connection. You also believe that working together on important projects, even if they're only chores around the house, and sharing athletic activities keep you happily bonded.

Male Scorpions born in 1950 like a woman who has wit and charm. Your lady is verbally adroit and her sex appeal comes out during casual conversation. She is so charming and interesting that just chatting with her leads to a wonderful good time. She's clever and intellectually involved and her interest in culture inspires you to develop your own. You feel relaxed and happy in her company and know that your friends envy you for capturing her heart.

Female Scorpios born in 1950 need a man who is both a free spirit and a responsible, down to earth sort of guy. Your fellow realizes that there's no substitute for play but he's a hard worker as well. He makes life fun and that increases your level of enjoyment in whatever you do together. You enjoy mutually stimulating conversation and his grasp of your feelings is a turn-on.

1950 SAGITTARIUS
From November 22, 21:03 through December 22, 10:12

♐ ## The Easy-going Lover

You're a gallant Sagittarius born in 1950, and to you a relationship should be passionate, devoted, and spiritual. You believe romantic connections exist for a purpose and you like to feel that you and your partner are connected emotionally, physically, and spiritually. Being receptive to each other's ideas and learning from each other sustain the relationship and keep it interesting. You'd hate to be trapped in a romance in which the partners were self-centered or manipulative.

You believe in peace and compromise, and if you know what your mate needs, it makes sense to you to try to make that happen. You like giving and receiving. You realize that a relationship is about doing what makes you both feel happy, just because giving happiness is such a wonderful way to live. Sharing fun and enjoying each other's company keep the love alive for you. Good feelings are most important to you, but they're indefinable and reside below the surface.

The mate who shares your spiritual approach to life can hold your interest. Being part of something greater than just yourself makes you feel you're going through life as part of a successful team. You love sharing tender moments and good conversation, and it's fun for you to try New Age techniques such as creative visualizations or meditations together. Common goals and a sense of mutual cooperation are also important.

Male Archers born in 1950 need a woman who is outgoing and friendly, and whose sparkle lights up a room. Your lady is charming and self-possessed. She's funny, but not a clown, and people admire her appearance as well as her point of view. Quiet devotion appeals to you and knowing she loves you will always keep her front and center in your heart.

Lady Sagittarians born in 1950 prefer a man who is macho enough to get things done, yet sensitive enough not to seem like a jerk. Your guy is kind and helpful, he's never full of himself, and he often puts other people's needs ahead of his own. He's never a blowhard, although down deep he has a steady sort of confidence as well as a cheerful spirit—and he's always a warm, good time.

Edith Piaf – The Little Bird

According to legend, she was born under a lamp post on the streets of Paris, abandoned by her alcoholic mother, and brought up in a brothel in Normandy by her grandmother. Whatever the truth, Edith Piaf's unconventional start on this earth was the beginning of a colorful and turbulent life.

By the age of eight, Edith was working alongside her acrobat father as a street entertainer. By fifteen she was making her own way in life as a street singer, and by eighteen she was pregnant by her live-in lover. He was the first in a long line of men that Edith Piaf devoured. The arrival of baby Marcelle spelled quarrels for the lovers and the relationship did not last. Neither did Marcelle—she died of meningitis at the age of two.

It was then that Edith's fortunes changed forever. Music impresario Louis Leplée spotted Edith singing on the streets of Paris. He booked her to perform in his club and gave her the name "Piaf," French slang for sparrow. A legend was created.

She was an instant hit. Her emotive voice moved people to tears and after her shows there was riotous applause. She could do no wrong—until Leplée was murdered in his apartment and Edith found herself a chief suspect. However, she was never charged with the crime. Her friends abandoned her and she sought solace in the arms of songwriter Raymond Asso. She soon left him and embarked on a series of tempestuous, doomed affairs. With each new man came a new life. When Edith got bored, she simply moved on.

By 1941 she was firmly established

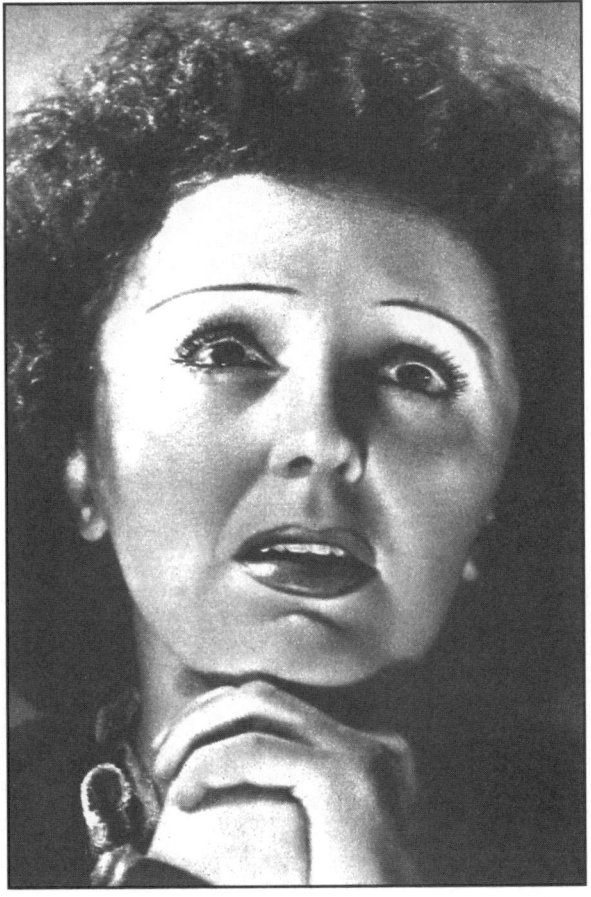

> *"Morality means living in a way that takes the fun out of life."*
>
> **EDITH PIAF**

as a star, commanding sell-out performances, and her lover *du jour* was Henri Contet. He introduced her to a seedy world, which she entered with relish. Renting an apartment over a brothel, she was the queen who held court over the underbelly of Parisian society, rubbing shoulders with stars, rogues, bohemian intellectuals, prostitutes, and villains. She knew how to party hard, and in style—always with a bottle of something strong by her side and a handsome man within her reach.

Then she met the man who was to be the love of her life—a married Moroccan boxer, Marcel Cerdan. She threw herself into the relationship with all her usual zeal and gusto. But it was all to end in tragedy when Cerdan was killed in a plane crash on his way to be with Edith in New York. She was devastated, and it was a love she would never get over.

Lonely, depressed, an alcoholic, and addicted to painkillers after a horrific car crash, Edith consoled herself as only she knew how. Cruising the bars of Paris, she found comfort in the arms of strangers.

The depression did not last long and in 1952 she married an old friend, Jacques Pills. After a few years of married life, shunning the limelight, Edith burst back on the scene with a new whirlwind cycle of lovers and parties.

The drink and the drugs had ravaged her body but had never deterred her in her pursuit of a good time. Edith died in October 1963 of cancer. Tens of thousands of fans flocked to pay their respects.

Passionate and spontaneous, Edith Piaf lived for the moment. Her wild abandon caused her much tragedy, but as she famously sang, "Non! Je ne regrette rien."

▶ READ ABOUT JUDY GARLAND, ANOTHER POPULAR SINGER, ON PAGE 219

1951

- ★ I LOVE LUCY
- ★ THE AFRICAN QUEEN
- ★ FROM HERE TO ETERNITY
- ★ CATCHER IN THE RYE
- ★ COLD, COLD HEART
- ★ TOO YOUNG

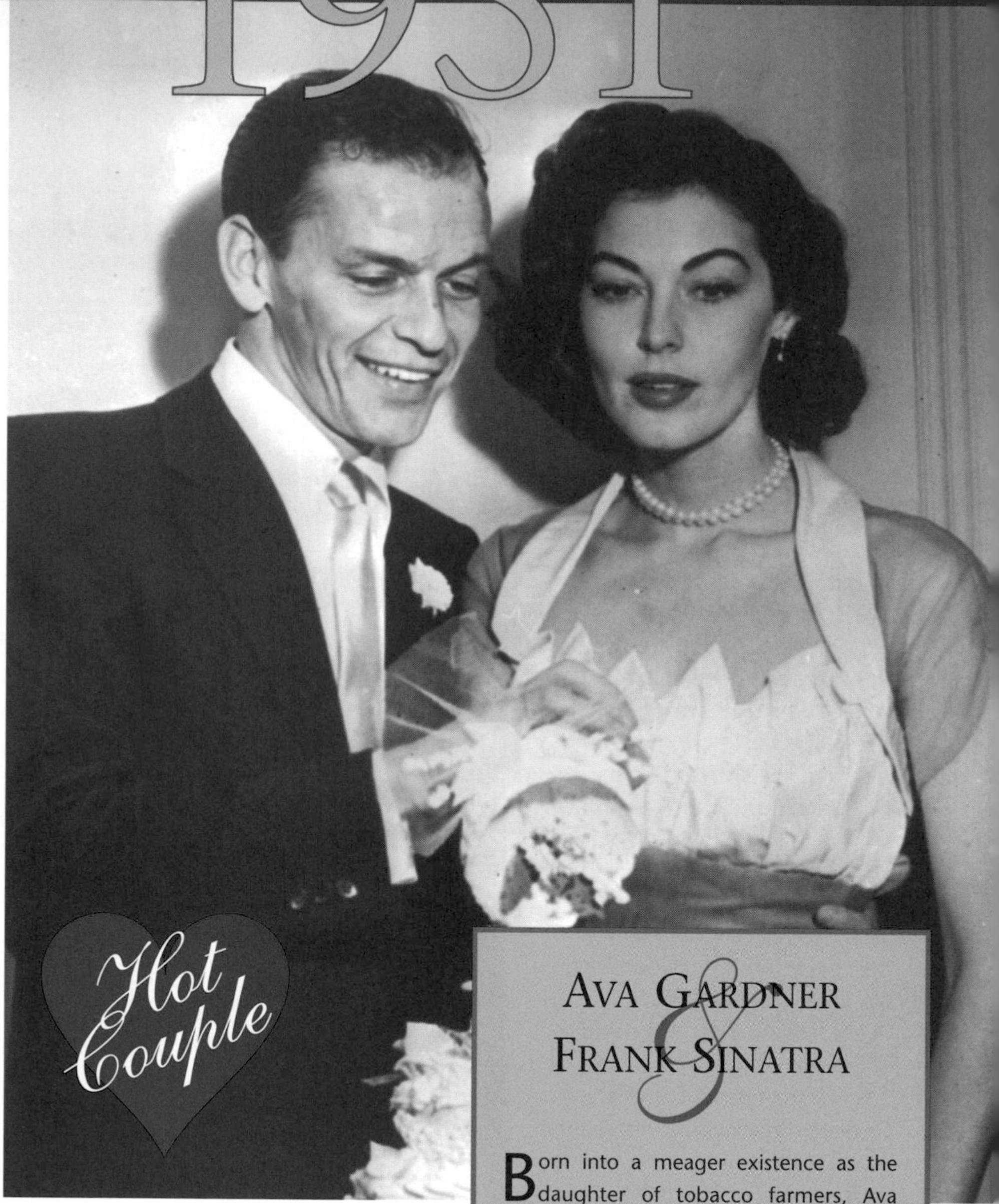

EVENTS

While Margaret Sanger, founder of Planned Parenthood, was urging development of oral contraceptives, radio stations were banning Dottie O'Brien's "Four or Five Times" and Dean Martin's "Wham Bam, Thank You Ma'am" for being too suggestive.

Janet Leigh *(Psycho)* married Tony Curtis, the Shah of Iran married Princess Soraya Esfandiari, and Liz Taylor divorced Conrad Hilton.

I Love Lucy debuted on TV and French writer Andre Gide died. He had caused a scandal in 1924 over publication of the first essay to plead for the recognition of homosexuality.

POP CULTURE

1951 was a year for movies that would become classics. In Humphrey Bogart's *The African Queen,* a boat captain and spinster pair up for a trip down an African river. *An American in Paris*, a Gene Kelly vehicle, tells the story of a poor American painter who's torn between the money of a patroness and the girl he loves—who happens to be the girlfriend of an acquaintance. In *A Place in the Sun*, adapted from the Dreiser novel *An American Tragedy*, a young man's prior romance with a working-class woman complicates his new affair with a wealthy woman. *A Streetcar Named Desire* features a sensitive Southern belle who retreats into fantasy.

In the bookstores people were buying *The Story of a King*, about the man who gave up the throne for love, the former King Edward VIII. Other must-reads included *From Here to*

Eternity by James Jones, the story of violent military life in a pre-World War II Pearl Harbor. *Catcher in the Rye*, by J. D. Salinger, later became a staple on high school reading lists—when it wasn't being banned for sexual content and vulgarity. Donald Webster Cory released *The Homosexual in America*, the first non-clinical work that described the lives of homosexuals, most of whom were still in the closet.

In 1951 Les Paul and Mary Ford had two hits on the charts—"How High the Moon" and "Mockin' Bird Hill." Other favorites were Perry Como's "If," Tony Bennett's "Cold, Cold Heart," Nat King Cole's "Too Young," and Rosemary Clooney's "Come On-A My House."

Hot Couple

AVA GARDNER & FRANK SINATRA

Born into a meager existence as the daughter of tobacco farmers, Ava Gardner lived out the ultimate rags-to-riches fantasy. When her brother-in-law posted a picture of her in his photography studio in Manhattan, a movie executive from MGM spied her stunning beauty.

When she married Frank Sinatra on November 7, he was at the lowest point in his career. Ol' Blue Eyes wasn't doing as well as he would later on, and often had to borrow money from Ava. They divorced in 1957. He kept a statue of Ava from *The Barefoot Contessa* until his wife, Barbara Marx, made him dispose of it.

SEE ALSO
▶ FRANK SINATRA *Page 211 & 270*

270

1951 CAPRICORN

From December 22, 1950 10:13 through January 20, 1951 20:51
(December 1951 Capricorns, see 1952 Capricorn)

♑ *The Stable Idealist*

You're a mystical Capricorn born in 1951, and you believe a relationship must be a positive combination of stability and true love. Devotion is very meaningful to you because you believe that once you give your heart, you can never take it back. Lifetime commitments are your frame of reference because you feel casual connections are a big waste of time.

Being able to relate harmoniously is another significant feature of your good relationship. You admit that a quarrel now and then is unavoidable, but you always want to try to get along and support each other. Intuition plays a role in your relationship—you can feel and know what each other is thinking and feeling, and that unconscious connection binds you even closer together. Being of one mind is another very important aspect of your good relationship. You feel that when you build a life together, it's good to share significant points of view.

A creative and dynamic partner has always appealed most to you. Someone who piques your interest with an unusual comment, a fascinating tale told at a party, or an invitation to share a mutual interest fits the mold for your ideal partner. You love looking for antiques, strolling along old streets, or visiting historical sites, and that provides an excellent backdrop for romance to begin or to endure.

Male Goats born in 1951 prefer a forward-minded woman who thinks with her head as well as her heart. Your lady is intelligent and practical, and even when her ideas are innovative, she explains how to make them workable. She is idealistic and romantic as well, and you enjoy being part of the dream world in her mind. She strikes you as a good mother, reliable partner, and someone you would always want in your life.

1951 Female Cappies need a strong, macho, take-charge kind of man. Your guy is a bit larger than life, and he always seems to take control of any situation. Fiercely masculine, he's a man's man and he doesn't expect you to giggle and be silly or overly dainty. Despite his strength, he's also sensitive and he understands how sentiment plays an important part in life.

CAPRICORN ZODIAC SIGN
YOUR LOVE PLANETS

YOUR ROMANTIC SIDE   p. 696
► **VENUS IN CAPRICORN**
Born Dec. 22, 1950 10:13 - Jan. 07, 1951 21:09
► **VENUS IN AQUARIUS**
Born Jan. 07, 21:10 - Jan. 20, 20:51

YOUR SEX DRIVE   p. 722
► **MARS IN AQUARIUS**
Born Dec. 22, 1950 10:13 - Jan. 20, 1951 20:51

YOUR CELEBRITY TWINS   p. 760
Find out the astrological similarities you have with famous people.

YOUR COMPATIBILITY   p. 780
Compare planets to find out how compatible you are in a relationship.

YOUR RELATIONSHIP KARMA   p. 824
► **SATURN IN LIBRA**
Born Dec. 22, 1950 10:13 - Jan. 20, 1951 20:51

DAVID NIVEN
English Actor
Mars in Capricorn

271

1951 AQUARIUS

From January 20, 20:52 through February 19, 11:09

♒ *The Balanced Romantic*

As an affectionate Aquarius born in 1951, your relationship must have just the right balance of closeness and freedom. You believe in loving with your whole heart and soul, but you also need space to pursue your own interests. A deep and emotionally satisfying connection with your mate is very important to you and you feel that once there's that genuine bond, you're mated for life.

Having fun with your mate is what life is all about for you. Caring passionately about the same things keeps your relationship close and happy. Being in one of those detached marriages where there's no common ground would not appeal to you at all. You believe in giving unselfishly as part of a good relationship and that each person should look out for the needs and fulfill the desires of the other. That way you each feel safe and happy, and the relationship flourishes.

A partner with depth and passion appeals most profoundly to you. You like to sense chemistry and compatibility and you realize that those things can't be quantified. A good opening gambit where you're concerned is to challenge you to a friendly competition or to discuss current events or the arts scene. Talking together and feeling that pull makes you want to learn more and in an ongoing relationship it keeps the magic alive.

Male 1951 Aquarians prefer a woman who is confident and outgoing. Your lady has spunk and charisma and there's something adorable about her. She is sexy in her own wholesome way and from the moment you met, you wanted to spend more time with her. Sometimes she's possessive, but you know that's just because she cares. Often she focuses more on your needs than her own and you just love that.

Female Aquarians born in 1951 feel a man should be sensitive and intuitive but not wishy-washy. Your guy is driven by his emotions but he also has courage and integrity. He understands that balance and cooperation are needed in a partnership, and he gives you the space you need and the respect you demand. He's funny, playful, and athletic and if you're down he knows just the right way to elevate your mood.

AQUARIUS ZODIAC SIGN
YOUR LOVE PLANETS

YOUR ROMANTIC SIDE   p. 696
► **VENUS IN AQUARIUS**
Born Jan. 20, 20:52 - Jan. 31, 20:13
► **VENUS IN PISCES**
Born Jan. 31, 20:14 - Feb. 19, 11:09

YOUR SEX DRIVE   p. 722
► **MARS IN AQUARIUS**
Born Jan. 20, 20:52 - Jan. 22, 13:04
► **MARS IN PISCES**
Born Jan. 22, 13:05 - Feb. 19, 11:09

YOUR CELEBRITY TWINS   p. 760
Find out the astrological similarities you have with famous people.

YOUR COMPATIBILITY   p. 780
Compare planets to find out how compatible you are in a relationship.

YOUR RELATIONSHIP KARMA   p. 824
► **SATURN IN LIBRA**
Born Jan. 20, 20:52 - Feb. 19, 11:09

DINAH SHORE
American Singer
Sun in Pisces

1951 PISCES
From February 19, 11:10 through March 21, 10:25

The Firecracker

You're a vivacious Pisces born in 1951 and your relationship must be exciting. You're much less focused on stability than many of your friends and you may have waited quite a while to make a permanent commitment. Marrying just for the sake of security has never appealed to you. Being able to have a good time is essential in your good relationship. Common interests you share and down time where you are each free to pursue your hobbies are equally important to you.

You do believe in true love and want to feel that enduring magic and the sense that you have connected with your one and only perfect soul mate. You have always tended to leap into relationships rather quickly and may have found yourself kissing a few frogs before finding the real thing. But ultimately you have faith that you can create the loving relationship that really matters to you, one in which you each accept and respect each other and share lots of laughs.

A sense of mystique has always been what attracted you to a partner and it's something you appreciate in an ongoing relationship as well. High energy appeals to you, so even if someone picks a quarrel, you can find a way to turn it into a love story, just like one of those movie plots where the protagonists first hate each other then fall in love. You like sharing outdoor activities, arts events and even a cruise to an exotic place.

Male Pisces born in 1951 like a woman who is a bit of a firecracker. Your lady is exciting and outgoing and she can probably change the oil in your car. There's no question that she's a no-nonsense woman and you don't mind at all if she doesn't even own a lipstick. She has her moments, though and she can be amazingly romantic and sensitive.

Female 1951 Fishies realize that a man can't be fenced in. Your guy has his own agenda and you find that fascinating about him. He does what he likes most of the time and you have fun making jokes about it. This fellow is funny, exciting and you always have a good time when you're together. He just knows how to make you laugh, and he loves surprising you in and out of bed.

1951 ARIES
From March 21, 10:26 through April 20, 21:47

The Passionate Sensualist

Mellow Aries born in 1951, your relationship must feel close and comfortable. A strong connection below the surface is important to you, so there's an unspoken bond in your relationship that gives you both understanding and resonance. It's not so much that you're obsessed with true love and finding the mate you were destined to love. In fact, you find that a little silly. You just want to be with someone who makes you feel cozy and warm on a long-term basis.

An intense attraction is important to you because you realize that no matter what goes wrong in life, that passion for each other will help you both heal your problems and remain together. Being able to accept and forgive each other is also important to you because you feel that mistakes in life are inevitable—and a good relationship endures despite them. Being appreciated for who you are and loving your mate for the same reason is always your goal.

A partner who plays hard to get appeals to you because you love the challenge of the hunt. In an ongoing relationship you enjoy social events and fine dining, arts events like concerts, and you adore sharing a candlelit meal where there's music and dancing. Not only is that romantic but it's sensual. The partner who will tease you a little, and give you a back rub and just the right degree of drama and chaos can claim your heart forever.

1951 male Rams like a woman who is earthy and sensual. Your lady loves to touch and even the way she dresses in soft silks, shimmering velvets and elegant jewelry make her seem feminine and caressable. This woman is passionate and her heart is deep. She makes no apology for her needs and expects you to fulfill them, but making love to her is always an experience you savor.

Female Aries born in 1951 prefer a man who is masculine yet also sensitive, sensual and sweet. Your guy has a mind of his own, but that doesn't mean he's unwilling to consider your feelings. He wants to be close to you and to share a life, so he understands the importance of compromise. He's intuitive about your needs and is an excellent lover because of that.

272

1951 TAURUS *From April 20, 21:48 through May 21, 21:14*

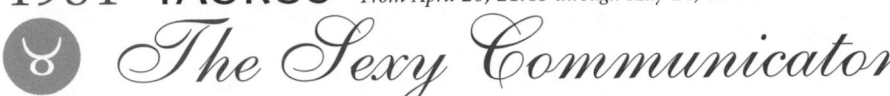

The Sexy Communicator

You're a determined Taurus born in 1951 and your relationship has to be both frothy and stable. You like to feel you are in control and have a handle on life, so you believe in commitment and stability. You don't like the idea of a safe relationship however and you'd never commit just to know you have a sure thing.

Romance is very important to you and you like to feel there's passion and sparkle in your relationship. Having fun, laughing, and talking to each other is what keeps your relationship happy and strong. Communication is essential in your relationship, not just because you feel it's important to share feelings, but because you love to talk and fall in love not just with your eyes and heart but with your ears as well. Having things in common to share and discuss keeps you happily together.

A partner who has something interesting to say has always appealed to you. You love it when you meet someone new—whether romantically or just as a friend, and you instantly click and find yourselves chatting away for hours about many mutually interesting

topics. The ability to continue doing that keeps your love alive. You enjoy attending arts events together, the theater, museums, and concerts. You also love feeling that zing of chemistry that tempts you to share impromptu trysts.

Male Bulls born in 1951 prefer a woman who is informed, intelligent, and interesting. Your lady is clever, she has all sorts of fun and worthwhile tidbits to share, and she's mysterious enough to keep you guessing. She is delicate and playful, frothy as whipped cream and she maintains her youthful outlook on life. If you're bossy or demanding, she forgives you and laughs about your quirks and when you're cranky, she cheers you up.

1951 Female Taureans like a man who's stable and a little stubborn. Your guy knows what he wants and although he's rarely flexible in his actions, he makes you feel safe and protected. His machismo appeals to you and even if you get embroiled in a few power struggles, that only serves to heighten the delicious sexual tension that attracted you to him in the first place.

TAURUS ZODIAC SIGN
YOUR LOVE PLANETS

YOUR ROMANTIC SIDE   p. 696
▶ **VENUS IN GEMINI**
Born Apr. 20, 21:48 - May 11, 1:40
▶ **VENUS IN CANCER**
Born May 11, 1:41 - May 21, 21:14

YOUR SEX DRIVE   p. 722
▶ **MARS IN TAURUS**
Born Apr. 20, 21:48 - May 21, 15:31
▶ **MARS IN GEMINI**
Born May 21, 15:32 - May 21, 21:14

YOUR CELEBRITY TWINS   p. 760
Find out the astrological similarities you have with famous people.

YOUR COMPATIBILITY   p. 780
Compare planets to find out how compatible you are in a relationship.

YOUR RELATIONSHIP KARMA   p. 824
▶ **SATURN IN VIRGO**
Born Apr. 20, 21:48 - May 21, 21:14

LESLIE CARON
French Actress
Venus in Gemini

1951 GEMINI *From May 21, 21:15 through June 22, 5:24*

The Loving Playmate

Playful Gemini born in 1951, you need a relationship that keeps you energized and active. "The couple that plays together stays together" is your motto, and you approve of a relationship based on fun and good times. And why not see it like that? As long as you continue to have fun together, you feel the relationship will last forever. The last thing you would want is a stable but dull attachment that provides security but little pizzazz.

Raising a happy family appeals to you, and right from the start you could envision a thriving clan laughing and playing together like a cheerful sitcom family. Good communication is an essential in your happy relationship, and by talking and sharing interesting ideas you also share warm feelings. Common interests are also important to you because then you and your mate have things to do together that appeal to both of you. To you, a relationship is more than a partnership—it's a love affair between best friends.

A playful partner who is upbeat and fun is always your first choice. Sharing picnics,

outdoor concerts, and theater in the park are just some of the things you enjoy doing together. You love to talk about current events or the arts, so a partner who is well-informed and articulate holds your interest. You like being involved in neighborhood events and could even feel romantic for a mate while leading a scout troop.

Male 1951 Geminis like a woman who is sweet and generous. Your lady is kind and considerate, and she loves doing nice things for other people, you included. She is a natural nurturer and children and pets adore her, old ladies find her charming, and even the crabbiest person brightens when she enters the room. You do, too, and it's an inner glow that warms your heart.

Female Geminis born in 1951 like a man who can put his money where his mouth is. He says what he means and does what he says. Your guy is straightforward and honest—although not always predictable. He changes his mind just often enough to maintain your interest. He's intelligent and creative, athletic and outgoing, and is often quite musical.

GEMINI ZODIAC SIGN
YOUR LOVE PLANETS

YOUR ROMANTIC SIDE   p. 696
▶ **VENUS IN CANCER**
Born May 21, 21:15 - June 07, 5:09
▶ **VENUS IN LEO**
Born June 07, 5:10 - June 22, 5:24

YOUR SEX DRIVE   p. 722
▶ **MARS IN GEMINI**
Born May 21, 21:15 - June 22, 5:24

YOUR CELEBRITY TWINS   p. 760
Find out the astrological similarities you have with famous people.

YOUR COMPATIBILITY   p. 780
Compare planets to find out how compatible you are in a relationship.

YOUR RELATIONSHIP KARMA   p. 824
▶ **SATURN IN VIRGO**
Born May 21, 21:15 - June 22, 5:24

274

GENE KELLY
American Dancer
Sun in Leo

1951 CANCER
From June 22, 5:25 through July 23, 16:20

The Happy Mate

Creative Cancer born in 1951, to you a relationship has to be comfortable, congenial, and chemical. That's right—chemistry! You believe there has to be a strong connection under the surface that draws you together and keeps you both happy in your relationship. Getting along harmoniously is important to you and that's another aspect of chemistry—if you're well suited, you feel things just fall into place. You would hate to strain and stress within a relationship. You feel either it works well or not at all.

Romance is another important dimension. You like tenderness, hearts and flowers, and the sense that you'd each go to the ends of the earth to please the other. Good communication is important to you too and you enjoy talking about everything because to you conversations are another source of fun. You choose to be in a relationship where you just click and that means even a casual ride in the car leads to good conversation and lots of merriment.

A partner who has a natural sparkle appeals most to you, and you find that as long as you can share lively verbal interactions, you're happy to pursue or continue the involvement. You appreciate the fact that a partner wants to be with you and making his or her interest known makes you feel cherished. Buying you a special gift, staring deeply into your eyes, and complimenting you on your style and flair are good ways into your heart.

Male Crabs born in 1951 need a woman who is luminous and exciting. Your lady has natural flair and she is charming and attractive. You're always pleased to introduce her to people you know because she is so appealing that everyone adores her. This woman is kind and generous, positive and cheerful, and she brightens your world.

1951 female Cancers like a man who balances restraint with unpredictability. Your guy is independent, but he also has a sense of responsibility. He has his own code of ethics, yet on some levels he seems a bit of a rebel, somewhat of a wild card, and that appeals to you because he keeps life from getting dull. He's a youthful, playful, energetic, and fun partner.

1951 LEO
From July 23, 16:21 through August 23, 23:15

The Congenial Collaborator

As a considerate Leo born in 1951, your relationship must be happy and congenial. Being sensitive to each other's feelings and needs is an essential aspect of your good relationship. You can't imagine how people survive in partnerships filled with animosity and screaming. Love to you is about nurturing, tender embraces, and the feeling that you would do anything to make your partner's life happy, successful, and warm.

The feeling that you're building something of value together bind, you closer within your relationship. You believe in hard work and mutual support, and together you are stronger as a team than either of you might be apart. You enjoy good conversation and often you discuss practical matters and brainstorm together to solve life's little problems. Your conversation is also laced with sweet endearments and little jokes that make your relationship rich and joyous.

A partner who is kind and thoughtful has always been your preference and you appreciate good taste, proper manners, and family values. Working on projects together appeals to you and a date to a home improvement store or a romance that blossoms while on a business trip together feels perfectly natural. Being a good team is what it's all about. You enjoy being treated to a healthy home-cooked meal and some good conversation.

Male Leos born in 1951 prefer a woman who is demure and tasteful. Her look is graceful and classical and she never worries about being in style. She sticks to her own choices and always looks elegant and well-turned out. This lady is helpful and kind, but she doesn't baby people. Her conversation sparkles and her personality is somewhat quirky, but that's because she's a true individual.

1951 Lady Lions feel a man should be sensitive, emotional and intuitive but never cowardly or wishy-washy. Your guy is multi-dimensional and a little complicated. He acts on instinct and is courageous and sometimes even impatient, but his feelings are easily hurt and he is articulate about expressing them. He has a spiritual side and an uncanny way of understanding what you're all about.

1951 VIRGO

From August 23, 23:16 through September 23, 20:36

♍ *The Literate Lover*

You're a romantic 1951 Virgo and your relationship must be passionate and pretty intense. You love all the drama of romance and the subtle things too, and your relationship has to be just as much fun as a romance novel. A relationship that maintains the same intensity and feeling of courtship it had at the start is just perfect, in your opinion. You feel that people get bored in marriages because they stop putting effort into wooing their mates. That's something you'd never do.

An intense connection suits you best. You want to feel those pangs of desire and to take turns sweeping each other off your feet. Good conversation is another plus, and you love stolen moments during the day when you can laugh and woo each other over the phone. Voicing your sentiments is a positive way you keep your relationship romantic, and you love to jot special messages in greeting cards sent for no reason at all.

A romantic and passionate partner is always your first choice. You appreciate it when someone goes to a little trouble to treat you to a special evening. You like luxury but creativity and good taste appeal to you more. A mate who will give you a special book, take you to a poetry reading, or find an extra special way to seduce you keeps you coming back for more.

1951 male Virgos like a woman who has her act together. Your lady is clever, skilled, and charming and she always knows what she's doing. She appears serene even at the busiest moment because she's so efficient everything is well in hand. To people who see her casually she is pretty and elegant but also demure. To you, she's subtle, and you see beneath the surface the sexy playmate who will do anything to please you.

Female Virgos born in 1951 prefer a man to have a little flash, a bit of flair, and a lot of pizzazz. Your guy is exciting and macho and you know that no matter what, he will always be there for you. This fellow is stable and reliable and he loves to play with you or the kids in your life. He is generous and kind but also demanding and sexy and he inspires the best fantasies you've ever imagined.

VIRGO ZODIAC SIGN
YOUR LOVE PLANETS

YOUR ROMANTIC SIDE — p. 696
▶ VENUS IN LIBRA
Born Aug. 23, 23:16 - Sept. 23, 20:36

YOUR SEX DRIVE — p. 722
▶ MARS IN LEO
Born Aug. 23, 23:16 - Sept. 23, 20:36

YOUR CELEBRITY TWINS — p. 760
Find out the astrological similarities you have with famous people.

YOUR COMPATIBILITY — p. 780
Compare planets to find out how compatible you are in a relationship.

YOUR RELATIONSHIP KARMA — p. 824
▶ SATURN IN LIBRA
Born Aug. 23, 23:16 - Sept. 23, 20:36

MONTGOMERY CLIFT
American Actor
Sun in Libra

275

1951 LIBRA

From September 23, 20:37 through October 24, 5:35

♎ *The Passionate Paramour*

As a sexy 1951 Libra, your relationship has to be intensely physical. To say that chemistry is important to you in a relationship is an understatement. You feel a sexual buzz below the surface in every encounter and you build a relationship because of that heated, magnetic pull that draws you together from the moment you meet. You can't imagine a relationship without chemistry, and a tepid attachment would be simply impossible for you.

Sharing, loving, and giving are other important aspects of your relationship. Being able to give and receive is very important to you and you feel that a good relationship allows two people to express their best selves through service and generosity to each other. Communication is essential as well because flirting is so much fun, and whether the conversation is light or serious, it draws you closer together within the relationship.

You really enjoy a challenge, and a partner who doesn't make it too easy for you is much more fun. You like being assertive and wooing a mate, and you like to work at gaining someone's affection. Sharing good conversation is a great opening gambit because you like to see what's under the surface. The current of energy flowing between you is what it's all about, and whether you're talking at work, chatting online, or socializing at a party, it's all about the chemistry.

Male Libras born in 1951 prefer a woman who is demure and restrained—up to a point. You like seeing a woman who might at first seem prim turn into a sexy tigress, and her sex appeal turns you on even more. Your lady is intelligent and helpful, and she will always offer a helping hand. She can be picky and she tries to restrain you when you go overboard.

Female 1951 Libras want a man to be intensely macho and sexy. Your guy is strong and assertive, and he seems quite capable of dominating everyone around him, although often he chooses to stand back and let others take the lead. He's quite magnetic, and he has this way of pushing you to take risks you've always wanted to try. His conversation is enthralling and when you need help, he's there.

LIBRA ZODIAC SIGN
YOUR LOVE PLANETS

YOUR ROMANTIC SIDE — p. 696
▶ VENUS IN LIBRA
Born Sept. 23, 20:37 - Oct. 24, 5:35

YOUR SEX DRIVE — p. 722
▶ MARS IN LEO
Born Sept. 23, 20:37 - Oct. 05, 0:19
▶ MARS IN LIBRA
Born Oct. 05, 0:20 - Oct. 24, 5:35

YOUR CELEBRITY TWINS — p. 760
Find out the astrological similarities you have with famous people.

YOUR COMPATIBILITY — p. 780
Compare planets to find out how compatible you are in a relationship.

YOUR RELATIONSHIP KARMA — p. 824
▶ SATURN IN LIBRA
Born Sept. 23, 20:37 - Oct. 24, 5:35

VIVIEN LEIGH
English Actress
Sun in Scorpio

276

1951 SCORPIO
From October 24, 5:36 through November 23, 2:50

The Security Seeker

You're a responsible Scorpio and your relationship is always about giving and sharing. You believe love is always about caring tenderly for a partner and making each other's lives easier, better, and more fulfilled. Kindness and generosity are very important to you in a relationship because it means that love is truly present. How you feel is important, but the way you both act is a better barometer of just how successful the relationship is, in your opinion.

Commitment is very important to you in a relationship. You want to know that there is mutual trust and a promise from the heart always to stay and take care of each other's needs. Without that, what do you have? You can't imagine how people go through life dating and playing the field when fidelity is so much more beautiful to experience. Building something worthwhile together is the backbone of your relationship. You want to create a solid home, a safe family, and a happy life.

Good manners and good taste have always been important to you in a partner. You appreciate so much when someone who cares for you shows those feelings in a kind and thoughtful gesture. Helping you out when you're in need, bringing you soup when you're sick, or giving you a healing massage are ways in which a lover might be endeared to you. You like working together on projects and even if it's hard work, it feels romantic because you share the load.

Male 1961 Scorpions prefer a woman who is solid and reliable. Your lady is demure and tasteful, and she always looks elegant and classical, never unrefined. She is skilled and intelligent and always sees a way to solve a problem or make someone in trouble feel better. You know where you stand with this woman and her devotion to you is steadfast and comforting.

Female Scorpios born in 1951 like a man to be down-to-earth and practical. Your guy is orderly and efficient and he always knows what's needed in any situation. He deals with life's little tribulations coolly and you admire the way he's always capable and calm. He is helpful and kind and no matter what you need, he pitches in.

1951 SAGITTARIUS
From November 23, 2:51 through December 22, 15:59

The Romantic Individualist

As an independent Sagittarius born in 1951, your relationship must give you the flexibility to express yourself. You care very much about freedom and change, so your good relationship can never smother you or fence you in too much. Commitment and stability are indeed important to you but only on your own terms. You like to feel that you and your partner are on the right track—that being together enhances your lives and that you're stronger as a couple than as individuals. Otherwise you'd rather not have commitment at all!

To you, a relationship is a tool for learning and personal growth. Not only do you learn about your mate, but by being together you learn about yourself and this process of self-discovery helps you make better choices in your life. Incisive conversation is important to you and you enjoy a relationship in which you're able to communicate about the deep issues on your mind. Love, devotion, and responsibility are also important, but because you care, not out of mere obligation.

You enjoy spending time with a mate who is secure enough to give you your own space and encourage your personal interests. Someone who gives you tickets to baseball camp or jewelry making class so that you can attend on your own is a partner who understands you and is endeared to you. You also like visiting art and architecture exhibits, traveling, and sharing casual social events.

Male Archers born in 1951 prefer a woman with an interesting level of complexity. You don't want to be able to unravel all her mysteries in one evening! Your lady loves freedom but she never flaunts convention. She's smart enough to follow her own course without stepping on any toes. She is stable in her affections but is never clingy or whiny.

Female Sagittarians born in 1951 expect a man to be complicated and multifaceted. Your guy is courtly and well mannered most of the time, but sometimes he just has to rebel and you are amused to observe him as he sets a few people on their ears. He prizes responsibility but refuses to be an automaton and he makes his choices with intelligence and wit.

'50s

Marlon Brando – Unpredictable Lover

Marlon Brando's love life was as outrageous and unpredictable off-screen as his anti-social roles were onscreen. In the 1940s he took lovers in droves when he was studying acting in New York, and this pattern continued during his early Hollywood career. His first marriage in 1957 to actress Anna Kashfi lasted a stormy two years, and his second marriage in 1960 was interrupted by several affairs. In 1962 he fell in love with the Tahitian actress Tarita Teriipia while they were filming *Mutiny on the Bounty*. Another lover from this era, screenwriter Pat Quinn, described her intoxication with Brando, "My God, he was beautiful. Even when we started our relationship—he was 41 and I was 28—he was still quite a specimen. He had that Greek-god countenance."

Although Brando made successful films through the end of the 20th century, many critics feel that his best years were between 1951 and 1954. This breakthrough phase began with his brutishly realistic portrayal of Stanley Kowalski in *A Streetcar Named Desire* and continued with explosive performances in *Viva Zapata*, *The Wild One*, and *On the Waterfront,* for which he won his first Oscar. In each of these pictures his smoldering sexuality and mumbling rebelliousness redefined the concept of a male movie star, as he made T-shirted angst cool before James Dean was a tragic teenager.

Marlon Brando was born during the New Moon in Aries, giving him the fighting spirit of this first sign. His Sun and Moon are further energized by a

Marlon Brando and Mary Murphy in *The Wild One*

> *"The story of my life is a search for love."*
>
> **MARLON BRANDO**

square to Mars, a combination that recognizes no limitations from traditional authority figures. With Aries and Mars so strongly placed in his horoscope he naturally played the tough guy, like the leather-clad biker in *The Wild One* who defiantly challenged moral standards. "What are you rebelling against?" asks a barmaid in this 1954 flick. Brando

responds, "What've you got?"

Uranus, the planet representing rebellion and personal independence, is located near the fourth house of the home and family, where his Sun and Moon lie. These planets inevitably create a tempestuous domestic scene. Brando's early home life was the very definition of dysfunctional. In his autobiography Brando writes about his father, "His blood consisted of compounds of alcohol, testosterone, adrenalin, and anger. He enjoyed telling me I couldn't do anything right." Brando concluded that his difficult childhood left him wanting "several women in my life at once, as an emotional insurance policy."

In addition to the two marriages, Brando created another set of children with Tarita, as well as with his former housekeeper Christina Ruiz. Violence has been a repeated theme in his own home life, which became headline news in 1990 when his eldest son shot and killed his half-sister's lover in Brando's mansion. Then, in 1995 his daughter Cheyenne, who had a history of drug abuse and mental problems, hanged herself.

Something happened to Brando after he achieved celebrity status. He went into seclusion for many years, became obese, and often criticized the acting profession. Many fans wonder what he could have been, building on the angry young man theme of the 1951-1954 period. Perhaps he spoke for all our failed hopes when, as Terry Malloy in *On the Waterfront*, he said, "You don't understand. I could have had class. I could have been a contender."

277

▶ READ ABOUT JAMES DEAN ON PAGE 309

1952

- ⍟ **BRIGITTE BARDOT**
- ⍟ **CHRISTINE JORGENSEN**
- ⍟ **THE QUIET MAN**
- ⍟ **SINGIN' IN THE RAIN**
- ⍟ **YOU BELONG TO ME**
- ⍟ **EAST OF EDEN**

EVENTS

In Britain, Alan Turing, the wartime codebreaker and computer pioneer, fell from grace after being charged with "gross indecency with males." His sentence involved being treated with hormones that caused impotence, and he commited suicide two years later.

The trial of Marie Besnard opened in France. She was accused of having poisoned her husband and eleven other people using arsenic. Ten years later she was acquitted after a long and passionate trial.

At age 18 Brigitte Bardot married director Roger Vadim, the man she met when she was only 15. She wore a handmade dress she designed herself. Designer Edith Piaf married Jacques Pills. Her friend and witness at the wedding, Marlene Dietrich, was dressed in black.

George Jorgensen, age 26 and a former GI, was transformed into Christine during multiple sex change operations in Denmark, an event that scandalized all America.

POP CULTURE

In the 1952 film, *The Quiet Man*—a romantic comedy—an Irish-American boxer falls in love with the red-haired sister of the town bully. *Singin' in the Rain* was a romantic musical with an on-screen couple struggling to change from silent films to "talkies." *Ivanhoe*, adapted from the Walter Scott classic, was a medieval tale of knights and their ladies. *The Importance of Being Earnest*, from the classic Oscar Wilde play, a high comedy of two young couples, disguises, and impersonations, debuted in Europe.

Long before the popular game show was the song "Wheel of Fortune." "You Belong to Me," "Glow-Worm," and "I Went to Your Wedding" were also hits, as was "Half As Much," sung by Rosemary Clooney.

The bestseller lists were headed by classic writers, including John Steinbeck with *East of Eden*, and Daphne du Maurier with *My Cousin Rachel*, the story of a man bewitched by a manipulative woman who may have killed her husband. Edna Ferber made the list too with *Giant*, the tale of a wealthy Texas ranger who marries an educated Virginia woman. Another love story, *The Saracen Blade*, set in the twelfth century tells the story of a serf who falls for the daughter of a baron.

Hot Couple

BRIGITTE BARDOT & ROGER VADIM

Actor/director/journalist Roger Vadim married actress/sex goddess Brigitte Bardot in 1952, four years before his film *And God Created Woman* would catapult her to stardom. He was known to be a womanizer and was later involved with Jane Fonda and Catherine Deneuve, gorgeous screen legends on a par with the sexy, sensual Bardot.

Although they were a sizzling, much-talked about couple, their marriage didn't last very long. Vadim would later say of Bardot: "From the moment I liberated Brigitte, the moment I showed her how to be truly herself, our marriage was all downhill." They were divorced in 1957.

SEE ALSO

▶ **CATHERINE DENEUVE** *Page 505*

▶ **JANE FONDA** *Page 441*

1952 CAPRICORN

From December 22, 1951 16:00 through January 21, 1952 2:37
(December 1952 Capricorns, see 1953 Capricorn)

The Sensitive Soul

Sometimes you may wonder if you fully deserve all of the good things that you're attracting. You may even have passed up more than one good relationship because of this. You tend to hold your feelings inside and, although you're strong, doing so could be your greatest weakness. A very reserved person, you cringe at the thought of being with someone who's flashy or a show-off in public, and you're sure to avoid spendthrifts and those with extravagant tastes. The truth is that within the sanctuary of the right relationship, you can open up dramatically!

Your best union upholds your personal values, supporting a strong work ethic and inborn caution to such a degree that everything becomes easier and sunnier. In the right setting you can be wonderfully warm and generous—qualities you long to express—and your firecracker dry wit can enliven a roomful of people. But first you must be totally relaxed.

Teamed with your ideal loving partner, you actually feel freer to show your true face, and you can see the world with much greater clarity.

The right person encourages you to "take your passion and make it happen." In return, you learn just how precious you are and how much you're cared for. After all, truly honest, down-to-earth, hardworking people like you are rare finds!

If you're a male Capricorn born in 1952, you're attracted to an idealistic lady who loves excitement and adventure. She's also good-natured, and insightful enough to break through any inhibitions and help you to unwind. Of course, the very ultimate unwinding occurs in the bedroom, after the ultimate in excitement! This woman knows what she's doing, and with her repertoire, and your energy, your Capricorn heart can truly melt.

For a 1952 female Capricorn, the man who's generous and has a strong sense of right and wrong is the match for you. He insists on an equal relationship when it comes to responsibilities, and can bring you contacts that help you in business. Your success is his success! Best of all, he's a true romantic, adept at unveiling and adoring everything about you, including your imperfections!

CAPRICORN ZODIAC SIGN
YOUR LOVE PLANETS

YOUR ROMANTIC SIDE   p. 696
▶ VENUS IN SCORPIO
Born Dec. 22, 1951 16:00 - Jan. 02, 1952 18:43
▶ VENUS IN SAGITTARIUS
Born Jan. 02, 18:44 - Jan. 21, 2:37

YOUR SEX DRIVE   p. 722
▶ MARS IN LIBRA
Born Dec. 22, 1951 16:00 - Jan. 20, 1952 1:32
▶ MARS IN SCORPIO
Born Jan. 20, 1:33 - Jan. 21, 2:37

YOUR CELEBRITY TWINS   p. 760
Find out the astrological similarities you have with famous people.

YOUR COMPATIBILITY   p. 780
Compare planets to find out how compatible you are in a relationship.

YOUR RELATIONSHIP KARMA   p. 824
▶ SATURN IN LIBRA
Born Dec. 22, 1951 16:00 - Jan. 21, 1952 2:37

279

1952 AQUARIUS

From January 21, 2:38 through February 19, 16:56

The World-Embracer

The whole world is your playground, 1952-born Aquarius! Your sphere of interest is much larger than any single relationship, encompassing just about everyone on the planet. When it comes right down to it, you may not even need a committed relationship. Still, there's something indefinably attractive about having a life partner and, despite your wanderlust, a long-term monogamous relationship can give your life a solid foundation.

The most rewarding relationship for you highlights the sharing of ideas, ideals, and global aspirations. Yours is a busy, eclectic lifestyle that may even accommodate a houseful of interesting, like-minded people at any hour of the day or night. Your lover welcomes them all!

The one who's right for you presents a brains-first image. She or he may not be the most stunningly attractive person on earth, but there's a strong magnetic pull and a sparking of the imagination that can't be denied. The way to hold your interest is to give you a long leash while also keeping your mind engaged. You want someone who is keenly intelligent and

intuitive about your needs, and your ideal partner maintains a fine balance between joint and solo activities. Implicit faithfulness clinches the "deal."

A male 1952 Aquarius thrives with an independent woman of strong mental and moral substance: airheads need not apply! Exterior physical beauty is not the main requirement, nor is stylish clothing or material possessions. Your ideal mate is, like you, an embracer of the world–someone who genuinely cares. Of course, you also need to know that under those baggy jeans is some sexy underwear, selected and worn specifically for you!

For female Aquarians born in 1952, the ideal partner is brainy, scrupulously honest, and has no desire to control you. Making space for all the freedom you require, he deeply respects your worldly engagements. And, when day is done and you're ready to relax, you can count on him for succor, soulful sex, and one terrific sense of humor! The meaning that you seek in the outside world pales in comparison to the heaven of your lover's embrace.

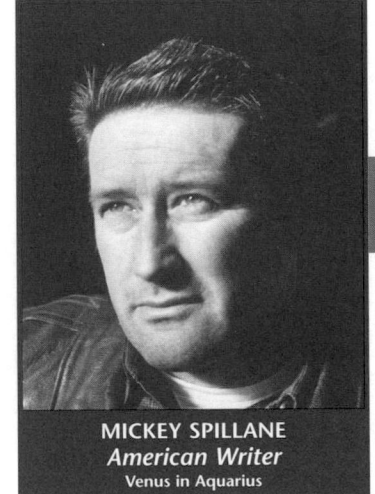

MICKEY SPILLANE
American Writer
Venus in Aquarius

AQUARIUS ZODIAC SIGN
YOUR LOVE PLANETS

YOUR ROMANTIC SIDE   p. 696
▶ VENUS IN SAGITTARIUS
Born Jan. 21, 2:38 - Jan. 27, 15:57
▶ VENUS IN CAPRICORN
Born Jan. 27, 15:58 - Feb. 19, 16:56

YOUR SEX DRIVE   p. 722
▶ MARS IN SCORPIO
Born Jan. 21, 2:38 - Feb. 19, 16:56

YOUR CELEBRITY TWINS   p. 760
Find out the astrological similarities you have with famous people.

YOUR COMPATIBILITY   p. 780
Compare planets to find out how compatible you are in a relationship.

YOUR RELATIONSHIP KARMA   p. 824
▶ SATURN IN LIBRA
Born Jan. 21, 2:38 - Feb. 19, 16:56

CYD CHARISSE
American Dancer
Sun in Pisces

280

1952 PISCES
From February 19, 16:57 through March 20, 16:13

The Love Artist

The last thing you need is a relationship that brings discord into your life, Pisces of 1952—and the first thing you need is one that brings peace. You're so attuned to what's around you that you pick up on the subtlest of feelings—which can be, by turns, helpful and unnerving! However, thanks to your kind and nurturing spirit, you make an ideal partner. A social creature, you're always up for a party or a dinner out, especially with your super-significant other, who also likes to live and eat well.

Although you're highly creative and artistic, these qualities don't always translate to high incomes. You prefer to work behind the scenes, avoiding routines, but your eclectic work habits may lead to an erratic cash flow that sparks worries. Having a life partner at your side, particularly one with a high-paying job, can go far to ease these tensions.

The heaven-sent mate handles your sensitive soul with kid-glove gentleness. There's a melding of intuition, understanding, and spirituality between you that creates a soft buffer against the sometimes-harsh experiences of life. You can share and come to terms with your feelings within the safe cocoon of this relationship. And when life seems especially trying, your partner understands that your pain is real and would never see it as a weakness. Such complete acceptance is both liberating and gently grounding.

As a Piscean male born in 1952, you may have waited until later in life to choose a lifetime partner. The woman you've waited for is a wise truth-lover who has no patience for the angst and drama of inflamed egos. Rather, she is cool and calm. She has lots of friends too, and her time with them gives you some much-needed hours alone. Together, you enjoy both peace AND dynamite lovemaking, born as much of reality as of fantasy!

Lady Pisceans born in 1952, your best male partner is highly ambitious and, as a result, likely to be well-to-do. He's self-reliant and exhibits a powerful, but not pushy, sex drive. No matter how wild or unusual your sexual fantasies, or how serene and transcendent, he's always eager to please!

1952 ARIES
From March 20, 16:14 through April 20, 3:36

The Passionate Adventurer

If anyone is "on" it's YOU, 1952 Aries! Your passion and zest for life attract you to where the action is, whether it's parasailing, mountain climbing, or being the only one in your party brave enough to sample the cow tongue in a Russian restaurant. To make this exciting lifestyle complete, you need someone who not only joins you in your fearless embrace of life but can even outpace you sometimes!

In your ideal relationship, the two of you are usually on the go, savoring new experiences while also "giving back" to those less fortunate. But it's in your alone-time that you shine most brightly. As strong and confident people, you are secure enough to relax into sex that is unrushed and intensely pleasurable for both of you. Such glorious moments may be enhanced by music and beautiful surroundings, which are important to you as well.

The one who captures your mind and heart is not afraid to take chances, to do things that take guts. It could be on the job, where your lover challenges unfair policies—or maybe that courage comes through as physical daring, as in zipping down an icy ski trail. Whatever it is, you'll be entranced by an independent and creative thinker who never ceases to amaze and tantalize. Your special someone also happens to love music and art just as much as you do. Flirting with others is to be avoided, however, as it could seriously jeopardize the relationship.

As a 1952 male Ram, you're probably drawn to a woman whose shy and demure public face is totally dropped, along with any trace of modesty, in the bedroom. Secure in your respect for her individuality and complexity, she gives herself to you entirely—body, mind, and soul. Never before have you experienced anything this complete!

Female 1952 Ariens, your perfect mate can be just as passionate and intense as you are. You catch his sexy vibe easily, especially when those eyes seem to be boring right through you! Is he reading your mind, picking up on your fantasies? He just might be! This loyal guy desires more than just your body, however. He will honor, cherish, and hold you dear for a lifetime.

1952 TAURUS
From April 20, 3:37 through May 21, 3:03

The Settled Epicure

Chances are, you're like most 1952 Taureans and have already settled in to a cozy and comfortable lifestyle. In any case, major change and rocking of the boat are not for you, and you probably take comfort in routines. Which is not to suggest any lack of excitement and growth within the parameters of your Taurean fortress. It's simply that you've come a long way, and have dropped anchor in a good place!

The relationship of your dreams is therefore a settled one, in synch with the security you've already established on your own. But it won't be predictable, for the heights of your passion have yet to be scaled!

Your ideal partner likes to work, invest, and save money with you, ever refining the sanctuary you call home. Neither of you like noise or discord, and the tranquility of your love nest is the perfect setting for deep, mutual exploration. Though your courtship may start out slowly, you'll be partners for life—settled, satisfied, yet never, ever bored! Independent and unclingy, you're also unquestionably loyal,

and both of you will be intensely focused on the other. And, the more you look, the more you'll see and sense. Like the petals of a rose, your sensuality unfolds over time, with exquisite fragrance and irresistibility.

One way to the heart of you male Taureans is through your stomach. Happily, your ideal ladylove enjoys creating sumptuous meals for you, complete with soft music and candlelight. She understands that under your quiet facade beats a romantic and libidinous heart. And, like you, she'll be more than ready for "dessert."

Most of you 1952 female Taureans can be won by a man who is quietly charming in public yet surprisingly sexual behind closed doors. Remember, he may have been set and settled for years now, but there are still plenty of empty spaces for you to fill. So many wonderful things to give to this receptive and hungry man! And who better suited to the job than an earthy Taurean like yourself! You can be sure he's "the one" every time those peaceful, easy feelings that are his trademark give way to an urgency that only you can satisfy.

TAURUS ZODIAC SIGN
YOUR LOVE PLANETS

YOUR ROMANTIC SIDE   p. 696
- ▶ VENUS IN ARIES
  Born Apr. 20, 3:37 - May 04, 8:54
- ▶ VENUS IN TAURUS
  Born May 04, 8:55 - May 21, 3:03

YOUR SEX DRIVE   p. 722
- ▶ MARS IN SCORPIO
  Born Apr. 20, 3:37 - May 21, 3:03

YOUR CELEBRITY TWINS   p. 760
- *Find out the astrological similarities you have with famous people.*

YOUR COMPATIBILITY   p. 780
- *Compare planets to find out how compatible you are in a relationship.*

YOUR RELATIONSHIP KARMA   p. 824
- ▶ SATURN IN LIBRA
  Born Apr. 20, 3:37 - May 21, 3:03

PEGGY LEE
American Singer
Sun in Gemini

281

1952 GEMINI
From May 21, 3:04 through June 21, 11:12

The Ingenious Innovator

You're a whirlwind of activity, 1952 Gemini, as you seamlessly coordinate the complexities of life. Happiest with several projects on the front burner, you blend family, business, and social pursuits with enviable ease. Though constantly "in flight," you are anything but flighty.

Routine and "same-old, same-old" are what you're NOT about, and your ideal relationship supports and renews this ever-fresh energy. Your flexibility and versatility spark many a fun time, be it at home, laughing the night away with your lover, or even at a soup kitchen, ladling out stew—and good cheer—to those in need. It is this expansiveness and generosity of spirit that make you so attractive.

In your most fulfilling relationship, you're seldom tied down—excess responsibility can feel like a millstone around your neck. Accordingly, your mate is independent, your intellectual equal, and great at managing money. With all those assets in a partner, you're free to be doing other things than balancing a checkbook. This can be a godsend! For here is someone who attends to the

sometimes-tedious aspects of life while also keeping the home and heart fires burning! At the same time, you are intrigued by your "organizer's" clever wit and repartee, which will keep you on your toes. You and your mate can create imaginative "games" to play, and bring them into reality if you wish.

If you're a 1952 Gemini male, you're attracted to the lady who can argue her points fiercely, yet leave good feelings all around. You are definitely up to the challenge, too, scoring plenty of points of your own as lively intellectual sparring draws you irresistibly closer. Inevitably, a "meeting of the minds" leads to a meeting of body and soul, where there's nothing left to debate!

The star-blessed match for you, 1952 Gemini woman, is a very stubborn fellow indeed. His opinions are strong, yet he's totally open-minded when it comes to really knowing and understanding YOU, inside and out. He would love to know what makes you tick! You may be rather mysterious, and a natural-born flirt, but you'll never forget where your heart lies.

GEMINI ZODIAC SIGN
YOUR LOVE PLANETS

YOUR ROMANTIC SIDE   p. 696
- ▶ VENUS IN TAURUS
  Born May 21, 3:04 - May 28, 19:18
- ▶ VENUS IN GEMINI
  Born May 28, 19:19 - June 21, 11:12

YOUR DRIVE AND MAGNETISM   P. 696
- ▶ MARS IN SCORPIO
  Born May 21, 3:04 - June 21, 11:12

YOUR CELEBRITY TWINS   p. 760
- *Find out the astrological similarities you have with famous people.*

YOUR COMPATIBILITY   p. 780
- *Compare planets to find out how compatible you are in a relationship.*

YOUR RELATIONSHIP KARMA   p. 824
- ▶ SATURN IN LIBRA
  Born May 21, 3:04 - June 21, 11:12

SUSAN HAYWARD
American Actress
Sun in Cancer

282

1952 CANCER
From June 21, 11:13 through July 22, 22:06

 ## The Paradise-Builder

Most 1952 "crabs" like yourself seek—and find—safe harbor in the refuge that is home. For here is where you feel most natural, secure, and creative, and you work to ensure that nothing enters in to disturb that peace. But no matter where you hang your hat, you're sure to nurture, calm, and protect all who enter your sphere of activity.

Your most satisfying union is one that enables you to care for others, whether at home or at work. Cancereans of either sex are notoriously excellent homemakers, creating surroundings that are both beautiful and comfortable. Time and expense are no objects when it comes to realizing this dream! And, my 1952 Cancerean friend, as one of the world's most sympathetic and empathic listeners, your home life fairly hums with the harmony of responsive interaction.

Your ideal partner appreciates these nurturing acts, and reciprocates with tender loving care. Whether you're cooking nutritious meals, tiling the bathroom, or planting petunias, your mate takes appreciative notice and may even join in, because you so much enjoy each other's company. Your concern for the safety and well-being of others is also returned in the thoughtfulness of your chosen one, who knows that little things mean a lot!

The very best match for you, 1952 male Crab, understands that your occasional moods are temporary—"time-out" to be respected and not taken personally. Your lady lets you withdraw from time to time, knowing that before long your mood will lift. You also know that she can be counted on to create happy times with family and friends, especially around the holidays, when her knack for entertaining really sparkles!

As a 1952 female Cancerean, the man for you is a trustworthy soul who loves home, family, and, unconditionally, you! He wins your love and complete respect with his sterling character and sweetly passionate ways. Although thoroughly "domesticated," your guy never ceases to surprise and inspire with his worldly wiles. Your lovemaking is as rife with possibilities as a tropical rainforest, constantly renewing you. In his arms is a cure for every ill!

1952 LEO
From July 22, 22:07 through August 23, 5:02

 ## The Loving Leader

The stars cast you as a leader, 1952 Leo, in just about everything you do. And in return for these lion-hearted efforts, you expect a little appreciation… or, better make that a lot of appreciation!

You're poised to receive wonderful treatment from an admiring true soul mate, someone who intuitively knows that admiration of your talents is the key to holding your heart. The "lion's share" of that person's time and attention may be what you're after, in return for which you are devoted and faithful. When that kind of attention is not forthcoming, however, you're fairly content to be alone, making do with the affection of pets, or perhaps getting your kudos at work. But, of course, what you really thrive on is a committed relationship with your one and only love.

You love to laugh, and to make love, and to shower your beloved with thoughtful gifts. Your partner deeply appreciates the joy that you give, and is honored to share a lifetime commitment. "The one" for you works hard at creating a warm and welcoming home, a haven to which your friends and associates are drawn. You love luxury, whether lavish or tastefully understated, and take pride in opening your "castle" to all comers. Most important, you know that your lover will always put you first. Not that you expect constant catering to your needs, or the sacrifice of your lover's own personal ambition. Rather, your partner achieves goals not directly related to you while still putting you ahead of everything else.

For a male Leo born in 1952, the female who keeps and captivates you can enjoy your leadership without feeling dominated. Though she moves in her own orbit, you are the sun of her universe, and her face is ever turned to you. Unselfishly motivated, she strokes your ego (and every inch of your body), while also lifting your spirit!

As a 1952 Lioness, you require that your man possess absolute integrity, sensitivity, and a unique sense of style. That you come first in his life is a given, and he is only too happy to oblige, whether in the bedroom or boardroom. Expecting the world, you get it—and then

1952 VIRGO

From August 23, 5:03 through September 23, 2:23

The Fastidious Romantic

Virgo of 1952, your attention to detail and need for order make you a wizard in the world of work, especially if you work with numbers or in a corporate or medical setting. Fastidiously clean and organized, your home can be visited at a moment's notice, without you needing to run around and hide the unwashed dishes or the brimming laundry basket. However, the well-organized life that gives you such comfort and control can sometimes cause problems in the not-so-tidy world of romance. You might even have been known put work ahead of pleasure, sometimes opting to forego romantic bliss for doing a good deed or finishing an important project.

At the same time, you're a secret romantic at heart, much to the delight of your lover! You can be bold and outspoken in expressing your love, as well as mysteriously subtle and full of poetic nuance. In love, you're an explorer and adventurer, blazing trails that fit none of the neat categories of your workaday world. Sexually, your ideal mate may take the lead initially, but only until it's clear you're both headed for the "promised land" of blissful unity.

A relationship with "the one" also bolsters your self-esteem, for now you are known and loved on many levels, not just for your worldly successes. It helps if your lover can meet you halfway in your need for an organized environment, helping you to relax and not be so hard on yourself. With this person, you see that life is good—smiles and laughter come much more easily.

You male Virgos born in 1952 are happiest with a partner skilled in the social graces, and you are proud to appear with her in public. She shares your appreciation of art and music, can converse knowledgeably about many topics, and is empathetically people-wise. Best of all, she is fine-tuned to you, a virtuoso at "playing" your mind and body!

Female 1952 Virgos appreciate a man who is bold and energized—and neat! He makes you laugh and your heart sing as you travel along uncharted paths to ever-greater intimacy. The man of your dreams not only picks up on your unspoken passions—he also picks up his socks!

VIRGO ZODIAC SIGN
YOUR LOVE PLANETS

YOUR ROMANTIC SIDE   p. 696
▶ VENUS IN LIBRA
Born Aug. 23, 5:03 - Sept. 03, 8:16
▶ VENUS IN LIBRA
Born Sept. 03, 8:17 - Sept. 23, 2:23

YOUR SEX DRIVE   p. 722
▶ MARS IN SCORPIO
Born Aug. 23, 5:03 - Aug. 27, 18:52
▶ MARS IN SAGITTARIUS
Born Aug. 27, 18:53 - Sept. 23, 2:23

YOUR CELEBRITY TWINS   p. 760
Find out the astrological similarities you have with famous people.

YOUR COMPATIBILITY   p. 780
Compare planets to find out how compatible you are in a relationship.

YOUR RELATIONSHIP KARMA   p. 824
▶ SATURN IN LIBRA
Born Aug. 23, 5:03 - Sept. 23, 2:23

DICK BUTTON
American Olympic Ice Skater
Mars in Virgo

283

1952 LIBRA

From September 23, 2:24 through October 23, 11:21

The Generous Peacemaker

You weigh in on the Libran scale as a thoroughly nice and sociable person! With your strong sense of right and wrong, you're willing to lend an ear, and sage counsel, to anyone with a problem. Your home environment reflects this balance in its peaceful organization and neatness, without which you can feel tense, or even ill. Any relationship you're in must be similarly balanced on the scales of openness and honesty.

Good at compromise, you meet your partner more than halfway—most of the time. There may be issues on which you won't budge, but generally you can bend, "working on the relationship" in a flexible and open-minded way. Whether male or female, you enjoy the shopping and organizing involved in romantic atmosphere-building, and are likely to provide your lover with the very best of food and drink. Once you have created just the right ambiance, your passions will overshadow all else.

Your most compatible partner, a hardcore realist like yourself, tends to gather as much information as possible before coming to conclusions. Socially conscious and concerned about the suffering of underdogs, you can make a happy difference, working side by side for humanitarian causes. The right person can also help you to make decisions without obsessing over outcomes—showing you that taking your "best shot" usually works better than worrying.

Your dream woman, male Libran of 1952, has the very same appetite for love and its myriad expressions that you do. Like you, she is passionately committed to the relationship and is an artist at the give-and-take of both daily living and lovemaking. Your pleasure is her pleasure, and vice versa. She just lets it happen! So much so that, afterwards, there is no doubt that you are "made for each other."

Female Librans born in 1952, you appreciate a strong partner to lean on, especially someone who is daring and adventuresome. You love new ideas, new places, new tastes—new everything!—and your man, with great zest and joie de vivre, takes you there! He's also willing to follow your lead in a lifetime of super-sensuous, super-attuned communion.

LIBRA ZODIAC SIGN
YOUR LOVE PLANETS

YOUR ROMANTIC SIDE   p. 696
▶ VENUS IN LIBRA
Born Sept. 23, 2:24 - Sept. 27, 17:35
▶ VENUS IN SCORPIO
Born Sept. 27, 17:36 - Oct. 22, 5:01
▶ VENUS IN SAGITTARIUS
Born Oct. 22, 5:02 - Oct. 23, 11:21

YOUR SEX DRIVE   p. 722
▶ MARS IN SAGITTARIUS
Born Sept. 23, 2:24 - Oct. 12, 4:44
▶ MARS IN CAPRICORN
Born Oct. 12, 4:45 - Oct. 23, 11:21

YOUR CELEBRITY TWINS   p. 760
Find out the astrological similarities you have with famous people.

YOUR COMPATIBILITY   p. 780
Compare planets to find out how compatible you are in a relationship.

YOUR RELATIONSHIP KARMA   p. 824
▶ SATURN IN LIBRA
Born Sept. 23, 2:24 - Oct. 23, 11:21

DYLAN THOMAS
Welsh Writer
Sun and Mars in Scorpio

1952 SCORPIO
From October 23, 11:22 through November 22, 8:35

♏ The Cautious Romantic

You're probably still not a big fan of change, 1952 Scorpio, but it's likely that time has taught you that it can be tonic—especially when it comes to the ever-changing expressions of love. You take relationships seriously, preferring to soldier on even when things aren't really working. Partly out of duty but also from fear of loss, you tend to hang in there, avoiding confrontation.

While it's in your nature to work hard at making things better, you've also come to understand that you can't always be in control. Being "top dog" may have once felt natural to you, but you've since learned the fine art of compromise. Your tendency to keep secrets may also be hard on a relationship. This secrecy comes from caution, though, and the right partner helps you to relax your hold on yourself. Loving warmth brings about a thaw, and your feelings flow more freely.

When it comes to love, no one is more intense than you are, Scorpio of 1952. Though caring little about the opinions of others, you do care—and deeply—about maintaining the high regard of your partner. You strive to be kind, fair, and generous, ever respectful of the dynamic and tantalizing differences between you. Occasionally you may rub each other the wrong way, but friction of the pleasant kind arises when you rub each other the right way, and your playtimes together are never dull!

Male 1952 Scorpions, you are cautious with your feelings, and think long and hard before putting your faith and trust in any one person. But the woman who does inspire a commitment brings great peace. Now that you can let down your guard, all of life seems less problematic. You learn that her love is the one thing in life that you can count on.

Female Scorpions born in 1952 put the permanent sting on the man who is goal-oriented and disciplined. The persistence he shows in wooing you also carries over into practical matters of planning and follow-through, at which he excels. He wants success, usually involving money, and works hard to get it. Powering much of this ambition is a volcanic sexual energy that only you can fully trigger!

1952 SAGITTARIUS
From November 22, 8:36 through December 21, 21:42

♐ The Space-Giver

Once, you might have been willing to drop everything and travel halfway around the world just to experience a sunset, Sagittarius of 1952. Suspicious of committed relationships, you cherished your freedom and independence. You still do, but now you're more settled than you were earlier in life, and more interested in having a home, and someone to come home to who doesn't fence you in.

Greeting you at the door these days is the mate who offers strong intellectual stimulation while giving you plenty of space. Frequent enlivening visits from family and friends help to ground you even further. Ever the optimist, you explore your common interests and concerns with a cheerfulness that makes you fun to be with. Especially gratifying is sharing with your mate intimate thoughts and impressions that no one else is privy to!

The best match for you also matches you in intelligence, keeping you on your toes mentally and challenging many of your assumptions. About important matters, however, such as your need for laughter and relaxation, you are in perfect agreement. You also share a free-spirited love of adventure that dovetails nicely with your equal love of a stable home. You know that after each "flight," a warm and stable nest awaits you!

Loyalty and devotion are very important to you, male Sagittarius of 1952. You're attracted to the woman who takes your relationship seriously, especially when it comes to stabilizing the finances. She's not a materialist, of course—she just has the interest and knack for money matters. Neither is she too serious. Like you, she loves a good joke, and has been known to roll on the floor with laughter. A roll in the hay with her is better yet, as humor melts into deep physical sharing.

Female Sagittarians born in 1952, you are happy with the guy who is a visionary, who sees the world as it is, will be, and should be. Bringing so many possibilities to your door, he inspires you to reexamine your views. Equally visionary in the bedroom, he seems to "just know," or intuit, what you have for years been longing for. He hits the bull's-eye every time!

'50s

Lucille Ball and Desi Arnaz

As their TV theme song, which was sung only once on their show, declared, life was heaven for the fictional Lucy and Ricky Ricardo, who would quarrel and love, making up again and again. Unfortunately, the passionate and turbulent marriage of Lucille Ball and Desi Arnaz failed to have the same happy Hollywood ending as the weekly episodes of their highly successful television series. Arnaz was plagued by alcoholism, a disease that affected both his real and TV family. Keith Thibodeaux who played the TV son Little Ricky said, "I can see why their marriage didn't make it ... as kids we'd definitely stay away from him when he was drunk."

Loved by millions of TV watchers through the generations, the *I Love Lucy* show still stands as one of the greatest shows ever to be broadcast over the airwaves. But, more than that, Lucy and Ricky's wacky escapades and endearing love affair became the model for an idealized happily married life for an impressionable and unsophisticated viewing audience in the early 1950s. Those same viewers would have quite a dose of reality when Lucille and Desi decided to divorce in 1960, just after filming the last episode of their much-loved TV show.

Reality and fiction were strangely intertwined for Lucille Ball and Desi Arnaz. In a remarkable coincidence, their second child was born on the very same night that Lucy Ricardo gave birth to her TV son Little Ricky. Lucy and Desi had met during the filming of *Too Many Girls* in 1940 and, after a whirlwind courtship, married later that year. And since Desi was known for both his drinking and his womanizing, "too many girls" was a primary factor that led to the Arnaz' divorce. For a Leo like Ball, who would always strive

to maintain her dignity, the thought of her husband with other women was certainly difficult to tolerate over the course of their twenty-year marriage. In her 1960 *TV Guide* interview, she admitted that she should have filed for divorce long ago. Even the fictional Lucy had a jealous streak and she constantly worried that Ricky might have a wandering eye.

Arnaz had Mars, the planet of masculinity and desire, standing together with his Pisces Zodiac sign, giving him a dreamy, steamy, and romantic quality that Lucy as well as millions of female fans around the world found irresistible. The quintessential "Latin Lover," Arnaz heated up the small screen with his sexually charged rendition of "Babalu" as well as his volatile temper. He'd often threaten and sometimes did take Lucy over his knee for a spanking and, though she would scream, one can't help but think she sort of enjoyed it. In the politically correct world of the 21st century, this behavior would be totally unacceptable for the first couple of television situation comedy. If their marriage was indeed the model for an entire generation's view of marriage, it is no wonder that so many of those unions ultimately ended in divorce.

Lucille Ball and Desi Arnaz were a unique and talented pair who created a television legacy that will surely stand the test of time. And though their marriage failed because of their all too human shortcomings, for new generations of TV lovers throughout the world, the Ricardos are happy, young, and in love forever.

"Am I happy? No. Not yet. I will be. I've been humiliated. That's not easy for a woman."

LUCILLE BALL
TV Guide interview, July 18, 1960

► READ ABOUT DEBBIE REYNOLDS AND EDDIE FISHER, ANOTHER ENTERTAINMENT COUPLE, ON PAGE 302

1953

- ✪ **MARILYN MONROE**
- ✪ **PRINCESS MARGARET**
- ✪ **CHRISTIAN DIOR**
- ✪ **SEXUAL BEHAVIOR IN THE HUMAN FEMALE**
- ✪ **RAGS TO RICHES**
- ✪ **PERRY COMO**

Hot Couple

EVENTS

1953 was a great year for Marilyn Monroe. Hugh Hefner's *Playboy* magazine debuted with a 50,000 circulation and the famous blonde on the cover. Uncertain if there would be a second issue, the cover contained no date. Marilyn made her TV debut on the Jack Benny show, and starred in the movie *Gentlemen Prefer Blondes.* She was later linked to President Kennedy, but in 1953 Jack was a senator, and marrying Jacqueline Bouvier.

Yvonne Chevallier was acquitted of shooting her husband, the mayor of New Orleans, after he asked for a divorce so he could marry his mistress.

In England the secret relationship between Princess Margaret and Peter Townsend, who was already married, was revealed. The Princess also introduced a new look, wearing high heels and smoking in public. Another new look came from Christian Dior, who invented the "short skirt" (just below the knees), creating a revolution in fashion. In an anti-feminist step, Leland Kirdel was quoted in *Coronet* magazine as saying, "The smart woman will keep herself desirable. It is her duty to be feminine and desirable at all times in the eyes of the opposite sex."

POP CULTURE

Big box-office draws were *Roman Holiday*, the story of an Italian princess who runs away to escape her royal duties and falls for an American reporter, and *Kiss Me Kate,* about a pair of divorced actors playing opposite each other in *The Taming of the Shrew.*

Topping the bestseller lists was Kinsey's *Sexual Behavior in the Human Female*. This blockbuster study of female sexual behavior caused an uproar. It reported that one-half of women were not virgins when they married and one-quarter of married women had had an affair by age forty. *The Natural Superiority of Women* caused controversy by stating that women are sexually, intellectually, biologically, and emotionally better than men.

At the top of the charts was "Vaya Con Dios," by Les Paul and Mary Ford. Tony Bennett crooned "Rags to Riches," and Patti Page charmed with "The Doggie in the Window." Perry Como had two hits—"Don't Let the Stars Get in Your Eyes" and "No Other Love."

MARTIN LUTHER KING *&* CORETTA SCOTT

African-American civil rights leader Martin Luther King, Jr. met his wife Coretta Scott while in Boston studying for his doctoral degree. She was studying voice at the New England Conservatory of Music. King couldn't have known how important his future marriage to Coretta would be to the US civil rights movement he founded.

They were married June 18, 1953 at her home in Montgomery, Alabama, where they decided to settle. They had four children together. After King was assassinated in 1968, Coretta continued his mission. She founded the Martin Luther King, Jr. Center for Nonviolent Social Change in Atlanta, Georgia.

SEE ALSO
▶ **DENZEL WASHINGTON** *Page 629*
▶ **J. F. KENNEDY** *Page 351*

1953 CAPRICORN

From December 21, 1952 21:43 through January 20, 1953 8:20
(December 1953 Capricorns, see 1954 Capricorns)

♑ The Private Sensualist

As a 1953 Capricorn, your relationship takes root in the fertile field of your solid and surprisingly emotional landscape. You seek an enduring, supportive mate—the one who helps you advance your career is kept close. Your traditional, family-oriented nature thrives with the support of a tight-knit clan. You revel in protecting and providing for the ones you love—giving useful gifts to others makes you feel needed. And though you tend to call the shots, you are a benevolent monarch with a tender heart.

If you appear aloof or reserved in public, it is a thin veil for your quirky sensibility and earthy sensuality. Once behind closed doors, you have an insatiable appetite for physical pleasures. Your emotional sensuality makes you a highly responsive and caring lover. For you power and success are still the most potent aphrodisiacs around, but you are also drawn to a mate with a mysterious or even slightly dangerous edge. The right partner is a stable one, who reassures your jealous side, but who can also bring your shadowy fantasies into the light.

You are endeared to those who lighten your load—an ideal mate lures you back from melancholia with subtle humor and patient encouragement. Asking you about your ancestral roots could spark an entire evening of captivating storytelling. A gracious charmer, skilled in the social arena, could be your most powerful ally. The one who expertly eases you into a relaxed state after a hard day of work wins your gratitude.

The 1953 male Goat grows more handsome with time with an equally enduring sex drive. A smoldering siren with a classic style and frisky sensual nature could win your heart. The right woman can lure you out of your emotional shell, and arouse your animal physicality. Only a true and loyal lover need apply.

For you 1953 female Capricorns, a man of substance and enduring virility makes the grade. You need a confident man who won't mind if you take charge on occasion. Your time is valuable, and a man who arrives late might miss his chance. The right man knows that the jewelry should be as genuine as his intentions.

CAPRICORN ZODIAC SIGN
YOUR LOVE PLANETS

YOUR ROMANTIC SIDE   p. 696
▶ VENUS IN AQUARIUS
Born Dec. 21, 1952 21:43 - Jan. 05, 1953 11:09
▶ VENUS IN PISCES
Born Jan. 05, 11:10 - Jan. 20, 8:20

YOUR SEX DRIVE   p. 722
▶ MARS IN PISCES
Born Dec. 21, 1952 21:43 - Jan. 20, 1953 8:20

YOUR CELEBRITY TWINS   p. 760
Find out the astrological similarities you have with famous people.

YOUR COMPATIBILITY   p. 780
Compare planets to find out how compatible you are in a relationship.

YOUR RELATIONSHIP KARMA   p. 824
▶ SATURN IN LIBRA
Born Dec. 21, 1952 21:43 - Jan. 20, 1953 8:20

DONNA REED
American Actress
Sun in Aquarius

1953 AQUARIUS

From January 20, 8:21 through February 18, 22:40

♒ The Unpredictable Friend

You 1953 Aquarians desire a deep, emotional bond with your partner, along with plenty of room for the spontaneous and unexpected to happen. Your friendliness attracts many, but your detached compassion seems to extend to all of humanity. Funny, gregarious, and a bit flirty, you enjoy many stimulating exchanges during the day. A broad, detached thinker, you might find it challenging to share your private feelings with others. When you find true love, your mysterious coolness melts into radiant warmth.

Your independence is fiercely protected—even in committed bonds, you breathe easier knowing that the exits are clearly marked. A witty conversationalist ranks high on your list, and your own repertoire of subjects is extensive. You love to shock, and may break with tradition by marrying outside your race or cultural background. After the foreplay of witty banter, you thrive in a sexual relationship with plenty of experimentation. Being friends first allows you to know your beloved as an individual. You might dream of merging souls with another person, but the reality likely falls short of your independent ideals.

Since sexual arousal begins in your mind, the right mate will captivate you with intellectual discussions. You admire the partner who has a cultivated knowledge and passionate interest in one subject. You revel in unique experiences—trying the fare of a new restaurant or seeing an art house movie might be appealing.

As a 1953 male Aquarius, you gravitate toward a free-spirited woman with passionate interests in life. The right woman will dazzle you with her sparkling wit and innovative sexuality. A kind, compassionate woman brings out your emotional sensuality. You are a progressive partner—your devotion to an undemanding mate grows.

You 1953 female Aquarians seem coolly detached, but your intimate partner knows that you're a big softie at heart. You desire a brilliant man who can give you space and knows when to offer praise to bolster your confidence. A spontaneous but gentle touch arouses your libido—the right man lures you with a skilled, steady hand.

AQUARIUS ZODIAC SIGN
YOUR LOVE PLANETS

YOUR ROMANTIC SIDE   p. 696
▶ VENUS IN PISCES
Born Jan. 20, 8:21 - Feb. 02, 5:53
▶ VENUS IN ARIES
Born Feb. 02, 5:54 - Feb. 18, 22:40

YOUR SEX DRIVE   p. 722
▶ MARS IN PISCES
Born Jan. 20, 8:21 - Feb. 08, 1:06
▶ MARS IN ARIES
Born Feb. 08, 1:07 - Feb. 18, 22:40

YOUR CELEBRITY TWINS   p. 760
Find out the astrological similarities you have with famous people.

YOUR COMPATIBILITY   p. 780
Compare planets to find out how compatible you are in a relationship.

YOUR RELATIONSHIP KARMA   p. 824
▶ SATURN IN LIBRA
Born Jan. 20, 8:21 - Feb. 18, 22:40

JEAN SIMMONS
English Actress
Venus in Pisces

288

1953 PISCES
From February 18, 22:41 through March 20, 22:00

The Spicy Sweetheart

As a 1953 Pisces, you want a relationship that generates an atmosphere of magic and wonder in your life. You thrive in a bond that offers loving intensity and supports your delightfully quirky imagination. Sentimental and caring, you idealize romance and long for many transcendent moments of ecstasy shared with your beloved. But though you have a dreamy side, your erotic passions are of a highly physical, earthy nature. With the right partner heaven and earth meet in the deep merging of your sexual selves.

Your heightened sensitivity becomes a gift, when you show discernment in your choice of a mate. Callous, superficial people can cause ripples in your otherwise serene waters. If you've made bad choices in the past, you've learned to shield yourself from the harsher vibrations of the world. Your faith in love is resilient—a thoughtful gift or remark can cause you to get teary-eyed. The one who wins your heart discovers that your imaginative creativity extends into the bedroom. Your changeable sensuality makes room for endlessly fascinating explorations into play and fantasy.

To win your heart the right partner must appeal to both your strength and your sensitivity. You shine in romantic scenarios such as taking a carriage ride in the park or spending the night in a moonlit castle. Subtle, graceful seductions slowly open your tender heart. Once smitten, you revel in innovation and will not shy from making sly provocations when the mood is just right.

As a male Pisces born in 1953, you are drawn to women with earthly passions and otherworldly charm. Your charisma draws a bold and creative woman—someone with an artistic bent keeps you fascinated. Variety satisfies your erotic curiosity, and a woman with theatrical flair in the bedroom makes your day.

If you are a female 1953 Pisces, you likely draw a strong, manly man, who wants to protect your timeless innocence. The ideal man brings you meaningful gifts and whispers sweet nothings in your ear. Vulnerability in a man is the ultimate turn-on for you. The ideal man can also help you make your dreams a reality.

1953 ARIES
From March 20, 22:01 through April 20, 9:24

The Insightful Truth-teller

If you are an Aries born in 1953, you are likely a straight shooter in all you do. Your ideal relationship is full of direct, open talks between you and your beloved. Your forceful nature calls for an equally agile sparring partner with whom to share high-spirited debates. You are deeply sympathetic to the troubles of others, but prefer a confident mate to a clinging vine. Your great stores of sunny energy attract partners able to bask in your glow as well as shine on their own.

You delight in a spontaneous partner open to new adventures—perhaps taking an exotic trip or discovering a new hobby together. You keep your intimate bonds evolving by initiating bold changes or gently addressing any barriers to intimacy. Your physical vitality and earthy sensuality enhances the closeness you feel in your relationship. And while your unique feisty temperament leads to the occasional disagreement, you have a knack for smoothing things over with charm and tact.

To inspire you is to win your heart. You enjoy a partner who ignites your lust for life and admires your razor sharp mind. Honesty is your policy, and you expect your mate to be truthful as well. The partner who makes you feel unique and doesn't mind playing follow the leader is kept close. You also warm up to the one who shelters you when you need quietude. In general, the companion who keeps your youthful spirit alive with the promise of new adventures wins your heart.

As a male Ram born in 1953, you are attracted to a sensual woman who can appreciate your timeless virility. A woman who strokes your ego with sincere compliments can quickly embolden you in uncertain situations. A steady partner with her own ambitions can share her strength with you. The wise woman knows that your bark is worse than your bite.

The female Ram of 1953 is a dynamic force of nature requiring a partner with great joie de vivre. You enjoy a mate who challenges your mind and tells you the latest jokes. An optimistic, extroverted man is the life of your party. Your libido is healthy and you revel in keeping passions at a boiling point.

1953 TAURUS *From April 20, 9:25 through May 21, 8:52*

The Affectionate Builder

The Taurean of 1953 is a relationship architect, able to build strong bonds of love that last. An impulsive side to your romantic nature is filtered through a practical outlook. You might be flirty and sensual by nature, but you ponder the big decisions of love carefully and over time. You are an idealist in love and tend to put your beloved on a pedestal. And yet, your down-to-earth persona is reassuring to potential partners. You can see people clearly and accept them for who they are.

Once bonded to a romantic partner, you are a loyal and responsive lover. Surprises thrill you and an unexpected romantic gesture meets a great reward. An abundant feast shared with the one you love feeds your soul. You may extend your love of earthly delights into the bedroom with aphrodisiacs, oils, candles, and other tools of seduction. With such resourcefulness you are likely to find all the excitement and variety you crave in any union.

You relax and shine in the presence of easygoing, considerate companions. Someone who asks to see your most highly prized possessions is met with great enthusiasm. You are both sentimental and experimental. You are just as likely to seize on an invitation to try a new culinary delight, as to return to a old favorite restaurant. Those with outdoorsy interests such as gardening or hiking could strike a chord with you. But your ideal mate knows to cut you a wide berth, allowing you to take your time in all matters.

If you are a male Taurus born in 1953, others may sense a wild and lusty past from the twinkle in your eye. The right woman knows how to arouse the primal sensuality lurking below your sensible façade. Your humor is understated, but physical gags delight you—a well-timed pratfall could have you rolling.

As a female Bull of 1953, you trust your instincts in matters of the heart. Your easy way with the man in your life wins his deep affection. But your partner must prove his mettle over time before it registers in your old-fashioned heart. A man who cherishes hearth and home and never takes you for granted is a winner in your book.

TAURUS ZODIAC SIGN
YOUR LOVE PLANETS

YOUR ROMANTIC SIDE   p. 696
▶ VENUS IN ARIES
Born Apr. 20, 9:25 - May 21, 8:52

YOUR SEX DRIVE   p. 722
▶ MARS IN TAURUS
Born Apr. 20, 9:25 - May 01, 6:07
▶ MARS IN GEMINI
Born May 01, 6:08 - May 21, 8:52

YOUR CELEBRITY TWINS   p. 760
Find out the astrological similarities you have with famous people.

YOUR COMPATIBILITY   p. 780
Compare planets to find out how compatible you are in a relationship.

YOUR RELATIONSHIP KARMA   p. 824
▶ SATURN IN LIBRA
Born Apr. 20, 9:25 - May 21, 8:52

JANE RUSSELL
American Actress
Sun in Gemini

289

1953 GEMINI  *From May 21, 8:53 through June 21, 16:59*

The Gracious Comedian

As a 1953 Gemini, your endless curiosity about your world enhances all your relationships. Your light, breezy style charms most people, and your social nature keeps your contact list growing. A party with close friends can be a showcase for your nimble wit and refined conversation. Your humor veers toward the delightfully devilish and you seek a mischievous partner who can delight you as well—a daily dose of tomfoolery can keep you amused. Your ideal mate has surprises in store for just the right moment.

Youthful in mind, body, and spirit, you thrive with a partner whose suitcase is always packed. A nomadic traveler at heart, you seek a partner to roam the planet with. You'll never be a caged bird—even in domestic situations, you have a gift for creating change and variety. Your mind is an ever-turning kaleidoscope of elusive thoughts and feelings—the ideal partner is the one who accepts you rather than tries to figure you out.

Engaging your mind is a good way to win your heart. You respond to postcards and letters with great flair and tenderness.

Someone who sends you newspaper clippings or inspiring anecdotes may begin a lifelong correspondence. The mate who knows how to soothe your frayed nerves is high on your list. A foot rub or gentle massage from your partner could melt tensions and bring out your playfully erotic nature.

You 1953 male Twins are masters at the art of seduction and seek a woman who can bewitch both your intellect and your libido. A sophisticated woman well-versed in many subjects makes a great dinner companion. Your ideal mate charms your brilliant mind through lively discussions and humorous stories. A vivacious partner can draw you out with laughter—all the way to the bedroom.

As a 1953 female Gemini, your witty banter brings out the playful side in most people. Conservative or rigid types can weigh you down—you thrive with progressive, flexible thinkers. A worldly man who can whisk you off to exotic destinations has the edge. Your changeable nature calls for a man who can hold on loosely, while promising never to let go.

GEMINI ZODIAC SIGN
YOUR LOVE PLANETS

YOUR ROMANTIC SIDE   p. 696
▶ VENUS IN ARIES
Born May 21, 8:53 - June 05, 10:33
▶ VENUS IN TAURUS
Born June 05, 10:34 - June 21, 16:59

YOUR SEX DRIVE   p. 722
▶ MARS IN GEMINI
Born May 21, 8:53 - June 14, 3:48
▶ MARS IN CANCER
Born June 14, 3:49 - June 21, 16:59

YOUR CELEBRITY TWINS   p. 760
Find out the astrological similarities you have with famous people.

YOUR COMPATIBILITY   p. 780
Compare planets to find out how compatible you are in a relationship.

YOUR RELATIONSHIP KARMA   p. 824
▶ SATURN IN LIBRA
Born May 21, 8:53 - June 21, 16:59

JAMES BALDWIN
American Writer
Sun in Leo

1953 CANCER
From June 21, 17:00 through July 23, 3:51

♋ The Devoted Homebody

If you are a Cancer born in 1953, you enjoy deeply intuitive connections to both family and friends. Your sentimental nature causes you to continually renew bonds from the past—your warmth and lively humor draws new companions. Your radiance peaks at big, festive gatherings, particularly during traditional holidays. You enjoy a relationship that grows in trust and love over time. Reminiscing with your partner keeps good memories alive—your steel-trap memory captures the nuances of life to be shared later.

You love a partner who likes to hold hands in public and cuddle in private. Your ideal relationship is a cushioned nest in which you can safely expose your most tender feelings. You have a tendency to nurse old wounds—the right partner finds that humor can usually lift your mood. Your sensuality is like a deep cave whose mysterious recesses require a brave and gentle spelunker. You shy away from domestic strife and know how to bring harmony back to a rocky situation.

A sure-fire way to win your affection is to serve you a home-cooked meal. You'll also appreciate any thoughtful or sentimental gift to add to your collection of mementos. You are protective in the company of more flippant or detached associates. You have a quirky, childlike openness to the world—the partner who can amuse you and spark your sense of wonder has the edge. Understanding and fidelity rank high, and you'll spoil a mate who is loyal and true.

If you are a male Cancer of 1953, your ideal woman protects your tender heart, while admiring your quiet masculinity. The serene woman with the Mona Lisa smile gives you the peace and stability you crave. Edgy and rough personalities send you into retreat. You align yourself with a kind-hearted companion who admires your compassionate ways.

As a 1953 female Crab, you approach life as a romantic daydreamer with a gift for turning those dreams into reality. You desire a man who is devoted to making you feel secure, while surprising you with spontaneous sexual advances. The man who knows that your beauty shines from the inside out has won your heart.

1953 LEO
From July 23, 3:52 through August 23, 10:44

♌ The Regal Celebrant

As a 1953 Leo, your romantic encounters are epic in proportion, and you've surely traversed the dramatic peaks and valleys of love. Your passions run red hot, and your impulsive libido has likely been refined to a smoldering magnetism. Any grand romantic plans usually include something hot and steamy, whether it's freshly boiled seafood or more provocative fare. You thrive on receiving praise and compliments, but ultimately seek a relationship of mutual adoration.

Though a fireball in love, you have a sensitivity that may take others by surprise. Your legendary confidence can falter at times, but a companion with kind, soothing words will easily prop you back up. If you swing toward arrogance or egotism, the right partner uses humor to remind you of your status as mere mortal. Mostly you see life sunny side up and desire a relationship that is festive and celebratory. Throwing lavish parties together can appeal to your house proud and generous nature.

Someone trying to win your affection might try inviting you to a cultural event, such as an art opening or movie premiere. A partner with a gift for the culinary arts could initiate an evening of sensory pleasures. You enjoy being showered with gifts—the more luxurious, the better. The one who rekindles your sexual spark is kept close at hand. You enjoy the art of seduction, especially to keep a long-time affair fresh—the lover who revels in uninhibited, joyful lovemaking wins your devotion.

If you are a 1953 male Leo, your heart is true to a woman you can admire on her own merit. Fit, active women with get up and go really get you going. You are bonded to the woman who has a colorful personality but a more natural style in make-up and hair. A spirited woman who can match your sexual drive completes your dream.

As a 1953 female Lion, your queenly ways win admirers and even wannabes of both sexes. You demand an attentive lover, and are ardently expressive in return. A brave-hearted man who never bows to your unique brand of bravado has the edge. You enjoy a bold, extravagant man who doesn't skimp on evenings out.

1953 VIRGO

From August 23, 10:45 through September 23, 8:05

The Serene Communicator

If you are a Virgo born in 1953, you desire a relationship of domestic comforts and stability, while also satisfying your passions. The cool façade you present to the world serves to protect a highly sensitive and hopeful heart. An ideal relationship reflects your love of routine and good old-fashioned hard work. You may thrive in a working partnership that allows you to work side-by-side during the day. Far from being all work and no play, you enjoy spontaneous playtimes with your mate.

Your intimate companion finds you can be generous and extravagant—a surprising contrast to your usually thrifty nature. You light up when engaged in conversation, perhaps discussing current events, books, or art. You find intelligence to be a sexy trait—and the talking may continue into the bedroom. A verbal lover fires up your libido, especially if there is a touch of tension as well. You feel a strong need, however, for your relationship to be tempered by peace and harmony.

Those trying to attract your attention should take care to present a tasteful, well-groomed appearance. You respond to someone who understands your initial need for privacy. You also admire people whose wholesome lifestyles give them a healthy glow. A practical gift for your home could win your affection. You much prefer an evening of tasteful refinement over chaotic, free-wheeling events.

For you 1953 male Virgoans, a vivacious woman who can lure you out of your shell makes a fine match. You are slow to trust and desire a companion who can stand the test of time. A make up-free, well-scrubbed, natural-looking woman attracts your simple tastes. Drama queens need not apply—you are drawn to an earthy, sensual woman with rock steady emotions.

As a female Virgo born in 1953, a man must prove his mettle before you could give him your heart. A clever and witty man stimulates your libido as sure as any aphrodisiac. You seek a patient man who cherishes the vulnerability beneath your detached reserve. The partner who appreciates your discerning intellect while arousing your primal sensuality is a sure thing.

VIRGO ZODIAC SIGN
YOUR LOVE PLANETS

YOUR ROMANTIC SIDE   p. 696
▶ VENUS IN CANCER
Born Aug. 23, 10:45 - Aug. 30, 1:34
▶ VENUS IN LEO
Born Aug. 30, 1:35 - Sept. 23, 8:05

YOUR SEX DRIVE   p. 722
▶ MARS IN LEO
Born Aug. 23, 10:45 - Sept. 14, 17:58
▶ MARS IN LIBRA
Born Sept. 14, 17:59 - Sept. 23, 8:05

YOUR CELEBRITY TWINS   p. 760
Find out the astrological similarities you have with famous people.

YOUR COMPATIBILITY   p. 780
Compare planets to find out how compatible you are in a relationship.

YOUR RELATIONSHIP KARMA   p. 824
▶ SATURN IN LIBRA
Born Aug. 23, 10:45 - Sept. 23, 8:05

ALAN LADD
American Actor
Sun in Virgo

291

1953 LIBRA

From September 23, 8:06 through October 23, 17:05

The Sophisticated Idealist

For you 1953 Librans, an ideal relationship has a deeply rooted permanence and traditional flavor. Add many moments of both subtle and extravagant romantic gestures and you stay smitten. You've refined and polished your social image over the years and have a more relaxed approach to being in the public eye. However, image is still important to you and you shine with a partner who fills you with pride. You desire a mate who shares both your ambition and your gift for keeping work light and fun.

You are a delightful mix of extroverted attention-seeking and extreme emotional self-containment. The right mate knows when to flatter and seduce, and when to leave you alone. There is a practical side to your nature that can eclipse your usually playful ways in love. You work hard, but the occasional weekend getaway in a lush, romantic setting can put you back in the mood. Wine and dine you, and you might just share the deeper layers of your sensual nature.

The lucky person who engages you in a rousing, sophisticated debate can win your admiration. You respond to a partner with good taste and personal style and charm. The one who works hard and plays hard, while maintaining a glamorous air, is aces with you. You might appear coolly detached at times, but a sweet romantic note or bouquet of flowers can quickly open your warm heart. An evening of subtle seduction stirs your dormant passions and you'll keep close anyone who is a match for your sexual prowess.

As a male Libra of 1953, you desire a feminine woman of grace and refinement. You are drawn to signs of classic luxury—long, flowing skirts and elegant fabrics turn your head. You appreciate a woman who knows how to create a romantic atmosphere. Oils, candles, and silky lingerie stir your imagination and your heart.

If you are a female 1953 Libra, you create a beautiful world that most men only dream of entering. A man with expensive tastes and a matching generosity ranks high. If he arrives at the door empty-handed, you might point him to the nearest florist. You seek a devoted man who enjoys your frolicsome sensuality.

LIBRA ZODIAC SIGN
YOUR LOVE PLANETS

YOUR ROMANTIC SIDE   p. 696
▶ VENUS IN LEO
Born Sept. 23, 8:06 - Sept. 24, 3:47
▶ VENUS IN LIBRA
Born Sept. 24, 3:48 - Oct. 18, 15:26
▶ VENUS IN LIBRA
Born Oct. 18, 15:27 - Oct. 23, 17:05

YOUR SEX DRIVE   p. 722
▶ MARS IN LIBRA
Born Sept. 23, 8:06 - Oct. 23, 17:05

YOUR CELEBRITY TWINS   p. 760
Find out the astrological similarities you have with famous people.

YOUR COMPATIBILITY   p. 780
Compare planets to find out how compatible you are in a relationship.

YOUR RELATIONSHIP KARMA   p. 824
▶ SATURN IN LIBRA
Born Sept. 23, 8:06 - Oct. 22, 15:35
▶ SATURN IN SCORPIO
Born October 22, 15:36 - Oct. 23, 17:05

BURT LANCASTER
American Actor
Sun in Scorpio

292

1953 SCORPIO
From October 23, 17:06 through November 22, 14:21

♏ *The Curious Explorer*

As a 1953 Scorpio, you thrive on intensity of emotion in a relationship, but also have a gift for restoring harmony. Some like it hot, and your tempestuous passions often reach a boiling point. You desire a relationship that stirs up your deep, watery emotions—a regular tsunami of erotic activities keeps you sexually satisfied. Mysterious and profound, you settle in with a partner who knows there is always more to discover. You seek a mate who is constantly shedding worn-out ways of thinking to arrive at deeper truths.

Your nature is paradoxical—you enjoy both times of independent co-habitation and times of intimate merging of souls. The ideal mate knows when you've hung up the Do Not Disturb sign and gives you some space. Your sexual approach is direct and forceful—faint-hearted lovers will never fare well with you. You thrive in a relationship full of lusty, uninhibited days and nights. If your intensity veers toward possessiveness, your innate sense of balance quickly sets things right again.

Someone trying to draw your attention might tell you a rich story with captivating characters—you also love to spin a good yarn. You'll spot insincerity in a flash and toying with your emotions is not advised. You enjoy a mate who doesn't always air dirty laundry—or pushes to hear yours. You cherish the ones who stand guard over your deepest secrets like a sentinel.

The 1953 male Scorpio has a smoldering intensity that is hard to resist. You desire a loyal woman with an equally voluptuous sensuality. Your passions are deep and intuitive—a bold, fiery feline with bedroom eyes could hit the mark. Your ideal mate can dazzle all the men at a party, and with a private glance, assure you of her endless devotion.

For you 1953 female Scorpios, only a strong-willed, fiercely loyal lover will do. You weed out players and fast-talkers in an instant—you shield your vulnerability from all but the most stalwart man. Your sexuality is like a strong undertow, and requires a man with equally powerful emotional tides. The virile man with endurance in the bedroom has it made.

1953 SAGITTARIUS
From November 22, 14:22 through December 22, 3:30

♐ *The Charismatic Playmate*

If you are a Sagittarius born in 1953, romance brings yet another chance to explore, experiment, and have fun. A relationship is the cherry on top of an already active life—a partner should hit the ground running to keep up with you. You radiate a casual, light-hearted approach to the adventure of love. But if you've sown wild oats, you've also known your share of deep, committed bonds. Your enthusiasm is contagious—you may thrive in marital bliss as long as it continues to satisfy your curiosity and wanderlust.

Ultimately, you desire a companion who mirrors your passion to roam the planet, absorbing new experiences. You enjoy a partner who is your best friend, a confidante to share your triumphs and trials with. You are easy-going and undemanding, but you might feel an uncomfortable tinge of jealousy in sticky situations. The assurance of a loving partner restores the luster to your crown and brings back your perennial smile. The comforts of home and hearth may grow on you, but your independent spirit will never be fully domesticated.

To light you up, someone might suggest a back-to-nature excursion, such as a safari to Africa or a rafting trip down the Amazon. The mate who engages you in philosophical discussions infused with humor wins high marks. Big open spaces are where you shine—you might enjoy an open-air concert or skating in the park. Any seductive gestures or sudden advances are likely to be met with a sly smile. Sexually, you are an active volcano and a ready and willing partner.

To lure you male 1953 Sagittarians, a woman should be prepared to satisfy your prowling nature. The wise woman knows how to fulfil your primal fantasies, while bewitching you with the sensual pleasures of a beautiful home. A quick-witted and spontaneous partner keeps your fires burning.

As a female 1953 Sagittarius, you have a youthful radiance that likely attracts men of all ages. You won't be a caged bird and prefer a man who doesn't try to change or tame you. The light but loyal heart draws you near. A nimble and experimental lover brings out your uninhibited erotic nature.

Marilyn Monroe

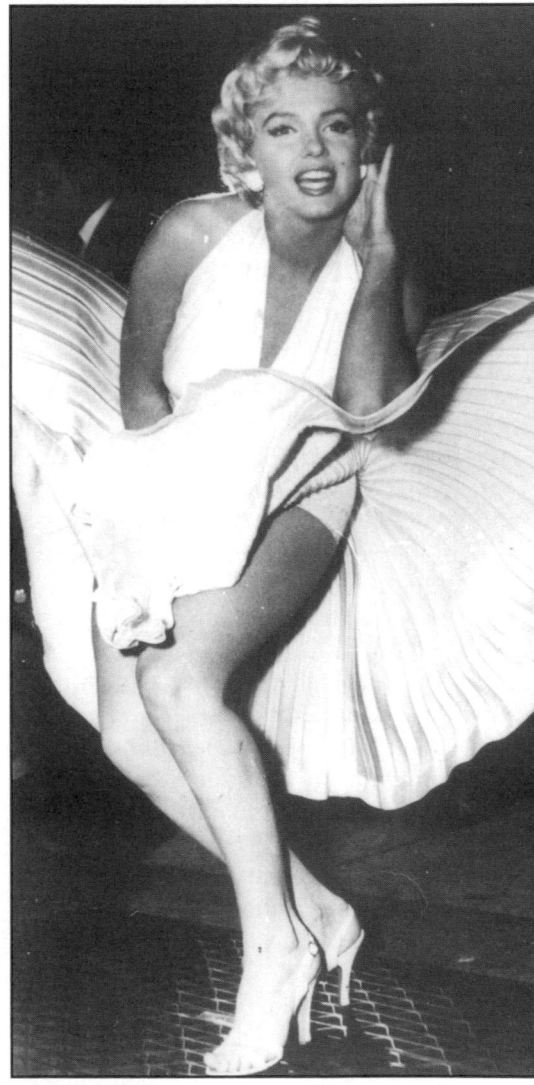

Without a doubt, Marilyn Monroe was the most famous sex symbol of the 20th century. This glorious goddess captured the public's imagination like no movie star ever did before or since, and we still talk about her stunning image, her myth, and her tragedy. She was bursting with animal magnetism, yet seemed vulnerable and innocent at the same time. Men fantasized about her, but she was the biggest dreamer of all.

She dreamed herself out of poverty and isolation, and once reminisced, "I used to think as I looked at the Hollywood night, 'there must be thousands of girls sitting alone like me, dreaming of becoming a movie star. But I'm not going to worry about them. I'm dreaming the hardest.'" By 1953 Marilyn was a big star. She made three hugely successful movies and began dating America's most beloved sports hero, Joe Di Maggio. Also that year, Hugh Hefner debuted his issue of *Playboy* magazine featuring her scandalously nude photo as the centerfold.

Marilyn Monroe was born a Gemini, and like many Geminis, she had two sides to her personality. The public face was bright, luminous even, and can be seen in her onscreen image that projected incredible voltage. Offscreen, and especially toward the end of her life, she was drug dependent, suffered from doomed marriages and affairs, and ended up committing suicide—although that little footnote blossomed into a conspiracy theory that she was murdered. Marilyn enchanted the world, yet couldn't find personal happiness.

She was born with Venus in Aries, a placement that enjoys flirting and showing off. That became a problem when she married Joe Di Maggio in January 1954. That relationship lasted only 286 days. Joe was jealous and had always hoped that Marilyn would give up her film career to become a housewife. The last straw came when she was filming one of Hollywood's most famous scenes for *The Seven Year Itch*—the billowing skirt as she stood over a subway grate. Joe was furious that hundreds of onlookers gleefully watched the many takes for that scene. Over and over her skirt flew up to reveal her panties. That night Joe and Marilyn fought furiously and then divorced a few weeks later.

Marilyn married the renowned playwright Arthur Miller in June 1956. Many thought this was a ridiculous match of "the beauty and the brain," but Marilyn said, "If I was nothing but a dumb blonde he wouldn't have married me, would he?" She courageously risked her own career by publicly supporting her husband when he refused to name names before the communist-hunting Congress. Marilyn always claimed she wanted children, but when she became pregnant, she continued to drink and take pills. She miscarried twice. Miller wrote the film script for her last movie, *The Misfits*, but by then the title described the state of their marriage. They divorced in January 1961.

She is reputed to have had a two-year affair with John F. Kennedy when he was President. Anyone watching her breathlessly sing "Happy Birthday, Mr. President" at Madison Square Garden in her semi-transparent, rhinestone gown might sense that they did indeed have a sexual relationship. Marilyn's mystique continues well after her death. While that gown sold at auction for $1.3 million, we will probably never know the truth about her affair with JFK.

> *"We are all born sexual creatures, thank God, but it's a pity so many people despise and crush this natural gift."*
>
> **MARILYN MONROE**

► READ MORE ABOUT MARILYN MONROE ON PAGES 294, 334, AND 351

1954

- ★ ROCK AND ROLL
- ★ COLETTE
- ★ JOE DI MAGGIO
- ★ BRIGADOON
- ★ HEY THERE
- ★ SH-BOOM
- ★ THE MAGNIFICENT OBSESSION

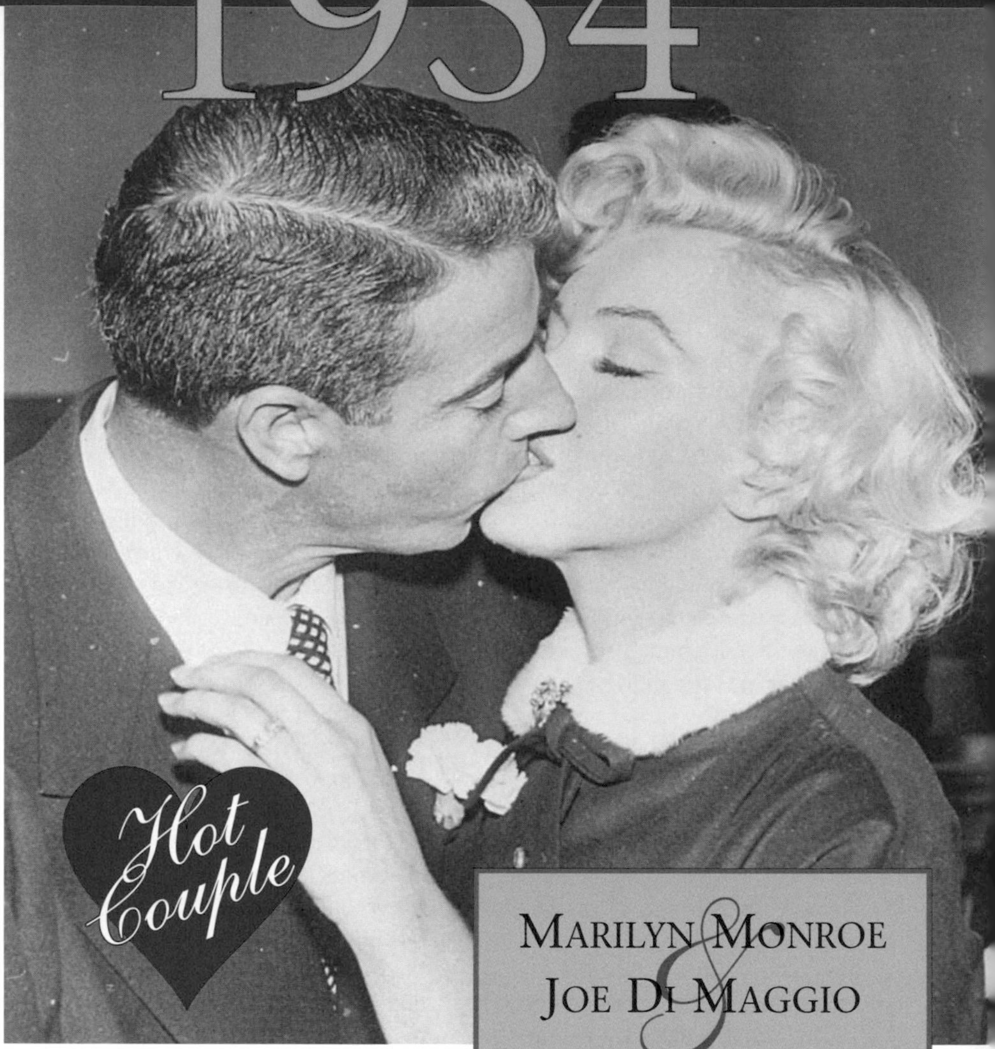

EVENTS

The British Home Office launched a campaign against obscene publications after an Interpol conference surmised that pornography was the root cause of sex crimes.

Across the Atlantic, US Representative Ruth Thompson tried to stifle rock and roll by introducing legislation meant to ban sending certain "pornographic" records through the mail. In the September 24th issue of Billboard, the editorial criticized rhythm and blues songs because of references to sex. Police in two states confiscated jukeboxes, starting a ban across the country.

Colette, author of *Gigi*, which was later made into a successful movie, died August 3.

Marilyn Monroe married baseball great Joe Di Maggio—the marriage lasted nine months. That same year Marilyn went to Korea to sing to the troops.

POP CULTURE

Director Vincente Minnelli gave us *Brigadoon*, a fantasy in which a traveler to Ireland discovers love in a town that comes alive only once every one hundred years. In *The Last Time I Saw Paris*, a writer stays in Paris after the liberation, falls in love, marries, and destroys it all with alcohol before eventually turning his life around. In *The Magnificent Obsession,* a man attempts to emulate the life of a local man who died, including falling in love with the man's wife, but only succeeds in causing more tragedy.

Eddie Fisher had two hits on the charts—"Oh! My Papa" and "I Need You Now." So did Rosemary Clooney, with "Hey There" and "This Ole House." The Crew-Cuts got people rockin' 'n' rollin' with "Sh-Boom," while the Chordettes set the pace for slow dancing with "Mr. Sandman."

The Mandarins by Simone de Beauvoir won France's highest literary award. In this fictionalized account of her real life and friends (Sartre, Camus, et al.), she portrays the Parisian intellectual society at the end of World War II and the feelings of a woman torn between love and her political conviction. Another book mixing fact and fiction was *Mary Anne* by Daphne du Maurier, an account of her great-great grandmother's time as a mistress to the Duke of York during the Napoleonic wars.

Hot Couple

MARILYN MONROE & JOE DI MAGGIO

Although their union only lasted nine months, the marriage of "Yankee Clipper" Joe Di Maggio to sexpot and screen legend Marilyn Monroe captured everyone's imagination. She was the famous blonde bombshell, and he was the quiet, gentlemanly baseball player. After he retired from baseball the year before, Di Maggio told a friend that he wanted to meet a glamorous woman. He found the holy grail of glamour in Marilyn Monroe.

It seemed to be an unlikely match, and although the marriage was brief, their friendship lasted forever. Di Maggio continued to send flowers to Monroe's gravesite for many years after she died in 1962.

SEE ALSO
► MARILYN MONROE *Page 293*

1954 CAPRICORN

From December 22, 1953 3:31 through January 20, 1954 14:10
(December 1954 Capricorns, see 1955)

♑ *The Free-spirited Sweetheart*

Oozing with charm and grace, you 1954 Capricorns are in great demand, both socially and romantically. Pals play a very important role in your life, and there's a good chance that a marriage could grow out of one of your friendships. You may feel a strong kinship with older, established people, and may wind up with a romantic partner who holds great distinction in a particular field. You like relationships that have an unusual stamp to them, and therefore do best with a unique and visionary mate.

Although you desire a lover who is accomplished, you have no desire to attach yourself to somebody else's star. You have big dreams of your own, and want a relationship that allows you to pursue them. It's very important for you to have a big measure of independence in marriage. You're one of those folks who would actually benefit from a marriage in which one of the partners travels a lot. The less constricted you feel, the more effusive you are toward your spouse. In your case, absence definitely makes the heart grow fonder!

Individualists never fail to capture your attention. You're a great admirer of anyone who feels no pressure to conform to the status quo. You also have quite an earthy sense of humor, and like a sexy joke that is in good taste. When it comes to lovemaking, you want a partner who always makes you feel desirable and attractive. Being ravished by hugs, kisses and passionate embraces makes your ego soar, and you never fail to respond in an enthusiastic manner.

You male Goats who were born in 1954 do best with a woman who is goal-oriented and confident. Nothing turns you on like a female who knows where she is going. You also delight in a partner whose dry sense of humor matches your own. Anyone who makes you laugh at your own foibles is a good match for you.

As a 1954 female Capricorn, you are happiest with a man who is volatile, mesmerizing, and lusty. You want a guy whose emotions run deep. Polite diplomats are not for you, because they leave you off-balance and uncertain. You far prefer a man who tells you what he likes and dislikes in no uncertain terms.

CAPRICORN ZODIAC SIGN
Your Love Planets

YOUR ROMANTIC SIDE   p. 696
▶ **VENUS IN CAPRICORN**
Born Dec. 22, 1953 3:31 - Jan. 20, 1954 14:10

YOUR SEX DRIVE   p. 722
▶ **MARS IN SCORPIO**
Born Dec. 22, 1953 3:31 - Jan. 20, 1954 14:10

YOUR CELEBRITY TWINS   p. 760
Find out the astrological similarities you have with famous people.

YOUR COMPATIBILITY   p. 780
Compare planets to find out how compatible you are in a relationship.

YOUR RELATIONSHIP KARMA   p. 824
▶ **SATURN IN SCORPIO**
Born Dec. 22, 1953 3:31 - Jan. 20, 1954 14:10

DANNY KAYE
American Comedian
Sun in Capricorn

295

1954 AQUARIUS

From January 20, 14:11 through February 19, 4:31

♒ *The Unique Romantic*

As a 1954 Aquarius, you are quite choosy when it comes to romance. Although you may have dated a great deal in your younger days, you probably held off making a serious commitment. You desire a partner who completely captivates you, from the top of your head to the tips of your toes. The connection between you may be more chemical than intellectual. You want a relationship that emits sparks!

You're quite a romantic person, but like to put a unique spin on the way you court your partner. For you, nothing kills a relationship quicker than neglecting those tender little intimacies that are so prevalent during the early stages of dating. Consequently, you may continually spring romantic surprises on your spouse long after you've said your vows. Your relationship may be many things, but it will never be boring! Unlike many people in love, you have no intention of changing your partner. Molding your spouse into some fantastic ideal is the last thing you would want.

A slow, steady process of seduction is the best way to reel you in. An admirer would be wise to first drop a few compliments your way, and then follow with admiring glances, and graduate to lingering touches to your arm or back. You love to prolong the suspense of courtship, and appreciate a suitor who sends shivers of anticipation down your spine every time you meet. In the bedroom, you enjoy being lightly caressed all over. This stimulates your already sensitive nerve endings, and never fails to put you in the mood for love.

As a 1954 male Water Bearer, your taste in women is as varied as your hobbies. You admire traditional, earthy types, as well as zany individualists. Tender, poetic females also appeal to you. Ultimately, however, you're looking for a partner with a strong animal magnetism that draws you in like a powerful magnet.

You female 1954 Aquarians like two kinds of guys. The first is the strong, silent type who always keeps you guessing. The second is an outgoing, enthusiastic man who is always up for an adventure. In the final analysis, you do best with a mate who is strong and masterful.

AQUARIUS ZODIAC SIGN
Your Love Planets

YOUR ROMANTIC SIDE   p. 696
▶ **VENUS IN CAPRICORN**
Born Jan. 20, 14:11 - Jan. 22, 9:19
▶ **VENUS IN AQUARIUS**
Born Jan. 22, 9:20 - Feb. 15, 7:00
▶ **VENUS IN PISCES**
Born Feb. 15, 7:01 - Feb. 19, 4:31

YOUR SEX DRIVE   p. 722
▶ **MARS IN SCORPIO**
Born Jan. 20, 14:11 - Feb. 09, 19:17
▶ **MARS IN SAGITTARIUS**
Born Feb. 09, 19:18 - Feb. 19, 4:31

YOUR CELEBRITY TWINS   p. 760
Find out the astrological similarities you have with famous people.

YOUR COMPATIBILITY   p. 780
Compare planets to find out how compatible you are in a relationship.

YOUR RELATIONSHIP KARMA   p. 824
▶ **SATURN IN SCORPIO**
Born Jan. 20, 14:11 - Feb. 19, 4:31

HARRY BELAFONTE
American Singer
Sun in Pisces

1954 PISCES
From February 19, 4:32 through March 21, 3:52

The Temperamental Paramour

Romantically, you 1954 Pisceans are a bit of a puzzle. One minute you're red hot with passion, and the next you're as cool as a cucumber. That's because your moods ebb and flow with the tides. You're a very sensitive person who does best with a partner who can anticipate your needs with just a glance. You want a relationship that supports your creative talents and thrives on sudden changes. Leading a conventional lifestyle may not suit you very well, as you could have quite a restless spirit.

Despite your impulsive ways, you're quite domestic, and desire a home in which everyone feels safe enough to express their feelings without reprisal. A partnership that thrives on plenty of communication would be best for you. You couldn't bear a mate who keeps resentments hidden. You'd rather have a heated argument than suffer in silence. Fortunately, you're a born problem-solver and enjoy hammering out solutions with the help of your spouse. Maintaining an open dialogue with your mate helps you to enjoy the fulfilling relationship you've always desired.

If someone wants to attract and keep your attention, they should compose a poem or song in your honor. You're very flattered by artistic tributes, and like the idea of being someone's creative inspiration. Nothing turns you on more than a lover who stares deeply into your eyes as a prelude to sex. You want to merge both souls and bodies with your partner, and appreciate a suitor who takes the time to know the real you before making the first move.

For a male Fish who was born in 1954, you seek a woman who is sensitive, expressive, and affectionate. You also admire women who are forthright and honest. A mate who is willing to discuss her feelings in an honest, constructive way is best suited to your straightforward sensibilities.

If you're a 1954 female Piscean, you are happiest with a man who is intelligent and authoritative. You want a partner whom you can look up to. A guy with questionable morals doesn't have much of a chance with you. A partner who serves as your spiritual advisor and creative champion is your ideal.

1954 ARIES
From March 21, 3:53 through April 20, 15:19

The Serious Suitor

Love is rarely taken lightly by you 1954 Rams. When you form a relationship, it's because you are utterly devoted to your mate's happiness. Casual dating is an alien concept for you, because there is nothing frivolous about the way you feel about your romantic partner. Consequently, you do best in a partnership that is founded on mutual respect and sincere admiration, rather than sheer sexual chemistry. You want a partner who is not only your lover, but your closest confidante.

You may have a tendency to idolize your partner, preferring to overlook their weak points and emphasize their strengths. Living up to your expectations can be a challenge, but the rewards are fantastic. You're an extremely romantic person, and love to cater to your lover's every whim. You enjoy making reservations at some secluded little hideaway at the spur of the moment. It simply isn't in your nature to take your spouse for granted.

A suitor would be wise to take a serious, respectful approach to you. You're not impressed by flirts, but you do appreciate someone who is able to articulate their interest in a respectful way. Expressing admiration for your ideas is a good beginning. You welcome the prospect of getting to know each other over a gourmet dinner at a sumptuous restaurant. It's a good idea to wait until the third date before making a pass at you. Once you've established a comfortable rapport, you enjoy making love in a dimly lit room with seductive music playing.

As a male 1954 Ram, you do best with a woman who is feisty, independent, and daring. A female who isn't afraid to risk life and limb for the sake of adventure really turns you on. You're also attracted to women who are tasteful and sensual. Above all, your partner should put your relationship first on her list of priorities.

Men who are optimistic and outgoing appeal most to you female Ariens who were born in 1954. You also admire ambitious, down-to-earth guys. A mate who helps, respects and encourages your goals is ideal. You want to be admired for your ambition, not scolded for it. Progressive-minded men really turn you on.

1954 TAURUS

From April 21, 15:20 through May 21, 14:46

The Wild Card

Most times, you 1954 Bulls are steady, serene, and soothing. Then, all of a sudden, you could be dancing on a tabletop with a lampshade on your head. Such unpredictable behavior may come as a shock to casual acquaintances, but it's not so surprising for your romantic partner. That's because they're accustomed to these periodic outbursts, and embrace them as part of your charm. There's a good chance that your relationships are characterized by long periods of calm, punctuated by short bursts of electricity. Consequently, you do best with a mate who is not only adaptable, but has a good sense of humor as well.

Although you want to create a secure foundation for your partner, you don't like it when your relationship falls into a boring routine. You want to feel free to explore new vistas and different lifestyles with your mate, even if it means leaving old patterns behind. A partnership that can sustain these kinds of sudden shifts is ideal for you. Not all of the changes you orchestrate are disruptive, though. You're also the type of lover who is apt to slip tickets for a luxury cruise beneath your mate's pillow on your anniversary.

Catching your eye can be complicated. You appreciate a person who appears to follow the rules but betrays a rebellious streak. Whispering an irreverent comment in your ear during a serious moment can really excite your interest. Sexually, you may be a bit shy and reserved, and thrive with a lover who encourages you with loving compliments and sighs of admiration. A suitor who is patient and persistent with you will eventually see you burst into flower in the bedroom.

Women who are grounded, comforting, and physically affectionate appeal to you as a 1954 male Bull. You also admire females who are witty and well read. A partner who is willing to follow wherever you lead is a perfect match for you.

You 1954 female Taureans want a man who is elegant, authoritative, and organized. A guy that makes you feel safe and secure always brings out the best in you. You do best with a mate who not only indulges your flights of fancy, but smiles on them too.

TAURUS ZODIAC SIGN
YOUR LOVE PLANETS

YOUR ROMANTIC SIDE — p. 696
► **VENUS IN TAURUS**
Born Apr. 20, 15:20 - Apr. 28, 22:02
► **VENUS IN GEMINI**
Born Apr. 28, 22:03 - May 21, 14:46

YOUR SEX DRIVE — p. 722
► **MARS IN CAPRICORN**
Born Apr. 20, 15:20 - May 21, 14:46

YOUR CELEBRITY TWINS — p. 760
Find out the astrological similarities you have with famous people.

YOUR COMPATIBILITY — p. 780
Compare planets to find out how compatible you are in a relationship.

YOUR RELATIONSHIP KARMA — p. 824
► **SATURN IN SCORPIO**
Born Apr. 20, 15:20 - May 21, 14:46

AUDREY HEPBURN
English Actress
Sun in Taurus

297

1954 GEMINI

From May 21, 14:47 through June 21, 22:53

The Dream Lover

Delightful to converse with and bewitching to behold, you 1954 Geminis are in a great deal of romantic demand. Jealous outsiders wish they could have a partner who is as sweet, charming, and attentive as you are. The secret to your appeal is an exalted view of love. You settle for nothing less than bliss when it comes to relationships. As a result, you are always looking for ways to make your mate feel desired and appreciated, even long after your bond has been established. You're apt to buy your lover sexy underclothes years after you've made your initial commitment in order to keep the passion alive.

You have an extremely healthy sexual appetite and put lovemaking high on your list of relationship priorities. Age actually increases your desire, and there's a good chance you'll be sexually active well into your golden years. A mate who welcomes your frequent amorous advances works best for you. You're a real social butterfly, and do best with a mate who enjoys entertaining as much as you do.

An admirer who seeks to win your heart should baby you a bit. You love it when somebody remembers the way you take your coffee or goes out of the way to find your favorite pastry. A lover who is self-assured and purposeful never fails to arouse your passion. You'll want a suitor who likes making love as much as you do, because you tend to like vigorous sex that can go on for hours. Therefore, it pays to be in shape before going after your affections!

Lots of different women appeal to you 1954 male Geminis. You appreciate females who are talkative and witty, as well as ladies who are shy and domestic. Women with a dramatic flair also appeal to you. Ultimately, you do best with a partner who works just as hard as you do to keep the romance alive in your relationship.

As a 1954 female who was born under the sign of the Twins, you want a man who is suave and sophisticated. Your knees probably turn to jelly when a man bends to kiss your hand. Selfish, insensitive types really turn you off. You benefit most from a partner who anticipates your needs and makes you feel like a queen.

GEMINI ZODIAC SIGN
YOUR LOVE PLANETS

YOUR ROMANTIC SIDE — p. 696
► **VENUS IN GEMINI**
Born May 21, 14:47 - May 23, 15:03
► **VENUS IN CANCER**
Born May 23, 15:04 - June 17, 17:03
► **VENUS IN LEO**
Born June 17, 17:04 - June 21, 22:53

YOUR SEX DRIVE — p. 722
► **MARS IN CAPRICORN**
Born May 21, 14:47 - June 21, 22:53

YOUR CELEBRITY TWINS — p. 760
Find out the astrological similarities you have with famous people.

YOUR COMPATIBILITY — p. 780
Compare planets to find out how compatible you are in a relationship.

YOUR RELATIONSHIP KARMA — p. 824
► **SATURN IN SCORPIO**
Born May 21, 14:47 - June 21, 22:53

EVA MARIE SAINT
American Actress
Sun in Cancer

298

1954 CANCER
From June 21, 22:54 through July 23, 9:44

The Unaffected Sweetheart

You 1954 Crabs have a candor that is terribly disarming. You're not interested in putting on some phony act to attract admirers. A relationship that is firmly rooted in truth is your greatest desire. You'd rather have your partner know about all your shortcomings from the outset than be disillusioned later. Fortunately, you possess so many wonderful qualities that your partner isn't likely to complain over your few faults. Your optimism, generosity, and enthusiasm are just a few of the reasons you are able to attract tremendous love and devotion.

Home and family are extremely important to you. Consequently, you do best with a spouse who devotes a lot of time and energy to domestic pursuits. Because you're a very giving person, you need a mate who is just as attentive about serving your needs. Lavish presents and tender words mean less to you than unselfish acts of devotion. Your love and affection only grows over time. You're not the type of person to leave your marriage at the first sign of trouble. Rather, you'll dig in your heels and work on your problems as a means to build a stronger relationship. You're good at enacting loving compromises.

Demonstrating strong, abiding affections is a surefire way to attract your attention. An admirer would be wise to brag about lifelong friendships and strong family ties. Although your sexual desires are considerable, you are a shy and hesitant lover. Therefore, a suitor would be wise to take the lead in the bedroom. Soft lips are a particular turn-on for you.

If you're a male Crab who was born in 1954, you respond to women who are bold, courageous, and magnetic. Women who have a sense of drama may hold a special attraction for you. Expressive, serious females also appeal to you. You do best with a partner who is faithful and family-oriented.

Men who prize financial and emotional security win favor with you 1954 female Cancereans. You admire a guy who can plan for the future and still manage to live in the present. Honest, open-minded males also thrill you. You want a mate who recognizes and celebrates your inner beauty.

1954 LEO
From July 23, 9:45 through August 23, 16:35

The Devoted Helpmate

As 1954 Leo, love is a continual source of fascination for you. Romance may be the primary motivating factor in your life, and yet you're puzzled by the power it holds over you. It's hard for you to be inspired unless you're in an exciting relationship. Therefore, you do best with a dynamic, adventurous partner who is always willing to try new things. At times, your relationship may experience thrilling peaks and troubling valleys, but you'd rather have an exciting bond than a stagnant one. Besides, you don't really mind getting into spats with your lover, because such tiffs invariably lead to passionate reconciliations.

Sometimes you'd rather remain silent than risk hurting your partner's feelings. A spouse who helps you articulate your emotions in a constructive way could open new worlds for you. For you, a good relationship is a means to self-improvement. You love it when your mate offers advice on how to handle problems or cope with stressful situations. Similarly, you love rendering assistance to your beloved, because this makes you feel needed. You do best in an equal partnership.

You don't mind it a bit when a suitor pursues you—in fact, you're flattered by the attention. A good way to win your heart is to display remarkable courage and daring. You particularly admire fierce athletes and ambitious business people. When it comes to sex, you enjoy a fun-loving, lighthearted approach. Anyone who is able to make you laugh while experiencing pleasure has an excellent chance of winning your lifelong devotion.

As a 1954 male Leo, you prefer women who are witty and perceptive. Coy types don't go over very well with you. You also enjoy females who are ladylike and refined. You do best with a mate who knows how to fire you up, both sexually and intellectually.

You female Lions who were born in 1954 want a man who is spontaneous and free-spirited. A guy with a flirtatious nature poses an exciting challenge for you, as you enjoy devising ways to keep their gaze firmly focused on you. Ultimately, you want a partner who fills your life with wonderful surprises.

1954 VIRGO

From August 23, 16:36 through September 23, 13:54

The Friendly Flirt

As a 1954 Virgo, you've been blessed with a silver tongue. You know exactly what to say to make a person blush with pleasure. A partner who is as adept in the art of flirting fills your life with constant pleasure and excitement. You want a relationship that regularly stimulates your imagination and inflames your passion. Although your sign is often associated with routines, you don't want a predictable relationship and you're always looking for new ways to put spice into your love life.

Sex should play a very big part in your relationship, as you have very powerful physical desires. You do very well with a mate who helps you forget your inhibitions in the bedroom. One way to dampen your enthusiasm in a relationship is to belittle your dreams. You've always been somewhat of a visionary, and dislike it when somebody tries to discourage you from meeting your goals. You reward an enthusiastic, supportive spouse with a lifetime of love and laughter. Making your partner laugh may be one of your greatest joys, and you can be perfectly willing to poke fun at yourself as a means to elicit a smile from your lover.

Saucy compliments and impertinent remarks never fail to make your eyes sparkle with excitement. You love a person who appears polite and solicitous while breaking all the rules. Your suitor should not be deceived by your own prim exterior—beneath that tailored shirt beats the heart of a lion!—and would be well advised to make a bold first move, because this lets you know that your admirer's desires are as powerful as your own.

Women who are lovely, gracious, and polite always win favor with you 1954 male Virgins. You also appreciate females with strong passions and smoldering desires. A mate who makes you feel like an irresistible sex symbol even when you're in a ratty bathrobe is a perfect match for you.

If you're a female Virgo born in 1954, you want a man who is comfortable in his own skin. You love a guy who exudes masculinity without resorting to aggressive behavior or boastful talk. A partner who can make you blush with one appreciative glance is your ideal.

VIRGO ZODIAC SIGN
YOUR LOVE PLANETS

YOUR ROMANTIC SIDE   p. 696
- ▶ **VENUS IN LIBRA**
Born Aug. 23, 16:36 - Sept. 06, 23:28
- ▶ **VENUS IN SCORPIO**
Born Sept. 06, 23:29 - Sept. 23, 13:54

YOUR SEX DRIVE   p. 722
- ▶ **MARS IN SAGITTARIUS**
Born Aug. 23, 16:36 - Aug. 24, 13:21
- ▶ **MARS IN CAPRICORN**
Born Aug. 24, 13:22 - Sept. 23, 13:54

YOUR CELEBRITY TWINS   p. 760
Find out the astrological similarities you have with famous people.

YOUR COMPATIBILITY   p. 780
Compare planets to find out how compatible you are in a relationship.

YOUR RELATIONSHIP KARMA   p. 824
- ▶ **SATURN IN SCORPIO**
Born Aug. 23, 16:36 - Sept. 23, 13:54

299

1954 LIBRA

From September 23, 13:55 through October 23, 22:55

The Operatic Suitor

You 1954 Librans express yourselves on a grand scale, especially when it comes to love. You think nothing of sending six dozen roses to your lover's office. Similarly, you may be willing to revamp your entire appearance as a means to please your beloved. Whatever form your devotion takes, it's sure to be met with gasps of delight. You love a relationship that is filled with big surprises, and enjoy building a reputation as an impulsive and generous lover. The person who built the Taj Mahal is your kind of romantic.

A mate who is impulsive and a little opinionated best suits your temperament. You dislike wondering what your lover is thinking, and prefer a partner who is willing to speak their mind without fear of censure. A relationship that is characterized by plenty of heated discussions holds your interest. If your spouse's spirits are low, you may clown around as a way to make your lover smile. Fortunately, it's hard to be in a bad mood when you're around, and your mate probably ends up laughing at your silly antics.

A suitor seeking your affections should be well-versed in the arts and current events. You've got an extremely active mind, and enjoy talking about the latest movies, books, and political upheavals. Savvy admirers turn you on. When it comes time to take things to a physical level, it helps to linger on initial contacts like handholding and gentle caresses. You want sex to progress to a powerful crescendo, like a beautiful piece of music.

As a male Libran who was born in 1954, you do best with a female who is diplomatic but decisive. You admire a woman who knows what she wants, and goes about getting it in a graceful way. A mate who is able to wind you around her little finger is perfectly suited to you. Secretly, you love being sweet-talked!

You 1954 female Librans appreciate men who are self-reliant but need nurturing. Although you would hate to play nursemaid to your partner, you probably enjoy fetching him cups of coffee and rubbing his feet as a means to brighten his day. You need a partner who lets you know that you make his life complete.

FRANCOISE SAGAN
French Writer
Mars in Libra

LIBRA ZODIAC SIGN
YOUR LOVE PLANETS

YOUR ROMANTIC SIDE   p. 696
- ▶ **VENUS IN SCORPIO**
Born Sept. 23, 13:55 - Oct. 23, 22:06
- ▶ **VENUS IN SAGITTARIUS**
Born Oct. 23, 22:07 - Oct. 23, 22:55

YOUR SEX DRIVE   p. 722
- ▶ **MARS IN CAPRICORN**
Born Sept. 23, 13:55 - Oct. 21, 12:02
- ▶ **MARS IN AQUARIUS**
Born Oct. 21, 12:03 - Oct. 23, 22:55

YOUR CELEBRITY TWINS   p. 760
Find out the astrological similarities you have with famous people.

YOUR COMPATIBILITY   p. 780
Compare planets to find out how compatible you are in a relationship.

YOUR RELATIONSHIP KARMA   p. 824
- ▶ **SATURN IN SCORPIO**
Born Sept. 23, 13:55 - Oct. 23, 22:55

RICHARD WIDMARK
American Actor
Venus in Scorpio

300

1954 SCORPIO
From October 23, 22:56 through November 22, 20:13

♏ *The Adoring Adventurer*

As a 1954 Scorpio, you're eager for your lover to expose you to new worlds. You've got a very curious mind, and want to enjoy a relationship that sharpens your desire for knowledge. A partner who doesn't question authority or the meaning of life is not for you. You do far better with a mate who uses travel, scholarship, and spiritual practices as a means to widen your mutual horizons. A relationship in which both partners are encouraged to grow and change with the times works best for you.

Someone who expresses no interest in other lands, cultures, and people has little appeal for you. There's a good chance that your marriage will involve a great deal of travel. Even if you aren't able to take lots of trips, you may enjoy watching movies set in a foreign locale with your spouse. A passionate person like you thrives on a vibrant sex life. You enjoy a mate who enjoys making love all night long. As far as you're concerned, sex is a means to join minds and spirits with your beloved.

If someone wants to get your interest and hold it for a lifetime, they should appeal to your intellect first. Although you're not a snob, you do enjoy discussing philosophical matters. Expressing an interest in law, religion, or politics is a good way to get your attention—and knowing a lot about them is sure to win your heart. As with all Scorpions, you are pretty highly sexed, although you don't like to get intimate with somebody until you know them well. A slow process of seduction works best with you. You melt when your admirer softly brushes your lips with theirs before actually kissing you.

Women who are inspirational and impassioned fare best with you 1954 male Scorpions. You also enjoy females who are well-traveled and knowledgeable about different cultures. Ultimately, you want a partner whose searing curiosity about life matches your own.

As a female 1954 Scorpio, you admire a man who is good-natured, sociable, and caring. A guy who is involved with humanitarian causes usually attracts your interest. You want a compassionate mate who is interested in the world, not just himself.

1954 SAGITTARIUS
From November 22, 20:14 through December 22, 9:23

 *The Tireless Lover*

A big ball of sexual energy—that's you, 1954 Sagittarius! You love making eyes at the opposite sex, and delight in flirtatious banter. You want a relationship that fills you with ecstasy, and use a whole manner of unusual methods to keep your partner interested. As a lover, you're unparalleled. Trying to keep up with you in the bedroom is fun but exhausting. Sex doesn't deplete you, it fills you with energy! Therefore, you are best suited to a partner who has terrific stamina.

You possess deep passions and profound dislikes, and benefit from a partner who can help you develop a more nuanced approach to life. It's easy for you to lose your cool, so you appreciate a soothing partner who can calm you down when you start seeing red. Ideally, you want a marriage in which you can give your mate excitement, while they provide you with perspective. Your spouse is sure to benefit from your lust for life, too, as it can be quite contagious. A relationship in which you're constantly encouraged to explore new challenges works best for you.

Expressing a desire for intimacy is a good way to attract your attention. You love the idea of merging souls with someone special, and your ears perk up when you hear an admirer speak in terms of "soul mates" and "karmic attractions." Sexually, you prefer light touches to forceful embraces. When a lover traces a repeated pattern on your back, it drives you wild with desire.

Women who are emotional, sensitive, and loyal thrill you 1954 male Archers. You appreciate a female who sympathizes with your fiery emotions. A mate who is able to channel your restless energy into worthy projects is ideal for you. You're also turned on by enticing women who can transform your frustration into sexual desire.

If you're a female Sagittarian born in 1954, you want a man who is aloof and somewhat detached, at least on the surface. You love melting a guy's reserve. Men preoccupied by their creative urges also appeal to you. When all is said and done, you do best with a partner who needs you to remind him of his passionate side. You're a born seductress!

Federico Fellini and Giulietta Masina

Nudity, prostitution, bisexuality, and orgies are boldly depicted in the late Italian moviemaker Federico Fellini's celluloid masterpieces. A visionary, his films are semiautobiographical, infused with a poetic intensity and a twisted absurd reality.

His voluptuous leading ladies exuding sexuality are at the heart of his movies. The signature scene in one of his best-known movies, *La Dolce Vita*, features the perfect Fellini fantasy woman—big-breasted beauty Anita Ekberg bathing in Rome's majestic Trevi Fountain. Set at the height of Italy's post-war economic boom, the movie explores the decadent workings of hedonistic Italian society. But its message was too much for the Catholic Church, which condemned it for painting an amoral and explicit picture of promiscuous guilt-free sex. But despite a turbulent scandal, *La Dolce Vita* went on to win the Palme D'Or at Cannes.

All of Fellini's leading ladies were startlingly striking sex kittens, oozing eroticism. This led many to suspect that he was just a dirty old rogue who lusted after young girls. But in truth, *il maestro*, as he was also known, was only ever in love with one woman—his wife.

Fellini was working with the Italian Radio Auditions Board during World War II when he met Giulietta Masina. An actress, Masina came to light with a radio play, written by her colleague—Fellini. The collaboration was electric—a year later they were married. It was the beginning of a long partnership, their love forming the building block on which their creative and artistic energies met.

Giulietta was not only Fellini's lover

and wife, she had become his muse, inspiration, and confidante. Fellini cast her in his movies, and her performances received as much critical acclaim as his directing. But the turning point was the 1954 movie *La Strada*, which propelled both of them into the international arena of world cinema. Critics raved about the movie, which is a touching tale of an innocent girl who is sold by her family to a violent strongman in a travelling circus. Fellini elicited from Masina a magnetic performance. Her Chaplinesque ability to be at once funny and tragic moved audiences to tears and laughter in the beat of a breath.

The movie won an Academy Award for Best Foreign Language Film and Fellini and Giulietta's fame was now assured and their recognition worldwide.

But like any married couple working together, their relationship could be explosive. Fellini and Masina were both deeply superstitious—they regularly

attended séances and consulted astrologers. Masina's interest in the supernatural was even more profound than that of her husband, and Fellini was inspired to make a movie about her spirituality and sixth sense. *Giulietta Degli Spiriti* in 1965 was his first color movie and is a journey into the psyche of a troubled woman who has visions. The film was a revealing portrait of the relationship between the husband and wife team, and the strain of scrutinizing their marriage sometimes proved too much—loud, passionate arguments were regular occurrences on the set.

Despite tantalizing temptations presented by the string of buxom starlets that graced his films, Fellini and Masina were with each other until death. Fellini died in October 1993 in Rome, the day after his fiftieth wedding anniversary. Giulietta died five months later. Her last words were, "I am going to spend Easter with Federico."

"We had the advantage, Federico and me, of being married young, so we became formed together."

MASINA
after Federico's death in 1993

301

▶ READ MORE ABOUT FELLINI'S FILMS AND LEADING MAN MASTROIANNI ON PAGE 367

1955

- ✪ JAMES DEAN
- ✪ MARILYN MONROE'S LEGS
- ✪ THE SEVEN YEAR ITCH
- ✪ MARJORIE MORNINGSTAR
- ✪ AUNTIE MAME
- ✪ BILL HALEY & HIS COMETS

EVENTS

Sexy *Rebel Without a Cause* star James Dean died. However, the young Elvis Presley was very much alive. Officials in San Diego and Florida warned Presley if he moved at all during his performances, he would be arrested on obscenity charges. He was not the only one facing censorship. New York banned the gigantic poster in Times Square showing Marilyn Monroe's legs, advertising the movie *The Seven Year Itch*.

Revlon no-smear lipstick came on the scene, assuring kissers there would be no tell-tale evidence. In Paris Christian Dior presented his new collection, the new *poitrine effacée*—the flat-chested flapper look. For once a woman's bustline was not emphasized.

POP CULTURE

Moviegoers loved *To Catch a Thief*, directed by Alfred Hitchcock. This lighthearted suspense/romance set on the French Rivera was full of twists. *The Seven Year Itch* was an account of a man's attempt not to give in to temptation when his wife goes on vacation and leaves him alone with the blonde (Marilyn Monroe) living upstairs. In the classic musical *Guys and Dolls* a gambler falls in love with a mission worker. In the French film *Les Diaboliques* the wife and the mistress murder the man who mistreats them—but the body mysteriously disappears.

Bookstores had no problem selling *Marjorie Morningstar* by Herman Wouk,

Hot Couple

the classic story about a teenage girl who wants to be an actress, to her parents' horror. *Auntie Mame* told of a boy who comes under the guardianship of his one-of-a-kind aunt. *Bonjour Tristesse* by Francoise Sagan was a French novel about a young girl who meddles in her father's romantic affairs—with deadly results. In *Ten North Frederick*, by John O'Hara, a 50-year-old man pushed into politics by his wife finds his principles are in question—he ends up with a mistress his daughter's age.

Bill Haley & His Comets had teens bopping to "Rock Around the Clock." Fats Domino belted out "Ain't That a Shame" and Tennessee Ernie Ford gave us the now classic "Sixteen Tons." Fans of Mitch Miller sang along with "The Yellow Rose of Texas."

DEBBIE REYNOLDS & EDDIE FISHER

When Debbie Reynolds married fellow singer Eddie Fisher on September 18, 1955, she was known as "America's Sweetheart." No one knew that their union would inspire one of the most infamous love triangles in Hollywood. They seemed to embody the ideal 1950s marriage when their daughter Carrie was born. She would become *Star Wars*' Princess Leia in the 1970s.

But all was not perfect in paradise. Fisher fell in love with Elizabeth Taylor, the widow of his recently deceased best friend, Mike Todd, and left Reynolds in 1958 for Liz. His affair with Taylor ruined his career and was considered the scandal of the decade.

SEE ALSO
▶ PAUL SIMON & CARRIE FISHER *Page 532*
▶ ELIZABETH TAYLOR *Page 399*

1955 CAPRICORN

*From December 22, 1954 9:24 through January 20, 1955 20:01
(December 1955 Capricorns, see 1956 Capricorn)*

♑ *The Romantic Rebel*

As a 1955 Capricorn, free love was in the wind when you came of age. With the sexual revolution in full swing, you were less likely to follow the usual traditional approach Capricorns take toward dating, sexual experimentation, and commitment. In a serious relationship you can be just as faithful and dependable as characters from the old TV show, *Father Knows Best*, but your choices are more likely to honor personal principle, as opposed to socially acceptable rules. You thrive in a relationship in which both partners support each other's freedom to make the most of their unique talents as individuals.

For you a committed partnership is all about teamwork. With your mate by your side you can face the world and make the most of all the opportunities that stretch out before you. Likely to be nurturing, compassionate, and emotionally expressive, you can be a caring lover to your partner and an indulgent parent to any children you may have. Once you reach a certain level of security and comfort, you may resist change and become a bit rigid—a development that can lead

to stagnation in your relationship and your personal growth. Open-mindedness and adaptability keeps your relationship going and growing over the long term. A passionate sex life keeps you feeling fresh and rejuvenated. Lovemaking may inspire a sense of awe and romance that never gets stale.

Atmosphere can strongly influence your mood. Scented candles, luscious colors, and music can soothe your soul and inspire you to make a love connection. Concerts and a night of dancing give you a romantic way to come together physically before the sex gets going.

The 1955 Capricorn man thrives with a woman who shares his dreams and aspirations. Whether she exudes a smoldering passion or an idealistic enthusiasm, you appreciate someone who can give you a good, swift, and loving kick in the rear to get you moving.

Female Capricorns born in 1955 like a man who is intuitive and kindhearted. Ideally, he expresses his feelings openly and is tuned in to your concerns. His eagerness to listen reassures you that you are precious to him.

CAPRICORN ZODIAC SIGN
YOUR LOVE PLANETS

YOUR ROMANTIC SIDE   p. 696
▶ **VENUS IN SCORPIO**
Born Dec. 22, 1954 9:24 - Jan. 06, 1955 6:47
▶ **VENUS IN SAGITTARIUS**
Born Jan. 06, 6:48 - Jan. 20, 20:01

YOUR SEX DRIVE   p. 722
▶ **MARS IN PISCES**
Born Dec. 22, 1954 9:24 - Jan. 15, 1955 4:32
▶ **MARS IN ARIES**
Born Jan. 15, 4:33 - Jan. 20, 20:01

YOUR CELEBRITY TWINS   p. 760
*Find out the astrological similarities you have
with famous people.*

YOUR COMPATIBILITY   p. 780
*Compare planets to find out how compatible
you are in a relationship.*

YOUR RELATIONSHIP KARMA   p. 824
▶ **SATURN IN SCORPIO**
Born Dec. 22, 1954 9:24 - Jan. 20, 1955 20:01

KIM NOVAK
American Actress
Sun and Venus in Aquarius

303

1955 AQUARIUS

From January 20, 20:02 through February 19, 10:18

♒ *The Impassioned Insurgent*

For you, Aquarius of 1955, a romantic relationship can kick off a whole new stage of growth in your life. Intimate partners can bring out different aspects of your personality and move you to take on new challenges. If a relationship when you were younger defied traditional mores, any opposition from parents or authority figures was likely to draw you closer to your mate. For you the position of "you-and-me-against-the-world enhances the passion of a romance.

You thrive in a relationship that succeeds in striking a balance between freedom and commitment, independence and interdependence, idealism and intimate needs. Ingenious Aquarians have what it takes to invent and re-invent their relationships as necessary to maintain that delicate balance over the long haul. Interestingly, the will that drives you to maintain the fine-tuning on your partnership comes from an irrational source—a deep, intense, and emotional attachment between you and your mate. Because it defies explanation, the passion you and your mate share fills your lovemaking with an aura of wonder and magic.

The way to the heart of the brainy Aquarian is through the intellect. Your favorite form of foreplay may be an intense conversation, the kind that keeps you up all night with flashes of insight that hit you like a lightning bolt. For you sex can be utterly mind-blowing when it is adventurous, a bit naughty, and includes lots of experimentation.

To appeal to the Aquarian man of 1955 a woman needs to have a minimum level of intellectual sophistication. The quality that captivates you, though, is a sweet, loving nature. Her delicate, romantic way assures you she will always love you, unconditionally. A taste for sexual exploration can excite your own penchant for discovery.

An ambitious, go-getting man can provide the intensity and excitement that the Aquarius woman of 1955 finds so thrilling. You adore someone who can turn you on to new ideas, trends, and challenges. With his brave, pioneering spirit, he can inspire you to strike out in pursuit of new frontiers of knowledge, possibility, and accomplishment.

AQUARIUS ZODIAC SIGN
YOUR LOVE PLANETS

YOUR ROMANTIC SIDE   p. 696
▶ **VENUS IN SAGITTARIUS**
Born Jan. 20, 20:02 - Feb. 06, 1:14
▶ **VENUS IN CAPRICORN**
Born Feb. 06, 1:15 - Feb. 19, 10:18

YOUR SEX DRIVE   p. 722
▶ **MARS IN ARIES**
Born Jan. 20, 20:02 - Feb. 19, 10:18

YOUR CELEBRITY TWINS   p. 760
*Find out the astrological similarities you have
with famous people.*

YOUR COMPATIBILITY   p. 780
*Compare planets to find out how compatible
you are in a relationship.*

YOUR RELATIONSHIP KARMA   p. 824
▶ **SATURN IN SCORPIO**
Born Jan. 20, 20:02 - Feb. 19, 10:18

ANNA MAGNANI
Italian Actress
Sun in Pisces

304

1955 PISCES
From February 19, 10:19 through March 21, 9:34

The Peaceful Partner

Pisces of 1955 provide a romantic partner with an island of peace and quiet in the middle of a crazy world. Your mate may have been attracted to your gentle way with people and your talent for staying serene under stress. You are not the type who gets a charge out of sparring with loved ones. In a disagreement you tend to give in, leaving an opponent feeling as if you've gone off to a secret, impenetrable place. You may have chosen a mate who learned quickly from experience that you respond better to sweet enticement than harsh compulsion. For you a relationship should be a harmonious sanctuary.

A deep, unspoken understanding may be the force that binds you to a partner over the years. You and your mate may have felt you were destined to find each other. And, like Cinderella's glass slipper, once you came together, it was a perfect fit. Indeed, a fairy tale sense of romance may fill your days and nights with a sense of magic. As you go through different phases in your life, you and your mate may keep courting, creating new ways to woo and wow each other.

Going out and having fun together lets you fall in love over and over. Sentimental gifts and gestures renew the good feelings you share and keep your sex life fresh and exciting.

In the bedroom you can be wild and sensual, responsive to pleasure-enhancing techniques, and even props. Creativity in entertainment and lovemaking captures your attention. You and your partner may especially enjoy going on a couples' weekend that allows you to explore new ways to satisfy each other.

The 1955 Piscean man treasures the woman who is stable and devoted, but who is constantly developing and revealing new and fascinating sides of herself. Like Sheherazade, she can provide you with a thousand-and-one ways to divert your mind and delight your senses.

The yearnings of the 1955 Piscean woman find satisfaction with a man who is an indulgent romantic. You may long for someone who is imaginative and thoughtful. Candy and flowers are nice, but you find it hard to resist the man who finds even more ingenious ways of winning you.

1955 ARIES
From March 21, 9:35 through April 20, 20:57

The Compassionate Companion

The thrill of the chase alone is not enough for the 1955 Aries. A nice reward should await you at the end of the pursuit. Only a very special someone can move you to shift into high gear, and you don't plow ahead mindlessly or on impulse. Whether you are wooing a new flame or romancing an existing one, the campaign usually begins with some detective work to find out what exactly gives your beloved a thrill. Then you formulate a plan for thrill delivery and carry it out. In winning over a sweetheart the thoughtfulness and determination you show is flattering, endearing, and just plain irresistible!

You are likely to lavish your mate with gifts, especially the kind you can enjoy together. Of course, it's great to see a partner wearing fine earrings or cuff links from you, and it's great to share a bottle of fine wine, a box of chocolates, or a bushel of fresh apples. Your attachment to your mate tends to be intense. When work, activities, or other friends claim your honey's time, it can make you feel neglected and sometimes even a little jealous. All is forgiven

in the boudoir, where the undivided attention of your mate rapidly makes up for any shortfalls.

With your strong sensuality, almost every part of your body, including your hair, can be sensitive to stroking and caressing. You may have a weakness for your partner's cologne. When you have to be away, you might carry an article of your mate's clothing. Breathing in the unique scent of a lover can bring on a rush of memories and good feelings.

The ideal woman for the 1955 Aries man is friendly and sympathetic. You brighten up with someone who notices the effort you put into realizing your goals. This lady makes it her business to give you a positive reaction. Gracious and devoted, she's delighted to follow your romantic lead.

A resourceful, productive man is ideally suited to the Aries woman of 1955. Likely to share your own affection for creature comforts, this guy has what it takes to make sure you'll always have the best. His sense of value and budgetary smarts enable you to live rich, without going broke.

1955 TAURUS
From April 20, 20:58 through May 21, 20:23

The Treasure Finder

For Taurus of 1955 the romantic world is your oyster, filled with pearls awaiting discovery. You give off a magnetic glow when you succeed in finding buried treasure in a place where no one would even think to look. The flea market or an estate auction can be a starting place for romance or the perfect venue for a hot date. You may have recognized a beloved partner as a diamond in the rough. Tending to go slow in a relationship gives you plenty of time to get to know someone and discover his or her inner beauty. Your nose for value and excellent timing enables you to provide a comfortable standard of living for yourself, your mate, and family.

You have plenty of energy to work on a relationship, but for you, the process doesn't feel like work. Much like the gardener nursing antique roses into prizewinning blooms, you enjoy tending to romance. Having a mate multiplies the joy of sharing life's challenges and victories and the abundance of the natural world. For you it's great to have someone to come home to talk to. You may also be a little chatty in the bedroom, because good communication allows you to thrill your mate and to receive the kind of attention that satisfies your own desires.

Pleasant sounds in general—birds chirping, raindrops on the window sill, soothing music—can ease you into the mood for lovemaking. Words of love deepen the intensity of your sexual connection with your mate. You can never tire hearing how special you are to your beloved.

The Taurus man of 1955 appreciates a woman who is ardently devoted. Even better than her word, this lady gets a thrill from proving her love through concrete acts. She does the things that matter to you. She showers you with favors, escorts you to important events, and hugs and caresses you wherever you go.

For the Taurus woman of 1955, a man with a melodious voice starts out with an advantage over all others. It's even better if he can sing, preferably softly, in your ear. The luscious sound he makes can make you melt. Of course, what he says is important. His words show he's charming, sentimental, and sincere.

TAURUS ZODIAC SIGN
YOUR LOVE PLANETS

YOUR ROMANTIC SIDE   p. 696
▶ VENUS IN PISCES
Born Apr. 20, 20:58 - Apr. 24, 15:12
▶ VENUS IN ARIES
Born Apr. 24, 15:13 - May 19, 13:34
▶ VENUS IN TAURUS
Born May 19, 13:35 - May 21, 20:23

YOUR SEX DRIVE   p. 722
▶ MARS IN GEMINI
Born Apr. 20, 20:58 - May 21, 20:23

YOUR CELEBRITY TWINS   p. 760
Find out the astrological similarities you have with famous people.

YOUR COMPATIBILITY   p. 780
Compare planets to find out how compatible you are in a relationship.

YOUR RELATIONSHIP KARMA   p. 824
▶ SATURN IN SCORPIO
Born Apr. 20, 20:58 - May 21, 20:23

DANIELLE DARRIEUX
French Actress
Sun and Venus in Taurus

1955 GEMINI
From May 21, 20:24 through June 22, 4:30

The Soulful Seeker

For Gemini of 1955 a serious romantic relationship is the pot of gold at the end of the rainbow, the successful outcome to a lifetime of encounters with a wide range of people. Still, finding that one special person, your soul mate, marks the beginning of a new adventure in intimacy and personal growth. With your idealistic outlook on love and romance you may look to relationships to increase the pleasure life has to offer. When the hard times inevitably come, you may be relieved to discover that you can rely on your mate to ease any burden and to keep your spirits strong.

You have plenty of natural talents that enhance the health and happiness of an intimate partnership. Because your nerves are delicate, you work hard to prevent conflict and discord. Your communication skills allow for a smooth flow of concerns, opinions, and preferences. You and your partner can talk any issue through before it escalates to anger. Your gift for creating harmonious relations extends to the bedroom, where you make love with a gentle sweetness. Born under the sign of the Twins, you have an instinctive sensitivity to another person's needs, a gift that keeps on giving to your grateful partner, who, need we add, is thrilled to return your favors.

An air of beauty and delicacy is the hallmark of romance and intimacy for you. To see your partner dressed up and ready to go out can give you a rush, second only to seeing your sweetheart dressed solely in candlelight. A soothing bath in the glow of the flames is a seductive entrée into daring intimacy.

A sensuous, serene woman is appealing to the 1955 Gemini man. When you're with someone who has a peaceful disposition, you look forward to coming home at night. Out on the town together, every treat and sight seems richer. Or you can stay home and let him spoil you.

The Gemini woman of 1955 adores the sentimental man who brings a fanciful outlook to ordinary events in life. Someone with a dreamy perspective can fill you with a romantic feeling. His heart is so tender, you can talk to him about anything and enjoy his reassuring insights.

GEMINI ZODIAC SIGN
YOUR LOVE PLANETS

YOUR ROMANTIC SIDE   p. 696
▶ VENUS IN TAURUS
Born May 21, 20:24 - June 13, 8:37
▶ VENUS IN GEMINI
Born June 13, 8:38 - June 22, 4:30

YOUR SEX DRIVE   p. 722
▶ MARS IN GEMINI
Born May 21, 20:24 - May 26, 0:49
Mars in Cancer
Born May 26, 0:50 - June 22, 4:30

YOUR CELEBRITY TWINS   p. 760
Find out the astrological similarities you have with famous people.

YOUR COMPATIBILITY   p. 780
Compare planets to find out how compatible you are in a relationship.

YOUR RELATIONSHIP KARMA   p. 824
▶ SATURN IN SCORPIO
Born May 21, 20:24 - June 22, 4:30

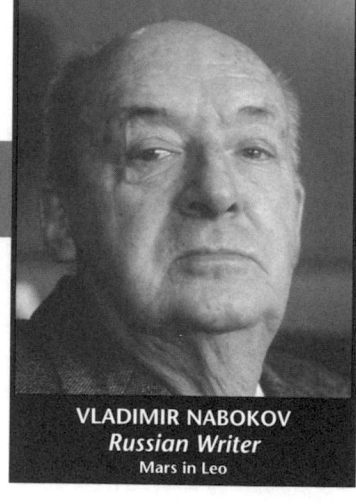

VLADIMIR NABOKOV
Russian Writer
Mars in Leo

1955 CANCER
From June 22, 4:31 through July 23, 15:24

 The Tender Guardian

The 1955 Cancer might have a soft spot for flowers and candlelight, but you believe that the proof of a lover's sincerity and devotion comes through deeds, over time. You may be all too aware that flattery and wooing can lull you into letting your guard down. If you've ever trusted someone and been burned, you may have become twice as shy. Such an experience may have taught you to protect your feelings until a lover proved worthy. Finding a partner who could lure you out of your shell may have been an enormous relief to you, because you're not quite yourself without someone to love. In a committed relationship you are a tender and generous lover, likely to shower your mate with romantic gifts and sentimental keepsakes.

Highly sensitive to your sweetheart's feelings, you may lash out fiercely at anything or anyone who would threaten or hurt someone you love. The trust and emotional support you and your mate share creates a rock solid foundation for the long-term stability of your relationship and family life. You and your mate may cast a reserved image in public, but in private the two of you can let it all hang out. The confidence you enjoy together lets you express your animal passions. You may enjoy some naughty tools for enhancing your pleasure, such as vibrators or other sex toys.

Your passion can perk up upon the mere sight of your mate in clothing that flatters the chest area or reveals a glimpse of cleavage. In lovemaking dwelling on this part of your body can set your excitement off like a rocket.

The Cancer man of 1955 appreciates a woman who is expressive and tender-hearted. Kind words can boost your mood and encourage you to do your best. Recognizing the preciousness and fragility of life, your ideal lady wouldn't dream of parting for the day without saying "I love you" first.

The Cancer woman born in 1955 finds contentment with a man who is responsible and passionate. He gives you the kind of care and attention that wins your trust and makes you feel safe. For him honoring commitments deepens his feelings of connection with the people dearest to him.

1955 LEO
From July 23, 15:25 through August 23, 22:18

The Cuddly Companion

In all your golden glory, Leo of 1955, you come across in a big way. Your powerful presence attracts admirers, and a love relationship can start when someone special notices you from across a crowded room and turns out to be your biggest fan. You may inspire strong reactions in others—for better or worse—and this makes it easy for you to sort out loyal devotees from drab killjoys. This strategy can have a downside. Like a luxury liner and a Venetian gondola that pass in the night, you could miss the chance for closeness with someone a bit different from "your type." You can have a great relationship with a mate who shies away from the limelight or instant romantic fireworks. To probe beyond first impressions, to really get to know someone—and to let them get to know you— can lead to a deep and wondrous bond.

With a loving mate you can reveal a deeper, more vulnerable side of your personality. Others may see you as courageous—and you are—but people forget that courage is only possible when you feel afraid. When you confide fears or doubts to a mate and receive reassurance and encouragement in return, you know your relationship is on rock solid ground. Depending on the romantic tone your partner sets in bed, you can be as cuddly as a kitten or as fierce as a tiger.

An exhibitionist streak may attract you to the risqué side of sex. Revealing clothing—on you or your lover—can stir your passions. You may also get thrills from fooling around in unusual places—an elevator, a theatre, an airplane, a swimming pool.

An introverted woman can present an intriguing challenge to the 1955 Leo man. Getting her to let down her guard can give you a triumphant feeling. Bringing out her adventurous side—which she's likely to have, or she wouldn't have been attracted to you—can make you feel delirious.

The Leo woman of 1955 appreciates a man who has a genius for making a spectacle of his love for you. Everyone likes material gifts, but you get a special thrill from a gesture that is dramatic, creative, and unique. His pride in having won you assures you that you've got a forever thing.

1955 VIRGO

From August 23, 22:19 through September 23, 19:40

The Subtle Pursuer

You, 1955 Virgo, are responsive and sensuous, with a subtle but compelling appeal. Indeed, you may have great success in getting partners to pursue you until you catch them. Because you may find it distasteful to openly chase a lover, you may seduce your sweetheart by unleashing your powers of enchantment and letting nature follow its course, straight to your doorstep. Your sign rules service, and you perform favors like no one else can. You have an acute sensitivity to what a partner needs and the ability to deliver—with every detail covered and sealed with a kiss. The attention you give can make your sweetheart feel special, loved, and eager to reciprocate.

In a long-term relationship you and your partner can establish a well-ordered lifestyle that allows you to feel peaceful and secure. It may be very important to you to have a hard-working and responsible mate, someone who can equally share in running your household and caring for your family. You may need to be mindful of certain expectations you may impose—not everyone does things the way you do. You can maintain harmony in your relationship by

taking care to openly communicate your needs and emphasize the issues most important to you. Telling your partner what you need in bed can bring on a rush of exhilaration.

You have a healthy taste for the finer things in life. You can't help but be delighted when a lover shows up with a few of your favorite things. Sharing luxuries with your mate can bring out your amorous yearnings and lead to hours of sensual indulgence.

The 1955 Virgo man feels most comfortable with a woman who is perceptive and understanding. You may be a stickler when it comes to values and purity of principles. You tend to have a lot of respect for the woman who can appreciate where you're coming from, even if she disagrees.

The man who is a logical, cool customer can be very sexy to the Virgo woman born in 1955. You admire someone who can analyze a problem and has the full confidence and competence to solve it. For you grace under pressure is the quality that makes a mate like this a real keeper!

VIRGO ZODIAC SIGN
YOUR LOVE PLANETS

YOUR ROMANTIC SIDE p. 696
▶ VENUS IN LEO
Born Aug. 23, 22:19 - Aug. 25, 18:51
▶ VENUS IN LIBRA
Born Aug. 25, 18:52 - Sept. 18, 22:40
▶ VENUS IN LIBRA
Born Sept. 18, 22:41 - Sept. 23, 19:40

YOUR SEX DRIVE p. 722
▶ MARS IN LEO
Born Aug. 23, 22:19 - Aug. 27, 10:12
▶ MARS IN LIBRA
Born Aug. 27, 10:13 - Sept. 23, 19:40

YOUR CELEBRITY TWINS p. 760
Find out the astrological similarities you have with famous people.

YOUR COMPATIBILITY p. 780
Compare planets to find out how compatible you are in a relationship.

YOUR RELATIONSHIP KARMA p. 824
▶ SATURN IN SCORPIO
Born Aug. 23, 22:19 - Sept. 23, 19:40

JOHN CAGE
American Composer
Sun and Venus in Virgo

307

1955 LIBRA
From September 23, 19:41 through October 24, 4:42

The Sweet Socialite

For you, Libra of 1955, casual mingling can be a stop along the way to romance and fulfillment in life. For you an active social life can lead to a fateful meeting with a soul mate, or it can provide an exciting and dynamic setting in which a romantic relationship can flourish. You are likely to have a talent for networking, matchmaking, and making lasting, and often intense, friendships. Because you can be a warm, elegant, and charming companion, you offer a partner the opportunity to meet new people, to enjoy a variety of entertaining pursuits, and to advance in his or her career.

The sign of Libra rules love and romantic relationships, and for you, being in a committed partnership can make you feel complete. A personal investment as deep as yours can bring out the best of your relationship skills—tact, diplomacy, and the ability to compromise. Sometimes, when your sixth sense tells you that something's wrong, you may overemphasize your partner's needs, at the expense of your own. Fairness tends to be very important to you, and any compromise should be fair to

both your partner and you. Likely to be an even-handed lover, you enjoy peak satisfaction only when you know you've brought your partner to the heights of ecstasy.

For you the lead-in to lovemaking should be beautiful—never raw, harsh, or crude. Fragrant flowers, mood music, and romantic whisperings can spark your passions. Gentle touching and soft, sweet kisses can progress into the deeper, prolonged intermingling of your bodies.

The Libran man born in 1955 fancies a woman who shows artistic refinement in her clothing, leisurely pursuits, and the atmosphere she creates at home. Creativity can stimulate or soothe you. Sensitive to your mood and needs, this lady can bring balance and harmony to your life.

An attentive man is a turn-on for the 1955 Libra woman. It can be a dream come true for you to have a partner who gets a kick out of spoiling you. Because you are a gracious partner, you are likely to respond to his generosity with your own thoughtful favors. Together you can create a never-ending cycle of kindness.

LIBRA ZODIAC SIGN
YOUR LOVE PLANETS

YOUR ROMANTIC SIDE p. 696
▶ VENUS IN LIBRA
Born Sept. 23, 19:41 - Oct. 13, 0:38
▶ VENUS IN SCORPIO
Born Oct. 13, 0:39 - Oct. 24, 4:42

YOUR SEX DRIVE p. 722
▶ MARS IN LIBRA
Born Sept. 23, 19:41 - Oct. 13, 11:19
▶ MARS IN LIBRA
Born Oct. 13, 11:20 - Oct. 24, 4:42

YOUR CELEBRITY TWINS p. 760
Find out the astrological similarities you have with famous people.

YOUR COMPATIBILITY p. 780
Compare planets to find out how compatible you are in a relationship.

YOUR RELATIONSHIP KARMA p. 824
▶ SATURN IN SCORPIO
Born Sept. 23, 19:41 - Oct. 24, 4:42

THELONIOUS MONK
American Musician
Venus in Scorpio

308

1955 SCORPIO
From October 24, 4:43 through November 23, 2:00

 ♏

The Passion Magnet

If only the Scorpio of 1955 could be cloned. Then everyone could enjoy a partner as dramatic, colorful, and romantic as you! For you passion is up there with air, food, water, and shelter. Clothing may be an essential need in life, but when you and your sweetheart are alone, the less you have on, the better. At every stage of a relationship, you can sweep a partner off his or her feet. Emotional intensity and sexual desire tend to be the forces that hold your relationship together over time, and you may devote a lot of energy and imagination to keep the feelings fresh and spicy.

Once a relationship falls into a regular groove, you are a devoted partner, in for the long haul. You may feel strongly that something about your mate is unique and special, and it may be hard to imagine ever feeling the same passion for anyone else. This feeling can enhance your loyalty and move you to express how precious your mate is to you. It can also make you become a bit possessive, especially if competing interests make claims on your partner's time. You can rest assured that your natural magnetism is an irresistible force, drawing a mate back home to your loving arms.

At its best lovemaking can lead to an out-of-body experience for you. Meditating together can lead you to explore ways of combining spirituality with sexuality. You and your mate might follow the Kama Sutra or Tantric practices. Your detective skills can also uncover more recent sex manuals designed for couples observing Western religions.

A woman who is open-minded and non-judgmental can be a great match for the 1955 Scorpio man. You feel best with a partner to whom you can tell everything, even your deepest, darkest thoughts and desires. As you confide more in her over time, your trust in her can grow, along with your passion.

A quiet, mysterious man can captivate the Scorpio woman of 1955. He can excite your desire to explore every facet of him. In some sense you may feel that you'll never know him completely, and that just makes him all the more intriguing to you. He can be a puzzle that you'll never tire of solving.

1955 SAGITTARIUS
From November 23, 2:01 through December 22, 15:10

♐ ## *The Tender Provocateur*

Full of charisma but approachable, wise but humble, the Sagittarian of 1955 is a fascinating and compelling partner. Your ability to put higher principles ahead of your own interests can make you an inspiring catch. A loving partnership may be sacred to you, and it may be a no-brainer to sacrifice selfish desires, especially if they threaten the dreams you share with your mate. You may have a strong need to help people, a force that can lead you and your mate to attain the highest form of relationship, one in which you share so much love for each other that the next natural step is to turn that love out into the world.

The engine that drives your relationship is the ability to speak frankly to each other on intellectual and personal matters. To some it may seem as if you're fighting, but you may just get a rise out of provoking each other. The public face of your relationship is likely to be quite different from how you interact in private. You may lavish each other with romantic gestures and share a tender, intuitive attachment that any attempt at understanding would only dampen. You are likely to enjoy another bond that is deeper still—sex. You may have a hearty sexual appetite, the satisfaction of which you and your partner may keep shrouded in secrecy.

Forbidden fruit can be highly enticing to you. If it's something that "nice people don't do," that may be all the more reason to try it. You might enjoy making love in naughty places, and you may be highly responsive to a suggestive mate.

The Sagittarius man of 1955 adores a woman who is sensual and lusty. If she seems cold and prudish to other men, you may feel all the more special for your ability to bring out her animal instincts. Once you have won her, you can trust that her devotion to you is solid and enduring.

The Sagittarius woman born in 1955 responds strongly to the man who exudes a smoldering passion. His powerful will can arouse your competitive spirit and stir your interest in him. His secrets are a treat well worth waiting for—you can spend hours pouring over the depth and complexity of his soul.

James Dean

Elia Kazan, director of early '50s screen idol James Dean, proclaimed "His great love was himself and he spent a good deal of his time off the set taking pictures of himself." But Kazan said this with affection, and later explained that the young actor needed coaxing because he was like a fretful, uncertain animal. "God, he gave everything he had," said Kazan. "There wasn't anything he held back." Kazan was directing the new arrival to Hollywood in Dean's first big picture, *East of Eden*, and it was on that set that Dean met and fell in love with the Italian actress Pier Angeli.

As an Aquarian, James Dean naturally was a spontaneous, inventive actor. He didn't like to memorize his lines but, like Marlon Brando, preferred to get into the mood of the scene and play it from there. While the technique came across well, it often upset his fellow actors who never knew what he would say next. Raymond Massey, who played the stern, religious father in *East of Eden*, didn't like Dean because of this unpredictability and demanded of Kazan to "make him read the lines the way they were written."

Perhaps the most important relationship for Dean was the difficult one with his own father, and those who were like his father. With his Mars in proud, bold Leo, he openly questioned authority figures and had little trouble conjuring up this feeling in his second movie *Rebel Without a Cause*. Offscreen he had a passion for motorcycles and sports cars and driving fast—recklessly fast. The legend of James Dean grew around his sudden death in a car accident. He had made only three feature films, with the last two appearing after his death on September 30, 1955.

Photographs of the accident scene flashed across most every newspaper in the US, and it seemed that the entire nation went into mourning. Within a few months over 400 James Dean fan clubs were established, and nearly a half century later fans were still visiting his gravesite. The most devout fans, known as the Deaners, held seances and described mystical communion with his spirit. They made love on his grave.

Some biographers claim that James Dean was gay or bisexual. One author claims evidence that points to seduction by a Methodist minister when Dean was a teenager growing up in Fairmont, Indiana. But it appears that he was madly in love with Pier Angeli. He once told a friend that "Pier is a rare girl. I respect her. Unlike most Hollywood girls, she's real and genuine." And she had a transforming effect on Dean. He began combing his hair for the first time and even wore a tuxedo when he escorted her to the premiere of *A Star Is Born*.

Dean was deeply hurt and disappointed when her mother broke up their affair because he wasn't Catholic. Angeli then married actor Vic Damone, who was both Italian and Catholic. Dean wasn't invited to the wedding, but sat sullenly on his parked sports car across from the church's entrance, nursing his wounded pride. Less than a year later, only days before his fatal car accident, Angeli paid Dean a visit. She told him that he was her only true love, and rumor has it that he cried through the night.

> *"I wouldn't marry her unless I could take care of her properly . . ."*
>
> **JAMES DEAN**
> **about his relationship with Pier Angeli**

▶ READ ABOUT MARLON BRANDO ON PAGE 277

1956

- ⊛ ELVIS PRESLEY
- ⊛ THE KING AND I
- ⊛ BUS STOP
- ⊛ TEA AND SYMPATHY
- ⊛ SINGING THE BLUES
- ⊛ PEYTON PLACE
- ⊛ PRINCESS GRACE

EVENTS

Britain's Blonde Bombshell Diana Dors secured a deal with Hollywood studio RKO after her role as a murderess in *Yield to the Night*. Unfortunately, the studio was already in its death throes, and after being cast in just two films, she returned to Britain.

Elvis Presley appeared on *The Ed Sullivan Show* and so shocked the TV host with his gyrating hips that the cameramen were instructed to show him from the waist up.

Grace Kelly became a princess when she married Prince Rainier of Monaco. Marilyn Monroe married Arthur Miller, her third husband. And when sex symbol Jayne Mansfield saw the recently crowned Mr. Universe in a revue, she told the waiter, "I'll have a steak—and the man on the left!"

POP CULTURE

There were two Kings in the movie theaters. Elvis in *Love Me Tender* and Yul Brynner in *The King and I*. Elvis played a soldier who comes back from the Civil War to find his girlfriend married to his brother. Brynner, as the King of Siam, falls in love with his children's English governess. Other box-office hits were *Bus Stop*—in which a rodeo rider falls in love with a singer and forces her to return with him to his Montana home—and the musical *Carousel*—where a carnival worker killed in a robbery can return to Earth for just one day. *Tea and Sympathy*, a progressive film for the time, dealt with a gay college student who gets sympathy from the headmaster's wife.

In spite of all the Presley hits, there was room for other artists. Guy Mitchell released "Singing the Blues," and Gogi Grant sang "The Wayward Wind." Other hits were "Memories Are Made of This" by Dean Martin and "My Prayer" by the Platters.

Grace Metalious's *Peyton Place*, a story of scandal and sex in a New England town, shocked the nation—or at least those who admitted reading it. The book *James Dean Returns* proved a sex symbol can be dead and still capture interest. It sold a half million copies. In Oakley Hall's *Mardios Beach* the protagonist uses women on his climb to the top.

Hot Couple

GRACE KELLY & PRINCE RAINIER

Grace Kelly, the exquisite American film actress and daughter of an American millionaire, met Prince Rainier III of Monaco at the Cannes film festival in 1955. The moment he saw her, he wanted her for his princess.

Kelly's career was skyrocketing, but she gave it all up to marry her prince. Her father paid the handsome dowry of two million dollars for this privilege. They wed in a civil ceremony and the next day drove the streets of Monte Carlo in an open-top car to celebrate with their subjects. In 1982, tragedy struck when Princess Grace drove her car over a cliff in Monaco.

SEE ALSO

▶ ALFRED HITCHCOCK Page 341

▶ LADY DI & PRINCE CHARLES Page 516

1956 CAPRICORN

From December 22, 1955 15:11 through January 21, 1956 1:47
(December 1956 Capricorns, see 1957 Capricorn)

♑ *The Untamed Amour*

It wouldn't do you justice, 1956 Capricorn, to describe you as the strong silent type. That's merely a first impression. You're no fool, and you're not about to reveal your true, untamed nature to casual friends or co-workers. Only the most devoted lover gets to enjoy the privilege of finding out just how deep and wild your still waters run. You can be a passionate partner, with an intensely magnetic appeal and a taste for sensuous, uninhibited fun. Being secretive and discreet can give you greater control over various situations in your life, including romantic affairs, but it can leave your mate feeling shut out from your affection and from decisions best made together. To entrust your needs to your mate might feel like jumping off a cliff, but once you take the plunge, you're likely to discover that the precipice is only one-foot-deep.

You may find it easier to open your heart with a nonjudgmental partner who understands you, empathizes with your feelings, and has faith in your ability to overcome any challenge. For you a relationship thrives on trust, and the more plunges you take, the stronger your love and commitment can grow. Ideally, you and your mate can become best friends, who also happen to have a burning desire for each other's bodies! When you're in the mood for love, you can woo your lover with subtle but thoroughly romantic determination.

You can be delightfully open to sexual suggestion and experimentation. Forbidden fruit can be thrilling for you, and you may have a hearty appetite for naughty sexual adventures. Stolen intimacy in risky places can arouse your rebellious passions.

The 1956 Capricorn man enjoys a woman who is friendly and even tempered. You appreciate someone who can keep a cool head in a crisis. With her analytic mind and positive attitude you can trust this woman to be a help in any situation.

Female Capricorns born in 1956 like the man who is strong and self-disciplined. You admire a man who says what he means and backs up his meaning with concrete action. His reliability and take-charge efficiency can inspire your confidence.

CAPRICORN ZODIAC SIGN
YOUR LOVE PLANETS

YOUR ROMANTIC SIDE   p. 696
► VENUS IN CAPRICORN
Born Dec. 22, 1955 15:11 - Dec. 24, 1955 6:51
► VENUS IN AQUARIUS
Born Dec. 24, 1955 6:52 - Jan. 17, 1956 14:21
► VENUS IN PISCES
Born Jan. 17, 14:22 - Jan. 21, 1:47

YOUR SEX DRIVE   p. 722
► MARS IN SCORPIO
Born Dec. 22, 1955 15:11 - Jan. 14, 1956 2:27
► MARS IN SAGITTARIUS
Born Jan. 14, 2:28 - Jan. 21, 1:47

YOUR CELEBRITY TWINS   p. 760
Find out the astrological similarities you have with famous people.

YOUR COMPATIBILITY   p. 780
Compare planets to find out how compatible you are in a relationship.

YOUR RELATIONSHIP KARMA   p. 824
► SATURN IN SCORPIO
Born Dec. 22, 1955 15:11 - Jan. 12, 1956, 18:46
► SATURN IN SAGITTARIUS
Born Jan. 12, 18:47 - Jan. 21, 1:47

311

SHIRLEY JONES
American Actress
Venus in Aquarius

1956 AQUARIUS

From January 21, 1:48 through February 19, 16:04

♒ *The Free Lover*

In love and relationships, Aquarius of 1956, you can be a law unto yourself. Unless you can see a rational reason for traditional rules or roles, you may cast them to the winds. The advantage is that you and your partner can happily enjoy tremendous freedom to develop your greatest potential as individuals. The disadvantage is that you and your partner may enjoy so much freedom, one or both of you may feel something is missing in your intimacy as a couple. For you a romance can begin with a rush of intoxicating passion that can lead you and your mate to idealize each other. But infatuation can be superficial and fleeting. You can turn romance into a lasting relationship by making a conscious decision to devote yourself to your mate.

Making the effort necessary to cultivate and renew romance over time can be a pleasure for you. Your principles and beliefs can provide a firm foundation for an enduring commitment. Telling the truth to each other may rank highest among your values, because you can't have trust without it. Likely to believe that love has more to do with actions than feelings, you may measure the amount of love in your life by how much you give—not by how much you get. Your tender empathy toward your mate creates a positive karmic cycle of mutual giving and generosity that extends to your love life.

Just as you value truthfulness in your relationship, frank talk about sex can be an enormous turn on for you. You may like a lover who brazenly tells you exactly what to do. Using blue language in the bedroom can arouse your rebellious impulses and inspire you to be as bad as your word.

The Aquarian man of 1956 appreciates a woman who is romantic and sensitive. You tend to be highly intellectual and may enjoy someone who can stimulate your imagination. With your ingenuity you can help her fulfill your wildest fantasies.

A gallant, philosophical man is a superb counterpart for the 1956 Aquarian woman. Your curiosity and flair for experimentation blend perfectly with his love of exploration and new ideas. With this partner in learning and love you can find true bliss.

AQUARIUS ZODIAC SIGN
YOUR LOVE PLANETS

YOUR ROMANTIC SIDE   p. 696
► VENUS IN PISCES
Born Jan. 21, 1:48 - Feb. 11, 7:45
► VENUS IN ARIES
Born Feb. 11, 7:46 - Feb. 19, 16:04

YOUR SEX DRIVE   p. 722
► MARS IN SAGITTARIUS
Born Jan. 21, 1:48 - Feb. 19, 16:04

YOUR CELEBRITY TWINS   p. 760
Find out the astrological similarities you have with famous people.

YOUR COMPATIBILITY   p. 780
Compare planets to find out how compatible you are in a relationship.

YOUR RELATIONSHIP KARMA   p. 824
► SATURN IN SAGITTARIUS
Born Jan. 21, 1:48 - Feb. 19, 16:04

ANTHONY QUINN
Mexican-American Actor
Venus in Pisces

312

1956 PISCES
From February 19, 16:05 through March 20, 15:19

 ## The Healing Helpmate

Likely to be idealistic and imaginative, 1956 Pisces, you may believe in the healing power of love. You may have a weakness for wounded birds, and the help you give to a friend in distress can lead to a romantic involvement. Able to see the best in others, you tend to come through in the clutch when a mate is down. Such a rescue impulse can make you an indispensable partner, but it can lead you to waste time and energy on a lost cause or to tolerate abuse. In your experience you may have had a few wake-up calls that taught you to trust your gut instincts about people and situations. Maturity tends to strengthen your awareness of the right time for drawing a line in the sand and saying no.

To be true in a relationship you have to be true to yourself and your own values. Because you can be a dreamer and a romantic, there is an innocence about you that needs to be shielded and cherished. Your empathy can be so intense, you may feel your mate's emotions as if they were your own. In a long-term commitment you thrive with a partner who respects your individuality and is protective of your sensitivity—someone who can get outraged at the mere idea of anyone taking advantage of your kindness. For you and your mate intimacy can take on fairy tale sweetness. With one kiss all problems seem to fade into the mist.

You may have a flair for drama and acting, and a night at the theatre or movies can stir your passions. In the bedroom you and your mate may enjoy role playing, enacting romantic scenarios, and fulfilling each other's fantasies.

For you the 1956 Piscean man, an ardent, energetic woman can be the answer to your prayers. It can be so exciting for you to be around someone who has the courage and gumption to take on any challenge. Her verve inspires you to push the outer envelope of your capabilities.

The 1956 Piscean woman tends to feel safe and secure with a devoted, take-charge man. His responsible nature and reliable follow-through assures you of his commitment and love for you. With this organized and capable man, you can establish a stable and orderly lifestyle.

1956 ARIES
From March 20, 15:20 through April 20, 2:42

The Deliberate Devotee

Fast, fiery, and furious is the Arien way in love and romance, but you, Aries of 1956, are unlikely to waste your energy on impulsive bursts of passion. You tend to have unusual stamina and good instincts for maintaining a relationship over the long term. You may be methodical and deliberate as you go about choosing a mate, courting, making a real commitment, and running your household and family life. At each stage of a relationship you may have a strong sense of the appropriate expectations and responsibilities for each partner. But without a steady source of romance and inspiration, carrying out your duties can leave you feeling empty. By showing appreciation for all the things you do, your mate can help you see obligations as acts of love. Such a perspective can turn your relationship into a rewarding source of joy.

Certain values—religious, philosophical, or spiritual—can provide an enduring and enriching bond between you and your partner. Your partnership thrives when the two of you can find a way to make every aspect of your life meaningful.

You and your partner may enjoy an easy free compatibility with an emotional attachment and physical attraction that comes to you instinctively. In the bedroom you may fall into a comfortable groove together, but you both may be interested in exploring new ways to keep sex fresh and exciting.

Sensual pleasures may be a staple in your intimate life. You may have a taste for fine foods, wine, soft music, rosy lighting, robust scents. Your sense of touch tends to be especially responsive. Stroking or a long massage can ease you into the mood for love.

The 1956 Arien man can hardly resist a woman who is gracious and loyal. You may appreciate someone who lavishes you with creature comforts and physical affection. With her robust style she provides you with many pleasant ways to expend your energy.

The Aries woman of 1956 adores a man who is ambitious and self-disciplined. You tend to be attracted to someone who is good at making things happen. With his efficiency and focus this man can inspire you to take on challenges that yield results.

1956 TAURUS

From April 20, 2:43 through May 21, 2:12

♉ *The Delightful Dish*

Your love life, 1960 Taurus, can be just like a big buffet, filled with a wide variety of dishes—all worth sampling. Casual dating can be fun for you, and you may have many friends and an active social life. You tend to get romantically involved with greater ease and speed than most Taureans, and in your day, you may have had more than one love interest going at a time. A penchant for sampling lovers can create some upset. Fortunately, you're likely to have a gift for expressing your intentions with tact and charm. Your breezy style allows you to avoid misunderstandings—a skill that can promote harmony in a long-term relationship.

You may keep a mate at a distance and hold your emotions in reserve until you feel certain that a partner is "the one." Once assured that a mate is trustworthy, you can overcome any reluctance to bare your soul. You tend to be a devoted partner, in it for the long haul. You bring an even-temper and poise to the usual ups and downs of a relationship and family life. For you and your mate the big buffet that is your love life shifts to the range of experiences that the two of you can enjoy together. A relationship allows you to share the wealth of the good earth, and you may eagerly lavish your mate with sensual pleasures.

Variety can be exciting for you, and you may appreciate a mate who tantalizes you with new flavors, scents, sounds, and sights. You may also have an enormous sexual curiosity and can enjoy experimenting with a range of daring techniques, positions, and pleasure-enhancers. Lotions, oils, and erotic accessories can increase your sensuous excitement.

The Taurean man of 1960 appreciates a woman who is charming and inquisitive—all the better to scout out things that can thrill you. With her, you can discover the outer expanses of your capacity for joy and return the favor many times over.

A man with a genius for romance can win the heart of the 1960 Taurean woman. For you, it really is the thought that counts. You tend to appreciate a partner whose gifts and gestures show just how well he knows you and how much he loves you.

CARROLL BAKER
American Actress
Sun in Gemini

313

1956 GEMINI

From May 21, 2:13 through June 21, 10:23

♊ *The Irrepressible Optimist*

It's no use hiding your feelings from your heartthrob, 1956 Gemini. Your sign rules communication, and any secrets you may have tend to betray themselves through your body language and often hilarious Freudian slips. With your passion, charm, and spontaneity you can capture the heart of a new love or keep a current sweetheart riveted. Likely to have a brilliant, creative mind, you may interpret your romantic prospects with unusual humor and optimism. If the odds of getting or staying together with the object of your affections are one-in-a-million, you might think, "So I've got a chance...." Where there's a will, there's a way. Such a sunny outlook enables you to keep a positive outlook when a relationship goes through any rough patches.

In a serious romance you have a wonderful gift for making things right when anything goes wrong. You may have an endearingly creative flair for delivering an apology, and your partner may let you off the hook way too easily. Perceptive and sensitive to a mate's feelings, you may have a good idea when not to press your luck. Making love to your partner allows you to feel your emotional attachment on such a deeply intuitive level, it can defy even your understanding.

Talking can be as good as sex for you, or at least a form of foreplay. A meaningful romantic relationship can blossom in a conversation that lasts until dawn. Having something to figure out can be stimulating. The mystery of your lover's body and her responses are enigmas that you may never lose interest in unraveling.

An imaginative, moody woman can be highly enticing to the 1956 Gemini man. Her intensity may intrigue you, and you may enjoy the challenge of getting in sync with her changeable feelings. She may rely on your cheery outlook and generously reward your ability to brighten her disposition.

The man with an electrifying intellect and strong intuition presents the 1956 Gemini woman with an irresistibly seductive combination. Not everyone can keep up with your mental pace, but with his original ideas and dead-on instincts, this fellow can push your outer envelope.

YUL BRYNNER
Russian Actor
Sun in Cancer

314

1956 CANCER
From June 21, 10:24 through July 22, 21:19

 The Perceptive Partner

With your affectionate disposition and seductive aura, Cancerian of 1956, you may lead a charmed love life. You may have an unusual talent for resolving conflicts, healing rifts, and getting a relationship on the right track—a gift that can enable you to accumulate good romantic karma, especially if you use it to help dear friends and family members. An exquisite sensitivity to other people's thoughts and feelings—bordering on psychic perception—allows you to anticipate a partner's needs. You tend to have a vivid imagination that lets you fulfill your sweetheart's fantasies with originality and dramatic impact. Your powers of concentration and willingness to listen can make your mate feel truly heard and respected.

Sweetly but compellingly persuasive, you tend to make it a pleasure for a mate to give you exactly what you want. When a partner proves exceptionally stubborn or is just fixing for a fight, the frustration you may feel can be overwhelming. In that case, you may fall back on the ultimate Cancerian strategy and beat a temporary retreat into your shell. After a cooling-down period, tempers tend to ease, and disputes tend to work themselves out. You can channel any heated passion that may remain by engaging in a long-celebrated custom for making up after an argument—lovemaking.

You may be a sentimental soul, tending to brighten at reminders of sweet occasions and any successes you and your mate have shared. You may be especially responsive when a mate shows thoughtfulness or affection toward someone who is dear to you, such as a parent or a child.

The Cancerian man of 1956 tends to feel most comfortable with a woman who is nurturing and tenacious. You appreciate someone who keeps you in mind as she goes through her daily routine. Her creativity in tending to your needs assures you of her devotion.

The Cancerian woman born in 1956 can find fulfillment with a man who is romantic and indulgent. You tend to enjoy someone with a gentle demeanor and a flair for creating a soothing atmosphere. Able to go with the flow of your moods, he can ease you into happiness.

1956 LEO
From July 22, 21:20 through August 23, 4:14

 The Animal Attraction

You have an electrifying appeal, Leo of 1956, and an unpredictability that can arouse a lover's urge to capture you. The first lesson for any mate who hopes to have half a chance of holding onto you is this—you cannot be owned. Held, yes, and you hope frequently, in strong, loving arms, but not held onto. You need a free reign, flexibility, and lots of breathing space in a relationship. You may be among the members of your generation who pioneered the alternative lifestyle. Any marriage for you is likely to be a highly original arrangement, tending to reflect your creativity in establishing a routine that allows you and your mate to express yourselves as individuals.

When you feel secure in your freedom, you can be a fiercely loyal partner. The key to success in your commitment is trust, ingenuity, and plenty of good, old-fashioned animal attraction. It takes a unique person to have the right chemistry for you and the ability to strike the kind of balance you need in a partnership. With that in mind, you may regard your partner as special, precious, and clearly irreplaceable. Together, you can be a powerful and charismatic team, able to work long and hard to realize your goals. The privacy of the bedroom allows you and your mate to fully experience the deep intensity of your bond.

Sex can be an intoxicating and even spiritual experience for you, an opportunity to dissolve into a feeling of oneness. You thrive with a mate who can minister to you with imagination and erotic abandon. You may enjoy unusual or exotic techniques.

A charming and intelligent woman can spark the interest of the 1956 Leo man. You appreciate a self-sufficient partner who can be savvy and seductive. Generous with support, she offers you the reliability and objectivity of a true friend and the passion of a true love.

The Leo woman of 1956 adores the man who encourages her to dream. You tend to be idealistic and a little rebellious, and you thrive with a man who casts sunbeams on your parade. With his lively imagination and romantic impulses this man makes it a pleasure to love him.

1956 VIRGO

From August 23, 4:15 through September 23, 1:34

The Steamy Sweetheart

As a 1956 Virgo, you've got an abundant supply of steamed heat to fuel your romantic engine. You thrive in a relationship that is founded on friendship and allows for a two-way flow of communication. When you need to vent your feelings, you and your mate may rely on each other for sympathy and an objective point of view. Sometimes physical affection is the best remedy for a build-up of bottled energy, and you may have a healthy sexual appetite. Your ability to harmonize the ease of friendship with the passion of romance enables you to have a well-rounded relationship, based on a realistic understanding of each partner's needs.

You tend to be idealistic about relationships, and are willing to work hard to be a reliable and supportive partner. When things don't go as expected in love or in life in general, you may become cranky and critical of your partner. Perfectionism tends to be a symptom that you're under a lot of stress. Being open to a mate's friendly feedback can help you to shift gears and get a healthy venting session under way. Emotional cooperation like this enables you and

your mate to maintain balance in your relationship over the long term. In the bedroom you may take pride in your ability to give your partner perfect service and satisfaction.

Working together on creative projects can enhance your emotional bond, renew your attraction for each other, and fire up your passion for sensual pleasures. Sharing erotic fantasies can give you and your mate new ideas to add to your store of information on how to thrill each other.

For the Virgo man of 1956, a tender, intuitive woman can be a comfortable companion. You tend to be most attracted to a lady who radiates with inner beauty and wisdom. With her ability to tune into your mood and preferences she enables both of you to enjoy the very best.

An intensely seductive man appeals to the Virgo woman born in 1956. With his flair for creating a romantic atmosphere, he can divert your attention from the demanding details of your routine. This man makes sure you get your recommended daily requirement of racy relaxation.

VIRGO ZODIAC SIGN
YOUR LOVE PLANETS

YOUR ROMANTIC SIDE   p. 696
▶ **VENUS IN CANCER**
Born Aug. 23, 4:15 - Sept. 08, 9:22
▶ **VENUS IN LEO**
Born Sept. 08, 9:23 - Sept. 23, 1:34

YOUR SEX DRIVE   p. 722
▶ **MARS IN PISCES**
Born Aug. 23, 4:15 - Sept. 23, 1:34

YOUR CELEBRITY TWINS   p. 760
Find out the astrological similarities you have with famous people.

YOUR COMPATIBILITY   p. 780
Compare planets to find out how compatible you are in a relationship.

YOUR RELATIONSHIP KARMA   p. 824
▶ **SATURN IN SCORPIO**
Born Aug. 23, 4:15 - Sept. 23, 1:34

315

DEBORAH KERR
Scottish Actress
Sun in Libra

1956 LIBRA

From September 23, 1:35 through October 23, 10:33

The Poised Powerhouse

Only your heartthrob may know for sure, 1956 Libra, what a force of nature you can be. At social gatherings you tend to carry yourself with subtle elegance and poise. As self-contained as you may be, though, you are likely to radiate with exuberant passion. Librans tend to avoid conflict, and sometimes, for fear of your partner's reaction, you may hold your tongue and temper about something important to you. Because you tend to be a high-energy person, stifling your feelings and concerns can create unhealthy stress for you and tension between you and your honey.

Relying on your natural gifts of diplomacy enables you to assert yourself with tact and sensitivity to your mate's feelings. With your humility and compassion you can work out fair compromises that benefit your relationship and take account of both partners' needs. A vigorous wellness regimen can be great for you and your relationship. Partnering up for regular exercise and outdoor activities allows you to enjoy time together, while feeling rosy, refreshed, and vital. Enchantingly seductive, you have an unusually imaginative approach to

wooing and intimacy. For you lovemaking can be a beautiful experience, and just to look at your partner may fill you with burning desire.

Likely to have an artistic temperament, you can be susceptible to poetic sweet nothings, whispered in your ears. Music can warm up your mood, and you may be highly responsive to rhythm. When you're out together dancing, cheek-to-cheek or otherwise, your romantic energy can soar to heavenly heights.

The Libra man born in 1956 enjoys a woman who has a sunny, regal bearing. You may enjoy making a striking impact when you go out together, and with this lovely lady you can count yourself among the beautiful people. Her languid sensuality can rouse your spirit and warm your heart.

An empathetic, sensitive man can be the perfect partner for the 1956 Libra woman. You can benefit from a having a mate who can tune into your mood and sense when there's something on your mind. With this caring man you can bare your soul and receive loving support.

LIBRA ZODIAC SIGN
YOUR LOVE PLANETS

YOUR ROMANTIC SIDE   p. 696
▶ **VENUS IN LEO**
Born Sept. 23, 1:35 - Oct. 06, 3:11
▶ **VENUS IN LIBRA**
Born Oct. 06, 3:12 - Oct. 23, 10:33

YOUR SEX DRIVE   p. 722
▶ **MARS IN PISCES**
Born Sept. 23, 1:35 - Oct. 23, 10:33

YOUR CELEBRITY TWINS   p. 760
Find out the astrological similarities you have with famous people.

YOUR COMPATIBILITY   p. 780
Compare planets to find out how compatible you are in a relationship.

YOUR RELATIONSHIP KARMA   p. 824
▶ **SATURN IN SCORPIO**
Born Sept. 23, 1:35 - Oct. 10, 15:12
▶ **SATURN IN SAGITTARIUS**
Born Oct. 10, 15:13 - Oct. 23, 10:33

KIRK DOUGLAS
American Actor
Sun in Sagittarius

1956 SCORPIO
From October 23, 10:34 through November 22, 7:49

♏ The Lucky Lover

You can be a serious love magnet, 1956 Scorpio. Tending to radiate with a sex appeal so powerful and hypnotic, admirers may flock to you. Falling in love can tempt you to lavish a heartthrob with extravagant gifts and favors, and you may make great sacrifices for the sake of your relationship. To avoid being taken advantage of you may have adopted strong personal standards that enable you to discriminate between an idle infatuation and a romance with serious potential. Over the years you may have become an excellent judge of character. Maturity and wisdom tend to make you lucky in love. Then again, religiously cultivating the honesty in your relationship allows you and your mate to make your own luck.

Your gift for healing and regenerating love creates a stable ground in which your partnership can take root. You are likely to have a strong instinct for the natural lifecycles of love, and this awareness allows you to ease the stress of any changes you and your mate may undergo over the years. When you sense that you and your mate are falling into the same-old same-old, you have the willpower and creativity to revive the romance and launch your relationship into a new and exciting phase. Through lovemaking you can invite your mate to join you in a fantasy world, filled with bustier-ripping passion.

Mystical or occult practices allow you to feel deeply in tune with your mate. You might enjoy Tantric sex, especially meditative exercises that allow you to breathe in sync with each other. A long massage can lift you to the peak of pleasure.

A woman who is gracious and artistic can be an attractive mate for the 1956 Scorpio man. You thrive with someone who gives high priority to the well-being of your relationship. With this lovely lady you can fill your life together with harmony and creative beauty.

A spiritual, compassionate man exudes a compelling power of attraction for the Scorpio woman of 1956. You can deeply relate to someone with a sense of wonder and awe about the world around you. With his ability to sense your feelings he strikes you as a true soul mate.

1956 SAGITTARIUS
From November 22, 7:50 through December 21, 20:58

♐ The Sincere Soul Mate

You may be a master in the art of flirting, 1977 Sagittarius. In social situations you can bubble over with energy, charm, and a sense of humor that can be infectious and utterly irrepressible. While you wouldn't dream of hurting a soul, you can sometimes get carried away, push a joke or philosophical argument a little too far, and overwhelm others—including your mate. Likely to be unusually sensitive to people's feelings, you can quickly pick up on any offense taken and make prompt amends. With your sunny, sincere, and well-meaning disposition, it would be virtually impossible—if not downright cruel—to reject an apology from you.

Your flirtatious appeal is unlikely to ruffle a serious partner. A committed relationship tends to bring out your sober, industrious side. Your devotion and instinctive honesty assures your mate of your trustworthiness and provides a rock-solid foundation for your relationship. You may have a one-track mind for the safety and security of your mate and loved ones. In the face of any threat to their health or happiness, you can be fiercely protective. The love you feel for your mate tends to energize you. You may have a poetic sensibility that allows you to notice the beauty in every day life and makes you a dreamy, romantic lover.

You may have a weakness for beauty, and a day at an art museum or a night at the theater can stir your ardor. For you lovemaking can be melodious. Music can strongly influence your mood, and you may love to cuddle in bed while harmonious tones reverberate around you.

The Sagittarius man of 1956 thrives with a woman who is soulful and intense. You appreciate someone who is driven by her romantic passions. With her aura of mystery this simmering seductress can entice you to embark on a never-ending expedition to explore her secrets.

The Sagittarius woman born in 1956 adores a man who is powerful and courageous. You admire a person who pursues his interests with intensity, especially when one of them is you. With his enthusiasm for trying new things every day with this bold man can be an amazing adventure.

Elvis and Priscilla Presley

In the 1950s, before Elvis Presley was known as "the King," he was called "Elvis the Pelvis" because of his blatantly sexual style of gyrating his hips when singing. Teenage girls swooned, and their fathers fumed. Elvis was a cultural phenomenon, but of all the women he could have had, the woman who first touched his soul was not yet a woman.

Elvis first laid eyes on Priscilla Beaulieu when she was only fourteen years old. Drafted into the Army, he was staying in an off-base house in West Germany, and she was the daughter of an Air Force captain stationed nearby. Elvis had parties at his house, and through a mutual friend, she was invited over. Later, after Priscilla left, Elvis said to his guitar man Charlie Hodge, "Did you see the structure of her face? It's almost like everything I've looked for in a woman in my life." For the next six months Cilla, as Elvis called her, was chauffeured back and forth to his house. She mingled with the other visitors until late in the evening when he gave her a secret signal. Then the two would go off to his bedroom for private talk and cuddling.

Back in the States, Priscilla began to adapt to his love of the nightlife. She began taking amphetamines and sleeping pills so she could stay up all night long with him. By 1963 Elvis convinced her parents that she should move to Memphis to finish high school while living at Graceland. In December 1966 he presented her with a 3½ carat diamond, and the two finally married on May 1, 1967 in Las Vegas. Exactly nine months later Priscilla gave birth to Lisa Marie Presley, and the new arrival changed the relationship between the two of them— their sex life became nonexistent.

There were rumors of Elvis' affairs, of

" *Well, sir, I happen to be very fond of her.*

I guess you might say I need someone to talk to."

ELVIS explaining his intentions to Priscilla's father

course, some going all the way back to before their marriage—most notably the one about Ann-Margret and their incredible "chemistry" in the film *Viva Las Vegas*—and more rumors of others stepping in to make sure the King's reputation wasn't sullied.

To counter Elvis' rumored affairs and his very real drugging, Priscilla had an affair with a karate teacher in the early '70s. When she filed for divorce in 1973 it was as though Elvis had been dealt a hard blow, one that shook him to the core. He couldn't (or wouldn't) tell her how he felt, but his true feelings showed up on stage in his songs, such as "Separate Ways" and "Hurt."

Even after the divorce, they never really ended the relationship. They would still call each other to talk as friends. But where Priscilla went on to create a successful life and business career for herself, Elvis continued his downward spiral until his death on August 16, 1977.

According to the medical examiner's report, it was a girlfriend, Ginger Alden, who found the King dead on the dressing room floor at Graceland.

A few years after his death, Priscilla Presley wrote in her memoirs about the early days with Elvis: "Blinded by love, I saw none of his faults or weaknesses. He was to become the passion of my life."

317

▶ READ ABOUT PAUL MCCARTNEY AND LINDA EASTMAN ON PAGE 416 ▶ READ ABOUT JOHN LENNON AND YOKO ONO ON PAGE 423

1957

- ⍟ OBSCENITY
- ⍟ JERRY LEE LEWIS
- ⍟ BY LOVE POSSESSED
- ⍟ SEXY REXY
- ⍟ AN AFFAIR TO REMEMBER
- ⍟ APRIL LOVE
- ⍟ WAKE UP, LITTLE SUSIE

EVENTS

In the US two lawsuits raised the issue of whether laws against obscenity were unconstitutional.

Elizabeth Taylor divorced her second husband, Michael Wilding and two days later married her third, Mike Todd. Jerry Lee Lewis raised eyebrows when he married his cousin Myra Gale Brown, age 13, while he was still married to his first wife.

In a high point in the fairy tale marriage of Grace Kelly and the Prince of Monaco, the new Princess gave birth to her first child, Princess Caroline. Oona Chaplin gave birth to her sixth child. Charlie Chaplin was 36 years older than his wife and proud of his fertility. Gina Lollobrigida gave birth to Milko II, baptized by the newspapers "the Eighth King of Rome." Despite all of these birthdays though, the first transmission of a live birth on British television created a scandal over voyeurism.

POP CULTURE

Readers were lapping up *By Love Possessed*, the story of an old-fashioned attorney trying to be objective about his world. *Compulsion* was based on the "Crime of the Century," the senseless 1924 Leopold-Loeb murder of Bobby Franks. In the French novel *Spoiled Children* a French girl finds love at an American college.

Director Billy Wilder scored again with *Love in the Afternoon*, in which a middle-aged playboy falls for the daughter of a private eye who's been hired to investigate him. *An Affair to*

Hot Couple

Remember debuted with a playboy and an engaged singer meeting on a cruise, but their plan to find each other six months later is disrupted when she is hit by a taxi and disabled. *The Garden of Eden*, a British nudist film, was shown in several theaters, the local authorities allowing it after deciding that nudity and sex were two different things.

Elvis Presley had the charts all sewn up with "All Shook Up," "Jailhouse Rock," and "Teddy Bear." "Love Letters in the Sand" and "April Love" were two ballad hits for Pat Boone. The Everly Brothers' hit "Wake Up, Little Susie," the story of a pair of teens falling asleep at a drive-in, was briefly banned in Boston.

REX HARRISON & KAY KENDALL

Rex Harrison was a notorious womanizer and was christened "Sexy Rexy" for his lothario-like antics. Before the British actor married actress Kay Kendall, he had already been involved in a sex scandal that purportedly led to the suicide of one of his prior co-stars. He divorced his first wife, actress Lilli Palmer, to marry the bubbly redhead, despite Kendall's terminal leukemia.

Kendall never knew she was sick, as Rex and her doctor conspired to keep it from her. She lived the good life until the end. Rex secretly longed to reconcile with his ex-wife after Kendall passed, but the spark was never re-ignited.

SEE ALSO
▶ HAROLD PINTER & ANTONIA FRASER *Page 515*

318

1957 CAPRICORN
From December 21, 1956 20:59 through January 20, 1957 7:38
(December 1957 Capricorns, see 1958 Capricorn)

♑ *The Amorous Sensualist*

Blessed with an abundant appreciation of beauty, you 1957 Goats are extremely tasteful. Your central motivation may be to enjoy a life filled with sensual pleasure. It's only natural, then, that you do well with a partner who's as refined and discerning as you are. When you join forces with a mate who enjoys gourmet food and fine wine, it is a wonderful means of doubling your pleasure. Maybe that's why you have taken such great care to find the perfect person with whom to share your life.

You probably have a high profile, and do best with a mate who is comfortable in the spotlight. A natural leader like you needs a partner who is able to uphold an image of dignity and respectability. To some degree, you expect your relationship to serve as a role model for others to follow. In your private life, you're wonderfully affectionate and amorous. Age probably won't slow you down in the bedroom. You're the kind of lover who gets better as you get older, and do best with a similar mate.

When somebody wants to catch your eye, they should understand that you are incredibly responsive to sensual stimulus. Therefore, your suitor would be wise to wear musky cologne whenever they are in your presence. Offering to share a gourmet lunch is also a wonderful means of getting acquainted with you. If things progress to an intimate level, your lover should understand that ardent caresses make you purr with pleasure. Foreplay isn't a luxury for you—it's a necessity!

As a 1957 male Goat, you are attracted to two types of women. The first is athletic, independent, and adventurous. The second is traditional, refined, and sensual. Whichever kind of female you like best, she should be enthusiastic and creative. You want a mate who fuels your own zest for life.

If you're a woman Capricorn who was born in 1957, you appreciate a man who is reliable, steady, and affectionate. You need to know where you stand with your mate, and resent males with roving eyes. Guys with deep, sexy voices turn you on, and you'd do very well with a partner who likes to whisper in your ear as a prelude to lovemaking.

CAPRICORN ZODIAC SIGN
YOUR LOVE PLANETS

YOUR ROMANTIC SIDE — p. 696
▶ VENUS IN SAGITTARIUS
Born Dec. 21, 1956 20:59 - Jan. 12, 1957 20:22
▶ VENUS IN CAPRICORN
Born Jan. 12, 20:23 - Jan. 20, 7:38

YOUR SEX DRIVE — p. 722
▶ MARS IN ARIES
Born Dec. 21, 1956 20:59 - Jan. 20, 1957 7:38

YOUR CELEBRITY TWINS — p. 760
Find out the astrological similarities you have with famous people.

YOUR COMPATIBILITY — p. 780
Compare planets to find out how compatible you are in a relationship.

YOUR RELATIONSHIP KARMA — p. 824
▶ SATURN IN SAGITTARIUS
Born Dec. 21, 1956 20:59 - Jan. 20, 1957 7:38

1957 AQUARIUS
From January 20, 7:39 through February 18, 21:57

♒ *The True Romantic*

You 1957 Aquarians are among the most sensitive folks in the zodiac. Your intuition is especially strong when it comes to romance. Somehow, you manage to gravitate toward people who share your dreamy, idealistic view of life. It's no wonder why your relationships have had a fairy tale quality to them! You want to live happily ever after with a soul mate who understands your needs on a psychic level. You want a symbiotic partnership.

You're quite a spiritual person and do best with a partner who shares your belief in a Higher Power. Performing volunteer work with your mate may be especially rewarding for you. Using love as a means to shut out the real world has never been your style. You'd rather fight injustices with the help of your mate. People with magnetic auras really turn you on, and your sex life will only be enhanced if you pair up with a dynamic, charismatic type. Power is a definite aphrodisiac for you.

If a suitor wants to attract or keep your interest, they should always be engaged in the world around them. Your idea of a great first date might be watching a controversial documentary. If the vibes between you are strong enough, you may propose discussing the film at a coffee shop afterwards. As to your sex life, you want a partner who is vocal and responsive. A lover who gives you constant encouragement and praise in the bedroom fills you with delight. You're also aroused by a partner whose lovemaking is masterful and assured.

As a male Water Bearer who was born in 1957, you are happiest with a woman who is elegant and proper. Women who wear their hearts on their sleeves make you distinctly uncomfortable. You also appreciate females who march to the beat of their own drummer. A courageous and independent partner is the perfect complement to your own forthright personality.

You 1957 female Aquarians do well with men who put a great emphasis on home life. Although you are quite outgoing and adventurous, it's important for you to maintain a comfortable and settled abode. A partner who seeks to create a harmonious domestic life suits you beautifully.

JOANNE WOODWARD
American Actress
Mars in Aquarius

AQUARIUS ZODIAC SIGN
YOUR LOVE PLANETS

YOUR ROMANTIC SIDE — p. 696
▶ VENUS IN CAPRICORN
Born Jan. 20, 7:39 - Feb. 05, 20:15
▶ VENUS IN AQUARIUS
Born Feb. 05, 20:16 - Feb. 18, 21:57

YOUR SEX DRIVE — p. 722
▶ MARS IN ARIES
Born Jan. 20, 7:39 - Jan. 28, 14:18
▶ MARS IN TAURUS
Born Jan. 28, 14:19 - Feb. 18, 21:57

YOUR CELEBRITY TWINS — p. 760
Find out the astrological similarities you have with famous people.

YOUR COMPATIBILITY — p. 780
Compare planets to find out how compatible you are in a relationship.

YOUR RELATIONSHIP KARMA — p. 824
▶ SATURN IN SAGITTARIUS
Born Jan. 20, 7:39 - Feb. 18, 21:57

319

JACK KEROUAC
American Writer
Sun in Pisces

1957 PISCES
From February 18, 21:58 through March 20, 21:15

♓ *The Sexual Healer*

As a 1957 Pisces, you indeed possess profound healing powers. According to you, love is the cure for all of the world's ills. That's why romantic relationships have played such an important part in your life. You're very attracted to people who are emotionally scarred in some way. Healing your mate's wounds is an exciting challenge for you. You do best in relationships that are fuelled by compassion and sympathy. Partnerships that involve lots of petty fights hold no interest for you.

Sex has a rejuvenating effect on you, so it's important that you pair up with somebody who has a reverent attitude toward lovemaking. You wouldn't do well in a relationship in which sex was treated as a mere form of recreation. A mate who sees physical intimacy as a means to connect on an emotional and spiritual level suits you very nicely. When your relationship is undergoing anxiety or tension, you may propose sex as a means to get all of your frustrations out. It's hard for you to retain resentments after merging with your partner.

Caring, generous acts never fail to attract your attention. A person who is determined to make the world a better place has a good chance of winning your affection. You're also quite interested in the arts, and are drawn to suitors who express themselves creatively. If someone wants to arouse your passion, they should take you out on the dance floor. Moving to music never fails to whet your sexual appetite.

As a male Piscean who was born in 1957, you appreciate females who are open-minded and humane. Materialistic women leave you cold. You far prefer a lady who gives thanks for her blessings, and seeks to share them with those less fortunate than herself. A woman with deep, soulful eyes never fails to make your heart pound.

You 1957 female Fish seek a man who knows his own mind. Wishy-washy guys drive you crazy. You do best with a partner who is extremely physical. Cerebral types who can't stand to bestow or receive affection leave you cold. You want a guy who not only loves to be hugged, kissed, and caressed, but is eager to return these favors.

1957 ARIES
From March 20, 21:16 through April 20, 8:40

♈ *The Solicitous Suitor*

As a 1957 Ram, you're always eager to perform a service for your beloved. Nothing gives you more pleasure than attending to your partner's needs, no matter how great or small. You're especially eager to make their sexual dreams come true, and want a relationship in which fantasies are taken seriously. You'd never laugh at your mate's desires, no matter how outlandish or strange. Similarly, you expect that your needs will be respected and valued by your partner. A relationship that is riddled with taboos would be difficult for you to sustain.

You want a partnership that makes you feel useful and needed. A cooperative person who often asks you for advice is your ideal partner. There's a good chance that your marriage will have elements of a student-teacher relationship. You have a strong attraction toward people who admire and respect your abilities, and enjoy dispensing wisdom to your romantic partner.

When somebody wants to win favor with you, they should ask you about your field of expertise. You're extremely flattered when people express interest in your work. You like to take the lead when it comes to sex, but a suitor can encourage you to make the first move by wearing red. Wearing this color in front of you is akin to waving a flag in front of a bull! A suitor with well-defined muscles also has a good chance with you, as you love athletic physiques.

As a 1957 male Ram, you enjoy a woman who is dynamic and energetic. You're quite physical yourself, and need a partner who can keep up with you, both in and out of the bedroom. Sweet, demure females also excite your imagination. Ultimately, you want a partner who welcomes your advice and likes to rest problems on your capable shoulders.

A man who is witty, smart, and interesting stands the best chance with you 1957 female Ariens. Dumb jocks really turn you off, as you want a partner who can provide you with plenty of stimulating conversation. You're not intimidated by a man who is reluctant to settle down. Restless types pose an exciting challenge for you. Nothing makes your pulse pound like a wild rebel!

1957 TAURUS
From April 20, 8:41 through May 21, 8:09

The Unwitting Dreamboat

You 1957 Bulls are rarely aware of your own charms. It simply never occurs to you that you could be an object of lust. However, if you would take a careful look around, you'd notice that several of your friends positively light up whenever you enter the room. Certain colleagues tend to blush in your presence. Even shopkeepers tend to stammer when waiting on you. Chalk it up to charisma! Luckily, you never use your sexual magnetism to manipulate or control people, and prefer relationships in which each partner has a particular sphere of influence.

There's a good chance that you prefer to hold court at home. You probably possess a great many domestic skills, and enjoy cooking and decorating to suit yourself. A partner who celebrates and appreciates these gifts is an ideal match for you. You have a respect for artists, and would do well with somebody who works in a creative field. A mate with a demanding career doesn't bother you, so long as they come straight home after a long day's work. You want to be the shelter from your spouse's storms.

If someone wants to catch your eye, they should exhibit some sort of creative talent. You are incredibly turned on by expressive people with vivid imaginations. It's possible that you're a little reserved sexually, and you would do well with a mate who takes a slow but steady pace toward lovemaking. High-pressure tactics won't work with you. Slow, persistent kisses along your neck never fail to drive you wild with passion.

Women who are tenacious, sentimental, and dependable appeal most to you 1957 male Bulls. You also appreciate females who are broad-minded and versatile. Above all, however, your partner must possess an artistic skill of some kind. Nothing turns you on like a lady who can conjure beauty out of thin air.

If you're a female Taurus who was born in 1957, you enjoy men who are quick-witted and versatile. You love a guy who has a snappy comeback for every remark. Men who are tender, protective, and sensitive also hold a special place in your heart. Ultimately, your partner must have a strong spiritual core.

321

1957 GEMINI
From May 21, 8:10 through June 21, 16:20

The Sentimental Homebody

Unlike Twins born in other years, you 1957 Geminis are firmly rooted to home. Your main focus may be maintaining a stable domestic environment in which a romantic relationship can thrive. Not surprisingly, you do best with a reliable and accomplished partner who is more interested in keeping the peace than in stirring up controversy. From your perspective, a strong relationship can be the one constant in an otherwise chaotic universe. Consequently, you're very selective when it comes to choosing a marriage partner.

The one area in which you are adventurous is sex. You're always willing to experiment with different techniques, and welcome a partner who is eager to expand their sexual horizons. You have a tendency to link sex with love, so one-night stands really are not for you. When you do settle down with your soul mate, though, all of your inhibitions melt away. It's easy for you to experiment when you're in the confines of a loving relationship.

Attracting your attention is as simple as bringing up a controversial issue. You love

stimulating debates, and you are often aroused by people who can defend their viewpoints in an ardent manner. Once a suitor engages you mentally, they should make their sexual attraction known. Often, you see people's interest in you as merely friendly. Once a suitor has captured your fancy, you're perfectly ready and willing to make the first move toward lovemaking.

You 1957 male Twins do well with women who are imaginative and exhilarating. Although you want a partner who enjoys a secure home life, she shouldn't be afraid to disagree with you. A spirited debate acts like an aphrodisiac on you. You're also drawn to dreamy, feminine types who express themselves through creative media like poetry, painting, and photography.

If you're a female Gemini who was born in 1957, you want a man who is a bit guarded about his emotions. You're flattered by a partner who only lets down his guard when he's in private with you. You also appreciate a guy with a goofy sense of humor, and you can be quite aroused when he breaks into a loud guffaw.

IAN FLEMING
English Writer
Sun in Gemini

MITZI GAYNOR
American Actress
Venus and Mars in Cancer

322

1957 CANCER
From June 21, 16:21 through July 23, 3:14

♋ The Good Provider

Nobody takes their romantic obligations more seriously than you do, 1957 Cancer. When you're in love, you do everything in your power to provide a secure and comfortable lifestyle for your partner. Being a good provider fills you with a sense of pride. You love showering your partner with luxuries, and may even defer marriage so that you can put together a nest egg for your future family. You want your relationship to rest on a secure foundation.

Although you are very money conscious, your first priority is your romantic relationship. You prize your partner above all else, and make sure that they are aware of your devotion. Expressing your love through actions and words is second nature to you. Nobody could ever accuse you of being a cold fish! For you, relationships are a way to close ranks against a world that is sometimes harsh and unfeeling. Therefore, you do best with a mate who views you as an ally instead of an adversary.

When somebody wants to catch your eye, they would be wise to demonstrate an interest in children. You have a special fondness for children, and respect people who are dedicated to their welfare. Once a suitor has made their romantic intentions clear, they make the first move. You tend to be a little shy in love. Planting a tender kiss on your lips in the moonlight is a wonderful way to capture your heart. Once your passion has been brought to the surface, you enjoy long, languorous lovemaking sessions that can last all night.

If you're a male Cancer who was born in 1957, you do best with a woman who is enchanting, scintillating, and dramatic. You really enjoy the company of a strong-willed woman. Moody, secretive, and introverted females also fascinate you. In the final analysis, you want a partner who makes you feel as though you're the only man for her.

A man who is goal-oriented, commanding, and passionate is perfect for you 1957 female Crabs. You adore a guy that exudes animal magnetism, and enjoy basking in the rays of his warm personality. A mate who demands lots of tender loving care is a perfect match for your nurturing soul.

1957 LEO
From July 23, 3:15 through August 23, 10:07

♌ The Anxious Romantic

Lively, colorful, and zany, you 1957 Lions are the life of the party. You're always looking for new ways to entertain the crowd. Sometimes you're so busy clowning for the masses that you put romance on the back burner. Once you do meet your soul mate, however, you'll focus all of your energies on him or her. Love is no laughing matter for you. When someone captures your heart, you feel slightly vulnerable.

Although you thrive in front of large groups of people, intimate encounters are a little daunting for you. It's hard for you to reveal your secrets and weaknesses to one person. Therefore, you do best in a relationship that is based on unconditional love. A partner that makes you feel comfortable and free in any setting is your ideal mate. You tend to be overly self-critical. Hopefully, your spouse will teach you to be more kind and forgiving towards yourself.

Anybody seeking your affection should go out of their way to put you at ease in an intimate setting. Bringing you your favorite drink or saving you a comfortable chair is a terrific way to break the ice. Romantically, you like to be the one who calls the shots. Therefore, your suitor would be wise to put themselves in a convenient position for a kiss when you're finally alone together. As a 1957 Leo, you like plenty of foreplay, so any admirer should remember this when your relationship heats up.

A wide variety of women appeal to you 1957 male Lions. You mainly enjoy females who are modest, discerning, and intelligent. Girls with brains really turn you on. You also like women who are elegant and attractive. Females who are generous and gifted also hold a special place in your heart. Mainly, though, you want a mate who will comfort you when you're down.

You female Leos who were born in 1957 like two types of men. The first is dominant and energetic, and the second is serious and intellectual. Whichever type of guy you pick to be your partner, he should take your creative talents seriously. You want to be recognized as a multi-faceted woman, and need an appreciative man who celebrates you as such.

1957 VIRGO
From August 23, 10:08 through September 23, 7:25

♍ *The Passionate Powerhouse*

When it comes to love, you 1957 Virgins bide your time carefully. You like to wait and watch for romantic interests who are best suited to your discerning temperament. Then, when you spot the right candidate, you can focus on the object of your desire like a laser. You view relationships as the ultimate enhancement to life. Finding a mate who deepens your appreciation for simple pleasures is very important to you. That's why you do best with a partner whose tastes are as refined and elegant as yours.

You were probably born with a great deal of restless energy. Having a secure home life can ease the tension that builds up inside. A mate who takes pleasure in making your home warm and inviting is ideal for you. There's a good chance that you're aggressive and outgoing in your professional life. Coming home to a loving partner will give you the necessary sustenance to meet all of your lofty work goals. For you, a good relationship is an excellent counterbalance to a challenging career.

A suitor who compliments you on your taste, celebrates your ambition, and admires your practicality should be able to seduce you in no time. You do well with a partner who is sure of themselves and likes to guide you into unfamiliar sexual territory. You're especially aroused by someone who wears spotless clothing, has shiny hair, and smells of soap. You've always equated cleanliness with sexiness. A person who uses foul language has very little chance with you, since you detest profanity.

Women who are stylish, sociable, and sensitive stand a good chance with you male Virgos who were born in 1957. You also admire a woman who has a strong hypnotic aura around her. Ultimately, you want a mate who is devoted and tender. It's also important for your woman to support your career ambitions.

If you're a 1957 female Virgo, you're looking for a man who is detail-oriented and attentive. You love it when a guy notices that you're wearing a new dress or that you've changed your hairstyle. A partner who recognizes your inner beauty, as well as your outward charms, is an ideal match for you.

VIRGO ZODIAC SIGN
YOUR LOVE PLANETS

YOUR ROMANTIC SIDE — p. 696
► VENUS IN LIBRA
Born Aug. 23, 10:08 - Sept. 14, 6:19
► VENUS IN SCORPIO
Born Sept. 14, 6:20 - Sept. 23, 7:25

YOUR SEX DRIVE — p. 722
► MARS IN LIBRA
Born Aug. 23, 10:08 - Sept. 23, 7:25

YOUR CELEBRITY TWINS — p. 760
Find out the astrological similarities you have with famous people.

YOUR COMPATIBILITY — p. 780
Compare planets to find out how compatible you are in a relationship.

YOUR RELATIONSHIP KARMA — p. 824
► SATURN IN SAGITTARIUS
Born Aug. 23, 10:08 - Sept. 23, 7:25

ALTHEA GIBSON
American Tennis Champion
Sun, Venus and Mars in Virgo

1957 LIBRA
From September 23, 7:26 through October 23, 16:23

♎ *The Enthusiastic Charmer*

You 1957 Librans are so darned positive, it's contagious! You're always looking at the bright side of things, and can whip up enthusiasm quicker than a pint of cream. You're especially idealistic when it comes to love. For you, romance is the highest goal to which to aspire. You're always thinking of new and exciting ways to pay tribute to your partner— is it any wonder that outsiders sigh with envy over your relationship? It's rare to see so much thought and effort go into a union. Fortunately, your excitement toward your partner is quite inspiring. Even the biggest cynic might be moved to buy their beloved a bouquet of flowers after watching you in action.

There's a good chance that you had a strong desire for marriage from a very early age. You view having a partner as a means to balance any weaknesses in your own personality. Similarly, you enjoy rounding out your mate's shortcomings. Apart, you are two halves of a broken coin. Together, you form something of lasting value. No wonder you place so much importance on relationships!

Anyone seeking to win your heart should demonstrate good taste. Bringing you to an elegant restaurant is sure to win points with you. Similarly, you like romantic but understated gestures. You'd prefer a single red rose to a pedestrian bouquet of daisies. Sexually, you like to be persuaded into the bedroom with soft but urgent kisses. You love being pursued, and enjoy it when your lover wears down your resistance.

As a 1957 male Libra, you appreciate a woman who is curious and adventurous. A female who likes to experiment in the bedroom won't meet with any protests from you. You're also drawn to zesty, free-spirited types. You do best with a mate who is open to new ideas, as this helps to keep your romance fresh and alive.

Men who are lively, intelligent, and persuasive are perfect for you 1957 female Librans. You want a guy who has a chivalrous air about him. Ideally, you'll find an attentive partner who continues to court you after 40 years of marriage. You're determined that the bloom will never fade from your relationship.

LIBRA ZODIAC SIGN
YOUR LOVE PLANETS

YOUR ROMANTIC SIDE — p. 696
► VENUS IN SCORPIO
Born Sept. 23, 7:26 - Oct. 10, 1:15
► VENUS IN SAGITTARIUS
Born Oct. 10, 1:16 - Oct. 23, 16:23

YOUR SEX DRIVE — p. 722
► MARS IN LIBRA
Born Sept. 23, 7:26 - Sept. 24, 4:30
► MARS IN LIBRA
Born Sept. 24, 4:31 - Oct. 23, 16:23

YOUR CELEBRITY TWINS — p. 760
Find out the astrological similarities you have with famous people.

YOUR COMPATIBILITY — p. 780
Compare planets to find out how compatible you are in a relationship.

YOUR RELATIONSHIP KARMA — p. 824
► SATURN IN SAGITTARIUS
Born Sept. 23, 7:26 - Oct. 23, 16:23

LEONARD BERNSTEIN
American Conductor
Mars in Scorpio

324

1957 SCORPIO
From October 23, 16:24 through November 22, 13:38

♏ *The Reclusive Romantic*

Deep, mysterious, and compelling, you 1957 Scorpions are a fascinating group. You prefer conducting your love life in private, and it may be years before associates learn your marital status. It's not that you're ashamed of your partner—it's just that you want to keep your relationship private and special. Subtle and discreet, you're not the type to engage in public displays of affection. You prefer expressing your ardent passion behind closed doors, where you can release your inhibitions without fear.

You want a partnership that has a mystical quality about it. In all probability, you feel a karmic link with your partner. Blessed with strong psychic powers, you have a knack for anticipating your mate's needs before they are ever articulated. You don't want a partnership in which everything has to be spelled out and discussed. You far prefer operating on instinct, especially when it comes to sex. Nothing thrills you more than discovering a new erogenous zone on your spouse's body.

If somebody wants to attract your attention, they should remark, "I can't help but feel that we've met somewhere before." The prospect of having known this person in a previous life will draw you into one of those deep conversations that you love so much. When it comes to lovemaking, you want a partner who is vocal and passionate. Quiet, repressed lovers only suppress your own ardor, and leave you vaguely dissatisfied. Your suitor should keep the details of your relationship a secret, even from their friends.

Women who are independent and opinionated greatly appeal to you 1957 male Scorpions. You relish the prospect of taming such a female. You also admire women who are ambitious and resilient. Shy, retiring types leave you cold. Ultimately, you want a partner who isn't intimidated by your forceful personality.

If you're a woman Scorpio who was born in 1957, you're looking for a guy who is affectionate, sentimental, and romantic. You do best with a partner who treats you like a rare and beautiful piece of sculpture. If there's anything you can't stand, it's being taken for granted.

1957 SAGITTARIUS
From November 22, 13:39 through December 22, 2:48

♐ *The Surprising Suitor*

There's a lot that doesn't meet the eye with you 1957 Archers. In public, you're driven, ambitious, and magnetic. In private, you're shy, retiring, and dreamy. It's a paradox that often comes as a surprise to your lover. You want a relationship that allows you to shake off all of the pressures associated with your job. Therefore, you do best with a playful partner who encourages your creativity and artistic impulses.

You're probably very spiritual and seek a relationship that is based on mutual faith. You're not averse to having philosophical debates with your partner, so long as you both respect each other's opinions. It's possible that you're a little secretive about your sexual desires. A mate who is able to intuit your physical needs is a perfect match for you. You may not articulate your love for your partner very often, but you do show it by providing a secure home. You're also quite helpful, and enjoy relieving your mate of mundane chores and irksome responsibilities.

In order to catch your attention, a suitor should inquire about your interests outside of work. Too often, people assume that a career-oriented person like you is completely obsessed with work. By acknowledging your wide range of interests, an admirer is sure to win favor with you. You're hesitant to reveal your true sexual nature until you're completely comfortable with your partner. Therefore, a suitor who demonstrates an open-minded attitude toward lovemaking has a good chance of winning your undying devotion.

You 1957 male Archers want a woman who is an experienced enchantress. A female who demonstrates masterful ability in the bedroom isn't intimidating—she's arousing! You also do well with a woman who is inventive and visionary. A partner who enjoys bringing out your hidden talents is an ideal spouse for you.

As a 1957 female Sagittarian, you do best with a man who is intense, mysterious, and sensual. You want a guy who will treat you with solicitous respect in public, and then ravish you in the bedroom. You want a mate who appreciates both your intellectual and your sexual charms.

Sophia Loren – An Exotic Legend

With her mesmerizing, noble beauty, Sophia Loren could have had just about any lover she wanted. She's co-starred with some of the world's most famous leading men, including Marcello Mastroianni, Gregory Peck, Cary Grant, John Wayne, Charlton Heston, Anthony Quinn, Clark Gable, and Marlon Brando. Loren turned away from these potential suitors by becoming involved with Italian producer Carlo Ponti, some 21 years her senior. This affair generated a huge scandal, since Ponti was already married and divorce in Italy was illegal.

Sophia Loren was born as an earthy Virgo, giving her plenty of common sense and a strong work ethic. Her Venus, the planet associated with love and beauty, is also in Virgo. It is enhanced by a strong connection with mystical, otherworldly Neptune. The Venus-Neptune pairing is especially favorable in an actress's chart, bestowing an aura of romantic transcendence, as if she were a goddess. Loren's natural, buxom beauty led her to a Rome Beauty Pageant when she was 16, where Carlo Ponti first spotted her.

By the end of the 20th century when she was at an age most would consider past her prime, Loren still radiated a magnificent charm and serenity. She has responsible Capricorn rising at her birth, a sign that often appears old during youth, but younger than usual in later years. Loren once explained this astrological phenomena in acting terms, "I was born old. I never really had a childhood. When I'm making a movie and have to appear sad, all I have to do

"I needed a father, a lover, a husband, a guide . . . Carlo is all four."

SOPHIA LOREN
of her husband Carlo Ponti

is go back to my memories."

Ponti was impressed with Loren's potential and wanted to help her career along. He changed her name (from Sofia Scicolone) and teamed her up with Marcello Mastroianni in the 1955 film *Too Bad She's Bad*. He also advised her to lose some weight and get a nose job, which she refused to do. The two fell in love, and in 1957 Ponti arranged to get a divorce by proxy in Mexico and then marry Loren. Italian authorities refused to recognize Ponti's divorce, and the couple was forced to leave the country to avoid bigamy charges.

While all this was going on, Loren was invited to play opposite Cary Grant in the 1957 Hollywood epic *The Pride and the Passion*. Now she was becoming an international star, and Cary Grant, who was 52 and married, fell in love with her. He asked her to marry him, but she turned him down, partly because they had different cultural backgrounds and partly because she was already involved with Ponti. "I needed a father, a lover, a husband, a guide," she said. "Carlo is all four."

Over the next few years Loren was typecast as a sex symbol. She realized that her talents weren't being fully appreciated. "I am not a sexy pot," as she put it so delightfully. She returned to Italy to make *Two Women*, a wrenching portrayal of her as a mother trying to protect her daughter from the horrors of war. This role brought her an Oscar for Best Actress in 1962. Now she had achieved recognition for her beauty and as a respected artist. In 1966 she legally married Ponti in France, and the two have remained partners ever since.

325

▶ READ ABOUT MASTROIANNI ON PAGE 367 ▶ READ ABOUT CARY GRANT ON PAGE 244 ▶ READ ABOUT CLARK GABLE ON PAGE 170 ▶ READ ABOUT MARLON BRANDO ON PAGE 277

1958

- ✪ MIKE TODD
- ✪ YVES SAINT-LAURENT
- ✪ BELL, BOOK, AND CANDLE
- ✪ INDISCREET
- ✪ LOLITA
- ✪ SIMONE DE BEAUVOIR
- ✪ ALL IN THE GAME

EVENTS

The British doctor Marie Stopes died. During her lifetime Stopes attracted much controversy due to her frank and unambiguous approach to sexual relations, combined with her pioneering advocacy of birth control.

In the US Elvis Presley was drafted into the Army, much to the horror of his many adoring fans.

Lana Turner's daughter stabbed Turner's boyfriend, Johnny Stompanato, in an incident later determined to be justifiable homicide.

Yves Saint Laurent, the 22-year-old who succeeded designer Christian Dior, presented his first collection. The "Trapeze" style created the new look of the season and was considered a triumph. Tights and pantyhose made their appearance and heralded in the era of the miniskirt.

POP CULTURE

Moviegoers watched *The Long, Hot Summer*, a film about a Mississippi patriarch who tries to set up his daughter with a drifter to insure he'll have grandchildren. *Bell, Book, and Candle* gave us a modern day witch with her sights and her spells set on a publisher who's engaged to her old competitor. *South Pacific* was a lush musical set in the Solomon Islands. The romantic comedy *Indiscreet* was one of the first films to deal with the previously taboo topic of intermarital affairs.

The bestselling novel *Lolita* sold one million copies. *Doctor Zhivago* by Boris Pasternak, later made into sweeping cinema, was a saga detailing the lives and loves of a large cast of characters during the Russian Revolution. It won a Nobel Prize for literature but the author was not allowed to accept it.

Anatomy of a Murder was about the trial of a man accused of murdering his wife's rapist. In *Memoirs of a Dutiful Daughter*, Simone de Beauvoir tells of her first encounter with her lover Jean-Paul Sartre.

Teens were bopping to "At the Hop" by Danny & the Juniors, and dreaming about the Everly Brothers and their "All I Have to Do Is Dream." Two novelty songs made the charts that year: "The Chipmunk Song" by David Seville and "The Purple People Eater" by Sheb Wooley. It's "All in the Game," a soft ballad by Tommy Edwards, rounded out the hits.

Hot Couple

ERICH MARIA REMARQUE & PAULETTE GODDARD

Before she married Remarque in 1958, Goddard was involved with Charlie Chaplin, and starred in his film *Modern Times*. Her marriage to Chaplin was a turbulent one, and it ended in divorce.

Remarque was a refugee from Nazi Germany, and the author of the novel *All's Quiet on the Western Front*. Goddard was known as one of the sexiest female leads in Hollywood. She had a mesmerizing quality that made men swoon. They were both classic in their own right. Only Goddard could win the heart of this serious-minded author. Five years after they were married, Remarque suffered a stroke. He died seven years later.

SEE ALSO
► CHARLIE CHAPLIN *Page 63*

1958 CAPRICORN

From December 22, 1957 2:49 through January 20, 1958 13:27
(December 1958 Capricorns, see 1959 Capricorn)

♑ *The Pragmatist*

In most areas of life, you tend to be quite serious and conservative, Capricorn of 1958. In relationships, however, you often show a more optimistic, adventurous side. Although you rarely throw caution to the wind and usually keep your feet planted firmly on the ground, you may be willing to take a few risks in love rather than always playing it safe. You might even surprise a few people with your unconventional approach to love.

Relationships could inspire you to do things you wouldn't have experienced otherwise. Perhaps some of your partners came from cultures, backgrounds, or socioeconomic groups that are different from yours. You tend to be open-minded and enjoy all sorts of people, not just those who are like you. Although you value stability and longevity, you might not feel it's necessary to stay with the same mate forever and could find monogamy a bit too restrictive. Even in a marriage or other committed relationship, you don't want things to become too predictable.

Although you can seem rather cool and aloof to those who don't know you intimately, in the bedroom you are anything but. Like most earth-sign folks, you just naturally understand the physical side of love. You also have a curious nature and are usually game to try something new. A curious, imaginative, uninhibited partner could find you to be an enthusiastic participant.

1958's Capricorn men are often fascinated by unconventional, independent women. You might prize brains over beauty, and appreciate someone who is a true original. Your ideal partner doesn't just go along to get along—she makes her own rules and doesn't mind making a few waves. A fair-minded woman with whom you can share lively discussions could get your vote.

Capricorn women of 1958 enjoy witty, fun-loving men who can teach them things and expand their horizons. Worldly types, adventurers, and men who like to travel also might appeal to your inquisitive side. A man who is generous with his time, money, and energy gets extra points. Someone who makes you laugh and feel young at heart could move to the front of your line of prospects.

CAPRICORN ZODIAC SIGN
YOUR LOVE PLANETS

YOUR ROMANTIC SIDE — p. 696
▶ **VENUS IN AQUARIUS**
Born Dec. 22, 1957 2:49 - Jan. 20, 1958 13:27

YOUR SEX DRIVE — p. 722
▶ **MARS IN SAGITTARIUS**
Born Dec. 22, 1957 2:49 - Jan. 20, 1958 13:27

YOUR CELEBRITY TWINS — p. 760
Find out the astrological similarities you have with famous people.

YOUR COMPATIBILITY — p. 780
Compare planets to find out how compatible you are in a relationship.

YOUR RELATIONSHIP KARMA — p. 824
▶ **SATURN IN SAGITTARIUS**
Born Dec. 22, 1957 2:49 - Jan. 20, 1958 13:27

EARTHA KITT
American Singer
Sun in Capricorn

327

1958 AQUARIUS

From January 20, 13:28 through February 19, 3:47

♒ *The Inventive Individualist*

Independent Aquarians of 1958 often march to a different drummer. Rather than playing the game of love according to established rules, you make your own rules and don't mind upsetting a few people in the process. You need to be free to do your own thing and aren't likely to let a partner clip your wings. Nor do you want a lover to depend on you too much. Your independent, unpredictable nature makes you a lively and interesting companion, though some conservative types might have trouble keeping up with you.

Friendship and equality are important to you, and you are usually most content with a partner you consider your peer. You dislike power struggles and prefer to share the perks and the responsibilities of a relationship. Ideally, you can help each other and bring out each other's best. Honest and fair-minded for the most part, you tend to approach love in a direct, uncomplicated, even-handed manner. However, you can be a bit brusque and detached at times, and could hurt a sensitive partner's feelings without meaning to.

Because your head usually rules your heart, you probably aren't especially romantic. You can be quite an inventive lover, however, and may like to experiment. Variety is the spice of life, in your book, and even in a monogamous relationship you try to keep your sex life fresh and exciting. You'd probably be happiest with a partner who stimulates you mentally as well as physically, and who can teach you a new trick or two.

Male Water Bearers born in 1958 enjoy bright, unconventional, somewhat quirky women. A partner who thinks for herself, takes chances, and doesn't look to others for approval could win your admiration. A friendly, outgoing personality is welcome, too. You may not be able to figure her out, but that's okay—you like surprises.

Female Aquarians of 1958 want partners who are their intellectual equals. Although you enjoy a man who shows you a good time, you also need someone you can rely on. An idealistic, forward-thinking mate might suit you well, but someone who is practical and realistic could help you bring your lofty ideas down to earth.

AQUARIUS ZODIAC SIGN
YOUR LOVE PLANETS

YOUR ROMANTIC SIDE — p. 696
▶ **VENUS IN AQUARIUS**
Born Jan. 20, 13:28 - Feb. 19, 3:47

YOUR SEX DRIVE — p. 722
▶ **MARS IN SAGITTARIUS**
Born Jan. 20, 13:28 - Feb. 03, 18:56
▶ **MARS IN CAPRICORN**
Born Feb. 03, 18:57 - Feb. 19, 3:47

YOUR CELEBRITY TWINS — p. 760
Find out the astrological similarities you have with famous people.

YOUR COMPATIBILITY — p. 780
Compare planets to find out how compatible you are in a relationship.

YOUR RELATIONSHIP KARMA — p. 824
▶ **SATURN IN SAGITTARIUS**
Born Jan. 20, 13:28 - Feb. 19, 3:47

PAUL NEWMAN
American Actor
Mars in Aries

1958 PISCES
From February 19, 3:48 through March 21, 3:05

The Imaginative Romantic

Romantic Pisceans of 1958 are inclined to idealize love and may have high hopes and expectations of relationships. With your vivid imagination and compassionate nature, you can see the good in others—and your faith in them might inspire them to become the best that they can be. You like to help people, whether it's by healing their wounds or serving as their Muse. Your generosity of spirit is one of your most endearing qualities. But sometimes you might delude yourself or give partners too much leeway, letting them take advantage of your kindness.

You might tend to focus on otherworldly considerations, rather than the here-and-now. Perhaps you seek a "match made in heaven"—or at least a partner who shares your spiritual path. A relationship with a creative individual, like yourself, could also suit you well. High-minded, caring, and supportive, you can elevate a partnership to its highest level. However, your expectations might be a bit unrealistic and could lead to disappointment.

You probably have a rich fantasy life, which can play itself out through your sexual encounters. With your colorful imagination, you could enliven any experience and give it a touch of glamour. You tend to be a romantic at heart and enjoy all the little things that make a big difference. A partner who takes you away from the humdrum of daily life could win your heart.

Idealistic, humanitarian women often appeal to Pisces males born in 1958. You value intelligence and independence in a partner, and might benefit from a relationship with someone who is less emotional and impressionable than you. Someone who can be your best friend and join you in your attempt to make the world a better place could be a good match for you.

Practical, patient, dependable men could be good choices for female Pisceans of 1958. You might also be attracted to strong, mature men who serve as teachers or father figures for you. Someone who takes care of the details of everyday life could be a real asset. A stable partner who has his feet firmly planted on the ground might be able to help you bring your dreams to fruition.

1958 ARIES
From March 21, 3:06 through April 20, 14:26

The Energetic Explorer

Like actress Mae West, if given a choice between two "evils," you'd probably pick the one you haven't tried yet, Aries of 1958. Your adventurous spirit keeps you questing for excitement and new experiences, in love and in life. When someone piques your interest, you are likely to pursue him or her with gusto and not let obstacles or disappointments deter you from your objective. Your enthusiasm is often short-lived, however, and if another tantalizing opportunity presents itself, you might shift gears and tear off in a different direction.

No matter how old you are, you retain a childlike wonder that can make you a delightful companion. Your idealism and zest for life can be infectious. Spontaneous and unpredictable, you need a lot of freedom in a relationship and don't want a partner to fence you in. Although you may be something of a loner, you might enjoy taking a lively partner along on your adventures.

Your ardor is easily ignited, but like a brush fire, it may burn out quickly. Although you can be an entertaining and energetic lover, you may not be very romantic or sensitive, sometimes showing more concern about your own satisfaction than your partner's. A lover will probably have to provide a good deal of stimulation—usually in the form of new experiences, risks, and challenges—to keep your attention from wandering.

Men born under the sign of the ram in 1958 are usually drawn to idealistic, imaginative women who are as changeable as they are and who keep them guessing. You probably prefer someone whose sights are set on the far horizon to one who is practical and domestic, for mundane matters tend to bore you. Your perfect partner shouldn't make herself too available, either, for you enjoy a good contest.

Unconventional, uninhibited men rate high with Aries women of 1958. You want a partner who is as independent as you are and doesn't make too many demands on you. Someone who can easily adapt to changing circumstances and who thrives on excitement could be a good match for you. He should also share your idealism, pioneering spirit, and sense of adventure.

1958 TAURUS

From April 20, 14:27 through May 21, 13:50

The Unabashed Romantic

Romantic and affectionate are good words to describe you, Taurus of 1958. You enjoy all those little touches that keep love alive—even if you've been with a partner for many years, you may still do special things to show him or her that you care. You appreciate a lover who dotes on you, too, by giving you thoughtful gifts, cooking your favorite meals, or bringing you flowers. Physical demonstrations of affection come naturally to you, and you probably like to hold hands or snuggle while watching old movies together.

Your romantic feelings are easily triggered, but your enthusiasm doesn't tend to wane once the novelty wears off. You can be a devoted partner and probably appreciate the stability, comfort, and security a long-term relationship affords. Stability needn't equate with boredom, however. Although you might be content with a few creature comforts and simple pleasures, you relish a bit of excitement and change now and again, just to add some spice to your love life.

You might like plenty of spice added to your sex life, for Tauruses are generally known for their lusty natures. You also tend to put a good-size helping of romance in your erotic encounters and could be something of an artist in the bedroom. A partner who wants to please you won't forget to pamper you and offer you lots of sensual delights, such as a massage or bubble bath.

Taurus men of 1958 may enjoy a sensitive, tender-hearted partner who is as romantic as they are. Artistic or musically inclined women could make good companions for you. But you might also have fun with a playful, feisty, outgoing woman who doesn't complicate love and just takes things as they come. You're a connoisseur of the physical form, so beauty and fitness are probably on your "must have" list.

Women born in 1958 under the sign of the bull are usually suckers for romance. A man who sings love songs to you or reads you poetry in bed could enchant you. Creative yourself, you could identify with artistic types and may enjoy being your partner's Muse. Sensitivity, kindness, and a good imagination are the keys to your heart.

LOUIS JOURDAN
French Actor
Sun in Gemini

329

1958 GEMINI

From May 21, 13:51 through June 21, 21:56

The Mercurial Mate

Some might call you fickle, Gemini of 1958, and you may have a roving eye. But that doesn't mean you can't care deeply about a partner or make a commitment to someone. You simply enjoy people and want to sample as many of life's delights as possible. All is grist for your romance mill. Every experience teaches you something, and you are probably an avid student.

So long as a partner doesn't make too many demands on you or limit your freedom too severely, you can be a lively and entertaining companion. Your keen imagination and wealth of information could fascinate a mate for many years. You can be quite affectionate, too, and may profess your love often, perhaps in poetry or song. You're not all fun and games, though—you have a serious side, too. Although you may appear cavalier about love, you can become very attached to a partner and might be heartbroken if a relationship doesn't work out.

Communication is your forte, and you enjoy a good conversation more than just about anything. Your ideal partner might regale you with amusing stories and share information with you on a wide range of topics. Most likely, you enjoy talking about sex, too, and usually don't hesitate to tell a lover what you want. Changeable by nature, you need lots of variety and appreciate someone who is willing to experiment.

Male Geminis of 1958 often seek stable, down-to-earth mates who can help to anchor them in the real world. A practical woman could provide a good counterpoint to your imaginative, intellectual personality. Sensual, affectionate types who are physically demonstrative might make you feel loved and needed. Someone who can cook and is good with kids gets bonus points.

1958's female Geminis may be attracted to rather idealistic, impractical types who can create beautiful fantasies for them. Men who are primarily concerned with their jobs and the mundane aspects of life probably bore you. You prefer someone with a bit of mystery or adventure in his soul, who sees life in a colorful and exciting way. A man who stands up for the underdog could get a standing ovation from you.

SANDRA DEE
American Actress
Mars in Cancer

1958 CANCER
From June 21, 21:57 through July 23, 8:49

The Changeable Companion

Cancers of 1958 may be homebodies at heart, but they have a bit of the adventurer in them, too. Unlike some Cancers born in other years, you might feel a need to get away from your loved ones periodically and do your own thing. You want to continue expanding your horizons, learning new things and adding to your repertoire of experiences. Perhaps you enjoy traveling—you might even meet a partner while on a trip—and may appreciate a worldly or knowledgeable mate who shares information with you.

Although you value security, you don't always play it safe in romance. You could have experienced some ups and downs in your love life as a result. You can be quite changeable and tend to act spontaneously, making decisions with your heart rather than your head. Your sensitive emotions are easily engaged and you can love deeply. When someone hurts your feelings, you may lash out with angry words. Your temper is usually short-lived, however, and you probably feel guilty if you cause a partner pain.

Your moods are likely to influence your libido—in an instant, you can change from passionate to sulky and withdrawn. Sometimes you might enjoy playing the aggressor; other times you can be rather passive. A partner needs to make you feel secure and valued by reassuring you that you're desirable and giving you plenty of TLC.

Intelligent women usually strike a chord with Cancer men of 1958. Even if she isn't educated, she should be clever, well-read, and able to converse on many subjects. A friendly, versatile partner who adapts easily to changing situations—and your own changeable moods—could be a good companion. You may find slender, agile, youthful women more attractive than voluptuous beauties.

Men of action often appeal to Cancer women born in 1958. You appreciate strong, decisive, assertive guys who know what they want and take it. No computer geeks or sensitive romantic types for you—you probably prefer "men's men," athletes, and adventurers. You might also be attracted to men who have a wild side, who can trigger your own sense of adventure and bring you out of your shell.

1958 LEO
From July 23, 8:50 through August 23, 15:45

The Proud Performer

You may not know exactly what you want until you see it, Leo of 1958, but once someone catches your eye you probably go all-out to win that person's favor. Usually, your charm, charisma, and confidence bring you success in romantic endeavors. An enthusiastic partner, you can be quite dramatic and colorful when it comes to showing you care. Perhaps you like to impress your lover with entertaining adventures and thoughtful gifts. But the greatest gift of all is your love—right, Leo?

Romantic and affectionate, you try to keep passion alive in a relationship, no matter how long you've been with your partner. Your sometimes unpredictable and spontaneous nature can make things interesting, too. However, you can be self-centered and might insist on having your own needs and desires met in a relationship, rather than seeing the union as an equal partnership. Although you are often fun-loving and optimistic, if a lover doesn't give you the respect you seek or hurts your pride, you might show your lion's teeth. In the bedroom, you may express your vitality

and enthusiasm with aplomb. You do your best to make each romantic interlude a memorable experience, and might even pride yourself on your performance. You like to be the best at whatever you do and can be quite an exciting lover. A partner can bring out your star quality by enacting your fantasies and lavishing you with praise.

A woman who devotes herself to you and your children could land the role of costar in the story of your life, male Leo of 1958. You appreciate a warm, caring, affectionate partner who knows how to create a comfortable home and safe haven for you. A woman who nurtures you with a lion's share of attention could gain your loyalty and protection.

Strong, stable, dependable men often make female Leos of 1958 purr. An easygoing mate with lots of patience, who strokes your ego and encourages your creativity, could be a good partner for you. You might find strong, hardy, even beefy guys sexier than sleek, model-slim ones. A man who's generous with his affection and money could win your seal of approval.

1958 VIRGO

From August 23, 15:46 through September 23, 13:08

The Supportive Mate

You may be modest about your relationship skills, Virgo of 1958, but those who know you intimately would probably give you rave reviews. Caring and compassionate, you make a sincere attempt to be kind, supportive, and helpful to your partner. Your loved ones rarely doubt your devotion, for you probably do lots of little things to show your affection. It might be easier for you to express your love in practical ways than with pretty words or emotional displays.

A loyal and dedicated mate, you aren't inclined to stray once you make a commitment. Through good times and bad, a partner can usually depend on you. You are probably the one who keeps your domestic life running smoothly and efficiently. When problems arise, you do what's necessary to fix them and are willing to put effort into making your relationships work. Some partners might even feel your expectations are too high, though, and give up because they can't meet your exacting standards.

Although you might appear rather reserved, you can be quite sensual and creative in the bedroom. You invest the same care into lovemaking as you do in other areas of life, and your attention to detail can make you a skillful lover. Your ideal partner won't take your affection and eagerness to please for granted, however—he or she should remember to compliment you on your expertise.

Discriminating Virgo men of 1958 might be swept off their feet by beautiful women. Glamorous, movie-star types and cover girls usually top your list—you like a partner who stands out in a crowd. You may also find creative women who have a dramatic flair appealing. Someone with a sunny disposition, who knows how to dress and entertain with style, could get your vote.

Female Virgos of 1958 usually give "thumbs up" to men who are as practical and dependable as they are, and might appreciate stay-at-home types with a domestic streak. A pleasant personality and affectionate nature are probably more important to you than good looks or status. You probably won't mind if he has money and property, however. Artistic or musical ability could be assets, too.

VIRGO ZODIAC SIGN
YOUR LOVE PLANETS

YOUR ROMANTIC SIDE   p. 696
- ▶ VENUS IN LEO
  Born Aug. 23, 15:46 - Sept. 09, 12:34
- ▶ VENUS IN LIBRA
  Born Sept. 09, 12:35 - Sept. 23, 13:08

YOUR SEX DRIVE   p. 722
- ▶ MARS IN TAURUS
  Born Aug. 23, 15:46 - Sept. 21, 5:25
- ▶ MARS IN GEMINI
  Born Sept. 21, 5:26 - Sept. 23, 13:08

YOUR CELEBRITY TWINS   p. 760
Find out the astrological similarities you have with famous people.

YOUR COMPATIBILITY   p. 780
Compare planets to find out how compatible you are in a relationship.

YOUR RELATIONSHIP KARMA   p. 824
- ▶ SATURN IN SAGITTARIUS
  Born Aug. 23, 15:46 - Sept. 23, 13:08

331

CHARLTON HESTON
American Actor
Sun in Libra

1958 LIBRA
From September 23, 13:09 through October 23, 22:10

The Diplomatic Lover

Love makes your world go round, Libra of 1958. Relationships are central to your happiness and you're rarely without a significant other. You aren't inclined to chase after partners, though—that's not your style. Instead, you prefer to make yourself attractive and wait for suitors to come court you. With your pleasing personality, grace, and savoir faire, you don't usually have to wait long.

You tend to intellectualize love, however, and might seem a bit detached or unemotional. Most likely, you want a partner you can socialize with, someone who is a friend and companion—too much intimacy or intensity could be uncomfortable for you. That doesn't mean you can't be a loyal and devoted mate, for you take your commitments seriously and can be content in a stable, long-term partnership. Because you dislike conflict and upsets, you often try hard to make your relationships work.

Probably not the lustiest of lovers, you are more inclined to express yourself through romantic gestures than with unbridled desire.

Your tastes tend to be rather conservative, and "kinky" might not even be in your vocabulary. Sex is probably most enjoyable to you within the context of a loving relationship and your interest may wane if you aren't getting along well with your partner. You respond best to tenderness and affection, and might recoil if a lover is pushy or crude.

"Ladies" generally attract Libra men of 1958. You want a woman you can take home to meet your mother. Flashy, tough, or overtly sexy women usually turn you off. You appreciate intelligence and poise in a partner, especially when combined with a pretty face and well-proportioned figure. Neatness, good manners, and a congenial personality are important, too.

Intelligent men "rule" in the opinion of most Libra women born in 1958. You want a partner who shares your interests and can engage you in stimulating conversations. Because you like to learn, a man who can teach you new things could be a good match for you. Slim, agile men who retain their boyish charm into their middle years might fit your image of masculinity.

LIBRA ZODIAC SIGN
YOUR LOVE PLANETS

YOUR ROMANTIC SIDE   p. 696
- ▶ VENUS IN LIBRA
  Born Sept. 23, 13:09 - Oct. 03, 16:43
- ▶ VENUS IN LIBRA
  Born Oct. 03, 16:44 - Oct. 23, 22:10

YOUR SEX DRIVE   p. 722
- ▶ MARS IN GEMINI
  Born Sept. 23, 13:09 - Oct. 23, 22:10

YOUR CELEBRITY TWINS   p. 760
Find out the astrological similarities you have with famous people.

YOUR COMPATIBILITY   p. 780
Compare planets to find out how compatible you are in a relationship.

YOUR RELATIONSHIP KARMA   p. 824
- ▶ SATURN IN SAGITTARIUS
  Born Sept. 23, 13:09 - Oct. 23, 22:10

JEANNE MOREAU
French Actress
Venus in Sagittarius

332

1958 SCORPIO
From October 23, 22:11 through November 22, 19:28

The Elusive Lover

Self-contained Scorpios of 1958 can seem a bit unapproachable at times, but that may inspire some people to take up the challenge and try to get close to you. Your air of mystery is quite intriguing. However, you value your privacy and rarely let anyone—even lovers and friends who have known you for years—see into your soul. Those who do manage to win your trust, however, can count on you to be a sincere and devoted partner. In fact, you might become so attached to those you care for that you can be possessive at times.

You tend to be an extremist in matters of the heart, either throwing yourself totally into a relationship or slamming the door in the face of love. Even when you are involved in a steady partnership, you probably experience many emotional highs and lows—the passionate reunions usually make up for the pain of the breakups. Power struggles can be an issue in your relationships, for you like to be the one in control most of the time.

On a passion scale of 1 to 10, you probably rank 11. You usually enjoy sex most when it includes a strong emotional component, however. Your tastes lean toward the exotic and you may be fascinated by things your culture considers "taboo." But you don't need a lot of partners to keep you satisfied. You'd probably prefer one significant other who doesn't censor you and who can match you in intensity and eroticism.

Male Scorpions of 1958 usually prefer partners who are as passionate and emotional as they are. Dark, sultry women have a better chance of lighting your fires than wholesome, blonde, cheerleader types. Your ideal partner will understand your tempestuous nature and not be reluctant to express her own powerful emotions. Above all, she must be faithful to you.

Scorpio women born in 1958 might seek mates who offer stability and security. Practical, earthy men can help balance your intense emotions and keep you on a steady course. A patient, easygoing personality is a plus. Artists, musicians, and other creative types often interest you, too. And let's not forget to include sensuality on your wish list, Scorpio!

1958 SAGITTARIUS
From November 22, 19:29 through December 22, 8:39

The Serious Seeker

Idealistic Sagittarians of 1958 may search the world for the perfect partner. Along the way, you have probably enjoyed your share of romantic liaisons. Your curiosity and desire to experience as much of life as you can might lead others to think you are a rolling stone. But unlike some Sagittarians, you can make a commitment to the right person, and once you find your ideal mate, you could become a happy husband or wife. You still might like to flirt, but you probably won't stray too far.

Most of the time, you maintain a cheerful, optimistic attitude toward love—and you can be a lively, entertaining companion. Occasionally, though, disappointments can damage your idealism—that's when you need a supportive partner to boost your flagging spirits. Whether your love grows stronger over time or begins to feel like a prison depends to some degree on how trusting and open-minded your partner is. You need to feel free to pursue your search for the truth, and a mate who joins you in your quest—or at least gives you a long leash—is likely to gain your respect.

You are usually a playful and affectionate lover, and your curiosity could lead you to try just about anything in pursuit of pleasure. At times, however, you might experience feelings of insecurity or inadequacy. An understanding partner can brighten your dark moments by taking a light-hearted approach to sex and keeping your attention focused on the future. For you, laughter is the best medicine.

Athletic women and outdoorsy types generally appeal to Sagittarian men born in 1958. You appreciate a partner who takes a broad view of life and doesn't sweat the small stuff. Someone who is as inquisitive and adventurous as you are, who likes to travel and never stops learning, could be a good mate for you.

Practical, realistic, dependable men can be excellent counterpoints to idealistic, changeable Sagittarian women of 1958. If he has money or a good job, so much the better. Creative types might delight you, too. A man who pampers you with beautiful gifts, good food, and lots of affection could keep you from wandering.

'50s

Lana Turner's Fatal Affair

On the night of April 4, 1958, cinema goddess Lana Turner's gangster lover Johnny Stompanato was killed in her Beverly Hills mansion by Cheryl Crane, Turner's 14-year-old daughter. She stabbed him to death. Within hours of the killing, newsstand tabloids flashed pictures of Stompanato dead on Turner's bedroom floor—and of Turner, looking beautiful and afflicted. The coroner's inquest was a must-see media spectacular, broadcast on television and radio. Appearing in the starring role was Lana Turner, giving the performance of her life in her daughter's defense.

Just a year before, Stompanato had wormed his way into Turner's heart, introducing himself under the false name of "Johnny Steel" and winning her over with daily deliveries of flowers, phone calls, music, and gifts. Turner, on the rebound from her fourth divorce, was vulnerable to such gentlemanly fawning. Even after she discovered his real name and his shady identity as a gigolo and part-time bag man for Hollywood racketeer Mickey Cohen, Turner succumbed to Stompanato's forbidden allure and his tall-dark-and-handsome good looks.

Anxious to preserve her reputation as the star of such Hollywood hits as *The Postman Always Rings Twice*, *The Bad and the Beautiful*, and *Peyton Place*, Turner avoided appearing in public with Stompanato, a situation that enraged him. The more Stompanato pressured Turner for a more prominent role in her life, the more she began to distance herself from him. As is common in cases of domestic violence, the relationship took a turn for the worse once Turner sought to end things. The conflict came to a head in England, where Stompanato had followed Turner while she was filming *Another Time, Another Place*.

Following a fight in which he shoved and choked her, Turner succeeded in having Stompanato deported to the US.

More beatings followed, including a brutal attack in March after the 1958 Academy Awards ceremonies. Nominated for her role as Constance Mackenzie in *Peyton Place*, Turner had again shunned Stompanato as her escort. On April 4, 1958, Turner's final attempt to end the relationship triggered another fight in her bedroom. Overhearing Stompanato as he threatened to cut her mother's face and harm her grandmother, Cheryl ran downstairs and returned to her mother's bedroom with a large carving knife. When Turner finally opened the door, Stompanato pushed past her. Cheryl plunged the knife into him and punctured his aorta. Stompanato bled to death on the bedroom floor.

The Los Angeles County Coroner concluded that Cheryl's fatal attack on Stompanato was justified to save her mother's life. Astrologers consider it to be a fated event. One method by which astrologers determine connections between various people is to lay their birth charts on top of one another. Certain heavenly bodies situated next to each other ("conjunct") or exactly opposite in position on the charts reveal strong connections. When the charts for Turner, Cheryl, and Stompanato are placed together, along with the chart for the day of the killing, astrologers can see why these three individuals are linked together. One prominent point is that the asteroid Astraea, which symbolizes difficult endings, makes close conjunctions with the lunar nodes, symbols of destiny. Astraea's position in the sky on April 4 was directly conjunct Stompanato's lunar node and Cheryl's Leo Zodiac sign. In other words, Cheryl was fated to end it all for Stompanato.

Lana Turner with ex-husband Steve Crane and daughter Cheryl

"It started with flowers ... it was to end with screaming headlines, in tragedy and death."

**LANA TURNER on her ill-fated relationship
with Johnny Stompanato**

▶ READ ABOUT ANOTHER MURDER SCANDAL IN HOLLYWOOD ON PAGE 24

-  BARBIE
- ⭐ LADY CHATTERLEY'S LOVER
- ⭐ SOME LIKE IT HOT
- ⭐ ROCK HUDSON
- ⭐ RETURN TO PEYTON PLACE
- ⭐ FRANKIE AVALON
- ⭐ COME SOFTLY TO ME

EVENTS

Mattel debuted the Barbie doll, the first non-baby doll on the American market, with 351,000 dolls sold the first year. Her impossible measurements led Barbie into controversy when feminists claimed it made young girls grow up to feel inadequate.

Thirty-one years after it was written, the book *Lady Chatterley's Lover* (about a married woman and her gamekeeper lover) was deemed obscene and banned from the US mails. Emily Wheelock Reed stood up against the Alabama state legislature in defense of a children's book that was about to be banned. *The Rabbit's Wedding* was said to promote miscegenation, interbreeding or marriage between different races.

Actor Alain Delon and Romy Schneider announced their engagement, but the pairing did not last. Delon abruptly broke with Romy to marry another woman. The relationship between playboy singer Sacha Distel and sexpot Brigitte Bardot went the same way when she surprised all by suddenly marrying someone else.

POP CULTURE

Some Like It Hot, starring Marilyn Monroe, broke a number of barriers because it included homosexuality, seduction, and sexual innuendo. *Pillow Talk* paired popular stars Rock Hudson and Doris Day. Animosity builds between an interior decorator and a playboy who ties up the phone all day—until they meet and he decides to add her to his list of conquests.

Return to Peyton Place by Grace Metalious hit the bookstores after Dell paid a record advance of $256,000 for it. In *Man with Two Wives,* a man's ordered life, complete with adoring wife, is turned upside down when his passionate first wife shows up. *Around the World with Auntie Mame* was the sequel to the original madcap novel and has Mame traveling and getting into trouble at each stop. In *Do you like Brahms?* by Françoise Sagan the heroine is torn between a stable and unfulfilling relationship and a passionate but unconventional lover.

DJs were spinning Bobby Darin's "Mack the Knife," the rousing "Battle of New Orleans" by Johnny Horton, and "Venus" by teen idol Frankie Avalon. Joining the charts were "The Three Bells," the Fleetwoods' "Come Softly to Me," and the Platters' "Smoke Gets in Your Eyes."

Hot Movie

SOME LIKE IT HOT

Some Like It Hot was the hottest film of the decade. It featured more ribaldry and debauchery than moviegoers had ever been exposed to. Tony Curtis and Jack Lemmon played musicians who ran from the mob while disguised as women. Marilyn Monroe spoofed her own dizzy blond persona with charm and finesse.

It was a screwball comedy, featuring speakeasies and gangsters, and was one of the highest grossing films of that era. Gender bending and sexual innuendo were considered highly indecorous in the late fifties, but that only made *Some Like It Hot* the inferno of success that it became.

SEE ALSO
▶ MARILYN MONROE *Page 293 & 294*

334

1959 CAPRICORN

From December 22, 1958 8:40 through January 20, 1959 19:18
(December 1959 Capricorns, see 1960 Capricorn)

♑ *The Practical Partner*

Love is serious business for you, Capricorn of 1959. You might even approach romantic relationships in much the same manner as you do business agreements. The old custom of arranged marriages probably makes some sense to you, for you understand the importance of pairing up with a mate who shares your values, comes from a similar background, and has many of the same goals you do. You might also appreciate someone whose personal, professional, or financial assets could enrich the relationship.

Security and stability are important to you—therefore, a steady, long-term partnership could suit you well. Once you make a commitment to someone, you do your best to keep it. You could be content with a mate who provides a comfortable lifestyle, and perhaps a few luxuries. And because you tend to be somewhat shy, a person who makes you feel safe, secure, and treasured has a good chance of winning your heart.

You enjoy all sorts of sensual pleasures, from good food to good sex. For the most part, however, your tastes aren't particularly exotic and your appetites can usually be satisfied by someone whose down-to-earth, uncomplicated approach matches your own. You may not be the most romantic lover, but your devotion and endurance make up for what some might consider a lack of imagination. No flash in the pan, you could continue to be quite a lusty lover long after your peers' fires have burned out.

An intelligent, capable, pragmatic woman who demonstrates competence at home and/or in the business world is likely to appeal to male Capricorns born in 1959. Maturity, too, is a plus in your book—giggly, gum-chewing airheads need not apply. Instead, you want a partner who behaves with dignity and knows how to handle herself in all situations.

Women born under the sign of the goat in 1959 are usually attracted to strong, silent types. You'll probably give your seal of approval to men who are good-natured and affectionate, but who aren't pushovers. You want a partner you can depend on, a no-nonsense guy who takes charge and solves problems. If he has money, so much the better.

CAPRICORN ZODIAC SIGN
YOUR LOVE PLANETS

YOUR ROMANTIC SIDE   p. 696
▶ **VENUS IN CAPRICORN**
Born Dec. 22, 1958 8:40 - Jan. 07, 1959 8:15
▶ **VENUS IN AQUARIUS**
Born Jan. 07, 8:16 - Jan. 20, 19:18

YOUR SEX DRIVE   p. 722
▶ **MARS IN TAURUS**
Born Dec. 22, 1958 8:40 - Jan. 20, 1959 19:18

YOUR CELEBRITY TWINS   p. 760
Find out the astrological similarities you have with famous people.

YOUR COMPATIBILITY   p. 780
Compare planets to find out how compatible you are in a relationship.

YOUR RELATIONSHIP KARMA   p. 824
▶ **SATURN IN SAGITTARIUS**
Born Dec. 22, 1958 8:40 - January 5, 1959, 13:33
▶ **SATURN IN CAPRICORN**
Born Jan. 5, 13:34 - Jan. 20, 19:18

WILLIAM S. BURROUGHS
American Writer
Sun and Venus in Aquarius

1959 AQUARIUS

From January 20, 19:19 through February 19, 9:37

♒ *The Unpredictable Idealist*

Water bearers of 1959 grew up when traditional attitudes about male-female roles, sexual expression, and relationships in general were changing. Thus, you independent people tend to be trend-setters and rule-breakers who like to do things your own way. You don't want anyone to tell you how to live or love, and you might take an anything goes attitude. Even if your relationships seem normal on the surface, there is probably something unconventional about them—and that keeps things interesting!

You need lots of freedom and might rebel if a partner tries to put too many limits or demands on you. Equality is important to you, too, and you probably won't be content to let another person call all the shots. You want a lover who respects your rights and encourages you to fulfill yourself. Your ideal partner will be able to teach you a thing or two, yet he or she should also value your intelligence. A creative individual who appreciates your wonderful imagination could find you a fascinating companion.

Always ready to try something you haven't tried before, you are eager to expand your romantic horizons—with one significant other or with a number of different partners. Idealistic about love, you quickly grow bored if things become too dull or routine. Although you may appear rather aloof, once someone gets to know you intimately, you are quite romantic and know how to infuse your relationship with a touch of magic.

1959's Aquarian men are usually fascinated by imaginative women who express themselves in colorful, original ways. Artists, musicians, and bohemian types may appeal to you. You have high expectations of your partner, and want a woman who combines intelligence with sensitivity, who is independent but not afraid to show her vulnerability.

Female water bearers born in 1959 generally feel comfortable with strong, stable men who can serve as anchors for you. An easy-going, down-to-earth guy could be a good compliment to your somewhat feisty, free-spirited nature. You might enjoy snuggling up to an affectionate "teddy bear"—as long as he doesn't hold on too tightly.

AQUARIUS ZODIAC SIGN
YOUR LOVE PLANETS

YOUR ROMANTIC SIDE   p. 696
▶ **VENUS IN AQUARIUS**
Born Jan. 20, 19:19 - Jan. 31, 7:27
▶ **VENUS IN PISCES**
Born Jan. 31, 7:28 - Feb. 19, 9:37

YOUR SEX DRIVE   p. 722
▶ **MARS IN TAURUS**
Born Jan. 20, 19:19 - Feb. 10, 13:56
▶ **MARS IN GEMINI**
Born Feb. 10, 13:57 - Feb. 19, 9:37

YOUR CELEBRITY TWINS   p. 760
Find out the astrological similarities you have with famous people.

YOUR COMPATIBILITY   p. 780
Compare planets to find out how compatible you are in a relationship.

YOUR RELATIONSHIP KARMA   p. 824
▶ **SATURN IN CAPRICORN**
Born Jan. 20, 19:19 - Feb. 19, 9:37

JACK BRABHAM
Australian Racing Champion
Sun in Aries

1959 PISCES
From February 19, 9:38 through March 21, 8:54

 ## *The Plucky Romantic*

Some people may be surprised when they discover that you gentle, peace-loving Pisceans of 1959 have a feisty, independent side, too. A partner who thinks he or she can manipulate or dominate you could be in for a rude awakening. Certainly, you are kind and compassionate, like all people born under the sign of the fishes, and you usually are willing to forgive many shortcomings in a lover. But if pushed too far, you might fight back—or seek calmer seas elsewhere.

You approach love with curiosity and a sense of adventure. Your quest for knowledge and new experiences may have brought many interesting people into your life. Perhaps you still find it difficult to commit yourself totally to one significant other, for you don't like limiting your options and might keep an eye out for the perfect partner. Inclined to idealize love, you may be seeking a soul mate who will fulfill your every dream and desire. As a result, you've probably encountered some disappointments as well as some grand romances along the way.

Lovers are often attracted not only to your friendly, playful personality, but to the aura of mystery you project as well. Your changeable nature can make it hard to figure you out—but that's part of your special appeal. You are probably happiest with a partner who offers you plenty of variety—sexually and otherwise—and who can introduce you to new ideas and experiences.

Active, physically fit, outdoorsy types often intrigue male Pisceans of 1959. You may find women who have a bit of the tomboy in them more attractive than curvaceous beauties. Above all, you value a partner who knows what she wants and isn't afraid to go for it. Independence, self-confidence, and daring rank high on your list of assets in a woman.

Pisces women born in 1959 prize intelligence in male partners, for you want to be able to engage in stimulating conversations on a variety of subjects with your lover. You also want a multifaceted individual with whom you can share your many interests. Someone who makes you laugh and who boosts your spirits when you feel blue could score high with you.

1959 ARIES
From March 21, 8:55 through April 20, 20:16

♈ ## *The Spirited Adventurer*

You adventurous Ariens of 1959 seek thrills and challenges in life and in love. If someone or something simply drops in your lap, you'll probably feel disappointed, for you enjoy the chase as much as the conquest. A partner who takes you on a merry quest, however, is likely to engage your ardor and your imagination.

Not the type to play it safe, you tend to approach romance with a playful spirit and don't mind going out on a limb now and again. Despite your seemingly indomitable self-confidence, though, you can experience a bit of frustration and pain when someone rejects your advances. A bit self-centered, you want what you want right now and might have trouble compromising or taking "no" for an answer. But you rarely let disappointments get you down for long—your curiosity and joie de vivre keep you in the game of love for as long as a partner is willing to play.

Like most rams, your passion is usually ignited quickly, and once your appetite is whetted, you tend to lack patience or finesse. Some of the finer points of romance could escape your notice, but you make up for it with enthusiasm. Unlike your fellow Ariens born in other years, you do have the ability to stick with the right partner and might appreciate the security of a steady relationship—once you've enjoyed your share of romantic adventures, that is.

Aries men of 1959 are frequently attracted to warm, affectionate, uncomplicated women who provide a comfortable home. Someone who can cook and has an easy-going disposition could keep you from roaming. You value stability in a partner, and like to know that your lover has eyes for you alone. When it's time to light your fire, sensual, voluptuous females can usually do it best.

Clever, quick-witted men are likely to win the heart of an Aries woman born in 1959. Writers, teachers, and people with good communication skills may appeal to you, for you enjoy partners who can stimulate you intellectually and expand your mental horizons. Your ideal mate should be as curious and spontaneous as you are, share your zest for life, and always be ready to try something new.

1959 TAURUS
From April 20, 20:17 through May 21, 19:41

The Affectionate Homebody

Your motto might be "Home is where the heart is," Taurus of 1959, for you are among the most domestic members of the zodiac. Family and loved ones come first in your book, and the people you care about know how important they are to you. A loyal partner, you do your best to create a comfortable and secure environment for those who are dearest to you. From an early age you probably sought a stable relationship rather than playing the field. You might even have married your high school sweetheart.

Practical in love (and other areas of life), your needs tend to be basic and realistic. You don't expect Prince Charming or some love goddess to satisfy your every wish. You could be content with a few creature comforts, an affectionate mate, and a healthy family. Patient and persevering, you rarely give up until you've achieved your aims. Once you set your sights on someone, you might woo that person with gifts and shower him or her with attention. You have a knack for making the object of your affection feel special.

The physical side of love is your specialty —not just sex, though that's certainly important to you, but all forms of sensual pleasure appeal to your earthy nature. Snuggling, touching, and other shows of affection nurture you and make your feel loved. A partner can please you by hugging you often, cooking your favorite meals, and giving you thoughtful presents.

Men born under the sign of the bull in 1959 often find smart, sociable women interesting, and you might not mind if your mate is brighter than you—as long as she doesn't let her intellectual and career goals interfere with family life. An affectionate, demonstrative, and dependable partner who likes to cook and is good with kids would probably suit you best.

Security is a priority for Taurus women of 1959, so your ideal partner should be able to provide that. Consequently, you may seek a mate who has money or at least a good job, so he can give you what you desire. Warm and loving family men rank high on your list, too—you don't want someone who's wedded to his work or away from home a lot.

TAURUS ZODIAC SIGN
Your Love Planets

YOUR ROMANTIC SIDE — p. 696
- ▶ **VENUS IN GEMINI**
Born Apr. 20, 20:17 - May 10, 15:44
- ▶ **VENUS IN CANCER**
Born May 10, 15:45 - May 21, 19:41

YOUR SEX DRIVE — p. 722
- ▶ **MARS IN CANCER**
Born Apr. 20, 20:17 - May 21, 19:41

YOUR CELEBRITY TWINS — p. 760
Find out the astrological similarities you have with famous people.

YOUR COMPATIBILITY — p. 780
Compare planets to find out how compatible you are in a relationship.

YOUR RELATIONSHIP KARMA — p. 824
- ▶ **SATURN IN CAPRICORN**
Born Apr. 20, 20:17 - May 21, 19:41

337

SIMONE SIGNORET
French Actress
Venus in Taurus

1959 GEMINI
From May 21, 19:42 through June 22, 3:49

The Curious Companion

Gregarious Geminis of 1959 are likely to have a wide circle of friends and loved ones—in some cases, these may be one and the same, for you want your lovers to be friends as well as romantic partners. Your collection of companions might be diverse or eclectic, for your innate curiosity and friendly nature attract all sorts of people to you. Because you are eager to learn new things and enjoy sharing ideas with others, you may choose partners who are seekers, just as you are.

Although you generally seem light-hearted and outgoing, you probably have a sensitive side, and your feelings—as well as your pride— could be hurt easily if a partner doesn't give you enough attention. Even if the relationship isn't a permanent one, you want to feel you are the center of your lover's universe—at least temporarily. But your changeable nature and resilience usually enable you to bounce back quickly from disappointments, moving on to the next person who catches your eye. Especially in your youth, you might have been a bit of fickle, and even if you settle down later

in life, you may still have fun flirting.

You appreciate brains as well as beauty in a lover—a partner can charm you with pretty words. Someone who has a vivid imagination and can make each romantic interlude seem fresh, fun, and exciting could hold your interest for a lifetime. If not, once the glamour and romance fade, you could grow restless and start looking around for a new playmate.

Male Geminis born in 1959 are usually fond of women who tend to your every need and make you feel special. You'd probably be happiest with a warm, affectionate, nurturing partner who provides a secure port in the storm for you. It helps if she likes children, too. Physical beauty, artistic talent, and a sense of style are icing on the cake.

Female Geminis of 1959 tend to be attracted to men who can protect and care for you—even if you are competent yourself, you may seek a partner who is a doting father figure. You want a mate you can be proud of, so someone who is handsome, charming, and successful might top your list of candidates.

GEMINI ZODIAC SIGN
Your Love Planets

YOUR ROMANTIC SIDE — p. 696
- ▶ **VENUS IN CANCER**
Born May 21, 19:42 - June 06, 22:41
- ▶ **VENUS IN LEO**
Born June 06, 22:42 - June 22, 3:49

YOUR SEX DRIVE — p. 722
- ▶ **MARS IN CANCER**
Born May 21, 19:42 - June 01, 2:25
- ▶ **MARS IN LEO**
Born June 01, 2:26 - June 22, 3:49

YOUR CELEBRITY TWINS — p. 760
Find out the astrological similarities you have with famous people.

YOUR COMPATIBILITY — p. 780
Compare planets to find out how compatible you are in a relationship.

YOUR RELATIONSHIP KARMA — p. 824
- ▶ **SATURN IN CAPRICORN**
Born May 21, 19:42 - June 22, 3:49

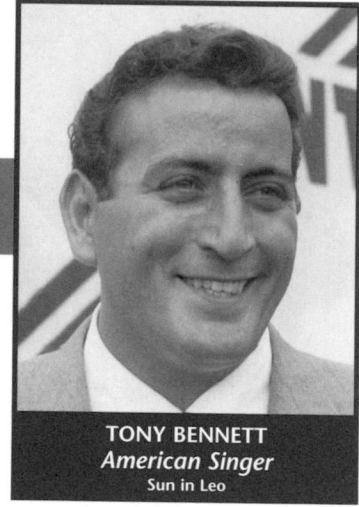

TONY BENNETT
American Singer
Sun in Leo

338

1959 CANCER
From June 22, 3:50 through July 23, 14:44

The Sensitive Caretaker

Sensitive Cancers of 1959 often wear your hearts on your sleeves, and your deep feelings can be easily hurt. When you give your love to someone, you expect it to be absolutely reciprocated—and you can be a bit possessive of your partners. Even if you know someone cares for you, you appreciate regular demonstrations of affection to reassure you that you truly matter. Whirlwind romances probably don't interest you—you prefer a stable, secure relationship with a devoted mate.

Home and family are priorities for you, and you probably won't feel fulfilled unless a relationship produces offspring. Quite likely, you lavish your children with the same loving care you give to your partner. A strong connection to family members and your heritage can provide you with a sense of security—and security is key to your happiness. Therefore, you may choose a mate whose financial assets, even status in the community, or family connections offer you the comfort and stability you crave.

Your sensuality is closely tied with your emotions. To arouse you physically a partner might need to stimulate your emotions first. Usually you need to feel secure with a partner before you are willing to open up to him or her. Deeply romantic, you appreciate a lover who takes time to court you, rather than rushing into bed—even if you've been together for years.

Competent, vital, self-confident women could be good compliments to many Cancer men born in 1959. A woman who capably handles responsibilities at home and/or work could earn your respect. You also want a loyal, loving partner who devotes herself to you and your children. Someone who is as beautiful inside as she is outside, and who demonstrates grace under fire gets highest honors.

Strong leaders appeal to most Cancer women of 1959, for they can provide the security and status you seek. A man must earn your love by showing he's worthy of your respect. Creative types could also strike a chord with you. You're not immune to handsome men and a sophisticated, romantic fellow could charm you, but you want someone with substance, not just a pretty face.

1959 LEO
From July 23, 14:45 through August 23, 21:43

The Discerning Dramatist

Leos born in 1959 seem to sizzle with electricity. As a result, people are often drawn to you by the dozens. Nevertheless, you tend to be discriminating in matters of the heart and usually choose your partners carefully. You know you have much to offer a mate and aren't likely to give yourself away too cheaply. You want a partner who values you highly and treats you like precious royalty. After all, your zodiac symbol is the king of beasts!

Generous toward those you care about (sometimes to a fault), you like to show lovers a good time and may shower them with gifts. You have a knack for turning a romance into a colorful drama. In return, you seek a partner's admiration and loyalty. And though your head can be turned by a pretty face now and again, you are usually loyal to your mate. You probably have high expectations of your lovers, and can be quite demanding at times. Perhaps you feel you are helping them to improve themselves, but not all partners will respond favorably to criticism, even if it is constructive.

Underneath your outward confidence, you might be just a bit uncertain about your desirability and need a lover to reinforce your ego. You adore attention and blossom when someone praises your looks, talent, or sexual prowess. A partner who flatters you and makes you feel important could find you to be an imaginative, sensitive, and romantic lover.

Male lions of 1959 usually prefer caring, compassionate women who take care of every need. You also appreciate someone who is practical and efficient, who can handle the mundane aspects of your life so you can devote yourself to the really important matters. She should be neat, trim, and pretty—but not so attractive that she outshines you.

1959's lionesses are often drawn to level-headed, pragmatic men who support your creativity, feed your self-esteem, and take care of the details. You want someone you can depend on, who will be there when you need him most. Common sense and business acumen are probably more important to you than good looks. A handyman who can fix anything could score high marks with you.

1959 VIRGO

From August 23, 21:44 through September 23, 19:07

The Adept Technician

You put great care into all you do, Virgo of 1959, including your relationships. You have a knack for soothing life's traumas, and with your kind and compassionate nature, you often make life easier for your loved ones. As a result, a partner can come to rely on you to fix whatever goes wrong, and you do so with competence. One of the ways you show you care is by doing things for him or her—whether it's repairing a leaky faucet, cooking a favorite meal, or putting cold compresses on a fevered brow.

You can tend to be somewhat shy and unassuming, often letting the other person take the lead and make many of the decisions. Although you can probably handle just about any challenge that comes your way, you may prefer to take a backseat to your partner, supporting and encouraging his or her ambitions. Meticulous, you carefully analyze a relationship's strengths and weaknesses so you can find ways to improve it. At times you can be too analytical, though, and lovers may worry they can't meet your high expectations.

An adept technician, your attention to detail most likely makes you a more than capable lover. You care about pleasing your partner and may refine your sexual skills to the nth degree. Your head often rules your heart, though, and you might see emotions as messy or impractical. Cleanliness, grace, and dependability probably impress you more than money, fame, or power.

Virgo men of 1959 often find shy, modest, sensitive women appealing. You value intelligence and competence, and might appreciate a woman who has a good head for business or an ability to run an orderly, efficient household. A mate who is much like you—practical, hard-working, and conscientious—is probably your best match.

Virgo women born during 1959 are usually attracted to refined, intelligent gentlemen who don't feel a need to prove their masculinity. Someone with good taste, good manners, and good breeding will usually win out over those who are brash, bold, or only beautiful. Healers, artists, and those who strive to make the world a better place could find a place in your heart, too.

VIRGO ZODIAC SIGN
YOUR LOVE PLANETS

YOUR ROMANTIC SIDE   p. 696
- ▶ **VENUS IN LIBRA**
  Born Aug. 23, 21:44 - Sept. 20, 3:00
- ▶ **VENUS IN LEO**
  Born Sept. 20, 3:01 - Sept. 23, 19:07

YOUR SEX DRIVE   p. 722
- ▶ **MARS IN LIBRA**
  Born Aug. 23, 21:44 - Sept. 05, 22:45
- ▶ **MARS IN LIBRA**
  Born Sept. 05, 22:46 - Sept. 23, 19:07

YOUR CELEBRITY TWINS   p. 760
Find out the astrological similarities you have with famous people.

YOUR COMPATIBILITY   p. 780
Compare planets to find out how compatible you are in a relationship.

YOUR RELATIONSHIP KARMA   p. 824
- ▶ **SATURN IN CAPRICORN**
  Born Aug. 23, 21:44 - Sept. 23, 19:07

DOROTHY DANDRIDGE
American Actress
Mars in Libra

339

1959 LIBRA

From September 23, 19:08 through October 24, 4:10

The Discriminating Partner

You invest a lot of energy into relationships, Libra of 1959. Unlike Libras born in other years, you don't vacillate in matters of the heart—you know what you want and go after it, rather than waiting for the other person to make the first move. If someone catches your attention, you may pursue that person intently—without being pushy, of course—using your charm, intelligence, and congeniality to win him or her over. With your friendly personality you often succeed in your quest for love.

In some ways your own identity might be linked with that of your partner, such that a relationship enables you to accomplish more and fulfill yourself in ways you couldn't do alone. Perhaps you feel incomplete if you don't have a significant other in your life. But even though you dislike being alone, you tend to be discriminating in your choice of partners. Although you may be willing to take a few chances on love, you aren't frivolous with your affection. You seek a lasting, committed partnership, and want to make sure the one you select is right for you in the long term.

Some might say you are overly analytical or emotionally detached, but your lovers would argue that you are an attentive and affectionate companion. You want to give pleasure as well as receive it, and may go to great lengths to satisfy your partner. Your own preferences tend to be rather conservative, however, and you might have to work at being more inventive, if that's what's called for.

Neat, orderly, conscientious women can be good mates for Libra men born in 1959. You need to be able to rely on your mate. You appreciate a partner who pays attention to details and understands your needs and idiosyncrasies. Good looks are usually less important to you than a good heart and a good mind.

Creative types often appeal to female Libras of 1959. Even if they aren't artists, writers, or musicians themselves, you expect them to have an appreciation of the finer things in life. Grace, tact, and good manners top your list—you don't like your partners to have many rough edges and macho men generally turn you off.

LIBRA ZODIAC SIGN
YOUR LOVE PLANETS

YOUR ROMANTIC SIDE   p. 696
- ▶ **VENUS IN LEO**
  Born Sept. 23, 19:08 - Sept. 25, 8:13
- ▶ **VENUS IN LIBRA**
  Born Sept. 25, 8:14 - Oct. 24, 4:10

YOUR SEX DRIVE   p. 722
- ▶ **MARS IN LIBRA**
  Born Sept. 23, 19:08 - Oct. 21, 9:39
- ▶ **MARS IN SCORPIO**
  Born Oct. 21, 9:40 - Oct. 24, 4:10

YOUR CELEBRITY TWINS   p. 760
Find out the astrological similarities you have with famous people.

YOUR COMPATIBILITY   p. 780
Compare planets to find out how compatible you are in a relationship.

YOUR RELATIONSHIP KARMA   p. 824
- ▶ **SATURN IN CAPRICORN**
  Born Sept. 23, 19:08 - Oct. 24, 4:10

LEE REMICK
American Actress
Sun in Sagittarius

1959 SCORPIO
From October 24, 4:11 through November 23, 1:26

♏ The Passionate Powerhouse

Few can match your personal magnetism, Scorpio of 1959, and it's probably safe to say that you make a lasting impression on nearly everyone you meet. Although some may be intimidated by your aura of power, others are drawn to your quiet strength—particularly the opposite sex. You also project a sense of mystery that can be most intriguing.

Because you are deeply emotional, you might attempt to control romantic situations and partners. You may have been hurt in the past and don't want to leave yourself open for another painful experience. Consequently, you might be quite particular in your choice of partners. When you do decide to trust someone and establish a relationship, you are inclined to give it your all and can be a sensitive, protective, and devoted mate. In fact, you could become so enmeshed in your partner that you would have trouble separating your own needs from his or hers, a condition that could produce jealousy and possessiveness.

Your sex appeal is hard to ignore, and regardless of how good-looking you are, you probably have no trouble attracting admirers. Sexual partners may find you to be a passionate and romantic lover, and the time they spend with you is likely to be quite exciting. You appreciate an imaginative, open-minded partner who can match your intensity and who is willing to push the outside of the envelope, for you don't like to set limits in intimacy.

Male Scorpions of 1959 are often drawn to gentle, unassuming women who bring out your protective side and make you feel powerful. Because you can be quite willful, you may be most content with someone who is adaptable and doesn't challenge your authority. A neat, orderly, even-tempered partner could provide a good balance in your somewhat turbulent life.

Women born in 1959 under the sign of the Scorpion usually admire men who are strong and passionate. You don't want someone who lets you push him around, and although you may have your share of romantic battles, that only makes things more exciting. Power, for you, is a heady aphrodisiac, and you value a partner who wields it capably.

1959 SAGITTARIUS
From November 23, 1:27 through December 22, 14:33

♐ The Entertaining Playmate

Fun-loving Sagittarians of 1959 often find yourselves at the center of social gatherings, amusing friends and loved ones with your delightful wit. Your optimism and outgoing nature make other people feel comfortable in your presence—you have a knack for brightening their spirits and making them forget their troubles. It's no surprise, therefore, that you tend to attract many partners who admire your spontaneity, sense of humor, and playfulness.

For the most part, you see relationships as a form of entertainment—and you really know how to show a lover a good time. Your expansiveness and curiosity might sometimes lead to excesses, however, and you might have to work hard to maintain a long-term, monogamous relationship. Your love of life and people keeps you questing for yet another adventure. You do have a serious side, but when opportunity knocks you usually open the door. Even if you have loved and left many partners over the years, you probably had fun and they are likely to hold fond memories of your time together.

Sex, too, might be something of a game for you and your playfulness can be refreshing to some people. But your free-spirited attitude might keep you from getting as close to your lovers as you'd like. Underneath your winsome ways, you do have a more passionate side and you can be quite romantic when you want to be. The right partner can encourage your idealism and imagination, perhaps by acting out your fantasies.

Feminine women usually appeal to Sagittarian men born in 1959. Although you admire strength, you might not find aggressive women or "jocks" particularly attractive. A friendly, good-natured partner would probably suit you well—but you could also find a tempestuous, sultry vixen irresistible.

Men who possess a depth and breath of knowledge and experience could capture the heart of a Sagittarian woman born in 1959. Someone who can bring you new experiences could win your favor. You enjoy an upbeat, outgoing partner, but you want him to have some substance, too. Your ideal mate is optimistic without being naive, and serious without being morose.

Hitchcock & His Blondes

"Blondes make the best victims. They're like virgin snow that shows up the bloody footprints."

ALFRED HITCHCOCK

Many of Hitchcock's movies contain recognizable elements of his style, one being that his leading lady is often portrayed as an icy young woman, and usually a blonde. Roger Ebert, the *Chicago Sun-Times* film critic, once wrote that Hitchcock's female characters "... reflected the same qualities over and over again..." Hitchcock's platinum women shared a classic beauty—symmetrical features and hair styled in sleek pageboys or pulled into place with a French twist, only to be disheveled along the way in some treacherous journey.

In film after film, Hitchcock also revealed that beneath the chilly exterior of his blondes was a deep sexual desire and erotic nature. In *To Catch a Thief* (1955), Grace Kelly is excited by the idea that Cary Grant might be a dangerous jewel thief. Taking him on a picnic, she asks demurely, "Do you want a leg or a breast?" There's a strong sexual insinuation that she's not just talking about the chicken.

Grace Kelly was perhaps known as the quintessential Hitchcock blonde. In fact, Hitchcock had Kelly in mind for *The Birds* (1963) and *Marnie* (1964), however, because of her marriage to Prince Rainier of Monaco, Kelly retired from the movie industry for good. Tippi Hedren, a pretty model who Hitchcock saw in a television commercial, became his new discovery. After a few weeks of filming *The Birds*, Hitchcock told the Associated Press, "Get a look at that girl, she's going to be good ... I think Svengali Hitch rides again." But during the filming of *Marnie*, in which Hedren plays a frigid kleptomaniac, Hitchcock's unwanted advances towards Hedren permanently damaged their relationship.

Other famous Hitchcock's blondes include Ingrid Bergman, who starred in one of his best-known films as a hedonistic sexual explorer, opposite Cary Grant, in *Notorious* (1945). In *Vertigo* (1958) Jimmy Stewart plays John Ferguson, a detective obsessed in remaking Kim Novak's mysterious brunette character into the blonde image of a dead woman. As noted in a 1996 review by film critic James Berardinelli, "Hitchcock scholars are in general agreement that John is a subconscious representation of the director—a man constantly striving for his own image of perfect female beauty."

The luminous blonde Eva Marie Saint made only one film with Hitchcock, but that turned out to be #40 on the American Film Institute's list of the top 100 Films of all time. In *North By Northwest* (1959), Saint plays an alluring secret agent who effortlessly seduces Cary Grant. On Alfred Hitchcock, Eva Marie Saint remarked: "[Hitchcock] said, 'I don't want you going back to... do[ing] movies where you wash the dishes looking drab in an apron. The audience wants to see their leading ladies dressed up.' He saw me as others didn't."

In *Psycho* (1960), Janet Leigh's transformation from immoral criminal to powerless victim in the bloody shower sequence won her an Oscar nomination and a Golden Globe Award. Early on in the film, Leigh wears white lingerie, yet once she becomes a thief, stealing $40,000, she's next seen in black, indicating her downward spiral into destruction. Almost forgotten in the horror flick is actress Vera Miles, the other icy blonde.

From the start of his career, Hitchcock preferred his blondes. And although there are seemingly many personal psychological aspects for this preference, Hitchcock felt that they always "make the best victims."

341

► READ ABOUT GRACE KELLY AND PRINCE RAINIER ON PAGE 310 ► READ ABOUT INGRID BERGMAN ON PAGE 203 ► READ ABOUT CARY GRANT ON PAGE 244

1960 -1969

THE SWINGING SIXTIES

The 1960s were a heady time of revolution in lifestyles, music, and civil rights, heralding a new age of sexual freedom.

The children of the conformist, sedate fifties came of age against the "youth quake" and later the backdrop of the Vietnam War, and rebellion expressed itself in clothing and hair styles, sex, drugs, and rock 'n' roll, and on into powerful, far-reaching political movements for social change. These ranged from the early '60s "mods" in London, where Mary Quant designed the miniskirt, to the later '60s hippies in San Francisco with their back-to-the-land communes and psychedelic drug manifestos. The decade that started with civil rights demonstrations proceeded to anti-war draft-card burnings, massive peace marches, and civil unrest throughout the world.

The US saw the assassination of President John Kennedy, and later his brother Robert and Martin Luther King. The early civil rights movement gave birth to Black Power. Riot and demonstrations flared, from the anti-war crusades on campuses, to the 1968 National Democratic Convention in Chicago, to the first demonstration for gay rights, known as the "Stonewall Riots," in New York City.

In France in May 1968, student rioters were joined by ten million workers, who shut down the economic machinery of the country for several weeks, while in August of that same year, Soviet tanks rolled into Prague to quash the reforms of the "Prague Spring" movement. Violence erupted on campuses from Japan to Italy to Mexico.

The "Pill" went on sale in Britain and, not long after, the government made it available for free on the national health service, kick-starting a new age of sexual freedom. Women worldwide saw legislation for reproductive choice, no-fault divorce, and equal rights in the workplace.

Music was eclectic, from the early stirring folk anthems of Bob Dylan and Pete Seeger, to the "British invasion" of the Beatles and the Rolling Stones, to Jimi Hendrix, Janis Joplin, and the gigantic 1969 Woodstock concert. The Beatles became spokesmen for a generation, segueing from the sweet, blues-influenced early "I Want to Hold Your Hand" to their seamless experimental masterpiece album *Sgt. Pepper's Lonely Hearts Club Band*. Broadway captured the energy of the times with *Hair*, in which peace-and-love hippies danced nude and sang about the "dawning of the Age of Aquarius."

Modern celebrity was ushered in by Andy Warhol's famous-for-being-famous "superstars" at the New York club Max's Kansas City and by Truman Capote's exclusive high-society Black and White Ball of 1966. The arts broke free of conventional forms and became improvisational and politicized—there were "happenings" in the street and jazz-poetry jams in packed clubs.

THE SILVER SCREEN
It was also a time of experimentation in film, from Polanski's *Repulsion* to Antonioni's *Blowup*, and Cassavetes' *Faces*. *Easy Rider* fused biker culture with the American road-trip movie tradition, while *Bonnie and Clyde* followed the wild, violent odyssey of an outlaw couple. *Midnight Cowboy*, about a hapless hustler in New York City, was the first major studio release with an "X" rating and went on to win the Academy Award for Best Picture. Alfred Hitchcock's cult classic *Psycho* produced the most famous shower scene ever shot and Stanley Kubrick's *Lolita*, adapted from Vladimir Nabokov's novel, depicted a man's obsession with a teenaged girl.

BETWEEN THE PAGES
A raft of previously censored novels saw the light of day in the 1960s, including Henry Miller's *Tropic of Cancer*, D.H. Lawrence's *Lady Chatterley's Lover*, and *Fanny Hill* by John Cleland. Feminist classics included Doris Lessing's *The Golden Notebooks* and Betty Friedan's *The Feminine Mystique*. Richard Brautigan's *Trout Fishing in America* and Kurt Vonnegut's *Slaughterhouse Five* both used

experimental form to explore complex social issues. Alan Watts pioneered the fusion of Eastern enlightenment with Western psychology in *The Book*. The sixties also saw the rise of the pop-psych and -sociology genre, with *Games People Play* and *Human Sexual Response*, and such titillating fictional counterparts as *The Chapman Report*.

PEOPLE
Edie Sedgwick embodied youth glamour, while Audrey Hepburn sparkled as free spirit Holly Golightly in *Breakfast at Tiffany's*. Sophia Loren, Elizabeth Taylor, Jacqueline Kennedy, Elvis Presley, and every one of the Beatles made news with their nuptials, as did Peter Sellers when he wed Britt Ekland.

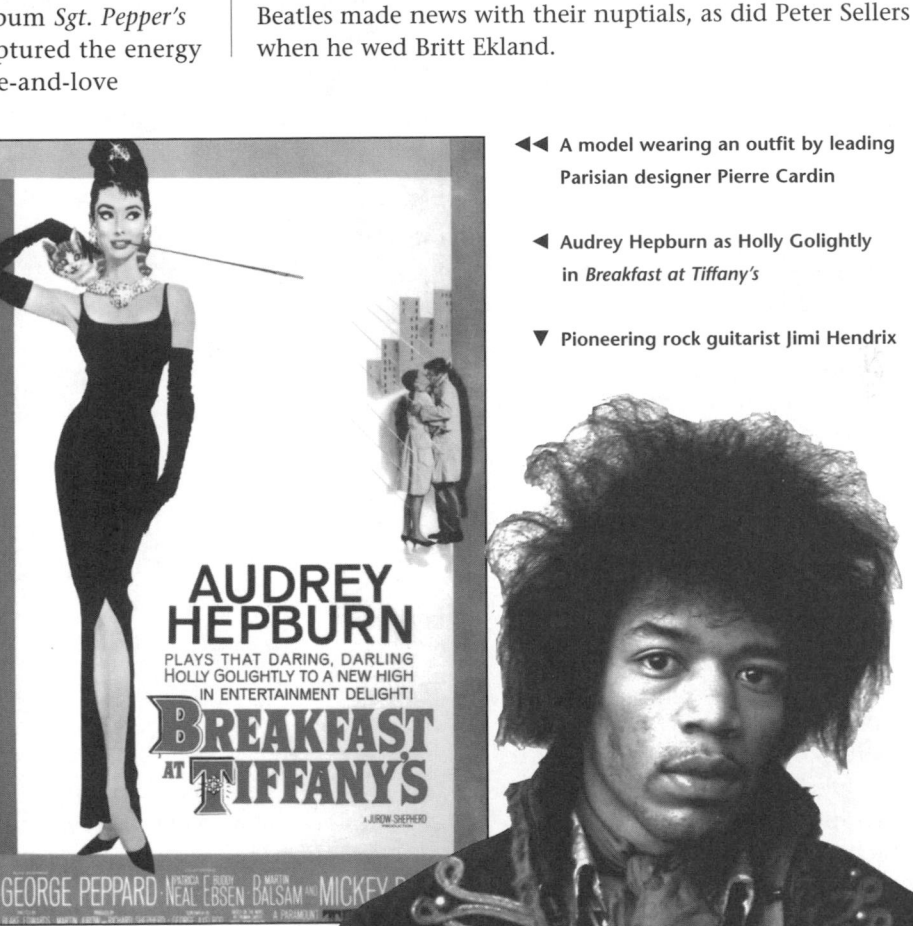

◄◄ A model wearing an outfit by leading Parisian designer Pierre Cardin

◄ Audrey Hepburn as Holly Golightly in *Breakfast at Tiffany's*

▼ Pioneering rock guitarist Jimi Hendrix

343

AUDREY HEPBURN PLAYS THAT DARING, DARLING HOLLY GOLIGHTLY TO A NEW HIGH IN ENTERTAINMENT DELIGHT!

BREAKFAST AT TIFFANY'S

A JUROW-SHEPHERD

GEORGE PEPPARD

1960

- ★ LUCILLE BALL AND DESI ARNAZ DIVORCE
- ★ BIRTH CONTROL PILL INTRODUCED
- ★ HITCHCOCK'S PSYCHO
- ★ NEVER ON SUNDAY
- ★ THE TWIST
- ★ UPDIKE'S RABBIT, RUN

EVENTS

1960 brought more celebrity divorces than nuptials, including Lucille Ball and Desi Arnaz and Vivien Leigh and Laurence Olivier, although Britain's Princess Margaret married photographer Anthony Armstrong-Jones at Westminster Abbey. Pope John XXIII warned that women with improper attire would be denied the Sacrament in all Catholic churches, while Sweden's Lutheran Church allowed women to be consecrated as priests for the first time. In London, Penguin Books, the publisher of D.H. Lawrence's banned *Lady Chatterley's Lover*, was acquitted of obscenity charges, and the book was finally reissued. The United States introduced the first commercially produced birth control pill, Enovid 10.

POP CULTURE

It was a terrific year for provocative films, including two about prostitutes—*Butterfield 8*, for which Elizabeth Taylor won an Oscar for her portrayal of a sophisticated call girl, and *Never On Sunday*, starring sultry Melina Mercouri as a vivacious yet dedicated Greek prostitute. Alfred Hitchcock's *Psycho* featured Anthony Perkins as a creepy, murderous motel clerk. In Billy Wilder's now-classic *The Apartment*, Jack Lemmon and Shirley MacLaine navigated the perils of corporate climbing and office romances. *L'Avventura (The Adventure)*, directed by Michelangelo Antonioni, involved the mysterious vacation disappearance of a young woman.

1960 was Elvis all the time, with his hits "It's Now or Never," "Are You Lonesome Tonight?" and "Stuck on You." "The Twist," recorded by Ernest "Chubby Checker" Evans, launched an international dance craze. Vocal groups harmonized "Save the Last Dance for Me" and "Cathy's Clown," while Britain's Cliff Richard mined the love theme with "Fall in Love with You" and "I Love You."

John Updike's acclaimed novel *Rabbit, Run* profiled a disillusioned man who leaves his family on a quest for meaning. *The Constant Image* by Marcia Davenport told of love and adultery among the upper classes in Milan. *The Chapman Report* by Irving Wallace supplied titillation in the guise of sociology as a fictional psychologist conducts sex surveys of randy suburban housewives.

Hot Couple

SAMMY DAVIS JR. & MAY BRITT

From the very beginning, the relationship between Sammy Davis Jr. and the gorgeous Swedish starlet May Britt caused a public outcry. Davis, a vocal supporter of presidential candidate John F. Kennedy, felt compelled to postpone his marriage to Britt until after the election. At the same time, Britt's movie contract was not renewed.

But they did marry on November 13, 1960, and for a time were happy. Britt sacrificed her career to marry Davis, only wanting a conventional marriage and children. But after holding together even through racist death threats and bad press, the marriage collapsed and they divorced in 1968.

SEE ALSO

▶ JOHN F. KENNEDY *Page 351*

▶ FRANK SINATRA *Page 211*

1960 CAPRICORN

From December 22, 1959 14:34 through January 21, 1960 1:09
(December 1960 Capricorns, see 1961 Capricorn)

♑ *The Practical Romantic*

The multi-faceted nature of your personality, 1960 Capricorn, can be intriguing to a partner, because there is always something new to discover about you. On the one hand, your mate may find you to be responsible, hard-working, and true to your commitments. On the other hand, you can be a big dreamer, oblivious to practicality, and happy to lose yourself in flights of creative or romantic fancy. If you feel you're being pigeon-holed into one role, you can become restless and volatile. You thrive in a relationship that allows you to give the fullest expression possible to the full range of your character traits.

If a partner fell in love with you when you were emphasizing one side of your personality, he or she may feel confused when the other side emerges. With your visionary gifts you can invite your mate to play a central role in creating a partnership that can strike a healthy balance between your competing impulses. For example, you might rely on your mate to suggest ways to put your dreams and fantasies to good use in improving your professional and financial

prospects together. And after a long day of being responsible and productive, you might sweep your sweetheart off his or her feet with romantic gestures that are imaginative and enchanting. You can be a very seductive lover with a happy-go-lucky charisma that is intoxicating.

A partner may learn quickly not to invite you to act on a dare, unless he or she expects you to go through with it. A bit of risk can be irresistible for you. Sexually adventurous, you may enjoy exploring all the possibilities being part of a couple allows.

The 1960 Capricorn man enjoys a woman who has a hearty sense of humor. You may have a somewhat ironic point of view, and you appreciate a lady with the smarts to get your jokes and to fire off a few of her own. Her lighter side makes every day life a pleasure.

Female Capricorns born in 1960 like a man who is far-sighted and practical. You admire someone who has the gumption to seize an opportunity. With his big picture perspective he can help you to weather any setbacks and stay focused.

CAPRICORN ZODIAC SIGN
YOUR LOVE PLANETS

YOUR ROMANTIC SIDE   p. 696
- ► VENUS IN SCORPIO
  Born Dec. 22, 1959 14:34 - Jan. 02, 1960 8:42
- ► VENUS IN SAGITTARIUS
  Born Jan. 02, 8:43 - Jan. 21, 1:09

YOUR SEX DRIVE   p. 722
- ► MARS IN SAGITTARIUS
  Born Dec. 22, 1959 14:34 - Jan. 14, 1960 4:58
- ► MARS IN CAPRICORN
  Born Jan. 14, 4:59 - Jan. 21, 1:09

YOUR CELEBRITY TWINS   p. 760
Find out the astrological similarities you have with famous people.

YOUR COMPATIBILITY   p. 780
Compare planets to find out how compatible you are in a relationship.

YOUR RELATIONSHIP KARMA   p. 824
- ► SATURN IN CAPRICORN
  Born Dec. 22, 1959 14:34 - Jan. 21, 1960 1:09

MELINA MERCOURI
Greek Actress
Mars in Capricorn

345

1960 AQUARIUS

From January 21, 1:10 through February 19, 15:25

♒ *The Spontaneous Sweetheart*

For you, the 1960 Aquarian, the "big bang" theory describes how a universe of passion can burst into your life. You may owe at least one great romance to love at first sight, or the proverbial bolt of lightning may have suddenly cast your feelings for a friend in a dramatically different light. For you spontaneity can be the very essence of romance, and you may prefer to let love evolve naturally, as if by magic. It can be a turn-off for you if a suitor or mate is trying too hard, and you may recoil if a mate pressures you to make a commitment. In defining the nature of your relationship and the role each partner plays, you may prefer to improvise, crossing each bridge as you get there.

With a mate who is self-sufficient, laid-back, and trusting, you prove over time to be a faithful and devoted partner. Your ideal relationship allows both partners plenty of freedom to grow and pursue their interests as individuals. Love, sex, and emotional attachment may be deeply personal subjects for you. Indeed, you may have been involved with a mate for a long time before letting others in

your life in on the big news. The privacy of the bedroom lets you open your body, heart, and soul to your mate. Enveloped in the magical feeling romance can inspire, you may lavish your lover with passionate attention.

Lovemaking can awaken for you a childlike fascination with discovery and experimentation. Sharing and acting out naughty fantasies can embolden you to bring your flair for innovation into the act. Trying out different techniques and positions can be electrifying, especially with sex toys.

The Aquarius man of 1960 appreciates a woman who is empathetic and wise. You tend to feel comfortable with someone who senses what you need without needing a lot of discussion. This lady can take care of you without overwhelming or smothering you.

A productive, goal-oriented man is a wonderful counterpart for the Aquarius woman of 1960. Busy with his own activities, he allows you the freedom to pursue your own. You may find that you can't wait to come home to such an intriguing partner.

AQUARIUS ZODIAC SIGN
YOUR LOVE PLANETS

YOUR ROMANTIC SIDE   p. 696
- ► VENUS IN SAGITTARIUS
  Born Jan. 21, 1:10 - Jan. 27, 4:45
- ► VENUS IN CAPRICORN
  Born Jan. 27, 4:46 - Feb. 19, 15:25

YOUR SEX DRIVE   p. 722
- ► MARS IN CAPRICORN
  Born Jan. 21, 1:10 - Feb. 19, 15:25

YOUR CELEBRITY TWINS   p. 760
Find out the astrological similarities you have with famous people.

YOUR COMPATIBILITY   p. 780
Compare planets to find out how compatible you are in a relationship.

YOUR RELATIONSHIP KARMA   p. 824
- ► SATURN IN CAPRICORN
  Born Jan. 21, 1:10 - Feb. 19, 15:25

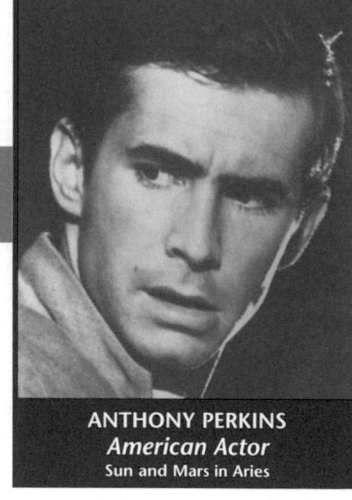

ANTHONY PERKINS
American Actor
Sun and Mars in Aries

346

1960 PISCES
From February 19, 15:26 through March 20, 14:42

 ## The Mysterious Mate

Likely to be a great romantic, 1960 Pisces, you may embrace life with a bustier-ripping passion. Rather than suffer the real world with all its warts and flaws, you have a gift for creating your own dreamy atmosphere with music, luscious décor, and fashionable touches that can be inviting to friends and seductive to lovers. Your friendships tend to be filled with romantic intensity, and your romantic partnerships tend to thrive on the harmony of friendship. For you all the world may be a stage, and you may share a passion for theatre with your mate. You may relate to each other with emotional intensity and drama.

While you can be tenacious in maintaining many friendships, you may conceal your deepest thoughts and feelings from all but your truest, closest friend—your mate. Allowing only your mate to be privy to the baring of your soul underscores the special nature of your relationship and seals with a kiss the enduring bond between you. Still, there are some secrets that you may never disclose, and from time to time your partner may sense you are holding back. Your mate may simply have to accept a certain degree of frustration as the trade-off for your perpetually mysterious allure and the ecstasy you provide in the bedroom.

Sharing fantasies and role playing can fill your sex life with interest, variety, and excitement. The more imaginative and eccentric your fantasies are, the more thrills you may derive from enacting them. Likely to have a weakness for rescuing a lover in distress, you tend to come through with extra compassion and tenderness when your partner is most in need.

For you, the 1960 Piscean man, an idealistic woman can be the answer to your prayers. It can be so liberating for you to be around someone who has the courage to reject the status quo. Her passion can inspire you to pursue your greatest aspirations.

The heart of the 1960 Piscean woman beats a little faster around a man who is ingenious and innovative. You tend to enjoy someone who can stimulate your mind with unusual ideas. His willingness to experiment can excite your own creativity.

1960 ARIES
From March 20, 14:43 through April 20, 2:05

The Winsome Warrior

For you, Aries of 1960, love truly can conquer all. If life puts you to the test in winning or keeping a lover, you may map out a problem-solving strategy with military-like precision. Friendly and clever, you have a winning appeal, and your impassioned persistence can soften the heart of the most reluctant partner. Dreaming up ingenious ways of wooing your mate, you may do some detective work behind the scenes to find out what your partner likes. With a seemingly effortless flair, you can succeed in making a partner's dreams come true.

Members of your sign tend to enjoy the thrill of the chase, but your days of playing the field may have been shorter than for most Ariens. Once you have met the right person, you tend to develop a deep, emotional attachment and become a faithful and supportive mate. Your sensitivity to your mate's emotions can be so intense, you may feel his or her pain as if it were your own. While such empathy can move you to treat your partner with extra care, it can sometimes lead you to interfere in his or her affairs. To avoid the possibility of intruding it would be wise to ask your partner if your help is needed before you intervene. In the bedroom you can be a tender lover, exquisitely attuned to your mate's sexual responses and preferences.

A romantic atmosphere tends to arouse your passions. Music, rich colors, and lighting can influence your mood. You and your lover may attend to each other's bodies with studious fascination, probing every area for a reaction and trying out different ways of achieving peak pleasure.

The 1960 Arien man can hardly resist a woman who is subtle and intriguing. She may be tender and generous with affection, and yet there is something about her that seems impossible to possess. Her mysterious allure arouses your hunter spirit and holds your interest.

The Aries woman of 1960 adores a man who is romantic and sensual. You tend to be attracted to high-powered partners, and this man simmers with intensity. His passion can energize you, and his zeal in finding ways to please you leaves no doubt as to his devotion.

1960 TAURUS

From April 20, 2:06 through May 21, 1:33

The Receptive Romantic

Romance makes the world go round for Taurus of 1960. Nothing energizes you like the feeling of falling in love. While most Taureans tend to take their time in getting involved, the rush of passion in a new relationship can weaken your resistance and pry your heart wide open. For you a romantic partnership provides a constant flow of inspiration that fuels your creativity and brings out the best in you. When your partner is away, you tend to feel not quite yourself, and the feeling that something is missing can be palpable. You may become possessive and suspicious, especially if you feel unsure of where you stand with your mate. A stable, long-term commitment brings you a comforting sense of security.

You may have an ingenious way of satisfying your need for commitment without sacrificing your craving for the intoxicating feeling of love freshly in bloom. Just as romance inspires your creativity, your creativity can inspire you to fall in love with your mate, over and over again. You may idealize your mate, and with every milestone that you and your partner reach over the years, your growth together provides new opportunities to discover more things to admire. You tend to express your admiration by lavishing your sweetheart with sensual pleasures.

You may have a mighty appetite for physical affection—in and out of the bedroom. Your skin may be quite sensitive. Holding hands, tender caressing, and soft kisses can be highly arousing for you. Lovely sights, pungent aromas, and delicious flavors tend to spark your passions. For you lovemaking is most exciting when it engages all of your senses.

The Taurean man of 1960 appreciates a woman who is serene but determined. You tend to feel most secure with someone who does not keep you guessing about her devotion to you. Her practical, no-nonsense style assures you of her affection.

A man with an imaginative approach to romance can win the heart of the 1960 Taurean woman. You can flourish with a partner who stirs your passions and sweeps you off your feet. With this captivating man you can make your dreams come true.

347

1960 GEMINI

From May 21, 1:34 through June 21, 9:41

The Hearty Butterfly

In many ways, 1960 Gemini, you are like a butterfly. In social gatherings you may flutter about, charming others and attracting admirers with your grace and wit. Early on in your life, you might have hopped from romance to romance, pausing only to take in what you needed in the moment. But just as the delicate butterfly has the stamina to fly cross entire continents, you too have the capacity for astounding endurance in a love relationship. A soul mate may have suddenly appeared to you, or you may have simply reached a point in your life when casual relationships lost interest for you, and you hungered for something more.

A serious romance allows you to explore the mysteries of your lover's soul, a process that offers you endless fascination. The very deep feelings a relationship can arouse in you may force you to stop and consider what matters most in life in general and to you in particular. You tend to be a thinking person, likely to make a conscious decision to commit yourself to your sweetheart. Once you make such a commitment, you may dedicate your heart, mind, and soul to keeping it. The devotion you and your mate have for each other makes your life meaningful, a dream-come-true for meaning-hungry Gemini. For you sex provides a way for you to express your appreciation for your partner.

You may love to talk in bed and appreciate a partner who is highly vocal in expressing preferences and pleasure. Variety keeps your sex life interesting, and you may generously reward a partner who comes up with new and unusual ideas to try out together.

A cheerful, clever woman can be highly enticing to the 1960 Gemini man. You enjoy a partner who can keep you on your toes. With her quick wit and eye for amusing associations she can keep you laughing. Her mischievous sense of fun ensures that you will never be bored.

The Gemini woman of 1960 can't resist the man who can keep up with her rapid pace. Someone with drive and initiative can energize and inspire you. His ability to turn you on to new interests can capture your imagination and leave you eagerly anticipating his next move.

DEAN MARTIN
American Singer
Sun and Mars in Gemini

PRINCESS MARGARET
British Princess
Sun in Leo

1960 CANCER
From June 21, 9:42 through July 22, 20:36

The Nurturing Homebody

Just as the crab carries its house on its back, dear Cancerian of 1960, home is where your heart is. Wherever you go, you bring a true moveable feast of nurturing affection with you that can sustain a relationship through lean times. Your sign rules feeding and tender loving care, and you are among the most indulgent of Cancers, lavishing your mate and any family you may have together with sensual pleasures and creature comforts. For you food can be love, and you may take it personally if a sweetheart rejects one of your generous proffers. Your mate can reassure you that the love you share is secure, no matter what.

Your feelings can color your perceptions and reactions, and you may rely on your mate for the occasional reality check. Good communication helps you make sense of your gut impulses and keep a healthy perspective. Your mate, in turn, may often consult you for your intuitive take on a situation and rely on your gift as an excellent judge of character. Being able to depend on each other is the cement that holds your relationship together for the long term. Your tender empathy for each other enables you and your mate to be the best of friends. For you physical affection can be one of the six essential food groups, best consumed in private.

You may respond well to the traditional trappings of romance—flowers, gifts, love notes, sentimental keepsakes. Going out and having fun with your mate can satisfy your craving for one-on-one closeness. Your partner may be your favorite dish, and you may savor the taste of your mate's body and kisses.

The Cancer man of 1960 tends to feel most comfortable with a woman who is doting and protective. You're happiest when you can look forward to coming home and being babied. Able to anticipate your every need, this lady makes you her number one priority.

The Cancer woman born in 1960 can find contentment with a man who can be earthy and practical. You feel safe and secure with someone who can lend you a strong shoulder. With this man you never want for opportunities to stop and smell the roses.

1960 LEO
From July 22, 20:37 through August 23, 3:33

The Playful Idealist

You exude a certain air of innocence, Leo of 1960, a quality that can make you an intriguing catch. You tend to be idealistic about love and relationships, and you may have had to kiss a few frogs before finding a match who could meet your royal requirements. Your innocence can attract an exploiter as easily as a protector, and experience may have won you the wisdom of knowing when to throw someone back into the pond. Since you can remember, you may have always dreamed of having a harmonious family life, with ample support for your mate and any children you may have. You thrive with a partner who cherishes the purity of your will and shares your hopes and dreams.

In general, Leos tend to have a healthy sense of self-worth, but for you, feeling good may depend on honorable behavior. You may expect no less from your mate. Mutual respect for each other and your commitment creates an enduring foundation for your love and home life. Beyond such serious matters, you and your mate are likely to share a passionate attraction to each other. Spending time together—going out for a romantic night on the town or enjoying an intimate night at home—keeps your relationship bubbly and spirited. You can be kittenish in the bedroom, enticing your mate with your warmth, sensuality, and languid beauty.

Likely to be a playful lover, you may adore a mate who can make you squeal with laughter. Teasing and fooling around can loosen you up and arouse your passions. Fantasy fulfillment and role-playing allow you to express your theatrical gifts with seductive flair.

An ardent and romantic woman can make the 1960 Leo man feel sexy and desirable. You appreciate a fiercely loyal partner who stands by you through thick and thin. Generous with praise, she encourages you in your undertakings and takes pride in being all yours.

The Leo woman of 1960 adores the man who can stimulate her intellect. Learning can be a great source of pleasure for you, and someone with a clever outlook can keep you entertained. With his mischievous sense of fun, this man can expose you to a wide variety of amusements.

1960 VIRGO

From August 23, 3:34 through September 23, 0:58

♍ The Discreet Sensualist

Y ou are likely to be very well put-together in appearance, 1960 Virgo, and your unique sense of style can convey a devil-may-care attitude that makes you approachable and touchable. You have a sexy, compelling presence that may seem to contradict the virginal reputation of your sign. You may exult in the attention, but you are not too shy to shoot down any unwelcome advances. You tend to be picky about choosing the right partner, and you're not likely to be interested in casual affairs. Once you're involved, that's it— you're a loyal, devoted mate, and your seductive gifts are strictly for the benefit of your partner.

A commitment can mean serious business for you, and you are willing to work hard to maintain the health and happiness of your relationship. Taking care of your mate is likely to be a pleasure for you, because it makes you feel needed and appreciated. A strong emotional attachment may bind you to your partner. While you tend to shy away from public displays of affection, you are likely to be much more open in private, where sharing your feelings with

a trusted partner can afford you a release. Sex also provides a welcome release for any built-up tensions. Free to let it all hang out in private, you may bring an athlete's vigor to lovemaking.

Sexy messages, discreetly delivered, can rev up your erotic engine. You may prefer to whisper in bed, but you've got a lot to say. You tend to enjoy a partner who comes to bed with a variety of ideas about how you might please each other, and you may be willing to try anything at least once.

For the Virgo man of 1960 a gentle, elegant woman can be utterly captivating. A lady with an understated appeal tends to be most attractive to you. In your admiring eyes she can become even more beautiful. In your loving arms she can become a seductive enchantress.

A charming, astute man appeals to the Virgo woman born in 1960. You tend to be sensitive to details and may have very particular preferences in many areas of life. With his ability to appreciate the fine points, he can ensure that you will always have the very best.

VIRGO ZODIAC SIGN
YOUR LOVE PLANETS

YOUR ROMANTIC SIDE   p. 696
- ▶ **VENUS IN VIRGO**
  Born Aug. 23, 3:34 - Sept. 02, 19:28
- ▶ **VENUS IN LIBRA**
  Born Sept. 02, 19:29 - Sept. 23, 0:58

YOUR SEX DRIVE   p. 722
- ▶ **MARS IN GEMINI**
  Born Aug. 23, 3:34 - Sept. 21, 4:05
- ▶ **MARS IN CANCER**
  Born Sept. 21, 4:06 - Sept. 23, 0:58

YOUR CELEBRITY TWINS   p. 760
Find out the astrological similarities you have with famous people.

YOUR COMPATIBILITY   p. 780
Compare planets to find out how compatible you are in a relationship.

YOUR RELATIONSHIP KARMA   p. 824
- ▶ **SATURN IN CAPRICORN**
  Born Aug. 23, 3:34 - Sept. 23, 0:58

YVES MONTAND
French Actor
Venus and Mars in Virgo

349

1960 LIBRA

From September 23, 0:59 through October 23, 10:01

♎ The Selfless Sweetheart

A century before you were born, 1960 Libra, great romantics declared that they would die for love. You are unlikely to be quite so melodramatic, but you might understand how someone could feel that way. Your love for a partner can be passionate and deep. You may be willing to sacrifice a great deal for the sake of a relationship or to help out your mate. Such noble instincts can hold things together through tough times, but too much self-denial can throw your partnership out of balance and leave you feeling neglected and resentful. You've got a good gut instinct for when a partnership is becoming one-sided. That's your cue to speak up and let your mate know how you feel and what you need. With your gifts of tact and diplomacy you can create a win-win solution.

While you tend to be generous with affection, you can also provide practical support for your goals as individuals and for your dreams as a couple. The romantic fireworks that got your relationship off the ground can turn into an emotional attachment that deepens over the years. For you lovemaking allows you to express

your feelings for your mate. In the privacy of the bedroom you can enjoy the undivided attention of your partner, and you may feel freer to open your heart and speak your mind.

You appreciate a lover who can gently initiate into the erotic mysteries of sex. Tender pillow talk can soften your resistance and stir your passions. Sensitive to your surroundings, soft music and lighting create a romantic atmosphere that puts you in the mood for love.

The Libra man born in 1960 enjoys a woman who is passionate and a little bit possessive. You tend to appreciate someone who makes you feel needed. Her intense desire for you can be pleasantly flattering, and the depth of her feelings assures you that your commitment is secure.

A nurturing, protective man can be a satisfying partner for the 1960 Libra woman. Because you are likely to have a refined sensibility, you may admire someone who treats you with courtesy and care. With his gentility and poise this gentleman can romance you in high style.

LIBRA ZODIAC SIGN
YOUR LOVE PLANETS

YOUR ROMANTIC SIDE   p. 696
- ▶ **VENUS IN LIBRA**
  Born Sept. 23, 0:59 - Sept. 27, 5:12
- ▶ **VENUS IN SCORPIO**
  Born Sept. 27, 5:13 - Oct. 21, 17:11
- ▶ **VENUS IN SAGITTARIUS**
  Born Oct. 21, 17:12 - Oct. 23, 10:01

YOUR SEX DRIVE   p. 722
- ▶ **MARS IN CANCER**
  Born Sept. 23, 0:59 - Oct. 23, 10:01

YOUR CELEBRITY TWINS   p. 760
Find out the astrological similarities you have with famous people.

YOUR COMPATIBILITY   p. 780
Compare planets to find out how compatible you are in a relationship.

YOUR RELATIONSHIP KARMA   p. 824
- ▶ **SATURN IN CAPRICORN**
  Born Sept. 23, 0:59 - Oct. 23, 10:01

JEAN SEBERG
American Actress
Sun in Scorpio

1960 SCORPIO
From October 23, 10:02 through November 22, 7:17

♏ The Unusual Companion

As a 1960 Scorpio, you may have a flair for the exotic in romance. Travel abroad can provide the perfect setting for you for starting an ardent love affair or rejuvenating a current relationship. You may have chosen a partner from a different country or cultural background. Likely to have an unusually creative mind and an unorthodox outlook, you tend to enjoy a relationship that expands your beliefs and challenges you to grow. Criticism can be very humiliating for you, and you may be reluctant to open up and share your unconventional views with just anybody. You may have spent a long time searching and waiting before you could find a nonjudgmental soul mate, someone with the empathy and gentle approach that could put you at ease. To feel that your mate truly understands you can be the answer to your prayers, bringing you enormous relief.

Because it takes a very special person to make you feel completely comfortable, you may regard your mate as a rare treasure. The sense that your partnership is unique tends to enhance your bond with your mate. You may believe that you and your partner were fated to meet, and your chemistry may have indicated that you already knew each other. For you making love to your partner involves not only the meeting of your bodies, but the also the interconnection of your souls.

You tend to be highly responsive to a mate who lavishes you with tender loving care. Selfless giving, with no strings attached, arouses a powerful passion in you. To make your mate writhe with pleasure can be delightful for you.

A woman who is open-minded and expressive can be an inspiring mate for you, the 1960 Scorpio man. You thrive with someone who can be a sounding board for your feelings and ideas. Her generosity and enthusiasm can boost your spirits and encourage you to fulfill your wildest fantasies.

A tender, passionate man exudes a hypnotic power of attraction for the Scorpio woman of 1960. The depth of your own feelings allows you to relate to someone who can be moody at times. You may have an irresistible impulse to probe the mysteries of his fascinating soul.

1960 SAGITTARIUS
From November 22, 7:18 through December 21, 20:25

♐ The Romantic Rival

As if by sheer magic, 1960 Sagittarius, a relationship can draw you in and draw out your greatest talents and achievements. You may gravitate to a mate with muse-like powers to arouse your creativity and sharpen your focus. Your receptivity to your partner makes you a caring and devoted lover—whatever the two of you may be in, you are in it together. Your sign rules gambling and risk, and while it can be thrilling to invest everything you've got in a promising venture, too much dependence in a romantic partnership can overload your partner with responsibility and strain your bond. Ideally, a relationship should enable you to pursue enriching friendships and opportunities for growth in the world.

The emotional and material rewards you gain from outside commitments can fortify your pride and independence. In turn, you can inspire your mate to pursue activities of his or her own. The moral support you provide each other lends balance and dynamism to your relationship and expands the resources that you can enjoy together. You may find it hard to resist a challenge. Seeing someone who admires your mate can provoke you to outperform any would-be competitor. The romantic investment you make in your sex life affords you a regular opportunity to hit the erotic jackpot.

You can be a lusty partner, open to trying anything once—or many times if it wins a big response. You may approach lovemaking with the vigor of an athlete and the curiosity of a mad scientist, experimenting with different positions and working up a sweat.

The Sagittarius man of 1960 thrives with a woman who is steadfast and focused. You appreciate someone who has faith in you and lets you know it. Her ability to see the practical possibilities of your ideas can inspire you to work hard to turn your visions into accomplishments.

The Sagittarius woman born in 1960 adores a man who is powerful but sensitive. You admire a person who has the courage to express his feelings and to let his tenderness show. He may not be macho in a conventional sense, but with him you feel as safe as if you were with Hercules himself.

John F. Kennedy – A Powerful Aphrodisiac

Born on May 29, 1917 at 3 pm in Brookline, Massachusetts, John F. Kennedy, a Gemini, was not only the first US President born in the twentieth century but the first President with real sex appeal. We know that his charismatic presence captivated millions of American voters who preferred the dazzling and sexy Kennedy charm to Vice President Richard Nixon's dour and serious demeanor in their televised Presidential debate. But was Kennedy's dynamic television appearance due to his naturally magnetic appeal or something more? In *RFK: A Candid Biography of Robert F. Kennedy*, author C. David Heymann writes that JFK attributed his success in the debate to a brief sexual encounter in a hotel closet with stripper Blaze Starr, fiancé of Louisiana Gov. Earl Long—who happened to be throwing a party in the next room.

With Jupiter, the planet of excess that gives a larger-than-life flair to whatever it touches, in Kennedy's eighth house of sex, death, and transformation, it is no wonder that his sexual encounters as well as his death have taken on near mythical proportions. In addition to Jupiter, Kennedy's Gemini Sun and Venus (the planet of love and attraction) also occupy the eighth house, adding to the sexual dynamism in the chart. Some attribute Kennedy's over-the-top sex drive to be a side effect of treatment for Addison's Disease, an illness related to the adrenal glands. Kennedy had the sign Libra rising in his horoscope, and that sign is said to govern the adrenals. And we've already connected Venus, the ruler of Libra, to the sex area of his chart.

Kennedy's alleged dalliance with Blaze Starr is only one of many reported sexual encounters attributed to the youthful and handsome Senator and President. His lovers are said to have included Angie Dickinson, Jayne Mansfield, Mafia party girl Judith

351

> *"Marriage means the end of a promising political career . . ."*
>
> SENATOR JOHN F. KENNEDY (prior to his marriage to Jacqueline)

Exner Campbell, and a multitude of airline stewardesses, secretaries, and aides. But Kennedy's most famous affair is the one he purportedly had with Marilyn Monroe, a fellow Gemini. Her breathless rendition of "Happy Birthday" at the President's televised 45th birthday party in 1962 has literally become one of the most celebrated moments of the decade, forever etched upon the memory of our collective consciousness. In fact, even John Kennedy, Jr. memorialized that infamous moment on a cover of his magazine, *George*, with Drew Barrymore posing as the sexy and seductive Monroe, despite the fact that the episode probably caused considerable embarrassment to his mother.

While he was alive, Kennedy's sexual escapades were kept secret. It was his marriage to the intelligent and ethereally beautiful Jacqueline that captured the attention of the world. Remember, he once quipped that he was the man who accompanied Jackie Kennedy to Paris. While he may have been politically savvy in many respects, JFK's perspective on the effect marriage would have on his political career or his sex life could not have been more wrong. With power as the ultimate aphrodisiac, Kennedy was able to seduce virtually any woman that he desired. And the American public's adoration of his young, attractive family certainly helped his political cachet. Though life in Camelot was far from a fairy tale, John and Jacqueline Kennedy remain one of the most fascinating couples in US history.

▶ READ ABOUT JACQUELINE KENNEDY ON PAGE 415 ▶ READ ABOUT MARILYN MONROE ON PAGES 293 AND 294 ▶ READ ABOUT FRANK SINATRA ON PAGE 211

1961

- ★ THE I.U.D.
- ★ WEST SIDE STORY
- ★ BREAKFAST AT TIFFANY'S
- ★ BLUE MOON
- ★ TROPIC OF CANCER
- ★ STRANGER IN A STRANGE LAND

EVENTS

1961 heralded a relaxation in sexual mores compared to the morally repressive 1950s. The Motion Picture Association of America approved changes in its code that would allow portrayals of homosexuality, if "treated with care, discretion, and restraint." The National Council of Churches, representing mainstream Christian denominations in the US, approved the practice of birth control and, in Buffalo, inventor Jack Lippes created the I.U.D. However, a birth control clinic in New Haven was shut down nine days after opening for violating Connecticut laws prohibiting the sale of birth control devices.

President Kennedy, on a State visit for talks with France's President de Gaulle, good-humoredly told journalists that his actual mission was to "escort Jacqueline Kennedy," wildly popular both at home and abroad. And on the celebrity love match front, a 79-year-old Pablo Picasso married his 37-year-old model, Jacqueline Roque.

POP CULTURE

Movies tended toward the sweeping epic, including classics *West Side Story*, a musical version of the Romeo and Juliet tale in which the star-crossed lovers hail from rival New York gangs, and *Splendor in the Grass*, Natalie Wood and Warren Beatty's struggle with sexual awakening in a repressive 1920s Midwest small town. This was also the year of *Breakfast at Tiffany's*, in which free-spirited Audrey Hepburn enchants bohemian New York.

Rock 'n' roll ruled the airwaves with such hits as Del Shannon's "Runaway," Dion's "Runaround Sue," and Chubby Checker's "Pony Time." But orchestral hits like Bert Kaempfert's "Wonderland at Night," crooned tunes like the Marcels' "Blue Moon," and novelty songs like the Tokens' "The Lion Sleeps Tonight" showed the continued public appetite for softer fare.

Bestseller lists reflected an evolving cultural adventurousness, including Robert Heinlein's science-fiction classic *Stranger in a Strange Land*, chronicling the adventures of an alien visitor, and Henry Miller's previously censored *Tropic of Cancer*, an earthy account of his years in 1930s Paris. Harold Robbins' *The Carpetbaggers* recast Howard Hughes' life story as a steamy saga, while Muriel Spark's *The Prime of Miss Jean Brodie* was about an eccentric, charismatic schoolmistress.

Hot Couple

PABLO PICASSO & JACQUELINE ROQUE

On March 2, 1961, when Picasso, one of the most famous artists of the century, married his model, secretary, and assistant, Jacqueline Roque, he was seventy-nine years old and still going strong. She was a mere thirty-seven. Although he was well known to be a charismatic ladies man, Picasso also had a reputation for treating his paramours poorly.

Picasso often said that there were two kinds of women—goddesses and doormats. This summed up his world view when it came to his wives. Roque and Picasso had a tumultuous, stormy relationship, but when he died in 1973, she was at Picasso's side.

SEE ALSO
► CHARLIE CHAPLIN *Page 63*

1961 CAPRICORN

From December 21, 1960 20:26 through January 20, 1961 7:00
(December 1961 Capricorns, see 1962 Capricorns)

♑ The Loyal Partner

Loyal and softhearted, Capricorn of 1961, you don't take relationships lightly, nor do you want to share them with the rest of the world. Your home is a warm, protective nest, and at the end of the day you want someone who waits with open arms and a listening ear, ready to rub your neck and back. Looking forward to those long, loving strokes gliding up and down your skin gets you through the day.

For you, love also has an unpredictable side, with twists and turns that leave you never knowing what tomorrow will bring. You love the excitement of exploring the side streets of your partner's sensitivity and emotions, just to see what you can find. That kind of exploration brings the two of you closer together and, as often as not, leads you into the bedroom for a long night of sensitive passion.

Anyone who wants to turn your head must be focused completely on you. The person who looks you straight in the eye and listens while you tell the story of your life gets through to you quickly. Your potential mate should have no qualms about a kiss or a hug in public, and may even declare their love for you from the rooftops. The madder and more eccentric love makes this person, the more attracted and enticed you'll be.

Women who dress conservatively in public but scantily at night suit your taste, 1961 Capricorn male. You are an absolute sucker for the lady who is unique, individualistic, and unafraid to be a bit shocking to knock you a bit off-balance, challenge your mind, and whet your sexual appetite. You may be somewhat slow to arouse, but once a woman who has pleasure on her brain gets under your skin, you can love the night away and still be ready for more.

The dreamboat who sends shivers up and down your spine, 1961 Capricorn lady, is a man of few words and a master of illusion. He can make you think he is independent, proud, and aloof, yet once you have him in a deliciously compromising position, he is ready to please you and pleasure you. He can even prepare gourmet meals, and for dessert, he'll make you feel sweet all over. Now that's a man to be reckoned with.

CAPRICORN ZODIAC SIGN
YOUR LOVE PLANETS

YOUR ROMANTIC SIDE   p. 696
- ▶ VENUS IN AQUARIUS
  Born Dec. 21, 1960 20:26 - Jan. 05, 1961 3:30
- ▶ VENUS IN PISCES
  Born Jan. 05, 3:31 - Jan. 20, 7:00

YOUR SEX DRIVE   p. 722
- ▶ MARS IN CANCER
  Born Dec. 21, 1960 20:26 - Jan. 20, 1961 7:00

YOUR POWER OF ATTRACTION   p. 760
Find out the astrological similarities you have with famous people.

YOUR COMPATIBILITY   p. 780
Compare planets to find out how compatible you are in a relationship.

YOUR RELATIONSHIP KARMA   p. 824
- ▶ SATURN IN CAPRICORN
  Born Dec. 21, 1960 20:26 - Jan. 20, 1961 7:00

1961 AQUARIUS

From January 20, 7:01 through February 18, 21:15

♒ The Movie Star

For you, Aquarius of 1961, love is like a romantic movie, sometimes bordering on the dramatic but always with a happy ending. By day, you walk hand-in-hand through exotic street scenes, while at night you dine at a sidewalk café, savoring a good French wine, topped with a dessert rich in chocolate. Later, your co-star carries you into the bedroom, where you make love until early morning, with wild sensual abandon.

Self-confident, eccentric, and extroverted, you want your relationships to have that extra dash and spice that you just can't get from your everyday routine. Since you usually go after what you want, it's unlikely your relationship will ever leave you bored. You can't wait to hear what your partner has in store for your next adventure, and the perfect situation is one in which neither of you runs out of fresh ideas.

Anyone who wants to get in on the fun of being your lover needs to look at life uncompromisingly, and the conformist who worries about what others think is not for you. A potential partner need not agree with your unconventional political and social ideals, but must admire them. Most important, your mate will know when to take the lead when the talking stops and the kissing starts, and when the passion is over, you won't have any doubt that you've been loved.

The woman of your dreams, Aquarius male of 1961, makes your head spin with the sound of her sultry voice and the touch of her silky hands. Though you believe in equality of the sexes, you will fall every time for the woman who lets you know how intelligent, strong, and handsome you are. While you know that she is twisting you around her little finger, you are more than happy to play her game, as long as you know she is here to stay.

The man you find most attractive, Aquarius female of 1961, is ambitious and on a straightforward career track, and he cannot be bought or sold. He stands up for his beliefs, and approaches life on his own terms. In matters of love, he knows how to be reliable, comforting, and sensual, so that he does best what you need most—keeps you happy, loved, and satisfied.

MARIE LAFORET
French Actress
Mars in Aquarius

AQUARIUS ZODIAC SIGN
YOUR LOVE PLANETS

YOUR ROMANTIC SIDE   p. 696
- ▶ VENUS IN PISCES
  Born Jan. 20, 7:01 - Feb. 02, 4:45
- ▶ VENUS IN ARIES
  Born Feb. 02, 4:46 - Feb. 18, 21:15

YOUR SEX DRIVE   p. 722
- ▶ MARS IN CANCER
  Born Jan. 20, 7:01 - Feb. 05, 0:21
- ▶ MARS IN GEMINI
  Born Feb. 05, 0:22 - Feb. 07, 5:24
- ▶ MARS IN CANCER
  Born Feb. 07, 5:25 - Feb. 18, 21:15

YOUR CELEBRITY TWINS   p. 760
Find out the astrological similarities you have with famous people.

YOUR COMPATIBILITY   p. 780
Compare planets to find out how compatible you are in a relationship.

YOUR RELATIONSHIP KARMA   p. 824
- ▶ SATURN IN CAPRICORN
  Born Jan. 20, 7:01 - Feb. 18, 21:15

354

WARREN BEATTY
American Actor
Sun in Aries

1961 PISCES
From February 18, 21:16 through March 20, 20:31

♓ The Powerful Charmer

For you, Pisces of 1961, relationships are like fairy tales, filled with damsels in distress, and dashing Prince Charmings on white chargers. Though you may be a bit of a dreamer, you are still realistic enough to know that you need that magical feeling, that ebb and flow of electricity when eyes meet eyes and lips touch in a long, extended kiss. Where love is concerned, you accept no compromises on quality and quantity.

Once you have that loving feeling, you can meet the world head-on, knowing that even if you fall flat on your face there is someone waiting in the wings to pick up the pieces. Rather than being someone who observes life sitting on the sidelines, you live it to the fullest, but you know that you do more, and you do it better, when you're with someone else.

Those who want to get your seal of approval should dare you to live your dreams, and be willing to offer realistic solutions and alternatives when things don't work out for you. A potential mate should call or arrive on time, be there for you through thick and thin, and do everything to win your trust, since it is trust that wins you over. And along with that trust comes those romantic, seductive moments with soft mood music and sweet words whispered in your ear.

The woman who best suits you, Pisces male of 1961, is independent, exciting, and even a bit unpredictable. Part of her charm lies in her ability to keep you guessing. She need not be verbal, or even logical, but what gives her appeal is an artistic edge and the way she dresses to the nines. What attracts you is the challenge of taking charge, taming her moods, and turning on the seductive charm to win her heart without saying a word.

1961 Pisces female, you are usually attracted to a man who is rugged, muscular, and very physically active. He is just as comfortable taking you dancing as he is sitting beside you on the living room sofa, watching a romantic comedy, or even a tearful chick flick. On the inside, this man needs to be vulnerable, sensitive, and cuddly, and, more than anything, you must be able to lean on him through thick and thin.

1961 ARIES
From March 20, 20:32 through April 20, 7:54

♈ The Devilish Tickler

Impulsive and passionate, Aries of 1961, you love taking risks, whether sampling new fare in an exotic restaurant or taking on a daring physical challenge. You will put everything on the line in order to make a relationship work, keeping the one you love happy at all costs. If being with someone does not make you feel on top of the world, you will give it up and find someone new.

You want to be involved with someone electrifying, someone who lets you know you're alive. This person laughs at the same things you do and responds to the same things that touch your heart. What you love most is to share that intuitive spark with someone, to read each other's minds without uttering a single word—especially when it comes to the things that arouse you both.

Anyone who wants to be part of your life needs to be both naughty and nice, ready for action the moment the two of you say hello. This person knows how to reach your soft spot, making you laugh with just a glance or a gesture. Tickling your funny bone is just a prelude to tickling those wonderful, forbidden spots that cause your entire body to sing with ecstasy, as you lose control in delicious passion.

The woman of your dreams, 1961 male Aries, is passionate about life, and, like you, will try hard to make your union succeed. When you are together, she focuses solely on you, making you feel as if you are the only man alive. She can have a heart-to-heart talk one day and engage in a political debate the next, always ready to match you on a mental level. But mostly, she is a tigress in the bedroom, and a darling little lamb when the lovemaking is over.

A man who is kindhearted, generous, and unafraid to show his sensitive sides strums your heartstrings, Aries lady of 1961. You have absolutely no use for guys who are detached and overbearing or who love the sound of their own voices. What turns you on is the man truly interested in anything that interests you and who can even prepare dinner for the two of you at the end of a long, hard day. And for dessert, he leads you into the bedroom, where your every wish is his command.

1961 TAURUS

From April 20, 7:55 through May 21, 7:21

The Pleasure Seeker

Taurus of 1961, you have that certain mysterious something that has the opposite sex eating out of your hands. Though you can have your pick of the lot, there is nothing for your true love to worry about once you commit to a loving partnership. You may still be flirtatious every now and again. That is not only part of your charm, but the edge that keeps your real relationship fresh and sensual.

For you, fun and seriousness are interchangeable, and you want someone who, like yourself, gives equal weight to both. One time, you might go on a "dirty" weekend, in a sleazy little motel making love and thrilling each other from head to toe. At other times you might want to be on a higher plane, perhaps strolling through local museums, taking in all the knowledge and culture you can. What is most important is simply being together.

The person who catches your eye and holds your attention is someone you know will be there for you no matter what. Due to your fast-paced life and the variety of interests that you have, you need someone who can manage your time for you, and help keep you on track. But while organization may be the cake, sensuality is the tasty icing—those soft fingers stroking your face and your chest, and that soft, enticing personal scent that follows you wherever you go.

As a 1961 male Taurus, you like a woman who is independent, successful, and sensual. You don't mind at all being seduced, so a woman who takes the lead both in the boardroom and the bedroom makes your knees weak and your senses sing. You are not particularly attached to old-fashioned male stereotypes, so a woman who takes turns being dominant and receptive will stay with you for years to come.

You, 1961 Taurus female, want a man who is strong, sensitive, and not attached to being in charge. He likes being at home, and if he can even take turns cooking (and cleaning), it is a real turn-on for you. But what arouses you most is what he can do for you when dinner is over. Sharing a hot tub, rubbing your back, and kissing your neck, will make this man the one for you for the rest of your life.

TAURUS ZODIAC SIGN
YOUR LOVE PLANETS

YOUR ROMANTIC SIDE — p. 696
▶ **VENUS IN ARIES**
Born Apr. 20, 7:55 - May 21, 7:21

YOUR SEX DRIVE — p. 722
▶ **MARS IN CANCER**
Born Apr. 20, 7:55 - May 06, 1:12
▶ **MARS IN LEO**
Born May 06, 1:13 - May 21, 7:21

YOUR CELEBRITY TWINS — p. 760
Find out the astrological similarities you have with famous people.

YOUR COMPATIBILITY — p. 780
Compare planets to find out how compatible you are in a relationship.

YOUR RELATIONSHIP KARMA — p. 824
▶ **SATURN IN CAPRICORN**
Born Apr. 20, 7:55 - May 21, 7:21

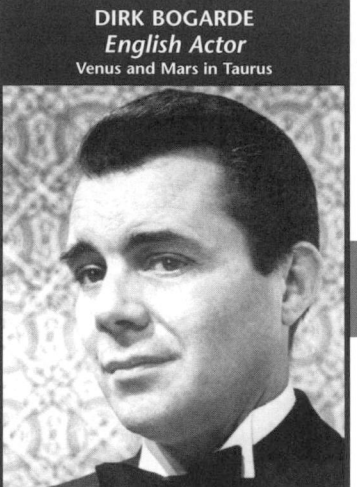

DIRK BOGARDE
English Actor
Venus and Mars in Taurus

355

1961 GEMINI

From May 21, 7:22 through June 21, 15:29

The Friendly Spirit

As a Gemini of 1961, you are friendly, outgoing, and spirited, and value the time you spend with your closest partner. For you, a relationship provides something your friendships do not—a space where you can weave dreams, live out fantasies, and speak a language you both understand. You can verbalize your deepest, hidden desires, unafraid to appear foolish, for in the eyes of someone you love, you are never silly, but always wonderful.

If your activities overwhelm you, and you end up spending fewer intimate hours than you'd like with the one you love, your partner knows how to get you away from it all. Your mate knows exactly what that takes for you to unwind and de-stress, beginning with undressing you with a sexy look, and ending with leading you behind closed doors where your desires will be completely awakened.

Anyone who enters your life needs to be a live wire, someone who can regale you with fabulous stories, party all night, and greet the dawn dancing. Someone who can lead the conversation and break the silences with a super-funny joke is just your type. In other words, the person who can match your own restless nature will win your heart, especially if that fun side is combined with lots of lovely sex and a deeply romantic heart.

As a 1961 Gemini male, you don't beat around the bush, and you even find it quite a turn-on when a woman is equally honest and forceful. In particular, flirtatious verbal banter gets your juices flowing, and makes you really energetic in the bedroom. You like a woman on your arm you can be proud of, and if she's on a career track, so much the better. She knows she can have it all, and have you, too.

The man you want to spend your life with, female Gemini of 1961, is restless yet vulnerable, athletic yet intellectual. Since you have so many interests, your ideal guy loves being with you, but has no trouble filling his time when you are not around. You want a compassionate, caring man, since loyalty means everything to you. He's someone who gets along with people, has lots of friends, and is sure to be comfortable in your world.

GEMINI ZODIAC SIGN
YOUR LOVE PLANETS

YOUR ROMANTIC SIDE — p. 696
▶ **VENUS IN ARIES**
Born May 21, 7:22 - June 05, 19:24
▶ **VENUS IN TAURUS**
Born June 05, 19:25 - June 21, 15:29

YOUR SEX DRIVE — p. 722
MARS IN LEO
Born May 21, 7:22 - June 21, 15:29

YOUR CELEBRITY TWINS — p. 760
Find out the astrological similarities you have with famous people.

YOUR COMPATIBILITY — p. 780
Compare planets to find out how compatible you are in a relationship.

YOUR RELATIONSHIP KARMA — p. 824
▶ **SATURN IN CAPRICORN**
Born May 21, 7:22 - June 21, 15:29

NATALIE WOOD
American Actress
Sun and Mars in Cancer

1961 CANCER
From June 21, 15:30 through July 23, 2:23

 The Airy Optimist

If love is anything at all, Cancer of 1961, it can free you from the dreariness of yesterday to give you hope for tomorrow. For you, love is like a spiritual journey, an experience you cannot put into mere words. Instead, a close and loving relationship makes you feel like you are floating on air, and that "lightness of being" frees your inhibitions in a way that nothing else can.

But romance is not all "up in the air" for you, as you recognize love's practical side—the often delicate work of reconciling two different sets of needs and interests. You are perhaps better than most at paying attention to this part of relationship, but you are even better about attending to the sensual side of things. Touching, tingling, and looking into one another's eyes are to you the essence of the spirit of love.

Someone who wants to be in your life does not need to be a fancy dresser or a great wit, as you are more interested in those inner qualities that sets him or her apart from the crowd. Among those qualities you find most attractive are an optimistic view of life and a tolerance for different viewpoints and opinions. These indicate someone who is not only open to possibilities, but also open to the possibilities in you.

If you're a 1961 Cancer man, you are attracted to a woman not at all obvious in looks or manner, a quiet type who might escape the notice of most other men. Along with that quiet, however, comes a nice, warm smile that tells you she appreciates you for who you are and will devote all of her time to you. She is not only an ideal partner, but the perfect lover—generous, giving, and erotic—and she only has eyes for you.

For the 1961 Cancer woman, the perfect guy is comfortable in any situation, but most comfortable when he's around you. He doesn't spend time being unhappy or dissatisfied. If something doesn't go his way, he picks up the pieces and immediately moves on. He is a born teacher, and wants to eagerly share with you the secret of his success. But mostly, he wants to share the secrets of his soul, and for that you will be eternally grateful.

1961 LEO
From July 23, 2:24 through August 23, 9:18

 The Positive Romancer

As a Leo of 1961, you're ever hopeful about the prospects for love in your life, and when you're involved in a relationship, you're ever hopeful about the things it will bring into your life. Optimistic and idealistic, you see the best in every romantic partnership, though you're willing to work for the best, at times when there may be problems.

A realist by day, and a romantic by night, you think of your relationship as an inspirational haven, and your partner as your muse, the one who feeds you a steady diet of creative ideas, fanciful daydreams, and passionate kisses. What sets your partnership apart is that you are willing to explore those options, transforming your nightly dreams into daily realities.

The person who wants a place in your life must show from the start that you won't be taken for granted. A vibrant yet playful personality always thrills you, and you are always in awe of great storytelling prowess. Add a smart, yet never ostentatious appearance, and you will definitely be there for the next round. Someone flighty and flirtatious will only turn your head in the other direction, as the person sincerely interested in you is the one who will ultimately win your heart.

For the Leo man of 1961, your ideal woman stands apart from the crowd. She has an unspoken understanding of who she is and where she is going. A pretty face and a well-turned figure will always catch your eye, but you prefer the intangible something that exists the first time you touch. Making love to this lady is truly an experience, but it is the heart-to-heart connection that transports those physical sensations to a place you have never been before.

If you're a 1961 Leo woman, your perfect man is someone who understands you instinctively, without the need for conversation or explanations. The first time you talk to him, you feel as if you've met someone who has known you all your life, who knows what you are thinking, and who appreciates those subtleties that no one else ever notices about you. And when the two of you touch, it's as if a life force passes between your fingertips.

1961 VIRGO
From August 23, 9:19 through September 23, 6:41

The Secret Lover

That old song "Secret Love" could have been written for you, Virgo of 1961, since you look at relationships as something intensely private and personal, almost like a religious experience that you share with no one, not even your closest friends. This is not because you have a secret life, but because you value the sensuality and intimacy you can achieve when the world is not there to intrude upon you.

What does go on behind the scenes are the sights and sounds of life between the sheets and making love as if the world stood still. Your impulse may be to keep out the world, but the happiness you gain from a fabulous relationship makes you want to share it with everyone you know. When you're in love with someone, you're in love with the world, facing each day with a smile on your face and a song in your heart.

Someone who wants to catch your eye should make you feel as if you are the only one in the room. Making direct eye contact, taking your hand in theirs, and listening to your every word are initial qualities that will attract your attention. Once that special someone gets a foot through the door, a potential mate will show you love, love, and more love, but in a special way that nobody else can.

If you're a 1961 Virgo man, your ideal woman likes to stay close to home and close to you. You want someone who puts you first, and her profession second, and you are not ashamed to say so. At the same time, you want someone equal to you in intelligence, assertiveness, and physical prowess, extending from the ski slopes to the bedroom. That may seem a tall order, but when she comes along, you will let her know every day how thankful you are she is there.

For the 1961 Virgo woman, the man of your dreams is the strong, silent type who always has a friendly word and a warm embrace to start your day. He's successful at what he does, but he knows when to stop, especially since that might cut into time he can spend with you. And the time when the two of you are together is close to being heaven on earth, because there's no lover quite so attentive, or quite so passionate.

VIRGO ZODIAC SIGN
YOUR LOVE PLANETS

YOUR ROMANTIC SIDE   p. 696
- ▶ VENUS IN CANCER
  Born Aug. 23, 9:19 - Aug. 29, 14:17
- ▶ VENUS IN LEO
  Born Aug. 29, 14:18 - Sept. 23, 6:41

YOUR SEX DRIVE   p. 722
- ▶ MARS IN LIBRA
  Born Aug. 23, 9:19 - Sept. 23, 6:41

YOUR CELEBRITY TWINS   p. 760
Find out the astrological similarities you have with famous people.

YOUR COMPATIBILITY   p. 780
Compare planets to find out how compatible you are in a relationship.

YOUR RELATIONSHIP KARMA   p. 824
- ▶ SATURN IN CAPRICORN
  Born Aug. 23, 9:19 - Sept. 23, 6:41

ANNA KARINA
Danish Actress
Sun and Mars in Virgo

357

1961 LIBRA
From September 23, 6:42 through October 23, 15:46

The Exquisite Entertainer

Creative, entertaining, and wildly erotic, Libra of 1961, you view relationships like a brightly colored tapestry, sharing experiences as warm and diverse as the colors of the rainbow. Your taste is exquisite, in art and in lovers, and you will not settle for anything less than the full gamut of what being madly in love allows. That means living your life together like a multi-media adventure in sight, sound, and touch that you and your partner can never get enough of. When you fall in love, you jump right in feet first, head later, but with every bit of your heart.

Anyone lucky enough to be with you knows that being in your company is like a wild, mysterious, and even raunchy joy ride. You take nothing for granted, and are ever attentive to make sure that your partner's needs and desires are met. Just as you enjoy life and living it to the fullest, you want everything large or small, happy or sad, that love has to offer.

Someone who wants to win your heart must be one of a kind, and, like a rare jewel, of the highest quality. Beneath the charming mannerisms (and those do count for something) a potential mate must prove to be worthy. For starters, your perfect partner must have a striking appearance, a warm, open personality, and when you feel warm hands touch you, you will know right away whether there is more where that came from.

For the 1961 Libra man, the woman you call your own has a great social sense, dresses well, and is a knockout to look at. You'd like her to have her own career, as long as it's not so demanding that you never spend time together. When night falls, you want the two of you together, and you want her there with the same thing that's on your mind—lots of hugs, kisses, and touching all over.

If you're a 1961 Libra lady, you have no problem setting your sights on someone who looks like a movie star, yet exudes the power of a CEO. That authority, combined with good looks and a winning personality, are just the ticket for you, and if that sounds like everything every woman wants, the difference is that you aren't too shy to ask for the best.

LIBRA ZODIAC SIGN
YOUR LOVE PLANETS

YOUR ROMANTIC SIDE   p. 696
- ▶ VENUS IN LEO
  Born Sept. 23, 6:42 - Sept. 23, 15:42
- ▶ VENUS IN VIRGO
  Born Sept. 23, 15:43 - Oct. 18, 2:57
- ▶ VENUS IN LIBRA
  Born Oct. 18, 2:58 - Oct. 23, 15:46

YOUR SEX DRIVE   p. 722
- ▶ MARS IN LIBRA
  Born Sept. 23, 6:42 - Oct. 01, 20:01
- ▶ MARS IN SCORPIO
  Born Oct. 01, 20:02 - Oct. 23, 15:46

YOUR CELEBRITY TWINS   p. 760
Find out the astrological similarities you have with famous people.

YOUR COMPATIBILITY   p. 780
Compare planets to find out how compatible you are in a relationship.

YOUR RELATIONSHIP KARMA   p. 824
- ▶ SATURN IN CAPRICORN
  Born Sept. 23, 6:42 - Oct. 23, 15:46

HORST BUCHHOLZ
German Actor
Sun in Sagittarius

1961 SCORPIO
From October 23, 15:47 through November 22, 13:07

♏ The Visionary Futurist

With that faraway look in your eyes, Scorpio of 1961, you are what some would call a visionary, looking to the future, appearing to be anywhere but here. For you, relationships provide a connection with the present, and the right person can entice you to live for today, while sharing dreams about tomorrow. A perfect union holds the key to the future, and sharing your life with someone until you reach maturity is as exciting a prospect as anyone could offer.

Despite your idealistic vision of love that often takes you to another sphere, you know that a successful partnership means listening to your partner's needs, wants, and especially, desires. When you are attentive to your love, you know that the real key is touching, intimacy, and lovemaking. This will bind you both and keep you together.

Someone who wants to attract your attention has a commanding presence when entering a room, putting you on notice that you don't always have to take the lead. You want that person to switch roles easily, since you are most drawn to someone who is kindhearted, gentle, and unafraid to show affection. The person with a warm touch, plus a good and caring heart, will win you every time.

If you're a 1961 Scorpio man, the first thing you notice about a woman is her smile and sense of humor. If she beams from ear to ear, and retorts quickly and lightheartedly, you know that she doesn't take herself or life too seriously, except in ways that really matter. You want someone who can subtly rub up against you at a party, teasing you lightly, but never giving away what she has in store for you when you are alone.

You, 1961 Scorpio woman, want the simple things—a good conversationalist with a self-deprecating sense of humor. This man takes you seriously, but he's not at all tied up in himself nor worried about his place in history. He is more concerned with how he rates with you, and how he improves your life by being part of it. Most important, you know the first time he envelops you in his warm embrace that this is where you want to be for the rest of your life.

1961 SAGITTARIUS
From November 22, 13:08 through December 22, 2:18

♐ The Forceful Powerhouse

You can be a powerful force, Sagittarius of 1961, in life and love alike. When you sweep into a room, you have a plan and a purpose, and people know you're there the moment you show up. The same thing holds true in love. When you set your sights on the one with whom you want to be romantically linked, you'll do everything you can to convince that special someone that you're the one.

Once you've won someone's heart and stirred their wildest fantasies, a potential mate has a difficult time imagining life without you. Connected by each other's hopes and dreams, you are more than willing to compromise where necessary to keep the relationship strong. Your eagerness to give to your partner is from genuine caring, not merely a strategy to make things go your own way.

Someone who wants your attention must engage you head-on, with a no-holds-barred approach to relating to you. The cagey, seductive type won't get too far, but the person who boldly steps right up and speaks the truth (especially about you) is the one you will want to spend time with. Someone attentive in all areas of life (and who woos you in each room of the house), but who gives you your personal space, is a surefire candidate for winning your heart.

As a 1961 Sagittarius man, you'll fall in love a woman who looks good, has an air of confidence about her, and who knows her own mind. You want someone who can be a partner in everything you do, working through major life decisions with you, offering the best advice she can muster. You're especially taken with someone who's not afraid to grab you and lead you off to the bedroom where she brings out the gentle beast in you.

If you're a 1961 Sagittarius lady, you like a man who is almost a force of nature, full of vigor, full of romance, and with a firm purpose that keeps him on any course he sets until he's achieved success. You never have to doubt where you stand with this man, and you never have to doubt that despite all his achievements, you're the center of his world. And when the two of you make love, he knows just how to touch you in all the right places.

'60s

Rock Hudson and Doris Day

No two stars were better suited to play contenders in the great battle of the sexes than Rock Hudson and Doris Day. Their first film together, the 1959 hit *Pillow Talk*, was known as a clean sex comedy—a bit racy for its time, but eventually earning $7.5 million and winning the Oscar for Best Original Screenplay. Audiences and critics alike were charmed by the snappy banter between the prudish professional Doris Day and the manipulative womanizer Rock Hudson.

At first Hudson was hesitant to make *Pillow Talk* because he had never made a comedy before, but the screenplay's clever, witty dialogue eventually brought him around. Besides, *Harvard Lampoon* had just given him the worst actor of the year award and he was ready for a change of direction. He enjoyed sharing the screen with Doris Day, and their fun-loving chemistry came across clearly while portraying the sparring, wholesome couple. He explained their success formula saying, "There's a tug-of-war over who's going to put it over on the other, who's going to get the last word, a fencing match between two adroit opponents who in the end are going to fall into bed together."

The Rock and Doris team became the top box-office draw in the early 1960s when they followed up with the 1961 hit *Lover Come Back*. Before playing the handsome ad man on the make, Hudson starred in many westerns as the tall, dark, leading man. With his Sun in the warrior sign of Scorpio and conjunct stern Saturn, he was playing parts that suited this more serious side of his personality. However, Hudson's Moon is in lighthearted, carefree Sagittarius, but this did not emerge until Doris Day came into his life. She brought out his playfulness, and he became what the Hollywood Reporter called "one of the best light comedians in the business."

Doris Day's sunny personality and wholesome goodness belie a difficult childhood. Severe illness and a car accident ended her hopes for a dancing career, but with her Sun and Venus in bold Aries, she charged back as a singer. By 1955 she had starred in a dozen fluffy musicals, and was voted by servicemen in Korea as "the girl we would most like to take a slow boat back to the States with." Her Venus is much enhanced by a trine to Mars in Sagittarius, giving her sex appeal and an easy rapport with men. This highly romantic Venus-Mars combination brought her starring roles with some of Hollywood's most attractive men, including James Stewart, Cary Grant, and Ronald Reagan.

Mars is our Inner Warrior, and Doris Day's Mars in Sagittarius attacked Rock Hudson's Moon. She tickled his funny bone. She called Rock "Roy Harold" on the set (because he was born Roy Harold Scherer, Jr.), and he returned the friendly insult by then calling her "Eunice." The biggest trouble they had was trying not to laugh because no matter how ridiculous their on-screen situations might appear to the viewer, to the players it was supposed to be a matter of life and death.

Another strong connection between their horoscopes is in the relationship sign of Libra. Hudson had the sign Libra rising at his birth, an indicator that he worked best in a partnership. For their third and final film together they played a married couple in the 1964 *Send Me No Flowers*. Later he would find success in the popular TV series *McMillan and Wife*. Sadly, he gained instant notoriety after his 1985 announcement that he had AIDS.

"The trouble we had was trying not to laugh..."

FROM *ROCK HUDSON: HIS STORY*
by Rock Hudson and Sarah Davidson

Doris Day's Saturn is found in Libra and gives her many insights and experiences into the nature of partnership. Even though she was married four times, with Saturn in Libra she knows what a partnership should be like. Her Saturn fitted neatly with Hudson's Rising Sign, undoubtedly prompting her to say, "We looked good together, we looked like a couple should look."

► READ ABOUT CARY GRANT ON PAGE 244   ► READ ABOUT DYAN CANNON AND CARY GRANT ON PAGE 384

1962

- ⊛ **MARILYN MONROE OVERDOSES**
- ⊛ **VATICAN II**
- ⊛ **KUBRICK'S LOLITA**
- ⊛ **DUKE OF EARL**
- ⊛ **LOVE ME DO**
- ⊛ **SEX AND THE SINGLE GIRL**

Hot Couple

EVENTS

Sexy siren Marilyn Monroe died at age 36 from an overdose of sleeping pills. The drug thalidomide, given as a sedative to pregnant women, was withdrawn from the market after being proven to cause birth defects. The Second Vatican Council, under Pope John XXIII, relaxed church doctrine on a number of points for the 20th Century, but held firm its position against contraception. In San Francisco, Tavern Guild, the first gay business association, was formed by bar owners to fight discrimination. Celebrity marriages included those of Sean Connery to actress Diane Cilento, and Mary Tyler Moore to TV executive Grant Tinker. Bad news, however, for film producer Carlo Ponti, found guilty of bigamy—he was already married under Italian law when he wed his second wife Sophia Loren.

POP CULTURE

Film gems of 1962 included *Long Day's Journey Into Night*, directed by Sidney Lumet and adapted from Eugene O'Neill's dysfunctional family drama, and *Lolita*, directed by Stanley Kubrick and adapted by Vladimir Nabokov from his novel about a seductive nymphet and an obsessed professor. Francois Truffaut's daring *Jules et Jim* chronicled a classic love triangle set in early 1900s Paris. Wholesome Americana could still be found in *The Music Man* film adaptation of the Broadway musical about a charming con man in a small Iowa town.

Pop music hits included "Big Girls Don't Cry," "Sherry," and "Soldier Boy." Gene Chandler's "Duke of Earl" made a big novelty splash, while teen idol Bobby Vinton schmaltzed "Roses are Red." Ray Charles's "I Can't Stop Loving You" is still a classic, as is Shirley Bassey's "What Now My Love." And the Beatles entered the scene with "Love Me Do."

Bestsellers included Katherine Anne Porter's *Ship of Fools*, about a multinational cast of characters onboard a cruise ship bound for Germany in 1931, and Doris Lessing's *The Golden Notebooks*, an early feminist classic about a progressive woman writer. James Baldwin broke new ground with *Another Country*, a story of interracial, bisexual, and homosexual affairs among a group of friends. Helen Gurley Brown trotted out glib, breathless advice modeled on her own glamorous life in *Sex and the Single Girl*.

SEAN CONNERY & DIANE CILENTO

When sexy Scottish superstar Sean Connery first met Australian actress Diane Cilento, it was on the set of the stage play *Anna Christie* in 1957. They were reunited during filming for the television version in 1960. They fell instantly in love and were married on November 30th, 1962, in Gibraltar. It was quite a year for Connery. He filmed his first James Bond flick, *Dr. No* in 1962.

Marriage wasn't their only collaboration. Diane published a novel called *Manipulator* in 1968, for which 007 designed the cover. Despite the fact that they worked well together, the couple divorced in 1973.

SEE ALSO

▶ THE BOND GIRLS *Page 687*

▶ ROMAN POLANSKI & SHARON TATE *Page 408*

1962 CAPRICORN
From December 22, 1961 2:19 through January 20, 1962 12:57
(December 1962 Capricorns, see 1963 Capricorn)

♑ *The Pragmatic Paramour*

Born during 1962, you, Capricorn, are extremely choosy in the relationship department—and you have every right to be. You're honest, trustworthy, and real—so naturally, you expect the same in return. You like a lover to be honest, reputable, and "together" in all matters. You also know what you don't like. If your prospective mate isn't self-disciplined, responsible, and confident—able to handle the checkbook, a portfolio, and a wine list with the same amount of expertise, that is—you're history.

Anyone who comes off as even the least bit scattered during the first few minutes of your encounter will lose your respect. And once that's gone, it's impossible to win it back. To keep your interest long-term, your ideal partner needs to be intelligent, patient, and organized, with a frugal, practical, and workable five-year plan.

While you're in The Interview Process—dating, that is—you'll insist on only well dressed, impeccably groomed, and intelligent companions with high-minded tastes like yourself. Forget that boring poetry recital as the two of you walk hand-in-hand along the beach. You're after solid substance. The real thing. In short, if you're going to invest your time and energy into a relationship, your partner had better be worth it.

If you're a 1962 Capricorn man, you're naturally attracted to women who are independent, scrupulously honest, and keenly perceptive. Your ideal partner needs to be comfortable in all social situations, with a wardrobe, vocabulary, and easy social refinement that will help impress any prospective clients. In short, she'll be your silent partner—in business as well as after lights out in the bedroom.

Female 1962 Capricorns want a partner who will absolutely be able to match and never be intimidated by your strengths and/or personal successes. He needs to be as supportive of your career as you are of his, intensely interested in your opinions, and totally secure emotionally. Oh, and sexy as well. In short, your mission, should you choose to accept it, is to search out a man who is equal parts James Bond and Richard Simmons.

361

CHARLES AZNAVOUR
French Singer
Mars in Aquarius

1962 AQUARIUS
From January 20, 12:58 through February 19, 3:14

♒ *The Independent Playmate*

Aquarians of 1962 are the most independent, rebellious, and impulsive of all those born under your sign in recent memory. Your search for a mate won't stop until you've found a true individual: someone who is unique, self-reliant, and perpetually spontaneous. In fact, if he or she forgets to call every now and then, you'll find it appealing, not unsettling.

You want quality rather than quantity when it comes to spending time with your lover, not constant attention. It's more important to find a kindred spirit—someone who, like you, has a life of their own, friends they won't forget just because they're romantically involved, and a humanitarian cause they're utterly devoted to.

Any hint of neediness, dependency, or possessiveness will totally turn you off—permanently. Your attention and your passion will only stay constant if you're intellectually fascinated with your lover at all times. If they play hard to get without meaning to, or if you have the sneaking suspicion that they could definitely live without you, you won't ever look elsewhere.

1962 male Aquarians see the ideal woman as someone who puts her career and professional interests first. The more fervently committed she is to what she believes in, the more you'll admire her—which is the only way your heart and your libido will ever become engaged. You won't tolerate a nag, or a jealous or obsessive lover—or anyone who shows up to meet you wearing the latest designer fashions. Your lady needs to look as individual on the outside as she is on the inside. And if her sexual tastes push the proverbial envelope just a tad, so much the better.

Because you're a 1962 Aquarius female, you're looking for a man who won't call too often, be too eager, or strike you as the least bit possessive. You'll only commit to someone who looks and acts totally different from anyone you've ever known, and that goes for his idea of a date, too. If he offers to take you hang-gliding or tornado-chasing, and en route, suggests that the two of you join the Mile-High Club, you'll definitely accept the invitation—over and over again.

URSULA ANDRESS
Swiss Actress
Sun and Venus in Pisces

362

1962 PISCES
From February 19, 3:15 through March 21, 2:29

The Rebellious Romantic

Born during the Sun's 1962 passage through Pisces, you arrived with a mixed bag of expectations in the department of relationships. Mr. or Ms. Right absolutely must be spontaneous, curious, bold, and honest at all times. The last thing in the world you want to discover is that your partner backs down on their opinions. And if you pick up a hint of artificiality or cowardliness, you'll disappear. Permanently.

You also need someone who's a true romantic at heart—but your idea of romance is a bit different from that of the average bear. Strength of purpose is a turn-on to you. In fact, the more your prospective lover seems eager to fight City Hall, the more interested you'll be in exploring far more intimate details. You'll go along to the demonstration, go door-to-door to circulate petitions, and happily stand out in the cold by their side, passing out Greenpeace brochures. You'll also make darn sure you turn up the thermostat when the two of you get home, in more ways than one.

To stay interested, you need to be with someone who's "real." The more genuine a prospective partner is at all times, and the more willing they are to go to bat for what they believe in, the longer you'll want to be a part of their life.

Male 1962 Pisceans are looking for a woman who's tough but tender, a tomboy who loves sports, but won't even try hide her tears while the two of you watch "Ghost." Once you're sure she really possesses that delicate inner balance, you won't hesitate to present her with a small velvet box. You'll either pop the question over dinner—which might be a hot dog at the hockey game—or dessert such as hand-dipped chocolate strawberries you're feeding each other in bed.

If you were born a female 1962 Piscean, confidence is a trait you absolutely must see in your lover. The perfect man for you is someone who literally can also wear many hats. If he enjoys the opera as much as a football game, happily accompanies you to the mall, and brings home interesting bedroom toys every now and then, the more irresistible you'll find him, and the more likely you'll be to commit.

1962 ARIES
From March 21, 2:30 through April 20, 13:50

The Aggressive Admirer

Born during 1962, you, Aries, are a force to be reckoned with on the outside, and a puppy dog on the inside. So if you sat down and made a list of what you really want in a partner, the traits you'd mention might seem contradictory to some. You're looking for someone equal parts action-hero, leading man or lady, and kindred spirit.

You need to respect their judgment, trust that they'll be faithful to you, and feel a deep emotional connection. Secretly, though, your biggest turn-on is a lover who keeps you wondering if there might not be a little something about them you'll never, ever know. Needless to say, keeping you interested is not an easy task, and it takes a very special person to pull it off. The first step is to impress you with courage under fire. If you spot someone who isn't backing down from a challenge, especially if you sense that under that brave front they're just a tiny bit afraid, you'll be fascinated and eager to learn what else is going on in there.

Once your curiosity has been aroused, you'll be excited in a number of ways and extremely assertive in pursuit of your lover. When it comes to luring someone into your boudoir, you'll be creative, direct, and eager to please. If all conditions are go, he or she will never know what it's like to be lonely, unappreciated, or afraid of anyone or anything. You'll never, ever stray.

Above all else, 1962 Aries men want a woman who's fiery and passionate, confident and assertive in bed and not at all afraid to challenge you, there or anywhere else. In short, you want a lover who's also a worthy opponent. If she lets you know from Day One that she expects equal time behind the steering wheel, figuratively and literally, you'll enthusiastically do what it takes to keep her.

1962 Aries females just won't settle for anything less than a real take-charge type, the classic "alpha male." He can't be uncertain of himself or easily intimidated, or you'll be history in a hurry. But what you really desire most is desire itself, brought to you courtesy of a man who's strong enough to make you feel like a woman.

1962 TAURUS
From April 20, 13:51 through May 21, 13:16

The Proud Partner

As a 1962 Taurus, you place a high value on patience, sensuality, and self-assurance. But there are other qualities you consider equally important in a relationship. For starters, you just can't stand being smothered or being bored, not for a single second. You do need someone who's extremely solid in every way. Solid, but not controlling, which translates into physical appeal, emotional stability, and financial self-sufficiency, all at once.

Some might say you're being unrealistic, that someone this "perfect" doesn't exist. But you know that's not true, and you won't settle for less, no matter how long it takes. You know you'll eventually meet someone who fits the bill, and that once that happens, complete and total commitment is what you'll offer and what you'll expect in return. Above all, you insist on emotional and physical fidelity. But if you're sure you've got it, you won't be the least bit jealous. What you will be is proud. Extremely proud.

Still, as faithful as you are, one of the best ways to keep you interested is for your partner to flirt just a bit. That's fine with you. In fact, you actually consider it healthy and even a type of foreplay, at times. In private, especially once the bedroom door closes, your partner needs to make you feel as if you're the only person in the world—basically because, to you, that's exactly what he or she is.

Male 1962 Taureans are in search of a woman who exudes sensuality, sexuality, and mystery, who makes you feel proud, content, and just a teeny bit smug. She should attract the eye of every man in the room, and hold that attention as she graciously excuses herself to make her way to you. Most importantly, she'll know instinctively by your glance from across the room when it's time to do just that.

If you're a female 1962 Taurus, you want a man who looks, acts, and makes love like a model for a Harlequin paperback book cover. He absolutely must be perceptive enough to fulfill your romantic fantasies in bed without your ever having to say a word, and so faithful that you'll never feel you need to ask where he's been.

TAURUS ZODIAC SIGN
YOUR LOVE PLANETS

YOUR ROMANTIC SIDE   p. 696
- ▶ VENUS IN TAURUS
Born Apr. 20, 13:51 - Apr. 28, 9:22
- ▶ VENUS IN GEMINI
Born Apr. 28, 9:23 - May 21, 13:16

YOUR SEX DRIVE   p. 722
- ▶ MARS IN ARIES
Born Apr. 20, 13:51 - May 21, 13:16

YOUR CELEBRITY TWINS   p. 760
Find out the astrological similarities you have with famous people.

YOUR COMPATIBILITY   p. 780
Compare planets to find out how compatible you are in a relationship.

YOUR RELATIONSHIP KARMA   p. 824
- ▶ SATURN IN AQUARIUS
Born Apr. 20, 13:51 - May 21, 13:16

363

1962 GEMINI
From May 21, 13:17 through June 21, 21:23

The Traditional Sensualist

Born during 1962, you, Gemini, are a different breed of Twin. Until you've got proof your potential companion can be trusted, you're a bit on the shy side. You're instinctively put off by anyone who's too much of a "player." If they're too busy flirting and paying attention to others to give you the attention and reassurance you need to feel secure, there won't be a second date. You're after a mate who'll put your feelings and your relationship at the very top of their priority list.

They've also got to be able to see behind your shy exterior because once you've committed your heart, you'll be far from shy in the boudoir. When you're in public together, you may be discreet and modest, but your lucky sweetheart will know a wonderful, delicious secret—that once the lights are out, you're a force to be reckoned with. You need someone steady as a rock who'll appreciate the constancy of your amorous and enthusiastic attention under the covers.

In fact, rather than wishing for a more active social life, your ideal mate much prefers a few more quiet evenings at home alone with you.

That type of tender loving care, along with a good selection of bubble bath, massage oil, and sexy CDs, will keep your passion alive and your interest running on high, long-term.

1962 Gemini men are looking for a woman who wants to stay home and assume the more traditional female role. You want a woman who'll be the perfect wife, homemaker, and mother, even as she exudes a quiet sensuality that inspires you to make your way home as soon as possible after you leave the office. That doesn't mean you won't give her the respect she deserves, only that she'll need to understand your need to provide for her.

If you're a 1962 Gemini woman, you want a mate you can devote yourself to entirely, someone who'll allow you to be the soft, sensual creature you really are, even as he asks for and respects your advice, opinions, and wisdom. If his attitude shows that he's the undisputed king of the castle—and the boudoir—yet he still makes you feel that you're the queen of his heart, you'll be his forever.

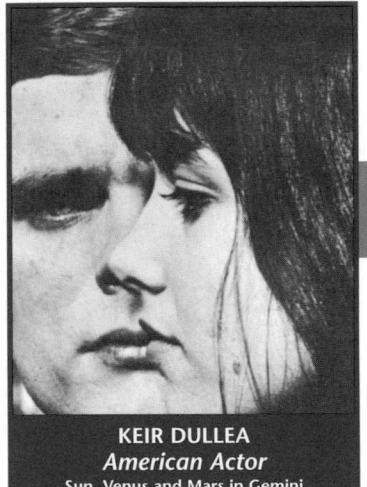

KEIR DULLEA
American Actor
Sun, Venus and Mars in Gemini

GEMINI ZODIAC SIGN
YOUR LOVE PLANETS

YOUR ROMANTIC SIDE   p. 696
- ▶ VENUS IN GEMINI
Born May 21, 13:17 - May 23, 2:45
- ▶ VENUS IN CANCER
Born May 23, 2:46 - June 17, 5:30
- ▶ VENUS IN LEO
Born June 17, 5:31 - June 21, 21:23

YOUR SEX DRIVE   p. 722
- ▶ MARS IN ARIES
Born May 21, 13:17 - May 28, 23:46
- ▶ MARS IN TAURUS
Born May 28, 23:47 - June 21, 21:23

YOUR CELEBRITY TWINS   p. 760
Find out the astrological similarities you have with famous people.

YOUR COMPATIBILITY   p. 780
Compare planets to find out how compatible you are in a relationship.

YOUR RELATIONSHIP KARMA   p. 824
- ▶ SATURN IN AQUARIUS
Born May 21, 13:17 - June 21, 21:23

SUE LYON
American Actress
Sun in Cancer

1962 CANCER   *From June 21, 21:24 through July 23, 8:17*

The Sentimental Dreamer

Born during 1962, Cancer, you arrived with a strong love of fantasy, romance, and the longing for a soul mate who'll dream and fantasize right along with you. Your ideal mate will happily spend Saturday evenings flipping through photo albums, treasure boxes, or scrapbooks, talking over the good times you've had, and the rest of the week searching for your next romantic getaway in a hidden stack of travel brochures.

If he or she brings up the subject of what the children will be named before you're actually married, you'll be absolutely positive you've found the right one. Of course, even after you've decided that you really want to spill your feelings and open your heart, you'll need someone who'll make you feel safe enough to do it.

To keep those home-fires burning—which is first and foremost for you—your ideal mate absolutely must be as fond of and creative at making magic together as you are. He or she should create an aura of mystery, enchantment, and magic wherever they happen to be. If the very thought of him or her leaves you breathless, it's all over. In short,

you're looking for the magnetism of a movie star, the allure of a sex symbol, and the substance of a tried-and-true friend.

Born a 1962 Cancer male, your ideal partner is a woman who'll instinctively understand your feminine side—and, more importantly, allow you to feel no less a man when you display it. She should be happy to share the cooking and child-care responsibilities with you, even as she praises you for your masculine qualities because she knows how much you enjoy caring for your family, not just at work, but also in a "hands-on" way.

If you're a 1962 Cancer woman, you need a man who's not afraid to show his heart to you and the rest of the world. You're drawn to men who are sympathetic, tolerant, and wholeheartedly compassionate, most especially when it comes to children, older folks, and animals. The more kind, sensitive, and loving he is—and that goes double for his behavior once the lights are out—the longer you'll want him to occupy the pillow next to yours in that comfy king-sized bed.

1962 LEO   *From July 23, 8:18 through August 23, 15:11*

The Lavish Lover

Leos born during 1962 are the ultimate "spoilers," as their lucky partners will happily attest. They're masters of pomp, ceremony, lavish gifts, and enjoying life, both in public and in private. You want to share all the best things in life with a lover, like chocolates, pillows, and surprise foot rubs that end up turning into long, amorous evenings. Your costar in the wonderfully romantic story of your lives should be able to deliver all this and more without looking like they're even trying.

You're looking for a very particular brand of lover. They need to possess an outer gentility, a knack for knowing even your most secret and intimate wishes, and high-end tastes in both departments. If he or she knows a fine bottle of wine from a cheap one, a designer suit from an off-the-rack copy, and a real-life Rolex from a knock-off, you'll be intrigued—and that's where it all starts for you.

But ultimately, there's a certain earthy sensuality and a quietly powerful attitude that will win your heart. Anyone who wants to keep your interest and your undivided amorous

attention needs to be able to satisfy you on many levels—but nobody would ever say it won't be well worth the effort. You're quality, and that's exactly what you deserve.

1962 male Leos are in search of a woman whose charm, elegance, and understated sensuality are fairly ooze out of her. Actual physical beauty is really secondary to you. You're far more interested in the way she carries and conducts herself. To keep you around long-term, your lady needs to be confident and self-assured-enough to put out a magnetic force field that's irresistible.

1962 lady Leos are looking for a modern-day night in armor, a confident, responsible figure who's a comfort and an inspiration to everyone he knows. He acts the part of "Head of the Household," but he knows who that really is—not a doubt in his mind—and that would be you. If he treats you like a queen in public, always makes you proud to be his, and never turns down an invitation to play hide-and-seek under the covers, he'll be the King of your heart permanently.

1962 VIRGO
From August 23, 15:12 through September 23, 12:34

♍ *The Super Partner*

As a 1962 Virgo, you need to be with a partner who has it all. Your sharp mind and keen intuition are indisputable, as is your expertise at problem solving, puzzles, and mysteries. So, first and foremost, you definitely need a partner who's a genuine intellectual challenge—highly intelligent, with detective skills and perceptive abilities that rival yours. You're interested in what's beneath the surface. In fact, you find a quick mind and finely tuned instincts much sexier than mere physical appearance.

Once your mind has been engaged and entertained, however, anyone who wants to keep you interested long-term also needs to be uncannily perceptive when it comes to your moods and needs. That same cerebral caliber needs to extend into the realm of the instinctive, as well.

Your ideal mate should intuitively understand not just what you say, but what you don't say. Your ideal lover has to be just as aware of your feelings as they are to your tastes in literature. Whether you're having a tender conversation or gazing into each other's eyes across the table, you need to be absolutely sure you're understood on a deep emotional level. Once those needs have been met, it's also imperative that your mate have a good career, with a prosperous financial future on the horizon. In short, you want it all, and nothing less, but you're more than willing to give the same in return.

1962 Virgo men are after a woman who can handle it all, from maintaining a successful career to planning an elegant dinner party for twenty, to keeping her children—and her husband, of course—happy, well cared for, and secure in her love. She needs to earn your respect and admiration by never wasting a single moment of her day, by being highly organized and efficient in all departments.

1962 Virgo women are looking for an intelligent, dutiful partner who puts home and family first and foremost on his priority list. If he's close to his own family and also manages to charm yours the first time he meets them, he'll keep you interested, in love, and eager to share the rest of your life with him and him alone.

VIRGO ZODIAC SIGN
YOUR LOVE PLANETS

YOUR ROMANTIC SIDE   p. 696
▶ VENUS IN LIBRA
Born Aug. 23, 15:12 - Sept. 07, 0:10
▶ VENUS IN SCORPIO
Born Sept. 07, 0:11 - Sept. 23, 12:34

YOUR SEX DRIVE   p. 722
▶ MARS IN CANCER
Born Aug. 23, 15:12 - Sept. 23, 12:34

YOUR CELEBRITY TWINS   p. 760
Find out the astrological similarities you have with famous people.

YOUR COMPATIBILITY   p. 780
Compare planets to find out how compatible you are in a relationship.

YOUR RELATIONSHIP KARMA   p. 824
▶ SATURN IN AQUARIUS
Born Aug. 23, 15:12 - Sept. 23, 12:34

CLIFF RICHARD
English Singer
Sun and Mars in Libra

365

1962 LIBRA
From September 23, 12:35 through October 23, 21:39

♎ *Steadfast and Passionate*

Born a 1962 Libra, you put loyalty, fidelity, and total commitment above anything else when it comes to choosing a mate. That means you need someone who you're absolutely sure you can trust, whether you're right there with them, or away on a business trip across the country. You'll know if your partner isn't being completely honest, too—that and a whole lot more.

Your perceptive abilities are unmatched when it comes to the one you love, so honesty is a very important thing to you. Your ideal mate will open up to you easily, and confide absolutely everything in you, no matter how insignificant or trivial it might seem to others. In return, you'll repay that honesty with your complete and total devotion—and there's no one who loves quite like a 1962 Libra.

To keep you interested, in addition to sharing their innermost thoughts with you, your mate must also be willing to give one hundred percent in the bedroom. You won't be satisfied with lovemaking that becomes routine or stale, either. You want variety, passion, and excitement, not to mention creativity. If your lover keeps scented massage lotions on hand or sprinkles the sheets with red rose petals, they stand an excellent chance of keeping both your heart and your ardor constant.

1962 Libra men want a woman they can be proud of—who'll make all eyes turn when she enters the room. If she glances back at others, however, you won't be amused. Your lady needs to be focused on you and you alone. This doesn't mean you're looking for a "love goddess," at least not physically. It's more important that she carry herself in such a way that she's attractive, alluring, and almost magically magnetic.

If you're a 1962 Libra lady, your ideal man is someone who exudes power and competence who always makes you proud to call him yours. He needs to be subtle, able to say more with his eyes than he'd want to with words. In fact, you prefer a man who's a bit on the quiet side, who's confident enough to never need to brag about personal details to his friends. Keeping intimate details of your relationship secret is an absolute must.

LIBRA ZODIAC SIGN
YOUR LOVE PLANETS

YOUR ROMANTIC SIDE   p. 696
▶ VENUS IN SCORPIO
Born Sept. 23, 12:35 - Oct. 23, 21:39

YOUR SEX DRIVE   p. 722
▶ MARS IN CANCER
Born Sept. 23, 12:35 - Oct. 11, 23:53
▶ MARS IN LEO
Born Oct. 11, 23:54 - Oct. 23, 21:39

YOUR CELEBRITY TWINS   p. 760
Find out the astrological similarities you have with famous people.

YOUR COMPATIBILITY   p. 780
Compare planets to find out how compatible you are in a relationship.

YOUR RELATIONSHIP KARMA   p. 824
▶ SATURN IN AQUARIUS
Born Sept. 23, 12:35 - Oct. 23, 21:39

CAPUCINE
French Actress
Venus in Sagittarius

366

1962 SCORPIO
From October 23, 21:40 through November 22, 19:01

♏ *The Sensual Romantic*

If you were born a 1962 Scorpio, your idea of the perfect relationship begins with a partner who's both sexual and sensual—creative, tender, and passionate, and utterly devoted to keeping the passion you share alive and well forever. In fact, what you really appreciate is a lover who knows exactly how to create the perfect atmosphere for love. Quiet music and soft candlelight are just the beginning.

Once your libido belongs to someone, your heart will be soon to follow, and it won't be going anywhere else in a hurry. You'll spare no expense to prove that point to your sweetheart, but you do expect the same in return. You've also never been afraid of a little drama in a relationship. You expect fireworks of all kinds, which means you really won't mind if an argument turns just a tad dramatic. In fact, a slamming door every now and then is a secret turn-on for you.

To keep you interested for the long haul, prospective lovers need to prove to you that they're up for the challenge, so anyone who keeps quiet, drives off, or refuses to argue will bore you in a minute. Your idea of being in love is having a relationship that's fiery, passionate, and never, ever dull. Once you know you've found it, your attention will never stray.

1962 Scorpio men want a woman who's quite bold—bold enough to suggest skipping lunch in favor of a romantic rendezvous. But she also needs to be subtle and able to communicate easily to you with her eyes. If she can deliver a glance from across the room at a party that's dragging on too long—one that tells you it's time for some quality time alone together—you'll be fascinated and hooked. For good.

You 1962 Scorpio ladies just won't settle for less than a man who's ardent, amorous, and willing to let you know in most lavish fashion that he belongs to you and you alone. A trail of pink rose petals that starts at the front door and leads upstairs to a candlelit bath will certainly do the trick, but your partner also needs to be your confidante. He needs to be the one you trust with your secrets, someone who'll also share his own with you.

1962 SAGITTARIUS
From November 22, 19:02 through December 22, 8:14

♐ *The Worldly Comic*

If you're a 1962 Sagittarius, you were born with a double dose of your sign's fondness for fun, knowledge, and socializing. When it comes to settling down, your ideal partner needs to be equal parts philosopher, stand-up comedian, and accomplished host. You want someone who enjoys meeting new people and traveling, both physically and intellectually. They need a great sense of humor and the ability to see the silver lining in even the darkest cloud.

Pessimism or an excess of caution in a lover will turn you off quicker than anything. In fact, the slightest trace of gloom or melancholy will have you running as far and as fast as your hooves will carry you. You also want someone around who's equally curious about the big questions, including politics, social trends, and belief systems. That doesn't mean you'll necessarily need him or her to always agree with you, however—only that they can hold their own in a discussion on any of those topics.

Keeping your mind happy and being an eager travel partner will raise your curiosity about what else is in there, and are the surest-fire ways to keep your attention constant. At home, it won't matter if you're holding hands, having yet another long chat at the kitchen table, or spending the evening pursuing a more tender connection, as long as you're doing it together.

1962 Sagittarius men need a woman who's your a friend, lover, and intellectual equal. She should share your interest in world events, happily laugh it up with lighthearted friends at a comedy club, and surprise you by revealing that she's wearing silky lingerie under her hiking outfit. And if she's equally comfortable in those boots as she is in high heels, she's definitely the one.

Female 1962 Sagittarians are restless and lively. The one thing they just can't stand is a couch potato. A man who lives his life vicariously in front of the television set won't interest you in the slightest—and you won't pretend he does. You're after a man who makes his own experiences and excitement, and isn't afraid to take a well-calculated risk—as long as there's fun involved.

Marcello Mastroianni

Despite the sheer variety of Marcello Mastroianni's over 150 cinematic roles, he is best known for his Latin Lover persona, which began with the 1960 film *La Dolce Vita*. In the early 1960s he emerged as the most in-demand actor in Europe, earning some 100 million lira per film, and working with Italy's finest filmmakers and famous actresses. His many awards include the British Film Academy's "Best Foreign Actor," two best actor awards at Cannes, and three Oscar nominations.

Mastroianni was born with his Sun in the partnership sign of Libra, and so naturally his most notable work came through his key relationships. After Federico Fellini cast him for the lead in *La Dolce Vita* as the womanizing gossip columnist surrounded by Rome's decadent, wealthy partygoers, the two collaborated in several more commercially successful films, including *8½*, *City of Women*, and *Ginger and Fred*. But it would be his relationships with beautiful women that caused the most stir. In 1961 he toured the US and defensively, perhaps humbly, claimed "I am not a sex addict." He said that Fellini had hired him because he had a "terribly ordinary face."

Mastroianni's Venus in Leo opposes his Mars in Aquarius, a combination that is constantly on the alert for potential romantic adventures. This Venus-Mars polarity produces strong sexual desire, yet is always unsatisfied and has little willingness to remain devoted to one person. Following the Italian custom of not divorcing, Mastroianni stayed married for 45 years, but had numerous love affairs. The most scandalous was probably with Catherine Deneuve, since they had a love child in 1972. In a more frank moment he explained, "For love and understanding, I turn to my wife. For

*"I love people and
I love life.
Perhaps that's why
life has loved me in
return."*

MARCELLO MASTROIANNI

love and sensuality, I have my lovers."

In 1961 Mastroianni starred in *Divorce Italian Style*. In this clever sex comedy he plays a Sicilian nobleman who devises a complex scheme to kill his wife so he can turn his attention to his beautiful cousin. The film closely reflects his own astrological profile, since his Venus is conjunct Neptune, the planet associated

with fantasy, imagination, and glamor. Mastroianni's Venus-Neptune conjunction conjures up images of ideal love and is mesmerized by absolute beauty and secret romance. With Mars in opposition to Venus and Neptune, Mastroianni's horoscope is built for romantic triangles, which he regularly fleshed out in both his film career and private life. We see in *Divorce Italian Style* this dynamic at work. The cousin is beautiful, yet unattainable, and the wife is in the way.

Beyond the scope of this film, his Venus-Neptune combination attracted some of Europe's most luscious actresses as co-stars—Gina Lollobrigida, Brigitte Bardot, Catherine Deneuve, and, most fruitfully, with Sophia Loren. Mastroianni and Loren came to symbolize the common Italian man and woman, whether they were married or in love. Loren's planets line up neatly with his, accounting for their competent teamwork. Most notably, her Mars in Leo is right on his Venus in Leo, making her the perfect foil for his own fantasies about women. In the sex comedies *Marriage Italian Style* and *Yesterday, Today, and Tomorrow*, their mutual sexual tension is dramatically played out to the delight of moviegoers everywhere.

Perhaps one of the sexiest scenes ever filmed was when Sophia Loren performed a striptease for Mastroianni in *Yesterday, Today, and Tomorrow*. Loren plays a high-priced prostitute who has to give up her best customer, a seminarian played by Mastroianni, to save his soul. In the famous scene, Loren's voluptuous carnality is slowly revealed to a wide-eyed Mastroianni. He sits watching her, his hand covering his mouth or biting his nails as she gets down to skimpy bra and panties. He can't believe his good fortune that he should be so lucky to receive this vision.

▶ READ ABOUT FEDERICO FELLINI ON PAGE 301 ▶ READ ABOUT SOPHIA LOREN ON PAGE 325 ▶ READ ABOUT CATHERINE DENEUVE ON PAGE 505

1963

- ✪ PROFUMO AFFAIR
- ✪ FEMININE MYSTIQUE
- ✪ ELIZABETH TAYLOR AS CLEOPATRA
- ✪ VIVA LAS VEGAS
- ✪ BLUE VELVET
- ✪ CITY OF NIGHT
- ✪ FANNY HILL

EVENTS

Britain was scandalized as British Secretary of War John Profumo resigned after admitting his affair with a 21-year-old former showgirl, who was also allegedly involved with a Soviet. Sylvia Plath committed suicide, two weeks after the publication of her novel *The Bell Jar*. The feminist movement in the United States was given voice by Betty Friedan's *The Feminine Mystique*. Flamboyant French chanteuse Edith Piaf died, while the Duke and Duchess of Argyll were granted a divorce on grounds that the duchess was notoriously promiscuous. For the first time, the BBC allowed mention of sex, religion, politics, and royalty in its comedy programs.

POP CULTURE

Films were on the frothy side in 1963 with the teen surfer flick *Beach Party* starring Frankie Avalon and Annette Funicello, and *Viva Las Vegas*, an Elvis Presley and Ann-Margret romantic musical comedy. The lavish, historical costume drama *Cleopatra*, starring real-life lovers Elizabeth Taylor and Richard Burton, drew huge audiences. Henry Fielding's classic class satire *Tom Jones*, about a bawdy 18th-century gentleman, got over-the-top film treatment. Great American directors produced lighter fare with Vincent Minnelli's *The Courtship of Eddie's Father*, about a widower with a matchmaking six-year-old son, and Billy Wilder's *Irma La Douce*, a Shirley MacLaine-Jack Lemmon vehicle about a hooker with a heart of gold.

American doo-wop groups sang "He's So Fine," "Walk Like a Man," and "My Boyfriend's Back," while the Beatles had hits with "She Loves You" and "From Me To You." Heartthrob Bobby Vinton sang "Blue Velvet," and Little Stevie Wonder made his debut. In the novelty category, who could forget "Dominique" by the Singing Nun?

Books exploring contemporary social and moral upheavals included David Storey's *Radcliffe*, about power and passion in a homosexual relationship, and John Rechy's *City of Night*, a sensitive portrayal of the world of male prostitutes, hustlers, and drag queens. Mary McCarthy's classic *The Group* chronicled the lives and aspirations of eight 1933 Vassar graduates. John Cleland's *Fanny Hill*, banned since 1750, shocked US readers with its faux-autobiographical account of an 18th-century London prostitute.

Sex Idol

STEVE McQUEEN

The epitome of cool, Steve McQueen was one of the sexiest leading men of the sixties. He wooed audiences with his rugged good looks and tough charm. In 1963 he made three films, including *The Great Escape*, in which he played a POW on the run from the Nazis. He was a man's man, doing his own stunts in chase scenes.

Racing cars was his deepest passion—and his eventual downfall. In 1979 McQueen was diagnosed with a rare form of lung cancer caused by asbestos exposure from insulated racing suits. He died of a heart attack in 1980.

SEE ALSO
- ▶ JAMES DEAN *Page 309*
- ▶ FAYE DUNAWAY *Page 458*

1963 CAPRICORN

From December 22, 1962 8:15 through January 20, 1963 18:53
(December 1963 Capricorns, see 1964 Capricorns)

The Dream Builder

The sign of Capricorn produces many leaders, and the 1963 Capricorn is no exception. Your particular brand of leadership flourishes within the context of partnership. You have a unique ability to take in the dreams of others, re-organize them in your mind, and breathe life into them in the real world. You have a big-picture perspective that enables you to see the greatest potential in any person or idea. Such an outlook is a wonderful complement to your ability to give concrete form to feelings, desires and ideals.

These talents make you a marvelous partner in a romantic relationship. A lover's wishes are your command. You can take romantic dreams and recast them on a rock solid foundation of love. From there, you and your partner can build an enduring edifice of devotion. Because your sign rules time and maturity, you treasure those things that gain in value over time. Commitment comes to you naturally and lends a comforting and secure structure, within which you and your beloved can experience all the phases of life. The idea of growing old together fills you with a deep sense of satisfaction.

Sharing fantasies can be wildly seductive for you. While you are the picture of propriety to the outside world, you have a bawdy side that you love to indulge in private. Your lovemaking may involve role-playing. One partner plays the gruff Cossack to the other partner's Muscovite countess—or the stoic cattle herd and the saloon can-can dancer. Did we mention that you have a healthy sex drive?

The 1963 male Mountain Goat wants a partner whose hopes and dreams open new expanses of potential and opportunity. You may fantasize about the mutual motivation you would enjoy as a partner in a power couple. Working together to fulfill your dreams is your idea of a perfect relationship.

Female Capricorns born in 1963 seek partners who can be both practical and idealistic. You admire integrity in a person and will settle for nothing less in a lifelong mate. Someone who keeps track of important details may appeal to you, given that you yourself are never content to do things halfway.

CAPRICORN ZODIAC SIGN
YOUR LOVE PLANETS

YOUR ROMANTIC SIDE — p. 696
- ▶ **VENUS IN SCORPIO**
  Born Dec. 22, 1962 8:15 - Jan. 06, 1963 17:34
- ▶ **VENUS IN SAGITTARIUS**
  Born Jan. 06, 17:35 - Jan. 20, 18:53

YOUR SEX DRIVE — p. 722
- **MARS IN LEO**
  Born Dec. 22, 1962 8:15 - Jan. 20, 1963 18:53

YOUR CELEBRITY TWINS — p. 760
Find out the astrological similarities you have with famous people.

YOUR COMPATIBILITY — p. 780
Compare planets to find out how compatible you are in a relationship.

LESSONS & CONNECTIONS — p. 824
- ▶ **SATURN IN AQUARIUS**
  Born Dec. 22, 1962 8:15 - Jan. 20, 1963 18:53

ROD TAYLOR
Australian Actor
Sun, Venus, and Mars in Capricorn

369

1963 AQUARIUS

From January 20, 18:54 through February 19, 9:08

The Thrill Seeker

Pushing limits is likely to be an instinctive activity for Aquarius of 1963, especially in your youth. Others may see you as a rebel, and you may have this image of yourself. Testing boundaries can be exciting, but it also affords you the comfort of knowing they are there. The idea of total, unbounded freedom can be terrifying, and living at the edges packs a potent thrill for you, much like bungee jumping. In early adulthood, you may have been drawn to "bungee-jumping" relationships, in which you ran off a symbolic cliff with partners who were dangerous or unsuitable. However deeply you may have plunged, you would ultimately bounce back and get out.

With age, a bungee cord (like everything else) loses its springiness. And with the wisdom that time brings, you are likely to enjoy greater and deeper satisfaction with a reliable and compassionate partner, as opposed to the expectation of escape. You may have fewer death-defying thrills, but you can appreciate the gifts of intimacy a partner brings. You will never lose your taste for new and stimulating experiences, especially in the boudoir. You are a giving and imaginative lover, eager to please your partner. When you connect sexually with someone you love, you may experience tenderness so intense it is electrifying.

To capture your attention, a lover should cater to your sense of adventure and lust for learning. Day trips and outings that expose you to exotic cultures and peoples arouse your interest and imagination. When a partner succeeds in stimulating your mind, the rest of you follows close behind.

The 1963 male Aquarian wants a partner who is both reliable and interesting. You would love to join hands with someone who can expand your horizons. Your ideal mate pushes you to keep growing and challenging yourself.

Female Aquarians born in 1963 seek partners who are ambitious and disciplined. High-energy people appeal to you on an instinctive level, but you really admire someone who can focus his or her energy through strategy and planning. That kind of "make-it-happen" competence can win your heart for life.

AQUARIUS ZODIAC SIGN
YOUR LOVE PLANETS

YOUR ROMANTIC SIDE — p. 696
- ▶ **VENUS IN SAGITTARIUS**
  Born Jan. 20, 18:54 - Feb. 05, 20:35
- ▶ **VENUS IN CAPRICORN**
  Born Feb. 05, 20:36 - Feb. 19, 9:08

YOUR SEX DRIVE — p. 722
- ▶ **MARS IN LEO**
  Born Jan. 20, 18:54 - Feb. 19, 9:08

YOUR CELEBRITY TWINS — p. 760
Find out the astrological similarities you have with famous people.

YOUR COMPATIBILITY — p. 780
Compare planets to find out how compatible you are in a relationship.

LESSONS & CONNECTIONS — p. 824
- ▶ **SATURN IN AQUARIUS**
  Born Jan. 20, 18:54 - Feb. 19, 9:08

SARAH MILES
English Actress
Mars in Aries

1963 PISCES
From February 19, 9:09 through March 21, 8:19

The Friendly Romantic

Pisces of 1963 is a magnanimous soul, generous, giving, and kind. Casual relationships can be more intense and meaningful for you than they usually are for others. Often speaking of friendships in affectionate terms, you may repeat the story of how you met a dear friend and "just fell in love." Sometimes you can be possessive about loved ones, and you may feel hurt and abandoned when someone falls out of touch with you. Likely to be a diligent card-sender and address-book-updater, you are tenacious in maintaining relationships over time and distance. You may also develop strong attachments to companion animals. As far as you're concerned, pets are just people who happen to come from a different species.

Sexual involvement may be the key factor distinguishing a romantic partner from the rest of your friends. It helps if he or she fits in and gets along famously with your crew. If not, a certain tension can develop, especially if your partner becomes jealous of your devotion to your buddies—or if your buddies feel you've abandoned them. With maturity, you are more likely to prefer someone who is like-minded, shares your dreams, and is in like Flynn with your pals. Lovemaking gives you the chance to delight your sweetheart with the pleasures of entering a private precinct of pleasure, reserved exclusively for the two of you.

You are highly responsive to romantic treats and overtures, especially those that arouse intense feelings. Music strongly influences your moods. Hearing one of your favorite songs can make you putty in a suitor's hands, especially if the song recalls a sentimental occasion.

The 1963 Pisces male seeks a partner who is romantic and sexy, but is also a best friend. You need someone who respects your separate needs as an individual. Sometimes you just need to be alone. A partner who understands this can win your gratitude and long-term devotion.

Female Pisceans born in 1963 seek partners who are generous and big-hearted. You can be so giving and concerned about others that it's nice to come home to someone who is happy to take care of you for a while.

1963 ARIES
From March 21, 8:20 through April 20, 19:35

The Ardent Pursuer

Ardent is the best description for Aries of 1963. That one word conveys the heat, enthusiasm, and tenderness of your personality. It describes the way you pursue a new love and the way you love in an established relationship. Like any Arien, you enjoy the thrill of the chase, but once you've pledged your love to one special person, you're content—indeed relieved—to chase after other goals. For you, the stability of a steady relationship allows you to expend your fiery energy in the pursuit of new opportunities for achievement and expansion in your life.

After a date, you are likely to hear, "I had a total blast with you." Such positive feedback is likely to continue throughout your life, from your mate, friends, and any children you may have. Pleasure outings enable you to bond with people dear to you. A photo album assembled during your most serious relationships would be filled with pictures recording romantic getaways and generous gifts. Your playful side is endearing to kids and downright sexy to an intimate partner. Sometimes you can be a big tease and may push your luck a little too far. Should a special someone's outrage snap you back to your senses, your compassionate instincts can take over. You are very good at soothing hurt feelings and smoothing over any ruffled feathers.

Perhaps you tease others because so enjoy being teased yourself. Friendly, playful sparring—verbal or physical—can be a big turn on for you. You respond very well to sexy, romantic overtures that allow you to blow off excess energy or emotional steam. A lover's quarrel can be like foreplay for you.

The Aries man of 1963 is likely to seek a woman who appears to be his opposite. She may seem quiet and understated, especially in comparison to your charismatic "bad" self, but you'll treasure her ability to keep you in line, usually by shooting you that one, unmistakable look.

Nothing less than a tiger will do for the 1963 Aries woman—except of course when that tiger is being a great big pussycat. You like a man who is feisty but sweet, competitive but not crazy, and independent but loyal.

1963 TAURUS

From April 20, 19:36 through May 21, 18:57

The Happy Hugger

Taureans are famous for their creature comforts, and romance is particularly comforting for Taurus of 1963. For you, relationships provide a sanctuary, where you can escape into the sensation of falling in love, the niceties of courtship, the feeling as if your fantasies are being fulfilled. Sweet gestures, treats, gifts, and other romantic notions—things like these give you so much pleasure, you are likely to include them as much as possible in any long-term relationship you may have. Your unusual mental creativity inspires you to come up with all kinds of new and fun ways to rejuvenate a relationship.

While partners certainly appreciate your hearts and flowers, your commitment to relationship romance maintenance serves your own self-interest. When you encounter aggravation in your workaday life, you're likely to absorb and store it as tension in your body. Happy relationship habits, including regular lovemaking, provide a welcome way to relieve any frustrations in your worldly affairs. Your emotional wellness regimen includes a mega-dosage of hugs from friends, family members, kids, pets. The best hugs of all, of course, are the ones you can get from an intimate partner, preferably when you're both alone and naked.

You are one seriously sensuous being. Just about every part of your body is susceptible to arousal. A lover seeking to turn you on should create a checklist of your senses and devise different ways to stimulate each one. Such a strategy could evolve into systematic plan to keep you deliriously distracted for months or even years. Now, that's one ideal relationship!

A woman with simmering passions has tremendous appeal for the 1963 Taurus male. Her mysteriousness can be delightfully absorbing for you. Solving the puzzle means unleashing a rush of feelings that can wash away any lingering stress or aggravation.

The 1963 Taurus woman appreciates a man who is compassionate and able to anticipate her needs. It's not like you expect anyone to read your mind. Still, when your guy shows up with flowers, after you've had a tough day at work, he's your hero.

TAURUS ZODIAC SIGN

YOUR LOVE PLANETS

YOUR ROMANTIC SIDE   p. 696
▶ VENUS IN PISCES
Born Apr. 20, 19:36 - Apr. 24, 3:38
▶ VENUS IN ARIES
Born Apr. 24, 3:39 - May 19, 1:20
▶ VENUS IN TAURUS
Born May 19, 1:21 - May 21, 18:57

YOUR SEX DRIVE   p. 722
MARS IN LEO
Born Apr. 20, 19:36 - May 21, 18:57

YOUR CELEBRITY TWINS   p. 760
Find out the astrological similarities you have with famous people.

YOUR COMPATIBILITY   p. 780
Compare planets to find out how compatible you are in a relationship.

YOUR RELATIONSHIP KARMA   p. 824
▶ SATURN IN AQUARIUS
Born Apr. 20, 19:36 - May 21, 18:57

SIDNEY POITIER
American Actor
Mars in Taurus

371

1963 GEMINI

From May 21, 18:58 through June 22, 3:03

The Sensuous Messenger

Plenty of fresh air is one of the essential food groups for Gemini of 1963. Because you are so perceptive, your nerves can become tense and frayed. When that happens, you need to step away, air yourself out, and rid yourself of all the noise, demands, and conflicting messages. In relationships, it is important for you to reserve a fair share of breathing space, where you can clear your mind and downshift those speedy mental processes. A partnership between equals is essential as you are likely to find it intolerable to be with someone who breathes down your neck.

You appreciate a quiet, steady partner who invites you to get away from it all and renew yourself. You may regard your time together as a sensuous sanctuary, where your sweetheart can help you gather up scattered energies and refocus them through your body. Born under the sign of the Messenger, you have a natural talent for making connections. Physical intimacy with a loving partner lets you tap into deeper levels of feeling and awareness. For you, the message is in the massage, especially one that begins with your shoulders, works through your arms and wrists, and kneads the kinks out of your hands and fingers. Releasing the tension from these sensitive spots sends currents of arousal throughout your body and onward to your mate.

Clever repartee never fails to stimulate you, but someone who truly cares about you will take you for a peaceful walk in the woods. With the wind blowing through your hair, birds chirping, and the sweet smell of damp soil and woodland flowers filling your head, your inner fluffy bunny comes to life.

The earth mother type may be irresistible to the 1963 Gemini man. This will be especially true if you tend to be head-centered and intellectual. You may seek a woman who can take care of you, from the neck down, and help you express your sensuality.

The man who understands and honors the 1963 Gemini woman's need for freedom can win her undying gratitude and devotion. You need a good listener, someone who encourages you to express yourself. Attention like that makes you feel truly loved.

GEMINI ZODIAC SIGN

YOUR LOVE PLANETS

YOUR ROMANTIC SIDE   p. 696
▶ VENUS IN TAURUS
Born May 21, 18:58 - June 12, 19:56
▶ VENUS IN GEMINI
Born June 12, 19:57 - June 22, 3:03

YOUR SEX DRIVE   p. 722
▶ MARS IN LEO
Born May 21, 18:58 - June 03, 6:29
▶ MARS IN VIRGO
Born June 03, 6:30 - June 22, 3:03

YOUR CELEBRITY TWINS   p. 760
Find out the astrological similarities you have with famous people.

YOUR COMPATIBILITY   p. 780
Compare planets to find out how compatible you are in a relationship.

YOUR RELATIONSHIP KARMA   p. 824
▶ SATURN IN AQUARIUS
Born May 21, 18:58 - June 22, 3:03

JILL ST JOHN
American Actress
Sun in Leo

1963 CANCER
From June 22, 3:04 through July 23, 13:58

The Passionate Correspondent

Cancereans tend to hold feelings inside and keep their thoughts to themselves, but Cancer of 1963 has passions so strong they demand expression. You have a wellspring of creative energy that you can channel through artistic projects and romantic pursuits. You and a partner can make beautiful music together, by taking in a concert on a date or actually performing in venues such as the shower, intimate fireside sing-a-longs, amateur events, or humming softly in each other's ear. Poetry and love letters can provide another way to let your feelings out and to hold a partner close, especially when circumstances require you to spend time apart.

You may dream of establishing a harmonious household, where you can entertain loved ones. You thrive in a relationship with a people-person, someone who is happy to officiate in your summer barbeque ritual and who understands your need to share ideas and activities with second family of supportive friends. In private, the two of you can draw together from a shared well of passion and inspiration. Some of your best conversations take place when you're in your lover's arms. When you're with "the one," lovemaking allows you to communicate on multiple levels—through your body, instinct, and spirit.

Because you are a sentimental soul, you respond strongly to little gifts and gestures that reflect meaningful experiences and feelings. When a partner notices something—however small—that matters to you, it makes you feel special, treasured, and very sexy.

The 1963 Cancer man appreciates a perceptive woman who has a sixth sense. Ideally, when her radar detects tension, she takes you aside tenderly, holds your hand, and gently asks, "Hey, what's up?" You can trust her implicitly to hold your feelings and vulnerability in her confidence.

The Cancer woman born in 1963 needs a man who is supportive and nurturing. When you vent about the aggravating people or events of the day, he validates your feelings—and your right to have them. His reliable presence and habits make you feel safe and protected, and his strong embrace always reassures you.

1963 LEO
From July 23, 13:59 through August 23, 20:57

The Childlike Companion

You are as likely as any Leo to love getting compliments, but as a Leo of 1963, you may also have an affinity for complements. That is, you may be attracted to people who have traits that are different from but match well with your own. Leos tend to see themselves as the center of the universe. To the extent you sport this trait, you are likely to attract a friend or lover who reminds you when it's time to think of other people. You may be drawn to older partners or to someone with an air of maturity. This is not to say that you are immature, but you may exude a childlike air. A certain innocence can color your overall perspective, and you enter into the mystery of partnership with a sense of wonder and awe. No degree of jadedness can inoculate someone from your enthusiasm.

The battle of the sexes may provide a friendly-but-provocative backdrop to your relationships. You may spar with a mate over the roles you play in your partnership or family, but the exchange is tends to be playful and good-humored. Open communication is a skill you're willing to work at, especially because it can provide such pleasant rewards in the bedroom. A little teasing can warm things up, and your affectionate, full-body response keeps the love flowing. You are all heart.

Sweet little nothings whispered in your ear, especially when they include compliments, can turn you on in a big way. You light up upon hearing how much someone likes or loves you, and it gets even better when that person goes on to list all the wonderful reasons why.

For the Leo man born in 1963, there is no greater ally than a woman who makes you look good to others. She knows the right time and place to raise issues, and she can be quite frank and firm with you in private. But you never doubt for a second her loyalty to you and your ambitions.

The 1963 Leo woman is likely to choose a man who is elegant and soft spoken. Proud to show her off in public, he treats her as his diva. If he is the head of the household, he takes care of everyone and everything quietly and competently, never calling attention to his authority.

1963 VIRGO
From August 23, 20:58 through September 23, 18:23

♍ The Lusty Disciplinarian

Virgos are known for their fastidiousness, and the Virgo of 1963 is no exception. You may maintain a very healthy routine, with orderly housekeeping, regular exercise and excellent nutrition. Your discipline in keeping such a regimen can benefit your partner and any family you may have. For you, clean living may also involve devoting a considerable amount of energy to the process of determining and standing up for your beliefs. Issues of right and wrong can be a prominent for the sometimes-judgmental Virgoan. You get along best with friends and partners whose ideals and goals harmonize well with yours. A relationship provides you with an opportunity to share a way of life that enables you and your sweetheart to pursue the best in life and to be at your best.

Because you came of age almost a decade after the Sexual Revolution, your attitude towards sexuality may reflect both your times and the freedom to make moral decisions as an individual. Whether or not you believe that sex is appropriate only within the context of marriage, the idea of marriage without sex may rank among your worst nightmares. Sexual compatibility is likely to be high on your list of desirable qualities in a mate. While you may insist on discretion and privacy, you can be delightfully earthy and lusty with a worthy partner.

Being right about a controversial subject or a disputed piece of information can feel intoxicatingly good to you. Accordingly, winning an argument can be a powerful aphrodisiac for you. A clever partner might enjoy challenging your views on a hot subject and letting you win the debate.

The 1963 Virgo man tends to go for the woman who is all-librarian on the outside but who conceals a simmering temptress beneath her squeaky-clean façade. You must be able to trust her to keep the many intimate secrets the two of you promise to accumulate together.

The Virgo woman born in 1963 may gravitate towards the man of great integrity and firm principle. His stability and predictability affords you a feeling of security. Within the safety of the structure he provides, you can relax into intimacy.

VIRGO ZODIAC SIGN
YOUR LOVE PLANETS

YOUR ROMANTIC SIDE   p. 696
- ▶ **VENUS IN LEO**
  Born Aug. 23, 20:58 - Aug. 25, 5:48
- ▶ **VENUS IN VIRGO**
  Born Aug. 25, 5:49 - Sept. 18, 9:42
- ▶ **VENUS IN LIBRA**
  Born Sept. 18, 9:43 - Sept. 23, 18:23

YOUR SEX DRIVE   p. 722
- ▶ **MARS IN LIBRA**
  Born Aug. 23, 20:58 - Sept. 12, 9:10
- ▶ **MARS IN SCORPIO**
  Born Sept. 12, 9:11 - Sept. 23, 18:23

YOUR CELEBRITY TWINS   p. 760
Find out the astrological similarities you have with famous people.

YOUR COMPATIBILITY   p. 780
Compare planets to find out how compatible you are in a relationship.

YOUR RELATIONSHIP KARMA   p. 824
- ▶ **SATURN IN AQUARIUS**
  Born Aug. 23, 20:58 - Sept. 23, 18:23

RACHEL ROBERTS
Welsh Actress
Sun and Venus in Virgo

373

1963 LIBRA
From September 23, 18:24 through October 24, 3:28

♎ The Artful Sweetheart

Libra of 1963 tends to have a sense for originality in artistic tastes and projects. You may interact with your environment in ways that are unusual, creative, and imaginative. You may be one of those people who can start with an ordinary living space, and, with just some paint, curtains, and modest accessories, dress it up into a lovely and harmonious atmosphere for love and family life. In your wardrobe and personal appearance, your elegant style makes an affecting impression.

The sign of Libra rules love and marriage, and you are likely to be blessed with particularly strong relationship skills. You understand instinctively that maintaining a long-lasting bond requires each partner to hold on loosely to the other. Preferring to shy away from harsh confrontations, you are unlikely to attempt to force any issues. You allow love to evolve naturally, through shared activities and recreational outings. Hand-holding and good night kisses are a step along the way to lovemaking, but no matter how long a relationship lasts, you never lose your affinity for tender touching and friendly caresses. You tend to measure the health of any relationship by the degree to which it allows each partner to grow and change over time, and you may expect sexual intimacy to follow a similar course.

Lovely gifts, particularly artfully-crafted trinkets and jewelry, can deepen your tender feelings for the giver. A courteous and generous gesture melts your heart. You like to be wooed and eased into lovemaking. Anything crude, vulgar, or overly direct is guaranteed to turn you off.

A quiet gentility in a woman intrigues the 1963 Libra man. You seek a partner who is lovely in an understated way. Loud makeup or loud habits of any sort are a big no-no for you. Ideally, your partner will be your co-creator of a beautiful family and lifestyle.

A man of power and influence can be highly attractive to the 1963 Libran woman. His resourcefulness and romantic sensibility provides a stimulating foil for your creative approach towards life. He can seduce you with subtle confidence and steamy sensuality.

LIBRA ZODIAC SIGN
YOUR LOVE PLANETS

YOUR ROMANTIC SIDE   p. 696
- ▶ **VENUS IN LIBRA**
  Born Sept. 23, 18:24 - Oct. 12, 11:49
- ▶ **VENUS IN SCORPIO**
  Born Oct. 12, 11:50 - Oct. 24, 3:28

YOUR SEX DRIVE   p. 722
- ▶ **MARS IN SCORPIO**
  Born Sept. 23, 18:24 - Oct. 24, 3:28

YOUR CELEBRITY TWINS   p. 760
Find out the astrological similarities you have with famous people.

YOUR COMPATIBILITY   p. 780
Compare planets to find out how compatible you are in a relationship.

YOUR RELATIONSHIP KARMA   p. 824
- ▶ **SATURN IN AQUARIUS**
  Born Sept. 23, 18:24 - Oct. 24, 3:28

RICHARD BURTON
Welsh Actor
Sun in Scorpio

374

1963 SCORPIO
From October 24, 3:29 through November 23, 0:48

 ## The Seductive Magician

The sign of Scorpio rules sex and passion, and the Scorpio of 1963 can be highly seductive. In your younger days, you may have unintentionally invited romantic interest from people who misinterpreted your manner of paying attention to others. You tend to look directly into people's eyes and to listen closely, with an intensity suggesting that you are weighing on every word. You don't mean to mislead anyone. It just takes some time for Scorpio wizards and enchantresses to master their magic. When you do set your sights on a particular person, you can be utterly captivating. You have a romantic aura that entices a lover to feel as if his or her deepest fantasies are coming true.

Through the years, you may have had a series of serious relationships with somewhat possessive partners who did their part to help you rein in any involuntary animal magnetism. In contrast to the sexy image you cast, you are actually very discriminating about dating and relationships. Protective of your innermost feelings, you are not one to open up with just anybody. Nor are you the type to settle for anything less than a committed relationship with a true soul mate. With that person, you enjoy the trust necessary to strip away your emotional armor and unleash your passion with volcanic intensity.

Sharing sexual secrets can be very exciting for you. When someone opens up to you about things they wouldn't share with others, it can be disarming and intriguing. Hearing naughty or even embarrassing details can make you feel very special and inspire you to share your own experiences and fantasies.

The Scorpio man of 1963 seeks a partner who can help him to improve himself and expand his reach and opportunities in the outside world. Ideally her ability to see your potential and her optimism about your prospects helps to boost your chances of success.

The Scorpio woman born in 1963 appreciates a man who can get her still waters flowing. When that guy makes you laugh, you may feel like you can conquer the world. Your ideal partner believes wholeheartedly in your talents and abilities as a leader.

1963 SAGITTARIUS
From November 23, 0:49 through December 22, 14:01

The Romantic Teammate

Sagittarius of 1963 is an imaginative, romantic soul. Your sign rules travel, and you may have a special affinity for flights of fancy. You can be like a big kid, aspiring to the farthest limits of your own imagination. You may have a Pied Piper quality about you, capturing children's attention with a flair for amazing storytelling. Because your sense of possibility and belief in others can be a compelling force, you may have great success in motivating a lover. Your unique air of authority inspires people's confidence in you. You could be a brilliant teacher and a powerful leader. Your package of talents can make you a wonderful partner, spouse, and parent.

With you, partners may feel encouraged to go back to school or to pursue courses of training that allow them to improve their professional prospects. For you, the whole of a relationship is greater than the sum of its partners. You are likely to be a firm believer in the power of teamwork. The emotional support you find and give in a relationship makes all things possible. Laughter is also likely to be an important component in your partnership, family life, and even the bedroom. A dash of silliness keeps you from taking yourself too seriously or over-dramatizing challenges. The sound of your true love's laughter is one of the most powerful aphrodisiacs for you.

Because your imagination is so strong, sharing intimate fantasies can be intriguing and absorbing. The delight of pleasing your partner inspires you to explore his or her secret desires. To fulfill them together can be an erotic epiphany for you.

A woman who is outgoing and self-motivated appeals to the 1963 Sagittarius man. Something about her drive can arouse your competitive tendencies. It's not that your ego compels you to outdo her achievements—her ambitions spur you to pursue your own greatest potentials.

The 1963 Sagittarius woman seeks a man who is resourceful and generous. Regardless of your financial situation, he can make you feel rich by encouraging you to appreciate the abundance you share in emotional support, health, and happiness.

Christine Keeler and John Profumo

They called it the scandal that almost brought down the British government in 1963. A slight exaggeration, perhaps, but the shenanigans between a streetwise showgirl, a society osteopath, and a high-ranking cabinet member had all the ingredients for a world-class scandal: beautiful women, spies, unrestrained sex, royalty, gangsters—the works.

It all started with Dr. Stephen Ward. Friend to the Royal Family and doctor to Winston Churchill, Ward was at home among the cream of society, even keeping a cottage on Lord Astor's luxurious estate, Cliveden. But the high-living osteopath liked to adjust more than backs—he was also fond of fixing up his famous friends with willing women, just for the mischief of it.

It was at Cliveden that Ward brought together two men and the showgirl in what would become the sex scandal of the '60s. Two parties were taking place within the grounds that weekend in July 1961. Guests at the grand manor included the very married Minister for War John "Jack" Profumo, a Conservative Party stalwart. But Ward, too, was entertaining, and among his group was his roommate, the 19-year-old London cabaret showgirl, Christine Keeler.

Ward had also befriended another showgirl who was a friend of Keeler's, Mandy Rice-Davies. Mandy, blonde and pixie-like, and Christine, auburn-haired and elegant, were favorites with Ward's swinging, wealthy pals. They fit easily into the scene at Lord Astor's, reputed to have been the scene of many an orgy.

Though the weekend began with two parties, it ended as one. During hijinks

Christine Keeler

around the pool, Profumo met Keeler—who was skinny dipping and couldn't reach her towel in time—and the flirtation began. The next day, another important player showed up. Ward's friend Eugene Ivanov, a Soviet naval attache, was an elegant playboy and suspected spy. Unbeknownst to the doctor, British Intelligence had his Russian friend under surveillance for a long time. And within days, the British Minister and presumed Soviet spy had a bit of risky business in common: both were sleeping with the fair Christine.

The amicable Ward liked to brag about couples he'd brought together, and it wasn't long until the government was warning Profumo to end the affair. Profumo wrote Keeler a letter calling it

quits. Unfortunately for him, Christine had other lovers, including two West Indian gangsters who, unlike the upper crust, weren't content to settle things with words.

In October 1962, in a Soho nightclub, one lowlife slashed the other's face in a fight over Christine. He then went into hiding and asked Christine to find him an attorney so he could give himself up. When she refused to help, he showed up at Ward's house and fired several shots into the door. Neighbors called the police, journalists soon followed, and several lives began to unravel.

As the GOP would hound President Clinton almost 40 years later, Profumo's opposition used his indiscretions to their advantage. Like Clinton, Profumo lied, telling the House of Commons on March 21, 1963, "There was no impropriety whatsoever in my acquaintance with Miss Keeler."

Sex may be the scandal but it's the lies that end careers. Three months later, Profumo was forced to resign. Still, he got off easy. Keeler went to jail. Charged with "living off immoral earnings of girls" and facing the loss of his reputation and freedom, Dr. Stephen Ward committed suicide with an overdose of sleeping pills.

Keeler and Rice-Davies were briefly the toast of London. Then they, too, faded into obscurity. In 1989, the film *Scandal*, starring John Hurt, Joanne Whalley, Ian McKellen, and Bridget Fonda, put Keeler in the news again. But the aging, unglamorous ex-showgirl was still bitter at being branded a prostitute. "I took on the sins of everybody," lamented the girl who just wanted to have fun.

375

▶ READ ABOUT SWINGING LONDON ON PAGE 383 ▶ READ ABOUT THE PRESIDENT CLINTON SEX SCANDAL ON PAGE 654

1964

- ⭐ THE BEATLES' "BRITISH INVASION"
- ⭐ GO TOPLESS!
- ⭐ BOND GETS PUSSY GALORE
- ⭐ MY FAIR LADY
- ⭐ OH, PRETTY WOMAN
- ⭐ CANDY

Hot Couple

EVENTS

The Beatles landed in New York amid teen hysteria—the "British Invasion" of the American music scene had begun. Scanty clothes made news worldwide as topless waitressing began in San Francisco, three London women were found guilty of indecency for wearing topless dresses, and Elke Sommer became the first woman to appear on a Spanish cinema screen in a bikini. Only a month after the Pope's scathing attack on the contraceptive pill, the first Brook Advisory Clinic opened, offering family planning to unmarried women in the UK. The UN warned that the world's population was increasing by 63 million every year. Elizabeth Taylor married Richard Burton, her *Cleopatra* co-star—for the first time. "Whiskey-a-Go-Go," the first disco, opened on L.A.'s Sunset Strip. And *Life* magazine challenged gay stereotypes with its photo spread of San Francisco's "Tool Box" leather bar.

POP CULTURE

1964 was a year for enduring films of variable quality, as Sean Connery's James Bond took on Pussy Galore in *Goldfinger*. Audrey Hepburn and Rex Harrison met cute in George Cukor's *My Fair Lady*, the musical version of George Bernard Shaw's *Pygmalion*. *Marriage Italian Style*, directed by Vittorio de Sica, depicted a businessman's long-time mistress's reaction to his betrayal.

The Beatles ruled the charts on either side of the ocean, with "I Want to Hold Your Hand," "Can't Buy Me Love," "I Feel Fine," and "She Loves You." But there were also classics with the Animals' groundbreaking "The House of the Rising Sun," Roy Orbison's "Pretty Woman," and the Supremes' "Baby Love." The Beach Boys' "I Get Around" evoked free-spirited California surf culture, while some people clung fiercely to the '50s message in the Dixie Cups' "Chapel of Love."

Bestsellers explored taboo themes: Christopher Isherwood's *A Single Man*, a day in the life of a middle-aged gay man; Kristin Hunter's *God Bless the Child*, an unflinching look at what it means to be a black woman growing up in the ghetto; and Terry Southern and Mason Hoffenberg's *Candy*, a satirical sex odyssey originally published (and banned for being pornographic and obscene) in France in 1958.

ALAIN DELON & NATHALIE DELON

Frenchman Alain Delon was desired by men and women, and dallied with both. Discovered when party-crashing the 1957 Cannes Film Festival, he became a star with *Plein Soleil (Purple Noon)*. The handsome playboy romanced international beauties and had a child with musician/model Nico. In 1964, he married gorgeous Nathalie. They were jet set favorites until 1968, when Delon's bodyguard was slain in a sex-and-drugs scandal that ruled the tabloids. Despite the fact that they were cleared of any connection, and though they had a young son, the Delons' marriage didn't survive the notoriety. Today, Delon is still acting and, yes, still drop-dead gorgeous.

SEE ALSO
▶ CATHERINE DENEUVE *Page 505*

1964 CAPRICORN

From December 22, 1963 14:02 through January 21, 1964 0:40
(December 1964 Capricorns, see 1965 Capricorn)

♑ *The Committed Partner*

You're a determined Capricorn born in 1964, and to you a relationship must be totally committed and focused. You believe in strong, long-lasting connections and you have no patience at all with frivolous romantic dalliance. In your opinion, life's too short. You're a team player, and a relationship is the ultimate team in which both people help each other to achieve mutually supported goals.

Good communication is essential to you. Being able to connect intellectually is crucial or else why would you bother staying with this person? Honest communication leads to a comforting sense of camaraderie and friendship, probably the most essential components of your relationship. Being able to depend upon your partner is another significant aspect of a strong relationship. You want to be there for the one you love, and expect to have that favor returned.

You have a distinct sense of your preferred "type" in every walk of life, and it's not so much what a mate might do, as what he or she is. To sustain your interest, your mate must be a true partner, on your side in every situation, ready to do battle for you, if need be. "You and me against the world," just might be your motto. You enjoy sharing social activities and like being active in your community. Pitching in together to host a charity event or even to make a good impression on the boss—that's what it's all about.

Male goats born in 1964 need a woman who is sparkling and communicative. From the moment you meet, she has what it takes to be your best friend. Your lady is a people-person, and her social skills come in handy when you need to favorably impress someone. Highly intelligent, your gal is keenly aware of what's going on. She is committed to you, and you know you can always count on her no matter what.

Female Capricorns born in 1964 expect a man to be assertive and intelligent. Your guy knows his own mind and he expresses his ideas aggressively, and with verve. He's strong and determined and an excellent leader, inspiring confidence in all whom he meets. He's achieved success in his field, and you feel instantaneously that he's your perfect partner.

CAPRICORN ZODIAC SIGN
YOUR LOVE PLANETS

YOUR ROMANTIC SIDE — p. 696
- ► VENUS IN CAPRICORN
  Born Dec. 22, 1963 14:02 - Dec. 23, 1963 18:52
- ► VENUS IN AQUARIUS
  Born Dec. 23, 1963 18:53 - Jan. 17, 1964 2:53
- ► VENUS IN PISCES
  Born Jan. 17, 2:54 - Jan. 21, 0:40

YOUR SEX DRIVE — p. 722
- ► MARS IN CAPRICORN
  Born Dec. 22, 1963 14:02 - Jan. 13, 1964 6:12
- ► MARS IN AQUARIUS
  Born Jan. 13, 6:13 - Jan. 21, 0:40

YOUR CELEBRITY TWINS — p. 760
Find out the astrological similarities you have with famous people.

YOUR COMPATIBILITY — p. 780
Compare planets to find out how compatible you are in a relationship.

YOUR RELATIONSHIP KARMA — p. 824
- ► SATURN IN AQUARIUS
  Born Dec. 22, 1963 14:02 - Jan. 21, 1964 0:40

TIPPI HEDREN
American Actress
Sun in Capricorn

377

1964 AQUARIUS

From January 21, 0:41 through February 19, 14:56

♒ *Seeker of Perfection*

As a responsible Aquarius born in 1964, you require a relationship that is passionate, supportive, and romantic. You believe in true love, and that each of us has a perfect partner—which is just the sort of relationship you want to have. You hate the idea of compromise, and want to be with your soulmate because you feel it's your destiny. Although responsibility is also important to you and you believe in loving and caring for someone, you feel that it has to be just right, or you'd rather keep looking.

Sensitivity is another important component of your relationship. You want to know and be known, and the only way to accomplish this goal is to be willing to open up and share everything, without feeling it's a risk. A little intuition is essential, and you feel that being able to know each other by means that can best be described as psychic is just another reasonable expectation of true love.

To sustain your interest, a mate must be intense, passionate, and sensitive. You want to feel that electrical buzz, the chemistry that holds everything in place, the connection that you know was somehow always meant to be. Tender moments of passion mean a lot, but so does sharing the serious responsibilities of life. That a mate will offer praise and give your spirits a boost is a big plus, because you like emotional support and compliments. You also like sharing romance—you'll willingly go dancing, sneak into a closet at a party for a quick kiss, or plan a trip around the world together.

Male Aquarians born in 1964 like a woman who is sensitive and passionate, yet also bold and outgoing. Your lady has a lot of pizzazz, and you appreciate those special qualities that make her so intense and interesting. Her love for you is boundless, and you feel happy simply because she's in the same room.

Female Aquarians born in 1964 like a man to be sensitive yet stable. Your guy has strong intuition and he's quite musical, so if you're crabby or feeling blue he just might sing you a tune to calm your nerves. He's dependable, and you know that if you ask him to do a favor, he will never forget to carry through.

AQUARIUS ZODIAC SIGN
YOUR LOVE PLANETS

YOUR ROMANTIC SIDE — p. 696
- ► VENUS IN PISCES
  Born Jan. 21, 0:41 - Feb. 10, 21:08
- ► VENUS IN ARIES
  Born Feb. 10, 21:09 - Feb. 19, 14:56

YOUR SEX DRIVE — p. 722
- ► MARS IN AQUARIUS
  Born Jan. 21, 0:41 - Feb. 19, 14:56

YOUR CELEBRITY TWINS — p. 760
Find out the astrological similarities you have with famous people.

YOUR COMPATIBILITY — p. 780
Compare planets to find out how compatible you are in a relationship.

YOUR RELATIONSHIP KARMA — p. 824
- ► SATURN IN AQUARIUS
  Born Jan. 21, 0:41 - Feb. 19, 14:56

REX HARRISON
English Actor
Sun in Pisces

1964 PISCES
From February 19, 14:57 through March 20, 14:09

 The Intense Romantic

You're a mystical Pisces born in 1964, and to you a relationship must be spiritual as well as passionate. You believe in deep and intense connections, and you're determined to be with the perfect partner. True love is not only important to you, it's your only frame of reference. You're not willing to settle for anything less.

Your relationship must be intensely passionate, although that doesn't mean that you constantly agree with your partner. A little friction seems quite normal to you and it's always a learning experience to debate—even to quarrel—because the intensity of your love connection leads to wonderful make-up sessions. The main thing you seek to share in a relationship is a sense of belonging and inner recognition, knowing that you are connected because you were meant to be together.

The partner who is ever fascinating sustains your interest. You believe that we each must continue to grow and change, and you support that aspect of your partner's individuality. Your partner endears him—or herself to you by returning the favor. You enjoy mutually fun interesting activities and may like playing instruments together, or at least dancing at home to the stereo. Traveling, discussing serious matters, and working together to make life better keep you committed.

Male Pisces born in 1964 desire a woman who is her own person. Your lady has a strong personality and she sparkles and shines. Her ideas are creative and unique, and it's fun to see the way she expresses herself. You enjoy her taste and love the way she looks. This gal is a free spirit who loves to get you involved in her attempts to try new things. She is strong enough to stand up to you, and reliable enough to be the perfect support system.

Female fishies born in 1964 need a man who is both strong and sensitive. Your guy has a spiritual bent and just seems to "know things." It's this otherworldly connection that gives him the drive and intensity that make him so strong. He is confident and self-assured and, though he can be annoyingly macho on occasion, he usually snaps to his senses before you get irritated—and while it still feels sexy!

1964 ARIES
From March 20, 14:10 through April 20, 1:26

 The Committed Sensualist

As an outgoing Aries born in 1964, your relationship must give you what you need without restricting your freedom. You believe strongly in individual self-expression but you also realize that compromises are necessary when two people merge lives. This can be like walking a tightrope, which you may find frustrating at times, but you also greatly value companionship and commitment, therefore you endeavor to achieve the necessary level of balance to make it all work out.

Interesting conversation is critical to you because you can't stand boredom—you'd rather talk to a stranger than be connected to someone whose dull wit numbs your brain. Sex appeal is also vitally important, and you realize that chemistry is a must when it comes to loves relationships. Commitment is another important dimension of your relationship, and your goal is to remain committed while also growing as individuals. That way, the relationship evolves and changes as you both do.

A partner who is both sexy and clever keeps you interested. You like being stimulated intellectually and physically, and maintaining an aura of fun and excitement is a wonderful way for your partner to keep the love alive. You enjoy being pampered, and a mate who will surprise you with breakfast in bed, followed by an exciting day at the auto races, is just right. If you can pencil in some time for hot and heavy passion, your day is made.

Male rams born in 1964 need a woman who is sensual and reliable. Your lady is yours alone—and you appreciate her commitment to you because it makes you feel safe, even on those days when you're your own worst enemy. This gal has a clever mind—she challenges you intellectually and appreciates the wit in your rejoinders. She is soft and sexy and it's easy to see what drew you to her.

Female Aries born in 1964 need a guy to be a bit of a firecracker. You like him to be hot and sexy and if he's a bit hasty and impatient, you don't mind at all because that seems so exciting to you. It's fun to share his dreams, to enjoy his spur of the moment schemes, and when he takes you in his arms, you swoon and shiver with delight.

1964 TAURUS
From April 20, 1:27 through May 21, 0:49

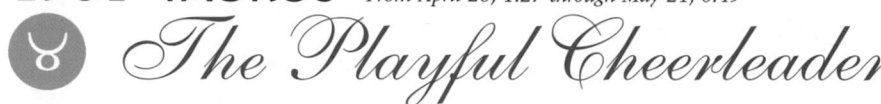

The Playful Cheerleader

You're a rip-roarin' Taurus born in 1964, and you demand a relationship as lively and fun as you are yourself. The good times you share have been your lifelong barometer of the quality of the relationship—if you can't share good times and enjoy each other's company, it's not worth continuing the involvement.

Good communication and sharing mutual goals are important to you as well, and in your relationship you expect to love and support each other no matter what. Being your partner's cheerleader and biggest fan is the most wonderful aspect of your relationship because it brings a sense of security and love. Mutual acceptance is very important to you as well. You want to give and receive positive feelings of love, joy and encouragement, and to grow as a person as a result of the support you share.

The partner who makes you laugh keeps you interested because you look forward to each new conversation, each day shared, and each idea you toss back and forth. A lively intellectual connection is the foundation on which you build love and commitment, but you also appreciate being nurtured and pampered. You love to play, and when your mate tickles you in bed, blindfolds you and takes you on a secret excursion, or challenges you to a game of Scrabble™, you know it can last forever.

Male bulls born in 1964 prefer a woman who is youthful, tender and reliable. Your lady is lots of fun, yet she's also totally committed to you. Her heart is completely yours, but she never smothers you or makes annoying demands. She understands that you're a big kid at heart, which is one of the things she loves about you. She is great with kids, loves pets, and knows how to nurture as well as play.

Female Taureans born in 1964 need a man who is optimistic, lively, and assertive. Your guy is outgoing and friendly. and he can match you word for word in any intellectual gambit. His flirting is fun and he knows how to tickle your fancy. No matter how many years you've shared, it always feels a little like a really great first date. He's your perfect playmate and you enjoy each new day you spend together.

TAURUS ZODIAC SIGN
YOUR LOVE PLANETS

YOUR ROMANTIC SIDE   p. 696
▶ **VENUS IN GEMINI**
Born Apr. 20, 1:27 - May 09, 3:15
▶ **VENUS IN CANCER**
Born May 09, 3:16 - May 21, 0:49

YOUR SEX DRIVE   p. 722
▶ **MARS IN ARIES**
Born Apr. 20, 1:27 - May 07, 14:40
▶ **MARS IN TAURUS**
Born May 07, 14:41 - May 21, 0:49

YOUR CELEBRITY TWINS   p. 760
Find out the astrological similarities you have with famous people.

YOUR COMPATIBILITY   p. 780
Compare planets to find out how compatible you are in a relationship.

YOUR RELATIONSHIP KARMA   p. 824
▶ **SATURN IN PISCES**
Born Apr. 20, 1:27 - May 21, 0:49

MUHAMMAD ALI
American Heavyweight Boxer
Mars in Taurus

379

1964 GEMINI
From May 21, 0:50 through June 21, 8:56

The Lively Lover

You're an adaptable Gemini and you demand a relationship that is multi-faceted. Tenderness and commitment are important aspects of your relationship, but that doesn't mean you expect it to be staid or predictable, because those qualities bore you. You want to feel that your love affair will continue all your life, and that even a long marriage will feel more like a romance than a pragmatic business arrangement.

Deep affection and sensuality are very important to you, and you enjoy a relationship in which each partner is free to express him or herself completely. Being free to experiment and try new things together really appeals to you and shows that the relationship is a success because there is both intimacy and a foundation of stability and trust. Good communication is also essential—of course, to you, that goes almost without saying. If you can't talk, what hope is there of anything else?

To sustain your interest, a partner must have a lively and outgoing personality of considerable depth. You enjoy being teased and engaged in conversation, and you appreciate a partner who knows you well enough to plan events that are sure to be hits. Spending time with children and pets is also appealing, and you like being home together as much as going out. Deeply spiritual, you might be interested in trying astral projection, or exploring your mutual past lives. There's bound to be a lot to discuss!

Male Geminis born in 1964 like a woman who is sensitive and sentimental, yet also independent and a little bit quirky. She has a sixth sense about you and understands better than anyone else what makes you tick. While having an agenda of her own, your lady also puts you at the center of her world, leaving no doubt that she will remain devoted forever.

Female Geminis born in 1964 need a man who is stable and reliable as well as spiritual and sensitive. Your guy is there when you need him, often intuiting what you need without your having to spell it out. His boyishness is charming and, although he's hasty sometimes, his instincts are trustworthy. He has disarming wit and lively conversation.

GEMINI ZODIAC SIGN
YOUR LOVE PLANETS

YOUR ROMANTIC SIDE   p. 696
▶ **VENUS IN CANCER**
Born May 21, 0:50 - June 17, 18:16
▶ **VENUS IN GEMINI**
Born June 17, 18:17 - June 21, 8:56

YOUR SEX DRIVE   p. 722
▶ **MARS IN TAURUS**
Born May 21, 0:50 - June 17, 11:42
▶ **MARS IN GEMINI**
Born June 17, 11:43 - June 21, 8:56

YOUR CELEBRITY TWINS   p. 760
Find out the astrological similarities you have with famous people.

YOUR COMPATIBILITY   p. 780
Compare planets to find out how compatible you are in a relationship.

YOUR RELATIONSHIP KARMA   p. 824
▶ **SATURN IN PISCES**
Born May 21, 0:50 - June 21, 8:56

GINA LOLLOBRIGIDA
Italian Actress
Sun in Cancer

380

1964 CANCER
From June 21, 8:57 through July 22,19:52

The Joyful Playmate

You're a playful Cancer born in 1964, and your relationship must be sexy and fun. Chemistry is very important to you and you like to feel a strong and passionate connection as a constant in the relationship. Mutual interests are also important to you because you love to talk and play together. A spirit of youthful bonhomie is what keeps you together, and if you couldn't share that you'd not be happy at all.

Communication is another significant issue, though sometimes you feel you're connecting below the surface. Just having good feelings and a general sense of understanding each other means more to you than having to iron out the details of your feelings, as though you were lawyers, coming to terms. Often, in talking about movies or television shows you may find yourselves using those discussions to make sense of your own relationship.

A partner who is youthful and playful keeps you interested. You love it when your mate flirts with you or prepares an impromptu event for you both to share. Doing things with children, sharing clever games, going bicycling or on picnics keep you young and in love. Sex is another way for you to be playful, and as long as you're laughing, kissing, and having fun in bed, the relationship can endure forever.

Male Crabs born in 1964 need a woman who is youthful and lots of fun. Your gal has a sort of cheerleader personality— you'd love to see her jumping up and down with those colorful pompoms. She's fun to talk to and everyone loves to be around her because she's so lively and cheerful. Kids delight in her and pets gravitate to her door. She has a sexy, womanly quality but also a sweet, girlish innocence, and that's a winning combination.

Female Cancers born in 1964 like a guy to be macho but not heavy-handed. Your guy knows what he wants but he sometimes changes his course, and that flexibility keeps you interested. Occasionally he can be domineering, but then he stops to make fun of himself, so you never quite know what you're going to get. This fellow is playful yet he's never a fool. He goes after what he wants and makes sure that you're satisfied—in and out of bed.

1964 LEO
From July 22, 19:53 through August 23, 2:50

The Sentimental Sweetheart

As an intellectual Leo born in 1964, your relationship must feel just right. You have strong spiritual discernment and know that how a connection feels below the surface is very important. You feel the relationship has to fit perfectly, like shoes. A sense of destiny brings you together and keeps you interested—you both feel that being together in a long-lasting relationship was meant to be. You would hate to be trapped in a casual involvement in which every day you wondered why you were still there.

Communication is also essential to you because being mentally stimulated is the spice of life. Being in a relationship where each partner feels the other is the most interesting person on earth really keeps you close and happy. You're willing to argue now and then and to share differing points of view, but as long as it's enthralling to discuss your ideas, the relationship endures.

A partner must be rather dreamy and romantic to sustain your interest. You like sharing mystical ideas and the whole attraction is decidedly otherworldly, which is just the way you like it. Being surprised is lots of fun and you enjoy being taken to New Age lectures, outrageous theater productions, and outré art galleries. You'll also happily visit a playground together, whether or not you have kids, because you love the happy squeals of children.

Male Leos born in 1964 crave a woman who is musical and romantic. Your lady could easily appear in Victorian robes and you would not consider it at all peculiar. She has a sensitive, timeless quality, and you sense in her the sort of spirit that inspires poets to pen sonnets. This woman is youthful and playful but also solid and reliable, and there's never any question about her loyalty to you.

Lady lions born in 1964 need a man who is sensitive and charming. He is intensely intelligent and always has something fascinating to say, which makes you review your own point of view. Yet there's more to your guy than talk. This fellow is kind and nurturing, and he has a way of wrapping you up in sweet, tender bear hugs that make you feel all's right with the world.

1964 VIRGO

From August 23, 2:51 through September 23, 0:16

The Devoted Mate

You're a nurturing Virgo born in 1964, and your relationship must be sweet, tender, and loving. Two people living to care for and please each other is your ideal for romantic perfection. A cozy sense of togetherness really appeals to you in a relationship, and being able to relax together and just be who you really are is what your love is all about. Being able to come home at the end of a long day and fall into your true love's arms sustains you both and makes you feel that you have made a perfect world all your own.

Fascinating conversation is the centerpiece of your relationship. Being interesting and intellectually engaged keeps you both so vital. You love to be in a relationship where each partner simply can't wait to share the latest idea and get riveting feedback. Building something together is what it's all about, and therefore your relationship must work on many levels— mind, body, heart and soul. Anything less you would consider a waste of time.

To sustain your interest, your partner must have a tender heart. Knowing that you share mutually warm feelings does a lot to keep you together. Of course, you love being given special presents and sharing intimate dinners, whether out at a fine restaurant or in your own kitchen. Even more wonderful, you love the idea of having and raising children. Being a team and being a family is what matters to you above all, and for that your mate must simply be the one you love.

Male Virgos born in 1964 seek out a woman who is tender and nurturing. Your lady is a mother at heart and always seems to know how to soothe your spirit and wipe away a tear. She is open and gentle, and loves reaching out to those in need. She loves spending time in the kitchen, whipping up treats, and she enjoys meditation as well.

Female Virgos born in 1964 are happiest with a man who is macho yet sensitive. His heart is open and generous, and he reaches out when someone is in need. Your guy is strong and, always feeling safe and secure, is readily available to help people. He's a sucker for the underdog, loves to play with kids, and can spin great yarns and recite tender poetry.

VIRGO ZODIAC SIGN
YOUR LOVE PLANETS

YOUR ROMANTIC SIDE — p. 696
▶ **VENUS IN CANCER**
Born Aug. 23, 2:51 - Sept. 08, 4:52
▶ **VENUS IN LEO**
Born Sept. 08, 4:53 - Sept. 23, 0:16

YOUR SEX DRIVE — p. 722
▶ **MARS IN CANCER**
Born Aug. 23, 2:51 - Sept. 15, 5:21
▶ **MARS IN LEO**
Born Sept. 15, 5:22 - Sept. 23, 0:16

YOUR CELEBRITY TWINS — p. 760
Find out the astrological similarities you have with famous people.

YOUR COMPATIBILITY — p. 780
Compare planets to find out how compatible you are in a relationship.

YOUR RELATIONSHIP KARMA — p. 824
▶ **SATURN IN PISCES**
Born Aug. 23, 2:51 – Sept. 16, 21:03
▶ **SATURN IN AQUARIUS**
Born Sept. 16, 21:04 - Sept. 23, 0:16

PETER SELLERS
English Actor
Sun and Mars in Virgo

1964 LIBRA
From September 23, 0:17 through October 23, 9:20

The Exhilarating Romantic

As an impetuous Libra born in 1964, your relationship must be exciting. You like being linked to someone who's up for rollicking good times but who occasionally makes you feel unsure about what's coming next. Even though you admit that sometimes this can be unnerving, you realize that, no matter what, you must follow your heart and your impulses.

You believe in true love and in destiny, and you want to share your life with that one perfect soulmate. Occasionally in the past, it's been a bit confusing because you believed you'd found that soulmate only to discover that it was all illusion and confusion. But those are the perils of aiming high, and you know that with age comes greater wisdom. This gives you a strong sense of confidence about the stability of your love life. You would never want to settle for a commitment just for the sake of being attached. You have to follow your special star.

A partner who is witty, charming, romantic, sensitive and even a little bit mystical can best sustain your interest. You like to admire that special sparkle in your mate and you're endlessly interested in discovering new rainbows inside him or her. You adore being teased and engaged verbally because there's always something new to explore. Formal-dress events are also appealing, and you love being wooed and ogled by candlelight.

Male Libras born in 1964 like a woman who is beautiful and exciting. This gal has to have a lot of pizzazz, and you enjoy seeing her in action. She crosses the room with verve and flair, twirls around the dance floor with style and panache, and makes you work to gain her attention. Your lady has an agenda and interests of her own, as well as a loving, generous heart and a ready smile.

Lady Libras born in 1964 need a man who is generous and sensitive. Your guy has strong intuition and can connect with other people on many deep levels. He is aware of your feelings and is ever ready to be there for you when you're in need. He's also quite musical and loves to whirl you around the dance floor. His ideas are original, and he expresses them with passion.

LIBRA ZODIAC SIGN
YOUR LOVE PLANETS

YOUR ROMANTIC SIDE — p. 696
▶ **VENUS IN LEO**
Born Sept. 23, 0:17 - Oct. 05, 18:09
▶ **VENUS IN VIRGO**
Born Oct. 05, 18:10 - Oct. 23, 9:20

YOUR SEX DRIVE — p. 722
▶ **MARS IN LEO**
Born Sept. 23, 0:17 - Oct. 23, 9:20

YOUR CELEBRITY TWINS — p. 760
Find out the astrological similarities you have with famous people.

YOUR COMPATIBILITY — p. 780
Compare planets to find out how compatible you are in a relationship.

YOUR RELATIONSHIP KARMA — p. 824
▶ **SATURN IN AQUARIUS**
Born Sept. 23, 0:17 - Oct. 23, 9:20

HONOR BLACKMAN
English Actress
Sun and Mars in Sagittarius

1964 SCORPIO
From October 23, 9:21 through November 22, 6:38

♏ *The Marrying Kind*

You're a gracious Scorpio born in 1964, and you need a relationship that is stable, reliable, and comfortable. You care very much about love and loving, and at the core of your relationship is the commitment to love and take care of each other forever. Stability means a lot to you and you take very seriously the marriage vow, "'Til death us do part." The thought of serial monogamy just strikes you as a huge mistake.

Living harmoniously within a relationship is very important to you because you believe in kindness and good manners. Knowing that you can count on each other is rewarding to you because it gives you the solid emotional foundation on which you can depend. Responsibility and devotion are number one in your book, and you love to let your mate know that you will always love, honor, and obey.

To sustain your interest, a partner must be committed to you and the relationship. Mutual devotion is what you seek, and you believe that as time passes you grow to love each other more. You appreciate being pampered by a partner who places your needs high up on the list of what's important. A thoughtful gift speaks volumes, and you love being given things to go in the home you share. You also enjoy working side by side on special projects and relaxing together as well.

Male Scorpions born in 1964 favor a woman who is generous, vivacious, and friendly. Your woman is kind and thoughtful, always willing to offer a helping hand. You appreciate her well-developed social graces and the effortless way she makes a home and brings comfort and cheer to all who enter it. This lady is elegant well-dressed, and well-spoken, and you love introducing her to your friends and colleagues.

Female Scorpios born in 1964 prefer that a man be responsible, solid, and stable. Your guy is the perfect dad and a reliable mate who changes a flat tire without furrowing his brow. When something needs doing around the house, he never procrastinates and he doesn't make excuses either—he just steps in and does what's necessary. His ideas are deep, and you always feel comfortable and safe when he's in the room.

1964 SAGITTARIUS
From November 22, 6:39 through December 21, 1949

♐ *The Love Slave*

You're an intense Sagittarius born in 1964, and your relationship must be passionate. You absolutely believe in true love and are willing to wait however long it may take to find it. Part of the reason you're such a romantic is that you also delight in independence and a lot of freedom, and you figure that it's much easier to "have it all" if you're with that one perfect soulmate.

Chemistry is something else that matters a great deal to you in a relationship. You'd never make a commitment just to settle down. You have to be absolutely riveted, passionately connected, and practically on fire with desire before you feel that this is the right relationship for you. Communication and good conversation are also important, but they don't supersede feelings below the surface. When it comes to a relationship, you believe intuition is the only true barometer of what's what.

A mate who makes you shiver and quiver with desire will sustain your interest. You need to know that there is an electrical connection so strong it will never fade. You may also discover that no matter how much you fight, sharing intense passion helps heal all wounds. Artful seduction is tops on your list of how to impress you and, even if it begins only with some harmless sexy flirtation, you love being a part of that runaway chemistry.

Male archers born in 1964 need a woman who is passionate and intense. Your lady is self-possessed and there's just something about her—an aura that is sexy and mystical. You sense there's much to know about her, and no matter how long you've been together, there's always something more to discover. This woman is unapologetic about her desires and she loves taking turns being the love slave.

Female Sagittarians born in 1964 prefer a man who is intelligent, articulate, sexy, and electrifying. Your guy is so intense he makes the floorboards shake just by walking across a room. He knows what he wants and isn't at all shy about sweeping you up in his arms and tossing you into bed. He's demanding and somewhat self-absorbed, but he's also considerate, helpful—and a phenomenal lover.

'60s

Swinging London

The world was ripe for a sexual revolution—and swinging London delivered. The London scene, which had been bubbling underground for a couple of years, burst out, spilling a groovy hot stew of fashion, music, film, sex, and scandal. This was a very British invasion.

Carnaby Street and the King's Road were the meccas of cool, the places to hang out, see, and be seen. Young girls paraded up and down with their thin plucked eyebrows, sharp asymmetric Vidal Sassoon haircuts, and tiny shift dresses. And Mary Quant was their patron saint. Small and doll-like, Quant unleashed her bottom-skimming mini on a generation looking to break boundaries. Kissing in public was cool and a new liberal attitude to sex was dawning. Drugs were *far out* and the mood was psychedelic. Experimenting with marijuana and LSD wasn't just considered fashionable—it was thought to be a deep,

worthy experience. Authorities were outraged, parents were appalled.

Models were no longer debutantes and aristocrats. Young Londoners like Jean Shrimpton stormed the pages of *Vogue*, and this was the year a fifteen-year-old, convent-educated waif was discovered—Twiggy was to become the highest paid model of the sixties, epitomizing swinging London.

Fashion photography wasn't all about selling clothes—it was now about expressing a mood. David Bailey was the master photographer, immortalizing the new London look and capturing the newfound freedom. In his 1964 collection *Box of Pinups*, Bailey featured a mixed bag of everything that London stood for—the likes of Lord Snowdon and the Krays stood side by side, causing an outrage. Royalty and gangland mobsters had never before shared the same space—now they were

sharing the same nightlife, in pursuit of pure hedonism.

Music mayhem was everywhere and the Kinks were one of the innovators. "You Really Got Me" was an instant hit and pioneer of a new heavy metal, with its signature distressed guitar sound.

And four lads from Liverpool with long pudding bowl mops were about to go stellar. The Beatles' "I Want to Hold Your Hand" shot to number one in America and their film *A Hard Day's Night* was released. They touched down in the US for a tour. Their popularity was sealed, their fame assured—Beatlemania had arrived.

For the bad boys and girls who didn't want to swallow the wholesome image of the Beatles, there were the Rolling Stones. In 1964, the Stones released their first album—this is the year they really made it big. Rubber-lipped, androgynous, and charismatic, lead singer Mick Jagger oozed sexuality and with his band injected a healthy dose of "sex, drugs, and rock 'n' roll" into the mix. His exploits were legendary and he was the rebel's perfect role model. Every disillusioned teenager flocked to see him strut in his leotard and frilly scarves, belting out his blues-inspired honky-tonk lyrics with an alluring apathy.

Marianne Faithfull epitomized the 1964 woman. A seventeen-year-old rock chick groupie, she was the convent-educated aristocratic girlfriend of Mick Jagger. Her innocent looks belied her appetite for drugs and sex—a life of decadence was just beginning.

1964 swinging London rocked the establishment and the repercussions reverberated around the world. Kick-starting youth into a new era of sexual freedom and experimentation, London was the epicenter of a new cultural revolution.

▶ READ ABOUT THE BEATLES ON PAGES 416 AND 423   ▶ READ ABOUT MICK JAGGER ON PAGE 434

1965

- ⊛ **THE BEAUTIFUL PEOPLE**
- ⊛ **MINISKIRT MANIA**
- ⊛ **CONTRACEPTION BECOMES CONSTITUTIONAL**
- ⊛ **REPULSION**
- ⊛ **SATISFACTION**
- ⊛ **YESTERDAY**
- ⊛ **GAMES PEOPLE PLAY**

Hot Couple

EVENTS

In 1965, the swinging '60s really hit their stride. "The Fifty Most Beautiful People" bash at Andy Warhol's famous Factory loft in New York heralded the modern idea of celebrity, and the scene's "It" girl was Edie Sedgwick, sultry muse to Bob Dylan and Lou Reed, who was featured in *Vogue* and *Life* as a "youthquaker." The miniskirt, designed in London by Mary Quant, had women baring thighs six inches above the knee, and the British government scrambling for a new way to tax women's dresses other than on skirt length. The first singles complex, in which apartment living resembled an organized party cruise, opened in California. And free love reached Connecticut when the US Supreme Court ruled an 1879 law banning contraceptives unconstitutional.

POP CULTURE

1965's outstanding films included David Lean's adaptation of Boris Pasternak's novel, *Doctor Zhivago*, a classic love story set in the Russian revolution, and Roman Polanski's powerful *Repulsion*, starring Catherine Deneuve as a deranged manicurist with serious issues about sex. Julie Christie received the Oscar for her performance in *Darling*, about an ambitious model in the swinging '60s. Frankie Avalon and Annette Funicello frolicked once more on the beach in *Beach Blanket Bingo*. In Mario Monicelli's *Casanova '70*, danger was the aphrodisiac of choice for an impotent man.

Rock music was entrenched, with "Satisfaction" from the Rolling Stones, "Turn! Turn! Turn!" from the Byrds, and the Beatles' "We Can Work it Out," "Yesterday," and "Help!" Pop hits included Sonny & Cher's "I Got You Babe," the Righteous Brothers' "You've Lost That Lovin' Feelin'," and Petula Clark's "Downtown."

Bestsellers included John Fowles' acclaimed *The Magus*, in which a young Englishman becomes ensnared in a game of political and sexual betrayal on a Greek island. For lighter fare, 1965 readers turned to Ian Fleming's James Bond thriller *The Man with the Golden Gun*, and Arthur Hailey's *Hotel*, about a cast of colorful characters at a luxury hotel in New Orleans. Eric Berne, M.D., the founder of transactional analysis, explained power games in interpersonal relationships in *Games People Play*, an early pop-psych self-help book.

CARY GRANT & DYAN CANNON

Cary Grant was a movie star's movie star. Even though he thought he was too old to play opposite Audrey Hepburn in the romantic thriller *Charade*, age differences didn't stop him in real life. He was thirty-three years older than steamy starlet Dyan Cannon when their sultry love affair began. They married on July 22, 1965.

Cannon left her acting career to be a wife to Grant and mother to their only child, Jennifer. But she could only sustain life as a homemaker for so long. The couple divorced in 1968. Cannon starred in the pop-culture classic *Bob & Carol & Ted & Alice* in 1969.

SEE ALSO
▶ **CARY GRANT** *Page 244*
▶ **HITCHCOCK & HIS BLONDES** *Page 341*

1965 CAPRICORN

From December 21, 1964 19:50 through January 20, 1965 6:28
(December 1965 Capricorns, see 1966 Capricorn)

♑ *The Romantic Explorer*

You 1965 Goats love nothing more than to mentally or physically explore new territory. It's no surprise, then, that you're very adventurous when it comes to love. For you, a relationship feels akin to an exciting journey. You're not sure whether the trip will be pleasant, but you are certain it will be enlightening. Some of your love interests may be your greatest teachers, which is why they hold such a special place in your heart, even after they have passed from your life.

You're in love with love and do best with a partner who shares your romantic sentiments. Sexually, you are a bit reserved, so it helps to have a mate who encourages you to lose your inhibitions. Once you feel comfortable with your beloved, you are willing to experiment in the bedroom. You enjoy making love in luxurious surroundings. After you have said your vows, you will always work hard to keep the romance alive in your marriage. It simply isn't in your nature to take your loved one for granted.

If somebody wants to attract your attention, they should express a love for the outdoors.

Earth signs like yours have a special connection to nature, and you feel a kinship with people who share this affinity. Propose an outdoor activity for the first date, whether it's a sumptuous picnic in the park or a hiking expedition through the mountains. Above all, be a good friend. As a 1965 Capricorn, you're more prone to develop romantic feelings toward a pal than a complete stranger.

For a male Capricorn born in 1965, your perfect mate is broadminded, enthusiastic, and humorous. You love girls who can laugh at themselves and aren't continually concerned about getting their hair mussed or their hands dirty. You also gravitate toward accomplished career women.

As a female Goat who was born in 1965, you appreciate a guy who is intelligent and discriminating. Men who take good care of their bodies also attract you, because you love lean, tight physiques. Ultimately, you want a partner who is a nice balance of intellectual and athletic. Too much of one quality and not enough of the other leaves you cold.

CAPRICORN ZODIAC SIGN
YOUR LOVE PLANETS

YOUR ROMANTIC SIDE   p. 696
▶ **VENUS IN SAGITTARIUS**
Born Dec. 21, 1964 19:50 - Jan. 12, 1965 7:59
▶ **VENUS IN CAPRICORN**
Born Jan. 12, 8:00 - Jan. 20, 6:28

YOUR SEX DRIVE   p. 722
▶ **MARS IN VIRGO**
Born Dec. 21, 1964 19:50 - Jan. 20, 1965 6:28

YOUR CELEBRITY TWINS   p. 760
Find out the astrological similarities you have with famous people.

YOUR COMPATIBILITY   p. 780
Compare planets to find out how compatible you are in a relationship.

YOUR RELATIONSHIP KARMA   p. 824
▶ **SATURN IN PISCES**
Born Dec. 21, 1964 19:50 - Jan. 20, 1965 6:28

LEE MARVIN
American Actor
Sun in Aquarius

1965 AQUARIUS

From January 20, 6:29 through February 18, 20:47

♒ *The Strategic Lover*

You 1965 Water Bearers view courtship as the ultimate game. It's great fun for you to figure out how to ensnare a love interest into your web of intrigue. Often, you'll spend months or weeks trying to figure out what makes the object of your affection tick. You need a partnership that places a heavy emphasis on intellectual stimulation. Somebody who keeps you guessing provides you with just such excitement. Your sexual appetite is directly affected by your mental activity. The more you think, the greater your sex drive. Your biggest erogenous zone is unquestionably the brain.

Despite all of your scheming and planning, your romantic motives are absolutely pure. You benefit from a partner with whom you can merge hearts and souls. Intimacy is very important to you. There's a good chance you keep a friendly distance with friends and family. That's because there's only one person with whom you want to share your entire being—your partner.

A person who is interested in winning your affection should plot their moves carefully. Asking

you to fill out a fun psychological test would surely pique your interest. You're very flattered when anybody tries to learn the hows and whys of your behavior. Sexy double-entendres also excite you, because they demonstrate a sensual nature that is close to your own. Suitors would be well advised to pause before answering any of your questions. This lends an air of mystery that you find quite intriguing.

You 1965 male Aquarians like women who are experienced and wise. As somebody who loves a challenge, you delight in a female who makes you feel off-balance and unsure. You also appreciate idealistic women who want to change the world for the better. Nothing turns you on like an ardent social crusader.

As a 1965 female Water Bearer, you want a man who is kind, attentive, and sensual. You've got a strong sexual appetite, and need a partner who likes to linger over you in bed. You can't abide selfish, boorish types. Maybe that's why your heart always skips a beat when a man helps you on with your coat or opens the car door for you.

AQUARIUS ZODIAC SIGN
YOUR LOVE PLANETS

YOUR ROMANTIC SIDE   p. 696
▶ **VENUS IN CAPRICORN**
Born Jan. 20, 6:29 - Feb. 05, 7:40
▶ **VENUS IN AQUARIUS**
Born Feb. 05, 7:41 - Feb. 18, 20:47

YOUR SEX DRIVE   p. 722
▶ **MARS IN VIRGO**
Born Jan. 20, 6:29 - Feb. 18, 20:47

YOUR CELEBRITY TWINS   p. 760
Find out the astrological similarities you have with famous people.

YOUR COMPATIBILITY   p. 780
Compare planets to find out how compatible you are in a relationship.

YOUR RELATIONSHIP KARMA   p. 824
▶ **SATURN IN PISCES**
Born Jan. 20, 6:29 - Feb. 18, 20:47

386

JULIE CHRISTIE
English Actress
Sun and Venus in Aries

1965 PISCES
From February 18, 20:48 through March 20, 20:04

The Attentive Partner

Whoever snags you as their soul mate is lucky indeed, 1965 Pisces. You're one of the most solicitous and thoughtful partners around. Making your mate happy is one of your primary goals in life. When you're not in a relationship, you're busy dreaming of what life will be like when your true love comes along. Ultimately, you do best with a partner who can complete you by adding fun and spontaneity to your life. When you do find the right person, it could be as though your life has been transformed from black-and-white to glorious Technicolor.

Although most Pisceans have very strong intuitions, yours is especially powerful. There's a good chance that many of your friends joke about your psychic abilities. You really have especially good instincts when it comes to romance. Ideally, your partner is detailed, organized, and down-to-earth. Such a person serves as a delightful counterbalance to your dreamy ways. In exchange, you enjoy bringing out your mate's creative side.

Suitors would be wise to demonstrate compassion in front of you. Helping little old ladies across the street, taking in a stray animal, or fixing a batch of homemade soup for a sick friend are all surefire ways to attract your attention. You're also attracted to low-key, modest types who underplay their accomplishments. Braggarts bore you senseless. You're more interested in the shy number who sits in the corner than the noisy jokester who commandeers the spotlight.

If you're a male Pisces who was born in 1965, you probably like women who are sensitive and giving. If there's anything you love, it's a woman who wants to find solutions rather than create problems. You also like intensely feminine types who can anticipate your every wish. You adore being waited on by your beloved, and return the favor by constantly doting on her.

You 1965 female Fish want a man who is receptive and sensuous. Your ideal partner is a guy who really listens to you, and remembers how you take your tea or who your favorite singer is. Repressed types pose a delicious challenge for you. You love to help a shy man lose his inhibitions.

1965 ARIES
From March 20, 20:05 through April 20, 7:25

The Giving Sweetheart

On the outside, you 1965 Ariens are a dynamic, daring lot. On the inside, however, you're quite soft and sweet. Only your romantic partner understands what a gentle soul you really are. Most of your friends and family would be astonished to learn how attentive and loving you are towards your mate. You're also a tender and thoughtful lover, and take careful note of your partner's likes and dislikes in the bedroom. Giving your mate sexual pleasure is a thrill for you.

You're quite an efficient person, and may look for a partner who would benefit from your organizational skills. A relationship that makes you feel useful and needed would benefit you tremendously. Being with an absent-minded partner who appreciates your help and compliments your skills is just heaven for you.

Winning a place in your heart is quite simple. All a suitor has to do is ask for your help, and then take your suggestions. Anyone showing a willingness to change and improve their lives wins favor with you. You also like creative, scatterbrained types who encourage your own imagination. A suitor who offers to show you how to paint, draw, or play music would likely attract your interest. Secretly, you may be a little uncertain of your creative talents, and would welcome a partner who brings out your artistic side.

As a 1965 male Arien, you're probably drawn to charming, temperamental women. Females who express strong opinions on everything from current events to the color of the walls arouse your passion. You're also very responsive to women who have a spiritual, haunting quality about them. You love coming to the rescue of a damsel in distress!

You 1965 female Rams like guys who are faithful, honest, and modest. You detest playing games, and love it when a guy goes out of his way to pay you a sincere compliment. Your favorite pick up lines are probably, "I'm not very good at this, but I couldn't help notice you from where I'm sitting. I just wanted to know, would you like to join me for lunch sometime?" With an approach like this, your bashful suitor could soon become your one-and-only.

1965 TAURUS

From April 20, 7:26 through May 21, 6:49

The Thoughtful Lover

As a 1965 Taurus, you've always got love on the brain. You're forever thinking about the special person in your life, whether real or imagined. Interestingly, your romances have a powerful effect on your work. When you're in a relationship, you're probably incredibly productive and filled with inspiration. You do best with a spouse who isn't threatened by your creative spurts. Consequently, you're bound to choose a marriage partner who enjoys pursuing their own hobbies. You need a free-flowing relationship that affords you lots of private time to do your own thing.

In general, you are quite enthusiastic about the prospect of love. It's hard for you to relate to folks who view romance in a cynical way. Maybe that's because you usually attract fun, upbeat partners. A relationship that thrives on laughter and spontaneity suits you best. Sexually, you are very impulsive, and enjoy making love whenever the mood seizes you. You do best with a responsive mate who is eager to follow your lead in the bedroom.

If someone wants to attract your attention, they should express an interest in the arts. You're probably very passionate about painting, dancing, or photography. Bringing up the subject of ESP is also a good idea, as you're intrigued by the idea of psychic phenomena. The best way to win your affection, though, is to always demonstrate compassion and sensitivity to others.

If you're a male Bull who was born in 1965, your tastes toward women probably run to the sensual type. You love a girl who treats herself to the finer things in life on a daily basis. You're also drawn to social, chatty females who can talk about anything from the environment to who is on the cover of the latest tabloid magazine.

You female Taureans of 1965 like men who are expressive, daring, and smart. Fast-talking jokesters appeal to your love of witty repartee. Men with refined tastes and polite manners also score big points with you. Your ideal guy knows how to order the perfect bottle of wine with a gourmet meal. You need a sensual partner who intends on living the good life with you.

TAURUS ZODIAC SIGN
YOUR LOVE PLANETS

YOUR ROMANTIC SIDE — p. 696
▶ VENUS IN TAURUS
Born Apr. 20, 7:26 - May 12, 22:07
▶ VENUS IN GEMINI
Born May 12, 22:08 - May 21, 6:49

YOUR SEX DRIVE — p. 722
▶ MARS IN VIRGO
Born Apr. 20, 7:26 - May 21, 6:49

YOUR CELEBRITY TWINS — p. 760
Find out the astrological similarities you have with famous people.

YOUR COMPATIBILITY — p. 780
Compare planets to find out how compatible you are in a relationship.

YOUR RELATIONSHIP KARMA — p. 824
▶ SATURN IN PISCES
Born Apr. 20, 7:26 - May 21, 6:49

OMAR SHARIF
Egyptian Actor
Venus in Gemini

1965 GEMINI

From May 21, 6:50 through June 21, 14:55

The Passionate Dynamo

Dynamic, ambitious, and restless, it's hard to pin down you 1965 Geminis. You're always looking toward the future and rarely take time to stop and smell the flowers. You're apt to do a lot of dating before you finally settle down, because you have so many interests. It could be hard for you to find a partner who consistently engages your mind and heart. Sexually, you are extremely inventive, and enjoy a relationship that welcomes plenty of experimentation. Inhibited, timid lovers hold little charm for you. You benefit most from an open-minded mate.

Because your heightened ambition could create a hectic public existence, it's very important for you to lead a tranquil personal life. Being with the right partner is they key to this mission. As far as you're concerned, the ideal partnership consists of blending two opposites. You do best with a mate whose primary focus is the home. You really admire people who are talented in the domestic arts, and benefit from a spouse who dedicates plenty of time to home and family.

Anybody interested in becoming your partner should invite you to a family function. You love observing the way other people's relatives relate and communicate. Alternately, they could invite you over to their place for a home cooked meal. Starting a conversation about sports or politics is also advised, as these may be two of your favorite topics. Expressing an optimistic view of life is always wise, as you can't abide dark, gloomy types.

If you're a male Twin who was born in 1965, you do best with a woman who is versatile and caring. You want a partner who is willing to take full control over the private aspects of your life together. This gives you the time and energy to focus on your professional life, while she takes care of things on the home front.

As a female 1965 Gemini, you want a man who is both smart and nurturing. Although you like intellectual guys, you're turned off by men who take an analytical approach toward everything. Finding a partner who likes to intersperse intense discussions with cuddling sessions would be ideal for you.

GEMINI ZODIAC SIGN
YOUR LOVE PLANETS

YOUR ROMANTIC SIDE — p. 696
▶ VENUS IN GEMINI
Born May 21, 6:50 - June 06, 8:38
▶ VENUS IN CANCER
Born June 06, 8:39 - June 21, 14:55

YOUR SEX DRIVE — p. 722
▶ MARS IN VIRGO
Born May 21, 6:50 - June 21, 14:55

YOUR CELEBRITY TWINS — p. 760
Find out the astrological similarities you have with famous people.

YOUR COMPATIBILITY — p. 780
Compare planets to find out how compatible you are in a relationship.

YOUR RELATIONSHIP KARMA — p. 824
▶ SATURN IN PISCES
Born May 21, 6:50 - June 21, 14:55

TERENCE STAMP
English Actor
Sun and Mars in Cancer

1965 CANCER
From June 21, 14:56 through July 23, 1:47

♋ The Expressive Suitor

Communication is the strong suit of 1965 Crabs. You have very little problem expressing yourself, which makes you an ideal sort of lover. Telling and showing your beloved just how much you care is no problem. There's a good chance you're a master at writing love letters and making tender gestures of affection. Meaningless flirtations are a waste of time for you, though. You'd rather read a good book than banter with somebody who doesn't really interest you.

You do best in a relationship that adds sweetness and levity to life. As someone who has a very childlike spirit, you benefit from a partner who shares your unbridled enthusiasm towards life. There's a good chance you have a strong affinity for children, and may pair up with somebody who wants to have several little ones with you. If you decide not to have children, you might decide to enter into a creative partnership with your beloved.

Adopting a playful attitude is a wonderful way to attract your attention. You're always drawn to people who treat life like one big playground. Proposing fun outings to the zoo, circus, or carnival would go over very well with you. You also have a delightfully goofy sense of humor, and like corny jokes. In the bedroom, you enjoy a partner who takes a playful approach toward lovemaking. Consequently, it's a good idea for your admirer to preface a kiss with a silly joke. You consider laughter to be the most powerful aphrodisiac ever.

You male Cancerians who were born in 1965 go for two types of women. The first type is sweet, shy, and sensual. The second is flamboyant, expressive, and passionate. Whichever kind of female you prefer, it's important that she's very affectionate. You thrive on hugs, kisses, and caresses, and need a partner who loves to cuddle.

As a female 1965 Crab, you want a man who is extremely intelligent. You love brainy types, and gravitate towards men who are either analytical or idealistic. Having a partner with whom to discuss ideas is essential for you. Uncommunicative guys drive you up the wall! Men with a wide variety of interests also turn you on.

1965 LEO
From July 23, 1:48 through August 23, 8:42

♌ The Lavish Lover

You 1965 Lions don't like to live by half measures. You'll make any sacrifice necessary to enjoy the best quality you can in merchandise, restaurants, and hotel rooms. Your generosity is legendary, and usually extends to your romantic partners. Nothing makes you happier than presenting your beloved with some gorgeous trinket of your affection. When you don't have money in your pocket, you still manage to live like a millionaire, because you're able to recognize and appreciate small blessings, too. If your soul mate shares your expansive view, you're sure to lead a rich and satisfying existence together.

Although you greatly prize creature comforts, you believe that the most important ingredient in life is love. Not having a mate can sometimes depress you. Fortunately, you're so warm and charming that you have little problem attracting suitors. You do best with a marriage partner who is sensual but firmly grounded in reality. You greatly benefit from a mate who loves luxury, but is able to budget for it at the same time. You appreciate a spouse who can plan ahead.

If somebody wants to impress you, they should pamper you for a change. You're always so busy bestowing gifts and compliments on others that it comes as a thrill when somebody returns the favor. You're extremely turned on by blatant displays of sexuality, so it's a good idea to wear form-fitting clothes in your presence. You appreciate anybody who takes good care of their physique, and likes to show it off!

As a 1965 male Lion, you have a pretty broad range of tastes when it comes to women. You like dramatic females as well as shy and reserved ones. Women who know how to dress fashionably also impress you. Ultimately, however, you want a partner who is appreciative, admiring, and loving.

You female Leos who were born in 1965 like men who are refined and have good taste. Any guy who demonstrates plenty of knowledge in art is well-suited to you. Rough, take-charge types make you very uncomfortable. You'd rather have a suave partner who is secure enough in his charms that he doesn't have to revert to macho behavior.

1965 VIRGO

From August 23, 8:43 through September 23, 6:05

The Discriminating Suitor

As a 1965 Virgin aren't the type to fall in love easily. In fact, you're apt to put off a romantic commitment for years, just so you can weigh your options. Growing up, the increasing divorce rate probably gave you pause about entering the marriage state too quickly. When you do settle down, you want it to be for life. Sexually, you do best in a relationship where your partner's loyalty and devotion is evident at all times. You feel uncomfortable with a mate who has roving eyes. Much to the delight of your partner, you get more comfortable with your sexual self as you get older.

Although you do take your partnerships very seriously, work can get in the way of your personal life. Forming a romantic attachment to a business partner might be an ideal arrangement for you, because your personal and private lives will fuse into a seamless whole. You do best in a marriage that values the ideas of work and service. Perhaps that's why you may choose a spouse who is involved with humanitarian causes. A relationship that helps you feel connected to the world at large is your ideal.

A good approach toward becoming your lover would be to ask you about your field of expertise. You're usually quite modest about your accomplishments, and welcome the change to expound on them. You're also impressed by an admirer who puts plenty of thought and effort into a date. When it comes time to make the first move, you appreciate a suitor who asks permission beforehand. This helps to melt your reserve.

Women who are tasteful and artistic greatly appeal to you 1965 male Virgins. You're very appreciative of girls with good manners. Dark, moody types also intrigue you. Ultimately, however, your partner must share your serious view of marriage. You're not the type to make a commitment lightly, and your mate shouldn't, either.

As a 1965 female Virgo, you want a man who is passionate and unpredictable. Although you may desire a secure and stable professional life, something deep inside you craves a thrilling personal relationship. A man who keeps you slightly off balance thrills you tremendously.

VIRGO ZODIAC SIGN
YOUR LOVE PLANETS

YOUR ROMANTIC SIDE   p. 696
▶ **VENUS IN LIBRA**
Born Aug. 23, 8:43 - Sept. 13, 19:49
▶ **VENUS IN SCORPIO**
Born Sept. 13, 19:50 - Sept. 23, 6:05

YOUR SEX DRIVE   p. 722
▶ **MARS IN SCORPIO**
Born Aug. 23, 8:43 - Sept. 23, 6:05

YOUR CELEBRITY TWINS   p. 760
Find out the astrological similarities you have with famous people.

YOUR COMPATIBILITY   p. 780
Compare planets to find out how compatible you are in a relationship.

YOUR RELATIONSHIP KARMA   p. 824
▶ **SATURN IN PISCES**
Born Aug. 23, 8:43 - Sept. 23, 6:05

VIRNA LISI
Italian Actress
Mars in Virgo

1965 LIBRA

From September 23, 6:06 through October 23, 15:09

The Perceptive Charmer

As a 1965 Libra, you've been blessed with a keen intuition that probably makes you a wonderful lover. You have a great sixth sense as to what your beloved needs to hear in order to feel sexy and appreciated. While your peers struggled with the opposite sex as teenagers, you may have had no difficulty at all finding dates. Your startling powers of observation help you to know when to make the first move, and when to hold back. That's an ability that nobody can teach. Luckily, you have this skill in abundance!

As far as relationships are concerned, you want a partner who takes on half the responsibilities of a household. Adhering to stereotypical gender roles is not important to you. What is essential is that your mate pitches in with the house or yard work whenever the need arises. A relationship in which both partners can communicate their feelings openly is your ideal. It's hard for you to deal with a partner who lets their resentments fester. You'd rather have your spouse voice their anger immediately, so you can work things out together.

Suitors who admire your talents have the best shot of getting a date with you. You're an extremely accomplished person and want to be recognized for your gifts. Dressing impeccably and having beautiful manners also makes a terrific impression on you. You're turned off by admirers who have an unkempt appearance. Taking you to some quiet, beautiful spot on your first date is a wonderful way to win your heart. You're very sensitive to beauty and admire people who share this sensibility.

As 1965 male Libran, you want a lady who is sexy and stubborn. Females who constantly defer decisions get on your nerves. You'd rather have a partner who knows her own mind. You're also drawn to athletic, outdoorsy types. Women with well-defined calf muscles really turn you on!

Men who are outgoing, friendly, and a little goofy really appeal to you 1965 female Librans. Guys who make you laugh always hold a special place in your heart. If your dream man likes to play sports, you'll only encourage him. You like a fellow with a trim physique.

LIBRA ZODIAC SIGN
YOUR LOVE PLANETS

YOUR ROMANTIC SIDE   p. 696
▶ **VENUS IN SCORPIO**
Born Sept. 23, 6:06 - Oct. 09, 16:45
▶ **VENUS IN SAGITTARIUS**
Born Oct. 09, 16:46 - Oct. 23, 15:09

YOUR SEX DRIVE   p. 722
▶ **MARS IN SCORPIO**
Born Sept. 23, 6:06 - Oct. 04, 6:45
▶ **MARS IN SAGITTARIUS**
Born Oct. 04, 6:46 - Oct. 23, 15:09

YOUR CELEBRITY TWINS   p. 760
Find out the astrological similarities you have with famous people.

YOUR COMPATIBILITY   p. 780
Compare planets to find out how compatible you are in a relationship.

YOUR RELATIONSHIP KARMA   p. 824
▶ **SATURN IN PISCES**
Born Sept. 23, 6:06 - Oct. 23, 15:09

SHIRLEY BASSEY
Welsh Singer
Mars in Scorpio

390

1965 SCORPIO
From October 23, 15:10 through November 22, 12:28

♏ ## The Romantic Philosopher

The epitome of the strong, silent type, you 1965 Scorpions probably aren't aware of just how sexy you really are. Blessed with considerable brains and creativity, you're usually preoccupied with some complicated project. The notion that you could be the object of anyone's desire seems totally crazy to you. Therefore, you benefit from a partner who is direct. Your mate should also take a straightforward approach to lovemaking with you, because it can be difficult for you to pick up on subtle techniques of seduction.

Beneath your contemplative façade beats the heart of a true romantic. A partner who appreciates your tender inner core brings out the best in you. You're also quite philosophical and enjoy discussing ethical, legal, and religious matters with your beloved into the wee hours of the night. You don't do well with a spouse who takes things at face value. You want to delve into life's mysteries, preferably with the help and support of your mate.

Admirers would be wise to approach you cautiously, because the direct approach tends to make you nervous. Asking for the directions to the library or bookstore are good ways to make your acquaintance. Bringing up subjects like philosophy or religion can also tempt you out of your shell. After initial contact has been made, your suitor should take care to ease you into a sexual relationship. It's important for you to feel emotionally comfortable with your partner before you're physically intimate together.

Women who are flirtatious and fun greatly appeal to you 1965 male Scorpions. Although you're somewhat shy, you can't help but admire a bubbly, vivacious female who is the life of the party. Elegant, refined women also arouse your passion. In the final analysis, however, you want a partner who takes love and marriage very seriously.

As a female Scorpio who was born in 1965, you want a guy who is philosophical and sophisticated. Shallow but good-looking men leave you cold. You want a partner who has a strong value system, and isn't afraid to discuss his feelings with you. Good conversation really turns you on.

1965 SAGITTARIUS
From November 22, 12:29 through December 22, 1:39

♐ ## The Fast Mover

You 1965 Archers don't let any grass grow under your feet when it comes to romance. If you see somebody you like, you'll probably move across the room with lightning speed to get their phone number. Sometimes your love interests are taken aback by your direct manner, but they'll soon come to appreciate it. That's because you don't play games with people's emotions. When you love somebody, you say it. Sweethearts rarely wonder where they stand when they are with you. Although you're not an especially emotive person, you do believe in being honest and upfront at all times.

There's a good chance that you have an optimistic attitude toward relationships. When you're in love, you tend to give your partner the benefit of the doubt. You're not the type of lover to harbor jealousies or nagging fears. Ideally, you want a partner who has plenty of intellectual curiosity. You do very well with a partner who takes pride in being a perpetual student. Close-minded or rigid people hold little charm for you.

You're very responsive to people who are stimulating conversationalists. Anybody who can talk about a wide variety of subjects is sure to win favor with you. A suitor who shares this outlook will probably hit it off with you. You're also quite spiritual, and are drawn to people whose actions are guided by a particular philosophy or creed. You don't mind who makes the first move in a relationship, as long as it's done fairly quickly. You hate prolonging sexual tension! Sexually, you have plenty of staying power.

As a 1965 male Archer, you're attracted to women who are brainy and detached. Females who ooze sexuality from every pore don't pose the exciting challenge that an aloof intellectual does. You also like women who harbor an earthy sensuality beneath a sophisticated veneer.

Loners often appeal to you female Sagittarians who were born in 1965. You love a man who sets himself apart from the crowd, thinking his own thoughts and dreaming his own dreams. You do well to team up with a partner who loves sex as much as you do. You've been known to wear out weaker guys!

Joe Orton – The Perverse Playwright

Carnaby Street, groupies, and sex-drugs-and-rock-'n'-roll made 1960s London a very happening scene. However, some things were still considered best left in the closet—things like promiscuous homosexuality. In this atmosphere of taboo, the outspokenness and barbed wit of writer Joe Orton made him a natural poster boy for gays in the 1960s. His boyish good looks and desire for attention didn't hurt, either. Born January 1, 1933, he burst upon the British literary scene like a wild, flashy comet with plays like *Entertaining Mr. Sloan* (1964) and *Loot* (1966), scathing satires of British complacency that brought the gay sensibility to the stage and screen.

A former actor, Orton met 25-year-old Kenneth Halliwell when both of them were students at the Royal Academy of Dramatic Art. Considering themselves married, the two set up housekeeping and both turned to writing. But their love and the isolation of being homosexual in a still uptight Britain soon became the only things they had in common, as Orton became the toast of London while Halliwell disintegrated into the resentful role of stay-at-home partner and unpublished author.

Handsome and impish, Orton loved stirring the pot. In 1962, both he and Halliwell were imprisoned for defacing more than 70 library books. To Orton, it was all a prank and a bit of conceptual art—the vandalism consisted of silly acts such as pasting a photo of a female nude over the author's likeness in an etiquette book. But other aspects of Orton's taste for risk and wild predilections were to lead to his death at his lover's hands.

He was a notorious, and proud, toilet trawler, haunting the public lavatories of the capital to revel in anonymous sexual encounters, a not uncommon practice among English gays at the time, who called it "cottaging." He didn't make a secret of his sexual appetites and kept detailed notes on his wanderings through the nighttime streets of London in search of sex with strangers. In those days, cruising was a dangerous pastime, and more than once, Orton put himself in risky situations, narrowly escaping both arrest and personal harm. For Orton, though, putting himself at risk was all part of the game.

In the end, it was all too much for the unhappy, unsuccessful Halliwell who, like a disgruntled housewife, envied his lover's success and despised his sexual infidelities. On August 9, 1967, Halliwell grabbed a hammer and bashed in his lover's skull. Then, as Orton lay dying, Halliwell swallowed 22 Nembutal sleeping pills and took his own life as well.

According to Halliwell's suicide note, found next to the playwright's journal, "If you read his diary, all will be explained," it said. "P.S. Especially the latter part."

In a trick of fate that Orton, with his perverse sense of humor, would have enjoyed, the coroner's office discovered that Halliwell had died first, thus making Orton his legal heir. If Orton had died first, all his books and papers would have gone to Halliwell's family, who admitted they would have destroyed everything. As it was, Orton's writings and satirical talent lived on.

His wit and words made him a star. His uninhibited lifestyle made him an icon. Together, they led to his brutal death. Orton died, as he had lived, in the headlines, his penchant for attention leading his biographer, John Lahr, to note that Orton was never rebellious without seeking attention and applause for his efforts. At his funeral, as he had requested, the Beatles' song "A Day in the Life" was played. Ironically, a film

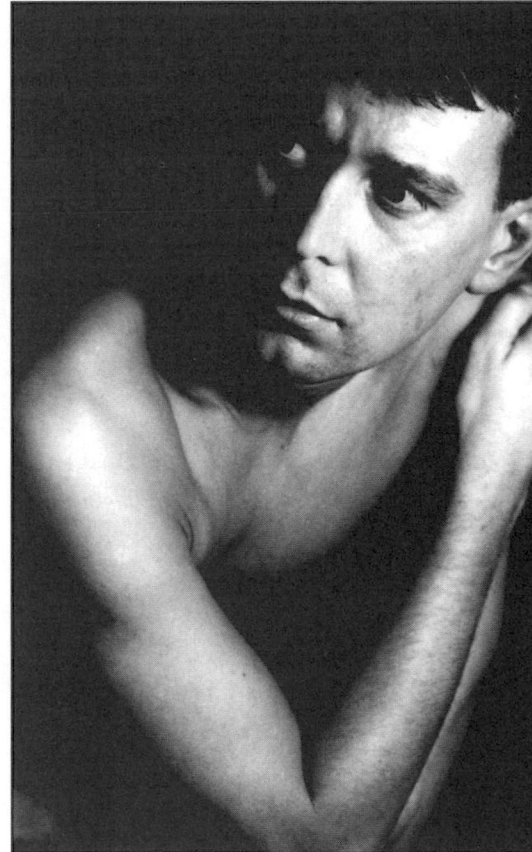

> *"I have high hopes of dying in my prime."*
>
> **ORTON'S DIARY, July 1967**

project between the Beatles and Orton had fallen through not long before, because the band was afraid Orton would write a screenplay too daring and sexual for their reputations. The outrageous life and tragic death of Joe Orton can be experienced in *Prick Up Your Ears*, Stephen Frears' 1987 film featuring bravura performances by Gary Oldman and Alfred Molina.

▶ READ ABOUT THE SWINGING LONDON SCENE ON PAGE 383   ▶ READ ABOUT THE BEATLES ON PAGES 416 AND 423

1966

Hot Couple

- ⊛ **NOW**
- ⊛ **"THE FUGITIVE" ACQUITTED**
- ⊛ **BLOWUP**
- ⊛ **UN HOMME ET UNE FEMME**
- ⊛ **WILD THING**
- ⊛ **UP ABOVE THE WORLD**
- ⊛ **HUMAN SEXUAL RESPONSE**

EVENTS

The National Organization for Women (NOW) was founded to help US women gain equal rights, Creative Playthings introduced the first anatomically correct male baby doll, and Germany legislated equal responsibility and separate assets for both partners in a marriage. Shenanigans included Frank Sinatra's Las Vegas marriage to Mia Farrow, 29 years his junior, and the acquittal of glamorous 47-year-old widow Candy Mossler and her 23-year-old nephew and lover for the murder of banking tycoon Jacques Mossler, clearing the way for her to inherit $28 million. Also acquitted was Dr. Sam Sheppard, at his second trial for the 1954 murder of his pregnant wife. Sheppard's first trial and conviction inspired the 1963 TV series *The Fugitive*. Timothy Leary, former Harvard psychology professor and prominent LSD advocate, was arrested on charges of narcotics possession.

POP CULTURE

1966 was the definitive year for the '60s-era film. *Alfie* starred Michael Caine as a pleasure-seeking playboy. In *Un Homme et Une Femme*, a widow and widower find love. Michelangelo Antonioni's stylized, atmospheric *Blowup* followed a London fashion photographer who may have inadvertently witnessed a murder. Elizabeth Taylor and Richard Burton played a married couple fiercely addicted to bitter recriminations in Mike Nichols' adaptation of the Albee play *Who's Afraid of Virginia Woolf?*

1966 created such enduring hits as The Mamas and the Papas' "Monday,

Monday," the Troggs' "Wild Thing," Lovin' Spoonful's "Summer in the City," and the Supremes' "You Can't Hurry Love." Novelty hits included "Winchester Cathedral," "Cherish," and "The Ballad of the Green Berets." The Beatles' "We Can Work It Out" was answered with "I'm a Believer" by their ersatz American imitators, the Monkees.

Bestsellers included *Valley of the Dolls* by Jacqueline Susann, in which three women navigate the world of showbusiness, and Harold Robbins' *The Adventurers*, about a high-society playboy, replete with graphic sex and violence. American expatriate writer Paul Bowles' sublime *Up Above the World* and Paul Scott's *The Jewel in the Crown* both explored the moral ambiguity of white Westerners' actions in third-world countries. *Human Sexual Response* by William Howard Masters and Virginia E. Johnson presented the results of research into the sex lives of 694 subjects.

FRANK SINATRA & MIA FARROW

Frank Sinatra, age 50 in 1966, sent shockwaves through Hollywood when he wed starlet Mia Farrow, age 21, on July 19. Sinatra, the crooning heartthrob, had been linked to some of the hottest stars of the era—Lana Turner, Marlene Dietrich, and Marilyn Monroe. His buddy Dean Martin summed up the unusual union in one sentence: "I've got scotch older than Mia Farrow." Although they divorced two years later in 1968, Sinatra remained a father figure for Farrow. Years later it was rumored that Ol' Blue Eyes offered to have 57-year-old Woody Allen's legs broken when Allen's affair with Farrow's adopted daughter, Soon-Yi Previn, age 22, was disclosed.

SEE ALSO

▶ **FRANK SINATRA** *Page 211*

▶ **AVA GARDNER AND FRANK SINATRA** *Page 270*

392

1966 CAPRICORN

From December 22, 1965 1:40 through January 20, 1966 12:19
(December 1966 Capricorns, see 1967 Capricorn)

♑ The Honest Observer

You have a distinct moral code that is individual, unconventional, and unshakable. You do not attach to people lightly, though everyone seems to want to attach to you! You expect your love relationship to have the same honesty, mutual respect, and breathing room as your closest friendship. The messy, needy, reactive parts of romance make you skittish, but if you are treated well and dealt with gently and tentatively, like a cat, you can eventually come to terms with the sometimes unappealing aspects of long-term love.

You must be involved with someone who inspires you, who you can look up to. You have plenty of friends so the person who you commit to must be ideal to you in some way. You expect your lover to have integrity and vision and to hold you to a tough, almost unreachable standard. You want to work hard in love and if things are too "easy" you sense that the relationship is lacking something essential.

You are extremely astute and perceptive though you usually don't hog center stage sharing your observations. But, if a potential lover shows keen insights about human nature and about you in particular, you are sure to be intrigued and enamored. You are very cerebral and tapped into the culture and will appreciate it if a potential lover can intelligently discuss the latest films, books, and news stories with you. And, beneath your humble, smart persona you possess dancing feet, so if someone wants to really get you going they should find a way to start moving across a dance floor with you!

1966 Capricorn men want women who are strong and dominating and who force them to be Great Men. You respond passionately to a woman who possesses a fierce hatred of injustice. A woman who isn't afraid to fight for you or with you will surely win your love.

Capricorn women born in 1966 want men who are ahead of their time and who work for themselves. You want a leader, not a follower and don't mind if he has an abrasive or arrogant edge. In fact, these qualities turn you on! You expect your man to be his own boss, and not easily dominated by her, his parents, or anyone.

CAPRICORN ZODIAC SIGN
YOUR LOVE PLANETS

YOUR ROMANTIC SIDE — p. 696
▶ VENUS IN AQUARIUS
Born Dec. 22, 1965 1:40 - Jan. 20, 1966 12:19

YOUR SEX DRIVE — p. 722
▶ MARS IN CAPRICORN
Born Dec. 22, 1965 1:40 - Dec. 23, 1965 5:35
▶ MARS IN AQUARIUS
Born Dec. 23, 1965 5:36 - Jan. 20, 1966 12:19

YOUR CELEBRITY TWINS — p. 760
Find out the astrological similarities you have with famous people.

YOUR COMPATIBILITY — p. 780
Compare planets to find out how compatible you are in a relationship.

YOUR RELATIONSHIP KARMA — p. 824
▶ SATURN IN PISCES
Born Dec. 22, 1965 1:40 - Jan. 20, 1966 12:19

1966 AQUARIUS

From January 20, 12:20 through February 19, 2:37

♒ The Dedicated Dreamer

You dedicate yourself with great effort to everything you do, whether it's at work, with your family, or in love. You don't take anything for granted. In fact you often expect that what's here today may be gone tomorrow. You are seeking a friend, a colleague, a fellow dreamer, and a sexy, sexy lover in a life partner. Nothing less will do! If you can't have it all in one person, you may want to spread yourself around and date many people. In love, you are a strange mix of hope and tentative trust. You've endured a lot of disappointments and are deeply vulnerable.

Your work is primary in your life so you must be involved with someone who feels the same way about their vocation. You have a knack for getting your loved one to work for you in some capacity. Power dynamics come up a lot in your love life. You enjoy analyzing this phenomenon.

If someone wants to get your attention they should be very earthy and comfortable in their body. You like to get right to the action and check out the sexual chemistry as soon as possible! You also appreciate a person who is a bit of a workaholic like you, and possesses a strong work ethic. If someone really wants to impress you they should take you to their place of business to show you what they do. You believe that working hard can change the world and will be awed by someone who shares this philosophy and backs it up with strong, concrete action.

1966 Aquarius men are looking for women who care deeply about the world around them. Humanitarians turn you on. You love to see a woman stand up for other people. Women who love animals and who fight for every kind of "underdog" also impress you guys. You also like a woman who is as interested in technology and science as you are.

Women born under the sign of Aquarius in 1966 are drawn to guys who are artistic and sensitive but driven about getting their creative vision out into the world. The dreamier he is the dreamier you get. But you need a man who will follow through on the promise of his dreams. You want a fellow who is not philosophically locked in to traditional male and female roles.

VANESSA REDGRAVE
English Actress
Sun in Aquarius

AQUARIUS ZODIAC SIGN
YOUR LOVE PLANETS

YOUR ROMANTIC SIDE — p. 696
▶ VENUS IN AQUARIUS
Born Jan. 20, 12:20 - Feb. 06, 12:45
▶ VENUS IN CAPRICORN
Born Feb. 06, 12:46 - Feb. 19, 2:37

YOUR SEX DRIVE — p. 722
MARS IN AQUARIUS
Born Jan. 20, 12:20 - Jan. 30, 7:00
MARS IN PISCES
Born Jan. 30, 7:01 - Feb. 19, 2:37

YOUR CELEBRITY TWINS — p. 760
Find out the astrological similarities you have with famous people.

YOUR COMPATIBILITY — p. 780
Compare planets to find out how compatible you are in a relationship.

YOUR RELATIONSHIP KARMA — p. 824
▶ SATURN IN PISCES
Born Jan. 20, 12:20 - Feb. 19, 2:37

MICHAEL CAINE
English Actor
Sun and Venus in Pisces

1966 PISCES
From February 19, 2:38 through March 21, 1:52

The Experimental Romantic

The only thing you are sure about in this life is that change is the only thing one can be sure about in life. You have many moods and the potential to swim in so many directions, little fish! In love you are a great experimenter and transformer. You change who you are just a little each time you fall in love. You are hard to pin down, even to yourself! After awhile you will settle into a stable relationship, but your head will always be in dreams.

You want your love life to be full of poetry and sensuality and beauty and may have a hard time settling into a mundane routine with your partner. You believe that love is meant to radically alter the heart and the senses, and you live up to your beliefs. You want a relationship that is passionate and dramatic and doesn't follow anyone's rules but your own. But you are always making up the rules as you go! You are totally honest about who you are, so you know that you have nothing to hide.

If someone wants to attract your attention they have got to talk on a divine and deeply felt level. Superficial conversation bores you. So does an emphasis on practicality. A potential lover who speaks in poetic, over-the-top language is bound to catch your ear and your eye. You are also a great music lover and will appreciate someone who is passionate about this art form as well. Sexy, slow dancing is always a sure-fire way to attract you. You also respond well to someone who can tell great stories and entertain a crowd.

As a 1966 Pisces male you are seeking a woman who will ground you a little and bring you down to earth, but without clipping your angelic wings. She should be creative but stable, since you tend to be all over the place. You want a woman who is tolerant of all people and who treats everyone fairly and respectfully.

Pisces women born in 1966 want men who live life on the edge and who are true to themselves at any cost. You appreciate a man who is physically active and perhaps competes in athletic competitions. You also likes guys who enjoy collaborating with you on artistic projects. You adore playful men.

1966 ARIES
From March 21, 1:53 through April 20, 13:11

The Independent Artiste

Unconventional and artistic, you are truly a visionary and a pioneer. As a 1966 Aries you are a very independent thinker and a true iconoclast. You do not want to fit anybody's cookie-cutter fantasy about what you should be. You refuse to fit into anyone else's mold. You're just not capable of that. Your spirit is strong and generous and because of this you detest all forms of pettiness. A lover who thinks big, lives large, and tries to create more beauty and meaning in the world is the one for you. You want a relationship that is an artistic and spiritual partnership, one in which you inspire your lover on the most profound levels and vice versa.

Sometimes you may feel like no one will live up to your high standards. But the deep, romantic voice inside you tells you that that just ain't so. You just have to hold onto your dreams and visions. Your intuition is strong, and when it comes to matters of the heart, your challenge is to really listen to what that inner voice tells you. You know that relationships are meant to teach you all about the power of faith and dreams.

To arouse your attention, a potential partner should engage in a discussion about art or music and the feelings they induce. Someone who can argue passionately with you about aesthetic matters but then wow you with a deep soulful, silent gaze is sure to interest you and keep your attention.

As a male Aries born in 1966 your ideal female partner is someone with a soaring imagination who thinks "outside the box." She has to be deeply compassionate about all living things, particularly animals and people who live in poverty. You want a woman who brings out the altruist in you.

As a 1966 Aries woman, you want a man who is unthreatened by powerful female energy. He must have a lot of physical and mental stamina in order to keep up with you. The more athletic he is the better. He must also possess a childlike spirit. If he is too set in his ways you will feel weighed down. You need a man who is strong enough to stand up to you but not so tough that he tries to control you and crush your will.

394

1966 TAURUS

From April 20, 13:12 through May 21, 12:31

The Gentle Powerhouse

In love, your motto is "Visualize the end result and work backwards." You are self-aware enough to know what you want from the relationship sector of your life, and practical enough to know how to get it. Still, you would never "just settle" for what's convenient in love. You possess a sensitive, refined nature and want to commit forever to a sensual and loyal mate. You hold out for the best. Patience is definitely one of your greatest virtues.

You demand strength from a partner but you can't stand pushiness. A lover with a gentle voice, smile, and touch makes your heart go pitter-pat. Endless chatter and silly surprises annoy you. You prefer deep affection and the stability of a day-to-day routine you can count on. Your home is your sanctuary and you won't feel completely at home unless you're sharing your space with a beloved partner.

If someone wants to catch your eye they've got to show you respect and take a delicate, persistent approach. You don't appreciate high drama. You prefer courtship to be slow and steady. Someone who shares your taste for quality food, fine fabrics, and the good things in life is sure to arouse your interest. But you are not decadent. You are impressed by someone who knows how to splurge on you and on themselves once in awhile, but who is wise enough to save for a rainy day.

As a 1966 Taurus male, you don't like wishy-washy or needy females. If she shares your love of fine food and is a great cook herself, all the better! You want someone who will stand by your side over the years. Women with a lot of mood swings scare you. You don't ask for much but when you do ask for something you expect to get it. The ideal woman for you intuitively understands what the "deal breakers" are in your relationship.

Women born under the sign of Taurus in 1966 are looking for men who are loyal and loving. You definitely won't judge a book by its cover. A lot of charm and big talk turn you off. You want a man who puts his money where his mouth is (and it doesn't hurt if he makes a good living too!) For you, actions speak much louder than words.

TAURUS ZODIAC SIGN
YOUR LOVE PLANETS

YOUR ROMANTIC SIDE   p. 696
- ▶ **VENUS IN PISCES**
  Born Apr. 20, 13:12 - May 05, 4:32
- ▶ **VENUS IN ARIES**
  Born May 05, 4:33 - May 21, 12:31

YOUR SEX DRIVE   p. 722
- ▶ **MARS IN TAURUS**
  Born Apr. 20, 13:12 - May 21, 12:31

YOUR CELEBRITY TWINS   p. 760
Find out the astrological similarities you have with famous people.

YOUR COMPATIBILITY   p. 780
Compare planets to find out how compatible you are in a relationship.

YOUR RELATIONSHIP KARMA   p. 824
- ▶ **SATURN IN PISCES**
  Born Apr. 20, 13:12 - May 21, 12:31

GEORGE PEPPARD
American Actor
Mars in Gemini

1966 GEMINI
From May 21, 12:32 through June 21, 20:32

The Realistic Genius

You are intellectually curious and possess an endless thirst for knowledge. Your mind is without a doubt where your desires begin. Relationships for you must be cerebrally stimulating. Verbal foreplay really gets you going! But, you have been burned too many times by smart lovers who are also erratic and hard to pin down. You are too sensual to bet on someone who is here today and gone tomorrow. You want a lover who will be with you forever, and a partnership where you'll always have things to talk about.

In order for you to be happiest in a relationship, you need a lover who is accessible enough for you to reach by phone and e-mail many times a day, but who is independent enough to not sit and wait for your calls and notes. You are an air sign, after all, and need to be on a long leash. Yet, there is a part of you that is thrilled to feel sensually and emotionally possessed by someone who loves you dearly.

To lure you out, a potential mate should suggest that you go to a dim sum or tapas restaurant together, or to a wine tasting. Your ideal date is one in which you can try lots of different delicious things, and sit and converse for hours on end! You are also highly turned on by someone who speaks many different languages. If a potential lover isn't bilingual (yet!) that's okay, but they should at least be able to turn a few sexy phrases in a foreign tongue.

A man born under the sign of Gemini in 1966 wants a woman who is affectionate in public and who is adept at the fine art of verbal flirting. You love to be teased and toyed with but in a playful not sadistic way. You like women who know what they want and aren't afraid to go for it. You also need a woman who will encourage you to be a success in your career.

1966 female Geminis want men who will intellectually challenge them. He's got to be well read and well-versed in the classics as well as areas of art, finance, literature, and a variety of subjects that he is interested in. You like men who are flexible and fun loving. Rigid guys who are married to their single routines annoy you. You appreciate spontaneity.

GEMINI ZODIAC SIGN
YOUR LOVE PLANETS

YOUR ROMANTIC SIDE   p. 696
- ▶ **VENUS IN ARIES**
  Born May 21, 12:32 - May 31, 17:59
- ▶ **VENUS IN TAURUS**
  Born May 31, 18:00 - June 21, 20:32

YOUR SEX DRIVE   p. 722
- ▶ **MARS IN TAURUS**
  Born May 21, 12:32 - May 28, 22:06
- ▶ **MARS IN GEMINI**
  Born May 28, 22:07 - June 21, 20:32

YOUR CELEBRITY TWINS   p. 760
Find out the astrological similarities you have with famous people.

YOUR COMPATIBILITY   p. 780
Compare planets to find out how compatible you are in a relationship.

YOUR RELATIONSHIP KARMA   p. 824
- ▶ **SATURN IN PISCES**
  Born May 21, 12:32 - June 21, 20:32

JACQUELINE SUSANN
American Writer
Sun and Venus in Leo

1966 CANCER
From June 21, 20:33 through July 23, 7:22

 The Homey Flirt

Born under the sign of Cancer in 1966, you are definitely the settle down kind. Yes, you love to flirt with any and all who cross your path, but underneath your charming façade, you are not at all fickle about what you want from your love life. Commitment and long-term loyalty mean everything to you. You idealize all aspects of home and family life, and deeply desire a meaningful marriage and a brood of beloved kids.

Yet you are addicted to mental stimulation and must have a mate who pushes you intellectually and encourages you to explore obscure areas of knowledge. You believe that all of life is about teaching and learning, and need to be in a relationship that allows you to stretch your mind and your emotional resources.

If someone wants to catch your eye they've got to have a subtle opening remark. You are an A+ student when it comes to the art of flirting, so hackneyed lines including "What's your sign?" will bore you silly. If a potential lover shares secret knowledge about a foreign land or an obscure event from history, it's sure to make you intrigued. Once you are ensconced in scintillating conversation, you are ripe for love. But a potential mate for you needs to be a solid citizen, too. You have long-term friends and roots and are suspicious of people who are all excitement and no stability.

A 1966 male Cancer is looking for a woman whose background and interests seem exotic or foreign in some way to him. "Vive la différence" is your motto. But underneath the initial cultural or cerebral differences you must know that you share the same family values. She must want to make a home with you and she must be interested in becoming friends with your relatives.

Women born under the sign of Cancer in 1966 want men who are never bored and know how to entertain themselves. If he's an avid reader with many unusual hobbies, all the better. He's also got to be easygoing and open to hanging out with all of your unusual friends. If he is taking classes in subjects that he's obsessed with, just as you are, you will surely feel that he is the yang to your yin.

1966 LEO
From July 23, 7:23 through August 23, 14:17

The Nurturing Exhibitionist

You are warm and cuddly and love to be in a relationship because you adore both giving and receiving affection. For you, there is no such thing as too much closeness. You love to hug and kiss constantly. A partner who is severely cold and restrained makes you sad. However, you love to unlock the hidden snuggle bunny beneath a lover's cool and enigmatic exterior. Your gift is for bringing out the best in people. You are a surrogate parent to everyone, and you like it that way. You love to feel needed.

You expect a relationship to be about complete loyalty and devotion. You can't stand being with someone who is on the fence or has one foot in and one foot out. You love to entertain at home or go to close friends' or relatives' homes for small gatherings. Your ideal situation is one in which you are entertaining close companions with story, song, or sassy jokes as your partner looks on adoringly.

If someone wants to attract, you they have to be able to both give and receive a compliment. Flattery is your Achilles' heel, but it does have to be rooted in truth. You are not an egotist but you do need a lot of attention! If a potential lover introduces you to close friends and family and is equally comfortable joining in with your circle, that bodes well for a long-term match. And with you, long-term is everything. You are not just looking for someone to date.

If you are a 1966 Leo male, you are looking for a woman who is tender and supportive and who believes in you one hundred percent. You can't stand detachment. You are enamored of women with strong beliefs and a strong moral code. Flightiness and "convenient" values make you insecure. You like a woman with an old-fashioned way about her, who on occasion will dress up like a 1940s movie star. You are a sucker for glamor.

As a 1966 Leo female you want a man who acts and dresses like a "real man." You don't like guys who are more vain than you are! Over the long haul, you appreciate a man who is sensitive and loving and who shows profound compassion and patience with your family and your children.

1966 VIRGO
From August 23, 14:18 through September 23, 11:42

The Physical Philanthropist

Virgos born in 1966 are deeply connected to the natural world and love to spend time outdoors. Sports and sunshine bring out your best so you must be with someone who shares these passions. You are not a run-around type and definitely expect a relationship to be monogamous and traditional. Any level of sneakiness or secrets in your love life make you so uncomfortable that you become physically ill. You are a worrier, so you need a partner you can trust who brings out your most noble qualities.

You are security-minded but not greedy. You want the simple good things in life and a big cushion to fall back on in the back, just in case. You expect your relationship to be an altruistic partnership in which both you and your lover give your time and money to causes that you believe in. You are high-minded, but at the same time you work hard to actually make the world a better place and will hold your partner to this same charitable standard.

You are not immediately open to new things, so a potential lover must put you at ease by emphasizing what you have in common before introducing you to unfamiliar areas. Anything that blends the physical with the spiritual, like gardening or yoga, intrigues you, for sure. A partner who suggests that you engage in one of these activities together is sure to make their mark on you.

1966 Virgo men want women who are traditional on the outside but who are naughty behind closed doors! The more buttoned-up a woman is, the more you enjoy unbuttoning her. You likes a lady who puts others before herself and who devotes a decent portion of her time to helping the needy. But when she is "off-duty," you love a woman to be as physically active and sporty as you are.

Women born under the sign of Virgo in 1966 are looking for men who are dignified and successful and not too turbulent and complex. You appreciate a man with a strong sense of right and wrong. At the same time, you respond to a man who is intensely passionate about his beliefs and would die for them. A guy who is unpretentious, down-to-earth and deeply soulful is sure to win your heart.

VIRGO ZODIAC SIGN
YOUR LOVE PLANETS

YOUR ROMANTIC SIDE   p. 696
- ▶ **VENUS IN LEO**
  Born Aug. 23, 14:18 - Sept. 08, 23:39
- ▶ **VENUS IN VIRGO**
  Born Sept. 08, 23:40 - Sept. 23, 11:42

YOUR SEX DRIVE   p. 722
- ▶ **MARS IN CANCER**
  Born Aug. 23, 14:18 - Aug. 25, 15:51
- ▶ **MARS IN LEO**
  Born Aug. 25, 15:52 - Sept. 23, 11:42

YOUR CELEBRITY TWINS   p. 760
Find out the astrological similarities you have with famous people.

YOUR COMPATIBILITY   p. 780
Compare planets to find out how compatible you are in a relationship.

YOUR RELATIONSHIP KARMA   p. 824
- ▶ **SATURN IN PISCES**
  Born Aug. 23, 14:18 - Sept. 23, 11:42

JAMES COBURN
American Actor
Sun and Venus in Virgo

397

1966 LIBRA
From September 23, 11:43 through October 23, 20:50

The Aesthetic Lover

You are in love with the arts and in love with love. But the older you get, the deeper you delve into the true meaning behind the outer beauty, in both realms. You expect your relationship to be refined and genteel, never crude and messy. In love, you desire a partner who appreciates high culture but who isn't too stuffy and pretentious to enjoy vegging out with takeout in front of the tube all night. You are a blend of hedonism and hard work, and want a lover who complements you in both those areas.

When it comes to relationships, no matter how many you've had, you remain naïve, utterly open, and vulnerable. Because of this you know that you must keep your protective pals around you. They can be your external screening device and will be sure to give the boot to liars and con artists. Once in love, you like constant conversation and togetherness.

If someone wants to attract you they've got to put time and energy into how they present themselves. You are not shallow but appearances do matter to you, which is why a well-groomed, stylish look is sure to light your fire. You are also intrigued by a person with a passionate interest in art. You are enamored by poetic metaphors and find the "literal" and down and dirty worlds too offensive to spend much time in. You like to keep your head just a little bit in the clouds, so a potential lover must rise up to meet you there.

As a 1966 Libra male you appreciate a woman who is whip-smart and possesses refined tastes. You have to be able to take her anywhere. A woman with social skills to spare makes your heart race. If she is artistic and spends her free time engaging in creative pursuits, all the better.

A 1966 female Libra needs a man who is a risk-taker but with a gentle, humble spirit. You want a guy you can put on a pedestal and worship, but who won't let your deep admiration go to his head. If he is charming and well versed in all forms of literature, music, and art, you are sure to be doubly lovey-dovey for him. You yearn for a man who is lyrical and urbane and as much of a hopeless romantic as you are.

LIBRA ZODIAC SIGN
YOUR LOVE PLANETS

YOUR ROMANTIC SIDE   p. 696
- ▶ **VENUS IN VIRGO**
  Born Sept. 23, 11:43 - Oct. 03, 3:43
- ▶ **VENUS IN LIBRA**
  Born Oct. 03, 3:44 - Oct. 23, 20:50

YOUR SEX DRIVE   p. 722
- ▶ **MARS IN LEO**
  Born Sept. 23, 11:43 - Oct. 12, 18:36
- ▶ **MARS IN VIRGO**
  Born Oct. 12, 18:37 - Oct. 23, 20:50

YOUR CELEBRITY TWINS   p. 760
Find out the astrological similarities you have with famous people.

YOUR COMPATIBILITY   p. 780
Compare planets to find out how compatible you are in a relationship.

YOUR RELATIONSHIP KARMA   p. 824
- ▶ **SATURN IN PISCES**
  Born Sept. 23, 11:43 - Oct. 23, 20:50

PETULA CLARK
English Singer
Sun in Scorpio

398

1966 SCORPIO
From October 23, 20:51 through November 22, 18:13

 *The Perceptive Prophet*

As a 1966 Scorpio you expect a relationship to be mutually challenging. You are astute at perceiving your lover's deepest motivations and you want your partner to delve just as deeply into your inner world. You love to play psychologist, but you are interested in more than just mental foreplay. You need someone with a deep spirit who is interested in the mind-body-soul connection. You are demanding and want "all or nothing at all," and you are willing to walk away if someone offers you only half of their heart.

You tend to obsess about your love life and have a surprising need for steady reassurance. You're not as confident as you appear! All of your insights don't always stop you from worrying that underneath it all, your partner doesn't love you enough. You needn't fear! You are a strong taste, but one that is intoxicating and easy to get hooked on.

To intrigue you, a potential lover could take one of two routes. You respond well to a straightforward show of integrity. Purity of spirit is a turn-on to you. Someone who does not even know how to play games will surely soothe your suspicious soul. Another way to attract you is by talking about dreams—daydreams as well as nocturnal ones. You are fascinated by the unconscious mind and have a hidden escapist streak. Talk of dreams is sure to loosen you up and help you to express your magical side in addition to your analytical nature.

As a 1966 Scorpio man, you need a woman who is not easily intimidated by critical language. She must be articulate and strong and able to absorb and appreciate your many opinions while offering her own ideas. She must be able to keep up with you and match your willpower.

A female Scorpion born in 1966 is most compatible with a guy who is tough but tender. You have no respect for men you can push around, yet you need an affectionate mate who snuggles with you for long periods of time and shows you with his body and his eyes that he is absolutely there for you. He must be able to take your many moods in stride and find goofy ways to make you laugh when you become stuck in a dark place.

1966 SAGITTARIUS
From November 22, 18:14 through December 22, 7:27

The Discerning Searcher

You are a mass of fascinating paradoxes and believe that the relationship area of your life will help you to sort out the mystery that is you! You are fun-loving and can stay up all night drinking and telling stories with the best of them. Yet you are convinced that life contains a deep core of spiritual meaning and you are obsessed with tapping into the Divine. But you are not gullible. You are a critical thinker who reads opposing points of view on every subject that matters to you—then you draw your own conclusions. You expect your mate to argue with you regularly while respecting your strongly held opinions.

You want your love relationship to be open. You know that you will change and grow in many impossible-to-predict ways as life goes on, and you realize that the same will be true for your lover. You value individual freedom over security-centered commitments. You're willing to take those risks and expect your partner to be secure and brave enough to do the same. To you, the phrase "don't ever change" is the death knell to a relationship.

If someone is trying to light your spark they should show an avid interest in foreign travel. You hate to stay in the same place for too long and feel the most alive (and randy!) when you are exploring new lands. A potential partner must also be free-spirited and not uptight and conventional. The phrase "I'm game for everything," is a major green light for you! A wild and exuberant laugh and fierce sense of humor to match get you aroused mentally and physically, too.

1966 Sagittarius males are drawn to women who are unafraid adventurers. Your ideal woman books her own flights to faraway places and packs light so that she can pick up and go at any time. Your fantasy is to follow her up a mountain or across a huge expanse of water.

Females born under the sign of Sagittarius in 1966 are attracted to men who are on the road to finding out what the meaning of life really is. A generous, curious heart combined with an open mind inside the package of a virile, athletic build will surely light your flame and keep it lit!

Elizabeth Taylor – The Loving Beauty

During the 1950s and well into the 1960s, Elizabeth Taylor was widely considered to be not only the most glamorous woman in Hollywood, but also the most beautiful woman in the world. She had been famous ever since *National Velvet* became a smash hit in 1944, and she was the first actress to receive a $1 million contract for her starring role in *Cleopatra* in 1963. Her life off screen oscillated between enchanting fairy tale and Greek tragedy, with a revolving door of famous husbands and lovers, drug and alcohol abuse, death, and scandal.

With her Sun in misty-eyed Pisces and her Moon in erotic, magnetic Scorpio, Taylor is keenly attuned to the inner world of feelings. When we see her dramatically expressing her passions, her joys, hopes, and yearnings, we instinctively grasp that she herself is deeply experiencing these emotions, and we are convinced that the role she is playing is real. And as those penetrating, sparkling eyes emanate a mysterious, enchanting energy from the screen, we know that she is something more than just a pretty face attached to a voluptuous figure.

Astrologically, this luminescent quality can be attributed to the celestial star Antares. This bright red star is on Taylor's Ascendant, the sign rising at the moment of her birth. This star has been known since ancient times to bring fame, honor, and tragedy when placed so prominently in the horoscope. Antares (derived from anti-Ares, or rival to Mars) inspires its natives to be bold and headstrong, and it gives an attraction for danger and adventure. Taylor's Venus, the planet associated with love and beauty, is found

Elizabeth Taylor in *Cleopatra*

in Aries, and this placement underscores her impulsive, courageous, and self-assertive temperament, especially when it comes to affairs of the heart.

Venus enhances Taylor's personal magnetism by the network of aspects to other planets in her chart. Venus is exactly conjunct Uranus, ensuring that her relationships would be exciting, spontaneous, and short-lived. Venus-Uranus turns to anything new and different, as it avoids the traditional, safe way of relating. Then Venus is favorably in trine aspect to Jupiter, a golden combination that easily attracts money, popularity, and good luck. Finally, and perhaps most significantly, Venus is adversely linked to Pluto, the planet governing intrigue, betrayal, and seduction.

At 17 Elizabeth Taylor was dating billionaire Howard Hughes, but then went on to marry the hotel scion Nicky Hilton the next year. That commitment lasted only a scandalous nine months. She then married actor Michael Wilding the following year and stayed with him for four years. While Taylor is best known for her torrid affair with Richard Burton, she says she was most happy with her third husband, director Mike Todd. She was devastated when he died in a plane crash on March 22, 1958— only four days before the Oscar ceremony (she was nominated for Best Actress for her role in *Raintree County*). Todd was flying his private plane named *The Lucky Liz*.

After this personal shock, Taylor developed a reputation for breaking up other peoples' marriages. She stole her fourth husband Eddie Fisher from Debbie Reynolds. Then, while she was still married, she met Richard Burton on the set of *Cleopatra*. He too was already married, but the two inflamed each other's passions, and they became involved in a simultaneous off- and on-screen romance. Neptune, the planet associated with drugs and alcohol abuse, is strongly placed in both their charts, giving them a tendency toward this self-destructive impulse.

However, not until they met each other did these inclinations become problematic. Taylor and Burton suffered from a Mars-Saturn affliction: his Mars squares her Saturn. This challenge begins with hot passion, but soon becomes a battle for mastery over the other, especially in the bedroom. They loved each other and they hated each other. They divorced and re-married each other, and then divorced again. Burton died on August 5, 1984, ending her last great love affair.

399

▶ READ ABOUT THE LOVE TRIANGLE BETWEEN ELIZABETH TAYLOR, EDDIE FISHER, AND DEBBIE REYNOLDS ON PAGE 302

1967

- ⭐ **ABORTION RIGHTS IN BRITAIN**
- ⭐ **INTERRACIAL MARRIAGE BAN RULED UNCONSTITUTIONAL**
- ⭐ **BONNIE AND CLYDE**
- ⭐ **THE GRADUATE**
- ⭐ **LIGHT MY FIRE**

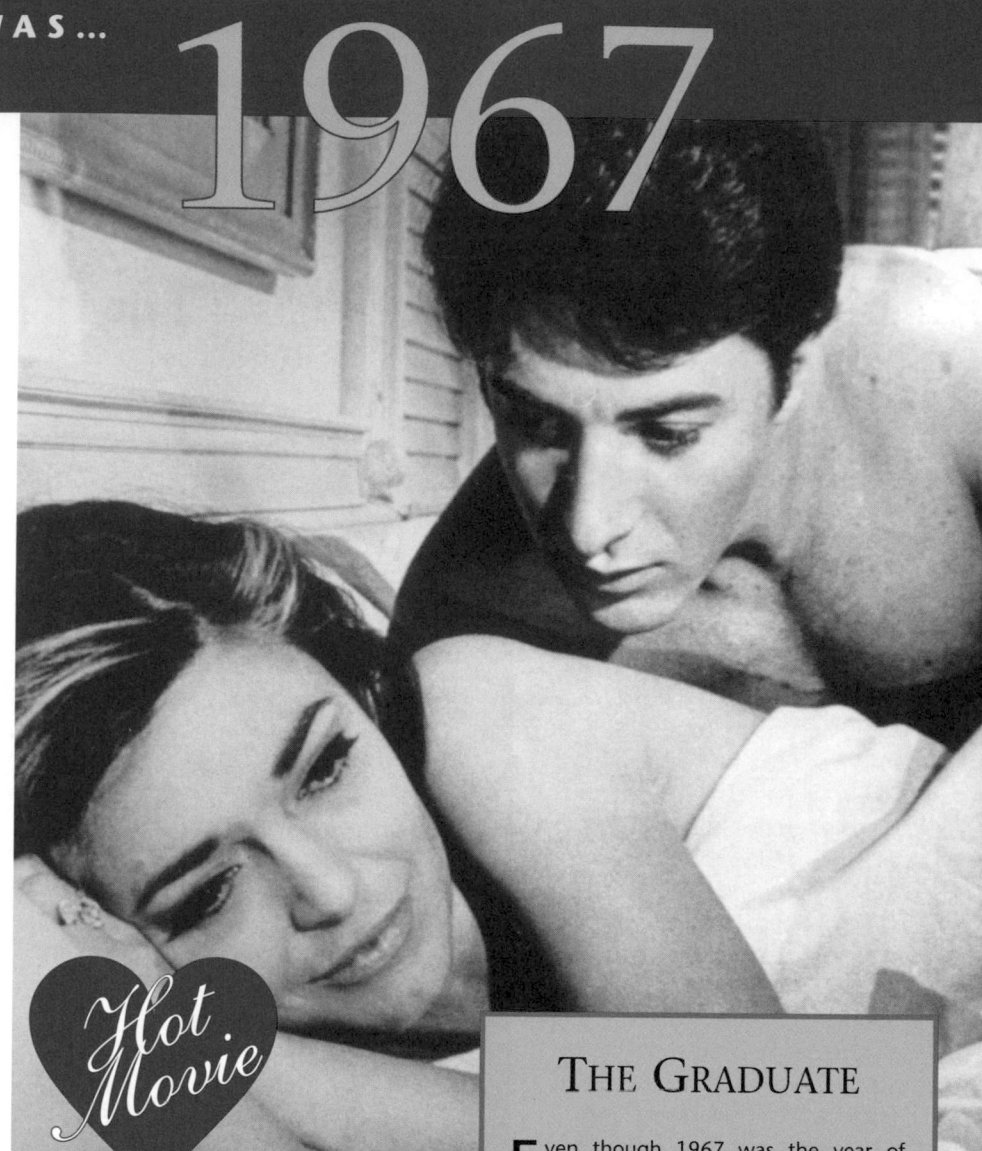

Hot Movie

EVENTS

1967 was a mixed year for equality and reproductive rights in Britain. The Sexual Offences Bill became law the same month that homosexual acts between adult men were permitted for the first time. Abortion was legalized, yet over half a million people signed a petition against it and the Society for the Protection of Unborn Children was formed. The US Supreme Court ruled that states couldn't ban interracial marriages—a ban then still in effect in sixteen states. Albert DeSalvo, the "Boston Strangler," confessed to the sexual molestation and murder of thirteen women, but was sentenced to life imprisonment on the lesser charges of rape. Couples heading to Las Vegas to get married included singer Elvis Presley and Priscilla Beaulieu, as well as actors Ann-Margret and Roger Smith.

POP CULTURE

Classic 1967 films included *Bonnie and Clyde*, with Faye Dunaway and Warren Beatty as an American folk-hero bank robbing couple. *Guess Who's Coming to Dinner* featured Sidney Poitier as the black doctor who disconcerts a middle-class white family, and *The Graduate* showed a young Dustin Hoffman having simultaneous affairs with a mother and daughter. In Luis Buñuel's *Belle de Jour*, Catherine Deneuve is a wealthy wife whose experiments with prostitution lead to tragedy.

The Beatles' seminal album *Sgt. Peppers Lonely Hearts Club Band* led to hits for the title track and "All You Need Is Love." The Doors sang "Light My Fire," the Turtles were "Happy Together," and "Ode to Billie Joe," whose lyrics suggested a strange crime, became an unlikely hit. "To Sir with Love," from the movie of the same name, was on the charts along with Nancy and Frank Sinatra's duet, "Somethin' Stupid."

Books ranged from the highly literary novel *The Eighth Day* by Thornton Wilder, the intertwined stories of two families, to the downright silly, such as *Phyllis Diller's Marriage Manual*. Another cultural figure turned author was director Elia Kazan, who later made a film of his 1967 autobiographical novel of midlife crisis, *The Arrangement*. Mary Stewart's *The Gabriel Hounds* told of the intrigue and romance a young Englishwoman finds in Lebanon.

THE GRADUATE

Even though 1967 was the year of flower power and free love, the movie *The Graduate* still managed to shock audiences. It was a groundbreaking film that explored the taboo relationship between an older woman and her recent college graduate young lover. Actress Anne Bancroft was Mrs. Robinson, a sexy suburban mother with designs on her neighbor, Benjamin Braddock, played by Hollywood newcomer Dustin Hoffman.

The film was a rather scandalous coming of age story, especially as Benjamin's girlfriend was Mrs. Robinson's daughter. When Benjamin said to his libidinous neighbor, "Mrs. Robinson, you're trying to seduce me," moviegoers gasped. But their provocative pairing was a road to movie success—it won nine Oscars.

SEE ALSO
▶ *SHAMPOO Page 466*

400

1967 CAPRICORN

From December 22, 1966 7:28 through January 20, 1967 18:07
(December 1967 Capricorns, see 1968 Capricorn)

♑ *The Practical Romantic*

At an early age, you already knew what you wanted—in life and in love—and you set out to get it, Capricorn of 1967. And, with your special combination of pragmatism matched with optimism, you've likely had your share of success, in both the boardroom and the bedroom. It might even be said that you take a serious, almost businesslike approach to love. Never pushy, you use dignity and charm—and an unexpected sense of humor—to attract partners, biding your time and persevering until you win them over. You are in it for the long haul, after all.

A traditionalist in many ways, you prefer a stable relationship with someone who can be a partner to you, rather than engaging in lots of frivolous affairs that never could develop into anything lasting. This doesn't mean you don't like excitement and variety, for nothing could be further from the truth. In fact, you can be quite adventurous and amorous, once you let down your guard. It's just that you want to delve into love's many mysteries with one special person, letting each shared experience lead to another that's even better.

You like to get to know your lover well enough that you feel comfortable together and can explore each other's sexual preferences without embarrassment or reservation. You realize that depth as well as breadth are important in a fulfilling sex life, and depth can only be achieved over time. Like the goat that is your zodiac symbol, you have a randy side, although you don't flaunt it publicly. But in private anything goes. A partner who wants to please you might appeal to your sensuality and your romantic nature, perhaps by giving you a full-body massage by candlelight.

Male Capricorns of 1967 enjoy women whom they can consider their equals. You prefer a strong, capable partner who knows her own mind and has her own style to someone who lets you call all the shots.

You women who were born under the sign of the goat in 1967 tend to be drawn to sophisticated, intelligent, sociable men who know what to wear, what wine to serve, and how to behave in any situation. Creative types might also earn a special place in your heart.

CAPRICORN ZODIAC SIGN
YOUR LOVE PLANETS

YOUR ROMANTIC SIDE   p. 696
► **VENUS IN CAPRICORN**
Born Dec. 22, 1966 7:28 - Jan. 06, 1967 19:35
► **VENUS IN AQUARIUS**
Born Jan. 06, 19:36 - Jan. 20, 18:07

YOUR SEX DRIVE   p. 722
► **MARS IN LIBRA**
Born Dec. 22, 1966 7:28 - Jan. 20, 1967 18:07

YOUR CELEBRITY TWINS   p. 760
Find out the astrological similarities you have with famous people.

YOUR COMPATIBILITY   p. 780
Compare planets to find out how compatible you are in a relationship.

YOUR RELATIONSHIP KARMA   p. 824
► **SATURN IN PISCES**
Born Dec. 22, 1966 7:28 - Jan. 20, 1967 18:07

KATHARINE ROSS
American Actress
Sun in Aquarius

401

1967 AQUARIUS

From January 20, 18:08 through February 19, 8:23

♒ *The Independent Idealist*

You have high ideals, in love as well as in other areas, Aquarius of 1967. Born when the flower children were touting love as the solution to the world's problems, you believe relationships should be based on more than convenience or sexual attraction. You want someone who complements you in every way, as a lover, creative partner, and friend. Even though you may have had your share of disappointments, you remain hopeful that love will find a way. More often than not, your optimism tends to produce favorable results, but sometimes other people might find it hard to meet up to your high expectations.

In your opinion, equality is essential to a successful relationship. You expect to "share and share alike" with your partner when it comes to childcare, finances, housework, decision making, and other areas. You see no reason for sexism or power games, and do your best to achieve balance. At times, though, balancing commitment with freedom might get tricky, for although you enjoy having a life together, you don't want to sacrifice your independence.

Open-minded about sex, you have a curious side that might lead you to experiment a bit. But underneath your free spirit beats the heart of a true romantic who longs for a soul mate. You probably aren't content to jump from bed to bed, and once you find the right person you can be true blue. However, you get bored easily, so a partner who wants to keep you must offer you lots of variety and surprises, perhaps by encouraging you to try things you've never tried before.

Aquarian males born in 1967 tend to seek imaginative partners who are interested in things beyond their everyday, domestic lives. A high-minded, compassionate woman who wants to make the world a better place is likely to intrigue you more than one whose goal is to settle down and raise a family.

Female Aquarians of 1967 often prize friendship above all else in a mate. An agreeable companion with whom you can socialize and exchange ideas could be your romantic ideal. It helps if he brings you flowers, takes you out to nice places, and knows something about the arts.

AQUARIUS ZODIAC SIGN
YOUR LOVE PLANETS

YOUR ROMANTIC SIDE   p. 696
► **VENUS IN AQUARIUS**
Born Jan. 20, 18:08 - Jan. 30, 18:52
► **VENUS IN PISCES**
Born Jan. 30, 18:53 - Feb. 19, 8:23

YOUR SEX DRIVE   p. 722
► **MARS IN LIBRA**
Born Jan. 20, 18:08 - Feb. 12, 12:19
► **MARS IN SCORPIO**
Born Feb. 12, 12:20 - Feb. 19, 8:23

YOUR CELEBRITY TWINS   p. 760
Find out the astrological similarities you have with famous people.

YOUR COMPATIBILITY   p. 780
Compare planets to find out how compatible you are in a relationship.

YOUR RELATIONSHIP KARMA   p. 824
► **SATURN IN PISCES**
Born Jan. 20, 18:08 - Feb. 19, 8:23

FRANCO NERO
Italian Actor
Mars in Aries

1967 PISCES
From February 19, 8:24 through March 21, 7:36

The Passionate Dreamer

You don't really believe in Knights in Shining Armor and Fairy Princesses, but you can still dream, can't you, Pisces of 1967? With your vivid imagination, you can transform whomever you're with into your romantic ideal and polish the most ordinary situation with a patina of glamour. Love, for you, is a magical experience that lifts you out of the mundane realm and transforms your life.

Most likely, your love life has seen some big ups and downs—and you could experience a few more. But that only makes it more interesting. Periodic crises can keep things from getting dull, and "dull" is the kiss of death to a relationship with you. Intensely emotional and passionate, you aren't the type to go into a romance halfway. Unless there's plenty of chemistry between you and another person, you probably won't stick around. When the right individual comes along, however, you put your heart and soul into the partnership.

Sex with you can be an electrifying experience. Eager to please and willing to try just about anything, you really know how to fan the flames to keep the fire blazing. Your lover shouldn't misinterpret your unabashedness as insincerity, though, for intimacy is a serious issue for you. You also have a "sixth sense" that enables you to connect with your partner at a deep level. In bed, you let your heart and body do the talking. It's no fun if you have to explain what you want to your partner—you expect that person to intuit your wishes and fulfill them.

An uninhibited woman with a sense of adventure is most appealing to Pisces men of 1967. Despite the fact that you can be a bit possessive, you find independent, outspoken women intriguing, perhaps because the combination sets off fireworks between you. Playfulness and sense of humor are assets, too, for they help to balance your rather serious nature.

Men of mystery are practically irresistible to Pisces women of 1967. You are drawn to intense, brooding types who exude sexuality and have a bit of the "bad boy" in them. A man who can take charge and rally in times of crisis will score extra points with you.

1967 ARIES
From March 21, 7:37 through April 20, 18:54

The Playful Adventurer

Love is a game for you, Aries of 1967, and you play to win. Nothing sparks your enthusiasm more than a challenge—some might argue that the chase is the most exciting part for you. Certainly you do enjoy a good contest and don't want the object of your affection to give in to you too easily—that would take the fun out of it! But you can be a devoted partner, once you find the right person. And when you spot that person, you quickly make your intentions known.

Your zest for life and your youthful exuberance make you a lively companion. Not easily discouraged, you bounce back from romantic "spills" and move on to the next opportunity. At times, though, you may be a bit selfish and self-centered, and might have trouble seeing your partner's side of things. You'll probably resist any attempts to "clip your wings," for instance, because you have a strong independent streak. As long as your mate respects your individuality, you are usually content to come home at night.

Sex is high on your list of priorities in a relationship. Some like it hot, and you are one of them. You have a powerful libido and aren't likely to wait around very long for a partner to warm up to you. In bed, as in other areas of life, you enjoy lots of stimulation. Your tastes are pretty straightforward, and for the most part you can dispense with romantic frills. Action, not talk, is the name of the game.

Men born under the sign of the ram in 1967 are often attracted to uncomplicated, down-to-earth women. She doesn't have to be bright or beautiful, but she should exude sensuality and have a pleasant personality. You're happiest with someone who tends to your physical needs and provides a comfortable, secure home life.

A man who knows how to handle himself in any situation can win the heart of an Aries woman born in 1967. You like a man to be strong, but not coarse or aggressive—the iron fist in the velvet glove, so to speak. Good looks and a sense of style are real plusses. You also enjoy a cheerful, outgoing companion who likes to go places and do things with you—no couch potatoes, please!

1967 TAURUS

From April 20, 18:55 through May 21, 18:17

The Cheerful Companion

Unlike most people born under the sign of the bull, you see change as a good thing, Taurus of 1967. Sure, you appreciate security and stability as much as the next person. But you don't limit yourself when it comes to romance and eagerly welcome new people into your life, knowing that they will bring you new experiences. As a result, you attract your share of admirers and your love life is rarely dull.

You don't like being alone and are happiest when you have a companion with whom you can share good times. Easygoing for the most part, you are willing to meet your partner more than halfway and do what you can to make a relationship flourish. In fact, you may be a bit too adaptable and generous at times. You're a lover, not a fighter, and you try to avoid discord whenever possible—you don't see any reason to waste time arguing when you could be having fun.

One of your favorite ways to have fun is making love. For you, sex is a natural and necessary part of life, like eating. Sex is also a form of self-expression. You use "body language" as a way to communicate with your partner—and you are fluent in it. And speaking of communication, talking about sex is a big turn-on for you. You're a real sucker for romance, too. A partner who whispers sweet words in your ear or reads love poems to you in bed can make you melt.

Intelligent women fascinate Taurus males born in 1967. You enjoy the company of someone you can talk to, who can introduce you to new ideas and teach you a few things. You probably know your way around the kitchen and have good taste in home decor, so your partner needn't be very domestic. But she'll receive high marks if she's a sociable, outgoing "people-person" who gets along well with your friends and family.

1967 Taurus women tend to be incurable romantics, so an old-fashioned gentleman who courts you has a good chance of winning your heart. The more graceful and intelligent he is about it, the better. Affectionate yourself, you want someone who enjoys all that "touchy-feely" stuff. A neat appearance and an agreeable disposition are icing on the cake.

TAURUS ZODIAC SIGN
YOUR LOVE PLANETS

YOUR ROMANTIC SIDE   p. 696
▶ **VENUS IN GEMINI**
Born Apr. 20, 18:55 - May 10, 6:04
▶ **VENUS IN CANCER**
Born May 10, 6:05 - May 21, 18:17

YOUR SEX DRIVE   p. 722
▶ **MARS IN LIBRA**
Born Apr. 20, 18:55 - May 21, 18:17

YOUR CELEBRITY TWINS   p. 760
Find out the astrological similarities you have with famous people.

YOUR COMPATIBILITY   p. 780
Compare planets to find out how compatible you are in a relationship.

YOUR RELATIONSHIP KARMA   p. 824
▶ **SATURN IN ARIES**
Born Apr. 20, 18:55 - May 21, 18:17

SHIRLEY MACLAINE
American Actress
Sun and Mars in Taurus

403

1967 GEMINI

From May 21, 18:18 through June 22, 2:22

The Inventive Analyst

Much of the time, your head rules your heart when it comes to relationships, Gemini of 1967. Generally, you take a rational approach to love and think things through before you act. Consequently, you are rarely swept off your feet. You may even make a list of each prospect's good and bad points before giving that person a "thumbs up." Instead of feeling your way along, you may spend a good deal of time analyzing each facet of your relationship.

Your outgoing personality is one of your most appealing traits, and draws many people to you. And like all Geminis, your insatiable curiosity may lead you to experiment with love in an attempt to experience as much as you can. Those of you born in 1967 aren't as fickle as other twins, though, and don't feel a need to sample every delicacy at love's smorgasbord. You want to be free to spend time with friends and pursue your many interests. But you can be faithful to a partner who offers you lots of variety, mental stimulation, an active social life, and good conversation.

Your curiosity and inventiveness can make you an interesting lover, for you are usually eager to try new things. You may even read books or watch videos to get ideas. However, you aren't particularly assertive and often wait for your partner to initiate sex. Talking about sex can get you in the mood and you might like your partner to regale you with favorite fantasies.

1967's Gemini men want to be nurtured and cared for by female partners. You like to curl up with a sensitive, compassionate woman who applies soothing balm to your wounds and makes you feel secure. An emotional, intuitive partner could help to balance your rational, intellectual nature. You might also be attracted to someone who's a bit of a homebody, who loves cooking and kids.

Women born in 1967 under the sign of the twins enjoy agreeable, friendly companions. You like intelligent men with whom you can share ideas as well as good times. Above all, though, you want a partner who puts you first in his life—someone who listens to you, remembers your birthday, and makes you feel special.

GEMINI ZODIAC SIGN
YOUR LOVE PLANETS

YOUR ROMANTIC SIDE   p. 696
▶ **VENUS IN CANCER**
Born May 21, 18:18 - June 06, 16:47
▶ **VENUS IN LEO**
Born June 06, 16:48 - June 22, 2:22

YOUR SEX DRIVE   p. 722
▶ **MARS IN LIBRA**
Born May 21, 18:18 - June 22, 2:22

YOUR CELEBRITY TWINS   p. 760
Find out the astrological similarities you have with famous people.

YOUR COMPATIBILITY   p. 780
Compare planets to find out how compatible you are in a relationship.

YOUR RELATIONSHIP KARMA   p. 824
▶ **SATURN IN ARIES**
Born May 21, 18:18 - June 22, 2:22

RICHARD HARRIS
Irish Actor
Mars in Cancer

1967 CANCER
From June 22, 2:23 through July 23, 13:15

The Devoted Homebody

Home is where your heart is, Cancer of 1967, and your desire for the security of home and family influences your decisions in relationships. Therefore, you are generally happiest with someone who shares your fondness for children and domestic life. Although you may have sown a few wild oats in your youth, you value commitment and tend to take a serious approach to love. The life of a bon vivant has little appeal for you—you'd rather enjoy the comfort and closeness of those nearest and dearest to you.

You attract many admirers, perhaps because you lavish such care and kindness on them. One of your finest qualities is your ability to make others feel safe, comfortable, and cherished. With those you love, your generosity and compassion know no bounds. Of course, you expect a partner's complete fidelity and devotion in return. You may run into a few problems now and again if a lover seeks more independence than you can accept, for your deep feelings are easily bruised. Like the crab, which is your zodiac symbol, you hold on tightly to those you care about.

Usually, you don't separate sex and love. For you, sex is best shared with a partner who really matters to you. You need to feel comfortable and secure with a person before you reveal yourself—then you can be a passionate and attentive lover. Very affectionate, you can never get enough stroking and snuggling. A partner who wants to win your heart must provide the emotional and physical closeness you crave.

For male crabs of 1967, beauty ranks high on your list of "must haves" in a partner. To be seen with woman who stands out in a crowd gives you a sense of pride. Of course, you also want your family and friends to approve of her. Therefore, you'll probably be most content with someone whose background is similar to yours.

Female Cancers of 1967 also prize good looks and style in a partner. It doesn't hurt if he has some status in the community, too. But dependability and financial stability are the most important considerations, for you want to be able to raise a family and enjoy the secure home life you desire.

1967 LEO
From July 23, 13:16 through August 23, 20:11

The Romantic Dramatist

You're in love with love, Leo of 1967—the drama of romance, the thrill of a new affair. Seeing yourself reflected in the eyes of an adoring partner flatters your ego and boosts your self-esteem. You relish all the accoutrements of romance and play the role of lover with real aplomb. You might even take a few tips from old movies and add them to your relationship repertoire.

Your charm is likely to draw many people to you. Regardless of how good looking you are, you project an image of confidence, power, and charisma that others find attractive. Lucky in love, you often make the first move and call the shots in relationships. As long as you are the dominant partner, you can be loyal and devoted to your mate. And to those who are fortunate enough to win your affection, you are usually quite generous, attentive, and protective.

Your sexual quotient tops the chart, for you combine passion with romance and imagination. Because you take pride in your ability to give your partner pleasure, you can be an unparalleled lover. As in other areas of life, you infuse your lovemaking with a touch of glamour and grandeur. You know the right setting can greatly enhance the experience— satin sheets, heart-shaped hot tubs, and mirrors on the ceiling (so you can watch your performance) might kindle your fires.

Lion "kings" born in 1967 tend to be quite selective when it comes to choosing a mate. You know you have much to offer the right person, and you expect her to be worthy of your love. Brains plus beauty make an irresistible combination, but you want her to be modest about her assets and not outshine you. Your ideal woman appears rather conservative and businesslike on the outside, but eagerly exhibits a kinky side in private.

Power, it's said, is the headiest aphrodisiac, and female Leos of 1967 would probably agree. A man who takes charge and commands the respect of others is likely to get the key to your heart. You might not mind if he's a bit possessive and controlling, so long as he shows you the attention and respect you deserve and lavishes you with beautiful gifts regularly.

1967 VIRGO
From August 23, 20:12 through September 23, 17:37

The Enticing Enigma

You present an image of mystery that intrigues others because they can't quite figure you out, Virgo of 1967. At first glance, you seem rather shy and reserved. But once people get to know you, they realize you are anything but meek. In fact, you possess an underlying intensity and uniqueness that give you an undeniable allure. Most of the time, you wait for others to come to you, rather than seeking them out. If you decide you want someone, though, you might patiently pursue that person's affection, leaving no stone unturned in the process.

You tend to be rather skeptical about other people's motives and may take your sweet time before letting someone get close to you. When it comes to choosing a mate, you are quite particular and don't like settling for second best. But once you open your heart, you can be a loyal and sensitive partner. Your lover had better not betray you, however, for you have a jealous streak a formidable temper when crossed.

Sexually, you are something of an enigma, too. Those who aren't on intimate terms with you may consider you to be cautious, restrained, even modest. But that's just because you like to keep your private affairs private, instead of flaunting your sexuality. Anyone lucky enough to be your lover knows you are both passionate and inspired in bed. Little things mean a lot to you and you really appreciate an attentive partner who notices and satisfies your every need.

Virgo males of 1967 appreciate women who are practical and efficient. She doesn't have to be beautiful, but a neat appearance is important. Anyone who's loud and flashy will probably get scratched off your dance card right away. An intelligent woman with a good head for business is more likely to get your vote, especially if she also has a kind heart and a gentle manner.

Although the virgin is Virgo's symbol, women born under this sign in 1967 are hardly prudes. In fact, you are probably drawn to men who exude sexuality and have a wild side to their natures. Your heart also goes out to a man who's not afraid to show his feelings, but only in private, please.

PETER FINCH
English Actor
Sun in Libra

1967 LIBRA
From September 23, 17:38 through October 24, 2:43

The Relationship Expert

Relationships are your forté, Libra of 1967, for your zodiac sign is ruled by Venus, the planet (and goddess) of love. Unless you are involved in a relationship, you aren't really happy, often viewing yourself as half of a couple rather than as an individual. You enjoy companionship and rarely lack admirers. With your pleasing personality and friendly nature, you can usually be found at the center of your social circle. You love attention, but have high standards and can be quite particular about your partners.

Because your sense of self is influenced by what others think of you, you may adjust your behavior to please your partner. Naturally cooperative and adaptable, you don't mind giving ground if it promotes peace and harmony. You'll go to great lengths to avoid a fight and try to keep things on a positive note as much as possible. But if another person places too many demands on you or tries to limit your freedom, you might rebel or become resentful.

Romance is your middle name, and all those pretty preliminaries—flowers, candlelit dinners, long walks on the beach—are usually the best ways to get you in the mood. Flattery, too, can work wonders with you, as you do have a vain side. For the most part, you prefer to take a lighthearted approach to sex and have fun with your partner. But with someone whose tastes are rather exotic, you can switch gears and turn up the heat.

You Libra men of 1967 enjoy the company of intelligent women who have a strong work ethic and a good head for business, like you. Neat, orderly, practical women might also win favor with you. Someone with a caring, compassionate nature, whom you can rely on in time of need could find herself first in line for your affection.

1967's Libra women find outgoing, fun-loving men most appealing—especially ones who have traveled widely and regale you with tales of adventure. You also want a partner who shares your penchant for socializing and entertaining, who likes dancing, dining, and good times. A sense of humor tops your list of priorities and you just can't resist a man who makes you laugh.

ANNIE GIRARDOT
French Actress
Sun, Venus and Mars in Scorpio

406

1967 SCORPIO
From October 24, 2:44 through November 23, 0:03

 The Sensual Intuitive

Love is a serious matter for you, Scorpio of 1967. You believe in the marriage vow "Til death do us part," and when you give your heart to someone, it's forever. You not only want a companion to share your life with, you'd like to merge body, mind, and soul with your mate. As a result, you are very choosy about the people you allow into your life and prefer to be alone rather than to settle for someone who doesn't meet your standards. Once you're in a relationship, you tend to be rather possessive and controlling, with a jealous streak as wide as the Mississippi River.

Security is high on your list of priorities in life, so a relationship must provide stability on many levels—emotionally, financially, and physically. Your ideal partner must be trustworthy and dependable—and it wouldn't hurt if this person had some money and/or a good job in the bargain. But that doesn't mean you want things to always be steady and predictable. Frequent changes in your routine and periodic emotional upheavals keep things exciting.

Your sex appeal is second to none and few can match you when it comes to performance. Your "sensual intuition" enables you to tune in to your partner's most secret wishes. You blend physical endurance with emotional intensity, a combination that makes sex with you an unforgettable experience. Of course, you need a lover who can keep up with you and who is willing to let you call the shots, not only in the bedroom but in most areas of the relationship.

Scorpio males born in 1967 prefer women who are ladies in public and "wild" women in the bedroom. A neat appearance, an ability to run a household efficiently, and a caring nature are the keys to your heart. Your ideal partner may be intelligent, but you don't want her to outshine you. Above all, she must respect your privacy.

Female Scorpions seek partners who are good providers and responsible parents. You need to be able to depend on your mate in good times and bad—not that you can't take care of yourself. Strong, silent types appeal to you. You also want someone who gets better with age, like fine wine.

1967 SAGITTARIUS
From November 23, 0:04 through December 22, 13:15

The Amorous Adventurer

When it comes to having fun, few people can match you, Sagittarius of 1967. Your clever wit and upbeat personality often place you at the center of any social gathering. You certainly know how to show a partner a good time! A relationship with you is likely to be a whirlwind of activity, as you rarely sit still for long—there are just too many things to do and places to go. If a congenial companion wants to accompany you, that's great, but woe be to anyone who tries to tie you down.

You want to enjoy as many experiences as you can, in love as well as in other areas of life. Consequently, you curious folks may have difficulty limiting yourself to one partner at a time. If a relationship doesn't work out, you chalk it up to experience and move on to the next adventure. Some people might accuse you of being indiscriminate, but most find your warm, open nature hard to resist. Of course, you can commit yourself to the right person for life, and that person for you is someone who respects your individuality.

You bring your curiosity and playfulness into the bedroom, too, where you take a freewheeling approach to sex. But you needn't stick to the bedroom for your amorous adventures—changing sites could provide the variety you crave. Always eager to learn, you appreciate a partner who can teach you new tricks and who is game to learn a few from you.

Although you Sagittarian men of 1967 may chafe at restrictions yourself, you might not mind a partner who only has eyes for you. A woman who isn't afraid to demonstrate her femininity could bring out your masculine qualities, so long as she isn't too fragile or dependent. A pleasant personality is certainly a plus, but she should have something going on beneath her sweet exterior—superficiality doesn't cut it with you.

Men who know their own minds are likely to capture the fancy of you Sagittarian women born in 1967. Someone who has common sense as well as intelligence could fill the bill. Although you appreciate a steady partner you can depend on, he can't be stodgy, for you like surprises and want a man who keeps you guessing.

The Summer of Love

Scott McKenzie's song "San Francisco" was a rallying cry to the youth of America that year. Already rebelling against parental authority and the establishment, angry about a war that was unofficial but was killing young soldiers just the same, they took to heart the Pied Piper's song and followed it—to San Francisco. A former Beatnik haven in the '50s, the Haight-Ashbury district of San Francisco became the main site of youth rebellion. With cheap rent and decent weather, the barefoot Flower Children of 1967 set out to make the Haight their proving ground for Utopia.

They brought with them the clothes on their back, the energy of youth, and a desire to change the world. Communes sprang up, the result of a desire to form a new type of family and live closely together. Anti-materialistic, anti-establishment, anti-war, and anti-violence, they shared food, attended peace rallies, and made love. They wore their hair long, their bellbottoms wide, and their shirts tie-dyed. Psychedelic posters decorated the walls: Make Love, Not War. Fed by local merchants, treated by the local free medical clinic, the hippies thought their carefree days would last forever.

The music that summer both reflected and fed upon the changing idealism and innocence of America's youth. The Monkee's "Daydream Believer" vied for airtime with Steppenwolf's "Born to Be Wild," Buffalo Springfield's "For What It's Worth," and the Beatles "A Day in the Life." That summer saw the birth and meteoric rise of a number of music groups. At a two-day concert in Mill Valley, California, festivalgoers could listen to bands such as the Byrds and Jefferson Airplane for a mere two dollars. As many others did, Jim Morrison, lead singer and songwriter for The Doors, took all the

newfound freedoms of the culture to the extreme. He fought against authority in his music and on the stage, living to the drumbeat of drugs, alcohol, and sex, and became a cultural icon before dying at age 27 of a heart attack.

But it was a hard life. The majority of Flower Children who made their way to communes were middle-class kids who'd grown up with at least a modicum of materialistic comfort. While it was materialism they were rebelling against, it was also what they were used to. The long-patient merchants of the area stopped being as giving. Landlords wanted cash for rent. Police presence was everywhere, and even picking flowers in a public park brought the wrath of the establishment. Venereal disease, homelessness, and hunger were rampant.

Many of the hippies along the Haight turned to drugs, adding overdose to the list of medical emergencies treated at the free clinics. LSD was the pharmaceutical of choice, especially after the pronouncement by the Beatles that they'd dropped acid. LSD promised enlightenment and was easy to find. Eastern religions became the cornerstone of their philosophy.

Then disillusionment set in. Having rejected social mores and family, all

1967 Woodstock

roads home seemed blocked and the future was murky.

The Summer of Love 1967 was an experiment in idealism, an attempt to change the world one sit-in, one flower, one peace sign at a time. History has tried unsuccessfully to label it a failure, a folly of misspent youth. But those there know it wasn't a failure. It was worse than that. It was an end of innocence.

▶ READ ABOUT THE BEATLES ON PAGES 416 AND 423   ▶ READ ABOUT JOHN PROFUMO AND CHRISTINE KEELER ON PAGE 375

1968

- ⍟ **SCUM ACTIVIST SHOOTS WARHOL**
- ⍟ **ROMEO AND JULIET**
- ⍟ **BARBARELLA**
- ⍟ **I HEARD IT THROUGH THE GRAPEVINE**
- ⍟ **I WANT IT NOW**

EVENTS

1968 saw such practical advancements for women as the marvelous invention of the epidural to relieve pain during childbirth, and British no-fault divorces in case of "irretrievable breakdown of marriage." However, the Roman Catholic Church insisted that every act of marital intercourse must remain physically open to the possibility of conception. Sheila Ann Thorns made news world giving birth to Britain's first sextuplets. In New York, Valerie Solanas, author of the Society for Cutting Up Men (SCUM) Manifesto, shot and wounded pop artist Andy Warhol. Jacqueline Kennedy, widow of slain US President John F. Kennedy, married Greek shipping magnate Aristotle Onassis.

POP CULTURE

In film, Franco Zeffirelli's *Romeo and Juliet* starred actual teenagers. John Cassavetes' *Faces*, about marital infidelity, became an instant independent film classic. Barbra Streisand made her film debut in *Funny Girl*, about comedienne Fanny Brice's life and loves. Jane Fonda played a futurist uber-babe in the campy, science fiction *Barbarella*. In *Buona Sera, Mrs. Campbell*, three World War II American fliers each believe they've fathered the same child. In Claude Chabrol's *Les Biches*, a wealthy woman picks up a young female street artist, then adds a male architect to the menage.

The Beatles' "Hey Jude," at seven-plus minutes the longest single ever released, topped both the US and UK

Hot Couple

charts. Marvin Gaye's "I Heard It Through the Grapevine" fused soul and blues, as did Otis Redding's "The Dock of the Bay." Herb Alpert's jazz influences produced "This Guy's in Love with You," and Simon & Garfunkel had a hit with "Mrs. Robinson," from the film *The Graduate*.

1968 novels included Kingsley Amis' *I Want It Now*, a satire reflecting the immorality of modern society, *The Nice and the Good* by Iris Murdoch, in which a suicide investigation reveals the complexities of love, and Angela Carter's *Several Perceptions*, in which a young nihilist seduces his best friend's mother. Gore Vidal's *Myra Breckinridge* was a stylish, satirical take on transsexuality and 1960s American culture. *Nicholas and Alexandra* by Robert K. Massie was a blockbuster history of the last Tsar of Russia that read like a novel.

ROMAN POLANSKI & SHARON TATE

On the first night they met, director Roman Polanski and gorgeous starlet Sharon Tate took LSD and slept together as the sun came up. They were married on January 20, 1968 in London. Famous guests littered the reception at the Playboy Club—Warren Beatty, Sean Connery, Rolling Stones Brian Jones and Keith Richards, Peter Sellers, Rudolf Nureyev, and Vidal Sassoon.

In a shocking twist, their whirlwind Hollywood romance was cut short. When Tate was just 26 years old and eight months pregnant with Polanski's child, she was brutally murdered by the Manson family. A devastated Polanski returned to Europe to mourn.

SEE ALSO

▶ **WARREN BEATTY** *Page 466*
▶ **CATHERINE DENEUVE** *Page 505*

1968 CAPRICORN

From December 22, 1967 13:16 through January 20, 1968 23:53
(December 1968 Capricorns, see 1969 Capricorn)

♑ The Intimate Eccentric

For the 1968 Capricorn, there is a time and place for everything–with emphasis on "everything." On first impression, you appear to be dutiful and hardworking–which, indeed, you are. But those admitted to your intimate circle know an individual of many facets, someone who is generous, eccentric, passionate, and tenderhearted. A magnetic personality is your secret weapon, as are your mystifyingly deep wells of energy.

Your attitude toward romance has never been obvious—to anyone except your beloved. You have plenty of work and activities to keep you absorbed and, quite appropriately unbeknownst to others, a significant other may toil alongside you. Because you're not the type to "let it all hang out" on your first meeting with someone, you've never been one to use dating services, personal ads, or singles events as a way of finding a mate. You feel much more comfortable pursuing interests that bring like-minded people into your sphere and allow you to get acquainted over time.

To attract your attention, a prospective partner should get involved in the activities that interest you, especially any charitable causes. You have deep sympathy for and generosity toward the needy, and your heart swells when someone shows that he or she shares those sympathies. Conversely, someone who thinks you are all business will just melt upon bearing witness to your tender, giving side.

The 1968 male Mountain Goat wants a woman who can strike a balance between freedom and commitment. While you enjoy the stability of a steady relationship, you are likely to feel uncomfortable with someone who looks exclusively to you to make all the decisions. For you, interdependence is what it's all about. You want an ally.

Female Capricorns born in 1968 appreciate men who are dependable and supportive but also open to change. You know that the secret to relationship success lies in the ability to grow through your separate stages together. The "separate-but-together" part is somewhat paradoxical, but the riddle and mystery of it all is what makes your relationships interesting and long lasting.

CAPRICORN ZODIAC SIGN
Your Love Planets

YOUR ROMANTIC SIDE   p. 696
▶ VENUS IN SCORPIO
Born Dec. 22, 1967 13:16 - Jan. 01, 1968 22:36
▶ VENUS IN SAGITTARIUS
Born Jan. 01, 22:37 - Jan. 20, 23:53

YOUR SEX DRIVE   p. 722
▶ MARS IN AQUARIUS
Born Dec. 22, 1967 13:16 - Jan. 09, 1968 9:48
▶ MARS IN PISCES
Born Jan. 09, 9:49 - Jan. 20, 23:53

YOUR CELEBRITY TWINS   p. 760
Find out the astrological similarities you have with famous people.

YOUR COMPATIBILITY   p. 780
Compare planets to find out how compatible you are in a relationship.

YOUR RELATIONSHIP KARMA   p. 824
▶ SATURN IN ARIES
Born Dec. 22, 1967 13:16 - Jan. 20, 1968 23:53

PATRICK MCGOOHAN
American Actor
Mars in Aquarius

409

1968 AQUARIUS

From January 20, 23:54 through February 19, 14:08

♒ The Independent Partner

For the 1968 Aquarian, true love sets you free. You need to have the space and the freedom to be true to yourself and to pursue the interests that matter most to you. For you, traditional, pre-conceived roles are boring, if not impossible to fulfill. You have too many ambitions to live up to someone else's expectations, especially those that have nothing to do with who you are as an individual.

You thrive in the kind of romance that allows you to share your passions. In fact, your involvement in a relationship may dawn on you, suddenly, in the midst of some utterly absorbing occupation. Just when you're enjoying yourself the most, you turn and notice how tenderly you feel toward a steady companion in your activities. The connection comes on effortlessly. You need someone who is attuned to the things that turn you on and exposes you to exciting experiences. Mutual acceptance of each other's quirks and eccentricities allows the bond to flourish.

You have an instant way of recognizing your ideal mate. When you both observe an incident or hear something, you can look at each other and know exactly what the other is thinking. The two of you may laugh out loud, leaving everybody else to wonder what the heck is going on. You gravitate towards someone who shows independent initiative, leadership qualities, and devotion to a cause. You just love to be around someone who makes things happen.

A woman who is trusting and independent appeals most to the Aquarius man of 1968. She never doubts your love, even as you both pursue a variety of interests in the world. Outside commitments reinforce the romance the two of you share in private, on an emotional and physical level.

For the 1968 Aquarius woman, the man who treasures your individuality is a keeper. Other people may see you as "different," but your true love sees you as unique and special. Your ideal partner accepts you as you are and encourages you to pursue and develop your distinctive talents. Within the boundaries of a relationship founded on mutual trust and respect, you enjoy a hearty and energetic sex life.

AQUARIUS ZODIAC SIGN
Your Love Planets

YOUR ROMANTIC SIDE   p. 696
▶ VENUS IN SAGITTARIUS
Born Jan. 20, 23:54 - Jan. 26, 17:34
▶ VENUS IN CAPRICORN
Born Jan. 26, 17:35 - Feb. 19, 14:08

YOUR SEX DRIVE   p. 722
▶ MARS IN PISCES
Born Jan. 20, 23:54 - Feb. 17, 3:17
▶ MARS IN ARIES
Born Feb. 17, 3:18 - Feb. 19, 14:08

YOUR CELEBRITY TWINS   p. 760
Find out the astrological similarities you have with famous people.

YOUR COMPATIBILITY   p. 780
Compare planets to find out how compatible you are in a relationship.

YOUR RELATIONSHIP KARMA   p. 824
▶ SATURN IN ARIES
Born Jan. 20, 23:54 - Feb. 19, 14:08

OLIVIA HUSSEY
English Actress
Sun in Aries

1968 PISCES
From February 19, 14:09 through March 20, 13:21

The Giving Soul

The 1968 Pisces is privy to a cosmic paradox about love—to get it, you have to give it away. And a wonderfully giving soul you are. You are not one to hide your feelings or be stingy with compliments or encouraging words. It is probably very important to you to always say, "I love you," before a dear one walks out the door or hangs up the phone. You are likely to have many male and female friends, but once a relationship crosses the line into romance, you are a faithful and loyal partner.

Mutual give-and-take is the engine driving your ideal relationship. For you, giving is its own reward, and this karmic dynamic attracts partners eager to return your favors. Although many Pisceans can get caught in the trap of one-sided giving and martyrdom, you have unusually strong boundaries and the ability to stand up for yourself should any would-be partner take advantage of your kindness.

To stir your romantic interest, an admirer or partner should go for it and seduce you. Gifts, sweet words, and thoughtful gestures dissolve your resistance, arouse your passions, and provoke your desire to reciprocate. You have a deep appetite for intense experiences. A night at the opera, a concert, or a moving cinema feature can be stimulating and even intoxicating for you. Your suitor should choose entertainment carefully, however, because you tend to absorb and reflect the mood and tone of what you see and hear.

The 1968 male Piscean longs for an intimate partner who can be his best friend and soul mate. Everything in life feels richer for you when you can share it with someone who is dear to you. You love to spoil your sweetheart and have a flair for romance. Without prompting, your special lady returns your favors and lets you know she is always on your side.

The female Piscean born in 1968 likes a man who is physically affectionate and works hard to honor commitments. You appreciate someone who combines high energy levels with discipline and focus. You are good at taking care of loved ones, but you need the assurance of knowing that your man has what it takes to take care of you.

1968 ARIES
From March 20, 13:22 through April 20, 0:40

The Compassionate Catch

Being diligent and pragmatic, you 1968 Ariens have what it takes to succeed in the business world while keeping a sizzling romance going in private. An exceptional capacity for discipline enables you to focus your abundant energies in productive and often lucrative ways. Your commanding presence and concrete accomplishments make you quite a catch. The most endearing aspects of your personality emerge in intimate quarters, where you can express your wonderfully tender, compassionate side. You may have enjoyed a series of stable relationships with partners who are suitable, but not "the one." Love at first sight blossoms into a committed romance with someone who just feels right, for reasons you can't begin to explain.

Someone who doesn't know you well might expect you to insist on a traditional relationship, but you are willing to be open-minded about lifestyle choices, especially where necessary to accommodate the needs of your partner. You can be a supportive partner in a power couple, enjoying the rewards of two careers and the excitement of shared challenges and new opportunities. Sex should be hot and passionate, as lovemaking has a way of refueling your strength.

You are most likely to let down your guard with someone who can see that there is much more to you than what you do or how much you have. Someone who virtually finishes your sentences and anticipates your needs fills you with a sense of magic.

Love has to be fresh, dynamic, and ever-evolving for the Arien man of 1968. You thrive with a woman who tunes into your feelings as they develop. When you're preoccupied with outside problems, you need someone to gently divert your attention and help you to let go. Her tender loving care pleases your body and boosts your spirits.

The 1968 Arien woman needs a partner who admires her ability to make things happen and get things done. You thrive with a man who makes it his business to know what you're up to and to do what he can to offer moral and practical support. You're never better at closing a deal than when you can look forward to a hearty celebration at home.

1968 TAURUS

From April 20, 0:41 through May 21, 0:05

The Earthy Dreamer

Taurus of 1968 walks with two feet firmly planted on the ground. In going about your business, that firm footing comes in handy, especially as you set about creating a comfortable lifestyle for yourself and your loved ones. You are practical, down-to-earth, and diligent, and these characteristics provide a healthy foundation for a relationship with someone who can bring out the soulful, intuitive side of your personality. Romance lifts you to elevations you'd never dream of in your workaday routine. Of course, that's the point of relationships for you—to enable you to escape from mundane concerns, to share your dreams, and make a deep, spiritual connection with another human being.

Having a certain degree of security in your relationship allows you to focus your attention on deeper desires. You may prefer intimate nights at home, where you can entertain each other with your own familiar supplies and furnishings. You enjoy your creature comforts, and the pleasure of sharing them with your partner can spark your animal passions. An intimate relationship allows you to strike the perfect balance between the worldly and mystical aspects of your life. You can realize this ideal in the act of lovemaking, when you and your partner express your mutual devotion through the intermingling of your bodies.

Your partner can reap nonstop rewards by catering to your hearty appetite for sensual pleasures. Vigorous physical activity can excite your passion while allowing you to blow off any excess tension. A bit of playful wrestling can be a fun and sexy lead-in to a night of lovemaking.

The 1968 Taurean man needs a woman who motivates him in a gentle way. You are much more responsive to the "carrot" than the "stick." You appreciate someone who inspires you to take on new challenges in your career and provides a soothing retreat at home.

Resourcefulness ranks high with the 1968 Taurean woman. Your ideal man shares your dreams of achieving financial security and establishing a gracious home and family life. With each little gift and favor, he lets you know how precious you are to him.

TAURUS ZODIAC SIGN
YOUR LOVE PLANETS

YOUR ROMANTIC SIDE p. 696
- ▶ **VENUS IN ARIES**
  Born Apr. 20, 0:41 - May 03, 6:55
- ▶ **VENUS IN TAURUS**
  Born May 03, 6:56 - May 21, 0:05

YOUR SEX DRIVE p. 722
- ▶ **MARS IN TAURUS**
  Born Apr. 20, 0:41 - May 08, 14:13
- ▶ **MARS IN GEMINI**
  Born May 08, 14:14 - May 21, 0:05

YOUR CELEBRITY TWINS p. 760
Find out the astrological similarities you have with famous people.

YOUR COMPATIBILITY p. 780
Compare planets to find out how compatible you are in a relationship.

YOUR RELATIONSHIP KARMA p. 824
- ▶ **SATURN IN ARIES**
  Born Apr. 20, 0:41 - May 21, 0:05

1968 GEMINI

From May 21, 0:06 through June 21, 8:12

The Thoughtful Charmer

The little things matter to Gemini of 1968. Your sharp mind keeps you attuned to the details that mean the most to loved ones—an important anniversary, a favorite color, a birthday, a lover's middle name. Your command of the fine points has a tremendous impact, especially when it shows up in gifts, favors, or sweet little love notes. Thoughtfulness like yours is a rare gift, one that enables you to make another person feel truly loved.

The way someone strides across a room can capture your attention, and with nothing more than that, you can fall in love. Relationships may have come on fast and furious for you in your youth. As you mature, playing the field can become repetitive and boring. A stable relationship frees you to explore the wonders of intimacy with a devoted lover, someone who can excite your mind and soothe your sensitive nerves. You are likely to find it infinitely more fascinating to discover all the various facets of a steady partner's personality and abilities. You can be chatty and charming, and an appreciative audience—someone with infectious laughter—can win you.

Because books and learning give you a thrill, you and your mate can enjoy hours of entertainment from erotic literature and sex manuals. Reading sexy stories aloud can make your passions surge. Reserving an honored place on the bed for an open sexual "workbook," the two of you can study and carry out practice exercises with gusto.

First impressions can be very seductive to the 1968 Gemini man, especially when you are young. For long term relationship success, you need a partner who is just as smart as you are. Keeping up with your snappy repartee keeps you interested. Having the insight to see through nonsense enhances your sense of trust and security in your ideal mate.

The female Gemini of 1968 loves a partner who admires her smarts and keeps her on her intellectual toes. In a serious relationship you need someone who is reliable but never boring. You thrive with a sweetheart who masters the art of watching out for you, without cramping your style or compromising your freedom.

DAVID HOCKNEY
English Artist
Venus in Gemini

GEMINI ZODIAC SIGN
YOUR LOVE PLANETS

YOUR ROMANTIC SIDE p. 696
- ▶ **VENUS IN TAURUS**
  Born May 21, 0:06 - May 27, 17:01
- ▶ **VENUS IN GEMINI**
  Born May 27, 17:02 - June 21, 3:19
- ▶ **VENUS IN CANCER**
  Born June 21, 3:20 - June 21, 8:12

YOUR SEX DRIVE p. 722
- ▶ **MARS IN GEMINI**
  Born May 21, 0:06 - June 21, 5:02
- ▶ **MARS IN CANCER**
  Born June 21, 5:03 - June 21, 8:12

YOUR CELEBRITY TWINS p. 760
Find out the astrological similarities you have with famous people.

YOUR COMPATIBILITY p. 780
Compare planets to find out how compatible you are in a relationship.

YOUR RELATIONSHIP KARMA p. 824
- ▶ **SATURN IN ARIES**
  Born May 21, 0:06 - June 21, 8:12

411

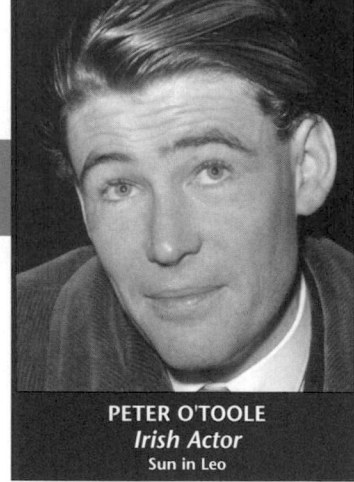

PETER O'TOOLE
Irish Actor
Sun in Leo

412

1968 CANCER
From June 21, 8:13 through July 22, 19:06

♋ The Adept Enchanter

As a Cancer of 1968, you wield the power of enchantment. You can look at anything, no matter how ordinary, and find something good about it. Because you can see the beauty in a person, you can make a lover feel beautiful. Your imagination is vivid, strong, and inspiring, and it helps you to make things better. Your ability to see the best in others attracts admirers and thrills a romantic partner. In romance, you uphold a vision of perfect love. Your ability to see the highest potentials in a relationship can inspire you to overcome tremendous obstacles and weather many a crisis.

Your emotions run deep and intense, and you can be graced and cursed with intuition so powerful, it borders on psychic insight. Sometimes it can be hard to distinguish between your feelings and those of your partner. With time and maturity, you become more grounded. Realistic feedback from your partner can help you to know which instincts you can trust. A relationship with a fellow enchanter can be your ideal. It's so exciting to find someone who shares your dreams and encourages you to pursue your ideals.

You have a weak spot for good old fashioned romance. Revisiting sentimental favorites—movies, songs, restaurants, vacation spots—can bring on a rush of pleasant memories and feelings. Sex can be an intensely emotional experience for you, and you enjoy peak pleasure when your mate speaks tender words of love.

To feel secure in a relationship, the Cancer man of 1968 needs a woman who respects his deep emotions and sensitivity. Your ideal mate will have a skin thick enough to weather occasional bouts of moodiness—but not so thick as to seem unsympathetic. Someone who is practical and trustworthy affords you the safety you need to let your feelings show.

A patronizing man is most unlikely to succeed with the 1968 Cancer woman. You need a mate who will never undermine you or suggest that your instincts are "crazy." Your ideal partner is stable and reliable, and you can rely on him as a gentle sounding board. Mindful of your tenderness, he tells you the truth in a way that is kind and reassuring.

1968 LEO
From July 22, 19:07 through August 23, 2:02

♌ The Hearty Lover

Leo of 1968, you have a regal bearing that is natural and simply charming. As far as people go, you are relatively uncomplicated. There is nothing pretentious in your manner—you are all heart. Your straightforward manner makes others feel secure because they know exactly where they stand. You want what you want when you want it, and if you're not happy, you'll say so. Sometimes you roar like a lion, but the storm passes quickly. Ten minutes later, you're back to being as endearing as a kitten.

Something about your flair for drama lets you get away with romantic behavior that would be a hangin' offense in someone not quite so adorable as you. You may have more lovers' quarrels than average, but they rarely escalate out of control. Besides, nothing about you is average. When your mate attracts admiration from others, you can swell with pride, but sometimes you might become a little jealous. An emotional venting session provides a healthy release of anger—and a wonderful excuse for making up. This is one of the best things about a relationship with you. It's never

boring. And once attached, you remain loyal and true. You offer the most exciting brand of relationship stability under the sun.

On the subject of seduction, you can be so susceptible to a good ego stroking, it's almost unfair. With age and wisdom, flattery only goes so far with you. Genuine admiration lends you a golden glow. One thing you'll never lose is your taste for romance, particularly when it involves giving you "the royal treatment."

A woman who strikes a dramatic figure makes a compelling partner for the 1968 Leo man. You enjoy an equal companion who can share the spotlight with you in public. You might not admit it, but you may prefer a mate who lords over you in the privacy of your lion's lair.

The female Leo born in 1968 needs a man who makes her feel like the queen she is. You need plenty of attention and physical affection, or your aura will droop like a sunken soufflé. Protective and loyal, but never jealous or possessive, your ideal mate is proud to let you shine in the spotlight.

1968 VIRGO

From August 23, 2:03 through September 22, 23:25

♍ *The Compatible Connoisseur*

Virgo of 1968 has an unusual capacity for excellence—a natural outgrowth of your keen sensitivity to detail—that provides a mate with countless reasons to thank the heavens for you. Because you dot every "i" and cross every "t," a partner can have total confidence in your ability to solve problems, handle complex chores, and take care of delicate matters with grace and finesse. Your mate probably wouldn't dream of facing with any challenge without first seeking your advice. Your talent for making life easier keeps a relationship running smoothly through the years.

Your nose for excellence enables you to share and intensify all kinds of pleasures in life. Your mate may have sweet memories of how you pointed out the unique beauty of a piece of music, the unusual talent of a certain athlete, or the special features of a fine wine. You may show a similar diligence in the bedroom, where you have a delightful curiosity about the fine points of your lover's sexual eccentricities. You and your mate could spend hours absorbed in exploring each other's bodies. Perfecting the art of launching your honey to the peaks of ecstasy may be one of your proudest achievements.

If someone wants to seduce you, he or she should serve up your favorite wine, gourmet dish, musical performance, or other delicacy—in accordance with your particular preferences. Whether your sweetheart gets it right or not, the display of maximum effort matters most to you. You won't even dream of how you might have done it yourself.

A woman of refined tastes appeals to the 1968 Virgo male. You like someone who finds your little quirks endearing. In many facets of your life, you have very definite preferences. You need someone who can have a good sense of humor about those few items that defy compromise on your part.

The Virgo woman of 1968 adores the man who gives her unconditional love. You can be so hard on yourself when you make a mistake, and he can nip that tendency in the bud—scooping you up in his arms and reminding you that while he admires all the things you do so well, it's you, just you, he loves.

VIRGO ZODIAC SIGN
YOUR LOVE PLANETS

YOUR ROMANTIC SIDE   p. 696
  ▶ **VENUS IN VIRGO**
  Born Aug. 23, 2:03 - Sept. 02, 6:38
  ▶ **VENUS IN LIBRA**
  Born Sept. 02, 6:39 - Sept. 22, 23:25

YOUR SEX DRIVE   p. 722
  ▶ **MARS IN LEO**
  Born Aug. 23, 2:03 - Sept. 21, 18:38
  ▶ **MARS IN VIRGO**
  Born Sept. 21, 18:39 - Sept. 22, 23:25

YOUR CELEBRITY TWINS   p. 760
  Find out the astrological similarities you have with famous people.

YOUR COMPATIBILITY   p. 780
  Compare planets to find out how compatible you are in a relationship.

YOUR RELATIONSHIP KARMA   p. 824
  ▶ **SATURN IN ARIES**
  Born Aug. 23, 2:03 - Sept. 22, 23:25

BRITT EKLAND
Swedish Actress
Sun, Venus, and Mars in Libra

413

1968 LIBRA
From September 22, 23:26 through October 23, 8:29

♎ *The Fantasy Lover*

In general, Librans tend to be artistically inclined, and this is certainly true for Libra of 1968. Music may hold a sacred place in your heart. Just a few bars of a song can conjure precious memories of loved ones and of special times in a relationship. Harmony is something you strive for in every aspect of your life, and especially in an intimate partnership. So often a relationship can be about competing wills, but you are a maestro of compromise and give-and-take.

Inspiration virtually wafts out of your pores. People cannot help but gravitate towards someone with an attitude as positive and uplifting as yours. A relationship with you provides a safe haven, away from the madness of the outside world. You would not have it any other way, as you automatically shy away from discord. Much like music, your presence soothes any savage beast lurking in your lover's heart. You may take spontaneous dance breaks in the privacy of your love nest, a very pleasant habit that can lead to spontaneous lovemaking.

You are very seductive and susceptible to seduction. To win your affections, a partner should notice and compliment you on what you're wearing. You are, after all, quite particular about and proud of your fashion choices, with emphasis on accessories. Your hair also provides another auspicious avenue—the sensation of fingers running through your locks can melt away any resistance.

The 1968 Libran man likes to be with a woman who looks and feels good to him. Traditional standards of beauty do not necessarily limit your choices. You also have an eye for a beautiful soul, and your ability to see inside your beloved strongly colors what you perceive on the outside. The warmth of her sweet smile may be your favorite feature.

A pragmatic man can be a comfort for Libran woman of 1968. You need a partner who can help you translate your soulful inspirations into concrete creations. Ideally your mate should be a practical, well-grounded, and earthy person. He may provide support for your career potential or help you to realize your sweetest dreams about love and marriage.

LIBRA ZODIAC SIGN
YOUR LOVE PLANETS

YOUR ROMANTIC SIDE   p. 696
  ▶ **VENUS IN LIBRA**
  Born Sept. 22, 23:26 - Sept. 26, 16:44
  ▶ **VENUS IN SCORPIO**
  Born Sept. 26, 16:45 - Oct. 21, 5:15
  ▶ **VENUS IN SAGITTARIUS**
  Born Oct. 21, 5:16 - Oct. 23, 8:29

YOUR SEX DRIVE   p. 722
  ▶ **MARS IN VIRGO**
  Born Sept. 22, 23:26 - Oct. 23, 8:29

YOUR CELEBRITY TWINS   p. 760
  Find out the astrological similarities you have with famous people.

YOUR COMPATIBILITY   p. 780
  Compare planets to find out how compatible you are in a relationship.

YOUR RELATIONSHIP KARMA   p. 824
  ▶ **SATURN IN ARIES**
  Born Sept. 22, 23:26 - Oct. 23, 8:29

SANDY DENNIS
American Actress
Mars in Sagittarius

414

1968 SCORPIO
From October 23, 8:30 through November 22, 5:48

♏ *The Sexual Powerhouse*

For Scorpio of 1968, there is no avoiding the prominent role that your sex drive plays in all of your affairs. It serves as a perpetual motion engine that drives your creativity and, of course, your sex life. You have a healthy appetite for sensual indulgence, and like certain movie stars, a simmering animal magnetism. You need to be mindful about sexual repression, which can throw you off-balance and leave you feeling angry, frustrated, or depressed. Physical intimacy is not, however, your only healthy outlet. By channeling the power of your burning desires, you can move mountains, let alone achieve your greatest ambitions.

Let's face the naked truth—you are a powerhouse. Tremendous energy like yours intrigues and attracts admirers. You can be a real heartthrob, a sex symbol. And yet—what you appear to be on the outside is very different from who you are on the inside. You'll admit only a privileged few to your inner circle, and a romantic partner is the most important person of all. Forging a mystical and physical connection with your mate, you can share your deepest secrets and yearnings.

You are not as susceptible to seduction as people might think, and you become even less so as you mature. Once your heart locks on one person, you throw away the key. The allure of mystery is something you do find irresistible. In a way, you hope you'll never completely know or understand your mate.

The Scorpio man born in 1968 seeks a woman who can indulge and satisfy his powerful appetite for passion and physical affection. A wilting lily will never do. Your ideal lady must be strong enough to keep up with your energy levels and gutsy enough to stand up to you. The woman who finds your intensity intoxicating is a keeper.

The man who adores powerful women is the answer to 1968 Scorpio woman's dreams. Heaven help the partner who tries to dominate you— unless the attempt occurs in the fun of private boudoir games. You simply must have someone worthy of your absolute trust, upon whom you can rely for support. You value the man who can be firm but gentle, honest but discrete.

1968 SAGITTARIUS
From November 22, 5:49 through December 21, 18:59

♐ *The Loyal Companion*

Although the sign of Sagittarius is associated with bachelorhood, the 1968 Sagittarian is unusually commitment-oriented. Blessed with a wise instinct about love and romance, you celebrate and encourage the individuality of each partner in a relationship. Your great respect for personal freedom allows you to make a commitment, not because you have to, but because that is what you want in your heart. And that heart of yours is loyal, steady, and constant. Together, you and your mate can enjoy a dynamic relationship that allows for change, growth, and expansion over the years.

In a serious romantic relationship, you may spend a lot of time on the road. Home is literally where your heart is, and you can provide a zone of comfort and intimacy wherever you go. Because travel requires constant problem solving, the experience tests and prepares the two of you for your journey together through life. In a long term relationship, getting away from it all gives you and your honey a chance to brush up on your relationship skills, especially lovemaking.

For any Sagittarian, heaping helpings of laughter is an essential ingredient in any relationship. You have a taste for the exotic and a marvelous sense of humor. Both are hot buttons for you in a seduction attempt. Should a would-be lover come belly dancing toward you—regardless of his or her gender or state of physical fitness—you'll find it hard to resist. At the very least, you and your pursuer will enjoy a good laugh and remember the day with a smiling fondness.

Emotional security and self-sufficiency are must-have qualities in the ideal woman for the Sagittarian man of 1968. You appreciate someone who can hold down the fort, at home or on the road. Your ideal mate trusts you implicitly, lends you a very long leash, and takes the little bumps and glitches in stride.

The 1968 Sagittarian woman responds well to a man who is willing to compromise. Working through problems together can be energizing for you and for the relationship in general. You appreciate a good listener who can be philosophical about the challenges you face.

Aristotle Onassis – The Ambitious Lover

The two most famous Greeks of the twentieth century, opera singer Maria Callas and shipping tycoon Aristotle Onassis, met for the first time at a gala in Venice in 1957. Though they were both already married, their relationship was scandalously consummated two years later onboard his magnificent yacht *Christina* with both their spouses and Winston Churchill among the jet-setting guests. Her love for him was probably the most precious gift he ever received, yet in 1963 he spurned her to pursue the prized Jacqueline Kennedy.

After several years of relentless wooing and intense financial negotiations, he succeeded in marrying the former First Lady in October 1968. While the tabloid press called her "Jackie O," Onassis insiders began referring to the "Jackie jinx." His shipping empire and numerous other holdings began a precipitous decline, and he turned back to Maria Callas when Jackie retreated to New York to be with her children. By the time he wanted Maria back his physical health failed him, and he died in 1975 before he could arrange a divorce from Jackie.

Onassis was born with his Sun in ambitious Capricorn and his Mars in the watery sign of Pisces. Mars forms a favorable trine aspect to Neptune, the king of the seas, and this combination naturally favors the building of a shipping fleet. Onassis became immensely wealthy, and in the 1950s was known as the King of Monte Carlo (much to the consternation of Prince Rainier) because of his controlling interest in the tiny country's casinos and hotels. From this port he would cruise around the Mediterranean, using his wealth and social connections to seduce high-profile women.

Maria Callas fell in love with Onassis right away, but fended off his advances

Aristotle Onassis with Maria Callas

415

for two years. The astrological indicator for love-at-first-sight is when one person's Venus aligns with the other's Uranus. Uranus represents the sudden rush of electrical excitement, and when in the presence of erotic Venus, the animal magnetism can become overwhelming. From the time they first began making love in August 1959, Maria wanted nothing more than to play the Greek wife. She let her singing career slip and wanted more than anything to have a baby with Onassis. According to the definitive account in Nicholas Gage's *Greek Fire*, a son was secretly born in 1960, but died on the same day, March 30, 1960.

In 1963 Onassis bought the Greek island of Skorpios after Prince Rainier rewrote the Monaco tax laws to get rid of his rival. By this time Ari was becoming interested in Jacqueline Kennedy, and managed to slip away from Maria to enjoy his seduction of Jackie. The first meeting between the American Queen (who was born with the Sun in regal Leo) and the

Greek Tycoon took place in early October 1963. Onassis invited her for a little cruise onboard the *Christina*, ostensibly to help her get over her depression following the loss of her newborn baby. JFK called Onassis an "international pirate" and sent his Secretary of Commerce, FDR Jr., as a chaperone.

At the end of the cruise Onassis presented her with a stunning farewell gift, a diamond and ruby necklace worth $50,000. When Jackie returned to Washington, she was raving about her trip but was greeted by a politically unacceptable amount of negative publicity. For several years, Onassis would jet back and forth between his two love interests, but Jackie and Ari finally married in 1968, shortly after Robert F. Kennedy's assassination. Only a week or two later, Onassis returned to the loving arms of Maria. Jackie's Rising Sign is Scorpio, making her marriage to Onassis on Skorpios a star-crossed getaway, filled with intrigue and betrayal.

► READ ABOUT PRINCE RAINIER ON PAGE 310   ► READ ABOUT JACQUELINE KENNEDY ON PAGE 351

1969

- ✪ **PORNOGRAPHY**
- ✪ **BED-IN**
- ✪ **STONEWALL RIOTS**
- ✪ **HAIR!**
- ✪ **EASY RIDER**
- ✪ **CRIMSON AND CLOVER**
- ✪ **PORTNOY'S COMPLAINT**

EVENTS

The US Supreme Court declared a Georgia anti-pornography law unconstitutional, *Penthouse* magazine began publishing, and when Denmark legalized pornography, a "Sex Fair" was held in Copenhagen. Beatles Paul McCartney and John Lennon both disappointed fans by marrying. Lennon spent his seven-day honeymoon in the presidential suite of the Amsterdam Hilton staging a "Bed-In" with bride Yoko Ono to protest against the Vietnam War. New York police raided the popular Greenwich Village gay bar Stonewall Inn, sparking days of protest now known as the Stonewall Riots.

Human eggs were fertilized in a test tube for the first time in Cambridge, where King's College announced that it would begin to admit women undergraduates. California enacted the nation's first "no-fault" divorce law. Britain's Princess Anne caused a stir when she danced onstage at the end of the nude musical *Hair*—fully clothed!

POP CULTURE

Films were catching up with the cultural landscape. Dennis Hopper's *Easy Rider* chronicled a motorcycle road trip through 1960s America. *Midnight Cowboy*, directed by John Schlesinger, found two lonely drifters lost in a bleakly portrayed New York. Frederico Fellini's *Satyricon* was a surreal odyssey through decadent ancient Rome. *Women in Love*, Ken Russell's adaptation of D.H. Lawrence's novel, explored the English class system through the love affairs of an artist and her sister.

It was the dawning of the Age of Aquarius, at least given the popularity of the musical *Hair* and the Fifth Dimension's anthem "Aquarius/Let the Sun Shine In." "In the Year 2525" painted a bleak future, while the Archies' "Sugar, Sugar" was pure bubblegum pop. Excellent and enduring songs included the Rolling Stones' "Honky Tonk Women," Sly & the Family Stone's "Everyday People," and the haunting "Crimson and Clover" by Tommy James & the Shondells.

Bestsellers included *Portnoy's Complaint* by Philip Roth, a comic coming-of-age novel about a sex-obsessed Jewish boy, and *Naked Came the Stranger* by 25 journalists calling themselves "Penelope Ashe" to see if a truly bad, but sex-filled, novel would sell—it did. In Margaret Drabble's *The Waterfall*, a poet gets involved with her best friend's husband. John Fowles' *The French Lieutenant's Woman* was a Victorian romance between lovers with complex emotional histories.

Hot Couple

PAUL MCCARTNEY & LINDA EASTMAN

American photographer Linda Eastman had already won critical acclaim for her work when she met Beatle Paul McCartney in 1967. Their union was an instant success. He would later write a song for his beloved called "Lovely Linda."

The couple were married at a registry office in London on March 12, 1969. Legions of young women were heartbroken by the event and pointed to Linda as the cause of the Beatles' breakup. In spite of fan harassment, theirs was one of the most enduring celebrity marriages of all time—spanning thirty years. Paul was devastated by her death from breast cancer in 1998.

SEE ALSO

▶ JOHN LENNON AND YOKO *Page 423*
▶ SWINGING LONDON *Page 383*

416

1969 CAPRICORN

From December 21, 1968 19:00 through January 20, 1969 5:37
(December 1969 Capricorns, see 1970 Capricorn)

♑ *The Intellectual Romantic*

As a hard-working Capricorn born in 1969, your relationship must provide you a safe haven where you can express yourself and have your needs met. You believe in romance and can often be quite sentimental where love is concerned. You're passionate and intense and demand a connection that rivets you, heart and soul. Why be involved in a romance that is merely tepid? All or nothing is your motto!

You need to feel understood and accepted, and in a relationship you expect limitations and restrictions to be put aside. Your bedroom is your oasis and you go there with your lover to cast aside the cares of the day. You want to be on a winning team and appreciate being able to feel that you are working together with your partner to build the life you both want.

To spark your interest, a mate must be creative and sexy because you believe that chemistry is essential. To maintain that interest, sex appeal is important but it's far from all you require. The mate who drags you to a computer show, an art gallery, or who tickles your toes when you lie together on the sand sparks your imagination. You need to feel an intellectual connection as well as a physical one, so a partner who engages you in clever conversation, who wants to share interesting activities, and whose idea of tomorrow meshes with your own is someone you're content to woo forever.

Male Goats born in 1969 prefer a woman who is tender, romantic, and sweet. She is loving and kind, open and warm and she snuggles you while you're sleeping. Your lady may not quite be mother nature yet, but you see those qualities in her and know that she is someone who can make a warm and wonderful home and raise a loving family. She's the one you fantasize about—whether in bed or in an apron. She's your dream girl!

Female Cappies born in 1969 appreciate a masculine man who is macho but also sensitive. He can be a bit domineering, but that seems sexy to you, particularly when he hoists you into his arms and tosses you into bed. Your guy is solid and strong and seems like someone who can hold his own in any sort of situation.

CAPRICORN ZODIAC SIGN
YOUR LOVE PLANETS

YOUR ROMANTIC SIDE   p. 696
▶ **VENUS IN AQUARIUS**
Born Dec. 21, 1968 19:00 - Jan. 04, 1969 20:06
▶ **VENUS IN PISCES**
Born Jan. 04, 20:07 - Jan. 20, 5:37

YOUR SEX DRIVE   p. 722
▶ **MARS IN LIBRA**
Born Dec. 21, 1968 19:00 - Dec. 29, 1968 22:06
▶ **MARS IN SCORPIO**
Born Dec. 29, 1968 22:07 - Jan. 20, 1969 5:37

YOUR CELEBRITY TWINS   p. 760
Find out the astrological similarities you have with famous people.

YOUR COMPATIBILITY   p. 780
Compare planets to find out how compatible you are in a relationship.

YOUR RELATIONSHIP KARMA   p. 824
▶ **SATURN IN ARIES**
Born Dec. 21, 1968 19:00 - Jan. 20, 1969 5:37

JON VOIGHT
American Actor
Sun in Capricorn

417

1969 AQUARIUS

From January 20, 5:38 through February 18, 19:54

♒ *The Sparkling Eccentric*

You're a dynamic Aquarius, born in 1969 and you require a relationship that is exciting, dynamic, and intense. You couldn't care less about getting tied up by commitment and never make choices just for the sake of convention. You have to start out riveted and stay interested to remain involved. A relationship is a playground for you and it's where you laugh, try new and outrageous ideas, and seek a kindred spirit.

Friendship and communication are the most important dimensions to you in any encounter, so your relationship must always feel like a connection with a best pal. You like to experiment and may want to try out an unconventional living situation. You feel that other people take life too seriously, and as long as consenting adults are involved, let the games begin.

The partner who is dazzling enough to gain your interest beyond a one night stand is a bit eccentric. You love good conversation and nothing is as much fun as comparing war stories in which you try to outdo each other with your romantic escapades. Sex appeal matters too, so a connection under the surface is important. A stranger who finds you attractive enough to walk up to you on the street and plant a kiss on your lips—well that stranger will quickly become a pal and perhaps a lover. Going roller blading or windsurfing, or trying astral projection together keeps your romance lively.

Male Aquarians born in 1969 like a woman who's quite a handful. She's assertive, demanding, knows what she wants, and doesn't stop till she gets it. Your lady is a real firecracker and you don't mind at all that her past rivals your own. It makes her far more appealing and as long as she's not a clinging vine you're content to keep her in your life.

Female 1969 Aquarians need a man to have enough sex appeal to keep you panting and enough sensitivity to make it all worthwhile. Your guy has great intuition and he knows that when he attempts lovemaking in a closet at a party, you'll respond with laughter and encouragement. He's a bit psychic, a great dancer, and sometimes he lets you be the one on top!

AQUARIUS ZODIAC SIGN
YOUR LOVE PLANETS

YOUR ROMANTIC SIDE   p. 696
▶ **VENUS IN PISCES**
Born Jan. 20, 5:38 - Feb. 02, 4:44
▶ **VENUS IN ARIES**
Born Feb. 02, 4:45 - Feb. 18, 19:54

YOUR SEX DRIVE   p. 722
▶ **MARS IN SCORPIO**
Born Jan. 20, 5:38 - Feb. 18, 19:54

YOUR CELEBRITY TWINS   p. 760
Find out the astrological similarities you have with famous people.

YOUR COMPATIBILITY   p. 780
Compare planets to find out how compatible you are in a relationship.

YOUR RELATIONSHIP KARMA   p. 824
▶ **SATURN IN ARIES**
Born Jan. 20, 5:38 - Feb. 18, 19:54

1 Read Your Sign   **2** Look Up Your Love Planets   **3** Go to Pages Shown

JEAN-PAUL BELMONDO
French Actor
Sun and Venus in Aries

418

1969 PISCES
From February 18, 19:55 through March 20, 19:07
The Committed Wanderer

If you're a forceful Pisces born in 1969, your relationship must provide you with the secure foundation you need to forge success out in the world. You believe strongly in commitment and in sharing a dream. You're romantic and your belief in destiny may have inclined you to make hasty commitments too early in life. You learned that it's important to be able to give your heart away to one person forever, and of course the key is in choosing the right recipient of that precious gift.

Your relationship reflects your sense of idealism, and you realize that by sharing your life with a partner you can grow and become your best self. You want to give and receive encouragement, support, and enduring affection. Trust and understanding are other aspects of romance you look for, and you are willing to put in all the necessary effort to create a relationship that thrives and endures.

To spark your interest, a mate must be outgoing and assertive. Wallflowers really aren't your type. A mate who challenges you to a footrace or who takes you for a motorcycle ride makes your blood rush, and then you enjoy wondering what's next. Traveling together really appeals to you, and a picnic in a nearby park is a great way to begin. Then if the chemistry is right, you'd be ready at a moment's notice to backpack across a foreign continent.

Male 1969 Pisces like a woman who is exciting yet stable. She has her own interests but doesn't mind including you. Her personality is strong and on a slow day she might change the oil in your car. Sometimes she's bossy but she always helps you out in a pinch. You know her heart is yours forever and you feel warm and cozy having her your corner.

Female Pisces born in 1969 enjoy the company of a happy wanderer. Your guy may be a traveling salesman, a bus driver, or just someone who's always on the go. You don't mind that he's sometimes gone because you have a life of your own as well. You like a man who's athletic, has good reflexes, and a universality of spirit. An occasional quarrel is okay as long as there are good sparks when you make up.

1969 ARIES
From March 20, 19:08 through April 20, 6:26
The Beautiful Dreamer

As a creative 1969 Aries, your relationship is usually a work in progress. You believe in commitment and in true love, and you wish they were easier to achieve. Your spirit is strong and fanciful, and that's why achieving a happy partnership is so important to you. You believe in love that lasts and you want to have a relationship that is just as magical as in the movies. Perhaps that's why you so strongly relate to the idea of happily ever after.

Freedom and self-expression are so very important to you, and so you feel that within a perfect relationship those elements are guaranteed. You know that each partner needs freedom, and that's just fine as long as you always hold each other tightly in your minds and hearts. You must be committed, but not tied down.

To gain and hold your attention, a partner has to spark your imagination. It's all right that you don't actually know the person at first, because if you find yourself fantasizing about that particular mate, then you realize it's worth getting to know him or her a little better.

Outdoorsy, active mates appeal most to you, so being invited to climb a mountain, to go hiking, dog walking, or to a volleyball tournament appeals to you. The couple that plays together, stays together!

Male 1969 Rams require a mate who is active and sexy, yet also reliable and imaginative. Spontaneity is very important to you, and you love being on the receiving end of her exciting ideas. Your lady has a spiritual side as well and there's something special about her—even though you can't quite describe what it is. She may be a bit older or more experienced, but she just touches you, heart and soul.

Female Aries born in 1969 like a man who is playful, outgoing, and athletic. You're willing to give but you don't want to be pinned to a man who is needy or whiny. He has to be independent and not expect you to be his slave. He is loving and friendly, likes kids and animals, and makes your life more fun than it was without him. You feel open and confident when he's around and you're willing to experiment a little in bed with him.

The Sex Machine

A determined Taurus born in 1969, your relationship is why you stop working and head home. You prize stability and success, but you'd never make a permanent commitment just to avoid loneliness. You believe in a strong and exciting connection with the right partner, and you realize that having a true love in your life gives you the strength to go out in the world and create success.

Being understood and encouraged is what a good romance is all about, and you go out of your way to share interesting ideas and hot passion. To you a romance contains all the riches that make life wonderful. Nothing is more rewarding than sharing exciting conversation with the person who knows you best and then coming home for a long night of sizzling lovemaking. You're multidimensional and you expect your relationship to have all the same positive elements that make you so special.

To capture your heart, a mate must first of all be interesting. Sex appeal is important, but the partner who makes you laugh or shares an idea you hadn't yet considered piques your imagination. That's where a lifelong commitment begins. Chemistry is another essential ingredient and that's something you recognize immediately. You just know who would be a sizzling partner and who wouldn't. A casual caress, the way your bodies glide together on the dance floor, or being offered a delectable treat is the first step toward romance.

Male 1969 Bulls prefer a woman who is outgoing, assertive, and very sexy. A woman who walks right up to you and makes a pass is a challenge you enjoy. Your mate is hot, youthful, sexy, and independent. She needs you to dazzle her sexually and intellectually, not to baby-sit her every move. You can be bossy and you need a woman who's an equal—whether you're vertical or horizontal.

Female Taureans born in 1969 require a man who is sexy, macho, and a bit domineering. He's an achiever and used to getting his own way, and when he orders you around it's a bit of a turn on. This guy is creative and intelligent, so everything he does is larger than life, which is just the right size for you.

The Social Chatterbox

You're a garrulous Gemini, born in 1969, and to you a relationship must be intellectually stimulating or you feel tied down. In your opinion, sharing ideas is the most important aspect of any relationship and you enjoy being with someone who stimulates your mind as well as your heart. A relationship must change and grow because you hate boredom and refuse to be involved with commitment just for the sake of security or continuity. You'd rather lead an unstable life than a humdrum one.

You believe in romance and in sexual attraction, and sometimes you fall in love at first sight. That feeling of being dazzled is what love is all about for you, and when you find a partner whose moods change often enough to keep you guessing, you're willing to settle down. Often you prefer playing the field.

You enjoy sharing a bike ride, a picnic in the country, or a trip to a museum, but the best way to pique your interest is to engage you in a lively debate. A rousing argument never turns you off because, although you're attached intellectually to the process, you're detached emotionally from the ideas. Someone who can hold their own with you will make you take a second look. You respond to chemistry, and while you're talking with a special someone, you begin to fantasize about romance and sex.

Male Geminis born in 1969 like a woman who is swift and smart. Dainty little creatures seem so wispy to you. Your ideal woman can hold up her end of the conversation and might drag you into the back seat of her car for some hasty lovemaking. An outdoor girl is always better than someone who likes staying at home. You live out in the world and want your companion to be lively, active, and sexy.

Female 1969 Geminis insist on a mate who is a clever wordsmith. Your guy is smart and funny and he loves to dazzle you with his ingenious ideas and wry sense of humor. He's laid back and outdoorsy, athletic but not terribly macho, and he adores doing fun things on the spur of the moment. You don't mind at all that he's fast to seduce you and slow to commit. That way you keep your options open.

TAURUS ZODIAC SIGN

Your Love Planets

YOUR ROMANTIC SIDE   p. 696
▶ **VENUS IN ARIES**
Born Apr. 20, 6:27 - May 21, 5:49

YOUR SEX DRIVE   p. 722
▶ **MARS IN SAGITTARIUS**
Born Apr. 20, 6:27 - May 21, 5:49

YOUR CELEBRITY TWINS   p. 760
Find out the astrological similarities you have with famous people.

YOUR COMPATIBILITY   p. 780
Compare planets to find out how compatible you are in a relationship.

YOUR RELATIONSHIP KARMA   p. 824
▶ **SATURN IN ARIES**
Born Apr. 20, 6:27 – Apr. 29, 22:23
▶ **SATURN IN TAURUS**
Born Apr. 29, 22:24 - May 21, 5:49

ARETHA FRANKLIN
American Singer
Mars in Gemini

419

GEMINI ZODIAC SIGN

Your Love Planets

YOUR ROMANTIC SIDE   p. 696
▶ **VENUS IN ARIES**
Born May 21, 5:50 - June 06, 1:47
▶ **VENUS IN TAURUS**
Born June 06, 1:48 - June 21, 13:54

YOUR SEX DRIVE   p. 722
▶ **MARS IN SAGITTARIUS**
Born May 21, 5:50 - June 21, 13:54

YOUR CELEBRITY TWINS   p. 760
Find out the astrological similarities you have with famous people.

YOUR COMPATIBILITY   p. 780
Compare planets to find out how compatible you are in a relationship.

YOUR RELATIONSHIP KARMA   p. 824
▶ **SATURN IN TAURUS**
Born May 21, 5:50 - June 21, 13:54

GENEVIEVE BUJOLD
French-Canadian Actress
Sun in Cancer

1969 CANCER
From June 21, 13:55 through July 23, 0:47

 *The Sensitive Magician*

As an imaginative Cancer born in 1969, your relationship must be a romantic oasis for your mind and heart. You're sensitive and creative, and believe in the magic that is love. Inspired by movies, fairy tales, and your own imagination, you work to create a dream relationship that exceeds what Hollywood can envision.

You insist on connecting on all levels with a mate. That way you can build a relationship that can grow and last. True love is important for you because you believe that it provides the foundation for personal freedom and self-expression. Your relationship must be the fertile ground that nourishes each participant and provides happiness, security, and comfort. You realize that this is a tall order, but settling for anything less just doesn't appeal to you. You know love is complicated, so you take your time in finding just the right person.

You are sensitive and respond to chemistry more readily than any ploy a potential suitor might try, but that doesn't mean you're not impressed when someone expresses interest in you. Of course you are! You just love being the object of desire! A mate who can make you laugh is on the right track, but you also enjoy sharing pleasant meals, as well as outdoor activities and athletic events. Holding hands in the movies is very romantic and you like planning long trips to exotic destinations and traveling together, too.

Male Crabs born in 1969 want a woman who is sensual, sexy, and romantic. You like the feminine aura she presents when she walks into a room, yet you also appreciate her independence and spunk. Your lady is a bit fanciful, believes in magic, and is totally passionate about the really special things in life—you included.

1969 Cancer females need a man to be independent, outgoing, confident, and a little unpredictable. He's insouciant and a bit of a bad boy, but that's just because sometimes he doesn't pay attention. Under the surface he has a good heart and will help an old lady cross the street. Your guy is clever and humorous, and he makes life sparkle a little brighter just by

1969 LEO
From July 23, 0:48 through August 23, 7:42

The Considerate Partner

Born as a 1969 Leo, you are focused and need a relationship that is stable and reliable. You care about doing things properly and you need to feel that there is someone in your life you can count on. Commitment is very meaningful to you, not just because it implies stability, but because it means ongoing love and devotion. You believe in romance and much tenderness, and you realize that love is meant to grow and endure.

Personal self-expression is always important to you, yet you believe in compromise as well. Being part of a couple means for you that sometimes your own personal desires and needs are less important than the good of the team. You want your needs met, but not at the expense of someone you love. You also care about building a strong foundation, and that means having a good marriage, a nice home, and a happy family.

To gain and hold your interest a mate really has to care about you and show a level of devotion equal to your own. Tenderness and sweet sentimental gestures endear you to a prospective partner, and on that you build a

solid future. Inviting you to cozy dinners, sharing soft conversation by the fire, or working together on neighborhood projects give you the strong sense of togetherness that is so emotionally satisfying.

Male Leos born in 1969 need a woman who is soft and gentle, sweet and kind, tender and nurturing. You feel a bond when you meet her and know she's a good mother, a best pal, and a great cook. She knows the way to your heart and puts lots of effort into making you feel loved and cherished. Children adore her, pets sit at her feet, and everyone who meets her says that she's special.

1969 Lady Lions want a man who is outgoing and sexy, yet also practical and down to earth. Your guy is smart and informative, and he has lots of useful information and practical skills. He is passionate about life yet also disciplined and controlled. He's the sort of guy you know can be counted on when there's a crisis and he shows you a good time when things are calm. You want a happy family, so he must be a solid citizen and reliable provider.

1969 VIRGO
From August 23, 7:43 through September 23, 5:06

The Scintillating Sensualist

As a 1969 Virgo, you are self-directed and goal-oriented, and your relationship has to meet your needs on many levels. You have strong ideas about the way a partnership must function, and you want your life to be orderly, stable, and consistent. Being with a congenial partner is very important to you because you prefer to avoid dissention and strife. That doesn't mean you're easygoing or a patsy, however. You know what's right and want life to match your ideas and ideals.

You believe in caring and commitment, and will go a long way to make sure your partner is happy. You expect the same consideration in return and know that the only way to build a long-lasting partnership is through cooperation and understanding. You can be generous as long as you feel appreciated. Passion is also very important to you, and as long as the chemistry is right, it's easier to make necessary compromises.

To hold and keep your interest, a mate must be intelligent. Engaging you in fascinating conversation is an excellent way to begin. You're impatient, though, and you don't want to talk about the weather. Sharing interesting ideas and useful information will always attract you. You might even meet someone special in an online chat room. You enjoy socializing and will happily accompany a partner to a charity event. Making a difference in the world is a good way to share something worthwhile.

Male 1969 Virgos want a partner who is beautiful, sexy, and alluring, but she must also have substance and stability. No bimbos for you! Your special woman knows who she is. Perhaps she's older and more experienced, but she also has a youthful, playful side. She has an intensely developed sexuality, but is also sensitive and demure.

Female Virgos born in 1969 want a man who is clever, verbally adroit, intelligent, and so sexy he singes the curtains just by entering the room. Macho men appeal to you and even if he's too bossy and demanding, you feel confident that you can hold your own with him. He makes his level of commitment to you very apparent, and you never have to wonder about his loyalty.

VIRGO ZODIAC SIGN
YOUR LOVE PLANETS

YOUR ROMANTIC SIDE   p. 696
- ▶ **VENUS IN CANCER**
  Born Aug. 23, 7:43 - Aug. 29, 2:47
- ▶ **VENUS IN LEO**
  Born Aug. 29, 2:48 - Sept. 23, 3:25
- ▶ **VENUS IN VIRGO**
  Born Sept. 23, 3:26 - Sept. 23, 5:06

YOUR SEX DRIVE   p. 722
- ▶ **MARS IN SAGITTARIUS**
  Born Aug. 23, 7:43 - Sept. 21, 6:34
- ▶ **MARS IN CAPRICORN**
  Born Sept. 21, 6:35 - Sept. 23, 5:06

YOUR CELEBRITY TWINS   p. 760
Find out the astrological similarities you have with famous people.

YOUR COMPATIBILITY   p. 780
Compare planets to find out how compatible you are in a relationship.

YOUR RELATIONSHIP KARMA   p. 824
- ▶ **SATURN IN TAURUS**
  Born Aug. 23, 7:43 - Sept. 23, 5:06

RAY CHARLES
American Singer
Sun in Virgo

1969 LIBRA
From September 23, 5:07 through October 23, 14:10

The Relaxed Romantic

As an optimistic Libra born in 1969, you expect your relationship to work out fortuitously, like everything else in your life. A relationship shouldn't be a source of strife or strain because life's too short. You believe in being sensitive and receptive, connecting with that perfect person, and living harmoniously together for a long time.

Communication, cooperation, and sex appeal are some of the essential qualities of your relationship. All for one and one for all is your motto, and you believe that working together to make your life happy brings you closer to each other and to eternal bliss. Giving is as important as receiving, and you enjoy being on both sides of the seesaw. Stability and commitment are essential, but not because they're required. Instead you just know when it's right, and then it makes sense to keep pedaling along, side by side.

Good communication is the way to capture—and then maintain—your interest. You love nothing more than a romantic evening of deep conversation while you gaze starry eyed at each other. A tasteful, considerate gesture is another way to win and keep your heart. Fixing you dinner with all your favorite foods, with soft music playing in the background, will definitely make you smile. And if the meal is followed by a sensual massage or foot rub with scented oils and candlelight, you'll be hooked.

Male Libras born in 1969 require a woman who is subtle, sensitive, and demure. There's no question that your lady is sexy, but she doesn't flaunt it with revealing clothing or unrestrained behavior in public. In the bedroom it's a different story, and you love seeing her other side emerge. She is kind and gentle and always offers a helping hand when you need it.

1969 Lady Libras choose a man who is clever and sparkling. His sense of humor never fails and he keeps you laughing and interested. He's stable and a hard worker, and you know he will always achieve his goals. Although he's a no-nonsense guy deep down inside, he still knows how to play—and communicate with you. He's sexy and strong but far from overbearingly macho.

LIBRA ZODIAC SIGN
YOUR LOVE PLANETS

YOUR ROMANTIC SIDE   p. 696
- ▶ **VENUS IN VIRGO**
  Born Sept. 23, 5:07 - Oct. 17, 14:16
- ▶ **VENUS IN LIBRA**
  Born Oct. 17, 14:17 - Oct. 23, 14:10

YOUR SEX DRIVE   p. 722
- ▶ **MARS IN CAPRICORN**
  Born Sept. 23, 5:07 - Oct. 23, 14:10

YOUR CELEBRITY TWINS   p. 760
Find out the astrological similarities you have with famous people.

YOUR COMPATIBILITY   p. 780
Compare planets to find out how compatible you are in a relationship.

YOUR RELATIONSHIP KARMA   p. 824
- ▶ **SATURN IN TAURUS**
  Born Sept. 23, 5:07 - Oct. 23, 14:10

GOLDIE HAWN
American Actress
Sun and Venus in Scorpio

422

1969 SCORPIO
From October 23, 14:11 through November 22, 11:30

The Starry-Eyed Lover

Because you're a communicative Scorpio, born in 1969, your relationship must have a strong intellectual dimension. Being with someone whose ideas interest you, whose views are simpatico, whose tastes mesh with your own, is the stuff of romantic perfection. You like a strong sense of friendship and camaraderie in any relationship, the ability to live in harmony and enjoy similar things.

You're romantic and you enjoy all the trappings and all the hearts and flowers, even if you make fun of them sometimes. Giving and sharing are equally important relationship dimensions, and you need to feel connected to someone who lavishes you with affection, just as you do in return. You believe in true love as well as in commitment, but you'd never force an involvement just to avoid solitude. Instead you wait until it feels just right before you say "I do."

To attract your interest, a partner must be charming, wooing you with a sparkling smile and a clever opening line. You enjoy social outings as well as charity events, and like being asked to dress up in formal clothes for a good

cause. Floating across a dance floor together lets you explore the magic and the chemistry rather quickly. To keep your attention, a partner will keep a steady stream of cultural events on the calendar.

Male 1969 Scorpions need a woman who sparkles, is charming, and yet has substance and a good head on her shoulders. Her taste is impeccable, she's adored by all who meet her, and she always has time to offer a hug to someone who needs it. Her sex appeal is subtle, but she always know the perfect way to seduce you, perhaps with a certain look across the room. She's fun to talk to and good at choosing presents for you.

Female Scorpios born in 1969 like a man to be macho and independent. Your guy is assertive and he expects to get his own way. You may have to compromise a bit, but you don't mind because he reminds you of a sexy movie star. He's socially adept, but also has a serious side. He doesn't have endless hours to devote to frivolity. Instead he does good works, and you love being at his side.

1969 SAGITTARIUS
From November 22, 11:31 through December 22, 0:43

The Amorous Idealist

Passionate 1969 Sagittarius, your romance must be intense. A complete merger of body, intellect, and soul is what you have in mind. You are deeply romantic and you believe in nothing less than true love. Meshing completely with your one true soul mate is your goal, and it gives meaning to every area of your life. A relationship for you must foster tenderness and gentleness in an atmosphere where both can open up and share complete intimacy. You want to know and be known, and be stimulated in every way, and shallower interactions don't interest you for a long term relationship.

You believe in independence as well as commitment, and you see no dichotomy there. When you're with a true love, you know it means that each person's individual needs are as perfectly met as are the needs of the two of you as a unit. Your perfect relationship demands balance and understanding, as well as the ability to communicate so that you both get what you need.

To gain your interest, a mate must have the right chemistry—and a bit of nerve. You

appreciate sex appeal and perk up when someone is gutsy enough to come up to you and make a pass. You enjoy being invited to concerts, dances, and movies. Drawing you in to intelligent conversations will pique your interest even more. But to truly win your heart, a would-be partner needs to offer you stability and a sense of home base along with the fun.

Male archers born in 1969 want a woman who is sensitive, romantic, idealistic, and sexy. She is part goddess and part little girl. She can rhapsodize endlessly about true love and about her favorite hobbies, then turn around and make on-target observations about the world. She definitely keeps you guessing. Even though she's soft and tender, she's also independent and gutsy.

Female 1968 Sagittarians want a man who is sexy, independent, helpful, kind, and sometimes a tyrant. He's often generous and magnanimous, but sometimes surprises you by insisting on having his own way. He's a willing partner in the spontaneous escapades you dream up, but provides solid grounding for you at the same time.

'60s

John and Yoko – Unconventional Idealists

Offbeat, unconventional, and utterly unique, John Lennon and Yoko Ono are the quintessential '70s couple. The couple met in 1967 at London's Indica Gallery, where Yoko was presenting some off her conceptual art. One piece involved a tall white ladder that went all the way up to the ceiling. Written on the ceiling in tiny letters was the word "Yes." John Lennon claims, "When I saw that piece, I knew I was in love."

At the time, Lennon was already married, but he found himself irresistibly pulled into Ono's orbit. Chalk it up to the stars. Not only were the couple's Sun signs highly compatible (John was a Libra and Yoko is an Aquarius), Lennon's Venus and Ono's Mars were in the same sign: Virgo. This combination makes for a very powerful attraction. In addition, people with a Venus-Mars link have a fated quality to their love. Their mutual sexual desire can make the air crackle with excitement.

Virgo is the sign of the Virgin. Interestingly, the first album Lennon and Ono made together was called Two Virgins. Perhaps the artists instinctively drew upon their astrological link when they chose the title.

John and Yoko married in 1969, causing shock waves around the world. An interracial romance was still daring in those days, but society was rapidly changing. Lennon and Ono embraced these changes and used them to showcase their favorite political causes. One such cause was world peace. In an effort to draw attention to the peace movement, the pair staged a "Bed-In for Peace" on their honeymoon, inviting the press in to their hotel suite. Reporters rushed to the scene, hoping to nab some steamy photos of the newlyweds. Instead, they found two benign-looking hippies clad in pajamas, eager to talk about pacifism.

The couple's marriage only added to the tensions that had been mounting for some time among the Beatles. Before Yoko arrived on the scene, John and Paul McCartney had collaborated very closely with their music. Rumors began that Yoko's presence created a wedge between them. The final blow was struck when Lennon announced, "I want a divorce from the Beatles" at an Apple Records meeting. Music fans were devastated when the Beatles confirmed in 1970 that they were officially broken up. The public accused Yoko of destroying their favorite group, and she became the target of many vicious jokes. John ignored the public's disapproval, stuck close to his wife, and concentrated on their creative and activist endeavors.

Being an unconventional Aquarian, in 1973 when her marriage to John began to show signs of wear, Yoko found a "unique" way to mend the rift. She set John up with a young girl named May Pang. Pang was instructed to be John's lover, caretaker, and companion while Yoko lived elsewhere. The separation lasted 18 months, after which the couple reunited and began trying for a baby. Yoko had several heartbreaking miscarriages, which served to strengthen the bond between her and John even more. She finally gave birth to a healthy baby boy named Sean in 1975. Lennon's first son Julian had been born during the Beatles' heyday, and the rock star had largely missed the boy's growing-up years. This time, John dropped out of the music scene for a while to became a full-time house husband, and Yoko took over the family business.

On December 8, 1980 an assassin's bullet struck down John in New York City. The once vilified Ono was hailed as a hero for the way she handled her grief. The praise was too little, too late for Yoko. She remarked bitterly, "For 10 years I was the devil. Now suddenly I'm an angel. Did the world have to lose John for people to change their opinion of me? It's unreal. If it brought John back, I'd rather be hated."

The cover of John and Yoko's last album remains the finest testament of the closeness of their relationship. It features a close-up of John putting a gentle kiss on Yoko's lips. The image evokes a song that Lennon wrote 10 years before, at the start of their journey together: "I don't believe in Beatles/I just believe in me/Yoko and me/And that's reality."

▶ READ ABOUT PAUL McCARTNEY ON PAGE 416   ▶ READ ABOUT THE BEATLES ON PAGE 383

1970 -1979

THE "ME" DECADE

The 1970s were times of stark

endings and exciting

beginnings. A prolonged

recession forced people to

reduce their expectations of

the "good life."

The 1970s ushered in a new era of global economic turbulence. Oil prices skyrocketed, making the 1970s the worst decade since World War II. After nearly ten years the Vietnam War finally came to an end. For the first time in history a US President, Richard M. Nixon, resigned. Women finally won the right to vote in Switzerland, while a "Black is Beautiful" campaign swept through African-American communities across the United States.

The widespread use of birth control pills allowed women to explore their sexuality without fear of pregnancy. Abortion was legalized in the United States and Italy.

Men were urged to throw off their macho exteriors and get in touch with their softer sides. Sensitive male film idols such as Robert Redford, Paul Newman, Jon Voight, and Dustin Hoffman got the lion's share of lead movie roles. In music James Taylor provided a soothing counterpoint to the machismo of Led Zeppelin's Robert Plant.

Homosexuals also demanded increased freedom and began living openly together. Even straight people experimented with members of their own sex. A new "gay chic" emerged and gender-bending stars such as David Bowie and Elton John taunted the public with "Is he or isn't he?"

THE SILVER SCREEN

At the movies *Love Story*, about a doomed love affair between two idealistic young people, struck a chord with the public. *Harold and Maude*, *Last Tango in Paris*, and *The Great White Hope* featured partnerships that defied convention.

A more open-minded attitude about sex emerged. The movie *The Boys in the Band* created a stir when it explored relationships within the homosexual community and *Le Souffle au Coeur* by Louis Malle caused its own scandal by depicting an incestuous moment between a mother and son.

Films also became more sexually explicit. Couples began watching pornographic movies such as *Deep Throat* and *Behind the Green Door* together, hoping to improve their lovemaking techniques.

Divorce rates surged and marriages declined as the decade wore on. Theaters featured films—*Up the Sandbox*, *The Stepford Wives*, and *Diary of a Mad Housewife*—about frustrated married women. *An Unmarried Woman* explored divorce from the female standpoint, while *Starting Over* showed the man's perspective. *Kramer vs. Kramer* dared ask if women are naturally better parents than men.

BETWEEN THE PAGES

The literary set also dealt with changing sexual values. Spicy novels *Once Is Not Enough* and *The Lonely Lady* flew off the shelves, and how-to books *The Joy of Sex* and *Everything You Wanted to Know About Sex but Were Afraid to Ask* did brisk business. E.M. Forster's *Maurice*, published after his death, explored homosexual love, and prolific British erotic author Jackie Collins wrote *The Bitch*, which would be made into a film with Jackie's sister Joan Collins as the star.

◀◀ John Travolta stars in
Saturday Night Fever

◀ Women campaign for
equal rights

▼ Farrah Fawcett's appearance in
Charlie's Angels elevates her to
sex symbol status

425

PEOPLE

The decade also produced some interesting couples. Among the pairings that raised eyebrows were entertainer Dinah Shore and actor Burt Reynolds, who was 19 years her junior, Beatle John Lennon and artist Yoko Ono, and Canadian Prime Minister Pierre Trudeau and his younger hip wife Margaret. Diana Spencer met Prince Charles for the first time—he described her as "very jolly."

The 1970s were also notable for romantic pairings in the music industry. Several couples—Sonny and Cher, Captain and Tennille, Paul and Linda McCartney, John and Yoko, and Ike and Tina Turner—hit the charts together.

Couples also broke up. Elvis and Priscilla Presley parted ways and Elizabeth Taylor and Richard Burton divorced for the second time.

Faye Dunaway's sleek glamour and Raquel Welch's stunning proportions captivated the men. Women sighed over John Travolta's dance moves, Sylvester Stallone's rugged looks, and Warren Beatty's roguish behavior.

Mick Jagger was the big-lipped, long haired, leotard-wearing lead singer of the Rolling Stones, oozing raw sex appeal. This was the decade he actually married one of his exploits, Bianca de Macias, who also bore him a child.

While many new sex symbols arrived on the scene, an enduring one left. Elvis Presley, the King of Rock and Roll, died on August 16, 1977 after years of prescription drug abuse had taken a toll on his body.

- ⊛ **GAY & LESBIAN RIGHTS**
- ⊛ **JIM MORRISON**
- ⊛ **WOMEN IN LOVE**
- ⊛ **DIARY OF A MAD HOUSEWIFE**
- ⊛ **MASTERS AND JOHNSON**
- ⊛ **LOVE STORY**
- ⊛ **THE JACKSON 5**

Sex Idol

EVENTS

1970 was an important year for women, equal rights, and romance and sex. In Britain, the Employment Secretary Barbara Castle reassured women that the bill proposing equal pay for men and women would not compromise a woman's maternity rights or cost her a job.

In the US, California became the first state to pass a no-fault divorce law, bringing divorce out of the closet. A new sense of sexual pride was born on the east coast, when thousands marched through New York City, demanding the repeal of laws that made homosexual acts between consenting adults illegal. New York enacted the most liberal abortion law yet, and the US Justice Department joined the fight against outdated mores, filing the first sexual discrimination lawsuit to challenge the practice of hiring based on gender.

Not everything in 1970 was about social issues, though. Celebrity marriages abounded. Joy Philbin agreed to be Regis' better half; Tipper and Al Gore wed; and musicians Barry Gibb, David Bowie, and Jim Morrison tied the knot too.

POP CULTURE

In the movie theaters viewers wept at *Love Story* and laughed at *Diary of a Mad Housewife*, a satire about a bored housewife and her egotistical husband. Another big hit was *The Great White Hope*, the story of the first African-American heavyweight contender

and the racial prejudice over his relationship with a white woman. In Britain Andy Warhol's film *Flesh* was seized by police on the grounds that it was obscene.

DJs spun The Jackson 5's "I'll Be There," The Partridge Family's "I Think I Love You," The Carpenters' "We've Only Just Begun," and Paul McCartney's first hit without the Beatles, "Maybe I'm Amazed."

Bestseller lists often express the interests of the public and 1970 was no exception. Three of the biggest books were *Human Sexual Inadequacy* by Masters and Johnson, *Everything You Always Wanted to Know About Sex but Were Afraid to Ask* by David Reuben, and *The Sensuous Woman* by "J"—the first how-to book with instructions on heightening sexual pleasure.

RYAN O'NEAL

Sexy leading man Ryan O'Neal lit up the screen with his sandy hair and boyish good looks opposite Ali MacGraw in 1970's smash hit, *Love Story*. He was nominated for an Oscar for his performance as Oliver Barrett IV, a Harvard law student and hockey jock who fell madly in love with a Radcliffe girl named Jennifer Cavilerri.

Although his stardom seemed set to take off in 1970, O'Neal's career sputtered before he could get out of the gate. He is now better known as the long-time partner of seventies TV bombshell Farrah Fawcett, with whom he lived until 1997.

SEE ALSO
▶ PAUL NEWMAN & JOANNE WOODWARD *Page 433*

1970 CAPRICORN
From December 22, 1969, 0:44 through January 20, 1970, 11:23 (December 1970 Capricorns, see 1971 Capricorn)

The Irresistible Charmer

The 1970 Capricorn has powers of persuasion that are impossible to resist. You know just what to say to catch someone's attention and win them over, and you enjoy pitting yourself against educated authority figures. No matter how sophisticated or experienced a person is, they just can't help but say yes to your requests. That's why you're often granted special favors that provide access to restricted people, places, and things. This is a favorable talent for romancing, for what better way to impress your date than getting an audience with royalty or rock stars?

Despite your success in the love department, you are very selective about whom you date. You want a mature, accomplished partner who is eager to build a life together. Casual affairs leave you cold, because they don't give you an opportunity to grow or expand. For you, sex and love go hand-in-hand. Once you do set your sights on someone, though, you will do anything and everything in your power to win them over.

You're not easily seduced, but here are some tips others can use to grab the 1970 Capricorn's attention—and heart. Your sign greatly appreciates classic taste and those who wear beautiful, tailored clothing. While suitors might find you aloof initially, that's only because you want to see if the other is willing to go the distance romantically. You like it when admirers are persistent in their attentions. Above all, you won't tolerate tardiness, even if it's just a casual date.

1970 male Goats are attracted to refined, sophisticated women with an earthy sexuality. You love it when women add feminine touches to a traditional look. The sight of a woman wearing seamed stockings with a business suit drives you wild. You also need a partner who is very affectionate behind closed doors. Public displays of affection make you uncomfortable, but you love to be petted and kissed in private.

1970 Capricorn females long for a man who is sensitive, artistic, and gentle. Big, hulking he-men leave you cold. Ultimately, you want a lover who anticipates your needs and encourages your own creativity.

GERMAINE GREER
Australian Feminist
Sun in Aquarius

1970 AQUARIUS
From January 20, 11:24 through February 19, 1:41

The Optimistic Suitor

Friendly, outgoing, and upbeat, the 1970 Aquarius is a popular figure indeed. You meet and make friends wherever you go, thanks to your effervescent attitude. Being in your company is like drinking champagne—your bubbly conversation makes people feel almost positively giddy. You'll never lack for admirers, and it's always easy for you to find a date, even late on Saturday night! In fact, you like the dating scene so much, it may be hard for you to settle down. There are so many interesting fish in the sea, and you're determined to meet as many of them as possible.

Romance is a source of amusement for you—it makes life fun and exciting. Love is quite a different story, though. When you do decide to devote your life to one partner, it's with the desire to build something that will last a lifetime.

The best way to catch the 1970 Aquarius's attention is to ask what they're reading. They're sure to respond with energy and enthusiasm—this sign loves to exchange information and explore new ideas. Be up on the latest trends, and know what cultural events are going on around town. If there's anything the 1970 Aquarius loves, it's taking in the latest show, exhibit, or concert. If you're totally stumped for ideas, ask them for directions to a nearby spot. There's a good chance this gentle humanitarian won't just tell you how to get to your destination—they'll take you there, chatting all the while.

Male Water-bearers born in 1970 like a wide variety of women. Ultimately, your ideal partner is creative, adventurous, and smart. You want a lover who is willing to try anything once, just for the sake of an experiment. It's a good idea to pair up with somebody who likes to tease and titillate. This never fails to work up your appetite for love.

Female 1970 Aquarians like men who are bold, aggressive, and daring. You want to be the only woman in your man's life, and disdain guys who are constantly ogling other ladies. You're enormously attracted to rugged, outdoorsy types. Occasionally, you'll be drawn to a sensitive artist, but only if he's extremely masculine to boot.

JEAN-CLAUDE BRIALY
French Actor
Sun and Venus in Aries

1970 PISCES
From February 19, 1:42 through March 21, 0:55

The Stubborn Sentimentalist

If you hear someone quietly sobbing in the back of the movie theater, it's probably the 1970 Pisces. It doesn't matter if you're watching *Gone with the Wind* or *Rambo*. You always find something touchingly beautiful in a story. That's because you view life as a fairy tale, a magical journey with a moral thrust. Movies help you to affirm this belief, which is why you have such exalted expectations of relationships. If your partnership doesn't resemble some Hollywood ideal, you suspect there's something wrong.

Fortunately, you have no trouble attracting hopeless romantics like yourself. That's because you're extremely psychic, and can sense when somebody shares your values. Occasionally, you get drawn to dark, desperate types who need to be rescued, but that gets boring after a while. Invariably, you resume your search for a Prince or Princess Charming who won't drag you down to the depths of despair.

If somebody wants to attract your attention, they should note your resemblance to a glamorous movie star. As far as you're concerned, that's the highest compliment you could ever receive. Alternately, they could express an interest in one of your many pets, or invite you to an animal rights fund-raiser. Discussing esoteric subjects like astrology, ESP, and telekinesis are also good ways to capture your interest.

Male Fish born in 1970 are attracted to two kinds of women. The first is a sensitive, artistic type who is quite mysterious and elusive. The second is a feisty, outgoing woman who loves a challenge. Either one of these women would suit you well, but hopefully, your partner would be both intuitive and tough. Diana, the beautiful goddess of the hunt, is your romantic ideal.

The 1970 female Pisces wants a protective, affectionate man. Your ideal partner will have a fine appreciation for the arts, but still enjoy athletic activities that keep him in shape. Above all, he should be a humanitarian. You can't abide crass, selfish types who only think of themselves. You want a partner who loves all creatures, great and small, so long as you're at the top of his list!

1970 ARIES
From March 21, 0:56 through April 20, 12:14

The Randy Detective

As a 1970 Aries, you want a relationship to exude elements of mystery and fascination. It's important for you to have a partner who keeps you guessing. You're not interested in a romance that makes you feel safe and secure—you'd rather have a mate who challenges you and reminds you that every day is a new adventure. It helps if your partnership also has an underlying spiritual component. That's because you view love as something sacred.

An active person, you've got a healthy sexual appetite and need a mate who can satisfy your physical needs as well as match your stamina in the bedroom. A steady relationship allows you to explore your sexual horizons in a safe context. However, you're more interested in unmasking your partner's sexual self than adding notches to your bedpost. Acting out sexy movie scenarios may be a favorite ways to melt your lover's reserve.

If somebody wants to attract your attention, they can do it in one of two ways. The first way is to initiate a provocative conversation with you. You like to be both stimulated and titillated. Nothing appeals to a 1970 Aries like a lively debate. Another approach is to tell you a sexy joke. You love to laugh, and appreciate a suitor who has an earthy sense of humor. Anybody with an alluring laugh is sure to win favor with you, too.

Male Rams born in 1970 like women who are vibrant, athletic and a little on the argumentative side. You're also drawn to females who are emotionally centered and physically sensual. Above all, you want a partner who is not afraid to take risks and likes excitement. You can't tolerate a mate who needs routine and wants to do the same thing night after night.

If you're a female 1970 Aries, you want a man who is physically demonstrative. You have no desire to warm up a cold fish. Men who are terrific conversationalists also turn you on. As far as you're concerned, mental and physical stimulation go hand-in-hand. One thing you can't stand is a whiner. Guys who endlessly complain make your blood boil. You prefer a man who rolls with the punches and lands on his feet.

1970 TAURUS

From April 20, 12:15 through May 21, 11:36

The Tasteful Romantic

The 1970 Taurus longs for a secure, stable, and sensual relationship above everything else. You're more than willing to wait for the love of your life to walk through the door, but until he or she does, you're apt to be a little lonely. That's because you consider love to be the absolute ultimate experience. Without romance, your life could be compared to a flower without its scent—beautiful to behold, but lacking in something essential.

Fortunately, it's not hard for a charming person like you to attract interested suitors. Chances are you've got a rich, melodious voice that puts a magic spell on practically everyone you meet. Nevertheless, when you do meet the right person, you take things nice and slow. As far as you're concerned, courtship is one of the most exciting phases of a relationship, and you aim to enjoy every precious second of it.

If somebody wants to seduce you, they've got their homework cut out for them. That's because you have subtle, refined tastes that can only be detected by paying close attention to your movements, patterns, and behavior. A person who presents you with your signature cologne, favorite plant, or preferred flavor of ice cream stands a good chance of becoming your lover. It's not the gift that's important to you—it's the thought that they had to put behind it.

A male Taurus born in 1970 is looking for a woman who is sexy in an understated way. Feminine touches like seamed stockings, musky perfume, or silk undergarments really get your motor running. You're not a big fan of stick-thin models—you'd rather have a girl who has a bit of meat on her bones. Witty conversationalists also bring out the best in you.

A female Taurus who was born in 1970 prefers a guy who is familiar with the game of love and knows how to flirt. The thrill of the chase is very important to you. If a man keeps you guessing and makes you feel slightly off-balance, that's a good sign. Above all, your mate must be smart. You're more interested in a man's brain than his body, although a nice physique certainly wouldn't hurt his chances with you!

TAURUS ZODIAC SIGN
YOUR LOVE PLANETS

YOUR ROMANTIC SIDE   p. 696
- ▶ **VENUS IN TAURUS**
  Born Apr. 20, 12:15 - Apr. 27, 20:32
- ▶ **VENUS IN GEMINI**
  Born Apr. 27, 20:33 - May 21, 11:36

YOUR SEX DRIVE   p. 722
- ▶ **MARS IN TAURUS**
  Born Apr. 20, 12:15 - May 21, 11:36

YOUR CELEBRITY TWINS   p. 760
  Find out the astrological similarities you have with famous people.

YOUR COMPATIBILITY   p. 780
  Compare planets to find out how compatible you are in a relationship.

YOUR RELATIONSHIP KARMA   p. 824
- ▶ **SATURN IN TAURUS**
  Born Apr. 20, 12:15 - May 21, 11:36

DOMINIQUE SANDA
French Actress
Venus in Taurus

429

1970 GEMINI

From May 21, 11:37 through June 21, 19:42

The Smart Sweetheart

Smart but shy, brash but nurturing, the 1970 Gemini is a delicious blend of opposites. Because you love to take creative risks, you yearn for home life that provides plenty of stability and security. And that's exactly where your romantic partner comes in. You need a lover who is willing to accept your varied interests, even if such interests separate you and your loved one every once and a while. Actually, there are certain advantages to spending a little time away from your loved one—it makes the reunions that much sweeter!

In love, you tend to be the aggressor in a relationship. As you have little patience waiting around for somebody else to make the first move, you're the one who usually takes the initiative. However, if you do find a suitor who is even more forward than you, it makes your pulse race. Nothing excites you more than a person who knows what they want and isn't afraid to go after it.

One of the best ways to win your affection is to shower you with a bit of pampering. You're more than capable of doing it yourself, but you enjoy being fussed over. It makes you feel special, and you are! Anybody interested in you would be wise to bring chicken soup when you're sick, have your favorite snack on hand at all times, or give you a massage in just the right spot! These tender little gestures have a way of winning your heart.

If you are a male 1970 Gemini, your tastes run to full-figured women who know how to cook. Basically, you're looking for a partner who is alternately sexy and nurturing, depending on your mood. She should be fairly intuitive, too, so that she can anticipate your needs. It gets too confusing when you're being seduced when you want to be babied, or vice-versa!

Female Twins who were born in 1970 want a big, protective man to lean on. Although you're quite adept at standing up for yourself, your heart simply melts when you see a man fighting for your honor. You also like a guy who treats you like a lady. If he helps you with your coat, opens the door for you, and lights your cigarette, there's hope for you as a romantic couple.

GEMINI ZODIAC SIGN
YOUR LOVE PLANETS

YOUR ROMANTIC SIDE   p. 696
- ▶ **VENUS IN GEMINI**
  Born May 21, 11:37 - May 22, 14:18
- ▶ **VENUS IN CANCER**
  Born May 22, 14:19 - June 16, 17:48
- ▶ **VENUS IN LEO**
  Born June 16, 17:49 - June 21, 19:42

YOUR SEX DRIVE   p. 722
- ▶ **MARS IN GEMINI**
  Born May 21, 11:37 - June 02, 6:49
- ▶ **MARS IN CANCER**
  Born June 02, 6:50 - June 21, 19:42

YOUR CELEBRITY TWINS   p. 760
  Find out the astrological similarities you have with famous people.

YOUR COMPATIBILITY   p. 780
  Compare planets to find out how compatible you are in a relationship.

YOUR RELATIONSHIP KARMA   p. 824
- ▶ **SATURN IN TAURUS**
  Born May 21, 11:37 - June 21, 19:42

FERNANDO REY
Spanish Actor
Mars in Leo

1970 CANCER
From June 21, 19:43 through July 23, 6:36

The Unapologetic Sensualist

Fine wine, gourmet food, and beautiful surroundings aren't luxuries for the 1970 Cancer—they're necessities! And your highly developed tastes extend to your romantic sensibilities. You're looking for a partner who looks like they've emerged straight from the pages of a fairy tale. Long, flowing locks and dreamy eyes are definite turn-ons for you, because such attributes help sustain the illusion that you're living out a romantic fantasy. Is it any wonder you love those old black-and-white movies in which everybody is dressed in fabulous costumes?

You can be a little shy about expressing your interest, preferring the other person to approach you first. If you are compelled to make the first move, it's likely to be pulled off in an amusing context. That's because you often use laughter as a means to protect yourself from rejection. Fortunately, however, you're a very charming character and it isn't too hard for you to attract suitors.

If someone wants to capture your heart, they should do it in grand style. Inviting you to the opera, ballet, or museum are all good bets, as you have a high appreciation for the arts. It's also a good idea to take you to any place that requires fancy attire—you adore getting dressed up! An elegant picnic with gourmet food is equally a good way to win your affection.

Male Crabs who were born in 1970 like women who are magnetic but tasteful. There's something very desirable about an immaculately dressed woman who appears to have total control at all times. Such a female poses an exciting challenge, because you'd like to make her lose that composure in the bedroom.

Female 1970 Cancers gravitate toward cuddly, protective men with warm hearts. It's also important for you to have a mate who knows how to spend money. Although you aren't a spendthrift, you do enjoy savoring the finer things in life. You'd rather have your mate save for a month to take you to a five-star restaurant than to bring you to some local fast food joint. In the bedroom, you need a mate who likes taking his time. As far as you're concerned, sex should be savored.

1970 LEO
From July 23, 6:37 through August 23, 13:33

The Dignified Swan

Suave, sophisticated, and sexy, the 1970 Leo can be a little intimidating! That's because you're very discriminating. Only the most confident lovers will make overtures toward you. That's truly a shame, because you do have an affinity for quiet types. If you're going to find your soul mate, you'd better make the first move. This probably suits you anyway, because you like to have the upper hand in relationships. Therefore, it's a good idea for you to seek a partner who welcomes your authoritative, protective influence.

Although many people might not know this, you have a strong spiritual side. You only show this facet of your personality to your closest friends and relatives. Finding someone who shares your reverent attitude is very important, because it's hard for you to relate to people who only view life from its material aspects. While you enjoy creature comforts just as much as the next person, they're utterly meaningless for you without a spiritual foundation.

Anybody wanting to seduce you should give you their full attention. Having a captive audience makes you feel warm, appreciated and loved. You're also not averse to being taken to expensive restaurants. Although you probably make a respectable income, it feels good when somebody else picks up the check for a change. Even if your suitor doesn't make a lot of money, they can always impress you with a fresh bouquet of flowers.

Male Lions who were born in 1970 want a woman they can show off. Your ideal mate will dress in high style and have a magnetic personality to match your own. Social graces are also important to you. Women with an air of propriety always manage to win your admiration.

The man best suited to a female Leo born in 1970 is passionate and adoring. You want to feel loved at all times, and delight in a partner who lavishes you with hugs and kisses. It doesn't hurt if he treats you like a queen, either. Let's face it, you love to be pampered! An occasional display of jealousy makes your pulse pound with joy. You like a man who is a little possessive. It makes you feel worthy and valued.

1970 VIRGO

From August 23, 13:34 through September 23, 10:58

The Long-term Lover

Hard working, diligent and determined, romance may seem like the last thing on the 1970 Virgo's mind. However, appearances can be deceiving. The fact is, you're an incredibly romantic person—it's just that you don't wear your heart on your sleeve. It takes you a long time to develop an attraction towards someone, but when you do, it's for keeps. As far as you're concerned, relationships are meant to last a lifetime. When you find somebody you want to spend your life with, you'll do anything to win their affection.

Emotionally, you are quite reserved. You prefer to show your love through actions, not words. This can be somewhat frustrating for your lover, so it's wise to get into the habit of saying "I love you," even if it goes against your nature. Hearing those three magic words will make a tremendous difference to your relationship. Writing love letters and poems to your beloved can also uplift and sustain your bond.

If somebody wants to seduce you, they should compliment you on your good taste. You pride yourself on your classic sensibilities, and feel a strong bond with folks who are able to recognize them. You also feel flattered when people ask you for help, because it allows you to show off your organizational abilities in a modest way. Appealing to the 1970 Virgo's desire to serve is a great strategy.

The 1970 male Virgo wants a woman whose passionate heart is masked by an elegant veneer. You're very attracted to women who wear sexy black underwear beneath feminine frills. Your ideal partner should be quite learned in at least one subject, as you're quite brainy yourself. Ultimately, you want your partner to stimulate both your mind and your body.

Women who were born in 1970 under the sign of Virgo want a vibrant, vital man. You want a partner who is going to add a dash of real dynamism to your life, without totally disrupting it. You're perfectly willing to drop everything and jet off for a romantic weekend in Paris, provided your mate has a stable source of income. Guys with athletic bodies also appeal to you, although you'd never admit this to your friends!

VIRGO ZODIAC SIGN
YOUR LOVE PLANETS

YOUR ROMANTIC SIDE   p. 696
- ► **VENUS IN LIBRA**
  Born Aug. 23, 13:34 - Sept. 07, 1:53
- ► **VENUS IN SCORPIO**
  Born Sept. 07, 1:54 - Sept. 23, 10:58

YOUR SEX DRIVE   p. 722
- ► **MARS IN LEO**
  Born Aug. 23, 13:34 - Sept. 03, 4:56
- ► **MARS IN VIRGO**
  Born Sept. 03, 4:57 - Sept. 23, 10:58

YOUR CELEBRITY TWINS   p. 760
Find out the astrological similarities you have with famous people.

YOUR COMPATIBILITY   p. 780
Compare planets to find out how compatible you are in a relationship.

YOUR RELATIONSHIP KARMA   p. 824
- ► **SATURN IN TAURUS**
  Born Aug. 23, 13:34 - Sept. 23, 10:58

431

1970 LIBRA

From September 23, 10:59 through October 23, 20:03

The Eccentric Romantic

The 1970 Libra is anything but conventional. Although you've been blessed with your sign's good taste and artistic abilities, you can manifest them in unusual ways. That's why you attract so many visionaries—they're drawn to your inventive sensibilities. Maybe that's why your relationships are a little unusual, too. You need the freedom in a relationship to explore your sudden whims. Otherwise, you feel restricted and claustrophobic.

This doesn't mean you can't have a rewarding partnership that lasts a lifetime. Rather, it means that you need a partner who isn't threatened by your independent spirit. A long-distance relationship can work very well for you, because it allows you to enjoy the constant companionship of a devoted lover without being tied to their side. You also might wind up with somebody who is much older or younger than you, or who appears to be your complete opposite. The more unusual the pairing, the happier you will be! You know you've met the perfect partner when people stop to stare at you.

If somebody wants to attract your attention, they should invite you to some far-out museum exhibit or concert. It doesn't matter if the work on display is good or not, so long as it provides plenty of food for thought. Suitors should also remember that you love things of beauty, so presenting you with a lovely but unusual painting, sculpture, or flower is a good move.

The 1970 male Libra needs a woman with a healthy sexual appetite. You're very attuned to the pleasures of the flesh, and want a partner who is willing to explore these temptations. Brunettes tend to turn your head, as you are drawn to their dusky mystery. You don't mind if your partner gets bossy with you—in fact, it kind of turns you on!

A female Libra who was born in 1970 wants a guy who knows how to dress. As far as you're concerned, sexual attraction should be a two-way street. You spend plenty of time fixing yourself up, so why shouldn't your suitor? A man with a faint dash of expensive cologne can drive you wild with desire, especially if he is wearing a silk shirt and designer shoes.

KAREN CARPENTER
American Singer
Mars in Libra

LIBRA ZODIAC SIGN
YOUR LOVE PLANETS

YOUR ROMANTIC SIDE   p. 696
- ► **VENUS IN SCORPIO**
  Born Sept. 23, 10:59 - Oct. 23, 20:03

YOUR SEX DRIVE   p. 722
- ► **MARS IN VIRGO**
  Born Sept. 23, 10:59 - Oct. 20, 10:56
- ► **MARS IN LIBRA**
  Born Oct. 20, 10:57 - Oct. 23, 20:03

YOUR CELEBRITY TWINS   p. 760
Find out the astrological similarities you have with famous people.

YOUR COMPATIBILITY   p. 780
Compare planets to find out how compatible you are in a relationship.

YOUR RELATIONSHIP KARMA   p. 824
- ► **SATURN IN TAURUS**
  Born Sept. 23, 10:59 - Oct. 23, 20:03

JAMES EARL JONES
American Actor
Venus in Sagittarius

1970 SCORPIO
From October 23, 20:04 through November 22, 17:24

♏ *The Passionate Idealist*

Ardent and principled, you're likely to find the 1970 Scorpio at a protest rally or voting drive. Born with a divine sense of purpose, you want to make good use of your valuable time on this planet. You're absolutely determined to transform the world, and in the process, yourself. As far as you're concerned, romance is but a small part of this exciting ride called life, albeit a thrilling one.

Without a doubt, your idealism extends to love. You want a partner you can not only respect, but worship. So long as you share the same values with your lover, it's easy to overlook their faults. Occasionally you use love as a means to shield yourself from the harsh realities of life. Sometimes you get so bogged down with social causes that you need a private haven from the world. Love can provide you with such a haven.

If someone wants to get your attention, they should bring up a controversial subject like religion or politics. You're eager to discuss such topics at length, and admire people who share your concern about the state of the world. You also like folks who ask psychologically probing questions, although you may not answer them right away. That's because you don't like revealing your secret self to others. Still, you're stimulated by people who express interest in getting to know this side of you.

Male Scorpios born in 1970 want a woman who is sexy, mysterious, and elusive. You love the thrill of the chase. The more a woman eludes your advances, the more interested you become. You're one man who isn't afraid of powerful women. In fact, you're aroused by them. The higher the social position a woman holds, the better it is for the male 1970 Scorpio.

1970 female Scorpios want a man who treats her like an equal. You're really turned off by power plays, and absolutely detest men who view women as inferior species. You know you've met someone special when a man asks you for advice, inquires after your opinions, and listens to your views on everything from science to sports to entertainment. Ideally, you want a brainy guy who is turned on by your intellectual strengths.

1970 SAGITTARIUS
From November 22, 17:25 through December 22, 6:35

♐ *The Sexy Mystic*

Love is a divine mystery to the 1970 Sagittarius. However, you have no intention of solving this mystery—you're content to enjoy love on its own terms. You're never happier than when you are in the midst of a heady love affair, and often have a faraway expression when thinking about the object of your affection. It's easy for you to fall in and out of love, and your friends get a great deal of amusement when you declare you've found "the one" for the sixth time in a year. However, you are capable of tremendous devotion, provided your partner shares your sense of delight and wonderment at just being alive.

Spiritual matters play a big role in your life, and you see romantic relationship as the purest expression of spirituality. Sex isn't dirty to you. On the contrary, it's a religion! You use it as a means to merge souls, and revel in the divine sense of intimacy that making love affords. The act of looking deeply into somebody's eyes gives you a sexual thrill, because it's akin to penetrating their soul.

If someone wants to seduce you, all they have to do is mention mysticism, the occult, or the supernatural. These subjects never fail to rivet your attention. It's easy for you to have an affinity for somebody who believes that life consists of more than three dimensions. You also admire people who are well traveled, so a suitor would be wise to show you photos from their latest trip.

A male Archer who was born in 1970 wants a woman who is passionate and demonstrative. You hate having to coax affection out of your partner. You'd rather be swept off your feet the moment you walk through the door. A woman with an element of danger about her excites your sensibilities. You never want to feel as though you're on safe ground with your partner. As far as romance is concerned, you want to live on the edge!

Female Sagittarians born in 1970 are attracted to men with strong intellects. You enjoy analyzing people and places with the object of your affection. It's especially exciting to meet a man who likes to verbally antagonize you. This is your favorite form of flirting.

432

Paul Newman and Joanne Woodward

In a film career that has spanned five decades, superstar Paul Newman most commonly portrays the antihero, the twinkly-eyed, charming heel that audiences always fall in love with. His nonconformist style and his eternally adolescent horseplay have never gone out of date, nor has his enduring relationship with his wife, actress Joanne Woodward. Bucking the Hollywood norm of numerous affairs and marriages, this couple has remained together since 1958. They regularly co-star in cinematic ventures, while offscreen their joint interests include political activism, charitable foundations, and a highly profitable gourmet food company.

Newman's first big break in the acting business was in 1953 when he was assigned a leading role in the Broadway play *Picnic*. Equally significant for his future was that Joanne Woodward had also signed up for the play. The two met and soon fell in love, but unfortunately for Newman, he was already married and had three kids. The next year Newman received a contract from Warner Brothers, and when he moved out to Hollywood he left his family behind. Newman divorced in 1957, and in 1958 he married Woodward, which was also the year they co-starred in *The Long, Hot Summer*. The extraordinary match-up between Newman and Woodward is reflected in how well their planets line up. Primarily, their fundamental mutual respect and support are shown by his Sun in Aquarius aligned with her Moon in Aquarius, at the same time that her Sun in Pisces aligns with his Moon in Pisces. Just as the Moon reflects the light of the Sun, they help each other shine.

With the beneficial planets Venus and Jupiter prominently placed in his horoscope, Newman has rightfully felt that he was born under a lucky star. In the movie, *Somebody Up There Must Like Me*, his portrayal of boxing champion Rocky Graziano received rave reviews. Newman's Mars in Aries gives him the spontaneous energy and courage that come across so clearly in film. His Mars is enhanced by a trine to Neptune, the planet of glamour and empathy. By 1969 when he and Robert Redford teamed up in *Butch Cassidy and the Sundance Kid*, Newman was well-known for creating driven, independent, likeable rogues.

Even when the script called for crafting a heartless character, Newman somehow made the audience like him. A good example is in *Hud* when the great actor Melvyn Douglas tells Newman, "You're an unprincipled man, Hud." But audiences did give a damn about Hud, just as they did when Newman played *Cool Hand Luke*, the alcoholic pool shark in *The Hustler*, and the psychologically wounded husband opposite Elizabeth Taylor in *Cat on a Hot Tin Roof*. We do care about Newman—he makes these flawed characters irresistibly glamorous.

Newman's Mars is in conflict with his Capricorn planets, a combination that often finds expression in anti-authoritarian attitudes. Time after time, we see Newman fight against the system, the odds, and tradition. This astrological tension carries over into his private life, and since the 1970s Newman has fought for a variety of liberal political causes. In 1978 Newman's son Scott died from a drug overdose, a tragedy that led to the creation of the Scott Newman Foundation, which aims to prevent substance abuse through education.

Since then Paul Newman and Joanne Woodward have worked together to fund AIDS research, support various environmental causes, and start the Hole in the Wall Gang Camp for children with cancer. This Aquarius-Pisces team is breaking all kinds of traditions, and especially Hollywood's reputation for multiple love affairs and marriages. He remains an incurable romantic. While filming the 1974 disaster flick *The Towering Inferno*, he took a break with Joanne by hiring a helicopter to fly off to a dinner served on a golf course green with a string quartet playing. In telling this story, Woodward said, "Wouldn't you know, looking up, we had flown right through a rainbow."

433

▶ READ ABOUT NEWMAN'S *CAT ON A HOT TIN ROOF* CO-STAR LIZ TAYLOR ON PAGE 399

- ⭐ DIVORCE LAWS
- ⭐ TOPLESS SUNBATHING
- ⭐ CARNAL KNOWLEDGE
- ⭐ CLINT EASTWOOD
- ⭐ ANAÏS NIN
- ⭐ BEE GEES
- ⭐ MELANIE

Hot Couple

EVENTS

1971 was a year of diametrical forces. The divorce laws and sexual values continued to loosen in some ways, but became more conservative in others. In Britain the Divorce Reform Act came into being, allowing legal separation on the grounds of "irretrievable breakdown of marriage." In the US, criminal laws in Idaho, Colorado, and Oregon were overhauled to include legalizing all private sexual acts between freely consenting adults, and the Defense Department removed the homosexual tendencies question from the medical-history form completed by draftees.

Meanwhile police on the French Riviera ordered hundreds of female sunbathers to put their bikini tops back on or face arrest, and in a crash program to drive sin out of New York's Greenwich Village and Times Square, authorities launched a full-scale war against prostitutes and sex shows with police raids resulting in jail terms, rather than the usual fines, for the first time.

POP CULTURE

Movies centered around relationships and sex. *Carnal Knowledge* chronicled the love lives of two college roommates. *The Summer of '42* followed a teen's crush on an older woman. *Klute* was a character study of the hidden sides of a prostitute's lifestyle. And Clint Eastwood's *Play Misty for Me* was a classic study of obsessive love.

Bookstores featured volumes catering to the romantic and sexual interests of their readers. Harold Robbins debuted *The Betsy*, a steamy account of a wealthy family in the auto manufacturing industry. *Any Woman Can! Love and Sexual Fulfillment for the Single, Widowed, Divorced … and Married*, by David Reuben, M.D., provided another sexual instruction manual for women. The 20th century's premier erotic writer Anaïs Nin released the fourth installment of her work *The Diary of Anaïs Nin: Volume IV, 1944-1947*. And *Maurice* by E. M. Forster, published posthumously, was about the platonic love affair between two gay Cambridge undergraduates.

Love songs that are still popular today abounded. The Bee Gees' "How Can You Mend a Broken Heart," Rod Stewart's "Maggie May," and Carole King's "It's Too Late" dominated the charts. On the lighter side, "Joy to the World" by Three Dog Night and "Brand New Key" by Melanie had people dancing and singing.

MICK JAGGER & BIANCA DE MACIAS

On May 12, 1971, rocker Mick Jagger married Nicaraguan socialite, model, and actress Bianca de Macias, on the Côte d'Azur in France. She was pregnant when they wed and their daughter, Jade, was born five months later. Prior to meeting Bianca, Jagger's torrid relationship with singer Marianne Faithfull was followed immediately by yet another affair that resulted in his first child, with actress Marsha Hunt.

Jagger was a notorious womanizer, and it was no different during his marriage to Bianca. She tolerated it for a time, but when his liaison with young Texas model Jerry Hall started in 1978, she filed for divorce.

SEE ALSO
▶ SWINGING LONDON *Page 383*

434

1971 CAPRICORN

From December 22, 6:36, 1970 through January 20, 1971, 17:12
(December 1971 Capricorns, see 1972 Capricorn)

The Pack Leader

Gregarious, outgoing, and tons of fun, the 1971 Capricorn is one of the most social signs around. Friendships are among your most important relationships, and it would be practically impossible for you to take on a lover who doesn't get along with your chums. Actually, there's a good chance that your life partner will start out as one of your best buddies. You're the kind of person who needs to like somebody before you fall in love. Once you've made a commitment, you'll continue to look on your beloved as a cherished friend.

Although you're too practical to be called romantic, you do harbor deep passions for the object of your affection. Public displays of affection are not your style. You'd rather express your devotion in private. Once you have your beloved alone, however, you don't hesitate to shower them with passionate embraces and heated kisses. You're a deeply sensual person who likes to linger over lovemaking. You prefer to work up slowly to the first sexual encounter. The longer the courtship phase of your relationship lasts, the happier you are. Nobody could accuse you of being a fast mover!

If somebody wants to attract your attention, they should express interest in humanitarian issues. You're committed to making the world a better place, so anyone who shares this commitment could be a wonderful match for you. Your suitor should enjoy going out in big groups, because you love to have your pals around at all times. Ultimately, this person should focus first on being a loyal friend to you.

Then, when a romance develops, your relationship will be stronger than ever. As a male Capricorn born in 1971, you are strongly attracted to friendly, outgoing women who are ready for adventure. Your ideal partner will pride herself on being "just one of the boys." You can't resist a prankster! Especially one who is a dynamo in the bedroom.

Female Goats born in 1971 are attracted to strong, powerful men. You just love those take-control types, and welcome putting problems into their capable hands. The man you love should have a strong sex drive to match your own.

CAPRICORN ZODIAC SIGN
YOUR LOVE PLANETS

YOUR ROMANTIC SIDE p. 696
▶ **VENUS IN SCORPIO**
Born Dec. 22, 1970 6:36 - Jan. 07, 1971 0:59
▶ **VENUS IN SAGITTARIUS**
Born Jan. 07, 1:00 - Jan. 20, 17:12

YOUR SEX DRIVE p. 722
▶ **MARS IN SCORPIO**
Born Dec. 22, 1970 6:36 - Jan. 20, 1971 17:12

YOUR CELEBRITY TWINS p. 760
Find out the astrological similarities you have with famous people.

YOUR COMPATIBILITY p. 780
Compare planets to find out how compatible you are in a relationship.

YOUR RELATIONSHIP KARMA p. 824
▶ **SATURN IN TAURUS**
Born Dec. 22, 1970 6:36 - Jan. 20, 1971 17:12

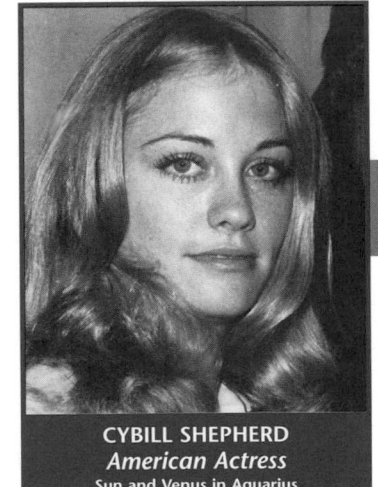

CYBILL SHEPHERD
American Actress
Sun and Venus in Aquarius

435

1971 AQUARIUS

From January 20, 17:13 through February 19, 7:26

The Self-conscious Suitor

The 1971 Aquarius is utterly adorable in love. You have a tendency to idealize the object of your affection, to the point perhaps of becoming afraid of expressing your admiration. As far as you're concerned, nobody is good enough for your one and only—not even you! However, once you are attracted to somebody, you usually work up your courage to ask for a date. It may take a few practice runs in front of the mirror but, eventually, your ardor will overcome your shyness.

At times you can be rather shy when it comes to romance, although you're an utter chatterbox with friends. To some extent, you expect your partner to read your mind. You're somewhat psychic yourself, so you often take your uncanny sixth sense for granted. Hopefully, you'll team up with someone who is as sensitive as you are. That way, you won't have to express your passion in words.

Anybody who wants to catch your fancy has their work cut out for them. You are drawn to individuals who set themselves apart from the crowd. Standing alone in the corner of a jam-packed party will usually do the trick. Voicing opposition to the popular opinion is also a good move. If there's anything that gets your pulse pounding, it's the sight of a cool rebel!

As a male Water Bearer who was born in 1971, you are looking for a brainy, worldly woman. Females with a highly developed sense of curiosity about other cultures are especially sexy to you. It definitely helps if she's well-traveled. You want a lover with whom you can sit up all night, talking about the meaning of life and speculating about the future. You use conversation as a prelude to lovemaking.

If you're a female 1971 Aquarius, you want a humorous, upbeat partner with whom to share your life. Any guy who can laugh at himself is sure to win favor with you. It helps if your love interest is athletic, for you cannot abide a couch potato. Finding a man who can bolster your self-confidence is essential. You possess many hidden talents. When you meet a man who both recognizes and celebrates these gifts, grab him and hold on tight. He's definitely a keeper!

AQUARIUS ZODIAC SIGN
YOUR LOVE PLANETS

YOUR ROMANTIC SIDE p. 696
▶ **VENUS IN SAGITTARIUS**
Born Jan. 20, 17:13 - Feb. 05, 14:56
▶ **VENUS IN CAPRICORN**
Born Feb. 05, 14:57 - Feb. 19, 7:26

YOUR SEX DRIVE p. 722
▶ **MARS IN SCORPIO**
Born Jan. 20, 17:13 - Jan. 23, 1:33
▶ **MARS IN SAGITTARIUS**
Born Jan. 23, 1:34 - Feb. 19, 7:26

YOUR CELEBRITY TWINS p. 760
Find out the astrological similarities you have with famous people.

YOUR COMPATIBILITY p. 780
Compare planets to find out how compatible you are in a relationship.

YOUR RELATIONSHIP KARMA p. 824
▶ **SATURN IN TAURUS**
Born Jan. 20, 17:13 - Feb. 19, 7:26

CLINT EASTWOOD
American Actor
Mars in Aries

1971 PISCES
From February 19, 7:27 through March 21, 6:37

The Starry-eyed Idealist

It's very easy to spot the 1971 Pisces in a crowd. You're the one who is always walking along with your head cocked to the side, as if listening to a friend that nobody else can see. There's a faint smile on your lips, even as you trip over cracks in the concrete and bump into fellow pedestrians. In other words, you're in a world of your own creation. It's a world where romance reigns supreme. Until you find your ideal lover, you're bound to remain in your self-created fantasy land. Why deal with real life when your imaginary one is so much nicer?

For you, love has always been a means to escape the harsh realities of life. You're looking for a partner who makes you feel sexy and lovable, even on your worst days. In exchange for their devotion, you'll overlook their every fault. You don't mind the occasional debate. In fact, you might tease your mate for the sole purpose of making up afterwards. You want love to take you from the depths of despair to the heights of joy. What's the fun of having a relationship if you always get along? You want a partnership that is spiced with plenty of pepper, even if it makes your eyes water occasionally.

Attracting your attention is fairly easy. Just quote some romantic poetry, preferably by Byron or Shelley. Piscean poets like Elizabeth Barrett Browning and Edna St. Vincent Millay also melt your heart. You're a sucker for compliments, so long as they're fanciful. For instance, you'd rather have your locks compared to a river of silk than to be told that your new hairstyle looks good.

Male Fish born in 1971 are drawn to women who are refined on the outside and free-spirited on the inside. You want a lover who is filled with surprises. A "what you see is what you get" type would leave you cold. Humble philanthropists really turn you on.

The 1971 woman Pisces wants a loving, protective man. You're a bit traditional when it comes to gender roles, and like to be cuddled and cherished by a masculine lover. It helps if your partner likes to make you laugh, as your sex drive undulates with your ever-changing moods.

1971 ARIES
From March 21, 6:38 through April 20, 17:53

The Romantic Explorer

The 1971 Aries has a positive outlook that is quite infectious. Perhaps that's why you make friends wherever you go. Like the Pied Piper, your following just grows and grows. And although you like lots of company, you're ultimately looking for one special relationship to make your life complete. You're one of those people who may be immune to romance for years. Then, suddenly you're at a party and you lock eyes with somebody from across a crowded room. From that moment on, you're hooked.

The idea of love at first sight is quite a believable concept for you. The most important thing for you in a relationship is that inexplicable chemistry that exists between lovers. If you don't feel an explosive bang from the moment you meet a person, you sense that a romantic relationship is not in the cards. Alternately, you could be platonic friends with somebody for years and years and then suddenly you're madly in love. Romance has a way of striking like lightning for the 1971 Aries.

In order for somebody to win your heart, they have to be unusual in some way. Whether it's a weird hat or an unconventional philosophy, there has to be something about your lover that is unique. A good way to grab your attention is to make some outrageous remark in public. Agitators never fail to seize your interest, and you're always looking for new ones to add to your sizable crowd of friends.

1971 male Rams want a woman with an unusual mind and a feminine body. You can't fall in love with somebody who is smart but slovenly. Alternately, it's hard for you to be attracted to a beautiful girl who doesn't have a thought in her head. It may take years and years for you to find your dream partner, but when you do, you'll do everything in your power to make her yours.

Women Ariens who were born in 1971 like the strong, silent type of man. You love a guy who keeps you guessing. The more elusive he seems, the more attracted you are. Ultimately, however, your partner should give you a measure of independence to pursue your own interests. You have no intention of living your life through somebody else.

1971 TAURUS
From April 20, 17:54 through May 21, 17:14

The Dogged Devotee

As a 1971 Taurus, you know what you want, and won't stop until you've achieved your goals. This dogged persistence is evident in your romantic style. Although you don't fall in love easily, you do fall hard. Once this happens, you'll move mountains to be with the object of your desire. Relationships are a serious business for you. You may even see them as a means of spiritual regeneration. A sensitive partner who seeks to heal your wounds with loving words and kind gestures would be an ideal match for you.

Fortunately, you're a very dynamic person and have no trouble attracting scores of admirers. You have a strong moral code that could cause you to get involved with a variety of political issues. It's very possible that you could meet your partner at a rally or protest of some kind. Your deep interest in social issues gives your personality a serious cast at times. That's why it's a good idea for you to get involved with somebody who shares your concerns, because such a partner will understand the reason for your solemn expression.

If somebody wants to become your one and only, they should show you their creative work. You have a profound admiration for artists, and may long to be more creative yourself. Anyone who recognizes and encourages your vivid imagination will win a special place in your heart. You also have a healthy sexual appetite, and enjoy the sight of a well-formed leg or a curvaceous backside. Form-fitting but classic clothing is a definite turn on for you.

Male Bulls who were born in 1971 have a wide range of tastes when it comes to women. Some of you like soft, feminine types, while others admire energetic athletes. Still others of you like earthy, Rubenesque creatures. Whatever physical type of woman you like, she must have a spiritual element to her.

The 1971 female Taurus gravitates towards two kinds of men. The first is authoritative and strong, and the second is smart and free-spirited. Whichever type you prefer, your partner should crave intimacy. You want a guy whose idea of love is merging hearts, souls, and minds with one special person.

TAURUS ZODIAC SIGN
YOUR LOVE PLANETS

YOUR ROMANTIC SIDE   p. 696
- ▶ **VENUS IN PISCES**
  Born Apr. 20, 17:54 - Apr. 23, 15:43
- ▶ **VENUS IN ARIES**
  Born Apr. 23, 15:44 - May 18, 12:47
- ▶ **VENUS IN TAURUS**
  Born May 18, 12:48 - May 21, 17:14

YOUR SEX DRIVE   p. 722
- ▶ **MARS IN CAPRICORN**
  Born Apr. 20, 17:54 - May 03, 20:56
- ▶ **MARS IN AQUARIUS**
  Born May 03, 20:57 - May 21, 17:14

YOUR CELEBRITY TWINS   p. 760
Find out the astrological similarities you have with famous people.

YOUR COMPATIBILITY   p. 780
Compare planets to find out how compatible you are in a relationship.

YOUR RELATIONSHIP KARMA   p. 824
- ▶ **SATURN IN TAURUS**
  Born Apr. 20, 17:54 - May 21, 17:14

DONALD SUTHERLAND
Canadian Actor
Venus in Gemini

437

1971 GEMINI
From May 21, 17:15 through June 22, 1:19

The Shy Sweetheart

You 1971 Geminis come in two varieties. Some of you are loners who protect your privacy like tigers. Others of you are serious souls who conduct your lives with grace and dignity. Whichever category you fit into, your attitude toward romance is the same. You view love as a means to connect with your partner on a spiritual level.

You can be quite shy at times and have difficulty mixing with a wide group of people. Dealing with folks on a one-on-one basis allows your delightful spirit to shine through. Once people get to know you, they realize that you're quite a deep person and very intuitive. That's why you gravitate toward spiritual souls who share your belief that there is more to life than the physical dimension. When you find your ideal mate, there's a good chance that you both will have a hard time separating fantasy from reality. That's just fine by you. You consider reality to be overrated, anyway.

Anybody who wants to win your heart should ask you about your dreams. Dreams are very important to you, because you feel that they

offer a tantalizing glimpse at one's psyche. A person who expresses interest in your night visions demonstrates that they want to know the real you. You also admire outgoing, adventurous people. If a friendly person invites you along on an unusual trip, you're bound to say yes.

Male Twins who were born in 1971 are looking for a domestic sort of woman who will engage their interest. You want to build a happy, welcoming home with your partner. Therefore, a woman who is a talented cook and likes to entertain a lot would be a good match for you. You also love good conversationalists, and could team up with a partner who is blessed with the gift of gab.

Women who were born in 1971 under the sign of Gemini want a man who is unique in some way. He could be a visionary artist, a passionate libertine, or a mad scientist—just as long as he thinks differently than other people. You secretly long to be the inspiration for a creative man's work. Fortunately, your optimism and enthusiasm can have a good effect on your partner's imagination.

GEMINI ZODIAC SIGN
YOUR LOVE PLANETS

YOUR ROMANTIC SIDE   p. 696
- ▶ **VENUS IN TAURUS**
  Born May 21, 17:15 - June 12, 6:57
- ▶ **VENUS IN GEMINI**
  Born June 12, 6:58 - June 22, 1:19

YOUR SEX DRIVE   p. 722
- ▶ **MARS IN AQUARIUS**
  Born May 21, 17:15 - June 22, 1:19

YOUR CELEBRITY TWINS   p. 760
Find out the astrological similarities you have with famous people.

YOUR COMPATIBILITY   p. 780
Compare planets to find out how compatible you are in a relationship.

YOUR RELATIONSHIP KARMA   p. 824
- ▶ **SATURN IN TAURUS**
  Born May 21, 17:15 - June 18, 16:10
- ▶ **SATURN IN GEMINI**
  Born June 18, 16:11 - June 22, 1:19

LEA MASSARI
Italian Actress
Venus in Cancer

438

1971 CANCER
From June 22, 1:20 through July 23, 12:14

♋ The Quirky Sentimentalist

The 1971 Cancer is an odd but adorable duck. You have a unique way of looking at things that sets you apart from the crowd. You may form passionate attachments for seemingly mundane things, like your favorite cereal or a certain pair of shoes. Fortunately, your sweet demeanor and goofy laugh are most endearing, and even your strangest preoccupations make people smile with affection. One thing is for sure—you're not like anybody else, and you like it that way!

Your attitude towards romance is, "I'm not exactly sure of what I want from love, but I'll know it when I see it." Consequently, you may spend many contented years on your own, happily buried in your work. Then, all of a sudden, you'll cross paths with somebody who seems hauntingly familiar. You won't remember exactly where you met, but you'll be compelled to find out. The connection you feel could very well be karmic. Soon, you'll be spending every spare moment with the object of your affection, delighting in their every word, movement, and gesture.

If someone wants to attract your attention,

they should make philosophical observations about silly matters, such as television comedies or pop stars. You love it when somebody attributes deep meaning to shallow matters, because it appeals to your sense of the absurd. Anybody who goes out of their way to baby you will also score big points, as you secretly loved to be coddled and pampered.

The 1971 male Crab wants a woman who combines sarcasm with sentiment. Although you love girls who like to poke fun at the system, you need a partner that also shares your deep love of tradition. A woman who is eager to form traditions with you is sure to capture your heart. You love observing anniversaries and personal milestones with the one you love, laughing at yourselves all the while.

Female Cancers who were born in 1971 like men who are unconventional and independent. You're not interested in teaming up with some cookie-cutter image of male sensuality. You're interested in how a guy thinks and what he believes. Intelligent contrarians never fail to make your pulse pound.

1971 LEO
From July 23, 12:15 through August 23, 19:14

♌ The Sensitive Sensualist

The 1971 Leo doesn't play around when it comes to romance. You're a very sensitive soul who takes tender words to heart. If someone pledges devotion to you, you expect that suitor to honor such a serious vow. It's possible that more than one lighthearted flirt has caused you heartache. You simply can't understand why someone would pelt you with compliments if they weren't entirely serious about getting into a relationship.

Although you may have experienced some disappointments in love, you wouldn't trade your romantic ideals for anything. Happily, a similarly sensitive soul should have no problem spotting you in a crowd. Often, you'll be wearing some rich, sumptuous fabric or wearing a bewitching fragrance. That's because you are a very sensual person, and delight in luxurious sights, sounds, scents, textures, and tastes.

When somebody wants to court you, they should think in terms of drama. A single, dew-covered rose tucked between the pages of your favorite book is sure to draw a delighted gasp from you. Similarly, a beautifully wrapped box

of gourmet chocolates will make a wonderful impression, as would a boxed set of CDs from your favorite recording artist. You appreciate any gift that combines luxury and forethought.

You 1971 male Lions want a woman who knows how to create a cozy atmosphere at home. It's very important for you to have a quiet retreat from the outside world. Ideally, your partner will possess talent in all the domestic arts, including cooking, cleaning, sewing, and entertaining. Make no mistake, however—you don't want a shrinking violet for a mate. You'd far prefer a lady who enjoys being seen on your arm.

Female Leos who were born in 1971 want a man who is vital, athletic, and adventurous. A guy who means what he says, and says what he means never fails to win your admiration. If a man tells you he will call the next day, he'd better do so, or you're apt to cut him loose. Men who play mind games are not for you. You need a partner who isn't afraid to say "I love you." If he's eager to back up his words with actions, that's even better.

1971 VIRGO

From August 23, 19:15 through September 23, 16:44

The Elusive Paramour

It's hard to pin down a 1971 Virgo. You're not the type of person to commit yourself to anyone or anything until you're completely sure of your heart. A "wait and see" attitude pervades everything you do. This can be quite frustrating for your admirers, who are eager to pull back the veil of mystery that exists between you and the rest of the world. You're not deliberately trying to be difficult—it's just hard for you to trust people until they've demonstrated their loyalty in some tangible way. Fortunately, your love of home and family makes you an excellent catch, and many suitors are eager to prove their worth to you.

Love for you is the foundation for a happy home. You probably want a mate who is interested in settling down and having plenty of children. Often when you date somebody you're trying to assess whether this person would be good with kids. You're perfectly willing to forego a relationship with a love interest that excites you personally but lacks the stabilizing influence that you feel is necessary in a potential parent.

Anybody seeking to win a special place in your heart should demonstrate a love of family. A person who proudly displays photos of relatives on their desk has a good chance of turning your head. The fastest way to seduce you is by inviting you over for a home-cooked meal. If your admirer's home is cozy, warm, and tasteful, your reserve will crumble and you'll ask for a second date.

Male Virgos who were born in 1971 want a partner who is patient. You don't want to be rushed into any decisions—especially marriage! Your dream girl will be ladylike and tasteful, and know how to handle a budget. Ultimately, you want a mate who yearns to settle down and create a happy, comfortable life together.

The 1971 female Virgo wants a partner who believes in the equality of the sexes. You're always impressed by men who know how to cook and clean, as well as fix cars. Guys that are intellectual also get your motor running. A heated debate is often a prelude to lovemaking for you, so it helps if your love interest is well-informed and likes to argue.

VIRGO ZODIAC SIGN
Your Love Planets

YOUR ROMANTIC SIDE   p. 696
- ▶ **VENUS IN LEO**
  Born Aug. 23, 19:15 - Aug. 24, 16:24
- ▶ **VENUS IN VIRGO**
  Born Aug. 24, 16:25 - Sept. 17, 20:24
- ▶ **VENUS IN LIBRA**
  Born Sept. 17, 20:25 - Sept. 23, 16:44

YOUR SEX DRIVE   p. 722
- ▶ **MARS IN AQUARIUS**
  Born Aug. 23, 19:15 - Sept. 23, 16:44

YOUR CELEBRITY TWINS   p. 760
Find out the astrological similarities you have with famous people.

YOUR COMPATIBILITY   p. 780
Compare planets to find out how compatible you are in a relationship.

YOUR RELATIONSHIP KARMA   p. 824
- ▶ **SATURN IN GEMINI**
  Born Aug. 23, 19:15 - Sept. 23, 16:44

JACKIE COLLINS
English Writer
Sun and Venus in Libra

1971 LIBRA
From September 23, 16:45 through October 24, 1:52

The Tempestuous Lover

It's evident that the 1971 Libra has deep emotions. You wear your heart on your sleeve all the time, especially when dealing with the opposite sex. You probably started to have crushes at a very early age, falling in and out of love regularly with various classmates. Flirtatious banter may be one of your favorite hobbies. You adore trading insults with love interests. The more you tease somebody, the better you like them. Dressing to attract attention is another means to draw somebody into your web of intrigue.

As far as you're concerned, romance should be a source of excitement, not contentment. You gravitate towards partners who have a talent for arousing your anger. A good, healthy squabble never fails to fuel your passion. Although you're quick to anger, you never stay mad for long. In fact, you usually wind up in your lover's arms shortly after a heated tiff. You love to kiss and make up!

Anyone seeking to turn your head should make a teasing remark about your distinctive appearance. That's sure to pique your interest.

Your ideal suitor will sprinkle genuine praise among sarcastic remarks. You're no masochist—it's important for you to be appreciated for your wit, intelligence, and sensitivity. If you feel that your suitor isn't treating you with the respect you deserve, you'll quickly end the union and move on to greener pastures.

1971 male Librans want a woman who can give as good as she gets. Any female who is adept at verbal sparring has an excellent chance with you. You also have a weak spot for dark, elusive types with an air of mystery. Predictable partners leave you cold. You want a woman who will constantly challenge you and excite you, both intellectually and sexually.

Women who were born in 1971 under the sign of the Scales love highly evolved men. You're seeking a guy who treats you like an equal partner and not a sex object. Of course, you love to be appreciated and admired for your allure, but what is more important is that your partner is captivated by your way of thinking. You do best with an intelligent mate who stimulates your mind.

LIBRA ZODIAC SIGN
Your Love Planets

YOUR ROMANTIC SIDE   p. 696
- ▶ **VENUS IN LIBRA**
  Born Sept. 23, 16:45 - Oct. 11, 22:42
- ▶ **VENUS IN SCORPIO**
  Born Oct. 11, 22:43 - Oct. 24, 1:52

YOUR SEX DRIVE   p. 722
- ▶ **MARS IN AQUARIUS**
  Born Sept. 23, 16:45 - Oct. 24, 1:52

YOUR CELEBRITY TWINS   p. 760
Find out the astrological similarities you have with famous people.

YOUR COMPATIBILITY   p. 780
Compare planets to find out how compatible you are in a relationship.

YOUR RELATIONSHIP KARMA   p. 824
- ▶ **SATURN IN GEMINI**
  Born Sept. 23, 16:45 - Oct. 24, 1:52

440

BJORN ANDRESEN
Swedish Actor
Venus in Sagittarius

1971 SCORPIO
From October 24, 1:53 through November 22, 23:13

♏ *The Passionate Spitfire*

Life is never boring when the 1971 Scorpio is on the scene! You're probably a person who looks at life in black-and-white terms—shades of gray don't exist for you. Consequently, you're either madly in love or have sworn off romance altogether. Your relationship status is bound to change quite frequently until you find your true love. You do believe in finding your one and only, and if you have to kiss a lot of frogs along the way, never mind—anything worthwhile requires a degree of sacrifice. At least, that's the way you think of love.

You usually don't mind it when your mate is angry at you. As far as you're concerned, anger is better than indifference. Sometimes you flirt as a means to get attention. Nothing thrills you more than to see your beloved's eyes blaze with passion. You're not above giving in to an occasional pout, especially if you think it will draw reassuring hugs and kisses.

A suitor who seeks your affection would be wise to take you seriously. If there's anything you detest, it's being patronized. Asking you for advice is always a good idea, as you pride yourself on having definite opinions. You're also attracted to folks who like to flaunt their sexuality in some way. Anybody who sports musky cologne, sheer fabrics, or a luxurious mane of hair has a good chance with you.

Men who were born in 1971 under the sign of Scorpio want a woman who is physically affectionate. You take sex very seriously, and need partner who is inventive and adventurous in the bedroom. You're also attracted to two polar opposites when it comes to types of women. One is reclusive and secretive, the other is outgoing and friendly. Whichever kind of mate you pick, though, she should have a healthy sexual appetite.

1971 female Scorpions enjoy intense, creative types. Your passions are always aroused by men who get carried away by their work. Whether your dream man is a performance artist or a poet is immaterial. The important thing is that he views life through a whimsical lens. You benefit most from a mate who makes you feel as though you're the only woman in the Universe.

1971 SAGITTARIUS
From November 22, 23:14 through December 22, 12:23

♐ *The Tongue-tied Romantic*

Friendly, funny, and fair, the 1971 Archer is in much demand. That's why it's such a puzzle that you can be so shy when it comes to love. Admirers are probably lined up around the corner to have an audience with you, but you're convinced that they'll be disappointed once they get you in an intimate setting. Actually, nothing could be farther from the truth. You are really a fabulous catch, and would be wise to work on your self-confidence a bit.

A reverent attitude towards marriage makes you very selective about your life partner. You want a mate who is adventurous but grounded. At times you can get carried away by flights of fancy, so it would help to have a partner who brings you back down to earth. You also want a secure, happy nest, but can be a bit of a spendthrift. Here is where a stable partner can help, too. Anybody who is good with a budget would be an excellent match for you, as they could help you attain your dream of having a beautiful home.

If somebody wants to turn your head, they should join a volunteer organization. You've got a very soft heart and love championing the underdog. A person who shares your humanitarian spirit would have a good chance of winning your affection. You also adore your family, and probably have one favorite relative. Your admirer would be well advised to invite this person along on a picnic or sports outing—you love going out in groups!

Male Sagittarians who were born in 1971 want a woman who is refined and hardworking. You greatly admire goal-oriented people, and seek a partner who has big dreams for herself and her family. It would also help if your mate were a bit aggressive sexually. You're quite passionate, but have a hard time making the first move. Any girl who likes to initiate lovemaking would get along swimmingly with you.

1971 female Archers like men who are sweet, idealistic, and affectionate. You long to merge souls with someone who is instinctive about your own emotional needs. At times you have difficulty expressing your true feelings, so it would help if you had a partner who is extremely intuitive.

Jane Fonda – The Sexy Revolutionary

Jane Fonda's movie career can be divided into three distinct phases, one for each of her three husbands. Her sex kitten style begins with French director Roger Vadim, and her more serious roles coincided with her partnership to political activist Tom Hayden. Her last cause-oriented phase found a sympathetic partner in media mogul Ted Turner. With Pluto, the planet of transformation, found in her seventh house of partners, each of Fonda's three husbands represented a powerful but fundamentally different influence on her life.

With her Sun and Venus in the adventurous sign of Sagittarius, Fonda found it easy to travel to Paris, the capital of New Wave filmmaking, to escape becoming just another Hollywood studio player. Among the movement's avant-garde directors was Roger Vadim, who had previously launched the careers of Brigitte Bardot and Catherine Deneuve. Beginning with the 1964 film *La Ronde*, Vadim transformed Fonda's image into a symbol for sexual freedom, hedonism, and sensual nudity.

Vadim's reputation as a Pygmalion found a willing participant with Jane Fonda, who in later years remarked, "I needed someone to teach me how to be a woman... And he taught me a lot, but it's a certain version of a woman." The two were married in 1965. Vadim's Saturn, the planet of control and authority, is right on Fonda's Venus, the love planet. He naturally shaped her into his preferred image of woman as seductress, with her wild, blond hair and risqué roles. The French press dubbed her the American Brigitte Bardot, while one appalled American critic called her "Miss Screen Nude of 1967."

The most famous film she made during this "sex kitten" phase was the 1968 sci-fi hit *Barbarella*, in which she plays a semi-clothed adventuress exploring strange new worlds and battling evil galactic forces. This movie fixed her sexy image in the public mind as she personified the free love ethic of the hippie counterculture. That same year Fonda became pregnant with her first child and witnessed the calamities of the French government. "In the streets there was revolution, and then there was my own revolution—which childbirth is," she said. "I was seeing people in the United States putting their lives on the line to try and end the war, and I realized I wanted to be there."

Fonda returned to Hollywood charged with radical activism. The first film she made after *Barbarella* was the realistic *They Shoot Horses, Don't They?* While her personal lifestyle had completely changed, the movie-going public was confused. Somehow she had transcended being a female body to begin expressing a political thesis. Roger Vadim complained that she had violated his idea of womanhood, and the two were soon divorced. "I prefer to be married to a soft and vulnerable woman rather than to an American Joan of Arc," he said.

In 1971 she sheared her golden hair for her role as a prostitute in the psychological thriller *Klute*, for which she received her first Oscar for Best Actress. In this picture her voice is strangely disembodied, reflecting the stark contrast between her naturally beautiful body and the shrillness of her radical political message. Her new nickname when she visited North Vietnam during the summer of 1972 was "Hanoi Jane." Earlier that year she met Tom Hayden, a well-known political radical. They married in January 1973, and she continued to make movies with messages, well-told stories that became box-office successes.

However, by the end of the eighties she divorced Hayden. Later she met Ted Turner and became his adoring wife. She was often photographed cheering at Atlantic Braves' games with the politically incorrect tomahawk chop. She and Turner were married from 1991 to 2000, during which time she remained a social activist, and specialized in making revisionist documentaries about the history of Native Americans. Turner provided the media outlet by duly showing them on his worldwide cable networks.

► READ MORE ABOUT JANE FONDA'S EX-HUSBAND, ROGER VADIM, ON PAGE 278

- ⊛ **SEXUAL IMPOTENCE**
- ⊛ **THE FBI**
- ⊛ **OPEN MARRIAGE**
- ⊛ **MARLON BRANDO**
- ⊛ **DEEP THROAT**
- ⊛ **ROBERTA FLACK**
- ⊛ **LEAN ON ME**

Hot Couple

EVENTS

In 1972 sexual laws and mores continued to be liberalized. The UK's Divorce Reform Act of the previous year resulted in an increase in divorce petitions. In the US, Pennsylvania passed a code legalizing premarital and extramarital sex, and Massachusetts ruled the law that prohibited the sale of contraceptives to single people unconstitutional.

All this sexual liberalization had a price attached, though. A study reported an increase in sexual impotence among young men—resulting from anxiety over the newly increased sexual freedom of women.

Other people were also concerned with the new sexual freedom. FBI Director J. Edgar Hoover demonstrated an intense interest in the sex lives of prominent Americans and set the FBI to investigating "who is sleeping with whom in Washington." And as in any decade, it's often two steps forward, one step back. Frank Zappa and the Mothers of Invention were prevented from performing in London because of the obscene content of their songs.

POP CULTURE

Sex-related books dominated bestseller lists. *Open Marriage: A New Lifestyle for Couples* by Nena and George O'Neill and *The Erotic Life of the American Wife* by N. Gittelson were very popular. Barbara Seaman's book, *Free and Female: The Sex Life of the Contemporary Woman* gave us a frank

look at the female orgasm in biological detail.

Movies got more explicit, too. *Last Tango in Paris* was the first graphically erotic story with a major star—Marlon Brando—and was banned when it came out. *Deep Throat* became one of the first pornographic films to break into mainstream America. After it was declared obscene in New York, the movie went on make $600 million and is one of the top-grossing films of all time. 1972 was also the year for *Harold and Maude*, the cult classic black comedy about a young man, obsessed with death, who falls in love with an octogenarian.

DJs played "The First Time Ever I Saw Your Face," by Roberta Flack, and "Lean On Me," by Bill Withers. Don McLean also broke onto the charts with his classic love song to the US—"American Pie."

ROBERT WAGNER & NATALIE WOOD

Their marriage in 1957 was reported as the most "glittering union of the 20th Century." But the first time around, stars Robert Wagner and Natalie Wood succumbed to the perils of Hollywood and divorced in 1962.

In ensuing years, they both married others but kept in touch. In 1971, they ran into each other in a restaurant. Suddenly the old feelings were back, as if they'd never been apart. They married for the second time aboard their yacht *Splendour* on June 16, 1972. Little did they know that their beloved boat would become the site of Wood's untimely death by drowning, in 1981.

SEE ALSO
▶ **WARREN BEATTY** *Page 497*

442

1972 CAPRICORN

From December 22, 1971, 12:24 through January 20, 1972, 22:58
(December 1972 Capricorns, see 1973 Capricorn)

♑ *The Relaxed Romantic*

You're a freedom-loving Capricorn born in 1972, and your relationship must be exhilarating. Friendship is the most essential dynamic in any relationship, and you always strive to know a person first as a friend before taking the involvement to the next level. A feeling that you're on the same wavelength is inspiring to you, and may be counted on to always draw you closer.

Personal freedom and independence are also vital to any good relationship. You don't want to feel tied down and you resent it when a partner attempts to tell you what to do. You feel that a good relationship allows each person to just go with the flow, to do what comes naturally. That way, you're each happy as individuals while also merging as a couple. You believe in commitment and yes, you want security, but you also quite wisely feel that fulfillment may mean waiting for the partner who suits you best.

To engage your interest, a prospective partner might invite you to attend a high-tech or computer show, or an outdoor event of some

sort. Cars and automobile racing may appeal to you, and even if you're just spectators, it gives you the chance to witness something exciting together while holding hands in the process. Sharing ideas is very important to you, and it's good to know that your partner always has something interesting to say. Because of this, you can envision a tie that grows, and will endure.

Male Capricorns born in 1972 like a woman who is clever and intelligent. Your gal has her own thoughts and opinions, and she loves to express them. The verve with which she does so gains her many friends and your unending interest. She has many useful skills, can probably fix your computer, and you may have met her online in a chat room.

Female goats born in 1972 expect a guy to be a self-starter. Lazy, stodgy, or slow do not describe your man! You notice that he may be too hasty, making decisions that are sometimes laughably rash, but you don't care because he's boyish, adorable, and sexy. He's also rather musical, a good dancer, and has a lucky way of wandering into the right situation at the right time.

CAPRICORN ZODIAC SIGN

YOUR LOVE PLANETS

YOUR ROMANTIC SIDE   p. 696
- ▶ **VENUS IN CAPRICORN**
  Born Dec. 22, 1971 12:24 - Dec. 23, 1971 6:31
- ▶ **VENUS IN AQUARIUS**
  Born Dec. 23, 1971 6:32 - Jan. 16, 1972 15:00
- ▶ **VENUS IN PISCES**
  Born Jan. 16, 15:01 - Jan. 20, 22:58

YOUR SEX DRIVE   p. 722
- ▶ **MARS IN PISCES**
  Born Dec. 22, 12:24 - Dec. 26, 18:03
- ▶ **MARS IN ARIES**
  Born Dec. 26, 1971 18:04 - Jan. 20, 1972 22:58

YOUR CELEBRITY TWINS   p. 760
Find out the astrological similarities you have with famous people.

YOUR COMPATIBILITY   p. 780
Compare planets to find out how compatible you are in a relationship.

YOUR RELATIONSHIP KARMA   p. 824
- ▶ **SATURN IN GEMINI**
  Born Dec. 22, 1971 12:24 - Jan. 10, 1972 3:39
- ▶ **SATURN IN TAURUS**
  Born Jan. 10, 1071 3:40 to Jan. 20, 1972 22:58

MICHAEL YORK
English Actor
Venus in Aquarius

1972 AQUARIUS

From January 20, 22:59 through February 19, 13:10

♒ *Fairy-tale Lover*

You're a sentimental Aquarius born in 1972, and your relationship must be passionate and romantic. Even though you're intelligent and communicative, you fall in love with your heart, not your head, and you need a fiery relationship to be magical rather than practical. You believe in romance and going a little off the deep end, which could mean a number of commitments before you actually find a suitable partner. Even if you must suffer a breakup, you feel that the passion you felt was worth what you had to endure after it ended.

You do believe in commitment, although what you really want is the fairy-tale, happily-ever-after type of ending that goes on to lifelong happiness. The nuts-and-bolts of romance don't interest you at all. You just want the sweet kisses, the tender sighs, and the sense that you've connected with your Prince or Princess Charming.

To engage your interest, a potential partner must be a bit dazzling. You want to feel that aura of romance and tenderness from the very moment you meet. Perhaps you're a movie buff

and if so, you mentally replay various romantic cinematic scenarios: you want to live a love story equally grand. Planned and even accidental meetings appeal to you, but it's also fun to be taken on a lark to cultural events, to buy a kiss at a charity fund-raiser, or to "relate" by crashing bumper cars at an amusement park.

Male Aquarians born in 1972 need a woman who is romantic, soft, and tender. Her eyes are misty and luminous, and in their depth you can see what's good about life. She's the sort of woman you know will always care about you making hot cocoa for you on a gloomy night, rescuing stray animals, and bringing out the best in children.

Female Aquarians born in 1972 want a guy who is speedy and exciting, a bit impatient and somewhat of a handful. You like a man who is macho. If he occasionally says inappropriate things, you don't care, because you can read what's in his heart. You like to be slightly overwhelmed, and his hastiness in pursuing you only makes the chase more exciting. He is also intelligent and has amusing things to say.

AQUARIUS ZODIAC SIGN

YOUR LOVE PLANETS

YOUR ROMANTIC SIDE   p. 696
- ▶ **VENUS IN PISCES**
  Born Jan. 20, 22:59 - Feb. 10, 10:07
- ▶ **VENUS IN ARIES**
  Born Feb. 10, 10:08 - Feb. 19, 13:10

YOUR SEX DRIVE   p. 722
- ▶ **MARS IN ARIES**
  Born Jan. 20, 22:59 - Feb. 10, 14:03
- ▶ **MARS IN TAURUS**
  Born Feb. 10, 14:04 - Feb. 19, 13:10

YOUR CELEBRITY TWINS   p. 760
Find out the astrological similarities you have with famous people.

YOUR COMPATIBILITY   p. 780
Compare planets to find out how compatible you are in a relationship.

YOUR RELATIONSHIP KARMA   p. 824
- ▶ **SATURN IN TAURUS**
  Born Jan. 20, 22:59 - Feb. 19, 13:10

RICHARD CHAMBERLAIN
American Actor
Sun in Aries

444

1972 PISCES
February 19, 13:11 through March 20, 12:20

 *The Committed Communicator*

As a stable Pisces born in 1972, you seek a relationship that gives you peace of mind. An enduring partnership that engages you both intellectually and emotionally is central to your happiness. You want to be connected to the right person and breakups are very difficult for you. You strive to maintain your relationships, and may still be in touch with a high-school sweetheart, whether as a lover or a friend.

You place a high premium on communication, having learned that most potentially disruptive differences in a relationship can usually be healed through honest and sensitive communication. Since giving and receiving love are of paramount importance in your life, you want to continuously reach out to your partner to be sure that your thoughts and feelings are being clearly expressed. Feeling free to interact socially with whomever you like is also important, but you'd never want to be with someone who felt that cheating or "open marriage" is tolerable.

To engage your interest, a partner must open up intellectually and share interesting thoughts—not just of an intellectual nature, but personal revelations that give you a glimpse inside the heart. You do enjoy being wooed, and you love being invited on picnics or other carefree outings. Spur-of-the-moment invitations are fun, but you also enjoy planning a special date for a long while. As a sensual being who loves being touched, one of the many ways to your heart is through your feet—via massage.

Male fish born in 1972 like a woman who knows what she wants. You may be the keeper of the ideas and of the flame, but it's up to her to add fuel to the fire, driving the relationship steadily forward. Her ideas and plans appeal to you as well, whether or not you actually carry them out. Outgoing and emotionally generous, she enjoys lavishing you with attention and affection.

Female Pisces born in 1972 need a man to be sensitive and intelligent, as well as stable and reliable. He is filled with interesting conversation and has his feet planted firmly on the ground. While not always motivated to go out, he's fun to snuggle with at home, content to spend time with you rather than go out with the guys. His devotion and dependability make him a keeper.

1972 ARIES
From March 20, 12:21 through April 19, 23:36

♈ *The Artistic Lover*

As a communicative Aries born in 1972, your relationship must offer lots of stimulating intellectual interaction and idealism in equal measure. Sometimes relationships confuse you because you believe in commitment and stability but also find that true passion is difficult to maintain. So how do you find that one perfect person who will inspire you to remain committed and starry-eyed? Interview, interview, interview!

Being able to play together is important to you, and you believe that sharing interests keeps a relationship vital. It's also essential that you change and grow, so there are always new worlds to discover with each other. You would hate to be trapped in a partnership with someone who stayed the same, year after year. You believe in flexibility, and thriving in an atmosphere where it's okay to change your mind.

To get your attention, a partner must be fascinating, ardent and intelligent. Stimulating conversation never ceases to thrill you, so your mate must be an attentive listener as well as a sparkling conversationalist. Someone who turns around on a bus or at the movies and cracks a joke is likely to end up in the seat next to yours. You also like art and cultural events, connecting with people who aren't just hobbyists but rather professionals in an artistic medium.

Male rams born in 1972 like a woman to be youthful, yet also mature and wise. She may be older than you are but she seems the same age, and her ideas are timeless. There's a musical lilt in her voice and she has mystical and flirty things to say. She's interested in commitment but never bosses you around, inspiring enough mystery between you to keep you guessing and on your toes.

Female Aries born in 1972 like a playful fellow who's sometimes goofy and a bit of a punster. He has an interest in culture and does things to surprise you. While he seems orderly in his approach to living, he's never a fussbudget. He loves having a good time but sometimes he's broke. You don't mind, though, because you realize that money is never the measure of a man. Although this man may be older than you are, he has a bit of a Peter Pan quality that makes him youthful and fun.

1972 TAURUS

From April 19, 23:37 through May 20, 22:59

The Love Slave

As a playful yet serious Taurus born in 1972, your relationship has to meet your needs—or you call it quits. Your love connection must be both sparkling and sexy, as you enjoy being tantalized and stimulated. You fall in love rather easily and may put it down to an addiction to chemistry. Still, since that emotional and sexual charge you feel is so enthralling, you don't mind at all being a bit of a "prisoner of love."

Emotional and physical compatibility are of utmost importance to you. You'd never agree to stay with a partner who was intellectually dull, or a dolt in the bedroom. You're always pushing to take it deeper and probe a little farther, continuously moving toward greater intimacy. You enjoy outrageous ideas and can be somewhat shocking, so you require a good-natured mate who can go along for the ride.

To engage your interest, the more scandalous the come-on, the better. Someone walking up to you at a party and intimating that you should have sex may excite you, whether you accept the offer or not. You just like the motive behind the gesture. Clever conversation stimulates you, and sharing ideas that people are normally too shy to reveal makes you want to know that person better. You also like competition, and a rousing game of Scrabble™ or a 5-mile run can get your juices flowing.

Male bulls born in 1972 like an intellectual woman who speaks her mind. Her talent for sharing sparkling jokes and observations lets you know that you're with an equal. Her point of view meshes with yours, she is liberal and sexy and appreciates your kinky side. Your lady loves to frolic with kids and play with pets, but at night she melts into your arms like a sultry sex goddess.

Female Taureans born in 1972 need a man to be intensely sexy and sometimes domineering. He can be pushy, but you don't mind because it's fun to see just how far you'll go together. You love hearing his outrageous ideas and find it fun to challenge him intellectually. Your guy seems like a man's man, and his strength gives you a sense of comfort and stability. You just know that he's a winner and that he'll reach his goals.

TAURUS ZODIAC SIGN
YOUR LOVE PLANETS

YOUR ROMANTIC SIDE — p. 696
- ▶ VENUS IN GEMINI
  Born Apr. 19, 23:37 - May 10, 13:50
- ▶ VENUS IN CANCER
  Born May 10, 13:51 - May 20, 22:59

YOUR SEX DRIVE — p. 722
- ▶ MARS IN GEMINI
  Born Apr. 19, 23:37 - May 12, 13:13
- ▶ MARS IN CANCER
  Born May 12, 13:14 - May 20, 22:59

YOUR CELEBRITY TWINS — p. 760
Find out the astrological similarities you have with famous people.

YOUR COMPATIBILITY — p. 780
Compare planets to find out how compatible you are in a relationship.

YOUR RELATIONSHIP KARMA — p. 824
- ▶ SATURN IN GEMINI
  Born Apr. 19, 23:37 - May 20, 22:59

DIANA ROSS
American Singer
Mars in Gemini

445

1972 GEMINI

From May 20, 23:00 through June 21, 7:05

The Sweet Snuggler

As a sensitive Gemini born in 1972, your relationship has to be serious and tender but not overwhelming or smothering. You take life and love very seriously and you believe in solid family values. Though capable of a strong marriage and happy family life, you still need your personal space. Your heart is mostly traditional, yet you also have a need to try new things and make them work. Yours is an inborn need to innovate while also remaining true to your promises and responsibilities.

Your relationship is a sweet oasis where you can go to give and receive love. It's the nest that holds and nurtures your heart, the solid foundation that gives you the confidence to go out into the world and create success. Intimacy and unfailing emotional support are important to you. You must be understood and loved for who you are. Support for self-expression and mutual goals are what bond you, but love is what keeps you together.

To gain your attention, a romantic partner can make a sweet gesture and sweep you off your feet. Being given a basket of home-baked cookies by an admirer makes you want to know more. Cooking together is also a passion. You love family activities and, even on a first date, will enjoy being brought home to meet the relatives. Volunteering is also a meaningful part of your life—perhaps even more so when working alongside the one you love.

Male Geminis born in 1972 need a woman who is a mother at heart. Soft and tender, gentle and loving, she knows how to cook your favorite treats and to make you laugh. She's made a cozy home and has the personality to match, and it just feels right to hug and snuggle her from the moment you meet. Your lady is generous and loving, a bit of a homebody and possibly even a tad plump.

Female Geminis born in 1972 want a man who is sensitive and emotional, independent yet also focused on the needs of others. He may sometimes be quirky, but his heart is always in the right place and he'd never do anything bad or hurtful. This guy is practical and serious, skilled and informed, someone who can teach you something useful and whip up a gourmet dinner, all in the same day.

GEMINI ZODIAC SIGN
YOUR LOVE PLANETS

YOUR ROMANTIC SIDE — p. 696
- ▶ VENUS IN CANCER
  Born May 20, 23:00 - June 11, 20:07
- ▶ VENUS IN GEMINI
  Born June 11, 20:08 - June 21, 7:05

YOUR SEX DRIVE — p. 722
- ▶ MARS IN CANCER
  Born May 20, 23:00 - June 21, 7:05

YOUR CELEBRITY TWINS — p. 760
Find out the astrological similarities you have with famous people.

YOUR COMPATIBILITY — p. 780
Compare planets to find out how compatible you are in a relationship.

YOUR RELATIONSHIP KARMA — p. 824
- ▶ SATURN IN GEMINI
  Born May 20, 23:00 - June 21, 7:05

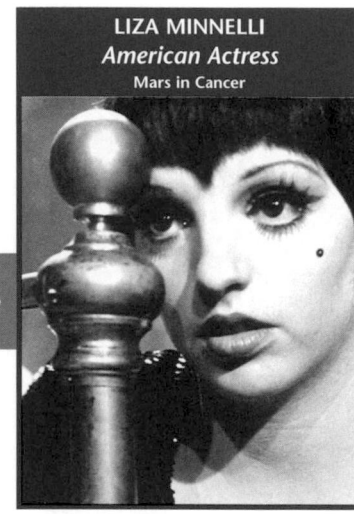

LIZA MINNELLI
American Actress
Mars in Cancer

446

1972 CANCER
From June 21, 7:06 through July 22, 18:02

The Security Seeker

You're a theatrical Cancer born in 1972, and your relationship must be stable and stimulating. As it's in your nature to give and give some more, the generosity of grand, romantic gestures elevates the romance and makes your heart sing. Commitment and obligation go hand in hand, and feeling responsible for each other gives you a sense of security.

You love children and are able to nurture a happy family. Having what it takes to be a good parent, you also consider parenting a rewarding dimension of any marriage. Great conversation and clear communication are also essential to maintaining intimacy and learning to satisfy each other's needs. Naturally trusting and trustworthy, you just know that your mate will always be there.

To gain your attention, a mate might share interesting details with you about a project that is personally meaningful. Fascinated by all that makes people tick, you're especially intrigued to glimpse the inner world of that special someone. You enjoy culture and may be professionally involved in the arts. It's always fun to share an evening at the theater, or even to work together with local thespians. Attending or planning a charity event is another way you can enjoy sharing meaningful, quality time.

Male crabs born in 1972 need a woman who is youthful but also mature. She may be older than you are but she remains playful and looks young for her age. She is dynamic, physically active, and intellectually stimulating. You can be sure she'll be an outstanding parent because she takes the responsibilities of love seriously. She is skilled and informed, and talking with her is always a pleasure.

Female Cancers born in 1972 need a man who is a bit larger than life. He's outgoing and generous, exciting to talk to, and he loves to laugh. He always goes the extra mile for people he loves and helps strangers just as readily. Your guy has lots to say and always makes his comments lively and interesting, sometimes sharing happy recollections of his childhood. He makes you feel protected and safe, and you love to snuggle contentedly in his arms.

1972 LEO
From July 22, 18:03 through August 23, 1:02

The Passionate Perfectionist

Because you're an intense Leo born in 1972, your relationship must be riveting. You need to feel a profound level of passion and commitment that warms you to your very soul. Although you participate in fun and pleasant social activities with lots of good pals, where romance is concerned, you believe that only one true love will do. If a connection doesn't hold you entranced, you assume you're with the wrong partner, and move on.

A connection of body, mind, and soul is what you want, and you will search endlessly for just the right person. Because chemistry is such a strong factor in your approach to love, you're quite susceptible to transitory attractions. However, you don't want a series of meaningless affairs. You just know it takes a while—possibly even an in-depth search—to find your perfect partner.

To gain your attention, a partner has to sizzle with excitement. You will notice the chemistry first of all and then you go from there. You appreciate assertiveness, and someone with the confidence to show interest in you gains high marks. Something as simple as a casual touch can make sparks fly and awaken you to a special connection. You enjoy physical people and may find true love while jogging through the park, climbing a Stairmaster at the gym, or even while shopping for workout clothes.

Male Leos born in 1972 go for a woman who is passionate and intense. She is incredibly sexy and her kisses make you quiver. You don't mind at all when she's a bit possessive because that makes your romance all the more exciting. Her insatiable interest in you just shows that she has good taste. Your lady is socially adept, likes children, shares interesting ideas and, most of all, she knows what she wants.

Lady Leos born in 1972 want a man to be a bit of a jock. All those rippling muscles are thrilling to behold as he's lifting the couch you're sitting on! Your guy is also assertive, never shying away from voicing his opinions and beliefs. You have no trouble at all imagining this courageous man as your proverbial knight in armor. Being his lady fair is your true calling, a role you'll want to play for a lifetime.

1972 VIRGO

From August 23, 1:03 through September 22, 22:32

The Solid Sentimentalist

As a goal-oriented Virgo born in 1972, your relationship must improve the quality of your life. You believe in basing your life on a solid foundation, and a strong relationship is part of that fundamental stability. A solid partnership helps you to cope with the challenges of daily life, providing comfort and a sense of control.

You're sentimental about love, and sometimes you admit to going over the edge, but you can also see that not every romantic liaison was meant to last. You find this frustrating but true. Your goal may even be to stop all the nonsense of dating and just make that commitment and settle down. If you haven't yet done so, it simply means that you haven't found—the Right One—but you're determined to keep on looking for as long as necessary until you can come face to face.

To capture your attention, a partner must have a special sort of pizzazz. You can't help enjoying it when someone offers you a homemade treat, or asks you out to a whimsical event. You'd like to believe that chemistry is enough when choosing a mate, but experience has proven otherwise. You know you should cast a pragmatic eye on any potential romance, and you're determined to do so. Someone who works well with you may be good choice, and you enjoy discussing practical matters as a prelude to love.

Male Virgos born in 1972 prefer a woman who is exciting and romantic. She likes to flirt and is a bit of a femme fatale. Your lady has a special mystique and she likes to flaunt it. Her taste is eccentric, but she has a down-home nurturing side, and you love being in the aura of her femininity. Her playfulness charms you and it's not hard to imagine her surrounded by spellbound children, bringing light and love to your world.

Female Virgos born in 1972 need a man who is practical, skilled, and down-to-earth. Your guy knows what he's doing and what he's saying, and you can count on him to bring order and direction to your life. He finds your eccentricities charming, and even when chaos ensues he'll skillfully glide into the fray and set matters straight. He's always there to help, and never shirks an extra chore.

VIRGO ZODIAC SIGN
YOUR LOVE PLANETS

YOUR ROMANTIC SIDE   p. 696
- ► **VENUS IN CANCER**
  Born Aug. 23, 1:03 - Sept. 07, 23:26
- ► **VENUS IN LEO**
  Born Sept. 07, 23:27 - Sept. 22, 22:32

YOUR SEX DRIVE   p. 722
- ► **MARS IN VIRGO**
  Born Aug. 23, 1:03 - Sept. 22, 22:32

YOUR CELEBRITY TWINS   p. 760
Find out the astrological similarities you have with famous people.

YOUR COMPATIBILITY   p. 780
Compare planets to find out how compatible you are in a relationship.

YOUR RELATIONSHIP KARMA   p. 824
- ► **SATURN IN GEMINI**
  Born Aug. 23, 1:03 - Sept. 22, 22:32

ROMY SCHNEIDER
Austrian Actress
Mars in Virgo

447

1972 LIBRA

From September 22, 22:33 through October 23, 7:40

The Passionate Aesthete

You're a strong-willed Libra born in 1972, and your relationship must be passionate, romantic, and stable. You love with your whole heart and soul, rejoicing in the beauty of a relationship that grows and endures. You love those sentimental commercials depicting long-married couples, and you just might turn out to be like them.

Getting what you want is essential to you, and you'll expend every effort to make it happen. You also have deep spiritual yearnings, and will work quite hard to realize a magical, mystical union. Give and take are the yin and yang of love, and you will always reach out to meet your mate's needs. And of course, you expect the same in return. Total commitment, belief in each other, and a selfless and enduring devotion are what you expect from love. Why would you settle for anything less? You wouldn't dream of it!

To sustain your affection, a partner must be thoughtful and kind. You appreciate all the grand, romantic gestures, but also take notice of the little things, such as being helped with minor inconveniences. You crave deep and meaningful interaction, so attending a meditation or New Age class, doing yoga together or practicing Reiki on each other may bring you close almost instantly. What you seek is intense and boundless intimacy, which is something you feel rather than do.

Male Libras born in 1972 want a woman who is kind, generous, and reliable. Your lady is the salt of the earth, and you know that no matter what happens, she'll be there for you. She's the sort of woman you could easily imagine in your life forever, as the better you know her, the more deeply you love her. She also has excellent taste, fitting seamlessly into your world as she goes all-out to entertain your friends and family.

Lady Libras born in 1972 require a fellow who is charming, passionate, and so sexy he puts movie stars to shame. Your guy radiates energy and charisma, making you swoon every time he enters the room. From the moment you meet, you may look into each other's eyes and just know how easy it would be to dissolve passionately into each other's arms. He's strong and secure, filling your world with love and happiness.

LIBRA ZODIAC SIGN
YOUR LOVE PLANETS

YOUR ROMANTIC SIDE   p. 696
- ► **VENUS IN LEO**
  Born Sept. 22, 22:33 - Oct. 05, 8:32
- ► **VENUS IN VIRGO**
  Born Oct. 05, 8:33 - Oct. 23, 7:40

YOUR SEX DRIVE   p. 722
- ► **MARS IN VIRGO**
  Born Sept. 22, 22:33 - Sept. 30, 23:22
- ► **MARS IN LIBRA**
  Born Sept. 30, 23:23 - Oct. 23, 7:40

YOUR CELEBRITY TWINS   p. 760
Find out the astrological similarities you have with famous people.

YOUR COMPATIBILITY   p. 780
Compare planets to find out how compatible you are in a relationship.

YOUR RELATIONSHIP KARMA   p. 824
- ► **SATURN IN GEMINI**
  Born Sept. 22, 22:33 - Oct. 23, 7:40

BILLY DEE WILLIAMS
American Actor
Mars in Sagittarius

1972 SCORPIO
From October 23, 7:41 through November 22, 5:02

♏ *The Social Butterfly*

For a romantic Scorpio like you, born in 1972, a relationship must feature lots of hearts and flowers. You believe in commitment, but you don't always get that far because it's so much fun to just socialize and date. Meeting new people is always a genuine thrill, but you've also come to see that casual social encounters are no substitute for having that one special person in your life. You love the idea of romance, the soft music and candlelit dinners, and you may be quite content to engage in serial dating until later in life.

Personal freedom is critically important to you, and must be one of the cornerstones of your relationship. You feel that each partner must develop independent interests, because then there's so much more to share when you're together. Communicating interesting ideas is essential to the health of your relationship.

To gain your attention a partner must be sparkling and romantic. Being swept off your feet on the dance floor, whispering sweet nothings as you glide along—such is the stuff of your romantic fantasies and, at long last, your romantic fulfillment! Dressing up and stepping out for a night on the town is a special delight with this gorgeous creature who looks so attractive and well-dressed. You admit that you're a sucker for a great face and body, and you have no plans to change that.

Male Scorpions born in 1972 seek out a woman who is pretty and charming, well versed in the social graces, and open to a commitment. You want to feel that your lady is intrigued at the prospect of being with you permanently, but you don't want to feel that she's chasing you down the street with a leash in her hand! Committed, but still open and free, is your preference. She is demure, but also sexy and liberated enough to be just a little kinky.

Many of you female Scorpios born in 1972 expect your man to be a bit of a free spirit. He's charming and outgoing—a social superstar—and you understand that a guy like this is hard to pin down. He's incredibly exciting and, blessed with excellent instincts and reflexes, is a talented and fashionably dressed dancer, who can also carry on a fascinating conversation. He may even be the sort to serenade you beneath your window with a guitar or violin!

1972 SAGITTARIUS
From November 22, 5:03 through December 21, 18:12

♐ *The Devoted Hedonist*

An unassuming Sagittarius born in 1972, you believe a relationship should be based on pleasure and devotion. Love and commitment come easily to you, and when the chemistry is right, the devotion usually follows. Giving and sharing affection mean the world to you as you bask in an atmosphere of contentment and joy. No matter how challenging life becomes, you always have this love to fall back on.

You need to know that you have someone in your corner, someone who will always go to bat for you. In exchange, you offer your whole heart and unending devotion. Passion and sexual compatibility are other important considerations. And, while there's no substitute for chemistry, you have the ability to see good in so many people that it's easy to maximize whatever chemistry you initially feel.

To gain your attention a partner must be sexy. Having sex appeal and a cheerful approach to living endears someone to you right away. You love it when you meet a person and mesh instantly, and the romantic prospect just seems to know things about you without having to ask. Long, deep conversations enthrall you, and a first date can be as simple as sitting on a couch and sharing opinions.

Male Sagittarians born in 1972 need a woman who is charismatic. She is sexy, and when she enters a room, heads turn. Her energy is cheerful and confident, her manner open and warm. You sense that, under the surface, there's far more to her than meets the senses. You love the mystique of her femininity and feel compelled to learn more about her. She's easy to be with and always leaves you wanting more.

Female archers born in 1972 aim for a man who's macho and strong, but not so bossy that he comes off as an archaic joke. He is sexy and knows how to pique your interest with a sense of humor about life and himself. He knows who he is and is smart enough not to take himself too seriously. Ever willing to share personal information, when you talk you know that real intimacy is happening. This guy works hard, even against difficult odds. He's someone you can admire—in and out of bed.

Sex in the '70s – Liberation, Lust, and Love

It was a time of government scandal and sexual revolution, and mainstream society around the world was flocking to movie houses to see the film about a sexually frustrated wife of a French Embassy official, who is encouraged by her husband to explore every possibility about sex.

In 1974, the French government lifted most film censorship, delighting the producers and distributors of porn, making films like *Emmanuelle* (1974) an unprecedented box-office triumph in Paris as well as an international success. *The Story of O* (1975), where a woman known only as "O" is introduced to the world of sadomasochism by her lover, was another "art porn" film that enjoyed similar notoriety.

And while European societies historically were more open to the portrayal of onscreen sex and sexuality, this was the first time in Hollywood history that movies like *Midnight Cowboy* (1969), which was rated X and won the Oscar, *Carnal Knowledge* (1970), and *Shampoo* (1975) took on more sexually explicit content. It was this public acceptance that paved the way for the pornography industry to enjoy what is now referred to as "The Golden Age of Film Porn."

Sliding progressively along the porn road are the hard-core porn films like *Deep Throat* (1972). Linda Lovelace was thrust into sexual megastardom with her starring role in this all-time classic, adult entertainment film. Co-starring Harry Reems, *Deep Throat* was a pioneering sex film that made Linda Lovelace's name one and the same with oral sex. After *Deep Throat*, Linda's name headlining a 1970s theater marquee guaranteed success, but while she appeared in several films after *Deep Throat*, she never again was the lead of a sex film.

Marilyn Chambers, another darling of

Linda Lovelace in hard-core porn film *Deep Throat*

449

> *"Our society loves violence and is ashamed of human sex . . ."*
>
> LINDA LOVELACE

the 1970s hard-core scene, was touted as the "All American Girl." Growing up in Connecticut, and with her wholesome good looks, Marilyn became a successful model—even posing as a young mother for Ivory Snow, whose proud slogan since the 1800s had been "99-44/100% pure." Her modeling career led her to Hollywood where eventually she made a decision that would change her life forever. Intrigued by the story of *Behind the Green Door* (1972), Marilyn told the *LA Times*, "... I really liked the fantasy involved. And I figured it might be my last chance at something really big."

The movie about "Gloria," a girl who is kidnapped and forced into exotic sex acts on stage, was a huge hit and led Chambers to another unforgettable performance in 1973 with *The Resurrection of Eve*. Taken together, the two movies allegedly made close to $30 million dollars. When Chambers signed on to do *Behind the Green Door* she was very savvy and negotiated 10% of the movie's box-office gross.

By the late 1970s, the face of pornography changed once again with the videocassette recorder, bringing soft- and hard-core porn into the home. Today, approximately 10,000 new video titles are released yearly, and pornography is available to anyone who has Internet access.

▶ FIND OUT MORE ABOUT *THE SUMMER OF LOVE* ON PAGE 407 AND *SHAMPOO* ON PAGE 466

1973

- ★ PREMARITAL SEX
- ★ SEXUAL DISCRIMINATION
- ★ THE WAY WE WERE
- ★ FEAR OF FLYING
- ★ JOY OF SEX
- ★ LET'S GET IT ON
- ★ CARLY SIMON

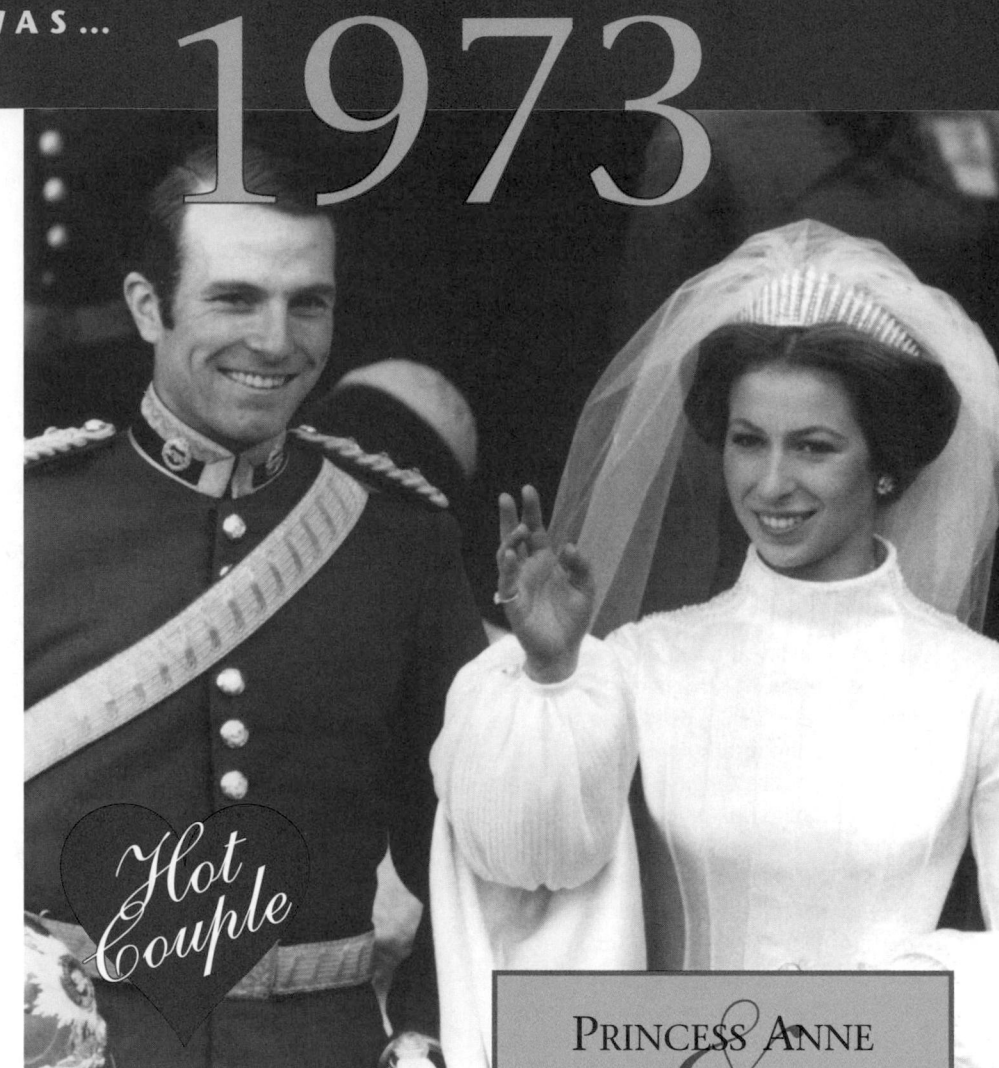

Hot Couple

EVENTS

In 1973, a Gallup Poll reported that Americans were significantly more tolerant toward premarital sex than they were at the end of the 1960s. However, the poll also revealed that the Puritan ethic still remained stronger in the United States than in Britain. One step ahead of the US, the British government proposed the Equal Opportunities Committee to investigate complaints of sexual discrimination in the workplace. But just how liberal was Britain at the time? Prominent ministers Earl Jellicoe and Lord Lambton were forced to resign after their liaisons with prostitutes were discovered.

In the US, the New York chapter of the National Organization for Women held a two-day Women's Sexuality Conference, the first to concentrate on physical liberation and sexual pleasure. Around the same time, the American Bar Association called for the removal of criminal penalties for sexual conduct of a noncommercial nature between consenting adults.

POP CULTURE

Moviegoers shed a few tears in 1973. *The Way We Were* paired Barbra Streisand and Robert Redford in a story of lovers who were just not meant to be. *Blume in Love* was a heartrending, often shocking tale of a lawyer willing to try anything to win back his wife. George Segal and Glenda Jackson helped us laugh again with the romantic comedy, *A Touch of Class*, about a couple struggling to find their way through an extramarital affair.

Fear of Flying, by Erica Jong, appeared on everyone's bookshelves in 1973 and described her idea of the ultimate sexual encounter. *The Joy of Sex*, with its title a take-off on the popular cookbook, *The Joy of Cooking*, was an uninhibited guide to lovemaking. In Jacqueline Susann's novel *Once Is Not Enough*, January Wayne searches the glamorous world of the entertainment industry for the perfect man.

Top love songs were "Killing Me Softly," by Roberta Flack, "My Love," by Paul McCartney & Wings, and "Let's Get It On," by Marvin Gaye. Carly Simon put down an arrogant lover with "You're So Vain" and kept everyone guessing as to who it was about.

PRINCESS ANNE & MARK PHILLIPS

Queen Elizabeth's daughter, the lovely and elegant Princess Anne, was a horse show-jumper in the 1970s. She led a very private life, and when rumors began to spread that she was involved with another show-jumper, the army officer Mark Phillips, Buckingham Palace denied it. Yet only weeks later, the Palace announced their engagement.

On November 14, 1973, there was a grand wedding procession along the streets of London, which were lined with thousands of well-wishers, while 27.8 million watched on television. This was a landmark event for the royal family, opening the door for royals to marry commoners. Despite this, the couple divorced in April 1992.

SEE ALSO

▶ QUEEN ELIZABETH & PRINCE PHILIP *Page 236*

▶ LADY DIANA & PRINCE CHARLES *Page 516*

1973 CAPRICORN
From December 21, 1972, 18:13 through January 20, 1973, 4:47
(December 1973 Capricorns, see 1974 Capricorn)

♑ The Ambitious Adventurer

Born in 1973, you're a particularly passionate breed of Capricorn. Never afraid of hard work or an impossible challenge, you believe the world is there to be conquered. In love, as in work, you have the same courageous, persistent attitude. You want someone who inspires you to push your own limits. You believe that a partnership is all about increasing the material as well as spiritual wealth of both people exponentially.

You are very earthy and your body dictates who you love more than your mind. Logic and common sense don't play much of a part in your romantic life. You know who you are attracted to and you simply must have that person at any cost. You don't mind having to fight for him or her—in fact you enjoy it! You possess a competitive streak and may get turned on by winning the love of someone who is torn between you and a lesser mate.

To get your attention, potential partners must be very involved in their own activities and must not hang on your every word. You prefer to do the chasing and are put off by people who are too accommodating or have too much time on their hands. Potential lovers can entice you by bending your ear about their obsessions and then moving on to talk to the other attractive, powerful people in the room!

As a male Capricorn, born in 1973 you need a female partner who is intense but flexible. You demand a lot of attention but also need a lot of space when career matters call. She must be willing to go with the flow, but yet she can't be wimpy. You expect a lot, but in return you want to give a woman the life of her dreams—spiritual adventures, exotic trips, passion, and material security. You must be with a woman who desires those things.

A female Capricorn born in 1973 needs a guy who is scholarly and masculine—who will teach you a lot about the spiritual as well as intellectual secrets of the universe. But he should also enjoy playing sports and staying out late! You likes a macho man, but he has to have a sense of humor about his manliness, too. You are wry and dry and must have a male mate who matches your wit and perceptiveness.

CAPRICORN ZODIAC SIGN
YOUR LOVE PLANETS

YOUR ROMANTIC SIDE   p. 696
▶ **VENUS IN SAGITTARIUS**
Born Dec. 21, 1972 18:13 - Jan. 11, 1973 19:14
▶ **VENUS IN CAPRICORN**
Born Jan. 11, 19:15 - Jan. 20, 4:47

YOUR SEX DRIVE   p. 722
▶ **MARS IN SCORPIO**
Born Dec. 21, 1972 18:13 - Dec. 30, 1972 16:11
▶ **MARS IN SAGITTARIUS**
Born Dec. 30, 1972 16:12 - Jan. 20, 1973 4:47

YOUR CELEBRITY TWINS   p. 760
Find out the astrological similarities you have with famous people.

YOUR COMPATIBILITY   p. 780
Compare planets to find out how compatible you are in a relationship.

YOUR RELATIONSHIP KARMA   p. 824
▶ **SATURN IN GEMINI**
Born Dec. 21, 1972 18:13 - Jan. 20, 1973 4:47

MARVIN GAYE
American Singer
Mars in Capricorn

451

1973 AQUARIUS
From January 20, 4:48 through February 18, 19:00

♒ The Brilliant Brooder

You are a deep thinker and believe that all of life's mysteries can be revealed and problems solved by a concentrated application of the mind. You get unnerved by people who are too clingy and emotional, because you are so cool and self-contained. Yet all your ruminating has convinced you that you need a fiery, passionate type of person to complement your restrained ways. When it comes to love, you are willing to struggle through confusion and drama to get to the Zen place you know awaits you—and your lover—on the other side.

You think of yourself as "easy," but really you are complex and enigmatic and impossible to predict. Just when you are settled into one way of being, you switch gears. You don't want someone who is solid like a rock. You believe love should be grandly impossible.

If potential partners want to snag your attention, they should turn their sexual intensity on full-tilt. Deep eye contact makes you deeply uncomfortable—yet you love that feeling. When a potential lover sets his or her sights on you and moves (physically and emotionally) closer and closer to you, you can't resist. You have a soft spot for people who are so confident that they would be willing to put it all on the line for you—and for love. You admire that kind of boldness and respond by melting into that person's arms.

If you are a male Aquarius born in 1973, you are particularly attracted to women who are haughty and diva-esque. You never lose your cool, but you are inexplicably turned on by a woman who loses her temper when arguing, cries during the opera, and gets a look of wild abandon on her face when she's dancing with you.

Female Aquarians born during 1973 are drawn to men who are pushy, wild, and don't need much sleep! Left to your own devices, you are happy to surf the Net for hours, then snuggle up with a complex book of philosophical science. But you can become highly romantic when a guy pulls you from your cerebral cocoon and drags you out to thrilling, circus-like places—from wild after-hours bars to maybe even the circus itself. You love a man with a loud, raucous laugh.

AQUARIUS ZODIAC SIGN
YOUR LOVE PLANETS

YOUR ROMANTIC SIDE   p. 696
▶ **VENUS IN CAPRICORN**
Born Jan. 20, 4:48 - Feb. 04, 18:42
▶ **VENUS IN AQUARIUS**
Born Feb. 04, 18:43 - Feb. 18, 19:00

YOUR SEX DRIVE   p. 722
▶ **MARS IN SAGITTARIUS**
Born Jan. 20, 4:48 - Feb. 12, 5:50
▶ **MARS IN CAPRICORN**
Born Feb. 12, 5:51 - Feb. 18, 19:00

YOUR CELEBRITY TWINS   p. 760
Find out the astrological similarities you have with famous people.

YOUR COMPATIBILITY   p. 780
Compare planets to find out how compatible you are in a relationship.

YOUR RELATIONSHIP KARMA   p. 824
▶ **SATURN IN GEMINI**
Born Jan. 20, 4:48 - Feb. 18, 19:00

BOB MARLEY
Jamaican Singer
Venus in Aries

452

1973 PISCES *From February 18, 19:01 through March 20, 18:11*
♓ The Ethereal Evader

You hate to be pinned down. You love to swim literally and figuratively in wide-open expanses of water. You want love to feel endless, dreamy, and surreal. The real world can get you down. You are happiest when you are swept away by love. Your dream is to put the moves on a potential partner in a fairy tale way. You might overcompensate sometimes for your extreme romanticism by pretending to be cynical, but that's just a cover-up.

You want to be with someone who believes in forever. You don't date, you mate! It is not in your power to hold back, even in the beginning of a relationship. Therefore, you need to be with someone who does not scare easily when you pour all your passion into them. Yet once you are deeply involved, you begin to treat your partner more as a friend than a lover. It is up to that person to then keep the romance alive, just as you did in the beginning. Once you are past the honeymoon stage, you may become a little evasive and pull away from your lover. You need someone who recognizes that this is just a defense—you are afraid you are going to lose what you love so much.

To capture your attention, the best bet is to quietly seduce you, maybe even act a little shy. Once you sense interest, you like to be the one to make the grand, over-the-top gesture. Treading the line between friendship and romance is likely to get your attention. You like to think that love was your discovery alone!

If you are a 1973 male born under the sign of Pisces, you need a woman who is feminine and ethereal on the outside, but who will behave like your rock of Gibraltar. You need a strong woman who has compassion for all your fears and sorrows. She must be kind-hearted through and through and hilariously funny, too!

Female Pisceans born during 1973 need men who are the strong, silent type. You like to be the wild and wacky one and prefer a guy who is bemused by your antics. You are comfortable sitting on the sidelines to watch and cheer him on. You have a weak spot for men who are ultra-sensual and give great foot and neck massages. If he's a great cook, even better!

1973 ARIES *From March 20, 18:12 through April 20, 5:29*
♈ The Versatile Romantic

As a 1973 Aries you are more aware of other people's moods and desires than the average Ram. You sense what a lover needs and you're ready to give it. Whether you smoke or not, you always carry a lighter in case someone needs it. You love to be the first one to say you can help. Your ideal of love is a rescue fantasy in which you do the rescuing. You love the idea of taking someone away from a dreary or torturous existence and introducing the world of fine wine, good conversation, and passionate love.

You expect a relationship to be filled with hours of togetherness every day. And within those hours you want to be able to show your honey off to the world and vice versa. You know those couples who make everyone else ill by fawning all over each other in public? Well, that's what you want your romance to be like!

If potential mates want to attract you, they should coyly suggest favorite places to kiss and canoodle in public. You will surely take the bait! Would-be lovers can't be too subtle, because you are a little oblivious—but in a cute way.

You are incredibly turned on by a good dancer and someone who knows how to order the perfect wine and meal at a four-star restaurant.

As a 1973 male Aries, you like a woman who is fit, athletic, and knows how to fight with you. Arguing about a movie or play can lead to passionate love-making, as quick as you can make a "thumbs up" or "thumbs down" sign. You like a woman with an adventurous spirit who will egg you on with the line, "What's the matter, scared to take me on?" You like a woman who is always running off to the next adventure, so you have to run after her. Something about the chase is ultra-romantic for you. You never want to conquer her—just to claim her as yours and yours alone.

1973 female Aries need men who are shameless flirts and know how to keep you stimulated right when you are on the verge of feeling restless and bored. You want a guy who is secure enough in his masculinity to be a little playful, silly, and just plain weird! You hate guys who are stiff and square, but you love an eccentric male.

1973 TAURUS

From April 20, 5:30 through May 21, 4:53

The Cuddly Loner

Born in 1973, you are a kind and gentle type of Taurus—more peaceful than the average strong-willed bull. Especially in matters of the heart, you would rather kiss and cuddle then bark and bicker. You want love to be fine and mellow. Yet, you've got rough edges and hate superficial people. That's why you desire a partner who will soften you and show you that at least one person in this world will be there for you unconditionally.

You don't need many people in your life and are content working and playing on your own. But, once you are exposed to love you get addicted! You believe that a romantic relationship should be insular, pure and utterly based on fidelity. You barely have patience and time for one lover, let alone many! And you expect your main squeeze to be thinking of you and you alone, too.

If would-be lovers want to catch your eye they should dress in quality fabrics that are soft to the touch, and wear subtle, attractive colognes. Your senses draw you to what you want. Also, you are a sucker for people with musical talent or who are big music aficionados. You love to slow dance and despite your pulled-together exterior you can melt in the arms of someone who is as sensual and sensitive to melodies as you are.

As a 1973 Taurus male, you want a woman who is secure enough in herself to hold back and not push you or try to control you, and that means in bed, too. You prefer to take the lead and appreciate a woman who is a great listener. You need her to fit into your life. However, once you are attached you become "Mr. Twosome" and are an absolute equal partner. But if she wants you, she's got to be patient and let you come to her—and then allow you the time to really trust her, too.

If you are a 1973 Taurus woman, you need a guy who is sincere and does not play games. He must be as straightforward as you are to earn your trust. You want a mate who is close to his family and friends and does not have to pick up a dictionary to know the meaning of the word "loyalty." Sexually, he has to be patient and slow-moving. You're in no rush, why should he be?

TAURUS ZODIAC SIGN
YOUR LOVE PLANETS

YOUR ROMANTIC SIDE — p. 696
- ► VENUS IN TAURUS
  Born Apr. 20, 5:30 - May 12, 8:41
- ► VENUS IN GEMINI
  Born May 12, 8:42 - May 21, 4:53

YOUR SEX DRIVE — p. 722
- ► MARS IN AQUARIUS
  Born Mar. 20, 5:30 - May 08, 4:08
- ► MARS IN PISCES
  Born May 08, 4:09 - May 21, 4:53

YOUR CELEBRITY TWINS — p. 760
Find out the astrological similarities you have with famous people.

YOUR COMPATIBILITY — p. 780
Compare planets to find out how compatible you are in a relationship.

YOUR RELATIONSHIP KARMA — p. 824
- ► SATURN IN GEMINI
  Born Apr. 20, 5:30 - May 21, 4:53

ERICA JONG
American Writer
Mars in Gemini

453

1973 GEMINI

From May 21, 4:54 through June 21, 13:00

The Intellectual Homebody

Born in 1973, you are a Gemini with a sentimental streak. You love spending time at home with your honey, talking, cuddling, and frolicking in bed. You are a playful lover who is tried and true through and through. But you also enjoy shuffling out of bed and getting on your computer to research your latest cerebral obsession—or staying in bed, reading an obscure novel, while your darling is still whispering sweet nothings in your ear.

You are faithful in body and expect your partner to be, too, but you also need someone who has a mind of his or her own and an avid desire to learn about complex subjects. A relationship must be a true meeting of the minds for you to feel satisfied and secure. You don't want someone who is tagging along after you at the library or bookstore. Potential lovers of yours will go to their own section, find their own intellectual stimuli, and then meet you for coffee and scintillating chat two hours later.

If prospective mates want to seduce you, they need to be able to out-analyze you. Sure, you know a lot of fascinating facts, but can you see the big picture—how all the details fits together and affect human behavior and the world at large? If someone can match you in minutia and trump you when it comes to drawing deep, meaningful conclusions, you've been snagged for keeps. Also, a potential lover should talk about sex. The brain is certainly your biggest sex organ and you like to get jazzed up verbally before your shoes even come off!

As a 1973 male Gemini you are seeking a woman who is quicker on the uptake than you are—and sassier! You are a very well-educated and curious guy. In other words, you're no slouch where smarts are concerned. Therefore, a female who is an avid reader and can call you on your memory gaps and misinformation is sure to make you delirious with passion.

You, a female 1973 Gemini, need a man who is well-balanced and just as interested in high culture as he is in the bottom line in business. You want a guy who can analyze current stock trends and play a mean jazz trumpet—or at least appreciate the sound of one.

GEMINI ZODIAC SIGN
YOUR LOVE PLANETS

YOUR ROMANTIC SIDE — p. 696
- ► VENUS IN GEMINI
  Born May 21, 4:54 - June 05, 19:19
- ► VENUS IN CANCER
  Born June 05, 19:20 - June 21, 13:00

YOUR SEX DRIVE — p. 722
- ► MARS IN PISCES
  Born May 21, 4:54 - June 20, 20:53
- ► MARS IN ARIES
  Born June 20, 20:54 - June 21, 13:00

YOUR CELEBRITY TWINS — p. 760
Find out the astrological similarities you have with famous people.

YOUR COMPATIBILITY — p. 780
Compare planets to find out how compatible you are in a relationship.

YOUR RELATIONSHIP KARMA — p. 824
- ► SATURN IN GEMINI
  Born May 21, 4:54 - June 21, 13:00

ROBERT DE NIRO
American Actor
Sun in Leo

1973 CANCER
From June 21, 13:01 through July 22, 23:55

The Faithful Firecracker

As a 1973 Cancer, you are a lot more fiery and reckless than typical moon children. You want love to be a fight and a struggle, and once you've experienced the requisite amount of drama, then you can settle down and make a home with your lover. Ultimately, you want love to be warm, cozy, and sweet, but you need to feel as if you've fought a war to get to that gentle, serene place.

You believe relationships should have a "you and me against the world" feeling. You would fight to the death to protect your loved one and expect the same kind of passionate loyalty in return. A relationship has to have an element of unpredictability and tenuousness in the beginning to keep your interest.

If someone wants to catch your eye, he or she needs to be in distress or crisis in some way. You love to bust in and offer assistance and play the role of gallant savior. If someone is too self-sufficient, you don't know what to do! Superficiality bores you, so if a potential lover tells you about the cinematic struggles of parents or siblings, and then promises to bring you home to meet them, you will surely feel fired up and fanatical about them. And that translates to the bedroom, too. Intimacy turns you on more than a cheap role in the hay. You must feel a deep protective bond toward the person you are sleeping with.

1973 Cancer men need women who are loud and loving. She can't be restrained or demure. She's got to have a lot of fire in her heart and the means and words to express the love that's in her soul. She should be outdoorsy, too. Your canoe was built for two and you want a partner with whom you can see the sights of the natural world.

A woman born under the sign of Cancer in 1973 is in need of a man who is aware of all his fears, but is willing to push past them to make his love life and his entire life into what he imagines. He's got to be a cock-eyed optimist who will pull you out of your negative moods, too. You want a man who will take on the world with you, and fight any obstacle to create a dreamy, protected home with you. He's got to love kids—and your parents, too!

1973 LEO
From July 22, 23:56 through August 23, 6:52

The Precise Sensualist

Your motto is "if you can't do something right, don't do it at all." You absolutely adore applying your talents to cooking, business, and relationships. You can take a diamond in the rough and turn it into a stunning jewel. When it comes to love, you need to feel needed. You believe that all relationships come with a give and take. You usually begin in giving mode and enjoy fixing up a lover whose life is in disarray. But once that job is done, you are like every other Leo—you love to be catered to!

Self-sufficiency is your strong suit and you don't really need someone to fix up your life. What you need a lover for is—well—loving! Sensuality is your weak spot. You crave affection like a puppy, and adore being stroked, fondled, and fussed over. You need a partner who will scrub your back, massage your toes, and cook you a gourmet meal—or take you out for one. Sexually, you are more into quality than quantity. You don't count notches on your belt, but you do remember the most incredibly romantic nights.

To get your attention a would-be lover must appeal to your two most dominant traits: your desire to be of service and your desired to be physically catered to. A potential lover should say: "I'm at a crossroads in my career and I don't know what move to make next." After you've come up with a game plan, the thank-yous must include a full-on, lingering bear hug that lasts for an hour and involve a lot of hair-stroking and back-rubbing.

If you are a male Leo born in 1973 you need a woman who embodies the extremes of saint and sinner—Madonna and whore. In other words, if she's lived a wild life already, she must be ready to settle down. If she's led a sheltered existence, she must want to cut loose and live large. And if she's a craftswoman who works with her hands, great!

As a 1973 Leo lady, you need a man who possesses the drive to be a leader in the world, but who has a soft enough heart to be a big teddy bear at home. Your man must leave his work at the office and pay attention to you all night long; and then get up early and set the world on fire all over again!

454

1973 VIRGO
From August 23, 6:53 through September 23, 4:20

The Experimental Contrarian

Born in 1973, you are a paradoxical and impossible-to-predict Virgo. You are highly romantic and need love like oxygen, but you also need to be discontented in your relationship to feel contented! You believe that romance must be constantly challenging and full of areas that need fixing. Bliss is not blissful for you—it stresses you out!

You want love to be meaningful, genteel, and as challenging as a Ph.D. dissertation. You believe that it takes a lifetime for two people to begin to understand each other's internal worlds. You are willing to work hard to understand and to be understood. You don't trust a relationship when it is too easy. And you want your lover to be willing to work with you to reach the heights of ecstasy and understanding. Sexually, you are a fan of the Kama Sutra, and are willing to try any position and any experience at least once. Your sensual nature could best be described as experimental.

To grab your attention a potential paramour should engage you in a philosophical debate.

You love to see someone's mind work, especially when it veers gracefully and passionately in directions where your own gray matter would never venture. You also enjoy all forms of narrative, so if potential lovers can brilliantly dissect the structure of a recently-read book, play, or movie that turned them on, then you will surely get turned on too. And for all your talking, you also love to cut loose and party. You like to get sexy with a would-be lover on the dance floor or anyplace in public. Your exhibitionistic streak is strong!

A 1973 Virgo man is looking for a woman who can argue like a debate team captain, get dirty on the ball field, and then clean up nicely and go to the theater. You like a girl with eclectic interests who rarely gives an inch and expects you to be the one to bend.

If you are a 1973 Virgo woman, you need a guy who possesses a "live and let live attitude." You want to know above all else that no matter how much you two may disagree over the little things, he loves you deeply and would never leave you over something cerebral or silly.

VIRGO ZODIAC SIGN
YOUR LOVE PLANETS

YOUR ROMANTIC SIDE — p. 696
▶ VENUS IN LIBRA
Born Aug. 23, 6:53 - Sept. 13, 9:04
▶ VENUS IN SCORPIO
Born Sept. 13, 9:05 - Sept. 23, 4:20

YOUR SEX DRIVE — p. 722
▶ MARS IN TAURUS
Born Aug. 23, 6:53 - Sept. 23, 4:20

YOUR CELEBRITY TWINS — p. 760
Find out the astrological similarities you have with famous people.

YOUR COMPATIBILITY — p. 780
Compare planets to find out how compatible you are in a relationship.

YOUR RELATIONSHIP KARMA — p. 824
▶ SATURN IN CANCER
Born Aug. 23, 6:53 - Sept. 23, 4:20

1973 LIBRA
From September 23, 4:21 through October 23, 13:29

The Subtle Seeker

Born in 1973, you are a Libra who believes love is an utter mystery to be revealed slowly and with suspense, just like a serial novel. You hate to find everything out right at the start. You prefer the thrill of discovering new and fabulous fun facts as the relationship progresses. You believe life is an adventure, and love is too. That's what inspires you to get up in the morning. For you relationships are more about the journey than the destination.

No one would ever guess by looking at your serene, pleasant Libran face how much the wheels behind your forehead are turning. You are always weighing each new bit of information. You use your sensual observation to draw new conclusions for the case you are making for or against a lover. You don't believe in commitment just for the sake of security. During each phase of the relationship you put your honey through yet another round of subtle, sometimes invisible tests. You can't bear a relationship to remain static.

If potential partners hope to woo you, they should engage you in esoteric conversation

about art or spirituality. Anyone who can communicate almost exclusively in analogies and metaphors is sure to float your boat! You are happiest debating over a good bottle of wine in a subdued aesthetically-appealing environment. You tend to be people-pleasing, but have a real soft spot for people who go out of their way to please you. If a potential lover strokes your back or offers you a foot massage, you will melt. You take this as a sign of this person's giving nature in bed.

If you are a Libra male born in 1973, you are seeking a woman who is passionate and intense with a mischievous streak. You are drawn to women who keep you guessing and who always hold a little something back. If she speaks in a low sexy, growl she will have you hooked right away.

As a woman born under the sign of Libra in 1973, you are looking for a man who is a good listener and thoroughly unshockable. He can't judge you or your wild assortment of friends—from nuns to ne'er-do-wells. So you need a man who is accepting of all kinds of people.

JACQUELINE BISSET
English Actress
Venus and Mars in Libra

LIBRA ZODIAC SIGN
YOUR LOVE PLANETS

YOUR ROMANTIC SIDE — p. 696
▶ VENUS IN SCORPIO
Born Sept. 23, 4:21 - Oct. 09, 8:07
▶ VENUS IN SAGITTARIUS
Born Oct. 09, 8:08 - Oct. 23, 13:29

YOUR SEX DRIVE — p. 722
▶ MARS IN TAURUS
Born Sept. 23, 4:21 - Oct. 23, 13:29

YOUR CELEBRITY TWINS — p. 760
Find out the astrological similarities you have with famous people.

YOUR COMPATIBILITY — p. 780
Compare planets to find out how compatible you are in a relationship.

YOUR RELATIONSHIP KARMA — p. 824
▶ SATURN IN CANCER
Born Sept. 23, 4:21 - Oct. 23, 13:29

455

LIV ULLMAN
Norwegian Actress
Sun in Sagittarius

1973 SCORPIO
From October 23, 13:30 through November 22, 10:53

♏ The Passionate Pal

As a 1973 Scorpio, it seems as though you are everybody's buddy. You know how to converse with all sorts of people on a myriad of topics. In love you want someone who is just as scintillating a conversationalist as five of your most interesting friends put together, but you have one caveat. Your lover must keep all your secrets and be willing to reveal all of his or hers to you. You believe in sharing your whole self with your loved one and demand the same emotional courage in return.

You are an over-the-top personality, one part flirt and two parts performer. You expect your relationship to be fluid enough to contain all your ever-morphing, larger-than-life personas. You want to be in a partnership that is fun and free-spirited but maintains a strong commitment at its core.

A good way for a would-be partner to grab your attention is to push right in and compete with a room full of other people who are already paying attention to you! You are rarely alone. You hate to compartmentalize and like everybody to get along with everybody. A potential lover should get friendly with your pals to win points. Sexually, you need a good lover to be confident, experimental, and erotic in bed and out. You like a partner who feeds you fruit in public and turns you on with words and looks.

As a Scorpio male born in 1973, you want a woman who is confident enough to challenge you and poke fun at you, but who is sensitive and respectful enough to never humiliate you (especially in public!) or question your core values. You like women who are well-traveled, who possess a taste for exotic food and exotic sex. You want a woman who will be your lover and best friend. Simply one or the other won't do.

As a female Scorpio born in 1973 you also want your man to be your best friend. He must channel his passion into one strong, bold career choice and one strong, bold woman—namely, you! You want a guy who is full of passion and surprises, but who is stable and reliable, too. If he has a playful, little boy quality and can make you laugh when you are angry, he will surely win and keep your heart.

1973 SAGITTARIUS
From November 22, 10:54 through December 22, 0:07

♐ The Sweet-natured Flirt

As a 1973 Sagittarian, you are hard to pin down. You love a challenge and expect a relationship to be risky and ripe with conflict. In fact, you induce conflict by fighting so hard to win the heart of the ones you love, and then you could act coy and seductive with all of that person's friends! Yet you are idealistic and good-hearted, and know where your values lie. You would never do anything to cross your own secret lines.

This breed of Sagittarian needs a lot of space to roam and a lot of "alone time" to just think. You are ponderers and philosophers and are always trying to learn more from books and from people. You want relationships to be learning experiences, too, and are very attracted to challenging types.

If you are trying to seduce 1973 Sags, start by flirting quietly and sweetly with them. Tousling their hair as if they are kittens or puppies is always a good trick. Then get into their mind. Put out for exploration one of your strange obsessions and let them wrap their head around it. They love learning about new things, so teach, teach, teach. (And if you can teach this Sag some new tricks in bed, he or she will repay your generosity by being a fabulous student!) And have patience with them as they preach. They may get fanatical about their beliefs, but they never stay set in their ways for long.

If you are a Sagittarian male born in 1973 you have a weak spot for women who are a little chilly on the outside and who keep you at bay for longer than most men could tolerate. You love to pull grand, original tricks out of your hat to impress your lady love. Once involved you need a lady with serious values and serious smarts. An idealistic intellectual is your ideal woman.

If you are a lady Sagittarius of 1973, you need a man who is adventurous and egotistical. For some reason self-deprecating guys turn you off. A self-made man with a touch of arrogance and a lot of generosity and altruism to balance out his vanity is your perfect guy. Men who are athletic and love horses—as well as the entire animal kingdom—also make your heart race.

Fanning the Feminist Flames

Although matriarchal societies are not unheard of, the world that we've known for thousands of years has been largely "a man's world." Until relatively recently, women have been seen as weak, helpless, less intelligent, tending to hysteria, and generally inferior. So men made sure to keep them at home, away from the strains of higher learning, careers, commerce, or anything that might disrupt the balance of power. A woman's best bet, for her own security and protection, was to be more or less owned by a man. The drive for Women's Liberation, and the birth of feminism, was long in coming.

Feminism, though, is not unique to our times. In his *Republic*, Plato looked critically at sex roles. Ibsen's famous play, *A Doll's House*, gave us the male-dominated Nora. Earlier feminist writers, such as Mary Wollstonecraft in 1792, railed against "domestic tyranny." Women are raised to be "the toys of men," she dared say. And although Abigail Adams had asked her husband John to "remember the ladies" in the Declaration of Independence, he somehow forgot. It wasn't until 144 years later that the 19th Amendment to the US Constitution finally gave women the right to vote. All the while, though, feminists, both male and female, were coming together, tilling the soil for change. "The burdens are hard on those who attack an almost universal opinion," lamented John Stuart Mill in an 1869 essay.

Feminist flames were fanned by the Abolitionist Movements in the US and the UK. Members of female anti-slavery

A Women's Liberation rally in New York

societies identified with the slaves they wished to liberate, determining that both causes, to succeed, required power. Finally, when a female delegation to London's World Anti-slavery Convention in 1840 was not allowed to speak, incensed women, including Americans Lucretia Mott and Elizabeth Cady Stanton, and Englishwoman Anne Knight, began to organize. In 1847, Knight published what is believed to be the first ever leaflet on women's suffrage. And in 1848, Mott and Cady Stanton were behind the historic milestone of the feminist movement, the Seneca Falls Convention, which demanded full legal equality for women in education,

commerce, property ownership, guardianship of children, and divorce laws.

Winning the vote in 1920 in the US and in 1928 in the UK was a major stride forward. But although the female war effort workers during WWII were respected, people remained divided on the question of "women's place" once the war was won. The '50s saw continuing discrimination in most major areas. Following the lead of Simone de Beauvoir's groundbreaking *The Second Sex* (1949), Betty Friedan awakened potential feminists with *The Feminine Mystique* (1963), boldly suggesting that feminine fulfillment went beyond housewifery and childbearing.

The Women's Liberation Movement finally exploded in the '60s and in 1970, Germaine Greer's *The Female Eunuch* challenged the male status quo head-on, condemning marriage as a form of legalized slavery. The book was an immediate bestseller and became the bible for the feminist movement of the '70s. In Britain feminist campaigning reached new heights and in 1973 the first feminist publishing house, Virago Press, was launched, publishing the major feminist thinkers of the time: Kate Millett, Eva Figes, Angela Carter and Lynne Segal. In the same year in the US, the Supreme Court's Roe v. Wade ruling secured abortion rights. Since then, "girl power" has increased exponentially as feminism's scope continues to broaden. *All* women stand together as sisters, yet with distinct challenges. "You've come a long way, baby," they might say, "but you still have some way to go!"

457

▶ READ ABOUT *SEX AND THE CITY*, THE TV SERIES ON TODAY'S SINGLE WOMEN, ON PAGE 679

1974

- ★ SEXUAL INTERCOURSE
- ★ MISS WORLD
- ★ THE GREAT GATSBY
- ★ EMMANUELLE
- ★ HAROLD ROBBINS
- ★ JOHN DENVER
- ★ HAVING MY BABY

EVENTS

Family planning became available to all British citizens in 1974. While the Italian government decided to keep the existing, more repressive, divorce laws, France relaxed its abortion laws. A US survey found that married couples engaged in sexual intercourse more often than those in the same age brackets did the previous decade. The increase was attributed to more widespread use of contraception, the availability of legal abortion, and increasing societal permissiveness and discussion of sex.

Although divorce had less of a stigma attached, the Miss World winner resigned her title, fearing she would be named and shamed in a divorce case. Divorce was no stranger to Elizabeth Taylor; she had married Richard Burton after several other husbands, but divorced him for the first time in 1974. They were later to remarry and divorce again.

POP CULTURE

Romance, at home and abroad, filled the screen in 1974. F. Scott Fitzgerald's *The Great Gatsby* was a tragic love story between the titular Gatsby and Daisy Buchanan. In *The Seduction of Mimi*, sex and politics drove the tale of a simple but obstinate Sicilian woman who migrates to the big city. *Emmanuelle* was about the initiation of a diplomat's young wife into the world of sex and sensuality. And in *The Girl from Petrovka*, an American journalist falls in love while on an assignment in the Soviet Union.

Hot Couple

Readers the previous year apparently hadn't had enough, so *More Joy: A Lovemaking Companion to the Joy of Sex* hit the shelves, and included more aspects of lovemaking, from massaging to swinging. Anaïs Nin continued to titillate with the fifth volume of her diary, covering 1947-1954, as she traveled from Acapulco to New York, attracting creative geniuses and lovers as she went. Three popular bestselling novelists—Harold Robbins, Irving Wallace, and Jackie Collins—also made the bestseller lists with *The Pirate*, *The Fan Club*, and *The Love Killers*.

1974 popular songs such as Barbra Streisand's "The Way We Were," John Denver's "Annie's Song," and Paul Anka's "Having My Baby" were geared toward the sentimental. "I Can Help" by Billy Swan lightened things up a bit.

FAYE DUNAWAY & PETER WOLF

Actress Faye Dunaway was introduced to musician Peter Wolf in San Francisco. The sophisticated honey-blond thespian may have seemed an odd match for the wild-looking, Bronx-born singer, but their friendship blossomed into romance. Before Faye, Wolf had only one other love—his beloved companion, Edie, who died in a car accident a few years before. Dunaway had other romances, such as high-profile liaisons with comedian Lenny Bruce and actor Marcello Mastroianni. Dunaway and Wolf married on August 7, 1974 and divorced four years later. Dunaway later said, "We were like two warriors, always moving forward and helping each other. He's still my special friend."

SEE ALSO
▶ MARCELLO MASTROIANNI *Page 367*

458

1974 CAPRICORN

From December 22, 1973, 0:08 through January 20, 1974, 10:45
(December 1974 Capricorns, see 1975 Capricorn)

♑ *The Amorous Iconoclast*

For 1974 Capricorn, unusual personal magnetism can be the secret to your success in business and romantic affairs. Your innovative ideas, methods, and achievements create a "buzz" that attracts people's interest and makes it exciting to be around you. An intimate partner may have started out as someone who heard about you, admired you from afar, and wanted to get to know you better. Up close and personal, you are just as compelling, able to keep an intimate partner on pins and needles, in anticipation of your next move.

Your ideas for pitching woo tend to be surprising, sometimes elaborate, romantic, and quite endearing. Your highly entertained mate—and his or her family—might describe you as "a real original." Reaching a certain level of accomplishment and independence is most important before you settle down, but once you find your soul mate, you are likely to put your relationship and home life ahead of career concerns. Family ties bring out your tender side. Providing for your mate and any family you may have can be a source of great pride for

you, and you may feel just as strongly about your ability to satisfy your sweetheart in bed. As sharp and businesslike as you may be in public, you can be a sexy beast in private.

Playful and physical, you make love with gusto. A partner who lets loose on you with full-bodied abandon can pump you up with exhilaration. A daring lover might engage you in an erotic game of hide-and-seek. What happens once you find each other is up to you.

The 1974 Capricorn man seeks a woman who can understand and get behind his visions and ideas. You are likely to be attracted to women who are interesting, active, and intelligent. Your ideal partner has "something going on," and her passions seem to fit intriguingly well with yours.

Female Capricorns born in 1974 like the man who is creative and handy. Your ideal man may cater to your taste for fine living by enhancing your home with hand-crafted bookcases, luscious gardens, and collectibles. His taste for sensuality and comfort makes you eager to spend time at home enjoying his creations.

CAPRICORN ZODIAC SIGN
YOUR LOVE PLANETS

YOUR ROMANTIC SIDE   p. 696
▶ **VENUS IN AQUARIUS**
Born Dec. 22, 1973 0:08 - Jan. 20, 1974 10:45

YOUR SEX DRIVE   p. 722
▶ **MARS IN ARIES**
Born Dec. 22, 1973 0:08 - Dec. 24, 1973 8:08
▶ **MARS IN TAURUS**
Born Dec. 24, 1973 8:09 - Jan. 20, 1974 10:45

YOUR CELEBRITY TWINS   p. 760
Find out the astrological similarities you have with famous people.

YOUR COMPATIBILITY   p. 780
Compare planets to find out how compatible you are in a relationship.

YOUR RELATIONSHIP KARMA   p. 824
▶ **SATURN IN CANCER**
Born Dec. 22, 1973 0:08 - Jan. 7, 1974 20:21
▶ **SATURN IN GEMINI**
Born Jan. 7, 20:22 to Jan. 20, 10:45

459

1974 AQUARIUS

From January 20, 10:46 through February 19, 0:58

♒ *The Uncaped Crusader*

Aquarius of 1974 tends to have a rather philosophical outlook on love and romance. Unlikely to blindly accept societal norms about dating, courtship, and marriage, you may have your own, strongly-held ideas about what a relationship should be like, what it should do for both partners, and what you want to get out of it. The relationship most likely to succeed for you is one that fits and supports your unique needs as an individual and allows you and your partner to improvise in terms of the roles you play and any obligations you may owe each other. Every relationship you have gives you an opportunity to test, renegotiate, and revise your beliefs in the light of experience.

Meeting your soul mate marks the beginning of a turning point in your life, an experience that can move you to throw your preconceived notions out the window. While you need never surrender your unique personality with all its glorious eccentricities and quirks—indeed, this is what endears you to a partner in the first place—the intimacy of your attachment tends to shift

your emphasis away from intellectual ideals and deeper, into the realm of tenderness, needfulness, love, and trust. In the privacy of the bedroom, you can relax and show your true feelings.

Sensuous indulgences stir up your animal passions and allow you to feel love in the most delightful way. Sexual experimentation can lead to electrifying interludes with your beloved. Trying new techniques and exploring each other's bodies brings you together in an explosive fusion of emotional and physical ecstasy.

Staying power appeals to the Aquarian man of 1974. You can flourish with a woman who is a steady and reliable friend. While she may lend a strong shoulder, you especially enjoy the innovative use she makes with the rest of her body and with yours.

An earthy, sensible man is a wonderful counterpart for the brainy Aquarian woman of 1974. You may rely on this man for his practical insight on your ideas. His reality checks enable you to avoid wasting time and energy by shifting your focus to matters in which you have a true personal stake.

MARTHE KELLER
Swiss Actress
Sun in Aquarius

AQUARIUS ZODIAC SIGN
YOUR LOVE PLANETS

YOUR ROMANTIC SIDE   p. 696
▶ **VENUS IN AQUARIUS**
Born Jan. 20, 10:46 - Jan. 29, 19:50
▶ **VENUS IN CAPRICORN**
Born Jan. 29, 19:51 - Feb. 19, 0:58

YOUR SEX DRIVE   p. 722
▶ **MARS IN TAURUS**
Born Jan. 20, 10:46 - Feb. 19, 0:58

YOUR CELEBRITY TWINS   p. 760
Find out the astrological similarities you have with famous people.

YOUR COMPATIBILITY   p. 780
Compare planets to find out how compatible you are in a relationship.

YOUR RELATIONSHIP KARMA   p. 824
▶ **SATURN IN GEMINI**
Born Jan. 20, 10:46 - Feb. 19, 0:58

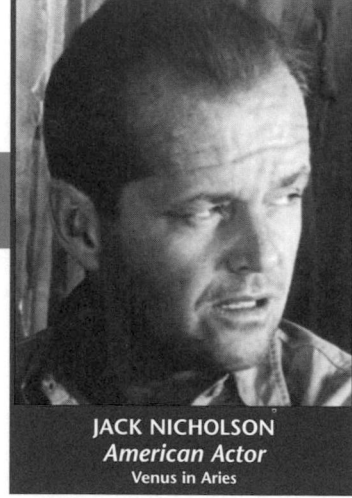

JACK NICHOLSON
American Actor
Venus in Aries

1974 PISCES
From February 19, 0:59 through March 21, 0:06

The Seductive Communicator

Pisces of 1974, you seem to instinctively know your way around relationships. You have a subtle magnetism that attracts admirers, and your flair for romance can draw a special person in even closer. Poetry, music, and fantasy may have a prominent role in your life, and sharing such pleasures makes a relationship with you a captivating and magical experience. A partner may gravitate to the soothing atmosphere you create with your almost psychic ability to anticipate a mate's thoughts and reactions. Because you are devoted and adaptable, you are able to weather any challenges that inevitably arise in a relationship. Because you can be so comforting and supportive, your partner is likely to run to you when he or she is going through a tough time.

Ultimately, you have the best kind of romance with someone who is on the same intuitive wavelength as you and who can prompt you to openly speak about those issues and concerns that matter to you and to the relationship. Expressing your feelings and needs enables you to tap into inner wells of strength, the depth and power of which may astonish you. Because you exude a hypnotic sexual aura, your seductive appeal provides another pleasurable avenue for getting your way.

Pleasing your partner has a lovely way of pleasing you. The best thing a lover can do is to make a clear show of appreciation for your little gifts and favors. Vocal responsiveness in bed is like cheerleading for you. Nothing turns you on like knowing that you are succeeding in making someone else feel good.

The 1974 Pisces man melts in the presence of a woman who is idealistic about romance. Having someone with whom to share your dreams is almost as good as making them come true. Your perfect mate is willing to do whatever it takes to create a life that reflects your highest ideals.

A chatty, charming man can make the Piscean woman of 1974 go weak at the knees. His sensitivity can be disarming and softens your heart. He may keep you on your toes with his mischievous sense of fun, a naughty streak that livens up lovemaking and keeps your romance hot and spicy.

1974 ARIES
From March 21, 0:07 through April 20, 11:18

The Pillow Talker

The Aries of 1974 is a leader and a trend setter. You may feel most comfortable around high-energy people who have no problem keeping up with your fast pace. While you enjoy having company as you take care of routine errands, you most appreciate someone who, like you, has a mission, completes it, and gets out of there! Anyone would feel lucky for the chance to run off with you. A romantic getaway gives you the chance to relax and give your sweetheart your undivided attention. With no work or responsibilities demanding your time, a fanciful and starry-eyed side of your personality can emerge. You may enjoy dancing, music, and lavishing your mate with sentimental keepsakes. Your relationship thrives when you make an intimate escape part of your daily routine.

The bonds of your relationship are stronger than they may appear. Just as air fans a fire, your romance thrives on freedom and breathing space. Mutual respect for each other's individuality is the cement that holds the two of you together. Open lines of communication are not just something you "should have." For you, talking to your beloved is a pleasure, filled with stimulating ideas and humorous word play. After a busy day out on your own, you probably can't wait to get home to tell your sweetheart all about it.

Pillow talk has a way of easing your pace while arousing your feelings of intimacy and connection. For you, communication can be the sexiest part of lovemaking. It turns you on to hear what feels good to your partner and to share what you like, in kind.

The ideal woman for the 1974 Aries man has a genius for keeping you in line, without calling attention to that fact. You wouldn't respect her enough to make her yours if you didn't suspect she was smarter than you. Of course, she would never point this out in public.

The Aries woman of 1974 appreciates a man who is powerful but fair. Because he has leadership qualities of his own, you may agree to divy up your life together into areas where one or the other of you is boss. A friendly competitiveness ensures that this partnership will never be boring.

460

1974 TAURUS

From April 20, 11:19 through May 21, 10:35

The Indulgent Caretaker

Spending cozy, intimate time with you, 1974 Taurus, is a pleasure not to be missed. Closeness with you is an especially precious gift because you can be very discriminating in choosing a romantic partner. You are unlikely to get serious until you've known someone for a long time, have allowed a sense of trust to develop together, and feel confident that the relationship can work. Any mate of yours can rest assured that he or she is very special to you. Once you've made a commitment, you can be a most indulgent, nurturing partner.

Actions tend to matter a lot more to you than mere words. You may not shower a partner with compliments and love notes, but just when he or she is about to complain, you show your feelings in a big way. A marriage proposal from you is likely to be as well-mapped-out and strategized as a battlefield attack plan, an effort that reveals the depth and intensity of your passion. In a long term relationship, you will go the extra mile to keep tabs on what your partner needs and to do whatever you can to help make your mate's

dreams come true. Through thick and thin, you show yourself to be as supportive and reliable as a best friend and as tender, sexy, and amorous as the most romantic lover.

Sentimental gifts and gestures can make you feel misty and eager for a hug. A little cologne dabbed on a lover's neck can create an irresistible target for kissing. For you, gentle hugging and kissing can steadily build into a steamy sexual encounter.

The Taurean man of 1974 appreciates a woman who communicates love on an intuitive level. You may not be highly verbal, but the two of you devise your own private body language for expressing affection. Your ideal woman escapes with you to a romantic isle that materializes whenever you two come together.

A tender nurturing man is ideal for the 1974 Taurean woman. You feel safe and secure with a man who cares about your needs and makes it his business to provide you with only the best. Feeding your heart, soul, and tummy, he knows how to keep every part of you satisfied. Your appreciation multiplies his own pleasure.

AL PACINO
American Actor
Venus and Mars in Gemini

1974 GEMINI
From May 21, 10:36 through June 21, 18:37

The Resilient Romantic

People born under the sign of Gemini tend to be very smart, thought-driven individuals, and the Gemini of 1974 shares these intellectual gifts. Likely to have a healthy curiosity about the world around you, you may exude a sense of magic and wonder in your approach to life—a breezy, charismatic quality that can capture the attention of others and captivate a partner. A romance with you is never boring. Getting to know your lover can fill you with exhilaration. And, as your experiences together bring out different facets of each other's personality, there is always something new to discover.

You are a bright and cheery partner, and your mate may cherish your ability to find something positive about almost any challenge you may face together. With your clever, agile mind, you can come up with playful ways to make loving fun. The foundation of your relationship comes from your heart. Your feelings of attachment to your sweetheart deepen over time. Spirituality opens another resource that can strengthen your bond with

your beloved. Even if you come from different traditions, you are open to sharing the best of both. Lovemaking brings the harmonious balance of your relationship to a soulful climax. Together with your mate, you derive the ultimate sexual pleasure in the intermingling of your bodies, feelings, and spirit.

A sweetly romantic soul, you are likely to have a soft spot for poetry, music, and fantasies. Words of love stir up your passions. Beautiful music can influence your mood, and you may have a favorite song that brings up sentimental feelings.

A woman who takes the initiative can be intriguing for the 1974 Gemini man. Her spontaneity and enthusiasm gives you the green light to unleash your charm and woo her. You have a soft spot for a sweet lady who responds to the romantic trappings of courtship.

The Gemini woman of 1974 can bond deeply with a romantic, creative man. You find it hard to resist someone who appeals to your imagination. Because your mind provides a pipeline to your heart, escaping to a realm of fanciful pleasures offers endless delight.

DIAHANN CARROLL
American Actress
Sun in Cancer

462

1974 CANCER
From June 21, 18:38 through July 23, 5:29

The Caring Guardian

Cancereans don't get enough credit for their skills as leaders, and the Cancer of 1974 is prominent among these under-recognized souls. You are likely to exude an air of authority that makes a partner feel safe and secure. In a relationship, it is your pleasure to take good care of your sweetheart. It's natural for you to be protective of your mate, but you may meet with resistance if a partner feels you are being too controlling. Because you have a keen sensitivity to a partner's feelings and thoughts, you can tune into any concerns that may arise, talk it over, and make any adjustments or accommodations needed to maintain harmony.

Your creativity in solving problems and striking compromises keeps your relationship dynamic and ever-growing. A loving home base provides you with a sense of balance and rootedness, from which everything else can flow. The stability of your relationship and the support of your mate frees you to pursue new ventures and challenges in life. The emotional bond between you gains in strength as the two of you draw from a deep, instinctive sense of

passion. The sign of Cancer rules feeding and breasts—in making love, you and your partner may virtually feed off of each other. Kissing sessions can be intense and prolonged, as if to draw the life force from your lover.

You may have a strong need to feel appreciated. Sometimes nothing more than a simple thank you for a thoughtful favor can swell your heart and put you in the mood for love. The partner who takes time to show appreciation for something you do all the time is in for a generous reward.

The Cancer man of 1974 may have a romantic weakness for a damsel in distress. You find it gratifying to help someone through a rough time. A woman with a clever mind and a sparkle in her eyes can make your heart skip a beat. Her smile can energize you.

A fiercely loyal man makes the 1974 Cancer woman feel safe and secure. Because you can be a homebody, you thrive with someone who warmly welcomes friends and family to your lair. At the same time, his sense of fun inspires you to go out and live it up!

1974 LEO
From July 23, 5:30 through August 23, 12:28

The Courtship Connoisseur

The 1974 Leo has a relationship skill that offers a lifetime of pleasure. You have a natural knack for the romantic date. The key ingredient in your recipe for courtship success is the way you light up when you're out on the town. A partner can't help but feel privileged to be out with you on a special trip. You have an intuitive ability to tune into your partner's feelings and reactions, making mental notes of your sweetheart's likes and dislikes. Your partner may feel that you know him or her better than anyone. You begin your most serious relationship with a passionate desire burning in your heart. Over time, your feelings relax into a deeper tenderness toward your mate.

If anything hurts or upsets your partner, you may feel the pain as if it were your own. You are a loyal and protective mate. Because the bonds of passion tend to be precious to you, giving it regular attention and nurturance is likely to be a high priority for you. Making time for intimacy with your sweetheart is an important part of your health and wellness regimen. Over the years, you are likely to

accumulate a vast well of knowledge about your partner's body, favorite techniques, and turn-ons. Your eagerness to try new things keeps lovemaking fresh and exciting.

You are a generous lover, eager to please and lavish your beloved with tokens of your appreciation. When someone wears or prominently displays a gift you have given, you light up like a sparkler. For you music, dancing, and poetry can be a form of exquisite foreplay.

A mild-mannered woman can become a fairy princess in the eyes of the 1974 Leo man. You bring out the best in your sweetheart and your relationship. Because you tend to idealize the woman you love, she feels more beautiful when she's around you. Like magic, she actually becomes more lovely.

The Leo woman of 1974 appreciates a man who remembers anniversaries, your birthday, and your favorite movie or food. Alone, each piece of information may be inconsequential, but when he makes it a reason for a special occasion, he lets you know how important you are to him.

1974 VIRGO *From August 23, 12:29 through September 23, 9:57*

The Fiery Friend

For you, Virgo of 1974, the best romantic relationships happen when a friendship catches fire. Members of your sign tend to be reserved and distrustful of relationships that start with lightning and fireworks on Day One. With a reliable friend, you can let your guard down over time. When friendship turns to love and desire, that comfortable companion can suddenly seem like someone completely new. Feelings of fondness and trust turn to deep warmth and attraction. Likely to be a creature of habit, you may thrive in a relationship that adds fun and romance to your routine—holding hands as you run errands and stealing kisses along the way.

For you, a serious relationship is all about give-and-take. Communication is important, but deeds should be as good as words. You may gravitate to a partner who is eager to take care of you. Good service is a Virgo specialty, so you're likely to return the favor. You tend to feel most secure in a partnership when you know you are needed. In the highest realization of your relationship's potential, you and your mate may devote yourselves to the service of others less fortunate than you. The love you direct outside your relationship comes back to strengthen your bond.

You slip into a more amorous frame of body when something, or someone, takes you out of your daily grind. If you can't take a day trip or an extended vacation, you might respond to a "day at the spa" in the privacy of your own home—with a special someone as your own personal massage therapist.

The 1974 Virgo man feels most comfortable with a woman who is empathetic and discreet. She may be a real lioness behind closed doors, but that's your private business. An understated sensuality satisfies your need for propriety while making you feel that you've happened upon a treasure.

Hard work, discipline, and tenderness appeal to the Virgo woman born in 1974. You are likely to care about community matters and appreciate someone who is happy to partner with you in efforts to improve your neighborhood and help others. A warm, friendly man is especially charming and endearing to you.

GORE VIDAL
American Writer
Sun and Mars in Libra

463

1974 LIBRA *From September 23, 9:58 through October 23, 19:10*

The Sweet Persuader

The 1974 Libra has some very powerful communication skills. With a glamorous personality and a magnetic aura, you can be extremely persuasive. The sheer pleasure of basking in your energy can draw admirers into your orbit. If the partner you desire does not happen to be among them, you can be even more compelling when you actively set about seducing someone. Once you've got a partner's attention, you can be quite the sweet talker, with a talent for saying exactly what a lover wants to hear—and wants to believe. A partnership with you can be magical. Harmonious relations are likely to be a priority, and you are likely to devote plenty of time and energy to keeping romance fresh.

As a relationship matures, your attachment to your sweetheart tends to deepen. Having a best friend and lover can bring you deep emotional satisfaction. Members of your sign often have artistic leanings, and you may create a lovely, peaceful atmosphere at home. You may woo your mate with music and poetry, rich with sentimental themes. When you are with a partner you love, your sex life is likely to be passionate, rich, and varied. As a lover, you are likely to have a light but well-aimed touch that teases your mate with anticipation.

When it comes to sex and seduction, you may leave a paper trail. That is, you may enjoy sending and receiving sexy notes, e-mails, cards, phone messages. The more "forbidden" the destination, i.e., to your mate at work, the bigger the kick you may get out of it, so long as the contents remain naughtily private.

The Libran man born in 1974 tends to go for a woman who is all business in public, but who is soft, tender, and sexy when you get her alone. She shouldn't be too available, even when your relationship is settled. You like to experience the thrill of the chase, again and again.

A take-charge man is a turn-on for the 1974 Libra woman. For you, an aura of power and influence can be very attractive. Negotiating the details of intimacy and love-making can provide you with an extremely delightful challenge. Your ideal man gets a kick out of letting you win.

FAYE DUNAWAY
American Actress
Mars in Sagittarius

1974 SCORPIO
From October 23, 19:11 through November 22, 16:37

 ♏

The Secret Believer

Born under a sign associated with great power and tremendous will, the Scorpio of 1974 abides by a higher law that can keep such forces within manageable limits. Spirituality may play an important role in your life and can provide the setting where true love finds you. Likely to have an active and creative mind, you can be very appealing to someone who follows a thoughtful path through life. You tend to thrive in a relationship that allows you to share the principles that give you direction and fill your days with meaning.

You're unlikely to share your innermost feelings with just anyone. Members of your sign tend to protect themselves by being secretive, and you have one very tender heart to protect. When you do open up with a love interest, it's a sign that you're in for the long haul. A serious commitment affords you the security to let down your guard and have some fun. Empathetic and supportive, you may enjoy spoiling your partner with romantic gifts. For you, lovemaking is best when you can truly surrender in a relationship based on trust and mutual caring. You may especially enjoy the wonder and mystery of getting to know your lover's body.

Because you are so cautious about letting your feelings show, your heart goes out to a lover who confides in you. You can find trading deep dark secrets to be profoundly arousing. One of the most profoundly intimate experiences you can have is to let your lover see your body and discover how exactly you respond to different kinds of stimulation.

A woman who is open to mystical experiences is a great match for the 1974 Scorpio man. You need a soul mate who understands that there is a layer of reality that we all see and a deeper layer with hidden meanings. Your ideal mate is eager to take your hand and explore the mysteries together.

Two different kinds of men can captivate the Scorpio woman of 1974. One has intense passions. You may feel uniquely qualified to help him channel all that energy. If two intensely passionate people are a crowd, you may prefer a gentle giant who can adapt his moods and temperament to yours.

1974 SAGITTARIUS
From November 22, 16:38 through December 22, 5:55

♐

The Affectionate Adventurer

Your ability to set and meet your own goals makes you an attractive target for Cupid's bow. A partner may be drawn to your sense of ambition and limitless opportunity. Likely to be romantic and affectionate, you may look forward to creating perfect love with a very special partner. A feeling of destiny may be a crucial element in your willingness to make a romantic commitment, and you may have waited to settle down until you felt you had found a true soul mate. Love can't be perfect all the time, but your willingness to aim high can fill your relationship with the most joy humanly possible.

Two of your least favorite words might be, "Yeah, but..." To your mind, anyone who would say that must lack imagination—a gift with which you are amply endowed. Your penchant for fantasy and romantic adventure can keep your relationship fresh and lively. You flourish with a partner who is eager to explore the world with you. For you, going places alone can feel like going nowhere at all. When you can share new experiences with a companion, everything feels more real. You may be equally adventurous as a lover. New sexual experiences can be as seductive as the lure of exotic cultures, and exploring your sweetheart's body can be as awe-inspiring as the Pyramids.

If pressed to pick the sexiest part of a lover, you're likely to pick his or her laughter. To laugh until it hurts may be your favorite form of foreplay. Speaking plainly about sex can spark your desire to turn all talk into more action.

The Sagittarius man of 1974 adores a daring woman who understands the necessity for taking the occasional risk. You can thrive with a lover who is inspiring and empathetic. When she senses that you are feeling tired or discouraged, she can safeguard your hopes and dreams like a treasure.

The Sagittarius woman born in 1974 appreciates a man who can help to give concrete form to her ideas in the real world. Because you tend to have a big-picture perspective, a partner with a mind for methods, planning, and resources can be your perfect complement. Together, you can't lose!

Raquel Welch – The Sex Goddess

During the 1960s and 1970s, Raquel Welch was one of the most popular celebrities in the world. After she appeared in the 1966 sci-fi hit *Fantastic Voyage*, she landed her most recognized starring role as Loana in *One Million Years B.C.* She became an instant international sex symbol based largely on the publicity posters for this movie, which showed her wearing a fur bikini. Still, very few people actually saw the movie. The dozens of films she made during this phase of her career generally tanked at the box office, and Welch felt trapped by her image. Her unrelenting ambition became to prove that she had much more to offer than mere beauty.

Raquel Welch was born with her Sun in hardworking, analytical Virgo, a fact that should alert the astrologically savvy that she is indeed much more than a static image. Her Virgo Sun is energized by a conjunction with assertive Mars, giving her plenty of drive and determination. This side of her is favorable for self-promotion but also for the occasional temperamental outburst. From time to time Welch would get into major disagreements with people. The most notable instance was in 1980 when she was chosen to star in John Steinbeck's *Cannery Row*. The studio claimed she was not attending morning rehearsals and that she insisted on doing her own hair and makeup, so she was fired. Welch sued and in 1986 won a multimillion dollar settlement. But she was blackballed from Hollywood for the next ten years.

Welch's image as a sex goddess comes from the feminine planets, the Moon

and Venus. Her Moon is in sexy, magnetic Scorpio and enormously charged by a square aspect to Pluto. This Moon-Pluto dynamic arouses extreme emotional states and a powerful desire nature. The raw animal instincts are just below the surface and project to the general public as intense sexuality. Venus, the planet associated with physical beauty, is well placed in her horoscope, so she naturally developed a voluptuous, captivating appearance. Before she was 18 she had already won several beauty contests. By the end of the century she made the number three spot on *Playboy* magazine's list of the top 100 sexiest stars of the twentieth century, behind Jayne Mansfield and Marilyn Monroe.

Welch felt disillusioned by becoming a fantasy figure, a sex icon, basically, an inanimate thing. She had ideas and ambitions about the making of movies, but no one would listen to her. "I would remember talking with directors and they would say, 'Could you just not think and have any ideas, please!' It kind of felt like doors were being closed to my soul," she explained. She decided to try new movie roles to increase her range as an actress. In 1969 she teamed up with Jim Brown, the former football star, in the movie western *100 Rifles*, which featured the first interracial love scene in a major Hollywood picture. Then in 1970 she portrayed an ambitious transsexual in *Myra Breckinridge*, but this one flopped, as did her next, self-produced film, *Hannie Caulder*.

Welch went to Las Vegas to launch a one-woman, whimsical show spoofing her own sexuality. The show went well, and this led to her being cast in *The Three Musketeers*, which also became a commercial success, and most importantly, for which she earned a Golden Globe Award for Best Actress. For the first time in her life she achieved the recognition she had been seeking. In 1982, banned from Hollywood due to her lawsuit, she went to Broadway to replace Lauren Bacall in *Woman of the Year*. The critics loved her, and ticket sells boomed. "After so many years, it finally gave me the legitimacy I was looking for," she said. "I was able to knock everybody's socks off because they didn't know I had all these cards up my sleeve."

▶ READ MORE ABOUT MARILYN MONROE ON PAGES 293 AND 294

- ⭐ **THE PILL**
- ⭐ **PHEROMONES**
- ⭐ **THE STORY OF O**
- ⭐ **WARREN BEATTY**
- ⭐ **CAPTAIN & TENNILLE**
- ⭐ **THAT'S THE WAY I LIKE IT**

EVENTS

A confidential report in Spain was leaked, divulging that the "Pill" was being used by more than half a million Spanish women. On the other side of the Atlantic, in the US, a study conducted by a Cornell University psychologist and published in *Psychology Today* magazine revealed that collegians were cohabiting in greater numbers than ever before.

Maybe part of the reason could be attributed to the aromatic "sex attractant" chemicals that researchers discovered in the vaginal secretions of women. These chemicals, known as pheromones, had been found in all animals, but their presence in humans, though suspected, had not been previously confirmed.

Continuing with the spice, Annabel Hunt hit the headlines as the first person in Britain to perform naked on television—she was participating in a nude opera version of *Ulysses*.

POP CULTURE

Popular films in 1975 ranged from the historic to the contemporary, from the hysterical to the intense. *Barry Lyndon* was a tale of an eighteenth-century rogue, and *L'Histoire d'O (The Story of O)* was the screen adaptation of the French erotic novel. *Shampoo* featured Warren Beatty as a hedonistic Beverly Hills hairdresser in this comedy of morals. In *Swept Away,* an uppity lady finds herself marooned on a deserted island with the hired help—romance and role reversals follow. Al Pacino was powerful in *Dog Day Afternoon,* portraying a gay man who robs a

Hot Movie

bank to finance his lover's sex-change operation.

Copies of *Looking for Mr. Goodbar* flew out of the bookstores as women read about the life of single Terry Dunn searching for Mr. Right in all the wrong places. Arthur Hailey's *The Moneychangers* gave us a steamy look at money, sex, power, and banking. *Ragtime*, E. L. Doctorow's tale of turn-of-the-century America, intrigued the public with its real-life characters and scandals.

On the juke box Captain & Tennille had us hustling to their hit "Love Will Keep Us Together." Other top tunes included Elton John's "Island Girl" and "Philadelphia Freedom," a Tony Orlando & Dawn rendition of "He Don't Love You," and KC & the Sunshine Band's "That's the Way (I Like It)."

SHAMPOO

When the wildly popular sex farce *Shampoo* erupted on the scene in 1975, charismatic leading man Warren Beatty's star was still on the rise. He played a notorious womanizing hairdresser bent on seducing dazzling temptresses Goldie Hawn, Lee Grant, and Julie Christie. He also produced and co-wrote the film.

Beatty had a real-life reputation as a ladies man, and this only made his on-screen antics even more mesmerizing. The film was a smash hit and earned him an Oscar nomination for the screenplay. Coming just before the dawn of the disco era, *Shampoo* heralded an age of decadence and self-indulgence.

SEE ALSO

▶ WARREN BEATTY *Page 497*

▶ ANNIE HALL *Page 482*

1975 CAPRICORN

From December 22, 1974, 5:56 through January 20, 1975, 16:35
(December 1975 Capricorns, see 1976 Capricorn)

♑ *The Psychic Sweet-talker*

As a 1975 Capricorn, you know how to give a compliment. That's because you have an uncanny ability to discern people's soft spots. Your flattering words usually win you a special place in society, and you're probably quite popular. There is a good chance that you'll do a fair amount of dating, refusing to settle down until your later years. Playing the field is simply too much fun! The longer you stay single, the greater your reputation will grow as a charming heartbreaker.

Eventually, however, you will want to find a life partner, and when that happens, you'll become very serious. Marriage is no laughing matter for you. You're intent on finding a mate who is willing to stick by you in both good times and bad. Sexually, you need a partner who puts you at ease with your body. You blossom with a lover who continually murmurs how sexy and alluring you are as you make love. You are easily aroused in luxurious environments, and may enjoy sex play in the bathtub.

Any suitor who seeks to capture your heart should express an interest in family. You deeply desire to have children, although you may not get started on this quest until later in life. It's also important to notice any little changes you've made. When somebody praises you for a new hairstyle or outfit, you understand that they are just as observant as you are. This is a definite plus in your book.

Two different kinds of women appeal to you 1975 male Goats. The first is controlled on the outside, but passionate on the inside. The second is social and smart. Whichever category your dream girl fits into, it's essential that she be witty, sophisticated, and irreverent. A rich, sexy laugh never fails to get your juices flowing.

As a female Capricorn born in 1975, you may have one masculine ideal. You're probably searching for an old-fashioned cowboy type—rough yet courteous, direct but fair-minded. Taking risks is sometimes scary for you, so it's a good idea to team up with a mate who helps you push past these fears. You can't abide snobs, and usually gravitate toward guys who have a wide variety of friends.

CAPRICORN ZODIAC SIGN
YOUR LOVE PLANETS

YOUR ROMANTIC SIDE — p. 696
▶ VENUS IN CAPRICORN
Born Dec. 22, 1974 5:56 - Jan. 06, 1975 6:38
▶ VENUS IN AQUARIUS
Born Jan. 06, 6:39 - Jan. 20, 16:35

YOUR SEX DRIVE — p. 722
▶ MARS IN SAGITTARIUS
Born Dec. 22, 1974 5:56 - Jan. 20, 1975 16:35

YOUR CELEBRITY TWINS — p. 760
Find out the astrological similarities you have with famous people.

YOUR COMPATIBILITY — p. 780
Compare planets to find out how compatible you are in a relationship.

YOUR RELATIONSHIP KARMA — P. 824
▶ SATURN IN CANCER
Born Dec. 22, 1974 5:56 - Jan. 20, 1975 16:35

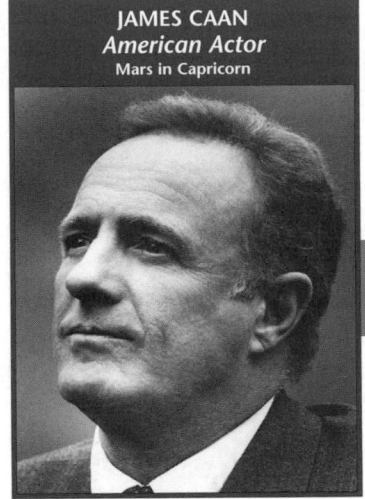

JAMES CAAN
American Actor
Mars in Capricorn

467

1975 AQUARIUS

From January 20, 16:36 through February 19, 6:49

♒ *The Diligent Suitor*

Love is a serious business to you 1975 Aquarians. You're not the type to play around with somebody's heart. When you seek a person's devotion, you do so in earnest. At times you're so intent on sealing the deal that you forget to put a dash of sugar into the proceedings. That's not because you don't have romantic instincts. Rather, you're just so anxious to win your beloved's heart that you forget to linger over the sweet opening moments of courtship.

You have a tendency to view relationships like a chemical equation. It fascinates you to think that two very dissimilar people can find joy and happiness together. You are turned on by a partner who has an experimental attitude toward sex. When it comes to making love, you prefer to explore unfamiliar territory than to go over the same old ground.

It's easy to attract your attention—just peruse a bunch of old trivia books! You love discussing strange facts, figures, and phenomena with folks. Anybody who expresses an interest in ESP, aliens, and the paranormal will probably connect with you. You're also quite distinctive looking and pride yourself on having your own personal style. A love interest that embraces your style is bound to find favor with you.

As a 1975 male Aquarius, you want a woman who has an insatiable lust for life. You're always excited by females who have a variety of hobbies. A girl whose life is her work holds no charm for you. Women who have a quirky or unusual outlook are especially attractive. You couldn't abide a mate who wants an average lifestyle.

If you're a woman Water Bearer who was born in 1975, you probably like men who are ambitious in a low-key sort of way. Nothing thrills you more than learning that the guy you're with runs his own business or holds political office. You want a man who is confident enough in his abilities that he doesn't have to brag about them. Guys with strong leadership qualities always appeal to you—there's such a powerful aura around these men. Ultimately, you want a mate who is so secure in his masculinity that he doesn't have to brandish it about like a sword.

AQUARIUS ZODIAC SIGN
YOUR LOVE PLANETS

YOUR ROMANTIC SIDE — p. 696
▶ VENUS IN AQUARIUS
Born Jan. 20, 16:36 - Jan. 30, 6:04
▶ VENUS IN PISCES
Born Jan. 30, 6:05 - Feb. 19, 6:49

YOUR SEX DRIVE — p. 722
▶ MARS IN SAGITTARIUS
Born Jan. 20, 16:36 - Jan. 21, 18:48
▶ MARS IN CAPRICORN
Born Jan. 21, 18:49 - Feb. 19, 6:49

YOUR CELEBRITY TWINS — p. 760
Find out the astrological similarities you have with famous people.

YOUR COMPATIBILITY — p. 780
Compare planets to find out how compatible you are in a relationship.

YOUR RELATIONSHIP KARMA — P. 824
▶ SATURN IN CANCER
Born Jan. 20, 16:36 - Feb. 19, 6:49

TIM CURRY
English Actor
Sun in Aries

1975 PISCES
From February 19, 6:50 through March 21, 5:56

The Sexy Idealist

It's hard to feel pessimistic around you Fish who were born in 1975. You're just so darned positive, especially when it comes to love! As far as you're concerned, love is the ultimate remedy for all the world's problems. Perhaps that's why you pursue relationships so ardently. For you, partnerships are a means to heal emotional and spiritual wounds. You have a tendency to fall in love hard, fast, and often.

You're never as attractive as when you're involved with some humanitarian cause. It's very important for you to bring peace and prosperity to impoverished and powerless people. Animals hold a special place in your heart, too, and there's a good chance you could meet your mate while working at a shelter, kennel, or veterinarian's office. If you don't have pets, it may be because your lifestyle is too unpredictable to keep one. In that case, you may meet your partner on one of your many exotic trips.

Demonstrating a serious interest in the arts is always an excellent way to get your attention. You love all forms of creative expression, and view artists as akin to gods. You're also moved by people who are sentimental. When it comes time to make the first move with you, your admirer would be wise to come to you with a dilemma of some sort. You love kissing somebody's tears away. Your compassion can move to ardor with some encouragement.

As a male Fish who was born in 1975, you admire a variety of women. You like shy, sporty, and sensual females, and have a hard time settling down with one partner. The woman who ultimately steals your heart will be a born nurturer. Deep down inside, you want to be pampered and coddled like a baby, and deeply appreciate any woman who is eager to do this for you.

Men with a strong social conscience are good partners for you 1975 female Pisces. You can't abide guys who aren't up on the latest news—they seem so shallow and callous. When you meet a man who combines sensitivity, compassion, and sex appeal, you know you've met your match. If your mate has artistic talent, so much the better. You're particularly turned on by musicians

1975 ARIES
From March 21, 5:57 through April 20, 17:06

The Lovable Mischief-maker

Trust you 1975 Aries to cook up some crazy scheme. You thrill getting into mischief, and seek a partner who enjoys your antics. Even when you overstep your boundaries, you are quick to apologize. It's hard to stay angry at you for long, which is why you probably count many former lovers among your friends. You don't like breaking ties with somebody just because the romance has gone out of your relationship.

What you really want from a partner is a friend with a clever mind to match your own. You delight in a mate who keeps you guessing about their motives. This desire for intrigue extends to your sex life. Nothing turns you on more than a partner who takes you by surprise in the bedroom. You like to make love as often as possible, and would benefit from a lover who shares your desire for frequent sex. Marriage will do nothing to cool your ardor. In fact, your physical desire for your spouse may deepen over the years. You do best with a partner who is completely devoted to you.

Therefore, anybody wanting to seek your attention would be wise to make some penetrating remark about your body language. You love it when people notice your quirks—it shows they are interested in getting to know the real you. Another surefire way to turn your head is to play a practical joke on you. You're sure to spend the next few days devising a way to return the favor. What better way to begin a romance?

Women with an earthy sense of humor always win favor with you 1975 male Rams. You're looking for a girl who can make you laugh at your own foibles. Ideally, your partner will have a razor-sharp mind that allows her to see many angles of a single situation or idea. According to you, smart women are not intimidating—they're stimulating!

If you're a female Arien who was born in 1975, you want a guy who is shy but devilish. You have a special fondness for men who sit quietly in the corner, laughing softly at everybody's antics. A self-conscious man poses an exciting challenge for you. You want a partner with hidden depths, and you will stop at nothing to draw a bashful man out of his shell.

1975 TAURUS
From April 20, 17:07 through May 21, 16:23

The Steadfast Lover

As a 1975 Taurus, you are one of the most determined signs in the entire zodiac. When you catch sight of something—or someone—you want, you'll stop at nothing to obtain it. This is especially true with regard to romance. You're quite inventive in courtship, and like wooing the object of your affection with unusual gestures like putting your phone number in a fortune cookie or spelling out your beloved's name in votive candles beneath their bedroom window.

Direct and outspoken, you don't waste any time expressing your love. There's a delicious intensity about your personality that is quite thrilling. Anybody who has held your gaze for more than ten seconds will sense that you are an extremely passionate lover. When it comes to relationships, you're looking for a partner who heightens your senses and brings an added force to life. If you get married, it will be anything but a conventional relationship. You want a partner who is willing to go to extremes with you, so you can experience life's distilled essence together.

The best way to attract your attention is through witty banter. You really admire folks who can offer snappy comebacks and sarcastic retorts at the drop of a hat. You're also drawn to folks who possess charm, grace, and poise. A good dancer never fails to win favor with you, especially when they offer to teach you some tricky moves. You like people with understated but classic taste—flashy types can make you quite uncomfortable.

Women who are intelligent and nurturing appeal most to you 1975 male Bulls. You're looking for somebody who will not only encourage your interests, but also reassure you when your pursuit of them becomes difficult. Any woman who is willing to make short-term sacrifices for long-term goals would be a good match for you.

As a female Taurus who was born in 1975, you want a man who is gentle, romantic, and spiritual. You're especially touched by guys who seem to need protection in some way, because such men bring out your considerable nurturing instincts. Pairing up with a sensitive artist would be an ideal arrangement for you.

TAURUS ZODIAC SIGN
Your Love Planets

YOUR ROMANTIC SIDE — p. 696
▶ **VENUS IN GEMINI**
Born Apr. 20, 17:07 - May 09, 20:10
▶ **VENUS IN CANCER**
Born May 09, 20:11 - May 21, 16:23

YOUR SEX DRIVE — p. 722
▶ **MARS IN PISCES**
Born Apr. 20, 17:07 - May 21, 8:13
▶ **MARS IN ARIES**
Born May 21, 8:14 - May 21, 16:23

YOUR CELEBRITY TWINS — p. 760
Find out the astrological similarities you have with famous people.

YOUR COMPATIBILITY — p. 780
Compare planets to find out how compatible you are in a relationship.

YOUR RELATIONSHIP KARMA — p. 824
▶ **SATURN IN CANCER**
Born Apr. 20, 17:07 - May 21, 16:23

ISABELLE ADJANI
French Actress
Venus in Gemini

469

1975 GEMINI
From May 21, 16:24 through June 22, 0:25

The Dashing Suitor

Exuberant is the word that best describes you 1975 Geminis. You've got a zest for life that is most refreshing. You love plunging into new situations headfirst, and that includes romance. It only takes you a second to fall in love, and when you do, watch out! You'll pursue the object of your affection with a daring ardor that is breathtaking. When folks see you in action, they're reminded that chivalry is not dead. It's as though you stepped straight from the pages of a fairy tale.

You are quite a popular figure and often meet love interests through friends. There's a good chance that everyone you know is eager to set you up with their cousin or best friend, simply because you're one of the nicest people around. No matter how you feel about a particular date, you manage to make them feel wonderful. That's because you're able to flatter folks without seeming insincere. When you meet someone who really bowls you over, though, it will be totally obvious. You tend to revert to crazy antics when you're in love, much like the class clown did back in grade school.

Anybody who is well-traveled has a good chance of winning your affection. You're totally captivated by tales of foreign lands and exotic cultures. Spiritually-minded people also find favor with you. Sexually, you desire a partner who views making love as a means of connecting on a profound level. You're generally not interested in hopping into bed with somebody for the sake of sheer physical pleasure. You want to join both minds and bodies with your dream lover.

You male Twins who were born in 1975 are attracted to women who are intense and creative. Passive types leave you cold, and you absolutely hate it when somebody plays hard-to-get with you. You want to know where you stand in your lover's life. If your partner is a bit eccentric, that's even better.

As a 1975 female Gemini, you want a friendly, outgoing man with leadership potential. A man who inspires your confidence never fails to attract your interest. You want a partner who will treat you like an equal and a friend, not just a sex object.

GEMINI ZODIAC SIGN
Your Love Planets

YOUR ROMANTIC SIDE — p. 696
▶ **VENUS IN CANCER**
Born May 21, 16:24 - June 06, 10:53
▶ **VENUS IN LEO**
Born June 06, 10:54 - June 22, 0:25

YOUR SEX DRIVE — p. 722
▶ **MARS IN ARIES**
Born May 21, 16:24 - June 22, 0:25

YOUR CELEBRITY TWINS — p. 760
Find out the astrological similarities you have with famous people.

YOUR COMPATIBILITY — p. 780
Compare planets to find out how compatible you are in a relationship.

YOUR RELATIONSHIP KARMA — p. 824
▶ **SATURN IN CANCER**
Born May 21, 16:24 - June 22, 0:25

MARISA BERENSON
American Actress
Mars in Cancer

470

1975 CANCER
From June 22, 0:26 through July 23, 11:21

The Conflicted Romantic

Accomplished, smart, and wise beyond your years, you 1975 Cancers are an impressive group. For all of your achievements, however, you are a little wistful when it comes to romance. There's a good chance that you chose ambition over love at a very early age. As you grow older, however, you'll seek a partner who shares your respect for hard work and love of tradition. Sexually, you benefit most from a lover who can bring you out of your shell. It may take a while for your mate to loosen you up, but when they do, the results will be spectacular! As a lover, you will get better as you get older.

You're very idealistic when it comes to love, and seek a partner who is tender, valiant, and true. It's your dream to settle down with somebody who appreciates the real you, instead of all the status and material trappings you're bound to accumulate. You want a relationship that provides you with a safe haven from the outside world. When you come through the front door after a hard day's work, you yearn to have someone to come running and leap into your arms, covering you with kisses.

If somebody wants to attract your attention, they'll exhibit talent in all of the domestic arts. Anybody who can cook and keep house is sure to win your profound respect and admiration. You also love nurturing types, and thrill when a special someone remembers that you like marshmallows in your hot chocolate or cinnamon on your French toast. People who possess an earthy sensuality particularly are especially attractive to you.

You 1975 male Crabs want a woman who enjoys keeping the home fires burning. You're very ambitious, but want to live in comfort. Therefore, a woman who loves cooking and keeping house is your ideal partner. It wouldn't hurt if she has a decorative flair—you want a home with a personal touch.

If you're a female Cancer born in 1975, you want a man who is affectionate, tender, and down-to-earth. You don't mind if your partner is assertive—it excites you when your man takes a stand. For the most part, however, you want somebody to cuddle with on cold winter nights and sultry summer days.

1975 LEO
From July 23, 11:22 through August 23, 18:23

The Sociable Flirt

There's no doubt about it, as a 1975 Leo you're one of the most charming folks around. You're always full of compliments, and have a knack for making grandmothers feel 16 years old and 16-year-old boys feel like men of the world. It's no surprise, then, that you're so successful in love. One word from you and the object of your affection melts like butter on a hot skillet. You fall in love quite easily and tend to idolize your partners, and this only adds to your charm. It's rare to meet somebody who is as romantic and idealistic as you in this day and age.

You want a relationship that makes you feel like the star of a colorful musical. In fact, you're not above singing in the rain or dancing with hat racks when you're infatuated with a person. Love has a transformative effect on you, and even the bleakest days seem sunny when your sweetheart is near. There's a good chance that you'll travel the world with your partner, rather than staying together in one place. Exotic surroundings will only fuel your passion.

Attracting your attention is easy. Just talk about the movies, theater, or music. You're passionately interested in the arts, and love discussing the latest trends. After a suitor has made initial contact with you, it's best that they become a little elusive. You love a challenge, and thrill in chasing down someone who has sparked your interest.

Women who are neat and meticulous in their appearance always win favor with you 1975 male Leos. You want a partner who is skilled but modest—nothing turns you on like a gifted worker who blushes with pleasure at a sincere tribute. A woman with high standards also bolsters your ego, because you know that by picking you as her mate, she's paying you the ultimate compliment.

As a female Lion who was born in 1975, you want a man who is intelligent and articulate. A stimulating conversation is akin to a sensual massage for you, and nothing puts you in the mood for love like a good debate. You also appreciate a man who likes the finer things in life. An intellectual mate who indulges you on a regular basis is ideal.

1975 VIRGO

From August 23, 18:24 through September 23, 15:54

The Uncontrolled Romantic

You 1975 Virgins are a lusty lot. Possessing big dreams and fiery passions, it takes everything in your power to remain cool, calm, and collected. You're especially carried away by love. Your ideal partner makes you feel as though you are the only person in the room, even when you're crammed together in a jam-packed stadium. A cozy relationship that has an exclusive feel about it makes you blossom with joy. You're not content to team up with somebody out of sheer loneliness.

Possessing terrific instincts, you trust your intuition to lead you to the right partner. Your first question upon meeting a potential love interest is, "Do I feel any chemistry between us?" If the answer is no, you'll nip things in the bud right away. You feel very strongly that there must be an initial sexual attraction between people in order for a romance to ensue. You're not terribly concerned if your partner doesn't share your interests. The important thing is that you respond to each other on physical, spiritual, and emotional levels.

It's best to take a direct approach when seducing you. You love a person who knows what they want and is willing to do anything to win their prize. Proposing a visit to an unusual or out-of-the-way spot also intrigues you. Dinner and a movie are all well and good, but you'd rather go on a date that excites your imagination and keeps you both a little off balance. Discussing controversial books and news items will also catch your attention, because you love provocative subjects.

As a male 1975 Virgo, you're looking for a woman who likes to be on display. It fills you with pride to walk into a room with a stunning female on your arm. If she has a distinctive way of dressing, boasts a gorgeous mane of hair, or wears a signature color, you're really hooked.

You female Virgins who were born in 1975 want men with brains. A writer, professor, philosopher, or scientist would be ideal for you. You're looking for a partner who is always on the go, because you've got a restless nature, too. A partner who is able to take you on exotic business trips would be heaven.

JOHN CAZALE
American Actor
Venus in Virgo

471

1975 LIBRA

From September 23, 15:55 through October 24, 1:05

The Hopeful Lover

As a 1975 Libra, you're one of the most optimistic folks around. This is especially true with regard to love. As far as you're concerned, love can solve any problem. Perhaps that's why you are so preoccupied with relationships. Although you're quite self-reliant, there's a good chance you feel somewhat incomplete without a partner. Therefore, you're always on the lookout for someone special. The prospect of joining hands and hearts with your soul mate is simply thrilling for you.

You have an intense and magnetic personality that attracts admirers to you like a flower draws bees. And while you are always quick to spot people's good points, you're very selective about whom you choose as a mate. Ultimately, you want a relationship that is as rare and precious as a flawless diamond. Settling down with somebody for the sake of companionship isn't your style. You're willing to keep digging in order to strike gold.

There are a few basic ground rules for anybody who wants to become your mate. First and foremost, your admirer must be open-minded. You can't abide prejudiced people. It helps if your suitor is well-traveled, because this demonstrates a curiosity about other cultures. When it comes time to make the first move with you, your admirer should move with the grace of a jungle cat. You can't abide awkward fumblers. A suave suitor who kisses you with bold assurance makes your heart pound with excitement.

As a 1975 male Libran, you're looking for a woman who has a regal air about her. Nothing turns you on like a girl with great posture and a sexy strut. You're also attracted to women who are observant and analytical. You love analyzing various people with your partner, and delight in her perceptive observations.

For the female Libran born in 1975, your perfect partner is smart and intuitive. You greatly appreciate a man who is able to challenge your intellect and anticipate your desires. You're probably the type of woman who would never consider going out with a guy that hates to read. Consequently, you'd be wise to look for your soul mate in a library or bookstore.

LEE GRANT
American Actress
Sun and Mars in Scorpio

472

1975 SCORPIO
From October 24, 1:06 through November 22, 22:30

 *The Prize Catch*

Original, steadfast, and adventurous, it's no wonder you 1975 Scorpions are so much in demand. Your drive and determination is tempered by a whimsical outlook that is quite captivating. People can't make up their minds whether you're a born executive or a creative genius. The truth is, you're both, which accounts for your incredible sex appeal. Picking your partner can be an exquisitely agonizing decision, because you probably have tons of admirers from which to choose.

You're seeking a relationship that will broaden your horizons and deepen your understanding of life. For you, love is the ultimate learning experience. That's probably why you seek a partner with an unusual background. Looking at life through their eyes will give you a fresh appreciation for different people, cultures, and countries. When it comes to making love, you do best with a partner who's as open-minded about their sexuality as they are about the world around them. You want a lover who encourages you to act out your wildest fantasies without reservation.

Anybody seeking to attract your attention would be wise to bring up subjects like religion and philosophy around you. You can especially be interested in the idea of an afterlife, and enjoy speculating about what existence is like beyond the Earth plane. Expressing a passion for various cultural art forms is also sure to grab your attention. You most likely are always interested in learning about people in foreign lands, and would welcome a partner who could enlighten you on this subject.

As a male Scorpion who was born in 1975, you're looking for a woman who is constantly looking to improve herself. A girl who sees life as the ultimate learning experience would be the perfect partner for you. Females well versed in the arts also appeal to you, and there's a good chance your life partner will possess creative talent.

You female 1975 Scorpios are looking for a brooding, passionate man who makes you feel like the heroine in a romance novel. It helps if your love interest enjoys the company of children, for you like fatherly, protective types, too.

1975 SAGITTARIUS
From November 22, 22:31 through December 22, 11:45

The Chivalrous Suitor

As a 1975 Sagittarius, you're probably one of the most honest and upright people in the world. You'd rather let somebody down gently than string them along with false hopes. Fortunately, you rarely get in compromising positions with lovers, because you're so forthright about your feelings. When you say "I love you," you mean it with every fiber of your being. Maybe that's why you tend to take your time picking out your perfect partner.

Romance is very important to you. There's a good chance that you'll be courting your spouse with wine, candy, and flowers well after your 30th wedding anniversary. You often use music as a prelude to lovemaking, and certain songs never fail to put you in the mood. You're looking for a partner who also delights in tender, sentimental gestures, and isn't afraid to make them towards you.

Lending you a favorite book of poetry or photography is a good way to win your heart. You love gaining insight to people through their artistic sensibilities. Giving sweet tokens of affection is also advised. A single flower left

on your desk or a funny cartoon clipped from the newspaper can make you smile all day. You like it when an admirer makes the first move with you. Any would-be lovers should be aware that you are extremely dynamic in the bedroom, and enjoy making love several times over the course of one night.

You 1975 male Sagittarians want a girl who is all sugar and spice and everything nice. Women who wear delicate frills and flowery fragrances always find favor with you. You also like females who possess a smoldering sensuality. Women with hidden dimensions fascinate you. Ideally, you want a partner who is prim and proper in public, but bold and passionate in private.

If you're a 1975 female Archer, you're probably looking for a man who is magnetic and dynamic. Bold businessmen and rugged athletes usually appeal to you, but you do have an occasional weakness for artistic types, too. The most important thing, though, is that your partner has a great spirit of adventure, and is eager to explore every hidden corner of the world with you.

The Rocky Horror Picture Show

Camp, kinky, cross-dressing gender-bending—and that's just the audience. Yes, it can only be the cult classic *The Rocky Horror Picture Show*.

An homage to hammy horror with a dash of sci-fi, a nod to Marvel comics, and lashings of rock 'n' roll, *The Rocky Horror Picture Show* isn't your average sing-along musical.

But then the plot isn't your average storyline. When a bit of car trouble leaves clean-cut preppie college kids Brad and Janet stranded in a rainstorm, they go to the nearest castle for help. Enter transvestite Dr. Frank-N-Furter, from the planet Transexual in the galaxy of Transylvania, who has just created the perfect man— prime hunk Rocky Horror. Brad and Janet discover the delights of sexual liberation in an orgy—quite literally—of song, dance, and suspenders. Outrageous and subversive? That was the point.

What started as an experimental play in a fringe theatre in London became a screen hit quicker than Frank-N-Furter could whip off Rocky's Y-fronts. Written by Richard O'Brien and originally entitled *They Came from Denton High*, the Rocky phenomenon began in June 1973 when music mogul Lou Adler, visiting from the States, happened to catch the show. Within 36 hours he had bought the American theatrical rights and by 1975 it was immortalized on the silver screen—with Adler as executive producer.

Tim Curry, who played Frank-N-Furter in the original theater version, slipped into his fishnets and stilettos for the film role. Susan Sarandon and Meatloaf injected the pizzazz star factor and even writer Richard O'Brien made an appearance as butler Riff Raff. But for all its rippling sexuality, the movie bombed. That is, until 18 months later, when a funny thing started happening in theaters across America. Every Saturday at midnight, throngs of cross-dressing,

Tim Curry as
Dr. Frank-N-Furter in *The Rocky Horror Picture Show*

garter-wearing folk were turning up to chant along at the film. *Rocky* legend has it that it all began in Greenwich Village when a guy started to shout back at the actors on the screen. His one-liners caught on quickly and soon everyone in the audience was participating, creating lines of their own.

From underground hit to out-of-the-closet smash, the show's followers were now as important as the show itself. Turning up in Basques, lacy thongs, and not much else, dressing the part became *de rigeur*. And no fan was a real fan without their props—newspaper hats, rubber gloves, rice, and toilet rolls all ready. There were even dance steps to learn for when "The Time Warp" song blasted out. This wasn't just audience participation—this was audience devotion.

Now over thirty years later, the same lines are yelled. Repartee can differ from theater to theater—the more diehard and adventurous the fans, the more risqué and titillating the comments. A quick (tame) guide for beginners—when Brad says he's going to hunt for a telephone and Janet replies that she's going with him, shout out, "That'll be a first." When Dr. Scott goes into the lab, throw a roll of toilet paper.

What started off as a '70s glammed-up, tongue-in-cheek, spoof horror, sexual romp has become an ageless bastion of over-the-top kitsch. And for anyone who is planning to go and is a "Rocky Virgin," there's only one rule—leave your chaste thoughts at home and prepare to be deflowered.

473

- ⊛ RENEÉ RICHARDS
- ⊛ "JIGGLE TV"
- ⊛ A STAR IS BORN
- ⊛ THE HITE REPORT
- ⊛ ROD STEWART
- ⊛ SILLY LOVE SONGS
- ⊛ PAUL SIMON

Hot Couple

EVENTS

Reputations were at stake in 1976 when then US presidential candidate Jimmy Carter admitted in a *Playboy* magazine interview that he had looked at women with lust and had committed adultery in his heart. Carter managed to win the election, but in Britain, Liberal leader Jeremy Thorpe resigned from the party after allegations he'd had a homosexual affair with a male model. Reneé Richards was barred from competing in women's professional tennis—because she was born Richard Raskin. Richards had legally become female after completing hormone replacement therapy and surgery. Richards later won her case and competed in the 1977 US Open.

Reputations were quickly made when the original TV drama *Charlie's Angels* premiered to high ratings. Starring Farrah Fawcett, Kate Jackson, and Jaclyn Smith, the series was also savaged by critics who viewed it as "family-style porn" and "jiggle TV." A poster of Farrah Fawcett sold 12 million copies, and her winged hairstyle became an overwhelming favorite with American women.

POP CULTURE

At the movies viewers were riveted to a third remake of *A Star is Born*. Barbra Streisand and Kris Kristofferson paired up for this classic rocky romance between an aging has-been and his up-and-coming bride. Other films chronicled well-known people, such as *The Incredible Sarah*, about French actress Sarah Bernhardt, and the Fellini film, *Casanova*, an account of the legendary lover, a Venetian nobleman.

Booksellers touted *The Hite Report: A Nationwide Study of Female Sexuality*, by Shere Hite. Novels that grabbed attention were Sidney Sheldon's *A Stranger in the Mirror*, about Toby Temple, a television superstar who woos a Hollywood starlet to a tragic end, and a Jacqueline Susann book, *Dolores*, a thinly veiled account of Jacqueline Kennedy Onassis.

The pop charts exploded with catchy love tunes, all done by well-known recording artists, such as Rod Stewart's "Tonight's the Night," Paul McCartney & Wings' "Silly Love Songs," Chicago's "If You Leave Me Now," and the Four Seasons' "Oh, What a Night." Elton John & Kiki Dee paired up for "Don't Go Breaking My Heart," and Paul Simon gave us "50 Ways to Leave Your Lover."

CHARLOTTE RAMPLING & JEAN-MICHEL JARRE

When young British actress Charlotte Rampling married hip French musician Jean-Michel Jarre on October 8, 1976, they were the celebrity couple of the moment. In that same year, she drew critical acclaim for her role as a femme fatale in the remake of Raymond Chandler's *Farewell, My Lovely*. Rampling and Jarre had a mansion in Versailles and opened it to all of their celebrity friends. They were glamorous jet-setters and truly in love.

The marriage lasted for many years, but began to dissolve in the late eighties. As a result, Rampling suffered a highly publicized nervous breakdown and entered a psychiatric institution.

SEE ALSO

▶ CATHERINE DENEUVE *Page 505*

▶ ROD STEWART & ALANA HAMILTON *Page 498*

474

1976 CAPRICORN

From December 22, 1975, 11:46 through January 20, 1976, 22:24
(December 1976 Capricorns, see 1977 Capricorn)

♑ *The Charismatic Diplomat*

As a 1976 Capricorn, you have the ability to get along with anyone and everyone. You are truly interested in what makes other people tick and are especially fascinated by people from other cultures. Because you are so sociable and such a great listener you are very much in demand as a date and a lover—and you know it! You act humbly, but inside you are secretly arrogant and know that if you turn on the charm and persistence you truly can have anyone.

In love you want it all—passion, intellectual stimulation, and long-term commitment. You need a partner who is comfortable in any setting because you tend to befriend influential people from varied backgrounds. You believe that a relationship is meant to increase both people's status in the world. You also believe that partners should be nurturing, yet firm with each other—you want to be told if you are ruining your life or making a big mistake! Honesty is something you put at the top of your list in a relationship.

A clever way for a would-be date to win your affection would be to make an observant remark, then another, then another. Great wit turns you on as nothing else can. You also like to look up to a lover—you do not want to be in a teaching role. You have a similar way of operating in bed and love it when a lover takes the lead and tells you what to do (in a sexy, not controlling way, of course!)

As a male Capricorn born in 1976, you're looking for a woman who can make you laugh and who can help you succeed in the business world. Even though you like to travel and learn about ways of life that are vastly different from your own, you are still pretty traditional at heart. You want to be with a woman who will be a great mother, but who has a youthful spark that marriage and kids won't dilute.

If you are a female Capricorn born in 1976, you are most compatible with a man who is an avid reader and fabulous talker. You love a guy who is well-versed in a myriad of relevant as well as obscure topics. If he has a professorial air about him and can be charming on the dance floor and at cocktail parties he will surely steal your heart.

CAPRICORN ZODIAC SIGN
YOUR LOVE PLANETS

YOUR ROMANTIC SIDE   p. 696
- ▶ **VENUS IN SCORPIO**
  Born Dec. 22, 1975 11:46 - Jan. 01, 1976 12:13
- ▶ **VENUS IN SAGITTARIUS**
  Born Jan. 01, 12:14 - Jan. 20, 22:24

YOUR SEX DRIVE   p. 722
- ▶ **MARS IN GEMINI**
  Born Dec. 22, 1975 11:46 - Jan. 20, 1976 22:24

YOUR CELEBRITY TWINS   p. 760
Find out the astrological similarities you have with famous people.

YOUR COMPATIBILITY   p. 780
Compare planets to find out how compatible you are in a relationship.

YOUR RELATIONSHIP KARMA   p. 824
- ▶ **SATURN IN LEO**
  Born Dec. 22, 1975 11:46 - Jan. 14, 1976 13:07
- ▶ **SATURN IN CANCER**
  Born Jan. 14, 13:08 to Jan. 20, 22:24

ELTON JOHN
English Singer
Venus in Aquarius

475

1976 AQUARIUS

From January 20, 22:25 through February 19, 12:39

♒ *The Volatile Idealist*

As a 1976 Aquarius, you are passionate about your beliefs and simply cannot bear to be around apathetic or bland people. They really depress you. You believe that we only have so much time in this life to do important, meaningful things, and you are intent on changing the world in your lifetime. You believe that relationships should be all about doubling the power of one and becoming an unstoppable, two-headed force for positive change in the universe.

You spend a lot of time preaching to the converted, and believe that your lover should be tolerant of all human beings—especially you! You need a lot of caretaking, even though you claim, "I'm easy." For you a relationship must have a feeling of life or death urgency, but yet it cannot get in the way of the altruistic work you have set out to do. You are full of paradoxes and expect your partner to be patient with you, rather than try to change you.

If someone is interested in catching your eye he or she must be versed in politics and the important issues of the day. Enthusiasm is the quality that attracts you the most, though. Being able to give an update of front-page stories is not enough. You respond to a person's show of inner and outer passions. You also love someone feisty, who takes the devil's advocate point of view. This keeps you on your toes. And you believe that if someone can keep you on your toes verbally he or she will be able to sweep you off your feet sexually! A verbal connection that is strong often leads to a physical union that is even stronger.

As a 1976 Aquarius male, you are most compatible with women who are serious about work and who possess a deep sense of values. She must come to you already a fully-developed person with passionate, intense beliefs and opinions. She must adapt to you, but never at the expense of her core integrity.

If you are a woman born under the sign of Aquarius in 1976, you are looking for a man who is funny and smart. You like a certain "everyman" quality in a guy, but beneath his unpretentious exterior he's got to be whip-smart and a quick study in any subject.

AQUARIUS ZODIAC SIGN
YOUR LOVE PLANETS

YOUR ROMANTIC SIDE   p. 696
- ▶ **VENUS IN SAGITTARIUS**
  Born Jan. 20, 22:25 - Jan. 26, 6:08
- ▶ **VENUS IN CAPRICORN**
  Born Jan. 26, 6:09 - Feb. 19, 12:39

YOUR SEX DRIVE   p. 722
- ▶ **MARS IN GEMINI**
  Born Jan. 20, 22:25 - Feb. 19, 12:39

YOUR CELEBRITY TWINS   p. 760
Find out the astrological similarities you have with famous people.

YOUR COMPATIBILITY   p. 780
Compare planets to find out how compatible you are in a relationship.

YOUR RELATIONSHIP KARMA   p. 824
- ▶ **SATURN IN CANCER**
  Born Jan. 20, 22:25 - Feb. 19, 12:39

JENNIFER O'NEILL
American Actress
Sun in Pisces

476

1976 PISCES
From February 19, 12:40 through March 20, 11:49

The Soulful Flirt

As a 1976 Pisces, you are debonair and sexy, and you know it. You are kind to animals and children, but you are passively brutal when flirting with the opposite sex. You simply have no boundaries! If you can attract attention from someone cute and interesting, you will. However, you really mean no harm. You are mischievous, not malevolent. You are looking for someone to tame you, but who is tolerant of your suave and sultry ways. You believe that a relationship is meant to be so inspiring that it can keep you from getting into trouble with anyone outside of it.

Deep down you are looking for a soul mate to redeem you, take you away from temptation, and distract you from your wicked ways. Love is like a religious experience for you—ecstatic and hellish all at once. You love the agony and the ecstasy of it all. You want love to be transcendent. You believe that your partner should be your muse and vice versa.

To intrigue you a potential lover has got to move fast because you have a short attention span. A loaded comment—something sexy and suggestive—will make you stop and listen. However, someone who is more crude than cute will turn you off.

As a 1976 Pisces man, you need a woman who is honest to a fault and will inspire the same kind of honesty in you. You like to put your lady on a pedestal, and so someone who is charitable and giving and always helpful to those less fortunate is sure to earn your admiration and amour. At the same time you like a woman who is sexually unrepressed and has unconventional values—but values, nonetheless—when it comes to matters of the heart.

If you are a female Piscean born in 1976, you need a man who is light-hearted and fun, who doesn't try too hard to possess you or pin you down—at least not at first. But you do need a man who will stay true to you and who will treat you as both a lover and a friend. He also can't be jealous because you need your guy friends around you, too. Sexually, you like a guy who is experimental in the sack, but who respects your comfort zones and doesn't push you to be wild and wily in bed all the time.

1976 ARIES
From March 20, 11:50 through April 19, 23:02

The Nurturing Pioneer

Born in 1976, you are strong and powerful, but you prefer to take care of others rather than dominate them. You love good food and good music and long for a special someone with whom you can share the sweet things in life. However, you are prone to melancholy by nature. When you are feeling depressed, you tend to isolate yourself, rather than seek out uplifting company. You have many moods and believe that a romantic relationship is what will keep you in balance.

You are extremely sensual and loving, once you trust someone, but in the beginning you may act a little cool and restrained. You believe that love should build over time, and then last a lifetime—if it's real. You are highly romantic and vulnerable, and therefore are skittish about taking emotional or sexual risks before you feel secure enough.

A would-be date has got to be patient and persistent. You tend to assume that everyone likes you—but only as a friend. This is because you are not as confident as you could be. Therefore, a strong show of affection and the obvious signs of interest are necessary. You love it when someone calls you on the phone or emails you a lot. The more contact the better. Also, you love to go to concerts. Once a potential lover has you out, listening or dancing to music, an impromptu make-out session should get you all fired up. You love surprises, and you love to kiss passionately in public!

As a 1976 male Aries, you need a woman who is open and honest about her feelings and who doesn't play games. You appreciate a woman who babies you a little, rubs your back when you're tired, and cooks your favorite meals for you. At the same time, you want to play knight in shining armor to her, and she has to be receptive to your heroic overtures.

If you are a female Aries born in 1976, you need a man who is flexible and detached, and who doesn't take your mood swings to heart. Your guy should push you to be your most adventurous self. He must be well-read so he can turn you on intellectually as well as sexually. You also like guys who are ultra-social, and who introduce you to new people.

1976 TAURUS
From April 19, 23:03 through May 20, 22:20

The Possessive Pleaser

Taureans are known to be quite sensual, but you are more overtly sexual than the average bull. You believe that a relationship begins with deep erotic attraction and that that is the glue that holds two people together. You put all your energy into showing your affection and making your partner feel sexy and attractive—and you expect the same in return. Once you are hooked on your lover, you hold on tight. You can be the jealous, possessive type, although you are incredibly subtle about showing that part of your nature. You like to spend all your free time with the one you love and believe that a separate vacation means you two are heading for separate beds. You are traditional and believe in building a stable family life with your beloved. You also believe that your relatives and your partner's relatives should mix together and mix often. You love spending time with the kids in the clan.

To woo you a potential lover has got to be very touchy-feeling with you—play with your hair, scratch your back, or give you a neck rub, for example. If he or she speaks in a low, sexy voice, and expresses an intimate connection with you quickly, you are likely to respond. Heavy eye contact and an invitation to an outdoorsy romantic place—such as a walk on the beach at sunset or a Sunday drive through the mountains—will get your heart racing. Romantic dates by day lead to fiery sex at night!

As a male Taurus born in 1976, you are most compatible with a woman who is highly romantic and not afraid to show her passion—for you! You may be too embarrassed to ask for the over-the-top gestures you really long for. She's got to know you well enough to lure you out of town for a surprise romantic weekend together, or to take tango lessons—anything that is sexy and sweet and meant for two and two alone!

If you are a lady Taurus born in 1976, you want a guy who is homey. You like guys who are masculine and real without a touch of vanity. Outdoorsy guys who love to fish, golf, and play all kinds of sports make you swoon. What gets you the most, though, is a guy who knows how to nurture a child.

TAURUS ZODIAC SIGN
YOUR LOVE PLANETS

YOUR ROMANTIC SIDE   p. 696
▶ VENUS IN ARIES
Born Apr. 19, 23:03 - May 02, 17:48
▶ VENUS IN TAURUS
Born May 02, 17:49 - May 20, 22:20

YOUR SEX DRIVE   p. 722
▶ MARS IN CANCER
Born Apr. 19, 23:03 - May 16, 11:09
▶ MARS IN LEO
Born May 16, 11:10 - May 20, 22:20

YOUR CELEBRITY TWINS   p. 760
Find out the astrological similarities you have with famous people.

YOUR COMPATIBILITY   p. 780
Compare planets to find out how compatible you are in a relationship.

YOUR RELATIONSHIP KARMA   p. 824
▶ SATURN IN CANCER
Born Apr. 19, 23:03 - May 20, 22:20

BARBARA STREISAND
American Singer
Sun in Taurus

477

1976 GEMINI
From May 20, 22:21 through June 21, 6:23

The Domesticated Explorer

You have a wild side, but are wise enough to express it in a constructive, not destructive, way. You love to travel and to learn about new ways of life. People from foreign cultures are interesting to you. At the same time, you are a settle-down kind of lover, and you know you are happiest when you are on your own home turf and snuggled up with the one you love. You are able to balance your adventurous brain with a solid, consistent lifestyle.

Love for you is about sharing ideas and being loyal to each other. Your ideal relationship has a brother-sister or a best friend type of dynamic. A couple of times a month you need fireworks and dark intensity, but the rest of the time you are happy with regular warm, sensual, and intellectual interaction with your partner.

Whoever wants to catch your eye has got to project a regal sense of dignity. You do not want to rescue anyone, nor do you need rescuing. Class and composure turn you on. You love to read, see movies, eat foreign food, and go to obscure cultural events, so if someone offers to take you to a comic book convention, followed by dinner at an African restaurant, followed by a late showing of a cult movie, you will definitely say yes. You love people who are original and not afraid to be perceived as offbeat. You also like a lover who puts on an exotic, funky soundtrack for you to make love by!

As a 1976 Gemini man, you are most compatible with a woman who is independent, confident and gentle in spirit. She must be soft in manner, but not a wimp. You can't stand being dominated or possessed and need a woman who is secure enough in your love that she won't demand hollow expressions of feeling from you.

If you are a female 1976 Gemini, you are best suited to a guy who is proud and articulate and who encourages you to develop your brilliant mind as much as possible. You want to appreciate a man who is your biggest cheerleader, but who isn't either parental or patronizing in his show of support. You also need a man who is generous, knows how to travel in style, and treats every kind of person with graciousness and respect.

GEMINI ZODIAC SIGN
YOUR LOVE PLANETS

YOUR ROMANTIC SIDE   p. 696
▶ VENUS IN TAURUS
Born May 20, 22:21 - May 27, 3:42
▶ VENUS IN GEMINI
Born May 27, 3:43 - June 20, 13:55
▶ VENUS IN CANCER
Born June 20, 13:56 - June 21, 6:23

YOUR SEX DRIVE   p. 722
▶ MARS IN LEO
Born May 20, 22:21 - June 21, 6:23

YOUR CELEBRITY TWINS   p. 760
Find out the astrological similarities you have with famous people.

YOUR COMPATIBILITY   p. 780
Compare planets to find out how compatible you are in a relationship.

YOUR RELATIONSHIP KARMA   p. 824
▶ SATURN IN CANCER
Born May 20, 22:21 - June 5, 5:10
▶ SATURN IN LEO
Born June 5, 5:11 to June 21, 6:23

JAMES BROLIN
American Actor
Sun in Cancer

1976 CANCER
From June 21, 6:24 through July 22, 17:17

The Cuddly Critic

As a 1976 Cancer, you have lots of opinions about everything, and are never shy about expressing them—to loved ones and strangers alike. You are very in touch with the critic inside you and believe that your lover should be open to taking your helpful hints. They are all given with good will. You want your romantic life to be meaningful and permanent. You are suspicious of people who play around or flirt too strongly. You can't stand unscrupulous behavior.

You are turned on by integrity and stability. Making a home with someone you love is what you are destined to do, and even if you resist settling down for awhile, you know deep in your soul that when you do, it will be for life. You want your love life to be a thing of beauty that you can brag to all your friends about. You see yourself as being one half of the ideal couple that everyone else uses as their romantic role model.

A potential paramour has to be very huggy and affectionate. Touch translates to your heart immediately. You love to get swept up into the fascinating and intricate details of another person's mind and world. You also like it when someone else takes the lead in bed. You are confident in your ability to express affection, but a little shy when it comes to making love, until you feel sure about what turns your partner on.

As a Cancer man born in 1976, you need a woman who is family-oriented, but ambitious outside the home, too. For all your nagging, you tend to be the disorganized one—which is why you are most compatible with a woman who knows how to start a project and see it through to the end. She has to be a good cook, too, but she must be tolerant of your picky eating habits!

Female Cancers born in 1976 respond to men who are hard-working and dedicated to making the world a better place. If he has an ecological bent or is deeply moved by the natural world, you are bound to be deeply moved by him. He has to be very physical—interested in sports and sex! You are very affectionate and will love it if he is prone to spontaneous public displays of affection. He should want to show you off.

1976 LEO
From July 22, 17:18 through August 23, 0:17

The Romantic Workaholic

You are a Leo on a mission. You always have a to-do list on your desk and in your head, and you tend to work harder than most to do your job and to help others do theirs. You are a natural leader and tend to gravitate toward positions of responsibility. Therefore, you need a lover who respects your work, but who knows how to get you to relax, and even get crazy sometimes! Secretly, you want to be lured away from your work.

You want a relationship to be a true partnership—in which you are the boss! You can't help taking the dominant role—it's your nature. Therefore, you are best suited to be with a person who is laid back and doesn't have big power issues. However, you also want a partner you can look up to who doesn't have much use for the limelight—thereby leaving center stage for you!

To get your attention, a potential lover has to express interest in one of your many work projects. Time is money to you, so a potential paramour has got to be able to exhibit intelligence, romantic interest in you, interest in your career, and about a hundred other good qualities in the first five minutes you meet! Basically, they have got to be so relaxed and cool that none of your tests will intimidate them. You also like it when someone cuts to the chase sexually and doesn't keep you wondering whether you are adored or not. Total worship of you in the sack is a must!

If you are a male Leo born in 1976, you need a woman who is full of fire and integrity. She has got to be able to express what her passions are, and they can't all be selfish hobbies. You love a woman who is on a mission to make the world a better place, one small action at a time.

As a female Leo born in 1976, you are most compatible with a man who is precise and consistent. He's got to say what he means and mean what he says, and—most important—follow through on his promises. If he is comfortable out of doors and is drawn to gardening and meditation, this is a plus. You need someone to help you fend off your anxiety. If he is an excellent masseuse, he will make you purr like a lioness for years to come.

1976 VIRGO

From August 23, 0:18 through September 22, 21:47

The Natural Mate

Most Virgos have reputations for being self-sufficient workaholics, but you are much more romantic and relationship-centric than the average virgin. You've always sensed deep inside that your relationship would either make you or break you, and you are right. Getting together with the right person and staying with that person will have a huge effect on your destiny. When it comes to love, you do believe in destiny and that something mystical and intangible is guiding your fate. In love you are the personification of absolute devotion.

You believe a relationship is more than just about companionship and attraction. Although you would never speak this way to anyone but your beloved, you are convinced that love is a cosmic connection that is so deeply spiritual, it's impossible to describe in generic Hallmark cliches or typical sound bites. You are absolutely faithful to the one you love and everyone senses that.

If someone is looking to catch your attention, he or she had better move fast because you are likely to get scooped up quickly. You respond to a soft-spoken demeanor that covers a deep, soulful strength. Your type definitely holds the "iron fist in a velvet glove." You are in tune with the natural world and you love flowers and plants. Someone who can speak knowledgeably on this subject and present you with a perfect plant that captures your personality will hook you easily. This kind of gesture gets you sexually aroused, too. You are thoughtful in bed and must have a partner who is, too.

If you are a 1976 Virgo male, you need an educated female lover. You love to learn from the one you love. You are also drawn to a woman who has an artistic bent. If she can expose you to artistic beauty by taking you to museums and perhaps painting your portrait, you will be smitten for life.

As a Virgo female born in 1976, you are drawn to men who are intelligent and opinionated by day, but soft and romantic by night. You need a man who is tender and thoughtful and who would never forget your birthday or anniversary. He's got to be able to speak using beautiful language, too.

PETER FRAMPTON
English Musician
Mars in Virgo

479

1976 LIBRA

From September 22, 21:48 through October 23, 6:57

The Sociable Sexpot

As a 1976 Libra, you know that you possess a very secret and sexy mojo. You are a natural entertainer, and love to throw parties and bring all sorts of unusual, seemingly incompatible, types together. You are also a great matchmaker. Witty and cosmopolitan as you can be, you can also be a wild animal when the guests leave and the lights go down.

You believe that relationships are meant to be exciting and full of thrills and intrigue. You will settle down eventually, but you need a lot of drama first. Romance brings out your creativity. When you are in love, you write, dance, sing, paint, and do pretty much whatever inspires you. You are never without a crush or someone who is crushed out on you.

To get your attention an interested lover has to pull out all stops to seduce you. If he or she has a "whatever" attitude, so will you. You respond to intense, whispered expressions of attraction and interest. Secrets and surprises are your weak spots. If someone lures you out one night to give you a surprise, and then presents you with a very personalized romantic gift—a mixed tape full of sexy love songs, perhaps—and then reveals the secret—I am wild about you—you will absolutely go wild yourself! Oh, wait until the evening is over! In bed you are a tiger, once you know you are desired.

As a 1976 Libra man, you are best suited to be with a woman who is tough, self-actualized, and not faint of heart. She has to have a strong ego to put up with your mischief and flirtatiousness. She also has to have a strong sense of right and wrong to teach you the same! You need a woman who can calm you down and show you that life—and love—do not have to go from one extreme to the other.

If you are a woman born under the sign of Libra in 1976, you are most compatible with a man who demands the best from you. You can be lazy and shady, but you want to be a good girl not a bad girl! If he can encourage you to finish what you've started—especially your education—and to express your strong artistic talent, you will do everything in your power to please him all the time, especially in bed!

JANE BIRKIN
English Actress
Sun and Mars in Sagittarius

1976 SCORPIO
From October 23, 6:58 through November 22, 4:21

♏ *The Extreme Dater*

Romantically, you know you are a late bloomer who will settle down at the very last minute, when you absolutely have to. You fall in love easily—with many people! You look at love as a grand adventure in which you may risk life and limb to gain the prize—the adoration of the one you want. However, once you get what you want, you don't always want it for long. You like to roam and to play and hate to feel someone is draining your huge reserves of physical and mental energy.

You want your love life to be colorful and can't stand being involved with someone who is addicted to routine and togetherness, just for the sake of togetherness. You like relationships best when they are a huge challenge, seemingly impossible. You have a strong ego and know you can eventually wear down the one you want and make that person come to you. You can spend hours and hours plotting, and you definitely prefer to be in the feline position in a romantic game of cat and mouse.

A would-be lover has to be a little wild and wily and do something bold, such as kiss you on the lips suddenly—and then run away! This turns you on immensely. You love a good game, and will definitely run after this mysterious stranger. You also are intrigued by people who are from foreign backgrounds or who have traveled to unusual places. Even just talking about traveling to an exotic locale will get you in the mood.

If you are a man born under the sign of Scorpio in 1976, you need a woman who is funny and fierce and will call you on your fibs and evasions every time! You need a woman you can respect, who has a huge sense of dignity and a lot of strong friends and family around her. You are drawn to women who are goal-oriented and who have secret mystical abilities or interest in the occult.

As a female Scorpio born in 1976, you need a guy who is competitive and bold. You like a man who is bigger than life and a bit of a performer. You also need him to be an emotional detective who will ferret out the keys to your true nature through penetrating, personal questions. His goal must be to know you completely.

1976 SAGITTARIUS
From November 22, 4:22 through December 21, 17:34

♐ *The Fun Mystic*

If you were born under the sign of Sagittarius in 1976, you have hidden intuitive powers that come to the surface when you are involved with the right person. You have spent much of your life searching for answers. Your early life is a series of adventures, but as you age, you might get more serious and soulful, and perhaps will become deeply obsessed with matters relating to God and spirituality. You believe that the right lover will help you connect all the seemingly unrelated dots in your life.

You are looking for a relationship that will test your limits and push you to be a much deeper person than you already are. You need to be with someone who is as at home in a pub, telling—or listening to you tell—great shaggy dog stories, as they are in a temple of any denomination, seeking out answers about the meaning of life. You are extreme in your needs and desires, and expect your partner to be able to switch gears without making much of a fuss. You absolutely detest pettiness and small-mindedness.

To grab your attention, an interested lover has to be generous to a fault, in spirit and with money. You love it when someone encourages a shy person to come out of his or her shell, and this moves you to be romantically attracted that much sooner. You are very perceptive about group dynamics and tend to get turned on by someone within a small crowd rather than in a more formal date setting.

As a 1976 male Sagittarius you are most suited to be with a woman who is ahead of her time, who possesses an inventive, scientific mind. She has got to be someone who thinks outside the box and who does not follow conventional rules. She should be highly verbal and a great friend, who is able to take some of your most diamond-in-the-rough pals under her generous wing.

If you are a lady archer born in 1976, you need a man who is noble and philosophical and who can spot hypocrisy a hundred miles away. You want a leader, not a follower, but it's okay if he marches to his own drummer and does not fit in with any particular group. You also like a man who enjoys camping and roughing it.

Robert Redford – A Talented Sex Symbol

Robert Redford, a dashing daredevil, was born with both his Sun and Mars in the courageous, creative sign of Leo, an ideal astrological signature for playing the lead in any cinematic drama. Some of his most popular movies highlight his Leonine radiant self-confidence to dramatize the hero's story of overcoming great odds to achieve victory. *The Candidate*, *Downhill Racer*, *All the President's Men*, *The Natural*, and his personal favorite *Jeremiah Johnson* are the best examples.

Redford's Mars is given a jolt by Uranus, the planet of radical independence. By the late 1950s Redford had dropped out of college and had taken to carousing, sleeping in jails, and drinking hard. Then he met Lola Jean Van Wagenen, an 18-year-old Mormon from Utah. He fell in love with her and her large, supportive family, something he never had and always missed when he was growing up. The two married in 1958 and remained together until 1985, an unusually lengthy history by Hollywood standards. Redford refuses to discuss his private life, but seems to blame himself for the breakup. "I got lost for a time" is his only comment on the subject.

Men with Mars-Uranus aspects are action-oriented and tend to be fascinated by dangerous situations. These traits are great for making adventure films, like *Out of Africa*, *The Sting*, and *Three Days of the Condor* or, more recently, *Havana* and *Sneakers*. While Hollywood capitalized on Redford's Mars-Uranus influence, Redford's private life is also characterized by the anti-establishment vibe of this planetary pairing. He loves to drive recklessly fast and barks his disdain for politics, which he says are "completely stymied by compromise, corruption, weakness, and ignorance."

Redford's wild streak is balanced by a

"People have been so busy relating to how I look, it's a miracle I don't become a self-conscious blob of protoplasm."

ROBERT REDFORD

passionate interest in the art of moviemaking. In 1979 Redford made his directorial debut with *Ordinary People*, which became a commercial success and earned him an Oscar for Best Director. He took pride in directing meticulously crafted pictures, including *A River Runs Through It*, *Quiz Show*, and *The Legend of Bagger Vance*.

While moviegoers will always remember him and buddy Paul Newman as the fun-loving outlaws in *Butch Cassidy and the Sundance Kid*, Redford has matured gracefully into a top-tier director and part-time environmental activist. In 1980 he founded the Sundance Institute to assist independent filmmakers, gathering them for retreats to sharpen their skills and prepare them for the tough business of moviemaking. The annual Sundance Film Festival is now widely considered the premier event for independent filmmakers.

With his Moon and Venus both in Virgo, Redford can become obsessed with details. When he was filming *The Horse Whisperer*, he had his crew inspect 300 ranches throughout the west in search of the movie's right locale, finally settling on a spread along Montana's Boulder River. He found experts to show him exactly how to wrangle horses.

His Venus in Virgo loves the innocence and cleanliness of the natural environment, which he began investing in after he married Lola. He bought land around Park City, Utah, and made this the staging ground for the annual Sundance Film Festival. While Hollywood wags say he has become a loner by moving out toward the wilderness, he describes his departure from the Los Angeles area in Virgo terms: "I watched green spaces turn into malls, and the smell of orange blossoms turn into exhaust fumes."

481

► READ ABOUT ROBERT REDFORD'S SEXY CO-STAR PAUL NEWMAN ON PAGE 433

1977

- ★ DIANA SPENCER
- ★ MARGARET TRUDEAU
- ★ ANNIE HALL
- ★ THE THORN BIRDS
- ★ DELTA OF VENUS
- ★ THE BEE GEES
- ★ YOU LIGHT UP MY LIFE

Hot Movie

EVENTS

Britain was in an uproar in 1977. First, a guardsman who raped a seventeen-year-old girl was set free by Justice Slynn, who claimed the guilty man merely "allowed his enthusiasm for sex" to overpower him. Then the magazine *Gay News* published a poem suggesting Jesus was homosexual and was fined £1000 for blasphemy. But all was not lost. Diana Spencer was first introduced to Prince Charles, who later described her as "very jolly."

Another relationship made headline news when the Canadian Prime Minister Pierre Trudeau and his First Lady, Margaret, announced their separation. Margaret had taken the unprecedented step of leaving a presiding head of state.

Although barred the previous year from competing in women's tennis, Reneé Richards' case went to the NY Supreme Court—and she won. It was ruled that after sex reassignment surgery, transsexuals legally became the opposite sex.

POP CULTURE

If the term had been coined then, people might have said 1977 was a year for chick flicks. Moviegoers rocked with laughter during *Annie Hall*, a quirky romance that won four Oscars and started a fashion trend. *The Goodbye Girl* launched Richard Dreyfus and touched viewers' hearts. *Looking for Mr. Goodbar* scared viewers—probably enough to curb some of the decade's earlier promiscuity.

Books from 1977 also made an impact. *The Thorn Birds* by Colleen McCullough followed three generations of the Cleary family—and one notably long-term but star-crossed romance between the heroine and a priest. *Oliver's Story* by Erich Segal, a sequel to *Love Story*, took up Oliver's quest for love and meaning following the death of his wife. On a lighter note, Anaïs Nin published her *Delta of Venus: Erotica*, and Jackie Collins' *Lovers and Gamblers* was released.

DJs gave frequent air time to "How Deep Is Your Love," by the Bee Gees, and "I Just Want to Be Your Everything," by younger brother Andy Gibb. Queen just wanted "Somebody to Love," and the Emotions wanted to give the "Best of My Love."

Debby Boone crooned "You Light Up My Life"—and people liked it. They also liked "Evergreen" from the film *A Star Is Born*.

ANNIE HALL

When Woody Allen created *Annie Hall* in 1977, he intended it as a meditation on love in the '70s. The neurotic, romantic adventures of Manhattan writer Alvy Singer (Allen) and his relationship with the ditzy Annie Hall, winsomely played by Diane Keaton, was one of the most memorable films of the decade.

Woody Allen wrote, directed, and starred in this groundbreaking film. He revolutionized the urban romantic comedy genre with innovative cinematic techniques, like speaking directly into the camera. And Diane Keaton's quirky wardrobe set the standard for fashion in 1977. *Annie Hall* won four Oscars, for Best Picture, Best Actress, Best Screenplay, and Best Director.

SEE ALSO
► WOODY ALLEN *Page 587*
► WARREN BEATTY *Page 497*

1977 CAPRICORN

From December 21, 1976, 17:35 through January 20, 1977, 4:13
(December 1977 Capricorns, see 1978 Capricorn)

♑ *The Discriminating Devotee*

Your sign is associated with Pan, the ancient horned Greek god, who presided over the Saturnalia, a raucous wintertime festival with wild dancing, feasting, drinking, even orgies. You may be reserved around acquaintances and can be quite discriminating about choosing lovers—only the best for you! Once you make a commitment, you can open up. With your bawdy sense of humor, generosity, and lusty sensuousness, you fill a relationship with much laughter and pleasure. You're not one to go out unless there's a quality attraction—a show, fine dining, a special event. You may prefer those intimate nights at home, where you and your mate can partake from a suite of creature comforts that tend to become richer and more luxurious as your resources increase over time.

You are a tender, romantic lover, and you get better with age. You may show some restraint in allowing a commitment to progress, and this can arouse a mate's impatience on issues such as meeting the parents, trading house keys, moving in together, getting engaged or married, having kids. You can ease any conflict by reassuring your partner that your love is true. It is simply the Capricorn way to build a firm foundation for love by allowing a relationship to grow slowly, without being hurried or forced. Once you cross the threshold of sexual intimacy, you are delightfully loose and uninhibited.

Sex with you can be like a two-person orgy, an unrestrained pleasure fest with food, wine, and games. You need someone who is unafraid to make a wild mess with you. To power down afterwards, you might share a bubble bath with wine, scented candles, and music.

The 1977 Capricorn man seeks a most compassionate woman. You may feel especially comfortable with someone who has a sixth sense for what is on your mind. With trust and deep affection for each other, you can enjoy a commitment as good as solid gold.

Female Capricorns born in 1977 like the man who is practical and generous. "Less talk and more action" is a formula that can win you over. His self-discipline assures you that he is a reliable partner, in command of his responsibilities.

1977 AQUARIUS

From January 20, 4:14 through February 18, 18:29

♒ *The Intimate Individualist*

Your first great love, Aquarius of 1977, may be with humanity in general or with a group that supports you in the passionate pursuit of certain goals and ideals. You may not be ready to make a serious romantic commitment until later in life. For all the satisfaction that outside causes can bring, you may find yourself longing for something more. To devote yourself to one person—and to experience that same devotion in return—can bring out a side of you that is finely attuned to the fragility of life and the preciousness of love. Family life, including any children you may have, can further expand your emotional sensitivity and capacity for joy. The triumphs may be smaller in scale—as compared to saving the world—but they are deeper in immediacy and personal meaning.

Friendship and trust are the forces that hold your relationship together. You thrive in an equal partnership, with a mate by your side to share common interests and enjoy a variety of activities. Ideally, your relationship enables and empowers both partners to pursue their own learning and personal growth as individuals.

The progress that you enjoy separately can make you stronger as a couple. Making love with your mate can allow you to escape into an exclusive realm of romance and sweetness. You can get utterly lost in your sweetheart's kisses.

You are open to intimate suggestion. When a lover turns you on to a certain song, a touching poem, or an interesting technique, you may be happy to continue in that vein. Aquarians tend to be somewhat rebellious, so you may get a big kick out of the idea (and act) of doing something naughty.

The Aquarian man of 1977 can be quite open to being romanced by woman. A little role change can make things interesting. You may be delightfully intrigued by a woman with an ethereal, spiritual aura, who seems to know something you don't.

A sensuous, take-charge man is a wonderful counterpart for the Aquarian woman of 1977. Your open-mindedness invites him to find things that can stimulate and excite you. His affectionate nature makes it easy to share your feelings with him.

JOHN TRAVOLTA
American Actor
Sun in Aquarius

RUDOLF NUREYEV
Russian Ballet Dancer
Sun in Pisces

484

1977 PISCES
From February 18, 18:30 through March 20, 17:41

The Hypnotic Heartthrob

A burning desire can set you, 1977 Pisces, apart from most members of your sign. When you want someone, you may pursue that person ardently, but with a twist. Smoldering with seductive energy, you may have a genius for getting someone to chase you until you catch him or her. Your hypnotic magnetism can attract a new partner or keep a current heartthrob riveted to your side. With you, a lover may feel transported to a distant time and place. It's as if you are the last two people on earth, and all your lover can see or care about is you. You can be very good at taking care of people, and your ability to make a mate feel like royalty may be a point of pride for you.

In a serious relationship, you may become virtually indispensable to your mate. This can make you feel secure with your partner, but if the balance tips too far away from the fulfillment of your needs, you can feel neglected and unappreciated. Because your partner may not share your intuitive gifts, you should get in the healthy habit of openly expressing your wishes and preferences. Sensual communication can hold your relationship together over the long term. Showing your partner what you desire, especially when it comes to lovemaking, sends a sexy request that any partner would be delighted to honor.

Impressionable and open to experimentation, you can become something of a mad scientist in the boudoir. Absorbed in devising new techniques for thrilling your partner, you may be willing to try just about anything once. Still, you are hardly an exhibitionist, and a caring partner must be sure to maintain the privacy you share.

For you, the 1977 Piscean man, a woman who pushes you to try new things can be a dream-come-true. You may find it easy to absorb her ambition. As she fills you with energy, you can go out in the world with renewed passion for any challenge.

The heart of the 1977 Piscean woman beats a little faster around a man who is a staunch individualist. The fact that he's not just anybody, and even a bit rebellious, can make you feel proud that he chose you and that your relationship is special.

1977 ARIES
From March 20, 17:42 through April 20, 4:56

The Compassionate Companion

The meeting between you, Aries of 1977, and a soul mate can be like an atomic collision, unleashing a chemical chain reaction in which passion fuses with intensity and ignites with explosive energy. For you, a relationship can blast off and zoom ahead at a dizzying pace. But, as the saying goes, the brightest light tends to burn out the fastest, and certainly, chemistry fades over time. The challenge for you and your mate is to make it through "the dying of the light" without rage or disillusionment and to adapt to a different, more regular pace. You have a powerful will that enables you to take control of your relationship and give it what it needs to hold together and grow over the long term.

Making a conscious effort to work on a relationship brings out the compassionate side of your personality. Your empathy for your partner's feelings makes it easier to compromise on issues and work out any problems. The give-and-take of a serious commitment enables you and your mate to revive and freshen the chemistry between you. Over time, your romantic intensity can transform into a passionate attachment that is deeper and more enduring. As a lover, you tend to be eager to fulfill fantasies and exquisitely sensitive to your partner's preferences and responses.

Absorbing your senses in imagery and sounds, a movie or adult video can trigger your susceptibility to romantic suggestion. Moments of stolen intimacy in the darkness of the movie theater can thrill you. Music has a similar ability to stir your passions and arouse your sexual impulses.

The ideal woman for the 1977 Arien man is earthy and sweet. When you're speeding through your day, she can stop you dead in your tracks with a delightful diversion. Her need for plenty of physical affection gives you many happy opportunities to vent your abundant energy.

The Arien woman of 1977 appreciates a man who is tender and romantic. His disarming compassion can inspire you to let down your guard, and his charm can be utterly intoxicating. His subtle, seductive style eases you into a comfortable state of rest and relaxation.

1977 TAURUS
From April 20, 4:57 through May 21, 4:13

The Sparky Suitor

A 1977 Taurean brings a volcanic quality to romance. On the surface, you may seem quiet and laid-back, but your heart is a hunk of burnin' love. Your ideal relationship is like Stromboli, the volcano that lights up the Sicilian night sky with steady-but-harmless showers of sparks. The intensity of a passionate attachment can energize you, and you may attract a partner who thrives on ardent devotion and lust. Communication between you and your mate can become animated and sometimes even argumentative, but the regular venting of feelings and desires rapidly dissipates any heat and keeps lines of communication wide open.

Like most Taureans, you may sometimes get jealous when another person or activity makes excessive demands on your mate's attention or time. A little bit of reassurance and understanding from your partner goes a very long way with you. Your relationship flourishes when you and your mate treat your commitment to each other as a number-one priority, the foundation for your future together and for a stable family life. Making time to go out and have fun together allows you renew your loving connection and keep the passion alive. Generous with physical affection, you may touch and hug your sweetheart often, without giving it a thought.

Sex provides a crucial channel for venting your fire power, and you may make love with athletic vigor, achieving peak satisfaction when you can work up a sweat. Frank conversation about intimate matters turns you on because it allows you to give and get exactly what you want. A sexual adventure in the great outdoors can be especially exciting for earthy Taurus.

The Taurean man of 1977 appreciates a woman who can take the initiative in a relationship. For you, a mate with strong ideas about what she wants adds spice to your love life. A lady with a flair for drama can capture your imagination.

A man with a creative approach to romance can win the heart of the 1977 Taurean woman. When it comes to gifts and entertainment, you may love a surprise. Your ideal man can come up with original ideas that keep you happily on your toes.

STEVIE WONDER
American Singer
Sun in Taurus

485

1977 GEMINI
From May 21, 4:14 through June 21, 12:13

The Intuitive Communicator

Endowed with a tender heart and a great mind, the Gemini of 1977 brings the gifts of intelligence and sensitivity to a romantic relationship. As is so often true for individuals born under the sign of the Twins, everything is better for you when you can share it with someone you love. Likely to have an intuitive sense for what's on your partner's mind, you can choose to go with your gut, or you may prompt your partner to tell you what's up and how you can be most supportive. Your talent for dual-level communication can keep your relationship running smoothly.

You are likely to have a multi-faceted personality, a quality that prevents a relationship with you from becoming boring or predictable. Sometimes you can be outgoing, at ease in social situations, happy to be a fun couple at parties with your mate. At other times you can be shy, preferring to stay home and keep your honey all to yourself. Because your sensitivity is so finely tuned, you may rely on your romantic connection as an escape from a frenetic world. Hugs and caresses can give your energy a boost, and you may renew yourself in a lover's embrace. While sex can provide a crucial channel for relating to your sweetheart, you may insist on keeping the details strictly private.

Mood-stirring expression can excite your passions. A great performance by a musician, dancer, or actor can be as intoxicating as the finest wine. Inspiring words—such as a brilliant speech or a lover's sweet nothings, whispered in your ear—can give you chills and utterly transport you.

An earthy, luscious woman can be highly enticing to the 1977 Gemini man. You enjoy a partner who helps you tune in to the pleasures of all your senses. Her erotic ideas can fill your sex life with a fascinating dynamism. This muse can inspire you to great feats of creativity.

The Gemini woman of 1977 can't resist the man who can make her laugh. You have a unique appreciation for someone with a clever mind, who challenges you to make fast and funny associations. On a dime, he can turn to romance and whisk you away on scintillating flights of fancy.

CAROL BOUQUET
French Actress
Sun in Leo

1977 CANCER

From June 21, 12:14 through July 22, 23:03

The Hand Holder

As a Cancerean born in 1977, you tend to instinctively blend romance with serious commitment. Not the type to play the field, you may have found it a relief when dating relationships have relaxed into a steady thing. You tend to develop a strong emotional attachment to a partner and are unlikely to break up for frivolous reasons. Your loyalty gives you the strength to be supportive of a partner in hard times. Indeed, you may be "the marrying kind," tending to evaluate partners based on whether they are suitable marriage material and not letting a relationship go very far if a partner seems reluctant to commit. The sign of Cancer rules family and parenting, and you may dream of having a joyful home life with a spouse and children.

You are likely to have an idealistic outlook on love and relationships. For you, marriage or a serious romantic partnership provides a stable ground in which two people can strive to reach to their greatest potential. The idea of sex as a duty may make you laugh. For you, sexual intimacy is the very essence of bliss in a committed relationship. You can be a very nurturing lover, eager to ply your mate with sensual delights. Food may play an integral role in lovemaking. You may seduce a partner with a fabulous meal or bring various fun edibles into the boudoir with you.

You may have a taste for public displays of affection. Out on a weekend stroll with your sweetheart, walking arm-in-arm or holding hands can make you feel wonderful. Steady touching and kissing stirs your passion and renews your sense of security in your relationship.

The Cancerean man of 1977 tends to feel most comfortable with a woman who is easygoing and sweet. Not easily ruffled, she finds your varying moods enriching and entertaining. Her warmth and responsiveness moves you to lavish tender loving care on her.

The Cancerean woman born in 1977 can find contentment with a man who can be both a lover and a best friend. A resourceful partner can afford you a sense of safety and security. Sharing the wealth of the good earth with him can be a dream come true for you.

1977 LEO

From July 22, 23:04 through August 23, 5:59

The Fantasy Fulfiller

Leos can often be childlike and flamboyant, but the Leo of 1977 has a more mature and understated presence. Your own star-quality charisma can enchant a roomful of strangers. Up close and personal, a lover is likely to find you to be delightfully humble and quite approachable, with a disarming sense of humor. Loyal and dutiful, you may often prove that you are as good as your word. Such reliability inspires trust and enhances your ability to keep a relationship going over the long term. You may have a gift for speaking with tenderness and insight. To your mate, your words can be a balm for flagging spirits.

In challenging times, pride may keep you from seeking support from your partner and lead you to feel needlessly isolated. A loving mate can gently remind you that it's no shame to accept help and that your own favors earn you many happy returns. This kind of give-and-take provides the foundation for a healthy, dynamic relationship. While you convey a dignified image in the public sphere, you are a delightfully romantic and imaginative lover in private. You may be quite verbal in the boudoir, and you and your partner may exchange and enact various fantasy scenarios. Your ability to fulfill your mate's desire can make you swell with excitement.

Finding sexy love notes can set your heart aflutter. You might get a kick out of having a secret admirer. For you, a bit of mystery and playfulness adds spice to romance. Creative little surprises in the course of your day can liven up a long-term relationship with sweetness and fun.

A youthful, mischievous woman helps the 1977 Leo man feel young at heart. You appreciate a partner who draws out the more whimsical aspects of your personality. Ideally, she should have a love of learning that enables the two of you to benefit from every life lesson.

The Leo woman of 1977 adores the man who stimulates her creativity. You need someone with a sharp mind, capable of making interesting and insightful observations. A charming companion on vacations and at cultural events, he can expose you to experiences that stir your imagination.

1977 VIRGO

From August 23, 6:00 through September 23, 3:28

The Spiritual Helpmate

Several people, including a romantic partner, may refer to you, Virgo of 1977, as their best friend. Empathetic and hardworking, you are likely to be a true helpmate. You may be the kind of person who goes all out to stand up for a friend, a loved one, or just about anyone who is in need. A habit of expressing your feelings directly and without reservation can endear you to a mate. Your honey may admire your courage in being so forthright. With your heart out there, on your sleeve, your mate may feel the urge to protect you. You thrive in a relationship that provides you with a soothing and secure retreat, where you can find comfort and renewal after giving so much of yourself in the world.

Spiritual compatibility can hold your partnership together over the years. While you and your mate may come from different religious backgrounds, what matters most is that you find ways to share inspiration and uplifting experiences together. Together, you may create your own personal rituals to guide you as your relationship grows and progresses. Sexuality can provide another path for establishing a soul connection with your mate. You may enjoy exploring and experimenting with the erotic customs of other cultures, such as the Kama Sutra and Tantrism.

You can be deeply responsive to the ambiance of your surroundings, and the chance to share sacred secrets can be enticing for you. Scented candles and soft music can transform an ordinary room into a sanctuary of love, where you and a partner can explore the eternal mysteries of sexual union.

For the Virgo man of 1977, a sunny, glamorous woman can be utterly enchanting. She is likely to reward you handsomely for the ease with which you express your admiration for her. To be needed, especially by the woman you admire, makes you feel just wonderful!

A man of sensitivity and refinement appeals to the Virgo woman born in 1977. He may have very particular tastes and needs, and you are likely to take pride in your ability to satisfy him. His emotional tenderness enables him to be the supportive friend and soul mate of your dreams.

VIRGO ZODIAC SIGN
YOUR LOVE PLANETS

YOUR ROMANTIC SIDE   p. 696
- ▶ **VENUS IN CANCER**
  Born Aug. 23, 6:00 - Aug. 28, 15:08
- ▶ **VENUS IN LEO**
  Born Aug. 28, 15:09 - Sept. 22, 15:04
- ▶ **VENUS IN VIRGO**
  Born Sept. 22, 15:05 - Sept. 23, 3:28

YOUR SEX DRIVE   p. 722
- ▶ **MARS IN GEMINI**
  Born Aug. 23, 6:00 - Sept. 01, 0:19
- ▶ **MARS IN CANCER**
  Born Sept. 01, 0:20 - Sept. 23, 3:28

YOUR CELEBRITY TWINS   p. 760
Find out the astrological similarities you have with famous people.

YOUR COMPATIBILITY   p. 780
Compare planets to find out how compatible you are in a relationship.

YOUR RELATIONSHIP KARMA   p. 824
- ▶ **SATURN IN LEO**
  Born Aug. 23, 6:00 - Sept. 23, 3:28

BARBARA BACH
American Actress
Sun and Venus in Virgo

487

1977 LIBRA

From September 23, 3:29 through October 23, 12:40

The Smooth Sweetheart

True to your sign, 1977 Libra, you tend to exude the very essence of elegance and refinement, but a romantic partner may rely upon you for your unwavering resolve and determination. While your sweetheart may appear to be boss to the outside world, in private the two of you may have a quiet understanding about who really rules the roost. Your sensitivity allows you to convey your will with empathy and respect for your mate's feelings. You have a comforting but persuasive way of communicating that enables you to get what you want while making your sweetheart feel great. Sometimes, you can be so smooth that your mate may be left wanting. In that case, you may need to strike a new compromise that weighs more in your sweetheart's favor.

For you, mutual respect and loyalty is the cement that holds a relationship together over the long term. You and your mate may strongly support each other's efforts to improve yourselves through education, travel, or even professional training. The growth you enjoy separately as individuals enables you to expand your ambitions and accomplishments as a couple. In the privacy of your bedroom, you may share your dreams and celebrate your triumphs. Making love can open a channel of physical communication that allows you to express your deepest feelings and desires.

Gourmet dining may bring you sensual pleasure, and a wine tasting can whet your appetite to share an intoxicating vintage. Having a partner feed you can be a tremendous turn on, especially in the privacy of home, where you can afford to get a bit messy.

The Libran man born in 1977 enjoys a woman who is meticulous in her appearance and perhaps a bit shy. Her reticence can be challenging for you, and you may find it exciting to pursue her. Like a rose, she may open petal-by-petal, thrilling you with each layer of her hidden beauty.

A generous, gregarious man can be a wonderful partner for the 1977 Libran woman. Taking care of friends and family may be very important to you, and his ease with others makes entertaining a pleasure. Ideally, he has a hearty sense of humor that keeps everybody smiling.

LIBRA ZODIAC SIGN
YOUR LOVE PLANETS

YOUR ROMANTIC SIDE   p. 696
- ▶ **VENUS IN VIRGO**
  Born Sept. 23, 3:29 - Oct. 17, 1:36
- ▶ **VENUS IN LIBRA**
  Born Oct. 17, 1:37 - Oct. 23, 12:40

YOUR SEX DRIVE   p. 722
- ▶ **MARS IN CANCER**
  Born Sept. 23, 3:29 - Oct. 23, 12:40

YOUR CELEBRITY TWINS   p. 760
Find out the astrological similarities you have with famous people.

YOUR COMPATIBILITY   p. 780
Compare planets to find out how compatible you are in a relationship.

YOUR RELATIONSHIP KARMA   p. 824
- ▶ **SATURN IN LEO**
  Born Sept. 23, 3:29 - Oct. 23, 12:40

OLIVIA NEWTON-JOHN
Australian Singer
Mars in Scorpio

1977 SCORPIO
From October 23, 12:41 through November 22, 10:06

 ## The Mystical Achiever

The 1977 Scorpio can be both a dreamer and an achiever, and the combination of these gifts enables you to create a great romance. For as long as you can remember, you may have longed for someone who shared your passions. Uniting with that person enables you to turn your greatest aspirations into goals and to realize those goals together. An intense relationship with a soul mate can make you feel more whole. For you, emotional intensity may be a necessary part of any love affair. Without it, you might lose interest and prefer to become "just friends."

Members of your sign are often interested in mysticism. A sign or sense of destiny may assure you that your mate is "the one." Intense passion can sometimes fade in the normal course of a partnership, and understanding this can prevent you from abandoning a relationship that holds long-term promise. Likely to be introspective, you may have an interest in psychology, and you and your mate might explore spirituality, both as a means of working through issues in your relationship and to promote your personal growth as individuals. For you, spiritual compatibility may go hand-in-hand with sexual desire, and when you come together with a partner, it may feel as if you are uniting on an ethereal plane, suffused with meaning that only the two of you can perceive or understand.

A little bit of drama can get your blood flowing. A night at the theater can be an exciting date for you. Some playacting in private can lead to a steamy love scene, with you and your mate in the starring roles.

A woman who is lovely and artistic can be an inspiring mate for the 1977 Scorpio man. Ideally, she will turn out to be your muse. You are a doer, and by applying her ideas in your projects, you can come up with wonderful creations and win her appreciation for you, the creator.

A sunny, optimistic man holds a magnetic power of attraction for the Scorpio woman of 1977. You may love someone who can shine a light onto the dark subjects that can so fascinate and consume you. Fiercely protective and a little bit possessive, he makes you feel precious.

1977 SAGITTARIUS
From November 22, 10:07 through December 21, 23:22

The Daring Dreamer

Dare to dream are words that may capture the philosophy of the 1977 Sagittarian. A dreamer who lives in the real world, you have the discipline and tenacity to pursue goals that may not come to fruition for years, decades, or even in your lifetime. Holding passionately to your convictions and aspirations, you may become part of an innovative movement. It's so important to have a romantic partner who is strongly supportive of you, as any pressure to compromise your ideals can create conflict in an affair. You flourish with someone who has the courage to make a difference and is unafraid to face some challenges for the sake of the vision you share.

Sagittarians tend to be irrepressibly and inspiringly truthful, another factor that can mean break-up or break-through in a serious relationship. Learning to be a bit more diplomatic allows you to speak your mind and spare your mate's feelings. Open-ended communication and mutual respect can hold your relationship securely together through the years. The intensity of your feelings can find its fullest expression in lovemaking. You are a generous, nurturing lover. Your mate's sexual satisfaction may be essential to your own contentment.

"Truth or Dare" is the ultimate sexy party game for you, and you may always go for the dare. Forbidden or risky activities can give you quite a thrill. Sagittarius rules exploration and discovery. Should you and your partner undertake intimate explorations that involve the risk of being "discovered," fate may reward you with a climactic result.

The Sagittarian man of 1977 thrives with a woman who is optimistic and open-minded. You appreciate someone with a big-picture perspective, who doesn't allow details to interfere with the goals you share. With this lovely lady by your side, you can overcome every obstacle.

The Sagittarian woman born in 1977 adores a man who is encouraging and unfailingly loyal. His warmth and humor can make you laugh off any setback in life. Able to inspire your fantasies and creativity, his fierce passion for learning can fill every day with wonder and pleasure.

The Disco Explosion

Flare-legged trousers with slick polyester shirts, cheeky hot pants and shiny spandex tube tops, big shoes and crazy boots. Permed, layered, and big hair (for both sexes). Rotating mirrored balls and multi-colored flashing lights, Donna Summer and The Village People. Doing the Hustle, the Bump, and the Bus Stop—oh happy memories. Those were the disco days—or nights. Love it or hate it, the hottest and arguably the most influential music trend of the decade, disco grew from its roots in New York underground nightclubs and house parties in the early '70s into a worldwide dance phenomenon.

This was the '70s. The nation was in an economic funk and youngsters were searching for a temporary escape from their low-paid jobs—if they had one! Disco was it. Unlike other types of music, it wasn't about raising social consciousness or staying in alone to review the meaning of life—it was about getting out, having fun, and dancing. Disco evolved into a lifestyle. Dancers wanted to be seen, and a spin under the disco ball was no casual dress affair. Colorful, outrageous clothes were a sight to behold. If you danced well and dressed right, you got lucky. In this era of escapism, cocaine was considered glamorous and was often described as the champagne or caviar of drugs. Alcohol consumption was high.

Disco brought much acclaim to the disc jockeys—the guys who played the records for a generation to dance to.

Nightclubs were the place to be and names like The Loft, Flamingo, the Gallery, and New York New York scored their mark in music history. Probably the best known of all was Studio 54. This was disco at its most extravagant—a place where stars mixed with eccentrics and the unknowns, a hothouse of beautiful people, endless cocaine, and sex. In a pre-AIDS, birth-controlled, promiscuous era of sexual and social excess, Studio 54 was the place to party.

If there was ever a good time to launch a film about a disco king dazzling audiences with his moves atop an under-lit kaleidoscopic dance floor, this was it. In 1977 *Saturday Night Fever* catapulted disco to even dizzier heights and made John Travolta a star in his role as Brooklyn dance ace Tony Manero. And in the unlikely event that you hadn't already heard of the Bee Gees, their success with Grammy winning "Stayin' Alive" would probably have done the trick.

This was a decade of wild abandon, and disco music provided the soundtrack to gay liberation and a decade obsessed with sexual freedom. Songs became anthems and danceable party classics such as "The Hustle," by Van McCoy, "I Will Survive," by Gloria Gaynor, "Rock The Boat," by the Hues Corporation, and "Ring My Bell," by Anita Ward—to name a few—were launched. It was disco, disco, disco. There was a National Disco Week, World Disco Dance Championships, a TV show (*Disco Step-By-Step*) dedicated to disco music and dance instruction, and even a Queen of Disco! It looked like disco was here to stay, but maybe partly due to what some described as "overkill," the late '70s saw a "Disco Sucks" backlash. Record sales dropped, but disco refused to die. It may have gone undercover and changed its name, but the beat still goes on.

489

▶ READ ABOUT *GREASE*, ANOTHER MOVIE STARRING JOHN TRAVOLTA, ON PAGE 490   ▶ READ ABOUT SWINGING LONDON, ON PAGE 383

- ✪ HOMOSEXUALITY
- ✪ JON VOIGHT
- ✪ GREASE
- ✪ SIDNEY SHELDON
- ✪ SCRUPLES
- ✪ ANDY GIBB
- ✪ THREE TIMES A LADY

EVENTS

In Manchester, in the UK, the birth of the first test tube baby, Louise Brown, dominated the headlines.

In the US, sex was still a big issue. The government announced it would finance sex-change operations. To qualify, candidates had to spend at least one year living as a member of the opposite sex. The New Jersey Senate approved a penal code that eliminated penalties for sexual conduct between consenting adults—including homosexuals.

Homosexuals were given attention in Florida, too. The Supreme Court of Florida ruled that homosexuality did not prevent a new lawyer from being accepted by the state bar. The court held that sexual preference did not in itself constitute a failure to meet the "good moral character" standards for practicing law in the state.

POP CULTURE

The movie theaters offered some serious fare. *Coming Home*, starring Jane Fonda and Jon Voight, followed a love triangle between a gung-ho Vietnam veteran, his wife, and the embittered paraplegic she comes to love. In *An Unmarried Woman,* a wife's comfortable existence is shattered when her husband declares his love for another woman.

Just for fun was *Grease*—with the Bee Gees (they wrote the hit song "Grease Is the Word"), John Travolta, and Olivia Newton-John. There was even more fun with *La Cage Aux Folles.* To save his son's upcoming marriage

into a conservative family, a gay man and his long-term partner try to conceal their lifestyle and ownership of a transvestite club.

Erotica and glitz dominated the bestseller lists. *The Early Diaries of Anaïs Nin, 1914-1920* were released. Sidney Sheldon's *Bloodlines* followed the beautiful daughter of the world's richest man. And *Scruples* by Judith Krantz was set in the ruthless world of high fashion and international movie making.

This was the year when almost every song on the charts belonged to either the Bee Gees or their younger brother, Andy Gibb. "Night Fever," "Stayin' Alive," and "Shadow Dancing" had lovers disco dancing, as did Chic's "Le Freak" and A Taste of Honey's "Boogie Oogie Oogie." The Commodores slowed it down a notch for slow dancers with "Three Times a Lady."

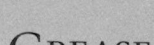

Hot Movie

GREASE

When the movie *Grease* opened to wide critical and audience acclaim in 1978, the chills were electrifying. It featured a cast of hot newcomers, including the sexy Australian Olivia Newton-John and the hunk star of TV's *Welcome Back, Kotter,* John Travolta. The sizzling scenes between these two budding idols became the stuff of screen legend.

It was a musical set in the fictional Rydell High. The Pink Ladies and the T-Birds were the Greek chorus behind the evolving romance between Danny and Sandy (Travolta and Newton-John). The last scene featured Sandy in the tightest pair of black satin jeans ever seen on screen till then.

SEE ALSO
▶ THE DISCO EXPLOSION *Page 489*

1978 CAPRICORN

From December 21, 1977, 23:23 through January 20, 1978, 10:03
(December 1978 Capricorns, see 1979 Capricorn)

♑ *The Dreamy Sexpot*

You 1978 Capricorns simply ooze sex appeal. When you're in the room, the temperature starts to rise. It's not as though you dress provocatively or fill your conversations with suggestive comments. You just have a certain animal magnetism that radiates in all directions. Although plenty of people may be interested in you romantically, you're quite selective when it comes to choosing a partner. You're willing to wait until the right mate comes along.

There has to be a spiritual link between you and your soul mate. You probably have a deep faith in humanity that is the guiding force in your life. Pairing up with someone who shares your optimistic view is very important. When it comes to sex, you do best in a committed relationship. It can be difficult for you to be physically intimate with a lover whose affections are inconsistent. You also enjoy plenty of intense, heavy foreplay.

Drawing your attention could be as simple as asking deep, probing questions about your personal life. Although you probably won't answer, it excites you to think that someone is interested in your private affairs. You're also attracted to suitors who give you the full measure of their attention. If there's anything you can't stand, it's a date with roving eyes. You expect to be their one and only focus. Lovers with an element of danger send shivers of delight down your spine. Therefore intense, brooding types definitely have a good chance with you.

You male 1978 Goats are looking for a woman who is dignified, romantic, and traditional. Females who are driven and ambitious really impress you. You're turned on by a woman who runs her own business, because her accomplishments would be a constant source of admiration for you. It's also important that your partner has a lusty bedroom manner, as your sexual appetite is considerable.

Men who are proud, passionate, and personable are your ideal as a 1978 female Capricorn. Your perfect mate likes to take charge in a romantic sort of way. Ideally, your partner will want to lavish you with loving gestures, beautiful gifts, and fun trips.

NICK NOLTE
American Actor
Sun and Venus in Aquarius

1978 AQUARIUS

From January 20, 10:04 through February 19, 0:20

♒ *The Steady Lover*

Proud, dignified, and serious, you 1978 Aquarians command respect wherever you go. There's a certain force to your personality that prompts folks to defer to your every decision. Naturally, your commanding presence can be a little intimidating for any romantic prospects. Fortunately, though, you have no problem taking the initiative when the right prospect comes along. In fact, you like taking the lead in romance, and in all other areas of life, too!

You're not the type of person to embark on a frivolous affair. Rather, you prefer teaming up with a partner in order to build a safe, secure life together. Even though you have unconventional views about many issues, you could be very conservative about relationships. There's a good chance that you will wait until later in life to settle down. It's also possible that you will marry someone who has plenty of sexual experience. The teacher-student fantasy may be an exciting idea. Playing it out with your mate can be a thrill.

Attending to your emotional needs is a sure-fire way for a suitor to win your approval. Often, you're so busy taking care of others that you put your own desires last. You're always gratified when somebody goes out of their way to make you feel comfortable. Escorting you to an exclusive or restricted club also wins points for you, because you like feeling privileged. You're also dazzled by people who can handle problems in a controlled, reassuring way.

As a male Water Bearer who was born in 1978, you're seeking a woman who is honorable, friendly, and intelligent. You particularly admire females who conduct their lives according to a core set of standards. Women who are sensitive and compassionate touch your heart. Ideally, you're looking for a partner who reminds you to live life on a high moral plane.

You 1978 women Aquarians want a man who is protective and reliable. Having a partner who lets you know where you stand at all times is very comforting for you. You're particularly drawn to guys who project an image of manly confidence in public, but display a gentle sensitivity in private.

JILL CLAYBURGH
American Actress
Venus in Aries

492

1978 PISCES
From February 19, 0:21 through March 20, 23:33

The Romantic Inspiration

You 1978 Pisceans combine generosity and whimsy in a delightful way. This reassuring quality may have drawn many romantic prospects your way. It's quite possible that certain friends have harbored crushes on you for years. Your dreamy outlook on life may have prevented you from noticing their admiring glances. Consequently, you do best with a mate who takes a direct approach toward everything in life, including relationship matters.

Your ideal relationship is one that infuses your life with energy and optimism. You want a partner who celebrates your creative urges. If there's anything you can't stand, it's a pessimist. Settling down with an adventurous mate will allow you to take advantage of life's many opportunities. Your adventurous spirit also extends to sex. As far as you're concerned, the bedroom is a place to explore, experiment, and invent. You do best with a lover who shares your open-minded attitude and seeks to explore new sexual territory with you.

An assertive lover who is eager to sweep you into a tide of romance is sure to win your heart. You're thrilled by dashing gestures of chivalry. Challenges to rivals, gallant sacrifices, and passionate public tributes make your pulse pound with pleasure. As a 1978 Pisces, you yearn to live out some cinematic ideal of love. Any suitor who provides you with this experience is sure to win your lifelong loyalty and devotion.

You male Fish who were born in 1978 are drawn to two distinct types of women. The first is a tender, romantic sort who believes that love is a transcendental experience. The second is a bold, daring kind of woman who likes to fight injustices. Ultimately, you're looking for a partner who is passionately invested in life.

As a female Fish who was born in 1978, you want a man who likes to take charge in an old-fashioned way. The guy who makes you swoon is a courtly gentleman who makes the first move. You love a guy who puts you on a pedestal and will do anything in his power to satisfy your needs, both emotional and sexual. Men who build up to a passionate crescendo really turn you on.

1978 ARIES
From March 20, 23:34 through April 20, 10:49

The Unpredictable Lover

Life is filled with surprises when you 1978 Rams are around! You love taking bold chances and thrilling risks, especially when it comes to love. Sometimes you view relationships as a divine power struggle. You're not especially intent on being in control all of the time, but you do enjoy engaging in a struggle for dominance. Nothing delights you like verbally sparring with your partner. In your perfect relationship there is an abundance of spicy repartee. The closer your relationship resembles an intricate chess match, the better.

Love isn't entirely fun and games for you, however. When you do settle down with someone special, you take your responsibility toward them very seriously. Keeping your mate sexually satisfied is important to you. Despite your lighthearted appearance, you're always taking mental notes on what your partner seems to like and dislike in bed. Nobody could ever accuse you of being a selfish lover. A healthy sex life is essential to your happiness. Consequently, you may spend a great deal of time and energy on meeting your soul mate's physical needs.

Entering a competition against you is the best way to win your affection. You consider it to be the ultimate compliment when somebody wants to measure their talents against yours. Expressing an open-minded attitude toward sex is also wise, as you are excited at the prospect of experimentation. Suitors who play hot and cold with you can also arouse your passion.

Women who are forceful and dynamic really turn you on as a 1978 male Aries. You're turned on by a girl who isn't afraid to push you aside and assume the driver's seat. If she has a sarcastic sense of humor, that's all the better. Your ideal partner will be alternately passive and aggressive in the bedroom, as you like switching roles.

You 1978 female Rams are looking for a man who is tough and sentimental at the same time. Your ideal guy is secure enough in his masculinity to shed an occasional tear at the movies. A man who approaches sex like a grand conquest excites your imagination. You'd love to be your mate's ultimate adventure.

1978 TAURUS

From April 21, 10:50 through May 21, 10:07

The Wistful Adventurer

As far as you 1978 Taureans are concerned, home is where the heart is. You take a great deal of pleasure from your domestic surroundings, and probably enjoy spending quality time with your friends and family. In fact, your home life may be so cozy that you look to relationships to provide you with excitement. At times, you may gravitate toward romantic interests who seem completely opposite from your close pals. A mate who is eccentric and daring suits you very well. You want an unconventional partnership.

Sex is a deep, meaningful experience for you. Therefore, you tend not to have romances with people who think making love is a form of recreation. When you find somebody who makes you feel transformed through the act of love, you cling tight to them. Marriage could occur quite suddenly for you, especially if you have an impulsive partner. As someone who is rather cautious by nature, you love it when your mate helps you get swept up in the moment.

If somebody wants to ask you out on a date, they should propose a venue that is unconventional. You're always eager to see places and things that are outside the realm of your normal experience. Getting along with your friends and family is also important, as these people play a vital role in your life. When it comes time to get intimate, your suitor should linger over foreplay. You like sex to build to a blissful crescendo.

As a 1978 male Taurus, you want a woman who is both sensual and intellectual. You love smart females who are attuned to their physical desires. A partner who is able to establish a serene home life but still eager to take exciting road trips is ideal for you. Although you do want a comfortable abode, it's important for you and your mate to occasionally explore the wilder side of life, too.

You 1978 female Bulls want a man who is a virtual love magnet. You've always been drawn to guys who radiate sex appeal. A partner who is as equally affectionate as he is attractive makes you extremely happy. Men who enjoy playing sports have a good chance with you, as you like a guy with a competitive spirit.

TAURUS ZODIAC SIGN
YOUR LOVE PLANETS

YOUR ROMANTIC SIDE   p. 696
- ▶ **VENUS IN TAURUS**
  Born Apr. 20, 10:50 - Apr. 27, 7:52
- ▶ **VENUS IN GEMINI**
  Born Apr. 27, 7:53 - May 21, 10:07

YOUR SEX DRIVE   p. 722
- ▶ **MARS IN LEO**
  Born Apr. 20, 10:50 - May 21, 10:07

YOUR CELEBRITY TWINS   p. 760
Find out the astrological similarities you have with famous people.

YOUR COMPATIBILITY   p. 780
Compare planets to find out how compatible you are in a relationship.

YOUR RELATIONSHIP KARMA   p. 824
- ▶ **SATURN IN LEO**
  Born Apr. 20, 10:50 - May 21, 10:07

DEBBIE HARRY
American Singer
Venus and Mars in Taurus

493

1978 GEMINI
From May 21, 10:08 through June 21, 18:09

The Idealistic Partner

Love is all daisies and buttercups for you 1978 Geminis. You're incredibly idealistic when it comes to romance, and insist that there's no greater goal to chase. Until you find your true love, you'll be on a constant quest to find him or her. There's a good chance you'll do a great deal of dating before you finally marry. That's fine with you. A gregarious person like you always enjoys meeting people. The only downside to dating is that so many people tend to fall in love with you, when you only feel friendship in return. It takes a magical person to capture your heart.

Your sex life probably has an intense, powerful quality. You only make love with partners with whom you have a strong chemistry. Jumping into bed for fun just isn't your style. When you do meet the right person, you'll feel transformed by your lovemaking together. It's essential for you to have a marriage that places a strong emphasis on sex, because you see it as the ultimate expression of love. If your relationship undergoes a period of abstinence, you worry that something is wrong.

Although you are quite easygoing and friendly, you like it when a suitor takes a strong, forceful approach toward you. A confident attitude is sure to attract your interest. Taking you to a sexy movie is well-advised, because you can be very impressionable. You're also turned on by deep, ardent kisses. Anybody who wants to become your partner should make sure that your first kiss together be passionate and romantic.

If you're a male Gemini who was born in 1978, your tastes toward women are quite varied. Intuitive, temperamental females pose an exciting challenge to you. You also like women who are regal and vibrant. Ultimately, however, you're looking for a partner who is as romantic and hopeful as you are. Pessimists really turn you off.

Two different types of men appeal to you 1978 female Geminis. The first is outgoing and virile. The second is the strong silent type. At rock bottom, though, you need a partner who has a strong moral code. You don't trust ruthless men who will do anything to get ahead.

GEMINI ZODIAC SIGN
YOUR LOVE PLANETS

YOUR ROMANTIC SIDE   p. 696
- ▶ **VENUS IN GEMINI**
  Born May 21, 10:08 - May 22, 2:02
- ▶ **VENUS IN CANCER**
  Born May 22, 2:03 - June 16, 6:18
- ▶ **VENUS IN LEO**
  Born June 16, 6:19 - June 21, 18:09

YOUR SEX DRIVE   p. 722
- ▶ **MARS IN LEO**
  Born May 21, 10:08 - June 14, 2:37
- ▶ **MARS IN VIRGO**
  Born June 14, 2:38 - June 21, 18:09

YOUR CELEBRITY TWINS   p. 760
Find out the astrological similarities you have with famous people.

YOUR COMPATIBILITY   p. 780
Compare planets to find out how compatible you are in a relationship.

YOUR RELATIONSHIP KARMA   p. 824
- ▶ **SATURN IN LEO**
  Born May 21, 10:08 - June 21, 18:09

CAROLE LAURE
French-Canadian Actress
Sun in Leo

494

1978 CANCER
From June 21, 18:10 through July 23, 4:59
The Impulsive Romantic

You 1978 Crabs love to get swept up in the tide of romance. Even when you're not with a partner, you like to surround yourself with sexy music, fresh flowers, and candlelight. Life seems harsh and unfriendly without these soft touches. Fortunately, you possess tremendous creative flair and can make even a drab environment feel comfortable and inviting with very little effort. A mate who appreciates these talents is ideal for you. You do best in a relationship that prizes beauty, comfort, and harmony above all else. Tumultuous pairings make you uncomfortable and threaten your security.

You're an intuitive and imaginative lover, and benefit from a partner who is eager for sexual experimentation. There's a good chance that you'll have quite an active love life before settling down with your soul mate. Marriage is a serious business for you, and you're likely to settle down with someone who has traditional ideas about this sacred institution. Joining up with a flighty person would not suit your temperament. You're better off with a mate who is dependable.

Anyone who expresses an open-minded attitude toward sex has a good chance of hitting it off with you. You can't abide prudes. If someone wants to ask you out on a date, they should propose going to an avant-garde film festival or a performance art exhibit. You love to see creative boundaries being pushed. It's a good idea to make the first move with you, because you enjoy being pursued.

You male Crabs who were born in 1978 have a variety of tastes when it comes to women. Females with a vibrant sexuality really excite you. You also like down-to-earth women with powerful intellects. Whichever kind of woman you choose as your life partner, she should be supportive and dependable.

As a 1978 female Cancer, you want a man who is unpretentious and discriminating. It's also important that your mate has a sharp intellect—brainless, brawny types hold no charms for you. If you meet a guy who likes helping around the house, he stands a good chance of becoming your life partner. You do not enjoy waiting on a couch potato.

1978 LEO
From July 23, 5:00 through August 23, 11:56
The Romantic Perfectionist

As 1978 Lion, you have very definite ideas about how romance should be conducted. You probably cringe when you see people proposing marriage on live television—what could be more embarrassing? Love is a very private matter for you. You won't make your move until the setting is absolutely right. Candlelit restaurants and secluded country inns are probably among your favorite venues for romance. You do best with a partner who has a similar sensibility toward courtship.

You have vivid sexual fantasies and enjoy playing them out with your partner. Sometimes it is difficult for you to communicate your desires verbally, which is why you will benefit from a mate who is sensitive and intuitive. It's possible that you confuse sex with love, and it hurts you very deeply when someone with whom you've been intimate takes the encounter casually. A sexual partner who shares your deep sense of commitment is ideally suited to your loyal heart. As far as marriage is concerned, you thrive with a spouse who is both a lover and a friend.

Direct, forthright suitors have the best chance of winning your affection. You are a little hesitant when it comes to asking for a date, so it's best that your admirer makes the first move. You're quite passionate, but need a persuasive lover who makes you forget your inhibitions. You love being caressed and massaged, and this is an excellent way to lead up to lovemaking with you. Seducing you with soft words and compliments also has a good effect on you.

If you're a male Lion who was born in 1978, you admire a demure but bright woman. Dramatic, showy types turn you off—you're more interested in a modest woman who lets her intellectual prowess speak for itself. Above all, you appreciate a mate who is as tasteful and discerning as you are.

As a 1978 female Leo, you want a man who is graceful but a little detached. Ardent, passionate guys make you feel intimidated. You'd rather team up with a guy who takes a cerebral approach to love. Men who know how to give compliments hold a soft spot in your heart—you love being appreciated and admired.

1978 VIRGO
From August 23, 11:57 through September 23, 9:24

♍ *The Practical Partner*

Sensible, thoughtful, and eager to please, you 1978 Virgins are pleasant companions. You're always anticipating people's needs and looking for ways to make life more comfortable. And although you're extremely giving, you're a little shy when it comes to romance. You might feel silly saying words of devotion to your beloved, and prefer writing anonymous love notes as a means of expressing your feelings. When you do find a partner who understands and respects your needs, you'll feel very blessed indeed.

Passionate, dramatic confrontations make you feel uncomfortable. You do best with a mate with whom you can reason. If your mate directs an angry outburst toward you, you're more likely than not to withdraw than retaliate. Therefore, it's a good idea for you to have a marriage partner who has excellent communication skills. When it comes to making love, you enjoy a partner who tells you what he or she needs in no uncertain terms. This makes it easy to cater to your mate's every sexual desire.

If someone wants to attract your attention, they should be gentle and persistent. You have a tendency to get flustered when a suitor expresses interest in you. If your admirer takes this into account, they should eventually be able to entice you out to a museum or concert. You have a profound appreciation for the arts, although you prefer quiet, dignified exhibits to loud, raucous displays. Soft, reassuring kisses are a great way to weaken your sexual reserve.

You male Virgos who were born in 1978 like women who are elegant. Ladylike manners and tasteful clothing never fail to make your pulse race. You also admire deeply creative women, although their mood swings can sometimes throw you off balance. Ultimately, you need a perceptive partner who knows when to exert pressure on you and when to take it off.

If you're a 1978 female Virgo, you want a man who is elegant and charming. Rough, behemoths fill you with distaste. Guys whose passions smolder just beneath the surface also intrigue you. Your ideal mate will treat you like a lady in public and an irresistible sex goddess in private.

VIRGO ZODIAC SIGN
YOUR LOVE PLANETS

YOUR ROMANTIC SIDE   p. 696
▶ **VENUS IN LIBRA**
Born Aug. 23, 11:57 - Sept. 07, 5:06
▶ **VENUS IN SCORPIO**
Born Sept. 07, 5:07 - Sept. 23, 9:24

YOUR SEX DRIVE   p. 722
▶ **MARS IN LIBRA**
Born Aug. 23, 11:57 - Sept. 19, 20:56
▶ **MARS IN SCORPIO**
Born Sept. 19, 20:57 - Sept. 23, 9:24

YOUR CELEBRITY TWINS   p. 760
Find out the astrological similarities you have with famous people.

YOUR COMPATIBILITY   p. 780
Compare planets to find out how compatible you are in a relationship.

YOUR RELATIONSHIP KARMA   p. 824
▶ **SATURN IN VIRGO**
Born Aug. 23, 11:57 - Sept. 23, 9:24

CHRISTOPHER REEVE
American Actor
Sun and Venus in Libra

495

1978 LIBRA
From September 23, 9:25 through October 23, 18:36

♎ *The Possessive Lover*

As a 1978 Libran, you love with your entire mind, body, and soul. You're an intensely passionate person who likes to push the romantic envelope. At times you'd lay down your life for your beloved—at others, you're tempted to strangle him or her. Love can bring extreme joy or turbulence to your life. That's just fine with you—you'd rather have a relationship of extremes than go along at an even keel. Ultimately, you thrive in a partnership that is exciting and a bit dangerous.

For you, sex is an essential component to a successful marriage. If the passion goes out of a relationship, you have no qualms about breaking ties and moving on. If you do stay with a marriage partner for the rest of your life, it will be because you've sustained a passion for one another. Staying together because it's convenient or comfortable is probably not an option for you. You need a marriage that is always vibrant and alive. Otherwise, what's the point?

Seducing you can be a delicious but torturous game. You love playing hot and cold with your admirers. If a suitor notices that

you've become distant and aloof, they should mirror your behavior. You absolutely can't stand to be ignored, and will quickly do everything in your power to recapture your admirer's interest. Displaying an ardent sexual appetite on the first date is also a good idea. Your physical needs are considerable, so you're looking for a partner who can keep up with you in the bedroom.

You men who were born in 1978 under the sign of the Scales want a dark seductress. Women who are passionate, intense, and sultry never fail to get your motor running. A girl who is quick to anger also excites you, as this shows she has strong feelings. Wishy-washy diplomats turn you off. You need a mate with fire in her veins!

Men who are mesmerizing and compelling are cut out for you 1978 female Librans. You've always gone for dark rebels, and quite a few have probably broken your heart. Your ideal man will combine ardent sensuality with protective love. You want to feel as though you totally belong to your partner, body and soul.

LIBRA ZODIAC SIGN
YOUR LOVE PLANETS

YOUR ROMANTIC SIDE   p. 696
▶ **VENUS IN SCORPIO**
Born Sept. 23, 9:25 - Oct. 23, 18:36

YOUR SEX DRIVE   p. 722
▶ **MARS IN SCORPIO**
Born Sept. 23, 9:25 - Oct. 23, 18:36

YOUR CELEBRITY TWINS   p. 760
Find out the astrological similarities you have with famous people.

YOUR COMPATIBILITY   p. 780
Compare planets to find out how compatible you are in a relationship.

YOUR RELATIONSHIP KARMA   p. 824
▶ **SATURN IN VIRGO**
Born Sept. 23, 9:25 - Oct. 23, 18:36

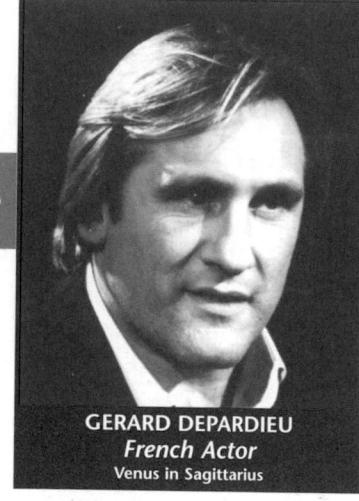

GERARD DEPARDIEU
French Actor
Venus in Sagittarius

496

1978 SCORPIO
From October 23, 18:37 through November 22, 16:04

♏ *The Purposeful Romantic*

You 1978 Scorpions have no problem overcoming obstacles. You're extremely inventive, and enjoy coming up with creative solutions to stubborn problems. This is especially true with regard to romance. If the object of your desire doesn't express interest in you at first, you're not fazed in the slightest. In fact, you're excited by their disinterest, and will do everything imaginable to turn their indifference into an unbridled passion. Fortunately, you're usually successful in these endeavors.

You have a strong need for a rewarding and harmonious marriage. Life can be turbulent for you, so you do best with a loving spouse who gives you support to withstand any upsets. When you're with a loving partner, your delightfully romantic nature comes out in full force. You're an incredibly devoted spouse, and will do everything imaginable to make your partner happy and fulfilled. You can't tolerate infidelity, though, and can be extremely possessive.

When somebody wants to become your lover, they should focus on your needs like a laser. You want to be the sole object of an admirer's desire, and enjoy displays of ardent devotion. A person who tattoos your name on an intimate part of their body would probably have a good chance of winning your heart. Impulsive gestures also touch you, and you're likely to smile with delight if your suitor breaks into a love song in a public place. Sexually, you want a partner whose lovemaking style could best be described as "torrid."

You male 1978 Scorpions want a woman who possesses powerful sensuality and magnetism. A girl who can hypnotize you by just looking into your eyes stands a good chance of becoming your lover. You also admire women who dress provocatively, at least in private. Finding a partner who alternately wants to be your sexual slave and master would be ideal.

As a 1978 female Scorpion, you're turned on by brooding, mysterious men. You love guys who betray their feelings through actions, not words. A man who punches the wall with frustration or sweeps you into a passionate embrace is sure to win your everlasting devotion.

1978 SAGITTARIUS
From November 22, 16:05 through December 22, 5:20

♐ *The Inspired Suitor*

Visionary, dreamy, and romantic, you 1978 Sagittarians are very satisfying lovers. You tend to put your partner on a pedestal and idealize their every word and action. No wonder so many want to be your one-and-only! It takes someone very special to win your heart, however. You benefit most from a partner with a divine sense of social justice, as well as a whimsical view of life. People with a childlike innocence are particularly attractive to you—you can't stand jaded, overly sophisticated types.

As far as marriage is concerned, you want an equal partnership with somebody who has their own interests. You won't last long with a partner who jealously watches your every move—you need freedom to grow and develop. Similarly, you're eager to encourage your spouse's ambitions and give your beloved all the necessary freedom to make his or her dreams come true. You want a marriage that is constantly evolving, and enjoy a mate who sees life as the ultimate adventure. Travel may play a big part in your marriage.

Suitors would be wise to win your friendship before asking you for a date. You're interested in learning a person's tastes and pursuits before beginning a romance. You're not averse to having a physical relationship with a friend, but if somebody wants to win your love, they should be open-minded, compassionate, and adventurous. It would also help if your admirer loves animals. You enjoy sex al fresco, and may be quite responsive to lovemaking attempts that are initiated outdoors.

As a male 1978 Archer, you want a woman who has deep feelings and enjoys a spirited debate. You love a female who can defend her opinions to the most vociferous opponents. Ideally, you're looking for a partner whose head is as powerful as her heart.

Men who are energetic and ambitious attract you 1978 female Sagittarians. You're very stimulated by guys who have big plans for the future—you want a mate who is going somewhere in life. If you have to choose, you'd rather have a man who errs on the side of quantity versus quality when it comes to making love. You have lots of energy to burn!

Warren Beatty – The Lusty Star

Ever since Warren Beatty debuted in the 1961 hit *Splendor in the Grass*, he's been known as a charming womanizer. At the time, he was having an affair with Joan Collins, but this ended when he moved in with costar Natalie Wood. As Beatty became a big celebrity in the '60s and '70s, he continued to have affairs with his costars, as well as rumored affairs with many other women. One of these was Carly Simon, who wrote the song "You're So Vain," which resulted in speculation about who the song was about. It would appear that his love life enhanced his creative efforts. By 1978 he took full control of his own destiny by directing, writing, producing, and starring in *Heaven Can Wait*, for which he received an unprecedented four Oscar nominations.

Warren Beatty was born an independent Aries, with his Sun found in his horoscope in the seventh house of partnerships. His best efforts emerge when he can bounce his lines off beautiful costars. He can be the bold, trailblazing pioneer when he has someone who appreciates and mirrors back to him his genius. We saw this most effectively in his first big hit, the 1967 gangster flick *Bonnie and Clyde*. Here he was both actor and producer and teamed up with Faye Dunaway to portray two Depression-era bank robbers. The movie's success owes itself to Beatty's realistic view of poor America, as well as the unprecedented last scene of slow-motion violence.

A great deal of Beatty's charm can be attributed to the marriage asteroid Juno, which is prominently positioned with his Ascendant, the sign rising at time of birth. Juno actually prefers to be in a committed relationship, but since in this horoscope it's opposite Saturn, the planet of restriction and

"This image people have of Warren Beatty bears no reality to me."

BEATTY referring to himself.

limitations, Beatty feels hemmed in by marriage. His older sister actress Shirley MacLaine says that he can't even commit to dinner. In 1975 Beatty spoofed his own playboy image by acting in and producing *Shampoo*, where he plays a bed-hopping hairdresser trying to juggle his lovers, played by actresses Goldie Hawn and Julie Christie. It was rumored that he had

real-life affairs with both these women.

Beatty's Mars further describes his tendency to wander. It's in the roaming sign of Sagittarius and forms a challenging aspect to Uranus, the planet of rebellion and independence. This Mars-Uranus combination is what makes Beatty such an iconoclast. In his personal life and in the roles he chooses to play, Beatty is a maverick. In the 1981 blockbuster *Reds*, Beatty stars as John Reed, the controversial American journalist who covered the Bolshevik Revolution. Beatty also wrote the script, directed, and produced the film, for which he received four Oscar nominations and won Best Director. His co-star, and new off-screen romantic partner, was Diane Keaton.

Despite his great success, Warren Beatty only appeared in 20 or so films by the end of the 20th century. By the 1990s he still attracted millions of moviegoers, most notably through two films featuring doomed antiheroes, the 1991 *Bugsy* and the 1998 *Bulworth*. But 1992 marked the end of an era, because Beatty married his *Bugsy* co-star Annette Bening. Perhaps Beatty at age 55 was finally settling down. The couple seem rock solid and have four kids. "I've been rejuvenated through my children," says Beatty. "I've never laughed or cried as much in my life than since I had my children."

In *Bulworth*, co-starring Halle Berry (and yes, there have been rumors), Beatty plays a Senator who provides a radical solution to America's racial problems. His re-election campaign features a rap song that promotes interracial sex as the way to remove all the color barriers.

It looks as though Beatty has finally found what he didn't even know he was looking for. He says of his wife Annette, "I was looking for someone to make me good. When I met her, I felt relief."

497

▶ READ MORE ABOUT WARREN BEATTY IN *SHAMPOO* ON PAGE 466

1979

- ⊛ ERIC CLAPTON
- ⊛ LINDA RONSTADT
- ⊛ 10
- ⊛ SEXUAL EXCITEMENT
- ⊛ SOPHIE'S CHOICE
- ⊛ DONNA SUMMER
- ⊛ I WILL SURVIVE

EVENTS

Public personalities and their relationships dominated the news. Jeremy Thorpe, former leader of the Liberal Party in the UK charged with plotting to kill his male lover, was acquitted. Susan Ford, 21-year-old daughter of former US president Gerald Ford, wed Secret Service guard Charles Vance, 37. Eric Clapton wed Patti Boyd, the ex-wife of Beatle George Harrison. Rod Stewart got hitched to Alana Hamilton. Jerry Brown, governor of California, hooked up with singer Linda Ronstadt. His relationship with her was viewed by the media as politically self-destructive and was widely credited for ruining his chances to run against Jimmy Carter in the 1980 US presidential election.

POP CULTURE

Moviegoers were mesmerized by Bo Derek in 10, with her beautiful figure and blonde cornrows. Meryl Streep gained attention for her role in *Kramer vs. Kramer*, an Academy Award winner about a couple's divorce and the effect of the custody battle on father and son. Neil Simon's *Chapter Two* was about a recently widowed author who woos and marries a recently divorced actress, only to find he can't forget his first wife.

By 1979 bookstores still had room on their shelves for books on human sexual response. *Sexual Excitement: Dynamics of Erotic Life* explored the nature of sexual excitement through a detailed examination of the erotic life of a single psychoanalytic patient. Glitz still had a place, too. *The Bitch* by Jackie Collins watches Fontaine Khaled shed her rich but restrictive husband for a life of champagne, designer clothes, and hot men—until she meets her match in Nico Constantine. *Sophie's Choice* by William Styron made an impact, too, and later went on to be made into a movie that helped lead actress Meryl Streep win an Oscar.

Disco still reigned. The Bee Gees topped the charts with "Too Much Heaven." Donna Summer had two hits—"Bad Girls" and "Hot Stuff." Gloria Gaynor made women feel stronger with "I Will Survive." Rod Stewart was still going strong, too. Most answered positively to his question "Do Ya Think I'm Sexy?" "Escape (The Pina Colada Song)" made some nod in agreement, and others laugh.

Hot Couple

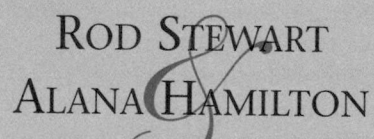

ROD STEWART & ALANA HAMILTON

Born in December 1945 in Highgate, London, British rock legend Rod Stewart began his career in the 1960s when he toured Europe as part of a small jazz group. He is well-known for his turbulent relationships with models and actresses.

A blonde himself, he has always had a thing for glamorous blonde women, and when he met George Hamilton's ex-wife, actress Alana Hamilton, he was instantly smitten. No one knew better than Stewart the premise of his album, *Blondes Have More Fun*. By the time they divorced in 1984, he was on to his next blonde, model Kelly Emberg.

SEE ALSO

▶ MICK JAGGER & BIANCA *Page 434*

▶ JEAN-MICHEL JARRE & CHARLOTTE RAMPLING *Page 474*

1979 CAPRICORN

From December 22, 1978, 5:21 through January 20, 1979, 15:59 (December 1979 Capricorns, see 1980 Capricorn)

♑ *The Ambitious Hero*

Deliciously sexy Capricorn of 1979, you aren't even aware of how attractive you are to the opposite sex! Which makes you even more attractive. Only "A-List" relationships—the absolute best—will satisfy you. Not willing to settle, you dream of being with someone who helps you to gain more knowledge, success, and prestige.

You're ambitious, strong, and noble, but believe you would be that much fiercer a presence in the world if you had someone fabulous by your side to do it all for. It's as if you're a good luck charm for the one you love. Still, you want someone to be just as lucky for you. You expect a relationship to be public as well as private. Showing off your beloved makes you as proud as a peacock. Mixing business with pleasure with the one you love and all your collective colleagues and connections gives you a big thrill. Your favorite kind of dates are at cocktail parties and big fundraisers where influential, in-the-know people gather. And that naturally includes you and your lover. You know that two can

conquer the world more easily than one.

A potential suitor should mention the latest hot clubs and places to go when conversing with a 1979 Capricorn. A would-be lover can't be a stay at home type. Talk of world travel, politics, and climbing the career ladder will give you a special tingle where it counts!

As a male Capricorn born in 1979 you need a woman who is confident enough to ask you out and to kiss you passionately first. She should egg you on to do wild, exciting, adventurous things, such as following her across the globe. In addition, a woman with a taste for luxury turns you on. You like to give expensive, sensual gifts that you can adorn your honey with—and seduce her out of!

As a 1979 Capricorn woman, you're most compatible with a man who is serious about his career and knows what he wants out of life. He should have a strong sense of purpose. If he is dominating in bed, you say, "That's a good thing." You like it when your man pulls you into a cab and whisks you home for a hot night between the sheets. Animal lust is a must for you!

CAPRICORN ZODIAC SIGN
Your Love Planets

YOUR ROMANTIC SIDE   p. 696
▶ **VENUS IN SCORPIO**
Born Dec. 22, 1978 5:21 - Jan. 07, 1979 6:37
▶ **VENUS IN SAGITTARIUS**
Born Jan. 07, 6:38 - Jan. 20, 15:59

YOUR SEX DRIVE   p. 722
▶ **MARS IN CAPRICORN**
Born Dec. 22, 1978 5:21 - Jan. 20, 1979 15:59

YOUR CELEBRITY TWINS   p. 760
Find out the astrological similarities you have with famous people.

YOUR COMPATIBILITY   p. 780
Compare planets to find out how compatible you are in a relationship.

YOUR RELATIONSHIP KARMA   p. 824
▶ **SATURN IN VIRGO**
Born Dec. 22, 1978 5:21 - Jan. 20, 1979 15:59

NASTASSJA KINSKI
German Actress
Sun in Aquarius

499

1979 AQUARIUS

From January 20, 16:00 through February 19, 6:12

♒ *The Mad Scientist*

Aquarius of 1979, you can be wildly experimental when it comes to romance, believing that a relationship is meant to be a grand exploration between two people in love. Part of you is like a scientist or observer in love—relationships seem impossible to figure out, yet are so exciting to apply your inventive mind and heart to. You know, intuitively, that life is meant to be lived with another person, even though underneath it all you are quite happy alone. A relationship with an intense person who knows how to give you enough space is your ideal.

You believe that a relationship should start with a meeting of the minds and be based on friendship and mutual respect. Vivid displays of emotion and sexuality titillate you, but make you undeniably nervous, too. In a relationship, you need a comfort level that allows you to express your emotions and longings openly. You want your ideal mate to bring you to a deep emotional and sexual place.

A potential suitor could get your attention by showing a true humanitarian nature. The would-be mate could tell you about a great

volunteer opportunity for the needy and push you to sign on for a shift. An interested suitor must show confidence enough to urge you to practice what you preach. It's a major plus if someone can converse with you about technology and spirituality.

As an Aquarius man born in 1979 you are attracted to women who are serious about their careers but who have a conscience too—not just an interest in commerce. She must be the maker of her own rules, and not someone who can be bossed around. She has the gumption to keep you on your toes and the subtle sexiness to seduce you out of your clothes!

If you are a woman born under the sign of Aquarius in 1979 you need a man who is ahead of his time and not afraid to go against convention to achieve his dreams and goals. He is an inspiration to you and someone who believes in himself completely. Confidence without cockiness is an aphrodisiac for you. You feel a passionate hunger for this kind of man and can't get enough of him emotionally, intellectually, or sexually.

AQUARIUS ZODIAC SIGN
Your Love Planets

YOUR ROMANTIC SIDE   p. 696
▶ **VENUS IN SAGITTARIUS**
Born Jan. 20, 16:00 - Feb. 05, 9:15
▶ **VENUS IN CAPRICORN**
Born Feb. 05, 9:16 - Feb. 19, 6:12

YOUR SEX DRIVE   p. 722
▶ **MARS IN CAPRICORN**
Born Jan. 20, 16:00 - Jan. 20, 17:06
▶ **MARS IN AQUARIUS**
Born Jan. 20, 17:07 - Feb. 19, 6:12

YOUR CELEBRITY TWINS   p. 760
Find out the astrological similarities you have with famous people.

YOUR COMPATIBILITY   p. 780
Compare planets to find out how compatible you are in a relationship.

YOUR RELATIONSHIP KARMA   p. 824
▶ **SATURN IN VIRGO**
Born Jan. 20, 16:00 - Feb. 19, 6:12

MALCOLM MCDOWELL
English Actor
Mars in Aries

1979 PISCES
From February 19, 6:13 through March 21, 5:21

The Sentimental Psychic

Your intuitive powers about the opposite sex are super-strong, although you don't always listen to those "inner voices." When it comes to love, you are the eternal optimist. You look for romance in a stranger's eyes and sometimes in the eyes of friends. Flirting is your forte, and once you find true love you flaunt it! You tend to be very affectionate and like to smother your beloved with kisses, hugs, and unexpected gifts. Holding back is not in your repertoire.

You expect a relationship to be passionate, mysterious, and deeply emotional. You love to surprise your partner with a spontaneous rendezvous, presents, and games, and love to be surprised yourself in return. But you also expect the one you love to be there for you each and every day through good and bad. Distance is not your thing, but closeness is, the more often the better.

A potential lover must behave in a charismatic and daring manner in order to catch your eye. The grand gesture is a good idea. Sending two dozen roses to your office, or sending a limo to pick you up for a weekend trip will surely make your heart flutter. A potential suitor should pay special attention to your erogenous zones such as your feet and your hair. Music and dance are great sources of joy for you, so an offer to take you to a concert or ballet will certainly move you to tears, before you even get the chance to say "yes." You have a deep, deep soft spot for children, animals, and helpless creatures, so someone who is kind to all will get under your skin (and under your sheets) very quickly.

If you are a male Pisces born in 1979 you need a woman who is sweet and giving, but who will not compromise her basic values to please you. Your perfect mate is an opinionated woman who is secure enough in her beliefs that she doesn't have to shout them out from the rooftops.

As a female Piscean born in 1979, your perfect partner is a strong man with soul. He expresses his feelings through artistic and musical means—and he gives great massages! He's very physical and creative, and may also share your interest in the psychic world.

1979 ARIES
From March 21, 5:22 through April 20, 16:34

The Sensitive Competitor

You are an especially romantic, refined, and evolved breed of Aries. You believe that love is all about giving and you long to find that special person you can lavish your affection and protection on. Ideally you prefer to hunt down and win the heart of the one you adore. You have an athlete's sense of fair play but you are ultra-competitive, too! "All's fair in love and war" is your motto. Love should be exciting, in your view.

Once you "win" your love's affection you may become just a tad complacent, unless your mate knows how to challenge you. Aries of '79, you are so brave of heart that you more than welcome challenges. Your ideal relationship is full of dramatic scenes that test your heroic qualities. If left by yourself, you believe, you might never know the courage you are capable of. Therefore, you expect your union to be one that brings out the grand warrior existing inside you.

A would-be suitor has to play hard to get to catch your attention. If a potential lover walks into a party with another date or leaves a conversation with you to talk to someone else, you will surely follow (or at least call the next day to ask for a date). A potential paramour could also talk about sports or working out, asking for your help in that area, which will surely make you spring into action.

As a man born under the sign of Aries in 1979, you need a woman who is gentle and kind, above all else. You need a cheerleader and a friend, someone who appreciates your noble qualities and isn't fooled by surface defenses, such as bravado or aloofness. If she follows a physical practice that the two of you can share together—such as karate or dance—all the better. A woman must speak through her body and not just her brain to make you happy over the long haul.

If you are a 1979 Aries woman, you need a man who has a great sense of humor. He is soulful when it counts, yet fun-loving too. He will pull you out of your work and force you to come out and play with him—and make out with him! He's adventurous and likes mountain climbing and sky diving, along with other "extreme" sports.

500

1979 TAURUS

From April 20, 16:35 through May 21, 15:53

The Cuddly Paramour

Born in 1979, you are a forceful and driven kind of Taurus. In your career you're single-minded and have a strong desire to win, and in love you have a similar "all or nothing at all" attitude. You are content to be alone rather than to be with the wrong person. As you see it, a relationship should make both people stronger, fiercer, and braver.

In your love life you need a certain amount of tradition and domestic security along with a daily dose of intensity. You want a relationship that is passionate but predictable. Erratic behavior and breaking up and getting back together again and again is torture for you. You are capable of committing one hundred percent and expect the other person to, as well. Once you are involved with someone on that deep level, you can be quite the cuddly sweetie pie, very affectionate and quick with a gentle touch.

A would-be suitor must let you think you are making all the moves and very subtly give you the right signals—eye contact, a gentle touch on your shoulder. A potential paramour should speak to you in a low voice and make you draw closer. If a lover-in-waiting can actually wait rather than push for a date, that is the best approach. This suitor should stay as physically close to you as possible, without overtly flirting with you. Subtlety and persistence are called for!

As a 1979 Taurus male, you need a woman who is her own person, who won't go out of her way to adapt her opinions or her life to yours. She is not impressed by your talk but by your actions, and she pushes you to challenge yourself deeply. But for all her strength she is soft and kind too—and a great cook. Comfort foods home cooked by your honey soothe your nerves.

If you are a woman born under the sign of Taurus in 1979 you need a man who is warm and passionate and who is not threatened by a strong woman. He views you as his equal and wants to be partners in the rough and tumble game of life with you. He has total integrity and a passion for living. Your ideal mate is soft-spoken with a sexy voice, and can talk you into his bed quietly...and frequently.

TAURUS ZODIAC SIGN
YOUR LOVE PLANETS

YOUR ROMANTIC SIDE   p. 696
▶ **VENUS IN PISCES**
Born Apr. 20, 16:35 - Apr. 23, 4:01
▶ **VENUS IN ARIES**
Born Apr. 23, 4:02 - May 18, 0:28
▶ **VENUS IN TAURUS**
Born May 18, 0:29 - May 21, 15:53

YOUR SEX DRIVE   p. 722
▶ **MARS IN ARIES**
Born Apr. 20, 16:35 - May 16, 4:24
▶ **MARS IN TAURUS**
Born May 16, 4:25 - May 21, 15:53

YOUR CELEBRITY TWINS   p. 760
Find out the astrological similarities you have with famous people.

IND YOUR MATCH   p. 780
Compare planets to find out how compatible you are in a relationship.

YOUR RELATIONSHIP KARMA   p. 824
▶ **SATURN IN VIRGO**
Born Apr. 20, 16:35 - May 21, 15:53

MARIE-FRANCE PISIER
French Actress
Sun and Venus in Taurus

501

1979 GEMINI

From May 21, 15:54 through June 21, 23:55

The Patient Thinker

You move at a slower pace than most Geminis, taking things one step at a time. In touch with the Earth, you know that Mother Nature intended for all creatures to have a mate. Love is about patience, you believe, and are willing to wait for the ideal love to come along. Working with your sweetie to make your relationship as ideal as possible can be your ultimate goal. As far as you're concerned, a relationship should be a challenge, yet fun at the same time, bringing a sparkle to your days. A relationship is meant to be icing on the cake for two people who are already full and happy individuals in their own right, in your view. Your ideal partnership provides companionship with someone who is independent and very much an individual, but who is also cuddly, warm, and affectionate. You believe that intimacy is the greatest perk of being in love, and you are right!

Someone trying to attract your attention has to be quick on the uptake because you are smart and subtle tand won't waste your wit and wisdom on anyone who is dense or worse—smug. A potential suitor needs to express, "I don't know anything about that, tell me more" in order to make you look twice. This paramour should jokingly hint that you may only know enough about a particular subject to provide cocktail party chatter and not much more! Feisty would-be suitors catch your eye!

As a male Gemini born in 1979, you need a lady who is extremely intelligent but who does not lead her life only "from the neck up." She is sensual, sexually expressive, and home-oriented. She has close ties to friends and family, which reassures you and makes you feel more rooted in your existence. Your ideal woman sticks to her guns and tells you passionately what she wants emotionally and physically.

As a female 1979 Gemini, you need a guy who is homey and happy to snuggle up with you and watch movies. Yet he must be active in the world, too. If he is intellectually passionate about something you will always be passionate about him. In bed, he is "the king of foreplay." He loves to kiss you and slowly worship your whole body.

GEMINI ZODIAC SIGN
YOUR LOVE PLANETS

YOUR ROMANTIC SIDE   p. 696
▶ **VENUS IN TAURUS**
Born May 21, 15:54 - June 11, 18:12
▶ **VENUS IN GEMINI**
Born June 11, 18:13 - June 21, 23:55

YOUR SEX DRIVE   p. 722
▶ **MARS IN TAURUS**
Born May 21, 15:54 - June 21, 23:55

YOUR CELEBRITY TWINS   p. 760
Find out the astrological similarities you have with famous people.

YOUR COMPATIBILITY   p. 780
Compare planets to find out how compatible you are in a relationship.

YOUR RELATIONSHIP KARMA   p. 824
▶ **SATURN IN VIRGO**
Born May 21, 15:54 - June 21, 23:55

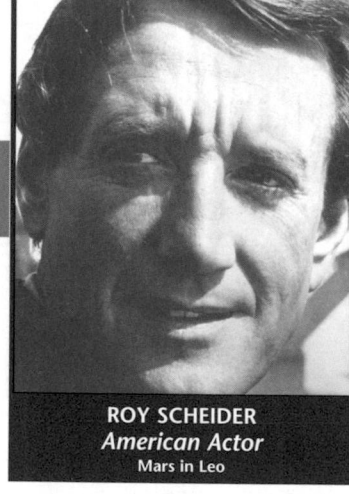

ROY SCHEIDER
American Actor
Mars in Leo

1979 CANCER
From June 21, 23:56 through July 23, 10:48

The Outgoing Traditionalist

As a 1979 Cancer you are full of life and possess a vivid, high-energy personality. Romance is a very important part of your life and you need to be in love in order to feel alive. You enjoy the game-like elements of dating. Getting inside the head of your partner and finding out what makes your special person tick is the key to your kind of relationship.

You believe that relationships should be lived both publicly and privately. It isn't enough for you to stay at home and stare into your lover's eyes (though you do like to do that too!) You also need to be out amongst friends and family with your honey. Integration is your key word and you need to be with someone who values their close relationships with parents, siblings, extended family, and friends as much as you do.

If a potential paramour wants to attract you, a quick and active approach is necessary because you never sit still for long. The would-be lover must be friendly enough to find a way into the conversation you are already having with someone else and impress you with wit and warmth. A hopeful lover must show a desire to make a real intimate connection with your body, mind, and soul. Merely flirting with you in a surface way won't cut it.

As a male Cancer born in 1979 you need a woman who is understanding and loving. She places a lot of emphasis on family and on communication. She does everything in her power to make herself and her own friends and family happy—from cooking their favorite meals to giving wise, non-judgmental advice—and she sets an inspiring example for you. She is a "regular gal" you can put on a pedestal.

If you are a lady born under the sign of Cancer in 1979, you are most compatible with a man who is intellectually stimulating—to you and himself as well. He is able to entertain himself when you are busy with your many activities. At heart, he's a family man whose favorite pastime is spending quality days and nights with you, and the members of your collective family. However, when you are alone together, he shows you a very intense side of his being, through his lovemaking.

1979 LEO
From July 23, 10:49 through August 23, 17:46

The Talky Purist

Even more than most Leos, you're extremely sociable and magnetic and draw the attention of many admirers. In fact, you love to be worshipped—but really just by your one and only. Your greatest quality is that you are utterly loyal to the one you love. Your very glamorous appearance attracts lots of notice—even when you dress down.

In your view, relationships are meant to be bigger than life and to last forever. You absolutely believe in soul mates and are as romantic as they come. Settling for a mundane relationship is not an option. Attention, affection, and verbal reassurance from the one you love are deal breakers for you if they're lacking in a relationship. Leo of '79, you must receive loads of adoration, and you are willing to give it back in return. Generosity is another wonderful trait of yours, and you expect the same from your beloved.

If someone wants to get your attention, flattery and eye contact are sure bets. A potential lover can woo you easily with words. But beyond commenting generously on your looks, vivacious personality, and many talents, a would-be mate must show grace, integrity, and above all good intentions. A suitor must express a strong moral code, and a belief in right and wrong. A lover in waiting must show a sincere desire for a genuine long-term relationship—not just a short conquest or fleeting good time.

As a male Leo born in 1979, you need a woman who doesn't mind giving the limelight to you. She is a little quiet and dignified, and conducts herself with a lot of class—and a little bit of sass at just the right times! In bed, your ideal woman is a real firecracker who drops her inhibitions with her clothes! You love trying to keep up!

As a 1979 Leo woman, your dream man is warm and affectionate and prone to saying he loves you—with words and thoughtful actions—several times a day. He can't help but call out your name in bed many times. He happily entertains your many loved ones with you. And he is one to give thoughtful little gifts when you least expect—or deserve—them! His willingness to please is one of his greatest traits.

502

1979 VIRGO

From August 23, 17:47 through September 23, 15:15

The Promise Keeper

Your motto can be, "If you're going to do something, do it right." This applies to your career, your hobbies, and your approach to love. Virgo of '79, you expect a relationship to move forward slowly, not impulsively. Old-fashioned courtship turns you on. However, once you are deeply involved, the mysterious and sexy parts of your nature come out and you begin to take more emotional and erotic risks. If your partner is willing to open up completely, you're game, too.

From your standpoint, a relationship should be private, deep, and full of promises that must be kept. You expect your partner to have the same values and basic goals as you do. This means that integrity and honesty are more important than anything else. You're turned off by lovers who are selfish and only concerned with the short run and immediate gratification.

To get your attention, a potential lover should take a genteel approach. Tried and true lines like, "Would you like to have dinner sometime?" and "I really enjoyed talking to you, may I call you up so we can chat more?"

are sure-fire hits. A workaholic with a sincere love of home and family will catch your eye. A lover in waiting should express a desire to play out in the sun, as you love the outdoors. Suggesting a walk on the beach is a good idea. A hopeful suitor could also get your attention by inviting you to a picnic or sporting event.

If you are a male Virgo born in 1979, your ideal woman soothes your nervous nature by pleasuring you with luxurious massages and good lovin' all night long. Then she might encourage you to go outside and play with her, rather than spend the whole day working and worrying. She is focused on her own work and is talented at making things with her hands, as well as using them to make your body feel fantastic!

As a female Virgo born in 1979, you are attracted to guys who are great storytellers. Your ideal man is earthy and athletic with no trace of vanity or pomposity. In bed, he is commanding and strong, but deeply emotional. His favorite pastime is looking deeply into your eyes as you make mad passionate love.

VIRGO ZODIAC SIGN
YOUR LOVE PLANETS

YOUR ROMANTIC SIDE   p. 696
▶ **VENUS IN LEO**
Born Aug. 23, 17:47 - Aug. 24, 3:15
▶ **VENUS IN VIRGO**
Born Aug. 24, 3:16 - Sept. 17, 7:20
▶ **VENUS IN LIBRA**
Born Sept. 17, 7:21 - Sept. 23, 15:15

YOUR SEX DRIVE   p. 722
▶ **MARS IN CANCER**
Born Aug. 23, 17:47 - Sept. 23, 15:15

YOUR CELEBRITY TWINS   p. 760
*Find out the astrological similarities you have
with famous people.*

YOUR COMPATIBILITY   p. 780
*Compare planets to find out how compatible
you are in a relationship.*

YOUR RELATIONSHIP KARMA   p. 824
▶ **SATURN IN VIRGO**
Born Aug. 23, 17:47 - Sept. 23, 15:15

KLAUS KINSKI
German Actor
Sun and Venus in Libra

503

1979 LIBRA

From September 23, 15:16 through October 24, 0:27

The Irresistible Sensualist

As a 1979 Libran, you are a mystery to yourself and to others. The desire for love drives everything you do. Romance is the one thing that is always on your mind and you expect a partner to treat you like a lover, not just a companion. Yes, you want to be swept off your feet, but in a subtle fashion. You want to share all with your mate, but you want some private space, too. There are times when you need to be alone and times when you need to spend every waking moment with your beloved. With you, there's no predicting what your mood will be—keeping a partner on his or her toes! Your romantic ways make you irresistible to the opposite sex!

In a relationship, you want your lover to surprise you and lift you to new heights of consciousness. At the same time, you want your mundane needs taken care of. A lover who cooks and cleans in sexy underwear is your ideal! In return, you long to lavish sexy words and affection on the person you desire most. You expect love to make your life fuller by a thousand-fold. Anyone can go to work or to

Mom's for a weekly Sunday dinner. What you want is a thrilling romance!

If a suitor wants to woo you, a would-be paramour had better study fine cuisine and Shakespeare's most moving sonnets. A potential lover should loosen you up and move closer to you with a delicious meal, expensive wine, and luxurious, sensual words. A tender but possessive touch of your lower back during conversation is apt to send you into a tailspin.

If you are a male Libran born in 1979, you need a woman who leaves sexy notes on your pillow and welcomes you home with French or Italian meals from her hands or the gourmet store. She also has a whip-smart mind and keeps up to date on politics and the arts, all the while gracing you with a sensual backrub.

As a female Libran born in 1979, your perfect guy is an ambitious man who is regal and prince-like in his demeanor and who treats you like a queen, especially in public. He is generous and ultra-respectful and giving towards your family and his own. At home, he is simply tender, sweet, and even-tempered.

LIBRA ZODIAC SIGN
YOUR LOVE PLANETS

YOUR ROMANTIC SIDE   p. 696
▶ **VENUS IN LIBRA**
Born Sept. 23, 15:16 - Oct. 11, 9:47
▶ **VENUS IN SCORPIO**
Born Oct. 11, 9:48 - Oct. 24, 0:27

YOUR SEX DRIVE   p. 722
▶ **MARS IN CANCER**
Born Sept. 23, 15:16 - Sept. 24, 21:20
▶ **MARS IN LEO**
Born Sept. 24, 21:21 - Oct. 24, 0:27

YOUR CELEBRITY TWINS   p. 760
*Find out the astrological similarities you have
with famous people.*

YOUR COMPATIBILITY   p. 780
*Compare planets to find out how compatible
you are in a relationship.*

YOUR RELATIONSHIP KARMA   p. 824
▶ **SATURN IN VIRGO**
Born Sept. 23, 15:16 - Oct. 24, 0:27

HANNA SCHYGULLA
German Actress
Venus in Scorpio

504

1979 SCORPIO
From October 24, 0:28 through November 22, 21:53

 The Secret Chaser

You were born with a question on your lips, Scorpio of 1979. You may not remember what that question was but you are sure it has something to do with the meaning of sexual relationships. Curiosity may have killed the cat but it is the quality that defines your life—especially your love life! You believe that love is all about plumbing the dark depths to figure out what makes a person's heart really beat. Secret knowledge is what you desire from a relationship.

You expect love to be fun, upbeat, inspiring, warm, and optimistic. You like to play sports with your beloved, and spend as much time as possible hiking and exploring the out-of-doors. And indoors, in the bedroom (the kitchen, the closet, wherever) you expect a lot of exploration and adventure, too! A union that is part cat-and-mouse, changing roles in the game of love, is your ideal.

To bring a glint to your eye, a would-be suitor should say something provocative and thought-provoking. A line with a sexual undertone that isn't too obvious is sure to make your ears perk up. However, if someone comes on too strongly, you will quickly be turned off. Moving towards you, then pulling away, then repeating the cycle again and again is the key to driving you mad with passion and curiosity. Emotionally, though, you must feel safe enough to be utterly vulnerable with your one true love, or else all the sexual heat in the world won't add up to much.

As a male Scorpio born in 1979, your perfect woman is devoted to important things like the environment, spirituality, and teaching children. However, she doesn't take your dramatic side too seriously. She sees through your minor mind games and cute, mischievous tricks, and encourages you to be as honest and emotionally brave as possible.

If you are a female Scorpio born in 1979, your ideal man is sure of himself and possesses a strong sense of right and wrong. He is a rare man who is a moral inspiration to you, but who also enjoys a good party! He is energetic in bed and makes you laugh with cute pillow talk one moment and sighs deeply with true longing the next.

1979 SAGITTARIUS
From November 22, 21:54 through December 22, 11:09

The Humble Seeker

You might not be certain what you're looking for in love, Sagittarius of 1979, but you know it is out there somewhere. Your dream relationship has an almost literary feel to it. Great stories inspire you, and you really do expect a relationship to be a "storybook romance," complete with seeking, finding, miscommunication, major conflicts, and of course a happy ending.

In your view, a relationship is meant to help you find the answers to deep, spiritual questions about life. In your opinion, an ideal partner is one you can search with, work with, teach, and learn from. You are very hard-working and conscientious and expect to be with someone who feels a moral obligation, as you do, to get big things done in life, one small, careful step at a time.

If someone is looking to attract you, this potential paramour must be ultra-obvious about it! You have too many things on your mind to pick up on subtle hints, and you are too humble to think that someone is actually coming on to you. Therefore, a would-be lover must touch you with meaning and tell you in a way that is authentic, not banal. A potential lover should be just as straightforward in a physical way, and must pay attention to all of your needs and your erogenous zones as well. A lingering hand on one of those areas will send a clear message to you!

If you are a Sagittarian man born in 1979, you are most compatible with a woman who knows her heart and mind well, and can communicate her needs to you clearly. She is interested in good causes, but most of all, in you. Although she too loves to read, she is the one who takes the book out of your hand at night and encourages you to talk about what's in your heart.

As a woman born under the sign of the Archer in 1979, you are best-suited to be with a man who is an avid student of nature, and an active lover who likes to "get with you" as often as possible. He knows what he wants (you!) and goes after you regularly—at home, on camping trips, even at the movies. He's like a randy teenager all the time, and lets you know that you are the one who makes him feel that way.

Catherine Deneuve – Talent and Chic

Behind the cool beauty of Catherine Deneuve lurks an eroticism that piques the imagination. Her svelte, enchanting figure is always sharply, but modestly dressed, as she gives the impression of promising much, but revealing so little. Deneuve has played offbeat leading ladies and has been in some pathological thrillers—she's starred as a part-time prostitute and a lesbian vampire, as well as playing a determined plantation owner in colonial French Vietnam. Her private life has likewise taken an unconventional twist. After having a child with her lover, French director Roger Vadim, in 1963, she married photographer David Bailey. They divorced in 1972, which was the same year she had a child with her Italian lover Marcello Mastroianni.

Catherine Deneuve was born with her Sun in the beauty-seeking sign of Libra and the ambitious, cautious sign of Capricorn on the Ascendant, the sign rising in the heavens at the time of her birth. The combination of these two contrive to give Deneuve the appearance and demeanor of detached beauty. Her understated elegance and beguiling reserve create an aura of mystery, but also serve as a shield. "It's like protection, like a shell or armor," she says. "Elegance can have a kind of comfort that feels protective." Yet behind the marvelously sculpted features, we sense hidden, darker passions, the kind that filmmaker Luis Bunuel unveiled in the 1967 classic *Belle de Jour*. Many Deneuve fans identify her most with the role she played in this film, a wealthy but bored housewife who takes a part-time afternoon job at a fashionable brothel.

Style comes from the planet Venus, and Deneuve has Venus in unpretentious

> *"Not being married was never a problem for me."*
>
> **CATHERINE DENEUVE**

Virgo. Venus in Virgo attracts through modesty. The famed fashion designer Yves Saint Laurent designed the clothes she wore in *Belle de Jour*, which began a long and mutually affectionate friendship between the two. Deneuve describes how these clothes set the seduction scenes: "It is much more erotic to see a woman with a modest dress, a trench coat and dark glasses. That's much better than going to meet a man with high heels, a plunging neckline, and a tight waist. It's more disturbing. It's sexually troubling."

Venus in Deneuve's horoscope becomes erratic and unpredictable by being in a square aspect to Uranus, the planet of rebellion and independence. This planetary pairing provides the excitement, the unseen potential behind the exquisite façade. While directors sought to flesh out the hidden meanings behind her fragile beauty, Deneuve herself was busy experiencing an unconventional romantic life. She fell in love with director Roger Vadim, and very much wanted to have his baby, but did not become one of his five wives. During the '60s and '70s she made five movies with Marcello Mastroianni and had his love child, Chiara, who became a reputable actress in her own right. "I was so in love with Marcello. He was really a wonderful man. He had such a sense of humor—such lightness and generosity and talent. He treated me very well, but, oh, did he have a flamboyant way of living."

The French public never had a problem with Deneuve's private life. She didn't become fodder for the scandal sheets as she might have in England or America. To the contrary, France exalted her. She became a celebrity spokesperson for Chanel perfume and later promoted her own fragrance. In the early '80s she was chosen to be France's "Marianne," the symbol of national feminine beauty. The honor means she had her likeness engraved on France's coins and stamps for all to enjoy and appreciate. And she continued to make excellent films through the end of the twentieth century, most notably the 1992 epic *Indochine*, for which she was nominated for an Academy Award for Best Actress.

505

▶ FIND OUT MORE ABOUT DENEUVE'S PARTNERS, ROGER VADIM ON PAGE 278 AND MARCELLO MASTROIANNI ON PAGE 367

1980 -1989

THE AGE OF GENERATION X

The decade of AIDS, high

divorce rates, and the PG-13

rating also brought us

Pac-man, *Flashdance* and

the New Romantics.

To the generation growing up in the 1980s, it was a time of Rubik's cubes, Dr. Pepper, MTV, computer technology, parental divorce, and the fear of AIDS.

The decade opened with the tragic murder of former Beatle John Lennon in front of his apartment building in New York City. The nation was stunned by the loss and grieved along with his widow, Yoko Ono. Another assassination attempt shocked the world when an obsessed fan of actress Jody Foster shot and wounded President Ronald Reagan.

In Britain, Margaret Thatcher was the Conservative Prime Minister, encouraging consumerism and conspicuous consumption, which gave birth to the Yuppie and a new (short-lived) era of promiscuity and decadence. Ostentation was the name of the game, even when it came to expressing sexuality, with cross-dressing Boy George leading the way.

On a more serious note, AIDS was lurking in the background. It took a while for authorities to confirm that the AIDS virus had been identified, and for years it was thought only to affect homosexuals. Jerry Falwell called AIDS a "gay plague," and Rock Hudson was the first known celebrity to die of AIDS. But the world was wrong. Everyone was at risk.

The divorce rate had risen to 50 percent by the 1980s and half of school-age kids lived between two households, shared by two sets of parents. As their parents and other concerned groups fought over lyrics and sexually explicit videos, a new rating, PG-13, was created to warn parents of sex, language, or violence in films.

But for every person trying to set rigid rules, there was another trying to bend or break them. Brooke Shields raised a few smiles as well as a few eyebrows with her Calvin Klein jeans ads. Meg Ryan did, too, with her public performance of an orgasmic experience in *When Harry Met Sally*. The Reverend Sun Myung Moon defied convention when he married more than 2,000 couples in New York, some strangers to each other. And an Arizona man tried to see how far he could push the envelope—with 105 wives, he was found guilty of polygamy.

Chartbusters in the early '80s included Madonna, Michael Jackson, Blondie, and Queen. Mid-decade gave us Foreigner, Dire Straits, and USA for Africa. Whitney Houston made her debut later, sharing the air waves with George Michael, Bon Jovi, the Bangles, and U2. In England, the New Romantics brought with them a new wave of music, with bands like Duran Duran and Human League under the spotlight.

THE SILVER SCREEN

Some movie soundtracks during this decade became as famous as the films they accompanied. *Urban Cowboy* made Gilley's Bar a household name, and "Looking for Love in All the Wrong Places" spawned a generation of line dancers. *The Blue Lagoon* gave us the hit "Endless Love," *Arthur* delivered "Arthur's Theme," and Joe Cocker and Jennifer Warnes sang the rousing "Up Where We Belong" from *An Officer and a Gentleman*. *Flashdance* gave us "Oh, What a Feeling," among others.

But not all movies were about the music. Some made us laugh (*Romancing the Stone* and *The Princess Bride*). Others moved us (*Children of a Lesser God* and *Sophie's Choice*), and still others such as *Fatal Attraction* made a lasting impression about rabbits as pets and cured some couples of infidelity.

BETWEEN THE PAGES
The 1980s was the decade for mainstream glitz and romance with authors Sidney Sheldon, Danielle Steel, Judith Krantz, Jackie Collins, and Harold Robbins dominating the bestseller lists year after year. With little room for anyone else, John Irving still managed to elbow in with *The Hotel New Hampshire*, as did Alice Walker with *The Color Purple*.

PEOPLE
Henry and Christina Ford got divorced, while Glenn Close got married but then divorced three years later. The very public marriage between Patty Duke and John Astin dissolved. And although Piano Man Billy Joel appeared to be happily married to his Uptown Girl, model Christie Brinkley, they also eventually broke up.

Royalty had its pairings and breakups, too. Grace Kelly's daughter Princess Caroline of Monaco divorced her husband, while her sister Princess Stephanie's marriage fared no better. Princess Di and Prince Charles married to huge fanfare—although theirs also became a failed marriage. The marriage of Prince Andrew and Sarah Ferguson went the same route.

◄◄ Billy Joel's "Uptown Girl" Christie Brinkley

▲ Rock Hudson, (right) seen here as Daniel Reece in *Dynasty*, dies of AIDS

▼ Richard Gere and Debra Winger in *An Officer and a Gentleman*

507

1980

- ★ MEL GIBSON
- ★ BROOKE SHIELDS
- ★ SOMEWHERE IN TIME
- ★ THY NEIGHBOR'S WIFE
- ★ JOHN LENNON
- ★ BLONDIE
- ★ ROCK WITH YOU

EVENTS

This was a banner year for celebrity marriages and divorces. Mel Gibson married Robyn Moore, French director Louis Malle married Candice Bergen, and tennis champion Bjorn Borg wed Mariana Simionescu.

Chip Carter, son of US President Carter, and his wife were divorced. Princess Caroline of Monaco's marriage to Philippe Junot was dissolved in a Monaco court. Her petition to the Vatican to annul the two-year marriage was not granted until 1992.

And while Brooke Shields titillated US audiences with her whispered TV commercial, "Nothing comes between me and my Calvins," the year ended with a terrible loss to the world. John Lennon was murdered in New York in front of his wife, Yoko Ono. She reportedly was so grief-stricken she could eat nothing but chocolate for a month.

POP CULTURE

Somewhere in Time with Christopher Reeve and Jane Seymour became almost an instant cult classic. In it the hero discovers he was the lover of an actress from another life—and finds a way to travel back in time to see her once more. *The Blue Lagoon* gave Brooke Shields the spotlight again with the story of two children surviving alone on a deserted island.

Bestselling books included Sidney Sheldon's *Rage of Angels*, a tale of ambition and passion with a brilliant young female lawyer pitted against the

Sex Idol

mob, and *Princess Daisy* by Judith Krantz, a romantic riches to rags and back to riches story. *Shelley: Also Known as Shirley*, gave us Shelley Winters' 500 pages of tell-all, with the "dirt" on the many stars she knew and sometimes loved, such as James Dean, Jimmy Stewart, Errol Flynn, Montgomery Clift, and Marlon Brando. *Thy Neighbor's Wife*, Gay Talese's report on American sexuality, was shocking to some when first published with its chronicle of American permissiveness before the age of AIDS.

John Lennon's last song, "Starting Over," poignantly filled the airwaves. Kenny Rogers had a hit with "Lady," Diana Ross with "Upside Down," and Blondie with "Call Me." Queen had two hits: "Crazy Little Thing Called Love" and "Another One Bites the Dust." Another favorite was "Rock with You" by Michael Jackson.

RICHARD GERE

The 1980 film *An American Gigolo* made heartthrob actor Richard Gere into a superstar. Adored for his romantic roles in *An Officer and a Gentleman* (1982) and *Pretty Woman* (1990), Gere, a founding member of Tibet House, has promoted humanitarian causes throughout his career. His 1991 marriage to supermodel Cindy Crawford sparked scandalous rumors about Gere's sexuality. They divorced in 1995. In 1999 *People* magazine declared Gere "The Sexiest Man Alive." Recent successes include his 2002 marriage to actress Carey Lowell, the birth of their son, Homer, and a Golden Globe award for his role in the 2002 movie, *Chicago*.

SEE ALSO
► JULIA ROBERTS *Page 653*
► CATHERINE ZETA-JONES *Page 688*

1980 CAPRICORN

From December 22, 1979 11:10 through January 20, 1980 21:48
(December 1980 Capricorns, see 1981 Capricorn)

♑ *The Playful Pal*

You're an outgoing Capricorn born in 1980, and to you a relationship must be a source of mutual happiness. You feel that friendship is an essential dimension to any relationship, particularly a romance, and you'd never want to be involved in a love affair with someone you wouldn't also want as a friend. Mutual support and encouragement provide you both with the emotional stability you thrive on.

Communication is very important to you, and your relationship must feature lots of interesting conversations. You enjoy sharing your ideas with your partner and receiving useful and inspiring feedback. Playfulness is another wonderful bonus in your relationship, and you've found that as long as you can kid around and make each other laugh, your problems will be that much easier to resolve.

The partner who has something meaningful to say will gain your attention most easily. You enjoy being sought out for good conversation by someone who appreciates and shares your sense of humor. Connecting with that one special person in a group setting is also a good idea because it's among your friends that you find the best pool of potential mates. Fun party times with these friends appeal to you, but you're just as interested in attending computer and high-tech fairs, making travel plans, and then setting sail! Your ideal partner shares many of these interests.

Male goats born in 1980 like a woman who is intelligent, sparkly, and independent. Your lady has a mind of her own and a clever way of expressing herself. She knows how to be a good friend and reaches out when she sees people in need. This gal has a bit of an eccentric streak but you like that because her quirkiness adds to her charm. Together, you can laugh and joke about everything.

Female Capricorns born in 1980 like a man who is effervescent and outgoing. Your guy is capable, competent, and careful in everything he does, but also has an impatient side and is a real self-starter. You enjoy talking with him and feel you will never grow tired of the amusing way he expresses himself. Together, you are cozy and comfortable.

CAPRICORN ZODIAC SIGN
Your Love Planets

YOUR ROMANTIC SIDE   p. 696
▶ **VENUS IN CAPRICORN**
Born Dec. 22, 1979 11:10 - Dec. 22, 1979 18:34
▶ **VENUS IN AQUARIUS**
Born Dec. 22, 1979 18:35 - Jan. 16, 1980 3:36
▶ **VENUS IN PISCES**
Born Jan. 16, 3:37 - Jan. 20, 21:48

YOUR SEX DRIVE   p. 722
▶ **MARS IN VIRGO**
Born Dec. 22, 1979 11:10 - Jan. 20, 1980 21:48

YOUR CELEBRITY TWINS   p. 760
Find out the astrological similarities you have with famous people.

YOUR COMPATIBILITY   p. 780
Compare planets to find out how compatible you are in a relationship.

YOUR RELATIONSHIP KARMA   p. 824
▶ **SATURN IN VIRGO**
Born Dec. 22, 1979 11:10 - Jan. 20, 1980 21:48

DOLLY PARTON
American Singer
Sun and Venus in Capricorn

1980 AQUARIUS

From January 20, 21:49 through February 19, 12:01

♒ *The Steadfast Romantic*

As an impetuous Aquarius born in 1980, your relationship must have lots of sparkle and excitement. You believe in having fun with the people you love! Your "better half" is also a peaceful and congenial soul who can help you to relax. Good communication is important to you, and if there's nothing to say, then clearly the relationship is not a keeper.

You also look for stability and commitment. Knowing that someone cares deeply for you provides a sense of security that you would otherwise not have. Being with someone you can't count on would make you very nervous indeed. You may discover that it's sometimes difficult to make a relationship work, and that compromise is often very necessary. By focusing on happiness, affection, and a positive view of life, you find that a relationship helps you both make the most of yourselves as partners and as individuals.

Offering you a challenge is one way to pique your interest. The partner who can stand up to you in a chess game, a challenging round of Jeopardy, or even a wicked game of miniature golf gains your admiration. You like good conversation, and when you're talking and laughing, it's obvious there's good potential for further interaction. You also like sharing athletic activities and working together on meaningful projects.

Male Aquarians born in 1980 prefer a woman who doesn't mind being vulnerable. Your lady is quite frank and open about her need for love, never acting aloof or "cool" to hide her tender side. She has a good sense of humor, sharing both laughs and interesting ideas with you as your bond grows increasingly strong and intimate. She is serious—"the real thing"—even when she's laughing, and she's never shallow or flighty.

Female Aquarians born in 1980 like a guy who can hold his own in any situation. He likes to laugh, and his jokes can make you fall on the floor in hilarity. He's assertive and outgoing, with a lot of personal confidence and charisma. When you need advice, he's right there to help, and will always pitch in willingly to lend a hand. He's careful, orderly, and, when it comes to romance, delightfully attentive.

AQUARIUS ZODIAC SIGN
Your Love Planets

YOUR ROMANTIC SIDE   p. 696
▶ **VENUS IN PISCES**
Born Jan. 20, 21:49 - Feb. 09, 23:38
▶ **VENUS IN ARIES**
Born Feb. 09, 23:39 - Feb. 19, 12:01

YOUR SEX DRIVE   p. 722
▶ **MARS IN VIRGO**
Born Jan. 20, 21:49 - Feb. 19, 12:01

YOUR CELEBRITY TWINS   p. 760
Find out the astrological similarities you have with famous people.

YOUR COMPATIBILITY   p. 780
Compare planets to find out how compatible you are in a relationship.

YOUR RELATIONSHIP KARMA   p. 824
▶ **SATURN IN VIRGO**
Born Jan. 20, 21:49 - Feb. 19, 12:01

DEBRA WINGER
American Actress
Venus in Aries

510

1980 PISCES
From February 19, 12:02 through March 20, 11:09

The Assertive Romantic

You're a high-energy Pisces, and your relationship must be exciting on many levels. True love is certainly your goal, but more than the hearts-and-flowers aspect of romance, you seek a strong, intense connection that feels magical and "meant to be". As a deeply spiritual person, your experience of love takes on many dimensions. You need to feel that your relationship is more than just dating, but a connection at a deep, soul level.

Being able to share affection without reservation is so important to you. You'd hate to be with a partner who was uptight or afraid of displays of affection. That would throttle you and take all the fun out of being in love. You like sharing an active lifestyle with your partner, one that brings you together in a variety of experiences. Having common interests keeps your relationship lively, and you fall more in love as a result of all you share.

To gain your attention, a partner has to be both upbeat and passionate. You love the idea of being intensely adored, and someone who has had a longstanding crush on you automatically gains points in your book. Being invited to do something very romantic appeals to you, so someone planning a date and keeping it all a surprise until you're whisked away strikes you as a wonderful gesture. You may also like going to car and boat shows, motivational seminars, and sports events even if you just spectate.

Male Pisces born in 1980 like a woman who is so exciting she's kind of a handful. To you, someone who is dynamic and intense is particularly interesting. Your lady isn't afraid to express her feelings or to share with you her gentle and tender side. She ardently believes in true love, and if she thinks you're the one, then watch out—she'll chase you forever!

Female fishies born in 1980 want a guy to be exciting, outgoing, athletic, and confident. Soft and wimpy guys are a real turn-off to you because you're so intense and passionate you insist on a guy who can meet you at your own level. Your fellow is clever, a fine communicator, and has lots of useful skills. Most of all, he cares about you and your needs.

1980 ARIES
From March 20, 11:10 through April 19, 22:22

The Excitement-Seeker

You're a volatile Aries born in 1980, and your relationship must be dynamic, fluid, and exciting—or you're out the door. You want to team up with someone who enhances your total experience of life. Of course, you believe in commitment and marriage, but excitement is much more what you're all about. You'd hate to be smothered by some humdrum partner who is determined to capture your heart and keep you a prisoner.

A relationship has to offer you more than just everyday pleasantries. A little friction may feel natural, and that means you can expect to quarrel sometimes, followed by make up sessions that make everything all right. You're not afraid of conflict—sometimes you may find that you relish it a bit too much! Passion and romantic attraction are absolutely essential to you. Without chemistry, what do you have? Nothing at all, in your opinion!

A partner who keeps you guessing can most easily attract and hold your attention. You don't always want to know what's coming next, and you may even forgive someone who stands you up on a first date because then you want to see what will happen next. Flirting really intrigues you, so a partner who sends subtle signals and keeps you guessing is much more exciting to you than someone whose heart can be easily won. You enjoy being invited to simple dinners or to classy events as long as they're not dull or stuffy.

Male rams born in 1980 want a woman who's exciting, unpredictable, sexy, and a bit complicated. You don't want to know from the moment you meet that she's yours for the taking. Working for her affection appeals more to you. Your lady has a stable side and the potential to be serious, but you know it will take a lot of patience to get her to settle down.

Female Aries born in 1980 like a man to have just the right degree of macho charisma. Your guy is determined, a strong leader, and sometimes he just goes off on his own tangent. You respect and accept that about him. He's also musical, loves to dance, and perhaps even plays an instrument. He is strong and protective, possibly reminding you of your favorite entertainer.

1980 TAURUS

From April 19, 22:23 through May 20, 21:41

The Romantic Individualist

Despite your independent nature, Taurus, you want your relationship to make you feel secure. You believe in true love and recognize that it's difficult to attain. Of course, this knowledge would never stop you from seeking your soulmate! You believe it's necessary to be with your perfect partner in order to create a happy and fulfilled life.

Independence and personal growth are other essential features of your ideal relationship, wherein each partner is encouraged to pursue personal interests and not be cast in the other's mold. Achieving a lifestyle that is independent, yet also coupled with a partner's, is your goal. Believing in your partner and establishing a level of trust are the underpinnings of this lifestyle. Fidelity is very meaningful to you, and you'd never think that independence included cheating—that's not your expectation at all!

Challenging you to a rousing debate is an excellent opening gambit for a partner who wants to pique your interest. An intense intellectual connection could signal the possibility of deeper involvement. You also enjoy music and are always up for attending a concert. Parties that help you to connect not just with a partner but with many interesting people are nourishing to your relationship as well.

Male bulls born in 1980 need a woman to be intelligent, loquacious, and interesting. Your gal reads and has something intelligent to say about pretty much everything. She likes art and culture, and by having her in your life, you open up to many new and exciting possibilities. This lady believes in true love, although she may have a few hard-luck stories to tell. She's still out there trying, and something about that touches your heart.

Female Taureans born in 1980 like a guy who is exciting, outgoing, and very sociable. He's the sort of audacious fellow who used to pull little girls' pigtails, and he still delights in showing off for an audience. His spiritual side is just as apparent, and you know his heart is in the right place. He's witty and determined to get his own way, sometimes sweeping you up into his arms for a waltz around the room.

TAURUS ZODIAC SIGN
YOUR LOVE PLANETS

YOUR ROMANTIC SIDE   p. 696
- ▶ VENUS IN GEMINI
  Born Apr. 19, 22:23 - May 12, 20:52
- ▶ VENUS IN CANCER
  Born May 12, 20:53 - May 20, 21:41

YOUR SEX DRIVE   p. 722
- ▶ MARS IN LEO
  Born Apr. 19, 22:23 - May 04, 2:26
- ▶ MARS IN VIRGO
  Born May 04, 2:27 - May 20, 21:41

YOUR CELEBRITY TWINS   p. 760
Find out the astrological similarities you have with famous people.

YOUR COMPATIBILITY   p. 780
Compare planets to find out how compatible you are in a relationship.

YOUR RELATIONSHIP KARMA   p. 824
- ▶ SATURN IN VIRGO
  Born Apr. 19, 22:23 - May 20, 21:41

BJORN BORG
Swedish Tennis Champion
Sun in Gemini

1980 GEMINI

From May 20, 21:42 through June 21, 5:46

The Team Player

As a sentimental Gemini born in 1980, your relationship must meet your needs on an emotional and intellectual level. You believe that more than just romance is at stake. If the relationship is to be a success, partners must be able to share important ideas, goals, and feelings. Being able to talk about your deepest needs and feelings means a lot to you, and so does discussing your philosophies and general ideas. It's through communication that a relationship really works, in your experience.

Romance is also important to you because you long for tenderness, devotion, and nurturing. Being able to envision having a home and family together could be a promising sign in your relationship because, although there is plenty of fun, the connection must be deeper than just fun to hold your interest. Sharing activities that excite you both keeps the spirit of love alive as you enthusiastically seek out new things to enjoy with your partner. Someone who has a lot to offer on many levels gains your interest quite easily. You realize that even if you're not destined to fall in love with this person, you still might become best pals. You're open enough to see what sort of connection might result from an invitation to a concert, a challenge to hit some baseballs in a batting cage, or even to attend a fifth-grade production of a classic musical.

Male Geminis born in 1980 like a woman who is sweet and sensitive, yet also clever and intellectual. Your gal has a soft, musical quality and she's very romantic. She loves to talk about love and connecting with a soulmate, and she so easily swoons at the latest love story or movie that she's just adorable. This lady has a desire for commitment, and you know she'll always go the distance for someone she loves.

Female Geminis born in 1980 like a guy to be clever and to have a penetrating intellect. His ideas are rich and complex, entrancing you with their brilliance. He's also outgoing and athletic, and it's a joy to watch that powerful, elegant body in action! Your fellow is brave and bold, ever ready to rush in when help is needed.

GEMINI ZODIAC SIGN
YOUR LOVE PLANETS

YOUR ROMANTIC SIDE   p. 696
- ▶ VENUS IN CANCER
  Born May 20, 21:42 - June 05, 5:43
- ▶ VENUS IN GEMINI
  Born June 05, 5:44 - June 21, 5:46

YOUR SEX DRIVE   p. 722
- ▶ MARS IN VIRGO
  Born May 20, 21:42 - June 21, 5:46

YOUR CELEBRITY TWINS   p. 760
Find out the astrological similarities you have with famous people.

YOUR COMPATIBILITY   p. 780
Compare planets to find out how compatible you are in a relationship.

YOUR RELATIONSHIP KARMA   p. 824
- ▶ SATURN IN VIRGO
  Born May 20, 21:42 - June 21, 5:46

HELEN MIRREN
English Actress
Sun in Leo

512

1980 CANCER
From June 21, 5:47 through July 22, 16:41

The Fated Nurturer

You're an accommodating Cancer born in 1980, and your relationship must feature much give-and-take. You believe in true love and want to be in a relationship where you and your partner are willing to go all-out for each other. The magic of romance is tremendously important to you and there has to be a sort of mystical connection between you and your love. Your sense of it being destined, or meant to be, gets you past any quarrels or small crises that may arise.

Good communication is another bright facet of your relationship. You discover that being able to share your thoughts with someone who is your intellectual equal brings you closer together and keeps life interesting. You enjoy being challenged intellectually by a partner on your own level and are enthralled by lively discussion and debate. Working together side by side toward mutual goals also matters very much to you. You want a partner in every sense of the word.

To spark your interest, a person who uses a clever intellectual approach will be rewarded with more than a smile. You love greeting cards and funny e-mails, perhaps even getting to know a potential partner online in a chat room. And because you enjoy cultural events and all things elegant and refined, you and your partner might want to visit an art gallery, take in a play, or even go ballroom dancing.

Male Cancers born in 1980 like a woman to be youthful and radiant. Your gal is perky and adorable, retaining her "cheerleader quality" for life. She is open and outgoing, warm and generous, and you just know she could make a cheerful lifelong companion. The fulfillment of your every romantic fantasy, this lady seems to have endless affection for you and gets along very well with children.

Female crabs born in 1980 need a guy who is an intellectual firecracker yet also practical and down-to-earth. Your guy speaks his mind and cares so much about what's good for you that often he pokes his nose into your business—but you know it's only because he worries about you. Steady and reliable, he always finishes what he starts and helps you to feel more confident about life.

1980 LEO
From July 22, 16:42 through August 22, 23:40

The Love-struck Romantic

As a strong-willed Leo born in 1980, your love life must be quite intense. You like a relationship that on the surface appears to be serene and casual, but that under the surface is actually quite magnetic, even hypnotic. Sharing these intense feelings for each other is what makes your relationship the central focus of your life, and what gives it the potential to endure.

A sense of gentle romance is also very enticing to you, and you need to feel there is some magic to the everyday interactions you share. Being able to laugh together and to make jokes about practically everything keeps you happy in a relationship. It's another way by which you both can tell that you do indeed have this deep, magical bond. What it may really come down to for you is chemistry. You want to be love-struck from the moment you meet, and to build a relationship on that electrical foundation of passion and intense emotion.

You're more apt to identify a potential partner based upon your own subtle feelings when you're in the same room than because of any opening gambit aimed at capturing your attention. You do enjoy meaningful conversation, so someone interested enough to draw you out appeals to you. And because you love music, attending a concert is a wonderful way to begin dating. Dancing offers another kind of romantic possibility because it gives you a real "feel" for the other person.

Male Leos born in 1980 seek a woman who is tender and romantic, yet with depth of passion and a rapier intellect. Your lady is larger than life in every way except for dress size. Actually, you don't mind at all if she's a little bit plump as long as she's magnetic and totally ravishing. She has a sexy, flirtatious manner, and the moment your eyes lock, your heart is hers.

Lady lions born in 1980 demand that a guy be strong and passionate—this macho fellow is ultra sexy! It's even possible that he reminds you of your favorite characters from movies and romance novels. He is as smart as he is sexy, constantly challenging you and making you laugh. You feel that perhaps you've known him in other lifetimes and that today he is your destiny.

1980 VIRGO

From August 22, 23:41 through September 22, 21:08

The Tempestuous Lover

You're a passionate Virgo born in 1980, and your relationship must be supremely exciting to hold your interest. You believe intensely in chemistry, and you may sometimes notice that your feelings are a little bit out of control. That just makes life more exciting! Connecting with and feeling those intense emotions are what makes your relationship so special: you feel that as long as you continue to share that sort of chemistry, you have a good chance of staying together.

You also believe in tenderness and nurturing, knowing that without them, a relationship has no real heart. Chances are, your relationship began as love-at-first-sight—a scenario not only beautiful in itself, but one that gives you a good story to tell about how you met! You expect to quarrel, but what you really enjoy is the making up.

A partner who does something outrageous gains your interest quickly because you want to delve more deeply to learn what's really going on. A sexy, almost lascivious gambit appeals to you and makes you feel like a character in a movie. You also enjoy simple interactions, so just taking a walk or sharing a pleasant lunch with someone new is may be better than a fancier date because that gives you time to talk to each other and feel the connection.

Male Virgos born in 1980 need a woman who is sweet and loving, never demanding or clingy. Your lady has a mind of her own and can stand up to authority, if need be. She expects you to chase her for quite a while—which is fine with you because it's so much fun. Though it's unnerving to be kept guessing about her feelings, it's also exciting. There is strong attraction between you, though, and you can feel her swooning from the moment you hold her in your arms.

Female Virgos born in 1980 like a guy to be strong, macho, and determined. Intelligent and sexy, he knows how to show his interest so there's never any confusion. You feel the love connection instantly, and, even if you know nothing about him, you sense that he's your guy. He has a bit of a history, maybe a bad-boy reputation, but that just makes him all the more alluring.

LUCIANO PAVAROTTI
Italian Singer
Sun in Libra

513

1980 LIBRA

From September 22, 21:09 through October 23, 6:17

The Amorous Space-Giver

As an independent Libra born in 1980, your relationship must be dynamic and exciting. You believe in trusting and sharing, preferring a relationship in which both partners give each other the necessary space. Independent interests are very important to you and provide plenty to report when you're together. That way, you avoid "smothering" overexposure.

Being encouraged to express your best and most interesting self is another positive aspect of your relationship. You like to feel that you know and understand each other better than anyone else, and whatever little quirks you each possess only add to the uniqueness that makes you a team. Passion and chemistry are two other very significant joys of your relationship. You need to feel it's exciting! Otherwise, you couldn't make sense of why you were there.

You most readily respond to partner who is attractive and sexy, and enjoy an obvious sexual attraction from the moment you meet. Being invited to a play or other theatrical event is a great way to kick things off. You'd also enjoy going to something a bit more outrageous—like seeing a belly dancer or an X-rated hypnotist. Flirting and having fun is what it's all about, and you may even enjoy carrying on a romance with someone you know online.

Male Libras born in 1980 prefer a woman who is beautiful and magnetic. Your lady has an allure that makes people notice her whenever she walks through a room. And, with her strong independent streak, she makes you work for her affection. This gal isn't aloof, however—she's just the sort of woman who has a mind of her own. She's helpful and kind, and knows how to be there for a friend in need.

Lady Libras born in 1980 need a man who is strong and macho yet also a little unpredictable. Below the surface you know he's rock-solid, no matter how flaky he occasionally appears. He's dynamic and energetic, radiating sex appeal that is electric and exciting. His mind is deep and he sees beneath the surface of things, sparking many penetrating conversations. He gives you your space, appreciating and championing the things about you that you like best.

BOB HOSKINS
English Actor
Sun in Scorpio

514

1980 SCORPIO
From October 23, 6:18 through November 22, 3:40

♏ *The Grand Romantic*

You're a romantic Scorpio born in 1980, and your romance must be chockfull of hearts and flowers. All the sentimental things that make love so thrilling add up to your idea of perfection in a relationship. You believe not only in true love and destiny, but in the idea that two people can live completely for each other—which is just what you want in your relationship.

Sharing interesting ideas is important to you, and you can spend endless hours on the phone with your partner, talking about "us." Your healthy relationship allows you to share just about everything. That way, you can know one another perfectly, better than any other person ever has before. You may have strong mutual interests, but even if you don't, you believe that you should both be willing to compromise. After all, sharing is more important than the specific thing you're actually doing. Being together always comes first in your relationship!

A partner who is sensitive and romantic gains your notice immediately because you feel so strongly simpatico. You love to stroll hand in hand on a beach, or perhaps take tango lessons. Asking you to a concert or dance is an auspicious beginning, but you also appreciate a grand romantic gesture. Someone who gutsily serenades you below your window, for instance, could make you wonder if perhaps this might be your long-lost soulmate.

Male Scorpios born in 1980 need a woman who is beautiful, charming, and romantic. Her soul is tender and her heart gentle, and you sense a soft sweetness about her. This gracious lady is also uncannily good at seeing life from various points of view, which helps her put people completely at ease. A natural at entertaining, she creates harmony, peace, and joy wherever she goes.

Female Scorpions born in 1980 need a guy who is sensitive. Your man has a spiritual side to his nature and is sometimes able to see life from your point of view. He loves music and dance and may sometimes even sweep you into his arms for a waltz around the room. He understands the need to compromise and is happiest when everyone else is feeling content.

1980 SAGITTARIUS
From November 22, 3:41 through December 21, 16:55

♐ *The Synergistic Sweetie*

You're a passionate Sagittarius, born in 1980, and your relationship must be sexy and romantic. You care very much about intimacy, believing that a relationship must allow you both to open up and share your deepest secrets without any threat of disapproval. An easy sense of chemistry is important, and it seems as if you just "connect" and belong together.

Cooperation and mutual support are also important to you in a relationship. Being on the same team helps you both feel stronger and safer, for by being together you accomplish more than you might by yourself. This also means you look out for each other, and if your partner is on the wrong track, of course you must speak up. That's what an honest relationship is all about, in your experience.

A partner who is deep—yet also cheerful and outgoing—gains your interest at once. You love being invited to a seminar, or to connect with someone of your own profession, because you have so much in common. You also like athletic contests, so playing volleyball on the beach, or even miniature golf, are good ways to get to know each other. Having something in common is a real facilitator, and a partner who wants to share your interests rates an early A-plus.

Male archers born in 1980 need a woman who is passionate and intense. Your special lady has a deep, mysterious quality, and you sense a strong, passionate connection right from the start. She is very sexy but also self-possessed, so you know you're dealing with a quality person with a lot on the ball. She is creative and fun-loving, a joy to share many of your interests with because she's open to new ideas and enjoys pleasing you.

Female Sagittarians choose a man who is practical and down-to-earth. Your guy should be determined and an achiever, because you need to feel proud of your partner and to know you can always count on him. This fellow may be a bit intense, sometimes a little hasty, occasionally bossy and domineering. But what you like about him is that he is masculine, a sort of no-nonsense guy. He's enjoyably sexy without being pushy or selfish, and he's often very creative.

Pinter's Women – A Bittersweet Romance

It's not surprising that creative women would help shape British playwright Harold Pinter's colorful life—he was born in 1930 under the Zodiac sign Libra, the sign of relationships, art, and women. Pinter met his first wife, Cancer actress Vivien Merchant, in 1953 while he was still a struggling young actor working under the name David Baron. Three years later, they reconnected as co-stars in *Motive for Murder* and married that same year. The newlyweds toured England together, performing at resorts and local theaters, but settled in London when Merchant became pregnant. In 1958, their only son, Daniel, was born.

Over the years Pinter gained success as a playwright, and in the 1960s Merchant starred in several of his plays. "Vivien was a hell of an actress and a woman of undoubted independence of mind," Pinter recalled. But as his acclaim grew, what had started out as a partnership of equals became lopsided. His marriage to Merchant began to break down and he commenced an affair with Joan Bakewell. In true Libran style, Pinter used his personal life and relationships to fuel his creativity and many critics believe some of his best screenplays, including *The Servant, Accident,* and *The Go-Between,* were written during this period.

In 1975, Pinter met Lady Antonia Fraser, a noted author of historical biographies and mysteries. Born under the meticulous sign of Virgo in 1932, Fraser is known for her attention to detail and her painstaking research for bestsellers such as *Mary Queen of Scots* (published in 1969). The refined and Oxford-educated Lady Antonia—a Catholic, mother of six children, married to the conservative politician and member of Parliament Sir Hugh

Harold Pinter and Lady Antonia Fraser on their wedding day

Fraser—seemed an unlikely match for the tough, taciturn, Jewish tailor's son who had openly proclaimed his passionate left-wing ideology since the US-backed coup against Chile's President Allende in 1973. However, her views were more closely akin to Pinter's than her husband's, and the pair grew more politically active and outspoken as their relationship developed.

In 1977, Pinter and Fraser began living together. The two writers' love affair generated steamy copy in the British press. Gossipmongers speculated whether the Catholic Lady Antonia would divorce her noted husband of 21 years to marry Pinter. According to Pinter, "People—the press—really wanted to destroy us." Fraser expressed surprise at the outcry in the tabloids and the public's intense interest in their relationship. "I look back on it in absolute amazement. We were two writers in our 40s who decided to live together. We weren't that interesting."

During that time, Pinter penned his play *Betrayal*, which many believed to be autobiographical despite his protestations. In large part, the public's fascination with the scandal contributed to the play's success, even though critics considered it to be one of Pinter's lesser works.

An angry Merchant sued for divorce, and in 1980 her marriage to Pinter ended. Shortly thereafter, Pinter married Lady Antonia and the couple has remained together contentedly ever since. Their love story's ending, however, isn't entirely happy. The relationship devastated both writers' previous spouses and caused an irreparable rift between Pinter and his son Daniel. Vivien Merchant succumbed to alcoholism and died still embittered in 1982. Sir Hugh Fraser's death followed in 1984 and his family blames Lady Antonia for the suffering that led to his demise.

515

"I don't idealize women. I enjoy them. I have been married to two of the most independent women it is possible to think of."

HAROLD PINTER in *New Statesman,* Nov. 8, 1999

► READ ABOUT FRANKLIN D. ROOSEVELT AND ELEANOR, ANOTHER DEVOTED COUPLE, ON PAGE 121

1981

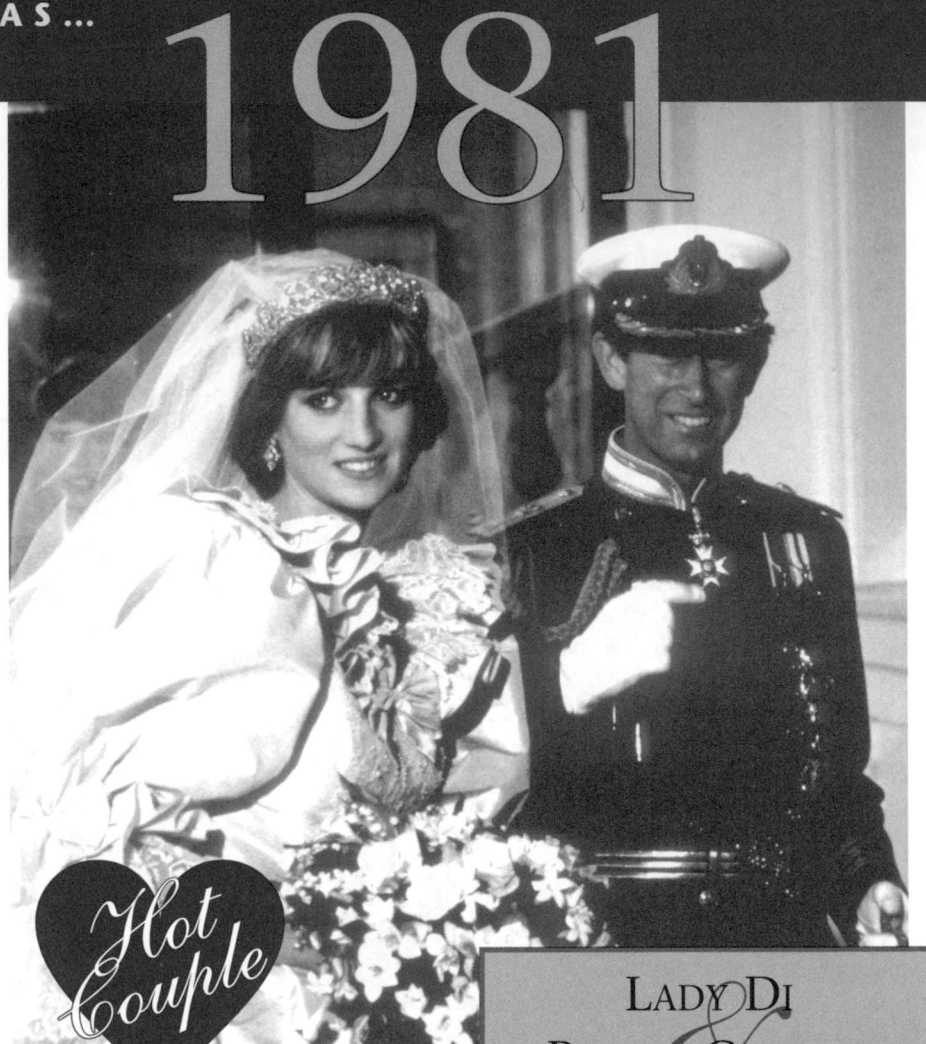

Hot Couple

- ⭐ **PRINCESS DI**
- ⭐ **LUKE AND LAURA**
- ⭐ **THE YORKSHIRE RIPPER**
- ⭐ **ON GOLDEN POND**
- ⭐ **MISS PIGGY'S GUIDE TO LIFE**
- ⭐ **DOLLY PARTON**
- ⭐ **BETTE DAVIS EYES**

516

EVENTS

Two fairy-tale weddings happened this year—one real, one fictional. In the UK Princess Di and Prince Charles filled television screens across the world with the royal wedding that captured the hearts and imagination of so many devoted fans. Four months later with almost as much hoopla, Luke and Laura wed on the US TV soap, *General Hospital*.

One year after a crazed fan shot John Lennon, John W. Hinckley, Jr., obsessed with Jody Foster and trying to get her attention, shot and wounded Ronald Reagan in Washington, D.C. In England Peter Sutcliffe, alias the Yorkshire Ripper, was sentenced to prison for life after having murdered thirteen prostitutes. In France Japanese student Issei Sagawa killed a young Dutchwoman and ate some pieces of her body. The press dubbed him the "Cannibal," and rightfully so.

POP CULTURE

Moviegoers were moved by Henry Fonda's performance with his daughter Jane in *On Golden Pond. Arthur* warmed hearts with the tale of an immature but rich drunkard, cared for by his fatherly butler, as he tries to grow up to keep the love of an outspoken shoplifter he helps. In *Modern Romance*, directed by Albert Brooks, a codependent couple can't seem to break away from their dysfunctional ways—but at least the sex is great.

From the bookshelves readers were

reaching for *Miss Piggy's Guide to Life*. "Call me Moi" begins this definitive, essential Miss Piggy (Superstar, Calendar Girl) self-help volume. Colleen McCullough's *An Indecent Obsession* made an impression with its damaged and decorated war hero who enters nurse Honour Langtry's life with tragic results. *The Hotel New Hampshire* by John Irving was an original family saga that combined black humor with sentiment and outrage at cruelty and injustice.

Three popular movies early in this decade provided us with hits songs as well. "Endless Love," sung by Diana Ross and Lionel Richie, was from the film of the same name. The film *Arthur* gave us "Arthur's Theme," sung by Christopher Cross. And Dolly Parton starred in *9 to 5* and released the title song, too. Other popular hits included Olivia Newton-John's "Physical" and Kim Carnes' "Bette Davis Eyes."

LADY DI & PRINCE CHARLES

July 29, 1981 marked the fairy-tale wedding of Lady Diana Spencer and Charles, Prince of Wales. She bore Charles two sons—William in 1982 and Harry in 1984—but Charles' indifference left her lonely, desperate, and suffering from bulimia.

Charles' longstanding affair with Camilla Parker Bowles moved Diana to pursue extramarital affairs. The couple separated in 1992 and divorced in 1996. Just as it appeared that she had found love with Dodi Al-Fayed, Diana's sudden death in a car crash on August 31, 1997 riveted world attention once again, to mourn the passing of the "Princess of People's Hearts."

SEE ALSO

▶ **PRINCESS ELIZABETH & PRINCE PHILIP** *Page 236*

▶ **PRINCE WILLIAM** *Page 672*

1981 CAPRICORN

From December 21, 1980 16:56 through January 20, 1981 3:35
(December 1981 Capricorns, see 1982 Capricorn)

The Logical Lover

Most 1981 Capricorns believe that people are meant to find their soulmates, and you are no exception. Although you are quite self-sufficient and don't mind being alone, you know that you will learn much more about yourself and the world by hooking up with the right partner—permanently. You expect a relationship to involve a lot of communication and a true intellectual connection. Arguing is fine, as long as neither party hits below the belt. Lovers should understand the power of their words, in your view.

While you are a deep believer in commitment, you will not tolerate being placed "in a box" by your partner. You know that no one will ever completely possess you and you are clear about that from the outset. A relationship that allows you to be a loyal lover while maintaining your autonomy is your ideal.

A potential lover hoping to catch your eye should engage you in a philosophical discussion about love. Anyone who canspeak passionately, yet objectively, and with humor, about the battle of the sexes is sure to arouse you. A would-be suitor could also present you with an analytical problem for you to solve. A chance to hone your logic skills gets your mind racing—and then your hormones follow suit.

If you are a man born under the sign of Capricorn in 1981, your ideal woman has a bawdy sense of humor and always knows what to say to pull you out of a blue or chilly mood. She can relate just as easily to the bus driver as to the head of a prestigious bank. She does not have a judgmental bone in her body. Your perfect woman is also willing to try anything once, in bed. She is playful and silly, and enjoys seducing you in public places.

As a female Capricorn born in 1981, the best fellow for you is smart and stubborn when it comes to sticking to his dreams. He's an absolute idealist and has the best intentions for himself and for you. This altruist pushes you to be your most noble self, and he practices what he preaches. Sexually, he is extremely communicative and loves to please. He asks you what turns you on and then aims to fulfill your every fantasy.

1981 AQUARIUS

From January 20, 3:36 through February 18, 17:51

The Receptive Connoisseur

Born in 1981, you are an Aquarius who is much more receptive and affected by other people than the average Water-Bearer. For you, a relationship is meant to change both parties deeply. Like the blending of chocolate and peanut butter, you see a relationship as two great tastes coming together and creating something unique and amazing in the process. Ideally, you want a relationship to sweep you into another way of life. You already know what you know, but with a lover you can discover new and incredible worlds—both physically and emotionally.

A relationship between two people who "yes" each other to death and always agree seems like a nightmare to you. If two people can't disagree, then they can't be passionate toward each other either, in your view. You expect a relationship to have some bumps in the roads, and some twists and turns, too. As long as both people believe in each other, any challenge is surmountable.

A would-be suitor should make a real effort to talk to you about the future. Sharing wishes and dreams is a sure-fire way to bond with you. A lover-in-waiting should also discuss artistic and aesthetic matters with you. The visual is your strongest sense, and you are turned on by a person who is observant on that level. A potential lover should also make heavy eye contact with you when speaking. That draws you in like nothing else.

If you are a male Aquarius born in 1981, your ideal woman is a contrarian who never takes anything at face value (including your views about the world). She likes to tackle difficult intellectual problems and she is absolutely addicted to helping others. Sexually, she is wild and free and has very few inhibitions. She likes to giggle and talk a lot in bed, too. She has a young spirit.

Your ideal man, 1981 female Aquarius, is sensitive and poetic and would not hurt a fly. His gentle nature makes him a magnet for children and animals—who love him like crazy. In bed, he is super-sexy and soulful and makes lovemaking a truly magical experience. In his career, he is quiet but centered, and does work that is creative and meaningful.

CAPRICORN ZODIAC SIGN
Your Love Planets

YOUR ROMANTIC SIDE   p. 696
▶ VENUS IN SAGITTARIUS
Born Dec. 21, 1980 16:56 - Jan. 11, 1981 6:47
▶ VENUS IN CAPRICORN
Born Jan. 11, 6:48 - Jan. 20, 3:35

YOUR SEX DRIVE   p. 722
▶ MARS IN CAPRICORN
Born Dec. 21, 1980 16:56 - Dec. 30, 1980 22:29
▶ MARS IN AQUARIUS
Born Dec. 30, 1980 22:30 - Jan. 20, 1981 3:35

YOUR CELEBRITY TWINS   p. 760
Find out the astrological similarities you have with famous people.

YOUR COMPATIBILITY   p. 780
Compare planets to find out how compatible you are in a relationship.

YOUR RELATIONSHIP KARMA   p. 824
▶ SATURN IN LIBRA
Born Dec. 21, 1980 16:56 - Jan. 20, 1981 3:35

JANE SEYMOUR
English Actress
Sun in Aquarius

517

AQUARIUS ZODIAC SIGN
Your Love Planets

YOUR ROMANTIC SIDE   p. 696
▶ VENUS IN CAPRICORN
Born Jan. 20, 3:36 - Feb. 04, 6:06
▶ VENUS IN AQUARIUS
Born Feb. 04, 6:07 - Feb. 18, 17:51

YOUR SEX DRIVE   p. 722
▶ MARS IN AQUARIUS
Born Jan. 20, 3:36 - Feb. 06, 22:47
▶ MARS IN PISCES
Born Feb. 06, 22:48 - Feb. 18, 17:51

YOUR CELEBRITY TWINS   p. 760
Find out the astrological similarities you have with famous people.

YOUR COMPATIBILITY   p. 780
Compare planets to find out how compatible you are in a relationship.

YOUR RELATIONSHIP KARMA   p. 824
▶ SATURN IN LIBRA
Born Jan. 20, 3:36 - Feb. 18, 17:51

KATHLEEN TURNER
American Actress
Mars in Pisces

518

1981 PISCES
From February 18, 17:52 through March 20, 17:02

The Flexible Fanatic

You love people and love to be in love and expect a relationship to be like a film or a fairytale. Maybe you aren't a "realist," but you are a real romantic. For you, a relationship must be dream-like and deep—a complete union of two hearts, minds, and souls. Giving all you have to the one you love is like second nature to you. You don't expect the same from your partner, but it's nice if you get it!

Relationships that are all about "tit for tat"— you give this much, and the other person matches it equally—are of no interest to you. You're inspired to give from your heart and expect the other person to have the same inclination. It's not about quantity for you, but quality. Of course, you have fine tastes and do enjoy a comfortable lifestyle. A relationship, you believe, should also help both parties to feel more secure in the concrete world.

If someone is looking to win your affection, this potential lover should engage you in a deeply personal conversation. Someone who is willing to reveal meaningful truths—from fears to hopes to dreams—will surely arouse your interest. Getting you in a dark, cozy setting helps, too. You are more likely to feel and act romantic if a potential suitor creates a charming environment—candles and wine will definitely help! Since you tend to "get into" things completely, a potential lover should find out what your latest obsession is—yoga, scuba diving, or whatever— and ask you as much as possible about this subject.

If you are a male Pisces born in 1981, your dream-woman is emotionally gentle but firm with you. She is your most ardent supporter but she is not afraid to tell you the truth, as long as it's for your own good. She is the one who helps plan your future, always looking ahead and offering support as you bring your dreams to fruition.

For female Pisces of 1981, the ideal man has a huge, kind heart. He is secure in his masculinity and doesn't have to prove anything to you or to the world. He enjoys music, dancing, and being near the water. He is deeply empathic and always the shoulder you can lean on when you're scared.

1981 ARIES
From March 20, 17:03 through April 20, 4:18

The Physical Powerhouse

You have energy to burn—physically, emotionally, and on every level. That's why you expect a relationship to keep you active, moving, and engaged in life even more than you would be on your own. For you a relationship involves doing lots of exciting things together, from international travel to competing in sporting events. Living a thrilling life together, full of adventure and surprise, is your idea of how a relationship must be. Playing it safe is not an option for you.

A relationship that involves sitting in front of the TV, or lying on the couch, reading all night, is of no interest to you. Two people need to bring out each other's passions in order for love to thrive, as far as you're concerned. It helps if both people are up-front about their goals and desires, right from the get-go. You don't want to have to read your partner's mind, or vice versa.

If a potential lover wants to capture your heart, a big display of enthusiasm might be the ticket. Someone who is too timid to show affection or desire is not for you. Asking you to go dancing or to a sporting event is a good idea, too. Anything that involves physical activity is of interest to you. A would-be suitor can woo you with sensual words and actions, too. You like to gauge sexual chemistry early on, so a hopeful lover would be wise to show an interest in your body as quickly and passionately as possible.

If you're a male 1981 Aries, your perfect mate is confident, full of life, and more than a little mischievous. She likes to play practical jokes and to tell funny stories. She is a people-person who often invites new friends over to chat. When it comes to inhibitions—well, she doesn't have any! She likes to let go and be loud and raucous in the bedroom.

As a female 1981 Aries, your choice is a "real man," through and through. He loves sports and he loves sex! In fact, sex is a little like a sport to him. He likes to seduce you as often as possible, and is quite spontaneous about lovemaking. In his career, he is ambitious and has a very strong entrepreneurial spirit. Being the boss is his goal.

1981 TAURUS

From April 20, 4:19 through May 21, 3:38

The Practical Artist

Security and sensuality are of equal importance to you, in life and in love. You expect a relationship to provide you with plenty of both. When you are involved with someone, you want to spend quality time together every day. For you, a long-distance relationship may be worse than no relationship at all. Cuddling on the couch after dinner with your honey, and talking in bed are your favorite activities. You believe that relationships are meant to be as simple and beautiful as a work of art. You don't like to overanalyze love.

You expect a relationship to be cozy and warm. Predictable is good, but boring is not. Your mind is incredibly creative and you have multiple artistic talents. Therefore, you appreciate a relationship that inspires you to express your refined sensibilities. What you cannot tolerate in a relationship are extremes, and abrupt changes. Life with a mate must be consistent—and consistently lovely.

If a potential partner wants to catch your eye, the best route is through your other senses. You are very sensuous and will respond intensely to a slow, warm touch. A would-be suitor who can soften you up with yummy food is also on the right track. And finally, your entire mood changes when sleek, sexy music plays, so a lover-in-waiting should definitely throw something subtle and seductive on the stereo.

The perfect mate for you, 1981 Taurus guy, is a cultured but down-to-earth woman who is just as comfortable at the opera as she is at a hockey game. She is funny and nurturing, and always makes everyone feel at home. On top of that, your ideal gal is a gifted gourmet. Sexually, she is tender and seductive, and loves to spend the whole night turning you on. Her favorite way to seduce you is by whispering her sexiest desires into your ear.

If you are a female Taurus born in 1981, your best guy is a straight shooter who says what he means and means what he says. He is a reliable, loving character who enjoys spending time at home. However, he likes to save up money for luxurious vacations—alone with you—in exotic places. Good food gets him giddy and romantic.

TAURUS ZODIAC SIGN
YOUR LOVE PLANETS

YOUR ROMANTIC SIDE   p. 696
▶ VENUS IN TAURUS
Born Apr. 20, 4:19 - May 11, 19:44
▶ VENUS IN GEMINI
Born May 11, 19:45 - May 21, 3:38

YOUR SEX DRIVE   p. 722
▶ MARS IN ARIES
Born Mar. 20, 4:19 - Apr. 25, 7:16
▶ MARS IN TAURUS
Born Apr. 25, 7:17 - May 21, 3:38

YOUR CELEBRITY TWINS   p. 760
Find out the astrological similarities you have with famous people.

YOUR COMPATIBILITY   p. 780
Compare planets to find out how compatible you are in a relationship.

YOUR RELATIONSHIP KARMA   p. 824
▶ SATURN IN LIBRA
Born Mar. 20, 4:19 - May 21, 3:38

GRACE JONES
Jamaican Singer
Sun and Venus in Taurus

519

1981 GEMINI

From May 21, 3:39 through June 21, 11:44

The Sexy Homebody

You want love to be full of secret surprises and plenty of delicious, private sensuality. Too dignified for public displays of affection, you like to save your sexiness for the home front and expect your partner to do the same. "You and me against the world" could be your motto. Entertaining a small group of fascinating people, on your turf, is preferable to going out to noisy clubs all night long. Ideally, you like to spend long, luxurious days all alone with your honey, in bed, in the tub—anywhere private and pleasurable.

Sexually, you expect a relationship to take you to deeply emotional places—but you want to get there slowly. Communication, on a physical as well as intellectual level, is immensely important to you. You find it annoying if someone plays games with you. You want to feel free to say what's in your heart and not be judged for it. In turn, you appreciate it when a lover does the same. Fighting makes you nervous and you really don't like to be around anyone who enjoys dramatic scenes. Calm discussions make you happy.

A would-be suitor looking to woo you should spend a lot of time just talking to you. A mental connection must be made before any lovemaking can take place! Inviting you over for a romantic, home-cooked meal is a good idea. Giving you a neck massage during the evening, or playfully mussing your hair can put you in a sexy mood.

As a 1981 male Gemini, your ideal woman has a wicked and wily sense of humor and does a lot of playful things to keep you mentally and physically aroused. She sends you flirty e-mails and leaves cute, funny notes on your pillow. She gives you plenty of space to tend to your hobbies but is always there for you at night.

If you are a female Gemini born in 1981, your perfect guy is easy to talk to and never too rushed to hug and kiss you—at great length. He has simple, classic tastes and isn't easily drawn in by distracting people. He knows what a great thing he's got in you and he makes the most of it. Reading and writing are a part of his everyday routine, and he loves to share his thoughts and reflections with you.

GEMINI ZODIAC SIGN
YOUR LOVE PLANETS

YOUR ROMANTIC SIDE   p. 696
▶ VENUS IN GEMINI
Born May 21, 3:39 - June 05, 6:28
▶ VENUS IN CANCER
Born June 05, 6:29 - June 21, 11:44

YOUR SEX DRIVE   p. 722
▶ MARS IN TAURUS
Born May 21, 3:39 - June 05, 5:25
▶ MARS IN GEMINI
Born June 05, 5:26 - June 21, 11:44

YOUR CELEBRITY TWINS   p. 760
Find out the astrological similarities you have with famous people.

YOUR COMPATIBILITY   p. 780
Compare planets to find out how compatible you are in a relationship.

YOUR RELATIONSHIP KARMA   p. 824
▶ SATURN IN LIBRA
Born May 21, 3:39 - June 21, 11:44

---

1 Read Your Sign   **2** Look Up Your Love Planets   **3** Go to Pages Shown

HARRISON FORD
American Actor
Sun in Cancer

520

1981 CANCER *From June 21, 11:45 through July 22, 22:39*
The Loyal Gadabout

As a 1981 Cancer, you need a lot of varied stimulation to keep you happy. For you, a relationship needs to be erotic, entertaining, and esoteric. However, as long as your partner is "present" on all the important levels—sexual, emotional, and intellectual—you are as loyal and loving as they come. You expect a union to be about shared interests and similar values. Opposites may attract but they don't last over the long haul together, as far as you're concerned.

Your ideal relationship is full of day-to-day camaraderie and fun, and occasional luxurious adventures together. Building a future together is what it's all about for you. Being involved with someone who is vague about what they want, or incapable of appreciating the little pleasures of daily life, is not for you. Taking spontaneous trips to museums, sporting events, concerts, etc., with the one you love is your idea of heaven. Sitting at home and complaining is your idea of the opposite place!

If a potential lover wants to catch your eye, a good way to do it is by talking about the latest places to go and films to sees. Cerebral discussions can lead to sensual snuggles together. Asking you to see a hot new show or to check out an interesting book are also good ways to pique your interest. Flirty dialogue makes your ears perk up, too.

For a 1981 Cancer man, the ideal woman is sure of herself and has a strong, confident, charismatic personality. She is your biggest fan and sings your praises to any and all who will listen. Glamorous and sophisticated, she knows how to dress for any occasion, without seeming to make much of a fuss. She is a class act who always seems poised and in control. Sexually, she is a hidden lioness ready to roar!

If you are a female Cancer born in 1981, your perfect man is a subtle and skilled lover who is open to expressing all sides of his nature—from tender to virile—in bed. His goal is to make you feel as comfortable with yourself as possible. He never judges and always makes you laugh and appreciate life. Intellectual he is, but he's also a regular guy who enjoys a night out with the boys.

1981 LEO *From July 22, 22:40 through August 23, 5:37*
The Gallant Lover

Matters of the heart are on your mind all the time. Even your nighttime dreams are about love. Therefore, you must be in a love relationship that is highly romantic and that makes you feel that you are vibrantly alive. Simple domesticity is not enough for you. You need to show the world how much you adore your partner, and are a big fan of splendid displays. In order for you to be happy in love, you need to be very public about your romantic relationship. Others may recognize how hard you fought to get the one you love, and then admire you both for working through the (often dramatic) challenges of your relationship. As long as your relationship is never humdrum, you are happy.

You can't stand being told what to do, and must always be the one who initiates changes in the relationship. Your wisdom and kindness are your greatest qualities, and they must be recognized by your partner. Presenting a united front to the world, as a couple is also very important to you.

If someone is looking to seduce you, your would-be lover has got to allow you to make at least some of the moves. Offering an extra ticket to a show is a good idea, because it gives you the opportunity to say, "Great, and I'll make us dinner beforehand." A potential partner should definitely try to get you on the dance floor, as you love to show off your moves! A karaoke bar is also a good suggestion, because you are such a talented and fun ham!

If you are a male Leo born in 1981, your perfect woman is a little demure and shy but knows what she wants. She lets you take the lead, but often whispers her thoughts and desires to you quietly. She is at one with nature and introduces you to parts of the great outdoors that you've never even noticed. Sexually, she is more experimental than you are and gently guides you to lose your inhibitions, one by one.

As a female Leo born in 1981, your ideal guy is a family man who is close to his parents and acts naturally with children. He is competitive in sports and possessive in love. He knows what he wants and goes for it. In bed, he shows the same drive and passion.

1981 VIRGO

From August 23, 5:38 through September 23, 3:04

The Subtle Seducer

Born in 1981, you are a very romantic breed of Virgo. For you, life is empty and full of longing without love in your life. You believe that you are at your best when you are united with that special someone. Relationships are meant to be gentle, sexy, and ultra-private unions, as far as you're concerned. What goes on behind closed doors is a very intimate and soulful matter. Therefore, you do not kiss and tell, and your partner had better not, either.

Partnerships that are full of fights, suspicion, and unnecessary drama are not for you. When it comes to romance, sweetness and daily sensuality are your cup of tea. And as long as you are with a like-minded partner, you are faithful for life. You are happiest when you are involved in a relationship that allows you to turn on your very subtle powers of seduction. By day, you may seem like a private, introverted person, but by night (with the right person), you are a tender tiger!

If someone wants to attract you, this would-be suitor must be subtle, like you. A softly spoken and coy remark about how good you smell or what a nice voice you have will surely send a signal. However, the potential lover should then let you make the next move. Getting together with you is like a tennis match; as both partners must keep the ball in the air. Dressing in soft, sensual fabrics could help a potential lover to catch not just your eye, but your touch!

If you are a male Virgo born in 1981, your ideal mate is an artistic and intelligent woman who also possesses a sharp sense of style. She is well-groomed and well-read, and generally a genteel, calm presence to be around. But, when she has a bee in her bonnet she can be quite a firecracker—which you love! This same passion shows up in the bedroom, where she is quite intense.

For 1981 Virgo females, the perfect man has a kind, gentle way about him and rarely if ever raises his voice. He is poised and gracious when entertaining friends, colleagues, and family. However, his favorite activity is spending quality time with you—just reading the Sunday paper, taking walks, and, of course, making love.

VIRGO ZODIAC SIGN
YOUR LOVE PLANETS

YOUR ROMANTIC SIDE — p. 696
▶ VENUS IN LIBRA
Born Aug. 23, 5:38 - Sept. 12, 22:50
▶ VENUS IN SCORPIO
Born Sept. 12, 22:51 - Sept. 23, 3:04

YOUR SEX DRIVE — p. 722
▶ MARS IN CANCER
Born Aug. 23, 5:38 - Sept. 02, 1:51
▶ MARS IN LEO
Born Sept. 02, 1:52 - Sept. 23, 3:04

YOUR CELEBRITY TWINS — p. 760
Find out the astrological similarities you have with famous people.

YOUR COMPATIBILITY — p. 780
Compare planets to find out how compatible you are in a relationship.

YOUR RELATIONSHIP KARMA — p. 824
▶ SATURN IN LIBRA
Born Aug. 23, 5:38 - Sept. 23, 3:04

ELVIS COSTELLO
Irish Singer
Sun in Virgo

521

1981 LIBRA

From September 23, 3:05 through October 23, 12:12

The Lusty Enigma

Relationships must have a certain amount of mystery to keep you intrigued, Libra of 1981. You love to be with someone who makes your heart race and who has the same butterflies-in-the-stomach reaction to you. However, you prefer to be the one who has just a tad more control when it comes to love. This means that you do like to fall, and fall hard, but you do not like to be in a relationship where you lose your ability to think clearly. You need space in a relationship, as well as closeness. Both people need time to do their own thing—from reading, to errands, to just plain loafing—without having to answer to a mate. Work must also be factored in to love, as you are very ambitious

Open displays of affection and lust are a necessary, daily requirement for you. You're wonderful about reassuring a partner how enamored you are, and you expect the same cuddling and cooing in return. It is very important for you to feel intellectually engaged with the person you're involved with. Some cerebral repartee is essential or you feel dulled and depressed. A meeting of the minds, mixed with unstoppable sexual chemistry, is your idea of ideal love.

If someone wants to catch your eye, this potential lover should turn up the charm to high. No, higher still! The suitor must make you feel like you're the only person who exists, in a roomful of people. Upping the conversational ante to subjects such as love and sex will also make you sit up and take notice. You like someone who takes risks with you.

If you are a male Libra born in 1981, your perfect woman is fiery and passionate. She will tell you exactly what she thinks and feels at all times. Holding back is not part of her repertoire. She is a sexual dynamo who gets turned on very easily. When she's in the mood, she's really in the mood! She is sporty and enjoys competitive outdoor games.

As a 1981 Libra woman, you want a guy who is sexy and smart. He doesn't waste time with people who lack vitality and ambition. He's quite driven when it comes to his career, but is even more focused on spending luxurious, quality time with you.

LIBRA ZODIAC SIGN
YOUR LOVE PLANETS

YOUR ROMANTIC SIDE — p. 696
▶ VENUS IN SCORPIO
Born Sept. 23, 3:05 - Oct. 09, 0:03
▶ VENUS IN SAGITTARIUS
Born Oct. 09, 0:04 - Oct. 23, 12:12

YOUR SEX DRIVE — p. 722
▶ MARS IN LEO
Born Sept. 23, 3:05 - Oct. 21, 1:55
▶ MARS IN VIRGO
Born Oct. 21, 1:56 - Oct. 23, 12:12

YOUR CELEBRITY TWINS — p. 760
Find out the astrological similarities you have with famous people.

YOUR COMPATIBILITY — p. 780
Compare planets to find out how compatible you are in a relationship.

YOUR RELATIONSHIP KARMA — p. 824
▶ SATURN IN LIBRA
Born Sept. 23, 3:05 - Oct. 23, 12:12

RICHARD PRYOR
American Comedian
Sun in Sagittarius

522

1981 SCORPIO
October 23, 12:13 through November 22, 9:35

♏ The Serious Smoothy

For you, 1981 Scorpio, relationships are meant to be savored and slowly enjoyed, like a delicious, gourmet meal. You love every aspect of love, from the anticipation, to the first kiss, to the commitment. The worst romantic scenario for you is the "quickie." Taking your time and enjoying the build up is half the fun for you. In bed, you are an intuitive expert at foreplay, and desire the same sort of spontaneous and slow seduction from your partner.

A relationship must be multilayered to interest you. The simple "good life" is not what you want. A complex, intense whirlwind of sex and emotion is! You are able to (literally) charm the pants off of anyone, but save your prowess for someone who is sensual and mature. In return, you like to feel as if your partner spends every waking moment thinking about you romantically, and planning new ways to turn you on and get to know you more deeply.

If someone wants to attract you, this potential lover must pay attention to verbal cues you give, and respond to your hints in a smart, subtle way. For instance, if you mention seafood, the suitor should find out whether it's crab or lobster you prefer, and then follow up by suggesting a cozy inn that serves the Epicurean aphrodisiac of your choice. Being observant, thoughtful, and bold goes far, if someone is looking to lure you in (and then) blow your mind!

As a 1981 Scorpio guy, your perfect woman is a workaholic who knows how to budget her time. She is thinking of her future and yours, and has lofty ambitions. However, she is realistic (and randy) enough to schedule plenty of time for loving between the two of you. Her serious nature inspires you to follow through on your goals.

If you are a female Scorpio born in 1981, your ideal man makes pleasing you a daily priority. When your neck is sore, he rubs it for you. If you mention a book that you need, he picks it up for you. But he is no pushover. When he has a serious concern, he discusses it with you and expects you to compromise. Your perfect mate has high standards for himself, for you, and for your relationship.

1981 SAGITTARIUS
From November 22, 9:36 through December 21, 22:50

♐ The Persuasive Philosopher

You view relationships almost as if they were chess matches. Strategy, sportsmanship, and patience are all of equal importance. Throw in a little luck and you've got love, as far as you're concerned! Romance may be baffling to you, but somehow you are compelled to figure out what makes a partnership tick. Therefore, a match that is too simple and laid-back leaves you bored and antsy. You prefer a union that has a lot of edge and perhaps a few (seemingly insurmountable) challenges.

Getting involved in a romance is easy for you, because when you turn on the charm, your wit and will are hard to resist. But in order for you to remain satisfied in a relationship, you need a partner who is your equal, who is just as philosophical and driven to learn as you are. It is this—the desire to understand love—that is at the heart of a relationship for you.

If someone is looking to win your affection, this potential suitor must be willing to talk, talk, talk, well into the night. Philosophical discussion is a favorite activity of yours, so a would-be lover must show powers of articulation and (verbal) energy. Another way to interest you is to suggest a night of bar- or party-hopping. Yes, you are cerebral, but you are fun-loving too! Therefore, a potential mate who is up for a raucous good time (and drags you out for one) is on the right track.

If you are a 1981 Sag man, your perfect woman is a gal with radical views who isn't afraid to stand up and fight for the underdog every chance she gets. She is kind to all animals, and is also passionate about environmental issues. She loves to spend time outdoors, especially hiking in the woods. And during those treks she loves to make passes at you!

As a female Sagittarian born in 1981, you choose a guy who's dedicated to his craft—whether it's building houses or playing the cello—and takes his work very seriously. Still, he leaves plenty of time to sit and talk with you for hours at a time. He is analytical and loves to dissect a dilemma from every possible angle. Sexually, he's Mr. Versatile and is always willing to try something new.

Diana – The Tragic Princess

Standing gawkily beside a car, shoulders slightly hunched, with the sun shining through her diaphanous skirt revealing long, lean legs, the first photo of Prince Charles' new girlfriend, Diana Spencer, ignited an intense curiosity in the public that was never to be extinguished.

A bashful and naïve 19-year-old, "Shy Di" was a virgin when she met the British heir to the throne. Prince Charles was her Prince Charming and despite having little in common, he proposed to her a year later. Their wedding was the society event of the decade, with millions watching around the globe.

Thrust under the media spotlight, she became the most photographed woman on the planet. Soon the reserved, stuffy, country-casual style was replaced with glitzy, fashionable designer gear and a new jet-set lifestyle. She was what the British public had been waiting for—a glamorous royal.

For the first few years all seemed well. She bore Charles two sons, William and Harry, and was a devoted mother. But before long, cracks began to show and her marriage became punctuated by a string of affairs. Charles re-ignited his acquaintanceship with his old flame and wife of a close friend, Camilla Parker Bowles. Diana fell passionately in love with the debonair cavalry officer James Hewitt.

Lonely and depressed, Diana threw all her energies into charity work. Her warm bedside manner and her bravery in championing taboo causes such as AIDS and drug addiction won her public sympathy. She became known as the "People's Princess" and made regular visits to hospitals.

However, the public didn't know the

Diana's first photocall as Prince Charles' new girlfriend

true extent of her despair until Andrew Morton's shockingly revelatory biography, *Diana: Her True Story*. In it Charles was vilified as a cold and uncaring husband, while Diana was a vulnerable victim driven to attempting suicide and living at the mercy of the royals. But the biggest revelation of them all was about to be exposed—Diana had collaborated with Morton in a calculating move aimed at humiliating Charles and the royal family.

Charles and Diana officially separated later that year, but Diana had one more trick up her sleeve. In a televised interview on the BBC, she disclosed details of their marriage, which later brought up questions about Charles'

"The very essence of compassion, of duty, of style, and of beauty."

DESCRIPTION OF PRINCESS DI
by her brother, Earl Spencer

523

suitability to rule. The Queen was incandescent with rage and in an unprecedented move requested the couple obtain a divorce. Diana finally broke free from the shackles of her marriage and in a final twist of the knife, the Queen ordered that she drop her royal prefix, HRH (Her Royal Highness).

Diana cut back on her official duties but still dedicated herself relentlessly to charity work. It was rumored that she had a number of affairs, and in the summer of 1997 she met the charismatic son of an Egyptian millionaire. Dodi Al Fayed was an international playboy and Diana was snapped holidaying aboard his luxury yacht. For the first time it appeared she had found happiness. But six weeks later they were both dead, killed in a car crash in Paris, fleeing pursuing paparazzi.

Diana Spencer may have looked like the perfect fairy-tale princess, but tragedy plagued her short life. Idolized by an adoring public, millions flocked from around the world to pay their respects in what was the most dramatic communal outpouring of grief in the history of Great Britain.

▶ READ ABOUT PRINCE WILLIAM ON PAGE 672

- ✪ PRINCESS GRACE
- ✪ REVEREND SUN MYUNG MOON
- ✪ AN OFFICER AND A GENTLEMAN
- ✪ THE COLOR PURPLE
- ✪ JACK AND DIANE
- ✪ PAUL MCCARTNEY

Hot Movie

EVENTS

While US congressional investigators looked into a male prostitution ring linked to Capitol Hill, France ruled that homosexuality was no longer an offense. In nearby Monaco, Princess Grace died in a car accident.

The Reverend Sun Myung Moon married 4,150 of his followers at Madison Square Garden in New York City. Many of the couples were complete strangers to each other.

The body of prostitute Wendy Caulfield, thought to be the first victim of the Green River serial killer, was found near Seattle. Michael Fagan, an unemployed London man, entered the room where Queen Elizabeth II was sleeping. Before security could arrive, he sat on the edge of her bed and said he just wanted "to tell her something important."

POP CULTURE

Richard Gere swept away moviegoers almost as much as Debra Winger in *An Officer and a Gentleman. Sophie's Choice* gave us an aspiring writer after World War II who becomes friends with a chemist and his Polish refugee girlfriend, Sophie. She brings mystery and horror to the story when she begins to reveal her past. In the gender-bender *Victor/Victoria*, Victoria, an opera singer, can't find a job until the day she transforms herself into Victor, a Polish count.

The Color Purple by Alice Walker became almost an instant classic. Its dramatic portrayal of an abused black

woman's struggle for empowerment got added to the reading lists of almost every college literature course. *Living, Loving, and Learning* was a collection of Dr. Buscaglia's informative and amusing lectures that he delivered worldwide between 1970 and 1981. In *The Name of the Rose*, it's the year 1327 and the most interesting things happen at night in the wealthy Franciscan Italian abbey where monks die easily and where a young savage woman can be seen naked.

John Cougar's ditty about "Jack and Diane" became an immediate hit. Joan Jett had us singing along with "I Love Rock 'n' Roll," as did Joe Cocker and Jennifer Warnes with "Up Where We Belong," from the film *An Officer and a Gentleman.* Paul McCartney and Stevie Wonder gave us a touching duet with "Ebony and Ivory."

VICTOR/VICTORIA

A woman pretending to be a man pretending to be a woman—this was the gender-bending premise for the 1982 movie *Victor/Victoria*. In this romantic musical comedy, Julie Andrews plays a desperately poor singer, Victoria, who poses as a female impersonator, Count Victor Grezhinski, in a Depression-era Paris cabaret. When a tough Chicago gangster, played by James Garner, develops a strange attraction to Grezhinski, the farce unfolds. The film earned seven Oscar nominations, including Andrews for best actress. Robert Preston and Leslie Ann Warren were nominated for their supporting roles as a gay nightclub owner and a gangster's moll.

SEE ALSO

▶ *SOME LIKE IT HOT* Page 334

▶ *EDDIE IZZARD* Page 661

1982 CAPRICORN

From December 21, 1981 22:51 through January 20, 1982 9:30
(December 1982 Capricorns, see 1983 Capricorn)

The Team Player

As a sociable Capricorn born in 1982, your relationship must be friendly, warm, and a thriving part of your social life. You believe in group attachments and you like being a couple within a group. That way it feels like a big, happy unit in which everyone shares a nice interaction. A warm sense of camaraderie is essential to you in a relationship because you need to feel an intellectual connection. You'd never become romantically linked with someone who wasn't also a pal. You connect with your heart, but also with your head, and that keeps you from being attracted to someone who isn't a good choice for you.

Good communication and generosity of spirit are other important dimensions of a good relationship. It's so essential for each of you to be on the other's team and that way it feels warm, happy, and loving. A relationship is about togetherness, but it's also about being a strong and happy individual. You feel the best relationships help a person grow stronger and more secure.

To attract your attention a person must first want to be your pal. Hanging out together in the same social circle is an easy avenue to romance, one you very much enjoy. You care about the state of the world and being invited to volunteer together can be very romantic. You're willing to wash cars to help a good cause and to get romantic while soaking each other with water.

Male Goats born in 1982 like a woman who is sparkling, friendly, and very outgoing. When in school, you probably had a crush on a cheerleader because of the spunky way she pranced around. You like smart women who have something interesting to say, and who don't mind showing their intellect. It's also nice to be lavished with hugs and kisses.

Female Cappies born in 1982 like a guy who is sensitive and romantic. Having good manners and social skills is important to you and you don't like it at all when men are rough or tacky. Your guy wants to please you and goes out of his way to see that you have a good time. He has an old-fashioned elegance and you feel that you connect as best friends as well as romantic partners.

ANNIE LENNOX
Scottish Singer
Sun in Capricorn

1982 AQUARIUS

From January 20, 9:31 through February 18, 23:46

The Old-fashioned Romantic

You're a loquacious Aquarius born in 1982, and to you a relationship is a foundation of security. You need closeness and trust and believe that a relationship binds you completely to the other person. Because you believe so strongly in love, you're often willing to put your own needs aside to make your partner happy. Sometimes it's frustrating because you often wonder if this is a one-sided arrangement, but you also realize that with the right mate there is the cooperation you find so essential.

Fidelity is another important dimension of a relationship and you would never want to be tied to someone you couldn't trust. Honor and commitment go hand in hand to you and you take a broken promise very seriously. A relationship has to be reliable and solid and you admire older people who've been together for decades. You'd like to duplicate that longevity in your own relationship.

To spark your interest a partner must be of good character, intelligent, solid, reliable, and sane. You can't resist sex appeal, though, and find it hard to say no when chemistry is involved. Someone who begins a lively or amusing conversation gains your attention quickly because you love a rousing debate. Conversations about your hopes and dreams for the future help you see if you're both on the same wavelength. You also enjoy dressing up and sharing courtly social events.

Male Aquarians born in 1982 like a woman who is old-fashioned. Her style is respectable and her clothes conservative. This woman must be taken seriously and you appreciate that about her. She's someone you'd marry—never a playgirl—although she has a smoldering, sexy quality that is very magnetic. She's a bit possessive, sometimes insecure, but always interesting.

Female Aquarians born in 1982 seek a man who is sensitive, yet responsible. He is socially adept, yet places a high priority on responsibilities. You can envision him becoming a big success, but still taking the time to care for his wife and family on an emotional level. He's good with people, knows how to make you laugh, and you feel he will always be trustworthy.

EDDIE MURPHY
American Actor
Sun and Venus in Aries

526

1982 PISCES
From February 18, 23:47 through March 20, 22:55

The Sentimental Sweetheart

You're a traditional Pisces born in 1982 and to you a relationship must provide a solid sense of commitment and hope for the future. Where love is concerned, you take a mature point of view and believe that responsibility, reliability, and dependability are just as important as romance is. Knowing you can depend on each other makes you feel secure and content about your relationship.

You can't understand people who take a casual attitude toward love or each other. To you that borders on heresy. Making a commitment to care for someone says a lot about who you are, and you'd never want to let a partner down. Passion and chemistry are also important to you in a relationship. A deep connection is what you seek. You want to feel confident that you can look toward the future and see the one you love right there by your side.

A partner who speaks up and offers a joke or clever remark gains your attention easily. You enjoy getting to know a person before beginning a relationship. You also appreciate art and culture, so it's fun for you to be invited to a movie, a concert, or even to a dance. Old-fashioned displays of romance strike a sentimental chord with you. You also care about chemistry, so feeling that intense connection makes you perk up instantly.

Male Pisces born in 1982 prefer a traditional woman who has her head on straight. She's down to earth and sensible, but she's also spiritual and sexy. You both have strong intuition and sometimes all it takes for a romance to begin is to gaze deeply into each other's eyes. You like that intoxicating aura of chemistry below the surface. Your lady is multi-dimensional and you feel she'll remain interesting as time passes.

Female Fishies born in 1982 need a man who is artistic and romantic, yet also stable and reliable. Your guy has a flair and is charming, yet he can mow the lawn and assemble a bookcase without losing his temper. You appreciate a ready wit and the ability to apply attention and patience to any responsibility. You like someone who shows maturity beyond his years and gives you a sense of comfort and caring.

1982 ARIES
From March 20, 22:56 through April 20, 10:06

The Convivial Companion

As a sociable Aries born in 1982, your love relationship must be a very passionate friendship. You enjoy social connections of all sorts, and it's rewarding for you to be part of a couple as well as part of a larger group of friends. That gives you many social outlets as well as a cozy sense of comfort and connection. Friendship is a very important dimension of any relationship because it means you are able to connect on many levels. You're bemused by couples who have only one thing in common.

Chemistry is also important to you and you want to be completely in love. Part of that equation is being understood and allowed to express your individuality completely. You would never be with someone who laid down too many rules or didn't appreciate you for yourself. Intense passion and ongoing devotion are also essential for you. You can't really help it—where love is concerned you want the whole package!

You find a partner with many facets to his or her personality worth a second glance. You connect first through good communication and you really appreciate the person who shows an interest by being a good listener. You also like sharing social events and aren't even adverse to being fixed up. You want to make a friend first. Talking about your feelings appeals to you and you might just connect with a true love online in a chat room.

Male Rams born in 1982 like a woman who is intellectual yet also spirited, passionate, and sensitive. Your lady has a strong sense of intuition and she may insist you've been lovers through previous lives. She can sometimes be possessive, but you know that's just because she finds you so entrancing that she can't control herself. To you that's sexy and appealing and you enjoy her spunk.

Female Aries born in 1982 need a guy who is polite, but who expresses his individuality without apology. You want your man to be as assertive as you are. However, he also must understand that you don't always want to be a dainty sex object. Establishing a good level of give and take and his willingness to give you the respect you deserve can keep you on even footing.

1982 TAURUS *From April 20, 10:07 through May 21, 9:22*

The Flirtatious Lover

As a sweet-talking Taurus born in 1982, your relationship must be congenial and relaxed. You like to feel that you're with someone who understands and appreciates you and that keeps the quarrels and strife to a minimum. You believe in freedom of self-expression, but it's also nice to consider the needs of your partner. That way you each feel happy and respected.

Getting along with your partner is important to you, but you also realize that an occasional lover's quarrel is inevitable. A small degree of friction translates into increased chemistry and you find that romantic—and even a little cinematic. You love the dance of romance and enjoy feeling that sense of veiled passion below the surface—right from the first moment you're introduced.

You appreciate a sparkling partner with pizzazz, and someone who flirts and teases piques your interest quickly. Being engaged in witty conversation is the perfect opener to you because it shows that you have some things in common. You also appreciate sentimental expressions of affection and love getting those tender greeting cards and emails. Sharing movies, cultural events, and romantic outings appeals to you and you love stopping for stolen kisses wherever you are.

Male Bulls born in 1982 like a woman who is sparkling and pretty. Smart and independent, she is always her own person. Your gal knows what she wants and she radiates good humor and sex appeal. She has a lot of passion deep inside her heart, but she has enough subtlety to keep you guessing, at least for a little while. She is creative, perhaps an artist, and your lady enjoys sharing interesting ideas as well as romantic outings and sweet kisses.

Females Taureans born in 1982 want their guy to be sexy and outgoing, magnetic, a bit too independent, but also thoughtful, kind, and courtly. He has good manners and if he makes an occasional faux pas, he has the wit and charm to apologize with a clever turn of phrase that always makes you laugh. The sweet, sentimental things he says touch your heart. Your fellow is sexy and he enjoys chasing you until you catch him.

TAURUS ZODIAC SIGN
YOUR LOVE PLANETS

YOUR ROMANTIC SIDE   p. 696
▶ **VENUS IN PISCES**
Born Apr. 20, 10:07 - May 04, 12:26
▶ **VENUS IN ARIES**
Born May 04, 12:27 - May 21, 9:22

YOUR SEX DRIVE   p. 722
▶ **MARS IN LIBRA**
Born Apr. 20, 10:07 - May 21, 9:22

YOUR CELEBRITY TWINS   p. 760
Find out the astrological similarities you have with famous people.

YOUR COMPATIBILITY   p. 780
Compare planets to find out how compatible you are in a relationship.

YOUR RELATIONSHIP KARMA   p. 824
▶ **SATURN IN LIBRA**
Born Apr. 20, 10:07 - May 21, 9:22

JESSICA LANGE
American Actress
Sun and Venus in Taurus

527

1982 GEMINI *From May 21, 9:23 through June 21, 17:22*

The Intellectual Sensualist

As a communicative Gemini born in 1982, your relationship must be intellectually stimulating as well as sensual. You need a relationship to provide a good overall connection so you can share ideas with that special someone. You'd never be with someone just because of chemistry, no matter how sexy that person appears. After all, talking is much too important.

You believe strongly in independence and feel partners must have the right to their own interests and ideas. Too many rules can be a turn off, and although you believe in total commitment, you feel that it's nice to have your own friends and social outlets. A positive sensual connection is also important because that's another way to communicate. You need your mind and your body stimulated.

The partner who has something fascinating to say is always going to gain your attention first. Tongue-tied people just don't appeal to you. Sharing fascinating ideas keeps you endlessly inspired and you might like connecting with someone whose interests in a technical field coordinate with your own. You also like being touched, and a partner who will give you an impromptu shoulder rub or pretend to read your palm as an excuse to hold your hand is sweet enough to make you want a little more.

Male Geminis born in 1982 like a woman who is soft and sensual. Your lady is gentle and tender and she touches your heart in many ways. You want to love and protect her and you appreciate it a lot when she makes you sweet treats or lavishes you with kisses. Your gal must also be intelligent because you need to be able to communicate. The interesting things she says stay with you even longer than the memory of those tender embraces.

Female Geminis born in 1982 need a guy who is a rip-roaring good time. Your fellow is smart and sparking and he keeps you interested. His comments are witty and intelligent and he's a great jokester and punster. He loves talking to you and never complains about the endless hours you spend together on the phone. He is socially adept and has a natural grace, and you appreciate his good manners and attention to detail.

GEMINI ZODIAC SIGN
YOUR LOVE PLANETS

YOUR ROMANTIC SIDE   p. 696
▶ **VENUS IN ARIES**
Born May 21, 9:23 - May 30, 21:01
▶ **VENUS IN TAURUS**
Born May 30, 21:02 - June 21, 17:22

YOUR SEX DRIVE   p. 722
▶ **MARS IN LIBRA**
Born May 21, 9:23 - June 21, 17:22

YOUR CELEBRITY TWINS   p. 760
Find out the astrological similarities you have with famous people.

YOUR COMPATIBILITY   p. 780
Compare planets to find out how compatible you are in a relationship.

YOUR RELATIONSHIP KARMA   p. 824
▶ **SATURN IN LIBRA**
Born May 21, 9:23 - June 21, 17:22

LIONEL RICHIE
American Singer
Venus in Cancer

528

1982 CANCER
From June 21, 17:23 through July 23, 4:14

♋ The Dependable Companion

You're a hard-working Cancer born in 1982 and your relationship must be easy-going and reliable. A sense of trust is very important to you because you feel it's essential to be able to count on someone you love. You believe in going all out in a relationship so that each partner is well taken care of. If that means compromise and occasional self-sacrifice is needed, so be it.

Romance is equally important, but you feel that if you're with the right person, romance just naturally flows. A sense of emotional connection and physical sparkle keeps the attachment happy and that's what really matters. Creative freedom is another aspect of a good relationship because it means that each person supports the goals and desires of the other. Being in a relationship where there is no support or cooperation would strangle you and you'd never let that happen.

An artistic person most easily gains your interest because you admire the creative process and find it endlessly interesting to discuss things such as art, movies, and writing. Intellectual stimulation is essential and you love connecting with a mentally compatible partner. Someone who offers to share an exciting book is a fun companion because then you have something to say to each other. You also enjoy going together to museums, receiving greeting cards, and being treated to a social event.

Male Cancers born in 1982 need a woman who is spunky and playful. You can imagine this gal a spry old lady of ninety, still active and lively, and as much fun as she was in grade school. Her ideas are fun to hear and she makes plans that really appeal to you. She's sexy to you, but nobody would ever call her a sexpot. That's what makes her more exciting and special—because it's personal.

Lady Crabs born in 1982 like a man who is courteous, sensitive, kind, and responsible. Your guy is hard working and serious but he's never all business. He likes socializing and knows how to impress you with his well-developed social graces. He's romantic, but he never goes off the deep end. You can imagine him in a happy family with lots of cheerful kids.

1982 LEO
From July 23, 4:15 through August 23, 11:14

♌ The Tender-hearted Romantic

You're a passionate Leo born in 1982 and to you a relationship must be tender, romantic, and totally committed. You believe in connecting on all levels and your feelings for each other must be genuine and deep. You'd never get taken in by good looks alone because you know it takes more than the externals to shape a tie that binds. A connection must start in the heart and be as strong in the soul—or else it's just marking time.

A romantic attraction is, of course, essential because nobody wants to be involved without some sparks. You know that the right partner stimulates you on all levels, though, and to you that's what a relationship is all about. A sense of caring and nurturing is another important aspect. Being each other's best friend, stalwart champion, and tender sweetheart is what you want.

Sweetness is what you most appreciate in a partner who wants to gain your attention. That someone would go out on a limb to attract and please you. You find that very endearing and you'd want to know that person better. Inviting you to a party or a picnic, to a playground to sit on the swings while the children laugh all around you, or taking you to a fancy dress up event are other ways you enjoy being wooed.

Male Leos born in 1982 like a woman who is tender and gentle, a mother at heart, someone who can nurture and snuggle. Your gal is great with kids, kind to old ladies and pets, and walks across the street to shake an acquaintance's hand. She knows when someone needs a hug and she's always there to give it. This lady is the sort of person who will be treasured all her life. All you want to do from the moment you meet her is wrap her up in your arms forever.

Lady Lions born in 1982 need a guy who is intense and magnetic. You like a passionate, macho man because you find him stimulating and sexy. Even if he's a little bossy, you know it's just because he cares so much about you. A family man is your type of fellow and you can envision creating a home together. He's sexy and creative and he loves pleasing you. You know that year after year you will be happy together.

1982 VIRGO

From August 23, 11:15 through September 23, 8:45

♍ The Impassioned Lover

You're a magnetic Virgo born in 1982 and your relationship must be passionate, intense, and spiritual. You believe in a connection on all levels, and a simple, casual, disposable romance doesn't interest you at all. True love is very important to you and that means a relationship in which both partners fall in love with heart and soul. There has to be a connection below the surface for it to be truly meaningful to you.

You can't help being attracted because of intense chemistry between you and a partner, and sometimes you've been known to convince yourself that it was true love when it was really just sexual attraction. No matter what, chemistry is important and to you a relationship must have that strong, unstoppable draw because that's what keeps it going when times get tough. A sense of mutual expectation is another important dimension to your relationship.

Sex appeal is often what sparks your interest first, so a partner who wants to woo you must be attractive and radiate a kind of mystique you find impossible to resist. You enjoy spiritual pursuits, so visiting an ashram together could prove to be an interesting time for you. You might also enjoy trying group meditations or even attending a séance. But what really knocks your socks off is that first deep, intense, no holds barred, ultra-passionate kiss.

Male Virgos born in 1982 need a woman who is glamorous, mysterious, and spiritual. Your lady has an aura about her and often people mistake her for an actress. She has natural charisma, a lot of pizzazz, and she's very sexy. This gal has a sense of herself and she takes over a room when she enters it. Her personal magnetism is intense, but under it all she's also kind, loving, and nurturing—every man's fantasy.

Female Virgos born in 1982 prefer a man to be strong, assertive, and determined. Your guy knows what he wants and he knows how to get it. He sweeps you up into his arms and you love the way he makes you swoon. There is a strong sense both of chemistry and destiny. You're positive you've been together in other lifetimes and that it's meant to be.

JULIE ANDREWS
English Actress
Sun in Libra

529

1982 LIBRA

From September 23, 8:46 through October 23, 17:57

♎ The Elegant Romantic

You're a romantic Libra born in 1982 and having harmony, tenderness, and positive interaction is most important to you in a relationship. Balance is an essential component of any relationship and you'd absolutely refuse to be part of any interaction that was marred by chaos or constant quarreling. Good manners are just too important to you and your relationship must be as genteel as you are.

Creativity is another positive element in a good relationship. Sharing good ideas and interesting points of view is always fun because, although you like harmony in a relationship, you're not adverse to a debate now and then—as long as voices remain calm. Chemistry brings another dimension to a good relationship in your opinion, but it's nothing flagrant or tacky. It's just a matter of two well-suited partners recognizing in each other the very thing that draws them together.

To gain your attention, a partner must use good manners. You love formal introductions and the days in which people stopped by and left engraved calling cards on silver trays really appeal to you. Attending a dance together is a nice way to meet because if you can dance comfortably with someone, there could be more there on which to build. You also like outdoor activities, so going for a walk on a pleasant day, strolling through an art fair or a park is a nice way to connect.

Male Libras born in 1982 need a woman who is pretty, well-mannered, and gracious. Your lady is emotionally balanced, although she does change her mind now and then. She is an excellent hostess and knows how to make everyone around her feel comfortable. She is sexy in her own way and often rather athletic, but she's never sweaty or unkempt looking.

Lady Libras born in 1982 need a man who is outgoing and uncomplicated. You don't want your guy to be too much of a fussbudget, but he mustn't be a clod either, just a regular nice guy with a bit of sexy sparkle. He has excellent social skills and is charming and friendly without making too big a deal of any situation. His presence calms you and you enjoy socializing with him as your partner.

BILLY IDOL
English Singer
Sun in Sagittarius

530

1982 SCORPIO
From October 23, 17:58 through November 22, 15:22

♏ *The Lovable Playmate*

You're a boisterous Scorpio born in 1982 and to you a relationship must be lots of fun. Playfulness is important in any interaction and you feel that the couple who plays together stays together. Socializing and going out together to mutually enjoyable places is the glue in your relationship. You love starting the day, planning some fun activities to share with your true love.

Personal freedom is another important component of togetherness in your opinion. Each person in a relationship must be allowed to follow his or her own path or else you don't see how all those dreams can be fulfilled. Helping each other to use your special talents and achieve success is a nice way to share a life. That means you're team players and want the best for someone you love. You believe there is enough love to go around so everyone who wants to can find happiness. You'd hate to be in a relationship where that wasn't the expectation.

The mate who is cheerful and outgoing gains your interest quite easily. Someone who is a people person the way you are finds a natural level of compatibility. You can pass many happy hours standing and chatting, joking and laughing, and just shooting the breeze. You enjoy many social opportunities and can even have fun on a water cooler break. You like dating and going out for a nice dinner or a casual walk. Even connecting at a business meeting could appeal to you.

Male Scorpions born in 1982 need a woman who is sparkling and charming. Your gal is often the life of the party and when she walks into a room, heads turn in her direction. She's adept at talking about pretty much everything and she always has an interesting opinion. Her kindhearted nature can cheer people up and she's always willing to lend a hand.

Females Scorpios born in 1982 prefer a man to be independent yet also solid and practical. Your guy is an achiever and an innovator and his ideas are clever and ground-breaking. He's easy going but also has his own priorities and he expects you to cooperate and be on his team. You admire that approach because he's always in your corner, too.

1982 SAGITTARIUS
From November 22, 15:23 through December 22, 4:37

♐ *The Beloved Giver*

You're a kind-hearted Sagittarius born in 1982 and to you a relationship must be congenial, supportive, and loving. You believe deeply in true love and want to find your soul mate and share a perfectly happy life. Sharing and caring are very important to you. It feels natural to reach out to the one you love and try to make your mate's life warm and happy.

Good communication is essential to you in a relationship and you enjoy being able to say just about anything to your partner. Deep and serious talks are always interesting, but it's also fun just to goof off and chat about any little thing on your mind. Your hopes and dreams seem so much more real when you can express them to someone who visualizes them as clearly as you do. Working together toward mutual goals matters to you too. It's all about loving and giving and you'd hate to be trapped in a shallow interaction where there wasn't deep, true love.

To stimulate your interest a partner might invite you to a concert or engage you in an interesting conversation. You always look below the surface, so it's more about how you feel when you're with this person than what happens around you. You like working together on mutually involving projects and you're interested in healing and making the world a better place. Taking a Reiki class and practicing on each other could bring you close very quickly and enhance your sexual connection.

Male Archers born in 1982 like a woman whose energy is soft and dreamy, but who has a clever mind and can share interesting points of view. Your lady is multi-dimensional. She is soft and loving, and maybe even a little psychic. She loves music and dancing, and she seems to know all about you and what you like. You find her a mystery worth exploring.

Female Sagittarians born in 1982 need a guy to be solid and strong. Macho men appeal to you because they have the sort of sexy charisma that keeps you interested. Your guy has clever, tender things to say, and he has a gentle side, too. You know he'd move mountains to make you happy and you feel safe and protected when you're in his company.

Joan Collins – Queen of the Small Screen

Outside of millionaire Donald Trump, no one epitomizes the glitzy and extravagant decade of the 1980s as much as actress Joan Collins. A contract player for 20th Century Fox (she was briefly considered for the leading role in *Cleopatra*), the beautiful and sexy brunette had fashioned a string of mostly forgettable films since first coming to Hollywood in 1955. But it was on American television that she managed to achieve true international fame, joining the cast of the evening soap opera *Dynasty* in 1981 as the Machiavellian "Alexis Carrington Colby."

Clad in a seemingly endless array of jewel-toned, Nolan Miller-designed shoulder-padded power suits and sequin-festooned gowns, "Alexis" schemed, manipulated, and slept her way to the top as the corporate and personal arch-rival of ex-husband "Blake Carrington" (John Forsythe). Her amoral character was the perfect foil for the too-sweet "Krystle," played by Linda Evans, and on more than one occasion the two glamorous, middle-aged beauties indulged in a primetime cat fight. *Dynasty* became one of the most talked about and top-rated shows of the decade, with *TV Guide* praising its "campy opulence."

Judging from Collins' autobiography *Past Imperfect*, as a young actress in Hollywood during the 1950s, the lovely British import had her choice of dates among the male population of Tinseltown. During her heyday in the film capitol she was even engaged to Warren Beatty for a brief time before he became involved with Natalie Wood. In later years, the combination of her TV character's onscreen antics and Collins' admissions about her own private life promoted a racy public image, though she also played the more sedate real-life roles of devoted mother (she has three children) and tireless worker for children's charities. In 1985 she married for the fourth time, to the much younger Peter Holm. This marriage lasted for only two years, but it made her the unofficial poster girl for older woman-younger man relationships.

Her Gemini Zodiac sign, as well as Venus in Gemini, accentuates a playful, lighthearted, and somewhat flippant attitude toward love and sex. Four of her five marriages (including one to fellow entertainer Anthony Newley) have ended in divorce, yet Joan has always managed to bounce back from heartbreak with her incredible optimism and sense of humor still intact. Geminis like talking about sex almost as much as they enjoy practicing it, and Collins' two tell-all autobiographies gleefully dished the dirt on her marriages and romances. And although once dubbed "the British open" for her allegedly promiscuous lifestyle, she claims to have turned down love affairs with the likes of Robert Kennedy, Frank Sinatra, and Dean Martin.

Joan's sister is the bestselling novelist Jackie Collins. Since the late 1980s, Joan herself has published four novels, including *Star Quality*, her most recent literary offering. Collins received the coveted Order of the British Empire (OBE) from Queen Elizabeth II in 1997 in recognition of her contribution to the arts and for her continuing charity work. Collins married for the fifth time in 2002 to a man 32 years her junior, Percy Gibson. As the author of several books on health and beauty, she has kept both her looks and her delightful sense of humor long past the age when most women—even movie stars!—have thrown in the towel on glamour.

"I hope he is the one — the last one!"

JOAN COLLINS speaking about her fifth and current husband, Percy Gibson

▶ READ ABOUT WARREN BEATTY ON PAGE 497 ▶ READ ABOUT ROBERT WAGNER AND NATALIE WOOD ON PAGE 442

1983

- ⭐ **POLYGAMY**
- ⭐ **GAY PLAGUE**
- ⭐ **FLASHDANCE**
- ⭐ **HOLLYWOOD WIVES**
- ⭐ **STING**
- ⭐ **BILLIE JEAN**
- ⭐ **TOTAL ECLIPSE OF THE HEART**

EVENTS

In the US an Arizona man—with 105 wives—was found guilty of polygamy. Harrison Ford and Melissa Mathison married but with an unhappy ending. They divorced 17 years later amid rumors that Ford's womanizing finally took its toll.

Reverend Jerry Falwell offended many when he described AIDS as a "gay plague."

The pope condemned artificial contraception again, while the US Supreme Court reaffirmed its 1973 Roe vs. Wade decision with rulings that limited a state's power to restrict access to legal abortions.

In the UK, Margaret Thatcher was re-elected Prime Minister, thanks in part to her government's successful war with Argentina over the Falkland Islands the year before.

POP CULTURE

Films that caught attention were *Flashdance*, with a female welder by day—and semi-exotic dancer by night—who dreams of a career in legitimate dance and a construction boss who helps make it happen, and *Yentl*, starring and directed by Barbra Streisand. Yentl disguises herself as a boy so she can study at an orthodox Jewish school, but her masquerade creates problems when she falls for a male student. In *Romantic Comedy*, compatible writing partners spend fifteen years together and share everything—except their beds.

Readers enjoyed *Changes*, by

Hot Couple

Danielle Steel, about a newly married couple experiencing pressure from their ready-made family. In *Hollywood Wives* the wives are a privileged breed of women with a ticket to ride gratis via a famous husband. *Talking with Your Child About Sex* provided a self-help book to make this subject easier to approach.

Before Sting went solo, there was the Police. Their "Every Breath You Take" made it to the top of the charts, as did Michael Jackson's rousing "Billie Jean" and "Beat It." Irene Cara had a hit with "Flashdance" from the movie of the same name, and Paul McCartney teamed up for another duet, this time with Michael Jackson in "Say Say Say." Kenny Rogers and Dolly Parton made another duo for "Islands in the Stream." Bonnie Tyler belted out "Total Eclipse of the Heart" and Men at Work gave us "Down Under." Yes sang "Owner Of a Lonely Heart" and Nena, "99 Luftballons."

PAUL SIMON & CARRIE FISHER

August 16, 1983 marked the wedding of singer-songwriter Paul Simon and Carrie Fisher, the actress best known as Princess Leia in the original *Star Wars* movies. The marriage was the culmination of a five-year romance. Fisher, who documented her struggles with drug addiction in her autobiographical novel, *Postcards From the Edge*, found Simon's rhythmic way with words to be soothing. Still, during the marriage, she took thirty painkiller pills a day to stave off the symptoms of her then undiagnosed manic-depression. The marriage, which lasted a mere eleven months, inspired the 1991 novel by Fisher, *Surrender the Pink*.

SEE ALSO
▶ DEBBIE REYNOLDS & EDDIE FISHER *Page 302*
▶ LUCILLE BALL AND DESI ARNAZ *Page 285*

532

1983 CAPRICORN

From December 22, 1982 4:38 through January 20, 1983 15:16
(December 1983 Capricorns, see 1984 Capricorn)

♑ *The Stable Wit*

Capricorn of 1983, you may seem a bit aloof to the world in general but, in a close relationship, your partner knows better. You may wait until you're older to settle down, unsure of yourself with the opposite sex, but it's within a love alliance that your heart and soul truly shine, revealing a delightfully dry sense of humor, a deep level of compassion, and a strong loyalty to your mate.

You're no stranger to hard work, and in your ideal relationship, you and your love strive together to create comfort and security. Unconventional and free-spirited, you're not one to follow all the rules—except the ones you make for yourself—and a partnership with you is likely to be a unique combination of traditional and New Age. When all is said and done at the end of the day, you're both likely to be found at home. If you do go out, you prefer a physical activity rather than a social one, and you're happiest when your partner is at your side, no matter what you're doing.

The one who wants to attract your notice might have to be blunt to make sure you don't miss it. A mere glance across the room won't do the trick because you're not likely to believe it's an attempt to flirt. Telling a joke, inviting you to a sports event, or soliciting your help with a worthwhile project will get your attention. To keep it, a would-be suitor will have to prove—over time—to be of good character and someone who lets you feel safe letting down your guard.

A 1983 Capricorn male needs a woman who knows how to laugh and have fun. She has a quirky side that shows up behind closed doors, tantalizing you endlessly. In public she's always a proper lady, which you find amusing. Doing volunteer work for the underprivileged is important to her, and you're happy to lend a hand.

For a Capricorn woman born in 1983, the ideal mate is steady, reliable, and loyal—and sexy. He melts your heart daily with his romantic gestures. It's easy for him to heat up your nights because he loves finding all your hot buttons, one after the other. With his love wrapped around you, it's hard to resist—and you don't want to.

CAPRICORN ZODIAC SIGN
YOUR LOVE PLANETS

YOUR ROMANTIC SIDE p. 696
▶ VENUS IN CAPRICORN
Born Dec. 22, 1982 4:38 - Jan. 05, 1983 17:57
▶ VENUS IN AQUARIUS
Born Jan. 05, 17:58 - Jan. 20, 15:16

YOUR SEX DRIVE p. 722
▶ MARS IN AQUARIUS
Born Dec. 22, 1982 4:38 - Jan. 17, 1983 13:09
▶ MARS IN PISCES
Born Jan. 17, 13:10 - Jan. 20, 15:16

YOUR CELEBRITY TWINS p. 760
Find out the astrological similarities you have with famous people.

YOUR COMPATIBILITY p. 780
Compare planets to find out how compatible you are in a relationship.

YOUR RELATIONSHIP KARMA p. 824
▶ SATURN IN SCORPIO
Born Dec. 22, 1982 4:38 - Jan. 20, 1983 15:16

ISABELLE HUPPERT
French Actress
Venus in Aquarius

1983 AQUARIUS

From January 20, 15:17 through February 19, 5:30

♒ *The Cosmic Lover*

You're idealistic, free-spirited, original, forward-looking, and independent, Aquarius of 1983, and you prefer your relationships to be the same way. In your perfect partnership there are no leashes and, if there are, a lot of slack keeps you from feeling tied down. That's not to say there's no excitement or passion that keeps you together. Rather it's the emotional involvement with global concerns that provides the glue for your relationship. That said, there's also a streak of the romantic in you that shows itself best when you've given your heart and you feel connected to your love in an almost cosmic way.

Your ideal pairing will find both of you working side by side for charitable causes, possibly involving children and animals. Or maybe you'll be elbow-to-elbow in the kitchen whipping up a foreign recipe you got off the Internet—for twenty friends who'll be stopping by later. You crave mental stimulation, and the perfect relationship fosters an environment where every day has a new mental adventure, even if it's just working the crossword puzzle together—in ink.

The would-be suitor who captures your attention is likely to be doing something kind and selfless for another. You'll approve with all your heart and may find yourself lingering and making excuses to be nearby—yet you may not realize for a long time that there is more to your connection than just Good Works. The one who keeps you coming back has to be intelligent, a bit offbeat, and positive.

1983 Aquarius men need a woman with a big heart. She knows she'll see you when she sees you, and that freedom makes you want to get home all the faster. Intuitive and demure, yet a bit wicked, she seems to read your mind—especially in the bedroom where the two of you experiment until dawn.

Aquarian females born in 1983 need a partner with his feet on the ground. He doesn't hesitate to tell you when your ideas are wacky, but he won't hold you back, either. He's a smart man in many ways, street-wise and able to handle whatever comes up. When he takes you in his arms, you forget the outside world even exists.

AQUARIUS ZODIAC SIGN
YOUR LOVE PLANETS

YOUR ROMANTIC SIDE p. 696
▶ VENUS IN AQUARIUS
Born Jan. 20, 15:17 - Jan. 29, 17:30
▶ VENUS IN PISCES
Born Jan. 29, 17:31 - Feb. 19, 5:30

YOUR SEX DRIVE p. 722
▶ MARS IN PISCES
Born Jan. 20, 15:17 - Feb. 19, 5:30

YOUR CELEBRITY TWINS p. 760
Find out the astrological similarities you have with famous people.

YOUR COMPATIBILITY p. 780
Compare planets to find out how compatible you are in a relationship.

YOUR RELATIONSHIP KARMA p. 824
▶ SATURN IN SCORPIO
Born Jan. 20, 15:17 - Feb. 19, 5:30

ROB LOWE
American Actor
Sun and Mars in Pisces

534

1983 PISCES
From February 19, 5:31 through March 21, 4:38

The Dreamy Paramour

In the ideal relationship, Pisces of 1983, both of you work to keep things forever fresh and exciting. Your favorite emotion is love, and the heady rush of a brand new love, replayed over and over, keeps both of you filled with passion for each other. Weekends at a borrowed lakeside cabin in the woods, weekly date nights where you linger over dessert with fingers touching, and walks under a full moon insure that you both stay foremost in the other's heart.

You're highly creative, and enjoy working alongside your partner as you explore music and art. Perhaps you'll share space in a painter's studio or photographer's darkroom. The connection you feel with your lover, combined with your idealistic nature, might find the two of you working together in a helping profession or with the underprivileged. In your perfect relationship, you are joined at the heart with your partner, and your lovemaking is a means of expressing your deepest feelings.

The one who wants to attract your attention has to play hard to get—at least at first. You love the thrill of the chase, and after making the initial bold overture, a would-be suitor needs to drop back and let you do the romancing. Someone who wants to keep your interest long term needs an intuitive streak when dealing with others and an understanding of what you're thinking without any words being spoken.

For Pisces males born in 1983, your ideal match has a dreamy look that belies a sharp mind. She may look like an angel, but when she speaks it's worth hearing. It might be a weekly dance class, a sci-fi reading group, or an astrology website, but she's likely to be in charge of something out of the ordinary.

A Pisces woman born in 1983 needs a man who has the soul of a poet. Whether or not he actually writes doesn't matter because he lives his life every day seeing things in ways that others don't. He shares his vision of the world with you, and fascinates you with his ideas. His creativity doesn't stop at the bedroom door—in fact that's where he shines the brightest when he takes you to places you've never before imagined.

1983 ARIES
From March 21, 4:39 through April 20, 15:49

The Sensual Daredevil

Bold, ambitious Aries of 1983, your most prominent characteristic is your courage. There's almost nothing you can't have once you make up your mind to have it—and that includes love. When you set your sights on a potential lover, you don't hold back in your quest to win love and affection. Once in a relationship, though, you frequently need to be reassured that you're desired. With the right partner you're confident enough to open your heart, setting the stage for a long alliance.

In your ideal relationship, you are paired up with someone who likes to take risks as much as you do. Physically strong with energy to burn, you want a mate who can keep up with you, whether you're mountain climbing or cuddling in an all-night love marathon. You're strongly attracted to money—how to get it and keep it—and your perfect mate will work alongside you to reach your mutual financial goals.

To attract your attention, a potential suitor will be doing something active or daring. If that's followed up with witty repartee (a slightly off-color joke will do, but only if it's whispered in your ear privately) the hooks will be in and you'll be intrigued. You're very sensual, and the one who wants to keep your interest will touch you—a lot. Even a hand on your shoulder as you talk will be enough to keep you focused and eager to learn more.

For Aries guys born in 1983, the ideal female is interested in charity work, is down-to-earth and practical, and has solid values. With strong opinions of her own, she can stand her ground with you, but doesn't hold a grudge when you disagree. She's not afraid to try new things, and that includes any sexy ideas you might have in or out of the bedroom.

Female Ariens born in 1983 like stable men. Your perfect man is hard working, but knows when to quit, leaving plenty of time for play—with you. He's a bit rugged and possessive, but knows he can't rein you in. He loves to talk and the two of you can spend hours happily chatting away. It's when the lights are off that his soft, sensual side appears, delighting and tantalizing you—over and over again.

1983 TAURUS *From April 20, 15:50 through May 21, 15:05*

The Patient Connoisseur

You love routine and stability, Taurus of 1983. It makes you comfortable if you know that tomorrow will be the same as today. This is the key for you—comfort. Because of that, you might delay seeking a permanent relationship. Once you decide that you want to be in a partnership you might find that the ideal one for you has those same qualities. No, you don't want a dull romance. Your ideal relationship offers you stability, but it also affords you opportunities to nourish and stimulate the senses. And, 1983 Taurus, when you commit your heart to someone, you're quite the romantic! Candlelight dinners and love notes become the new routine—because you're in love.

You have a sharp intellect and may enjoy discussing worldwide current events with your mate. The two of you love to share your day and plan your tomorrows wrapped in each other's arms. Your home, no matter where it is, is your castle, and you take care to see that it's as luxurious as possible. Having friends over for enjoyable, relaxed evenings while you and your partner act as co-hosts is the best

way the two of you work as a team.

A would-be suitor who wants to get your attention can do it in the kitchen. A gourmet meal on a table set with fresh flowers, followed by relaxing on a sofa with plump cushions is sure to please you. Add some quiet background music, and maybe a shoulder massage, and you'll be hooked. Enjoying pleasurable activities that explore sound, texture, and taste will keep your relationship humming.

The 1983 Taurus male wants a partner who's smart. Not only does she keep you on your mental toes with jokes and puzzles, but she's well thought of in her daily pursuits. She matches you love note for love note, and doesn't hesitate to dim the lights to set the tone for the evening.

A Taurus woman born in 1983 wants a guy who isn't going to be stopped by obstacles. Like you, he has goals and is determined to reach them. He lets you know in small and large ways how much he loves you, whether it's taking your deposit to the bank or reading poetry while you amorously lie with your head in his lap.

TAURUS ZODIAC SIGN
YOUR LOVE PLANETS

YOUR ROMANTIC SIDE — p. 696
▶ **VENUS IN GEMINI**
Born Apr. 20, 15:50 - May 09, 10:55
▶ **VENUS IN CANCER**
Born May 09, 10:56 - May 21, 15:05

YOUR SEX DRIVE — p. 722
▶ **MARS IN TAURUS**
Born Apr. 20, 15:50 - May 16, 21:42
▶ **MARS IN GEMINI**
Born May 16, 21:43 - May 21, 15:05

YOUR CELEBRITY TWINS — p. 760
Find out the astrological similarities you have with famous people.

YOUR COMPATIBILITY — p. 780
Compare planets to find out how compatible you are in a relationship.

YOUR RELATIONSHIP KARMA — p. 824
SATURN IN SCORPIO
Born Apr. 20, 15:50 - May 6, 19:20
▶ **SATURN IN LIBRA**
Born May 6, 19:21 - May 21, 15:05

BOY GEORGE
English Singer
Sun in Gemini

535

1983 GEMINI *From May 21, 15:06 through June 21, 23:08*

The Chatty Partner

Quick, witty Gemini of 1983, your most perfect relationship could sneak up on you when you're not looking. There you are, happily debating a favorite topic with a member of the opposite sex you've known for a while and—boom, a flash of emotion leaves you speechless. But only for a moment. You recover quickly, but the truth will be in your heart. In your ideal partnership the two of you are first connected mentally. You'll love spending time with your mate in a wide variety of activities, the more the merrier, but you may have to keep your calendars on matching electronic day planners to keep them all straight.

The home you share with your partner will be Grand Central Station at times, with people from all walks of life stopping by. The two of you sometimes have trouble finding time to be alone together, but when you do, you discover one of life's truths—the brain is the sexiest organ of all. Your lovemaking is a rollicking good time, with lots of laughter and experimentation.

Someone who wants to catch your eye will do it verbally. A conflicting opinion to something

you've just said or some verbal repartee is sure to make you smile. If you think you have something to learn, all the better. Keeping your attention is harder, but a potential mate who's involved in a number of projects, has a challenging vocabulary, and some worthy goals is likely to be the one you'll stick with.

A 1983 Gemini male needs an independent partner with a down-to-earth plan for success. She's lively, warm, and friendly, and may even have a number of guy pals. But her heart belongs to you. She's absolutely trustworthy, and that stills any little doubts you might have. You're a secret, sensual romantic, and your ideal gal is the delighted recipient of your loving massages.

For a female 1983 Gemini, only a happy mate will do. He's positive and upbeat, always ready to put a good slant on negative events. While he may not lavish you with expensive gifts, the ones he brings lets you know how well he understands you. He isn't clingy or demanding, but gives you all the freedom you need.

GEMINI ZODIAC SIGN
YOUR LOVE PLANETS

YOUR ROMANTIC SIDE — p. 696
▶ **VENUS IN CANCER**
Born May 21, 15:06 - June 06, 6:03
▶ **VENUS IN LEO**
Born June 06, 6:04 - June 21, 23:08

YOUR SEX DRIVE — p. 722
▶ **MARS IN GEMINI**
Born May 21, 15:06 - June 21, 23:08

YOUR CELEBRITY TWINS — p. 760
Find out the astrological similarities you have with famous people.

YOUR COMPATIBILITY — p. 780
Compare planets to find out how compatible you are in a relationship.

YOUR RELATIONSHIP KARMA — p. 824
▶ **SATURN IN LIBRA**
Born May 21, 15:06 - June 21, 23:08

MERYL STREEP
American Actress
Sun and Venus in Cancer

536

1983 CANCER
From June 21, 23:09 through July 23, 10:03

The Contented Romancer

You love home and family, Cancer of 1983. Your vision of the ideal relationship includes a happy domestic life with a loving mate and a fat bank account for security. Together you work to build a solid foundation, a peaceful environment where your love can flourish and safety is assured. For you all happiness springs from that, and, with a partner at your side, you can settle into a life of contentment.

Romance is at the heart of your loving partnership, and you are a true romantic. You like to give—and receive—flowers, sweet notes, and all the old-fashioned expressions of love. Walking hand-in-hand under a full moon? Of course. Cuddling on the couch while you watch old movies? Certainly. Lavishing attention on friends and family, and grand gestures, especially if they involve surprises, are right up your alley, too. You and your mate can spend hours happily working side by side to create the perfect celebration, with one of you snapping photos for the album. Sound traditional? Yes, and you love it, especially when you're the recipient of all the attention.

The one who catches your eye could be doing a genealogy family tree at the library or bidding on an heirloom at an antique auction. Add a love of animals and kids, and you'll be intrigued. Feed you a home cooked meal in soft surroundings, and you'll be hooked, especially if the would-be suitor lets you know where you stand and doesn't make you guess about any romantic intentions.

For a 1983 male Crab, your ideal partner is skilled in the home arts, but also has a profession. She's likely to be working with the elderly or the disadvantaged, or perhaps with children. But she might be a physician or scientist, too. No matter what she does, though, her main focus is on making the world a better place.

The 1983 Cancer female needs a man who is morally sound, gentle, artistic, and a bit independent. He's trustworthy, but he has his own interests apart from yours. You're the recipient of his talents, though, whether he sketches a drawing for your wall or builds a china cabinet for your mother's crystal stemware.

1983 LEO
From July 23, 10:04 through August 23, 17:06

The Touchy-Feely Realist

When you think about your ideal relationship, Leo of 1983, it's likely you think of forever. You have a good sense of who and what you are, and know that a lifelong commitment with one you love will provide a solid base for your life. A partnership with a compatible mate who also believes in hard work is the way you'll get the material things you want. You'll want the best for your family, whatever it costs. You're a touchy-feely sign, and your relationship will be warmed by daily doses of genuine affection and approval.

You're a realist, but you're also an optimist. The future is bright, you believe, and will be filled with fun, friends, and leisure. When you travel together, hopefully as often as finances will allow, you'll want the very best in accommodations. Being needed is high on your list, and you and your mate could find yourselves on the board of directors for a charity organization or youth sports league. You're in demand socially because of your wit and the class you bring to any gathering, and you'll love attending functions with your

equally classy partner at your side.

You're attracted to strong personalities, and the one who catches your eye is likely to be giving a speech or leading a group. If you're singled out for recognition, your interest will be piqued. A potential mate who wants to keep your attention needs to listen carefully to every word you say, eyes locked on yours as though you are the only person that matters.

For the 1983 Leo male, the idea partner loves home life as much as you do. She's very supportive—and appreciative—of all you do. She is active in the community or works in a prestigious field, but knows when to quit and focus her attention on you. You purr like a contented cat under her gentle hands.

A female Lion born in 1983 loves to get presents, and your ideal guy knows just what you like. Perhaps a gift certificate to a day at the spa where you can be pampered? He stands up to you, but is always considerate of your desires. He can read your body like a book and keeps you simmering, even when you're nowhere near the bedroom.

1983 VIRGO
From August 23, 17:07 through September 23, 14:41

♍ The Quiet Dramatist

Meticulous, caring Virgo of 1983, you might find it hard to stick with the daily routines of a long relationship—unless you find the ideal partner. To keep from falling into a boring rut, you and your partner will have to try to make sure every day is just a little bit different—and fun. In your ideal love alliance, you and your mate see eye-to-eye on the most important things, which makes you willing to compromise on the others. You prefer a quiet home life, but are pleased to play co-host with your partner when friends stop by for some intelligent chat and a great meal.

You're careful with money, preferring to have it as security, but you're generous with your lover. The two of you might have a beautiful garden where you grow veggies to share with a community food bank. Or perhaps you will jointly run a catering company, allowing you to feed others while making a dollar at the same time. With your love of culture and your flair for drama, the two of you may be part of the local theater scene, working together to acquire props or even taking acting parts.

Anyone who wants to capture your attention must do it quietly. No brazen displays in public, please! A potential mate must be open enough to get past your initial shyness. Giving you tickets to a comedy improv or asking you questions about investing will spark an interest. A suitor will have to prove over time to be responsible and stable—and in love with you.

A 1983 Virgo male needs a non-demanding partner who understands that chaos and drama in large doses can make you nervous. A happy, positive gal who has established values will teach you to relax. At the same time she appreciates your methodical ways, and lets you know it. She thinks you're sexy, and loves touching you—all over.

For a female Virgo born in 1983, a rule-breaker can keep your life exciting. He's responsible and would never hurt anyone, but he comes out with zinging one-liners that keep you in stitches. Possibly a member of the medical profession, his heart is in the right place. He loves surprising you with gifts you wouldn't buy for yourself.

VIRGO ZODIAC SIGN
YOUR LOVE PLANETS

YOUR ROMANTIC SIDE   p. 696
▶ **VENUS IN VIRGO**
Born Aug. 23, 17:07 - Aug. 27, 11:42
▶ **VENUS IN LEO**
Born Aug. 27, 11:43 - Sept. 23, 14:41

YOUR SEX DRIVE   p. 722
▶ **MARS IN LEO**
Born Aug. 23, 17:07 - Sept. 23, 14:41

YOUR CELEBRITY TWINS   p. 760
Find out the astrological similarities you have with famous people.

YOUR COMPATIBILITY   p. 780
Compare planets to find out how compatible you are in a relationship.

YOUR RELATIONSHIP KARMA   p. 824
▶ **SATURN IN LIBRA**
Born Aug. 23, 17:07 - Aug. 24, 11:52
▶ **SATURN IN SCORPIO**
Born Aug. 24, 11:53 - Sept. 23, 14:41

MARTINA NAVRATILOVA
Czech Tennis Champion
Sun in Libra

1983 LIBRA
From September 23, 14:42 through October 23, 23:53

♎ The Flattering Flirt

Friendly, flirtatious Libra of 1983, you are in love with the idea of love. You're one of the best natural flirts in the zodiac because you know how to flatter members of the opposite sex and make them adore you. But as much as you love the chase, at some point you'll be ready for a committed partnership because deep down inside you hate to be lonely. For all the attention you receive in social situations, sometimes it isn't enough, and you want the love of one special person.

Your ideal relationship will be a melding of two hearts that beat as one. With your mate at your side, you'll design a very attractive home that will become your oasis, a stress-free place to regroup. It's likely the two of you will be active in community affairs, perhaps on the local arts council or participating in a literacy program. You seek balance in all things, and in your ideal partnership the two of you will be willing to talk things out and compromise where necessary so both of you can get what you need. Setting romantic scenes and surprising the other with gifts, you'll find ways

to keep the love fires burning.

To get your attention a would-be suitor must be classy, cheerful, and attractive. If there are artistic leanings, or a musical talent, so much the better. Inviting you to a poetry reading or special cooking class will make you curious enough to stick around and take a second look.

1983 male Libras gravitate to women who come with a readymade set of friends and acquaintances. She's popular in a number of circles and loves showing you off. You never have to worry about being embarrassed in public because she's quite the lady. Under that gorgeous exterior, though, is a sharply analytical mind that keeps you on your toes.

Lady Librans born in 1983 need a guy who has a bit of an edge. He might be a closet romantic, something only you see in private, and he might prefer not to constantly be with your friends. His unique way of looking at the world intrigues you, and you can't help but adore him for the protective love he wraps around you. He makes you feel safe and oh, so sexy.

LIBRA ZODIAC SIGN
YOUR LOVE PLANETS

YOUR ROMANTIC SIDE   p. 696
▶ **VENUS IN LEO**
Born Sept. 23, 14:42 - Oct. 05, 19:34
▶ **VENUS IN VIRGO**
Born Oct. 05, 19:35 - Oct. 23, 23:53

YOUR SEX DRIVE   p. 722
▶ **MARS IN LEO**
Born Sept. 23, 14:42 - Sept. 30, 0:11
▶ **MARS IN VIRGO**
Born Sept. 30, 0:12 - Oct. 23, 23:53

YOUR CELEBRITY TWINS   p. 760
Find out the astrological similarities you have with famous people.

YOUR COMPATIBILITY   p. 780
Compare planets to find out how compatible you are in a relationship.

YOUR RELATIONSHIP KARMA   p. 824
▶ **SATURN IN SCORPIO**
Born Sept. 23, 14:42 - Oct. 23, 23:53

537

DAVID BOWIE
English Singer
Venus in Sagittarius

538

1983 SCORPIO
From October 23, 23:54 through November 22, 21:17

The Secret Romantic

Many people might not believe this about you, Scorpio of 1983, and you might not want to admit it, but deep down inside you are a true romantic. That's not to say you wear your heart on your sleeve. Instead you keep your soft side hidden—until you find yourself in a loving relationship. The recipient of your affections will feel the full force of your attention. Rather than socialize in groups, you and your mate will find yourselves wanting to be alone with each other much of the time. You love to talk about life and death, and probe your lover's inner psyche, and the two of you could see many dawns after endless nights exploring each other's mind—and body.

You believe in karma—what goes around, comes around—and you and your mate won't turn down too many opportunities to help someone else. But you need to guard your energy output and like your home life to be quiet and restful, a place where the two of you can relax and recharge your batteries. And, you want to see the fruits of your labors around you in the form of material things.

To attract your attention a suitor needs to give off vibes that are calming and centered and on target. Your interest will be piqued by someone who appears to see through your attempts to flirt—you'll want to know more! The one who wants to keep your interest will never tell you all their personal secrets at once, letting them be discovered slowly over a lifetime.

A 1983 male Scorpion needs a woman who can't be tamed. She knows who she is and will resist any attempts to change her. Home is where she likes to be, and wants you at her side. She's wildly passionate about you, and welcomes your lovemaking with open arms— and throws in a few ideas of her own—leaving you little room for jealousy.

For 1983 female Scorpions a highly intelligent man with a good reputation will earn your loyalty. He's kind and genuinely aims to please. But he's no pushover. With matters of the heart, he won't be toyed with— no flirting with others allowed. You won't mind that, however, because he knows all the sexy tricks in the world to keep the passions hot.

1983 SAGITTARIUS
From November 22, 21:18 through December 22, 10:29

The Adoring Adventurer

A permanent long-term relationship might be the last thing on your mind, Sagittarius of 1983. You're just too busy having fun, the world at your door! But at some point The One will come along, and you'll be hooked. Adventure is your middle name and your partnership will be based on a mutual love of life and exploration. In your vision of the ideal situation, you and your mate are always on the go, hand in hand, seeking whatever is around the next corner. But you require a home base of some kind—nothing fancy—but a place to return to.

With the one who's captured your heart you can be quite sweet and sensitive. The two of you can sit staring into each other's eyes—until one of you cracks a joke and you both dissolve into laughter. Still, the idea of understanding your partner—as well as everyone else in the world—may lead you and your mate to study the psychic arts, and together you might discover things you wouldn't have been found on your own.

The one who catches your eye probably will

be in the middle of telling you an interesting factoid you didn't already know. The mental click you hear is the sound of your radar locking on—and you'll want to learn more. If the suitor is into travel, animals, astrology, current events, business, sports, or any of a hundred other topics, and then invites you for coffee, you might not surface again for days—or forever. The suitor who keeps your attention has an energy level, both mental and physical, to match yours.

A 1983 male Archer appreciates a female with a sparkle in her eye and a throaty laugh. She's half pal, half lover, and all woman. She can go into sexy vixen mode at the drop of a hat—or any other article of clothing—and has an imagination that even surpasses yours. Though she may have a wild streak, she also loves quiet times and prefers to spend them with you.

A female born in 1983 under the sign of Sagittarius likes a partner with opinions. He'll woo you with sweet words and challenge you with his worldly view. He's physically active, but not a fitness fanatic. He loves sports for the sheer joy of movement.

Goth – The Dark Side

Emerging in the late seventies as a rebellious backlash to the glammed-up glitz of disco, the Gothic movement's origins were British and rooted in punk. By 1983 a new subculture was born and the word Goth became synonymous with a funereal style and a morbid attitude.

Taking inspiration from early 19th century literature, the Goths' fascination for all things macabre and supernatural permeated every facet of their lives. Bram Stoker's *Dracula* and Mary Shelley's *Frankenstein* were the bibles of Gothic reading, and at the helm of the modern renaissance was Anne Rice. Updating the vampire genre, she brought sepulchral glamour to the "undead," reinventing them as twisted heroes and antiheroes in a world of tragic romanticism. Set against rich, ravishing backdrops and exploring themes such as the curse of immortality, Rice's books throb with carnal seduction and homoeroticism. Her work quickly raised her to the status of Queen of Gothic expressionism, a position from which she still reigns.

Unsurprisingly, Goth life only really began when the sun went down. Club interiors were transformed to mimic the dank, arched, gargoyle-strewn Gothic architecture of 12th century cathedrals and castles. Fashion followed fetish with vampires and witches as muses. Leather, lace, and velvet were used to create a bold, erotic look drenched in sullen sensuality. And the color was, of course, black. In a cross-dressing blurring of gender roles, boys and girls dressed from head-to-toe in all shades of ebony, with black makeup applied to eyes, lips, and nails, set against a corpse-like complexions of powdered white faces. Christian or pagan symbols were obligatory, with either crucifixes or Egyptian Ankhs as the must-have accessory. Although most Goths declared themselves atheist, religious overtones were an essential part of the Gothic obsession with the more sombre periods in man's past.

Among the Gods of Gothic music were Joy Division, Bauhaus, The Damned, and Sisters of Mercy, who fused poetic, lugubrious lyrics with an intense dark metal sound. The mood was mystical and apocalyptic, embracing all that was alternative, dark, and underground. The drink to enjoy the music to was a Snakebite and Black, a lethal half-and-half mix of beer and cider served with a dash of blackcurrant—added more for aesthetic reasons than to enhance taste.

One of the first films to capture the Gothic moment was *The Hunger*. Now a cult classic, it brought to celluloid the sexual undertones of vampirism that had always been hinted at but never before presented quite so overtly. In a stylish, visual feast of gothic gloom, the androgynous David Bowie played the part of a pale-faced vampire, finally faced with death after two hundred years. Catherine Deneuve was his lustful partner, a vampiress hungry for blood and sex, and Susan Sarandon, the innocent victim, was attacked in a steamy lesbian shower scene. The film was a bloodbath of killing, frenzied "feeding," and sex.

Morose yet arousing, sinister yet seductive, Goths ventured into the darkness in search of beauty and meaning in the barren landscape of death. Living at the fringes of acceptable behavior, they were often misunderstood and ridiculed, and even accused of Satanism and witchcraft. Nevertheless, Goth culture found a devoted following and flourished into an international movement. Masters of their worlds, Goths were never going to be slaves to the living.

539

Brad Pitt in *Interview With the Vampire*

"Death, depression, angst, and despair — welcome to the dark world of the Goths."

▶ READ ABOUT CATHERINE DENEUVE ON PAGE 505 ▶ READ ABOUT SUSAN SARANDON ON PAGE 579

1984

- ⊛ **AIDS**
- ⊛ **VANESSA WILLIAMS**
- ⊛ **BOY TOY**
- ⊛ **ROMANCING THE STONE**
- ⊛ **WOMEN COMING OF AGE**
- ⊛ **WHAT'S LOVE GOT TO DO WITH IT**
- ⊛ **PHIL COLLINS**

EVENTS

This was the year a stunned public received official confirmation that the AIDS virus had been identified.

In the US old nude photos of Vanessa Williams, the newly crowned Miss America, surfaced in *Penthouse* magazine, and she was forced to resign her title. The PG-13 movie rating was created to warn parents of sex, language, or violence in films. After a complaint by Wal-Mart, PolyGram Records changed the cover of the Scorpions' "Love At First Sting" album. The original featured a partially nude couple locked in an embrace, the man giving the woman a tattoo on her thigh.

In the UK the charity single "Do They Know It's Christmas," in aid of Ethiopian famine victims, became the highest selling single of all time.

POP CULTURE

Moviegoers were thrilled with the Michael Douglas/Kathleen Turner pairing in *Romancing the Stone*. The storyline gave us a romance novelist who lives out her fantasies when she travels to Colombia to rescue her sister. She meets up with a sexy adventurer who must choose between love and a priceless jewel. *Splash* was another kind of romance, pairing a young businessman with the girl of his dreams—who turns out to be a mermaid. Gene Wilder both starred in and directed *The Woman in Red*, about a happily married man who gets into trouble when, egged on by his

Hot Couple

unfaithful friends, he pursues a beautiful model.

At the bookstores people were reading "*...And Ladies of the Club*," which centered on the members of a book club and their struggles to understand themselves, each other, and the tumultuous world they live in. Jane Fonda, with Mignon McCarthy, released *Women Coming of Age*, an open and upbeat approach to suggestions on diet, exercise, sexuality, and self-image. In her autobiography, *The Life and Hard Times of Heidi Abromowitz*, we got an inside look at Joan Rivers.

Madonna made her entrance onto the pop scene with "Like a Virgin," and Tina Turner made her comeback with "What's Love Got to Do with It?" Other hits were Boy George's "Karma Chameleon," Kenny Loggins' "Footloose," and Phil Collins' "Against All Odds." Van Halen's "Jump" and Stevie Wonder's "I Just Called to Say I Love You" were also popular.

ANDREW LLOYD WEBBER & SARAH BRIGHTMAN

At a 1981 audition for the musical *Cats*, the show's creator, Andrew Lloyd Webber, could not help but notice a young lady with blue hair and the voice of an angel—Sarah Brightman. She won the small role of Jemima in the show and, most significantly, Lloyd Webber's heart. Although wed to others when they met, Brightman and Lloyd Webber divorced their spouses and married on March 22, 1984.

During the marriage Lloyd Webber created a series of starring roles for Brightman in *Phantom of the Opera*, *Requiem*, and *Aspects of Love*. The couple were divorced in 1990 but remain loving friends.

SEE ALSO
▶ BETTY GRABLE & HARRY JAMES *Page 204*
▶ REX HARRISON & KAY KENDALL *Page 318*

1984 CAPRICORN

From December 22, 1983 10:30 through January 20, 1984 21:04 (December 1984 Capricorns, see 1985 Capricorns)

♑ *The Refined Romantic*

Suave, sophisticated, and understated, you 1984 Capricorns appear older and wiser than your contemporaries. Your smooth, worldly attitude is extremely attractive, and it's likely that you have a sizable following of admirers. Because you're so self-contained, however, you may not be aware of how popular you really are. You're not interested in the casual dating scene, anyway. You want a serious relationship in which both partners come to understand each other intuitively. Unless you feel an instinctive pull toward a love interest, you're not likely to embark on a romance.

Beneath your cool façade pulses a smoldering sensuality. Sexually, you're a little reserved until you find a partner you can trust and respect. When you find your true love, you'll unleash an earthy sensuality that is nothing short of breathtaking. Outside of the bedroom, you place strong emphasis on friendships and appreciate a partner who does the same. Maintaining an intimate group of friends gives your romantic partnership the secure grounding you crave. You appreciate a sociable lover who supports and encourages your friendships.

Asking for your help is a surefire way to attract your attention. Creative scatterbrained types really turn you on. You love it when you're called upon to organize an admirer's life. Expressing admiration for your hard work and ambition is also a good means to win your heart. Too often your diligence is taken for granted, so you really appreciate it when a suitor recognizes and celebrates it. When it comes time to take your relationship to the physical stage, your admirer would be wise to make the first move. Slow, passionate caresses always light your fire.

A woman who is bright, humane, and friendly is the ideal partner for you male Goats who were born in 1984. Even though you can be quite conservative, you appreciate a lady who is open-minded and adventurous.

As a 1984 female Capricorn, you want a man who is motivated, hardworking, and tasteful. You're also attracted to observant, passionate guys. A partner who is focused on making you happy is your ideal.

KATARINA WITT
German Figure Skating Champion
Venus and Mars in Capricorn

541

1984 AQUARIUS

From January 20, 21:05 through February 19, 11:15

♒ *The Successful Sweetheart*

As a 1984 Aquarius, you are determined to achieve success in both your personal and professional lives. You want a relationship that can endure the glare of the spotlight, because you intend on spending most of your time there. A mate who enjoys supporting you from behind the scenes is best suited to you. It also helps if your partner enjoys leading an unconventional lifestyle—you often prefer to swim against the social tide. Ultimately, you want a partnership that affords you both personal freedom and emotional stability. A stifling, tempestuous union is not for you.

Sometimes you get so wrapped up in your work that you can actually forget about sex. A lover who puts you in touch with your physical needs can open exciting new worlds for you. Although you probably consider the brain to be the sexiest organ in the human body, you do enjoy it when your partner tries to find your other erogenous areas. As an extremely spiritual person, you need a partner who shares your deep belief that there is more to life than meets the eye. Performing charitable works with your mate is a good way to strengthen your bonds of devotion.

A serene, sedate admirer who appreciates your originality is sure to grab your interest. Because you're so restless, you gravitate toward potential partners who make you feel calm and reassured. If there's anything you can't stand, it's a conventional thinker. You're extremely turned on by folks who look to the future for inspiration. A suitor planning to make a romantic overture toward you should remember that you enjoy the element of surprise. An unexpected kiss is sure to get an enthusiastic response from you.

If you're a male Water-Bearer born in 1984, you want a woman who is kind-hearted, idealistic, and athletic. You're also attracted to ladies who are imaginative but practical. A down-to-earth mate is your ideal.

Men who are tenacious, honorable, and passionate never fail to excite you 1984 female Aquarians. You want a guy who is determined to get ahead without stepping on other people. A principled partner brings out the best in you.

MARGUERITE DURAS
French Writer
Sun and Venus in Aries

542

1984 PISCES
From February 19, 11:16 through March 20, 10:23

The Philosophical Flirt

Although you 1984 Pisceans are reflective and spiritual, you're also quite fun-loving, too. This is especially true with regard to romance. Just because you're a deep thinker doesn't mean you have no interest in love. In fact, you can be one of the most flirtatious characters around. You want to know what makes people tick and you occasionally use flattering compliments to gain insight into potential love interests. You're also extremely social and often embark on romances with friends. Fortunately, you're an extremely considerate mate and usually manage to maintain friendships with former sweethearts. You want a joyous relationship.

You have very high standards when it comes to making love. It's highly unlikely that you'd have sex with someone for sheer fun. If you're going to have a physical relationship with somebody, it's because you respect and love your partner. There's a good chance you take a great interest in social causes, and appreciate a partner who shares your humanitarian instincts. You love mixing with big crowds of people, so it helps if your mate is as gregarious as you are. Ultimately, however, you want a lover who strives to make the world a better place.

A suitor with a curious mind is sure to win your approval. You're really turned on by people who are perpetual students of life. Creative types also attract you, and it's quite likely your life partner will have considerable talent in one of the arts. Many of your friends would be surprised to learn that you are rather aggressive in romance and enjoy making the first move. Your admirer should know that you are extremely receptive to experimental sexual techniques.

If you're a male Fish born in 1984, you want a woman who is independent but tender-hearted. You're also drawn to romantic, intuitive ladies. A partner who devotes her life to humanitarian causes could be your ideal.

As a 1984 female Pisces, you enjoy a man who is passionate, committed, and uncompromising. You don't have the slightest interest in wishy-washy types. A mate who treats life as a crusade is a perfect match for you.

1984 ARIES
From March 20, 10:24 through April 19, 21:37

The Sexy Suitor

You 1984 Rams are an incredibly sexy bunch, and you know it! Your gaze has an intensity that is positively exhilarating, as your legions of admirers can attest. And although you could probably have your pick of suitors, you prefer to settle down with one special person. You want an intimate relationship that is based on passion, devotion, and above all, trust. Fortunately, you're probably very intuitive, and have good instincts when it comes to selecting a romantic partner. An admirer who is in need of emotional healing speaks to your heart, since you're an extremely compassionate person. For you love is the remedy.

Making love is practically a religion to you. Your physical and spiritual needs are closely intertwined. Meaningless sex has no interest for you. You need a lover who treats your union as sacred. Because you have natural leadership abilities, it helps if your mate is comfortable with yielding the spotlight to you. Even though you enjoy being the center of attention, there is little chance that your lover will feel jealous of your adoring public.

That's because you're such an affectionate, attentive partner.

A well-traveled suitor wins your admiration and respect. You appreciate an adventurer who is eager to explore unfamiliar cultures and exotic lands. Expressing a passion for a particular hobby also excites you. It would be difficult for you to relate to an admirer who didn't feel strongly about at least one subject. When you're drawn to a love interest, there is nothing to stop you from making the first move. Your admirer would be wise to remember that you have been blessed with incredible stamina and might enjoy making love for hours.

Women who are fragile, sensitive, and pretty appeal to you 1984 male Rams. You also enjoy feisty, athletic ladies. Ultimately, you seek a partner who wants to merge her soul with yours. Aloof types leave you cold.

If you're a female Aries who was born in 1984, you want a man who is mysterious, self-controlled, and devastatingly sexy. A partner who makes you feel like a gorgeous heroine in a dark romance is your ideal.

1984 TAURUS
From April 19, 21:38 through May 20, 20:57

The Passionate Partner

Caring, considerate, and compassionate, you 1984 Bulls make wonderful romantic partners. Sharing comes naturally to you and you enjoy performing kind little services for your mate. You want a relationship that is stable but exciting. A down-to-earth lover with a strong romantic streak is your idea. If you avoid the temptation to rely too heavily on your partner, there is an excellent chance that you will have a long and prosperous marriage. Thankfully, you have good negotiating skills and can find a solution to virtually any partnership problem. You do especially well with a mate who is imaginative, insightful, and intellectually curious.

Sexually, you are quite adventurous, and enjoy playing out your fantasies. A lover who is playful and spontaneous gives you a thrill. At times you may go through periods of abstinence, simply because you're so focused on your thoughts. Teaming up with a mate who reminds you of your physical needs helps you to live a more balanced lifestyle. One of the best ways to achieve intimacy with your partner is to take a class together. Studying the same subject will give your relationship an intellectual flavor that can be most rewarding.

An admirer who is gentle, sympathetic, and friendly is sure to catch your eye. Such a person is a perfect foil for your witty banter. Inviting you to a sporting match or a debate is a good idea because you probably enjoy watching heated competitions. You also appreciate a suitor who dresses well and has personal finesse. Although you prefer to be the aggressor in love, your admirer would be wise to encourage you with flirtatious remarks. It's virtually impossible for you to resist a sexy challenge.

If you're a male Taurus born in 1984, you want a woman who is strong, motivated, and outspoken. You're also attracted to earthy, sensual types. A smart, giving mate who makes you laugh is your ideal.

Quietly ambitious, perceptive men really excite you 1984 female Bulls. Although you dislike overtly aggressive men, you do admire an enterprising guy who pursues what he wants with dogged persistence.

TAURUS ZODIAC SIGN
YOUR LOVE PLANETS

YOUR ROMANTIC SIDE — p. 696
► VENUS IN ARIES
Born Apr. 19, 21:38 - May 02, 4:52
► VENUS IN TAURUS
Born May 02, 4:53 - May 20, 20:57

YOUR SEX DRIVE — p. 722
► MARS IN SCORPIO
Born Apr. 19, 21:38 - May 20, 20:57

YOUR CELEBRITY TWINS — p. 760
Find out the astrological similarities you have with famous people.

YOUR COMPATIBILITY — p. 780
Compare planets to find out how compatible you are in a relationship.

YOUR RELATIONSHIP KARMA — p. 824
► SATURN IN SCORPIO
Born Apr. 19, 21:38 - May 20, 20:57

RUTGER HAUER
Dutch Actor
Mars in Gemini

1984 GEMINI
From May 20, 20:58 through June 21, 5:01

The Loving Diplomat

As a 1984 Gemini, you are always looking for ways to form harmonious relationships. This is especially true with regard to romance. A tempestuous union would not suit you at all. You prefer a mate who is as kind, thoughtful, and cooperative as you are. That doesn't mean you can't have the occasional argument. In fact, you enjoy a spirited debate. But you have no intention of picking fights with your partner when, you could be making love instead. You really dislike unnecessary confrontations.

For you sex is never better than when it's with someone you love and respect. It may be hard for you to conceive of having a physical encounter with a casual acquaintance. A partner who shares your idealistic view about sex brings out the best in you. You have a serious attitude toward work and service, and appreciate a partner who is deeply involved in a charitable cause. Teaming up with somebody who doesn't have a social conscience would not offer you much fulfillment. Although you're very compassionate, you're also fun-loving and enjoy a mischief-making mate.

Anyone who is interested in you should be aware that you can fall in love at the drop of a hat, and are extremely spontaneous in your affections. Demonstrating an optimistic attitude toward life is a surefire way to win your affection. You can't help feel a kinship with someone who shares your joyous outlook. A suitor with unconventional beliefs is also intriguing—you are drawn to folks who march to the beat of a different drummer. An unpredictable character like you is bound to make the first move in a relationship. Your partner should know that you are intensely sensual and passionate in the bedroom.

Women who are creative, easy-going, and determined are irresistible to you 1984 male Geminis. You're also drawn to energetic, witty ladies. You want a partner who appreciates your relaxed approach to life.

As a female Gemini born in 1984, you enjoy a man who is romantic but practical. You can't stand flighty guys who say one thing and then do another. A reliable partner who makes you feel loved would be your ideal.

GEMINI ZODIAC SIGN
YOUR LOVE PLANETS

YOUR ROMANTIC SIDE — p. 696
► VENUS IN TAURUS
Born May 20, 20:58 - May 26, 14:39
► VENUS IN GEMINI
Born May 26, 14:40 - June 20, 0:47
► VENUS IN CANCER
Born June 20, 0:48 - June 21, 5:01

YOUR SEX DRIVE — p. 722
► MARS IN SCORPIO
Born May 20, 20:58 - June 21, 5:01

YOUR CELEBRITY TWINS — p. 760
Find out the astrological similarities you have with famous people.

YOUR COMPATIBILITY — p. 780
Compare planets to find out how compatible you are in a relationship.

YOUR RELATIONSHIP KARMA — p. 824
► SATURN IN SCORPIO
Born May 20, 20:58 - June 21, 5:01

543

BRUCE SPRINGSTEEN
American Singer
Mars in Leo

1984 CANCER
From June 21, 5:02 through July 22, 15:57

The Diligent Admirer

You 1984 Crabs are never sexier than when you are hard at work. There is something so appealing about your commitment to doing a good job. Because you are so absorbed in your duties, you may not realize the full extent of your allure. However, if you take the time to look around, you'll probably see several admirers just begging for your attention. When you do decide to embark on a relationship, it will be because you care for your partner with all of your heart. Casual relationships are not your style.

Your responsibilities could make it difficult for you to loosen up in the bedroom. A lover who makes you lose your inhibitions adds exciting new dimensions to your life. As you get older, it will be easier to embrace your sexual self. You deeply desire a harmonious household, and seek a spouse who has a talent for creating a relaxing atmosphere. At times you can be very set in your domestic routines and would consequently benefit from a mate who encourages you to be more spontaneous. A partnership in which you provide security while your mate generates passion is ideal for you.

An organized, down-to-earth admirer has a good chance of catching your eye. Such a person makes you feel safe and secure—which is tremendously comforting. Entertaining storytellers also win a special place in your heart because you love to laugh. You tend to be a little shy about making the first move toward a relationship. Any admirer of yours would be wise to take a tender, comforting approach toward you. It's easier for you to proceed with a physical relationship when you know where you stand with your partner. Urgent caresses usually put you in the mood for love.

If you're a male Cancer born in 1984, you want a lady who is sociable, sensitive, and insightful. Women who are generous, magnetic, and sensual also excite you. You need a partner who reminds you of your sex appeal.

As a 1984 female Crab, you appreciate a man who is passionate, expressive, and generous. You can't abide stingy guys. A mate who makes you feel safe and protected enough to take risks is your ideal match.

1984 LEO
From July 22, 15:58 through August 22, 22:59

The Intuitive Lover

As a 1984 Leo, you are wise to trust your romantic instincts. That's because you have a sixth sense about what your partner wants and needs to be happy. You probably have no problem expressing your deepest emotions, and enjoy paying tribute to your partner with songs, poems, and letters. It's easy for you to fall in and out of love, but the partner who wins your heart permanently should be generous, friendly, and adventurous. Cautious types tend to dampen your enthusiasm. As far as you're concerned, a relationship should encourage both partners to take risks and live life to the fullest.

When it comes to making love, you are ardent but tender. For you sex is the ultimate blend of physical and spiritual pleasure. You appreciate a warm, affectionate lover with few sexual hang-ups. As somebody with a strong intellectual curiosity, you do best with a mate who is similarly eager to learn as much as possible. You wouldn't last long with a partner who is good-looking but empty-headed. At times you may be prone to the blues and would benefit from a cheerful partner who encourages you to adopt a more optimistic outlook.

A frank, open admirer has a good chance of catching your eye. You dislike folks who play games, especially when it comes to romance. Athletic, vivacious types also appeal to you. Anybody who invites you camping or hiking is sure to win your affection. You also enjoy sociable suitors who have friends from all walks of life. Your admirer should wait for you to make the first move because you have a knack for picking just the right moment for a passionate encounter. Stroking your hair is sure to make you purr with delight.

Women who are warm, enthusiastic, and magnetic appeal greatly to you 1984 male Lions. You also appreciate shy, helpful, and kind-hearted ladies. You need a partner who is eager to bask in the warm rays of your love.

As a 1984 female Lion, you enjoy a deeply perceptive, imaginative man. A guy who can read your mind by just looking into your eyes gives you a thrill. Your ideal match is a mate who strives to know you inside and out.

1984 VIRGO  *From August 22, 23:00 through September 22, 20:32*

♍ *The Adoring Homebody*

Generous and nurturing, you 1984 Virgos enjoy looking after those you love. You want a relationship that satisfies your need to be needed. A partner who gives you confidence in exchange for tenderness would be your ideal match. Domestic life is very important to you and you appreciate a mate who prefers spending a quiet evening at home to attending a big rollicking party. Still, it wouldn't hurt for you to team up with a sweetheart who encourages you to come out of your shell every once in a while. Having your beloved by your side makes it easier for you to meet people and socialize.

You have plenty of sexual curiosity, and are always looking for new ways to excite your partner. A lover who is willing to experiment in the bedroom brings out the best in you. Although you may appear to be cool and detached in public, you're actually quite sensual and earthy in private. You wouldn't want a partnership that centers only on intellectual pursuits. A mate who enjoys sensual pleasures such as good food, beautiful music, and gorgeous scenery helps to enhance your appreciation of life.

Expressing an interest in nature is a good way to catch your eye. You probably love the great outdoors and respect an admirer who shares this passion. A generous, open-minded suitor also has a good chance of winning your heart. You can't abide self-interested folks who never think about anybody else's welfare. When it comes to making the first move, you're wonderfully romantic, but a bit shy. A suitor who moves to kiss you may be pleasantly surprised by your enthusiastic response. Nothing thrills you more than making love in the shower.

As a male Virgo born in 1984, you want a woman who is smart, self-motivated, and witty. You're also drawn to females who are sentimental, affectionate, and stylish. A partner who boosts your self-confidence is best suited to you.

Men who are outgoing, emotional, and friendly excite you 1984 female Virgos. You love a guy who isn't afraid to wear his heart on his sleeve. An optimistic mate who keeps you in a positive mindset is your perfect match.

VIRGO ZODIAC SIGN
YOUR LOVE PLANETS

YOUR ROMANTIC SIDE — p. 696
▶ **VENUS IN VIRGO**
Born Aug. 22, 23:00 - Sept. 01, 5:06
▶ **VENUS IN LIBRA**
Born Sept. 01, 5:07 - Sept. 22, 20:32

YOUR SEX DRIVE — p. 722
▶ **MARS IN SAGITTARIUS**
Born Aug. 22, 23:00 - Sept. 22, 20:32

YOUR CELEBRITY TWINS — p. 760
Find out the astrological similarities you have with famous people.

YOUR COMPATIBILITY — p. 780
Compare planets to find out how compatible you are in a relationship.

YOUR RELATIONSHIP KARMA — p. 824
▶ **SATURN IN SCORPIO**
Born Aug. 22, 23:00 - Sept. 22, 20:32

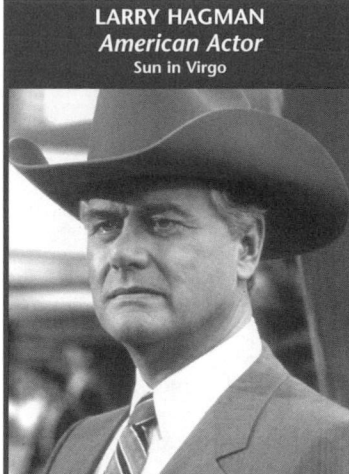

LARRY HAGMAN
American Actor
Sun in Virgo

545

1984 LIBRA  *From September 22, 20:33 through October 23, 5:45*

♎ *The Smooth Talker*

You 1984 Librans are a bunch of silver-tongued devils! You know just what to say to make a love interest blush with pleasure. Because you're so adept at the art of flirting, it can be difficult for you to settle down. There are so many attractive fish in the sea that it's hard to pick just one. Your ideal partner is smart, sexy, and somewhat elusive. Nothing excites you more than playing hard-to-get. A partnership that always keeps you slightly off balance is your ideal. As far as you're concerned, romance is more about excitement than stability!

Although you enjoy sex, you don't take it too seriously. For you making love is a means to have fun. A lover who shares this lighthearted attitude is best suited to you. Even if you're not overly concerned about sexual fidelity in a relationship, it is important for you to be honest with your partner. A mate who is open-minded and nonjudgmental brings out the best in you. You're also comfortable in a relationship that has a creative dimension to it. Pairing up with an artistic mate gives you a great deal of inspiration.

Expressing interest in music is an excellent way to get your attention because this is probably one of your greatest passions in life. A good conversationalist is also bound to impress you. Shy, retiring types make you feel awkward and uncomfortable. Your suitor would be wise to make a strategic withdrawal after you've gone on one or two dates. Nothing whets your appetite for romance like an elusive admirer! When it comes time to take your relationship to the physical level, your partner should make the first move. You especially enjoy having your back stroked.

If you're a male Libran born in 1984, you appreciate a woman who is sultry, seductive, and mysterious. You're also turned on by witty, intellectual types. A mate who makes you work for her affections is your perfect match.

As a 1984 female Libran, you want a man who is athletic but brainy. Tough but tender guys also excite you. Ultimately, you want a well-rounded partner who appeals to the many facets of your own complex personality.

LIBRA ZODIAC SIGN
YOUR LOVE PLANETS

YOUR ROMANTIC SIDE — p. 696
▶ **VENUS IN LIBRA**
Born Sept. 22, 20:33 - Sept. 25, 16:04
▶ **VENUS IN SCORPIO**
Born Sept. 25, 16:05 - Oct. 20, 5:44
▶ **VENUS IN SAGITTARIUS**
Born Oct. 20, 5:45 - Oct. 23, 5:45

YOUR SEX DRIVE — p. 722
▶ **MARS IN SAGITTARIUS**
Born Sept. 22, 20:33 - Oct. 05, 6:01
▶ **MARS IN CAPRICORN**
Born Oct. 05, 6:02 - Oct. 23, 5:45

YOUR CELEBRITY TWINS — p. 760
Find out the astrological similarities you have with famous people.

YOUR COMPATIBILITY — p. 780
Compare planets to find out how compatible you are in a relationship.

YOUR RELATIONSHIP KARMA — p. 824
▶ **SATURN IN SCORPIO**
Born Sept. 22, 20:33 - Oct. 23, 5:45

TINA TURNER
American Singer
Sun and Venus in Sagittarius

1984 SCORPIO
From October 23, 5:46 through November 22, 3:10

♏ ## The Brooding Romantic

As a 1984 Scorpion, you don't take romance lightly. You want a relationship that is profound, meaningful, and spiritual. There is no such thing as a casual date for you. You need a partner who wants to build a future together. Serious but sexy, you probably attract admirers wherever you go. Fortunately, you have great instincts when it comes to romance. When you find somebody who shares your values and interests, you waste no time in forging a relationship. You're too smart to let a promising love interest slip through your fingers.

Sexually, you can be extremely intense. You think nothing of making love for hours on end. Pairing with a lusty partner who has plenty of stamina is a wise idea. Casual sex doesn't interest you in the slightest. When you merge bodies with your lover, you are also blending souls. A partner who has a practical approach to money can counterbalance your more whimsical attitude. Although you enjoy the finer things in life, you need a mate who is able to conserve your resources for rainy days. You're also quite spiritual and value a spouse who prizes inner peace over material wealth.

Demonstrating knowledge of history is an excellent way to win your heart. You feel a kinship with an admirer who looks back at the past to make sense of the present. Any suitor who is able to make you laugh is also a good romantic candidate because you can take things too seriously at times. Your love interest should trust you to make the first move toward a physical relationship. It's important to remember that you enjoy masterful lovers who make you quake with desire. The more passionate your partner is in the bedroom, the better.

Women who are noble, principled, and confident give you 1984 male Scorpions a thrill. You're also drawn to shrewd, witty, and resourceful ladies. You need a partner who worships and adores you in equal amounts.

As a 1984 female Scorpio, you want a man who looks cool but has a fiery temperament. You're also attracted to eccentric guys with tender hearts. A mate who is a blend of opposites could win your lifelong devotion.

1984 SAGITTARIUS
From November 22, 3:11 through December 21, 16:22

⚹ ## The Sweet Visionary

Dreamy, idealistic, and generous, you 1984 Sagittarians are a romantic bunch. You always see the good sides of people, especially your loved ones. A partnership that is based on mutual adoration is your idea of heaven. You have no interest in changing your lover. When you embark on a relationship, it is with total acceptance of your partner's entire being. If that means overlooking character flaws, so be it. You greatly benefit from a compassionate but practical mate who can bring you back down to earth from time to time.

When it comes to sex, you believe that variety is the spice of life. You are extremely creative in the bedroom, and enjoy a partner who is as open-minded as you are. At times, however, you can get so wrapped up in your sexual fantasies that you forget to act on them. Therefore, it's wise to pair with a lover who encourages you to translate your thoughts into actions. Nagging fears have a way of undermining your confidence, so it's also important that your beloved encourages you to discuss what's on your mind. The more open the channels of communication are between you, the better your relationship will flourish.

A smart, curious suitor is sure to get your attention. You probably feel a strong bond with anyone who has a thirst for knowledge. You're also attracted to people who have a strong understanding of current events. Although you're spontaneous in your social life, you can be a little reserved when it comes to sex. Therefore, it's wise for your admirer to make the first move. A good way to loosen you up is to tell a joke before planting a passionate kiss on your lips.

If you're a male Archer born in 1984, you want a woman who is deeply romantic, traditional, and practical. You're also attracted to independent, intelligent females. A mate who celebrates your idealism brings out the best you have to offer.

Men who are open-minded, unconventional, and progressive excite you 1984 female Sagittarians. You can't bear stuffy guys with set ideas about how a woman should act. You far prefer a partner who enjoys every aspect of your unique personality

546

'80s

Don Johnson – The Hip Don Juan

From a very young age, Don Johnson knew he had a promising future with women. By the time he was sixteen, he was living with a twenty-five-year-old woman and presumably learning the finer techniques of advanced lovemaking. Along the way to becoming one of filmdom's most infamous Don Juans, he starred in some classic B movies and became an international celebrity when he landed the role of Sonny Crockett, the hip, pastel-clad detective in TV's *Miami Vice*.

Don Johnson's first feature film in 1970, *The Magic Garden of Stanley Sweetheart*, made him a cult star, and he used every ounce of his new-found celebrity status to hit the Hollywood party scene and bed pretty girls. The age of free love brought Johnson two marriages (both ended after a few months), romances with rock stars, actresses, and at least one beauty queen—and a few more movies. In 1973 Johnson was filming with Tippi Hedren, who had starred in Alfred Hitchcock's *The Birds*, when he first met her teenage daughter Melanie Griffith.

In 1976 Johnson proposed to Griffith on her 18th birthday, and the two flew to Las Vegas for a quickie ceremony. The marriage was meant to save their deteriorating affair, which had been going on for three years. In a later interview, Johnson admitted that he had slept with a former beauty pageant winner the night before his wedding. It wasn't a surprise when the marriage failed in a short time. Then, when Johnson was dating singer Tanya Tucker, he met actress Patti D'Arbanville and began a serious four-year relationship with her.

That affair produced a child, which in turn inspired Johnson to join Alcoholics

Don Johnson and Philip Michael Thomas in *Miami Vice*

Anonymous. Johnson had always been a hard drinker. He told a reported that before he went on the wagon a typical day's intake included "beer, a few martinis, several bottles of wine, and some good Napoleon brandy after dinner." Cleaning up his act also prepared him for the audition for *Miami Vice*, which became an instant hit. Johnson's style became the rage for male fashion: three-day stubble, white trousers, and pastel T-shirts.

Naturally, Johnson found himself much in demand from the opposite sex. He began an affair with Barbra Streisand, and the two recorded the romantic duet "Till I loved You." During this affair Johnson rekindled his relationship with Melanie Griffith, and in 1989 they remarried. Hollywood's Cutest Couple decided to leave Southern California to avoid the temptations of cocaine and alcohol and

relocated to Aspen, Colorado. Don Johnson became a father again, and Melanie was telling reporters she felt like a princess.

Fast forward to 2003. Johnson had fallen off the wagon, divorced Griffith in 1996, and made some bad movies. His career made another comeback with the hit TV show *Nash Bridges*, a San Francisco clone of *Miami Vice*. His fifth marriage to socialite Kelley Phleger in 1998 produced another child, and to date he has remained clean. However, difficulties returned when Johnson was pulled over at the Swiss-German border for a routine search and was found with $8 billion in cash. News media around the world reported it as a money laundering operation, but no charges were filed. Johnson denied it, saying "I am not going to sit idly back and be slandered and accused of things which are beneath my character."

► READ ABOUT MELANIE GRIFFITH ON PAGE 638

1985

- ⍟ CHRISTIE BRINKLEY
- ⍟ ROCK HUDSON
- ⍟ ROBERT REDFORD AND MERYL STREEP
- ⍟ DANIELLE STEEL
- ⍟ WE ARE THE WORLD
- ⍟ THE POWER OF LOVE

Hot Couple

548

EVENTS

1985 was the year for censorship, especially in the music arena. In the US the Recording Industry Association of America (RIAA) struck a deal with the National PTA and the PMRC (Parents Music Resource Center) to create a parental warning sticker to be placed on albums containing graphic depictions of sex and/or violence. But it was not all bad for musicians. Piano Man Billy Joel married his "Uptown Girl," model Christie Brinkley.

Live Aid, a concert featuring the biggest names in music including Queen and Madonna, was broadcast worldwide. The event raised millions for Ethiopian famine victims.

Catholic associations in France joined the censorship wagon when they banned the film *Hail Mary*, the modern story of Mary, a mechanic's daughter pregnant by Joseph, a taxi driver, despite a platonic relationship.

Actor Rock Hudson became the first major public figure to die from AIDS.

POP CULTURE

Out of Africa, starring Robert Redford and Meryl Streep, drew crowds with its poignant story and spectacular photography. *The Purple Rose of Cairo* was about a battered woman who escapes through movies—but the line between fantasy and reality gets blurred. In *The Jewel of the Nile* romance novelist Joan Wilder is back in the world of murder, foreign intrigue...and love. *Witness* starred Harrison Ford, a Philadelphia cop

whose life is altered while trying to help an Amish woman and her son who witnessed a murder.

The eighties were dominated by mainstream romance authors such as Sidney Sheldon (*If Tomorrow Comes*), Danielle Steel (*Secrets and Family Album*), and Jackie Collins (*Lucky*). Elvis Presley's ex-wife released her autobiography, *Elvis and Me*, a revealing story of the relationship between Elvis and his starstruck bride, Priscilla. Big in France was *The Wedding (Les Noces Barbares)*, a violent and painful tale of hope and revenge within a dysfunctional French family.

Although attempts were made to ban music lyrics, some musicians banded together for charitable purposes. "We Are the World" resulted from a grouping of dozens of famous singers calling themselves USA for Africa. Other recording artists were singing about love. Foreigner sang "I Want to Know What Love Is," and Huey Lewis and the News sang about "The Power of Love."

MADONNA & SEAN PENN

Conditions did not augur well for the wedding of Hollywood bad boy Sean Penn and "Material Girl" Madonna Ciccone, on August 16, 1985. In response to paparazzi hovering in helicopters, Penn scrawled curse words on a beach near the wedding site. The couple's 1986 movie, *Shanghai Surprise*, turned out to be a box office flop. Jailed for 30 days in 1987 for punching a photographer, Penn had even bigger problems with Madonna's skyrocketing music career, including her world tour that year. The couple divorced in 1989. Penn married Robin Wright in 1996, and Madonna married director Guy Ritchie in 2000.

SEE ALSO

▶ MADONNA *Page 555*
▶ TOM CRUISE & NICOLE KIDMAN *Page 590*

1985 CAPRICORN

From December 21, 1984 16:23 through January 20, 1985 2:57
(December 1985 Capricorns, see 1986 Capricorn)

♑ The Intense Realist

You 1985 Capricorns meet potential romantic encounters with serious intensity. You may be impulsive in speech and manner, but when love looms, you put your game face on. As you strategize your life and career, you may have an ideal mate in mind. But, while waiting for your future dream companion, you won't deny yourself the pleasures of today's company. You may enjoy close family ties, but are eager to make your mark in the world before starting your own. Why settle down, when there are so many mountains yet to climb?

Some may initially underestimate how much you care, since you mask your feelings so well. If you appear aloof or restrained, inwardly, you have an ocean of depth waiting to be navigated. Your hidden passions can be stirred into a powerful hurricane of emotion with the right partner. Moody jealousy may emerge if you are unsure of your partner's devotion. A little reassurance goes a long way with you, and the loving mate understands your need for emotional security.

The fastest way to your heart is through laughter—a well told joke lifts you out of any dark mood, and being around high-spirited people brings out your dry humor and congenial nature. Appealing to your physical sensual nature and draws you out of your shell. A scrumptious dinner punctuated by engaging conversation makes for a memorable evening out. Once triggered, your passions are aggressively playful, and are best contained within a bond of love and trust.

As a 1985 male Capricorn, you attract sophisticated women with a reserve of inner strength. Women with classic style, such as tailored suits or long skirts, catch your eye. The woman who offers unsolicited admiration fills an unspoken need. Your public shyness diminishes with a spontaneous woman who has social ease.

For you 1985 female Goats, only a rugged individualist will do. You like to be the boss, but a strong-willed man can provide a challenging friction. A serious man who respects your ambitious nature, while offering true devotion, has the edge. If he comes bearing flowers or chocolates, he finds a tender, receptive heart.

CAPRICORN ZODIAC SIGN
YOUR LOVE PLANETS

YOUR ROMANTIC SIDE   p. 696
▶ VENUS IN AQUARIUS
Born Dec. 21, 1984 16:23 - Jan. 04, 1985 6:22
▶ VENUS IN PISCES
Born Jan. 04, 6:23 - Jan. 20, 2:57

YOUR SEX DRIVE   p. 722
▶ MARS IN AQUARIUS
Born Dec. 21, 1984 16:23 - Dec. 25, 1984 6:37
▶ MARS IN PISCES
Born Dec. 25, 1984 6:38 - Jan. 20, 1985 2:57

YOUR CELEBRITY TWINS   p. 760
Find out the astrological similarities you have with famous people.

YOUR COMPATIBILITY   p. 780
Compare planets to find out how compatible you are in a relationship.

YOUR RELATIONSHIP KARMA   p. 824
▶ SATURN IN SCORPIO
Born Dec. 21, 1984 16:23 - Jan. 20, 1985 2:57

BOB GELDOF
Irish Live Aid Organizer
Sun in Capricorn

549

1985 AQUARIUS

From January 20, 2:58 through February 18, 17:06

♒ The Cool Observer

If you are an Aquarius born in 1985, you delight in having many unusual friends and admirers. Your endless fascination with human behavior makes you an avid people-watcher. Sitting in a café with a good book allows you to glance up occasionally and watch the parade of humanity. Others are drawn to your easygoing, affable persona—you crackle with wit and levity. With interest in everyone you meet, you exude an intriguing air of detached friendliness. Your romances usually brew from your established associations.

When friends become something more, it generally has the feel of a happy accident. You can sometimes guard your intense feelings under a mask of aloofness. Once bewitched by a special someone, your true depths are revealed. You show your sentimental streak in the small, thoughtful gifts you give to your beloved. In a romantic link, you can be surprisingly emotional during intimate moments. Your independent spirit attracts light, though perhaps mostly short relationships. Yet, your original bonds of friendship never go cold.

The person trying to catch your eye should try a little sophistication and glamour. You are drawn to suitors with refined tastes, but who still manage to stand out in a crowd. Eclectic people with unusual interests spark your interest— tattoos and other adornments may strike your fancy. Moody or wet blanket types cause you to run for cover—you prefer to keep it light. A highly intelligent mate is as verbal in social situations as you are.

For you 1985 male Aquarians, the right romantic partner is also a loyal friend. A woman who stimulates your mind with new ideas stays ahead of the game. If she makes you laugh, she has the edge. Your natural curiosity may lead you to experimentation—an uninhibited woman can learn happily alongside you.

As a 1985 female Aquarius, your unpredictable nature demands a mate who can go with the flow. You prize men who are spontaneous, quick-witted, and simply fun to be with. Men who don't try to fence you in are trusted companions. You thrive with a free-thinking man with a strong sensual appetite.

AQUARIUS ZODIAC SIGN
YOUR LOVE PLANETS

YOUR ROMANTIC SIDE   p. 696
▶ VENUS IN PISCES
Born Jan. 20, 2:58 - Feb. 02, 8:28
▶ VENUS IN ARIES
Born Feb. 02, 8:29 - Feb. 18, 17:06

YOUR SEX DRIVE   p. 722
▶ MARS IN PISCES
Born Jan. 20, 2:58 - Feb. 02, 17:18
▶ MARS IN ARIES
Born Feb. 02, 17:19 - Feb. 18, 17:06

YOUR CELEBRITY TWINS   p. 760
Find out the astrological similarities you have with famous people.

YOUR COMPATIBILITY   p. 780
Compare planets to find out how compatible you are in a relationship.

YOUR RELATIONSHIP KARMA   p. 824
▶ SATURN IN SCORPIO
Born Jan. 20, 2:58 - Feb. 18, 17:06

MIRANDA RICHARDSON
English Actress
Sun in Pisces

1985 PISCES
From February 18, 17:07 through March 20, 16:13

The Fiery Intuitive

As a 1985 Pisces, your appearance may be sweet and gentle, but when you see what you want, you boldly go for it. Your impulsive romantic nature may cause you to leap before you look, more than a few times. The thrill of the chase, and the first glow of a promising love, make you come alive. You have a generous, expansive approach to romance that creates a magical feeling of connection. The sting of heartbreak may make you more discerning over time—you deserve a mate who returns your affections with equal enthusiasm.

If you are bold and assertive in love, you also have a shy, sensitive private nature. You long to draw your beloved close and create an atmosphere of warmth and trust. Your lush imagination gives you a great advantage in the dating scene—you may be reserved, but you're never boring. You're likely know all the hot spots around town, and are always primed for a lively party. However, the ideal relationship includes nights at home, as well, perhaps cuddling while watching classic movies.

To win your affection, a suitor should initially play a little hard to get because you enjoy being the initiator in a drawn out game of seduction. Dinners out allow you to share the sensual pleasures of eating with good company. You also warm to a mate who surprises you with trinkets—a sentimental gift appeals to your romantic heart. The one who cherishes you understands your need to take things slow—you are modest and a bit old-fashioned when it comes to romantic encounters.

For the 1985 male Pisces, only an uninhibited, theatrical woman will do. A fashion chameleon with many sides to her nature, she will provide you with much entertainment. You desire a woman full of mysteries to be revealed over time, the femme fatale who always keeps you guessing.

If you are a female Pisces born in 1985, you want to be swept away by a dazzling Prince. Strong, confident men envelop you in a protective atmosphere, and mentally curious guys keep you entertained. Demanding males may drain your emotional well, however—you thrive with the right mix of solitude and social activities.

1985 ARIES
From March 20, 16:14 through April 20, 3:25

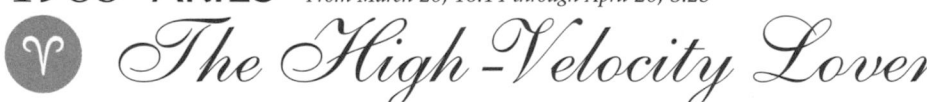

The High-Velocity Lover

As a 1985 Aries, you move swiftly and come alive in a big group of energetic and courageous companions. You were born with star quality and a smoldering intensity that often makes you the trendsetter among your peers. To keep things interesting, you seek a talented ensemble of supporting players of both sexes around you. You are frank and open in sexual matters, and are energized when others share that quality. When romance enters your life, you are often consumed by the passion you feel for your beloved. But more often than not, the flames that burned brightly in the morning can be spent ashes by nightfall.

Your innocently changeable behavior in love can befuddle more steadfast hearts, and you may leave behind more than a few broken ones. You feel your losses intensely, but then quickly move on to new, fresh encounters. As you get older, you are likely to form deeper and longer-lasting bonds. But for now, your sights are set on creating excitement, and you tend to stir up things rather than discover what's to be learned from restful calm. Down the road you may be ready to experience the stability that you've resisted.

Someone who wants to hold your attention should avoid laying all their cards out on the table. You respond to a suitor who is daringly provocative and endlessly fascinating. Direct and at times, argumentative, you are stimulated by a clash of minds. A fiery partner with a dramatic, changeable nature makes every day new and exciting.

As a 1985 male Ram, you are attracted to a woman who has confidence in her own ideas and abilities. Disagreements are like foreplay for you, so a playful debater with a heart of gold could light you up. You desire to be with a stunning partner, but may struggle with jealousy while dating a head-turner.

The 1985 female Aries is a fire starter in relationships, and desires a man who can fan the flames. You usually call the shots and need a man who admires your take-charge attitude. An ambitious guy who spends time with his buddies gives you the space you crave. You want a man to treat you like a diva, without becoming a doormat.

1985 TAURUS

From April 20, 3:26 through May 21, 2:42

The Devoted Sensualist

If you are a Taurus born in 1985, you are impulsive in matters of the heart, but are also dreaming of finding that one true forever love. These opposing forces may bring you more than your share of romantic drama. Others immediately see your sincerity, as well as your raw, primal sensuality. Your great physical vitality cannot be put on hold, and you may enjoy lusty times while waiting for your ideal mate. Your fantasy life is likely to be rich and imaginative, and a fertile world of ideas for future playful encounters.

You may not be one to gush about your heartfelt emotions, and others may underestimate the intensity of your affections. Your warmth comes through your generous and unexpected gift giving. When deeply smitten, your heart is loyal and true. Though jealousy may grip you in your private moments, your cooler head usually prevails. Your fiery passions are paired with a practical sensibility, giving you the ability to ride out any relationship storm. You exude a stable presence that can lead to domestic peace later in life.

To win your cautious heart, a potential mate should settle in for the long haul. You shine around people who enjoy your company in quiet moments, as well as the high times. If someone laughs heartily at your jokes, they might stand a chance. A suitor who revels in sensual pleasures as much as you do will stay at the top of your list.

For you 1985 male Taureans, you are drawn to women who have a natural approach to beauty, and a classic style to match it. A woman who can whip up a hearty meal, while making you feel relaxed and comfortable, has made a good start. You could melt with a woman who is experienced in the healing arts, such as massage. If she makes you want to conquer the world for her, she's the one.

The 1985 female Bull is drawn to traditional romantic activities such as walking on the beach or relaxing in front of the fire. An outdoorsy man could appeal to your earthy sensibility. If he is savvy with money, you might be intrigued. Your sensual self emerges around men who appreciate the hidden depths of your femininity.

BILLY JOEL
American Singer
Sun, Venus, and Mars in Taurus

551

1985 GEMINI

From May 21, 2:43 through June 21, 10:43

The Playful Dilettante

As a 1985 Gemini, you seek light-hearted romantic encounters that will satisfy your restless curiosity. Your dazzling persona lures many potential mates, and you have a casual attitude toward romance that others find intriguing. Dating is often fun for you, because you are electrified and energized by new situations. You know how to charm and seduce, and you revel in the gaze of adoring eyes. Love is a game that you play well, though perhaps not for very long. You may enjoy a string of exciting partners, while saving your own tender heart for that the ideal mate you see in your mind's eye.

Your dual nature baffles more conventional folk, who may not understand your elusive emotional nature. Like a rare and fragile exotic bird, you must never be pinned down to a heavy romantic entanglement. When you do get snared in the darker aspects of love, you emerge armed with more knowledge of your paradoxical nature. You seek a fellow whirling dervish who matches your zest for life and promises to make each day a new adventure.

The secret to winning your heart is simply holding your attention. You are attracted to a sexy mind full of humorous anecdotes. A stimulating conversation on anything from the latest art exhibit, to celebrity gossip, to political debate, can generate mental sparks. Someone making the moves should titillate your sexual curiosity, as well. You are open to novelty in all you do, and a flexible and experimental mate wins extra points.

The 1985 Gemini male attracts chameleon-like women with flair for accentuating their beauty. You seek the one woman in a million who can still surprise you long after the honeymoon period is over. A vivacious woman open to exploring new vistas with you can keep you mentally charged. Your ideal mate is your best friend, a companion in new adventures.

The 1985 Gemini female delights the many male admirers in her orbit with her zest for living. You walk tall with a worldly man of cultivated interests by your side. A successful suitor will stimulate your mind and arouse your body, while slowly forming a deeper bond.

ISABEL ALLENDE
Chilean Writer
Sun in Leo

552

1985 CANCER
From June 21, 10:44 through July 22, 21:35

 The Tenacious Sentimentalist

As a 1985 Cancer, you crave romantic bonds held together by deep love and mutual trust. Stability is a turn-on for you, and the lucky partner who provides that can reveal the oceanic depths beneath your cool façade. You desire a relationship that is going somewhere—casual players and superficial charmers are quickly weeded out of your world. Love is the drug for you, and your steel trap memory churns on images of past, present, and even future loves.

For those who get past your formidable front door, a garden of sensual delights awaits. With a devoted partner, you can be a covert flirt whose smoldering embers suddenly build to five-alarm fires. Since your passions can easily ignite jealousy, you may want to avoid those with the roving eye. For you, betrayals in love may take longer to heal, but you learn over time how to be more discerning. You want total devotion from your beloved, and someone who can admire and protect your empathic sensitivity.

To win your heart, a suitor should pay attention to your very subtle clues and be poised for the right moment to take action.

You revel in being admired and shine in the warmth of approval. But false flattery will get nowhere with you, and your ability to sense insincerity is highly refined. An overzealous suitor chases you away, while the patient one is amply rewarded.

The 1985 male Crab wants to protect and cherish his beloved. You attract intuitive women who respond to your deeply nurturing and sympathetic nature. Because you sense things about people, you're best paired with an emotionally rich partner. A woman who has won your trust, while stirring up your erotic imagination, is a keeper for you.

The 1985 female Crab exudes an intoxicating mix of sweetness and sensuality that can drive men wild. Yet your old-fashioned heart is cautious, and it takes a patient man to win your trust. Rugged or detached men hold no sway for you. Artistic types with a sentimental streak spark your interest. You seek a gentle giant whose love can help you forget the wounds of the past and live happily ever after in the present.

1985 LEO
From July 22, 21:36 through August 23, 4:35

 The Illuminating Celebrant

You 1985 Leos have a knack for being the life of the party, and you tend to attract sunny, outgoing companions. You believe that romantic relationships should always enhance the glow of your own moving spotlight. Regular admiration bolsters your confidence and fires up your sex drive. You desire a buoyant partner who has a changeable persona, and perhaps a few secrets in the closet, because mystery and theatrics stir your imagination. You shine with an ambitious mate that you can brag about to your friends. In private, you radiate warmth that keeps your lover from having any interest in straying.

You thrive in a group of adventurous friends of both sexes. And since you crave variety, chances are that there are many pots simmering on your romantic stove. From subtle flirtations to bold advances, you are mastering the art of seduction. But if a special one bewitches your heart, your loyalty is true blue. The mate who only has adoring eyes for you will avoid stirring up your jealousy. You can love with the devotion of an ardent fan, as long as it is reciprocated.

To claim your affections, a suitor should prepare to flatter and seduce. Your romantic heart responds to grand gestures, such as a midnight serenade under your window, or surprise tickets to see live music. An invitation to a masquerade ball or theme party would not be turned down—you revel in playing out fantasies. The mate who goes all out to provide your favorite kind of evenings wins your heart.

As a 1985 male Leo, you need to display your peacock feathers from time to time. You appreciate women who likewise adorn themselves with special touches, such as dangling earrings or flowers in the hair. A feisty, free-spirited woman who moves with abandon on the dance floor could catch your eye.

If you are a female Leo born in 1985, you are an agile actress at heart looking for your ideal leading man. Handsome, talented, witty, powerful—you want a winner in your life. A man who is generous with his money and affections has made a good start. Your libido ignites with men who pursue you with bold confidence.

1985 VIRGO *From August 23, 4:36 through September 23, 2:06*

The Gregarious Advisor

As a 1985 Virgo, romantic connections evolve naturally from your jam-packed daily life. Your usually calm personality is prone to sudden bursts of enthusiasm, and cheerful companions are kept close. Some may be drawn to your receptivity, but then find that their romantic maneuvers are met with a sudden aloof, detached reaction. This ability to shield your emotions works to your advantage—you never like to wear your heart on your sleeve. Some may be intrigued by your enigmatic ways, and yearn to discover your deeper nature.

Along with an air of mystery, you have a solid, down-to-earth outlook that draws many friends and lovers. Your rock steady self-possession often causes others to look to you for advice. You gravitate toward trustworthy people that you can confide in, as well. A mate with similar interests can accompany you to a class or excursion. Romance could also find you at the work place, since that is often where you prove yourself. Happy, spontaneous companions can distract you from your habit of worrying too much.

For someone trying to catch your eye, the best advice is to take an understated approach. Your wholesome nature draws those with interests in health and the outdoors. You don't like probing, aggressive suitors, and will likely rebuff more impulsive types. Good old-fashioned hand holding in a darkened cinema suits you just fine. Once in love, your passions bring color to your sensual explorations—trust in a relationship allows your feelings to deepen.

If you are a 1985 male Virgo, you exude a rugged manliness that many women find irresistible. Physically strong women who have sporty inclinations draw your attention. A woman with one or two passionate interests gets you going. The earthy gal with common sense, and a lusty appetite for the pleasures of life, has it made.

For you females born a Virgo in 1985, only a man of substance and integrity will do. Glitz and glam don't impress you—well-groomed men with classic style catch your discerning eye. The patient man who sees beyond your cool exterior, finds a tender, affectionate heart.

VIRGO ZODIAC SIGN
YOUR LOVE PLANETS

YOUR ROMANTIC SIDE   p. 696
▶ VENUS IN CANCER
Born Aug. 23, 4:36 - Aug. 28, 3:38
▶ VENUS IN LEO
Born Aug. 28, 3:39 - Sept. 22, 2:52
▶ VENUS IN VIRGO
Born Sept. 22, 2:53 - Sept. 23, 2:06

YOUR SEX DRIVE   p. 722
▶ MARS IN LEO
Born Aug. 23, 4:36 - Sept. 10, 1:30
▶ MARS IN VIRGO
Born Sept. 10, 1:31 - Sept. 23, 2:06

YOUR CELEBRITY TWINS   p. 760
Find out the astrological similarities you have with famous people.

YOUR COMPATIBILITY   p. 780
Compare planets to find out how compatible you are in a relationship.

YOUR RELATIONSHIP KARMA   p. 824
▶ SATURN IN SCORPIO
Born Aug. 23, 4:36 - Sept. 23, 2:06

553

WILLIAM HURT
American Actor
Mars in Libra

1985 LIBRA *From September 23, 2:07 through October 23, 11:21*

The Diligent Charmer

You 1985 Librans exercise a cautious curiosity before plunging into romantic relationships. You are delightfully social by nature, and you attract colorful friends who share your interests. Not much into solitude, you like doing things with a partner. With so many connections, there are usually a few secret crushes among them. If romance brews with a classmate or exercise partner, you go with the flow. Your ambitious, diligent nature keeps you involved in your work—the right mate will help you get ahead in life.

To strangers, you might appear friendly, but in a coolly detached way. Getting to know you takes time, and you expect people to win your trust. You warm more easily up to people who are good listeners—a thorough debate of some world event stimulates your mind. A tendency to hunt for flaws in other people may be a defense against being vulnerable to the wrong person. Over time, you will be more willing to take a few risks and surrender to imperfect love. In an atmosphere of acceptance, your deeper passions find expression.

When romance blooms, you want to feel special—buying you an expensive dinner in a high class restaurant could appeal to your lavish tastes. The right mate knows what's going on in town, and enjoys going with you to the latest events, even purchasing tickets ahead of time. Thoughtful gifts on anniversaries appeal to your sentimental nature. You have an old-fashioned outlook when it comes to romance—the worthy partner takes it slow, building trust over time first.

As a male 1985 Libra, you seek sophisticated women who are verbally expressive. Worldly women from another cultural background have an edge with you, and you enjoy being seen with a fashionably dressed partner. A feminine woman who teases you with a subtle glance stirs your senses.

The female 1985 Libra knows that confidence is an aphrodisiac—you thrive with a man at home in the public eye. Strong, silent types may intrigue you, but ultimately you need someone you can talk to about everything. Suave, sweet-talkers who keep it light and romantic win your discriminating heart.

LIBRA ZODIAC SIGN
YOUR LOVE PLANETS

YOUR ROMANTIC SIDE   p. 696
▶ VENUS IN VIRGO
Born Sept. 23, 2:07 - Oct. 16, 13:03
▶ VENUS IN LIBRA
Born Oct. 16, 13:04 - Oct. 23, 11:21

YOUR SEX DRIVE   p. 722
▶ MARS IN VIRGO
Born Sept. 23, 2:07 - Oct. 23, 11:21

YOUR CELEBRITY TWINS   p. 760
Find out the astrological similarities you have with famous people.

YOUR COMPATIBILITY   p. 780
Compare planets to find out how compatible you are in a relationship.

YOUR RELATIONSHIP KARMA   p. 824
▶ SATURN IN SCORPIO
Born Sept. 23, 2:07 - Oct. 23, 11:21

WHOOPI GOLDBERG
American Actress
Sun in Scorpio

554

1985 SCORPIO
From October 23, 11:22 through November 22, 8:50

The Magnetic Artist

As a 1985 Scorpio, you gravitate toward those with similarly inquisitive hearts and minds. Curious by nature, you have many deeply rooted, intense connections with others. You enjoy relationships you can dive into, practically merging with the object of your affections. Your instinctive ability to attract gives you the advantage—you can be gregarious and flirty one moment, and sensual and magnetic the next. Yet you have secretive ways about you, revealing only what you want others to see.

You can spot a fake a mile away, and seek out relationships with authentic, original, even eccentric people. Dark, brooding artists satisfy a yearning to go exploring beneath the surface of things. You thrive with a mate you can truly talk to, someone who can share the secrets of their psyche. When you've set your sights on someone, you can be direct, and even aggressive. Once hooked, you might be tempted to hold on too tightly to your beloved. But when you learn to give others the freedom you need yourself, your relationships will deepen.

To catch your eye, someone might tell you a bizarre, mysterious story. Engaging your emotional mind in an exchange of tall tales is a good way to keep you intrigued. Wishy-washy types don't amuse you—you like focused, opinionated people who speak up. You shine in a relaxed atmosphere where your sharp intellect has something to explore, and a suitor needs to provide that to keep your interest.

For you 1985 male Scorpios, a headstrong woman with a style of her own is your ideal. Bold, creative pioneers with exploration on their minds have a distinct edge. False flattery doesn't get far with you—a woman should mean what she says and say what she means. You are a very physically active person and require a dynamic, healthy partner.

As a 1985 female Scorpio, you demand absolute loyalty from your chosen man. If a man you're seeing sizes up the other women in the room, he will soon find himself alone. A manly man with tender sensitivities responds well to your emotional nature. If he can surrender to the sensual moments you share, he has it made.

1985 SAGITTARIUS
From November 22, 8:51 through December 21, 22:07

The Lighthearted Voyager

If you are a Sagittarius born in 1985, you seek challenge and fun in your romantic exploits. There is no time for heavy entanglements just yet—you're too busy exploring your world. You have parties to attend and exciting new friends to meet around every corner. An urge to travel might send you abroad, where romance could bloom under an exotic sky. Or you may find love closer to home, with romantic partners who often begin as friends. It helps if they share your curiosity and zest for life.

With so much going on, you are bound to meet plenty of interesting people. Your sharp sense of humor and broad interests captivate those around you. Friends revel in your light-hearted, carefree outlook, and you are rarely without companionship. When romance finds you, it may have the flavor of friendship for awhile. Even your closest friends may be surprised to learn of a deepening bond. A secretive side, paired with your casual demeanor, may keep people guessing, including your beloved.

To turn the tide from friendship to something more romantic, a suitor should be easygoing in their approach. Would-be mates who are clever and witty, with an exciting way of telling stories, keep you entertained. You enjoy relaxed atmospheres, such as an outdoor café or a picnic in the woods. Sporty or outdoor types have the energy and stamina to keep up with you. Your curiosity about sensual pleasures demands a mate with a similar experimental approach.

For you 1985 male Sagittarians, a vivacious woman with passionate interests suits you just fine. Active women who also need freedom and independence intrigue you. Heart-wrenching scenes have no appeal for you—you desire women who move forward quickly from disappointments. A woman with interests of her own keeps you on your toes.

As a 1985 female Sagittarius, your blunt, honest style calls for a man of matching directness. You want to learn from your mate— men with penetrating minds hold your attention. Athletic types who love the great outdoors can match your vitality. If he is a playful flirt with bold, dashing moves, he's got it made.

Madonna – Unlike a Virgin

The Material Girl was born Madonna Louise Ciccone, but ever since her first album "Madonna" was released in July 1983, that's how she's been known. While fame and wealth came relatively easily to Madonna, she had a much more difficult time finding a comfortable partner. Her four-year marriage to Sean Penn began as a great adventure, but was marred by his volatile temper and the question of her faithfulness.

With her Sun and Venus in the royal sign of Leo, Madonna easily assumes the role of the diva. When she first met Sean Penn, it was much like a queen meeting an admirer. She was filming for her 1985 video *Material Girl*, and Penn had been invited by the director to watch the shoot. She stood at the top of a staircase, and as she looked down to descend, saw him, and later claimed that she had a fantasy that they would fall in love and get married. Within weeks the two agreed to do just that. On Madonna's 27th birthday, August 16, 1985, they wed in Malibu.

Between 1983 and 1985 Madonna's star rose quickly as she became the unchallenged queen of pop music. She made her first movie, *Desperately Seeking Susan*, and another bestselling album, "Like a Virgin." Earning some $20 million annually, she became one of the country's richest female entertainers.

Penn and Madonna made the film *Shanghai Surprise* together. He played a hustler salesman in this picture, but the critics gave it thumbs down, and it sank at the box office. The stinker was an omen for their marriage too, as Madonna began hanging out with comedienne Sandra Bernhard. Sean felt he had to

"I'm a very passionate person, and when you really love someone, the sex and love is going to be great."

MADONNA, to *People* magazine

compete with Sandra for his wife's attention, and several reports indicate that Madonna and Sandra were lovers. Penn and Madonna had a huge fight in December 1988, and a month later were divorced.

Yet Madonna's love life never missed a beat. In 1989 Madonna landed a starring role in Warren Beatty's film *Dick Tracy*, and the two briefly became lovers. Over the next few years Madonna had a secret relationship with her bodyguard Jim Albright and the rapper Vanilla Ice, both about a decade younger than she. Albright ended their three-year affair when he realized that her friends were also her lovers. "She'd never been faithful to one man—period," he said. "She told me that. She is only loyal to herself." A few months later Madonna spotted Carlos Leon while jogging in Central Park one day. She arranged a meeting, and within the next two years the couple had a baby girl known as Lourdes. They then went their separate ways.

In August 2000, Madonna delivered her second baby, a boy named Rocco whose father, Guy Ritchie, is 10 years younger than the queen of pop. The two were married during a quiet and exclusive ceremony in Scotland in December 2000. Nowadays the couple split their time between their 1,200-acre estate in England and their Beverly Hills mansion working on creative projects and playing with their two children. Nevertheless, there are speculations about the state of their marriage. Likewise, the release of Madonna's latest album is colored by controversial and mixed reviews. It remains to be seen what our Material Girl has up her sleeve. Time will tell the luck of her stars.

555

▶ READ ABOUT WARREN BEATTY ON PAGE 497 ▶ READ ABOUT SEAN PENN ON PAGE 548

1986

- ⭐ PRINCESS STEPHANIE
- ⭐ ARNOLD SCHWARZENEGGER
- ⭐ CHILDREN OF A LESSER GOD
- ⭐ PRETTY IN PINK
- ⭐ KITTY KELLEY
- ⭐ WHITNEY HOUSTON
- ⭐ PAPA DON'T PREACH

EVENTS

It was a year spotlighting royalty. After only one year of marriage, Princess Stephanie Grimaldi, the daughter of Princess Grace, divorced her husband who was caught having an affair with a cabaret singer in Belgium. In the UK, Prince Andrew and Sarah Ferguson were married and then became the Duke and Duchess of York. Wallis Simpson, the Duchess of Windsor, died. King Edward VIII had abdicated his throne to marry her.

US royalty was also highlighted when Arnold Schwarzenegger married Maria Shriver (a Kennedy relative) in front of 450 guests in Hyannis, Massachusetts.

The US Supreme Court ruled 5 to 4 that homosexual activity between consenting adults in the privacy of the home is not protected by the Constitution. The second international conference on AIDS opened in Paris and two thousand researchers and clinicians attended. In Ireland, 60 percent of the voters decided against allowing divorce.

POP CULTURE

Children of a Lesser God was a notable film about a dedicated teacher of the deaf struggling to reach a woman who would rather stay within the safe confines of the hearing-impaired. Appealing to the younger set, *Pretty in Pink* was about a preppie student who learns to stop listening to his shallow friends and goes after the pretty but poor girl he really likes. *A Room with a View*, based on E.M. Forster's 1908 novel, took a look at Edwardian manners, courtship, and love.

Kitty Kelley got attention with *His Way: The Unauthorized Biography of Frank Sinatra*, the book Sinatra tried but failed to stop. Pat Conroy's *The Prince of Tides*, later made into a movie, was about a middle-aged protagonist who, with the help of a sympathetic female psychiatrist, confronts repressed horrors from his South Carolina family's past.

Whitney Houston had two big hits on the charts this year in "Greatest Love of All" and "How Will I Know." Other pop favorites were Madonna's "Papa Don't Preach," the Bangles' "Walk Like an Egyptian," and Patti LaBelle and Michael McDonald with "On My Own." Dionne & Friends contributed to the charts with the sentimental "That's What Friends Are For."

Hot Movie

9½ WEEKS

Kinky sexual experimentation fuelled the dangerous allure of the 1986 movie *9½ Weeks*, a story of a sadomasochistic relationship between two sophisticated New Yorkers. In one famous scene, Kim Basinger closes her eyes while Mickey Rourke plies her with a variety of foods and douses her face and thighs with honey. Later, the two have sex in a rainy alley stairway while a storm spout drenches them. In other scenes, Basinger performs a titillating striptease, and Rourke forces Basinger to crawl to him. The depiction of violent, obsessive eroticism pushed the outer limits of mainstream acceptability for its time.

SEE ALSO

► SEX IN THE '70S *Page 449*

► CATHERINE MILLET *Page 695*

1986 CAPRICORN

From December 21, 1985 22:08 through January 20, 1986 8:45 (December 1986 Capricorns, see 1987 Capricorn)

♑ *The Sentimental Sweetheart*

You're a passionate Capricorn born in 1986, and you want a relationship that has a good balance between chemistry and commitment. A solid connection with a partner is very important to you and even when you were in grade school going to a first dance, you had to feel that you were with someone who was special to you. Although it's fun to be with a partner who is super popular, you'd rather be with someone for whom you have tender feelings.

Sharing similar tastes and outlook are meaningful to you because then you feel you're with someone who makes sense in your life. You care very much about being able to talk about the things that matter to you, and you enjoy sharing intellectually challenging ideas with a partner. Having a steady who has respect worthy plans for the future is also important. You couldn't care less about a casual, frivolous attachment, and it's fun for you to joke about the people you know who pretend to be in love but are really just kidding themselves.

A clever joke or lively intellectual challenge is an excellent opening gambit when someone wants to gain your attention. You enjoy meeting someone new in elegant surroundings. Connecting at a wedding or country club type atmosphere feels special and it gives you a sense of what sort of future you might have.

If you're a male Goat born in 1986, you like a girl who is pretty and well-groomed. A tasteful appearance is very attractive to you and you'd never choose someone with a blue streak dyed in her hair. Your sweetie is down-to-earth and practical, and she has a good head on her shoulders. She knows what she wants and works hard to get it. Even though she's quite sane, she has lots of personal sparkle and you just know her kisses are sweet.

As a female Cappie born in 1986, you find attractive guys who are magnetic and a bit intense. The captain of the debate team or the guy voted most likely to succeed could be your perfect prom date because you feel you've chosen someone who has a future. He's the sort of fellow the girls squeal and whisper about and you suspect some day he'll be a solid husband.

1986 AQUARIUS

From January 20, 8:46 through February 18, 22:57

♒ *The Best Pal*

As a sociable Aquarius born in 1986, you feel a relationship should first of all be a good friendship. When you think about the people who have mattered most to you so far in your life, it's the quality of the friendship you've shared that really stands out. Being able to play together and enjoy each other's ideas and company makes any relationship more special, and that's what you seek from a steady companion.

Fun is very important to you now and it always will be. Sharing good times with someone special makes the moment more memorable. You feel that it's nice to be with a partner whose ideas coordinate with your own. Having a good sense of reality and knowing what's important is meaningful to you, and you love the idea of a relationship in which you both pitch in and work to make the world a better place.

Because you enjoy such a strong social circle, you have probably often become involved romantically with someone who was already a best pal. Sometimes it was just a crush but you knew it could lead to more with a little effort. A friend who seeks you out to share a private idea or to ask your opinion on something is on the right track because you love those cozy, personal moments. A lively competition is another way to win your heart, whether at the Monopoly board or the Ping Pong table.

As a male Aquarian born in 1986, you like a girl who is a true individual. She has her own ideas and always expresses them with intelligence and sparkle. This sweetie has tons of friends and she always stops to lend a hand when one is needed. Even though she's popular, she's not shallow or silly, and you feel she will make a difference not only in your life but in the world in which she lives.

If you're a female Aquarian born in 1986, you feel a boy should be playful and exciting but not a goof off. Your guy has the right degree of responsibility to make him a success at life but he's not stodgy or boring. He has a winning smile and a merry twinkle in his eye but under it all is a warm heart and a good sense of humor. He's a good leader and has an interesting point of view.

GARY OLDMAN
English Actor
Venus and Mars in Aquarius

557

JON BON JOVI
American Singer
Sun and Venus in Pisces

558

1986 PISCES
From February 18, 22:58 through March 20, 22:02

The Thrill Seeker

You're a dramatic Pisces born in 1986, and you feel a relationship must be exciting. You compare your life and loves to television and the movies and want to be involved just as cinematically. It's very easy for you to get crushes on new people, and so far your relationships may have been very short. But you have plenty of years ahead, so enjoy playing the dating game now. You can easily envision the someday when you and your mate will be the most thrilling couple on the block.

Chemistry is an essential component of your relationship. You need to feel that buzz for someone you like, and you may even start out hating the one you grow to love which is better for you because it's more exciting that way. To you, a relationship should be a little unpredictable. You don't like boring and aren't that determined to have a commitment. You know you're interesting and can always get a date, so you might just be willing to leave going steady to people who aren't as adept at flirting as you are.

A challenging, exciting partner is what you like, and if you meet in some crazy dramatic way, so much the better. You like being invited to concerts, picnics, and outdoor theme parks. When someone comes up to you and tells you something interesting and outrageous, you respond favorably. A kid has to be clever to get your attention—and having a unique appearance or even a motorcycle is a plus!

If you're a male Pisces born in 1986, you like girls who are musical and mysterious. Your sweetie keeps you guessing and you're never quite sure where you stand with her. She is sentimental and thoughtful, but sometimes she turns around and does something just a little bit shocking. You admire the way she tells off teachers now and then!

As a female Fishie born in 1986, you prefer a guy who is rebellious, like the bad boys in your favorite movies. Your fellow is outdoorsy and he loves to play with dogs and horses. He's athletic but not obsessive about it and he is always cheerfully playful. This guy cares about the underdog and is really sweet, even when he's pretending to be bad.

1986 ARIES
From March 20, 22:03 through April 20, 9:11

The Intuitive Sweetheart

As a multi-faceted Aries born in 1986, you require a relationship as complicated as you are. Strong mental and spiritual connections are tops on your list of what's important. Being able to hook up intellectually is essential to you if a partnership is to go anywhere at all. You feel you both must be interested in and interesting to each other. A sense of simpatico—an emotional connection below the surface—is also essential to you because you are sensitive and need that unspoken bond.

A mutual attraction is another important aspect of a good relationship and you feel there just has to be a sense of energy between you for there to be any real meaning in your involvement. You want to feel something deep and meaningful with a partner and that's what chemistry is all about. You can be quite mystical and can easily imagine that you were madly in love in other lifetimes, and that's just the sort of magical connection you seek.

You appreciate a partner clever enough to challenge you with a cunning remark, and rapid-fire repartee often leads to the beginning of a new romance. You enjoy being invited to concerts, dances, and costume parties, and even a charity car wash would appeal to you if the right person asked. You trust your instincts when choosing a date, and ultimately it comes down to how you feel about the person rather than the event you might share.

As a male Ram born in 1986, you like a girl with spunk. Your gal has interests of her own and she's quite distinctive about expressing herself. She may be the lead cheerleader or a future ballerina. Either way, people know who she is and she's admired for her special abilities. This sweetie likes people, is outgoing, but is also controlled and sensible.

If you're a female Aries born in 1986, you prefer a boy who is a solid achiever. Your fellow is down to earth and practical and he understands what's important in life. This guy is on the path to success, but he's not pushy or overbearing. He has a sensitive side and likes music and dance, and even though your parents approve and think he's a good guy, you do too!

1986 TAURUS

From April 21, 9:12 through May 21, 8:27

The Sweet Talker

You're a lively Taurus born in 1986, and your relationship must be intellectually stimulating and fun. You can imagine a lifetime commitment and you might even be certain that the crush of the moment is your perfect true love. That's because you believe in stability and reliability, and want to know that you can count on the person you consider your closest partner. A relationship without trust wouldn't appeal to you at all.

Laughing and playing together keeps you happy now and you imagine that it will keep you young in the future. Sharing goofy times with friends, chatting for hours on the phone or online, and tucking sweet little greeting cards and notes into each other's backpacks at school reinforces the closeness and pleasure in your relationship. Having a sweetheart gives you a sense of confidence, and you enjoy being able to be there for each other.

The sweet and clever things a date says are what matter most to you. Good conversation and amusing remarks are important, but it's when someone is able to express deeper sentiments that it really touches your heart. You are a bit of a media junkie, so you love discussing books and movies, and enjoy being invited to events that make you think and stretch your mind. It's that feeling of excitement when you know you will see your special someone that keeps you coming back.

If you're a male Bull born in 1986, you like a girl who has pizzazz. This sweetie is clever and pretty and your friends think she's really cool. Your gal always has a lot to say—sometimes she talks your ear off—but mostly you find her remarks interesting and you want to hear more. She is fascinated by your stories and just by knowing her you feel your life is more exciting and fun.

As a female Taurean born in 1986, you prefer a boy who has a good balance of spunk and reliability. Your fellow is dependable and trustworthy, a bit of a boy scout, but he's also cheerfully playful and never takes himself too seriously. He's willing to pitch in when there's a crisis and you know that he will grow up to be the sort of man who can always be trusted.

TAURUS ZODIAC SIGN
YOUR LOVE PLANETS

YOUR ROMANTIC SIDE   p. 696
  ► VENUS IN TAURUS
  Born Apr. 20, 9:12 - Apr. 26, 19:09
  ► VENUS IN GEMINI
  Born Apr. 26, 19:10 - May 21, 8:27

YOUR SEX DRIVE   p. 722
  ► MARS IN CAPRICORN
  Born Apr. 20, 9:12 - May 21, 8:27

YOUR CELEBRITY TWINS   p. 760
  Find out the astrological similarities you have with famous people.

YOUR COMPATIBILITY   p. 780
  Compare planets to find out how compatible you are in a relationship.

YOUR RELATIONSHIP KARMA   p. 824
  ► SATURN IN SAGITTARIUS
  Born Apr. 20, 9:12 - May 21, 8:27

CHRISTOPHER LAMBERT
French Actor
Mars in Gemini

559

1986 GEMINI
From May 21, 8:28 through June 21, 16:29

The Tenderhearted Romantic

As a deep and sentimental Gemini born in 1986, you seek a connection on an emotional level. To you, love is all about feelings, and even though you believe intellectual interaction is important, what matters most is the tenderness you hold in your heart for that special someone. In your relationship, there has to be a sense of closeness and a feeling that you've known each other forever. Whatever you want to say is acceptable because you are with someone you can always love and trust.

Laughing and playing together is fun for you now and it will always be a significant part of the relationship you build in the future. Even though you're still young, you can imagine building a home and a family and you want to be surrounded by happy, loving children and a warm and tenderhearted mate. To you a relationship is about finding that one perfect person who was destined always to be your very best friend and staying together forever.

A sweet, caring gesture can gain your interest rather easily. A date who brings you an ice cream cone, shows you a memento of the past, or reveals a sentimental detail strikes you as someone you'd like to know better. You enjoy doing casual things together, and a stroll by the seaside or a quiet talk in the corridor at school can help you learn more about this person who wants to capture your heart.

Male Geminis born in 1986 like a girl to be sentimental, soft, and pretty. Your sweetheart is as compassionate as she is gentle, and she will stop to help a younger child, rescue a lost puppy, or help a granny cross the street. Her eyes are shining and within them you see a person you could love and trust forever. She has a way of making you feel good about yourself and your possibilities for the future.

Female Geminis born in 1986 want a guy to be agile and interesting. Your fellow has lots of charm and wit, and he's a good guy through and through. You know things about him that other people don't, and the secrets you share bring you closer. This boy is certain to be a big success, but you know he will never let fame and fortune go to his head.

GEMINI ZODIAC SIGN
YOUR LOVE PLANETS

YOUR ROMANTIC SIDE   p. 696
  ► VENUS IN GEMINI
  Born May 21, 8:28 - May 21, 13:45
  ► VENUS IN CANCER
  Born May 21, 13:46 - June 15, 18:51
  ► VENUS IN LEO
  Born June 15, 18:52 - June 21, 16:29

YOUR SEX DRIVE   p. 722
  ► MARS IN CAPRICORN
  Born May 21, 8:28 - June 21, 16:29

YOUR CELEBRITY TWINS   p. 760
  Find out the astrological similarities you have with famous people.

YOUR COMPATIBILITY   p. 780
  Compare planets to find out how compatible you are in a relationship.

YOUR RELATIONSHIP KARMA   p. 824
  ► SATURN IN SAGITTARIUS
  Born May 21, 8:28 - June 21, 16:29

---

1 Read Your Sign   **2** Look Up Your Love Planets   **3** Go to Pages Shown

SHEENA EASTON
Scottish Singer
Mars in Cancer

1986 CANCER
From June 21, 16:30 through July 23, 3:23

 The Sympathetic Sweetheart

You're a supportive Cancer born in 1986, and you seek a relationship in which you each take care of the other. Kindness and nurturing are very important to you in an emotional interaction, and you always want to know you can count on the one who also counts on you. Love is very serious to you, and you wish you could meet your true love right now and spend your whole life with one beloved partner. Playing the field is less appealing to you than commitment.

Being able to share mutual goals is another positive feature of your ideal relationship. You want to work side by side with a partner and give each other feedback, encouragement, and advice. Even though you're serious about love, you also feel fun and play have an important role within a relationship. Being able to laugh together and give each other a hug on good and bad days keeps you both feeling happy.

You enjoy being the object of affection and will give a potential date a chance to make a good impression. A ready wit captures your attention, especially someone who can regale you with funny stories. You enjoy pitching in together on projects and don't mind collecting food for the needy as part of a date. Kind gestures mean a lot, and the date who brings you a treat or tells you how to solve a problem at school is your kind of person.

As a male Cancer born in 1986, you like a girl to be pretty but not overly vain or self-centered. Your sweetie is thoughtful and is always willing to look out for the needs of those she loves. This gal is serious, but can also be quite playful and she never stands on ceremony. Sometimes she's independent and other times she reaches out for a hug, but you like the challenge of discerning her mood of the day.

If you're a female Crab born in 1986, your guy has a lot of joie de vivre. He's cheerful and outgoing and he always has time for a friend. This boy is never lazy and you admire his determination to succeed at school and in life. He probably already has a plan for his future, and you hope it includes you. He's good at being organized and he always gets things done on time.

1986 LEO
From July 23, 3:24 through August 23, 10:25

The Balanced Lover

As a dynamic Leo born in 1986, you desire a relationship that is practical but also magical. You believe in true love and want to find that one special someone who is your destiny. That doesn't mean you're out of touch about life— even at this age you realize that love must also be a solid partnership of two people who care for and pitch in to help each other. Of course without romance and magic, all the collaboration in the world is meaningless, and you realize that a good relationship must have both.

Being on the same team is very important to you because you see the value of willingly helping each other to live better lives. That doesn't mean you should smother each other because you wouldn't like that at all. You just like being able to take for granted that someone who loves you will always be in your corner.

You appreciate creativity and the date who uses a unique approach in asking for a date might be lucky enough to win your favor. Having the nerve to serenade beneath your window, dressing up to deliver a singing telegram, or even inviting you to a younger sibling's piano recital are some of the ways a date could gain your attention. You enjoy working alongside a partner and will enthusiastically participate in a pep rally, a charity drive at school, or the prom committee.

If you're a male Lion born in 1986, you like a girl who is a little unpredictable. She seems one way but then she turns around and surprises you. These variable dimensions of her personality make her much more exciting. Your sweetie is a good friend but she's not vain enough to be part of the in-crowd. She has a mind of her own and believes in true love and romance, but she's far from a sure thing.

As a female Leo born in 1986, you like boys who are stable, hardworking, and on the track to success. You have your own agenda and the guy for you will always be supportive and as interested in your goals as you are in his. This fellow has a quiet sort of confidence and the ability to get just about everyone in his corner. He's an excellent leader and has values you can trust and admire.

1986 VIRGO
From August 23, 10:26 through September 23, 7:58

♍ The Ardent Romantic

You're a passionate Virgo born in 1986 and your relationship must feature intensity of feeling. Even though you can be quite practical and intelligent, you want to be involved in a romance where you can let yourself get carried away on a tidal wave of emotion. Something bland and colorless doesn't appeal to you now, nor will it ever. At any given moment, you probably have several crushes on schoolmates, a few more on movie or rock stars, and perhaps also an actual steady who wonders if your heart is really true.

This is the time in your life to enjoy all that romance, and you don't feel bad that you can't help playing the field. You have an active fantasy life and one day it will come in handy when you make a genuine commitment. Then you will want to forge a relationship in which you have joined your heart, body, mind, and soul with the perfect soul mate.

The excitement you feel and the gleam you see in a partner's eyes are all you need to become interested in someone new. Something as simple as a casual brushing of fingertips, a secret whispered close into your ear, or a stolen, impromptu kiss can set your heart thundering. You like the drama and mystery of wondering if you will actually get together and that's far more interesting than the date itself!

As a male Virgo born in 1986, you like a dynamic girl with lots of energy. Heads turn as your gal walks through a room and every guy you know wants to date her. She is creative and exciting and you know that there are tremendous depths to her, intellectually and emotionally. She's already had many interesting experiences despite her age and you love spending hours alone trying to unravel her mysteries.

If you're a female Virgo born in 1986, your ideal guy is someone who can meet you on your own level. He's strong and determined and he appreciates the special qualities inside you. There's a real sense of chemistry between you and when he holds you in his arms, you can feel his heart pounding inside his shirt. You love to imagine all sorts of exciting, romantic scenarios with the two of you as the central figures.

VIRGO ZODIAC SIGN
YOUR LOVE PLANETS

YOUR ROMANTIC SIDE   p. 696
▶ VENUS IN LIBRA
Born Aug. 23, 10:26 - Sept. 07, 10:14
▶ VENUS IN SCORPIO
Born Sept. 07, 10:15 - Sept. 23, 7:58

YOUR SEX DRIVE   p. 722
▶ MARS IN CAPRICORN
Born Aug. 23, 10:26 - Sept. 23, 7:58

YOUR CELEBRITY TWINS   p. 760
Find out the astrological similarities you have with famous people.

YOUR COMPATIBILITY   p. 780
Compare planets to find out how compatible you are in a relationship.

YOUR RELATIONSHIP KARMA   p. 824
▶ SATURN IN SAGITTARIUS
Born Aug. 23, 10:26 - Sept. 23, 7:58

SIGOURNEY WEAVER
American Actress
Sun in Libra

1986 LIBRA
From September 23, 7:59 through October 23, 17:1

♎ The Passionate Paramour

As an intense Libra born in 1986, you feel that a relationship must feature a strong and passionate connection. To you, romance is the heart and soul of an ideal partnership, and you want to be madly in love every single day of your life. You can't help it when you get crushes on people you find attractive, and you spend many idle moments in fantasy about what will happen when you finally do connect. You're just a romance novel waiting to happen!

Loving and being loved are the most important things in your life. You hate the idea of breakups, and want to feel safe and secure within your relationship. That could mean you've been going steady since third grade! Because you're deep beyond your years, you can imagine marrying very early and being with one true love all your life. But you also know you'll grow and change as time goes by, and you try to take it slow with that all-important lifelong commitment.

You love to connect intellectually via lively conversation because as you're talking, you have a chance to focus on those intense feelings below the surface. If you feel that potential zing and heady rush of emotion, you're willing to stop and spend some time learning more about the person who stimulates you. Being touched and walking hand in hand rank high on your list. You also appreciate a mate who's thoughtful enough to offer you a nice gift, but when it comes down to giving away your heart, it's the kiss that matters.

If you're a male Libra born in 1986, you like a girl who has depth and a zest for life. Your sweetie seems older than she is, and you know she's capable of deep devotion. When this gal loves someone, she never lets go and you feel comforted by knowing that no matter what, there will always be a place for you in her heart.

As a female Libra born in 1986, you prefer boys who are more mature than the usual teen. In fact, you may get crushes on older men because you like that confident macho quality that comes only with experience. Your fellow is deep and reliable and he takes your arm and holds you hand in a way that makes you feel safe and loved.

LIBRA ZODIAC SIGN
YOUR LOVE PLANETS

YOUR ROMANTIC SIDE   p. 696
▶ VENUS IN SCORPIO
Born Sept. 23, 7:59 - Oct. 23, 17:13

YOUR SEX DRIVE   p. 722
▶ MARS IN CAPRICORN
Born Sept. 23, 7:59 - Oct. 09, 1:00
▶ MARS IN AQUARIUS
Born Oct. 09, 1:01 - Oct. 23, 17:13

YOUR CELEBRITY TWINS   p. 760
Find out the astrological similarities you have with famous people.

YOUR COMPATIBILITY   p. 780
Compare planets to find out how compatible you are in a relationship.

YOUR RELATIONSHIP KARMA   p. 824
▶ SATURN IN SAGITTARIUS
Born Sept. 23, 7:59 - Oct. 23, 17:13

ISABELLA ROSSELLINI
Italian Actress
Mars in Scorpio

562

1986 SCORPIO
From October 23, 17:14 through November 22, 14:43

♏ *The Soulmate Seeker*

You're a passionate Scorpio born in 1986, and you want a relationship that thrills you intensely. Falling in love is the best feeling in the world to you, and you can't help responding to the overwhelming rush that you feel is the heart and soul of any relationship. It isn't just romance and the sweet cloud of tenderness that makes a relationship real to you, but you also seek the gentler feelings of being connected, a comfy closeness that is reassuring.

Being able to communicate about everything is important to you in a relationship, but often the deepest information is left unspoken. You seek a psychic connection with a mate in which you automatically know what each other is feeling and thinking. Casual alliances don't appeal to you at all, and although you might be tempted to form a crush on someone based on instantaneous attraction, ultimately you will always choose a relationship that has stronger potential.

A person who shares your points of view knows how to gain your attention. Casual conversations that have an aura of magic and mystery leave you wondering what else might happen with this new partner. You love it when someone trusts you enough to share a secret or deeply personal detail. Doing casual, friendly things like hanging out at a party or an after school club are the perfect first dates.

As a male Scorpion born in 1986, you like a girl who speaks to your heart and imagination. You fantasize about a girlfriend and wonder just what she's like deep inside. Your gal is exciting and dynamic and you always feel better just because she's in the room. She's feminine but not flowery and there is no better feeling than holding her in your arms and kissing her.

If you're a female Scorpio born in 1986, your guy is strong and macho. He's what you'd call a man's man, even though he's still a teen. There's something about him that tickles your imagination and you can easily envision a long future as his girlfriend. He's generous and helpful and can be counted on to pitch in when a good deed is needed. His friends love him and you like being part of his clique.

1986 SAGITTARIUS
From November 22, 14:44 through December 22, 4:01

♐ *The Supportive Sweetheart*

You're a devoted Sagittarius born in 1986, and you prefer a relationship that is comfortable, close, and congenial. Being able to love someone who loves you back is quite a gift and you feel that a relationship is all about snuggling down into a warm, supportive interaction. Being there for each other is top on your list of importance in any partnership and you'd never want to share yourself with someone who wasn't totally in your corner.

Good communication is another facet of your relationship and you feel that being able to talk about feelings and ideas really brings you closer. Your creative side is enhanced through a relationship and you enjoy spending time with a partner whose ideas inspire you. Not only do you believe in true love and strong past life connections, you feel there is a psychic bond in any good relationship, allowing your intuition to tell you how to nurture and love each other.

A sentimental gesture is an excellent opening gambit where you're concerned. A partner who sends you a card or gives you a handpicked flower—even if it's a weed—is someone who sees your sensitive side. You love being engaged in exciting conversation, and if a date offers to help you with a school project or to explain something you don't quite get, you appreciate the attention. You love hugs and attending a dance together allows you to embrace to music.

If you're a male Archer born in 1986, you like a girl who is as deep and sensitive as you are. Your sweetie has a good heart and she just seems to know what people are thinking and feeling. You can see in her eyes deep sympathy and understanding and you suspect she knows much more about you than you're willing to tell. This gal is very magnetic and her kisses make your heart pound.

As a female Sagittarian born in 1986, your guy is a real people person. He's sensitive and emotional but also spunky and serious. He knows when something needs to be done and he pitches right in. Your fellow is good at offering support and understanding but he's not wimpy or wishy-washy. He works hard and likes to play sports and go dancing.

Tom Cruise – Hollywood's Top Gun

Tom Cruise and Kelly McGillis in *Top Gun*

With good looks and a personality that was brimming with self-confidence, Tom Cruise became Hollywood's number one box-office draw in the 1980s and '90s. His engaging sexuality, irresistible grin, and love for action attracted moviegoers and made him a star.

Tom Cruise's love life seems to have gotten started around the same time as his acting career. His big break was a starring role in the 1983 comedy *Risky Business*. He and his leading lady, Rebecca De Mornay, quickly became off-screen lovers and stayed together for about three years. Aside from a previous high school romance, this was Cruise's first venture into matters of the heart. During this same period, he made his mark on the screen playing a navy fighter pilot in the 1986 adventure *Top Gun*, and a pool hustler with Paul Newman in *The Color of Money*.

The next woman in his life was Mimi Rogers, whom Cruise met at a dinner party. They married in 1987. It was Mimi who introduced Tom to the Church of Scientology, a controversial spiritual teaching that is often said to be a religious cult. To this day, Cruise remains an active member. He's unapologetic about his devotion to Scientology. "It's something that has helped me to be able to live the kind of life that I'm living and work toward being the kind of person that I want to be," he said. Cruise and Rogers divorced in 1990. She found it too difficult having her own identity with a star of Cruise's magnitude. No doubt their difficulties were also due in no small part to his meeting and working with Nicole Kidman.

Co-starring in the film *Days of Thunder*, Kidman and Cruise exuded real chemistry both on and off the set. Cruise described his encounter with Kidman in esoteric terms. Their meeting was "that special connection when you recognize your soul mate...it was as if a whole new life had started for me." And Nicole Kidman was equally expressive, saying "I was never going to get married. Never. But he was just the most incredible, unusual man I'd ever met." With Cruise's *Rain Man* co-star Dustin Hoffman as his best man, Cruise and Kidman exchanged vows on Christmas Eve 1990.

He and Nicole adopted two children, and both remain attentive parents. "I become an angry bear when it comes to my kids and wife," he said. "I just do my work and live my life and love my family." For ten years Cruise and Kidman seemed to have it all, as both stars were succeeding on their own terms and still managing to share life together as a family. Toward the end of the '90s rumors were spreading that Cruise was gay, and that he needed coaching to film the sex scenes with Kidman in Stanley Kubrick's 1999 *Eyes Wide Shut*. Cruise responded swiftly and vehemently, filing multi-million dollar lawsuits and getting retractions from magazines.

In 2001 the couple went through a highly publicized divorce and neither Kidman nor Cruise have revealed why they separated. Perhaps it was his latest love affair with Penelope Cruz, or Kidman's "friendship" with fellow Australian Russell Crowe. Perhaps their competing schedules or competing religious values were factors. Whatever the reasons, both continue separately to manage successful careers and come to terms with their ruptured family.

563

▶ READ ABOUT NICOLE KIDMAN ON PAGE 590 ▶ READ ABOUT PAUL NEWMAN ON PAGE 433 ▶ READ ABOUT DUSTIN HOFFMAN ON PAGE 400

1987

- ★ DONNA RICE
- ★ CONDOM COMMERCIALS
- ★ PATRICK SWAYZE
- ★ FATAL ATTRACTION
- ★ SHIRLEY MACLAINE
- ★ I KNEW YOU WERE WAITING
- ★ U2

EVENTS

A bit of scandal made the headlines when *The Miami Herald* reported that US Democratic presidential candidate Gary Hart, a married man, had spent the night with model Donna Rice—thus ending Hart's race for the top US office. Jim Bakker resigned from PTL (Praise The Lord) network after the revelation he had cheated on his wife in 1980.

Condom commercials began airing on radio for the first time, while Pope John Paul II officially rejected artificial procreation and condemned the techniques of in-vitro fertilization.

Censorship reared its head again in the US when a clerk was arrested in Florida for selling a copy of a 2 Live Crew album to a fourteen-year-old boy—authorities considered the album offensive because of explicit lyrics.

POP CULTURE

Moviemakers had something for everyone this year. For the romantic dance lovers there was *Dirty Dancing*, set in a Catskills holiday camp and starring Patrick Swayze as the handsome dance instructor with a heart of gold. Quite a few men got a scare watching *Fatal Attraction*, about a married man who hooks up with a woman who can't stand to be ignored. In the cult classic *The Princess Bride*, Buttercup and Westley romp through one adventure after another to find that true love, indeed, conquers all.

Danielle Steel topped the bestseller lists with two titles: *Kaleidoscope* and

Fine Things. *It's All in the Playing*, by Shirley MacLaine, the fifth volume chronicling the author's personal odyssey, tied her explorations into reincarnation with her romance with an unidentified married British politician. *The Sacred Night* was about the life of a Moroccan girl raised as a boy who renounces her role as only son after her father's death.

George Michael had two hits with "Faith" and "I Knew You Were Waiting," a duet he cut with Aretha Franklin. Whitney Houston also had two with "I Wanna Dance with Somebody" and "Didn't We Almost Have It All." U2 was not to be outdone. Their two were "I Still Haven't Found What I'm Looking For" and "With or Without You." Los Lobos did a successful remake of the 1950s hit "La Bamba."

Hot Couple

DIAHANN CARROLL & VIC DAMONE

On January 3, 1987, Diahann Carroll married Vic Damone, the velvety-voiced crooner of the hit, "I Have But One Heart." Carroll, best known as the first black woman to play the solo lead in a television series, starred in *Julia* (1968-1971).

While her nine-year marriage to Damone, her fourth husband, was interracial, it was Carroll's first marriage in 1956 to Monte Kay, also a white man, that was considered bold at the time. In 1959, Carroll commenced a torrid affair with Sidney Poitier. Although both she and Poitier divorced their spouses to be together, their stormy relationship ended in 1967.

SEE ALSO

▶ KATHARINE HEPBURN & SPENCER TRACY *Page 251*
▶ PAUL SIMON AND CARRIE FISHER *Page 532*

1987 CAPRICORN

From December 22, 1986 4:02 through January 20, 1987 14:39
(December 1987 Capricorns, see 1988 Capricorns)

♑ *The Committed Darling*

You're a congenial Capricorn born in 1987, and you want to create a comfortable relationship in which you feel happy. Getting along well with each other is not only important to you, it's imperative. You don't enjoy quarreling and you feel loving someone means you can cooperate without strife. You feel there should just be a natural, easy sort of connection that exists right from the moment you meet and lasts forever.

Chemistry is another aspect of a positive connection, and you enjoy feeling that buzz when you're in the room with someone and you really connect. To you that's what love is all about. Deep communication below the surface seems quite normal to you because you feel a psychic bond will be present in a good relationship. You each know what the other is thinking and feeling and when a hug is needed. Trust, honor, and commitment are what you seek, and you'd like to have a long and happy marriage with a perfect soul mate.

A date who is subtle and surprising appeals to you and you love it when someone creeps up, covers your eyes, and whispers, "Guess who!" You like the sense that you're sharing a secret world where only the two of you speak the language, so your heart is really set afire by those long, lingering conversations, sweet sighs, and soulful gazing into each other's eyes.

If you're a male Capricorn born in 1987, you like a girl you can trust. Someone flighty or changeable doesn't appeal to you at all. You want to feel you're giving your heart to a stable girl who will treat you right. Your sweetie is emotional and intense, yet also sometimes reserved and you know there are so many dimensions to her it will be a fascinating experience seeing them revealed.

As a female Cappie born in 1987, your guy is sensitive and musical. He's not shy, though, and when he sneaks below your window to play a sweet serenade, your heart flutters. This guy has plenty of spunk, but he never loses sight of the feelings of other people and he tries to understand your thoughts and opinions. He has magical eyes and a lilting voice and you feel calmer when he's in the room.

CAPRICORN ZODIAC SIGN
YOUR LOVE PLANETS

YOUR ROMANTIC SIDE   p. 696
▶ VENUS IN SCORPIO
Born Dec. 22, 1986 4:02 - Jan. 07, 1987 10:19
▶ VENUS IN SAGITTARIUS
Born Jan. 07, 10:20 - Jan. 20, 14:39

YOUR SEX DRIVE   p. 722
▶ MARS IN PISCES
Born Dec. 22, 1986 4:02 - Jan. 08, 1987 12:19
▶ MARS IN ARIES
Born Jan. 08, 12:20 - Jan. 20, 14:39

YOUR CELEBRITY TWINS   p. 760
Find out the astrological similarities you have with famous people.

YOUR COMPATIBILITY   p. 780
Compare planets to find out how compatible you are.

YOUR RELATIONSHIP KARMA   p. 824
▶ SATURN IN SAGITTARIUS
Born Dec. 22, 1986 4:02 - Jan. 20, 1987 14:39

KEVIN COSTNER
American Actor
Sun in Capricorn

565

1987 AQUARIUS

From January 20, 14:40 through February 19, 4:49

♒ *The Convivial Companion*

As a restrained Aquarius born in 1987, you want a relationship that is reliable and stable, but not smothering. Being able to trust the person you love and to assume a sense of continuity is very important to you. You try to maintain all your relationships and are probably still close to your best friend from elementary school. Camaraderie and friendship are tops on your list of what's important. You'd never choose a partner just because of chemistry or an attractive appearance. There has to be more of a real bond for you.

You need to express your feelings honestly, and being in a good relationship means you have someone who respects, enjoys, and understands you. That way you're both comfortable being yourselves and you grow as a result of the interaction. Playfulness is a quality you appreciate now and you always will. Talking, laughing, and sharing fun activities keep you happily together.

An intelligent remark is a good way to gain your interest, and if you can continue a lively debate for a while, you figure there might just be something there. You like that a date has taken the time to know your interests, and being invited to an outdoor event such as a car race, miniature golf, or horseback riding really appeals to you. Sitting on a date's couch and feeling awkward does not!

As a male Aquarian born in 1987, your perfect girl is charming, outgoing, active and fun, but she also has a serious side. She's playful and loves to be involved in all the most fascinating school activities, but she recognizes the importance of working hard at school and doing her best. Your gal likes to help other people and she has many ideas about how to improve the neighborhood and the world.

If you're a female Aquarian born in 1987, you feel a guy should be exciting and somewhat unpredictable. The idea that your fellow is a little bit wild, sort of a bad boy, appeals to you, yet you admit you also want him to be steady and sure and to have a good head on his shoulders. Your guy is impetuous but not stupid! He kisses you impulsively, but he's never irresponsible with your heart.

AQUARIUS ZODIAC SIGN
YOUR LOVE PLANETS

YOUR ROMANTIC SIDE   p. 696
▶ VENUS IN SAGITTARIUS
Born Jan. 20, 14:40 - Feb. 05, 3:02
▶ VENUS IN CAPRICORN
Born Feb. 05, 3:03 - Feb. 19, 4:49

YOUR SEX DRIVE   p. 722
▶ MARS IN ARIES
Born Jan. 20, 14:40 - Feb. 19, 4:49

YOUR CELEBRITY TWINS   p. 760
Find out the astrological similarities you have with famous people.

YOUR COMPATIBILITY   p. 780
Compare planets to find out how compatible you are.

YOUR RELATIONSHIP KARMA   p. 824
▶ SATURN IN SAGITTARIUS
Born Jan. 20, 14:40 - Feb. 19, 4:49

STEPHEN SONDHEIM
American Composer
Sun and Venus in Aries

1987 PISCES
From February 19, 4:50 through March 21, 3:51

The Passionate Paramour

You're a complicated and dynamic Pisces born in 1987, and you need a relationship that is challenging and stimulating. A superficial, bland tie is simply not for you. You need to feel an intense and passionate connection, one that fires your imagination and sets your heart to thundering. Despite relishing the ups and downs of amour, you also value commitment and stability. You want to know that the person you love will return your feelings and stick around for the long haul.

You don't mind at all if there's a little friction between yourself and a loved one because you find those little quarrels stimulating. Being able to talk on a deep and intimate level is also important. By communicating honestly you're both able to express what's really in your hearts and on your minds. This helps you establish that you share mutual ideals and have so much in common that you're motivated to remain close.

You don't always set much stock in first impressions when choosing a date. Some of your closest relationships have begun with a challenge or a quarrel, and you just love those movies in which the two people start out fighting and end up in each other's arms. A little combat is interesting and you enjoy being challenged to a rousing debate, a stimulating game of Scrabble™, or a contest of wits.

If you're a male Pisces born in 1987, you want a girlfriend who is also your best pal. Your sweetie is a true individual and she expresses herself with sparkle and flair. Her nature is cheerful and positive, and she always has a way of giving you a much-needed boost when you're down. She's industrious and skilled, intelligent and well-read, and you love talking for hours with her about anything and everything.

As a female Fishie born in 1987, you like a guy who knows his own mind. People who are wishy washy and waffle about bore you to pieces, and you certainly wouldn't want to kiss anyone like that! Your fellow is a little bit stubborn, but he regrets it immediately when he steps on your toes. He cares so much that he just wants what's best for you and is determined to make that happen.

1987 ARIES
From March 21, 3:52 through April 20, 14:57

The Artistic Aficionado

As a sensitive Aries born in 1987, you need a relationship filled with tenderness and affection. You want to feel close to that special someone and to know that all the love in your heart is returned. Casual attractions don't appeal to you because you believe in commitment, true love, and enduring affection. Even now you want to be in a steady relationship and perhaps you're still dating the first person who won your heart.

Chemistry is very important to you because you have such intense feelings, and without that energy and electricity you feel there's no genuine connection at all. There has to be a real sense of excitement and you feel that if you have that, any relationship is bound to last and remain thrilling. While you believe that honest communication is essential, you also know that the real connection happens below the surface and requires sort of a psychic buzz shared between you and your sweetheart.

Creative people are your favorite and you appreciate it when someone makes a special effort to gain your attention. A secret Valentine (any day of the year), a note slipped into your locker at school, or a treat left on your desk creates an aura of mystery that you just love. You enjoy art and music and sharing a concert or museum trip can be the perfect atmosphere for falling in love.

As a male Ram born in 1987, you like a girl who is sweet and tenderhearted. Her eyes are glowing and dewy and you can gaze into them for hours on end. Your gal is compassionate and helpful and it seems as though the whole world beats a path to her door for advice and consolation. She is artistic and musical and you feel she has enough talent to become a big star.

If you're a female Aries born in 1987, you prefer a guy who is agile and athletic. Your fellow is lively and exciting and he's always fun to be around. Because he's so intent on being entertaining, you try many new and interesting activities. He has a quick wit and good sense of humor and you never know what he's going to say next. Whether or not he's your boyfriend forever, you hope he'll always be your friend.

1987 TAURUS

From April 20, 14:58 through May 21, 14:09

The Prankster Playmate

Y ou're a lively Taurus born in 1987, and you require a relationship stimulating enough to maintain your interest. Although you can be quite romantic and you do believe in true love, you also find stability without passion a total bore. You'd never make a commitment just to have a partner because that would ultimately smother you.

Being able to play and laugh with someone is what you feel a good relationship is all about, because that lively spirit of fun makes you both feel happy. You have a youthful nature, and you most likely will always feel this way. When you marry, it will be to someone who likes to have as much fun as you do. Chemistry and sparkle are also important to you. Life should be fun and exciting in your opinion, and you love those heady feelings when you meet someone new and all is potential and imagination.

The partner who makes a bold move gains your attention—and admiration. Daredevil antics in school may not go over well with the teachers, but they sure make you laugh. Often

you don't want for a date to pursue you because you're so affectionate and impulsive, you're likely to be the one on the chase. You love to visit amusement parks, play sports, and go exploring new places. Sharing those things with a new date makes life sweet.

If you're a male Bull born in 1987, you like a girl who is outgoing and exciting. No shy violets for you! Your gal speaks right up, shares her opinions, and she might even be bold enough to grab you and smother you with kisses—right in the hallway at school! She loves to party and has tons of friends, and even though she's always the leader of the pack, she has time to chat with you about your dream car.

As a female Taurus born in 1987, you enjoy an impulsive guy with a firecracker wit and the ability to pull funny pranks without looking too guilty. Your fellow loves to play and have fun, but he's not a total slob—he does realize the importance of being reliable and he wants to be a success. You enjoy chasing him until he notices you. Then you have lots of fun watching him act goofy and listening to his many stories.

TAURUS ZODIAC SIGN
YOUR LOVE PLANETS

YOUR ROMANTIC SIDE   p. 696
- ► VENUS IN PISCES
  Born Apr. 20, 14:58 - Apr. 22, 16:06
- ► VENUS IN ARIES
  Born Apr. 22, 16:07 - May 17, 11:55
- ► VENUS IN TAURUS
  Born May 17, 11:56 - May 21, 14:09

YOUR SEX DRIVE   p. 722
- ► MARS IN GEMINI
  Born Apr. 20, 14:58 - May 21, 3:00
- ► MARS IN CANCER
  Born May 21, 3:01 - May 21, 14:09

YOUR CELEBRITY TWINS   p. 760
Find out the astrological similarities you have with famous people.

YOUR COMPATIBILITY   p. 780
Compare planets to find out how compatible you are in a relationship.

YOUR RELATIONSHIP KARMA   p. 824
- ► SATURN IN SAGITTARIUS
  Born Apr. 20, 14:58 - May 21, 14:09

CHER
American Actress
Sun in Taurus

567

1987 GEMINI
From May 21, 14:10 through June 21, 22:10

The Mystical Mate

A s a communicative Gemini, you like to feel your relationship was meant to be. A dynamic connection with a partner is much more interesting to you than some tepid hearts and flowers. You want to feel drawn to the person you love in an intense, passionate, heart-pounding way. You can be quite willful and determined, and if you feel you have found the right person, you will pursue that relationship for a long, long time. To you that's just another dimension of true love!

Lively communication really appeals to you and it's so much fun to argue and debate. You'd never want to be with some great looking dummy because you don't think love can happen if your brain is asleep! You need emotional and intellectual stimulation and feel once your mind, body, heart and soul are involved, the relationship is bound to work out well. Commitment and devotion are the way to go, in your opinion, and you feel that once you find the right partner one thing naturally leads to another.

Those potentially intense, electric feelings

are the first things you notice about any new date, and if there's an instantaneous, mystical connection, you're willing to race ahead. Someone attractive and magnetic who strokes your hand softly—perhaps pretending to read your palm—who blows kisses in your ear, or who challenges you to a debate is imaginative enough to gain your interest.

As a male Gemini born in 1987, you like a girl who is soft and pretty, and the sensual way she moves inspires many a fantasy. She is elegant and beautiful, and her style is pretty but conservative. She has a soft, resonant voice and magic happens when you look into her eyes. There's a certain calmness to her, but she always has something lively and interesting to say.

If you're a female Gemini born in 1987, you prefer to spend time with a guy who is deep and sensitive. Your fellow is quite emotional and he acts on instinct most of the time. He understands the feelings of other people and often knows their secrets, too. He's attached to his family but never a wimp. His quiet strength gives you confidence—and a thrill too.

GEMINI ZODIAC SIGN
YOUR LOVE PLANETS

YOUR ROMANTIC SIDE   p. 696
- ► VENUS IN TAURUS
  Born May 21, 14:10 - June 11, 5:14
- ► VENUS IN GEMINI
  Born June 11, 5:15 - June 21, 21:10

YOUR SEX DRIVE   p. 722
- ► MARS IN CANCER
  Born May 21, 14:10 - June 21, 21:10

YOUR CELEBRITY TWINS   p. 760
Find out the astrological similarities you have with famous people.

YOUR COMPATIBILITY   p. 780
Compare planets to find out how compatible you are in a relationship.

YOUR RELATIONSHIP KARMA   p. 824
- ► SATURN IN SAGITTARIUS
  Born May 21, 14:10 - June 21, 21:10

TONI MORRISON
American Writer
Mars in Cancer

1987 CANCER
From June 21, 22:11 through July 23, 9:05

The Quirky Romantic

You're an unpredictable Cancer born in 1987, and you demand a relationship that keeps you on your toes. Even at your young age you admit that life and love are complicated and you readily agree that a relationship must have a good combination of freedom and stability to hold your attention. Of course you want security, and you believe in commitment and happiness, but you wonder if that's possible in these modern times.

You feel that what makes a relationship last is when each partner can grow and change and share the freedom of personal self-expression. Flexibility and acceptance mean a lot to you, and in return for a nonjudgmental partnership you offer support and devotion. What you don't want is a rigid attachment in which each person expects life to be the same day after day. To you that's just unrealistic.

A quirky and unpredictable invitation gets your attention right away. Someone clever enough to leave a series of clues for you to find—on the way to a sporting event, computer fair, or blind date—might just be your perfect partner. A deep and insightful conversation is an excellent beginning, and as you learn more about how this person's mind works, you want to discover other things as well.

If you're a male Crab born in 1987, you like a girl who isn't predictable. One day she's serious and the next a total rebel, and that makes life exciting to you. Your girl is lively and intelligent and her opinions are always worth hearing. She expresses herself with verve and because of what she says, life makes a lot more sense. She is idealistic and romantic and she gazes into your eyes in a way that makes you want to kiss her.

As a female Cancer born in 1987, you prefer a boy to be courageous and bold. Your guy is helpful and pleasant, and he has no problem stepping in when there's a problem—or an underdog in trouble. He's always looking out for your best interests and tries hard to please you. This fellow is strong and athletic, although sometimes he trips over his own feet then cracks a joke. He inspires confidence and the feeling that someday he'll make his mark.

1987 LEO
From July 23, 9:06 through August 23, 16:09

The Elegant Romantic

As a loving Leo born in 1987, you want a relationship that is reliable but not dull. Commitment and stability are very important to you because you feel happy and secure to know that the person you love will always love you back. That feeling of closeness and continuity is very meaningful and you hope to have a long, happy marriage some day. Even though you need stability, you would not opt to connect with the wrong partner just to guarantee security because that just wouldn't feel right to you.

You feel that a playful, lively interaction is the heart and soul of a relationship. Caring for each other is wonderful, but it's also nice just to goof off and laugh and joke—being compatible on that level is absolutely necessary. An attractive appearance also matters to you, and you can imagine some day being the most appealing couple in your circle.

The partner with taste and class enough to offer you a formal invitation to an elegant event really appeals to you. Even if it's a first date, you love the idea of getting all dressed up in formal clothes. Perhaps you've been to more proms than anyone in your class! You also appreciate when someone takes the time to learn your taste and brings you a thoughtful gift.

As a male Lion born in 1987, you like a girl who is beautiful and elegant. A gorgeous blonde is just your type, although you won't sneer at a gorgeous redhead or brunette. Your girl is all lady and you admire her style and flair. She's right on top of the latest fashions and you're always proud to have her on your arm. She is kind and helpful, stops to look after the needs of younger kids, and makes you feel adored.

If you're a female Leo born in 1987, you like a solid guy who has spunk. Your fellow is calm and controlled yet also somewhat unpredictable. He has courage and principles and you always feel safe in his company. Because he has a playful streak you have fun together, and the conversations and laughter you share are the subject of much gossip with your girlfriends. This guy is generous and thoughtful, may be rich, and loves to give you gifts.

568

1987 VIRGO

From August 23, 16:10 through September 23, 13:44

The Subtle Sweetheart

You're a restrained Virgo born in 1987, and you want a relationship that is sane and affectionate. Really caring for the welfare of someone you love is very meaningful to you, and being in a relationship where you can look after each other's needs is so fulfilling. You love being able to pitch in and help a partner make the best of every opportunity and you feel that sort of mutual support and caring is the best aspect of romance.

Stability is very important to you and you believe wholeheartedly in commitment. You feel that a promise is definitely not made to be broken! You want to share compatible outlooks, tastes, and preferences because what's the point in fighting over the little things? Being with someone who is a good match is what you seek. Knowing you're right for each other allows you to make a commitment with confidence and to build a long and satisfying relationship.

A kind gesture is often the best way to your heart. In fact, when you have a crush on someone, you show your affection by helping that person out. The date who is willing to pitch in with a complicated school project—even if it's boring—or who won't mind keeping you company when you're stuck doing something around the house—is just your sort of person. You also appreciate a nice shoulder rub.

If you're a male Virgo born in 1987, you like a girl who is solid, sane, and pretty. Your sweetie isn't silly or frivolous because she has too good a head on her shoulders for that. She is tasteful, refined, and subtle, and you find that endlessly endearing. Because she is so intelligent, her ideas are fascinating, and she often suggests useful shortcuts that appeal to you. She is reliable and upstanding, but she loves a secret kiss that nobody can observe.

As a female Virgo born in 1987, your guy is the salt of the earth. Useful and organized, he knows what he's doing. You admire his skills and the careful way he approaches every task. He's hard-working and puts a lot of effort into making you happy. No matter how busy you are, he never minds helping, and he holds you tightly when you feel blue.

VIRGO ZODIAC SIGN
YOUR LOVE PLANETS

YOUR ROMANTIC SIDE   p. 696
▶ **VENUS IN VIRGO**
Born Aug. 23, 16:10 - Sept. 16, 18:11
▶ **VENUS IN LIBRA**
Born Sept. 16, 18:12 - Sept. 23, 13:44

YOUR SEX DRIVE   p. 722
▶ **MARS IN VIRGO**
Born Aug. 23, 16:10 - Sept. 23, 13:44

YOUR CELEBRITY TWINS   p. 760
Find out the astrological similarities you have with famous people.

YOUR COMPATIBILITY   p. 780
Compare planets to find out how compatible you are in a relationship.

YOUR RELATIONSHIP KARMA   p. 824
▶ **SATURN IN SAGITTARIUS**
Born Aug. 23, 16:10 - Sept. 23, 13:44

ROSAMUNDE PILCHER
Scottish Writer
Sun in Virgo

569

1987 LIBRA

From September 23, 13:45 through October 23, 23:00

The Profound Partner

As an affectionate Libra born in 1987, you desire a relationship that balances just the right degree of devotion and independence. You can't help being a genuine romantic, and you wouldn't want to be otherwise, but you also feel that a good relationship allows each person the freedom to express personal quirks and true individuality. You believe that having to stifle your personality wouldn't lead to happiness at all, no matter how much in love you were.

A deep and passionate connection is also quite important to you because you believe in stability where love is concerned. Giving your heart is a serious matter and you are determined to do that only when the partner is just right for you. That way you have a secure bond that feels wonderful and long-lasting. Intimacy is also important and that means having the freedom to open up and share your thoughts and feelings without fear of reprisals or ridicule.

You can't help responding to all the trappings of romance, so when someone brings you flowers, offers a sweet compliment, or takes your hand beneath the moonlight, your heart skips a beat. But to retain more than momentary interest, a date has to show you a deep and serious side. There has to be some meaningful conversation and a sense of emotional potential that you both feel. You also like quirky gestures and a joke now and then, just to keep things lively.

As a male Libra born in 1987, you like a girl with substance. Your sweetie is beautiful and elegant, but she's more than just a pretty face. She has deep feelings and when you're in her presence your own emotions feel deeper and more profound. You always think of marriage when you're around her and suspect she would make some lucky guy the perfect wife.

If you're a female Libra born in 1987, your special sweetheart is genteel but also quirky. This boy has good taste and personal refinement. His manners are excellent and he'd never taunt or embarrass you. But he also has a goofy side and loves to play. Sometimes he tells silly stories, and now and then he twirls you around in a dance step for no reason at all.

LIBRA ZODIAC SIGN
YOUR LOVE PLANETS

YOUR ROMANTIC SIDE   p. 696
▶ **VENUS IN LIBRA**
Born Sept. 23, 13:45 - Oct. 10, 20:48
▶ **VENUS IN SCORPIO**
Born Oct. 10, 20:49 - Oct. 23, 23:00

YOUR SEX DRIVE   p. 722
▶ **MARS IN VIRGO**
Born Sept. 23, 13:45 - Oct. 08, 19:26
▶ **MARS IN LIBRA**
Born Oct. 08, 19:27 - Oct. 23, 23:00

YOUR CELEBRITY TWINS   p. 760
Find out the astrological similarities you have with famous people.

YOUR COMPATIBILITY   p. 780
Compare planets to find out how compatible you are in a relationship.

YOUR RELATIONSHIP KARMA   p. 824
▶ **SATURN IN SAGITTARIUS**
Born Sept. 23, 13:45 - Oct. 23, 23:00

JOHN LONE
Chinese Actor
Venus in Scorpio

1987 SCORPIO

From October 23, 23:01 through November 22, 20:28

♏ ## The Fun Lover

You're a playful Scorpio born in 1987, and you enjoy a relationship that brings fun and pleasure into your life. Being able to relax with someone is important to you and you feel that fitting together like the pieces of a puzzle is what a real relationship is all about. You love the idea of a relationship in which you laugh, joke, and hold hands just because you care for each other and life is wonderful. Stress and strain do not belong in your happy romance.

A deep intellectual connection is also very rewarding, and you feel it's just great to be able to speak and be understood by someone who absolutely gets you. Intuition is another dimension of your relationship, and you find that by tuning into the mind and heart of your special sweetheart, you can understand that person much better. You love the idea that your partner can do the same for you because then it feels like a bond that can never be broken.

You enjoy casual social events as much as dressier ones, and it's fun for you to be invited to a party where you can sway to the music and enjoy standing around talking to a date about anything and everything. Mysteries appeal to you, so you enjoy discussing local events and trying to solve a crime together. You like dancing and a quiet, romantic evening alone feels quite magical—and very grown up!

If you're a male Scorpion born in 1987, you like a girl who has depth and intelligence. Your sweetie has wisdom beyond her years and it's always interesting to you to hear her point of view. When she's willing to share some of her experiences, you feel that you're seeing deep inside her mind and that's a wondrous vision. She's pretty and friendly and knows how to inspire you.

As a female Scorpio born in 1987, you like a charming, outgoing guy with excellent manners. Your honey is a lovely person and everyone you know enjoys his company. He has grace and elegance but he's no wimp. This fellow is a strong leader and he can inspire everyone you know to follow his lead. He is courageous, never backs down from a problem, sometimes seems a bit hasty, but he's always lots of fun.

1987 SAGITTARIUS

From November 22, 20:29 through December 22, 9:45

♐ ## The Dedicated Sweetheart

As an intense Sagittarius you want to be in a relationship that is close and feels reliable. Despite that you're a playful person, you feel a relationship is serious, and you need commitment and security. Being with someone you trust to remain devoted to you is very important, and that way you have a support system in your life. A sense of simpatico is the quality you seek in a relationship because then there is that wonderful feeling of closeness and belonging. You also respond to strong chemistry, and though you might be tempted, you try never to become involved when there's nothing more than a mere attraction.

Casual flings may sound cool to some people, but in your heart you know you want to be married for a long, long time. Right now you're young, so you choose going steady over marriage and even that relationship feels very important to you. You wish you could marry your steady and be happy forever, but you have the wisdom to realize that making such a serious commitment requires maturity and experience. You seek substance in a partner, so before you agree to date someone new, you have to feel that you know that person. Careful conversation is the only way to accomplish that goal. You enjoy sharing serious activities, club memberships, charity volunteer work, and even a soda break at your after-school job. You also like a quick hug or stolen kiss.

As a male Archer born in 1987, you prefer a serious girl who has something meaningful to say. Your gal is mature beyond her years, and she's in touch with the many accomplishments she hopes to achieve in the future. She is a reliable person, beloved by all the adults who know her, and someone the kids at school come to when they need help.

If you're a female Sagittarian born in 1987, your guy is intense and passionate. He has this dark, brooding quality about him, and looking into his eyes is both magical and scary. It's as though he hypnotizes you with his glance and reminds you of all the romantic movies you've seen. He is strong and macho, yet also sensitive, and he knows how you're feeling and what you need.

Mel Gibson – Tough, Sexy Hero

A rarity among Hollywood celebrities, Mel Gibson is a devoted family man and husband. And this is no run-of-the mill celebrity. Mel Gibson commands some $25 million per film, making him one of the highest paid actors in the business. With his rugged handsome looks and action hero roles, he has been cast opposite some of the most alluring cinematic goddesses on the screen, but seems to have refrained from any off-screen hanky-panky. He married Australian nurse Robyn Moore in 1980, and at last count they have produced seven children and have a solid relationship. "She's my Rock of Gibraltar," Gibson says.

His own upbringing provided a good role model for a stable family life. He himself is the sixth of eleven children. American born, his father moved the family to Australia in 1968, worried that his children might be drafted into the US Army. It was actually thanks to family that Gibson initially got into acting. One of Gibson's sisters, without his knowledge, submitted an application for him to the National Institute of Dramatic Art in Sydney. He decided to audition and was accepted, even though he had had no previous acting experience.

However, Gibson says that he owes his big break to a fat lip he got in a barroom brawl just before a 1979 movie audition for the leading role in Mad Max. "I was a mess," he said. "I had stitches in my head. I was peeing blood. I couldn't see." When Gibson showed up for the audition, he was sporting the exact beat-up look the director George Miller was looking for in his post-apocalyptic tale.

Two subsequent movies, Peter Weir's Gallipoli and Miller's The Road Warrior (the Mad Max sequel) made Gibson a rising star and thrust him into the

Mel Gibson and Danny Glover in *Lethal Weapon*

international scene. But it was in his role as a journalist (co-starring with Sigourney Weaver) in Weir's *The Year of Living Dangerously* that Gibson first showed his sex appeal and charisma onscreen. It is not by chance that he was the first to receive *People* magazine's billing as the "Sexiest Man Alive" and has also been on the "50 Most Beautiful People in the World" list numerous times.

But life also has had its downside for Gibson, who has battled with alcoholism. At one point early on in his career, he and his wife decided to take some time off from Hollywood. They returned to Australia where they bought a ranch, and Gibson learned to raise cattle.

Then in 1987, he teamed up with Danny Glover to make the hit *Lethal Weapon*. The movie proved to be such a success that three sequels followed, and Gibson's portrayal of the slightly psychotic undercover cop became a popular screen character. Gibson started his own production company, and in 1995 directed and starred in the Oscar-winning epic *Braveheart*. His action-hero status was then neatly balanced by the romantic comedy *What Women Want*, co-starring Helen Hunt.

Over the course of his career, Gibson has proven that he is a talented man who can act, direct, and produce. He seems to have come to terms with the pressures of fame but admits that he found it something of a torment for a while. He has learned that his life is a delicate balance between going full tilt on with his career and spending quality time with his wife and kids.

571

▶ READ ABOUT STEVE MCQUEEN, ANOTHER ROUGH AND TUMBLE SEX ICON, ON PAGE 368

- ⊛ **PRINCE**
- ⊛ **JIMMY SWAGGART**
- ⊛ **BABY M**
- ⊛ **TOM CRUISE**
- ⊛ **WORKING GIRL**
- ⊛ **ANNE RICE**
- ⊛ **BILLY OCEAN**

Sex Idol

EVENTS

Retailers across the world refused to carry Prince's album "Love Sexy" because the record's cover contained a nude, albeit unrevealing, photograph of Prince. In Denmark a law was passed that granted equal rights to homosexuals.

In the US Jimmy Swaggart admitted to consorting with prostitutes while Robin Givens filed for divorce from fighter Mike Tyson.

The court battle over Baby M ended with custody awarded to the father rather than the surrogate mother.

In the UK, the Acid House scene began, much to the distate of the press and media, as young people began to experiment with a drug called ecstacy and party in open areas such as fields or beaches. Despite widespread derision, this scene heralded the arrival of dance music and young people adopted the "Smiley Face" as their emblem.

POP CULTURE

Cocktail, starring Tom Cruise, gave us a great sound track and an American bartender in Jamaica who spurns a potential soul mate for a rich, older woman—only to realise true love can be its own reward. *Working Girl* brought attention to Melanie Griffith in her role as a secretary who stumbles on an opportunity to move up the ladder—and take her arrogant boss' boyfriend with her. *A Fish Called Wanda* showcased Jamie Lee Curtis, a beautiful con artist who falls in love with the man she's trying to con.

In *The Queen of the Damned* by Anne Rice, the third book in the Vampire Chronicle series, Lestat interrupts the 6,000-year sleep of Akasha, Queen of the Damned, who is bent on ridding the earth of male violence. In the French novel *Le Zèbre*, a husband tries to seduce his wife with anonymous letters to see how she'd react to a secret platonic affair with a stranger. In *Gracie: A Love Story*, George Burns tells the story of his life with Gracie Allen, the woman who was smart enough to become the dumbest woman in show business.

Michael Jackson was still scoring with his "Man in the Mirror." Steve Winwood had a hit with his "Roll With It." Rick Astley promised "Never Gonna Give You Up," and Billy Ocean sang "Get Outta My Dreams, Get into My Car." George Michael also had a hit with "One More Try."

FLORENCE GRIFFITH JOYNER

At the 1988 Olympics in Seoul, Florence Griffith Joyner turned in world record-smashing sprints for the gold medal in the 100 and 200 meter events. Coached by her husband, 1984 Olympic triple-jump gold medallist, Al Joyner, "Flo-Jo," as she was known to her adoring fans, was famous for her supermodel-calibre beauty and flamboyant fashion sense.

With her long, multicolored fingernails, one-legged leotards and shimmering, hooded running suits, Flo-Jo inspired the design for the 1988 US Olympic Team uniform. Tragically, she died at age 39, following a heart seizure. Known as "The Fastest Woman on Earth," Flo-Jo's world records still stand.

SEE ALSO

▶ **AMELIA EARHART** *Page 106*

▶ **JANE FONDA** *Page 441*

1988 CAPRICORN

From December 22, 1987 9:46 through January 20, 1988 20:23
(December 1988 Capricorns, see 1989 Capricorn)

♑ *The Snuggly Sweetheart*

You're a stable Capricorn born in 1988, and you want to fall totally in love with your best friend. You believe in passion, but what really means something to you is that great feeling of being close to someone who is your very best pal. Romance is very exciting to you and it's so much fun to go to school dances and stand around whispering with your friends about that special someone who's caught your eye. You can imagine only too well being the coolest couple in the school, and staying together all the way past graduation.

Being able to trust someone is very important to you. It wouldn't feel good at all to be in a relationship in which you had to worry about cheating. A friend wouldn't do that and a true love shouldn't either. There's a steady rhythm about being with someone who's good for you and that's something you understand very well. Your intuition tells you when a relationship is right and then you work to make it last.

You love computers and other high tech gadgets, and working together with a prospective date on a school project feels comfortable to you. If you can find something in common with a romantic partner, then it becomes easier to connect. You can talk about songs you downloaded, how to email pictures, or what's on television. Even if it doesn't turn into a full-blown romance, at least you're content knowing you've grown closer to a friend.

If you're a male Capricorn born in 1988, you prefer girls with style and flair. Of course, you fall madly in love with the hot women on television—who wouldn't—but in your life you need someone who's interesting and quirky. The girl you like best is smart and eloquent and she has such fascinating viewpoints that sometimes you change your own mind.

As a female Cappie born in 1988, you like a guy who knows his own mind, has solid ethics, and always acts upon his beliefs. Sometimes he's intense and sometimes playful, but you always feel safe and comfortable in his presence. Your fellow appreciates you for your best qualities and shares your interests. You have similar outlooks and want to improve the world.

CAPRICORN ZODIAC SIGN
YOUR LOVE PLANETS

YOUR ROMANTIC SIDE   p. 696
▶ **VENUS IN AQUARIUS**
Born Dec. 22, 1987 9:46 - Jan. 15, 1988 16:03
▶ **VENUS IN PISCES**
Born Jan. 15, 16:04 - Jan. 20, 20:23

YOUR SEX DRIVE   p. 722
▶ **MARS IN SCORPIO**
Born Dec. 22, 1987 9:46 - Jan. 08, 1988 15:23
▶ **MARS IN SAGITTARIUS**
Born Jan. 08, 15:24 - Jan. 20, 20:23

YOUR CELEBRITY TWINS   p. 760
Find out the astrological similarities you have with famous people.

YOUR COMPATIBILITY   p. 780
Compare planets to find out how compatible you are in a relationship.

YOUR RELATIONSHIP KARMA   p. 824
▶ **SATURN IN SAGITTARIUS**
Born Dec. 22, 1987 9:46 - Jan. 20, 1988 20:23

BRUCE WILLIS
American Actor
Venus in Aquarius

573

1988 AQUARIUS

From January 20, 20:24 through February 19, 10:34

♒ *The Mystical Mate*

As an idealistic Aquarian born in 1988, you believe in love, romance and passion. You can easily imagine falling madly in love while shipwrecked on a deserted island, and to you that sounds very cool. A relationship should be all magic and fireworks in your opinion, and you feel that if you can connect with your soul mate, you will have true love. Anything less than that doesn't really interest you.

Because you're so romantic, you form crushes very easily, and that's not such a bad thing because it helps you define what love is— what works for you and who is right for you. Of course, if your crush doesn't return your affection, that can be very hard on you, but you hope one day to have a relationship that is a perfect balance of destiny and caring. Chemistry is another important aspect of a relationship, and those intense, knot-in-the-stomach sort of feelings are the way you know it's love.

The grand romantic gesture really appeals to you and when a potential date starts a rumour that you're involved, keeps circling your home on a bike, or dedicates a song to you on the radio, your interest is quickly aroused. Someone bold enough to serenade outside your window would really win your heart. You love going to dances and parties together, strolling outdoors hand in hand and talking about everything that's on your mind.

As a male Aquarian born in 1988, you like a girl who is musical, creative and mystical. You find it interesting when she insists you were sweethearts in a past life and you love hearing her ideas for the next blockbuster movie. Your honey follows her instincts in life, is sensitive and emotional, and you gladly give her a hug when she's blue. She's soft and kisses you shyly.

If you're a female Aquarian born in 1988, your guy is casual and outgoing. He loves to play with animals and is most comfortable when outdoors. This fellow is a great jokester and he always knows how to make you laugh. Life never seems too serious when you listen to his point of view, yet he also has deep wisdom and caring. You can imagine many great adventures with him at your side.

AQUARIUS ZODIAC SIGN
YOUR LOVE PLANETS

YOUR ROMANTIC SIDE   p. 696
▶ **VENUS IN PISCES**
Born Jan. 20, 20:24 - Feb. 09, 13:03
▶ **VENUS IN ARIES**
Born Feb. 09, 13:04 - Feb. 19, 10:34

YOUR SEX DRIVE   p. 722
▶ **MARS IN SAGITTARIUS**
Born Jan. 20, 20:24 - Feb. 19, 10:34

YOUR CELEBRITY TWINS   p. 760
Find out the astrological similarities you have with famous people.

YOUR COMPATIBILITY   p. 780
Compare planets to find out how compatible you are in a relationship.

YOUR RELATIONSHIP KARMA   p. 824
▶ **SATURN IN SAGITTARIUS**
Born Jan. 20, 20:24 - Feb. 13, 23:59
▶ **SATURN IN CAPRICORN**
Born Feb. 13, 24:00 - Feb. 19, 10:34

GLENN CLOSE
American Actress
Sun and Mars in Pisces

574

1988 PISCES
From February 19, 10:35 through March 20, 9:38

The Devoted Date

You're an impassioned Pisces born in 1988, and you like a relationship that is affectionate and intense. Tepid love stories are not for you! You believe in loving with your whole heart and you want to be adored in return. Other people may call it chemistry, but you call it electricity—that intense feeling when you meet someone and you just know you were meant to be together. That's exactly what you want to have in a relationship!

Commitment is very important to you because you know that once you've both pledged your love, it's safe to share those deep, intense feelings without feeling shy. You want to be able to shout about how you feel and not appear foolish in doing so. Being able to talk to each other about anything and everything makes you feel that not only do you have a good relationship, but that you've connected with just the right person.

The romantic partner who comes up to you and engages you in a fascinating discussion really knows how to get your attention. Even if it seems like a quarrel at first, you don't mind because you like a passionate verbal exchange. A sensitive, affectionate gesture also appeals to you. Being given a flower or a compliment, sharing a dance or a concert, or just talking about life makes you feel you're creating a genuine connection.

If you're a male Pisces born in 1988, you like a girl who isn't shy about showing her affection. Your sweetie will take your hand, squeeze your arm, and give you a hug for no reason at all. You know where you stand with her and that makes you feel safer in opening up. Sometimes she's a bit hasty in declaring her affection, but that's okay with you—it makes you feel desirable.

As a female Fishie born in 1988, your guy is sensitive, yet also practical. He has a quiet sort of strength and usually knows the best way to accomplish any goal. This fellow is analytical and he has lots of useful information, but he also follows his instincts and trusts his impulses. Your sweetie seems mature and responsible and he has an eye to the future. It's fun to discuss goals for success and to hear his point of view.

1988 ARIES
From March 20, 9:39 through April 19, 20:44

The Creative Partner

As an amorous Aries born in 1988, you just love romance and want a relationship that is exciting. You need to feel magic, pizzazz and sparkle, and you've probably been falling madly in love since primary school. For you life without a significant other just isn't as sweet, so you always want to have a steady. You expect one day to be happily married to someone who is your perfect, true love.

You appreciate art and music and enjoy sharing those common interests with a partner. That way you have lots to say to each other and the relationship remains lively and interesting. You feel that a relationship is a happy little lifeboat in which you two can paddle along, sharing funny stories about people at school, and collaborating on creative projects. You can easily envision yourself as an adult in a marriage that is also a business partnership with that same "you and me against the world" mentality.

A partner must be creative and interesting to gain your attention, and even before you actually meet, you might have admired this person's artistic or musical style from a distance at school. You trust what feels right, and a casual or even accidental encounter during which you share a few amusing words can be enough to launch you into a relationship.

As a male Ram born in 1988, you like a girl who knows what she wants and has the courage to go after it. Having a gal pursue you is a big kick, though usually you're so busy chasing girls that it's hard to tell who's running in which direction. Your sweetie is smart and creative and she has things to say that are never run of the mill. You enjoy her impulsiveness and her kisses.

If you're a female Aries born in 1988, you like a guy who knows how to be macho and assertive. Your fellow has a well-developed point of view and he's never shy about expressing his ideas. He likes sports and often seems more comfortable hanging out with his pals than in the dating scene. You don't mind, though, because you'd rather have a normal, self-conscious guy than some silly ladies' man. When he takes your hand in his, you know he means it.

1988 TAURUS

From April 19, 20:45 through May 20, 19:56

The Perky Partner

You're a communicative Taurus and you need a relationship filled with zing and excitement. A lively intellectual connection is as important to you as a sense of attraction because your interest in someone begins in your mind. You like to know that there's something to say. Standing around with a date and fumbling to begin a conversation doesn't appeal to you at all.

Interacting on a creative level is also important to you because that ensures that you will remain fascinated and stimulated by each other. You're an excellent collaborator and you consider a relationship a partnership in which emotions should combine with ideas. You feel that chemistry contains a sort of mutual sparkle that makes you both light up while you're in the other's presence. To you that is the best part of a relationship because it inspires you to become interesting individuals while remaining best pals.

You know exactly what appeals to you when you meet someone and can easily imagine an adult relationship with a sweetheart who sparks your imagination. A clever joke or amusing double entendre is the perfect opening gambit for a partner who wants to steal your heart. You love walking along, talking, sharing ideas, or even just ducking into a fast food place to hang out with friends and enjoy each other's company.

If you're a male Bull born in 1988, you like a girl with wit. Your sweetie may be sporty or head of the debate team, but whatever she does, people like and find her interesting. She's slender, will always remain youthful, and you can imagine her much unchanged fifty years into the future. There's always a book in her backpack and she loves greeting cards and email.

As a female Taurus born in 1988, your fellow is macho. Even though he's still a boy, he seems like a man's man and you can envision him growing up to be a very protective mate. Your guy can seem quirky at times—his taste is often hilariously eccentric and he has amazing, visionary ideas. You love the way he kids around to make you laugh, and the straightforward way he reaches out when he wants to hold your hand.

TAURUS ZODIAC SIGN
YOUR LOVE PLANETS

YOUR ROMANTIC SIDE   p. 696
▶ **VENUS IN GEMINI**
Born Apr. 19, 20:45 - May 17, 16:25
▶ **VENUS IN CANCER**
Born May 17, 16:26 - May 20, 19:56

YOUR SEX DRIVE   P. 722
▶ **MARS IN AQUARIUS**
Born Apr. 19, 20:45 - May 20, 19:56

YOUR CELEBRITY TWINS   p. 760
Find out the astrological similarities you have with famous people.

YOUR COMPATIBILITY   p. 780
Compare planets to find out how compatible you are in a relationship.

YOUR RELATIONSHIP KARMA   p. 824
▶ **SATURN IN CAPRICORN**
Born Apr. 19, 20:45 - May 20, 19:56

STEFFI GRAF
German Tennis Champion
Sun in Gemini

575

1988 GEMINI

From May 20, 19:57 through June 21, 3:56

The Romantic Rebel

As a dynamic Gemini, you need a relationship that keeps you emotionally involved and intellectually connected. Although you admit that you fall in love rather quickly, you also realise that some depth is necessary in your interaction for it to be a real relationship. You believe in destiny and in finding the right partner, and you hope that your intuition will point you toward your soul mate. Right now you're just trying partners on for size!

Being able to talk about ideas and to share information makes you feel closer in a relationship. You could never be with someone who is dumb, no matter how attractive. The freedom to pursue your own hobbies will always be necessary in your relationship. You don't think two people need to be shackled together to be in love because outside interests are necessary to keep you both stimulated. Changing and growing together is a wonderful thing, but you also feel it's worthwhile in a relationship to grow as individuals, too.

You like spunk and even a bit of outrageousness in a partner, so when someone pulls a daft stunt to get your attention, you're totally impressed. If a date shoves a book in your face and says, "You gotta read this," you like knowing your sweetie wants an intellectual exchange. Whispering and passing notes in the library is another fun way to get your attention.

As a male Gemini born in 1988, you like a girl who is intelligent, raucous and unpredictable. Conventional girls with little pink bows in their hair bore you. You'd far rather spend time with a rebel who has too many earrings and challenging opinions. Your gal loves to play jokes, she always has a witty remark, and sometimes you just don't know where you stand with her.

If you're a female Gemini born in 1988, your favourite guy is sensitive, but also macho. He has an uncanny way of knowing what you're feeling and thinking, and he always reaches out to help you if you're down. Even though he's rather intuitive and sometimes you're sure he's psychic, your sweetie isn't wimpy at all. He's strong and you feel his presence—and his kisses—can be quite healing.

GEMINI ZODIAC SIGN
YOUR LOVE PLANETS

YOUR ROMANTIC SIDE   p. 696
▶ **VENUS IN CANCER**
Born May 20, 19:57 - May 27, 7:35
▶ **VENUS IN GEMINI**
Born May 27, 7:36 - June 21, 3:56

YOUR SEX DRIVE   p. 722
▶ **MARS IN AQUARIUS**
Born May 20, 19:57 - May 22, 7:41
▶ **MARS IN PISCES**
Born May 22, 7:42 - June 21, 3:56

YOUR CELEBRITY TWINS   p. 760
Find out the astrological similarities you have with famous people.

YOUR COMPATIBILITY   p. 780
Compare planets to find out how compatible you are in a relationship.

YOUR RELATIONSHIP KARMA   p. 824
▶ **SATURN IN CAPRICORN**
Born May 20, 19:57 - June 10, 5:07
▶ **SATURN IN SAGITTARIUS BORN** *June 10, 5:08 - June 21, 3:56*

JODIE FOSTER
American Actress
Mars in Leo

576

1988 CANCER
From June 21, 3:57 through July 22, 14:50

The Sweet Talker

You're a chatty Cancer born in 1988, and good conversation is the cornerstone of your relationship. You love to snuggle on the couch with someone special and talk about anything and everything. If you had a scrapbook, it would be a tape recorder on which you could capture some of the most memorable sound bites from your own sweetest love story. Sharing silence does not appeal to you at all, not when there's so much to discuss.

You feel that compromise is an important part of any relationship and if people were less selfish, relationships would endure. Being with someone who is as willing as you are to share and co-operate is top of your list. Mutual interests are also important to you in a relationship because the more things you have in common, the less sacrifice is needed. Wanting to share adventures and pleasures is as important to you as exchanging ideas.

Your relationships usually begin with a long, fascinating conversation, and even if you're just fantasising about a crush on someone, you love to make up the dialogue you each might speak.

A date who says sweet things is always memorable to you, and when you think back to the precise moment in which you fell in love, it's always the tender remarks you recall. You also enjoy sharing bike rides, boat trips and parties with mutual friends.

If you're a male Crab born in 1988, your special girl is clever and amusing. She may talk too much, but because her comments are so astute and fascinating, you don't mind at all. She is spry and playful, may be rather athletic, although she's rarely disciplined and often changes her mind. Your sweetie loves the current fashion, carries books and magazines wherever she goes, and everyone you know loves her company.

As a female Cancer born in 1988, you like a guy who is intuitive, hard working, yet also a rebel. Your fellow knows what he wants, but sometimes he's too shy to go after it. Then you give him a nudge and he feels more confident. He is often unpredictable, delightfully creative and very individualistic, but still he tries to fit in at school and to get good grades.

1988 LEO
From July 22, 14:51 through August 22, 21:53

The Security Seeker

As a co-operative Leo born in 1988, you want a close relationship in which you both help and support each other. Being an independent individual is always important, but it also feels right to you to be part of a team. That way you learn balance. You also feel that a little self-sacrifice is warranted in a relationship, but that each person should love and give equally.

You want to share strong, deep feelings and a positive sense of intimacy with a partner. Knowing that you're loved, accepted and appreciated makes you feel good about yourself and even more in love with your sweetheart. Security is very important to you and you will always want to feel safe within a committed relationship. Even now you're happier with a steady partner to count on and love, but you know that the real thing takes time and maturity to find.

You appreciate a date who makes an effort to know what appeals to you because even a small gesture is very meaningful. You love impromptu outings in which you follow mutual whims and just enjoy each other's company. You consider an excellent date something as simple as a trip to the playground where you squeeze onto the swings and talk as you float up into the sky. It's also fun to stroll through a shopping centre, listen to music or visit a beach.

As a male Leo born in 1988, a girl who is rather complicated and difficult to unravel appeals to you a great deal more than someone who is straightforward and dull. Your best girl is a bit intense, definitely emotional and sometimes seems a little needy—which causes you to wonder what's going on deep inside. She is artistic and creative and has an interesting point of view that never fails to surprise you.

If you're a lady Lion born in 1988, you like a guy who is assertive and macho, but not so sure of himself that he's a joke. Your fellow has a sweet innocence and a sentimental way of looking at the world, although he would deny that if you pointed it out. He's quite musical and he loves to serenade you, perhaps even with songs he wrote himself. He's also exciting and his kisses make you swoon.

1988 VIRGO

From August 22, 21:54 through September 22, 19:28

The Ardent Romantic

You're a passionate Virgo born in 1988, and you want a relationship that touches your heart and thrills your soul. Virgo may be a practical sign, but in love you're impetuous and romantic, and being too practical is the farthest thing from your mind. Sometimes you fall in love at first sight and it's very easy for you to chase a crush, but in your heart you really want one true love with whom you can share your life forever. You're probably in love with someone right now, and maybe you even fantasise about marrying that person, but we know you won't do that too quickly!

Loving and nurturing someone you adore is the essence of a relationship for you, and you look forward to a perfect bond in which you and a mate are devoted to each other. Building a happy family is another aspect of a good relationship—even when you were a small child you liked to play house. You feel that a family provides the warmest and most supportive atmosphere in which to love and be loved, and also one in which each person can express his or her individuality.

Chemistry is always the number one reason why you respond to someone who wants to date you. If you feel that electricity, you want to proceed. You do appreciate a tender glance, loving gesture, or thoughtful invitation. Someone who can show love easily is just your sort of person. On a date you'd enjoy a family gathering, sporting event, concert, or even a dress-up occasion.

If you're a male Virgo born in 1988, frivolous girls don't appeal to you at all. You prefer someone sweet and tender, soft and cuddly, and whose eyes light up when you enter the room. Your sweetie is beautiful, luminous and sometimes glamorous. But the best thing about her is her gentle heart and the way she opens her arms for a hug.

As a female Virgo born in 1988, you want to be excited by the guy in your life. Tepid nerds need not apply! Your fellow is strong and domineering, yet sensitive enough not to spend too much time with his foot in his mouth. He's emotional, a little psychic and a true individual, and he's also able to understand you and your needs.

VIRGO ZODIAC SIGN
YOUR LOVE PLANETS

YOUR ROMANTIC SIDE p. 696
▶ **VENUS IN CANCER**
Born Aug. 22, 21:54 - Sept. 07, 11:36
▶ **VENUS IN LEO**
Born Sept. 07, 11:37 - Sept. 22, 19:28

YOUR SEX DRIVE p. 722
▶ **MARS IN ARIES**
Born Aug. 22, 21:54 - Sept. 22, 19:28

YOUR CELEBRITY TWINS p. 760
Find out the astrological similarities you have with famous people.

YOUR COMPATIBILITY p. 780
Compare planets to find out how compatible you are in a relationship.

YOUR RELATIONSHIP KARMA p. 824
▶ **SATURN IN SAGITTARIUS**
Born Aug. 22, 21:54 - Sept. 22, 19:28

BARBARA TAYLOR BRADFORD
English Writer
Mars in Virgo

577

1988 LIBRA

From September 22, 19:29 through October 23, 4:43

The Thoughtful Romantic

As a loving Libra born in 1988, you want a relationship that features just the right degree of give and take. Balance is quite important to you and knowing that you can get along harmoniously with a partner is very comforting. Compromise is always necessary, and you find that within a good partnership, you learn more about yourself and your needs as a result of the concessions you make for your loved one's feelings. You think there's too much quarrelling in the world and you prefer to avoid it by being considerate.

Acceptance and understanding are traits important to you because you believe that a relationship is a source of growth as well as happiness, and being free enough to share your deepest emotions makes you feel secure. Nurturing and being cared for in return are also meaningful and that way you know that you're genuinely loved.

A grand romantic gesture is often the way to your heart. You just can't help enjoying the process of being wooed! A potential date who offers you a sweet gift, a helping hand, or a

particularly meaningful compliment is likely to find the keys to your heart. You enjoy attending carnivals, sporting events and you're not even adverse to pitching in and working at a charity event while on a date.

As a male Libra born in 1988, you want to spend time with a girl who is outgoing and exciting. Your little sweetie has spunk and you love that about her. She is affectionate and caring and will always be in your corner when you're in need. This girl can be very glamorous, but she's not about the latest fashion because she's clever enough to have style of her own. She is pretty and popular, and you feel happier when she's in the room.

If you're a female Libra born in 1988, your favourite fellow is rather complicated. Sometimes he seems quite self-centred, but just as you start to get annoyed, he displays his sensitive side. He really doesn't want to hurt your feelings and will apologise if he does. You like that he's exciting and dramatic and can be so romantic that when he takes you in his arms, it's almost like being in a fairy tale or movie.

LIBRA ZODIAC SIGN
YOUR LOVE PLANETS

YOUR ROMANTIC SIDE p. 696
▶ **VENUS IN LEO**
Born Sept. 22, 19:29 - Oct. 04, 13:14
▶ **VENUS IN VIRGO**
Born Oct. 04, 13:15 - Oct. 23, 4:43

YOUR SEX DRIVE p. 722
▶ **MARS IN ARIES**
Born Sept. 22, 19:29 - Oct. 23, 4:43

YOUR CELEBRITY TWINS p. 760
Find out the astrological similarities you have with famous people.

YOUR COMPATIBILITY p. 780
Compare planets to find out how compatible you are in a relationship.

YOUR RELATIONSHIP KARMA p. 824
▶ **SATURN IN SAGITTARIUS**
Born Sept. 22, 19:29 - Oct. 23, 4:43

JOHN MALKOVICH
American Actor
Sun and Venus in Sagittarius

578

1988 SCORPIO
From October 23, 4:44 through November 22, 2:11

♏ The Mannerly Mate

You're a genteel Scorpio born in 1988, and your relationship must be harmonious and romantic. You don't want to struggle, quarrel, or complain. You're much happier when there's intimacy in combination with good manners. Looking out for what makes a partner happy is as important to you as being happy yourself and, along with politeness, makes for the best kind of relationship.

You admit freely that romance can be a lot of work, but you don't mind because you feel a relationship is something worth working at. Life just doesn't fall into place— you're more than willing to get out there and build a happy partnership. Responsibility is important to you because you realise that love isn't just about tender emotions. It's about nurturing, caring for, and supporting one another. Love isn't all drudgery, though, and you adore the sweet little romantic touches that can make love special.

Attending elegant parties would appeal very much to you and you'd enjoy being with a partner who has the grace and charm to share such a special event. Dressing up, dancing to soft music and whispering little secrets in each other's ears are things that make life more special and are the turning point in any true romance. If you can whirl around the dance floor successfully and comfortably, you see potential for a relationship.

If you're a male Scorpion born in 1988, the girl of your dreams is classically pretty. Good taste really matters to you and you could hardly envision yourself madly in love with someone crass and tacky. No way! Your sweetheart is elegant, well mannered and liked by everyone. She has much personal sparkle, but she's subtle too. She always knows just the right thing to say and do.

As a female Scorpio born in 1988, you can envision spending the rest of your life with a guy who is a good leader, assertive, outgoing and dynamic, yet self-controlled when necessary. Your fellow has a strong personality and he makes an immediate impression. He has an appreciation for work and for music and you feel he's complicated in the very best way. He can be serious and romantic!

1988 SAGITTARIUS
From November 22, 2:12 through December 21, 15:27

♐ The Passionate Playmate

As an intense Sagittarian born in 1988, you gravitate toward relationships filled with almost cinematic levels of passion and drama. Love is what it's all about to you, and there has to be that compelling, intense connection or else what hope is there of building anything worthwhile? You believe in true love and lifetime commitments, and that's why you don't find casual entanglements all that hard to resist. Of course, you're not crazy, and as a teen, you know that marriage isn't on your agenda for a long while—but you do like fantasising about the future.

Personal self-expression is important to you, and you feel that a good relationship will provide you with the necessary acceptance and freedom to be the great person you are. You are always willing to afford that same courtesy to a partner. Mutual interests are another strong, binding factor. If you have similar preferences, it's easier to stay connected to each other.

A deep and meaningful glance may not seem all that significant, but to you it's the way to your heart. Staring into someone's eyes gives you a sense of whether or not any true connection could ever emerge. You like casual activities and interesting conversations, but really they're just the trappings for your romance. If your hands brush and sparks fly, you perk up and take notice. What it's all about are the feelings just below the surface!

As a male Archer born in 1988, you gravitate toward females who seem more like women than girls. Your lady is intense, passionate and she knows her own mind and heart. She is in touch with all those deep feelings and has no problem reaching out for what she wants. She might just grab you in the corridor at school and plant a sweet kiss right on your lips.

If you're a female Sagittarian born in 1988, you expect a guy to be rather complicated. Sometimes he's erratic and even selfish, and just as you're about to write him off, he turns sensitive, considerate and charming. At least he's never dull! Your sweetie is interesting, his ideas are always fun to hear, and he's a hard worker with many useful skills.

Sensual, Sexy Susan Sarandon

Susan Sarandon is a rare creature in Hollywood—a woman who has gotten better with maturity. At an age—late-fifties—where other female stars have been relegated to minor roles, she is still one of the hottest chicks around.

It was while married to drama student Chris Sarandon that she realised she might have a future in acting when an agent signed both of them. After taking small parts that forced her to hone her craft, Sarandon starred with Robert Redford in 1975 in *The Great Waldo Pepper*—the perfect launch to a likely golden career.

That same year she turned around and took a part in an offbeat musical film, *The Rocky Horror Picture Show*, thereby beginning a pattern of selecting a variety of roles to keep from being typecast. She played Janet Weiss, an innocent who is corrupted by a transvestite when she and her fiance stop for the night at a spooky castle. This low-budget flick became a cult classic for its over-the-top gender-bending and sexual risk taking.

A few years later, she got a role in Louis Malle's *Pretty Baby*, and then in his *Atlantic City*, which earned her an Academy Award nomination. Her personal life also underwent changes during this period. She divorced her husband Chris, although she kept his name, and began dating Malle. Later she dated Sean Penn, who is fourteen years younger, followed by a relationship with Italian director Franco Amurri, eight years younger, with whom she has a daughter.

In 1983 Sarandon appeared in *The Hunger* playing the lover of a bisexual vampire, followed by a role in *The Witches of Eastwick*, a film that brought her further into the Hollywood arena with the likes of Jack Nicholson and

579

Cher. By this time, she was holding her own against the big stars and decided to actively pursue the next role she was interested in, the leading lady in *Bull Durham*. Needless to say, she got the part.

She also won the heart of her *Bull Durham* co-star, Tim Robbins. The two have been together since 1988, living with their two sons and Sarandon's daughter. As with Sarandon's other love interests, Robbins is also younger, by eight years. Both are Libras, but it's likely that Robbins' Mercury in Scorpio combined with Sarandon's Scorpio Venus is what keeps things percolating between them in more ways than one. Beginning with war protests in the sixties, Sarandon (now joined by Robbins) has been a vocal activist for numerous issues and causes. Speaking out for what she

believes in and against what she doesn't, Sarandon has garnered considerable press for such issues as the imprisonment of Haitians for having AIDS.

Sarandon has continued to grab gutsy roles, such as Louise in *Thelma and Louise*, which netted her a nomination for Best Actress. Sarandon's Louise gave life to a woman's road trip flick that shattered norms and raised the bar, giving women the option of violence. But it was Tim Robbins' *Dead Man Walking* (1995) that finally brought Sarandon an Oscar for her role as Sister Helen Prejean, a nun who helps a death-row convict as his time dwindles.

Sarandon is still very active and on the scene. Actor, mother, committed partner and social activist, she continues to prove that being sexy and vibrant has nothing to do with age.

▶ READ ABOUT SEAN PENN AND HIS BRIEF MARRIAGE TO MADONNA ON PAGE 548 ▶ READ ABOUT GOTH CULTURE ON PAGE 539

1989

- ⍟ MTV
- ⍟ ABORTION
- ⍟ THE PAMELA BORDES AFFAIR
- ⍟ WHEN HARRY MET SALLY
- ⍟ GILDA RADNER
- ⍟ JANET JACKSON
- ⍟ WE DIDN'T START THE FIRE

EVENTS

Even at the end of the decade attempts at censorship were still going strong. In the US, Cincinnati tried to shut down the homoerotic art show of famous photographer Robert Mapplethorpe, and a Pepsi commercial set to Madonna's song "Like A Prayer" was pulled after one airing because religious groups were offended by the song's video. MTV instilled a policy that a lyric sheet must accompany all videos submitted to the network so the network could reject videos that endorsed violence, drugs, alcohol, or explicit depictions of sexual practices. The US Supreme Court ruled 5 to 4, upholding a Missouri law that placed state restrictions on abortion, stopping short of overturning the historic 1973 Roe vs. Wade decision.

In what the press dubbed "The Pamela Bordes Affair," a call girl employed by the House of Commons made London tremble. The first marriages between homosexuals were legally celebrated in Denmark.

POP CULTURE

When Harry Met Sally—and one scene in particular—spawned a decade's worth of moaning shampoo ads. *Always* is a classic love triangle, with a twist—one character is dead and must learn to let go while helping the new man take his place. In *Sea of Love*, a detective compromises an investigation and endangers his life when he falls in

Sex Idol

love with a suspected serial killer. *The Fabulous Baker Boys* showcased the Bridges brothers as two piano-playing brothers who hire a beautiful singer to spice up their act, but jealousies threaten their new success.

Two autobiographies and one biography made the best seller lists. *It's Always Something* by Gilda Radner, covered her career, her marriage to Gene Wilder and her struggle to battle the cancer that ended her life. Roseanne Barr authored *Roseanne: My Life as a Woman*, and *A Woman Named Jackie* gave us an intimate look at the fairy-tale life of Jacqueline Bouvier Kennedy Onassis.

Although Michael Jackson was quiet this year, his sister Janet had a hit with "Miss You Much." Madonna was still going strong with "Like a Prayer," and Billy Joel belted out "We Didn't Start the Fire." Paula Abdul sang "Straight Up" and Phil Collins cut "Another Day in Paradise."

MICHELLE PFEIFFER

Who knew Michelle Pfeiffer could sing? In *The Fabulous Baker Boys* (1989) in a role turned down by Madonna, Pfeiffer revealed her exceptional vocal talents. Starring as a sexy torch singer—accompanied by a pair of bickering brothers (played by real-life brothers Jeff and Beau Bridges)—Pfeiffer proved she was much more than just another gorgeous face. Her performance garnered Pfeiffer's second Oscar nomination. The first was for *Dangerous Liaisons* (1988).

Pfeiffer wed *thirtysomething* star Peter Horton in 1981. The couple divorced in 1989. She married *Ally McBeal* producer David Kelly in 1993, and today Pfeiffer continues to be one of Hollywood's hottest stars.

SEE ALSO

▶ MADONNA *Pages 548 & 555*
▶ RITA HAYWORTH *Page 228*

1989 CAPRICORN

From December 21, 1988 15:28 through January 20, 1989 2:06 (December 1989 Capricorns, see 1990 Capricorn)

The Focused Mate

Ever since you were young, Capricorn of 1989, you've always liked to sink your teeth into anything that interests you—whether a project at school, or a fascinating new hobby. As you mature, you will always be going somewhere, moving ahead while others are marking time on the road of life. When it comes to being in love and being with another person, your attitudes will be much the same, except that you will be moving ahead and moving on with that person, the two of you trying to find your way together.

Falling in love means that you focus on just one person, because in that area of your life you likely won't want to see a lot of change. You expect that whether you get involved in a very close relationship or a marriage, it will last and last, and the two of you will sink your teeth into it the way you do everything else.

The person who wants to catch your eye needs a lot of energy to do so because you'll always be a moving target. If you meet someone who seems to have boundless enthusiasm and who likes to participate in a lot of varied activities, you're probably going to be drawn to that person. Attraction isn't everything, though—anyone who wants to hold onto you needs to show an enthusiasm for the things you're doing and an interest in helping you do them.

For the 1989 Capricorn male, the kind of lady you're likely to end up marrying is someone who always seems to have a smile on her face, a song in her heart and a good idea of where she is going. She will love to talk to you for hours on end, listening to your ideas and your plans and offering suggestions on how they can work better. She will probably have a very sweet romantic side, and she'll be the kind of girl who likes long walks and holding hands.

If you're a 1989 Capricorn female, you could well end up paired with a very dynamic man who seems very much in control of his own life and destiny. Even though he probably will be a self-made type, he is into sharing, too, especially if you want to help in his work and help him fulfil his cherished dreams. But he also likes nice quiet times around the house.

AMY TAN
American Writer
Sun in Aquarius

581

1989 AQUARIUS

From January 20, 2:07 through February 18, 16:20

The Eclectic Darling

You love spending time alone or chatting on your computer, Aquarius of 1989, almost as much as you love joining clubs and socialising with friends. Some people may think you are a loner and others may consider you a social butterfly. When it comes to love, you will never have to choose being one or the other, because you will be loved for the totality of who you are. You will be in love with love, and with the idea of having a loving partner.

You will likely see a relationship as kind of a window on the rest of the world, with your true love showing you things in the world outside yourself you might not otherwise see. You can also be a window into a world of imagination and exploration for your partner. Together the two of you will help each other see things that neither one alone could.

To attract your attention someone who is interested in you needs to reach out and touch your mind, intriguing you with stories of travels, personal adventures, or future journeys you could take together. You're not much interested in flirtation, and anyone who tries

that out on you will just get a very cold shoulder. What you most appreciate in someone is a good mind and a real liking for people, something you'll know on your very first date.

If you're a 1989 Aquarius male, your perfect girl will be a real people person, someone who likes to mingle and who has an address book full of the names of her many friends and acquaintances. When she sweeps into a room, she will turn heads, because she will bring a refreshing sparkle that people notice and appreciate. You'll be more than proud to be with her, and though you'll love going out with her, you will love being alone together more than anything.

The perfect mate for you, 1989 Aquarius female, will at first glance remind you of someone you've seen on film. He may not be quite as handsome as a real movie star, but he will have a way about him that makes people take notice. Even though he will love to take you out and show you the town (and show you off as well), more than anything he loves his quiet time with you, and you alone.

ELLEN BARKIN
American Actress
Sun in Aries

1989 PISCES
From February 18, 16:21 through March 20, 15:27

The Soulful Dreamer

From the time you were very young, Pisces of 1989, you've always had big dreams of things you want to do, places you would like to see and perhaps even of a lavish lifestyle to go along with it. You like the idea of being rich and famous, but at the same time you also envision someone next to you to share the good times. And not just anyone, but a special someone you're sure you will meet one day.

In reality, your glamorous dreams are only a setting for your real goal, which is to have a soul mate, someone you intuitively understand and who intuitively understands you. As you grow up, you may from time to time meet people with whom you sense this kind of connection. But you'll know when the real thing comes along, when the two of you make plans for the future the moment you meet.

If someone wants to attract you, the first requirement is something a person can't fake—that inner intuition that makes you feel there is something right and familiar about this person. More than that, you will like someone who is open, honest and who shows an ability to share

and to sacrifice when necessary. Making you laugh or talking honestly about real emotions will clue you in that this person may be the one.

If you're a 1989 Pisces male, the future girl of your dreams will be someone with the perfect combination of that intuitive spark, the ability to enjoy herself and a warm and welcoming personality. She will want very much to share your dreams with you, but won't be shy about asking you to share hers as well. Working out how each of you can realise these dreams and doing it together will probably be your favourite activity.

The 1989 Pisces female will know her perfect man the minute he walks in the room. He won't be the kind of guy who draws everyone's attention, but he'll have a certain sensitive quality about him that will tell you there's more to him than most people see at first glance. His innate cheerfulness and his ability to understand you better than most people will lift you high when you're up emotionally, and keep you from falling too far down when you have the blues.

1989 ARIES
From March 20, 15:28 through April 20, 2:38

The Adoring Leader

You may not always be quite sure of what you'd like to be someday, Aries of 1989, but you have always felt that it will be exciting and special, and something everyone will take notice of. The bold approach you'll take to life will match the bold approach you take to love. When you're out on your own, you'll always know just what you want and how to get it, and the same will be true in your close relationships.

You like to be the leader where any kind of partnership is concerned, and this will be at least as true in romantic relationships as anything else. That doesn't mean that you see being together with someone you love as a one-sided proposition. You like to share, and as you mature, you will want to make joint decisions with the one you love. Sharing your life means sharing everything in your eyes, though you will probably take the lead more often than not.

Anyone who wants to attract your attention needs to give you centre stage, yet must also know how to challenge you in a gentle and friendly way, thus making you earn that lead position. The person who wants to win you has

to show you that life will be interesting when the two of you are together. Gentle kisses, good conversation and weekend outings to new places are a wonderful way to start.

The girl of your dreams, Aries male of 1989, will be someone who can be brassy and sassy, but with a touch of humour and a contagious laugh. She will back you up in everything you do, but also will tell you when she sees a better way for you to accomplish your goals. Even though you're pretty much the top dog in the relationship, you do need someone who's not afraid to remind you that you sometimes make mistakes and that you're as human as anyone else.

If you're an Aries female of 1989, your perfect man knows who he is and where he's going, but isn't afraid to share the road ahead with you. He will admire your ability to speak up and say what's on your mind, and will always listen to your ideas, your advice and your opinions. He's someone who sees you as his best friend and a girl he admires as much as he loves.

1989 TAURUS
From April 20, 2:39 through May 21, 1:53

The Steady Sweetheart

You're a very focused person, Taurus of 1989, someone who from a very young age has been able to stick to a task and see it all the way through to the end. You like the feeling of completeness you get from taking a project, large or small, from the planning stages to the final steps, as well as the satisfaction you get from knowing you have created something important. This same ability will stand you in good stead in your future relationships.

Just as you see everything you do as deserving of your complete attention and devotion, you will also feel the same when it comes to loving another person—nothing should be left to chance. In many ways you're old-fashioned and you won't easily understand people who seem to move from one romance to the next without much thought or care. For you romantic commitment means just what it says.

Anyone who would like to come into your life needs to understand this point—which means that flirting with you from across the room, as harmless as that may seem, is not the way to get your heart. You will like that kind of attention as much as anyone, but you'll be more interested in someone you can get to know close up and in a more serious way. The person who can engage your eyes, your mind and your heart all at the same time is the one you'll choose.

Your dream girl, 1989 Taurus male, has soulful eyes, a lovely face and an even more beautiful heart. From the moment you meet her, you will know that she's the kind who works hard at any commitment she makes, especially one as important as a commitment to the most important person in her life. She'll take you seriously, but she'll also be good at keeping you from being too serious. No one will be able to make you laugh the way she will.

For the 1989 Taurus female, the man you're likely to share your life with will be someone who has a vision of where he wants to be and how he wants to get there. Even though he's serious about his plans, he wants to include you in them, and will adjust those plans to take your ideas into consideration. He'll be the kind of person you can count on always.

TAURUS ZODIAC SIGN
Your Love Planets

YOUR ROMANTIC SIDE   p. 696
- ▶ **VENUS IN TAURUS**
  Born Apr. 20, 2:39 - May 11, 6:27
- ▶ **VENUS IN GEMINI**
  Born May 11, 6:28 - May 21, 1:53

YOUR SEX DRIVE   p. 722
- ▶ **MARS IN GEMINI**
  Born Mar. 20, 2:39 - Apr. 29, 4:36
- ▶ **MARS IN CANCER**
  Born Apr. 29, 4:37 - May 21, 1:53

YOUR CELEBRITY TWINS   p. 760
Find out the astrological similarities you have with famous people.

YOUR COMPATIBILITY   p. 780
Compare planets to find out how compatible you are in a relationship.

YOUR RELATIONSHIP KARMA   p. 824
- ▶ **SATURN IN CAPRICORN**
  Born Mar. 20, 2:39 - May 21, 1:53

DANIEL DAY-LEWIS
English Actor
Sun and Venus in Taurus

583

1989 GEMINI
From May 21, 1:54 through June 21, 9:52

The Spiritual Romantic

When love comes your way, Gemini of 1989, it is likely to be both exciting and a bit vexing. On the one hand, it will open up new vistas for you, giving you a new understanding of the world and perhaps even a vision of the possibilities for your own future. On the other hand, it will often knock you off course, making you shift gears and change plans when you least expect it.

Love gives you inspiring and spiritual feelings, making you think it involves a power greater than yourself, as if the cosmos has touched you somehow. Since others tend to see it in a more earthbound and practical way, you will have to use your charm, appeal and great instincts to combine your uplifting view with someone else's simple need for companionship. Once you have had some experience and made some adjustments, anyone you fall in love with will be lucky indeed.

The person who would like to get your attention, and perhaps even win your heart, is the one who will show you first a lighthearted, even humourous side, and then a more serious, committed side after you get to know each other. You like someone who can throw you a little off balance, yet catch you before you fall with a smile or a funny story. Once you know you can have fun with this person, you'll be ready for whatever comes next.

The 1989 Gemini male needs the kind of girl who loves to have fun and be funny, but is also sincere and even bookish, at times. Though she'll be very adept at dealing with people, especially in social situations, she also has a spiritual side. You'll love nothing more than to explore that aspect of her. She needs to be by herself at times to think and to meditate, but only for a while, because she needs being together with you much more.

For the 1989 Gemini female, the type of man you're likely to become involved with is someone who may be a little more worldly than you, someone who is able to handle the details of every day life so you don't have to bother with them yourself. He's generous and helpful, but most of all, he understands your spiritual needs. You'll never feel safer than when you're with him.

GEMINI ZODIAC SIGN
Your Love Planets

YOUR ROMANTIC SIDE   p. 696
- ▶ **VENUS IN GEMINI**
  Born May 21, 1:54 - June 04, 17:16
- ▶ **VENUS IN CANCER**
  Born June 04, 17:17 - June 21, 9:52

YOUR SEX DRIVE   p. 722
- ▶ **MARS IN CANCER**
  Born May 21, 1:54 - June 16, 14:09
- ▶ **MARS IN LEO**
  Born June 16, 14:10 - June 21, 9:52

YOUR CELEBRITY TWINS   p. 760
Find out the astrological similarities you have with famous people.

YOUR COMPATIBILITY   p. 780
Compare planets to find out how compatible you are in a relationship.

YOUR RELATIONSHIP KARMA   p. 824
- ▶ **SATURN IN CAPRICORN**
  Born May 21, 1:54 - June 21, 9:52

1989 CANCER From June 21, 9:53 through July 22, 20:44

The Devoted Healer

KENNETH BRANAGH
Irish Director
Mars in Cancer

You have always been devoted to those you care about, Cancer of 1989, and as you mature, you will instinctively know how to give and receive love unselfishly. Relationships will be a healing experience, a way to bring two people together and bring out their best. You tend to place other people's needs before your own, showing how to help others without asking anything in return—a quality that will benefit your future relationships.

As much as you love doing for others, you have an entirely private side, one filled with creative expression, especially music, that is for you and you alone. Because of this the more any partnership is filled with music, the better it will be. You'll be happiest if you're with someone who can attend concerts with you or simply create a romantic environment by making your own music together.

To attract you someone will have to brim with brilliance and creativity from head to toe. Doing something wildly romantic such as reciting a love poem out loud, writing a song just for you, or sending you a well-written love letter will have you interested and asking for more. You will especially appreciate someone who can prepare a wonderful home-cooked meal or take you to a great restaurant you would never find on your own.

The girl for you, 1989 Cancer male, will be dynamic and always raring to go. Assertive, attractive and full of energy, this take-charge woman will be proud to have you on her arm, and probably will organise your life so you never have to worry about anything practical again. With your giving nature you will bring out her softer side, and the times you are alone together will be spent creating your own romantic moments.

Demonstrative guys who express their love freely are the ones who will tickle your fancy, 1989 Cancer female. You will be attracted to original, inventive men, so the more outlandish he is in what he wears, what he says and where he takes you, the better. At a moment's notice he's liable to show you how much he loves you by taking you off for a wonderful weekend to a place you would never think of on your own.

1989 LEO *From July 22, 20:45 through August 23, 3:45*

The Imaginative Romantic

As you approach adulthood, Leo of 1989, you will naturally become more and more excited about the prospects that love can bring. You just love imagining yourself falling into a storybook romance when you least expect it, as your eyes meet a stranger's eyes and you both know on the spot you are right for each other. Though such scenes may be just your imagination talking, you always have the hope that they will happen for real.

Caring, generous, yet direct in expressing your feelings, you believe that in a relationship you should be able to talk freely about everything you think and feel. You will want your beloved to be someone who allows you to speak from your heart, and who admires you for your honesty. In the perfect partnership you take centre stage, and your partner is there to applaud when you succeed and to support you when you do not.

The person who wants to catch your eye must be able to walk into a room and make everyone take notice—especially you. You don't like beating around the bush, so someone who can match your directness and your intelligence and is not overly sensitive will suit your needs perfectly. You also like an observant person, the type who, when you least expect it, might give you a gift of something you mentioned only casually.

You want a girl, Leo male of 1989, who has lots of personality. By day, she is sweet and sensitive and an intent listener. At night, she is a real dynamo who loves dancing, partying and being out and about with you. She should be nice to look at, but also warm and cuddly, the type you like to come home to. Most important, she thinks that whatever you say and do is wonderful.

The man you daydream about, Leo female of 1989, is tall, dark and handsome. He loves the finer things in life—good food, nice clothes and expensive holidays—and he wants to make sure that you live the good life as well. You want someone with a good heart, and as extravagant though he may be, he must also be very giving. He will give a good friend the shirt off his back, and he will be very generous in the amount of love he gives to you.

1989 VIRGO

From August 23, 3:46 through September 23, 1:19

The Fanciful Realist

As you ponder your future, Virgo of 1989, you often think about what your life will be like when you find the right person with whom to share your joys and tears. For you the perfect relationship would be with someone who yearns for the simple life. The two of you could live in a scenic and secluded spot, high on a hill and you'd fill your time with walking, reading and being as close as two people in love could possibly be.

Although life is rarely that kind of picture postcard, you do feel love has to come close to that for you to be your happiest. Easygoing and idealistic, you will be a romantic perfectionist who won't settle for anything less than your fantasies dictate. You will also be realistic enough to know that good things don't happen so easily, so if you find someone who shares some of your romantic dreams, you'll be ready to become involved without a second thought.

The person who'll complete your life and whom you will notice the moment your eyes meet needs to have a look of mystery. If someone can hit you with just the right facial expression and firm and direct eye contact, then you know that this person is for you. You won't want someone chatty and clever, because you're interested in more than socialising and superficial companionship.

For you, 1989 Virgo male, the perfect female will not waste time with superficialities, as she'll get serious very quickly, a quality that fits in with your own personality. She will be comfortable living an urban lifestyle and can talk about any topic, from politics to literature to rock music. But she'll love that quiet time with you, and she'll love the way you make her feel warm and needed.

The perfect man, 1989 Virgo female, will be easy on the eyes, and even nicer to come home to. He is a gentle sort, and also a gentleman with manners that hark back to a more chivalrous era. This man is so sensitive and kind that you'll have to pinch yourself to make sure he is real. He might be a bit impatient and even slightly jealous, but as long as he is outdoors and interested in you, he will be happy—and so will you.

BROOKE SHIELDS
American Actress
Mars in Virgo

585

1989 LIBRA
From September 23, 1:20 through October 23, 10:34

The Pleasure Seeker

You, Libra of 1989, have always been easygoing and thoughtful, the one to whom others look if they want calm in the midst of a storm. You take most things in stride, rarely becoming agitated when events do not go your way. As you mature, these qualities will become even stronger, and your recipe for a happy life will consist of sharing simple pleasures—beautiful art, good music and walks in the rain—with the one you love.

A relationship will let you give someone else all the good things you have received. Being close to someone will also help you learn and grow as a person. You're the one your friends always come to when they want to feel good because you so easily lift their gloomy moods. In the same way you'll extend your patience, loving nature and unconditional love to your partner.

The one who wins your heart must first and foremost show a real love of people and, like you, must truly be interested in the unique qualities of all individuals. You'll definitely notice someone at ease with people and who never lets the conversation get lost in uncomfortable silence. Anyone who has these qualities, perhaps with a good portion of charm, has a good chance of catching your eye.

Your dream girl, Libra male of 1989, has to have "fun" written all over her, and yet still retain an aura of mystery. You do not want someone who tells you all about herself at your first meeting, but you do want someone who never fails to surprise you with her observations and her ability to find the new and different in the old and familiar. Mostly, she is someone warm and giving, and the person she is most generous with is you.

The man who moves mountains for you, Libra female of 1989, does indeed have physical strength, and will keep you going from morning till night. You just love hunky musclemen, but to keep romance alive for years to come, he must be brainy and eclectic in his tastes. He is easy to please and in his element wherever you go and whatever you do—from a rugged camping trip, to watching a romantic video. Being together with you will be the best thing in his life.

KAZUO ISHIGURO
Japanese Writer
Sun and Venus in Scorpio

586

1989 SCORPIO
From October 23, 10:35 through November 22, 8:04

 ## The Strong-Willed Partner

Probing, strong-willed and wildly creative, you, Scorpio of 1989, have lived a charmed life thus far—you are already used to having almost anything you want come true. These things have not been handed to you, but come with concentration, a bit of effort and a great deal of willpower. As you mature, those qualities will help you succeed in life, giving you strength to move heaven and earth to make someone fall in love with you.

With an almost photographic memory and an eye toward the future, you view partnership as a panorama of life itself, and you will want to pack everything into the experience. You can almost see yourself walking along a beach with someone you love, watching the waves roll ashore and dreaming away the remains of the day as you watch the sun set. That truly reflects your ideal.

The person who wants to share your life will have staying power, a strong personality and even stronger convictions. Someone whose mind changes several times an hour or is always accommodating is definitely a turn-off for you.

You want someone flexible enough to try the things you like, just as you expect to explore your partner's interests. Taking turns sharing in that way means that your beloved blends strength and generosity, two qualities you admire most.

A girl who is affectionate with a great sense of humour and winning smile is the one for you, 1989 Scorpio male. Your ideal woman will know how to step aside when you want privacy and will flap her wings when it's time for a night on the town. Your special someone will have an independent lifestyle, but when the two of you are together, she will shower you with hugs and kisses and more love than you could ever want.

Your dream guy, 1989 Scorpio female, will know how to charm everyone he meets, and charm them he does. But he will never give you cause to be jealous, because he will let you know over and over that he loves you, and his actions speak louder than words ever could. He never keeps you waiting, surprises you with gifts and flowers and above all, he makes you laugh whenever you're down.

1989 SAGITTARIUS
From November 22, 8:05 through December 21, 21:21

The Enthusiastic Adventurer

You, Sagittarius of 1989, like to view life as an unfolding adventure, and your dreams of the future may run the gamut from being an astronaut to starring on the Broadway stage. Whatever you do, including falling in love, will be done with intensity and with an equal measure of enthusiasm and idealism.

You love discovering what makes another person tick from inside out, and what keeps any relationship fresh will be finding intriguing, new things about each other all the time, even after you've been together for years and years. Sharing glorious daydreams means you will both take turns paying attention to daily details you would rather not have to deal with. And yet, even doing that together will become an adventure, if the two of you can be lighthearted and loving at the same time.

You will be completely enamoured by someone who has a quick wit, holds the conversation and most of all, can look you straight in the eye, even in a crowded room, and make you feel as if you are the only one there. Anyone who can transfix you like that is

certainly someone who looks at life with the same fervour as you. Once this first phase is over, the key to continuing on is to feel warm and fuzzy all over, at all times, whether you are dancing or simply watching television and laughing out loud.

There is a girl out there, Sagittarius male of 1989, who has a twinkle in her eye, a reserved smile and a zest for life that will surpass anything you might have hoped for in a partner. This special woman loves beautiful things, and can escort you to a department store and dress you in style. She doesn't look so bad herself, and her heart is big, filled with love for you.

That special guy who will make your heart skip a beat, Sagittarius female of 1989, reminds you of a dashing swashbuckler or any heroic figure clad in uniform and laden with medals. He is athletic, daring and may even like fast cars or flying his own planes. While he will bring excitement into your life, he will, underneath it all, love and protect you, letting you know all the while that you are the one who excites him most.

'80s

Deconstructing Woody Allen

In 1989 director Woody Allen released *Crimes and Misdemeanours*, a film in which the main character commits adultery and murder and gets away with it. In 1992, news broke of Woody Allen's affair with Soon-Yi Previn, the 21-year-old adopted daughter of Allen's longtime partner, Mia Farrow. Because Allen is famous for weaving autobiographical content throughout his films, this shocking development provoked many to re-examine his prior movies for some clue as to the director's state of mind leading up to and during the affair.

Born Allan Stewart Konigsberg on December 1, 1935, in Brooklyn, New York, Woody Allen began writing comedy in 1953. A dropout from NYU Film School, he worked as a television comedy writer during the 1950s and as a stand-up comedian in the 1960s. Allen's lifetime pursuit of psychoanalysis began in 1959. While his newfound insights may have precipitated his 1960 divorce from his first wife, Harlene Rosen—they were married in 1954—the subject of psychoanalysis became a recurring subject throughout Allen's films, central to his cinematic persona as the quintessential neurotic New York intellectual.

In 1966, *What's Up, Tiger Lily?* gave Allen his first breakthrough as a movie writer and director. In 1971, Allen enjoyed his first smash hit, *Bananas,* with leading lady Louise Lasser, whom Allen married in 1964 and divorced in 1969. Allen's habit of casting his real-life love interests, even after they had broken up, continued with Diane Keaton, who first starred in *Sleeper* (1973). *Annie Hall* (1977) garnered Oscars for Keaton as Best Actress, Allen as Best Director and for Best Picture and Best Screenplay. Keaton returned to Allen's films in *Manhattan Murder Mystery* (1993) when she took over the lead female role from

Mia Farrow, after the revelation of Allen's affair with Farrow's daughter.

Farrow had become Allen's artistic and romantic muse in 1980. She created memorable roles for him in ten films, including, *A Midsummer Night's Sex Comedy* (1982), *The Purple Rose of Cairo* (1985) and *Hannah and Her Sisters* (1986). During their twelve-year relationship, Farrow and Allen adopted two children, Moses and Dylan, and had one biological son, Satchel. The couple never married and maintained separate Manhattan apartments on either side of Central Park. In *Husbands and Wives* (1992), a film released as the Soon-Yi scandal broke, audiences watched with rapt attention as the marriage between Allen's and Farrow's characters came apart on screen.

Farrow's role as Halley Reed in *Crimes and Misdemeanours* marked the last time she played opposite Allen as an object of

romantic desire. In the film, a highly respected ophthalmologist murders his vindictive mistress to keep her from revealing their affair to his wife and ruining his comfortable life. At the time Allen was making the film, Soon-Yi was about 18 years old. One can only wonder whether Allen's cinematic meditation on crime, morality and the existence of God reflected his deepest thoughts about his desire for Farrow's daughter and the consequences that would follow once he acted on it.

In a bitter court battle, Farrow charged Allen with sexually abusing their daughter, Dylan. Although no criminal charges were issued, he lost custody and visitation rights to Moses, Dylan and Satchel. In 1997 Allen and Soon-Yi married and later adopted two daughters. Having made a slow comeback in public acceptability, Allen continues to make movies.

587

▶ READ ABOUT MIA FARROW ON PAGE 392

1990 -1999

THE NARCISSISTIC NINETIES

The 1990s, a time of

hedonism and spiritual

crisis, brought us a long

way in terms of tolerance.

*F*ollowing the end of the Cold War, a period of relative peace and prosperity allowed people to focus on more personal pursuits. Celebrities commanded huge salaries and media attention while the AIDS crisis and the Internet transformed everyday life for millions.

Fashions were slick and edgy, irony was in, and postmodernism had crept from the ivory tower to art, architecture, and cuisine. At the same time, the New Age movement blossomed, from esoteric therapies and alternative health treatments to aromatherapy candles, crystals, and yoga. And success was the goal of many in the 1990s—the age of cell phones, power breakfasts, and twenty-something dot-com millionaires.

The Internet transitioned from a few networked computers to a true World Wide Web accessed by tens of millions every day to email friends, read the latest news, chat, or find love. Subcultures and special interest groups found kindred spirits unfettered by distance. News (and rumors) could spread almost instantaneously, and people professed their deepest love to partners they had never met. Cyber sex was safer, and sometimes more romantic, than the real thing. This revolutionary technology brought a new set of perils. Sensational headlines trumpeted tawdry cases of stalkers, even killers, targeting victims via the Internet. Internet pedophiles became the latest fear for parents. And an irrational exuberance gripped investors who poured hundreds of millions of dollars into Internet startups.

AIDS, once a rare, stigmatized disease, became a worldwide health crisis.

Another movement of the 1990s was semantic: politically correct language. Sensitivity to cultural and racial diversity, stemming from liberal, multicultural concerns, went mainstream, after decades of the acceptance of racist and sexist slurs. Multiculturalism also found root in a new breed of backpacking travelers—hundreds of thousands of twenty-somethings started taking time off in between their studies to roam the world.

Celebrity was never more celebrated. Breathless reportage followed stars' breakthroughs, breakdowns, and breakups. Mariah Carey, Jennifer Lopez, Michael Jackson, and Jennifer Aniston provided grist for the mill. The union of Nicole Kidman and Tom Cruise perhaps epitomized the decade, as they adopted children, pursued their acting careers, and endured tabloid gossip, but would prove to last only a decade. Illicit affairs, divorce, and revelations plagued the British royal family, their exploits meticulously covered by the press. Princess Diana admitted to an affair, as did her husband Charles, and "Fergie," the Duchess of York, was caught having her toes sucked by a Texan.

Manufactured, shrewdly marketed pop, in the form of boy bands and girl bands, dominated the charts with the Spice Girls leading the way.

Celine Dion burst in on the scene, Whitney Houston burned brightly and then faltered, and rap went from a subculture of the street to a multibillion-dollar industry. Grunge, an alternative rock style that came out of Seattle, briefly influenced haute couture and forever changed music. Club music thrived in the form of house, trance, and industrial styles. As the dance drug ecstasy swept through clubs in the world, in Britain the "E" Generation was the biggest youth movement since rock 'n' roll. All-night open air raves playing techno and house music were banned by the British government and the yellow smiley face became the symbol of "Acid House" music.

◄◄ A rollerblader inspects a Versace advertisement, Miami Beach

▲ A "rave" in full swing

▼ Mariah Carey visits London to promote her new album *Rainbow*

THE SILVER SCREEN

Movies seemed to come in two flavors: Hollywood blockbusters and offbeat art-house gems. Pedro Almodóvar, Todd Haynes, Tim Burton, and Jane Campion directed stunning and original films, while *Titanic*, *Jurassic Park*, *Independence Day*, and *A Few Good Men* raked in box-office bucks.

BETWEEN THE PAGES

Talk show host Oprah Winfrey started a book club, catapulting select literary works to bestsellerdom. Other standouts of the decade included John Berendt's *Midnight in the Garden of Good and Evil*, Frank McCourt's *Angela's Ashes*, and Cormac McCarthy's *All the Pretty Horses*. Andrew Morton's *Diana: Her True Story* caused a scandal in England, revealing Prince Charles as a heartless husband and Diana as a vulnerable, suicidal anorexic, but the biggest revelation was that the Princess had collaborated with Morton.

PEOPLE

Princess Diana and Mother Teresa died within a week of each other, President Clinton's affair with Monica Lewinsky rocked America, Hugh Grant was caught with prostitute Divine Brown, Demi Moore's pregnant body adorned the cover of *Vanity Fair*, and Gianni Versace was murdered in Miami.

- ✪ CENSORSHIP
- ✪ PRETTY WOMAN
- ✪ HENRY & JUNE
- ✪ VOGUE!
- ✪ OPPOSITES ATTRACT
- ✪ IRON JOHN
- ✪ POSSESSION

EVENTS

Censorship made headlines. In the US an exhibition of Robert Mapplethorpe's edgy photography triggered obscenity charges against the Contemporary Arts Center of Cincinnati as well as decency standards for federal arts funding (later upheld by the Supreme Court), which prohibited "depictions of sadomasochism, homoeroticism, the sexual exploitation of children, or individuals engaged in sex acts." After a group of major directors decried "a new era of McCarthyism in the arts," the Motion Picture Association of America added the rating "NC-17" (no children under 17) to differentiate films containing strong adult themes or images from "X"-rated pornography. The FDA approved the five-year time-release contraceptive drug Norplant. Heartthrob Tom Cruise married rising star Nicole Kidman. Sex symbols Ava Gardner and Greta Garbo died. Switzerland made 14 the age of consent, and France prohibited the sale of dangerous aphrodisiac "poppers."

POP CULTURE

The year's top romantic films included *Ghost*, in which death proves no obstacle for true love, and *Pretty Woman*, which catapulted Julia Roberts to stardom as a streetwalker with a heart of gold. Tim Burton's *Edward Scissorhands* offered an offbeat parable of social conformity and redemptive love. *Longtime Companion* was the first mainstream drama dealing with the AIDS epidemic. *Henry & June*, a racy art

film based on Anais Nin's account of her tumultuous affair with Henry Miller in 1930s Paris, received the first age restricted viewing.

Sinead O'Connor sang an ethereal cover of Prince's "Nothing Compares 2 U." Pop icon Madonna made drag queen vamping "Vogue" and defended her explicit "Justify My Love" video (banned by MTV) on ABC's *Nightline*. Paula Abdul sang "Opposites Attract." Roxette sang "It Must Have Been Love," and Michael Bolton asked "How Am I Supposed to Live Without You?"

People were reading glittery blockbuster novels from Sidney Sheldon, Danielle Steel, Jackie Collins, and Anne Rice. Robert Bly's *Iron John: A Book About Men* sparked a firestorm over the nature of manhood. In *Possession: A Romance* by A.S. Byatt (winner of the Booker Prize), competing scholars uncover a secret affair between two long-dead poets and repeat history by falling in love. Pierrette Fleutiaux's prizewinning *We Are Eternal* explored the incestuous love between a brother and a sister.

Hot Couple

TOM CRUISE & NICOLE KIDMAN

On Christmas Eve 1990, heartthrob Tom Cruise (*Top Gun*) and Australian beauty Nicole Kidman wed in Telluride, Colorado, after a courtship begun while co-starring in *Days of Thunder*. The couple adopted two children and battled persistent tabloid rumors that Cruise was sterile, gay, or impotent. Cruise filed for divorce in February 2001 amid whispers of his involvement with *Vanilla Sky* co-star Penelope Cruz, as well as criticism of his more fervent Scientology beliefs.

Kidman, while devastated, went on to star in both the lavish musical *Moulin Rouge* and as Virginia Woolf in *The Hours*, for which she won a best actress Oscar.

SEE ALSO

▶ TOM CRUISE *Page 563*

▶ DAVID BECKHAM & VICTORIA ADAMS *Page 662*

1990 CAPRICORN

From December 21, 1989 21:22 through January 20, 1990 8:01
(December 1990 Capricorns, see 1991 Capricorn)

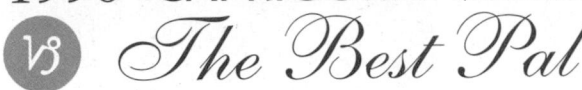

♑ *The Best Pal*

You're a communicative Capricorn born in 1990, and you like to share romantic feelings with someone who is also a friend. Being able to relax together is important to you—dating is scary enough without feeling you always have to be on your best behavior. You can imagine being grown and falling madly in love with someone who has always been your best friend. That way you can hang out together, be part of a group where you both fit in, and enjoy life as a couple that's well connected.

You enjoy sharing all sorts of interesting conversations with potential dates. It's exciting to hear a new take on something and you feel you can grow as a result of these meaningful intellectual interactions. Sharing fun and good times is always what you seek and you'd much rather be with someone whose taste and preferences are compatible with your own than to fall madly in love with an exotic stranger.

An interesting idea cleverly expressed is the best way for someone to get your attention. That makes it easier for you to talk with each other and feel comfortable. Being invited to a party is lots of fun for you, even if you're meeting the host for the first time. You love socializing in a group atmosphere. You also enjoy sharing outdoor events, picnics, campfire sing-alongs, hay rides, and long hikes.

If you're a male Goat born in 1990, you think those ultra-feminine girls with high heels and too much makeup are silly. You'd much rather spend time with a girl who sees you as a friend. Your favorite gal is sparkly and clever and she has interesting ideas that are new to you. She has a whole clique of friends, but she's never stuck up, and when you discuss things about school with her, she listens attentively.

As a female Cappie born in 1990, you like an outdoorsy, athletic guy best. Your fellow is cheerful and uncomplicated and he has a wonderful heart. He can see so many different points of view and he seems to have something in common with everyone. He loves to play, befriends every dog he meets, and he will hang upside down for ages on the parallel bars just to win a dare.

CAPRICORN ZODIAC SIGN
YOUR LOVE PLANETS

YOUR ROMANTIC SIDE   p. 696
▶ **VENUS IN AQUARIUS**
Born Dec. 21, 1989 21:22 - Jan. 16, 1990 15:22
▶ **VENUS IN CAPRICORN**
Born Jan. 16, 15:23 - Jan. 20, 8:01

YOUR SEX DRIVE   p. 722
▶ **MARS IN SAGITTARIUS**
Born Dec. 21, 1989 21:22 - Jan. 20, 1990 8:01

YOUR CELEBRITY TWINS   p. 760
Find out the astrological similarities you have with famous people.

YOUR COMPATIBILITY   p. 780
Compare planets to find out how compatible you are in a relationship.

YOUR RELATIONSHIP KARMA   p. 824
▶ **SATURN IN CAPRICORN**
Born Dec. 21, 1989 21:22 - Jan. 20, 1990 8:01

LAURA DERN
American Actress
Sun in Aquarius

1990 AQUARIUS

From January 20, 8:02 through February 18, 22:13

♒ *The Romantic Individualist*

As an idealistic Aquarian born in 1990, you feel life and love can be quite unpredictable. To you love is a serious thing and it's about more than just a date for a school dance. You want to feel you really care about someone who will love you for a long time, and that together you will build a solid partnership. Of course, you know that once you're older, this will be a less difficult goal. Right now you enjoy palling around with people who are pleasant companions.

Some people call you a rebel, but you know you're just a strong individual, and you feel that a good relationship will allow you to continue to express yourself just as you do now. Someone who loves you will adore you all the more because of your special qualities and you prize those distinctive traits in friends and romantic partners.

Working together on a school project is a great way for you to notice someone as more than just a friend. You pick right up on the shy glances, stammers, and casual brushing of hands. When you can combine your energy effectively with a partner's, there's always hope that it could turn romantic. A good joke is a great ice breaker, and you've used that yourself when you wanted to turn a head or two.

As a male Aquarian born in 1990, you like nice, normal girls who have interesting things to say. Your favorite sweetie is soft and pretty, but she never looks like something out of a weird fashion magazine. She is smart and practical, and if you are confused about something, she often has the perfect approach to make sense of the problem. Under the surface you know she's very romantic and idealistic, but she's also shy, so she doesn't always let on how she feels.

If you're a female Aquarian born in 1990, your type of guy is practical but a rebel. You like his down-to-earth points of view and often he knows the perfect way to help you get exactly what you want. He works hard, but can be quite stubborn, and if he doesn't get his way, sometimes he gives the teacher a hard time. He really does want to succeed, but he just can't help being a boy and you admire that about him.

AQUARIUS ZODIAC SIGN
YOUR LOVE PLANETS

YOUR ROMANTIC SIDE   p. 696
▶ **VENUS IN CAPRICORN**
Born Jan. 20, 8:02 - Feb. 18, 22:13

YOUR SEX DRIVE   p. 722
▶ **MARS IN SAGITTARIUS**
Born Jan. 20, 8:02 - Jan. 29, 14:09
▶ **MARS IN CAPRICORN**
Born Jan. 29, 14:10 - Feb. 18, 22:13

YOUR CELEBRITY TWINS   p. 760
Find out the astrological similarities you have with famous people.

YOUR COMPATIBILITY   p. 780
Compare planets to find out how compatible you are in a relationship.

YOUR RELATIONSHIP KARMA   p. 824
▶ **SATURN IN CAPRICORN**
Born Jan. 20, 8:02 - Feb. 18, 22:13

ALAN RICKMAN
English Actor
Sun and Venus in Pisces

592

1990 PISCES
From February 18, 22:14 through March 20, 21:18

The Unwavering Mate

You're a supportive Pisces born in 1990, and you want a relationship filled with affection and devotion. To you a relationship is the ultimate team on which each person wants to make sure the other feels loved and nurtured. Being a team player means working side by side to keep the relationship happy and successful, and also to help each other fulfill goals.

Commitment is very important to you now and always will be. You just can't imagine relationships in which one person sells the other out or is unfaithful. You believe wholeheartedly in loyalty and you intend to stay best friends forever with the people you've loved since grammar school. That same devotion will apply in the future when you make that lifetime commitment to marry your true love. To you something of value must last forever, and that's what love is all about.

You are a lively conversationalist and you love it when someone shows an interest in you by engaging you in an exciting discussion. Even if it seems like a debate or an argument, you know it's just an energetic exchange of ideas. You are also impressed when someone cares enough to pitch in and help you with a chore or school project or to do a good deed for you. A kindly gesture means a lot because, not only does it show affection, but also the character of the person involved.

If you're a male Pisces born in 1990, being with a girl who is trustworthy is tops on your list. You'd never want to admit you like a girl and then catch her gossiping and giggling with her silly friends. Your girl is sensitive to your feelings and she treats you with respect. She's a serious person and she's quite down to earth. This sweetie is responsible, but not boring, and she's very easy to be with.

As a female Fishie born in 1990, a stable fellow with good character is always your sort of partner. Your guy is solid, practical, and reliable, and everyone trusts him to act mature and responsible. He is in touch with his goals for the future and knows just what he wants to achieve out of life. Even though he's quite serious, he also has a great sense of humor.

1990 ARIES
From March 20, 21:19 through April 20, 8:26

The Passionate Partner

As an intense Aries born in 1990, you want to fall madly in love. You might even be deeply in love right now, despite your young age. You can't help it—it just feels natural to you to want a relationship. You're a passionate person and loving someone is what gives meaning to your life. Friendship and compatibility are very important to you in a relationship. It's good to feel comfortable with someone instead of all awkward and shy.

An emotional connection is the only part of a relationship that matters to you. Being able to share ideas, talk creatively, and brainstorm together will bring you closer to a special sweetheart. Even if you just gab about school, what's on television or the movie you want to see on the weekend, you feel it's a meaningful interaction. Sharing mutual ideals is important to you also. That way you can build a relationship in which you both work to make the world a better place.

You admire someone nervy enough to come right out and admit an interest in you, so you'd give a few brownie points even before the first conversation. Hanging out together with a group of friends is the ideal environment for romance to begin. You can sit together at the movies and wonder if you really do like each other until one of you is brave enough to make the first move!

As a male Ram born in 1990, you are drawn to girls with deep emotions. Although you are fascinated by pretty much every female out there, you feel most connected to girls who are magnetic and intense, like you are. Your girl has depth and passion and everything she does is with feeling. Her ideas are interesting and insightful and you feel you're a more worthwhile person just because she sees you as special.

If you're a female Aries born in 1990, your favorite guy knows how to be a good friend. He loves sharing his interests and wants you to hang out with him and his pals. You're always impressed with his ideas and the clever way his mind works. Your fellow is creative and intelligent and a real whiz with computers. He's a little awkward about romance, but you just know he's a good kisser.

1990 TAURUS

From April 20, 8:27 through May 21, 7:36

The Devoted Darling

You're an idealistic Taurus born in 1990, and nothing less than true love will do for you. Being in a relationship in which you're both devoted to each other is your dream, and you hope one day to start a long, wonderful marriage. Even now, you're really involved in the lives of your friends and you can't help wanting the very best for them. It doesn't make sense to you at all that some people can be so uncaring and casual about feelings. You'd never do that. You believe compromise and commitment are the necessary components in a relationship.

You really want to know what your date thinks about anything and everything, and good communication makes a relationship more special to you because it gives you real insights into your sweetheart's inner world. Sharing creative and artistic pursuits also appeals to you within a relationship. You can envision yourself years from now, married and being a chic couple who patronize the arts.

An invitation to a play, movie, or concert is the perfect first date, and even if you're going just as friends, you're content because you can connect quite easily with those deeper feelings below the surface. As you stroll together through the neighborhood, a shopping mall, or on the way home from school, there are opportunities to gaze into each other's eyes and that is very thrilling and electric for you.

If you're a male Bull born in 1990, your best sweetheart is passionate and creative. This girl is a whirlwind of energy and you find her endlessly exciting. Her ideas are clever and original, she has many special talents, and you can envision her being a big star in the future. She's never shy about sharing her feelings, whether they're loving ones or she's sounding off about something that annoys her. She sure has lots of spunk!

As a female Taurus born in 1990, your guy is sensitive and artistic. He loves music and can probably draw, paint, or compose songs. School dances with him are more fun because he's not shy and gawky about dancing the way the other boys are. Your fellow has many passions and he cares deeply about other people.

TAURUS ZODIAC SIGN
YOUR LOVE PLANETS

YOUR ROMANTIC SIDE   p. 696
- VENUS IN PISCES
Born Apr. 20, 8:27 - May 04, 3:51
- VENUS IN ARIES
Born May 04, 3:52 - May 21, 7:36

YOUR SEX DRIVE   p. 722
- MARS IN AQUARIUS
Born Apr. 20, 8:27 - Apr. 20, 22:08
- MARS IN PISCES
Born Apr. 20, 22:09 - May 21, 7:36

YOUR CELEBRITY TWINS   p. 760
Find out the astrological similarities you have with famous people.

YOUR COMPATIBILITY   p. 780
Compare planets to find out how compatible you are in a relationship.

YOUR RELATIONSHIP KARMA   p. 824
- SATURN IN CAPRICORN
Born Apr. 20, 8:27 - May 21, 7:36

MARIAH CAREY
American Singer
Mars in Taurus

593

1990 GEMINI
From May 21, 7:37 through June 21, 15:32

The Intellectual Companion

As a lively Gemini born in 1990, your ideal relationship provides independence and security. You need to be loved, but without being smothered. Closeness is very important to you and you feel comforted by the knowledge that a special someone will be there in your life, loving you day after day. It's the same now with friendships—you take comfort in the ones that endure. But you never want to feel you're joined at the hip with anyone. No matter how long you've been close to someone, there will always be things to do on your own.

Being able to share interesting ideas is another must in your relationship. You need intellectual stimulation, and you believe that a strong mental bond is what keeps a relationship lively. You don't have to agree with each other—a debate is just as satisfying as agreeing—you just have to be able to talk. While differing points of view are acceptable, you feel that to make a relationship work, you must share mutual interests.

You love a riddle or other verbal challenge, and the person who tickles your brain is likely to gain your attention. You like being known and understood, so the potential date who offers a genuinely meaningful compliment or observation about you is on the right track. You enjoy sharing exciting activities such as car races and athletic events, or something more sedate, a trip to the movies or dinner out.

As a male Gemini born in 1990, a girl has to have special qualities to make you sit up and take notice. She can be lively and assertive, a fast talker with lots to say, or artistic and moody. As long as she seems distinctive, she appeals to you. Your sweetie needs security and she requests a hug on occasion, even if all you are right now is best friends.

If you're a female Gemini born in 1990, you're attracted to boys who are creative and unpredictable. You like being surprised, and not knowing what your guy will do next makes life more fun for you. This fellow has some special talents, and it's interesting to see the way his mind works. You don't always agree with his ideas, but you enjoy debating them with him.

GEMINI ZODIAC SIGN
YOUR LOVE PLANETS

YOUR ROMANTIC SIDE   p. 696
- VENUS IN ARIES
Born May 21, 7:37 - May 30, 10:12
- VENUS IN TAURUS
Born May 30, 10:13 - June 21, 15:32

YOUR SEX DRIVE   p. 722
- MARS IN PISCES
Born May 21, 7:37 - May 31, 7:10
- MARS IN ARIES
Born May 31, 7:11 - June 21, 15:32

YOUR CELEBRITY TWINS   p. 760
Find out the astrological similarities you have with famous people.

YOUR COMPATIBILITY   p. 780
Compare planets to find out how compatible you are in a relationship.

YOUR RELATIONSHIP KARMA   p. 824
- SATURN IN CAPRICORN
Born May 21, 7:37 - June 21, 15:32

VINCENT PEREZ
Swiss Actor
Venus in Cancer

594

1990 CANCER
From June 21, 15:33 through July 23, 2:21

♋ The Fun Lover

You're a sociable Cancer born in 1990, and you need intellectual stimulation and lots of good fun in a relationship. Hanging out, chatting with your pals is your favorite activity, and you see a relationship as a natural extension of that. Being with someone, holding hands, laughing and telling jokes, and sharing all that as part of a group—that's the way you envision a perfect relationship working out.

You love cozy chats, marathon phone conversations, and getting a greeting card for no reason at all. That's what makes you feel close to a sweetheart. Of course, you believe in deep love and nurturing as part of any relationship, but you also believe that independence and freedom are important. Your goal is to create a relationship with a balance. You recognize that compromise is necessary in romance and in friendship, too, but you also feel there shouldn't be so much compromise that you end up feeling stifled. A potential partner who knows just the right thing to say gains your interest very quickly. A combination of words that can touch your heart is what you seek. You enjoy all sorts of invitations and would happily take a stroll to nowhere with someone interesting. You like browsing through book stores and discussing favorite books, going on bike rides, visiting museums, and talking on the phone as ways to get to know each other.

If you're a male Crab born in 1990, you get all warm and fuzzy over girls who are clever and articulate. A girl who can speak her mind is just your type, and you love spending hours sharing opinions in lively repartee. Your sweetie is cheerful, lively, and she loves to read. She might even be a cheerleader. Her spunky personality makes her good company and she makes you laugh.

As a female Cancer born in 1990, your guy is active, but can tend toward snap judgments, although he tries to control himself. He loves impromptu plans and you find his company very exciting because he's so unpredictable. Under the surface he is a responsible person and he always tries to be helpful and hard working. You might say he's a boy scout with pizzazz.

1990 LEO
From July 23, 2:22 through August 23, 9:20

♌ The True Lover

As an idealistic Leo born in 1990, you want true love with the partner who is your perfect mate. Even now you're picky about friendships and tend to gravitate only toward those people who genuinely touch your heart. Someday you expect to be madly in love and you get crushes rather easily because you see so many special qualities in lots of different people. You feel that with time and experience you will be able to discern who your true love is and then you want to stay married forever. You'd never make a commitment unless it was for real.

A sense of partnership is important to you in all relationships. Being comfortable together and feeling that you fit and belong makes it much easier to create a healthy and happy relationship. Communication is one dimension of that perfect fit. You feel that not only is good verbal interaction necessary, but that you should also have a finely developed psychic bond, because then and only then do you really understand each other. Even now you use your strong intuition to understand your pals better.

An invitation from the heart appeals to you more than anything else. Someone who invites you to share a special family event, a picnic, or just a casual lunch in the school cafeteria shows affection and that's what you care about. Offering you an ice cream cone or a beloved book works well, too!

As a male Leo born in 1990, your favorite girl is soft, tender, and sweet. She's a cozy and comfortable person and if you hug her, she hugs you back. She's a natural nurturer and she loves to look after smaller children and pets. Her eyes are luminous and glowing, and every time you're together your heart is filled with tenderness. You just know you will have special feelings for her forever.

If you're a female Lion born in 1990, your special guy is practical, logical, and stable. But sometimes he's downright stubborn. When you point this out, though, he's usually willing to compromise. He's artistic and musical and you can imagine him expressing genuine talent professionally in the future. That's why you like him—he's a temperamental artist!

1990 VIRGO
From August 23, 9:21 through September 23, 6:55

♍ The Deep Romantic

You're a creative Virgo and you require lots of chemistry and excitement in a relationship. You're the romantic type, and even in elementary school you often fell madly in love. As you get older, you realize that those feelings are quite thrilling, and you know you want to have that electricity permanently in your life as an adult. Right now you'd just like to hold hands, kiss, and have a few dates!

You take love seriously and want to find the one right person for you. Because you're so romantic, you realize that true love is the only thing that matters, not playing the field. Being able to connect on a deep and serious level is what you want. You feel that love should have an idealistic dimension and that everyone should be willing to sacrifice for love and a partner's happiness, whenever necessary. It's all part of the thrill of loving.

A grand, romantic gesture is your favorite opening gambit. You thrill to a bold person who walks over to you at a school dance and whispers that you are the most exciting person in the room. You enjoy a little mystery and magic, too. Beginning a relationship with a quarrel when the sparks fly, then ending up all starry-eyed for each other is your idea of a great way to fall in love.

If you're a male Virgo born in 1990, your girl is intense and romantic. You find her incredible depth of emotion quite appealing because you know how wonderful it will feel to have all that affection aimed at you. She is artistic and creative and she loves music, theater, and movies—something you can share. This trendsetter is endlessly fascinating and you love to hear the amazing things she has to say.

As a female Virgo born in 1990, you prefer a boy who is intelligent, verbally astute, and physically agile. Your guy may be captain of both the basketball team and the debate team! He's cheerful and relentlessly optimistic, and he always has fascinating comments to make about everything and everyone. He likes culture and art and is an avid reader. Even if you don't agree with everything he says and does, you still find him a stimulating companion.

JOHNNY DEPP
American Actor
Mars in Virgo

595

1990 LIBRA
From September 23, 6:56 through October 23, 16:13

♎ The Sparkling Sweetheart

As a companionable Libra born in 1990, you seek a relationship that is romantic and fun. You love those old musicals in which a couple danced with glamour and élan, and to you that is the epitome of what a relationship should be—elegant and beautiful. You absolutely adore the trappings of romance and can't understand why everyone doesn't realize that life is better lived by candlelight and soft music. It's so sad when a relationship becomes dull and the participants lead humdrum lives. You will never let that happen to you.

Sharing mutual interests is imperative to you because that gives you something to do as a couple. You can easily envision a life as an adult married couple in which you give and attend sparkling, sophisticated parties and wear glamorous clothes. You feel that being able to play together is a strong indicator that you have enough in common to make a relationship work. Of course, there is more to you than violins in the background of life. You believe in more than glamour. You believe in true love, and that's what you want for yourself—to merge your heart and your life with that of your one perfect partner.

The date who hands you a beautiful rose—or leaves one on your doorstep—really gets your attention. You love a romantic opening gambit. You adore the idea of being invited to a fancy dress-up event like a cotillion or prom, and you don't mind at all if you're not that well acquainted. What better way is there to learn about each other? You enjoy strolling through museums or art galleries, browsing book stores, and walking down a pretty street hand in hand.

As a male Libra born in 1990, you prefer to spend time with a girl who is beautiful and elegant. Your sweetie is musical and she's a wonderful dancer. There's something in her eyes so tender and romantic, you can just imagine capturing her heart and keeping it forever.

If you're a female Libra born in 1990, intelligence is tops on your list of requirements for a male companion. Your guy is clever and witty and he always makes you laugh. He loves adventures and takes you to fascinating places.

SINEAD O'CONNOR
Irish Singer
Sun and Venus in Sagittarius

1990 SCORPIO
From October 23, 16:14 through November 22, 13:46

The Romantic Optimist

You're an affectionate Scorpio and you believe love and attraction are the key to any relationship. Even though you're young, you already know that love is all about the magic you feel when in the company of a certain special someone. It doesn't happen every day or with everyone, so you feel it's smart to make the most of romance when it strikes. Devotion to the one you love means so much and you want to create a relationship in which you can each look out for the other's needs and best interests. Selfishness belongs nowhere in your relationship!

Being able to laugh and play together keeps things light, and you agree that a little frivolity goes hand in hand with depth of feeling because it keeps things balanced. Commitment is quite natural to you—you feel that where there is love, there is commitment, even when it's unspoken. You also believe that true love comes with acceptance and support, and that a mutual emotional boost allows each of you to become your best possible self.

A deep smoldering glance really speaks to your heart. Often few words need be uttered because when there's a real connection, you understand each other with a single gaze. Of course, you can't be silent forever and you enjoy a fun conversation that lets you both joke, laugh, and discuss the secrets of everyone around you.

If you're a male Scorpion born in 1990, you feel very comfortable with a girl who has depth and passion. Dull or tepid girls are boring to you, and you'd much prefer to spend time with someone who seems a bit old for her years. Your sweetie is affectionate and generous—she looks out for your needs and interests, and when you're together, you can't stop thinking about kissing her.

As a female Scorpio born in 1990, your favorite fellow is a regular chatterbox and he always has something fascinating to say. He loves jokes, limericks, and riddles, and you have a great time laughing together. This guy is peppy and cheerful, and if you have a problem, he has a way of making everything seem better. He's a good teacher and he knows so many people, he's like a party on wheels.

1990 SAGITTARIUS
From November 22, 13:47 through December 22, 3:06

The Easygoing Playmate

As a playful Sagittarian born in 1990, you believe romance should be fun. Other people make love too heavy a topic and you think that's why so many people divorce nowadays. You want to start out as playmates and stay that way as long as you're happy together. To you a relationship should be filled with pleasure, adventure, and excitement, not drudgery and arguments.

A good intellectual connection is another way to guarantee a successful relationship. You want to be able to share your thoughts and feelings with a partner whose verbal skills are on par with your own. That way you always remain endlessly fascinating to each other. You can understand the importance of complete commitment, although it's not tops on your list of requirements in a relationship. Instead, you feel it makes more sense to allow each person to express his or her individuality. Otherwise what would there be to say at the end of a day?

You like a partner nervy enough to come up with a wild and crazy come-on to show interest in you. Being dragged to a party where neither of you knows a soul could be lots of fun, visiting a restaurant and pretending not to speak English is appealing, or going on a scavenger hunt is a wacky way to get to know each other. You're not all eccentricity, though, and you're just as content to meet someone new while playing with your pooch.

As a male Sagittarian born in 1990, you prefer a girl with a good sense of adventure. Even if she's never been out of the state, your gal knows there's a whole wide world out there and she loves to talk about all the exotic places she wants to visit. You might even fantasize about backpacking together to the most distant port. She has a kind heart, speaks up for the underdog, does good deeds when she can, and doesn't have a jealous bone in her body.

If you're a female Archer born in 1990, you like to spend time with a guy who's smart enough to know his own mind, and flexible enough to change it. Your fellow is smart and aware, can communicate information with flair, and because he doesn't take life too seriously, loves to play and joke.

Michael Hutchence – A Rock 'n' Roll Tragedy

The bad boy of Australian rock, Michael Hutchence had the potent mix of looks, talent, and charisma needed to be a star and live the rock 'n' roll lifestyle. And boy, did he live it.

Born in Sydney, he moved with his family to Hong Kong when he was four and it was there that his love of music began. Moving back to Australia eight years later, his studies took second place as his singing developed into a fully fledged passion. Together with his school mate Andrew Farriss, he formed a band, which was eventually named INXS. By 1987 they were international stars, packing stadiums around the world and rubbing shoulders with the elite.

On stage Hutchence's performances were electric. Offstage he oozed a raw magnetic sex appeal that made him irresistible to women. And like any self-respecting rocker, he made full use of it, bedding scores of beautiful babes. For the press, his intoxicating combination of star quality and playboy womanizing proved perfect gossip fodder, and a media frenzy followed his every step. On the surface Hutchence seemed to lap up the attention. But tragically—and unbeknownst to his friends and family—he never learned to deal with the intrusion, and depression haunted him throughout his life.

His first high-profile relationship was with the then squeaky clean pop princess, Kylie Minogue. But with Hutchence introducing her to a world of drugs and debauchery, a sexier, raunchier Kylie emerged. The media had a field day, accusing Hutchence of

"Fame makes me feel wanted and loved, anybody wants that."

MICHAEL HUTCHENCE

corrupting the young singer. But thanks to his roving eye and weakness for women, the relationship was not to last. Because of his infidelities they parted, but remained good friends.

Within a couple of months he had moved on to his next glamour puss, in the shapely form of Danish supermodel Helena Christensen. By now the public was hooked on his exploits and the press made sure they delivered, snapping the attractive couple wherever they went. The relationship seemed to be going strong—until Hutchence made a fateful appearance on a popular television breakfast show.

Paula Yates was the peroxide-blonde vixen of British TV, interviewing stars on a luscious pink bed in her trademark provocative manner. She had briefly interviewed Hutchence in the '80s and had been smitten ever since. Now over a decade later and with her marriage on the rocks, the sexual chemistry was instant. The couple were mesmerized, falling deeply in love, with Paula declaring to the world that he had the "Taj Mahal of crotches." It was a relationship that was to change their lives forever.

But now the press had become vicious, taunting Hutchence for leaving a supermodel for an older, married mother. The couple also had to deal with Paula's husband, Bob Geldof, and his rage, which manifested itself in a long and bitter custody battle for their children. Hutchence became entangled in the mess, turning to drink and drugs for solace and sliding into a deep depression. Paula gave birth to his child, Heavenly Hiraani Tiger Lilly, but a year later Michael Hutchence was found dead—hanging naked with a belt round his neck, in a hotel room in Sydney. The pressure had proved too much. Paula never recovered from the grief and was found dead three years later of an apparent heroin overdose.

▶ READ ABOUT KURT COBAIN AND COURTNEY LOVE ON PAGE 621

1991

- ANITA HILL
- CONDOMS AND AIDS
- JULIA CALLS IT OFF
- THELMA AND LOUISE
- SEX YOU UP
- NO GREATER LOVE
- AMERICAN PSYCHO

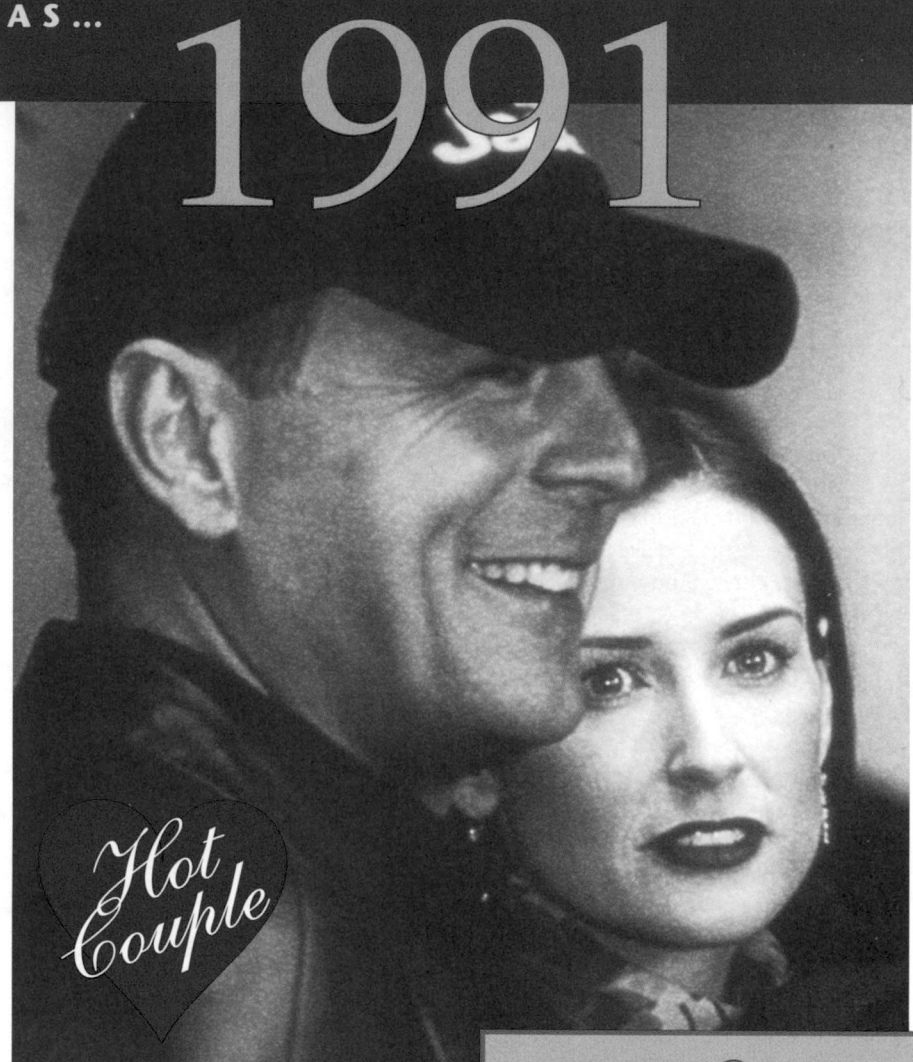

Hot Couple

EVENTS

In the US, law professor Anita Hill accused Supreme Court nominee Clarence Thomas of sexual harassment in a series of stormy congressional hearings. One-third of the women responding to a *McCall's* magazine survey reported unsatisfactory sex lives, rating unsatisfying sex more stressful than housework. Edith Cresson was elected Prime Minister, the first time a woman had held the position in France. Fox became the first network to allow condom advertising, condoms were distributed to New York City high school students as part of an AIDS prevention initiative, and 2,500 "Bikini Condoms" for women were stolen from a New Jersey manufacturer. Basketball legend "Magic" Johnson announced he had AIDS. Operation Rescue staged a month-long anti-abortion protest outside a Wichita, Kansas clinic that even conservative President George Herbert Bush called "excessive." Three days before her wedding to Kiefer Sutherland, Julia Roberts canceled the ceremony. Arlette Schweitzer became a surrogate mother for her daughter, thus giving birth to her own twin grandchildren.

POP CULTURE

The year's films included Disney's animated musical *Beauty and the Beast* and *Father of the Bride*, a remake of the Spencer Tracy classic featuring Steve Martin as the father not quite ready to admit his daughter is all grown up. In Barbra Streisand's *The Prince of Tides*, based on the Pat Conroy novel, a man helps his suicidal twin sister's psychiatrist understand their Southern gothic upbringing. In Ridley Scott's gal-pal road trip movie *Thelma and Louise*, an Arkansas waitress and a housewife ditch their no-good men, kill a would-be rapist, and go on the lam.

Color Me Badd sang "I Wanna Sex You Up," EMF had smash-hit "Unbelievable," Christian rocker Amy Grant sang "Baby Baby," and the C & C Music Factory dance floor anthem promised "Gonna Make You Sweat."

Bestsellers included Alexandra Ripley's *Scarlett: The Sequel to Margaret Mitchell's "Gone with the Wind,"* and Danielle Steel's *No Greater Love* about a woman's courage after her parents and fiancé are killed on the Titanic. Serial killers and urban love mixed in Mary Higgins Clark's *Loves Music, Loves to Dance* and Bret Easton Ellis's *American Psycho*, set amid the excess and glitter of 1980s New York.

BRUCE WILLIS & DEMI MOORE

Raven-haired beauty and actress Demi Moore married the charming, sexy, and jocular movie star Bruce Willis in 1987. They were one of the hottest Hollywood couples of the late eighties and early nineties, famous for publicizing their love for one another and making their marriage into fodder for the tabloids.

In 1991, when Moore was seven months pregnant with their second child, she shocked the world by appearing nude on the cover of *Vanity Fair*. She posed for the magazine again in 1992, this time covered in body paint. Despite their repeated public declarations of love, they were divorced in 2000.

SEE ALSO
► FAYE DUNAWAY & PETER WOLF *Page 458*
► BONNIE & CLYDE *Page 137*

1991 CAPRICORN

From December 22, 1990 3:07 through January 20, 1991 13:46
(December 1991 Capricorns, see 1992 Capricorn)

♑ *The Dedicated Worker*

Capricorn of 1991, you are a determined and diligent worker who is able to set a goal and achieve it. And, as you mature, it is likely that you will welcome taking on new responsibilities. Your friends and loved ones are able to count on you to live up to your promises. In fact, dependability is one of your most admirable traits and it is likely to be a wonderful advantage for you when it comes to relationships.

Even though you can be quite serious, you also have a marvelous sense of humor. You are often able to spot the interesting and quirky things about a situation that others will usually miss. This ability to see what isn't readily apparent to others makes you quite attractive and charming to the opposite sex. Others will be irresistibly drawn to your fresh, offbeat perspective and they will find that being with you is an undeniably stimulating and inspiring experience.

Though you are generally cautious, you also have a bold streak. You definitely enjoy a challenge and might be intrigued by daring activities such as snowboarding or hang-gliding.

If someone wants to get your attention, they need to be willing to go out on that precarious edge with you. But, if they really want to capture your heart, they also need to be able to be as seriously committed as you are to making a mark on the world.

The perfect female for the 1991 Capricorn male is someone who is highly independent and resourceful. She is likely to be a standout in any crowd, someone who has lots of friends and enjoys social gatherings. And, because you place such an importance on financial success and security, you want someone who has the grace, intelligence and sophistication to help you to achieve your grand ambitions.

For you, 1991 Capricorn female, the perfect male is someone who is solid and reliable but who also is creative and perceptive. You want someone who is able to share his feelings with you and who wants to probe the your innermost mysteries. He needs to be deep, thoughtful, and able to understand that you are a sensitive creature who requires faithfulness and loyalty from a partner.

CAPRICORN ZODIAC SIGN
Your Love Planets

YOUR ROMANTIC SIDE — p. 696
- ▶ **VENUS IN CAPRICORN**
  Born Dec. 22, 1990 3:07 - Jan. 05, 1991 5:02
- ▶ **VENUS IN AQUARIUS**
  Born Jan. 05, 5:03 - Jan. 20, 13:46

YOUR SEX DRIVE — p. 722
- ▶ **MARS IN TAURUS**
  Born Dec. 22, 1990 3:07 - Jan. 20, 1991 13:46

YOUR CELEBRITY TWINS — p. 760
  Find out the astrological similarities you have with famous people.

YOUR COMPATIBILITY — p. 780
  Compare planets to find out how compatible you are in a relationship.

YOUR RELATIONSHIP KARMA — p. 824
- ▶ **SATURN IN CAPRICORN**
  Born Dec. 22, 1990 3:07 - Jan. 20, 1991 13:46

ANTHONY HOPKINS
Welsh Actor
Sun and Venus in Capricorn

599

1991 AQUARIUS

From January 20, 13:47 through February 19, 3:57

♒ *The Empathetic Idealist*

A curious blend of radical non-conformity and compassionate idealism, 1991 Aquarian, you want to make the world a better place. You have strong ideas about how things should be done and you can't wait to put those ideas into practice. When it comes to relationships, you try to be fair and impeccably just in your dealings and people appreciate you for your trustworthiness.

Sometimes you may try just a bit too hard to be different and you might do crazy things just for their "shock" value. But, as you mature, you are likely to transform into a person who simply does his own thing without being concerned what others may think. Graced with an inventive and original imagination, you seek to maintain your individuality in a relationship. Others are likely to find your independent streak very appealing and will enjoy your unconventional ways.

You are brilliantly creative and you enjoy any activity that allows your imagination to run wild and free. Art and music especially pique your interest and anyone who is interested in

getting to know you better needs to like them as well. An afternoon listening to alternative rock or visiting a modern art exhibit is sure to delight you. But, to really win your heart, a prospective partner will need to share your humanitarian ideals.

For you, 1991 Aquarian male, the perfect female is sensitive, sweet, and caring. Though you want someone who is reasoned and rational, you also want someone who is kindhearted and able to empathize on an emotional level. Because you really value your freedom, you also need someone who will not try to smother you in a relationship. It helps if she shares your attitudes about being able to spend time apart and has a variety of her own interests.

The ideal male for the 1991 Aquarian female is one who is a communicator. You want to be with someone who is your intellectual equal and who shares your love of knowledge. It's likely that he will be quite versatile, enjoying many hobbies and interests. And you want someone who is a bit unpredictable and able to keep you guessing about what he'll do next.

AQUARIUS ZODIAC SIGN
Your Love Planets

YOUR ROMANTIC SIDE — p. 696
- ▶ **VENUS IN AQUARIUS**
  Born Jan. 20, 13:47 - Jan. 29, 4:43
- ▶ **VENUS IN PISCES**
  Born Jan. 29, 4:44 - Feb. 19, 3:57

YOUR SEX DRIVE — p. 722
- ▶ **MARS IN TAURUS**
  Born Jan. 20, 13:47 - Jan. 21, 1:14
- ▶ **MARS IN GEMINI**
  Born Jan. 21, 1:15 - Feb. 19, 3:57

YOUR CELEBRITY TWINS — p. 760
  Find out the astrological similarities you have with famous people.

YOUR COMPATIBILITY — p. 780
  Compare planets to find out how compatible you are in a relationship.

YOUR RELATIONSHIP KARMA — p. 824
- ▶ **SATURN IN CAPRICORN**
  Born Jan. 20, 13:47 - Feb. 6, 18:55
- ▶ **SATURN IN AQUARIUS**
  Born Feb. 6, 8:56 - Feb. 19, 3:57

GEENA DAVIS
American Actress
Venus in Pisces

600

1991 PISCES
From February 19, 3:58 through March 21, 3:01

The Fervent Believer

Blessed with both faith and enthusiasm, 1991 Pisces, you were born to shoot for the stars. You are a bit of a visionary and have an uncanny ability to be slightly ahead of the curve when it comes to what is fashionable or trendy. This same instinctual gift is rather useful for you when it comes to understanding what other people want and need. As a result, you are a natural in relationships, always willing to try to see the other's point of view.

Impulsive and fiery, you enjoy having a variety of people in your life and you may even be a bit fickle. You have a great deal of personal magnetism in addition to a reckless, devil-may-care quality that others find inexplicably charming. There are no limits or boundaries to what you are willing to share with another, and your aim is to really get under another person's skin in order to feel things as they do.

Easily bored, you like to be around people who can inspire you and feed your desire for interesting and varied experiences. If someone wants to capture your interest, they need to show that they are fun loving and capable of switching gears at a moment's notice. You like to keep things loose and flexible and if someone becomes too demanding or rigid, you will promptly run in the other direction.

Your perfect female, 1991 Pisces male, is someone who is effervescent and exciting. You like a challenge and it is important that she know how to keep you on your toes. But you also have a sensitive and dreamy side and you need a partner who can relate to your need for romance. Most importantly, she should know how to lift your spirits and demonstrate that she has confidence in your ability to attain your dreams.

1991 Pisces female, your ideal male is someone who wants to travel and explore all that the world has to offer. You are not afraid to think big and you need someone who is optimistic and has a positive outlook on life. He should be willing to risk everything in order to reach a cherished goal. But you also want someone who believes in the basic goodness of others and can find joy in simple and heartfelt moments.

1991 ARIES
From March 21, 3:02 through April 20, 14:07

The Relaxed Genius

Aries of 1991, you often appear to be a mass of contradictions. Though you have a quick and brilliant intellect, you may be flooded with so many impulses that you find it hard to act upon any one thought. And, while you are quite energetic and enjoy a variety of activities, you have more than a few moments when all you want to do is stay home and relax in front of the TV. You have some very traditional attitudes, yet you are also someone who tends to question authority.

When it comes to your romantic relationships, you may find that your paradoxical behavior will bewilder your partners. Because you take nothing for granted, others are attracted to your inquiring and rebellious nature. You love the idea of being in love and once you get to know yourself well, you will be able to commit to another. But, until you've explored all the facets of your own personality, you are also likely to be interested in having relationships with many different people.

You are an individual with very strong convictions and you will not hesitate to fight for what you believe. Others are inspired by your enthusiasm and someone who wants to get to know you better might be smart to join your latest cause. Or they may appeal to your more self-indulgent side and suggest spending the afternoon at the mall checking out all the latest trends.

For the 1991 Aries male, the ideal female is someone who has a practical nature and a good deal of inner strength. You need someone one who can be loyal, devoted, and will help you to fulfill your vast potential. She also needs to be a clear thinker, someone who can help you sort out all of your fabulous ideas and assist you in concentrating your energy in a positive direction.

1991 Aries female, your perfect male is sensitive, intuitive, and smart. You want someone who has a good deal of confidence and can find his way out of any difficult situation with ease and grace. He should be someone that you can trust to be your friend and ally through thick and thin. But, most of all, he needs to be spontaneous and free, ready to approach life with heart and soul.

1991 TAURUS

From April 20, 14:08 through May 21, 13:19

The Captivating Charmer

You have a way with words, 1991 Taurus, and it is important to you that those around you understand your thoughts and feelings. You derive a great deal of satisfaction from your ability to sway others to your thinking and, likewise, those who can do the same impress you. This give-and-take in communication will be the foundation of your relationships and you will endear yourself to others by both your willingness to listen and your readiness to share your own feelings in return.

In addition to your ability to relate on a mental level, your mesmerizing charm also makes you a very sought after romantic partner. Being around you can be downright magical for you possess more than your fair share of charisma. You seem to know just how to smile, walk, and talk in order to be noticed. And it's not that you're a show-off or loud. Understated and elegant, others simply can't help but to be enthralled by you.

Though you are very charming, you may nonetheless be reluctant to make the first move in a relationship. You don't like to risk rejection and you prefer a potential partner to show that they would welcome your attention. And, because you take commitment rather seriously, you are not likely to jump in too quickly. If someone really wants you, they need to take the time to be your friend first and demonstrate that they have a calm demeanor and a patient approach to relationships.

For the 1991 Taurus male, the perfect female is someone who is lively and spontaneous and adds excitement to every activity. It's likely that she will have a variety of interests and be the type of person who loves to be on the go. Above all, you want someone who has a good sense of humor and a lighthearted attitude towards life.

1991 Taurus female, your ideal male is someone who sees the beauty in life. He is the type of person who hears the sounds of nature as a melodic symphony and looks at you as one of the universe's most perfect creations. Most of all, your ideal partner has an enormous capacity for love and can give you the opportunity to respond with your own tenderness and affection.

TAURUS ZODIAC SIGN
YOUR LOVE PLANETS

YOUR ROMANTIC SIDE   p. 696
▶ **VENUS IN GEMINI**
Born Apr. 20, 14:08 - May 09, 1:27
▶ **VENUS IN CANCER**
Born May 09, 1:28 - May 21, 13:19

YOUR SEX DRIVE   p. 722
▶ **MARS IN CANCER**
Born Apr. 20, 14:08 - May 21, 13:19

YOUR CELEBRITY TWINS   p. 760
Find out the astrological similarities you have with famous people.

YOUR COMPATIBILITY   p. 780
Compare planets to find out how compatible you are in a relationship.

YOUR RELATIONSHIP KARMA   p. 824
▶ **SATURN IN AQUARIUS**
Born Apr. 20, 14:08 - May 21, 13:19

PAULA ABDUL
American Singer
Sun in Gemini

601

1991 GEMINI
From May 21, 13:20 through June 21, 21:18

The Truth Seeker

Gemini of 1991, you have a natural gift for conversation and a desire to learn all that there is about life. While others may sometimes see you as superficial or glib, the fact is that you are fervently interested in solving this puzzle we call life. You are not satisfied with perfunctory answers to important questions. Your path is to deeply explore all the possibilities until you get to the bottom of the matter.

This philosophy will most certainly color your relationships and you will not be content with a bond that does not go beyond surface attraction. Though you are quite capable of being flirtatious and will probably have your share of casual dates, you really want a partnership that will be all encompassing, one in which you can explore the depths of another's soul. And, when you find your true love, it is likely to be a life changing experience for both you and for your partner.

Unusual and innovative subjects absolutely intrigue you. Since you may be especially interested in areas such as the occult and science fiction, someone who wants to get your attention might suggest taking in the latest sci-fi flick. You love to unravel a mystery and a prospective partner can really capture your heart by engaging your mind in a seemingly unsolvable riddle. And, if they are smart, that riddle will be all about who they are and what makes them tick.

The ideal female for the 1991 Gemini male is someone you can connect to physically, mentally, emotionally, and spiritually. The spiritual component can never be underestimated for, without it, you may never be truly satisfied. It's important that she has a down-to-earth, nurturing quality about her and that she be able to relate to people with varying backgrounds and interests.

1991 Gemini female, your perfect male is someone who is bold and courageous, willing to aggressively go after what he wants. But you also want a person who can harmonize with your own goals and ideals and who appreciates your philosophical tendencies. Most of all, you want someone who has integrity and knows what it means to be true to oneself.

GEMINI ZODIAC SIGN
YOUR LOVE PLANETS

YOUR ROMANTIC SIDE   p. 696
▶ **VENUS IN CANCER**
Born May 21, 13:20 - June 06, 1:15
▶ **VENUS IN LEO**
Born June 06, 1:16 - June 21, 21:18

YOUR SEX DRIVE   p. 722
▶ **MARS IN CANCER**
Born May 21, 13:20 - May 26, 12:18
▶ **MARS IN LEO**
Born May 26, 12:19 - June 21, 21:18

YOUR CELEBRITY TWINS   p. 760
Find out the astrological similarities you have with famous people.

YOUR COMPATIBILITY   p. 780
Compare planets to find out how compatible you are in a relationship.

YOUR RELATIONSHIP KARMA   p. 824
▶ **SATURN IN AQUARIUS**
Born May 21, 13:20 - June 21, 21:18

1 Read Your Sign   **2** Look Up Your Love Planets   **3** Go to Pages Shown

RIVER PHOENIX
American Actor
Sun and Mars in Leo

1991 CANCER
From June 21, 21:19 through July 23, 8:10

The Passionate Player

Magnetic and loving, 1991 Cancer, you relish being at the center of attention. Although you may be a bit shy, you desperately want to be noticed and, at heart, you have the personality of a movie star. Guileless and somewhat naïve, you are quite interested in learning all you can about how to relate in a one-to-one relationship. But, because of your tremendous need for approval, you can easily be fooled by insincere flattery and attention from those who are less than honest.

Your stellar quality is likely to extend to your intimate relationships and you may find that you are overwhelmed with people who will be attracted to you. To your dismay, those closest to you may often misread your signals or misunderstand your intentions and see you as someone who is self-centered, an attention seeker. In truth, all you really want is to be loved and to give your heart to another without fear or reservation.

A lover of drama, you really enjoy film and theatre. For you, a perfect evening is one in which you witness a performance that really inspires you emotionally and one in which you will come away with a better understanding of the human condition. Potential partners should not only share your interests but also have a desire to reveal themselves spiritually and emotionally. You will only give your heart to a person who you believe to be your soul mate—that one person who completes you in a very special way.

For you, 1991 Cancer male, the perfect female partner is someone of whom you will be proud and will want to have as an exciting co-star. She needs to be loyal and optimistic and as fiercely protective of you as you are of her. And, most importantly, you want to be able to trust her implicitly and so you need someone who will not disappoint or deceive you.

Your ideal male, 1991 Cancer female, is nothing short of Prince Charming. You have a tendency to idealize your partner and so you can be easily disenchanted if he falls short of your high expectations. But your true love will be someone who will try, nonetheless, to give you the adoring attention you so desire.

1991 LEO
From July 23, 8:11 through August 23, 15:12

The Jovial Perfectionist

Born to spread warmth and happiness wherever you go, 1991 Leo, you have a good deal of dignity and grace. But you also have a strong need to be flawless and to do or say the right thing. Your quest for perfection stems from your desire to please others and your fear that you may fall short of some impossible standard. The truth is that you are the one that has set the bar so high and others will love you simply because you are a person who is deeply sincere and completely honorable.

In relationships, you may find that you expect as much from others as you do from yourself. This may prevent you from enjoying people as they are. Once you overcome the tendency for such exacting standards, you will find that you can accept yourself and others—warts and all. Then, all of the quirks that human beings inevitably exhibit may be seen with loving humor rather than as devastating inadequacies. As a result, you will find a new freedom to live and love without hesitation.

More than anything, you love to be useful. Detail-oriented, you are a master of organization and you have a place for everything. If someone wants to get your attention, they might invite you to help them plan a party or organize an outing to a sporting event. But, to really capture your heart, they need to demonstrate that they have a burning desire to be socially responsible as well as have a healthy respect for planet earth.

1991 Leo male, your perfect female is someone who has a strong desire to be the best that she can be. But, even though she may empathize with your need for perfection, it is equally as important that she be able to help you lighten up and not take life so seriously. Most of all, she should be willing to gently overlook your shortcomings so that you can finally learn to accept yourself.

For you, 1991 Leo female, the ideal male is industrious and organized and has a strong desire to serve humanity. It is important for you to be able to respect your partner in addition to loving him. You want a person who is inherently decent and who is willing to work with others for the common good.

1991 VIRGO

From August 23, 15:13 through September 23, 12:47

The Benevolent Critic

Virgo of 1991, you are a remarkable blend of generosity and warmth tempered by caution and pragmatism. You also can't seem to make up your mind on which you'd rather be—spontaneous but impractical or discerning yet uptight. Eventually, you'll learn that you can be impulsive without becoming totally unrealistic and that you can be judicious without falling into rigidity. And, while you're maturing, you are apt to have a lot of fun experimenting with how to strike a balance that is comfortable for you and those you love.

In relationships, you may find that you are very giving and may even be in danger of losing yourself in order to please another. Sensitive and intuitive, you will instinctively know what your partner wants and you quite naturally will want to fulfill every desire. Blessed with remarkable insight, others are attracted to you because you seem to know them so well. And you may use your considerable communication skills to help them feel comfortable and secure in a relationship.

You have an innate sense of what is good and you seek the highest quality in people as well as in your possessions. In order to get your attention, an individual needs to behave in an appropriate and inoffensive manner. Since you don't like to make a mistake, you certainly don't want to be around someone who is careless or unthinking. But, to really cement a relationship with you, a potential partner simply needs to be warm and genuine and able to approach others without pretension.

The ideal female for the 1991 Virgo male is someone who is not afraid to say what she thinks. You need a mate that will not only bolster your confidence but also give you the freedom you need to make your own decisions. Most of all, you want someone that will help you to show your love without fear or mistrust.

1991 Virgo female, your perfect male is ambitious, imaginative, and interested in self-improvement. Like you, he needs to pay attention to detail and have an appreciation for how things look and feel. Finally, he probably will be a bit of a maverick, someone with his own unique style and manner.

VIRGO ZODIAC SIGN
YOUR LOVE PLANETS

YOUR ROMANTIC SIDE   p. 696
▶ **VENUS IN LEO**
Born Aug. 23, 15:13 - Sept. 23, 12:47

YOUR SEX DRIVE   p. 722
▶ **MARS IN VIRGO**
Born Aug. 23, 15:13 - Sept. 01, 6:37
▶ **MARS IN LIBRA**
Born Sept. 01, 6:38 - Sept. 23, 12:47

YOUR CELEBRITY TWINS   p. 760
Find out the astrological similarities you have with famous people.

YOUR COMPATIBILITY   p. 780
Compare planets to find out how compatible you are in a relationship.

YOUR RELATIONSHIP KARMA   p. 824
▶ **SATURN IN AQUARIUS**
Born Aug. 23, 15:13 - Sept. 23, 12:47

KEANU REEVES
American Actor
Sun in Virgo

1991 LIBRA

From September 23, 12:48 through October 23, 22:04

The Unconventional Pacifist

You like to keep things on an even keel, 1991 Libra, and you may spend a good deal of energy making sure that your life is balanced. When you are young, you may find that balance by going to extremes. But, as you grow older, you will learn how to create a harmonious and peaceful environment for yourself and for those around you. You may find change confusing and upsetting yet, at heart, you are a bit of a renegade who really enjoys creating order out of chaos.

Ingenious and innovative, others are attracted to your sparkling personality and zany antics. Because you are so adept at seeing both sides of an issue, you may have a difficult time in making a decision and may be easily swayed by the opinions of others. However, as you mature, this same attribute will help you to understand your partner's point of view and you are likely to become quite expert at the give-and-take necessary to make a relationship succeed.

More than most, you really believe that life is more fun if you have a special someone along to keep you company. Witty and intelligent, you really enjoy smart conversations, whether as a participant or an observer. You also love the arts, especially theatre, concerts, and dance, so a potential partner might find it advantageous to splurge on tickets to such an event. It's even better if they can keep it a surprise since you feel that doing things on the spur of the moment makes them so much more exciting.

For you, 1991 Libra male, the ideal female is one who is reserved and intelligent. You want a relationship that will be a partnership of equals with your mate as your advisor as well as your soul mate. Therefore, it is important for her to have a good deal of analytical ability so that she can help you make decisions in your personal and business life.

1991 Libra female, your perfect male is logical, perceptive, and a fine judge of human character. It's like that he will treasure you in a very special way—not as a possession but as a valued friend and helpmate. Most of all, he is fair and just, someone whom people will trust with their deepest secrets.

LIBRA ZODIAC SIGN
YOUR LOVE PLANETS

YOUR ROMANTIC SIDE   p. 696
▶ **VENUS IN LEO**
Born Sept. 23, 12:48 - Oct. 06, 21:14
▶ **VENUS IN VIRGO**
Born Oct. 06, 21:15 - Oct. 23, 22:04

YOUR SEX DRIVE   p. 722
▶ **MARS IN LIBRA**
Born Sept. 23, 12:48 - Oct. 16, 19:04
▶ **MARS IN SCORPIO**
Born Oct. 16, 19:05 - Oct. 23, 22:04

YOUR CELEBRITY TWINS   p. 760
Find out the astrological similarities you have with famous people.

YOUR COMPATIBILITY   p. 780
Compare planets to find out how compatible you are in a relationship.

YOUR RELATIONSHIP KARMA   p. 824
▶ **SATURN IN AQUARIUS**
Born Sept. 23, 12:48 - Oct. 23, 22:04

603

MONICA SELES
Yugoslavian Tennis Champion
Sun in Sagittarius

1991 SCORPIO
From October 23, 22:05 through November 22, 19:35

♏ ## The Powerful Sage

Wise beyond your years, 1991 Scorpio, you have a way of looking beneath the surface and finding the real meaning in any situation. Blessed with incredible powers of discernment as well as strong philosophical leanings, you can usually ferret out the truth of the matter. You are never satisfied with surface explanations, and you may exasperate those around you with your need to know every single detail. As you grow, your faith in your own perceptions will grow and so will your confidence as a counselor and advisor.

When it comes to relationships, it is likely that you will use these strengths to mesmerize those of the opposite sex. Your potential for attracting others is enormous and your mysterious and intriguing demeanor will easily captivate them. Intense and profound, you will have great insight into most people and you may give a stranger the impression that you've known them all your life. Once you are involved with someone, you won't shy away from exploring the deep recesses of their souls.

It's not likely that you will ever be swept away too easily. It takes you a while to trust another and a potential date would be wise to give you time to proceed at your own pace. You are naturally suspicious and doubting, so you don't appreciate insincere flattery. If someone wants to compliment you, they best make sure that their words of appreciation are truthful and earnest.

Your ideal female, 1991 Scorpio male, is brilliant, charming, and fun to be around. You want someone who can keep up with you intellectually but is a lighter counterpart to your ponderous way of thinking. It's best if she has an optimistic and trusting nature so she can also balance your inborn skepticism. Most of all, you want a partner that you can trust to be loyal and devoted to you.

For you, 1991 Scorpio female, the perfect male is someone that you will not be able to dominate or control. Yet it is vital that he not seek to control you either. Once you find the person that matches your strength and can love you unconditionally, you will undoubtedly be a faithful and committed partner.

1991 SAGITTARIUS
From November 22, 19:36 through December 22, 8:53

♐ ## The Enthusiastic Scholar

You have an unquenchable thirst for knowledge 1991 Sagittarius, and you may even become what's known as a perennial student. Learning is like breathing for you—as necessary to your well being as food and water. Likewise, you may also be a teacher, disseminating your wisdom to anyone willing to listen. However, you need to be careful not to get lost in your lofty ideas and disregard your need to relate to people in an ordinary, every-day way.

When it comes to romantic relationships, you may very well be a lifelong learner. Others are fascinated by your inquisitive mind and your wide-eyed, childlike zest for gathering new experiences. Your open and frank approach to life is totally refreshing and, as a result, members of the opposite sex will find you rather alluring. It will be quite normal for you to wander from relationship to relationship in your youth in order to find out firsthand what you need in order to make a lasting commitment.

You have a special fondness for history, philosophy, and religion—an invitation to attend a lecture on any of those topics would be especially suitable. Travel is another fond desire of yours and you will certainly enjoy exploring the four corners of the planet with another. But, if physical travel is out of the question, a friend or partner might want to simulate a night in an exotic destination replete with all the trimmings—costumes, décor and, of course, the appropriate cuisine.

For you, 1991 Sagittarius male, your perfect female is a person who is serious-minded and has a profound understanding of human nature. You also need someone who can make each day seem like the birth of a new and exciting adventure. Finally, you want a person who can be a companion on your journey through life.

1991 Sagittarius female, you want a relationship that will grow and that will allow you to develop to your fullest potential. Your ideal male is someone who is relaxed and easygoing and who sees life as a mystical and magical ride. But most of all, you want a man who is honest and idealistic and who has a burning desire for acquiring wisdom.

'90s

The Spanish Underworld of Almodóvar

All Pedro Almodóvar has ever wanted to do is make movies. Growing up in impoverished rural Spain, trips to the cinema were an escape from his strict religious schooling by Franciscan Fathers—an experience that irreparably soured his view of Catholicism and provided a complex underlying theme for much of his work.

Desperate to learn the art of filmmaking, at the age of sixteen he waved good-bye to his family and humble roots and headed, penniless, for the throbbing Spanish capital, Madrid, with a single-minded, dogged drive and ambition to realize his ultimate goal—to makes movies. Unable to enroll in the national film school—the fascist dictator Franco had closed it—Almodóvar decided to educate himself in the ways of the world. Throwing himself head-first into the deep, pulsating underbelly of city life, he soaked up the essence of counter-culture in Madrid. Unabashedly gay, he explored his sexuality with gusto. He was a member of a transvestite punk-rock group, he drew X-rated comic books, and he began acting in avant-garde theatre groups where he mixed with raw, young talent, such as Antonio Banderas, with whom he would later work. Pedro's flamboyant sexuality filtered into his work, with his films depicting gender-bending characters and perverse sexual habits.

After a series of odd jobs, he landed a "proper" job, working for Madrid's National Telephone Company, where he stayed for several years. Naturally, this was all part of the bigger plan, saving up money from his wages to buy a movie camera, with which he started making daring and innovative short films. Before long he was a leading light in the Spanish pop culture movement known as "La Movida." Almodóvar found himself right in the middle of a cultural revolution—freedom burst onto post-Franco Spain in an explosion of artistic and sexual expression, with a verve and fervor never experienced before. Chronicling the hedonistic excesses of a country liberated after years of repression, the flamboyant, young Almodóvar reflected the mood of the times—his films were audacious and daring, kinky and offbeat, exposing the middle classes and giving the lonely and disenfranchised, living on the fringes of society, a voice. And all this with a heavy dose of black, dark humor.

By 1980 he had made his first feature, the bold and brash *Pepi, Luci, Bom, and Other Girls on the Heap*. Gaining cult status, it propelled him onto the international scene where his popularity rocketed. With the more conventional comedy, *Women on the Verge of a Nervous Breakdown*, he had his first worldwide hit—it was to become the most successful film in Spanish box-office history and was nominated for a best foreign film Oscar.

More controversial films followed. *Tie Me Up! Tie Me Down!* was given an X-rating by American censors, who were scandalized by Almodóvar's liberated and all-too-graphic depiction of urban Spanish society. Almodóvar, outraged by this infringement on his freedom of expression, joined campaigners and launched a legal battle to fight the rating, which rendered his work pornographic. They were victorious, and a new rating was born—the NC-17.

With heroin-addicted nuns, broken-hearted transsexuals, explicit gay sex, and murderous matadors all jostling for attention, Pedro Almodóvar tenderly and comically depicts the kitsch, the outrageous, and the eccentric. He is, by far, the most important filmmaker to emerge from post-Franco Spain.

605

"I grew up, suffered, gained weight, and developed myself in Madrid. And I underwent many of these changes in time with the city. My life and films are bound to Madrid, like the heads and tails of the same coin."

PEDRO ALMODÓVAR

▶ READ ABOUT ANTONIO BANDERAS ON PAGE 638

1992

Sex Idol

- ⭐ WOODY, MIA, AND SOON-YI
- ⭐ MURPHY BROWN
- ⭐ FERGIE AND DIANA IN THE TABLOIDS
- ⭐ THE CRYING GAME
- ⭐ SAVAGE NIGHTS
- ⭐ SEX
- ⭐ A RETURN TO LOVE

EVENTS

Woody Allen's affair with Mia Farrow's teenage adopted daughter, Soon-Yi Previn, sparked a very public and nasty custody battle between Woody and Mia over their children. In America three made-for-TV movies sensationalized the tawdry tale of "Long Island Lolita" Amy Fisher (16) who shot her older, married lover's wife. Vice President Dan Quayle accused single mother sitcom character Murphy Brown of promoting bad family values. Longtime personal and professional partners William Masters and Virginia Johnson (*Human Sexual Response*) and Tammy Faye and Jim Bakker (scandal-ridden Praise the Lord televangelists) both divorced. UK royal couples the Duke and Duchess of York and Diana and Charles legally separated. In the "Blood Affair," the French Ministry of Health faced accusations of negligence in addressing blood transfusion HIV contamination risks. The Anglican Church allowed women to be ordained as priests.

POP CULTURE

Brit-pop act Right Said Fred's "I'm Too Sexy" and funky California rockers Red Hot Chili Peppers' "Under the Bridge" were hits. Sir Mix-a-Lot celebrated the derriere in "Baby Got Back." Eric Clapton's memorial ballad "Tears In Heaven" won a Grammy. Glam girl group En Vogue taunted "My Lovin' (You're Never Gonna Get It)," and sassy trio TLC sang "Baby-Baby-Baby." Tarnished

ex–Miss America Vanessa Williams shined with "Save the Best for Last."

Steamy thriller *Basic Instinct* featured Sharon Stone as the seductive prime suspect in her ex-boyfriend's murder. Neil Jordan's *The Crying Game* combined politics and gender-bending love. Eighties icon Boy George sang the hit title song. *The Lover* was based on Marguerite Duras' autobiographical chronicle of a passionate love affair between a fifteen-year-old girl and an older Chinese man in 1920s Indochina. Writer-director Cyril Collard died from AIDS just a few days before his bittersweet film *Savage Nights* won a César.

Madonna's eyebrow-raising book *Sex* featured Steven Meisel's provocative, stylish photos of an often-nude Madonna and friends. *Mixed Blessings* by Danielle Steel followed three couples facing fertility and trust issues. Naura Hayden's *How to Satisfy a Woman Every Time...And Have Her Beg for More* promised how-to instructions for men. Marianne Williamson's *A Return to Love* revisited her *A Course in Miracles* theme that releasing fear makes room for love and miracles.

SHARON STONE

Smart, sexy Sharon Stone was born in 1958 and modeled before breaking into acting. In 1992 her status as a femme fatale was sealed in Basic Instinct, the steamy thriller in which she plays the prime suspect in her ex-boyfriend's murder. In its famous interview scene, Stone, sans undies, crosses her legs, giving the lead detective Nick Curran (Michael Douglas) an eyeful.

A Buddhist and a human rights advocate, Sharon Stone continues to light up the red carpet. In 1998, she married newspaper editor Phil Bronstein and adopted a baby boy. In 2001, she suffered a minor, unexpected brain hemorrhage, but has made a full recovery.

SEE ALSO

▶ SUSAN SARANDON *Page 579*

▶ CATHERINE ZETA-JONES *Page 688*

1992 CAPRICORN

From December 22, 1991 8:54 through January 20, 1992 19:31 (December 1992 Capricorns, see 1993 Capricorn)

The Super Sweetheart

Capricorns born in 1992 will have high expectations for their relationships. Perhaps you have a famous celebrity couple already in mind as your model of romantic perfection. A marriage much like your parents' or other couple in your extended family may appeal to you as you get older. When you do find the love of your life, you'll take your commitment to this person seriously. You're a natural caretaker, and your lucky partner will always feel pampered and very loved. You're especially good with money.

You have great ambitions and therefore need a mate that will be enthusiastic and supportive of your career. It's likely that you will travel widely during your lifetime and you'll need to be with a partner who likes to go exploring with you. You sometimes don't have much patience with people who can't keep up! You believe in living life to its fullest and will want an active companion by your side. Any person that is self-centered, lazy, or indifferent to the world around them will not win your affections.

In order to keep you interested, your special honeybunch will need to dazzle you with his or her knowledge of the latest trends and current events. Your significant other will have to make sure not to let your love life become boring. You'll want a sweetheart that you can discuss everything with. You're very sociable, so your darling should like to hang out with groups of your friends and, of course, with your family, too.

The perfect match for a 1992 Capricorn guy is a happy-go-lucky, intelligent, and independent girl. She will become a friend first before you have any romantic involvement or perhaps one of your close friends will introduce you to her. She'll love the great outdoors and be active in one or more sports. Your true love will become your best companion.

If you're a 1992 Capricorn girl, you'll be attracted to guys that are self-confident and athletic, with a good sense of humor. The one you choose to be your life-partner will be hesitant to show his feelings for you. You may have to find a way to let him know you're interested before he'll ask you out.

607

1992 AQUARIUS

From January 20, 19:32 through February 19, 9:42

The Patient Pal

When considering romance, 1992 Aquarians will need lots of time to figure out the score. You'll enjoy talking about love in general, but you can be shy about getting involved with the opposite sex. You won't be in a hurry to find just the person to share your life. You'll fall in love with someone that has already become a good friend, after you've gotten to know the person well. You care a lot about what your crowd thinks of whom you date and won't get too excited about anyone that doesn't fit in with them. A familiar, dependable face is the one you'll find most attractive.

You'll be patient and understanding with your partner. You know that everyone has flaws and you'll love your sweetheart's little eccentricities. Your communication skills are superior and you'll love being with a sweetheart that enjoys long conversations. It will be easy for you and your true love to talk about your differences and reach a compromise. You're sincere in all that you do and this makes mutual respect between you and your darling possible.

The lucky one that wins you over should not be a romantic slug. You require attention, and lots of it. You'll be happy with intimate shows of affection, frequent phone calls, and unexpected gifts. You'll love it if you and your partner can make a popular ballad "your song." It will make you happy to share your interest in the movies and the arts with the one you love. The thing you'll value most about being with your significant other is the enduring friendship.

Aquarian males born in 1992 will be attracted to outgoing girls that are easy to get to know. The one you'll love best may ask you out first. You'll adore her self-confidence and the fact that the two of you have mutual interests. She'll be super-smart and really helpful in your studies or work.

Handsome, hardworking guys are appeal most to Aquarian girls born in 1992. Your special love is ambitious. He sets high goals and can be relentless in achieving them. You'll admire his maturity and serious nature. However, he'll always find time for romance and will never neglect you.

KRISTI YAMAGUCHI
American Ice Skating Champion
Mars in Aquarius

1 Read Your Sign **2** Look Up Your Love Planets **3** Go to Pages Shown

JENNIFER SAUNDERS
English Actress
Mars in Aries

1992 PISCES
From February 19, 9:43 through March 20, 8:47

 ## A Genuine Gem

Pisces born in 1992 will lead interesting romantic lives. You'll have great expectations for the person that you want to share your life with. In fact, you may even draw up a list of the qualities you'll want to find in your true love. It's possible that you'll set such high standards that it will be difficult for anyone to measure up! There will be a few types of people that will be lopped off your list of potential partners permanently. You will never be happy with anyone that is critical of you, has a sullen disposition, or lacks great imagination. You're thoughtful and polite, and need to be with a partner that will treat you with gentleness.

Once you're drawn to someone special, however, you'll throw away the list and love that person just as they are. Any faults that you do discover in your lover will be accepted. Your intuition and instincts will carry you through from there, and your heart will tell you when you've made a good choice. You'll be true to your darling and always sincere. Your devotion to your loved one will be complete and lasting.

You'll never keep your sweetheart in the dark about what you need in the relationship. To keep you happy, your favorite admirer should be sensitive to your changing emotions. You're very sentimental and will like it when your angel makes a big deal out of your birthday and anniversary. You also love to receive gifts for no reason at all!

Pisces males born in 1992 will be attracted to girls that have an air of mystery about them. The one you like the best may seem mature for her age and have lots of responsibilities while she's young. She is not so easy to get to know and may keep you guessing about how she feels about you. When you do get acquainted, you'll discover you have many things in common.

The 1992 Pisces female looks twice at guys that are serious and somewhat aloof. The one that fascinates you the most will be unpredictable but, once you get to know him, he's a real charmer. He'll have lots of great ideas about how to make the world a better place. You'll admire him for his dedication to good causes.

1992 ARIES
From March 20, 8:48 through April 19, 19:56

♈ ## The Daring Darling

For the Aries born in 1992, love will be a wonderful adventure. You bring your unique personal style to everything you do and this will include your romantic life. You're so independent that you won't have any great need to choose a partner. This will give you an advantage in your relationship because you'll wait until you find just the right person to settle down with. While you're still looking, you'll have a number of practice partnerships that will help you zero in on exactly the kind of mate that you'll find happiness with. With some experience behind you, you'll find the perfect one for you.

Once you do fall in love, you'll want your sweetheart to be your best friend and playmate. You'll need a lover that's willing and able to drop everything and take off on a big trip with you on a whim. Although you'll be respectful of your loved one's feelings, you're likely show your affection through your actions rather than by displays of emotion. The gifts you choose for the one you love may be more amusing than romantic. You'll never get tied down with

anyone that is boring, narrow-minded, lacking in self-confidence or humorless.

No matter how far your travels take you from your partner, you'll keep coming back to the one that is fun to be with. You'll like it when your special person introduces you to new entertainment or activities. To keep your attention, it's important that your partner have fresh ideas, too. You'll want to be with someone that encourages you, and doesn't hold you back.

Illusive and mysterious women will appeal to the male Aries born in 1992. Your best girl will not be easy to win over but, when you do, you'll be satisfied that she's a great prize. She'll be tender and caring but also brave and excited about life and love.

Intellectual men with curious minds will have the most appeal to Aries females born this year. Perhaps he'll be a scientist or in some other cutting-edge occupation. Your special guy will love to talk and tell you all about his innovative ideas. You'll be his inspiration to do great things because he'll want to please you.

1992 TAURUS

From April 19, 19:57 through May 20, 19:11

The Fabulous Flirt

The relationship strength of 1992 Taureans lies in their great kindness and loyalty. You will be an excellent partner because you have a gentle disposition and will be fiercely devoted to your significant other. When you fall in love, you'll make the needs of your sweetheart equal to your own. You welcome change and will look for ways to cooperate with your mate. As a sentimental romantic, you'll try to keep the sparks flying, too. You'll love to flirt and tease and pamper your darling.

You won't rush into any long-term commitments and will be very particular about who you get involved with. Anyone that seems to be stuck in a rut and going nowhere won't gain your affections. People with ambition will please you. You'll have some significant life goals by then and will want to be with a partner that supports your dreams for the future. It's possible that you and your mate will establish a business together. You'll be one another's helpmates and a great working team!

Practical matters aside, you'll be happiest in a good old-fashioned, Hollywood style, love-that-lasts-forever marriage. The one you care for will keep the illusions alive by doing all those super courtship rituals that make celebrity life so appealing. You'll want to be wined and dined and taken to exclusive places on dates. Gifts are good too, and they should come often and be expensive. Fortunately, you'll also like other tokens of love and will be pleased to receive a hug or a love letter from your beloved.

As a male Taurus born in 1992, you'll be attracted to perky, playful girls. The one you'll know best may have been a cheerleader or involved in a physically demanding sport. She'll be sure of herself and not at all shy. You'll find her assertiveness appealing and her happy attitude a real treat.

Gentle, sensitive, and caring men will catch the hearts of 1992 Taurus women. Your favorite fella won't give up until he's won your heart. His persistence will charm you, but mostly you'll care about him for his loving ways. Everyone that knows your true love will agree that he's a sweetheart.

TAURUS ZODIAC SIGN
YOUR LOVE PLANETS

YOUR ROMANTIC SIDE   p. 696
▶ **VENUS IN ARIES**
Born Apr. 19, 19:57 - May 01, 15:40
▶ **VENUS IN TAURUS**
Born May 01, 15:41 - May 20, 19:11

YOUR SEX DRIVE   p. 722
▶ **MARS IN PISCES**
Born Apr. 19, 19:57 - May 05, 21:35
▶ **MARS IN ARIES**
Born May 05, 21:36 - May 20, 19:11

YOUR CELEBRITY TWINS   p. 760
Find out the astrological similarities you have with famous people.

YOUR COMPATIBILITY   p. 780
Compare planets to find out how compatible you are in a relationship.

IYOUR RELATIONSHIP KARMA   p. 824
▶ **SATURN IN AQUARIUS**
Born Apr. 19, 19:57 - May 20, 19:11

609

1992 GEMINI

rom May 20, 19:12 through June 21, 3:13

The Happy Communicator

Love for a 1992 Gemini will really be something to talk about when you're older. You'll never tire of discussing your romantic involvements with your friends, both before and after you make a commitment. When you're with your significant other, you'll want to go over every little detail of the relationship. To you, love won't be real until you hear the right words. You'll avoid getting too cozy with a person that doesn't like to share his or her feelings. Anyone that gives you the silent treatment won't be able to hold your affections.

After you get to know absolutely everything about your special love, you'll be happy to settle into a solid partnership. Home and family will become a priority and the one you care for most will share these values. Your superior communication skills will make it easy for you to resolve any challenges with the one you love. You're curious and interested in what your partner has to say and will consider all sides of any issue.

Your sweetheart will need to do more than just listen to keep you happy. You'll expect other kinds of attention, too. Because you're so sociable, you'll be thrilled when your partner takes you to parties and other fun happenings. You love nice things and will really appreciate receiving gifts. They don't have to be pricey but there should be lots of them. Sentimental cards and other written expressions of love will make your heart sing.

Down-to-earth, "girl-next-door" types will appeal to Gemini males born in 1992. Your darling will perhaps be someone you grew up with or that lives in your neighborhood. She'll be beautiful and have a lovely voice that enchants you. Your partner will be practical and will encourage you to build your bank account.

Athletic guys that are a little rebellious will catch the eye of 1992 Gemini girls. Your perfect partner will be easy to pick out of the crowd. He'll always be doing something absolutely different from everyone else. This guy will become a good friend first before you begin dating. He won't be too easy to figure out but this will only make him more interesting to you.

MICHAEL ONDAATJE
Canadian Writer
Mars in Gemini

GEMINI ZODIAC SIGN
YOUR LOVE PLANETS

YOUR ROMANTIC SIDE   p. 696
▶ **VENUS IN TAURUS**
Born May 20, 19:12 - May 26, 1:17
▶ **VENUS IN GEMINI**
Born May 26, 1:18 - June 19, 11:21
▶ **VENUS IN CANCER**
Born June 19, 11:22 - June 21, 3:13

YOUR SEX DRIVE   p. 722
▶ **MARS IN ARIES**
Born May 20, 19:12 - June 14, 15:55
▶ **MARS IN TAURUS**
Born June 14, 15:56 - June 21, 3:13

YOUR CELEBRITY TWINS   p. 760
Find out the astrological similarities you have with famous people.

YOUR COMPATIBILITY   p. 780
Compare planets to find out how compatible you are in a relationship.

YOUR RELATIONSHIP KARMA   p. 824
▶ **SATURN IN AQUARIUS**
Born May 20, 19:12 - June 21, 3:13

WHITNEY HOUSTON
American Singer
Sun and Venus in Leo

610

1992 CANCER
From June 21, 3:14 through July 22, 14:08

A Homegrown Cutie

As a 1992 Cancer, you'll be quite a catch for one lucky partner. You'll be the type that everyone will want to come home to—a thoughtful, kind, and loving mate that knows how to keep your darling happy. Because you're so sensitive and caring, your significant other will always feel understood and emotionally supported. You'll take your marriage vows seriously and make your sweetheart's needs equal to your own. However, you will also be self-protective of your own interests, sometimes withdrawing into your shell! You'll lead an active life outside the relationship and expect that your significant other will be accepting of this. Anyone that doesn't will make you feel disappointed in the long run.

When you begin to socialize with the opposite sex, you'll hang out with groups of your friends. It's likely that, when you get serious about someone, it will be one of these people you'll have known for a very long time. This will be important to you because you'll prefer to share your life with someone that has a similar background and values as you do. The history that you have together will be a very strong and lasting bond.

You'll want to be able to fall in love with your partner over and over again. The person that you settle in with can keep the romance in your heart forever by putting you on a pedestal and making you feel adored. You'll need a sweetheart who will be there for you when needed and that's also a good listener. You'll have a rich, imaginative inner life that you'll share with a dependable, accepting lover.

Shy, modest, and romantic girls appeal to Cancer guys born in 1992. Your one very special gal will be so lovely to look at that your friends will envy you. She'll have a wonderful but unusual way of expressing herself and several little idiosyncrasies that you'll find fascinating.

If you're a Cancer female born this year, you'll be drawn to sweet guys that have a lifestyle similar to your own. He'll be very good with children, animals, and all things connected with the earth. The Right One will bring you flowers a lot and worship the ground you walk on.

1992 LEO
From July 22, 14:09 through August 22, 21:09

The Ambitious Companion

The romantic life of a 1992 Leo will be very unique. For the early part of your adult life, your career will be your priority. You'll meet lots of potential partners and have a great time with them, too. However, your job will receive most of your attention—until you find the perfect sweetheart. When this happens, there'll be no doubt in your mind that fate has blessed you. You won't have to put your worldly ambitions on hold in order to be in this relationship. Rather, the one you care for will share your goals and understand that fulfilling them means spending some time apart.

Having avoided permanent involvement with the ones that weren't sensitive to your aspirations, you'll become a devoted and loving mate. There will be nothing too good for your darling. You'll want to share all you have with this person that makes you so happy. You'll be generous and attentive with your significant other. When your work takes you far away, you'll make sure the love of your life doesn't feel neglected. You'll never miss a day of intimate phone calls and other expressions of loving devotion.

Good partnerships are a two-way street and you'll consider the needs of your future true love. You'll give your heart every day to the one that proves to be faithful and true. To keep your interest, he or she should be dependably thoughtful and full of fun. The companionship of your special love is valuable to you. You'll want a sweetie that will travel with you and also enjoy quiet times at home.

A particular type of woman will appeal to Leo men born in 1992. She'll be beautiful, bright, and a real romantic. Having overcome many personal challenges in the past, she's going to be self-reliant and confident of her own talents and abilities. You'll admire her for her staying power.

Leo women of the 1992 variety will have an attraction for men with determination and stamina. Your one and only has high moral standards and great dreams for your future together. It's possible that he'll become wealthy. Your guy values his material comforts and will help you make a home that's happy.

1992 VIRGO

From August 22, 21:10 through September 22, 18:42

♍ *The Lucky Lover*

The romantic prayers of discriminating 1992 Virgos will be answered. Although you'll still be shy and reserved when you're older, your particular relationship style will make you appealing to a partner that is just perfect for you. You'll be lucky in many areas of your life, but most especially in love. You'll have lots of infatuations and are likely to fall in love at first sight several times. However, there'll be certain qualities that you'll look for in a mate and some will turn you off. You'll eventually reject any potential lovers that are either extremely boring or so outrageous that they embarrass you in public. That will never do!

When you and your dear heart meet, you'll both know that it's a good match. This relationship won't feel like work. The two of you will have an easy compatibility that your friends will envy. You'll have special ways of making your partner feel cared for. You'll fill his or her life with gifts from your heart—daily tokens of affection and big surprises on special occasions, all done with your exceptional good taste.

You'll remain happily in love with one that respects your inner life and is considerate of your feelings. Left to your own devices, you'll work too much and forget how to play, and your perfect partner will help you relax and have a good time. As one of the earth signs, you like to be touched. Your mate will show that you are loved by giving you lots of hugs and kisses.

For 1992 Virgo guys, happy girls that are optimistic about the future are most appealing. The one you care for may be from a different background than you are and possibly from a foreign country. You'll like to be with her because she'll has fascinating interests to share with you that will expand your life in many ways.

Curious, clever, and humorous guys are attractive to 1992 Virgo females. Your special man will be a great conversationalist and you'll love hearing his ideas. The two of you won't always agree but you'll respect one another's opinions. His sense of humor will keep you laughing. He'll consider you his best friend and confidante.

VIRGO ZODIAC SIGN
YOUR LOVE PLANETS

YOUR ROMANTIC SIDE — p. 696
▶ **VENUS IN VIRGO**
Born Aug. 22, 21:10 - Aug. 31, 16:08
▶ **VENUS IN LIBRA**
Born Aug. 31, 16:09 - Sept. 22, 18:42

YOUR SEX DRIVE — p. 722
▶ **MARS IN GEMINI**
Born Aug. 22, 21:10 - Sept. 12, 6:04
▶ **MARS IN CANCER**
Born Sept. 12, 6:05 - Sept. 22, 18:42

YOUR CELEBRITY TWINS — p. 760
Find out the astrological similarities you have with famous people.

YOUR COMPATIBILITY — p. 780
Compare planets to find out how compatible you are in a relationship.

YOUR RELATIONSHIP KARMA — p. 824
▶ **SATURN IN AQUARIUS**
Born Aug. 22, 21:10 - Sept. 22, 18:42

JEREMY IRONS
English Actor
Sun in Virgo

611

1992 LIBRA

From September 22, 18:43 through October 23, 3:56

♎ *The Relationship Wizard*

Like any good Libra, those born in 1992 know a lot about love. You'll have the additional advantage of being able to make those romantic dreams come true. Since you're so sociable, it's unlikely that you'll ever be alone on a Friday night during your dating years. You'll get lots of experience in matters of the heart. You'll make friends with the opposite sex so easily, that you'll learn all about life from their perspective, too. When you finally make a commitment to your darling, you'll have figured out just how to make the partnership work and this will be greatly to your advantage.

Along the way, you'll weed out anyone that was pessimistic, unrefined, or a slug. It's likely that you'll transform the life of your loved one significantly. Your upbeat attitude will bring joy to your lover's days. Through the years, you'll always do your best to remain attractive and desirable. The one you care for will be delighted to have you by his or her side, and the times you spend together will be quite magical.

Your darling can keep your interest in the romance active by always being willing to discuss your differences. You like to get your issues out in the open and find ways to reach a compromise. You'll always know that your sweetheart is listening to your feelings and that he or she will be emotionally supportive. Love and lasting friendship will be almost indistinguishable for you at times. You'll want to know that you can count on your partner to be there for you at all times.

Male Librans born in 1992 will be drawn to mysterious, intuitive girls that are not so easy to get to know. The beauty that you'll desire the most will be quietly self-assured and confident. She'll be involved in her own interests and will lead you on quite a chase before she lets you catch her.

If you're a female born in 1992, you'll be attracted to men that are much like your dad. Your darling will be very nurturing and protective with you, always giving you the feeling that you're loved and special. He'll be sentimental and never forget a birthday, anniversary, or the day you met.

LIBRA ZODIAC SIGN
YOUR LOVE PLANETS

YOUR ROMANTIC SIDE — p. 696
▶ **VENUS IN LIBRA**
Born Sept. 22, 18:43 - Sept. 25, 3:30
▶ **VENUS IN SCORPIO**
Born Sept. 25, 3:31 - Oct. 19, 17:46
▶ **VENUS IN SAGITTARIUS**
Born Oct. 19, 17:47 - Oct. 23, 3:56

YOUR SEX DRIVE — p. 722
▶ **MARS IN CANCER**
Born Sept. 22, 18:43 - Oct. 23, 3:56

YOUR CELEBRITY TWINS — p. 760
Find out the astrological similarities you have with famous people.

YOUR COMPATIBILITY — p. 780
Compare planets to find out how compatible you are in a relationship.

YOUR RELATIONSHIP KARMA — p. 824
▶ **SATURN IN AQUARIUS**
Born Sept. 22, 18:43 - Oct. 23, 3:56

STEPHEN REA
Irish Actor
Sun and Mars in Scorpio

612

1992 SCORPIO
From October 23, 3:57 through November 22, 1:25

♏ *The Playful Flirt*

You'll experience relationship fun throughout your life as a 1992 Scorpio. Lots of possible partners will desire you, and you'll become very aware of your powers to attract members of the opposite sex. You may believe that you can play the field forever! This will change once you meet and fall in love with your soul mate. When you finally give your heart to your true love, you'll continue to be a playful partner. You'll love to flirt and joke and tease your sweetie because that's how you'll show affection. Underneath all the lighthearted banter, however, you'll be seriously in love.

Obviously, you won't settle down with anyone that lacks a sense of humor or that doesn't respond to your fun approach to romance. Individuals that are overly sensitive and bad-tempered will never win your love. You will develop deep and lasting emotional ties with your life partner. As you get older, you'll become better at expressing your feelings. In the meantime, your actions will loudly declare that you are devoted to your darling. You'll be present to your sweetheart in unique but loving ways.

Your significant other will not have a hard time trying to find ways to please you. You'll like all the traditional ways of saying, "I love you!" including receiving gifts on special occasions. It will make you happy if your partner is not too easy to figure out, too. You especially like the challenge of solving a real mystery. You will want to be with someone who is sociable and knows how to throw a good party.

As a Scorpio man born in 1992, you'll like to be around women that are optimistic and fun loving. You may find your special gal far from home or in a foreign country. She'll share your lust for life and be your adoring companion. In some important way, your sweet love will be a real asset for you.

Exotic men that are experienced travelers will attract 1992 Scorpio women. You'll fall hard for the guy that has a unique way of expressing himself. It's likely that he'll be well educated and always up-to-date on current events. You'll share an interest in films, music, and the arts.

1992 SAGITTARIUS
From November 22, 1:26 through December 21, 14:42

♐ *The Positive Playmate*

Emotional security is the relationship goal of Sagittarians born in 1992. It will be important for you to know exactly whom you can count on and for what. When you settle down with your significant other, it will be someone that is tested and true over time. When you first get together, you'll be impressed with the way your darling quietly meets his or her obligations. You'll share everything and have a strong devotion to your sweetie's well-being. At times, your own contentment will depend on making your true love happy. You'll approach life and love with great enthusiasm and playfulness and need someone who is your intellectual equal.

Quite naturally, you'll be turned off by anyone those behavior is erratic or undependable, especially with finances. You'll want to be with a lover that is spontaneous and fun loving, but not out-of-control. You'll adore acting as your significant other's personal guide through many unique adventures. Your darling will never be disappointed in you either. Once you give your heart, you'll make the partnership your priority.

Your passion for your mate will never dwindle so long as you know you're loved. You'll need lots of demonstrations that you're desirable. The one that cares for you will keep finding new ways to show you that you matter a lot. You'll become bored with a routine rather easily and want to go new places and see new things with your partner.

For male Sagittarians born in 1992, the quest for an ideal mate will be a priority. You'll be most attracted to a woman that is slightly older and well established in her career. She'll have an unusual occupation, perhaps in the sciences or the arts. Your best gal will be a good conversationalist but love walking with you most of all.

Sagittarian girls born in 1992 will like guys that are not afraid to express their emotions. You may meet your special man while far from home and be attracted to his kind, nurturing ways. He'll be interested in hearing about your feelings and be respectful of your strong opinions. Your dear heart will become your best friend and lover.

Pamela Anderson – Baywatch Beauty

Pamela Anderson is best known for looking great in a bathing suit on television, for her tattoos, her breast implants (and later their removal), as well as for getting involved with "bad boy" types. But long before she became a *Baywatch* bombshell, Pamela Anderson was a star in her native Canada. In fact, she seemed destined for fame at birth. The first baby born on Canada's centennial anniversary, she became known as the "Centennial Baby." As a teenager she was "discovered" at a football game while wearing a tight Labatt's beer T-shirt. Her picture was broadcast on the stadium's TV screen and a new star was born. She was signed to a contract as a Labatt's spokesmodel.

She was only twenty-two when she came to Los Angeles, where she posed for the first of many *Playboy* covers. With her beauty, athletic grace, and alluring figure, she was a natural attention-getter—a series of stunning *Playboy* pictorials and videos showcased her physical assets.

In 1991 she won the role of "Tool Time" girl Lisa on the ABC show *Home Improvement*. It was through this part that she came to the attention of David Hasselhoff, who signed the curvaceous blonde for season three of *Baywatch*. It didn't take long for Anderson to make her mark as "C.J."

On New Year's Eve 1994, she met Motley Crue drummer Tommy Lee at a party in New York City. He immediately licked her face and asked for her phone number. He pursued her relentlessly, and six weeks later they were married in a beach ceremony, with Pamela wearing a white bikini. The couple proudly showed off their tattooed wedding rings to photographers. They then received unsolicited attention when their honeymoon video turned up on numerous Internet porn sites. It was stolen by a contractor who had worked in their basement.

Despite her glitzy image, Pamela embodies the natural shyness of her Cancer Zodiac sign. She admits, "I have this phobia—I don't like mirrors. And I don't watch myself on television. If anything comes on with me in it, I leave the room." Venus in showy Leo and Mars in narcissistic Libra explain the more flamboyant elements of her persona.

In 1995, hoping to make the jump to movie stardom, Anderson starred in *Barb Wire*, a sci-fi thriller where she didn't have to do much more than wear cleavage-baring black leather and chase an occasional "bad guy." In 1998 she served as executive producer and star of *V.I.P.*, a syndicated TV show.

Although she suffered a miscarriage while working on the film, Pamela later had two sons with Lee. The couple had a much-publicized breakup in 1998, then reunited the following year. But there were serious problems with the marriage, including Lee's arrest for alleged felony spousal abuse.

She and Tommy Lee split for good in 2000, when he was sentenced to 3 years probation and random court-ordered drug testing. Pamela sought custody of their children, claiming that Lee was a poor role model, "particularly when he is using alcohol." According to Lee, he is now clean and sober and poses no threat to his children.

Fortunately, Pamela has moved on. Since breaking up with Lee, Pamela has been linked with male model Marcus Schenkenberg, video producer Stavors Merjos, and Detroit-born rapper Kid Rock.

613

"It is great to be a blonde. With low expectations it's very easy to surprise people."

PAMELA ANDERSON

► READ ABOUT MAE WEST ON PAGE 129

1993

- ✪ BOBBITT'S REVENGE
- ✪ DON'T ASK, DON'T TELL
- ✪ ANGELS IN AMERICA
- ✪ ANYTHING FOR LOVE
- ✪ SLEEPLESS IN SEATTLE
- ✪ MARS AND VENUS
- ✪ THE MORNING AFTER

EVENTS

In the US, Lorena Bobbitt chopped off her philandering husband's penis with a butcher knife. Surgeons reattached the member and John Wayne Bobbitt became a minor porn star. President Clinton unveiled his compromise "Don't ask, don't tell" policy for gays in the military. Outspoken birth control advocate Joycelyn Elders became the first African American and second female US Surgeon General. Tony Kushner's epic AIDS parable, *Angels in America*, swept Broadway's Tony Awards and won the Pulitzer Prize. "King of Pop" Michael Jackson vehemently denied the charge of fondling a 13-year-old boy and settled out of court. The FDA imposed a moratorium on silicone breast implants. Researchers at George Washington University successfully cloned human embryos. A Steffi Graf fan stabbed tennis star Monica Selles on the court in Germany.

POP CULTURE

Hit songs included Mariah Carey's "Hero" and Janet Jackson's "Again." Britain's UB40 set "Can't Help Falling In Love" to a reggae beat. Silk invited "Freak Me." Movie star and rocker Meat Loaf drew the line with "I'd Do Anything for Love (But I Won't Do That)."

Sleepless in Seattle featured Meg Ryan and Tom Hanks as a couple who meet, bicker, and fall hard. *Groundhog Day* trapped cynical weatherman Bill Murray in a time loop until he learns to love. Robin Williams cross-dressed as his own kids' nanny in *Mrs. Doubtfire*. Angela Bassett gave an acting tour-de-force as hard-luck singer Tina Turner in *What's Love Got to Do With It*. Anthony Hopkins beautifully portrayed a repressed English butler's misplaced loyalty and love in *The Remains of the Day*. Jane Campion's *The Piano* chronicled a tragic arranged marriage in 19th-century New Zealand.

In Laura Esquivel's magical novel *Like Water for Chocolate*, a woman barred by family obligations from her true love pours her emotions into food preparation. David Guterson's *Snow Falling on Cedars* told of tragic interracial love amid the internment of Puget Sound's Japanese families. John Gray's pop-psych *Men Are from Mars, Women Are from Venus* argued that men and women speak fundamentally different emotional languages. Katie Roiphe's controversial *The Morning After* attacked campus feminism and questioned the idea of date rape.

Sex Idol

BRAD PITT

Hot-hot-hot actor Brad Pitt, he of the impish grin, has twice been named *People* magazine's "Sexiest Man Alive." By 1993, he had sizzled on the screen in *Thelma and Louise*, and even matched Tom Cruise's star power in *Interview with the Vampire*. He's earned acclaim for subsequent roles in *Twelve Monkeys*, *Seven*, and *Fight Club*.

But legions of female fans are more interested in the heartthrob's romantic availability. Unfortunately for them, Pitt prefers serial monogamy. His high-profile relationships include three years with Juliette Lewis, a tabloid-pleasing engagement with Gwyneth Paltrow, and his 2000 marriage to *Friends* star Jennifer Aniston.

SEE ALSO

1993 CAPRICORN

From December 21, 1992 14:43 through January 20, 1993 1:22
(December 1993 Capricorns, see 1994 Capricorn)

♑ *The Sensitive Protector*

You are highly sensitive to other people and tune into their moods easily. That's why you will generally choose a partner who is as emotional and caring as you are, and who expects a relationship to be mutually nurturing. Romance for you will start with a soulful connection, even more than a physical attraction. Looking into someone's eyes and seeing the deep, beautiful person inside is your special gift. No one could ever call you superficial, and you could never last long with someone who is shallow or one-dimensional.

For you, love will be all about fighting for the honor and happiness of the one you adore. Being that special someone's protector and cheerleader is the role that you will be happiest in. Because your nature is so noble and giving, you will surely receive the kind of loyalty and intense affection that you deserve. Your courageous nature will inspire your sweetheart to be just as brave.

A potential suitor will have to show kindness and depth from the get-go. You judge someone by how that person treats others. Therefore, generosity and gentle ways are total turn-ons for you. Showing you pictures of pets, family, and friends will give you a bird's-eye view of a potential partner's capacity for "heart connections."

As a male 1993 Capricorn, the ideal partner for you will be someone who is in tune with all forms of music and art. This girl will be a real dreamer who is not afraid to go after her dreams—no matter how many people say it's "impossible." Her artistic nature will inspire you to channel your deep sensitivity into a creative practice. She will most likely have big, deep, soulful eyes that bespeak an endless pool of love.

If you are a female Capricorn born in 1993, your perfect guy will be someone who is close to his family and who enjoys spending time with kids. He is patient, loving, and very protective towards you and anyone he cares for deeply. Most likely, he will enjoy water sports and will open a whole new world to you by showing you the mysteries of the seas. He is apt to have a cuddly, teddy bear way about him.

HOLLY HUNTER
American Actress
Venus and Mars in Aquarius

1993 AQUARIUS

From January 20, 1:23 through February 18, 15:34

♒ *The Responsible Rebel*

Born in 1993, you are a very subtle version of your sign, Aquarius. Yes, you are a philosophical seeker who views every relationship as an experiment, but you are also a passionate creature with deep longings for love. Undoubtedly, you will seek out relationships that test your emotional limits. Your huge capacity for growth is one of your greatest characteristics, and your mate will surely appreciate this quality.

What you will have little tolerance for are people who complain, "You don't understand me," but who do little to make themselves understood. Communication is your strong suit, and the person you get involved with must be equally adept at language. For you, romance will be like the greatest friendship in the world—but better. Just as you love to spend hours with your friends, you will look forward to spending quality time just hanging out and "being" with your sweetheart.

If someone is looking to catch your eye, a good approach is to engage you in a spirited discussion of current events. You have very strong opinions about politics, sports, movies, and pretty much all other subjects of the day. A would-be suitor who is willing to argue with you and push you to reconsider your points of view will surely make you very intrigued. Romance begins in your mind, so a potential partner can interest you quickly by challenging you to a little game of verbal fencing.

As an Aquarian male born in 1993, your ideal female is the kind of girl who "eats challenges for breakfast." She is sporty and full of energy and probably enjoys pushing her own limits as an athlete. Emotionally, she is loyal and fierce and will always make you feel like you are number one, and passionately adored.

If you are a female Aquarius born in 1993, your perfect guy will be tough on the outside—maybe a rock-and-roll or athletic type—but deeply sensitive on the inside. He will be completely trustworthy and will make you feel at home and safe whenever you are with him. Yet his nature is mysterious, and you will enjoy the slow, unfolding process of getting to really know him, and vice versa.

EMMA THOMPSON
English Actress
Sun in Aries

616

1993 PISCES
From February 18, 15:35 through March 20, 14:40

The Thoughtful Dreamer

As you grow older, Pisces of 1993, you will develop into quite a "catch" for the suitor lucky enough to discover you. Your way in romance will be to secretly do wonderful, loving things for your partner. Perhaps you will gather your honey's friends and family and throw your sweetheart a surprise birthday party. (And during all the other days of the year, you will be equally thoughtful, endearing, and generous.)

Because your nature is so innocent (in the best sense), you simply must be with someone who believes in love, and in you, one hundred percent. Opening up your heart completely is the only way you will know how to be with someone romantically, and you'll expect the same in return. For you, a relationship will be a highly emotional experience, with a lot of deep proclamations of love, and a lot of physical affection. You are the ultimate romantic.

If someone wants to grab your attention, a potential honey must pay a lot of attention to you. You are so giving by nature that the person who lavishes time, energy, and gifts on you will surely get the prize—you! A would-be suitor who shows passion for a hobby—like music, art, or even magic—could really intrigue you. You love to see someone get obsessive about their interests. Also, you love people and enjoy attending all kinds of parties, so inviting you to lots of cool gatherings is another good way to get "on their radar."

As a 1993 Pisces guy, your ideal girl will be a born optimist who believes not just in talking about her dreams, but in living them. This kind of active energy will bring out the best in you, and make you want to follow through on your dreams and desires. She is likely to be outspoken and unaffected by peer pressure.

If you are a 1993 female Pisces, your perfect guy will be affectionate and loyal. He will proudly hug and kiss you in public, and let the whole world know that you belong to him. He will enjoy camping and going to the beach. His dearest quality will be that whenever you are afraid, one touch and one kind word from him will make you feel that "It's going to be all right." And so it will.

1993 ARIES
From March 20, 14:41 through April 20, 1:48

The Energetic Optimist

As a 1993 Aries, you believe that people are more good at heart than bad, and that every person has the potential to do great things in this world. As you age, you will bring this type of nurturing, faith-filled energy to your relationships. Members of the opposite sex will want to be around you because you are so fearless about romance, so willing to expose the depths of your soul to the one you love. This quality rubs off on others and makes you "the one to be with."

For you, a relationship will have to be active and positive. Sitting around watching TV is not your idea of togetherness. Going out to parties, sporting events, and other highly social gatherings is what you will enjoy day to day with a partner. You have an almost endless supply of energy and "can-do" spirit, and will need to be with someone who matches you (or tries to)!

If someone wants to win your affection, this would-be partner must be willing to take a risk. You respond strongly to confidence, so a line like "I've always had a crush on you," will blow you away. When someone risks embarrassment to win you, you will be moved and attracted. A love-interest-in-waiting should also be spontaneous. A last-minute invitation to see a cool movie or concert, or to go skating, could excite you enough to make you say "yes."

As a male 1993 Aries, your type of girl will always tell you the truth but could never be described as "brutally honest." She is sensitive enough to intuit your moods, and nurture you when you are feeling down, but strong enough to say, "Come on! We're going out to have fun!" She will always have new and exciting interests which she will want to share with you. Together, you'll learn about the world.

If you are a female 1993 Aries, your ideal guy will be soulful, strong, and sweet. He's a combination ladies' man and man's man. He is highly competitive in school and work arenas, as well as on the sports field. Yet, at heart, he is a tender, gentle fellow, who can't bear the thought of hurting another. He will be drawn to you like a flame, and will never take you for granted.

1993 TAURUS

From April 20, 1:49 through May 21, 1:01

♉ *The Determined Firecracker*

Born in 1993, you are a fiery breed of bull. You have tons of stamina and energy—the first one up in the morning, and the last to go to bed at night. As you grow you will seek out relationships that are intense, vivid, and full of drama. You will be attracted to daring, risk-taking types who aren't afraid to "go for the gold" in love and in life. Physically, you will be drawn to strength and speed, and will probably become involved with someone who is active in competitive sports.

For you, a relationship will have to be exciting and fast-moving. You will most likely go after the person you want—you are determined, and never give up. But once you are involved, you will need a lot of "action" within the union. Reliability is one of your greatest traits, and you will need that in a partner, too. However, once you two are together, there has to be an "anything can happen" vibe in the air. Once you are with the one you love, you believe, miracles can occur. And you will prove yourself right!

If someone wants to interest you, a good approach is to be physically expressive with you. You are very affectionate and blossom when a potential partner shows feelings through touch. Laid-back tunes also put you in a romantic mood. If a potential suitor sets up a low-key but seductive environment, you are apt to respond with smiles and hugs.

As a Taurus guy born in 1993, your ideal girl will be confident and pure of heart. She believes in herself and in you, and has no patience for shady, manipulative people. She helps the needy and sets a good example for others, but she is no "Pollyanna." This girl's got a wild streak, too, and loves to dance late into the night and do daredevil activities—from white-water rafting to skydiving!

If you are a female Taurus born in 1993, you will be swept away by a guy who is noble and fearless. He's definitely the old-fashioned "knight in shining armor" type. He will most likely have a masculine demeanor combined with sexy, longish hair and long eyelashes. Although he may look like a heartthrob, rest assured that he's only got eyes for you.

LIAM NEESON
Irish Actor
Sun and Venus in Gemini

617

1993 GEMINI

From May 21, 1:02 through June 21, 8:59

♊ *The Mushy Magician*

If you are a Gemini born in 1993, you are full of wonder—part wizard, part artist, part genius—and all romantic. For you, a relationship will be soppy sweet and tender. Showing love is easy for you. In fact, just the thought of your beloved may make you teary-eyed. But in addition to your grand romantic heart, you possess a brilliant mind and need to be with someone who matches wits with you. Sometimes you have so many great ideas you don't know which one to address first. That's why it will be helpful to you, as you grow, to be with someone who is decisive and pushes you to choose one of your passions and "go for it."

A romantic relationship has got to be cinematic and a little bit over-the-top to keep you happy. Reading poetry, writing songs for each other, kissing for hours—these are all elements of what will make the romance of your dreams. You couldn't bear to be with someone who is restrained and cold. Warmth and a flair for the theatrical make your heart sing.

If someone is looking to attract your attention, a good way to do so is by asking you out to the movies, a play, or a concert. You love a good story and a dramatic spectacle. Talking about adventure/fantasy books and comic books, or enjoying real-life adventures will also turn you on! A potential honey who shows a devil-may-care attitude will also interest you. You love a prankster with a great sense of humor. You also will respond to a would-be suitor who matches you when it comes to knowledge of pop culture and history trivia.

As a 1993 Gemini male, your favorite type of female will be a real music buff who turns you on to all sorts of cool bands. She may be a musician herself. She is sensual and relaxed and loves to spend long, romantic days and nights with you.

If you are a 1993 Gemini female, your ideal guy will be a bit of a show-off, but that will be part of his charm. He knows how to keep an audience entertained, whether he's telling a funny story or dancing or singing. He may sweep you off your feet on a regular basis. Bringing you beautiful flowers is something he will always do for you.

TOM HANKS
American Actor
Sun in Cancer

618

1993 CANCER
From June 21, 9:00 through July 22, 1950

The Witty Flirt

Born in 1993, you are as loyal and loving as most other Cancers, but your charm level is so high that you can't help but flirt with all who will respond! You are merely being playful, and all members of the opposite sex will know it. But you can't help but exchange witty repartee and longing looks with a good number of partners. However, the person that you settle down with when you are older will be a real match for you in the charm and romance department. You believe that a relationship should be just as fun and meaningful in public as in private. That's why you will probably end up with someone who is an outgoing "people person" and who brings out that side of your nature even more.

Humor and goodwill are the foundations that your relationship will be built on. You can't stand it when someone makes you feel guilty just for being yourself, and you would never try to throw a wet blanket over someone else's big spirit. However, when you are with someone who is as secure and life-loving as you are, you will know that you are in the right relationship—the one that will last forever.

If someone wants to get your attention, a good way to do so is by being just as flirty, funny, and silly as you are. A would-be mate with a whimsical sense of humor will surely capture your heart. You also respond strongly to people who are good in groups and can relate to many different types of people. You are turned on by people with a strong fashion sense.

As a male 1993 Cancer, your type of girl will be well-versed in numerous subjects—from music to movies to ancient history. She has many intellectual pursuits—books she loves, theories she tries to figure out—and she loves to share them with you. Her way is independent, but she always makes time to listen to you, and hug and kiss you!

If you are a female 1993 Cancer, you will be drawn to guys who are outdoorsy and love to be around animals. He will be good with kids, and patient with demanding adults, too! He will bring out your homey side and make the idea of staying home and cooking and cuddling together seem like heaven.

1993 LEO
From July 22, 19:51 through August 23, 2:49

The Supportive Tiger

Born in 1993, you are more low-key than your fellow lions. But beneath your serene surface, a passionate tiger is ready to pounce and play. When you find the right mate, you come to life. A love relationship gives you purpose, and brings out your most noble, protective, and intense characteristics. As you grow, you will begin to seek out romantic relationships that inspire you to do great things with your life. Left on your own, you may be a little shy and unsure. But when you have someone to fight for, to impress, and to do amazing things for, that is when you will feel your life really has begun.

For you, a relationship cannot be cool or detached. Just dating will not do it for you. It's pure love or nothing at all, as far as you're concerned. You have a very active dream life and will know if you are with the right person from the beginning. Destiny, it seems, may play a part.

If someone is looking to catch your eye, this potential suitor should make an effort to get to know you on a deep level. You are turned off by superficiality and turned on by meaningful, emotional dialogue. Asking you on a very formal date is also a good move. Going to dinner, a show, and dancing will make you thrilled and "in the mood for love." Someone who knows how to date you "with style" is on the right track.

As a male 1993 Leo, your ideal girl will be the shy and demure type. By night, she will love to spend plenty of one-on-one time with you and those in your inner circle. Hard work is what will keep her busy by day. She believes that we all have a purpose on this earth, and will do a lot to make the world a better place. Most likely, she will possess a strong dedication to the environment.

If you are a female 1993 Leo, your type of guy will be intellectual, thoughtful, and somewhat soft-spoken. He's athletic and strong too, but will not have to make a big show to prove his strength. He will have many fascinating hobbies and a great memory—especially for important things like your birthday, your favorite song, etc. He will also be charitable and giving—of time and money.

1993 VIRGO

From August 23, 2:50 through September 23, 0:22

The Subtle Seducer

You are apt to grow up to be quite a heartbreaker, Virgo of 1993. You possess the giving, thoughtful traits that make you a great friend, and the charming, romantic personality that makes you a great bet in a relationship. For you, a relationship must be a balance of intellectual connection and physical attraction. You must be able to communicate with your partner. Someone who sulks in a corner or storms off in a huff is not for you. A relationship must be calm and consistent, yet there must also be tremendous sparks between you and your partner in order for you to feel satisfied.

Once you are involved, you'll love to spend long, lazy days with your honey. Just knocking around—taking hikes, seeing movies, talking for hours over a cappuccino—that's when a relationship is best for you.

If someone is looking to catch your eye, the best way is to be straightforward and just start up a conversation with you. You are incredibly approachable and unpretentious and will talk to anyone about anything. You also have a soft spot for people who are really good listeners.

If someone has the ability to say just a few words and draw you out emotionally, even just a little bit, you will be quite enamored! You are also very tuned in to the olfactory sense, so a subtle but yummy and spicy scent on a potential partner's neck could make you follow your nose!

If you are a male Virgo born in 1993, your type of girl will be a little haughty and diva-esque. She knows what she wants and isn't afraid to ask for it. However, she is loyal and loving and never turns her high attitude on you. She is super-protective towards those she cares for and is particularly good with children and animals. She is likely to have long, luxurious hair and sultry eyes.

If you are a female 1993 Virgo, your ideal guy is precise and detail-oriented. He likes to get the job done right and is ultra-responsible and hard-working. He puts just as much time, thought, and effort into his relationship with you. His special romantic gift is for knowing exactly the right kind of flowers to bring you to suit your mood.

VIRGO ZODIAC SIGN
YOUR LOVE PLANETS

YOUR ROMANTIC SIDE — p. 696
▶ VENUS IN CANCER
Born Aug. 23, 2:50 - Aug. 27, 15:47
▶ VENUS IN LEO
Born Aug. 27, 15:48 - Sept. 21, 14:21
▶ VENUS IN VIRGO
Born Sept. 21, 14:22 - Sept. 23, 0:22

YOUR SEX DRIVE — p. 722
▶ MARS IN LIBRA
Born Aug. 23, 2:50 - Sept. 23, 0:22

YOUR CELEBRITY TWINS — p. 760
Find out the astrological similarities you have with famous people.

YOUR COMPATIBILITY — p. 780
Compare planets to find out how compatible you are in a relationship.

YOUR RELATIONSHIP KARMA — p. 824
▶ SATURN IN AQUARIUS
Born Aug. 23, 2:50 - Sept. 23, 0:22

619

1993 LIBRA

From September 23, 0:23 through October 23, 9:36

The Serious Lover

You will definitely grow into a "relationship type of person," Libra of 1993. Although you will enjoy time on your own, it is truly with another person that you begin to "find yourself." For you, a relationship needs to have an artistic element. Your ideal is a partner who will go with you to plays, concerts, and readings. Talking about art and creating beautiful things together will be your idea of romantic heaven.

High-pressure people with possessive streaks drive you crazy. You are at your best when you are in a laid-back relationship where the roads are wide open and you and your darling can travel anywhere you please, anytime you please. Physical attraction has to be there, but you are not a "looks snob." You are particularly turned on by good skin and good manners! More than anything, you will want to be in a relationship with someone who is your equal. In true Libra fashion, you need a balanced partnership, where both people share similar interests and values.

If someone wants to catch your attention, subtly taking your hand should do the trick. You

are very in touch with body language, too. A would-be suitor who whispers in your ear or manages to pull you away from your crowd of friends to ask you something "important" is on the right track. Privacy and subtlety are the keys.

As a 1993 Libra male, your type of girl is quiet and classy. She rarely loses her cool, but she does have a hot and sultry side. She loves to dance and rock out to great music—with you. She is cultured and sophisticated on the one hand, but on the other, she enjoys a raucous good time. Most likely she has excellent bone structure and a restrained but commanding presence.

If you are a 1993 Libra female, your ideal guy is sexy and sure of himself. He has a private streak and may be hard to get to know at first, but you hold the key to his heart and can unlock his secrets. He is loyal to the extreme and a true ally to those he loves. When he doesn't like someone, he makes it known. His eyes are deep wells of emotion. Your perfect guy may also have an interest in the psychic world.

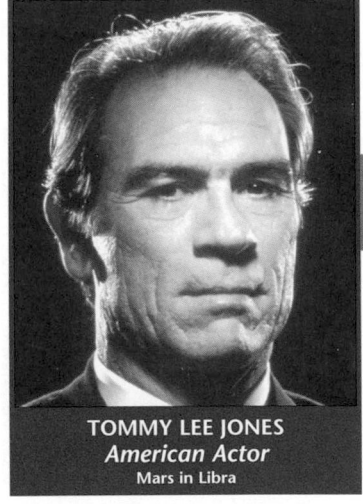

TOMMY LEE JONES
American Actor
Mars in Libra

LIBRA ZODIAC SIGN
YOUR LOVE PLANETS

YOUR ROMANTIC SIDE — p. 696
▶ VENUS IN VIRGO
Born Sept. 23, 0:23 - Oct. 16, 0:12
▶ VENUS IN LIBRA
Born Oct. 16, 0:13 - Oct. 23, 9:36

YOUR SEX DRIVE — p. 722
▶ MARS IN LIBRA
Born Sept. 23, 0:23 - Sept. 27, 2:14
▶ MARS IN SCORPIO
Born Sept. 27, 2:15 - Oct. 23, 9:36

YOUR CELEBRITY TWINS — p. 760
Find out the astrological similarities you have with famous people.

YOUR COMPATIBILITY — p. 780
Compare planets to find out how compatible you are in a relationship.

YOUR RELATIONSHIP KARMA — p. 824
▶ SATURN IN AQUARIUS
Born Sept. 23, 0:23 - Oct. 23, 9:36

JULIE DELPY
French Actress
Sun and Venus in Sagittarius

620

1993 SCORPIO   *From October 23, 9:37 through November 22, 7:06*

 ♏ *The Mystical Poet*

Unlocking the secrets of the universe, and of the heart, will be your great goal as you grow up, Scorpio of 1993. No small challenges for you, in life and in love. You want to dive into the depths, not swim in shallow waters. Clearly, your love life will be dramatic and intense. There will never be a dull moment. Your ideal relationship will be one in which you and your partner explore each other's minds, bodies, and souls completely. At the same time, you will want to be with someone who brings out your artistic streak, and who possesses a way with words and images, too.

Poets have been writing about love for thousands of years, and you have the heart of a poet. For you, a relationship must be a deep and divine mystery explored by two people. You love to uncover the secret workings of your partner's mind. In fact, you may enjoy creating your own secret "love language" with your honey. What you can't stand is this: A person who is completely dry and unromantic. You believe in magic. Your partner must too.

If someone is looking to capture your heart, the best approach is to be a bit mysterious. You love to uncover the truth, so if someone drops hints of romantic interest, but leaves it to you to follow through, then you will! You also like to go to atmospheric, dark places to talk and to cuddle.

As a 1993 Scorpio male, your ideal girl is a blend of softness and strength. She is the famed "iron fist in a velvet glove." She likes it when you take charge, and pick where to go and what to do, but when she has a strong opinion she does not hold back. Her visual sense is strong and she probably has great talent as a painter or photographer. Naturally, you are her favorite subject and Muse.

If you are a 1993 Scorpio female, your kind of guy is strong and smart. He won't allow anyone to push him around, because he is so sure of himself. Ambition is a strong trait he possesses, but he also likes to spend time just holding you and dreaming. This is the kind of guy that you can trust with your life. When he says you can count on him, he means it—absolutely.

1993 SAGITTARIUS   *From November 22, 7:07 through December 22, 20:25*

♐ *The Eager Explorer*

You want to understand all facets of human nature, Sagittarius of 1993. Your way is through experience. Just reading about love in books and seeing it in the movies is not enough for you. As you grow up, love relationships will become extremely important to you. Your type of romance will probably involve travel and adventure. Perhaps one (or more) of your great loves will hail from a foreign land. That would suit you fine, as you will greatly enjoy learning about other cultures—their food, music, and courtship rituals.

For you, true love is like a bone-chilling, heart-warming, and always thrilling escapade. When you are much older you will settle into a harmonious, domestic arrangement, but during your early dating years you will need to be free. If a partner tries to own you, and dictate your every move, you cannot take it. You must be treated with respect and trust, not caged. When you are given room to breathe in a relationship, you thrive. You also do well when you are involved with someone who likes to do outdoorsy things as often as possible.

If someone is looking to catch your eye, a good approach would be to ask you to do something athletic. "Extreme" sports were made for you. You also have a real silly streak, so funny date plans like karaoke, comedy clubs, or amusement parks should also light your fire.

If you are a male Sag born in 1993, your ideal girl is fiery, unpredictable, and utterly fascinating. She has many incredible talents and is enthusiastic about exploring them all. She will tell you exactly what she thinks, so be prepared. But she will teach you a lot about your own potential and about love. Her sexy way of walking will probably be the first thing you notice about her.

As a female Sagittarius born in 1993, you'll choose a guy with a tremendous sense of humor. He will always make you laugh and will never take himself too seriously. However, he is a deep person, too. This guy enjoys studying ancient history and comparative religion. He considers himself a seeker and a student of life. His athletic body will be just an added bonus!

Kurt and Courtney – Rocking Together

When Kurt Cobain and Courtney Love got together in latter part of 1991, he was on the verge of stardom. As singer, songwriter, and guitarist for Nirvana, a Seattle grunge band, Cobain was taking Nirvana and grunge music to a new level. His poetic lyrics and haunting onstage screams spoke to a young generation for its defiant and rebellious attitude toward mainstream society. Nirvana's album "Nevermind" had gone gold and would sell 10 million albums worldwide. Love herself, also a musician, had a female neopunk band, Hole. Although they weren't successful, her group had presented themselves as worthy musicians.

Over the course of just a few months, the lives of this grunge couple underwent substantial change. Love became pregnant, put her career on hold, became superstar Kurt Cobain's wife, and began planning for a family with her husband. It was a surprising scenario for two with such little experience in family stability and values. They both came from broken homes, and neither was hesitant to verbalize the emotional scarring that incurred through their dysfunctional family upbringings.

Their courtship and marriage received much media exposure, especially with their wild and reckless behavior. Indulging in pharmaceutical recreation seemed a favorite pastime. Love, known for her shocking and sometimes crass behavior, was quoted in *Vanity Fair* as saying she had taken heroin for a couple of months with Cobain while pregnant. Afterward both she and Cobain issued a statement about the article's inaccuracies. Nevertheless, after their daughter, a healthy Frances Bean Cobain, was born on August 19, 1992, they were investigated by the Los Angeles Child Protective Services and had to fight for her custody.

Cobain, who struggled for years with his addiction problems, also suffered from bipolar disorder and an unexplained chronic stomach pain. For a while, he seemed to have found happiness in his conjugal lifestyle, as he revealed in a *Rolling Stone* interview, "I'm just happier than I've ever been. I finally found someone that I am totally compatible with."

Love returned to music. Hole was offered a contract by Geffen Records, which also managed Nirvana, resulting in much speculation about the deal, Love's talent, and her true feelings for Cobain.

Meanwhile, Cobain's difficulty in accepting the magnitude of his success further fed his drug addiction, and life began to spin out of control. Rumors spread that his condition was affecting the band. There were also problems on the home front. In one incident, Cobain was taken to the county jail for allegedly assaulting his wife during a domestic dispute over his possession of guns. The case was dismissed, but three guns were removed from their home.

In March of '94 while both were abroad touring with their respective bands, Cobain experienced what was called "an accidental overdose." The couple returned together to the States to seek help, but on April 8th, Cobain was found dead in his home by his own hand, having put a shotgun to his head. High amounts of heroin and Valium were in his body.

The music world mourned its loss. During a public vigil, Love read a portion of Cobain's suicide note, which divulged his inner turmoil, fatigue, and disillusionment with life. Love, outspoken as always, openly expressed her pain, anger, and guilt. She asked the fans to chant. "Say 'You're a f—ker.' And then say you love him."

"It's like Evian water and battery acid." And when you mix the two? "You get love!"

KURT COBAIN in an interview with *Rolling Stone* talking about the couple's chemistry

▶ READ ABOUT SAMMY DAVIS, JR. AND MAY BRITT ON PAGE 344 ▶ READ ABOUT PAUL McCARTNEY AND LINDA EASTMAN ON PAGE 416

1994

- ⭐ **KERRIGAN-HARDING RIVALRY**
- ⭐ **ANNA NICOLE SMITH**
- ⭐ **O.J. SIMPSON ARRESTED**
- ⭐ **CHARLES CONFESSES**
- ⭐ **ALL FOR LOVE**
- ⭐ **FOUR WEDDINGS...**
- ⭐ **IMMORTAL BELOVED**

Sex Idol

EVENTS

The Violence Against Women Act (US) tightened penalties for sex offenders and provided services for victims of rape and domestic violence. Olympic figure skater Nancy Kerrigan was attacked and injured during practice in a sabotage plot hatched by rival Tonya Harding's ex-husband. "Playmate of the Year" Anna Nicole Smith (26) wed billionaire J. Howard Marshall II (89). He died 18 months later and she entered protracted litigation over his estate. Football legend and actor O.J. Simpson was arrested for the murder of his wife and her friend after a surreal car chase broadcast live on television. The television sitcom *Friends* premiered, and the ensemble cast became the decade's cultural icons. The Colorado Supreme Court found the state's anti-gay rights measure unconstitutional. In the UK Prince Charles spilled the beans about his private life on TV. He admitted to having been unfaithful to Diana and to "liking" Camilla Parker Bowles.

POP CULTURE

Ace of Base's string of hits included "The Sign." Boyz II Men promised "I'll Make Love to You." Canadian chanteuse Celine Dion belted out "The Power of Love." Toni Braxton could "Breathe Again." Bryan Adams, Rod Stewart, and Sting lent star power to "All for Love." French rapper MC Solaar was anything but "Obsolete."

Tom Hanks won an Oscar as *Forrest Gump*, a simple man who finds loyal friends, great wealth, and inner peace while navigating major 20th century historical moments. In Mike Newell's lighthearted British comedy, a group of friends search for love and meaning at *Four Weddings and a Funeral*. *Immortal Beloved* explored the passionate life of Ludwig van Beethoven. In Claude Chabrol's *Hell (L'Enfer)*, a stressed-out hotel manager develops paranoid delusions that his wife is unfaithful.

In Jane Hamilton's novel *A Map of the World*, a family is shattered by the drowning of a child and allegations of sexual abuse. Danielle Steel's *Wings* followed the dramatic life of a female aviator between World Wars I and II. *Politically Correct Bedtime Stories* by James Finn Garner retold twelve fairy tales in a humorous send up of "PC" language. Comedian and *Mad About You* star Paul Reiser shared wit and wisdom about relationships in *Couplehood*.

ELLE MACPHERSON

Lithe, six-foot Australian supermodel Elle MacPherson was "discovered" while on a 1982 ski vacation. 1994 marked the fourth *Sports Illustrated* swimsuit issue cover for "The Body," who has also graced Victoria's Secret catalogs, a *Playboy* spread, and her own line of calendars, intimate apparel, and fitness videos.

For six years during the 1980s, Elle appeared in every issue of *Elle* magazine—perhaps because her then-husband, Gilles Bensimmon, was its creative director. She subsequently dated Sean Penn and was engaged to the same London playboy Claudia Schiffer bedded and almost wedded. Elle is now happily settled with Swiss financier Arpade Busson, with whom she has two children.

SEE ALSO

▶ MICHELLE PFEIFFER *Page 580*

▶ SEAN PENN *Page 548*

1994 CAPRICORN

From December 22, 1993 20:26 through January 20, 1994 7:06
(December 1994 Capricorns, see 1995 Capricorns)

♑ *The Charismatic Presence*

If anyone is destined to be a strong presence and charismatic leader, you, Capricorn of 1994, certainly have that potential more than most. On the road to maturity, you will discover early on that you have the power to influence others, often just through the force of your personality. When you fall in love, you will do so with deep emotion and complete concentration, knowing that whomever you set your eyes on is the only one for you.

From the moment you vie for that person's heart, you will keep to your course, gently but relentlessly, until you succeed. Your real goal, though, will not be just to win someone's heart, but to experience the joy of sharing and of matching your life to someone else's. There is likely to be an almost competitive air in your relationships, though in a friendly way that will keep both of you alert and active.

The person who manages to catch your eye has to be both spirited and confident—no shrinking violet types for you. You will be quite aware that your personality is strong and that your presence makes people take notice, so

you'll need someone who can match you and challenge you on this level, as well as physically and intellectually. Once your interest is sparked, the softer side of both of you can slowly emerge.

In your future musings about the perfect girl, 1994 Capricorn male, you'll no doubt dream about someone beautiful to look at, who loves cultural pursuits, and who can introduce you to the finer things in life. At the same time, she will be wildly interested in your activities that show off your physical strength and endurance. She will be warm and affectionate, yet also be a challenge when she wants to be.

You will want a guy, 1994 Capricorn female, who is assertive yet gentle, hunky yet softhearted. The perfect male is one who will always defend you and come to your aid if someone hurts your feelings, yet at the same time someone not afraid to cry in a sad movie. You'll want someone like a white knight out of a fairy tale, but tenderhearted, and because you are determined to get what you want, you just might find him.

DREW BARRYMORE
American Actress
Mars in Capricorn

623

1994 AQUARIUS

From January 20, 7:07 through February 18, 21:21

♒ *The Questioning Teacher*

As a 1994 Aquarius, you are already quite precocious, always asking questions, and even questioning the answers. You want to learn about everything under the sun, and as you mature, you may gravitate toward being a real scholar and a wonderful teacher—both in school and outside of it.

When you find love, these qualities will work well for you, as you'll want to teach your partner about everything that interests you, from the latest technology to music to politics. You are also someone who will be completely open about your feelings, easily revealing your deepest fears and highest aspirations, once you've found the right person. In return, you will be a truly attentive companion, one who is eager to learn everything about the one you love.

Catching your eye will be easy, though winning your heart can take time. The person interested in you will need to show you a good mind, especially one that knows many things that you have yet to learn. But the follow-up to that, the thing that will hold your interest for keeps, is hearing words that show you a softer,

sensitive side and some real emotional depth. In other words, someone who wants you must reach both your mind and your heart at the same time.

The gal of your dreams, 1994 Aquarius male, will be beautiful from without and within. You'll like both brains and beauty, and the perfect girl exudes both of these the moment she walks into the room, along with a certain individuality that distinguishes her from anyone you have ever met. She can be conservative or unconventional, but underneath it all, she'll need to be compassionate, kind, and loving whenever you're together.

For the 1994 Aquarius female, there will be nothing like a guy who is clever and quirky, one who'll tell the most outlandish stories that have other people laughing so hard they don't know what to do. He really is a show-off and loves being the center of attention. But when you're alone, a different person will emerge—one who is a fabulous listener, a homebody, and someone who lets you know that when he is next to you, there is nowhere else he needs to be.

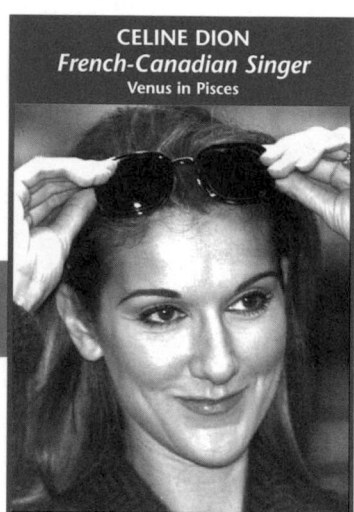

CELINE DION
French-Canadian Singer
Venus in Pisces

1994 PISCES
From February 18, 21:22 through March 20, 20:27

The Inspirational Artist

As you head into the future, Pisces of 1994, you'll look forward to a life filled with artistic inspiration, where others sing your praises for the marvelous things you create. Amidst the accolades, you'll hope to find a supportive partner, one who doesn't need your company all the time, and who'll do whatever it takes to help you to be your absolute best— even if it means giving you all the space and solitude you need.

For you, a relationship will be a way for two people to support one another's dreams, even if that means they must be apart from time to time. If you can find a partnership that lives up to those idealistic longings, then even when you are apart, you will be connected in spirit. And when you are together, you will be as affectionate and loving as two people can be. Love will provide encouragement and a safe haven where each of you can live up to the best you each offer.

You are intuitive and instinctual, and if someone wants to arouse your interest, there will need to be instant chemistry, or else you will quickly move on to something else. If you come alive the moment your eyes meet each other, and you feel like electricity is flowing through your veins, then you'll know that the relationship has endless possibilities. What will make it work between you and a potential sweetie is that you'll be able to laugh at the same jokes and cry at the same sad movies.

The gal who will capture your heart, 1994 Pisces male, will be someone with an artistic soul and a compassionate manner. She will love animals, especially those in need, and will care about people in a way that will amaze you. She'll have time for everyone and everything, but never run out of energy and time for you.

The guy who will make you walk around with a constant smile on your face, 1994 Pisces female, will be a smooth talker with a brilliant, innovative mind. This will be someone you could just sit with for hours, listening to everything he knows about history, politics, art, and music. Besides being inspirational, he will be soft, cuddly, and supportive of all your artistic endeavors.

1994 ARIES
From March 20, 20:28 through April 20, 7:35

The Imaginative Storyteller

From the time you were very young, Aries of 1994, you have been a great storyteller, able to do anything from writing imaginative prose to exaggerating an inconsequential incident into a fascinating tale. As you reach adulthood, that talent for weaving stories and telling anecdotes will attract others to you and help you form a romantic connection.

That wonderful talent for making life interesting means your relationships will be both fun and exciting, as the magic spell that you, an incurable romantic, can weave around another person may be too hard for most to resist. That mystical look in your eye, coupled with a sensitivity to what your partner wants, will make the life the two of you lead the envy of everyone you meet.

The person who wants to get your attention, and keep it, should simply look you straight in the eye and make you feel as if you are the only one in a crowded room. The more focused someone will be on you, the more you will return the interest, and in equal measure. This person must be attractive and dynamic and have a multitude of talents that you can enjoy, and enjoy telling others about.

Your image of the most wonderful girl in the world, 1994 Aries male, will be that of someone who's a soft touch when it comes to showing compassion to all her friends, family, and the world at large. You will be proud having someone by your side you can boast about, and you will not be afraid to be affectionate in front of your friends. More than that, she will love doing spontaneous, romantic things like taking moonlit walks, having candlelight dinners, or just staying at home as long as she is cuddling with you.

When you dream about the man who will sweep you off your feet, 1994 Aries female, he'll be a cross between a cute, youthful pop star who will serenade you, and a rugged he-man who will rescue you from a dire or dangerous situation. Such is the scope of your fantasy, but what matters most is that the man you will spend your life with will be unique, daring, and willing to try anything, as long as it pleases you—a true romantic daredevil.

1994 TAURUS
From April 21, 7:36 through May 21, 6:48

The Treasure Seeker

Slow-paced, artistic, yet unpredictable, Taurus of 1994, you have already begun moving to the beat of a different drummer—but one that is not always tapping out the same rhythm. Though on one day you may be lagging behind everyone else, on the very next your thoughts are racing towards the future. As you mature, you will continue to have your own sense of how and when things should be done.

When it comes to relationships, you will also have your own unique sense of timing. You might snap up a lasting romance at a young age if you think you found the "one," or you may wait a bit longer till the right person comes along. When you do fall, it will certainly be for keeps. The love you are looking for is like a rare jewel, and you will respect, admire, and treasure that person, since you'll know for sure what a unique individual you've found.

For someone to catch your eye, it will have to be done in a way that makes an immediate impression on you. The special someone you're looking for must have the right looks, sense of humor, creative tastes, and innovative mind that immediately bowls you over. Someone who happens to be very shy or really reserved, or who takes time in revealing secrets, will only waste your time.

The perfect gal for you, 1994 Taurus male, will be quick-witted and restless, and will get you moving in whatever direction you want to go. She'll be eclectic in her artistic and musical tastes, and as comfortable at a rock concert as listening to chamber music. You'll just love someone who can put you in a romantic mood at a moment's notice, who loves sharing an ice cream in the park, or walking along the beach in the middle of winter.

When you think about your dream guy, 1994 Taurus female, what will pop into your head first is someone who is an energetic go-getter, a great male who can switch moods in a matter of moments and thus keep you guessing. He might be hooked up to the computer one moment, and hugging you and kissing you the next. This is part of his charm, and the way he and you will always keep your love and life together fresh and exciting.

TAURUS ZODIAC SIGN
Your Love Planets

YOUR ROMANTIC SIDE   p. 696
► **VENUS IN GEMINI**
Born Apr. 20, 14:08 - May 09, 1:27
► **VENUS IN CANCER**
Born May 09, 1:28 - May 21, 13:19

YOUR SEX DRIVE   p. 722
► **MARS IN CANCER**
Born Apr. 20, 14:08 - May 21, 13:19

YOUR CELEBRITY TWINS   p. 760
Find out the astrological similarities you have with famous people.

YOUR COMPATIBILITY   p. 780
Compare planets to find out how compatible you are in a relationship.

YOUR RELATIONSHIP KARMA   p. 824
► **SATURN IN AQUARIUS**
Born Apr. 20, 14:08 - May 21, 13:19

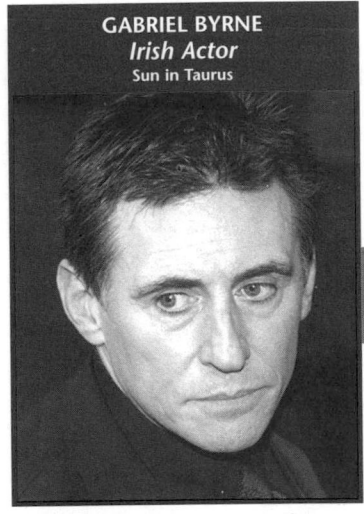

GABRIEL BYRNE
Irish Actor
Sun in Taurus

625

1994 GEMINI
From May 21, 6:49 through June 21, 14:47

The Talkative Chameleon

Sympathetic, talkative, and inquisitive, Gemini of 1994, you are completely fascinated by people, and the skills you exhibit in accommodating others from the earliest years show that you will have no difficulty succeeding in life on a variety of fronts. As an adult, communicating with people of diverse backgrounds will impact your ability to lead others and be a personable friend and fascinating partner.

By the time you and your beloved meet, you will be ready to travel throughout the world, testing out all your language skills, as well as your chameleonic ability to fit in wherever you go. The right partner will find that most appealing, and together you can create a life that will be one continuous adventure, discovering new people, places, and ideas. On the home front, your curiosity will extend to discovering as much about each other as two people possibly can.

Anyone who contemplates sharing your life's journey must have a vibrant personality without a hint of shyness, someone who will let you know right away that traveling is either an overwhelming passion or a secret longing waiting to come true. Once you know you have that in common, you will make sure you're dealing with someone who is not vain, and who cares deeply about humanity, perhaps even participating in volunteer activities.

The female who will win your heart, 1994 Gemini male, loves the great outdoors, never worrying about whether her hair is out of place, as long as it is blowing in the wind. But she'll be a homebody, too, and love nothing more after a full day of skiing or skating than to cook a really great meal just for you—from scratch. Then for dessert, she will put on some mood music, and fall right into your arms.

Dreaming about the perfect male, 1994 Gemini female, will elicit visions of someone who likes getting his hands dirty either pulling weeds in the garden or playing touch football with the rest of the guys. You'll really like someone who has some rough edges, but who can change at a moment's notice from being tough to being a big teddy bear, one who will warm you up in any weather.

GEMINI ZODIAC SIGN
Your Love Planets

YOUR ROMANTIC SIDE   p. 696
► **VENUS IN CANCER**
Born May 21, 13:20 - June 06, 1:15
► **VENUS IN LEO**
Born June 06, 1:16 - June 21, 21:18

YOUR SEX DRIVE   p. 722
► **MARS IN CANCER**
Born May 21, 13:20 - May 26, 12:18
► **MARS IN LEO**
Born May 26, 12:19 - June 21, 21:18

YOUR CELEBRITY TWINS   p. 760
Find out the astrological similarities you have with famous people.

YOUR COMPATIBILITY   p. 780
Compare planets to find out how compatible you are in a relationship.

YOUR RELATIONSHIP KARMA   p. 824
► **SATURN IN AQUARIUS**
Born May 21, 13:20 - June 21, 21:18

NATALIE PORTMAN
American Actress
Venus in Cancer

1994 CANCER
From June 21, 14:48 through July 23, 1:40

♋ *The Mystical Romancer*

As you grow older, Cancer of 1994, you may start thinking of love as an almost mystical experience, a connection between two people that seems to take them far outside the bounds of space and time. Even as you mature past the time when you experience your first love, you'll feel the same, and this will help to shape your romantic life through the years. Anyone who has you as a partner will truly be lucky, as you'll take such relationships seriously and try very hard to make them as good as they can be.

Once you've established a bond with someone, it stays with you no matter what, and you won't be easily daunted by the kinds of problems two people sometimes have when they're together. You will always feel there's a way to smooth out the rough spots, and even up the edges. Your optimism and your sensitivity will give others hope in many situations, but most especially in your romantic relationships.

The person whose mind is set on winning you will need to recognize your positive and intuitive nature, so a cheery face and a pleasant sense of humor are important. Someone who comes off as flighty and flirty will be a complete turn-off—you need a sign that this person will go the distance. That may be laughing at all your jokes, or simply using body language to show that you have a high approval rating.

As a 1994 Cancer male, you're likely to find your perfect lady in someone who likes to keep to a fairly small circle of friends and family, with you as the centerpiece. She will be somewhat on the serious side, less interested in frivolous entertainment than in reading a good book. But mostly she will be interested in everything that is important to you and will say so with her eyes and her smile.

If you're a 1994 Cancer female, you will find your match in a man who is a bit more dignified than the average. He will have a sensitive and intuitive side to him, but that will be the side that he will share only with you. He'll be the perfect companion to have with you on every occasion, though his favorite times are likely to be those when he and you are walking hand in hand.

1994 LEO
From July 23, 1:41 through August 23, 8:43

♌ *The Caring Communicator*

You may not be very talkative, Leo of 1994, but as you mature, you will become a good communicator who can always find a new way to express old truths. You will be the type who can find the silver lining behind every cloud, and that will make you a natural for soothing hurt feelings and bruised egos. When friends are mad at each other, you're the one they will call on to help them find a way to patch things up.

This attitude typifies the way you feel you should relate to other people, and it will especially apply to that someone you may fall in love with someday. With you, there is always a way to be happy and never a reason to stay mad for long. You will always make sure that the two of you work at the good things and solve your problems as soon as you become aware of them. You'll expect no less from the person you love.

Someone who wants to make you take notice will need to show you a positive, sunny disposition, one not just made up of fast superficial smiles. Beyond that, you'll need to know that this is someone with a sincere and deep interest in people, who sees others as individuals, not stereotypes. A suitor should love doing things on the spur of the moment and will show you as much by taking you for an unplanned drive in the country, or surprising you with tickets to a sold-out concert.

The perfect lady for you, 1994 Leo male, will be someone who knows how to laugh, but won't be afraid to cry. While she won't be self-indulgent about her feelings, she will never be afraid to show them to you. She will see your life together as a real partnership that will have to last through good times and sad times, with the two of you giving all the best you have to each other. More than anything, she'll know how to have fun.

As a 1994 Leo female, you're likely to find love with a man who has a strong character and a softhearted side he may show only to you. He'll be good at finding things for the two of you to do together, from walks in the rain to trips to exotic places. And no one will love to surprise you more than he does, especially with little thoughtful gifts.

1994 VIRGO *From August 23, 8:44 through September 23, 6:18*

The Playful Partner

You've always been independent and content to be on your own, Virgo of 1994, and as you reach adulthood you will be more social, becoming almost playful in how you relate. You may even earn the reputation as a friendly practical joker and the life and soul of the party. When it comes to relationships, you will be a lighthearted partner, one who can provide comic relief when your mate is sad. You won't be afraid to show true feelings, since you know your beloved will cheer you up if necessary.

For you, relationships mean sharing everything—hopes and dreams, balancing each other's moods. When one of you is down, the other will be up. When one of you wants to be a couch potato, the other will scoop you away for the day, or even the weekend. And when you're feeling tired, your partner will find a way to your heart with a warm hug.

Simple flirtation is often the best way to get your attention, as the unexpectedness will knock you out of your mental grooves. But that's just the introduction, so behind the looks and winks, someone interested in you has to show you a gentle and inviting side, with a heart that is kind and a mind that you're certain knows many intriguing facts about subjects you hope to learn about.

The perfect female, 1994 Virgo male, will be pleasant and charming, and understand perfectly what a partnership is all about. She'll be turned-off by inflated egos and will keep yours intact by being completely irresistible. This gal will be so much fun to be around that you will look forward to getting out and about with her as much as you can. She will know how to talk to you on a level that reaches both your heart and your mind.

The kind of guy you will fall in love with, 1994 Virgo female, will be someone who'll love to do things on the spur of the moment and will entertain you with his interesting stories and amusing anecdotes. He will love sharing his hopes and ideas with you, never failing to ask your opinion, and never failing to take it seriously. Mostly, you will love being together, in summer sunshine, or winter darkness, as long as you are close and cuddly.

VIRGO ZODIAC SIGN
YOUR LOVE PLANETS

YOUR ROMANTIC SIDE   p. 696
▶ **VENUS IN LEO**
Born Aug. 23, 15:13 - Sept. 23, 12:47

YOUR SEX DRIVE   p. 722
▶ **MARS IN VIRGO**
Born Aug. 23, 15:13 - Sept. 01, 6:37
▶ **MARS IN LIBRA**
Born Sept. 01, 6:38 - Sept. 23, 12:47

YOUR CELEBRITY TWINS   p. 760
Find out the astrological similarities you have with famous people.

YOUR COMPATIBILITY   p. 780
Compare planets to find out how compatible you are in a relationship.

YOUR RELATIONSHIP KARMA   p. 824
▶ **SATURN IN AQUARIUS**
Born Aug. 23, 15:13 - Sept. 23, 12:47

HUGH GRANT
English Actor
Sun in Virgo

627

1994 LIBRA  *From September 23, 6:19 through October 23, 15:35*

The Elusive Charmer

As you move towards adulthood, Libra of 1994, the double-sided nature of your personality will become crystal clear. Your social face will reflect a pleasant, accommodating personality—charming, sweet-talking, and eager to please. Your private side will lead you toward creative spaces and a private language that only you and your partner will understand.

Though the arts will be paramount in your life, you will definitely not be the starving artist type. You'll like the finer things in life way too much, and the key to your dream partnership will be having enough for a lovely home and the means to travel the world. Your both may even take turns supporting each others' creative drive, as long as one of you, in turn, earns the daily bread. For you, this will describe the perfect relationship, each of you helping each other when you want to do your own thing.

Attracting you will be easy, but keeping you interested will take a little more work. You have such a varied mind that initially you may be more attracted by the novelty of someone's appearance or lifestyle than anything else. Once that novelty wears off, in order to keep your attention, your beloved will need to somehow let you know that the real you is obvious, that the inner you has been revealed—and you are wonderful just as you are.

The perfect gal for you, 1994 Libra male, will match your wide variety of interests and perhaps introduce you to a few things that you haven't yet experienced. She will love you and appreciate you even more for not fitting into some convenient mold. You will tend to live the most interesting part of your life in the outside world, so she will balance that by giving you a home life that is relaxing and a love that makes your emotions soar.

If you're a 1994 Libra female, you'll need a man who is perhaps a bit quieter and more introspective than you. He will calm you and soothe you when the world seems to be conspiring to get you down, and yet at the same time he will awaken your mind and your senses. And there will be no one you can have fun with like you can with him.

LIBRA ZODIAC SIGN
YOUR LOVE PLANETS

YOUR ROMANTIC SIDE   p. 696
▶ **VENUS IN LEO**
Born Sept. 23, 12:48 - Oct. 06, 21:14
▶ **VENUS IN VIRGO**
Born Oct. 06, 21:15 - Oct. 23, 22:04

YOUR SEX DRIVE   p. 722
▶ **MARS IN LIBRA**
Born Sept. 23, 12:48 - Oct. 16, 19:04
▶ **MARS IN SCORPIO**
Born Oct. 16, 19:05 - Oct. 23, 22:04

YOUR CELEBRITY TWINS   p. 760
Find out the astrological similarities you have with famous people.

YOUR COMPATIBILITY   p. 780
Compare planets to find out how compatible you are in a relationship.

YOUR RELATIONSHIP KARMA   p. 824
▶ **SATURN IN AQUARIUS**
Born Sept. 23, 12:48 - Oct. 23, 22:04

MORGAN FREEMAN
American Actor
Mars in Scorpio

1994 SCORPIO
From October 23, 15:36 through November 22, 13:05

♏ *The Crowd Lover*

You will always be in tune with people, Scorpio of 1994, and the more people around you, the happier you will be. From the time you were young, you may have loved being where the crowds are, not as the center of attention, but as one of those mingling and enjoying the scene. As much as you love crowds, however, when it comes to romance, you're going to want to only be with one person.

When you meet someone who might make a good romantic partner, this individual may have some rather unique qualities. As a keen observer of people, you will notice their similarities and differences, and as you grow and mature, you will have studied many people with many varying lifestyles. You won't set impossibly high standards for romance, but if you can find someone who's a little bit different from that crowd you love so much, you'll be hooked.

Anyone who has an interest in you will need to show you something that's a little bit off the beaten track, whether it's a point of view, a creative style, or perhaps an artistic talent. The best way to approach you will be in a crowded social scene where there's a lot going on. If someone comes up to you just brimming with fun and energy and begins to talk to you about life and love, or perhaps asks you to dance, you'll be intrigued.

If you're a 1994 Scorpio male, the girl who wins your heart will have lots of verve and an exciting way of entering the room. Though she may not be as social as you, she will love nothing more than going out on the town with you, whether it's to a party or perhaps to a quiet night of dining and talk. She may have some unique talent or ability, but even if not, there will be something indefinable about her that will always keep you interested.

For the 1994 Scorpio female, that wonderful guy who'll be part of your life is the type that will sweep you off your feet when you first meet him. But even if his entrance into your life comes without much fanfare, he'll be someone with a mysterious quality that intrigues you. You will listen to him for hours and never get tired, just as he will never tire of you.

1994 SAGITTARIUS
From November 22, 13:06 through December 22, 2:22

♐ *The Best Friend*

When you reach adulthood, Sagittarius of 1994, you may at times think you weren't cut out for love, even though nothing could be further from the truth. Since you're the kind who will set goals and strive patiently to reach them, your intensity may give a misleading message that you find others a distraction. You may first have a few flings, but your kindness and loving nature will make it difficult for you not to end up with a romantic partner sooner or later. Once you find that special someone, you will happily settle into a comfortable groove with that one unique person.

You may have some difficulty knowing when work ends and play begins, but as you mature, you will definitely know the difference. Having fun with someone you love means having a best friend to talk to when you're down, and a warm companion when you want to just hold hands, stroll through the city, or run in the park.

Whoever might want to attract your attention in order to get to know you should approach you on the serious side first. Fun can come later, but someone really intent on turning your head will need to study you a little and perhaps talk to you about your latest project or interest. Once you've opened up on that level, your heart will be sure to follow.

Your dream girl, 1994 Sagittarius male, may be a bit different than most, but she'll be just as disciplined and focused as you are, perhaps even sharing some of the same goals. She may appear aloof to some, but she'll mainly show that side of herself to people she doesn't know well—or doesn't care to know. In reality, she will be quite warm and open, with an intense interest in other people, though most especially an interest in you.

The guy for you, 1994 Sagittarius female, will stand out from the crowd, sometimes because he'll be right out in front of it somewhere. He will definitely go down paths not followed by the average person, and often will be in the lead on issues of the day, as well as fashions and trends. You'll find him intriguing on a lot of different levels, but most certainly he'll inspire you in a romantic way.

Denzel Washington – A Charismatic Star

By the end of the 1990s, Denzel Washington was on every director's A-List and getting the ethereal $20 million per film salary that marked him as having arrived. He has that mysterious presence, a recognizable aura of strength and focus that the camera loves. Of the many characters he's played in the past twenty-five years, he's always a proud African-American man and always in control. Women love it, and men admire it. He's charismatic, handsome, and consistently leaves the audience with a vivid impression, making him one of Hollywood's best bets for a box-office hit.

Denzel Washington's powerful public image reflects what he's built in his private life. He has one of the most successful marriages in Tinseltown, having been married to Pauletta Pearson since 1980. They and their four children find enough quality time together in spite of his intense work schedule. The couple's mutual faith and their spiritual awareness keep them focused on family priorities. Still, being Mrs. Denzel Washington has to be one of the toughest jobs in town. But Pauletta is not the aggrieved spouse that the tabloids suggest. She is a vibrant, confident woman who has admitted "Yes, women come on to my husband. But it's also ridiculous because they don't know him. They know a character, an image, a movie star that they've made bigger than life ... I take it as a compliment, because they know he's with me." Denzel says that what he most appreciates about Pauletta is "her strength, her friendship, and the way we laugh together."

Washington first met his wife while they were both playing roles in the 1977 TV movie about Olympian runner Wilma Rudolph. They didn't hit it off right away, but six months later a mutual friend set them up, and the rest is history. The 2,500 people who showed up for their wedding were there to congratulate Pauletta, a starlet with a lot of potential. She was a trained pianist performing regularly in New York theatrical productions, while he was just one of many actors on a TV show called *St. Elsewhere*. Paulette gave up acting when she became pregnant with their first child in 1983. It was around that time when Washington realized he could make a living as an actor.

Julia Roberts is one of Denzel's biggest fans. When she was picked to play the lead in the 1993 legal thriller *The Pelican Brief*, the director asked her who she wanted to be her co-star. Without hesitation she said Denzel Washington, but the problem was that the author of the story, John Grishman, hadn't imagined the leading man as African American. Nor could he imagine it in the film version. However, Roberts' star power won the day, and Washington took the role.

This movie has another unpublished sidebar—the interracial love scenes between Roberts and Washington were deleted. She was upset at being blamed for not kissing him and declared, "Don't I have a pulse? Of course I wanted to kiss Denzel. It was his idea to take the damn scenes out." Washington explained that he didn't want to offend some moviegoers, especially black women. Back in 1989 when he was watching a screen test for *The Mighty Quinn*, he had an onscreen kiss with Mimi Rogers (an attractive white woman). Black women in the audience responded with loud boos—and black women have been his core audience.

At the 2002 Academy Awards, Washington won an Oscar for playing a corrupt cop in *Training Day*—the first Best Actor prize for an African American since Sidney Poitier in 1964. When asked about racial prejudice in Hollywood, he said, "There's been a lot of talk about race ... this is an award to an actor."

▶ READ ABOUT JULIA ROBERTS ON PAGE 653

- ★ SIMPSON VERDICT
- ★ NIGHTMARES OF DEPRAVITY
- ★ JENNY JONES SURPRISE
- ★ HUGH GRANT BLOWS IT
- ★ SEAL
- ★ BRAVEHEART
- ★ CHOICES

Hot Couple

EVENTS

The US was riveted by the televised murder trial of football legend O.J. Simpson, and 150 million people watched the October 3 acquittal. Pope John Paul characterized contemporary society as "steeped in elements of hedonism, self-centeredness, and sensuality." Republican Presidential candidate Bob Dole denounced the entertainment industry for producing "nightmares of depravity drenched in violence and sex." Carol Shaya-Castro was dismissed from the New York City Police Department for posing both nude and in uniform for *Playboy*.

After his male "secret admirer" was revealed on the *Jenny Jones Show*, Jonathan Schmidt shot and killed him. The World Health Organization estimated 1,025,073 AIDS cases worldwide. French actress Isabelle Adjani gave birth to the son of ex-lover Daniel Day-Lewis. Up-and-coming British actor Hugh Grant was arrested for having sex with a prostitute on Sunset Strip. Ireland's referendum legalizing divorce passed by only 9,163 votes.

POP CULTURE

Coolio's "Gangsta's Paradise" combined rock and rap. Seal's debut album included "Kiss from a Rose." R&B girl trio TLC had hits with "Waterfall" and "Creep." The Cranberries combined sweet harmonies and dreamy Celtic melodies in "No Need to Argue." Monica sang "Don't Take It Personal (Just One of Dem Days)."

Mel Gibson was *Braveheart*, the 13th-century Scottish independence leader, William Wallace. In *Waiting to Exhale*, based on Terry McMillan's novel, four black professional women endure no-good men and life's upheavals. *While You Were Sleeping* featured Sandra Bullock in a complicated misunderstanding over a fiancé in a coma. *The Bridges of Madison County* was based on the 1993 bestseller about the life-altering four-day love affair between an Iowa housewife and a *National Geographic* photographer. In *French Twist*, a womanizing husband gets his comeuppance when a lesbian falls in love with his wife.

Danielle Steel continued to dominate bestseller lists with *Five Days in Paris*, a bittersweet story of adulterous love, and *Lightning*, about a married couple coping with the woman's breast cancer. In Mary Lee Settle's *Choices*, a Southern society woman born in the 1920s becomes a political and social activist. John Gray's *Mars and Venus in the Bedroom* recommended monogamy and mutual respect to ensure "God's gift"—great sex.

WILL SMITH & JADA PINKETT

Will Smith was already a household name from his rap albums as the "Fresh Prince" with DJ Jazzy Jeff, his fish-out-of-water sitcom *The Fresh Prince of Bel-Air*, and his role in *Independence Day*. Jada Pinkett was a petite bombshell who unsuccessfully auditioned in 1990 to play Will's girlfriend on *Fresh Prince*. The two began dating in 1995 and married on New Year's Eve 1997.

The stylish Hollywood power couple are the doting parents of two (Will also has a son by his first wife). They left the 2002 Academy Awards when their daughter fell ill even though Will was up for Best Actor in *Ali*.

SEE ALSO

1995 CAPRICORN

From December 22, 1994 2:23 through January 20, 1995 12:59
(December 1995 Capricorns, see 1996 Capricorn)

♑

The Sharing Crusader

As a Capricorn of 1995, you may spend many youthful hours reading impressive biographies of ordinary people who changed the world, and then dream you are like them. Your visions of greatness can be pursued once you reach adulthood, especially when you realize that none of these people would have accomplished these goals without someone at their side acting as staunch supporter, trusted confidante, and objective advisor.

You will have qualities like these in mind as you search for the one with whom you want to spend your life. Together you can map out plans to do great things, such as attending political rallies or even working together on your favorite candidate's campaign. If you cannot change the world, then you will try to make a difference in the community where you live. Together the two of you might even be known as the "crusading couple," a label you will wear with pride.

The person who will arouse your romantic interest must be as outspoken as you. If the initial conversation veers toward superficiality,

you will walk the other way. If you sense passion, conviction, and dedication, it will whet your curiosity and arouse your emotions. The more intense someone is, the more intense is the promise of love between you and that person.

Your ideal gal, 1995 Capricorn male, will have eyes so expressive she speaks countless words with just a glance, an infectious laugh, and an ear-to-ear grin that knocks you off your feet. She will have a commanding presence and when she speaks, you are amazed at how people take notice and listen—even those with whom she disagrees. When you are alone, you find her irresistible, and the more you're around her, the more you never want to let her go.

Your perfect guy, 1995 Capricorn female, will have the soul of an artist and the intellect of a genius. One minute he may be hard at work, solving the world's problems, and the next he is acting like a romantic fool, hugging you ecstatically or catching your eye with longing looks. When you have a guy like this who combines every quality you dream about, you are his for the taking.

CAPRICORN ZODIAC SIGN
YOUR LOVE PLANETS

YOUR ROMANTIC SIDE — p. 696
► VENUS IN SCORPIO
Born Dec. 22, 1994 2:23 - Jan. 07, 1995 12:06
► VENUS IN SAGITTARIUS
Born Jan. 07, 12:07 - Jan. 20, 12:59

YOUR SEX DRIVE — p. 722
► MARS IN VIRGO
Born Dec. 22, 1994 2:23 - Jan. 20, 1995 12:59

YOUR CELEBRITY TWINS — p. 760
Find out the astrological similarities you have with famous people.

YOUR COMPATIBILITY — p. 780
Compare planets to find out how compatible you are in a relationship.

YOUR RELATIONSHIP KARMA — p. 824
► SATURN IN PISCES
Born Dec. 22, 1994 2:23 - Jan. 20, 1995 12:59

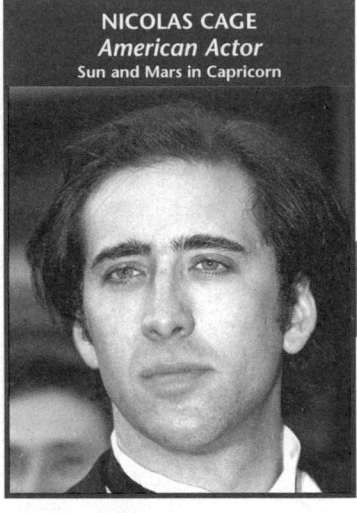

NICOLAS CAGE
American Actor
Sun and Mars in Capricorn

631

1995 AQUARIUS

From January 20, 13:00 through February 19, 3:10

♒

The Relentless Enthusiast

You, Aquarius of 1995, have an enormous amount of enthusiasm about life, with a real desire to break down barriers and get to the heart of things. As you mature, you will continue to focus on pursuing your goals, and this relentless attitude will extend to your view of love. Once you find the right person, you will follow your heart until the match is made.

Your parents may not have had a conventional relationship, and this may mean certain independence in your own relationships. You will tend to be attracted to those who are pursuing goals that may require a great deal of time away from home and family, such as a personal path to artistic greatness or a unique spiritual pursuit. You'll be willing to give someone like that the freedom to follow such goals, expecting the same in return, with both of you knowing you're together in mind and in spirit.

The one who will appeal to you is not concerned with trendy clothes or flirtatious talk. You want someone who has a variety of interests such as reading good literature, following

current events, or indulging a passion for sports, and will introduce you to new and intriguing pursuits that differ from yours, but that you can get involved in nonetheless.

An athletic, physically-fit gal who has that red-cheeked, wind-blown look will get you, 1995 Aquarius male, excited about going out and about on days that are perfect for trips to the beach or driving in the country. You will just love making her happy, and even if you have to sacrifice hours away from the computer screen, it will be worth seeing the smile on her face. What you want, she wants, and what she wants, you will give her along with lots of love.

Your idea of a special guy, 1995 Aquarius female, is someone who will hug you for no reason except to show how much he cares. He will be generous to a fault, passionate about his beliefs, and will be able to make you laugh at any time of day or night. You want a man who will be giving, affectionate, and able to express his feelings, even cry, when appropriate. You are always there for him, happy or sad, as he is for you.

AQUARIUS ZODIAC SIGN
YOUR LOVE PLANETS

YOUR ROMANTIC SIDE — p. 696
► VENUS IN SAGITTARIUS
Born Jan. 20, 13:00 - Feb. 04, 20:11
► VENUS IN CAPRICORN
Born Feb. 04, 20:12 - Feb. 19, 3:10

YOUR SEX DRIVE — p. 722
► MARS IN VIRGO
Born Jan. 20, 13:00 - Jan. 22, 23:47
► MARS IN LEO
Born Jan. 22, 23:48 - Feb. 19, 3:10

YOUR CELEBRITY TWINS — p. 760
Find out the astrological similarities you have with famous people.

YOUR COMPATIBILITY — p. 780
Compare planets to find out how compatible you are in a relationship.

YOUR RELATIONSHIP KARMA — p. 824
► SATURN IN PISCES
Born Jan. 20, 13:00 - Feb. 19, 3:10

JULIETTE BINOCHE
French Actress
Sun and Mars in Pisces

632

1995 PISCES
From February 19, 3:11 through March 21, 2:13

The Idyllic Friend

Throughout your childhood, you, Pisces of 1995, will spend many idyllic hours in the company of friends enjoying a range of activities, from participating in team sports to playing computer games. You will love being sociable, and as you mature and venture out into the world of higher education, you will probably join clubs, be involved in group events, and look forward to meeting new people.

You may even meet the love of your life at a social engagement or party, someone with whom you can plan a future together. But any relationship you seek must balance your wide circle of friends and endless activities with them against wonderful shared moments alone together. You and your partner will love planning romantic getaways and innovative excursions, from touring ancient ruins to river rafting. The more exciting and fun-filled your life is, the happier you will be together.

Anyone who will catch your eye must have a great sense of humor and even like a good old-fashioned prank every now and again. This person should be able to swap funny stories with you, letting you know that the same things tickle your funny bones. While laughter will never make or break a good relationship, it is one ingredient that lets you know that if hardships come along, you will find your way out of them soon enough.

A woman of few words yet with strong loyalties will be the one for you, 1995 Pisces male. Words are not as vital as the commitment she will make to her family and friends, and she will always come to the aid of those she loves. She will always stand behind you as your staunchest supporter, even if privately you agree to disagree. With that gal at your side you will surely be the envy of all your friends.

You dream about a guy who can teach you a thing or two about leading a healthful life, 1995 Pisces female. This man is dynamic, handsome, and wants to accompany you everywhere, whether to the theater or a football game. When he is with his friends, he lets them know you are the love of his life, and when you are alone, he takes you in his arms and whispers it in your ear.

1995 ARIES
From March 21, 2:14 through April 20, 13:20

The Motivated Mate

Self-motivated, forthright, and independent, you, Aries of 1995, will always follow the beat of your own drummer. Throughout your life, you will want to stand out, and will do so by making your own decisions rather than following the rest of the crowd. When it comes to love, you will also follow your own lead, and most likely will fall in love with someone who is unique and whose inner beauty will immediately be apparent to you.

Once you have set your sights on your true love, nothing will prevent you from making this person deliriously happy, because you are certain to be a mate who is affectionate, unselfish, and never at all boring. You will feel that relationships allow you to be spontaneous, and this in turn will help you to transform ordinary activities such as going to the beach or hiking in the woods into daylong romantic adventures.

Someone who wants to attract you needs to be vivacious and enthusiastic with a bubbly personality, a zest for life, and an authentic interest in knowing everything about you and all your friends. This person's inquisitive quality will be almost childlike, reacting to everything you do with absolute awe and wonder. You won't have any choice but to fall in love with the person whose fascination is focused solely on you.

The gal you'll dream about, 1995 Aries male, will provide you, the great wanderer, with just the anchor you need. She will listen intently to all your dreams, and in addition to cheerleading them along, she will lend you some practical tips on how they can come true. Her spontaneous hugs and kisses make you the envy of all your friends, but the best part of all is that away from the crowds, she is yours and yours alone.

Your ideal guy, 1995 Aries female, will be one who is responsible, productive, and in complete control during the work week. But once the weekend comes, he is playful, daring, and right where you want him—at your beck and call. You will love both sides of this man, and you will be under his spell, whether he is playing the dashing charmer or demure pussycat who loves cuddling on the sofa next to you.

1995 TAURUS
From April 20, 13:21 through May 21, 12:33

The Fairy Tale Dreamer

As you move into adulthood, Taurus of 1995, you will always find a little piece of beauty in every situation and in everyone you meet. The unique gift you have for turning mundane moments into magical ones will carry over into your romantic life. When you finally find your real true love, you will strive to have a fairy tale life together, with the two of you playing the leading characters.

Every day you will try to do something out of the ordinary for your mate, perhaps by serving breakfast in bed or buying a special gift just to see the surprise and delight on your partner's face. You will make sure you celebrate every birthday with a sentimental present and a romantic vacation—a different one every year. Nothing will ever be too good for the person you love and for that special relationship in your life.

The person who wants to hold your interest will have to be down to earth, and will know how to speak directly to you without being either too forward or intimidating. You will like to take things slowly, especially where love is concerned, but you will also want someone who, like yourself, is not afraid to show affection. After you meet this genuinely warm human being, it won't take you long to see the romantic possibilities.

For you, Taurus male of 1995, the perfect gal will be passionate about life and love, and almost everything that comes her way, from her favorite dessert to her favorite song to her favorite guy—you. She will understand you so well that she will know exactly what to do to make you happy, even when you're not quite sure what that is yourself. She especially knows that being there for you, day in and day out, is what you want most of all.

Your ideal guy, Taurus female of 1995, will constantly amaze you with the way he can do so many different things at one time. He will never let life get him down and will be able to provide a positive attitude for you and talk you out of any mood you might fall into. Exciting and unpredictable, his goal in life is to make you happy, and you can always count on him to come up with crazy, new ways to do that.

TAURUS ZODIAC SIGN
YOUR LOVE PLANETS

YOUR ROMANTIC SIDE   p. 696
► VENUS IN PISCES
Born Apr. 20, 13:22 - Apr. 22, 4:06
► VENUS IN ARIES
Born Apr. 22, 4:07 - May 16, 23:21
► VENUS IN TAURUS
Born May 16, 23:22 - May 21, 12:33

YOUR SEX DRIVE   p. 722
► MARS IN LEO
Born Apr. 20, 13:22 - May 21, 12:33

YOUR CELEBRITY TWINS   p. 760
Find out the astrological similarities you have with famous people.

YOUR COMPATIBILITY   p. 780
Compare planets to find out how compatible you are in a relationship.

YOUR RELATIONSHIP KARMA   p. 824
► SATURN IN PISCES
Born Apr. 20, 13:22 - May 21, 12:33

JOANNA LUMLEY
English Actress
Sun in Taurus

633

1995 GEMINI
From May 21, 12:34 through June 21, 20:33

The Knowledge Seeker

As a Gemini of 1995, you will be moved ahead in life by your thirst for knowledge and your strong desire to find it anywhere you can, especially from the people you meet. Your friends, acquaintances, and associates will be your real teachers, and you will always feel that the more you listen to their insights and experiences, the better able you will be to make the choices that lie ahead.

Your best teacher will be the person you go through life with. That special someone will serve as your tour guide, showing you how to be the best you can possibly be, and introducing you to a way of viewing the world that constantly amazes you. You will return the favor by sharing your own experiences and everything you know with your romantic other.

Anyone who wants to be your life partner must be intelligent and have a burning desire to learn and grow. You will know this is the one by a certain curiosity that shows itself easily in conversation with a willingness to explore every facet of any question. If that certain someone looks at you lovingly and admiringly and you are suddenly speechless with a silly smile on your face, you know that this person has touched your heart.

You want a gal, 1995 Gemini male, who is extraordinarily patient, determined, with a persistence that will consistently amaze you. She will look up to you and will consider you to be her greatest friend and most trustworthy teacher. This lady will love accompanying you to lectures, museums, concerts, and anything else that is both enjoyable and educational. Mostly though, her smile will always seem to say, "Thank you for coming into my life!"

The guy who challenges you to be the best you can be is the one who will win your heart, 1995 Gemini female. Your dreamboat can use words to transport you to foreign places without ever leaving home and can make you feel at home wherever you do travel together. With such a charming guy as your escort, you will be the envy of all those you meet. But when you are alone with him, those little boy looks arouse your desire to hold him and hug him and never let go.

GEMINI ZODIAC SIGN
YOUR LOVE PLANETS

YOUR ROMANTIC SIDE   p. 696
► VENUS IN TAURUS
Born May 21, 12:34 - June 10, 16:18
► VENUS IN GEMINI
Born June 10, 16:19 - June 21, 20:33

YOUR SEX DRIVE   p. 722
► MARS IN LEO
Born May 21, 12:34 - May 25, 16:08
► MARS IN VIRGO
Born May 25, 16:09 - June 21, 20:33

YOUR CELEBRITY TWINS   p. 760
Find out the astrological similarities you have with famous people.

YOUR COMPATIBILITY   p. 780
Compare planets to find out how compatible you are in a relationship.

YOUR RELATIONSHIP KARMA   p. 824
► SATURN IN PISCES
Born May 21, 12:34 - June 21, 20:33

GEORGE CLOONEY
American Actor
Mars in Leo

1995 CANCER
From June 21, 20:34 through July 23, 7:29

 ## The Private Communicator

As an intuitive Cancer of 1995, you will surely develop a certain instinct about what life can bring you, and you may not take kindly to those who disagree. Once you've set your sights on something or someone, you will be relentless in pursuing that goal, even if it means sampling a lot of different things so you will, indeed, know what you want.

Maturing into your dating years, you probably won't settle on just one person for quite a while, as you go about playing the field. However, once you get a good idea of what kind of romantic partner would be best for you, that field will begin to narrow quickly, and it won't take long for you to settle on "the one," to the exclusion of all others.

Someone who wants to win your heart will make sure that even the first time you meet, you can find a quiet spot away from the noise and the crowds so you can communicate and slowly discover that you share the same interests and even the same temperament. If each of you seems to finish each other's sentences and responds very naturally to the ebb and flow of the other person's feelings, this romance will have possibilities. Once you establish a rapport, simple activities such as long walks and quiet romantic movies will seal the deal.

The lady for you, 1995 Cancer male, will melt your heart the moment you fall in love with her at first sight. She will be perky, clever, and talkative without interrupting you or stepping on your toes. This gal dotes on your every word, and her romantic feelings will be deep, indeed, the kind of love that shows itself in small and quiet ways, without need for shouting from the rooftops or giving extravagant gifts.

The love of your life, 1995 Cancer female, will be the best communicator you've ever met. This guy will be able to talk to you for hours on end, but will also be good at conveying his thoughts, ideas, and feelings to others with ease, whether in groups or one at a time. When it comes to intimate moments together, he won't be so big on words, but his warm embrace and the touch of his hand on your face will tell you all you need to know.

1995 LEO
From July 23, 7:30 through August 23, 14:34

The Entertaining Performer

As a Leo of 1995, you have a talent for rounding up your friends and putting on a fabulous show, even directing and starring in amateur skits in your back yard. When you grow up, you may even try out for the professional stage. When it comes to relationships, you will continue to aim for the limelight, doing all that you can to win over your one true love.

Nothing will give you greater pleasure than escorting your beloved to the theater, opera, or ballet, and preserving those magical moments for days to come. You love entertaining each other and your favorite activities might be acting out the parts of your favorite love story or lip-synching tunes from a Broadway musical. As long as you and your partner are never bored, you will never tire of being together.

Anyone who wants to attract you should be high-spirited, outgoing, and a patron of the arts. You don't want someone too reserved, but neither do you want this person to come on too strong. Instead, you want to find ways to take it slowly and get to know each other at a steady pace. If your smiles and long glimpses into one another's eyes speak a thousand words, without uttering any, you may have found the one you've been waiting for.

The perfect lady, 1995 Leo male, is smart, independent, and with a flair for style—one that makes her attractive to almost every man she meets. While that may make you a bit jealous, it will keep you on your toes. You will always strive to treat her like a queen, and in exchange, you will earn her unconditional love, respect, and admiration. This lady is not someone you will want to let go, and she won't ever want to leave either.

As a 1995 Leo female, you will set your sights on a guy who will be sensitive, soft-spoken, and will like to create a romantic mood with your favorite music—from jazz to rock. He loves the outdoors, and more than anything, loves introducing you to physical activities you would never attempt on your own. Once he gets you outside, he will draw you out of yourself with his loving ways, making it possible for you to express your innermost feelings.

1995 VIRGO

From August 23, 14:35 through September 23, 12:12

The Deliberate Dreamer

You'll always be a bit of a dreamer, Virgo of 1995, but most people don't realize you are also quite a visionary. You've always gone about your activities inconspicuously, and instead of hanging out in the schoolyard, you are usually the one off in the corner with the faraway look, dreaming the dream quietly, and working out in your mind how to achieve it, little by little.

As you mature, you will go about a romantic relationship in much the same way. You're not likely to play the field because you will have your heart set on finding just the right one. Once you do, the two of you will become inseparable, able to read each other's minds and finish each other's thoughts. You will plan for that type of intensity, and if your visions become reality, you'll be sure to find your soul mate.

Someone who wants to attract you should break the ice by doing something silly and charming, like buying you an ice cream cone or taking you to a Karaoke bar. Once that person has made you crack a smile or introduces you to something new, you'll find your heart opening up to them. Seeing someone in unguarded moments is when a good heart and true sincerity show through best.

Your dream lady, Virgo male of 1995, will be a creative type who has the ability to write or to paint or even to act out a part on stage. That kind of creativity will always sweep you away into another world that you may not know too well on your own, and it helps to make her a constant mystery and delight to you. People who see you together may marvel that two people apparently so different can be so much in love, but you know that's because your hearts beat as one.

The perfect guy for you, Virgo female of 1995, will be someone who's very good at getting other people to set their differences aside and work together. That talent has an obvious application to your situation, as well, because he will be able to keep the two of you on an even keel through even the roughest times. He is an independent type who needs his space, but his favorite space most all of the time is around you.

ALICIA SILVERSTONE
American Actress
Sun and Mars in Libra

635

1995 LIBRA

From September 23, 12:13 through October 23, 21:31

The Romantic Realist

As you grow older, Libra of 1995, you will blossom from a kid with wondrous daydreams into an adult who believes that some of them can actually come true. While others will stay lost in those daydreams, you will find ways to integrate the world of romance into your every day life, never letting the practical demands muscle in on those moments that you will devote to the two of you being together.

You'll be the best partner anyone could want because you'll take nothing about romance for granted. You love the hugs and kisses and the sweet words, and will be generous with all three. Most important, you will also instinctively know that little things such as not working too hard and taking time out for weekend getaways or the occasional exotic vacation will do more to keep the two of you together than mere hearts and flowers could ever do by themselves.

The straightforward approach works best for anyone who would like to catch your eye. Someone who will immediately say hello and ask you out for coffee will get more than a casual glance from you. If that special person expresses a caring attitude toward friends, family, and those in need, you will know there lies a good heart, one who knows how to nurture and care for a relationship to help it grow.

The girl of your dreams, Libra male of 1995, has all her bases covered. She can organize your lives with no trouble at all and leave plenty of time for simple pastimes such as cuddling on the sofa, eating popcorn, and watching your favorite video. She will have soulful eyes and a generous heart that is as truly romantic as anyone's heart could be. A smile and an "I love you" from her can keep you going all day long!

Your ideal man, Libra female of 1995, is spontaneous, exciting, yet forceful and influential when he needs to be. He makes people sit up and take notice when he speaks, but underneath the tough exterior seen by most people is the softest and sweetest heart, one that is reserved just for you. With you he is always sympathetic, always a listener, and keeps you safe and warm in his loving arms.

ETHAN HAWKE
American Actor
Sun and Venus in Scorpio

636

1995 SCORPIO
From October 23, 21:32 through November 22, 19:00

♏ *The Pleasing Puzzler*

Inquisitive, adventurous, and playful, you, Scorpio of 1995, always pose the type of questions that others, including parents and teachers, don't always have quick answers to. As you mature, you'll continue to leave people knitting their brows and scratching their heads over some puzzle you've set before them, and it will have a fascinating effect on your romantic life.

People in love often don't ask questions, and you will meet your romantic match in that special someone who isn't thrown off balance by your quizzes and conundrums. Once in love, you will quickly learn that some areas of life are best enjoyed and not questioned. In any event, your tendency to turn things upside down and take them apart will make you an irresistible, exciting, and unpredictable partner, one who aspires to surprise your mate every day.

Anyone who wants to attract you will delight in being enigmatic and playing hard to get. This special person will have good looks and a pleasant personality, and will give you the feeling that there's something deep, fascinating, and intriguing lurking beneath the surface. Anyone who really likes you and wants to get something started will let you make the first move, and once you do, you will tell by the sound of your voices laughing together you have found the right one.

Your ideal mate, 1995 Scorpio male, will make life exciting through a constant, yet loving, test of wits and wills. It will be a friendly contest, but she will know how to keep your mind working and your heart racing just a little faster than it otherwise might. This stimulating give-and-take will always keep your romance exciting and new, and you will never take this lady for granted or stop telling her how wonderful she is.

The man of your dreams, 1995 Scorpio female, is a dynamo, yet never shy about letting others know just what his boundaries are when they're around him. His strength of character and his physical strength will really make you love him, especially when he shows his gentle side to you. If you have a dream to follow, this man will support you all the way.

1995 SAGITTARIUS
From November 22, 19:01 through December 22, 8:16

♐ *The Fanciful Explorer*

You have always wanted to grow up fast, Sagittarius of 1995, and sometimes your brain works overtime, contemplating everything you will do once you reach adulthood. Even at a young age, you will give your dreams a realistic edge, and inject fantasy into your everyday life. Once you mature and your attention turns to romance, you will feel that while love is in the hearts and minds of two people, it also lives in the real world.

Your relationship will allow you to expand your horizons by doing new things and meeting interesting people. You will enjoy hiking, bicycling, and taking long, nature walks together, as much as you love visiting European cathedrals or attending a lecture at the local library. Most important will be exploring the vast world, holding each other tightly, and smiling adoringly at each other from across the room.

Anyone who wants to pique your interest and get your heart to skip a beat will exude confidence, intelligence, and will regale you with wonderful stories the moment you meet. This person will be larger than life, but without batting an eye, will know instinctively when to get quiet, and give the floor over to you. In that instant you will know the timing is perfect and that romance is definitely in the air.

The wonderful lady who will change your life, 1995 Sagittarius male, is great at organizing all the myriad activities you do together, yet may be more of a dreamer than you are. While you're focused on the here and now, she can lift your eyes to gaze at a distant and inspiring future where the possibilities are endless. Together, the two of you are much more than either could ever be alone, and you both know it.

The guy of your dreams, 1995 Sagittarius female, will never be a slave to routine and can transform a day trip or night on the town into an exotic adventure. When it comes to the romantic side of your life together, the hugs and kisses will make your mind and spirit soar along with your heart. His heart will be as steady and as faithful as your own, and he will be equally committed to a life of love and sharing.

Heidi Fleiss – The Madam of Tinseltown

She didn't look like a madam. Or like the head of a million-dollar business either. In fact, when she first came to the attention of the general public, Heidi Lynne Fleiss, then in her late twenties, didn't look much different than the typical southern California coed—tan, fit, impeccably dressed in casual clothes. Growing up in a privileged family—her father Paul, a noted pediatrician, is the doctor who delivered Madonna's first child—Heidi was smart and enterprising even as a young girl, running a self-described "babysitting empire" by the time she was thirteen.

She graduated to bigger and better things, and from 1991 until her arrest in June 1993, Fleiss ran the biggest and most glamorous prostitution ring Hollywood had ever seen. Her "girls" were young and gorgeous, a cross-section of exotic and girl-next-door types to satisfy any sexual appetite. Her clients were rumored to be some of the industry's most powerful players, including studio heads, financial kingpins, and major stars. Arrested by the Los Angeles Police Department at her home, Fleiss' story immediately became front page news. The common feeling at the time was that perhaps Fleiss, a prominent doctor's child, and not quite actress material, reinvented herself as a madam.

Although the O.J. Simpson trial was transfixing America at roughly the same time, Fleiss' was still a high-profile case, given the scandalous nature of the rich and famous world she had access to. While the rest of the country hungered after the names in Heidi's infamous "little black book," Hollywood honchos and hotshots were shaking in their designer duds, fearing reprisals. Heidi, however, took the high road. She didn't voluntarily "out" anybody.

Actor Charlie Sheen of *Platoon* and *Wall Street* fame was one of the few high-profile individuals who became linked to the story. Called to testify, the star admitted that he had spent in excess of $50,696 for the services of "Heidi's girls."

Sheen, known as one of Hollywood's "bad boys," had a history of questionable behavior. In 1990, his then girlfriend Kelly Preston broke off their engagement because Sheen accidentally shot her in the arm. (Preston later wed John Travolta.) Sheen's post-Fleiss notoriety included drug busts followed by periods of rehabilitation. He is currently clean and sober.

Heidi's guilty conviction for pandering was changed to not guilty in 1996 by an appeals court. But because of her prior conviction for tax evasion, resulting from unreported "madam" income, she was sentenced to 37 months in California's Dublin Federal women's prison. Released to a halfway house after 20 months for "good behavior," Fleiss—3 days later—requested a return to prison to finish out her sentence. No reason was given for the request. She was released for good behavior in March 1999.

Since her release, Fleiss has penned a book on "sex tips," plus *Pandering: The Scrapbooks of Heidi Fleiss*, which was published early in 2003.

Heidi is a Capricorn, which helps to explain her uncommon business acumen. Capricorns are the financial heavyweights of the Zodiac. Having both her Venus and Mars in Aquarius shows a detached attitude toward sex. We can see this when Fleiss once told an interviewer that she didn't know "what the big deal" was about sex. Quite a comment from a woman who had earned her livelihood plying the flesh trade!

637

"Why would a movie star pay for sex? It eliminates a lot of hassle…there's no emotional attachment, not at first, and you don't have to go out and put together a string of lies and deceit to satisfy a desire"

CHARLIE SHEEN about being a client

▶ READ ABOUT SHOWGIRL CHRISTINE KEELER ON PAGE 375

- ★ RENT
- ★ UNWELCOME TOUCHING
- ★ MACARENA
- ★ THE ENGLISH PATIENT
- ★ SECRETS & LIES
- ★ LARRY FLYNT
- ★ STELLA'S GROOVE

638

Hot Couple

EVENTS

In the US, *Rent*, a contemporary musical *La Boheme* exploring bisexuality, AIDS, and the avant-garde, swept Broadway's Tony Awards and won the Pulitzer. The "Defense of Marriage" act denied federal recognition of same-sex marriages. Conflicting legal rulings marked pornography and censorship in cyberspace as a pivotal issue of the information age. A six-year-old boy was sent home from a North Carolina school for "unwelcome touching"— kissing a classmate on the cheek. Dolly the sheep became the world's first adult clone. Madonna gave birth to daughter Lourdes. Lisa Marie Presley divorced Michael Jackson. British royal couples and tabloid perennials Charles and Diana, and Fergie and Andrew, finally divorced. Margaux Hemingway, 41, overdosed—thirty-five years to the day after her famous grandfather's suicide. Belgium was horrified by a pedophile serial killer. Denny Mendez, 18, became the first black Miss Italia.

POP CULTURE

Mariah Carey had a hit with "One Sweet Day" while Celine Dion sang "Because You Loved Me." Singer-songwriter Tracy Chapman's "Give Me One Reason" and Los Del Rio's "Macarena" were hits.

The English Patient stunningly rendered Michael Ondaatje's novel about a tragic adulterous affair during World War II. In *The First Wives Club*, three women exact sweet revenge on their ex-husbands. In Mike Leigh's *Secrets & Lies*, a young, upscale black woman discovers that her birth mother is a working-class white woman. Lars von Trier's intense *Breaking the Waves* explored the psychological damage to a young couple after a tragic accident. *Kama Sutra: A Tale of Love* told a tale of seduction, revenge, and class division in 16th-century India. Milos Forman's *The People vs. Larry Flynt* profiled the struggles of *Hustler* magazine's publisher against censorship and drug addiction.

Terry McMillan's *How Stella Got Her Groove Back* found a 42-year-old divorced mom rejuvenated by a Jamaican fling. Basketball star Dennis Rodman's memoir was *Bad As I Wanna Be*. In Marie Darrieussecq's satirical *Pig Tales*, a young beautician slowly metamorphoses into a pig. In Danielle Steel's *Malice*, a woman faces a shocking degree of adversity—including incest, patricide, prison, blackmail, and a tabloid smear campaign about her sordid past.

ANTONIO BANDERAS & MELANIE GRIFFITH

Melanie Griffith, daughter of Tippi Hedren, was linked in an on-again, off-again melodramatic romance with older actor Don Johnson from the time she was fourteen. Antonio Banderas was a serious, and seriously sexy, Spanish actor who often starred in Pedro Almodóvar's films and had learned English for his role in 1992's *The Mambo Kings*. Both were still married to others when they met on the set of *Too Much* in late 1995; and both divorced pronto in order to marry one another in May of 1996.

Their daughter Stella was born in September of that year, nine months after they'd met.

SEE ALSO

▶ DON JOHNSON *Page 547*

▶ BRUCE WILLIS AND DEMI MOORE *Page 598*

▶ VIC DAMONE AND DIAHANN CARROLL *Page 564*

1996 CAPRICORN

From December 22, 1995 8:17 through January 20, 1996 18:51
(December 1996 Capricorns, see 1997 Capricorn)

♑ *The Visionary Idealist*

As you mature, Capricorn of 1996, being in love often will be both a dream and an adventure for you. Anyone lucky enough to share romantic times with you will be taken on a long, interesting journey to wonderful places where you'd never hope to go on your own. Even when you are younger, you can easily envision a future of sharing and caring with a special person.

As someone who is very attentive to the needs of those around you, from brothers or sisters to playmates, you really are the best kind of friend and the best kind of partner that anyone could want to have. When someone you love happens to be a little bit down in the dumps, you're always the one there with a cheery word and a warm and friendly hug. When someone you know is happy, you're there to back that person up and to make the good times even better.

If someone wants to be the special person in your life, the main requirement will be to be truthful and sincere. You're not much interested in anyone who is not really interested in you.

But you're willing and ready to go to the ends of the earth for someone who thinks a lot of you, and isn't afraid to say so. That's the kind of person you can learn a lot just from being with, and can have fun with in almost any situation.

Your perfect female, if you're a 1996 Capricorn male, has a really nice smile, and a truly pretty face, but may also be the kind of girl who has a talent such as singing or dancing. You like other people to know that the two of you are a special item, because she really is something to see. And the quiet time that the two of you spend together, talking about your innermost feelings, is always worth waiting for.

For a 1996 Capricorn female, the kind of guy you will be attracted to is not necessarily the popular type, though he has something extra that people do notice. He might be good at sports, or other physical activities, but more than anything else, he is really smart and lots of fun to talk to. You can learn more about his heart by the way the two of you stare into one another's eyes and hold hands, since his feelings run as deep as your own.

CAPRICORN ZODIAC SIGN
YOUR LOVE PLANETS

YOUR ROMANTIC SIDE — p. 696
▶ **VENUS IN AQUARIUS**
Born Dec. 22, 1995 8:17 - Jan. 15, 1996 4:29
▶ **VENUS IN PISCES**
Born Jan. 15, 4:30 - Jan. 20, 18:52

YOUR SEX DRIVE — p. 722
▶ **MARS IN CAPRICORN**
Born Dec. 22, 1995 8:17 - Jan. 08, 1996 11:01
▶ **MARS IN AQUARIUS**
Born Jan. 08, 11:02 - Jan. 20, 18:52

YOUR CELEBRITY TWINS — p. 760
Find out the astrological similarities you have with famous people.

YOUR COMPATIBILITY — p. 780
Compare planets to find out how compatible you are in a relationship.

YOUR RELATIONSHIP KARMA — p. 824
▶ **SATURN IN PISCES**
Born Dec. 22, 1995 8:17 - Jan. 20, 1996 18:52

EMILY WATSON
English Actress
Sun in Capricorn

639

1996 AQUARIUS

From January 20, 18:52 through February 19, 9:00

♒ *The Love Leader*

As you grow up, you'll realize that few people can match your energy, whether in life or in love, Aquarius of 1996. You'll be the kind of person who doesn't hesitate to commit yourself to something you believe in, and once you have, nothing will hold you back from reaching whatever goal you've set for yourself. If that goal happens to be a loving relationship with another person, then you will be firmly set on track.

When you fall in love, you will nearly always take the lead and be the one who has the last word when joint decisions are made. This is not because you think you know better than the other person, but because you feel responsible and protective. While this can be a noble thing, it can also be a problem. If you fall into the pattern of thinking that you always know best, such a mindset could lead you to ignore your partner's needs and feelings.

Though you'll often take the leadership role, the person who will most attract you will probably be someone independent and decisive, just like you. You find this person highly

intriguing, as nothing about the way you two relate will be simple, and each day will present a challenge. But the real key to someone winning your heart is that your beloved will know when to be firm and when to yield to your wishes.

If you're a 1996 Aquarian male, you are most likely to fall in love with a lady who was a bit of a tomboy when she was younger, someone active, energetic, and not afraid to stand up for herself and her own interests. She is not the shy type, nor someone who looks as if she stepped out of the pages of a magazine. She will look you straight in the eye, and has a smile that can melt your heart in an instant.

For the 1996 Aquarian female, the perfect guy will be someone always there when you need him, and someone who always knows what to do. You like to be your own boss, but you won't mind sharing the honor with the male in your life, since he's a sensitive type who loves holding hands and taking long walks in the park. Once he has sealed his commitment with a hug and a kiss, he will stay the course through thick and thin.

AQUARIUS ZODIAC SIGN
YOUR LOVE PLANETS

YOUR ROMANTIC SIDE — p. 696
▶ **VENUS IN PISCES**
Born Jan. 20, 18:53 - Feb. 09, 2:30
▶ **VENUS IN ARIES**
Born Feb. 09, 2:31 - Feb. 19, 9:00

YOUR SEX DRIVE — p. 722
▶ **MARS IN AQUARIUS**
Born Jan. 20, 18:53 - Feb. 15, 11:49
▶ **MARS IN PISCES**
Born Feb. 15, 11:50 - Feb. 19, 9:00

YOUR CELEBRITY TWINS — p. 760
Find out the astrological similarities you have with famous people.

YOUR COMPATIBILITY — p. 780
Compare planets to find out how compatible you are in a relationship.

YOUR RELATIONSHIP KARMA — p. 824
▶ **SATURN IN PISCES**
Born Jan. 20, 18:53 - Feb. 19, 9:00

EWAN MCGREGOR
Scottish Actor
Sun in Aries

1996 PISCES
From February 19, 9:01 through March 20, 8:02

The Unshakable Artist

More than anything, Pisces of 1996, you'll find that you like to feel you're in control of the situations around you, and as a result may not easily commit where loving relationships are concerned. You will take your time with this part of your life, not because you are afraid of commitment, but because once you're involved you want it to last. After you've established yourself in a marriage or romantic relationship, wild horses couldn't make you change.

Your certainty that you and your true love are right for each other will be unshakable, but it can make you so optimistic that you ignore little problems that can grow into big ones. Naturally sensitive, sympathetic, and a good listener, you usually can overcome this tendency. You'll be the most attentive partner anyone could ever hope for.

Someone who wants to win your heart will first appeal to that sensitive and artistic side of your nature by revealing his or her own creative side as soon as you meet. He or she might strike up a conversation about music or art, and if it turns out you share the same interests, the possibilities for true love are endless.

As a Pisces 1996 male, the female you will seek out looks great, smells nice, and wows you the moment she puts her hand in yours. Time spent together includes cuddles at movies and sharing hot chocolate on cold wintry days. You'll want someone who can build a good home life with you and may sacrifice some personal hopes and dreams if necessary. Most of all, you want someone who can share with you all your thoughts, hopes, and fears at the level of your deepest emotions.

For the 1996 Pisces female, the perfect male will have the ability to take all your worries and make them disappear. As you are a bit of a worrier, someone with a good sense of humor can get you out of those moods before they take hold. Along with that, you need someone sensitive and sympathetic like yourself, a person who can listen as well as converse. What you'll look forward to most are those shared moments when your eyes meet his, and his soft touch melts away all your troubles and cares.

1996 ARIES
From March 20, 8:03 through April 19, 19:09

The Sensitive Communicator

As you mature, you will be quite bold when it comes to relationships, Aries of 1996, and most likely you'll initiate most that you become involved in. But that does not mean you'll be pushy or demanding—rather, you will be a firm believer in the give-and-take of being in love.

You'll always be the first to listen when your partner needs to talk, and in return you'll expect nothing less. The essence of two people being together is the way the two take care of one another, and an outpouring of affection is one way to show you care. You'll want to understand what your partner is all about, and you will go to any lengths to make sure you grasp everything you can about that person. Few people you meet will ever be that caring or as loyal.

Anyone interested in you will need to know that flirtations are a turn-off, as are other superficial gestures that you are sure to notice. Though you'll appreciate someone well-groomed and good-looking, these things are only important if they reflect what's on the inside. The look in someone's eye, and the way your true love holds you in strong, caring arms, will let you know that this person won't ever leave your side.

If you're a 1996 Aries male, the female of your dreams will be someone who has no use for traditional male-female stereotypes. You may take the lead, starting the relationship, but your ideal partner will take it in a meaningful direction. She'll be a fun-loving soul whose idea of romance consists of moonlight walks along the beach or bicycle rides in the country. She will be firm and decisive when that's called for and yielding and agreeable when that's the ticket.

For the 1996 Aries female, the ideal man will see things in you that no one else can and will fully know your talents and potentials. You're not always sure you can do what you set out to, but with this man by your side, one who loves you for who you really are, you won't have to worry about where you're going and how you get there. He can look like a movie star or just an average guy, but as long as he has heart, he's the one for you.

1996 TAURUS

From April 19, 19:10 through May 20, 18:22

The Worldly Romantic

When you are older, 1996 Taurus, some people may think you set a price on love, but your values will run deeper than that. You'll learn that the true meeting of two hearts is more lasting than anything money could buy, although you will have a keen eye on love's practical side. You'll grasp only too well that if money is tight or in short supply, even the best love match can be permanently spoiled.

When everything worldly is in place, you'll be free to be yourself, and free to express love from the depths of your heart. Despite your practical nature, you truly are a romantic, and want nothing more than to be madly in love. The pleasure you'll get from partnering with someone as romantic as yourself, as the two of you explore the true extent of each other's hearts, minds, and souls, has no equal.

The one who wants to win your heart and mind should be an all-around nice person, both spontaneous and practical at the same time. You have simple tastes and just need to see that someone has a good heart, a direct way of speaking, and is even more intent on listening to every word you say. A nod, the touch of a hand, and a light kiss on the forehead will take you to seventh heaven.

The perfect lady for the 1996 Taurus male will be one who likes small pleasures such as walks in the rain or an evening spent cozied up on the living room sofa watching romantic movies. You'll like someone best who is a bit of a homebody, because that's what you are yourself, but also someone who can go over the family accounts with you to keep that part of your life orderly. She will be pretty, but it will be more vital that her beauty is more than skin deep.

The 1996 Taurus female will need a man who is all business when he's out in the world, and all Mr. Big Gushy Romantic when he's at home. A guy who knows his way around in the world and his way to your heart with surprise gifts and spontaneous love notes left around the house will make you sit up and take notice. If he is the lovey-dovey type, unafraid to show affection privately and publicly, he will just about make you swoon.

TAURUS ZODIAC SIGN
YOUR LOVE PLANETS

YOUR ROMANTIC SIDE   p. 696
▶ **VENUS IN GEMINI**
Born Apr. 19, 19:10 - May 20, 18:22

YOUR SEX DRIVE   p. 722
▶ **MARS IN ARIES**
Born Apr. 19, 19:10 - May 02, 18:15
▶ **MARS IN TAURUS**
Born May 02, 18:16 - May 20, 18:22

YOUR CELEBRITY TWINS   p. 760
Find out the astrological similarities you have with famous people.

YOUR COMPATIBILITY   p. 780
Compare planets to find out how compatible you are in a relationship.

YOUR RELATIONSHIP KARMA   p. 824
▶ **SATURN IN ARIES**
Born Apr. 19, 19:10 - May 20, 18:22

KRISTIN SCOTT-THOMAS
English Actress
Venus in Taurus

641

1996 GEMINI

From May 20, 18:23 through June 21, 2:23

The Glamour Gatherer

As you mature, you'll be attracted to glitz and style in most things, Gemini of 1996, and when it comes to love, there will be no exception. Your ideal relationship will be one that excites you and entertains you every day and in every way possible. You're not the dull homebody type, so you expect that any romantic partnership you're involved in will be on public display. Because the two of you will show off your affection, other people may be in awe of you both.

Despite this, you won't be interested in just superficial glamour, but rather the kind that comes from the truly exciting sparks that two highly interesting people can make fly when they get together. Underneath all the glitter, you'll want someone you can love deeply, someone who will love you deeply in return. If it takes time to find the perfect match who makes your life complete, you'll have all the patience in the world.

Whoever wants to win your heart must be a person of taste and style, a classy person who catches the eye of everyone when entering the room. But this person also needs to be truly interested in you, and willing to invest some time in finding out who you are and what you are all about. A warm smile, a warmer wit, and a really warm heart will finally do the trick to lure someone into your world.

If you're a 1996 Gemini male, your ideal will be a cross between a high-fashion model, a movie actress, and a romantic poet. She'll be the kind of person who seems to walk right up and grab you by the lapels just by smiling at you from across the room. If you meet a lady who makes you forget your name or what day it is before the first word is even spoken, chances are that she's the one.

The perfect man for a 1996 Gemini female is a self-confident, well-dressed male of substance and means, someone who loves to have fun and show you off out in public. At the same time, he has to have a deeply romantic and sympathetic side, and be someone willing to listen to you when you have worries, fears, or problems. He's always there for you, whether for a night out on the town, or a heart-to-heart talk.

GEMINI ZODIAC SIGN
YOUR LOVE PLANETS

YOUR ROMANTIC SIDE   p. 696
▶ **VENUS IN GEMINI**
Born May 20, 18:23 - June 21, 2:23

YOUR SEX DRIVE   p. 722
▶ **MARS IN TAURUS**
Born May 20, 18:23 - June 12, 14:41
▶ **MARS IN GEMINI**
Born June 12, 14:42 - June 21, 2:23

YOUR CELEBRITY TWINS   p. 760
Find out the astrological similarities you have with famous people.

YOUR COMPATIBILITY   p. 780
Compare planets to find out how compatible you are in a relationship.

YOUR RELATIONSHIP KARMA   p. 824
▶ **SATURN IN ARIES**
Born May 20, 18:23 - June 21, 2:23

BILLY CRUDUP
American Actor
Sun, Venus and Mars in Cancer

642

1996 CANCER *From June 21, 2:24 through July 22, 13:18*
The Flirtatious Joker

As a Cancer of 1996, you possess a youthful charm and jovial manner that tells people right up front just what kind of person you are. Those who know you recognize you from your infectious laugh, your flirtatious manner, and that faraway look in your eye. You love being the center of attention, and it makes you feel good when people warm to your charm and your wit.

Those qualities are at the top of the list of things that will attract romantic attention from others. Your positive attitude will be at the core of how you relate to another person, and you will feel that your part in a relationship is to keep your partner's spirits up, no matter what. Just as your partner can depend on you, you'll want to depend on your partner, and, more than that, you'll like the safe, secure feeling of knowing someone is always there for you.

Anyone who wants to be part of your life will have to match you word for word, joke for joke, because you'll want someone with a quick, but gentle, wit. If someone's sense of humor puts you at ease, soon the two of you will almost seem to read each other's minds. But it's the way someone takes your hand that will tell you that this person's heart is in the right place, and in the end, that is what really counts.

The female who'll make your life complete, 1996 Cancer male, has a vibrant personality and says whatever she wants to say, whenever she wants to say it. Not only will she wow all your friends, but on a physical level she will be an absolute knockout. This does not mean she has to be model thin, or dress in a spiffy manner, but she does have to have her own distinct look, one that will make you the envy of everyone who meets her.

For you, 1996 Cancer female, the male of your dreams is someone who can juggle many activities at one time, so that his professional and personal life do not intrude on each other. He is an achiever—a mover and a shaker—someone you are proud to be next to and to call your own. At the same time, he feels like a warm teddy bear when you hold him close, and when he is at your side, there is nobody else who matters.

1996 LEO *From July 22, 13:19 through August 22, 20:22*
The Loving Achiever

As a Leo of 1996, you are intent on finding your own way in life. Even when you fall flat on your face, you take great pride in picking up the pieces, sorting them out, and heading back into the fray once more. For you a relationship will be the perfect—even necessary—place for you to do that sorting.

Your perfect partner will always give you support, encouragement, and advice, whether you succeed or fail. You will not need words to let your partner know you will always be there—your warm, loving arms around your loved one's shoulders is all the assurance anyone needs. Because you are always listening to a distant drum that no one else quite hears, you'll need someone to keep you tuned in to the world around you and to help you tune that world out when it becomes necessary.

Anyone who wants to come into your life for the long haul has to be all ears from the moment the two of you meet. You love having an audience, even an audience of one, and your very special partner has to be that patient and attentive audience, even when you tell the same story once too often. Once you sense you've met a good listener with an open mind, open heart, and open arms that make you feel warm, that person is already halfway through the door to your heart.

The female who will sweep you off your feet, 1996 Leo male, wants to know everything about you and will never hesitate to listen to what is on your mind. Though she may have to pry things out of you at times, she'll know exactly how to get you to open up, even if you're not ready to talk. Someone intellectual, yet witty, kind, yet discriminating has just what you look for in a female companion.

Your Prince Charming, 1996 Leo female, is somewhat impish, yet secure in the way he looks at the world, ready and willing to stand up for what he believes in. Compassionate and unselfish, he will sacrifice almost anything for those he loves. This perfect someone supports you in spirit, helps you around the house and, most important for you, is physically warm and exciting, making you content in a way nothing else ever can.

1996 VIRGO

From August 22, 20:23 through September 22, 17:59

The Rosy Romantic

As a Virgo of 1996, you'll enter adulthood with a blend of responsibility, and yet be known to your friends as happy-go-lucky and oodles of fun. You will tend to see the world through rose-colored glasses, and you'll always be upbeat and optimistic that life will turn out fine. You'll have the same positive view of relationships, but you'll also see them as a way to balance your cheerful outlook with a dose of reality. And you'd like to count on your partner to do that for you.

A loving relationship will bring you together with someone who can be your soul mate, your helpmate, and your friend at the very same time. Included in that package is someone who will warm you when you are cold, and whose soft hands hold your hands in a firm, protective, yet loving clasp.

Someone who is really healthy and very physically fit will turn you on like nobody else, because you instinctively know you share in common your love of the outdoors. Once you have met your physical match, you will be completely under his or her spell, especially if a

love of music is thrown in as an added passion. Your tastes may be at opposite ends, but the responses that music ignites will lure you straight into this person's heart forever.

Your type of female, Virgo male of 1996, will let you know right up front who she is and what it is she wants out of life. She will find you the most attractive guy in the world and is the first to claim you as her own. This woman will fight for you, and once she knows that you will fight right back for her, she'll be in your corner every step of the way. You are her Adonis, so she listens to your every word and will have eyes only for you.

Your ideal male, Virgo female of 1996, will be someone who is cute, cuddly, and shy enough that it becomes part of his overall charm, yet he definitely knows how to assert himself in a strong manner. He has a remarkable sense of timing, and when he needs to take control, his hypnotic eyes can lure you wherever he wants to go. That strength, along with his spontaneity and his seductive charm, will truly make him the one for you.

VIRGO ZODIAC SIGN
YOUR LOVE PLANETS

YOUR ROMANTIC SIDE   p. 696
▶ **VENUS IN CANCER**
Born Aug. 22, 20:23 - Sept. 07, 5:06
▶ **VENUS IN LEO**
Born Sept. 07, 5:07 - Sept. 22, 17:59

YOUR SEX DRIVE   p. 722
▶ **MARS IN CANCER**
Born Aug. 22, 20:23 - Sept. 09, 20:01
▶ **MARS IN LEO**
Born Sept. 09, 20:02 - Sept. 22, 17:59

YOUR CELEBRITY TWINS   p. 760
Find out the astrological similarities you have with famous people.

YOUR COMPATIBILITY   p. 780
Compare planets to find out how compatible you are in a relationship.

YOUR RELATIONSHIP KARMA   p. 824
▶ **SATURN IN ARIES**
Born Aug. 22, 20:23 - Sept. 22, 17:59

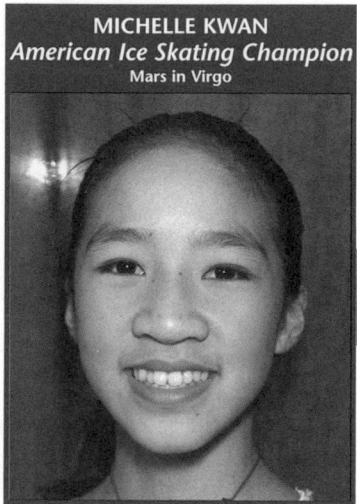

MICHELLE KWAN
American Ice Skating Champion
Mars in Virgo

643

1996 LIBRA

From September 22, 18:00 through October 23, 3:18

The Soft Touch

For you, Libra of 1996, relationships are a journey through time, where you can explore your past, enjoy the present, and plan for a wonderful future—which you know you would never find on your own. Caring, loving, yet a touch insecure, you will come to feel that life lived alone is only half a life. You'll do so much better with someone at your side, who can fill in all the gaps in your life.

You'll always look forward to seeing your partner at the end of the day, and you'll be thinking about this person throughout the day. When you are alone together, you won't be able to think of anything sweeter than the love you both share. The more hours you live that love, exchanging looks, trading passionate kisses, the better you will feel about having found your true soul mate.

You are one of the most feeling people around, and you'll be able to tell instantly if someone will stay in your life by the way that person takes your hand the first time you meet. A soft, yet firm touch lets you know that there is the right combination of

sensitivity and self-confidence, two qualities that are a must in your book. If the hands feel right, then you know that a sense of humor, a warm personality, and a caring heart are part of the package.

For the male Libra of 1996, there will be nothing more enticing than a woman who has her own sense of flair and a unique personality. You won't even mind if she is a bit outspoken, since that is part of her charm. Two things that make this woman unmistakably yours are her creative talents and her sharp mind, a unique combination that means she is so special, you could not stand to pass her up.

The man who wins your heart, Libra female of 1996, has a character all his own, and yet still conforms to good old-fashioned values such as earning a good living, providing for his family, and, most important, being completely honest. This is a fellow you will always be proud of. Other than that, you still want someone who could have stepped out of the "age of chivalry" and always makes you feel like a princess whose dashing prince has finally arrived.

LIBRA ZODIAC SIGN
YOUR LOVE PLANETS

YOUR ROMANTIC SIDE   p. 696
▶ **VENUS IN LEO**
Born Sept. 22, 18:00 - Oct. 04, 3:21
▶ **VENUS IN VIRGO**
Born Oct. 04, 3:22 - Oct. 23, 3:18

YOUR SEX DRIVE   p. 722
▶ **MARS IN LEO**
Born Sept. 22, 18:00 - Oct. 23, 3:18

YOUR CELEBRITY TWINS   p. 760
Find out the astrological similarities you have with famous people.

YOUR COMPATIBILITY   p. 780
Compare planets to find out how compatible you are in a relationship.

YOUR RELATIONSHIP KARMA   p. 824
▶ **SATURN IN ARIES**
Born Sept. 22, 18:00 - Oct. 23, 3:18

RALPH FIENNES
English Actor
Venus in Scorpio

1996 SCORPIO
From October 23, 3:19 through November 22, 0:48

♏ *The Passionate Poet*

You just love initiating dramatic situations, Scorpio of 1996, and the more intense and spectacular your relationships are, the more attractive they will be for you. If your connection does not have the drama and passion of a panoramic love story on the silver screen, then it will remain second-rate in your eyes. While that may place a lot of pressure on your partner to be extroverted all the time, it also means that neither of you will ever let your life together be dull or boring.

For you, the world itself is a creative stage, and you see your relationship as a means to take advantage of all that life offers. You just love immersing yourself in concerts, movies, and live performances, but it will mean a whole lot more when you have a partner with whom you can enjoy everything, since the excitement of each wonderful event lives on as a shared memory.

If that special someone wants to be part of your world, there must be eye-to-eye contact the moment you meet. Anyone who is shy, anyone who cannot meet the world head-on, need not even apply. You are a strong personality, and you will need someone with an even stronger one to share center stage. Once you know you've found the person who can match you, the real fun can begin.

Your favorite female type, Scorpio male of 1996, should be an impeccable dresser and look absolutely fabulous, whether the two of you are attending a formal affair or going hiking in the woods. Good looks are a real turn-on to you, and the woman who feels just as warm and cuddly as her enticing appearance might imply is the one who will get to you every time. What will make this match-up permanent is that she will always stand by you, no matter what happens.

For you, Scorpio female of 1996, a man who has a keen intellect combined with a creative spirit will be most fascinating to you. You want someone who has the feverish creative soul of a poet, someone who loves to recite love sonnets, and perhaps even compose some especially for you. The sound of his lilting voice, just the thought of his lips on yours, will send shivers up and down your spine.

1996 SAGITTARIUS
From November 22, 0:49 through December 21, 14:05

♐ *The Inspiring Transformer*

Inspiring, enthusiastic, and adventurous, you, Sagittarius of 1996, will always know exactly what you want in life, from career goals to the perfect partner. And even if the person who wins your heart in the end doesn't fit your preconceived image, you will try to see perfection nonetheless. Turning lemons into lemonade is your trademark, and you see your relationships as great challenges, where any challenge can be met, and conquered.

You would love nothing more than transforming fearful, lazy couch potatoes into adventurous athletes, and turning film fanatics into opera or ballet aficionados. For you relationships are two people who are completely interested in one another's lives, and just as you want to introduce the person you spend your time with to everything you are passionate about, you also want to immerse yourself in what interests your partner.

The person who will weave inroads into your life must be open-minded and eager to try new things. If the one you are with goes to an exotic restaurant and orders the strangest dish on the menu, you know that person definitely has a chance with you. Even more important is that your beloved must truly be interested in what you have to say and willing to respect your opinions, whether agreed with or not.

Women who are passionate, talkative, and physically active are the ones who will make your heart skip a beat, Sagittarius male of 1996. The moment your ideal woman walks through the door, your body will start to tingle, you'll feel a little dizzy, and you won't be able to refrain from kissing and hugging her. You'll know she is yours, if she is intuitive and responds to all those signs in exactly the way you wish she would.

The man who will complete your life, Sagittarius female of 1996, is someone who is a little bit restless, very intellectual, and has a heart of gold. Once you turn your attention to him, that nervous energy will suddenly transform into passion from which there is no turning back. This is a man who will trust you implicitly, and that in itself makes you feel as if you are on top of the world.

'90s

Hugh and Liz – True Friendship

When Jay Leno asked Hugh Grant on his *Tonight Show* "What were you thinking?" he was asking the question that the world wanted to know. It reflected everyone's amazement at the news that Grant had been arrested a month earlier, charged with soliciting oral sex with Hollywood hooker Divine Brown. In subsequent personal appearances on other popular shows, the good-looking and affable Grant apologized for his mistake, turning a potential public relations nightmare into a manageable cause célèbre.

The general feeling of astonishment was occasioned by the fact that Grant was engaged to one of the world's great beauties, actress-model Elizabeth Hurley. Though she had been in a few films, Hurley was largely unknown until she appeared at the London premiere of *Four Weddings and a Funeral* on the arm of Hugh Grant. The beautiful Hurley was provocatively attired in a black Versace gown with the side seams completely split and held together by safety pins. Soon afterwards she signed an exclusive modeling contract with Estee Lauder. Grant's arrest and the publicity surrounding it catapulted her into even greater prominence. He told the press, "She's been very supportive and we're going to try to work it out."

Which they apparently did, because despite the public embarrassment her fiancé's sexual faux pas caused her, Elizabeth Hurley stuck by him. The couple even followed through on plans to launch a film production company together, Simian Films. Later that year Hurley produced and Grant starred in the psychological thriller *Extreme Measures*. For a while it looked as if the two would eventually marry.

It's no surprise that the couple managed to combine romance, friendship, and a working relationship. He is a communicative Virgo while she is a talkative Gemini. The fact that he has Mars in Gemini and she has Mars in Virgo suggests a strong bond.

Proving that she could be funny as well as sexy, Elizabeth starred as the "shagelicious" Vanessa Kensington in *Austin Powers: International Man of Mystery* (1997) and as the Devil incarnate in *Bedazzled*. In 1999 she tried her hand at producing once again with *Mickey Blue Eyes*, starring fiancé Hugh Grant.

The couple continued to be seen together for the next few years, but by May 2000 they ended their thirteen-year relationship. Although rumors circulated about new romantic interests for both Grant and Hurley, all the couple would say was that the relationship had ended amicably and they remained "friendly."

In 2001, Hurley announced she was pregnant, asserting that the father was Hollywood producer Stephen Bing. He refuted her claim that the two of them had an "exclusive" relationship and demanded a DNA test to prove paternity. When the results showed he was the father, he apologized to Hurley through the press and offered her child support, which she refused, saying it was "not wanted or welcome." Her son

Damian was born in April 2002.

Despite having gone their separate ways, Grant and Hurley remain close friends. When a popular British magazine misquoted her, saying that Grant was "less than adequate in bed," the actress retaliated by insisting she'd never made such a remark. "I have never said anything mean about him and I never would because I truly love him."

Still a bachelor, Grant has talked about giving up acting and settling down to married life—if he can find the right woman.

▶ READ ABOUT ROD STEWART AND ALANA HAMILTON ON PAGE 498

1997

- ⍟ **ELLEN COMES OUT**
- ⍟ **PRINCESS DIANA DIES**
- ⍟ **HOW DO I LIVE**
- ⍟ **WANNABE**
- ⍟ **JEWEL**
- ⍟ **THE FULL MONTY**
- ⍟ **MEMOIRS OF A GEISHA**

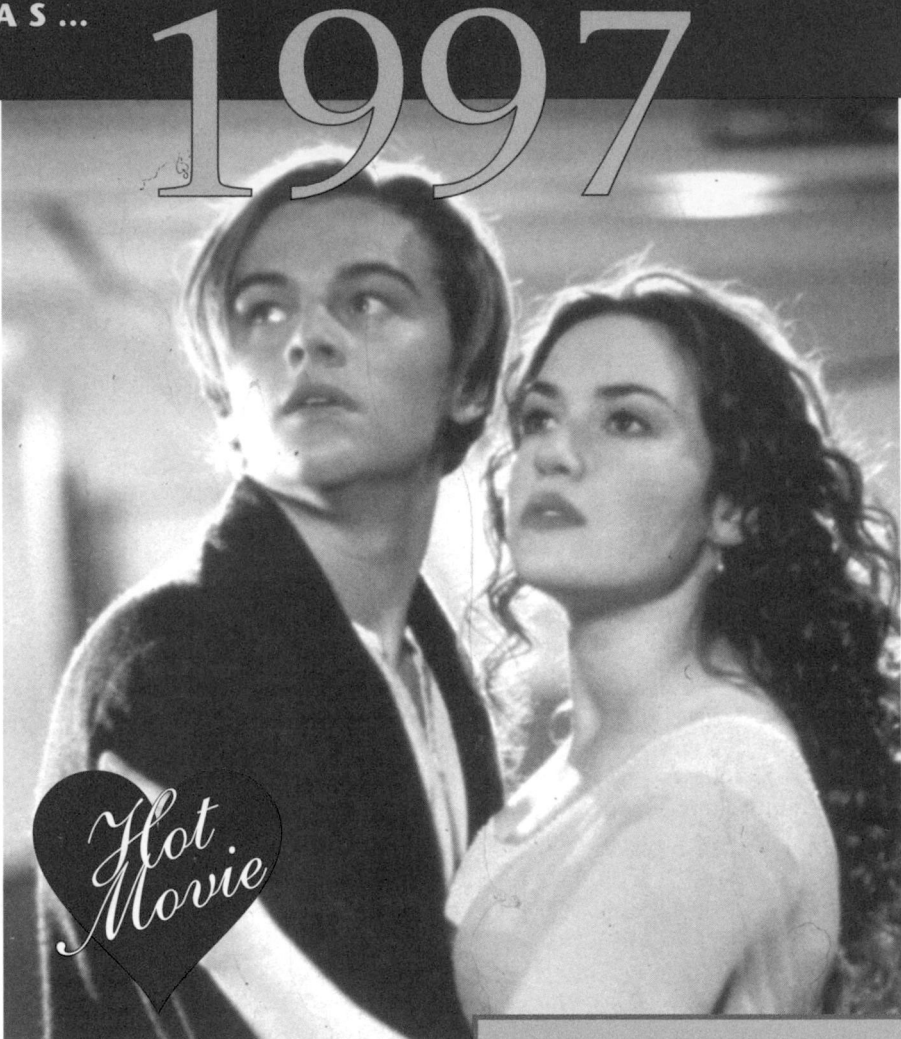

Hot Movie

EVENTS

New triple-drug combination therapy proved successful in reducing levels of HIV in infected patients. Bobbi McCaughey gave birth to the first living septuplets, conceived with fertility drugs. On US television comedienne Ellen DeGeneres outed herself—and her sitcom character, Ellen. Television sportscaster Marv Albert was fired from NBC amidst a tawdry sex scandal. Michael Jackson and wife Debbie Rowe named their son Prince Michael Junior (and later, their second son became Prince Michael II). Steamy honeymoon videos of *Baywatch* star Pamela Anderson and husband Tommy Lee appeared all over the Internet. Designer Gianni Versace was murdered in Miami. Princess Diana died in a car accident in Paris.

POP CULTURE

Country cutie LeAnn Rimes' "How Do I Live" topped the charts. Toni Braxton pleaded "Unbreak My Heart." Puff Daddy boasted "Can't Nobody Hold Me Down." R. Kelly's monster hit was "I Believe I Can Fly." Britain's Spice Girls sang "Wannabe," and newcomer Jewel sang "You Were Meant for Me."

Titanic, written and directed by James Cameron, recounted a tale of forbidden love aboard the doomed ship. In P.J. Hogan's *My Best Friend's Wedding*, Julia Roberts goes to extreme lengths to sabotage her ex-lover's wedding. In *The Full Monty*,

six unemployed steelworkers put a striptease act together—although they can't dance, aren't handsome, and get arrested for indecency before their triumphant one-night gig. In Ang Lee's *The Ice Storm*, narcissism and debauchery beget tragedy for two suburban Connecticut families. In *The Wings of the Dove*, based on the Henry James novel, a turn-of-the-century British woman concocts a scheme for her penniless lover to marry a dying heiress. *The Sweet Hereafter*, directed by Atom Egoyan and based on Russell Banks' novel, chronicled how a school bus accident rips apart a small Canadian town.

In Sidney Sheldon's *The Best Laid Plans*, a spurned lover later uses her media empire to wreak vengeance on the now-President. In Arthur S. Golden's *Memoirs of a Geisha*, Chiyo rises above abuse and malevolent competitors to the pinnacle of geisha society, even as that whole world collapses in the wake of World War II.

TITANIC

They claimed it was unsinkable. The survivor on Hollywood's *Titanic* was true love. A 1912 Romeo and Juliet, Rose (Kate Winslet) and Jack (Leonardo DiCaprio) were doomed lovers right from the start. Jack was a stowaway, a free-spirited gypsy soul who fell instantly in love with the fair-skinned and blue-blooded Rose.

An iceberg in the Atlantic would signal the end to their steamy, intense love affair. The *Titanic's* fate was sealed in the deep reaches of the sea, and so was Rose and Jack's "happily ever after." He gave up his life so that she could live. And their love lived on.

SEE ALSO

▶ **THE COMING OF AGE** *Page 12*

▶ **KURT COBAIN** *Page 621*

▶ **JOHN AND YOKO** *Page 423*

1997 CAPRICORN

From December 21, 1996 14:06 through January 20, 1997 0:41
(December 1997 Capricorns, see 1998 Capricorn)

The Spiritual Pragmatist

As you mature, Capricorn of 1997, you will blossom into someone who is spiritual yet pragmatic, artistic yet frugal. Anyone with whom you will eventually share good and bad times might be in for a roller coaster ride—but a pleasant one at that. You'll be able to talk about your hopes for earning money one minute, and then declare your love an hour later.

In a relationship you will come to feel comfortable revealing your many facets, producing an air of romantic excitement and spontaneity that is likely to intrigue the lucky person who shares your life. You want a partner who can offer support and, when need be, a seal of approval in the form of a kiss and hug. You believe in going for everything life offers, and though you will learn to take the bitter with the sweet, you'll expect that the sweet part will prevail in the end.

You are a believer in honesty and the basic goodness of people, and you'll be able to tell in a flash from the way someone looks you straight in the eye whether or not you've found a person whose values and integrity suit your own. Someone who makes you giggle when you least expect it, even when you are in a serious mood, gets your attention every time. Anyone who has the right values, makes you laugh, and also enjoys spiritual pursuits could easily sweep you off your feet.

The woman who will eventually make your life complete, Capricorn male of 1997, is someone who is athletic, physically fit, and loves doing anything that keeps her outside. Unusual and challenging physical activities such as bungee jumping or rock climbing may not be things you would attempt, but you'll be in awe of a partner who does these things on her own.

Your future soul mate, Capricorn female of 1997, is enterprising and relentless when it comes to succeeding in his chosen field. This man will be ambitious and a leader, and will have enough self-confidence to go back for more if he happens to lose a round in the game of life. At home, though, he will be a soft touch and a gentle soul who leaves his ego in the marketplace and gives all his attention to you at home.

CAPRICORN ZODIAC SIGN
YOUR LOVE PLANETS

YOUR ROMANTIC SIDE   p. 696
► **VENUS IN SAGITTARIUS**
Born Dec. 21, 1996 14:06 - Jan. 10, 1997 5:31
► **VENUS IN CAPRICORN**
Born Jan. 10, 5:32 - Jan. 20, 0:42

YOUR SEX DRIVE   p. 722
► **MARS IN VIRGO**
Born Dec. 21, 1996 14:06 - Jan. 03, 1997 8:09
► **MARS IN LIBRA**
Born Jan. 03, 8:10 - Jan. 20, 0:42

YOUR CELEBRITY TWINS   p. 760
Find out the astrological similarities you have with famous people.

YOUR COMPATIBILITY   p. 780
Compare planets to find out how compatible you are in a relationship.

YOUR RELATIONSHIP KARMA   p. 824
► **SATURN IN ARIES**
Born Dec. 21, 1996 14:06 - Jan. 20, 1997 0:42

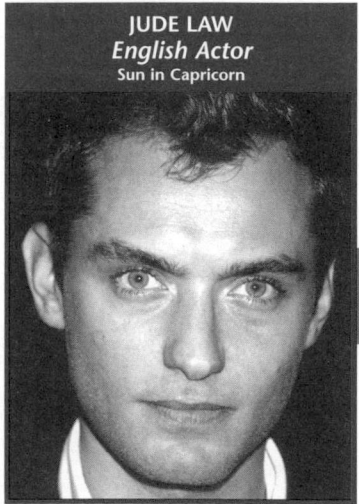

JUDE LAW
English Actor
Sun in Capricorn

647

1997 AQUARIUS

From January 20, 0:43 through February 18, 14:51

The Humanitarian Lover

Those who will come to know you well, Aquarius of 1997, will probably agree that your most endearing quality is your true belief that love conquers all, and that nothing in your wildest dreams will equal the feeling of your beloved's arms around you. For you a harmonious relationship will be one that will make you a happier, more productive human being. You'll sincerely believe that, as long as the feelings you both share run as deep as the ocean, your relationship will survive rough waters.

As you go through life, you will view partnerships as a place to grow and change through experiencing compassion and love. You and your mate will see yourselves as a clinging vine with your arms entwined around each other in both friendship and in affection. The deep feeling you are able to experience with your partner may even make the two of you the envy of others.

Anyone wishing to be part of your life will have to make you laugh from the moment you meet. You will always be grateful to those who can put you in a lighthearted mood, and they will find their way into your heart easily. People who are generous will also be attractive, and the more someone wants to give to you and to others, the more you will want to take that person into your own heart.

The female who will change your life, 1997 Aquarius male, loves children, animals, and anyone who needs her tender, loving care. Aside from her good nature, she will be smart, organized, and want nothing more than to plan a future with someone who thinks as she does. When this woman takes you in her arms, you will feel as if your troubles are a thing of the past and the future lies brightly ahead.

For you, 1997 Aquarius female, the male in your life will be comforting yet independent. He may look like a hunky body builder, a type you like, but underneath his muscular appearance will lie a heart as gentle as a summer breeze. This dreamboat is quite athletic, and does not enjoy being idle for too long. He can get you moving when you want to take it easy, and he is like a cuddly teddy bear when you fall into his arms at night.

AQUARIUS ZODIAC SIGN
YOUR LOVE PLANETS

YOUR ROMANTIC SIDE   p. 696
► **VENUS IN CAPRICORN**
Born Jan. 20, 0:43 - Feb. 03, 4:27
► **VENUS IN AQUARIUS**
Born Feb. 03, 4:28 - Feb. 18, 14:51

YOUR SEX DRIVE   p. 722
► **MARS IN LIBRA**
Born Jan. 20, 0:43 - Feb. 18, 14:51

YOUR CELEBRITY TWINS   p. 760
Find out the astrological similarities you have with famous people.

YOUR COMPATIBILITY   p. 780
Compare planets to find out how compatible you are in a relationship.

YOUR RELATIONSHIP KARMA   p. 824
► **SATURN IN ARIES**
Born Jan. 20, 0:43 - Feb. 18, 14:51

RUSSELL CROWE
Australian Actor
Sun in Aries

648

1997 PISCES
From February 18, 14:52 through March 20, 13:54

The Rainbow Seeker

As you mature into a sensitive, creative adult, Pisces of 1997, you may go through numerous relationships before you find that pot of gold at the end of the rainbow. You may travel far and wide to experience life to the fullest. Along the way you'll meet many different types so you can eliminate what you don't want, and be sure of what you do.

Once you do notice that special person, you may be quite assertive to woo that person into your life. For you relationships will be a means for you to be forthright, sometimes in contradiction to that demure side of you that most people will come to know and love. Your ideal partner will know how to temper your moods, perhaps able to give you a prearranged signal telling you to retreat, or letting you know with understanding nods that the time is right to be direct.

For someone to attract you, your beloved will need to think hot chocolates in winter and tall lemonades in summer. You will be most drawn to someone whose body is muscular, yet shapely, and whose skin reflects that this person loves being outside, but is sensible enough to stay out of the sun. Your biggest turn-on will be someone who is both physically and emotionally healthy, who is not afraid to show you and the rest of the world how he or she feels with affectionate hugs and kisses.

Your ideal partner, Pisces male of 1997, will be a combination of soft femininity and savvy know-how. She will be gentle, warm, and will love meeting new people all the time. You will be proud when you are with her, because people love her jovial manner and how interested she truly is in what other people say. Mostly, you just love how she is interested in you, and the way she lightly kisses you tells you so.

When the perfect male slips into your life, Pisces female of 1997, you will know him by his strong presence, the way he takes the lead and makes decisions for you. At other times, he will instinctively know when to be chivalrous and let you take the starring role. He will be an equal opportunity lover, and sharing everything is what he will promise you for the rest of your life.

1997 ARIES
From March 20, 13:55 through April 20, 1:02

The Attractive Extrovert

Headstrong and passionate as a child, you, Aries of 1997, will continue to take life by the horns as you continue into adulthood. As with everything else in life, when love comes calling, you'll always go with that warm, fuzzy feeling in your heart, even when your mind tells you to move slowly. You will always follow your instincts because they will usually take you to the right places.

For you relationships will be formed first on the basis of deep attraction, as eyes meet eyes with longing stares. Soon, your conversations will begin to mesh so that you can actually end each other's sentences. At that point, you will know that you have not merely found a friend, but a confidante, and not merely a sweetheart, but someone with whom you can spend the rest of your life.

Anyone who might want to grab your attention will need to share your very eclectic interests, which might run the gamut from taking spontaneous weekend trips to traveling halfway around the world to exotic locales. You will love the person who gets excited about planning future activities and who loves ice skating in winter and swimming in summer. Anyone whose athleticism matches yours will be someone with whom you can't wait to exchange kisses and cuddles.

A female who is extroverted, yet not competitive, bubbly, yet serious when she needs to be, is the one who will excite your heart and mind most, 1997 Aries male. As you mature, you will appreciate someone with those qualities plus great looks and an even finer mind. She should be sharp as a tack and discerning about people, able to distinguish the genuine from the phony types at a glance.

When you visualize your perfect guy, 1997 Aries female, he will be someone who has the practical side of life covered, and—unromantic as it may seem—can fix things (such as cars and computers) with ease and skill. On a more fanciful note, he will cheer you up when you are down, and will have endless surprises up his sleeve, the better to keep you entertained. Just the touch of his hand on your face and that warm, protective embrace will make you feel as if you're in heaven.

1997 TAURUS

From April 20, 1:03 through May 21, 0:17

The Accommodating Suitor

Accommodating and down to earth, you, Taurus of 1997, will probably spend your formative years learning to help others as well as making other people feel good about themselves. That is just the kind of all-around nice person you are, and as you mature that trait will make someone special realize what a great "catch" you are.

When looking into your eyes, your partner will see beauty reflected there, and in return that will make your beloved want to do anything to make life wonderful for you. The thoughtful things each of you will do for the other will make your relationship different from other, more ordinary ones. You will feel that the point of two people being together is to be totally involved and totally committed.

Someone who wants to make a lasting impression on you will have to have a very common-sense attitude toward life, mixed with idealistic plans for the future. This person will need to speak plainly but thoughtfully and with great sensitivity to others—someone who is direct, abrasive, or self-involved will turn you off. The one who will want your heart will not be afraid to touch you when speaking to you, and the body language will be as warm and as open as is the heart.

The female who will claim that special place in your life, 1997 Taurus male, will love art, music, and most anything that is aesthetically pleasing to the senses. That quality alone will show you have a lot in common with this girl, so you will never have to worry about becoming restless or bored with one another. She will be soft-spoken, will have infinite patience, and will always think positively. She'll teach you to do the same.

You, 1997 Taurus female, will want your male partner to have boundless energy, so he can be the perfect companion and role model, someone who will get you outside into the sunshine when you feel like holing up inside. When it's rainy, your future mate will find nothing more romantic than curling up with you on the sofa, perhaps in front of a warm fire, to read books you both enjoy or to watch a romantic movie—which, for sure, will put you in the mood for love.

KATE WINSLET
English Actress
Mars in Gemini

649

1997 GEMINI

From May 21, 0:18 through June 21, 8:19

The Inspiring Raconteur

You have many inspirational qualities that will stay with you as you move into adulthood, Gemini of 1997, especially in creative areas such as art and music. You will always attract others who have such talents and who will share your love of the finer things in life. For you a relationship will be a means of building a dream with someone else who shares both your interests and deepest aspirations.

You will want your future partner to help you create a place where you are free to continue dreaming—and to follow a path toward that dream without being daunted by distractions you might encounter along the way. In your mind partners should always be there to support each other's efforts, even when plans and dreams do not turn out as you expect.

You will not be that difficult to please, so the person who wants to be part of your life will simply need to look into your eyes, smile, and listen sincerely and intently to what you have to say. A kiss and hug of approval will also go a long way with you. The smile and the hugs will need to be authentic, though, as the biggest turn-off for you is the dishonesty of doing things simply to get a reaction.

Being empathetic to those less fortunate, coupled with intellectual depth and sensitivity, are qualities you will find most attractive in a female, Gemini male of 1997. If she is an artist or musician or at least responds to the same type of music you do, she surely is going to win your heart. You will know she's in sync with you if she's unafraid to show affection spontaneously, whether in public or when the two of you are alone.

The male who will make your heart do flip-flops, Gemini female of 1997, will be kind, considerate, and sensitive to what you need most, and without your ever having to ask for it.

You'd like someone who can be the life of the party, and who will fit comfortably into any scene. When the two of you are alone, he will put his arms around you when you least expect it. Saying "I love you" will be something he will not have to think twice about, and you will be happy to hear him say it over and over again.

J.K. ROWLING
English Writer
Sun in Leo

1997 CANCER
From June 21, 8:20 through July 22, 19:14

♋ *The Idealistic Partner*

You will never be known as a practical person, Cancer of 1997, and even as you grow up, you tend to be idealistic about the world situation and about love. You will probably idealize anyone you have a crush on, and you will view any partner as a cut above everyone else. This is a good thing, because love often leads to looking past our partner's imperfections to the good inside. Thus, you innately understand something important about being in love that so many others spend a lifetime learning.

At the same time, you will also see problems and imperfections, but your goal will always be to help smooth those things out and make them better. This is, in fact, what you hope the perfect partnership can do—always make everything right.

The best thing those who want to interest you can do is to be themselves. You will not be the type who cares for pretentious people or hoity-toity attitudes about life. You love all things that are down-to-earth, and because of that, you'll always steer clear of partners who you feel are hiding their hearts. You will really look for someone who laughs a lot and can engage you one to one in open, friendly, and heartfelt conversation.

If you're a 1997 Cancer male, you will want a female who is open and honest, and who likes to do the same things you like to do. Though you are someone who enjoys solitary activities such as writing, Internet surfing, or playing music, you still will want someone who can share nearly everything with you. From long walks on the beach—holding hands of course—to spending a day just hanging around the house, you will feel that all of those moments are better when they're done together.

For the 1997 Cancer female, the perfect guy stands out from the crowd because, even though he may like sports and going out with his friends, he'll primarily be interested in you. Those other things are just diversions, while the time he spends with you will complete his life. You will never have to wonder where you stand with him—he will always tell you what's on his mind. And where you're concerned, what's on his mind is always good.

1997 LEO
From July 22, 19:15 through August 23, 2:18

♌ *The Horizon Searcher*

As you move toward adulthood, you, Leo of 1997, will discover that there are very few people whose views on love and romance match your own. You look forward to finding love that fills that soft, mushy place in your heart, as well as something that broadens your horizons. Being with another person opens your eyes and helps you to see much further than you ever could alone.

You will never want to waste time when it comes to this very important part of your life. You may even hold off becoming involved until you finish your education and are sure that you've found someone who is a good match for you and your interests. You'll want to choose someone who actually finds it exhilarating discussing everything from rock music to politics. When you find the right person, you'll be truly committed and as faithful as anyone could be.

If someone wants to win your heart, then the key will be to reach both your mind and your heart. Sensitivity and a deep caring nature will get your attention more than anything else, but what really matters is an interest in learning and culture, just for its own sake. Whether you are brought up in a small town or big city, you will come to feel that the world has much more to offer than you can see by yourself, so anyone who can take you outside of yourself and your world will fascinate you.

The 1997 Leo male most wants to be with a female who sees love and marriage as a kind of journey made by two people, a journey in which the sky is the limit. You really like someone who can be cuddly, for sure, but who also loves to travel and to read and, more than anything else, to do these things with you. Life with her will be so much of an adventure that each and every day will be an exciting and breathtaking experience, never boring.

For the 1997 Leo female, the right fellow will be a restless type, someone who is always looking over the next horizon. He will have big dreams and the capacity for making those big dreams realities. With you at his side he will surely have the right formula for making those dreams—which include you—come true.

1997 VIRGO

From August 23, 2:19 through September 22, 23:55

The Misty Romantic

As skilled as you will be talking in detail about a variety of subjects, Virgo of 1997, you will be equally modest and shy when expressing your feelings to others. Wrapped up in your world of computers and other mental pursuits, you may get so used to being the brainy one you might actually forget how charming you actually are and how attractive you might be to the opposite sex. Though you will tend to be practical about matters of the heart, wanting everything in place before giving yourself to someone else, you will definitely be convinced otherwise when the right person comes along.

Your emotions run as deep as anyone else's, and for you, the perfect relationship, the one you dream about, will be with someone who helps you put your thinking mind to rest. This special someone will also get you excited about taking vacations together, where you can lie in the sun and cuddle on the beach, or warm each other by the fire after attacking the ski slopes.

If someone wants to grab your eye and win your heart, the way to do so will be to appeal to your romantic soul. Anyone who has a misty look combined with a friendly manner will get your attention in a minute; you may be slow to commit, but you're quickly intrigued and will come back for more. Combine that misty romanticism with a good mind and a warm heart, and you may not be able to resist.

If you're a 1997 Virgo male, you will love a gal who is entirely your opposite in many ways. Because you are practical, you will want someone whimsical, who will take your hand in hers, and lead you on an unknown adventure. You want a woman whose hand you can hold during a romantic walk, and who will read love poetry with you by a warm winter fire.

As a 1997 Virgo female, you'd really like to find someone who can support you in style, so you are not pressured to earn lots of money. Someone financially well off, or at least ambitious enough so that a secure future is guaranteed, will open the door. To stay permanently he must not worry too much about the future—leaving the two of you free to cuddle in your warm little love nest.

VIRGO ZODIAC SIGN
YOUR LOVE PLANETS

YOUR ROMANTIC SIDE   p. 696
> **VENUS IN LIBRA**
Born Aug. 23, 2:19 - Sept. 12, 2:16
> **VENUS IN SCORPIO**
Born Sept. 12, 2:17 - Sept. 22, 23:55

YOUR SEX DRIVE   p. 722
> **MARS IN SCORPIO**
Born Aug. 23, 2:19 - Sept. 22, 23:55

YOUR CELEBRITY TWINS   p. 760
Find out the astrological similarities you have with famous people.

YOUR COMPATIBILITY   p. 780
Compare planets to find out how compatible you are in a relationship.

YOUR RELATIONSHIP KARMA   p. 824
> **SATURN IN ARIES**
Born Aug. 23, 2:19 - Sept. 22, 23:55

MARTINA HINGIS
Swiss Tennis Champion
Sun in Libra

651

1997 LIBRA

From September 22, 23:56 through October 23, 9:14

The Gift Giver

As a child, Libra of 1997, you've probably always made a habit of breaking open your piggy bank to buy birthday presents for those you love. Reaching adulthood will increase your generosity—you have a weak spot for anyone you feel strongly about. When you fall in love you might just spend and spend on your partner. This comes from your truly generous and thoughtful nature, and if you wind up with someone more frugal than yourself, you will use your originality to surprise your partner with trinkets less expensive, but directly from the heart.

Your ultimate goal will not be to spend money as such, but rather to make someone you love feel good with little surprises. When you become romantically involved, you will probably continue to do what you did as a child—always looking for little things to give, little gestures to make that person's day just a little brighter.

Someone who wishes to attract your attention can also give you little presents, because you like to receive as much as you like to give. Besides that, you will want someone in your life who's generous of heart and mind, someone who's very thoughtful, good-hearted, and puts others before self. These are qualities you value in anyone, and certainly in the person you might be inclined to love.

You do have a perfect female in mind, 1997 Libra male, and though she might be the quiet type who attracts little attention, she will have every bit of yours and you will have every bit of hers. She will be both a romantic and a homebody, and she will like nothing better than feathering the love nest that the two of you build for each other. She won't need to be included in everything you do, as long as you let her know she's at the heart of your heart.

As a 1997 Libra female, the male who will attract your attention will prefer to be with you rather than without you, as he will love nothing more than talking to you, cuddling with you, and generally experiencing life together with you. Despite this, he will understand that you need your quiet time alone, and he'll have no problem making sure you get what you need.

LIBRA ZODIAC SIGN
YOUR LOVE PLANETS

YOUR ROMANTIC SIDE   p. 696
> **VENUS IN SCORPIO**
Born Sept. 22, 23:56 - Oct. 08, 8:24
> **VENUS IN SAGITTARIUS**
Born Oct. 08, 8:25 - Oct. 23, 9:14

YOUR SEX DRIVE   p. 722
> **MARS IN SCORPIO**
Born Sept. 22, 23:56 - Sept. 28, 22:21
> **MARS IN SAGITTARIUS**
Born Sept. 28, 22:22 - Oct. 23, 9:14

YOUR CELEBRITY TWINS   p. 760
Find out the astrological similarities you have with famous people.

YOUR COMPATIBILITY   p. 780
Compare planets to find out how compatible you are in a relationship.

YOUR RELATIONSHIP KARMA   p. 824
> **SATURN IN ARIES**
Born Sept. 22, 23:56 - Oct. 23, 9:14

ROBERTO BENIGNI
Italian Actor
Sun in Scorpio

1997 SCORPIO
From October 23, 9:15 through November 22, 6:47

♏

The Warm Teaser

Competitive and sensitive, your view of relationships, Scorpio of 1997, will likely be an interesting one. You tend to see love, or even friendship, between two people as a kind of contest, a challenge that, after all is said and done, will bring out the best in both of you. As you mature, you will probably be attracted to people with whom you can verbally spar, even when you disagree, and after the conversation is over, kiss and hug as two people should who are fond of, and even in love with, each other.

You're the type who may be considered a bit of tease with people you care for, though this is always done with a twinkle in your eye. In turn, you welcome being teased back—but ever so lightly, with humor and with love. You will never hesitate to let those you love know how you really feel deep down. You are a really good companion, and will come to be very attentive in love.

Someone who wants to attract you and to win your heart will need to have a good sense of humor, a ready wit, and a laugh that makes others want to laugh, too. Along with that will come a good understanding of when to be funny and when to be serious. When that serious time comes, you want to be around someone who can listen to you and bring a smile to your face just by caring.

As a 1997 Scorpio male, your ideal will center on a girl who is not only funny, but also fun, and the kind you'll be proud to be seen with in public. It will help if she's a sharp dresser and a looker, but these things won't mean much unless the sense of humor and the ability to have fun are there. And there will be no one who is warmer and more affectionate when the two of you are together—she will find you irresistible.

For the 1997 Scorpio female, the man you want is the handsome fellow who can tell a story that suits almost any occasion—without ever repeating himself. He will never let your life be boring, and will always be there to share your joys and to cheer you up when you're down. He is the kind of guy that every woman at the party wishes was hers. A warm smile, a warm hug, and a warm word. That's him in a nutshell.

1997 SAGITTARIUS
From November 22, 6:48 through December 21, 20:06

♐

The Infatuated Intellect

As you mature, your serious side will emerge—and will get you to the top of your class, Sagittarius of 1997. When it comes to falling in love, you will probably get all giddy and lose complete control—but in a very good way. Romance of the head over heels variety will likely come easily to you, and you may find yourself walking around in a daze at times, thinking of that person who has captured your heart. You just love that delicious, dizzying feeling of infatuation.

Even though you can at times be in love with love, you are not likely to be a real heartbreaker—you will know the difference between the feeling of love and the real thing. For you that real thing will mean caring and commitment, and you will know more than most how much time and patience that can take. When you've found the real thing, you will put your whole being into it.

The person who wants to win your heart will need to be more than a pretty face with a winning smile—though that helps. This person must have depth and substance. Having fun at a party is okay, but you really want to know what is in someone's heart and mind. You will want to be around someone you can talk with on a variety of subjects, share a laugh with, and even unburden your heart to. Mostly, you will want someone whose bear hugs make your hair stand on end.

The 1997 Sagittarius male wants a companion who is intelligent, witty, and fun to be with. It will be all right if she's the independent type who can run her own business, or even someone with a powerful career such as in medicine or law. You'll be there for her even when you are busy, and you will want her to be warm and affectionate when the two of you are together.

You, 1997 Sagittarius female, may daydream about a man who has everything wrapped into one package—movie-star handsome, great conversationalist with a good education, and willing to share domestic duties without grumbling. If he isn't quite the looker you'd like him to be and doesn't have a PhD, you'll still love him if he has an interesting mind and a heart focused only on you.

Julia Roberts – Hollywood's Pretty Woman

Julia Roberts charmed film viewers in the modern fairy tale *Pretty Woman* as the Hollywood hooker with a heart of gold. The winsome actress flashed her trademark smile, took a bubble bath, and looked gorgeous, while still managing to prove she could act—as her Oscar nominated performance suggests.

Even though she is widely considered to be one of the best-looking actresses working in films today, Roberts is not the conventional Hollywood beauty. Tall and somewhat gangly, with hazel eyes, curly hair, and an infectious smile, she seems to personify the charm and sparkle of a pretty coed more than a Tinseltown glamour girl. Critics have often compared her to Audrey Hepburn—a coltish, somewhat unconventional beauty who looks as fabulous in capri pants (or in Julia's case, jeans) as in designer duds. Long regarded as "America's Sweetheart" of romantic comedies (*I Love Trouble, Runaway Bride, My Best Friend's Wedding*), Roberts proved that she could make audiences believe her in dramatic roles, too (*Sleeping With the Enemy, The Pelican Brief,* and *Mary Reilly*). But it was in *Erin Brockovich* (2000) that she really showed her range as an actress. She played the lead in the type of film that Hollywood loves to give awards for as a real-life, feisty heroine who uncovers a utilities company scandal that is costing the residents of a California town their health and in some cases even their lives. Roberts won both the Golden Globe and the Academy Award as Best Actress for her performance in that film.

Her love life has provided the tabloid press with numerous romances and endless chances for speculation. She has broken engagements to Dylan

"I'm too tall to be a girl. I never had enough dresses to be a lady. I wouldn't call myself a woman. I'd say I'm somewhere between a chick and a broad."

JULIA ROBERTS

McDermott and Keifer Sutherland, and married and divorced singer Lyle Lovett. In between she has managed to be linked romantically with actors Jason Patric, Benjamin Bratt, Matthew Perry (Roberts did a guest spot on *Friends*), and Oscar winner Daniel Day-Lewis. When Roberts suddenly ditched her engagement to Sutherland, she seemed to be imitating a real-life runaway bride. The public furor over her broken romance, coupled with the stresses of her celebrity status, caused Julia's career to stumble temporarily. But hits such as *My Best Friend's Wedding* and *Notting Hill* in the late '90s returned her to popularity.

Soon afterward she became the highest paid actress in history, earning $20 million for *Erin Brockovich*. Now considered one of the most powerful players in Hollywood, Roberts has managed to retain her "girl next door" image despite her complicated romantic history. Some of this behavior can be explained by the astrological stars.

Roberts is a Scorpio, and women with this Zodiac sign are extremely intense, with a need to be in the driver's seat when it comes to romance. Power is always an issue with Scorpio. Women of this sign are sometimes considered to be promiscuous, but actually they are simply looking for that one special guy. The influence of Roberts' Venus in Virgo and Mars in Capricorn suggests that the actress believes in permanence and stability where love is concerned. In Julia's own words, "I believe that two people are connected at the heart… there are no boundaries or barriers if two people are destined to be together…" In July 2002, the actress tied the knot with cameraman Daniel Moder at her New Mexico ranch.

► READ ABOUT JULIA ROBERTS' CO-STAR IN *THE PELICAN BRIEF,* DENZEL WASHINGTON, ON PAGE 629

1998

Hot Story

- ★ SEX AND HATE CRIMES
- ★ VIAGRA
- ★ TRULY MADLY DEEPLY
- ★ NICE AND SLOW
- ★ SHAKESPEARE IN LOVE
- ★ SOMETHING ABOUT MARY
- ★ IN THE MEANTIME

EVENTS

In the US, the fatal beating of Matthew Shepard, a gay Wyoming student, sparked outcry over hate crimes. Schoolteacher Mary Kay Letourneau, 36, pregnant for the second time by her 14-year-old student, was sent to prison for child rape. Male impotence drug Viagra became a pharmaceutical phenomenon, fueled by ads emphasizing "performance" and featuring celebrity NASCAR drivers and former senator Bob Dole. NuShawn Williams, 21, was indicted in New York after knowingly exposing dozens of women to HIV during unprotected sex. Actress Carmen Electra and basketball star Dennis Rodman impulsively—and briefly—wed in Las Vegas after a night of partying. Scandal ensued when Israeli transsexual Dana International (formerly Yaron Cohen) won the Eurovision Song Contest. Denmark listed 4,337 legally married homosexual couples.

POP CULTURE

Rival single-name pop divas Brandy and Monica teamed up for "The Boy Is Mine." Shania Twain sang "You're Still the One." Usher took it "Nice & Slow." Other hits included Savage Garden's "Truly Madly Deeply," Destiny's Child's "No, No, No," and Madonna's "Ray of Light" and "Frozen."

Gwyneth Paltrow starred as the secret lover, muse, and leading lady of *Shakespeare in Love*. Business rivals Meg Ryan and Tom Hanks fell in love via email in *You've Got Mail*. Obsessive love led to madcap escapades in the Farrelly brothers' *There's Something About Mary*. In *Black Cat, White Cat*, a small-time hustler in Yugoslavia tries to marry his son to the daughter of a gangster he owes money to.

In Helen Fielding's novel *Bridget Jones's Diary*, a thirtysomething London woman looks for love in all the wrong places. Gayl Jones's *The Healing* illuminated issues facing black women in contemporary America via a Kentucky woman's personal odyssey. In *You Belong to Me* by Mary Higgins Clark, a call-in radio show psychologist unwittingly becomes involved with a serial killer. *In the Meantime: Finding Yourself and the Love You Want* claimed that cleaning your emotional, spiritual, and mental "house" clears the way for true love. Danielle Steel's *Mirror Image* involved a high-society identical twin switcheroo. *The Vampire Armand* by Anne Rice followed a character from *Interview with the Vampire* from 15th-century Kiev chronicling the glamour and tragedy of life as a vampire.

THE BILL & MONICA SHOW

When the scandalous story of their involvement broke in January 1998, US President Bill Clinton denied having sex with "...that woman, Ms. Lewinsky...." But Monica, a 25-year-old White House intern, admitted having had oral sex with Clinton when it was revealed that her conversations on the subject had been tape recorded by a dubious "friend."

Clinton was impeached by Congress for perjury and obstruction of justice in the Lewinsky matter, but finished his term with high public approval ratings. Monica went on to make an HBO TV special, started her own business designing handbags, and even presented a high-profile dating game show.

SEE ALSO

▶ PROFUMO SCANDAL *Page 375*

▶ JOHN F. KENNEDY *Page 351*

1998 CAPRICORN

From December 21, 1997 20:07 through January 20, 1998 6:45
(December 1998 Capricorns, see 1999 Capricorn)

♑ *The Loyal Friend*

Throughout your life, Capricorn of 1998, those who cross your path will think of you as cool, calm, and collected, ever the loyal friend, and always the sensible one. While that may describe your outward appearance, beneath the surface you will be quite daring, exciting, and often prone to taking risks.

For you, relationships will be a way to experience life from a completely different perspective, and your ideal partner will be someone totally different from you. While you may be off bungee jumping or skydiving, the one you love may be enjoying more refined pursuits such as the opera or the ballet. What you will have in common is a love of indulging in each other's differing passions as a way of showing your affection and respect for each other. And on the purely romantic side of things, you will love the times you spend with each other.

Your eyes will light up if you overhear a good-looking person talking with interest and conviction about social issues and current events. You will find the combination of looks and intelligence highly attractive, and it will make you want to get to know that person. If you find out that you share the same pet issues, or have the same crusading spirit, there is no doubt that you will have a long future together.

The gal who will make you take notice, 1998 Capricorn male, is completely unpredictable, but in an exciting way. She sees the world through her own eyes without worrying what other people think. You really admire her bold, unconventional way of looking at things, even when it clashes with your own point of view. And, keeping in character, she will be affectionate when you least expect it, making you love her all the more.

Your dream guy, 1998 Capricorn female, has more friends and engagements than he will ever have time for in this lifetime. And even though it means you will see him less than you might like to, during the times you are together you will delight in his joyous attitude toward life, and the nonjudgmental, loving way he treats everyone he meets. If just a little of that rubs off on you, you will never let him go.

CAPRICORN ZODIAC SIGN
YOUR LOVE PLANETS

YOUR ROMANTIC SIDE   p. 696
▶ VENUS IN AQUARIUS
Born Dec. 21, 1997 20:07 - Jan. 09, 1998 21:02
▶ VENUS IN CAPRICORN
Born Jan. 09, 21:03 - Jan. 20, 6:45

YOUR SEX DRIVE   p. 722
▶ MARS IN AQUARIUS
Born Dec. 21, 1997 20:07 - Jan. 20, 1998 6:45

YOUR CELEBRITY TWINS   p. 760
Find out the astrological similarities you have with famous people.

YOUR COMPATIBILITY   p. 780
Compare planets to find out how compatible you are in a relationship.

YOUR RELATIONSHIP KARMA   p. 824
▶ SATURN IN ARIES
Born Dec. 21, 1997 20:07 - Jan. 20, 1998 6:45

IAN MCKELLEN
English Actor
Mars in Aquarius

655

1998 AQUARIUS

From January 20, 6:46 through February 18, 20:54

♒ *The Inventive Devotee*

Inventive and brilliant, you, Aquarius of 1998, will be drawn to computers and other gadgets like a fish takes to water. You will be so fascinated with how things work that you may simply spend hours taking them apart and putting them back together. If anything breaks down, you often will be the one, even at a very young age, who will know how to fix it.

When it comes to relationships, you will be just as fascinated with how your partner's mind works, though in this case "taking it apart" by asking questions and listening intently to everything from childhood experiences to dreams for the future. The love of your life will be absolutely thrilled at your undivided attention and by the comments and insights that you offer. Your intensity and devotion will let your partner respond in kind, making this area of your life always interesting and never dull.

The one you will notice in a crowd will be vivacious and talkative, someone who never seems to lack for something interesting to say. This person will want to know everything about you, and will intuit exactly when and how to focus the conversation completely on you. The special individual who has perfect timing, a good mind, great sensitivity, and an eye for beauty will make you come back for more and more.

Your dream gal, 1998 Aquarius male, will have soulful eyes and a mysterious smile that speaks a thousand words—but words that only you will understand, creating an unspoken bond between you that will be apparent from the moment you first meet. She will be soft-spoken and compassionate, yet will let you know what she thinks and feels without any hesitation. And what she wants, first and foremost, is for you to be together.

The perfect guy for you, 1998 Aquarius female, will be sweet, sensitive, and receptive to everything you want and need. He is a true competitor on the playing field, though he loves lighthearted fun and games when he is with you. His goal in life is to keep you happy, and he will express this in the form of play, in an almost childlike way. You will be lucky to have someone like him by your side.

AQUARIUS ZODIAC SIGN
YOUR LOVE PLANETS

YOUR ROMANTIC SIDE   p. 696
▶ VENUS IN CAPRICORN
Born Jan. 20, 6:46 - Feb. 18, 20:54

YOUR SEX DRIVE   p. 722
▶ MARS IN AQUARIUS
Born Jan. 20, 6:46 - Jan. 25, 9:25
▶ MARS IN PISCES
Born Jan. 25, 9:26 - Feb. 18, 20:54

YOUR CELEBRITY TWINS   p. 760
Find out the astrological similarities you have with famous people.

YOUR COMPATIBILITY   p. 780
Compare planets to find out how compatible you are in a relationship.

YOUR RELATIONSHIP KARMA   p. 824
▶ SATURN IN ARIES
Born Jan. 20, 6:46 - Feb. 18, 20:54

CATE BLANCHETT
Australian Actress
Venus in Aries

656

1998 PISCES
From February 18, 20:55 through March 20, 19:54

The Hopeful Helper

Compassionate, kindhearted, and generous, Pisces of 1998, you will attract people to you when they need advice or a sympathetic ear. As a child, you may do things like giving away your old toys or clothes to those less fortunate. As an adult, you will likely devote a portion of both your personal and professional life to helping others.

When you fall in love, you will listen to your heart and dive right in, providing loving support for your partner through good times and bad. In return, your true love will be there to comfort you, helping you in your compassionate endeavors and allowing you to pour out all your hopes, fears, and dreams. Together, you may work on various community or humanitarian causes, and your common desire to help others will draw you together all the more.

You will be attracted to the type of person who can enter any room, or walk down any street, and instantly have everyone's attention. This could be due to a knockout appearance, a fabulous fashion sense, or just a commanding presence. Underneath all of the charm and magnetism, you have to see a kind face, hear a soothing voice, and find a definite inner warmth the first time your hands touch.

You will just adore a straightforward, no-nonsense gal, 1998 Pisces male. By day, she will be serious and very ambitious, approaching the world head-on with no pretensions. Once the sun sets, though, she will let her hair down and have fun—from partying with friends to dancing until dawn at a neighborhood club. She is extraordinarily accommodating, and whether you are out in public or viewing a romantic video at home, her preference ever and always is to be with you.

A guy who would rather serve you a home cooked meal by candlelight than watch the football game on TV will definitely be the one for you, 1998 Pisces female. Hardly a pushover, he is more of a doer than a spectator, a man's man who will spend many hours playing outdoor sports with friends or lifting weights in the gym. All that pumping iron and physical activity will only make him more relaxed and totally attentive when you are together.

1998 ARIES
From March 20, 19:55 through April 20, 6:56

The Goal-Oriented Dynamo

Nobody will ever want to get in your way, Aries of 1998, once you put your shoulder to the wheel and start pushing ahead. A ball of dynamite, you will always be single-minded, focused, and determined in whatever you do, whether that means making the best grades, getting into the finest schools, or successfully pursuing the one you love.

Being with someone you love who feels the same way about you will seem like your reward for the effort you exert in all walks of life. Never one to take anything for granted, you will try to earn that love over and over with things like front row tickets to your partner's favorite concert or reservations in the most expensive restaurant in town. Pleasing your beloved will be your greatest joy, and when you know you've succeeded in doing this, you will feel like a champion who has won first prize.

Anyone who wants to be a permanent fixture in your life needs to match you in intelligence, wit, and physical energy. You will be intrigued with someone who speaks foreign languages, or who uses unique words to describe a simple event, yet without seeming erudite or stuck-up. If that special person's eyes light up as the conversation turns to a favorite subject, you will see just the kind of enthusiasm that will make you fall, and fall hard.

The gal who will stimulate your heart and soul, 1998 Aries male, is her own person, one who leaves her own stamp on life, from the way she dresses to her outspoken views. She is not one to become involved with "group think," and you will be amazed at how she can speak her mind, never worrying about the opinions of others, while remaining thoughtful and sensitive. Those qualities will make you hold on to her tight.

You will just love a guy, 1998 Aries female, who is calm and confident, and can say the right things at just the right time. He is a real outdoors person and is so persuasive that even you will look forward to fishing trips and pitching a tent. Once he enters your life, the only thing that will matter is being close to him in thought and in deed, learning to appreciate whatever makes him happy.

1998 TAURUS
From April 20, 6:57 through May 21, 6:04

The Exotic Voyager

You have the heart of a poet, Taurus of 1998, and you will look toward the future with both reality and imagination. While people may label you a dreamer and secretly smile at the goals and plans you reveal to them, your perfect partner will be on the same wavelength and help turn your fantasies into realities that you both can share.

Your childhood wish to travel the world may come true with a partner by your side. Nothing could be more romantic in your eyes than honeymooning down the Nile River or hopping on the Orient Express. Even if you do not manage to see all those exotic places, you and your mate can dream of them as you cook international cuisine, see a foreign film, or learn to say "I love you" in as many languages as you can.

The person with the key to your heart will make perfect eye contact with you even during your very first conversation. You will know by the way you both listen eagerly to each other that there is real chemistry brewing between you. Your tastes need not be the same, as long as the two of you are willing to try anything

the other loves. That desire to know everything about someone means you've found a candidate to win your heart.

The gal who will make you swoon, 1998 Taurus male, has an allure that you cannot put your finger on, but the more you know her, the more you realize how much more there is to learn. She may be complex, but she is also charming, clever and witty, and loves anyone, like you, who can challenge her to think greater thoughts. In return, she will bring those qualities out in you, and for that you will want to be with her for the rest of your lives.

The man in your life, 1998 Taurus female, will cut a dashing, adventurous figure, with just the right combination of sensitivity, strength, and panache. You will always feel safe when you are in his arms and will never doubt that he will be there for you in good times and in bad. Though he could command crowds of friends if he wanted, actually he will be a bit of a loner who feels that you are the only one who can understand the workings of his heart, mind, and soul.

TAURUS ZODIAC SIGN
YOUR LOVE PLANETS

YOUR ROMANTIC SIDE   p. 696
- ▶ **VENUS IN PISCES**
  Born Apr. 20, 6:57 - May 03, 19:15
- ▶ **VENUS IN ARIES**
  Born May 03, 19:16 - May 21, 6:04

YOUR SEX DRIVE   p. 722
- ▶ **MARS IN TAURUS**
  Born Apr. 20, 6:57 - May 21, 6:04

YOUR CELEBRITY TWINS   p. 760
Find out the astrological similarities you have with famous people.

YOUR COMPATIBILITY   p. 780
Compare planets to find out how compatible you are in a relationship.

YOUR RELATIONSHIP KARMA   p. 824
- ▶ **SATURN IN ARIES**
  Born Apr. 20, 6:57 - May 21, 6:04

657

1998 GEMINI
From May 21, 6:05 through June 21, 14:02

The Friendly Networker

As a Gemini of 1998, you will be outgoing, friendly, and good at connecting and networking with all types of people. Though most will see you as forthcoming, you will see yourself as somewhat reserved, a person of relatively few words, but of deep, perceptive thoughts. You will feel that most people can say what they need to with their actions as well as their words.

When you fall in love, you might not write gushy notes to your beloved, but there will be no doubt what your true feelings really are. You will convey the depth of your love by being loyal to a fault, never even playfully flirting with anyone other than your one true love. You will not be the jealous type either, allowing your partner plenty of trust, independence, and, most of all, the certainty of knowing your love is eternal.

Anyone who wants you for a mate should convey honesty, integrity, with a sense of humor thrown in the mix. If you discover a shared passion for the performing arts, you will be completely smitten in a matter of moments.

You'll know for sure that you're on your way to a lasting and satisfying relationship after a magical night at the theater, followed by spending long hours in heartfelt conversation, pouring out your soul.

The gal for you, 1998 Gemini male, will have a knack for getting you to change your mind, or at least see her point of view, on just about anything. That's how charming and persuasive she is, and you will do almost anything to make her happy and see that fabulous smile light up the room. Just as you are interested in everything she does, so will she be, and you will never doubt for a moment her love for you.

The man of your dreams, 1998 Gemini female, will be charismatic and dynamic, in both physical appearance and intellectual pursuits. He is always active and busy, and while you will teach him the value of quiet contemplation, he will make sure you stay physically fit, so each of you will add something important to the other's life. He will never be modest about telling you how much he loves you, or what you mean to him, whether with words, or his warm embrace.

JOSEPH FIENNES
English Actor
Sun and Mars in Gemini

GEMINI ZODIAC SIGN
YOUR LOVE PLANETS

YOUR ROMANTIC SIDE   p. 696
- ▶ **VENUS IN ARIES**
  Born May 21, 6:05 - May 29, 23:31
- ▶ **VENUS IN TAURUS**
  Born May 29, 23:32 - June 21, 14:02

YOUR SEX DRIVE   p. 722
- ▶ **MARS IN TAURUS**
  Born May 21, 6:05 - May 24, 3:41
- ▶ **MARS IN GEMINI**
  Born May 24, 3:42 - June 21, 14:02

YOUR CELEBRITY TWINS   p. 760
Find out the astrological similarities you have with famous people.

YOUR COMPATIBILITY   p. 780
Compare planets to find out how compatible you are in a relationship.

YOUR RELATIONSHIP KARMA   p. 824
- ▶ **SATURN IN ARIES**
  Born May 21, 6:05 - June 9, 6:12
- ▶ **SATURN IN TAURUS**
  Born June 9, 6:13 - June 21, 14:02

JENNIFER LOPEZ
American Singer
Sun and Mars in Leo

1998 CANCER
From June 21, 14:03 through July 23, 0:54

♋ The Natural Companion

Like a magnet, Cancer of 1998, you will draw people from all walks of life to you, and without very much effort at all. Those around you will always sense that you have a sincere interest in them, and, as you mature, you may find that people often trust and confide in you, feeling that you will never judge them and that you will guard their secrets well.

Your winning ways with people will ultimately endear you to your true love, as you are a faithful friend, loyal partner, and a natural companion. Not only will your mate find it easy to trust and open up to you, but you will be completely candid about your own feelings as well. This will encourage a wonderful closeness that can make simple things like walking hand in hand on the beach, or feeding the ducks in the park, moments you will always remember.

Someone who wants to get to know you should listen intently to everything you say, without the need to always interject a thought or a comment. You will really appreciate it when someone engages you in conversation and then asks you about yourself, your personal interests, and your hopes for the future. This person's idea of a romantic evening involves simply communing under the stars on a clear night, without having to say a single word.

The lady of your dreams, 1998 Cancer male, will be an intuitive sort, someone who can communicate with you on a deep, soulful level. Just being together in ordinary situations will make you feel like you can anticipate the other's every word and motion—that your thoughts are one thought, and your hearts beat as one. Though the two of you can (and will) talk for hours, you love those times you are together in silence most of all.

Your best guy, 1998 Cancer female, will be active and enthusiastic but will reserve most of his energy for those times when you are together. He loves spending as many hours of the day with you, even if you wind up just driving down long country roads with no destination in sight. Mostly he will be attentive to everything you want, making sure you're never lacking for kisses, hugs, or his winning smile.

1998 LEO
From July 23, 0:55 through August 23, 7:58

♌ The Dream Spinner

You, Leo of 1998, will be a teller of tales and a spinner of dreams—traits that may show up almost from the time you began to talk. At your best, you will be able to create an almost magical environment around you that puts others in a positive frame of mind. You will do this by being a positive person yourself and also by using your whimsical stories to make others forget their troubles.

When it comes to the close relationships in your life, you will always keep you and your partner focused on the future when you come upon the occasional rough patch in your lives together. You have a truly romantic soul, so when you find the right person, you will make sure that love lasts for a lifetime. Selecting special days for each other, when the world belongs only to you, is one way of reminding each other what truly counts.

Exchanging ideas, opinions, and even personal dreams in a private environment is the best way to see if someone will fit into your future plans. You might extend an invitation to share a potluck dinner or to watch a special TV program together that will be of interest to both of you. If you discover a positive attitude that equals your own, then true love will surely blossom.

The gal for you, 1998 Leo male, will have a feisty side that you find both charming and amusing. She'll stand up easily to people twice her size, though always with a smile and a wink that puts them off balance. This lady will have such an intuitive understanding of you that you may think she can read your mind. You will never have quite so much fun with anyone as you do with her, and her ability to knock you off your feet with just a kiss will constantly amaze you.

The man who will be your soul mate, 1998 Leo female, is a strong, focused, and determined type who shows that strength in a gentle way. You'll never worry for a minute when you're with him, as you know you can count on him to care for you and protect you against anything and anyone. And he will have no match when it comes to sweet, loving passion, as you'll find out in those moments just meant for the two of you.

1998 VIRGO

From August 23, 7:59 through September 23, 5:36

The Close Connection

As a Virgo of 1998, you will always have nice, comforting words for everyone around you, and your soft-spoken ways will win you many friends. From childhood through adulthood, your life is likely to revolve around those close companions whom you can depend upon, as well as have fun with. When you meet your one true love, you will both agree that a life without friends to support and surround you is only a life half-lived.

The perfect evening will be to join your "circle" for dinner spiced with different opinions and viewpoints about a range of subjects—from politics to the arts. After spending a lively evening with people you love, the two of you will feel even more connected to each other. At other times, you and your soul mate will want to be alone—talking, walking hand in hand, or watching sunsets.

You are always intrigued by someone who is at ease in a crowd and has a way of easily connecting with people, whatever their likes or dislikes may be. Anyone who can take you to a crowded club and then get you to dance the night away will surely be high on your list of people you want to get to know better. If you can in turn introduce this person to some of your preferred pursuits, you may just find that you are falling in love.

Your favorite gal, Virgo male of 1998, is likely to be a bit of a talker, and you will enjoy nothing more than hearing her funny stories and witty observations on life. She's very much like you on one level, as she will never have a bad word for anyone and is the soul of helpfulness. Talk or no talk, when you're all by yourselves, there will be no more romantic pair of love birds than you two.

For you, Virgo female of 1998, your man will be a more down-to-earth type than most people you know, and someone who is quiet and retiring yet never boring. He is not a glib talker, nor does he like superficial chatter, but when he speaks he will say just the right thing at the right time. He will spend hours drumming up romantic scenarios, and when he gives you a hug and a kiss, you'll know for sure that no one will love you more than he does.

VIRGO ZODIAC SIGN
YOUR LOVE PLANETS

YOUR ROMANTIC SIDE   p. 696
- ▶ **VENUS IN LEO**
  Born Aug. 23, 7:59 - Sept. 06, 19:23
- ▶ **VENUS IN VIRGO**
  Born Sept. 06, 19:24 - Sept. 23, 5:36

YOUR SEX DRIVE   p. 722
- ▶ **MARS IN LEO**
  Born Aug. 23, 7:59 - Sept. 23, 5:36

YOUR CELEBRITY TWINS   p. 760
Find out the astrological similarities you have with famous people.

YOUR COMPATIBILITY   p. 780
Compare planets to find out how compatible you are in a relationship.

YOUR RELATIONSHIP KARMA   p. 824
- ▶ **SATURN IN TAURUS**
  Born Aug. 23, 7:59 - Sept. 23, 5:36

GWYNETH PALTROW
American Actress
Sun in Libra

1998 LIBRA

From September 23, 5:37 through October 23, 14:58

The Deep Romantic

You certainly will appreciate the finer things in life, Libra of 1998, but you will never be one to superficially chase the latest fashions and trends. You will know what has value and what doesn't, and will truly know the difference between being in love and just being infatuated with a good-looking face. Anyone you fall in love with will be lucky enough to share all your deepest feelings, hopes, and dreams.

In a romantic relationship, you will always treat your true love like royalty, with a constant shower of small gifts and a watchful attentiveness to your mate's feelings and needs. When you are in love you will never do things in half measures, so if you cannot afford expensive presents, you will choose something so sentimental that it will bring tears of joy to your partner's eyes. Even a week's vacation will transform into an exciting, creative journey, whether it is close to home or across the ocean.

A person who wants to attract you should have a sense of good looks and elegance that shows both in clothes and accessories. You will want someone whose beauty is more than skin deep, so style and flair must be accompanied by an air of confidence, real intelligence, and, finally, sharing the same vision of romantic simplicity from moonlit walks to a quiet evening in front of the fireplace.

The girl of your dreams, 1998 Libra male, will share your tastes and interests, but she'll be fiercely independent and will stand up for her dreams against any and all comers. You will be one of her dreams, and once you are hers, she will never let anything come between you. This passionate lady will love nothing more than holding you close and being alone together with you.

The guy you love, 1998 Libra female, will have more energy than any ten people you know and will always have love in abundance waiting for you. You will get a kick out of cheering him on the ball field with his friends or watching as he builds something with his hands in a basement workshop. When it comes to romance, he will love nothing more than to whisk you off in his arms and carry you off to your own private love nest.

LIBRA ZODIAC SIGN
YOUR LOVE PLANETS

YOUR ROMANTIC SIDE   p. 696
- ▶ **VENUS IN VIRGO**
  Born Sept. 23, 5:37 - Sept. 30, 23:12
- ▶ **VENUS IN LIBRA**
  Born Sept. 30, 23:13 - Oct. 23, 14:58

YOUR SEX DRIVE   p. 722
- ▶ **MARS IN LEO**
  Born Sept. 23, 5:37 - Oct. 07, 12:27
- ▶ **MARS IN VIRGO**
  Born Oct. 07, 12:28 - Oct. 23, 14:58

YOUR CELEBRITY TWINS   p. 760
Find out the astrological similarities you have with famous people.

YOUR COMPATIBILITY   p. 780
Compare planets to find out how compatible you are in a relationship.

YOUR RELATIONSHIP KARMA   p. 824
- ▶ **SATURN IN TAURUS**
  Born Sept. 23, 5:37 - Oct. 23, 14:58

659

BEN STILLER
American Actor
Sun and Mars in Sagittarius

1998 SCORPIO
From October 23, 14:59 through November 22, 12:33

♏ ## *The Joyful Personality*

Few people will ever match you for the sheer joy you bring into a room, Scorpio of 1998, and while you may become more serious as you mature, your sunny personality will still be the most identifiable thing about you. You like to be liked, and you will always have a good word to say about everyone you meet—even when others find it difficult to do so. The gift you have for remaining positive and cheering people up will be a most attractive and endearing trait and will have the opposite sex breaking down your door.

Since you may put yourself second from time to time, your partner will be there to remind you that you are always number one and will encourage to you to say what you think and feel, even if the two of you do not always agree. You may even learn to like heated discussions, especially if they end with the two of you kissing and making up.

Someone who brims with confidence and has a fun-loving attitude will always arouse your interest. Anyone wearing a frown will be a definite turn-off. If that special someone wants you to go for a nature walk, do a bit of serious hiking, or attempt rock climbing, you will be convinced that sharing a love of the outdoors is definitely a way for romance to blossom.

Your dream lady, 1998 Scorpio male, will share your ability to smooth over people's troubled feelings, so that the two of you could make a very compatible (and happy) match. You just love a real sharp dresser with a lot of originality, depending more on perfect taste rather than on designer labels. She will be generous and kind, as you are, so in between the hugs and kisses, each of you will shower the other with small gifts and much love.

The perfect man for you, 1998 Scorpio female, will be extroverted and forthright. He has a lot of initiative and never needs to be nudged or nagged to do anything from running errands to celebrating your birthday. He loves competing in sports events but is not consumed by it, as most of his attention is reserved for you. When he takes you in his warm embrace, you know that you are safer than you could ever be anywhere else.

1998 SAGITTARIUS
From November 22, 12:34 through December 22, 1:56

♐ ## *The Secure Leader*

You always appear to know what you want, Sagittarius of 1998, and you will be willing to do whatever it takes to get it. This certainty about who you are and where you are going makes you a natural leader, whether at school, in the community, or the world at large. When it comes to relationships, you will win your true love's heart by taking the lead, and your certainty will assure your partner that your feelings are true and lasting.

When you are truly in love, you will act like a kid showing off Christmas presents. You will think nothing of announcing that you are walking on air, nor introducing your mate to everyone you know. You're not all talk by any means, and you will love the close contact found in quiet, more intimate settings, from romantic dinners for two to finding a secluded spot in the mountains.

Anyone who wants to grab your attention, should be a bit mysterious, without being secretive, with a charming, warm manner that makes you want to get to know this person on a much deeper, more intimate level. Inviting you to a group activity where you will get to know each other in a "safe" environment is a good way to start. If you talk endlessly and passionately about the things you love, you will see your smile light up the other person's eyes and know that you are meant to be together.

The perfect lady for you, 1998 Sagittarius male, will be reserved and quiet, at least on the surface. Underneath that calm restraint, you will know her as someone with a quick wit and a real sense of fun, and she will fill your time with her infectious laughter and adorable smile. Romantically, she will be very affectionate, always near you where she can give you a little pat or a peck on the cheek.

Your soul mate, 1998 Sagittarius female, will be just a bit of a daredevil, even to the point of doing things like hang gliding or racecar driving as a hobby. He is devoted to you and will even temper his activities if he thinks they will worry you or make you nervous, as he will be most concerned with you, your feelings, and your needs. No one will be as loving to you as he is.

Eddie Izzard – The Accidental Transvestite

Cross-dressing camp comedian with a penchant for lipstick and nail varnish, Eddie Izzard's quick-fire left-field vision of the world has people clutching their sides in uproarious laughter.

It's not just his humor that's unusual. Although he was born in Yemen in 1962, his family returned to Great Britain soon afterward. They moved around the country until tragedy struck when Izzard was six—his mother died of cancer and he was packed off to boarding school.

In his teens he discovered the unorthodox nature of his sexuality—he was a transvestite. Studying accounting and math at the university seems a strange choice for an eccentric teenager who was once caught stealing make-up—for his own personal use—and who had an overwhelming desire to perform. Not surprisingly, his heart wasn't in his studies and he was kicked out of the program.

He was then free to follow his real dream, and he took to the streets of London as an entertainer, with quirky acts (riding a six-foot unicycle while attempting to free himself of handcuffs was a favorite) and a fast-paced stand-up routine.

In 1981 he decided he was finally ready to face a stiffer audience. He entered the Edinburgh Fringe Festival and unleashed his surreal wit on an unsuspecting world. His perceptive, tangential social commentary— dexterously delivered in a rapid stream of consciousness that even hecklers found difficult to interrupt—caused a sensation. News of the comic who could make you laugh about subjects as mundane as jam and cats began to spread.

So did news of his attire—for he dressed in women's clothes. The press and public became obsessed with his

sexuality. Was he a transsexual or a drag queen? Was he gay? Was this just a gimmick? The truth is that he is decidedly heterosexual, something that the pubic found hard to understand given his sartorial leanings. He simply likes wearing women's clothes. But the fact that he would not reveal the identity of his long-term girlfriend, nor discuss his relationship with her, made him even more intriguing and elusive. And calling himself a "male lesbian" only helped to further fascinate people.

But his droll comedy overshadowed his high heels, ensuring him continuing celebrity status. His sharp intellect paved the way for much of his material, commenting on politics and history with a Monty Pythonesque edge. A vociferous Europhile, he toured France, performing in French, and he now has his sights on a tour of Europe, naturally all in the local languages—whether he can speak them or not.

As his popularity grew so did his international reputation and his collection of awards. With his show *Dress to Kill*, he had also broken into America. By the mid '90s he was a star, managing to realize his other childhood ambition of being an actor. He made his screen debut in 1996, alongside Robin Williams and Bob Hoskins in *The Secret Agent*, and

in 1998—a prolific year for him—he starred in two major movies, *The Avengers* and *Velvet Goldmine*.

Stand-up performer, actor, social commentator—whatever guise Eddie Izzard decides to take, he is, without doubt, an experimental comic genius and pioneer of a new wave of alternative comedy. His theatrical style, offbeat look at the world, and sharp observational digressions have made him a Comedy King. Albeit a cross-dressing one.

▶ READ ABOUT EDDIE'S SURREAL WIT ABOUT HITLER'S MARRIAGE ON PAGE 220 ▶ READ ABOUT *THE ROCKY HORROR PICTURE SHOW* ON PAGE 473

- ★ DATE-RAPE DRUG
- ★ KENNEDY CURSE
- ★ COLUMBINE
- ★ LA VIDA LOCA
- ★ AMERICAN BEAUTY
- ★ BOYS DON'T CRY
- ★ WHITE OLEANDER

EVENTS

In the US, the Supreme Court of Vermont upheld equal protection rights of same-sex couples, and France expanded rights for all unmarried couples. Fifteen-year-old Samantha Reid died after the date-rape drug GBH (gamma-hydroxybutyrate) was slipped into her drink at a party. Television's *Blind Date* combined voyeurism with snarky thought-bubble commentary (a la *Pop-Up Video*). John F. Kennedy Jr., his wife, and her sister were lost at sea when the plane he was piloting disappeared near Martha's Vineyard. Over 48 million people watched Barbara Walters' interview with former White House intern and Clinton sex-scandal temptress Monica Lewinsky. Radio shock-jock Howard Stern was in hot water after joking about the Columbine High School shootings. "Barbie" turned 40. The world's population hit six billion. Royal nuptials included Caroline of Monaco and Prince Ernst-August of Hanover, Britain's Prince Edward and Sophie Rhys-Jones, and Belgium's crown prince Philippe and Mathilde d'Udekem.

POP CULTURE

Sexy nymphets ruled. Christina Aguilera sang "Genie in a Bottle" and Britney Spears urged "Baby One More Time." Resilient star Cher sang "Believe." Ricky Martin swiveled his hips to stardom in "Livin' La Vida Loca."

In *American Beauty*, a seemingly picture-perfect suburban family spirals into tragedy when the parents' midlife crises manifest themselves as increasingly bizarre behavior. *Runaway Bride* starred Julia Roberts, whose real-life adventures in near-marriage echoed the film's story. *Boys Don't Cry* told the true, tragic story of a girl who passes as a boy in a small Nebraska town. In Stanley Kubrick's final film, *Eyes Wide Shut*, Tom Cruise and Nicole Kidman explore the boundaries of sex, morality, and fidelity. Pedro Almodóvar's *All About My Mother* followed a bereaved mother's odyssey into her colorful past in Barcelona.

In Maeve Binchy's novel *Tara Road*, two women trade houses for a summer and discover the other's deepest secret. *White Oleander* by Janet Fitch is told through the eyes of a teenage girl who grows up in foster homes after her mother is jailed for murder. In Anita Shreve's *The Pilot's Wife*, a widow discovers that her husband had been leading a double life. In Nicholas Sparks' sentimental *Message in a Bottle*, two emotionally scarred people learn to love again.

Hot Couple

662

DAVID BECKHAM & VICTORIA ADAMS

What could be more paparazzi-perfect than that Britain's top footballer and spiciest pop star woo and wed? The gorgeous, glamorous duo were each at the top of their game—he as Manchester United's sexiest scorer, she as "Posh Spice" of the chart-topping Spice Girls—when she saw him from the stands in March 1997.

Their July 1999 wedding at an Irish castle was mobbed by fans and ringed by guards—even their baby son, Brooklyn, needed a security tag. They've since had a second child, Romeo, and Victoria has gone solo, career-wise, that is. Beckham continues to score, on and off the field, and was picked to captain England in the 2002 World Cup.

SEE ALSO
▶ WILL SMITH & JADA PINKETT *Page 630*

1999 CAPRICORN

From December 22, 1998 1:57 through January 20, 1999 12:36
(December 1999 Capricorns, see 2000 Capricorns)

♑ *The Magical Heartthrob*

Love and romance will always hold an aura of glamour for you, Capricorn of 1999, from fairy tales to teen heartthrobs to Hollywood movies. When you do become involved in a romantic relationship, you are likely to view two people together as something that must have a certain magic to it to know it's the real thing. When you are in love, you'll make sure the magic is there right from the beginning.

During your growing years, you'll find that you enjoy the times when you are together with friends in a beautiful atmosphere. Once you've reached adulthood, this same kind of atmosphere is the one in which you will enjoy being with that one particular person you love and respect the most. You can be in love, of course, without all of that, but you enjoy it more when the environment around you is just right.

If someone wants to catch your eye, the first requirement will be that extra something in personal appearance that tells you this is someone fashionable and elegant. However, while appearance is a good start, those who have a chance of winning your heart need to

have some depth to go with the elegance. Someone you can have a long, personal conversation with, sharing your deepest feelings, is just the right type.

For the 1999 Capricorn male, the female you're most likely to be with in a permanent relationship has the qualities of looks and elegance mentioned above, as well as the ability to talk to you one on one, long into the night. Along with that, however, you will be looking for someone who is generous to a fault, not just to you, but also to those less fortunate. She will be someone who likes to volunteer her time to worthy causes, even though most of her time is reserved for you.

As a 1999 Capricorn female, you'll be drawn to a guy who is handsome (maybe even movie-star quality), well-dressed, well-spoken, and madly in love with you. Even though he could be very much the independent type, he is someone that people find they can count on when the going gets roughs. He certainly will be there for you, and could win awards for his attentiveness to your every need.

RICKY MARTIN
Puerto Rican Singer
Venus in Aquarius

663

1999 AQUARIUS

From January 20, 12:37 through February 19, 2:46

♒ *The Happy Cheerleader*

You're an optimist, Aquarius of 1999, and even when people around you are gloomy, you will always be looking over the next hill and around the next bend for that better tomorrow you know is sure to be out there. That attitude will also show in your personal relationships, especially those of the romantic variety. You'll never let those you love be sad because you feel there is always something to look forward to.

You won't just look at realities through rose-colored glasses, though, and as you come of age, you will learn how to see potential problems just as easily as you see opportunities. However, you will feel that any problem can be solved—if you just put forth the effort. When you are involved with another person in a loving way, you work hard to keep these relationships on a steady course.

Anyone who wishes to attract your attention will need to show a sunny disposition and an ability to take the hard knocks of life without flinching. Neatness counts with you, as well, and though you'll never be interested in the

clothes horse who has to spend lots of money on fancy outfits, you do like someone who possesses a good appearance. A sense of humor is a must, too, because you appreciate a good laugh more than most.

If you're a 1999 Aquarius male, your ideal mate will be someone who radiates an inner glow of confidence. Her outer appearance will include a winning smile. Others will find it difficult to be unhappy around this lady because she is always teasing, making little jokes, and just generally keeping people on the edge of a laugh at all times. She will be someone you can really truly share life with, both the little personal moments and the big, important events.

The guy for you, 1999 Aquarius female, will seem to have boundless energy, combined with a boundless concern for you. Even though he is likely to have a really busy life in the outside world, when he is around you, he will cheer you when you're up, and lift you when you're down. Probably no one you know will be funnier than this fellow, and every time you laugh with him, it will warm your heart with love.

ANNETTE BENING
American Actress
Mars in Pisces

1999 PISCES
From February 19, 2:47 through March 21, 1:45

 The Glowing Enthusiast

No one will be able to set any boundaries for you, when it comes to romance, Pisces of 1999. Though others may concern themselves with what love is or isn't, for you it will be an indefinable glow, something you will recognize when you find it. That will be more than enough for you, and as you grow up and experience everything from infatuation to true lasting love, you will enjoy the experience without thinking much about it—or worrying what others think as well.

This will make you a spontaneously romantic person. But perhaps, when you are younger and less experienced, this might bring you some problems. As you mature, though, you will develop into someone who can give love spontaneously without setting any conditions on it. You may tend to idealize your relationships, but this in turn will give them a positive quality that makes them very durable.

Those who want to win you need to reach that warm spot in your heart, where you feel that indefinable glow you're keeping an eye out for. This is, of course, a bit of a challenge, because it means someone has to go beyond just flirting or looking good. What it will take is an ability to show a sincere interest in you, something that comes from within and is more than skin deep.

The gal for you, Pisces male of 1999, will be someone who's not afraid to love and be loved in return. She won't have any emotional hang-ups about committing herself to someone she knows she truly belongs with, and once she's hooked up with you, she won't look back. Along with that, however, she'll also likely be a very talented and creative individual, something you value almost as much as emotional sincerity.

As a 1999 Pisces female, you'll come to envision an ideal man as a fellow who is emotionally honest and doesn't become all tangled up in his own feelings. More than anything, he will want to share all aspects of his life with you, from socializing, to traveling, to long conversations about your innermost hopes and frustrations. You won't ever have to question your love when he is around, because he fills you with love from sunrise to sunset.

1999 ARIES
From March 21, 1:46 through April 20, 12:45

The Passionate Poet

As you become an adult, Aries of 1999, love will bring out the creative artist in you, a side that might otherwise stay hidden. Being in love is something that is likely to make you want to sing, shout, and perhaps even write a love poem or two. Some folks almost always seem to take love for granted, but it's unlikely you ever will.

When you fall in love and cultivate a romantic yet mature, exclusive relationship with one other special person, that creative urge will show up when you least expect it. You might simply write something beautiful, or just whisper lovely thoughts in your partner's ear. Feeling love for someone will give you an inner joy and peace, and you will want to share that feeling with your loved one.
Someone who wants to attract your interest needs to know how to loosen you up and relax you. Romantic feelings will most often catch you when you're off-guard and not expecting them. All it may take is a walk in the park or perhaps the sharing of a movie that makes you laugh and washes your little everyday worries away. Getting to you at this level will take some subtle effort, but the payback for the other person will always be worth it.

If you're a 1999 Aries male, your perfect romantic partner will likely be a lady who seems to know you better than you could ever know yourself. From the first time you meet her you may feel she can somehow sense your thoughts and feel your emotions. But in truth, she's just sensitive and has a very deep interest in you and your well-being. It will seem as if no one would ever be able to match her as a companion, and you'll love every moment you spend with her.

For the 1999 Aries female, the fellow who sweeps you off your feet will possibly be a creative type, someone who not only brings out your own creative streak, but may also help you to channel it. He will probably be a close match for your own interests, maybe even sharing many even your hobbies—which means that the two of you will spend more time together than apart. More than anything, he will be someone who is protective of you and considerate of your every need.

1999 TAURUS

From April 20, 12:46 through May 21, 11:51

The Irresistible Heart

As you mature and become an adult, Taurus of 1999, there will be something about you that others are bound to find completely irresistible. It will not be movie star looks or even your nice physique and great taste in clothes that will draw people to you. Underneath your pleasant manner will be an inner sweetness, a true heart of gold, and a sincere interest in others. Those who sense this in you will want to be friends for life, and much much more.

That interest in other people is something that will probably become evident when you are very young, but as you become older it will also show in the way you relate to others on a romantic level. For you just being with people you like is a great thing, but being with someone you love is something extra special and you give such relationships all of your time and attention. Anyone you love will know it for sure.

Someone who wants to grab your attention will need to reach you, not on the outside, but on the inside. That nice image you project, that attracts others to you, has more beneath it than shows on the surface, including joy and sadness, hopes and worries. Someone who can sense these things, and who is able to talk to you at that level will have no trouble in gaining your interest—and perhaps in winning your heart.

A 1999 Taurus male will find a perfect match in a girl who has both a stunning appearance and a good and honest heart. Those two things together will easily melt your own heart and make you putty in her hands. She will not, however, be interested in molding you into something else, but rather in knowing you for just who you are. She will be just as romantic as you, and in love with loving you.

For the 1999 Taurus lady, the male of your dreams will have a sensitive side that you will know the first time you meet him, even though others may not see it at all. To others he will seem like an average guy, but you will find him to be extremely generous and deeply romantic. While he is around, you will never have to worry because he will make sure that all is right in the world the two of you live in together.

TAURUS ZODIAC SIGN
YOUR LOVE PLANETS

YOUR ROMANTIC SIDE   p. 696
▶ VENUS IN GEMINI
Born Apr. 20, 12:46 - May 08, 16:28
▶ VENUS IN CANCER
Born May 08, 16:29 - May 21, 11:51

YOUR SEX DRIVE   p. 722
▶ MARS IN SCORPIO
Born Apr. 20, 12:46 - May 05, 21:31
▶ MARS IN LIBRA
Born May 05, 21:32 - May 21, 11:51

YOUR CELEBRITY TWINS   p. 760
Find out the astrological similarities you have with famous people.

YOUR COMPATIBILITY   p. 780
Compare planets to find out how compatible you are in a relationship.

YOUR RELATIONSHIP KARMA   p. 824
▶ SATURN IN TAURUS
Born Apr. 20, 12:46 - May 21, 11:51

ANDRE AGASSI
American Tennis Champion
Sun in Taurus

665

1999 GEMINI
From May 21, 11:52 through June 21, 19:48

The Thrill Seeker

Where love and romance are concerned, Gemini of 1999, you are likely to be someone who will take it to the absolute limit. When you've come of age in the world, no one is likely to find you and your romantic partner sitting quietly in the living room, sipping tea, and reading poetry. For you will love to be out in the world, whether on the road on trips to exotic places, or in the wilderness, matching yourself against the elements.

You are someone who will like to feel your blood pumping as you test your wits, strength, and endurance against everything you can think of. Once you find someone to share your life with, you will want to share these thrills with that person. Both the sharing and the great thrill of love itself will give you more than you could ever find alone.

It should be pretty obvious that anyone who will want to attract you should be a person who is ready, willing, and able to live life with great zest and gusto. This person needs the same ability to stay the course as you have and must be able to match your pace and your rhythm, no matter what situation the two of you are in. You won't need a talker as much as a doer, someone who doesn't need too many words to express deep feelings.

The Gemini male of 1999 will be able to find a great match with the gal who is a physical type, someone who will like being outside much more than she will like being inside. Even though she might enjoy roughing it, however, she will be completely feminine—someone who can climb a mountain by day and dress up at night. When it is time to shut the world out and for the two of you to be in your own world, together, she is the best companion anyone could have.

A fellow who is rugged, and ruggedly handsome, will be just to your taste, Gemini female of 1999. There is no question that you will like someone who will not want to sit around the house, and even though you won't mind if he has time away on his own, more often than not he will take you along on his adventures. He will be warm, caring, and the kind of guy who can keep you on track, no matter how you are feeling.

GEMINI ZODIAC SIGN
YOUR LOVE PLANETS

YOUR ROMANTIC SIDE   p. 696
▶ VENUS IN CANCER
Born May 21, 11:52 - June 05, 21:24
▶ VENUS IN LEO
Born June 05, 21:25 - June 21, 19:48

YOUR SEX DRIVE   p. 722
▶ MARS IN LIBRA
Born May 21, 11:52 - June 21, 19:48

YOUR CELEBRITY TWINS   p. 760
Find out the astrological similarities you have with famous people.

YOUR COMPATIBILITY   p. 780
Compare planets to find out how compatible you are in a relationship.

YOUR RELATIONSHIP KARMA   p. 824
▶ SATURN IN TAURUS
Born May 21, 11:52 - June 21, 19:48

MAEVE BINCHY
Irish Writer
Venus and Mars in Cancer

1999 CANCER
From June 21, 19:49 through July 23, 6:43

The Mature Dreamer

As a Cancer of 1999, you will always appear more mature than expected for your age, wondering about a distant future while others are looking forward only to the next day. In the romance department you may hope for a life that includes an extended family of friends because you thrive on social situations and always notice how others relate to those you love.

For you relationships bring out the best in the people involved, so you will want to be with a partner who can learn and grow with you. Because you are at times too direct and at other times at a loss for words, you also will need a partner who will let you know when you need to listen and when you need to speak up for yourself. Together, the two of you will learn the meaning of being close, and you'll treasure your moments together.

Anyone who wants to catch your attention can do so the easy way, by flirting shamelessly with you. You will admire those who dare to do and say what you would not, so you certainly will notice someone who is a bit flamboyant—as long as you sense some sincerity behind it. Getting your attention and keeping it are two different things, however, so after the flirting you will need someone who can be serious and seriously interested in you.

The gal for you, 1999 Cancer male, will instinctively know how to put you at ease when you are feeling uncomfortable. Telling a joke that will make you laugh, making little faces, or imitating some bit of movie dialogue the two of you find amusing are all ways to bring a smile to your face and to ease your tension. When you meet the lady who can tickle your funny bone, you'll know she's the one for you.

1999 Cancer female, you will just adore guys who speak eloquently yet with authority, who are the soul of diplomacy in any situation. The guy you will love to have by your side also helps you relate to the public and may lightly nudge you if you speak too loudly or go on for too long. But he truly can nudge your heart in a romantic way, and he is always there to let you know that he cares, every hour and every minute of the day.

1999 LEO
From July 23, 6:44 through August 23, 13:50

The Daydreaming Globetrotter

Whenever you look toward the future, Leo of 1999, you will feel as if you are looking out into a great unknown full of exciting possibilities. Independent yet emotional, you will often daydream about being a globetrotter, discovering parts of the world you have only seen in films or read about in books. You probably will always envision someone alongside you in your journeys, someone with whom you will share your wonderful experiences, and who will lead you down the road toward great accomplishments.

As much as you will love such adventurous daydreams, more exciting than that will be the possibility of creating a place you can call home. You have great hopes of making an impact on the world, with someone by your side to help you do that. Without that anchor you may feel that your great ideas will stay afloat with no way to implement them.

The person who seems to have all the answers and whose smile lights up the room is someone who will excite your interest. Along with that brilliance, there must be sensitivity and kindness for you to take this relationship beyond the getting to know you phase. Someone who can look into your eyes, smile, and perhaps touch your hand in just the right way is a person you'll want to know better.

The female who fits your dream image, 1999 Leo male, is likely to be a bit quirky with a personality and character all her own. You love independent types, and the more out of the ordinary she seems, the more in love you'll be. This is someone who will want to be your best friend. Whether happy or sad, you'll be able to talk to her about anything on your mind, including any secrets you want to share.

A guy who is outgoing, enthusiastic, and just a tad handsome (without being drop-dead gorgeous) is the kind who will make your heart skip a beat, 1999 Leo female. You will find that his physical energy matches your own, and his erudite, clever, and witty manner can make you tingle all over. You will never be attracted—at least not for long—to mere pretty boys, and as you grow and develop, you will come to appreciate an attractive mind and big heart.

1999 VIRGO

From August 23, 13:51 through September 23, 11:30

♍ *The Inquisitive Butterfly*

As you mature, Virgo of 1999, you will change from someone who is a bit self-conscious around the opposite sex into someone who is a social butterfly, more than eager to spread your wings. For you a great relationship involves two people getting to know everything about each other. Your inquisitive approach to relating to others may be a bit daunting for those you meet, but it will serve you well as you search for someone to share your life with.

Industrious, creative, and loving, you will come to understand that the most successful relationships are those in which two people communicate freely. This will be in your mind when you are trying to establish a good connection between you and someone you love. You know that without openness and honesty, even about small differences, you will never get past the handshakes and into the hugs.

Anyone who wants to catch your eye for more than a brief moment should be a bit talkative and know how to make you feel immediately at ease. Your biggest turnoff is someone whose silence seems to soak up all the good feelings in a room. More than talk, however, this person needs to have an intuitive understanding of you, a way of treating you that makes you feel the two of you are old friends right from the first time you meet.

Your dream girl, Virgo male of 1999, can be best described as someone with an indefinable something that keeps you interested and intrigued. She will have real character and a true inner beauty that gives her a unique quality all her own. She will love showing you off at public functions, and she will definitely love to brag about you to her friends and family.

The guy who will win your heart, Virgo female of 1999, is someone who may seem reserved and even secretive to those who don't know him well. But for you he will open up the mysteries of his heart and his soul from the first time you meet. He will be interested in the human condition and concerned with helping others. His compassion and his need to change the world for the better are qualities you not only admire but also want to be around all the time.

VIRGO ZODIAC SIGN
YOUR LOVE PLANETS

YOUR ROMANTIC SIDE   p. 696
▶ **VENUS IN LEO**
Born Aug. 23, 13:51 - Sept. 23, 11:31

YOUR SEX DRIVE   p. 722
▶ **MARS IN SCORPIO**
Born Aug. 23, 13:51 - Sept. 02, 19:28
▶ **MARS IN SAGITTARIUS**
Born Sept. 02, 19:29 - Sept. 23, 11:31

YOUR CELEBRITY TWINS   p. 760
Find out the astrological similarities you have with famous people.

YOUR COMPATIBILITY   p. 780
Compare planets to find out how compatible you are in a relationship.

YOUR RELATIONSHIP KARMA   p. 824
▶ **SATURN IN TAURUS**
Born Aug. 23, 13:51 - Sept. 23, 11:31

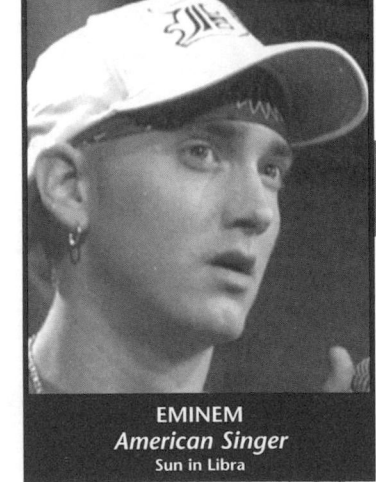

EMINEM
American Singer
Sun in Libra

667

1999 LIBRA

From September 23, 11:31 through October 23, 20:51

♎ *The People Pleaser*

Friendly, fun-loving, and aiming to please, you, Libra of 1999, will always seem to want to be part of a group. At times down the road, this might make some people think you are too focused on doing what is popular rather than on what is good for you. However, as you move on to adulthood, this becomes a valuable quality to help you learn how to make somebody who loves you happy. What you really want most, especially in your loving relationships, is for everyone to be happy together.

For you love makes the world go around, so you will sacrifice almost anything else to be with someone who accepts you as you are and returns your love. Your idea of a perfect relationship is one in which two people, whether they're rich, poor, or in between, share simple joys such as walking in the park hand in hand or cooking pancakes on a Sunday morning. As long as the two of you are together, nothing else really matters.

The key to winning your heart lies in a certain twinkle in the eyes or a welcoming little look reserved only for you. Facial expressions and body language say more to you than words ever could, so before you let someone get close, you want to know you do not need to converse to get your feelings across. Having established that, if you can be sure that this person believes in loyalty and commitment, the two of you have made a match.

The gal who makes your heart skip a beat, Libra male of 1999, will very likely be independent, bold, and self-confident. It makes you feel good to be around someone who is so dynamic, and who is willing to lay everything on the line for her ideals. And one of her most closely held ideals would be the love that the two of you share, something she will never let you doubt.

A nice-looking guy who is even-tempered, sensitive, and soft-spoken is the one you daydream about, Libra female of 1999. And you will love whatever comes along with the qualities you treasure most. He can be a rough-and-tumble type who likes touch football with the guys, or just someone quiet and bookish. If wishes come true, you'll love him with all your heart.

LIBRA ZODIAC SIGN
YOUR LOVE PLANETS

YOUR ROMANTIC SIDE   p. 696
▶ **VENUS IN LEO**
Born Sept. 23, 11:32 - Oct. 07, 16:50
▶ **VENUS IN VIRGO**
Born Oct. 07, 16:51 - Oct. 23, 20:51

YOUR SEX DRIVE   p. 722
▶ **MARS IN SAGITTARIUS**
Born Sept. 23, 11:32 - Oct. 17, 1:34
▶ **MARS IN CAPRICORN**
Born Oct. 17, 1:35 - Oct. 23, 20:51

YOUR CELEBRITY TWINS   p. 760
Find out the astrological similarities you have with famous people.

YOUR COMPATIBILITY   p. 780
Compare planets to find out how compatible you are in a relationship.

YOUR RELATIONSHIP KARMA   p. 824
▶ **SATURN IN TAURUS**
Born Sept. 23, 11:32 - Oct. 23, 20:51

CHRISTINA AGUILERA
American Singer
Sun and Venus in Sagittarius

1999 SCORPIO
From October 23, 20:52 through November 22, 18:24

♏ *The Ardent Perfectionist*

As you mature, Scorpio of 1999, you will begin to see that the world is made up of so many different types of people that it makes your head spin to think of all the possibilities. It may not be too easy to imagine there is just one special person out there for you, someone who will share your interests and make you feel romantically and emotionally fulfilled so that you will never be interested in anyone else. But there surely is such a person, as you will eventually come to understand.

Later on, you may believe that the right person will feel just exactly as you do. Once you realize that the fun and excitement of a relationship comes from the differences between two people just as much as from their similarities, then that fun can begin. And though you do have a bit of a perfectionist streak, in the end you will probably be the most tolerant of the other person's differences, as anyone could be.

To keep you interested your perfect match has to be someone who is mesmerized by your stories, your manner, and everything else about you. This person will be patient and will know how to make you feel you are truly number one. More than anything, you like a challenge, so anyone who really wants to win your heart will leave just a little unsaid—some mystery in the air for you to pursue.

The perfect lady for you, 1999 Scorpio male, is going to be a real straight shooter. She will have no time for pretension and will let you know when you are being just a little too full of yourself. You love every minute of it, though, because you know that no one will really understand as much about you as she does—and will still love you for it anyway.

You will fall head over heels for a guy who is cute and cuddly, 1999 Scorpio female, someone who will love to put his arms around you just to show you how much he cares. You'll be a sucker for him, if he shows his feelings freely, especially when he cries with you at a sad movie or laughs out loud when he is happy. Your ideal is also an outdoorsy type, someone who loves to be outside with you. That may be a tall order, but dreams do come true.

1999 SAGITTARIUS
From November 22, 18:25 through December 22, 7:43

 The Faithful Independent

As you get older, Sagittarius of 1999, you will continue to be the independent sort, and one who seems to raise multi-tasking to an art form. You will have so many different interests, ranging from cultural to political to social, that your life will always seem complete, whether you are in a relationship or not. Any partner you do have, therefore, will be unique in one way or another, and someone who will allow you a good deal of independence.

Even though the road you will travel in life might pull you and your partner apart for stretches of time, your time together will be more than special. With you it will definitely turn out to be true that "absence makes the heart grow fonder," and you will see a relationship as a series of absences punctuated by shorter, but wonderfully romantic, periods of togetherness.

Someone who wants to find a permanent place in your heart will appeal to your imagination and your love of adventure. Regaling you with wonderful travel stories or fictional tales of roads not traveled will steal your heart and awaken your senses. This will build a common bond between you very quickly, and if these stories are accompanied by a pleasant personality and a love of independence that matches your own, the deal will be sealed.

The gal of your dreams, 1999 Sagittarius male, will be equally comfortable pitching a tent and camping out in the woods, attending a lecture, or screaming her head off at a rock concert. She will have eclectic tastes and will know what it takes to be a good companion, a better friend, and even better partner. If the two of you are apart, she will never complain, and when you return, no welcome will be warmer than hers.

If you're a 1999 Sagittarius female, the guy who will win your heart will have to be charming and have a great personality and a real sense of fun and adventure. He will love trying out new things with you, going out together and acting like two kids in love— giggling out loud, sharing ice cream cones, going to the zoo, and anything else that make you feel eternally young and that your love will last forever.

Britney Spears – Growing Up with Justin

One of the most watched transitions of the 1990s was the evolution of Britney Spears' public image from her debut on *The Mickey Mouse Club*, to bubble gum pop princess, to her sexually charged videos. As Britney grew up, fans also watched the evolution of her relationship with Justin Timberlake of the popular boys band 'N Sync. The two met on the set of *The Mickey Mouse Club* when she was 12 and he was 13. They reconnected in 1998 when Britney appeared as the opening act for 'N Sync, and they became a twosome for the next four years.

The two young stars were also favorite fodder for the tabloids, with one of the most persistent questions about whether Britney was still a virgin. In her 1999 debut album *... Baby One More Time*, which sold 13 million copies and made her an instant international star, Britney displayed her All-American charm, a kind of Barbie doll-like innocence and natural beauty. And she touted a '90s kind of restraint following the AIDS epidemic in that she vowed to not have sex until she was married. Did she keep her promise?

By the year 2000 Britney was undergoing a Madonna-like reinvention that began with a flesh-colored outfit for MTV that made her appear nearly nude, and a skin-tight red catsuit for her video *Oops!...I Did it Again*. The transition caught many teen fans and their mothers by surprise, but the young adult world

was taking notice. Pepsi signed Britney to a major contract that brought her $10 million, and *Forbes* magazine gave her the number one spot on its "Celebrity 100" issue. Meanwhile, she and Justin bought a mansion in California's ritzy Mulholland Estates, though neither would admit that they were anything more than friends and housemates.

By March 2002 they were giving signals that they were no longer together. The tabloids announced the certainty of their split, though Justin's mother phrased it more diplomatically. She said they were just two kids who have an intense relationship, and when things go wrong, that's intense, too. Justin hit the dance floors from one coast to the other, while Britney went on tour. But she was clearly troubled. She was getting moody, and during an outdoor concert in Mexico she walked out after only four songs. After she and Justin split up in 2002, it became more obvious that they did have a close relationship, but an uncomfortable one plagued by the demands of their mutual careers and the constant pressure from the paparazzi.

The public Britney was getting even more sexually explicit. While Britney was touring in Germany, she commented in front of a chocolate museum that "chocolate for me is just like an orgasm." The love scenes she acted out in her next video *Don't Let Me Be the Last to Know* were performed with a 23-year-old model, but her mother/manager cut the most provocative parts out so it would be more acceptable to the general public. When asked if she was still a virgin, she said, "Who really cares if I've had sex? It's nobody's business. Trust me, I'm not going to have a press conference to announce it. If I mess up, I'm human. If I have a drink or I'm with someone, I'm human. I'm no different than anyone else my age."

669

▶ READ ABOUT MADONNA ON PAGE 555

2000 -2002

MILLENNIUM MADNESS

After September 11,

the world would never be

the same, with a climate of

fear driven by terrorism and

the threat of war.

*U*nprecedented worldwide celebration marked the beginning of a new millennium, amid hopes for a fresh beginning, for peace and a better world for all people. But on Sept. 11, 2001 tragedy struck—19 Islamic fundamentalists hijacked four domestic flights in the US and flew the planes into symbols of American strength: both towers of the World Trade Center and the Pentagon. Passengers aboard the fourth plane attempted to fight back, and the plane crashed into a Pennsylvania field. Over 3,000 people were killed in the attacks, and the US suffered a great loss of innocence—it could no longer feel invulnerable.

The victims included citizens of many nations as well as hundreds of firefighters and rescue personnel who were killed as the World Trade towers collapsed. The compelling televised images horrified people everywhere, and, in response, there was a massive outpouring of support and generosity for New York City and to the US. Within the US, hundreds of millions of dollars were raised by charities and a celebrity telethon, and a special bureau had to be created to distribute the flood of donations for the firefighters. There was also, amid the shock and grief, a sense of community, solidarity, and love.

Other countries tempered their support with some criticism of the US' historical role in the world, especially as the US launched a war on al-Qaeda and the Taliban in Afghanistan.

What seemed to be in the realm of science fiction— the cloning of human beings—became a possible reality. Apart from the famous "Dolly," the cloned sheep, various other animal clones had been been very short lived. Scientists managed to isolate and grow human embryonic stem cells in the laboratory. Eager to be able to produce human cells for valuable research for therapeutic uses, they were opposed by pro-life groups and church leaders. In March 2001, Italian gynacologist Severino Antinori, who operated a fertility clinic in Rome, announced he would attempt human cloning to help infertile couples who could not have children by any other method. In August of that year, the United States House of Representatives voted to ban all human cloning and rejected an amendment to the bill that would have permitted human cloning for stem cell research. But in 2002, scientists in the UK were given the go-ahead to create human embryo clones under controlled conditions for the purposes of therapeutic research.

On television, "reality TV" flourished, after a ground-breaking British show called *Big Brother* went stellar— resulting in the format being sold around the world and spawning dozens of spin-offs. Beginning with the first season of *Survivor*, American television networks released a flood of shows in which "real" people competed in often horrifying contests for large amounts of cash or humiliating competitions for love. In the winter of 2002, *Joe Millionaire*, a show in which a bevy of beauties vied to win the love of a construction worker posing as a multimillionaire, drew record-breaking numbers of viewers.

◀ Spanish flamenco dancer Joaquin Cortés, also known for his romance with supermodel Naomi Campbell

◀◀ Carrie-Anne Moss stars as Trinity in the sci-fi blockbuster *The Matrix*

▼ Madonna and Guy Ritchie

671

THE SILVER SCREEN

Big movies of the young century included Roman Polanski's *The Pianist*, the historical epic *Gladiator* with Russell Crowe in the tile role, the French film *Amelie*, and the Coen brothers' offbeat *O Brother, Where Art Thou?* Ang Lee's sweeping epic *Crouching Tiger, Hidden Dragon* gave Chinese cinema and martial arts a new lease on life and picked up many awards.

BETWEEN THE PAGES

The decade has already produced some excellent literature, including Michael Chabon's *The Amazing Adventures of Kavalier & Clay*, Jonathan Franzen's *The Corrections*, Kazuo Ishiguro's *When We Were Orphans*, and Ian McEwen's *Atonement*.

PEOPLE

New York mayor Rudi Giuliani became a popular and reassuring presence in the aftermath of the 9/11 terrorist attacks. But celebrity still ruled, with "bachelorette" Trista Rehn, fallen virgin nymphet Britney Spears, and Irish renegade heartthrob Colin Farrell. And while one celebrity marriage began—Madonna married director Guy Ritchie in a Scottish castle—another ended, with the bitter and public divorce of Tom Cruise and Nicole Kidman. Cruise was promptly linked with Penelope Cruz, Spanish actress and co-star in his film *Vanilla Sky*. People were still eager for every detail of Michael Jackson's bizarre life and Jennifer Lopez's love life. Musical tastes were varied and eclectic with everything from rap's bad boy Eminem to sultry jazz vocalist Norah Jones.

- ✪ LOVE BUG
- ✪ INTERNET DATING
- ✪ BABY BANK
- ✪ SANTANA
- ✪ CROUCHING TIGER, HIDDEN DRAGON
- ✪ ALMOST FAMOUS
- ✪ RELATIONSHIP RESCUE

EVENTS

The Love Bug computer virus spread via email attachments titled "I love you." Texas A&M student Kerry Kujawa was killed by a man posing as a female student on the Internet. Despite such dangers, millions worldwide used chat rooms, messaging, and personals sites to find love. The FDA approved RU-486, the so-called "abortion pill." Hamburg opened a "baby bank" where unwanted babies could be left for adoption. The Italian newspaper *Libero* caused an uproar by publishing the names of sex offenders. Meg Ryan ditched husband Dennis Quaid for Australian leading man Russell Crowe. The affair lasted six months. Hot Hollywood commodities Angelina Jolie, 24, and Billy Bob Thornton, 44, married, sported matching tattoos, and wore vials of one another's blood. Celebrity lesbian couple Ellen DeGeneres and Anne Heche broke up. Madonna married director Guy Ritchie at Scotland's Skibo Castle.

POP CULTURE

Santana's Grammy-winning comeback album included "Smooth" and "Maria Maria." Matchbox 20's "Bent," Lonestar's "Amazed," Atomic Kitten's "Whole Again," Destiny's Child's "Say My Name," and Faith Hill's "Breathe" were all hits.

In the offbeat comedy *Nurse Betty*, Renee Zellweger is a delusional soap opera fan and witness to a murder. In *All the Pretty Horses*, based on Cormac McCarthy's novel, a dispossessed young Texas rancher finds love and terrible

Sex Idol

injustice in 1940s Mexico. In Ang Lee's *Crouching Tiger, Hidden Dragon*, a warrior and the woman he secretly loves embark on a quest in feudal China. Cameron Crowe's semiautobiographical *Almost Famous* was about a teen writer's loss of innocence amid sex, drugs, and rock 'n' roll. In *Chocolat*, Vianne and her daughter open a chocolate shop in a rural French village, but clash with the locals when Vianne takes up with an Irish gypsy.

In Christina Schwarz's *Drowning Ruth*, a rural Wisconsin girl grows up in the shadow of a terrible family secret. In *Relationship Rescue*, "Dr. Phil" (of Oprah fame) applies his seven-step strategy to transform troubled partnerships. In Elizabeth Bailey's historical romance *The Veiled Bride*, a young woman agrees to marry wealthy Lord Raith. A Los Angeles artist has strange relationships with a young slacker and an older businessman in Steve Martin's *Shopgirl*.

PRINCE WILLIAM

Britain's Prince William turned 18 on June 21, 2000. Second in line for the throne after his father, Prince Charles, the handsome, athletic, bright William attracts the press—and teenage girls. He won respect and sympathy for his dignity after the tragic death of his mother, Princess Diana, in a 1997 car accident.

William graduated from prestigious Eton, and now attends Scotland's St. Andrew's University, where, as he says, "I like to keep my private life private." His adoring female fans will just have to content themselves with official royal portraits and daydreams of becoming the lucky lady who gets to marry this dashing prince.

SEE ALSO
- ▶ PRINCESS DIANA *Page 523*
- ▶ PRINCE CHARLES & PRINCESS DIANA *Page 516*

2000 CAPRICORN

From December 22, 1999 7:44 through January 20, 2000 18:22
(December 2000 Capricorns, see 2001 Capricorn)

The Prestige Seeker

You Capricorns born in 2000 will know the real thing when you see it. You'll be able to spot a diamond in the rough, and will just as easily spot the perfect mate. It won't be all about sparks of passion with you goats—it'll be about working hard in a relationship to keep it healthy. Stability will be your most notable asset, and for you, stability will mean the money needed to raise a family.

Keeping tradition alive, you'll revel in old-fashioned values and long for times that were less complicated on the dating front. You'll have a quaint view of sex as well, placing rose peddles on the four-poster bed and using light caresses to seduce your lover. If you don't feel as though your partner lives up to their potential, you'll lose interest. You Capricorns will strive to be the pillar of society, so you'll want a mate with whom you are proud to build a community and a home.

In order to attract your attention, a potential suitor will have to opt for a business look. The more impeccably dressed they are, the more points with you they'll score with you. The best bet for a memorable date with you will probably be a cultural event or a museum exhibit. If someone proves that they know about Picasso's Blue Period, you'll be impressed and you'll jump at the chance to enter a relationship with that person.

When you male 2000 Capricorns grow up, you could well be attracted to the woman all men want—the flirty, autonomous type that seems elusive but idealistic at the same time. She could be sporty, but spiritual at the same time. Her time might be spent with her many friends, but when you two are alone, her witty sense of humor will have you laughing and lighthearted.

As a female 2000 Capricorn, you'll be attracted to the whimsical romantic type of man—the artist who has chosen to struggle because he has a creative vision. You'll most likely be drawn to men who are sensitive because they allow you to show a softer side few are able to see. The future will reveal that you also can be attracted to a man who is well traveled and who allows you to see the world through his eyes.

CAPRICORN ZODIAC SIGN

YOUR LOVE PLANETS

YOUR ROMANTIC SIDE   p. 696
► VENUS IN SCORPIO
Born Dec. 22, 1999 7:44 – Dec. 31, 1999 4:53
► VENUS IN SAGITTARIUS
Born Dec. 31, 1999 4:54 - Jan. 20, 2000 18:22

YOUR SEX DRIVE   p. 722
► MARS IN AQUARIUS
Born Dec. 22, 1999 7:44 - Jan. 04, 2000 3:00
► MARS IN PISCES
Born Jan. 04, 3:01 - Jan. 20, 18:22

YOUR CELEBRITY TWINS   p. 760
Find out the astrological similarities you have with famous people.

YOUR COMPATIBILITY   p. 780
Compare planets to find out how compatible you are in a relationship.

YOUR RELATIONSHIP KARMA   p. 824
► SATURN IN TAURUS
Born Dec. 22, 1999 7:44 - Jan. 20, 2000 18:22

TIGER WOODS
American Champion Golfer
Sun in Capricorn

673

2000 AQUARIUS

From January 20, 18:23 through February 19, 8:32

The Offbeat Intellectual

As an Aquarian born in 2000, when you grow up, you may discover you are searching for a relationship that is honest and intellectually stimulating. Because your mind will constantly be in full throttle, you will need someone who can challenge you with deep thoughts, forcing you to find truth in your life. And although you might act rashly at times in order to stir up the humdrum, you'll really want someone who will stick with you.

Your unique sense of humor might be offbeat to some, but those that'll appreciate your quirky remarks will soon see you can find humor in almost any situation. You might even bring your quirky sense of humor into the bedroom. Tickle fights under the covers could be prelude to foreplay. A respectful relationship is the only kind for you, and if you find your partner's actions hypocritical, you'll drop them like a bad cliché.

For you to notice someone, they'll need the will to stand up for their beliefs as well as fight for society's good in general. Whether they'll be fighting for peace or for animal rights, they will certainly spark your interest if they take action for a cause. You'll want someone who has a variety of interests. They should be able to match your energy level and always have a fresh topic to talk about or a new approach to an old problem.

More than likely you 2000 Aquarian men will chose to date the class president instead of the head cheerleader. You'll find that you like for your women to be ambitious, strong, and oh so classy. You may prefer your woman to be fairly conservative with her affections in public, but in private you will want your woman to tie you down and show you who's boss.

If you're an Aquarian woman born in 2000, you'll want your man to bring you roses on your birthday and shower you with small love gifts the rest of year as well. As you mature, your romantic nature may make you attracted to gentle, sensitive men, but these guys better know how to bring home the bacon and fry it up in a pan to keep you happy. You'll find your man's whimsical side will allow you to try a variety of quirky activities in and out of the bedroom.

AQUARIUS ZODIAC SIGN

YOUR LOVE PLANETS

YOUR ROMANTIC SIDE   p. 696
► VENUS IN SAGITTARIUS
Born Jan. 20, 18:23 - Jan. 24, 19:51
► VENUS IN CAPRICORN
Born Jan. 24, 19:52 - Feb. 18, 4:42
► VENUS IN AQUARIUS
Born Feb. 18, 4:43 - Feb. 19, 8:32

YOUR SEX DRIVE   p. 722
► MARS IN PISCES
Born Jan. 20, 18:23 - Feb. 12, 1:03
► MARS IN ARIES
Born Feb. 12, 1:04 - Feb. 19, 8:32

YOUR CELEBRITY TWINS   p. 760
Find out the astrological similarities you have with famous people.

YOUR COMPATIBILITY   p. 780
Compare planets to find out how compatible you are in a relationship.

YOUR RELATIONSHIP KARMA   p. 824
► SATURN IN TAURUS
Born Jan. 20, 18:23 - Feb. 19, 8:32

BENICIO DEL TORO
Puerto Rican Actor
Sun, and Venus in Pisces

2000 PISCES
From February 19, 8:33 through March 20, 7:34

The Practical Dreamer

You'll grow to find that your gentle demure temperament is a gift you'll bring to all your relationships. You'll probably never lose that childlike wonderment of love leading to a romantic, dreamy nature, allowing you to fall in love easily. Throughout your life you might find you'll forge lifelong karmic connections with a variety of people. Sex for you will be all about bonding, and therefore you might find yourself wanting to linger in the moment.

Although you may be shy when it comes to initiating relationships, if someone makes their feelings known, you'll be able to take that leap and open your heart. You might become one of those people that doesn't really have a "type" that lights your fire physically, but you will probably pick partners based on religious philosophy and upbringing. You will also need a patient partner that allows you enough space to pursue creative projects.

In order for someone to have a lasting relationship with you, they'll have to trust the bonding process and be patient. If they focus on the future of the relationship instead of the here and now, they'll eventually watch you walk away. Even though you won't be open to people pushing you into commitments, you will want a partner who's open to evolving and slowly developing a steady, lasting connection.

You 2000 Piscean men may dream of setting up house with the perfect white picket fence, but what you'll dream and what you want might clash, so eventually you'll look for a mate that's flexible and multifaceted. She'll have to be in touch with her femininity and have an extremely vivid imagination—a bird of flight. On the other hand, she'll have to be a bit demanding like a spoiled rock-star, allowing you to feel needed and soothe her.

You female Pisceans born this year will never lose sight of the fairy tales you were once told and may pine away for the knight in shining armor. In reality, you'll want your guy to be there to bail you out. You'll want to be able to rely on your man when life seems totally chaotic, and want a strong willed man who knows what he wants and pursues it wholeheartedly.

2000 ARIES
From March 20, 7:35 through April 19, 18:38

The Successful Seducer

In years to come you may find that you love the initial excitement and possibilities of new relationships. But after that first date, you might find yourself losing interest unless there's a real possibility of a long-term thing. You'll be searching for passion, and will want someone who appeals to you both physically as well as financially—meaning they had better have a polished look without having to spend a fortune to pull it off.

Aries love the chase, so until you find "a winner" you might adopt the motto, "Don't hate the player, hate the game." In the bedroom you'll be sexually strong, wanting to put your all into that magical moment. You will probably know exactly what type of person you do want and have a mental checklist of the qualities your mate should have. So, when you do find Mr. or Mrs. Right, you'll know pretty quickly and dive right into a full-fledged relationship, getting fairly comfy fast.

You'll look for someone who's sensual and faithful. If their eye roams, forget it. In order for someone to keep your interest they'll need to focus their attention on you and not the "hottie" next door. They'll have to have nimble hands and need to make sure there's plenty massage oil in the house. It's also good if they're ambitious and not only able to pursue their own career, but be supportive of yours as well.

As a male Aries of the year 2000, you'll like your lady to be outgoing and social. You'll want to be able to pal around with her. She should be able to throw on a pair of jeans and a T-shirt and be comfortable hanging out with the guys. You might want your woman to have business sense and be able to chat with you about the stock market and your investments.

When you 2000 Aries girls grow up, you might want to marry a banker. At the very least, you'll definitely want a man of sophistication and taste who knows a bit about investing, a bit about diamonds, and bit about art collecting. You'll also want a man who's willing to return your feelings immediately— you won't want to play games and guess how your guy's feeling. You'll want to know right then and there.

674

2000 TAURUS

From April 19, 18:39 through May 20, 17:48

The Forever Faithful

As you grow older, you'll find that you're able to nurture relationships into steadfast, solid partnerships. Your cautious nature will cloak a warm heart, and you'll tend to reveal yourself slowly. Just like a fine wine, your love will age nicely over time. Sexually you'll prefer the erotic striptease approach to the all out impulsive caught-in-the-moment method. You'll prefer to go at your own pace and get to know your partner slowly.

You might find at times that you enjoy teasing your lover and laying it on a bit too thick, coaxing them to come to you and enjoying how they succumb to your looks and charm. You'll want to feel physically radiant when you're with your partner, and they should take the time to notice small changes to your appearance or compliment your new duds, since highlighting your outer appearance is how you'll show them what's inside your heart.

Your earthy nature will attract people whose feet are firmly planted on the ground. You'll want someone who is practical about love. Your mate should value hard work and want to share the fruits of their labor with you. Since you'll appreciate luxurious items, your mate should have good taste and realize that money is to be spent on things that enhance the enjoyment of life.

You boys born as 2000 Taureans will grow into men who not only appreciate a good home cooked meal, but worship the woman that feeds you tasty treats. You'll love nature and want your partner to have a green thumb as well. She should be comfortable around the house and proud of providing a fairly conservative, nurturing home with a prizewinning rose garden, of course.

As a female 2000 Taurus you'll want your guy to spur you with witty conversation. You'll want your man to be a jack-of-all-trades, and if playing a musical instrument is part of his repertoire, all the better. Your relationships might be freer than most, because at times your man might have lots of projects going on simultaneously. But this will allow you to be both a friend and lover, giving you time to play together, which will be followed by days of deep bonding.

TAURUS ZODIAC SIGN
YOUR LOVE PLANETS

YOUR ROMANTIC SIDE — p. 696
► VENUS IN ARIES
Born Apr. 19, 18:40 - May 01, 2:48
► VENUS IN TAURUS
Born May 01, 2:49 - May 20, 17:48

YOUR SEX DRIVE — p. 722
► MARS IN TAURUS
Born Apr. 19, 18:40 - May 03, 19:17
► MARS IN GEMINI
Born May 03, 19:18 - May 20, 17:48

YOUR CELEBRITY TWINS — p. 760
Find out the astrological similarities you have with famous people.

YOUR COMPATIBILITY — p. 780
Compare planets to find out how compatible you are in a relationship.

YOUR RELATIONSHIP KARMA — p. 824
► SATURN IN TAURUS
Born Apr. 19, 18:40 - May 20, 17:48

KYLIE MINOGUE
Australian Singer
Sun, Venus, and Mars in Gemini

675

2000 GEMINI

From May 20, 17:49 through June 21, 1:47

The Incurable Flirt

You'll thrive on change, so if you find that your mate is becoming boring or stuffy in any way, you'll immediately flit over to the next prospective suitor. You'll have many to choose from when it comes to finding a partner because people will be drawn to your gregarious demeanor. Sexually speaking, you'll use flattery and poetry to get a partner in the mood, and you'll communicate freely when it comes to telling your lover exactly what pleases you.

Since you'll probably always be on the go, you'll encounter lots of possible dating scenarios. Whether it's taking a class or attending a party, your dance card will always be full. With so many potential partners and so little time, the challenge for you will be deciding who to keep and who to toss. Perhaps you'll find that you'll want to keep them all and play the field for a while, but when you meet your intellectual match, you'll know you have a winner.

The ideal mate for you will understand your innate need for social interaction and will not be jealous of the many friends you keep. Actually, if they encourage you to go out on your own at times, then they'll stand a chance of keeping your heart for good. You'll need someone with a healthy ego who doesn't pout when you're not at home. They'll have to understand your voracious appetite for stimuli and be grateful that you've allowed them to tag along for the ride.

You Gemini males born in 2000 will want your woman to be flirty and fun. She should have a curious nature about her. You will probably want someone who is charming and knows how to talk you up. She should be the Judy to your Punch, and in fact, if she's able to play off your banter and have fun with your words, she'll turn you on for good.

As a female 2000 Gemini, you'll want your man to go, go, go. He should not be afraid to take you to parties and introduce you to his friends. You'll want to meet all of his buddies and establish friendships with all of your man's cohorts, but you'll expect the same in return from him. He should be willing to accompany you and take the time to get to know your friends.

GEMINI ZODIAC SIGN
YOUR LOVE PLANETS

YOUR ROMANTIC SIDE — p. 696
► VENUS IN TAURUS
Born May 20, 17:49 - May 25, 12:14
► VENUS IN GEMINI
Born May 25, 12:15 - June 18, 22:14
► VENUS IN CANCER
Born June 18, 22:15 - June 21, 1:47

YOUR SEX DRIVE — p. 722
► MARS IN GEMINI
Born May 20, 17:49 - June 16, 12:29
► MARS IN CANCER
Born June 16, 12:30 - June 21, 1:47

YOUR CELEBRITY TWINS — p. 760
Find out the astrological similarities you have with famous people.

YOUR COMPATIBILITY — p. 780
Compare planets to find out how compatible you are in a relationship.

YOUR RELATIONSHIP KARMA — p. 824
► SATURN IN TAURUS
Born May 20, 17:49 - June 21, 1:47

PENELOPE CRUZ
Spanish Actress
Mars in Cancer

676

2000 CANCER
From June 21, 1:48 through July 22, 12:42

The Caring Communicator

As you mature and express your sensitive temperament, you'll find gentle souls that understand your caring heart and empathetic nature. Kindness is something you'll want to foster in all your relationships. Communicating gently with forethought will become an integral part of your partnerships, so before you express yourself you'll want time to digest your feelings. Sexually you'll be soft and want to make sure there's plenty of time to spoon and cuddle after sex. You might find that you'll have a need now and then to talk about how your relationship's progressing.

You might be protective of your mate, wanting to shelter him or her from the world, and in fact some of the most romantic times you'll have might take place at home, weathering out a thunderstorm in front of the fireplace. A jet-setter might not be the best match for you, since you'll form strong emotional attachments to your partner and will want to be able to reach out (and even make physical contact) on daily basis.

For someone to attract your attention they'll have to be able to intuit your moods. They should know what to say to make you feel safe and be able to be there emotionally when you need them. Your partner shouldn't snap at people—they should always be considerate. They should have an appreciation for quite nights spent cuddling on the couch.

As a male Cancer born in 2000, you might look for a woman just like good ol' mom. She should want to pamper you, but at the same time she should make you feel strong, and make you feel as though you truly are "the man of the house." She should be able to reassure you of her love, and what better way than candlelight dinners waiting for you when you come home.

As a female Cancer born in 2000, you might like for your man to be warm and truly in touch with his feminine side. He should be comfortable going to a chick-flick and crying alongside his woman. The best way for him to show you how much he cares would be pitching in and helping with the housework. He should be gentle and know that the best way to heat up the bedroom is with lilac scented candles.

2000 LEO
From July 22, 12:43 through August 22, 19:47

The Loving Entertainer

You'll long for a large family since you'll love children and the sound of laughter and play. Family will be something you'll take pride in and you'll want to showcase your mate whenever possible. When it comes to partnerships, you will want to shower your mate with affection, and love it when they do the same in return. Holding hands in public will be something you're all for. Your flamboyant nature will make relationships with you exciting and it might always seem as though there is a drama brewing on the love front.

Demonstrative in love, you'll want to show your mate how much you love them with physical caresses and material trinkets. You might make large plays for a potential mate's attention, charming them and eventually winning their heart. A huge surprise proposal at the Super Bowl or renting the entire symphony to serenade you and your partner are examples of how you'll show you care. Nothing will be too bold for you when it comes to love.

In order for you to send someone a dozen roses delivered by a singing Panda, they'll have to be charming and something of a social climber. You won't have time to deal with wallflowers, so you'll opt for the life of party—someone with whom you can share the limelight. Strong personalities attract you—people who take risks and love life.

As a male born as a 2000 Leo, you will be drawn to the hostess with the mostest. You'll want a party girl. She should be self-confident. She should be sexy, know it, and flaunt it, but she should also have a romantic side, too. Little love notes, a naughty midday call at the office ... these will be things that she'll do to make you wild with passion and eager to get home.

You 2000 Leo ladies will definitely demand that your lover make large plays for your affections. Your guy should like to dress up, go out, and paint the town red. You'll need your partner to be very romantic and shower you with affection and gifts and not be afraid to shout his love from the rooftops. Your guy might be somewhat of a sportsman too, either watching or playing games that involve physical contact.

2000 VIRGO

From August 22, 19:48 through September 22, 17:27

The Perfect Partner

As a 2000 Virgo, you'll be on the search for the perfect mate with a list of relationship deal breakers, but this list will wane as you get older and you'll begin to rely on your instincts. You might find that you'll become quite passionate and warm up to individuals who will allow you to truly be yourself. You'll find the longer you know your mate, the more interested you'll be in experimenting in the bedroom, spicing up your sexual style.

You won't enter relationships with hidden agendas. Your intent will always be charitable and you'll always be willing to give to another—your relationships will be based on giving. As you get more comfortable in a particular partnership, you'll be able to ask for things from your mate, accepting generosity from them as well, which opens the door to a relationship that is based on mutual giving and receiving.

To attract your attention, someone must notice the details and watch their P's and Q's because if they mess up, you'll know. The one you'll be interested in won't be late or wishy-washy, and will never try to pull the wool over your eyes ... you'll spot it immediately. Your potential partner will be exact and always follow through. You'll find that your perfect mate is curious and always ready to share knowledge.

You Virgo guys born in 2000 will be attracted to the more reserved type of woman. She won't need bells and whistles to catch your eye. You'll like her classic beauty and she'll have more refined taste than usual. That's not to say you won't care how your gal dresses or how she presents herself—quite the opposite. She'll know what's in style. She'll have impeccable manners, never eat with her fingers, or interrupt someone mid sentence.

You Virgo women born in 2000 will want your man to regale you with stories. You'll want a man who'll come home from battle with tall tales of the open seas. He should be a bit of a showman and make you feel like the beautiful assistant at his side who gets her own applause for helping before the curtain falls. You'll enjoy the excitement he provides and love the attention he demands.

VIRGO ZODIAC SIGN
YOUR LOVE PLANETS

YOUR ROMANTIC SIDE   p. 696
▶ **VENUS IN VIRGO**
Born Aug. 22, 19:49 - Aug. 31, 3:34
▶ **VENUS IN LIBRA**
Born Aug. 31, 3:35 - Sept. 22, 17:27

YOUR SEX DRIVE   p. 722
▶ **MARS IN LEO**
Born Aug. 22, 19:49 - Sept. 17, 0:18
▶ **MARS IN VIRGO**
Born Sept. 17, 0:19 - Sept. 22, 17:27

YOUR CELEBRITY TWINS   p. 760
Find out the astrological similarities you have with famous people.

YOUR COMPATIBILITY   p. 780
Compare planets to find out how compatible you are in a relationship.

YOUR RELATIONSHIP KARMA   p. 824
▶ **SATURN IN GEMINI**
Born Aug. 22, 19:49 - Sept. 22, 17:27

Stephen Fry
English Writer
Sun and Mars in Virgo

677

2000 LIBRA

From September 22, 17:28 through October 23, 2:46

The Sophisticated Mate

As you Librans mature, your refined tastes will be challenged and one day you might even surprise yourself by being be much more emotional in relationships with lovers than with family or friends. Dramatic and charming, you'll almost always get the one who catches your eye. You Libras will be hard to resist. Sexually you'll look at your lovemaking as a work in progress, always trying new and better ways to bring passion to its highest level.

Although Librans are known for their indecisiveness, 2000 Librans will know when they've been hooked for good. When someone complements you in a relationship and there's a perfect balance of charm and mystery, you'll be prepared to make a commitment. And it's partnerships you'll crave, choosing to be with another rather than be alone. You might decide to keep your relationship under wraps a bit, causing others to wonder what you and your partner do alone together, especially at night.

In order for someone to attract your attention, they'll have to play Inspector Clouseau. The more intriguing someone is, the more appealing they'll become to you. Since you 2000 Librans will be attracted to an aloofness that allows room for your imagination to roam, playing a little hard to get wouldn't be such a bad idea for a suitor, because then the guessing isn't over. The trick for someone to pique your curiosity will be for them to always have an air of intrigue.

Born as a 2000 Libran male, you might find yourself drawn to the mysterious woman who wears sunglasses at all times and doesn't spill her guts on the first date. You'll enjoy knowing she has a secret past and will encourage her to share it, as long as it's only with you. You'll like for your lady to have an intensity that spurs dramatic passion in the bedroom.

All you 2000 Libran ladies will want your guy to get ahead the old-fashioned way—hard work and sweat. Namedroppers won't impress you gals, and you won't care so much who your man knows. It's who he is that'll really matter. You might be inclined to align yourself with the underdog, valuing the man who got ahead and beat the odds.

LIBRA ZODIAC SIGN
YOUR LOVE PLANETS

YOUR ROMANTIC SIDE   p. 696
▶ **VENUS IN LIBRA**
Born Sept. 22, 17:28 - Sept. 24, 15:25
▶ **VENUS IN SCORPIO**
Born Sept. 24, 15:26 - Oct. 19, 6:17
▶ **VENUS IN SAGITTARIUS**
Born Oct. 19, 6:18 - Oct. 23, 2:47

YOUR SEX DRIVE   p. 722
▶ **MARS IN VIRGO**
Born Sept. 22, 17:28 - Oct. 23, 2:47

YOUR CELEBRITY TWINS   p. 760
Find out the astrological similarities you have with famous people.

YOUR COMPATIBILITY   p. 780
Compare planets to find out how compatible you are in a relationship.

YOUR RELATIONSHIP KARMA   p. 824
▶ **SATURN IN GEMINI**
Born Sept. 22, 17:28 - Oct. 16, 0:45
▶ **SATURN IN TAURUS**
Born Oct. 16, 0:31 - Oct. 23, 2:47

BJORK
Icelandic Singer
Sun in Scorpio

678

2000 SCORPIO
From October 23, 2:47 through November 22, 0:18

♏ *The Intense Igniter*

You won't be one to take relationships lightly. Even those that don't last a lifetime will touch your soul in an indelible way. You won't ever forego passion in a relationship, either. If there's not a palpable spark, you might look elsewhere for love. But when someone does ignite your fire, woe Nelly! You won't be likely to back down when it comes to pursuing the hottie you have your eye on, and if they don't return your smile, you'll try even harder to capture their heart.

You'll want to know everything about your lover. Asking them questions about their past will lead to lots of late night conversations. You'll feel as though knowing your mate inside and out is an integral part of intimacy. In fact, you might not even plant a kiss without knowing your lover very well. Your partner's tics and habits will fascinate you and you'll fall in love not only with your lover's appearance but with their psyche as well.

In order to attract your attention, suitors should probe, asking you questions about your dreams and childhood experiences. They should want to strip away the layers of their ego and be interested in exploring the roots of their persona. You'll need someone who's extremely sexy and willing to be a bit naughty in the bedroom. And if they're able to shock you every once in a while, even better.

As a 2000 Scorpio man, you won't want your lady to sit at home. You'll want someone autonomous and independent. She should have the ability to speak her mind and might even harbor strong opinions about those in your close circle. Since she'll be able to express herself directly, you'll always know where you stand with her and where the relationship is going.

As a 2000 Scorpio lady, your guy will be cooperative and function well in a couple. In fact, he would rather be seen as a couple and probably prefer to socialize as a couple, so you might forgo twosome time for going out with others. But when he invites others over for a game of Scrabble don't serve beer and chips. Your man will have a sophisticated palate and prefer a Brie and fruit plate be served to your guests.

2000 SAGITTARIUS
From November 22, 0:19 through December 21, 13:36

♐ *The Roaming Romancer*

When you're older, you might encounter all sorts of people on your travels, leading to many relationships with a variety of types. You might even try your hand at romancing people from other countries or cultures, dipping your toes in the international sea of love. Since you'll be a gypsy at heart, before you know it you might have a long-distance relationship on your hands. Actually, you'll do quite well in relationships that allow space, no matter if the space is physical or emotional.

When the time comes for you to settle down, you will want a partnership that embodies a religious or philosophical bond as a basis for being together. You will look for someone who engages you in conversation. You might want your mate to not only be a lover, but a buddy as well. You show your love with spontaneous gestures, like packing a bottle of wine and a blanket, and then whisking your partner away on a romantic camping trip.

In order to attract your attention, a potential suitor will have to look at life as one big adventure. They shouldn't bother you with little details. They must have a great sense of humor and laugh at all your jokes. They must be able to indulge in life's greater pleasures, like Ben & Jerry's ice cream eaten on silky satin sheets while watching a movie on a big screen TV with surround sound.

You 2000 Sag men might attract women who have a bit of a wild side, but it will be well hidden under their business attire. She might be reserved when she's in her work mode, but when she's home she'll let her hair down. She might participate in activities that others find bizarre, like midnight séances or underwater polo.

For you 2000 Sag girls, having your guy on your arm will make the world will feel right. He'll be quite a charmer, pulling out your chair for you when you sit down to eat and bringing roses home to you when you've had a rough day. He'll be quite a looker, so your friends may be jealous, but your parents will probably love him. He'll act like perfect gentleman, always ready to smooth over stressful situations with witty words and practical advice.

HBO's *Sex and the City*

Can four smart, successful, and sexually adventurous women find love, happiness, and the perfect designer outfit in modern-day Manhattan? That's the essential question posed by *Sex and the City*, HBO's hit series featuring cute-but-chic Carrie (Sarah Jessica Parker), insatiable Samantha (Kim Cattrall), emotionally buttoned up Miranda (Cynthia Nixon), and Charlotte (Kristin Davis), the hopeless romantic. Together these four best friends traverse the social terrain generally reserved for men, and manage to look fabulous while doing it. Featuring engagingly contemporary storylines, deliciously risqué dialogue, and drop-dead gorgeous clothes, *Sex and the City* breaks new ground and entertains all at the same time.

From the top of her newest and most chic Roberto Cavalli outfit to the soles of her favorite Manolo Blahnik shoes, sex-and-lifestyles columnist Carrie Bradshaw epitomizes both the heart and existential angst of *Sex and the City*. Based loosely on the experiences of *New York Observer* sex columnist Candace Bushnell, the series debuted on HBO in June 1998 and became an instant hit.

Sipping Cosmopolitans and tossing off *bon mots* of dating wisdom, the glamorous foursome dish, dialogue, and debate their love lives with sassy cynicism and the occasional wistful quip. Bold Samantha has some of the best lines—"You mean to tell me you've been dating this guy for three weeks and you haven't seen his balls yet?" she mocks Charlotte. And when discussing her well-endowed lover with Carrie, "You dated Mr. Big and I'm dating Mr. TOO Big!" But there are plenty of pithy comments to go around, apt and often hilarious phrases—"orgasm alert," "Modelizers" (men who only date models), and clever

Sarah Jessica Parker

"So what are we going to do? Sit around bars, sipping Cosmos and sleeping with strangers when we're eighty?"

SARAH JESSICA PARKER as Carrie Bradshaw

epithets for men like "spring-roll guy," "the man with no soul," and the infamous "Mr. Pussy."

But *SATC* does more than simply narrate (and poke fun at) the dating and mating habits of New York's most eligible singles. Arguably the cultural descendant of *Julia*, *That Girl*, and *The Mary Tyler Moore Show*—programs that broke feminist ground in their day—the series treads the gulf between romance and sex with skill and wit. Yet there is something inherently old fashioned in the questions Carrie poses in her weekly column, ("Is it better to 'fake it' than to be alone?" "Have we missed the boat?" "What constitutes cheating?"). There is even an homage to MTM in the show's opening credits as Parker does a Mary-style pivot.

Carrie's off-again, on-again relationship/friendship with Mr. Big (Chris Noth), an archetypical Manhattan power player in the world of high finance, has given *SATC* some of its best moments as Carrie seeks to navigate the treacherous yet exhilarating undercurrents of Manhattan's dating scene. And though she later found "true love" with Aidan (John Corbett), an unaffected furniture designer, Carrie's inherently liberated libido wanted out and she broke the engagement, becoming a single girl once again. This is, after all, a show with a feminist heart.

A valentine to the city of New York, the Emmy and Golden Globe-winning *Sex and the City* offers a glimpse into a lifestyle we might all like to inhabit, if only occasionally. Each week women—and men—who are single, married, or somewhere in between find humor and truth in the witty, sexy, and occasionally heartbreaking exploits of four stylishly coiffed and coutured protagonists and their scintillating TV world.

STAR OF *JULIA*, DIAHANN CARROLL, ON PAGE 564 ▶ READ ABOUT SEX IN THE '70S - LIBERATION, LUST & LOVE ON PAGE 449

2001

- ★ 9/11
- ★ POWER OF PRAYER
- ★ CRUISE AND CRUZ?
- ★ FALLIN'
- ★ HALLE BERRY'S OSCAR
- ★ MOULIN ROUGE!
- ★ IN THE BEDROOM

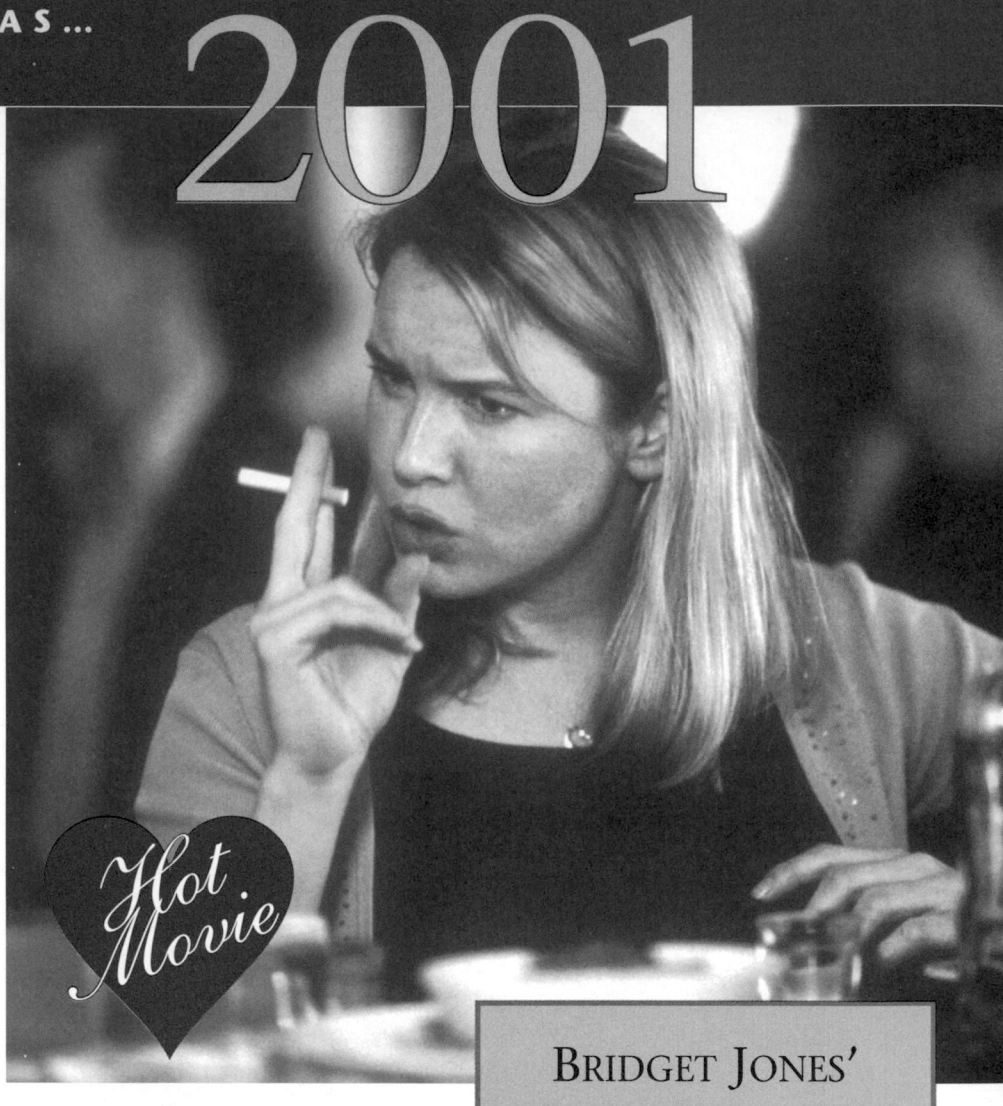

Hot Movie

EVENTS

In the wake of the 9/11 terrorist attacks on New York and Washington, many people turned to "apocalypse sex" or "Armageddon sex" for life-affirming stress relief. There were also widespread reports of ex-lovers and ex-spouses reestablishing contact. *The Journal of Reproductive Medicine* published findings that women undergoing fertility treatments (in-vitro fertilization and embryo transfers) had a 50 percent pregnancy rate, twice that of a control group, when anonymous strangers prayed for their success. Gary Condit was grilled by *Primetime Live*'s Connie Chung about the disappearance of Chandra Levy, a young Washington intern with whom the married California representative was having an affair. "Real Doll" was swamped with orders for life-sized, highly realistic "love dolls," sold on their website for $6,000. Germany's courts upheld legislation allowing same-sex marriages. Following a nasty, public breakup, Tom Cruise and Nicole Kidman divorced amid rumors linking Cruise with Spanish siren Penelope Cruz.

POP CULTURE

Alicia Keys' "Fallin'" won Song of the Year at the Grammys. People were listening to Jennifer Lopez's "I'm Real," Janet Jackson's "All for You," Lenny Kravitz's "Again," and former Spice Girl Geri Halliwell's cover of "It's Raining Men."

Halle Berry won an Oscar for her portrayal of the wife of a death-row inmate in *Monster's Ball*. In Baz Luhrmann's lavish musical *Moulin Rouge!*

Nicole Kidman is a cabaret star in bohemian 1900s Paris. Jennifer Lopez falls for the bridegroom whose lavish wedding she is organizing in *The Wedding Planner*. A family is torn apart in Todd Field's *In the Bedroom*. In *Charlotte Gray*, directed by Gillian Armstrong, a young Scottish woman joins the French Resistance after her lover is shot down over France.

Nora Roberts' *Midnight Bayou* was a Southern gothic romance replete with an old, possibly haunted mansion and a steamy love story between its new owner and a mysterious local woman. *Narcissus in Chains* by Laurell K. Hamilton featured vampire hunter Anita Blake, her otherworldly lovers, and a kidnapping at a vampire dive. Jacqueline Baird's *Marriage at His Convenience* was about an opportunistic cad and the woman who loves him. In Danielle Steel's *The Kiss*, a deadly bus accident accompanies a momentous first kiss.

BRIDGET JONES' DIARY

Striking a chord with women everywhere, *Bridget Jones' Diary* was the chick-flick hit of 2001. Adapted from Helen Fielding's original novel, the movie followed our heroine's sojourns into the familiar world of dating, bad jobs, and, most importantly, "singletons" verses "smug marrieds." The female audience was also kept happy by the presence of Hugh Grant in a wonderfully salacious role and Colin Firth as Bridget's true love Mark Darcy.

A twist to the tale was that a Texan was chosen to play the role of UK home counties' Bridget and yet Reneé Zellweger piled on weight, put on support pants, and adopted a plummy London accent with gusto. A sequel is rumored to go into production in 2003.

SEE ALSO

▶ HUGH GRANT *Page 645*

▶ CATHERINE ZETA-JONES *Page 688*

2001 CAPRICORN

From December 21, 2000 13:37 through January 20, 2001 0:16
(December 2001 Capricorns, see 2002 Capricorn)

♑ The Intuitive Healer

When looking toward the future, Capricorn of 2001, you may see yourself involved in the healing arts, helping others achieve mental and physical well-being. You will almost certainly possess a combination of both knowledge and intuition—that uncanny ability to assess what ails someone, and to pinpoint the remedy. With relationships, those same instincts will help you to choose the most compatible partner and improve the quality of both your lives.

Your perfect fit will be with someone who, like yourself, loves exploring ways to stay healthy and fit. Your dream vacation might be going to a fabulous spa where you relax in herbal baths, take invigorating walks, drink fresh fruit and vegetable juices, and best of all get massaged to your heart's delight. Being healthy together might not be romantic to some people, but to you and your ideal partner, nothing else will quite match up.

The person who will catch your eye must be attractive, have oodles of energy, and love outdoor sports. With your astute intuition, you'll know the moment your eyes meet that you are meant for each other. Anyone who smokes cigarettes, drinks too much, or likes heavily fried foods will be a complete turn-off, though you won't mind leading the way if someone wants you to help break bad habits.

The gal who'll most suit you, 2001 Capricorn male, is health-conscious, physically fit, and extraordinarily athletic without ever detracting from her femininity. She'll be at home in any setting, and be equally social and gregarious, as well as pensive and introspective. This girl will adapt to whatever you need when your moods suddenly change, and what's more important, she won't even mind.

For you, 2001 Capricorn female, you will know how your perfect guy feels just by looking into his expressive eyes. Feelings are one thing, and his mysterious and intriguing thoughts will be another, and you'll find it challenging trying to figure out what's on his mind, since he's not too talkative. You'll never mind doing all the talking, since you'll always know that you're in his heart when he takes you in his arms.

CAPRICORN ZODIAC SIGN
Your Love Planets

YOUR ROMANTIC SIDE   p. 696
- ▶ VENUS IN AQUARIUS
  Born Dec. 21, 2000 13:37 - Jan. 03, 2001 18:14
- ▶ VENUS IN PISCES
  Born Jan. 03, 18:15 - Jan. 20, 0:16

YOUR SEX DRIVE   p. 722
- ▶ MARS IN LIBRA
  Born Dec. 21, 2000 13:37 - Dec. 23, 2000 14:36
- ▶ MARS IN SCORPIO
  Born Dec. 23, 2000 14:37 - Jan. 20, 2001 0:16

YOUR CELEBRITY TWINS   p. 760
Find out the astrological similarities you have with famous people.

YOUR COMPATIBILITY   p. 780
Compare planets to find out how compatible you are in a relationship.

YOUR RELATIONSHIP KARMA   p. 824
- ▶ SATURN IN TAURUS
  Born Dec. 21, 2000 13:37 - Jan. 20, 2001 0:16

JUSTIN TIMBERLAKE
American Singer
Sun and Mars in Aquarius

681

2001 AQUARIUS

From January 20, 0:17 through February 18, 14:27

♒ The Ardent Artist

There are no two ways about, Aquarius of 2001—you are likely to be a very creative person. As you mature, you may take up an occupation that involves your artistic talents, creating something new and different out of the old. This certainly will be true in your romantic life, as you will see relating to another person at that level as something that brings all of your natural talents into play.

Even the most natural fit between you and your mate may have a few rough edges, but through talking openly and expressing your feelings every step of the way, your relationship will continue to last and grow. You will both be able to draw on your ability to find the new in the old, and to turn potential problems into wonderful possibilities. And that, of course, means your creative soul will help to support your romantic heart.

If those who would like to attract you understand that part of you, they will know that they need to touch on your love of beauty and your creative cinterests. The easiest way will be to focus conversation on cultural events of one kind or another, perhaps even inviting you to a play, a concert, or an art exhibit. While common interests help, you must see some spontaneity, the ability to throw caution to the winds, at least at times, and have fun.

You, 2001 Aquarius male, will find your perfect mate in a lady who can have fun, isn't bound by convention, and can also think (and converse) at a very deep level. By nature, in everything you do, you'll always look behind the superficialities, and think of what is really behind them. You'll need someone who can see the world in that way as well, bringing you new observations and insights as you live your lives together.

If you're a 2001 Aquarius female, you will find a man who is, more than anything, a listener, someone who takes you seriously and is sincerely interested, even fascinated, in your ideas and your creative pursuits. He will be joined with you on a very deep and intuitive level, perhaps understanding you better than anyone else can. And you will never feel more loved than when you are in his arms.

AQUARIUS ZODIAC SIGN
Your Love Planets

YOUR ROMANTIC SIDE   p. 696
- ▶ VENUS IN PISCES
  Born Jan. 20, 0:17 - Feb. 02, 19:14
- ▶ VENUS IN ARIES
  Born Feb. 02, 19:15 - Feb. 18, 14:27

YOUR SEX DRIVE   p. 722
- ▶ MARS IN SCORPIO
  Born Jan. 20, 0:17 - Feb. 14, 20:06
- ▶ MARS IN SAGITTARIUS
  Born Feb. 14, 20:07 - Feb. 18, 14:27

YOUR CELEBRITY TWINS   p. 760
Find out the astrological similarities you have with famous people.

YOUR COMPATIBILITY   p. 780
Compare planets to find out how compatible you are in a relationship.

YOUR RELATIONSHIP KARMA   p. 824
- ▶ SATURN IN TAURUS
  Born Jan. 20, 0:17 - Feb. 18, 14:27

682

RENEE ZELLWEGER
American Actress
Venus in Aries

2001 PISCES
From February 18, 14:28 through March 20, 13:31

The Inner Companion

If anything, Pisces of 2001, your romantic nature may be in a world apart from many other things you do. There is an almost secret side that may actually be the "real" you, and it is not something you will share easily except through writing your thoughts down in journals, poems, stories, or essays. When you become romantically involved with someone, you will see that almost as a welcome break from your literary endeavors.

Just as your inner life may be quite unique, your outer romantic life will seem very conventional. You will see love primarily as pleasant companionship with someone who accepts you for who you are without having any visions of "improving" you somehow, though you do want someone who can support your writing. And this kind of acceptance is just exactly what you will offer in return when you fall in love.

The best way for someone interested in you to find the key to your heart will be to look deeply into your eyes. If you see warmth, compassion, and sincerity exuding from the person across from you, then your interest will be aroused. Since you have to be reminded to be sociable, your true love will win points by taking you by the hand, and leading you to a club meeting, party, or other group activity.

Your ideal mate, 2001 Pisces male, will be someone who loves being home, and who shares your interest in simple pleasures and pastimes. She will know how to fill in all the gaps in your life, from creating an intimate, romantic atmosphere to preparing a gourmet meal. She will know your moods beforehand by the creases in your face, or the puckering of your lips. Mostly, she will be supportive, never questioning your need for time alone to work on your thoughts and ideas.

You, 2001 Pisces female, will fall in love with a man who will be a little more in tune with your inner world than most people. He will always be a listener rather than a critic, and since he will be supportive of your thoughts and intuitions, you will be free to be creative in ways you never dreamed of. You will be there with a warm hug, a friendly smile, and never a discouraging word.

2001 ARIES
From March 20, 13:32 through April 20, 0:36

The Fast-paced Competitor

As you move through life, Aries of 2001, you will have so many interests that others may never come close to matching your speed and your spirit. The grass won't grow under your feet, as you will always be ready to explore a new path. When you reach the age at which you begin to form relationships, the same rapid change may characterize that part of your life, at least for a while.

As you grow, learn, and develop your people skills, you will begin to focus less on the possibilities of a new romance every day, and more on finding that special person who can keep up with you, and even urge you on to a faster pace. Your first requirement for love is that it brings excitement into your life. The more fun it is, and the more challenging, the more to your liking it will be.

Someone who wants to attract your attention and win your heart should be physically fit, and have as much energy as you do, so much so that you might even have to exert yourself just to keep up. Anyone who challenges you in this way, and who promises to show you new worlds you haven't yet explored will have the key to your heart. Taking you along and showing you the ropes in this new world will be the best way to use that key.

You, 2001 Aries male, will find true romance with the girl who shares your many interests and who can match and exceed you in pursuing them. She will be challenging without making the contest all or nothing, as she'll love the thrill of a friendly competition just as much as you will. Her life will be just as portable as yours, as the two of you will always seem to be on the road to yet another adventure, wondering what is just beyond the next hill.

The ideal man for you, 2001 Aries female, will add thoughtfulness and introspection to your life, something that will complement your more outward orientation to the world. When you weary from trying to keep up with your own fast pace, he will always be there with a kind word and a way of turning your thoughts to other things. A hug from him, a little kiss, and the love light in his eyes are all you need to make things right.

2001 TAURUS
From April 20, 0:37 through May 20, 23:44

The Inspiring Innovator

You will never take much for granted, Taurus of 2001, and you will nearly always like to have a say in anything you're involved with. Someday when you're grown up, others will think of you as a dynamic type who is good at inspiring others, especially when that means convincing them to give up old habits and try new things. Your innovative ways will make you a natural in a romantic relationship, as you will never be one to let things fall into dreary and familiar patterns.

To you, being in love and spending each day with a special person will be an exciting prospect. You'll genuinely love people in general and will be endlessly fascinated with the ways in which they are different from you, whether in viewpoint or tastes. When you become romantically involved with another person, it will both stimulate your mind and further enrich your store of experiences.

Anyone who wants to appeal to you and win your heart will need to find a way to put you off balance, though gently of course. Someone with a sense of fun that includes practical jokes or the ability to tell outrageous stories with unexpected punch lines will have a good chance to score with you. Beyond that, this person must show you a sense of being directed toward a goal that you find appealing and interesting.

The perfect lady for you, 2001 Taurus male, will be someone who can provide a feeling of security that balances out your natural tendency to go for the new and different in everything. She will provide you with that one little part of your life that is always familiar, and changes but little, yet at the same time she'll love your forward-looking nature and admire your innovative abilities. She will always be there, with a warm smile and a loving embrace.

For you, 2001 Taurus female, the best guy will be someone who has a good mind with a lot of depth, perhaps including an interest in philosophical subjects. He'll always find a way to get you out of a blue mood, and his thoughtful approach to things will show you new worlds you never dreamed of. No one will be more supportive, and more loving than he.

TAURUS ZODIAC SIGN

YOUR LOVE PLANETS

YOUR ROMANTIC SIDE   p. 696
▶ VENUS IN ARIES
Born Apr. 20, 0:37 - May 20, 23:44

YOUR SEX DRIVE   p. 722
▶ MARS IN SAGITTARIUS
Born Apr. 20, 0:37 - May 20, 23:44

YOUR CELEBRITY TWINS   p. 760
Find out the astrological similarities you have with famous people.

YOUR COMPATIBILITY   p. 780
Compare planets to find out how compatible you are in a relationship.

YOUR RELATIONSHIP KARMA   p. 824
▶ SATURN IN TAURUS
Born Apr. 20, 0:37 - Apr. 20, 21:59
▶ SATURN IN GEMINI
Born Apr. 20, 22:00 - May 20, 23:44

VENUS WILLIAMS
American Tennis Champion
Sun and Venus in Gemini

683

2001 GEMINI
From May 20, 23:45 through June 21, 7:38

The Benevolent Heart

A sunny personality, a benevolent disposition, and a steady manner will always be your most enduring traits, Gemini of 2001. You will always see the good in other people and thus expect the best from them, though you will be realistic enough to know that many will not live up to those expectations. Since you will have an optimistic view, you will always feel that if others don't always give you their best at first, eventually they will come around.

This attitude will help you handle the superficiality that often comes with the early years of dating, and may lead you to explore wonderful relationship possibilities with those who need a little guidance and inspiration from you. In return, your partner will extend emotional support and kindness, so that you will always have that self-confidence that allows you to succeed in life.

Anyone wishing to get close to you and win your heart will need to show you the very thing you expect of them—a personal best that includes a real sincerity and a truly warm heart. Someone using a helpless demeanor as a ploy to get your attention won't fool you for long. Aside from that inner best, you will also like someone who is happiest being happy and having fun in a spontaneous and carefree way.

The kind of gal you will end up with, Gemini male of 2001, will be one who is as positive as you are about people in general, and may even be better than you at spotting the phonies. She will be very protective of you and won't hesitate to speak her mind, especially when she feels you may be off on a wrong path. Her idea of fun will be being with you, anytime and anywhere, whether it cuddling by the fire in winter, and swimming in summer.

Your perfect guy, Gemini female of 2001, will be sensitive, thoughtful, and a bit withdrawn when compared to you. Though he will like people as much as you do, he may not need to be around them as much as you, since his best companion (other than you, of course) is his own thoughts. He will have a romantic side that shows itself in spontaneous gifts and little affectionate moments that make your heart soar.

GEMINI ZODIAC SIGN

YOUR LOVE PLANETS

YOUR ROMANTIC SIDE   p. 696
▶ VENUS IN ARIES
Born May 20, 23:45 - June 06, 10:25
▶ VENUS IN TAURUS
Born June 06, 10:26 - June 21, 7:38

YOUR SEX DRIVE   p. 722
▶ MARS IN SAGITTARIUS
Born May 20, 23:45 - June 21, 7:38

YOUR CELEBRITY TWINS   p. 760
Find out the astrological similarities you have with famous people.

YOUR COMPATIBILITY   p. 780
Compare planets to find out how compatible you are in a relationship.

YOUR RELATIONSHIP KARMA   p. 824
▶ SATURN IN GEMINI
Born May 20, 23:45 - June 21, 7:38

RUPERT EVERETT
English Actor
Venus and Mars in Cancer

684

2001 CANCER
From June 21, 7:39 through July 22, 18:26

 The Steady Individual

You're very much an individual, Cancer of 2001, and as you grow, others may not be able to define you in any conventional or standard way. It may take you a while longer than most to find a groove in which to fit your life, but once you find your direction, you will stick to it and do anything you can to stand up for your beliefs.

The same might be true of your romantic relationships, as you may fall in love quite easily, and choosing a partner might make you feel like a kid in a candy store. But even if you can't make up your mind for a long while, eventually you will find someone who is very different from the crowd, and that will be the one for you. And once you've committed your heart, you will do everything to make things work.

Someone who wants more than a casual fling will need to show you a good heart and an inner sense of stability. This may be with a casual remark about those less fortunate, or by participating in something that you alone like to do. Anyone who has a very distinct sense of self, and a good idea of where to go in life, will arouse your interest, as well your curiosity. If you like the same music, and like the same food, you know that you have a better than average chance of being right for each other.

For you, Cancer male of 2001, the girl you'll end up with should be the intellectual type, with an interest in the cultural scene and the arts. She will introduce you to people, things, and ideas that you might not otherwise come across, due to your more practical orientation. Her idea of real fun with you will be to be outdoors, running, hiking, camping, and perhaps exchanging a few kisses under the moonlight.

Your dream guy, 2001 Cancer female, will be a fellow who seems to have a boundless supply of energy and a will to win that's second to none. Even though you may not be able to keep up with him at times, there will be no need to worry, as even when he's out there winning battles in the world, his thoughts will always be with you. Competitive he may be, but certainly faithful, and when he's with you, you will never doubt this for a minute.

2001 LEO
From July 22, 18:27 through August 23, 1:27

The Mature Idealist

Sensitive, intelligent, and idealistic, Leo of 2001, you will always seem mature for your age, and as you grow into adulthood you will continue to act older and wiser than your years. Even as a child, you will be able to reach out to others and will have a gift for knowing what to say to make people feel better. You will develop a keen insight into what makes people tick, making others want to be around you.

As easy as it will be for you to connect intimately with people, you are also a perfectionist and want everything in life to fit like a glove. Romantically, you will want a perfect lifetime partner who can be your best friend, confidante, and advisor. Once you set your eyes on the person you think is the right one, you will work very hard to make sure that your relationship is just as perfect as the one you've chosen.

For you, a loving relationship will be for keeps, so when you meet someone who is fickle, flighty, or changeable from one moment to the next, you will walk the other way. On the other hand, you will be most attracted to someone who does not put on any airs, and who is sincere and truthful from the instant you both start your first conversation. As your eyes meet, and you continue to make direct contact as you speak, your love will definitely be sealed.

The gal who is witty, clever, and has everyone's eye when she walks into a room will melt your heart, 2001 Leo male. As a true romantic, you won't think of anything more wonderful than to be humbled by love, and to place the woman of your dreams on a pedestal, set apart from the rest of the world. The more regal, intelligent, and beautiful your dream girl is, the more you will strive to be worthy of her love.

The guy who will keep you awake at night, 2001 Leo female, will have the capacity to sweep you off your feet, and make the world go away every time you are in his arms. You will have a soft spot for the masculine, competitive type, the one who excels in whatever he does, whether it's business or sports or just a friendly card game. But what is most important to him is that he excels with you.

2001 VIRGO

From August 23, 1:28 through September 22, 23:05

The Soul Mate

As a Virgo of 2001, you might spend your formative years gazing at a computer screen, often losing yourself online, and fascinated by all the information there at your fingertips. You will be able to converse on almost every subject under the sun, but may be in reverse gear and on the shy side when it comes to expressing your innermost feelings.

Of course, you will dream about falling madly in love like everyone else, but you'll feel that love must transcend childhood fantasies and be more than two people flirting and giggling. When your soul mate comes along, words won't be necessary since you will be communicating on a heart-to-heart level—reading each other's mind, and completing each other's thoughts. And when you are apart, you will wear your partner's heart right on your sleeve.

The person who will catch your fancy is someone not put off by your reserved nature, and will have unique ways to make you feel at ease from the moment you meet. Anyone who has the same taste in movies, laughs at the same jokes, and loves to do simple things like going to the zoo or walking in the park is someone you will want to consider as a long-term partner. You won't be difficult to please, except for your main requirement—someone whom you know you can trust to always be faithful.

You, 2001 Virgo male, will love gals who are down-to-earth, honest to a fault, and whose direct manner may at times be a little shocking. Those qualities will make you love her all the more, for you'll know that you never have to guess about what will make her happiest. She will tell you with her eyes when you are being insensitive, and will show you with her loving arms when she sees you as the sweetest guy in the world.

The guy who wins your heart, 2001 Virgo female, is the kind who will bring you flowers for no reason at all, except that he loves you. He will be a full-fledged romantic, and honest enough to apologize when he has said something to hurt your feelings. The man at your side will always remind you that love is a two-way street, and there is nobody more compassionate or willing to help others.

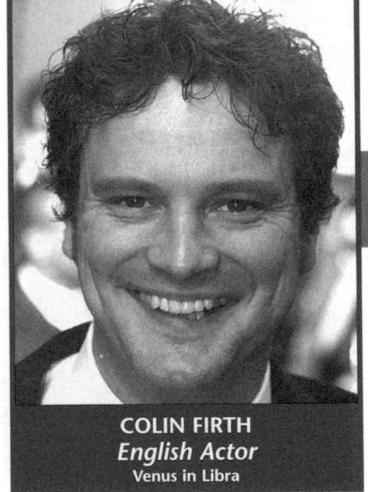

COLIN FIRTH
English Actor
Venus in Libra

685

2001 LIBRA

From September 22, 23:06 through October 23, 8:26

The Loving Linguist

As you journey toward adulthood, Libra of 2001, you will imagine yourself doing all sorts of fabulous things with your life—traversing the globe, speaking multiple languages, maybe even becoming a great humanitarian and leaving your mark on the world. So many dreams to live out, yet never enough time to do it all—especially for someone who often needs a little push in the right direction.

That's why sharing your life with someone equally adventurous will be so important to you. Your perfect partner will take you by the hand, and lead you into the light to show you the world you dream of. Together, you will enjoy life's pleasures—from exotic vacations and exciting friends to simple things like sharing a breathtaking sunset in your own back yard.

Anyone who wants your attention will need to turn on the charm as soon as you meet, as you'll always be quick to fall for someone who flatters you. Perhaps they'll take you to a fancy restaurant and treat you as if you were the only one in the room. To win your heart, the person vying for your affection should love your sense of humor, be a great conversationalist, and be ready to sample everything that interests you, from going to a Broadway musical to learning how to ski.

The gal who will steal your heart, 2001 Libra male, will be passionate about what she believes and at the same time will listen to others before finally making up her mind. She'll be eclectic in her tastes and as comfortable hanging around the house in blue jeans as she'll be going to the opera in formal attire. Mostly, this perfect female will be all yours, and she will hug and kiss you whenever the mood hits her, just to let you know where her heart is.

Your idea of the perfect guy, 2001 Libra female, will be the strong, silent type, one who speaks volumes with his intense stare, and who you know will be there for you in the good times and the bad. Masculine, yet unafraid to show his true feelings, he'll love sharing home cooked meals that remind him of his youth, as much as walking hand in hand through the park, showing the world how much he loves you.

AALIYAH
American Singer
Venus in Sagittarius

686

2001 SCORPIO
From October 23, 8:27 through November 22, 6:01

♏ The Creative Hobbyist

Creative and artistic, Scorpio of 2001, you will enjoy any hobby that lifts you to another realm and helps you escape into your own fantasy world. Your vivid imagination will always be your best friend, and whenever things get you down, you'll turn to your art, music, or writing to lift your spirits. And when you get older, love will do the same for you, lifting you to heights you never could have imagined.

Relationships will provide a way for you and your partner to create a world all your own. Intense and passionate, you may see your romantic moments as a larger than life musical where the main characters burst into song every time they express their deepest emotions. You will obviously not be singing and dancing your way through life, though love may make you feel as if you're walking on air.

Someone who wants to attract you will need to dress smart, smell just great, and brim with individuality. You'll love the artistic type who wants to join you on an exciting life adventure lived according to your own set of rules. More

than that, you'll be looking for someone kindhearted and gentle, someone who will let you know from the way your eyes meet and your hands touch that you belong together.

The gal of your dreams, 2001 Scorpio male, will be devoted to making you happy and pleasing you, while at the same time following her own independent creative path. She'll be someone who will want to know everything about you, and will try to appreciate everything you love, even when it is not her taste. She will go with you to a football game or action movie, just to be part of your life. And you will do the same in return.

For you, 2001 Scorpio female, that special guy will be a great blend of masculine jock and sensitive sweetheart. By day, he may like hanging out with his friends and doing "man" things like racing cars or playing ball, but once the sun goes down, he is all yours, and he will love doing whatever you've planned for your perfect evening. Whether you dance till dawn, or snuggle on the sofa, this guy will be all yours, and his warm embrace will tell you so.

2001 SAGITTARIUS
From November 22, 6:02 through December 21, 19:22

♐ The Laughing Lover

One thing you're already noted for, Sagittarius of 2001, is your contagious and cheerful attitude, smiling from ear to ear over the simplest things. As you grow you'll be able to find humor in almost any situation, and your ability to laugh even in the face of sadness will make you a partner that anyone would be proud to have.

For you, laughter will be the key to keeping any relationship you have alive and fresh. The infectious lighthearted manner you'll share will make both of you a popular couple and the centerpiece around which your social circle revolves. Sharing happiness and good times with your friends will reinforce your love and make the time when the two of you are alone even more precious.

Anyone who wants you to take notice will need to show an intense interest in how you view life and love, perhaps by engaging you in deep conversation that covers everything from politics to personal feelings. Once you know this person is not superficial or self-involved, you will look for a nice smile and sparkling eyes

that show an offbeat sense of humor. And if this person doesn't mind acting like a lovesick school kid in public, you'll have found the answer to all your dreams.

For you, 2001 Sagittarius male, the gal who can put you in your place when you are just a bit boastful and full of yourself will be a real asset. You'll want a mate who can serve as a mirror to tell you freely, without judgment, when you are being generous and compassionate—and when you might be condescending without intending to be. Give that gal good looks and a sharp wit, and you'll be all hers.

The guy who will be yours for life, 2001 Sagittarius female, is a ball of energy, with so many friends and activities that you can barely keep track of him. He will introduce you to cultural activities you've not been exposed to from jazz concerts to scholarly lectures. He is a true Renaissance man, and the more eclectic his tastes, the more fascinating he will be. Of course, he will always find time to be alone with you, take romantic walks on the beach, and do everything he can to make you smile.

2000s

The Bond Girls – Brains, Beauty, and Bikinis

Exotic locales, amazing gadgets, breathtaking stunts, and last-minute rescues are staples in every James Bond adventure. But the greatest appeal, at least for men, has always been the beautiful and bodacious Bond "girls."

Ian Fleming's literary creation, James Bond, Agent 007, debuted in the novel *Casino Royale*, published in 1953. President John F. Kennedy's admission that he always kept a few Ian Fleming books on his beside table helped to popularize the James Bond novels, but it was Hollywood that really brought the Bond phenomena—and the Bond Girls—to the world.

Since the producing team of Albert R. Broccoli and Harry Saltzman brought *Dr. No* to the screen in 1962, gorgeous women have been a staple of the genre. In the years since, nineteen more 007 films have been released with five different "Bonds" and a bevy of beautiful girls to charm, lure, deceive, frustrate, and match wits with Britain's most famous secret agent. James Bond has been seduced on screen by beauties ranging from the stunning Ursula Andress to the strongly captivating Halle Berry. And while no woman is quite his match, many of these sexy ladies have tangled with him as successfully on the other end of a gun as they have between the sheets.

The actresses who portray Bond Girls are often the popular actresses of the time (Honor Blackman, Maud Adams, Tanya Roberts, Teri Hatcher, and Sophie Marceau). There are those who were slightly past their prime of celebrity (Diana Rigg, Jill St. John, and Britt Ekland), and a few who virtually cut their acting teeth—at least in American films—portraying Bond

Halle Berry in *Die Another Day*

"I'm afraid you've caught me with more than my hands up!"

SEAN CONNERY as James Bond in
Diamonds Are Forever

Girls (Claudine Auger, Izabella Scorupco, and Jane Seymour). Halle Berry holds the distinction of being the only Oscar-winning actress (so far) to appear in a Bond movie, proving once and for all that beauty must be accompanied by brains.

Over the years the James Bond films have managed to survive and even transcend cultural changes such as feminism, the fall of Communism, and the onset of "political correctness." Not surprisingly, the Bond Girls have changed, too. Once characterized by "cutesy" names just this side of the censor—who could forget "Pussy Galore," "Octopussy," "Kissy Suzuki," or "Holly Goodhead"—they have evolved into more subtle representations of lust and menace (Sophie Marceau was "Elektra King" in *The World Is Not Enough* and Halle Berry played "Jinx" in *Die Another Day*).

Just what constitutes being a Bond Girl? Sometimes, such as the ill-fated "Jill" in *Goldfinger* or "Plenty O'Toole" in *Diamonds are Forever*, she is strictly a sex object. At other times she matches his skill and daring, and the sexual tug-of-war becomes as much a battle of wits as a battle of the sexes. Sometimes a woman begins as his adversary but ends up his accomplice in thwarting whatever evil individual or organization he is fighting—the exotic Grace Jones as "May Day" in *A View to a Kill* and Michelle Yeoh as "Wai Lin" in *Tomorrow Never Dies*.

Bond Girls always reflect the prevailing tastes and types. Certainly they are gorgeous, glamorous, and leggy, and always show lots of cleavage. But whether portrayed as a sex kitten, tigress, or brainy adversary, Bond Girls give James a run for his money—and always look fabulous doing it!

687

▶ READ ABOUT SEAN CONNERY ON PAGE 360

- ⭐ **PEDOPHILE PRIESTS**
- ⭐ **THE BACHELOR**
- ⭐ **J-LO AND BEN**
- ⭐ **BRUCE AND EMINEM**
- ⭐ **BIG FAT GREEK WEDDING**
- ⭐ **BITCH IN THE HOUSE**

Sex Idol

EVENTS

The Catholic Church in the US was rocked by media revelations that it had tacitly shielded pedophile priests from detection and prosecution. President George W. Bush's "marriage initiative" funded programs encouraging low-income women to marry. Girls attending a California school dance were asked to lift their skirts for a "thong check"—thongs were forbidden, partly because of "freaking" or "booty dancing," simulating the thrusting and grinding motions of sex. On television's voyeuristic reality show *The Bachelor*, 25 bachelorettes competed to become the fiancée of one bachelor. A European court upheld France's prohibition of adoption by homosexual couples, but Britain's House of Commons voted that unmarried, gay, and lesbian couples could adopt children. Pop's teen idols Britney Spears and Justin Timberlake broke up. Singer-dancer-actress Jennifer Lopez told ABC's Diane Sawyer that she was engaged to Ben Affleck. Jochen Wolf, a former Brandenburg state minister, was found guilty of trying to hire a contract killer to murder his wife after his mistress committed suicide.

POP CULTURE

Norah Jones' award-winning album "Come Away With Me" opened with the hit "Don't Know Why." Bruce Springsteen's "The Rising" was an emotional meditation on 9/11. Progressive rock group Magnetic Fields performed their entire double-CD *69 Love Songs* at Lincoln Center. Rap's breakout star Eminem released *The Eminem Show*.

In the smash independent film *My Big Fat Greek Wedding*, a woman defies her traditional Greek family to marry a WASPy English teacher. A selfish bachelor learns about love with the help of a child in *About a Boy*. Michael Apted's *Enigma* set a brainy love story amid the code-breaking operations at Bletchley Park during WWII.

The Bitch in the House collected angry essays on the issues facing contemporary women. David Gauntlett's *Media, Gender, and Identity* explored gender identity and the phenomenon of "girl power." In Amanda Boulter's *Around the Houses*, Anna has a tiny baby, a female lover, and a gay husband. In Alice Sebold's *The Lovely Bones*, a murdered 14-year-old girl watches her bereaved family from Heaven. *The Christmas Train* by David Baldacci followed a disillusioned journalist's adventure-filled train trip across country and his reunion with an old flame.

CATHERINE ZETA-JONES

Born to working-class parents in Wales, Catherine starred in *Annie* by eleven and was declared a has-been by British tabloids at twenty-four. *The Mask of Zorro* (with Antonio Banderas) proved them wrong. The statuesque brunette dated Simply Red's Mick Hucknall and was engaged to actor Angus MacFadyen.

American fans had just begun to flock to the beauty before she married high in the Hollywood hierarchy. Her *Traffic* co-star Michael Douglas was the lucky man. Their first child pre-dated the 2000 wedding, and Zeta-Jones was again eight months pregnant as she accepted her Best Supporting Actress Oscar for the 2002 movie *Chicago* in March 2003.

SEE ALSO

▶ ANTONIO BANDERAS *Page 638*

▶ LOUISE BROOKS *Page 95*

▶ MICHELLE PFEIFFER *Page 580*

2002 CAPRICORN

From December 21, 2001 19:23 through January 20, 2002 6:02

The Irresistible Charmer

It won't take long for people to realize that you are a born salesperson, Capricorn of 2002, or that you can make people want things they didn't even know they wanted. This will be apparent early in your life, when you persuade your parents to buy you something special or convince a playmate to play the game that you choose. When you mature, this quality will carry into your romantic life as you go about making the object of your affection feel the same way about you.

There's a way about you, a certain charm that few can resist once you turn it on. While you may use this charm to play the field, once you've settled on that special someone, you'll turn that power on to create a magical world only the two of you will share. You might weave your spell in the mountains, on the beach, or as you stroll hand in hand in the moonlight.

If someone wants to attract you, the best way to do it is to beat you at your own game, by giving you a sales pitch you can't ignore, much less refuse. The person who comes right up to you, looks straight into your eyes and says, "Let's talk," will take the right first step. To complete the scenario, a witty, scintillating conversation that goes on for hours will have you wanting more and more.

The gal who lights up your life, 2002 Capricorn male, will be very much like you, with many of the same interests and the ability to charm just about everyone she meets. It's likely that the two of you will arrange your lives so that you can be together most of the time, if only because both of you feels more alive when the other is around. You'll know for sure when you meet this one that she is the one for you.

If you're a 2002 Capricorn female, your dream guy will be someone quite a bit different from you, though in touch and in tune with you at an intuitive level. The two of you may have an ongoing conversation in which both of you can generally finish what the other is saying. Romantically and emotionally, you will be just as much in synch, and even though your outward interests may differ, inwardly both of you will find no better match than the other.

CAPRICORN ZODIAC SIGN
Your Love Planets

YOUR ROMANTIC SIDE   p. 696
- ▶ **VENUS IN SAGITTARIUS**
  Born Dec. 21, 2001 19:23 - Dec. 26, 2001 7:25
- ▶ **VENUS IN CAPRICORN**
  Born Dec. 26, 2001 7:26 - Jan. 19, 2002 3:42
- ▶ **VENUS IN AQUARIUS**
  Born Jan. 19, 3:43 - Jan. 20, 6:02

YOUR SEX DRIVE   p. 722
- ▶ **MARS IN PISCES**
  Born Dec. 21, 2001 19:23 - Jan. 18, 2002 22:53
- ▶ **MARS IN ARIES**
  Born Jan. 18, 22:54 - Jan. 20, 6:02

YOUR CELEBRITY TWINS   p. 760
Find out the astrological similarities you have with famous people.

YOUR COMPATIBILITY   p. 780
Compare planets to find out how compatible you are in a relationship.

YOUR RELATIONSHIP KARMA   p. 824
- ▶ **SATURN IN GEMINI**
  Born Dec. 21, 2001 19:23 - Jan. 20, 2002 6:02

2002 AQUARIUS

From January 20, 6:03 through February 18, 20:13

The Determined Dreamer

You always seem to know where you're going, Aquarius of 2002, and people who aren't sure of themselves or their direction in life may have a hard time keeping up with you. You will always have a commanding presence and an inventive side that very few can match. Even when you harbor secret doubts, nobody else will know it. When it comes to love, your "creative certainty" will stand you in very good stead.

When you encounter your soul mate, you will know how you feel, especially when you start envisioning your life together and dreaming the same "impossible" dreams. If you are as determined together as you are apart, you may actually wind up climbing Mt. Everest or going on an African safari. But even if you don't, you will have a wonderful time planning it and dreaming about it.

Someone who wants to attract you needs to let you take the lead and let you know they are interested in finding out everything about you, perhaps by asking you a question like, "Where do you see yourself ten years from now?" The person who looks at you with soulful eyes and bated breath while you recount your personal vision, will be the one who has a good chance of catching your eye and winning your heart.

The right lady for you, Aquarius male of 2002, will be someone who will share your hopes and ideals, so that you can do things as a team from start to finish. She will want to spend time on the road traveling to exotic places, learning different languages, and meeting people with different customs and values. So wonderfully social and curious is she that you will be always thankful for everything you will learn from her, just being at her side.

Your perfect guy, Aquarius female of 2002, will be a take-charge type in many areas of his life, but he considers you his equal and your lives together as a true partnership. He may not make the other girls turn their heads, but that is fine with you. You want this unselfish, compassionate, and exciting man all to yourself, since he knows how to spice up your life with hugs, kisses, and romantic days that would make others envious—if only they knew.

CHRISTIAN BALE
English Actor
Sun in Aquarius

AQUARIUS ZODIAC SIGN
Your Love Planets

YOUR ROMANTIC SIDE   p. 696
- ▶ **VENUS IN AQUARIUS**
  Born Jan. 20, 6:03 - Feb. 12, 1:18
- ▶ **VENUS IN PISCES**
  Born Feb. 12, 1:19 - Feb. 18, 20:13

YOUR SEX DRIVE   p. 722
- ▶ **MARS IN ARIES**
  Born Jan. 20, 6:03 - Feb. 18, 20:13

YOUR CELEBRITY TWINS   p. 760
Find out the astrological similarities you have with famous people.

YOUR COMPATIBILITY   p. 780
Compare planets to find out how compatible you are in a relationship.

YOUR RELATIONSHIP KARMA   p. 824
- ▶ **SATURN IN GEMINI**
  Born Jan. 20, 6:03 - Feb. 18, 20:13

QUEEN LATIFAH
American Singer
Sun in Pisces

2002 PISCES
From February 18, 20:14 through March 20, 19:16

The Enchanting Optimist

Spontaneous, vivacious, and wildly optimistic, you, Pisces of 2002, will go through life like Peter Pan—never wanting to grow up or settle down. You would rather spend your life following incredible dreams, thinking that if you do, your life will have a storybook ending. For you, relationships will be a way to find someone to lead you through life's journey, with you providing the endless optimism while your partner serves as the anchor that keeps you from going too far, too fast.

While your manner may be irritating to some of the hard, cold realists of the world, most people, including your beloved, will find you absolutely enchanting, and when you doing something romantic on the spur of the moment, like inundating your true love with chocolates, flowers, or expensive gifts, it just might seem that you really are living in a wonderland.

Someone who wants to attract you should reveal sensitivity and imagination the moment you meet. Asking you what you like to read, or finding out you love the same rock group and you've even been to the same concerts are great ways of getting your attention. After that, getting you to respond spontaneously and in a silly way will help you to open up and let the other person's heart in.

The girl who will win you for life, 2002 Pisces male, will look absolutely smashing when she enters the room whether she is dressed in designer clothes or something off the rack from a neighborhood store. She appreciates the finer things in life, though she is really modest, and would never demand them for herself. She has a lovely smile and a terrific laugh, and makes every day a romantic adventure. Her warm embrace tells you that you're more than man enough for her, and the only one she needs in life.

The guy for you, 2002 Pisces female, is one whose down-to-earth nature contrasts well with your more flashy style. He will be soft-spoken and someone able to make his point in just a few words. You will bring out his affectionate side, which is just as quiet and direct as his way of talking, and he will never let you doubt for a minute his love for you.

2002 ARIES
From March 20, 19:17 through April 20, 6:21

The Sensitive Communicator

Enterprising, passionate, and sensitive, Aries of 2002, you are a born communicator, blessed with an ability to say just the right things at all the right times. Your wonderful gift will also make you a visionary, one who comes up with dynamic ideas and musters the support of others to carry them out. As you are both inspirational and practical, you will also listen carefully and closely to others, something that will greatly enhance all your relationships.

Anyone who becomes romantically involved with you will know that you are sensitive to the feelings and needs of your partner, but also open about your own feelings and needs. You will instinctively know that two people's total acceptance of each other lies at the heart of love. As long as the two of you can talk with each other just as much as you hug and kiss, you will be together for life.

Someone who wants to attract you may not have to try too hard, as all it takes is openness, honesty, and some good conversation. You will be taken with anyone who is direct, even outspoken, and who does not stand on ceremony when it comes to taking the lead in asking for a date. Someone saying "Hi, I'd really like to get know you," will tell you that you're dealing with someone who has the confidence and the sincerity to win your heart.

Your perfect match, Aries male of 2002, will be a lady who combines a wild, sophisticated side with one that is practical and down-to-earth. A simple thing like going to the movies and sharing a bucket of popcorn with her will be a pleasant romantic adventure. She will make your life fun-filled and exciting, and in return, when you hold her in your arms you will let her know that she is safe and secure with you.

The man of your dreams, 2002 Aries female, will be someone who startles and surprises you with his daring and action-oriented ways. He loves to try new things, and won't hesitate taking on great challenges that others might shy away from. The best thing about him is the way in which he communicates his feelings, especially when it comes to saying those three little words, "I love you!"

2002 TAURUS
From April 20, 6:22 through May 21, 5:29

The Compassionate Speaker

If anything can be said about you, Taurus of 2002, it will be that you will always try to say precisely what's on your mind, but in a way that is truthful, tactful, and especially considerate of other people's feelings. When it comes to your relationships, it won't take you too long to let the person you love know how you feel, and your ability to say what you mean and mean what you say will take you straight to the heart of your one true love.

For you, relationships are a way of ruminating together about the nature of the stars, the heavens, and the universe, in addition to expressing through both word and deed how you feel about one another. You will learn soon enough that speaking the language of love requires truth and subtlety in equal measures, and you will both understand the beauty of both.

Anyone who wants to win your heart can do so by showing a creative, inspirational side. Quoting a fabulous love poem, acting out a scene from a great play or movie, or perfectly humming the tune of a song you adore will simply sweep you off your feet. If underneath that panache lies someone who is genuine and cares about humanity—from the downtrodden to the people next door—you have someone who holds the key to unlocking your heart.

Your perfect lady, 2002 Taurus male, will match your straightforward nature, but has a wild and creative element that you find intriguing. Where you are cautious, she will be daring, and where you are accommodating, she may be a bit combative, but always in a way that is lighthearted and loving. You are just crazy about the fact that opposites attract as much as you love what you have in common—being together for the rest of your lives.

Your soul mate, 2002 Taurus female, will love interacting with people of all walks of life, and you will revel in being exposed to all his diverse interests, experiencing things you would never think of doing like gourmet cooking or going to comedy clubs. He will never be shy in showing his affection, and will take you in his arms and tell you he loves you at the most unpredictable—but always perfect—moments.

TAURUS ZODIAC SIGN
YOUR LOVE PLANETS

YOUR ROMANTIC SIDE   p. 696
▶ **VENUS IN TAURUS**
Born Apr. 20, 6:22 - Apr. 25, 17:57
▶ **VENUS IN GEMINI**
Born Apr. 25, 17:58 - May 20, 13:27
▶ **VENUS IN CANCER**
Born May 20, 13:28 - May 21, 5:29

YOUR SEX DRIVE   p. 722
▶ **MARS IN GEMINI**
Born Apr. 20, 6:22 - May 21, 5:29

YOUR CELEBRITY TWINS   p. 760
Find out the astrological similarities you have with famous people.

YOUR COMPATIBILITY   p. 780
Compare planets to find out how compatible you are in a relationship.

YOUR RELATIONSHIP KARMA   p. 824
▶ **SATURN IN GEMINI**
Born Apr. 20, 6:22 - May 21, 5:29

ENRIQUE IGLESIAS
Spanish-American Singer
Sun in Taurus

691

2002 GEMINI
From May 21, 5:30 through June 21, 13:24

The Directed Pursuer

As you mature, Gemini of 2002, you will encounter very few people who are as determined, fast-paced, or as directed as you, or who have that same ability to focus on what they want and pursue it with an absolute vengeance. When it comes to love, you will do the same, and when you set your sights on the one who makes your heart skip a beat, you'll go about capturing your true love's heart, never resting until it's done.

Once you are victorious, you will stop running full speed ahead and slow down long enough to apply sweetness, flattery, and lots of romantic mood setting. You will think nothing of surprising your true love with candlelight dinners, soft music, and close, slow dancing. What's even nicer is that after you decide to spend your lives together, you will continue the honeymoon every day of the week.

The person who wants to win your heart should not come on like gangbusters, as that will arouse your suspicions more than your emotions. The one interested in you should be somewhat reserved while the two of you get to know each other. Once you discover that you like the same kind of music, laugh at the same jokes, and even love the same vacation spots, you will know that you are both on the same track with each other.

Your perfect mate, 2002 Gemini male, will be sensitive, subtle, and able to compromise with ease so that both of you are satisfied and happy. This is all to the good, as you will really need someone like this to act as a counterweight to your straightforward and dynamic approach to life. This great gal will be less concerned with getting somewhere than enjoying things in the here and now, something that will make your romantic life together a wonderful experience.

The guy who will knock you off your feet, 2002 Gemini female, will be the most supportive person you could ever find, and during those rare moments when your determination fails you, he will help you get back on track and keep going. His warmth and positive energy will radiate from him, and those romantic moments you share together are times when he will make you feel like a queen.

GEMINI ZODIAC SIGN
YOUR LOVE PLANETS

YOUR ROMANTIC SIDE   p. 696
▶ **VENUS IN CANCER**
Born May 21, 5:30 - June 14, 20:16
▶ **VENUS IN LEO**
Born June 14, 20:17 - June 21, 13:24

YOUR SEX DRIVE   p. 722
▶ **MARS IN GEMINI**
Born May 21, 5:30 - May 28, 11:43
▶ **MARS IN CANCER**
Born May 28, 11:44 - June 21, 13:24

YOUR CELEBRITY TWINS   p. 760
Find out the astrological similarities you have with famous people.

YOUR COMPATIBILITY   p. 780
Compare planets to find out how compatible you are in a relationship.

YOUR RELATIONSHIP KARMA   p. 824
▶ **SATURN IN GEMINI**
Born May 21, 5:30 - June 21, 13:24

SALMA HAYEK
Mexican Actress
Venus in Leo

692

2002 CANCER
From June 21, 13:25 through July 23, 0:15

The Sensitive Introspective

Sensitive, introspective, and serious, you, Cancer of 2002, will have extremely simple needs where your romantic life is concerned. You will want someone whom you can love, who loves you back, and who shares your love of solitude and the simple and uncomplicated pleasures of life, especially a romantic relationship.

In the morning, you may savor waking up and watching the sunrise together, or serving your partner breakfast in bed. At night, you will wish on shooting stars together as you take long, romantic walks. But the best part of being with someone you love will be simply spending time together day after day, whether you share activities or just work quietly on personal projects in adjoining rooms. As long as both of you know that the other is somewhere close, the rest of the world can go away. You will always have each other—forever.

Anyone who will want to make it to first base with you should do whatever it takes to transport you to an otherworldly place. Someone whose enchanting looks and inviting smile keeps you transfixed will have a chance of breaking through your outer shell. A warm, intelligent, and generous human being will make the biggest hit with you.

The gal you will obsess about, 2002 Cancer male, may not be classically beautiful, but she is an absolute knockout nonetheless. When she walks into a room, most people will think they have never seen anyone more fascinating. Just knowing that others find her irresistible will make you feel powerful and proud to be seen with her. Her beauty will not be skin deep, since she is a compassionate soul, one who will bring the absolute joy of her generosity into your life.

You will go through life, 2002 Cancer female, dreaming about a guy who will treat you like absolute royalty. This is someone who thinks you are wonderful no matter what you say or do, and who will always support all your endeavors, even those that he does not share with you. What he does know for sure is that he wants to give you the world, and will do whatever it takes to see you smile or to hear you tell him how much you love him.

2002 LEO
From July 23, 0:16 through August 23, 7:17

The Take-Charge Lover

As a Leo of 2002, your sharp mind, keen intellect, and take-charge nature means people will pay attention whenever you speak. You will be a charismatic figure throughout life, and even as a child, you will easily be the leader among your friends, the one who has the best ideas and knows how to carry them out. As an adult, you will have your choice of career, from attorney, to star reporter, to community organizer.

When it comes to love, you will find it easy to charm those of the opposite sex, but the one who finally captivates you has to be special. You will make love challenging, a game of matching wits one moment and being mushily romantic the next. Enthusiastic about living life to the fullest, you and your partner will always be on the go, sharing wonderful experiences hand in hand.

Anyone who wants to grab your attention must have a way with words and a mind as quick and flexible as yours. Verbal connections are, for you, just as important as physical attraction, and you will know right away if this person is a match for you. Minds are important, but the follow-through must be warm eyes that look straight at yours and a smile that conveys warmth and generosity, as these will win you for sure.

You will want a girl, 2002 Leo male, who doesn't mind letting you take center stage. She will not have an ounce of jealousy, and will never feel that she has to compete with you. You can have all the glory since a great deal of her pride will come from being with you. While she may defer to you in the things that you are good at, she will be multi-talented and highly creative herself. Mostly, though, she is in love with you, and her warmth will tell you so always.

The guy of your dreams, 2002 Leo female, will be strikingly good-looking, charming, and ready to take you on trips to both the known and the unknown. He will be able to recite beautiful love poems to you, and have you rolling on the floor with a corny joke a moment later. While all this sounds absolutely perfect, you will also be aware of his flaws, yet will love him unconditionally through good times and bad.

2002 VIRGO
From August 23, 7:18 through September 23, 4:55

The Talented Soul

As you go through life, Virgo of 2002, you will be so multi-talented that you will have a hard time not letting it go to your head. Equally masterful in areas such as computer technology or graphic design, you may not be as discriminating when it comes to love—you may find yourself simply falling head over heels for almost everyone you meet.

Since you see the good in everyone, you will always be able to find something loveable in each of them. It may be a person's heart, sense of humor, or even a spectacular appearance. Once you discover all those traits rolled into one special person, you will know without having to think twice that the right one has definitely come along. Only then will you establish a unique relationship based on shared dreams of love and adventure.

You will tend to fall for someone whose desire to do something good in the world shines through the moment you meet. Unless a good soul lies behind the nice appearance, you will never be the type to be impressed with a beautiful face, flamboyant clothes, or lots of money. Your love will be clinched once you hold hands, as the firm, loving grasp will tell you in a second that this special someone is the one you have always envisioned.

Your dream gal, 2002 Virgo male, will know what is on your mind without ever asking. When you return home after a long day, she will instinctively know what to do to get you in a loving mood—from a warm hello to preparing your best comfort food to playing your favorite music. She will have marvelous instincts and will always know when to listen intently, or when she can have the floor with all the attention coming from you.

Your perfect guy, 2002 Virgo female, will have a way with words that makes you the envy of all your friends. He will leave you little love notes, whisper beautiful things in your ear, and read you wonderful poetry that he may even compose himself. When you are feeling down, he has the just the right words to get you on your feet, and in those quiet, reflective moments, he will also know when he needs no words at all. Those times are the best of all.

VIRGO ZODIAC SIGN
YOUR LOVE PLANETS

YOUR ROMANTIC SIDE   p. 696
- ▶ **VENUS IN LIBRA**
  Born Aug. 23, 7:18 - Sept. 8, 3:05
- ▶ **VENUS IN SCORPIO**
  Born Sept. 8, 3:06 - Sept. 23, 4:55

YOUR SEX DRIVE   p. 722
- ▶ **MARS IN LEO**
  Born Aug. 23, 7:18 - Aug. 29, 14:38
- ▶ **MARS IN VIRGO**
  Born Aug. 29, 14:39 - Sept. 23, 4:55

YOUR CELEBRITY TWINS   p. 760
Find out the astrological similarities you have with famous people.

YOUR COMPATIBILITY   p. 780
Compare planets to find out how compatible you are in a relationship.

YOUR RELATIONSHIP KARMA   p. 824
- ▶ **SATURN IN GEMINI**
  Born Aug. 23, 7:18 - Sept. 23, 4:55

MATT DAMON
American Actor
Sun in Libra

693

2002 LIBRA
From September 23, 4:56 through October 23, 14:18

The Passionate Persuader

Throughout your formative years, Libra of 2002, you will undoubtedly earn yourself a reputation for being understanding and objective, the one who sees both sides of a story and will give an opinion based on facts, not on personal feelings. As you mature, you will continue to be wonderfully adept at conflict resolution, and any romantic partner you have will marvel at your ability to nip possible disagreements right in the bud.

Add that quality to your warmth, generosity, and idyllic view of love, and you will know why others will swarm around you like bees do to honey. While you may find something to love in all those who are attracted to you, there is only one who will touch you in a deep place that all the others cannot. When that happens, you will know you have truly found your mate, and you will pledge your love for the rest of your life.

The one who will arouse your passion has a way of looking at you that can melt you in a second. Following that comes a melodious voice that rings in your ear like beautiful music, and words that are poetic and modest. Given all that perfection, you will want to know that the person is real, down-to-earth, and honest in order for the two of you to go through life together.

The gal who will complete your life, 2002 Libra male, loves taking adventurous trips and is unafraid to try new things or visit new places. If you asked, she would fly with you to the Amazon, or perhaps accompany you to the French Riviera, and all on a whim. She will be just as comfortable reading quietly as going skydiving, as long as you are close by. But mostly she will go anywhere to be alone with you where you can shut out the world and simply be in love.

More than anything, 2002 Libra female, you want a guy who can always make you laugh—even when you feel that the world has let you down. When he smiles, you will just melt, and that twinkle in his eye makes you just want to hold him and hug him until you both cannot take it anymore. Of course, he has to be a really nice person, one you can introduce to anyone, someone who will be loved by all, especially by you.

LIBRA ZODIAC SIGN
YOUR LOVE PLANETS

YOUR ROMANTIC SIDE   p. 696
- ▶ **VENUS IN SCORPIO**
  Born Sept. 23, 4:56 - Oct. 23, 14:18

YOUR SEX DRIVE   p. 722
- ▶ **MARS IN VIRGO**
  Born Sept. 23, 4:56 - Oct. 15, 17:38
- ▶ **MARS IN LIBRA**
  Born Oct. 15, 17:39 - Oct. 23, 14:18

YOUR CELEBRITY TWINS   p. 760
Find out the astrological similarities you have with famous people.

YOUR COMPATIBILITY   p. 780
Compare planets to find out how compatible you are in a relationship.

YOUR RELATIONSHIP KARMA   p. 824
- ▶ **SATURN IN GEMINI**
  Born Sept. 23, 4:56 - Oct. 23, 14:18

694

JULIANNE MOORE
American Actress
Sun in Sagittarius

2002 SCORPIO

From October 23, 14:19 through November 22, 11:54

♏ *The Curious Cuddler*

For you, curious and unrelenting Scorpio of 2002, life may be defined as a series of journeys that you begin as a young child and continue on through adolescence and adulthood. You will ponder all the possibilities that life has in store for you—from your profession to your friendships to your spiritual quests—and you'll think about going to the ends of the earth to experience all that life has to offer.

When it comes to love, you will never have to go far to find it, since you will freely give love and consideration to all you meet. People will want to be around you in hopes that they too will absorb that wonderful feeling. That very special someone you meet someday will reach that secret place in your heart in a way that nobody else can. When you are with your true love, even an ordinary night for dinner and a movie will seem like a magical and memorable time.

You will be attracted to the type of person who expresses feelings and thoughts in ways that go beyond words. While you love passionate conversations about the arts, social issues, or even the latest medical breakthrough, you are looking for someone who can be perfectly content and joyful saying nothing, just being around you. Someone who comes on loud and strong, and engages in superficial chitchat will be a complete turn-off to you.

The perfect gal for you, 2002 Scorpio male, will be loving, kind, and affectionate. This wonderful woman will teach you how to love unconditionally, and will never comment on how late you are, or on how much time you spend away from her. She knows that when you are not with her, she is on your mind, and that when you are with her, your kisses and hugs will tell her you are totally hers.

If you could conjure up the guy who will make your life complete, 2002 Scorpio female, he would be one part handsome hunk, and one part caring, Good Samaritan, the kind who loves animals and children, and who will give anyone the shirt off his back. He will know instinctively when to give you your space, and when to give you a great big cuddle to let you know that he cares only for you.

2002 SAGITTARIUS

From November 22, 11:55 through December 22, 1:14

♐ *The Inspirational Mentor*

Adventurous, inspirational, and honest to a fault, you, Sagittarius of 2002, have much to look forward to as you transform from an inquisitive, precocious child into an idealistic and intellectual adult. You will always be mature for your years, and you will seem to have the answers to life's most puzzling riddles, even when young. This "wisdom" will make you someone who can be an outstanding teacher, or a brilliant politician.

When it comes to love, you will be smart enough to defer to that special someone, who will make you forget about your overactive brain for a while and show you how to "feel the love." In return, you will expand your partner's horizons, playing the roles of lover, friend, and mentor all at the same time. With both of you teaching the other about life on so many levels, it will be what many call the perfect relationship.

Anyone who wants to be in your life must have a sharp mind and a great wit, and be able to converse with you about everything under the sun. You just love someone who is your equal in terms of intellect and learning, as it helps to broaden your own knowledge. For you, the ideal relationship is one in which you share everything, including mental interests.

Your special gal, 2002 Sagittarius male, will be a ball of dynamite on all levels. When she wants your attention, she will turn off your computer, make you put down the books, and lead you outside, perhaps to an ice skating rink in winter or a crystal blue lake in summer. And you will have no choice but to go along, since the reward will be having this lady, with her warm embrace and her winning smile, all to yourself.

The guy who will make your life complete, 2002 Sagittarius female, will be charming and good-looking, and will look fabulous whether he is sitting around the house in jeans or dressing up for a formal affair. While looks count for a lot, what counts more will be his penetrating mind and his bottomless heart. He always seems to have the answers to all your doubts, along with a hug and a kiss. When you are in his arms you will know that everything will be all right.

1 Read Your Sign   **2** Look Up Your Love Planets   **3** Go to Pages Shown

2002s

The Sex Life of Catherine M.

Fat men, thin men, hairy men, ugly men, beautiful men ... Catherine Millet has had them all, in every position conceivable, in every orifice penetrable, and in every location possible.

In June 2001, an unassuming, conservatively dressed French woman in her fifties published an autobiographical book that rocked respectable French society. Within a year, *The Sex Life of Catherine M* was an international phenomenon, selling over 400,000 copies in France, translated into over twenty languages, and shocking readers across the globe with the graphic details of its author's promiscuous, licentious adventures.

And boy, was she adventurous. By day Millet was—and is—a respectable art curator, the editor of a highbrow French art magazine, and a member of the Paris intelligentsia. But by night Millet would abandon herself to her every fantasy, specializing in orgies, delighting in anonymous, nameless sex with—quite literally—hundreds of men, sometimes four—yes, four!—men at a time in, among other places, art galleries, cemeteries, saunas, sex clubs, trucks, washrooms, train platforms, and atop autos in a frenzy of "delicious giddiness." Such was her prolificacy that she can only recall forty-nine of the hundreds of men she had sex with, although this may have something to do with her favorite position—let's just say that looking a lover in the eyes might have proved a bit tricky.

And all these lascivious antics were often done in collaboration with her husband. Married for ten years to the writer and photographer Jacques Henric and living together for twenty years, theirs, needless

> *"Many women have fantasies about this kind of sex. I happened to play them out."*
>
> CATHERINE MILLET,
> from *The Observer*, May 2002

to say, was an open relationship. Although they've been monogamous for the past eight years, Henric's name litters the pages. When he wasn't playing a starring role in the proceedings—he is the only man openly identified in the book—he

often organized her illicit, multiple liaisons, secretly watching from the sidelines.

Millet's carnal memoirs inspired Henric to publish his version and vision of her libidinous life. *Légendes de Catherine M* is a collection of naked photos of Millet exposing herself in public places, with a risqué cover photo featuring Millet's famous, round, peachy *derriere*.

Brought up Catholic, as a child she wanted to be a nun. Her chaste ambitions were not to last. Only two weeks after losing her virginity, at eighteen, she experienced her first taste of group sex. She was hooked and she was insatiable. An awkward and shy young woman, the dating game intimidated and overwhelmed her. She cringed at pre-sex niceties and found dining or holding conversations excruciating when all she wanted to do was get straight down to business. Which is exactly what she did.

Writing in a detached manner, her prose is stylish and elegant as she reveals everything but her emotions. This is a coldhearted account of cold-blooded sex without feeling, a detached itemization, a passionless yet provocative romp through the murky depths of seedy sex. For Catherine Millet, her quest for sex was about satisfaction.

Loved and hated in equal measure, the book arouses strong reactions and virulent discussion. Is it simply glossy pornography masquerading as erudite writing, or is it an artistic literary masterpiece? Is Millet a pioneering libertine, an unwitting victim, or a raving nymphomaniac? Whatever conclusions readers reach, one thing's for sure: this lady certainly ain't repressed.

695

▶ READ ABOUT SEX IN THE '70S ON PAGE 449

YOUR ROMANTIC SIDE

Venus, the Planet of Love

In Roman mythology, Venus was the goddess of love and beauty. In astrology, Venus is the planet of relationships, particularly romantic partnerships. By looking at your Venus sign, you can discover your "love quotient"—the way you express affection, your capacity to give and receive love, your attitudes about relationships, what you look for in a partner, and how you are likely to relate to someone you love. Venus shows your sensual nature too—what gives you pleasure and how you go about making yourself attractive to a lover. A "feminine" planet, Venus in a man's birth chart also suggests the traits he finds most appealing in a woman—his feminine ideal. In a woman's chart, Venus describes her feelings about herself as a woman—the feminine qualities she chooses to portray and the characteristics she wants to be appreciated for. Your personal Venus Sign is the place where Venus was positioned in the sky at the time of your birth. You'll find your personal Venus Sign on your Zodiac Sign page. It is located in the column called **Your Love Planets** and listed under **Your Romantic Side**. Please read on to find out more.

INSTRUCTIONS

HERE'S HOW TO READ ABOUT YOUR ROMANTIC SIDE.

1 Find your Zodiac Sign reading.

2 Look beside your Zodiac Sign for **Your Love Planets**. Under **Your Romantic Side**, you'll find your Venus Sign.

3 Look at the index below. Locate your Zodiac sign across the top and then your Venus Sign on the left hand side column. Where the two lines intersect is a page number. Turn to this page to read all about **Your Romantic Side**.

Note: Keep all your Astrological Love Information handy by jotting down the page numbers of your Birth Year Events, Zodiac Sign, and Venus Sign.

Example

If you were born on June 3, 1964, you would be a Gemini with a Venus in Cancer. What kind of lover are you as a Gemini with Venus in Cancer? On the index below you will find that page 704 reveals everything about **Your Romantic Side**.

YOUR ROMANTIC SIDE PAGE INDEX

HOW TO USE THIS INDEX
• Locate your Zodiac Sign across the top.
• Find your Venus Sign.
• Turn to the page indicated where the two lines intersect to read all about **Your Romantic Side**.

VENUS SIGN	ARIES	TAURUS	GEMINI	CANCER	LEO	VIRGO	LIBRA	SCORPIO	SAGITTARIUS	CAPRICORN	AQUARIUS	PISCES
ARIES	p. 699	p. 699	p. 699								p. 698	p. 698
TAURUS	p. 700	p. 701	p. 701	p. 701								p. 700
GEMINI	p. 702	p. 702	p. 703	p. 703	p. 703							
CANCER		p. 704	p. 704	p. 705	p. 705	p. 705						
LEO			p. 706	p. 706	p. 707	p. 707	p. 707					
VIRGO				p. 708	p. 708	p. 709	p. 709	p. 709				
LIBRA					p. 710	p. 710	p. 711	p. 711	p. 711			
SCORPIO						p. 712	p. 712	p. 713	p. 713	p. 713		
SAGITTARIUS							p. 714	p. 714	p. 715	p. 715	p. 715	
CAPRICORN								p. 716	p. 716	p. 717	p. 717	p. 717
AQUARIUS	p. 719								p. 718	p. 718	p. 719	p. 719
PISCES	p. 721	p. 721								p. 720	p. 720	p. 721

YOUR ROMANTIC SIDE

Your Venus in Aries

L ove, for you, is an exciting contest. You might even view lovers as opponents to be conquered and prefer those who present a challenge. In your opinion, a bit of tension in a relationship keeps things from getting dull, and you probably don't want your love life always to be smooth and easy.

You like to be the dominant partner and are usually the one to make the first move. When you meet an appealing person, you waste no time letting him or her know you care. However, your attention span is rather short, and you might lose interest if the object of your desire doesn't provide enough thrills. Always on the look out for something new, you might change partners once the novelty wears off.

Sex may be more important to you than affection. Not particularly romantic, you can be an electrifying lover—but none of that touchy-feely stuff!

With Your AQUARIUS Zodiac Sign

A relationship with you could be a walk on the wild side. For you, love is an adventure and you eagerly embrace new experiences and challenges. Your quest for excitement could cause you to change partners frequently, thwart societal conventions, or choose a lover who keeps you guessing.

A peaceful, secure, harmonious partnership might bore you silly. You need lots of change and stimulation—even some conflict or chaos. More cerebral than emotional, you enjoy a bit of mental jousting and don't take differences of opinion to heart. A heated debate with a lover can actually be a form of foreplay for you.

You don't feel a need to be joined at the hip with a partner. Instead, you want plenty of room to pursue your individual interests, friendships, and activities. A relationship with you might be like a fireworks display—colorful and thrilling, but lacking real substance or permanence.

With Your PISCES Zodiac Sign

Your idealism is refreshing and infectious, and you have a way of bringing out the best in those you love. A champion of the underdog, you can see value in people that they may not recognize in themselves. Even if love disappoints you, you'll probably retain your youthful hopefulness throughout your life.

Underneath your gentle exterior is an adventurous, playful, and bawdy nature that might only be fully expressed through relationships. You may be timid in many areas, but in love you are willing to take risks. Consequently, you might enjoy some exciting, perhaps tempestuous romances. Even a long-term relationship may be punctuated by many ups and downs.

You tend to be compassionate and forgiving—but only to a point. A partner who pushes you too far could experience your quick anger. Usually, you give people the benefit of the doubt, but you don't have much patience with bad behavior.

698

▶ READ ABOUT YOUR ROMANTIC COMPATIBILITY *on p. 780* ▶ LOOK FOR YOUR CELEBRITY VENUS TWINS *on p. 767*

Your
Venus
in Aries

With Your **ARIES** Zodiac Sign

You are nothing if not spontaneous in matters of the heart. Like a brush fire, your affection is easily ignited and bursts rapidly into a major conflagration. But your passion may die down just as suddenly unless a partner continues to fan your flames with new thrills. Routine is like a bucket of ice water and can quickly douse your ardor.

You thrive on challenges and enjoy a good contest. A partner who is too "easy" might not interest you for long. You respect someone who can stand up to your strong personality, and who doesn't let you call all the shots. Perhaps you even find a periodic joust stimulating.

With your fun-loving and daring nature, you probably appreciate a partner who is a "playmate." Someone with whom you can share your favorite sport or who eagerly accompanies you on your wild adventures could be an ideal companion for you.

With Your **TAURUS** Zodiac Sign

Your approach to love tends to be straightforward and rather uncomplicated. You probably don't understand why other people seem to go through so many ups and downs in their relationships. Easygoing, friendly, and, for the most part, upbeat, you look for the best in your partners and usually find it.

Sex is likely to rank high on your list of priorities in a relationship. With your strong libido and adventurous nature, you may be inclined to push the outside of the erotic envelope and could be a dynamic lover. If the sex is good, you might not care too much if you and your partner are on the same wavelength or otherwise.

Although closeness and stability in a relationship are important to you, you need to be able to be your own person, too. A relationship that satisfies your physical needs and doesn't make too many demands on you could last forever.

With Your **GEMINI** Zodiac Sign

Your curiosity might lead you to explore all sorts of relationships— and you probably have lots of fun in the process. You approach love with enthusiasm, without trying to control how matters will proceed. Exploring new romantic territory fascinates you, and you want to see as much as possible.

With your playful, outgoing personality, you've probably had many romantic opportunities. But your restlessness could prevent you from sticking with one partner for long. You can be a delightful companion and enjoy sharing your many ideas and interests with a lover—so long as he or she offers you plenty of excitement and stimulation.

You don't usually get too deeply invested in relationships. If things don't work out, you might shed a few tears, but quickly move on to the next adventure. In your opinion, life's too short for angst and there are always more flowers in the field to pluck.

▶ **READ ABOUT YOUR ROMANTIC COMPATIBILITY** *on p. 780* ▶ **LOOK FOR YOUR CELEBRITY VENUS TWINS** *on p. 767*

Your Venus in Taurus

Few people are as warm and affectionate as you, Venus in Taurus. Sensual and earthy, you enjoy all sorts of physical pleasures, from good food to good sex. You express your affection in a tactile, hands-on manner, such as snuggling in front of the TV, holding hands, or giving your partner a back rub.

You like companionship and are usually happiest in a stable, committed relationship. Once you give your heart to someone, that person can depend on your love to last a lifetime. You don't need a lot of variety—you prefer one partner to many and tend to be a faithful, devoted mate. You could be possessive, though, and might not want to allow your partner much freedom.

Generous—sometimes to a fault—you like to shower those you love with thoughtful gifts and cook their favorite meals. For you giving is as important as getting.

With Your PISCES Zodiac Sign

Although you tend to be idealistic about love, you don't overlook the realities of life. You enjoy creature comforts and know you can't live on love alone. Even if you fall head over heels for someone, you usually keep your feet close to the ground.

Rather shy and passive, you usually wait for love to come to you rather than pursuing it. Once it finds you, it usually sticks around. You tend to give a relationship your all—with so much invested, you aren't likely to let go easily. A stable relationship can provide a sense of security for you.

Sensual and affectionate, you enjoy adding to your romantic repertoire. With your rich imagination, you have a real talent when it comes to setting the stage for love. You may enjoy a partner who is as creative as you—together you can form a relationship that's an artistic masterpiece.

With Your ARIES Zodiac Sign

You know what you want in love and don't hesitate to go for it. Once you set your sights on someone, you pursue the object of your desire with great zeal. With your special combination of drive and persistence, you stand a good chance of winning in the game of love.

Your sunny nature and optimism can make you a delightful companion. You want to experience all the good things life has to offer and enjoy sharing many of them with a congenial partner. A mate who can be both a lover and a "buddy" to you is probably your romantic ideal.

You have a strong independent streak and are inclined to want your own way much of the time. Sometimes you may have trouble seeing a partner's point of view. However, you can be a faithful mate, so long as the relationship offers you plenty of stimulation and excitement.

► READ ABOUT YOUR ROMANTIC COMPATIBILITY on p. 780   ► LOOK FOR YOUR CELEBRITY VENUS TWINS on p. 767

Your Venus in Taurus

With Your TAURUS Zodiac Sign

Few people appreciate sensory pleasures as much as you do—anything that feels good might be okay in your book.

Not just sex, but all types of physical contact appeal to you—hugging, kissing, and massages are among your favorite ways to show affection.

Although you can be quite romantic, your relationship considerations tend to be practical. Security and stability are important to you; therefore, you are likely to seek a partner who can provide the creature comforts you cherish. Some might call you materialistic, but you probably don't see any reason to fall in love with a poor person if a rich one is available.

Perhaps you even view your partner as a possession, and you usually hold on tightly to the things you love. A loyal and devoted mate, you are willing to give a great deal to your loved ones, but you expect their fidelity in return.

With Your GEMINI Zodiac Sign

Some might say you want to have your cake and eat it, too. For although you prize your freedom, you also seek stability in a relationship. Perhaps you'd like to be footloose yourself, but expect fidelity from your mate.

Your friendly nature may attract many companions, and even if you're in a committed relationship you might enjoy spending time with people besides your significant other. Although you have a fickle and flirtatious side, you can be a devoted and caring partner. With an equally gregarious partner, you could enjoy an active and entertaining social life.

Love, for you, is likely to be a body and mind experience. Mentally oriented, you want to share your ideas and interests with your partner. But you also have a sensual side and could see sex as a wonderful way to communicate with the one you love. A romantic friendship—with benefits—might be your ideal.

With Your CANCER Zodiac Sign

Home is where your heart is, and you probably can't think of anything more idyllic than snuggling in front of the fire with your lover after savoring a gourmet meal together. Quite the sensualist, you appreciate all sorts of sensory delights and are happiest when you can combine two or more—such as good food and good sex.

Although some people say that the best things in life are free, you probably don't believe that. You enjoy your creature comforts and seek security, on every level, in a relationship. Not that you only look at a lover's wallet, but you want to be able to provide a stable existence for your family—and for yourself.

You don't take love lightly and give yourself completely to your mate. Jealous and possessive of your lover, you expect fidelity in return. When you establish a partnership, you nurture it with plenty of tender loving care.

▶ READ ABOUT YOUR ROMANTIC COMPATIBILITY on p. 780   ▶ LOOK FOR YOUR CELEBRITY VENUS TWINS on p. 767

Your Venus in Gemini

Communication is probably the most important ingredient in a relationship with you. You take an intellectual approach to love and want to share ideas with a lover who is also a friend. On your list of desirable qualities in a mate, intelligence will usually outrank good looks, status, or money.

Infinitely curious, you may find it difficult to be faithful to one person—you're afraid you'll miss out on something if you make a commitment. Like a butterfly, you might flit from flower to flower, wanting to sample everything life has to offer.

You probably like to talk about love and sex and might tell your mate "I love you" a dozen times a day. Perhaps you enjoy writing love letters to your partner. A lover who reads love poems to you in bed could win your heart. In your case, the mind truly is the most sensitive erogenous zone.

702

With Your ARIES Zodiac Sign

Your lover probably doesn't have to guess whether or not you care—you make your feelings known in no uncertain terms. You might even tell a partner you love him or her a dozen times a day.

Always on the lookout for new experiences, you value a partner who can teach you things and expose you to exciting adventures. You want to get as much out of life and love as possible. You also enjoy sharing your many interests and activities with a companion who is as lively, outgoing, and curious as you are.

Your curiosity, however, could lead you to be a bit promiscuous or to change partners frequently once the initial excitement begins to wane. Even if you're in a monogamous relationship, you probably still like to look and flirt. The game of love is such fun that playing it could keep you youthful into your senior years.

With Your TAURUS Zodiac Sign

Both body and mind are important to you, and you appreciate a partner who combines brains with beauty. You want to be able to talk to your lover—and one of your favorite subjects is probably sex. Someone who teaches you new tricks could get your seal of approval.

Outgoing and good-natured, you make friends easily and probably have your share of admirers. And because you are both sensual and curious, you might enjoy experimenting sexually. Although you value loyalty and stability, your commitment to a partner might not last forever; therefore, serial monogamy could be your pattern.

Even though you may seek security, you don't want to give up your freedom in the bargain. A partner who tries to rein you in could stifle your playful, lighthearted charm. But while you might feel it's okay if you "hang loose," you probably won't like it if your mate plays around!

► READ ABOUT YOUR ROMANTIC COMPATIBILITY *on p. 780* ► LOOK FOR YOUR CELEBRITY VENUS TWINS *on p. 767*

Your Venus in Gemini

With Your GEMINI Zodiac Sign

You love to talk about love. Perhaps you enjoy conversing with friends about the ins and outs of romance, or spend hours chatting with a significant other. You might even find romance online. Unless you can communicate with your lover, you probably won't be happy.

Gemini is the sign of the twins, and you may be quite capable of carrying on more than one relationship simultaneously. You have so many interests—and so many sides to your personality—that it might be hard for you to limit yourself to just one person. And because you tend to see relationships as opportunities for learning, you may need several partners to satisfy your thirst for knowledge and experience.

You tend to intellectualize about relationships and don't usually form strong, emotional attachments. If love gives you a tumble, you "get back on the horse" and ride off in search of a new romance.

With Your CANCER Zodiac Sign

Despite your rather shy and sensitive nature, you don't shy away from love. Instead, you can be quite friendly and might not hesitate to initiate a conversation with someone who strikes your fancy. With your special blend of sociability and vulnerability, you may attract many admirers.

Your loved ones don't have to guess how you feel about them— you let them know, in word and deed, how much they mean to you. Compassionate and nurturing, you might enjoy cooking for your partner or doing little things around the house to please him or her. Perhaps you try to create a safe, secure, and comfortable "nest" for your family.

You know that good communication is important in a relationship. Quite likely you possess a unique ability to communicate verbally and intuitively. With your heart and mind working in tandem, you can form a dynamic and enduring connection with a partner.

With Your LEO Zodiac Sign

You have what it takes to write the book of love. Eager to be the center of attention, you enjoy entertaining others with your wit and charm. Relationships might be one of your favorite subjects, and you can probably keep lovers and friends amused for hours with your clever anecdotes.

Flattery counts with you— someone who wants to please you should shower you with compliments. You are usually forthcoming with praise for your partner as well. You have a knack for making a lover feel special, and you expect the same in return. Some of your lines might even come from old movies or love stories, and a romance with you isn't likely to be lacking in drama.

Brains as well as beauty are important to you, and you appreciate a partner who has both. But you might not like it if your mate is brighter or better-looking than you!

▶ READ ABOUT YOUR ROMANTIC COMPATIBILITY *on p. 780*   ▶ LOOK FOR YOUR CELEBRITY VENUS TWINS *on p. 767*

Your Venus in Cancer

Quality is more important than quantity to you. You value security in relationships and need a partner you can trust completely. Because home and family are important to you, you want a mate with whom you can settle down—when you give your heart to someone, it's for keeps.

Deeply emotional and very sensitive, you invest yourself completely in your relationship. The idea of infidelity is probably unthinkable for you. You could tend to be possessive of the one you love, but you don't expect more of your partner than you are willing to give yourself.

It's natural for you to nurture those you love and you may show your affection by cooking your mate's favorite meals. You enjoy physical closeness as well as emotional closeness, touching your lover often to reinforce the bond between you. Ideally, you'd like to merge with your partner—body, mind, and soul.

With Your TAURUS Zodiac Sign

A real homebody, you may feel that love just naturally leads to establishing a home and family together. As a result, you take relationships seriously—casual love affairs could seem to be either a waste of time or destabilizing. Security is all-important to you.

A close and abiding relationship can serve as your axle and give meaning to the rest of your life. You are probably more concerned with depth than breadth in matters of the heart. Once you make a commitment, your partner can rely on you to be there through good times and bad.

Your devotion isn't exactly selfless, though—there are usually some strings attached. You tend to subscribe to traditional values and expect undying loyalty and fidelity from your mate. Although you're willing to give as much as you demand, your possessiveness and "Siamese twin" approach to love could suffocate free spirits.

With Your GEMINI Zodiac Sign

Both your heart and mind seek fulfillment through relationships — you want depth as well as breadth in love. Communication is important to you, too, and your unique combination of intelligence and intuitiveness lets you form a special connection with a lover.

Your friendly and flirtatious personality might lead those who don't know you well to think you are superficial in romantic matters. But underneath your casual demeanor beats a sensitive and passionate heart. At times, you may seem to be two different people, but that keeps things interesting.

You might even use your clever wit and playful attitude as a way to keep people at arm's length—until you are sure they're sincere, that is—because you know how deeply you can be hurt if a love affair doesn't work out. A lover who passes your scrutiny, however, is likely to find you are a warm, compassionate, and entertaining partner.

704

▶ READ ABOUT YOUR ROMANTIC COMPATIBILITY on p. 780   ▶ LOOK FOR YOUR CELEBRITY VENUS TWINS on p. 767

Your
Venus
in Cancer

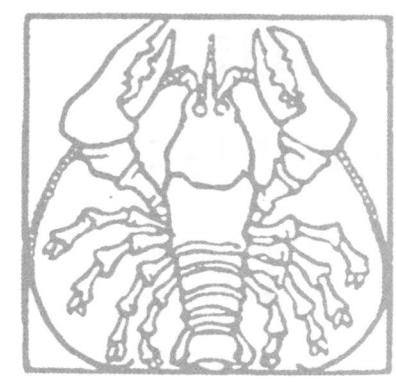

With Your **CANCER** Zodiac Sign

You wear your heart on your sleeve, and your sensitive feelings are easily bruised. As a result, you may be cautious about love and relationships. Maybe you expect people to prove their trustworthiness before you open the door to your heart and let them enter your life. Your deep emotions might make you feel vulnerable, and you need to know you can rely on your partner to be faithful.

Security is important to you, and you might derive a sense of security from a stable family life. Most likely you are fond of children and see them as the center of a relationship—unless your partnership gives you offspring, you might not feel fulfilled.

Affectionate and caring toward those you love, you may shower them with demonstrations of your devotion, perhaps by cooking their favorite meals. Peer relationships, though, might seem foreign to you—you prefer to "baby" your mate.

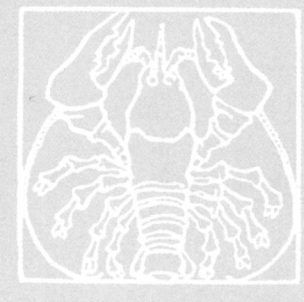

With Your **LEO** Zodiac Sign

Usually you appear to be the epitome of self-confidence, but in relationships you tend to be a bit shy. Because your feelings are so sensitive and deep, you don't want to go too far out on a limb and risk getting hurt. But if a partner shows you the devotion and loyalty you crave, you'll blossom.

Home and family are important to you, and you may be very proud of your loved ones. You might find reasons to brag about your partner—you could be his or her biggest fan. In return, you appreciate a mate who is supportive of you and who picks you up when you're feeling blue.

You want to be a star in your partner's eyes, and you'll often go to great lengths to please him or her. Although you may be a bit demanding at times, you rarely expect more than you're willing to give.

With Your **VIRGO** Zodiac Sign

It would be hard to find a more helpful and caring partner than you. You enjoy doing things for loved ones and work hard to make their lives easier. Whether you're tending the hearth fires or bringing home the bacon—or both—you do your best to build a secure relationship and domestic life.

At times, your head and heart may be at odds. You might like to stand back and analyze a partnership as if it were a spreadsheet, but your emotions sometimes get the upper hand. In a stable relationship, you can overcome feelings of insecurity and "go with the flow."

Sensitive and passive, you might let a partner call the shots—at least it appears that way from the outside. Like the puppet master, however, you're probably the one who holds the strings and keeps things running smoothly. You aren't pushy, but you usually get your way.

► **READ ABOUT YOUR ROMANTIC COMPATIBILITY** *on p. 780*   ► **LOOK FOR YOUR CELEBRITY VENUS TWINS** *on p. 767*

Your Venus in Leo

You appreciate beauty and drama and can elevate love to an art form. Perhaps you throw yourself into romance with such enthusiasm that you seem to be playing a role in an opera. Amore can also stimulate your creative juices, and you might paint a lover's portrait or sing love songs to him or her.

Generous, you may enjoy buying lovers beautiful gifts or taking them out to the best places. But your generosity isn't entirely selfless—you want your partner to show you the adoration and respect you deserve. You'll treat a mate like royalty, but you expect the same in return.

Because appearances are important to you, good looks are usually high on your list of "must haves" in a partner. Somewhat vain yourself, you can be won over with a little flattery. A lover who wants to stimulate your ardor will make you feel like a star.

With Your GEMINI Zodiac Sign

The words "I love you" are music to your ears, and you want your partner to say them to you often—and then follow up with a few compliments, for praise is the fastest way to make your heartstrings hum. And what could be better than a lover who sings romantic songs or reads love poems to you?

You enjoy the drama of being in love and might make a big show of romance. However, there could be more show than substance to your affection, for your feelings may not run very deep. You can be a delightful and charming companion, though, and despite a tendency to be a bit flirtatious, you are usually loyal to your mate.

Romance can stimulate your creativity, and you may express your affection in many colorful, imaginative ways. Perhaps your partner serves as your Muse. Your relationship could be your own personal romance novel.

With Your CANCER Zodiac Sign

You love being the center of your lover's attention. In other areas of life, your innate shyness might keep you in the background, but in matters of the heart, you like being in the limelight. All those little romantic overtures—flowers, candlelight dinners, thoughtful gifts—make you feel valued.

Your home is your castle and you enjoy holing up there with your loved ones. Security is important to you, but although your home may also be your fortress, it's probably a cozy one. Creating a beautiful home and a comfortable domestic life might be one of the ways you show your partner you care.

With your artistic sensibility, you have a knack for creating drama in your relationship. Your theatrics aren't all show, however—you are capable of deep affection and loyalty. Although your tendency toward moodiness could produce some ups and downs, you know how to keep romance alive.

▶ READ ABOUT YOUR ROMANTIC COMPATIBILITY *on p. 780* ▶ LOOK FOR YOUR CELEBRITY VENUS TWINS *on p. 767*

Your
Venus
in Leo

With Your **LEO** Zodiac Sign

For you, love is a many splendored thing. You love starring in the drama of your own life—and you want an attractive co-star to share the stage with you. Sometimes, though, you might get so caught up in the glamour of being in love that you forget about the day-to-day business of relating.

Appearances matter to you, and you might not consider signing on with an unattractive partner. At times, your lover might even feel like a beautiful accessory. Perhaps you enjoy going out on the town, seeing and being seen by the "right" people. You do know how to show someone a good time and make a partner feel special. Of course, you want to be adored in return.

Your creativity can enrich your relationship, and you might write sonnets or paint beautiful pictures for your mate. Whatever you turn your attention to becomes a work of art.

With Your **VIRGO** Zodiac Sign

Your heart has its own reasons! When it decides to take charge, it may nudge your usual shy, cautious personality aside and urge you to go for the gold. Love can bring out your best, and you might express your romantic feelings in creative or colorful ways.

Because you tend to be rather reserved, a partner who is more outgoing and courageous could be a good complement to you. You might also appreciate someone who can serve as your benefactor or protector. Modest and unassuming, you may let your mate be the dominant member of the partnership.

Perhaps you are attracted to creative people or those who garner respect from their peers. You want a partner you can be proud of, someone whose looks, status, or talent set him or her apart from the crowd. You could be content to stand on the sidelines, cheering your partner on to greatness.

With Your **LIBRA** Zodiac Sign

Love is your stage, and you usually perform best when in a relationship. In fact, you might not feel fulfilled unless you can share your life with someone special. Generous with your affection, you may be quite demonstrative toward your partner. You thrive on attention, too, and want your mate to shower you with loving words and gestures.

Your artist's eye can add drama and color to a relationship. Because you love beauty, you appreciate an attractive partner. However, a relationship with you might lack depth or true feeling. You seek companionship and congeniality, but usually try to avoid anything unsettling or unseemly.

Friendly and outgoing, you enjoy a partner with whom you can go places and do things. Someone who boosts your social status could be a plus. A relationship may enhance your creativity, confidence, and charisma, enabling you to succeed in ways you couldn't achieve on your own.

▶ READ ABOUT YOUR ROMANTIC COMPATIBILITY *on p. 780*   ▶ LOOK FOR YOUR CELEBRITY VENUS TWINS *on p. 767*

Your Venus in Virgo

You tend to take a practical approach to relationships and rarely let your heart rule your head. Glamour, excitement, and romance might not be very important to you. Instead, you want a partner you can depend on, someone who works hard and displays common sense.

Although you may not expect your lover to be a perfect "10," he or she should be neat, clean, and well-mannered. Slovenliness is a real turn-off for you.

You do your best to keep a partnership running smoothly. Considerate and compassionate, you try to take care of your mate's every need, and you can make yourself indispensable. It's important for you to feel needed, and you may show your love by cooking, cleaning, or fixing things around the house. At times your loved ones may feel you are a bit critical, but that's probably just your way of helping them to be their best.

With Your CANCER Zodiac Sign

Storybook romances probably don't hold much appeal for you—you are more interested in having a stable, practical, enduring relationship. You do your best to keep your partnership functioning smoothly and efficiently on a daily basis.

Few people are more caring and compassionate than you, and you may devote yourself totally to your loved ones. Rather than telling them you care, you express your love by doing things for them. It's important for you to know that your partner needs you, and you might strive to make yourself indispensable.

That's not to say you aren't romantic, for you enjoy affection and amorousness as much as anyone. But you tend to be cautious and critical, at least in the beginning, and might not exhibit your deep feelings until you feel you can trust a partner. Once you establish a relationship, though, your mate can depend on you through thick and thin.

With Your LEO Zodiac Sign

In most areas of life, you act with confidence and trust that things will turn out well. In relationships, though, you might be more analytical and cautious—even a bit shy—because you don't want others to judge or reject you.

You tend to be critical of partners and might have high expectations of them. Perhaps you seek the perfect lover and only consider those who meet your high standards. Or you could be a bit exacting in a relationship, so that your mate feels pressured by your demands. From your perspective, however, your intention is to help people become the best they can possibly be.

Because you like to be the center of attention, you might be happiest with someone who doesn't hog the spotlight. You enjoy acting as protector and benefactor and can behave quite magnanimously toward a partner who is content to play a supporting role.

▶ READ ABOUT YOUR ROMANTIC COMPATIBILITY *on p. 780* ▶ LOOK FOR YOUR CELEBRITY VENUS TWINS *on p. 767*

Your Venus in Virgo

With Your **VIRGO** Zodiac Sign

You can fix just about anything, from a broken faucet to a broken heart. Fixing your partner could be a labor of love for you. Eager to help those in need, you might find someone with a few flaws more attractive than someone who has it all together. In a relationship, you're probably the one who takes care of problems and makes the partnership work.

Analytical and meticulous, you tend to think your emotions rather than feeling them. Although you are sensitive and kind, you can seem rather dispassionate, and some people might find it hard to live up to your expectations.

Your job may occupy a prominent spot in your life, and you might fall into the "all work, no play" category. Someone whose career path is similar to yours, who can be your business partner as well as a romantic partner, could be a good match for you.

With Your **LIBRA** Zodiac Sign

In relationships you tend to be a perfectionist, and you aren't likely to settle for someone who doesn't meet your standards just because you hate to be alone. Even after you find Mr. or Ms. Right, you may still notice a few flaws and try to fix them.

At times, your lover may feel you are too critical or that your expectations are too high. From your perspective, though, improving someone shows you care. And you do tend to dote on your mate, doing all sorts of little things to make his or her life better. Few people are more attentive and caring than you.

You can be easily influenced by your partner's opinion. Perhaps you let your lover sit in the power seat—you might not mind playing a supporting role in the relationship. Although you can be "high maintenance" at times, you uphold your end of the bargain, too.

With Your **SCORPIO** Zodiac Sign

You're not one to hit the dating bars. Instead, your rather shy, sensitive nature generally causes you to retreat from the madding crowd and seek the company of a few trusted companions. Discriminating and cautious, you don't give your heart to just anyone, and you take your time getting to know someone before you make a commitment.

Once you do partner up, you give yourself wholeheartedly. Even so, you can be quite critical of your mate—but you might be deeply hurt if he or she criticizes you. You want other people to approve of you—although you probably won't reveal this—and as a result, you might try to hide your emotional vulnerability behind a mask of indifference.

It's important for you to feel you are in a position of power and control. A mate who doesn't challenge your authority, who demonstrates support and encouragement, could win your undying devotion.

▶ **READ ABOUT YOUR ROMANTIC COMPATIBILITY** *on p. 780* ▶ **LOOK FOR YOUR CELEBRITY VENUS TWINS** *on p. 767*

Your Venus in Libra

Love makes your world go around, and you are rarely without a significant other. Perhaps you think of yourself as half of a partnership rather than an individual. You might even stay in an unfulfilling relationship because you can't bear to be alone.

You rely on your natural powers of attraction to draw partners to you. Once you make a commitment, you usually keep it. Although you might not be the most passionate lover, giving your partner pleasure pleases you and you rarely say no.

Highly romantic, you enjoy the trappings of love—moonlit walks on the beach and candlelight dinners are the stuff your fantasies are made of. You're a lover, not a fighter, and eschew discord of any kind. To keep a relationship running smoothly you can be too quick to compromise. You dream of living happily ever after and do your utmost to make it come true.

With Your LEO Zodiac Sign

You rarely have to look for love—it finds you. Because you make love a priority and invest lots of energy in making yourself attractive, you probably have many admirers. Companionship is important to you and you don't like being alone. Good-natured and outgoing, you may enjoy entertaining —a partner who is as sociable and charming as you is an asset.

A romantic at heart, you delight in all the trappings of love. But your relationship may have more form than substance. You want a partnership in which both parties live happily ever after, and you might not delve too deeply into areas that could make waves.

You tend to look to partners to validate you and might not feel complete unless you are in a relationship. Generous and affectionate, you go to great lengths to please the one you love. Your lover's eyes are the mirrors through which you see yourself.

With Your VIRGO Zodiac Sign

Love is important to you, but that doesn't mean you let your heart call the shots. In fact, you tend to be quite rational about choosing a mate. Unlikely to be swept off your feet, you may approach romantic partnerships in much the same way as you would a business arrangement.

A neat and orderly relationship is more comfortable for you than one that's highly emotional, chaotic, or intensely passionate. Sensitive and easily upset, you want things to be congenial between you. When differences arise, you'd rather acquiesce or compromise than fight.

You might expect your partner to be neat and orderly, too, and are offended by slovenly types. You value an attractive appearance and good manners, but your checklist of "must haves" probably doesn't stop there. Some might feel you are too critical, but perhaps you see a relationship as a "work in progress" and are continually refining it.

▶ READ ABOUT YOUR ROMANTIC COMPATIBILITY on p. 780   ▶ LOOK FOR YOUR CELEBRITY VENUS TWINS on p. 767

Your Venus in Libra

With Your LIBRA Zodiac Sign

Romance is in your blood. For you, a life without love might not seem worth living. As a result, you are rarely without a significant other and may believe you can't have it all unless you're with someone.

Your charm and congeniality are likely to attract many admirers. If given a choice of more than one partner, however, you could vacillate until one of them gives up and moves on. Once you form an alliance with someone, you give it your all, even if it means adapting yourself to fit that person's expectations and lifestyle.

Relationships could be considered your calling or your art form, for you devote such care and attention to them. You might even pride yourself on your romantic "savoir faire." Love can stimulate your creativity, and your partner might serve as your Muse. Those of you who are artists might choose love and relationships as your subject matter.

With Your SCORPIO Zodiac Sign

An uncanny blend of passion and detachment, secrecy and sociability, you present an intriguing challenge for partners who may have trouble figuring you out. Sometimes you're indecisive, other times you can be jealous and possessive. However, your sex appeal and romantic nature usually make it all worthwhile.

You are likely to be quite particular when choosing a partner and don't take relationships lightly. Love is serious business for you and you invest heavily in it. You might even view your partner and yourself as two halves of a whole and could feel set adrift if a relationship fails.

Often you are given to extremes. But in relationships you usually try to keep things on an even keel and don't want your lover to put you through too much emotional turmoil. You might appreciate a partner who can smooth out the bumps in your life and establish balance out of chaos.

With Your SAGITTARIUS Zodiac Sign

Lady Luck is usually on your side in the game of love, and you rarely lack companionship. With your outgoing and cheerful personality, you might have enough adoring fans to fill a stadium. Your biggest dilemma could be choosing from among the options available to you.

Fun-loving and sociable, you aren't inclined to snuggle up in front of the TV with a partner—you want to be out and about. A relationship with you is likely to be filled with activities—everything from sporting events to art openings might be on your agenda—and you appreciate a lover who can keep up with you.

Domestic responsibilities and the day-to-day business of a relationship might not interest you much, though. You want your love life to be light and easy and usually try to steer clear of unpleasant, challenging, or emotional situations. In your love story, everyone lives happily ever after.

▶ READ ABOUT YOUR ROMANTIC COMPATIBILITY on p. 780   ▶ LOOK FOR YOUR CELEBRITY VENUS TWINS on p. 767

Your Venus in Scorpio

Love isn't a partnership for you, it's a merger. You want to erase all the boundaries between you and your mate to become one in body, mind, and soul. No one takes love more seriously than you do. Although you may have your share of lovers, what you really want is a deeply committed relationship that lasts forever.

Once you overcome your natural reserve, you can be a passionate and romantic partner. Sex may be important to you, but it's really just a way of being close to your lover, a physical demonstration of your powerful emotions.

Because you devote so much of yourself—and know how deeply you can be hurt if things don't work out—you tend to be quite jealous and possessive. You may not give the people you care about much breathing room, but they rarely doubt your affection because your love knows no bounds.

With Your VIRGO Zodiac Sign

Sensitive and reclusive, you usually "play your cards close to your vest" where relationships are concerned. You don't grant many people access to your inner sanctum, and someone who meets up to your high standards is lucky indeed, for you are a most loyal and devoted mate.

Few things escape your scrutiny. You pay careful attention to a partner's likes, dislikes, and idiosyncrasies, and often you do your best to accommodate to them. But you might also keep a list of a mate's shortcomings and attempt to perfect these. A natural psychiatrist, you probably analyze your relationship in depth in order to understand the interaction between you and how to improve it.

People may underestimate your intensity. Although you have an analytical bent, in relationships your heart leads the way. You may appear mild-mannered, but looks can be deceiving—the iron fist in the velvet glove could best describe you.

With Your LIBRA Zodiac Sign

You're inclined to be easygoing, sociable, and rather detached — but you may be drawn to people who are anything but. Instead, you might attract intensely emotional, passionate, and private partners who both excite and baffle you.

Love could even be a "proving ground" for you and put you through some tumultuous or transformative experiences. Perhaps relationships reveal your inner nature and provide important growth opportunities for you. You might even meet your "shadow" in the form of your partner.

Casual flings might not interest you much. For you, a relationship is a serious matter and once you commit yourself to someone, you intend to make the partnership last. You don't like being alone, and you probably couldn't bear to know your lover is with someone else. People who don't know you intimately may believe you are superficial, but your feelings run deep, and a romance with you could be quite intense.

▶ READ ABOUT YOUR ROMANTIC COMPATIBILITY on p. 780   ▶ LOOK FOR YOUR CELEBRITY VENUS TWINS on p. 767

Your
Venus
in Scorpio

With Your SCORPIO Zodiac Sign

Passion is your middle name. A relationship that's safe, comfortable, and peaceful might bore you to death. You need lots of drama and emotional ups and downs to keep your batteries charged. Love with you could be likened to a storm, full of thunder and lightning—even a hint of danger might appeal to you.

Not very trusting or optimistic, you approach love with skepticism and may check out a partner carefully before getting involved. You tend to be quite secretive yourself, however, and don't want a lover to invade your privacy. The dark side of human behavior fascinates you, particularly where sex is concerned. You might be attracted to someone with an air of mystery or someone who wields power, overtly or covertly.

Although a relationship with you probably won't be easy, few people can generate the intense, emotional excitement you do. Other people's love lives seem pale by contrast.

With Your SAGITTARIUS Zodiac Sign

Your sunny disposition and outgoing personality may lead people who don't know you intimately to think you don't take love seriously. But once Cupid's arrow strikes, you're hooked.

In relationships, you may dispense with your usual laissez-faire attitude and behave in a more possessive and controlling manner. Perhaps you are fascinated by people who exhibit emotional intensity and an air of mystery, even though they might also perplex you.

You like to have a long leash, but probably won't stray too far from home. Although you might be a bit flirtatious—and even have a casual fling—you aren't likely to jettison a basically sound relationship. Perhaps your relationship serves as an anchor for you, enabling you to sail off in search of adventure, knowing you can always return to a secure port.

With Your CAPRICORN Zodiac Sign

You like to think you are in control of all areas of your life and try to keep things functioning in an orderly fashion. But when you fall in love, all that rational, common-sense stuff goes right out the window—you can't micro-manage your powerful feelings. Relationships can help you connect with your own emotional depths.

Sensual and passionate, you need a lover whose libido and desire for true intimacy match your own. You don't take love lightly and probably aren't interested in the social or intellectual aspects of a relationship. A strong sexual and emotional connection is more important to you than being with someone who shares your interests, goals, or ideas.

A relationship with you probably won't be light and easy, for you can be moody and pessimistic at times. But you are determined to make love last and are willing to give it all you've got.

▶ **READ ABOUT YOUR ROMANTIC COMPATIBILITY** *on p. 780* ▶ **LOOK FOR YOUR CELEBRITY VENUS TWINS** *on p. 767*

Your Venus in Sagittarius

You could probably write the Book of Love, because you're eager to learn as much as you can through your relationships, and equally eager to share what you know with your partners. Love for you is an adventure, and you approach it with optimism, enthusiasm, and curiosity.

With your friendly, outgoing personality you probably attract many admirers. You'd rather not limit yourself to one person, though—life is full of possibilities and you don't want to miss out on any of them. You like to show partners a good time and may enjoy dancing, traveling, or attending athletic events with them. Doing things in a big way suits you fine, and you can be quite generous toward those you love.

Your "easy come, easy go" attitude lets you rebound quickly from romantic disappointments. Idealistic in love, you believe there's someone else waiting on the horizon—and there usually is.

With Your LIBRA Zodiac Sign

You can often be found at the center of any social gathering, and your friendly, easygoing nature breaks down barriers to romance. People find it easy to be with you—you have a knack for making them feel positive about themselves. You believe in the goodness of love, and your faith is usually rewarded.

You're looking for fun in a relationship and don't want to have to work hard at it. You probably won't put up with a romance that's too emotionally demanding, chaotic, or limiting for long. Life's too short to be unhappy, and with your optimistic, outgoing personality, you don't usually have to look far for your next partner.

Your relationships, however, tend to lack depth and might fall into the category of affectionate friendships rather than deeply emotional romances. Having someone to go places and do things with is probably more important to you than grand passion.

With Your SCORPIO Zodiac Sign

You tend to be cautious and selective about the people you let close to you, but when romance comes knocking you usually open the door. Love lights up your mysterious and sometimes dark personality like a beacon shining in the night. The right partner can help you overcome your reclusive nature and expand your horizons.

Of course you take relationships seriously—but you probably won't die of a broken heart if a love affair ends. You possess an inner resilience and a deep-rooted belief that all will work out, which lets you rise from the ashes like the phoenix.

You are an intriguing mix of dark and light, especially in matters of the heart. Perhaps your relationships combine elements of both comedy and tragedy. You can be a charming and witty companion, but there's nothing superficial about you. The person who shares your life can enjoy the best of both worlds.

714

▶ **READ ABOUT YOUR ROMANTIC COMPATIBILITY** *on p. 780* ▶ **LOOK FOR YOUR CELEBRITY VENUS TWINS** *on p. 767*

Your
Venus
in Sagittarius

With Your SAGITTARIUS Zodiac Sign

Some might call you a rolling stone, for you rarely settle down for long. With your restless nature, you may have trouble making long-term commitments to anything or anyone—there's just too much to see and do.

You probably like to travel and might enjoy taking trips to faraway places with a significant other. You could even meet your mate on a trip or hook up with someone from another country. A partner who introduces you to new experiences or broadens your understanding of the world could be a good match for you.

Your idealism might lead you to search the globe for the perfect lover. Or, you may romanticize your partner and be disappointed if he or she turns out to have feet of clay. Coping with day-to-day realities just isn't your thing—if a relationship makes too many demands on you, you might ride off into the sunset.

With Your CAPRICORN Zodiac Sign

Some say you can't teach an old dog—or goat, in this case—new tricks, but that's not true of you. In relationships, you are usually willing to stretch a bit and can be fairly broad-minded. You might appreciate a partner who introduces you to new experiences and ideas—you may even pair up with someone from another country or culture. Traveling with a partner could be a fun way to expand your horizons.

You tend to be rather shy and might be surprised to discover that so many people find you interesting and attractive. A fun-loving, extroverted partner can bring you out of yourself and perhaps encourage you to be more playful, sociable, and daring, especially in your later years.

Fortunate experiences in love can boost your optimism and counteract your innate skepticism. Even if things don't always work out as you'd hoped, you aren't afraid to try again.

With Your AQUARIUS Zodiac Sign

Optimistic and adventurous, you approach relationships with an open mind and an open heart. You enjoy companionship and, with your friendly, upbeat personality, you attract an ever-expanding circle of friends and lovers. However, you are inclined to idealize the concept of love and might prefer to spend more time chasing your dream than settling down in a real-life partnership.

Future-oriented, you rarely waste time reminiscing about the past or lamenting old relationships that didn't work out. Once a romance is over, you move on and don't look back. You don't usually harbor regrets or resentment and try to remain friends with former mates.

An inventive and imaginative lover, you like to put a fresh spin on romance so that your partner never knows quite what to expect. Hungry for new experiences, you are eager to try things you haven't tried before. If routine sets in, you might look elsewhere for excitement.

715

▶ **READ ABOUT YOUR ROMANTIC COMPATIBILITY** *on p. 780* ▶ **LOOK FOR YOUR CELEBRITY VENUS TWINS** *on p. 767*

Your Venus in Capricorn

716

Practical in love, you may handle affairs of the heart much as you do business relationships. In your opinion, a partnership is a long-term investment that's not to be entered into impulsively, and you want a mate you can depend on.

You may not be as cold or detached as you sometimes appear, but your natural caution and reserve usually keep you from falling head over heels. Actually, you tend to be shy and often wait for the other person to make the first move. Cautious and discriminating, you generally aren't interested in one-night stands—you prefer a relationship that will get better with time.

Your serious approach to love might cause you to wait until relatively late in life to tie the knot. You value maturity in a partner and might choose someone older than yourself — you want someone to take care of you, not the other way around.

With Your SCORPIO Zodiac Sign

You're not inclined to spend time in a relationship unless it's going to last. Playing the field doesn't interest you. From an early age you probably wanted to find the right mate and settle down. Your no-nonsense approach lets you dispense with game-playing and find someone who takes love as seriously as you do.

Selective, even a bit skeptical, you aren't likely to fall for a pretty face or charming personality— you're much too practical. Instead, you value people who are hard-working, dependable, and resourceful. Someone who is financially secure could be an asset, too. As a result, you might marry late in life or choose a partner who's older than you.

In private, you may shed your cautious and aloof exterior and reveal your sensual side. Like the proverbial tortoise, you take your time and don't rush into romance. But with your steady determination, you usually end up a winner.

With Your SAGITTARIUS Zodiac Sign

You are a unique combination of idealism and pragmatism, especially when it comes to matters of the heart. Although you may entertain fantasies about the perfect lover, you know that love isn't really the way it's portrayed in the movies.

Because you tend to think big, you might sometimes represent yourself in an overly glorified way. But even though you may have a bit of blarney in you, you usually don't stretch the truth too far and a partner can rely on you to fulfill your promises.

A steady, enduring relationship probably suits you better than a James Bond lifestyle. You need adventure, but you need security, too. A stable domestic life might give your curious mind and questing spirit freedom to soar and explore. A partner who can help you bring your vision down to earth and transform your dreams into realities could be a good match for you.

▶ READ ABOUT YOUR ROMANTIC COMPATIBILITY on p. 780   ▶ LOOK FOR YOUR CELEBRITY VENUS TWINS on p. 767

Your
Venus
in Capricorn

With Your CAPRICORN Zodiac Sign

You may have started thinking about marriage while other kids were still playing doctor. Mature and serious, you probably haven't wasted much time at the dating game. With your practical attitude toward love, you carefully examine partners' plusses and minuses — you might even do a spreadsheet to determine who is the best investment!

You don't expect perfection — you're a realist, after all. You value someone who is responsible, hardworking, and loyal. And you offer the same qualities in return. Your mate can rely on you to uphold your commitments and to do your utmost to build a stable, lasting relationship. Someone who can be your partner in business as well as in love could be a good match for you.

You probably aren't the most romantic lover, but you are more sensual than you appear. What you lack in glamour, you more than make up for with dependability and endurance.

With Your AQUARIUS Zodiac Sign

Although you value your independence, you don't like being alone. You probably have many companions but few who are really close. Usually you're open-minded about relationships and respect other people's preferences, but your own love life tends to be rather traditional. So long as a partner doesn't try to keep you under his or her thumb, you can be content in a monogamous relationship.

Not especially romantic, you pay attention to the day-to-day business of a relationship. Financial issues, career goals, and other real-life matters are considerations in choosing a partner. You aren't likely to run off with someone who only has dreams in his or her pocket.

Within the security of a stable relationship, you can feel safe to experiment and explore. You may appreciate a partner who takes care of the practical, mundane aspects of your life, freeing you up to pursue your intellectual, humanitarian, or creative goals.

With Your PISCES Zodiac Sign

No matter how attractive and talented you are, you may see yourself as a wallflower. You want a meaningful relationship and have much to offer a partner, but your sensitive feelings are easily hurt, and you might be afraid to take a chance on love. Perhaps you undervalue yourself and don't quite understand what others see in you.

Shy and reclusive, you may only allow a few, special people into your life. You value peace and quiet—too much activity can drain or upset you. Usually you'd rather hole up with a significant other than maintain a busy social agenda.

Although idealistic and romantic yourself, you enjoy the company of someone who is grounded and practical. As a result, you might gravitate toward a partner who is more mature, realistic, or financially stable than you. A steady relationship could provide the secure foundation you need to pursue your creative dreams.

717

▶ READ ABOUT YOUR ROMANTIC COMPATIBILITY *on p. 780* ▶ LOOK FOR YOUR CELEBRITY VENUS TWINS *on p. 767*

Your Venus in Aquarius

When it comes to love, "Vive la difference" could be your motto. With your open-minded approach to relationships, you might enjoy all sorts of people from all walks of life. Money, fame, and good looks may not matter much to you. What's important is that your lover is also your friend.

You need a lot of freedom in a relationship, and even in a marriage you don't want to be "joined at the hip." Jealousy and power struggles don't have much place in your life. Nor do you subscribe to sexist stereotypes. You want a partnership to be just that—a partnership in which both of you are on an equal footing.

You thrive on change and grow bored with routine. New experiences and ideas stimulate you, and you know how to put a fresh spin on love. A partner who wants to keep your attention should keep you guessing.

With Your SAGITTARIUS Zodiac Sign

A free spirit, you are always on the lookout for adventure, and enjoy partners who expand your range of experience. A seeker in every way, you like to experiment with love and generally hold an "anything goes" attitude. As a result, you've probably had your share of unconventional romantic liaisons—and you wouldn't want it any other way.

Your companions are likely to include a broad spectrum of people from many cultural backgrounds and walks of life. You take an open-minded approach to relationships and might be content to remain single or to have an open marriage. An "Ozzie and Harriet" lifestyle isn't for you.

Not particularly emotional or sensual, you might be more concerned with brotherly love than romantic love. At times, you may seem a bit too forthright or self-centered, but you never intend to hurt anyone. You simply believe in speaking your mind and doing your own thing.

With Your CAPRICORN Zodiac Sign

You may not be willing to take many risks in life, but love is one area where you might enjoy a bit of adventure. Relationships can help you lighten up and loosen up. Those who know you intimately probably realize you're not as rigid and conservative as you appear.

Of course, you aren't likely to throw caution to the wind—you want a partnership to be grounded in reality. In matters of the heart, you have the ability to blend idealism with pragmatism and can form a relationship that is stable but not stodgy or stifling.

Perhaps you find unconventional, free-spirited types interesting because they show you a side of life you might not venture into otherwise. You may also value their ability to question authority and reject the conventions you tend to let guide you. With the right partner, you can look to the future without abandoning the past.

▶ READ ABOUT YOUR ROMANTIC COMPATIBILITY on p. 780 ▶ LOOK FOR YOUR CELEBRITY VENUS TWINS on p. 767

Your
Venus
in Aquarius

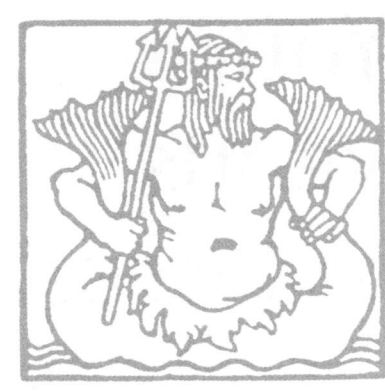

With Your AQUARIUS Zodiac Sign

When it comes to love, you march to a different drummer. Society's conventions and other people's opinions probably don't matter much to you—you follow your own rules. Your companions are likely to be an interesting and diverse group, made up of people of different ages, races, and cultural backgrounds—the more unusual the better.

You need lots of independence and aren't likely to put up with jealousy, possessiveness, or someone who is overly dependent on you. Even in a marriage or live-in situation, you enjoy going places and doing things alone or with people other than your primary partner.

Intelligence is more important to you in a mate than good looks, money, or status. Fairness and equality are among your most cherished ideals. You believe in balancing and sharing goals, responsibilities, and pleasures with a lover who is also a friend. Sexist stereotypes have no place in your life!

With Your PISCES Zodiac Sign

Often you have your head in the clouds and might base relationships on ideals rather than reality. With your compassionate spirit, you value those who share your spiritual, humanitarian, or political interests and hope that together you can accomplish something worthwhile. You tend to see partners as you want them to be, rather than as they are.

Although rather shy, you like people and probably have many companions who admire your imaginative, offbeat personality. A partner who is more outgoing and sociable than you are could serve as an "ice breaker" to bring you out of yourself. Unconventional, creative types usually appeal to you too—you don't want a "one size fits all" relationship.

Affectionate, but not particularly sensual, your curiosity might be piqued by unconventional sexual practices. You could find the idea more appealing than the real thing, however. Quite likely, your passion is more emotional and intellectual than physical.

With Your ARIES Zodiac Sign

You need wide open spaces in your relationships—you probably won't let a partner fence you in or put a brand on your flank. Sure, you enjoy companionship—and with your outgoing, free-spirited nature you probably attract many people who'd like to saddle up with you. But even within a committed relationship you want to have time for your own friends, interests, and activities.

Your willful, independent nature might cause you to be a bit reckless at times, and you are often intrigued by relationships that offer plenty of excitement. Easily bored, you need lots of stimulation and adventure. You don't necessarily have to change partners regularly, but if your love life gets too predictable you might do something to shake it up a bit.

Not particularly romantic, you'd probably rather go skydiving with a partner than snuggle by the fire. Most importantly, your lover should also be your friend.

▶ READ ABOUT YOUR ROMANTIC COMPATIBILITY on p. 780   ▶ LOOK FOR YOUR CELEBRITY VENUS TWINS on p. 767

Your Venus in Pisces

I dealistic in relationships, you may seek the perfect lover, a soul mate who can fulfill your every fantasy. Perhaps you believe love can solve all problems and take you away from the harshness of everyday life. For you love can be an almost mystical experience in which reality plays only a small part.

720

You have a soft heart and tend to be very kind and compassionate toward those you love. Creative people, like yourself, may attract you and you could enjoy playing their muse. At times, however, you may be too forgiving and allow partners to take advantage of your gentle, generous nature.

Sensitive and emotional, your deep feelings are easily engaged—and easily wounded. You also have a strong romantic streak and may try to pattern your relationships after old movies with happy endings. With your wonderful imagination you can make even the most ordinary relationship glamorous and exciting.

With Your CAPRICORN Zodiac Sign

Generally practical and realistic, you tend to romanticize love. Perhaps you look to a partner to take you away from the demands of everyday life. Or you might put a lover on a pedestal and expect that person to be perfect.

Shy and sensitive, you are selective about the company you keep and can be something of a recluse. Fear of rejection could keep you from reaching out to other people. You'd probably rather spend quiet evenings with a significant other or a few close friends than go out on the town.

Creative people might intrigue you, for they don't seem as concerned about material issues as you are. An artistic partner could help you get in touch with your own creative side. Even if you don't consider yourself an artist, you are supportive of your loved ones and might enjoy helping an imaginative mate to manifest his or her vision.

With Your AQUARIUS Zodiac Sign

You want to make the world a better place—and what better way to do that than with a like-minded partner? You seek a soul mate to share your creative, spiritual, and humanitarian goals. Your idealism might keep you searching for the perfect lover, regardless of how many times you've been disappointed.

You tend to believe in the goodness of humankind and can be rather naive at times. Willing to forgive others' failings, you can be a compassionate and supportive partner—but you might also let people take advantage of you. Perhaps you ignore the realities of a situation and are more concerned with what could be than what actually is.

Artistic people who inspire your own creativity probably appeal to you, and you may include a variety of imaginative, avant-garde types among your many companions. Money, status, and security aren't very important to you—your focus is on otherworldly issues.

▶ READ ABOUT YOUR ROMANTIC COMPATIBILITY *on p. 780* ▶ LOOK FOR YOUR CELEBRITY VENUS TWINS *on p. 767*

Your Venus in Pisces

With Your **PISCES** Zodiac Sign

For you, love is the stuff of poetry, songs, and fairy tales. Because you tend to view relationships through rose-colored glasses, you might not see yourself or your partner very clearly. The mundane aspects of a relationship probably don't matter much to you. As long as you can enjoy romantic bliss together and keep your dreams alive, you're happy.

Kindhearted and compassionate, you create a safe harbor for those you love. You soothe their pain and boost their spirits. But your search for perfection may result in disappointment sometimes if a lover doesn't meet up to your expectations.

With your vivid imagination, you can create a wonderland that is far richer and, in your mind, more real than the physical world you inhabit. Perhaps you also embellish your love life with qualities that aren't apparent to other people. A partnership with you is more than the sum of its parts.

With Your **ARIES** Zodiac Sign

You tend to fall in love at first sight—and you do it quite often. When you spot someone who interests you, you waste no time making your feelings known. In your haste, however, you might rush into a partnership without assessing the situation fully.

Idealistic in relationships, you enjoy the excitement and glamour of romance. Perhaps you see yourself as a storybook hero rescuing damsels in distress, or a heroine whose love enables your prince to achieve greatness. You want to be your partner's champion and vice versa. A relationship that contains an element of gallantry or tragedy might appeal to you.

Even in a long-term partnership, you may hold onto your fantasies—it's more fun that way. You don't want reality to intrude and burst your romantic bubble. With your childlike optimism and your wonderful imagination, you can create a "never-never land" where the passion never dies.

With Your **TAURUS** Zodiac Sign

You possess a rare and special ability to combine the earthly realm with the spiritual one in your romantic life. Both body and soul get into the act, so that love becomes a multidimensional and inspired experience for you. Although your sensual nature appreciates the physical side of love, you tend to be idealistic and might not feel completely fulfilled unless a relationship engages your deep emotions as well.

You are generally passive and rarely initiate relationships—but once you establish a partnership, you hold on with a firm grip. Kindhearted and generous, you are usually willing to give a great deal in order to make a relationship work. Sometimes you can be a bit too compassionate and forgiving, though.

Highly creative, you can infuse a partnership with richness and imagination. The romance might never go out of a relationship with you. Love could even be your favorite art form!

▶ READ ABOUT YOUR ROMANTIC COMPATIBILITY *on p. 780* ▶ LOOK FOR YOUR CELEBRITY VENUS TWINS *on p. 767*

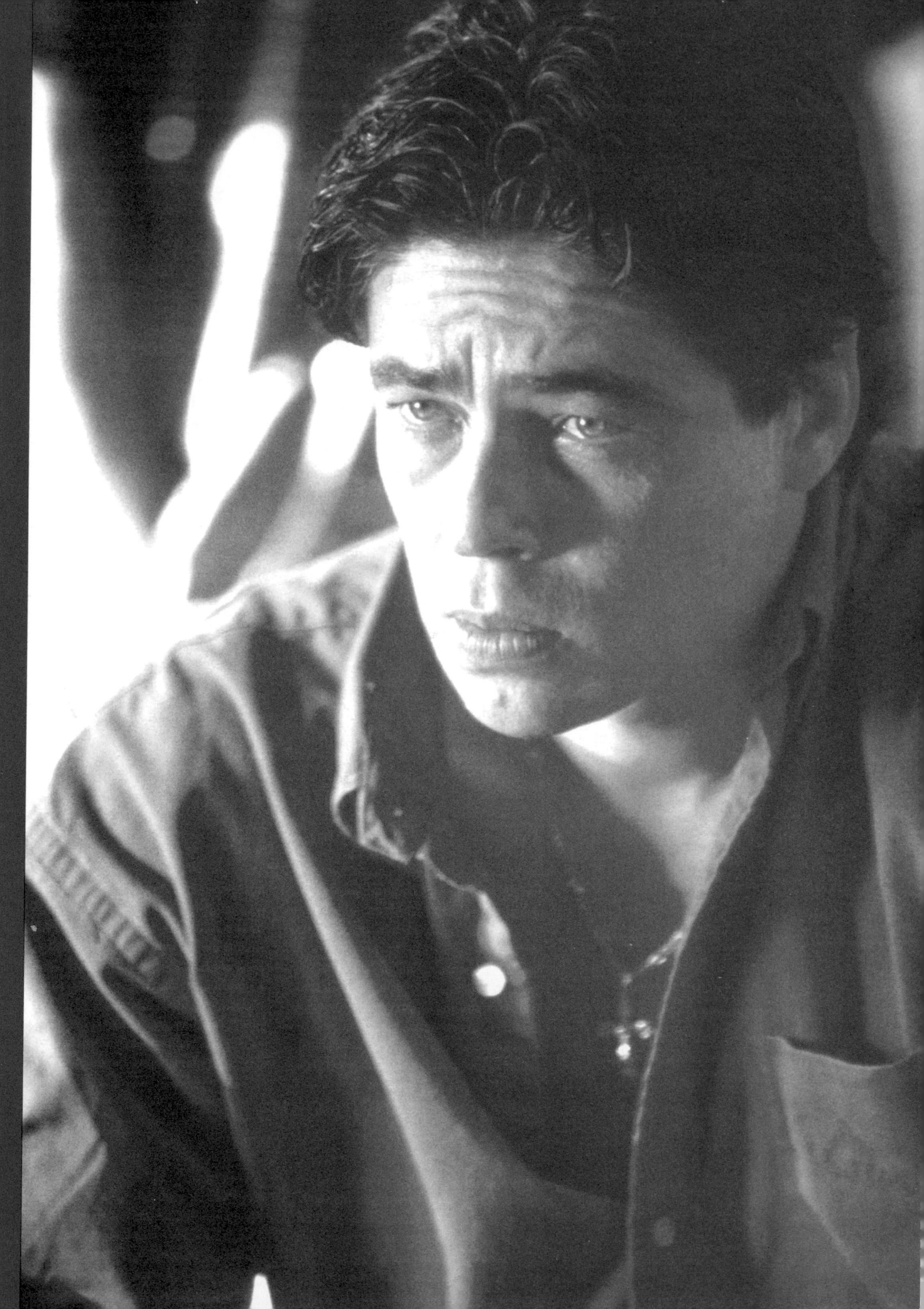

YOUR SEX DRIVE

Mars, the Planet of Sex

In Roman mythology, Mars was the god of war. In astrology, Mars is the planet of action—it shows how you assert yourself and go after what you want in life and love. It's also the planet of passion and drive—in relationships, your zodiac Mars Sign reveals what you desire, what fuels your fires and how you seek to satisfy your lust. The embodiment of sexual energy, Mars indicates your "sexual quotient"—how you express your sexuality, your attitudes toward sex, what turns you on, and how strong your libido is. A

"masculine" planet, Mars in a woman's birth chart also suggests the male traits she finds most attractive—her ideal man. In a man's chart, Mars describes the masculine qualities he wants people to value in him and how he displays his masculinity. Your personal Mars Sign is the place where this planet was positioned in the sky at the time of your birth. You'll find your personal Mars Sign on your Zodiac Sign page. It is located in the column called **Your Love Planets** and listed under **Your Sex Drive**. Please read on to find out more.

INSTRUCTIONS

HERE'S HOW TO READ ABOUT YOUR SEX DRIVE.

1 Find your Zodiac Sign reading.

2 Look beside your Zodiac Sign for **Your Love Planets**. Under **Your Sex Drive**, you'll find your Mars Sign.

3 Look at the index below. Locate your Zodiac Sign across the top and then your Mars Sign on the left hand side column. Where the two lines intersect is a page number. Turn to this page to read all about **Your Sex Drive**.

Note: Keep all of your Astrological Love Information handy by jotting down the page numbers of your Birth Year Events, Zodiac Sign, and Mars Sign.

Example

If you were born on June 3, 1964, you would be a Gemini with a Mars in Taurus. What type of sexual desires do you have as a

Gemini with Mars in Taurus? On the index below you will find that page 727 reveals everything about **Your Sex Drive**.

YOUR SEX DRIVE PAGE INDEX

HOW TO USE THIS INDEX
- Locate your Zodiac Sign across the top.
- Find your Mars Sign on the column to the right.
- Turn to the page indicated where the two lines intersect to read about **Your Sex Drive**.

MARS SIGN	ARIES	TAURUS	GEMINI	CANCER	LEO	VIRGO	LIBRA	SCORPIO	SAGITTARIUS	CAPRICORN	AQUARIUS	PISCES
ARIES	p. 724	p. 724	p. 724	p. 724	p. 725	p. 725	p. 725	p. 725	p. 726	p. 726	p. 726	p. 726
TAURUS	p. 727	p. 727	p. 727	p. 727	p. 728	p. 728	p. 728	p. 728	p. 729	p. 729	p. 729	p. 729
GEMINI	p. 730	p. 730	p. 730	p. 730	p. 731	p. 731	p. 731	p. 731	p. 732	p. 732	p. 732	p. 732
CANCER	p. 733	p. 733	p. 733	p. 733	p. 734	p. 734	p. 734	p. 734	p. 735	p. 735	p. 735	p. 735
LEO	p. 736	p. 736	p. 736	p. 736	p. 737	p. 737	p. 737	p. 737	p. 738	p. 738	p. 738	p. 738
VIRGO	p. 739	p. 739	p. 739	p. 739	p. 740	p. 740	p. 740	p. 740	p. 741	p. 741	p. 741	p. 741
LIBRA	p. 742	p. 742	p. 742	p. 742	p. 743	p. 743	p. 743	p. 743	p. 744	p. 744	p. 744	p. 744
SCORPIO	p. 745	p. 745	p. 745	p. 745	p. 746	p. 746	p. 746	p. 746	p. 747	p. 747	p. 747	p. 747
SAGITTARIUS	p. 748	p. 748	p. 748	p. 748	p. 749	p. 749	p. 749	p. 749	p. 750	p. 750	p. 750	p. 750
CAPRICORN	p. 751	p. 751	p. 751	p. 751	p. 752	p. 752	p. 752	p. 752	p. 753	p. 753	p. 753	p. 753
AQUARIUS	p. 754	p. 754	p. 754	p. 754	p. 755	p. 755	p. 755	p. 755	p. 756	p. 756	p. 756	p. 756
PISCES	p. 757	p. 757	p. 757	p. 757	p. 758	p. 758	p. 758	p. 758	p. 759	p. 759	p. 759	p. 759

ZODIAC SIGN

◄◄ BENICIO DEL TORO, ACTOR

Your Mrs in Aries

Sex is a game for you, Mars in Aries, and you play with gusto. You enjoy the chase as much as the conquest, and might be disappointed if your partner gives in too easily. Easily bored, you may lose interest unless a relationship continues to offer you plenty of challenges.

Somewhat self-centered, at times you might be more concerned with your own pleasure than your partner's. You don't usually mean any harm, however, and your playful, exuberant nature makes it hard to stay mad at you for long.

You need lots of stimulation and excitement and may be eager to try just about anything. Although your sex drive is strong, you might not be very sensual or affectionate. Few people can match your enthusiasm, but you may lack staying power or finesse. You probably like taking the lead and have no trouble asking your partner to satisfy your wildest desires.

724

With Your ARIES Zodiac Sign

Your love style is not for the faint at heart. When someone catches your eye, you ignite like a sparkler—you dazzle brilliantly but can fizzle out quickly without the right stimulation. You enjoy being the playful pursuer, and the right partner preserves the illusion of being the elusive prey.

Fast and furious lovemaking keeps you energized—a rousing debate can be a prelude to a vigorous tussle in the bedroom. An evening spent matching wits sharpens your mind and is a potent aphrodisiac. The right partner can match your aggressive flirtations, and frank, direct attitude toward sexuality.

But your fiery heart has a softer side once intimacy is established. There is a childlike innocence to your frequent bursts of enthusiasm. Your generosity toward your lover comes through in your spontaneous gift-giving or unexpected moments of daytime seduction. Sunny and open, your libido stands at alert both day and night.

With Your TAURUS Zodiac Sign

Your approach to love carries an urgent fervor that makes your lover feel quite desirable. Your magnetism emits signals from the start, but you can't be rushed. A slow, steady seduction may ignite to a raging passion quite suddenly. Yet your meteoric intensity is grounded in an earthy sensuousness.

Your delight in the senses often finds its way into the kitchen—preparing a feast with your lover can be hearty foreplay. Playfully feeding each other may heighten the ecstasy.

You are capable of ravishing your lover in every sense—the right mate cultivates an enduring simmer rather than a burned-out flame.

Once smitten, your generosity shines through in subtle and obvious ways. Shopping for unique treasures with your lover allows you to be the big spender. Your frequent initiation of lovemaking is a priceless gift in any bond. You have the stamina to gratify your lover morning, noon, and night.

With Your GEMINI Zodiac Sign

You're likely a shameless flirt, and while single, may keep many kettles on the stove—sampling what's available brings you the variety you crave. You captivate your suitors through witty conversation and a refreshing, devil-may-care attitude. Since you revel in the unexpected, you make dazzling first impressions.

Being friends with your lover is important to you, and your cultivated interests make you a charming companion. You travel light, and are always up for a spontaneous day-trip or shopping expedition. Sitting at a sidewalk café with your lover puts you in the mood and makes quiet room for the dance of seductive suggestion.

When subtle innuendo breaks through to urgent desire, your passions burn like a flaming meteor. You meet the challenge of new love with an enthusiasm for the thrill of erotic discovery. If the hint of routine emerges in your lovemaking, you quickly stir things up with spontaneous play or fantasy.

With Your CANCER Zodiac Sign

Your aloof reserve toward your love interest is punctuated by sudden power surges of ardent passion. But since impetuous leaps are often hazardous to your sensitive heart, you make bold moves only toward a sure thing. The fiery lust that runs in your veins finds full expression in the warmth of an enduring relationship.

A subtle power to charm and seduce gives you smoldering charisma when you need it most. You shine with a mate who also exudes confidence—walking arm-in-arm with your sexy lover makes you beam. An enchanting evening on the town can be the pretense for an evening-long seduction.

Your nurturing nature emerges in long-time bonds, making you a cuddly catch. Spontaneous gestures of affection make you a highly demonstrative mate—nights spent nestling on the couch at home suit you just fine. Giving sentimental mementos out of the blue shows the depths of your devotion.

▶ READ ABOUT YOUR SEXUAL COMPATIBILITY on p. 802   ▶ DISCOVER YOUR CELEBRITY MARS TWINS on p. 770

Your Mars in Aries

Sex is a game for you, Mars in Aries, and you play with gusto. You enjoy the chase as much as the conquest, and might be disappointed if your partner gives in too easily. Easily bored, you may lose interest unless a relationship continues to offer you plenty of challenges.

Somewhat self-centered, at times you might be more concerned with your own pleasure than your partner's. You don't usually mean any harm, however, and your playful, exuberant nature makes it hard to stay mad at you for long.

You need lots of stimulation and excitement and may be eager to try just about anything. Although your sex drive is strong, you might not be very sensual or affectionate. Few people can match your enthusiasm, but you may lack staying power or finesse. You probably like taking the lead and have no trouble asking your partner to satisfy your wildest desires.

With Your **LEO** Zodiac Sign

Like a shooting star across the night sky, you are a fiery spectacle that lights up any social gathering. Your sense of fun often places you at the center of a circle of admirers. Colorful personalities appeal to your theatrical nature—sharp dressers with attitude promise the excitement of a lusty challenge.

You're a big risk taker in love and may take a few hard tumbles from the lofty perch of infatuation. Though your pride may be wounded, you rebound from love's trials with remarkable speed. Your dazzling swiftness and jubilant approach to life graces you with magnetic charisma to burn.

Going to lively parties and arty events infuses your nights with glamour. The ideal mate radiates a sunny glow and doesn't mind following your lead. Passionate lovemaking brings ecstatic moments of sheer delight. Your natural generosity shines in the bedroom, and your enthusiasm frees the inhibitions of any lover.

With Your **VIRGO** Zodiac Sign

Good clean fun energizes your fiery libido—your enthusiastic pursuit of sensual pleasure has a wholesome quality that attracts natural-minded lovers. Your erotic side smolders like a dormant volcano. Once erupted, you go to any lengths to impress your love interest—you especially like to display your physical prowess.

In the throes of passion your cool reserve melts into sizzling intensity. You can charm and seduce your beloved with the ardor of a lovesick teenager. The thrill of new romance lights you up from within, giving you a radiant glow. The ideal lover grounds this intensity in a stabilizing daily routine.

Your strong physical vitality thrives on high-energy, lusty lovemaking. Any moments of shy inhibition are swiftly overcome in the embrace of a fun-loving mate. Showering together after exercise creates an intimate atmosphere. Two squeaky clean bodies fresh from the playing field can then unite in blissful abandon.

With Your **LIBRA** Zodiac Sign

When dating, you're like an enthusiastic kid at the fair. You're captivated by each colorful spectacle, but soon you'll be moving on to the next dazzling attraction. You crave spirited lovers who seem just out of reach—even in longtime bonds, you enjoy a lover who plays a little hard to get.

You flirt with abandon—gaining admirers can be a game to you, and more reserved types may find that cloying or insincere. You tend to show wildly contrasting shades of anger, from red-hot fury, to the dull pinks of passive aggression. You can be slyly seductive about getting what you want.

With an uninhibited lover, your libido lights up with the urgency of a five-alarm fire. You enjoy waking your lover up in the night with sweet and tender caresses. Smoldering kisses are your trademark and often lead to ecstasy. As long as the fireworks continue, you're hooked.

With Your **SCORPIO** Zodiac Sign

Though you may break a heart or two in your single days, it's likely that most ex-lovers think of you with wistful amazement. The adrenaline surge of new romance often causes you to career forward with reckless abandon, and few can match your smoldering charisma. Your fiery initiative in love demands a nimble sparring partner.

You shine in an atmosphere of playful competition but can become fiercely jealous once heart ties are formed. Your libido shoots off sparks when aroused by physical chemistry. The lover who wilts under your penetrating gaze quickly loses favor—you prefer sure-footed matches to more timid playmates.

An unflagging stamina can lead to hours of late-night amour. For you, lovemaking can be a thrilling, climactic catharsis, and your potent virility requires a partner of great stamina. An evening of breathless adventure can lead to passionate foreplay and culminate in a meteor shower of sexual fireworks.

▶ READ ABOUT YOUR SEXUAL COMPATIBILITY *on p. 802*　　▶ DISCOVER YOUR CELEBRITY MARS TWINS *on p. 770*

Your Mars in Aries

Sex is a game for you, Mars in Aries, and you play with gusto. You enjoy the chase as much as the conquest, and might be disappointed if your partner gives in too easily. Easily bored, you may lose interest unless a relationship continues to offer you plenty of challenges.

Somewhat self-centered, at times you might be more concerned with your own pleasure than your partner's. You don't usually mean any harm, however, and your playful, exuberant nature makes it hard to stay mad at you for long.

You need lots of stimulation and excitement and may be eager to try just about anything. Although your sex drive is strong, you might not be very sensual or affectionate. Few people can match your enthusiasm, but you may lack staying power or finesse. You probably like taking the lead and have no trouble asking your partner to satisfy your wildest desires.

With Your **SAGITTARIUS** Zodiac Sign

A whirl of excitement surrounds you, and you're always on the move—a longtime mate can often be more like a comrade in mutual adventure. Your impetuous, active nature propels you forward into feats of romantic daring. While single, your recklessness can draw you into many a humbling entanglement.

The volcanic heat you generate can lead to simmering warmth—or destructive explosions. When dating, you may enthusiastically leap toward lovers, and your exit may be just as abrupt. As you begin to take things slowly, you discover the subtle, layered sensuality that emerges in a more stable bond.

Slowing things down can keep your red-hot libido at a steady boil. You're a walking incendiary device, capable of setting fire to the most fatigued lover. Your stamina often makes you ready for late-night amour—you enjoy waking up your lover with all-over kisses and erotic touch that sizzles with fiery potency.

With Your **CAPRICORN** Zodiac Sign

Your fiercely competitive nature translates to daredevil flirtation on the dating scene. Bold and fiery, you may intimidate more reserved types—you come on strong and have the sexual stamina to back it up. However, you're more cautious about forming emotional ties and might leave a few befuddled lovers behind.

Once intrigued, you are a patient and determined suitor with sunny charm. You blend eager affection with subtle seduction in your tried and true approach. You may not always follow through once you've won a lover's favor—the wise suitor learns to slow things down to avoid becoming more of your unfinished business.

Your need to dominate makes you a lusty, aggressive lover. Your youthful looks grow more attractive with age, and your physical desire never wanes. A provocative look or playful squeeze ignites your combustible libido. Catching you in the sleepiness of the wee hours makes for sensuous lovemaking.

With Your **AQUARIUS** Zodiac Sign

You give off warmth everywhere you go, attracting many suitors with your fiery charisma. An attraction that creates mental sparks may quickly ignite your physical lust. You enjoy being the aggressive force in a game of seduction— you tend to make impulsive gestures, then restlessly move on to other interests.

A whirlwind romance leaves you breathless with excitement—traveling with a lover doubles the fun of any adventure. The ideal lover is a sparring partner who challenges your intellect. You hold loosely to romantic ties, and you may find it hard to keep promises made in the heat of passion.

You have no qualms about exploring the edges of the sexual frontier or busting through taboo, and your curiosity may lead you to experiment with erotic fantasy and sexual technique. You can be carefree and emotionally detached when it comes to lovemaking. Tender moments of intimacy come during the sleepier hours.

With Your **PISCES** Zodiac Sign

You have a quiet charisma, with the courage to take bold actions in love. You blaze a lusty trail to satisfy the urges of your fiery sex drive. Yet you can be vulnerable in romance and quickly pull back into solitary retreat. At times you may ignite a wildfire that overwhelms your deeply sensitive nature.

Your chameleon-like nature makes you both a cuddly homebody and an enthusiastic aficionado of nightlife. A provocative evening of theater or film stirs your colorful imagination. You enjoy dashing around town with your beloved, building the sexual tension through shared excitement.

Bringing music into the bedroom can add to the mood of the moment. Soft, fluttery kisses around the head and face wake up your finer sensuality. You may often be full of bravado but show a tender and gentle side during lovemaking. Your hot-blooded passion gives you endless stamina for a night of pleasure.

▶ READ ABOUT YOUR SEXUAL COMPATIBILITY on p. 802   ▶ DISCOVER YOUR CELEBRITY MARS TWINS on p. 770

Your Mars in Taurus

Some might say you are led around by your libido, and it's probably true that sex is rarely far from your thoughts. You have an innate understanding of the physical side of life and may invest a good deal of energy into satisfying your body's demands.

Your approach to sex is uncomplicated and direct. For you sex is as fundamental as eating—and just as necessary. Consequently, any warm body might suffice. Because you feel comfortable with your own body and probably don't have a lot of hang-ups, you can be a marvelous lover. Few people can match you when it comes to endurance.

Your tastes tend to be straightforward and unimaginative—you don't need a lot of frills to entice you. But pleasing your partner is important to you, so you are usually willing to follow a lover's lead. Your motto might be "if it feels good, do it."

YOUR SEX DRIVE

727

With Your **ARIES** Zodiac Sign

You dive right into earthly pleasures with an irresistible mix of languid sensuality and bold aggressiveness. If your sensual nature seems accessible, there are also cavernous depths to explore. This magnetism attracts many, but few are actually chosen—your heart waits for true love with the patience your libido sometimes lacks.

The pleasures of the senses extend to the kitchen, and your palate is one of your erogenous zones. Preparing a sumptuous meal with your lover provides tactile action with plenty of shared sensual moments. Creating an atmosphere of relaxed comfort opens you to exploration—oils and candles enhance the experience.

The right mate understands your playful physicality and uncomplicated approach to lovemaking. Emotional tangles don't snare you for long—you need to keep moving forward to feel alive. An old-fashioned pillow fight can get you laughing again. And the tenderness you reveal in sensual moments can heal any rifts.

With Your **TAURUS** Zodiac Sign

Still waters run deep, and your settled persona stands in contrast to your playfully lusty libido. Your desire for touch makes your skin hungry—the right mate knows how to satisfy your need for tactile sensuality and affection. You may be slow to act, but you make up for it with your all-night endurance.

Your cuddly earthiness gives you a direct approach to physical pleasure. Long hugs and lingering kisses show your partner where your heart lies. Your lack of inhibitions can relax any partner—erotic delicacies and a blindfold heighten the ecstasy. A natural innocence enhances your ease with primal pleasures.

Spending time outdoors with your partner can bring a glow to your cheeks. Making love in a woodsy setting takes you to an intimate Eden of earthly delights. Sharing an evening of exquisite music or theater fills your heart—the ideal mate shares your love of artistic beauty.

With Your **GEMINI** Zodiac Sign

With your contagious enthusiasm for earthly pleasures you lure your lover into a world full of sensory stimulation. Your enlivening presence cheers up those around you—the right lover keeps you lifted with plenty of adoring affection. An encouraging squeeze from your beloved renews your physical bond.

You may be gregarious and open, but you don't easily rush into a loving union. Wise suitors entertain your mind, while proving their worthiness over time. You like to be wined and dined—a sophisticated lover with refined tastes holds your interest. If cool flirtation turns to smoldering passion, the game has begun.

Your desire for touch makes you eager to explore ways to heighten the ecstasy. Your changeable nature keeps your lover guessing—one moment you give a playful peck on the cheek, then approach with deep, soulful kisses. Sensual oils and scented candles draw more senses into the atmosphere of seduction.

With Your **CANCER** Zodiac Sign

You prefer subtlety to flashy courtship rituals—slow and steady movement toward intimacy builds a bridge to your guarded heart. The right mate senses your need for tender touch and emotional bonding. Your fluctuating moods require a lover with keen intuition—a well-timed hug or kiss can alter your entire outlook.

Sharing the comforts of home with your beloved sets the stage for sensual pleasures. You enjoy venturing out to gather provisions for an entire weekend spent in your cozy nest. Preparing a scrumptious feast together evokes an atmosphere of voluptuous abundance. You thrive in a homey sanctuary of domestic bliss.

The right lover cultivates a warm feeling of safety—your lusty libido emerges fully only when deep trust has been established. Anniversaries and special days may be celebrated with evenings of candle-lit dinners and erotic massage. Your primal desires find expression through highly attuned emotions and a vital physicality.

Your Mars in Taurus

Some might say you are led around by your libido, and it's probably true that sex is rarely far from your thoughts. You have an innate understanding of the physical side of life and may invest a good deal of energy into satisfying your body's demands.

Your approach to sex is uncomplicated and direct. For you sex is as fundamental as eating—and just as necessary. Consequently, any warm body might suffice. Because you feel comfortable with your own body and probably don't have a lot of hang-ups, you can be a marvelous lover. Few people can match you when it comes to endurance.

Your tastes tend to be straightforward and unimaginative—you don't need a lot of frills to entice you. But pleasing your partner is important to you, so you are usually willing to follow a lover's lead. Your motto might be "if it feels good, do it."

With Your **LEO** Zodiac Sign

Your earthy sensuality is spiced with a flair for the dramatic. Using casual touch you engage your whole body in flirtations. You usually don't mind grand displays of public affection. A sexy lover's wandering hands show the world a glimpse of the sensual banquet you enjoy behind closed doors.

The first moments of intimacy with a new lover crackle with fiery intensity. Managing your combustible libido with cautious reserve gives your courtship a rhythm of charge and retreat. You enjoy the thrill of new sights and sounds with your beloved. Trying exotic cuisine or sampling wines appeals to your refined palate.

In private you can be quite the playful exhibitionist—your regal air is undiminished by a lack of clothing. The ideal lover adores your naked body and matches your physically affectionate ways. You prefer the wholesome and unadorned—all-natural erotic oils add to the pleasure of a loving massage.

With Your **VIRGO** Zodiac Sign

You desire to build sexual bonds on a solid foundation whose strength stands the test of time. Initial contact with a love interest may reveal your tentative caution—you prefer a slow seduction based on a rational assessment of common traits. Finding a compatible mate opens the door to deeper sensual exploration.

Sharing outdoor adventures is one way to test the mettle of a suitor. You seduce in the non verbal language of the physical body, and chemistry ultimately directs your libido. You relish experiences that engage all your five senses—preparing and devouring a feast together can bring many moments of pure pleasure.

With a loyal lover you communicate freely through tender touch. Soulful dancing allows you to match your partner's rhythm—which can enhance lovemaking. You might introduce healthy aphrodisiacs to add dimension, but usually prefer keeping it simple. You adore your lover's natural smells and revel in playful nudity.

With Your **LIBRA** Zodiac Sign

You respond to a slow, elegant courtship that builds toward a peak of physical desire. The gradual path to intimacy creates many chances to reveal your romantic heart—surprise gifts and candlelit dinners make for memorable landmarks. Establishing a relaxed, comfortable rhythm sets the tone for a rich, satisfying affair.

You can present a congenial façade, while tensions build to the point of eruption—physical intimacy can often bring resolution to a domestic conflict. Trying celebrated aphrodisiacs together appeals to your heightened senses. Telling each other made up erotic stories in scrumptious detail makes for a fun bedtime ritual.

Sex makes you come alive, and you're at home in the warmth of a loving bond. Long, rapturous foreplay brings your richly layered earthiness to the surface. You shiver with anticipation during a slow exploration of your lover's body—sensual massage can become central to your lovemaking and create liberating intimacy.

With Your **SCORPIO** Zodiac Sign

Though you may present a laid-back air, intimates know there are oceanic depths to explore. You respond to bold suitors in a sexually relaxed but intensely emotional courtship. The joy of sensate pleasure may draw you into an affair, but only a kinship with mysteries to explore keeps you interested.

The foolhardy suitor who mistakes you for easy prey soon learns not to trifle with your heart. Once trust is lost, you can become stubbornly unforgiving and may close the door too soon. For you, trust comes from surrendering with your beloved to moments of ecstasy, both lighthearted and richly layered.

Preparing exotic feasts, bathing, and cuddling all satisfy your delightfully hedonistic tastes. You respond sensuously to a lover who speaks to your animal nature. Your seduction may include sexy treats, such as provocatively placed edibles. Bedtime touch from head to toe lulls you into intimacy with a passionate edge.

▶ READ ABOUT YOUR SEXUAL COMPATIBILITY *on p. 802*   ▶ DISCOVER YOUR CELEBRITY MARS TWINS *on p. 770*

Your Mars in Taurus

Some might say you are led around by your libido, and it's probably true that sex is rarely far from your thoughts. You have an innate understanding of the physical side of life and may invest a good deal of energy into satisfying your body's demands.

Your approach to sex is uncomplicated and direct. For you sex is as fundamental as eating—and just as necessary. Consequently, any warm body might suffice. Because you feel comfortable with your own body and probably don't have a lot of hang-ups, you can be a marvelous lover. Few people can match you when it comes to endurance.

Your tastes tend to be straightforward and unimaginative—you don't need a lot of frills to entice you. But pleasing your partner is important to you, so you are usually willing to follow a lover's lead. Your motto might be "if it feels good, do it."

With Your SAGITTARIUS Zodiac Sign

Physical pleasure and erotic touch gives your energy a kick, and your cheerful openness attracts many lovers. While single, you may approach settled relationships with caution, choosing more playful affairs. You can be boldly direct about sexual matters and thrive with an equally uninhibited mate.

You need lots of kissing and cuddling to feel secure, and at times, you may run roughshod over more delicate feelings. The right mate understands the urgency of your primal desires. Making love in a natural setting sparks your wild passions—on terra firma, you can become a stalking animal on a lusty hunt.

Slow, languid massage relaxes you into the deeper rhythms of your earthy sensuality. In the silence of a quiet environment, you can tune into the nuances of stimulating touch. For you, lovemaking can also be lighthearted fun—laughing in bed with your partner can be a cathartic prelude to deeper intimacy.

With Your CAPRICORN Zodiac Sign

Initially, you may show cool reserve toward your love interest, and you protectively guard your intense passions. With an architect's eye for structure, you want romantic ties that have lasting appeal. Slow, steady moves toward intimacy give you time to test the enduring strength of what you're creating.

Though you may not show affection at first, your lover may sense the depth of your innate sensuality. In moments of shared silence, your animal physicality can be felt as a formidable presence. The ideal lover seduces the rich layers of your slumbering passions through patient, relaxed touch.

For you, sex can be an erotic feast of the senses—flavored oils, edible delicacies, and luscious fabrics all add to the soothing atmosphere. The pleasure of lovemaking can often be the glue that ties you to your lover—a vigorous tussle in the bedroom can resolve conflicts that arise and restore loving intimacy.

With Your AQUARIUS Zodiac Sign

Your love style is full of enigmatic contradictions, and you may demand complete freedom, while clinging possessively to your lover. You swing between orgiastic delight in the senses and a more austere approach. Your clever mind usually has a clear-eyed view of your quirks and revels in presenting yourself humorously.

Emotional appeals may be vexing, causing you to escape suddenly into aloofness. While single, you may prefer casual friendships with the fringe benefits of erotic play—the ideal suitor doesn't mind keeping things light. Your hearty appetite for tactile, sensory pleasure leads you toward a banquet of the senses.

You bring fun and spontaneity to the bedroom—you might enjoy sharing edible aphrodisiacs to enhance arousal. Languid caresses moving to more sensitive areas electrify your nervous system because your whole body is an erogenous zone. You enjoy the delicious tension built by teasing, tantalizing foreplay.

With Your PISCES Zodiac Sign

Although you may present an easygoing, calm exterior, you can also be a very private person. Your smoldering magnetism attracts many, but you are not one to leap into love. You're a sensualist with a need for profound connection. With the right mate, you unite body and soul in earthly pleasures.

You have a gift for relaxation and an enviable ability to enjoy each moment. For you the longings of the body are natural, and you need lots of physical affection. Holding hands or walking arm-in-arm brings you closer. In your friskier moments, you may have trouble keeping your hands to yourself.

You bring a starry-eyed wonder to lovemaking that creates enchantment in the bedroom. Nibbling on aphrodisiacs brings more of the senses into play. Sensuality begins with touching, and you like to slowly explore you lover's entire body. You revel in creating a secret erotic language to initiate a seduction.

▶ READ ABOUT YOUR SEXUAL COMPATIBILITY on p. 802   ▶ DISCOVER YOUR CELEBRITY MARS TWINS on p. 770

Your Mars in Gemini

730

You channel lots of energy into communication, and probably one of your favorite topics is sex. Perhaps you like to regale others with stories of your amorous exploits and are curious to hear the secrets of their intimate lives. Some might say you'd rather talk about it than do it.

Your inquisitive nature could lead you to experiment with different partners and sexual styles. Because you don't want to miss out on anything, you might be rather indiscriminate. Gemini is the sign of the twins, so you may find a ménage à trois intriguing.

Your mind is your most sensitive erogenous zone, and you probably like having a partner describe what he or she wants, in detail. Perhaps you enjoy erotic literature. Phone sex might be one of your turn-ons, too. Your oral nature could also find expression through oral sex—if you can stop talking long enough, that is!

With Your **ARIES** Zodiac Sign

The mate who engages your restless and brilliant intellect has a chance of keeping you entranced. Wildly social and endlessly curious, you thrive with a partner who matches your interest in what's happening in the world—the stimulating fire of one of you quickly ignites the other, and vice versa.

Dressing to the hilt and stepping out to catch a theatrical premiere could begin an evening of extravagant fun. Provocative glances and flirtations may flavor any critique of the evening's entertainment. Dining together in front of big windows for people-watching satisfies a need to observe the public spectacle.

If the mind is aroused, the sensual body follows—you can be a nimble, innovative lover. The right mate relaxes your sensitive nerves into the present moment with soothing words and gentle touches. Fantasy may become part of your repertoire and a trusting bond can allow a role-playing game to give expression to your many sides.

With Your **TAURUS** Zodiac Sign

Your changeable loving style can be satisfied within a trusting, stable bond. You have a taste for experimentation—the right mate assures you of fidelity, while tantalizing you with the promise of the unexpected. The occasional spontaneous quickie can be enough to gratify your restless but loyal heart.

You can be a delightfully verbal lover, turning subtle innuendo into a masterful tool of seduction. Enjoying matching wits with your lover, you can sometimes be a stubborn orator. You express your desires most powerfully when aroused both physically and mentally—the right partner summons both to the surface.

A craving for order could extend to your sex life—you might make a list of all the delicious things you're going to do to your lover. Trying every known aphrodisiac through history appeals to your need for variety. A picture book of erotica may become a reference manual for lusty bedtime reading.

With Your **GEMINI** Zodiac Sign

Trying to snare you with heavy seduction is like catching a butterfly with rough hands—the right lover knows you need plenty of space to show your dazzling colors. You enchant many with your breezy style and chameleon-like persona. Naturally flirtatious, you draw adoring eyes like bees to honey.

Your dual sensual nature may be hard to fathom at first—a nimble lover knows when to kiss and cuddle and when to stand back.

You need to spread your zest for living around and thrive with a partner who holds on lightly. Even in cherished bonds, you exude a playful friendliness that keeps things in flux.

Verbal enticements have a big impact on you—a well-crafted, sexy note can generate electrifying excitement. An evening out may include a progression of tantalizing erotic language. Whispering sweet nothings in bed engages your mind and your body. A soft touch opens the way for deeper pleasures.

With Your **CANCER** Zodiac Sign

In a sexual bond with deep emotional roots your expansive mind is free to roam. Initially, you dazzle suitors with a breezy lightness and casual sensuality that enlivens the air around you. Yet even as you thrive in the midst of a social buzz, your watchful heart observes and takes notes on possible love connections.

Your quirky humor electrifies any romantic dalliance—your contagious laughter softens even the most stoic of hearts. The ideal mate enjoys your witty banter and delights you with flirty word play in return. An intellectual rapport creates a merging of the minds, setting the stage for sparking the libido.

Expressing your lusty desires verbally connects the sacred with the playfully profane. Your bright mind conjures sexy nicknames for your beloved—which can evolve into fun role-playing. You enjoy exchanging provocative notes and whispering sweet nothings—your fluency in the language of love keeps bonds fresh.

▶ READ ABOUT YOUR SEXUAL COMPATIBILITY *on p. 802*   ▶ DISCOVER YOUR CELEBRITY MARS TWINS *on p. 770*

Your Mars in Gemini

You channel lots of energy into communication, and probably one of your favorite topics is sex. Perhaps you like to regale others with stories of your amorous exploits and are curious to hear the secrets of their intimate lives. Some might say you'd rather talk about it than do it.

Your inquisitive nature could lead you to experiment with different partners and sexual styles. Because you don't want to miss out on anything, you might be rather indiscriminate. Gemini is the sign of the twins, so you may find a ménage à trois intriguing.

Your mind is your most sensitive erogenous zone, and you probably like having a partner describe what he or she wants, in detail. Perhaps you enjoy erotic literature. Phone sex might be one of your turn-ons, too. Your oral nature could also find expression through oral sex—if you can stop talking long enough, that is!

With Your **LEO** Zodiac Sign

You're an unabashed flirt with a quick wit who thrives on excitement in romance. A riveting storyteller, you bewitch others with your tales—the best ones place you in the starring role. You know how to schmooze at a cocktail party or local event, always staying alert to the spark of desire.

Meeting new people provides food for your curious soul. The ideal lover has many shades of personality to discover. You can become restless with inhibited, reserved types—you shine with someone who matches your unquenchable lust for life. Your evening may begin with fine dining and last into the wee hours.

Once happily exhausted from a night on the town, you enjoy easing into relaxation with your lover. A calming bath winds you down and is lovely when shared in intimacy. Your way with words extends to lovemaking—playfully talking dirty to your beloved evokes a lusty atmosphere.

With Your **VIRGO** Zodiac Sign

Variety is the spice of your love life, but you steer clear of empty glamour. Your curiosity and diverse interests bring you into contact with throngs of potential lovers. The right lover holds your attention by dazzling you with witty charm and bright ideas, while also creating a bond built on mutual respect.

Once smitten, you bewitch your lover by establishing regular intimate dialogue. An afternoon phone call becomes a mini mental vacation of shared passion. Exchanging ideas brings you closer—you delight in reading your beloved's favorite novel. A hearty debate can be foreplay for your vital hungry mind.

You respond amorously to relaxed and comfortable sex games. The tactile pleasure of flavored oils and sweet treats on your lover's body propels your innovative sensuality. A gentle massage eases your hurried mind into deeper calm, making way for your elusive emotions to join in the erotic celebration.

With Your **LIBRA** Zodiac Sign

The hint of desire may cause entire scenarios to unfold in your vivid imagination. Your mind works overtime scheming ways to win the object of your affection. You charm with flirty playfulness and a casual air, and while single, you may cultivate several affairs to keep your options open.

You're easily bored and find it hard to settle down with one person. For you, sowing your wild oats means staying free to sample every erotic pleasure. A courtship of endless fascination keeps your restless, distracted mind from wandering—the spontaneous lover with charisma to burn has a fighting chance.

When your lusty thoughts meet delicious reality, you've struck gold. In a dynamic bond, you relax into deeper sensuality. A little pillow talk adds sweetness to the moment—you shine while captivating your lover with verbal affection. Teasing your lover with a peacock feather adds a touch of magic and beauty.

With Your **SCORPIO** Zodiac Sign

Your uniquely curious mind needs the freedom to roam, and you may resist the impulse to settle into a deeper bond. Like the dazzling butterfly, it seems unnatural to pin you down and place you inside a decorative box. The ideal lover dashes alongside you to greater excitement, from impromptu parties to midnight movies.

Once smitten, your restlessly frenetic mind settles into an intense singularity of focus. You may overwhelm your beloved with your zealous, probing approach—the subject of your investigation may feel quite picked apart and exposed. Yet your curiosity is what enables you to truly understand your beloved.

You bring a detective's shrewdness to your quest to please your mate. Every inch of your lover's body becomes a subject of sensual inquiry. You rebel at any glimpse of routine in lovemaking—playful wonder gives your technique a delightful spontaneity. Erotic reading matter makes for great sex.

▶ READ ABOUT YOUR SEXUAL COMPATIBILITY on p. 802   ▶ DISCOVER YOUR CELEBRITY MARS TWINS on p. 770

Your Mars in Gemini

You channel lots of energy into communication, and probably one of your favorite topics is sex. Perhaps you like to regale others with stories of your amorous exploits and are curious to hear the secrets of their intimate lives. Some might say you'd rather talk about it than do it.

Your inquisitive nature could lead you to experiment with different partners and sexual styles. Because you don't want to miss out on anything, you might be rather indiscriminate. Gemini is the sign of the twins, so you may find a ménage à trois intriguing.

Your mind is your most sensitive erogenous zone, and you probably like having a partner describe what he or she wants, in detail. Perhaps you enjoy erotic literature. Phone sex might be one of your turn-ons, too. Your oral nature could also find expression through oral sex—if you can stop talking long enough, that is!

732

With Your **SAGITTARIUS** Zodiac Sign

Your eyes twinkle with the excitable thoughts of a brilliant mind. Because your attention span can spread across cultures and continents, fixing your gaze on one lover can be challenging. You're like a traveling vaudeville act whose colorful spectacle draws a crowd but keeps on moving.

While single, you may have more than one lover at a time, since variety of experience gives you a thrill. Outdoor amour appeals to your need to expand into wide-open spaces. Spontaneous flings in an exotic destination spice up any trip. Traveling with a mate satisfies both the gypsy and the lover in you.

For you, playful fantasy may be a way to keep the imagination engaged in acts of pleasure. Sharing a warm bath or reading erotica in bed can help you wind down. Your high-strung nature becomes an asset in the bedroom—a tantalizing, light touch down your body electrifies your nervous system.

With Your **CAPRICORN** Zodiac Sign

Your witty charm and way with words often make you the life of the party, and you easily attract interesting suitors. If overcome momentarily by shyness, telling jokes and funny stories can bolster your confidence. You're openly playful and flirty, but it often takes years to truly know you.

You find a nimble mind a highly desirable quality in a lover, and your eyes stay twinkling in a bond with plenty of stimulation. While single, you may have more than one lusty playmate—variety and change give your restless spirit a thrill. The trustworthy lover with spontaneous, innovative moves has staying power.

Your detached, cool nature may initially resist surrendering to the chaos of freely expressed passion. Lighthearted fun in the bedroom brings out your uninhibited sensuality. Your excitable nature responds well to subtle touch, and soaking together in an aromatic bath can sink you into deeper nuances of pleasure.

With Your **AQUARIUS** Zodiac Sign

You can electrify a room with your witty charm and pithy observations, and your social ease gives you a wide circle of friends. While the glamour of romance may be a snap for you, sharing intimacy may be more challenging. Initially, you prefer a lover with a casual approach.

You're a playful flirt but rarely take it further. If a bond shows signs of growing humdrum, you'll either shake things up or be on your way. Such an unpredictable nature as yours needs plenty of room to move around. The concept of open relationships might appeal to your freedom-loving ways.

Variety in sexual expression ignites your curious libido. Taking time to relax in a warm bath calms your frenetic mind and eases you into a deeper, sensual rhythm. You enjoy a lively verbal rapport in the bedroom—sexy exchanges that rival any literary fantasy add fuel to the erotic fire.

With Your **PISCES** Zodiac Sign

You can be wildly social, collecting friends and admirers at every party you attend. You can hold a listener spellbound and are often a great mimic. Someone who piques your intellectual curiosity captures your interest. But it takes the hint of magic, or a feeling of kindred spirits, to open your tender heart.

You may dance around the edges of deeper romance, holding someone at a safe distance. Witty suitors who share your open, youthful outlook capture your interest—you instinctively protect yourself from abrasive or harsh suitors. For you, a strong, loyal partner can be a steadying anchor with whom to explore intimacy.

Your nimble fluency with sexy language makes you a seductive flirt. Laughing and talking in bed can be exhilarating foreplay. Whispering sweet nothings or naughty phrases can be playful fun during lovemaking. Soothing massage calms your acute nerves and sinks you into calmer layers of sensuality.

▶ READ ABOUT YOUR SEXUAL COMPATIBILITY *on p. 802*   ▶ DISCOVER YOUR CELEBRITY MARS TWINS *on p. 770*

Your Mars in Cancer

S ex without emotion might seem empty to you. Although you have a strong sensual nature, you may feel satisfied only with a partner you care about. Before you can relax and let down your guard, you need to feel safe and comfortable with your lover and know that you won't get hurt if you reveal your vulnerability.

Sensitive and emotional, you want lots of romance and affection with your sex. Hugging, touching, and other preliminaries are important to you. It helps if a partner says "I love you" often, too.

You enjoy creature comforts and security; therefore, spontaneous romps in the great outdoors might not appeal to you much. A real homebody, you probably prefer sex in your own bed and aren't very adventurous. Although some people with Mars in Cancer may try to prove their attractiveness through sexual exploits, most prefer a monogamous relationship with someone they love.

With Your **ARIES** Zodiac Sign

Your fiery libido may be quick on the trigger, but you don't always let it show. Your aloof air may be intoxicating to those in hot pursuit. Once sure of someone's affection, you can suddenly reveal a surprising sensitivity. You thrive with an intuitive partner who can sense your emotional rhythms.

With a refined partner you freely navigate both the calm and turbulent waters of love and desire. Taking morning showers or luxurious baths together brings you physically closer to your beloved in a playful way. Indulging your mate with a tender massage and being caressed in return can be gratifying.

You can be deadly serious and absurdly humorous by turns—the ideal mate shares your tragi-comic outlook. A flair for the dramatic brings a theatrical edge to your lovemaking. With laughter as a sensual lubricant between you, acting out a love scene from a favorite movie provides endless amusement.

With Your **TAURUS** Zodiac Sign

Your tender sensuality unfolds in a protected lover's nest of comfort and stability. Good food and great sex satisfy your hearty, primal desires—you're at your radiant best while cuddling in your cozy den with your lover. You enjoy cooking a big dinner together, generating savory smells that fill the house.

With such a tactile libido, sensory pleasures like sharing succulent fruits in bed could turn into an erotic free-for-all. You cherish physical closeness and use it as path to emotional release and merging. Sexy music and scented candles provide a soothing backdrop for slow, gentle lovemaking.

Your generosity shines through when love takes hold—shopping with your mate satisfies your need to accumulate. You give sentimental gifts to remind your lover of intimate moments. Fixing up a home together brings energy to your bond—sneaking in breaks for spontaneous "rolls in the hay" is the icing on the cake.

With Your **GEMINI** Zodiac Sign

While your vibrant personality brings you much attention, you hold out for sensual pleasure with the emotions involved. You may be a flirty smooth talker, but your sincerity is never in doubt—you exude a friendly warmth that makes people smile. Hosting a lavish party adds to your collection of happy memories.

You enjoy festive gatherings, especially with close family and friends. Being the center of attention has its charm, but you shine brightest in the adoring arms of your beloved. Yet your journey to the bedroom may take a circuitous route—you blend subtle seduction with the energizing milieu of social events.

A mischievous look between you may initiate a clandestine moment of private pleasure. You may seem distracted, but your intuitive antennae are sensing every nuance of your lover's body language. You give and receive many mixed messages before letting the dam of passionate desire burst through.

With Your **CANCER** Zodiac Sign

Using your discerning eye and remarkable intuition, you seek high and low for the right mate to enter your love nest. A hint of mysterious depths catches your fancy—you're interested in a lover with a fertile emotional landscape. Your subtle advances and tantalizing retreats begin the game of seduction.

You shine in unhurried moments with your lover—sharing a lazy afternoon in the park makes room for the nuances of emotional intimacy. Time spent near the water brings out your languid sensuality—soaking in a hot tub can evoke blissfully cozy togetherness. You're open to desire in a mood of calm and relaxation.

Once enamored, you sink into rich and passionate rhythms of lovemaking. Your refined senses respond to aphrodisiacs such as succulent fruits and herbal elixirs. The glow of candles adds to the atmosphere of comfort. Tender touch and a childlike sense of wonder give you an intoxicating openness.

▶ READ ABOUT YOUR SEXUAL COMPATIBILITY on p. 802   ▶ DISCOVER YOUR CELEBRITY MARS TWINS on p. 770

2 Your Mars in Cancer

Sex without emotion might seem empty to you. Although you have a strong sensual nature, you may feel satisfied only with a partner you care about. Before you can relax and let down your guard, you need to feel safe and comfortable with your lover and know that you won't get hurt if you reveal your vulnerability.

Sensitive and emotional, you want lots of romance and affection with your sex. Hugging, touching, and other preliminaries are important to you. It helps if a partner says "I love you" often, too.

You enjoy creature comforts and security; therefore, spontaneous romps in the great outdoors might not appeal to you much. A real homebody, you probably prefer sex in your own bed and aren't very adventurous. Although some people with Mars in Cancer may try to prove their attractiveness through sexual exploits, most prefer a monogamous relationship with someone they love.

With Your **LEO** Zodiac Sign

Though you bring an exuberant flair to the rituals of mating, your true feelings often remain a carefully guarded secret. Your charm and humor put people at ease—a gift for playing host makes you a central figure in your tight-knit circle. The ideal lover seduces you slowly but with great fanfare.

You enjoy a courtship filled with grand and meaningful moments. Having big events to look forward to brings you happiness in the present. Cultivating a string of fun shared memories bonds you to your lover. A romantic day may begin with lighthearted play and evolve into a seductive evening at your favorite restaurant.

Pleasures of hearth and home may include silky sheets and other luxurious fabrics. The colorful homey atmosphere you create in the bedroom matches your amorous enthusiasm for sensual delights. You are gifted at soothing your partner from daily stress with tender caresses and joyful lovemaking.

With Your **VIRGO** Zodiac Sign

You don't care much for needless fireworks or turbulence in romance. You observe a potential lover from afar before diving into the drama of an affair. Loud, aggressive people turn you off, and you shy away from casual players seeking a one-night stand. Your earthy libido responds to warm sincerity and subtle advances.

The ideal lover exudes a soothing, tranquil serenity. Settling into a stable union sets the stage for exploring deeper sensuality. The pleasure of vigorous lovemaking releases daily tension from your sensitive body. Regular sexual intimacy shifts the daily cloud of worry to the bliss of transcendent desire.

Your mind creates endless fantasies starring you and your sexy lover. Though you prefer simple pleasures of lovemaking to more exotic play, introducing a thrilling change can stir the red-hot passions between you. The soft glow of candles and familiar scents evoke a homey comfort that opens your heart.

With Your **LIBRA** Zodiac Sign

Though you appear as if romance is all fun and games, you play for keeps in matters of the heart. You're a masterful flirt with an affability that inspires loyalty and many close ties. The ideal lover intuits your moods and matches your emotional sensuousness—tender respect unlocks your deeper passions.

You rebuff harsh or insensitive suitors, desiring only to create a cozy oasis of shared bliss—you navigate the choppier waters of love with a gutsy resolve to restore peace. Spending a night watching a classic romance stirs your sentimental passions. Thoughtful gifts win your favor, regardless of monetary value.

You may assume your beloved reads minds, and too much silence can create a widening gulf between you. You gain much from overcoming shyness and showing your lover your lusty desire. But for you, holding hands in a darkened cinema can evoke as much intimacy as rapturous sexual union.

With Your **SCORPIO** Zodiac Sign

In romance, you guard your true intentions until you've observed a love interest from every angle. Initially, you may confound suitors with your enigmatic mix of personal magnetism and mysteriously shrouded emotions. Your magnanimous warmth shines through, and over time you slowly reveal your sensitive heart.

Direct, invasive people quickly learn not to bang loudly on your front door—the ideal lover tunes into the subtle nuances of your inner world. Your watery depths can become a destructive tsunami when a relationship turns sour. A courtship rhythm of subtle advance and retreat gives you time to test the waters.

In a cozy twosome, your seductive prowess finds a nourishing home. Your appetite for pleasure grows as your trust does. Long, sensual hugs and lingering kisses become slow foreplay that builds to a dramatic climax. Your great capacity for empathy inspires you to create a comforting, sensual atmosphere for tender intimacy.

▶ READ ABOUT YOUR SEXUAL COMPATIBILITY *on p. 802* ▶ DISCOVER YOUR CELEBRITY MARS TWINS *on p. 770*

734

Your Mars in Cancer

Sex without emotion might seem empty to you. Although you have a strong sensual nature, you may feel satisfied only with a partner you care about. Before you can relax and let down your guard, you need to feel safe and comfortable with your lover and know that you won't get hurt if you reveal your vulnerability.

Sensitive and emotional, you want lots of romance and affection with your sex. Hugging, touching, and other preliminaries are important to you. It helps if a partner says "I love you" often, too.

You enjoy creature comforts and security; therefore, spontaneous romps in the great outdoors might not appeal to you much. A real homebody, you probably prefer sex in your own bed and aren't very adventurous. Although some people with Mars in Cancer may try to prove their attractiveness through sexual exploits, most prefer a monogamous relationship with someone they love.

With Your **SAGITTARIUS** Zodiac Sign

Delightful paradox best describes your approach to sexual desire. You can be carefree in romance one moment and urgently serious the next. You yourself may be shockingly blunt but quickly recoil from an insensitive, harsh suitor. Initially, you hide the intensity of your feelings behind a jovial but refined mask.

If you enjoy a string of monogamous affairs, each one is likely to be richly emotional and memorable. When intrigued, you move in cautiously from all sides, like a surefooted dancer with one eye checking out the audience response. With encouragement, you begin to reveal your deep desire for enduring love.

Sensuous and gentle, your demonstrative nature emerges in a stable relationship. Tender kisses in the sleepy hours wake up your lusty libido. The cherished moments of lovemaking may come after a time of separation. And though you may travel far afield, the intimacy you share becomes your cozy sanctuary.

With Your **CAPRICORN** Zodiac Sign

Though you may appear stoic to the outside world, your intimates know you're a cuddly bear. You can't be rushed into new romance— your sensitivity means you're playing for high stakes. Your hard shell may give you the edge in public matters, but you thrive with a partner who helps you shed your mask.

A dignified courtship suits you best—an elegant dinner and sophisticated entertainment make for a fine evening. You also revel in cozy nights at home with your beloved. You have sharp intuition, and can sense how your lover feels. Sexual tension builds with a partner who picks up on nonverbal cues.

Romantic evenings of subtle seduction are likely to stir up your earthy passions. Your languid moves make you a sensuous lover of great emotional depth. For you, the real thing is better than any fantasy—you enjoy simple but meaningful expressions of desire over flashy theatrics.

With Your **AQUARIUS** Zodiac Sign

Not one to broadcast your intentions, you cast an invisible net to enchant your heart's desire. Gregarious and warm, you drop subtle hints to gauge the depth of someone's affections. You can be cuddly and loving, but at times you can be emotionally distant. A sensitive mate offers security, without caging you in.

You are naturally cautious about diving into romance. When dating, you shine in relaxed, casual settings. A cozy restaurant with soft music and dim lighting frees you to share your private thoughts. Feeling close enough to confide in your beloved increases your appetite for physical intimacy.

You thrive with a sensual lover who can surrender to the spontaneous moment. You enjoy lovemaking that takes advantage of the unexpected, rather than slipping into a routine. Emotional depth counts more to you than grand choreography, and a heartfelt hug is just as likely to linger in your memory.

With Your **PISCES** Zodiac Sign

With antennae tuned in to the hidden nuances of life, you often appear hesitant or shy. You are simply observing the scene, always aware of subtle mood shifts around you. You delight in sharing the absurdities of life and have strong comic gifts. Extremely warmhearted, you expect loyal adoration in return.

Your artistic temperament thrives with other creative souls, and you tend to shy away from cold-eyed materialists. If you are slippery to those trying to pin you down, you open colorfully in a happy bond. You may remain enigmatic, making advances, only to slip away into nourishing solitude.

For you, lovemaking opens you to vast nuances of emotion and sensation. Your theatrical flair can emerge in fantasy or role-playing in the bedroom. The richness of emotion matters more than expert technique. Music often makes the moment richer—you also enjoy bringing favorite foods into love play.

▶ READ ABOUT YOUR SEXUAL COMPATIBILITY *on p. 802*   ▶ DISCOVER YOUR CELEBRITY MARS TWINS *on p. 770*

Your Mars in Leo

736

Y̌ou enjoy being a star—especially in bed. The more adoration your partner shows you, the better your performance is likely to be. At times you may seem to be playing a role, but you really do have a passionate side—and a very affectionate one, too.

Even though you can tend to be self-centered, you are usually willing to go the extra mile to make sure your partner is satisfied as well. Knowing you are a good lover boosts your ego, and you might be quite proud of your sexual prowess. Of course, it helps if your partner praises your skill.

With your dramatic nature, you probably like to make something of a production of sex—sumptuous settings and erotic clothing might entice you. Strategically placed mirrors that let you watch your performance could be a turn-on, too. You might even have fun making your own X-rated home videos.

With Your **ARIES** Zodiac Sign

Your impulsive approach to love is complemented by a regal, confident pride. You'll pursue someone with vigor as long as your love object sends many admiring glances back in your direction. The steps of seduction may change many times with each taking turns leading the dance. Your spontaneity makes for endless thrills.

With such highly combustible materials at hand, it doesn't take much to spark your passions. Yet you crave much more than physical satisfaction—lovemaking should be a transcendent experience of oneness with your beloved.

One way to arouse your sexual appetite is through provocative language in the bedroom. Big, showy gestures of love, such as flowers or unexpected gifts, are fuel for your fire. Chances are you're rarely bored by a routine sex life—initiating impromptu moments of devil-may-care lovemaking keeps things fresh and new.

With Your **TAURUS** Zodiac Sign

You shine when your lover is generous with sincere and heartfelt compliments. You especially like to be admired for your sexual prowess—your sensory lovemaking style initiates a powerful nonverbal intimacy in your relationships. Once drawn out, your libido moves with the slow force of a regal but fierce feline.

A rapturous audience makes all the difference for you—you'll dazzle with a striptease, as long as your lover is transfixed.

Your voice has a deep, majestic resonance that melts the resistance of any reluctant lover. You enjoy lavish nights out, especially if the food and entertainment are memorable.

A theatrical flair emerges in the privacy of your bedroom. The right mate gives you room to be the strutting peacock and admires your colorful displays. Your need to dominate may trigger arguments, which can lead to making-up with playful abandon. Your lover knows you're a big softie underneath it all.

With Your **GEMINI** Zodiac Sign

Your dramatic flair turns heads when you pass by and you know how to use your charisma to work a room. You love the feelings stirred up by the first few dates, when the air bristles with erotic anticipation. The ideal mate continually rekindles that initial spark to keep that brand-new feeling between you.

Though your sunny extroversion makes you a natural flirt, you don't necessarily want your lover to have a wandering eye. Stolen kisses and public affection remind you of your lover's ardent passion. You enjoy being pampered by your lover—a sensual massage or breakfast in bed brings out your generosity in return.

Receiving a love letter worthy of any epic romance satisfies your need for grand gestures of devotion. Your wardrobe may hold many sexy outfits to match your many moods. You are wildly spontaneous, knowing just how to sneak in rejuvenating erotic moments all through the day.

With Your **CANCER** Zodiac Sign

Though it may not always show, you long to be adored by your beloved. Once your outer shell is softened, your lover gains access to a secret garden of earthly pleasures. The ideal mate matches your playful abandon in love, taking care not to trample on your vulnerable heart.

Your passions are juicy and voluptuous—you move from soulful kisses to fiery lovemaking with a natural grace and rhythm. In an enduring bond you find the stability you need for loving theatrics in the bedroom. Sexy attire and toys are fun props, but the drama evolves from the highly emotional choreography.

The right mate intuits when it's time to cuddle and when to step back and let you shine in the spotlight. You crave attention—getting dressed up together can cause you to sizzle with anticipation. Being admired while arm in arm with your faithful lover caps an evening of subtle seduction.

▶ READ ABOUT YOUR SEXUAL COMPATIBILITY on p. 802   ▶ DISCOVER YOUR CELEBRITY MARS TWINS on p. 770

Your Mars in Leo

Y ou enjoy being a star—especially in bed. The more adoration your partner shows you, the better your performance is likely to be. At times you may seem to be playing a role, but you really do have a passionate side—and a very affectionate one, too.

Even though you can tend to be self-centered, you are usually willing to go the extra mile to make sure your partner is satisfied as well. Knowing you are a good lover boosts your ego, and you might be quite proud of your sexual prowess. Of course, it helps if your partner praises your skill.

With your dramatic nature, you probably like to make something of a production of sex—sumptuous settings and erotic clothing might entice you. Strategically placed mirrors that let you watch your performance could be a turn-on, too. You might even have fun making your own X-rated home videos.

With Your **LEO** Zodiac Sign

For you love is a vibrant carnival and you don't want to miss any of the thrilling rides. Friendly and flirty, you bring a childlike joy to romance. Your generous spirit is a magnet for attracting affairs of royal grandeur. High-energy and amorous play give your lovemaking a touch of theatrical drama.

Your lover is a muse for your volcanic creativity—the ideal mate keeps your weighty ego propped up with loving adoration. Heartfelt compliments draw you further out into the spotlight. With a lover who triggers your spontaneity, your bedroom becomes a place where you freely strut your stuff.

Wearing sexy attire makes you eye candy for the adoring gaze of your beloved. You set the stage for sensual pleasure with flickering candles and erotic novelty. A peacock feather becomes a tantalizing teaser in your imaginative hands. Acting out fantasies engages your entire being in the game of seduction.

With Your **VIRGO** Zodiac Sign

A lover with smoldering charisma and dashing style appeals to your artistic sensibility. The first flush of romance holds special allure—you bring colorful pageantry to any courtship. You are drawn to sunny personalities, and the ideal lover radiates a joy for living that keeps you entertained.

Your search for perfect love may never bear fruit, but you eventually accept the lovable humanness of your mate. Laughing about shortcomings helps ease any tensions—your humor is a tonic for everyday stress and can bring you closer. A night of sophisticated comedy adds ammunition to your joke arsenal.

You bring a theatrical flair to the bedroom—sexy intimate apparel of silky fabrics makes you irresistible. After an absence from your lover, you find clever ways to renew your bond with a seductively loving welcome. You scratch a sexual itch by introducing new rituals and positions to your lovemaking repertoire.

With Your **LIBRA** Zodiac Sign

For you, sensual pleasure finds its fullest expression in a love affair of mythic proportions. Even the most casual dalliance may have a grand narrative in your private imagination. As star of your own tragicomic romance, you seek a worthy lover to share the spotlight and ignite your smoldering passions.

Your regal assurance and lighthearted charm draw many admirers, but you tend to hold people at arm's length. Your fiery libido awakens during festive evenings of dinner and dancing as long as adoring eyes stay fixed on you. Your lover can at times become simply a mirror for your mighty ego.

Making love in lavish comfort appeals to your refined taste—you're not likely to grab a quickie in a rain-soaked alley. Acting out love scenes draws out your colorful, theatrical presence. Rather than explore kinky variations, you prefer to heighten the ecstasy of lovemaking with memorable moments of foreplay.

With Your **SCORPIO** Zodiac Sign

Though the slightest provocation can ignite your fiery libido, you don't let that show to strangers. Your friendly ways shield an emotional depth that gives you a mysterious persona revealed to an intimate few. You may take a remote observer's stance in new situations, but your contagious lust for life always shines through.

Your all-or-nothing approach to love assures that intimacy will be grand and memorable. Your craving for attention, along with an insatiable sexual appetite, requires an attentive, brave-hearted lover. You enjoy winning over your beloved with lavish gifts and won't shy from showing your devotion with big spectacles.

Play and spontaneity bring a festive atmosphere to your bedroom. Sensuality can be a celebration with the right mate—you can spend an entire weekend in bed and emerge revitalized. Your ravenous hunger to reach cathartic peaks can start a wildfire of passion that quickly spreads to your lover.

▶ READ ABOUT YOUR SEXUAL COMPATIBILITY *on p. 802* ▶ DISCOVER YOUR CELEBRITY MARS TWINS *on p. 770*

Your Mars in Leo

738

You enjoy being a star— especially in bed. The more adoration your partner shows you, the better your performance is likely to be. At times you may seem to be playing a role, but you really do have a passionate side— and a very affectionate one, too.

Even though you can tend to be self-centered, you are usually willing to go the extra mile to make sure your partner is satisfied as well. Knowing you are a good lover boosts your ego, and you might be quite proud of your sexual prowess. Of course, it helps if your partner praises your skill.

With your dramatic nature, you probably like to make something of a production of sex—sumptuous settings and erotic clothing might entice you. Strategically placed mirrors that let you watch your performance could be a turn-on, too. You might even have fun making your own X-rated home videos.

With Your **SAGITTARIUS** Zodiac Sign

While enjoying single life, you may dive into affairs at breakneck speed with an affinity for love in grand style. Whirlwind romances are your specialty, and your daredevil antics may overwhelm more timid lovers. You live for amusement in all forms, and your friendly openness can attract all manner of fun.

Your enter a room with a regal assurance, which some may interpret as haughty. Your bravado can inspire you to take foolhardy risks in love, often with an all-or-nothing payoff.

You live life in glorious color, and your impulsive, hot-blooded nature makes you an irresistible lover and a delightful mate.

Great physical strength gives you endurance into the wee hours. All over tickling can be great foreplay with a playful lover. Making love may be strenuous, dramatic, and exuberant—you push toward that ultimate catharsis of ecstatic union. Luxurious fabrics and sexy attire add theatrical spice to the bedroom.

With Your **CAPRICORN** Zodiac Sign

Your proud, regal nature can turn wildly flirtatious when passions are ignited. You present a dazzling image of confidence, even when it is really only bravado. You make each affair a celebration of life's pleasures—when smitten, you enjoy spoiling your beloved with fancy dinners and lavish gifts.

From tango dancing to exotic fusion cuisine, you'll try anything once. For you, big parties are a chance to show off an attractive lover. You crave adoration and

respect, and a mate with a wandering eye triggers your fiery jealousy. You can be a devoted lover and expect the same loyalty in return.

You spare no expense to make your bedroom a place of beauty and comfort. You like to surprise your mate with erotic spectacles—greeting your lover in sexy attire, or less, sparks an evening of naughty fun. Sharing an over-the-top bubble bath puts you in a light, playful mood.

With Your **AQUARIUS** Zodiac Sign

For you, romance should be full of excitement and glamour. You enjoy parties and are especially drawn to fiery, charismatic people. When interested, you turn on the charm with sparkling wit and sunny warmth. You revel in the open adoration you attract and respond with generous affection.

Spending money on your beloved comes naturally to you—you also enjoy planning big surprises, such as breakfast in bed. From trying unusual cuisine to catching the

premiere of a film, sharing memorable times is what binds you to a lover. Your lust for life extends to the bedroom, where you revel in sensual pleasures.

An attentive lover with an original approach keeps you intrigued. Lighting a dozen candles in the bedroom or splurging on silky attire satisfies your desire for lavish theatrics. Your sheer delight in lovemaking can be contagious—a playful, energetic lover with physical stamina can keep up with you.

With Your **PISCES** Zodiac Sign

You bring frisky play and an open heart to any romance—you radiate vitality and are drawn to fiery, confident suitors. Shining when surrounded by admirers, you are gifted at sunny, light flirtation. But beneath that dazzling exterior lies a sensitive, hopeful heart that waits for true love.

The first flush of mutual attraction inspires your generous, impulsive nature—you may try to treat your lover by paying for everything. Surprising your lover with a sentimental

present gives you a special thrill. You take big risks for a worthy mate and may find it hard to let go of lost love.

Your talent in the art of seduction can lead to wild abandon in the bedroom. A lingering bath together after a night of decadent fun relaxes you and awakens desire. You respond to visual entertainment, such as a sultry striptease. Steamy, dramatic lovemaking makes you feel vitally alive.

▶ READ ABOUT YOUR SEXUAL COMPATIBILITY *on p. 802* ▶ DISCOVER YOUR CELEBRITY MARS TWINS *on p. 770*

Your Mars in Virgo

Virgo is the sign of the virgin, but that doesn't mean you aren't interested in sex. You probably just don't like to make a big display of your sensuality. Outwardly, you might seem rather modest, but in the bedroom you can exhibit your innate earthy side.

Your tendency to be critical may create sexual problems. Sometimes it might be difficult for you to relax and enjoy yourself, for your perfectionism can cause you to judge yourself and your partner too much. However, your manual dexterity and attention to detail could enable you to be a skillful lover.

Because neatness is important to you, you probably want your partner to be squeaky clean. Your environment, too, should be free of dirt and distractions. At times you may appear a bit prudish, and work, family, or other demands can diminish your ardor. But your lover knows the cooling trend is only temporary.

With Your **ARIES** Zodiac Sign

Active mental sparring fires up your lusty nature—the stimulation of an edgy debate bonds you to your partner. Your discriminating eye weeds out all but the most coolly sophisticated company around. Once you've met an intellectual equal, your daring, aggressive side kicks in, and the games begin in earnest.

Your literate seduction may include reading love poetry to one another in bed. Walking arm in arm to cultural events gives you ample time for a meeting of the minds. You might enjoy a lazy morning spent pouring over the Sunday paper, teaming up to finish the crossword puzzle, then making love on the crinkled newsprint.

Your approach to pleasure may be refined, but your primal urgency reminds your lover of your hot-blooded passions lurking below the surface. Vigorous exercise with your partner arouses your body and your sexual appetite.

With Your **TAURUS** Zodiac Sign

Your heightened sensory perception gives you a refined appreciation of the little things in life. You ease into intimacy slowly and don't like to be pursued vigorously. Natural lovers who stay fit and healthy catch your lusty eye. You prefer the unadorned scent of your lover's body to synthetic enhancements.

If you're modest at first, the patient mate knows how to awaken your hidden desires. Fantasy and theatrics in the bedroom are not your style—you crave transcendent, uncomplicated lovemaking. You're interested in a thoughtful and enduring sexual union that serves as an anchor for your ordered life.

Far from becoming dull, the layers of your earthy sensuousness unfold on solid, fertile ground. Your lovemaking becomes a mini vacation from the daily worries of your life. Your movements are refined and your voice is soothing. Tuning into your lover in an atmosphere of relaxed silence helps you find your sexual rhythm.

With Your **GEMINI** Zodiac Sign

With such brilliant thoughts swirling around in your own head, you can't help being aroused by mental stimulation. Electrifying conversations lift you from mundane cares—a lover who makes you laugh draws our your naughty side. Your libido answers the call of desire, but your practical side may hold back.

A surprise gift of erotic toys might thrill you one day and shock you the next. You hide a bashful reserve behind a flurry of dashing about—the patient lover learns to respect your enigmatic sensuality. Reading sophisticated erotica in bed merges your literate mind with primal desires.

Leaving provocative notes on your lover's pillow appeals to your need for a shared language of intimacy. Private words become rich with meaning when whispered in the ear of your beloved. Sharing a warm bath with your beloved relaxes your restless mind and sinks you into deeper layers of your earthy sensuality.

With Your **CANCER** Zodiac Sign

Your approach to love may appear cautious and reserved—you're not one to leap into romance recklessly. Some may find you picky, but you simply want to hold out for the very best. You quickly weed out nefarious players, and because many suitors follow your trail, only rarely do you need to initiate a campaign of seduction.

Though sometimes aloof with strangers, your disarming warmth shines through as trusting bonds are formed. You prefer getting to know potential lovers slowly through sharing common pursuits. A natural reserve may make first sexual encounters somewhat tentative. A loyal mate unlocks your instinctive erotic nature.

Getting physical with your beloved takes you on a mini vacation from your mundane worries. You appreciate simple pleasures—a single candle or bowl of grapes fits nicely in your bedroom. Rather than swirl in tempestuous passions, you prefer to cultivate an enduring bond in harmony with your daily routine.

▶ READ ABOUT YOUR SEXUAL COMPATIBILITY on p. 802   ▶ DISCOVER YOUR CELEBRITY MARS TWINS on p. 770

Your Mars in Virgo

Virgo is the sign of the virgin, but that doesn't mean you aren't interested in sex. You probably just don't like to make a big display of your sensuality. Outwardly, you might seem rather modest, but in the bedroom you can exhibit your innate earthy side.

Your tendency to be critical may create sexual problems. Sometimes it might be difficult for you to relax and enjoy yourself, for your perfectionism can cause you to judge yourself and your partner too much. However, your manual dexterity and attention to detail could enable you to be a skillful lover.

Because neatness is important to you, you probably want your partner to be squeaky clean. Your environment, too, should be free of dirt and distractions. At times you may appear a bit prudish, and work, family, or other demands can diminish your ardor. But your lover knows the cooling trend is only temporary.

With Your **LEO** Zodiac Sign

Your bubbly demeanor attracts many suitors, but you stick to high ideals before diving into carnal pleasures. The temptation of the casual affair holds little allure for you. A lover with fickle ways offends your royal constitution—you desire an attentive mate who cherishes both the mundane and transcendent moments.

Your tastes may be extravagant, but you prefer to keep it simple in the bedroom. Natural fibers and smells appeal to you over synthetic enhancements. You pursue healthy fun such as taking an exercise class with your mate. Going out dancing gets the blood pumping and draws out your earthy sensuality.

Those in your intimate sphere know the true depths of your passion. When the mood strikes, you know how to build sexual excitement. A slow striptease for your lover's eyes only reveals the performer behind your reserve. Your cool façade softens in the embrace of a respectful lover.

With Your **VIRGO** Zodiac Sign

Even when sparked by desire, your aloofness can eclipse your enigmatic sensuality. Your hidden passions are stirred by a sure, steady suitor—you only reveal the deeper layers over time. The promise of true love fuels your fantasies, and once in love, you soften into the ease of intimacy.

Little is left to chance in your love life—you rest easy when a night out has been pre-planned. Making reservations at a quiet refined restaurant appeals to your organized mind. Lifted from worry, you can fully dwell in the moment. You savor each morsel of food and each nuance of the night's entertainment.

A lover who distracts you from daily cares discovers a well of passionate earthiness. Sharing a playful bath sets a mood of relaxation. You employ your active mind in the bedroom by researching sexual techniques. Reading classic erotica while snuggling with your lover appeals to your literate tastes.

With Your **LIBRA** Zodiac Sign

A slow, artful seduction appeals to your dignified nature. You may be drawn to expressive lovers but are easily over-whelmed by aggressive ardor. The right lover will admire your hesitation to throw caution to the wind, though it may seem restrained. You cultivate a life rooted in the real world.

The suitor who presents a dazzling appearance appeals to you. Not one to actively hunt for love, you play the pursued in any affair. The wise lover respects your need for distance—you may entertain with enthusiasm one day and beat a hasty retreat into protected solitude the next.

You enjoy small touches in the bedroom, such as fresh flowers and clean linens. Your refined olfactory senses can make you a bit of a neat freak, and your lover should come to you smelling squeaky clean. "Less is more" describes your love style—you prefer simple touch to showy theatrics.

With Your **SCORPIO** Zodiac Sign

It takes time for your true affection to emerge—a slow, steady move to intimacy suits your discriminating tastes. Your penetrating mind draws you toward equally deep thinkers who take pride in their work lives. You shine when being helpful and thrive when your intense ardor is enthusiastically returned.

Because you shoulder many burdens, the ideal lover draws you away from worry and into the earthy, erotic body. You can be easily distracted with mundane chores—the patient lover tries to mix business with pleasure. You may bend over backwards to help your beloved and thrive with an equally devoted partner.

You learn to trust a lover willing to engage in liberating physical and emotional wrestling matches. Overcoming initial inhibitions may be a challenge whenever intimacy arises. For you, vigorous lovemaking can be cathartic in a loving bond. A patient, seductive lover sets the stage for slow, relaxed foreplay.

▶ READ ABOUT YOUR SEXUAL COMPATIBILITY *on p. 802*   ▶ DISCOVER YOUR CELEBRITY MARS TWINS *on p. 770*

Your Mars in Virgo

Virgo is the sign of the virgin, but that doesn't mean you aren't interested in sex. You probably just don't like to make a big display of your sensuality. Outwardly, you might seem rather modest, but in the bedroom you can exhibit your innate earthy side.

Your tendency to be critical may create sexual problems. Sometimes it might be difficult for you to relax and enjoy yourself, for your perfectionism can cause you to judge yourself and your partner too much. However, your manual dexterity and attention to detail could enable you to be a skillful lover.

Because neatness is important to you, you probably want your partner to be squeaky clean. Your environment, too, should be free of dirt and distractions. At times you may appear a bit prudish, and work, family, or other demands can diminish your ardor. But your lover knows the cooling trend is only temporary.

With Your SAGITTARIUS Zodiac Sign

If you seem reticent to plunge headlong into romance, it may be that you are simply planning a subtle attack. While dating, you may be wary of sharing your life with someone—you'll commit only to a sure thing with practical benefits. Your reserve hides your simmering desires, and a wise lover senses so much more.

Your meticulous outline for romance may be hastily shelved for the evening when passions flare. In the heat of the moment, your private inhibitions fade away, revealing a tender earthiness. A courtship that begins with intellectual excitement grows deeper when physical intimacy draws you closer.

Your athletic vigor makes you a nimble lover with hearty appetites. Once the wheels are greased, your libido may grow used to large doses of pleasure. An afternoon quickie brings out your childlike openness to being naughty. Playful amour in a cascading shower satisfies your lust for good, clean fun.

With Your CAPRICORN Zodiac Sign

Your serious demeanor weeds out reckless suitors and those with casual intentions—your self-contained persona may remain something of an enigma, even to longtime lovers. Physical chemistry may not be enough to lure you into an affair. You seek a mate whose life ambitions and daily routine complement your own.

When dating someone new, you may carefully guard your emotions—a patient suitor knows you need time to feel secure. You enjoy taking charge and may plan outings in advance, down to the last detail. Your affection begins to shine through over time, and your hidden passion for earthy pleasure surfaces.

Your true depths are only revealed in the intimacy of an enduring bond. A verbal rapport can bridge the distance with sexy talk when you are separated. Talking softly in bed can create tender moments of togetherness. Languid, sensuous touch begins the foreplay and heightens the ecstasy during lovemaking.

With Your AQUARIUS Zodiac Sign

Your gregarious personality attracts many friends, and romance may bloom from within that lively circle. When conversing with a trusted companion, your eyes are sparkly, your attention rapt. You're at home discussing art, music, and film—you may find it harder to show affection or reveal your deeper feelings.

You initially shy away from public displays of affection and prefer establishing a mental rapport at first. Playful adventure lifts you out of the mundane—a spontaneous visit to an amusement park could bring you closer. Your self-contained nature may make you seem indifferent to sensory delights—the wise mate knows sexy ways to whet your appetite for the pleasures of intimacy.

For you, sexual arousal begins with subtle flirtation, leading to provocative suggestion. Relaxation draws out your elusive passions. An erotic massage awakens the earthy richness of your sensuality. Erotic play and teasing builds delicious tension that heightens lovemaking.

With Your PISCES Zodiac Sign

You're not likely to jump through hoops to impress a love interest. Cool and remote, at times you may appear too busy for romance—a patient suitor settles in for a slow, steady courtship. Although you prefer building an honest rapport based on common interests, a touch of magic doesn't hurt.

Your mercurial charm helps you form strong intellectual ties—you can be brightly witty in relaxed company. An effusive hug in public may overwhelm your modest nature, and you shy away from heavy emotional swamplands. With an ordered life, you can ease into moments of deeper intimacy with your beloved.

Your moves are subtly seductive, and you can melt a lover with your sly, gentle smile. An invigorating shower can be playful foreplay—a sensuous massage using natural oils brings you closer to lusty physicality. Playful talking in bed can calm your restless mind and arouses your slumbering passions.

▶ READ ABOUT YOUR SEXUAL COMPATIBILITY on p. 802   ▶ DISCOVER YOUR CELEBRITY MARS TWINS on p. 770

Your Mars in Libra

742

Romance and sex tend to be integrally entwined for you, and you probably enjoy sex best when it's part of a loving, stable relationship. Therefore, you aren't likely to be promiscuous or frivolous with your affection. When single, you choose your partners with great care.

Peace-loving, you might shut down if there's any discord between you and your partner. You want everything to be nice and that includes your environment. Cleanliness, comfort, and congeniality all contribute to your enjoyment of sex. A romantic ambiance—candlelight, soft music, affectionate gestures, and loving words—can help to get you in the mood.

Not particularly spontaneous or passionate, you probably tend to be rather traditional and conservative sexually. As a result, you might reject anything you consider "kinky." However, your desire to please your partner could lead you to put your personal preferences aside. Making your lover happy makes you happy, too.

With Your **ARIES** Zodiac Sign

Your sensual style is full of delightful contradictions. You move toward your lover with the concentration of a big cat stalking prey. The next moment finds you conversing in a jovial but detached way. The right mate has the dexterity to switch gears to match your sexual rhythm and understand your enigmatic ways.

You thrive in the delicious moments of tension between you and your lover. Your refinement can never completely eclipse your animal lustiness. Saying the occasional sexy four-letter word to your partner can be liberating. Teasing with naughty suggestions can up the ante in the art of seduction.

Though inwardly you long to break all the rules, you generally stick with the tried and true. You're mostly aroused by dignified lovemaking, but the occasional free-for-all romp satisfies a primal craving. A trusting bond makes room for that pinch of erotic spice that brings full expression to your desires.

With Your **TAURUS** Zodiac Sign

If you're restless for physical affection, you know how to turn on the charm. You can summon out the hidden primal nature lurking underneath the façade of any sophisticated persona. You express your desires in a dignified, even poetic way. Once you've bewitched your lover, you bring out the big guns.

This gift for sparking the mind while seducing the body can lead to explosive lovemaking. You might enjoy reading well-crafted erotic stories to your lover to get the juices flowing. Creating sensuous comfort in your bedroom may include luxurious fabrics and plump grapes in a bowl close at hand.

You bring body and mind together in an artful way. An evening out with your mate to watch exquisite physical performances appeals to this innate talent. Your own idealism of love finds expression in the earthy reality of lusty union—heaven and earth meet in the arms of your cherished beloved.

With Your **GEMINI** Zodiac Sign

You long to be swept off your feet in high style—romance and sensuality cannot be separated in your book. Active and vital in other areas, you prefer being pursued in the game of love. You thrive in the midst of a whirl of social happenings. The ideal mate builds trust, while matching your exuberant pace.

You may be the life of the party, but in loving intimacy you reveal your true face. Charming rituals of your courtship may include candlelight dinners or spontaneous weekend getaways. Beauty and comfort gratify your refined sensibility—fresh flowers and a tasteful décor make your bedroom a dignified sanctuary.

Your dexterity with words makes language your most powerful tool of seduction. A phone call or email to a lover near or far renews intimate bonds. You respond to spontaneous gestures of romance—a lover's provocative look triggers the fiery spark of your impulsive sexuality.

With Your **CANCER** Zodiac Sign

The promise of intimacy sparks your instinctively fiery libido but in a detached affair, your flames flicker out. Without an intuitive bond, the vibrancy of an initial attraction grows lackluster. A tendency to rush into passionate affairs is tempered through experiences that bruise the tender heart.

You bring refinement to erotic desire and delight in the romance of courtship. The ideal lover wines and dines you, while maintaining a dignified air. Time spent surveying the local arts scene helps you find common intellectual interests. You enjoy a mix of public and private activities with your beloved.

Even while out on the town, you reach for intimate touch—holding hands or cuddling in the dark of the cinema merges your two worlds. A bedroom with romantic flavor makes it your sacred space for transcendent lovemaking. Heaven is brought down to earth when your sensual desires are heightened by moments of emotional union.

▶ READ ABOUT YOUR SEXUAL COMPATIBILITY *on p. 802*   ▶ DISCOVER YOUR CELEBRITY MARS TWINS *on p. 770*

Your Mars in Libra

Romance and sex tend to be integrally entwined for you, and you probably enjoy sex best when it's part of a loving, stable relationship. Therefore, you aren't likely to be promiscuous or frivolous with your affection. When single, you choose your partners with great care.

Peace-loving, you might shut down if there's any discord between you and your partner. You want everything to be nice and that includes your environment. Cleanliness, comfort, and congeniality all contribute to your enjoyment of sex. A romantic ambiance—candlelight, soft music, affectionate gestures, and loving words—can help to get you in the mood.

Not particularly spontaneous or passionate, you probably tend to be rather traditional and conservative sexually. As a result, you might reject anything you consider "kinky." However, your desire to please your partner could lead you to put your personal preferences aside. Making your lover happy makes you happy, too.

With Your **LEO** Zodiac Sign

Your libido ignites in the presence of an intense lover with a dignified gentility. A fiery suitor with a steadfast heart piques your interest. Your sexual appetite quickly flickers out with a distracted partner. Being treated like royalty seems your due—the right lover knows how to shower you with gifts and attention.

Sharing an evening of refined entertainment puts you in a jovial, relaxed mood. You enjoy setting the stage for magical moments of lovemaking. An erotic bath together surrounded by scented candles envelops you in illuminated bliss. Spreading rose petals across your bed heightens the romance of the evening.

Such enthusiasm for sensual pleasure can keep you and your lover engaged for an entire weekend. You enjoy planning excursions to exotic locations that provide a stunning backdrop for love. Lusty moments bring out your impulsive nature—initiating a spontaneous quickie shows your lover you're wild at heart.

With Your **VIRGO** Zodiac Sign

Your gift for artful seduction gives you a quality-over-quantity approach to seeking love's pleasures. Your discriminating tastes lead you to dignified affairs that last. You have a knack for making great first impressions, often catching many suitors in your net—you usually have your pick of many admirers.

A lover who showers you with genuine praise holds your attention. You enjoy a grand courtship with all the symbolic gestures such as flowers and chocolate. You enjoy refined entertainment and enlivening nights on the town. Underneath that casual flirtatiousness you hope to plant the deep roots of love.

You create a setting for romance that engages all the senses. The right music can mirror and add to the erotic tone of the evening. Traveling to inspiring places with a cozy feel brings you closer to your beloved. Your elusive passions emerge in full glory when surrounded by comfort and beauty.

With Your **LIBRA** Zodiac Sign

In the game of seduction, your charm makes the air around you crackle with excitement. You enjoy being a luminous object of desire, with many admirers in hot pursuit. Seeing your magnificence reflected in your suitor's eyes makes you beam, but your affections can swiftly change once you've won their heart.

Charismatic lovers with social confidence appeal to your ambitious nature. You thrive in a solid partnership and enjoy spending time with other couples. An elegant dinner party brings the chance to display your suave mate. Your idealistic heart opens to the magic of romance, often making sex an afterthought.

You have an instinct to please your beloved sexually and can draw out hidden passion. Though a vigorous tussle may be in your repertoire, you recoil from crude and unrefined expressions of physical love. You tend to remember the setting and the moods evoked during lovemaking, rather than details of technique.

With Your **SCORPIO** Zodiac Sign

A well-orchestrated seduction gets farther with you than any casual, reckless advance. For you the glamour of romance can be intoxicating—you prefer poetic expressions of love to primal urgency. When enamored, your clever mind conjures artful ways to add erotic ambiance to any setting.

Behind that social charm, you exert great influence on your lover. The undertow of your desire is always reshaping your relationship. Feisty clashes with your lover can energize you, especially if they bring a change. The road to deep understanding opens you to great heights and turbulent lows.

Making love after an argument can be a peak experience that renews your intimacy. Reading from sexy picture books can initiate refreshing experimentation—from flavored sensual oils to a teasing feather, you're open to pleasure enhancing props. Slow, skillful touch raises your temperature to a fever pitch.

▶ READ ABOUT YOUR SEXUAL COMPATIBILITY *on p. 802*   ▶ DISCOVER YOUR CELEBRITY MARS TWINS *on p. 770*

Your Mars in Libra

Romance and sex tend to be integrally entwined for you, and you probably enjoy sex best when it's part of a loving, stable relationship. Therefore, you aren't likely to be promiscuous or frivolous with your affection. When single, you choose your partners with great care.

Peace-loving, you might shut down if there's any discord between you and your partner. You want everything to be nice and that includes your environment. Cleanliness, comfort, and congeniality all contribute to your enjoyment of sex. A romantic ambiance—candlelight, soft music, affectionate gestures, and loving words—can help to get you in the mood.

Not particularly spontaneous or passionate, you probably tend to be rather traditional and conservative sexually. As a result, you might reject anything you consider "kinky." However, your desire to please your partner could lead you to put your personal preferences aside. Making your lover happy makes you happy, too.

With Your **SAGITTARIUS** Zodiac Sign

Though keeping your options open appeals to your freewheeling nature, you thrive in a partnership. The social whirl you dwell in brings many chances to satisfy your romantic inclinations. As the one usually pursued, you need only radiate your natural charm. Your only problem might be deciding whom you desire most.

Casting a wide net attracts many, and you may make promises you can't always keep. You're turned off by judgmental people—you prefer a dignified but unpretentious lover. You enjoy a setting of casual elegance—the ideal date is as relaxed at the most expensive restaurant as at an outdoor picnic.

You tend to want profound moments of erotic pleasure but are not particularly intense. You enjoy laughing and telling erotic stories in bed—the light touch of a feather across your body brings shivers of excitement. After plenty of closeness, you are ready for the fireworks of intimate lovemaking.

With Your **CAPRICORN** Zodiac Sign

You bring glamour to any courtship and appreciate an artful seduction full of romance. An elegant lover who wines and dines you in classy places has the edge. Your refined sensibility leads you to hint provocatively rather than make overt suggestions. The ideal lover picks up on your subtle advances.

Being the object of pursuit suits you best, and you don't care to chase after a reluctant lover. Domestic strife easily turns you off—you prefer the calm of a peaceful bond. Your sensual imagination can be stirred with an attentive lover, and the right music gets you in the mood.

Your libido can be impulsive and urgent at times. Your erotic feelings may run hot and cold—the wise lover makes the most of your wilder moments. Loving massage opens you to steamy passions that well up from deep within. Your sexual response grows steadier as your relationship deepens.

With Your **AQUARIUS** Zodiac Sign

Graced with a brilliant mind and plenty of social charm, you usually don't have to pursue a love interest. You cultivate many kinds of interactions, and have a knack for unlocking a lover's passions. You can be impulsive when attraction hits—finding true love may be an ideal that keeps you yearning for something better.

You have refined tastes, and enjoy a sophisticated, well-dressed lover—crude or insensitive people don't linger long in your intimate sphere. Outgoing and humorous, you thrive in the world of ideas. You may often seem above the fray of human entanglements, and enjoying sensual pleasures brings you down to earth.

Talking during lovemaking may come naturally to you—engaging your imagination through erotic language can be thrilling. Creating the right atmosphere with candles and oils appeals to your love of romance. Your frenetic energy responds to foreplay of slow, soothing massage and light, tender kisses.

With Your **PISCES** Zodiac Sign

You can be a smooth talker, flirting with a casual ease. In the first throes of an affair, you may be emboldened to take reckless leaps and make dramatic declarations. After such exposure, you may beat a hasty retreat. If you seem fickle, it may be a result of these impulsive moods.

While single, you enjoy dabbling in romantic adventure and are hard to pin down. You're drawn to well-dressed suitors with exquisite taste and refined manners. You prefer harmony over chaos, eschewing crowds for intimate, cozy settings—a dignified evening can be a prelude to graceful lovemaking.

Turning your bedroom into a shrine of pleasure appeals to your extravagant desires—luscious fabrics and succulent fruits are just two ways to beautify your lair. You're gifted at crafting provocative notes for your lover's pillow or pocket. The depth of emotion matters to you more than form or technique.

▶ READ ABOUT YOUR SEXUAL COMPATIBILITY on p. 802   ▶ DISCOVER YOUR CELEBRITY MARS TWINS on p. 770

744

Your Mars in Scorpio

Scorpio is known as the sex sign of the zodiac, and sex is probably your natural milieu. With your innate animal magnetism you probably attract plenty of admirers. Your keen intuition can let you tap into a partner's deepest desires and satisfy them.

You aren't interested only in the physical side of sex, however—the emotional side matters, too. Sex can even be a transcendent, spiritual experience for you. What you'd really like is to merge with your lover, and physical intimacy allows you to get close to your partner.

Your fascination with sex could lead you to explore all sorts of erotic activities. Taboo areas intrigue you, so practices that more modest types eschew might turn you on. You tend to be an extremist and may enjoy exploring the dark side of sexuality. Power and control could play a part in whetting your appetite—for you, sex is power.

With Your **ARIES** Zodiac Sign

Nobody can resist your smoldering charms, and you may have the notches on your belt to prove it. If past lovers stood befuddled as you swiftly made your exit, regrets are likely few—not many can match your explosive passions and deeply felt sensuality. You fix intensely on your beloved with sunny intensity.

Falling in love sends you deep into the bliss of sexual union, but a restless heart keeps you on the move. If your libido sometimes leads the way, you've learned to discriminate as well. Once in love, you wear your heart on your sleeve—a surprising vulnerability that may be humbling to your ego.

The right partner knows how to stand up to the unpredictable volatility that fuels you without putting out your fire. Playful power struggles in the bedroom can release pent up aggressions. Tempestuous lovemaking channels intense emotions into steamy moments that bring you together.

With Your **TAURUS** Zodiac Sign

Your smoldering magnetism may attract many, but your sensual nature finds expression in the privacy of an intimate bond. Once smitten, your cautious approach gives way to open seduction. You know how to ignite the fires of love—your penetrating gaze has a mesmerizing effect on those who fall under the spell.

Casual affairs hold little interest for you because you tend to dive deeply into the layers of your lover's soul. The right mate assures you of devotion by offering plenty of sensual delights. Generous amounts of physical affection act on your jealous moods like a tonic.

Your quiet reserve masks a determined will—you simply save your energy for worthwhile pursuits. When aroused, your physical stamina keeps your lover satisfied through the night. A virile mate with mysteries to unravel keeps you close. An affair with you may be tempestuous and steamy, but it will never be boring.

With Your **GEMINI** Zodiac Sign

You may seem to skim happily on the surface of love with sudden plunges into oceanic depths of sensuality. A great listener, you study a potential lover before making any bold moves. Your witty observations on life and love and hypnotically provocative gaze provide a natural platform for casual flirtations.

For you an attractive mind dazzles with light humor as well as probes into deeper waters. Long, meandering conversations with your ideal mate include both the serious and the silly. You crave independence of thought; sharing an afternoon together while both of you are engaged in solitary pursuits is typical.

Once smitten, your passions are let loose—you have a hearty sexual appetite that seeks variety in the bedroom. Sharing new discoveries together can be foreplay for your curious heart. You entice your lover with sultry verbal suggestions. Erotic play and sensual oils add spicy fun to your lovemaking.

With Your **CANCER** Zodiac Sign

The emotional intensity you employ to fulfill desires makes for many thrilling encounters. Like a stalking tiger, you roam a party or festive gathering with penetrating eyes and a curious mind. One smoldering look sends out a flirty but cautious vibe to sexy suitors in your orbit.

Using your keen intuitive powers, you can usually snag a winner. A lover who approaches in a slow, unassuming manner has the edge. You dip a toe into the wading pool of love before diving into the ocean—a little voice warns you to navigate carefully the choppy waters resulting from the dark side of passion.

Once smitten, you delight your lover with days of affection and nights of delicious lovemaking. You shine in retreat from the cacophony of the outside world. Sharing deep pleasure with your beloved renews your spirits—exchanging erotic stories can be tantalizing foreplay for a night of sensuality.

▶ READ ABOUT YOUR SEXUAL COMPATIBILITY *on p. 802*   ▶ DISCOVER YOUR CELEBRITY MARS TWINS *on p. 770*

Your Mars in Scorpio

Scorpio is known as the sex sign of the zodiac, and sex is probably your natural milieu. With your innate animal magnetism you probably attract plenty of admirers. Your keen intuition can let you tap into a partner's deepest desires and satisfy them.

You aren't interested only in the physical side of sex, however—the emotional side matters, too. Sex can even be a transcendent, spiritual experience for you. What you'd really like is to merge with your lover, and physical intimacy allows you to get close to your partner.

Your fascination with sex could lead you to explore all sorts of erotic activities. Taboo areas intrigue you, so practices that more modest types eschew might turn you on. You tend to be an extremist and may enjoy exploring the dark side of sexuality. Power and control could play a part in whetting your appetite—for you, sex is power.

With Your **LEO** Zodiac Sign

You've explored the dark, hidden side of love, always emerging with a renewed enthusiasm for erotic pleasures. With flashy charisma and a smoldering charm, you draw intrigue like bees to honey. Behind that penetrating gaze, your intuitive mind seeks to discover the motives behind your lover's every action.

You yearn to unlock the mysteries of your lover's psyche—the shadowy depths hold a certain fascination for you. Long, ambling walks together create space to dive to those depths and resurface with new insights. You enjoy checking out the latest film epic or thriller in the fantasy world of the darkened movie house.

When an insatiable appetite meets playful enthusiasm, you have a combustible libido on your hands. You bring an emotional intensity to lovemaking that astounds more timid souls. An active sex life creates an outlet for pent-up aggressions, and intimacy becomes a celebration of your love and affection.

With Your **VIRGO** Zodiac Sign

An air of secrecy guards your private passions from all but a chosen few. Even so, others sense the invisible tentacles of your smoldering sensuality. At social events you magnetize with your probing intellect and humorous insight into human behavior. You respond to a suitor who listens rapturously to your oratory.

You exist in a shroud of mystery, and a potential lover may find it hard to gauge your true feelings. Observing a suitor in a variety of situations shows you more pieces of the puzzle. Before long you are revealing the unfathomable depths and explosive passions behind the stoic mask.

You are an imaginative lover who thrives on plenty of affectionate touch—erotic massage can be relaxing, arousing foreplay. Highly demonstrative, you seize every chance to satisfy your hearty sexual appetite. In a trusting bond your fiery libido soars—you become the playful love slave who aims to please.

With Your **LIBRA** Zodiac Sign

While dating, you enjoy the inherent mystery in seducing a new lover—unraveling the secrets of a dark stranger gives you a thrill. Intrigue, and even danger, takes you to the edge of your intense passions. However, one severe tumble from heartbreak or power struggles can lead you toward calmer, more balanced affairs.

Though you often conceal your true feelings, your hearty sexual appetite often brings the extremes of emotion to the surface. Simply following the whims of your libido can whip up an unexpected maelstrom. Luckily, you're also blessed with a gift for knowing how to smooth out the rough edges.

Pleasing your lover comes easily to you, but you are slow to fully surrender to your wild passions. You respond hungrily to erotic touch, especially the delights of oral stimulation. Teasing your erogenous zone stirs up a frenzy of excitement that only orgiastic peaks of lovemaking will satisfy.

With Your **SCORPIO** Zodiac Sign

When unattached, your hypnotic charisma draws many, but few enter your inner sanctum. Though highly social, you tend to listen raptly as others reveal their souls. You shrewdly observe potential lovers, often from a safe distance. Underneath the cool façade lies a hot-blooded sex drive and tender vulnerability.

You make calculated, decisive moves toward your object of desire. During a courtship, you may pull back behind your stoic wall many times. The wise lover knows you're worth the wait and gives you breathing room. For you, trust forms slowly, as you dare to risk revealing the layers of your complex psyche.

You're an agile lover whose intense inner chaos finds release through strenuous lovemaking. Acting out lusty fantasies can be a creative outlet for volatile passions. Arousal may begin with a full body erotic massage, which makes you scream with anticipation. Your enthusiastic zeal for physical intimacy can be contagious.

▶ READ ABOUT YOUR SEXUAL COMPATIBILITY *on p. 802*   ▶ DISCOVER YOUR CELEBRITY MARS TWINS *on p. 770*

746

Your Mars in Scorpio

Scorpio is known as the sex sign of the zodiac, and sex is probably your natural milieu. With your innate animal magnetism you probably attract plenty of admirers. Your keen intuition can let you tap into a partner's deepest desires and satisfy them.

You aren't interested only in the physical side of sex, however—the emotional side matters, too. Sex can even be a transcendent, spiritual experience for you. What you'd really like is to merge with your lover, and physical intimacy allows you to get close to your partner.

Your fascination with sex could lead you to explore all sorts of erotic activities. Taboo areas intrigue you, so practices that more modest types eschew might turn you on. You tend to be an extremist and may enjoy exploring the dark side of sexuality. Power and control could play a part in whetting your appetite—for you, sex is power.

With Your SAGITTARIUS Zodiac Sign

Though you're a fireball of emotional energy, you often hold back like a watchful predator. While single, your devilish charm draws many suitors—you may privately observe and plan a strategy of seduction while joining in lively fun. You use artful flirtation to lure the most reserved lover out of their shell.

For you, romance can be a series of playful adventures that are often high velocity activities. With a free-spirited partner, vigorous dancing becomes the most delicious foreplay around. You thrive when your intense emotions find expression, rather than stay submerged—sexual release can make you feel completely reborn.

Your appetite for earthly pleasures grows as you get older. When others are winding down in life, your libido grows more demanding. Your imagination stays engaged with classic erotica, such as the Kama Sutra. Lovemaking may begin with slow, sensual touch and move toward a more urgent expression of desire.

With Your CAPRICORN Zodiac Sign

Cool-eyed reserve marks your initial approach to romance, and only a courageous, confident suitor stays in the game. You may want to observe a potential love interest from a safe distance. You don't waste time with casual flirtation—you mainly seek the profound closeness and enduring stability of a loving bond.

Your intentions are well hidden, and you may enjoy the intrigue of a secret love affair. Ambitious and capable, at times you may channel your enormous drive solely into furthering your career. The ideal lover supports your need for advancement, while relaxing you away from mundane concerns.

When alone with your beloved, you are an affectionate and generous lover. A born sensualist, you come alive in the arms of a lover with tender, skillful hands. The dramatic catharsis of lovemaking restores your vital energies and opens you to deep intimacy. Frequent, lusty tussles keep you feeling happy and alive.

With Your AQUARIUS Zodiac Sign

On the surface, you can be openly flirty but with an alluring sensuality that seems elusive. Your intensity is like an ocean with a powerful undertow—you can subtly cast a spell on those around you. Your moods swing to extremes—you may captivate many at a party but happily leave on your own.

Even close friends may not always know how you really feel. Though your passions are unpredictable, few can match the fiery passion of your lustier moods. You may shine like a radiant sun on your beloved one moment, then suddenly turn toward solitary pursuits. The ideal lover goes with the flow.

Behind closed doors, you can surrender to your primal desires. Long, generous hugs create an intimate atmosphere after a long day apart from your beloved. You enjoy initiating midnight or early morning lovemaking—your hypnotic gaze can arouse a sleepy lover to a state of alertness.

With Your PISCES Zodiac Sign

At a lively party, you're often the one telling funny stories while surrounded by a rapt audience. Your hypnotic gaze lures suitors, and your kind warmth keeps them hooked. If insecurity causes doubts to surface, you try to keep your cool. Your curious interest in others keeps you probing, while your own secrets stay hidden within.

You enjoy unraveling a dark mystery and may be drawn to secretive, slightly dangerous lovers. Long walks together give you time to dive into deliciously complex life stories. Such emotional intensity may flare up into domestic skirmishes—your moods can be explosive and as colorful as any fireworks display.

One glance from your sultry bedroom eyes may be enough to trigger a quickie moment of private pleasure. Slow, erotic massage leading to delicate teasing of erogenous zones builds aching sexual tension. The boiling passions that simmer under the surface find cathartic release through vigorous lovemaking.

► READ ABOUT YOUR SEXUAL COMPATIBILITY *on p. 802*   ► DISCOVER YOUR CELEBRITY MARS TWINS *on p. 770*

Your Mars in Sagittarius

For you, sex is fun—it's as simple as that. You tend to see sex as a game, and you don't take it too seriously.

An adventurer, you are eager to expand your erotic horizons and probably want to explore all sorts of sexual practices. When single, you may be rather indiscriminate in your choice of partners. Your restless nature can make it difficult for you to commit yourself to someone—that might limit your freedom too much.

Your curious nature could lead you to be something of a voyeur. You may enjoy hearing about other people's sex lives or even watching from the sidelines. Versatility is likely to be your strong point, and you're willing to try just about anything. Although you might lack deep emotions at times, you can be an entertaining lover and have a knack for making your partner laugh—your lover rarely leaves your bed unhappy.

748

With Your **ARIES** Zodiac Sign

You can crave spontaneous affairs that burn brightly, if not always for very long. You make dazzling first impressions, and may, at times, have several suitors at your beck and call. You can be brazen and flirty with a playful innocence that places you alongside all wild creatures found in nature.

Sexy talk flows from your mouth like a raging river—you're not one to hold back provocative thoughts. The sound of laughter may be heard from your bedroom, as you share a joke or two. Once aroused, your libido is like firebombs igniting, giving you stamina well into the night.

You enjoy breaking a sweat with your partner—an evening on the dance floor can be a prelude to vigorous lovemaking. Taking part in sports with a lover gets your blood pumping. And you're always ready for tomfoolery—a sultry glance exchanged while doing mundane chores can trigger an intimate moment.

With Your **TAURUS** Zodiac Sign

Your active, energized libido seeks plenty of playful fun with a loyal lover. In a stable bond you can happily explore new and novel ways to enhance pleasure—having a treasure chest of sexy toys and clothes nearby ignites your passions. With the right mate you are a fearless explorer at the edges of the sexual frontier.

Even the smallest suggestion of erotic touching sparks your fire—an evening of subtle teasing adds to the anticipation. You are aroused most by seductive gestures of physical contact with your lover. An evening out together can begin the tantalizing erotic dance of nonverbal suggestion you share with your mate.

Your flirty side may bring you close to edgy situations—a slightly wandering eye seems at odds with your steadfast nature. The right partner satisfies your lusty restlessness while creating a setting of relaxed comfort. Sharing vigorous, sporty activities brings you closer together.

With Your **GEMINI** Zodiac Sign

You are open to the exhilaration of sexual desire, but don't want your bonds to slow you down. Sensual pleasure is only one way to have fun—you move through life eager to experience it all. While your passion burns brightly with an innocent openness, the key to your heart may be well guarded.

Sharing a belly laugh with your lover fires up your lusty libido. Possessive or melancholy types rain on your parade—you want a mate who is also a friend. The right lover frequently stands back, knowing that like many great works of art, you are best viewed from a few steps away.

Your mind is encyclopedic, but you're always eager to learn more. The lover who piques your intellect may soon hold you in a sensual embrace. You pride yourself on innovation in your approach to lovemaking—your spontaneous moves keep your partner alert.

With Your **CANCER** Zodiac Sign

The ideal lover showers you with adoration and knows how to keep the flames of excitement flickering happily. You're a homebody with a touch of the thrill seeker—you enjoy a mate who lovingly lures you into uncharted territory. Others revel in your flirty persona, and your home is often a festive meeting place.

Being the life of the party presents many chances for romance. Your thirst for adventure puts you on the front lines—you often meet richly intriguing characters. Vigorous activities put fire in your libido. From sharing a common sport to flying a kite, you love running alongside your mate.

You bring volatility to the bedroom and astound lovers with your endurance. A little dancing can be a playful prelude to lovemaking—working up a sweat satisfies your appetite for physical action. When assured of your lover's loyalty, your uninhibited sensuality radiates a glow of spontaneous fun.

▶ READ ABOUT YOUR SEXUAL COMPATIBILITY on p. 802　▶ DISCOVER YOUR CELEBRITY MARS TWINS on p. 770

Your Mars in Sagittarius

For you, sex is fun—it's as simple as that. You tend to see sex as a game, and you don't take it too seriously.

An adventurer, you are eager to expand your erotic horizons and probably want to explore all sorts of sexual practices. When single, you may be rather indiscriminate in your choice of partners. Your restless nature can make it difficult for you to commit yourself to someone— that might limit your freedom too much.

Your curious nature could lead you to be something of a voyeur. You may enjoy hearing about other people's sex lives or even watching from the sidelines. Versatility is likely to be your strong point, and you're willing to try just about anything. Although you might lack deep emotions at times, you can be an entertaining lover and have a knack for making your partner laugh—your lover rarely leaves your bed unhappy.

With Your **LEO** Zodiac Sign

Uninhibited exuberance marks your love style, and you attract plenty of playmates to satisfy your restless spirit. You shine at festive parties, particularly if you're the guest of honor. The sound of your laughter is contagious—the ideal lover keeps you charmed with funny stories and interesting anecdotes.

Always on the move, you enjoy sharing traveling adventures with your mate. Trying the cuisine of other cultures fills you with delight. Lackluster places and people weigh heavily on your spirit—you are sparked by colorful personalities who live with great gusto. Sexual expression evolves naturally from your joie de vivre.

You express passion ardently, tumbling into bed with your lover after a day of happy exertion. If you seem nonchalant about sex, it simply reflects a natural, free-spirited attitude. You inspire independence in a bond by holding on loosely. Secretly, you long to be swept away by a rapturous love affair.

With Your **VIRGO** Zodiac Sign

A lust for wholesome pleasure and sporty fun draws those with similarly active lives. Your casual approach to romance draws an eclectic mix of potential lovers. You prefer a lover who begins as a friend—you may be a daredevil when it comes to sexual exploration, but you show a cautious reticence when forming deeper ties.

Spending time outdoors sparks your love of nature and animal physicality. A challenging camping trip provides a colorful backdrop to exploring primal desires. A shared interest in healthy living brings you closer—you're just as likely to indulge in a fruit smoothie as a fancy cocktail.

Your fiery sensuality simmers just below the surface, making you always ready for a spontaneous quickie. Being amorous in the first moments of morning sets a lively tone to the day. Sexy talk liberates your quick wit and a dash of playful humor lifts you out of mundane worries.

With Your **LIBRA** Zodiac Sign

While single, your need to roam may lead you into experimental adventures—you have luck attracting interest while traveling or in unusual situations. When dating, you may plunge into new affairs with dizzying speed, often making just as swift an exit. Finding an enduring love settles your restless nature.

Your open sensuality responds to a light, playful touch, and you stay cheerful with a partner who values peace in the home. A harmonious bond emboldens you to take big risks in other areas of your life. Because you wither as a caged bird, you thrive in a dynamic partnership with plenty of freedom to soar.

A quest for new experiences gives your lovemaking a spontaneous edge. Experimenting with new positions appeals to your highly vigorous approach. You enjoy sharing an invigorating shower, followed by the intimacy of an erotic massage—a special focus on the thighs heightens the pleasure.

With Your **SCORPIO** Zodiac Sign

While single, your restless spirit and lusty libido inspire you to generously spread your amorous gifts far and wide. Playful openness makes you a magnet for the romantic experience you desire. Fly-by-night trysts in unlikely places may give you much to boast about, as evidence of your sexual prowess.

A lively courtship may begin with vibrant discussion about art, politics and current events. You enjoy philosophizing, and become animated with a responsive, clever mate.

You're an outrageous flirt but may become jealous when the tables are turned. Once smitten, your eyes stay fixed on your cherished lover.

You can be creative when it comes to stating your desires—sending provocative love letters can put your passions into fiery words of longing. A graceful striptease fans the flames—you generally move freely and with few inhibitions. Pleasing your mate gives you a rush, and you rarely miss your mark.

▶ READ ABOUT YOUR SEXUAL COMPATIBILITY *on p. 802*   ▶ DISCOVER YOUR CELEBRITY MARS TWINS *on p. 770*

Your Mars in Sagittarius

For you, sex is fun—it's as simple as that. You tend to see sex as a game, and you don't take it too seriously.

An adventurer, you are eager to expand your erotic horizons and probably want to explore all sorts of sexual practices. When single, you may be rather indiscriminate in your choice of partners. Your restless nature can make it difficult for you to commit yourself to someone— that might limit your freedom too much.

Your curious nature could lead you to be something of a voyeur. You may enjoy hearing about other people's sex lives or even watching from the sidelines. Versatility is likely to be your strong point, and you're willing to try just about anything. Although you might lack deep emotions at times, you can be an entertaining lover and have a knack for making your partner laugh—your lover rarely leaves your bed unhappy.

750

With Your SAGITTARIUS Zodiac Sign

Wildly experimental, you view romantic ties as another chance to gain knowledge. You thrive with a vibrant mate who can run alongside you, without slowing you down with heavy emotional baggage. The ideal lover expands your intellectual horizons, while coaxing out your elusive emotionality.

Your nonchalance can be seen as a sign that you don't care for deeper connection. At the first sign of routine or boredom, you're often the first to shake things up.

Feeling free to roam is a top priority and vital to your well-being. Paradoxically, in a loose-knit union, you can begin to form an enduring bond.

Both sporty activities and sexual expression give you a chance to let off steam. Soaking with your lover in a scented bath eases you into relaxed sensuality. Your fiery aggression finds a healthy outlet in the pursuit of orgiastic lovemaking, and your zeal for strenuous lovemaking can be contagious.

With Your CAPRICORN Zodiac Sign

You're a bit of a paradox when it comes to romance. You can be playful and flirty one moment, and utterly serious the next. You may want to indulge in a rapturous, spontaneous affair, but become shy when making it a reality. You'd love to dive into reckless adventure, but you're also concerned with more practical matters.

While single, your restless nature may send you rushing into lusty experimentation. You can enjoy freewheeling, energetic affairs in

exotic locales. Making solid emotional commitments may take longer, and you can be surprisingly reserved when professing deep, amorous feelings.

Fulfilling your sexual longings in a stable bond makes room for unlimited discovery. You enjoy trying new ways to add to sensual pleasure, perhaps with naughty toys. High-energy lovemaking takes you to orgiastic peaks—this catharsis brings richly layered moments of emotional intimacy to your bond.

With Your AQUARIUS Zodiac Sign

You're a friend to many, and your sparkling exchanges can often lead to playful flirtation. Having fun comes easily to you, and you actively seek new adventures. Romance often begins as a marriage of the minds, but you fiercely guard your independence. To outsiders your affairs may appear more like friendships.

You have a trusting nature, but can grow more discerning over time. Preferring to keep things light, you shine brightly as part of a

comedy duo. Often disappearing into solitude for several days, you give mixed signals to a mate. But you return renewed and ready for more intelligent hedonism.

Telling jokes and funny stories arouses your libido as nothing else does. You initiate lovemaking like a house on fire, with energy and stamina to burn. Your spontaneity can make every time a fresh experience. Mellow foreplay relaxes your frenetic energy and heightens the pleasure.

With Your PISCES Zodiac Sign

You meet romance with an innocent exuberance that can make a potential lover's heart race. An immediate rapport may be enough to lure you into a casual, playful affair. You can show blind faith in love, but your discernment grows refined with experience. While single, you may dash from one romantic adventure to the next.

High-velocity fun gets your blood pumping—sharing sports or exercise with a lover appeals to your active nature. A mellow

walk of dreamy handholding may be fine, with ample room for sudden leaps of enthusiasm. After the exertion of the day, your bright, alert eyes quicken at the slightest sexual provocation.

Your candor in the bedroom brings hidden desires out into the open. For you, fantasy makes lovemaking more colorful and arouses your vivid imagination. Your changeable nature makes you a spontaneous, uninhibited lover—you may initiate an afternoon delight to satisfy urgent desires.

▶ READ ABOUT YOUR SEXUAL COMPATIBILITY on p. 802   ▶ DISCOVER YOUR CELEBRITY MARS TWINS on p. 770

Your Mars in Capricorn

Although you may seem cool and controlled on the outside, those who know you intimately know you have a randy side and a natural appreciation for the physical part of love. It might take a while for you to get over your natural reserve, but once you warm up, you are anything but shy.

Endurance is likely to be your forté. You probably feel no need to rush things. Careful and methodical, you may follow a set of established steps in order to reach your goal. Inclined to stick with what you already know rather than exploring new territory, you handle all the basic moves with competence.

Your stamina is probably one of your strongest assets—your lover can depend on you to satisfy his or her needs. Even in your later years, you are likely to retain your lustiness—a younger partner may be amazed at your sexual prowess.

With Your **ARIES** Zodiac Sign

Your sensual nature may swing from fiery passion to reserved detachment. Behind closed doors, the ideal mate knows how to use touch to lure out the sexy beast. You work hard and play hard—stroking you the right way can release all that daily tension. A generous lover knows that a loving massage makes you purr.

Once mellowed, you can be playfully aggressive in the game of seduction. A little roughhousing in the bedroom lets you flex your muscles—you prefer earthy, physically strong lovers with an uncomplicated approach to lovemaking. If you are fierce at times, you are also vulnerable and tender when the moment arises.

Your senses are refined, and you enjoy preparing and savoring a culinary feast with your lover. You let down your guard in relaxed company—sharing stories with your beloved draws you closer. Your humor comes in bright flashes that soften any intimate encounter.

With Your **TAURUS** Zodiac Sign

The suitor who tries to impress you with smooth moves and clever words likely evokes your aloof poker face. You don't like flirty games, nor will you take reckless risks to seduce. You want to assess all your options even before choosing a playmate—you make cautious, steady steps toward your object of desire.

While you take time to act, your imagination is fertile ground for elaborate fantasies that fulfill your deepest desires. The right lover doesn't rush you until you are ready, sensing a big pay off in the end. Brewing below that cool exterior is a sensuous, affectionate nature that unfolds over time.

Your appreciation of refinement finds expression in classy places, such as the opera or symphony. A creative, generous lover sparks your offbeat humor with funny stories and jokes. Spinning yarns and tall tales in bed can open your heart. A loving massage draws out your sensual earthiness.

With Your **GEMINI** Zodiac Sign

You can flirt with finesse, but you're not one to lose your head in a game of seduction. Any potential romantic partners undergo a rigorous interview process cleverly disguised as casual dating. Your outgoing manner attracts a diverse circle of friends, but only a few enter your most private sphere.

In public you prefer reserved expressions of warmth, such as a lingering touch on the arm or shoulder. Putting on your best finery for a night of culture and refinement satisfies your proud nature. Walking arm in arm gives you time to share funny stories or simply enjoy the silent moments together.

With your cherished lover you exhibit the earthy side of your lusty libido. Alone together, you shower your lover with physical affection. You initiate spontaneous encounters with a few sexy words and a steamily passionate touch. The privacy of your bedroom allows you to drop your mask, revealing a playful sensuality.

With Your **CANCER** Zodiac Sign

An air of dignified reserve describes your love style—you cut an imposing figure to many who try to catch your fancy. You repel flighty and superficial types with a cool look or raised eyebrow. But the lucky few who gain your hard-won trust are amply rewarded with enduring loyalty and affection.

Though you're not one to gush about your private feelings, you hold your beloved close to your heart. You thrive in domestic routine and enjoy preparing meals with your mate.

Your cuddly, demonstrative side shows in stolen kisses and spontaneous hugs. You love surprising your mate with sentimental gifts. Staying at home watching movies gives you time to relax and renew your intimacy after a stressful day. A slow, erotic massage releases you from worldly concerns. Your earthy sensuality anchors any turbulence that arises between you and your lover. Your tender touch reveals the sensitivity you keep guarded.

▶ READ ABOUT YOUR SEXUAL COMPATIBILITY *on p. 802*   ▶ DISCOVER YOUR CELEBRITY MARS TWINS *on p. 770*

Your Mars in Capricorn

Although you may seem cool and controlled on the outside, those who know you intimately know you have a randy side and a natural appreciation for the physical part of love. It might take a while for you to get over your natural reserve, but once you warm up, you are anything but shy.

Endurance is likely to be your forté. You probably feel no need to rush things. Careful and methodical, you may follow a set of established steps in order to reach your goal. Inclined to stick with what you already know rather than exploring new territory, you handle all the basic moves with competence.

Your stamina is probably one of your strongest assets—your lover can depend on you to satisfy his or her needs. Even in your later years, you are likely to retain your lustiness—a younger partner may be amazed at your sexual prowess.

With Your **LEO** Zodiac Sign

Though your passions are red-hot, you bring an air of caution to the courtship dance. Not willing to settle for less, you restrain mere lust for the promise of a grander affair. Casual flings quickly lose their appeal—you gravitate toward a confident lover who exhibits an enduring stability and undying devotion.

The thrill of new romance softens your cool reserve. When infatuation grabs hold, you dazzle your beloved with enthusiastic, fiery advances. Hitting the town in regal style appeals to your desire to roam around in the spotlight. Being admired as a power couple satisfies your quest for worldly success and respect.

Tender caresses and erotic massage mellow you into a relaxed sensuality—your earthy erotic nature is nourished by regular sexual release. The sanctuary of your bedroom becomes an intimate setting for your surprisingly sexy performances. Your affectionate nature seeks a lofty perch to show off your most private moves.

With Your **VIRGO** Zodiac Sign

Though you're private with your deepest feelings, you're wildly affectionate in a seasoned affair. Your cool exterior takes time to melt—the patient lover draws out your passions with a measured approach. The casual suitor who tries to sweep you off your feet with empty promises gets swiftly swept out the door.

You're likely to find romance while plotting your success. A lover with similar work interests makes a supportive companion. Your desire for material abundance leads you to a mate who enhances your life and offers practical support. A solid, confident lover contributes to your plan to enrich your personal empire.

In the comfort of hearth and home your tender passions erupt with playful abandon. Regular erotic massage renews your bond and connects you to your lusty physicality. Your bedroom reflects your affinity for simple, classic style—warm lighting and finely woven fabrics evoke an atmosphere of traditional charm.

With Your **LIBRA** Zodiac Sign

You may have extravagant tastes in some areas, but frivolous flings hold no appeal for you. Shrewd in life and love, you have the patience to wait for a loyal lover who fits into your master plan. You can feel pressured to achieve worldly success before merging lives in a committed bond.

You're an enigmatic study in contrasts—you may be lively in intimate company, but clam up around strangers. You can be cuddly and affectionate at times and mysteriously secretive at other times—a trusting partner won't take your cold shoulder personally. Part of your appeal may be that you defy easy definition.

Like a fine wine, your earthy sensuality grows richer and more layered over time. The lover who strokes your ego finds ample rewards—when emotionally secure, your appetite for sexual pleasure increases. You eschew gadgets and frilly bedclothes for simple but tasteful expressions of your love.

With Your **SCORPIO** Zodiac Sign

You're a contemplative loner who takes time before settling into a committed bond. Intensely loyal to a chosen few, you don't waste time on superficial relationships. For you, success and power are aphrodisiacs—you are drawn to a talented mate who can further your lofty ambitions.

Your wry humor and penetrating gaze can intimidate even the most courageous suitors. Others can see from the start that you won't be dominated in any way. You call the shots, and the right lover knows when to go with the flow. Initially you may look for compatibility in a mate over sexual chemistry.

The slow-moving, patient lover eases you into moments of relaxed sensuality—you don't like to be rushed into an ecstatic embrace. Sweet talk can draw out your hidden cuddliness and prime you for erotic play. In a stable bond, your appetite for earthy pleasure grows to a lustily insatiable hunger.

▶ READ ABOUT YOUR SEXUAL COMPATIBILITY *on p. 802*   ▶ DISCOVER YOUR CELEBRITY MARS TWINS *on p. 770*

Your Mars in Capricorn

Although you may seem cool and controlled on the outside, those who know you intimately know you have a randy side and a natural appreciation for the physical part of love. It might take a while for you to get over your natural reserve, but once you warm up, you are anything but shy.

Endurance is likely to be your forté. You probably feel no need to rush things. Careful and methodical, you may follow a set of established steps in order to reach your goal. Inclined to stick with what you already know rather than exploring new territory, you handle all the basic moves with competence.

Your stamina is probably one of your strongest assets—your lover can depend on you to satisfy his or her needs. Even in your later years, you are likely to retain your lustiness—a younger partner may be amazed at your sexual prowess.

With Your SAGITTARIUS Zodiac Sign

You may be outwardly flirty on the dating scene, but you show calculated judgment before diving into an affair. Getting past your protective armor takes time, and the wise suitor plays it calm, cool, and collected. You're impressed by a confident lover with a healthy appetite for erotic pleasure.

A courtship may begin with a series of casual, friendly chats over dinner. An easy rapport draws out your playful humor and far-reaching interests. Your enthusiasm for initiating spontaneous pleasure is soon revealed. Once smitten, your libido stands at the ready—the slightest provocation can ignite an evening of seduction.

Your quietly passionate approach to sexual desire begins as a spark and quickly grows to a raging wildfire. An impulsive, joyful quickie can bring much needed lightness to the work day. You take pride in your sexual prowess—after lovemaking, you enjoy reaping the rich, loving rewards of a grateful lover.

With Your CAPRICORN Zodiac Sign

Your cautious persona can resemble a fortress, cozy on the inside but formidable to outsiders. You bring shrewd caution and discernment to romance and might look for tangible reasons to pursue a love interest. With feet firmly rooted on the ground, you're looking for a faithful lover with a quiet confidence.

Spending time outdoors with your beloved draws out your wildly amorous nature. Cultivating a comfortable, sensual atmosphere at home gives you the space to relax. Tender hugs and soulful looks let your lover know you care. Your seduction style is subtle but powerful—your intimacy builds slowly through shared experience.

When you let down your guard, you can be quite loving and passionate. Erotic massage energizes all the cells in your highly sensitive body. Your lusty appetite for pleasure and physical stamina grow more active as you get older. Lovemaking can communicate the love you can't express in words.

With Your AQUARIUS Zodiac Sign

A cool reserve and calculated moves may best describe your approach to romance. You rarely surrender to chaotic emotion and are not likely to make wild pronouncements of love. You hide any shyness in social situations with your quirky wit—you are proud and ambitious, often making romantic alliances that bolster your career.

While admirers are many, you may find it challenging to reveal yourself intimately. A patient suitor builds your trust slowly through low-key experiences. Sharing interests, such as collecting antiques or gardening, can lead to happily productive times. You can be quietly persistent in forming solid bonds.

Home is where you begin to unwind, and your deeper sensuality emerges. A loving massage wakes up your formidable passion. Your tendency to dominate extends to the bedroom where you initiate moments of lusty amour. Boldly confident in your sexual prowess, you don't mind a little rough-and-tumble lovemaking.

With Your PISCES Zodiac Sign

Initially, you may observe a love interest with the cool eye of a practical realist. You wonder if you are compatible, and if you could share a stable life together. You're drawn to ambitious, confident suitors—once smitten, you can indulge your romantic nature with dreamy imaginings and sentimental gift giving.

You may be the strong, silent type in a courtship—the ideal suitor knows when to offer subtle, sincere affection. Initially, you prefer quiet admiration from your beloved to over-the-top, gushing sentiment. Your lusty passion may not be on display, but it can be a steady, enduring flame that never flickers out.

In private, your cuddly warmth creates many moments of treasured intimacy. Your libido may need a little coaxing after a workday, but once ignited, has stamina to burn. Music and candles create a classy atmosphere for refined lovemaking. Foreplay of slow, erotic massage draws out your earthy sensuality.

▶ READ ABOUT YOUR SEXUAL COMPATIBILITY *on p. 802*　▶ DISCOVER YOUR CELEBRITY MARS TWINS *on p. 770*

Your Mars in Aquarius

Anything new, different, or unusual intrigues you—especially when it comes to sex. Your open-minded, unconventional nature could lead you to explore all sorts of erotic pleasures, and you might be most interested in practices that are a bit way out. You like to experiment and can be quite an inventive lover.

Easily bored, you need lots of excitement and change. Perhaps you've had your share of lovers and believe that variety is the spice of life. Independence is important to you, but you can be faithful to a mate, as long as that person offers you plenty of versatility, freedom, and stimulation.

You tend to intellectualize about sex and probably aren't very passionate or affectionate. With your fascination with technology, you might enjoy sex toys and gadgets. For you sex is an adventure, and as soon as one thrill is over, you're ready to move on to the next.

754

With Your ARIES Zodiac Sign

You value your personal freedom above all and may not always like the binds implied by a sexual union. Ironically, this slippery, out-of-reach quality makes you a magnet for many potential lovers. You enjoy variety in the bedroom—a free-spirited, uninhibited mate puts the twinkle in your eye and the fire in your libido.

A vibrant intellectual rapport with your lover begins to unlock your elusive, detached sensuality. Once intrigued, you come on strong, shooting rapid-fire mental volleys—the ideal mate rises to the challenge of your cerebral foreplay. Your lusty humor cracks open the serious moments with the lubrication of laughter.

Your sexual imagination is powerful, if not always fully accessible—the right mate makes your mental fantasies come true. An eclectic lover with a chameleon-like nature could bring you the variety you crave. You enjoy exploring the very latest with your partner in everything from entertainment to sensual enhancements.

With Your TAURUS Zodiac Sign

A dazzling mind starts the seduction and physical attraction seals the deal. You are energized in the company of a sparkling wit—when combined with a healthy sexual appetite, your temperature rises. Keeping things light and friendly in the beginning allows you to set a comfortable pace.

If you are emotionally elusive at first, your physical warmth always shines through. Preparing a meal with your lover brings savory smells and the chance for a few seductive kisses. You love to experiment, both in the kitchen and the bedroom. Using sweet treats to adorn the body creates a sensual feast.

Using your magnetic voice to seduce your lover gets the juices flowing. Once lured into a sensual bond, your desires have a playfulness that can be gratified by all forms of erotic touch. You are a nimble explorer of the physical terrain but always eager to climb new peaks of ecstasy.

With Your GEMINI Zodiac Sign

The ideal lover brings you alive from the inside, and mental challenges are sure to put the shine in your eyes. Your endless curiosity gives you an engaging personality—the right lover shares your passion for lively, animated discussion. You rarely run out of fascinating topics to share with a responsive lover.

Taking time to relax with your mate opens the door to sensual pleasure. Erotic massage turns the focus on the body, giving your restless mind a mini vacation. Sensual enhancements bring variety to the bedroom—sexy toys and suggestive attire add spice to your already wildly creative lovemaking.

You thrive with plenty of room to move—you don't respond well to demands. Shared moments of solitude such as reading in bed satisfy your need for mental freedom. You move swiftly from passionate fervor to detached aloofness—the right lover accepts your changeable nature and goes with the flow.

With Your CANCER Zodiac Sign

The suitor who engages your imaginative mind has one foot in the door. From the arts to current politics you shine when exchanging ideas with others. Add a dash of humanitarian compassion, and you're hooked—electric conversation is an entry point, but it takes a kind heart to make it far with you.

Lively talk is peppered with humor in your love affairs. The ideal suitor laughs at the absurdity of life—telling jokes and funny stories enlivens your spirits. The fun extends to the bedroom, where you are playfully innovative. In a loving bond, you make room for the unexpected in your sex life.

Your bright mind conjures new approaches so that each time is fresh and spontaneous. Your light sensuality eventually deepens to reveal great emotional depth. Sharing tea and sympathy creates an atmosphere of mutual support. What remains unspoken finds expression in the private moments of lovemaking.

▶ READ ABOUT YOUR SEXUAL COMPATIBILITY on p. 802   ▶ DISCOVER YOUR CELEBRITY MARS TWINS on p. 770

Your Mars in Aquarius

Anything new, different, or unusual intrigues you—especially when it comes to sex. Your open-minded, unconventional nature could lead you to explore all sorts of erotic pleasures, and you might be most interested in practices that are a bit way out. You like to experiment and can be quite an inventive lover.

Easily bored, you need lots of excitement and change. Perhaps you've had your share of lovers and believe that variety is the spice of life. Independence is important to you, but you can be faithful to a mate, as long as that person offers you plenty of versatility, freedom, and stimulation.

You tend to intellectualize about sex and probably aren't very passionate or affectionate. With your fascination with technology, you might enjoy sex toys and gadgets. For you sex is an adventure, and as soon as one thrill is over, you're ready to move on to the next.

With Your **LEO** Zodiac Sign

Your gregarious ways lure an eclectic mix of potential lovers to your side. Your sparkling wit and riveting stories hold others spellbound. For you the fire of desire is lit first in the mind—you are drawn to original thinkers and creative free spirits. Lively parties give you the chance to flirt and mingle with abandon.

Large gatherings and festive events become the stage for the elusive flames of passion to ignite. Finding a special someone among the crowd energizes you to pull out all the stops. You make dating a playful adventure—you enjoy discovering new hot spots or surprising your lover with extravagant gifts.

You're not one to muck around in emotional swamplands—you prefer a romance of friendly lightness. Your detached coolness toward fulfilling desires turns into a smoldering urgency with a sexy mate. Your infectious delight in erotic pleasure can evolve into loving fantasy in the bedroom.

With Your **VIRGO** Zodiac Sign

Your eyes may sparkle toward a potential lover with friendly interest, but the secrets of your heart may remain maddeningly elusive. You absorb new ideas with a ravenous hunger and find your first connections are of the mind. Deep down, you believe in true love and hold out for a lover to match your ideal.

Going to events that stir the intellect bring you closer to your lover. Running an errand together brings flirty fun while taking care of business. You need solitude to fill your creative well—the compatible mate admires your fierce independence. You make unexpected gestures that reveal your true devotion.

If you are aloof in public, you're simply waiting to show your affection in private. The witty lover who makes your head spin with new ideas diverts you from petty concerns. Your earthy libido responds to slow, sensuous foreplay moving into an evening of spontaneous lovemaking.

With Your **LIBRA** Zodiac Sign

The quirky loner at the party may intrigue you enough to initiate a flirtatious volley of probing questions. Your gregarious intellect reaches out to many, stimulated by each bright spot of mental rapport. Having a steady partner appeals to you, but initially you prefer a detached, sometimes platonic affair.

Your elusive coolness can often be misjudged as an uncaring stance—you simply need time before exposing your true feelings. Aggressive, unrefined suitors can cause you to put up a remote, impenetrable wall. The right lover begins as a friend, with the bond growing more intimate through shared experience.

Once you find a worthy love, you dive deep into sensual pleasures with the enthusiasm of a child. You're a generous lover with a trick or two up your sleeve. You merge spontaneous impulses with innovative dexterity during uninhibited lovemaking. Your lusty lover joins you in the liberating act of creative intimacy.

With Your **SCORPIO** Zodiac Sign

You enjoy bursting through the barriers of sexual propriety or stultifying routine and look for equally uninhibited lovers. While playing the field, you may enjoy the novelty of fly-by-night trysts and erotic experimentation. Lovers often begin as friends, but the intensity of your smoldering emotions can't lie dormant for long.

A cool detachment best describes your initial approach to romance—you may let a good thing slip away by insisting to everyone, including your beloved, that you are "just friends." The ideal lover doesn't mind being one of many interests and respects your ferocious independence—you simply can't be backed into a corner.

Once smitten, you cautiously delve into the deeper waters of intimacy. When your spontaneity finds roots in a trusting union, your red-hot libido keeps the fire stoked. Your unpredictable nature drives you to make provocative gestures. An impromptu quickie in the morning is nourishment for your day.

▶ READ ABOUT YOUR SEXUAL COMPATIBILITY *on p. 802*   ▶ DISCOVER YOUR CELEBRITY MARS TWINS *on p. 770*

Your Mars in Aquarius

Anything new, different, or unusual intrigues you—especially when it comes to sex. Your open-minded, unconventional nature could lead you to explore all sorts of erotic pleasures, and you might be most interested in practices that are a bit way out. You like to experiment and can be quite an inventive lover.

Easily bored, you need lots of excitement and change. Perhaps you've had your share of lovers and believe that variety is the spice of life. Independence is important to you, but you can be faithful to a mate, as long as that person offers you plenty of versatility, freedom, and stimulation.

You tend to intellectualize about sex and probably aren't very passionate or affectionate. With your fascination with technology, you might enjoy sex toys and gadgets. For you sex is an adventure, and as soon as one thrill is over, you're ready to move on to the next.

756

With Your **SAGITTARIUS** Zodiac Sign

Though you enjoy many friendly connections, you often approach love with a cool detachment. Verbal rapport can initially lure you into an amorous dalliance. The ideal lover makes no emotional demands and is playfully adventurous—you are caring, but even within a marriage, you rebel against the accepted norms of coupling.

Not particularly sentimental, you are drawn to original thinkers and unconventional people. You have the courage to follow your heart over the taboos of culture and race when choosing a mate. When discord enters a loving union, you often contribute a clear-eyed objectivity, as if looking down from a lofty plateau.

For you, the mere hint of sexual activity activates shivers of restless excitement. You enjoy wild love play that is spontaneous and whimsical. Sexy talk during lovemaking inspires you to greater heights of erotic pleasure. The roaming hands of your lover can light you up with electrified intensity.

With Your **CAPRICORN** Zodiac Sign

In life and love, you'd rather take the road less traveled. You prefer navigating the terrain of romance without a map, following your intuition and your spontaneous impulses. Though your open, friendly personality lures many interesting suitors, you are very particular about whom you get involved with.

Your inner reserve makes you an affable but often solitary person. You try to resist the messier entanglements that sexual union can bring, and you rebuff lovers who want to take control.

Spending time apart fills your well, giving you more to share upon your return, and you may surprise your lover by frequently escaping.

Your quicksilver mind leads to innovative, original moves in the bedroom, especially bold approaches, such as taking off your lover's clothes with graceful skill. Relaxed moments open you to more languid sensuality—your earthy, slumbering passions are privately revealed in the intimate darkness of the night.

With Your **AQUARIUS** Zodiac Sign

Your excitable personality gives off sparks that inspire those around you. You can be a wily flirt, knowing just how to create an atmosphere of playful banter. With a network of eccentric friends, you tend to look for the good in people. You ease into romance by keeping it friendly and light.

Making people laugh comes easily to you, and you don't mind being the center of attention. You shine at lively parties, but you're also a loner often absorbed in creative work. You demand freedom to abruptly follow an inspiring idea, leaving lovers in the lurch. The right suitor supports your genius, while encouraging moments of intimacy.

Your originality gives you the courage to try anything, especially in the bedroom. Exotic potions and oils might intrigue you, and you're electrified by sexy talk. Hyper wildness leads to unexpected moves and sudden changes. You are a flexible, nimble lover with skillful ways to heighten pleasure.

With Your **PISCES** Zodiac Sign

Your head may seem blissfully in the clouds, but you absorb everything about those you meet. Your infinite curiosity leads you to reach out to many, sincerely wanting to understand them. By casting such a wide net, you are bound to form romantic ties. Yet you often remain enigmatic to those in your intimate sphere.

The ideal lover exudes a mysterious manner that merits further investigation. You admire original, creative thinkers who understand your need to cultivate your own solitary pursuits. A bond of two free spirits, with good times of light fun and engaging talk, may grow to deeper closeness.

Soothing your high-strung nerves opens you to a more relaxed sensuality. Holding hands while watching a film eases you into the intimacy of touch. A luxurious foot rub can electrify your entire body with pleasure. Your lover can expect the unexpected, as you surrender to the creative moment of lovemaking.

▶ READ ABOUT YOUR SEXUAL COMPATIBILITY *on p. 802*   ▶ DISCOVER YOUR CELEBRITY MARS TWINS *on p. 770*

Your Mars in Pisces

Your interests may lie more in the ethereal realm than the physical one, and you might not have a very strong libido. However, once your imagination is stimulated, your body is likely to follow.

Fantasy probably plays a large part in your sex life. You can use your innate creativity to devise all sorts of exotic pleasures—you might even see sex as an art form or an escape from your everyday routine. Deeply romantic, you enjoy candlelight, soft music, and beautiful surroundings for your amorous adventures. Taking a bath with a lover could be a favorite treat.

You tend to be idealistic about love and sex, and might seek perfection in your partner and in yourself. Unless you feel an emotional connection with your lover, you may not find sex very fulfilling. Perhaps you are seeking a spiritual union that connects you and your partner in body, mind, and soul.

With Your **ARIES** Zodiac Sign

Tenderhearted, you long to be swept off your feet and right into a loving embrace. There is an emotional depth to your sensuality that few can fathom. Your fiery sex drive is tempered by deep longings, resulting in an irresistibly sexy aura. You thrive in a sanctuary of earthly pleasure with your beloved.

Within a sheltered haven your fantasies find expression. Your imagination can transport you to exotic places and times without leaving the bedroom. Music, poetry, and candles all add dimension to the experience. Your genius is in merging the sacred and profane in an unforgettable way.

Your awareness of the invisible dance between you and your lover sets a tone of dignified reverence. You enjoy holding hands in the dark of the cinema or sitting together in a quaint café. Your warmth shows in your openly affectionate nature—frequent hugs keep you physically connected to your lover.

With Your **TAURUS** Zodiac Sign

You're at your friskiest in the safety of the familiar. Creating a comfy love nest with your mate sets the stage for erotic play to unfold. You know how to elevate relaxation to an art form—the ideal mate has an added calming effect. In a solidly built sanctuary your true depth emerges.

You revel in the carnival of the senses—the pleasure of food brings delicious moments with your lover. A masterful foot rub lets you come alive in mysterious ways.

Taking a bubble bath with your lover is the perfect prelude to delight. An evening of seduction ends with rapturously intuitive lovemaking.

You gravitate toward beauty in all its forms and have a wide-eyed wonder about the natural world. Exploring the outdoors with your lover brings you closer. Playfully sharing the absurdity of life puts the twinkle in your eye—laughing together brings the moments of intimacy you cherish.

With Your **GEMINI** Zodiac Sign

A vibrant social life connects you to an eclectic mix of people. You cast a wide net in the hopes that your ideal lover will be snared. Once smitten, you envelop your lover in an atmosphere of deeply felt sensuality. Together you create a world of private jokes and subtle innuendo that keeps you enchanted.

Unusual dates make you smile—a day strolling around a carnival or street fair provides endless amusement. Time spent near the ocean connects you to your deep desires—the intimacy of a shared bubble bath has a similar effect. Your libido rises in proportion to the quality of tender regard in your relationship.

The slightest flirtation triggers lusty images on your mental plane. Your openness increases the odds that the sexy scenarios dancing across your imagination may come true. You're bewitched by fantasy, both at the cinema or theater, and in the privacy of your bedroom.

With Your **CANCER** Zodiac Sign

Love is the ultimate turn-on for you, and the trappings of romance stir your erotic passion. The clever suitor appeals to your sentimental heart with thoughtful gifts and spontaneous surprises. An evening out may begin at an intimate café with dim lights and progress to the enchantment of the theater or movie house.

Falling for someone brings out your emotional sensuality. Once smitten, you begin to create a shared sanctuary with your beloved. The bedroom becomes a haven with soft lighting and sensuous bedding. You're gifted at selecting just the right mood music for an evening of amorous seduction.

More than a physical act, lovemaking for you involves mind, body, and soul. Your eyes are the portals through which you exchange infinite shades of feeling with an intuitive mate. Your vibrant imagination may lead you to playful fantasy, but you also enjoy the simple pleasures of a lingering hug or kiss.

▶ READ ABOUT YOUR SEXUAL COMPATIBILITY *on p. 802* ▶ DISCOVER YOUR CELEBRITY MARS TWINS *on p. 770*

Your Mars in Pisces

Your interests may lie more in the ethereal realm than the physical one, and you might not have a very strong libido. However, once your imagination is stimulated, your body is likely to follow.

Fantasy probably plays a large part in your sex life. You can use your innate creativity to devise all sorts of exotic pleasures—you might even see sex as an art form or an escape from your everyday routine. Deeply romantic, you enjoy candlelight, soft music, and beautiful surroundings for your amorous adventures. Taking a bath with a lover could be a favorite treat.

You tend to be idealistic about love and sex, and might seek perfection in your partner and in yourself. Unless you feel an emotional connection with your lover, you may not find sex very fulfilling. Perhaps you are seeking a spiritual union that connects you and your partner in body, mind, and soul.

With Your **LEO** Zodiac Sign

When your amorous daydreams meet lusty reality, sparks fly. Without trying you cast a seductive net to those around you. What may begin with a playful flirtation ripens into a deeply sensuous bond. The soft flames of your passion give an otherworldly quality to your affairs, making you hard to forget.

A night out with your beloved may start at an intimate café where the two of you can soak in the atmosphere. Your affinity for fantasy can lead you to the delights of the theater or movie house. When gentle regard forms, your libido responds in kind. A tender squeeze and knowing look can further the seduction.

You envelop your lover in a glow of warm affection—your wildly imaginative lovemaking resembles spontaneous play. Luxury in the bedroom may include fine fabrics and aromatic candles. Setting the stage with beautiful things provides the proper backdrop for your highly emotional sensuality.

With Your **VIRGO** Zodiac Sign

You may speak of serendipity and a divine hand guiding you toward your true love. Though your dreamy nature casts an invisible web of seduction, your feet are firmly on the ground. You desire to merge sexual pleasure with spiritual union—an uninhibited lover who celebrates the sacredness of the body piques your interest.

You enjoy a creatively romantic suitor—dazzling you with poetry or a compilation of hand-picked music sets the right mood for a grand courtship. You crave serenity and peaceful moments together, shying away from combative or aggressive lovers. Walking with your beloved near the ocean evokes your tidal sensuality.

The patient lover discovers ardor hidden beneath that mysterious air. Your body language in the bedroom is languid and dignified. When making love, you dive into deep intimacy. Though ready with imaginative moves, you often veer toward simple but passionate lovemaking.

With Your **LIBRA** Zodiac Sign

While dating, you dive into the intensity of a love affair, often losing interest when gritty reality or emotional conflict creeps in. Your dreamy, romantic nature propels you to find your "other half." Holding to fantastical ideals can sometimes keep you from enjoying the lovable humans that you so easily attract.

The surge of passion you feel in love's first glow may be directed more to love itself than the beloved. Over time your lofty, abstract notions of your mate settle into a more balanced view. You can bridge the gap with plenty of humor and by emphasizing the physical attraction between you.

Erotic pleasure evokes transcendent moments, and nothing delights you more than a foot massage—using scented oils engages all your senses. Comfort and luxury in the bedroom draw out your relaxed sensuality. You have a knack for intuiting your lover's desires and finding ways to satisfy them.

With Your **SCORPIO** Zodiac Sign

You have a dreamy demeanor and gentle approach to fulfilling desires, but an aggressive, rushed suitor soon sees the stinger hidden underneath your softness. A romantic, respectful mate appeals to your refined sensibility—you retreat into solitude behind a stoic wall when threatened by the harsher realities of the world.

A gruff partner melts quickly in your warm embrace—the ideal mate grows comfortable with moments of intense emotional nakedness. Your craving for togetherness can become stale and stifling to your beloved, if you neglect your own rich interests. You turn on the sexy charm in the sanctuary of a rich relationship.

Your soothing sensuality can have a relaxing effect on any lover. A chameleon-like flair for drama gives you a talent for role-playing or acting out fantasies. You have an almost telepathic sense of how to arouse your partner—once sparked, your tireless libido spurs you on to ecstatic lovemaking.

▶ **READ ABOUT YOUR SEXUAL COMPATIBILITY** on p. 802   ▶ **DISCOVER YOUR CELEBRITY MARS TWINS** on p. 770

Your Mars in Pisces

Your interests may lie more in the ethereal realm than the physical one, and you might not have a very strong libido. However, once your imagination is stimulated, your body is likely to follow.

Fantasy probably plays a large part in your sex life. You can use your innate creativity to devise all sorts of exotic pleasures—you might even see sex as an art form or an escape from your everyday routine. Deeply romantic, you enjoy candlelight, soft music, and beautiful surroundings for your amorous adventures. Taking a bath with a lover could be a favorite treat.

You tend to be idealistic about love and sex, and might seek perfection in your partner and in yourself. Unless you feel an emotional connection with your lover, you may not find sex very fulfilling. Perhaps you are seeking a spiritual union that connects you and your partner in body, mind, and soul.

With Your **SAGITTARIUS** Zodiac Sign

You form strong attachments and have a healthy lust for sexual pleasure. Your dreamy approach often creates a courtship of enchanted wonder. Being amazed at love's power is part of your charm, and the magic of romance is more than a cliché to you. You create a haven of togetherness that can be intoxicating.

The ideal mate understands your highly intuitive loving style. Exotic vacations and weekend getaways lift you out of the mundane environment and make for memorable intimacy. The deeply sensuous quality of your expressive nature goes well with the urgency of your physical desires.

You don't want to rush to the dessert before you've had a satisfying meal of tender foreplay. You appreciate the light strokes and soft kisses of a lover with a slow hand. Cuddling, along with a foot massage, can be tantalizing foreplay. Play and fantasy engage your imagination, as well as your body.

With Your **CAPRICORN** Zodiac Sign

If you are starry-eyed in romance, you can also be a stoic realist—the ideal lover knows how to charm both sides. You respond to the magic in love, such as serendipitous meetings. A romantic courtship stirs your libido—an enchanting evening may include listening to an outdoor symphony, or walking arm in arm.

Often you hide restless emotions behind a serene exterior. The ideal lover senses your infinite moods and intuits your desires. Your instincts make it hard to deceive you, at least not for long. The merging of your sensuous nature with your strong passions creates a ravenous sexual appetite.

You respond to the loving touch of a gentle lover. Taking time for slow foreplay opens all your senses to the ecstatic experience. Play and fantasy find expression in the comfort of your bedroom. Your lovemaking reveals your spontaneous creativity—you swing from moments of wild passion to tender calm.

With Your **AQUARIUS** Zodiac Sign

When intrigued by someone, you may quickly conjure vivid images of the two of you together. The idea of falling in love inspires your imagination, but you tend to play it cool at first. Your casual, friendly approach to courtship makes you seem nonchalant, hiding your deeper feelings.

You expect love to draw you into an adventure of discovery and enjoy unraveling the mysteries of a love interest. You have many friends and try to avoid becoming merged with a partner. The ideal lover accepts your faraway look as part of your quirky charm, as you often seem a million miles away.

In a loving bond, your daydreams can become fantasies played out in your bedroom. You respond sensually to gentle caresses and find special pleasure in a calming foot massage. Creating a dreamy atmosphere with oils and candles relaxes you into the moment, and sexy music adds to the fun.

With Your **PISCES** Zodiac Sign

Your approach to love can be as complex as nature itself, and as simple as that of a child. Your wide-eyed wonder and tender sensitivity can make close friends very protective of you. Yet you know how to enchant a suitor through subtle seduction—your changeable personality makes you an endlessly fascinating mystery.

You reach out to many with warm compassion and are shockproof and tolerant—the ideal mate admires these intangible qualities. Because you absorb nuances around you, you are easily overwhelmed, leading to crankiness and sharp words. Time for quiet reflection away from troubles refreshes your spirit.

The ebb and flow of your emotions finds expression in gentle, heart-felt lovemaking. You value tender moments of exquisite intimacy over routine, rushed expressions of physical desire. Long after the shy, furtive first time together, you expect to be searched for like a priceless treasure, different each time.

▶ READ ABOUT YOUR SEXUAL COMPATIBILITY *on p. 802*   ▶ DISCOVER YOUR CELEBRITY MARS TWINS *on p. 770*

YOUR CELEBRITY TWINS

Steffi Graf Miles Davis Ray Charles, Ursula Andress Tina Turner Aretha Franklin, born March 25, 1942 Muhammad Ali Erica Jong Isabel Allende Peter Frampton Annie Lennox Bjorn Borg Antonio

Steffi Graf Miles Davis Ray Charles, Ursula Andress Tina Turner Aretha Franklin born March 25, 1942 Muhammad Ali Erica Jong Isabel Allende Peter Frampton Annie Lennox Bjorn Borg Antonio Banderas Jon Bon Jovi Tom Cruise Johnny Depp Juliette Binoche Keanu Reeves Russell Crowe J.K. Rowling Nicole Kidman Celine Dion, Aries Halle Berry Cate Blanchett Steffi

Your Celebrity Twins

Jude Law, Capricorn of 1972

Marilyn Monroe, Gemini of 1926

Which celebrities share your Astrological Love Profile? In this section, find **Your Celebrity Twins**—find out about famous people who have the same **Romantic Side** as you, the same **Sex Drive** and **Relationship Karma**.

And if you wish to have more fun, write down the Astrological details of your favorite celebrity, and check in the **Compatibility** section, how you would get along in a relationship. Check out the celebrities gathered here by their Zodiac Signs as well as their Venus, Mars, and Saturn Signs!

INSTRUCTIONS

HERE'S HOW TO READ ABOUT YOUR CELEBRITY TWINS.

1 Find your Zodiac Sign Reading.

2 Look on to the right or left hand side of your Zodiac Sign for **Your Love Planets**. Under **Your Romantic Side**, you'll find Your Venus Sign. Under **Your Sex Drive**, your Mars Sign. Finally, under **Your Relationship Karma**, your Saturn Sign. Keep this personal Astrological Love Information handy.

3 In the next pages, discover the Celebrities who share your astrological profile—**Your Celebrity Twins.**

Your Celebrity Zodiac Twins on p. 762
Your Celebrity Venus Twins on p. 767
Your Celebrity Mars Twins on p. 770
Your Celebrity Saturn Twins on p. 773
Famous Couples Compatibility on p. 776

4 Have fun discovering the compatibility between you and your favorite celebrities! Check out their **Love Planets**. Go to the **Your Compatibility** section on page 780 to see how well you would get along in every aspect of a love relationship with them!

Example
If you were born on June 3, 1964, you are a Gemini with a Venus Sign in Cancer, a Mars Sign in Taurus, and a Saturn Sign in Pisces. Consulting this Celebrity Twins Section, you would find out that you have the same Zodiac Sign as Judy Garland, Marilyn Monroe, and more. You share the same Venus Sign with Clint Eastwood, Elizabeth Hurley, Keanu Reeves, and others. Salvador Dali, Mick Jagger, John F. Kennedy, and Madonna have their Mars Sign in Taurus—like you. Your Saturn Sign in Pisces is the same as Josephine Baker, Warren Beatty, and Alain Delon.

Your Celebrity Zodiac Twins

Aries

VICTORIA ADAMS, *born April 17, 1974*
FATTY ARBUCKLE, *born March 24, 1887*
ELLEN BARKIN, *born April 16, 1954*
CLYDE BARROW, *born March 24, 1909*
WARREN BEATTY, *born March 30, 1937*
JEAN-PAUL BELMONDO, *born April 9, 1933*
JACK BRABHAM, *born April 2, 1926*
DIRK BOGARDE, *born March 28, 1921*
MARLON BRANDO, *born April 3, 1924*
JEAN-CLAUDE BRIALY, *born March 30, 1933*
MAY BRITT, *born March 22, 1933*
JAMES CAAN, *born March 26, 1939*
MARIAH CAREY, *born March 27, 1970*
RICHARD CHAMBERLAIN, *born March 31, 1935*
CHARLIE CHAPLIN, *born April 16, 1889*
JULIE CHRISTIE, *born April 14, 1941*
JOAN CRAWFORD, *born March 23, 1904*
RUSSELL CROWE, *born April 7, 1964*
TIM CURRY, *born April 19, 1946*
BETTE DAVIS, *born April 5, 1908*
DORIS DAY, *born April 3, 1922*
CELINE DION, *born March 30, 1968*
MARGUERITE DURAS, *born April 4, 1914*
PETER FRAMPTON, *born April 20, 1950*
ARETHA FRANKLIN, *born March 25, 1942*
JAMES GARNER, *born April 7, 1928*
MARVIN GAYE, *born April 2, 1939*
BILLIE HOLIDAY, *born April 7, 1915*
LESLIE HOWARD, *born April 3, 1893*
OLIVIA HUSSEY, *born April 17, 1951*
ELTON JOHN, *born March 25, 1947*
SHIRLEY JONES, *born March 31, 1934*
ERICA JONG, *born March 26, 1942*
CHRISTOPHER LAMBERT, *born March 29, 1957*
ANDREW LLOYD WEBER, *born March 22, 1948*
ALI MACGRAW, *born April 1, 1938*
ELLE MACPHERSON, *born March 29, 1963*
EWAN MCGREGOR, *born March 31, 1971*
STEVE MCQUEEN, *born March 24, 1930*
TOSHIRO MIFUNE, *born April 1, 1920*
EDDIE MURPHY, *born April 3, 1961*
GARY OLDMAN, *born March 21, 1958*
GREGORY PECK, *born April 5, 1916*
ANTHONY PERKINS, *born April 4, 1932*
MARY PICKFORD, *born April 8, 1892*
DEBBIE REYNOLDS, *born April 1, 1932*
PAUL ROBESON, *born April 9, 1898*
DIANA ROSS, *born March 26, 1944*
OMAR SHARIF, *born April 10, 1932*
SIMONE SIGNORET, *born March 25, 1921*
BESSIE SMITH, *born April 15, 1894*
STEPHEN SONDHEIM, *born March 22, 1930*

CONSTANCE TALMADGE, *born April 19, 1898*
EMMA THOMPSON, *born April 15, 1959*
SPENCER TRACY, *born April 3, 1900*
SARAH VAUGHAN, *born March 27, 1924*
BILLY DEE WILLIAMS, *born April 6, 1937*
TENNESSEE WILLIAMS, *born March 26, 1911*
MICHAEL YORK, *born March 27, 1942*

Taurus

ANDRE AGASSI, *born April 29, 1970*
ARLETTY, *born May 14, 1898*
FRED ASTAIRE, *born May 10, 1899*
RICHARD BARTHELMESS, *born May 9, 1895*
ANNE BAXTER, *born May 7, 1923*
DAVID BECKHAM, *born May 2, 1975*
CATE BLANCHETT, *born May 14, 1969*
GABRIEL BYRNE, *born May 12, 1950*
CHER, *born May 20, 1946*
JILL CLAYBURGH, *born April 30, 1944*
GEORGE CLOONEY, *born May 6, 1961*
GARY COOPER, *born May 7, 1901*
JOSEPH COTTEN, *born May 15, 1905*
BING CROSBY, *born May 2, 1904*
PENELOPE CRUZ, *born April 28, 1974*
SALVADOR DALI, *born May 11, 1904*
DANIELLE DARRIEUX, *born May 1, 1917*
DANIEL DAY-LEWIS, *born April 29, 1957*
SANDRA DEE, *born April 23, 1944*
SANDY DENNIS, *born April 27, 1937*
BILLIE DOVE, *born May 14, 1903*
DAPHNE DU MAURIER, *born May 13, 1907*
SHEENA EASTON, *born April 27, 1959*
QUEEN ELIZABETH, *born April 21, 1926*
DUKE ELLINGTON, *born April 29, 1899*
ELLA FITZGERALD, *born April 25, 1917*
HENRY FONDA, *born May 16, 1905*
GLENN FORD, *born May 1, 1916*
MARTHA GRAHAM, *born May 11, 1894*
ALANA HAMILTON, *born May 18, 1945*
AUDREY HEPBURN, *born May 4, 1929*
KATHARINE HEPBURN, *born May 12, 1907*
ADOLF HITLER, *born April 20, 1889*
ENRIQUE IGLESIAS, *born May 8, 1975*
BIANCA JAGGER, *born May 2, 1945*
BILLY JOEL, *born May 9, 1949*
GRACE JONES, *born May 19, 1952*
KAY KENDALL, *born May 21, 1926*
JESSICA LANGE, *born April 20, 1949*
HAROLD LLOYD, *born April 20, 1893*
JOANNA LUMLEY, *born May 1, 1946*
SHIRLEY MACLAINE, *born April 24, 1934*

JAMES MASON, *born May 15, 1909*
JOAN MIRO, *born April 20, 1893*
MAE MURRAY, *born May 10, 1889*
VLADIMIR NABOKOV, *born April 22, 1899*
JACK NICHOLSON, *born April 22, 1937*
LAURENCE OLIVIER, *born May 22, 1907*
RYAN O'NEAL, *born April 20, 1941*
OONA O'NEILL, *born May 13, 1926*
MAUREEN O'SULLIVAN, *born May 17, 1911*
AL PACINO, *born April 25, 1940*
EVA PERON, *born May 7, 1919*
MICHELLE PFEIFFER, *born April 29, 1958*
MARIE-FRANCE PISIER, *born May 10, 1944*
TYRONE POWER, *born May 5, 1913*
SERGEI PROKOFIEV, *born April 23, 1891*
ANTHONY QUINN, *born April 21, 1915*
ROBERTO ROSSELLINI, *born May 8, 1906*
CORETTA SCOTT KING, *April 27, 1927*
DOROTHY SEBASTIAN, *born April 26, 1903*
DAVID O. SELZNICK, *born May 10, 1902*
SIMONE SIMON, *born April 23, 1910*
JAMES STEWART, *born May 20, 1908*
BARBRA STREISAND, *born April 24, 1942*
MARGARET SULLAVAN, *born May 16, 1911*
NORMA TALMADGE, *born May 6, 1893*
BARBARA TAYLOR BRADFORD, *born May 10, 1933*
ALICE B. TOKLAS, *born April 30, 1877*
RUDOLPH VALENTINO, *born May 6, 1895*
FATS WALLER, *born May 21, 1904*
ORSON WELLES, *born May 6, 1915*
DEBRA WINGER, *born May 16, 1955*
STEVIE WONDER, *born May 13, 1950*
PAULA YATES, *born April 24, 1960*
RENEE ZELLWEGER, *born April 25, 1969*

Gemini

PAULA ABDUL, *born June 19, 1962*
PIER ANGELI, *born June 19, 1932*
CHARLES AZNAVOUR, *born May 22, 1924*
CARROLL BAKER, *born May 28, 1931*
JOSEPHINE BAKER, *born June 3, 1906*
ANNETTE BENING, *born May 29, 1958*
MAEVE BINCHY, *born May 28, 1940*
BJORN BORG, *born June 6, 1956*
JOAN COLLINS, *born May 23, 1933*
TONY CURTIS, *born June 3, 1925*
VIC DAMONE, *born June 12, 1928*
JOHNNY DEPP, *born June 9, 1963*
KEIR DULLEA, *born May 30, 1936*
ISADORA DUNCAN, *born May 26, 1877*
CLINT EASTWOOD, *born May 31, 1930*
RUPERT EVERETT, *born May 29, 1959*

▶ FIND YOUR CELEBRITY VENUS TWINS ON PAGE 767 ▶ FIND YOUR CELEBRITY MARS TWINS ON PAGE 770

Joseph Fiennes
Gemini 1970

DOUGLAS FAIRBANKS, *born May 23, 1883*
JOSEPH FIENNES, *born May 27, 1970*
IAN FLEMING, *born May 28, 1908*
ERROL FLYNN, *born June 20, 1909*
MORGAN FREEMAN, *born June 1, 1937*
FEDERICO GARCIA LORCA, *born June 5, 1898*
JUDY GARLAND, *born June 10, 1922*
BOY GEORGE, *born June 14, 1961*
PAULETTE GODDARD, *born June 3, 1911*
BENNY GOODMAN, *born May 30, 1909*
STEFFI GRAF, *born June 14, 1969*
DASHIELL HAMMETT, *born May 27, 1894*
LILLIAN HELLMAN, *born June 20, 1905*
JUDY HOLLIDAY, *born June 21, 1921*
ELIZABETH HURLEY, *born June 10, 1965*
LOUIS JOURDAN, *born June 19, 1919*
JOHN F. KENNEDY, *born May 29, 1917*
NICOLE KIDMAN, *born June 21, 1967*
PEGGY LEE, *born May 26, 1920*
THOMAS MANN, *born June 6, 1875*
JEANETTE MACDONALD, *born June 18, 1903*
HERBERT MARSHALL, *born May 23, 1890*
DEAN MARTIN, *born June 17, 1917*
PAUL MCCARTNEY, *born June 18, 1942*
MALCOLM MCDOWELL, *born June 13, 1943*
IAN MCKELLEN, *born May 25, 1939*
KYLIE MINOGUE, *born May 28, 1968*
MARILYN MONROE, *born June 1, 1926*
LIAM NEESON, *born June 7, 1952*
VINCENT PEREZ, *born June 10, 1962*
PRINCE PHILIP, *born June 10, 1921*
NATALIE PORTMAN, *born June 9, 1981*
PRISCILLA PRESLEY, *born May 24, 1945*
PRINCE RAINIER, *born May 31, 1923*
LIONEL RICHIE, *born June 20, 1949*
ISABELLA ROSSELLINI, *born June 18, 1952*
JANE RUSSELL, *born June 21, 1921*
ROSALIND RUSSELL, *born June 4, 1907*
FRANCOISE SAGAN, *born June 21, 1935*
JEAN-PAUL SARTRE, *born June 21, 1905*
KRISTIN SCOTT-THOMAS, *born May 24, 1960*
BROOKE SHIELDS, *born May 31, 1965*
WALLIS SIMPSON, *born June 19, 1896*
IGOR STRAVINSKY, *born June 17, 1882*
IRVING THALBERG, *born May 30, 1899*
KATHLEEN TURNER, *born June 19, 1954*
ALIDA VALLI, *born May 31, 1921*
VENUS WILLIAMS, *born June 17, 1980*
WILLIAM BUTLER YEATS, *born June 13, 1865*

Cancer

ISABELLE ADJANI, *born June 27, 1955*
PAMELA ANDERSON, *born July 1, 1967*
JAMES BROLIN, *born July 18, 1940*
YUL BRYNNER, *born July 7, 1915*
PEARL BUCK, *born June 26, 1892*
GENEVIEVE BUJOLD, *born July 1, 1942*
DICK BUTTON, *born July 18, 1929*
JAMES CAGNEY, *born July 17, 1900*
ALEXANDER CALDER, *born July 22, 1898*
LESLIE CARON, *born July 1, 1931*
DIAHANN CARROLL, *born July 17, 1935*
JEAN COCTEAU, *born July 5, 1889*
BILLY CRUDUP, *born July 8, 1968*
TOM CRUISE, *born July 3, 1962*
OLIVIA DE HAVILLAND, *born July 1, 1916*
PRINCESS DIANA, *born July 1, 1961*
DUKE OF WINDSOR, *born June 23, 1894*
HARRISON FORD, *born July 13, 1942*
JOHN GILBERT, *born July 10, 1895*
TOM HANKS, *born July 9, 1956*
DEBBIE HARRY, *born July 1, 1945*
SUSAN HAYWARD, *born June 30, 1918*
ERNEST HEMINGWAY, *born July 21, 1899*
HERMAN HESSE, *born July 2, 1877*
DAVID HOCKNEY, *born July 9, 1937*
LENA HORNE, *born June 30, 1917*
FRIDA KAHLO, *born July 6, 1907*
MICHELLE KWAN, *born July 7, 1980*
JANET LEIGH, *born July 6, 1927*
GINA LOLLOBRIGIDA, *born July 4, 1927*
COURTNEY LOVE, *born July 9, 1964*
SUE LYON, *born July10, 1946*
LEA MASSARI, *born June 30, 1933*
VIVIEN MERCHANT, *born July 22, 1929*
ANNE MORROW, *born June 22, 1906*
CAMILLA PARKER BOWLES, *born July 17, 1947*
LUIGI PIRANDELLO, *born June 28, 1867*
ERICH MARIA REMARQUE, *born June 22, 1898*
GINGER ROGERS, *born July 16, 1911*
EVA MARIE SAINT, *born July 4, 1924*
JENNIFER SAUNDERS, *born July 6, 1958*
TERENCE STAMP, *born July 22, 1938*
BARBARA STANWYCK, *born July 16, 1907*
MERYL STREEP, *born June 22, 1949*
DONALD SUTHERLAND, *born July 17, 1934*
DOROTHY THOMPSON, *born July 9, 1893*
PRINCE WILLIAM, *born June 21, 1982*
NATALIE WOOD, *born July 20, 1938*
KRISTI YAMAGUCHI, *born July 12, 1971*

Leo

ISABEL ALLENDE, *born August 2, 1942*
PRINCESS ANNE, *born August 15, 1950*
LOUIS ARMSTRONG, *born August 4, 1901*
JAMES BALDWIN, *born August 2, 1924*
LUCILLE BALL, *born August 6, 1911*
ANTONIO BANDERAS, *born August 10, 1960*
COUNT BASIE, *born August 21, 1904*
TONY BENNETT, *born August 3, 1926*
HALLE BERRY, *born August 14, 1968*
ELEANOR BOARDMAN, *born August 19, 1898*
CAROLE BOUQUET, *born August 18, 1957*
CLARA BOW, *born July 29, 1905*
SARAH BRIGHTMAN, *born August 14, 1960*
JOHN CAZALE, *born August 12, 1935*
COCO CHANEL, *born August 19, 1883*
MAURICE CHEVALIER, *born August 12, 1888*
MAE CLARK, *born August 10, 1910*
BILL CLINTON, *born August 19, 1946*
ROBERT DE NIRO, *born August 17, 1943*
NATHALIE DELON, *born August 1, 1941*
AMELIA EARHART, *born July 24, 1897*
EDNA FERBER, *born August 15, 1885*
EDDIE FISHER, *born August 10, 1928*
ZELDA FITZGERALD, *born July 24, 1900*
ROBERT GRAVES, *born July 24, 1895*
MELANIE GRIFFITH, *born August 8, 1957*
ANN HARDING, *born August 7, 1901*
ALFRED HITCHCOCK, *born August 13, 1899*
DUSTIN HOFFMAN, *born August 8, 1937*
WHITNEY HOUSTON, *born August 9, 1963*
ALDOUS HUXLEY, *born July 26, 1894*
MICK JAGGER, *born July 26, 1943*
EMIL JANNINGS, *born July 23, 1884*
GENE KELLY, *born August 23, 1912*
JACQUELINE KENNEDY, *born July 28, 1929*
BARBARA LA MARR, *born July 28, 1896*
CAROLE LAURE, *born August 5, 1951*
MONICA LEWINSKY, *born July 23, 1973*
JENNIFER LOPEZ, *born July 24, 1970*
MYRNA LOY, *born August 2, 1905*
MADONNA, *born August 16, 1958*
PRINCESS MARGARET, *born August 21, 1930*
HELEN MIRREN, *born July 26, 1945*
ROBERT MITCHUM, *born August 6, 1917*
COLLEEN MOORE, *born August 19, 1900*
MAUREEN O'HARA, *born August 17, 1920*
PETER O'TOOLE, *born August 2, 1932*
SEAN PENN, *born August 17, 1960*
RIVER PHOENIX, *born August 23, 1970*
ROMAN POLANSKI, *born August 18, 1933*
WILLIAM POWELL, *born July 29, 1892*
QUEEN MOTHER, *born August 4, 1900*

▶ FIND YOUR CELEBRITY VENUS TWINS ON PAGE 767   ▶ FIND YOUR CELEBRITY MARS TWINS ON PAGE 770

Your Celebrity Zodiac Twins

ROBERT REDFORD, *born August 18, 1936*
J.K. ROWLING, *born July 31, 1965*
NORMA SHEARER, *born August 10, 1900*
SYLVIA SIDNEY, *born August 8, 1910*
JILL ST. JOHN, *born August 19, 1940*
JACQUELINE SUSANN, *born August 20, 1918*
MAE WEST, *born August 17, 1892*

Virgo

LAUREN BACALL, *born September 16, 1924*
BARBARA BACH, *born August 27, 1947*
ANNE BANCROFT, *born September 17, 1931*
INGRID BERGMAN, *born August 29, 1915*
LEONARD BERNSTEIN, *born August 25, 1918*
JACQUELINE BISSET, *born September 13, 1944*
JOAN BLONDELL, *born August 30, 1906*
CHARLES BOYER, *born August 28, 1897*
JOHN CAGE, *born September 5, 1912*
RAY CHARLES, *born September 23, 1930*
AGATHA CHRISTIE, *born September 15, 1890*
JAMES COBURN, *born August 31, 1928*
CLAUDETTE COLBERT, *born September 13, 1903*
SEAN CONNERY, *born August 25, 1930*
DOLORES COSTELLO, *born September 17, 1903*
ELVIS COSTELLO, *born August 25, 1954*
COLIN FIRTH, *born September 10, 1960*
ANTONIA FRASER, *born August 27, 1932*
STEPHEN FRY, *born August 24, 1957*
GRETA GARBO, *born September 18, 1905*
MITZI GAYNOR, *born September 4, 1931*
RICHARD GERE, *born August 31, 1949*
ALTHEA GIBSON, *born August 25, 1927*
HUGH GRANT, *born September 9, 1960*
LARRY HAGMAN, *born September 21, 1931*
SALMA HAYEK, *born September 2, 1966*
JEREMY IRONS, *born September 19, 1948*
JEAN-MICHEL JARRE, *born August 24, 1948*
TOMMY LEE JONES, *born September 15, 1946*
ANNA KARINA, *born September 22, 1940*
ALAN LADD, *born September 3, 1913*
PETER LAWFORD, *born September 7, 1923*
D.H. LAWRENCE, *born September 11, 1885*
MARGARET LOCKWOOD, *born September 15, 1916*
SOPHIA LOREN, *born September 20, 1934*
FRED MACMURRAY, *born August 30, 1908*
FREDRIC MARCH, *born August 31, 1897*
H.L. MENCKEN, *born September 12, 1880*
ARISTOTLE ONASSIS, *born September 21, 1906*
MICHAEL ONDAATJE, *born September 12, 1943*
JESSE OWENS, *born September 12, 1913*
DOROTHY PARKER, *born August 22, 1893*
MARK PHILLIPS, *born September 22, 1948*

ROSAMUNDE PILCHER, *born September 22, 1924*
JADA PINKETT, *born September 18, 1971*
KEANU REEVES, *born September 2, 1964*
FERNANDO REY, *born September 20, 1917*
RACHEL ROBERTS, *born September 20, 1927*
MICKEY ROURKE, *born September 16, 1950*
PETER SELLERS, *born September 8, 1925*
CHARLIE SHEEN, *born September 3, 1965*
RAQUEL WELCH, *born September 5, 1940*

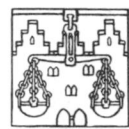

Libra

RENEE ADOREE, *born September 30, 1898*
PEDRO ALMODOVAR, *born September 25, 1951*
JULIE ANDREWS, *born October 1, 1935*
JEAN ARTHUR, *born October 17, 1900*
BRIGITTE BARDOT, *born September 28, 1934*
ERIC BENET, *born October 15, 1966*
CONSTANCE BENNET, *born October 22, 1905*
DIANE CILENTO, *born October 5, 1933*
MONTGOMERY CLIFT, *born October 17, 1920*
JACKIE COLLINS, *born October 4, 1939*
E.E. CUMMINGS, *born October 14, 1894*
MATT DAMON, *born October 8, 1970*
LINDA DARNELL, *born October 16, 1923*
CATHERINE DENEUVE, *born October 23, 1943*
MICHAEL DOUGLAS, *born September 25, 1944*
BRITT EKLAND, *born October 6, 1942*
T.S. ELIOT, *born September 26, 1888*
EMINEM, *born October 17, 1972*
SERGEI ESENIN, *born October 3, 1895*
WILLIAM FAULKNER, *born September 25, 1897*
PETER FINCH, *born September 28, 1916*
CARRIE FISHER, *born October 21, 1956*
F. SCOTT FITZGERALD, *born September 24, 1896*
JOAN FONTAINE, *born October 22, 1917*
GREER GARSON, *born September 29, 1904*
JANET GAYNOR, *born October 6, 1906*
BOB GELDOF, *born October 5, 1954*
GEORGE GERSHWIN, *born September 26, 1898*
DIZZY GILLESPIE, *born October 21, 1917*
ELINOR GLYN, *born October 17, 1864*
GRAHAM GREENE, *born October 2, 1904*
RICHARD HARRIS, *born October 1, 1930*
HELEN HAYES, *born October 10, 1900*
RITA HAYWORTH, *born October 17, 1918*
CHARLTON HESTON, *born October 4, 1924*
MARTINA HINGIS, *born September 30, 1980*
MIRIAM HOPKINS, *born October 18, 1902*
TREVOR HOWARD, *born September 29, 1913*
HOWARD HUGHES, *born September 24, 1905*
FANNIE HURST, *born October 18, 1889*
BUSTER KEATON, *born October 4, 1895*

DEBORAH KERR, *born September 30, 1921*
KLAUS KINSKI, *born October 18, 1926*
MARIE LAFORET, *born October 5, 1939*
TOMMY LEE, *born October 3, 1962*
JOHN LENNON, *born October 9, 1940*
CAROLE LOMBARD, *born October 6, 1908*
JOHN LONE, *born October 13, 1952*
MARCELLO MASTROIANNI, *born September 26, 1924*
LINDA MCCARTNEY, *born September 24, 1941*
THELONIOUS MONK, *born October 11, 1917*
YVES MONTAND, *born October 13, 1921*
ANTONIO MORENO, *born September 26, 1887*
MARTINA NAVRATILOVA, *born October 18, 1956*
OLIVIA NEWTON-JOHN, *born September 26, 1948*
EUGENE O'NEILL, *born October 16, 1888*
GWYNETH PALTROW, *born September 28, 1972*
BONNIE PARKER, *born October 1, 1910*
LUCIANO PAVAROTTI, *born October 12, 1935*
GEORGE PEPPARD, *born October 1, 1928*

Gwyneth Paltrow
Libra 1972

JUAN PERON, *born October 8, 1895*
WALTER PIDGEON, *born September 23, 1897*
HAROLD PINTER, *born October 10, 1930*
SOON-YI PREVIN, *born October 8, 1970*
JOHN PROFUMO, *born October 19, 1912*
CHRISTOPHER REEVE, *born September 25, 1952*
ANNE RICE, *born October 4, 1941*
IRENE RICH, *born October 13, 1891*
CLIFF RICHARD, *born October 14, 1940*
TIM ROBBINS, *born October 16, 1958*
MICKEY ROONEY, *born September 23, 1920*
ELEANOR ROOSEVELT, *born October 11, 1884*
SUSAN SARANDON, *born October 4, 1946*
ROMY SCHNEIDER, *born September 23, 1938*
LIZABETH SCOTT, *born September 29, 1922*
ALICIA SILVERSTONE, *born October 4, 1976*
PAUL SIMON, *born October 13, 1941*
WILL SMITH, *born September 25, 1968*
BRUCE SPRINGSTEEN, *born September 23, 1949*
DR. MARIE STOPES, *born October 15, 1880*
GORE VIDAL, *born October 3, 1925*
SIGOURNEY WEAVER, *born October 8, 1949*
CORNEL WILDE, *born October 13, 1915*
HELEN WILLS MOODY, *born October 6, 1905*

► FIND YOUR CELEBRITY VENUS TWINS ON PAGE 767   ► FIND YOUR CELEBRITY MARS TWINS ON PAGE 770

KATE WINSLET, *born October 5, 1975*
P.G. WODEHOUSE, *born October 15, 1881*
CATHERINE ZETA-JONES, *born September 25, 1969*

Scorpio

ROBERTO BENIGNI, *born October 27, 1952*
BJORK, *born November 21, 1965*
BETTY BRONSON, *born November 17, 1906*
LOUISE BROOKS, *born November 14, 1906*
RICHARD BURTON, *born November 10, 1925*
PRINCE CHARLES, *born November 14, 1948*
PETULA CLARK, *born November 15, 1932*
AARON COPLAND, *born November 14, 1900*
DOROTHY DANDRIDGE, *born November 9, 1923*
ALAIN DELON, *born November 8, 1935*
LEONADO DI CAPRIO, *born November 11, 1974*
JODIE FOSTER, *born November 19, 1962*
MARTHA GELLHORN, *born November 8, 1908*
ANDRE GIDE, *born November 22, 1869*
ANNIE GIRARDOT, *born October 25, 1931*
WHOOPI GOLDBERG, *born November 13, 1955*
LEE GRANT, *born October 31, 1927*
ETHAN HAWKE, *born November 6, 1970*
GOLDIE HAWN, *born November 21, 1945*
BOB HOSKINS, *born October 26, 1942*
ROCK HUDSON, *born November 17, 1925*
KAZUO ISHIGURO, *born November 8, 1954*
LEATRICE JOY, *born November 7, 1893*
GRACE KELLY, *born November 12, 1929*
VERONICA LAKE, *born November 14, 1919*
HEDY LAMARR, *born November 9, 1913*
BURT LANCASTER, *born November 2, 1913*
VIVIEN LEIGH, *born November 5, 1913*
VIRNA LISI, *born November 8, 1936*
MELINA MERCOURI, *born October 31, 1920*
DEMI MOORE, *born November 11, 1962*
GEORGIA O'KEEFFE, *born November 15, 1887*
PABLO PICASSO, *born October 25, 1881*
EZRA POUND, *born October 30, 1885*
CLAUDE RAINS, *born November 10, 1889*
STEPHEN REA, *born October 31, 1946*
JULIA ROBERTS, *born October 28, 1967*
HILARY RODHAM CLINTON, *born October 26, 1947*
ROY SCHEIDER, *born November 10, 1932*
JEAN SEBERG, *born November 13, 1938*
DYLAN THOMAS, *born October 27, 1914*
TED TURNER, *born November 19, 1938*
EVELYN WAUGH, *born October 28, 1903*

Sagittarius

CHRISTINA AGUILERA, *born December 18, 1980*
WOODY ALLEN, *born December 1, 1935*
KIM BASINGER, *born December 8, 1953*
PAUL BERN, *born December 3, 1889*
JANE BIRKIN, *born December 14, 1946*
HONOR BLACKMAN, *born December 12, 1927*
KENNETH BRANAGH, *born December 10, 1960*
HORST BUCHHOLZ, *born December 4, 1933*
MARIA CALLAS, *born December 3, 1923*
NOEL COWARD, *born December 1, 1899*
SAMMY DAVIS, JR., *born December 8, 1925*
FRANCES DEE, *born November 26, 1907*
JULIE DELPY, *born December 21, 1969*
JOE DI MAGGIO, *born November 25, 1914*
KIRK DOUGLAS, *born December 9, 1916*
IRENE DUNNE, *born December 20, 1898*
JANE FONDA, *born December 21, 1937*
GEORGE VI, *born December 14, 1895*
BETTY GRABLE, *born December 18, 1916*
GLORIA GRAHAME, *born November 28, 1923*
CORINNE GRIFFITH, *born November 24, 1894*
FLORENCE GRIFFITH JOYNER, *born December 21, 1959*
TOM HAYDEN, *born December 11, 1939*
VAN HEFLIN, *born December 13, 1910*
BILLY IDOL, *born November 30, 1955*
CELIA JOHNSON, *born December 18, 1908*
DON JOHNSON, *born December 15, 1949*
WASSILY KANDINSKY, *born December 4, 1866*
DOROTHY LAMOUR, *born December 10, 1914*
JOHN MALKOVICH, *born December 9, 1953*
JEAN MARAIS, *born December 11, 1913*
RICARDO MONTALBAN, *born November 25, 1920*
JULIANNE MOORE, *born December 3, 1960*
FRANCO NERO, *born November 23, 1941*
SINEAD O'CONNOR, *born December 8, 1966*
EDITH PIAF, *born December 19, 1915*
BRAD PITT, *born December 18, 1963*
CARLO PONTI, *born December 11, 1912*
RICHARD PRYOR, *born December 1, 1940*
LEE REMICK, *born December 14, 1935*
DIEGO RIVERA, *born December 13, 1886*
GILBERT ROLAND, *born December 11, 1905*
MONICA SELES, *born December 2, 1973*
FRANK SINATRA, *born December 12, 1915*
BRITNEY SPEARS, *born December 4, 1981*
BEN STILLER, *born November 30, 1965*
TINA TURNER, *born November 26, 1939*
LIV ULLMAN, *born December 16, 1939*
KATARINA WITT, *born December 3, 1965*

Capricorn

AALIYAH, *born January 16, 1979*
MUHAMMAD ALI, *born January 17, 1942*
DANA ANDREWS, *born January 1, 1909*
NILS ASTHER, *born January 17, 1897*
VILMA BANKY, *born January 9, 1898*
SHIRLEY BASSEY, *born January 8, 1937*
HUMPHREY BOGART, *born December 25, 1899*
DAVID BOWIE, *born January 8, 1947*
NICOLAS CAGE, *born January 7, 1964*
DYAN CANNON, *born January 4, 1937*
CAPUCINE, *born January 6, 1931*
PABLO CASALS, *born December 29, 1876*
RUTH CHATTERTON, *born December 24, 1893*
KEVIN COSTNER, *born January 18, 1955*
BEBE DANIELS, *born January 14, 1901*
MARION DAVIES, *born January 3, 1897*
SIMONE DE BEAUVOIR, *born January 9, 1908*
GERARD DEPARDIEU, *born December 27, 1948*
MARLENE DIETRICH, *born December 2, 1901*
FAYE DUNAWAY, *born January 14, 1941*
FEDERICO FELLINI, *born January 20, 1920*
JOSE FERRER, *born January 8, 1909*
RALPH FIENNES, *born December 22, 1962*
HEIDI FLEISS, *born December 30, 1965*
KAY FRANCIS, *born January 13, 1899*
AVA GARDNER, *born December 24, 1922*
MEL GIBSON, *born January 3, 1956*
CARY GRANT, *born January 18, 1904*
WILLIAM HAINES, *born January 2, 1900*
TIPPI HEDREN, *born January 19, 1935*
PAUL HENREID, *born January 10, 1908*
ANTHONY HOPKINS, *born December 31, 1937*
JAMES EARL JONES, *born January 17, 1931*
DANNY KAYE, *born January 18, 1913*
DIANE KEATON, *born January 5, 1946*
MARTIN LUTHER KING, JR., *born January 15, 1929*
EARTHA KITT, *born January 17, 1927*
JUDE LAW, *born December 29, 1972*
ANNIE LENNOX, *born December 25, 1954*
RICKY MARTIN, *born December 24, 1971*

Martin Luther King Jr.
Capricorn 1929

▶ FIND YOUR CELEBRITY VENUS TWINS ON PAGE 767   ▶ FIND YOUR CELEBRITY MARS TWINS ON PAGE 770

Your Celebrity Zodiac Twins

SARAH MILES, *born December 31, 1941*
HENRY MILLER, *born December 26, 1891*
POLA NEGRI, *born January 3, 1897*
JOE ORTON, *born January 1, 1933*
DOLLY PARTON, *born January 19, 1946*
ELVIS PRESLEY, *born January 8, 1935*
LUISE RAINER, *born January 12, 1910*
HANNA SCHYGULLA, *born December 25, 1943*
MOIRA SHEARER, *born January 17,1926*
ROD STEWART, *born January 10, 1945*
ALFRED STIEGLITZ, *born January 1, 1864*
ROD TAYLOR, *born January 11, 1930*
HELEN TWELVETREES, *born December 25, 1908*
JON VOIGHT, *born December 29, 1938*
DENZEL WASHINGTON, *born December 28, 1954*
EMILY WATSON, *born January 14, 1967*
RICHARD WIDMARK, *born December 26, 1914*
ANNA MAY WONG, *born January 13, 1905*
TIGER WOODS, *born December 30, 1975*
JANE WYMAN, *born January 4, 1914*
LORETTA YOUNG, *born January 6, 1913*

Aquarius

BJORN ANDRESEN, *born January 26, 1955*
JENNIFER ANISTON, *born February 11, 1969*
GEORGE BALANCHINE, *born January 22, 1904*
CHRISTIAN BALE, *born January 30, 1974*
JOHN BARRYMORE, *born February 14, 1882*
MARISA BERENSON, *born February 15, 1946*
EVA BRAUN, *born February 6, 1912*
BERTOLT BRECHT, *born February 10, 1898*
WILLIAM S. BURROUGHS, *born February 5, 1914*
COLETTE, *born January 28, 1873*
RONALD COLMAN, *born February 9, 1891*
GEENA DAVIS, *born January 21, 1956*
JAMES DEAN, *born February 8, 1931*
LAURA DERN, *born February 10, 1967*
MIA FARROW, *born February 9, 1945*
FARRAH FAWCETT, *born February 2, 1947*
CLARK GABLE, *born February 1, 1901*
STEPHANE GRAPELLI, *born January 26, 1908*
KATHRYN GRAYSON, *born February 9, 1922*
GERMAINE GREER, *born January 29, 1939*
RUTGER HAUER, *born January 23, 1944*
MICHAEL HUTCHENCE, *born January 22, 1960*
EDDIE IZZARD, *born February 7, 1962*
JAMES JOYCE, *born February 2, 1882*
MARTHE KELLER, *born January 28, 1945*
NASTASSJA KINSKI, *born January 24, 1961*
JACK LEMMON, *born February 8, 1925*
SINCLAIR LEWIS, *born February 7, 1885*
CHARLES LINDBERGH, *born February 4, 1902*

Vanessa Redgrave
Aquarius 1937

IDA LUPINO, *born February 4, 1914*
NORMAN MAILER, *born January 31, 1923*
BOB MARLEY, *born February 6, 1945*
LEE MARVIN, *born February 19, 1924*
JUNE MILLER, *born January 28, 1902*
CARMEN MIRANDA, *born February 9, 1909*
JEANNE MOREAU, *born January 23, 1928*
TONI MORRISON, *born February 18, 1931*
PAUL NEWMAN, *born January 26, 1925*
NICK NOLTE, *born February 8, 1941*
KIM NOVAK, *born February 13, 1933*
MERLE OBERON, *born February 19, 1911*
YOKO ONO, *born February 18, 1933*
CHARLOTTE RAMPLING, *born February 5, 1945*
VANESSA REDGRAVE, *born January 30, 1937*
DONNA REED, *born January 27, 1921*
KATHARINE ROSS, *born January 29, 1940*
FRANKLIN D. ROOSEVELT, *born January 30, 1882*
JANE SEYMOUR, *born February 15, 1951*
CYBILL SHEPARD, *born February 18, 1950*
JEAN SIMMONS, *born January 31, 1929*
GERTRUDE STEIN, *born February 3, 1874*
AMY TAN, *born February 19, 1952*
SHARON TATE, *born January 24, 1943*
JUSTIN TIMBERLAKE, *born January 31, 1981*
JOHN TRAVOLTA, *born February 18, 1954*
LANA TURNER, *born February 8, 1921*
ROGER VADIM, *born January 26, 1928*
CONRAD VEIDT, *born January 22, 1893*
ROBERT WAGNER, *born February 10, 1930*
VIRGINIA WOOLF, *born January 25, 1882*

Pisces

URSULA ANDRESS, *born March 19, 1936*
DESI ARNAZ, *born March 2, 1917*
DREW BARRYMORE, *born February 22, 1975*
HARRY BELAFONTE, *born March 1, 1927*
JOAN BENNETT, *born February 27, 1910*
JULIETTE BINOCHE, *born March 9, 1964*
JON BON JOVI, *born March 2, 1962*

GEORGE BRENT, *born March 15, 1904*
MICHAEL CAINE, *born March 14, 1933*
KAREN CARPENTER, *born March 2, 1950*
MADELEINE CARROLL, *born February 26, 1906*
CYD CHARISSE, *born March 8, 1921*
GLENN CLOSE, *born March 19, 1947*
KURT COBAIN, *born February 20, 1967*
NAT KING COLE, *born March 17, 1919*
BETTY COMPSON, *born March 19, 1897*
CINDY CRAWFORD, *born February 20, 1966*
BENICIO DEL TORO, *born February 19, 1967*
SERGE DIAGHILEV, *born March 19, 1872*
ROBERT DONAT, *born March 18, 1905*
JOHN GARFIELD, *born March 4, 1913*
JEAN HARLOW, *born March 3, 1911*
REX HARRISON, *born March 5, 1908*
HOLLY HUNTER, *born March 20, 1958*
ISABELLE HUPPERT, *born March 16, 1955*
WILLIAM HURT, *born March 20, 1950*
HARRY JAMES, *born March 15, 1916*
JENNIFER JONES, *born March 2, 1919*
CHRISTINE KEELER, *born February 22, 1942*
JACK KEROUAC, *born March 12, 1922*
QUEEN LATIFAH, *born March 18, 1970*
ROB LOWE, *born March 17, 1964*
DOROTHY MACKAILL, *born March 4, 1903*
ANNA MAGNANI, *born March 7, 1908*
GIULIETTA MASINA, *born February 22, 1920*
JESSIE MATTHEWS, *born March 11, 1907*
CARSON MCCULLERS, *born February 19, 1917*
PATRICK MCGOOHAN, *born March 19, 1928*
EDNA ST. VINCENT MILLAY, *born February 22, 1892*
GLENN MILLER, *born March 1, 1904*
LIZA MINNELLI, *born March 12, 1946*
MICHELE MORGAN, *born February 29, 1920*
CONRAD NAGEL, *born March 16, 1897*
ANAIS NIN, *born February 21, 1903*
DAVID NIVEN, *born March 1, 1909*
RUDOLF NUREYEV, *born March 17, 1938*
JENNIFER O'NEILL, *born February 20, 1948*
SIDNEY POITIER, *born February 20, 1927*
MAURICE RAVEL, *born March 7, 1875*
MIRANDA RICHARDSON, *born March 3, 1958*
ALAN RICKMAN, *born February 21, 1946*
VITA SACKVILLE-WEST, *born March 3, 1892*
DOMINIQUE SANDA, *born March 11, 1948*
ANN SHERIDAN, *born February 21, 1915*
DINAH SHORE, *born February 29, 1916*
MICKEY SPILLANE, *born March 8, 1918*
JOHN STEINBECK, *born February 27, 1902*
SHARON STONE, *born March 10, 1958*
ELIZABETH TAYLOR, *born February 27, 1932*
KURT WEILL, *born March 2, 1900*
BRUCE WILLIS, *born March 19, 1955*
PETER WOLF, *born March 7, 1946*
JOANNE WOODWARD, *born February 27, 1930*

▶ FIND YOUR CELEBRITY VENUS TWINS ON PAGE 767   ▶ FIND YOUR CELEBRITY MARS TWINS ON PAGE 770

Your Celebrity Venus Twins

Venus in Aries

JENNIFER ANISTON
FRED ASTAIRE
ANNE BAXTER
HARRY BELAFONTE
JEAN-PAUL
 BELMONDO
ANNETTE BENING
CATE BLANCHETT
JEAN-CLAUDE BRIALY
GABRIEL BYRNE
MARIAH CAREY
JULIE CHRISTIE
JILL CLAYBURGH
GEORGE CLOONEY
NAT KING COLE
JOSEPH COTTEN
BING CROSBY
DORIS DAY
SANDRA DEE
SANDY DENNIS
DAPHNE DU MAURIER
MARGUERITE DURAS
DUKE ELLINGTON
MIA FARROW
HENRY FONDA
MORGAN FREEMAN
JOHN GARFIELD
MARTHA GRAHAM
ALANA HAMILTON
DASHIELL HAMMETT
JEAN HARLOW
REX HARRISON
AUDREY HEPBURN
KATHARINE HEPBURN
LESLIE HOWARD
BIANCA JAGGER
JENNIFER JONES
KAY KENDALL
CHRISTOPHER
 LAMBERT
QUEEN LATIFAH
HAROLD LLOYD
ALI MACGRAW
DOROTHY MACKAILL
ANNA MAGNANI
BOB MARLEY
LEE MARVIN
STEVE MCQUEEN
EDNA ST. VINCENT
 MILLAY

LIZA MINNELLI
JOAN MIRO
MARILYN MONROE
EDDIE MURPHY
JACK NICHOLSON
RUDOLF NUREYEV
LAURENCE OLIVIER
JENNIFER O'NEILL
OONA O'NEILL
TYRONE POWER
PRISCILLA PRESLEY
CHARLOTTE
 RAMPLING
VITA SACKVILLE-WEST
DAVID O. SELZNICK
DINAH SHORE
STEPHEN SONDHEIM
ELIZABETH TAYLOR
LANA TURNER
ALIDA VALLI
KURT WEILL
ORSON WELLES
DEBRA WINGER
STEVIE WONDER
PAULA YATES
RENEE ZELLWEGER

Venus in Taurus

FATTY ARBUCKLE
CARROLL BAKER
ELLEN BARKIN
WARREN BEATTY
JULIETTE BINOCHE
DIRK BOGARDE
MARLON BRANDO
RICHARD
 CHAMBERLAIN
CHARLIE CHAPLIN
CYD CHARISSE
JEAN COCTEAU
GARY COOPER
BETTY COMPSON
TIM CURRY
SALVADOR DALI
DANIELLE DARRIEUX
DANIEL DAY-LEWIS
JOHNNY DEPP
PRINCESS DIANA
ROBERT DONAT

DUKE OF WINDSOR
DOUGLAS FAIRBANKS
ELLA FITZGERALD
JAMES GARNER
BOY GEORGE
STEFFI GRAF
DEBBIE HARRY
LILLIAN HELLMAN
ADOLF HITLER
JUDY HOLLIDAY
HARRY JAMES
BILLY JOEL
GRACE JONES
JESSICA LANGE
PEGGY LEE
ANDREW LLOYD
 WEBBER
ROB LOWE
THOMAS MANN
JAMES MASON
PAUL MCCARTNEY
IAN MCKELLEN
MAE MURRAY
CONRAD NAGEL
RYAN O'NEAL
PRINCE PHILIP
MARIE-FRANCE PISIER
PRINCE RAINIER
DEBBIE REYNOLDS
PAUL ROBESON
JANE RUSSELL
ROSALIND RUSSELL
DOMINIQUE SANDA
JEAN-PAUL SARTRE
KRISTIN SCOTT-
 THOMAS
SIMONE SIGNORET
CONSTANCE
 TALMADGE
NORMA TALMADGE
BARBARA TAYLOR
 BRADFORD
IRVING THALBERG
ALICE B. TOKLAS
SPENCER TRACY
SARAH VAUGHAN
FATS WALLER
PRINCE WILLIAM
BILLY DEE WILLIAMS
TENNESSEE WILLIAMS
WILLIAM BUTLER
 YEATS

Venus in Gemini

ISABELLE ADJANI
ANDRE AGASSI
ARLETTY
RICHARD
 BARTHELMESS
DAVID BECKHAM
CLARA BOW
JAMES BROLIN
YUL BRYNNER
GENEVIEVE BUJOLD
DICK BUTTON
LESLIE CARON
CHER
JOAN COLLINS
RUSSELL CROWE
TONY CURTIS
VIC DAMONE
BETTE DAVIS
KEIR DULLEA
ISADORA DUNCAN
AMELIA EARHART
SHEENA EASTON
GLENN FORD
HARRISON FORD
BENNY GOODMAN
TOM HANKS
SUSAN HAYWARD
DAVID HOCKNEY
OLIVIA HUSSEY
ENRIQUE IGLESIAS
FRIDA KAHLO
JACQUELINE KENNEDY
JOHN F. KENNEDY
MICHELLE KWAN
JANET LEIGH
COURTNEY LOVE
MYRNA LOY
JOANNA LUMLEY
HERBERT MARSHALL
VIVIEN MERCHANT
KYLIE MINOGUE
HELEN MIRREN
LIAM NEESON
AL PACINO
GREGORY PECK
ANTHONY PERKINS
EVA PERON
MARY PICKFORD
LUIGI PIRANDELLO
ISABELLA ROSSELLINI

ROBERTO ROSSELLINI
JENNIFER SAUNDERS
CORETTA SCOTT KING
DOROTHY SEBASTIAN
OMAR SHARIF
BROOKE SHIELDS
WALLIS SIMPSON
DONALD SUTHERLAND
RUDOLPH VALENTINO
VENUS WILLIAMS

Venus in Cancer

ISABEL ALLENDE
PIER ANGELI
PRINCESS ANNE
CHARLES AZNAVOUR
JOSEPHINE BAKER
JAMES BALDWIN
TONY BENNETT
MAEVE BINCHY
BJORN BORG
CHARLES BOYER
PEARL BUCK
JAMES CAGNEY
MAE CLARK
BILLY CRUDUP
OLIVIA DE HAVILLAND
BILLIE DOVE

CLINT EASTWOOD
RUPERT EVERETT
JOSEPH FIENNES
ZELDA FITZGERALD
IAN FLEMING
ERROL FLYNN
ANTONIA FRASER
FEDERICO GARCIA
 LORCA
JUDY GARLAND
MITZI GAYNOR
PAULETTE GODDARD
ERNEST HEMINGWAY
HERMAN HESSE
DUSTIN HOFFMAN
LENA HORNE
ELIZABETH HURLEY
ALDOUS HUXLEY
EMIL JANNINGS
JEAN-MICHEL JARRE
FRED MACMURRAY
FREDRIC MARCH
DEAN MARTIN
LEA MASSARI
COLLEEN MOORE
MAUREEN O'SULLIVAN
PETER O'TOOLE
CAMILLA PARKER
 BOWLES
VINCENT PEREZ
NATALIE PORTMAN
WILLIAM POWELL
THE QUEEN MOTHER
KEANU REEVES
LIONEL RICHIE

Kylie Minogue, Venus in Gemini

▶ FIND YOUR CELEBRITY ZODIAC TWINS ON PAGE 762   ▶ FIND YOUR CELEBRITY MARS TWINS ON PAGE 770

Your Celebrity Venus Twins

EVA MARIE SAINT
NORMA SHEARER
SYLVIA SIDNEY
BARBARA STANWYCK
JAMES STEWART
JILL ST. JOHN
IGOR STRAVINSKY
MERYL STREEP
MARGARET SULLAVAN
KATHLEEN TURNER
RAQUEL WELCH
MAE WEST
KRISTI YAMAGUCHI

ANNE MORROW
OLIVIA NEWTON-JOHN
JESSE OWENS
GWYNETH PALTROW
MARK PHILLIPS
WALTER PIDGEON
ROSAMUNDE PILCHER
ERICH MARIA
   REMARQUE
FRANCOISE SAGAN
JACQUELINE SUSANN
DOROTHY THOMPSON

Venus in Leo

PAULA ABDUL
PAMELA ANDERSON
LAUREN BACALL
LEONARD BERNSTEIN
COCO CHANEL
MAURICE CHEVALIER
TOM CRUISE
WILLIAM FAULKNER
PETER FINCH
EDDIE FISHER
GRETA GARBO
SALMA HAYEK
CHARLTON HESTON
MARTINA HINGIS
ALFRED HITCHCOCK
WHITNEY HOUSTON
HOWARD HUGHES
JEREMY IRONS
LOUIS JOURDAN
ANNA KARINA
NICOLE KIDMAN
ALAN LADD
BARBARA LA MARR
MONICA LEWINSKY
MARGARET
   LOCKWOOD
GINA LOLLOBRIGIDA
CAROLE LOMBARD
SUE LYON
JEANETTE MACDONALD
MADONNA
MARCELLO
   MASTROIANNI
MALCOLM MCDOWELL

Venus in Virgo

PEDRO ALMODOVAR
JULIE ANDREWS
LOUIS ARMSTRONG
JEAN ARTHUR
BARBARA BACH
LUCILLE BALL
ANNE BANCROFT
ANTONIO BANDERAS
BRIGITTE BARDOT
COUNT BASIE
INGRID BERGMAN
HALLE BERRY
CAROLE BOUQUET
SARAH BRIGHTMAN
JOHN CAGE
ALEXANDER CALDER
DIAHANN CARROLL
JOHN CAZALE
JAMES COBURN
DOLORES COSTELLO
ALAIN DELON
NATHALIE DELON
CATHERINE DENEUVE
ROBERT DE NIRO
EMINEM
SERGEI ESENIN
EDNA FERBER
CARRIE FISHER
ALTHEA GIBSON
JOHN GILBERT
LEE GRANT
ROBERT GRAVES
MELANIE GRIFFITH
ANN HARDING
HELEN HAYES
TREVOR HOWARD

FANNIE HURST
MICK JAGGER
BUSTER KEATON
GENE KELLY
DEBORAH KERR
CAROLE LAURE
PETER LAWFORD
JOHN LENNON
JENNIFER LOPEZ
SOPHIA LOREN
ROBERT MITCHUM
YVES MONTAND
ANTONIO MORENO
MARTINA
   NAVRATILOVA
MAUREEN O'HARA
MICHAEL ONDAATJE
BONNIE PARKER
LUCIANO PAVAROTTI
SEAN PENN
JUAN PERON
ROMAN POLANSKI
ROBERT REDFORD
CLIFF RICHARD
JULIA ROBERTS
RACHEL ROBERTS
GINGER ROGERS
ELEANOR ROOSEVELT
MICKEY ROURKE
J.K. ROWLING
TERENCE STAMP
EVELYN WAUGH
SIGOURNEY WEAVER
HELEN WILLS MOODY
KATE WINSLET
P.G. WODEHOUSE
NATALIE WOOD
CATHERINE ZETA-JONES

Venus in Libra

ERIC BENET
CONSTANCE BENNETT
JACQUELINE BISSET
JOAN BLONDELL
ELEANOR BOARDMAN
PRINCE CHARLES
PETULA CLARK
BILL CLINTON
JACKIE COLLINS
SEAN CONNERY

AARON COPLAND
ELVIS COSTELLO
E.E. CUMMINGS
MICHAEL DOUGLAS
BRITT EKLAND
T.S. ELIOT
COLIN FIRTH
F. SCOTT FITZGERALD
STEPHEN FRY
GREER GARSON
RICHARD GERE
MARTHA GELLHORN
HUGH GRANT
LARRY HAGMAN
RITA HAYWORTH
MIRIAM HOPKINS
BOB HOSKINS
GRACE KELLY
KLAUS KINSKI
MARIE LAFORET
VERONICA LAKE
HEDY LAMARR
BURT LANCASTER
D.H. LAWRENCE
VIVIEN LEIGH
PRINCESS MARGARET
H.L. MENCKEN
GEORGIA O'KEEFFE
DOROTHY PARKER
RIVER PHOENIX
PABLO PICASSO
JADA PINKETT

CLAUDE RAINS
CHRISTOPHER REEVE
IRENE RICH
TIM ROBBINS
MICKEY ROONEY
ROY SCHEIDER
PETER SELLERS
CHARLIE SHEEN
WILL SMITH
CORNEL WILDE

Venus in Scorpio

RENEE ADOREE
PAUL BERN
JANE BIRKIN
HONOR BLACKMAN
RAY CHARLES
AGATHA CHRISTIE
DIANE CILENTO
MONTGOMERY CLIFT
MATT DAMON
LINDA DARNELL
LEONARDO DI CAPRIO
KIRK DOUGLAS
RALPH FIENNES

JODIE FOSTER
AVA GARDNER
JANET GAYNOR
BOB GELDOF
GEORGE VI
GEORGE GERSHWIN
ANNIE GIRARDOT
ELINOR GLYN
BETTY GRABLE
GRAHAM GREENE
FLORENCE GRIFFITH
   JOYNER
RICHARD HARRIS
ETHAN HAWKE
GOLDIE HAWN
KAZUO ISHIGURO
CELIA JOHNSON
TOMMY LEE JONES
DOROTHY LAMOUR
TOMMY LEE
ANNIE LENNOX
JOHN LONE
LINDA MCCARTNEY
THELONIOUS MONK
DEMI MOORE
ARISTOTLE ONASSIS
EUGENE O'NEILL
GEORGE PEPPARD
HAROLD PINTER
SOON-YI PREVIN
JOHN PROFUMO
RICHARD PRYOR
LEE REMICK
FERNANDO REY
ANNE RICE
HILARY RODHAM
   CLINTON
SUSAN SARANDON
ROMY SCHNEIDER
HANNA SCHYGULLA
LIZABETH SCOTT
ALICIA SILVERSTONE
BRUCE SPRINGSTEEN
ALFRED STIEGLITZ
DR. MARIE STOPES
TED TURNER
GORE VIDAL
JON VOIGHT
DENZEL WASHINGTON
RICHARD WIDMARK
TIGER WOODS

Veronica Lake, Venus in Libra

► FIND YOUR CELEBRITY ZODIAC TWINS ON PAGE 762   ► FIND YOUR CELEBRITY MARS TWINS ON PAGE 770

Venus in Sagittarius

AALIYAH
CHRISTINA AGUILERA
BJORN ANDRESEN
DANA ANDREWS
GEORGE BALANCHINE
KIM BASINGER
ROBERTO BENIGNI
DAVID BOWIE
BETTY BRONSON
LOUISE BROOKS
CAPUCINE
PABLO CASALS
KEVIN COSTNER
NOEL COWARD
DOROTHY
  DANDRIDGE
BEBE DANIELS
FRANCES DEE
JULIE DELPY
GERARD DEPARDIEU
JOE DI MAGGIO
IRENE DUNNE
FARRAH FAWCETT
FEDERICO FELLINI
JOSE FERRER
JANE FONDA
JOAN FONTAINE
KAY FRANCIS
DIZZY GILLESPIE
WHOOPI GOLDBERG
GLORIA GRAHAME
CARY GRANT
GERMAINE GREER
CORINNE GRIFFITH
RUTGER HAUER
VAN HEFLIN
MICHAEL HUTCHENCE
JAMES EARL JONES
WASSILY KANDINSKY
JUDE LAW
VIRNA LISI
NORMAN MAILER
JOHN MALKOVICH
JEAN MARAIS
MELINA MERCOURI
JEANNE MOREAU
SINEAD O'CONNOR
JOE ORTON
EDITH PIAF
EZRA POUND

STEPHEN REA
DIEGO RIVERA
GILBERT ROLAND
JEAN SEBERG
PAUL SIMON
DYLAN THOMAS
TINA TURNER
HELEN TWELVETREES
ROGER VADIM

Venus in Capricorn

WOODY ALLEN
CHRISTIAN BALE
VILMA BANKY
BJORK
HUMPHREY BOGART
EVA BRAUN
HORST BUCHHOLZ
RICHARD BURTON
MARIA CALLAS
RONALD COLMAN
CINDY CRAWFORD
JAMES DEAN
FAYE DUNAWAY
CLARK GABLE
ANDRE GIDE
TOM HAYDEN
ANTHONY HOPKINS
ROCK HUDSON
BILLY IDOL
LEATRICE JOY
DIANE KEATON
SINCLAIR LEWIS
GIULIETTA MASINA
HENRY MILLER
RICARDO
  MONTALBAN
JULIANNE MOORE
TONI MORRISON
FRANCO NERO
PAUL NEWMAN
DOLLY PARTON
BRAD PITT
CARLO PONTI
ELVIS PRESLEY
MONICA SELES
ANN SHERIDAN
FRANK SINATRA
BRITNEY SPEARS
BEN STILLER

AMY TAN
ROD TAYLOR
JUSTIN TIMBERLAKE
LIV ULLMAN
CONRAD VEIDT
KATARINA WITT
VIRGINIA WOOLF
JANE WYMAN

Venus in Aquarius

MUHAMMAD ALI
DESI ARNAZ
JOHN BARRYMORE
JOAN BENNETT
MARISA BERENSON
JACK BRABHAM
KENNETH BRANAGH
GEORGE BRENT
BERTOLT BRECHT
WILLIAM S.
  BURROUGHS
JAMES CAAN
NICOLAS CAGE
DYAN CANNON
KAREN CARPENTER
RUTH CHATTERTON
GLENN CLOSE
MARION DAVIES
SAMMY DAVIS, JR.
SIMONE DE BEAUVOIR
SERGE DIAGHILEV
MARLENE DIETRICH
HEIDI FLEISS
ARETHA FRANKLIN
MEL GIBSON
KATHRYN GRAYSON
WILLIAM HAINES
TIPPI HEDREN
PAUL HENREID
HOLLY HUNTER
ISABELLE HUPPERT
WILLIAM HURT
EDDIE IZZARD
ELTON JOHN
DON JOHNSON
SHIRLEY JONES
ERICA JONG
JAMES JOYCE
CHRISTINE KEELER
EARTHA KITT
JACK LEMMON

IDA LUPINO
ELLE MACPHERSON
RICKY MARTIN
JESSIE MATTHEWS
CARSON MCCULLERS
SARAH MILES
GLENN MILLER
CARMEN MIRANDA
MICHELE MORGAN
POLA NEGRI
DAVID NIVEN
NICK NOLTE
KIM NOVAK
GARY OLDMAN
YOKO ONO
LUISE RAINER
MAURICE RAVEL
MIRANDA
  RICHARDSON
FRANKLIN D.
  ROOSEVELT
MOIRA SHEARER
CYBILL SHEPARD
MICKEY SPILLANE
GERTRUDE STEIN
JOHN STEINBECK
SHARON STONE
SHARON TATE
ROBERT WAGNER
EMILY WATSON
BRUCE WILLIS
MICHAEL YORK
LORETTA YOUNG

Venus in Pisces

VICTORIA ADAMS
URSULA ANDRESS
NILS ASTHER
CLYDE BARROW
DREW BARRYMORE
SHIRLEY BASSEY
JON BON JOVI
MAY BRITT
JAMES BROLIN
MICHAEL CAINE
MADELEINE CARROLL
KURT COBAIN
COLETTE
JOAN CRAWFORD
PENELOPE CRUZ
GEENA DAVIS

Britney Spears, Venus in Capricorn

BENICIO DEL TORO
LAURA DERN
CELINE DION
QUEEN ELIZABETH
PETER FRAMPTON
MARVIN GAYE
STEPHANE GRAPELLI
BILLIE HOLIDAY
DANNY KAYE
MARTHE KELLER
JACK KEROUAC
MARTIN LUTHER
  KING, JR.
NASTASSJA KINSKI
CHARLES LINDBERGH
SHIRLEY MACLAINE
PATRICK MCGOOHAN
EWAN MCGREGOR
TOSHIRO MIFUNE
JUNE MILLER
VLADIMIR NABOKOV

ANAIS NIN
MERLE OBERON
MICHELLE PFEIFFER
SIDNEY POITIER
SERGEI PROKOFIEV
ANTHONY QUINN
VANESSA REDGRAVE
DONNA REED
ALAN RICKMAN
DIANA ROSS
KATHARINE ROSS
JANE SEYMOUR
SIMONE SIMON
JEAN SIMMONS
BESSIE SMITH
ROD STEWART
BARBRA STREISAND
JOHN TRAVOLTA
PETER WOLF
ANNA MAY WONG
JOANNE WOODWARD

► FIND YOUR CELEBRITY ZODIAC TWINS ON PAGE 762   ► FIND YOUR CELEBRITY MARS TWINS ON PAGE 770

Your Celebrity Mars Twins

Mars in Aries

BJORN ANDRESEN
URSULA ANDRESS
FATTY ARBUCKLE
ARLETTY
GEORGE BRENT
MADELEINE CARROLL
CYD CHARISSE
NAT KING COLE
RONALD COLMAN
KEVIN COSTNER
JOAN CRAWFORD
RUSSELL CROWE
E.E. CUMMINGS
VIC DAMONE
DANIELLE DARRIEUX
NATHALIE DELON
SERGE DIAGHILEV
DUKE OF WINDSOR
CLINT EASTWOOD
DOUGLAS FAIRBANKS
ELLA FITZGERALD
FEDERICO GARCIA
    LORCA
PAULETTE GODDARD
STEPHANE GRAPELLI
CORINNE GRIFFITH
ALANA HAMILTON
ALDOUS HUXLEY
SHIRLEY JONES
JESSICA LANGE
JANET LEIGH
MONICA LEWINSKY
NORMAN MAILER
LINDA MCCARTNEY
MALCOLM MCDOWELL
SARAH MILES
GLENN MILLER
FRANCO NERO
PAUL NEWMAN
ANTHONY PERKINS
PRISCILLA PRESLEY
ANTHONY QUINN
LUISE RAINER
ANNE RICE
KATHARINE ROSS
JENNIFER SAUNDERS
KRISTIN SCOTT-
    THOMAS
MONICA SELES
OMAR SHARIF

WALLIS SIMPSON
PAUL SIMON
SIMONE SIGNORET
CONRAD VEIDT
ORSON WELLES

Mars in Taurus

PAULA ABDUL
MUHAMMAD ALI
PIER ANGELI
CHRISTIAN BALE
LUCILLE BALL
JOAN BENNETT
TONY BENNETT
DIRK BOGARDE
KENNETH BRANAGH
MARIAH CAREY
CHARLIE CHAPLIN
BING CROSBY
TOM CRUISE
SALVADOR DALI
BETTE DAVIS
ROBERT DE NIRO
CELINE DION
REX HARRISON
DEBBIE HARRY
ADOLF HITLER
ISABELLE HUPPERT
OLIVIA HUSSEY
MICK JAGGER

Madonna, Mars in Taurus

BILLY JOEL
CHRISTINE KEELER
JOHN F. KENNEDY
KLAUS KINSKI
EARTHA KITT
BARBARA LA MARR
QUEEN LATIFAH
JACK LEMMON
ALI MACGRAW
SHIRLEY MACLAINE
MADONNA
ANNA MAGNANI
RUDOLF NUREYEV
VINCENT PEREZ
EVA PERON
SIDNEY POITIER
GINGER ROGERS
DAVID O. SELZNICK
BRUCE WILLIS

Mars in Gemini

VICTORIA ADAMS
ANDRE AGASSI
NILS ASTHER
JOSEPHINE BAKER
ANTONIO BANDERAS
JOHN BARRYMORE
ANNE BAXTER
HARRY BELAFONTE
ELEANOR BOARDMAN

EVA BRAUN
SARAH BRIGHTMAN
YUL BRYNNER
JAMES CAGNEY
ALEXANDER CALDER
COCO CHANEL
JAMES COBURN
BETTY COMPSON
SEAN CONNERY
MARION DAVIES
DANIEL DAY-LEWIS
CATHERINE DENEUVE
KEIR DULLEA
JOSEPH FIENNES
COLIN FIRTH
EDDIE FISHER
F. SCOTT FITZGERALD
ZELDA FITZGERALD
ARETHA FRANKLIN
ELINOR GLYN
HUGH GRANT
RUTGER HAUER
LENA HORNE
LESLIE HOWARD
ERICA JONG
LOUIS JOURDAN
JAMES JOYCE
MARTIN LUTHER
    KING, JR.
CHRISTOPHER
    LAMBERT
ALAN LADD
HAROLD LLOYD
COURTNEY LOVE
PRINCESS MARGARET
DEAN MARTIN
KYLIE MINOGUE
JOAN MIRO
HELEN MIRREN
MAE MURRAY
CONRAD NAGEL
POLA NEGRI
MICHAEL ONDAATJE
PETER O'TOOLE
JESSE OWENS
AL PACINO
CAMILLA PARKER
    BOWLES
SEAN PENN
GEORGE PEPPARD
PRINCE PHILIP
NATALIE PORTMAN
SERGEI PROKOFIEV
QUEEN MOTHER
ERICH MARIA
    REMARQUE
LIONEL RICHIE

TIM ROBBINS
FRANKLIN D.
    ROOSEVELT
DIANA ROSS
ROBERTO ROSSELLINI
HANNA SCHYGULLA
JEAN SIMMONS
SIMONE SIMON
JAMES STEWART
MERYL STREEP
BARBRA STREISAND
NORMA TALMADGE
ALIDA VALLI
FATS WALLER
DEBRA WINGER
KATE WINSLET
TIGER WOODS
VIRGINIA WOOLF
MICHAEL YORK

Mars in Cancer

ISABELLE ADJANI
RENEE ADOREE
BARBARA BACH
RICHARD
    BARTHELMESS
MARISA BERENSON
INGRID BERGMAN
MAEVE BINCHY
WILLIAM S.
    BURROUGHS
RAY CHARLES
JILL CLAYBURGH
JEAN COCTEAU
BILLY CRUDUP
PENELOPE CRUZ
TONY CURTIS
TIM CURRY
SANDRA DEE
MARGUERITE DURAS
SHEENA EASTON
RUPERT EVERETT
EDNA FERBER
IAN FLEMING
ANTONIA FRASER
JAMES GARNER
MITZI GAYNOR
RICHARD GERE
GEORGE GERSHWIN
RICHARD HARRIS

AUDREY HEPBURN
JUDY HOLLIDAY
TREVOR HOWARD
DIANE KEATON
NASTASSJA KINSKI
HEDY LAMARR
BURT LANCASTER
CAROLE LAURE
D.H. LAWRENCE
TOMMY LEE
VIVIEN LEIGH
IDA LUPINO
JEAN MARAIS
LIZA MINNELLI
COLLEEN MOORE
JULIANNE MOORE
TONI MORRISON
ANNE MORROW
EDDIE MURPHY
DOLLY PARTON
PABLO PICASSO
HAROLD PINTER
MARIE-FRANCE PISIER
PRINCE RAINIER
KEANU REEVES
ALAN RICKMAN
JANE RUSSELL
CORETTA SCOTT KING
NORMA SHEARER
TERENCE STAMP
DONALD SUTHERLAND
EMMA THOMPSON
RUDOLPH VALENTINO
SIGOURNEY WEAVER
P.G. WODEHOUSE
PETER WOLF
NATALIE WOOD
JANE WYMAN

Mars in Leo

PEDRO ALMODOVAR
JEAN ARTHUR
FRED ASTAIRE
CARROLL BAKER
BRIGITTE BARDOT
COUNT BASIE
HALLE BERRY
JOAN BLONDELL
JAMES BROLIN
GENEVIEVE BUJOLD

► FIND YOUR CELEBRITY ZODIAC TWINS ON PAGE 762   ► FIND YOUR CELEBRITY VENUS TWINS ON PAGE 767

CAPUCINE
CHER
GEORGE CLOONEY
GARY COOPER
AARON COPLAND
JAMES DEAN
IRENE DUNNE
DUKE ELLINGTON
RALPH FIENNES
JOAN FONTAINE
GLENN FORD
HARRISON FORD
JODIE FOSTER
KAY FRANCIS
GREER GARSON
BOY GEORGE
JOHN GILBERT
DIZZY GILLESPIE
ROBERT GRAVES
GOLDIE HAWN
SALMA HAYEK
HELEN HAYES
MIRIAM HOPKINS
HARRY JAMES
JAMES EARL JONES
WASSILY KANDINSKY
ANDREW LLOYD
  WEBBER
GINA LOLLOBRIGIDA
JENNIFER LOPEZ
SOPHIA LOREN
JOANNA LUMLEY
ELLE MACPHERSON
PAUL MCCARTNEY
THELONIOUS MONK
DEMI MOORE
ANTONIO MORENO
VLADIMIR NABOKOV
JENNIFER O'NEILL
RIVER PHOENIX
GREGORY PECK
EDITH PIAF
EZRA POUND
ROBERT REDFORD
FERNANDO REY
HILARY RODHAM
  CLINTON
DOMINIQUE SANDA
ROY SCHEIDER
DINAH SHORE
FRANK SINATRA
BRUCE SPRINGSTEEN
JILL ST. JOHN
IGOR STRAVINSKY
IRVING THALBERG
DOROTHY THOMPSON
CORNEL WILDE

Mars in Virgo

ISABEL ALLENDE
JEAN-PAUL
  BELMONDO
ERIC BENET
CAROLE BOUQUET
JEAN-CLAUDE BRIALY
MAY BRITT
DICK BUTTON
GABRIEL BYRNE
MICHAEL CAINE
LESLIE CARON
MAE CLARK
PETULA CLARK
JOAN COLLINS
MATT DAMON
BEBE DANIELS
LINDA DARNELL
OLIVIA DE HAVILLAND
JOHNNY DEPP
PRINCESS DIANA
BILLIE DOVE
AMELIA EARHART
PETER FRAMPTON
STEPHEN FRY
CLARK GABLE
JANET GAYNOR
ALTHEA GIBSON
GRAHAM GREENE
MELANIE GRIFFITH
ERNEST HEMINGWAY
ELIZABETH HURLEY
FANNIE HURST
EMIL JANNINGS
DON JOHNSON
ANNA KARINA
GENE KELLY
JACQUELINE KENNEDY
DEBORAH KERR
MICHELLE KWAN
VERONICA LAKE
PETER LAWFORD
VIRNA LISI
CAROLE LOMBARD
SUE LYON
FRED MACMURRAY
LEA MASSARI
VIVIEN MERCHANT
YVES MONTAND
KIM NOVAK
GEORGIA O'KEEFFE

ARISTOTLE ONASSIS
YOKO ONO
JOE ORTON
GWYNETH PALTROW
DOROTHY PARKER
LUIGI PIRANDELLO
SOON-YI PREVIN
CLAUDE RAINS
IRENE RICH
ROMY SCHNEIDER
DOROTHY SEBASTIAN
PETER SELLERS
BROOKE SHIELDS
SYLVIA SIDNEY
WILL SMITH
BRITNEY SPEARS
MICKEY SPILLANE
BARBARA TAYLOR
  BRADFORD
RAQUEL WELCH
VENUS WILLIAMS
STEVIE WONDER

Mars in Libra

PAMELA ANDERSON
LOUIS ARMSTRONG
KIM BASINGER
PAUL BERN
JACQUELINE BISSET
CHARLES BOYER
BETTY BRONSON
LOUISE BROOKS
RICHARD BURTON
JOHN CAGE
MARIA CALLAS
DYAN CANNON
KAREN CARPENTER
DIAHANN CARROLL
RICHARD
  CHAMBERLAIN
BILL CLINTON
DOROTHY
  DANDRIDGE
LAURA DERN
MICHAEL DOUGLAS
BRITT EKLAND
EMINEM
SERGEI ESENIN
WILLIAM FAULKNER

FEDERICO FELLINI
MARTHA GELLHORN
WHOOPI GOLDBERG
GLORIA GRAHAME
ANN HARDING
ETHAN HAWKE
SUSAN HAYWARD
TIPPI HEDREN
ALFRED HITCHCOCK
BOB HOSKINS
WHITNEY HOUSTON
WILLIAM HURT
JEAN-MICHEL JARRE
TOMMY LEE JONES
LEATRICE JOY
BUSTER KEATON
NICOLE KIDMAN
PEGGY LEE
JOHN LENNON
JEANETTE
  MACDONALD
DOROTHY MACKAILL
JOHN MALKOVICH
FREDRIC MARCH
H.L. MENCKEN

ANAIS NIN
SINEAD O'CONNOR
BONNIE PARKER
JUAN PERON
WALTER PIDGEON
ROMAN POLANSKI
ELVIS PRESLEY
JOHN PROFUMO
CLIFF RICHARD
RACHEL ROBERTS
J.K. ROWLING
FRANCOISE SAGAN
JEAN SEBERG
CYBILL SHEPARD
ALICIA SILVERSTONE
DR. MARIE STOPES
TED TURNER
GORE VIDAL
EMILY WATSON
PRINCE WILLIAM
ANNA MAY WONG

Mars in Scorpio

DANA ANDREWS
JENNIFER ANISTON
PRINCESS ANNE
ANNE BANCROFT
SHIRLEY BASSEY
LEONARD BERNSTEIN
CLARA BOW
PABLO CASALS
JOHN CAZALE
RUTH CHATTERTON
MAURICE CHEVALIER
DIANE CILENTO
KURT COBAIN
CLAUDETTE COLBERT
COLETTE
DOLORES COSTELLO
JOSEPH COTTEN
SAMMY DAVIS, JR.
BENICIO DEL TORO
LEONARDO DI CAPRIO
JOSE FERRER
PETER FINCH
HENRY FONDA
MORGAN FREEMAN
MEL GIBSON
ANNIE GIRARDOT
LEE GRANT
KATHRYN GRAYSON
GERMAINE GREER
LARRY HAGMAN
VAN HEFLIN
LILLIAN HELLMAN
MARTINA HINGIS
DAVID HOCKNEY
DUSTIN HOFFMAN
ROCK HUDSON
BILLY IDOL
JEREMY IRONS
CELIA JOHNSON
GRACE JONES
GRACE KELLY
JUDE LAW
MARGARET
  LOCKWOOD
MYRNA LOY
GIULIETTA MASINA
TOSHIRO MIFUNE
HENRY MILLER
MICHELE MORGAN
LIAM NEESON

Robert Redford, Mars in Leo

▶ FIND YOUR CELEBRITY ZODIAC TWINS ON PAGE 762   ▶ FIND YOUR CELEBRITY VENUS TWINS ON PAGE 767

Your Celebrity Mars Twins

OLIVIA NEWTON-JOHN
MAUREEN O'HARA
MARK PHILLIPS
RICHARD PRYOR
STEPHEN REA
VANESSA REDGRAVE
ELEANOR ROOSEVELT
ISABELLA ROSSELLINI
MICKEY ROURKE
SUSAN SARANDON
JEAN-PAUL SARTRE
CHARLIE SHEEN
JACQUELINE SUSANN
AMY TAN
DYLAN THOMAS
HELEN TWELVETREES
JON VOIGHT

EDNA ST. VINCENT
  MILLAY
CARMEN MIRANDA
JACK NICHOLSON
NICK NOLTE
EUGENE O'NEILL
LUCIANO PAVAROTTI
CARLO PONTI
MAURICE RAVEL
CHRISTOPHER REEVE
MICKEY ROONEY
VITA SACKVILLE-WEST
MOIRA SHEARER
ALFRED STIEGLITZ
BEN STILLER
SHARON TATE
JOHN TRAVOLTA
EVELYN WAUGH
BILLY DEE WILLIAMS
HELEN WILLS MOODY
LORETTA YOUNG
RENEE ZELLWEGER

Mars in Sagittarius

JULIE ANDREWS
WARREN BEATTY
JANE BIRKIN
HONOR BLACKMAN
CATE BLANCHETT
PRINCE CHARLES
AGATHA CHRISTIE
MONTGOMERY CLIFT
NOEL COWARD
GEENA DAVIS
DORIS DAY
SANDY DENNIS
JOE DI MAGGIO
FAYE DUNAWAY
T.S. ELIOT
GRETA GARBO
JUDY GARLAND
GEORGE VI
ANDRE GIDE
STEFFI GRAF
FLORENCE GRIFFITH
  JOYNER
RITA HAYWORTH
HOWARD HUGHES
JACK KEROUAC
DOROTHY LAMOUR
HERBERT MARSHALL
LEE MARVIN
JESSIE MATTHEWS

Mars in Capricorn

AALIYAH
CHRISTINA AGUILERA
WOODY ALLEN
VILMA BANKY
ELLEN BARKIN
CLYDE BARROW
DREW BARRYMORE
ROBERTO BENIGNI
CONSTANCE BENNETT
BJORK
HUMPHREY BOGART
DAVID BOWIE
MARLON BRANDO
BERTOLT BRECHT
HORST BUCHHOLZ
JAMES CAAN
NICOLAS CAGE
ELVIS COSTELLO
ALAIN DELON
GERARD DEPARDIEU
MARLENE DIETRICH
KIRK DOUGLAS
DAPHNE DU MAURIER
MIA FARROW
MARVIN GAYE

BOB GELDOF
BETTY GRABLE
WILLIAM HAINES
JEAN HARLOW
KATHARINE HEPBURN
MICHAEL HUTCHENCE
FRIDA KAHLO
DANNY KAYE
MARTHE KELLER
JOHN LONE
THOMAS MANN
BOB MARLEY
EWAN MCGREGOR
MELINA MERCOURI
RICARDO MONTALBAN
JEANNE MOREAU
DAVID NIVEN
MERLE OBERON
LAURENCE OLIVIER
MARY PICKFORD
BRAD PITT
CHARLOTTE
  RAMPLING
MIRANDA
  RICHARDSON
DIEGO RIVERA
JULIA ROBERTS

ROSALIND RUSSELL
LIZABETH SCOTT
BARBARA STANWYCK
ROD STEWART
SHARON STONE
ROD TAYLOR
ROGER VADIM
SARAH VAUGHAN
RICHARD WIDMARK
KATARINA WITT
CATHERINE ZETA-
  JONES

Michael Hutchence, Mars in Capricorn

Mars in Aquarius

CHARLES AZNAVOUR
LAUREN BACALL
JON BON JOVI
JACK BRABHAM
PEARL BUCK

JULIE CHRISTIE
JACKIE COLLINS
FRANCES DEE
ISADORA DUNCAN
QUEEN ELIZABETH
FARRAH FAWCETT
HEIDI FLEISS
JOHN GARFIELD
CARY GRANT
CHARLTON HESTON
HOLLY HUNTER
KAZUO ISHIGURO
EDDIE IZZARD
MARIE LAFORET
SINCLAIR LEWIS
CHARLES LINDBERGH
JAMES MASON
MARCELLO
  MASTROIANNI
PATRICK MCGOOHAN
IAN MCKELLEN
JUNE MILLER
GARY OLDMAN
RYAN O'NEAL
ROSAMUNDE PILCHER
JADA PINKETT
WILLIAM POWELL
LEE REMICK
GILBERT ROLAND
ANN SHERIDAN
BESSIE SMITH
JUSTIN TIMBERLAKE
ALICE B. TOKLAS
ROBERT WAGNER
MAE WEST
TENNESSEE WILLIAMS
JOANNE WOODWARD
KRISTI YAMAGUCHI

Mars in Pisces

DESI ARNAZ
GEORGE BALANCHINE
JAMES BALDWIN
DAVID BECKHAM
ANNETTE BENING
JULIETTE BINOCHE
BJORN BORG
GLENN CLOSE
SIMONE DE BEAUVOIR

CINDY CRAWFORD
JULIE DELPY
CARRIE FISHER
ERROL FLYNN
JANE FONDA
AVA GARDNER
BENNY GOODMAN
MARTHA GRAHAM
DASHIELL HAMMETT
TOM HANKS
TOM HAYDEN
PAUL HENREID
HERMAN HESSE
BILLIE HOLIDAY
ANTHONY HOPKINS
ENRIQUE IGLESIAS
BIANCA JAGGER
ELTON JOHN
JENNIFER JONES
KAY KENDALL
ANNIE LENNOX
ROB LOWE
RICKY MARTIN
CARSON MCCULLERS
STEVE MCQUEEN
MARILYN MONROE
MARTINA
  NAVRATILOVA
OONA O'NEILL
MAUREEN O'SULLIVAN
MICHELLE PFEIFFER
TYRONE POWER
DONNA REED
DEBBIE REYNOLDS
PAUL ROBESON
EVA MARIE SAINT
JANE SEYMOUR
STEPHEN SONDHEIM
GERTRUDE STEIN
JOHN STEINBECK
MARGARET SULLAVAN
CONSTANCE
  TALMADGE
ELIZABETH TAYLOR
SPENCER TRACY
KATHLEEN TURNER
LANA TURNER
TINA TURNER
LIV ULLMAN
DENZEL WASHINGTON
KURT WEILL
PAULA YATES

▶ FIND YOUR CELEBRITY ZODIAC TWINS ON PAGE 762   ▶ FIND YOUR CELEBRITY VENUS TWINS ON PAGE 767

Your Celebrity Saturn Twins

Saturn in Aries

PAMELA ANDERSON
DANA ANDREWS
JENNIFER ANISTON
CLYDE BARROW
JOAN BENNETT
HALLE BERRY
JAMES CAAN
JACKIE COLLINS
BILLY CRUDUP
BETTE DAVIS
SANDY DENNIS
CELINE DION
JOSE FERRER
IAN FLEMING
ERROL FLYNN
MORGAN FREEMAN
MARVIN GAYE
MARTHA GELLHORN
BENNY GOODMAN
GERMAINE GREER
TOM HAYDEN
DAVID HOCKNEY
DUSTIN HOFFMAN
CELIA JOHNSON
NICOLE KIDMAN
MARIE LAFORET
CAROLE LOMBARD
ALI MACGRAW
FRED MACMURRAY
JAMES MASON
IAN MCKELLEN
H.L. MENCKEN
KYLIE MINOGUE
CARMEN MIRANDA
DAVID NIVEN
RUDOLF NUREYEV
LUISE RAINER
JULIA ROBERTS
KATHARINE ROSS
ROMY SCHNEIDER
JEAN SEBERG
SIMONE SIMON
WILL SMITH
TERENCE STAMP
JAMES STEWART
DR. MARIE STOPES
TED TURNER
TINA TURNER
HELEN TWELVETREES
LIV ULLMAN

JON VOIGHT
NATALIE WOOD
RENEE ZELLWEGER

Saturn in Taurus

ANDRE AGASSI
MUHAMMAD ALI
LUCILLE BALL
JOHN BARRYMORE
MAEVE BINCHY
CATE BLANCHETT
EVA BRAUN
JAMES BROLIN
MARIAH CAREY
JULIE CHRISTIE
MAE CLARK
MATT DAMON
NATHALIE DELON
JULIE DELPY
FAYE DUNAWAY
DOUGLAS FAIRBANKS
JOSEPH FIENNES
ARETHA FRANKLIN
JOHN GARFIELD
PAULETTE GODDARD
STEFFI GRAF
JEAN HARLOW
ETHAN HAWKE
VAN HEFLIN
ERICA JONG
JAMES JOYCE
ANNA KARINA
DANNY KAYE
CHRISTINE KEELER
QUEEN LATIFAH
JOHN LENNON
JENNIFER LOPEZ
LINDA MCCARTNEY
EWAN MCGREGOR
SARAH MILES
FRANCO NERO
NICK NOLTE
MERLE OBERON
RYAN O'NEAL
MAUREEN O'SULLIVAN
AL PACINO
BONNIE PARKER
RIVER PHOENIX
PABLO PICASSO
CARLO PONTI

SOON-YI PREVIN
RICHARD PRYOR
ANNE RICE
CLIFF RICHARD
GINGER ROGERS
FRANKLIN D.
    ROOSEVELT
SYLVIA SIDNEY
PAUL SIMON
JILL ST. JOHN
IGOR STRAVINSKY
BARBRA STREISAND
MARGARET SULLAVAN
RAQUEL WELCH
TENNESSEE WILLIAMS
P.G. WODEHOUSE
VIRGINIA WOOLF
MICHAEL YORK
LORETTA YOUNG
CATHERINE ZETA-
    JONES

Saturn in Gemini

VICTORIA ADAMS
ISABEL ALLENDE
CHRISTIAN BALE
GENEVIEVE BUJOLD
WILLIAM S.
    BURROUGHS
JOHN CAGE
COCO CHANEL
JILL CLAYBURGH
SANDRA DEE
CATHERINE DENEUVE
ROBERT DE NIRO
MARGUERITE DURAS
BRITT EKLAND
EMINEM
HARRISON FORD
RUTGER HAUER
BILLIE HOLIDAY
BOB HOSKINS
TREVOR HOWARD
MICK JAGGER
EMIL JANNINGS
GENE KELLY
ALAN LADD
DOROTHY LAMOUR
BURT LANCASTER
JUDE LAW

MONICA LEWINSKY
SINCLAIR LEWIS
IDA LUPINO
JEAN MARAIS
RICKY MARTIN
PAUL MCCARTNEY
MALCOLM MCDOWELL
MICHAEL ONDAATJE
JESSE OWENS
GWYNETH PALTROW
JADA PINKETT
MARIE-FRANCE PISIER
TYRONE POWER
JOHN PROFUMO
ANTHONY QUINN
ELEANOR ROOSEVELT
DIANA ROSS
HANNA SCHYGULLA
ANN SHERIDAN
SHARON TATE
ORSON WELLES
RICHARD WIDMARK
JANE WYMAN
KRISTI YAMAGUCHI

Saturn in Cancer

FATTY ARBUCKLE
DESI ARNAZ
DREW BARRYMORE
DAVID BECKHAM
MARISA BERENSON
INGRID BERGMAN
JACQUELINE BISSET
YUL BRYNNER
CHER
PENELOPE CRUZ
TIM CURRY
DANIELLE DARRIEUX
OLIVIA DE HAVILLAND
LEONARDO DI CAPRIO
JOE DI MAGGIO
KIRK DOUGLAS
MICHAEL DOUGLAS
MIA FARROW
EDNA FERBER
PETER FINCH
ELLA FITZGERALD
GLENN FORD
BETTY GRABLE
ALANA HAMILTON

DEBBIE HARRY
GOLDIE HAWN
ENRIQUE IGLESIAS
BIANCA JAGGER
HARRY JAMES
DIANE KEATON
MARTHE KELLER
JOHN F. KENNEDY
HEDY LAMARR
D.H. LAWRENCE
MARGARET LOCKWOOD
JOANNA LUMLEY
SUE LYON
BOB MARLEY
DEAN MARTIN
CARSON MCCULLERS
LIZA MINNELLI
HELEN MIRREN
DOLLY PARTON
GREGORY PECK
EDITH PIAF
EZRA POUND
PRISCILLA PRESLEY
CHARLOTTE RAMPLING
ALAN RICKMAN
DIEGO RIVERA
MONICA SELES
DINAH SHORE
FRANK SINATRA
ROD STEWART
DYLAN THOMAS
CORNEL WILDE
PETER WOLF

Saturn in Leo

BARBARA BACH
LEONARD BERNSTEIN
JANE BIRKIN
DAVID BOWIE
CHARLIE CHAPLIN
MAURICE CHEVALIER
BILL CLINTON
GLENN CLOSE
JEAN COCTEAU
NAT KING COLE
T.S. ELIOT
FARRAH FAWCETT
JOAN FONTAINE
DIZZY GILLESPIE
SUSAN HAYWARD
RITA HAYWORTH
ADOLF HITLER
LENA HORNE
JEAN-MICHEL JARRE
BILLY JOEL
ELTON JOHN
JENNIFER JONES
TOMMY LEE JONES
LOUIS JOURDAN
JESSICA LANGE

Drew Barrymore, Saturn in Gemini

▶ READ ABOUT YOUR RELATIONSHIP KARMA ON PAGE 825

Your Celebrity Saturn Twins

ANDREW LLOYD
    WEBBER
HERBERT MARSHALL
ROBERT MITCHUM
THELONIOUS MONK
ANTONIO MORENO
MAE MURRAY
GEORGIA O'KEEFFE
EUGENE O'NEILL
JENNIFER O'NEILL
CAMILLA PARKER
    BOWLES
EVA PERON
STEPHEN REA
FERNANDO REY
HILARY RODHAM
    CLINTON
DOMINIQUE SANDA
SUSAN SARANDON
ALICIA SILVERSTONE
MICKEY SPILLANE
JACQUELINE SUSANN
KATE WINSLET
TIGER WOODS

774

Saturn in Virgo

AALIYAH
PRINCESS ANNE
PAUL BERN
DIRK BOGARDE
PEARL BUCK
GABRIEL BYRNE
KAREN CARPENTER
CYD CHARISSE
PRINCE CHARLES
AGATHA CHRISTIE
MONTGOMERY CLIFT
RONALD COLMAN
GERARD DEPARDIEU
FEDERICO FELLINI
PETER FRAMPTON
RICHARD GERE
JUDY HOLLIDAY
FANNIE HURST
WILLIAM HURT
OLIVIA HUSSEY
JEREMY IRONS
DON JOHNSON
DEBORAH KERR
MICHELLE KWAN
VERONICA LAKE
CAROLE LAURE
PEGGY LEE
GIULIETTA MASINA
MELINA MERCOURI
TOSHIRO MIFUNE
EDNA ST. VINCENT
    MILLAY
HENRY MILLER
RICARDO MONTALBAN
MICHELE MORGAN
OLIVIA NEWTON-JOHN
MAUREEN O'HARA
PRINCE PHILIP
MARK PHILLIPS
MARY PICKFORD
WILLIAM POWELL
SERGEI PROKOFIEV
DONNA REED
IRENE RICH
LIONEL RICHIE
MICKEY ROONEY
MICKEY ROURKE
JANE RUSSELL
VITA SACKVILLE-WEST
CYBILL SHEPARD
SIMONE SIGNORET
BRUCE SPRINGSTEEN
MERYL STREEP
LANA TURNER
ALIDA VALLI
SIGOURNEY WEAVER
MAE WEST
VENUS WILLIAMS

Eva Marie Saint, Saturn in Libra

Saturn in Libra

CHRISTINA AGUILERA
PEDRO ALMODOVAR
CHARLES AZNAVOUR
JAMES BALDWIN
ANNE BAXTER
ROBERTO BENIGNI
MARIA CALLAS
RUTH CHATTERTON
DOROTHY
    DANDRIDGE
LINDA DARNELL
DORIS DAY
DUKE OF WINDSOR
AVA GARDNER
JUDY GARLAND
ELINOR GLYN
MARTHA GRAHAM
GLORIA GRAHAME
KATHRYN GRAYSON
DASHIELL HAMMETT
CHARLTON HESTON
MARTINA HINGIS
LESLIE HOWARD
ALDOUS HUXLEY
GRACE JONES
LEATRICE JOY
JACK KEROUAC
PETER LAWFORD
HAROLD LLOYD
JOHN LONE
NORMAN MAILER
JOAN MIRO
YVES MONTAND
LIAM NEESON
DOROTHY PARKER
NATALIE PORTMAN
PRINCE RAINIER
CHRISTOPHER REEVE
ISABELLA ROSSELLINI
EVA MARIE SAINT
LIZABETH SCOTT
JANE SEYMOUR
BESSIE SMITH
BRITNEY SPEARS
ALFRED STIEGLITZ
NORMA TALMADGE
AMY TAN
DOROTHY THOMPSON
JUSTIN TIMBERLAKE
CONRAD VEIDT
PRINCE WILLIAM
STEVIE WONDER
WILLIAM BUTLER
    YEATS

Saturn in Scorpio

ISABELLE ADJANI
BJORN ANDRESEN
LAUREN BACALL
ELLEN BARKIN
KIM BASINGER
RICHARD
    BARTHELMESS
TONY BENNETT
BJORN BORG
CHARLES BOYER
JACK BRABHAM
MARLON BRANDO
RICHARD BURTON
ELVIS COSTELLO
KEVIN COSTNER
TONY CURTIS
MARION DAVIES
SAMMY DAVIS, JR.
AMELIA EARHART
QUEEN ELIZABETH
SERGEI ESENIN
WILLIAM FAULKNER
F. SCOTT FITZGERALD
BOB GELDOF
GEORGE VI
MEL GIBSON
JOHN GILBERT
WHOOPI GOLDBERG
ROBERT GRAVES
CORINNE GRIFFITH
TOM HANKS
ROCK HUDSON
ISABELLE HUPPERT
BILLY IDOL
KAZUO ISHIGURO
WASSILY KANDINSKY
BUSTER KEATON
KAY KENDALL
KLAUS KINSKI
BARBARA LA MARR
JANET LEIGH
JACK LEMMON
ANNIE LENNOX
JOHN MALKOVICH
FREDRIC MARCH
LEE MARVIN
MARCELLO
    MASTROIANNI
MARILYN MONROE
POLA NEGRI
PAUL NEWMAN
OONA O'NEILL
JUAN PERON
WALTER PIDGEON
ROSAMUNDE PILCHER
LUIGI PIRANDELLO
PETER SELLERS
MOIRA SHEARER
WALLIS SIMPSON
JOHN TRAVOLTA
KATHLEEN TURNER
RUDOLPH VALENTINO
SARAH VAUGHAN
GORE VIDAL
DENZEL WASHINGTON
BRUCE WILLIS
DEBRA WINGER

Saturn in Sagittarius

RENEE ADOREE
ARLETTY
FRED ASTAIRE
VILMA BANKY
HARRY BELAFONTE
ANNETTE BENING
HONOR BLACKMAN
ELEANOR BOARDMAN
HUMPHREY BOGART
CAROLE BOUQUET
KENNETH BRANAGH
BERTOLT BRECHT
DICK BUTTON
ALEXANDER CALDER
JAMES COBURN
BETTY COMPSON
NOEL COWARD
VIC DAMONE
GEENA DAVIS
DANIEL DAY-LEWIS
IRENE DUNNE
DUKE ELLINGTON
CARRIE FISHER
EDDIE FISHER
ZELDA FITZGERALD
KAY FRANCIS
STEPHEN FRY
FEDERICO GARCIA
    LORCA
GEORGE GERSHWIN
ALTHEA GIBSON
ANDRE GIDE
LEE GRANT
MELANIE GRIFFITH
WILLIAM HAINES
HELEN HAYES
ERNEST HEMINGWAY
ALFRED HITCHCOCK
HOLLY HUNTER
GRACE KELLY
JACQUELINE
    KENNEDY

▶ READ ABOUT YOUR RELATIONSHIP KARMA ON PAGE 825

MARTIN LUTHER
  KING, JR.
EARTHA KITT
CHRISTOPHER
  LAMBERT
GINA LOLLOBRIGIDA
MADONNA
PATRICK MCGOOHAN
VIVIEN MERCHANT
COLLEEN MOORE
JEANNE MOREAU
VLADIMIR NABOKOV
CONRAD NAGEL
MARTINA
  NAVRATILOVA
GARY OLDMAN
GEORGE PEPPARD
MICHELLE PFEIFFER
SIDNEY POITIER
QUEEN MOTHER
ERICH MARIA
  REMARQUE
MIRANDA
  RICHARDSON
TIM ROBBINS
RACHEL ROBERTS
PAUL ROBESON
JENNIFER SAUNDERS
CORETTA SCOTT KING
NORMA SHEARER
JEAN SIMMONS
SHARON STONE
CONSTANCE
  TALMADGE
IRVING THALBERG
ROGER VADIM

Saturn in
Capricorn

LOUIS ARMSTRONG
JEAN ARTHUR
CARROLL BAKER
ANNE BANCROFT
ANTONIO BANDERAS
SARAH BRIGHTMAN
JAMES CAGNEY
CAPUCINE
LESLIE CARON
RAY CHARLES
PETULA CLARK
GEORGE CLOONEY

COLETTE
SEAN CONNERY
GARY COOPER
AARON COPLAND
BEBE DANIELS
JAMES DEAN
SERGE DIAGHILEV
PRINCESS DIANA
MARLENE DIETRICH
SHEENA EASTON
CLINT EASTWOOD
RUPERT EVERETT
COLIN FIRTH
ANTONIA FRASER
CLARK GABLE
JAMES GARNER
MITZI GAYNOR
BOY GEORGE
ANNIE GIRARDOT
HUGH GRANT
FLORENCE GRIFFITH
  JOYNER
LARRY HAGMAN
ANN HARDING
RICHARD HARRIS
AUDREY HEPBURN
MIRIAM HOPKINS
MICHAEL HUTCHENCE
JAMES EARL JONES
NASTASSJA KINSKI
CHARLES LINDBERGH
PRINCESS MARGARET
STEVE MCQUEEN
JUNE MILLER
JULIANNE MOORE
TONI MORRISON
EDDIE MURPHY
SEAN PENN
ANTHONY PERKINS
HAROLD PINTER
ROY SCHEIDER
KRISTIN SCOTT-
  THOMAS
DAVID O. SELZNICK
STEPHEN SONDHEIM
JOHN STEINBECK
ROD TAYLOR
EMMA THOMPSON
SPENCER TRACY
ROBERT WAGNER
KURT WEILL
JOANNE WOODWARD
PAULA YATES

Geena Davis, Saturn in Sagittarius

Saturn in
Aquarius

PAULA ABDUL
PIER ANGELI
GEORGE BALANCHINE
BRIGITTE BARDOT
COUNT BASIE
JEAN-PAUL
  BELMONDO
CONSTANCE BENNETT
JULIETTE BINOCHE
JON BON JOVI
GEORGE BRENT
JEAN-CLAUDE BRIALY
MAY BRITT
HORST BUCHHOLZ
NICOLAS CAGE
MICHAEL CAINE
DIANE CILENTO
CLAUDETTE COLBERT
JOAN COLLINS
DOLORES COSTELLO

JOAN CRAWFORD
BING CROSBY
TOM CRUISE
SALVADOR DALI
JOHNNY DEPP
ROBERT DONAT
BILLIE DOVE
RALPH FIENNES
JODIE FOSTER
GRETA GARBO
GREER GARSON
CARY GRANT
GRAHAM GREENE
TIPPI HEDREN
WHITNEY HOUSTON
HOWARD HUGHES
EDDIE IZZARD
SHIRLEY JONES
TOMMY LEE
SOPHIA LOREN
ROB LOWE
JEANETTE
  MACDONALD
DOROTHY MACKAILL
SHIRLEY MACLAINE
ELLE MACPHERSON
THOMAS MANN
LEA MASSARI

GLENN MILLER
DEMI MOORE
ANAIS NIN
KIM NOVAK
YOKO ONO
JOE ORTON
PETER O'TOOLE
VINCENT PEREZ
BRAD PITT
ROMAN POLANSKI
ELVIS PRESLEY
MAURICE RAVEL
DEBBIE REYNOLDS
GILBERT ROLAND
DOROTHY SEBASTIAN
OMAR SHARIF
GERTRUDE STEIN
DONALD
  SUTHERLAND
ELIZABETH TAYLOR
BARBARA TAYLOR
  BRADFORD
FATS WALLER
EVELYN WAUGH
HELEN WILLS MOODY
ANNA MAY WONG

Saturn in
Pisces

WOODY ALLEN
URSULA ANDRESS
JULIE ANDREWS
JOSEPHINE BAKER
SHIRLEY BASSEY
WARREN BEATTY
ERIC BENET
BJORK
JOAN BLONDELL
CLARA BOW
BETTY BRONSON
LOUISE BROOKS
DYAN CANNON
DIAHANN CARROLL
MADELEINE CARROLL
PABLO CASALS
JOHN CAZALE
RICHARD
  CHAMBERLAIN
KURT COBAIN
JOSEPH COTTEN
CINDY CRAWFORD

RUSSELL CROWE
SIMONE DE BEAUVOIR
FRANCES DEE
ALAIN DELON
BENICIO DEL TORO
LAURA DERN
KEIR DULLEA
DAPHNE DU MAURIER
ISADORA DUNCAN
HEIDI FLEISS
HENRY FONDA
JANE FONDA
JANET GAYNOR
STEPHANE GRAPELLI
REX HARRISON
SALMA HAYEK
LILLIAN HELLMAN
PAUL HENREID
KATHARINE HEPBURN
HERMAN HESSE
ANTHONY HOPKINS
ELIZABETH HURLEY
FRIDA KAHLO
VIRNA LISI
COURTNEY LOVE
MYRNA LOY
ANNA MAGNANI
JESSIE MATTHEWS
ANNE MORROW
JACK NICHOLSON
SINEAD O'CONNOR
LAURENCE OLIVIER
ARISTOTLE ONASSIS
LUCIANO PAVAROTTI
ROBERT REDFORD
VANESSA REDGRAVE
KEANU REEVES
LEE REMICK
ROBERTO ROSSELLINI
J.K. ROWLING
ROSALIND RUSSELL
FRANCOISE SAGAN
JEAN-PAUL SARTRE
CHARLIE SHEEN
BROOKE SHIELDS
BARBARA STANWYCK
BEN STILLER
ALICE B. TOKLAS
EMILY WATSON
BILLY DEE WILLIAMS
KATARINA WITT

▶ READ ABOUT YOUR RELATIONSHIP KARMA ON PAGE 825

Famous Couples Compatibility

DOUGLAS FAIRBANKS — MARY PICKFORD
Born May 23, 1883 — *Born April 8, 1883*
Zodiac Sign Gemini — Zodiac Sign Aries
Venus in Taurus — Venus in Gemini
Mars in Aries — Mars in Capricorn
Saturn in Taurus — Saturn in Virgo

ISADORA DUNCAN — SERGEI ESENIN
Born May 26, 1877 — *Born October 3, 1895*
Zodiac Sign Gemini — Zodiac Sign Libra
Venus in Gemini — Venus in Virgo
Mars in Aquarius — Mars in Libra
Saturn in Pisces — Saturn in Scorpio

GEORGE VI — QUEEN MOTHER
Born December 14, 1896 — *Born August 4, 1900*
Zodiac Sign Sagittarius — Zodiac Sign Leo
Venus in Scorpio — Venus in Cancer
Mars in Sagittarius — Mars in Gemini
Saturn in Scorpio — Saturn in Sagittarius

SINCLAIR LEWIS — DOROTHY THOMPSON
Born February 7, 1885 — *Born July 9, 1893*
Zodiac Sign Aquarius — Zodiac Sign Cancer
Venus in Capricorn — Venus in Leo
Mars in Aquarius — Mars in Leo
Saturn in Gemini — Saturn in Libra

CHARLES LINDBERGH — ANNE MORROW
Born February 4, 1902 — *Born June 22, 1906*
Zodiac Sign Aquarius — Zodiac Sign Cancer
Venus in Pisces — Venus in Leo
Mars in Aquarius — Mars in Cancer
Saturn in Capricorn — Saturn in Pisces

NORMA SHEARER — IRVING THALBERG
Born August 10, 1900 — *Born May 30, 1899*
Zodiac Sign Leo — Zodiac Sign Gemini
Venus in Cancer — Venus in Taurus
Mars in Cancer — Mars in Leo
Saturn in Sagittarius — Saturn in Sagittarius

JEAN HARLOW — PAUL BERN
Born March 3, 1911 — *Born December 3, 1889*
Zodiac Sign Pisces — Zodiac Sign Sagittarius
Venus in Aries — Venus in Scorpio
Mars in Capricorn — Mars in Libra
Saturn in Taurus — Saturn in Virgo

DUKE OF WINDSOR — WALLIS SIMPSON
Born June 23, 1894 — *Born June 19, 1896*
Zodiac Sign Cancer — Zodiac Sign Gemini
Venus in Taurus — Venus in Gemini
Mars in Aries — Mars in Aries
Saturn in Libra — Saturn in Scorpio

CLARK GABLE — CAROLE LOMBARD
Born February 1, 1901 — *Born October 6, 1908*
Zodiac Sign Aquarius — Zodiac Sign Libra
Venus in Capricorn — Venus in Leo
Mars in Virgo — Mars in Virgo
Saturn in Capricorn — Saturn in Aries

ERNEST HEMINGWAY — MARTHA GELLHORN
Born July 21, 1899 — *Born November 8, 1908*
Zodiac Sign Cancer — Zodiac Sign Scorpio
Venus in Cancer — Venus in Libra
Mars in Virgo — Mars in Libra
Saturn in Sagittarius — Saturn in Aries

KATHARINE HEPBURN — SPENCER TRACY
Born May 12, 1907 — *Born April 3, 1900*
Zodiac Sign Taurus — Zodiac Sign Aries
Venus in Aries — Venus in Taurus
Mars in Capricorn — Mars in Pisces
Saturn in Pisces — Saturn in Capricorn

BETTY GRABLE — HARRY JAMES
Born December 18, 1916 — *Born March 15, 1916*
Zodiac Sign Sagittarius — Zodiac Sign Pisces
Venus in Scorpio — Venus in Taurus
Mars in Capricorn — Mars in Leo
Saturn in Cancer — Saturn in Cancer

EVA BRAUN — ADOLF HITLER
Born Feburary 6, 1912 — *Born April 20, 1889*
Zodiac Sign Aquarius — Zodiac Sign Taurus
Venus in Capricorn — Venus in Taurus
Mars in Gemini — Mars in Taurus
Saturn in Taurus — Saturn in Leo

QUEEN ELIZABETH — PRINCE PHILIP
Born April 21, 1926 — *Born June 10, 1921*
Zodiac Sign Taurus — Zodiac Sign Gemini
Venus in Pisces — Venus in Taurus
Mars in Aquarius — Mars in Gemini
Saturn in Scorpio — Saturn in Virgo

DAVID O. SELZNICK — JENNIFER JONES
Born May 10, 1902 — *Born March 2, 1919*
Zodiac Sign Taurus — Zodiac Sign Pisces
Venus in Aries — Venus in Aries
Mars in Taurus — Mars in Pisces
Saturn in Capricorn — Saturn in Leo

INGRID BERGMAN — ROBERTO ROSSELLINI
Born August 29, 1915 — *Born May 8, 1906*
Zodiac Sign Virgo — Zodiac Sign Taurus
Venus in Virgo — Venus in Gemini
Mars in Cancer — Mars in Gemini
Saturn in Cancer — Saturn in Pisces

AVA GARDNER — FRANK SINATRA
Born December 24, 1922 — *Born December 12, 1915*
Zodiac Sign Capricorn — Zodiac Sign Sagittarius
Venus in Scorpio — Venus in Capricorn
Mars in Pisces — Mars in Leo
Saturn in Libra — Saturn in Cancer

BRIGITTE BARDOT — ROGER VADIM
Born September 28, 1934 — *Born January 26, 1928*
Zodiac Sign Libra — Zodiac Sign Aquarius
Venus in Virgo — Venus in Sagittarius
Mars in Leo — Mars in Capricorn
Saturn in Aquarius — Saturn in Sagittarius

MARTIN LUTHER KING, JR. — CORETTA SCOTT KING
Born January 15, 1929 — *Born April 27, 1927*
Zodiac Sign Capricorn — Zodiac Sign Taurus
Venus in Pisces — Venus in Gemini
Mars in Gemini — Mars in Cancer
Saturn in Sagittarius — Saturn in Sagittarius

MARILYN MONROE — JOE DI MAGGIO
Born June 1, 1926 — *Born November 25, 1914*
Zodiac Sign Gemini — Zodiac Sign Sagittarius
Venus in Aries — Venus in Sagittarius
Mars in Pisces — Mars in Sagittarius
Saturn in Scorpio — Saturn in Cancer

DEBBIE REYNOLDS — EDDIE FISHER
Born April 1, 1932 — *Born August 10, 1928*
Zodiac Sign Aries — Zodiac Sign Leo
Venus in Taurus — Venus in Leo
Mars in Pisces — Mars in Gemini
Saturn in Aquarius — Saturn in Sagittarius

GRACE KELLY — PRINCE RAINIER
Born November 12, 1929 — *Born May 31, 1923*
Zodiac Sign Scorpio — Zodiac Sign Gemini
Venus in Libra — Venus in Taurus
Mars in Scorpio — Mars in Cancer
Saturn in Sagittarius — Saturn in Libra

REX HARRISON — KAY KENDALL
Born March 5, 1908 — *Born May 21, 1926*
Zodiac Sign Pisces — Zodiac Sign Taurus
Venus in Aries — Venus in Aries
Mars in Taurus — Mars in Pisces
Saturn in Pisces — Saturn in Scorpio

ERICH MARIA REMARQUE — PAULETTE GODDARD
Born June 22, 1898 — *Born June 3, 1911*
Zodiac Sign Cancer — Zodiac Sign Gemini
Venus in Leo — Venus in Cancer
Mars in Gemini — Mars in Aries
Saturn in Sagittarius — Saturn in Taurus

▶ READ ABOUT YOUR ROMANTIC AND SEXUAL COMPATIBILITY ON PAGES 781 & 802

SAMMY DAVIS, JR. | **MAY BRITT**

Born December 8, 1925 | *Born March 22, 1933*

Zodiac Sign Sagittarius | Zodiac Sign Aries

Venus in Aquarius | Venus in Pisces

Mars in Scorpio | Mars in Virgo

Saturn in Scorpio | Saturn in Aquarius

SEAN CONNERY | **DIANE CILENTO**

Born August 25, 1930 | *Born October 5, 1933*

Zodiac Sign Virgo | Zodiac Sign Libra

Venus in Libra | Venus in Scorpio

Mars in Gemini | Mars in Scorpio

Saturn in Capricorn | Saturn in Aquarius

STEVE MCQUEEN | **ALI MACGRAW**

Born March 24, 1930 | *Born April 1, 1938*

Zodiac Sign Aries | Zodiac Sign Aries

Venus in Aries | Venus in Aries

Mars in Pisces | Mars in Taurus

Saturn in Capricorn | Saturn in Aries

ALAIN DELON | **NATHALIE DELON**

Born November 8, 1935 | *Born August 1, 1941*

Zodiac Sign Scorpio | Zodiac Sign Leo

Venus in Virgo | Venus in Virgo

Mars in Capricorn | Mars in Aries

Saturn in Pisces | Saturn in Taurus

CARY GRANT | **DYAN CANNON**

Born January 18, 1904 | *Born January 4, 1937*

Zodiac Sign Capricorn | Zodiac Sign Capricorn

Venus in Sagittarius | Venus in Aquarius

Mars in Aquarius | Mars in Libra

Saturn in Aquarius | Saturn in Pisces

MIA FARROW | **FRANK SINATRA**

Born February 9, 1945 | *Born December 12, 1915*

Zodiac Sign Aquarius | Zodiac Sign Sagittarius

Venus in Aries | Venus in Capricorn

Mars in Capricorn | Mars in Leo

Saturn in Cancer | Saturn in Cancer

ROMAN POLANSKI | **SHARON TATE**

Born August 18, 1933 | *Born January 24, 1943*

Zodiac Sign Leo | Zodiac Sign Aquarius

Venus in Virgo | Venus in Aquarius

Mars in Libra | Mars in Sagittarius

Saturn in Aquarius | Saturn in Gemini

PAUL MCCARTNEY | **LINDA MCCARTNEY**

Born June 18, 1942 | *Born September 24, 1941*

Zodiac Sign Gemini | Zodiac Sign Libra

Venus in Taurus | Venus in Scorpio

Mars in Leo | Mars in Aries

Saturn in Gemini | Saturn in Taurus

Mick Jagger, Leo and Bianca Jagger, Taurus

RYAN O'NEAL | **FARRAH FAWCETT**

Born April 20, 1941 | *Born February 2, 1947*

Zodiac Sign Taurus | Zodiac Sign Aquarius

Venus in Taurus | Venus in Sagittarius

Mars in Aquarius | Mars in Aquarius

Saturn in Taurus | Saturn in Leo

MICK JAGGER | **BIANCA JAGGER**

Born July 26, 1943 | *Born May 2, 1945*

Zodiac Sign Leo | Zodiac Sign Taurus

Venus in Virgo | Venus in Aries

Mars in Taurus | Mars in Pisces

Saturn in Gemini | Saturn in Cancer

NATALIE WOOD | **ROBERT WAGNER**

Born July 20, 1938 | *Born February 10, 1930*

Zodiac Sign Cancer | Zodiac Sign Aquarius

Venus in Virgo | Venus in Aquarius

Mars in Cancer | Mars in Aquarius

Saturn in Aries | Saturn in Capricorn

PRINCESS ANNE | **MARK PHILLIPS**

Born August 15, 1950 | *Born September 22, 1948*

Zodiac Sign Leo | Zodiac Sign Virgo

Venus in Cancer | Venus in Leo

Mars in Scorpio | Mars in Scorpio

Saturn in Virgo | Saturn in Virgo

FAYE DUNAWAY | **PETER WOLF**

Born January 14, 1941 | *Born March 7, 1946*

Zodiac Sign Capricorn | Zodiac Sign Pisces

Venus in Capricorn | Venus in Pisces

Mars in Sagittarius | Mars in Cancer

Saturn in Taurus | Saturn in Cancer

CHARLOTTE RAMPLING | **JEAN-MICHEL JARRE**

Born February 5, 1945 | *Born August 24, 1948*

Zodiac Sign Aquarius | Zodiac Sign Virgo

Venus in Aries | Venus in Cancer

Mars in Capricorn | Mars in Libra

Saturn in Cancer | Saturn in Leo

ROD STEWART | **ALANA HAMILTON**

Born January 10, 1945 | *Born May 18, 1945*

Zodiac Sign Capricorn | Zodiac Sign Taurus

Venus in Pisces | Venus in Aries

Mars in Capricorn | Mars in Aries

Saturn in Cancer | Saturn in Cancer

RICHARD GERE | **CINDY CRAWFORD**

Born August 31, 1949 | *Born February 20, 1966*

Zodiac Sign Virgo | Zodiac Sign Pisces

Venus in Libra | Venus in Capricorn

Mars in Cancer | Mars in Pisces

Saturn in Virgo | Saturn in Pisces

PAUL SIMON | **CARRIE FISHER**

Born October 13, 1941 | *Born October 21, 1956*

Zodiac Sign Libra | Zodiac Sign Libra

Venus in Sagittarius | Venus in Virgo

Mars in Aries | Mars in Pisces

Saturn in Taurus | Saturn in Sagittarius

SARAH BRIGHTMAN | **ANDREW LLOYD WEBER**

Born August 14, 1960 | *Born March 22, 1948*

Zodiac Sign Leo | Zodiac Sign Aries

Venus in Virgo | Venus in Taurus

Mars in Gemini | Mars in Leo

Saturn in Capricorn | Saturn in Leo

MADONNA | **SEAN PENN**

Born August 16, 1958 | *Born August 17, 1960*

Zodiac Sign Leo | Zodiac Sign Leo

Venus in Leo | Venus in Virgo

Mars in Taurus | Mars in Gemini

Saturn in Sagittarius | Saturn in Capricorn

VIC DAMONE | **DIAHANN CARROLL**

Born June 12, 1928 | *Born July 17, 1935*

Zodiac Sign Gemini | Zodiac Sign Cancer

Venus in Gemini | Venus in Virgo

Mars in Aries | Mars in Libra

Saturn in Sagittarius | Saturn in Pisces

TOM CRUISE | **NICOLE KIDMAN**

Born July 3, 1962 | *Born June 21, 1967*

Zodiac Sign Cancer | Zodiac Sign Gemini

Venus in Leo | Venus in Leo

Mars in Taurus | Mars in Libra

Saturn in Aquarius | Saturn in Aries

DEMI MOORE | **BRUCE WILLIS**

Born November 11, 1962 | *Born March 19, 1955*

Zodiac Sign Scorpio | Zodiac Sign Pisces

Venus in Scorpio | Venus in Aquarius

Mars in Leo | Mars in Taurus

Saturn in Aquarius | Saturn in Scorpio

▶ READ ABOUT YOUR ROMANTIC AND SEXUAL COMPATIBILITY ON PAGES 781 & 802

Famous Couples Compatibility

BRAD PITT
Born December 18, 1963
Zodiac Sign Sagittarius
Venus in Capricorn
Mars in Capricorn
Saturn in Aquarius

JENNIFER ANISTON
Born February 11, 1969
Zodiac Sign Aquarius
Venus in Aries
Mars in Scorpio
Saturn in Aries

ANTONIO BANDERAS
Born August 10, 1960
Zodiac Sign Leo
Venus in Virgo
Mars in Gemini
Saturn in Capricorn

MELANIE GRIFFITH
Born August 8, 1957
Zodiac Sign Leo
Venus in Virgo
Mars in Virgo
Saturn in Sagittarius

WILL SMITH
Born September 25, 1968
Zodiac Sign Libra
Venus in Libra
Mars in Virgo
Saturn in Aries

JADA PINKETT
Born September 18, 1971
Zodiac Sign Virgo
Venus in Libra
Mars in Aquarius
Saturn in Gemini

DAVID BECKHAM
Born May 2, 1975
Zodiac Sign Taurus
Venus in Gemini
Mars in Pisces
Saturn in Cancer

VICTORIA ADAMS
Born April 17, 1974
Zodiac Sign Aries
Venus in Pisces
Mars in Gemini
Saturn in Gemini

ERIC BENET
Born October 15, 1966
Zodiac Sign Libra
Venus in Libra
Mars in Virgo
Saturn in Pisces

HALLE BERRY
Born August 14, 1968
Zodiac Sign Leo
Venus in Virgo
Mars in Leo
Saturn in Aries

CATHERINE ZETA-JONES
Born September 25, 1969
Zodiac Sign Libra
Venus in Virgo
Mars in Capricorn
Saturn in Taurus

MICHAEL DOUGLAS
Born September 25, 1944
Zodiac Sign Libra
Venus in Libra
Mars in Libra
Saturn in Cancer

F. SCOTT FITZGERALD
Born September 24, 1896
Zodiac Sign Libra
Venus in Libra
Mars in Gemini
Saturn in Scorpio

ZELDA FITZGERALD
Born July 24, 1900
Zodiac Sign Leo
Venus in Cancer
Mars in Gemini
Saturn in Sagittarius

GEORGIA O'KEEFFE
Born November 15, 1887
Zodiac Sign Scorpio
Venus in Libra
Mars in Virgo
Saturn in Leo

ALFRED STIEGLITZ
Born January 1, 1864
Zodiac Sign Capricorn
Venus in Scorpio
Mars in Sagittarius
Saturn in Libra

GERTRUDE STEIN
Born February 3, 1874
Zodiac Sign Aquarius
Venus in Aquarius
Mars in Pisces
Saturn in Aquarius

ALICE B. TOKLAS
Born April 30, 1877
Zodiac Sign Taurus
Venus in Taurus
Mars in Aquarius
Saturn in Pisces

CHARLIE CHAPLIN
Born April 16, 1889
Zodiac Sign Aries
Venus in Taurus
Mars in Taurus
Saturn in Leo

OONA O'NEILL
Born May 13, 1926
Zodiac Sign Taurus
Venus in Aries
Mars in Pisces
Saturn in Scorpio

FRANKLIN D. ROOSEVELT
Born January 30, 1882
Zodiac Sign Aquarius
Venus in Aquarius
Mars in Gemini
Saturn in Taurus

ELEANOR ROOSEVELT
Born October 11, 1884
Zodiac Sign Libra
Venus in Virgo
Mars in Scorpio
Saturn in Gemini

BONNIE PARKER
Born October 1, 1910
Zodiac Sign Libra
Venus in Virgo
Mars in Libra
Saturn in Taurus

CLYDE BARROW
Born March 24, 1909
Zodiac Sign Aries
Venus in Pisces
Mars in Capricorn
Saturn in Aries

GRETA GARBO
Born September 18, 1905
Zodiac Sign Virgo
Venus in Leo
Mars in Sagittarius
Saturn in Aquarius

JOHN GILBERT
Born July 10, 1895
Zodiac Sign Cancer
Venus in Virgo
Mars in Leo
Saturn in Scorpio

JEAN COCTEAU
Born July 5, 1889
Zodiac Sign Cancer
Venus in Taurus
Mars in Cancer
Saturn in Leo

JEAN MARAIS
Born December 11, 1913
Zodiac Sign Sagittarius
Venus in Sagittarius
Mars in Cancer
Saturn in Gemini

FRIDA KAHLO
Born July 6, 1907
Zodiac Sign Cancer
Venus in Gemini
Mars in Capricorn
Saturn in Pisces

DIEGO RIVERA
Born December 13, 1886
Zodiac Sign Sagittarius
Venus in Sagittarius
Mars in Capricorn
Saturn in Cancer

HUMPHREY BOGART
Born December 25, 1899
Zodiac Sign Capricorn
Venus in Capricorn
Mars in Capricorn
Saturn in Sagittarius

LAUREN BACALL
Born September 16, 1924
Zodiac Sign Virgo
Venus in Leo
Mars in Aquarius
Saturn in Scorpio

EVA PERON
Born May 7, 1919
Zodiac Sign Taurus
Venus in Gemini
Mars in Taurus
Saturn in Leo

JUAN PERON
Born October 8, 1895
Zodiac Sign Libra
Venus in Virgo
Mars in Libra
Saturn in Scorpio

LUCILLE BALL
Born August 6, 1911
Zodiac Sign Leo
Venus in Virgo
Mars in Taurus
Saturn in Taurus

DESI ARNAZ
Born March 2, 1917
Zodiac Sign Pisces
Venus in Aquarius
Mars in Pisces
Saturn in Cancer

FEDERICO FELLINI
Born January 20, 1920
Zodiac Sign Capricorn
Venus in Sagittarius
Mars in Libra
Saturn in Virgo

GIULIETTA MASINA
Born February 22, 1920
Zodiac Sign Pisces
Venus in Capricorn
Mars in Scorpio
Saturn in Virgo

JAMES DEAN
Born February 8, 1931
Zodiac Sign Aquarius
Venus in Capricorn
Mars in Leo
Saturn in Capricorn

PIER ANGELI
Born June 19, 1932
Zodiac Sign Gemini
Venus in Cancer
Mars in Taurus
Saturn in Aquarius

ELVIS PRESLEY
Born January 8, 1935
Zodiac Sign Capricorn
Venus in Capricorn
Mars in Libra
Saturn in Aquarius

PRISCILLA PRESLEY
Born May 24, 1945
Zodiac Sign Gemini
Venus in Aries
Mars in Aries
Saturn in Cancer

SOPHIA LOREN
Born September 20, 1934
Zodiac Sign Virgo
Venus in Virgo
Mars in Leo
Saturn in Aquarius

CARLO PONTI
Born December 11, 1912
Zodiac Sign Sagittarius
Venus in Capricorn
Mars in Sagittarius
Saturn in Taurus

JACQUELINE KENNEDY
Born July 28, 1929
Zodiac Sign Leo
Venus in Gemini
Mars in Virgo
Saturn in Sagittarius

JOHN F. KENNEDY
Born May 29, 1917
Zodiac Sign Gemini
Venus in Gemini
Mars in Taurus
Saturn in Cancer

MARCELLO MASTROIANNI
Born September 26, 1924
Zodiac Sign Libra
Venus in Leo
Mars in Aquarius
Saturn in Scorpio

CATHERINE DENEUVE
Born October 23, 1943
Zodiac Sign Libra
Venus in Virgo
Mars in Gemini
Saturn in Gemini

▶ **READ ABOUT YOUR ROMANTIC AND SEXUAL COMPATIBILITY ON PAGES 781 & 802**

778

JOHN PROFUMO
Born October 19, 1912
Zodiac Sign Libra
Venus in Scorpio
Mars in Libra
Saturn in Gemini

CHRISTINE KEELER
Born February 22, 1942
Zodiac Sign Pisces
Venus in Aquarius
Mars in Taurus
Saturn in Taurus

ELIZABETH TAYLOR
Born February 27, 1932
Zodiac Sign Pisces
Venus in Aries
Mars in Pisces
Saturn in Aquarius

RICHARD BURTON
Born November 10, 1925
Zodiac Sign Scorpio
Venus in Capricorn
Mars in Libra
Saturn in Scorpio

JOHN LENNON
Born October 9, 1940
Zodiac Sign Libra
Venus in Virgo
Mars in Libra
Saturn in Taurus

YOKO ONO
Born February 18, 1933
Zodiac Sign Aquarius
Venus in Aquarius
Mars in Virgo
Saturn in Aquarius

PAUL NEWMAN
Born January 26, 1925
Zodiac Sign Aquarius
Venus in Capricorn
Mars in Aries
Saturn in Scorpio

JOANNE WOODWARD
Born February 27, 1930
Zodiac Sign Pisces
Venus in Pisces
Mars in Aquarius
Saturn in Capricorn

WARREN BEATTY
Born March 30, 1937
Zodiac Sign Aries
Venus in Taurus
Mars in Sagittarius
Saturn in Pisces

ANNETTE BENING
Born May 29, 1958
Zodiac Sign Gemini
Venus in Aries
Mars in Pisces
Saturn in Sagittarius

DON JOHNSON
Born December 15, 1949
Zodiac Sign Sagittarius
Venus in Aquarius
Mars in Virgo
Saturn in Virgo

MELANIE GRIFFITH
Born August 8, 1957
Zodiac Sign Leo
Venus in Virgo
Mars in Virgo
Saturn in Sagittarius

SUSAN SARANDON
Born October 4, 1946
Zodiac Sign Libra
Venus in Scorpio
Mars in Scorpio
Saturn in Leo

TIM ROBBINS
Born October 16, 1958
Zodiac Sign Libra
Venus in Libra
Mars in Gemini
Saturn in Sagittarius

MICHAEL HUTCHENCE
Born January 22, 1960
Zodiac Sign Aquarius
Venus in Sagittarius
Mars in Capricorn
Saturn in Capricorn

PAULA YATES
Born April 24, 1960
Zodiac Sign Taurus
Venus in Aries
Mars in Pisces
Saturn in Capricorn

PAMELA ANDERSON
Born July 1, 1967
Zodiac Sign Cancer
Venus in Leo
Mars in Libra
Saturn in Aries

TOMMY LEE
Born October 3, 1962
Zodiac Sign Libra
Venus in Scorpio
Mars in Cancer
Saturn in Aquarius

KURT COBAIN
Born February 20, 1967
Zodiac Sign Pisces
Venus in Pisces
Mars in Scorpio
Saturn in Pisces

COURTNEY LOVE
Born July 9, 1964
Zodiac Sign Cancer
Venus in Gemini
Mars in Gemini
Saturn in Pisces

HUGH GRANT
Born September 9, 1960
Zodiac Sign Virgo
Venus in Libra
Mars in Gemini
Saturn in Capricorn

ELIZABETH HURLEY
Born June 10, 1965
Zodiac Sign Gemini
Venus in Cancer
Mars in Virgo
Saturn in Pisces

BRITNEY SPEARS
Born December 4, 1981
Zodiac Sign Sagittarius
Venus in Capricorn
Mars in Virgo
Saturn in Libra

JUSTIN TIMBERLAKE
Born January 31, 1981
Zodiac Sign Aquarius
Venus in Capricorn
Mars in Aquarius
Saturn in Libra

ANTONIA FRASER
Born August 27, 1932
Zodiac Sign Virgo
Venus in Cancer
Mars in Cancer
Saturn in Capricorn

HAROLD PINTER
Born October 10, 1930
Zodiac Sign Libra
Venus in Scorpio
Mars in Cancer
Saturn in Capricorn

VIVIEN MERCHANT
Born July 22, 1929
Zodiac Sign Cancer
Venus in Gemini
Mars in Virgo
Saturn in Sagittarius

WOODY ALLEN
Born December 1, 1935
Zodiac Sign Sagittarius
Venus in Capricorn
Mars in Capricorn
Saturn in Pisces

SOON-YI PREVIN
Born October 8, 1970
Zodiac Sign Libra
Venus in Scorpio
Mars in Virgo
Saturn in Taurus

MIA FARROW
Born February 9, 1945
Zodiac Sign Aquarius
Venus in Aries
Mars in Capricorn
Saturn in Cancer

ANAIS NIN
Born February 21, 1903
Zodiac Sign Pisces
Venus in Pisces
Mars in Libra
Saturn in Aquarius

HENRY MILLER
Born December 26, 1891
Zodiac Sign Capricorn
Venus in Capricorn
Mars in Scorpio
Saturn in Virgo

JUNE MILLER
Born January 28, 1902
Zodiac Sign Aquarius
Venus in Pisces
Mars in Aquarius
Saturn in Capricorn

BILL CLINTON
Born August 19, 1946
Zodiac Sign Leo
Venus in Libra
Mars in Libra
Saturn in Leo

HILARY CLINTON
Born October 26, 1947
Zodiac Sign Scorpio
Venus in Scorpio
Mars in Leo
Saturn in Leo

MONICA LEWINSKY
Born July 23, 1973
Zodiac Sign Leo
Venus in Leo
Mars in Aries
Saturn in Gemini

ARISTOTLE ONASSIS
Born September 21, 1906
Zodiac Sign Virgo
Venus in Scorpio
Mars in Virgo
Saturn in Pisces

MARIA CALLAS
Born December 3, 1923
Zodiac Sign Sagittarius
Venus in Capricorn
Mars in Libra
Saturn in Libra

JACQUELINE KENNEDY
Born July 28, 1929
Zodiac Sign Leo
Venus in Gemini
Mars in Virgo
Saturn in Sagittarius

PRINCE CHARLES
Born November 14, 1948
Zodiac Sign Scorpio
Venus in Libra
Mars in Sagittarius
Saturn in Virgo

PRINCESS DIANA
Born July 1, 1961
Zodiac Sign Cancer
Venus in Taurus
Mars in Virgo
Saturn in Capricorn

CAMILLA PARKER BOWLES
Born July 17, 1947
Zodiac Sign Cancer
Venus in Cancer
Mars in Gemini
Saturn in Leo

▶ READ ABOUT YOUR ROMANTIC AND SEXUAL COMPATIBILITY ON PAGES 781 & 802

YOUR COMPATIBILITY

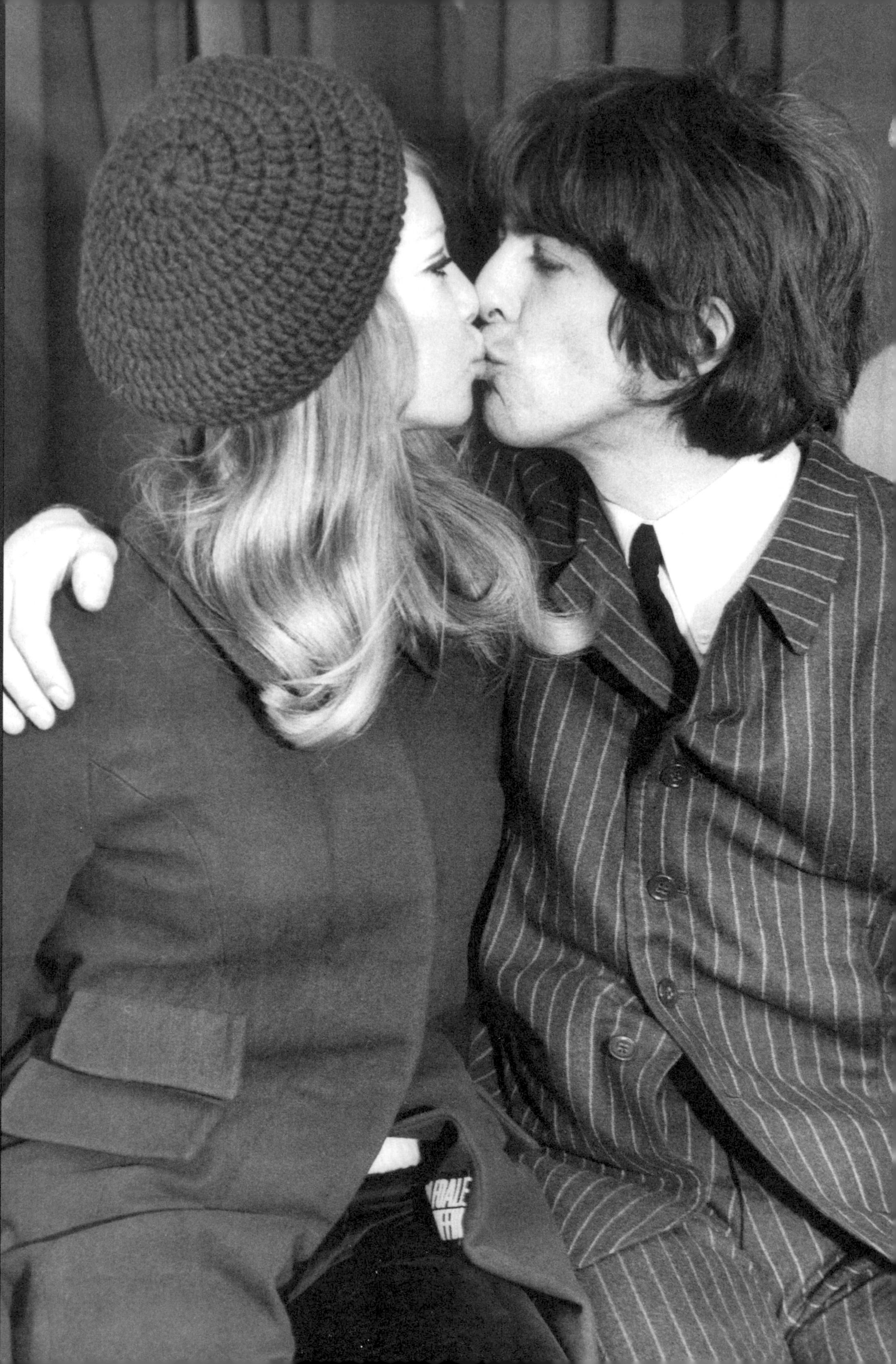

How do you say "I love you?" Do you and your partner speak the same language of love? Do you satisfy each other's needs for affection and romance? Or do the two of you seem to pass like ships in the night, unable to read each other's signals?

Each of us expresses our loving feelings in a unique way, according to the position of Venus in the birth chart. If your Venus Sign is compatible with your partner's Venus Sign, the two of you have similar attitudes about love and romance, and you can give and receive affection to each other harmoniously. You just naturally "feed" each other the love you require to be happy and fulfilled in the relationship. But if your Venus Sign isn't in tune with your partner's Venus Sign, one or both of you may feel unappreciated or misunderstood. Even though you may love one another, you have trouble showing your love in a way your partner can accept. In this section, you'll discover how your capacity for romance interacts with your partner's, and how you can enhance the love in your relationship.

INSTRUCTIONS

HERE'S HOW TO READ ABOUT YOUR ROMANTIC COMPATIBILITY.

1 Find your Zodiac Sign reading.

2 Look beside your Sign for **Your Love Planets**. Under **Your Romantic Side**, you'll find your Venus Sign.

3 Look up your partner's Zodiac Sign and Venus sign.

4 Look at the index below. Locate your Venus Sign and your Partner's Venus Sign. Where the two intersect, there is a page number. Turn to it to read all about **Your Romantic Compatibility**.

Note: Keep all of your Astrological Love Information handy by jotting down the page numbers of your Birth Year Events, Zodiac Sign, and Venus Sign and your Partner's Birth Year Events, Zodiac Sign and Venus Sign.

Example

If you were born on June 3, 1964, you would be a Gemini with a Venus in Cancer. If your partner was born on January 31, 1964, his or her Zodiac Sign would be Aquarius with a Venus in Pisces. Locate your Venus in Cancer and your partner's Venus in Pisces on the chart below. What type of romantic qualities does this relationship have? Where the two lines intersect you will find the page number of **Your Romantic Compatibility**. In this example, the Romantic Compatibility Reading is found on page 792.

YOUR ROMANTIC COMPATIBILITY PAGE INDEX

PARTNER'S VENUS SIGN

YOUR VENUS SIGN	ARIES	TAURUS	GEMINI	CANCER	LEO	VIRGO	LIBRA	SCORPIO	SAGITTARIUS	CAPRICORN	AQUARIUS	PISCES
ARIES	p. 782	p. 782	p. 782	p. 782	p. 783	p. 783	p. 783	p. 783	p. 784	p. 784	p. 784	p. 784
TAURUS		p. 785	p. 785	p. 785	p. 785	p. 786	p. 786	p. 786	p. 786	p. 787	p. 787	p. 787
GEMINI			p. 787	p. 788	p. 788	p. 788	p. 788	p. 789	p. 789	p. 789	p. 789	p. 790
CANCER				p. 790	p. 790	p. 790	p. 791	p. 791	p. 791	p. 791	p. 792	p. 792
LEO					p. 792	p. 792	p. 793	p. 793	p. 793	p. 793	p. 794	p. 794
VIRGO						p. 794	p. 794	p. 795	p. 795	p. 795	p. 795	p. 796
LIBRA							p. 796	p. 796	p. 796	p. 797	p. 797	p. 797
SCORPIO								p. 797	p. 798	p. 798	p. 798	p. 798
SAGITTARIUS									p. 799	p. 799	p. 799	p. 799
CAPRICORN										p. 800	p. 800	p. 800
AQUARIUS											p. 800	p. 801
PISCES												p. 801

HOW TO USE THIS INDEX
- Find your Venus Sign.
- Locate your Partner's Venus Sign.
- Turn to the page indicated where the two lines intersect to read about **Your Romantic Compatibility**.

◄◄ PATTI BOYD AND GEORGE HARRISON

Your Romantic Compatibility

Venus in **ARIES** matched with Venus in **ARIES** ♈♈

Love runs hot in this match! It can be a relief to finally find a sweetheart who has no problem keeping up with your fast pace. Together you may be a real power couple, with intense passions and interests that allow you to energize and inspire each other. You can always rely on your mate to tell you to "Go for it!"

The things that turn both of you on tend to be similar, and a preference for instant gratification can enhance your pleasure. Still, you can end up butting heads on those rare occasions when you both want different things.

Managing any clash of wills is the greatest challenge in this relationship. Providing a way to vent excess energy, occasional sparring sessions can be good for your bond. Because you both tend to be very direct, you can lay your cards on the table and work out a compromise. Yet none of your sports ever keeps you from action in bed.

Venus in **ARIES** matched with Venus in **TAURUS** ♈♉

The thrill of the chase energizes this bond, and your relationship tends to move forward in bursts of passion. While one partner may plunge into a new phase of love, the other may prefer to go slow—a difference that challenges the pursuer and raises the excitement level between you.

As the partnership develops, it helps to work out a rhythm together, as you to adapt to the other's varying paces in romance and life in general. While one partner hustles to take care of business, the other offers an enticing refuge of peace and serenity.

When one of you gets in a rut, you can rely on your mate to give you an extra motivational boost. The love you share tends to be intense, and a healthy taste for pleasure provides a satisfying result. The two of you may enjoy finding new ways to indulge each other's senses. Fulfilling each other's sexual desires can be a lifetime preoccupation in this relationship.

782

Venus in **ARIES** matched with Venus in **GEMINI** ♈♊

Passion develops quickly in this relationship, as you are both likely to pursue love and life at a fast pace and to give each other plenty of fuel for love's fire. Your wills blend harmoniously here, as one partner is usually delighted to follow the other partner's lead along the road to romantic fulfillment.

You can be best friends as well as lovers, but if emotions become too intense, one partner may bolt. Such a departure tends to be only temporary, and because you are both likely to have a variety of outside interests, you can afford each other a comfortable amount of freedom and breathing room.

Your conversations can be animated, flirtatious, and sometimes even heated. A playful, humorous spirit helps to diffuse tensions and keep tempers from flaring too hot. Curiosity and the pursuit of new trends and experiences can enliven your bond with wonder and fascination.

Venus in **ARIES** matched with Venus in **CANCER** ♈♋

This relationship can thrive on two fronts. As a couple, you may draw from a bank of shared talents that can bring advancement in the world and security at home. You are both leaders and can get along famously, provided you have a clear understanding of who's the boss in public and who rules the roost behind closed doors.

Emotional issues may be your greatest challenge. Strong feelings may first emerge in heated outbursts. Your talent bank includes a gift for unearthing the true feelings beneath any anger. Talking things over allows you to deepen your attachment.

Your household is likely to be a safe, stable, and nurturing haven that allows the more outgoing partner to relax and refuel. Such a supportive home base can be a launching pad for outside pursuits that bring abundant fruits of success back into the relationship and any family you may have.

► LOOK UP YOUR RELATIONSHIP KARMA *on p. 824* ► DISCOVER THE RELATIONSHIP KARMA YOU SHARE WITH CELEBRITIES *on p. 760*

Venus in **ARIES** matched with Venus in **LEO** ♈♌

While you may both have strong wills, a competitive streak in one partner is more likely to win the admiration—not the opposition—of the other. Together, you are a highly spirited, courageous, and unbeatable team. Loyalty is the ironclad bond that holds you together through any challenge.

Both of you have a minimum daily requirement of loving admiration. If one partner becomes overly occupied with other interests or, heaven forbid, other people, the potential for ego clashes rises. So long as you shower each other with attention and give due respect to each other's needs, things should run smoothly.

You may enjoy an easy, playful intimacy that flows naturally and instinctively. Outdoor recreation is a must, as it allows you to expend excess energy and to reinforce your emotional and physical attachment. This is a highly affectionate match, and you may often reach out unconsciously to stroke and embrace each other.

Venus in **ARIES** matched with Venus in **VIRGO** ♈♍

At the outset of this relationship, you may regard each other as alien but fascinating beings. The more methodical partner may find the fearless impulsivity of the other to be refreshing and exhilarating. The more outgoing partner may enjoy the luxury of knowing that all minor details will be taken care of.

To make this match work over time, you simply must reach an understanding that you are both very different people with different priorities, but together you can complement each other beautifully. You each have the ability to make your sweetheart more effective and to enrich your relationship with abundance and success.

A healthy lifestyle is the perfect goal for you to share. One mate can get you both motivated, while the other can reinforce your discipline to maintain a hearty regimen. Because you're both hard workers, joint projects inspire mutual admiration, stir your passions, and enhance your closeness.

Venus in **ARIES** matched with Venus in **LIBRA** ♈♎

Mutual respect and cooperation provide a middle ground in this relationship, allowing opposing personality traits to blend together in harmony. Physical attraction tends to fuel a powerfully passionate chemistry between you. While one of you may exude elegance and beauty, the other virtually radiates with charisma and raw, animal magnetism.

To establish a healthy flow of communication, the two of you may need to reconcile your very different styles of expression. The more tactful but indirect mate may come to appreciate that frank talk leaves no one guessing. And if one partner comes across in a harsh way, a softer delivery can make a message easier to absorb.

You may both feel instinctively that you can learn a lot from each other. An overly selfless partner can enjoy greater assertiveness and contentment. And any "me-first" tendencies in the other partner can give way to the benefits of teamwork and deeper intimacy.

Venus in **ARIES** matched with Venus in **SCORPIO** ♈♏

Passion lends a steamy undercurrent to this match-up. Physical attraction can bubble up and explode in a burst of erotic interest and excitement. A healthy respect for each other's strengths exerts a powerful draw. You may both feel that you've finally met your match—someone who doesn't put up with nonsense.

Lover's quarrels can become heated and intense, and while one partner may enjoy getting everything out in the open, the other may shut down, withdraw, and come up with a quietly devastating punishment. You both have wills of steel, but most of the time it pays to let the strong, silent mate prevail.

The rewards of yielding and making up tend to be generous and deep, and they feel oh so good. You can trust that the intimate secrets of your relationship will never travel beyond the four corners of your bedroom. Unbending determination makes this love affair last.

4

YOUR COMPATIBILITY

783

▶ LOOK UP YOUR RELATIONSHIP KARMA *on p. 824* ▶ DISCOVER THE RELATIONSHIP KARMA YOU SHARE WITH CELEBRITIES *on p. 760*

Your Romantic Compatibility

Venus in **ARIES** matched with Venus in **SAGITTARIUS** ♈♐

Enthusiasm and laughter fan the flames of this high-spirited romance. The two of you tend to love the same things, but for different reasons. As a result, this relationship can be one win-win scenario after another. For example, you may both love competition. One mate seeks the thrill of victory. The other enjoys peak performance. Win-win!

Neither of you is likely to shy away from risk-taking. The upside is that you can enjoy massive payoffs when things go well. The downside is that, with your fearlessness and hunger for excitement, you can get each other into big trouble. Together, though, you can withstand enormous setbacks because you both adore a challenge and have the optimism to try, try again.

An active lifestyle keeps your partnership fresh and moving forward. There is always something new and fascinating to explore. Direct, frank, and truthful, you may just plain like each other!

Venus in **ARIES** matched with Venus in **CAPRICORN** ♈♑

You can be the kind of power couple that stays together forever while outsiders scratch their heads and wonder how two such completely different people can get along so well. Let them scratch! What you have here can be the perfect delegation of individual talents. Together you make each other more efficient, effective, and successful.

Before this relationship hits its stride, one mate's impulsivity and initiative may hit the other partner's wall of conservatism and deliberation. You can overcome this obstacle with a compromise that promises action while giving practical considerations their due. By combining forces, you can become a lean, mean focused team, able to make your dreams come true.

While you may seem cool and impersonal in public, you two are likely to be all over each other in private. When the time and place is right, your passion for each other can be physical, sensual, and uninhibited.

Venus in **ARIES** matched with Venus in **AQUARIUS** ♈♒

A passion for anything new and enthusiasm for the future can spark the flame of this romance. Sharing the courage to buck trends and start your own, you may treasure the support and understanding you can give each other. Friendship comes naturally in this match, and plenty of freedom can be the wind beneath your wings of love.

You both may feel strongly about doing things "your way," which is fine, as long as you both agree. Should you get stuck in a stubborn disagreement, you have the creativity to find a new and innovative solution.

Respect for each other's unique gifts and individuality is the glue that holds you together. Each mate has a talent for making the other feel special. Intimacy opens another realm of wonder and experimentation. Likely to push the outer envelope of erotic pleasure, you can ensure that every time feels like the first time.

Venus in **ARIES** matched with Venus in **PISCES** ♈♓

A protective impulse may get this relationship going. The brave champion rushes out to save a darling-in-distress, but, as this romantic fantasy plays itself out, the lovers may come to wonder, "Just who is rescuing whom?" Over time this relationship brings out each partner's hidden strengths and deepest vulnerabilities.

In this combination, one partner may be more openly willful, and problems can arise if the other mate feels bullied or overpowered. Coming to blows rarely ever happens. Rather, the more passive partner will seem to vaporize into thin air, leaving the other to swing at shadows—a very powerful strategy indeed.

The great karmic lesson in this partnership is that love conquers all, and compassion and empathy can heal all rifts. You may feel drawn to each other by a mysterious, seductive force. The intimacy you share can provide the most exquisite out-of-body experiences your body ever had.

► LOOK UP YOUR RELATIONSHIP KARMA *on p. 824*   ► DISCOVER THE RELATIONSHIP KARMA YOU SHARE WITH CELEBRITIES *on p. 760*

Venus in **TAURUS** matched with Venus in **TAURUS**

Venus in Taurus times two makes for an easy, peaceful match. Ensconced in the comfort of each other's company, neither of you may see any great need to venture out again—at least not until you exhaust your joint supply of creature comforts. Because you share an instinctive understanding of what gives each other pleasure, you may indulge your mate as liberally as you indulge yourself.

The biggest problem with this match is that you may get along great, but the spark can fade. Or a stubborn disagreement may turn into a stagnant standoff. You may need to make a conscious effort to bring some passion and flexibility into this relationship.

Because you both tend to be aware of your motivational challenges, you can sympathetically prod each other to loosen up, get out, and live a little. Steadfast devotion and a preference for stability can hold you together through thick and thin.

Venus in **TAURUS** matched with Venus in **GEMINI**

In this relationship, sweetness comes in a rainbow assortment of flavors. The pleasure of sharing a variety of sensory treats can get this romance going and provide a constant source of entertainment and excitement as times goes by.

The subject of change can be a sticking point for you two. While too much of the same-old, same-old can be fatally boring to one partner, the other may like things just the way they are. It helps to remember the things you like and value about your mate's opposing traits.

The easy adaptability one mate enjoys can make it more fun and less frightening to face change together, and the serenity and stability of one partner can soothe the sometimes fragile nerves of the other. Communication is important, so long as you judge it by its quality—not its quantity. Even if words are few, they are sure to be said with love.

Venus in **TAURUS** matched with Venus in **CANCER**

Just as the earth cradles the moon in its orbit, you two belong together. Night–time moon gazing and a cuddle is a surefire way to refresh your romance, but make sure to begin or end your evening with a good meal. It's likely that one mate expresses affection by cooking for or feeding loved ones, while the other adores consuming tasty treats. It's a perfect match!

You have to dig to find areas where you two might clash. Sometimes one partner may not be sufficiently sensitive to the other's moods and feelings. But that doesn't mean your sweetie doesn't care!

The more volatile mate can turn up the volume enough to be heard, and unless you cross a high-level, red-flag boundary, your big peaceful lug of a heartthrob will absorb the wave and respond with consoling sympathy. Tending to each other's comfort is a high and pleasant priority in this partnership.

Venus in **TAURUS** matched with Venus in **LEO**

A cozier couple is hard to find! Warmth, loyalty, and fond adoration bind you together. Because you offer each other a wealth of creativity, you can lavishly indulge each other's taste for the good life. Your household is likely to be richly furnished, affording a life of comfort for the two of you and any family you may have.

You both tend to be rather strong-willed, and a difference in opinion can lead to a stubborn standoff. The more dramatic partner is likely to force the situation to a resolution, which usually boils down to a need to feel not just respected, but openly appreciated and admired.

Generosity with gifts, kind sentiments, and tender gestures comes easily to both of you. Liberal doses of physical affection can keep your romance moving along happily and neither of you is afraid to be demonstrative. The rallying cry for this love affair is: "Only the best for my sweetheart!"

▶ LOOK UP YOUR RELATIONSHIP KARMA *on p. 824*   ▶ DISCOVER THE RELATIONSHIP KARMA YOU SHARE WITH CELEBRITIES *on p. 760*

Your Romantic Compatibility

Venus in **TAURUS** matched with Venus in **VIRGO** ♉♍

This match makes a lot of "sense"—in terms of sensibility, common sense, and sensuality. You may share a practical sensibility that makes it easy to define and prioritize goals. Together you may value an uncomplicated relationship, based on the common sense virtues of caring, compatibility, and honesty. Sensual pleasures provide an erotic undercurrent to your attachment.

The relationship can run into some static if one partner insists on imposing certain habits or standards or the other.

Usually, the more laidback mate will consent to the lifestyle choices of the more particular sweetheart, so long as the latter agrees to handle—without resentment or reproach—any extra work that making things "just-so" requires.

Because you are both earthy types, sharing the natural wealth of our home planet allows you to nourish your bodies, your senses, and your romance. Refreshing time outdoors, in the woods or gardening, can stir your passions.

Venus in **TAURUS** matched with Venus in **LIBRA** ♉♎

The art of love finds many different means of expression in this match. For one mate, it is a craft, a way to invest romantic meaning into everyday actions and objects. For the other mate, it is high art—the creation of a harmonious environment and painstaking attention to a beloved's happiness.

Without careful communication and understanding of each other's needs, your respective styles can clash. The earthy, hands-on approach of one mate can overwhelm

the other mate's preference for a certain delicacy and gentility. Because you both tend to be patient, tolerant people, you can talk things through and do what's necessary to ensure a mutual comfort level.

Abundant creativity graces this relationship. One partner tends to have the practical resourcefulness to give concrete support in bringing the beautiful visions of the other to realization. Together you make an inspiring team, able to make your sweetest dreams come true.

Venus in **TAURUS** matched with Venus in **SCORPIO** ♉♏

Sensuality is a keynote of your partnership and you seem to have an innate understanding of how to please each other. You tend to agree that if it feels good, do it. The sparks really fly when you're together, and you like to turn the heat up high.

At times, you might find yourselves on opposite sides of the field, so to speak, perhaps where money or friends are concerned. Because you can both be quite stubborn and willful, compromise may be tricky. Your partnership

may be punctuated by frequent fights, followed by passionate reunions.

Your relationship is likely to have plenty of "glue." Even though you may have your differences, you aren't likely to give up on love and can stick together through good times and bad. Despite that, your partnership might encounter jealousy and possessiveness. Because you both value commitment and loyalty, a union between you could last a lifetime.

Venus in **TAURUS** matched with Venus in **SAGITTARIUS** ♉♐

A passion for abundance can draw these two very different personalities together. One partner may be a magnet for lucky breaks, but as a team, you tend to enjoy a greater ability to make your own luck. While you might take risks to get ahead, the more conservative partner in this match is likely to be busy in the background, hedging your bets.

Your relationship can succeed, provided you balance one mate's need for changing scenery with the other's

need for security. Quality time together allows you to ante-up into your shared bank of affection and trust. The honesty of the more adventurous partner makes it easier for the more sedentary mate to patiently hold down the fort.

This match allows you to bring the exotic treasures of the world into your home. And as you journey through life together, you can be assured of traveling in comfort and style.

► LOOK UP YOUR RELATIONSHIP KARMA *on p. 824* ► DISCOVER THE RELATIONSHIP KARMA YOU SHARE WITH CELEBRITIES *on p. 760*

Venus in **TAURUS** matched with Venus in **CAPRICORN**

An easy compatibility provides this relationship with a rock-solid foundation. Both of you tend to value commitment, stability, and security, but you also know how to have lots of fun. In intimate moments, you may growl affectionately with animal passion and generously indulge each other's sensuous desires.

The only problems you may have together are what at least one of you might term as "problems we like to have." That is, you may get along so famously, your comfortable groove could, over time, become a ditch. Because both of you are diligent workers, you can make the conscious effort necessary to keep your romance fresh and lively.

As a team, you can enjoy resourcefulness, determination, and wonderful creativity. The gifts you share give you a leg up over other couples in climbing the ladder of success—not that you're competitive, but you do like to have the very best.

Venus in **TAURUS** matched with Venus in **AQUARIUS**

To some, you may be "The Odd Couple." But you're both unlikely to care what others think, especially when you're in love. You might even feel that oddness is a hoot! Together you have such a wide range of different traits and talents, you can cover all your partnership bases. While one mate handles practical, day-to-day needs, the other can envision great possibilities for your future.

To get this relationship really going, you need just one person to tell you, "It'll never work." You can both be rather, well, stubborn and defiant. If you make this trait work for you, your love will be on solid ground.

Having a common cause allows you to share your passion for an issue and for each other. Sometimes it can be lonely to march to your own drummer, but both of you know how to make your sweetheart feel unique, special, and precious.

Venus in **TAURUS** matched with Venus in **PISCES**

This relationship is sweeter than a chocolate bonbon with a soft marshmallow center. The love you share can be full of tenderness. While one partner may be a sensitive softie, the other generously provides support, security, and calm protection. You are lovers, not fighters, and this profoundly peaceful partnership can suit you perfectly.

Because you both tend to avoid confrontation, communication between you can sometimes break down. For fear of upsetting or worrying your mate, one or both of you may hesitate to raise a subject that's bothering you. When it finally comes out, your partner's gentle concern and willingness to help may make you realize how silly it was to hold back.

What one mate brings in seductiveness, the other rewards with a luscious sensuality. You may love to soothe each other's senses with music, movies, good eating and drinking, and taking in the beauty of the great outdoors.

Venus in **GEMINI** matched with Venus in **GEMINI**

One night the two of you talk until dawn. The next thing you know, your grandchildren are getting married, and the conversation is still going strong. Needless to say, for this chatty couple, things tend to go very, very fast. It may seem as if you've found your long-lost twin in curiosity, mischief-making, intellectual passion, and word play.

Both of you can be so perceptive that your nerves can sometimes get rattled and raw. While it is hard to be comforting to your mate when you're in such a state, you can more than respect each other's need for quiet time. You might share techniques and establish some ground rules for powering down your active minds after a long day.

Cheerful, social, and fun loving, you may share a sense of humor that allows you to weather hard times. Learning from everything as your love grows, your light-hearted approach allows you to thrive together.

▶ LOOK UP YOUR RELATIONSHIP KARMA *on p. 824* ▶ DISCOVER THE RELATIONSHIP KARMA YOU SHARE WITH CELEBRITIES *on p. 760*

Venus in **GEMINI** matched with Venus in **CANCER** ♊♋

Intellect meets intuition in this love affair, and brilliant imagination is its offspring. While one of you tends to be a thinker, your sweetheart may be more in tune with feelings. You two can come up with amazingly creative ways to romance each other.

A failure of communication can cause you to be hard on each other. One mate is too moody and defensive. The other is shallow and hyper-rational. Whoa! Understanding the different ways you perceive things can help you to find a way to connect.

Non verbal communication may be the best way for both of you to express what's on your mind or in your heart. Making love says it all for you two. Both of you are actually quite sensitive and perceptive. Listening to each other is a skill that can strengthen your bond and make it last. It's easy to reach out, compromise, and respond with generosity when you feel you've been truly heard.

Venus in **GEMINI** matched with Venus in **LEO** ♊♌

The fun never ends in this match because you can entertain each other endlessly. With one mate's charismatic warmth and the other's witty way with words, you may be an A-List couple at parties and group outings. High-spirited friendship can provide a lasting foundation for your relationship.

Conflicting demands for freedom and loyalty may sometimes cause friction. One mate tends to thrive on loving attention, while the other can be a bit of a social butterfly. The best compromise allows either partner to maintain a wide range of pals, so long as you have an unmistakable and frequently reaffirmed understanding that your sweetheart is Numero Uno, special, the very best, beyond compare.

The commitment you share tends to be stable, but you can adapt well to new circumstances and challenges. Sharing a passion for learning and a gift for teaching, you can turn each other on to new, stimulating experiences.

Venus in **GEMINI** matched with Venus in **VIRGO** ♊♍

A passion for knowledge can arouse your interest in each other. While one partner has an earthy, practical outlook, the other tends to focus on concepts and ideas. Such differing viewpoints can make your mate seem all the more fascinating and your relationship all the more absorbing.

The steady habits of one partner can conflict with the other's penchant for variety and frequent changes of pace. Because you're both good communicators, you can minimize any discord over your varying styles by openly discussing your needs. From there you can work out a compromise that allows for flexibility within stable boundaries.

A common sensitivity to the tiniest details of any subject allows you to share big thrills together. You may enjoy parsing out what is so exceptional about a vintage wine, a book, or a musical number. Attention to the little things and kind favors can make for an enduring bond.

Venus in **GEMINI** matched with Venus in **LIBRA** ♊♎

Something about this romance can feel like you've gained entrée into the rarified atmosphere of a vintage champagne musical, with snappy repartee and an ego-boosting air of sophistication. Sparkling, thought-provoking conversation may seduce you into submission. Only the finest words are spoken here, as neither of you would dream of fouling your flirtation with vulgarity.

Still, something about both of you can seem unreachable. To avoid breezing right past each other, you may reach a point where one of you has to stop playing mind games and come out with it: "I love you. I want to be with you." Then you have to agree and shake on it.

The two of you can get along famously, enjoying a natural flow of friendship, communication, and mutual fascination. A sense of beauty may fill your intimate moments with enchantment. Highly creative as partners, you can elevate affection to a fine art.

▶ LOOK UP YOUR RELATIONSHIP KARMA *on p. 824*   ▶ DISCOVER THE RELATIONSHIP KARMA YOU SHARE WITH CELEBRITIES *on p. 760*

Venus in **GEMINI** matched with Venus in **SCORPIO** ♊♏

How is it possible for an attraction to bloom between someone so light, open, and chatty and another person so intense, brooding, and secretive? It's a mystery. The two of you may enjoy a romantic alchemy that fires up your passions as surely as it defies explanation.

One mate in this union may have a talent for bending the truth, while the other can be suspicious and distrustful. Still, both of you "just know" when the other

is fudging, so you either won't bother fibbing, or you'll both laugh it off. A dark sense of humor may be a healing, compelling force in your relationship.

Nothing is what it seems in this partnership, and only the two of you can understand. The seemingly "superficial" partner may enjoy exclusive access to shadowy depths of the other's soul. Together you may enjoy long, absorbing conversations that lighten heavy feelings and make life meaningful.

Venus in **GEMINI** matched with Venus in **SAGITTARIUS** ♊♐

This union of two curious, open-minded souls allows both partners to more than satisfy each other's cravings for a variety of stimulating experiences and adventures. Your most romantic dates may involve frequent day trips, and as the bond between you grows, you are likely to embark on distant journeys that test and build your relationship skills.

One mate can be a sweet talker and a bit of a truth-bender, while the other can be overwhelmingly blunt. But romance can blur a fib into a spell of amorous

imagination. And should someone "open mouth and insert foot," your mate is likely to dissolve into a laughing fit and let the incident pass, without recrimination.

Your shared bank of intellectual talents and optimism allows you to turn trivial pursuits into goal-oriented action. While you may benefit from a wealth of worldly wisdom, the belief that generosity begins at home can bring your commitment an abundance of intimate rewards.

789

Venus in **GEMINI** matched with Venus in **CAPRICORN** ♊♑

The two of you can be like two ships passing on the sea of love—one a luxury ocean liner, the other a turbo-powered speedboat. If you happen to weigh anchor on a common shore, though, you may be in for the most surprising love affair of your life—one filled with laughter and devilish fun.

The different speeds at which you operate can be a challenge. One mate works slowly and diligently towards long-term and lasting goals. The other

wants—and usually gets—instant gratification. Overcoming this obstacle allows you to discover all kinds of ways in which your varying traits can complement each other.

The flightier mate may long for the stability and faithful commitment that the more grounded partner can provide. And the more serious mate may truly appreciate the wild humor and playfulness this partnership inspires. Together, you can enjoy the best of all worlds.

Venus in **GEMINI** matched with Venus in **AQUARIUS** ♊♒

In this meeting of the minds, friendship is a no-brainer. Likely to regard your mate as your intellectual equal, the two of you may enjoy an electrifying exchange of ideas. Any flirtation tends to involve ingenious word play, and nimble mental gymnastics can be a potent form of seduction that leads to deeper emotional and physical connections.

Both of you can be too smart for your relationship's own good. One mate may take an opposing point of

view, just for the fun of it, and the other can be stubbornly self-righteous. To maintain harmony, you may have to agree that sometimes it's better to be loved than to be right.

A playful, experimental approach to love and romance keeps things interesting. Together, you may try anything once. Able to give each other plenty of freedom, you can cling to each other lightly, which is just how both of you like it.

▶ LOOK UP YOUR RELATIONSHIP KARMA *on p. 824* ▶ DISCOVER THE RELATIONSHIP KARMA YOU SHARE WITH CELEBRITIES *on p. 760*

Your Romantic Compatibility

Venus in **GEMINI** matched with Venus in **PISCES**   ♊♓

Two shape-shifting and entertaining lovers come together in this match—one equipped with a mystical gift for casting illusions, the other with the power of magic words. Fascination and curiosity fuel the seductive power of your bond.

Making a commitment stick can be the main challenge in this union. Either of you can be elusive, for fear of being hurt or due to a skittering attention span. Because both partners tend to be sensitive, you are likely to avoid quarrels and discord. Talk to each other. For two people as nonjudgmental as you, communication can flow smoothly. By clarifying your needs, you can build a bridge of intimacy.

Whether you need to shield tender emotions or soothe a bad case of sensory overload, you may appreciate the comforting sanctuary this relationship offers. After a long hard day, the two of you can escape to a private island of romantic delights.

Venus in **CANCER** matched with Venus in **CANCER**   ♋♋

Taking care of each other is the common bond in this relationship, and both partners tend to express love by being nurturing and protective. Sharing meals may get high priority. After all, you are both likely to be very much family-oriented. Marriage and children is often the ultimate objective of this match-up.

With two givers in this union, the greatest challenge for each of you is to get used to being a receiver sometimes. This may sound like the kind of problem you'd like to have, but it may not be easy. Letting someone take care of you requires giving up control, at least temporarily.

Then again, being pampered into submission is a wonderful way to go. You may both work hard to create a secure and cozy home life. Instinctively sensitive to each other's feelings, you make it safe for your mate to open up and express needs and affection, especially when it comes to creative bedroom self–expression.

Venus in **CANCER** matched with Venus in **LEO**   ♋♌

In this match-up, one partner might purr, "I want to take care of you," while the other might sing, "You make me feel so young...." The love you feel for each other can arouse great tenderness and concern for your mate's well-being. You may enjoy entertaining friends and family at home where you can offer cozy accommodations.

A parent-child dynamic best describes how you relate to each other. Should one mate get too comfortable as the object of attention, the other may feel pigeonholed in the care-giving role. A period of silent treatment or a lover's quarrel can move you to restore a fair balance in roles.

The shyer mate in this match can benefit from the warm encouragement your sweetheart provides. You tend to be protective of each other with respect to the outside world, but when you're alone, you may play together like a couple of kids.

Venus in **CANCER** matched with Venus in **VIRGO**   ♋♍

This is as near to perfect as a match-up can get. Both partners tend to feel their best when serving and caring for a loved one. As a result, each of you gets to enjoy first-rate material and emotional nurturance. Together, you can have a dream lifestyle in which your health, safety, and all-around well-being receives diligent and tender attention.

In this partnership, painstaking attention to detail is a sign of deep affection. You do need to take care not to pick at each other if something fails to meet your standards. Both partners tend to have feelings that bruise easily. It helps to remember that your way is not always the only right way.

You are both likely to be very private people, and it can be a great comfort to have an ally with whom you can close ranks against the world. Trust cloaks this relationship in ironclad security. Deep feelings keep you in love through thick and thin.

▶ LOOK UP YOUR RELATIONSHIP KARMA *on p. 824*   ▶ DISCOVER THE RELATIONSHIP KARMA YOU SHARE WITH CELEBRITIES *on p. 760*

Venus in **CANCER** matched with Venus in **LIBRA**

Consideration for each other's needs and feelings is the keynote of this relationship. Both partners tend to take the initiative in making sure the other is happy, and you may make a point of being gentle and kind in your interactions. As a result, communication between you tends to be easy and smooth.

Neither of you likes to fight, and that can be good or bad. Reluctant to confront anything unpleasant, you may both end up harboring resentments and being passive-

aggressive. Ultimately, you'll reach the point of breakup or breakthrough, a state that can move you to tap your abundant creativity and imagination in overcoming conflicts together.

You may enjoy good taste in every sense of the phrase. Fine wining and dining may serve as a favorite way to bond and stir up romantic feelings. Indulging each other lavishly allows both of you the pleasure of giving and receiving.

Venus in **CANCER** matched with Venus in **SCORPIO**

Intuitive understanding runs so deep in this relationship, it borders on psychic perception. To know what your sweetheart needs or thinks at any given moment, the two of you hardly even need to speak. You may throw each other smoldering, passionate looks that can draw you together like magnets.

While one mate can be a bit moody, the other can sometimes plunge into a dark funk. In such a downward spiral, you may both feel powerless to pull

out by yourselves. Strong ties to friends and family can give your relationship an extra boost of support in challenging times and help you turn the emotional tide in your favor.

Physical affection in this relationship is usually rich with feeling and tenderness. When either partner feels insecure, the other usually knows exactly how to put any such worries to bed. Together you two can more than satiate any hunger for love and intensity.

Venus in **CANCER** matched with Venus in **SAGITTARIUS**

Although one mate may be a homebody and the other a happy wanderer, this couple can travel quite well together. Romantic journeys may be central to your bond, be they weekend escapes, exotic vacations, or a walk around the block. You may both share a gift for stuffing high-class hotel accommodations into a knapsack-sized space.

One mate's need for assurance of your commitment can spark impatience or an overly blunt response. You don't want to bruise each other's feelings or smother a

sweetheart's need for freedom. With trust and understanding—and you are both truthful, trustworthy types—the differences between you can be complementary strengths.

One partner can hold down the fort while the other scours the world for treasures to bring home and share. Your life together can be a moveable feast. You are both generous souls, eager to indulge each other. Nothing is too good for your baby.

Venus in **CANCER** matched with Venus in **CAPRICORN**

This match makes for a traditional power couple. One partner tends toward public prominence, while the other is the power behind the throne. Both of you can be fiercely protective of your privacy, a zone that allows you to share sides of your personalities that no one else will ever see.

You each tend to be big on control and can get good and cranky if a mate attempts to micromanage you, especially in your respective

zone of authority. It's good to agree, straight off the bat, to delegate certain responsibilities to one mate or the other, not to interfere, and never to criticize each other in front of others.

The affection you share tends to be intense and surprisingly uninhibited. Both of you are uniquely able to give your sweetheart the commitment and security that makes it safe to express deep feelings and let it all hang out.

▶ LOOK UP YOUR RELATIONSHIP KARMA *on p. 824*   ▶ DISCOVER THE RELATIONSHIP KARMA YOU SHARE WITH CELEBRITIES *on p. 760*

Your Romantic Compatibility

Venus in **CANCER** matched with Venus in **AQUARIUS** ♋ ♒

This is a great relationship for two people who long for an escape from the rough and tumble of a cruel world. No matter how misunderstood and lonely you may feel, your mate can understand and sympathize. You both share an unlimited imagination, and being able to share your wildest dreams can fuel your passion for each other.

Different expectations about exclusivity and intimacy can cause some conflict. Too much time out with friends or a non-committal approach to love can leave one mate in the cold. If you want this relationship to last, you simply cannot over emphasize the unique importance of your connection to each other.

Thus assured, the more private of the two of you can afford the other mate an infinite amount of slack. Your home may be an inviting place for friends and socializing. The time you share alone, after everyone leaves, is precious and sacred.

Venus in **CANCER** matched with Venus in **PISCES** ♋ ♓

A primal, wordless connection between you drives a steady stream of passion. You can share such sweet vivid dreams together, and you are both caring people. To find a lover who speaks the language of emotion frees you to gush forth with intensity and appreciation.

You may be accustomed to reading each other's mind, but problems can arise if you misinterpret your mate's signals. Because both of you tend to withdraw from conflict, you can end up in a standoff. Each partner is so empathetic, it's a shame to lose time this way. Talking together is always better than you expected and can help you avoid misunderstandings in the first place.

The chemistry between you is utterly soul stirring and awe-inspiring. For the two of you, physical intimacy is filled with feeling. Together, you can enjoy heart-to-heart conversations that leave no doubt as to the strength and security of your commitment.

Venus in **LEO** matched with Venus in **LEO** ♌ ♌

Of all couples in love, you are easily the most striking. Friends may often comment how good you look together. Playful and full of warmth, the two of are fun to be with. An active social life can bring compelling drama to your relationship, along with many opportunities to see, be seen, and make the scene.

Both of you tend to need a lot of attention and adoration, but if you become too self-absorbed, the partnership can become strained to the breaking point. The golden rule can be an all-purpose answer. Treat your mate as you would like to be treated yourself.

You can both be lavishly generous with loved ones. Just make sure to include your sweetheart in the equation. A little bit of approval, recognition, and encouragement goes a very long way in this relationship. Your creative ways with romance allow you to enjoy a wealth of pleasure.

Venus in **LEO** matched with Venus in **VIRGO** ♌ ♍

The two of you can make this a perfect match or a perfect disaster. One of you tends to thrive on being appreciated, and the other is a first-class appreciator, able to pick up and elaborate on the fine points of what makes your mate so wonderful—a list of virtues that your mate will never tire of hearing. Perfect!

If you allow the relationship to become all about one partner, though, the magic can fade. The lower-profile mate may become critical and judgmental. When the spotlight turns into a microscope, the once-adored, golden glory can lose heart and interest.

Doing a lot of favors and working behind the scenes can be satisfying, but the partner who does this needs a fair share of intimate attention and approval. Fortunately, the more outgoing mate can more than compensate with warmth, encouragement, and infinite generosity. Mutuality can make this relationship work.

► LOOK UP YOUR RELATIONSHIP KARMA *on p. 824*   ► DISCOVER THE RELATIONSHIP KARMA YOU SHARE WITH CELEBRITIES *on p. 760*

Venus in **LEO** matched with Venus in **LIBRA** ♌♎

You are likely to be the couple that everyone wants at their party. Elegant and charismatic, gregarious and warm, you can attract attention and a wide range of friends and admirers. Your tastes tend to run rich, but never pretentious. Enjoying the finest in wining, dining, and entertainment may be a staple of your romantic life.

Maintaining equality in your relationship may be important but challenging. And while one mate may press for a solid commitment, the other may be somewhat indecisive, although always in a pleasant, however maddeningly evasive way. These problems tend to dissolve when both partners agree to make communication and compromise a high priority in the relationship.

For you, living in the lap of luxury can mean a relationship flush with loving generosity and playful affection. Both gloriously creative, you can encourage each other in expressing your ideas and filling your life together with beauty and romance.

Venus in **LEO** matched with Venus in **SCORPIO** ♌♏

The built-in challenges of this relationship can spark the flames of passion. You are both high-powered lovers with tremendous wills. A hypnotic sense of chemistry may draw you together. The noble courage of one partner can present the other with an intriguing invitation to play.

Lovers' quarrels between you two can look like the clash of the titans. One mate may roar with fury while the other douses the fire with verbal blows that cut to the core. After licking your wounds, you can reunite, find forgiving salvation in each other's arms, and start anew.

Such power struggles may be a key element in the attraction between you. Stubborn but heartfelt devotion can hold you together over the long term. The bottom line is that you just thrill each other. The high drama you generate can satisfy any cravings you may have for intensity of feeling and deeply penetrating pleasure.

793

Venus in **LEO** matched with Venus in **SAGITTARIUS** ♌♐

This match-up triggers a gold rush of laughter, fun, and passion. Enough is never enough for either partner, and you may spoil each other with lavish treats, favors, and affection. No one is likely to say no to adventure—in travel, entertainment, or intimacy—as you are both brave souls who revel in risk. Together, you may take a lucky gamble in love.

While you are both true to the core, you may learn that the truth sometimes hurts, particularly if it's conveyed in blunt observations. One mate's sunny exterior can veil a tender heart that bruises easily. It is possible to show sensitivity, without having to kowtow to another's ego.

You're both highly resilient, and for the most part it's easy to laugh off the little bumps and rough patches along the way. Few couples are more cheery and optimistic, especially when love deals you such a royal flush.

Venus in **LEO** matched with Venus in **CAPRICORN** ♌♑

To climb the ladder of success, it helps to be able to see where you're going, and in the sunshine of this love match, you need never lose your way. Your potential to be great assets to each other may draw you together. One mate sparkles with charisma and creativity, while the other conveys a take-charge air of competence and self-assurance.

Because you both have rather different styles, you can sometimes lose patience with your mate's preoccupations. All work and no play can make for a dull partner, but all play and no work can make for a slew of unfulfilled goals. Sharing your dreams allows you to get excited about all you can accomplish as a team.

You both place great value on fidelity and keeping your word. Your mutual honor and confidence ensures a relationship based on honesty and trust. Loyalty seals your commitment for the long term.

▶ **LOOK UP YOUR RELATIONSHIP KARMA** *on p. 824*   ▶ **DISCOVER THE RELATIONSHIP KARMA YOU SHARE WITH CELEBRITIES** *on p. 760*

Your Romantic Compatibility

Venus in **LEO** matched with Venus in **AQUARIUS**

Love can strike you two like a bolt out of the blue, and you may gravitate towards each other like magnets with opposing charges. A mutual appreciation for each other's talents as individuals may provide a friendly foundation for your relationship. You may feel that your mate is the one person who can truly appreciate just how unique and special you are.

While one mate tends to be self-oriented, the other tends to care about humanity in general.

This difference can lead to accusations of selfishness versus impersonality. Understanding the virtue of being true to yourself can provide you with a way out of the impasse.

You may both be rebellious, and so long as you're on the same side, such tendencies can be thrilling and entertaining. Making a heartfelt commitment to serve others together allows you to share in expressing the highest form of love a couple can give.

Venus in **LEO** matched with Venus in **PISCES**

As the leading players in the theater of love, you two can stage quite a steamy romance. Each partner has an enchanting flair for drama that keeps this relationship endlessly engaging and entertaining. Your mate may sweep you off your feet with a flourish, or you might seduce your sweetheart into submission with a come-hither expression.

Prima donna tendencies might put a damper on passion. A mate's overwhelming demands for approval

can bring the action to a grinding halt. And if the other gets sulky and doesn't want to play, you both miss out on the fun. A little empathy and generosity towards your sweetheart can get things rolling again.

Each partner has what it takes to be a great audience as well as a star. You can both be wonderfully supportive and encouraging towards your mate. With amazing creativity, you can entice each other with intrigue, mystery, and excitement.

Venus in **VIRGO** matched with Venus in **VIRGO**

As two of a Venusian kind, you may know certain secrets about each other that would be neither obvious nor readily shared with other lovers. You may appear prim, prudent, and discreet, but your sweetheart can detect an enticingly, earthy sensuality about you. Because you both tend to be fastidious where love and romance is concerned, you can enjoy the comfort of being with a kindred spirit.

You're usually able to anticipate each other's particular

needs, but nobody's perfect. Sometimes you may find yourselves picking at each other, especially in stressful situations. Both of you tend to be perceptive and self-aware, so you should be able to snap out of it, figure out what's really bothering you, and fix it.

A gift for adaptability enables the two of you to make the little adjustments that a healthy partnership requires. Willingness to work together can ensure the longevity of your relationship.

Venus in **VIRGO** matched with Venus in **LIBRA**

Exquisite taste may trigger the initial attraction in this match-up, and you may enjoy treating each other to the finest in dining, drinking, and cultural entertainment. Because you share a preference for delicacy, good manners are likely to be a hallmark of your partnership. You may subtly seduce each other through elegantly sexy attire and gentle attention to a sweetheart's desires.

Disagreements can arise as to the usefulness of

criticism as a means of expressing affection. People of goodwill can differ over whether it's better to be truthful or to be nice. Both of you may have well-intentioned designs for making over your mate, but it's best to approach such a project with subtlety and tact.

The flow of conversation tends to sparkle with insight and engaging wit. Neither partner needs to be reminded to take the other's wishes into account, an advantage that lends harmony to your bond.

► LOOK UP YOUR RELATIONSHIP KARMA *on p. 824* ► DISCOVER THE RELATIONSHIP KARMA YOU SHARE WITH CELEBRITIES *on p. 760*

Venus in **VIRGO** matched with Venus in **SCORPIO**

Yours is a love that runs deep and pure. Intensely private and discreet, the two of you can create your own intimate realm where you can safely expose your innermost feelings, forbidden thoughts, and passionate sensuality. The trust and attraction you share allows you to know each other in a way that no one else can possibly imagine.

Once you've gained access to your mate's tender side, an irresistible compulsion may move you to start fiddling around and make—or at least suggest—some changes.

This is a no-no. Both of you are highly sensitive and can instantly erect a steel plate wall to shut off criticism, judgments, or attempts at control.

Acceptance, understanding, and unconditional love work best in this relationship. Fierce honesty meets with appreciation here, so long as you are talking about your own feelings, perceptions, and needs. Feedback should be given on a strictly "take-what-you-need-and-leave-the-rest" basis.

Venus in **VIRGO** matched with Venus in **SAGITTARIUS**

This relationship often follows a traditional model, in which a fiery, outgoing suitor takes on the challenge of drawing out a shy, hard-to-get, but intriguing sweetheart. The pursuer may be under the impression that beneath the understated exterior lies a treasure trove of goodies, just waiting to be discovered. Such an assumption would be correct.

Your outward styles tend to be very different, and the thundering approach of one mate can be overwhelming

to someone more bashful. A cat-and-mouse dynamic can energize the passion between the lovers. Ultimately, the admirer's optimism, sincerity, and persistence win the day and the approval of the more wary mate.

Both partners can offer each other a wealth of benefits. You both tend to express affection through generous giving. While one mate may lavish a beloved with material goods and hearty encouragement, the other is likely to serve, with caring favors and hard work.

Venus in **VIRGO** matched with Venus in **CAPRICORN**

This partnership brings the satisfaction of finally meeting the person who shares your high standards and has the work ethic to live up to them. You are both practical, no-nonsense types, frugal and sensible when necessary, and lusty and sensual when no one else is looking.

Because you tend to see so eye to eye, there is very little potential for conflict here. Both mates tend to appreciate each other's steady diligence. Sometimes

your living or loving habits can become too rigid, and pressure can arise to let go of the old ways and start thinking outside the box.

Leaving "the box" can be a little scary, but it tends to keep the relationship fresh and moving forward. You are both very private people, modest and respectful of propriety. When you're alone, though, you can let loose with an animal passion so wild it would shock you if it weren't so instinctive.

Venus in **VIRGO** matched with Venus in **AQUARIUS**

A lively exchange of ideas can get this relationship going and keep things interesting. You may appreciate each other's contrasting perspectives. One mate can envision possibilities while the other tends to analyze things from a practical standpoint. The imagination and vast knowledge you share can make you extremely effective in realizing your goals together.

You are both cool customers who can deal with relationships and sexuality with a rather clinical

objectivity. Taking an experimental approach to intimacy can be intriguing and entertaining for both of you. Still, you may need to make an extra effort to bring some earthy warmth and romance into your love life.

Serving a cause together is something that can add passion to your relationship. You both share genuine concern for others. At the same time, the two of you may enjoy the occasional pleasure of getting away from the rat race and renewing your bond.

▶ LOOK UP YOUR RELATIONSHIP KARMA *on p. 824* ▶ DISCOVER THE RELATIONSHIP KARMA YOU SHARE WITH CELEBRITIES *on p. 760*

Venus in **VIRGO** matched with Venus in **PISCES** ♍♓

This fantasy match-up is for real. The dreamy aspirations of one mate can come in for a soft landing in the practical possibilities envisioned by the other. Together you are a couple of idealists, able to contribute the imagination, clear thinking, and hard work necessary to make your dreams come true.

Your ability to envision a perfect world together can exert a magnetic attraction between the two of you. But, directed at each other, perfectionism can

wound sensitive feelings. Each of you wants nothing better than to please the other. Protecting the tenderness of your attachment needs to be a high priority in this partnership.

Between the romantic seductiveness of one mate and the sweet sensuality of the other, you can enjoy a magical partnership. The logical incisiveness of one partner can bring out the best in a sweetheart's creativity. You can inspire and care for each other beautifully.

Venus in **LIBRA** matched with Venus in **LIBRA** ♎♎

Love doesn't get any sweeter than it does in this romance. Both of you tend to be expert in showing consideration for your mate's needs and feelings. Conversation tends to proceed with great delicacy and tact, as neither of you is likely to tolerate harsh words or in-your-face confrontations.

An outsider watching you make decisions together might get dizzy. The two of you tend to go around and around, touching on all possibilities and making a

painstaking effort not to offend each other. For you, the process of negotiation can be pleasant in and of itself, but at some point you have to just choose.

The two of you are likely to enjoy an elegant lifestyle, with a harmonious household and a glamorous social calendar packed with events and parties. You tend to be an attractive couple and can make quite an impression as you indulge each other in the finest dining and cultural entertainment.

Venus in **LIBRA** matched with Venus in **SCORPIO** ♎♏

Bustier-ripping passion meets hearts-and-flowers romance in this affair. The enchanting chemistry between you can inspire great creativity. Grace abounds between you and can motivate both partners to overcome their inhibitions and take a loving leap of faith. If one of you has been hurt before, this partnership can grant you a new lease on life.

Good manners and courteous customs alone won't cut the romantic mustard. Emotional honesty really matters in this relationship. Besides, it's impossible to

keep your true feelings hidden from an intuitive mate. Opening up and showing all sides of your self can enhance the trust and increase the staying power of your bond.

Once these two partners make a commitment, it is as good as etched in stone. No matter what kinds of challenges you may face, the healing power of love is on your side. Together you can enjoy many nights of hedonistic pleasure.

Venus in **LIBRA** matched with Venus in **SAGITTARIUS**

Glamour, social engagements, travel—all this can be yours in this infinitely stimulating match-up. You two may be a must-invite couple at parties, where you can mingle freely and charm everybody with your elegance and good humor. A love for exotic art and culture can provide another source of endless entertainment.

While you both share a passion for truth and justice, your different styles in pursuing these virtues can clash at times. The more outspoken partner can benefit from a

few lessons in tact and diplomacy, and the more well-mannered mate may come to appreciate the advantages of being direct and upfront.

The mental sparks between you can be enough to keep you awake nights, trading ideas and laughing until you can't breathe. You are both very indulgent lovers, eager to lavish each other with romantic favors. Together you can take aim at the stars and realize your highest aspirations.

▶ LOOK UP YOUR RELATIONSHIP KARMA *on p. 824* ▶ DISCOVER THE RELATIONSHIP KARMA YOU SHARE WITH CELEBRITIES *on p. 760*

Venus in **LIBRA** matched with Venus in **CAPRICORN** ♎ ♑

Power can be the aphrodisiac that draws the two of you together. One mate tends to take good care of material needs. Only the best will do for a sweetheart! The other partner may be more of a people person, ensuring the health and happiness of your relationship and bringing you the benefits of a sparkling social life, networking, and community.

With understanding and acceptance, you can cope with differing romantic styles. Rather than protest a partner's resistance to "mushy love stuff," you can find ample evidence of love in measures taken to assure your security or in a mate's presence and support on important occasions.

Just the same, to say "I love you" can go a very long way to reinforce good feelings. You are both well-mannered people but may generously indulge each other in private. Devoted to commitment, you can make your relationship a delightful labor of love.

Venus in **LIBRA** matched with Venus in **AQUARIUS** ♎ ♒

Friendly flirting can turn into a vibrant love affair for this pair. The intellectual firepower each of you brings to the equation can make for absorbing conversations. Able to capture each other's imagination with creative possibilities, the two of you may be compelled to start making plans for a fabulous future.

Both of you can fall in love with a beautiful idea, and following through on your plans may be a bit of a challenge. Still, your airy noncommittal natures allow you to come and go freely, while maintaining good feelings. Regular, repeated contact allows you can crank up the desire and will to take your relationship to the next level of feeling and commitment.

The two of you may enjoy a varied and exciting social life. One-on-one intimacy for you is marked by a gentle, easy compatibility. Treating each other fairly can be the key to lasting harmony.

Venus in **LIBRA** matched with Venus in **PISCES** ♎ ♓

An atmosphere of gentle harmony prevails in this relationship. The partners tend to treat each other with great care and delicacy. The tender language of emotion is spoken here, and you may go to great pains to avoid offending your sweetheart's sensitivities. Each mate has a unique gift for inspiring a beloved's creativity.

You both tend to avoid conflict, and fear of a partner's reaction can keep you from raising various concerns. When issues are allowed to brew, they can create tension, and one or both of you may sulk or withdraw. Keep in mind your fear of confrontation is almost always more severe than the reality.

Both of you are highly sympathetic listeners, eager to help, please, and support your mate. Free-flowing communication is the life blood of this relationship, as it allows you to avoid misunderstandings. Together you can share comfort, passion, and the wealth of your imagination.

Venus in **SCORPIO** matched with Venus in **SCORPIO** ♏ ♏

An irresistible impulse draws the two of you together. Physical attraction may strike you immediately and is likely to remain a powerful force throughout the life of your relationship. You may feel as if you have finally found your true soul mate, the one person who can understand you intimately, wordlessly, completely.

You both have gargantuan wills, and when they conflict, it can seem as if you've plunged into a life-or-death struggle. If worries and anger are allowed to stew, you can hurt each other deeply. The urgency of your feelings makes it a first-order priority to keep lines of communication open and constantly flowing.

The creativity between you can be energizing beyond compare. It can be an immense relief to be with someone as intensely passionate as you are. In your lover's arms, you may feel reborn. Mutual respect is the mortar that holds you two together over time.

► LOOK UP YOUR RELATIONSHIP KARMA *on p. 824*   ► DISCOVER THE RELATIONSHIP KARMA YOU SHARE WITH CELEBRITIES *on p. 760*

Your Romantic Compatibility

Venus in **SCORPIO** matched with Venus in **SAGITTARIUS**   ♏ ♐

A hypnotic fascination energizes this partnership, as if you've been given the chance to explore the best of all worlds. One mate throws open the door to active adventure, inviting you to encounter exotic cultures and wondrous experiences. The other partner can lead you through a portal into the mysterious passions of the soul.

While you may share a passionate commitment to truth seeking, overly blunt talk can offend tender sensitivities. It is important for you to agree to keep the details of your intimate affairs strictly secret. A philosophical outlook and sense of humor helps to keep things light and fills this partnership with exuberance.

A sense of danger may make this relationship all the more enticing, as both of you tend to exult in the thrills of risk-taking. You probably can't help but be intrigued by each other. Together you can plunge into the abundance of life with intensity.

Venus in **SCORPIO** matched with Venus in **CAPRICORN**   ♏ ♑

In this classic collaboration, willpower meets the material means to make it happen, with god-like effectiveness. The two of you can be deadly serious, and whatever you set your powerhouse minds on together, you can have—or else! When no one is looking, you can get absolutely wicked pleasure from each other.

It can be hard to pull out of a heavy mood when you are both feeling down. Still, you two specialize in rising to the occasion in tough challenges. When too much idle time goes by, one of you can snap the other out of it through sheer determination.

You both tend to be intensely private people, and your intimate life together can be delightfully naughty, bordering on lurid. Behind closed doors, you may drop all inhibitions and go at each other with an animal passion. Dark but sidesplitting humor allows you to keep things light.

Venus in **SCORPIO** matched with Venus in **AQUARIUS**   ♏ ♒

When two powerful personalities such as you come together, the passion and intensity can be electrifying. The prospect of exploring the intriguing mysteries of intimacy may attract you to each other. Having a meaningful life may be a mutual goal, and this relationship can more than deliver on that promise.

To make your commitment secure, you simply must have a baseline understanding that your connection is the most unique, special, and important of all. A sense of profound trust between you allows both mates to pursue outside friendships and activities without triggering jealousy or fears of abandonment.

This match-up can be a powerful antidote to loneliness and isolation. Your bond allows you to extend yourselves emotionally and in the world. On your sweetheart's arm, you may enjoy greater courage to expand your social life. At home, you can gain the sense of connection and understanding that may elude you in the crowd.

Venus in **SCORPIO** matched with Venus in **PISCES**   ♏ ♓

Once submerged in the sea of love, neither of you may see any need to come back up for air. Emotionally, you are perfectly matched. One mate can effortlessly accommodate the other's need for total immersion in love and affection. And when the most seductive personality in creation meets the other most seductive personality in creation, physical attraction is a given.

As nice as it may be, if you stay isolated together for too long, you're likely to start getting on each other's nerves. At some point, one or both of you may start to itch for renewed contact with the outside world.

The stimulation you receive out on the town and with other people gives you plenty of material to talk about when you go home to debrief each other about your adventures. Your spiritual life tends to be as incredibly rich as the creativity you inspire in each other.

► LOOK UP YOUR RELATIONSHIP KARMA *on p. 824* ► DISCOVER THE RELATIONSHIP KARMA YOU SHARE WITH CELEBRITIES *on p. 760*

Venus in **SAGITTARIUS** matched with Venus in **SAGITTARIUS**

When Venus falls twice in the sign of the Centaur, unbridled passion follows. In this eight-legged romp, no one will ever tell you to hold your horses. Rather, you two happy wanderers are likely to gallop wherever your lust for life—and each other—takes you. Together you can enjoy the best in wining, dining, and cultural refining.

A Las Vegas wedding would be one ultimate adventure—(there are many)—for you two romantic risk-takers. Because you both tend to be gamblers, you can win big and lose big. You'll either have to agree on some limits and boundaries or consent to accept setbacks without blame or recrimination.

Tremendous optimism and luck are gifts you may share, and you can rely on your resilience to help you take any ups and downs in stride. A fabulous sense of humor and a philosophical outlook hold you together throughout this thrilling journey.

Venus in **SAGITTARIUS** matched with Venus in **CAPRICORN**

If you're looking for a relationship to help you get ahead in life, you've come to the right mate. When it comes to defining and meeting goals, this combination can't be beat. The awesome focus you share can inspire instant and mutual admiration. You may feel freer to take risks you never dreamed of and heartened by results you might never have achieved on your own.

You've both made a bit of a trade-off by choosing a partner whose traits can be opposite to your own. One's fearless impulses may seem reckless. The other's conservative restraint may seem miserly. It helps to remember the greater benefits you gain by having talents that can complement each other.

The two of you may share a fabulous sense of humor, and laughing together may be a potent aphrodisiac. In private, you may enjoy an orgiastic enthusiasm for naughty horseplay and sensory indulgence.

Venus in **SAGITTARIUS** matched with Venus in **AQUARIUS**

For this dynamic duo, a spirited exchange of intellectual derring-do can spark the flames of passion. Your mate's ingenious insights may strike you like a bolt of lightning. Together you may enjoy an exciting social life, with many friends and stimulating outings.

The high-flying mental acrobatics in this partnership can be thrilling. Once things settle into a groove, though, a sense of emotional attachment can be lacking. To give this relationship "legs," the two of you need to cultivate intimacy. You both tend to be deeply devoted to the truth, and your soulful sincerity can inspire tender empathy.

Sharing your dreams can bind your hearts together, as you can assure each other that nothing is impossible. You are both idealistic adventurers, eager to take on the world together. The prospect of exploring each other's mind, body, and soul can exert a powerful attraction. With steady encouragement, your love can grow.

Venus in **SAGITTARIUS** matched with Venus in **PISCES**

Generosity is the keynote for this combination, as both of you tend to lavish a sweetheart with sentimental keepsakes, sensual pleasures, and thoughtful favors. Because each partner's personality has many facets, exploring each other can be as fascinating and intriguing as an expedition to an exotic isle.

You may both agree that honesty is essential to a healthy relationship, but you may differ on what exactly that means. One mate may put a beautiful spin on hard cold facts, and the other may sometimes wield truth like a blunt instrument. To be sure you're "on the same page," tact and gentle consideration for each other's feelings can help.

Travel can be a favored activity, and the two of you are likely to be accomplished escape artists. Whether you fly to distant lands or wander through landscapes painted in your dreams, your journeys together may be filled with romance and magic.

▶ LOOK UP YOUR RELATIONSHIP KARMA *on p. 824* ▶ DISCOVER THE RELATIONSHIP KARMA YOU SHARE WITH CELEBRITIES *on p. 760*

Your Romantic Compatibility

Venus in **CAPRICORN** matched with Venus in **CAPRICORN** ♑ ♑

To be with someone every bit as capable and accomplished as yourself can be an enormous relief. With a take-charge confidence and a clear sense of what belongs where, the two of you may feel that your relationship stands as the last bastion of sanity and order in a crazy, mixed-up world.

Both of you like to be in control, and it may be hard to resist the urge to micromanage your mate. To avoid conflict it's best to delegate responsibilities in your

relationship. Letting go and having faith in your sweetheart's abilities allows you to fully enjoy the benefits of this most competent match-up.

Once you both come to truly trust each other, this bond is unbreakable. Your respect for commitment and for each other boosts your chances for romantic success. Though you may not poetically state your love, it is forever true. In private, you may share humor and a wild sensuality that makes all your hard work worthwhile.

Venus in **CAPRICORN** matched with Venus in **AQUARIUS** ♑ ♒

When these two visionaries unite, great things become possible. Your ability to "think outside the box" together can make inspiring sparks that turn into romantic fireworks. A sense of shared aspiration can excite and magnetize the two of you. Once concrete results start showing up, the roots of this romance can become firmly established.

One partner may launch into all-out revolt if the other insists on being the boss in this relationship. To have peace together, you may have to agree to divide up

certain aspects of your life into little fiefdoms, where one mate's say is law—usually because the other mate could not care less.

You can exert a steadying influence on each other, without having to sacrifice your need for change and growth. Your relationship grants you the stability of progress that comes gradually over time. The intimacy you share tends to be lusty, refreshingly playful, and long lasting.

Venus in **CAPRICORN** matched with Venus in **PISCES** ♑ ♓

This is one comforting combination. Dreamy imagination, sometimes adrift at sea, can find a safe, secure mooring. You may love what you get from each other. The diligent worker can come home to a sanctuary of soothing serenity. A partner with tender sensibilities can relax into a relationship in which trust is the rule.

Practical concerns may get different priority from each of you, but you're unlikely to fight about it, and it's not worth fighting about anyway. Rather, one

mate may wither and withdraw if the other presses the issue. The one who cares the least is likely to simply let the other mate handle the business in the family.

The realm of sensuality is where this relationship comes alive. The seductive sweetness of your bond can make you hunger for each other. Together you can enjoy an ardent passion that sparks your creativity and inspires your devotion.

Venus in **AQUARIUS** matched with Venus in **AQUARIUS** ♒ ♒

For these two romantic nonconformists, it can be a tremendous relief to be with a kindred spirit. Love may have struck you like a lightning bolt, just as your friendship was getting comfortable. Likely to be intellectual equals, you have an instant basis for mutual respect. You may sense that you are somehow different from (and better than) other couples.

The two of you are unlikely to have any problem with each other's need for freedom. Just as suddenly as your

romance ignited, though, it can slip back into a friendship. To give this relationship staying power—and growing power—you may need to make a conscious effort to nurture intimacy.

Sparring over issues can excite your passions, but opening up about things that matter personally can open up a whole new emotional dimension to your attachment. Sharing your dreams and deepest desires can bless your partnership with staying power.

800

► LOOK UP YOUR RELATIONSHIP KARMA *on p. 824* ► DISCOVER THE RELATIONSHIP KARMA YOU SHARE WITH CELEBRITIES *on p. 760*

Venus in **AQUARIUS** matched with Venus in **PISCES** ♒♓

Life can be a dream for two idealistic souls like you. With your different perspectives—one intuitive, one logical—you may engage each other in long and fascinating conversations. Imagining a perfect world together can compel you to make a modest attempt at fixing things, with a loving relationship that can provide an escape from all the corruption and ugliness outside.

You may find it challenging to relate to each other on certain levels. One mate's cool, analytic temperament may leave the other hungering for closeness. Patience can be a virtue here. Fortunately, the partner with the greater emotional needs also tends to have the most powerful seductive pull.

The two of you are likely to experiment with a wide variety of romantic diversions. Caring deeply for others is a trait you are both likely to share, and aiding others together allows you to experience the highest form of love.

Venus in **PISCES** matched with Venus in **PISCES** ♓♓

Once upon a time, two lovers found themselves living in a fairy tale. This relationship, with all its hearts, flowers, and rosy romance, is for real. When you two seductive spirits come together, you can entertain each other endlessly. Understand each other? You're more likely to read each other's mind!

While the two of you are busy enjoying music, theater, and other such crucial occupations, practical matters can slide. Eventually one or both of you may have to come back to earth and take care of business. One partner usually takes more responsibility than the other, but recriminations are not likely to be a problem.

Both of you take care of each other in your own ways. An abundance of empathy keeps this relationship running smoothly. Shared spirituality can provide an enduring foundation for your commitment. Your deep attachment can fill your days together with creativity, playful escapes and magic.

► LOOK UP YOUR RELATIONSHIP KARMA *on p. 824* ► DISCOVER THE RELATIONSHIP KARMA YOU SHARE WITH CELEBRITIES *on p. 760*

YOUR COMPATIBILITY

Your Sexual Compatibility

(SEE YOUR ROMANTIC COMPATIBILITY ON PAGE 780)

What turns you on? Does your partner light your fire or throw cold water on the flames? Do your bodies dance to the same rhythm or are you out of step with each other's sexual needs? Do you bring out the animal in one another?

Each of us expresses our passion in special, distinct ways, according to the sign our Mars is in. If your Mars Sign is compatible with your partner's Mars Sign, you have the ability to spark each other's lust and satisfy one another's deepest desires. You just naturally pick up on each other's cues and know what gives one another pleasure. You find the same things stimulating. You make beautiful music together. But if your Mars and your partner's Mars are at odds, you may frustrate one another or experience tension when you are together. Perhaps your sexual cycles aren't the same, or one person's libido is stronger than the other's. In this section, you'll see how your sexual quotient and your partner's interact, and learn how you can turn up the heat in your relationship.

INSTRUCTIONS

HERE'S HOW TO READ ABOUT YOUR SEXUAL COMPATIBILITY.

1 Find your Zodiac Sign reading.

2 Look beside your Zodiac Sign for **Your Love Planets**. Under **Your Sex Drive**, you'll find your Mars Sign.

3 Look up your partner's Zodiac Sign and Mars Sign.

4 Look at the index below. Locate Your Mars Sign and your Partner's Mars Sign. Where the two lines intersect, there is a page number. Turn to this page to read all about **Your Sexual Compatibility**.

Note: Keep all of your Astrological Love Information handy by jotting down the page numbers of your Birth Year Events, Zodiac Sign, and Mars Sign and your Partner's Birth Year Events, Zodiac Sign, and Mars Sign.

Example

If you were born on June 3, 1964, you would be a Gemini with a Mars in Taurus. If your partner was born on January 31, 1964, he or she would be an Aquarius with a Mars in Aquarius. On the chart below, locate Mars in Taurus and Mars in Aquarius. Where the two lines intersect you will find the page number of **Your Sexual Compatibility**. What type of sexual sizzle does this pairing have? In this example, the Sexual Compatibility Reading is found on page 809.

YOUR SEXUAL COMPATIBILITY PAGE INDEX

PARTNER'S MARS SIGN

YOUR MARS SIGN	ARIES	TAURUS	GEMINI	CANCER	LEO	VIRGO	LIBRA	SCORPIO	SAGITTARIUS	CAPRICORN	AQUARIUS	PISCES
ARIES	p. 804	p. 804	p. 804	p. 804	p. 805	p. 805	p. 805	p. 805	p. 806	p. 806	p. 806	p. 806
TAURUS		p. 807	p. 807	p. 807	p. 807	p. 808	p. 808	p. 808	p. 808	p. 809	p. 809	p. 809
GEMINI			p. 809	p. 810	p. 810	p. 810	p. 810	p. 811	p. 811	p. 811	p. 811	p. 812
CANCER				p. 812	p. 812	p. 812	p. 813	p. 813	p. 813	p. 813	p. 814	p. 814
LEO					p. 814	p. 814	p. 815	p. 815	p. 815	p. 815	p. 816	p. 816
VIRGO						p. 816	p. 816	p. 817	p. 817	p. 817	p. 817	p. 818
LIBRA							p. 818	p. 818	p. 818	p. 819	p. 819	p. 819
SCORPIO								p. 819	p. 820	p. 820	p. 820	p. 820
SAGITTARIUS									p. 821	p. 821	p. 821	p. 821
CAPRICORN										p. 822	p. 822	p. 822
AQUARIUS											p. 822	p. 823
PISCES												p. 823

HOW TO USE THIS CHART
- Find your Mars Sign.
- Locate your Partner's Mars Sign.
- Turn to the page indicated where the two lines intersect to read about **Your Sexual Compatibility**.

◄◄ *THE GRADUATE* STARRING ANNE BANCROFT & DUSTIN HOFFMAN

Your Sexual Compatibility

Mars in **ARIES** matched with Mars in **ARIES**

It just doesn't get much more fiery than this. You make love, argue, and make up, all with the same degree of intensity. It is precisely the tempestuous nature of this relationship that makes it so much fun.

With all of its high drama your love life may bear a close resemblance to a romance novel. But the two of you know that any partnership needs stability, too, to thrive and grow. Knowing that you can count on each other's loyalty and support in good times and difficult times makes you feel deeply connected.

Even though both love and sexual attraction seems to come easily to this relationship, you are likely to work very hard at keeping the romance alive by being spontaneous. Giving each other "naughty but nice" gifts on Valentine's Day or on other special occasions is just one way of keeping the spirit of love alive the whole year 'round. Most of all, keep it physical!

Mars in **ARIES** matched with Mars in **TAURUS**

Your union is characterized by strong sexual attraction and a great deal of affection. The passion between the two of you burns long and hot, like smoldering embers. People can tell you are in love by just observing you walking hand in hand down the street.

For you sharing is a powerful and magnetic force in the partnership. Being able to confide sexual fantasies to each other and then act upon them forges a deeply satisfying love life. While you understand that great sex alone doesn't make a relationship work, you also believe that no couple can be truly happy unless there is plenty of sexual chemistry.

Because of the intense feelings that exist between you, even minor misunderstandings can give rise to attitudes of jealousy on occasion. This emotion has the potential to be troublesome, but a spirit of genuine love keeps you from staying angry for very long.

Mars in **ARIES** matched with Mars in **GEMINI**

Your union is punctuated with a lot of giggles and some good-natured teasing. You use humor as a way of getting closer, and even if this approach may not work for other couples, it certainly works for you. Even when there are periods of stress in the relationship, you know that a few gentle and well-placed jokes will break the tension.

If there is any drawback to your partnership, it is an inability to confront issues realistically. Sometimes you prefer to leave things unsaid rather than risk an argument, but it is better to trust each other enough to make a few criticisms now and then.

Your lovemaking requires updated novel approaches to keep it lively, which is what your sex life thrives on. The two of you believe in making time to be together, no matter how busy your individual schedules may be. As far as you are concerned, the measure of true love is what you are willing to give up for it.

Mars in **ARIES** matched with Mars in **CANCER**

You have the kind of relationship that seems to embody all the best qualities of being in love—passion, understanding, and the ability to ignore differences in habits and opinions while being able to celebrate the piquancy these bring to your union.

Being able to depend on one another in any situation helps to develop an attitude of trust that makes the sexual elements of your partnership marvelous. Because you derive so much satisfaction from talking things out, there is very little left unsaid between you. That level of sensitivity has a ripple effect that makes itself felt in every area of your life together. Needless to say, it is an extremely powerful influence for the good.

If there is a drawback to your partnership, it is possibly that too much emotionalism overrides practicality at times. But even when you do have arguments, you forgive each other quickly, without holding a grudge.

▶ LOOK UP YOUR RELATIONSHIP KARMA *on p. 824* ▶ DISCOVER THE RELATIONSHIP KARMA YOU SHARE WITH CELEBRITIES *on p. 760*

Mars in **ARIES** matched with Mars in **LEO** ♈♌

There is so much drama in this planetary pairing that your relationship sometimes resembles a TV soap opera. But even when the emotion meter is turned up too high, the feelings are honest and sincere. You believe you were made for each other, and that your union is special on every level.

You are a glamorous couple, and you usually manage to turn heads whenever you are out. There is something about the way you look at each other that lets everyone else in the room know you are madly in love.

There may seem to be as much dissent as agreement in this relationship—as much criticism as kissing—but it doesn't detract from your happiness one bit. You simply have a very vocal relationship in which the two of you feel perfectly comfortable speaking your mind. It's exactly that kind of passion and commitment that makes you the perfect couple.

Mars in **ARIES** matched with Mars in **VIRGO** ♈♍

You are a very passionate couple, and you enjoy stealing an occasional kiss in public or engaging in a little affectionate cuddling at the table of your favorite restaurant. Spontaneity is just one of the ways you show how much you love each other. How you feel about one another seems to be written on your faces. In the bedroom, your ardor knows no bounds—you'll do anything together!

At times it is easy for you to get caught up in the minutiae and day-to-day aspects of a partnership, such as who is responsible for what chores and whose job it is to pick up the dry cleaning. But these details in no way detract from the romance.

There is nothing superficial going on here—this is a serious and mature relationship. You feel you can depend upon each other to tell the truth and be supportive regarding all major decisions that confront you as a couple—now, as well as in the future.

Mars in **ARIES** matched with Mars in **LIBRA** ♈♎

Communicating on a verbal as well as nonverbal level is an important element of your success as a couple. This truth is you simply love being together. You believe that sharing life's minor moments has its charms, too, because that is what makes it possible to appreciate the larger moments.

Tempers can flare easily in this relationship, causing the two of you to snap at each other, or even blame the other for things that are wrong between you.

Fortunately, you meet most of the stress in this romantic partnership with common sense and a level-headed approach to the problem.

You are a playful and inventive pair who believes in communicating your wants and desires to each other. The two of you never tire of trying new things in and out of the bedroom. Thanks to this attitude, your relationship stays fresh and spontaneous, no matter how long you are together.

Mars in **ARIES** matched with Mars in **SCORPIO** ♈♏

Alternately stormy and sensual, this relationship has a lot of emotional resonance. This closeness benefits greatly from an unspoken communication, and at times it may seem you can read each other's thoughts. It is this amazing connection that gives both depth and sweetness to the relationship.

Because your feelings are deep, there can be occasions when you are seriously at odds, even about sexual habits and needs. You certainly understand that to really enjoy each other sexually, you need to be comfortable with your own sexuality. Fortunately, being able to be totally open and honest with each other minimizes the problem that not communicating well can cause.

Permanence is an important factor in your life as a couple. The two of you take a long-term view of your relationship, and you revel in the knowledge you are together—not only today—but for the rest of your lives.

► LOOK UP YOUR RELATIONSHIP KARMA *on p. 824* ► DISCOVER THE RELATIONSHIP KARMA YOU SHARE WITH CELEBRITIES *on p. 760*

Mars in **ARIES** matched with Mars in **SAGITTARIUS** ♈♐

When it comes to romantic fireworks, your relationship really is in a class by itself. Because you are both very high-strung and impulsive, there are probably times when you simply do not see eye to eye. But happily these times are overshadowed by those occasions when the two of you are in complete accord about everything else.

You know how to have a lot of fun as a couple, sexually and in all other ways. There is a certain amount of competition between you that manages to keep things from becoming dull or too predictable. It is this good-natured rivalry that helps to sweeten your sex life.

Once you accept that too much arguing can have a negative impact on the relationship, you might choose to agree to disagree about some things. But that doesn't detract in any way from your basic good compatibility and sexual "sizzle."

Mars in **ARIES** matched with Mars in **CAPRICORN** ♈♑

Although you may not make a big show of affection in public, you certainly qualify as a hot couple behind closed doors. You have a sophisticated kind of relationship that doesn't require constant verbal assurances of love. You believe that doing thoughtful things for one another is every bit as much an affirmation of love as actually speaking those three little words.

At times stubbornness or just the need to be "right" in an argument can have a negative impact on your relationship, causing the two of you to sulk and walk away, rather than talk things out. Or you may choose to make up by making love before you have really settled any differences.

Knowing you can depend on each other to be there in difficult as well as joyous times is one of the elements that keep this relationship fresh and interesting for both of you.

Mars in **ARIES** matched with Mars in **AQUARIUS** ♈♒

There is a quirky kind of vibe to this romance that makes it special. Not only are you lovers, you are likely to be best friends, too—the sort who can make even a shared bowl of popcorn and a late night movie on TV a romantic experience.

While the essence of any fulfilling partnership is being able to appreciate differences, there are many times when those same differences can seriously divide you. When that happens it is easy to wonder just how the two of you ever got together in the first place.

Romantically, you put a great deal of attention into the preliminaries of love, knowing that if you can satisfy each other in these ways, all the rest will be perfection. Words play a big part in how you relate to one another sexually. Fantasy scenarios and erotic conversation help to put you in a sexy mood. Passions sizzle when you play kinky tricks.

Mars in **ARIES** matched with Mars in **PISCES** ♈♓

Even if the two of you may not seem to have what it takes to be one of those "happily ever after" couples, your romance does possess its own form of special magic. Showing your love in thoughtful little ways through a compliment, a surprise gift or a passionate kiss helps to validate the relationship. Sexually, you know how to strike sparks.

Differences in how you see things only help to make the relationship stronger and more exciting. Who wants to be together when there are no challenges or reasons to kiss and make up after a fight? Being at opposite ends of an idea actually gives this partnership more spiritual resonance.

Even in the slow periods there is a lot going on between you, and the enthusiasm to keep things new and special accomplishes just that. Some relationships lose potency with age, but yours just keeps on getting better and better.

▶ LOOK UP YOUR RELATIONSHIP KARMA *on p. 824*   ▶ DISCOVER THE RELATIONSHIP KARMA YOU SHARE WITH CELEBRITIES *on p. 760*

Mars in **TAURUS** matched with Mars in **TAURUS**

Although you may not have a lot of flash as a couple, the two of you sure know how to keep each other feeling on top of the world. Your sex life may lack some variety, but it certainly isn't missing heat, and what some couples might consider boring is actually a turn-on for you.

If there is a drawback to your togetherness, it could be a tendency to take the relationship for granted simply because it is so good. Making an

effort to appreciate each other in both big and small ways keeps this from happening too much to affect the partnership.

For you fine dining is often a prelude to a romantic evening. You appreciate the aesthetic link between great food and great sex. There is so much sensual understanding between the two of you that conversation is often less important than a passionate embrace.

Mars in **TAURUS** matched with Mars in **GEMINI**

There is nothing one-dimensional about this partnership. The two of you enjoy sharing a joke as much as sharing a kiss and seem able to remake the relationship over into anything you want it to be, any time you wish. The sense of freedom provided by this kind of understanding makes your togetherness both strong and special.

Naturally, as every other couple does, you have arguments at times, and it is a tribute to your being

generally so in sync that these are few and far between. At times when you do fight, sarcasm can be a negative means of expression.

The key to your long-term happiness is having a very clear image of just who you are as a couple. Trust and loyalty are major issues for this planetary pairing, and having these core needs met allows the passion and excitement between you to flourish. Sensual and raunchy sexual fantasy trips help as well.

Mars in **TAURUS** matched with Mars in **CANCER**

There is a great deal of empathy and affection in this relationship. You often seem to anticipate each other's thoughts and actions without being told, and you may even finish one another's sentences at times. For you the act of truly knowing one another is a big part of the wonderful gift that comes about as a result of true emotional intimacy.

Control issues have the power to cause problems in this union. Because you are both stubborn and often

unwilling to make compromises, there may be times when the relationship seems to reach an emotional impasse. Fortunately, you usually manage to iron things out.

Even though your attitude toward romance is serious and committed, you do not lose sight of the fact that being together is also about having fun. You know how to make each other feel special in ways that run the gamut from physical passion to spiritual oneness.

Mars in **TAURUS** matched with Mars in **LEO**

You are the sort of couple who believes that a relationship is a living, breathing entity that requires both work and attention. Boredom is never an issue with the two of you because you work very hard to keep things interesting.

Although there is so much positive energy in your relationship, the two of you can't expect your life together to be a bed of roses. You both see yourself as being "right" much of the time, creating tension in the

partnership and bringing out your individual ego issues. Although these problems tend to be transitory, they can cause feelings of anger and disappointment to pull you in opposite directions.

Even though you are a couple that likes to socialize, you prefer spending much of your time alone together. Whether it is a passionate night of lovemaking or a comfortable evening watching TV, you are two who crave togetherness.

▶ LOOK UP YOUR RELATIONSHIP KARMA *on p. 824* ▶ DISCOVER THE RELATIONSHIP KARMA YOU SHARE WITH CELEBRITIES *on p. 760*

Your Sexual Compatibility

Mars in **TAURUS** matched with Mars in **VIRGO**

For the two of you sex doesn't have to be flashy. You actually prefer slow-burning embers to fireworks. You are one of those deeply sensual couples that enjoys keeping each other warm on cold winter nights. Besides all the great sexual feelings, this planetary pairing offers a true meeting of the minds.

There may be times when all this passion works to a disadvantage and a little bit of restlessness sets in. At such times it is easy to take the partnership for granted, simply because it usually runs so smoothly. One way or another, you are able to reignite those romantic sparks.

This is not one of those high-maintenance relationships with a lot of demands and false expectations on both sides. The two of you can appreciate the value of a union in which contentment is looked upon with favor and the communication is virtually effortless.

Mars in **TAURUS** matched with Mars in **LIBRA**

Your expectations about love as a couple waver between self-indulgence and idealism. No matter how compelling the sexual magnetism may be, you two never lose sight of the part romance plays in making love. Even at its most sensual, there is always a feeling of affection in this planetary pairing that makes you friends as well as lovers.

Your attitudes seriously conflict at times, and when this happens it may feel as if all the joy has gone out of your togetherness. When you feel as if the romance has become routine, you can spice things up by making love in an exotic location or indulging in a little fantasy role-playing.

Emotional harmony between the two of you is vital for equal enjoyment. Working this out could become a major issue at times, but it is worth the effort. When it works well, there is not only equality, there is pure joy.

808

Mars in **TAURUS** matched with Mars in **SCORPIO**

There is an incredible amount of passion in this partnership. You don't hold back in your search for total sensual fulfillment and sexual nirvana. This isn't just a love affair—this is a true blending of souls.

Always searching for the balance of power in the relationship, you can experience deep emotions, so much so that it can even hurt. Jealousy is a problem between you that won't always go away, and there are even times when you seem to be as much rivals as lovers. But you manage to work it out because you know how incredible the two of you are together.

Soulful and intense, you enjoy long lovemaking sessions, stirring protestations of love, and dramatic shows of affection. This is a relationship that is hot, rapturous, and filled with the kind of intensity that is generally reserved only for operatic plotlines and X-rated movies.

Mars in **TAURUS** matched with Mars in **SAGITTARIUS**

You make a great couple in social situations because the two of you look so good together. Sexually, you are even more compatible, although one of you likes to move at a faster pace. Your love life is a yummy combination of golden oldies and plenty of new refrains. Either way, you certainly make some very sweet harmonies together.

Because you are such a sensual couple, there can be a frequent tendency to rely a little too much on sex to fix any problems that come into the relationship. Talking things out in detail rather than just jumping into bed right away makes your relationship better and more complete.

When all is said and done, this is a partnership that is meant to last. That is because you do your best to keep improving on what is already a pretty good thing. In love, as in everything else, it is true that practice makes perfect.

▶ LOOK UP YOUR RELATIONSHIP KARMA *on p. 824* ▶ DISCOVER THE RELATIONSHIP KARMA YOU SHARE WITH CELEBRITIES *on p. 760*

Mars in **TAURUS** matched with Mars in **CAPRICORN** ♉♑

In good times or bad, you have the kind of togetherness that really lasts. The two of you don't expect things to run smoothly all the time, and when problems come up, as they inevitably do, the solid foundation you have built through trust and hard work keeps things from falling apart. This is something you can rely on to work.

The potential weaknesses of this union are the same as the strengths. Too much concentration on externals and not enough on the emotional pulse of your togetherness can sometimes cause the romantic sparks to dwindle. Scheduling "spontaneous" romantic trysts every now and then helps keep things hot.

You have a clearly defined relationship, and yet the two of you are not willing to leave it at that. You believe that to remain strong, your partnership needs to adapt to new circumstances, grow, and even change with time.

Mars in **TAURUS** matched with Mars in **AQUARIUS** ♉♒

This relationship is an offbeat blend of oppositions and contradictions—which is precisely what makes it so emotionally intoxicating and fun. There is plenty of passion—with a capital "P"—as well as a great deal of teasing and good humor. You two know that laughter has the ability to promote intimacy between sexual partners.

Because stubbornness and holding a grudge after an argument is a factor in this relationship, compromise can be difficult to achieve. Fortunately, there is also enough love, respect, and common sense to keep these problems to a minimum.

Your romantic partnership is sparked by a lot of common interests and shared values. You know how to have fun on many levels, although romance is usually at the top of the list. Happily, the two of you also recognize the need to emphasize various aspects of your partnership to keep things interesting.

Mars in **TAURUS** matched with Mars in **PISCES** ♉♓

The passion in this relationship has the quality of sensual indulgence, something akin to gorging on hot fudge sundaes and not worrying about the calorie count. Keeping things interesting in the bedroom is never a problem for the two of you. If anything, the longer you are together, the better things are likely to get.

At times a little too much physical passion can keep you from making some needed adjustments in other areas of the relationship. No matter how rewarding great sex is, there are other avenues of togetherness that need to be explored.

The kind of chemistry your partnership has is unusual—both intense and tender. You do not believe in demanding too much from each other. It is much more about "giving" than "getting." In many ways this planetary meld is better suited than any other to be a couple in the most personal sense of the word.

Mars in **GEMINI** matched with Mars in **GEMINI** ♊♊

This planetary pairing is as festive and bubbly as twin servings of pink champagne. At times the level of conversation can be reminiscent of a Noel Coward play. As for the rest of the time, you have a marvelous tendency to play engaging practical jokes on each other that reveal your genuine fondness.

You aren't really comfortable with intense feelings and prefer to keep the relationship lighthearted and emotionally breezy. The downside to this can be an inability to deal with more intense issues between you, somewhat limiting your emotional closeness when you need it most.

The lovemaking between you two is joyful and uninhibited. You have fun trying new things in the bedroom because, as far as you are concerned, too much of the same thing is boring, no matter how good it might be. As a result, you probably have a few "how-to" books on your nightstand!

▶ LOOK UP YOUR RELATIONSHIP KARMA *on p. 824*   ▶ DISCOVER THE RELATIONSHIP KARMA YOU SHARE WITH CELEBRITIES *on p. 760*

Your Sexual Compatibility

Mars in **GEMINI** matched with Mars in **CANCER**   ♊♋

For the two of you romance is so much better when accompanied by friendship. In fact, your union seems to embody the best of both worlds and can flourish with the proper encouragement. You can find happiness in the small things—sleeping late on the weekend, having a lazy brunch, then spending an entire day together. Whether you're shopping, at the movies, or just sitting on the couch holding hands and kissing, you are in a romantic's paradise.

There are times when you neglect to give each other enough space, and the relationship can seem to become demanding, even claustrophobic. Retaining outside friendships and interests helps keep these negative feelings at bay.

The two of you understand that in today's busy and complicated world, romance isn't something that renews itself over and over again—it has to be made a priority. That is what you manage to accomplish, and it certainly works.

Mars in **GEMINI** matched with Mars in **LEO**   ♊♌

You are one of those tempestuous couples that seem to argue a lot, but for the most part, that is just because you don't believe in leaving anything unsaid. You feel that the more you communicate, the better the relationship will be, and basically, your union appears to benefit from this approach. For the two of you silence is so much worse than a fight.

Of course, with this attitude you do run the risk of hurting each other's feelings from time to time. On

these occasions there is a chance that the partnership can be negatively impacted by sarcasm and finger-pointing.

The best thing about this planetary partnership is the amazing energy that is created by your togetherness. Sparks seem to fly when you simply look at one another. This kind of chemistry is priceless and is one of the reasons that your relationship came into being.

Mars in **GEMINI** matched with Mars in **VIRGO**   ♊♍

Refinement and good taste characterize your relationship. You can be extremely passionate, but there is also a great deal of respect and affection in this union. You believe that getting there is half the fun, and can appreciate preludes to lovemaking just as much as you do the main event.

Communication is a crucial element in your partnership. Not only do you rely a good deal on verbal stimuli to get in the mood, it is also a big part

of how you relate to each other in nonsexual situations. When there are spats, you can make up by talking things out in detail. Even awkward moments can be defused by a little playful humor or some witty quips.

Intelligence is a powerful aphrodisiac for you, but the two of you are happiest when the words and the music of love and sex are melded into a glorious symphony of emotion.

Mars in **GEMINI** matched with Mars in **LIBRA**   ♊♎

This is one of those King and Queen of the prom relationships that people on the outside pretend to dislike but secretly envy. You certainly are a fun couple, and it is obvious to just about everyone that you have great chemistry together.

Because you are a talkative pair, there are probably times when a battle of words is not only lively, but unnecessarily sarcastic. You don't really want to hurt each other's feelings, but a need to

get to the bottom of an issue can create a witty banter that sometimes turns nasty.

You believe in love with a light touch, and as a result, your relationship is likely to be characterized by many shared interests and activities, as many of them intellectual in nature as romantic. For you partnership means just that. You want to be equals, friends, lovers, and you won't settle for anything less.

► LOOK UP YOUR RELATIONSHIP KARMA *on p. 824*   ► DISCOVER THE RELATIONSHIP KARMA YOU SHARE WITH CELEBRITIES *on p. 760*

Mars in **GEMINI** matched with Mars in **SCORPIO** ♊♏

You make a charismatic pair of lovers. There is a strong intuitive link between the two of you that borders on ESP. Being able to anticipate each other's ideas or actions can lend a special dimension to the relationship. That loyalty plays a big part in your union, adding strength and longevity to it.

One problem you may experience at times is the inability to talk things out calmly. Part of the intensity you feel is likely to kick up some emotional dust that can make it hard for either of you to admit being wrong—or even being sorry.

Although in many ways this is a partnership of opposites, you always know how to keep each other happy in the bedroom. This is a relationship in which absolutely nothing is held in reserve. The excitement is limitless, and you always give top priority to time spent together in private. There are no limits to what you will do to pleasure each other.

Mars in **GEMINI** matched with Mars in **SAGITTARIUS** ♊♐

This partnership is all about equality. The two of you need to feel as if you have an equal stake in the relationship. Otherwise, it is not as satisfactory for either of you in the bedroom. Some couples may be able to have a great sex life even when other areas of the union are less than happy, but this is not the case for you.

Even minor periods of conflict can put a damper on your love life. During times when you may be fighting, you are likely to spend some time apart. Maybe that is the reason you strive to keep the relationship working so well.

When the romance is hot and heavy between the two of you, every aspect of your togetherness is good as well. Working toward common goals can only make things get better between this planetary pairing as time goes on. Making sure your time together is diverse and fast paced is key to keeping love alive.

Mars in **GEMINI** matched with Mars in **CAPRICORN** ♊♑

Yours is a unique, complex partnership with many facets and interesting characteristics. You know that it is not just about romance or sex or any other single thing. The pride you have in your partnership is in making it reflective of as many areas of life as possible. You believe in sharing more than just a love life.

However, the tough thing for both of you is that distractions and negatives in your relationship can be a wet blanket for your passions, causing you to pull apart, at least until the problem is resolved. When you communicate well, however, it can keep the fires burning in all areas of your relationship.

For the most part, you seem to be one of those fortunate pairs whose sex life just keeps getting better the longer you are together. Part of your pleasure comes from feeling emotionally safe and totally at ease with each other.

Mars in **GEMINI** matched with Mars in **AQUARIUS** ♊♒

There are a lot of strong, positive feelings in this relationship. But there is plenty of physical fun, too. Language turns you both on, and verbal cues have a definite link to making your sex life playful and fun. Naughty talk, erotic stories, and even some fantasy role-playing all do their part in keeping things fresh and interesting.

This planetary pairing depends a great deal on variety to keep the romantic momentum going. Because of that, there are times when outside demands—busy schedules, for one—make it hard or even impossible to take the relationship in a new direction.

Yours is a sophisticated partnership that doesn't require constant self-analysis and examination. The two of you know what you want from this union, and as long as you are willing to spend the time and effort keeping each other interested, you are sure to be happy as well.

► LOOK UP YOUR RELATIONSHIP KARMA *on p. 824*   ► DISCOVER THE RELATIONSHIP KARMA YOU SHARE WITH CELEBRITIES *on p. 760*

Your Sexual Compatibility

Mars in **GEMINI** matched with Mars in **PISCES**   ♊♓

The keynote to your success as a couple is a sense of humor. Together you really know how to have a good time, whether the two of you are out at a social gathering, dancing and partying, or at home, snuggling under the covers, locked in each other's arms.

There are some dips in the relationship, times when it seems as if you have done it all and seen it all. During such periods it can be hard to inject some new excitement into the partnership. Another drawback can be fatigue—there are nights when you are too tired to make love so you simply go through the motions. Being able to weather these challenges proves your emotional investment in the union.

Paying attention to all the positive aspects of your togetherness keeps things happy and relaxed—which is what you like. This is not an intense relationship but it is an enthusiastic one.

Mars in **CANCER** matched with Mars in **CANCER**   ♋♋

Security is the bedrock of this relationship. One of the reasons you are so happy together is because you give one another a sense of emotional safety that is life-enhancing. Lying in bed holding each other, while a "serenity" candle burns on the nightstand, is just the sort of prelude to passion that characterizes your union.

However, there are times when this relationship can get too needy, with both of you expecting the other to fulfill emotional wants that are next to impossible. Understanding that no one individual can be all things to a partner helps you deal with this unrealistic expectation.

Respect for each other's feelings shows up in every aspect of your partnership. You aren't the kind of couple that can say hurtful things and then blithely make things up between the sheets. For you lovemaking to be meaningful needs to be a beautiful extension of your day-to-day love and happiness.

Mars in **CANCER** matched with Mars in **LEO**   ♋♌

When it comes to sensuality, your relationship is at the top of the class. It is a love that has as its touchstone a shared and powerful sensitivity. You know how to give each other what you want without even using words. While you enjoy engaging in lots of activities together, you never lose sight that your function as a couple is primarily to make each other happy in every way possible.

Hurt feelings and bruised egos can sometimes be a consequence of the outspoken communication you two share. It is good to have an open dialogue, as long as the verbal exchanges don't lack respect.

One of the things that enables your relationship to keep getting better and better is an open-minded approach to your togetherness. The two of you are not afraid that disagreements or differences of opinion are symptomatic of trouble or boredom.

Mars in **CANCER** matched with Mars in **VIRGO**   ♋♍

Although the sex is an intense element of this relationship, the romance is tempered with tenderness, affection, and respect. You see this as a lifetime partnership, something to be valued and cherished. You know it can get even better with time, so you don't expect everything to happen all at once. As your time together grows, you know the relationship will deepen.

The two of you have your differences, there is no doubt about that, and at times they can create problems. But because your togetherness possesses so many positive qualities, there is enough leeway for the two of you to agree to disagree about minor issues.

There is a strong spiritual component working in this planetary pairing. The two of you may even feel as if you have known each other before in another existence. This kind of esoteric bond not only fortifies the relationship, it gives it a unique dimension.

▶ LOOK UP YOUR RELATIONSHIP KARMA *on p. 824*   ▶ DISCOVER THE RELATIONSHIP KARMA YOU SHARE WITH CELEBRITIES *on p. 760*

Mars in **CANCER** matched with Mars in **LIBRA**

You have the sort of relationship in which it is easy to relax and just be yourselves. This in no way takes away from the passion between the two of you. In fact, it adds to it. Being able to draw on shared values, experiences, and points of view gives you the security to fully express yourself in every way, including sexually.

If there is a downside to this relationship, it could be a lack of enthusiasm for trying new things. The two of you can get so accustomed to everything being perfectly fine just the way they are that you don't understand the value of change. And change in the bedroom is vital here.

One of the things that cements your togetherness is your willingness to let individual concerns take a backseat to what is right for the relationship. You don't let ego issues get in the way, proving that for both of you being a couple is what it's all about.

Mars in **CANCER** matched with Mars in **SCORPIO**

You know one another on such an emotionally intimate level that it is almost spooky. For you love is often an unspoken thing, a feeling as deep and profound as the ocean. You do not believe that the kind of passion you share can be defined by words, even words of love.

Unfortunately, during times when the two of you are at odds, the bad feelings can be just as intense. This is especially true if there is a subtle rivalry going on between you. Remembering that love doesn't struggle for dominance but searches for equality helps you keep any major disagreements in perspective.

When you look into each other's eyes, you feel as if you can read the answer to all of life's mysteries there. The sensual fulfillment that comes from a truly committed relationship is beautiful and rare, and in this union, you have found it.

Mars in **CANCER** matched with Mars in **SAGITTARIUS**

This partnership has enormous mutual respect—and mutual lust! That is really the key to keeping the relationship so happy. You know better than to assume that things will always run so smoothly, and in truth you wouldn't want them too. You enjoy the sparks kicked up by a good argument, knowing that nothing that miniscule can do permanent damage to this union.

But there are times when fears about your future as a couple cause problems, and on such occasions the two of you may be particularly sensitive to any bumpy patches in the relationship. These are periods when it may be possible to draw on the strengths that are the foundation of your romance.

But despite any minor glitches, this planetary pairing is just about as good as it gets. You manage to have it all—rapturous romance plus unyielding loyalty. What more can you ask?

Mars in **CANCER** matched with Mars in **CAPRICORN**

This is one of those relationships that never seems to grow old. No matter how long the two of you are together, there is a freshness about your partnership that keeps both of you interested. You are an affectionate pair who kiss and hold hands in public, never worrying about what other people might think or say.

Sometimes there are communication problems in your union because of an unwillingness to face unpleasant facts or confront difficult issues. Left unresolved over a period of time, this can turn into a bad habit that is hard to break and negatively impact on your togetherness. There can also be arguments about who has control over finances.

Loyalty plays a big part in your relationship. The two of you have a sense of "us against the world" at times, knowing that no matter what disappointments life may have in store, you can always depend on one another.

► LOOK UP YOUR RELATIONSHIP KARMA *on p. 824* ► DISCOVER THE RELATIONSHIP KARMA YOU SHARE WITH CELEBRITIES *on p. 760*

Your Sexual Compatibility

Mars in **CANCER** matched with Mars in **AQUARIUS**

Differences really cause the sparks to fly in this partnership, but that is just the way you want it. The two of you have no desire to be one of those cookie-cutter couples who have the same opinions. You probably feel it is your very differences that help to make the togetherness so special.

Because you are accommodating of each other's feelings, it can be difficult for the two of you to be completely honest, even where sexual likes and dislikes are concerned. But things improve, sexually and in every other way, when you both have the courage and conviction to say what you feel.

This is a relationship that truly has the potential to grow into something even more special as time goes on. The more you learn about one another, the sweeter the togetherness becomes, allowing you to have a union that is both sexually satisfying and emotionally rewarding.

Mars in **CANCER** matched with Mars in **PISCES**

Empathy and sensitivity are the hallmarks of this planetary pairing. In fact, this relationship is as close to being one made in heaven as they come. You relate to one another in an almost mystical fashion, feeling a soul-kinship that goes far beyond the limitations of love. This emotional closeness helps to make your sex life extraordinary.

There are times when this understanding seems to work against you, and the relationship becomes too comfortable for its own good. When you grow too accustomed to these harmonious feelings you may stop trying to grow and improve as a couple. If this happens, the partnership can lose its spice.

One of the positive things about this partnership is your ability to sense each other's needs without having to talk things out first. Love like this doesn't happen at random, and you probably feel as if the two of you were destined to be together.

814

Mars in **LEO** matched with Mars in **LEO**

Your romantic relationship has almost as much boisterous energy as a brass band. The two of you are madly in love and you want everyone around you to know it. This is a very attractive partnership with movie-star type glamour.

But all of that tempestuous passion can also translate to some disagreements on occasion. The two of you do everything in a big way—even argue! You both want to be in charge, and that can lead to trouble. But you don't hold grudges and enjoy making up after a fight. The bigger the argument, the more intense your reconciliation is.

This partnership has a great deal of enthusiasm and positive energy. You understand that individual egos must sometimes be sacrificed for the good of the relationship. Even if you have been together for a long time, you seem able to keep the sexual attraction as hot as when you first met.

Mars in **LEO** matched with Mars in **VIRGO**

As a couple you manage to achieve a comfortable balance between emotional and physical attraction. You are conscious of working on friendship issues in your relationship. For the two of you, being friends as well as lovers really works, and it does not detract from the sexual chemistry you enjoy.

On the downside, sometimes the two of you worry that you are no longer as "hot" as you were in the past. You may have unrealistic expectations about your appearance. But you keep things in perspective if you realize that comparing the past with the present has little real meaning or value.

You have an image of what you wish to be as a couple and you continually strive to attain the embodiment of that image. You see yourselves as a very happening duo, and regardless of your age or amount of years together, that is what you want to remain.

► LOOK UP YOUR RELATIONSHIP KARMA *on p. 824* ► DISCOVER THE RELATIONSHIP KARMA YOU SHARE WITH CELEBRITIES *on p. 760*

Mars in **LEO** matched with Mars in **LIBRA** ♌♎

Glamour, romance, passion—together you have it all, and more. This is one of the best suited of all planetary pairings. You look great together and always seem to give the impression that the two of you are having a wonderful time, no matter what you are doing.

There are occasions when ego can get in the way of the relationship, and when this happens, it can be hard to reach a compromise. At such times discussions can cause more problems than they can solve, especially if both of you are convinced you are right.

But for the most part, romance has the edge over any problems that might crop up. Sexually, there is plenty of heat happening in this relationship. Optimism about your life together and the vision to set far-ranging goals suggests that the two of you will be happy together for a long, long time.

Mars in **LEO** matched with Mars in **SCORPIO** ♌♏

The passion index for this relationship is always set on "high." The sexual vibe between you is explosive—the emotional equivalent of TNT. It doesn't matter how long you have been together, either. With so much emotion invested in your togetherness, there is very little chance that the passion will lose its intensity.

Few things cause as much trouble as arguing over finances, and this is likely to be a bone of contention between the two of you. This is particularly true if one of you is continually looking to control the money, using it as a means to control the relationship.

There are some very basic, almost old-fashioned values underpinning this relationship. Foremost among them is loyalty, which practically defines the partnership for both of you. Knowing that you have each other's continued support makes this a union that will be both sexually and emotionally satisfying today, tomorrow, and well into the future.

Mars in **LEO** matched with Mars in **SAGITTARIUS** ♌♐

With this planetary combination, the passion just doesn't stop. You are one of those madly in love couples that everyone else wishes they were on occasion. You always seem to be having a good time when you are out in public. But it is when you are alone that the fireworks really start.

There is a lot of well-intentioned joking that goes on between the two of you, yet at times the humor can turn sharp and sarcastic, and you can hurt each other's feelings. Also, because you are such a fiery pair, there are bound to be some raucous arguments once in a while that spill into bedroom mayhem.

Not the sort of couple who is always content to sit at home on a Saturday night, you love going out for an evening to eat, to dance, or maybe just people watch. Whatever you do, you enjoy the romance and sociability of one another's company.

Mars in **LEO** matched with Mars in **CAPRICORN** ♌♑

You can be one another's "trophy" as well as each other's best friend. The wonderful thing about this planetary pairing is that it has so many possibilities and definitions. You can have as much fun eating out or going to the movies together as you can taking a luxury cruise. You simply enjoy being together in every way.

Like most couples, there are occasions when you reach an impasse. For the two of you this usually means that you refuse to see each other's point of view. While this in itself isn't an issue for concern, the stubbornness with which you both cling to your opinions can be a source of resentment.

Although there is plenty of romance in this relationship, you don't depend on love and sex alone to make it work. You both realize that without some genuine understanding and true affection, no relationship is likely to last.

▶ LOOK UP YOUR RELATIONSHIP KARMA *on p. 824* ▶ DISCOVER THE RELATIONSHIP KARMA YOU SHARE WITH CELEBRITIES *on p. 760*

Your Sexual Compatibility

Mars in **LEO** matched with Mars in **AQUARIUS**

There is incredible chemistry in this union of opposites. Although the two of you have a tendency to zigzag emotionally at times, this adds rather than detracts from your success as a couple. The two of you seem to thrive on controversy, knowing that it helps to keep the passion in high gear.

One of the problems in this relationship can be a sense of unreality where money is concerned. You both love to spend the coin of the realm, and that can lead to a bad case of "who's watching the budget?" Unless somebody takes control, you could find yourselves knee-deep in debt, and that is a sure–fire passion-killer.

There is absolutely nothing predictable about this planetary pairing, and you wouldn't have it any other way. You enjoy the good times and the bad times together, because you understand that it takes both to give a relationship strong meaning.

Mars in **LEO** matched with Mars in **PISCES**

Sensitivity, caring, and a strong physical attraction are the characteristics of this romantic relationship. Even if your personalities are very different, it is unlikely that there will be a negative impact on the partnership. Being able to learn from each other and grow as a couple is what you are all about.

Of course, there are times when the antagonism level rises to a pitch that creates disputes and perhaps even some noisy arguments. During these periods sarcasm could get in the way of understanding each other. There may also be occasions when you use sex as a way to make up—which doesn't really solve anything.

The best thing about this planetary pairing is that you can never stay angry at one another for long. You can even laugh about the disagreements, feeling they have actually served to bring the two of you closer than you were before.

Mars in **VIRGO** matched with Mars in **VIRGO**

This is a friendship as well as a love affair. You want to be intimate in many ways, and sexual intimacy is only a part of that. The intellectual chemistry between you is fierce and exciting, and it fuels everything else in this partnership.

From a negative perspective it is very easy for you to be overly critical of each other, making insensitive remarks as a result. You prize perfection and hold each other to a high standard. The biggest challenge is allowing yourselves to relax in the relationship. Being able to get from romance to reality can be rough, but once it happens this partnership is better off.

On the flip side, you will bend over backwards to please one another, willing to put yourselves second to each other and for the good of the relationship. For you, happiness means feeling close and sharing all the good times as a team.

Mars in **VIRGO** matched with Mars in **LIBRA**

This is a very sophisticated partnership that also has the potential to be highly sensual. For the two of you being in tune emotionally isn't just a prerequisite for passion, it is a real turn-on. You love being able to predict what each other will think or say. And this kind of synergy does a great deal to enhance your love life.

At times there can be a little too much leaning on one another, causing some emotional claustrophobia in the relationship. In the short-term it is not really a problem, but if allowed to continue in this manner for too long, it can invalidate the trust and respect you have for each other.

While you aren't a bold couple, you don't mind showing a little affection in public, as long as it is in good taste. For the most part, you are content to keep your private feelings private. In your boudoir, there are no holds barred.

▶ LOOK UP YOUR RELATIONSHIP KARMA *on p. 824* ▶ DISCOVER THE RELATIONSHIP KARMA YOU SHARE WITH CELEBRITIES *on p. 760*

Mars in **VIRGO** matched with Mars in **SCORPIO** ♍ ♏

As a couple, you give off an exciting vibe. There is a lot of earthy sexuality in this relationship, and the two of you are always looking for ways to spice things up even more in the bedroom. While you don't shy away from the tried and true, both of you enjoy indulging in exotic sensual pleasures every now and then.

There isn't a lot of leeway allowed in this relationship. You hold each other to high standards and expect unqualified loyalty and support from each other. Any deviation can cause ripples of uncertainty in your union.

But such misunderstandings are relatively rare, and most of the time the relationship is clicking on all cylinders. And while it isn't just about sex, you believe that as long as things remain happy and compatible between the sheets, there is far less likelihood of outside events creating problems for the two of you.

Mars in **VIRGO** matched with Mars in **SAGITTARIUS** ♍ ♐

The differences between the two of you mean far less than the powerful sexual attraction that draws you together. You are a magnetic pair who feels as if you were meant to be together. It doesn't matter what age you are or how long you have been a couple—this combination is magical.

As a couple, communication is not your strong suit. You tend to rely on nonverbal messages, including lovemaking, to speak for you. For this reason there are times when you may be at odds and not willing to talk things out. When the two of you don't take the trouble to express your feelings, you can end up being annoyed at one another. This can lead to long sexual dry spells.

You have a lot of fun together, and it doesn't just revolve around what goes on in the bedroom. As long as you can find ways to spend time together, you make a happy and harmonious pair.

Mars in **VIRGO** matched with Mars in **CAPRICORN** ♍ ♑

You may not be openly demonstrative, but the two of you are an extremely passionate couple behind closed doors. There is an earthy kind of sexual attraction at work in this partnership, an unspoken vibe that is as alive and exciting as the day you two met.

As a couple, the status quo can be a bit too important to you, and there are times when you care too much about how your relationship appears to those on the outside. Being concerned about a relationship image in no way corresponds to the actual state of your partnership.

Even though you lap up sexual pleasures, this is more than just a physical relationship. The two of you have a genuine affection for one another that transcends your sexual togetherness. You know the value of a balanced partnership, and are willing to put your efforts toward making it even better in the future than it is today.

Mars in **VIRGO** matched with Mars in **AQUARIUS** ♍ ♒

Though you have very different natures, this partnership is emotionally fulfilling and relatively trouble-free. Depending on how long the two of you have been together, you may have already learned to complement each other's personality in a comfortable balancing act of give-and-take that bolsters the relationship.

The disagreements you do have are likely to be about very basic things, and you may be unwilling to discuss them, preferring to sulk alone and in silence. Neither of you likes to argue, so it often seems easier to ignore problems when they come, even if that is not the wisest way to handle things.

For the most part, however, the two of you fit together like adjoining pieces of a puzzle. Love, sensual pleasures, and a satisfying dose of good old-fashioned romance is just what you need to keep this relationship as happy and successful in the future as it is now.

▶ LOOK UP YOUR RELATIONSHIP KARMA *on p. 824* ▶ DISCOVER THE RELATIONSHIP KARMA YOU SHARE WITH CELEBRITIES *on p. 760*

Your Sexual Compatibility

Mars in **VIRGO** matched with Mars in **PISCES** ♍♓

Yours is the sort of relationship that can weather problems, changes, and even differences of opinion. That is because you have a relatively idealistic view of what a romantic partnership should be. In this day and age that may seem naïve, but for the two of you it works—and how!

If this planetary pairing does have a problem, it is likely to be because of emotional demands. It can become a habit for the two of you to look to each other to fulfill every wish, every need. That can put too much stress on the relationship and even create an "us against them" mentality. Isolating yourselves this way can hurt rather than help your togetherness to flourish.

The loyalty and emotional support that you give to each other is the foundation of your relationship. Sexually, you have tremendous compatibility, and things just seem to get better as time goes on.

Mars in **LIBRA** matched with Mars in **LIBRA** ♎♎

If there is such a thing as the perfect "Valentine couple" it is the two of you. Your relationship is true love personified, and even though sex is an important element of your togetherness, it is much more about romance, and that is spelled with a capital "R."

However, the risk that is possible in this union is one of superficiality. You want everything to run smoothly and work out well, and if it doesn't, the relationship can flag. Working hard to add reality as well as glamour to your partnership makes it even better. Keeping your sex life new, creative, and vibrant helps too.

But when it comes right down to it, this is one of those fairy tale, happily-ever-after stories. The two of you don't believe that permanence equals boredom. You want to be as much in love twenty years from now as you are today, and you believe that keeping the romance alive makes that possible.

Mars in **LIBRA** matched with Mars in **SCORPIO** ♎♏

Passionate, smoldering, charged with feeling, this planetary partnership is about as volatile and exciting as they come. This is an incredibly rich and complicated relationship with so many emotional ups and downs that there are probably times when the two of you feel as if you have stepped from the pages of a particularly torrid romance novel.

You are a dramatic pair. You argue, sometimes bitterly, but always make up before too much time has gone by. The one drawback to your partnership is that this emotionalism can be exhausting. There are times when you avoid confrontation because you don't want to go through all the hoopla associated with an argument.

The two of you have eyes only for each other, but the strong connection you feel between you is more than just physical. It is as if the two of you are opposite sides of a coin, unable to be separated.

Mars in **LIBRA** matched with Mars in **SAGITTARIUS** ♎♐

The "fun" quotient for this romantic relationship is extremely high. The two of you are lovers, playmates, best friends—fellow travelers on the path of life who know how to have a great time together. You don't believe that a relationship should have to be "work." For you it is meant to be as effortless as an exchange of ideas.

There are times when the partnership may run off track because of a lack of attention to practical matters, and the romance can wane as a result. But when you give yourselves a chance to discover deep meaning to your togetherness, you find that it is actually about more than just being in love.

The good news is that, even when you do fight, there are rarely any bad feelings between the two of you. This amiable, good-natured attitude helps keep things happy, no matter what else might be going on between you.

► LOOK UP YOUR RELATIONSHIP KARMA *on p. 824* ► DISCOVER THE RELATIONSHIP KARMA YOU SHARE WITH CELEBRITIES *on p. 760*

Mars in **LIBRA** matched with Mars in **CAPRICORN** ♎♑

This is a very classy planetary pairing—a relationship of intellectual and romantic equals. Yet this is by no means a tame relationship. You may give the appearance of being very cool, but when the two of you are alone together, that reserve is sure to be replaced by passionate abandon.

At times when you disagree, look out! Tempers flare and nasty words are likely to get tossed around freely. The two of you are very good at holding grudges, which suggests that forgiveness doesn't come easily to either of you. Thankfully, there are far more good times than acrimonious ones.

One of the reasons you work so well as a couple is because you tend to have the same sort of long-range goals, as well as the ability to look at the world in much the same way. Given all the other great things about this relationship, this is the icing on the cake.

Mars in **LIBRA** matched with Mars in **AQUARIUS** ♎♒

The two of you understand one another on a level that goes far beyond the reaches of romance. In fact, you have the kind of relationship that can be both physically exciting and emotionally comfortable. Being able to keep this equilibrium is a tribute to how much you love and value each other.

There are times when your relationship becomes too predictable and you are inclined to stir things up a little, especially in the bedroom. You can be too analytical about love sometimes, and when that happens you need to break free of your usual patterns and try new ways of expressing your love.

You don't lose sight of the fact that communication is one of the most valuable tools you have as a couple. You both believe in sharing your thoughts on just about everything, secure in the knowledge that everything you share brings you just that much closer.

Mars in **LIBRA** matched with Mars in **PISCES** ♎♓

Even though from the outside your partnership may seem to be based on somewhat superficial factors, there is actually a very strong spiritual element at work in this relationship. This in no way detracts from the sexual chemistry between the two of you. In fact, this adds to it.

Possessiveness can be a real problem in this partnership, especially if the feelings of jealousy are not dealt with in a forthright manner. It is also possible that when there are arguments, unresolved issues could lead to periods of anger and resentment.

The two of you are not constantly voicing your feelings for one another, but that is because you don't need to. In this relationship words are less important than the feelings you are able to generate. The powerful emotions expressed by something as simple as a glance or an embrace tell all that there is to know.

Mars in **SCORPIO** matched with Mars in **SCORPIO** ♏♏

This is one of those push-and-pull relationships where the sex is so great that it seems to be worth the challenges that may arise. The two of you can clash emotionally at times, which is why there are so many sexual sparks. This relationship works best when you allow it to transcend the realm of sexual love into something that goes beyond the mere physical.

Sometimes jealousy and possessiveness can be a problem. You love each other so much that you don't want to share each other with friends or family members. Because of all the emotion involved, this kind of togetherness can be tiring on occasion.

But when things are working well, you feel incredibly connected. There are strong bonds of sensuality, loyalty, and psychological understanding. You know what is in each other's heart, and you continually strive to know and appreciate one another emotionally as well as physically.

▶ LOOK UP YOUR RELATIONSHIP KARMA *on p. 824* ▶ DISCOVER THE RELATIONSHIP KARMA YOU SHARE WITH CELEBRITIES *on p. 760*

Your Sexual Compatibility

Mars in **SCORPIO** matched with Mars in **SAGITTARIUS**   ♏ ♐

There is a great deal of lively energy in your relationship—one of the elements that makes your life together so exciting. You don't believe in complicating a romantic partnership with lots of stuffy rules. As far as the two of you are concerned, you prefer to make things up as you go along.

At times when you don't see eye to eye you probably have very animated arguments, and you might even throw things once in a while. At other times both of you may choose to be icy and uncommunicative. Happily, this impasse never lasts for too long.

Sexually, you couldn't be better together. You are not the sort of people who have a bunch of "how to" books on the bedside table—you don't need them! In fact, the two of you could doubtless author a few such spicy texts. Your sex life is alternately intense, romantic, and just plain fun.

Mars in **SCORPIO** matched with Mars in **CAPRICORN**   ♏ ♑

This is a romantic partnership that runs hot and cold. When everything is going well, the two of you are on cloud nine, and it is hard to imagine that things could ever be any better.

Of course, when you are going through difficult times, it can be hard for you to understand why you are together! A show of temper in an argument is nothing new for this planetary pairing. But because the relationship is such a passionate one, the two of you are always able to make up after any disagreement.

Sexually, you are an intense pair. There is a kind of magnetism between you that shows in the simplest acts, such as holding hands or looking into each other's eyes. You love with profound feeling and don't mind showing it. When people see the two of you together, they know they are seeing a couple deeply in love.

Mars in **SCORPIO** matched with Mars in **AQUARIUS**   ♏ ♒

This relationship can be alternately passionate and calm, easygoing and complicated—in fact, anything but predictable. For the two of you, a partnership is at its best if there are plenty of fireworks between you on a regular basis.

Sometimes it can be difficult for each of you to keep from trying to take control of the relationship. When one can't hold back, there are likely to be brief periods of anger or even estrangement. Happily, you are simply too much in love to stay angry for very long. And you would rather experience a few bumps along the road than become bored with this union.

One of the best things about your togetherness is your ability to remake the relationship on a regular basis. The two of you know that things can go stale if nothing changes, so you do your best to keep each other on your toes no matter who is in charge.

Mars in **SCORPIO** matched with Mars in **PISCES**   ♏ ♓

This is the sort of romantic partnership that legends are made of. Passion, eroticism, and a soul link that makes the two of you feel as if you could be happy only together—this relationship has it all. One of the best things this union has going for it is the ability to transform the ordinary limits of romance into something grander.

Often, the greater the passion, the greater chance there is for hurting one another's feelings. Everything about this pairing is so intense that even the slightest disagreement can lead to disillusionment and severely bruised egos.

Fortunately, the two of you don't really have to work on this relationship in the same way that other couples do. In fact, it is almost as if the closeness you share creates some wonderful kind of mystical ESP that keeps you close in spirit, even during times when you may be separated by distance.

▶ LOOK UP YOUR RELATIONSHIP KARMA *on p. 824*   ▶ DISCOVER THE RELATIONSHIP KARMA YOU SHARE WITH CELEBRITIES *on p. 760*

Mars in **SAGITTARIUS** matched with Mars in **SAGITTARIUS**

It just doesn't get any better than this! Your relationship is free-spirited, gregarious, and just plain fun. You enjoy doing things together and are able to make even the most ordinary circumstances seem like something out of a romantic movie. For the two of you laughter is practically an aphrodisiac.

Despite all this, or maybe because of it, there are periods when too much of a good thing is exactly that, and boredom can be the result. Also, because the two of you are so accustomed to the good times, you can be somewhat spoiled about working at the relationship.

Unlike many pairings that seem to resist or even fear change, yours has the ability to go through many transformations and remain strong. If anything, your togetherness seems to improve with age. A sense of permanence built through love and trust cannot be disrupted by any circumstances, good or bad.

Mars in **SAGITTARIUS** matched with Mars in **CAPRICORN**

It was probably the sexual chemistry that drew the two of you together in the first place, but chances are the relationship is about more than just that. It may be intense, but you also know that such passion can be short-lived. You want the kind of togetherness that confirms your love, now and in the future.

Stubbornness can be a real problem in this relationship. Because there are a lot of differences in tastes, opinions, and even values, at times it can be very difficult to get along. Fortunately, the high level of respect you feel for each other helps you to overcome this.

But, at the end of the day, you two would rather argue and disagree with each other, than have smooth sailing with anybody else. That is the measure of a great partnership, and one of the things that keeps you coming back on a daily basis.

Mars in **SAGITTARIUS** matched with Mars in **AQUARIUS**

This is a melding of personalities, a true blending of souls. It is very probable that you have the same philosophy of life, the same goals, perhaps even the same core values. No doubt this emotional and spiritual connection had a big part in drawing you to each other. It is rare, something most couples wish they had.

As in many relationships with partners in such accord, there can come a time when the two of you begin to take each other for granted. At those times the fact that you are so happy together can actually work against you, because it may be difficult to set relationship goals and personal boundaries.

In the best of times this partnership purrs along, remarkably happy. And although the sexual chemistry may not be the strongest element working between you, it is powerful enough to keep both of you coming back for more!

Mars in **SAGITTARIUS** matched with Mars in **PISCES**

There is a sweet naiveté about this partnership that others envy. The two of you are friends as well as lovers—it's obvious in the way you look at one another and finish each other's sentences. Whether dressed to the nines at a social event or just grabbing a burger at a fast-food restaurant, the two of you give off a vibe that says plainly to everyone "we belong together."

Because your relationship is so casual and effortless, there can be times when you don't give it the attention and energy it deserves. On those occasions the two of you might even worry that you are falling out of love.

But this partnership is at its best when you are not concerned about what signals you are sending to each other. Then you can relax in the comfort and security that is afforded only by a relationship in which romance and friendship exist together.

► LOOK UP YOUR RELATIONSHIP KARMA *on p. 824*   ► DISCOVER THE RELATIONSHIP KARMA YOU SHARE WITH CELEBRITIES *on p. 760*

Your Sexual Compatibility

Mars in **CAPRICORN** matched with Mars in **CAPRICORN**

Yours is a partnership that is built on many things, including a shared appreciation for all of the finer things in life. You enjoy making love in expensive and luxurious surroundings where the two of you can indulge your senses as a prelude to a night of sensual and physical delights.

Sometimes materialism can be a dividing point in your partnership. The two of you can get so caught up in the trappings of your togetherness—what you own—that you lose contact with the things about being together that matter the most.

The strong points of your union are understanding and a desire for permanence. You probably think alike and have similar values. One of the reasons you are willing to work hard on the relationship is because you are committed to staying together. For both of you, that is the measure of how worthwhile your union really is.

Mars in **CAPRICORN** matched with Mars in **AQUARIUS**

There is a great deal of raw, kinetic energy to this planetary pairing. You have plenty in common to draw you together, yet there are enough differences to make things interesting. In fact, one problem you never have to worry about as a couple is getting bored. In sex, in conversation, and even in the everyday details of life, you manage to keep each other interested and excited.

One of the few drawbacks to this relationship is that the two of you may be too stubborn to compromise on both big and small issues. When you let pride get in the way, it can mean hurt feelings and the inability to forgive.

Unlike some couples, the two of you never run out of things to talk about. Keeping each other intellectually stimulated goes a long way toward making the relationship a success on every other level.

Mars in **CAPRICORN** matched with Mars in **PISCES**

You are a profoundly nurturing couple, always interested in taking care of each other in every way. This is a real love match and the romance isn't likely to wane, regardless of circumstances or how long the two of you have been together.

There is a great deal of humanitarian bonding to this pair, for you are as likely to show great concern for others as well as for each other. At times there is a lack of sensual understanding for what the other wants, especially if there is not a clear channel of communication between you.

Yet there is an emotional resonance to this partnership that goes far deeper than sexual chemistry. You understand the concept of being truly, deeply in love. You have strong ties to each other that seem to reflect a karmic bond. No matter how many differences you have, your understanding of love is the same.

Mars in **AQUARIUS** matched with Mars in **AQUARIUS**

Physical attraction may have brought you together, but there is just as much intellectual compatibility going on in this planetary pairing, and that is where the relationship really soars. The two of you share ideas and opinions. It doesn't matter if you agree or not, because this is a partnership that thrives on communication and the occasional dose of controversy.

If there is a problem in this relationship, it is that the two of you have trouble showing affection. Even when there is plenty of passion between you, simple things such as holding hands or saying "I love you" may not be a part of your romantic agenda.

Sexually, you enjoy trying new things and are unlikely to shy away from being bold—in fact, the more provocative your sex life is, the better you like it. For you, inventiveness is every bit as important as the passion itself, maybe even more.

▶ LOOK UP YOUR RELATIONSHIP KARMA *on p. 824* ▶ DISCOVER THE RELATIONSHIP KARMA YOU SHARE WITH CELEBRITIES *on p. 760*

Mars in **AQUARIUS** matched with Mars in **PISCES** ♒♓

You are a charismatic couple, irresistibly drawn to one another. It doesn't matter if you have been together for a week, a month, or a decade—the magic is there and it is extremely powerful.

Of course, no couple is perfect, so at times there are certain to be misunderstandings between the two of you. On these occasions you are more likely to withdraw and be sullen and uncommunicative. Loud arguments are not your style as a couple. When angry, you simply

prefer your own space.

The two of you don't depend on words to communicate everything you feel. At times, just a glance or a brief touch can say everything that needs saying. But you aren't strictly a soulful couple. You work hard to stay attractive for one another. Just because the love and respect are there doesn't mean you stop paying attention to the physical aspects of your relationship.

Mars in **PISCES** matched with Mars in **PISCES** ♓♓

There is so much intuition and unspoken communication constantly working between the two of you, that it often feels as if you have known each other all of your lives. You seem to know each other's thoughts before they are even voiced. This ability creates an emotional closeness, a link that helps to define the relationship.

Naturally, there are times when this sense of closeness can become stifling. On such occasions it is

difficult for both of you to keep your individuality from being swallowed up by the relationship. Pursuing interests and hobbies that are independent of the union gives you the freedom that you require.

Your sex life is greatly enhanced by the powerful spiritual connection that you share. Pure physical passion simply is not enough for the two of you because you need to feel emotionally bonded in order to have the kind of togetherness you both want.

► LOOK UP YOUR RELATIONSHIP KARMA *on p. 824* ► DISCOVER THE RELATIONSHIP KARMA YOU SHARE WITH CELEBRITIES *on p. 760*

YOUR RELATIONSHIP KARMA

Saturn, the Planet of Karma

Have you ever felt like you've known someone forever, even though you've just met for the first time? Do you believe your relationship was somehow "meant" to be? Do certain things in your life and your relationship seem to be "fated"?

"Karma" is a term that refers to conditions that are rooted in previous lifetimes. According to the concept of reincarnation, we all live many times, and we meet up with certain people again and again in each lifetime. The people we feel closest to are probably people we've known for many incarnations and who have played important roles in many of our past lives. Therefore, your present partner is likely to be someone you've been close to in previous lifetimes. You've chosen to be together now in order to teach each other important life lessons. How you relate to one another now may stem from actions, behaviors, or experiences you had together in a previous existence. In this section, you'll discover your karmic purpose in this lifetime and see how you and your partner can grow through your relationship.

INSTRUCTIONS

HERE'S HOW TO READ ABOUT YOUR RELATIONSHIP KARMA.

1 Find your Zodiac Sign reading.

2 Look beside your Zodiac Sign for **Your Love Planets.** Under **Your Relationship Karma,** you'll see your Saturn Sign.

3 Look up your partner's Zodiac Sign.

4 Look at the index below. Locate your Partner's Zodiac Sign and your Saturn Sign. Where the two lines intersect, is the page of **Your Relationship Karma** Reading.

Note: Keep all of your Astrological Love Information handy by jotting down the page numbers of your Birth Year Events, Zodiac Sign, and Saturn Sign and your Partner's Birth Year Events and Zodiac Sign.

Example
If you were born on June 3, 1964, you would be a Gemini with Saturn in Pisces. If your partner was born on January 31, 1964, his or her Zodiac Sign would be Aquarius. Locate your Saturn in Pisces and your Partner's Zodiac Sign Aquarius on the chart below. What type of lessons and past life connections does this relationship have? The two intersect on page 863 for this example of **Your Relationship Karma.**

YOUR RELATIONSHIP KARMA PAGE INDEX

YOUR SATURN SIGN	ARIES	TAURUS	GEMINI	CANCER	LEO	VIRGO	LIBRA	SCORPIO	SAGITTARIUS	CAPRICORN	AQUARIUS	PISCES
ARIES	p. 828	p. 828	p. 828	p. 828	p. 829	p. 829	p. 829	p. 829	p. 830	p. 830	p. 830	p. 830
TAURUS	p. 831	p. 831	p. 831	p. 831	p. 832	p. 832	p. 832	p. 832	p. 833	p. 833	p. 833	p. 833
GEMINI	p. 834	p. 834	p. 834	p. 834	p. 835	p. 835	p. 835	p. 835	p. 836	p. 836	p. 836	p. 836
CANCER	p. 837	p. 837	p. 837	p. 837	p. 838	p. 838	p. 838	p. 838	p. 839	p. 839	p. 839	p. 839
LEO	p. 840	p. 840	p. 840	p. 840	p. 841	p. 841	p. 841	p. 841	p. 842	p. 842	p. 842	p. 842
VIRGO	p. 843	p. 843	p. 843	p. 843	p. 844	p. 844	p. 844	p. 844	p. 845	p. 845	p. 845	p. 845
LIBRA	p. 846	p. 846	p. 846	p. 846	p. 847	p. 847	p. 847	p. 847	p. 848	p. 848	p. 848	p. 848
SCORPIO	p. 849	p. 849	p. 849	p. 849	p. 850	p. 850	p. 850	p. 850	p. 851	p. 851	p. 851	p. 851
SAGITTARIUS	p. 852	p. 852	p. 852	p. 852	p. 853	p. 853	p. 853	p. 853	p. 854	p. 854	p. 854	p. 854
CAPRICORN	p. 855	p. 855	p. 855	p. 855	p. 856	p. 856	p. 856	p. 856	p. 857	p. 857	p. 857	p. 857
AQUARIUS	p. 858	p. 858	p. 858	p. 858	p. 859	p. 859	p. 859	p. 859	p. 860	p. 860	p. 860	p. 860
PISCES	p. 861	p. 861	p. 861	p. 861	p. 862	p. 862	p. 862	p. 862	p. 863	p. 863	p. 863	p. 863

PARTNER'S ZODIAC SIGN

HOW TO USE THIS CHART
- Find your Saturn Sign.
- Locate your Partner's Zodiac Sign.
- Turn to the page indicated where the two lines intersect to read about **Your Relationship Karma.**

◄◄ LADY DI AND PRINCE CHARLES ON THEIR WEDDING DAY

Reincarnation
Fated, Meant-to-Be Love
That Feeling of Destiny

It usually begins with a deep, unbroken glance. Eyes locked, you stand transfixed in the grip of something you can't describe—an emotion you can't define, a feeling of knowing that makes no real sense. Between the two of you there is some sort of recognition, even though you never have met. Of course we all know the feeling of déjà vu, that sense of having done something before, having walked a certain street before, having lived through one of life's moments before. This is a similar feeling, but it is stronger and more perplexing, perhaps because it always leads to love.

"I fell in love with her from the first moment we met," said a widower at his beloved wife's funeral.

"We had nothing in common at all, yet Daddy and I both felt it, felt we knew each other, and it was comfortable for us both," confided a mother to her daughter on the eve of her child's wedding.

"It was a scary breakup," shared the divorcee, *"but then I met him, and it was like coming home. It was crazy but we just knew."*

All these people have one thing in common. They share that intense feeling of destiny, a sense that their romance was meant to be. Feelings so strongly right at the beginning of a romance can rarely be explained any other way, so we say it's fated love, a love meant to be.

The Sanskrit word, namaste, can be translated as "my soul greets your soul" or "the divine within me honors the divine within you." The phenomenon that occurs in those passionate lovers' glances is one soul recognizing another.

When you look deep into another's eyes and feel that sense of knowing, of deep familiarity, you are living the principle of namaste—you are recognizing a soul with whom your soul has walked, lived, and loved before.

With the acceptance of the principle of reincarnation comes the belief that when the body dies, your soul returns to a great ocean of spirit from which it came. After a time and in accordance with the spiritual laws of karma, your soul will return to earth, along with other familiar spirits, once again to experience existence as a human being

According to the laws of karma, each life we live has a purpose, a life lesson, a desire for growth. Just as a child goes through school, we live our lives, desiring evolution, reaching for perfection, for the beauty of universal love. But life on earth moves very slowly and life lessons often take more than one lifetime. It is said we repeat those same lessons with those same souls who are a part of the very lesson itself. This is one reason why it feels comfortable to be with some souls, to love to the death others, to nurture and parent some—and to hate, despise, and even murder others. That is the complex beauty of life on the earth plane.

Lisa fell in love with Kevin almost at first sight. They sat at a table, on a blind date, and she gazed into his handsome face listening to him talk. By the second date she was entranced. His kisses induced a state she likened to a trance; his lovemaking made her feel hypnotized. He was the love of her life and it was as close to ecstasy as Lisa had ever come. Each day Lisa awoke in a cloud of joy, of perfect happiness, and her heart was flooded with love. She felt herself floating, drunk with passion, and could envision a perfect life with Kevin forever.

Kevin, on the other hand, had never been in love. He was a ladies' man, and he adored the scent, feel, touch, and softness of women. It was his intense appreciation for all that is feminine that lulled Lisa into a sense of security. Surely he must love her as she loved him. He was too enthralled by everything she did, too charmed watching her apply makeup, too adoring in bed, too thrilled by the sound of her voice. What else could it mean?

In short order, Lisa found out what it meant. Chasing women was Kevin's hobby, and there were other women he had yet to try. Devastated, broken hearted, too weak to think, Lisa retreated to her bed to mourn the end of the romance after Kevin left her without an explanation.

Although Lisa healed eventually, she was scarred by the experience and retreated from the dating game for a long time. What helped her most was finding out about the karma she and Kevin had shared. In lifetime after lifetime, he had broken her heart! Once in the 17th century, she was a working-class girl and Kevin a titled gentleman who trifled with her. In that life his abandonment prompted her to go to distant lands where help for the sick was needed. She soon found herself a fatality of the disease she had come to fight.

Lisa had actually lost her life because of a broken heart! In learning that she came to several conclusions. She had a deep and wonderful capacity for loving—which made her very special indeed. But she also learned she must take charge of her heart, not give it away so capriciously, nor should she let a broken heart be fatal. Lisa had to be the master of her own fate and discovering the details of her past life meant-to-be love helped her find the strength to go on and love again.

Amy met a boy while still in school, and they had been friends for a long while before they became lovers. He helped her through a breakup with an uncaring boyfriend. She helped him deal with an ex who was stalking him. Then one day they tumbled into bed together, and their friendship turned to love.

Unlike the boys in her past, there was little drama involved. Jay was there day after day, still in her life, still loving her. But Amy was concerned because Jay came from a different culture than her own, and her strict parents were sure to break apart the romance. More than a year went by and Amy still hadn't introduced Jay to her parents. Finally, she took the plunge and was amazed when not only did nothing happen, her parents actually liked the boy she planned to marry and treated him like a son. Until Amy uncovered her past life connections with Jay, she had no idea why!

Amy and Jay had been together many times before and were comfortable with each other every time. In one ancient life she was a young servant girl and he the son of an emperor. When he fell in love with her, she became his wife and was accepted in that life as one of the family. Who was the emperor? Her current father! So no wonder this strict dad accepted the boy she was sure he would hate—Jay had been his beloved son many lifetimes before.

One way to learn about your own past life connections is to explore your Saturn, which is the planet of karma and earthly life lessons. By seeing how your Saturn combines with your partner's Zodiac Sign, you can gain some insights into the life lessons you've come together to learn and what you each need from the other. You can understand some possible mutual past lives and gain some insights into the love you share today. ∎

Your Saturn in Aries

One of your goals in this lifetime is to learn to be a better leader. Your Saturn in Aries means that, in other lives, it was very difficult for you to be proactive. Perhaps you sat and "fiddled while Rome burned," or took some other course of action you regret. Now you want to reach out for what you need with more certainty, assertiveness, and determination.

Are you shy about love? Have you ever fallen for someone and thought, gee, that person would never go for me, prompting you not to take any risk at all? Chances are you took just that approach in other lifetimes. Now you want to make up for that inaction by learning that it's better to take a risk and lose than to never have tried at all.

Be assertive now. Don't be shy. Reach for that brass ring, whatever it is, and let people know you're in the game.

With Your Partner's **ARIES** Zodiac Sign

You can't help admiring your mate for being such a firecracker. In your heart you appreciate the lack of caution with which your sweetie approaches romance, and you enjoy that sensation of being swept off your feet. But you may also worry, because sometimes you wonder where the relationship is actually taking you.

Your need for security prompts your partner to make grand and sweeping promises, but you wonder how they are different from the general intentions voiced by your mate in the earliest days of your relationship. You've been partners in other lifetimes and are working now to create a solid union based on commitment and trust.

There is a mutual sense of obligation between you, and it feels very natural to share resources like money and a home. You're a team, and that gives you both a good feeling because you've always known this is a serious relationship.

With Your Partner's **TAURUS** Zodiac Sign

There is a kind of soft and mystical connection between you. It's very comfortable for you to experience your mate's calm and sensual approach to love, because it feels unhurried and peaceful. There is no rush, and that increases your sense of security in the partnership. It was easy to connect when you first met because you didn't have to struggle or worry.

If you've had a difficult day, your mate is right there, ready to snuggle and give you some emotional support. It's warm and sweet to sink into each other's arms. With that warm and loving connection, your life feels easier and safer. You know that your sweetheart will always provide a cozy nest, no matter what happens to you in the outside world.

Your past life experiences together may reflect a love relationship or marriage that was complicated by loss or controversy.

With Your Partner's **GEMINI** Zodiac Sign

Your Gemini mate's natural speed appeals to you because you see how much fun life can be when you follow your impulses. Your mate is certain life should never be taken too seriously, and you find this approach rather comforting. It means that if you attempt something and it doesn't quite work out, there will always be other chances to begin again without recrimination. It's nice to be flexible!

There is an ease and steadiness between you without any sensation of burden or too much obligation. It just feels comfortable to connect, and neither of you worries too much about where it is leading. Perhaps you were best friends in other lifetimes and now it's easy to lend each other a helping hand in times of need.

You share mutual respect and want to help each other with your individual goals. You each feel you can make a valuable contribution to the other's life.

With Your Partner's **CANCER** Zodiac Sign

Sometimes you wonder about the way your mate follows all those natural inclinations so easily. To you, that shows courage of conviction, which is something you admire very much. Yet you worry a little because your partner is rather difficult to understand. Little is spoken, and you have to take everything on faith. You wish you could define the relationship a little more clearly, but that is hard to do.

Yet the abiding affection your partner feels for you is abundantly clear. It's comforting to you to be involved with someone whose emotions are so deep and steady. You feel sheltered in that intense love. Perhaps you two were child and parent in other lifetimes and there was obligation, security, and respect. Now you want to be equals, so you're working to balance the sense of give-and-take between you.

This relationship helps you learn trust and acceptance.

▶ LOOK UP YOUR ROMANTIC AND SEXUAL COMPATIBILITY ON PAGES 780 & 802

Your Saturn in Aries

One of your goals in this lifetime is to learn to be a better leader. Your Saturn in Aries means that, in other lives, it was very difficult for you to be proactive. Perhaps you sat and "fiddled while Rome burned," or took some other course of action you regret. Now you want to reach out for what you need with more certainty, assertiveness, and determination.

Are you shy about love? Have you ever fallen for someone and thought, gee, that person would never go for me, prompting you not to take any risk at all? Chances are you took just that approach in other lifetimes. Now you want to make up for that inaction by learning that it's better to take a risk and lose than to never have tried at all.

Be assertive now. Don't be shy. Reach for that brass ring, whatever it is, and let people know you're in the game.

With Your Partner's **LEO** Zodiac Sign

Your Leo mate has many wonderful qualities that you admire. The ability to love with a generous heart is very beautiful to behold. You feel that you can always count on this partner, no matter what. Your sweetheart has a steady approach to life and the willingness to keep on plugging away. It shows you that with confidence and commitment, so much can be accomplished.

You connect easily and the relationship feels friendly and comfortable, no matter how long you've been involved. You want to help and support each other and find that it is quite natural to be in each other's corner, no matter what. There's a great deal of acceptance and approval between you, and it never feels as though one of you is demanding something the other cannot provide.

You have shared many lifetimes as friends and perhaps even lovers, and now you are comfortable together.

With Your Partner's **VIRGO** Zodiac Sign

Life feels very manageable when your Virgo mate is involved. You admire your sweetie's ability to organize and handle details. It gives you a sense of confidence about the things you must tackle on your own. You don't have to ask for help with this partner because it's always forthcoming, so you feel safe and loved.

When there is something in life that is difficult, your mate will give you an honest assessment of the situation. That helps you see things from a different perspective. Because your partner has the ability to break a situation down into smaller components, you feel that you have a helpmate who can make a real difference in your life. This methodical approach gives you a better handle on the things in life about which you lack confidence.

Friends as well as lovers in a past life together, you and your mate learned the value of honest communication.

With Your Partner's **LIBRA** Zodiac Sign

You find it difficult to be as assertive as you need to be, and your Libra mate is frequently indecisive. Your sweetie often makes one choice and then does an about-face. This is something you find quite frustrating! You often find yourself telling your partner to hurry up and make a decision and then to stick with it. You want to feel secure, not in the middle of a whirlwind!

Your mate feels that sometimes you are too autocratic and that your demands for certainty can be a little annoying. Perhaps in other lifetimes you were parent and child, or teacher and student, or involved in a May-December romance. Now it seems as though you're making demands on your mate, and your beloved has to find a sense of balance, always an issue for Libra, in order for the relationship to work positively.

Together you stabilize and help each other to be more reliable.

With Your Partner's **SCORPIO** Zodiac Sign

The intensity and deep level of conviction displayed by your Scorpio partner is very impressive to you because you see how life can be lived when one is willing to risk everything for passion and impulse. Your mate never hedges a bet, and you feel that this is a good life lesson for you. Yes, sometimes things don't work out, but in putting forth genuine effort based on a personal choice, there can be integrity and honesty.

Because your Scorpio partner is so stable, you feel confident and connected. It seems as though your relationship will always endure, and that gives you a sense of hope for the future. Even if you were slow to make romantic advances, the overwhelming passion displayed by your partner gave you the courage to reach out for love.

In an earlier incarnation together you might have been closer through a situation involving physical danger.

▶ LOOK UP YOUR ROMANTIC AND SEXUAL COMPATIBILITY ON PAGES 780 & 802

Your Saturn in Aries

One of your goals in this lifetime is to learn to be a better leader. Your Saturn in Aries means that, in other lives, it was very difficult for you to be proactive. Perhaps you sat and "fiddled while Rome burned," or took some other course of action you regret. Now you want to reach out for what you need with more certainty, assertiveness, and determination.

Are you shy about love? Have you ever fallen for someone and thought, gee, that person would never go for me, prompting you not to take any risk at all? Chances are you took just that approach in other lifetimes. Now you want to make up for that inaction by learning that it's better to take a risk and lose than to never have tried at all.

Be assertive now. Don't be shy. Reach for that brass ring, whatever it is, and let people know you're in the game.

With Your Partner's **SAGITTARIUS** Zodiac Sign

There is something heartwarming about your Sagittarian mate. This person is filled with joy and enthusiasm and never worries about appearances. Your partner can just reach out to anyone without apprehension. You admire that very much and feel that if you could do that, your own life would be better.

Being a risk-taker comes easily to your sweetie, and you want to be more of a risk-taker yourself. The key is in realizing that when things go wrong, it's easy enough to dust yourself off and try again. Your partner exemplifies that approach to life. Chances are you were good friends or happy school chums in other lifetimes, and it feels quite natural for you to maintain that youthful joie de vivre now. You're comfortable together and you enjoy each other's company.

Offering each other encouragement and support brings you both into harmony and provides security.

With Your Partner's **CAPRICORN** Zodiac Sign

You're not always sure what you want or what steps to take, but your Capricorn partner has a sort of grit and determination that helps you achieve focus. This mate is goal-oriented, and you find that very interesting. It's useful to see the way your partner envisions the steps to any goal because that helps you understand what it's possible to do.

You're always there pushing your mate to grow and achieve more, and sometimes it feels that you're more active as the partner behind the scenes than you are focusing on your own goals. But that's all right because it just seems natural for you to boost your mate up that ladder of success. Perhaps you were a beloved teacher or even employer in other lifetimes, and now you care so much about what your partner can do.

You are the wind beneath your beloved's wings!

With Your Partner's **AQUARIUS** Zodiac Sign

Your Aquarian mate is always so sure of absolutely everything. Have you ever met anyone with such intense courage of conviction? Perhaps not, and maybe that's why you admire this partner so much. Sheer force of belief can move mountains, and that's what makes this sweetheart such a force for change and achievement.

You can really connect with your partner's points of view and are willing always to go to bat for your mate. It feels that together you can make a real difference in the world. If you're afraid to take a step, your mate gives you a pep talk and you feel comfortable charging forward with your beloved's seal of approval. You connect very positively in the world of intellect and ideas and find that together you are stronger than either of you could ever be alone.

Perhaps in other lifetimes you collaborated on intellectual projects, and now you inspire each other to think deeper thoughts.

With Your Partner's **PISCES** Zodiac Sign

The quiet shyness of your Pisces mate causes you to think about contemplation. You know what it's like to rush into making choices and to worry later that you're on the wrong track. On the other hand, because your mate is so sensitive, you can well understand the frailties of indecision. Life is complicated, and this is something you both sense.

You appreciate the tender, nurturing side of your partner, particularly when you're having a difficult time and are racked with worry. The love you are given really speaks to your heart and then you feel safer, calmer, and more secure. This relationship gives you hope for the future and the sense that a gentle heart can be a good thing as long as you don't allow anyone to trample it.

In a past life you and your mate may have shared a relationship that was forced to end prematurely.

▶ LOOK UP YOUR ROMANTIC AND SEXUAL COMPATIBILITY ON PAGES 780 & 802

Your Saturn in Taurus

S aturn in Taurus reflects a karmic need to learn to trust your heart. In other lifetimes, you've given your all and have been disappointed. Things have not worked out as you'd hoped, so you began to fudge your choices. So much fear developed that you did things half-heartedly, without the level of commitment needed. With that approach, success was very hard to attain.

In past lives, you married not for true love, but for other reasons, perhaps security. You may have fallen madly in love with someone but were afraid to join hands with that person, fearful that having a mutual destiny would somehow derail your life. But in making the safe choice, you were disappointed.

In this lifetime, it's your challenge to turn that inclination around and to make brave choices that reflect what your heart actually needs. This is not the time to sell out. Live for love!

With Your Partner's **ARIES** Zodiac Sign

Your Aries mate acts on impulse, never worrying about the consequences, and that can be quite useful for you to observe. Your tendency to worry about the choices you make causes you to try to hedge all bets, but as you see your mate's resilience even in the face of unwise decisions, you try to become more courageous.

It feels a little scary to be with someone who begins something and may not finish it, because then you worry about security issues within the relationship. But it's also helpful to realize that not everything begun must be continued forever. In life there are some easy outs! Your mate feels secure having you around, because you are left to clean up the messes, something that annoys you but teaches a positive lesson.

Your past life link may be as acquaintances who worshipped one another from afar but were unable to get together.

With Your Partner's **TAURUS** Zodiac Sign

Stability is a good and valuable thing and you see that exemplified so clearly in your Taurus mate. This person is always there, sticks to a promise, and is determined to never let you down. It feels wonderful to experience a heart so stable and so committed.

From the moment you met, the relationship felt serious. Both of you intuited that you could count on this partnership and each other. Although you have difficulty trusting your instincts, you see in your partner what can happen in life when there's a commitment. Life can get messy, but there is always time to chip away at whatever problems exist. Things can be fixed with time and effort. For you, that is a positive lesson about how to give a situation your all without worrying it will blow up in your face.

In other lifetimes you were close partners and now you endeavor to be the same.

With Your Partner's **GEMINI** Zodiac Sign

The best thing about your Gemini partner is also the worst thing! You don't know whether to rejoice or be terrified by someone who floats without an anchor from one plan to another. The idea that you can change your mind at any time is quite seductive, yet somehow you feel you must surely be on the wrong track when you take that approach.

It is sometimes necessary in life to make commitments to people, ideas, and beliefs, and you are working hard to do that. But it's also useful to realize that not every moment of life is written in stone and your Gemini mate teaches you that very clearly. Perhaps in other lifetimes you challenged each other to lively debates, and now you help each other see different points of view.

Your fears and insecurities come out with this mate, and then you can acknowledge and vanquish them.

With Your Partner's **CANCER** Zodiac Sign

Passion and depth of feeling are very strong in your Cancer mate, and you love knowing where you stand in the relationship. That someone can adore and nurture you on a daily basis makes you feel special and secure. Even when you are facing life's challenges, struggling through a difficult moment, or wrestling with doubt and insecurity, you always take comfort in knowing you are loved.

In other lifetimes you two were close and an easy sense of camaraderie developed. You could share your feelings without fear of recrimination, and you do the same thing now. Even when you are most severely critical of yourself, you know your partner will provide a hug and some words of encouragement, and that gives you hope for the future.

There is a level of devotion and forgiveness between you that allows you both to go out into the world and conquer your demons.

▶ LOOK UP YOUR ROMANTIC AND SEXUAL COMPATIBILITY ON PAGES 780 & 802

Your Saturn in Taurus

Saturn in Taurus reflects a karmic need to learn to trust your heart. In other lifetimes, you've given your all and have been disappointed. Things have not worked out as you'd hoped, so you began to fudge your choices. So much fear developed that you did things half-heartedly, without the level of commitment needed. With that approach, success was very hard to attain.

In past lives, you married not for true love, but for other reasons, perhaps security. You may have fallen madly in love with someone but were afraid to join hands with that person, fearful that having a mutual destiny would somehow derail your life. But in making the safe choice, you were disappointed.

In this lifetime, it's your challenge to turn that inclination around and to make brave choices that reflect what your heart actually needs. This is not the time to sell out. Live for love!

With Your Partner's **LEO** Zodiac Sign

Your Leo sweetheart's natural flamboyance appeals to you because of the confidence displayed. Your mate acts from the heart and never stops to think or inflict censorship. You see how comfortable and fun life can be without worry or shyness, but you also provide the voice of reason and good taste in the union when your partner seems to be going over the top.

You inspire your sweetie to make the most of every opportunity and to create a larger success in life, but you also make demands that are occasionally hard to follow. Your lover wants the freedom to enjoy life, but you insist on waiting until the time is right or the chores are done. Compromise and mutual understanding are the keys to harmony.

Perhaps in another life you were an employer or teacher and it was your job to help your sweetheart attain maturity and success.

With Your Partner's **VIRGO** Zodiac Sign

Because your Virgo mate always knows just the right way to accomplish any task, it seems easier to make the most of mutual opportunities. You admire the fearless way your sweetie approaches any problem and the determination to do things just so. But your tendency to hedge your bets sometimes causes quarrels with your partner. Your mate never wants to do that and complains when you seem to lack the courage of your convictions.

It can be quite useful for your partner to see life through the various points of view you provide. That allows further refinement to his or her absolute vision. And it is helpful for you to see that choosing a platform and sticking to it is a good way to live.

Perhaps in other lifetimes you were friends or colleagues coming from different cultures or lifestyles, and you had to come to a mutual accommodation.

With Your Partner's **LIBRA** Zodiac Sign

What happens when two people who can't make up their mind try to build a life together? Compromise, conversation, and change. Your Libra mate is changeable to the extreme, leaving you to wonder what will be the choice du jour with this partner. In seeing the way that he or she waffles over any decision, you recognize the liabilities inherent in not making choices, or in not sticking with the choices you make.

You want to relax more and enjoy life, but often you worry about seeming lazy. Your Libra partner's capacity for pleasure and fun is extensive—you see how beautiful life is when you make the most of every opportunity to frolic. Your mate spends money more frivolously than you feel is reasonable, but you see from this partner that pleasure is important and that resources are there at your disposal.

In an earlier life you might have been best friends.

With Your Partner's **SCORPIO** Zodiac Sign

With your Scorpio mate, you want to know for sure that you are loved. You need to feel that ongoing sense of devotion and of commitment, but sometimes your partner protests, regarding this as a show of neediness. Your mate may have more money than you, and your reliance on those resources can cause problems until you work out the financial terms of your relationship.

To you, the union felt serious right away— you always knew there was a strong potential for permanence. Your lover took a bit longer to make that commitment, and that too was a source of stress for you. In another lifetime you may have been involved in a May-December romance in which you were the younger love partner. Because of all the passion you shared, you were an excellent couple, but not genuine partners.

In this lifetime, you're working to be lovers who are also equals.

▶ LOOK UP YOUR ROMANTIC AND SEXUAL COMPATIBILITY ON PAGES 780 & 802

Your Saturn in Taurus

Saturn in Taurus reflects a karmic need to learn to trust your heart. In other lifetimes, you've given your all and have been disappointed. Things have not worked out as you'd hoped, so you began to fudge your choices. So much fear developed that you did things half-heartedly, without the level of commitment needed. With that approach, success was very hard to attain.

In past lives, you married not for true love, but for other reasons, perhaps security. You may have fallen madly in love with someone but were afraid to join hands with that person, fearful that having a mutual destiny would somehow derail your life. But in making the safe choice, you were disappointed.

In this lifetime, it's your challenge to turn that inclination around and to make brave choices that reflect what your heart actually needs. This is not the time to sell out. Live for love!

With Your Partner's **SAGITTARIUS** Zodiac Sign

Life often seems overly serious to you and you tend to worry too much about your perceived imperfections and shortcomings. Your Sagittarian mate is just the opposite. This partner lives in the moment, relishes each day, and makes the most of everyone and everything. When something goes wrong you feel anguish, but in seeing your mate shrug and move on, you find a better approach to even life's more serious problems.

You feel that it's important to recognize the truly significant issues in life, and you help your mate do that, too. You would like to be responsibility-free, and sometimes you want to run away from problems, but a nagging little voice in your head tells you not to.

It is very possible that in a previous existence, or perhaps several of them, the two of you were lovers involved in a series of difficult personal challenges that caused you to grow in wisdom together.

With Your Partner's **CAPRICORN** Zodiac Sign

Determination, resolve, and commitment are issues you're working on in this lifetime, and you see those qualities exemplified very well in your Capricorn mate. This partner never quits, never says die, and is willing to go down with the ship if necessary. To you, this is astonishing and extremely praiseworthy. Having the courage of your convictions is a real challenge, and your mate has tons of this wonderful quality, making it easier for you to see ways in which you too can be more brave and determined.

Perhaps in other lifetimes your partner was a mentor who offered guidance and encouragement to you. Now it seems that you're doing that for each other. By being each other's support system, life seems easier and more fulfilling.

Sharing and cooperation are very important to both of you. They come quite naturally when you're with each other.

With Your Partner's **AQUARIUS** Zodiac Sign

Your Aquarian love is rather freewheeling, and you seek to stabilize your mate's life. You need much more security than your lover does, and you try always to make sure you share a commitment that will endure. Your sweetheart feels this pressure and may sometimes resist, causing you to press harder for assurances.

You worry over financial matters while your mate tends to be more frivolous with your resources. Compromise and communication are needed. Perhaps in another lifetime you were business partners and, because of different sensibilities, you lost money and your home or livelihood. Now there is a sense of emotional imbalance, which you are seeking to repair. With love and trust, you begin to heal together.

As you express trust in your partner's devotion and responsibility to you, your mate becomes more reliable and trustworthy. Then you feel safe and have more faith.

With Your Partner's **PISCES** Zodiac Sign

If nobody makes a choice in your household, what happens? Other people decide your fate! These are issues you and your Pisces mate deal with. You both care about making a good impression and the feelings of other people, so sometimes it's tricky for you to function as a team and do what's best for everyone concerned. Neither of you want to be responsible for the difficult, hard-nosed decisions.

In observing each other, you see that it can be useful to take a stand and let the chips fall where they may. Otherwise, you have to cooperate to extricate yourselves from situations in which neither of you wants to be. It's a matter of learning balance and assertiveness, and that can be good for both of you.

Your mate may have been your spiritual teacher or guru in an earlier existence, helping you to attain wisdom through study.

► LOOK UP YOUR ROMANTIC AND SEXUAL COMPATIBILITY ON PAGES 780 & 802

Your Saturn in Gemini

Learning to develop a sense of intellectual discrimination is very important with Saturn in Gemini. While your tendency may be to enjoy casual intellectual pursuits, reading pulp fiction, or watching mindless television just like most of us, it's your task in this lifetime to elevate your standards and focus on more serious mental activity. That way you can use your mind and make a better living.

In this lifetime, you are learning to focus on what matters. As a schoolchild, it was always a struggle to focus on your homework when other more fun pursuits called to you. But discipline was essential, and if you forced yourself to work hard and earn good grades, you were a happier child, and that led to being a more successful adult.

Using your intellect is important, and there is always a place for casual entertainment, but in this lifetime you don't want to become too immersed in it. Look for quality instead!

With Your Partner's **ARIES** Zodiac Sign

It takes a little while for you to plug into what your Aries partner is really saying. This mate has a penchant for making hasty assumptions and swift promises, and at the beginning of your relationship, that was quite exciting and what you needed. But as time together passed, you began to wise up and ask yourself if your mate could really be counted on to deliver on all those promises.

Not taking things at face value is a skill you're both learning—having that in common brings you closer together. Through careful communication, you each learn more about each other and what defines your time together. Because your Aries sweetie is so passionate and hasty, you often get pulled into activities you might prefer to avoid, so that sharpens your degree of discrimination.

In a previous incarnation you and your mate may have been teacher and student.

With Your Partner's **TAURUS** Zodiac Sign

Although it can be frustrating at times, you find that with your Taurus partner, you learn a great deal about personal values. Your mate understands the need for security and is determined to earn enough money for a solid and stable lifestyle. Some days you'd rather play hooky and loll on the couch with a paperback, but your partner gives you a nudge and inspires you to become more responsible.

When you think back to the days when your bank account was empty and you had to sit on tacky old chairs, you recognize the value of your mate's insistence on working hard and managing money well. Perhaps in other lifetimes this mate was your financial advisor or a mentor who tried to teach you the value of a dollar. It seems that the same is true in this lifetime!

Your sweetie helps you be more responsible, and you teach your partner to try new things.

With Your Partner's **GEMINI** Zodiac Sign

Your Gemini partner loves to talk about anything and everything, and you find this trait quite enthralling. You love hearing your sweetie's point of view about movies, books, and television shows, and it helps sharpen your own intellect. Through all the good conversation you share, your relationship grows and becomes more fun.

But sometimes you feel that your partner doesn't quite express ideas or feelings in a way that is reliable or precise, and you act as editor, fine-tuning the comments you hear. The relationship has always felt serious to both of you, and it seems that you are much more solid as individuals through teaming up together. You take turns giving each other input about projects and ideas, and when one of you has the urge to slack off, the other speaks up and demands responsible action.

In a past life you may have been best friends.

With Your Partner's **CANCER** Zodiac Sign

The value of security is one thing you learn from your Cancer partner. This mate requires a cozy home and people to love. Building a secure family base is what your mate is all about and being a part of it gives you a warm, happy feeling. You don't always choose to think about tomorrow or to plan ahead, but with this partner you learn how important it is to do so.

Sometimes your tendency is to brush off your worries and ignore serious situations by burying your nose in the television. With this partner, you can't do that because your mate is so focused on security that any problems that occur must be handled immediately. This helps you learn the value of prioritizing.

The karmic differences in your individual paths suggest that in your past lives together you were rivals who needed to learn how to appreciate each other's unique qualities.

▶ LOOK UP YOUR ROMANTIC AND SEXUAL COMPATIBILITY ON PAGES 780 & 802

Your Saturn in Gemini

Learning to develop a sense of intellectual discrimination is very important with Saturn in Gemini. While your tendency may be to enjoy casual intellectual pursuits, reading pulp fiction, or watching mindless television just like most of us, it's your task in this lifetime to elevate your standards and focus on more serious mental activity. That way you can use your mind and make a better living.

In this lifetime, you are learning to focus on what matters. As a schoolchild, it was always a struggle to focus on your homework when other more fun pursuits called to you. But discipline was essential, and if you forced yourself to work hard and earn good grades, you were a happier child, and that led to being a more successful adult.

Using your intellect is important, and there is always a place for casual entertainment, but in this lifetime you don't want to become too immersed in it. Look for quality instead!

With Your Partner's **LEO** Zodiac Sign

It's always great fun for you to attend local plays, to see new movies the day they open, and to read new books. Your Leo partner loves being part of the glittering world of show business, and together you enjoy many cultural activities. Are they all worth your time and attention? Indeed!

You learn something very important as a result of being a culture hound—you learn to develop a critical eye. Perhaps in other lifetimes you were writer and performer, giving each other encouragement and critiques, even if you rarely got raves from the local critics.

You seem witty and self-assured on the surface, but your Leo mate knows that you need lots of attention, encouragement and tender loving care. Just the realization that you are loved and emotionally supported goes a long way toward making you feel secure in the relationship. Permanence is more important to you than you realize.

With Your Partner's **VIRGO** Zodiac Sign

Most days you're ready to admit that your Virgo partner can really get on your nerves by being so picky and precise. Does everything always have to be just so? You don't always think so, and often the bone of contention in your relationship is about your need to just relax in front of the television or with a silly movie, while your mate insists on quality selections.

You can be quite persuasive, though, and your insistence on trying new things really does help your partner open up to other possibilities. Everything in life doesn't have to be a masterpiece to be enjoyable, and you teach this to your partner. Perhaps in other lifetimes you were the young student and your mate a teacher too set in old ways.

That often seems the case these days, as you teach your mate to be more flexible, and as he or she helps you focus more on quality than quantity.

With Your Partner's **LIBRA** Zodiac Sign

Whether or not you like all your Libra mate's friends, you very much enjoy being part of your beloved's social whirl. It's fun for you to meet new people and share activities. Most of the time you don't analyze the situation too much, you just enjoy it. But when you stop to think about your social life, you realize that your mate has organized and refined your pleasures.

You also admire the ease with which your Libra partner communicates with people.

This mate always knows the right thing to say. When you're fumbling for a phrase, you envision your lover and try to think of what your partner would say in such a situation. Grace and elegance of speech is something you want to learn, and your mate is an excellent role model.

Perhaps in other lives your mate was your mentor who helped you achieve social success. You could have come together through an arranged marriage.

With Your Partner's **SCORPIO** Zodiac Sign

Depth and passion are two of your Scorpio lover's best traits, and you admire the courage of conviction they represent. The only problem could be that your sweetheart sees you as being short on intellectual curiosity. You're curious, of course, but to your mate some of your interests may seem a bit frivolous and some of your conversation mere chatter.

Perhaps in other lifetimes you wanted to share your ideas with the world, and your partner was too critical and kept revising your work. These days it seems that the same thing is happening! It's up to both of you to connect on an emotional level and to listen to what's being felt, rather than said. This can be a challenge for you both.

Through interacting with your Scorpio sweetheart, your conversation becomes more interesting and more sparkling, and you become a pro at entertaining.

► LOOK UP YOUR ROMANTIC AND SEXUAL COMPATIBILITY ON PAGES 780 & 802

Your Saturn in Gemini

Learning to develop a sense of intellectual discrimination is very important with Saturn in Gemini. While your tendency may be to enjoy casual intellectual pursuits, reading pulp fiction, or watching mindless television just like most of us, it's your task in this lifetime to elevate your standards and focus on more serious mental activity. That way you can use your mind and make a better living.

In this lifetime, you are learning to focus on what matters. As a schoolchild, it was always a struggle to focus on your homework when other more fun pursuits called to you. But discipline was essential, and if you forced yourself to work hard and earn good grades, you were a happier child, and that led to being a more successful adult.

Using your intellect is important, and there is always a place for casual entertainment, but in this lifetime you don't want to become too immersed in it. Look for quality instead!

With Your Partner's **SAGITTARIUS** Zodiac Sign

In your romance with your Sagittarian partner, it sometimes feels as though nobody is minding the store. You both enjoy living and playing around, and that can mean nobody is focused on the pragmatic details of life or the relationship. You often feel that your mate should be focused on more reasonable pursuits—it sometimes feels like a quarrel when you offer suggestions on being more practical.

In other lifetimes, perhaps you were the older sibling, trying to offer some guidance to an unruly younger sibling. Now it feels to your partner that you're making demands that are too heavy. How secure are you both in the relationship? That is an issue you debate often. You want to know that there is a commitment, but you worry that your partner wants more freedom than feels comfortable to you.

You each must learn to respect the other's choices, whether or not they make sense to you.

With Your Partner's **CAPRICORN** Zodiac Sign

There is always something for you to think about when considering your Capricorn partner's no-nonsense approach to living. Everything seems so real, so well defined, and so important! To you, that is quite amazing. Your mate never seems to make a false move, and when the occasional thing goes wrong, how can it be as serious as it seems?

This mate gives you a real sense of balance, because although you seldom see life as seriously as your mate does, you also realize that being a bit more structured and practical is a good idea. As you reflect on your own choices, you realize that you could accomplish so much more if you were to emulate your partner now and then.

In a past life experience together the two of you may have had your love affair thwarted by domineering family members who found it an unsuitable match.

With Your Partner's **AQUARIUS** Zodiac Sign

There's nothing like being in the presence of an idealistic genius to give your own outlook a new frame of reference. Your Aquarian mate is determined to make the world a better place, and when you listen to that well-articulated point of view, you wonder if you've ever really considered your own opinions in that much depth.

Your mate has much knowledge and many skills that you also admire. You realize that it's worthwhile to learn something carefully and to use what you learn. It's also useful to be able to share what you know with other people, which is something you can inspire your partner to do. Just knowing and believing are never enough. You realize it's also essential to be able to express yourself in ways people can understand, and this is something you share with your sweetheart.

Perhaps in a past life you were literary intellectuals, comparing notes.

With Your Partner's **PISCES** Zodiac Sign

You and your gentle Pisces sweetheart have some very nice things in common. You're both accepting and willing to try new things without making prior judgments. That keeps your life together interesting because it means you venture without prejudice into cutting-edge theater and galleries, and you listen to the hippest hip-hop.

Because your mate is so intuitive, even when you're just repeating jokes from a bubble gum wrapper, the emotional subtext is very clear. If you don't always say what you mean, it doesn't matter because your partner knows what's in your heart. You appreciate your lover's special talents and are always there, nudging, offering encouragement, and hoping your sweetie can realize more goals.

Perhaps in another life you were friends who worked hard on each other's behalf. Now you are doing the same thing, pulling for each other and offering occasional artistic critiques when necessary.

▶ LOOK UP YOUR ROMANTIC AND SEXUAL COMPATIBILITY ON PAGES 780 & 802

Your Saturn in Cancer

Being loved and nurtured is very important to you, but with Saturn in Cancer, you are learning that if you're ruled by need, you often will be disappointed by the people on whom you're counting to meet those needs. Every child wants to be mothered, and you understand that impulse only too well. Perhaps in other lifetimes you weren't nurtured as you should have been, and as a result you felt insecure.

In this lifetime, there is a strong desire to be cared for, and that means you reach out for attention and affection. But if you are so needy that you reach out indiscriminately, you probably won't get what you're seeking. So now you have to choose the people who are capable of nurturing you properly, and whose lives you can enrich as well.

Security is always worth having, but in this lifetime, it's your challenge to gain security without paying too high an emotional price.

With Your Partner's **ARIES** Zodiac Sign

When you first met your Aries mate, it was easy to feel swept away on a tide of passion. All those thrilling remarks and promises made you feel that you'd never again have to worry about love. But later on you began to wonder, "Were those promises made from the heart, or were they just the product of grand impetuosity?"

You need security, and sometimes your Aries partner feels a little smothered by your demands for commitment and attention. Together you have to work to find a little balance so that you feel safe and your lover doesn't feel smothered. It's likely that in other lifetimes you wooed your partner, who was an attractive sex object. Now you often feel the same thing is happening!

From you, your partner learns to develop sensitivity to your feelings. You learn that security can never come from someone else. You must find it in your own heart.

With Your Partner's **TAURUS** Zodiac Sign

It's quite easy for you to be seduced by your Taurus mate. Your partner's desire for security and stability is very enticing to you. From the moment you met, it felt as though he or she could help you get what you really need. Sometimes that's a very good thing because you feel safe and cozy in this person's arms.

But if you should connect with a Taurus who really isn't good for you, perhaps because he or she is controlling, it will be very hard to let go because all that security and commitment are such a big draw. Perhaps in other lifetimes you were the sought-after sex object and your partner offered you more financial security than love.

In this lifetime, it's your challenge to go after all those things you need and to build a solid life based on love, rather than money. You learn that money without love is no real security at all. Family counts here, too.

With Your Partner's **GEMINI** Zodiac Sign

It can be a real challenge for you to connect with your Gemini partner because you're always wondering if your needs are being met. What is the real level of commitment your partner is offering you? You're never quite sure. You feel a nagging urge to define the terms of the relationship, perhaps to the extent that your mate feels a little smothered.

You really want to know you're building a solid home and family, but on some level you wonder if together you and this lover really have the knack to do so. It requires some communication and a lot of self-confidence. This is one of those situations in which you learn multiple lessons. The more faith you develop in love, the greater your sense of security.

The love link between you and your mate probably extends to a past lifetime when the two of you shared a powerful secret.

With Your Partner's **CANCER** Zodiac Sign

Your Cancer partner is an excellent role model for you. It's so easy to see what's truly important by the way this mate lives. Family, love, home, tenderness, and caring are what this lover is all about. In just observing your sweetie's gentle heart, you see how to make better choices.

From the moment you met, it felt serious and important—you easily envisioned the home and family you could create together. Even if you were just friends at first, you kept after your beloved until you connected romantically because you just knew you belonged together.

In other lifetimes you may have been mates, but perhaps the relationship didn't work out perfectly. You might have needed different things. This time you're working to be true partners who can give each other the necessary devotion that signals true love. A little sacrifice might be indicated, but you feel it's worth it.

▶ LOOK UP YOUR ROMANTIC AND SEXUAL COMPATIBILITY ON PAGES 780 & 802

Your Saturn in Cancer

Being loved and nurtured is very important to you, but with Saturn in Cancer, you are learning that if you're ruled by need, you often will be disappointed by the people on whom you're counting to meet those needs. Every child wants to be mothered, and you understand that impulse only too well. Perhaps in other lifetimes you weren't nurtured as you should have been, and as a result you felt insecure.

In this lifetime, there is a strong desire to be cared for, and that means you reach out for attention and affection. But if you are so needy that you reach out indiscriminately, you probably won't get what you're seeking. So now you have to choose the people who are capable of nurturing you properly, and whose lives you can enrich as well.

Security is always worth having, but in this lifetime, it's your challenge to gain security without paying too high an emotional price.

With Your Partner's **LEO** Zodiac Sign

Trust is so important in a relationship and you've learned much about that from your Leo mate. You feel it's risky sometimes to give your heart to another person, but your Leo always wants to do what's right, so you feel that you're involved with a quality person who is trustworthy.

You may have had some issues about choosing a partner well, and perhaps your heart got a little singed in the past. When you met this mate, you felt that you were connecting with someone you could respect and admire. Although your Leo is good at making a longstanding commitment, you both may have to work together to manage mutual resources.

Money is a bit of an issue between you because you worry about the future but aren't sure what's necessary to secure it, and your partner likes to enjoy the good life, right now, today. A working compromise is called for here.

With Your Partner's **VIRGO** Zodiac Sign

One of the most touching qualities about your Virgo partner is the way he or she always rushes in to help someone in need. To you, this exemplifies the way a loving heart functions. From observing your sweetheart in action, you understand so much better the way family members and friends pitch in and help each other.

Perhaps in another life you were an abandoned child, lost and alone, and your mate offered some food, a kindness, or a place to rest your head. Could be your lives merged only for a short time, but your soul always remembered how meaningful is kindness to a stranger, and you resolved to connect more closely in a future life.

Now you are together and you're working hard to pull for each other, to be best friends, and to function as the helpmate you each need to make the most of every opportunity.

With Your Partner's **LIBRA** Zodiac Sign

Casual social interactions appeal to you, but at the end of a sparkling evening, you wonder what you really got out of it. This is the issue you work on with your Libra mate. You seem always to need more depth, a greater sense of definition from each encounter, and often your partner is content just to enjoy a pretty moment without making too much of it.

Your tendency is to nudge your mate to work at understanding just what the connection with your friends really means—who is more and who is less important in your lives. Your partner helps you see something quite useful—that you don't have to be joined at the hip to get something from another person. You can socialize casually and still feel you've done something positive.

In other lifetimes, you were probably just as different as you are today, and through your interaction you grew as individuals.

With Your Partner's **SCORPIO** Zodiac Sign

You both love and fear your Scorpio mate. It's so compelling and assuring to merge with someone capable of making a lifetime commitment with such absolute confidence, yet you wonder, "Can this really make sense?" You know it's what you want, but still it scares you a little. It's as if your partner knows a secret that you don't, and you must go on sheer faith—something that is very difficult for you.

Security is always an issue with you, and if you're with the wrong partner, it can be very hard to sever the tie, especially if the mate is saying, "Hey, we belong together." Sometimes you wonder if even a good relationship will end, but you know that's just your fear of abandonment talking.

A previous incarnation may have seen your mate in the role of your guardian or staunch protector in some way. Now you can both be fighting a tendency to get into a parent–child relationship because of this.

► LOOK UP YOUR ROMANTIC AND SEXUAL COMPATIBILITY ON PAGES 780 & 802

Your Saturn in Cancer

B eing loved and nurtured is very important to you, but with Saturn in Cancer, you are learning that if you're ruled by need, you often will be disappointed by the people on whom you're counting to meet those needs. Every child wants to be mothered, and you understand that impulse only too well. Perhaps in other lifetimes you weren't nurtured as you should have been, and as a result you felt insecure.

In this lifetime, there is a strong desire to be cared for, and that means you reach out for attention and affection. But if you are so needy that you reach out indiscriminately, you probably won't get what you're seeking. So now you have to choose the people who are capable of nurturing you properly, and whose lives you can enrich as well.

Security is always worth having, but in this lifetime, it's your challenge to gain security without paying too high an emotional price.

With Your Partner's **SAGITTARIUS** Zodiac Sign

There's an exciting, youthful buzz about your Sagittarian partner, and you find that very appealing. This person makes you feel that life is sweet and that worry is completely unnecessary. Sometimes you can just enjoy the fun you share and not worry at all about anything challenging or scary. So what if you chose to live together and never marry? Are children really necessary? It's very easy to share those carefree thoughts with your mate.

But under the surface a nagging desire to button up your life comes through and then you demand a reckoning. Being the mellow sort, your Sagittarian may agree to commit, and if so, that gives you comfort. The problem is, you wonder if anyone is actually the driver in the vehicle of this relationship.

The karmic tie between you and your mate harkens back to a past life where your mate faced danger in order to secure your safety.

With Your Partner's **CAPRICORN** Zodiac Sign

Capricorns often need someone to help them remember to focus on personal matters with as much commitment as they give to their careers. In your relationship, that's your job. You are absolutely committed to giving your all to your mate, and if that means offering help, advice, or exceptional tender loving care, you're willing to do so.

But what really matters is the way you insist on building a strong personal foundation between you. Even in the early days of your relationship, you were always there, offering a calm presence so that everything wouldn't fall apart. And even when you'd resolved to break it off, you just wouldn't quit on this partner.

Sometimes you feel like your lover's guidance counselor, and perhaps you played that role in other lifetimes. It's not a one-way street, though, because you develop greater strength and resilience by being the emotional leader in the relationship.

With Your Partner's **AQUARIUS** Zodiac Sign

A desire to help the world is a noble thing, and your Aquarian mate has so many admirable plans to make a difference that you really feel your heart melt. Help and kindness have strong meaning for you, and you find it as rewarding to do a good deed as to be the recipient of one.

There's a real sense of connectedness and brotherhood in the philosophies of your mate, and you can see how being that committed is a very good thing. Sometimes you feel that nobody is taking care of you, and you sense that your mate would always want to do so.

A fear of abandonment from a past life trauma can leave you feeling scared and alone. Perhaps in another lifetime you were away at school and your partner was the headmaster or headmistress. You wanted to gain favor and be noticed as special, but you also got a warm feeling of belonging to the group of kids in your mate's care.

With Your Partner's **PISCES** Zodiac Sign

Your Pisces love can be the sweetest person on Earth! You appreciate so much all the tender sentiments that are lavished upon you. You recognized from the moment you met that it would be quite hard not to want a lifetime commitment from this devoted partner.

Yet you also worried a little. Could you really give as much back as was being given to you? Were you ready to make a serious commitment, and would you be happy with this partner? In short, you were scared, and when you stopped to think about it, you realized that the depth of your mate's love was a little frightening.

Perhaps in another lifetime you were lovers, but you chose to go away, or it could be that circumstances pulled you apart, and you felt some guilt as a result. Now you want to repay that devotion and to live up to your mate's positive expectations.

▶ LOOK UP YOUR ROMANTIC AND SEXUAL COMPATIBILITY ON PAGES 780 & 802

Your Saturn in Leo

Some people chase quite naturally after their heart's desires, but for you this is difficult. You aren't always perfectly sure of what you want and need, and even if you do know, sometimes you're hesitant to reach for it. Often you blame it on shyness, but you know you need to be more assertive.

In other lifetimes you made half-hearted efforts because you were too scared to go after what you wanted, which led to some regrets in old age. Perhaps you were madly in love with someone very special, and even though there was a spark between you, you were fearful, shy, and lacking confidence, so you never pursued the object of your affection. You learned that it's better to have loved and lost than never to have tried at all!

In this lifetime, you're working to have the courage of your convictions. Reach out for love and for life!

With Your Partner's **ARIES** Zodiac Sign

Your Aries mate is brash, bold, and unapologetic, and you absolutely love that. Even though your partner tends to crash and burn a lot, you still admire so much the certainty of conviction present in every act and deed. Life seems so easy and uncomplicated when viewed through your mate's eyes. You want something? Well, go get it! What could be simpler?

Your tendency is to see potential problems, and that can be very useful to your mate. You offer guidance, words of wisdom, and a little foresight that reduces the negative consequences of your partner's too hasty action. This is a real relationship of balance and give-and-take. You each see in the other things you can use and emulate.

Perhaps in other lifetimes you were business or romantic partners whose differences enhanced your similarities. Now you give each other stability and confidence.

With Your Partner's **TAURUS** Zodiac Sign

Even though you sometimes hesitate to admit it, your Taurus mate's stubbornness is very appealing to you. Yes, you occasionally want to throttle your partner for sticking to an idea or plan about which you have grave doubts, but you are very impressed with the courage of conviction displayed.

When you think about your own choices, you recognize how much more easily swayed you are than your mate. Of course flexibility is often a good thing, but in observing your partner's level of commitment, you realize that if you had displayed more steadfastness in certain areas of your life, you would have gotten more of what you wanted and deserved.

In this regard, your mate is a real inspiration. Perhaps in other lifetimes you were soldiers and it was only your partner's determination that kept you both alive. Now you feel that you're much more likely to realize your heart's desires with this partner at your side.

With Your Partner's **GEMINI** Zodiac Sign

There are many avenues to any destination, and you learn a great deal about flexibility from your Gemini partner. Life seems so simple when you adopt your mate's values—as long as you have good books, a television, and a phone, life can be very pleasant. You seldom see your Gemini anguish over anything, and that gives you a sense of peace.

You are learning in this lifetime about the importance of specific choices, and that's something you communicate to your mate. Frivolous conversation is just as good to your sweetie as a meaningful exchange, but when you point out that time is being squandered, your partner gives more thought to his or her choices.

Perhaps in another lifetime you were the shy teacher who put more effort into helping your student achieve important goals than you did toward your own aims. Now you also learn through teaching.

With Your Partner's **CANCER** Zodiac Sign

What's the difference between your Cancer partner and a teddy bear? Not much! Both are extremely loveable and huggable, and you admire the way your mate offers open arms to anyone in need of a snuggle. When you feel shy or withdrawn, you just look at your partner's emotional honesty.

It's rewarding to see someone brave enough to shout out, "You hurt my feelings." Although you know your mate has some secrets, you still feel that this is the way you should be—open and loving and tenderhearted, without worrying about rejection. Yes, you realize this isn't entirely true—your mate does worry about being rebuffed, but those fears never block this partner from reaching for love.

Perhaps in another lifetime, your mate wanted to marry you, but you were uncertain about making the commitment. Maybe you felt a lack of security, but later on you came to wish you'd accepted.

▶ LOOK UP YOUR ROMANTIC AND SEXUAL COMPATIBILITY ON PAGES 780 & 802

Your Saturn in Leo

Some people chase quite naturally after their heart's desires, but for you this is difficult. You aren't always perfectly sure of what you want and need, and even if you do know, sometimes you're hesitant to reach for it. Often you blame it on shyness, but you know you need to be more assertive.

In other lifetimes you made half-hearted efforts because you were too scared to go after what you wanted, which led to some regrets in old age. Perhaps you were madly in love with someone very special, and even though there was a spark between you, you were fearful, shy, and lacking confidence, so you never pursued the object of your affection. You learned that it's better to have loved and lost than never to have tried at all!

In this lifetime, you're working to have the courage of your convictions. Reach out for love and for life!

With Your Partner's **LEO** Zodiac Sign

Your Leo partner has so many wonderful qualities you admire, but on some level, the thing you like best is the ability to be theatrical, flamboyant. You tend always to censor yourself, and you really would love just to get out there and sing with the karaoke, dance with abandon, or wear flashy clothes. Even when you're being the voice of reason and asking your mate to show a little decorum, secretly you're applauding.

You realize that there's more to your mate than pizzazz. This partner knows how to love and is willing to go to bat for you. Your welfare is just as important to your partner as his or her own, and you find that deeply endearing.

It is likely that in a previous life your Leo mate "rescued" you from an unhappy relationship, and that as a result you still react to him or her with a mixture of gratitude and romantic awe.

With Your Partner's **VIRGO** Zodiac Sign

Whenever you feel a little hesitant or scared or shy, your Virgo mate has the sweetest way of stepping in and building your confidence. Nobody knows you as thoroughly as this partner, and although sometimes your Virgo can inflict rather deadly criticism, there is also the laundry list of what's right about you that your mate easily reels off.

"You can do it because..." your partner will say, and with that brilliant analysis you feel much more confident about tackling whatever the problem is. If you were incapable, your mate would surely share that fact to save you disgrace. So, this mate is your security blanket.

In other lifetimes, your partner may have been a beloved teacher, prodding you to succeed on a grander level, or the director when you were an actor. It just feels right to be prodded and guided by this partner because you share much trust.

With Your Partner's **LIBRA** Zodiac Sign

You and your Libra partner share an avid interest in the arts. Whether your involvement is professional or more casually attuned to a hobby, it's fun for you to discuss each aspect of a cultural event. Through these conversations, you share more than interesting points of view. Your own artistic ability is enhanced and developed.

Being more creative, and taking your talents more seriously, are two of the things you are working on in this lifetime.

Perhaps you're not Picasso or Sarah Bernhardt. But you have an inner spark, and that is something you want to nourish. Your Libra partner helps you do so and, because this mate has such a high level of taste and refinement, you know you can learn so much.

In other lifetimes you may have been partners in a creative profession, and you learned as much together by your failures as your successes. Now you are natural friends.

With Your Partner's **SCORPIO** Zodiac Sign

The question you ask yourself when comparing your approach to life with that of your Scorpio partner is how much can you really allow yourself to love. Would you be willing to love to the end of time, and could you give your life for love? Somehow, it's never tepid between you and this partner. In being together, you're inspired to review your choices and see how you measure up.

Right from the moment you met, you hoped your Scorpio would notice you, want you, and cherish you, but it never seemed that any of the choices were up to you. You could wish, but then you had to wait to be chosen. Now you still feel that the power lies more with your partner than with you, but you also gain something that way.

A possible past life experience as star-crossed lovers makes your life together now all the more sweet!

▶ LOOK UP YOUR ROMANTIC AND SEXUAL COMPATIBILITY ON PAGES 780 & 802

Your Saturn in Leo

Some people chase quite naturally after their heart's desires, but for you this is difficult. You aren't always perfectly sure of what you want and need, and even if you do know, sometimes you're hesitant to reach for it. Often you blame it on shyness, but you know you need to be more assertive.

In other lifetimes you made half-hearted efforts because you were too scared to go after what you wanted, which led to some regrets in old age. Perhaps you were madly in love with someone very special, and even though there was a spark between you, you were fearful, shy, and lacking confidence, so you never pursued the object of your affection. You learned that it's better to have loved and lost than never to have tried at all!

In this lifetime, you're working to have the courage of your convictions. Reach out for love and for life!

With Your Partner's **SAGITTARIUS** Zodiac Sign

You care quite a bit about decorum and good taste because you never want to be the brunt of anyone's scorn. Because your Sagittarius mate is such a carefree live wire, you often act as a stabilizing force. Your suggestions help your mate behave in a more reasonable manner.

But you learn something from your partner, too. You see that it's possible to live just as you choose, and that if someone doesn't like your actions, you can simply shrug and ignore them. This can be very liberating! You admire your mate's ability to not let other people cause stress or annoyance.

You take yourself quite seriously and your mate enjoys teasing you about this at times. This good-natured ribbing could reflect a past life experience together where the two of you were childhood friends who grew up together and your mate, older and wiser than you, was your idol.

With Your Partner's **CAPRICORN** Zodiac Sign

One of your karmic lessons in this lifetime is to learn stability and commitment, and that comes from believing in yourself and your goals. Your Capricorn mate is a wonderful role model because this partner never gives up and will work to exhaustion to make a goal a reality. As you observe this raw determination, you begin to see that it is possible to do the same.

You and your mate are both drawn to the principles of austerity, and you may both be so frugal that a friend has to speak up and suggest that you let go a little and enjoy life more. That idea may make sense from an outside point of view, but you and your mate are relatively comfortable living an ordered life with few frivolities.

Perhaps in another life you used obligations to your mate to prevent you from chasing a dream. Don't do that again in this one!

With Your Partner's **AQUARIUS** Zodiac Sign

Even though you sometimes quarrel about the right way to accomplish your goals, you admire the way your Aquarian mate displays intense courage of conviction. This partner is absolutely sure about everything and will stop at nothing to make an important point. This to you is very impressive. When you have to make a hard choice, you remind yourself of your mate's determination.

Sometimes your Aquarius has wild and crazy ideas, and you provide the voice of reason. Your calmness and ability to see through a situation to potential problems helps your partner make needed adjustments. You may also provide professional contacts who can help your mate with career expansion. Knowing you helps your partner grow both personally and professionally.

Perhaps in other lifetimes you were the trusted advisor who helped keep your mate on the straight and narrow. You're still the stable one, but you're willing to change a little!

With Your Partner's **PISCES** Zodiac Sign

Trust is a wonderful quality, and you enjoy the way your Pisces mate looks at the world with open, trusting, optimistic eyes. Going through life expecting the best is very difficult for you, but your mate's rose-colored glasses give you a new vista on life. It's nice to feel that things can work out, and even if they don't, you realize this is a better attitude.

Your mate's tendency to stop and smell the flowers is another beautiful trait that you admire. It's nice to be part of a life with someone who is determined to focus on what's good and beautiful.

The sense of trust that you have placed in your mate probably relates to an earlier incarnation where you two were together as students. In that time together you may have had to depend on him or her to enlighten you about life's great spiritual mysteries. In this life you revel in the tenderness you receive.

▶ LOOK UP YOUR ROMANTIC AND SEXUAL COMPATIBILITY ON PAGES 780 & 802

Your Saturn in Virgo

Your task in this lifetime is to achieve the balance of a healthy mind in a healthy body. In other lifetimes you were very single-minded. Either you were an intellectual who did little but think—perhaps in a withered body—or you were completely physical, going through your days mindlessly existing and thinking only when absolutely necessary.

Now you must strive for the rewards of living completely. You want to be an intellectually vibrant person living happily in a healthy body. This can take some discipline, because you now tend to go overboard in certain areas. Perhaps you like to binge on treats and leave the consequences until tomorrow. "All things in moderation" should be your goal.

Hard work is another major karmic lesson. What you build in this life takes time and effort. Now you must learn to stick with something until it produces the return you initially desired.

With Your Partner's **ARIES** Zodiac Sign

There's something very comfortable to you in the way your Aries mate races into life without forethought or a planning. Although you like acting on impulse and following your own urges, you often wonder if this is the sensible route to any reasonable destination.

This behavior feels comfortable to you because it's similar to your own approach in other lifetimes. It is what you're trying to learn to change! That's not to say that your Aries partner is always wrong. But a little bit of thought before action is a good way to live, and together you can learn this through experience.

You have a deep sense of admiration for your Aries mate's personal courage in facing challenges. In other lives together you may have been rescued by him or her at a time of extreme danger, or perhaps there was an occasion when you were inspired by this person's bold courtship of you.

With Your Partner's **TAURUS** Zodiac Sign

Sharing your life with a Taurus partner produces a sense of coziness and comfort for you. Together you work to make your world secure, organized, and sane. You both trust in the other, having confidence that as a team you can be happier and safer than you might be if apart. It's comfortable for you to make a commitment to each other.

When you observe your mate's love of food and pleasure you can easily connect, and you may be great eating buddies. But if either of you has a weight problem, you can also pull together to find a healthier approach to eating and a buddy system of exercise.

In other lifetimes you may have been good friends, always willing to pitch in and help each other in times of need. Even today, you recognize and support each other's best qualities and pitch in to minimize mutual frailties.

With Your Partner's **GEMINI** Zodiac Sign

Sometimes you feel that your Gemini mate is all talk and little productive action, and that makes you ponder the best way to go through life. You often try to provide a stabilizing influence for your partner, and although there may be some complaints about your tendency to monitor every thought and decision, your mate does learn to be more precise from you.

You learn the importance of productive intellectual action, and that purposeful thought is more useful than idle daydreaming. A good mind requires stimulation, and your partner is always interesting to you because of the sheer volume of information that he or she can share. Then you move forward and use that knowledge.

In other lifetimes, you may have been your mate's teacher, director, or coach, and as you analyzed your partner's tendencies, you made suggestions about how to use their talents more effectively.

With Your Partner's **CANCER** Zodiac Sign

Your Cancer partner's tendency to act on pure impulse and emotion seems quite bold and courageous to you, but on some level you want to make life more organized and less chaotic. You always feel there should be some sort of to-do list operating in your lives, and that your mate just wants to follow momentary impulses. Together you can be much more of a force for success.

The challenge for you is to assert some level of control without seeming overly critical, as if you are trying to set some sort of agenda. There is a tendency for your partner to handle issues in a passive-aggressive way that exacerbates rather than solves problems. You have so much to give one another, but playing "games" can hold you back.

In another lifetime you may have been your partner's older sibling or teacher, helping your mate to make sense of life.

▶ LOOK UP YOUR ROMANTIC AND SEXUAL COMPATIBILITY ON PAGES 780 & 802

Your Saturn in Virgo

Your task in this lifetime is to achieve the balance of a healthy mind in a healthy body. In other lifetimes you were very single-minded. Either you were an intellectual who did little but think—perhaps in a withered body—or you were completely physical, going through your days mindlessly existing and thinking only when absolutely necessary.

Now you must strive for the rewards of living completely. You want to be an intellectually vibrant person living happily in a healthy body. This can take some discipline, because you now tend to go overboard in certain areas. Perhaps you like to binge on treats and leave the consequences until tomorrow. "All things in moderation" should be your goal.

Hard work is another major karmic lesson. What you build in this life takes time and effort. Now you must learn to stick with something until it produces the return you initially desired.

With Your Partner's **LEO** Zodiac Sign

Your heart opens up when you see how kind and generous your Leo mate is. There is great value in helping another person, even a stranger, and you can see from your partner's deeds how good life can be when you're there for someone else.

Pleasure is one of the particular specialties of Leo, and your partner's ability to enjoy life to the fullest is lots of fun to share. When you experience that love of opulence, good food, and over-the-top social events, you have a truly wonderful time. Yet sometimes you wonder if all this makes sense. You are trying to learn balance in this lifetime, and those extreme Leo tendencies are not in keeping with this life lesson. This, too, is part of the karma with this partner.

Perhaps in an earlier lifetime together your Leo mate allowed you entrée into a higher social strata that otherwise would not have been open to you.

With Your Partner's **VIRGO** Zodiac Sign

There are many mutual benefits to be derived from this partnership. Your Virgo sweetie is practical, organized, and efficient, and those are traits you are working to gain. In being together, you can easily see how manageable life is in the hands of someone that capable. Discipline and austerity are two other Virgo traits you may learn from your mate.

Your relationship seemed quite serious from the moment you met, and somehow you both knew you had a reason to be together. Virgo is one of those bachelor signs, and your mate's tendency to be picky may be the reason he or she was still available when you met. Maybe you were determined and persistent, and along the way won that coveted heart.

Perhaps in other lifetimes you were colleagues but not lovers, and there was always an unanswered attraction between you. Now there is an element of partnership on more levels.

With Your Partner's **LIBRA** Zodiac Sign

The need to find balance is something you share with your Libra love. Learning to make the right choices is always a Libra issue, and in a way it's your issue too as you seek to find harmony in your life. Because your partner cares so much about being attractive and having a fulfilling social life, you see how important it is to take care of your body and your mind.

It feels quite comfortable for both of you to work together to create a gracious lifestyle. There is much organizing necessary when entertaining, and by working together to plan a party or other event, you practice some of those useful Virgo traits like efficiency, thoroughness, and attention to details.

Perhaps in other lifetimes you were both creative, artistic types but you couldn't accomplish as much because neither of you was practical. Now you're working to become more down-to-earth.

With Your Partner's **SCORPIO** Zodiac Sign

Willpower is a very impressive trait that your Scorpio mate possesses in spades. This is someone who can stick to a course of action—or a diet—for as long as necessary. You admire this quality, and wish you could do that, too. In observing your partner's unwavering resolve, you begin to see that it's not as difficult as you imagine to develop determination.

Part of your quest to learn balance results in an interesting life lesson—you learn that flexibility can be a big asset. If you can't reach a goal one way, try a different route. This is something you can share with your Scorpio sweetie to help him or her release a fixed idea beyond its usefulness.

Perhaps in other lifetimes you were comrades, business partners, or adventurers who, because of your combined skills and talents, were able to increase your chances of mutual survival.

▶ LOOK UP YOUR ROMANTIC AND SEXUAL COMPATIBILITY ON PAGES 780 & 802

Your Saturn in Virgo

Your task in this lifetime is to achieve the balance of a healthy mind in a healthy body. In other lifetimes you were very single-minded. Either you were an intellectual who did little but think—perhaps in a withered body—or you were completely physical, going through your days mindlessly existing and thinking only when absolutely necessary.

Now you must strive for the rewards of living completely. You want to be an intellectually vibrant person living happily in a healthy body. This can take some discipline, because you now tend to go overboard in certain areas. Perhaps you like to binge on treats and leave the consequences until tomorrow. "All things in moderation" should be your goal.

Hard work is another major karmic lesson. What you build in this life takes time and effort. Now you must learn to stick with something until it produces the return you initially desired.

With Your Partner's **SAGITTARIUS** Zodiac Sign

The soul of a free spirit lives inside your Sagittarian sweetheart, and you enjoy that positive energy and outlook. Expecting life to be wonderful can lead to a much happier day. You can have many good times together. But often it's up to you to be the serious one.

Learning to be more practical, you have to work on compromise if this partner won't give up on leaving things to chance. Here you must take charge. For you, taking charge in this relationship can be quite useful.

As you pitch in and work harder at your shared life, you learn that you have more of a knack for leading and compromising than you previously thought. And you savor and enjoy the freedom of spirit this Sagittarius can provide if you allow yourself this blessing.

In other lifetimes you may have been soldiers of fortune, going where the wind took you.

With Your Partner's **CAPRICORN** Zodiac Sign

There's always the question of the right way to accomplish any task between you and your Capricorn mate. You work well together, though, and find that you can learn much from each other. Your sweetie's approach to life is organized and goal-oriented, which you find quite intriguing. Your desire to make sense of every situation helps your partner when incisive analysis is needed.

Your mate's innately austere nature is interesting for you to observe. You learn how to make the most of every opportunity and even from each loaf of bread —your mate never wants to waste a crumb.

Perhaps in other lifetimes you were the apprentice in your partner's shop, and you learned every detail of a business from this mate. Now you provide support and a stabilizing influence as your partner gives you insights into the best way to accomplish any goal.

With Your Partner's **AQUARIUS** Zodiac Sign

Your Aquarian sweetheart is one of the most intellectual people you've ever met. It's interesting for you to observe the inner workings of this mate's mind, because you see how a person can carry thought into reality. When you pause to contemplate this, you realize that although your mate has interesting ideas, sometimes they're not quite practical because they're so idealistic in nature.

As you come to this conclusion, you work to develop your own mode of thinking and making sense of the world. That helps you learn the skill of using your mind for practical purposes. Your efforts in this direction can be quite inspiring for your mate because as you debunk his or her ideas, new and better notions can take their place.

Perhaps in past lifetimes, you were impassioned scholars who loved to bounce ideas off each other. Now you act similarly, and you each learn the power of thought.

With Your Partner's **PISCES** Zodiac Sign

There is a sense of mutual obligation and caring between you and your Pisces sweetheart. From the moment you met, you felt it was a serious relationship and that somehow you were meant to look after this person and see that everything was always all right. You feel the need to help organize your mate.

Your partner felt the pull immediately also, and sensed your need for love and attention. In fact, it may have felt too serious too quickly to your mate, and he or she might have resisted the tug of the relationship for a long while. Life is less casual for your Pisces when you're around, and this mate has to try harder to live up to your expectations.

In other lifetimes, you may have been involved in a May-December romance where one of you took care of the other. Now you're trying to be equals. Don't be so serious that you forget about having fun.

▶ LOOK UP YOUR ROMANTIC AND SEXUAL COMPATIBILITY ON PAGES 780 & 802

Your Saturn in Libra

There is a karmic need to repay old relationship debts with Saturn in Libra. Although you would never be intentionally cruel today, it's quite possible that in other lives you abandoned loved ones or failed to live up to your responsibilities. This created a residue of distrust and karmic debt.

Now, although you don't deserve it at all, sometimes lovers leave you with no explanation whatsoever. It can be one of those gut-wrenching scenarios where someone runs out on a casual errand and is never heard from again. The way to handle such a situation is to send love to the person and just forgive and let go. That way, the karma is broken and you never have to deal with this problem again.

With love comes obligation, so be willing to give to those you love with no strings attached. If you give more than you take, do it without resentment.

With Your Partner's **ARIES** Zodiac Sign

Your Aries mate was always so assertive and determined to woo you that you found it very exciting to be the object of this partner's affections. But you can't help wondering if it's safe to trust and just believe the relationship will endure. At the beginning, this was a very intense issue and you kept demanding that your sweetie slow down a little. Only over time do you feel safe.

Learning romantic responsibility may be a serious issue for both of you and in this lifetime, you're working on that together. It's unwise to promise "forever" right at the beginning of a relationship, because then you can never know if that promise makes sense or can be kept.

Yet you both knew from the start that this was a serious connection and you both had an investment in seeing where it would go. You've probably been mates in other lifetimes, but you keep trying to realize true love.

With Your Partner's **TAURUS** Zodiac Sign

You feel a sense of comfort in knowing just how stable and committed is your Taurus mate's heart. When this person loves you it is forever, and you feel much safer with this partner than with many others in your past.

Your expectation is that somehow love affairs will crash and burn, and perhaps your past is littered with broken hearts. When you met your Taurus love, you felt that this was your chance to heal. No matter how a romance works out, this partner seems able to love forever. Such depth of commitment assumes there will be time to repair the problems, to confront the issues, and to find your way back into each other's heart.

Even if there were problems between you in other lifetimes, there was also a spirit of forgiveness and devotion, and that is something you want to experience again in this life.

With Your Partner's **GEMINI** Zodiac Sign

Stability and commitment are qualities you need, and often you wonder if you can really have that with your Gemini partner. Because your sweetie is so flexible and can enjoy the company of just about anyone at all, your tendency is to be insecure, particularly early in the relationship, about the level of devotion you can expect.

It's not such a bad thing to be with a mate who forces you to confront your insecurities, and that's what happens in this relationship. As you face your worries you learn that no matter whom you love, there are never any guarantees. You have to live for today, enjoy the moment, and trust that you will be able to endure or enjoy whatever comes tomorrow.

The phenomenal communication that you and your mate have between you reflects an earlier life together when you may have been youngsters together, sharing adolescent secrets.

With Your Partner's **CANCER** Zodiac Sign

There is a question of whose needs will be met between you and your Cancer partner. You both feel a sense of obligation to the other that is quite serious, but often neither of you feels that you can count on the other for what you might need. Negotiations and open communication are very important.

You adore the gentle and tender heart your Cancer sweetie shows to everyone in your world. Nobody is sweeter or snugglier. Yet sometimes you feel that this mate is just too needy and that there is a well you can never fill up. Yet you do feel a sense of security with this partner, and that is very important to you.

In other lifetimes you may have been lovers who were unfaithful to each other, and now you're working to build trust and commitment. It's necessary now to put yourself in each other's place to develop genuine understanding.

▶ LOOK UP YOUR ROMANTIC AND SEXUAL COMPATIBILITY ON PAGES 780 & 802

Your Saturn in Libra

There is a karmic need to repay old relationship debts with Saturn in Libra. Although you would never be intentionally cruel today, it's quite possible that in other lives you abandoned loved ones or failed to live up to your responsibilities. This created a residue of distrust and karmic debt.

Now, although you don't deserve it at all, sometimes lovers leave you with no explanation whatsoever. It can be one of those gut-wrenching scenarios where someone runs out on a casual errand and is never heard from again. The way to handle such a situation is to send love to the person and just forgive and let go. That way, the karma is broken and you never have to deal with this problem again.

With love comes obligation, so be willing to give to those you love with no strings attached. If you give more than you take, do it without resentment.

With Your Partner's **LEO** Zodiac Sign

Leos try very hard to always be trustworthy and honorable, and you find these qualities very appealing. By seeing how much your Leo partner tries to create a respectable image and to do good rather than ill, you see how important it is to stick to your own code of ethics.

With a generosity of spirit that is touching, your mate tries hard to look out for your best interests. You have always felt that this is someone you can love and trust.

In return for your sweetie's devotion, you want to be protective and supportive, and you intend to always be as helpful as you can in any and every situation.

You share a great deal of encouragement and admiration, and that has been ongoing for many lifetimes. You have been good friends in the past—an energy that continues today so that you can express your best selves. Telling each other often of your love fills a need for both your souls.

With Your Partner's **VIRGO** Zodiac Sign

Your Virgo partner is determined to be responsible, and loves to leap in and solve problems—even for strangers—because it feels good to keep the world spinning smoothly. You often think about these qualities and wonder what it all means. You can see that kindness is what life's all about, and are learning how valuable it is to be willing to put someone ahead of yourself.

You learn from your Virgo sweetie that being selfish never feels that great,

and that often a little self-sacrifice is better than the reverse. Yet because this mate is never whiny or clingy, there is ample space between you. You'd not dream of taking him or her for granted, and you're content in the relationship because you never feel smothered.

You continue to learn from your Virgo sweetheart, a pattern that is repeated from an earlier incarnation when you were a student in his or her charge.

With Your Partner's **LIBRA** Zodiac Sign

Libra is, of course, the heart and soul of romance, and seeking love is the number one Libra pastime. It's interesting for you to hear the war stories of your sweetheart, because you would assume that a person so gentle and attractive would have had an easy time with love. But no, balance is an issue you both have, which means that much of the time you're seeking equilibrium rather than enjoying it.

Romance is important, but there's more

to love than that, and you and your mate learn this together. This relationship seemed serious from the start—somehow you both felt that you were completing some destiny in connecting with each other.

You shared love affairs in other lifetimes, but somehow never managed to elevate your passions to true love. Now you're working to offer each other affection combined with devotion that is genuine and unshakable.

With Your Partner's **SCORPIO** Zodiac Sign

What is the real meaning of love? Isn't it to care more for a loved one than you do for yourself? This is something you can learn from your Scorpio sweetheart. This mate's ability to love beyond the edge of time is phenomenal, and you sensed right from the start that this is someone who is willing to give love and commitment forever.

To love is to become one, to have every area of your soul merge, and to care so

much for the other person's welfare that there's little time to worry about yourself. This is the sort of life-altering devotion you sense you can share with your Scorpio partner, although it scares you a little to consider all of the ramifications.

The strong tie you share now could be the result of an earlier lifetime when the two of you were in love and yet unable to make a life together. Don't let a hidden fear of separation touch your love now.

▶ LOOK UP YOUR ROMANTIC AND SEXUAL COMPATIBILITY ON PAGES 780 & 802

Your Saturn in Libra

There is a karmic need to repay old relationship debts with Saturn in Libra. Although you would never be intentionally cruel today, it's quite possible that in other lives you abandoned loved ones or failed to live up to your responsibilities. This created a residue of distrust and karmic debt.

Now, although you don't deserve it at all, sometimes lovers leave you with no explanation whatsoever. It can be one of those gut-wrenching scenarios where someone runs out on a casual errand and is never heard from again. The way to handle such a situation is to send love to the person and just forgive and let go. That way, the karma is broken and you never have to deal with this problem again.

With love comes obligation, so be willing to give to those you love with no strings attached. If you give more than you take, do it without resentment.

With Your Partner's **SAGITTARIUS** Zodiac Sign

The easygoing nature of your Sagittarian sweetie appeals to you because it feels as though life together can be uncomplicated and unthreatening. Your mate is less demanding than many of the partners you've had in the past, and you never feel you're swimming in waters that are too deep for you.

You share an easy sense of camaraderie and feel that you can look after each other without worrying about inconvenience or strain. If your mate needs something, you're willing to put some effort into helping, and you find it fun to pitch in and provide a helping hand. Because you're there, your mate feels happier and more secure.

In other lifetimes you were probably good friends and you feel just as comfortable with each other now. There is no sense of urgency or concern that you could ever let the other down. You just enjoy the relationship and feel content expressing yourselves.

With Your Partner's **CAPRICORN** Zodiac Sign

Sometimes you wonder if you're in the right relationship when dealing with your Capricorn sweetheart. This person can be so career-oriented that you often feel that the relationship is happening in some alternate plane. Can you really get what you need on an emotional level? This is what you ask yourself.

On the other hand, there are few demands, and you usually feel secure in your partner's affections. This mate counts on you and rarely has a roving eye, so you don't worry about being abandoned for another. You often provide career aid and advice, feeling good about being instrumental in helping your partner achieve much-deserved success.

In other lifetimes you may have been business partners who worked together successfully. Now it's more difficult because you're also trying to be lovers, and the emotional dimension seems so complicated. It takes caring and communication—as well as commitment.

With Your Partner's **AQUARIUS** Zodiac Sign

Your Aquarian mate's ability to sustain so many ongoing friendships seems quite wonderful but it makes you wonder if there is safety in numbers. You're never sure if you can put all your eggs in one basket and rely on one person to attend to your needs for a lifetime. But if you had a support system as your partner does, you would feel safer.

This is a useful lesson to learn. Friendship is an important dimension of any relationship, and if you had romances that crashed and burned in the past, you can probably see that they would have had a better chance of survival if you had also been friends, instead of just lovers.

The fact that the two of you can communicate on many different levels is the legacy of other lifetimes together where you may have depended upon one another for a livelihood or a community responsibility. You shared equally in this situation.

With Your Partner's **PISCES** Zodiac Sign

Your Pisces mate has two interesting qualities—the ability to "be there" for just about the whole world, and the tendency to run away when emotionally overloaded. You can really relate to both. You know how important it is to love and be loved, and you want to give your all to someone you love. Yet often you feel smothered, and when that happens you wonder if it's time to leave.

As leaving a mate is a karmic issue for you, it helps you see this tendency in someone else. You realize that what's necessary is some sort of coping mechanism by which you can come through for a loved one without becoming so overloaded you want to flee. When you accomplish this, you feel much more secure about your ability to sustain a happy relationship.

In a past incarnation the two of you may have been close friends, involved in a religious undertaking together.

▶ LOOK UP YOUR ROMANTIC AND SEXUAL COMPATIBILITY ON PAGES 780 & 802

Your Saturn in Scorpio

I t's easy to feel separate and alone here on the earth plane when we assume that our being begins and ends with the flesh that seems to define our identity. There is more to you than your body, however, and it's your task in this lifetime to try to reconnect on a spiritual level.

Perhaps in other lifetimes you have been a libertine, having sex indiscriminately for physical pleasure. Now you know there is much more to sex than orgasm. That act of extreme pleasure is also the means by which two people can connect on a spiritual level—blending souls and experiencing true ecstasy. In merging on all levels with a true love, you also connect with God.

That is what you're trying to realize in this lifetime. Your need is to find the courage to open your soul to others and to feel the universal vibration that defines us all.

With Your Partner's **ARIES** Zodiac Sign

Isn't it easy to be with your Aries mate? This person takes everything pretty much at face value and there are few complications when it comes to sex. The Aries motto is, "Forget tomorrow—let's enjoy today!" On many levels this approach appeals to you because you can simply float through the relationship, enjoying life.

But you also feel that your connection is incomplete. You know there is more to life and love, and you seek a deeper involvement.

This can lead to discussions about the relationship and where you're going with it. No conversation can solve the problem, though, because what you need is to find each other's soul and connect that way. One approach may be through joint meditation or creative visualizations.

In other lifetimes you probably were lusty animals in bed together. Now you want to elevate that lust to a connection that rocks your souls.

With Your Partner's **TAURUS** Zodiac Sign

There is a great deal you and your Taurus mate may learn from each other, and perhaps that's why there was such a strong sense of destiny from the moment you met. This partner's unhurried, detail-oriented, sensual style of lovemaking can be a natural springboard to transcendent sex.

You can connect with each other on so many levels that developing true intimacy seems natural. Through all the time you spend physically naked, arousing each other's bodies, it becomes more comfortable to bare your soul as well. That is the pathway to true intimacy in which you each know everything about the other. Being seen and known is quite liberating, and very rewarding spiritually.

The strongly sexual bond the two of you share now is doubtless based on your experiences together in past lifetimes where you lusted after one another but were unable to consummate your love.

With Your Partner's **GEMINI** Zodiac Sign

You have a sense of indefinable karmic memory when connecting with your Gemini partner. Although you may rarely have played the field in this lifetime, hearing your mate's war stories strikes a real chord in you. You can understand how someone can be fulfilled by various types of interactions with a number of people rather than one intense tie.

Yet in acknowledging this mate's past, you also recognize the insecurity it creates in your own heart. Could your partner really

make a lifetime commitment to you when there are so many equally enticing choices out there in the marketplace? This is what you asked yourself when you first met, and when there are difficult periods in the relationship, you ask that question again. Only time and experience can prove to you that you're safe and your mate is committed.

Perhaps in other lifetimes you were casual lovers, and now you want to be something deeper.

With Your Partner's **CANCER** Zodiac Sign

On many levels, you realize that your Cancer sweetheart is an excellent role model. This mate can love so deeply and so intensely! You realize how wonderful it is to be on the receiving end of this sort of selfless devotion. It's easy to see how loving someone so deeply can bring you together in a way that touches your soul.

Your needs are as important to your mate as his or her own, and you sense that, should any harm come to you, it would be

as devastating to your mate as a personal injury. That is one strong indicator of true love.

Your ability to feel safe with this partner reflects trust built up over the experiences of many lifetimes together where you took turns being dependent upon one another. Now you are able to bring that sense of security into your daily life as partners and lovers. Nurturing each other is the cornerstone of your relationship.

► LOOK UP YOUR ROMANTIC AND SEXUAL COMPATIBILITY ON PAGES 780 & 802

Your Saturn in Scorpio

I t's easy to feel separate and alone here on the earth plane when we assume that our being begins and ends with the flesh that seems to define our identity. There is more to you than your body, however, and it's your task in this lifetime to try to reconnect on a spiritual level.

Perhaps in other lifetimes you have been a libertine, having sex indiscriminately for physical pleasure. Now you know there is much more to sex than orgasm. That act of extreme pleasure is also the means by which two people can connect on a spiritual level—blending souls and experiencing true ecstasy. In merging on all levels with a true love, you also connect with God.

That is what you're trying to realize in this lifetime. Your need is to find the courage to open your soul to others and to feel the universal vibration that defines us all.

With Your Partner's **LEO** Zodiac Sign

An ability to enjoy pleasure is something you share with your Leo partner. It's very nice to experience the best that money can buy, and you like the opulence that seems important to your mate. But you're always reaching for something more.

You knew from the moment you met that casual sex would never be enough. Early on, you wanted to feel there was a connection and a commitment, and you pressed quite hard for that. To you, this relationship felt serious more quickly than it did for your partner.

But your Leo is a steady person, and you always knew that once a commitment was made it would last, and that gave you a sense of security.

In another lifetime you may have been involved in an arranged marriage, and now that it's voluntary you want it to be more profound and special, a connection of body, mind, and spirit.

With Your Partner's **VIRGO** Zodiac Sign

The no-nonsense, all-or-nothing approach of your Virgo mate helps you learn the value of substance. This is one mate who would rather remain celibate than embark on a pointlessly casual fling, and you admire that sort of determination. Life is much less messy with your mate at the helm, and you want to emulate some of those fine qualities.

When you think about what you have with this person, it makes you proud because you know you've won the heart of a quality mate and that together you can create a valuable relationship.

In another lifetime, you may have seemed frivolous to your mate, and therefore your proposal was declined. Now you're working to add depth to your demeanor and expression of love. You find that your mate is a mentor, guiding you toward much that is good, and that in the bedroom each act of love becomes increasingly profound.

With Your Partner's **LIBRA** Zodiac Sign

Your Libra love lives and breathes romance, and that is quite enchanting. Each day you're together you enjoy the trappings of amour, and it feels magical. This storybook romance appeals to you, whether or not you've made an actual lifetime commitment.

Your Libra partner wants ongoing romance, but this mate may have a bit of a history where love is concerned—to him or her, falling in love is more enthralling than managing a day-to-day relationship.

You understand this only too well, and through time shared, you can learn whether or not this romance will go the distance.

In other lifetimes you may have been casual partners, friendly cohabitants, or mates in short-lived romances. Now you're trying to work harder to build and maintain a relationship. That means more honesty, more vulnerability, and more intimacy. This takes work and a commitment to stay together.

With Your Partner's **SCORPIO** Zodiac Sign

You knew from the moment you met your Scorpio sweetheart that you were swimming in waters much deeper than you were used to. This mate has intensity of passion and extreme depth of emotion, and although you admire those things very much, they're also a little scary.

You are trying to learn those very qualities, and you've felt right from the start that there was destiny for you to complete with this partner. Intimacy can be quite thrilling, and each time your mate pushes you to try something a little riskier in the bedroom, you know you're doing it not just for the pleasure, but for the closeness that comes of allowing yourself to be vulnerable.

In other lifetimes, your mate may have loved you more than you deserved and somehow you didn't quite come through. Now you want to re-establish trust and learn to give each other exactly what you need.

▶ LOOK UP YOUR ROMANTIC AND SEXUAL COMPATIBILITY ON PAGES 780 & 802

Your Saturn in Scorpio

I t's easy to feel separate and alone here on the earth plane when we assume that our being begins and ends with the flesh that seems to define our identity. There is more to you than your body, however, and it's your task in this lifetime to try to reconnect on a spiritual level.

Perhaps in other lifetimes you have been a libertine, having sex indiscriminately for physical pleasure. Now you know there is much more to sex than orgasm. That act of extreme pleasure is also the means by which two people can connect on a spiritual level—blending souls and experiencing true ecstasy. In merging on all levels with a true love, you also connect with God.

That is what you're trying to realize in this lifetime. Your need is to find the courage to open your soul to others and to feel the universal vibration that defines us all.

With Your Partner's SAGITTARIUS Zodiac Sign

Honesty in a relationship is very important to you, and although your Sagittarian mate can be quite freewheeling, this is a completely honest partner. If your sweetheart wanted an open relationship, you would hear about it, rather than being subjected to dishonesty or secret trysts that could break your heart.

Because this mate never makes a big deal about anything, it's much easier for you to admit your frailties and open up about whatever secrets from your past you haven't shared with other partners. It just feels comfortable to come clean. Your willingness to do this also helps your partner to share more, and together you build a closer relationship.

You enjoy all the many hours of deep conversation you share and feel that somehow together you can explore all the mysteries in the universe. In a past lifetime together you may have been lovers who triumphed over vastly different backgrounds.

With Your Partner's CAPRICORN Zodiac Sign

You and your Capricorn partner have something in common—the need to work harder at making a deep emotional relationship strong and meaningful. This mate believes in commitment and a solid family unit but, because of pressing career obligations and goals, may not always be available for the intimacy you need to develop.

On the other hand, you each feel that you can help the other in many areas of life, and you're both loyal. You want to be supportive and to help each other generate success. If you can take the lead emotionally, and reach out for greater intimacy, that can help the relationship tremendously.

In other lifetimes you may have been good friends, but there was always a bit of emotional distance between you, perhaps because of the customs of the times. Now it seems more important to open up, to share your inner thoughts and feelings.

With Your Partner's AQUARIUS Zodiac Sign

Your Aquarian partner is a good friend to all, including you, and you appreciate this generous approach to relationships. Because friendships often carry a connection that lasts for many decades, if not a lifetime, there can be great intimacy building through shared experience. But you may also sense a wall between yourself and your partner—and other people in your lover's life as well.

You may also feel that it's up to you to encourage your mate to share more of the personal details with you, and to open up and become more vulnerable on an emotional level. Perhaps you initiate conversations about where the relationship has been, and where it's headed. Your mate may feel this is a bit heavy-handed, so there are always romantic negotiations under way.

In other lifetimes you were probably friendly acquaintances, but now you want to grow closer so that at some point the relationship can turn into love.

With Your Partner's PISCES Zodiac Sign

The nonjudgmental way your Pisces sweetheart approaches life and your relationship gives you confidence and a real sense of emotional support. No matter what your vulnerabilities, you feel that this partner is one person with whom you can open up in a risk-free environment.

This mate's tenderness and gentle heart show you how love can feel and inspire you to offer greater depth of affection in return. Because you receive so much emotional support from this mate, it's been easier for you to envision a lifetime commitment to this partner than to lovers from your past.

Your Pisces partner appreciates your involvement in the relationship and feels more secure as a result of your continuing devotion. In a previous life the two of you might have engaged in a secret love affair. Being able to show your love now causes your feelings to grow and inspires true intimacy.

► LOOK UP YOUR ROMANTIC AND SEXUAL COMPATIBILITY ON PAGES 780 & 802

Your Saturn in Sagittarius

We all stand upon the foundation of our individual beliefs, and in this lifetime it's your task to define those philosophies for yourself. It's your karmic task in this lifetime to determine what principles are most genuinely your own and to build your life upon that system. Much deep thought is needed!

852

Perhaps in other lifetimes you simply accepted what you were told without considering it for yourself. Now it's up to you to decide what makes sense, what ideas truly resonate for you, and what's worth incorporating into your personal system of beliefs. With this approach you have a more solid way to go through life and find yourself better able to avoid risky situations and negative people.

Now it's up to you to find the true meaning of life as it makes sense to you. That way you can find inner peace and outer joy.

With Your Partner's **ARIES** Zodiac Sign

The fiery, self-starting nature of your Aries partner can be quite inspirational to you. This is one person who rarely takes at face value something heard. Your mate wants to originate ideas, not follow someone else's! Seeing this in action can be quite inspirational to you.

It is exhilarating to be able to voice an opinion and not worry about the consequences, just as your mate does. When you enter into lively conversation together, you know that no matter what you say, it will be accepted as your opinion and there will be no consequences—whether you're right or wrong. This makes your verbal exchanges freer and more fun. It's liberating to realize that you can disagree completely and still adore each other.

In other lifetimes you may have been in love but unable to marry because of religious differences. Now you can be together, regardless of whether or not you share completely congruent philosophies.

With Your Partner's **TAURUS** Zodiac Sign

Your Taurus partner is so down-to-earth that life seems simple and blissfully uncomplicated from his or her point of view. There's something comforting about being with someone who can enjoy life on its most basic level.

Your mate's ability to make sense of life is reliable, as often it's just a matter of identifying the obvious. Even though Taurus may be a bit shy, this partner doesn't hesitate about reaching for something that matters, and you find this admirable. As you find your mate acting on instinct you do the same and are happy with the results.

What it says is that when you trust your heart, good can result. That's exactly the life lesson you're learning this time around. That may not have been the case in a previous incarnation together when stricter social codes kept the two of you apart despite a powerful sense of attraction between you.

With Your Partner's **GEMINI** Zodiac Sign

Good conversation is practically guaranteed with your Gemini partner, and that keeps the relationship lively. Although this mate loves to talk about anything and everything, often the discussion can lack depth. But when you broach a serious subject, as you usually do, you find yourself connecting with someone who keeps you on your toes.

Intellectual interaction is very important in this relationship because it helps each of you define who you are as individuals and as a couple. You felt from the moment you met that this was someone you wanted to know better. There was just this burning itch to talk. Even if all you do is discuss current events, you find the interaction worthwhile because it helps you express your ideas and define your ideology.

In other lifetimes you may have been colleagues, but lacked a real intellectual rapport. Any tendency to join forces and blindly follow someone else is being changed now through intellectual interaction.

With Your Partner's **CANCER** Zodiac Sign

A mate who relies totally on instinct seems a bit scary to you, but also brave and admirable. That's how you see your Cancer partner. This is someone who connects with his or her heart and is never afraid to take action based upon personal beliefs. It's quite interesting for you to observe this process happening.

You're not always sure what you're feeling or even thinking, and sometimes you must work to articulate those things before they're completely clear to you. But your mate charges forward on pure impulse, with little thought of consequences. You can see how a lioness would do the same to defend her cubs, and you'd like to be more like this yourself.

You appreciate the healing force of your Cancer partner's love. It reflects a pattern that has developed over several lifetimes where you were in the care of your mate who was a healer.

► LOOK UP YOUR ROMANTIC AND SEXUAL COMPATIBILITY ON PAGES 780 & 802

Your Saturn in Sagittarius

We all stand upon the foundation of our individual beliefs, and in this lifetime it's your task to define those philosophies for yourself. It's your karmic task in this lifetime to determine what principles are most genuinely your own and to build your life upon that system. Much deep thought is needed!

Perhaps in other lifetimes you simply accepted what you were told without considering it for yourself. Now it's up to you to decide what makes sense, what ideas truly resonate for you, and what's worth incorporating into your personal system of beliefs. With this approach you have a more solid way to go through life and find yourself better able to avoid risky situations and negative people.

Now it's up to you to find the true meaning of life as it makes sense to you. That way you can find inner peace and outer joy.

With Your Partner's **LEO** Zodiac Sign

The steadiness and determination with which your Leo mate approaches life appeals to you. Your partner is stable and devoted. You admire that level of constancy because to you it means courage of conviction. Although this partner isn't terribly argumentative or involved in passionate religious or philosophical debates, he or she can find what makes sense and have confidence in those beliefs.

This is what you want to do for yourself.

It's interesting to discuss ideas and beliefs with your mate because you genuinely want to know his or her viewpoint. Through sharing cultural activities, you spark fascinating discussions that help you both define the world in which you live together.

The highly dramatic and sensual nature of your love affair denotes a pattern established in a past lifetime where you and your Leo mate were involved as professional collaborators in an operatic or acting group.

With Your Partner's **VIRGO** Zodiac Sign

Although your Virgo mate is occasionally flexible, this is one person who is almost always positive about the right way to go about any task. Your mate has the courage of conviction as well as purity of mind and heart. If your partner is certain about something, there can be no stopping him or her, and you feel this is admirable because you recognize that many people would give in when faced with other people's objections.

Your conversations are quite fascinating, and you both feel that you give the other insights and valuable guidance. The way your Virgo stops to analyze each person and event makes you see that it's quite possible to get a clear take on any situation.

In other lifetimes your mate may have been the teacher who tried to encourage you to come to wise conclusions after carefully weighing all the facts of the matter.

With Your Partner's **LIBRA** Zodiac Sign

Your Libra partner cares so much about fitting in and belonging to the social strata that he or she makes a strong effort to be attractive, acceptable, and congenial. Sometimes you wonder if this modus operandi could lead to unoriginal viewpoints. You know it feels good to go with the flow, but you also realize that it's important sometimes to take a stand.

In observing your mate's excellent manners and grasp on decorum, you see how

rewarding it is to be surrounded by congenial people. Good manners are pretty much the Libra motto. This partner can express pretty much any point of view with taste and class. You realize that you can indeed be free to assert your ideas—even concepts that challenge your listener—if they're shared with respect.

The two of you are playmates and friends as well as lovers, a pattern repeated over many lifetimes where you bonded strongly.

With Your Partner's **SCORPIO** Zodiac Sign

Scorpio is a sign that trusts absolutely in instinct and the heart, and you learn the value of this approach from your mate. Despite the fact that your partner makes decisions on instinct and always holds fast to a system of belief that works for him or her, this mate is not usually all about converting nonbelievers.

Your partner is inclined to let those all-important beliefs remain private, and you see the value in this, too. You can live your life as

you choose, based on your own principles, without involving other people, and this is something your Scorpio mate shows you. So much of life and thought remains internal, and that's just fine. A rousing discussion is always interesting, but you also see from your mate that what most defines us all is often unspoken.

Perhaps in other lifetimes, religious beliefs forced you to be secret lovers. Now you can do as you please.

► LOOK UP YOUR ROMANTIC AND SEXUAL COMPATIBILITY ON PAGES 780 & 802

Your Saturn in Sagittarius

We all stand upon the foundation of our individual beliefs, and in this lifetime it's your task to define those philosophies for yourself. It's your karmic task in this lifetime to determine what principles are most genuinely your own and to build your life upon that system. Much deep thought is needed!

Perhaps in other lifetimes you simply accepted what you were told without considering it for yourself. Now it's up to you to decide what makes sense, what ideas truly resonate for you, and what's worth incorporating into your personal system of beliefs. With this approach you have a more solid way to go through life and find yourself better able to avoid risky situations and negative people.

Now it's up to you to find the true meaning of life as it makes sense to you. That way you can find inner peace and outer joy.

With Your Partner's SAGITTARIUS Zodiac Sign

Intellectual curiosity is a wonderful quality exemplified by your Sagittarian mate. This partner is always interested in learning about new lifestyles, systems of belief, and philosophies. You find it fascinating to observe how your mate becomes involved in exploring these ideas as they're presented.

This partner manages to fit in just about everywhere, and it's amazing to see how well your mate can connect with people who are so different, even if there's no common language. Perhaps you've felt insecure about traveling to distant places or even strange neighborhoods, but from your mate you learn that we all have things in common and that new people can be a wonderful and exciting adventure.

You've known from the start that this mate has much to teach you. In a past life you and your mate probably roamed the world together as a pair of adventurous lovers and best friends.

With Your Partner's CAPRICORN Zodiac Sign

Both of you have a worldly view of life, though at times you seem to be working from a completely opposing game plan. Therefore, though you share a forward-looking nature, you view things from a separate and unique perspective. You see opportunities as a gift to be explored. Your Capricorn mate sees them as a responsibility to be earned. Together you are able to accomplish difficult goals that would severely test or even end other relationships.

Status is important to Capricorn, who is likely to be motivated by monetary success and feel insecure without it. You are equally happy living the good life, but a more carefree attitude toward attaining material things can be a bone of contention between the two of you.

In past life experiences together you may have been the teacher or mentor and your mate the student, though in this life those roles are likely to have been reversed.

With Your Partner's AQUARIUS Zodiac Sign

There is no such thing as an Aquarian without a philosophy of living, as you've learned only too well with this mate. Your sweetheart has something to say about absolutely everything, and you can see how easy it is not only to develop a personal platform for yourself, but for everyone on the planet.

Although your mate's ideals may be more social than spiritual, you still find it a tonic to be around someone so definite. You would like to be more like that yourself. Yet you recognize that if you acquiesce to his or her strong opinions, your mate will do all your thinking for you.

The strong conviction that underlies your most valued beliefs is probably shared by your mate, and this is one of the things that makes your love so dynamic. In a past life together you may have been writers or revolutionaries working together for a social or political cause.

With Your Partner's PISCES Zodiac Sign

One of the most interesting qualities about your Pisces mate is the natural psychic ability that allows this partner to connect very closely with the spirit world. Your sweetheart goes on instinct, but also admits that sometimes those instincts are not personal but rather the result of otherworldly guidance.

You love the idea that there are positive forces out there to help you. Being with your Pisces partner helps you develop this sort of understanding, and the ability to have total faith in the existence of spirit is very comforting. Trusting that things will work out is one of your partner's greatest strengths, and you find this a wonderfully fulfilling way to look at the world.

Perhaps in another lifetime your mate was a daring explorer and you the less secure sidekick, and by following his or her path, you learned that going on trust is the best way to approach life—and adventures.

► LOOK UP YOUR ROMANTIC AND SEXUAL COMPATIBILITY ON PAGES 780 & 802

Your Saturn in Capricorn

Learning to build a solid success slowly over time is your karmic challenge in this lifetime. In other lives, you've had early success but squandered it, and now it takes more effort to build the career you want. Your tendency is to reach for something quick and easy, but as you soon discover, that seldom works out.

It's unwise for you to be a dilettante, learning skills only partially and then leaping to the next challenge before you've truly completed the first one. It can result in your being pushed back to square one. In other lifetimes you may have been considered a huge success, but lost love or happiness in your pursuit of fame and fortune. Now you have a slight fear of success as a result.

It's your challenge to learn that success is what you make of it. Choose a career—and a relationship—and stick with it until you succeed.

With Your Partner's **ARIES** Zodiac Sign

You and your mate have a great deal in common. You're both inclined toward hasty action and changes of mind. Your Aries mate often feels ready to abandon a project—or a relationship—when the going gets tough. You can relate strongly to that inclination.

You suspect, though, that another approach would be a better choice. You recognize that sometimes you must stick with something a little longer, and in communicating this to your partner, you learn it yourself. You can be a stabilizing influence in your mate's life, and the more you play this role, the better you become at steadying your own efforts.

In other lifetimes you may have been foolhardy soldiers or adventurers, racing around each corner without a thought to your safety. Perhaps your mate perished as a result of your impetuosity. Now you want to serve and protect your partner.

With Your Partner's **TAURUS** Zodiac Sign

Nobody has more determination and downright stick-to-itiveness than your Taurus partner. This mate sets sail on a course of action and never reverses direction. When your Taurus makes a commitment, it might as well be written in stone! This is someone who may still be employed at the same job first begun at eighteen.

For you this is a real lesson in what can be accomplished over time when determination and commitment are present. You see that sometimes bad patches come along, but when a person works through them, good times return. This observation gives you a great deal more faith in life. You learn that you too could take this road, and you try much harder to be stable because of the influence of your mate.

In other lifetimes, your mate may have been a teacher who tried to get you to avoid shortcuts and follow your true path.

With Your Partner's **GEMINI** Zodiac Sign

When you feel like quitting your job, running out on responsibilities, or taking shortcuts, your Gemini mate is usually quite supportive. This is someone who understands the perils of boredom and who believes in change. You feel safe under this mate's influence, because if you make choices that seem a little iffy, there are few recriminations.

But on some level you suspect this isn't the best course of action. Your doubt prompts you to initiate discussion about whether you're truly on the right track. As you and your mate consider the situation, it becomes increasingly clear what you should do, and then you're more likely to make the right choice, rather than the easy one.

Your mate has wit but you have common sense, which serves your partnership well. In a past life together your roles may have been reversed, with you as the more lighthearted partner and your mate as the serious one.

With Your Partner's **CANCER** Zodiac Sign

Because your Cancer mate needs so much love and security, this partner is very good at commitment. Whether it's a job or a relationship, your sweetie knows how important stability is. You sensed from the moment you met that this was someone you could always count on, and you wanted to be there for your partner as well.

The longer you are together, the more respect you have for your mate. You see what can be accomplished with time and effort, and find that with the love and support of your Cancer mate you can achieve more. When you seek advice about your best course of action, your partner is right there, offering support and encouragement. That just naturally steers you in a good direction.

In other lifetimes your partner may have been a teacher, coach, or even a beloved parent. In addition to being your lover now, your mate is also your mentor.

▶ LOOK UP YOUR ROMANTIC AND SEXUAL COMPATIBILITY ON PAGES 780 & 802

Your Saturn in Capricorn

Learning to build a solid success slowly over time is your karmic challenge in this lifetime. In other lives, you've had early success but squandered it, and now it takes more effort to build the career you want. Your tendency is to reach for something quick and easy, but as you soon discover, that seldom works out.

It's unwise for you to be a dilettante, learning skills only partially and then leaping to the next challenge before you've truly completed the first one. It can result in your being pushed back to square one. In other lifetimes you may have been considered a huge success, but lost love or happiness in your pursuit of fame and fortune. Now you have a slight fear of success as a result.

It's your challenge to learn that success is what you make of it. Choose a career—and a relationship—and stick with it until you succeed.

With Your Partner's **LEO** Zodiac Sign

Pride is a strong and motivating factor for your Leo mate, who needs to feel validated and appreciated at almost every turn. It is your nature to be willing and happy to let exciting Leo shine while you provide the stability in the background. Your mate is accustomed to basking in the limelight, and even though that's not your style, there is an amazing synergy of purpose created between you.

Yet you would be a saint if at times you did not feel socially eclipsed by your more flamboyant partner. You probably see this pattern of inequality as something you don't care enough about to challenge. For example, you are likely to have more, perhaps deeper, friendships with people, even though your nature precludes a surfeit of social attachments.

Perhaps in other lifetimes the two of you were drawn together, depending on your opposing characteristics for strength.

With Your Partner's **VIRGO** Zodiac Sign

Nobody works harder than your Virgo partner. To this person, it doesn't matter what other people say and think. Your mate answers to a higher authority! As you observe your Virgo's tendency to work until the dropping point in order to live up to his or her own high standards, you are very impressed. You realize that not only is this someone you always want in your corner, but this is the way you should be, too.

It is incomprehensible to your mate that anyone should begin something and then leave it unfinished. If ever you flake out, you're sure to receive a number of lectures about how to complete the project. You may even come home to find your mate finishing what you've left undone.

The deep bond you feel in this relationship could signify a past life where the two of you grew old together.

With Your Partner's **LIBRA** Zodiac Sign

Your Libra mate's love of pleasure and romance can be quite charming, but this is often someone who chooses lifestyle over career, and that can mean you share the same tendencies. You do suspect that it's not a good idea to spend all your time and energy planning fancy dress-up events, particularly if your bank account won't support such pursuits.

If so, then it's up to you to play the bad guy, working with your mate to institute more responsible policies. This can be an excellent learning experience for you as well. And in your efforts to be more serious, you communicate this to your mate, causing your partner to become a tad more practical.

In other lifetimes you may have been great pals, mutual pranksters, or irresponsible lovers who focused only on pleasure. In this lifetime you can have love and fun, but not without responsibility.

With Your Partner's **SCORPIO** Zodiac Sign

Because Scorpio is a sign that does everything intensely, you can see from your mate that it's possible to have a passionate love life, a pleasurable day-to-day existence, and a fulfilling career. The key is personal investment and commitment, and you learn a great deal about these worthwhile qualities by watching your mate live up to responsibilities.

Stability is another Scorpio trait, and you recognize that you might have achieved more if you'd shown the same degree of stamina expressed by your partner. Because it's so interesting and useful for you to witness your mate in action, you may feel as though your love life is also a class in life lessons.

In other lifetimes your partner may have been someone whose success you admired greatly, someone you wished to have as a mentor. Now you're working to provide mutual affection and support, and to offer each other unwavering devotion.

▶ LOOK UP YOUR ROMANTIC AND SEXUAL COMPATIBILITY ON PAGES 780 & 802

Your Saturn in Capricorn

L earning to build a solid success slowly over time is your karmic challenge in this lifetime. In other lives, you've had early success but squandered it, and now it takes more effort to build the career you want. Your tendency is to reach for something quick and easy, but as you soon discover, that seldom works out.

It's unwise for you to be a dilettante, learning skills only partially and then leaping to the next challenge before you've truly completed the first one. It can result in your being pushed back to square one. In other lifetimes you may have been considered a huge success, but lost love or happiness in your pursuit of fame and fortune. Now you have a slight fear of success as a result.

It's your challenge to learn that success is what you make of it. Choose a career—and a relationship—and stick with it until you succeed.

With Your Partner's SAGITTARIUS Zodiac Sign

You'd like to believe that everything will always work out fine, no matter what, and you envy your Sagittarian mate that optimism. But somehow you wonder if that's the case. When you stop to think about it, you recognize that you are trying to build something, and if you aren't, you sense that you want to be.

Eventually, you learn that you can create something worthwhile only with time and effort, but this may be a difficult lesson.

You'd rather spend time with your partner, having picnics, playing with your pets, and discussing the deeper meanings of life. The problem is that you know down deep that you want material comforts, while your mate seldom cares about material matters.

It feels like there is so much history between you and your Sagittarian partner that it's likely in some past lifetime the two of you were involved in an intense, if ill-fated love affair.

With Your Partner's CAPRICORN Zodiac Sign

You're so impressed by your Capricorn mate's ability to focus nonstop on the process of achieving success that early in the relationship you probably offered yourself as an apprentice. It's hard for you to envision yourself with the same determination. You may wonder if it's some sort of career fever possessed by your mate that you lack.

No, it's not! Your partner is simply expressing the qualities that you want to develop for yourself. After all, you didn't come

together by accident. It felt serious from the start, and you sensed immediately that this partner really had something important to teach you.

Your determination to make the relationship work, no matter what, was the dawning of commitment, which is a positive thing for you to learn. This knowledge expresses an unspoken energy left over from a past life when you may have been unable to live up to that promise.

With Your Partner's AQUARIUS Zodiac Sign

You have in common with your Aquarian mate a respect for stability, commitment, and responsibility. You share the same ethics and you each want to do what's right as often as you can. Although your partner is stable, this mate is rarely focused completely on career or success. Instead, it seems much more important to him or her to make the world a better place.

You see this as an admirable trait, often fantasizing about all the good you would do if

you had wealth at your disposal. Because you want to make the world a better place, you become more committed to achieving success and greater disposable income. There are many good things about having money and power, and your mate's kind heart inspires you to discover them.

The strong physical attraction between you and your mate could reflect a previous existence together as young sweethearts, unable to marry.

With Your Partner's PISCES Zodiac Sign

In those dark moments when you wish you could fling it all aside and plunge forward into something new and more immediately rewarding, your Pisces mate is right there, offering you love and support. This partner has endless faith in you and often shares the belief that you can do anything you set your mind to.

This is deeply comforting for you, and whether you choose to stick with something difficult or race ahead toward something new,

you feel safer in this world having a partner who makes no judgments about your choices. As you share more time together, you want to live up to your mate's faith and positive expectations of you.

The understanding that you and your mate share and the unconscious sense of accommodation you give one another could be rooted in a past lifetime as family members or distant relatives bound by common values and beliefs.

▶ LOOK UP YOUR ROMANTIC AND SEXUAL COMPATIBILITY ON PAGES 780 & 802

Your Saturn in Aquarius

Of course we must all take care of ourselves, and there is no need to apologize for doing so. But it's also worthwhile to be able to put personal needs aside in deference to what's best for someone else. With Saturn in Aquarius, you are learning to be less selfish and more selfless.

In other lifetimes, you took too much without thinking of the needs of others. Perhaps you owned vast resources and paid your workers badly, or put them in danger. Maybe you were one of those kings who overtaxed the poor. Could be you were a corrupt politician! Now it's up to you to develop a social consciousness.

We are all connected, and by reaching out a helping hand to a single individual, you can elevate the universal vibration. In this lifetime, you need to do more to make the world a better place.

With Your Partner's **ARIES** Zodiac Sign

Aries is the "me-me-me sign," and all people born under this sign are meant to focus on themselves. When your Aries mate insists on doing what he or she wants, there is no karmic foul being committed. But you can't help wishing your mate would offer you more consideration and recognition.

In noticing this, you do yourself a great service because you learn more about your own life lessons. It is better when one person notices another's needs and offers to meet them without prodding. On a simple level, that's the basis for good manners. But on a complex level, it's the beginning of universal love.

As you and your mate negotiate your relationship over the years, you both learn to give and take. In a past life with your mate you may have been overly demanding, and now it's your turn to be the more giving and understanding partner. Can you do this even when your Aries is being bossy?

With Your Partner's **TAURUS** Zodiac Sign

Your Taurus mate needs to create a secure financial future. Although your partner seems placid, there may be a lot of worry beneath the surface about financial matters, and that is why it's always so urgent to focus on money. In a way, this is equally comforting to you because it makes you feel that you will be safe and cared for, no matter what.

Still, you can't help but feel that too much concentration on material matters obscures other important dynamics in the relationship that are equally controversial. Because you are both very set in your ways, it is hard to merge points of view or reconcile core values, especially if the two of you have political or religious differences.

In an earlier incarnation together, you may have been on extremely different social or economic levels that kept you from playing out your relationship in a fulfilling way.

With Your Partner's **GEMINI** Zodiac Sign

No matter how deeply your Gemini mate loves you, there is always a strong need to interact with other people. It's never about free love or casual sex. This mate needs a range of intellectual and emotional stimulation. Your level of personal self-assurance may be tested by your partner's desire to seek out other people.

If you're secure, you don't mind it when your mate spends time with friends. You realize that these encounters are soul-building opportunities for your partner, providing something valuable to share with you. And because you know this mate is itchy to talk—and that you alone can't provide all the stimulation—you see that socializing is definitely in your partner's best interest.

In a past incarnation together, you may have been abandoned by your partner, and that causes you unconscious fear now. But learning to trust that what you have in the present is real and good helps you feel safe.

With Your Partner's **CANCER** Zodiac Sign

Even as a child, your Cancer partner easily identified with those in need and felt their pain. A natural impulse to help feed the hungry, care for troubled children, and adopt lost pets continues to this day. You admire the tender and caring heart this demonstrates.

In observing your mate's impulse to help the needy and the suffering, what you see is an intense form of empathy. Your partner feels their pain and wants to allay it. This is one of the strongest reasons why people are compelled to do good. You know the adage about walking a mile in someone else's shoes!

Because of your partner's sensitivity to other people's feelings and needs, you become more attuned to the problems of those around you. Your dependence on your sweetheart's kindness harkens back to a previous existence when you were involved in a humanitarian project together.

▶ LOOK UP YOUR ROMANTIC AND SEXUAL COMPATIBILITY ON PAGES 780 & 802

Your Saturn in Aquarius

Of course we must all take care of ourselves, and there is no need to apologize for doing so. But it's also worthwhile to be able to put personal needs aside in deference to what's best for someone else. With Saturn in Aquarius, you are learning to be less selfish and more selfless.

In other lifetimes, you took too much without thinking of the needs of others. Perhaps you owned vast resources and paid your workers badly, or put them in danger. Maybe you were one of those kings who overtaxed the poor. Could be you were a corrupt politician! Now it's up to you to develop a social consciousness.

We are all connected, and by reaching out a helping hand to a single individual, you can elevate the universal vibration. In this lifetime, you need to do more to make the world a better place.

With Your Partner's **LEO** Zodiac Sign

Extravagance and the desire to live the good life are among Leo's more challenging traits, but generosity and kindness are among the best. Somehow your Leo mate finds a way to combine all these tendencies and can be an incredible force for good. All those fancy dress-up charity events are created by people like your mate, and they raise buckets of money for the needy.

There's something about your partnership that attunes both of you to the wish to do this. Perhaps it's unspoken, but somehow the two of you together are a stronger force for good than either of you could be alone. You inspire each other to be altruistic and charitable.

In past lifetimes you may have been quite frivolous, luxury-loving libertines until some shattering event forced you to a reckoning. Now you feel more responsible, living your lives for your own pleasure as well as for the good of other people.

With Your Partner's **VIRGO** Zodiac Sign

Virgo may be the most helpful sign of all. While many people provide aid for accolades and glory, your mate does it to make the world hum to a smoother rhythm. Perhaps the compulsion for order is selfish, but pitching in wherever a need is spotted elevates the universal vibration.

You appreciate knowing your partner stands ready to work until your problems are solved. It's great having someone in your corner, and you know that not even a thank-you is required. As you observe this behavior, you think about ways you can return the favor.

It feels good to give back to someone who gives to you. In a previous life you and your Virgo mate may have been crusaders for justice and the betterment of people less fortunate. Perhaps you loved one another, but in a selfless, impersonal way. Now you are able to build something better on that foundation.

With Your Partner's **LIBRA** Zodiac Sign

Good manners, kindness, and consideration are Libra traits, and nobody is a better host. Seeing to the needs of other people in a social situation comes naturally to your mate. Of course, hosting an elegant soiree isn't quite on a par with curing the ailing poor or feeding the hungry, but it's still about focusing on the needs of someone other than oneself.

You can see the value in this kind of consideration, and you learn a sort of personal finesse from watching your mate in action. Something rather synergistic happens in your partnership, and you both grow and learn. As a result, your mate is drawn more into the social expression of humanitarianism, and you are likely to lose some of your more superficial attitudes.

In other lifetimes you may have been close friends whose social class precluded awareness of the needy. Now you're learning to live in the real world.

With Your Partner's **SCORPIO** Zodiac Sign

Your Scorpio partner tends to concentrate on a few close relationships while remaining closed to new or more casual contacts. You find this interesting because you see so many wonderful qualities in your partner, and you know how well liked he or she could be.

Your influence can be very helpful in bringing new people and ideas to the partnership. You have a curiosity about things you don't know and are often compelled to forge bonds with new people. This helps your mate release some of that shy secretiveness and open up a bit more.

Your Scorpio is someone who will fight to the death for a loved one, and you admire this depth of commitment. Perhaps in a previous lifetime you were sexually attracted to one another, but because of the strict social rules of the day yours was a forbidden love.

▶ LOOK UP YOUR ROMANTIC AND SEXUAL COMPATIBILITY ON PAGES 780 & 802

Your Saturn in Aquarius

Of course we must all take care of ourselves, and there is no need to apologize for doing so. But it's also worthwhile to be able to put personal needs aside in deference to what's best for someone else. With Saturn in Aquarius, you are learning to be less selfish and more selfless.

In other lifetimes, you took too much without thinking of the needs of others. Perhaps you owned vast resources and paid your workers badly, or put them in danger. Maybe you were one of those kings who overtaxed the poor. Could be you were a corrupt politician! Now it's up to you to develop a social consciousness.

We are all connected, and by reaching out a helping hand to a single individual, you can elevate the universal vibration. In this lifetime, you need to do more to make the world a better place.

With Your Partner's **SAGITTARIUS** Zodiac Sign

Because material things mean so little to your Sagittarius partner, this person will gladly give a stranger the metaphorical shirt off his or her back. How can someone be so generous and nonchalant about personal resources, you wonder. It's all about emotional security. That sunny, positive outlook displayed by your mate comes from faith in the universe. Your partner expects things to work out, and usually they do.

Most people are selfish because they fear they will be neglected in some way or another. Not your Sagittarius mate! This person feels a part of the stream of life and knows that security and sustenance will be provided. That's why your mate so gladly offers your possessions, your home, or your dinner to anyone in need.

You love your Sagittarian mate's flair for drama and showmanship. This may reflect an earlier incarnation when the two of you were lovers as well as theatrical colleagues.

With Your Partner's **CAPRICORN** Zodiac Sign

Although your Capricorn mate often seems obsessed in that nonstop drive to attain wealth and success, this partner has a genuine commitment to the community and family unit. Your mate seldom wants to hoard wealth. Rather, there is a positive desire to build something secure—a home, happy family, and harmonious community.

If you get totally enmeshed in your Capricorn's compulsion to build this solid personal base, you may have less time available to help other people. What you learn from this partner is just what qualifies as help and how you can make a difference in your world in various ways. Reaching out is reaching out!

Perhaps in other lifetimes you were business partners, totally involved in your own financial gain. Now you want to adopt a more universal approach. This helps not only you, but shows your mate the greater meaning of success.

With Your Partner's **AQUARIUS** Zodiac Sign

Your Aquarian mate is the best karmic role model you could possibly find. Nobody is more committed to helping other people or improving the world. This mate befriends every stranger and gets personally involved in the lives of those pals who might need a helping hand. It's fascinating to listen to your partner's theories about how to fix the ailing planet. So much thought goes into them.

Upon observing this well-meaning commitment to good works, you notice something interesting. Your partner never feels alone in the world. This person feels a connection to everyone and everything. Helping others is the same thing as helping yourself. This is what you are trying to learn in this lifetime.

Perhaps in other lives you were frivolous and your mate was a committed member of society who wouldn't give you a second glance. Now you're close partners and you become a better and more sensitive person for this association.

With Your Partner's **PISCES** Zodiac Sign

Like a sponge absorbing water, your Pisces mate easily absorbs the feelings and worries of other people. Although it can be wearying for your partner to handle, it naturally creates a state of empathy and caring. That's why your Pisces is so willing to help people.

Although we are separate beings in our flesh, on the spirit level we are all connected, and your mate feels this bond very strongly. The problems of the world are also your partner's concerns. So something must be done! On a personal level this is also true—no matter what you're feeling or needing, this partner wants to offer a hug and a helping hand.

Feeling connected to others is a wonderful experience. It makes your world a safer and richer place. The sensitivity of your love for one another suggests a previous lifetime where one of you was cared for by the other.

▶ LOOK UP YOUR ROMANTIC AND SEXUAL COMPATIBILITY ON PAGES 780 & 802

Your Saturn in Pisces

You have felt separate and alienated for many lifetimes, but now you are reaching back into the universal oneness. With Saturn in Pisces, it's important for you to learn the freedom to express what's in your heart—your abilities and talents. The way to do that is through openness to spirit.

Great art is energy channeled in from spirit and translated into words, images, or sounds to which people can relate. Art is powerful, not just because of the intense emotions it can stir, but because it helps people feel the inspiration felt by the artist at the time of creation. This is what you're working on in this lifetime.

In other lives you were artistic but sold out because you were afraid to hold fast to your vision. Now you no longer want to compromise. You want to feel the rainbows of spirit flow through you so you can be authentic, creative, and loving.

With Your Partner's **ARIES** Zodiac Sign

The passion of Aries! Has anyone in your life ever been more bold or self-assured? You learn so much from the way your partner courageously makes personal choices with nary a glance back. You can see the beauty of life when there's never a worry about the consequences of action. That is the way to be an artist—and a lover!

Your tendency is to go more slowly, to second-guess, to wonder if you're on the right track, and sometimes that can be quite paralyzing where creative work is concerned. It can also hold you back romantically because you endlessly debate: Should I hold a hand, offer a kiss, declare my affections?

In an earlier life together you were probably kept apart due to being from rival political or philosophical factions. In this life you can use that lesson to achieve a greater understanding in your relationship.

With Your Partner's **TAURUS** Zodiac Sign

You and your mate have hesitation in common. Because your Taurus partner is so stable, it takes a long while for this mate to make a commitment to anything. There is always the fear that once something is begun, the choice may turn out to have been a bad one. Your mate seems to see choices as being irreversible.

When you think about it, you realize that this sort of hesitation can be quite crippling because it holds you back from trying new things. Most things in life can be started and ended—there is always choice. So there should be more hope and passion about beginnings than fear of being trapped without end.

You want to take more chances, and you encourage your mate to be a risk-taker, too. You can be quite good for each other. In other lives you may have been involved in a creative venture that only bold steps could save.

With Your Partner's **GEMINI** Zodiac Sign

It's always interesting to discuss books, art, and music with your partner, because not only do you enjoy each other's company, you share ideas and grow artistically. In contemplating the impact of a work of art, you see the various elements that define it. Being a critic can't teach you to be an artist, of course, but it can give you better awareness of the building blocks of creativity.

Your Gemini partner's scattershot approach to intellectual activity might need some direction. This is someone who will read just about anything, watch any television show, and see any movie. That's being a communications junkie, and through your influence, your mate begins to consider whether these things are worth the time they take to experience.

In other lifetimes, you may have been the critic and your partner the artist, writer, or actor whose creative efforts were refined by your sensibilities.

With Your Partner's **CANCER** Zodiac Sign

One of the most stirring things about your Cancer partner is the ability always to feel and express feelings. This is one person who's never out of touch with his or her heart. Instead, your sweetie's emotions are like a locomotive, driving every thought, word, and deed.

You recognize that this is a good way to be because it's pure, honest, and genuine, and you want to possess these qualities yourself. You don't always recognize or understand your own feelings, but by observing your Cancer mate, you work harder to do so.

Pure emotion is not only important to your psyche—it's also a good barometer of what's going on around you. By obeying your gut instincts, you know whom to trust, love, or avoid. This is also something you can learn from your mate. In other lifetimes you may have been lost in the wilderness together and only gut instincts ensured your survival.

▶ LOOK UP YOUR ROMANTIC AND SEXUAL COMPATIBILITY ON PAGES 780 & 802

Your Saturn in Pisces

You have felt separate and alienated for many lifetimes, but now you are reaching back into the universal oneness. With Saturn in Pisces, it's important for you to learn the freedom to express what's in your heart—your abilities and talents. The way to do that is through openness to spirit.

Great art is energy channeled in from spirit and translated into words, images, or sounds to which people can relate. Art is powerful, not just because of the intense emotions it can stir, but because it helps people feel the inspiration felt by the artist at the time of creation. This is what you're working on in this lifetime.

In other lives you were artistic but sold out because you were afraid to hold fast to your vision. Now you no longer want to compromise. You want to feel the rainbows of spirit flow through you so you can be authentic, creative, and loving.

With Your Partner's **LEO** Zodiac Sign

Leo is a very creative and artistic sign, but seldom wants to do anything that looks silly. So your Leo mate always seeks balance between self-expression and what's appropriate to maintain the respect of friends and loved ones. This modus operandi is exactly what you seek to learn.

You want to be able to take risks and express yourself without fear of making yourself vulnerable. In fact, on some levels, you want to go beyond self-censorship or the worry that others might lose respect for you. But for now, it's comforting to you to adopt your mate's approach to self-expression—share your lights without looking like a fool.

In other lifetimes you both may have been much wilder and crazier, acting out a number of insane stunts while the world laughed. If you were artists, you were certainly too outrageous for the times in which you lived!

With Your Partner's **VIRGO** Zodiac Sign

Although your Virgo mate has excellent taste and refined sensibilities, the tendency to be analytical often outweighs any artistic leanings. This approach may be quite comfortable to you because nobody can make sense of a situation like your sweetheart, and in hearing whatever interpretation is being offered, you feel safer.

But when it comes to the raw act of creation, you don't always get the best advice from this mate. Art can be messy, brutal, and sometimes even ugly, and your partner generally doesn't like life to be this intense. Yet your sweetie does feel a kind of raw, earthy passion, and together you can let go sexually and emotionally.

In other lifetimes, this partner may have been a teacher who helped you learn skill and technique, but whom you outgrew artistically. Now you are working to be partners who can share every aspect of life without stepping on each other's sensibilities.

With Your Partner's **LIBRA** Zodiac Sign

Your Libra is an art lover with whom you can enjoy many outings to museums, art galleries, plays, concerts, and movies. While your mate wants to discuss how well a work of art met certain critical criteria, you are looking to see how deeply it affected you emotionally.

It's possible that by discussing artistic merits with your partner, you can dissect something and move closer to its essence. That is a worthwhile intellectual activity and very stimulating to the relationship because it keeps you both involved with the other's mind. But you must always try to go beyond that. What do you feel? That's always the question you must ask yourself.

Your ability to learn from your Libran mate reflects many past lives together when he or she may have been your tutor or mentor, showing you the ways of the world and helping you climb the ladder of success.

With Your Partner's **SCORPIO** Zodiac Sign

Nobody trusts more profoundly in instinct than your Scorpio mate. This person goes almost completely by the gut and makes every choice in life based upon emotion. There is a sort of raw courage here, and you admire this very much, although you often wonder if you could do this yourself. It would feel like being on automatic pilot, and you wonder if you have that much trust.

This is exactly what you're working to develop. Your karma in this lifetime is to learn the beauty of being on auto-pilot, and how well that works when you're aware of your connection to spirit. When your spirit guides are working with you, it's as though you're being propelled through life toward your greatest good. That's quite similar to the way your Scorpio mate lives.

In other lifetimes your mate may have saved you from perishing in very dangerous circumstances. The courage displayed created an enduring sense of trust.

▶ LOOK UP YOUR ROMANTIC AND SEXUAL COMPATIBILITY ON PAGES 780 & 802

Your Saturn in Pisces

You have felt separate and alienated for many lifetimes, but now you are reaching back into the universal oneness. With Saturn in Pisces, it's important for you to learn the freedom to express what's in your heart—your abilities and talents. The way to do that is through openness to spirit.

Great art is energy channeled in from spirit and translated into words, images, or sounds to which people can relate. Art is powerful, not just because of the intense emotions it can stir, but because it helps people feel the inspiration felt by the artist at the time of creation. This is what you're working on in this lifetime.

In other lives you were artistic but sold out because you were afraid to hold fast to your vision. Now you no longer want to compromise. You want to feel the rainbows of spirit flow through you so you can be authentic, creative, and loving.

With Your Partner's **SAGITTARIUS** Zodiac Sign

Your Sagittarian mate has deep respect for all sorts of spiritual endeavors. Nobody is more interested in different cultures and forms of personal expression. No matter where in the world you go together, your mate feels comfortable and at ease. That's because the Sagittarian recognizes the true brotherhood of man and the universal spirit inside us all.

You are working in this lifetime to experience the same thing. Being flooded with spiritual energy brings a deep sense of bliss. No wonder your partner is so cheerful and mellow! That "What, me worry?" attitude can be a great approach to art and life.

You learn a positive way of living from this mate. But your partner learns something, too. You and your Sagittarian mate really know how to have fun together. In a past existence you may have been part of a group of strolling players, traveling the countryside.

With Your Partner's **CAPRICORN** Zodiac Sign

The nuts and bolts of life are what your Capricorn mate is all about. Everything must come down to one plus one. This philosophy can be very reasonable and comfortable for you because it seems to diminish the risks that threaten to derail you.

But you are supposed to be learning to follow your instincts and take risks. This is an emotional process, and although your mate is sometimes a risk-taker, it's usually after an exhaustive analytical process. So for you to complete your karma, you need to go in the opposite direction of your mate. Will this mess up your relationship? Not at all! Your mate provides a sense of stability and commitment, and that gives you the safety net you need.

You're freer to pursue artistic and spiritual interests without worrying as much about acquiring your daily bread. In this lifetime and others, your mate may have been your patron.

With Your Partner's **AQUARIUS** Zodiac Sign

Aquarius is the ultimate intellectual sign, and your mate's approach to life is often overly mental and dispassionate. This partner is moved much more by ideas than by feelings. Perhaps you can relate strongly to this approach to living, and maybe it comes quite naturally to you. If so, you're learning to be more emotional—in order to create balance.

Despite the somewhat unemotional approach to life, your partner can be a great risk-taker. Your sweetie is absolutely sure about the right way to do anything and wants to change the world for the better. As you watch the way your lover insists on a specific ideology, plan, or philosophy, you can see how a deep level of commitment and personal confidence can produce a fire in the belly.

You feel an intellectual kinship with your lover that dates from an earlier incarnation together as members of a tightly knit philosophical group.

With Your Partner's **PISCES** Zodiac Sign

That tremulous, emotional, follow-the-instincts quality of your Pisces mate is just what you're trying to learn in this lifetime. Your mate has the soul of an artist, whether he or she is creative or not. You share that passion for all that stirs the emotions and is beautiful.

It's fun for you to attend an artistic event with this partner because the slightest level of sentimentality can trigger a flood of tears, followed by embarrassed giggles. You can see from your mate's easy emotional responses how cathartic it can be to just let your feelings flow.

This relationship felt serious to you right from the start, and you sensed that there was much you could learn from your Pisces. In other lifetimes your mate may have taken fearless artistic or romantic risks while you stood by and worried, counseling caution. Now you seek love and enlightenment from your sweetheart.

▶ LOOK UP YOUR ROMANTIC AND SEXUAL COMPATIBILITY ON PAGES 780 & 802